CONTEMPORARY NOVELISTS

Contemporary Writers Series

Contemporary Dramatists
Contemporary Literary Critics
Contemporary Novelists
(including short story writers)
Contemporary Poets
Contemporary Popular Writers
Contemporary Southern Writers
Contemporary Women Poets
Contemporary World Writers

CONTEMPORARY NOVELISTS

SEVENTH EDITION

PREFACE TO THE SEVENTH EDITION

DAVID MADDEN

EDITORS

NEIL SCHLAGER

AND

JOSH LAUER

St J

ST. JAMES PRESS

AN IMPRINT OF THE GALE GROUP

DETROIT • NEW YORK • SAN FRANCISCO
LONDON • BOSTON • WOODBRIDGE, CT

Neil Schlager and Josh Lauer, *Editors*

Kristin Hart, *Project Coordinator*

Michelle Banks, Erin Bealmear, Laura Standley Berger, Joann Cerrito, Jim Craddock,
Steve Cusack, Nicolet V. Elert, Miranda Ferrara, Jamie FitzGerald, Melissa Hill,
Laura S. Kryhoski, Margaret Mazurkiewicz, Carol A. Schwartz, Christine Tomassini, Michael J. Tyrkus
St. James Press Staff

Peter M. Gareffa, *Managing Editor, St. James Press*

Mary Beth Trimper, *Manager, Composition and Electronic Prepress*
Evi Seoud, *Assistant Manager, Composition Purchasing and Electronic Prepress*
Dorothy Maki, *Manufacturing Manager*
Rhonda Williams, *Buyer*

Kenn Zorn, *Product Design Manager*
Mike Logusz, *Graphic Artist*

ISBN 1-55862-408-2
ISSN 1531-2232

Printed in the United States of America

St. James Press is an imprint of Gale Group
Gale Group and Design is a trademark used herein under license
10 9 8 7 6 5 4 3 2 1

CONTENTS

PREFACE	PAGE vii
EDITORS' NOTE	xiii
BOARD OF ADVISERS	xv
CONTRIBUTORS	xvii
LIST OF ENTRANTS	xxi
CONTEMPORARY NOVELISTS	**1**
NOTES ON ADVISERS AND CONTRIBUTORS	1083
NATIONALITY INDEX	1103
TITLE INDEX	1109

PREFACE

Beginning at the beginning, "novel" means, obviously, a new thing. The universal definition has been, more or less, that it brings a piece of news about places, people, and ideas.

The Death of the Novel and the Death of Reading

From the beginning, its health has been in doubt, and rumors of its death have dogged its history. If in the new millennium, rumors persist that the novel is no longer new—that it is old and as good as dead—perhaps, just to be certain, we ought to take its pulse now as a precaution against premature burial.

And while we are at it, shouldn't we also take the pulse of the reader, in the corporate sense—"the reader is dead" being the latest variation on the notion of the death of the novel?

Like "God is dead," "the novel is dead" was, on its inception, a lame-brained metaphor. A detailed chronology of the novel reveals, in every era, not only its liveliness, but its well-earned right to the term "novel."

On the contemporary scene, however, it can perhaps be said that there are no master novelists, male or female, and no masterpieces. If that is true, is that sad? I can't bring myself to think so. As a young writer, I had my heroes, and, at 67, I revere them still: James Joyce, Joseph Conrad, Thomas Wolfe, Ernest Hemingway, Virginia Woolf, Ralph Ellison, William Faulkner, Katherine Anne Porter, Carson McCullers, Wright Morris. They are dead, as are many who were once my contemporaries. But we who are left survive in that which is immortal—the art of fiction itself—while interesting subjects, such as war, love, and crime, and trends, such as the epic, the naturalistic, and the psychological novel, come and go in reader interest. The House of Fiction, Henry James assured us, has many windows and many doors. Readers have entered the front and the back doors and looked out through those many different windows with a sense of fiction's sameness and diminished creative power only if they have insisted on reading the same kinds of writers, genres, subjects, themes, and styles over and over again.

"Make It New!"

For the history of the novel is a history, almost decade by decade, of reinvigoration through innovation, in conception, style, and structure. Compared to the public awareness at mid-century of such innovative novelists as James Joyce and Gertrude Stein, readers today are not mindful of innovation, as such. Even so, the accomplishments of innovators of today are no less impressive for being unacknowledged by the general public or critics. In 1934, in *The ABC of Reading*, Ezra Pound exhorted both writers and readers to "Make it new!" Well, what is new? A rather perverse argument is that the novel has offered little "news that stays news" since 1760, when *Tristram Shandy*'s shelf life began. A more profitable view of the state of the novel is that, on the evidence, it is business as usual in the House of Fiction. And business is vigorous and good.

Forces That Both Debilitate and Reinvigorate the Novel

Paradoxically, the very forces perceived to contribute to the prophesied death, or at least debilitation, of the novel and of the reader actually also reinvigorate and keep both very much alive today. As long as we focus with shivering obsessiveness on one or a nexus of forces, we run the risk of becoming transfixed, victims of a self-fulfilling prophecy. But if we consider all the forces and link our concern about their negative effects with a discovery of their positive effects, we may see that out of the fires that consume arise Phoenixes of more than one species.

In an era when the catch phrase is the death of reading itself, a list of all the forces that threaten the death of the novel fails to convince when we look at the well-read works of the past twenty years by such "new" novelists as: Susan Straight, Connie Porter, Robert Olen Butler, Andrei Codrescu, Alice Walker, Allen Wier, Richard Ford, Robert Morgan, Martin Amis, T. C. Boyle, Louise Erdrich, Amy Tan, John Irving, Thomas Keneally, Ernest Gaines, Charles Johnson, Bobbie Ann Mason, Barry Hannah, Steven Millhauser, Cormac McCarthy, Toni Morrison, Salman Rushdie, and Leslie Silko. True, many older novelists, with five or so successful novels on record, can't get published anymore—a crying shame. But now Internet reprints from Barnes and Noble and on-demand reprints from the Authors' Guild will eventually keep many excellent novels in print, both popular and innovative. And on the publishing scene, it is true that too few magazines publish short stories, because most magazines, like television channels, target specialized audiences. But more stories than ever are being published, mostly in literary quarterlies.

We are blessed with a phalanx of forces that develop and shape writers and readers and that pose both dark and bright prospects. On the dark side, the litany of long-active forces reads this way: the specter of environmental disaster; the plague of epidemics; the population time bomb; atomic annihilation; competition for world markets; diminishing faith in the political process. Cross-genre and media fertilization, cross-cultural assimilation, the creative turmoil of technological innovations, economic globalization, political strife or coalitions, religious discord or tolerance, and the relativism of shifting philosophical visions are negative and positive forces acting upon the progress and fate of fiction.

Readers have become television addicts, but while the proliferation of channels on cable television threatens to fragment the interests of viewers so finely that the diminution of a common experience for the reading of fiction may seem fatal to the novel, television—which is after all little more than radio with pictures—is now a conservative force. The most fundamentally revolutionary invention since the printing press, the major new force of unknown, but knowable, consequences, is the Internet, with the traffic hazards of the Information Superhighway, but with the potential to facilitate a major step in the way we perceive human experience. More specifically, the litany of dark and bright forces claims that readers and writers are taught literature by young teachers who at the notion of masters and masterpieces turn pale, who seem to hate literature more than they love cultural criticism and who work to replace "dead white male classic writers" with politically correct up-to-the-minute writers who foster discussion of issues on race, class, gender, post-colonialism, Freudianism, and Marxism. But actual sales in literature textbooks reveal that traditional fiction remains the vibrant core of curricula. Yes, students read less, but imagine the readers of the Harry Potter series as readers and writers of tomorrow. Yes, even young writers read less, but they write more: fiction, poetry, imaginative nonfiction, screenplays, and even stage plays. Those who write, we may expect, will eventually read. Most writers are now learning how to write in college and come out of the same workshop pedagogy, but there are signs of more variety in teaching strategies.

Most agents are inaccessible to new writers, but more small publishers are looking for emerging talent. The new editors must be more adept at sales and marketing than the art of fiction, but sometimes their ignorance is a blessing. Huge publishers cannibalize each other and smaller ones perish, but others rise and fall. Huge bookstore chains brutally compete, while small bookstores fade away, but Internet book sales have created a healthy chaos out of which we may hope some good may come.

There is far more of everything today on the literary scene. More literary magazines, small presses, critical journals, creative writing courses, writers conferences, than ever before. In the last two decades, societies devoted to the study and appreciation of Richard Wright, Thomas Wolfe, Carson McCullers, William Faulkner, Eudora Welty, Robert Penn Warren, even living writers, Cormac McCarthy, for instance. One of the conventional reasons why we should study literature, especially the classics, is that it reflects the society in which it was written. That justification has always struck me as half-assed, to borrow from Candide. The more complete reason is that literature both reflects and affects society, directly, as in *Uncle Tom's Cabin* by Harriet Beecher Stowe and *The Jungle* by Upton Sinclair, indirectly or more subtly, as in *Huckleberry Finn* and *A Catcher in the Rye*. In some literature courses today, the emphasis is upon how the reflection is distorted and the effect is negative. But the imagination and the visionary temperament have also created other worlds.

A piece of bad news is, some argue, that it is in the nature of the novel that it depicts and thus perpetuates the conflict among those dark forces. But the piece of good news is that novels also assimilate and domesticate those forces and thus give impetus to bright forces as well. Some writers—Ronald Sukenick in *The Death of the Novel* and John Barth in *Lost in the Funhouse*, for instance—even deal in their fiction with the undying question of the death of the novel.

Literary Fiction and Popular Genres

The universal type of the novelist wears a ragged Harlequin costume, on each patch of which is the name of a genre, a type, or a trend. The popular genres mutated during the last century, from bringing the news about the epic West, then the asphalt jungle, then the unknown universe, then the realm of the occult, until the West, the mean streets, outer space, and the bizarre have become relatively domesticated. Today, the territory ahead is fantasy, with resonant connotations of spiritualism. For most popular genres and types of novels there is a serious or literary counterpart, especially in innovative fiction. The Popular Culture Society has, for 35 years now, encouraged the serious examination of that interplay.

My survey into deepest Barnes and Noble reveals that not even the spirit of John Wayne can keep the Western in the saddle, even though the spirit of Louis L'Amour is there, but virtually alone, on two long shelves. But Larry McMurtry and Cormac McCarthy carry us beyond even Walter Van Tilburg Clark, while the very few Western movies showing up these days fail to compare well with *The Ox-Bow Incident*. Crime novels participate in a popularity sustained by television and the movies. If John Grisham, Elmore Leonard, and James Lee Burke are not the masters that Hammett, Chandler, and Cain were, they, like the late Ross Macdonald, transmit their own power. Historical romances flood both new and used book stores, but no Charlotte Brontë or even Daphne Du Maurier counterparts are found among the serious fiction titles; we are mindful, however, that the Civil War novels of Jeff Shaara, Charles Frazier, and Madison Jones help keep up interest in that defining moment in American history. Science fiction is holding its own, but no literary figures like Aldous Huxley, George Orwell, or Arthur C. Clarke are imagining other worlds either, while it is movies such as *Star Wars* and television series such as *Star Trek* that set the standard in the public consciousness.

Among more literary genres, we note that political novels are few. Except for the Civil War novel, now in its glory, the clamor of war novels, even Vietnam novels, is seldom heard. Two relatively new genres are novels in which the author pays homage to one of the giants, Hemingway, Dickens, Brontë, Poe, Twain, and Melville by taking up where they left off or by imagining new adventures for their characters, even minor ones; and the antiquarian novel, in which old genres such as the Gothic Romance are revisited by writers such as Joyce Carol Oates generally identified as literary, not genre-bound. Religious subjects and themes are appearing with surprising frequency, but no Graham Greene has yet appeared. Business and medical novels, purely as such, are being written to be used as textbooks in those disciplines.

The energy and pervasiveness of the once-marginalized ethnic novel have come in as a tidal wave that started building out in the sea of the 1960s: Chicano, Native American, African American, Irish, and Middle Eastern and oriental writers living in England. And far more women novelists are considered major in the literary sense, for instance, Toni Morrison, Mary Lee Settle, Susan Sontag, Muriel Spark, Elizabeth Spencer, Edna O'Brien, Rosellen Brown, Anne Tyler, Ellen Gilchrist, Mavis Gallant, and Diane Johnson.

Other Forms of Artistic Expression

A diagnosis of the state, health, and venturesomeness of the novel becomes clearer when we compare it with other literary genres and other forms of art, none of which seem dead, some of which, however, seem to be dying at the rind but are still vital at the core. From the 1950s on, there were highly visible innovations in the fields of drama, movies, music, dance, and painting. Movies and the theater are far less venturesome, more conventional overall, now than they were in the 1950s and 1960s. But even comic-strip sex and violence action movies are almost as sophisticated in the making as movies based on such novels as *The English Patient*. The adaptation of movies from the works of Shakespeare, Austen, Dickens, Forster do well. Having seen the movie, people today less often say, "I don't have to read the novel"; they say, "Can't wait to read the novel." That fabulous invalid, the theater, stages mostly musicals, revivals of musicals, but the lights go up on few new plays by playwrights of the stature of Tennessee Williams, Arthur Miller, and Edward Albee while aging innovators such as Sam Shepard and Harold Pinter are taken gratefully for granted. But theater is to literature as baseball is to basketball—too slow for most folks. Innovations in both serious and popular music have just about played out. Hiphop and Rap mutants dominate, corrupting the language, but Rap revels in a love of words, while music videos train young viewers to be receptive to innovative techniques in movies and in fiction as well. Interactive relationships among all media have never been as symbiotic as now.

Although all forms, genres, and modes of artistic expression do today as the novel often does—pursue randomness at a fast pace—the subjects, themes, and techniques of innovative fiction, and all other arts, have been masterfully, thoroughly, and forever assimilated, domesticated by popular culture. Novels can no longer hope to shock, disorient, confuse readers into new perspectives on human experience. But the novel has a firm place in this myriad, as no more and no less venturesome than most other forms and ahead of most; in its place, the novel provides many kinds of experiences in many different aesthetic venues. Asian, French, Indian, Chinese, Japanese, South American novelists do not seem to deviate to any notable extent from these generalizations.

The Contemporary Appeal of the Commonplace

Perhaps to see more clearly how the new derives from innovative masterworks of the past, from Sterne to Joyce, one might look at the novels of Chinua Achebe, Rudolfo Anaya, Julian Barnes, John Barth, Don DeLillo, Raymond Federman, Barry Hannah, Steve Katz, Richard Kostelanetz, Frederick Busch, Ernest Gaines, Charles Johnson, Allen Wier, Toni Morrison, Steven Millhauser, Thomas Pynchon, Ronald Sukenick, Gilbert Sorrentino, Kurt Vonnegut, Jr., Rudolph Wurlitzer. They keep our eye on venturesomeness, but bless those novelists who are conventional, in the best sense, in the Trollope sense: Louis Auchincloss, Margaret Atwood, Russell Banks, Charles Frazier, George Garrett, Saul Bellow, R. V. Cassill, John Knowles, Hortense Calisher, Norman Mailer, Gore Vidal, Alice Munro, Reynolds Price, Philip Roth, Eudora Welty, Ann Beattie.

If the Laurence Sternes disrupt the smooth history of the novel, even 600 or so years after its birth, the Anthony Trollopes sustain the flow. Both types are in our lives today, but the perception is of a Trollopian era. Novelists and readers have come a long way from Flaubert's "mot juste," through Joyce's multifaceted style, through Wolfe's rhapsodic but simple style, and Hemingway's simple but complex style, to William Gass, who holds the fort, a lonely outpost under the banner of style: "I don't write novels, I write words." Lacking the distinctiveness of Joyce, Wolfe, and Hemingway, the style of most of the best novelists today is relatively commonplace but effective.

Perhaps the perennial appeal of the commonplace, the ordinary, in style, subject, locale, and form derive from writer-reader fatigue from contending with the same forces that both threaten and invigorate the novel. Conventional novelists satisfy a craving for escape—not out of readers' own lives into other places, other times, and the lives of an exotic other, which the various popular genres provide—but deeper into the ordinary lives they live, or wish to live, and a craving for enlightenment about that life.

The history of the novel shows that even the most innovative, avant garde, or experimental novelists venture out only to discover and cozy down into a niche. If one looks at the most venturesome novel by D. H. Lawrence, John Barth, William Gaddis, James Joyce, Virginia Woolf, William Burroughs, Gertrude Stein, Andre Gide, Thomas Pynchon, Julio Cortazar, Vladimir Nabokov, Allain Robbe-Grillet, and John Hawkes, and then looks at all their others, one may discern a certain sameness. Few new voices prove to be polyphonic. Faulkner stands out as an innovator whose restless temperament imagined forms for four or five novels distinctively different from each other.

The terms innovative, avant garde, and experimental do not all mean the same thing; all three are useful for their nuanced differences; "innovative" is perhaps a better word than "experimental" or "avant garde" for use as a generalization, but a word that might embrace all three and might apply to some extent to the contemporary scene is "venturesome." Venturesomeness is just as prevalent today as it ever was. That readers are not as aware of this quality in the newest novels may only mean that variety describes the novel today in a climate of change so great and rapid we seldom pause, as we speed along on the Information Superhighway, to assess and elevate novelists to the status of venturesome masters of the form.

It has been my intention neither to excoriate nor to extol the state of the novel. If I am wrong, I can only hope not to live long enough to be counted among the mourners. If I am right, I can hope that a myriadminded perspective among writers and readers will keep the novel alive for at least a thousand years.

How Will the Novel Survive in the New Millennium?

Another recurrent question about the novel presupposes that the novel is indeed alive:

> What might we predict for its future? Until recently, I have always felt that speculation about a form so protean is boring. But the context in which the novel must continue to develop will itself be far more protean. Such a very general and brief survey as I have been conducting is doomed to hostile reception by those readers impatient with generalizations per se and those devotees of any one genre, trend, or critical perspective. I can only plead a desire to venture into the realm of myriadmindedness, which is the theme of my generalization about the future of novelists and readers. As writer, critic, and as one who professes in creative writing workshops and in literature classes, I have always felt comfortable with a multitude of terms, even labels, of concepts and generalizations, mindful of their transitory power to illuminate and to propel one on into another realm of emotion, imagination, and thought.

What can the novel venture to achieve in this new millennium? Since the assignment I have given myself is to look back from the shifty horizon of the new millennium, permit me here at the end to pose a possibility for the future of writers and readers and for the novel, the deserving form that we must, working together, keep alive. Having claimed that writers today are just as venturesome as writers of any other era, I claim now that too few readers have ever been so venturesome as to meet novelists more than halfway. Even well-intentioned readers often mistake relatively fresh controversial subjects and themes for innovativeness in form, style, and technique, when they are merely being venturesome as readers. Serious readers of the future will have to learn, I imagine, how to read, just as writers must learn how to write, to paraphrase Mark Harris.

The question then arises, what new thing might the novelist write that would thrive only with a new kind of readership? The one major technique that, in the not so long history of the novel, has never realized its potential is the omniscient point of view, "omniscient" more as in God than even in Fielding, Dickens, Wolfe, Conrad, Tolstoy, Hardy, or Mann, none of whom ever came near consciously, deliberately exploring the possibilities. Which are what? At this point in time, only God knows. Recall the many applications of the Latin prefixes "omni" and also "multi" and "poly" and the possibilities begin to proliferate and to activate the intellectual imagination.

One of the problems is choreographic. How is the venturesome novelist of the future to keep all time and space and the characters there moving rhythmically at the still point of the dance, of art? It's a mystery, and a task, but a mystery worth contemplating and a task that may prove to be exhilarating for the new writer and the new reader.

After omniscience, what else do I have in mind? Myriadmindedness. Coleridge called Shakespeare myriadminded, and if you think about it, so were Da Vinci and other Renaissance minds, right on up through James Joyce, William Faulkner (I first heard the word applied to him) and Robert Penn Warren (I now apply the word to him) in the last century (no one comes to mind in this new century). But those minds do not really demonstrate what I mean by the word. By myriadmindedness, as a description of the future of the novelist whom I envision, I mean no longer monominded, but more positively, I mean, at first, having "the ability to hold two opposed ideas in the mind at once and still retain the ability to function," as F. Scott Fitzgerald said in, significantly enough, *The Crack-Up*. But beyond that, myriadmindedness is the ability to achieve simultaneity, and in the novel that means what it means in painting: two elements, interactive, functioning at once, just as all the reds and yellows in a painting simultaneously activate the viewer's perception.

Just as the surviving novelists of the future will have to cultivate myriadmindedness to depict the multivalent milieu of our lives, the reader will have to cultivate the ability to respond consciously to the development of two elements simultaneously. Writers and readers are active in the same global cultural complexities. Today, however, most writers and their readers are satisfied with cultivating their own gardens, little victory gardens that nourish small neighborhoods. Just as magazines and cable networks target specialized audiences, the novel, even the literary novel that aspires to the immortality of art, works a small audience.

My prediction is that mankind, with the imperative aid of computers and their continual development of expanding capabilities, will pursue the development of an ability first to perceive and contemplate and process intellectually two things simultaneously, and then maybe twenty years later, three things—an achievement that will constitute the first major breakthrough in human learning since man learned to use fire and hand tools. Then four things, with the goal of continuing that development process forever. The cultivation of the omniscient point of view and simultaneity in the novel will serve the more general venturesome purpose and long process of developing myriadmindedness and will even—I envision hopefully—lead the way. I can make that claim because the novel, from its nativity, has been the only human activity in which emotion, imagination, and intellection have been presented omnisciently in a focused, conscious manner. All novels, taken together, have provided readers, throughout the past five or six centuries, with a manifold view of humankind. We look to the new millennium horizon for that writer who will set an example of myriadmindedness for us all.

—David Madden

EDITOR'S NOTE

The selection of writers included in this book is based on the recommendations of the advisers listed on page xiii.

The entry for each writer consists of a biography, a complete list of separately published books, and a signed essay. In addition, entrants were invited to comment on their work.

Original British and United States editions of all books have been listed; other editions are listed only if they are first editions. All uncollected short stories published since the entrant's last collection, plus others mentioned by the entrant, have been listed; in those cases where an uncollected story was originally published in a magazine and later in an anthology, we have tended to list the anthology. As a rule all books written about the entrant are listed in the Critical Studies section; the reviews and essays listed have been recommended by the entrant.

We would like to thank the entrants and contributors for their patience and cooperation in helping us compile this book.

BOARD OF ADVISERS

CONTRIBUTORS

Lisa Abney
Rima Abunasser
Maureen Aitken
Stephen Akey
Walter Allen
Richard Almonte
Patricia Altner
Richard Andersen
Susan Ang
Mar Asensio-Aróstegui
Alvin Aubert
Harold Augenbraum

Jane S. Bakerman
John Clement Ball
William C. Bamberger
John Barnes
Bob Batchelor
Ian A. Bell
Samuel I. Bellman
Bruce Bennett
Bernard Bergonzi
Tammy Bird
Earle Birney
William Bittner
William Borden
Elmer Borklund
Malcolm Bradbury
M.E. Bradford
Eckhard Breitinger
Peter Brigg
Juliette Bright
W.S. Broughton
Lloyd W. Brown
Richard Brown
Lynne Bryer
Harry Bucknall
Jackie Buxton
Keith Byerman

Mary Cadogan
Cynthia Cameros
Frank Campenni
Michela Canepari-Labib
Victoria Carchidi
D.D.C. Chambers
Michael A. Chaney
Shirley Chew
Paul Seiko Chihara
Laurie Clancy
Anderson Clark
Sam Coale
Loretta Cobb
Tom Colonnese
Judy Cooke

Richard Corballis
John Cotton
F. Brett Cox
Ralph J. Crane
Susan E. Cushman
Edmund Cusick

Helen Daniel
Terence Dawson
Doreen D'Cruz
Leon de Kock
Marc Delrez
Peter Desy
Susie deVille
Adam Dickinson
Peter Dickinson
R.H.W. Dillard
Paul A. Doyle
Dorothy Driver
Deborah Duckworth
Andy Duncan
Patricia Keefe Durso
Josh Dwelle
Klay Dyer

Ursula Edmands
Chester E. Eisinger
Geoffrey Elborn

Mark A.R. Facknitz
Peter Ferran
Keith Ferrell
John W. Fiero
Ruel E. Foster
Jill Franks
Anne French
Warren French
Melvin J. Friedman
Lucy Frost
John Fuegi

David Galloway
Tim Gauthier
Stephannie S. Gearhart
David Geherin
James Gindin
D.C.R.A. Goonetilleke
Lois Gordon
Pat Gordon-Smith
Hedwig Gorski
Marian Gracias
Colin Graham
Suzanne Disheroon Green
Sinda Gregory
George Grella

Jessica Griffin
Prabhu S. Guptara
Laurie Schwartz Guttenberg
Tracie Church Guzzio

Jay L. Halio
James B. Hall
Joan Wylie Hall
John Hanrahan
Jennifer Harris
June Harris
James A. Hart
Sue Hart
Thomas Hastings
David M. Heaton
John Herbert
Michelle Hermann
Katharine Hodgkin
Janis Butler Holm

Van Ikin

Louis James
A. Norman Jeffares
David K. Jeffrey
Annibel Jenkins
Ron Jenkins
Rosemary E. Johnsen
William A. Johnsen

H.R.F. Keating
Margaret Keith
Wendy Robbins Keitner
Fiona Kelleghan
Sandra Kemp
Burton Kendle
Jake Kennedy
Liam Kennedy
Tabish Khair
Robert F. Kiernan
Bruce King
Celia M. Kingsbury
Connie Ann Kirk
H. Gustav Klaus
Marcus Klein
Jerome Klinkowitz
Judson Knight
Judith C. Kohl
James Korges
Iva Korinkova
Marta Krogh

Suzanne Lane
Ryan Lankford

Josh Lauer
Mary M. Lay
Robert Lecker
Thomas LeClair
Chris Leigh
Michal Lemberger
Peter Lewis
Stanley W. Lindberg
Jack Lindsay
Jennifer Livett
Devoney Looser
Gail Low
John Lucas
Robert E. Lynch

Andrew Macdonald
Gary D. MacDonald
Gina Macdonald
Clinton Machann
David Madden
Veronica Makowsky
Irving Malin
Paul Marx
Lawrence Mathews
Roland Mathias
John McCormick
Frederick P.W. McDowell
Margaret B. McDowell
John McLeod
Ian McMechan
Kevin McNeilly
John Mepham
Patricia Merivale
Robert E. Mielke
D. Quentin. Miller
Stephen Milnes
Radhika Mohanram
David Montrose
Gerald Moore
Harry T. Moore
Robert A. Morace
Anne Morddel
Laura Moss
Eric Muirhead
Graham J. Murphy
Heather Murray

Janna Z. Nadler
Shyamala A. Narayan
W.H. New
Judie Newman
Leslie Norris
Maril Nowak
Robert Nye

Liam O'Brien
D.J. O'Hearn
John O'Leary
James Ortego

Malcolm Page
Joseph Parisi
Marian Pehowski
Tom Penner
George Perkins
Lisa A. Phillips
Marge Piercy
Jan Pilditch
Sanford Pinsker
Marco Portales
John Povey
Cathy Kelly Power
Jeremy Poynting
Joanna Price
Elizabeth Purdy
Lyn Pykett

Isabel Quigly

Arthur Ravenscroft
Sandra Ray
John M. Reilly
Jessica Reisman
H. Winston Rhodes
Alan Riach
Karen Robertson
Marilyn Rose
Christine Roth
S.A. Rowland
Trevor Royle
Alan Rubin
Louis D. Rubin, Jr.

Geoff Sadler
Hana Sambrook
David Sanders
Stewart Sanderson
William J. Schafer
Neil Schlager
Lynda D. Schrecengost
Roberta Schreyer
Linda Semple
Michele S. Shauf
Alan R. Shucard
Melissa Simpson
Victoria A. Smallman
Angela Smith
Christopher Smith
Curtis C. Smith
Andy Solomon
Eric Solomon
Tabitha Sparks
Jane W. Stedman
Caroline Steemson
Mark Stein
Carol Simpson Stern
James R. Stevens
Brian Stonehill
Victor Strandberg
J.R. Struthers
W.J. Stuckey
Maggi R. Sullivan
Judith Summers
Fraser Sutherland
John Sutherland
Dean Swinford
Arlene Sykes

Shana Tacon
Sharon Talley
Anna-Marie Taylor
John Thieme
Roger Thompson
Drew Tidwell
Chris Tiffin
Philippa Toomey
Shirley Toulson
Nicolas Tredell
C.W. Truesdale
Richard Tuerk
Penny van Toorn

Aruna Vasudevan
Thomas A. Vogler

Tobias Wachinger
William Walsh
Val Warner
Diane Watson
Harold H. Watts
Perry D. Westbrook
Leonard Wilcox
Margaret Willy
Janet Wilson
Bill Witherup
George Woodcock
Tim Woods
Michael Woolf
J.J. Wylie

Leopoldo Y. Yabes

Steven Zani
Heather Zwicker

CONTEMPORARY NOVELISTS

LIST OF ENTRANTS

Chinua Achebe
Peter Ackroyd
Glenda Adams
Richard Adams
Ama Ata Aidoo
Brian Aldiss
James Aldridge
Sherman Joseph Alexie
André Alexis
Dorothy E. Allison
Lisa Alther
Elechi Amadi
Martin Amis
Mulk Raj Anand
Rudolfo A. Anaya
Barbara Anderson
Jessica Anderson
I. N. C . Aniebo
Michael Anthony
Ayi Kwei Armah
Jeannette Armstrong
Thea Astley
Margaret Atwood
Louis Auchincloss
Paul Auster

Murray Bail
Paul Bailey
Beryl Bainbridge
Elliott Baker
J. G. Ballard
Russell Banks
John Banville
Leland Bardwell
A. L. Barker
Pat Barker
Julian Barnes
Wilton Barnhardt
Andrea Barrett
Stan Barstow
John Barth
Frederick Barthelme
Jonathan Baumbach
Richard Bausch
Nina Bawden
Gregory Dale Bear
Ann Beattie
Stephen Becker
Mary Beckett
Sybille Bedford
Madison Smartt Bell
Saul Bellow
Gregory Albert Benford
John Berger
Thomas Berger
Doris Betts
Rachel Billington
Maeve Binchy
Neil Bissoondath
Clark Blaise
Fred Bodsworth
Dermot Bolger
Vance Bourjaily
John Bowen
George Bowering
Edgar Box
William Boyd
Clare Boylan
T. Coraghessan Boyle
Edward P. Bradbury
Malcolm Bradbury
Ray Bradbury
David Bradley
John Ed Bradley
Melvyn Bragg
Sasthi Brata
André Brink
Erna Brodber
Christine Brooke-Rose
Anita Brookner
Rita Mae Brown
Rosellen Brown
Wesley Brown
Frederick Buechner
Lois McMaster Bujold
James Lee Burke
Bonnie Burnard
Alan Burns
Janet Burroway
Frederick Busch
Octavia Estelle Butler
Robert Olen Butler, Jr.

Hortense Calisher
Philip Callow
Henry Calvin
Marion Campbell
Curt Cannon
Peter Carey
R. V. Cassill
Brian Castro
Frank Cauldwell
David Caute
Jerome Charyn
Upamanyu Chatterjee
Alan Cheuse
Mark Childress
Shimmer Chinodya
Carolyn Chute
Sandra Cisneros
Arthur C. Clarke
Austin C. Clarke
William Cobb
Andrei Codrescu
Jonathan Coe
J. M. Coetzee
Barry Cole
Isabel Colegate
Hunt Collins
James Colvin
Shane Connaughton
Pat Conroy
David Cook
William Cooper
Robert Coover
Douglas Coupland
Peter Cowan
William Trevor Cox
P. J. Coyne
Jim Crace
Harry Crews
Michael Crichton
E. V. Cunningham
Michael Cunningham

David Dabydeen
Fred D'Aguiar
Blanche d'Alpuget
Edwidge Danticat
Lionel Davidson
Liam Davison
Jennifer Dawson
Louis de Bernières
Ralph de Boissière
Len Deighton
Samuel R. Delany
Nicholas Franklin Delbanco
Don DeLillo
Anita Desai
Boman Desai
Shashi Deshpande
Joan Didion
Chitra Banerjee Divakaruni
Stephen Dixon
E. L. Doctorow
J. P. Donleavy
Ellen Douglas
Michael Douglas
Dale Sara Dowse
Roddy Doyle
Margaret Drabble
Robert Drewe
C. J. Driver
Marilyn Duckworth
Alan Duff

Maureen Duffy
Elaine Dundy
Nell Dunn
John Gregory Dunne
Dorothy Dunnett
Wilma Dykeman

Clyde Carlyle Edgerton
Stevan Eldred-Grigg
Janice Elliott
Alice Thomas Ellis
Bret Easton Ellis
Trey Ellis
James Ellroy
David Ely
Buchi Emecheta
Louise Erdrich
Walter Ericson
Ahmed Essop
Percival L. Everett

Zoë Fairbairns
Nuruddin Farah
Beverley Farmer
Howard Fast
Sebastian Faulks
Irvin Faust
Elaine Feinstein
Eva Figes
Timothy Findley
Tibor Fischer
Thomas Flanagan
Shelby Foote
Richard Ford
Margaret Forster
Frederick Forsyth
David Foster
John Fowles
Janet Frame
Ronald Frame
Dick Francis
Michael Frayn
Gillian Freeman
Marilyn French
Bruce Jay Friedman
Kinky Friedman
Abby Frucht

Ernest J. Gaines
Mavis Gallant
Janice Galloway
Kenneth Gangemi
Cristina Garcia
Alex Garland
Helen Garner
George Garrett
William H. Gass
William Gay
Maggie Gee
Maurice Gee
Zulfikar Ghose
Amitav Ghosh
Kaye Gibbons
Graeme Gibson
William Gibson
Ellen Gilchrist
Brian Glanville
Douglas Glover
Gail Godwin
Herbert Gold
William Goldman
Nadine Gordimer
Giles Gordon
Mary Gordon
Phyllis Fay Gotlieb
Robert Gover
Patricia Grace
Winston Graham
Shirley Ann Grau
Alasdair Gray
Stephen Gray
Joanne Greenberg
Kate Grenville
John Grisham
Winston Groom
Doris Grumbach
Albert Guerard
Romesh Gunesekera
Sunetra Gupta
Allan Gurganis
Abdulrazak S. Gurnah
David Guterson

Arthur Hailey
Russell Haley
James B. Hall
Rodney Hall
Marion Halligan
Hugo Hamilton
Jane Hamilton
Clifford Hanley
Barry Hannah
Ezra Hannon
Mark Harris
Wilson Harris
Jim Harrison
Elizabeth Harrower
Veronica Hart
Nicholas Hasluck
Jon Hassler
Marianne Hauser
Shirley Hazzard
Dermot Healy
Roy A. K. Heath
Ursula Hegi
Mark Helprin
Aidan Higgins
Tomson Highway
Oscar Hijuelos
Carol Hill
Susan Hill
Thomas Hinde
Barry Hines
Edward Hoagland
Russell Hoban
Jack Hodgins
Harry Summerfield Hoff
Alice Hoffman
Desmond Hogan
Alan Hollinghurst
Hugh Hood
Christopher Hope
Nick Hornby
Janette Turner Hospital
Elizabeth Jane Howard
Maureen Howard
Jeffrey Hudson
David Hughes
Keri Hulme
Emyr Humphreys
Evan Hunter
Kristin Hunter

Michael Ignatieff
Witi Ihimaera
David Ireland
John Irving
Kazuo Ishiguro
Festus Iyayi

Mick Jackson
Dan Jacobson
Howard Jacobson
Kelvin Christopher James
P. D. James
Tama Janowitz
Gish Jen
Robin Jenkins
Ruth Prawer Jhabvala
Charles Johnson
Colin Johnson
Denis Johnson
Diane Johnson
Stephanie Johnson
Jennifer Johnston
Elizabeth Jolley
Gayl Jones
Glyn Jones
Gwyneth A. Jones
Madison Jones
Marion Patrick Jones
Mervyn Jones
Erica Jong
Neil Jordan
Ivar Jorgenson
Arun Joshi
Gabriel Josipovici
Ward Just

Johanna Kaplan
Steve Katz
Dan Kavanagh
Jackie Kay
Victor Kelleher
William Melvin Kelley
Maeve Kelly
James Kelman
Randall Kenan
Thomas Keneally
A. L. Kennedy
William Kennedy
Ken Kesey
Fiona Kidman
Benedict Kiely
Jamaica Kincaid
Francis King
Stephen King
Thomas King
Johanna Kingsley
Barbara Kingsolver
Maxine Hong Kingston
W. P. Kinsella
John Knowles
Calvin M. Knox
Elizabeth Knox
C. J. Koch
Joy Kogawa
Bernard Kops
William Kotzwinkle
Robert Kroetsch
Hanif Kureishi

George Lamming
John Lange
John le Carré
Chang-rae Lee
Sky Lee
Ursula K. Le Guin
Alan Lelchuk
Elmore Leonard
Doris Lessing
Jonathan Lethem
Ira Levin
Norman Levine
Catherine Lim
Penelope Lively
David Lodge
Earl Lovelace
Alison Lurie
Morris Lurie

Ann-Marie MacDonald
Bernard MacLaverty
David Madden
Deirdre Madden
Jamal Mahjoub
Norman Mailer
Clarence Major
David Malouf
Hilary Mantel
Kamala Markandaya
Wallace Markfield
Daphne Marlatt
Owen Marshall
Paule Marshall
Adam Mars-Jones
Richard Marsten
Carole Maso
Bobbie Ann Mason
Allan Massie
Hilary Masters
Peter Mathers
Harry Mathews
Jack Matthews
Peter Matthiessen
Elizabeth Mavor
William Maxwell
Ed McBain
Patrick McCabe
Cormac McCarthy
Sue McCauley
Alice McDermott
Roger McDonald
Joseph McElroy
Ian McEwan
John McGahern
Patrick McGrath
Thomas McGuane, III
Jay McInerney
Terry McMillan
Larry McMurtry
James McNeish
Candia McWilliam
Gita Mehta
Pauline Melville
Barbara Mertz
John Metcalf
Anne Michaels
Barbara Michaels
Leonard Michaels
Stanley Middleton
Alex Miller
Steven Millhauser
Susan Minot
Mark Mirsky
Rohinton Mistry
Julian Mitchell
Timothy Mo
N. Scott Momaday
Rick Moody
Michael Moorcock
Lorrie Moore
Frank Moorhouse
Toni Morrison
John Mortimer
Nicholas Mosley
Walter Mosley
Mudrooroo
Bharati Mukherjee
Val Mulkerns
John Munonye
Alice Munro
Gerald Murnane
Albert L. Murray

Chaman Nahal
V. S. Naipaul
R. K. Narayan
Mudrooroo Narogin
Gloria Naylor
Njabulo S. Ndebele
Jay Neugeboren
Ngugi wa Thiong'o
Eilis Ní Dhuibhne
Lawrence Norfolk
Howard A. Norman
Robert Nye

Joyce Carol Oates
Edna O'Brien
Tim O'Brien
Joseph O'Connor
Julia O'Faolain
Andrew O'Hagan
Ben Okri
Tillie Olsen
Stewart O'Nan
Michael Ondaatje
David Osborne
Vincent O'Sullivan
Cynthia Ozick

Grace Paley
Charles Palliser
Tim Parks
Anne Perry
Kathrin Perutz
Jerzy Peterkiewicz
Elizabeth Peters
Harry Mark Petrakis
Caryl Phillips
Jayne Anne Phillips
Mike Phillips
Marge Piercy
David Plante
James Plunkett
Richard Powers
David Pownall
Terry Pratchett
Reynolds Price
Richard Price
David Profumo
E. Annie Proulx
James Purdy
Thomas Pynchon

Anne Rampling
Robert Randall

Frederic Raphael
Piers Paul Read
John Rechy
Ishmael Reed
Desmond Reid
Ruth Rendell
Anne Rice
David Richards
Mordecai Richler
Tom Robbins
Michèle Roberts
Kim Stanley Robinson
Marilynne Robinson
Peter Robinson
Mary Robison
Daphne Rooke
A. N. Roquelaure
Judith Rossner
Philip Roth
Arundhati Roy
Bernice Rubens
Jane Rule
Michael Rumaker
Salman Rushdie
Joanna Russ

Nayantara Sahgal
Lisa St. Aubin de Teran
Garth St. Omer
J. D. Salinger
James Sallis
Ferrol Sams, Jr.
Thomas Savage
Susan Fromberg Schaeffer
Budd Schulberg
Rosie Scott
I. Allan Sealy
Carolyn See
Hubert Selby, Jr.
Will Self
Shyam Selvadurai
Vikram Seth
Mary Lee Settle
Jeff Shaara
Maurice Shadbolt
Tom Sharpe
Wilfrid Sheed
Carol Shields
Anita Shreve
Bapsi Sidhwa
Clancy Sigal
Leslie Marmon Silko
Robert Silverberg

Mona Simpson
Andrew Sinclair
Khushwant Singh
F. Sionil Jose
Carolyn Slaughter
Jane Smiley
Emma Smith
Lee Smith
Ray Smith
Rosamond Smith
Jane Somers
Susan Sontag
Gilbert Sorrentino
Wole Soyinka
Muriel Spark
Alan Spence
Colin Spencer
Elizabeth Spencer
C. K. Stead
John Steffler
Michael Stephens
Neal Stephenson
Bruce Sterling
Daniel Stern
Richard G. Stern
Robert Stone
Randolph Stow
Susan Straight
William Styron
Ronald Sukenick
Susan Swan
Graham Swift

Amy Tan
Emma Tennant
Shashi Tharoor
Alexander Theroux
Paul Theroux
Audrey Thomas
D. M. Thomas
Lawrence Thornton
Colin Thubron
Gillian Tindall
Peter Tinniswood
Miriam Tlali
Colm Toíbín
Barbara Trapido
Rose Tremain
William Trevor
Joanna Trollope
Frank Tuohy
Anne Tyler

Barry Unsworth
John Updike
Edward Upward

Guy Vanderhaeghe
Peter Vansittart
M. G. Vassanji
Gore Vidal
Helena Maria Viramontes
Noel Virtue
William T. Vollmann
Kurt Vonnegut, Jr.

David Wagoner
Dan Wakefield
Alice Walker
David Foster Wallace
Marina Warner
Keith Waterhouse
David Watmough
James Welch
Fay Weldon
Irvine Welsh
Eudora Welty
Albert Wendt
Mary Wesley
Anthony C. West
Paul West
William Wharton
Edmund Valentine White, III
John Edgar Wideman
Rudy Wiebe
Allen Wier
Marianne Wiggins
Michael Wilding
Damien Wilkins
John A. Williams
Connie Willis
A. N. Wilson
Jeanette Winterson
Tim Winton
Larry Woiwode
Tom Wolfe
Tobias Wolff
Charles Wright
Rudolph Wurlitzer

James Yaffe
Lois-Ann Yamanaka
Helen Yglesias
Al Young
Sol Yurick

A

ACHEBE, Chinua

Nationality: Nigerian. **Born:** Albert Chinualumogu in Ogidi, 16 November 1930. **Education:** Government College, Umuahia, 1944–47; University College, Ibadan, 1948–53, B.A. (London) 1953. **Family:** Married Christiana Chinwe Okoli in 1961; two sons and two daughters. **Career:** Talks producer, Lagos, 1954–57, controller, Enugu, 1958–61, and director, Voice of Nigeria, Lagos, 1961–66, Nigerian Broadcasting Corporation; chairman, Citadel Books Ltd., Enugu, 1967. Senior research fellow, 1967–73, professor of English, 1973–81, and since 1984 professor emeritus, University of Nigeria, Nsukka. Visiting professor, 1972–75, and Fulbright Professor, 1987–88, University of Massachusetts, Amherst; visiting professor, University of Connecticut, Storrs, 1975–76; Regents' Lecturer, University of California, Los Angeles, 1984; Visiting Distinguished Professor of English, City College, New York, 1989, visiting professor, Stanford University, 1990. Charles P. Stevenson Professor of Literature, Bard College. Founding editor, Heinemann African Writers series, 1962–72 and since 1970 director, Heinemann Educational Books (Nigeria) Ltd., and Nwankwo-Ifejika Ltd. (later Nwamife), publishers, Enugu; since 1971 editor, *Okike: An African Journal of New Writing*, Nsukka; since 1983 governor, Newsconcern International Foundation, London; since 1984 founder and publisher, *Uwa Ndi Igbo: A Bilingual Journal of Igbo Life and Arts*. Since 1998 goodwill ambassador, United Nations Population Fund. **Awards:** Margaret Wrong Memorial prize, 1959; Nigerian National trophy, 1960; Rockefeller fellowship, 1960; Unesco fellowship, 1963; Jock Campbell award (*New Statesman*), 1965; Commonwealth Poetry prize, 1973; Neil Gunn International fellowship, 1974; Lotus award for Afro-Asian writers, 1975; Nigerian National Merit award, 1979; Commonwealth Foundation award, 1984. Litt.D.: Dartmouth College, Hanover, New Hampshire, 1972; University of Southampton, 1975; University of Ife, 1978; University of Nigeria, 1981; University of Kent, Canterbury, 1982; University of Guelph, Ontario, 1984; Mount Allison University, Sackville, New Brunswick, 1984; Franklin Pierce College, Rindge, New Hampshire, 1985; University of Ibadan, 1989; Skidmore College, Saratoga Springs, New York, 1990; D. Univ.: University of Stirling, 1975; Open University, Milton Keynes, Buckinghamshire, 1989; LL.D.: University of Prince Edward Island, Charlottetown, 1976; D.H.L.: University of Massachusetts, 1977; Westfield College, London, 1989; Georgetown University, Washington, D.C., 1990; doctor of letters, honoris causa, Trinity College, Connecticut, 1999. Honorary Fellow, Modern Language Association (USA), 1975; member, Order of the Federal Republic of Nigeria, 1979; Honorary Member, American Academy, 1982; Fellow, Royal Society of Literature, 1983. **Member:** University of Lagos Council, 1966; chairman, Society of Nigerian Authors, 1966, and Association of Nigerian Authors, 1982–86; member, Anambra State Arts Council, 1977–79; Pro-Chancellor and Chairman of Council, Anambra State University of Technology, Enugu, 1986–88. Since 1981 member of the Executive Committee, Commonwealth Arts Organization, London; since 1983 member, International Social Prospects Academy, Geneva; since 1984 director, Okike Arts Center, Nsukka. Served on diplomatic missions for Biafra during Nigerian Civil War, 1967–69; deputy national president, People's Redemption Party, 1983. **Address:** P.O. Box 53, University of Nigeria, Nsukka, Anambra State, Nigeria.

PUBLICATIONS

Novels

Things Fall Apart. London, Heinemann, 1958; New York, McDowell Obolensky, 1959; introduction by Kwame Anthony Appiah, New York, Knopf, 1992.
No Longer at Ease. London, Heinemann, 1960; New York, Obolensky, 1961.
Arrow of God. London, Heinemann, 1964; New York, Day, 1967.
A Man of the People. London, Heinemann, and New York, Day, 1966.
Anthills of the Savannah. London, Heinemann, 1987; New York, Doubleday, 1988.
The African Trilogy. London, Picador, 1988.

Short Stories

The Sacrificial Egg and Other Stories. Onitsha, Etudo, 1962.
Girls at War. London, Heinemann, 1972; New York, Doubleday, 1973.

Poetry

Beware, Soul-Brother and Other Poems. Enugu, Nwankwo-Ifejika, 1971; revised edition, Enugu, Nwamife, and London, Heinemann, 1972; revised edition, as *Christmas in Biafra and Other Poems*, New York, Doubleday, 1973.
Another Africa (essay and poems), photographs by Robert Lyons. New York, Anchor Books, 1998.

Other (for children)

Chike and the River. London and New York, Cambridge University Press, 1966.
How the Leopard Got His Claws, with John Iroaganachi. Enugu, Nwamife, 1972; New York, Third Press, 1973.
The Flute. Enugu, Fourth Dimension, 1977.
The Drum. Enugu, Fourth Dimension, 1977.

Other

Morning Yet on Creation Day: Essays. London, Heinemann, and New York, Doubleday, 1975.
In Person: Achebe, Awoonor, and Soyinka at the University of Washington. Seattle, University of Washington African Studies Program, 1975.
The Trouble with Nigeria. Enugu, Fourth Dimension, 1983; London, Heinemann, 1984.
The World of the Ogbanje. Enugu, Fourth Dimension, 1986.
Hopes and Impediments: Selected Essays 1965–1987. London, Heinemann, 1988; New York, Doubleday, 1990.

The University and the Leadership Factor in Nigerian Politics. Enugu, ABIC, 1988.

A Tribute to James Baldwin. Amherst, University of Massachusetts Press, 1989.

The Voter, adapted by Ivan Vladislavic. Johannesburg, South Africa, Viva Books, 1996.

Home and Exile. New York, Oxford University Press, 2000.

Contributor, *The South Wind and the Sun*, edited by Kate Turkington. Johannesburg, South Africa, Thorold's Africana Books, 1996.

Contributor, *Order and Chaos.* Chicago, Great Books Foundation, 1997.

Editor, *The Insider: Stories of War and Peace from Nigeria.* Enugu, Nwankwo-Ifejika, and Chatham, New Jersey, Chatham Booksellers, 1971.

Editor, with Jomo Kenyatta and Amos Tutuola, *Winds of Change: Modern Stories from Black Africa.* London, Longman, 1977.

Editor, with Dubem Okafor, *Don't Let Him Die: An Anthology of Memorial Poems for Christopher Okigbo.* Enugu, Fourth Dimension, 1978.

Editor with C.L. Innes, *African Short Stories.* London, Heinemann, 1985.

Editor, *Beyond Hunger in Africa: Conventional Wisdom and a Vision of Africa in 2057.* Nairobi, Heinemann Kenya, and London, Currey, 1990.

*

Bibliography: In *Africana Library Journal* (New York), Spring 1970; *Chinua Achebe: A Bibliography* by B.M. Okpu, Lagos, Libriservice, 1984; *Chinua Achebe* by C.L. Innes, Cambridge University Press, 1990.

Critical Studies: *The Novels of Chinua Achebe* by G.D. Killam, London, Heinemann, and New York, Africana, 1969, revised edition, as *The Writings of Chinua Achebe,* Heinemann, 1977; *Chinua Achebe* by Arthur Ravenscroft, London, Longman, 1969, revised edition, 1977; *Chinua Achebe* by David Carroll, New York, Twayne, 1970, revised edition, London, Macmillan, 1980, 1990; *Chinua Achebe* by Kate Turkington, London, Arnold, 1977; *Critical Perspectives on Chinua Achebe* edited by Bernth Lindfors and C.L. Innes, London, Heimemann, and Washington, D.C., Three Continents Press, 1978; *Achebe's World: The Historical and Cultural Context of the Novels of Chinua Achebe* by Robert M. Wren, Washington, D.C., Three Continents Press, 1980, London, Longman, 1981; *The Four Novels of Chinua Achebe: A Critical Study* by Benedict C. Njoku, Bern, Switzerland, Lang, 1984; *The Traditional Religion and Its Encounter with Christianity in Achebe's Novels* by E.M. Okoye, Bern, Switzerland, Lang, 1987; *Chinua Achebe* by C.L. Innes, Cambridge, Cambridge University Press, 1990; *Reading Chinua Achebe: Language and Ideology in Fiction* by Simon Gikandi, London, Currey, 1991; *Approaches to Teaching Achebe's ''Things Fall Apart''* edited by Bernth Lindfors, New York, Modern Language Association of America, 1991; *Chinua Achebe: A Celebration* edited by Kirsten Holst Petersen and Anna Rutherford, Oxford, England, Heinemann, 1991; *Chinua Achebe: New Perspectives* by Umela Ojinmah, Ibadan, Spectrum, 1991; *Reading Chinua Achebe: Language and Ideology in Fiction* by Simon Gikandi, London, Currey, 1991; *Gods, Oracles and Divination* by Kalu Ogbaa, Trenton, N.J., Africa World Press, 1992; *Art, Rebellion and Redemption* by Romanus Okey Muonaka, New York, Lang, 1993; *South Asian Responses to Chinua Achebe* edited by Bernth Lindfors and Bala Kothandaraman, New Delhi, Prestige Books International, 1993; *Chinua Achebe, the Importance of Stories* (videocassette), 1996; *International Symposium for Chinua Achebe's 60th Birthday.* Ibadan, Nigeria, Heinemann Educational Books, 1996; *Colonial and Post-Colonial Discourse in the Novels of Yom Sangsop, Chinua Achebe, and Salman Rushdie* by Soonsik Kim, New York, P. Lang, 1996; *Form and Technique in the African Novel* by Olawale Awosika, Ibadan, Nigeria, Sam Bookman, 1997; *Chinua Achebe: A Biography* by Ezenwa-Ohaeto, Bloomington, Indiana University Press, 1997; *Conversations with Chinua Achebe* edited by Bernth Lindfors, Jackson, University Press of Mississippi, 1997; *A Teacher's Guide to African Narratives* by Sara Tallis O'Brien, Portsmouth, New Hampshire, Heinemann, 1998.

Chinua Achebe comments:

I am a political writer. My politics is concerned with universal human communication across racial and cultural boundaries as a means of fostering respect for all people. Such respect can issue only from understanding. So my primary concern is with clearing the channels of communication in my own neighborhood by hacking away at the thickets that choke them.

Africa's meeting with Europe must be accounted a terrible disaster in this matter of human understanding and respect. The nature of the meeting precluded any warmth of friendship. First Europe was an enslaver; then a colonizer. In either role she had no need and made little effort to understand or appreciate Africa; indeed she easily convinced herself that there was nothing there to justify the effort. Today our world is still bedeviled by the consequences of that cataclysmic encounter.

I was born into the colonial era, grew up in the heady years of nationalist protest and witnessed Africa's resumption of independence. (It was not, however, the same Africa which originally lost her freedom that now retained it, but a different Africa created in the image of Europe—but that's another story.) So I have seen in my not very long lifetime three major eras in precipitate succession, leaving us somewhat dazed. My response as a writer has been to try to keep pace with these torrential changes. First I had to tell Europe that the arrogance on which she sought to excuse her pillage of Africa, i.e., that Africa was the Primordial Void, was sheer humbug; that Africa had a history, a religion, a civilization. We reconstructed this history and civilization and displayed it to challenge the stereotype and the cliché. Actually it was not to Europe alone that I spoke. I spoke also to that part of ourselves that had come to accept Europe's opinion of us. And I was not alone nor even the first.

But the gauntlet had barely left our hands when a new historic phase broke on us. Europe conceded independence to us and we promptly began to misuse it, or rather those leaders to whom we entrusted the wielding of our new power and opportunity did. So we got mad at them and came out brandishing novels of disenchantment. Actually we had all been duped. No independence was given—it was never given but taken, anyway. Europe had only made a tactical withdrawal on the political front and while we sang our anthem and unfurled our flag she was securing her iron grip behind us in the economic field. And our leaders in whose faces we hurled our disenchantment neither saw nor heard because they were not leaders at all but marionettes.

So the problem remains for Africa, for black people, for all deprived peoples and for the world. And so for the writer, for he is like the puppy in our proverb: that stagnant water in the potsherd is for none other but him. As long as one people sit on another and are deaf to their cry, so long will understanding and peace elude all of us.

* * *

Chinua Achebe established his reputation with *Things Fall Apart,* one of the first novels to be published in post-independence Africa. It was admired for many reasons, notably the tragic profundity of its theme and the insights it offered on traditional Ibo life. Western critics also approved of Achebe's acceptance of the formal conventions of the genre even while he proved that the English language could be modified to express the very different African cultural context. This book became both archetype and classic, and many budding authors have attempted to emulate Achebe without demonstrating his competence. *Things Fall Apart* has been translated into many languages and is an established text in schools. It has sustained extensive critical examination and yet its poignant story still retains its capacity to move the reader.

Achebe's declared intention was to provide evidence that traditional African life was not the primitive barbarism that was the common judgment of the colonialists. Set in the early period of the initial British intrusion into Nigeria, the novel shows a society which, if not perfect, had structure and dignity; where human relations had order and security. Into this world came the foreigner and ''things fall apart.'' The title, taken from Yeats, makes a subtle comment on the theme, because it expresses some degree of inevitability rather than calculated cause. Perhaps neither side could foresee the consequences of actions which seemed entirely reasonable within their own context. Though setting straight the record, this is not an anti-colonialist novel in the simplistic sense. Achebe discerns a terrifying truth, that when powerful worlds clash, even the best of men are defeated and only the accommodators prosper. Okonkwo exemplifies all the virtues of his people, but he is too harsh and inflexible to tolerate the inescapable changes. His friend Obierika is a far weaker but more sensible person. He survives, like others who yield their honor and adapt, preferring prosperity at the cost of their heritage. While understanding that this is a reasonable decision, which in time created the society which Achebe inherits, he clearly indicates where honor rests. Okonkwo is ''the greatest man.''

Three further novels form a tetralogy which covers Ibo history from the first arrival of the British to the violent coup of 1966. Though third to be published, it is *Arrow of God* which carries on the historical sequence. Its theme is similar to that of *Things Fall Apart.* Ezeulu, a distinguished village man, this time a high priest, finds himself in conflict with the now established British administration, a conflict activated as much by ignorance as malice. Angered by imprisonment and the failure of his people to assist him, Ezeulu imposes harsh penalties upon them. At last their misery is so acute they turn to the Christian missionaries who are preaching a less oppressive religion. With a terrible irony the priest's fierce battle to sustain the tribal god causes his destruction. Again there is the depiction of strength, admirable in itself, but too harsh to see the advantage and necessity of compromise. The man who most exemplifies traditional virtues, just like Okonkwo, brings about their destruction along with his own. In a further plot twist, Ezeulu sends his son to learn the ways of the white missionaries. He does not anticipate the conversion of the boy who then denies his heritage and begins to exemplify the cultural ambivalence and generational opposition which education inescapably brings.

The other two novels examine this dualistic situation. The revealing title of *No Longer at Ease* comes from T.S. Eliott. Obi, a bright, eager young man, is sent to England to study and returns to the luxury of the high Civil Service appointment previously reserved for the British. He is confident and optimistic, feeling he represents the hopes for a better Nigeria which will flourish under the direction of this new class of youthful, educated, and therefore honest and efficient administrators. In fact his position imposes peculiar strains. A salary, huge by village standards, proves insufficient to live the European life expected of him. His indifference, even scorn, of the values of his tradition, learned during his time in England, offends his people who had funded him. Obi is exposed as an alien and becomes uncomfortable and ineffective in both worlds. He drifts into taking bribes and is soon as corrupt as those he used to despise. He is an inept crook, however, and is charged and imprisoned. At one level this is a depressing tale. If someone as decent as Obi succumbs, can anyone succeed in improving conditions in Nigeria? The cynical colonial characters express only passing surprise, gloating to find their prejudice confirmed: ''All Africans are corrupt.'' Achebe has something much deeper to communicate. Given this history and these conditions, how is it possible for even the idealist to maintain his integrity? In the final analysis when the struggle with the system destroys even the best, who shall be blamed? It is a contemporary application of the issue raised in the two historical novels.

The situation in *A Man of the People* is even more depressing. It reflects the terrible political deterioration which Nigeria has suffered since independence. ''The Man,'' is Nanga, a brutally corrupt politician who nevertheless manages to remain both popular and successful. The novel examines this disastrous paradox. The term ''man of the people'' seems to indicate an admirable figure. Then, as Nanga's vile deeds are revealed, the reader reverses his judgment. How can a crook be ''of the people?'' In an ending of shattering pessimism, Achebe seems to accept that people as greedy and immoral as these deserve such a man who does nothing more than exploit their own similar values; envy not accusation motivates the voters. The dedicated intellectual, Odili, is drawn not as the hero come to redeem his people, but as an arrogant and incompetent fool. His ideas are far more remote from the people's than Nanga's. Corruption they understand, merely wishing to share in it; idealism seems absurd and irrelevant. Naively unpolitical Odili is defeated and in the dismal conclusion makes off with the funds committed to his election campaign, justifying his theft with typical intellectual rationalizations. The nation falls into chaotic violence.

Achebe's pessimism was prescient. Social cohesion in Nigeria disintegrated. When the disastrous civil war broke out he was a prominent participant on the Biafran side. These efforts so preoccupied him and induced so deep a discouragement that since 1966 his output has been slender. From the battle came some short stories which realistically depicted the sufferings—and the continuing corruption—within the cause to which he had dedicated himself with such idealism and hope. His most poignant comments on the war are in the poems of *Beware, Soul-Brother.*

In 1987 a new novel appeared. *Anthills of the Savannah* addresses the same themes. The decades of independence have brought only minimal reasons for hope. Ruling governments have oscillated between corrupt citizens and violent army generals. For the first time Achebe chooses to disguise the setting by inventing a fictional state, Kangan. The rulers and their practices are closely modeled on the actual atrocities of Amin's Uganda. This may be intended to universalize the African situation, or indicate that Achebe can no longer bear to contemplate directly the misery to which his own country has come. But there are some flickers of hope. Interestingly enough, it is the female characters who display strength and assurance through the corruption and violence.

Perhaps Achebe has begun to lose confidence in the generation which he has served. Nevertheless, his early quartet stands as a masterly achievement that will inform generations of readers of the disasters colonialism brought to Africa—sometimes with benign intentions. The tragic realization in the books of the human misery that results from massive social and economic change brings to the mind the Wessex novels of Hardy.

—John Povey

ACKROYD, Peter

Nationality: British. **Born:** London, 5 October 1949. **Education:** St. Benedict's, Ealing, 1960–67; Clare College, Cambridge, 1968–71; Yale University, New Haven, Connecticut (Mellon fellow), 1971–73. **Career:** Literary editor, 1973–77, and joint managing editor, 1978–81, the *Spectator,* London; chief book reviewer, the *Times,* London, from 1986; editor, president, and CEO, Tuttle Publishing; editor, Element Books, 1996–97, CEO, 1997–99. Lives in London. **Awards:** Maugham award, 1984; Whitbread award, for biography, 1985, for fiction, 1986; Royal Society of Literature Heinemann award, for non-fiction, 1985; *Guardian* Fiction prize, 1985. Fellow, Royal Society of Literature, 1984. H.D.L.: Exeter University, 1993. **Agent:** Anthony Sheil Associates, 43 Doughty Street, London WC1N 2LF, England.

PUBLICATIONS

Novels

The Great Fire of London. London, Hamish Hamilton, 1982; Chicago, University of Chicago Press, 1988.
The Last Testament of Oscar Wilde. London, Hamish Hamilton, and New York, Harper, 1983.
Hawksmoor. London, Hamish Hamilton, 1985; New York, Harper, 1986.
Chatterton. London, Hamish Hamilton, 1987; New York, Grove Press, 1988.
First Light. London, Hamish Hamilton, and New York, Grove Weidenfeld, 1989.
English Music. London, Hamish Hamilton, 1991; New York, Knopf, 1993.
The House of Doctor Dee. London, Hamish Hamilton, 1993.
Dan Lemo and the Limehouse Golem. London, Sinclair Stevenson, 1994; as *The Trial of Elizabeth Cree,* New York, Doubleday, 1995.
Blake. London, Sinclair Stevenson, 1995; New York, Knopf, 1996.
Dan Leno and the Limehouse Golem. London, Minerva, 1995.
The Plato Papers: A Prophecy. New York, Doubleday/Nan A. Talese, 2000.

Uncollected Short Stories

''The Inheritance,'' in *London Tales,* edited by Julian Evans. London, Hamish Hamilton, 1983.
''Ringing in the Good News,'' in *The Times* (London), 24 December 1985.

Poetry

London Lickpenny. London, Ferry Press, 1973.
Country Life. London, Ferry Press, 1978.
The Diversions of Purley and Other Poems. London, Hamish Hamilton, 1987.

Other

Notes for a New Culture: An Essay on Modernism. London, Vision Press, and New York, Barnes and Noble, 1976.
Dressing Up: Transvestism and Drag: The History of an Obsession. London, Thames and Hudson, and New York, Simon and Schuster, 1979.
Ezra Pound and His World. London, Thames and Hudson, and New York, Scribner, 1981.
T.S. Eliot (biography). London, Hamish Hamilton, and New York, Simon and Schuster, 1984.
Dickens (biography). London, Sinclair Stevenson, and New York, Harper Collins, 1990.
The Life of Thomas More. London, Chatto and Windus, 1998.
Foreword, *Thomas Chatterton and Romantic Culture,* edited by Nick Groom. New York, St. Martin's Press, 1999.
Editor, *PEN New Fiction.* London, Quartet, 1984.
Editor, *The Picture of Dorian Gray,* by Oscar Wilde. London, Penguin, 1985.
Editor, *Dickens' London: An Imaginative Vision.* London, Headline, 1987.

* * *

By the time Peter Ackroyd published his first novel in 1982, he was already well known in the literary world as a poet, critic, literary theorist, and cultural historian. Since his début as a novelist he has further enhanced his reputation as a non-fiction writer, first with his award-winning biography of T.S. Eliot and more recently with his imaginatively daring biographies of Charles Dickens, William Blake, and Thomas More. Before the appearance of his first novel, it seemed that his writing career was likely to develop in the fields of literary criticism and biography, but with ten novels in quick succession between 1982 and 1999 he has established himself as one of the most gifted and imaginative English novelists to have emerged during the recent past.

Ackroyd's polemical book, *Notes for a New Culture,* contains a relentless attack on the parochialism and impoverishment of contemporary English culture, especially literature and the academic literary establishment; he makes clear his intellectual allegiance to Continental (primarily French and German) models and theories descending from such figures as de Sade, Nietzsche, Mallarmé, and Husserl, in opposition to what he sees as the stultifying tradition of empiricism, positivism, and humanism still dominant in English artistic and intellectual life. He insists on the autonomy and formal absoluteness of language, on the way in which language constitutes meaning only within itself, and he therefore challenges the philosophical basis of orthodox realistic fiction, regarding its conventions as no longer having any validity for the modern writer. As might be expected, his novels are not conventionally realistic, but his innovative approach to fiction has not led him into the cul-de-sacs of hyper-selfconscious experimentalism or navel-gazing phenomenology. On the contrary, each novel possesses a strong narrative drive and is highly readable, demonstrating that Ackroyd has not felt the need to reject storytelling in order to develop his own type of literary fiction.

There is an element of deception in the title of Ackroyd's novels, especially as the first four, *The Great Fire of London, The Last Testament of Oscar Wilde, Hawksmoor,* and *Chatterton* could be the titles of historical or biographical studies rather than works of fiction. The fire in *The Great Fire of London* is not that of 1666, but an apocalyptic fictional one that begins with the burning of a film set for a screen adaptation of *Little Dorrit.* As if to substantiate his theoretical point that writing emerges from other writing rather than from life, Ackroyd draws on Dickens's novel in many ways, thus emphasizing the fictionality of his own fictional world, however realistic it may appear in some respects. Ackroyd's novel is centrally concerned with the perpetual human activity of creating fictions in life as well as in art. The short opening section of *The Great Fire of London,* ''the story so far,'' outlines the plot of *Little Dorrit* and ends: ''although it could not be described as a true story, certain events have certain consequences''—including, of course, the writing of Ackroyd's novel. Dickens's eponymous heroine and the novel itself feature prominently in the minds of many of Ackroyd's characters, including Spenser Spender (a filmmaker, with two poets' names who is determined to put the novel on the screen), Rowan Phillips (a Cambridge don currently working on Dickens), and Audrey Skelton (a telephone operator who is possessed by the spirit of Little Dorrit during a séance). The setting of much of *Little Dorrit,* the Marshalsea Prison, also provides a link between the two novels because its site is visited by several of Ackroyd's characters. With its panorama of London in the 1980s from left-wing activists to gay bars, *The Great Fire of London* is at least as much a London novel as *Little Dorrit.* Ackroyd's narrative structure, in which several strands begin in parallel and gradually intertwine and coalesce, is itself derived from Dickens's methods and techniques, especially in his later novels such as *Little Dorrit.* By using one of the greatest of English novels as his point of departure, Ackroyd inevitably takes the risk of being unflatteringly compared with Dickens, but *The Great Fire of London* must be taken on its own terms, not Dickens's, and as such it is an exuberant, inventive, and accomplished piece of writing.

Ackroyd's second novel draws its inspiration from the life of an important late Victorian writer. *The Last Testament of Oscar Wilde* is the testament that Wilde himself did not write but that Ackroyd has written for him in the form of a journal-cum-memoir covering that last few months of Wilde's life in Paris in 1900. The book therefore purports to be Wilde's autobiographical confessions in the tradition of writing that connects St. Augustine with Rousseau and De Quincey. To write *The Last Testament of Oscar Wilde* Ackroyd must have steeped himself in Wilde's biography as well as his writing, and presumably could have written yet another study of the man and his work. Instead Ackroyd has chosen the freedom of fiction to enter imaginatively into Wilde's mind as he lives through his last weeks in France and simultaneously offers an explanation of his famous rise and infamous fall. The obvious danger with a novel of this type, not only about an historical personage but written from his point of view, is that readers will be tempted to compare the ''facts'' with the fictional re-creation, but this would be to approach the novel in far too literal-minded a way. As a fictional character, Ackroyd's Wilde cannot be the historical Wilde: for all its ''factual'' content, *The Last Testament of Oscar Wilde* is primarily a work of the imagination about the relationship between the artist and the world and about the difference between fictional and historical truth.

The skill with which Ackroyd creates a style and tone of voice for his narrator and sustains it throughout *The Last Testament of Oscar Wilde* is a remarkable technical achievement, but it pales beside the ludic and verbal virtuosity of *Hawksmoor,* in which he plays far more elaborate games with fact and fiction, history and imagination. The title is the name of Sir Christopher Wren's most distinguished assistant, Nicholas Hawksmoor, the great architect responsible for some of London's finest churches (referred to in *The Great Fire of London*), but in the novel these churches are attributed to Nicholas Dyer while Hawksmoor himself is a modern Detective Chief Superintendent investigating a series of murders in the East End. Although *Hawksmoor* contains characters who belong to history and draws heavily on various historical sources, it is not an historical novel in the usual sense; indeed, it radically subverts the conventions of historical fiction. In a concluding note Ackryod states that ''this version of history is my own invention'' and that ''any relation to real people, either living or dead, is entirely coincidental.'' The six odd-numbered chapters in a book in which numerology plays a significant part are set in the early 18th century and are narrated by Dyer in a contemporary idiom, complete with old spellings and the initial capitalization of many words. Although a builder of churches, Dyer is secretly a Satanist and devotee of black magic, as well as being an opponent of the new scientific empiricism of the Royal Society. He dedicates his buildings to the dark powers by ensuring a human sacrifice in connection with each one. The six even-numbered chapters, set two and a half centuries later, provide a third-person narration of the bizarre and puzzling killings associated with the same churches and of Hawksmoor's attempt to track down the culprit. Ackroyd creates mystery and suspense, but unlike orthodox writers of crime and detection he does not provide a solution. Despite the time shift between the two narratives, they flow smoothly into each other and run strictly in parallel. The last words of the first chapter are also the first words of the second chapter. For example, the name of Dyer's first sacrificial victim is the same as that of the first person murdered in the twentieth-century narrative. Time dissolves so that the modern policeman is, in a sense, investigating crimes of the past. One of Ackroyd's central concerns is the human continuity associated with place, specifically the East End of London, in spite of all the changes wrought by the passage of time. *Hawksmoor* is as multi-layered as the archaeological heritage beneath the baroque churches built by Dyer. The dazzling erudition and ingenuity of Ackroyd's third novel bring to mind such authors as Borges, Nabokov, Pynchon, and Eco without seeming derivative in the pejorative sense.

Like *The Last Testament of Oscar Wilde, Chatterton* fictionalises the last part of an important literary figure's life, but in other respects, especially its handling of time and form, this novel is much closer to *Hawksmoor,* and is equally rich in internal echoes and cross-references. Like Ackroyd himself, the ''marvellous boy'' Thomas Chatterton was a master of pastiche and ''faking,'' and it is easy to understand why Ackroyd should have been attracted by the fictional, rather than the biographical, possibilities offered by this extraordinary eighteenth-century poet. Chatterton committed suicide in 1770 while still in his teens, and for his Romantic successors his bizarre and tragic death ensured his status as a martyr in the cause of Art and Poetry. At a time when there was a great revival of interest in the Middle Ages, Chatterton was one of several poets who adopted a medieval style and presented their literary pastiches not as ''imitations'' but as authentic poetry of the past which they had unearthed. Chatterton attributed his ''Rowley'' poems to a fifteenth-century monk. However only some sections of the novel are set in the eighteenth century, with Chatterton either speaking in his own voice or being described. Much of the novel concerns a modern and frequently comic quest by a young poet and a much older woman novelist to discover the truth about Chatterton's death. An eighteenth-century manuscript provides these literary detectives with clues suggesting that Chatterton's suicide was itself faked and that he survived under another name. Interwoven with the eighteenth-century and twentieth-century narratives are sections set in Victorian England dealing with Henry Wallis's famous and highly romanticised painting of Chatterton's death (1856), for which the model was George Meredith, then himself a young poet. In this intricately structured novel about the reality of literature and art and the fictionality of reality, Ackroyd continues to explore the main themes of *Hawksmoor,* but the pervasive issues of plagiarism and faking focus particular attention on the ambiguity of art (''a lie that tells the truth'') and its relationship with life, which is no less ambiguous.

Ackroyd's 1989 novel, *First Light,* is his longest and arguably his most ambitious, but after *Hawksmoor* and *Chatterton* it seems disappointing. This is not because *First Light* is any less readable then its two predecessors. Again there is a mystery to be investigated—an archaeological one—and this provides a strong narrative drive. The problem arises from the task Ackroyd sets himself—to resuscitate pastoral romance by writing a modern version of it. Iris Murdoch is another writer who has attempted to revivify pastoral and romance, and *First Light* is more Murdochian than Ackroyd's earlier novels, but both novelists experience considerable difficulty in reconciling pastoral conventions with the contemporary world without being fey. The excavation of a Neolithic passage grave in a rural backwater of the West Country—indeed of Hardy's Wessex—is what brings a fairly large and diverse cast of characters together in a lavishly textured story of intrigue, comedy, and pathos. A further dimension is added by the astronomical investigation of a giant star at a nearby observatory, which parallels the archaeological probe into the past. Literary allusions, especially to Hardy's fiction, abound in Ackroyd's imaginative exploration of time, history, space, and landscape, yet the total effect is more precious and etiolated than in the two city novels that preceded *First Light.*

Ackroyd has said that he is not interested in realism in the novel, and has further developed in his next two novels, *English Music* and *The House of Doctor Dee,* a genre in which fact and fiction are equally intertwined. This choice suggests that the traditional confines of fiction are inadequate to express what Ackroyd wants to say. In both novels Ackroyd has incorporated historically ''dead'' people, who talk to the living fictional characters with the purpose of giving meaning to some quest of his ''living'' characters. As a writer who particularly projects what he has to say through other voices, he has been likened to a ventriloquist, or a ''polyquilivist.'' *The Music of England* refers to composed music, but also to landmarks in the whole of English literature, painting, and architecture. The novel provides an idiosyncratic survey of these arts, brought together in a total harmony through the imagination of Timothy Harcombe, an old bachelor, who recalls his boyhood life in the early 1920s. At night in alternating chapters, Timothy in either sleep or dream or trance, talks to historical and fictional characters and interacts with them as real people. The historical figures represent an unbroken link in ''the great tradition'' in English artistic creativity. Blake, for example, has him ''write'' a Song of Albion, naming English poets up to the end of the nineteenth century who have been conscious of this English heritage. Ackroyd's choice of those who defend the ancient springs is of course a subjective one, and few would include the very minor Ernest Dowson, nor really expect Blake (if he could have read him) to admire him at all.

Pastiche is again a strong feature in *The House of Doctor Dee,* set, like *English Music,* in Clerkenwell, London, where the area is at least as important as the characters. At times Ackroyd seems to have made it more so, letting the atmosphere of shady back streets block the light that would develop his characters more fully. The discovery by Matthew Palmer, a historical researcher, that a house he has inherited from his father once belonged to the Elizabethan astrologer, Dr. John Dee, is only the loose framework of the novel. Yet the framework, as in all Ackroyd's novels, is not limited to a simple structure or time scale and depends on a cumulative effect of rapid change of scene, period, and minutiae of often apparently irrelevant detail for the total effect. It is the means for informing the reader, amongst much else, about Dr. Dee, black magic, and Palmer's father, who it transpires had a sexual relationship with a transvestite. Matthew as a character hardly matters, but what he explores does.

Dan Lemo and the Limehouse Golem was publicised as a departure for Ackroyd and described by the publisher as ''a ground-breaking commercial entertainment.'' If it is taken at face value as an imitation of the Victorian crime novel, it indeed succeeds very well, with its search for the perpetrator of horrifically detailed serial killings. Inexact clues point suspicion at all of the main characters, but deliberately Ackroyd provides no solution. Many of the characters are not what they seem to be and have double identities. Lambeth Lizzie, hanged for the murder of her husband, may or may not have been guilty, but she wore men's clothes, while the eponymous Dan Lemo, a rather repulsive music-hall artist, is a female impersonator. The whole question of reality and appearance is raised by the use of ''golem'' of the title, a ''mythical creature able to dissolve in thin air'' but which takes its identity by absorbing the souls of others. *Dan Lemo and the Limehouse Golem* is a wild theatrical extravaganza, but Ackroyd justifies his insistence that the reader question everything in it by quoting from Oscar Wilde's *The Truth of Masks:* ''Truth is independent of facts always, inventing or selecting them at pleasure. The true dramatist shows us life under the condition of art, not art in the form of life.''

Except for *The Last Testament of Oscar Wilde, Milton in America* is the only one of Ackroyd's novels to take place in a setting other than England. *Milton in America* is a novel predicated on the possibility that John Milton, the English poet, fled England near the end of the Commonwealth, and ended up in New England. Divided into two sections, ''Eden,'' and ''Fall,'' the novel employs an extended metaphor of Milton himself enacting the role of Lucifer the fallen angel in the historical Milton's *Paradise Lost:* forced to leave heavenly England, and make his way in the savage hell of New England. The novel traces John Milton's ascendancy as the leader of a settlement named New Milton, whose population evinces all the worst characteristics of the Puritanism, including the burning of suspected witches, overt hatred of Catholics, racism, sexism, homophobia, among others. Ackroyd brilliantly utilizes the American genre of the utopian-community novel (one thinks of Hawthorne's *The Blithedale Romance* and Morrison's *Paradise*) to his own ends. Here, religious hypocrisy, embodied in the character of Milton, is shown to lead to horrific ends.

Returning to his setting of choice, London, Ackroyd's latest novel, *The Plato Papers,* once again breaks new ground. Instead of his usual trope of seeing the past mirrored in the present, Ackroyd sets his new novel in a London of the very distant future, circa A.D. 3700.

In this London, angels are everyday members of society, and people have ancient Roman-and Greek-sounding names like Ornatus, as well as Sparkler and Madrigal, that might come from the Victorian music hall stage. The plot in this shortest of Ackroyd's novels revolves around a character named Plato, who is the chief orator of the city of London. Plato's job is to explain to the citizens of London their past. It has always been difficult to see Ackroyd directly in his characters, but with Plato, we are finally able to see the author writing himself directly into a character. Plato, whose hilarious misreadings of canonical writers of the distant past like Dickens (claimed as author of Darwin's *Origin of the Species*) and Freud (claimed as a stand-up comedian) are good examples of the literary technique of defamiliarization. Re-writing the story of Plato (the philosopher) and the Cave, Ackroyd has his future-Plato visit another cave, which turns out to be the earth as we know it, circa 1999. Like Milton in *Milton in America* (who goes off for six weeks into the wilderness), *The Plato Papers* ends with Plato self-banished from his beloved London, accused by his society of corrupting young people by teaching that there is an alternate reality. Readers of Ackroyd's ten novels have come to know and appreciate the nuances of this alternate reality.

—Peter Lewis, revisions by Geoffrey Elborn and Richard Almonte

ADAMS, Glenda

Nationality: Australian. **Born:** Sydney, 1939. **Education:** University of Sydney, B.A. (honours) 1962; Columbia University, New York, M.S. 1965. **Family:** Has one daughter. **Career:** Writing Workshop instructor, Columbia University, New York, and Sarah Lawrence College; fiction writing teacher at University of Technology, Sydney; associate director, Teachers and Writers Collaborative, New York, 1973–76. **Awards:** Miles Franklin Literary award, 1987; *Age* Fiction Book of the Year, 1990; National Book Council award for fiction, 1991. **Member:** Australian Society of Authors; Australian Writers Guild. **Agent:** Goodman Associates, 500 West End Ave., New York, New York 10024, USA. **Address:** Department of English, Columbia University, New York, New York 10027, USA.

Publications

Novels

Games of the Strong. Sydney, Angus and Robertson, 1982; New York, Cane Hill Press, 1989.
Dancing on Coral. New York, Viking, and Sydney and London, Angus and Robertson, 1988.
Longleg. Sydney, Angus and Robertson, 1990; New York, Cane Hill Press, 1992.
The Tempest of Clemenza. New York, Angus & Robertson, 1996.

Short Stories

Lies and Stories. N.p., 1976.
The Hottest Night of the Year. Sydney, Angus and Robertson, 1979; New York, Cane Hill Press, 1989.

Plays

Pride, 1993.
Wrath, 1993.
The Monkey Trap. Sydney, Australia, Griffin Theatre, 1998.

*

Manuscript Collection: Australian Defense Force Academy, University of New South Wales, Canberra, Australia.

* * *

Born in Sydney, Glenda Adams left an Australia she found too restrictive in 1964 and lived in New York for many years before finally returning to her home country in what she sees as the completion of a personal odyssey. Her first collection of short pieces, written and published in various periodicals in the United States, was *Lies and Stories,* but *The Hottest Night of the Year,* which includes seven stories from the first collection together with more recent work, was the first book to establish her reputation. Most of the stories are written in the first person and concern vulnerable or alienated female protagonists, who fiercely insist nevertheless on retaining their individuality and independence. The first six stories seem to be set in Sydney (though the setting is not always named) and deal with the experience of childhood and adolescence. Running through them is a note of implicit protest against the mistreatment of women. This emerges clearly in "The Music Masters," with its bitterly misognynistic father, and is carried on in several stories about the early days of marriages in which husbands invariably dismiss and behave condescendingly toward their new wives. The later stories are more playful and whimsically self-conscious in form. "Twelfth Night, or The Passion," for instance, shows the narrator determinedly exercising her option to have an improbably happy ending, whereas "Reconstruction of an Event" ostentatiously flaunts its different narrative possibilities. The stories are written in a deceptively simple style and marked often by a bizarre kind of humour and almost surreal disconnectedness, qualities that will emerge in Adams's later fiction.

Games of the Strong is, in retrospect, Adams's least characteristic novel. Written in the genre of the dystopian novel (a surprisingly ubiquitous one in Australian fiction) it describes an impoverished police state; dissidents are expelled to "The Island," where they are left to die, where poverty is rampant, and where no one is to be trusted. Its heroine, Neila, is hardly political at all and is mostly concerned to discover the truth about her parents' deaths (allegedly in a car accident), but slowly she is drawn into resisting the injustices and inequalities she sees all around her. It is a world that is full of betrayals and one in which, although she insists constantly on her own weakness ("I have no valour," "I am a coward and did not want to get hurt"), Neila develops into another of Adams's sturdily independent female protagonists. Perhaps the most puzzling aspect of the novel is its allegorical intention or lack of it. There is only one reference to this world, a brief mention of David Oistrakh playing a Beethoven concerto, but there are several contemptuous observations on outside democratic powers that willingly tolerate the excesses of "The Complex."

Adams came into her own as a writer, however, with her two recent novels. *Dancing on Coral,* which won the Miles Franklin Award for the best Australian novel of the year, is a very funny and witty novel, its style built around a sense of derangement, non sequiturs, and conversations not connecting or at cross purposes. Lark Watters (who had appeared briefly in one of Adams's early stories) grows up in Sydney during the 1960s and falls in love with Solomon Blank, but he wins a scholarship in America. Then she is attracted to an American named Tom Brown. She and Donna Bird, her rival for Tom's attentions, embark on a freighter bound for the United States, but en route Lark, tormented by her dominant companion, allows her to be left behind when the ship sails.

The novel is in part a satire on what the author sees as a decade of silliness. It is peopled by grotesques, like the German captain of the freighter and Lark's father, who is building a coffin for himself and who indulges in trivial pursuits, such as learning how to get around London and memorising all the stops on the air route from Sydney to London. Underneath the comedy the serious point is being made, through a letter that Lark's mother writes to her saying that her father has disappeared: "Too, before I left on my holiday he said to tell you, you have made your own way in this tricky world. You have done it all yourself. There has not been much help from us, I am aware." Bereft of both lover and husband at the end, Lark is finally free to be her own person.

Independence is also a theme of *Longleg,* Adams's most disturbing novel. William Badger is ten when the novel opens shortly after the war and is fearful that his mother—beautiful, young, and dissatisfied with the country she lives in and with everything else—will leave him, which she does. When she eventually returns she is a different woman, from whom William closes himself off. We see William then at various stages of his life and in various places as he grows through relationships with women as if to gain the security he has never had—with Meg Meese, who takes him cave exploring with her Trogs; Tillie Pepper and her group of radical activists, the Pan-European Barbarians; and Amanda, the married woman he falls in love with until finally he realizes the truth of what the most sympathetic of the Barbarians had said to him: "I think you can always recognize when you have to take a new path and when you should stay where you are." It is a brilliantly inventive novel and in its protagonist, William, Adams has created her most sympathetic character.

Certain types appear constantly in Glenda Adams's fiction: the vulnerable adolescent or young woman often just married; the older, sophisticated woman who is a threat to the bride; idiosyncratic or irresponsible parents. Her principal characters are questers seeking to find the identity so many people leave undiscovered; even the constant name-changing is a symbol of their uncertainty. Voyages dominate her two most recent novels, which are both very funny and at times poignant.

—Laurie Clancy

ADAMS, Richard (George)

Nationality: British. **Born:** Newbury, Berkshire, 9 May 1920. **Education:** Bradfield College, Berkshire, 1933–38; Worcester College, Oxford, 1938–39, 1946–48, B.A. in modern history 1948, M.A. 1953. **Military Service:** Served in the British Army, 1940–46. **Family:** Married Barbara Elizabeth Acland in 1949; two daughters. **Career:** Worked in the Ministry of Housing and Local Government, London, 1948–68; Assistant Secretary, Department of the Environment, London, 1968–74. Writer-in-residence, University of Florida, Gainesville, 1975, and Hollins College, Virginia, 1976. President, Royal Society for the Prevention of Cruelty to Animals, 1980–82 (resigned). Independent Conservative parliamentary candidate for Spelthorne, 1983. **Awards:** Library Association Carnegie medal, 1972; *Guardian* award, 1973. Fellow, Royal Society of Literature, 1975. **Agent:** David Higham Associates Ltd., 5–8 Lower John Street, London W1R 4HA. **Address:** 26 Church Street, Whitechurch, Hampshire RG28 7AR, England.

PUBLICATIONS

Novels

Watership Down. London, Collings, 1972; New York, Macmillan, 1974.
Shardik. London, Allen Lane-Collings, 1974; New York, Simon and Schuster, 1975.
The Plague Dogs. London, Allen Lane-Collings, 1977; New York, Knopf, 1978.
The Girl in a Swing. London, Allen Lane, and New York, Knopf, 1980.
Maia. London, Viking, 1984; New York, Knopf, 1985.
Traveller. New York, Knopf, 1988; London, Hutchinson, 1989.
Tales from Watership Down, with decorations by John Lawrence. New York, Knopf, 1996.

Fiction (for children)

The Bureaucats. London, Viking Kestrel, 1985.

Poetry

The Tyger Voyage (for children). London, Cape, and New York, Knopf, 1976.
The Ship's Cat (for children). London, Cape, and New York, Knopf, 1977.
The Legend of Te Tuna. Los Angeles, Sylvester and Orphanos, 1982; London, Sidgwick and Jackson, 1986.

Other

Voyage Through the Antarctic, with Ronald Lockley. London, Allen Lane, 1982; New York, Knopf, 1983.
A Nature Diary. London, Viking, 1985; New York, Viking, 1986.
The Day Gone By: An Autobiography. London, Hutchinson, 1990; New York, Knopf, 1991.
Editor, *Occasional Poets: An Anthology.* London, Viking, 1986.

Other (for children)

Nature Through the Seasons, with Max Hooper. London, Kestrel, and New York, Simon and Schuster, 1975.
Nature Day and Night, with Max Hooper. London, Kestrel, and New York, Viking Press, 1978.
The Watership Down Film Picture Book. London, Allen Lane, and New York, Macmillan, 1978.

The Iron Wolf and Other Stories (folktales). London, Allen Lane, 1980; as *The Unbroken Web,* New York, Crown, 1980.
Editor, *Grimm's Fairy Tales.* London, Routledge, 1981.
Editor, *Richard Adams's Favourite Animal Stories.* London, Octopus, 1981.
Editor, *The Best of Ernest Thompson Seton.* London, Fontana, 1982.

*

Richard Adams comments:

(1991) I can only say, like Trollope, that I am an entertainer, and the essence of fiction is that the reader should wish to turn the page.

* * *

Originally published as a book for children, *Watership Down* made Richard Adams's name as a novelist by becoming one of the leading bestsellers of the 1970s. Set in the rabbit world of the English countryside, it is primarily an adventure story, original in conception, but with excellent natural descriptions and evocations of such human virtues as courage, loyalty, and modesty. The story begins when a peaceful rabbit warren in Berkshire is destroyed by a new housing development and a party of young bucks escape, thanks to the ability of one of their number, Fiver, to foresee the future. What follows is an odyssey to find a new home, during which the rabbits encounter many strange and terrifying adventures. Danger comes from human beings, poisoned fields, machines, and also from another group of rabbits led by the despotic General Woundwort. ''In combat he was terrifying, fighting entirely to kill, indifferent to any wounds he received himself and closing with his adversaries until his weight overbore and exhausted them. Those who had no heart to oppose him were not long in the feeling that here was a leader indeed.'' Eventually, the rabbits achieve their goal but have to fight a fiercely contested battle to protect their new territory.

Adams, a senior civil servant when he wrote *Watership Down,* admitted that many parts of the novel were created as stories to please his children during long car journeys and that much of the factual information came from R.M. Lockley's study *The Private Life of the Rabbit,* but his work is very much a fictional unity. Some critics have suggested that *Watership Down* is an allegory on man's indifference to the natural life of his planet and, taken that way, it presents a grimly satirical view; but the novel is best seen as part of the fantastic strain in English literature, in line with the work of C.S. Lewis, J.R.R. Tolkien, and Kenneth Grahame.

In his second novel, *Shardik,* Adams shifted his center of literary influences to the adventure genre of H. Rider Haggard and John Buchan. The action and setting are timeless and the background imaginary—the Beklan empire which has been over-run, and its inhabitants, the Ortelgans, enslaved. When a large bear is driven from their forests, the Ortelgans take him to be an ancient bear-god called Shardik. With his help they are able to drive off their oppressors and are returned to power. Kelderek, ''a simple foolish fellow,'' becomes king of the Ortelgans but idleness and luxury lures him into wickedness. Once again the country is threatened but is redeemed by Shardik's blood sacrifice. Although Adams centered most of his attention on the bear, the humans are real enough and his ability to create an imaginary world may be considered the novel's great strength. In parts overwritten—a trap for any adventure novel—*Shardik* is, nevertheless, a powerful statement about man's inhumanity to man.

Adams was more successful when he returned to the animal world in *The Plague Dogs,* which is, among other things, a hard-hitting attack on the world of animal research. Snitter, a thoroughbred terrier, and Rowf, a mongrel, escape from a government research station in the Lake District and the novel is an account of their adventures to keep out of man's way before they escape to the mystical Isle of Dog. As in *Watership Down,* Adams gives his animals human characteristics but they are not men in dogs' guise. When Snitter and Rowf decide to live off the land, for example, it is a fox who teaches them the necessary tricks and they have difficulty understanding his thick local dialect. When they are seen, men appear only as the enemy and the animals themselves have little understanding of their world.

Although he has also written adventure novels in the style of *Shardik,* Adams is at his happiest in the animal world. The Arcadian worlds of the rabbits' Berkshire and the dogs' Lake District are peopled by an organized society of idealized, largely peaceful animals, but this is not simple anthropomorphism. The animals might be able to speak and to rationalize like human beings but they have not lost their animal characteristics. The rabbits of *Watership Down* even have the remnants of an ancient rabbit language with its own words like *n-Frith* for noon and *hrududu* for tractor or any other man-made machine. It is his ability to create the rabbits and dogs as sensible and sensitive creatures and not as animals-in-man's-clothing or as lovable furry creatures which gives Adams his greatest strength as a novelist.

In 1996, a full twenty-two years after the publication of *Watership Down,* Adams returned to the setting of his greatest success with *Tales from Watership Down.* This collection of nineteen intertwined stories forms an extended narrative concerning the further adventures of Hazel, Bigwig, and all the other memorable characters of the first book. El-ahrairah returns as well, still larger than life; but *Tales from Watership Down* also sees the appearance of a new hero from a new warren—and thus the grand cycle of the rabbits' lives continues.

—Trevor Royle

AIDOO, (Christina) Ama Ata

Nationality: Ghanaian. **Born:** Abeadzi Kiakor, Ghana, 1942. **Education:** University of Ghana, Legon, B.A. (honours) 1964; Stanford University, California. **Career:** Lecturer in English, University of Cape Coast, Ghana, 1970–82; Minister of Education, 1982–83; writer-in-residence, University of Richmond, Virginia, 1989; chair, African Regional Panel of the Commonwealth Writers' prize, 1990, 1991; professor of English, University of Ghana, Cape Coast. **Awards:** Fulbright scholarship, 1988; Short Story Prize, Mbari Press. **Address:** University of Ghana, Department of English, Cape Coast, Ghana.

Publications

Novels

Our Sister Killjoy; or, Reflections from a Black-Eyed Squint. London, Longman, 1977; New York, NOK, 1979.
Changes: A Love Story. London, Women's Press, 1991; New York, Feminist Press at the City University of New York, 1993.

Short Stories

No Sweetness Here. London, Longman, 1970; New York, Doubleday, 1971.
The Eagle and the Chickens and Other Stories. Engu, Nigeria, Tana Press, 1986.
The Girl Who Can and Other Stories. Accra, Ghana, Sub-Saharan Publishers, 1997.

Plays

The Dilemma of a Ghost (produced Legon, 1964; Pittsburgh, 1988). Accra, Longman, 1965; New York, Macmillan, 1971.
Anowa (produced London, 1991). London, Longman, and New York, Humanities Press, 1970.

Poetry

Someone Talking to Sometime. Harare, Zimbabwe, College Press, 1985.
Birds and Other Poems. Harare, Zimbabwe, College Press, 1987.
An Angry Letter in January and Other Poems. Coventry, England, Dangaroo Press, 1992.

Other

Dancing Out Doubts. Engu, Nigeria, NOK, 1982.
Contributor, *Contemporary African Plays*, edited and introduced by Martin Banham and Jane Plastow. London, Methuen, 1999.
Contributor, *The Cambridge Guide to Women's Writing in English*, edited by Lorna Sage. New York, Cambridge University Press, 1999.

*

Critical Studies: *Ama Ata Aidoo: The Dilemma of a Ghost* (study guide) by Jane W. Grant, London, Logman, 1980; *The Art of Ama Ata Aidoo: Polylectics and Reading Against Neocolonialism* by Vincent O. Odamtten, Gainesville, University Press of Florida, 1994; *Emerging Perspectives on Ama Ata Aidoo* edited by Ada Uzoamaka Azodo and Gay Wilentz, Trenton, New Jersey, Africa World Press, 1999.

* * *

Christina Ama Ata Aidoo's greatest strength is her ability to mix humor and hope with the serious issues of gender and social conflict. Her protagonists are caught in situations that are beyond their power to change; however, these characters' resistance to traditional roles and beliefs make them vibrant within these prescribed roles. Ghanaian critic Vincent Odamtten warns against using the terms of the (Western) liberal humanist tradition to describe the roles of these women: ''individuality'' and ''independence'' do not do justice to the different needs of African woman, he cautions. Their need for community, he believes, is greater than Western women's, and what they seek are relationships of equality with their men, not the wherewithal to live without them. Although this view is itself biased by Odamtten's own cultural and gender identity, it does appropriately state that Aidoo's protagonists seek fulfillment within their existing relationships rather than trying to live without men's love.

Aidoo's keen sense of drama is conveyed in both dramatic scripts and novels through witty, realistic, idiomatic dialogue and through careful juxtaposition of scenes that tell a story in pictures. In both plays, *Anowa* and *The Dilemma of a Ghost*, there are two sets of doubles to the main characters, whose scenes parallel the themes of the main duo. Characters called ''Boy'' and ''Girl'' bicker, slap, and insult the representative of the opposite sex, just as their grown-up counterparts do. The second set of doubles is the grandparent pair. Each play illustrates a social problem through the viewpoints of three generations. Aidoo surprises expectations through *chiasmus*: the grandfather figure speaks for the female protagonist's point of view, while the grandmother upholds the traditional view.

The plays discuss the social problems of gender roles and capitalism imposed on an agrarian society. *The Dilemma of a Ghost* features a strong woman married to a weak man who becomes corrupted by his own greed. When he decides to own slaves, she loses her mind because her values and love have been corrupted beyond her capacity of acceptance. In the contemporary setting of *Anowa*, on the other hand, the strong female protagonist is an African American who marries into a Ghanaian family. Her pivotal argument with his society is her belief in her right to delay childbirth. A side issue, which would provide an element of hilarity onstage, is that she smokes and drinks. The real issue of the play, however, is the imbalance of the day-to-day marital relationship: caught between the strong wills of mother and wife, the husband doesn't know who he agrees with. He wants whatever is easiest, not being able to make his own moral choices.

While Aidoo's dramas would make exciting stage productions because of their idiom, color, and tension, the novels make more entertaining reading. *Our Sister Killjoy*, written in 1966, is a precursor to the 1991 novel, *Changes: A Love Story*, in the same way that the play *Dilemma* foresees *Anowa*. The first novel tells the story of a sixteen-year-old Ghanaian girl who travels to Germany and London on an international government program for youth. The titular character, Sissie, earns her negative epithet of ''killjoy'' because she doubts the motives behind government programs such as student loans and grants to study abroad. Instead of celebrating the opportunity to expand their horizons, she deplores the suffering of her black brothers and sisters who live at poverty level in cold, unfriendly London, while deluding themselves that they are privileged to enroll in white education factories. Sissie urges them to return to Africa, to apply their skills to its economy instead. Many of her most ''successful'' compatriots are willfully blind to the horror they have bought into: soul-destroying white capitalism.

Sissie's idealism is touching, but it is not her only moral quality. The scene in which she ''loses her innocence'' is forceful and makes her seem cynical beyond her years. In rejecting a young German woman's love, Sissie observes her own enjoyment in causing pain to another. The reader wants her to connect her own enjoyment of power to her political ideas about white supremacy, to realize that she could be as abusive of power as a white person, but she does not make the connection.

Changes is the more polished novel: both narrator and protagonist are more mature. The protagonist, Esi, illustrates that, although the modern Ghanaian woman can ''emancipate'' herself by divorce, and obtain both love and independence by becoming another man's second wife, it is not enough. Although Esi's new lover is considered progressive in his views because he wants to honor her freedom and equality, his social status as an African male with the right to have many wives and girlfriends makes him different from Esi. Entirely honest in portraying the conflict between the need for love and the need for independence, *Changes* suggests that one thing that will not change, even if social structures do, is women's need for loving attention. Aidoo's characters are wise about gender differences; they do not blame everything on "the system" but recognize fundamental differences between men and women.

—Jill Franks

ALDISS, Brian (Wilson)

Nationality: British. **Born:** East Dereham, Norfolk, 18 August 1925. **Education:** Framlingham College, Suffolk, 1936–39; West Buckland School, 1939–42. **Military Service:** Served in the Royal Corps of Signals in the Far East, 1943–47. **Family:** Married Margaret Manson in 1965 (second marriage; divorced 1997); four children, two from previous marriage. **Career:** Bookseller, Oxford, 1947–56; literary editor, Oxford *Mail,* 1958–69; science-fiction editor, Penguin Books, London, 1961–64; art correspondent, *Guardian,* London, 1969–71. President, British Science Fiction Association, 1960–65; co-founder, 1972, and chair, 1976–78, John W. Campbell Memorial award; co-president, Eurocon Committee, 1975–79; chair, Society of Authors, London, 1978–79; member, Arts Council Literature Panel, 1978–80; president, World SF, 1982–84. Since 1975 vice-president, Stapledon Society; since 1977 founding trustee, World Science Fiction, Dublin; since 1983 vice-president, H.G. Wells Society; since 1988 vice-president, Society of Anglo-Chinese Understanding; since 1990 council member, Council for Posterity. Since 1991 managing director, Avernus Ltd. **Awards:** World Science Fiction Convention citation, 1959; Hugo award, 1962, 1987; Nebula award, 1965; Ditmar award (Australia), 1970; British Science Fiction Association award, 1972, 1982, 1986, and special award, 1974; Eurocon award, 1976; James Blish award, for non-fiction, 1977; Cometa d'Argento (Italy), 1977; Jules Verne prize, 1977; Pilgrim award, 1978; John W. Campbell Memorial award, 1983; International Association for the Fantastic in the Arts award, for scholarship, 1986; Eaton award, 1986; World SF President's award, 1988; Kafka award, 1991. Guest of Honour, World Science Fiction Convention, London, 1965, 1979. Fellow, Royal Society of Literature, 1990. **Agents:** Robin Straus, 229 East 79th St., New York, New York 10021, USA; Michael Shaw, Curtis Brown, Haymarket House, 28/29 Haymarket, London SW1Y 4SP, England. **Address:** Hambelden, 39 St. Andrews Road, Old Headington, Oxford OX3 9DL, England.

Publications

Novels

The Brightfount Diaries. London, Faber, 1955.
Non-Stop. London, Faber, 1958; as *Starship,* New York, Criterion, 1959.
Vanguard from Alpha. New York, Ace, 1959; as *Equator* (includes "Segregation"), London, Digit, 1961.
Bow Down to Nul. New York, Ace, 1960; as *The Interpreter,* London, Digit, 1961.
The Male Response. New York, Galaxy, 1961; London, Dobson, 1963.
The Primal Urge. New York, Ballantine, 1961; London, Sphere, 1967.
The Long Afternoon of Earth. New York, New American Library, 1962; expanded edition, as *Hothouse,* London, Faber, 1962; Boston, Gregg Press, 1976.
The Dark Light Years. London, Faber, and New York, New American Library, 1964.
Greybeard. London, Faber, and New York, Harcourt Brace, 1964.
Earthworks. London, Faber, 1965; New York, Doubleday, 1966.
An Age. London, Faber, 1967; as *Cryptozoic!,* New York, Doubleday, 1968.
Report on Probability A. London, Faber, 1968; New York, Doubleday, 1969.
Barefoot in the Head. London, Faber, 1969; New York, Doubleday, 1970.
The Hand-Reared Boy. London, Weidenfeld and Nicolson, and New York, McCall, 1970.
A Soldier Erect; or, Further Adventures of the Hand-Reared Boy. London, Weidenfeld and Nicolson, and New York, Coward McCann, 1971.
Frankenstein Unbound. London, Cape, 1973; New York, Random House, 1974.
The Eighty-Minute Hour. London, Cape, and New York, Doubleday, 1974.
The Malacia Tapestry. London, Cape, 1976; New York, Harper, 1977.
Brothers of the Head. London, Pierrot, 1977; New York, Two Continents, 1978.
Enemies of the System. London, Cape, and New York, Harper, 1978.
A Rude Awakening. London, Weidenfeld and Nicholson, 1978; New York, Random House, 1979.
Brothers of the Head, and Where the Lines Converge. London, Panther, 1979.
Life in the West. London, Weidenfeld and Nicolson, 1980; New York, Carroll and Graf, 1990.
Moreau's Other Island. London, Cape, 1980; as *An Island Called Moreau,* New York, Simon and Schuster, 1981.
The Helliconia Trilogy. New York, Atheneum, 1985.
  Helliconia Spring. London, Cape, and New York, Atheneum 1982.
  Helliconia Summer. London, Cape, and New York, Atheneum, 1983.
  Helliconia Winter. London, Cape, and New York, Atheneum 1985.
The Horatio Stubbs Saga. London, Panther, 1985.
The Year Before Yesterday. New York, Watts, 1987; as *Cracken at Critical,* Worcester Park, Surrey, Kerosina, 1987.
Ruins. London, Hutchinson, 1987.
Forgotten Life. London, Gollancz, 1988; New York, Atheneum, 1989.
Dracula Unbound. London, Grafton, and New York, Harper Collins, 1991.
Remembrance Day. London, HarperCollins, and New York, St. Martin's Press, 1993.
Somewhere East of Life. London, HarperCollins, and New York, Carroll and Graf, 1994.

Short Stories

Space, Time, and Nathaniel: Presciences. London, Faber, 1957; abridged edition, as *No Time Like Tomorrow,* New York, New American Library, 1959.
The Canopy of Time. London, Faber, 1959; revised edition, as *Galaxies Like Grains of Sand,* New York, New American Library, 1960.
The Airs of Earth. London, Faber, 1963.
Starswarm. New York, New American Library, 1964; London, Panther, 1979.
Best Science Fiction Stories of Brian Aldiss. London, Faber, 1965; as *Who Can Replace a Man?* New York, Harcourt Brace, 1966; revised edition, Faber, 1971.
The Saliva Tree and Other Strange Growths. London, Faber, 1966.
Intangibles Inc. London, Faber, 1969.
A Brian Aldiss Omnibus 1–2. London, Sidgwick and Jackson, 2 vols., 1969–1971.
Neanderthal Planet. New York, Avon, 1970.
The Moment of Eclipse. London, Faber, 1970; New York, Doubleday, 1972.
The Book of Brian Aldiss. New York, DAW, 1972; as *The Comic Inferno,* London, New English Library, 1973 .
Excommunication. London, Post Card Partnership, 1975.
Last Orders and Other Stories. London, Cape 1977; New York, Carroll and Graf, 1989.
New Arrivals, Old Encounters: Twelve Stories. London, Cape, 1979; New York, Harper, 1980.
Foreign Bodies. Singapore, Chopmen, 1981.
Seasons in Flight. London, Cape, 1984; New York, Atheneum, 1986.
The Magic of the Past. Worcester Park, Surrey, Kerosina, 1987.
Best Science Fiction Stories of Brian W. Aldiss (not same as 1965 book). London, Gollancz, 1988; as *Man in His Time,* New York, Atheneum, 1989.
A Romance of the Equator: Best Fantasy Stories. London, Gollancz, 1989; New York, Atheneum, 1990.
A Tupolev Too Far. London, HarperCollins, 1993; New York, St. Martin's Press, 1994.
The Secret of This Book: 20 Odd Stories, illustrations by Rosamund Chorley and Brian Aldiss. New York, HarperCollins, 1995.

Plays

Distant Encounters, adaptation of his own stories (produced London, 1978).
SF Blues (produced London, 1987).

Television Play: *Life* (*4 Minutes* series), 1986.

Poetry

Pile: Petals from St. Klaed's Computer. London, Cape, and New York, Holt Rinehart, 1979.
Farewell to a Child. Berkhamsted, Hertfordshire, Priapus, 1982.
At the Caligula Hotel. London, Sinclair Stevenson, 1995.
At the Caligula Hotel and Other Poems. London, Sinclair-Stevenson, 1995.
Songs from the Steppes of Central Asia: The Collected Poems of Makhtumkuli: Eighteenth Century Poet-Hero of Turkmenistan (versified by Aldiss, based on translations by Youssef Azemoun). Caversham, Berkshire, England, Society of Friends of Makhtumkuli, 1995.

Other

Cities and Stones: A Traveller's Jugoslavia. London, Faber, 1966.
The Shape of Further Things: Speculations on Change. London, Faber, 1970; New York, Doubleday, 1971.
Billion Year Spree: A History of Science Fiction. London, Weidenfeld and Nicolson, and New York, Doubleday, 1973.
Science Fiction Art, illustrated by Chris Foss. New York, Bounty, 1975; London, Hart Davis, 1976.
Science Fiction as Science Fiction. Frome, Somerset, Bran's Head, 1978.
This World and Nearer Ones: Essays Exploring the Familiar. London, Weidenfeld and Nicolson, 1979; Ohio, Kent State University Press, 1981.
Science Fiction Quiz. London, Weidenfeld and Nicolson, 1983.
The Pale Shadow of Science (essays). Seattle, Serconia Press, 1985.
... And the Lurid Glare of the Comet (essays). Seattle, Serconia Press, 1986.
Trillion Year Spree: The History of Science Fiction, with David Wingrove. London, Gollancz, and New York, Atheneum, 1986.
Science Fiction Blues (selections), edited by Frank Hatherley. London, Avernus, 1988.
Bury My Heart at W.H. Smith's: A Writing Life. London, Hodder and Stoughton, 1990.
The Detached Retina. Liverpool, Liverpool University Press, 1995.
Foreword, *Blood Read: The Vampire as Metaphor in Contemporary Culture,* edited by Joan Gordon and Veronica Hollinger. Philadelphia, University of Pennsylvania Press, 1997.
The Twinkling of an Eye, or, My Life as an Englishman. New York, St. Martin's, 1999.
Foreword, *Soft as Steel: The Art of Julie Bell* by Nigel Suckling. New York, Thunder's Mouth Press, 1999.
Editor, *Penguin Science Fiction.* London, Penguin, 1961; *More Penguin Science Fiction,* 1963; *Yet More Penguin Science Fiction,* 1964; 3 vols. collected as *The Penguin Science Fiction Omnibus,* 1973.
Editor, *Best Fantasy Stories.* London, Faber, 1962.
Editor, *Last and First Men,* by Olaf Stapledon. London, Penguin, 1963.
Editor, *Introducing SF.* London, Faber, 1964.
Editor, with Harry Harrison, *Nebula Award Stories 2.* New York, Doubleday, 1967; as *Nebula Award Stories 1967,* London, Gollancz, 1967.
Editor, with Harry Harrison, *All about Venus.* New York, Dell, 1968; enlarged edition, as *Farewell, Fantastic Venus,* London, Macdonald, 1968.
Editor, with Harry Harrison, *Best SF 1967* [to *1975*]. New York, Berkley and Putnam, 7 vols., and Indianapolis, Bobbs Merrill, 2 vols., 1968–1975; as *The Year's Best Science Fiction 1–9,* London, Sphere, 8 vols., 1968–1976, and London, Futura, 1 vol., 1976.
Editor, with Harry Harrison, *The Astounding-Analog Reader.* New York, Doubleday, 2 vols., 1972–1973; London, Sphere, 2 vols., 1973.
Editor, *Space Opera.* London, Weidenfeld and Nicolson, 1974; New York, Doubleday, 1975.

Editor, *Space Odysseys.* London, Futura, 1974; New York, Doubleday, 1976.

Editor, with Harry Harrison, *SF Horizons* (reprint of magazine). New York, Arno Press, 1975.

Editor, with Harry Harrison, *Hell's Cartographers: Some Personal Histories of Science Fiction Writers.* London, Weidenfeld and Nicolson, and New York, Harper, 1975.

Editor, with Harry Harrison, *Decade: The 1940's, The 1950's, The 1960's.* London, Macmillan, 3 vols., 1975–1977; *The 1940's* and *The 1950's,* New York, St. Martin's Press, 2 vols., 1978.

Editor, *Evil Earths.* London, Weidenfeld and Nicolson, 1975; New York, Avon, 1979.

Editor, *Galactic Empires.* London, Weidenfeld and Nicolson, 2 vols., 1976; New York, St. Martin's Press, 2 vols., 1977.

Editor, *Perilous Planets.* London, Weidenfeld and Nicolson, 1978; New York, Avon, 1980.

Editor, with others, *The Penguin Masterquiz Book.* London, Penguin, 1985.

Editor, with Sam J. Lundwall, *The Penguin World Omnibus of Science Fiction.* London, Penguin, 1986; New York, Penguin, 1987.

Editor, *My Madness: The Selected Writings of Anna Kavan.* London, Pan, 1990.

Editor, *Mini Sagas from the Daily Telegraph Competition.* Stroud, Gloucestershire, Sutton, 1997.

*

Bibliography: *Brian W. Aldiss: A Bibliography 1954–1984* by Margaret Aldiss, San Bernardino, California, Borgo Press, 1991.

Manuscript Collections: Bodleian Library, Oxford University; Dallas Public Library.

Critical Studies: ''Generic Discontinuities in SF: Brian Aldiss' *Starship*'' by Fredric Jameson, in *Science-Fiction Studies* (Terre Haute, Indiana), vol. 1, no. 2, 1973; *Aldiss Unbound: The Science Fiction of Brian W. Aldiss* by Richard Mathews, San Bernardino, California, Borgo Press, 1977; *Apertures: A Study of the Writings of Brian Aldiss* by Brian Griffin and David Wingrove, Westport, Connecticut, Greenwood Press, 1984; article by Aldiss in *Contemporary Authors Autobiography Series 2* edited by Adele Sarkissian, Detroit, Gale, 1985; *A Is for Brian: A 65th Birthday Present for Brian W. Aldiss from His Family, Friends, Colleagues, and Admirers* edited by Frank Hatherley, London, Avernus, 1990.

Brian Aldiss comments:

(1991) With *Somewhere East of Life*, I have completed the Squire Quartet, which opened with *Life in the West.* These novels cover a great extent of territory, from the United States to Singapore and Turkmenistan, from Stockholm to Sicily. Always my native county of Norfolk, East Anglia, serves as a sort of fulcrum. Family affairs are set against the slow decline of the West and the abrupt demise of the Soviet Union.

An idea of how much I might encompass was brought home to me while writing the three Helliconia novels in the early to mid-1980s: *Helliconia Spring*, *Helliconia Summer*, and *Helliconia Winter.* I have never experienced that great divide some people detect between science fiction and the ordinary contemporary novel; this probably reflects my reading and the company I keep.

I write every day and always have done—not invariably for publication. My SF presents a spectrum moving from extreme surreal situations in the early novels to events merely colored by an incipient future. By the time I wrote *Report on Probability A* and *Barefoot in the Head,* I had already moved away from the confines of genre fiction.

Happily, my contemporary novels have been about as successful as the more imaginative ones. Recent pleasures include having a volume of critical essays and a selection of my poems published. I'm now working on a large-scale autobiographical ''thing''—an unlicked cub as yet—which will contain my experience of and meditations on war.

To be able to write is a slice of great golden fortune.

* * *

The great contribution Brian Aldiss has made to the art of science fiction is to help to raise it to the point where it is now accepted, by all but the chronically bigoted, as a literary form worthy of serious consideration. I suspect that this has much to do with the fact that Aldiss has always looked upon himself primarily as a novelist rather than as a writer of SF, and he has written several novels other than those on science-fiction themes.

His first full length science-fiction novel was *Non-Stop,* which was based on the almost classic SF theme of a giant space-ship adrift in space. As a piece of storytelling, it is first class, and it displays all the excellences that are to be found in his later work: the ability to establish by carefully selected detail a convincing atmosphere of place and time, and a logical development of situations so that even the most outlandish become acceptable to the reader. In *Hothouse*, for example, Aldiss creates a world dominated by vegetation where we can sense the continual and overwhelming growth, even breathe the vegetable air, and in *Greybeard* the experience of being in post-atomic Oxford is remarkably vivid. But in *Non-Stop*, while the exploration of the ship (once built by giants) by Roy Complain and his companions has parallels with the sense of awe and wonder experienced by the Old English poets when they encountered the ruins of Roman cities, the space ship becomes a microcosm of Earth which, too, can be seen as a giant ship itself endlessly adrift in space, and the exploration develops into a search for destination and purpose.

A quality which informs Aldiss's work, and which should not be overlooked, is his sense of humor. In *Non-Stop* one aspect of this can be seen in his pursuit of the idea that in the future psychology will develop its own theology and superstitions and replace our present religions. It is a plausible thesis and at the same time an amusing one, and often Aldiss's humor helps to save his SF novels from the over-seriousness that has engulfed other practitioners in this genre. It has been responsible too for the excellent humorous novels. The logical consequences of the invention and universal use of an ''Emotional Register'' are used in *The Primal Urge* to create a fantastic and hilarious story.

Since the late 1960s Aldiss has striven to extend the boundaries of his art. In *Report on Probability A* he attempted the first SF anti-novel, a study in relative phenomena which proved a *tour de force,* and in *Barefoot in the Head* he produced another ''first,'' where groups of poems and ''pop-songs'' reflect and comment on the preceding prose chapters. In a Europe reeling psychodelically from an attack by an Arab state with Psycho-Chemical Aerosol Bombs, Chateris, the hero of *Barefoot in the Head*, gradually absorbs the acid-head poison in the atmosphere to find himself a new Messiah. As social and thought patterns disintegrate so does the language, and Aldiss develops a stunning-punning prose reminiscent of the verbal pyrotechnics of Joyce's *Finnegans Wake.* At the same time he creates a nightmare world reflecting trends observable in the situation already with us.

Though not strictly within a discussion of Aldiss's novels, we should not overlook his collections of short stories, *Space, Time, and Nathaniel* and *The Canopy of Time*, of which he is justly proud. The Horatio Stubbs series constitutes a fictional autobiography covering the years from the 1930s to the 1960s, where through the sexual and spiritual development of Horatio are examined certain aspects of the poverty of English middle-class life. The first, *The Hand-Reared Boy*, begins with Horatio as a boy, his masturbatory fantasies and his first sexual encounters. The direct and extremely realistic style of the first part of this novel might not be to everyone's taste, but it flowers into a most beautifully controlled story of Horatio's first and hopeless love for an older woman. In the second novel, *A Solder Erect*, we find Horatio still hard at it in the army and serving in India and Burma where his sexual and social education is broadened. The coarse brutality of wartime soldiering in the Far East is accurately and brutally portrayed, but redeemed by humor and set in contrast with Horatio's growing awareness of values beyond the more immediately erotic, a theme continued and brought to conclusion in the third novel in the series, *A Rude Awakening*, where Horatio encounters the Dutch, Indian, Japanese, Chinese, and Indonesian forces in Sumatra and finds himself with two girls.

On the SF side, Aldiss's *Frankenstein Unbound* breaks new ground again. As a result of the indiscriminate use of nuclear weapons within the ambits of the Earth-Lunar system the infrastructure of space is seriously damaged to the point where time and space go ''on the brink.'' The consequent ''time shifts'' find Joe Boderland suddenly transported to Switzerland in the year 1816 where he encounters not only Mary Shelley, the creator of Frankenstein, but Frankenstein himself in a world where reality itself is equally unstable and the dividing line between the real and the imagined world has become confused. In this situation Boderland finds himself unsure of his own role, and it is the discovery and fulfillment of his mission which constitutes the central theme of the narrative. It is a measure of Aldiss's powers as a novelist that he persuades the reader of the *reality* of this fantastic situation. The theme, I suspect, was suggested by his researches into the origins of science fiction which he undertook to produce his history of the genre, *Billion Year Spree* (and now *Trillion Year Spree*), and in which he makes a powerful case for Mary Shelley's *Frankenstein* as the first true SF novel.

More recent novels increase one's admiration for Aldiss's versatility and unflagging powers of invention. *Brothers of the Head*, the story of Siamese twin boys with a third dominant head which becomes increasingly demanding, is a brilliant if disturbing excursion into the macabre, while *The Malacia Tapestry* almost defies definition. Set in an age-old city state, riddled with rival philosophies, under the spell of magicians, and where change is forbidden, it presents the reader with a panorama of dukes, wealthy merchants, thespians, courtesans, spongers, and soldiers. What we are never sure of is whereabouts in the time scale we are. Is it a medieval town? Then just a glimpse of something tells us no. An alternative world? But never explicitly so. The way in which Aldiss makes this totally imaginary world a reality is remarkable, a superb example of how to induce the suspension of disbelief.

Given Aldiss's run of the gamut of fictional styles and structures it was almost inevitable that sooner or later he would attempt a saga. In *The Helliconia Trilogy* he does just that and in inventing an entire solar system with its own history, dynasties, religions, mythologies, and cultures it is one of epic proportions. While parallels with life on Planet Earth can be observed, the chief and fundamental difference is in the length of Helliconia's seasons. Centuries long the whole of life changes as the seasons wear on, dormant life forms emerge and dynasties rise and fall. At the heart of this, nevertheless, is the struggle between the Humans and the Phagors, and a stroke of genius is to have hovering in the background an Earth Observation Platform which is itself declining into disaster, thus adding a further perspective to this cosmic vision. The other remarkable aspect of Aldiss's invented universe is that it is not, as is so often the case in science fiction, an ideal world held up in criticism of our own. Helliconia's history is as messy, corrupt, illogical, and confused as Earth's. If there is a message it is in Helliconia's acceptance of and adjustment to its even harsher physical environment, while the Earth Platform's disaster is directly related to Earth's attempt to over-control its environment.

The books themselves, *Spring*, *Summer*, and *Winter*, are full of action and incident: picaresque journeys, hierarchical struggles, natural disasters, feats of endurance, bravery, loyalty and affection, and dynastic warfare which make them each, in an old-fashioned phrase, a gripping read. They are in addition a remarkable achievement.

Aldiss moved on from the massive achievement of Helliconia to yet another achievement. Back to Earth and the mainstream novel his *Forgotten Life* is another remarkable example of Aldiss's ability to assemble and organize a mass of material, in this case ranging over 50 years and three continents. In a sense the novel can be seen as a sort of intellectual whodunit, a cerebral voyage of discovery.

In the novel Clement Winter, who is married to a successful author of fantasy novels, comes into the possession of his brother Joseph's letters and diaries. In going through these in order to find and comprehend a pattern in his brother's life, Clement comes to review and assess his own. Aldiss calls upon his own experiences in pre-war Suffolk, wartime Burma and Sumatra, and his life as a writer in Oxford.

The real stuff of autobiography comes in *Bury My Heart at W.H. Smith's*. This is, not surprisingly, a wide-ranging story, haunted by wartime experience in Burma. True to its title Aldiss's autobiography is marked by a lightness of touch, and a cheerful friendly modesty. The story it tells is an intriguing one.

In the mid- to late 1990s Aldiss, then entering his eighth decade, proved himself still highly active. He published a story collection (*The Secret of This Book*, 1995), two books of poems (*At the Caligula Hotel* and *Songs from the Steppes of Central Asia*, both 1995), a biography (*The Twinkling of an Eye, or, My Life as an Englishman*, 1999), and assorted other works.

—John Cotton

ALDRIDGE, (Harold Edward) James

Nationality: Australian. **Born:** White Hills, Victoria, 10 July 1918. **Education:** Swan Hill High School; London School of Economics. **Family:** Married Dina Mitchnik in 1942; two sons. **Career:** Writer, Melbourne *Herald* and *Sun*, 1937–38, and London *Daily Sketch* and *Sunday Dispatch*, 1939; European and Middle East war correspondent, Australian Newspaper Service and North American Newspaper

Alliance, 1939–44; Tehran correspondent, *Time* and *Life,* 1944. **Awards:** Rhys Memorial prize, 1945; World Peace Council gold medal; International Organization of Journalists prize, 1967; Lenin Memorial Peace prize, 1972; Australian Children's Book Council Book of the Year award, 1985; *Guardian* award, for children's book, 1987. **Agent:** Curtis Brown, 28/29 Haymarket, London SW1Y 4SP, England. **Address:** 21 Kersley Street, London SW11, England.

PUBLICATIONS

Novels

Signed with Their Honour. London, Joseph, and Boston, Little Brown, 1942.
The Sea Eagle. London, Joseph, and Boston, Little Brown, 1944.
Of Many Men. London, Joseph, and Boston, Little Brown, 1946.
The Diplomat. London, Lane, 1949; Boston, Little Brown, 1950.
The Hunter. London, Lane, 1950; Boston, Little Brown, 1951.
Heroes of the Empty View. London, Lane, and New York, Knopf, 1954.
I Wish He Would Not Die. London, Bodley Head, 1957; New York, Doubleday, 1958.
The Last Exile. London, Hamish Hamilton, and New York, Doubleday, 1961.
A Captive in the Land. London, Hamish Hamilton, 1962; New York, Doubleday, 1963.
The Statesman's Game. London, Hamish Hamilton, and New York, Doubleday, 1966.
My Brother Tom. London, Hamish Hamilton, 1966; as *My Brother Tom: A Love Story,* Boston, Little Brown, 1967.
A Sporting Proposition. London, Joseph, and Boston, Little Brown, 1973; as *Ride a Wild Pony,* London, Penguin, 1976.
Mockery in Arms. London, Joseph, 1974; Boston, Little Brown, 1975.
The Untouchable Juli. London, Joseph, 1975; Boston, Little Brown, 1976.
One Last Glimpse. London, Joseph, and Boston, Little Brown, 1977.
Goodbye Un-America. London, Joseph, and Boston, Little Brown, 1979.
The True Story of Lola MacKellar. London, Viking, 1992.

Short Stories

Gold and Sand. London, Bodley Head, 1960.

Uncollected Short Stories

"Braver Time," in *Redbook* (New York), May 1967.
"The Unfinished Soldiers," in *Winter's Tales 15,* edited by A.D. Maclean. London, Macmillan, 1969; New York, St. Martin's Press, 1970.
"The Black Ghost of St. Helen," in *After Midnight Ghost Book,* edited by James Hale. London, Hutchinson, 1980.

Plays

The 49th State (produced London, 1947).
One Last Glimpse (produced Prague, 1981).

Television Plays: Scripts for *Robin Hood* series.

Other

Undersea Hunting for Inexperienced Englishmen. London, Allen and Unwin, 1955.
The Flying 19 (for children). London, Hamish Hamilton, 1966.
Living Egypt, photographs by Paul Strand. London, MacGibbon and Kee, and New York, Horizon Press, 1969.
Cairo: Biography of a City. Boston, Little Brown, 1969; London, Macmillan, 1970.
The Marvelous Mongolian (for children). Boston, Little Brown, and London, Macmillan, 1974.
The Broken Saddle (for children). London, MacRae, 1982; New York, Watts, 1983.
The True Story of Lilli Stubek (for children). South Yarra, Victoria, Hyland House, 1984; London, Penguin, 1986.
The True Story of Spit MacPhee (for children). Ringwood, Victoria, Viking, and London, Viking Kestrel, 1986.

*

Critical Studies: "The Necessity of Freedom: A Discussion of the Novels of James Aldridge," in *Overland* (Melbourne), November 1956; "It All Comes Out Like Blood: The Novels of James Aldridge," in *Australians* by John Hetherington, Melbourne, Cheshire, 1960; "Man of Action, Words in Action" by Eric Partridge, in *Meanjin* (Melbourne), 1961; "The Heroic Ordinary" by Evelyn Juers, in *Age Monthly Review* (Melbourne), February 1987; *Workers and Sufferers: Town v. Self in James Aldridge's St. Helen Novels,* London, Australian Studies Centre, 1987, and "My Brother Tom: My Other Self," in *Orana* (Sydney), February 1989, both by Michael Stone.

* * *

James Aldridge left Australia when quite a young man as a war correspondent; and this fact has largely determined the material and the angle of approach in his work. He went through the Greek campaign and wrote two books based directly on his experiences in it. Here his method was strongly affected by Hemingway; but the books were saved from being mere imitations by the genuine freshness and truth of his presentation. He was learning how to build a narrative full of stirring events and based on historical developments which he knew at first-hand, and at the same time to link the story with the personal problems and struggles of his protagonists. With his next book, a collection of stories, came a break from the Hemingway influence. What he had gained from his apprenticeship was now integrated in his own method and outlook. The tales showed how well he was able to grasp situations with very diverse settings and convincingly to define aspects of national character in a compact form. Still drawing on his wartime experiences as a correspondent, he wrote *The Diplomat*, an ambitious large-scale work, dealing with both the Soviet Union and the region of the Kurds in northern Mesopotamia. With much skill he explored the devious world of diplomacy in the postwar world, making the issues concrete by their basis in the difficult national question of the Kurds. Aldridge emerged as an important political novelist. He showed himself able to handle complicated political themes without losing touch with the essential human issues. The political aspects were removed from triviality or narrowness by being linked with the painful struggles of the protagonist to understand the world in which he found himself an actor. Thus what gave artistic validity to the work, beyond any particular conclusions reached in the search for truth, was the definition of that search itself.

In *The Hunter* Aldridge next refreshed himself by dropping all large themes and turning to Canada in a work more concerned with immediacies of experience: his theme was the world of the hunter, a direct relationship to nature, and he showed he could conjure up a dimension of sheer physical living. But it was perhaps significant that when he turned from the theme of contemporary history and politics, it was to the sphere of nature, not to everyday life in some specific society. For good and bad, his uprooting through the war had made him into a novelist of the large national conflicts of his age. His material had thus been born of his journalism, but in transforming it to fiction he overcame the journalistic limitations and was able to penetrate to deep human issues. He saw problems in terms of real people, and has never been guilty of inventing puppets to represent national or political positions.

He turned again to the Near East, in *Heroes of the Empty View*, *I Wish He Would Not Die*, and *The Last Exile*, in which he took up the problems of the Arab world, with special reference to Egypt. He was helped by having many direct connections and sources of information; but despite his sympathy for the Arabs he did not oversimplify issues or make his works into tracts for a particular point of view. The stories clarified events and deepened the reader's understanding of the human beings entangled in vast conflicts. In his later works he returned to the question of the Soviet Union, but with less force and artistic success than in *The Diplomat* or the books on the near East. It would be hard to point to any contemporary novelist who has dealt more directly with international political problems in the second half of the twentieth century. Certainly it would be difficult to find one who has done so with such success, uniting a warm sympathy for the persons about whom he writes with, in the last resort, a true artistic detachment.

—Jack Lindsay

ALEXIE, Sherman Joseph, Jr.

Nationality: American. **Born:** Spokane, Washington, 7 October 1966. **Education:** Gonzaga University, 1985- 87; Washington State University, B.A. 1991. **Awards:** Poetry fellow, Washington State Arts Commission, 1991; National Endowment for the Arts, 1992; winner, Slipstream's fifth annual chapbook contest, March 1992; American Book Award, 1996. **Address:** P.O. Box 376, Wellpinit, Washington 99040, U.S.A.

PUBLICATIONS

Novels

Reservation Blues. New York, Atlantic Monthly Press, 1995.
Indian Killer. New York, Atlantic Monthly Press, 1996; New York, Warner Books, 1998.

Short Stories

The Lone Ranger and Tonto Fistfight in Heaven. New York, Atlantic Monthly Press, 1993; New York, Harper Perennial, 1994.
The Toughest Indian in the World: Stories. New York, Atlantic Monthly Press, 2000.

Poetry

I Would Steal Horses. Niagara Falls, New York, Slipstream, 1992.
The Business of Fancydancing: Stories and Poems. Brooklyn, New York, Hanging Loose Press, 1992.
First Indian on the Moon. Brooklyn, New York, Hanging Loose Press, 1992.
Old Shirts & New Skins. Los Angeles, University of California American Indian Studies Center, 1993.
Water Flowing Home: Poems. Boise, Idaho, Limberlost Press, 1994.
Seven Mourning Songs for the Cedar Flute I Have Yet to Learn to Play. Walla Walla, Washington, Whitman College Press, 1994.
The Summer of Black Widows. Brooklyn, New York, Hanging Loose Press, 1996.
The Man Who Loves Salmon. Boise, Idaho, Limberlost Press, 1998.
One Stick Song. Brooklyn, New York, Hanging Loose Press, 1999.

Play

Smoke Signals, with introduction and notes by the author, New York, Hyperion, 1998.

* * *

Sherman Alexie, whose works repeatedly underscore the importance of retaining tribal connections, draws on the oral, religious, and political traditions of his Spokane/Coeur d'Alene Indian heritage. The wandering story lines of his novels reflect non-mainstream organizational structures, approaches, and attitudes as they shift time settings (mythical, historical, and modern), place, and person to gradually reveal tribal, family, and personal connections in keeping with the Native American philosophical framework, the web of life. As in oral tradition, Alexie's narratives aim for sudden, brief insights as connections that initially elude readers gradually take meaningful shape over time; their humor is dark, and their goal, in part, is to debunk what Alexie sees as political and cultural myths. Alexie, who began his writing career as a small press poet, asserts that, for the reservation Indian, imagination, given impetus by anger, is the only way to survive a life of despair worsened by alcoholism, abuse, poverty, diabetes, and economic dead ends.

''Distances,'' one of 22 intertwined stories from *The Lone Ranger and Tonto Fistfight in Heaven* (1993), typifies the crossover vision of intersecting times as Alexie's modern characters successfully reenact the failed nineteenth-century Plains Indian Ghost Dance. Historically, the dance was a desperate attempt to make whites disappear and to return the land to a pre-Columbian utopian state, yet it failed, bringing down on the heads of its practitioners the full weight of the U.S. Cavalry. Alexie's dystopian vision captures the futility of yearning for a return to the past: if modern technology and anyone with white blood were willed away, as the Ghost Dance promised, who and what would be left on the reservations? The assimilated would be without homes or transportation, food or clothing. In Alexie's apocalyptic tale tribes would be separated into the ''Skins,'' or reservation Indians, and the "Urbans," or Indian outsiders, but such precautions would fail because even the pure bloods carry in their bloodstreams the taint of white diseases, so many would sicken and die. Even though hunter-gatherers who have been dead a thousand years are reborn, and their women give birth to salmon, life remains a dead end for Native Americans. At the close of *Indian Killer* (1998), the main character, who is possibly a schizophrenic serial killer, leads Seattle's native street people in a Ghost Dance that depopulates Seattle.

The Lone Ranger and Tonto Fistfight in Heaven and *Reservation Blues* (1994) illustrate the interconnectedness of life through three shared interlocking central characters: storyteller and self-proclaimed visionary Thomas Builds-the-Fire and his companions Junior and Victor, a former reservation-wide basketball hero and a semi-reformed alcoholic. (These young men appear in the 1998 film *Smoke Signals*, loosely based on the two novels.) *Reservation Blues* places pop music (blues and rock-and-roll) in the role of traditional storytelling as Thomas and his friends, aided by the magic guitar of legendary bluesman Robert Johnson, form the band Coyote Springs and recreate the world through their music. Before their recording session with U.S. Cavalry generals Sheridan and Wright, reincarnated as recording executives, the young musicians seek a vision on a mountain presided over by Big Mom, a Spokane Indian mystic whose personal history has been forever marked by the slaughter of 900 horses by the United States Cavalry in 1861. Since Mom has been the spiritual guide of Janis Joplin, Jimi Hendrix, and Benny Goodman, among others, the American blues, infused with the Indian spirit, echoes the "Reservation Blues" of the title. Alexie playfully and critically juxtaposes New Age groupies with the plight of a fishing people stuck in a land where all the rivers have been dammed. In *The Lone Ranger*, the reservation storyteller, like the Coyote Band and like their creator, uses his art to recreate the world and make daily life less bleak. As Thomas accompanies Victor to bring Victor's dead father's pickup and ashes home, the road that leads away from home also leads back to the past and forward to the future; the native Creation story, the mother goddess, and Coyote link all in the web of life.

Indian Killer (1998), a murder mystery of sorts, includes a cast of characters whose personal histories intersect in Seattle, Washington, in the late 1980s. The novel relies on an intentionally confrontational narrative voice, that of a displaced urban Indian, ironically named John Smith, whose adoption has left him without tribal roots and with no way to regain the tribal knowledge that Alexie believes is essential to his identity, despite his foster parents' attempts to educate him about native ways. A disturbed schizophrenic, he is beset on every side by racial and cultural stereotypes: white liberals suffering collective guilt for past wrongs; redneck Indian haters; homeless native drunks; cruel fathers. Alexie offers hazy visions of white doctors ripping John from his Indian mother's womb and armed men rushing him to his white adoptive parents. In retaliation for his foster parents' inadequacy, Smith kills and scalps random whites, though greedy rednecks are responsible for the most publicized death he is accused of (hence the intentional confusion inherent in the title: an Indian who kills or a killer of Indians?). Alexie mocks whites who universalize and romanticize Indians into something they are not, and he sympathizes with Indian characters like Maria, who runs a mobile sandwich kitchen for homeless Indians and attacks the white myths promulgated in local university courses. The detective story's genre conventions (investigating a crime, establishing culpability) take second place to Alexie's message that well-meaning whites cannot make up for their ancestors' genocide and that it is too late to rectify past wrongs: What has been destroyed—the native way of life and belief—can never be fully regained. Thus, many of his Indians are alcoholics and drug abusers, madmen, or ineffectual poseurs.

Alexie's first two works of fiction balance alienation and defeatism with laughter, but his third focuses only on gratuitous acts of violence and self-destruction. His collection of short stories *The Toughest Indian in the World* (2000), with its heartbreaking tales of hope and love amid pain and chaos, seems to be an emotional counter to the negativism of *Indian Killer*. Alexie offers readers vivid images of reservation life, some irreverent humor, and a distinctive perspective that he particularizes as his own Spokane/Coeur d'Alene voice. He admits that his characters contain bits and pieces of himself, and he worries that, given the statistical brevity of the lives of reservation males, his time of creativity is limited.

—Gina Macdonald

ALEXIS, André

Nationality: Canadian. **Born:** Trinidad, 1957. **Family:** One daughter. **Career:** Playwright, radio writer, poet, and writer of fiction. **Awards:** Trillium Book Award, 1999. **Agent:** c/o McClelland & Stewart, Inc., 481 University Avenue, Toronto, Ontario M5G 2E9 Canada. **Address:** Toronto, Ontario, Canada.

Publications

Novels

Childhood: A Novel. New York, Henry Holt, 1998.

Short Stories

Despair and Other Stories of Ottawa. Toronto, Coach House Press, 1994; published as *Despair and Other Stories,* New York, Henry Holt, 1999

Other

Lambton Kent: A Play. Toronto, Gutter Press, 1999.

* * *

Inclined towards experimental and avant-garde modes in his plays and performance-art collaborations, André Alexis in his fiction both represents and disturbs the familiar surfaces of banal, quotidian reality. His prose is emotionally cool but vivid and surprising in its images; his narrative world alternates—often in the same paragraph—between the mundanely recognizable and the outrageously, nightmarishly fantastical. Describing his fictional terrain as "the shifting ground between the imagined life and the life that you live in from day to day," he invites readers to question their assumptions about the normal and the abnormal, the real and the unreal, the remembered and the lived.

His début book, *Despair and Other Stories of Ottawa*, is an unsettling collection of macabre tales set mostly in the placidly prosperous Canadian capital where Alexis grew up, having moved to Canada from Trinidad at age three. Beneath Ottawa's apparently dull, institutional exterior Alexis reveals dream-worlds of flesh-biting ''Soucouyants,'' bar patrons holding their own severed heads in their laps, and worms that, when swallowed, cause a boy and his father to write fine poetry until the burgeoning annelids destroy them. At times nauseating, at times darkly humorous, Alexis's playful stories wallow in the grotesque, but the weirdly degenerative physical conditions and lurid sexual scenarios they describe seem not so much comments on bodily vulnerabilities and (im)possibilities as mental and aesthetic exercises—discomfiting workouts for the writer's (and the reader's) imagination. More cerebral than referential, more performative than political, Alexis's narratives are often deliberately solipsistic and self-reflexive; when the street addresses mentioned in diverse stories all include the number 128, or when one story's characters are all named either André Alexis or Andrée Alexis, the author's role as presiding consciousness and metaphysical provocateur becomes as important a subject as anything actually ''happening'' in the stories.

Much the same can be said of Alexis's meditative first novel, *Childhood*, though it sheds the stories' *outré* preoccupations in favor of a firmer grounding in the psychologically and ontologically familiar. Addressing themes of loss, absence, the meaning of love, and the slipperiness of memory, the novel depicts 40-year-old Thomas MacMillan's search for knowledge and understanding of some fascinating but puzzling others, especially the mother who abandoned him at birth. But his introspective narrative of childhood relations turns out to be primarily a quest for the self; ''The way to Katarina and Henry [his mother and her lover] is through me,'' he writes, but the reverse is also true. Having experienced as a child a variety of bewildering deceptions, dislocations, and power struggles, Thomas attempts to reconstruct his memories and order his life; his narrative activity is often displaced by his list-making habit and penchant for diagrams, graphs, and footnotes, all of which rather endearingly, if absurdly, endeavor to explain his world to himself and the enigmatic ''you'' to whom the novel is addressed. His four section titles—''History,'' ''Geography,'' ''The Sciences,'' and ''Housecleaning''—and his relentlessly analytical cast of mind reinforce the impression of an idiosyncratic man struggling nobly to gather the loose strands of his self into a coherent pattern.

One of Alexis's points in this quietly lyrical novel is that the search to make sense of the past and the self that has emerged from it—a well-worn theme of Canadian and international literature—is unavoidably subjective; any construct that results is but one of an infinite number of possible variations. The past is always framed and contaminated by present conditions, and the same story told a year later will be a different one. As Alexis has said in an interview, ''all versions of the self are provisional, time-based, and evanescent, but all of these versions are also true, however briefly.'' In its muted attentiveness to place (Petrolia, Ontario, and Ottawa), to daily minutiae and to delicate maneuverings in intricate relationships, *Childhood* paints a compelling, if rather narrow, fictional portrait. And although it shares the first book's even, unflashy prose and tone of controlled detachment, it nonetheless resonates emotionally to a degree that the stories do not (nor seem to want to do).

Alexis rejects fashionable labels such as ''magic realist,'' ''surrealist,'' or ''postmodern'' that might seem to describe his work. And while his Trinidadian roots could place him within West Indian and African-Canadian literary traditions, he accepts these affiliations reluctantly, noting that such writing was not formative to his artistic and intellectual development. As literary influences he cites a diverse group that includes Samuel Beckett, Jorge-Luis Borges, Italo Calvino, Raymond Queneau, Leo Tolstoy, and Marcel Proust, along with the Canadian writers Norman Levine, bpNichol and Margaret Avison. His sensibility is often described as ''cosmopolitan,'' which may be code for ''European''; it is notable that the issues of race and racism, exile and displacement that vex so many African-Canadian and African-American writers are virtually absent from Alexis's work. Trinidadian origins, when they are mentioned at all, are typically treated as simple facts of a character's background rather than as sources of anxiety or conflict; their visible difference from the Canadian mainstream goes unnoticed or unremarked by most of Alexis's characters. Whether this represents a denial or a transcendence of the racialized consciousness that his peers' writing so often reflects, Alexis's quirky fiction seems destined to follow its own singular path through the contemporary literary landscape.

—John Clement Ball

ALLISON, Dorothy E.

Nationality: American. **Born:** Greenville, South Carolina, 11 April 1949. **Education:** Florida Presbyterian College (now Eckerd College), B.A. 1971; New School for Social Research, M.A. **Family:** Companion of Alix Layman; children. **Awards:** Lambda Literary awards, 1989 and 1999. **Agent:** Frances Goldin, 305 East Eleventh Street, New York, New York 10003, U.S.A. **Address:** Box 112, Monte Rio, California 95462, U.S.A.

Publications

Novels

Bastard out of Carolina. New York, Dutton, 1992.
Cavedweller. New York, Dutton, 1998.

Short Stories

Trash. Ithaca, New York, Firebrand Books, 1988.

Poetry

The Women Who Hate Me. Brooklyn, New York, Long Haul Press, 1983.
The Women Who Hate Me: Poetry 1980–1990. Ithaca, New York, Firebrand Books,1991.

Other

Skin: Talking About Sex, Class and Literature. Ithaca, New York, Firebrand Books, 1994.
Two or Three Things I Know for Sure. New York, Dutton, 1995.
Introduction, *The Redneck Way of Knowledge: Down-Home Tales,* by Blanche McCrary Boyd. New York, Vintage Books, 1995.
Foreword, *My Dangerous Desires* by Amber L. Hollibaugh. Durham, North Carolina, Duke University Press, 2000.
Contributor, *Lesbian Words: State of the Art,* edited by Randy Turoff. New York, Masquerade Books, 1995.
Contributor, *Ida Applebroog: Nothing Personal, Paintings 1987–1997* by Ida Applebroog. New York, Distributed Art Publishers, 1998.

Contributor, *This Is What Lesbian Looks Like,* edited by Kris Kleindienst. Ithaca, New York, Firebrand Books, 1999.
Contributor, *The Beacon Best of 1999: Creative Writing by Women and Men of All Colors,* edited by Ntozake Shange. New York, Beacon Books, 1999.
Contributor, *The Mammoth Book of Modern Lesbian Short Stories,* edited by Emma Donoghue. New York, Carroll & Graf, 1999.
Contributor, *The Vintage Book of International Lesbian Fiction: An Anthology,* edited by Naomi Holoch and Joan Nestle. New York, Random/Vintage, 1999.

* * *

Dorothy Allison was born in 1949, to a teenage unwed mother in South Carolina. This fact is central to Allison's literary sensibility, which often takes up the themes of illegitimacy and poverty, marginalization and the rebellion it inspires. Like the writer herself, Allison's characters fashion themselves out of their painful circumstances, not in spite of them.

Out of her impoverished and abusive background, Allison made her way to college on a National Merit Scholarship, and by her early twenties she was living in a feminist commune in Tallahassee, Florida. There she began to take her writing seriously, and in 1988 her first book, *Trash*, a collection of short stories, was published by a small press. Shortly thereafter, a book of poetry, *The Women Who Hated Me*, appeared and heightened Allison's reputation in the gay and lesbian literary community.

Allison's first mainstream success came with *Bastard Out of Carolina*, which was well received by critics and was nominated for the National Book Award. It was also optioned and produced as a TV-movie, though not without controversy. The incest and violence at the narrative core of *Bastard* frightened off some broadcast executives, but the movie did eventually air on cable television.

A semi-autobiographical novel, *Bastard Out of Carolina* centers around a young girl, Ruth Anne (''Bone'') Boatwright, growing up as ''poor white trash'' in the small-town South of the 1950s. In addition to her decidedly Southern gift for colorful and resonant dialogue, Allison's characterization drives the novel. We meet the Boatwright aunts, uncles, and cousins and through them Allison convincingly constructs a microcosm through which to view, and to understand, the deeper psychologies of dispossession and violence. The signs of rural poverty—a surfeit of liquor, sex, and quarreling—are there, to be sure, but Allison probes beneath the conventional shorthand to show us ''the poor'' as people rather than an abstraction. Even more important, and chillingly, she also de-abstracts incest, bringing to the scenes between Bone and her stepfather, Daddy Glen, a disturbingly convincing realism.

Allison's fiction fits well into the category somewhat narrowly defined as Southern Gothic, and she counts one of the style's foremost progenitors, Flannery O'Connor, as her most important literary ancestor. But Allison's sensibility in fact relates to two broad strands in American literature: the first, James Baldwin, Tennessee Williams, Carson McCullers, and what she calls ''the whole critical tradition of southern outlaw writers, the queer, disenfranchised and expatriate novelists''; and the second, contemporary working-class novelists such as Sapphire, Terry McMillan, and Jewelle Gomez and work that otherwise shares Allison's feminist preoccupations—the poetry of Audre Lorde and Adrienne Rich, for instance. Indeed, it is not surprising that Allison the novelist would turn to poetry for inspiration. Her prose often reaches the lyrical decibels, and she has said that her novels and stories sometimes begin as poems that, through the editing process, unfold themselves into narrative strands.

In her second novel, *Cavedweller*, Allison leaves behind the autobiographical impulse of *Bastard* and invents the story of Delia Byrd, a rock-n-roller who escapes domestic violence and makes it to California, only to return to Cayro, Georgia, a decade later to struggle with alcoholism and craft a new life. *Cavedweller* is an epic narrative that traces familiar themes in Allison's work—especially maternal love and spiritual hunger.

Allison is also the author of a collection of essays, *Skin*, and a memoir adapted from a performance piece, *Two or Three Things I Know for Sure*.

—Michele S. Shauf

ALTHER, Lisa

Nationality: American. **Born:** Lisa Reed in Kingsport, Tennessee, 23 July 1944. **Education:** Wellesley College, Massachusetts, 1962–66, B.A. 1966. **Family:** Married Richard Alther in 1966; one daughter. **Career:** Editorial assistant, Atheneum Publishers, New York, 1966; staff writer, Garden Way Publishers, Charlotte, Vermont, 1969–72; visiting lecturer, St. Michael's College, Winooski, Vermont, 1980; book reviewer for newspapers and magazines. Lives in Hinesburg, Vermont. **Address:** c/o Watkins-Loomis Inc., 133 E. 35th St., No.1, New York, New York 10016, U.S.A.

Publications

Novels

Kinflicks. New York, Knopf, and London, Chatto and Windus, 1976.
Original Sins. New York, Knopf, and London, Women's Press, 1981.
Other Women. New York, Knopf, 1984; London, Viking, 1985.
Bedrock. New York, Knopf, and London, Viking, 1990.
Five Minutes in Heaven. New York, Dutton, and London, Viking, 1995.

Uncollected Short Stories

''Encounter,'' in *McCall's* (New York), August 1976.
''The Art of Dying Well,'' in *A Collection of Classic Southern Humor,* edited by George William Koon. Atlanta, Peachtree, 1984.
''Termites,'' in *Homewords,* edited by Douglas Paschall. Knoxville, University of Tennessee Press, 1986.
''The Politics of Paradise,'' in *Louder than Words,* edited by William Shore. New York, Vintage, 1989.

Other

Non-Chemical Pest and Disease Control for the Home Orchard. Charlotte, Vermont, Garden Way, 1973.
Introduction, *Tess of the D'Urbervilles: A Pure Woman* by Thomas Hardy. New York, Signet Classic, 1999.

Contributor, *Ladies Laughing: Wit as Control in Contemporary American Women Writers,* edited by Barbara Levy. Amsterdam, Netherlands, Gordon and Breach, 1997.

Contributor, *The Best of the Best: 18 New Stories by America's Leading Authors,* edited by Elaine Koster and Joseph Pittman. New York, Signet, 1998.

Contributor, *Beyond Sex and Romance?: The Politics of Contemporary Lesbian Fiction*, edited by Elaine Hutton. Women's Press, 1999.

*

Critical Studies: "Condemned to Survival: The Comic Unsuccessful Suicide" by Marilynn J. Smith, in *Comparative Literature Studies* (Urbana, Illinois), March 1980; "Alther and Dillard: The Appalachian Universe" by Frederick G. Waase, in *Appalachia/America: The Proceedings of the 1980 Appalachian Studies Conference* edited by Wilson Somerville, Johnson City, Tennesse, Appalachian Consortium Press, 1981; article in *Women Writers of the Contemporary South* edited by Peggy Whitman Prenshaw, Jackson, University Press of Mississippi, 1984.

* * *

Lisa Alther comments with shrewdness, insight—and a hefty measure of irony—upon American types, their trendy habits, and their dreams. Typical though they be, Alther's protagonists are, nevertheless, fully realized individuals who are sometimes despairing, prickly, dense, or self-destructive, but who are also unfailingly interesting folk, often surprisingly courageous survivors. These factors, along with Alther's keen sense of place, her clever manipulation of point of view, and her exploitation of various levels of comedy are the chief strengths of *Kinflicks*, *Original Sins*, and *Other Women*.

Alther's manipulation of point of view contributes to the sprawling effect of her bulky novels even as it helps control them. The picaresque *Kinflicks* alternates between third-person narration of the present moment as Ginny Babcock Bliss keeps vigil at her mother's deathbed, and first-person flashbacks which hilariously and satirically recount Ginny's penchant for redesigning herself to suit those who successively dominate her affections—parents, gum-chewing football hero, motorcycle hood, lesbian reformer, snow-mobile salesman, disturbed Viet vet, baby daughter. Ultimately, alone but rather more determined, she sets out to suit herself. The distancing effect of Ginny's memories facilitates the bald, raucous humor of the book for, in effect, Ginny is laughing at herself *with* her readers; the detachment of the third-person narrator in the alternate chapters legislates against melodrama or shallow sentimentality.

Though *Original Sins* is told in the third person, major sections allow readers to share the consciousness of five protagonists. Members of a huge extended family, sisters Emily and Sally Prince, brothers Jed and Raymond Tatro, and Donny Tatro are inseparable as children, but are later driven apart by circumstances of sex, social class, personal ambition, and race (Donny is black). A *bildungsroman, Original Sins* depicts youngsters who believe they can do anything, becoming adults who often wonder if anything worthwhile can be done—yet they never stop trying. *Other Women*, a "delayed *bildungsroman,*" also uses the third person throughout and shifts between the consciousness of its protagonists, Carolyn Kelley, a single mother whose lesbian relationship is dissolving, and her therapist, Hannah Burke. As Hannah counsels Carolyn toward acceptance of herself, adulthood, and responsibility, some of her own very old, deep wounds begin to heal, and the novel concludes with a note of genuine hope symbolized by the women's developing friendship. In *Other Women* and *Original Sins*, the availability of each protagonist's thought processes lends immediacy and realism as it arouses empathy. Readers may not fully endorse the protagonists' decisions, but they remain involved and concerned with the characters because their motivations are so clearly drawn. Suitably, the humor in these novels is quieter, developing more from quirks of personality and wry social comment than from the slapstick situations of *Kinflicks*.

Because both *Kinflicks* and *Original Sins* are set primarily in Tennessee, her home state, Alther has been dubbed a regionalist. She recognizes the influence of fellow Southerner Flannery O'Connor upon her literary sensibilities and freely acknowledges the usefulness and attraction of the "ready-made social context" available to Southerners writing about their area (see her article "Will the South Rise Again?," *New York Times Book Review,* 16 December 1979). It is equally important, however, to note that Alther's settings range across the eastern United States. Her assessment of college life on a New York City campus, her stringent portrayal of the power struggles among supposedly egalitarian Northern civil rights workers (*Original Sins*), her lovingly drawn Vermont landscapes in *Other Women*—as well as her acknowledgment that conducting a private life privately is just as difficult in any closed Northern community as it is in a Southern one (*Kinflicks*)—attest to her understanding of several locales and make explicit the wide scope of her social commentary. In this way, Alther differs a bit from regionalists who imply rather than dramatize the larger applications of their social comment.

Considered by many to be a feminist writer, Alther focuses primarily upon contemporary American women, giving great attention to the limitations thrust upon them, but she also details their self-imposed restrictions and stresses the need for each to assume responsibility for her own life. In an interview with Andrew Feinberg (*Horizon,* May 1981), she commented, "People are assigned roles because of their external characteristics and then are forced to play them out ... unless they are lucky enough to figure out what is going on and get out." The process of getting out, always painful, sometimes unsuccessful, is the motivational force in Alther's plots and functions as effectively for several male characters as it does for females. Alther's awareness that despite the deep social divisions which exist between many contemporary women and men, there are also shared problems—such as the constrictions of traditionalism, the desire to escape from parents' demands, the difficulties of assimilation into another cultural-geographic region—demonstrates the universality of feminist fiction just as her humor reveals that feminist writers can treat serious subjects without being deadly dull. By modifying critical categories, Lisa Alther produces novels incorporating strong plots and intriguing characterizations with effective social commentary.

The latter part of the 1990s saw nothing new in the way of extended fiction from Alther; however, she continued to pursue a wide-ranging career as reviewer, critic, and commentator. Her efforts included offerings as diverse as an introduction to an edition of Thomas Hardy's *Tess of the D'Urbervilles;* a discussion included in *Beyond Sex and Romance?: The Politics of Contemporary Lesbian Fiction*; and a July 1999 piece in the *Women's Review of Books* about a trip back to her home in east Tennessee. As with much of the world in the information age, Alther found that television, film, and the

Internet had greatly increased the sense of connection between this once-isolated region of Tennessee and the outside world.

—Jane S. Bakerman

AMADI, Elechi

Nationality: Nigerian. **Born:** Aluu, 12 May 1934. **Education:** University College, Ibadan, 1955–59, B.Sc. in mathematics and physics 1959. **Military Service:** Served in the Nigerian Federal Army, 1963–66, 1968–69. **Family:** Married Dorah Ohale in 1957; eight children. **Career:** Government survey assistant, Calabar, 1953–55, and surveyor, Enugu, 1959–60; science teacher in mission schools, Oba and Ahoada, 1960–63; principal, Asa Grammar School, 1967; administrative officer, 1970–74, and permanent secretary, 1975–83, Government of Rivers State, Port Harcourt; writer-in-residence and Dean of the Faculty of Arts, College of Education, Port Harcourt, 1984–87; Commissioner of Education, 1987–89, and Commissioner of Lands and Housing, 1989–90, Rivers State. **Awards:** International Writers Program grant, University of Iowa, 1973; Rivers State Silver Jubilee Merit award, 1992. **Address:** Box 331, Port Harcourt, Nigeria.

PUBLICATIONS

Novels

The Concubine. London, Heinemann, 1966.
The Great Ponds. London, Heinemann, 1969; New York, Day, 1973.
The Slave. London, Heinemann, 1978.
Estrangement. London, Heinemann, 1986.

Plays

Isiburu (in verse: produced Port Harcourt, Nigeria, 1969). London, Heinemann, 1973.
Peppersoup (produced Port Harcourt, Nigeria, 1977). Included in *Peppersoup, and The Road to Ibadan,* 1977.
The Road to Ibadan (produced Port Harcourt, Nigeria, 1977). Included in *Peppersoup, and The Road to Ibadan,* 1977.
Peppersoup, and The Road to Ibadan. Ibadan, Onibonoje Press, 1977.
Dancer of Johannesburg (produced Port Harcourt, Nigeria, 1979).

Other

Sunset in Biafra: A Civil War Diary. London, Heinemann, 1973.
Ethics in Nigerian Culture. Ibadan and London, Heinemann, 1982.
Translator, with Obiajunwo Wali and Greensille Enyinda, *Okwukwo Eri* (hymnbook). Port Harcourt, Nigeria, CSS Printers, 1969.
Translator, *Okupkpe* (prayerbook). Port Harcourt, Nigeria, CSS Printers, 1969.

*

Critical Studies: *The Concubine: A Critical View* by Alastair Niven, London, Collings, 1981; *Elechi Amadi: The Man and His Work* by Ebele Eko, Ibadan, Kraft, 1991; *Elechi Amadi at 55 (Poems, Short Stories and Papers)* edited by W. Feuser and Ebele Eko, Ibadan, Heinemann, 1994; *Four Fathers of African Fiction: A Critique of Artistic Flares and Flaws in the Major Works of Amos Tutuola, Cyprian Ekwensi, Chinua Achebe, and Elechi Amadi* by Felix Edjeren, Eregha, Nigeria, Ughelli, 1998.

Elechi Amadi comments:

(1991) I like to think of myself as a painter or composer using words in the place of pictures and musical symbols. I consider commitment in fiction a prostitution of literature. The novelist should depict life as he sees it without consciously attempting to persuade the reader to take a particular viewpoint. Propaganda should be left to journalists.

In my ideal novel the reader should feel a sense of aesthetic satisfaction that he cannot quite explain—the same feeling he gets when he listens to a beautiful symphony. For those readers who insist on being taught, there are always things to learn from a faithful portrayal of life in a well-written novel.

* * *

From his first appearance as a novelist, with *The Concubine* in 1966, Elechi Amadi established himself as a unique figure in African fiction. He was not alone in attempting to convey the day-to-day texture of traditional, pre-colonial life in an African village: Chinua Achebe's *Things Fall Apart* had already done this, at least to an extent. But he distinguished himself by not offering any explicit contrasts between that traditional world and the one that replaced it. Whereas *Things Fall Apart* and many other African novels are concerned, in part at least, with the coming of the white man and the effect of that event, Amadi's novels have never emphasized alien influences at all. The action of any of his three novels could have taken place either five years or a century before the colonial intrusion upon the area. Likewise the dilemmas that confront and finally destroy his heroes or heroines derive entirely from the beliefs, practices, and events of their indigenous culture.

The Concubine was followed by *The Great Ponds* and *The Slave.* Although not thematically related, all three novels take place in what is recognizably the same Ikweore environment. The action of all three appears to turn upon the working out of a fate that falls on the characters from outside; yet it would be meaningless, in the eyes of this traditional and god-fearing community, to call such a fate unjust. Iheoma, heroine of *The Concubine,* is powerless to avert her spiritual marriage to the sea-king, a union that prevents her having any successful human relationships. Her attraction thus becomes a fatal one, resulting in the deaths of all those who seek to free her from her condition. Likewise, the hero of *The Slave* leaves the shrine of Amadioha to which his late father was bound as an *osu* (cult-slave), and appears to have right on his side in arguing for his emancipation, since he was not actually conceived there. Nevertheless, his brief career in freedom has an obstinately circular form, curving through initial success to a series of disasters that bring him, friendless and alone, back to the shrine he had so hopefully deserted.

Amadi has maintained a nicely judged ambiguity about the meaning of these events, leaving the reader to determine that meaning instead. The society of which he writes would have rejected—and perhaps still rejects—any clear distinction between the natural and spiritual orders of existence. These interpenetrate to such an extent that man cannot demand the mastery of his fate through will alone. The highest he can aspire to is to know his fate and tune his soul to its acceptance. Tragedy springs as much from failure to do this, as from the nature of that fate itself.

—Gerald Moore

AMIS, Martin (Louis)

Nationality: British. **Born:** Oxford, 25 August 1949; son of Kingsley Amis. **Education:** Exeter College, Oxford, B.A. (honors) in English 1971. **Family:** Married 1) Antonia Phillips in 1984 (divorced 1996), two sons; 2) Isabel Fonseca in 1998, one daughter; one daughter from an earlier relationship.**Career:** Editorial assistant, *Times Literary Supplement,* London, 1972–75; assistant literary editor, 1975–77, and literary editor, 1977–79, *New Statesman,* London. Since 1979 full-time writer. Lives in London. **Awards:** Maugham award, 1974. **Agent:** Andrew Wylie, New York, New York U.S.A.

PUBLICATIONS

Novels

The Rachel Papers. London, Cape, 1973; New York, Knopf, 1974.
Dead Babies. London, Cape, 1975; New York, Knopf, 1976; as *Dark Secrets,* St. Albans, Hertfordshire, Triad, 1977.
Success. London, Cape, 1978; New York, Harmony, 1987.
Other People: A Mystery Story. London, Cape, and New York, Viking Press, 1981.
Money: A Suicide Note. London, Cape, 1984; New York, Viking, 1985.
London Fields. London, Cape, 1989; New York, Harmony, 1990.
Time's Arrow; or, The Nature of the Offence. London, Cape, and New York, Harmony, 1991.
The Information. New York, Crown Publishing, 1995.
Night Train. New York, Harmony Books, 1997.

Short Stories

Einstein's Monsters: Five Stories. London, Cape, and New York, Harmony, 1987.
Heavy Water and Other Stories. New York, Harmony Books, 1999.

Plays

Screenplays: *Mixed Doubles,* 1979; *Saturn 3,* 1980.

Other

Invasion of the Space Invaders. London, Hutchinson, 1982.
The Moronic Inferno and Other Visits to America. London, Cape, 1986; New York, Viking, 1987.
Visiting Mrs Nabokov and Other Excursions. London, Cape, 1993; New York, Harmony, 1994.
Introduction, *The Adventures of Augie March* by Saul Bellow. New York, Knopf, 1995.
Experience: A Memoir. New York, Hyperion, 2000.

*

Bibliography: *Bruce Chatwin, Martin Amis, Julian Barnes: A Bibliography of Their First Editions* by David Rees, London, Colophon Press, 1992.

Critical Studies: *Venus Envy* by Adam Mars-Jones, London, Chatto and Windus, 1990; *Martians, Monsters, and Madonna: Fiction and Form in the World of Martin Amis* by John A. Dern, New York, P. Lang, 2000.

Theatrical Activites: Actor: **Film**—*A High Wind in Jamaica*, 1965.

* * *

The buzz surrounding the release of his much anticipated memoir *Experience* has confirmed Martin Amis's standing as one of the most important contemporary English-language writers. Published in May 2000, *Experience* is a candid self-portrait of 51-year-old Amis's life, much of which has been played out in public, particularly in the press in his native Britain: his leaving his wife of almost 10 years and his two sons to take up with an American woman; his firing his agent and wife of best friend Julian Barnes in order to secure a more lucrative—some would say extravagant—advance for *The Information;* his torturous bout of dental reconstruction; and—most importantly—his complex relationship with his most famous critic and one of England's most important writers of the postwar era, his father Kingsley.

In fact, Amis's fiction has often been defined by its relationship to—and difference from—that of his father. Whereas Kingsley's writing adheres to the aesthetic conventions of realism which aspire to narrative objectivity, Martin's novels exemplify the postmodern aesthetic in which narratives call attention to themselves as fictions through the presence of an intrusive narrative voice which is often indistinguishable from that of the author. The themes pervasive in much of Amis's work—self-reflexivity, self-consciousness, epistemological and ontological uncertainty—exemplify the themes of postmodernism and the postmodern novel.

Published in 1973, when Amis was only 24, *The Rachel Papers* anticipates Amis's concern in future novels with literary and cultural self-consciousness. It is the story of Charles Highway, an articulate and arrogant 19-year-old reflecting on and trying to make sense of his life as he prepares to enter Oxford University—and adulthood. His story is centered around his seduction of Rachel, whom he meets while in London to attend a cram school for Oxford. As Highway's relationship with Rachel develops, his recognition of her corporeality is in contraposition to his fondness for language, in which he ultimately finds more abandon than sex. Generally well-received when it was first published, *The Rachel Papers* has become one of Amis's best known novels for its witty and candid representation of the transformation from adolescence to adulthood.

In *Dead Babies,* which followed in 1975, two groups of characters—the repulsively self-indulgent upper class English set of Quentin Villiers and his wife Celia, and the extremely drug-and-sex crazed Americans—team up for a weekend orgy of self-destruction that is not quite *self*-destruction since it is hurried on by the manipulative malignity of the mysterious ''Johnny'' who turns out to be none other than an alter ego of one of the ''Appleseed Rectory'' ravers. This narrative trickery, which allows Amis the freedom to ask questions about good and evil, about psychology and identity, and about the rules of narrative writing, without being stuffy or discursive, became a trademark of subsequent fictions.

Both *Success* and *Other People* disappointed certain reviewers, though for different reasons; the former, perhaps, because of its entrapment in some of Amis's obsessions and the latter, perhaps, because it attempted to break away from these obsessions and into new ground. In *Success,* Gregory Riding is another resident in the vicinity of what Philip Larkin called ''fulfillment's desolate attic.'' He is more repellingly self-infatuated than Charles Highway, but—even despite his incestuous affair with his sister—less purely evil than Quentin Villiers. As the wheel of fortune turns, he loses his superhuman abilities with women and goes poetical and mad. Terry, his foster brother and erstwhile dupe, conversely ends up top dog. The novel is written as a dialogue alternating the narratives of the foster-brothers and subtly contrasting their points of view.

The amnesiac displacement of Mary Swan's sensibility that colors the narrative of *Other People,* might be thought of as providing some sort of continuity with Gregory's ending of *Success.* This displaced sensibility provides an opaque window through which we see the world of the novel and its events. These include Mary's escape from the hospital, her stay with a group of tramps and with the alcoholic family of one of them, until this relative domestic security is broken up by the violent Jock and Trev. Mary moves on to a hostel and then to a job as a waitress and a place in a squat where she manages a brief relationship with Alan en route to the world of ordinary domesticity, of the ''other people,'' Prince, the apparently friendly policeman comes with the hints of her previous identity as a sexually predatory girl called Amy Hide, who may or may not have been murdered by a mysterious Mr. Wrong. By the end Mary seems to have rediscovered her old self but only, perhaps, in the sense that she has died into a cyclical afterlife or else returned from the death of the novel into her previous life. The novel's epilogue, in the voice of its intrusive narrator, further draws together hints that Prince may in fact be Mr. Wrong and that either or both may be identical with the narrator, who seems to aggrieved at something Mary has done to him and to be ultimately responsible for her death-in-life. Much of this is deliberately left unresolved and was condemned as incomprehensible by some readers. *Other People* is consequently Amis's most underrated novel. It demands but also rewards much careful re-reading and, while it is not as funny as his other books, its concerns are close to the lucid center of his art.

The attempt to explore the relationship of narrator to the character and to establish a new and compelling metaphor of narratorial complicity becomes a central thread of *Money* and also of Amis's 1989 work, *London Fields.* In *Money,* the narrator is a grotesque high-and-low-life television commercial director called John Self, who jets backwards and forwards across the Atlantic trying to put together a deal to direct his first feature film. Meanwhile, his precarious life falls apart as sexual, financial, and literary plots become entangled in a series of schemes of which Self turns out not to be the perpetrator, as he supposed, but the victim. *Money* is perhaps Amis's most exemplary postmodern novel, addressing the tenuous distinction between reality and make-believe, high culture and low culture, as well as the uncertainty about gender roles and the place of women in contemporary society. *Money* also questions the nature of free will in postmodern society, evidenced in Self's pathological suspicion that he is being manipulated by forces that he cannot apprehend. This issue is further complicated by the appearance in the book of Martin Amis, the writer Self hires to work on his screenplay. Amis the character's musings about the relationship between the author and the characters he creates represents the kind of self-reflexivity and the blurring of the distinction between art and life that define postmodern writing.

Keith Talent, the protagonist of *London Fields,* is still more at home in a west London pub than Self and has an equally well-developed taste for the bad. The opening statement ''Keith Talent was a bad guy …'' offers an apparently incontrovertible condemnation of his horrible taste for playing darts, more horrible appetite for video pornography, and completely dreadful habit of saying ''Cheers!'' and ''innit'' on all occasions. But Keith, repulsive though he is, is to be upstaged in the novel, both by its postmodern *femme fatale* Nicola Six and by the grander evil of the narrator Samson Young, whom she lures into being the instrument of her planned self-destruction. In some ways, *London Fields* is a recasting of some of the ideas in *Other People* according to the lessons learned in writing *Money.* It has an undercurrent—new since Amis's post-nuclear stories *Einstein's Monsters*—of global crisis and eco-consciousness. We are invited to ''imagine the atomic cloud as an inverted phallus and Nicola's loins as ground zero.'' Language glitters again and identity is a hall of mirrors and, like his darting surrogate, Amis is a master of the devastating finish.

The Jewish-American background of the narrator of *London Fields* (described in the novel's racy idiolect as a ''four-wheel Sherman'') may have anticipated the theme of *Time's Arrow,* whose title had been a provisional title for the previous book. Also reminiscent of the two previous books is Amis's determination to take on the most enormous of the social issues of the 20th century: here it is the Nazi Holocaust and its aftermath. *Time's Arrow* is Amis's most ambitious technical achievement to date and is, indeed, one of the most extraordinary narrative experiments in existence, almost unprecedented outside of the science fiction of Philip K. Dick. The novel is written in reverse time, tracing a typical American suburban scene of the present back to the concentration camp Auschwitz, where its narrator, Odilo Unverdorben, has been an official. Some readers have complained that the cleverness and showiness of the time experiment detracts from the seriousness of the subject, but this need not be so. Read in the tradition of an experimental and historically traumatized novel like Kurt Vonnegut's *Slaughterhouse Five* or else backed-up by the critiques of rationalist intellectual constructions provided by postmodernist theoreticians like Theodor Adorno, the disturbances created by the novel's form and by its horrific subject matter hang nightmarishly together.

If *Time's Arrow* might have led us to expect a development away from the brilliant satire of the early novels towards a more sober and mature seriousness in Amis's work, then *The Information* must represent something of a disappointment. It is a book that euphorically condemns middle-age but which is surely itself written out of a deeply repressed fear of aging and its disillusionments. In *The Information,* Amis turns his gaze toward a kind of 40-year-old alter ego called Richard Tull—a novelist who is quite pathetically unsuccessful and who ekes out a modicum of literary income and of self-respect from the occasional review. For the most part, it must be said, Amis's reviewers took this chastening portrait of their craft in fairly good part. While Tull vegetates in the ruins of his ego and ambition, his arch rival Gwyn Barry strides from success to success. Only further disappointments greet Tull, and what the novel calls ''the information'' is his growing sense of vacuity and despair. Amis is quite relentlessly brilliant here, once again, on the compromises to and erosions of literary ambition that are brought on by domesticity and by the loss of a sentimentally cherished but unattainable ideal. Tull is, in some ways, the most fully fleshed, and the most convincing of all of Amis's postmodern grotesques, and he would quite probably have been the most congenial if the author had once relaxed and allowed him to peep out from beneath the high steel-capped heels of his satire. Neither he, nor the author, seem to contemplate for a moment the redeeming possibility that literary success is neither the only nor the absolute in human values; perhaps much in postmodern culture would lead us to the same conclusion.

Night Train, Amis's ninth and most recent novel, was published in 1997 to mixed reviews, criticized by some for sparseness of style and, as John Updike has said, for its ''post-human'' quality. *Night Train* is the story of the jaded, tough-talking female detective Mike Hoolihan whose pointed unsentimentality is shaken by the apparent suicide of her boss's daughter Jennifer, whose grisly death seems incongruous with her charmed life. At her boss's request, Mike undertakes to find Jennifer's killer, as it seems unlikely that her death would have been self-inflicted in light of her personal and professional successes, as well as her apparent optimism and benignity. Mike's investigation yields some startling revelations about her own identity and, more generally, about the development of the female identity in the postmodern world, a theme that is pervasive in much of Amis's work. Perhaps more significantly, *Night Train* explores the issue of motive in postmodernity, another theme important to Amis's work. In typical Amis fashion, *Night Train* bucks the conventions of genre, offering a detective story in which motive itself becomes the suspect.

In addition to his memoir *Experience* and the nine novels, Amis has published the short story collections *Einstein's Monsters* and *Heavy Water and Other Stories* as well as numerous essays, many of which have been collected in *Invasion of the Space Invaders, The Moronic Inferno and Other Visits to America,* and *Visiting Mrs. Nabokov and Other Excursions.*

—Richard Brown, updated by Alan Rubin

ANAND, Mulk Raj

Nationality: Indian. **Born:** Peshawar, 12 December 1905. **Education:** Khalsa College, Amritsar; Punjab University, 1921–24, B.A. (honours) 1924; University College, University of London, 1926–29, Ph.D.; Cambridge University, 1929–30; League of Nations School of Intellectual Cooperation, Geneva, 1930–32. **Family:** Married 1) Kathleen Van Gelder in 1939 (divorced 1948); 2) Shirin Vajifdar in 1950, one daughter. **Career:** Lecturer, School of Intellectual Cooperation, Summer 1930, and Workers Educational Association, London, intermittently 1932–45; has also taught at the universities of Punjab, Benares, and Rajasthan, Jaipur, 1948–66; Tagore Professor of Literature and Fine Art, University of Punjab, 1963–66; Visiting Professor, Institute of Advanced Studies, Simla, 1967–68. Fine Art Chairman, Lalit Kala Akademi (National Academy of Art), New Delhi, 1965–70. Since 1946 editor, *Marg* magazine, Bombay: editor and contributor, *Marg Encyclopedia of Art,* 136 vols., 1948–81; since 1946 director, Kutub Publishers, Bombay. Since 1970 President of the Lokayata Trust, for creating a community and cultural centre in Hauz Khas village, New Delhi. **Awards:** Leverhulme fellowship, 1940–42; World Peace Council prize, 1952; Padma Bhushan, India, 1968; Akademi prize, for *Morning Face,* 1970; Sahitya Academy award, 1974; Birla award; distinguished writer award, State Goverment of Maharashtra, India. D.Litt: University of Delhi, University of Patiala, University of Andhra, University of Benaras, and University of Kanpur. Fellow, Indian Academy of Letters. **Address:** 25 Cuffe Parade, Bombay 400 005, India.

Publications

Novels

Untouchable. London, Wishart, 1935; New York, New York Liberty Press, n.d.; revised edition, London, Bodley Head, 1970.
The Coolie. London, Lawrence and Wishart, 1936; as *Coolie,* London, Penguin, 1945; New York, Liberty Press, 1952; revised edition, London, Bodley Head, 1972.
Two Leaves and a Bud. London, Lawrence and Wishart, 1937; New York, Liberty Press, 1954.
The Village. London, Cape, 1939.
Lament on the Death of a Master of Arts. Lucknow, Naya Sansar, 1939.
Across the Black Waters. London, Cape, 1940.
The Sword and the Sickle. London, Cape, 1942.
The Big Heart. London, Hutchinson, 1945; revised edition, edited by Saros Cowasjee, New Delhi, Arnold-Heinemann, 1980.
Private Life of an Indian Prince. London, Hutchinson, 1949; revised edition, London, Bodley Head, 1970.
Seven Summers: The Story of an Indian Childhood. London, Hutchinson, 1951.
The Old Woman and the Cow. Bombay, Kutub, 1960; as *Gauri,* New Delhi, Orient, 1976; Liverpool, Lucas, 1987.
The Road. Bombay, Kutub, 1961; London, Oriental University Press, 1987.
Death of a Hero. Bombay, Kutub, 1963.
Morning Face. Bombay, Kutub, 1968; Liverpool, Lucas, and East Brunswick, New Jersey, Books from India, 1986.
Confession of a Lover. New Delhi, Arnold-Heinemann, 1976; Liverpool, Lucas, 1988.
The Bubble. New Delhi, Arnold-Heinemann, 1987; Liverpool, Lucas, 1988.

Short Stories

The Lost Child and Other Stories. London, J.A. Allen, 1934.
The Barber's Trade Union and Other Stories. London, Cape, 1944.
The Tractor and the Corn Goddess and Other Stories. Bombay, Thacker, 1947.
Reflections on the Golden Bed. Bombay, Current Book House, 1947.
The Power of Darkness and Other Stories. Bombay, Jaico, 1958.
Lajwanti and Other Stories. Bombay, Jaico, 1966.
Between Tears and Laughter. New Delhi, Sterling, 1973.
Selected Short Stories of Mulk Raj Anand, edited by M.K. Naik. New Delhi, Arnold-Heinemann, 1977.
Tales Told by an Idiot: Selected Short Stories. Mumbai, Jaico Publishing House, 1999.

Play

India Speaks (produced London, 1943).

Other

Persian Painting. London, Faber, 1930.
Curries and Other Indian Dishes. London, Harmsworth, 1932.
The Golden Breath: Studies in Five Poets of the New India. London, Murray, and New York, Dutton, 1933.
The Hindu View of Art. Bombay, Asia Publishing House, and London, Allen and Unwin, 1933; revised edition, Asia Publishing House, 1957.
Letters on India. London, Routledge, 1942.
Apology for Heroism: An Essay in Search of Faith. London, Drummond, 1946.
Homage to Tagore. Lahore, Sangam, 1946.
Indian Fairy Tales: Retold (for children). Bombay, Kutub, 1946.
On Education. Bombay, Hind Kitabs, 1947.
The Bride's Book of Beauty, with Krishna Hutheesing. Bombay, Kutub, 1947; as *The Book of Indian Beauty,* Rutland, Vermont, Tuttle, 1981.
The Story of India (for children). Bombay, Kutub, 1948.
The King-Emperor's English; or, The Role of the English Language in the Free India. Bombay, Hind Kitabs, 1948.
Lines Written to an Indian Air: Essays. Bombay, Nalanda, 1949.
The Indian Theatre. London, Dobson, 1950; New York, Roy, 1951.
The Story of Man (for children). New Delhi, Sikh Publishing House, 1952.
The Dancing Foot. New Delhi, Ministry of Information, 1957.
Kama Kala: Some Notes on the Philosophical Basis of Hindu Erotic Sculpture. London, Skilton, 1958; New York, Lyle Stuart, 1962.
India in Colour. Bombay, Taraporevala, London, Thames and Hudson, and New York, McGraw Hill, 1959.
More Indian Fairy Tales (for children). Bombay, Kutub, 1961.
Is There a Contemporary Indian Civilisation? Bombay, Asia Publishing House, 1963.
The Story of Chacha Nehru (for children). New Delhi, Rajpal, 1965.
The Third Eye: A Lecture on the Appreciation of Art. Patiala, University of Punjab, 1966.
The Humanism of M.K. Gandhi: Three Lectures. Chandigarh, University of Panjab, 1967(?).
The Volcano: Some Comments on the Development of Rabindranath Tagore's Aesthetic Theories. Baroda, Maharaja Sayajirao University, 1968.
Roots and Flowers: Two Lectures on the Metamorphosis of Technique and Content in the Indian-English Novel. Dharwar, Karnatak University, 1972.
Mora. New Delhi, National Book Trust, 1972.
Author to Critic: The Letters of Mulk Raj Anand, edited by Saros Cowasjee. Calcutta, Writers Workshop, 1973.
Album of Indian Paintings. New Delhi, National Book Trust, 1973.
Folk Tales of Punjab. New Delhi, Sterling, 1974.
Seven Little-Known Birds of the Inner Eye. Rutland, Vermont, Tuttle, 1978.
The Humanism of Jawaharlal Nehru. Calcutta, Visva-Bharati, 1978.
The Humanism of Rabindranath Tagore. Aurangabad, Marathwada University, 1979.
Maya of Mohenjo-Daro (for children). New Delhi, Children's Book Trust, n.d.
Conversations in Bloomsbury (reminiscences). New Delhi, Arnold-Heinemann, and London, Wildwood House, 1981.
Madhubani Painting. New Delhi, Ministry of Information and Broadcasting, 1984; Oxford, Oxford University Press, 1995.
Pilpali Sahab: Story of a Childhood under the Raj (autobiography). New Delhi, Arnold-Heinemann, 1985.
Poet-Painter: Paintings by Rabindranath Tagore. New Delhi, Abhinav, 1985.
Homage to Jamnalal Bajaj: A Pictorial Biography. Ahmedabad, Allied, 1988.
Amrita Sher Gill: An Essay in Interpretation. New Delhi, National Gallery of Modern Art, 1989.
Kama Yoga. New Delhi, Arnold, and Edinburgh, Aspect, n.d.
Chitralakshana (on Indian painting). New Delhi, National Book Trust, n.d.
Afterword, *The Panorama of Jaipur Paintings* by Rita Pratap. New Delhi, D. K. Printworld, 1996.
Afterword, *Price of Partition: Recollections and Reflections* by Rafiq Zakaria. Mumbai, Bharatiya Vidya Bhavan, 1998.
Afterword, *V. K. Krishna Menon: A Biography* by K. C. Arora. New Delhi, Sanchar Publishing House, 1998.
Editor, *Marx and Engels on India.* Allahabad, Socialist Book Club, 1933.
Editor, with Iqbal Singh, *Indian Short Stories.* London, New India, 1947.
Editor, *Introduction to Indian Art,* by A.K. Coomaraswamy. Madras, Theosophical Publishing House, and Wheaton, Illinois, Theosophical Press, 1956.
Editor, *Experiments: Contemporary Indian Short Stories.* Agra, Kranchalson, 1968.
Editor, *Annals of Childhood.* Agra, Kranchalson, 1968.
Editor, *Grassroots.* Agra, Kranchalson, 1968(?).
Editor, *Tales from Tolstoy.* New Delhi, Arnold-Heinemann, 1978.
Editor, with Lance Dane, *Kama Sutra of Vatsyayana* (from translation by Sir Richard Burton and F.F. Arbuthnot). New Delhi, Arnold-Heinemann, and Atlantic Highlands, New Jersey, Humanities Press, 1982.
Editor, with S. Balu Rao, *Panorama: An Anthology of Modern Indian Short Stories.* New Delhi, Sterling, 1986; London, Oriental University Press, 1987.
Editor, *Chacha Nehru.* New Delhi, Sterling, 1987.
Editor, *Aesop's Fables.* New Delhi, Sterling, 1987.
Editor, *The Historic Trial of Mahatma Gandhi.* New Delhi, National Council of Educational Research and Training, 1987.
Editor, *The Other Side of the Medal,* by Edward Thompson. New Delhi, Sterling, 1989.
Editor, *Sati: A Writeup of Raja Ram Mohan Roy about Burning of Widows Alive.* New Delhi, B.R. Publishing, 1989.
Editor, *Splendors of Himachal Heritage.* New Delhi, Abhinav Publications, 1997.

*

Bibliography: *Mulk Raj Anand: A Checklist* by Gillian Packham, Mysore, Centre for Commonwealth Literature and Research, 1983.

Critical Studies: *Mulk Raj Anand: A Critical Essay* by Jack Lindsay, Bombay, Hind Kitabs, 1948, revised edition, as *The Elephant and the Lotus,* Bombay, Kutub, 1954; "Mulk Raj Anand Issue" of *Contemporary Indian Literature* (New Delhi), 1965; *An Ideal of Man in Anand's Novels* by D. Riemenschneider, Bombay, Kutub, 1969; *Mulk Raj Anand: The Man and the Novelist* by Margaret Berry, Amsterdam, Oriental Press, 1971; *Mulk Raj Anand* by K.N. Sinha, New York, Twayne, 1972; *Mulk Raj Anand* by M.K. Naik, New Delhi, and

London, Arnold-Heinemann, and New York, Humanities Press, 1973; *Anand: A Study of His Fiction in Humanist Perspective* by G.S. Gupta, Bareilly, Prakash, 1974; *So Many Freedoms: A Study of the Major Fiction of Mulk Raj Anand* by Saros Cowasjee, New Delhi and London, Oxford University Press, 1978; *Perspectives on Mulk Raj Anand* edited by K.K. Sharma, Atlantic Highlands, New Jersey, Humanities Press, 1978; *The Yoke of Pity: A Study in the Fictional Writings of Mulk Raj Anand* by Alastair Niven, New Delhi, Arnold-Heinemann, 1978; *The Sword and the Sickle: A Study of Mulk Raj Anand's Novels* by K.V. Suryanarayana Murti, Mysore, Geetha, 1983; *The Novels of Mulk Raj Anand: A Thematic Study* by Premila Paul, New Delhi, Sterling, 1983; *The Wisdom of the Heart: A Study of the Works of Mulk Raj Anand* by Marlene Fisher, New Delhi, Sterling, 1985; *Studies in Mulk Raj Anand* by P.K. Rajan, New Delhi, Arnold, 1986; *Mulk Raj Anand: A Home Appraisal* edited by Atma Ram, Hoshairpur, Punjab, Chaarvak, 1988; *The Language of Mulk Raj Anand, Raja Rao, and R.K. Narayan* by Reza Ahmad Nasimi, New Delhi, Capital, 1989; *Mulk Raj Anand: A Short Story Writer* by Vidhya Mohan Shethi, New Delhi, Ashish, n.d; *Six Indian Novelists: Mulk Raj Anand, Raja Rao, R.K. Narayan, Balachandran Rajan, Kamala Markandaya, Anita Desai* by A. V. Suresh Kumar, New Delhi, Creative Books, 1996; *Mulk Raj Anand: The Journalist* by Gita Bamezai, New Delhi, Kanishka Publishers, 2000.

Mulk Raj Anand comments:

I began to write early—a kind of free verse in the Punjabi and Urdu languages, from the compulsion of the shock of the death of my cousin when she was nine years old. I wrote a letter to God telling him He didn't exist. Later, going through the dark night of another bereavement, when my aunt committed suicide because she was excommunicated for interdining with a Muslim woman, I wrote an elegy. Again, when I fell in love with a young Muslim girl, who was married off by arrangement, I wrote calf love verse. The poet-philosopher, Muhammad Iqbal, introduced me to the problems of the individual through his long poem ''Secrets of the Self.'' Through him, I also read Nietzsche to confirm my rejection of God. After a short term in jail, my father, who was pro-British, punished my mother for my affiliations with the Gandhi Movement. I went to Europe and studied various philosophical systems and found that these comprehensive philosophies did not answer life's problems. I was beaten up for not blacklegging against workers in 1926, in the coal-miner's strike. I joined a Marxist worker's study circle with Trade Unionist Alan Hutt, and met Palme-Dutt, John Strachey, T.S. Eliot, Herbert Read, Bonamy Dobrée, Harold Laski, Leonard Woolf. During that time I fell in love with a young Welsh girl painter, Irene, whose father was a biologist. For her I wrote a long confession about the break-up of my family, the British impact, and my later life. Nobody would publish the narrative. So I began to rewrite portions, as allegories, short stories, and novels. On a tour with Irene, in Paris, Rome, Vienna, Berlin, Brussels, I discovered Rimbaud, Gide, and Joyce. My first attempt at a novel was revised in Gandhi's Sabarmati Ashram in Ahmedabad, but was turned down by 19 publishers in London. The 20th offered to publish it if E.M. Forster wrote a Preface. This the author of *A Passage to India* did.

Since the publication of this first novel, I have written continuously on the human situation in the lives of people of rejects, outcasts, peasants, lumpen, and other eccentrics, thrown up during the transition from the ancient orthodox Indian society to the self-conscious modernist secular democracy.

I believe that creating literature is the true medium of humanism as against systematic philosophies, because the wisdom of the heart encourages insights in all kinds of human beings who grow to self-consciousness through conflicts of desire, will, and mood. I am inclined to think that the highest aim of poetry and art is to integrate the individual into inner growth and outer adjustment. The broken bundle of mirrors of the human personality in our time can only become the enchanted mirror if the sensibility is touched in its utmost pain and sheer pleasure and tenderest moments. No rounded answers are possible. Only hunches, insights, and inspirations and the *karuna* that may come from understanding.

The novelist's task is that of an all-comprehending ''God,'' who understands every part of his creation, through pity, compassion, or sympathy—which is the only kind of catharsis possible in art. The world is itself action of the still center. The struggle to relate the word and the deed in the life of men is part of the process of culture, through which illumination comes to human beings. The world of art is communication from one individual to another, or to the group through the need to connect. This may ultimately yield the slogan ''love one another,'' if mankind is to survive (against its own inheritance of fear, hatred, and contempt, now intensified through money-power, or privileges, and large-scale violence of wars) into the 21st century, in any human form.

*   *   *

Mulk Raj Anand is the champion of the underdog. All his novels deal with the underprivileged sections of Indian society. He was the first Indian novelist to make an untouchable the hero of a novel. *Untouchable* describes one day in the life of 18-year-old Bakha, who is treated as dirt by all Hindus just because his profession is to clean latrines. Artistically it is the most perfect of Anand's earlier novels. The distinction of Anand's writing lies in capturing Bakha's work ethic—Bakha tackles his odious job with a conscientiousness that invests his movements with beauty. The next novel, *Coolie*, has a wider canvas and is more diffuse in structure. Munoo, a young orphan, works at a variety of odd jobs at Daulatpur, Bombay, and Simla till he dies aged 15 of tuberculosis brought on by undernourishment. Munoo is exploited not because of caste but because he is poor. *Two Leaves and a Bud* is about the plight of the laborers in a tea plantation in Assam; the novel fails because Anand's approach is too simplistic; the English owners are shown as unmitigated villains. Anand's next work was a trilogy with the young Lal Singh as hero. *The Village* is an authentic picture of a typical Punjabi village, and shows the adolescent Lal Singh rebelling against the narrow superstitions of the villagers—he goes so far as to cut his hair, unthinkable for a Sikh. *Across the Black Waters* shows Lal as a soldier fighting in the trenches of Flanders in World War I; his contact with the French makes him realize that the white races too are human, and not demigods like the British in India. *The Sword and the Sickle* shows Lal engaged in revolutionary activities in India after eloping with the village landlord's daughter; it is not as well written as the earlier two volumes.

Anand is a prolific writer, and has written a large number of extremely varied short stories. They reveal his gift for humor, and deal in a lighter vein with the problems that engage him in his novels—the exploitation of the poor, the impact of industrialization, colonialism, and race relations. One of Anand's best novels, *The Big Heart*, deals with the traditional coppersmiths who feel threatened by mechanization. The large-hearted Ananta tries to weld them into a trade union; he tells them that it is not the machines but the owners who exploit them, but he dies in a scuffle before his ideals can be realized.

The Old Woman and the Cow (republished as *Gauri*) takes up the plight of another underprivileged section of society—women. The heroine, Gauri, is sold to an old money-lender by her own mother out of economic necessity. Gauri re-enacts the *Ramayana* myth of Sita by staying for some time in the house of the old banker, just as Sita had to stay with Ravana. Gauri is reunited with her husband Panchi just as Sita was reunited with Rama, and Panchi rejects her later, just as Rama rejected the pregnant Sita because of social pressures. At this point, Anand gives a new turn to the old myth: unlike Sita who bore her sufferings meekly, Gauri rejects her cowardly husband and goes on to build a new life for herself. The story is well conceived and the use of the myth original, but the writing is hurried and slipshod, the harangues on social justice not organic to the plot. *Private Life of an Indian Prince*, a study of a neurotic maharajah, is confused and disorganized; some critics, however, have defended the narrative as a true reflection of the hero's psyche, and consider it Anand's best novel.

Anand is now at work on an ambitious seven-volume autobiographical novel, *The Seven Ages of Man*. *Seven Summers*, published more than four decades ago, is a lyrical account of early childhood, primarily from the child's point of view. *Morning Face* describes the life of the protagonist, Krishan Chander Azad, up to the age of 15, and we get a vivid picture of the brutality that once passed for school-teaching. *Confessions of a Lover* deals with Krishan's undergraduate days at Khalsa College, Amritsar. The novel is not only a moving human document, it is an authentic account of life in the Punjab in the 1920's, and records the ferment caused by Gandhi's *satyagraha*. The fourth volume, *The Bubble*, covers the period 1925–29; it shows Krishan as a student in England, obtaining a Ph.D. degree. He falls in love with Irene Rhys, and pours out his feelings by writing a long novel (just as Anand did in real life). Most of Anand's works have a linear structure, but *The Bubble* departs from this convention. It is in the form of letters, diary entries, and excerpts from the novel Krishan is writing; it also includes numerous philosophical discussions. The life of an Indian student in England of the time, and particularly Krishan's loneliness, are impressively portrayed. But, like *Morning Face* and *Confessions of a Lover*, *The Bubble* is too long (600 pages). If only the ''outpourings'' had been sensitively edited, *The Bubble* would have been Anand's best work, and a triumph in terms of technique.

The forthcoming *And So He Plays His Part* is the fifth volume of *The Seven Ages of Man*. Anand observes in his ''Afterwords'' (*sic*), ''As the forthcoming novel entitled *And So He Plays His Part* is seven novels in one, I have decided to issue it in parts, beginning with *Little Plays of Mahatma Gandhi*, as work in progress, symbolic of my departure from the accepted form.'' This ''novel'' is in the form of 15 scenes of a drama, framed by a long letter to Irene and a postscript to this letter, and shows the hero Krishan Chaner Azad living in Gandhi's ashram at Sabarmati, working on a novel with an untouchable as hero. All the characters, including historical figures like Gandhi and Subhas Chandra Bose, speak the same bad English, and the exclamation mark seems to be the only punctuation in their speeches. The innumerable mistakes of spelling and grammar (perhaps the printer is to blame) make it difficult for the reader to appreciate Anand's new perspective on Mahatma Gandhi.

Anand attempts to capture the ambiance of Punjabi life by literally translating words and phrases, but this device does not always succeed. Readers outside the Punjab may find it difficult to make anything of phrases like ''there is no talk,'' and ''May I be your sacrifice.'' However, Anand is successful in presenting a vivid picture of the Punjabi peasant and the problems of the poor. The range of his novels is impressive, covering not only the Punjab but life in towns like Bombay and Simla, the trenches of Flanders, and the tea gardens of Assam. His concern for the underdog does not take the form of communism—he is above all a humanist, and his humanism embraces all aspects of life, from contemporary slums to ancient Indian art and philosophy.

—Shyamala A. Narayan

ANAYA, Rudolfo A(lfonso)

Nationality: American. **Born:** Pastura, New Mexico, 30 October 1937. **Education:** Albuquerque High School, graduated 1956; Browning Business School, Albuquerque, 1956–58; University of New Mexico, Albuquerque, B.A. in literature 1963, M.A. in literature 1968, M.A. in guidance and counseling 1972. **Family:** Married Patricia Lawless in 1966. **Career:** Teacher, Albuquerque public schools, 1963–70. Director of Counseling, 1971–73, associate professor 1974–88, professor of English, 1988–93, and since 1993, professor emeritus, University of New Mexico. Lecturer, Universidad Anahuac, Mexico City, Summer 1974; teacher, New Mexico Writers Workshop, Albuquerque, summers 1977–79. Associate editor, *American Book Review,* New York, 1980–85. Since 1989 founding editor, *Blue Mesa Review,* Albuquerque. Vice-president, Coordinating Council of Literary Magazines, 1974–80. **Awards:** Quinto Sol prize, 1971; University of New Mexico Mesa Chicana award, 1977; City of Los Angeles award, 1977; New Mexico Governor's award, 1978, 1980; National Chicano Council on Higher Education fellowship, 1978; National Endowment for the Arts fellowship, 1979; Before Columbus Foundation award, 1980; Corporation for Public Broadcasting Script Development award, 1982; Kellogg Foundation fellowship, 1983; Mexican Medal of Friendship, 1986. D.H.L.: University of Albuquerque, 1981; Marycrest College, Davenport, Iowa, 1984. **Address:** 5324 Canada Vista N.W., Albuquerque, New Mexico 87120, USA.

PUBLICATIONS

Novels

Bless Me, Ultima. Berkeley, California, Quinto Sol, 1972.
Heart of Aztlán. Berkeley, California, Justa, 1976.
Tortuga. Berkeley, California, Justa, 1979.
The Legend of La Llorona. Berkeley, California, Tonatiuh-Quinto Sol, 1984.
Lord of the Dawn: The Legend of Quetzalcoatl. Albuquerque, University of New Mexico Press, 1987.
Alburquerque. Albuquerque, University of New Mexico Press, 1992.
Zia Summer. New York, Warner, 1995.
Jalamanta: A Message from the Desert. New York, Warner, 1996.
Rio Grande Fall. New York, Warner Books, 1996.
Shaman Winter. New York, Warner Books, 1999.

Short Stories

The Silence of Llano. Berkeley, California, Tonatiuh-Quinto Sol, 1982.

Uncollected Short Stories

''The Captain,'' in *A Decade of Hispanic Literature.* Houston, Revista Chincano-Riqueña, 1982.
''The Road to Platero,'' in *Rocky Mountain* (St. James, Colorado), April 1982.
''The Village Which the Gods Painted Yellow,'' in *Nuestro,* January-February 1983.
''B. Traven Is Alive and Well in Cuernavaca,'' in *Cuentos Chicanos,* revised edition. Albuquerque, University of New Mexico Press, 1984.
''In Search of Epifano,'' in *Voces.* Albuquerque, El Norte-Academia, 1987.

Plays

The Season of La Llorona (produced Albuquerque, 1979).
Who Killed Don Jose? (produced Albuquerque, 1987).
The Farolitos of Christmas (produced Albuquerque, 1987). New York, Hyperion, 1995.

Screenplay (documentary): *Bilingualism: Promise for Tomorrow,* 1976.

Poetry

The Adventures of Juan Chicaspatas. Houston, Arte Publico Press, 1985.

Other

A Chicano in China. Albuquerque, University of New Mexico Press, 1986.
Flow of the River. Albuquerque, Hispanic Culture Foundation, 1988.
The Anaya Reader. New York, Warner, 1995.
Maya's Children: The Story of La Llorona, illustrated by Maria Baca. New York, Hyperion Books for Children, 1997.
Farolitos for Abuelo, illustrated by Edward Gonzales. New York, Hyperion Books for Children, 1998.
My Land Sings: Stories from the Rio Grande, illustrated by Amy Cordova. New York, Morrow Junior Books, 1999.
Roadrunner's Dance, illustrated by David Diaz. New York, Hyperion Books for Children, 2000.
An Elegy on the Death of Cesar Chavez, with illustrations by Gaspar Enriquez. El Paso, Texas, Cinco Puntos Press, 2000.
Contributor, *Muy Macho: Latin Men Confront Their Manhood,* edited by Ray Gonzales. New York, Anchor, 1996.
Contributor, *The Floating Borderlands: Twenty-Five Years of U.S. Hispanic Literature,* edited by Lauro Flores. Seattle, University of Washington Press, 1999.
Contributor, *Saints and Sinners: The American Catholic Experience through Stories, Memoirs, Essays, and Commentary,* edited by Greg Tobin. New York, Doubleday, 1999.
Editor, with Jim Fisher, *Voices from the Rio Grande.* Albuquerque, Rio Grande Writers Association, 1976.
Editor, with Antonio Márquez, *Cuentos Chicanos.* Albuquerque, New America, 1980; revised edition, Albuquerque, University of New Mexico Press, 1984.
Editor, with Simon J. Ortiz, *A Ceremony of Brotherhood 1680–1980.* Albuquerque, Academia, 1981.
Editor, *Voces: An Anthology of Nuevo Mexicano Writers.* Albuquerque, El Norte-Academia, 1987.
Editor, with Francisco A. Lomeli, *Atzlan: Essays on the Chicano Homeland.* Albuquerque, El Norte-Academia, 1989.
Editor, *Tierra: Contemporary Short Fiction of New Mexico.* El Paso, Texas, Cinco Puntos Press, 1989.
Foreword, *Dictionary of Hispanic Biography,* edited by Joseph C. Tardiff and L. Mpho Mabunda. Detroit, Gale, 1996.
Translator, *Cuentos: Tales from the Hispanic Southwest, Based on Stories Originally Collected by Juan B. Rael,* edited by José Griego y Maestas. Santa Fe, Museum of New Mexico Press, 1980.

*

Manuscript Collection: Zimmerman Library, University of New Mexico, Albuquerque.

Critical Studies: ''Extensive/Intensive Dimensionality in Anaya's *Bless Me, Ultima*'' by Daniel Testa, in *Latin American Literary Review* (Pittsburgh), Spring-Summer 1977; ''Degradacion y Regeneracion en *Bless Me, Ultima*'' by Roberto Cantu, in *The Identification and Analysis of Chicano Literature* edited by Francisco Jimenez, New York, Bilingual Press, 1979; *Chicano Authors: Inquiry by Interview* edited by Juan Bruce-Novoa, Austin, University of Texas Press, 1980; *The Magic of Words: Rudolfo A. Anaya and His Writings* edited by Paul Vassallo, Albuquerque, University of New Mexico Press, 1982; article by Anaya, in *Contemporary Authors Autobiography Series 4* edited by Adele Sarkissian, Detroit, Gale, 1986; *Rudolfo A. Anaya: Focus on Criticism* edited by César A. González-T., La Jolla, California, Lalo Press, 1990 (includes bibliography by Teresa Márquez); *Keep Blessing Us, Ultima: A Teaching Guide for Bless Me, Ultima by Rudolfo Anaya* by Abelardo Baeza, Austin, Texas, Easkin Press, 1997; *Conversations with Rudolfo Anaya,* edited by Bruce Dick and Silvio Sirias, Jackson, University Press of Mississippi, 1998; *A Sense of Place: Rudolfo A. Anaya: An Annotated Bio-Bibliography* by Cesar A. Gonzalez, Berkeley, University of California Press, 1999; *Rudolfo A. Anaya: A Critical Companion* by Margarite Fernandez Olmos, Westport, Connecticut, Greenwood Press, 1999.

Rudolfo A. Anaya comments:

(1995) I was born and raised in the eastern llano, plains country, of New Mexico. I spent my first 14 years in Santa Rosa, New Mexico, a town bisected by the Pecos River and Highway 66. My ancestors were the men and women of the Rio Grande Valley of the Albuquerque area who went east to settle the llano.

The llano was important for grazing sheep, and yet there were along the Pecos river little farming communities. My mother's family comes from such a small Hispanic village, Puerto de Luna. The most important elements of my childhood are the people of those villages and the wide open plains, and the landscape.

In my first novel, *Bless Me, Ultima*, I used the people and the environment of my childhood as elements of the story. Like my protagonist, Antonio, my first language was Spanish. I was shaped by the traditions and culture of the free-wheeling cow punchers and sheep herders of the llano, a lifestyle my father knew well, and was also initiated into the deeply religious, Catholic settled life of the farmers of Puerto de Luna, my mother's side of the family.

The oral tradition played an important role in my life. I learned about story from the cuentistas, the oral storytellers. It is a tradition one often loses when one moves into print, but its elements are strong and as valuable today as they have been historically. I want my literature to be accessible to my community, and I want it to reflect the strands of history which define us.

Because the Mexican American community has existed within the larger Anglo American society since the 19th century, and legally since 1848, our place in the history of this country is unique. We have a long history in the southwest, in the western United States. That history is generally not well known. Cultural identity is important to us as a way to keep the values and traditions of our forefathers intact.

In the 1960s the Mexican Americans created a social, political, and artistic movement known as the Chicano Movement. As a writer, I was an active participant in that movement. My second novel, *Heart of Aztlán*, deals with themes in the Chicano Movement. The novel explores a return to Mexican mythology. Chicano artists and writers like me returned to Mexican legends, mythology, and symbolism to create part of our Chicano expression.

When I was 16 I hurt my back and stayed a summer in a hospital. In *Tortuga,* I explored some of the consequences of that stay. The hero of the story is a young man who must find some redemption in suffering. The mythopoeic forces which had influenced my first two novels also are at work in the healing process which the protagonist must undergo.

Western writers reflect their landscape. We cannot escape the bond we have to our environment, the elements, especially water. As a Chicano writer I am part of a community which for the first time in our contemporary era has produced enough literary works to create a literary movement. Prior to the 1960s western literature was written about us, but seldom by us. Now the world has a truer insight into our world; the view is now from within as more and more Chicano and Chicana writers explore their reality.

Recently my work has taken a turn, and I have written my first murder mystery, *Zia Summer*. Although the form has certain requirements, often called the formula of a murder mystery, I have found the genre an interesting way to communicate my ideas. As an insider into Nuevo Mexicano (New Mexico) culture, I explore the cultural history of the region. I want my work to reflect the values of those ancestors who have lived in the Rio Grande Valley for so many centuries.

I am very interested in the spiritual values that are my inheritance, both from the Spanish/Mexican heritage and from the Native American side. As a mestizo, a person born from these two broad streams (or more correctly, from *many* inheritances), I want to create a synthesis, a worldview. I use the murder mystery genre as a tale of contemporary adventure, but the story within is laden with the cultural depth and richness that is our way of life. Ancestral values are the substratum of my work, as they have always been. I hope this new type of ''adventure'' fiction creates a mirror for our contemporary journey, a point of discussion of our world view.

This turn in my writing has been most enjoyable. The page-turning quality of the murder mystery allows me to have fun. Yes, fun. A writer should enjoy his work in spite of the cost. Each one of us suffers his own pain. But the new form also has a serious intent. It still allows me the deeper exploration that is part of my search for meaning.

An example of this continuing journey of knowledge is a novella called *Jalamant, the Prophet*, which I wrote in 1994. The continuing clarity of the worldview I was exploring in the murder mystery series became strong enough to require a coalescing in this philosophical work.

So nothing is lost to the writer. There is a pattern, and the communication to the reader continues in new forms.

* * *

Rudolfo A. Anaya is best known for a trilogy of novels published during the 1970s. Although *Bless Me, Ultima*; *Heart of Aztlán*; and *Tortuga* offer separate worlds with different characters, there are suggestions and allusions in the second and third novels that loosely connect the three works.

Bless Me, Ultima, a first-person narrative, details the childhood and coming of age of young Antonio Marez, a boy who grows up in the rural environs of Las Pasturas and Guadalupe, New Mexico, in the late 1940s and early 1950s. Behind almost every experience and adventure Antonio undergoes there is Ultima, a ''cuarandera'' who comes to live with the Marez family at the start of the novel. She is a miracle-worker who heals the sick through her extensive knowledge of the herbs and remedies of the ancient New Mexico settlers. Guided by her unseen but pervasively felt presence, Antonio moves through a series of incidents that show him the greed, evil, and villainy of men. The novel is significant mainly because it introduces characters and a type of writing not seen before in Chicano literature.

Heart of Aztlán, despite winning the Before Columbus Foundation American Book award, fared less well than its predecessor. The main character is Clemente Chavez, a farmer who loses his land at the start of the narrative and is forced to move into a barrio in Albuquerque. In the city, the Chavez family see their teenage children lose themselves in drugs, sex, and violence. Prompted by a desire to preserve his family, Clemente undertakes a soul-searching quest for an identity and a role for himself and the Chicanos in the barrio. The writing here is noticeably more labored than in *Ultima*. The book ends with a Chicano march against the oppressive Santa Fe Railroad, an attempt to provide a fictive analogue to the Chicano consciousness-raising efforts of the 1970s.

In *Tortuga*, Anaya engagingly captured life in a sanitarium for terminally ill teenagers. There is plenty happening in this labyrinthine ward in the desert, and the novel shows that Anaya is particularly adept at plausibly instilling life, vigor, and reasons to live into characters abandoned by society.

Anaya has also published work in other genres. For some time he has been interested in using the media to advance the interests of Spanish-speaking American citizens, and in 1976 he wrote a screenplay, *Bilingualism: Promise for Tomorrow*, which was produced as a documentary and aired on prime-time television. He is a tireless promoter of Chicano and other ethnic literatures and has edited a number of anthologies.

The Adventures of Juan Chicaspatas is something of a departure: a 48-page mock-heroic epic poem that employs the same type of search motif used in *Heart of Aztlán*. Anaya's tone and attitude here are quite different from that of his earlier work. In *Heart of Aztlán*, he was seriously engaged in creating a language appropriate to rendering one character's quest for self-definition, but *Juan Chicaspatas* (literally, John Smallfeet) is written in the language of the ''vatos locos,'' or crazy barrio Chicanos who jest at virtually everything. In passing, Anaya pointed out that there are ''many tribes of Chicanos,'' which suggests that there are different languages as well. The prime message of the sixteenth-century Aztlán goddess is: ''Go and tell your people about Aztláan. Tell them I live. Tell them the españoles will come and a new people will be born. Tell them not to become like the tribes of the Anglos, and remind them not to honor King Arthur. Tell them their Eden and their Camelot are in Aztlán. Their covenant is with the earth of this world.'' Anaya's message had not changed, but now the appeal was made not to the more middle-class Chicanos as in the earlier work, but in a language closer to that of Alurista and Sergio Elizondo, two other writers who take great relish in Chicano slang.

A writer given to prodigious output, Anaya in the late 1990s produced two novels for adults (*Rio Grande Fall* and *Shaman Winter*) as well as numerous books for children, along with nonfiction works and contributions to anthologies.

—Marco Portales

ANDERSON, Barbara

Nationality: New Zealander. **Born:** Barbara Lillian Romaine, 14 April 1926. **Education:** Woodford House secondary school, 1939–43; University of Otago, Dunedin, 1944–46, B.A. 1946; Victoria University, Wellington, 1979–83, B.A. 1983. **Family:** Married Neil Anderson in 1951; two sons. **Career:** Science teacher, Samuel Marsden Collegiate School, Wellington, 1947, Hastings Girls' High School, 1961, and Queen Margaret's College, Wellington, 1964–67; medical laboratory technologist, public hospitals in Napier, 1948–51, and Wellington, 1972–78. **Awards:** Queen Elizabeth II Arts Council grant, 1988, 1991; Victoria University fellowship, 1991; Goodman Fielder Wattie award, for *Portrait of the Artist's Wife,* 1992. **Agent:** Caroline Dawnay, Peters Fraser and Dunlop, 503–504 The Chambers, Chelsea Harbour, Lots Road, London SW10 0XF. **Address:** 36 Beauchamp Street, Karori, Wellington, New Zealand.

Publications

Novels

Girls High. Wellington, Victoria University Press, 1990; London, Secker and Warburg, 1991.

Portrait of the Artist's Wife. Wellington, Victoria University Press, and London, Secker and Warburg, 1992; New York, Norton and Norton, 1993.

All the Nice Girls. Wellington, Victoria University Press, 1993; London, Cape, 1994.

The House Guest. Wellington, New Zealand, Victoria University Press, 1995.

Proud Garments. Wellington, New Zealand, Victoria University Press, 1996.

Long Hot Summer. Wellington, New Zealand, Victoria University Press, 1999.

Short Stories

I Think We Should Go into the Jungle. Wellington, Victoria University Press, 1989; London, Secker and Warburg, 1993.

The Peacocks: And Other Stories. Wellington, New Zealand, Victoria University Press, 1997.

Uncollected Short Stories

''I Thought There'd Be a Couch,'' in *Vital Writing: New Zealand Stories and Poems, 1989–90.* N.p., Godwit Press, 1990.

''We Could Celebrate,'' in *Speaking with the Sun.* Sydney, Allen and Unwin, 1991.

Play

Gorillas (produced Wellington, 1990).

Radio Plays: *Eric,* 1983; *Impossible to Tell,* 1984; *Hotbed,* 1984; *Close Shave,* 1988; *The Couch,* 1988; *Backwards Glance,* 1990.

* * *

Barbara Anderson may not have been published until she was in her sixties, but since beginning, the works have tumbled over themselves to be released to a growing readership. Anderson explores the inner workings of everyday lives, with all their incongruities and foibles, making the reader witness to the often contradictory nature of family life and romantic love. The short stories in her first published work, *I Think We Should Go into the Jungle* are an eclectic collection, demonstrating a variety of thematic interests that defy easy categorization. Anderson's technique, however, is more easily definable. She often constructs her stories out of the tension of unlikely conjunctions and juxtapositions. Gaps found in the strange marriage of extraordinarily disparate ideas provide the reader with the space for creative intervention, which is a prerequisite for any story's completion. In Anderson's view, the story is not entirely an authorial product. It is produced through the combined efforts of reader and writer. Anderson has described herself as a devotee of the ''fleeting-glimpse school of short fiction'' and it is these glimpses which take the reader on a journey behind the scenes in ordinary lives that in the writing are never merely ordinary, in fact they teem with imaginative inconsistencies which Anderson paints with a characteristic wry humor and attention to detail.

The last two stories of *I Think We Should Go into the Jungle* anticipate the characters and locale of her second work, *Girls High.* Anderson's shift into the discontinuous narrative structure of *Girls High,* is signposted via the episodic variety of ''School Story,'' which anticipates the plural points of view employed in *Girls High.* Like the minimalist plotting of *Girls High,* ''School Story'' is held together by the rivalry of Miss Franklin and Miss Tamp. In the final story in *I Think We Should Go into the Jungle,* ''Fast Post,'' Anderson inaugurates what would be a recurring theme in *Girls High* as well as later novels, namely, the proximity of sex and mortality.

In *Girls High,* Anderson has devised a work that falls between a collection of short stories and a novel. There is a fixed cast of characters, a unifying locale, the school, although not all the happenings occur in the school, and temporal progression from the first staff meeting of the year to the final event of the school year, the Leavers' Play. Having paid her respects to certain nominal unities, Anderson trusts her work to the diverse consciousnesses inhabiting her book. The titles of all the stories, except the first and last, indicate that what we are witnessing is filtered through individual characters. For instance one title reads, ''Miss Franklin Remembers the Smell of Pepper,'' and another, ''Mr. Marden Thinks about Carmen.'' The syntax of the titles scarcely varies, consisting of subject, abstract verb, and object. An emphasis on introspection allows Anderson to avoid spatial and temporal confinement as the memories and thoughts of her characters often travel well out of range of the school and the present. Anderson seems to be suggesting that the banality of the quotidian, which is often within immediate view, is a deceptive front that hides significant depths.

The stories in *Girls High* proceed as much through their gaps as through their revelations, like those in *I Think We Should Go into the Jungle,* and in the later collection of short stories *The Peacocks.* One aspect of the discontinuities in *Girls High* is that character is not a fixed constant, but the discrepant outcome of the interplay of different points of view. Anderson's choice of play for the school leavers, *Mother Courage,* perhaps serves as a covert retrospective comment on how her characters are situated vis-à-vis the reader. The many angles trained on any particular character discourage identification and ensure, if not alienation, at least a dispassionate distance. The minimalist but clumsy plot of *Girls High* confirms Anderson's discomfort with and incapacity for a too ready rationalization of life, a theme which continues through her later novels.

In 1992 Anderson published *Portrait of the Artist's Wife,* which won New Zealand's prestigious Wattie Award in the same year. This novel extends Anderson's thematic preoccupation with the uneasy balance between relationships and creativity, one that becomes increasingly prevalent in her later novels. *Portrait of the Artist's Wife* opens with a posthumous book launch and ends with the death of the author of that book, Jack McCalister. What lies between these two events is the story of Sarah, and of Jack, and of a relationship that spans forty tumultuous years. From a shared 1950s childhood in ''the Bay,'' these two escape their families as teenagers and set up house in Wellington, attempting to juggle his writing and her art with a lack of money and the inconvenience of an impending baby which preempted the registry office wedding. In the ensuing years Anderson's novel illuminates the selfishness of her characters in their singular pursuits of creativity, he as a writer, she as an artist, and their ability to be terrible together but even worse when apart. In London on a writing fellowship with their 18-year-old daughter Dora, Sarah discovers she is pregnant again at 36. The situation is made more difficult in view of a recent reconciliation between Jack and Sarah after acts of betrayal, adultery, and desertion. When Sarah suggests to Jack that the baby might not be his, his supreme confidence in his masculine domination of the relationship is evident. He pauses, then dismisses the suggestion outright, telling Sarah that not only is the child his, it will be a girl and she will be named Emily. At Emily's birth his ''I told you'' claims even this event as his own. Anderson depicts with clarity the shifting roles of wife, mother, and mainstay of the family Sarah is forced to undertake, and the battle between these roles and her desires as an artist, while Jack, despite brief bouts of parental and spousal concern, carries on an archetypal life of drinking, infidelity, and fiction. This reconciling of personal artistic desire with family obligations is a recurring theme, which Anderson explores from many angles in her writing.

Critics of Anderson's work often focus on the untidy nature of plot in her novels. However, in sacrificing the neatness of a plot that has one or two central characters as the primary focus, Anderson draws together a cast of extras who loom largely and do sometimes threaten to overshadow the main events. A feature in all Anderson's writing is her vivid characterization, so that even minor players are finely drawn, often remaining with the reader long after the novel is read. There is Mrs. Leadbetter, the politician's wife in *Portrait of the Artist's Wife,* consulting her notebook of notable people, where a crossed out name means a dead wife. In *Proud Garments* there is Carla, the regal Italian mistress who never leaves Milan but whose presence reaches beyond the grave. Or consider Wilfred Q. Hughes, who keeps the dresses of his three dead wives hanging in a shed and displays them proudly to visitors in *The House Guest.* Dead women's stories are often crucial to the plots of Anderson's novels. In *The House Guest* it is the ghost of a woman writer (Wilfred Q. Hughes's third wife) who provides both the novel's title and the mystery to be unraveled. However, it is the unconnected deaths of Robin's childhood sweetheart wife, Lisa, and elderly Miss Bowman that open the novel out into an exploration of the ephemeral connections of discordant lives that is Anderson's oeuvre.

In *Long Hot Summer,* Anderson returns to ''the Bay'' where she herself grew up, and to the 1930s, in a beachside story of family summers and racial tensions firmly located in the temporal milieu of early twentieth-century New Zealand. The filmic plot of this novel means that once again the cast of extras are vibrantly depicted, while the film itself (''Lust in the Dust'') provides the plot device which enables Anderson to anchor the themes of belonging, desire, and racism which circle through the novel. The two narrators are mother and daughter, and their differing perspectives on the events of the summer give the reader a sometimes comic, sometimes painful reminder of the distances between child and grownup. Ann and Lorna's dreams, musings and betrayals preoccupy them, and their interspersed accounts of the summer at Laing's Point provide counterpoints in commentary. They are witnesses as members of the Laing family assert their Maori heritage, and as the relationship develops between Isabel Clements and Tam Ropata, crossing color barriers and giving voice to seldom spoken but deeply held racist views.

The eventual departure of 'Bel and Tam provides the novel with its penultimate filmic moment, that of the riders in silhouette against the skyline on a ridge, a clichéd off-into-the-sunset moment which is almost saved from bathos by the final moments of the novel.

It is in the junctures between cliché and originality that Anderson writes her extraordinary stories. Anderson resists moral commentary in her novels, instead she lays out the often messy moments of relationships and family for the readers to recognize and to judge for themselves. The gift of observation makes Anderson a novelist who weaves a story leaving spaces for the reader to add their own colors, but the gaps that she leaves do not diminish the reading, rather they provide spy holes for the reader to press up against with their own eyes.

—Doreen D'Cruz, updated by Shana Tacon

ANDERSON, Jessica (Margaret)

Nationality: Australian. **Born:** Jessica Margaret Queale, Gayndah, Queensland, 25 September 1916. **Education:** State schools in Brisbane; Brisbane Technical College art school. **Family:** Married and divorced twice; one daughter from first marriage. **Awards:** Miles Franklin award, 1979, 1981; New South Wales Premier's award, 1981; *The Age* Book of the Year award, 1987. Lives in Sydney. **Agent:** Elaine Markson Literary Agency, 44 Greenwich Avenue, New York, New York 10011, USA.

PUBLICATIONS

Novels

An Ordinary Lunacy. London, Macmillan, 1963; New York, Scribner, 1964.
The Last Man's Head. London, Macmillan, 1970.
The Commandant. London, Macmillan, and New York, St. Martin's Press, 1975.
Tirra Lirra by the River. Melbourne, Macmillan, 1978; London and New York, Penguin, 1984.
The Impersonators. Melbourne, Macmillan, 1980; as *The Only Daughter,* New York and London, Viking, 1985.
Taking Shelter. Ringwood, Victoria, New York, and London, Viking, 1990.
One of the Wattle Birds. Ringwood, Victoria, Australia, Penguin Books, 1994.

Short Stories

Stories from the Warm Zone and Sydney Stories. New York, Viking, 1987; London, Viking, 1988.

Plays

Radio Plays: *The American,* 1966, *The Aspern Papers,* 1967, and *Daisy Miller,* 1968, all from works by Henry James; *The Maid&quoteright;s Part,* 1967; *The Blackmail Caper,* 1972; *Quite Sweet, Really,* 1972; *Tirra Lirra by the River,* 1975; *The Last Man's Head,* from her own novel, 1983; *A Tale of Two Cities* (serial), from the novel by Dickens; *Outbreak of Love* (serial), from the novel by Martin Boyd.

*

Manuscript Collections: Mitchell Library, Sydney; Australian National Library, Canberra.

Critical Studies: ''Tirra Lirra by the Brisbane River,'' in *Literature in Northern Queensland,* vol. 10, no. 1, 1981, and ''A Rare Passion for Justice: Jessica Anderson's *The Last Man's Head,*'' in *Quadrant* (Sydney), July 1988, both by Donat Gallagher; ''The Expatriate Vision of Jessica Anderson'' by Elaine Barry, in *Meridian* (Melbourne), vol. 3, no. 1, 1984; interview with Jennifer Ellison, in *Rooms of Their Own,* Ringwood, Victoria, Penguin, 1986, and with Candida Baker, in *Yacker 2,* Woollahra, New South Wales, Pan, 1987; ''Jessica Anderson: Arrivals and Places'' by Alrene Sykes, in *Southerly* (Sydney), March 1986; article by Gay Raines, in *Australian Studies* (Stirling, Scotland), no. 3, 1989; *Fabricating the Self: The Fictions of Jessica Anderson* by Elaine Barry, St. Lucia, Queensland, Australia, University of Queensland Press, 1996; *A Study Guide to Jessica Anderson's Tirra Lirra by the River* by Valerie McRoberts, Ballarat, Australia, Wizard Books, 1998.

Jessica Anderson comments:

The settings of my seven works of fiction relate neatly to the three places where I have spent my life: mostly Sydney, a substantial portion of Brisbane, and a dash of London.

Now that I intend to write no more fiction, I can appreciate the pleasure I had in writing those seven books, and discount the pain, by realising how disappointed I would be if I had failed to produce them. That is not to say that I am wholly satisfied, but that I worked to my full capacity, and am pleased to have had this chance of deploying my imagination, observation, and experience.

* * *

In one of the more quietly startling moments of Jessica Anderson's *Tirra Lirra by the River*, Nora, the elderly narrator/protagonist, tells the reader almost off-handedly that in middle age she tried to commit suicide. One reason for the attempt was the failure of a facelift operation, and she links this with the horrifying revelations coming out of postwar Germany: ''... if I leap to explain that the weakness resulting from six bronchial winters, and the approach of menopause, left me morbidly defenceless against the postwar revelations of the German camps, it is because I am ashamed to admit that in the same breath as that vast horror, I can speak of the loss of my looks.''

Anderson's novels do not tackle broad social, political or historical issues head-on. Rather, the large event, the major issue, is always in the background, while her characters move in a world where small personal experiences, experiences which are as nothing on a world scale, profoundly influence them.

Tirra Lirra by the River is one of three novels by Anderson which begins with a woman arriving in Australia from ''overseas.'' In *The Commandant* the woman is 17-year-old Frances, arriving from Ireland in the 1830s to live with her sister and brother-in-law, Captain Patrick Logan, the commandant of the title, who is remembered in Australian history as a fanatical and brutal disciplinarian, loathed by the convicts under his charge in the penal settlement at Moreton Bay. Frances initially takes on the traditional role of innocent observer, until events make her unwillingly responsible for a young convict receiving 50 lashes—thus drawing her into ''the system.'' In *Tirra Lirra by the River* and *The Impersonators*, however, the role of one-who-arrives is more complex: both elderly Nora (*Tirra Lirra*) and middle-aged Sylvia (*The Impersonators*) are Australians returning home after many years of absence in Europe, bearing the accretions and conflicts of two cultures. The arrivals in these three books provide a promising opening, with their inherent possibilities of movement and change; yet they also provide a direct entry into several of Anderson's major themes. (Her two earlier novels, *An Ordinary Lunacy* and *The Last Man's Head,* open with smaller-scale but nonetheless portentous visits.)

Anderson is fascinated by the tug between the old culture (Europe) and the new (Australia). In her novels, arrival is always part of a longer journey, an inner journey as well as a physical one, and thus relates to the acquiring of wisdom and the conflicting desires for flight and sanctuary. To arrive at an unfamiliar place normally sharpens one's awareness of environment, and descriptions of place—particularly of houses, and the harbour and gardens of Sydney, shown as being deeply part of the consciousness of the women characters in particular—are among the strengths of Anderson's later novels.

Tirra Lirra by the River, the most highly regarded of Anderson's works, has in fact appeared in three forms: as a short story, as a radio play, and finally as a prize-winning novel. By no means overtly feminist, it has been praised by feminist critics as showing the difficulties of women's lives from the point of view of a woman born early in the century. As the title suggests, the novel has links with Tennyson's poem, ''The Lady of Shallott.'' In the poem, the Lady, generally accepted as artist or perhaps anima, lives secluded in a tower on an island, weaving her magic web and watching the world indirectly through a mirror. When she hears Lancelot pass by, singing, she looks down for the first time on the ''real'' world; the mirror cracks, the web flies out the window, and the lady, dying, floats in her boat down to Camelot. Nora relates to the Lady in a quite complex way, which has at its base the idea of her as artist seeing the world indirectly, through the mirror of a culture (European) not her own. The process begins when she is a child, and she sees how a flaw in the glass of a window transforms the appearance of ordinary sticks, stones, and blades of grass into the magical landscape—with rivulets, castles, and lakes—of her story books. Enchanted, she fails even to see the ''real river'' near her home. After a failed marriage, she goes to London, working there for many years making theatre costumes; finally, she returns to Australia, and, like the Lady of the poem, faces the ''real:'' for her, suppressed memories, mistaken beliefs, a real river instead of the river running down to Camelot, and the discovery that embroidered hangings she made before she left Australia are the most promising things she ever did. Like the Lady, she becomes very sick, but unlike the Lady, she recovers, and the novel ends with her globe of memory (one of the recurrent images of the book) in full spin, with no dark sides hidden. Anderson habitually tests and qualifies her themes, and in *Tirra Lirra* Nora's spiritual/physical journey is counterbalanced by the lives of other women, who are partly defined, though not judged, by the journeys they make—or do not make.

As noted above, *The Impersonators,* a more diffuse and less successful book than *Tirra Lirra,* takes as its point of departure the return of Sylvia after nearly 20 years away. Here the conflict is framed in terms of what appears to be the cultural richness of Europe and the raw discontinuity of Australia; implicit is the question whether Australians who have been abroad to centers where culture is more securely consolidated are under an obligation to ''come home and use what they've learned.'' In the end Sylvia, like Nora accepting that which for her is ''real,'' recognizes that she has been yearning over ''other people's rituals,'' and decides to stay in Sydney with her lover. An equally important theme is signalled by the title of the book: in the materialistic, fractured Sydney of 1977, when the story is set, most of the characters are in some sense impersonators, living part of their lives behind protective masks. Anderson's portrait is sharp-eyed and unsentimental, but compassionate rather than satirical. In 1994, she followed up her earlier works with *One of the Wattle Birds*, and throughout the 1990s her writing continued to receive critical attention in Australia.

—Alrene Sykes

ANIEBO, I(feanyichukwu) N(dubuisi) C(hikezie)

Nationality: Nigerian. **Born:** Nigeria in 1939. **Education:** Government College, Umuahia; University of California, Los Angeles, B.A., C.Phil., M.A. **Military Service:** Joined the Nigerian Army in 1959: attended cadet schools in Ghana and England; officer in the United Nations peace-keeping force in the Congo; at Command and General Staff College, Fort Leavenworth, Kansas; fought on the Biafran side in the Nigerian civil war; discharged from army, 1971. **Career:** Currently, Senior Lecturer in English, University of Port Harcourt. **Address:** Department of English, University of Port Harcourt, P.M.B. 5523, Port Harcourt, Rivers State, Nigeria.

PUBLICATIONS

Novels

The Anonymity of Sacrifice. London, Heinemann, 1974.
The Journey Within. London, Heinemann, 1978.
Rearguard Actions. Ibadan, Nigeria, Heinemann Educational Books, 1998.

Short Stories

Of Wives, Talismans and the Dead. London, Heinemann, 1983.
Man of the Market: Short Stories. Port Harcourt, Pam Unique, 1994.

Uncollected Short Stories

''The Jealous Goddess,'' in *Spear* (Lagos), October 1963.
''My Mother,'' in *Sunday Times* (Lagos), 22 December 1963.
''The Ring,'' in *Nigeria Magazine* (Lagos), December 1964.
''The Peacemakers,'' in *Nigeria Magazine* (Lagos), December 1965.
''Shadows,'' in *Black Orpheus 20* (Lagos), 1966.
''Mirage,'' in *Nigeria Magazine* (Lagos), March 1966.
''The Outing,'' in *Happy Home and Family Life* (Lagos), May 1972.
''Happy Survival, Brother,'' in *Ufahamu* (Los Angeles), vol. 7, no. 3, 1977.

* * *

Since 1963 I.N.C. Aniebo has been the author of a steady succession of short stories written for various periodical publications, a selection of them at last appearing as *Of Wives, Talismans and the Dead* in 1983. Most of them deal with the problems of Igbo people in Eastern Nigeria trying to cope with the transition from rural to urban living and with other pressures of accelerating social change, including that most hectic of such changes, war itself. The commonest experience in Aniebo's fiction is the bewilderment that results from lack of trust in other people and lack of faith in the efficacy of the gods, whether traditional African or imported Christian. He often plunges his characters into some variety of spiritual emptiness or near-despair after they have been betrayed by those closest to them in childhood, adolescence, work, or marriage. The acrid taste of defeat is perhaps Aniebo's most distinctive contribution to West African literature in English—his ability to record convincingly instances of human strength wilting and shriveling, usually as the indirect outcome of large social processes. If Aluko's writing captures the comedy of Nigerian life acclimatizing itself to the modern world, and Achebe's the tragedy of it within an historical perspective, and Soyinka's the human spirit refusing to be broken by it, then what Aniebo records is the intense pain that afflicts people when social change halts, trips, nonpluses, or defeats them.

In the story ''Dilemma,'' the priestess addresses her wayward son: ''The earth has never changed. The winds still continue to blow, the rains to fall, and men to be born and die. Only little things that don't matter change. Don't say because things change, you'll stop believing in God and believe in the Devil.'' Her words pronounce the traditional wisdom that many Nigerians today mock, or cannot accept, or covet, when it appears in others, or deliberately reject for the pursuit of personal ambition and the acquisition of consumer goods. Aniebo, however, presents such evaporation of faith not as an ordinary clash-of-cultures matter but as the heavy price that Nigerians pay for entry into the modern world. While it is more pervasive in large towns, like Port Harcourt in the novel *The Journey Within*, it characterizes also the stories in *Of Wives, Talismans and the Dead*, most of which are set in rural Igbo villages. Thus, in the privacy of their tender incestuous love, widowed father and devoted daughter and only surviving child, in ''Maruma,'' find the true fulfillment of giving to another, but when her pregnancy makes their love public, their having broken a powerful social taboo destroys first their relationship and then themselves and their line. Yet, years later, their ruined, crumbling compound is symmetrically matched at the other end of the village by another as desolate, whose respectable and fecund owners had committed no ''abomination.'' This even-handed ''leveling'' at the end of the story is the author's explicit comment, and it makes one wonder whether the dark views of the human condition that many of Aniebo's characters express aren't also his own, as in the war story, ''In the Front Line'': ''The war had proved that no matter what one did or worshipped one died all the same, and more often than not like a rat.'' Similarly, in the thoughts of Cristian Okoro in *The Journey Within*: ''... his family had fought for survival, always getting up after a fall, always continuing to fight after a defeat. So, was life merely a getting-up after a fall?''

Aniebo's first published book, *The Anonymity of Sacrifice*, is a novel about the bitterness of successive Biafran ''falls'' during the Nigerian Civil War. It is a collection of very vivid, rapidly sketched illustrations of, admittedly, some heroic improvisations against great odds, but chiefly of betrayals, misunderstandings, personal defeats, frustration, and distrust, with the estrangement of the two major characters, and their pointless deaths, inadequately exploited novelistically. While the details of the narrative do indeed convey disillusion and corruption, there is little sense of their being worked into a firm design, and the title promises more significance than the book delivers.

The second novel, *The Journey Within*, is altogether more relaxed in execution, but again more ambitious in the endeavor than in the realization. It is centered upon the stories of two marriages, one traditional, the other Christian. In probing, to some depth, the joys, sorrows tensions, struggles, love, and hatred that are generated between husband and wife, Aniebo is clearly arguing that marriage (whatever its kind) is a very thorny experience. Unfortunately, by making the two marriages progressively less distinctive, he throws away the opportunity to break his larger theme with finer shades and more delicate ironies. Yet the novel is full of sardonic instances of human folly, as individuals seek their own fulfillments in an urban environment of free and selfish enterprise. While there is much mature observation of love and sexuality, some of the scenes between lovers are rendered with more mere titillation than the tone of the narration elsewhere strives after.

The collection of short stories is certainly the most successful of Aniebo's books, for under the pressure of brevity and pithiness, his particular gift, the rapid but accurate sketching of a scene without having to sustain its implications across a large design, is revealed as professional and complete in its own right. In the novels his transitions from one emotion to another are often incongruous, but in the stories he can move without inhibition or oddity across a gamut of emotions—anger at the exploitation of dockers in ''Rats and Rabbits,'' self-confidence without moral crutches in ''Godevil'' (intentionally ambiguous as ''Go devil'' or ''God evil''?), self-gratification in ''Moment of Decision,'' the horror of murder within the family in ''The Quiet Man'' and ''A Hero's Welcome,'' and, rarely, the consolation of faith in ''Four Dimensions.'' The bleakness of Aniebo's vision is tempered, in his best writing, by a wry ironic sense that does not exclude muted compassion.

—Arthur Ravenscroft

ANTHONY, Michael

Nationality: Trinidadian. **Born:** Mayaro, 10 February 1932. **Education:** Mayaro Roman Catholic School; Junior Technical College, San Fernando, Trinidad. **Family:** Married Yvette Francesca in 1958; two sons and two daughters. **Career:** Lived in England, 1954–68; journalist, Reuters news agency, London, 1964–68; lived in Brazil, 1968–70; assistant editor, Texaco Trinidad, Pointe-à-Pierre, 1970–72. Since 1972 researcher, National Cultural Council (now Ministry of Culture), Port-of-Spain; broadcast historical radio programs, 1975–1989; University of Richmond, VA, teacher of creative writing, 1992. **Address:** 99 Long Circular Road, St. James, Port-of-Spain, Trinidad.

Publications

Novels

The Games Were Coming. London, Deutsch, 1963; Boston, Houghton Mifflin, 1968.
The Year in San Fernando. London, Deutsch, 1965; Portsmouth, New Hampshire, Heinemann, 1996.
Green Days by the River. Boston, Houghton Mifflin, and London, Deutsch, 1967.
Streets of Conflict. London, Deutsch, 1976.
All That Glitters. London, Deutsch, 1981.
Bright Road to El Dorado. Walton-on-Thames, Surrey, Nelson, 1982.
The Becket Factor. London, Collins, 1990.
In the Heat of the Day. Portsmouth, New Hampshire, Heinemann Educational Publishers, 1996.

Short Stories

Sandra Street and Other Stories. London, Heinemann, 1973.
Cricket in the Road and Other Stories. London, Deutsch, 1973.
Folk Tales and Fantasies. Port-of-Spain, Columbus, 1976.
The Chieftain's Carnival and Other Stories. London, Longman, 1993.

Other

Glimpses of Trinidad and Tobago, with a Glance at the West Indies. Port-of-Spain, Columbus, 1974.
Profile Trinidad: A Historical Survey from the Discovery to 1900. London, Macmillan, 1975.
The Making of Port-of-Spain 1757–1939. Port-of-Spain, Key Caribbean, 1978.
First in Trinidad. Port-of-Spain, Circle Press, 1985.
Heroes of the People of Trinidad and Tobago. Port-of-Spain, Circle Press, 1986.
The History of Aviation in Trinidad and Tobago 1913–1962. Port-of-Spain, Paria, 1987.
A Better and Brighter Day. Port-of-Spain, Circle Press, 1987.

Towns and Villages of Trinidad and Tobago. Port-of-Spain, Circle Press, 1988.

Parade of the Carnivals of Trinidad 1839–1989. Port-of-Spain, Circle Press, 1989.

The Golden Quest: The Four Voyages of Christopher Columbus. London, Macmillan Caribbean, 1992.

Historical Dictionary of Trinidad and Tobago. Lanham, Maryland, Scarecrow Press, 1997.

Editor, with Andrew Carr, *David Frost Introduces Trinidad and Tobago.* London, Deutsch, 1975.

*

Critical Studies: In *London Magazine,* April 1967; ''Novels of Childhood'' in *The West Indian Novel and Its Background* by Kenneth Ramchand, London, Faber, and New York, Barnes and Noble, 1970; *Green Days by the River* by Linda Flynn and Sally West, Oxford, Heinemann Educational, 1989.

Michael Anthony comments:

I see myself principally as a storyteller. In other words, I am not aware that I have any message. I think both the past life and the fascination of landscape play a most important part in my work.

My infancy has been very important in my literary development and so far almost everything I have written—certainly my novels—are very autobiographical.

It is strange that I have never had the desire to write about England, although I spent 14 years there. To some people, judging from my writing alone, I have never been out of Trinidad. And this is true in some sort of way.

I feel a certain deep attachment to Trinidad and I want to write about it in such a way that I will give a faithful picture of life here. But when I am writing a story I am not aware that I want to do anything else but tell the story.

* * *

Michael Anthony's most successful novels are set in southern Trinidad, and deal with the experiences of childhood and youth. Each is simple in structure. When Anthony has stepped outside that framework, as he does in *Streets of Conflict,* and attempted explicit social comment, the results have not always been successful.

His first novel, *The Games Were Coming,* subtly explores the need for a balance between restraint and joyful abandon. In a society where order has been imposed by force, and the idea of celebration therefore takes on political undertones, these are important issues. The story contrasts the cycling championships, for which the novel's hero, Leon, is training with self-denying discipline, and the approach of carnival, which is associated with ''fever,'' ''chaos,'' and ''release.'' Leon becomes so obsessed by the need for restraint that he neglects his girlfriend, Sylvia, and nearly loses her. She in turn suffers for failing to know herself. She prides herself on being cool, controlled, and pure, but is embarrassed by indelicate thoughts that spring unbidden to her mind. She disapproves of carnival, but is willing to ''jump-on'' at night when no one will see. She ignores these promptings of sexual energy, and as a result is swept away by her feelings—and by Leon's neglect—into the arms of her calculating middle-aged employer. Anthony suggests a resolution of these forces, first in the character of Leon's younger brother Dolphus, who is attracted equally to the games and to carnival, and second by a subtle pattern of imagery that hints at the complementary quality of these events. Thus the ''madness and wildness'' of jouvert morning is shown as the energy disciplined into the ''richness and splendor'' of Grand Carnival.

The Year in San Fernando is also much more than a sensitive novel about growing up. Although Anthony scrupulously adhered to the unfolding perceptions of 12-year-old Francis, from puzzled naiveté towards the growth of sympathetic understanding, what he created in the novel is a richly textured and moving portrayal of the growth and disappearance of what is human. Set against the passage of the seasons is Francis's relationship with Mrs. Chandles, the old woman for whom he is brought as a companion from his impoverished village home in return for his board and schooling. Initially, she is all dominant will, a self-contained, bitter old lady who treats Francis as a virtual slave. When the year begins, he is cowed and passive, scarcely more than a bundle of sensations. As the year passes, however, he observes how Mrs. Chandles's spirit and flesh wilt in the drought of crop-season, and comes to understand the reasons for her ill-temper. At the same time, Francis's self is growing powerfully as he begins to acknowledge his feelings, both positive and negative. There is a brief season of rain when Mrs. Chandles is released from her pain and the two meet as open and giving personalities. But then as Francis continues his growth to personhood, the personality of Mrs. Chandles disintegrates, and she begins to die. There is more for Francis to learn than his part in the cycle of life and death, and this is contained in a puzzling comment Mrs. Chandles makes. Throughout the dry season he has painstakingly tended her shriveling flowers, and oiled and massaged her protesting limbs. She comments on his ''willing mind'' and tells him that she ''connected willingness of mind with sacredness.'' It is through this ''sacredness'' that Francis redeems his year in San Fernando from time.

None of Anthony's other novels quite achieves the same degree of understated but unflawed art. *Green Days by the River* evokes another passage from adolescent freedom to adult responsibility in the countryside around Mayaro. Despite the beauty of its prose, the novel seems to escape from Anthony's control. The central relationship is Shellie, a youth, and Mr. Gidharee, an Indian farmer who lures him into marriage with his daughter. Here the meeting is complicated by its Trinidadian ethnic resonances. In portraying Gidharee as a creolized Jekyll who charms Shellie into his confidence, and an Indian Hyde who sets his dogs to savage him as a warning of what will happen if he fails to marry his daughter, Anthony unavoidably appears to be making a veiled statement about ethnic relations. Two kinds of irony tangle. One is the dramatic irony that Shellie fails to see the twig being limed to catch him, the other is the irony of Shellie's racial innocence when so much of Gidharee's behavior adds up to a Creole stereotype of the Indian as an economic threat. The second irony leads to inconsistencies in the portrayal of Shellie, who is bright and sensitive in all respects except in his dealings with Gidharee, where he appears spineless and impercipient. It is hard to know in a somewhat evasive novel quite what Anthony intended.

Two attempts to deal with broader social issues have met with limited success: *Streets of Conflict,* was inconsistent, and the plot of *In the Heat of the Day* seemed weighted by the heavy message Anthony intended for it to carry. *All That Glitters,* by contrast, found Anthony in territory more suited to his abilities. The story centers around the growing awareness of young Horace Lumpers regarding the complications of the adult world around him, and specifically the jealousies and deceptions provoked by the return of his sophisticated Aunty Roomeen to the village of Mayaro. In a more intense way than in any earlier novel, Anthony focused on a child's attempt to discern whether people were being sincere or false. Words such as trickster, genuine, hypocrite, acting, and feigned serve as leitmotifs in the text, and Horace has to learn that being adult means wearing different faces. This play on truth and falsity is linked through the novel's two complementary mottoes (''Gold Is Where You Find It'' and ''All That Glitters'') to Anthony's most conscious exploration of the nature of his art. The distinction is caught in the contrast between Horace's joy in discovering through writing what he thinks and feels—when he writes about the golden day with the fishermen or the sordid saga of the stolen golden chain—and the way that the adult clichés used by his teacher Myra tend to embalm experience. Nevertheless, for all her circumlocutions, she recognizes the child's magical directness, and it is her advice, ''Make it colorful and vivid—and true,'' which both Horace and Michael Anthony follow.

—Jeremy Poynting

ARMAH, Ayi Kwei

Nationality: Ghanaian. **Born:** Takoradi in 1938. **Education:** Achimota College, Accra; Groton School, Massachusetts; Harvard University, Cambridge, Massachusetts, A.B. in social studies; Columbia University, New York. **Career:** Translator, *Révolution Africaine* magazine, Algiers; scriptwriter for Ghana Television; English teacher, Navrongo School, Ghana, 1966; editor, *Jeune Afrique* magazine, Paris, 1967–68; teacher at Teacher's College, Dar es Salaam, and universities of Massachusetts, Amherst, Lesotho, and Wisconsin, Madison. **Address:** c/o Heinemann Educational, Ighodaro Road, Jericho PMB 5205, Ibadan, Oyo State, Nigeria.

PUBLICATIONS

Novels

The Beautyful Ones Are Not Yet Born. Boston, Houghton Mifflin, 1968; London, Heinemann, 1969.
Fragments. Boston, Houghton Mifflin, 1970; London, Heinemann, 1975.
Why Are We So Blest? New York, Doubleday, 1972; London, Heinemann, 1975.
Two Thousand Seasons. Nairobi, East African Publishing House, 1973; London, Heinemann, 1979; Chicago, Third World Press, 1980.
The Healers. Nairobi, East African Publishing House, 1978; London, Heinemann, 1979.
Osiris Rising: A Novel of Africa Past, Present, and Future. Pogenguine, Senegal, Per Ankh, 1995.

Uncollected Short Stories

''A Short Story,'' in *New African* (London), December 1965.
''Yaw Manu's Charm,'' in *Atlantic* (Boston), May 1968.
''The Offal Kind,'' in *Harper's* (New York), January 1969.
''Doctor Kamikaze,'' in *Mother Jones* (San Francisco), October 1989.

Other

Contributor, *The South Wind and the Sun: Stories from Africa,* edited by Kate Turkington. Johannesburg, South Africa, Thorold's Africana Books, 1996.
Translator, *Zaire, What Destiny?,* edited by Kankwenda Mbaya. Oxford, England, ABC, 1993.
Translator, *Senegambia and the Atlantic Slave Trade* by Boubacar Barry. New York, Cambridge University Press, 1998.

*

Critical Studies: *The Novels of Ayi Kwei Armah: A Study in Polemical Fiction* by Robert Fraser, London, Heinemann, 1980; *Ayi Kwei Armah's Africa: The Sources of His Fiction* by Derek Wright, London, Zell, 1989; *Resistance in Postcolonial African Fiction* by Neil Lazarus, New Haven, Yale University Press, 1990; *Critical Perspectives on Ayi Kwei Armah* edited by Derek Wright, Washington D.C., Three Continents, 1992; *The Novels of Ayi Kwei Armah* by K. Damodar Rao, New Delhi, Prestige, 1993; *Form and Technique in the African Novel* by Olawale Awosik, Ibadan, Nigeria, Sam Bookman, 1997; *Ayi Kwei Armah: The Telling of the Way* by Olawale Awosika, Benin City, Nigeria, Ambik Press, 1997; *The Existential Fiction of Ayi Kwei Armah, Albert Camus, and Jean-Paul Sartre* by Tommie L. Jackson, Lanham, Maryland, University Press of America, 1997; *Post-Colonial African Fiction: The Crisis of Consciousness* by Mala Pandurang, Delhi, Pencraft International, 1997; *Ayi Kwei Armah, Radical Iconoclast: Pitting Imaginary Worlds Against the Actual* by Ode S. Ogede, Westport, Connecticut, Heinemann, 1999.

* * *

Ayi Kwei Armah's masterly control over language forces his reader to suspend his disbelief, however reluctant he may be to do so. The comic or horrific distortion of what is nearly recognizable reality in the first three novels has extraordinary imaginative power.

The title of the first novel refers to an inscription which the central character, known only as ''the man,'' sees on a bus. By implication it refers back to the Teacher's story of Plato's cave, where the one man who escapes from the cave and returns to tell his fellow sufferers of the beautiful world outside is thought to be mad by those in the ''reassuring chains.'' The man is anonymous because he is regarded as mad in his society, modern Accra. His family suffers from his refusal to take bribes in his position as a railway clerk, and his honesty is incomprehensible to ''the loved ones.'' His former friend, Koomson, has become a Minister through corruption, and, though the regime of which he is a part falls, an equally corrupt one takes its place. The fusion of styles in *The Beautyful Ones* can be seen in the first few pages, which give a realistic account of a bus journey but also introduce the controlling symbol in the novel, that of money as decay, or excrement. The bus conductor smells a cedi note and finds it has ''a very old smell, very strong, and so very rotten that the stench itself of it came with a curious, satisfying pleasure.'' This anticipates the comic and horrible way in which Koomson has to escape the new regime, by wriggling through a latrine. The depravity of the society is suggested by the manner in which a young man confesses he has made money in a lottery ''in the embarrassed way of a young girl confessing love;'' if he escaped from his society the man would only mirror his broken pencil sharpener, whose handle ''sped round and round with the futile freedom of a thing connected to nothing else.''

Armah's ability to invest apparently insignificant objects or scenes with meanings is clear in *Fragments*. Early in the novel there is a detailed account of the destruction of a mad dog by a man with a gross sexual deformity, while the little boy who loves the dog looks on helplessly. It is so vivid that it prepares the reader for the destruction of the central character, Baako, who returns to Ghana from New York wanting to write film scripts because ''Film gets to everyone.'' He finds that his society wants material evidence of his ''been-to'' status. The new element in this novel is represented by Naana, Baako's blind grandmother, who is the voice of the traditional culture. Traditional ceremonies, such as Baako's baby nephew's outdooring, have lost their spiritual significance and become an opportunity for ostentation and avarice; the plot suggests that Naana's fears for the baby as the victim of this irreligious display are justified, for he dies in the course of it. The fragments of the title seem to be the members of the new society, placed within the opening and closing sections of the novel which express Naana's sense of meaningful community. The only other hopeful element is the growing love between Baako and the sensitive Puerto Rican, Juana.

Why Are We So Blest? is a more fragmented novel than *Fragments*, jumping between three narrators with no obvious narrative line, though we eventually discover that Solo, a failed revolutionary, is using the notebooks of Aimée, a white American, and Modin, a Ghanaian, intercut with his own text. The savage irony of the title is sustained throughout the novel, which lacks the cynical comedy of the two previous works and is much more overt in its distortion of reality. All the white women in the novel prey on the black men: Modin, a student who drops out of Harvard to go to Laccryville in North Africa as a would-be revolutionary, is used primarily by Aimée, who epitomizes the sexual sickness of all the white women. She is frigid when she meets Modin, and uses him as an object to stimulate her sexual fantasies of intercourse with a black servant. Modin's attempt to liberate her into a fuller sensitivity destroys him. The horrific scene, in which Aimée is raped and Modin castrated by white men, fully enacts Aimée's fantasy. She is sexually aroused and kisses Modin's bleeding penis, asking him to say that he loves her. Solo sees Modin as an African who does not know ''how deep the destruction has eaten into himself, hoping to achieve a healing juncture with his destroyed people.''

Armah's most recent novels are historical. *Two Thousand Seasons* is written in a new style, in its repetitiveness and long leisurely sentences suggesting that it is folk myth: ''With what shall the utterers' tongue stricken with goodness, riven silent with the quiet force of beauty, with which mention shall the tongue of the utterers begin a song of praise whose perfect singers have yet to come?'' Its narrator is not identified, though he participates in the action. The violation of his people's way of life by Arab and then European invaders is depicted powerfully but the ideal of ''the way, our way'' remains nebulous. *The Healers* is stylistically much more vigorous, and is set at a precise time in the past, during the Second Asante War. The idea of ''inspiration'' is gradually defined in the course of the novel as being a healing and creative force which can only work slowly, and Armah perhaps sees himself as one of those prophesied by Damfo in the novel, ''healers wherever our people are scattered, able to bring us together again.''

—Angela Smith

ARMSTRONG, Jeannette

Nationality: Canadian (Okanagan). **Born:** Penticton (Okanagan) Indian Reservation, British Columbia, Canada, 1948. **Education:** Okanagan College; University of Victoria, British Columbia, Canada, B.F.A. **Career:** Since 1989 director, En'owkin School of International Writing, Okanagan, British Columbia.

PUBLICATIONS

Novels

Slash. Penticton, British Columbia, Theytus, 1987; revised edition, 1998.

Whispering in Shadows. Penticton, British Columbia, Theytus Books, 1999.

Poetry

Breathtracks. Penticton, British Columbia, Theytus, 1991.

Other

Enwhisteetkwa; Walk in Water (for children). Penticton, British Columbia, Theytus, 1982.

Neekna and Chemai (for children), illustrated by Barbara Marchand. Penticton, British Columbia, Theytus, 1984.

The Native Creative Process: A Collaborative Discourse, with Douglas Cardinal. Penticton, British Columbia, Theytus, 1992.

We Get Our Living Like Milk from the Land: Okanagan Tribal History Book. Penticton, British Columbia, Theytus, 1993.

Contributor, *Speaking for the Generations: Native Writers on Writing,* edited by Simon J. Ortiz. Tucson, University of Arizona Press, 1998.

Contributor, *Native North America: Critical and Cultural Perspectives: Essays,* edited by Patricia Monture-Angus and Renee Hulan. Chicago, LPC Group, 1999.

*

Critical Studies: *Momaday, Vizenor, Armstrong: Conversations on American Indian Writing* by Hartwig Isernhagen. Norman, University of Oklahoma Press, 1999.

* * *

Following in the footsteps of her great aunt, Hum-Ishu-Ma (Mourning Dove/Christine Quintasket, 1888–1936), author of *Cogewea, The Half-Blood* (1927) and *Coyote Stories* (1933), Jeannette Armstrong published the first novel by a First Nations woman in 1985. With the publication of the novel, *Slash,* Armstrong established a place for writing by contemporary Native Canadian women along with Beth Brant's *Mohawk Trail,* Maria Campbell's *Halfbreed,* Beatrice Culleton's *In Search of April Raintree,* and Ruby Slipperjack's *Honour the Sun.* Now in its eight printing, *Slash* is an important novel that traces out a young Native Canadian man's struggles with colonialism, racism, and a self-identity that doesn't fit easily into ''assimilated,'' ''traditional,'' or ''Pan-Indian'' categories. In addition to her work as a novelist, Armstrong is also a political activist, sculptor, writer of children's books, and educator. Born on the Penticton Indian Reserve in British Columbia, she maintains strong links to her Okanagan community, which is reflected in the novel *Slash.*

Armstrong's novel foregrounds key issues in the political, cultural, and linguistic struggles of Native Americans in both Canada and the United States in the late 1960s and early 1970s, such as the birth of the American Indian Movement, changes in the Canadian Indian Act, the takeover of Department of Indian Affairs (DIA) and Bureau of Indian Affairs (BIA) offices, and the Wounded Knee occupation. Set primarily in British Columbia, Armstrong's title character, Thomas Kelasket, who is nicknamed "Slash" while serving time in prison, demonstrates how these events are linked, although geographically and culturally distant and distinct. Armstrong wants to examine how Native Americans, particularly young people, can confront what she calls their "postcolonial" situation, the double bind resulting from existence under the dominant white culture, on the one hand, and a desire to preserve important aspects of their own aboriginal communities, on the other.

Armstrong's novel is a bildungsroman, a fictional autobiography tracing the growth of a single main protagonist as he struggles with social and psychological pressures to maintain a positive sense of identity and community in a rapidly changing world. The novel is framed by two poems, one entitled "For Tony," which describes a man much like Slash, and an untitled concluding poem, as well as a "Prologue" in which Slash reminisces about his own progress from childhood innocence, through a self-destructive adolescence, to a mature state of understanding and an "Epilogue" in which Slash reflects on his adulthood and his reasons for relating his story, namely to assist young people like his son. The novel's four long chapters begin with "The Awakening," in which a 14-year-old Slash first comes to realize that being Indian in Canada means either occupying a space which is entirely antithetical to white Canadian values or adopting an "assimilated" identity and becoming what Homi Bhabha has called "almost white but not quite." Interestingly, Armstrong is able to convey a sense of the young adolescent's inner struggles by using dialogue a teenager of the 1960s and 70s might employ. For example, Slash and his friends use terms such as "chicks," "Mary Jane," and "Bro." In the second and third chapters, "Trying It On" and "Mixing It Up," the protagonist recounts his various experiences as a drug dealer, convict, activist, vagrant, and prodigal son. Slash tries on various roles and identities, shifting restlessly from place to place, focusing on his own inability to come to terms with what it means to be an Native person in North America. The final chapter, "We Are a People," draws the loose threads of Slash's life together as he struggles to make sense of his identity as an Okanagan community member and activist in many Native struggles, as well as his new roles of father, husband, and widower. In so doing, Armstrong elucidates complex notions of sovereignty, self-recognition, and treaty rights.

The three names he uses throughout the novel suggest these kinetic and multiple senses of self. "Thomas/Tommy," his Anglo-Celtic Christian birth name, indicates both his relationship to his family—his parents and siblings call him Tommy—and the assimilative force of the dominant Canadian culture; "Slash," a nickname he's given by his first love, Mardi, after a drug-related bar brawl in Vancouver, represents the angry, cynical warrior self; and an undisclosed Okanagan name, which, according to Slash, is given ceremonially to tribal members after birth, suggests his relationship to the larger Okanagan community in British Columbia and the close ties he maintains with individuals living on his own reserve.

In addition to being a bildungsroman, the novel follows another popular literary form, the picaresque, or traveler's tale, since its narrative consists of a loosely knit series of events involving numerous characters, many of whom do not recur in the rest of the text. For most of the narrative, Slash wanders from place to place—his reserve to Vancouver, Ottawa to Toronto, the Pine Ridge Reservation to Washington, D.C.—although he returns periodically to visit with his family in British Columbia. In moving through these cycles of relocation, Slash better understands his place in the world as an activist struggling for Native rights in general as well as his role as a member of a specific Native community. These connections are very important, especially when his father, who is suffering from medical problems, is healed by a visit from a medicine person from another tribe, although the Kelasket family typically doesn't trust outsiders.

Slash is somewhat polemical in its style; that is, Armstrong (who, as director of the En'owkin Centre in Penticton, is deeply involved in Native Canadian education) wants to employ her fiction to make clear, strong political statements about the contemporary state of Native Canada. And despite the fact that the main protagonist is a young man, the novel is also profoundly feminist. Slash is respectful of the women in his life and at one point proclaims, "It's really the women who keep things smooth ... We learned early from our mothers and grandmothers that it is women who are the strength of the people."

Slash confronts the personal and social issues that young First Nations people face and offers hope for improvement through education and self-discovery. The text moves forward from frustration and anger through activism to self-and communal-affirmation, but this path is not so neatly drawn or simple. Slash engages the welter of events and ideologies in contemporary history and projects a vital, current role for First Nations people in that history, a role played out in the narrative by the title character himself. This novel may prove to be one of the most important twentieth-century works of fiction by a Canadian author, as it addresses the historical origins of racism and colonialism and its contemporary manifestations in First Nations communities, as well as elucidating Native Canadians' struggle for the recognition of sovereignty with a rich and distinct First Nations' voice.

—Kevin McNeilly, updated by Michelle Hermann

ASTLEY, Thea

Nationality: Australian. **Born:** Thea Beatrice May Astley in Brisbane, Queensland, 25 August 1925. **Education:** The University of Queensland, Brisbane, 1943–47, B.A. 1947. **Family:** Married Edmund John Gregson in 1948; one son. **Career:** English teacher in Queensland, 1944–48, and in New South Wales, 1948–67; senior tutor, then fellow in English, Macquarie University, Sydney, 1968–85. Lives near Sydney. **Awards:** Commonwealth Literary Fund fellowship, 1961, 1964; Miles Franklin award, 1963, 1966, 1973; Moomba award, 1965; *Age* Book of the Year award, 1975; Patrick White award, 1989; *Age* Book of the Year award, 1996. **Agent:** Elise Goodman, Goodman Associates, 500 West End Avenue, New York, New York 10024, U.S.A.

PUBLICATIONS

Novels

Girl with a Monkey. Sydney, Angus and Robertson, 1958; New York, Penguin, 1987.
A Descant for Gossips. Sydney and London, Angus and Robertson, 1960.
The Well-Dressed Explorer. Sydney and London, Angus and Robertson, 1962; New York, Penguin, 1988.
The Slow Natives. Sydney, Angus and Robertson, 1965; London, Angus and Robertson, 1966; New York, Evans, 1967.
A Boat Load of Home Folk. Sydney and London, Angus and Robertson, 1968; New York, Penguin, 1983.
The Acolyte. Sydney and London, Angus and Robertson, 1972; in *Two by Astley,* New York, Putnam, 1988.
A Kindness Cup. Melbourne, Nelson, 1974; in *Two by Astley,* New York, Putnam, 1988.
An Item from the Late News. St. Lucia, University of Queensland Press, 1982; New York, Penguin, 1984.
Beachmasters. Ringwood, Victoria, Penguin, 1985; New York, Viking, 1986.
It's Raining in Mango: Pictures from a Family Album. New York, Putnam, 1987; London, Viking, 1988.
Two by Astley [includes *A Kindness Cup*]. New York, Putnam, 1988.
Reaching Tin River. New York, Putnam, 1990.
Coda. New York, Putnam, 1994; London, Secker and Warburg, 1995.
The Multiple Effects of Rainshadow. New York, Viking, 1996.
Drylands: A Book for the World's Last Reader. Ringwood, Victoria, Australia, Viking, 1999.

Short Stories

Hunting the Wild Pineapple. Melbourne, Nelson, 1979; New York, Putnam, 1991.
Vanishing Points. New York, Putnam, 1992; London, Minerva, 1995.
Collected Stories. St. Lucia, Queensland, Australia, University of Queensland Press, 1997.

Uncollected Short Stories

"Cubby," in *Coast to Coast.* Sydney, Angus and Robertson, 1961.
"The Scenery Never Changes," in *Coast to Coast.* Sydney, Angus and Robertson, 1963.
"Journey to Olympus," in *Coast to Coast.* Sydney, Angus and Robertson, 1965.
"Seeing Mrs. Landers," in *Festival and Other Stories,* edited by Brian Buckley and Jim Hamilton. Melbourne, Wren, 1974; Newton Abbot, Devon, David and Charles, 1975.
Contributor, *Amnesty,* edited by Dee Mitchell. Port Melbourne, Victoria, Minerva, 1993.

Other

Editor, *Coast to Coast 1969–1970.* Sydney, Angus and Robertson, 1971.

*

Thea Astley comments:

(1972) My main interest (and has been through my five published and current unpublished novels) is the misfit. Not the spectacular outsider, but the seedy little non-grandiose non-fitter who lives in his own mini-hell. Years ago I was impressed at eighteen or so by *Diary of a Nobody,* delighted by the quality Grossmith gave to the non-achiever and the sympathy which he dealt out. My five published novels have always been, despite the failure of reviewers to see it, a plea for charity—in the Pauline sense, of course—to be accorded to those not ruthless enough or grand enough to be gigantic tragic figures, but which, in their own way, record the same *via crucis.*

* * *

Thea Astley is one of the most widely respected novelists in Australia, despite the fact that she has never received the kind of sustained critical attention that has been given to some of the country's newer female writers. Born in Queensland into a Catholic family, she long ago abandoned the Church but freely acknowledges its influence. Her language is rich in religious terminology and metaphor, yet she tends mostly to see religious life itself as containing tensions that lie immediately beneath its surface and eventually erupt in destructive forms. Politically to the left, her writing is nevertheless marked by formal, cultural, and, in many respects, ethical conservatism. She is also one of Australia's wittiest and shrewdest novelists, and she plots carefully for dramatic effect and exciting finales.

Astley's first three novels are apprentice works, though they contain the seeds of many of her later ideas, but with *The Slow Natives,* which won for her the first of a record four Miles Franklin awards, she established her reputation. In this novel the author chooses not to follow the fate of one or two particular characters, as she did in her early work, but to move freely among a group, switching attention omnisciently from one to another. Almost all the characters suffer from some form of spiritual aridity; in Astley's vision, there often seems nothing between repression, and empty or even corrupt sexuality. At times the novel sounds uncannily like Graham Greene in tone: "we carry our own hells within," a priest tells another character, and a moment later he uses the exact term from Greene: "They'll think I'm a whisky priest."

A Boat Load of Home Folk takes up several of the same themes but looks back also to the early *A Descant for Gossips* in its concentration on the torments of adolescence. It is peopled by as sorry and defeated a lot as the previous novel and in fact, several of the peripheral characters reappear and play a more central role. Again, sexual repression, but more generally an inability to love, lies at the heart of the problem with most of the characters. As Father Lake puts it, "God save me, God save me ... from a lack of love." The novel is also noteworthy for a magnificently climactic cyclone as well as for the blossoming of a comic talent which had been present earlier but here achieves an anarchic, even surreal quality.

The Acolyte is Astley's own favorite among her novels. Like several other Australian novels—Patrick White's *The Vivisector,* for example—it takes up the notion of the artist as a destroyer of human lives, feeding off the flesh of lesser mortals in the service of his sacred art. Unlike White, however, Astley is interested less in the artist figure himself than in the mortals who are helplessly attracted to him and allow themselves to become his sacrificial victims.

A Kindness Cup and *An Item from the Late News* are both violent and angry novels. The former is based on an incident that took place at The Leap, Queensland, in the second half of the nineteenth century when a group of blacks were massacred. The small town of The Taws is celebrating the progress it has made over the last two decades and has invited former citizens back for a week of reunion. The question, which is eventually answered in the negative, is whether the town can finally acknowledge the injustices it perpetrated in the past. *An Item from the Late News* deals once again with a person who has returned to the town years after a series of tragic events in order to expunge her guilt. As in *A Kindness Cup* the strong characters are evil bullies, while the others exhibit at most a kind of weak tolerance. The novel takes place against the ironical background of Christmas, just as *A Kindness Cup* uses the New Year.

Coming in between these two grimmest of her novels, *Hunting the Wild Pineapple* is a wonderfully funny, anarchic collection of stories, as if the author feels she can let her hair down in the shorter, more open form of the story in contrast to her meticulously plotted novels. Astley has in fact written quite a lot of short fiction as the publication of her *Collected Stories* in 1997 revealed. Most of the stories are related by Keith Leverson, whom we left as a young boy at the end of *The Slow Natives* in hospital with his leg amputated. Now middle-aged, Leverson is ''a monopod self-pitier'' but also a man who has become accustomed to observing others rather than living himself and his perceptions are shrewd, sardonic, witty. Mostly, the observation is of ''this second-rate Eden,'' Astley's familiar northern Queensland, the area ''north of twenty and one hundred and forty-six,'' and of the drop-outs and hippies who inhabit it. In contrast to the sympathetic way she had treated tortured adolescents in earlier novels, Astley through Leverson views these young people with a sort of benign contempt.

Beachmasters breaks new ground in that it is set outside Australia and is quite overtly political. A group of natives on the Pacific island of Kristi, somewhere near to the north of Australia, stage a brief-lived revolt against the English and French powers which govern it. Their bizarre rebellion is described in a quite Conradian way, in terms that are both absurdly farcical on the one hand and profoundly sad on the other. For all the comic elements in the rebellion, Astley's treatment is full of outrage. The sub-title of her eleventh book of fiction, ''Pictures from the Family Album,'' is revealing as to how the novel works. *It's Raining in Mango* comes complete with a brief family tree and in fourteen episodes takes the history of the Laffey family from the time of the arrival of Cornelius and his wife up to roughly the present and the fourth generation. Ironically juxtaposed against their loosely structured history is that of a line of blacks—''Bidiggi'' (known later as Bidgi the Mumbler) born in the 1860s, father of Jackie Mumbler, grandfather of Charley Mumbler and great-grandfather of Billy Mumbler.

Although the social concerns that inform all of Astley's work are present in *Reaching Tin River* they are more muted. The novel deals more directly with the relations between the sexes and is an unusually personal work, the pain internalized rather than directed outwards in the form of moral outrage. It is the story of the quest by Belle for her mother, and perhaps ultimately for herself. *Reaching Tin River* is an oddly moving novel. If there is a limitation to Astley's writing, it takes the form of a lack of emotional range. She is moved to anger far more often than anything deeper. This novel is quite desolate in parts, as well as being extremely funny in others. There is a wonderful evocation of Astley's favorite hunting ground of northern Queensland and its small towns with their absurd names.

Vanishing Points consists of two novellas which implicitly comment on one another. As the title suggests, they are linked by the protagonists' search for a means of escape and retreat from the world as a way of rediscovering meaning in it for themselves. The epigraph to each of the three sections of Astley's short novel *Coda* concerns itself with newspaper reports of old people being abandoned and left to fend for themselves by their children—granny dumping. In the course of the novella we learn about the life of Kathleen Hackendorf, her marriage, her friend Daisy who is now dead but whom she still sees and speaks to everywhere, and finally the treachery of her daughter and her politician husband. In Astley's later works the female characters rebel and stand up for themselves more and more, as if they have finally worked out that life has been dealing them a bum hand. Kathleen is never more attractive than when she is being rude to people who patronize her.

Like *A Kindness Cup, The Multiple Effects of Rainshadow* is based on a specific historical incident and again it is filled with a sense of outrage at the unjust treatment meted out to black people in Australia. Structurally complex, ranging widely in time and character, the novel takes the same despairing view of black-white relations in Australia as *It's Raining in Mango,* suggesting the cyclic and repetitive nature of the violence which befalls Aboriginal people, even though some characters such as a Catholic priest attempt to make a stand. Associated with the theme of endemic racism is Astley's increasingly overt preoccupation with feminism, though feminist issues have always been present in some form or other in her novels.

Drylands confirms the direction in which most of Astley's recent work has been going. Its eloquent subtitle is ''a book for the world's last reader'' and in its account of three generations Astley is able to pour all her dislike of what she believes contemporary Australia and especially contemporary Australian males have become. She deplores her society's racism, its sexism, the decline of country towns and country values, its lack of interest in culture, the illiteracy of its youth and especially their preference for loud, mindless rock over classical music. None of these concerns is new in her work but never has she written so stridently and despairingly, if with ferocious energy, about them. Despite her increasing pessimism, however, Astley's later writing has lost none of its wit, sharp-eyed observation, and relish in the absurdities of egotism. Her body of work is unmatched by that of any contemporary Australian novelist except perhaps Thomas Keneally.

—Laurie Clancy

ATWOOD, Margaret (Eleanor)

Nationality: Canadian. **Born:** Ottawa, Ontario, 18 November 1939. **Education:** Victoria College, University of Toronto, 1957–61, B.A. 1961; Radcliffe College, Cambridge, Massachusetts, A.M. 1962; Harvard University, Cambridge, Massachusetts 1962–63, 1965–67. **Family:** Married; one daughter. **Career:** Lecturer in English, University of British Columbia, Vancouver, 1964–65; instructor in English, Sir George Williams University, Montreal, 1967–68; teacher of creative writing, University of Alberta, Edmonton, 1969–70; assistant professor of English, York University, Toronto, 1971–72. Editor and member of board of directors, House of Anansi Press, Toronto, 1971–73. Writer-in-residence, University of Toronto, 1972–73, University of Alabama, Tuscaloosa, 1985, Macquarie University, North

Ryde, New South Wales, 1987, and Trinity University, San Antonio, Texas, 1989; Berg Visiting Professor of English, New York University, 1986. President, Writers Union of Canada, 1981–82, and PEN Canadian Centre, 1984–86. **Awards:** E.J. Pratt medal, 1961; President's medal, University of Western Ontario, 1965; Governor-General's award, 1966, 1986; Centennial Commission prize, 1967; Union League Civic and Arts Foundation prize, 1969, and Bess Hogkin prize, 1974 (*Poetry,* Chicago); City of Toronto award, 1976, 1989; St. Lawrence award, 1978; Radcliffe medal, 1980; Molson award, 1981; Guggenheim fellowship, 1981; Welsh Arts Council International Writers prize, 1982; Ida Nudel Humanitarian award, 1986; Toronto Arts award, 1986; Los Angeles *Times* Book award, 1986; Arthur C. Clarke Science-Fiction award, for novel, 1987; Humanist of the Year award, 1987; National Magazine award, for journalism, 1988; Harvard University Centennial medal, 1990; Trillium award, for *Wilderness Tips,* 1992, for *The Robber Bride,* 1994; Trillium award for excellence in Ontario writing, 1995; Commonwealth Writer's prize, 1994, Sunday Times award for literary excellence, 1994, both for *The Robber Bride.* Chevalier dans L'Ordre des arts et des lettres, 1994; Giller prize 1996; Medal of Honor for Literature (National Arts Club), 1997. D.Litt.: Trent University, Peterborough, Ontario, 1973; Concordia University, Montreal, 1980; Smith College, Northampton, Massachusetts, 1982; University of Toronto, 1983; Mount Holyoke College, South Hadley, Massachusetts, 1985; University of Waterloo, Ontario, 1985; University of Guelph, Ontario, 1985; Victoria College, 1987; University of Leeds, 1994; McMaster University, 1996. LL.D.: Queen's University, Kingston, Ontario, 1974. Honorary degree from Oxford University, Oxford, England, 1998. Companion, Order of Canada, 1981. Fellow, Royal Society of Canada, 1987; Honorary Member, American Academy of Arts and Sciences, 1988. **Agent:** Phoebe Larmore, 228 Main Street, Venice, California 90291, U.S.A. **Address:** c/o Oxford University Press, 70 Wynford Drive, Don Mills, Ontario M3C 1J9, Canada.

PUBLICATIONS

Novels

The Edible Woman. Toronto, McClelland and Stewart, and London, Deutsch, 1969; Boston, Little Brown, 1970; New York, Bantam Books, 1996.
Surfacing. Toronto, McClelland and Stewart, 1972; London, Deutsch, and New York, Simon and Schuster, 1973.
Lady Oracle. Toronto, McClelland and Stewart, and New York, Simon and Schuster, 1976; London, Deutsch, 1977.
Life Before Man. Toronto, McClelland and Stewart, 1979; New York, Simon and Schuster, and London, Cape, 1980.
Bodily Harm. Toronto, McClelland and Stewart, 1981; New York, Simon and Schuster, and London, Cape, 1982.
The Handmaid's Tale. Toronto, McClelland and Stewart, 1985; Boston, Houghton Mifflin, and London, Cape, 1986.
Cat's Eye. Toronto, McClelland and Stewart, 1988; New York, Doubleday, and London, Bloomsbury, 1989.
The Robber Bride. Toronto, McClelland and Stewart, New York, Doubleday, and London, Bloomsbury, 1993.
Alias Grace. New York, Nan A. Talese, 1996.
The Blind Assassin. New York, Nan A. Talese, 2000.

Short Stories

Dancing Girls and Other Stories. Toronto, McClelland and Stewart, 1977; New York, Simon and Schuster, and London, Cape, 1982.
Encounters with the Element Man. Concord, New Hampshire, Ewert, 1982.
Murder in the Dark: Short Fictions and Prose Poems. Toronto, Coach House Press, 1983; London, Cape, 1984.
Bluebeard's Egg and Other Stories. Toronto, McClelland and Stewart, 1983; Boston, Houghton Mifflin, 1986; London, Cape, 1987.
Unearthing Suite. Toronto, Grand Union Press, 1983.
Hurricane Hazel and Other Stories. Helsinki, Eurographica, 1986.
Wilderness Tips. Toronto, McClelland and Stewart, New York, Doubleday, and London, Bloomsbury, 1991.
Good Bones. Toronto, Coach House Press, 1992; London, Bloomsbury, 1993; published as *Good Bones and Simple Murders.* New York, Nan A. Talese/Doubleday, 1994.
In Our Nature: Stories of Wilderness, edited by Donna Seaman. New York, Dorling Kindersley, 2000.

Uncollected Short Stories

''When It Happens,'' in *The Editors' Choice 1,* edited by George E. Murphy, Jr. New York, Bantam, 1985.
''Theology,'' in *Harper's* (New York), September 1988.
''Kat,'' in *New Yorker,* 5 March 1990.
''Weight,'' in *Vogue* (New York), August 1990.
''Hack Wednesday,'' in *New Yorker,* 17 September 1990.
Contributor, *Fiction,* edited by R. S. Gwynn. New York, HarperCollins, 1993.
Contributor, *Myths and Voices: Contemporary Canadian Fiction,* edited by David Lampe. Fredonia, New York, White Pine Press, 1993.

Plays

Radio Plays: *The Trumpets of Summer,* 1964.

Television Plays: *The Servant Girl,* 1974; *Snowbird,* 1981; *Heaven on Earth,* with Peter Pearson, 1986.

Poetry

Double Persephone. Toronto, Hawskhead Press, 1961.
The Circle Game (single poem). Bloomfield Hills, Michigan, Cranbrook Academy of Art, 1964; introduction by Sherrill Grace. Toronto, House of Anansi, 1998.
Talismans for Children. Bloomfield Hills, Michigan, Cranbrook Academy of Art, 1965.
Kaleidoscopes: Baroque. Bloomfield Hills, Michigan, Cranbrook Academy of Art, 1965.
Speeches for Doctor Frankenstein. Bloomfield Hills, Michigan, Cranbrook Academy of Art, 1966.
The Circle Game (collection). Toronto, Contact Press, 1966.
Expeditions. Bloomfield Hills, Michigan, Cranbrook Academy of Art, 1966.
The Animals in That County. Toronto, Oxford University Press, 1968; Boston, Little Brown, 1969.
Who Was in the Garden. Santa Barbara, California, Unicorn, 1969.

Five Modern Canadian Poets, with others, edited by Eli Mandel. Toronto, Holt Rinehart, 1970.
The Journals of Susanna Moodie. Toronto, Oxford University Press, 1970; Boston, Houghton Mifflin, 1997.
Oratorio for Sasquatch, Man and Two Androids: Poems for Voices. Toronto, Canadian Broadcasting Corporation, 1970.
Procedures for Underground. Toronto, Oxford University Press, and Boston, Little Brown, 1970.
Power Politics. Toronto, Anansi, 1971; New York, Harper, 1973; second edition published as *Power Politics: Poems,* Concord, Ontario, Anansi, 1996.
You Are Happy. Toronto, Oxford University Press, and New York, Harper, 1974.
Selected Poems. Toronto, Oxford University Press, 1976; New York, Simon and Schuster, 1978.
Marsh, Hawk. Toronto, Dreadnaught, 1977.
Two-Headed Poems. Toronto, Oxford University Press, 1978; New York, Simon and Schuster, 1981.
True Stories. Toronto, Oxford University Press, 1981; New York, Simon and Schuster, and London, Cape, 1982.
Notes Towards a Poem That Can Never Be Written. Toronto, Salamander Press, 1981.
Snake Poems. Toronto, Salamander Press, 1983.
Interlunar. Toronto, Oxford University Press, 1984; London, Cape, 1988.
Selected Poems 2: Poems Selected and New 1976–1986. Toronto, Oxford University Press, 1986; Boston, Houghton Mifflin, 1987.
Selected Poems 1966–1984. Toronto, Oxford University Press, 1990.
Poems 1965–1975. London, Virago Press, 1991.
Morning in the Burned House. Toronto, McClelland and Stewart, Boston, Houghton Mifflin, and London, Virago, 1995.
Eating Fire: Selected Poetry 1965–1995. London, Virago, 1998.

Other (for children)

Up in the Tree. Toronto, McClelland and Stewart, 1978.
Anna's Pet, with Joyce Barkhouse. Toronto, Lorimer, 1980.
For the Birds. Toronto, Douglas and McIntyre, 1990.
Princess Prunella and the Purple Peanut, illustrated by Maryann Kovalski. New York, Workman, 1995.

Other

Survival: A Thematic Guide to Canadian Literature. Toronto, Anansi, 1972.
Days of the Rebels 1815–1840. Toronto, Natural Science of Canada, 1977.
Second Words: Selected Critical Prose. Toronto, Anansi, 1982; Boston, Beacon Press, 1984.
Margaret Atwood: Conversations, edited by Earl G. Ingersoll. Princeton, New Jersey, Ontario Review Press, 1990.
Strange Things: The Malevolent North in Canadian Literature. New York, Oxford University Press, 1995.
The Labrador Fiasco. London, Bloomsbury, 1996.
A Quiet Game: And Other Early Works, edited by Kathy Chung and Sherill Grace, with illustrations by Kathy Chung. Edmonton, Alberta, Juvenilia Press, 1997.
Two Solicitudes: Conversations (with Victory-Levy Beaulieu), translated by Phyllis Aronoff and Howard Scott. Toronto, McClelland and Stewart, 1998.
Introduction, *Women Writers at Work: The Paris Review Interviews,* edited by George Plimpton. New York, Modern Library, 1998.
Contributor, *The Case Against ''Free Trade'': GATT, NAFTA, and the Globalization of Corporate Power,* edited by Ralph Nader. San Francisco, Earth Island Press, 1993.
Editor, *The New Oxford Book of Canadian Verse in English.* Toronto, New York, and Oxford, Oxford University Press, 1982.
Editor, with Robert Weaver, *The Oxford Book of Canadian Short Stories in English.* Toronto, Oxford, and New York, Oxford Univeristy Press, 1986.
Editor, *The Canlit Food Book: From Pen to Palate: A Collection of Tasty Literary Fare.* Toronto, Totem, 1987.
Editor, with Shannon Ravenel, *The Best American Short Stories 1989.* Boston, Houghton Mifflin, 1989.
Editor, *Barbed Lyres.* Toronto, Key Porter, 1990.
Editor, with Barry Callaghan, *Gwendolyn MacEwen.* Toronto, Exile Editions, 1994.
Editor, with Robert Weaver, *The New Oxford Book of Canadian Short Stories in English.* New York, Oxford University Press, 1995.
Foreword, *The Book Group Book: A Thoughtful Guide to Forming and Enjoying a Stimulating Book Discussion Group,* edited by Ellen Slezak. Chicago Review Press, 1995.

*

Bibliography: ''Margaret Atwood: An Annotated Bibliography'' (prose and poetry) by Alan J. Horne, in *The Annotated Bibliography of Canada's Major Authors 1–2* edited by Robert Lecker and Jack David, Downsview, Ontario, ECW Press, 2 vols., 1979–80.

Manuscript Collection: Fisher Library, University of Toronto.

Critical Studies: *Margaret Atwood: A Symposium* edited by Linda Sandler, Victoria, British Columbia, University of Victoria, 1977; *A Violent Duality* by Sherrill E. Grace, Montreal, Véhicule Press, 1979, and *Margaret Atwood: Language, Text, and System* edited by Grace and Lorraine Weir, Vancouver, University of British Columbia Press, 1983; *The Art of Margaret Atwood: Essays in Criticism* edited by Arnold E. Davidson and Cathy N. Davidson, Toronto, Anansi, 1981; *Margaret Atwood* by Jerome H. Rosenberg, Boston, Twayne, 1984; *Margaret Atwood: A Feminist Poetics* by Frank Davey, Vancouver, Talonbooks, 1984; *Margaret Atwood* by Barbara Hill Rigney, London, Macmillan, 1987; *Margaret Atwood: Reflection and Reality* by Beatrice Mendez-Egle, Edinburg, Texas, Pan American University, 1987; *Critical Essays on Margaret Atwood* edited by Judith McCombs, Boston, Hall, 1988; *Margaret Atwood: Vision and Forms* edited by Kathryn van Spanckeren and Jan Garden Castro, Carbondale, Southern Illinois University Press, 1988; *The Novels of Margaret Atwood and Anita Desai: A Comparative Study in Feminist Perspectives* by Sunaina Singh, New Delhi, Creative Books, 1994; *Various Atwoods: Essays on the Later Poems, Short Fiction, and Novels,* edited by Lorraine M. York, Concord, Ontario, Anansi, 1995; *The Influence of Painting on Five Canadian Writers: Alice Munro, Hugh Hood, Timothy Findley, Margaret Atwood, and Michael Ondaatje* by John Cooke, Lewiston, New York, Edwin Mellen Press, 1996; *Margaret Atwood* by Coral Ann Howells, New York, St. Martin's, 1996; *Re/membering Selves: Alienation and Survival in the Novels of Margaret Atwood and Margaret Laurence* by Coomi S. Vevaina, New Delhi,

Creative Books, 1996; *Margaret Atwood: A Biography* by Nathalie Cooke, Toronto, ECW Press, 1998; *The Red Shoes: Margaret Atwood Starting Out* by Rosemary Sullivan, Toronto, HarperFlamingo Canada, 1998; *Margaret Atwood Revisited* by Karen F. Stein, New York, Twayne, 1999; *Margaret Atwood,* edited by Harold Bloom, Philadelphia, Chelsea House, 2000.

* * *

In interviews, Margaret Atwood has often commented that when she started writing in the late 1950s and early 1960s, ''Canadian literature'' was considered a contradiction in terms. Arguably, as a novelist, poet, critic, and literary/political activist, Atwood has done more to put Canada on the literary map than any other author. While Atwood is an accomplished poet—and the interconnections between her poetry, short fiction, and her longer works are both rich and complex—it is primarily as a novelist that she has gained an international reputation. Her first novel, *The Edible Woman,* establishes a preoccupation that remains central in all her subsequent fiction: power politics, and in particular, sexual politics. Excavating their layered histories and formative childhood experiences, Atwood explores and exposes the unequal power relations that shape and inhibit the lives of her female protagonists. Novel by novel, she extends the scope and the complexity of this examination in an astute commentary on North American social and cultural politics and an unflinching recognition of our all too human capacity to both inflict and sustain harm. Although Atwood refuses any designations that may pigeonhole her as a writer, her work is clearly feminist, and distinctively Canadian.

While Atwood's first three novels are quite different in form and tone—anti-comedy, mythic quest, and Gothic spoof—they are united by their focus on the individual effects of a society that encourages women to collude in their own objectification. The three protagonists: Marian in *The Edible Woman,* the significantly unnamed narrator in *Surfacing,* and Joan Foster in *Lady Oracle,* all experience (or witness) the transformations demanded by gendered social norms, with their illusory promise of a happily ever after. Atwood's heroines, however, are not the stuff of which fairy tales or costume gothics are made. Thus, *The Edible Woman* traces the ambivalent responses of Marian MacAlpin (who, ironically, works for a market research firm), to her upcoming marriage to a young, rising lawyer. Here, Atwood links the economy of a consumer society with women's place in the economy of the marriage market for Marian's engagement to Peter marks her transition from subject consumer to object consumed as she becomes entrapped by his conservative expectations of regulation femininity. As Peter, the epitome of a shrink-wrapped husband-to-be, starts subjecting Marian to his ideal wife makeover, Marian experiences an increasing sense of her self as an object, an alienation that is textually signaled by the movement from first- to third-person narration. While she generally acquiesces to Peter's demands, her unconscious rejection of this process is played out quite literally in terms of consumption: Marian's body begins to refuse food. This rejection begins with steak, but as the wedding day approaches her rebellion escalates in a symbolic identification with any edible object. Finally, she flees her own engagement party before she is trapped forever in the menacing photographic frame of Peter's desires. Her return to subject status is marked by the baking of an edible woman; presenting this cake surrogate to her shocked fiancé, she rejects both his marriage proposal and his objectifying construction of her. Eating the cake herself, she moves from consumed victim to autonomous consumer.

Atwood's second novel develops many of the thematic concerns of her poetry in evocative prose. Like *The Edible Woman, Surfacing* presents a woman disabled by the consequences of her ''marital'' experience, but the protagonist's journey from psychic and emotional paralysis to unified agency has a powerful mythic dimension that the earlier novel lacks. With three companions, the narrator returns to the landscape of her childhood—a remote cabin on a lake in Northern Quebec—to search for her missing father. She is ambivalent about revisiting the scene of her past, because it reminds her of a more immediate event, the loss of her child in a recent divorce. It is an experience that has left her anaesthetized, cut off from her emotions by a form of mind/body split, and her memories are so painful that she represses them in willful amnesia. The quest in search of her father, however, triggers a quest of self-discovery, as the narrator's history refuses to remain submerged; she is haunted by memories of her parents, a marriage that never was, and her complicity in the abortion of her child. Eventually, she is forced to confront her specters when a dive below the lake surface becomes a symbolic dive into her own unconscious. Abandoning her manipulative companions, she ritualistically sheds all vestiges of a language and culture that has led her into self-betrayal and murder. Alone on the island, she undergoes a shamanistic cleansing madness, ultimately surfacing with a newfound sense of self. The novel's conclusion resonates with Atwood's contemporaneous thematic guide to Canadian literature, *Survival.* Poised to return to the world that she has left, the narrator's vision leaves her with a resolution that speaks to her experience as both a Canadian and as a woman: ''This above all, to refuse to be a victim.''

Lady Oracle comes as something of a light relief as Atwood's concerns with metamorphosis and identity are given a comic spin. With a protagonist whose many incarnations give new meaning to ''a.k.a.,'' Atwood parodies the conventions of romance and of the gothic in an exploration of the damaging effects of mass-produced fantasies for women. Joan Foster is the ultimate escape artist whose identity is made up of a number of different personae. Ostensibly, she is Joan Foster, self-effacing wife of an ineffectually radical husband, but she is also Joan Foster, celebrated author of a volume of feminist poetry. Secretly, she is Louisa K. Delacourt, author of some fifteen costume gothics. Lurking in the background is a freakish circus clown figure, the Fat Lady, a lingering self-conception from her years as an overweight, unloved child. When, under threat of blackmail, Joan's various lives are in danger of converging, she fakes her own drowning and flees to Italy. These personae, however, continue to surface as she completes her latest Harlequinesque offering, *Stalked By Love,* in an ironic and unconscious identification with her heroine's predicament. For all its droll comedy—Atwood even includes parodic autobiographical asides—*Lady Oracle,* like *The Edible Woman,* contains a serious message. Although Joan's recognition of her situation is debatable, the novel demonstrates the debilitating consequences for women of the beauty myth and the conventional romance plot.

Life Before Man is Atwood's bleakest exploration of relations between the sexes, and her most atypical novel to date. Although popular with readers, it has been less well received by critics, partly because of its uncharacteristic pessimism. Set in a claustrophobic one-mile radius of metropolitan Toronto, the novel is dominated by a central symbolic locale, the dinosaur exhibit at the Royal Ontario Museum. Atwood's specimens are emotionally isolated characters involved in a love triangle: Elizabeth, whose icy, self-control is a product of a dreadful childhood; Nate, her indecisive, politically disillusioned husband; and Lesje, a dreamy paleontologist who becomes Nate's lover. Covering a precisely dated two-year span, and structured by the alternating perceptions of the participants in this banal *ménage à trois, Life Before Man* traces the frustrated interactions of characters who cannot connect. Events in the novel are unrelentingly quotidian; even the dramatic suicide of Elizabeth's lover occurs before the story opens. Lesje's obsession with prehistory focuses the novel's exploration of time and extinction, since the age of the dinosaurs provides a metaphysical conceit for the eyeblink of human existence in cosmic terms. Perhaps, Atwood implies, we are only in the middle of a lengthy evolutionary process; certainly, the changes undergone by the three protagonists are minimal at best. Since they are products of social milieu that is all too recognizable as our own, ''life before man'' suggests that at this historical moment ours is a condition that is not yet fully human.

Challenged about the apparent hopelessness of *Life Before Man,* Atwood asserts the writer's responsibility to bear witness to the world around her. Moving her examination of power politics into an international arena, Atwood's next two novels, *Bodily Harm* and *The Handmaid's Tale,* translate this commitment into a moral imperative. Here, Atwood outlines the interconnected nature of various oppressions for the protagonists' personal circumstances are literally or symbolically associated with systemic abuses of power. Initially, both Rennie Wilford in *Bodily Harm* and Offred in *The Handmaid's Tale* are complacently assured of their own political neutrality, in the mistaken belief that violence happens elsewhere to other people. They quickly learn, however, that immunity is a political myth. Rennie becomes embroiled in the after-effects of British and American foreign policy, while Offred exists in a chilling aggregate of historical and contemporary events pushed to their logical extreme: a totalitarian theocracy whose seeds lie in America's Puritan history. Both take up the challenge of documenting their experiences, bearing witness to the brutal realities of the worlds that they inhabit. The novels are saved from didacticism, however, by their narrative strength and the ironic observations of the protagonists who demonstrate that history, especially personal history, is never reducible to simplistic black and white categorizations.

Bodily Harm's protagonist is a journalist of sorts, but her work centers on surfaces rather than depths: Rennie writes trivial lifestyle pieces for city magazines. Her own insulated lifestyle, however, is disrupted by a malignant tumor. After a mastectomy, and subsequent abandonment by her lover—a more sinister version of Peter in *The Edible Woman*—she flees to a Caribbean island attempting to escape her feelings of violation and a life that has become too horrifically real. Structured associatively, rather than chronologically, *Bodily Harm* demonstrates Atwood's talent for mining the multilayered possibilities of metaphorical language as she links sexism with imperialism, cancer of the female body with cancer of the body politic. The fragmented narrative echoes Rennie's own sense of dismemberment. Like the narrator in *Surfacing,* she is alienated from the body that has betrayed her, a divorce that symbolically complements her inability to connect with others. Thus, she refuses to engage with the political situation in her island getaway, preferring instead to remain a professional tourist. When the island is shaken by a political coup, however, Rennie is dragged unwillingly into the thick of it. Witnessing the brutal torture of a defenseless prisoner, and the equally viscous beating of her friend and cellmate, Lora, Rennie starts making some personal and political connections. Finally, she realizes the illusory nature of her belief in her own political exemption, and of the pressing need for massive involvement. Clearly, Atwood's own involvement with Amnesty International marks this novel, for Rennie's projected response to the Canadian officials who release her and request her silence is a telling resolution: ''In any case she is a subversive. She was not one once but now she is. A reporter. She will pick her time; then she will report.''

The Handmaid's Tale—Atwood's first sustained prose foray into speculative fiction—struck many as a radical departure, but it is merely a versatile variation in her ongoing exploration of the intersections of sex and power. It is also the novel that best exemplifies her understanding of the political, a term that she defines as ''who's allowed to do what to whom, who gets what from whom, who gets away with it and how.'' Revisioning Orwell's *1984* in feminist terms, Atwood creates the Republic of Gilead, a dystopian projection extrapolated from current trends. Although some critics derided its plausibility, the path of American affairs since the novel's publication makes *The Handmaid's Tale* read like prophetic realism. In Atwood's not-too-distant patriarchal future, New England has been taken over by right-wing Christian fundamentalists whose family values involve the state-enforced reduction of women to economic and biological functions, justified by selective readings of the Old Testament. As one of the few fertile women in a polluted world, the protagonist's role is that of a surrogate mother; she is a handmaid, ritually impregnated by the paternalistic Commander whose name she bears. Offred's ''now'' is partially explained by the memories that both pain and sustain her in a series of flashbacks to a past very similar to our own present. Then, Offred's chosen absence from history offered freedom; in Gilead this imposed absence constitutes historical erasure. Thus, her account documents her struggle to maintain her identity in a society that refuses to acknowledge it. Prohibited from access to pens or books, Offred's precocious command of language proves central to her self-preservation. And of course Offred is constructing and preserving her identity through the fragmented story that she relates, thus her text is strewn with postmodern allusions to the role of the reader in that process. As a subversive reporter on experience, Offred's plea for an audience becomes all the more pressing in the light of the ironic historical notes that conclude the novel.

With *Cat's Eye, The Robber Bride,* and *Alias Grace,* Atwood returns to the Toronto setting of her earlier work to explore public and private histories, and the vicissitudes of female friendships. In many ways, *Cat's Eye* is also a return to the territory covered in *Surfacing,* not only in its autobiographical echoes, but also in its exploration of time and memory. Both present an artist protagonist reluctant to examine her personal and historical depths, who eventually wrestles with her inner demons in a psychic exorcism, but *Cat's Eye*'s complexities are more subtle and more fully realized. The novel is retrospective both in form and content. A retrospective exhibition brings a grudging Elaine Risley back to the city of her childhood in a return that initiates an imaginative narrative retrospective of her own supposedly forgotten past. A child of the 1940s and 1950s, (like Atwood), her reflections render the Toronto scene in every minute detail, thus *Cat's Eye* functions not only as memoir, but also as a social document of post-war Canadian culture. The dramatic center of the novel lies in Elaine's childhood experience of victimization at the hands of her three best friends, and in her ambivalent feelings about the chief agent of her feminine indoctrination and torment, Cordelia. As Atwood presents it, the world of little girls is not marked by sugar and spice, but rather by the same power politics that characterize adult life. Artistic insight is offered, however, in the paintings that are the key to Elaine's unresolved anxieties, and ultimately her attempt to master her past in a visionary blend of revenge and forgiveness, love and loss. *Cat's Eye* is perhaps Atwood's most profound achievement for here she, like her protagonist, transforms the scattered details of a life into unified work of art.

If *Cat's Eye* ventures into the uncharted terrain of malicious little girls, then *The Robber Bride* plumbs the depths of female sexual competitiveness. Here, Atwood braids the contrasting histories and perceptions of three battle-scarred ''veterans''—Charis, Tony, and Roz—whose weaknesses are exploited by a machiavellian seductress. In a comic gender inversion of Grimm's tale, the titular villain is Zenia, a protean *femme fatale* who invades the protagonists' lives only to make off with the booty—their men. Indeed, warfare is the dominant motif, for Zenia's sexual terrorism is played out against a backdrop of past and present military conflict. As in *Bodily Harm,* the personal and the political are intricately intermingled. *The Robber Bride* also develops Atwood's characteristic concern with formative influences and female identity since Zenia, like Cordelia in *Cat's Eye,* functions not only as an antagonist, but also as a *doppelgänger* for each of the characters. Although each woman's point of view is symmetrically apportioned, it is Tony—the text's literal and figurative historian—whose perspective frames the novel. Musing on the ambiguous promise of History's explanatory power, and its relation to the inexplicability of Zenia, it is she who wonders whether the evil that Zenia represents may not also be a part of us.

With *Alias Grace,* her most recent novel, Atwood contributes to the contemporary boom in historical fiction, even as she indulges the fascination with ''bad girls'' that marks her previous two novels. Raiding the nineteenth-century archive, Atwood presents the richly evoked history of Canada's answer to Lizzie Borden: the ''celebrated murderess,'' Grace Marks, convicted of abetting the murder of her Tory employer and his housekeeper/mistress. A Zenia who is allowed to tell her own story, Grace calmly exposes the contradictory constructions of her character, and unsettles the conventional expectations of Simon Jordan, the ambitious doctor who hopes to make his reputation by curing her apparent amnesia about the case. Like the imprisoned handmaid, Grace's tale is her only power and she wields her ability with consummate skill; she is as adept at storytelling as she is at the female art of quilt-making, the novel's dominant, somewhat overdetermined metaphor. Grace Marks's narrative voice is quintessential Atwood—dispassionate, laconic, devastating in its acuity—but, much like the historians who consider the handmaid's tale, Simon Jordan cannot ''hear'' its political import or register his own complicity in the unequal class and gender system that her story so subtly exposes. Exhibiting the same prurient interest in Grace's case as the salivating public (and, implicitly, the reader), Simon longs for the gory details; an ever enigmatic Grace provides an uncompromisingly detailed account of the social and economic circumstances that may (or may not) have led a housemaid to murder. Although *Alias Grace* contains a ''revelation'' that demonstrates Atwood's continued attraction to the psychological possibilities afforded by the gothic mode, even this sensational conclusion is ambiguous. Ultimately, the question of Grace Marks's guilt or innocence is subordinated to a more telling exposé of the power politics that constitute Atwood's abiding concern. In this, her first extended exploration of Canada's past since *The Journals of Susanna Moodie,* Atwood reiterates and historicizes the central tenet of her moral vision: our human potential to be both a victim and victimizer and our responsibility to be neither.

—Jackie Buxton

AUCHINCLOSS, Louis (Stanton)

Nationality: American. **Born:** Lawrence, New York, 27 September 1917. **Education:** Groton School, Massachusetts, graduated 1935; Yale University, New Haven, Connecticut, 1935–38; University of Virginia Law School, Charlottesville, LL.B. 1941; admitted to the New York bar, 1941. **Military Service:** Served in the United States Naval Reserve, 1941–45: Lieutenant. **Family:** Married Adele Lawrence in 1957; three sons. **Career:** Associate lawyer, Sullivan and Cromwell, New York, 1941–51; associate, 1954–58, and partner, 1958–86, Hawkins Delafield and Wood, New York. Since 1966 president of the Museum of the City of New York. Trustee, Josiah Macy Jr. Foundation, New York; former member of the Executive Committee, Association of the Bar of New York City. **Awards:** New York State Governor's award, 1985. D.Litt.: New York University, 1974; Pace College, New York, 1979; University of the South, Sewanee, Tennessee, 1986. **Member:** American Academy. **Agent:** Curtis Brown, 10 Astor Place, New York, New York 10003. **Address:** 1111 Park Avenue, New York, New York 10128, U.S.A.

Publications

Novels

The Indifferent Children (as Andrew Lee). New York, Prentice Hall, 1947.

Sybil. Boston, Houghton Mifflin, 1951; London, Gollancz, 1952.

A Law for the Lion. Boston, Houghton Mifflin, and London, Gollancz, 1953.

The Great World and Timothy Colt. Boston, Houghton Mifflin, 1956; London, Gollancz, 1957.

Venus in Sparta. Boston, Houghton Mifflin, and London, Gollancz, 1958.

Pursuit of the Prodigal. Boston, Houghton Mifflin, 1959; London, Gollancz, 1960.

The House of Five Talents. Boston, Houghton Mifflin, 1960; London, Gollancz, 1961.

Portrait in Brownstone. Boston, Houghton Mifflin, and London, Gollancz, 1962.

The Rector of Justin. Boston, Houghton Mifflin, 1964; London, Gollancz, 1965.

The Embezzler. Boston, Houghton Mifflin, and London, Gollancz 1966.

A World of Profit. Boston, Houghton Mifflin, 1968; London, Gollancz, 1969.

I Come as a Thief. Boston, Houghton Mifflin, 1972; London, Weidenfeld and Nicolson, 1973.

The Partners. Boston, Houghton Mifflin, and London, Weidenfeld and Nicolson, 1974.

The Winthrop Covenant. Boston, Houghton Mifflin, and London, Weidenfeld and Nicolson, 1976.

The Dark Lady. Boston, Houghton Mifflin, and London, Weidenfeld and Nicolson, 1977.

The Country Cousin. Boston, Houghton Mifflin, and London, Weidenfeld and Nicolson, 1978.

The House of the Prophet. Boston, Houghton Mifflin, and London, Weidenfeld and Nicolson, 1980.

The Cat and the King. Boston, Houghton Mifflin, and London, Weidenfeld and Nicolson, 1981.

Watchfires. Boston, Houghton Mifflin, and London, Weidenfeld and Nicolson, 1982.

Exit Lady Masham. Boston, Houghton Mifflin, 1983; London, Weidenfeld and Nicolson, 1984.

The Book Class. Boston, Houghton Mifflin, and London, Weidenfeld and Nicolson, 1984.

Honorable Men. Boston, Houghton Mifflin, 1985; London, Weidenfeld and Nicolson, 1986.

Diary of a Yuppie. Boston, Houghton Mifflin, 1986; London, Weidenfeld and Nicolson, 1987.

The Golden Calves. Boston, Houghton Mifflin, 1988; London, Weidenfeld and Nicolson, 1989.

Fellow Passengers: A Novel in Portraits. Boston, Houghton Mifflin, 1989; London, Constable, 1990.

The Lady of Situations. Boston, Houghton Mifflin, 1990; London, Constable, 1991.

Tales of Yesteryear. Boston, Houghton Mifflin, 1994.

The Education of Oscar Fairfax. Boston, Houghton Mifflin, 1995.

Her Infinite Variety. Boston, Houghton Mifflin, 2000.

The Embezzler. New Brunswick, New Jersey, Transaction, 2000.

Short Stories

The Injustice Collectors. Boston, Houghton Mifflin, 1950; London, Gollancz, 1951.

The Romantic Egoists: A Reflection in Eight Minutes. Boston, Houghton Mifflin, and London, Gollancz, 1954.

Powers of Attorney. Boston, Houghton Mifflin, and London, Gollancz, 1963.

Tales of Manhattan. Boston, Houghton Mifflin, and London, Gollancz, 1967.

Second Chance. Boston, Houghton Mifflin, 1970; London, Gollancz, 1971.

Narcissa and Other Fables. Boston, Houghton Mifflin, 1983.

Skinny Island: More Tales of Manhattan. Boston, Houghton Mifflin, 1987; London, Weidenfeld and Nicolson, 1988.

False Gods. Boston, Houghton Mifflin, 1992; London, Constable, 1993.

Three Lives. Boston, Houghton Mifflin, 1993; London, Constable, 1994.

The Collected Stories of Louis Auchincloss. Boston, Houghton Mifflin, 1994.

The Atonement, and Other Stories. Boston, Houghton Mifflin, 1997.

The Anniversary and Other Stories. Boston, Houghton Mifflin, 1999.

Play

The Club Bedroom (produced New York, 1967).

Other

Edith Wharton. Minneapolis, University of Minnesota Press, 1961.

Reflections of a Jacobite. Boston, Houghton Mifflin, 1961; London, Gollancz, 1962.

Ellen Glasgow. Minneapolis, University of Minnesota Press, 1964.

Pioneers and Caretakers: A Study of 9 American Women Novelists. Minneapolis, University of Minnesota Press, 1965; London, Oxford University Press, 1966.

Motiveless Malignity (on Shakespeare). Boston, Houghton Mifflin, 1969; London, Gollancz, 1970.

Henry Adams. Minneapolis, University of Minnesota Press, 1971.

Edith Wharton: A Woman in Her Time. New York, Viking Press, 1971; London, Joseph, 1972.

Richelieu. New York, Viking Press, 1972; London, Joseph, 1973.

A Writer's Capital (autobiography). Minneapolis, University of Minnesota Press, 1974.

Reading Henry James. Minneapolis, University of Minnesota Press, 1975.

Persons of Consequence: Queen Victoria and Her Circle. New York, Random House, and London, Weidenfeld and Nicolson, 1979.

Life, Law, and Letters: Essays and Sketches. Boston, Houghton Mifflin, 1979; London, Weidenfeld and Nicolson, 1980.

Three "Perfect Novels" and What They Have in Common. Bloomfield Hills, Michigan, Bruccoli Clark, 1981.

Unseen Versailles. New York, Doubleday, 1981.

False Dawn: Women in the Age of the Sun King. New York, Doubleday, 1984.

The Vanderbilt Era: Profiles of a Gilded Age. New York, Scribner, 1989.

J.P. Morgan: The Financier as Collector. New York, Abrams, 1990.

Love Without Wings: Some Friendships in Literature and Politics. Boston, Houghton Mifflin, 1991.

Deborah Turbeville's Newport Remembered: A Photographic Portrait of a Gilded Past. New York, Abrams, 1994.

The Style's the Man: Reflections on Proust, Fitzgerald, Wharton, Vidal, and Others. New York, Scribner, 1994.

Deborah Turbeville's Newport Remembered: A Photographic Portrait of a Gilded Past (text), photography by Deborah Turbeville. New York, Henry N. Abrams, 1994.

The Man Behind the Book: Literary Profiles. Boston, Houghton Mifflin, 1996.

La Gloire: The Roman Empire of Corneille and Racine. Columbia, South Carolina, University of South Carolina, 1996.

Woodrow Wilson. New York, Viking, 2000.

Afterword, *High Society: The Town and Country Picture Album, 1846–1996,* edited by Anthony T. Mazzola and Frank Zachary. New York, Abrams, 1996.

Contributor, with others, *A Century of Arts and Letters: The History of the National Institute of Arts and Letters and the American Academy of Arts and Letters as Told, Decade by Decade, by Eleven Members,* edited by John Updike. New York, Columbia University Press, 1998.

Foreword, *New York Novels* by Edith Wharton. New York, Modern Library, 1998.

Foreword, *The Age of Innocence* by Edith Wharton. New York, Modern Library, 1999.

Editor, *An Edith Wharton Reader.* New York, Scribner, 1965.

Editor, *The Warden, and Barchester Towers,* by Trollope. Boston, Houghton Mifflin, 1966.

Editor, *Fables of Wit and Elegance.* New York, Scribner, 1975.

Editor, *Maverick in Mauve: The Diary of a Turn-of-the-Century Aristocrat,* by Florence Adele Sloane. New York, Doubleday, 1983.

Editor, *The Hone and Strong Diaries of Old Manhattan.* New York, Abbeville Press, 1989.

Introduction, *Cattle Boat to Oxford: The Education of R. I. W. Westgate: Edited from His Letters, Diaries, and Papers* by Sheila Margaret Westgate. New York, Walker, 1994.

Introduction, *Jean Christophe* by Romaine Rolland. New York, Carroll & Graf, 1996.

Introduction, *The Reef* by Edith Wharton. New York, Scribner, 1996.

*

Bibliography: *Louis Auchincloss and His Critics: A Bibliographical Record* by Jackson R. Bryer, Boston, Hall, 1977.

Manuscript Collection: University of Virginia, Charlottesville.

Critical Studies: *The Novel of Manners in America* by James W. Tuttleton, Chapel Hill, University of North Carolina Press, 1972; *Louis Auchincloss* by Christopher C. Dahl, New York, Ungar, 1986; *Louis Auchincloss: The Growth of a Novelist* by Vincent Piket, Nijmegan, Netherlands, European University Press, 1989, New York, St. Martin's Press, and London, Macmillan, 1991; *Louis Auchincloss: A Writer's Life* by Carol W. Gelderman, New York, Crown, 1993.

Louis Auchincloss comments:

(1972) I do not think in general that authors are very illuminating on their own work, but in view of the harshness of recent (1970) reviewers, I should like to quote from a letter of Edith Wharton in my collection. It was written when she was 63, ten years older than I now am, but the mood is relevant. She is speaking of critics who have disliked her last novel: ''You will wonder that the priestess of the life of reason should take such things to heart, and I wonder too. I never have minded before, but as my work reaches its close, I feel so sure that it is either nothing or far more than they know. And I wonder, a little desolately, which.'' Mrs. Wharton's work was far from its close, and I hope mine may be!

* * *

Louis Auchincloss is among the few dedicated novelists of manners at work in contemporary America. He is a successor to Edith Wharton as a chronicler of the New York aristocracy. In this role he necessarily imbues his novels with an elegiac tone as he observes the passing beauties of the city and the fading power of the white Anglo-Saxon Protestants of old family and old money who can no longer sustain their position of dominance in the society or their aristocratic ideals. His principal subject is thus the manners and morals, the money and marriages, the families and houses, the schools and games, the language and arts of the New York aristocracy as he traces its rise, observes its present crisis, and meditates its possible fall and disappearance. The point of vantage from which he often observes the aristocracy is that of the lawyer who serves and frequently belongs to this class.

The idea of good family stands in an uneasy relation to money in Auchincloss's fiction. Auchincloss dramatizes the dilemma of the American aristocracy by showing that it is necessary to possess money to belong to this class but fatal to one's standing within the class to pursue money. People who have connections with those who are still in trade cannot themselves fully qualify as gentlemen, as the opportunistic Mr. Dale in *The Great World and Timothy Colt* shows. On the other hand, Auchincloss is clearly critical of those aristocrats like Bertie Millinder or Percy Prime who do nothing constructive and are engaged simply in the spending of money. Auchincloss recognizes that the family is the most important of aristocratic institutions and that its place in its class is guaranteed by the conservation of its resources. This task of preserving the family wealth falls to the lawyers, and his fiction is rich in the complexities, both moral and financial, of fiduciary responsibility; *Venus in Sparta* is a novel in point. The paradox that Auchincloss reveals but does not seem sufficiently to exploit is that the conservative impulse of the aristocracy, which emphasizes the past, is concerned ultimately with posterity, which of course emphasizes the future.

Auchincloss does, however, fully exploit the conflict between the marriage arranged for the good of the family, often by strong women, and romantic or sexual impulses that are destructive of purely social goals, as *Portrait in Brownstone* illustrates. Sex and love are enemies to the organicism of conservative societies, in which the will of the individual is vested in the whole. Auchincloss observes the workings of this organic notion in the structure of family and marriage as well as in institutions like the school and the club where a consensus judgment about value and behavior is formulated and handed down. Such institutions preserve a way of life and protect those who live by it from those on the outside who do not. *The Rector of Justin* is the most obvious of Auchincloss's novels to deal with an institution, or with a man as an institution, that performs this function.

Auchincloss's fiction does more than present us with a mere record of the institutions that support the American aristocracy. The dramatic interest in his novels and whatever larger importance may be accorded them lies in his recognition that the entire class is in jeopardy and that individual aristocrats are often failures. The closed, unitary life of the aristocracy is sometimes threatened by outsiders—Jews, for example, as in *The Dark Lady* and *The House of the Prophet*—who must be repelled or at worst absorbed. Sometimes Auchincloss sees problems arising within the context of aristocracy itself, as when individual will or desire comes in conflict with the organicism; perhaps Rees Parmalee, in *Pursuit of the Prodigal*, makes the most significant rebellion of all Auchincloss's characters, but he is rejecting a decadent aristocracy and not aristocracy itself. Auchincloss is severely critical of the idea of the gentleman when it is corrupted by allegiance to superficial qualities, like Guy Prime's capacity to hold his liquor or to behave with virile cordiality in *The Embezzler*. But the real failures are those aristocrats who suffer, as so many of Auchincloss's male characters do, from a sense of inadequacy and insecurity that leads them to self-destructiveness. They are not strong and tough-fibered, as so many of the women are; they seem too fastidious and over-civilized, and they are failing the idea of society and their class. In this way, and in others, Auchincloss regretfully chronicles the passing of the aristocracy, which cannot sustain its own ideals in the contemporary world: *A World of Profit* is the most explicit recognition of this failure.

Auchincloss has made his record of the New York aristocracy in a style which is clear and simple, occasionally elegant and brilliant, and sometimes self-consciously allusive. He has a gift for comedy of manners, which he has not sufficiently cultivated, and a fine model in Oscar Wilde. Other influences upon him include Edith Wharton, in ways already mentioned; Henry James, from whom he learned the manipulation of point of view, and the faculty of endowing things, art objects for example, with meaning; and St. Simon, a memorialist who did for the French court what Auchincloss wishes to do for Knickerbocker New York. Yet among his faults as a novelist, especially evident because of the particular genre he has chosen, is a failure to give the reader a richness of detail; he does well with home furnishings but is far less successful with the details of institutions. Furthermore, he sometimes loses control of his novels and permits action to overwhelm theme. The most serious criticism to be made of his work is that while he does indeed pose moral dilemmas for his characters, he too easily resolves their problems for them. He does not sufficiently convey a sense of the bitter cost of honesty or courage or moral superiority, a continuing difficulty for him, as *The Country Cousin* demonstrates.

This same ethical conflict is seen in *Three Lives*, which, like Gertrude Stein's work of the same title, consists of three novellas disclosing the lives of three characters from the same stratum of society. Being Auchincloss rather than Stein, his characters are three New Yorkers born to wealth around the turn of the century. In *Tales of Yesteryear*, we see as well an assortment of characters of wealth and privilege who suffer a hardening of the heart as a result of their station in society. In several tales, members of the older generation look back over their lives with quiet regret, suggesting that wealth and power do not bring contentment. From this collection come some of the stories in Auchincloss's fiftieth book, *The Collected Stories of Louis Auchincloss*. Here readers find a full range of Auchincloss, from one of his earliest stories, the perfectly composed ''Maud,'' to his most recent ''They That Have the Power to Hurt.''

He has given us, on balance, a full enough record of upper-class life in New York, but he has fallen short of the most penetrating and meaningful kinds of social insight that the best of the novelists of manners offer.

—Chester E. Eisinger, updated by Sandra Ray

AUSTER, Paul

Nationality: American. **Born:** Newark, New Jersey, 3 February 1947. **Education:** Columbia University, New York, B.A. 1969, M.A. 1970. **Family:** Married 1) Lydia Davis in 1974; 2) Siri Hustvedt in 1981; two children. **Career:** Has had a variety of jobs, including merchant seaman, census taker, and tutor; creative writing teacher, Princeton University, New Jersey, 1986–90. **Awards:** Ingram Merrill Foundation grant, for poetry, 1975, 1982; PEN Translation Center grant, 1977; National Endowment for the Arts fellowship for poetry, 1979, and for creative writing, 1985; Cheavlier de l'Ordre des Arts et des Lettres, 1992; Prix Medicis Etranger, 1993; Independent Spirit Award, 1996. **Address:** c/o Viking, 375 Hudson Street, New York, New York 10014, U.S.A.

Publications

Novels

Squeeze Play (as Paul Benjamin). London, Alpha-Omega, 1982; New York, Avon, 1984.
The New York Trilogy. London, Faber, 1987; New York, Penguin, 1990.
City of Glass. Los Angeles, Sun and Moon Press, 1985.
Ghosts. Los Angeles, Sun and Moon Press, 1986.
The Locked Room. Los Angeles, Sun and Moon Press, 1987.
In the Country of Last Things. New York, Viking, 1987; London, Faber, 1988.
Moon Palace. New York, Viking, 1989; London, Faber, 1990.
The Music of Chance. New York, Viking, 1990; London, Faber, 1991.
Leviathan. New York, Viking, and London, Faber, 1992.
Mr. Vertigo. New York, Viking, and London, Faber, 1994.
Timbuktu. New York, Holt, 1999.

Uncollected Short Story

''Auggie Wren's Christmas Story,'' in *New York Times*, 25 December 1990.

Plays

Eclipse (produced New York, 1977).

Screenplays: *Smoke*, Miramax Films, 1995; *Blue in the Face* (with Wayne Wang), Miramax Films, 1995; *Lulu on the Bridge: A Film*, New York, Holt, 1998.

Poetry

Unearth: Poems 1970–72. Weston, Connecticut, Living Hand, 1974.
Wall Writing: Poems 1971–75. Berkeley, California, Figures, 1976.
Fragments from Cold. New York, Parenthèse, 1977.
Facing the Music. New York, Station Hill, 1980.
Disappearances. New York, Overlook Press, 1988.

Other

White Spaces. New York, Station Hill, 1980.
The Art of Hunger and Other Essays. London, Menard Press, 1982; expanded edition, New York, Penguin, 1997.
The Invention of Solitude. New York, Sun, 1982; London, Faber, 1988.
Ground Work: Selected Poems and Essays 1970–1979. London, Faber, 1990.
Smoke and Blue in the Face: Two Films. New York, Hyperion, 1995.
The Red Notebook and Other Writings. Boston, Faber and Faber, 1995.
Why Write? Providence, Rhode Island, Burning Deck, 1996.
Hand to Mouth: A Chronicle of Early Failure. New York, Holt, 1997.
Introduction, *Hunger* by Knut Hamsun, translated by Robert Bly. New York, Noonday Press, 1998.
Introduction, with David Cone, *Things Happen for a Reason: The True Story of an Itinerant Life in Baseball* by Terry Leach with Tom Clark. Berkeley, California, Frog, 2000.
Contributor, *Edward Hopper and the American Imagination* by Deborah Lyons and Adam D. Weinberg, edited by Julie Grau. New York, Norton, 1995.
Editor, *The Random House Book of Twentieth-Century French Poetry*. London, Random House, 1982; New York, Vintage, 1984.
Editor and translator, *The Notebooks of Joseph Joubert: A Selection*. San Francisco, North Point Press, 1983.
Translator, *A Little Anthology of Surrealist Poems*. New York, Siamese Banana Press, 1972.
Translator, *Fits and Starts: Selected Poems of Jacques Dupin*. Weston, Connecticut, Living Hand, 1974.
Translator, with Lydia Davis, *Arabs and Israelis: A Dialogue*, by Saul Friedlander and Mahmoud Hussein. New York, Holmes and Meier, 1975.

Translator, *The Uninhabited: Selected Poems of André de Bouchet.* Weston, Connecticut, Living Hand, 1976.

Translator, with Lydia Davis, *Jean-Paul Sartre: Life Situations.* New York, Pantheon, 1977; as *Sartre in the Seventies: Interviews and Essays,* London, Deutsch, 1978.

Translator, with Lydia Davis, *China: The People's Republic 1949–76,* by Jean Chesneaux. New York, Pantheon, 1979.

Translator, with Françoise Le Barbier and Marie-Claire Bergère, *China from the 1911 Revolution to Liberation.* New York, Pantheon, 1979.

Translator, *A Tomb for Anatole,* by Stéphane Mallarmé. San Francisco, North Point Press, 1983.

Translator, *Vicious Circles,* by Maurice Blanchot. New York, Station Hill, 1985.

Translator, *On the High Wire,* by Philippe Petit. New York, Random House, 1985.

Translator, with Margit Rowell, *Joan Miró: Selected Writings.* Boston, Hall, 1986.

Translator and author of foreword, *Chronicle of the Guayaki Indians* by Pierre Clastres. New York, Zone Books, 1998.

Translator, with others, *The Station Hill Blanchot Reader,* edited by George Quasha. Barrytown, New York, Station Hill, 1999.

*

Critical Studies: *Review of Contemporary Fiction,* vol. 14, no. 1, Spring 1994 (entire issue devoted to Auster); *Beyond the Red Notebook: Essays on Paul Auster* edited by Dennis Barone, Philadelphia, University of Pennsylvania Press, 1995.

* * *

Paul Auster has frequently been called a ''postmodern'' novelist, perhaps in part because critics do not know what else to call a writer whose works include metaphysical detective stories, a dystopian fantasy, an extravagant *bildungsroman,* and an ambiguous parable of fate and chance. To the extent that the term denotes an ironic stance towards language and its uses, Auster is indeed postmodern; yet without surrendering this irony or foregoing the advantage of self-conscious narration, he has moved to a greater expansiveness of form and content. His later novels have not been hampered by embarrassment at asking big questions about the possibility of self-knowledge and personal redemption; rather, they have conceded to the reader the unmediated pleasures of character and story.

Such pleasures are rather scant in *The New York Trilogy*, the epistemological mystery novels that established Auster's reputation. What entertainment they provide is almost wholly cerebral: the delectation of intellectual puzzles that have little or no relation to a reality beyond the texts themselves. *City of Glass*, the first volume, is about a mystery novelist named Quinn whose attempt to live the life of the kind of hardened gumshoe he writes about ends in a tragic muddle. Not the least of the novel's ontological jokes is that the detective for whom Quinn is mistaken is named Paul Auster. Auster himself, or a simulacrum of him, appears in a scene in which the increasingly desperate Quinn goes to him for advice. Interrupted while composing an essay on the vanishing narrators of *Don Quixote,* Auster is unable to help; he is a writer, not a private investigator. This Paul Auster, however, is not the author of *City of Glass*. The ''actual'' author, it turns out, is a former friend of Auster's who heard the story from him and is convinced that Auster has ''behaved badly throughout.''

Ghosts extends the paradoxes about identity and fictive creation into a world of Beckett-like abstraction and austerity. White hires Blue to watch Black, who does little but write and watch back: ''Little does Blue know, of course, that the case will go on for years.'' Not even violence can finally break this stasis, and as the narrator says at the end, ''we know nothing.''

A reader may get the feeling that *The New York Trilogy* is too clever for its own good, that Auster engages knotty intellectual issues partly to evade more troubling emotional ones. *The Locked Room*, the concluding volume, is nothing if not clever, yet it reveals a new openness in Auster's sensibility. The Paul Auster-like narrator is a young writer of promise whose life is taken over by the appearance, or disappearance, of his *doppelgänger* Fanshawe, his best friend from his youth. Fanshawe is presumed dead but has left his manuscripts in the care of the narrator, who sees them through publication and to a literary acclaim far surpassing that of his own work. As Fanshawe's appointed biographer, the narrator embarks on an obsessive investigation into the mystery of his friend's life, thereby discovering much about himself as about Fanshawe, for the lines separating their two identities are naturally convergent. *The Locked Room* may be no more than a game, but the stakes, which do not preclude the anguish that attends existential doubts about one's identity, are considerably higher than those in *City of Glass* and *Ghosts*.

The presence of a controlling author is not insisted upon in *In the Country of Last Things*, a nightmarish tale of total social breakdown in an unnamed city-state that could be New York some years in the future. This does not mean, however, that in this work Auster has resolved all doubts about the problematic relationship of language to reality. The narrator, a young woman named Anna Blume, comes to the city in search of a lost brother, only to be trapped in its round of violence, despair, and physical and spiritual poverty. She keeps a journal (the text of the novel) full of reflections on the inadequacy of words to describe a world where people scavenge viciously for garbage or plot their own suicides. Yet Anna, her lover, and her two remaining friends retain their decency if not their dignity. The truly lost, Auster suggests, may be those who have given up on language itself.

Language acquires a renewed immediacy and momentum in *Moon Palace*, one of Auster's most entertaining novels, and among his best. Its immensely complicated plot concerns the adventures of Marco Stanley Fogg, an orphan in the best Dickensian tradition, whose modest inheritance runs out in his senior year at Columbia University, consigning him— for reasons obscure even to himself— to a season of homelessness and near starvation in Central Park. Just before the weather turns cold, he is rescued by his former college roommate and a young Chinese woman who becomes the love of his life. Soon thereafter he takes a job as an amanuensis to an eccentric and irascible old cripple whose wild stories of his youth as a painter and subsequent adventures in the old West Marco faithfully transcribes. Finally Marco meets up with the old man's estranged son, now a middle-aged and obese professor of history who has taught at a succession of second-rate colleges. In the end Marco loses everything: father, father-figure, and his loving girlfriend and their child, yet his excruciating education has not been wasted. The novel ends with Marco watching the moon rise from a California beach and thinking, ''This is where I start … this is where my life begins.''

Auster's accustomed self-referentiality and playing up of literary patterns and allusions once again reveal the artifice that underlies any fictive representation of reality, but the emphasis in *Moon Palace* is on the reality, not the artifice. The more improbable the events described, the more bizarre the cast of characters, the more the reader is inclined to believe. Marco wonders if old Thomas Effing's outlandish reminiscences can possibly be true, but they are as true as they need to be: true to Effing's private wounds and world, true to the chaotic social reality of America in the 20th century, true to the novel's themes of personal loss and recovery, of the endless invention of the self.

What *The Music of Chance* is ''about'' is rather less clear. As fluidly written as *Moon Palace*, it begins as a fairly straightforward account of the squandering of a family inheritance by a 35-year-old ex-fireman named Jim Nashe; but about halfway through, it shifts into a Kafka-like parable in which Nashe and a young gambler named Jack Pozzi are trapped on the estate of a pair of rich and sinister eccentrics and forced to build a huge wall from the rubble of a castle disassembled and shipped overseas from Ireland. Nashe grows in moral stature as his difficulties increase, but the chances that determine his fate are ordained by the author, who ends the novel with a fatal car crash that is at once wholly arbitrary and perfectly logical. Although Auster's intelligence, humor, and inventiveness are evident throughout, the novel's realist and allegorical tendencies tend to work against one another. *The Music of Chance* remains rather opaque, but it also demonstrates Auster's engagement with issues much larger than those that concerned the hermetic fabulist of *The New York Trilogy*.

The 1995 film *Smoke*, directed by Wayne Wang from a screenplay by Auster, succeeded in bringing the author's work before a larger, though still highly selective, audience. The story, of intersecting lives and the struggle for intimacy, also revealed him in a much more emotional light than his previous, more cerebral, works. In line with this increased openness, during this period Auster published *Hand to Mouth*, a reminiscence on his early challenges as a writer. He also began moving deeper into the world of film, and in 1997 directed his first picture, *Lulu on the Bridge*.

—Stephen Akey

B

BAIL, Murray

Nationality: Australian. **Born:** Adelaide, South Australia, 22 September 1941. **Education:** Norwood Technical High School, Adelaide. **Family:** Married Margaret Wordsworth in 1965. **Career:** Lived in India, 1968–70, and in England and Europe, 1970–74. Member of the Council, Australian National Gallery, Canberra, 1976–81. **Awards:** *The Age* Book of the Year award, 1980; National Book Council award, 1980; Victorian Premier's award, 1988. **Address:** c/o Faber and Faber, Inc., 50 Cross St., Winchester, Massachusetts 01890, U.S.A.

PUBLICATIONS

Novels

Homesickness. Melbourne, Macmillan, 1980; London, Faber, 1986; New York, Farrar, Straus, and Giroux, 1999.
Holden's Performance. London, Faber, 1987.
Eucalyptus. New York, Farrar, Straus, and Giroux, 1998.

Short Stories

Contemporary Portraits and Other Stories. St. Lucia, University of Queensland Press, 1975; as *The Drover's Wife,* London, Faber, 1986.

Uncollected Short Stories

"Healing," in *New Yorker,* 16 April 1979.
"Home Ownership," In *Winter's Tales 27,* edited by Edward Leeson. London, Macmillan, 1981; New York, St. Martin's Press, 1982.

Other

Ian Fairweather. Sydney, Bay, 1981.
Longhand: A Writer's Notebook. Fitzroy, Victoria, McPhee Gribble, 1989.
Editor, *The Faber Book of Contemporary Australian Short Stories.* London, Faber, 1988.
Editor, *Fairweather.* Queensland, Australia, Art and Australia Books, 1994.

* * *

Murray Bail is, with Peter Carey and Frank Moorhouse, one of the chief innovators in the tradition of the Australian short story and is especially associated with its revival in the early and mid-1970s. Since then he has established a reputation as one of Australia's most original and distinctive novelists. Bail's first book was a collection of short stories titled *Contemporary Portraits and Other Stories.* The first of many tricks is that there no story called "Contemporary Portraits." The collection was later republished as *The Drover's Wife and Other Stories.* Bail's interest in the relationship between language and reality is present in all the stories and especially "Zoellner's Definition." "The Drover's Wife" is a rewriting of Henry Lawson's classic story. Bail's version is a monologue by the deserted husband, based on a famous painting by Russell Drysdale. The story "Portrait of Electricity" contains the seeds of Bail's first novel, *Homesickness.* A great man is defined in terms of the various examples and pieces of evidence of his existence contained in a museum devoted to him, beginning with an ashtray and culminating in an example of his excrement. The stories display the strange mixture of surrealist fantasy and broad satire of Australian mores that characterizes all of Bail's work.

The motif of the museum is taken up in *Homesickness,* a funny, inventive, highly intelligent novel. Bail's obsession is with mythologizing what he sees as so far an unmythologized and therefore unpossessed country. A group of travelers from Australia set out to tour the world. As they do so they shift about and continually form new groups, new liaisons. At the same time they visit a series of museums, each of which seems a kind of paradigm of the culture it represents. The museum in Quito, Ecuador, for instance, is a Museum of Handicrafts. Many of the artifacts are British anachronisms, symbolic of the occupation of the country in the nineteenth century. In New York they see a reenacted mugging. In London there is a Museum of Lost and Found Objects. There are many internal and self-referential jokes, witty aphorisms, characters with figurative names. There is a little African boy whose name is Oxford University Press and who, asked what he wants to be when he grows up, says "A tourist." Throughout all the wit and ingenuity Bail's concerns emerge with striking consistency. His interest in nationality is only part of his larger interest in identity, which is also central to the novel's motifs of tourism, museums, homesickness ("They could hear Sasha being homesick in the basin") and national differences: at one stage the party go into a series of cliches about national identity that lasts for three pages. And in turn concern with identity merges into concern with language and the relationship between language and experience.

Holden's Performance is again an attempt to mythologize Australia. As the controlling metaphor for the previous novel had been Australians circling the world looking for themselves and their home, so in this it is Australia's national car and icon, General Motors' Holden; the title refers to both "Australia's own car," as it used to be advertised, and the protagonist, Holden Shadbolt, who is made a deliberately representative figure. The novel covers his career from his birth in 1932 to the mid-1960s when he departs for the United States. The motif of the car is carried skillfully through to the final pages of the novel, which are a summary of the character of Holden and by implication of the national identity: "Ability to idle all day. Slight overheating," etc.

Bail makes it clear in all sorts of ways that in documenting the career of Holden he is also documenting the history of Australia from the 1930s, and even earlier, to the mid-1960s and the end of the reign of the Prime Minister, R. G. Menzies, whom he calls in the novel R. G. Amen. At one point in the novel we are told of Hoadley, the ambassador to Egypt, that "More than most ambassadors it seems he had this obsession for building bridges—between men and city, city and country, words and action, the imagination and fact." The same is true of the author. The preoccupation with language is evident to the point where Bail says that there is a ''solidarity of words and objects,'' and this is one thing he tries to show. Holden literally eats words—newsprint: ''What did Holden's early growth consist of? Words, words: a flawed gray-and-white view of the world.'' His health suffers as a result of the many errors in the newspapers he digests.

Bail's most recent novel, *Eucalyptus,* won him a number of literary awards. It opens with a discussion of the desertorum or Hooked Mallee, one of several hundred species of Eucalyptus, Australia's national tree. But almost immediately this turns into parodic speculations on the national character: ''And anyway the very word, desert-or-um, harks back to a stale version of the national landscape and from there is a more or less straight line onto the national character, all those linings of the soul and the larynx, which have their origins in the bush, so it is said, the poetic virtues (can you believe it?) of being belted about by droughts, bushfires, smelly sheep and so on; and let's not forget the isolation, the exhausted shapeless women, the crude language, the always wide horizon, and the flies.'' All this—the preoccupation with myths of the Australian character, the self-referentiality, the investing of physical objects with figurative qualities—is familiar in Bail's work. What is surprising is that beneath all its game-playing and cerebrality, Eucalyptus is an unexpectedly human and even tender novel.

This account of a farmer who offers the hand of his spectacularly beautiful daughter to the man who can correctly name each of the five hundred species of eucalyptus tree he has planted on his property is a love story, a fairy tale and also, to a certain extent, a detective story in which the author plants clues as carefully as his protagonist plants his beloved trees. The husband and suitor of the beautiful Ellen are both good men in their own ways but their masculinity is bound up, in an Australian way, with emotional inhibition. In contrast, the femininity of the ''speckled'' Ellen is constantly stressed and she is associated with water, with softness and flexibility, with nature. As the fable of the storytelling stranger who finally wins her suggests, she is the young woman held captive by an ogre, thinking constantly of ways to escape. That she eventually does so is suggested in the closing paragraph of this wonderful novel.

Bail's intense interest in the visual arts led to his writing a biography of the Australian painter Ian Fairweather. He is also the author of *Longhand: a Writer's Notebook,* which offers fascinating insights into his own artistic practice.

—Laurie Clancy

BAILEY, Paul

Nationality: British. **Born:** Peter Harry Bailey in Battersea, London, 16 February 1937. **Education:** Sir Walter St. John's School, London, 1948–53; Central School of Speech and Drama, London, 1953–56. **Career:** Actor, 1956–63. Literary Fellow, University of Newcastle-upon-Tyne and University of Durham, 1972–74; visiting lecturer, North Dakota State University, Fargo, 1977–79. **Awards:** Maugham award, 1968; Arts Council award, 1968; Authors' Club award, 1970; E.M. Forster Award (U.S.A.), 1974; Bicentennial Arts fellowship, 1976; Orwell Memorial prize, for essay, 1978. Fellow, Royal Society of Literature, 1982. **Address:** 79 Davisville Road, London W12 9SH, England.

Publications

Novels

At the Jerusalem. London, Cape, and New York, Atheneum, 1967.
Trespasses. London, Cape, 1970; New York, Harper, 1971.
A Distant Likeness. London, Cape, 1973.
Peter Smart's Confessions. London, Cape, 1977.
Old Soldiers. London, Cape, 1980.
Gabriel's Lament. London, Cape, 1986; New York, Viking, 1987.
Sugar Cane. London, Bloomsbury, 1993.
Kitty and Virgil. Woodstock, New York, Overlook Press, 2000.

Plays

A Worthy Guest (produced Newcastle-upon-Tyne, 1973; London, 1974).
Alice (produced Newcastle-upon-Tyne, 1975).
Crime and Punishment, adaptation of a novel by Dostoevsky (produced Manchester, 1978).

Radio Play: *At Cousin Harry's,* 1964.

Television Play: *We Think the World of You,* with Tristram Powell, 1980.

Other

An English Madam: The Life and Work of Cynthia Payne. London, Cape, 1982.
An Immaculate Mistake: Scenes from Childhood and Beyond (autobiography). London, Bloomsbury, 1990; New York, Dutton, 1992.
Editor, *The Oxford Book of London.* New York, Oxford University Press, 1995.
Editor, *First Love.* London, Orion, 1999.

*

Theatrical Activities: Actor: **Plays**—roles in *The Sport of My Mad Mother* by Ann Jellicoe, London, 1958; *Epitaph for George Dillon* by John Osborne and Anthony Creighton, London, 1958; and other plays.

Paul Bailey comments:

(1991) I write novels for many reasons, some of which I have probably never consciously thought of. I don't like absolute moral judgments, the ''placing'' of people into types—I'm both delighted and appalled by the mysteriousness of my fellow creatures. I enjoy ''being'' other people when I write, and the novels I admire most respect the uniqueness of other human beings. I like to think I show my characters respect and that I don't sit in judgment on them. This is what, in my small way, I am striving for—to capture, in a shaped and controlled form, something of the mystery of life. I am writing, too, to expand and stimulate my own mind. I hope I will have the courage to be more ambitious, bolder and braver in my search for the ultimately unknowable, with each book I write.

* * *

Paul Bailey's first novel, *At the Jerusalem*, has been rightly acknowledged as one of the outstanding literary debuts of the 1960's in England, and among the reasons why it attracted attention when it appeared was that it departed so markedly from our usual expectations of first novels—autobiographies in thin disguise. What came as a surprise was to find a first novel by a young man in his twenties about old age and its attendant tribulations. Yet Bailey's achievement did not, of course, lie in merely writing about the elderly and their problems, but in doing so with such sympathetic understanding and sensitivity while maintaining sufficient detachment and objectivity to avoid any trace of sentimentality. There is no falsification, no whimsy, none of that awkwardness and emotional uncertainty that tend to afflict writers when dealing with the old. Bailey's depiction of an old people's home, the Jerusalem of the title, and especially of the central character, Mrs. Gadny, whose fairly rapid decline after entering the home is charted, carries complete conviction. Quiet and unpretentious as *At the Jerusalem* is, it is also an extraordinary feat of the imagination.

In retrospect, we can now see that *At the Jerusalem* introduced many of the themes and preoccupations which have come to be integral components of the Bailey world: isolation, suffering, death, suicide, old age, the pain of loss, psychological collapse, role-playing in an attempt to bear or ward off reality. If *At the Jerusalem* is mainly a study of disintegration—Mrs. Gadny's fate is to be taken to a mental hospital—Bailey's second novel, *Trespasses*, partly set in a mental hospital, is about an attempt at reintegration after personal breakdown and fragmentation. Surprisingly for a Bailey novel, *Trespasses* ends on a note of muted optimism, but much of the book is pervaded by anguish, leading to suicide in the case of one character and mental collapse in the case of another. Technically, *Trespasses* is much more adventurous work than the fairly orthodox and straightforward *At the Jerusalem*. Some sections of the novel are collages of short, fragmented monologues, appropriate enough for the subject but demanding considerable concentration and imaginative involvement on the part of the reader, who has to construct the total picture from the pieces like a jig-saw puzzle. This intricate cross-cutting between different minds is a most economical way of revealing characters and events; narrated in a conventional way, the novel would be very much longer and far less intense than it is, and the technique justifies itself as the pieces finally cohere into a highly organized pattern.

Bailey's pursuit of poetic concentration, a concomitant of his increasing technical sophistication and artistic discipline, is taken a stage further in his third novel, *A Distant Likeness*. Like *Trespasses*, the novel is fragmented and elliptical so that the reader again has to work hard to piece the information together. Bailey is almost as sparing of words as Webern was of musical notes. The book, about a policeman in charge of a murder investigation, is another study in disintegration, resulting in this case from the policeman's inner contradictions. Many critics have felt the ''distant likeness'' to be between the policeman and the murderer, but the sentence from Simone Weil's *Notebooks* that provides the novel with its title, ''Privation is a distant likeness of death,'' is perhaps the key to the interpretation of this complex book. Bailey's subject is privation, and it appears in various forms. *A Distant Likeness* has been compared to *Crime and Punishment,* but Bailey's novel is not so much like Dostoevsky as a distillation of a super-refined Dostoevskian essence. The extreme compression can be likened to T.S. Eliot's miniaturization of epic form in *The Waste Land,* a parallel that suggests itself because of similarities between the imagery of the two works.

After the minimalist austerity and purity, as well as human bleakness, of *A Distant Likeness*, Bailey altered course somewhat, producing a much more relaxed novel in a comic, even picaresque, vein, *Peter Smart's Confessions*. Here the Dickensian side of his talent, evident but not prominent in his earlier books, is given freer rein, although he maintains his usual technical and stylistic control, never wasting words. *Peter Smart's Confessions* is a kind of *bildungsroman,* dealing with the development of a sensitive and artistic boy surrounded by philistinism and other forms of paralyzing opposition. Yet much of the interest lies in the gallery of eccentrics and extraordinary characters with whom Peter comes into contact rather than in Peter himself. The later stages of the novel are more desultory and less subtle than the brilliant first half, but the novel as a whole opened up new possibilities for Bailey.

Old Soldiers is his most completely satisfying novel since *At the Jerusalem* and is also about old age, the two main characters being men in their seventies with unforgettable memories of World War I—hence the title. Technically, the novel is not as ''difficult'' as *Trespasses* or *A Distant Likeness*, but it resembles them in its brevity, imagistic density, and dependence on suggestion rather than statement. As usual, much is left unsaid. Bailey's treatment of the two very different men, who are nevertheless drawn together after their paths cross, again reveals one of his central concerns as a novelist to be the essential isolation of human beings, the way in which everyone lives and dies alone. He exposes the vulnerable core at the heart of all individuals, the strategies by which people try to disguise their vulnerability and protect themselves from the daily assault of reality, including the inevitability of death. This marks him as a descendant of Conrad, a novelist he greatly admires. Yet if Bailey peels away the deceptions and self-deceptions, the masks and pretenses, by which his characters live, he does so with enormous sympathy for their predicament. Bailey respects the uniqueness of individuals, and possesses the true novelist's fascination with people of every description.

Since *Old Soldiers* in 1980, Bailey has undertaken a great deal of literary journalism and broadcasting, become an important advocate of Italian literature, and written a couple of non-fiction books, but has published only two novels, *Gabriel's Lament* and *Sugar Cane*. This is by far his longest work of fiction and encompasses over 40 years of English life, from the early years of World War II on. The lament of the title is Gabriel Harvey's belated expression of grief at the age of 40 when, in the closing stages of the novel, he discovers the truth about his mother's disappearance nearly 30 years earlier in 1950. What Gabriel learns in Minnesota when he opens a strange bequest from his father, a box of letters, is that his mother Amy had committed suicide within a few weeks of leaving home, supposedly to take an extended holiday. Although Gabriel has become a religious scholar and successful author, much of his life—his adolescence and adulthood—has been profoundly affected by Amy's mysterious absence as well as by the overbearing presence of his outrageously eccentric father, Oswald, one of Bailey's most brilliant creations and a comic character of Dickensian stature. Thirty-five years older than his wife, Oswald, whose lifestyle is transformed by an unexpected financial windfall, eventually reaches the Shavian age of 94. In one sense, the story of his life that Gabriel unfolds is one of loneliness and perplexity, but it is also hilariously funny at times because of Oswald's unpredictable behavior and speech. Oswald may make Gabriel suffer, but he simultaneously makes the reader laugh. Bailey achieves a delicate synthesis of the tragic and the comic in *Gabriel's Lament*, which like his other novels succeeds in widening our sympathies and extending our imaginations.

—Peter Lewis

BAINBRIDGE, Beryl (Margaret)

Nationality: British. **Born:** Liverpool, 21 November 1934. **Education:** Merchant Taylors' School, Liverpool; ballet school in Tring, Hertfordshire. **Family:** Married Austin Davies in 1954 (divorced 1959); one son and two daughters. **Career:** Actress with repertory theaters in Liverpool, Windsor, Salisbury, London, and Dundee, 1949–60; cellar woman in a bottle factory, London, 1970; clerk, Gerald Duckworth Ltd., publishers, London, 1961–73. Presenter, *Forever England* television series, 1986. Since 1987 weekly columnist, London *Evening Standard*. **Awards:** *Guardian* Fiction prize, 1974; Whitbread award, 1977. D. Litt.: University of Liverpool, 1986. Fellow, Royal Society of Literature, 1978; Whitbread Award, 1996; W.H. Amith Award, 1998; Commonwealth Eurasian Prize, 1998. **Address:** 42 Albert Street, London NW1 7NU, England.

PUBLICATIONS

Novels

A Weekend with Claude. London, Hutchinson, 1967; revised edition, London, Duckworth, 1981; New York, Braziller, 1982.
Another Part of the Wood. London, Hutchinson, 1968; revised edition, London, Duckworth, 1979; New York, Braziller, 1980.
Harriet Said. London, Duckworth, 1972; New York, Braziller, 1973.
The Dressmaker. London, Duckworth, 1973; as *The Secret Glass,* New York, Braziller, 1974.
The Bottle Factory Outing. London, Duckworth, 1974; New York, Braziller, 1975.
Sweet William. London, Duckworth, 1975; New York, Braziller, 1976.
A Quiet Life. London, Duckworth, 1976; New York, Braziller, 1977.
Injury Time. London, Duckworth, 1977; New York, Braziller, 1978.
Young Adolf. London, Duckworth, 1978; New York, Braziller, 1979.
Winter Garden. London, Duckworth, 1980; New York, Braziller, 1981.
Watson's Apology. London, Duckworth, 1984; New York, McGraw Hill, 1985.
Filthy Lucre. London, Duckworth, 1986; published as *Filthy Lucre, or the Tragedy of Ernest Ledwhistle and Richard Soleway: A Sotry.* London, Flamingo, 1988.
An Awfully Big Adventure. London, Duckworth, 1989; New York, Harper Collins, 1991.
The Birthday Boys. London, Duckworth, 1991; New York, Carrol and Graf, 1994.
The Dolphin Connection. North Blackburn, Victoria, Australia, CollinsDovePublishers, 1991.
Every Man for Himself. New York, Carroll and Graf, 1996.
Master Georgie: A Novel. New York, Carroll and Graf, 1998.

Short Stories

Mum and Mr. Armitage: Selected Stories. London, Duckworth, 1985; New York, McGraw Hill, 1987.
Collected Stories. London, Penguin Books, 1994.

Plays

Screenplays: *Sweet William,* 1980.

Television Plays: *Tiptoe Through the Tulips,* 1976; *Blue Skies from Now On,* 1977; *The Warrior's Return* (*The Velvet Glove* series), 1977; *Words Fail Me,* 1979; *The Journal of Bridget Hitler,* with Philip Saville, 1981; *Somewhere More Central,* 1981; *Evensong* (*Unnatural Causes* series), 1986.

Other

English Journey; or, The Road to Milton Keynes. London, Duckworth, and New York, Braziller, 1984.
Forever England: North and South. London, Duckworth, 1987.
Something Happened Yesterday. London, Duckworth, 1993.
Foreword, *Scott's Last Expedition: The Journals* by Robert Falcon Scott. New York, Carroll and Graf, 1996.
Contributor, *Colin Haycraft, 1929–1994: Maverick Publisher,* edited by Stoddard Martin. London, Duckworth, 1995.
Editor, *New Stories 6.* London, Hutchinson, 1981.

*

Critical Studies: *Ironic Formula in the Novels of Beryl Bainbridge* by Elizabeth Wennö, Göteborg, Sweden, Acta Universitatis, 1993.

Beryl Bainbridge comments:

(1976) As a novelist I am committing to paper, for my own satisfaction, episodes that I have lived through. If I had had a camera forever ready with a film I might not have needed to write. I am not very good at fiction .... It is always me and the experiences I have had. In my last three novels I have used the device of accidental death because I feel that a book has to have a strong narrative line. One's own life, whilst being lived, seems to have no obvious plot and is therefore without tension.

I think writing is a very indulgent pastime and I would probably do it even if nobody ever read anything.

I write about the sort of childhood I had, my parents, the landscape I grew up in: my writing is an attempt to record the past. I am of the firm belief that everybody could write books and I never understand why they don't. After all, everyone speaks. Once the grammar has been learnt it is simply talking on paper and in time learning what not to say.

* * *

With the exception of *Sweet William* and *Winter Garden*, most of Beryl Bainbridge's novels have been centered on a death or act of violence. Her novels are also overshadowed by generalized violence, usually World War II. *The Dressmaker* evokes the Liverpudlian home front during the war, and *An Awfully Big Adventure* that city's postwar seediness. The title story and others in *Mum and Mr. Armitage* are set in the immediate postwar period. So is *A Quiet Life*, with German prisoners-of-war waiting to be repatriated, and *Harriet Said* slightly later, amid vivid memories of Italian prisoners-of-war. In *A Weekend with Claude*, an elderly Jewish woman finds herself unable to forget the concentration camps—the same camps that obsess the ''Commandant'' of the campsite in the earlier version of *Another Part of the Wood*. Since *Young Adolf* takes as its conceit the idea that Hitler might have lived in Liverpool in 1909, the book's very conception foreshadows the Holocaust and the war. *Winter Garden* is set against the Cold War; *Injury Time* draws on a background of terrorism and armed crime in contemporary London; and another London novel, *The Bottle Factory Outing*, relies for its effect on the build-up of a violently foreboding atmosphere in and around the bottle factory, without any political cause. *Watson's Apology* examines a clergyman's murder of his wife; it is based on an actual case of 1871. Bainbridge's novels in fact work largely by the build-up of violent atmosphere, drawn from both external circumstances and the characters themselves; this typically erupts in a death, albeit apparently accidental.

In *A Weekend with Claude*, the central act of violence is a shooting, innocuous in its effect whatever its intention. Like her second novel, *Another Part of the Wood*, which Bainbridge also later rewrote, it lacks the taut spareness which distinguishes her work from *Harriet Said* on.

Harriet Said presents a double-edged moral quandary: not only is the killing accidental, but the murdered person is a 13-year-old. On one level, the book is an amusing portrayal by a girl of her friend's sexuality and unnatural ''wisdom'': ''We both tried very hard to give our parents love, and security, but they were too demanding.'' In *The Dressmaker* a young girl's pathetic first love for an American G.I. tragically unfolds against the stark symbolism of the dressmakers' work, while the dressmaker ''dreamed she was following mother down a country garden, severing with sharp scissors the heads of roses.'' Through the more flamboyant black comedy of *The Bottle Factory Outing* flickers the rare lyricism that as elsewhere in Bainbridge's work is a measure of her Joycean acceptance of her characters. This lyrical quality derives from the setting; the garden in *A Weekend with Claude* has become Windsor Great Park in the later novel. But the death precludes total acceptance.

In *Sweet William*, a girl living in a London bedsit falls disastrously in love with the Don Juan of the title, a philandering playwright who moves nonchalantly among the human wreckage he creates. Outstanding here is the portrait of the girl's mother; reacting to her vicious pettiness, the daughter is all the more vulnerable to William. *A Quiet Life* again focuses on what children become in reaction to their parents, and hints that those children may pass on the same qualities to their own children, who will in turn react against them. Bainbridge begins several novels with a Chapter 0; here, as brother and sister meet 15 years later, she both begins and ends with this device—as in *An Awfully Big Adventure*.

Injury Time depicts the unorthodox dinner party of a middle-aged quartet, accidentally taken as hostages in a siege, to the special embarrassment of a married man caught dining with his mistress. Beneath the black comedy, both the mean and generous impulses of the two main characters come through in all their ambivalence.

Young Adolf is Bainbridge's most ambitious book, with the tension deriving from the reader's knowledge of what is to come, historically. Against this scenario, details such as the brown shirt made for the penniless Adolf by his sister-in-law—so that ''he needn't sit wrapped in a blanket while his other one was in the wash''—are intensely black comedy.

Winter Garden hilariously follows an accident-prone civil servant masquerading as an artist in order to accompany his mistress in a delegation to the Soviet Union. In *Watson's Apology* Bainbridge traces a 26-year-old marriage to suggest how the Reverend Watson came to murder his wife. Contemporary documents are used in a narrative remarkable for its authentic reconstruction of Victorian London, culminating in moving impressions of the aged Watson.

Bainbridge wrote *Filthy Lucre* in 1946, at the age of 11, and several short stories in *Mum and Mr. Armitage* touch on the generation gap. Like many novelists, with stories Bainbridge takes risks not ventured in novels, as for instance in the surreal ''The Man Who Blew Away'' and ''Beggars Would Ride.'' The setting of a *Peter Pan* production in ''Clap Hands, Here Comes Charlie'' is extended in *An Awfully Big Adventure*. Sixteen-year-old assistant stage manager Stella understands nothing of the doomed homosexual loves surrounding her, and virtually nothing of the equally doomed heterosexual loves, yet she is the catalyst for the inevitable act of violence.

Even in Bainbridge's earlier novels, the mandatory act of violence often seemed superfluous; this immensely gifted novelist's use of the device has become, to some extent, formulaic.

The 1995 film production of *An Awfully Big Adventure*, directed by Mike Newell and starring Hugh Grant, Alan Rickman, and Georgina Cates, extended the exposure of the author's works to a larger audience. It was not the only time in the 1990s when her career touched on the world of film, though in the other case the relationship was quiet coincidental. In 1996 Bainbridge earned the Whitbread Novel Award for *Every Man for Himself*, a fictionalized account of the *Titanic* disaster; at the same time, director James Cameron was filming his own fictionalized version of the tragedy, which would win the Academy Award for best picture two years later.

—Val Warner

BAKER, Elliott

Nationality: American. **Born:** Buffalo, New York, 15 December 1922. **Education:** Indiana University, Bloomington, B.S. 1944. **Military Service:** Served in the United States Army Infantry, 1943–46. **Career:** Writer for television programs *U.S. Steel Hour* and *Robert Montgomery Show;* script supervisor, *Zero One* series, BBC Television, London. **Address:** c/o Viking, 375 Hudson Street, New York, New York 10014, USA.

Publications

Novels

A Fine Madness. New York, Putnam, and London, Joseph, 1964.
The Penny Wars. New York, Putnam, 1968; London, Joseph, 1969.
Pocock and Pitt. New York, Putnam, 1971; London, Joseph, 1972.
Klynt's Law. New York, Harcourt Brace, and London, Joseph, 1976.
And We Were Young. New York, Times, 1979; London, Joseph, 1980.
Unhealthful Air. New York, Viking, 1988.

Doctor Lopez. London, Holofernes, 1995.
Percy, Bob, and Assenpoop. Van Nuys, California, Sacred Beverage Press, 1999.

Short Stories

Unrequited Loves. New York, Putnam, and London, Joseph, 1974.

Plays

The Deliquent, The Hipster, and The Square (broadcast, 1959). Published in *The Delinquent, The Hipster, The Square, and the Sandpile Series,* edited by Alva I. Cox, Jr., St. Louis, Bethany Press, 1962.

Screenplays: *A Fine Madness,* 1966; *Luv,* 1967; *Viva Max,* 1970; *Breakout* (with Howard B. Kreitsek and Mark Norman). Columbia Pictures, 1975.

Radio Plays: *The Delinquent, The Hipster, and The Square,* 1959.

Television Plays: *The Right Thing,* 1956 (U.K); *Crisis in Coroma* (*U.S. Steel Hour*), 1957; *The Entertainer,* from play by John Osborne, 1976; *Malibu,* from novel by William Murray, 1983; *Lace,* 1984, and *Lace II,* 1985, from novel by Shirley Conran.

*

Manuscript Collection: Indiana University, Bloomington.

* * *

Elliott Baker's first novels, *A Fine Madness* and *The Penny Wars*, demonstrate a diversity of ideas and themes but focus on moral and psychological growth and the life of the imagination. They are comic views of modern America informed by an underlying sense of tragedy or tragic potential. Baker's later works continue to present this tension.

A Fine Madness depicts the triumph of an artist, a kind of American Gulley Jimson, over the forces of conformity and death-in-life. Samson Shillitoe, a working-class hero, a Blakean poet driven by powerful artistic and sexual urges, is pursued and seized by a group of psychiatric experimenters. He is analyzed, institutionalized, and lobotomized but emerges whole, sane, and uncastrated, his creative (and procreative) energies intact. Baker uses his inside knowledge of modern psychotherapy to show the artist at war with a mechanical world and the mechanized minds of clinical psychology. Shillitoe is obsessed by imagination, driven by forces beyond his control. He is amoral, anti-social, unconcerned with ''adjustment'' or mental health. The psychologists view him only as a specimen, a sample of neurosis or psychosis. Shillitoe's view triumphs: he conceives and produces an epic-sized poem and his common-law wife conceives his child. Life and creation vanquish death and destruction.

In *The Penny Wars* Baker creates a nostalgic vision of adolescence on the eve of World War II. Tyler Bishop, another rebel, grows up in 1939 in squalor and confusion of values. An unreconstructed liberal, Tyler worries about the Nazis while America's smugness and isolationism seem invincible, worries about his budding sexuality, worries about the world he will inherit. Himself a WASP, he stands up for Jews and Negroes, fights bigotry and ignorance—and loses. Through a series of social confrontations, Tyler begins to find his way toward a self-sufficient individualism.

Unrequited Loves, a set of related novellas, documents the youth (1939–45) of a persona named ''Elliott Baker,'' especially initiations into love and sex. Each story is a comic odyssey wherein the young man discovers the battles and truces in the war between men and women. It is Baker's most genial and optimistic book, focusing the nostalgia of *The Penny Wars* on our national pastimes—love, war, baseball, growing up.

Pocock and Pitt is a satirical exploration of identity and childhood in the modern world. Wendell Pocock, American middle-class victim of repeated heart attacks, becomes Winston Pitt, British worker in an organ bank. A pawn in an international espionage duel, he discovers genuine love and redemption after exhausting the cold consolations of history and philosophy. The novel develops the slapstick mediations of *A Fine Madness* and widens Baker's scope to the state of the whole modern world.

Klynt's Law is a *tour de force* in combining genres—a satirical ''college novel,'' a thriller of Las Vegas criminal shenanigans, a study of parapsychology and gambling compulsions. In it, Tobias Klynt (a.k.a. Kleinmann), an archetypal *klutz,* breaks with his shrewish wife, his university career, and the straight world to put the paranormal talents of four students to work on roulette wheels. They have evolved the perfect ''system'' to beat Las Vegas but fail to understand that gambling is not for winners. The irony is alternately black and farcical, and, as in all good gambling stories, winners are losers.

The same is true in *And We Were Young*, which traces four ex-rifle-squad members in the red-scare years after World War II. A tangle of coincidences—or synchronistic ironies—brings them together in New York City, where each betrays his youthful desires and beliefs in the enveloping glaciers of the Cold War. The book extends Baker's picture of the generation that grew up with World War II, begun in *The Penny Wars* and *Unrequited Loves*, and develops his vision of our society as it changed radically in a new internationalist world.

In *Unhealthful Air* Baker updates F. Scott Fitzgerald's Pat Hobby stories, by way of Damon Runyon. The novel follows the adventures of a devious, cynical Hollywood scriptwriter and gambler, Corey Burdick, who becomes entangled with a horserace-fixing syndicate, an Ozark nymphet, and her brutal husband. The book deals wittily with movie-TV *clichés* and the way our lives imitate the ''art'' of the movies. At one point, Burdick wonders in exasperation, ''Was there any act of man that hadn't already appeared on the motion picture screen?'' Using his native wit, Burdick manages to survive the ''unhealthful air'' of Los Angeles—and even to prosper.

—William J. Schafer

BALLARD, J(ames) G(raham)

Nationality: British. **Born:** Shanghai, China, 15 November 1930. **Education:** Leys School, Cambridge; King's College, Cambridge. **Military Service:** Served in the Royal Air Force. **Family:** Married Helen Mary Matthews in 1954 (died 1964); one son and two daughters. **Awards:** *Guardian* Fiction prize, 1984; James Tait Black Memorial prize, 1985. **Agent:** Margaret Hanbury, 27 Walcot Square,

London SE11 4UB. **Address:** 36 Old Charlton Road, Shepperton, Middlesex TW17 8AT, England.

PUBLICATIONS

Novels

The Wind from Nowhere. New York, Berkley, 1962; London, Penguin, 1967.
The Drowned World. New York, Berkley, 1962; London, Gollancz, 1963.
The Burning World. New York, Berkley, 1964; revised edition, as *The Drought,* London, Cape, 1965.
The Crystal World. London, Cape, and New York, Farrar Straus, 1966.
Crash. London, Cape, and New York, Farrar Straus, 1973.
Concrete Island. London, Cape, and New York, Farrar Straus, 1974.
High-Rise. London, Cape, 1975; New York, Holt Rinehart, 1977.
The Unlimited Dream Company. London, Cape, and New York, Holt Rinehart, 1979.
Hello America. London, Cape, 1981.
Empire of the Sun. London, Gollancz, and New York, Simon and Schuster, 1984.
The Day of Creation. London, Gollancz, 1987; New York, Farrar Straus, 1988.
Running Wild. London, Hutchinson, 1988; New York, Farrar Straus, 1989.
The Kindness of Women. London, Harper Collins, 1991; New York, Farrar, Straus, and Giroux, 1991.
Rushing to Paradise. New York, Picador USA, 1995.
Cocaine Nights. London, Flamingo, 1996; Washington, D.C., Counterpoint, 1998.

Short Stories

The Voices of Time and Other Stories. New York, Berkley, 1962; London, Orion, 1992.
Billenium and Other Stories. New York, Berkley, 1962.
The Four-Dimensional Nightmare. London, Gollancz, 1963; published as *The Voices of Time*, London, Phoenix, 1998.
Passport to Eternity and Other Stories. New York, Berkley, 1963.
Terminal Beach. London, Gollancz, 1964; abridged edition, New York, Berkley, 1964; London, Phoenix, 1993.
The Impossible Man and Other Stories. New York, Berkley, 1966.
The Disaster Area. London, Cape, 1967.
The Day of Forever. London, Panther, 1967.
The Overloaded Man. London, Panther, 1967.
Why I Want to Fuck Ronald Reagan. Brighton, Unicorn Bookshop, 1968.
The Atrocity Exhibition. London, Cape, 1970; as *Love and Napalm: Export USA,* New York, Grove Press, 1972; published in expanded, annotated, illustrated edition under original title, with author's annotations, San Francisco, RE/Search Publications, 1990.
Chronopolis and Other Stories. New York, Putnam, 1971.
Vermilion Sands. New York, Berkley, 1971; London, Cape, 1973.
Low-Flying Aircraft and Other Stories. London, Cape, 1976.
The Best of J.G. Ballard. London, Futura, 1977.
The Best Short Stories of J.G. Ballard. New York, Holt Rinehart, 1978; with introduction by Anthony Burgess, New York, Holt, 1995.
The Venus Hunters. London, Panther, 1980.
News from the Sun. London, Interzone, 1982.
Myths of the Near Future. London, Cape, 1982.
Memories of the Space Age. Sauk City, Wisconsin, Arkham House, 1988.
War Fever. London, Collins, 1990; New York, Farrar Straus, 1991.

Other

A User's Guide to the Millennium: Essays and Reviews. New York, Picador USA, 1996.
Contributor, *Isaac Asimov Presents the Great SF Stories #22 (1959),* edited by Isaac Asimov and Martin H. Greenberg. New York, DAW Books, 1991.
Contributor, *Isaac Asimov Presents the Great SF Stories #24 (1962),* edited by Isaac Asimov and Martin H. Greenberg. New York, DAW Books, 1992.
Contributor, *The Playboy Book of Science Fiction,* edited by Alice K. Turner. New York, HarperPrism, 1998.

*

Bibliography: *J.G. Ballard: A Primary and Secondary Bibliography* by David Pringle, Boston, Hall, 1984.

Critical Studies: *J.G. Ballard: The First Twenty Years* edited by James Goddard and David Pringle, Hayes, Middlesex, Bran's Head, 1976; *Re/Search: J.G. Ballard* edited by Vale, San Francisco, Re/Search, 1984; *J.G. Ballard* by Peter Brigg, San Bernardino, California, Borgo Press, 1985; *Out of the Night and into the Dream: A Thematic Study of the Fiction of J.G. Ballard,* New York, Greenwood Press, 1991; *Out of the Night and into the Dream: A Thematic Study of the Fiction of J.G. Ballard* by Gregory Stephenson. Westport, Connecticut, Greenwood Press, 1991; *The Angle Between Two Walls: The Fiction of J.G. Ballard* by Roger Luckhurst. New York, St. Martin's Press, 1997.

J.G. Ballard comments:

I believe that science fiction is the authentic literature of the 20th century, the only fiction to respond imaginatively to the transforming nature of science and technology. I believe that the true domain of science fiction is that zone I have termed inner space, rather than outer space, and that the present, rather than the future, is now the period of greatest moral urgency for the writer. In my own fiction I have tried to achieve these aims.

* * *

As in the case of his acknowledged partial inspiration Graham Greene, J.G. Ballard seems to divide his distinguished canon into novels and ''entertainments'': serious, experimental prose which expands narrative possibilities, and productions which are, aesthetically, less rigorous. In the former category, one would find in chronological order *The Drowned World, The Crystal World, The Atrocity Exhibition, Crash, The Unlimited Dream Company, Empire of the Sun, The Day of Creation, The Kindness of Women,* and

Rushing to Paradise. Ballard's ''entertainments'' include *The Wind from Nowhere, The Drought,* the short story cycle *Vermilion Sands, Concrete Island, High-Rise, Hello America, Running Wild,* and *Cocaine Nights.* Ballard's voluminous short fiction could profitably be divided along similar lines, with far greater debate concerning what works best. Ballard's own selection of his best fiction is very reliable: sympathetic readers of Ballard will share his enthusiasm for ''The Voices of Time'' and ''The Terminal Beach.'' Nonetheless, he has consistently produced rewarding short prose since the last exhaustive anthology, most of which has been collected in *Low-Flying Aircraft, The Venus Hunters, Myths of the Near Future, War Fever,* and *A User's Guide to the Millennium.* These collections of essays and reviews provide a useful glimpse into the process by which Ballard transforms his opinions on issues into powerful symbolic topographies.

However, such divisions merely recapitulate the divisions which characterize most criticism of Ballard's work. Our task should not be to categorize Ballard's output but to understand how these works operate. Both novels and ''entertainments'' are involved in creating imaginary landscapes that anticipate the full extent of the horrors of contemporary life. Ballard's works, which range from elaborate evocations of erotic car crash fantasies (*Crash*) to deep-sea still lifes of submerged cities (*The Drowned World*) create and explore physical and psychological places which, for Ballard, stem from the unconscious desires of capitalist culture. For this reason, Ballard's work may seem intimidating to the uninitiated. Beginning with an ''entertainment'' before venturing into the major canon will allow the reader to acclimate to Ballard's grasping imagination, his densely ironic voice, and genuine moral vision.

Empire of the Sun provides the kindest entry into the major canon. This novel is both boy-book, a work written for adults about childhood, and war memoir. Jim, the protagonist, has received inevitable comparisons with his author. Both were interred in Japanese prisoner-of-war camps in China during World War II; Ballard admits these related events were his own in the foreword. As a result, *Empire of the Sun* allows the credulous to ''solve'' the case of J.G. Ballard. The young author's separation from his parents, radical dislocation, and struggle for survival produce the traumatic scene of the Ballardian text: a world of flat affect where setting predominates over character and action (unless a generic formula is being ruthlessly parodied), a landscape littered with aircraft fuselages, automobiles, miasmas, and tarmac, all aching to burn under the silent, bone-revealing glare of the Nagasaki explosion Jim witnesses in the ontological climax of the novel: ''the light was a premonition of his death, the sight of his small soul joining the larger soul of the dying world.'' Thus begins the death-in-life of Jim Ballard.

This youth, our mythic construction of the ideal Ballard-author, grows up to become a science-fiction writer: the world he experienced did not match the conventions of nineteenth-century fiction, so he turned to visions of the future, reading pulp magazines while an airman in Canada. W. Warren Wager in *Terminal Visions* offers us a helpful paradigm for reading Ballard's science fiction and experimental canon through time. Ballard, roughly, has moved from an obsession with feminized natural landscape in the quartet of so-called disaster novels (the world imperiled by the four elements, approximately), through an obsession with homoeroticized technological artifacts (*The Atrocity Exhibition* through *High-Rise*), to an achieved polymorphous perversity (*The Unlimited Dream Company*). Only after this long therapeutic journey could he return to the traumatic scene that collapsed all of these impulses into a single event. Furthermore, Ballard's own statements posit this progressive impulse in his work which, paradoxically, regresses from more distant future worlds to our present world of apartment complexes and flyovers, and ultimately to his Shanghai past. *Empire of the Sun* gives the critic marvelous ammunition for familiarizing an unsettling fictional presence. The affect-less Ballardian voice, similar to that of William S. Burroughs, can be traced to the peculiar traumas of the Japanese camps.

Such reductive remarks could have passed for an accurate assessment of Ballard's work until he returned to the fantastic after *Empire of the Sun* with more recent works such as *The Day of Creation, Running Wild, Rushing to Paradise,* and *Cocaine Nights.* But even before these publications one was suspicious about this narrative of the career. Something is lost in the neatness of it all; most notably, the inescapable belatedness of the recent mainstream work. We read it in the light of Ballard's earlier science fiction and experimental writing: the cramped cubicles of Lunghau C. A. C. irresistibly invoke the locales of ''Billenium'' and *High-Rise.* Ballard values the fabulative powers of science fiction too greatly to allow his summating work to stand outside them. The ultimate joke on the reader may be that *Empire of the Sun* is history revealed as the ultimate science fiction text, especially as Ballard writes either. As Gould remarks in ''Low-Flying Aircraft,'' ''The ultimate dystopia is the inside of one's own head.'' *Empire of the Sun* is an immense and real achievement, but only partially enlightening as an end result of Ballard's journey as a writer. Other, less reductive structures can be suggested to illuminate Ballard's strategies.

One of the most helpful perspectives for enjoying Ballard can be located in Roland Barthes's *Mythologies,* which explains the social significance of a linguistic decoding of contemporary symbols and popular culture figures. For Barthes, myth is a secondary order of signification, a higher code of accepted meaning. The image of an oak tree in an insurance company advertisement, by a theft of the sign, becomes a signifier of longevity, dependability, etc. The artist has two strategies for attacking the conventional accretions of myth: she or he, according to Barthes, can either restore to physical objects their uncanniness and historicity or create a third order of signification by looking behind the myth for its concealed signification.

A fairly plausible case can be made that Ballard has always attacked conventional signification, progressing from Barthes's first strategy to an increasing use of his second strategy. The early novels restore to things their non-mythic materiality. This is exemplified by the significance accorded the heightened elemental powers in the quartet, as well as the technological flotsam and jetsam blown about or floating by. Likewise, the crystallization process in *The Crystal World* provides an almost perfect allegory of the defamiliarization of bourgeois nature.

But Ballard has been honing his skills at discovering the third order of signification, which emphasizes the ironic undercurrent inherent in the significatory process, since *The Wind from Nowhere.* One of the few nice things one can say about this work—produced in two short weeks, it remains Ballard's worst novel—is that it knows at all points that it's formulaic junk, a parody of the ''cozy catastrophe'' John Wyndham school of disaster writing. Its successor, *The Drowned World,* employs similar methods through its transparent allusiveness. However, *The Drowned World* also questions its own generic confines: it is a disaster fiction that reveals an awareness of the narrative and symbolic structures underlying disaster fiction. For Ballard and his protagonist Kerans, disaster is concealed psychic opportunity. In the clearly indicated ''happy'' ending of the work, Kerans embraces the destructive principle, the chthonic, by heading south into greater heat.

As in most later Ballard, such self-destruction is always a symbolic invitation to transformation, a relentless reiteration that the old social, political, and biological orders are quickly mutating into a new form inherently hostile to humanity. In Michel Foucault's terminology, we are in a shifting episteme: writers like Ballard and Burroughs most clearly anticipate the shape of the end result of such a shift. Their strategies are those of survival. Ballard reveals in *Empire of the Sun* that ''a code within a code'' always intrigued Jim. He would always watch bridge games for this reason; later, such skills would keep him alive. The same applies for Ballard. This decoding process, often embedded in allegorical tableau, allows Ballard to predict, and thereby prevent, possible futures.

In *The Atrocity Exhibition,* Ballard's talents as a reader of bourgeois myth emerge strikingly. The book dissects some of the psychoanalytic significance behind the overdetermination of 1960s culture: television coverage of the Vietnam war, the assassination of John F. Kennedy, Marilyn Monroe, the automobile, cancer victims all converge in a terrifying psychedelic phantasmagoria of image, redeemed, like *Naked Lunch,* only by its abiding ironic humor, its Swiftian critical distance, and its undeniable prophecy. The obsessional accuracy of this series of ''condensed novels'' has aged remarkably well, as a chapter title like ''Why I Want to Fuck Ronald Reagan'' indicates.

For some readers, *Crash* is even more difficult, a semiological anatomy of the automobile accident that exchanges breadth (in *The Atrocity Exhibition*) for depth of analysis. As in the later *Empire of the Sun,* Ballard toys with the reader by giving the narrator his own name. Ballard the character's quest for ''the keys to a new sexuality born from a perverse technology'' horrifies, delights, and enlightens. At his best, Ballard's imagination risks the unimaginable, even as his clunky, chunky prose—with its transparent allusions and similes, its hard-boiled rhythms, and its vague redundancies—acquires a paradoxical grace all its own: a bombed-out, flat affect poetry that perfectly ensnares our era. His sinister replication of medical school textbook argot in this second phase assures us Ballard has a good ear; he knows exactly what effects he's achieving in this minatory technological pornography.

Ballard's recent polymorphous phase has given us some of his finest writing, in *The Unlimited Dream Company, Empire of the Sun,* and *The Kindness of Women* and his funniest in the overlooked *Hello America.* Lately, his quest for ultimate reality has passed through autobiographical incident to the ultimate contemporary reality: television. It remains an interesting question who's influencing whom: Ballard or Baudrillard, the cool rhetoric of ''hyperreality,'' the triumphant televisual simulacrum. One suspects Ballard is the influence here, since Baudrillard has written on *Crash,* while Ballard seems uninterested in theory when interviewed. Be that as it may, I have been alluding to many postmodern theorists here because Ballard's practice so overtly complements their observations. Since at least *The Atrocity Exhibition* and short stories like ''Motel Architecture'' and ''The Intensive Care Unit'' in *Myths of the Near Future,* Ballard has been interested in the alternate gestalt of televisual reality. In this stage, the simulational triumphs completely over the real. In *The Day of Creation,* a fantastic river appears in Africa, created out of the embodied wish fantasies of Mallory, the main character. He alternately wishes to destroy and preserve his creation, to drift down it and to explore its source. It is what Deleuze and Guattari would deem a ''smooth space,'' a zone of easy movement and free play that comes suspiciously to resemble the world inside our VCRs. One character, Senger, carries a broken camera and ''films'' an ''imaginary documentary.'' When they drift rapidly downstream, the scenery looks like ''a reversed playback.'' As Senger explains to Mallory, ''Television doesn't tell lies, it makes up a new truth… . Sooner or later, everything turns into television.'' Baudrillard couldn't have said it better.

By the time we get to *Running Wild,* a tale of videotaped violence and suburban mayhem that intentionally resembles a children's book, Ballard can revise reality through his simulations, as when the narrator compares some of the deadly children's journals to ''*Pride and Prejudice* with its missing pornographic passages restored.'' The tone throughout all of Ballard, finely honed in the most recent books, is the creepy-funny both/and double register of postmodernism, the mood of any Jack Nicholson or Dennis Hopper performance. Is Ballard writing satire? Social criticism? Whimsy? Yes.

The Kindness of Women is his most remarkable achievement along these thematic lines. This novel-autobiography hybrid is a sequel to *Empire of the Sun* and a virtual retrospective gallery exhibition of all the major phases discussed above: for example, the chapter called ''The Exhibition'' returns to the interests of *Crash*; the first three chapters rework *Empire of the Sun.* This book, if not his most accessible, is nonetheless the most thorough introduction available to Ballard's fictional project. And it offers a powerful culmination of his meditations on media and simulation. The climax of the book is his participation in Stephen Spielberg's filming of *Empire of the Sun.* Ironically, Spielberg chose to film the British section of Shanghai in Sunningdale, a residential area fifteen minutes away by car from Shepperton (a distant suburb of London where Ballard has lived for the last 35 years). As Ballard notes in his annotations to the *Re/Search* magazine reissue of *The Atrocity Exhibition,* ''I can almost believe that I came to Shepperton 30 years ago knowing unconsciously that one day I would write a novel about my wartime experiences in Shanghai, and that it might well be filmed in these studios. Deep assignments run through all our lives; there are no coincidences.'' *The Kindness of Women* unifies all of Ballard's lifelong obsessions and enables him to return full circle to his childhood, now made more real as Hollywood film: ''All the powers of modern film had come together for this therapeutic exercise.'' Echoing Samuel Beckett's wish to leave ''a stain upon the silence,'' Ballard sees his true immortality as a blurred image in the film, which is all that remained of his cameo appearance after final editing: ''this seemed just, like the faint blur which was all that any of us left across time and space.''

One story in his latest short fiction collection *War Fever* also deserves mention in this regard, the hilarious ''Secret History of World War 3.'' It zanily prophesies a change in the Constitution enabling Ronald Reagan to serve a third term in the 1990s. His fading health comes to dominate the national consciousness so much that his vital signs scroll across all channels, his bowel movements deserve special news bulletins, and a brief nuclear exchange goes unnoticed by distracted viewers. Ballard was obviously thinking of Reagan's polyp operation, but the story anticipates the bloated media spectacles which increasingly dominate the public realm.

This assessment of the link between media culture, with its numerous sects and factions, and the natural world is developed in *Rushing to Paradise.* Here, as in his more recent *Cocaine Nights,*

Ballard works consciously within the satirical tradition. *Rushing to Paradise* emphasizes the failures inherent in attempts to manufacture the utopian. In this sense, Ballard focuses on extremism and factionalism as forces that are as powerful as the four elements in his disaster quartet. As a result, Ballard shifts his focus from descriptions of imaginary places to detailed examinations of character. This movement is likewise evident in *Cocaine Nights,* with its emphasis on the lurid depravity of the rich on holiday. Such shifts indicate a new stage in Ballard's writings. These more recent novels operate like collections of prose such as *A User's Guide to the Millennium* in their more overt commentaries on the social aspects of contemporary culture.

Ballard will undoubtedly continue to grow along the amazing and original course he has charted. Much of his supposed classism and racism seems unfounded; his use of formulaic heroines, though periodic and appropriate for his gender-bound, extreme loners, has drawn greater and more justified criticism from feminists. Recent stories like ''Having a Wonderful Time'' and ''The Smile'' and the character of Noon in *The Day of Creation* adumbrate his own interest in correcting these misperceptions. Thematically, he will continue to gesture towards a problematic social transformation, hoping for its arrival but uncertain of its shape, wishing for it to resemble the community in his utopian *Vermilion Sands,* but, ever the survivor, willing to settle for anything shy of Eniwetok. As long as we avoid choosing the latter (and perhaps for a bit on the day after if we do not manage that), Ballard will continue to interest us as our bravest explorer of the psychic contours of post-nuclear humanity, the fabulist chronicler of our overlooked median strips. Somehow this maverick presence has become one of the most important and distinguished writers of English prose working today. His metaphors will haunt any reader; he dares to articulate what only the most obscure regions of our animal brain contemplate: desires for nuclear apocalypse, for incestuous sex, for participating in auto wrecks. Above all, Ballard maps these impulses, creating narrative places which reveal the innate connections between events and desires.

—Robert E. Mielke, updated by Dean Swinford

BANKS, Russell (Earl)

Nationality: American. **Born:** Newton, Massachusetts, 29 March 1940. **Education:** Colgate University, Hamilton, New York, 1958; University of North Carolina, Chapel Hill, 1964–67, A.B. 1967 (Phi Beta Kappa). **Family:** Married 1) Darlene Bennett in 1960 (divorced 1962), one daughter; 2) Mary Gunst in 1962 (divorced 1977), three daughters; 3) Kathy Walton in 1982 (divorced 1988); 4) Chase Twichell in 1989. **Career:** Mannequin dresser, Montgomery Ward, Lakeland, Florida, 1960–61; plumber, New Hampshire, 1962–64; publisher and editor, Lillabulero Press, and co-editor, *Lillabulero* magazine, Chapel Hill, North Carolina, and Northwood Narrows, New Hampshire, 1966–75; instructor, Emerson College, Boston, 1968 and 1971, University of New Hampshire, Durham, 1968–75, and New England College, Henniker, New Hampshire, 1975 and 1977–81. Since 1981 has taught at New York University and Princeton University, New Jersey. Lives in Princeton. **Awards:** Woodrow Wilson fellowship, 1968; St. Lawrence award, 1975; Guggenheim fellowship, 1976; National Endowment for the Arts grant, 1977, 1982; Merrill Foundation award, 1983; Dos Passos prize, 1985; American Academy award, 1986. **Agent:** Ellen Levine Literary Agency, 432 Park Avenue South, Suite 1205, New York, New York 10016. **Address:** c/o Ellen Levine Literary Agency, Suite 1801, 15 E. 26th Street, New York, New York 10010, U.S.A.

PUBLICATIONS

Novels

Family Life. New York, Avon, 1975.
Hamilton Stark. Boston, Houghton Mifflin, 1978.
The Book of Jamaica. Boston, Houghton Mifflin, 1980.
The Relation of My Imprisonment. Washington, D.C., Sun and Moon Press, 1983.
Continental Drift. New York, Harper, and London, Hamish Hamilton, 1985.
Affliction. New York, Harper, 1989; London, Picador, 1990.
The Sweet Hereafter: A Novel. New York, HarperCollins, 1991; London, Picador, 1992.
Rule of the Bone. New York, HarperCollins, 1995.
Cloudsplitter. New York, HarperFlamingo, 1998.

Short Stories

Searching for Survivors. New York, Fiction Collective, 1975.
The New World. Urbana, University of Illinois Press, 1978.
Trailerpark. Boston, Houghton Mifflin, 1981.
Success Stories. New York, Harper, and London, Hamish Hamilton, 1986.
The Angel on the Roof: The Stories of Russell Banks. New York, HarperCollins, 2000.

Uncollected Short Stories

''Indisposed,'' in *Prime Number,* edited by Ann Lowry Weir. Urbana, University of Illinois Press, 1988.
''The Travel Writer,'' in *Antioch Review* (Yellow Springs, Ohio), Summer 1989.
''Xmas,'' in *Antaeus* (New York), Spring-Autumn 1990.

Poetry

15 Poems, with William Matthews and Newton Smith. Chapel Hill, North Carolina, Lillabulero Press, 1967.
30/6. New York, The Quest, 1969.
Waiting to Freeze. Northwood Narrows, New Hampshire, Lillabulero Press, 1969.
Snow: Meditations of a Cautious Man in Winter. Hanover, New Hampshire, Granite, 1974.

Other

The Invisible Stranger: The Patten, Maine, Photographs of Arturo Patten (text), photographs by Arturo Patten. New York, HarperCollins, 1999.
Introduction, *Gringos and Other Stories* by Michael Rumaker. Rocky Mount, North Carolina, North Carolina Wesleyan College Press, 1991.

Introduction, *A Tramp Abroad* by Mark Twain. New York, Oxford University Press, 1996.

Contributor, *The Autobiographical Eye,* edited by Daniel Halpern. Hopewell, New Jersey, Ecco Press, 1993.

Editor, with Michael Ondaatje and David Young, *Brushes with Greatness: An Anthology of Chance Encounters with Greatness.* Toronto, Coach House Press, 1989.

* * *

Novelist, poet, and short story writer Russell Banks experienced early in life an abundance of pain, denial, and adventure that would later profoundly influence his writing. In 1989 Banks told interviewer Wesley Brown: ''I can see my life as a kind of obsessive return to the 'wound' ... Going back again and again trying to get it right, trying to figure out how it happened and who is to blame and who is to forgive.'' Revisiting past memories is apparent early in Banks's career as is seen in his collections of poetry, including *15 Poems, 30/6, Waiting to Freeze,* and *Snow: Meditations of a Cautious Man in Winter.* And, although Banks does not consider himself to be much of a poet, these collections are significant because in his poetry we see the presence of the themes he later develops in his short story collections, including *Searching for Survivors, Success Stories,* and *Trailerpark,* and in his novels. Banks addresses several recurring issues in these three genres, notably the joys and sorrows of life in New England, race relations in the Caribbean and America, conditions of the working class, American family struggles, and repressed childhood memories.

Family Life, Banks's first novel, is a relatively short text that rejects traditional methods of narration and characterization and attempts instead, in what some consider to be a postmodern move, to make the reader aware of the artifice of writing. In spite of the fragmented story, however, Banks presents a cogent tale that engages the reader. Set in an imaginary kingdom, the novel focuses on the events surrounding King Egress, the Hearty; his wife Naomi Ruth; and their sons, Dread, Orgone, and Egress, Jr. Some critics suggest that *Family Life,* though about a family in a fantasyland, indicts the contemporary American family. The story's self-centered, displeased parents and children who are drifting through their teen years rather lethargically do, in fact, appear to support this claim. The novel is difficult to categorize, as it might be deemed anything from a fable to a satire, and was called by some critics an ''experimental novel,'' though Banks rejects this label along with others that are sometimes bestowed upon the book.

Banks's second novel, *Hamilton Starks,* is another text that is concerned with the art of writing, using the story of a character known as ''A.'' (but later called ''Hamilton Starks'' by the story's main narrator) to track the process of composing a novel. Throughout *Hamilton Starks* many people construct their own unique and often discordant versions of Starks's character by presenting lengthy monologues, stories-within-stories, and even some their own writings about Starks. Because of these various viewpoints, the story suggests that Starks's life, and perhaps everyone's life, is disconnected and fragmented; there is no inherent ''self'' to discover or to rely upon.

The ''relation'' was a genre practiced by imprisoned seventeenth-century Puritans and written to testify to the ways their faith was tested and so strengthened when they were jailed. Banks's third novel, *The Relation of My Imprisonment,* was modeled after this genre. The novel tells of a coffin maker who is imprisoned for twelve years when he continues his trade after a law has been established prohibiting the work. The prisoner, now considered to be a heretic, narrates his experiences in prison, which include acts of debauchery, obsessive thoughts about food, drink, and money, and even attempts at in-depth self-analysis. The book, some critics suggest, though partly concerned with Puritan Dissenters in England, ultimately confronts the metaphorical imprisonment of contemporary Americans, who, like the narrator, are fragmented and so suffer a loss of self.

As he departs somewhat from the formal experimentation in his first three novels, *The Book of Jamaica* marks Banks's move toward realism and his intensified preoccupation with class issues. Set in Jamaica, the book tells the story of an American professor, who is left unnamed until he is befriended by the Maroons and then is called ''Johnny''—a term of affection they bestow upon him. The novel focuses on the professor's experiences while studying the Maroons, a group descended from slaves, who in the seventeenth and eighteenth centuries revolted against their British and Spanish owners. ''Johnny,'' who narrates his own tale, is burdened by his systematic style of thinking and believes that his feelings of alienation will be quelled if only he can remake himself and become more like the Jamaicans. However, in spite of his attempts to become like the Jamaicans, ''Johnny'' realizes that race, economics, and culture ultimately separate America and the Caribbean.

Fostering realism in each chapter, but using metafictional techniques in the novel as a whole, Banks's *Continental Drift* manages to combine two seemingly dissimilar tales, one of a white working-class American man, Bob DuBois, and one of Vanise Dorsinville, an impoverished black Haitian single mother who attempts to escape to America in order to have a better life. DuBois, an oil-burner repair man living in New Hampshire, realizes his dissatisfaction with his life—''He is alive, but his life has died''—and so decides to pursue the American dream by moving his family to Florida so he can work in his brother's liquor store. Though DuBois's situation appears at first to be rather grim, as his tale is juxtaposed with Vanise's, DuBois's world begins to look as if it is one of wealth and comfort. The two stories in *Continental Drift* are linked by the suggestion that humanity's movements are similar to the movements in nature—nearly imperceptible, though constantly occurring and ultimately inescapable—and by the description of the drifting quality of life in twentieth century America.

Banks's next three novels, *Affliction, The Sweet Hereafter,* and *Rule of the Bone,* might be thought of as the result of his marked shift away from the postmodern techniques of his early work and toward ''gritty'' realism. These three novels are similar in terms of style and theme; each uses a first person narrative and each is concerned, at some level, with the traumas of childhood and the American family.

Affliction, made into a movie in 1997 starring Nick Nolte, Sissy Spacek, James Coburn, and Willem Dafoe, explores the inner life of Wade Whitehouse and his struggle to escape ''the tradition of male violence'' and alcoholism in his working-class family. Set in a fictional town in New Hampshire—''a town people sometimes admit to having come from but where almost no one ever goes''—the novel is narrated by Wade's brother Rolfe, who has escaped the family by being its first member to attend college, and who, because he is ultimately implicated in the family's life, becomes preoccupied with interpreting Wade's psyche. Rolfe's narrative, though elevated and insightful, reveals that he too finds it nearly impossible to flee his family's cycle of brutality. Some critics have argued that Rolfe's narrative is clumsy and implausible because there is no way he might know all of Wade's thoughts at any given moment as the story suggests he does. Still, others argue that without Rolfe as mediator, the story would lack psychological intensity because Wade himself could not articulate his own inner feelings as can his brother.

Banks demonstrates the versatility of the first person narrative in *The Sweet Hereafter,* a novel about a school bus accident that claims the lives of fourteen children in a fictional town in upstate New York, as he presents the story from four unique points of view: Dolores Driscoll, the bus driver responsible for the accident; Billy Ansel, a parent of two children who died in the crash; Mitchell Stephens, a New York City lawyer who believes that ''[t]here are no accidents''; and Nichole Burnell, an eighth grader who is left paralyzed after the crash. The novel, ultimately, is concerned with the status of children in America and examines who is to blame, and who is to forgive. Atom Egoyan recently filmed an adaptation of *The Sweet Hereafter,* which was nominated for two Oscars and won three Cannes Film Festival awards.

Banks's *Rule of the Bone* has been hailed by some as a contemporary *Huck Finn* or *Catcher in the Rye* because of its troubled protagonist's first person narrative. Primarily concerned with the events that contribute to fourteen-year-old Chappie Dorset's maturation, the novel includes his encounters with family, politics, religion, money, sex, drugs, and his development of self. Abused by his stepfather, Ken, and ''heavy into weed,'' Chappie runs away from home, takes on a new identity as he renames himself ''Bone,'' and learns several life lessons from an illegal Jamaican alien, I-Man, and an abandoned, abused young child, Rose. Eventually, Bone decides to go to Jamaica with his mentor, I-Man, where he meets his biological father, who, much to Bone's dismay, does not live up to the boy's expectations. Some critics have praised the novel in its entirety, though others have critiqued its chapters set in Jamaica for their improbable events and simplistic moral conclusions. Still, the novel is concerned with criticizing the irrational and selfish world of adults, while it glorifies the endurance of youth. And again, as in *Affliction* and *The Sweet Hereafter,* Banks critiques the nuclear family.

Banks's most recent novel, *Cloudsplitter,* is a fictionalized account of Owen Brown, son of John Brown, who led his followers to murder pro-slavery groups in Kansas and claimed to have received orders from God to attack Harper's Ferry in 1859. The book acquaints the reader with several historical figures, including Frederick Douglass and Ralph Waldo Emerson, but its main focus is on Owen's tale of his father's life and its effects on their family. Although this novel, which Banks researched for several years, seems to diverge from his previous subject matter, Banks's main concerns—a son haunted by the memory of his father, the obsessive return to the ''wound,'' family relationships, and racial issues—are apparent in *Cloudsplitter.*

—Stephannie Gearhart

BANVILLE, John

Nationality: Irish. **Born:** Wexford, 8 December 1945. **Education:** Christian Brothers School, and St. Peter's College, both Wexford. **Family:** Married Janet Dunham in 1969; two sons. **Career:** Copy editor, *Irish Press,* Dublin, 1970–83. Since 1989 literary editor, *Irish Times,* Dublin. **Awards:** Allied Irish Banks prize, 1973; Arts Council of Ireland Macaulay fellowship, 1973; Irish-American Foundation award, 1976; James Tait Black Memorial prize, 1977; *Guardian* Fiction prize 1981; Guinness Peat Aviation award, 1989. **Agent:** Sheil Land Ltd., 43 Doughty Street, London WC1N 2LF, England.

Publications

Novels

Nightspawn. London, Secker and Warburg, and New York, Norton, 1971.
Birchwood. London, Secker and Warburg, and New York, Norton, 1973.
Doctor Copernicus. London, Secker and Warburg, and New York, Norton, 1976.
Kepler. London, Secker and Warburg, 1981; Boston, Godine, 1983.
The Newton Letter: An Interlude. London, Secker and Warburg, 1982; Boston, Godine, 1987.
Mefisto. London, Secker and Warburg, 1986; Boston, Godine, 1989.
The Book of Evidence. London, Secker and Warburg, 1989; New York, Scribner, 1990.
Ghosts. London, Secker and Warburg, and New York, Scribner, 1993.
Athena. London, Secker and Warburg, and New York, Scribner, 1995.
The Untouchable. New York, Knopf, 1997.

Short Stories

Long Lankin. London, Secker and Warburg, 1970.

Uncollected Short Stories

''The Party,'' in *Kilkenny Magazine,* Spring-Summer 1966.
''Mr. Mallin's Quest'' and ''Nativity,'' in *Transatlantic Review* (London), Autumn-Winter 1970–71.
''Into the Wood,'' in *Esquire* (New York), March 1972.
''De rerum natura,'' in *Transatlantic Review 50* (London), 1975.
''Rondo,'' in *Transatlantic Review 60* (London), 1977.

Plays

Screenplay: *Reflections,* 1984; *The Broken Jug (After Kleist),* 1994.

Other

Introduction, *Ormond, a Tale* by Maria Edgeworth. Belfast, Appletree Press, 1992.
Introduction, *The Deeps of the Sea and Other Fiction* by George Steiner. Boston, Faber and Faber, 1996.
Contributor, *Arguing at the Crossroads: Essays on a Changing Ireland,* edited by Paul Brennan and Catherine de Saint Phalle. Dublin, New Island Books, 1997.

*

Manuscript Collection: Trinity College, Dublin.

Critical Studies: ''John Banville Issue'' of *Irish University Review* (Dublin), Spring 1981; *John Banville: A Critical Introduction* by Rudiger Imhof, Dublin, Wolfhound Press, 1989, Chester Springs, Pennsylvania, Dufour, 1990; *John Banville, A Critical Study* by

Joseph McMinn. New York, Macmillan, 1991; *The Supreme Fictions of John Banville* by Joseph McMinn, New York, Manchester University Press, 1999.

* * *

John Banville writes about writing. His characters are marionettes, entangled in self-reflexive explorations of the relationship between creation and reality. Banville's fiction is full of borrowings, from Marvell to Sir Arthur Eddington, yet it is saved from intellectualism and narcissism by its disciplined structure and Nabokovian narrative voice, deliberately uneasy and emotionally strained.

Its third-person narrative distinguishes *Long Lankin* from Banville's later books. Like *Dubliners,* this debut collection presents different stages in the lives of Irish characters in sets of episodic stories dealing with childhood, adolescence, and adulthood respectively. "The Possessed," a novella, is added as a coda. Each story centres on two dispossessed characters who frustrate each other's initial sense of freedom and end up in a state of arrest, wholly unable to fathom the "whatness of things." Ominously prominent background noises and shadows continually hint at Long Lankin, the leper from the old English ballad, whose cure depended on a ritual murder. He materializes in the novella as Ben White and radically upsets the tenor, chronology, and fictional level of the book. White's transformation into "Black Fang" intermediates his appearance in two preceding stories: in "Summer Voices" as a boy, bullied by his sister and fascinated with death; and in "Island" as an unproductive writer who stares at Delos and is accused of murder by his demanding girlfriend. In "The Possessed," Ben demands a blood-sacrifice for creative freedom, metaphorically kills his sister by severing their—almost incestuous—ties, and lifts himself to the status of implied author, unleashing a savagery that reflects the author's urge to finish off the book.

Nightspawn is a sequel to "The Possessed" and exploits the metafictional effects of coalescing hero, narrator, and writer. Ben imitates Yeats, Prufrock, and Shelley, and in the best *nouveau roman* tradition he soon becomes a pawn in his own cliché thriller. His Greek island gets crowded with his stock characters who emotionally involve White beyond his narrative control and are to blame for the novel's doubles, double plots, and obscurity. Eager to get to "the real meat," but checked by "the conventions," White becomes the first of Banville's Beckettian heroes who must go on, or perish in silence and who are doomed at the end to return to the first sentence.

In *Birchwood,* Banville refutes many of his fabulations. Gabriel Godkin, the narrator, is once again autocratic and conditioned by his own narrative. His genre is the Irish big house with all its familiar trappings and stock characters. There are slapstick humour and morbid fun: Granny Godkin finds her end in the summerhouse by spontaneous combustion. Intermingled with the big house is the external world of romance, Prospero's circus, which Gabriel joins on his quest for a sister who is in fact an imaginative character created to deprive him of his inheritance by the aunt who proves to be his mother. Gabriel's anachronistic narrative is determined by his "search for time misplaced"; like the antics of Birchwood's grandfather clock, it transcends boundaries of time as deftly as Proust's *Recherches.* But the book's shifting frames of reference are firmly fixed in its philosophical observation that the expression of the memories of things is at best a two-dimensional mirror-image in which much is consistently reversed.

In his classical tetralogy, Banville translates his fascination for the relationship between creation and reality into eminent scientists' quests for truth. He even appends bibliographies with references to works on theoretical physics. In *Doctor Copernicus,* Duke Albrecht claims that he and Copernicus are "the makers of ... supreme fictions." And indeed, Coppernigk is time and again likened to Wallace Stevens in order to show how science is art and how art cannot express truth, but only embody it. Coppernigk's quest leads from conceptualization to cognition, a unification with his anti-self, his syphilitic brother Andreas who repeats verbatim Eddington's "We *are* the truth." Although the book recreates the cruelty and stench of the Renaissance, it is not an historical novel. Copernicus is a protégé of a writer's consciousness which is informed by Einstein, Kierkegaard, Wittgenstein, Max Planck, Yeats, and Stevens—who are all quoted in a pandemonium of opposing philosophical contentions. Banville feels free to introduce a map-cap, manic depressive paranoid called Rheticus, who claims responsibility for Copernicus's *De Revolutionibus,* lies like mad, lays bare the irrational undertones of the book and provides a delightfully comic interlude. Ultimately *Doctor Copernicus* is another metafiction; all characters may be figments of Copernicus's own mind; and he, in turn, acts and thinks as part of the literary creation. Every book of the novel is a closed entity, revolving within itself and resolving in a restatement of the first paragraph, with the very last sentence being a return to the very first. The narrative reads like a fugue, but despite its insistence on form it is immensely realistic in its depiction of a nightmarish era, where total chaos is just around the corner.

The structure of *Kepler* is a reflection of the hero's belief that "in the beginning is the shape." The five chapters are shaped like the polygons that Kepler envisaged within the intervals of the six planetary orbits; the sections acrostically spell out the names of famous scientists, and the shifts of time in each section reflect Kepler's discovery that the planets move in ellipses. In his Quixotic quest for a truthful order, Kepler the man becomes conditioned by the entropy that Kepler the scientist creates, with a paradoxical anti-hero as the result.

At the basis of *The Newton Letter* lies von Hofmannsthal's *Ein Brief;* the Nabokovian first sentence aptly reads "Words fail me, Clio." The epistolary form grants the narrator more autonomy than any of Banville's protagonists and emphasizes his treacherous subjectivity. The novel is the satire of the tetralogy and details the consequences of immersing an historian with a Newtonian mechanistic view in the common world of the big house, where Goethe's humanity reigns supreme. The hero is constantly baffled and blinded, misinterprets the inhabitants of Ferns and is Banville's most convincing example that truth is perhaps inhuman.

The Book of Evidence and *Athena* exploit even further than Banville's previous work the fragile span between reality and the need to believe and live in illusion. The first person narrative of Frederick Montgomery in *The Book of Evidence* is a confessional monologue of an art expert awaiting trial for murdering a young female servant, who caught him stealing a Dutch masterpiece, *A Portrait of a Woman with Gloves*, from a friend. He killed her simply because she was in the way. Montgomery, a gentleman and non-criminal type, has to make sense of his crimes, to discover the impulse that drove him to them. Articulately written, Montgomery's recollections of his past include scenes of viewing life from within, through windows, as if he had been imprisoned all his life. This feature continues when he appears in *Athena.* Montogmery, out of prison, changes his name to Morrow, but becomes no less self-obsessed.

Banville's imaginative description of the *Portrait of a Woman with Gloves*, as seen by Montgomery, goes beyond what is on the canvas. Montgomery is able to brilliantly invent details of the life and circumstances of a long-dead woman in the portrait, but of the living woman he killed, he realises later, he cannot be forgiven because ''I never imagined her vividly enough, that I never made her be there sufficiently, that I did not make her live. I could kill her because for me she was not alive.'' *Athena* develops Montgomery/Morrow's difficulties of identity in a scenario that is a fantastic play of words and images. Figures from *The Book of Evidence* recur, but slightly altered, and even the one solid character, described with a blend of humour and pathos, Morrow's dying aunt, is a fraud. Acting as a kind of subliminal commentary, paintings are described and analysed to reflect on Morrow's psyche and his pursuit of love via an imagined recreation of the murdered servant. In *The Book of Evidence* Montgomery declared that his task was to bring her back to life and that he would from then on be ''living for two''; he later remarks in *Athena* ''She had been mine for a time … from the start that was supposed to be my task: to give her life.'' Gombrich notes of Belli's *Pygmalion* ''that his quest was 'for forms more perfect and more ideal than reality,''' which pinpoints Morrow's obsession and his tragic dual state of mind. Banville's handling of this extremely complex theme is faultless, for his great ability is to project us into the psychotic world of Montgomery/Morrow, and to share his confusion without question.

—Peter G.W. van de Kamp, updated by Geoffrey Elborn

BARDWELL, Leland

Nationality: Irish **Born:** Leland Hone, India, 1928. **Education:** Alexandra School, Dublin; London University, 1950s. **Family:** Married 1) Michael Bardwell in 1940s (separated 1950s), three children; 2) Finton McLachlan in 1959, three sons. **Career:** Various jobs, London and Paris, 1940s; playwright and writer for radio, Ireland, 1960s; poetry editor, *Force 10* magazine, County Sligo, Ireland. **Address:** County Sligo, Ireland.

PUBLICATIONS

Novels

Girl on a Bicycle: A Novel. Dublin, Irish Writers Co-operative, 1977.
That London Winter. Dublin, Co-op Books, 1981.
The House. Dingle, Ireland, Brandon, 1984.
There We Have Been. Dublin, Attic Press, 1989.

Short Stories

Different Kinds of Love. Dublin, Attic Press, 1987.

Poetry

The Mad Cyclist. Dublin, New Writers' Press, 1970.
The Fly and the Bed Bug. Dublin, Beaver Row Press, 1984.
Dostoevsky's Grave: Selected Poems. Dublin, Dedalus, 1991.
The White Beach: New and Selected Poems, 1960–1998. Cliffs of Moher, Ireland, Salmon Publishing, 1998.

Plays

Thursday. Dublin, Trinity College, 1972.
Open Ended Prescription. Dublin, Peacock Theatre, 1979.
Edith Piaf. Dublin, Olympia Theatre, 1984.

Other

Contributor, *Ms. Muffet and Others: A Funny, Sassy, Heretical Collection of Feminist Fairytales.* Dublin, Attic Press, 1986.
Editor, with others, *The Anthology.* Dublin, Co-Op Books, 1982.

* * *

Over the past four decades Leland Bardwell has been an important and popular presence in Irish writing. As a poet, dramatist, short story writer, and novelist, Bardwell has consistently produced work that is noted for its complexity, creativity, detail, and craftsmanship. Originally a poet, Bardwell turned to prose in the 1970s as a means of supporting her family. *Girl on a Bicycle*, set in 1940s Ireland, was her first novel and it introduced several of the themes that continue to resurface in Bardwell's subsequent writing. Through the character of a young Protestant woman attempting to negotiate life—ultimately unsuccessfully—in a new Catholic state, Bardwell explores both the reality of being Protestant in England, and what it means to be an individual caught up in the momentum of historical change. In both of these central thematic questions, Bardwell's own experience is evident: Protestant herself, born in colonial India and brought to Ireland at the age of two, she has not only lived through the violent political upheaval of twentieth-century Ireland, but also survived being bombed while living in London during World War II. As a former extramural student at London University, Bardwell has been able to situate these experiences in relation to the ancient history she studied, and furthermore realize their potential for literary and mythic treatment, as evident in much of her poetry, where she often incorporates mythical and historical figures in poems that signify the contemporary present.

Bardwell's best-known novel to date, *The House*, and her latest novel, *There We Have Been*, continue to probe questions of history, memory, relationships, personal identity, and Protestantism. Both of these novels reveal Bardwell's ability to convincingly create and then mine the psyches of individual characters, and the kinds of personal crises that underlie their everyday lives. In *The House* a middle-aged Irish Protestant man who has been living in England returns to his family home in Ireland. When confronted with the physical space of his history, memories of his childhood refuse to be contained, forcing him to confront the history of his emotional relationships as well. Those factors that are supposed to define him as an individual—familial ties, religion, etc.—are revealed to be both problematic and tenuous, and Bardwell's protagonist must reconsider just what and who has made him what he is. *There We Have Been* features a similar return by a protagonist to a childhood home. Just as the farm Diligence Strong returns to has been neglected, so too have her memories of, and questions about, the personal past. In struggling with the presence of her emotionally distant brother and the memories of a sister whose death has never been satisfactorily understood, Diligence must strip away the fabrications families and individuals construct in an attempt to perpetuate the illusion of coherence in their lives.

That Bardwell situates a return to home as the crucial generative action of each book suggests how fundamental she believes space and place, as mitigated by history, to be in the formation of individuals. Furthermore, it underscores how central she understands memory to be as an ordering principle of the imagination, a theme that recurs in her poetry. For Bardwell, the individual is always in some way in the process of ''returning,'' whether it be a physical return, an emotional one, or both. In 1998 Bardwell published her fourth book of poetry, *The White Beach: New and Selected Poems, 1960–1998*, which is resonant with returns. Divided into four sections, each of which chronicles one of the four decades during which she has been writing, the collection poetically documents the personal and political developments of Bardwell's life to date, demonstrating their inextricability. Her poetry, so deeply personal in its reflections on her relationships and experiences, nevertheless veers away from egocentrism, documenting those she has encountered and been moved by with equal sensitivity and clarity, particularly the lives of other women. This anticipated poetic overview of four decades' experience and literary output is expected to be followed by an equally anticipated new novel.

—Jennifer Harris

BARKER, A(udrey) L(ilian)

Nationality: British. **Born:** St. Paul's Cray, Kent, 13 April 1918. **Education:** Schools in Beckenham, Kent, and Wallington, Surrey. **Career:** Worked for Amalgamated Press, London, 1936; reader, Cresset Press, London, 1947; secretary and sub-editor, BBC, London, 1949–78. Member of the Executive Committee, English PEN, 1981–85. **Awards:** Atlantic award, 1946; Maugham award, 1947; Cheltenham Festival award, 1963; Arts Council award, 1970; South East Arts award, 1981; Society of Authors travelling scholarship, 1988. Fellow, Royal Society of Literature, 1970. **Agent:** Jennifer Kavanagh, 44 Langham Street, London W1N 5RC, England. **Address:** 103 Harrow Road, Carshalton, Surrey SM5 3QF, England.

PUBLICATIONS

Novels

Apology for a Hero. London, Hogarth Press, and New York, Scribner, 1950.
A Case Examined. London, Hogarth Press, 1965.
The Middling: Chapters in the Life of Ellie Toms. London, Hogarth Press, 1967.
John Brown's Body. London, Hogarth Press, 1969.
A Source of Embarrassment. London, Hogarth Press, 1974.
A Heavy Feather. London, Hogarth Press, 1978; New York, Braziller, 1979.
Relative Successes. London, Chatto and Windus, 1984.
The Gooseboy. London, Hutchinson, 1987.
The Woman Who Talked to Herself. London, Hutchinson, 1989.
Zeph. London, Hutchinson, 1992.
The Haunt. London, Virago Press, 1999.

Short Stories

Innocents: Variations on a Theme. London, Hogarth Press, 1947; New York, Scribner, 1948.
Novelette with Other Stories. London, Hogarth Press, and New York, Scribner, 1951.
The Joy-Ride and After. London, Hogarth Press, 1963; New York, Scribner, 1964.
Lost upon the Roundabouts. London, Hogarth Press, 1964.
Penguin Modern Stories 8, with others. London, Penguin, 1971.
Femina Real. London, Hogarth Press, 1971.
Life Stories. London, Chatto and Windus, 1981.
No Word of Love. London, Chatto and Windus, 1985.
Any Excuse for a Party: Selected Stories. London, Hutchinson, 1991.
Contributor, *Seduction: A Book of Stories,* edited by Tony Peake. New York, Serpent's Tail, 1994.

Play

Television Play: *Pringle,* 1958.

Other

Introduction, *Hester Lilly, and Other Stories* by Elizabeth Taylor. London, Virago, 1990.

* * *

The theme of A.L. Barker's work is the ambivalence of love and the dangers of egoism. She examines those relationships that exist between victor and victim, he who eats and he who is eaten. This material is handled lightly and skillfully; she has the satirist's ability to select detail, placing her characters socially as well as psychologically. Her territory covers childhood, the worlds of the outcast and the ill, and the impoverished lives of the lonely. She is close to the English tradition of the comic novel and like Angus Wilson, a major writer in this genre, she often indulges in caricature.

Many of her short stories reveal a fondness for the macabre, introducing elements of horror into the midst of apparent calm. Her first collection, *Innocents,* begins with a study of a boy testing his courage in swimming; he becomes involved in a scene of adult violence that is far more dangerous to him than the tree-roots in his river. Innocence in these stories is seen as inexperience, as the blinkered vision of the mad and as the selfishness of the egoist. *Lost upon the Roundabouts* is a further exploration of these ideas, and contains two very fine short stories, ''Miss Eagle'' and ''Someone at the Door.''

The central characters in Barker's novels are parasites, dependent on other people for a sense of their own identity. For Ellie in *The Middling* love means ''turning another person into a colony of myself.'' Charles Candy, the central character of *Apology for a Hero,* loves his wife Wynne ''because she could give him himself.'' After Wynne's death he acquires a housekeeper and finds that ''when he was with her he felt located.'' He meets death on a reckless voyage, persuaded that sea-trading will, at last, show him the real Mr. Candy.

The egoist in *A Case Examined* is Rose Antrobus, the chairman of a charity committee with the power to allocate money either to a destitute family or to the church hassock fund. Rose has always insulated herself against suffering. She remembers a childhood friend, Solange, whom she credits with the understanding of despair: Solange provokes violence, she feels, by her own wickedness. This fantasy is shattered by a visit to Paris and a meeting with the real Solange, whose account of Nazi persecution shakes Rose into compassion. A bridge has been made between the worlds of the two women, between the petty and the tragic, and the committee decision is altered accordingly.

Femina Real is an entertaining set of portraits, nine studies of the female character. In many of the situations an apparent vulnerability hides an underlying strength. A frail woman dominates those around her: adolescence vanquishes middle-age; a ten-year-old cripple turns the tables on the man holding her prisoner. As always, Barker's clear prose style matches the accuracy of her observations. *The Haunt,* which Barker completed just before she was struck by a debilitating illness in 1998, marked a departure in that, unlike earlier works, this one is not an ''articulated novel'' of short stories, or even an extended short story, but rather a fully realized narrative. The haunting of the title refers not to ghosts, of which there are plenty in earlier writings, but rather to the act or experience of being haunted—a phenomenon she treats as something to be enjoyed and treasured, not feared. Indeed, Barker's is a talent to be treasured as well.

—Judy Cooke

BARKER, Pat(ricia)

Nationality: British. **Born:** Thornaby-on-Tees, England, 1943. **Education:** LSE, B.Sc.1965. **Family:** Married David B. Barker in 1978; two children. **Career:** Has taught further education. **Awards:** Fawcett prize, for *Union Street;* Booker Prize, 1995, for *The Ghost Road.* **Agent:** Curtis Brown Associates, 162–168 Regent Street, London W1R 5TA, England.

Publications

Novels

Union Street. London, Virago, 1982; New York, Putnam, 1983.
Blow Your House Down. London, Virago, and New York, Putnam, 1984.
The Century's Daughter. London, Virago, and New York, Putnam, 1986.
The Man Who Wasn't There. London, Virago, 1989; New York, Ballantine, 1990.
Regeneration. London, Viking, 1991; New York, Dutton, 1992.
The Eye in the Door. London, Viking, 1993; New York, Dutton, 1994.
The Ghost Road. London, Viking, 1995; Boston, Compass, 1995.
The Regeneration Trilogy. London, Viking, 1996.
Another World. London, Viking, 1998; New York, Farrar, Straus, and Giroux, 1999.

*

Film Adaptation: *Stanley and Iris,* from the novel *Union Street.*

* * *

Union Street was Pat Barker's first novel, and at once marked her as a powerful voice in objective realism. She had tried writing middle-class fiction but was encouraged by Angela Carter to write of her own working-class roots. Set in an unnamed northern England industrial town, *Union Street* consists of seven interlinked stories, each named after a working-class woman. These form a graphic account, in their own idiom, of women whose lives are circumscribed by poverty and violence. The first chapter, which is the longest, describes a childhood typically shared by the older characters, describing circumstances that account for their attitudes as adults. Kelly Brown, an intelligent 11-year-old, is hardly cared for by her mother, who has been abandoned by her husband. Playing truant, Kelly roams the streets at night, and on one such occasion she is raped. This she conceals from her mother, and in the end, determined not to be defeated, she is even more strongly compelled to wander alone. Barker treats Kelly entirely sympathetically, so that when the girl vandalizes a middle-class house and her own school, the reader feels compassion rather than disgust at her actions. She encounters an old woman in a park who has chosen to abandon her house to avoid being put in an old people's home. The woman will die in the cold, and this experience encourages Kelly to return to her mother.

The speech patterns of the characters are authentically northern English working-class, and the story of *Union Street* reveals bigotry caused by ignorance, overt racism, unwanted pregnancies, and a close society united and also torn apart by appalling social conditions. Running like a thread through all the chapters is the strong Iris King, whose capable way of organizing her own life while helping others provides hope in the midst of misery. The novel, which is cyclical, ends with the story of Alice Brown, a confused, senile woman who believes that nineteenth-century workhouses still exist, and has saved against the indignity of a pauper's funeral. In doing so she is half-starved, and even after a severe stroke she refuses to go to a home. Knowing she will be forcibly moved and not allowed to end her days in her own house, she decides to die in the open. She is the woman Kelly met at the beginning of the novel, and Alice's reflections of her own past emphasize the unchanging patterns of life.

Barker's skill was confirmed by her *Blow Your House Down,* a fictional reconstruction of prostitution and a Yorkshire Ripper prototype. More successful was *The Century's Daughter,* which covers a period of 80 years and has a large cast of characters, some of whom might have strayed from *Union Street.* In a sense a fictional history of the century, the most poignant section is about the sufferings of men in the trenches of World War I and the effect their deaths have on their families. It was a subject that fascinated Barker, and one which she made her own in a trilogy about the Great War.

The fictional treatment of World War I was the domain of the male writer until Susan Hill broke new ground with *Strange Meeting.* Barker's Regeneration trilogy—comprised of *Regeneration, The Eye in the Door,* and *The Ghost Road*—uses a mixture of fiction and facts about W. H. R. Rivers, an army doctor, and his shell-shocked patients at the Craiglockhart War Hospital in Edinburgh. The patients, who have to be cured before they are sent back to the front—probably to be killed—include several familiar names, in particular Wilfred Owen and Siegfried Sassoon. There is also William Prior, a completely fictional creation who appears in all three novels.

Regeneration—the regeneration of nerves, that is—examines in microscopic detail the horrific mental disorders caused by trench warfare. Much of the historical detail is already familiar, but Barker gives it a new perspective by providing a background to the soldier's lives. Prior's mental disturbance is exacerbated by his past relationship with his violent father; his reversion as an adult to his childhood ways of escape by ''changing'' to another personality is a persistent theme in the series. Originally working-class but now an army officer, he is what the middle and upper classes snobbishly label as a ''temporary gentleman.''

He is, however, acceptable for sex, and the second novel opens with a gay sex scene between him and an upper-class officer, whose hidebound class consciousness will gradually be eroded. Barker expands on the facts of a genuine cause célèbre of a female pacifist wrongly imprisoned on trumped-up evidence she was plotting to kill Lloyd George. Her version of this real character is called Beattie Roper, and Beattie tests the loyalties of Prior, the intelligence officer called in to question her. It so happens she is his lifelong friend, and thus he finds himself on the one hand wanting to prove evidence against an agent provocateur in order to help her, and on the other hand pulled by his own strongly nonpacifist convictions.

Another figure in *The Eye in the Door* is a lunatic who sets out to expose homosexuals, libeling an actress by implying that she is a lesbian, and attempting to nail an M.P. for the same crime. All the characters feel watched, by conscience or under suspicion, and the ''eye in the door'' is the glass in a cell through which the inmate is constantly scrutinized. Implicit in the entire series, however, is the eye of the author scrutinizing her own society, an idea that becomes more apparent in *The Ghost Road.* As Prior returns to the front, newly patched up by Rivers and on his way to new horrors—horrors that seem particularly absurd in light of the fact that the war is drawing to a close—Rivers thinks back on his earlier work among the headhunters of Melanesia. The same British Empire now engaged in acts of wholesale slaughter on the battlefields of France, it seems, had earlier outlawed headhunting among the natives of its colony. Barker presents these two facts with a minimum of comment, thus only serving to heighten the topsy-turvy moral landscape of her characters' world.

—Geoffrey Elborn

BARNES, Julian (Patrick)

Pseudonym: Dan Kavanagh. **Nationality:** British. **Born:** Leicester, 19 January 1946. **Education:** City of London School, 1957–64; Magdalen College, Oxford, 1964–68, B.A. (honours) in modern languages 1968; also studied law. **Family:** Married Pat Kavanagh in 1979. **Career:** Editorial assistant, *Oxford English Dictionary* supplement, 1969–72; contributing editor, *New Review,* London, 1977–78; assistant literary editor, 1977–79, and television critic, 1977–81, *New Statesman,* London; deputy literary editor, *Sunday Times,* London, 1980–82; television critic, the *Observer,* London, 1982–86; London correspondent, *The New Yorker,* 1990–94. Lives in London, England. **Awards:** Somerset Maugham award, 1981; Faber Memorial prize, 1985; Médicis Essai prize (France), 1986; American Academy award 1986; Gutenberg prize (France), 1987; Premio Grinzane Cavour (Italy), 1988; Prix Fémina (France), 1992; Shakespeare prize (Hamburg), 1993. Chevalier de l'Ordre des Arts et des Lettres, 1988. **Agent:** Peters Fraser and Dunlop, 503–504 The Chambers, Chelsea Harbour, Lots Road, London SW10 0XF, England.

PUBLICATIONS

Novels

Metroland. London, Cape, 1980; New York, St. Martin's Press, 1981.
Before She Met Me. London, Cape, 1982; New York, McGraw Hill, 1986.
Flaubert's Parrot. London, Cape, 1984; New York, Knopf, 1985.
Staring at the Sun. London, Cape, 1986; New York, Knopf, 1987.
A History of the World in 10 1/2 Chapters. London, Cape, and New York, Knopf, 1989.
Talking It Over. London, Cape, and New York, Knopf, 1991.
The Porcupine. London, Cape, and New York, Knopf, 1992.
Cross Channel. New York, Knopf, 1996.
England, England. New York, Knopf, 1999.

Novels as Dan Kavanagh

Duffy. London, Cape, 1980; New York, Pantheon, 1986.
Fiddle City. London, Cape, 1981; New York, Pantheon, 1986.
Putting the Boot In. London, Cape, 1985.
Going to the Dogs. London, Viking, and New York, Pantheon, 1987.

Uncollected Short Stories

''The 50p Santa'' (as Dan Kavanagh), in *Time Out* (London), 19 December 1985–1 January 1986.
''One of a Kind,'' in *The Penguin Book of Modern British Short Stories,* edited by Malcolm Bradbury. London and New York, Viking, 1987.
''Shipwreck,'' in *The New Yorker,* 12 June 1989.

Other

Letters from London: 1990–1995. London, Picador, and New York, Vintage, 1995.
Introduction, *The Reef* by Edith Wharton. New York, Knopf, 1996.
Contributor, *The Mammoth Book of Twentieth-Century Ghost Stories,* edited by Peter Haining. New York, Carroll and Graf, 1998.
Contributor, *The Penguin Book of Twentieth-Century Essays,* edited by Ian Hamilton. London, Penguin, 2000.
Translator, *The Truth About Dogs,* by Volker Kriegel. London, Bloomsbury, 1988.

*

Critical Studies: *Understanding Julian Barnes* by Merritt Moseley, Columbia, South Carolina, University of South Carolina Press, 1997; *Language, History, and Metanarrative in the Fiction of Julian Barnes,* New York, Lang, 2000.

* * *

The much-quoted glowing tribute paid to Julian Barnes by Carlos Fuentes has given him the reputation—by no means entirely undeserved—of being the most literary, the most intellectual and above all the most international of British contemporary novelists. Barnes's fluency receives frequent acclaim, and indeed, this prolific writer's most successful experiments in literary form can be most closely compared to his Italian, French, and South American contemporaries. Yet along with such international strains, however, there is something specifically English deeply interfused in his work.

His first novel, *Metroland,* published in 1981 when Barnes was 35, owes a great deal to the language and traditions of English poetry. Philip Larkin (himself later to praise Barnes) is quoted on occasions and the poet's steady, empirical temperament and suburban stoicism can be sensed behind the narrative. The plot centers around a young Englishman, Christopher Lloyd, who visits France during the revolts of 1968 and has a brief affair with a French girl. The novel immediately demonstrates Barnes's aptitudes as both meticulous stylist and careful recorder of closely observed detail. Its three balanced scenes, which echo Flaubert's *Éducation sentimental* in many ways, are equally vivid and imaginative: the adolescent pranks of clever schoolboys Chris and his friend Toni; Chris's belated and intelligently unsentimentalized sexual initiation in Paris; and the suburban idyll of Chris's subsequent marriage, to which Toni's rather phony iconoclasm is compared. These values may seem anti-extremist to the point of being smug, but the scenes are very convincing.

Graham Hendrick in *Before She Met Me* ditches his safe, nonsexual first wife for a sportier, younger model (Ann) who suits him better at first, until her previous life as a minor, sexy starlet soon becomes the subject of his obsessive fascination. While reminiscent of Nabokov's Humbert Humbert, Hendrick is also a typical Barnes protagonist, rather academic in temperament (he might be Chris Lloyd 10 years on) and catalogues Ann's past life and celluloid affairs meticulously until the supposed trail leads him back to the brash novelist host Jack Lupton at whose house he has first met her. This fact finally makes Hendrick lose his cool and leads him to the carefully planned murder and suicide he has devised in order to punish her.

If these two early novels were promising in that they revealed much of Barnes's wit and psychological sensitivity, *Flaubert's Parrot,* being both a tribute to his acknowledged master and model, Flaubert, and one of the most outstanding contributions to British postmodernism, is Barnes's master work. This prize-winning, widely acclaimed 1984 novel combines the semi-academic protagonist Geoffrey Braithwaite and his interest in the complexities of marital love with a brilliant, well-informed, creative exploration of the French writer's life and work, which ultimately questions the philosophical nature of all history and knowledge. It is one of only a handful of novels written in England whose inventiveness in form has kept pace with what has been such an intellectually stimulating period in literary theory and criticism. The postmodern problematizing of any attempt to reconstruct historical truth is moderated, though, as the novel presents a plethora of ideas and invention that make it by no means only abstract or intellectual. If Hendrick in *Before She Met Me* constructs like a detective the data he obsessively imagines, Braithwaite's attempt to find the authentic parrot that sat on Flaubert's desk while *Un Coeur simple* was written (while at the same time rationalizing his wife's suicide), is doomed to fail, because every trace he finds is inevitably subjective. So the narrator-detective's own writing pushes more and more into the center of the novel.

Barnes's other identity as crime writer Dan Kavanagh (complete with mildly racist fictional biography) was the worst kept literary secret of the 1980s, casually announced in the cult literary magazine *Quarto* and then blown wide open when ''Kavanagh'' appeared on a front cover portrait in the *London Review of Books,* and when Barnes married the literary agent Pat Kavanagh. The first two immensely entertaining novels featuring his bisexual ex-cop Duffy (*Duffy* and *Fiddle City*), with the Soho sex clubs of the former and the airport smuggling of the latter providing vivid low-life detail, were as successful in their way as *Metroland* was in its. But by the time of *Putting the Boot In* and *Going to the Dogs,* with *Flaubert's Parrot* as the new yardstick, the joke and the material have worn a little thin. In the contemporary fiction scene a successful highbrow novel may well outsell a supposedly ''popular'' crime thriller, so profit alone is not sufficient motive. The Duffy novels (reflecting the grand topic of the impossibility of the detective putting together the single pieces to get the overall picture) helped give Barnes some ''street-cred'' and may also have served to keep his desire to be sensational out of his input into literature.

Structurally, Barnes's heterogeneous 1986 novel *Staring at the Sun* is (like *Metroland*) a triptych. The boldness of its form, its long time-perspectives and its compelling central metaphor (of a pilot who, due to an accident of flying, experiences sunrise twice) make it another accomplished novel of ideas. It highlights three moments in the life of Jean Sergeant: as a naive 17-year-old during World War II entering a sexually-closeted marriage; as a mother in her mid-fifties in 1984, who takes off on a trip to explore the wonders and wisdoms of the world; and finally as a widow on the eve of her 100th birthday in the twenty-first century, when all the answers to life's questions (at least those questions to which answers are possible) are stored on the General Purposes Computer within a program that (depending on your degree of credulity or skepticism) is called either The Absolute Truth or TAT.

Barnes's *A History of the World in 10 1/2 Chapters* (the allusion, of course, is to H.G. Wells's classic of Edwardian optimism *A Short History of the World*) confronts history with postmodern theories of representation to produce the most successful yet of his novels. Its ten chapters, each a tour de force, describe a succession of critical moments from our culture and history where nothing less is at stake than human survival itself. Noah's Ark from the point of view of a woodworm and then in subsequent searches for the historical record of Ararat; a semi-academic Barnes protagonist lecturing on a Mediterranean cruise but caught up in a terrorist hijack; a girl who may be inventing her story to protect herself from emotional trauma; Gericault's *Raft of the Medusa,* first imagined as history and then brilliantly analyzed as art, all lead up to a curiously empty achieved heaven at the end of survival's quest, in which Leicester City Football Club nauseatingly win the F.A. Cup year after year and a hearty breakfast is served every morning. Simultaneously playful and serious, yet packed with suggestive detail, the book presents a world that is imagined through the postmodern concept of ''fabulation,'' one in which everything is subtly related to everything else by metaphor and analogy rather than by causal succession, a world only comprehensible in terms of the ''primal metaphor'' of sea voyage and survival. Its lush parenthetical celebration of love—the half chapter at the core of the novel—links English poetry and postmodernism since, to return to Larkin's ''almost'' truth: ''what will survive of us is love.''

Talking It Over is an effortlessly structured sequence of monologues that tells of the love triangle of the three principal speakers: boring banker Stuart; unpredictable TEFL teacher Oliver; and the rather simple-minded social-work-trained picture restorer Gillian, who comes between them. At first Stuart's schoolboy friendship for Oliver is hardly threatened by his love for and marriage to Gillian but love soon triangulates and transfers and Stuart gets left out in the cold.

Though both men vigorously deny it, the male-bonding is obviously a powerful undercurrent, but love itself (''a system for getting someone to call you darling after sex,'' Stuart cynically concludes), the inevitability of repeated patterns, and the wonderful tendency of language (gestured at in the title) to turn something into something else are the smoothly handled themes. *Talking It Over,* Barnes's entry to the nineties, returns to a realistic idiom while deftly absorbing some well-documented trends in the sociology of contemporary love: frankly capitalistic and commercial metaphors; the intensification of romantic affection during a period when marital break-up is almost the norm; background details regarding telephone pornography and AIDS. It returns to many of the things Barnes has done successfully in the earlier novels and does them better still, though one wonders why he didn't have a go at writing it as a play.

The Porcupine, a novella, and Barnes's seventh work of fiction written under his own name, appeared in 1992 as a very timely response to the political upheavals that occurred in the former Eastern Bloc countries. Whilst Romania made the biggest headlines of the day, Barnes took Bulgaria as his subject and produced an economical yet convincing portrait of a society in the crisis of ideological revolution. Several aspects of *The Porcupine,* such as its meticulous descriptive pace, its Eastern European setting, its hints of Kafka, and the tenor of its concern with issues of gender as well as those of politics suggest a comparison with the work of his contemporary Ian McEwan. Again central, now politically crucial, is the attempt to evaluate competing claims to the truth in a postmodern cultural environment where all unitary claims are to be questioned. The two competing claims to truth in this situation are those of Stoyo Petkanov, the old party man and leader of the country for the past 33 years who now has to defend the whole of the past Communist regime and its ideals in the face of the new drive toward capitalism and its spokesman, the new Prosecutor General, Piotr Solinsky. Petkanov is the ready-made villain of the piece, but Barnes lets us in on his point of view, so that by the end of the trial we have warmed to him as a man of a certain kind of integrity and achievement. We are left in no doubt that, in the real world, politics is stronger than justice and that the best location for justice—poetic justice in its original sense—may lie in the balance and dialogue of the novel itself.

The next book to be published in 1995 was a collection of journalistic pieces Barnes had written as London correspondent of the *New Yorker,* where all of them originally appeared. Although the title *Letters from London: 1990–1995* seems a bit odd as the last letter dates from August 1994, the book, detailed, fresh, and often funny, is another masterpiece. Covering a variety of things his American metropolitan readership might find of interest regarding Britain—Thatcher's fall, the poll tax, the Rushdie affair, and the caprices of the Royal Family—Barnes manages never to bore his readers, even when focusing on abstruse matters like chess tournaments and maze-making or on half-forgotten scandals. The letters show Barnes—as in *The Porcupine*—to be a sensitive political writer, concerned with the state of Britain in times of a dawning change in power. For all its freshness, however, the book also reveals a gloomy—especially towards the end—and rather weary Barnes, deploying the image of the political clock being ''rehung on the wall at a completely different angle.''

If France—its locations, language, and literature—figures largely in most of Barnes's books, the 1996 short story collection *Cross Channel* is the monumentalization of the writer's love affair with Britain's continental next-door neighbor. All ten stories link Britain to France in some way, spanning the seventeenth century to the year 2015. Barnes is at his best here, exposing the respective and mutual stereotypes in a wonderfully ironic way. The major ''French'' topics that appear, from *amour fou* to the *Tour de France,* are pitted against very ''English'' characters—the self-righteously austere composer Leonard Verity in ''Interference,'' the frigidly lewd Uncle Freddy in ''Experiment,'' the late nineteenth century tourist-explorers Emily and Florence in ''Hermitage,'' and Barnes himself as ''an elderly Englishman'' of sixty-nine years in the concluding story ''Tunnel.'' In this last piece, which sees the narrator, traveling on the Eurostar in less than three hours from London to Paris, torn between nostalgia and self-directed cynicism, all these different views on the notoriously problem-riddled Anglo-French relationship are eventually linked together, as the elderly Englishman leaves ''the tunnel of memory,'' and ''when he returned home, began to write the stories you have just read.'' Perhaps this is Barnes's answer to the question that the protagonist in the Great War story ''Evermore'' poses and that pervades the whole collection: ''She wondered if there was such a thing as collective memory, something more than the sum of individual memories.''

In his most recent novel, *England, England,* Barnes returned to post-postmodernist territory, though not in terms of stylistic devices, but as far as the topic is concerned. The tycoon Sir Jack Pitman, as grotesque as powerful a character, mobilizes forces to realize his one last great idea: a transformation of the Isle of Wight into a quality tourist resort, gathering all the quintessences of England—that is, replacements and replica of Stonehenge and Bronte-country, a half-size Big Ben, Manchester United, and Robin Hood. ''The Project'' recycles the five-star sites of England's past as simulacra in the third millennium, following exclusively the logic of the market. Sir Jack's team is busy advertising ''England, England'''s quality leisure, searching for a logo or convincing the Royal Family to move to the Isle's replica of Buckingham Palace. The decline of ''Olde England'' into a place of yokeldom about to be forgotten by the world is the logical consequence of Barnes's dark satire. The book, however, is more interested in the effects the vast success of ''The Project'' has on human relationships. Martha Cochrane, the Appointed Cynic in Sir Jack's team and the protagonist proper of the novel, engages in a capital power struggle with her employer. In a world where the replica easily outmatches the original, Martha's search for real love remains futile. Yet the book ends on a note of melancholy, with Martha in the country formerly known as England, nostalgic for a past she has never known. *England, England* confirms once again Julian Barnes's status as one of Britain's top novelists, refined in style and controlled in structure. We can only look forward to his next delightful masterpiece.

—Richard Brown, updated by Tobias Wachinger

BARNHARDT, Wilton

Nationality: American. **Born:** Winston-Salem, North Carolina, 25 July 1960. **Education:** Michigan State University, B.A. 1982; Oxford University, M. Phil. 1989. **Agent:** Henry Durlow, Harold Ober and Associates, 425 Madison Avenue, New York, New York 10017, U.S.A. **Address:** c/o St. Martin's Press, Inc., 175 Fifth Avenue, New York, New York 10010, U.S.A.

PUBLICATIONS

Novels

Emma Who Saved My Life. New York, St. Martin's Press, 1989.
Gospel. New York, St. Martin's Press, 1993.
Show World: A Novel. New York, St. Martin's Press, 1998.

* * *

Wilton Barnhardt is an epochal novelist, targeting phases, periods, decades. In his first novel, *Emma Who Saved My Life*, Gil narrates his twenties-life through the 1970s (Barnhardt was born in 1960, so these historical backdrops are archival, not personal). There is a beginning chapter which grounds time present in Evanston, post-1984 (although Barnhardt stays well away from the resonances of that year) then successive chapters devoted to his New York years from 1974 through 1983. Gil fled college for New York, and an acting career. He moves in with Lisa, a girl he had a crush on in college, and her unusual friend Emma, whom he falls in love with as well.

This is a narrated book, with characters who are friends because they tell funny stories about themselves to each other. Gil's story is about trying to rise up through menial roles and depressing insights into the theatre world. We get a thorough review of Brooklyn life which is balanced between fun and depression. Gil eventually reaches a level of success which his friends credit, but he also realizes that he is not a great talent, which turns him back home.

Part of the novel's quality is its durable self-regulation. Gil finds himself pursued by a woman well beyond his usual company, who does everything thoroughly and stylishly. He doesn't understand her interest in him, but it doesn't destabilize him either. At a party she gives, he meets an old boyfriend of hers she has invited as well, who makes him see that his time is nearly up. In one of the most somber points in the book, Gil finds out from him that Connie has herpes. Gil doesn't pretend it doesn't hurt him, but he also tells us that it formalizes his nonsexual friendship with Emma.

Finally, Gil does not chew the curtains as he realizes he is only acting at acting. He takes one last look at New York with Emma, and concludes back in the present time of the book's composition, as he and his wife wait for their baby in Evanston.

One could not anticipate the gargantuan *Gospel* from anything Barnhardt had written, yet it too can be seen as a chronicle of an epoch, of the Gulf War period as the ''End Times'' prophesied by all the religions of Abraham. Lucy Dantan is a graduate student in theology at the University of Chicago. The chair of her department sends her to Oxford (there are no fellow faculty he would trust) to bring back Dr. O'Hanrahan, an emeritus faculty and former chair whose drinking and quixotic scholarship threatens the reputation of his department. O'Hanrahan is on the trail of the lost gospel of Matthias. Religious, political, and academic agents follow him (and her) to Oxford, County Antrim, Florence, Assisi, Rome, Puglia, Athens, Holy Mt. Athos, Piraeus, Jerusalem, Aswan, the Nile, Khartoum, Gonder, Addis Ababa, and The Promised Land (a PTL-type college-hospital-retirement village in Philadelphia, Louisiana). Each group chasing them seeks the lost gospel to change the world for the last time. Yet the individual scholars and learned theologians surrounded by vested interests are mostly full of concern and forgiveness for each other. Lucy and O'Hanrahan gradually come to trust in each other.

Beginning the novel, and interspersed within these chapters, are sections of the lost gospel, a homely and despairing account of his trial of faith the disciple Matthias (who replaced Judas) dictates to be sent to his brother Josephus.

A recurring narrative device of a divine voice speaking back to Lucy and O'Hanrahan's silent ruminations, which at times runs the danger of descending into the George Burns ''Oh God'' shtick, becomes impressive at the end. Although there are erudite footnotes to Matthias's gospel detailing the Church's rewriting of Sophia, the female principle of wisdom, into the (male) Holy Spirit, and the novel's dedication to Barnhardt's mother and two other female relatives at the beginning, it is not until the end of this long novel that we fully understand that it is Sophia (not the Father) whose voice they hear.

Show World, Barnhardt's latest novel, features the 1990s, when the economy has insured that those usually hired last will be first: Humanities majors are perfect for the worlds of Washington and Hollywood, where nothing is made, everything is public, hyped, shown. Samantha Flint escapes Missouri by going to Smith College, remaking herself. Her college roommate Mimi Mohr approves her skeptical understanding of public identities, and introduces her to the spectacle of Manhattan. Samantha follows her there after graduating, entering the world of public relations.

A contact she makes with a senator at a charity affair in New York gets too much publicity for her client, embarrassing her boss who sent her there in her place, but the senator makes her his legislative director after she has served on his staff a few years in Washington. When he announces his retirement, she realizes she can not give up the public power, and she signs on as legislative director for the man who wins his seat, a right-wing yahoo whose signature causes against homosexual rights and other liberal interests are compromised by his son's accidental death within an autoerotic cult at military school.

When her senator ignores her advice for a speech that could transcend his difficulties, she gives him over to the scandal press, which finishes her in Washington. She follows Mimi out to Hollywood, but her growing dependence on drugs matches the destructive and suicidal culture of Hollywood agency culture. She marries a client of Mimi's as a cover for his homosexuality, but she cares as little for him as anyone else. When her husband dies in a homosexual orgy in a Las Vegas hotel, she becomes the hunted victim of the public attention she has managed throughout her life, and her body finally detonates under the conflicting effects of the drugs she uses. Before it chronicles Samantha's life beginning at Smith in 1978, the novel began with a note from Samantha to Mimi dated 1998, mailing her the file of everything she has ever written, and it effectively closes with an essay dated 1978, which she decided not to present to her college writing class as too self-revelatory: a pastoral afternoon playing as hard as she can with her rural cousins, holding hands.

—William Johnsen

BARRETT, Andrea

Nationality: American. **Born:** 16 November 1954. **Education:** Union College, Schenectady, New York, 1974, B.S. in Biology. **Career:** Faculty, Northlight Writers' Conference, Moorhead, Minnesota, 1988–89, and Mount Holyoke Writers' Conference, 1991–93;

senior fiction fellow, New York State Summer Writers' Institute, Skidmore College, 1993; faculty, Warren Wilson MFA Program for Writers, 1993–98, 2000; faculty, Yellow Bay Writers' Workshop, University of Montana, 1995, Bread Loaf Writers' Conference, 1996–97, 1999, and Napa Valley Writers' Conference, 1996; adjunct lecturer, University of Michigan, 1995. Visiting writer, Saint Mary's College, California, 1998, and University of Virginia, 1999. **Awards:** National Endowment for the Arts fellowship, 1992; Peden prize for best short fiction, Missouri Review, 1995; Distinguished Story citation, *Best American Short Stories*, 1995; fiction prize, The Southern Review, 1996, Los Angeles Times Book Prize, finalist, 1996, and National Book Award, 1996, all for *Ship Fever and Other Stories;* Pushcart prize, 1997, for ''The Forest''; Guggenheim fellowship, 1997; Salon Magazine book award, 1998, American Library Association Notable Book, 1999, and Lillian Fairchild award, 1999, all for *The Voyage of Narwhal.* **Agent:** c/o Wendy Weil Literary Agency, 232 Madison Avenue, Suite 1300, New York, New York 10016 USA. **Address:** 243 Berkeley Street, Rochester, New York 14607, USA.

Publications

Novels

Lucid Stars. New York, Delta/Delacorte Press, 1988.
Secret Harmonies. New York, Delacorte Press, 1989.
The Middle Kingdom. New York, Pocket Books, 1991.
The Forms of Water. New York, Pocket Books, 1993.
The Voyage of the Narwhal. New York, W. W. Norton, 1998.

Short Stories

Ship Fever and Other Stories. New York, W. W. Norton, 1996.

Uncollected Short Stories

''Secret Harmonies,'' in *Northwest Review* (Eugene, Oregon), vol. 23, no. 3, 1985.
''Animal Magic,'' in *Prairie Schooner* (Lincoln, Nebraska), vol. 61, no. 1, 1987.
''Here at the Starlight Motel,'' in *Michigan Quarterly Review* (Ann Arbor), vol. 26, no. 4, 1987.
''Escaped Alone to Tell,'' in *Willow Springs* (Cheney, Washington), no. 24, 1989.
''The Seducer,'' in *Mademoiselle* (New York), October 1989.
''The Church of New Reason,'' in *American Short Fiction* (Austin, Texas), no. 1, 1991; reprinted in *American Voices: Best Short Fiction by Contemporary Authors,* selected by Sally Arteseros, New York, Hyperion, 1992.
''The Forms of Water,'' in *American Short Fiction* (Austin, Texas), no. 6, 1992.
''The Littoral Zone,'' in *Story* (Cincinnati, Ohio), Spring 1993; reprinted in *The Norton Anthology of Short Fiction,* edited by R.V. Cassill and Richard Bausch, 6th edition, New York, W. W. Norton, 2000.
''Out Here,'' in *American Short Fiction* (Austin, Texas), no. 12, Winter 1993.
''The English Pupil,'' in *Southern Review* (Baton Rouge, Louisiana), January 1994; reprinted in *The Second Penguin Book of Modern Women's Short Stories,* London, Viking, 1997.
''The Behavior of the Hawkseeds,'' in *Missouri Review* (Columbia), vol. XVII, no. 1, 1994; reprinted in *The Best American Short Stories, 1995,* edited by Jane Smiley, Boston, Houghton Mifflin, 1995.
''Agnes at Night,'' in *Story* (Cincinnati, Ohio), Fall 1994.
''The Marburg Sisters,'' in *New England Review* (Middlebury, Vermont), Fall 1994.
''Rare Bird,'' in *The Writing Path 1: Poetry and Prose from Writers' Conferences,* edited by Michael Pettit, University of Iowa Press, 1995.
''Soroche,'' in *Story* (Cincinnati, Ohio), Autumn 1995.
''The Mysteries of Ubiquitin,'' in *Story* (Cincinnati, Ohio), Summer 1996.
''The Forest,'' in *Ploughshares* (Boston, Massachusetts), Winter 1996; reprinted in *The 1998 Pushcart Prize XXII: Best of the Small Presses, an Annual Small Press Reader,* Wainscott, New York, Pushcart Press, 1997.
''Blue Dress,'' in *I've Always Meant to Tell You: Letters to Our Mothers,* edited by Constance Warloe, New York, Pocket Books, 1997.
''Breathing Under Ice,'' in *Outside,* October 1998.
''Theories of Rain,'' in *Southern Review* (Baton Rouge, Lousiana), Summer 1999.
''The Door,'' in *Story* (Cincinnati, Ohio), Autumn 1999.
''Servants of the Map,'' in *Salmagundi* (Saratoga Springs, New York), Fall 1999–Winter 2000.
''Why We Go,'' in *New York Times Magazine,* 6 June 1999.

Other

Introduction, *The Widow's Children* by Paula Fox. New York, W. W. Norton, 1999.
Introduction, ''Paula's Case'' by Willa Cather, in *The Norton Anthology of Short Fiction,* edited by R.V. Cassill and Richard Bausch, 6th edition, New York, W. W. Norton, 2000.
Introduction, *Weird and Tragic Shores: The Story of Charles Francis Hall, Explorer* by Chauncy Loomis, New York, Modern Library, 2000.

* * *

Andrea Barrett writes highly researched literary fictions that explore human character and relationships through the language and lens of science. Her work has been critically acclaimed and, with her fifth and sixth publications, popularly successful. Her works have progressed from close-in, intimate portraits of modern-day American families to stories that encompass a wider scope in history, geography, and theme. In *Lucid Stars* and *Secret Harmonies* Barrett focused on the struggles and quest for selfhood of young female characters within the contexts of dysfunctional families. With *The Middle Kingdom* and *The Forms of Water* she moved out to engage other characters and places, while continuing to examine and illuminate the relationships of individuals to one another, to the world, and to themselves with notable intelligence and depth. Barrett's next work, the collection of stories entitled *Ship Fever*, moved her character-driven writing into a more complex realm of history and science, a journey that the novel *The Voyage of the Narwhal* continued.

Voyage of the Narwhal, in telling the story of a nineteenth century sailing expedition to the Arctic and its consequences, recasts classical adventure narrative through the experiences of characters not generally heard from in such texts. Barrett unfolds the journey through the eyes of several characters, but chiefly those of Erasmus Darwin Wells, a reticent, disappointed naturalist, and Alexandra, a woman of scientific mind who longs to go on an expedition but remains at home in Philadelphia as companion to Erasmus's sister. The journey is as much into the complicated landscapes of human ambition, desire, and regret as it is into the expanse and detail of the harsh, beautiful environment of the Arctic, life aboard ship, and life as a woman in the mid-nineteenth century. Erasmus and Alexandra are both of a scholarly mind, interested in understanding how life, in the articulation of living flora and fauna, works; they are, like many of Barrett's characters, people who name and order the world in order to illuminate and know it. In opposition to Erasmus is the leader of the expedition, a young man who, in his lack of will to see or understand anything but his own ambition—in which he resembles the traditional protagonists of classical adventure narratives—cuts a course that leaves loss and death in its wake.

Though Barrett expresses surprise that people view *Voyage of the Narwhal* as an adventure tale, she does admit that she sees both science and writing as a sort of adventure, and physical exploration as an excellent metaphor for both. She is fascinated with the history of science, its language and way of viewing the world, and this is reflected in all her work, though nowhere so keenly and successfully as in *Voyage of the Narwhal* and the short stories in *Ship Fever*, each a thoughtful meditation on science and scientists, whether historic or contemporary.

This preoccupation, not yet fully realized, is nevertheless evident in her earlier works. A tradition of astronomy, of naming the stars, and charting and exploring the heavens as a means of charting one's life, is handed on from one generation to the next and one side of a broken family to the other by the women in *Lucid Stars*. The language of music, of composers, and of secret musical codes is the thread that weaves together the characters in *Secret Harmonies*. It is science that brings together the protagonist of *The Middle Kingdom* and her husband and brings them to China, and it is science and medicine that in part bring her together with Dr. Yu, the Chinese woman who helps her turn her life around.

The influence of scientists like Charles Darwin and Gregor Mendel, of nineteenth-century scientific journals and naturalists' texts, is evident not only in Barrett's themes and characters but in the thoroughgoing research and meticulous observation of detail in her writing. This meticulousness, which is so potent in *Voyage*, on occasion makes her earlier novels seem too slow and fails to provide a sense of meaningful result or insight, rather like a failed experiment. It is in the turn to scientists, naturalists, and people consumed by theories and phenomenon of the observable world as her protagonists that Barrett's work gains its most rewarding power and intensity.

Examining Barrett's short stories in connection to *Voyage of the Narwhal* reveals further nuances of her preoccupation with the themes of science and imagination with regard to what might be termed the chemistry of self as her particular field of inquiry. In "Theories of Rain" a girl raised by two women who write science texts for children correlates the phenomena of mist, rain, meteor showers, and various relationships and behaviors of the scientific men in her life as though she is reading barometric pressures in order to form an understanding of her life. In "The English Pupil" the Swedish naturalist Carolus Linnaeus, who developed modern taxonomy, loses the names and order of his own life as the chemistry of his brain loses cohesion. In "Rare Bird" the character of Sarah Anne Billopp, an ornithologist who sets out to refute a theory of Linnaeus's, foreshadows the character of Alexandra in *Voyage of the Narwhal* in that she, too, in following her mind's passion, breaks from the traditional female role she had been occupying.

Barrett is a writer of unfailing intelligence and integrity with a knack for getting inside her characters' minds and emotions. Her earlier work, focusing largely on the struggles of women to find their place in life, is at times uneven, but she has secured a place for herself in literature with works that bring together science and imagination with history and character in insightful, rewarding narratives. Her writing is marked by a clear prose and authoritative detail. Her language articulates theories of self and human relations in which the desire to realize order out of chaos, to name and understand life, emotions, and the world around them makes her characters very human indeed.

—Jessica Reisman

BARSTOW, Stan(ley)

Nationality: British. **Born:** Horbury, Yorkshire, 28 June 1928. **Education:** Ossett Grammar School. **Family:** Married Constance Mary Kershaw in 1951; one son and one daughter. **Career:** Draftsman and sales executive in the engineering industry, 1944–62. Lives in Hawath, West Yorkshire. **Awards:** Writers Guild award, 1974; Royal Television Society award, 1975. M.A.: Open University, Milton Keynes, Buckinghamshire, 1982. Honorary Fellow, Bretton Hall College, Wakefield Yorkshire, 1985. **Agent:** Lemon Unna and Durbridge Ltd., 24 Pottery Lane, London W11 4LZ, England.

PUBLICATIONS

Novels

A Kind of Loving: The Vic Brown Trilogy. London, Joseph, 1981.
- *A Kind of Loving.* London, Joseph, 1960; New York, Doubleday, 1961.
- *The Watchers on the Shore.* London, Joseph, 1966; New York, Doubleday, 1967.
- *The Right True End.* London, Joseph, 1976.

Ask Me Tomorrow. London, Joseph, 1962.
Joby. London, Joseph, 1964.
A Raging Calm. London, Joseph, 1968; as *The Hidden Part,* New York, Coward McCann, 1969.
A Brother's Tale. London, Joseph, 1980.
Just You Wait and See. London, Joseph, 1986.
B-movie. London, Joseph, 1987.
Give Us This Day. London, Joseph, 1989.
Next of Kin. London and New York, Joseph, 1991.

Short Stories

The Desperadoes. London, Joseph, 1961.
The Human Element and Other Stories, edited by Marilyn Davies. London, Longman, 1969.
A Season with Eros. London, Joseph, 1971.

A Casual Acquaintance and Other Stories, edited by Marilyn Davies. London, Longman, 1976.
The Glad Eye and Other Stories. London, Joseph, 1984.

Plays

Ask Me Tomorrow, with Alfred Bradley, adaptation of the novel by Barstow (produced Sheffield, 1964). London, French, 1966.
A Kind of Loving, with Alfred Bradley, adaptation of the novel by Barstow (broadcast 1964; produced Sheffield, 1965). London, Blackie, 1970.
An Enemy of the People, adaptation of a play by Ibsen (produced Harrogate, Yorkshire, 1969). London, Calder, 1977.
Listen for the Trains, Love, music by Alex Glasgow (produced Sheffield, 1970).
Stringer's Last Stand, with Alfred Bradley (produced York, 1971).
We Could Always Fit a Sidecar (broadcast 1974). Published in *Out of the Air: Five Plays for Radio,* edited by Alfred Bradley, London, Blackie, 1977.
Joby, adaptation of his own novel (televised 1975). London, Blackie, 1977.
The Human Element, and Albert's Part (televised 1977). London, Blackie, 1984.

Radio Plays: *A Kind of Loving,* from his own novel, 1964; *The Desperadoes,* from his own story, 1965; *The Watchers on the Shore,* from his own novel, 1971; *We Could Always Fit a Sidecar,* 1974; *The Right True End,* from his own novel, 1978; *The Apples of Paradise,* 1988; *Foreign Parts,* 1990.

Television Plays: *The Human Element,* 1964; *The Pity of It All,* 1965; *A World Inside* (documentary), with John Gibson, 1966; *A Family at War* (1 episode), 1970; *Mind You, I Live Here* (documentary), with John Gibson, 1971; *A Raging Calm,* from his own novel, 1974; *South Riding,* from the novel by Winifred Holtby, 1974; *Joby,* from his own novel, 1975; *The Cost of Loving,* 1977; *The Human Element,* 1977; *Albert's Part,* 1977; *Travellers,* 1978; *A Kind of Loving,* from his own novels, 1981; *A Brother's Tale,* from his own novel, 1983; *The Man Who Cried,* from the novel by Catherine Cookson, 1993.

Other

Editor, *Through the Green Woods: An Anthology of Contemporary Writing about Youth and Children.* Leeds, E.J. Arnold, 1968.

*

Stan Barstow comments:

Came to prominence about the same time as several other novelists from North of England working-class backgrounds, viz. John Braine, Alan Sillitoe, David Storey, Keith Waterhouse, and saw with satisfaction, and occasional irritation, the gains made in the opening up of the regions and the ''elevation'' of the people into fit subjects for fictional portrayal absorbed into the popular cultures of the cinema and TV drama series and comedy shows. Still, living in the provinces and using mainly regional settings, consider myself non-metropolitan oriented. The publication of some of my work in the U.S. and its translation into several European languages reassures me that I have not resisted the neurotic trendiness of much metropolitan culture for the sake of mere provincial narrowness; and the knowledge that some of the finest novels in the language are ''regional'' leads me to the belief that to hoe one's own row diligently, thus seeking out the universal in the particular, brings more worthwhile satisfactions than the frantic pursuit of a largely phony jet-age internationalism.

(1995) As I review this comment in 1995, reading flourishes, yet the mainstream literary novel has a harder time than ever in the world of the ''celebrity'' novel, where fortunes are regularly made by doing badly what others have spent their working lives trying to do well.

* * *

It is never easy for the author of a best-selling first novel to come to terms with its success. All too often, publishers demand a sequel, or at the very least another novel written in the same vein, in an attempt to recreate the formula. Stan Barstow is one of the few novelists who has managed to keep intact the mold of their first success and then to have built upon it. Following the appearance of *A Kind of Loving* in 1960, he created a trilogy around Vic Brown, the driven central character who finds himself struggling against the odds in a tough and no-nonsense world. Written at the tail-end of the 1950s, when Britain was entering its first sustained period of postwar prosperity, it is very much a novel of its times. It also reflected a sense of proletarian evangelism: it was as if Barstow was desperate to write about real lives and real events, things normally ignored by the literary world at the time. Although the background was supplied by the potentially grim northern town of Cressley, this was not a joyless fortress but a living place whose inhabitants had created a close-knit community. In many ways too, Cressley was a metaphor for what was happening at the time, as its population seemed to be unaware of the shift that was slowly eroding their existences. Vic is told this in terms that could be said to be prophetic: ''But we're all living in a fool's paradise, that all. A fool's paradise, Vic. Full employment and business booming? It just isn't possible, lad. Don't say I didn't warn you when the crash comes.''

Barstow's ability to grasp the moment and record it in fictional terms is typical of the way in which he attacks a novel. Tom Simpkins, caught up in a love affair in *A Raging Calm,* is aware of the possibilities that lie outside his own existence and wants to enjoy them but is also painfully aware of the inhibitions that have helped to shape his life and to give meaning to his sense of morality. (Here it is worth acknowledging that Barstow is particularly responsive to all the complexities for romantic and physical love and does not shirk from attempting to understand the motives for adultery, broken affairs, divorce and unhappiness.) With his ability to allow the narrative to unfold through the development of his main characters, it is little wonder that *A Raging Calm* was later transformed into an equally successful television play.

That Barstow was content to remain within the confines of a world which he knew best—the West Riding of Yorkshire—and with characters whom he understood—the working class of northern England—has been made abundantly clear by his later output. His trilogy of novels about the Palmer family during World War II is a good example—*Just You Wait and See, Give Us This Day,* and *Next of Kin.* The setting of the small Yorkshire town of Daker, another close-knit community of millhands and colliers, is a resonant background for a wide range of ordinary people who find themselves caught up, willy-nilly, in the maelstrom of war. By far the most notable of these is Ella, a mature 23-year-old who comes to prominence in *Give Us This Day*—the anxieties and hardships she has to face give the meaning to the book's title. A young war bride, she discovers that marriage means having to cope with the absence of her husband Walter as she struggles to make a home which they can enjoy once the war is over. Without ever descending into sentimentality, Barstow carefully recreates the tender embarrassment that invades their lives when they meet, and one of the novel's highlights is a firmly constructed set-piece scene in which Walter comes home on leave and the young couple have to rediscover one another all over again.

Mature and single-minded beyond her years, Ella is the still presence at the novel's center, and around her the other characters act almost like a chorus to record the desperate events of a world—their world, in the town of Daker—that has been plunged into war. One of the most memorable moments in the novel is Barstow's description of a mass air-raid on Sheffield that Ella and her mother witness from a train. ''None of the pain and loss in her life had prepared her for the vast faceless malice of last night; for sitting in that train while the sky lit up, the bombs fell, the ground shook beneath her. And all the time, behind, in the middle of it, people they knew, whom they had only just left behind.''

In its successor, *Next of Kin*, an older Ella has to struggle even harder to preserve her independence and to adjust to the privations of being a war widow. Although she revives a relationship with a former lover, Howard Strickland, he remains a shadowy figure who only brings new pressures into her life. As in the previous two novels, a key feature is Barstow's unerring ability to bring alive the atmosphere of life in a northern provincial town. A born storyteller, Barstow also underscores all his writing with a genuine love for the characters he has created.

B-movie finds Barstow breaking new ground with a short novel written in the manner of a 1950s crime thriller. Opening with the murder and robbery of a pawnbroker in a Northern town, it shifts focus to the two leading characters, young men on holiday in Blackpool. As the two friends form relationships with local girls and news filters through of the murder in their home town, the tension rises and events move to a shocking conclusion. The fact that most readers would recognize the murderer at an early stage does not in any way detract from the power of the plot, core of which is the changed relationship between close friends who are suddenly revealed as strangers, and the life-and-death decisions that are forced upon them.

B-movie, like the Palmer trilogy, is an excellent example of its form, but in both works Barstow transcends genres to produce something of his own. His writing refuses to fit into pigeon-holes, remaining what it has always been, tough and honest and true to itself.

—Trevor Royle, updated by Geoff Sadler

BARTH, John (Simmons)

Nationality: American. **Born:** Cambridge, Maryland, 27 May 1930. **Education:** The Juilliard School of Music, New York; Johns Hopkins University, Baltimore, A.B. 1951, M.A. 1952. **Family:** Married 1) Ann Strickland in 1950 (divorced 1969), one daughter and two sons; 2) Shelly Rosenberg in 1970. **Career:** Junior instructor in English, Johns Hopkins University, 1951–53; instructor, 1953–56, assistant professor, 1957–60, and associate professor of English, 1960–65, Pennsylvania State University, University Park; professor of English, 1965–71, and Butler Professor, 1971–73, State University of New York, Buffalo; Centennial Professor of English and Creative Writing, Johns Hopkins University, 1973–91, professor emeritus, 1991—. **Awards:** Brandeis University Creative Arts award, 1965; Rockefeller grant, 1965; American Academy grant, 1966; National Book award, 1973. Litt. D.: University of Maryland, College Park, 1969; F. Scott Fitzgerald Award, 1997; PEN/Malamud Award, 1998; Lannan Literary Awards lifetime achievement award, 1998. **Member:** American Academy, 1977, and American Academy of Arts and Sciences, 1977. **Agent:** Wylie Aitken and Stone, 250 West 57th Street, New York, New York 10107. **Address:** c/o Writing Seminars, Johns Hopkins University, Baltimore, Maryland 21218, U.S.A.

Publications

Novels

The Floating Opera. New York, Appleton Century Crofts, 1956; revised edition, New York, Doubleday, 1967; London, Secker and Warburg, 1968.

The End of the Road. New York, Doubleday, 1958; London, Secker and Warburg, 1962; revised edition, Doubleday, 1967.

The Sot-Weed Factor. New York, Doubleday, 1960; London, Secker and Warburg, 1961; revised edition, Doubleday, 1967.

Giles Goat-Boy; or, The Revised New Syllabus. New York, Doubleday, 1966; London, Secker and Warburg, 1967.

Letters. New York, Putnam, 1979; London, Secker and Warburg, 1980.

Sabbatical: A Romance. New York, Putnam, and London, Secker and Warburg, 1982.

The Tidewater Tales: A Novel. New York, Putnam, 1987; London, Methuen, 1988.

The Last Voyage of Somebody the Sailor. Boston, Little Brown, 1991.

Once Upon a Time: A Floating Opera. Boston, Little Brown, 1994.

Short Stories

Lost in the Funhouse: Fiction for Print, Tape, Live Voice. New York, Doubleday, 1968; London, Secker and Warburg, 1969.

Chimera. New York, Random House, 1972; London, Deutsch, 1974.

Todd Andrews to the Author. Northridge, California, Lord John Press, 1979.

On with the Story: Stories. Boston, Little, Brown, 1996.

Other

The Literature of Exhaustion, and The Literature of Replenishment (essays). Northridge, California, Lord John Press, 1982.

The Friday Book: Essays and Other Nonfiction. New York, Putnam, 1984.

Don't Count on It: A Note on the Number of the 1001 Nights. Northridge, California, Lord John Press, 1984.

Further Fridays: Essays, Lectures, and Other Nonfiction, 1984–1994. Boston, Little Brown, 1995.

Contributor, *Innovations: An Anthology of Modern and Contemporary Fiction*, edited by Robert L. McLaughlin. Normal, Illinois, Dalkey Archive Press, 1998.

Introduction, *Not-Knowing: The Essays and Interviews of Donald Barthelme* by Kim Herzinger. New York, Random House, 1997.

*

Bibliography: *John Barth: A Descriptive Primary and Annotated Secondary Bibliography* by Josephy Weixlmann, New York, Garland, 1976; *John Barth: An Annotated Bibliography* by Richard Allan Vine, Metuchen, New Jersey, Scarecrow Press, 1977; *John Barth, Jerzy Kosinski, and Thomas Pynchon: A Reference Guide* by Thomas P. Walsh and Cameron Northouse, Boston, Hall, 1977.

Manuscript Collection: Library of Congress, Washington, D.C.

Critical Studies: *John Barth* by Gerhard Joseph, Minneapolis, University of Minnesota Press, 1970; *John Barth: The Comic Sublimity of Paradox* by Jac Tharpe, Carbondale, Southern Illinois University Press, 1974; *The Literature of Exhaustion: Borges, Nabokov, and Barth* by John O. Stark, Durham, North Carolina, Duke University Press, 1974; *John Barth: An Introduction* by David Morrell, University Park, Pennsylvania State University Press, 1976; *Critical Essays on John Barth* edited by Joseph J. Waldmeir, Boston, Hall, 1980; *Passionate Virtuosity: The Fiction of John Barth* by Charles B. Harris, Urbana, University of Illinois Press, 1983; *John Barth* by Heide Ziegler, London, Methuen, 1987; *Understanding John Barth* by Stan Fogel and Gordon Slethaug, Columbia, University of South Carolina Press, 1990; *A Reader's Guide to John Barth* by Zack Bowen, Westport, Connecticut, Greenwood Press, 1994; *John Barth and the Anxiety of Continuance* by Patricia Tobin. Philadelphia, University of Pennsylvania Press, 1992; *Death in the Funhouse: John Barth and the Poststructuralist Aesthetics* by Alan Lindsay, New York, P. Lang, 1995; *Transcending Space: Architectural Places in Works by Henry David Thoreau, E.E. Cummings, and John Barth* by Taimi Olsen, Lewisburg, Pennsylvania, Bucknell University Press, 2000.

* * *

John Barth is often called one of the most important American novelists of the twentieth century. He combines the kind of experimentation associated with postmodernist writing with a mastery of the skills demanded of the traditional novelist. A progression toward postmodernism may be traced in his works from the more traditional treatments of his earlier books—*The Floating Opera*, *The End of the Road*, and *The Sot-Weed Factor*—to the wild experimentation that characterizes such works as *Giles Goat-Boy*, *Chimera*, *Letters*, and especially *Lost in the Funhouse*. In *Sabbatical*, he returns to the more traditional kind of narrative, with the added postmodernist twist that the novel itself is supposed to be the work produced by the two central characters in it. In *The Tidewater Tales*, too, the novel is supposed to be the work of one of the central characters. In fact, *The Tidewater Tales* combines many of the elements of postmodern fiction, including an awareness of itself as fiction, with the strong story line associated with more traditional novels. Barth's works after *Tidewater Tales*—*The Last Voyage of Somebody the Sailor* and *Once Upon a Time*—also involve many elements of postmodernist fiction, especially *Once Upon a Time*, in which the narrator constantly reminds the reader that the work is a piece of fiction.

Although Barth denies that he engages in experimentation for its own sake, the stories in *Lost in the Funhouse* give that appearance. Subtitled *Fiction for Print, Tape, Live Voice,* the work marks Barth's embrace of the world of the postmodern in which fiction and reality, and fictitious characters and the authors that produce them, become indistinguishable and in which consistent suspension of disbelief becomes almost impossible. Barth's insistence that some of the stories in this "series," as he calls it, were not composed "expressly for print" and thus "make no sense unless heard in live or recorded voices" is questionable, since they are in print and presumably the author did compose them in written form. Nonetheless, they show Barth's versatility with various fictional forms. Still, even if Barth really intended a story like "Echo," the eighth in the series, only for live or recorded voice, it is difficult to determine whether it is profound or merely full of gimmickry.

Barth calls *Letters* "an old time epistolary novel," yet it is anything but old-fashioned. In this monumental work, the author himself becomes a fictitious character with whom his "fictitious drolls and dreamers," many of whom are drawn from Barth's earlier works, correspond concerning their often funny yet sometimes horrifying problems. The letters they exchange gradually reveal the convoluted plot that involves abduction, possible incest, and suicide. That postmodernism may have reached a dead end in this book is something Barth himself seems to have recognized with his return to a more traditional form in *Sabbatical*, a novel with an easily summarizable plot involving clearly defined characters. *The Tidewater Tales*, too, has a very strong story line, yet like *Letters*, it has some characters familiar from other works by Barth, including the "real" authors of *Sabbatical*. It also includes a thinly disguised version of Barth himself, called Djean, familiar from *Chimera*, as well as many characters from other pieces of literature, including Ulysses and Nausicaa (also known as the Dmitrikakises), Don Quixote (called Donald Quicksoat), and Scheherazade, who is more closely modeled on the Scheherazade of Barth's *Chimera* than on the heroine of the *Arabian Nights*.

Along with Barth's movement from modernism to postmodernism may be traced a movement from what he calls "the literature of exhaustion" to what he calls "the literature of replenishment." The antiheroes of his earlier works—Todd Andrews, Jake Horner, and Ebenezer Cooke—give way to the genuinely heroic protagonist of *Giles Goat-Boy*, a book of epic dimensions containing a central figure and plot modeled largely on myths of various heroes, both pagan and Christian. This work may prove to be one of the most important pieces of literature of the twentieth century. The central character, Giles himself, may be lacking a human father (quite probably he was fathered by the computer that controls the world of the novel). As the book unfolds, he proceeds without hesitation to fulfill his typically heroic destiny to "*Pass All Fail All.*" Whatever victories he achieves are, of course, ambiguous, and his existence is left in doubt.

The part of the book involving the actual narrative of events in the life of George Giles is entitled "*R. N. S. The Revised New Syllabus of George Giles OUR GRAND TUTOR* Being the Autobiographical and Hortatory Tapes Read Out at New Tammany College to His Son *Giles (,) Stoker* By the West Campus Automatic Computer and by Him Prepared for the Furtherment of the Gilesian Curriculum." It contains a kind of comic, cosmic new testament, a collection of sacred-profane writings designed to guide future students in the university world in which the body of the novel is set. Narrating the life and adventures of George Giles, the goat-boy of the title, it recounts his intellectual, political, and sexual exploits. The introductory material to the ''Revised New Syllabus,'' consisting of a ''Publisher's Disclaimer,'' with notes from Editors A through D and written by ''The Editor-in-Chief''; the ''Cover-Letter to the Editors and Publisher,'' written by ''This regenerate Seeker after Answers, J. B.''; the ''Posttape'' as well as the ''Postscript to the Posttape,'' again written by J. B.; and the ''Footnote to the Postscript,'' written by ''Ed.,'' are all part of this fiction.

From the paralysis of a Jacob Horner in *The End of the Road* to the action of a Giles is a long stride. Horner is paralyzed, he claims, because he suffers from ''cosmopsis,'' ''the cosmic view'' in which ''one is frozen like the bullfrog when the hunter's light strikes him full in the eyes, only with cosmopsis there is no hunter, and no quick hand to terminate the moment—there's only the light.'' An infinite number of possibilities leads to a paralyzing inability to choose any one. The same kind of cosmic view, however, causes no problem for George Giles, who, when unable to choose between existing possibilities, unhesitatingly creates his own, as he does when he first leaves the barn to seek his destiny in the outside world. Heroically, George realizes that he ''had invented myself as I'd elected my name,'' and he accepts responsibility not only for himself but also for his world.

In *Sabbatical* and *The Tidewater Tales*, Barth draws heavily on the folklore of the Chesapeake Bay and the CIA. In the former, he writes of the end of a year-long sailing voyage taken by Fenwick, an ex-CIA agent, and Susan, a college professor, in order to decide what they will do with their lives. Their problem's resolution seems trite and unconvincing, but their path toward that resolution is interesting. Like *Chimera*, *Sabbatical* is a twentieth-century fairy tale, ending with the statement that the two central characters ''lived/Happily after, to the end/Of Fenwick and Susie. . . .*'' The rhyme is completed in the footnote: ''*Susan./Fenn.'' Obviously, in this work too it is often difficult to distinguish gimmickry and profundity. Sentimentality also pervades *The Tidewater Tales*, essentially the story of the ending of Peter Sagamore's writing block, as he and his pregnant wife travel the Chesapeake Bay on their sailboat named *Story.*

The Last Voyage of Somebody the Sailor is set partially and *Once Upon a Time* is set mostly on the Chesapeake Bay. Both are pieces of fantasy, the former loosely structured on the seven voyages of Sinbad the Sailor as told by Scheherazade in *1001 Arabian Nights.* Both are also structured, Barth claims in *Once Upon a Time*, on the hero quest, which he calls the Ur-myth. In fact, in *Once Upon a Time*, the narrator, who may also be the author, says that all of his works since *The Sot-Weed Factor* are variations on the Ur-myth, even though he claims not to have known about the myth when he wrote *The Sot-Weed Factor*.

Both *The Last Voyage of Somebody the Sailor* and *Once Upon a Time* draw largely on the author's life, so much so that the latter repeats many things from the former. The latter pretends to be autobiography masquerading as fiction, but it may be fiction masquerading as autobiography. At any rate, it recounts what its narrator claims both is and is not Barth's early life, his education, his two marriages, his teaching career, and the writing of his books and stories.

Barth then is one of the most important figures in twentieth-century American literature. He has consistently been at the forefront of literary experimentation, consequently producing works occasionally uneven and, as a result of his particular type of experimentation, occasionally too self-consciously witty. Still, he has produced some works that are now ranked and probably will continue to be ranked among the best of this century.

—Richard Tuerk

BARTHELME, Frederick

Nationality: American. **Born:** Houston, Texas, 10 October 1943; brother of the writer Donald Barthelme. **Education:** Tulane University, New Orleans, 1961–62; University of Houston, 1962–65, 1966–67; Johns Hopkins University, Baltimore (teaching fellow; Coleman Prose award, 1977), 1976–77, M.A. 1977. **Career:** Architectural draftsman, Jerome Oddo and Associates, and Kenneth E. Bentsen Associates, both Houston, 1965–66; exhibition organizer, St. Thomas University, Houston, 1966–67; assistant to director, Kornblee Gallery, New York, 1967–68; creative director, BMA Advertising, Houston, 1971–73; senior writer, GDL & W Advertising, Houston, 1973–76. Since 1977 professor of English, director of the Center for Writers, and editor of *Mississippi Review,* University of Southern Mississippi, Hattiesburg. Visual artist: exhibitions at galleries in Houston, Norman, Oklahoma, New York, Seattle, Vancouver, Buenos Aires, and Oberlin, Ohio, 1965–74. **Awards:** National Endowment for the Arts fellowship, 1979; University of Southern Mississippi research grant, 1980. **Address:** Box 5144, Hattiesburg, Mississippi 39406, U.S.A.

Publications

Novels

War and War. New York, Doubleday, 1971.
Second Marriage. New York, Simon and Schuster, 1984; London, Dent, 1985.
Tracer. New York, Simon and Schuster, 1985; London, Dent, 1986.
Two Against One. New York, Weidenfeld and Nicolson, 1988; London, Viking, 1989.
Natural Selection. New York, Viking, 1990.
The Brothers. New York, Viking, 1993.
Painted Desert. New York, Viking, 1995.
Bob the Gambler. Boston, Houghton Mifflin, 1997.

Short Stories

Rangoon. New York, Winter House, 1970.
Moon Deluxe. New York, Simon and Schuster, 1983; London, Penguin, 1984.
Chroma and Other Stories. New York, Simon and Schuster, 1987; London, Penguin, 1989.

Uncollected Short Stories

''Cooker,'' in *New Yorker,* 10 August 1987.
''Law of Averages,'' in *New Yorker,* 5 October 1987.
''Shopgirls,'' in *Esquire* (Japanese edition, Tokyo), August 1988.
''War with Japan,'' in *New Yorker,* 12 December 1988.
''Driver,'' in *New American Short Stories 2,* edited by Gloria Norris. New York, New American Library, 1989.

"With Ray and Judy," in *New Yorker,* 24 April 1989.
"Domestic," in *Fiction of the Eighties,* edited by Gibbons and Hahn, Chicago, *TriQuarterly,* 1990.
"The Philosophers," in *Boston Globe Magazine,* 22 July 1990.
"Margaret and Bud," in *New Yorker,* 15 May 1991.
"Jackpot," in *Frank Magazine,* 1992.
"Retreat," in *Epoch,* 1993.

Other

Trip (text), photographs by Susan Lipper. New York, Powerhouse, 1999.
Double Down: Reflections on Gambling and Loss (with Steven Barthelme). Boston, Houghton Mifflin, 1999.

* * *

Frederick Barthelme's early fiction—*Rangoon* and *War and War*—is self-consciously experimental, overly influenced (and greatly overshadowed) by the far more successful work of writers such as his older brother Donald. It was not until more than a decade later, in the 17 stories that comprise *Moon Deluxe,* that he would begin writing the kind of fiction that would establish him as one of the most interesting of contemporary American writers.

Barthelme's stories have the familiar look of the real world; they are meticulously detailed in such matters as the make and color of the cars the characters drive, the brand names of the products they buy, the names of the places where they live and the restaurants where they eat. On the other hand, they are eerily vague and indistinct about such matters as their location (the general setting is the Sun Belt states along the Gulf Coast), background information about the characters' jobs, their past—sometimes even their own names. Barthelme's fictional world is filled with real objects but empty of meaningful experience; his characters talk about things, but seldom about things that matter.

The stories are typically narrated in present tense by men in their late thirties, either single or divorced, who live alone. Like Camus's Meursault, they report events in a detached, disengaged, almost affectless manner. (Several of the stories are told in second person, which distances the narrator even from himself.) Passive individuals, these men are watchers rather than doers; it is usually the women who are the aggressors, the men responding almost willy-nilly to their advances. These characters reveal so little of their real selves that they are virtually interchangeable from one story to another.

The emptiness of the characters' lives, and the dead tone in which the tales are narrated, combine to make a powerful statement about the loneliness that infects the lives of many who inhabit the modern shopping malls, fast food restaurants, and singles apartment complexes of contemporary suburban America. However, by presenting incidents and dialogue with a decidedly comic touch, Barthelme avoids making his stories as bleak as his characters' lives. The stories also transmit a strong sense of expectation, an unsettling feeling that something dramatic is about to happen (it seldom does). In *Moon Deluxe* the dull and the routine seem charged with mystery.

Second Marriage is a brilliant comedy of contemporary social and sexual manners, rich in offbeat characters and wickedly funny dialogue. The novel tells the story of a man named Henry (no last name) whose ex-wife Clare moves in with him and his current wife Theo. The two women soon discover they like each other more than they like Henry, so they ask him to move out. The book records with wry humor his goofy experiences following his eviction by his wives.

Henry is in many ways a typical Barthelme character: decent but ineffectual, he finds himself pushed aside, a casualty of the sexual revolution; bewildered, he passes the time watching TV, vacuuming his apartment, cleaning the refrigerator, aimlessly reading magazine articles he doesn't understand. One activity that usually rouses him from his torpor is eating, a favorite pastime for all of Barthelme's characters. None of them especially savors food; going out to eat is simply something to do, a safe way of filling up time, though the fast food they routinely consume is as lacking in nutrition as the tentative relationships they stumble in and out of.

Martin, the narrator of *Tracer,* moves into the Florida motel-condo operated by his wife Alex's sister Dominica following the breakup of his marriage. He is soon sleeping with Dominica, which complicates matters when both Alex and Dominica's estranged husband Mel show up. Out of this tangled web of relationships Barthelme fashions another of his quirky comedies of modern life.

Tracer is rich in details, incidents, and dialogue which underscore Barthelme's favorite themes of displacement and failed connections. The central symbol of the novel is a P-38 Night Fighter plane which, like Martin, has come to rest on Dominica's property like a lost bird. The dialogue, composed largely of humorous yet pointless monologues, conversational non-sequiturs, and misunderstood statements, is as disconnected as the characters' lives. Even incidents (such as the bizarre episode involving a stranger who takes out a gun and inexplicably begins shooting at the P-38) seem to have become unglued from any sort of logical context.

Two Against One presents another familiar Barthelme triangle. Following a six-month separation, Elise returns to husband Edward on his 40th birthday with a novel suggestion: she wishes to invite her former lover Roscoe, whose wife has been killed in a traffic accident, to move in with the two of them. Sex is not the motivating factor; some sort of connection is. Like the rest of Barthelme's aimless and confused heroes, Edward is uncertain what he should do; though not entirely opposed to the idea, he does not know whether he likes it either.

Like *Tracer, Two Against One* moves beyond the spare, elliptical quality of Barthelme's earlier fiction. The characters are also portrayed with more empathy, less scorn. They may not have any of the answers, but in contrast to many of their earlier counterparts, they are at least yearning for answers and taking tentative (albeit unorthodox) steps towards finding them.

The aimlessness that afflicts Barthelme's characters, and that is often the source of much of the humor in his books, takes on a decidedly darker hue in *Natural Selection.* Peter Wexler concludes that he is not terribly happy in his marriage to his second wife, Lily. Wandering the malls and haphazardly driving the freeways temporarily provides a comforting outlet for his uneasiness, as these activities commonly do for Barthelme's characters. But this time the resolution of his marital dilemma comes unexpectedly: in the final scene of the novel, a late-night drive on the freeway with his wife results in a fatal traffic accident. Thus the heartbreak that usually lurks just beneath the comic surface in Barthelme's novels surfaces with sudden impact.

Barthelme is a poet of the mundane who combines the satirist's knack for exposing the ridiculous in contemporary society with a photographer's ability to capture the quotidian details of everyday life. His fiction, situated somewhere between good-humored social satire and documentary realism, both captures the absurdity and celebrates the wonder of the ordinary.

During the late 1990s, he produced two additional works—a novel and a work of narrative nonfiction—that amply illustrate the close relation between the ordinary and extraordinary in the world of Barthelme. *Bob the Gambler* concerns a Texas architect, Ray Kaiser, drawn into the world of Gulf Coast casinos. For him, losing becomes not a tragedy but a kind of adventure: ''I sort of felt it was more exhilarating to lose a lot than to win a little. Losing meant you had to play more, try harder.'' Barthelme's acquaintance with his subject matter was far more than academic, as revealed in *Double Down: Reflections on Gambling and Loss,* cowritten with brother Steven (*And He Tells the Horse the Whole Story*). In the course of researching *Bob the Gambler,* Barthelme visited a number of casinos; and following the death of their parents, as the Barthelmes reveal, both became full-fledged gambling addicts who ''would have been willing to win, but ... were content to lose.'' The owners of the Grand Casino in Gulfport, Mississippi, however, did not buy this account: they filed suit against the Barthelmes for conspiring with a blackjack dealer to rig games. Indicted in September 1997, the brothers faced up to two years in prison before the Mississippi State Circuit Court dismissed the charges in August 1999.

—David Geherin

BAUMBACH, Jonathan

Nationality: American. **Born:** New York City, 5 July 1933. **Education:** Brooklyn College, New York, 1951–55, A.B. 1955; Columbia University, New York, 1955–56, M.F.A. 1956; Stanford University, California, 1958–61, Ph.D. 1961. **Military Service:** Served in the United States Army, 1956–58. **Family:** Married 1) Elinor Berkman in 1956 (divorced 1967), one son and one daughter; 2) Georgia A. Brown in 1968 (divorced 1990), two sons. **Career:** Instructor, Stanford University, 1958–60; instructor, 1961–62, and assistant professor, 1962–64, Ohio State University, Columbus; assistant professor, New York University, 1964–66; associate professor, 1966–70, 1971–72, and since 1972 professor of English, Brooklyn College, City University of New York. Visiting professor, Tufts University, Medford, Massachusetts, 1970–71; University of Washington, Seattle, 1978–79, 1985–86; Brown University, Providence, Rhode Island, 1994. Film critic, *Partisan Review,* New Brunswick, New Jersey, and Boston, 1974–83. Co-founder, 1974, co-director, 1974–78, and currently member of the Board of Directors, Fiction Collective, New York; chair, National Society of Film Critics, 1982–84. **Awards:** *New Republic* award, 1958; Yaddo grant, 1963, 1964, 1965; National Endowment for the Arts fellowship, 1967; Guggenheim fellowship, 1978; Ingram Merrill Foundation fellowship, 1983. **Agent:** Ellen Levine Literary Agency, 432 Park Avenue South, Suite 1205, New York, New York 10016. **Address:** Brooklyn College, Department of English, Bedford Avenue and Avenue H, Brooklyn, New York 11226, U.S.A.

PUBLICATIONS

Novels

A Man to Conjure With. New York, Random House, 1965; London, Gollancz, 1966.
What Comes Next. New York, Harper, 1968.
Reruns. New York, Fiction Collective, 1974.
Babble. New York, Fiction Collective, 1976.
Chez Charlotte and Emily. New York, Fiction Collective, 1979.
My Father More or Less. New York, Fiction Collective, 1982.
Separate Hours. Boulder, Colorado, Fiction Collective 2, 1990.
Seven Wives: A Romance. Boulder, Colorado, Fiction Collective 2, 1994.
D-Tours. Normal, Illinois, FC2, 1998.

Short Stories

The Return of Service. Urbana, University of Illinois Press, 1979.
The Life and Times of Major Fiction. New York, Fiction Collective, 1987.

Uncollected Short Stories

''You Better Watch Out,'' in *Seems* (Sheboygan, Wisconsin), Fall 1978.
''Neglected Masterpieces III,'' in *Columbia* (New York), 1986.
''The History of Elegance,'' in *Columbia* (New York), April 1988.
''Low Light,'' in *Fiction International* (San Diego), Spring 1990.
''The Mother Murders,'' in *Witness* (Farmington Hills, Michigan) Summer-Fall 1990.
''The Man Who Invented the World,'' in *Film Comment* (New York), February 1991.
''Men at Lunch,'' in *Boulevard,* Fall 1991.
''Stills from Imaginary Movies,'' in *Film Comment,* May-June 1991.
''The Villa Mondare,'' in *Mississippi Review,* Spring 1992.
''The Reading,'' in *Boulevard,* Spring 1993.
''Outlaws,'' in *Georgetown Review,* Fall 1993.
''Bright Is Innocent,'' in *Iowa Review,* September 1994.
''His View of Her View of Him,'' in *Boulevard,* Spring 1995.

Play

The One-Eyed Man Is King (produced New York, 1956).

Other

The Landscape of Nightmare: Studies in the Contemporary American Novel. New York, New York University Press, 1965; London, Owen, 1966.
Editor, with Arthur Edelstein, *Moderns and Contemporaries: Nine Masters of the Short Story.* New York, Random House, 1968; revised edition, 1977.
Editor, *Writers as Teachers/Teachers as Writers.* New York, Holt Rinehart, 1970.
Editor, *Statements: New Fiction from the Fiction Collective.* New York, Braziller, 1975.
Editor, with Peter Spielberg, *Statements 2: New Fiction.* New York, Fiction Collective, 1977.

*

Manuscript Collection: Boston University Library.

Critical Study: *The Life of Fiction* by Jerome Klinkowitz, Urbana, University of Illinois Press, 1977; *Writing in a Film Age: Essays by*

Contemporary Novelists edited by Keith Cohen, Boulder, University Press of Colorado, 1991.

Jonathan Baumbach comments:

Novels are an attempt to make sense out of experience and to make experience out of sense, to eschew the illusion of verisimilitude, to give form to what never existed, not to imitate life but to re-invent it out of language, to imagine the processes of the imagination, to imagine the imagining of the processes of the imagination, involved with cinema, dream, and memory, and the underground landscape of their conjunction.

No theory informs the work. It is what it comes to. My fiction is the illusion of itself.

* * *

A helpful preface to Jonathan Baumbach's fiction is his critical study, *The Landscape of Nightmare: Studies in the Contemporary American Novel.* Baumbach is representative of a new style of novelist (which includes Ronald Sukenick, Jerzy Kosinski, and William H. Gass), having earned a graduate degree before writing fiction himself. Baumbach's thesis, that ''To live in this world, to live consciously in this world in which madness daily passes for sanity is a kind of madness in itself,'' describes a problem for literary art against which he poses his own fiction as solution. ''Unable to believe in the surface (the *Life* magazine reality) of our world,'' he argues, ''the best of the post-Second-World-War novelists have taken as their terrain the landscape of the psyche.'' Yet for that ''landscape of nightmare'' writers such as Bernard Malamud and William Styron were still using techniques more appropriate to social realism. In his own work Baumbach has striven to find a new style suitable for the innovative fiction he writes. As he emphasized to an interviewer in 1973, ''I'm not just using the dream in the traditional sense, in the psychological sense where it's an almost compacted parable, with special symbols. I'm just trying to find another way of getting at reality. I mean, my sense is that the conventional novel, for me, anyway, is on its way to a dead end. And I'm trying to get at the way things are in a way that no one has ever seen them before.''

Baumbach's first novel, *A Man to Conjure With,* synthesizes various trends outlined in his critical study. Much like William Styron's *Lie Down in Darkness,* Baumbach's work has a protagonist who moves simultaneously backward and forward in time, carefully orchestrating revelations of plot and character so that the present is gradually understood in a plausible and convincing way. As a result, the narrative is assembled as a psychological collage; only in the protagonist's final act do all the elements become clear. Baumbach's technical achievement has been to find a structural form that reflects this psychological state: a thoroughly spatial novel.

What Comes Next is a more tightly written exploration of this same structural theme. Again the situation is psychological: a young college student, beset by sexual and parental problems, is ''flipping out,'' and Baumbach's novel expresses this confusion by its very form. Violence erupts on every page, though primarily as mental device, since it is usually sparked by newspaper headlines and fantasized incidents. The book organizes itself as a literal landscape of nightmare, as all reference points for the character's reality are located within his own disjointed perceptions. As far as temporal narrative, ''what comes next'' is created from the workings of his mind.

Baumbach's subsequent work has been even more strongly experimental. His third novel, *Reruns,* abandons plot and character entirely in favor of dream-like images from movies rerun page by page. *Babble,* a novel made up of several ''baby stories'' written through the mid-1970s, is more playful but no less daring in its technical achievement. In order to explore the workings of narrative, Baumbach records the stories his infant son allegedly tells him (''His second story is less fresh than the first, though of greater technical sophistication''; ''The robot is after him again, this time disguised as a soda vending machine. 'You can't have any Coke,' the robot says, 'until you wash your face.'''). Once more Baumbach has become the critic in order to fashion a new mode for fiction.

Technical resources for Baumbach's developing style of fiction are discussed in his introduction to *Writers as Teachers / Teachers as Writers.* Here, speaking as both a fiction writer and a literary critic, he reveals that in creative writing classes one can ''talk to the real person, the secret outlaw hiding out in the 'good' student.'' This outlaw quality distinguishes the narrative artist, whose genius is to be in touch with himself or herself, with the personal voice inside that overcomes the ''strategies of evasion'' which in fact cover up the idiosyncratic qualities of expression (and therefore of beauty and insight). Such expression cannot be taught, but can only be developed in a context whereby the writer-to-be discovers his or her own talent. The strategies for doing this reflect Baumbach's own experiments in fiction: overcoming the fear of being foolish, learning that it is less important to understand something than appreciating how to live with it, and getting to know how to exist in a community with one's readers. In the process, one must fight against ''years and years of systematic depersonalization to get at what's unique and alive.'' Consequently Baumbach and his contributors emphasize the importance of finding one's personal voice, a strategy that informs the later contributions to a fiction anthology Baumbach co-edited, *Moderns and Contemporaries,* the second edition of which features personally vocal stories by Grace Paley (also a contributor to the writing book) and Donald Barthelme.

Throughout the 1970s Baumbach continued to experiment with various structures for fiction, including the sub-genre parodies, movie mythologies, and dreamlike obsessions featured throughout his story collection *The Return of Service.* But it is his fifth novel, *Chez Charlotte and Emily,* which displays his greatest facility as a writer. Ostensibly the device by which a bored husband and wife communicate with each other (by proposing a narrative and then critiquing it), the novel is actually an excuse (à la *The Canterbury Tales*) for the telling of stories. Freed from the necessity of plausible context, Baumbach is able to spin out fantasies of shipwreck, sexual adventure, intrigue, and the complexity of human relationships—all as pure writing, justified by the arrangement of the couple's critical debate. Soon the two contexts, critical and fictional, merge—as they must, Baumbach would argue, for it is through works of the imagination that we preserve our consciousness of the world.

His sixth novel, *My Father More or Less,* experiments with forms of intertextuality to make this same point. Alternately narrated by Tom Terman and by a third-person narrator reflecting the actions of his father Lukas, the novel shows how Tom's visit to his father in London is shaped by the son's memory of his earlier abandonment, while the father's own coming to terms with his son, his mistress, and his employer becomes interwoven with the detective-story screenplay he's been working on. Lukas only superficially controls his film narrative, as its development toward the protagonist's death is impelled by the pressure of events unfolding in Terman's life. But these same events are enriched by the textual experience with his script. At times the writer's role takes over, as when Terman extricates himself from an unhappy situation by ''writing himself a few lines of dialogue.'' For his part, Tom finds himself in a film script situation enhanced by the fact that actual movies have been shot on location in his father's house; but when events threaten, he is able to telephone his father for a rescue, much like a character calling upon the author for relief. That the father is creator of the son helps establish the naturalized quality of Baumbach's narrative. Although as experimentally intertextual as the most sophisticated literary experiments, *My Father More or Less* reads as accessibly as the most realistic fiction, indicating that Baumbach has found a useful device for bringing innovative fiction back within the literary mainstream.

Comfortable in his style that melds both tradition and innovation, Baumbach uses a range of familiar materials in the stories of *The Life and Times of Major Fiction* to show how fresh techniques for presentation are available to the writer who both knows the tricks of the trade and appreciates how readers will appreciate their use. His particular genius is displayed in ''Mr. and Mrs. McFeely at Home and Away,'' based as it is on characters from a popular children's show who are, in their televised roles, the quintessence of familiarity, while their lives off-screen are shown as offering a challenge to the imagination, given that on TV the audience's imagining has been done for them. In similar manner, the challenge to write a story about basketball produces ''How You Play the Game,'' an exercise in trying to make a narrative out of what is in essence merely a situation. The author, who is a character in his own story by virtue of having been asked in the first line to write it, struggles to make life as interesting as art, and succeeds only by following the most rudimentary role of fantasy: placing himself in the actual game.

A similar strategy informs *Separate Hours,* Baumbach's novel in which the long relationship of husband and wife becomes problematic for a novel, because its telling is complicated by the fact that each is a psychotherapist possessed of an entire battery of systems for just such interpretation. As in the basketball story, there are thus two streams to the narrative: action and interpretation. Problems result when one turns into the other. That each character wishes to be the narrator creates a dilemma for the reader in search of a story to be trusted. The dual nature of this and of all narrative is Baumbach's continuing interest, also evident in his experiments at combining photos and text as ''stills from imaginary movies.'' *D-Tours* returns to the idea of a story-within-a-story, but does so in a manner much simpler than that which readers of Baumbach have become accustomed: this novel is more clearly a series of interrelated stories, united by the character of Max Million, who skips blithely between genres, situations, incidents, and even planets.

—Jerome Klinkowitz

BAUSCH, Richard

Nationality: American. **Born:** Fort Benning, Georgia, 18 April 1945. **Education:** George Mason University, B.A. 1973; University of Iowa, M.F.A. 1975; also attended Northern Virginia Community College. **Military Service:** U.S. Air Force, survival instructor, 1966–69. **Family:** Married Karen Miller; two sons, three daughters. **Career:** Worked as singer-songwriter and comedian; professor, George Mason University, Fairfax, Virginia, 1980—. **Awards:** National Endowment for the Arts grant, 1982; Guggenheim Fellowship, 1984; Lila Wallace Reader's Best Writer's Award, 1992; Academy Award in Literature (American Academy of Arts and Letters), 1993. **Agent:** Harriet Wasserman, Russell & Volkening, Inc., 551 Fifth Avenue, New York, New York 10017, U.S.A. **Address:** Department of English, George Mason University, 4400 University Drive, Fairfax, Virginia 22030–4443, U.S.A.

PUBLICATIONS

Novels

Real Presence: A Novel. New York, Dial Press, 1980.
Take Me Back: A Novel. New York, Dial Press, 1981.
The Last Good Time. New York, Dial Press, 1984.
Mr. Field's Daughter: A Novel. New York, Linden Press/Simon & Schuster, 1989.
Violence. Boston, Houghton Mifflin/Seymour Lawrence, 1992.
Rebel Powers. Boston, Houghton Mifflin/Seymour Lawrence, 1993.
Good Evening Mr. and Mrs. America, and All the Ships at Sea. New York, HarperCollins, 1996.
In the Night Season: A Novel. New York, HarperFlamingo, 1998.

Short Stories

Spirits and Other Stories. New York, Linden Press/Simon & Schuster, 1987.
The Fireman's Wife and Other Stories. New York, Linden Press/Simon & Schuster, 1990.
Rare and Endangered Species: A Novella and Stories. Boston, Houghton Mifflin/Seymour Lawrence, 1994.
Aren't You Happy for Me? and Other Stories. London, Macmillan, 1995.
The Selected Stories of Richard Bausch. New York, Random House, 1996.
Someone to Watch Over Me: Stories. New York, HarperFlamingo, 1999.

Other

Afterword, *Appalachee Red: A Novel* by Richard Andrews. Athens, University of Georgia Press, 1987.
Introduction, *The Sound of Writing,* edited by Alan Cheuse and Caroline Marshall. New York, Anchor Books, 1991.
Introduction, *The Old Forest and Other Stories* by Peter Taylor. New York, Modern Library, 1995.
Foreword, *Bad Man Blues: A Portable George Garrett* by George Garrett. Dallas, Texas, Southern Methodist University Press, 1998.
Contributor, *Love in Full Bloom,* edited by Margaret Fowler and Priscilla McCutcheon. New York, Ballantine Books, 1994.
Contributor, *Off the Beaten Path: Stories of Place,* edited by Joseph Barbato and Lisa Weinerman Horak. New York, North Point Press, 1998.
Editor, with R. V. Cassill, *The Norton Anthology of Short Fiction.* New York, W. W. Norton, 2000.

*

Critical Studies: *Contemporary Literary Criticism,* Volume 51, Detroit, Gale, 1989; *Contemporary Authors Autobiography Series,* Volume 14, Detroit, Gale, 1992; *Dictionary of Literary Biography,* Volume 130, *American Short-Story Writers Since World War II,* Detroit, Gale, 1993.

* * *

Real Presence begins with a man answering an employment advertisement only to discover that the company that placed the ad is not only no longer hiring—it has all but gone out of business. From such prosaic beginnings, the novel centers upon a literally heartsick priest who becomes the unwilling benefactor to the erstwhile job-hunter and his family of five wild children and an eternally beset and very pregnant wife. This, with its Southern setting, its identifiable symbolism, its cast of seeming grotesques, and its dramatic crisis of faith, is, as one reviewer put it, ''Flannery O'Connor country.'' But the author of *Real Presence* would soon, in later works, pull himself out of the long shadow thrown by the author of *Wise Blood.*

As a novelist, Richard Bausch is an unabashed humanist. His writing is far from the satirical social surveys of Tom Wolfe or the metafictional virtuosities of John Barth. Nor is he, like O'Connor, a metaphysical tester of souls. Instead, over the course of eight novels and four acclaimed collections of short fiction, Bausch has focused his own talents on that most cliched, and thus undervalued, of fictional constructs—character.

Bausch deploys an unadorned and direct, but unusually supple, style of narration that eschews overt affect for simple description and depiction. Telling details and evocative incidents accrete until discernible personalities emerge. *The Last Good Time* begins with several pages describing the quotidian routine of an old widower who lives alone in a small apartment. But Bausch does not create static portraits; he is as rigorous as an anthropologist in filling in the context of circumstance under which his characters are formed. Taking E. M. Forster's epigraph to ''only connect'' as his aesthetic manifesto, Bausch excels at portraying lives in the process of living. The routine of the elderly man in *The Last Good Time* is shown to have deep roots in the man's past, but it must soon give way when his life is irrevocably altered by the intrusion of a young prostitute.

If Bausch's mastery of literary characterization is unquestionable, his choice of character has created considerable critical acrimony, for Bausch has chosen to focus his meticulous imagination on creating ordinary people living ordinary lives. Critics often fault Bausch's choice of subject matter as uninteresting, which may help explain why his work does not enjoy a wider readership. *Take Me Back*, Bausch's second novel, may have suffered from being marketed as the story of a marriage sundered by alcoholism and mental illness. But the achievement of this particular novel is that Bausch has, through scrupulous attention to the portrayal of the emotional lives of his characters, breathed real life into such stereotypical clay. The alcoholic husband, a professional failure, slowly emerges as nobly, if imperfectly, loyal to his wife, a former musician whose decline into insanity is portrayed with pathos.

It is not that Bausch is incapable of literary experimentation; the structures of all his novels are as organically complex with memory and rumination as they are largely linear in chronology. But *Mr. Field's Daughter*, Bausch's fourth novel, is also formally complex, interspersing its mostly third-person narration with chapters entitled ''Certain Testimony'' that contain the first-person voices of the book's two main characters, an older man and his grown daughter, both of whom must cope with the damage her elopement has caused to their relationship even as they disagree with how to deal with the daughter's estranged and vengeful husband.

Even when Bausch creates the most extraordinary circumstances, as he does in *In the Night Season*, in which a young widow and her son become the target of vindictive and murderous smugglers thinly disguised as white-supremacist militia-men, Bausch maintains a tight focus on the emotional reactions of his characters. The more sensational elements of his plots are harnessed tightly to this aim. That is, the significance of such extraordinary events, like the armed robbery that Connally, the protagonist, survives in *Violence*, is secondary to their aftermath. The real violence of *Violence* lies in the way that physical trauma begets emotional damage in perpetrators as well as victims. In this novel, the end of a physical act of violence marks only the beginning of its many victimizations, and Bausch explores the unfolding consequence of the fatal robbery with what seems to be an unerring eye for the confusions and surges of passion that roil throughout his characters' interactions. As Connally changes from shocked victim to inadvertent hero to ostensible avenger in the wake of the crime, Bausch describes each transformation from within Connally's perceptions. What matters for Bausch is not the depiction of a sensational event; it is the artful creation of real feeling.

The Russian formalist Victor Shklovsky maintained that the purpose of art was to knowingly shift perceptions so as to make familiar objects seem new again. Bausch most effectively employs this maxim in *Rebel Powers*, his sixth novel and his most ruminative one, in which a middle-aged bookseller, tellingly named Thomas, remembers and relates the failed marriage of his parents following his father's imprisonment for a petty crime. Taking the familiar elements of an alienated husband and wife, the travails of single parenting, and a young man's coming-of-age, Bausch attempts artistic alchemy, this time with a plot that partakes of nothing more extraordinary than the theft of a typewriter. Still, *Rebel Powers* is, in its dogged resistance to encapsulation, Bausch's least ordinary book. Again and again in this novel, Thomas posits, then rejects, easy explanations for the events he narrates, and this unwillingness to pass summary judgement focuses attention on the principals involved rather than on the culpability of their actions. Clearly, the placement of blame is seen as a barrier to connection and compassion with Thomas's parents, a discernible lesson that, once distilled, nevertheless diminishes (and is antithetical to) this particular incarnation of the Bauschian aesthetic. What is important are the lives portrayed, not the parables thus gleaned, and Thomas's relentless remembrance, executed without indictment, becomes a book-length manifestation of filial love.

Bausch's only overt comedy is his seventh novel, *Good Evening Mr. and Mrs. America, And All the Ships At Sea*, a bildungsroman set in 1963 in Washington D.C., where Walter Marshall, a nineteen-year-old innocent, is enrolled in the D'Allessandro School for Broadcasting, but he has developed political, even presidential, aspirations because of his adoration of the assassinated President John F. Kennedy. Walter then undergoes romantic and moral maturation through a series of comic developments that disabuse him of his dreams.

For all the bleakness and despair and disillusionment that Bausch introduces into the lives of his literary constructs, he nevertheless ends all of his novels on a note that is, if not hopeful, at least an acknowledgement that life endures, like the Dilsey section of Faulkner's *The Sound and The Fury.* It is a gesture aimed at addressing the wider world outside each novel, enfolding it back into the universe out of which Bausch has scrupulously worked to distill and clarify his narratives and his aesthetic ends. For Walter Marshall, the end of

Good Evening Mr. and Mrs. America, And All the Ships At Sea is a tragicomic one as Walter, wiser for all the buffetings his ideals have taken, still manages to muster enough noble aspiration to seek out a better place based on an idealized past, ''where concern for what was right mattered, and people were what they seemed to be ... where the war was being fought for freedom, and where the conflict was definite, the enemy clear.'' In short, the novel ends with Walter resolving to enlist in the Vietnam War.

—J.J. Wylie

BAWDEN, Nina

Nationality: British. **Born:** Nina Mabey in London, 19 January 1925. **Education:** Ilford County High School; Somerville College, Oxford, B.A. 1946, M.A. 1951; Salzburg Seminar in American Studies, 1960. **Family:** Married 1) H.W. Bawden in 1946, two sons (one deceased); 2) the broadcast executive A.S. Kark in 1954, one daughter. **Career:** Assistant, Town and Country Planning Association, 1946–47; Justice of the Peace for Surrey, 1968–76. Regular reviewer, *Daily Telegraph*, London. **Awards:** *Guardian* award, for children's book, 1976; *Yorkshire Post* award, 1976. Fellow, Royal Society of Literature, 1970. CBE (Commander of the British Empire). **Member:** PEN Executive Committee, 1968–71; President, Society of Women Writers and Journalists. **Agent:** Curtis Brown, 162–168 Regent Street, London W1R 5TB. **Address:** 22 Noel Road, London N1 8HA, England; or, 19 Kapodistriou, Nauplion 21000, Greece.

Publications

Novels

Who Calls the Tune. London, Collins, 1953; as *Eyes of Green,* New York, Morrow, 1953.
The Odd Flamingo. London, Collins, 1954.
Change Here for Babylon. London, Collins, 1955.
The Solitary Child. London, Collins, 1956; New York, Lancer, 1966.
Devil by the Sea. London, Collins, 1957; Philadelphia, Lippincott, 1959; abridged edition (for children), London, Gollancz, and Lippincott, 1976.
Just Like a Lady. London, Longman, 1960; as *Glass Slippers Always Pinch,* Philadelphia, Lippincott, 1960.
In Honour Bound. London, Longman, 1961.
Tortoise by Candlelight. London, Longman, and New York, Harper, 1963.
Under the Skin. London, Longman, and New York, Harper, 1964.
A Little Love, A Little Learning. London, Longman, 1965; New York, Harper, 1966.
A Woman of My Age. London, Longman, and New York, Harper, 1967.
The Grain of Truth. London, Longman, and New York, Harper, 1968.
The Birds on the Trees. London, Longman, and New York, Harper, 1970; Thorndike, Maine, Thorndike Press, 1995.
Anna Apparent. London, Longman, and New York, Harper, 1972.
George Beneath a Paper Moon. London, Allen Lane, and New York, Harper, 1974; as *On the Edge,* London, Sphere, 1985.
Afternoon of a Good Woman. London, Macmillan, 1976; New York, Harper, 1977.
Familiar Passions. London, Macmillan, and New York, Morrow, 1979.
Walking Naked. London, Macmillan, 1981; New York, St. Martin's Press, 1982.
The Ice House. London, Macmillan, and New York, St. Martin's Press, 1983.
Circles of Deceit. London, Macmillan, and New York, St. Martin's Press, 1987.
Family Money. London, Gollancz, and New York, St. Martin's Press, 1991.
A Nice Change. London, Virago Press, 1997.

Fiction (for children)

The Secret Passage. London, Gollancz, 1963; as *The House of Secrets,* Philadelphia, Lippincott, 1964.
On the Run. London, Gollancz, 1964; as *Three on the Run,* Philadelphia, Lippincott, 1965.
The White Horse Gang. London, Gollancz, and Philadelphia, Lippincott, 1966.
The Witch's Daughter. London, Gollancz, and Philadelphia, Lippincott, 1966.
A Handful of Thieves. London, Gollancz, and Philadelphia, Lippincott, 1967.
The Runaway Summer. London, Gollancz, and Philadelphia, Lippincott, 1969.
Squib. London, Gollancz, and Philadelphia, Lippincott, 1971.
Carrie's War. London, Gollancz, and Philadelphia, Lippincott, 1973.
The Peppermint Pig. London, Gollancz, and Philadelphia, Lippincott, 1975.
Rebel on a Rock. London, Gollancz, and Philadelphia, Lippincott, 1978.
The Robbers. London, Gollancz, and New York, Lothrop, 1979.
Kept in the Dark. London, Gollancz, and New York, Lothrop, 1982.
The Finding. London, Gollancz, and New York, Lothrop, 1985.
Princess Alice. London, Deutsch, 1985.
Keeping Henry. London, Gollancz, 1988; as *Henry,* New York, Lothrop, 1988.
The Outside Child. London, Gollancz, and New York, Lothrop, 1989.
Humbug. London, Gollancz, and New York, Clarion Books, 1992.
The Real Plato Jones. London, Gollancz, 1993; New York, Clarion Books, 1994.
Granny the Pag. New York, Clarion Books, 1996.
Off the Road. New York, Clarion, 1999.

Other (for children)

William Tell. London, Cape, and New York, Lothrop, 1981.
St. Francis of Assisi. London, Cape, and New York, Lothrop, 1983.
In My Own Time. London, Virago Press, 1994; New York, Clarion Books, 1995.

*

Critical Study: Article by Gerda Seaman, in *British Novelists since 1960* edited by Jay L. Halio, Detroit, Gale, 1983.

Nina Bawden comments:

I find it difficult to comment on my adult novels. I suppose one could say that the later books, from *Just Like a Lady* onwards, are social comedies with modern themes and settings; the characters moral beings, hopefully engaged in living. People try so hard and fail so often, sometimes sadly, sometimes comically; I try to show how and why and to be accurate about relationships and motives. I have been called a ''cryptomoralist with a mischievous sense of humor,'' and I like this description: it is certainly part of what I aim to be.

This quotation, from the *Christian Science Monitor,* though not the most flattering, might be useful:

> Nina Bawden is a writer of unusual precision who can depict human foibles with an almost embarrassing accuracy. Yet for all that she centres dead on target, there is always a note of compassion in her stories. The light thrown on her characters, clear though it is, is no harsh spotlight. It is a more diffuse beam that allows one to peer into the shadows and see causes even while it focuses on effects.

* * *

The world of the English middle classes is the focal point for most of Nina Bawden's fiction. In *The Birds on the Trees*—a key novel in her development—she observes life as she sees it, centering on an entirely believable middle-class family, with children who puzzle and dismay their parents, because these are the people she sees every day, and these are the children who interest and baffle her, too. She captures the capricious intensity of sibling love, rivalry, and loyalty; she is reluctant to pin blame and quick to display compassion; she is also logical enough to offer no easy solutions, but sufficiently warm-hearted to include realistic sprinklings of hope. Above all, she brings a sympathetic ear to the cadences of everyday speech, a virtue which heightens the intensity of the plot—a story of alienation and the betrayal by the pampered Toby of his vain self-righteous parents.

Her no-nonsense, no-holds-barred approach to contemporary social problems is taken a stage further in *Walking Naked,* a chillingly precise novel about people unable to come to grips with the worlds they inhabit. Laura is a novelist whose method of dealing with difficulties is to retreat into the realm of her imagination. These problems are induced by guilt—guilt about her parents, her first marriage, her son who is in jail, her friends, and her present husband. ''I write because I am afraid of life,'' is her easy palliative to life's ills. Now life is taking its revenge. In the course of one fraught day Laura struggles to come to terms with what she has made of her life, to strip away the layers of anxiety which give her nightmares that her house is falling down about her ears, to avoid the self-deception which has made a mockery of her art, to walk naked and alone. The timescale gives the novel a sharp narrative vigor and the dialogue is always slyly intelligent and believable, but what gives *Walking Naked* its authority is Bawden's precise analysis of middle-class mores and the way in which they are brought to bear on a woman's life.

As in all her later fiction Bawden excels at revealing the tensions and hidden currents at work beneath the calm and humdrum exteriors of her characters. She is no mere moralist; rather, the matter of relationships is her main concern. In *The Ice House,* a caustic glance at the complexities of modern marriage, friendship, and loyalty, she examines the unlikely friendship of Daisy and Ruth who have been friends since their schooldays. As girls, Daisy was boisterous and extroverted; Ruth withdrawn and frightened, a victim of an overbearing father. Thirty years later Ruth has a successful career and, on the surface at least, has a happy marriage; Daisy, though, is less content. When a tragedy rocks the lives of the two women and their families, its repercussions force them out of uneasy self-deception into a new and painful reality which they both have to accept. *The Ice House* is an unusual and subtle novel about familiar themes—love, marriage, friendship, adultery—in which the emotional lives of the two female protagonists are viewed with a mixture of sympathy and disconcerting accuracy. No less tangled are their moral confusions and the task of unraveling them gives the novel its central narrative line. To her adult novels Bawden has brought psychological depth and a humorous focus on human moods, resignations and self-deceptions, tempered only by her powers of observation and discrimination.

Nina Bawden is one of the very few authors who will admit to making a conscious adjustment to writing for children. She has said: ''I consider my books for children as important as my adult work, and in some ways more challenging.'' In all her children's novels childhood is seen with a special clarity, and she has the gift of understanding her subject. *The Peppermint Pig,* for example, explores the reactions of a family of Edwardian children to their new and reduced circumstances, and it is through their eyes that we see their reactions to the world around them. We can understand their hopes and fears, their relationships with each other and with the adult world: this is felt most clearly in a profound episode dealing with the inevitable death of Johnny, the children's pet pig.

Off the Road and *Granny the Pag* are both for children, though the former represents something of a departure for Bawden. Set in the year 2040, the book concerns 11-year-old Tom, who joins in his grandfather in seeking the latter's childhood home. In their world, it is a journey fraught with danger, one that takes them through ''the Wall'' and into a forbidden region called ''the Wild.'' The subject matter of *Granny the Pag* is far more down-to-earth. A ''Pag,'' as narrator Cat (or Catriona) explains, is ''someone who can make things happen,'' and her flamboyant grandmother—who rides a motorcycle and wears leather—certainly is one. No wonder, then, that when Cat's self-indulgent and emotionally distant parents decide that they want to take on raising her themselves, she chooses to stay with her grandmother. Bawden's secret is that her sympathy for her characters never flags—she thereby retains the readers' sympathies, too.

—Trevor Royle

BEAR, Gregory Dale

Nationality: American. **Born:** San Diego, California, 20 August 1951. **Education:** San Diego State College (now University), A.B. 1969. **Family:** Married 1) Christina Nielsen in 1975 (divorced 1981); 2) Astrid Anderson in 1983, one son, one daughter. **Career:** Worked in bookstores, a planetarium, and as a freelance teacher in San Diego, California. **Awards:** Nebula Award (Science Fiction Writers of America), best novelette and best novella, 1984, best short story, 1987, best novel, 1994; Hugo Award, best novelette, 1986, best short story, 1987; Prix Apollo, 1986. **Agent:** Richard Curtis, 171 East 74th Street, New York, New York 10021, U.S.A. **Address:** 506 Lakeview Road, Alderwood Manor, Washington 98037, U.S.A.

PUBLICATIONS

Novels

Hegira. New York, Dell, 1979.
Psychlone. New York, Ace, 1979.
Beyond Heaven's River. New York, Dell, 1980.
Strength of Stones. New York, Ace, 1981.
Corona (*Star Trek* novel). New York, Pocket Books, 1984.
The Infinity Concerto. New York, Berkeley, 1984.
Eon. New York, Bluejay Books, 1985.
Blood Music. New York, Arbor House, 1985.
The Serpent Mage. New York, Berkeley, 1986.
The Forge of God. New York, Tor Books, 1987.
Eternity. New York, Warner Books, 1988.
Hardfought (bound with *Cascade Point* by Timothy Zahn). New York, Tor Books, 1988.
Queen of Angels. New York, Warner Books, 1990.
Heads. Legend, 1990.
Anvil of Stars. New York, Warner Books, 1992.
Songs of Earth and Power (includes *The Infinity Concerto* and *The Serpent Mage*). Legend, 1992.
Moving Mars. New York, Tor Books, 1993.
Legacy. New York, Tor Books, 1995.
/ (pronounced ''slant''). New York, Tor Books, 1997.
Dinosaur Summer. New York, Warner Aspect, 1997.
Foundation and Chaos. New York, HarperPrism, 1998.
Darwin's Radio. New York, Ballantine, 1999.
Star Wars: Rogue Planet. New York, Del Rey, 2000.

Short Stories

The Wind from a Burning Woman. Sauk City, Wisconsin, Arkham House Publishers, 1983.
Sleepside Story. New Castle, Virginia, Cheap Street, 1987.
Early Harvest. New England Science Fiction Association, 1988.
Tangents. New York, Warner Books, 1989.
Sisters. Pulphouse, 1992.
The Venging. Legend, 1992.
Bear's Fantasies: Six Stories in Old Paradigms. Newark, New Jersey, Wildside Press, 1992.

Other

The White Horse Child (computer file). Union City, California, Ebook, 1992.
Introduction, *Psycho Shop* by Alfred Bester and Roger Zelazny. New York, Vintage Books, 1998.
Contributor, *Isaac Asimov's War,* edited by Gardner Dozois. New York, Ace Books, 1993.
Contributor, *Far Futures,* edited by Gregory Benford. New York, Tor, 1995.
Contributor, *Skylife: Space Habitats in Story and Science,* edited by Gregory Benford and George Zebrowski. New York, Harcourt Brace, 2000.
Editor, with Martin H. Greenberg, *New Legends.* New York, Tor, 1995.

* * *

Greg Bear is widely considered to be among the best of his generation's science fiction writers. Specifically, Bear is felt to have made major contributions to the reinvigoration of ''hard'' science fiction—that is, science fiction in which the science, however speculative or far-fetched, is solidly grounded in reality. Additionally, Bear recognized during the 1980s the vast changes that were taking place in the biological sciences, building several of his most important books around biological themes and extrapolations. *Blood Music* was among the first novels to deal with nanotechnology, the science of engineering machines, and in this case intelligent life forms—at the microscopic and submicroscopic levels. The novel also dealt with information engineering, a theoretical field which argues that the manipulation of information itself can affect the structure of the universe; information engineering is also at the heart of Bear's award-winning novel *Moving Mars.* His duo of novels, *Queen of Angels* and */* (pronounced ''Slant''), along with the short novel, *Heads,* explore the effects of nanotechnology on a world transformed almost beyond recognition. *Queen of Angels* is Bear's most overtly experimental and ambitious novel. More recently he used many of his biological themes and concerns in a thriller, *Darwin's Radio.*

Bear has always displayed an enthusiastic willingness to stretch and experiment. Other than books that are direct or indirect sequels to each other, he has rarely repeated himself in theme or approach. His early stories and novels (he sold his first short story when he was 16) explore classic science fictional themes and settings—alien planets, mysterious structures, and the nature of religion and power. Bear is also a talented visual artist—his work has graced the covers of science fiction magazines and the reprint edition of one of his own novels—and even his earliest works were enhanced by a dramatic visual sense.

In 1985 Bear hit his stride as a writer, publishing two novels, *Blood Music* and *Eon,* that attracted substantial attention and established him as a mature novelist. The science fiction community noted the arrival of a major writer. *Blood Music* was nominated for the Hugo and Nebula, leading science fiction awards; the previous year a shorter version of the story won the Hugo and Nebula, while another work, the visionary and experimental *Hardfought,* won a Nebula. Another story, the heartbreaking ''Tangents,'' won the 1987 Hugo and Nebula awards.

While biology has been the focus of much of Bear's major work, his other 1985 novel, *Eon,* demonstrated his mastery of materials more traditionally associated with science fiction: vast sweeps of time and space. *Eon,* and its sequels, *Eternity* and *Legacy,* explore a vast structure whose interior offers access to other times and places. Although more recent historical developments have outdated some of *Eon*'s underpinnings—primarily the conflict between the United States and the Soviet Union—the readability and ongoing popularity of this novel and its sequels is preserved by Bear's ability to communicate a true sense of wonder at the size and mystery of the universe, as well as his well-developed storytelling abilities and insights into characters.

Another pair of linked novels, *The Forge of God* and *Anvil of Stars,* likewise explore the vastness of space. The first novel deals with destruction of the Earth, and culminates in a sequence of images, as our planet dies, that are among the most haunting and tragic in all of science fiction. The sequel is a more straightforward revenge story, although Bear declines to offer his characters—or his readers—any easy answers or triumphs.

Following his own literary triumphs of the 1980s, Bear grew more overtly experimental and published in 1990 what many consider his finest achievement—*Queen of Angels*. Set in a world so transformed by nanotechnology as to be alien to us, this stylistically audacious novel is a tale of crime and punishment, and of the role and responsibility of the artist in society. Using typography, invented jargon and slang, news clips, and other narrative devices, Bear not only tells a story, he also immerses the reader in his transformed world to a degree unusual in science fiction (or, for that matter, any other type of fiction). However, other books set in the *Queen of Angels* world—*/* and *Heads*—employ more traditional narrative tools.

Following *Queen of Angels*, Bear seemed to concentrate on extending the range of his speculations rather than his stylistic experiments. Always a clear and often a poetic writer, Bear focused his energies in the 1990s on novels that revisited many of his—and science fiction's—grand themes, but did so in literary modes more accessible to general readers than *Queen of Angels*. His novel *Moving Mars*, won the 1994 Nebula, and was one of the first of the decade's wave of large ''Mars novels.'' The novel functions admirably as both an adventure story and as an investigation of the informational nature of our universe. Its broad speculations are among the boldest in recent science fiction.

Although it is for his science fiction that Bear is best known, he has published some fantasy, most notably the novels that form the sequence *Songs of Earth and Power*. Again wrestling with the nature and responsibilities of the artist, this novel sequence is among Bear's most effective, if least known, works.

Rarely forgetting that novelists are also entertainers, Bear has written more than a few works that might be classed solely as ''entertainments.'' Chief among them is his novel *Dinosaur Summer*, a loving look at the motion pictures of the 1930s and 1940s, the role of science fiction itself in shaping our view of the world, and the process by which a boy becomes a man. *Dinosaur Summer* is perhaps the most purely delightful of Bear's works.

He has also joined in exploring the science fictional universes of other writers, most notably Isaac Asimov's legendary Foundation universe. Along with Gregory Benford and David Brin (together referred to by science fiction fans as ''the killer Bs,'') Bear participated in the creation of a new Foundation trilogy, linked to Asimov's great sequence of stories and novels. Bear's contribution was the novel *Foundation and Chaos*.

Another novel set in a universe not his own is *Star Wars: Rogue Planet*, an adventure tale set in the Jedi universe of George Lucas's *Star Wars* films. *Rogue Planet* was a major international bestseller.

Despite diversions in the Foundation and Star Wars universes, as the twenty-first century loomed Bear seemed determined to continue breaking new ground, setting himself new challenges. His novel *Darwin's Radio* synthesized much of his biological thinking and speculation, with Bear's provocative ideas about evolution couched in a taut plot. Although the book reads like a straightforward medical-scientific thriller of the sort that Michael Crichton or Robin Cook might write, the level of speculation and characterization underlying the story is far deeper than is common in suspense fiction. Bear's speculations, indeed, attracted some attention from the professional scientific community. The novel's sensibility was likewise informed by those virtues that have been hallmarks of Bear's pure science fiction—verisimilitude, thoroughness of research, seamless integration of science and plot, and careful and clear writing.

If not the sort of coterie-gathering literary breakthrough that *Queen of Angels* was, *Darwin's Radio* nonetheless sent a clear signal that Bear intended to continue breaking new ground and opening new territory, both for science fiction and for himself. He has been one of the key figures in science fiction over the past two decades, and bids fair to become one of science fiction's most effective literary ambassadors to the larger reading world.

—Keith Ferrell

BEATTIE, Ann

Nationality: American. **Born:** Washington, D.C., 8 September 1947. **Education:** American University, Washington, D.C., B.A. 1969; University of Connecticut, Storrs, 1970–72, M.A. 1970. **Family:** Married 1) David Gates in 1973 (divorced), one son; 2) Lincoln Perry. **Career:** Visiting assistant professor, 1976–77, visiting writer, 1980, University of Virginia, Charlottesville; Briggs Copeland Lecturer in English, Harvard University, Cambridge, Massachusetts, 1977–78. **Awards:** Guggenheim fellowship, 1977; American University Distinguished Alumnae award, 1980; American Academy award, 1980; L.H.D., American University, 1983. Member of the American Academy and Institute of Arts and Letters since 1983. **Agent:** International Creative Management, 40 West 57th Street, New York, New York 10019, U.S.A. **Address:** c/o Janklow and Nesbit, 598 Madison Avenue, New York, New York 10022–1614, U.S.A.

PUBLICATIONS

Novels

Chilly Scenes of Winter. New York, Doubleday, 1976.
Falling in Place. New York, Random House, 1980; London, Secker and Warburg, 1981.
Love Always. New York, Random House, and London, Michael Joseph, 1985.
Picturing Will. New York, Random House, and London, Cape, 1990; New York, Vintage, 1991.
Another You. New York, Knopf, 1995.
My Life, Starring Dara Falcon. New York, Knopf, 1997.

Short Stories

Distortions. New York, Doubleday, 1976.
Secrets and Surprises. New York, Random House, 1978; London, Hamish Hamilton, 1979.
Jacklighting. Worcester, Massachusetts, Metacom Press, 1981.
The Burning House. New York, Random House, 1982; London, Secker and Warburg, 1983.
Where You'll Find Me and Other Stories. New York, Linden Press, 1986; London, Macmillan, 1987.
What Was Mine and Other Stories. New York, Random House, 1991.
Park City: New and Selected Stories. New York, Knopf, 1998.

Other

Spectacles (for children). New York, Workman, 1985.
Alex Katz (art criticism). New York, Abrams, 1987.

Americana, photographs by Bob Adelman. New York, Scribner, 1992.

Editor, with Shannon Ravenel, *The Best American Short Stories 1987.* Boston, Houghton Mifflin, 1987.

*

Theatrical Activities: Actress: **Play**—Role in *The Hotel Play* by Wallace Shawn, New York, 1981.

* * *

Chilly Scenes of Winter and *Distortions* were published simultaneously, and, to Ann Beattie's consternation, she was quickly celebrated as the chronicler of the disillusioned 1960s counterculture. She was praised as an objective observer of the ennui and disillusion of the postlapsarian love children, the generation that turned on in the 1960s but totally dropped out in the 1970s. Of this Beattie said: ''That's a horribly reductive approach… . What I've always hoped for is that somebody will then start talking more about the meat and bones of what I'm writing about,'' and one shares Beattie's sentiment. While it is true that many of her stories use the manners and jargon of the post-counterculture era as a backdrop—particularly its songs and culture heroes—these details function in much the same way as Raymond Carver's Pacific Northwest, or Donald Barthelme's New York City. They create a concrete setting from which larger human dilemmas may be extracted—in Beattie's case, the difficulties of adjusting to the modern world, the growing distance between one's youthful dreams and present responsibilities, and, most particularly, the fragility and difficulty of sustaining relationships and the despair of loneliness. What also persists in Beattie's fiction, at least until *Love Always,* is a focus on the common human decency and bonds of friendship that survive even the worst of times. Despite their personal circumstances, Beattie's men and women extend themselves to others.

Since the mid-1980s, Beattie has taken a more negative and less sympathetic or ironic and detached view toward members of the generation who became aging, careless, and smug Yuppies. *Picturing Will,* while focusing on the problems of balancing career and parenthood, reveals entirely new concerns. As the title suggests, Beattie is not only interested in parenthood and children (here a boy named Will) but in the responsibilities incurred by human will, along with the contingencies determined by an impersonal fate.

Chilly Scenes of Winter, more than any of her subsequent works, details the dreams and values of the 1960s. It concerns a 27-year-old disaffected love-child, Charles, despairing over his girlfriend Laura's return to her husband. Instead of pursuing her, the helpless Charles busies himself with a cast of needy people—his childhood friend Sam, his suicidal mother, and ex-girlfriend Pamela (now experimenting with lesbianism), and his helplessly naive sister Susan. When he at last learns that Laura has left her husband he visits her, and they prepare to sail into the sunset.

Beattie treats the loss of optimism and first love as by-products of the 1960s youth culture. She also studies, through Charles and Sam, the aimlessness and ennui of the 1970s lost generation. ''You could be happy … if you hadn't had your eyes opened in the sixties,'' is repeated throughout. Beattie retains a characteristic detachment—a balance between an objective (sometimes critical) and affectionate (sometimes mocking) portrait of the times. Charles, for example, is wistful toward the past. Everyone has died, he repeats—not just Janis Joplin and Brian Jones, but also Jim Morrison's widow Pamela, Amy Vanderbilt, Adele Davis, and maybe even Rod Stewart (about whom, of course, he is wrong). Elsewhere, the world-weary Charles and Sam lament that times have grown worse, because ''women put their brassieres back on and want you to take them to Paul Newman movies.'' Beattie has a wonderful sense of humor.

The dreamer Charles, out of place in any time or locale, is afraid of the present; he is also obsessed with illness and death, and, like many others in the book, he longs to be a child again. But his earnestness, sympathy, and kind generosity are redemptive. Even so, the novel ends bitterly. Sam gets a new and ugly dog, ''a terrible genetic mistake,'' as Charles observes, and one can't help thinking the same of his own reunion with Laura.

The stories in *Distortions* focus on the empty relationships of married and single couples, on the urgent need for companionship and definition that drives most people. Especially moving are the figures in ''Dwarf House,'' ''The Parking Lot,'' ''A Platonic Relationship,'' ''Snakes' Shoes,'' and ''Vermont.'' Although these characters are only peripherally aware of their drab lives, the reader feels deeply for them. More fully portrayed are the characters in *Secrets and Surprises,* men and women once again trapped in unfulfilling jobs and personal relationships. A more affluent group, they are into gourmet cooking, jogging, health foods, weekends in the country, and the usual fare of the 1970s upper-middle-class mobile society. What they share is a deep sense of emptiness, although friendship and pets (particularly dogs) are once more their only comfort. Some of Beattie's most memorable evocations of loneliness and yearning are in the title story, ''A Vintage Thunderbird,'' ''A Reasonable Man,'' ''Distant Music,'' and ''The Lawn Party.'' Lines that summarize a lifetime—like one character's remark that people smile because they don't understand each other—underscore the collection. These people are trapped but they lack self-pity; they are lost but they still extend a hand.

An even more sophisticated society inhabits *The Burning House,* but it is the juxtaposition of loneliness and selflessness that continues to move the reader. Little occurs in the way of change, although there are occasional moments of muted insight; once again, the stories are evocations of mood, descriptive of states of being. There also remains very little trace of the 1960s past. Of particular interest is the title story and ''Learning to Fall,'' where Beattie concretizes two characters' remarks: ''What will happen can't be stopped,'' and ''I'm sick of hearing how things might have been worse, when they might also have been better.'' ''Girl Talk'' is about two women, one young, unmarried, and pregnant, and the other, the unborn child's grandmother, who is many times married, wealthy, still beautiful but no longer capable of bearing children. It is about how ''pain is relative.'' ''The Cinderella Waltz,'' one of Beattie's most evocative stories, is about the complex of emotions exchanged between a mother and daughter and their estranged husband/father and his new male lover.

Falling in Place, Beattie's second novel, portrays the limited control one has over one's destiny and how life just seems to fall in place. Once again, Beattie measures the fragility of relationships, here focusing on the disintegration of a family and the guilt that falls to both parents and children. The book lacks a traditional plot; rather, Beattie shifts from character to character and then combines events from each chapter into brief italicized mood interludes. Set in Connecticut and New York in the summer of 1979, the novel focuses on the surrogate emotional relationships each member of the John Knapp family sets up. The climax revolves around the son's quasi-accidental shooting of his sister and how the family members finally face one another—things fall into place. Although the book ends with a positive resolution, like *Chilly Scenes of Winter,* it is bitter and the prognosis for future happiness is bleak.

Love Always, Beattie's third novel, marks a change in style and vision. Less detached, satiric, and sympathetic, her indictment of her materially successful, world-weary people is more pronounced. The book opens at a Vermont retreat, where the sophisticates of a trendy New York magazine, *Country Daze,* have gathered. Lucy Spenser, for example, under the pseudonym Cindi Coeur, writes both the letters and answers for a tongue-in-cheek Miss Lonelyhearts column. Lucy's niece, 14-year-old Nicole, who joins the group, is a TV actress who portrays an adolescent alcoholic on a popular soap opera. The brilliance of the novel results from Beattie's intertwining how the real-life Vermont group is defined not just by the bucolic fantasy of country life espoused by the magazine but also by the fantasies and grim truth of the Miss Lonelyhearts column, as well as the melodramatic, selfish, and sometimes cruel world of television and Hollywood soaps. The so-called real characters in the novel—infertile in every sense of the word—are as needy and blighted as any portrayed by the printed word or on screen. These characters also lack, one should note, the compassion and generosity that have characterized Beattie's earlier people.

The short stories in *Where You'll Find Me* are terse, minimalist profiles of Beattie's familiar 1960s and 1970s types, once again estranged from themselves and others. Now successful doctors, lawyers, and Indian chiefs, they have the money, possessions, and social respect that go along with their time, place, and economic efforts. But they suffer the losses that accompany people of their status and age, such as divorce, illness, and death. Beattie's focus is the enormous disparity between external success and inner emptiness. All the same, these figures retain our sympathy. ''People and things never really get left behind,'' remarks one, very much aware that human connection remains possible.

Picturing Will confronts the next, logical question. Can one have it all: ambition, success, and a child? And if so, how does one deal with the eventualities of divorce, missing fathers, potential stepfathers, and—always of central concern—the young child? Will is the five- and later six-year-old abandoned child of a scurrilous, selfish, and violent father. His mother, clearly the more caring parent, is torn between career and motherhood. It is her lover, Mel, who truly parents and completely loves Will. The novel is divided into three sections that reflect each family member's point of view: interwoven through these, in addition, is yet another commentary that functions as the authorial voice, in matters of true responsibility and a child's deepest needs. The commentary is, in fact, from Mel's diary.

If Beattie's earlier characters were passive products of a specific social, cultural, and political world, the figures here are personally responsible for their own lives, despite the vagaries of fate. But Beattie never loses her sense of humor. Mel, for example, remarks on the responsibilities of fatherhood: ''Do everything right, all the time, and the child will prosper. It's as simple as that, except for fate, luck, heredity, chance, the astrological sign under which the child was born, his order of birth, his first encounter with evil, the girl who jilts him in spite of his excellent qualities.''

The fragility of human relationships and their inevitable disintegration—between friends, spouses, children and parents—is once again Beattie's subject in *What Was Mine.* ''You Know What,'' the ironic title of one story, could well characterize many of the others: characters speak on slightly tangential levels that are sufficiently askew to guarantee miscommunication. Mothers and fathers worry over children—whose lives justify worry—but the quality and definition of that worry is frequently inappropriate. In ''Horatio's Trick,'' a 19-year-old college student criticizes his mother for being too intimidated by him to directly ask about his life. Beattie acknowledges the son's disturbance: ''She was just sitting there, scared to death.'' The title piece tells of another son whose father died after World War II, and whose mother, true to the father's memory, lived with but never married ''Uncle Herb.'' Ethan, the son, now a young man, loves Herb as a father, but they are forced to separate when the mother, ''irrationally angry,'' decides she no longer wants him in the house. Herb tries to console the son with advice to listen to Billie Holiday's records, study Vermeer's paintings, and ''look around'' and ''listen.'' He explains that ''What to some people might seem the silliest sort of place might be, to those truly observant, a temporary substitute for heaven.'' One makes due with what one has at hand. The deep compassion in Beattie's portrayals of these necessary accommodations, along with her exquisite evocation of the emptiness and loneliness in both the self and world, continue to place her among the best fiction writers in America today. One is haunted by lines such as the following, exchanged between two 14-year-old boys: ''We both suffered because we sensed that you had to *look* like John F. Kennedy in order to *be* John F. Kennedy.''

The plot of *Another You* involves an exceedingly complex set of relationships between characters Marshall, Sonja, McCallum, Cheryl, Sarah, Livan, and Tony. Marshall remains the central figure, however, and throughout the story he is dogged by the awareness of a secret involving his past. Eventually the reader learns what this secret is, but Marshall never does. Darcy Fisher, who goes by the stage name of Dara Falcon, also has a secret, and this provides part of the allure that draws Jean Warner, the narrator of *My Life, Starring Dara Falcon,* to her. This book represents a shift for Beattie: not only is it her first coming-of-age story, but it relies less on the details of the 1970s (Jean in the 1990s tells the story as a flashback) than on the powerful relationships of its characters.

—Lois Gordon

BECKER, Stephen (David)

Also writes as Steve Dodge. **Nationality:** American. **Born:** Mount Vernon, New York, 31 March 1927. **Education:** Harvard University, Cambridge, Massachusetts, 1943–47, B.A. 1947; Yenching University, Peking, 1947–48. **Military Service:** Served in the United States Marine Corps, 1945. **Family:** Married Mary Elizabeth Freeburg in 1947; two sons and one daughter. **Career:** Instructor, Tsing Hua University, Peking, 1947–48; teaching fellow, Brandeis University, Waltham, Massachusetts, 1951–52; lecturer, University of Alaska, College, 1967, Bennington College, Vermont, 1971, 1977, 1978, University of Iowa, Iowa City, 1974, and Hollins College, Virginia, 1986. Since 1987 professor of English, University of Central Florida, Orlando. Editor, Western Printing Company, New York, 1955–56. **Awards:** Paul Harris fellowship, 1947; Guggenheim fellowship, 1954; National Endowment for the Arts grant, for translation, 1984. **Agent:** Russell and Volkening Inc., 50 West 29th Street, New York, New York 10001. **Address:** 880 Benchwood Dr., Winter Spring, Florida 32708, U.S.A.

PUBLICATIONS

Novels

The Season of the Stranger. New York, Harper, and London, Hamish Hamilton, 1951.
Shanghai Incident (as Steve Dodge). New York, Fawcett, 1955; London, Fawcett, 1956.
Juice. New York, Simon and Schuster, 1958; London, Muller, 1959.
A Covenant with Death. New York, Atheneum, and London, Hamish Hamilton, 1965.
The Outcasts. New York, Atheneum, and London, Hamish Hamilton, 1967.
When the War Is Over. New York, Random House, 1969; London, Hamish Hamilton, 1970.
Dog Tags. New York, Random House, 1973; London, Barrie and Jenkins, 1974.
The Chinese Bandit. New York, Random House, 1975; London, Chatto and Windus, 1976.
The Last Mandarin. New York, Random House, and London, Chatto and Windus, 1979.
The Blue-Eyed Shan. New York, Random House, and London, Collins, 1982.
A Rendezvous in Haiti. New York, Norton, and London, Collins, 1987.

Uncollected Short Stories

''To Know the Country,'' in *Harper's* (New York), August 1951.
''The Town Mouse,'' in *The Best American Short Stories 1953,* edited by Martha Foley. Boston, Houghton Mifflin, 1953.
''A Baptism of Some Importance,'' in *Story.* New York, McKay, 1953.
''Monsieur Malfait,'' in *Harper's* (New York), June 1953.
''The New Encyclopaedist,'' in *The Year's Best SF 10,* edited by Judith Merril. New York, Delacorte Press, 1965.
''Rites of Passage,'' in *Florida Review* (Orlando) Autumn 1984.

Other

Comic Art in America: A Social History of the Funnies, the Political Cartoons, Magazine Humor, Sporting Cartoons, and Animated Cartoons. New York, Simon and Schuster, 1959.
Marshall Field III: A Biography. New York, Simon and Schuster, 1964.
Translator, *The Colors of the Day,* by Romain Gary. New York, Simon and Schuster, and London, Joseph, 1953.
Translator, *Mountains in the Desert,* by Louis Carl and Joseph Petit. New York, Doubleday, 1954; as *Tefedest,* London, Allen and Unwin, 1954.
Translator, *The Sacred Forest,* by Pierre-Dominique Gaisseau. New York, Knopf, 1954.
Translator, *Faraway,* by André Dhôtel. New York, Simon and Schuster, 1957.
Translator, *Someone Will Die Tonight in the Caribbean,* by René Puissesseau. New York, Knopf, 1958; London, W.H. Allen, 1959.
Translator, *The Last of the Just,* by André Schwarz-Bart. New York, Atheneum, and London, Secker and Warburg, 1961.
Translator, *The Town Beyond the Wall,* by Elie Wiesel. New York, Atheneum, 1964; London, Robson, 1975.
Translator, *The Conquerors,* by André Malraux. New York, Holt Rinehart, 1976.
Translator, *Diary of My Travels in America,* by Louis-Philippe. New York, Delacorte Press, 1977.
Translator, *Ana No,* by Agustín Gomez-Arcos. London, Secker and Warburg, 1980.
Translator, *The Forgotten,* by Elie Wiesel. New York, Schoken, 1995.
Translator, *The Last of the Just,* by Andre Schwarz-Bart. Woodstock, New York, Overlook Press, 2000.

*

Critical Study: By Becker, in *Contemporary Authors Autobiography Series 1* edited by Dedria Bryfonski, Detroit, Gale, 1984.

* * *

Equally distinguished as a translator, a biographer, a commentator on the popular arts, and a novelist, Stephen Becker brings to his fiction a breadth of experience with world culture and human behavior which yields moral complexity and psychological verity in his work. Two major themes intertwine through his novels—the problems of justice and the necessity for self-knowledge and self-fulfillment.

Beginning most clearly with *Juice,* Becker concentrates on the moral and social complexities of law and justice, continuing this theme in *A Covenant with Death* and *When the War Is Over.* The problem Becker's protagonists face is to distinguish between the arbitrary and mechanical justice of the law and true human justice. The rigidity and absoluteness of law collide with human values—especially the need for expiation, mercy and compassion. The characters' dilemma is to choose between true justice and simple retribution and to use the mechanism of blind justice to solve difficult moral problems. Against this theme is developed another—an existential concept of the self, men struggling with themselves, with nature and with circumstances to become fully alive and functioning beings. This theme is isolated most clearly in *The Outcasts,* which describes a group of engineers building a bridge deep in a primeval jungle. There they must overcome the indifferent force of nature, their own weaknesses, their fears and prejudices.

In *Juice* the theme of human and mechanical justice arises when the central character, Joseph Harrison, kills a pedestrian in an auto accident. His friends and employer try to use the law and the power of money and position (''juice'') to white-wash the occurrence, while Harrison demands an absolute judgment to redeem his error. The tensions between views of law and truth reshape Harrison's whole existence. In *A Covenant with Death* a young judge is confronted with a difficult decision in a murder case; through detective work, insights into motivation and a complete understanding of the limits of the law, Judge Lewis is able to render a humane verdict and still satisfy the meaning of law. The forces of procrustean and draconian legalism are averted through the judge's efforts, through an intense moral revaluation which ultimately changes the judge's own life. In this novel, humanity triumphs through the action of the law.

The tragedy of the law is exposed in *When the War Is Over,* Becker's most satisfying novel. It is the story of the last victim of the

Civil War, a boy executed as a Confederate guerrilla long after hostilities had ceased. The moral struggle is embodied in Lt. Marius Catto, a young career officer caught between a genuine love of peace and justice and a natural inclination toward the arts of war. He works to prevent General Hooker from wreaking vengeance through law on the boy but fails and is left scarred and embittered by disillusionment. The novel, based on historical fact, is a brilliant reconstruction of the time and place and an intense scrutiny of moral and social values. It convincingly examines the mechanism of military order, social justice and our conflicting views of violence and law. The story uncovers basic contradictions in our organization of legal murder.

Dog Tags is another densely detailed chronicle of man at war and his ability to survive it humanly and intelligently. It focuses on Benjamin Beer, a Jew wounded in World War II and later interned in North Korea. His response to war is to become a skilled and humane doctor, as if in expiration for the universal crime of war. His life is a moral struggle for self-knowledge and understanding of man's limitless potentials; ''You're worried about good and bad,'' he says, ''well, I'm worried about good and evil.'' In his quest, Benjamin learns his own abilities and limitations and achieves peace and grace within himself.

The Chinese Bandit, The Last Mandarin, and *The Blue-Eyed Shan* are finely-wrought and highly atmospheric Asian tales which focus on the collision of Western adventurers with oriental culture. Each story details the effect of American mercenaries in search of action in China and Southeast Asia after World War II and develops the moral and social conflicts between the two cultures through tales of violence and individual struggles for survival. The landscape and social patterns of a changeless East are refracted through the sensibilities of self-sufficient and resourceful Americans who find themselves alone in the crowds of the orient.

In *A Rendezvous in Haiti,* Becker returns to the U.S. Marines as a focus for a romantic adventure. The novel follows a young Marine lieutenant, Robert McAllister, and his fiancée during a rebellion in Haiti in 1919. McAllister, a veteran of the brutality of World War I, must single-handedly rescue his fiancée from the rebels (and the romantic spell of a mysterious rebel chieftain), crossing the island and its dense jungles. The story, like Becker's earlier Conradian romances, is rich with authentic period details and feeling and also comments seriously on American political and cultural imperialism and adventurism.

Becker's examination of society's structure and limitations and his portrayal of men seeking ''grace under pressure'' is a significant contribution to contemporary fiction. The existential premises of the works—individuals finding meaning inside the arbitrary bounds of social order—reflect our acceptance of the civilization we have built.

—William J. Schafer

BECKETT, Mary

Nationality: Northern Irish. **Born:** Belfast, Northern Ireland, 28 January 1926. **Education:** Attended St. Mary's Training College. **Family:** Married Peter Gaffey in 1956; three sons, two daughters. **Career:** Teacher at primary schools in Belfast, Northern Ireland, 1945–56. **Awards:** Arts Award (Ireland *Sunday Tribune*), 1987. **Agent:** Nat Sobel, Nat Sobel Associates, Inc., 146 East 19th Street, New York, New York 10003, U.S.A. **Address:** 24 Templeville Drive, Dublin, Ireland.

PUBLICATIONS

Novels

Give Them Stones. New York, Beech Tree Books, 1987.

Short Stories

A Belfast Woman and Other Stories. Swords, County Dublin, Ireland, Poolbeg Press, 1980.
A Literary Woman. London, Bloomsbury, 1991.

Other

Orla at School (for children), illustrated by Carol Betera. Swords, County Dublin, Ireland, Poolbeg Press, 1991.
A Family Tree, illustrated by Ann Kennedy. Swords, County Dublin, Ireland, Poolbeg Press, 1992.

* * *

Mary Beckett's two collections of short stories, *A Belfast Woman* and *A Literary Woman*, and her novel *Give Them Stones*, have earned her a place as one of contemporary Ireland's finest writers. The people she writes about are ordinary, and their lives mundane. Against the backdrop of Irish political dissonance and the constant, random threat of violence, their lives are shaped by a tragic undertone of loss and compromise. Beckett's writing is spare, and often disconcerting. Her Ireland is a crumbling edifice where life must go on, often at a great price, and the nation's political and public traumas are replayed in the family again and again, between the generations and between men and women. Beckett, a former primary school teacher and writer for the BBC, is a Roman Catholic whose non-partisan portrait of Ireland shows it to be a country with no victorious sides.

The thankless position of women, particularly those in the lower middle-class, comprises Beckett's focus in many of her short stories and in *Give Them Stones*. Beckett writes about women living on the precipice between middle-class respectability and lower-class suffering. As Frank McCourt has popularized in *Angela's Ashes,* the entrapment of Irish women due to the common stresses of (primarily male) alcoholism and unemployment create a nation of beleaguered wives, and Beckett's are no exception. They desire national unity not out of deeply felt political convictions, but out of a desire to more easily live their lives and better protect their children. The women in Beckett's stories offer case studies of the chronically depressed, told with the graceful hand of a poet.

Beckett's stylistic influences are an earlier generation of British women writers, including Rosamund Lehman, Elizabeth Taylor, and Muriel Spark, who like Beckett, deftly and economically capture the details of private, interior lives. She also shares the polite detachment of Anita Brookner, but Beckett's heroines seem one step closer to madness, fraught as they are by random IRA raids, fires, and harassment. Beckett's overarching tone of compromise is lifted, when least expected, by a sharp wit that counteracts the bleakness of the lives of these women and men, and infuses her stories with the calmness sometimes possible in the heart of a crisis.

Beckett's first collection of stories, *A Belfast Woman*, anticipates her later works in its recurrent theme of women learning to adapt to disappointing lives. One woman resents demands made on her with a telling reflection upon her place in the world: ''I'm a woman. I'm supposed to be passive. I've got three small children. I'm expecting another.'' This woman's catalogue of troubles extends naturally from the assertion of her gender, and like many of her fictional counterparts, she endures by resignation rather than courage. The small acts of rebellion of many of Beckett's women are characterized not so much by bravery but by desperation, and for the protection of someone else—husband, children, or parents.

The resigned tone of *A Belfast Woman* is repeated in *Give Them Stones*, but Beckett's novel is an extraordinary document of one woman's struggle against the oppressive tide of poverty and political oppression. The longer narrative structure suits Beckett well, as she recounts in detail heroine Martha Hughes's life, from childhood through middle age. As with many of the women in Beckett's stories, Martha is a strong woman surrounded by weak men. Her father cannot find work and dies young, after virtually neglecting his family in favor of his political loyalties. Her brother is another disappointment, a ne'er-do-well killed young by the IRA. Martha decides to marry the passive but affable Dermot Hughes largely because his family house includes a well-appointed kitchen. Martha finds in this kitchen her deliverance from a lifetime of waiting for Dermot to provide for her and their children (which he does so only intermittently). Using her talent for baking, Martha sells bread from home to her neighbors, all while caring for Dermot, an unsympathetic mother-in-law, and her four sons.

But Martha's determination to take her life into her own hands is hardly a statement of empowerment. Her efforts to earn money are a mark of her desperation, and the aching fatigue that comes from her work is a predominant theme in the novel. In the only form of defiance she has access to, Martha refuses to sell her bread to IRA soldiers after experiencing their harassment and witnessing their haphazard murder of a young neighbor boy. The ending of *Give Them Stones* is unexpected because uplifting, and with it Beckett shows her talent for making narrow lives the subject of greatness, and for finding hope, love, and forgiveness in improbable places.

In *A Literary Woman*, stories mostly set in Dublin, Beckett expands her range by weaving in and out of these tales the maddening presence of an anonymous letter writer, a self-proclaimed ''watcher'' or ''well-wisher'' who takes it upon herself to write incriminating letters, anonymously. This woman, revealed in the titular story, translates neighbors' problems into misinformed and misbegotten rumors—a dead child motivates the charge of infanticide, a distant wife is accused of alcoholism. These letters unsettle their recipients, and the malevolence of the ''literary woman'' documents a noxious public spirit, a local version of Ireland's larger, political and religious enmity. These stories surprise and unnerve the reader in ways that inspire new attention to the seemingly plainest of people and events. Their canny ability to unsettle the simple domestic worlds that Beckett illustrates suggest that no private life, however modest, is without its private dramas and illicit secrets.

Critics have almost universally singled out Mary Beckett as an important chronicler of life in modern Ireland, and as a writer with a uniquely lyrical prose style. *Give Them Stones* has been called a ''small miracle'' and ''immensely readable,'' and was awarded Ireland's *Sunday Tribute* 1987 Arts Award for Literature.

—Tabitha Sparks

BEDFORD, Sybille

Nationality: British. **Born:** Sybille von Schoenebeck in Charlottenburg, Germany, 16 March 1911. **Education:** Privately in Italy, England, and France. **Family:** Married Walter Bedford in 1935. **Career:** Worked as a law reporter: covered the Auschwitz trial at Frankfurt for the *Observer,* London, and the *Saturday Evening Post,* Philadelphia, 1963–65, and the trial of Jack Ruby at Dallas for *Life,* New York, 1964. Vice-president, PEN, 1979. **Awards:** Society of Authors traveling scholarship, 1989. Fellow, Royal Society of Literature, 1964. O.B.E. (Officer, Order of British Empire), 1981. **Address:** c/o Greene and Heaton, 37 Goldhawk Rd., London W12 8Q0, England.

PUBLICATIONS

Novels

A Legacy. London, Weidenfeld and Nicolson, 1956; New York, Simon and Schuster, 1957.

A Favourite of the Gods. London, Collins, and New York, Simon and Schuster, 1963.

A Compass Error. London, Collins, 1968; New York, Knopf, 1969.

Jigsaw: An Unsentimental Education. London, Hamish Hamilton, and New York, Knopf, 1989.

Uncollected Short Stories

''Compassionata at Hyde Park Corner,'' in *23 Modern Stories.* New York, Knopf, 1963.

''Une vie de chateau,'' in *New Yorker,* 20 February 1989.

Other

A Visit to Don Otavio: A Mexican Journey. London, Gollancz, and New York, Harper, 1953; revised edition, New York, Atheneum, 1963; as *A Visit to Don Otavio: A Traveller's Tale from Mexico,* London, Collins, 1960.

The Best We Can Do: An Account of the Trial of John Bodkin Adams. London, Collins, 1958; as *The Trial of Dr. Adams,* New York, Simon and Schuster, 1959.

The Faces of Justice: A Traveller's Report. London, Collins, and New York, Simon and Schuster, 1961.

Aldous Huxley: A Biography. London, Chatto and Windus-Collins, 2 vols., 1973–74; New York, Knopf, 1 vol., 1974.

As It Was: Pleasures, Landscapes, and Justice. London, Sinclair Stevenson, 1990.

In Conversation with Naim Attallah. London, Quartet Books, 1998.

*

Critical Studies: By Evelyn Waugh, in *Spectator* (London), 13 April 1956; V.S. Pritchett, in *New Statesman* (London), 11 January 1963; P.N. Furbank, in *Encounter* (London), April 1964; Bernard Levin, in

London *Daily Mail,* 12 September 1966; Constantine FitzGibbon, in *Irish Times* (Dublin), 19 October 1968; introductions to *A Favourite of the Gods* and *A Compass Error,* both London, Virago Press, 1984, and article in *London Magazine,* January 1991, all by Peter Vansittart; Robert O. Evans in *British Novelists since 1900* edited by Jack I. Biles, New York, AMS Press, 1987; David Leavitt in *Voice Literary Supplement,* June 1990; Gilbert Phelps in *Folio Quarterly* (London), Winter 1990; Anne Sebbaix in *Daily Telegraph,* 4 February 1995.

* * *

The stature of Sybille Bedford's first and still her finest novel, *A Legacy,* suggests Thomas Mann's *Buddenbrooks,* or the historical theme of Hermann Broch's *The Sleepwalkers.* All three writers are continental in their attention to the effects of historical event on the flow of family life and time. If Bedford lacks the philosophical dimension of Mann or the high and heavy seriousness of Broch, she possesses instead energy, gaiety, and a refreshing comic sense that seem unmistakably British.

What stays in the mind long after a reading of *A Legacy* is not the Prussia or Baden of 1810–1913 in which it is set, but characters, scenes, and individual sentences of fine prose. Bedford's best characters are improbable but memorable for her objective treatment of them. Johannes von Feldon once danced with a bear at a fair, became autistic from the brutality of his military academy, then a decorated, still autistic captain of cavalry. Julius von Felden, a central figure in the chronicle, is nominally Catholic, briefly a diplomat, member of the Jockey Club in Paris, collector of bibelots, and devoted to his monkey and two chimpanzees, whom he treats as human beings. He marries into the Merz family of Berlin, astonished that they are nominally Jewish rather than Catholic, but content to accept their over-stuffed largesse. The elder Merzes are wealthy philistines given to large, frequent meals and to generosity to their feckless offspring and their children, who acquire ''the habit of being rich.'' The tragicomedy of the two families and their incompatible histories combine into a plot involving legacies, marriages, fornications, and displacements. The death of Julius's Merz wife, Melanie, a dim, determined girl, leads to his marriage to an Englishwoman, Caroline Trafford, a beautiful, fickle, interesting wife and, briefly, mother. The actual legacies are frittered away, and the figurative legacy of Caroline to Julius is a German house and a precocious daughter, who supposedly is narrator. The chronicle is mainly narrated in the third person.

A Favourite of the Gods, set in Italy, might appear to be a departure from *A Legacy,* but it is not. Often called ''Jamesian'' for its account of a wealthy American girl who marries a corrupt Roman minor aristocrat, it is James-like only in theme. The Italians here are caricatures, uttering ''Già'' and ''Meno male,'' while Anna the American is such only by description. Over-filled with incident, the novel relates the education of Constanza, Anna's daughter, who is brought up in Edwardian England when Anna cannot stomach her husband's adultery. Again people eat and drink fabulously, fall in and out of loves and beds, while potted history is served in chunks: ''Meanwhile, Mussolini marched on Rome.'' History here, as in the later *A Compass Error* and *Jigsaw,* is outlined, reported, but the characters do not actually live and have their fictional reality in that history. Constanza marries Simon Herbert, the author's least convincing character. A pacifist by conviction, he nevertheless is commissioned and sent to the trenches, emerging promptly with a convenient wound. A brilliant career follows, and an arranged divorce from Constanza permits his marriage to a press tycoon's daughter. Simon dies young. Constanza's daughter, Flavia, is born in 1914; after the war, Contanza moves from lover to lover but remains unmarried and at odds with Anna, the dowager-heroine. Wonderful episodes occur, but the novel suffers from a weak structure and a surfeit of raw matter.

Flavia is the narrator of *A Compass Error,* the structure of which is pure disaster. Left alone at 17 in Provence to swot for entrance to Oxford, Flavia engages in a lesbian affair and consumes some 53 pages of this brief novel to recapitulate in monologue to her lover the entire contents of *A Favourite of the Gods.* A psychologically improbable plot involving Constanza's last chance at marriage to a French intellectual unfolds. Flavia is again precocious, a great imbiber of claret, and intellectually ambitious as well as bisexual. Plot tends to falsify chronicle, which has its own twists and turns.

Jigsaw is a novel only by courtesy. Despite some novelistic touches, it is transparently personal memoir, as well as an explanation of the structural difficulties of the two preceding novels. We are back in the territory of *Legacy,* with the story of young Billi's (for Sybille) early years at Feldkirch with her father, the impoverished Julius, eating smoked mutton but drinking the rare clarets surviving from better days. Like Flavia, like Constanza, she moves as a young girl to London, then to Provence, and the dubious tutelage of her egotistical, beautiful, self-indulgent mother, who declines into poverty and drug addiction. Again the text is packed with incident, with essays on wine and politics, but now with actual historical figures: Aldous and Maria Huxley; Cyril Connolly, Roy Campbell, Ivy Compton-Burnett among them. Again a precocious girl aspires to university and fails, but a writer's career beckons (that distinguished career as travel writer and reporter which has also been Bedford's). Characters and entire episodes are lifted from the preceding narratives, but the story is frankly her own, with elements of confession and muted justification. Although eminently readable, the whole fails to do justice to splendid parts.

Bedford's affinity is perhaps not with Mann or Broch, but with Huxley and Compton-Burnett, whom she imitates, and with Molly Keane, who tells over and again the same story with elegant and delightful variations, comic turns with tragic overtones.

—John McCormick

BELL, Madison Smartt

Nationality: American. **Born:** Williamson County, Tennessee, 1 August 1957. **Education:** Princeton University, New Jersey, A.B. (summa cum laude) in English 1979; Hollins College, Virginia, M.A. 1981. **Family:** Married Elizabeth Spires in 1985; one daughter. **Career:** Writer-in-residence, Goucher College, Towson, Maryland, 1984–86, 1988–89; lecturer, YMHA Poetry Center, New York, 1984–86; visiting lecturer, University of Iowa Writers Workshop, Iowa City, 1987–88; lecturer, Johns Hopkins University Writing Seminars, Baltimore, Maryland, 1989–91. **Awards:** Lillian Smith award, 1989; Guggenheim fellowship, 1991; Maryland State Arts Council award, 1991; Howard Foundation fellowship, 1991; Robert Penn Warren award for the Fellowship of Southern Writers, 1995. **Agent:** Vivienne Schuster, John Farquharson Ltd., 162–168 Regent Street, London W1R 5TB, England; or, Jane Gelfman, John Farquharson Ltd., 250 West 57th Street, New York, New York

10107. **Address:** Department of English, Goucher College, Towson, Maryland 21204, U.S.A.

PUBLICATIONS

Novels

The Washington Square Ensemble. New York, Viking Press, and London, Deutsch, 1983.
Waiting for the End of the World. New York, Ticknor and Fields, and London, Chatto and Windus, 1985.
Straight Cut. New York, Ticknor and Fields, 1986; London, Chatto and Windus, 1987.
The Year of Silence. New York, Ticknor and Fields, and London, Chatto and Windus, 1987.
Soldier's Joy. New York, Ticknor and Fields, 1989.
Doctor Sleep. San Diego, Harcourt Brace, 1991.
Save Me, Joe Louis. San Diego, Harcourt Brace, 1993.
All Souls' Rising. New York, Pantheon, and London, Granta, 1995.
Ten Indians. New York, Pantheon Books, 1996.
Master of the Crossroads. New York, Pantheon Books, 2000.

Short Stories

Zero db and Other Stories. New York, Ticknor and Fields, and London, Chatto and Windus, 1987.
Barking Man and Other Stories. New York, Ticknor and Fields, 1990.

Other

The History of the Owen Graduate School of Management. Nashville, Tennessee, Vanderbilt University, 1988.
Narrative Design, a Writer's Guide to Structure. New York, W.W. Norton, 1997.

* * *

Madison Smartt Bell's special province is the sensuousness of desperation, the aesthetic hideaways in which the disenchanted, disenfranchised, and dysfunctional seek refuge from storms raging in their own minds. That has been clear from his first novel, *The Washington Square Ensemble,* whose tangle of first-person narratives follows a gang of urban heroin dealers through a jungle of violence and sin.

The violence and frantic edge-running of Bell's novels invite comparison with the early novels of Robert Stone. Both writers probe the grimy underbelly of life and characters balanced precariously between suicide and murder. But as dark as Bell's tales may be, rays of affirmation seep in, unlike Stone's. For Stone's characters, the darkening world offers little chance to wrench from it a life. But for Bell's, the moral condition of the world is either static or cyclic rather than entropic. There are dusks, but there are also dawns. In that way, Bell's world may be truer than Stone's, and less soul-deadening.

Bell's characters are in quest of redemption and rebirth. They'll blow bullet holes in traditional moral tablets, as do Stone's, but they seem more eager to pick up a pen and write new ones than to cling to the pistol.

This quest appears in Bell's 1985 novel, *Waiting for the End of the World,* the story of a plot to detonate a nuclear device under New York. Larkin, an associate member of a cell led by the profoundly maladjusted psychiatrist Simon Rohnstock, has the unenviable position of human trigger for the weapon—a kind of guerrilla Valhalla entirely appropriate to Bell's message, for the author seems to suggest that only gestures of immense proportion can have any lasting impact in an age of mass lassitude.

Ultimately, collective will disintegrates as Rohnstock decides that this venture might be just the vehicle to propel him to para-political supremacy, and Larkin begins to doubt his own purpose. By this stage however, the focus has shifted towards the novel's other themes: Larkin has ''adopted'' Tommy, the child victim of vicious ritualistic abuse, and is being pursued by the boy's demented father—a dark avenging angel. Descending into the detritus of New York society, Bell unifies several quasi-religious sub-texts, blending a spate of spontaneous combustions, elements of Russian Orthodoxy, and a liberal dose of Satanism. The subsequent action takes on mystic overtones—Tommy's real name is revealed to be Gabriel, and he, previously mute, manifests visionary powers and a voice suitable to their expression. Larkin's own spectacular fate is just one of many impressive flashes of invention that litter a script which is both a convincing study of personal motivation and an accomplished semi-allegorical interpretation of late twentieth-century malaise.

Straight Cut reveals a clear movement towards order. Bell follows the rivalry between Tracy Bateman and Kevin Carter, former friends and colleagues in an independent film-making company that has been their cover for drug smuggling. Kevin and Tracy represent two sides of the same nature, one scheming and manipulative, the other intuitive and unambiguous; platonically in love with each other and both in love with Tracy's estranged wife Lauren. The real interest of the book lies not in the high-tension plot twists, but in the duel between intellect and instinct, a tussle kept alive brilliantly by Bell's rapid scene shifting and neat line in tough-guy backchat.

The Year of Silence fuses multiple narrative perspectives, offering a series of individual reactions to Marian's death from an overdose. Friends, lovers, and nodding acquaintances are all struggling desperately to come to terms with a world bereft of her presence. In truth, only Gwen, Marian's cousin, has by the end of the book reached a compromise, and we leave her in the sanctuary of a white clapboard holiday home, preparing to restart her life. The loss of a ''flair for transforming the tacky into something transcendent'' is to be mourned, but whether it quite merits the indulgence of a whole book is questionable. Depending on your preference, Bell either offers a stunning essay on the idolization of vacuousness or fails to evoke sufficient sympathy for Marian for us to feel much moved by the bleatings of the bereaved.

If *The Year of Silence* lacks completeness, almost all of the pieces in *Zero db* are the finished article: polished, absorbing, and of a consistently high standard. This is Bell in virtuoso form, producing an utterly compelling range of voice and concern, and throwing off the shades of Faulkner and Poe which have coloured his previous technical and imaginative achievements. ''Today Is a Good Day to Die'' is a memorable highlight, and, happily, in ''Triptych I'' and ''Triptych II'' we are at last afforded a real insight, from an insider, into life on a Tennessee hog farm.

In *Soldier's Joy,* Thomas Laidlaw returns from Vietnam to his family's now-deserted farm outside Nashville. A loner, Laidlaw wants little more than peace, freedom to roam the landscape, and time to hone his considerable talents as a bluegrass banjo player. He's been half a world away dispensing and avoiding death.

Tennessee seems the ideal place to heal from a disorienting war. Bell's minutely observed description make Laidlaw's deliberate actions feel like Nick Adams returning to the Big Two-Hearted River, his farm an arcadian balm to his senses. Then comes Laidlaw's reunion with his black childhood friend and Vietnam comrade Rodney Redmon, and Laidlaw learns he has simply left one war zone for another. *Soldier's Joy* is a tale of life lived close to the bone. Once again Bell tenses his muscular grip on the feel and meaning of violence, wrenching a piece of literary art from a plot whose outline could sound like that of a television movie.

In *Doctor Sleep,* Bell weaves an arresting if uneven tapestry. Its several threads unfurl from three closely observed days and nights in the life of Adrian Strother. Four years earlier, Adrian had sworn off both heroin and New York City and moved to London. Now he works as a hypnotist, ''a sort of psychological repairman,'' whose most interesting client, Eleanor Peavy, suffers multiple personalities: prim Miss Peavey by day, prostitute Nell by night.

She is the least of Adrian's problems. Wracked by insomnia, he walks London's streets where a serial killer brutally murders little girls. Mistaken for his friend Stuart (a born-again former addict now forming a heroin self-help center), Adrian is stalked by thugs and abducted by London's chief heroin distributor. When drug traffickers are not hunting him, he's hunting them under pressure from Scotland Yard. On free nights, he moonlights as a stage hypnotist at a burlesque club or works out at a tae kwon do studio and spars with his West Indian friend Terence after class in the dark.

Back in Adrian's flat, his pet boa constrictor is losing color and won't eat, and Adrian's neglected girlfriend Clara has left him for the fourth time. Nicole—the dazzling former call-girl Stuart battered and Adrian secretly married—is in London, maybe to pick up with Adrian again or maybe to ask him for a divorce. All the while, Adrian reflects obsessively on the Hermetic mysticism of Renaissance philosopher Giorano Bruno. Little wonder Adrian cannot sleep.

As far removed from the Tennessee hills, glacial pacing, and third-person restraint of *Soldier's Joy* as *Doctor Sleep* is, the two books feel strongly linked. Like returning soldier Thomas Laidlaw, Adrian seldom eats and never sleeps, has thematically important attachments to both his male friends and his animals, and is painfully reticent about his feelings. Most importantly, like Laidlaw just back from Vietnam, Adrian is a solitary figure in need of healing.

There is nothing new about that. Since his first novel, *The Washington Square Ensemble,* with its cluster of heroin dealers, Bell has always written with conspicuous sympathy for the alienated and the bruised. He searches for characters beaten down by a combination of life and poor choices, whose hearts (to paraphrase a line of Spires's) are a bit off-center, yet who desire affirmation. At some point, a moment flickers where new choice is possible, and they choose to move toward grace, often amid religious symbolism.

As the elements of *Doctor Sleep* bond artfully together—as Eleanor Peavey's pathology links to the vicious child murders which tie to the London drug lord who bears on Adrian's work with Scotland Yard and Adrian's need to face the truth which joins him in spirit to Eleanor Peavey—perhaps the most important element turns out to be Adrian's fasting snake. Adrian feels a Jungian connection to it and keeps it ''in honor and acknowledgment of the snake in'' himself. The boa constrictor will not eat for the same reason Adrian cannot sleep: he is undergoing a dramatic metamorphosis.

Bell may not always hide the symbolic seams where plot and philosophy join, he can oversensationalize an ending, and his fascination for characters from society's dingiest creases does put off some readers. But in *Doctor Sleep* he once again artfully blends perceptiveness, a deadpan mastery of the grotesque, and a startling profundity of mind.

Though Bell meanders between the beatific Appalachian rurality of his childhood, the decaying gothic grandeur of the New York that nursed from him his first novel, and foggy London, he is, in fact, a regional writer. His region is the misty border buffering purgatory from hell in the sootiest creases of contemporary society. In *Save Me, Joe Louis,* 23-year-old Macrae walks that border. He is AWOL from the army and living in New York's Hell's Kitchen. He hasn't enjoyed much of anything since his teen years in Tennessee when he was in love, without knowing it, with a spirited photographer named Lacy.

Petulant and lost, Macrae often takes ''a wring fork in the criss-cross trails of conversation'' and blindly strews mines along his own path. He forms unfortunate attachments, one to a prostitute whose pimp decides to blow half her head off. Macrae's most dangerous alliance is with his increasingly unstable partner-in-crime Charlie, whose rationale—''Ain't nobody cares that much what you do''—faintly recalls Flannery O'Connor's Misfit. After they've made New York too hot for their comfort by forcing people to withdraw and turn over money from their ATMs, they head south to Baltimore where they add a third partner, a benign young black man named Porter, fresh off a jail term for a bar fight that turned inadvertently gory. The three hold up an armored bank truck, but police arrive, bullets fly, and the trio heads full speed for Macrae's father's farm outside of Nashville.

Were trigger-happy Charlie not with him, Macrae might at last feel he's returned from far east of Eden. There's the potential for a wholesome life in Tennessee. Adjacent to Macrae's land is the farm of Thomas Laidlaw, the hero of *Soldier's Joy.* Not only is Laidlaw there, still playing banjo with his bluegrass band and still with Adrienne Wells, but the beautiful Lacy has returned home from art school in Philadelphia. That she still loves Macrae is clear to everyone but him, who keeps stumbling aimlessly in restless confusion. After a robbery attempt which they botch even worse than the Baltimore fiasco, Macrae, Charlie, and Porter flee to the South Carolina coast. There it grows obvious that Macrae may have outlived his usefulness to Charlie, and that the book's final page won't be big enough to hold both of them.

In *Save Me, Joe Louis,* Bell once again invites us to care about characters who offer scarcely an inch of ground to build affection on. Yet once again, by combining subtle technique and native compassion, he succeeds, walking sympathetically among contemporary thieves and moral lepers with a charity that either converts or shames his readers. *All Souls' Rising* is the most intensely historical of Bell's works, drawing on a time and place unfamiliar to many American readers—Haiti during its struggle for independence in the late 1700s and early 1800s. The book was a finalist for the National Book Award, but *Ten Indians* was less well-received. With its diffuse plot surrounding Mike Derlin, a white professional who inexplicably opens a martial arts school in the black projects of Baltimore, it ran the risk of losing focus. Yet *All Souls' Rising* has proven that Bell can paint beautifully on a large canvas, without losing a sense of the entire picture.

—Ian McMechan, updated by Andy Solomon

BELLOW, Saul

Nationality: American. **Born:** Lachine, Quebec, Canada, 10 June 1915; grew up in Montreal; moved with his family to Chicago, 1924. **Education:** Tuley High School, Chicago, graduated 1933; University of Chicago, 1933–35; Northwestern University, Evanston, Illinois, 1935–37, B.S. (honors) in sociology and anthropology 1937; did graduate work in anthropology at University of Wisconsin, Madison, 1937. **Military Service:** Served in the United States Merchant Marine, 1944–45. **Family:** Married 1) Anita Goshkin in 1937 (divorced), one son; 2) Alexandra Tschacbasov in 1956 (divorced), one son; 3) Susan Glassman in 1961 (divorced), one son; 4) Alexandra Ionescu Tulcea in 1975 (divorced 1986); 5) Janis Freedman in 1989, one daughter. **Career:** Teacher, Pestalozzi-Froebel Teachers College, Chicago, 1938–42; member of the editorial department, ''Great Books'' Project, *Encyclopaedia Britannica,* Chicago, 1943–44; freelance editor and reviewer, New York, 1945–46; instructor, 1946, and assistant professor of English, 1948–49, University of Minnesota, Minneapolis; visiting lecturer, New York University, 1950–52; Creative Writing Fellow, Princeton University, New Jersey, 1952–53; member of the English faculty, Bard College, Annandale-on-Hudson, New York, 1953–54; associate professor of English, University of Minnesota, 1954–59; visiting professor of English, University of Puerto Rico, Rio Piedras, 1961; Romanes Lecturer, 1990. Since 1962 professor and chairman, 1970–76, Committee on Social Thought, University of Chicago; now Gruiner Distinguished Services Professor. Co-editor, *The Noble Savage,* New York, then Cleveland, 1960–62. Fellow, Academy for Policy Study, 1966; fellow, Branford College, Yale University, New Haven, Connecticut. **Awards:** Guggenheim fellowship, 1948, 1955; American Academy grant, 1952, and gold medal, 1977; National Book award, 1954, 1965, 1971; Ford grant, 1959, 1960; Friends of Literature award, 1960; James L. Dow award, 1964; International Literary prize, 1965; Jewish Heritage award, 1968; Formentor prize, 1970; Nobel Prize for Literature, 1976; Pulitzer prize, 1976; Neil Gunn International fellowship, 1977; Brandeis University Creative Arts award, 1978; Malaparte award (Italy), 1984; Scanno award (Italy), 1988; National Book award, for lifetime achievement, 1990; Lifetime Cultural Achivement Award (YIVO Institute for Jewish Research), 1996. D.Litt.: Northwestern University, 1962; Bard College, 1963; Litt.D.: New York University, 1970; Harvard University, Cambridge, Massachusetts, 1972; Yale University, 1972; McGill University, Montreal, 1973; Brandeis University, Waltham, Massachusetts, 1973; Hebrew Union College, Cincinnati, 1976; Trinity College, Dublin, 1976. Chevalier, 1968, and Commander, 1985, Order of Arts and Letters (France); Commander, Legion of Honor (France), 1983. **Member:** American Academy, 1970. **Agent:** Harriett Wasserman Literary Agency, 137 East 36th Street, New York, New York 10016. **Address:** Committee on Social Thought, University of Chicago, 1126 East 59th Street, Chicago, Illinois 60637, U.S.A.

PUBLICATIONS

Novels

Dangling Man. New York, Vanguard Press, 1944; London, Lehmann, 1946.
The Victim. New York, Vanguard Press, 1947; London, Lehmann, 1948.
The Adventures of Augie March. New York, Viking Press, 1953; London, Weidenfeld and Nicolson, 1954; with an introduction by Martin Amis. New York, Knopf, 1995.
Henderson the Rain King. New York, Viking Press, and London, Weidenfeld and Nicolson, 1959.
Herzog. New York, Viking Press, 1964; London, Weidenfeld and Nicolson, 1965.
Mr. Sammler's Planet. New York, Viking Press, and London, Weidenfeld and Nicolson, 1970; with an introduction by Stanley Crouch. New York, Penguin Books, 1996.
Humboldt's Gift. New York, Viking Press, and London, Secker and Warburg, 1975.
The Dean's December. New York, Harper, and London, Secker and Warburg, 1982.
More Die of Heartbreak. New York, Morrow, and London, Alison Press, 1987.
The Actual. New York, Viking, 1997.
Ravelstein. New York, Viking, 2000.

Short Stories

Seize the Day, with Three Short Stories and a One-Act Play (includes *The Wrecker*). New York, Viking Press, 1956; London, Weidenfeld and Nicolson, 1957; published as *Seize the Day*, with an introduction by Cynthia Ozick, New York, Penguin Books, 1996.
Mosby's Memoirs and Other Stories. New York, Viking Press, 1968; London, Weidenfeld and Nicolson, 1969.
Him with His Foot in His Mouth and Other Stories. New York, Harper, and London, Secker and Warburg, 1984.
A Theft. New York and London, Penguin, 1989.
The Bellarosa Connection. New York and London, Penguin, 1989.
Something to Remember Me By: Three Tales. New York, Viking, and London, Penguin, 1991.
The American Short Story: A Collection of the Best Known and Most Memorable Short Stories by the Great American Authors (contributor), edited by Thomas K. Parkes. New York, Galahad, 1994.

Uncollected Short Stories

''The Mexican General,'' in *Partisan Reader,* edited by William Phillips and Philip Rahv. New York, Dial Press, 1946.
''Dora,'' in *Harper's Bazaar* (New York), November 1949.
''A Sermon by Dr. Pep,'' in *The Best American Short Stories 1950,* edited by Martha Foley. Boston, Houghton Mifflin, 1950.
''The Trip to Galena,'' in *Partisan Review* (New York), November-December 1950.
''Address by Gooley MacDowell to the Hasbeens Club of Chicago,'' in *Nelson Algren's Book of Lonesome Monsters,* edited by Nelson Algren. New York, Lancer, 1962; London, Panther, 1964.
''The Old System,'' in *Playboy* (Chicago), January 1968.
''Burdens of a Lone Survivor,'' in *Esquire* (New York), December 1974.

Plays

The Wrecker (televised 1964). Included in *Seize the Day,* 1956.
Scenes from Humanitas: A Farce, in *Partisan Review* (New Brunswick, New Jersey), Summer 1962.

The Last Analysis (produced New York 1964; Derby, 1967). New York, Viking Press, 1965; London, Weidenfeld and Nicolson, 1966.

Under the Weather (includes *Out from Under, A Wen,* and *Orange Soufflé*, produced Edinburgh and New York, 1966; as *The Bellow Plays,* produced London, 1966). *A Wen* published in *Esquire* (New York), January 1965; in *Traverse Plays,* edited by Jim Haynes, London, Penguin, 1966; *Orange Soufflé* published in *Traverse Plays,* 1966; in *Best Short Plays of the World Theatre 1968–1973,* edited by Stanley Richards, New York, Crown, 1973.

Television Plays: *The Wrecker,* 1964.

Other

Dessins, by Jesse Reichek; text by Bellow and Christian Zervos. Paris, Editions Cahiers d'Art, 1960.

Recent American Fiction: A Lecture. Washington, D.C., Library of Congress, 1963.

Like You're Nobody: The Letters of Louis Gallo to Saul Bellow, 1961–62, Plus Oedipus-Schmoedipus, The Story That Started It All. New York, Dimensions Press, 1966.

Technology and the Frontiers of Knowledge, with others. New York, Doubleday, 1973.

The Portable Saul Bellow, edited by Gabriel Josipovici. New York, Viking Press, 1974; London, Penguin, 1977.

To Jerusalem and Back: A Personal Account. New York, Viking Press, and London, Secker and Warburg, 1976.

Nobel Lecture. Stockholm, United States Information Service, 1977.

Conversations with Saul Bellow, edited by Gloria L. Cronin and Ben Siegel. Jackson, University Press of Mississippi, 1994.

It All Adds Up: From the Dim Past to the Certain Future. New York, Viking, 1994.

The Collected Essays of Ralph Ellison (preface), edited by John F. Callahan. New York, Modern Library, 1995.

Foreword, *Sixty Years of Great Fiction from Partisan Review*, edited by William Phillips. Boston, Partisan Review Press, 1997.

Foreword, *Clean Hands: Clair Patterson's Crusade against Environmental Lead Contamination*, edited by Cliff I. Davidson. Commack, New York, Nova Science Publishers, 1998.

Editor, *Great Jewish Short Stories.* New York, Dell, 1963; London, Vallentine Mitchell, 1971.

*

Bibliographies: *Saul Bellow: A Comprehensive Bibliography* by B.A. Sokoloff and Mark E. Posner, Norwood, Pennsylvania, Norwood Editions, 1973; *Saul Bellow, His Works and His Critics: An Annotated International Bibliography* by Marianne Nault, New York, Garland, 1977; *Saul Bellow: A Bibliography of Secondary Sources* by F. Lercangée, Brussels, Center for American Studies, 1977; *Saul Bellow: A Reference Guide* by Robert G. Noreen, Boston, Hall, 1978; *Saul Bellow: An Annotated Bibliography* by Gloria L. Cronin, New York, Garland, 2nd edition, 1987.

Manuscript Collections: Regenstein Library, University of Chicago; University of Texas, Austin.

Critical Studies (selection): *Saul Bellow* by Tony Tanner, Edinburgh, Oliver and Boyd, 1965, New York, Barnes and Noble, 1967; *Saul Bellow* by Earl Rovit, Minneapolis, University of Minnesota Press, 1967, and *Saul Bellow: A Collection of Critical Essays* edited by Rovit, Englewood Cliffs, New Jersey, Prentice Hall, 1975; *Saul Bellow: A Critical Essay* by Robert Detweiler, Grand Rapids, Michigan, Eerdmans, 1967; *The Novels of Saul Bellow* by Keith Michael Opdahl, University Park, Pennsylvania State University Press, 1967; *Saul Bellow and the Critics* edited by Irving Malin, New York, New York University Press, and London, University of London Press, 1967, and *Saul Bellow's Fiction* by Malin, Carbondale, Southern Illinois University Press, 1969; *Saul Bellow: In Defense of Man* by John Jacob Clayton, Bloomington, Indiana University Press, 1968, revised edition, 1979; *Saul Bellow* by Robert R. Dutton, New York, Twayne, 1971, revised edition, 1982; *Saul Bellow* by Brigitte Scheer-Schäzler, New York, Ungar, 1973; *Saul Bellow's Enigmatic Laughter* by Sarah Blacher Cohen, Urbana, University of Illinois Press, 1974; *Whence the Power? The Artistry and Humanity of Saul Bellow* by M. Gilbert Porter, Columbia, University of Missouri Press, 1974; *Saul Bellow: The Problem of Affirmation* by Chirantan Kulshrestha, New Delhi and London, Arnold-Heinemann, 1978, Atlantic Highlands, New Jersey, Humanities Press, 1979; *Critical Essays on Saul Bellow* edited by Stanley Trachtenberg, Boston, Hall, 1979; *Quest for the Human: An Exploration of Saul Bellow's Fiction* by Eusebio L. Rodrigues, Lewisburg, Pennsylvania, Bucknell University Press, 1981; *Saul Bellow* by Malcolm Bradbury, London, Methuen, 1983; *Saul Bellow's Moral Vision: A Critical Study of the Jewish Experience* by L.H. Goldman, New York, Irvington, 1983; *Saul Bellow: Vision and Revision* by Daniel Fuchs, Durham, North Carolina, Duke University Press, 1984; *Saul Bellow and History* by Judie Newman, New York, St. Martin's Press, and London, Macmillan, 1984; *A Sort of Columbus: The American Voyages of Saul Bellow's Fiction* by Jeanne Braham, Athens, University of Georgia Press, 1984; *On Bellow's Planet: Readings from the Dark Side,* Rutherford, New Jersey, Fairleigh Dickinson University Press, 1985, and *Herzog: The Limits of Ideas,* London, Maxwell Macmillan, 1990, both by Jonathan Wilson; *Saul Bellow* by Robert F. Kiernan, New York, Crossroad Continuum, 1988; *Saul Bellow and the Decline of Humanism* by Michael K. Glenday, London, Macmillan, 1990; *Saul Bellow: Against the Grain* by Ellen Pifer, University Park, Pennsylvania State University Press, 1990; *Saul Bellow: A Biography of the Imagination* by Ruth Miller, New York, St. Martin's Press, 1991; *Saul Bellow at Seventy-Five: A Collection of Critical Essays* edited by Gerhard Bach, Tubingen, Narr, 1991; *Saul Bellow* by Peter Hyland, New York, St. Martin's Press, 1992; *Saul Bellow: A Mosaic* compiled by Aharoni et al., New York, Lang, 1992; *Character and Narration in the Short Fiction of Saul Bellow* by Marianne M. Friedrich, New York, Lang, 1993; *Saul Bellow: The Feminine Mystique* by Tarlochan Singh Anand, Jalandhar, India, ABS, 1993; *Quest for Salvation in Saul Bellow's Novels* by Kyung-Ae Kim, Frankfurt am Main, Lang, 1994; *Saul Bellow and the Struggle at the Center* edited by Eugene Hollahan, New York, AMS Press, 1994; *The Critical Response to Saul Bellow,* edited by Gerhard Bach. Westport, Connecticut, Greenwood Press, 1995; *Handsome Is: Adventures with Saul Bellow: A Memoir* by Harriett Wasserman. New York, Fromm International, 1997; *Prophets of Recognition: Ideology and the Individual in Novels by Ralph Ellison, Toni Morrison, Saul Bellow, and Eudora Welty* by Julia Eichelberger, Baton Rouge, Louisiana State University Press, 1999; *Small Planets: Saul Bellow and the Art of Short Fiction,* edited by Gerhard Bach and Gloria L. Cronin, East Lansing, Michigan State University Press, 2000; *A Room of His Own: In Search of the*

Feminine in the Novels of Saul Bellow by Gloria L. Cronin, Syracuse, New York, Syracuse University Press, 2000.

* * *

Saul Bellow is widely recognized as America's preeminent living novelist. His fiction, which is as intellectually demanding as it is imaginatively appealing, steadfastly affirms the value of the human soul while simultaneously recognizing the claims of community and the demoralizing inauthenticity of daily life. Refusing to give in to the pessimism and despair that threaten to overwhelm American experience, Bellow offers a persistently optimistic, though often tentative and ambiguous, alternative to postmodern alienation. In their struggle to understand their past and reorder their present, his protagonists chart a course of possibility for all who would live meaningfully in urban American society.

Reflecting the stylistic influence of Flaubert, Bellow's first two novels, *Dangling Man* and *The Victim*, are brief and disciplined works, darker in mood and less intellectually complex than the later fiction but featuring protagonists who anticipate later Bellovian heroes both in their introspection and in their resistance to urban apathy. The first novel to display Bellow's characteristic expansiveness and optimism, *The Adventures of Augie March* presents a dazzling panorama of comically eccentric characters in a picaresque tale narrated by the irrepressible title character, who defends human possibility by embracing the hope that ''There may gods turn up anywhere.'' Subsequent novels vary in tone from the intensity of *Seize the Day* to the exuberance of *Henderson the Rain King* to the ironic ambiguity of *Herzog*, but all explore the nature of human freedom and the tensions between the individual's need for self and society. Augie March, Tommy Wilhelm, Eugene Henderson, and Moses Herzog all yearn to redeem themselves by finding the beauty in life. By creating these highly individualistic characters and the milieu in which they move, Bellow reveals the flashes of the extraordinary in the ordinary that make such redemption possible and rejects the attitude that everyday life must be trivial and ignoble.

This redemption of the self paradoxically requires the surrender of the self. Nowhere is this fact more vividly portrayed than in *Henderson the Rain King*. Driven in the beginning by a relentless inner voice that repeats, ''I want! I want!,'' Henderson's egoistic absorption in his material success ironically alienates him from himself. Fleeing civilization to seek fundamental truths in the wilderness of Africa, he discovers the loving relationship that humans need with nature and with each other and symbolically surrenders his self by accepting responsibility for a lion cub and an orphan child.

In their quest to find the love that gives meaning to life, Bellow's protagonists must also come to terms with death. The message Bellow conveys in almost all of his novels is that one must know death to know the meaning of life and what it means to be human. Henderson overcomes his fear of death when he is buried and symbolically resurrected in the African king Dahfu's experiment. Similarly, in *Seize the Day*, Tommy Wilhelm confronts death in a symbolic drowning. Charlie Citrine in *Humboldt's Gift* echoes Whitman in viewing death as the essential question, recognizing that it is only through death that the soul can complete the cycle of life by liberating itself from the body. Bellow's meditations on death darken in *Mr. Sammler's Planet* and *The Dean's December*. While the title character in *Mr. Sammler's Planet* awaits the death of the person he most values in the world, Bellow contemplates the approaching death of Western culture at the hands of those who have abandoned humanistic values. *The Dean's December* presents an apocalyptic vision of urban decay in a Chicago totally lacking the comic touches that soften Charlie Citrone's portrait of this same city as a ''moronic inferno'' in *Humboldt's Gift*. With *More Die of Heartbreak* and the recent novellas, however, Bellow returns to his more characteristic blend of pathos and farce in contemplating the relationship between life and death. In the recent *Ravelstein*, Bellow once again charts this essential confrontation when Chick recounts not only his best friend's death from AIDS but also his own near-death experience from food poisoning. Through this foreground, in a fictionalized memoir to his own friend Allan Bloom, Bellow reveals the resilient love and tenderness that offer the modern world its saving grace.

Because Bellow refuses to devalue human potential in even his bleakest scenarios, his novels often come under attack for their affirmative endings. Augie hails himself as a new Columbus, the rediscoverer of America; Henderson, while triumphantly returning home with his new charges, dances with glee, ''leaping, leaping, pounding, and tingling over the pure white lining of the grey Arctic silence.'' Herzog inexplicably evades his fate, emerging from the flux of his tortured mind to reclaim his sanity and his confidence in the future. Yet, the victories of Bellow's heroes are not unqualified, but rather as ambiguous and tenuous as is the human condition itself. As a new Columbus, Augie speaks from exile in Europe; in holding the orphan child, Henderson recalls the pain of his separation from his own father; by renouncing his self-pity and his murderous rage at his ex-wife Madeleine, Herzog reduces but does not expiate his guilt. Nonetheless, these characters earn whatever spiritual victory they reap through their pain and their refusal to succumb to doubt and cynicism. Through their perseverance in seeking the truth of human existence, they ultimately renew themselves by transcending to an intuitive spiritual awareness that is no less real because it must be taken on faith.

In all of Bellow's works, an appreciation of the cultural context in which his protagonists struggle is essential to understanding these characters and their search for renewal. Bellow's vision centers almost exclusively on Jewish male experience in contemporary urban America. Proud of their heritage, his heroes are usually second-generation Jewish immigrants who seek to discover how they can live meaningfully in their American present while honoring their ties to the past. Much of their ability to maintain their belief in humanity despite their knowledge of the world can be attributed to the affirmative nature of the Jewish culture. Bellovian heroes live in a WASP society in which they are only partially assimilated. However, as Jews have done historically, they maintain their concern for morality and community despite their cultural displacement.

Though in some ways separated from American society, Bellow's protagonists also strongly connect their identity with America. Augie begins his adventures by claiming, ''I am an American, Chicago born—Chicago, that somber city.'' Almost all of Bellow's novels take place in an American city, most often Chicago or New York. Through his depiction of urban reality, Bellow anchors his novels in the actual world, and he uses the city as his central metaphor for contemporary materialism. Although recognizing the importance of history and memory, Bellow's novels maintain a constant engagement with the present moment. His characters move in the real world, confronting sensuous images of urban chaos and clutter that often threaten to overwhelm them. Looking down on the Hudson River, Tommy Wilhelm sees ''tugs with matted beards of cordage'' and ''the red bones of new apartments rising on the bluffs.'' Sammler denounces contemporary New Yorkers for the ''free ways of barbarism'' that they practice beneath the guise of ''civilized order, property rights [and] refined technological organization.'' In *Humboldt's Gift*, which is replete with images of cannibalism and vampirism, Charlie Citrone sees *Von Trenck*, the source of his material success, as ''the blood-scent that attracted the sharks of Chicago.'' Acknowledging the influence of the city on his fiction, Bellow himself has remarked, ''I don't know how I could possibly separate my knowledge of life such as it is, from the city. I could no more tell you how deeply it's gotten into my bones than the lady who paints radium dials in the clock factory can tell you.'' However, although the city serves to identify the deterministic social pressures that threaten to destroy civilization, Bellow's heroes refuse to become its victims and instead draw on its latent resources of vitality to reassert their uniquely American belief in individual freedom, as well as their faith in the possibility of community.

Except for Clara Velde in *A Theft*, the protagonists in Bellow's novels and novellas are all male. The Bellovian hero typically seeks erotic pleasure, emotional security, and egoistic confirmation from the women in his life. In marriage, his relationships with women are conflicted, and he often retreats from his role as husband to a sensuous but selfish and demanding wife who paradoxically represents both his yearning for happiness and society's pressure to relinquish the freedom so essential to his self-realization. In contrast to the complex shadings that delineate his male characters, Bellow's females are often interchangeable and serve roles of little dramatic import. However, although the author has come under increasing criticism for his superficial treatment of women, his depiction of women and male-female relationships serves to reinforce the psychological crisis that each protagonist must negotiate to achieve peace and fulfillment.

Stylistically, Bellow's fiction reflects some of the same tensions that his protagonists seek to balance. His concern with social and personal destruction has been traced to European writers such as Flaubert, Dostoevsky, Kafka, Sartre, and Camus. But Bellow's fiction also has many ties to the American literary tradition. His neo-transcendentalism, his identification with America, and the loose form of his most acclaimed novels link him most obviously to Emerson and Whitman. An intensely intellectual writer who peppers his novels with allusions, Bellow draws on many cultural traditions in his analysis of both the sources of American experience and its present manifestations. His fiction fully documents the decline of Western civilization without conceding its demise, and the ambiguity and tenuousness of even his most positive endings balance sadness and comic skepticism with the steadfast faith that the artist can effect coherence and order out of the chaos of modern experience. For his achievement in confronting the modern existential dilemma with compassion and humor, Bellow's place in twentieth-century American literary history seems assured.

—Sharon Talley

BENFORD, Gregory Albert

Also writes as Sterling Blake. **Nationality:** American. **Born:** Mobile, Alabama, 30 January 1941. **Education:** University of Oklahoma, B.S. 1963; University of California, San Diego, M.S. 1965, Ph.D. 1967. **Family:** Married Joan Abbe in 1967; one son, one daughter. **Career:** Fellow, Lawrence Radiation Laboratory, Livermore, California, 1967–69, research physicist, 1969–71, consultant; assistant professor, University of California, Irvine, 1971–73, associate professor, 1973–79, professor of physics, 1979—. **Awards:** Woodrow Wilson fellowship, 1963–64; National Science Foundation grant, 1972–76; Nebula award, Science Fiction Writers of America, 1975, 1981; Office of Naval Research grant, 1975, 1982; Army Research Organization grant, 1977–82; British Science Fiction Association award, 1981; John W. Campbell award, World Science Fiction Convention, 1981; Ditmar award for International Novel, 1981; Air Force Office of Scientific Research grant, 1982; California Space Office grant, 1984–85. **Address:** Department of Physics, University of California, Irvine, California 92717, U.S.A.

PUBLICATIONS

Novels

Deeper Than the Darkness. New York, Ace, 1970; revised as *The Stars in Shroud,* New York, Putnam, 1979.
Jupiter Project (for children). Nashville, Thomas Nelson, 1975; second edition, 1980.
If the Stars Are Gods (with Gordon Eklund). New York, Putnam, 1977.
In the Ocean of Night. New York, Dial, 1977.
Find the Changeling (with Gordon Eklund). New York, Dial, 1980.
Shiva Descending (with William Rotsler). New York, Avon, 1980.
Timescape. New York, Simon & Schuster, 1980.
Against Infinity. New York, Simon & Schuster, 1983.
Across the Sea of Suns. New York, Simon & Schuster, 1984.
Time's Rub. New Castle, Virginia, Cheap Street, 1984.
Artifact. New York, Tor, 1985.
Of Space-Time and the River. New Castle, Virginia, Cheap Street, 1985.
In Alien Flesh. New York, Tor, 1986.
Heart of the Comet (with David Brin). New York, Bantam, 1986.
Great Sky River. Toronto, Bantam, 1987.
Under the Wheel (with others). Riverside, New York, Baen, 1987.
We Could Do Worse. Abbenford Associates, 1988.
Tides of Light. Toronto, Bantam, 1989.
Beyond the Fall of Night (with Arthur C. Clarke). New York, Putnam, 1990.
Centigrade 233. New Castle, Virginia, Cheap Street, 1990.
Chiller (under pseudonym Sterling Blake). New York, Bantam, 1993.
Furious Gulf. New York, Bantam, 1994.
Sailing Bright Eternity. New York, Bantam, 1995.
Foundation's Fear. New York, HarperPrism, 1997.
Cosm. New York, Avon Eos, 1998.
The Martian Race. New York, Warner Books, 1999.
Eater: A Novel. New York, Avon Eos, 2000.

Short Stories

In Alien Flesh. New York, T. Doherty Associates, 1986.
Matter's End. New Castle, Virginia, Cheap Street, 1991.

Other

Deep Time: How Humanity Communicates Across Millennia (nonfiction). New York, Avon, 1999.
Foreword, *Last and First Men: A Story of the Near and Far Future* by Olaf Stapledon. Los Angeles, J. P. Tarcher, 1988.
Introduction, *Look Away* by George Alec Effinger. Eugene, Oregon, Axolotl Press, 1990.
Contributor, *Again, Dangerous Visions,* edited by Harlan Ellison. New York, Doubleday, 1972.
Contributor, *Threads of Time: Three Original Novellas of Science Fiction,* edited by Robert Silverberg. Nashville, Thomas Nelson, 1974.
Contributor, *Universe 4,* edited by Terry Carr. New York, Random House, 1974.
Contributor, *New Dimensions 5,* edited by Robert Silverberg. New York, Harper, 1975.
Contributor, *Universe 8,* edited by Terry Carr. New York, Doubleday, 1978.
Contributor, *Universe 9,* edited by Terry Carr. New York, Doubleday, 1979.
Contributor, *Synergy: New Science Fiction,* edited by George Zebrowski. San Diego, Harcourt Brace Jovanovich, 1988.
Contributor, *Isaac Asimov's War,* edited by Gardner Dozois. New York, Ace Books, 1993.
Contributor, *Roads Not Taken: Tales of Alternate History,* edited by Gardner Dozois and Stanley Schmidt. New York, Del Rey/ Ballantine Books, 1998.
Contributor, *Science Fiction Theatre,* edited by Brian Forbes. Scottsdale, Arizona, Quadrillion Media, 1999.
Editor, with Martin H. Greenberg, *Hitler Victorious: Eleven Stories of the German Victory in World War II.* New York, Berkeley Publishing, 1987.
Editor, *The New Hugo Winners: Award-Winning Science Fiction Stories,* Volume 4. New York, Wynwood Press, 1989–1997.
Editor, with Martin H. Greenberg, *What Might Have Been, Volume 4: Alternate Americas.* New York, Bantam, 1992.
Editor, *Far Futures.* New York, Tor, 1995.
Editor, with George Zebrowski, *Skylife: Space Habitats in Story and Science.* New York, Harcourt Brace, 2000.

*

Critical Studies: *Dream Makers: The Uncommon People Who Write Science Fiction: Interviews by Charles Platt,* by Charles Platt, New York, Berkeley Books, 1980; *Bridges to Science Fiction,* Carbondale, Southern Illinois University Press, 1981; *Across the Wounded Galaxies: Interviews with Contemporary American Science Fiction Writers,* edited by Larry McCaffery, Urbana, University of Illinois Press, 1990.

* * *

Gregory Benford is an important American science fiction writer who is also a physicist of some distinction. The combination of large literary ambition and an ongoing scientific career (he is a professor of physics at the University of California, Irvine) has given Benford's work a depth of scientific speculation that is unsurpassed among writers of his generation. Beginning with his first novel, *Deeper Than the Darkness*, Benford has explored again and again the nature of intelligence in the universe, the place of Homo sapiens in that universe, and the role of science within the larger human culture. Benford's scientific career informs his work not only with the rigor of scientific knowledge that underlies his fiction, but also with the process of doing science, of science as a living profession. To find a body of fiction that so carefully and consistently explores the scientific impulse one would have to look at the novels of C.P. Snow from the generation preceding Benford, or those of Richard Powers from a generation later.

Benford's southern roots are also central to his literary work. Born in Alabama in 1941, Benford was greatly influenced by the works of William Faulkner. Faulkner's stylistic innovations and experiments continue to echo in Benford's often poetic and occasionally stream-of-consciousness prose; Benford's 1983 novel, *Against Infinity* was an homage to Faulkner's ''The Bear.'' Benford's familiarity with the main currents and voices of modern literature are reflected throughout his work.

Equally clear is his familiarity with and understanding of the nature of science fiction and its place in the body of literature. Benford's insights into science fiction's tropes and traditions enable him continually to explore and extend those traditions even as he introduces new and fresh themes of his own. His early novel for young readers, *Jupiter Project*, was a clear homage the works of Robert A. Heinlein, the most influential science fiction writer of the twentieth century. In essays and criticism Benford has presented a clear and sharp understanding of the literary opportunities and limitations of science fiction.

His early work—his first short story appeared in 1965—in fact seems in retrospect to be exploratory, with science fiction itself, and the nature of Benford's own abilities, the territory being explored. He worked frequently with collaborators, and on more than one occasion revisited earlier works, revising, for example, *Deeper Than the Darkness* as *The Stars in Shroud*, making it a richer and more textured (if slightly less youthfully exuberant) novel.

Never a prolific short story writer, Benford displayed a comfort at novella-length works, and by the late 1970s was using long stories to create a backdrop for a fictional cycle concerned with human contact with non-human intelligence. These early works were assembled as a novel, *In the Ocean of Night*, in 1977.

Even as Benford's novellas displayed an increasingly distinctive voice—and while simultaneously pursuing a full-time and intensive scientific and teaching career—he was creating the novel that would elevate him from his promising beginnings to a position of importance within science fiction. *Timescape*, published in 1980, transcended all of Benford's work to that date, and remains, simply, the finest and most ambitious literary portrait of scientists at work ever to emerge from science fiction, and one of the best in all of literature. The complex story of a polluted, dying earth, and the scientist who slowly becomes aware of messages from the future that hold the key to saving the planet, *Timescape* was a mature, balanced, provocative, and occasionally sly work. Ultimately moving and in many ways profound, *Timescape* presented Benford's view of the universe's indifference to our existence and the ways in which our approach to that indifference shapes us as a species. It was a remarkable and award-winning performance, and is one of the cornerstones of his career.

But Benford embarked on an even more ambitious literary voyage, one that began with the novella-sequence of *In the Ocean of*

Night. The story of astronaut Nigel Walmsley's encounter with and alteration by a non-human intelligence in the near future would provide the foundation for a cycle of novels that would take two decades for Benford to complete and would become, along with *Timescape*, his major contribution to science fiction. This was the ''Galactic Center'' saga, a sequence of six novels that move from the near future to the farthest, that employ a variety of literary experiments and techniques to present and explore the nature of intelligent life, and an unequalled portrait of cosmology as it is presently understood.

The non-human intelligence encountered by Walmsley turns out to be machine, rather than organic, in nature. The next novel in the sequence, *Across the Sea of Suns*, deals with Walmsley's voyage in search of the intelligence that altered him, and with the invasion of earth by beings inimical to human existence. The ambiguous ending of the second novel promised further revelations of Walmsley's destiny, but the next novel in the sequence, *Great Sky River*, jumped into the far future to tell the story of a family's flight through a brilliantly realized cosmology, pursued by machine intelligences. Succeeding as both literary fiction and rousingly adventurous hard science fiction, *Great Sky River* raised the bar for portrayals of alien intelligence, and broke much ground in the exploration of machine consciousness and the interface between humans and machines.

Two years later Benford pushed the Galactic Center novels even farther with *Tides Of Light.* Once more Benford's beleaguered humans—the Family—are locked in a death struggle with overwhelmingly powerful machines, against a vast galactic backdrop. It was becoming clear as the work emerged that Benford was drawing on his scientific knowledge to create fiction in which the universe itself, in addition to the novels' humans and non-humans, was a major character. Few works of science fiction have offered so concrete and poetic a ''sense of wonder'' at the physical universe's sheer size and strangeness: collapsing stars, whorls and eddies of space-time, bleak planetary vistas, and a lush sensuousness all work together to immerse the reader in Benford's vision.

Nor was the Galactic Center series—or his scientific work—enough to occupy Benford's energies. Always interested in suspense fiction, he turned to the field himself with *Artifact*, a thriller with an archaeological theme. Another suspense novel, *Chiller*, was published in 1993 under the pseudonym Sterling Blake. Collaborations over two decades included work with Gordon Eklund, William Rotsler, Mark O. Martin, and David Brin. The most notable of Benford's collaborative works was *Heart of the Comet*, with Brin, the story of an expedition to Halley's Comet. Benford collected his short stories in two volumes—*In Alien Flesh* and *Matter's End.*

After a five-year hiatus from the sequence, Benford returned in 1994 to the Galactic Center, and once again he raised the series' stakes. *Furious Gulf* follows the fleeing Family toward the True Center, toward ever larger revelations and speculations. Nigel Walmsley, ancient beyond words now, returns to the series as Benford tightens the spring of suspense and presents stunning cosmological speculations. With *Sailing Bright Eternity* Benford completed the Galactic Center cycle. This novel, which would perhaps seem inscrutable to readers unfamiliar with the preceding volumes, offered a level of surprise and surprisingly emotional, even visionary, transcendence for those who had made the entire journey. In long passages of prose that is essentially poetic, making use of a range of typographical and stylistic techniques, Benford achieved a true ending to his saga, one that presents the reader with an all but heartbreaking sense of intelligence's dual fragility and persistence in an uncaring universe. The Galactic Center sequence is one of science fiction's major accomplishments.

After completing the sequence, Benford turned to less ambitious—but no less entertaining or provocative—novels. *The Martian Race* was a rigorous look at the challenges a human expedition to Mars might face. His thematically related novels, *Cosm* and *Eater* used the form and structure of the thriller to explore questions of scientific responsibility and high-level physics. Along with David Brin and Greg Bear (the trio known as science fiction's ''Killer Bs''), Benford wrote one of the three novels of the ''Second Foundation Trilogy,'' set in the universe created by Isaac Asimov. Benford has also edited or co-edited several anthologies of science fiction stories. Benford's *Beyond The Fall of Night* was both a collaboration with Arthur C. Clarke and a sequel to Clarke's own first novel.

Prolific in nonfiction—both scientific and journalistic—Benford has since the mid-1990s contributed a science column to *The Magazine of Fantasy & Science Fiction,* as well as a variety of thoughtful and insightful essays on science fiction and science to numerous publications. His 1999 nonfiction book *Deep Time* explained trans-millennial communications strategies to non-scientific audiences. In 1990 he was awarded the United Nations Medal in Literature, and in 1995 he received the Lord Foundation award for his scientific accomplishments. For Japanese broadcaster NHK he wrote and hosted portions of a late-1980s scientific program, *A Galactic Odyssey,* which, despite a large investment, never aired.

Now in the fourth decade of an extraordinarily prolific career, Benford shows few signs of any diminution of ambition or ability. If his recent novels have operated on a less cosmic scale than his major works, they nonetheless display a still-gathering command of character and psychological insight. Perhaps most interesting about his recent work is Benford's effort to reach out to a larger audience than that of science fiction per se. Should that audience discover him, their attention will be rewarded many times over by this boldest of literary speculators.

—Keith Ferrell

BERGER, John (Peter)

Nationality: British. **Born:** Stoke Newington, London, 5 November 1926. **Education:** Central School of Art and the Chelsea School of Art, London. **Military Service:** Served in the Oxford and Buckinghamshire Infantry, 1944–46. **Family:** Married twice; three children. **Career:** Painter and drawing teacher, 1948–55; contributor, *Tribune* and *New Statesman,* both London, 1951–60; television narrator, *About Time,* 1985, and *Another Way of Telling,* 1989. Artist: exhibitions at Wildenstein, Redfern, and Leicester galleries, London, Denise Cade gallery, New York, 1994. **Awards:** Booker prize, 1972; *Guardian* Fiction prize, 1972; James Tait Black Memorial prize, 1973; New York Critics prize, for screenplay, 1976; George Orwell Memorial prize, 1977; Barcelona Film Festival Europa award, 1989;

Lannan Foundation award, 1989; Australian State prize, 1989. **Address:** Quincy, Mieussy, 74440 Taninges, France.

PUBLICATIONS

Novels

A Painter of Our Time. London, Secker and Warburg, 1958; New York, Simon and Schuster, 1959.
The Foot of Clive. London, Methuen, 1962.
Corker's Freedom. London, Methuen, 1964; New York, Pantheon, 1993.
G. London, Weidenfeld and Nicolson, and New York, Viking Press, 1972.
Into Their Labours (trilogy in one volume). New York, Pantheon, 1991; London, Granta, 1992.
Pig Earth (short stories). London, Writers and Readers, 1979; New York, Pantheon, 1980.
Once in Europa (short stories). New York, Pantheon, 1987; Cambridge, Granta, 1989.
Lilac and Flag: An Old Wives' Tale of a City. New York, Pantheon, 1990; Cambridge, Granta, 1991.
To the Wedding. New York, Pantheon, and London, Bloomsbury, 1995.
Photocopies. New York, Pantheon Books, 1996.
King, a Street Story. New York, Pantheon Books, 1999.

Plays

Jonas qui aura 25 ans en l'an 2000 (screenplay), with Alain Tanner. Lausanne, Cinémathèque Suisse, 1978; translated by Michael Palmer, as *Jonah Who Will Be 25 in the Year 2000,* Berkeley, California, North Atlantic, 1983.
A Question of Geography, with Nella Bielski (produced Marseille, 1984; Stratford-on-Avon, 1987; London, 1988). London, Faber, 1987.
Les Trois Chaleurs (produced Paris, 1985).
Boris, translated into Welsh by Rhiannon Ifans (produced Cardiff, 1985).
Goya's Last Portrait: The Painter Played Today, with Nella Bielski. London, Faber, 1989.

Screenplays, with Alain Tanner: *La Salamandre* (*The Salamander*), 1971, *Le Milieu du monde* (*The Middle of the World*), 1974, and *Jonas* (*Jonah Who Will Be 25 in the Year 2000*), 1976; *Play Me Something,* with Timothy Neat, 1989.

Poetry

Pages of the Wound: Poems, Photographs, Drawings by John Berger. London, Circle Press, 1994.

Other

Marcel Frishman, with George Besson. Oxford, Cassirer, 1958.
Permanent Red: Essays in Seeing. London, Methuen, 1960; as *Towards Reality,* New York, Knopf, 1962.
The Success and Failure of Picasso. London, Penguin, 1965; New York, Pantheon, 1980.
A Fortunate Man: The Story of a Country Doctor, photographs by Jean Mohr. London, Allen Lane, and New York, Holt Rinehart, 1967.
Art and Revolution: Ernst Neizvestny and the Role of the Artist in the U.S.S.R. London, Weidenfeld and Nicolson, and New York, Pantheon, 1969.
The Moment of Cubism and Other Essays. London, Weidenfeld and Nicolson, and New York, Pantheon, 1969.
The Look of Things, edited by Nikos Stangos. London, Penguin, 1972; New York, Viking Press, 1974.
Ways of Seeing, with others. London, BBC-Penguin, 1972; New York, Viking Press, 1973.
A Seventh Man: Migrant Workers in Europe, photographs by Jean Mohr. London, Penguin, and New York, Viking Press, 1975.
About Looking. London, Writers and Readers, and New York, Pantheon, 1980.
Another Way of Telling (on photography), with Jean Mohr. London, Writers and Readers, and New York, Pantheon, 1982.
And Our Faces, My Heart, Brief as Photos. London, Writers and Readers, and New York, Pantheon, 1984.
The White Bird, edited by Lloyd Spencer. London, Chatto and Windus, 1985; as *The Sense of Sight,* New York, Pantheon, 1986.
Keeping a Rendezvous. New York, Pantheon, 1991; London, Granta, 1992.
Isabelle: A Story in Shots (with Nella Bielski). Chester Springs, Pennsylvania, Dufour Editions, 1998.
Contributor, *Happiness and Discontent.* Chicago, Great Books Foundation, 1998.
Translator, with Anya Bostock, *Poems on the Theatre,* by Bertolt Brecht. London, Scorpion Press, 1961; as *The Great Art of Living Together: Poems on the Theatre,* Bingley, Yorkshire, Granville Press, 1972.
Translator, with Anya Bostock, *Helene Weigel, Actress,* by Bertolt Brecht. Leipzig, Veb Edition, 1961.
Translator, with Anya Bostock, *Return to My Native Land,* by Aimé Césaire. London, Penguin, 1969.
Translator, with Lisa Appignanesi, *Oranges for the Son of Asher Levy,* by Nella Bielski. London, Writers and Readers, 1982.
Translator, with Jonathan Steffen, *After Arkadia: The Wickerwork Tram and The Barber's Head,* by Nella Bielski. London, Viking, 1991.

*

Critical Studies: *Seeing Berger: A Revaluation of Ways of Seeing* by Peter Fuller, London, Writers and Readers, 1980, revised edition as *Seeing Through Berger,* London, Claridge Press, 1988; *Ways of Telling: The Work of John Berger* by Geoff Dyer, London, Pluto, 1986.

* * *

From his 10 years as art critic for the *New Statesman* through to his present storytelling narratives concerning AIDS and homelessness, John Berger has been constantly experimenting with various perspectives, voices, and kinds of writing. But certain qualities remain constant in all of his mixed-genre writing: the seriousness of tone and attitude toward human life; the conviction that ''seeing comes before words'' (*Ways of Seeing*); the determination to show how the ways of the modern capitalist world distort and destroy lives and imaginations; the spirit of affirmation of, and faith and hope in, possibilities of the creative imagination and humans' capacity as social animals to recognize the roots of value and meaning and to bring about change. As an oppositional and interdisciplinary thinker, Berger sees writing as a social act and writes not out of any particular tradition, but out of his rational and humane Marxist convictions, mitigated somewhat over the years by broader philosophical investigations.

His first three novels are set in the London of the 1950s and 1960s. *A Painter of Our Time* uses the world of an émigré to explore the crossroads of culture and politics. It arose out of Berger's art critical essays of the 1950s and out of his experiences with people he knew in the art world, particularly certain émigré artists. The novel sets Hungarian painter and scientific socialist Janos Lavin's artistic and political ideals against modern London's cynical and opportunist art business, with which he must deal, and explores his isolation as an exile with no suitable context in which to work.

Berger ''thought about [his next three novels] quite consciously in terms of British society'' (interview with Diane Watson, May 1988). He maintains that bourgeois society ''underdevelops'' consciousness and life on an individual level, and empathy consistently informs his fictional portraits of those whose lives are most ''underdeveloped,'' from his examination of those disabled by modern British society, to those ignored or dismissed by Marxism, such as the peasants about whom he writes in his trilogy *Into their Labours.*

In *The Foot of Clive* Berger departs permanently from the world of art in his fiction, and dramatizes the minutiae of the daily actions and the subconscious impulses of six men from across the class strata who are patients in a hospital ward. The lack of a collective dream and the void left by the society's destruction of a coherent heroic image informs the quality of life and relations in the ward, a microcosm of British society. Prevented from action, they lead a passive, static existence; all they can do is think, talk, and feed off their fears.

In *A Fortunate Man,* Berger's most moving work of non-fiction, he describes the situation of ''wholesale cultural deprivation''; in *Corker's Freedom*—his most underrated novel—he *illuminates* the situation by examining the consequences of this deprivation for one particular individual, Corker, the owner of an employment agency and a self-proclaimed ''traveller.'' Mainly by depicting the contours of Corker's self-consciousness, the novel traces several days in his awakening to what he feels to be his true potential and his struggle to liberate himself from his sister and from his society's expectations of him.

Berger's best known work of fiction, *G.,* closes out the phase of works written from inside the society of which he is most critical; it looks backwards to ideas and struggles of previous work and forwards to the solving of questions it raises about writing and to other possibilities of philosophical—mainly existential and phenomenological—and ideological perspective. This highly technically experimental novel grapples with the living of two kinds of time, historical and subjective, elucidates the workings of memory, and documents the historical preconditions that make a Don Juan possible: the novel is set in the period between the late nineteenth century and the beginning of World War I. *G.* is grounded in *Ways of Seeing,* particularly in its consideration of sexual appetite and social roles as determined by political, historical, and cultural contexts. Its global resonance is brought about by the author's imaginative identification with not only particular individuals, but with a historical period of a continent, with a revolutionary class, and with women. The mysterious, cosmopolitan Don Juan figure, G., has brushes with all that is vital about his period in history, but is interested in engaging with nothing but moments of liberation through sexual passion.

Berger described his ''thinking about narrative'' as ''having become tighter and more traditional'' after *G.* (''The Screenwriter as Collaborator,'' interview in *Cineaste,* no. 10, 1980), and he turned his attention to a culture whose perspective predates that of progress and capitalism. Throughout the three-part project *Into Their Labours*—comprised of *Pig Earth, Once in Europa,* and *Lilac and Flag,* each of which addresses a different stage of this process—he acts as a witness to the disintegration of traditional French peasant work, perspective, and experience, and adopts a storytelling voice and narrative style. In storytelling, Berger has found a language that speaks of and from lived experience, in opposition to that which reflects and perpetuates the constraints and limitations of bourgeois society. He values the art of storytelling for its ability to situate people, individually and collectively, in history, and as a kind of narrative that feeds and answers to imaginative and metaphysical experience. This rich and lyrical trilogy contains some of his best writing, particularly in *Once in Europa,* a book of love stories that turn on the mystery and amplitude of intimacy.

Berger's penchant for poetic declarations, coupled with his characteristic humanism, lends his fiction a strong sense of the aphoristic and even the allegorical. In his latest two novels, *To the Wedding* and *King: A Street Story,* Berger mobilizes a markedly sensual, erotically charged prose to once again explore the nature of political and physical resistance. *To the Wedding,* for example, is narrated by a blind storyteller who literally ''hears'' the novel. Berger deftly turns the reader into a ''listener of voices'' and the effect of the work, so rife with similes and preoccupied with both ancient and modern poetry, is beguilingly lyrical. The plot concerns the trauma of a young woman who contracts AIDS and, specifically, the uncovering of her past and the past of her family and friends as they journey to her wedding. Berger's specific descriptions of the physical body combating the AIDS virus constitute a terrible but revealing analogy of political struggle. When Nino, the protagonist, is eventually diagnosed the narrator confronts the utter bleakness of her situation and asks: ''How to change nothing into everything?'' It is a jarring and resolutely Berger-esque question—and one that *King,* Berger's most recent fiction, takes up directly.

King's eponymous protagonist—ostensibly a dog—is a sort of roving watch-mutt, not to mention a first-rate yarn-spinner, for a group of homeless squatters living on a motorway-bordering wasteland. Early on in the novel, King interrupts his own narrative to relate a brief parable about a sparrow trapped inside a house. As King explains, the bird eventually finds its way back into the air and then releases a chirp of joy. *King* itself, the reader recognizes, is a meditation about freedom and also, fundamentally, about the political responsibilities of the storyteller. Though *King* is essentially a tragic, even pessimistic novel—the squatters are, in the end, violently removed from the land—such is Berger's gift that his multi-vocal reportage seems to survive the community's destruction.

As unflinchingly brutal as Berger's descriptions of dispossession and human evil can be, the very act of writing remains—Berger convinces one of this—a sign of profound hope. Throughout his evolution from one of Britain's best social realists to master storyteller, his aim remains consistent: to point to possibilities of disalienation. And while his fiction moves increasingly in the direction of philosophical speculation and metaphysical rumination, it loses none of its political impact. Thus the small, seemingly insignificant sparrow engaged in its heroic escape comes to resonate and challenge the most dire, most bleak of closures. As Berger writes in his essay ''The White Bird'': ''Under the fallen boulder of an avalanche a flower grows.''

—Diane Watson, updated by Jake Kennedy

BERGER, Thomas (Louis)

Nationality: American. **Born:** Cincinnati, Ohio, 20 July 1924. **Education:** The University of Cincinnati, B.A. 1948; Columbia University, New York, 1950–51. **Military Service:** Served in the United States Army, 1943–46. **Family:** Married Jeanne Redpath in 1950. **Career:** Librarian, Rand School of Social Science, New York, 1948–51; staff member, *New York Times Index,* 1951–52; associate editor, *Popular Science Monthly,* New York, 1952–54; film critic, *Esquire,* New York, 1972–73; writer-in-residence, University of Kansas, Lawrence, 1974; Distinguished Visiting Professor, Southampton College, New York, 1975–76; visiting lecturer, Yale University, New Haven, Connecticut, 1981, 1982; Regents' Lecturer, University of California, Davis, 1982. **Awards:** Dial fellowship, 1962; Western Heritage award, 1965; Rosenthal award, 1965. Litt.D.: Long Island University, Greenvale, New York, 1986. **Agent:** Don Congdon Associates, 156 Fifth Avenue, Suite 625, New York, New York 10010, U.S.A.

PUBLICATIONS

Novels

Crazy in Berlin. New York, Scribner, 1958.
Reinhart in Love. New York, Scribner, 1962; London, Eyre and Spottiswoode, 1963.
Little Big Man. New York, Dial Press, 1964; London, Eyre and Spottiswoode, 1965.
Killing Time. New York, Dial Press, 1967; London Eyre and Spottiswoode, 1968.
Vital Parts. New York, Baron, 1970; London, Eyre and Spottiswoode, 1971.
Regiment of Women. New York, Simon and Schuster, 1973; London, Eyre Methuen, 1974.
Sneaky People. New York, Simon and Schuster, 1975; London, Methuen, 1980.
Who Is Teddy Villanova? New York, Delacorte Press, and London, Eyre Methuen, 1977.
Arthur Rex: A Legendary Novel. New York, Delacorte Press, 1978; London, Methuen, 1979.
Neighbors. New York, Delacorte Press, 1980; London, Methuen, 1981.
Reinhart's Women. New York, Delacorte Press, 1981; London, Methuen, 1982.
The Feud. New York, Delacorte Press, 1983; London, Methuen, 1984.
Nowhere. New York, Delacorte Press, 1985; London, Methuen, 1986.
Being Invisible. Boston, Little Brown, 1987; London, Methuen, 1988.
The Houseguest. Boston, Little Brown, 1988; London, Weidenfeld and Nicolson, 1989.
Changing the Past. Boston, Little Brown, 1989; London, Weidenfeld and Nicolson, 1990.
Orrie's Story. Boston, Little Brown, 1990.
Meeting Evil. Boston, Little Brown, 1992.
Robert Crews. New York, Morrow, 1994.
Suspects. New York, William Morrow and Company, 1996.
The Return of Little Big Man. Boston, Little, Brown, 1999.

Short Stories

Granted Wishes. Northridge, California, Lord John Press, 1984.

Uncollected Short Stories

''Professor Hyde,'' in *Playboy* (Chicago), December 1961.
''A Monkey of His Own,'' in *Saturday Evening Post* (Philadelphia), 22 May 1965.
''Fatuous Fables,'' in *Penthouse* (London), March 1973.
''Envy,'' in *Oui* (Chicago), April 1975.
''The Achievement of Dr. Poon,'' in *American Review 25,* edited by Theodore Solotaroff. New York, Bantam, 1976.
''Tales of the Animal Crime Squad,'' in *Playboy* (Chicago), December 1980.
''The Methuselah Factor,'' in *Gentlemen's Quarterly* (New York), September 1984.
''Planet of the Losers,'' in *Playboy* (Chicago), November 1988.
''Gibberish,'' in *Playboy* (Chicago), December 1990.
''Personal Power,'' in *Playboy* (Chicago), December 1992.

Play

Other People (produced Stockbridge, Massachussetts, 1970).

*

Film Adaptations: *Little Big Man*, 1970; *The Neighbors*, 1981; *The Feud*, 1989.

Bibliography: ''Thomas Berger: Primary and Secondary Works'' by James Bense, in *Bulletin of Bibliography* 6(2), 1994.

Manuscript Collection: Boston University Library.

Critical Studies: ''Bitter Comedy'' by Richard Schickel, in *Commentary* (New York), July 1970; ''Thomas Berger's *Little Big Man* as History'' by Leo Oliva, in *Western American Literature* (Fort Collins, Colorado), vol. 8, nos. 1–2, 1973; ''Thomas Berger's Elan'' by Douglas Hughes, in *Confrontation* (New York), Spring-Summer 1976; ''The Radical Americanist'' by Brooks Landon, and ''The Second Decade of *Little Big Man*'' by Frederick Turner, both in *Nation* (New York), 20 August 1977; ''Berger and Barth: The Comedy of Decomposition'' by Stanley Trachtenberg, in *Comic Relief* edited by Sarah Blacher Cohen, Urbana, University of Illinois Press, 1978; ''Thomas Berger Issue'' (includes bibliography) of *Studies in American Humor* (San Marcos, Texas), Spring and Fall 1983; ''Reinhart as Hero and Clown'' by Gerald Weales, in *Hollins Critic* (Hollins College, Virginia), December 1983; ''Laughter as

Self-Defense in *Who Is Teddy Villanova?,*'' in *Studies in American Humor* (San Marcos, Texas), Spring 1986, and ''A Murderous Clarity: A Reading of Thomas Berger's *Killing Time,*'' in *Philological Quarterly* (Iowa City), Winter 1989, both by Jon Wallace; *Thomas Berger* by Brooks Landon, Boston, Twayne, 1989; *Critical Essays on Thomas Berger* edited by David W. Madden, New York, G. K. Hall, 1995.

Thomas Berger comments:

I write to amuse and conceal myself.

* * *

Thomas Berger's novels exhibit an extraordinary comic sensibility, a satiric talent for wild caricature, and a concern for the quality of middle-class life in middle America. His novels chronicle the decline and fall of the Common Man in 20th-century America and meticulously detail the absurdities of our civilizations. Berger is one of the subtlest and most accurate parodists writing today, with a flawless sense of style and proportion that is charged with comic vitality.

His Reinhart saga (*Crazy in Berlin, Reinhart in Love, Vital Parts,* and *Reinhart's Women*) follows Carlo Reinhart from adolescence to middle age, detailing his career as a soldier in occupied Germany, a GI Bill student, and a failed wage-slave and decrepit father in the bewildering America of the 1980s. Reinhart epitomizes the failure of good intentions. A believer in the American Dream as purveyed in magazines, high-school classrooms, and advertisements, Carlo is a constant victim of deceit and fraud. Like the Good Soldier Schweik, Carlo takes the world at face value and assumes that appearance is reality; unlike Schweik, Carlo is guileless and incapable of hypocrisy, so he is perpetually victimized and disillusioned. The comedy arises in the gulf between Carlo's expectations and his experience.

In *Crazy in Berlin* Carlo is swept up in conspiracy, involved with spies and criminals dividing the spoils of the fallen Nazi state. A good-natured slob and summer soldier, Carlo survives, but he is driven to murder and madness, shattered not by war but by the lunacy of peace. The novel exudes the bitter ironies of sophisticated slapstick comedy, similar to Preston Sturges's films. Carlo, a bewildered, optimistic average man, is driven mad by the Hobbesian nightmare of Occupied Germany.

The second novel, *Reinhart in Love,* continues the mock-heroic saga. Carlo returns to the purported normality of peace-time America to continue college on the GI Bill. Again he is duped, exploited, and betrayed as Orlando himself, charged with cosmic love: ''*Reinhart was in love with everything.*'' But as his boss tells him, the world is still a Hobbesian jungle, with every man's hand raised against his fellows: ''life, real life, is exactly like the fighting, except in the latter you use guns and therefore don't destroy as many people.'' The novel ends with Carlo married by deception to a shrew, failed even at suicide and bereft of ideals and ambitions, ready to move upward and onward.

Vital Parts moves ahead 20 years to reveal Reinhart still married to his shrew and father to a fat, mooning daughter and a vicious ne'er-do-well son. He has failed at every capitalistic venture, lost his hair and youth, gained debts and a paunch. Again in suicidal despair, he becomes involved in a bizarre cryogenics scheme—to immortality via technology. He becomes the guinea pig in a scheme to freeze and revive a human being. Carlo feels he has little to choose between an absurd life, an absurd death, and a remote hope of immortality.

In *Reinhart's Women,* Carlo achieves a degree of peace with his wife and daughter, as he takes on a new role as a gourmet cook. Berger makes Carlo here less the ever-ready butt of slapstick and more the master of his destiny, as if Carlo were growing in later middle age into himself. The book's comedy is mellower and less acerbic than the view of corrupt post-World War II culture from which Berger began the saga.

In *Little Big Man* Berger also uses mock-heroic satire, here on the elaborate mythology of the Old West. A tale of cowboys and Indians told from *both* views, the novel describes the only white survivor of the Battle of the Little Big Horn—111-year-old Jack Crabb, victim of Indian attacks, Indian, Indian-fighter, gunfighter, gambler, con man, etc. The novel follows the ''half-man, half-alligator'' tradition of frontier humor, bursting with gigantic hyperbole. It is also a detailed, convincing picture of prairie life, both with the Cheyenne (the ''Human Beings'') and with the white settlers. The violence, squalor, and monotony of life in raw nature are as intensely realized as the farce. Jack Crabb is a frontier Carlo Reinhart, with the same insecurities, the same propensities for confusion and cowardice, the same common humanity.

Arthur Rex may be the finest redaction of the legend since Malory. It is a labor of love for pure story and style in which Berger's brilliant prose is honed like Excalibur itself. A straightforward rendering of the Arthurian material, the novel is a tribute to romance, adventure, and storytelling as the roots of our literature. Berger makes the characters come sharply alive in vigorous, dramatic scenes and retains the mixture of exuberance and nostalgia which defines the ancient cycle.

A theme inherent in Berger's work is that of metamorphosis—transformation, counterfeiting, deception, the shiftiness of reality. *Who Is Teddy Villanova?, Nowhere,* and *Neighbors* focus on this theme. Detective fiction and cold-war thrillers are parodied in the first two novels, which follow the hapless adventures of Russel Wren, an inept semi-pro detective who is constantly overwhelmed by violent events beyond his perception. *Who Is Teddy Villanova?* caricatures the conventions of the tough-guy detective novel, and *Nowhere* brilliantly combines the spy story and the utopian romance. An atmosphere of bizarre paranoia suffuses both installments of the Wren romance. In *Neighbors* the same mode is applied to suburban realities. Earl Keese, prone to hallucinations, is subjected to a series of emotional and mental assaults by a man and woman who move in next door. The story turns on paradoxes and illusions, an increasingly grotesque feeling that things are never what they seem. In Berger's view, our culture has crashed through the looking glass, where absurdity rules all and everything turns by subtle and malicious irony into its opposite.

Sneaky People and *The Feud* also anatomize middle-class American life; both are set in the 1930s and deal with the peculiar conflation of acquisitiveness and sexuality which creates the ethos for the people-next-door culture described in *Neighbors.* A mixture of healthy cynicism and obvious nostalgia makes the narratives attractive as satires on the conventional American success story. *The Houseguest* extends the comedy of domestic paranoia that shaped *Sneaky People, Neighbors,* and *The Feud.* In his usual absurdist/surrealist manner, Berger constructs a Kafkaesque novel of invaded hospitality and territorial hostility.

Being Invisible and *Changing the Past* mine Berger's fantastic-speculative vein. Each is a cautionary tale about power—one on the old idea of the presumed powers of invisibility, the other a ''three wishes'' story of a man granted the power to relive his life. The novels are fables on the vanity of human wishes and the inevitability of overreaching. Their comedy mirrors serious concerns with the ethics of power, the intractability of ego and the illusory nature of freedom and choice.

In *Orrie's Story* Berger retells the Orestes legend as a contemporary, post-Vietnam fiction. Less successfully than in the majestic *Arthur Rex,* he reinvents the past to illumine our complex present. *Suspects,* Berger's twentieth novel, is a murder mystery busy with extraneous details, as though the author was not content to offer up something so ordinary as a good, solidly suspenseful read. It came on the heels of *Robert Crews,* which found him on familiar ground: the tale of a hapless figure who ultimately finds a place for himself—if not a full understanding of his circumstances—in the midst of a larger drama. As its title suggests, the protagonist is a Robinson Crusoe type, and his ''Friday'' is a woman running away from her abusive husband. With *The Return of Little Big Man,* Berger stepped onto even more familiar territory. The book finds the unflappable Jack Crabb at age 112, witnessing events ranging from the shootout at the O.K. Corral (predictably, this time Wyatt Earp is the villain, not the Clanton brothers) and the appearance of Buffalo Bill and Annie Oakley in London, where Queen Victoria attends their Wild West Show.

—William J. Schafer

BETTS, Doris

Nationality: American. **Born:** Statesville, North Carolina, 4 June 1932. **Education:** Woman's College, Greensboro, North Carolina, 1950–53; University of North Carolina, Chapel Hill, 1954. **Family:** Married Lowry M. Betts in 1952; one daughter and two sons. **Career:** Journalist, *Statesville Daily Record,* 1950–51; *Chapel Hill Weekly and News Leader,* 1953–54; *Sanford Daily Herald,* 1956–57. Editorial staff, *N.C. Democrat,* 1961; editor, *Sanford News Leader,* 1962. Lecturer of creative writing, 1966–74, associate professor of English, 1974–78, professor of English, 1978–80, and since 1980 Alumni Distinguished Professor of English, University of North Carolina. Director, freshman-sophmore English, 1972–76; Fellows program, 1975–76; assistant dean, honors program, 1979–81; and faculty chair (elected), 1980–83, University of North Carolina. Visiting lecturer, Duke University, 1971; member of the board, 1979–81, and chair, 1981, Associated Writing Programs, National Endowment for the Arts. **Awards:** G.P. Putnam-U.N.C. Booklength Fiction prize, 1954; Sir Walter Raleigh Best Fiction by Carolinian award, 1957, for *Tall Houses in Winter,* 1965, for *Scarlet Thread;* Guggenheim fellowhsip, 1958; North Carolina Medal, 1975, for literature; Parker award, 1982–85, for literary achievement; John dos Passos award, 1983; American Academy of Arts and Letters Medal of Merit, 1989, for short story; Academy award, for *Violet.* Honorary D.Litt.: Greensboro College, 1987, and University of North Carolina, 1990; D.H.L., Erskine College, 1994. **Member:** National Humanities Center, 1993. **Agent:** Russell and Volkening, 50 West 29th Street, New York, New York 1001, USA. **Address:** c/o English Department, CB# 3520, University of North Carolina, Chapel Hill, North Carolina 27599–3520, USA.

Publications

Novels

Tall Houses in Winter. New York, Putnam, 1954; London, Gollancz, 1955.
The Scarlet Thread. New York, Harper, 1964.
The River to Pickle Beach. New York, Harper, 1972; New York, Simon and Schuster, 1995.
Heading West. New York, Knopf, 1981.
Souls Raised from the Dead. New York, Knopf, 1994.
The Sharp Teeth of Love. New York, Knopf, 1997.

Short Stories

The Gentle Insurrection. New York, Putnam, 1954; published as *The Gentle Insurrection and Other Stories.* Baton Rouge, Louisiana State University Press, 1997.
The Astronomer and Other Stories. New York, Harper, 1966; Baton Rouge, Louisiana State University Press, 1995.
Beasts of the Southern Wild. New York, Harper, 1973; published as *Beasts of the Southern Wild and Other Stories.* New York, Scribner, 1998.

*

Film Adaptation: *Violet,* adaptation from her own short story *''The Ugliest Pilgrim.''*

Manuscript Collection: Boston University, Boston.

Critical Studies: *The Home Truth of Doris Betts,* North Carolina, Methodist College Press, 1992; *Doris Betts* by Elizabeth Evans, New York, Twayne, 1997.

* * *

Doris Betts's writing is deeply informed by her religious sensibility, not in a dogmatic or didactic sense but in the way of one who asks important questions about good and evil, life and death, and who finds meaning in the universe and in the ways people respond to it. The biblical story of Job's much-tried faith could be considered a touchstone for Betts, and her fiction concerns similar trials in the 20th-century South, particularly North Carolina. Her earliest work tends to probe these philosophical questions in a somewhat programmatic way, as in ''Mr. Shawn and Father Scott'' in her first collection of short stories, *The Gentle Insurrection.* But four decades later in her novel, *Souls Raised From the Dead,* Betts's mature insights and highly developed techniques make her work incandescent with wisdom about the human condition.

In her second novel, *The Scarlet Thread,* Betts uses the experiences of the rapidly rising and dissolving Allen family of a North Carolina mill town to probe questions of human suffering. Through Thomas, the middle child, Betts explores the origins of evil. Thomas, from childhood on, exhibits anger and cruelty that culminate in the physical and mental abuse of his fragile wife, Nellie. One naturally wonders what made Thomas so, and one could respond that it was his belief that his siblings were ''favored'' both by life and their parents; his feelings of frustration and powerlessness were alleviated only through the power of cruelty. Betts, though, does not allow us to accept such a simplistic causal chain because Thomas's childhood and family are at least as good, and probably better, than those of most people around him, particularly the ''mill children'' and even his own siblings. His sister, Esther, responds to a jilting by leaving town and founding a new life. His brother, David, an artist in a world of philistines, pulls himself out of a life of drift backed by his parents' money to accept the challenge of learning the art of stone carving. Betts seems to suggest that even though all meet adversity in one sense or another, it is the individual's response to it that reveals whatever happiness is possible.

Betts's third novel, *The River to Pickle Beach,* continues to engage the question of human suffering through the contrasting responses of a married couple, Jack and Bebe Sellars. Jack responds to life's uncertainties with reserve and caution. He learns, plans, and avoids as much as he can, but his anxieties about the future will not let him enjoy the present; when he and Bebe embark on a new life as managers of a small beach resort, his fear of the impending visit of the owner's retarded relations blocks his own exhilaration at their new venture. It also prevents him from sharing Bebe's pleasure in the world of ocean and beach since Bebe meets life with optimism and joy, despite such disappointments as her childlessness. Jack's old army buddy, Mickey McCane, however, uses his rough childhood as the son of a disappearing and whoring mother to justify his need for power through the sexual degradation of women. When Bebe rejects his advances, Mickey does not learn that his demeaning attitude bars him from any meaningful relations with women but instead seeks the phallic power of guns on the easy target of the physically and mentally defective visitors whom, he subconsciously fears, represent his real self.

Abduction by a criminal who calls himself Dwight Anderson is the trial for North Carolina librarian Nancy Finch in Betts's fourth novel, *Heading West.* What started as a kidnapping becomes an opportunity for Nancy to escape not only Dwight but her self-made bonds to her elderly mother, epileptic brother, and spoiled sister. Nancy chooses to ''head west'' with him, bypassing some possibilities of escape, since she seems to fear her trivialized servitude to her family more than this dangerous criminal; she is learning that all he can do is kill her quickly as opposed to the slow death her ''normal'' life has become. She tests herself through her grueling flight from Dwight in the Grand Canyon and emerges victorious; he plunges to his death in an attempt to make himself feel powerful by controlling her with taunts and threats. Throughout her captivity, Nancy has attempted to find out what made Dwight so manipulative, affectless, and dehumanized—essentially to confront the problem of evil—and she continues to investigate his background as she heads back east alone. She learns that he was the ''bad twin'' raised by a crazed and begging grandmother; his brother, however damaged, has remained law-abiding. Again, Betts suggests that it is not circumstances, but the response to them that makes the man or woman and that even the horrors of an abduction have the potential for good in one who can learn from them.

What many would regard as the ultimate horror or evil, the death of a child, is Betts's subject in her fifth novel, *Souls Raised from the Dead.* Over the course of the novel, lively, intelligent Mary Grace Thompson dies of chronic renal failure, and those around her are tested like Job. As she always has, Mary Grace's mother escapes into her narcissistic world of men, mobility, and beauty rituals. Her father, Frank, a policeman who has seen much evil and suffering, must come to terms with Mary's illness, an adversary that cannot be confronted and vanquished by physical force. Unlike Mary's mother, Frank overcomes his tendency to avoid emotional situations in order to stand by Mary and to meet his commitments to life and work, friendships and family. His mother, Tacey, has always been a religious woman, but now her faith meets and surmounts, however tentatively, its ultimate challenge, surviving a grandchild who should have survived her. As this novel so painfully yet inspiringly suggests, for Betts we all have the potential to be ''souls raised from the dead'' no matter how life—and our situations in it—deny our circumstances.

—Veronica Makowsky

BILLINGTON, (Lady) Rachel (Mary)

Nationality: British. **Born:** Rachel Mary Pakenham, Oxford, 11 May 1942; daughter of the writers Lord Longford and Elizabeth Longford; sister of the writer Antonia Fraser. **Education:** University of London, B.A. (honors) in English 1963. **Family:** Married the film and theatre director Kevin Billington in 1967; two sons and two daughters. **Career:** Freelance writer; reviewer for *Financial Times* and *Evening Standard,* both London, and *New York Times;* columnist, *Sunday Telegraph,* London. **Agent:** David Higham Associates Ltd., 5–8 Lower John Street, London W1R 4HA, England. **Address:** The Court House, Poyntington, Nr. Sherborne, Dorset DT9 4LF, England.

PUBLICATIONS

Novels

All Things Nice. London, Heinemann, 1969.
The Big Dipper. London, Heinemann, 1970.
Lilacs Out of the Dead Land. London, Heinemann, 1971; New York, Saturday Review Press, 1972.
Cock Robin; or, A Fight for Male Survival. London, Heinemann, 1972.
Beautiful. London, Heinemann, and New York, Coward McCann, 1974.
A Painted Devil. London, Heinemann, and New York, Coward McCann, 1975.
A Woman's Age. London, Hamish Hamilton, 1979; New York, Summit, 1980.
Occasion of Sin. London, Hamish Hamilton, 1982; New York, Summit, 1983.
The Garish Day. London, Hamish Hamilton, 1985; New York, Morrow, 1986.
Loving Attitudes. London, Hamish Hamilton, and New York, Morrow, 1988.

Theo and Matilda. London, Macmillan, 1990; New York, HarperCollins, 1991.
Bodily Harm. London, Macmillan, 1993.
Magic and Fate: Being the Not Quite Believable Adventures of Sissie Slipper. London, Macmillan, 1996.
Perfect Happiness. London, Sceptre, 1996.

Uncollected Short Stories

''One Afternoon,'' in *Winter's Tales 1* (new series), edited by David Hughes. London, Constable, and New York, St. Martin's Press, 1985.
''The Photograph,'' in *Winter's Tales 2* (new series), edited by Robin Baird-Smith. London, Constable, and New York, St. Martin's Press, 1986.

Plays

Radio Plays: *Mrs. Bleasdale's Lodger,* 1976; *Mary, Mary,* 1977; *Sister, Sister,* 1978; *Have You Seen Guy Fawkes?,* 1979.

Television Plays: *Don't Be Silly,* 1979; *Life after Death,* 1981.

Other (for children)

Rosanna and the Wizard-Robot. London, Methuen, 1981.
The First Christmas. London, Collins Harvill, 1983; Wilton, Connecticut, Morehouse Barlow, 1987.
Star-Time. London, Methuen, 1984.
The First Easter. London, Constable, and Grand Rapids, Michigan, Eerdmans, 1987.
The First Miracles. London, Collins Harvill, 1990; Grand Rapids, Michigan, Eerdmans, 1991.

Other

The Great Umbilical, Mother Daughter Mother. London, Macmillan, 1994.

* * *

On a surface level the novels of Rachel Billington reflect the conventions of the upper-class comedy of manners. Her works are invariably set within an aristocratic milieu, their central characters a privileged churchgoing elite of country or London gentry, whose condescension towards the lower orders seems a natural response. Billington's books are distinguished by an adroit use of language, personalities revealed through conversations that display a keen, often caustic wit. Yet beneath the outward show of humor lurks a strong tendency to violence, which manifests itself in the conflicts of obsessional love.

In *All Things Nice* and *The Big Dipper* the wit and comedy predominate, these early novels emerging as vehicles for the author's stylistic skills. *Lilacs Out of the Dead Land* is both deeper and more dark. April, the younger daughter of moneyed parents, travels to Italy with her married lover. During their time together, she is forced to reassess their relationship in the context of her elder sister's death. The infatuation that draws her to the lover is slowly countered by the fear of being smothered by his love. As the tension builds inside her, events move swiftly to the cathartic act of violence. More complex and unsettling than its predecessors, *Lilacs Out of the Dead Land* shows considerable narrative skill, the author switching fluently from April's time with her lover to scenes with her parents, at the school where she teaches, and her last encounter with her sister. Dialogue fits the dovetailed scenes, each character perfectly matched by his or her patterns of speech. This novel is an early indication of the psychological depths that lie under the surface glitter of Billington's work.

Beautiful and *Cock Robin* are lighter, but accomplished creations, the elegant prose and polite behavior merely masking the pathological impulses deeper down. *Cock Robin* centers on the male narrator's passion for three girls at his university, all of them seemingly unattainable. The book follows the four of them in their careers, where the young man gradually emerges as the dominant figure, while the three goddesses prove to be tragic failures. The bitchy wit is in evidence, the story itself eminently credible, if marked by a heartless gloss. In *Beautiful,* obsessive passion again appears as a destructive force. Lucy, the flawless, amoral heroine of the novel, has thus far been able to shape the world in her image as it revolves around her. Alex, the discarded lover unwilling to let go, threatens to shatter that world and its fake stability: ''Lucy prided herself on her understanding of the human psyche; with the unmentionable exception of Alex, no one had ever stepped out of the role in which she had cast them.'' Once more the course is set for a violent resolution. A light, tautly written work, with short terse scenes and skilful dialogue, *Beautiful* shows the author at her most assured, the hard sheen of the surface and the murky underlying depths in perfect balance.

A Painted Devil is altogether more sinister, revealing Billington's vision at its grimmest. Obsessional love is again the agent of destruction, embodied in Edward, the negative central character. A painter of genius, Edward draws unquestioning adoration from his wife and friends, while giving nothing in return. His cold, remote personality, its inhuman quality symbolized by his hatred of physical love, is subtly glimpsed in conversation and unuttered thoughts. In *A Painted Devil* the glittering crust of civilized behavior is thin indeed, the novel becoming increasingly horrific as one tragedy follows another. Cruellest of all Billington's works, it is nevertheless a memorable achievement.

A Woman's Age is a new departure, the comedy of manners forsaken for an epic novel spanning a period of 70 years. It focuses mainly on the figure of Violet Hesketh, who survives a difficult childhood and broken marriages to find a successful career in politics. A mammoth undertaking, the novel shows its author's ability to convey the essence of the passing years, but one cannot help feeling that it lacks the bite and conviction of some of her shorter works, and it is in the latter that her main strength as a writer lies.

With *Occasion of Sin* is another experiment, this time a contemporary retelling of Tolstoy's *Anna Karenina;* Billington's account of the lawyer's wife who falls for a computer software executive follows the original closely, both in characters and incidents, but avoids too slavish an interpretation, particularly in some of its solutions. A worthy variant of the classic novel, the depth of this novel's theme is matched by a highly effective use of language, with Billington's mastery of dialogue well to the fore. *The Garish Day* is an ambitious saga covering two generations of diplomats at the time of the British Raj. A similar epic approach is taken in *Theo and Matilda,* where the lovers of the title are explored in various incarnations, through Saxon, Tudor, and Victorian periods to the present day. Their adventures are set against the background of Abbeyfields, whose landscape changes with the centuries from monastery to manor house, lunatic asylum, mental hospital, and finally "des res." Billington handles her epic materials with style and conviction, and Theo and Matilda must be judged the most impressive of her large-scale works.

Loving Attitudes centers on the confrontation between the successful media professional Mary Tempest and her unacknowledged daughter, the product of a youthful love affair. Their unexpected meeting leads Mary to a reassessment of her marriage and family, and to a fresh exploration of that earlier love. The gradual unfolding of the tangle of relationships is accomplished neatly and without strain, the characters sensitively portrayed as they are forced to confront the consequences of their actions.

Bodily Harm, a more powerful, disturbing novel, opens with a brutal knife attack on a young woman by a total stranger in a London shop. The girl survives and her attacker is jailed, but the passage of time draws them inexorably back together. Their slow recovery and rehabilitation, the reasons behind the attack, and the eventual resolution are achieved with masterly skill, action presented from the alternating viewpoints of the two protagonists, the climactic scene approached with a sequence of brief snapshot images and incidents. *Bodily Harm* ranks with the finest of Billington's work and is clear proof of her ability to blend stylistic flair with increasingly complex themes.

—Geoff Sadler

BINCHY, Maeve

Nationality: Irish. **Born:** Dublin, 28 May 1940. **Education:** Holy Child Convent, Killiney, County Dublin; University College, Dublin, B.A. in education. **Family:** Married Gordon Snell in 1977. **Career:** History and French teacher, Pembroke School, Dublin, 1961–68. Since 1968 columnist, *Irish Times,* Dublin. **Agent:** Christine Green, 2 Barbon Close, London WC1N 3JX, England.

PUBLICATIONS

Novels

Light a Penny Candle. London, Century, 1982; New York, Viking, 1983.
Echoes. London, Century, 1985; New York, Viking, 1986.
Firefly Summer. London, Century, 1987; New York, Delacorte Press, 1988.
Circle of Friends. London, Century, 1990; New York, Delacorte Press, 1991.
The Copper Beach. London, Orion, 1992; New York, Delacorte Press, 1993.
The Glass Lake. London, Orion, 1994; New York, Delacorte Press, 1995.
Evening Class. New York, Delacorte Press, 1996.
Tara Road. New York, Delacorte Press, 1996.

Short Stories

Central Line. London, Quartet, 1978.
Victoria Line. London, Quartet, 1980.
Dublin 4. Dublin, Ward River Press, 1982; London, Century, 1983.
London Transports (includes *Central Line* and *Victoria Line*). London, Century, 1983; New York, Dell, 1986.
The Lilac Bus. Dublin, Ward River Press, 1984; London, Century, 1986; New York, Delacorte Press, 1992.
Silver Wedding. London, Century, 1988; New York, Delacorte Press, 1989.
Dublin People. Oxford, Oxford University Press, 1993.
This Year It Will Be Different and Other Stories: A Christmas Treasury. New York, Delacorte Press, 1996.
The Return Journey. New York, Delacorte Press, 1996.

Plays

End of Term (produced Dublin, 1976).
Half Promised Land (produced Dublin, 1979).

Television Plays: *Deeply Regretted By—,* 1976; *Echoes,* from her own novel, 1988; *The Lilac Bus,* from her own story, 1991.

Other

My First Book. Dublin, Irish Times, 1978.
Maeve's Diary. Dublin, Irish Times, 1979.
Dear Maeve: Writings from the "Irish Times." Dublin, Poolbeg Press, 1995.
Aches and Pains, illustrated by Wendy Shea. New York, Delacorte Press, 2000.
Contributor, *Ladies' Night at Finbar's Hotel,* edited by Dermot Bolger. New York, Harcourt, 2000.

*

Maeve Binchy comments:

I write novels and stories set within my own experience of time and place, but they are not autobiographical. They mainly touch on the emotions of women and the aspirations and hopes of young Irishwomen growing up in the relatively closed society of Ireland in the 1950s and 1960s.

* * *

Maeve Binchy's best-selling novels set in mid-century Ireland alternate in form between works that focus on one woman or a pair of friends and collections of interlocking stories organized in a posy or grand chain. This was a form she developed early in *The Lilac Bus,* a collection on a group of passengers who travel home from Dublin every weekend, and repeats in *The Copper Beach* and *Silver Wedding.* Binchy's work is marked by her understanding of the social and economic structure of small Irish county towns—the grid of shopkeepers, doctors, lawyers, and hotel keepers who serve and order the community under the omnipresent supervision of the church.

Binchy's work, though marketed as romances, by no means fits that category precisely. Binchy, a longstanding columnist for *The Irish Times,* presents a realistic picture of the lives of women ordered within the rigidities of Catholic orthodoxy that forbid divorce and abortion. In her work, women's survival is predicated on the creation of powerful, though informal, networks of alliance and friendships that survive the vicissitudes of pregnancy, forced marriage, and alcoholism.

Such sociological accuracy does not support the illusions of romance. Although Benny, the large, only daughter of over-protective shopkeepers, in *Circle of Friends,* does win the love of the handsome soccer hero of the university, she painfully discovers his insubstantiality. The romance pattern of other novels is complicated by Binchy's decision to pursue her heroines' lives after the altar. In *Echoes,* the heroine's triumphant marriage to the doctor's son is succeeded by a first year of domestic unhappiness, postpartum depression, and despair. In *Light a Penny Candle,* the heroine, safely married, in a quarrel pushes her husband down the stairs and kills him. In both novels, the promise of a safe haven in marriage is complicated by Binchy's clear insight into the painful restrictions of domesticity.

Although women's friendships, formed often at eight or ten, last through adolescent love, courtship, marriage, abortion, domestic violence, and encompass even murder, systems of political, religious, and social authority remain controlled by men. Binchy's heroines struggle against, but do not entirely triumph over these circumstances. Binchy is too aware of particular constraints on Irish women's lives to allow easy rewards. In *Echoes* the conventional Bildungsroman features an intelligent heroine Clare, aged ten, who enters an essay competition. We await the triumphant rise of the sweetshop owner's daughter. Yet the necessary boundaries around Clare's triumphs are suggested by the echoing story of the teacher who encourages her. Angela O'Hara was once a successful student. She, like Clare, won a scholarship, yet was inexorably pulled back to Castlebay by the domestic responsibilities for an ailing mother that devolve on an unmarried daughter in an Irish family. Add to that boundary of success for an intellectual woman, the unavailability of contraception, and Binchy has created a life for her heroine more realistically limited than the popular romance usually provides.

Light a Penny Candle traces the story of two women whose friendship began when Elizabeth arrived in a small Irish town as a wartime evacuee. The loyalty of the childhood friendship of Aisling and Elizabeth is deepened through the vicissitudes of feminine experience—an abortion in London, a lover who will never marry, an alcoholic husband, and an unconsummated marriage. The pattern of their lives is shaped by the men they marry, until, in a frightening, though not fully confronted moment, the Englishwoman, Elizabeth, pushes her husband down the stairs and kills him accidentally. The silence of her best friend over the manslaughter she has witnessed demonstrates the depth of female bonding. In *Light a Penny Candle,* Binchy suggests that this violent accident may be nurtured by the stifling restraints of bourgeois marriage. Elizabeth's mother dies in an insane asylum after a violent attack on her husband. Her mother's murder of her lover is the secret that isolates Leo from her friends in *The Copper Beach.*

Firefly Summer, combining the two forms, centers on the successful marriage of Kate and John Ryan, a marriage that survives the appalling, almost casual, accident that cripples Kate for life, and links that story with the varied responses in the village to the building of a luxury hotel in a Georgian mansion burned in the Troubles. Binchy is particularly clear about the restraints on economic change, the wariness of envy, the precautions against feuds, the aggression that flares in petty vandalism. These are the ties that restrict initiative, yet smooth social friction. The central characters survive, their lives shadowed by great losses. Binchy's willingness to acknowledge in her novels a sense of a world without purpose—''It was never meant to be like this. Pointless tragedy, and confusion everywhere''—creates a dense picture of Irish life in the 1950s and 1960s.

The most captivating figure, if not the firmly established protagonist, of *Evening Class* is Nora O'Donoghue, known to her students as Signora. Despite her somewhat questionable past as the lover of a married Sicilian, Aidan Dunne invites her to help make his program of adult education classes—hers is ''Introduction to Italian''—a success. Those who fall under her spell refuse to judge Signora, as is the case (needless to say) with Binchy herself. Ria Lynch of *Tara Road* is on the other end of the affair triangle, finding herself abandoned by her successful developer husband in favor of his young pregnant lover. This sense of loss provides the occasion for a temporary trade of houses with Marilyn Vine, an American whose son has just died, and in the end each woman helps the other find meaning in her misfortune.

—Karen Robertson

BISSOONDATH, Neil

Nationality: Canadian (emigrated from Trinidad in 1973). **Born:** Devindra Bissoondath, Trinidad, West Indies, 19 April 1955. **Education:** York University, Toronto, B.A. in French 1977. **Career:** Teacher of English and French, Inlingua School of Languages, Toronto, 1977–80; teacher of English and French, Language Workshop, Toronto, 1980–85. **Awards:** McClelland and Stewart award for fiction, 1986, and National Magazine award, 1986, both for ''Dancing.'' **Address:** c/o Macmillan of Canada, 39 Birch Ave., Toronto M4V 1E2, Canada.

Publications

Novels

A Casual Brutality. Toronto, Macmillan, 1988; New York, Potter, 1989.

The Innocence of Age. Toronto, Knopf, 1992.

The Worlds within Her. Toronto, Knopf Canada, 1998.

Short Stories

Digging Up the Mountains. Toronto, Macmillan, 1985; New York, Viking, 1986.

On the Eve of Uncertain Tomorrows. Toronto, Dennys, and New York, Potter, 1990.

Other

Selling Illusions: The Cult of Multiculturalism in Canada. N.p., n.d.

* * *

Neil Bissoondath's writing takes readers into marginalized social and geographical territories, without ever moving far outside the conventions of literary realism. This combination of the exotic and the familiar has attracted a wide readership extending from North America to Europe, where his works have been translated into French and German.

Given his family history of double migration from India to Trinidad to Canada, it is not surprising that his narratives often focus on migrant experiences of displacement, uncertainty, isolation, cultural dislocation, and adaptation. These themes dominate many of the stories in *Digging Up the Mountains* and *On the Eve of Uncertain Tomorrows.* Of particular interest in such stories as "Christmas Lunch," "Veins Visible," "Security," and "The Power of Reason" is Bissoondath's alertness to the complexity of gender relations in multicultural contexts, and to differences between women's and men's respective experiences of migration and cultural adaptation.

Episodes of apparently random violence witnessed by Bissoondath in his early years in Trinidad find a place in his first novel *A Casual Brutality.* Narrated in the first person, the novel is a colonial Bildungsroman. The protagonist's inner journey towards maturity and understanding is bound up with a physical journey from a small Third World island to a metropolitan center of Western culture. Although the fictional island of Casaquemada resembles Trinidad in certain respects, Bissoondath's aim is not to recount a specific epoch in Trinidad's history, but rather to draw on episodes that took place in various West Indian countries. This desire to internationalize and universalize his stories, and to avoid analysis of specific historical episodes and political struggles, has attracted severe criticism from certain quarters.

Over time, Bissoondath's focus has shifted away from Trinidad toward his Canadian experiences and concerns. The title story of *On the Eve of Uncertain Tomorrows* penetrates the limbo world of a diverse group of fugitives from political violence and economic oppression who anxiously await the outcome of their applications for refugee status in Canada. "Uncertain Tomorrows" exposes the ethnocentricity of the legal criteria for granting refugee status, and the biases institutionalized in the court process. "The Power of Reason" emphasizes the gender-specificity of migrant experiences. Because equality of opportunity for women is often contingent upon their race and nation of origin, Canada's vertical mosaic has its own distinctive pink ghettos. Monica, an immigrant woman who cleans house for a white professional woman, has daughters who also work hard to take advantage of the opportunities gained through migration. Monica's sons, by contrast, either laze in front of the television or hang out on the street, mimicking the young Black American males they see on television. To Monica, her sons are complete strangers. The cultural gulf that opens up in many migrant families between the generations is compounded by a gap between gender roles.

Yet as *The Innocence of Age* suggests, migration is not a necessary prerequisite either to intergenerational conflict or to cultural alienation within the family. In Bissoondath's second novel, a father and son live in entirely different worlds, although both have always resided in Toronto. Except for the fact that its two main characters are Anglo-Canadian, and have no familial connection with another country, *The Innocence of Age* conforms in virtually every respect to the thematic and structural paradigms of "ethnic fiction." This would be a quintessential immigrant novel, were it not for the fact that its central characters are not immigrants. By writing an "ethnic novel" centering on people customarily perceived as "non-ethnic," Bissoondath effectively "ethnifies" Canada's dominant cultural group.

With each successive publication, it becomes increasingly clear that Bissoondath's novels and short stories occupy a place beside his interviews, newspaper and magazine articles, and his book on multiculturalism, *Selling Illusions: The Cult of Multiculturalism in Canada*—all contribute to the debate on Canadian multiculturalism. Irrespective of their geographical settings, which range from Trinidad to Europe and Japan as well as Canada, Bissoondath's works comment on the conditions under which the category of "multicultural writing" is constructed, and they critique the institutional circumstances under which "multicultural texts" are produced, interpreted, and evaluated. Bissoondath's literary practices and aesthetic values are entirely consistent with his critical stance on Canadian multiculturalism. By exploring what he sees as universal human themes, emotions, and experiences, Bissoondath endeavors to build and strengthen forms of mutual understanding and social cohesion that he would like to see asserted more strongly throughout Canadian society.

—Penny van Toorn

BLAISE, Clark (Lee)

Nationality: Canadian. **Born:** Fargo, North Dakota, United States, 10 April 1940; became Canadian citizen, 1973. **Education:** Denison University, Granville, Ohio, 1957–61, A.B. 1961; University of Iowa, Iowa City, 1962–64, M.F.A. 1964. **Family:** Married Bharati Mukherjee, *q.v.,* in 1963; two sons. **Career:** Acting instructor, University of Wisconsin, Milwaukee, 1964–65; teaching fellow, University of Iowa, 1965–66; lecturer, 1966–67, assistant professor, 1967–69, associate professor, 1969–72, and professor of English, 1973–78, Sir George Williams University, later Concordia University, Montreal; professor of Humanities, York University, Toronto, 1978–80; Professor of English, Skidmore College, Saratoga Springs, New York, 1980–81, 1982–83. Visiting lecturer or writer-in-residence, University of Iowa, 1981–82, Saskatchewan School of the Arts, Saskatoon, Summer 1983, David Thompson University Centre, Nelson, British Columbia, Fall 1983, Emory University, Atlanta, 1985, Bennington College, Vermont, 1985, Columbia University, New York, Spring 1986, and New York State Writers Institute, Sarasota Springs, New York, Summer 1994 and 1995; exchange professor, Meiji University, Japan, 1994. Currently, adjunct professor, Columbia University, New York. **Awards:** University of Western Ontario President's medal, for short story, 1968; Great Lakes Colleges Association prize, 1973; Canada Council grant, 1973, 1977, and travel grant, 1985; St.

Lawrence award, 1974; Fels award, for essay, 1975; *Asia Week* award, for non-fiction, 1977; *Books in Canada* prize, 1979; National Endowment for the Arts grant, 1981; Guggenheim grant, 1983. D.Litt.: Denison University, 1979. **Agent:** Janklow and Nesbit, 598 Madison Ave., New York, New York 10022.

PUBLICATIONS

Novels

Lunar Attractions. New York, Doubleday, 1979.
Lusts. New York, Doubleday, 1983.
If I Were Me. Erin, Ontario, Porcupine's Quill, 1997.

Short Stories

New Canadian Writing 1968, with Dave Godfrey and David Lewis Stein. Toronto, Clarke Irwin, 1969.
A North American Education. Toronto and New York, Doubleday, 1973.
Tribal Justice. Toronto and New York, Doubleday, 1974.
Personal Fictions, with others, edited by Michael Ondaatje. Toronto, Oxford Unversity Press, 1977.
Resident Alien. Toronto and New York, Penguin, 1986.
Man and His World. Erin, Ontario, Porcupine's Quill, 1992.

Plays

Screenplays: *Days and Nights in Calcutta,* with Bharati Mukherjee, 1991.

Other

Days and Nights in Calcutta, with Bharati Mukherjee. New York, Doubleday, 1977; London, Penguin, 1986.
The Sorrow and the Terror: The Haunting Legacy of the Air India Tragedy, with Bharati Mukherjee. Toronto, Viking, 1987.
I Had a Father. New York, Addison-Wesley, 1993.
Editor, with John Metcalf, *Here and Now.* Ottawa, Oberon Press, 1977.
Editor, with John Metcalf, *78* [*79, 80*]: *Best Canadian Stories.* Ottawa, Oberon Press, 3 vols., 1978–1980.

*

Manuscript Collection: Calgary University Library, Alberta.

Critical Studies: *On the Line,* Downsview, Ontario, ECW Press, 1982, and *Another I: The Fiction of Clark Blaise,* ECW Press, 1988, both by Robert Lecker; article by Blaise in *Contemporary Authors Autobiography Series 3* edited by Adele Sarkissian, Detroit, Gale, 1986.

Clark Blaise comments:

(1981) My fiction is an exploration of threatened space; the space has been geographically and historically defined as French-Canada and French-America (New England), as well as extremely isolated areas of the deep South. Most of my fiction has been concerned with the effects of strong and contrasting parents, with the memory of Europe and of Canada, and the very oppressive reality, rendered minutely, of America. I am concerned with nightmare, terror, violence, sexual obsession, and the various artistic transformations of those drives. The tone of the work is not gothic or grotesque, however; I am devoted to the close observation of the real world, and to hold the gaze long enough to make the real world seem distorted. My work is also involved with the growth of the mind, the coming on of ideas about itself and the outside world. I would agree with critics who see my work as courting solipsism, and much of my own energy is devoted to finding ways out of the vastness of the first person pronoun.

* * *

Clark Blaise's short stories and novels are marked by their preoccupation with the tensions between a host of metaphorical extremes. Blaise is attracted to raw experience, spontaneous impulse, grotesque realism, uncultured thought: simultaneously, he is a polymath who needs reason, order, intellect, and learning in order to survive. For Blaise, these two worlds can never coincide; yet his fiction is driven by the strategies he employs in his attempt to *make* them coincide. The most obvious strategy involves doubling and superimposition. Blaise's characters are often two-sided, and their stories detail, through extended use of archetype and symbol, a profound desire to discover an integrated and authentic self. A list of the authors who influenced Blaise—including Pascal, Flaubert, Proust, Faulkner, and Céline—suggests that his work is philosophical, realistic, epic, eschatological, and existential. It is important to note this range, if only because Blaise has been viewed as a purely realistic writer involved with the tragic implications of his age. This perspective seems curious when one considers the extent to which Blaise's stories become self-conscious explorations of their own mode of articulation. Their ultimate reality is internal, psychological, personal, and self-reflective. To trace Blaise's growing preoccupation with this self-reflective mode is to describe the evolution of his fiction.

A North American Education, Blaise's first collection of linked short stories, is marked by the multi-leveled revelation of the fears, obsessions, and aesthetic values informing its three central narrators. In the final group of tales—''The Montreal Stories''—Norma Dyer begins to comment on the cosmopolitan milieu he inhabits from the removed and condescending perspective of an intellectual elitist who appears to be in full, if arrogant, control. But as the three stories comprising this section develop, panic sets in; the distanced third-person perspective of the opening eventually gives way to a revealingly fragmented first-person mode that details Dyer's personal and narrative collapse as he confesses that ''I who live in dreams have suffered something real, and reality hurts like nothing in the world.'' In the ''Keeler Stories'' we hear the confessions of ''a writer, a creator'' who ''would learn to satisfy himself with that.'' But here, as in the closing ''Thibidault Stories,'' Blaise makes it clear that his narrators will never be satisfied with their creations, or with themselves. Yet they continue to deceive themselves in the belief that ''anything dreamt had to become real, eventually.''

The dreams shared by Blaise's narrators are always highly symbolic and archetypal in form, a conclusion supported by even the most cursory reading of Blaise's second short story collection, *Tribal Justice*. Here, in some of his richest and most evocative fiction, Blaise returns again and again to his narrators' meditations on their art. If there is a paradigmatic Blaise story—one that reveals the various tensions I have described—it is surely ''Grids and Doglegs.'' It begins with its narrator recalling his interest in creativity, maps, education, history, archaeology, and cultural life; but no sooner is this interest articulated than it is ruthlessly undercut by hints of isolation and impending doom. Other stories—I think particularly of ''Notes Beyond a History'' and ''At the Lake''—are framed by the same kind of divided opening, and by the same suggestion that the narrator who inhabits that opening is psychologically split.

Blaise's first two books established him as one of the finest short story writers in Canada at the very time he decided to explore a different genre. While *Lunar Attractions* proved that Blaise could master the novel form, it also demonstrated that his fundamental attraction to self-reflective writing remained central to his art. After all, *Lunar Attractions* is a semi-autobiographical account of a writer's development: David Greenwood insists on seeing himself in every aspect of his creation, so much so that his fiction becomes an intricate confession about his failure to get beyond himself. Yet *Lunar Attractions* is by no means purely solipsistic: it is a book about our times, about growing up in our times, and about the symbols and systems we use to explain our lives. Blaise has written that he wanted ''to create the portrait of the authentically Jungian or even Freudian whole mind,'' which ''sees every aspect of the natural and historical world being played out in its own imagination, and it literally creates the world that it sees.''

These words suggest that for Blaise the writer can never be merely a recorder or even the interpreter of events. He must give form to experience and must be responsible to that form. The nature of this responsibility is the focus of Blaise's second novel, *Lusts*. Here the nature of writing is explored through Richard Durgin's struggle to understand the suicide of his wife, a successful poet who challenged Durgin's assumptions about the social and political implications of art.

If Rachel is Richard's ''other self'' then her death is doubly significant: it suggests that Blaise may have overcome the personal divisions that kept his successive narrators from becoming whole. Does this mean that he has found the integrated self he has sought throughout his work? A forthcoming volume of autobiographical essays may answer this question. But Blaise has written autobiography before—most notably in *Days and Nights in Calcutta*—only to return to the story of his personal and aesthetic search. The search is essential to his art, for the quality of his writing—its permutations, obsessions, and complex use of voice—is tragically dependent on Blaise's constant inability to find himself or his final story.

—Robert Lecker

BODSWORTH, (Charles) Fred(erick)

Nationality: Canadian. **Born:** Port Burwell, Ontario, 11 October 1918. **Education:** Port Burwell public and high schools. **Family:** Married Margaret Neville Banner in 1944; two daughters and one son. **Career:** Reporter, St. Thomas *Times-Journal,* Ontario, 1940–43; reporter and editor, Toronto *Daily Star* and *Weekly Star,* 1943–46; staff writer and editor, *Maclean's Magazine,* Toronto, 1947–55. Since 1955 freelance writer. Director and former president (1965–67), Federation of Ontario Naturalists: leader of worldwide ornithological tours. Since 1970 honorary director, Long Point Bird Observatory; chair of the Board of Trustees, James L. Baillie Memorial Fund for Ornithology, 1975–89; editor, Natural Science of Canada series, 1980–81. **Awards:** Doubleday Canadian Novel award, 1967. **Agent:** Curtis Brown, 10 Astor Place, New York, New York 10003, U.S.A. **Address:** 294 Beech Avenue, Toronto, Ontario M4E 3J2, Canada.

PUBLICATIONS

Novels

Last of the Curlews. Toronto and New York, Dodd Mead, 1955; London, Museum Press, 1956; foreword by W. S. Merwin, afterword by Murray Gell-Mann, illustrated by Abigail Rorer, based on original drawings by T.M. Shortt. Washington, D.C., Counterpoint, 1995.

The Strange One. Toronto and New York, Dodd Mead, 1959; London, Longman, 1960.

The Atonement of Ashley Morden. Toronto and New York, Dodd Mead, 1964; as *Ashley Morden,* London, Longman, 1965.

The Sparrow's Fall. Toronto, McClelland and Stewart, New York, Doubleday, and London, Longman, 1967.

Other

The People's Health: Canada and WHO, with Brock Chisholm. Toronto, Canadian Association for Adult Education, 1949.

The Pacific Coast. Toronto, Natural Science of Canada, 1970.

Wilderness Canada, with others. Toronto, Clarke Irwin, 1970.

*

Critical Studies: Introduction by James Stevens to *Last of the Curlews,* Toronto, McClelland and Stewart, 1963; article in *The Oxford Companion to Canadian History and Literature* edited by Norah Story, Toronto, New York, and London, Oxford University Press, 1967; Don Gutteridge, in *Journal of Canadian Studies* (Peterborough, Ontario), August 1973; Olga Dey, in *Canadian Author and Bookman* (Toronto), Fall 1981; article in *A Reader's Guide to the Canadian Novel* by John Moss, Toronto, McClelland and Stewart, 1981.

Fred Bodsworth comments:

(1991) The major part of my work has been novels linking human and animal characters in a fiction format with strong natural history content and wilderness backgrounds. The nature storyteller who uses birds or mammals in fictional situations treads a narrow path if he wishes to be scientifically authentic and portray them as they really are. On the one hand, he has to personalize his animal as well as his human characters or he simply has no dramatic base for his story.

Yet if the personalizing of animal characters goes too far and begins turning them into furry or feathered people—the nature writer's sin of anthropomorphism—the result is maudlin nonsense that is neither credible fable nor fiction. I enjoy the challenge of presenting wildlife characters as modern animal behavior studies are showing them to be—creatures dominated by instinct, but not enslaved by it, beings with intelligence very much sub-human in some areas yet fascinatingly superhuman in others. Out of the blending of human and animal stories comes the theme that I hope is inherent in all my books: that man is an inescapable part of all nature, that its welfare is his welfare, that to survive he cannot continue acting and regarding himself as a spectator looking on from somewhere outside.

* * *

Fred Bodsworth, writing in imaginative, uncomplicated prose, has used the Canadian shield of pine-tree laden granite for the setting of his novels. He calls it ''a benign land sometimes amiable, even indulgent, but at other times a land of perverse hostility.'' These sparsely Indian-populated lands provide a unique characteristic which distinguishes Canada from its gargantuan neighbor to the south. Bodsworth is then readily identifiable as a Canadian novelist.

The strength of his writing is the skillful portrayal of characters who are dependent upon the milieu and the forces within it. He is able to make his birds and humans unpredictable because of unforeseen but crucial subtleties in the environmental settings. Bodworth's naturalist and ornithological knowledge fosters such keen insight. Atook, a native hunter in *The Sparrow's Fall*, seems doomed because Christian myth interferes with his hunting prowess. But the will to survive, which resides in all his characters, eventually causes Atook to cast aside his alien beliefs and adjust to his natural surroundings.

Last of the Curlews is his most stimulating and moving novel. Bodsworth reveals the brutal and senseless slaughter of a bird that has not developed a fear of the earth's most irrational creature, man. In sensitive prose, the tiny bird becomes personalized but not human; thus he avoids sham. The theme of this novel has increased in importance since its writing because of the growing awareness of our threatened environment.

Although Bodsworth commits the occasional transgression by allowing his creatures to reason, it does not seriously detract from his animal characters.

In *The Strange One*, he adroitly interweaves the mating of an alien Hebridean Barra goose with a native Canada goose and the love of a young biologist for a Cree maiden, who has been socialized in the whiteman's world. Indian-white miscegenation is as old as Canada itself and this theme intertwined with the geese is unusual in Canadian literature. Bodsworth is the first to write about it. The parallel between man and bird in this novel clearly reveals the interrelationship of man with animal when Rory, the scientist, follows what appear to be almost instinctual feelings, disregards social convention and returns to the beautiful Cree, Kanina.

The Strange One and *The Atonement of Ashley Morden* involve what may be melodramatic relationships between men and birds, but the two themes are drawn together skillfully, and are quite effectively written. An underlying theme in both these novels, as well as the others, is the complicated, often contradictory behavior of men contrasted with the logical, conditioned instincts of animals and birds.

In the context of Canadian literature, Bodsworth is one of the leading traditional novelists.

—James R. Stevens

BOLGER, Dermot

Nationality: Irish. **Born:** Finglas, Ireland, 6 February 1959. **Education:** Attended Beneavin College Secondary School. **Family:** Married Bernadette in 1988; two children. **Career:** Founder and editor, Raven Arts Press, Finglas, Ireland, 1979–92; executive editor, New Island Books, 1992—. **Awards:** A. E. Memorial Prize, 1986; Macaulay Fellowship, 1987; Samuel Beckett Award; Stewart Parker BBC Award; Edinburgh Fringe First Award; A. Z. Whitehead Prize. **Agent:** A. P. Watt, 20 John Street, London WC1N 2DR, England.

PUBLICATIONS

Novels

Night Shift. Dingle, Ireland, Brandon, 1985.
The Woman's Daughter. Dublin, Raven Arts Press, 1987; expanded edition, New York, Viking, 1991.
The Journey Home. New York, Viking, 1990.
Emily's Shoes. New York, Viking, 1992.
A Second Life. New York, Viking, 1994.
Father's Music. London, Flamingo, 1997.

Plays

The Lament for Arthur Cleary. Dublin Theatre Festival, 1989.
Blinded by the Light. Dublin, Abbey Theatre, 1990.
In High Germany. Dublin Theatre Festival, 1990; Dublin, New Island Books, 1999.
The Holy Ground. Dublin, Gate Theatre, 1990.
One Last White Horse. Dublin Theatre Festival, 1991.
A Dublin Quartet (contains the plays *The Lament for Arthur Cleary, In High Germany, The Holy Ground,* and *One Last White Horse*). London, Penguin, 1992.
The Dublin Bloom. Philadelphia, Annenberg Theatre, 1994; published as *A Dublin Bloom: An Original Free Adaptation of James Joyce's Ulysses.* London, Nick Hern Books, 1995.
April Bright; and Blinded by the Light: Two Plays. London, Nick Hern Books, 1997.
The Passion of Jerome. London, Methuen, 1999.

Poetry

The Habit of Flesh. Dublin, Raven Arts Press, 1979.
Finglas Lilies. Dublin, Raven Arts Press, 1980.
No Waiting America. Dublin, Raven Arts Press, 1981.
Internal Exiles. Mountrath, Ireland, Dolmen Press, 1986.
Leinster Street Ghosts. Dublin, Raven Arts Press, 1989.
Taking My Letters Back: New and Selected Poems. Dublin, New Island Books, 1998.

Other

A New Primer for Irish Schools (nonfiction, with Michael O'Loughlin). Dublin, Raven Arts Press, 1985.

Contributor, *The Crack in the Emerald: New Irish Plays,* edited by David Grant. London, Nick Hern Books, 1994.

Editor, *Manna in the Morning: A Memoir 1940–1958* by Madeleine Stuart. Dublin, Raven Arts Press, 1986.

Editor, *The Dolmen Book of Irish Christmas Stories.* Mountrath, Ireland, Dolmen Press, 1986.

Editor, *The Bright Wave: Poetry in Irish Now.* Dublin, Raven Arts Press, 1986.

Editor, *16 on 16: Irish Writers on the Easter Rising.* Dublin, Raven Arts Press, 1988.

Editor, *Invisible Cities: The New Dubliners: A Journey through Unofficial Dublin.* Dublin, Raven Arts Press, 1988.

Editor, *Invisible Dublin: A Journey through Dublin's Suburbs.* Dublin, Raven Arts Press, 1991.

Editor, *Francis Ledwidge: Selected Poems.* Dublin, New Island Books, 1992.

Editor, *Wexford through Its Writers.* Dublin, New Island Books, 1992.

Editor, *The Picador Book of Contemporary Irish Fiction.* London, Picador, 1993.

Editor, with Aidan Murphy, *12 Bar Blues.* Dublin, Raven Arts Press, 1993.

Editor, *Ireland in Exile: Irish Writers Abroad.* Dublin, New Island Books, 1993.

Editor, *Selected Poems* by Padraic Pearse. Dublin, New Island Books, 1993.

Editor, *The Vintage Book of Contemporary Irish Fiction.* New York, Vintage Books, 1995.

Editor, with Ciaran Carty, *The Hennessy Book of Irish Fiction.* Dublin, New Island Books, 1995.

Editor, *Greatest Hits: Four Irish One-Act Plays.* Dublin, New Island Books, 1997.

Editor and contributor, *Finbar's Hotel.* London, Picador, 1997.

Editor and contributor, *Ladies' Night at Finbar's Hotel.* San Diego, Harcourt, 2000.

*

Critical Studies: *No Mean City? The Image of Dublin in the Novels of Dermot Bolger, Roddy Doyle, and Val Mulkerns* by Ulrike Paschel, New York, P. Lang, 1998.

* * *

Dermot Bolger is one of the most remarkable products of Ireland's institution of universal secondary education in 1968, which produced a wider population of readers and writers of fiction independent of the universities and, arguably, the necessary number for a national audience for a national literature apart from the imaginative needs of England and America. This new guild of fiction readers and writers is necessarily Bolger's age and younger, which may account for the freedom with which Bolger described the ''suburban underbelly'' (Fintan O'Toole's sensational phrase) of Dublin. Bolger began writing convincingly not only of this class, but to this class.

Critics who early on disparaged the ''Finglas school of writing'' missed the utopian element never far from Bolger's writing and his work as a publisher. *Night Shift*, Bolger's first novel, describes the working conditions of eighteen-year-old Donal Flynn, who works the press at a factory, and lives with his young wife in a caravan at the bottom of her parent's garden. Donal's conflict is a common one, the competing loyalties to the wild freedom of his mates and his love for Elizabeth. Like all of Bolger's work, the story line is distinctive, arresting, and heading creatively for surprises.

Although she tries, Elizabeth can hardly fit herself to the rude male humor and dissolute behavior of Donal's friends. They are sympathetically portrayed, and the reader is given a full tour of the working class youth culture north of the Liffey, but at the same time is ready to agree with Donal that it is more than time to go home.

Donal does go home the morning after a final farewell to his youth, to find that Elizabeth is in the hospital. In her frenzied worry and despair over her husband's absence, she has fallen down the stairs, losing their baby. Donal tells her that he has come home to her to love her better, but his irresponsible self-absorption that has caused her such pain has taught her that she needs to take care of herself better. She hands him her ring and leaves him.

Bolger compares more than favorably with the self-absorbed quality of masculinity of other famous first-novel portraits of the artist like *Sons and Lovers* and *Portrait of the Artist As a Young Man* itself. The ethos of *Night Shift* is startling and inexorable: a young man even genuinely repentant can lose the love of a good woman, forever.

The Woman's Daughter first appeared in 1987, consisting of what are now Part I and sections of Part III of the final 1991 version. There is the abuse of more than one woman's daughter to follow, and the parallels and connections between stories and times are not merely formal. Bolger's characters are authentically haunted by people from the past. The poetry (*Leinster Street Ghosts*) and drama (*The Lament for Arthur Cleary*) of this period begin colluding with the fiction in considering hauntings as well as haunting each other: poems turning into plays and novels. The last narrator of *The Woman's Daughter* accepts in all their names the imperative of past voices: ''let us live on again through you, don't cast us into the darkness where our names and lives will have all meant nothing.''

The Journey Home shares with *Nightshift* the setting of suburban and north of the Liffey Dublin and a complex narrative sequence. Despite the title, the resonances are more public than domestic. Bolger borrows from postwar Italian film the metaphor of sexual perversion standing for political perversion to scandalize an Irish public inured to corruption. Perhaps the most sensational of his novels, it begins and concludes with Hano and Katie on the run from the police, because Hano has avenged his friend Shay's death by killing one of the notorious and politically influential Plunkett family. Solely in this novel Bolger offers a short glossary at the beginning, annotating Irish political and street slang.

Emily's Shoes risks the untouchable status of fiction that speaks for the dispossessed and voiceless by focusing on a child growing up with real problems but manifested in a fetish (for shoes) that has been used to ridicule psychological theory since Freud. It is up to the reader to decide if Bolger has transcended the stereotype to reach the boy's pain.

A Second Life is perhaps Bolger's greatest novel. It begins with Sean Blake's spirit floating above the nearby Botanical Gardens while seeing his body below in a car accident. We gradually realize that he is having a near-death experience. As Blake reluctantly recuperates he follows two spiritual hauntings: he tries to find his biological mother who gave him up for adoption, and to identify a face he saw when he was near death, a face that is associated with the past history of the Botanical Gardens. The novel also follows Sean's mother, who ''hears'' the crash in Dublin although she lives in England. As Sean works his way back to her, the novel brings her story forward, how she was forced into an institution for unwed mothers, forced to give up her child.

Sean ultimately gives up the search for the mysterious face from someone else's life to work harder on sorting out his own. Painfully, he finds his mother's identity a few days after she has died, still waiting for him to find her, but there is a magnificent reconciliation scene at the end, when Sean takes his family to the graves of his grandparents who cast his mother out, and releases his mother's ashes there. Like many of Bolger's novels, his feeling for the collective psyche of Ireland is uncanny. The novel was being published just as there was a long-delayed public investigation in Ireland of how women were hidden away in institutions for real or imaginary sins.

Tracey Sweeney is the narrator of *Father's Music*. We begin with her relationship with a married Irishman Luke Duggan who has left behind his family's notoriety in Dublin to run tile shops in London. Unknown to Luke, Tracey is herself half-Irish; her mother married an itinerant sean-nós singer three times her age while on a trip to Ireland, but he left her shortly after Tracey was born. Gradually uncovered is a damaging week in Tracey's past, when her mother took her back to Ireland to escape her restrictive parents, to perhaps find her husband. While in Dublin her mother stopped using the medication that kept her from succumbing to her depression. Tracey, aged eleven, is able to slip away from her mother in the streets of Dublin. She runs with a group of traveler children supporting themselves on what they can steal or scam, but she is sexually assaulted by a man before her grandfather comes to Dublin to bring her and her mother back to England.

The reader is as uncertain as Tracey herself whether to trust her middle-aged Irish lover. At times he seems to love her, at times he seems to be using her to screen a major crime. The novel profits from Bolger's longstanding involvement in traditional Irish music, as it follows Tracey's attempt to find her father. Luke is murdered before her eyes in the west of Ireland when they are close to finding her father. As the novel ends, Tracey, wrung nearly empty by all the pain, sits in a pub listening to her father. As if in a dream, she is recognized both by the pub owner and her father as her mother's child.

Temptation shares with Bolger's earlier work only the author's intention to imagine the real lives and intimate responsibilities of others in an arresting and unpredictable narrative. Alison, her husband Peadar, and their three children, go for their annual holiday at a hotel on the coast of Ireland south of Dublin. We first review the family's anticipation. Later, we discover that Alison's father, who once worked in the kitchen in Fitzgeralds, began the association of holidays there in Alison's mind by taking the family there once.

Peadar is preoccupied with his responsibilities as a headmaster; Alison has been waiting all term to tell him that she had a benign tumor removed from her breast. Peadar is called back suddenly when the construction company building an addition to the school goes bankrupt. Alison is left alone with her children for their five-day holiday, making her think more than once, ''I gave up my happiness to make another person happy.''

As deftly as ever Bolger wires a series of shocks to the reader. Chris, an old acquaintance who was in love with Alison twenty years before but who timidly deferred to Peadar, shows up at Fitzgeralds. Having recognized him after a bit, we follow Alison as she tries to match him with a wife and children from among the other guests, but she is told later that he lost them in a car accident. He is there to try to make some peace with the memory of his family before he leaves Ireland forever.

His presence makes Alison wonder about her life with Peadar. After several intense encounters, and a final episode where she saves Chris from drowning himself, Alison awaits her husband, ''her lover [who] would be here in the morning for her'' to take her and her children back home. One must admire the felt stress and importance of elementary kinships that run across the considerable range of class and experience Bolger has presented in his novels, from working class Finglas to a posh hotel at Rosslare.

—William Johnsen

BOURJAILY, Vance (Nye)

Nationality: American. **Born:** Cleveland, Ohio, 17 September 1922. **Education:** Bowdoin College, Brunswick, Maine, B.A. 1947. **Military Service:** Served in the American Field Service, 1942–44, and in the United States Army, 1944–46. **Family:** Married Bettina Yensen in 1946; three children (one deceased). **Career:** Instructor at the Writers Workshop, 1957–58, and associate professor, 1960–64, 1966–67, 1971–72, University of Iowa, Iowa City; visiting professor, 1977–78, and professor, 1980–85, University of Arizona, Tucson. Member, United States Department of State mission to South America, 1959. Distinguished Visiting Professor, Oregon State University, Corvallis, Summer 1968. **Awards:** American Academy of Arts and Letters award, 1993. D.Litt, Bowdoin College, 1993. **Agent:** William Morris Agency, 1350 Avenue of the Americas, New York, New York 10019, U.S.A.

Publications

Novels

The End of My Life. New York, Scribner, 1947; London, W.H. Allen, 1963.

The Hound of Earth. New York, Scribner, 1955; London, Secker and Warburg, 1956.

The Violated. New York, Dial Press, 1958; London, W.H. Allen, 1962.

Confessions of a Spent Youth. New York, Dial Press, 1960; London, W.H. Allen, 1961.

The Man Who Knew Kennedy. New York, Dial Press, and London, W.H. Allen, 1967.

Brill among the Ruins. New York, Dial Press, 1970; London, W.H. Allen, 1971.

Now Playing in Canterbury. New York, Dial Press, 1976.

A Game Men Play. New York, Dial Press, 1980.

The Great Fake Book. New York, Weidenfeld and Nicolson, 1987.
Old Soldier. New York, Fine, 1990.

Uncollected Short Stories

''The Poozle Dreamers,'' in *Dial* (New York), Fall 1959.
''Fractional Man,'' in *New Yorker,* 6 August 1960.
''Goose Pits,'' in *New Yorker,* 25 November 1961.
''Varieties of Religious Experience,'' in *The Esquire Reader,* edited by Arnold Gingrich and others. New York, Dial Press, 1967.
''A Lover's Mask,'' in *Saturday Evening Post* (Philadelphia), 6 May 1967.
''The Amish Farmer,'' in *Great Esquire Fiction,* edited by L. Rust Hills. New York, Viking Press, 1983.
''The Duchess,'' in *Stand One,* edited by Michael Blackburn, Jon Silkin, and Lorna Tracy. London, Gollancz, 1984.

Plays

$4000: An Opera in Five Scenes, music by Tom Turner (produced Iowa City, 1969). Published in *North American Review* (Cedar Falls, Iowa), Winter 1969.

Other

The Girl in the Abstract Bed (text for cartoons). New York, Tiber Press, 1954.
The Unnatural Enemy (on hunting). New York, Dial Press, 1963.
Country Matters: Collected Reports from the Fields and Streams of Iowa and Other Places. New York, Dial Press, 1973.
Fishing by Mail: The Outdoor Life of a Father and Son, with Philip Bourjaily. New York, Atlantic Monthly, 1993.
Editor, *Discovery 1–6.* New York, Pocket Books, 6 vols., 1953–1955.

*

Manuscript Collection: Bowdoin College Library, Brunswick, Maine.

Critical Studies: *After the Lost Generation* by John W. Aldridge, New York, McGraw Hill, 1951, London, Vision Press, 1959; by Bourjaily in *Afterwords* edited by Thomas McCormack, New York, Harper, 1969; *The Shaken Realist* by John M. Muste, Baton Rouge, Louisiana State University Press, 1970.

* * *

Vance Bourjaily's first three novels trace the effects of World War II on his generation of Americans, people who were undergraduates at the time of Munich and Benny Goodman's rendition of ''I Got It Bad and That Ain't Good.'' In the looser structure of his fourth book, *Confessions of a Spent Youth,* the war becomes one of several stages in the narrator's growing up, and Bourjaily attempts moods, situations, humor, and introspection that had not entered his more rigid earlier work. The novels that have followed this pivotal book have displayed a remarkable variety of subject and technique without gaining for Bourjaily the popularity or critical recognition that many have thought his due over the past 35 years.

The End of My Life recalls another slender novel of wartime ambulance service, Dos Passos's *One Man's Initiation—1917.* Skinner Galt, Bourjaily's hero, is another young man who believes in a few friends; any larger society or more complex idea repels him. He accounts for this emptiness by sifting through his slight reading and slighter experience to understand why he has ''no principles, no truths, no ethics, no standards.'' *The Hound of Earth* is a parable of American responsibility for nuclear power, which describes the last days of the seven-year flight of an atomic scientist, who has left his work and family because these ties constantly remind him of the people he has helped to kill. In his reduced fugitive existence, he is run down by a ''hound of earth,'' a nagging humanitarian impulse that makes him perform small acts of kindness to everyone he meets. *The Violated,* a far more ambitious novel, shows how four characters violate those whom they would love, and are, in turn, violated in the emptiness of their rapacious lives. The child of one of them (or perhaps two of them) plays the lead and directs other children in her own production of *Hamlet* before the parents, who sit as so many kings and queens stupefied or weary until when ''frightened with false fire,'' a Claudius rises to end the show. This most sustained and complicated of Bourjaily's early plots thus ends with his first striking outburst of fictional invention.

Confessions of a Spent Youth is a retelling of *The End of My Life* that relieves the narrator, Quincy Quince, of the burden of philosophical exposition and allows him to reminisce easily about his young life; friendships, drinking, brushes with drugs, his loves, and his war service. The autobiographical element, admitted by Bourjaily, is clearest in Quincy's statement that ''to recall is a pleasure,'' for these stories show the writer let loose with craft he had begun to tap with the children's play in *The Violated.*

In *The Man Who Knew Kennedy* Bourjaily examines the crises that overtake two friends in the months following the President's assassination. The connection between history and private lives is not altogether clear. Kennedy, according to the narrator, was killed by the psychotic force of someone writhing out of an abyss of frustration. A generation's illusions of invulnerability were smashed on impact. The gifted, graceful victim of this novel is, on the other hand, destroyed by his inexplicable ties to a woman as depraved as she is helpless. The man had traded on his talent instead of developing it, while the surviving friend realizes that he is the stronger of the two for such reasons as his ''making necessary items out of wood—not fibreglass.'' *Brill among the Ruins* is Bourjaily's richest novel, and Brill, a middle-aged lawyer from a small town in southern Illinois, is his most fully realized character. He stands among two kinds of ruins, the hard bargain of his life and the archaeological sites of Oaxaca, developing on that line an understanding of himself that finally arrests his flight from responsibility. The accounts of digging are superb, surpassed only by the hunting scene where Brill alone ''sculls'' for ducks along the banks of the Mississippi before dawn.

A Game Men Play concerns yet another combat veteran, this one a poetic, reflective man trained as a killer and conditioned as a victim. *Is there anything at all that I can do?* he wires an old friend and tormentor upon learning of a family catastrophe. What he could or could not do to help is lost in the novel's (perhaps deliberate) loose ends, although the last glimpse of him in exile is utterly clear, recalling an incident decades before when he helped free the inmates of a German death camp and confronted their ragged warden: '''bitte ...' He was the last man Chink killed in the Second World War. Chink did not stop to wonder if the man was asking for his life or for his death.'' If not Bourjaily's great novel, *A Game Men Play* is closer than the others to his summing up.

Bourjaily, always devoted to jazz, moved to New Orleans in the mid-1980s when he wrote widely read articles and further sharpened the already distinctive language of his fiction. *Old Soldier*, a novella, celebrates a bond between brothers, the title character and his AIDS-ridden sibling, against a background of jazz argot and a few piped Highland melodies. *The Great Fake Book*, another story of a young man's search for his father, takes its title and particular inspiration from ''Songs for Professional Musicians,'' which is explained to the hero, thus: ''Now if you know you chords, you kin fake 'bout any song you'd ever want to play from just this one book here.'' Most of the narrative moves through sketches by the father bearing the titles of old standards, transitions aided by the son's notes. At its best, the novel is the ''working book of magic spells'' the father and son took their fake book to be.

—David Sanders

BOWEN, John (Griffith)

Nationality: British. **Born:** Calcutta, India, 5 November 1924. **Education:** Queen Elizabeth's Grammar School, Crediton, Devon; Pembroke College, Oxford (editor, *Isis*), 1948–51; St. Antony's College, Oxford (Frere Exhibitioner in Indian Studies), 1951–53, M.A. in modern history 1953; Ohio State University, Columbus, 1952–53. **Military Service:** Served in the Mahratha Light Infantry, 1943–47: Captain. **Career:** Assistant editor, *Sketch* magazine, London, 1953–56; copywriter, J. Walter Thompson Company, London, 1956–58; head of the copy department, S.T. Garland Advertising, London, 1958–60; script consultant, Associated Television, London, 1960–67; drama producer, Thames Television, London, 1978–79, London Weekend Television, 1981–83, and BBC, 1984. Since 1991 member of the board, Authors Licensing and Copyright Society. **Awards:** Society of Authors travelling scholarship, 1986. **Agent:** (fiction) Elaine Greene Ltd., 37 Goldhawk Road, London W12 8QQ; (theatre) Margaret Ramsay Ltd., 14-A Goodwin's Court, London WC2N 4LL. **Address:** Old Lodge Farm, Sugarswell Lane, Edgehill, Banbury, Oxfordshire OX15 6HP, England.

Publications

Novels

The Truth Will Not Help Us: Embroidery on an Historical Theme. London, Chatto and Windus, 1956.

After the Rain. London, Faber, 1958; New York, Ballantine, 1959.

The Centre of the Green. London, Faber, 1959; New York, McDowell Obolensky, 1960.

Storyboard. London, Faber, 1960.

The Birdcage. London, Faber, and New York, Harper, 1962.

A World Elsewhere. London, Faber, 1965; New York, Coward McCann, 1967.

Squeak: A Biography of NPA 1978A 203. London, Faber, 1983; New York, Viking, 1984.

The McGuffin. London, Hamish Hamilton, 1984; Boston, Atlantic Monthly Press, 1985.

The Girls: A Story of Village Life. London, Hamish Hamilton, 1986; New York, Atlantic Monthly Press, 1987.

Fighting Back. London, Hamish Hamilton, 1989.

The Precious Gift. London, Sinclair Stevenson, 1992.

No Retreat. London, Sinclair Stevenson, 1994.

Uncollected Short Stories

''Another Death in Venice,'' in *London Magazine,* June 1964.

''The Wardrobe Mistress,'' in *London Magazine,* January 1971.

''Barney,'' in *Mae West Is Dead,* edited by Adam Mars-Jones. London, Faber, 1983.

''The Rabbit in the Garden,'' in *Critical Quarterly* (Manchester), Summer 1987.

Plays

The Essay Prize, with A Holiday Abroad and The Candidate: Plays for Television. London, Faber, 1962.

I Love You, Mrs. Patterson (produced Cambridge and London, 1964). London, Evans, 1964.

The Corsican Brothers, based on the play by Dion Boucicault (televised 1965; revised version produced London, 1970). London, Methuen, 1970.

After the Rain, adaptation of his own novel (produced London, 1966; New York, 1967). London, Faber, 1967; New York, Random House, 1968; revised version, Faber, 1987.

The Fall and Redemption of Man (as *Fall and Redemption,* produced London, 1967; as *The Fall and Redemption of Man,* produced New York, 1974). London, Faber, 1968.

Silver Wedding (televised 1967; revised version, produced in *We Who Are about to ...,* later called *Mixed Doubles,* London, 1969). London, Methuen, 1970.

Little Boxes (including *The Coffee Lace* and *Trevor*) (produced London, 1968; New York, 1969). London, Methuen, 1968; New York, French, 1970.

The Disorderly Women, adaptation of a play by Euripides (produced Manchester, 1969; London, 1970). London, Methuen, 1969.

The Waiting Room (produced London, 1970). London, French, 1970; New York, French, 1971.

Robin Redbreast (televised 1970; produced Guildford, Surrey, 1974). Published in *The Television Dramatist,* edited by Robert Muller, London, Elek, 1973.

Diversions (produced London, 1973). Excerpts published in *Play Nine,* edited by Robin Rook, London, Arnold, 1981.

Young Guy Seeks Part-Time Work (televised 1973; produced London, 1978).

Roger, in *Mixed Blessings* (produced Horsham, Sussex, 1973). Published in *London Magazine,* October-November 1976.

Florence Nightingale (as *Miss Nightingale,* televised 1974; revised version, as *Florence Nightingale,* produced Canterbury, 1975). London, French, 1976.

Heil Caesar!, adaptation of *Julius Caesar* by Shakespeare (televised 1974). London, BBC Publications, 1974; revised version (produced Birmingham 1974), London, French, 1975.

Which Way Are You Facing? (produced Bristol, 1976). Excerpts published in *Play Nine,* edited by Robin Rook, London, Arnold, 1981.

Singles (produced London, 1977).

Bondage (produced London, 1978).

The Inconstant Couple, adaptation of a play by Marivaux (produced Chichester, 1978).

Spot the Lady (produced Newcastle-upon-Tyne, 1981).
The Geordie Gentleman, adaptation of a play by Molière (produced Newcastle-upon-Tyne, 1987).
The Oak Tree Tea-Room Siege (produced Leicester, 1990).

Radio Plays: *Digby* (as Justin Blake, with Jeremy Bullmore), 1959; *Varieties of Love* (revised version of television play *The First Thing You Think Of*), 1968; *The False Diaghilev,* 1988.

Television Plays: created the *Garry Halliday* series; episodes in *Front Page Story, The Power Game, Wylde Alliance,* and *The Villains* series; *A Holiday Abroad,* 1960; *The Essay Prize,* 1960; *The Jackpot Question,* 1961; *The Candidate,* 1961; *Nuncle,* from the story by John Wain, 1962; *The Truth about Alan,* 1963; *A Case of Character,* 1964; *Mr. Fowlds,* 1965; *The Corsican Brothers,* 1965; *Finders Keepers,* 1967; *The Whole Truth,* 1967; *Silver Wedding,* 1967; *A Most Unfortunate Accident,* 1968; *Flotsam and Jetsam,* 1970; *Robin Redbreast,* 1970; *The Guardians* series (7 episodes), 1971; *A Woman Sobbing,* 1972; *The Emergency Channel,* 1973; *Young Guy Seeks Part-Time Work,* 1973; *Miss Nightingale,* 1974; *Heil Caesar!,* 1974; *The Treasure of Abbot Thomas,* 1974; *The Snow Queen,* 1974; *A Juicy Case,* 1975; *Brief Encounter,* from the film by Noel Coward, 1976; *A Photograph,* 1977; *Rachel in Danger,* 1978; *A Dog's Ransom,* from the novel by Patricia Highsmith, 1978; *Games,* 1978; *The Ice House,* 1978; *The Letter of the Law,* 1979; *Dying Day,* 1980; *The Specialist,* 1980; *A Game for Two Players,* 1980; *Dark Secret,* 1981; *Honeymoon,* 1985.

Other (for children)

Pegasus. London, Faber, 1957; New York, A.S. Barnes, 1960.
The Mermaid and the Boy. London, Faber, 1958; New York, A.S. Barnes, 1960.
Garry Halliday and the Disappearing Diamonds [Ray of Death; Kidnapped Five; Sands of Time; Flying Foxes] (as Justin Blake, with Jeremy Bullmore). London, Faber, 5 vols., 1960–1964.

*

Manuscript Collection: Mugar Memorial Library, Boston University; (television works) Temple University Library, Philadelphia.

Critical Studies: *Postwar British Fiction,* Berkeley, University of California Press, 1962, and "The Fable Breaks Down," in *Wisconsin Studies in Contemporary Literature* (Madison), vol. 8, no. 7, 1967, both by James Gindin.

Theatrical Activities: Director: **Plays**—At the London Academy of Music and Dramatic Art since 1967; *The Disorderly Women,* Manchester, 1969, London, 1970; *Fall and Redemption,* Pitlochry, Scotland, 1969; *The Waiting Room,* London, 1970. Actor: **Plays**—In repertory in North Wales, summers 1950–51; Palace Theatre, Watford, Hertfordshire, 1965.

John Bowen comments:

(1996) I have always been interested in problems of form. Thus, in my first novel, *The Truth Will Not Help Us,* I wanted to try to tell a story of an historical occurrence of 1705 in Britain in terms of the political atmosphere and activities in the U.S.A. in 1953; in both these years political witch-hunting caused injustice and harm to innocent persons. My second novel, *After the Rain,* began as an attempt to do for science fiction what Michael Innes had done for the detective story: I failed in this attempt because I soon became more interested in the ideas with which I was dealing than in the form, and anyway made many scientific errors. My third novel was straightforwardly naturalistic, but in my fourth, *Storyboard,* I used an advertising agency as a symbol of a statement about public and private life, just as Zola used a department store in *Au Bonheur des Dames.* In my fifth novel, *The Birdcage*, I attempted to use a 19th-century manner—the objective detachment of Trollope, who presents his characters at some distance, displays and comments on them. In my sixth novel, *A World Elsewhere*, the hero, himself a wounded and needed politician, is writing a fiction about Philoctetes, the wounded archer, and until he has found his own reasons for returning to political life in London, cannot conclude his fiction, because he does not see why Philoctetes should allow himself to accompany Odysseus to Troy. In *Squeak*, the biography of a pigeon I once helped to rear, the story is told sometimes from Squeak's point of view, sometimes from that of her owners. In *The McGuffin* I tried to tell the story as the first-person narrative of one of the characters *inside* the kind of film Hitchcock might have made, the character himself being a reviewer of films. The same interest in different problems of form can be seen in my plays—the first Ibsenesque, the second borrowing from Brecht, Pirandello, and the Chinese theatre, the third a pair of linked one-acters, designed as two halves of the same coin, the fourth an attempt to rework the myth of *The Bacchae* as Sartre, Giraudoux, and Anouilh had used Greek myths, and to blend verse and prose, knockabout comedy, high tragedy, and Shavian argument. My full-length play *The Corsican Brothers* (an expansion of my earlier television play) has songs set within the play to music pirated from 19th-century composers, and I tried to make, from the melodramatic fantasies of Dumas and Dion Boucicault, a kind of Stendhalian statement about a society based on ideas of honour. In two of my television plays, *Miss Nightingale* and *The Emergency Channel*, I experimented with a narrative method that was associative, not lineal.

In this commentary, I am more confident in writing of form than of theme. One's themes are for the critics to set out neatly on a board: one is not always so clearly conscious of them oneself. There is a concern with archetypical patterns of behaviour (therefore with myth). There is a constant war between reasonable man and instinctive man. There is the pessimistic discovery that Bloomsbury values don't work, but that there seem to be no others worth holding. There is a statement of the need for Ibsen's "Life Lie" even when one knows it to be a lie, and Forster's "Only connect" becomes "Only accept" in my work. There is, particularly in *The McGuffin*, a concern with—and sorrow over—the ways in which human beings manipulate others of their kind.

I believe that novels and plays should tell a story, that the story is the mechanism by which one communicates one's view of life, and that no symbolism is worth anything unless it also works as an element in the story, since the final symbol is the story itself.

Inasmuch as the influences on one's style are usually those writers whom one has discovered in one's adolescence and early twenties, I might be said to have been influenced as a novelist by Dickens, Trollope, E.M. Forster, Virginia Woolf, E. Nesbit, P.G. Wodehouse, and Evelyn Waugh—perhaps a little also by Hemingway and Faulkner. As a playwright, I have been influenced by Ibsen, Chekhov, Shaw, Pirandello, Anouilh, Giraudoux, and Noel Coward.

Most of these names, I am sure, would be on any lists made by most of my contemporaries.

* * *

John Bowen has always been an intelligent and didactic novelist. His first novel, *The Truth Will Not Help Us*, uses a story of English seamen charged with piracy in a Scottish port in 1705 as a metaphor for the political evil of assuming guilt by rumor or association. *A World Elsewhere* uses the myth of Philoctetes as a parallel to complicated speculation about hypocrisy and engagement in contemporary political life. *The Birdcage* contains a long essay giving an account of the history and development of commercial television; and a defense of advertising as not necessarily more corrupt than any other institution in urban, capitalistic society introduces *Storyboard*. Although Bowen's fictional lessons are invariably complex and thoughtful, the author's presence is always visible, as he arranges, blocks out, and connects the material. Myth is made pointedly and explicitly relevant; symbols, like the lovebirds in *The Birdcage* or the breaking of a bronze chrysanthemum at a funeral in *The Centre of the Green*, sometimes seem attached heavy-handedly and literally. Bowen always acknowledges his own presence in his fiction, at times addressing the reader directly and becoming playful and intelligently skeptical about the complexities that prevent him from making any easy disposition of the characters and issues he has developed. The author is conspicuously articulate and instructive, but he does not attempt to play God; in fact, the dangers of human substitutions for a nonexistent or unknowable deity comprise part of the message of *After the Rain* and the skepticism underlying *The Birdcage* and *A World Elsewhere*.

Bowen's novels contain sharply memorable and effective scenes: the retired colonel expressing his style and his strength through his garden in *The Centre of the Green*, the nocturnal trip around Soho in which a character is beaten in *The Birdcage*, the picnic on a Greek island in *A World Elsewhere*. Often the best scenes involve a witty and comic treatment of dramatic conflict between two characters involved in close relationship, like the familial and sexual relationships in *The Centre of the Green* and *Storyboard*, the brilliantly handled quarrel between two contemporary London lovers who have lived together too long that takes place in the Piazza San Marco in *The Birdcage*, or the play with switching gender identities in *The McGuffin*. Bowen's comedy, however, no matter how strident initially, invariably turns into sympathy for his characters because they are unable to be more dignified or to match their own conceptions of a fuller humanity. This characteristic switch from satire to sympathy is emblematic of most of Bowen's fiction which works on reversals, on dramatically presented and thematically central violations of expected conclusions. The simple, muscle-flexing athlete, not the expected sensitive intellectual, finally defies and defeats the tyrant who would make himself God in *After the Rain*. Humanity and integrity appear in just those places most easily and generally thought the most corrupt in modern society in *Storyboard*. The family in which all members seem, superficially, most selfish and isolated can understand and respect each other in *The Centre of the Green*. This engagingly perverse positivism is often applied to social or political clichés, as in the forceful and complicated treatment of E. M. Forster's ''Only connect'' in *The Birdcage* or the ramifications on ''politics is the art of the possible'' developed in *A World Elsewhere*. Such clichés, in Bowen's fictional world, never honestly express the concerns or dilemmas of the characters who use them so glibly, although they may yet be partially true in ways the characters never intend and can seldom comprehend. The fact that people, in Bowen's novels, generally haven't a very good idea of what they're about is no warrant for denying their humanity or their capacity to invoke sympathy.

In the mid-1960s, Bowen turned to writing and producing plays for stage and television. Some of these, like adaptations of Euripides' *The Bacchae,* Shakespeare's *Julius Caesar,* and Dion Boucicault's *The Corsican Brothers,* compress the use of myth and symbol in dramatic confrontations, and suggest darker and more tragic versions of experience than do the novels. In the mid-1980s, after nearly 20 years away from novels, Bowen published two, *Squeak* and *The McGuffin*. Both depend on formal devices, dramatic fictional artifice. In *Squeak*, this artifice involves the reconstruction of the knowable world through the carefully limited attention to a pigeon's perspective. *The McGuffin* refers to Hitchcock's term for a device in his films that triggered the action without itself being part of the plot, such that one could review the story and find an inconsistency at the heart of it. These novels function less as implicit social commentary than do some of Bowen's earlier ones, although beneath the wit, they still convey humane and thoughtful lessons concerning the need to accept human deficiency and to respect forms of being, in oneself and in others, that one could not have initially imagined. During the late 1980s and 1990s, Bowen produced three more novels: *The Girls*, *Fighting Back*, and *The Precious Gift*, a mystery.

—James Gindin

BOWERING, George

Nationality: Canadian. **Born:** Keremeos, British Columbia, 1 December 1935. **Education:** University of British Columbia, B.A. 1960, M.A. 1963; also studied at University of Western Ontario. **Military Service:** Aerial photographer, Royal Canadian Air Force, 1954–57. **Family:** Married Angela Luoma in 1962; one daughter. **Career:** Instructor and later assistant professor, University of Calgary, Calgary, Alberta, 1963–66; instructor and writer-in-residence, Sir George Williams University, Montreal, Quebec, 1967–68, assistant professor of English, 1968–72; professor of English, Simon Fraser University, Burnaby, British Columbia, 1972—. **Awards:** Governor-General's Award, 1969, 1980. **Address:** Department of English, Simon Fraser University, 8888 University Drive, Burnaby, British Columbia, V5A 1S6, Canada.

PUBLICATIONS

Novels

Mirror on the Floor. Toronto, McClelland & Stewart, 1967.
A Short Sad Book. Vancouver, Canada, Talonbooks, 1977.
Concentric Circles. Coatsworth, Canada, Black Moss Press, 1977.
Burning Water. New York, Beaufort Books, 1980.
Eneaux troubles. Editions Quinze, 1982.
Craft Slices. Ottawa, Canada, Oberon Press, 1985.
Caprice. New York, Viking, 1987.
Errata. Red Deer, Canada, Red Deer College Press, 1988.

Harry's Fragments: A Novel of International Puzzlement. Toronto, Coach House Press, 1990.
Shoot! Toronto, Key Porter Books, 1994.
Parents From Space. Montreal, Roussan Publishers, 1994.
Diamondback Dog. Montreal, Roussan, 1998.

Short Stories

A Place to Die. Ottawa, Canada, Oberon Press, 1973.
Flycatcher and Other Stories. Ottawa, Canada, Oberon Press, 1974.
Protective Footwear: Stories and Fables by George Bowering. Toronto, McClelland & Stewart, 1978.
The Rain Barrel and Other Stories. Vancouver, Canada, Talonbooks, 1994.

Poetry

Sticks and Stones. Vancouver, Canada, Tishbooks, 1963.
Points on the Grid. Contact Press, 1964.
The Man in Yellow Boots. Mexico City, El Corno Emplumado, 1965.
The Silver Wire. Quarry Press, 1966.
Baseball: A Poem in the Magic Number 9. Toronto, Coach House Press, 1967.
Rocky Mountain Foot: A Lyric, a Memoir. Toronto, McClelland & Stewart, 1968.
Two Police Poems. Vancouver, Canada, Talonbooks, 1968.
The Gangs of Kosmos. House of Anansi, 1969.
Touch: Selected Poems 1961–1970. Toronto, McClelland & Stewart, 1969.
Sitting in Mexico. Beaven Kosmos, 1970.
George, Vancouver: A Discovery Poem. Toronto, Weed Flower Press, 1970.
Geneve. Toronto, Coach House Press, 1971.
Autobiology. New Star Books, 1972.
The Sensible. Toronto, Massasauga Editions, 1972.
Layers 1–13. Toronto, Weed Flower Press, 1973.
Curious. Toronto, Coach House Press, 1973.
In the Flesh. Toronto, McClelland & Stewart, 1974.
At War with the U.S. Vancouver, Canada, Talonbooks, 1974.
Allophanes. Toronto, Coach House Press, 1976.
The Catch. Toronto, McClelland & Stewart, 1976.
Poem and Other Baseballs. Coatsworth, Canada, Black Moss Press, 1976.
The Concrete Island: Montreal Poems, 1967–1971. Montreal, Vehicule Press, 1977.
Another Mouth. Toronto, McClelland & Stewart, 1979.
Particular Accidents: Selected Poems. Vancouver, Canada, Talonbooks, 1980.
West Window: The Selected Poetry of George Bowering. Toronto, General Publishing, 1982.
Ear Reach. Alcuin Society, 1982.
Smoking Mirror. Edmonton, Canada, Longspoon, 1982.
Kerrisdale Elegies. Toronto, Coach House Press, 1984.
Seventy-One Poems for People. Red Deer, Canada, Red Deer College Press, 1985.
Delayed Mercy. Toronto, Coach House Press, 1986.
Urban Snow. Vancouver, Canada, Talonbooks, 1991.
George Bowering Selected: Poems 1961–1992. Toronto, McClelland & Stewart, 1993.
Blonds on Bikes. Burnaby, Canada, Talonbooks, 1997.

Other

How I Hear "Howl" (essay). Montreal, Sir George Williams University, 1968.
Al Purdy (monograph). Toronto, Copp Clark Publishing, 1970.
Three Vancouver Writers (criticism). Toronto, Coach House Press, 1979.
A Way with Words (criticism). Ottawa, Canada, Oberon Press, 1982.
The Mask in Place: Essays on Fiction in North America. Winnipeg, Canada, Turnstone Press, 1982.
Imaginary Hand: Essays. Edmonton, Canada, NeWest Press, 1988.
Contributor, *Solitary Walk: A Book of Longer Poems.* Toronto, Ryerson Press, 1968.
Contributor, *The Human Elements: Second Series,* edited by David Helwig. Ottawa, Canada, Oberon Press, 1981.
Contributor, *Approaches to the Work of James Reaney,* edited by Stan Dragland. Downsview, Canada, ECW Press, 1983.
Contributor, *The Oberon Reader.* Toronto, HarperCollins, 1991.
Editor, *Vibrations: Poems of Youth.* Toronto, Gage Educational Publishers, 1970.
Editor, *The Story So Far.* Toronto, Coach House Press, 1971.
Editor, *Great Canadian Sports Stories.* Ottawa, Canada, Oberon Press, 1979.
Editor, *Fiction of Contemporary Canada.* Toronto, Coach House Press, 1980.
Editor, *Selected Poems: Loki Is Buried at Smoky Creek* by Fred Wah. Vancouver, Canada, Talonbooks, 1980.
Editor, *My Body Was Eaten by Dogs: Selected Poems of David McFadden* by David McFadden. Toronto, McClelland & Stewart, 1981.
Editor, *The Contemporary Canadian Poetry Anthology.* Toronto, Coach House Press, 1982.
Editor, *Sheila Watson and The Double Hook.* Ottawa, Canada, Golden Dog Press, 1985.
Editor, with Linda Hutcheon, *Likely Stories: A Postmodern Sampler.* Toronto, Coach House Press, 1992.
Editor, with Michael Ondaatje, *An H in the Heart: A Reader.* Toronto, McClelland & Stewart, 1994.

*

Critical Studies: *Out-posts: Earle Birney, Bill Bissett, George Bowering, Nicole Brossard, Paul Chamberland, Raoul Duguay, B. P. Nichol, Claude P. Lokin (Peloquin): Interviews, Poetry, Bibliographies and a Critical Introduction to 8 Major Modern Poets* by Caroline Bayard and Jack David, Erin, Canada, Press Porcepic, 1978; *A Record of Writing: An Annotated and Illustrated Biography of George Bowering* by Roy Miki, Vancouver, Canada, Talonbooks, 1989; *George Bowering: Bright Circles of Color* by Eva-Marie Kroller, Vancouver, Canada, Talonbooks, 1992.

George Bowering comments:

(2000) There is a distinction between "the reader" and the person who is holding the silent book and reading it.

Sometimes I go so far as to say that the "author" and the "reader" are characters in my story. (The implications are interesting if you extend this structure to speeding tickets and marriage certificates.)

How often you or I have read something in criticism or theory about "the reader," and realized that this construct is as distinct from us as is Patrick Henry or Spider Robinson.

Anyone knows that literature is an idea but reading is what you do. Literature can't hurt you but reading can.

(I am of course in my own ant-trap here, because no matter what I do, the ''you'' I am talking about is not the person reading these words, are you?)

So that construct that certain critics like to write about, ''the reader,'' can't do anything about what is written. But if you are reading a book you can intervene. You can invent a reading.

You can always skip page 35. You can read from the last page to the first. You can stick pages from a pornographic novel between Northrop Frye's sheets. You can call the narrator of Atwood's second novel Agnes. Or you can intervene simply by reading the way you read.

The person who wrote the book can't stop you. The ''author'' can't, either. And the ''reader'' doesn't know you exist.

A lot of what they call ''reflexive'' writing is simply the result of the writer trying to be you. You are the ground of the so-called postmodern. You know, our high school English teachers really knew all this, but they didn't think that it was the kind of thing they were supposed to be teaching us. We knew it, too, but we didn't think we were supposed to think about such things during the high school English game.

* * *

A prolific and award-winning poet, provocative (though not always discerning) critic, and longtime gadfly on the Canadian literary scene, George Bowering is a prose writer whose oeuvre includes short fiction (notably *Protective Footwear: Stories and Fables*), a novella (*Concentric Circles*), and several novels, beginning with the forgettable *A Mirror on the Floor*, which was followed a decade later by what he has called a ''historical-geographical'' novel, *A Short Sad Book*. Recognized as much for its theorizing of, and challenges to, the traditional novel form, this later book established Bowering as a fiction-maker determinedly wary of realism and of traditional relationships between the increasingly static and institutional conditions of narrative and the telling of stories and spinning of yarns. With sections dedicated to a postmodern imploding of many of the clichés that continue to dominate the Canadian cultural imagination (including ''Canadian Geography'' and the drive to canonize ''The Pretty Good Canadian Novel''), *A Short Sad Book* set the stage in many ways for Bowering's next novel, *Burning Water*, for which he was awarded the prestigious Governor General's Award for Fiction despite generally weak and even negative reviews.

A metafictional exploration of the process and product of a novelist (named George Bowering) who travels to Italy in order to write a historical novel about Captain George Vancouver's cartographic colonization of the land mass that would become Canada's west coast, *Burning Water* demands its readers to confront often challenging questions about the ideological implications of art and artifice, about the assumptions informing Western traditions of language and narrative, and about the employment of history (as story, as ''fact,'' as political tool). Foregrounding Bowering's playful wit and propensity for wordplay (puns, for instance, abound in the book), the novel is also very much concerned with illuminating the mechanisms by which language is appropriated and deployed as an instrument of domination, especially as it comes to be wielded by hyper-masculine imperial powers. Developing a framed story that focuses, in part, on the intense, and ultimately fatal shipboard rivalry that builds between Vancouver and the ship's surgeon Menzies, Bowering shows how language (the textual, the oral, the cartographic) is the single most precious commodity sought after by the various constituencies from both the new and the old world.

Densely intertextual, openly parodic, and self-consciously reflexive, *Burning Water* prepared readers for Bowering's next two novels, *Caprice* and the less successful *Shoot!*. Once again taking their cues from stories and events from Canada's past, both books mark an affiliation, too, with the convention-laden genre of the classic American dime-store western. Subverting or reconfiguring the traditional strategies of stereotyping women and indigenous peoples, as well as the still popular romanticization of the outlaw gunslinger, Bowering's Canadian ''west'' is clearly a horizon marked by difference, a not-so-wild place where the reductive and the formulaic are laid bare for critical scrutiny.

Populated mainly by baseball- and peace-loving artists and writers (and by the occasional character from the earlier novels), it is a geocultural space, too, where language is the center of much attention as the traditional reticence of the wild west of Louis L'Amour and Zane Grey is inverted. It is a place where a love of language is not positioned as a weakness or flaw, but as a strategy for survival and source of intellectual and spiritual guidance. When Bowering's titular female hero, Caprice, finds herself trapped in a classic ''western'' quest to track down the killer of her brother, for example, she finds solace in the volumes of romantic poetry that fill her saddle bags and in the lines from Faust that she recites as she rides the hills of Western Canada. Similarly, the infamous (and hauntingly youthful) McLean gang, the protagonists of *Shoot!,* are read and sung to by the compassionate young wife of the warden, in whose jail they are eventually incarcerated en route to the gallows.

Although they can never sustain the complexities that distinguish such notable antecedents as Thomas Berger's *Little Big Man,* E.L. Doctorow's *Welcome to Hard Times,* or fellow Canadian Robert Kroetsch's *The Studhorse Man,* Bowering's novels do succeed in raising intriguing and seductive questions about now familiar poststructuralist constellations of language, power, sex, and discipline; questions that entertain and disabuse as readers weave their way through the polyphony of voices sounding in these fictions—from the musicality of first nation's storytellers to self-mythologizing spinners of tall tales to the minimalist dialogue of ranchmen and gunslingers. Bristling with subtle (and not so subtle) ironies, these are intelligent and generally well-crafted novels that do warrant reading and attention.

—Klay Dyer

BOX, Edgar

See VIDAL, Gore

BOYD, William

Nationality: British. **Born:** William Andrew Murray Boyd, Accra, Ghana, 7 March 1952. **Education:** Gordonstoun School, Elgin, Morayshire; University of Nice, France, diploma 1971; University of Glasgow, M.A. (honours) in English and philosophy 1975; Jesus College, Oxford, 1975–80. **Family:** Married Susan Anne Wilson in

1975. **Career:** Lecturer in English, St. Hilda's College, Oxford, 1980–83. Television critic, *New Statesman,* London, 1981–83. Lives in Chelsea, London. **Awards:** Whitbread award, 1981; Maugham award, 1982; Rhys Memorial prize, 1982; James Tait Black Memorial prize, 1990. Fellow, Royal Society of Literature, 1983; Sunday Express Book of the Year award, 1993. **Agent:** Lemon Unna and Durbridge Ltd., 24 Pottery Lane, London W11 4LZ, England.

PUBLICATIONS

Novels

A Good Man in Africa. London, Hamish Hamilton, 1981; New York, Morrow, 1982.
An Ice-Cream War. London, Hamish Hamilton, 1982; New York, Morrow, 1983.
Stars and Bars. London, Hamish Hamilton, 1984; New York, Morrow, 1985.
The New Confessions. London, Hamish Hamilton, 1987; New York, Morrow, 1988.
Brazzaville Beach. London, Sinclair Stevenson, 1990; New York, Morrow, 1991.
The Blue Afternoon. London, Sinclair Stevenson, 1993; New York, Knopf, 1995.
Armadillo. New York, Knopf, 1998.

Short Stories

On the Yankee Station and Other Stories. London, Hamish Hamilton, 1981; New York, Morrow, 1984; revised edition, London, Penguin, 1988.
The Destiny of Nathalie ''X''. London, Sinclair Stevenson, 1995; published as *The Destiny of Nathalie X and Other Stories.* New York, Knopf, 1997.

Plays

School Ties (includes the TV plays *Good and Bad at Games* and *Dutch Girls,* and an essay). London, Hamish Hamilton, 1985; New York, Morrow, 1986.
Care and Attention of Swimming Pools, and Not Yet Jayette (produced London, 1985).

Screenplays: *Stars and Bars,* 1988; *Aunt Julia and the Scriptwriter,* 1990; *Mr. Johnson,* 1990; *Chaplin,* 1992; *A Good Man in Africa,* 1994.

Radio Plays: *On the Yankee Station,* from his own story, 1985; *Hommage to A.B.,* 1994.

Television Plays: *Good and Bad at Games,* 1983; *Dutch Girls,* 1985; *Scoop,* from the novel by Evelyn Waugh, 1987.

Other

Introduction, *Martin Chuzzlewit* by Charles Dickens. New York, Knopf, 1994.

* * *

But for *An Ice-Cream War,* William Boyd would be firmly labelled an exponent of that familiar comic genre, the accident-prone hero novel, as practised by, among others, Kingsley Amis (*Lucky Jim*), Anthony Burgess (the Enderby series), and Tom Sharpe (the Wilt series). Both *A Good Man in Africa* and *Stars and Bars* feature protagonists—Morgan Leafy and Henderson Dores, respectively—entrusted with crucial assignments only to be hampered and finally thwarted by proliferating complications. Foreign locations enable Boyd to add occasional culture shock to their predicaments.

Morgan Leafy is a minor diplomat stationed in a provincial backwater in the ''not-very-significant'' West African nation of Kinjanja. For three years, his stupefying boredom has been palliated only by readily available alcohol and sex. Then, unexpectedly, his boss, Fanshawe, deputes him to cultivate, on behalf of H.M. Government, a local politician (Samuel Adekunle) who is a bigwig in the party set to win Kinjanja's forthcoming elections. At the same time, Morgan begins to court Priscilla, Fanshawe's attractive daughter. Initially, the outlook seems promising: both Adekunle and Priscilla respond to Morgan's overtures. Subsequently, things deteriorate inexorably. Distractions and indignities dog him. Through a misunderstanding, he loses Priscilla to a hated underling. Then he finds himself being blackmailed by Adekunle. To secure his silence, Morgan must suborn an expatriate Scot, Dr. Murray, who is obstructing a lucrative swindle the politician hopes to transact. Unfortunately, Murray is a model of rectitude: Morgan's proposition only worsens matters. In the final pages, though, providence apparently rescues him.

Henderson Dores is an art expert who has recently left England to join the fledgling New York branch of Mulholland, Melhuish, a London auction house. Already he has become simultaneously involved with two alluring, imperious women: his former wife, Melissa, with whom he is discussing remarriage, and his mistress, Irene. Henderson's assignment entails travelling to the Deep South to talk Loomis Gage, a reclusive millionaire, into letting Mulholland, Melhuish handle the sale of his paintings: a coup that would ''signal their arrival.'' Inconveniently, Bryant, Henderson's teenage stepdaughter-to-be, invites herself along, thereby jeopardising his plans to meet Irene while away. Then the Gage household proves to be chock-full of confusing and/or intimidating oddballs. Nevertheless, braving the violent opposition of Gage's elder son and assorted misadventures, Henderson brings matters to a successful conclusion. Gage, however, promptly suffers a fatal coronary, leaving him with only an unwitnessed oral agreement. Furthermore, Bryant announces her intention of eloping with Duane, the son of Gage's housekeeper. Abducting Bryant, Henderson decamps to New York. After further misadventures, the novel closes with him fleeing a vengeful Duane. By this time, Henderson has lost his job (perhaps temporarily) and both his women (probably permanently). The paintings, meanwhile, have been destroyed.

Stars and Bars contains various inventive comic flights, but several others seem decidedly routine, poking fun at soft targets like American speech, American cuisine (especially the downhome kind), radio ''sermonettes,'' country and western music. Elsewhere, bedroom farce ensues when Henderson and Irene rendezvous at Atlanta's swishest hotel. *A Good Man in Africa* generally avoids such lapses into the familiar. In addition, the world created in *Stars and Bars* is distinctly cartoon-like: Henderson is a two-dimensional character whose pratfalls provide entertainment alone. Morgan's mishaps also arouse some sympathy: the reader discerns his real desperation as Adekunle turns the screw, his pricks of conscience at engaging, albeit unavailingly, in corruption.

At one stage in Julian Barnes's *Flaubert's Parrot* the narrator proposes that certain types of fiction be no longer written, including "... novels about small hitherto forgotten wars in distant parts of the British Empire, in the painstaking course of which we learn ... that war is very nasty indeed." *An Ice-Cream War* is clearly one of the novels that has prompted this injunction: it is set mainly in East Africa during World War I, when the adjacent British and German colonies became a secondary battlefield. The description, though, is unjust: Boyd's point about the nature of war is a deeper one—he believes that literature has not only glossed over the bloodiness of war, but also its contingency.

Boyd's humour is altogether more grim here than in his other novels. Destiny is again antipathetic towards his characters, but the tricks of fate are now brutal rather than mischievous. An incongruous episode in *Stars and Bars* concerns Henderson's discovery that his father's death during World War II occurred when he was struck by a tin of pineapple chunks dropped from a supply plane. In *An Ice-Cream War*, death and injury from comparably absurd causes are commonplace; accident rather than design is throughout the motive force behind events. One of the principal characters, Captain Gabriel Cobb, takes part in the sea-borne invasion of German East Africa, during which military order and discipline degenerate into chaos. Later, as an escaping POW, he is killed by German askaris who have misunderstood their commander's orders. In the novel's penultimate section, Gabriel's revenge-bent younger brother, Felix, tracks down the commander only to find that he has just died from influenza. Elsewhere, Felix and his brother-in-law are severely wounded in training botch-ups.

The action of the novel is witnessed through several centres of consciousness. The main ones—in addition to Gabriel and Felix—are (in Britain) Gabriel's wife, Charis, and (in Africa) an American planter, Temple Smith, whose martial activities are simply a means of continuing his quest to recover a prized farm machine confiscated by the Germans. *An Ice-Cream War* is easily Boyd's most substantial work, even if he rather overdoes the ironies and also perpetrates some false notes, notably the employment—decidedly old-hat—of a Scottish sergeant with an impenetrable accent.

The stories in *On the Yankee Station* do not represent Boyd at his best. Several might have been written for the glossy magazine market. The remainder feature some fine ideas, but they are developed perfunctorily and without the stylistic verve of the novels. "Next Boat from Douala" and "The Coup," however, are noteworthy for the presence of Morgan Leafy, while "Hardly Ever" deals with the public school world also explored in the screenplay of *School Ties*.

The New Confessions might be regarded as a forerunner of a type of self-examination, to be intensified in *Brazzaville Beach*. A fictitious, rumbustious "autobiography" of an outrageous Scotsman, John James Todd, presents a man, both "vile and contemptible" and "generous and selfless," with a self-deprecatory humour. Boyd's skill in sweeping rapidly through years and across continents matches a range of challenging situations that confront Todd, who eventually comes to terms with his life at age seventy.

Without any escape route of humour, *Brazzaville Beach* is the self-probing of Hope Clearwater, a woman trying to understand her life in England and Africa, burdened by incomprehensible tragic events. How much is she to blame, she asks? Firmly believing that "the unexamined life is not worth living," hers is one she insists has to be told honestly. The review is relayed in non-chronological episodes, between England, with the remembered life of her husband, his madness and suicide, and Africa, where she discovers that the chimpanzees she is to study are involved in a murderous war with each other. The novel operates as an allegory, for it is set within the Biafran war of 1963. Neither the death of her husband, the killings of the chimpanzees (some she was forced to shoot herself), or the human civil war could be avoided. Hope Clearwater's husband died because of a compulsive need to prove life by rigid mathematical formula, and his parallel figure in Africa nearly destroys Hope Clearwater because of his blindness to facts, which threaten to wreck a theory and his lifework. Simply being, Boyd argues, has rules, but they are not inflexible in a system that selects survivors. Hope's questioning, her "selections, willed and unwilled ... of infinite alternatives and choices," resolve through flexible mathematics, as defined by Pascal. It does not matter if theories could be fully proved as long as they worked. "Intuition," Hope finally learns, rates "higher than vigorous proof."

The stories in *The Destiny of Nathalie X* are populated by an array of international characters, from the African filmmaker of the title piece to the Vietnamese writer in another story, to a variety of others, all united in their sense of exile—whether literal or internal. A sense of exile likewise pervades the world of Lorimer Black, protagonist of *Armadillo*. Despite his Anglicized name and his innocuous job as an insurance adjuster, Black is the descendant of gypsies, and as the tale unfolds he finds his exile deepening: first he loses his job, then other events assail him. Throughout the book is an abiding sense of London, a city Boyd observes so carefully one would think that he, too, came from somewhere else.

—David Montrose, updated by Geoffrey Elborn

BOYLAN, Clare

Nationality: Irish. **Born:** Dublin, 1948. **Education:** Convent schools in Dublin. **Family:** Married Alan Wilkes in 1970. **Career:** editor, *Young Woman,* Dublin, 1969–71; staff feature writer, *Dublin Evening Press,* 1973–78; editor, *Image,* Dublin, 1981–84. Regular book reviewer and feature writer for *Sunday Times,* London, *Irish Times,* Dublin, *Evening Standard,* London, *New York Times, Los Angeles Times, The Guardian,* London, *Cosmopolitan, Vogue,* and *Good Housekeeping.* Lives in Kilbride, County Wicklow. **Awards:** Journalist of the Year award, 1973. **Agent:** Gill Coleridge, Rogers Coleridge and White Ltd., 20 Powis Mews, London W11 1JN, England.

Publications

Novels

Holy Pictures. London, Hamish Hamilton, and New York, Summit, 1983.

Last Resorts. London, Hamish Hamilton, 1984; New York, Summit, 1986.

Black Baby. London, Hamish Hamilton, 1988; New York, Doubleday, 1989.

Home Rule. London, Hamish Hamilton, 1993; as *11 Edward Street,* New York, Doubleday, 1994.

Room for a Single Lady. London, Little, Brown, 1997.

Short Stories

A Nail on the Head. London, Hamish Hamilton, 1983; New York, Penguin, 1985.
Concerning Virgins. London, Hamish Hamilton, 1989.
That Bad Woman. London, Little Brown, 1995.
Another Family Christmas: A Collection of Short Stories. Dublin, Poolbeg, 1997.

Other

The Literary Companion to Cats. London, Sinclair Stevenson, 1994.
Editor, *The Agony and the God, Literary Essays.* London and New York, Penguin, 1994.
Contributor, *Ladies' Night at Finbar's Hotel*, edited by Dermot Bolger. New York, Harcourt, 2000.

*

Clare Boylan comments:

My novels deal with the confrontative and revelatory nature of sexual relationships, the anarchy of innocence, and the difference between male and female morality. In my novels the random and exploitative nature of maternal love is a recurrent theme. Overall, there is the sense of a wonderful life in which the characters are not equipped to participate and the dark motifs are explored through humor and irony.

* * *

The novels and stories of Clare Boylan follow the search of lonely individuals for love and fulfillment in a hostile environment. Events are often viewed through the eyes of children or the elderly, each intimidated by an increasingly threatening world. Her writing embraces all aspects of life from the comic and grotesque to the tragic, and displays a rare ability to approach routine situations from unexpected angles. In *Holy Pictures* the society of adults dominates. To Nan and Mary, growing up in Dublin in 1925, the world of their elders is marked by rules specifically designed to thwart the dreams of the young, its rigidity typified by the old-fashioned corset produced in their father's factory. Nan, coming painfully to adolescence in a strict convent school, is lured by the dream-world of the cinema and the cut-out pictures of movie stars she worships at a distance. She and Mary long to escape the drab life allocated to them, glimpses of freedom coming only briefly as in Nan's dance as the fairy at a school concert. ''She was a star, elevated as the lovely ladies of America who wore coatees of mink and ermine and walked on spirals of celestial stairs.'' Such dreams break down before the blind indifference and rejection of the adult world. The author presents these rites of passage without sensationalism, deftly contrasting the innocence of the girls against the often-grotesque figures of their elders. Touches of humor lighten the story, but only serve to emphasize its prevailing darkness. Boylan's outwardly simple style conceals the depth of her insights, visual imagery subtly utilized in family photographs, pictures of film stars, and the religious cards Mary handles like talismans. These provide a focus for the dreams of the two girls, calling out the purest qualities in their worshippers. *Last Resorts* reverses the vision of *Holy Pictures*, its single-parent heroine dominated by the selfish needs of teenage children. Harriet longs for the easy domesticity taken from her by the desertion of her husband. ''Contentment was more nourishing than joy. Being in love was not very peaceful.'' Snatching vainly at happiness with a married lover, and faced by the return of her husband with a fresh set of demands, Harriet is forced to choose between the comfort of others and her own freedom. Boylan portrays her struggles in a restrained prose whose quietness occasionally startles with sharp single-line images. Set in the present in a more exotic location than *Holy Pictures, Last Resorts* explores the same basic theme.

Home Rule moves further into the past, describing the fortunes of the Anglo-Irish Devlin family in Dublin in about 1900. With memorable skill Boylan evokes the colorful, squalid city underworld, its casual violence and cruelty. The reader follows the efforts of Daisy Devlin and her siblings to break out from their grim slum tenement with its dissolute father and deluded mother. Daisy escapes only to fall for the handsome, feckless Cecil Cantwell, whose ill-fated business schemes with ''the Cantwell corset'' recall the use of this rigid, imprisoning symbol in *Holy Pictures*. Daisy's adventures, and those of her family, are movingly recounted, the author blending humor and pathos with a threatening, atmospheric darkness.

Recent novels show continuing exploration of the form, and fresh psychological perceptions. In *Black Baby* Boylan re-enters the modern world, where an African child ''adopted'' by a young middle-class convent girl comes to Dublin to find her now aging ''mother.'' The contrasting characters of large, assertive, life-enhancing Dinah and the sad, withdrawn pensioner Alice, who at her ''daughter's'' prompting makes her own bid for independence, engage the reader's interest and sympathy, the imaginative plot matched by lively dialogue and description. Towards the end the action veers into the surreal, and the conclusion (for this reader at least) is something of a disappointment. This is a pity, because in all other respects *Black Baby* is a brilliant example of Boylan's ability to find an unexpected slant on everyday life, and in places is as witty and poignant as anything she has written.

Room for a Single Lady sees the novelist at her best. Rose Rafferty's journey from childhood to adolescence in the Dublin of the 1950s is beautifully evoked, and the book is crammed with the usual lively cast of characters. Rose's glamorous mother downtrodden by domesticity, her old-fashioned father with his doomed ''get-rich-quick'' schemes, her sisters Bridie and Katie, all live in the memory. More striking still are the procession of lodgers whose different personalities hold out to Rose the promise and the perils of the world outside. Through them, and her family, Rose confronts love and loss, the taboos of sex and incest, from the shocking experiences of Minnie and Mo to the slapstick ''affair'' of Katie and the milkman ''Norman Wisdom.'' Boylan's first-person narrative abounds in wonderful one-liners—a Christmas turkey lies in the pantry ''like a great reclining nude,'' a bird savaged by the cat flaps feebly ''like a wasp stuck in jam,'' Christmas itself approaches ''like a big, lighted cruise liner.'' Through Rose's eyes, the reader experiences the excitement and terror of entering the adult world, and the bittersweet loss of innocence as childhood passes. (''That summer when nothing happened seemed the end of time intensely lived.'') *Room for a Single Lady* has all Boylan's finest qualities, and shows her writing at its most inspired.

Equally impressive but far more harrowing is *Beloved Stranger*, where Boylan confronts the problems of aging. The lives of a devoted elderly couple are totally disrupted when shortly before their golden wedding the husband falls victim to senile dementia. The disintegration of the handsome, self-assured Dick Elliott—made crueler still by rare moments of lucidity—is viewed through the eyes of his wife and middle-aged daughter, who find themselves struggling to accept this unforeseen catastrophe. Quietly and without sentimentality Boylan outlines the distress of Lily as she sees her beloved husband change to a violent, aggressive stranger, and shows how she and her daughter Ruth at last come to terms with his madness and death. With today's aged population increasing steadily, and in a world where care homes are a growth industry, Boylan depicts the heartbreak that afflicts so many ordinary lives. With *Room for a Single Lady, Beloved Stranger* marks the peak of its author's achievement so far.

Boylan's talents are equally evident in the shorter forms. Her earliest collection of stories, *A Nail on the Head*, describes the pursuit of love in its many manifestations. ''The Wronged Woman'' reveals the differing views of a husband by his two wives, while ''Bad Natured Dog'' deftly points out the gulf between appearance and reality. Boylan ranges from the throwaway humor of ''Ears'' to the macabre atmosphere of ''For Your Own Bad'' and ''Mama,'' the grotesque characters worthy rivals to those of *Holy Pictures*. With *Concerning Virgins* the emphasis is on naivete and innocence, where in a variety of encounters her ''virgins'' meet and adapt to the demands placed upon them. The author moves easily from the wry humor of ''Venice Saved'' to the nightmare scenario enacted by two young girls in ''The Picture House,'' and once more displays her gift for the unexpected in striking imagery and frequent twists of plot. The same is true of *That Bad Woman*, perhaps her best collection to date, where Boylan again provides a new perspective on familiar themes. In different stories she compels pity for a music-hall artist jailed for sex with an under-age girl, and casts fresh light on the feelings of the young woman who steals a child. Things are not always what they seem, Boylan seems to be telling us. The liberating affair of ''That Bad Woman'' has a surprising aftermath, while in ''It's Her'' the insistent phone-calls of the nagging ex-wife prove to have a deeper, more tragic purpose. Like her novels, Boylan's stories show keen insights and a heightened, inspired use of language, her understated style creeping stealthily up to startle the unwitting reader. Here, as elsewhere in her fiction, she avoids happy endings, her vision of life presented as a continually absorbing process, still to be resolved.

—Geoff Sadler

BOYLE, T. Coraghessan

Nationality: American. **Born:** 2 December 1948. **Education:** State University of New York, Potsdam, B.A. in English and history 1968; University of Iowa, Iowa City, M.F.A. in fiction 1974, Ph.D. in British literature 1977. **Family:** Married Karen Kvashay; one daughter and two sons. **Career:** Assistant professor, 1978–82, associate professor, 1982–86, and since 1986 professor of English, University of Southern California, Los Angeles. **Awards:** Coordinating Council of Literary Magazines award, 1977, for fiction; National Endowment for the Arts grant, St. Lawrence award, 1980, for *Descent of Man; Paris Review*'s Aga Khan prize, 1981, for fiction; *Paris Review,* John Train prize, 1984, for humor; Commonwealth Club of California, silver medal award, 1986, for *Greasy Lake,* gold medal, 1988, for *World's End;* Guggenheim fellowship, 1988; PEN/Faulkner Novel of the Year award, 1988, for *World's End;* O'Henry award, 1988, for ''Sinking House,'' 1989, for ''The Ape Lady in Retirement;'' Prix Passion novel of the year, 1989, for *Water Music;* National Academy of Arts and Letters Howard D. Vursell memorial award, 1993, for prose excellence; Prix Medicis Etranger, 1997. D.H.L.: State University of New York, 1991. **Member:** Literature panel, National Endowment for the Arts, 1986–87. **Agent:** Georges Borchardt, 136 East 57th Street, New York, New York 10022, U.S.A.

PUBLICATIONS

Novels

Water Music. Boston, Little Brown, 1982; London, Gollancz, 1982.
Budding Prospects: A Pastoral. New York, Viking, and London, Gollancz, 1984.
World's End. New York, Viking, 1987; London, Macmillan, 1988.
East Is East. New York, Viking, 1990; London, Cape, 1991.
The Road to Wellville. New York, Viking, and London, Granta, 1993.
The Tortilla Curtain. New York, Viking, 1995.
Riven Rock. New York, Viking, 1998.
A Friend of the Earth. New York, Viking, 2000.

Short Stories

The Descent of Man. Boston, Little Brown, 1979; London, Gollancz, 1980.
Greasy Lake and Other Stories. New York and Harmondsworth, Viking, 1985.
If the River Was Whiskey. New York, Viking, 1989.
The Collected Stories of T. Coraghessan Boyle. London, Granta, 1993; published as *T.C. Boyle Stories: The Collected Stories of T. Coraghessan Boyle.* New York, Viking, 1998.
Without a Hero. New York, Viking, and London, Granta, 1994.
Santa Barbara Stories, edited by Steven Gilbar. Santa Barbara, California, John Daniel, 1998.

*

Film Adaptations: *The Road to Wellville,* 1994.

Critical Studies: *Passion and Craft: Conversations with Notable Writers,* edited by Bonnie Lyons and Bill Oliver. Urbana, University of Illinois Press, 1998.

* * *

A fictionist who delights in equal measures of the irreverent and the satiric, the ironical twist and the serious meditation, T. Coraghessan Boyle has been linked with writers such as Thomas Pychon and John Barth. What more accurately defines the arc of Boyle's career, however, is his persistent juggling of the mundane and the surreal. The result is not only stories filled with surprises; they are also balanced adroitly between the dazzle of invention and the systematic undercutting of the ordinary.

Boyle's earliest stories gave hints of longer, more ambitious novels to come. For example, ''Heart of the Champion'' (1975), focuses on popular TV canine/icon Lassie and her love affair with a sex-starved coyote; ''A Women's Restaurant'' concerns itself with a male protagonist's obsession with a women-only eatery. Seventeen of Boyle's stories from this period were collected in *The Descent of Man,* the title derived from a story about a woman's liaison with a chimpanzee who dotes on Nietzsche.

Water Music, his first novel, cobbles Mungo Park, the Scottish explorer, with a fictional counterpart named Red Rise. Their comic adventures in Africa are both informed by Park's actual expeditions of 1795 and 1805 and given a comic dimension by Rise's exploits as an irrepressible con man. What intrigued most critics, however, was the sheer verbal energy of Boyle's polysyllabic style. Here, in short, was a young, go-for-broke writer to reckon with.

Budding Prospects confirmed the suspicions that Boyle is a comic novelist potentially of the first rank. Felix Nasmyth, the novel's laconic protagonist, is a disillusioned teacher who finds himself entangled in a scheme to grow marijuana, and thus grow rich. For Nasmyth, the prospect of untold riches dances around his head like sugarplum fairies. The rub, alas, is that Nasmyth has a long track record as a quitter:

> I've always been a quitter. I quit the boy scouts, the glee club, the marching band. Gave up my paper route, turned my back on the church, stuffed the basketball team … I got married, separated, divorced. Quit smoking, quit jogging, quit eating red meat.

Ironically enough, the dope farm teaches the disillusioned teacher the lesson of hard work; and even when one of his associates, a fast-talking former CIA agent, skips off with the profits, it really doesn't matter. The money that had mattered so greatly at the beginning is no longer the center of Nasmyth's new, improved life.

Although Boyle continues to publish collections of short fiction (*Greasy Lake and Other Stories, If the River Was Whiskey,* and *Without a Hero*), the formula of bizarre action superimposed on seemingly normal settings has grown both predictable and limited. There is little doubt that Boyle has a way with the one-liner, much less that his short stories make for an engaging read. But, added together, they lack the heft one expects from a writer of his talent.

With *World's End,* however, the larger, more expansive canvas of the novel brought him the wide critical regard he apparently craves. Set in the Hudson River Valley of New York, *World's End* tells the interlocking tale of three families over ten generations. In a series of collisions, simultaneously literal and figurative, the past meets the present and historical mistakes are reenacted once again. An inescapable destiny thus shapes Boyle's most ambitious and aesthetically accomplished novel thus far. By contrast, *The Road to Wellville* has its comic way with an easier target: the health-food sanitarium run by cereal king John Harvey Kellogg. The high jinks that went on in Battle Creek, Michigan, during the early 1900s become an extended analogy for present-day food fads. Flimflammers are, of course, an abiding subject in American humor, and *The Road to Wellville* is a worthy enough contribution to that tradition. One turns its pages laughing, which is more than one can say of the novel's film version.

Boyle has yet to settle down as a serious writer, but those who keep their eye on contemporary American literature's best prospects know his name and look forward to his next books with anticipation.

—Sanford Pinsker

BRADBURY, Edward P.

See MOORCOCK, Michael

BRADBURY, Malcolm (Stanley)

Nationality: British. **Born:** Sheffield, Yorkshire, 7 September 1932. **Education:** West Bridgford Grammar School, Nottingham, 1943–50; University College, Leicester, 1950–53, B.A. in English (1st class honours) 1953; Queen Mary College, University of London (research scholar), 1953–55, M.A. in English 1955; Indiana University, Bloomington (English-Speaking Union fellow), 1955–56; University of Manchester, 1956–58, Ph.D. in American Studies 1962; Yale University, New Haven, Connecticut (British Association for American Studies fellow), 1958–59. **Family:** Married Elizabeth Salt in 1959; two sons. **Career:** staff tutor in literature and drama, Department of Adult Education, University of Hull, Yorkshire, 1959–61; lecturer in English, University of Birmingham, 1961–65. Lecturer, 1957–67, senior lecturer, 1967–69, reader in English, 1969–70, professor of American studies, 1970–95, and since 1995 professor emeritus, University of East Anglia, Norwich. Visiting professor, University of California, Davis, 1966; visiting fellow, All Souls College, Oxford, 1969; visiting professor, University of Zurich, 1972; Fanny Hurst Professor, Washington University, St. Louis, 1982; Davis Professor, University of Queensland, Brisbane, 1983; visiting professor, Griffith University, Nathan, Queensland, 1983, University of Birmingham, 1989, University of Hull, 1994; University of Nottingham, 1996. Series editor, Stratford-upon-Avon Studies, for Arnold publishers, London, 1971–84, and Contemporary Writers series for Methuen publishers, London. **Awards:** American Council of Learned Societies fellowship, 1965; Royal Society of Literature Heinemann award, 1976; Rockefeller fellowship, 1987; Emmy award, for television series, 1988; Monte Carlo Television Festival award, 1991. D.Litt.: University of Leicester, 1986; University of Birmingham, 1989; University of Hull, 1994. Fellow, Royal Society of Literature, 1973; Honorary Fellow, Queen Mary College, 1984. C.B.E. (Commander, Order of the British Empire), 1991. **Agent:** Curtis Brown, 4th Floor, Haymarket House, Haymarket, London SW1Y 4SP, England; or, 10 Astor Place, New York, New York 10003, U.S.A. **Address:** School of English and American Studies, University of East Anglia, Norwich, Norfolk NR4 7TJ, England.

PUBLICATIONS

Novels

Eating People Is Wrong. London, Secker and Warburg, 1959; New York, Knopf, 1960.

Stepping Westward. London, Secker and Warburg, 1965; Boston, Houghton Mifflin, 1966; New York, Penguin, 1995.

The History Man. London, Secker and Warburg, 1975; Boston, Houghton Mifflin, 1976.

Rates of Exchange. London, Secker and Warburg, and New York, Knopf, 1983.

Cuts: A Very Short Novel. London, Hutchinson, and New York, Harper, 1987.

Doctor Criminale. London, Secker and Warburg, and New York, Viking Penguin, 1993.
To the Hermitage. London, Picador, 2000.

Short Stories

Who Do You Think You Are? Stories and Parodies. London, Secker and Warburg, 1976; augmented edition, London, Arena, 1984.

Plays

Between These Four Walls (revue), with David Lodge and James Duckett (produced Birmingham, 1963).
Slap in the Middle (revue), with others (produced Birmingham, 1965).
The After Dinner Game, with Christopher Bigsby (televised 1975). Included in *The After Dinner Game,* 1982.
Love on a Gunboat (televised 1977). Included in *The After Dinner Game,* 1982.
Standing In for Henry (televised 1980). Included in *The After Dinner Game,* 1982.
The Enigma, from the story by John Fowles (televised 1980). Included in *The After Dinner Game,* revised edition, 1989.
The After Dinner Game: Three Plays for Television. London, Arrow, 1982; revised edition (includes *The Enigma*), London, Arena, 1989.
Inside Trading: A Comedy in Three Acts. Portsmouth, New Hampshire, Heinemann, 1997.

Radio Plays: *Paris France* (documentary), 1960; *This Sporting Life,* with Elizabeth Bradbury, from the novel by David Storey, 1974; *Scenes from Provincial Life* and *Scenes from Married Life,* with Elizabeth Bradbury, from the novels by William Cooper, 1975–1976; *Patterson,* with Christopher Bigsby, 1981; *Congress,* 1981; *See a Friend This Weekend,* 1985.

Television Plays: *The After Dinner Game,* with Christopher Bigsby, 1975; *Stones* (*The Mind Beyond* series), with Christopher Bigsby, 1976; *Love on a Gunboat,* 1977; *The Enigma,* from the story by John Fowles, 1980; *Standing In for Henry,* 1980; *Blott on the Landscape* series, from the novel by Tom Sharpe, 1985; *Porterhouse Blue* series, from the novel by Tom Sharpe, 1987; *Imaginary Friends* series, from the novel by Alison Lurie, 1987; *Anything More Would Be Greedy* series, 1989; *The Gravy Train* series, 1990; *The Green Man* series, from the novel by Kingsley Amis, 1990; *The Gravy Train Goes East* series, 1992; *Cold Comfort Farm,* from the novel by Stella Gibbons, 1995.

Poetry

Two Poets, with Allan Rodway. Nottingham, Byron Press, 1966.

Other

Phogey! How to Have Class in a Classless Society. London, Parrish, 1960.
All Dressed Up and Nowhere to Go: The Poor Man's Guide to the Affluent Society. London, Parrish, 1962.
Evelyn Waugh. Edinburgh, Oliver and Boyd, 1964.
What Is a Novel? London, Arnold, 1969.
The Social Context of Modern English Literature. Oxford, Blackwell, and New York, Schocken, 1971.
Possibilities: Essays on the State of the Novel. London, Oxford University Press, 1973.
The Outland Dart: American Writers and European Modernism (lecture). London, Oxford University Press, 1978.
All Dressed Up and Nowhere to Go (revised editions). London, Pavilion-Joseph, 1982.
The Expatriate Tradition in American Literature. Durham, British Association for American Studies, 1982.
Saul Bellow. London, Methuen, 1983.
The Modern American Novel. Oxford and New York, Oxford University Press, 1983; revised edition, 1991.
Why Come to Slaka? London, Secker and Warburg, 1986; New York, Penguin, 1988.
My Strange Quest for Mensonge: Structuralism's Hidden Hero. London, Deutsch, 1987; New York, Penguin, 1988.
No, Not Bloomsbury (essays). London, Deutsch, 1987; New York, Columbia University Press, 1988.
The Modern World: Ten Great Writers. London, Secker and Warburg, 1988; New York, Viking, 1989.
Unsent Letters: Irreverent Notes from a Literary Life. London, Deutsch, and New York, Viking, 1988.
From Puritanism to Postmodernism: The Story of American Literature, with Richard Ruland. London, Routledge, 1991.
The Modern British Novel. London, Secker and Warburg, 1994.
Dangerous Pilgrimages: Transatlantic Mythologies and the Novel. London, Secker and Warburg, 1995; New York, Viking, 1996.
Editor, *Forster: A Collection of Critical Essays.* Englewood Cliffs, New Jersey, Prentice Hall, 1966.
Editor, *Pudd'nhead Wilson, and Those Extraordinary Twins,* by Mark Twain. London, Penguin, 1969.
Editor, *E.M. Forster: A Passage to India: A Casebook.* London, Macmillan, 1970.
Editor, with Eric Mottram, *U.S.A.,* in *The Penguin Companion to Literature 3.* London, Penguin, and New York, McGraw Hill, 1971.
Editor, with James McFarlane, *Modernism 1890–1930.* London, Penguin, 1976; Atlantic Highlands, New Jersey, Humanities Press, 1978.
Editor, *The Novel Today: Contemporary Writers on Modern Fiction.* Manchester, Manchester University Press, and Totowa, New Jersey, Rowman and Littlefield, 1977; revised edition, London, Fontana, 1990.
Editor, with Howard Temperley, *Introduction to American Studies.* London, Longman, 1981; revised edition, 1989; third edition, New York, Longman, 1998.
Editor, *The Red Badge of Courage,* by Stephen Crane. London, Dent, 1983.
Editor, *The Penguin Book of Modern British Short Stories.* London, Viking, 1987; New York, Viking, 1988.
Editor, with others, *Unthank: An Anthology of Short Stories from the M.A. in Creative Writing at the University of East Anglia.* Norwich, University of East Anglia Centre for Creative and Performing Arts, 1989.
Editor, *The Sketch Book of Geoffrey Crayon, Gent,* by Washington Irving. London, Dent/Everyman, 1993.

Editor, *The Blithedale Romance,* by Nathaniel Hawthorne. London, Dent/Everyman, 1993.
Editor, *Present Laughter: An Anthology of Modern Comic Short Stories.* London, Weidenfeld and Nicolson, 1994.
Editor, *The Marble Faun,* by Nathaniel Hawthorne. London, Dent/ Everyman, 1995.
Editor, *Class Work: An Anthology of 25 Years of Creative Writing at UEA.* London, Hodder and Stoughton, 1995.
Editor, *The Atlas of Literature.* New York, Stewart, Tabori & Chang, 1996.

*

Critical Studies: ''Fictions of Academe'' by George Watson, in *Encounter* (London), November 1978; ''Images of Sociology and Sociologists in Fiction'' by John Kramer, in *Contemporary Sociology* (Washington, D.C.), May 1979; ''The Business of University Novels'' by J.P. Kenyon, in *Encounter* (London), June 1980; ''Malcolm Bradbury's *The History Man:* The Novelist as Reluctant Impresario'' by Richard Todd, and interview with Todd, in *Dutch Quarterly Review* (Amsterdam), vol. 2, 1981–1983; interviews in *The Radical Imagination and the Liberal Tradition* edited by Heide Ziegler and Christopher Bigsby, London, Junction, 1982, with Ronald Hayman, in *Books and Bookmen* (London), April 1983, with Alastair Morgan, in *Literary Review* (London), October 1983, and in *Novelists in Interview* by John Haffenden, London, Methuen, 1985; article by Melvin J. Friedman, in *British Novelists since 1960* edited by Jay L. Halio, Detroit, Gale, 1983; *The Dialogic Novels of Malcolm Bradbury and David Lodge* by Robert A. Morace, Carbondale, Southern Illinois University Press, 1989; article by Richard Todd, in *Post-War Literatures in English: A Lexicon of Contemporary Authors,* Bouhn Stafleu, Holland, 1994.

Malcolm Bradbury comments:

(1996) I suppose my fiction—six novels and a volume of short stories, as well as many television scripts and film screenplays, and three ''television novels''—roughly follows the pattern, the styles and cultural and moral concerns, that have run through British fiction over the now five decades over which I've been writing. I began writing fiction in the 1950s when, in the period after the defeat of fascism, and in the aftermath of the Holocaust and the nuclear bomb, the novel in Britain moved back toward social and moral realism. In the wake of those events, there was also a strong concern with the problems affecting liberal and humanistic values. In fact if my books do possess one consistent theme (I believe they do), then that is their concern with the problems of liberalism, humanism, and general moral responsibility in the late 20th-century world.

In my earlier novels (*Eating People Is Wrong*, *Stepping Westward*), the central characters are concerned if confused moral agents, liberals not in the political but the moral sense, trying to do a reasonable amount of good in a difficult world, generally with comic, ironic or near-tragic results. I wrote *Eating People is Wrong* when I was 20 and was a university undergraduate, fascinated by the liberal universe of academic life, a place of often confused humanism and idealistic goodwill. I revised it a little later to make it more a retrospective general portrait of intellectual life in the British 1950s. With *Stepping Westward*, the result of several years in American universities as a graduate student, and about an American campus in the troubled years of anti-liberal sentiment that came from the witch-hunting of Senator McCarthy, I became interested in the different transatlantic meanings of liberalism, and I also began to explore my sense that humanism was in conflict with the hard realities of cold war politics and also with an age of materialist obsessions, self-seeking, and desire.

That theme is treated with a far harsher irony in *The History Man*, set in British academic life in the aftermath of the student revolutions of 1968. Its central character, Howard Kirk, is a radical sociologist who believes he is the spokesperson of a Marxist revolutionary process—history itself—that will still sweep away everything in its path; he tries to seduce his students and his colleagues into his bed and into the radical future. It is an ironic and a somewhat dark novel, as its liberal characters become incompetent in the face of inhumane theory and ideology. My next novel, *Rates of Exchange*, written at the beginning of the 1980s, is somewhat more hopeful. Dealing with various visits to Eastern European countries and my feeling that the rigid grid of the Marxist state was being increasingly undermined by the playfulness of language and the enduring power of the human imagination, it is set in an imaginary Eastern European state, Slaka, which is undergoing a language revolution. Its central character is a magical realist novelist, Katya Princip, who uses fiction to break free of ideology—and who in a later incarnation (see further on) becomes president of the country after it finally throws off its Stalinism. Like a number of British novelists I had also by now become fascinated by the opportunities of television drama in Britain. My next book, *Cuts: A Very Short Novel*, deals with this. A comedy about the making of what proves an abortive television series in the monetarist years of Mrs Thatcher's 1980s, it is about cuts in two senses: the cuts to British services that happened in the New Conservative 1980s, and the filmic technique of cutting.

Since some of these books are set in or around universities, I have often been thought of as a ''campus novelist,'' and described as a progenitor of what is now called ''the university novel.'' This is true to a point: I was a first-generation university student fascinated by the strangeness of the academic and intellectual world, and so made it fictional country. I have also spent most of my adult life teaching in universities in a number of countries; I am a professor of American studies and a teacher of creative writing, though now part-time; I have written a good deal of literary criticism, and been influenced by it. So my first book is set in a British redbrick in the 1950s, when it was a place of social change; my second is set on American campus near the Rockies at the start of the 1960s when it seemed a place of liberation; my third is set in a British new university as the 1960s died and the 1970s began, and radical hopes were beginning to be replaced by hard economic realities. I see them more as books about their decades, their themes, ideas, emotions, hypocrisies, intellectual fashions, and preoccupations; a university environment means that I can write about historically self-conscious and self-critical characters, the types who most interest me. I most see myself as a comic novelist, mixing satirical and ironic social and intellectual observation with play and parody. If I started writing in a time when the British novel was both thematically and technically provincial, I have tried to break out of that and become a more cosmopolitan, international, and technically elaborate writer. In *Rates of Exchange*, for example, I sought to find not only a larger subject matter, the question of what ideology we seek to live by in the late 20th century, but also a different language; in fact much of the novel exploits the technique of using English spoken by non-native speakers as its tone of voice.

My books have thus changed considerably over the years (and will continue to do so), but so has British fiction, which during the later 1960s and 1970s grew far more cosmopolitan and technically varied. As writer and critic, I have been very interested in postmodern experiment and found many of my more recent influences abroad. From *The History Man* onward, my books became harsher in tone, more elaborate technically, and they challenge some of the traditional ideas of character, realism of presentation, and moral confidence with which British novels have so often been written. *Rates of Exchange* thus deals with the problem of the British writer who uses a language deeply changed by its modern role as a lingua franca, and a world where stories become less reassuring and more ambiguous. This probably makes some of my later works rather more ironic, parodic, and less companionable, though I also think it makes them better. During the 1980s, for various reasons, I also found myself using the form of what I think of as the ''television novel,'' that is, novel-like forms and ideas written and produced as television series. I liked television's immediacy, its rich techniques, its fast narrative pace. *Anything More Would Be Greedy*, a six-part series for Anglia Television, is about a group of students growing older, richer, and ever more cynical in Mrs Thatcher's entrepreneurial Britain; while *The Gravy Train* and *The Gravy Train: The Economic Miracle* (forthcoming) are both four-part drama series for Channel 4, dealing ironically with the European Community as it reaches toward the great late 20th century dream of European integration. The second series is once again about Slaka, after the fall of the Berlin Wall, and its attempts under President Katya Princip to join the mysterious entity of ''Europe.''

So my concerns and interests have widened. My sixth novel, *Doctor Criminale*, is a comedy about a tainted philosopher who has been a powerful intellectual influence during the Cold War period, and is now being seen as the philosopher of the Nineties. It's my attempt to deal with the great transformation that came with the end of the 45-year Cold War era, and to capture the climate as the new century, indeed a new millennium, approaches. I have continued to write regularly in a wide variety of media—books, television, film, and radio—and both in fiction and non-fiction, especially literary criticism and, increasingly, journalism. Having now retired from university teaching—mostly recently the teaching of creative writing—and working as a full-time writer, I am, though, returning ever more refreshed to the novel. I still think of it as my primary and essential form—an ever-changing form that inevitably alters a good deal in history for any writer who isn't chiefly concerned with perpetuating the popular genres or simply providing entertainment.

I view my books as works of comic and satirical observation, which amongst other things explore both the decades in which they're set, and the changing moods and modes of fiction. Socially they explore the moral 1950s, the radical 1960s, the cautious 1970s, the entrepreneurial 1980s, and now the nervous and increasingly cynical 1990s. In form they shift from moral comedy to harder irony, where the comic more nearly touches the tragic. I stay fascinated by fiction's fictionality, and regard all our forms of exploring knowledge as forms of fiction-making, which is one reason why I regard the novel as central. Since it acknowledges its fictionality, and often explores its own method and declares its own scepticism, it stays at best one of our chief ways of discovering and naming the world. At the same time it depends on a sense of truth, a feeling for reality, a response to the authentic experience of individual humanity. And, if my books are satirical explorations of current confusion, pain, and inauthenticity, they hardly (as some critics have said) betoken the end of humanism. In fact the novel belongs with the spirit of ''liberalism,'' in the better sense of that word: the challenging of ideologies, intellectual fashions and inhuman systems or theories through sympathy and the imagination. Which is why I think the novel is always under challenge, but is far from dead.

* * *

Ever since the 1959 publication of his first novel, *Eating People Is Wrong*, Malcolm Bradbury has been regarded as an extremely witty satirist, lampooning topical phenomena and issues. He excels in group scenes: the cautiously wild and slap-stick university party that mixes faculty and students in *Eating People Is Wrong*; the American faculty committee meeting to choose a writer-in-residence that begins *Stepping Westward* and is ironically contrasted with the concluding one a year later; the department meeting that combines haggling over procedure, trivia, several forms of self-seeking, and genuine academic concerns in *The History Man*; the adult education class that was apparently cut from *Eating People Is Wrong* and, in revised form, printed in the collection of *Who Do You Think You Are?*; the guest lectures of and alcoholic lunches for the English linguist on a two-week tour of the country in ''central Eastern Europe'' that prides itself on ''clean tractors'' and a ''reformed watercress industry'' in *Rates of Exchange*. All these pieces bring people, representing various points of view on some current question of politics or communal definition, into sharp, comically outrageous conflict or misunderstanding.

Bradbury often castigates a whole contemporary milieu through scenes like the ''with-it,'' consciously ''existential'' party, a license for free self-definition, arranged by the ''new university'' sociologist, Howard Kirk, in *The History Man*. Bradbury also exploits his talent for mimicry of current attitudes, modes of speech (like the variety of ways to mangle English in *Rates of Exchange*), and the style and themes of other writers. A long section of *Who Do You Think You Are?*, for example, contains astringent parodies of Snow, Amis, Murdoch, Braine, Sillitoe, and others, along with less biting and salient echoes of Angus Wilson and Lawrence Durrell. The use of Amis (with whose early work Bradbury's has often been compared) is particularly resonant. Like Amis, Bradbury sometimes includes characters from one fiction in another, like the free-loving psychologist, Flora Beniform, who is both Howard Kirk's uncommitted mistress in *The History Man* and a central character on the television panel concerning modern sexual mores satirized in the story ''Who Do You Think You Are?'' As an in-joke, Bradbury even appropriates the Amis character who doesn't appear, the fraudulent L.S. Caton used in a number of novels until Amis finally killed him off in *The Anti-Death League*. Bradbury makes him a professor, scheduled to visit Benedict Arnold University in the U.S. to give a lecture on the ''angry young men,'' who never arrives. In spite of all the critical comparisons and interlocking references, Bradbury's satire is different from Amis's, Bradbury generally more concerned with issues and ideas, less implicitly committed to pragmatic success in the world or, until the recent *Rates of Exchange*, to mocking various forms of contemporary incompetence.

Much of Bradbury's fiction takes place within a university setting: the provincial red-brick during the 1950s in *Eating People Is Wrong*, the American university in the flat wilderness of the Plains states in *Stepping Westward* the new south coast university in 1972 in *The History Man*. Yet, as Bradbury himself has rightly insisted, the applications of his fiction extend beyond the university, just as the implications of his moral treatments of contemporary experience are far from slapstick comedy. In *Stepping Westward* the Englishman, James Walker, who becomes writer-in-residence at the ''moral supermarket'' of the American university, begins with his own ''decent modest radicalism'' and tries to extend himself to assimilate more of the modern world, looking for ''sense and design.'' The plot depends on Walker's public refusal to sign an American loyalty oath, part of his English ''faith in unbelief,'' and the America he finds is one of ''violence and meaninglessness and anarchy.'' In *The History Man* Howard Kirk, seen far less sympathetically than James Walker is, seeks ''liberation'' and ''emancipation'' in the new university for himself and others, ignoring or condescending to his old friend, Beamish, a rather bumbling locus of value in the novel, who claims ''there is an inheritance of worthwhile life in this country.'' In this novel, written entirely in the rush of the present tense, Kirk chooses instead to redevelop the town, to lie, to manipulate others in the name of the ''now'' and the ''new,'' and to ignore the voice of a young English teacher who sees her function as simply reading and talking about books. In both novels Bradbury's moral focus is clear and searching, although it sometimes seems slightly provincial. He attacks the self-seeking, the self-deceptive, and the meretricious, like a career academic named Froelich who becomes chairman in *Stepping Westward* and Kirk himself in *The History Man*. Yet some of Bradbury's work has more complexity and distance than outlining the moral framework might suggest. Sometimes, as in *The History Man,*, which ends with Kirk's wife deliberately pushing her arm through the window, an act of self-destruction like that more ambivalently performed by Beamish at an earlier party, or in a short story entitled ''A Very Hospitable Person,'' the satire seems brittle, almost cruel, in denying the central figures any humanity or self-doubt. At other times, as in an excellent story called ''A Breakdown,'' about a student having a futile affair with a married man in Chesterfield who runs off to Spain to punish herself, or as in *Stepping Westward*, where James Walker recognizes that America has defeated him, that, in spite of all his morality, he could not really handle his own freedom to define himself, Bradbury's perspective is more sympathetic without diluting the moral concern. A prefatory note to *Rates of Exchange* characterizes the novel as ''a paper fiction, offered for exchange'' that illustrates ''our duty to lie together, in the cause, of course, of truth.'' Beneath its comic texture of constant mutual misunderstanding and incompetence (sometimes overdone), Bradbury sensitively questions the comfortable assumption of virtue or truth in any of the various national, political, intellectual, or sexual languages that form systems of human exchange.

Bradbury's commitment to liberal humanism has always been tempered by a willingness to test its continuing viability against various cultural, political, and economic challenges. And nowhere is that willingness more clearly evident than in *Doctor Criminale*. This witty fiction about fashionable literary theory, as well as the fashion for literary theory, is also, appropriately enough, Bradbury's most self-consciously intertextual novel to date, drawing on an impressive array of literary precedents which include his own *Rates of Exchange*, *Cuts*, and two Gravytrain television series as well as his friend David Lodge's *Small World,* an updating of the campus novel for an age of the global campus. But in many respects the work *Doctor Criminale* draws on most is F. Scott Fitzgerald's ''symbolist tragedy,'' *The Great Gatsby,* ''about the struggle of the symbolic imagination to exist in lowered historical time, and about that symbol's inherent ambiguity, its wonder and its meretriciousness,'' as Bradbury wrote in *The Modern American Novel.*

Doctor Criminale is, of course, a comedy, not a tragedy, and its subject is theory's, not the symbol's, essential ambiguity. Bradbury's Nick Carraway is the hapless, anachronistlc Francis Jay, a verbal man and naive liberal humanist adrift in the visual culture of entrepreneurial England. And his Gatsby is a man no less able to inspire wonder in his admirers, the supercritic and celebrity thinker Bazlo Criminale. Criminale, the ''text'' Jay sets out to decode, proves a most elusive quarry. As mysterious as Eliot's famous MacCavity the Cat, he seems less a person than a floating signifier who exists largely as a collection of mutually exlusive interpretations, or signifieds. He is alternately a philosopher who has declared the end of philosophy and a master mystifier pulling books and articles out of his theoretical hat; perhaps a spy, though maybe a double agent, an ardent Communist or, what is just as likely, an ardent anti-Communist. Above all he is a version of the late Yale deconstructionist, Paul de Man, who posthumously became the subject of intense controversy following the discovery of articles he had written during the Nazi occupation. Like de Man, Criminale seems to be a man at best ''flexible'' and at worst ''a moral disappointment.'' Bradbury's jokey magical mystery tour of the political, economic, and literary landscape at the end of the Cold War and on the eve of the European Community, thus, does more than just delight; it also ''problematizes'' both fashionable theory and old-fashioned liberal humanism by having each ''interrogate'' the other. However, *Doctor Criminale* does more than illuminate their relative strengths and weaknesses; in examining theory in a specific historical context, Bradbury also examines many of the defining features of the culture in which theory has been so ardently promoted and just as strenuously resisted.

During the late 1990s, Bradbury did not produce any novel-length fiction; rather, he directed his attention toward drama, offering up plays (including *Insider Trading*) and an adaptation of Stella Gibbons's *Cold Comfort Farm* for the 1996 film directed by John Schlesinger. He also edited anthologies and wrote about the subject he has experienced both from outside and inside, literature.

—James Gindin, updated by Robert A. Morace

BRADBURY, Ray(mond Douglas)

Nationality: American. **Born:** Waukegan, Illinois, 22 August 1920. **Education:** Los Angeles High School, graduated 1938. **Family:** Married Marguerite Susan McClure in 1947; four daughters. **Career:** Since 1943 full-time writer. President, Science-Fantasy Writers of America, 1951–53. Member of the Board of Directors, Screen Writers Guild of America, 1957–61. Lives in Los Angeles. **Awards:** O. Henry prize, 1947, 1948; Benjamin Franklin award, 1954; American Academy award, 1954; Boys' Clubs of America Junior Book award, 1956; Golden Eagle award, for screenplay, 1957; Ann Radcliffe award, 1965, 1971; Writers Guild award, 1974; Aviation and Space Writers award, for television documentary, 1979; Gandalf award, 1980. D.Litt.: Whittier College, California, 1979. **Agent:** Harold Matson Company, 276 Fifth Avenue, New York, New York 10001. **Address:** c/o Bantam, 666 Fifth Avenue, New York, New York 10103, U.S.A.

Publications

Novels

Fahrenheit 451. New York, Ballantine, 1953; London, Hart Davis, 1954; with a new foreword by the author, Thorndike, Maine, G. K. Hall, 1997.
Something Wicked This Way Comes. New York, Simon and Schuster, 1962; London, Hart Davis, 1963.
Death Is a Lonely Business. New York, Knopf, 1985; London, Grafton, 1986.
A Graveyard for Lunatics: Another Tale of Two Cities. New York, Knopf, and London, Grafton, 1990.
The Smile. Mankato, Minnesota, Creative Education, 1991.
Green Shadows, White Whale. New York, Knopf, and London, HarperCollins, 1992.
Quicker Than the Eye. New York, Avon Books, 1996.
Driving Blind. New York, Avon Books, 1997.
With Cat for Comforter, illustrated by Louise Reinoehl Max. Salt Lake City, Utah, Gibbs Smith, 1997.
Dogs Think That Every Day Is Christmas, illustrated by Louise Reinoehl Max. Salt Lake City, Utah, Gibbs Smith, 1997.
Ahmed and the Oblivion Machines: A Fable, illustrated by Chris Lane. New York, Avon Books, 1998.

Short Stories

Dark Carnival. Sauk City, Wisconsin, Arkham House, 1947; abridged edition, London, Hamish Hamilton, 1948; abridged edition, as *The Small Assassin,* London, New English Library, 1962.
The Martian Chronicles. New York, Doubleday, 1950; as *The Silver Locusts,* London, Hart Davis, 1951.
The Illustrated Man. New York, Doubleday, 1951; London, Hart Davis, 1952; New York, Avon Books, 1997.
The Golden Apples of the Sun. New York, Doubleday, and London, Hart Davis, 1953.
The October Country. New York, Ballantine, 1955; London, Hart Davis, 1956; with a new introduction by the author. New York, Ballantine Books, 1996.
Dandelion Wine. New York, Doubleday, and London, Hart Davis, 1957; New York, Avon Books, 1999.
A Medicine for Melancholy. New York, Doubleday, 1959.
The Day It Rained Forever. London, Hart Davis, 1959.
The Machineries of Joy. New York, Simon and Schuster, and London, Hart Davis, 1964.
The Vintage Bradbury. New York, Random House, 1965.
The Autumn People. New York, Ballantine, 1965.
Tomorrow Midnight. New York, Ballantine, 1966.
Twice Twenty Two (selection). New York, Doubleday, 1966.
I Sing the Body Electric! New York, Knopf, 1969; London, Hart Davis, 1970; published as *I Sing the Body Electric and Other Stories,* New York, Avon Books, 1998.
Bloch and Bradbury, with Robert Bloch. New York, Tower, 1969; as *Fever Dreams and Other Fantasies,* London, Sphere, 1970.
(*Selected Stories*), edited by Anthony Adams. London, Harrap, 1975.
Long after Midnight. New York, Knopf, 1976; London, Hart Davis MacGibbon, 1977.
The Best of Bradbury. New York, Bantam, 1976.
To Sing Strange Songs. Exeter, Devon, Wheaton, 1979.
The Stories of Ray Bradbury. New York, Knopf, and London, Granada, 1980.
The Last Circus, and The Electrocution. Northridge, California, Lord John Press, 1980.
Dinosaur Tales. New York, Bantam, 1983.
A Memory of Murder. New York, Dell, 1984.
The Toynbee Convector. New York, Knopf, 1988; London, Grafton, 1989.

Plays

The Meadow, in *Best One-Act Plays of 1947–48,* edited by Margaret Mayorga. New York, Dodd Mead, 1948.
The Anthem Sprinters and Other Antics (produced Los Angeles, 1968). New York, Dial Press, 1963.
The World of Ray Bradbury (produced Los Angeles, 1964; New York, 1965).
The Wonderful Ice-Cream Suit (produced Los Angeles, 1965; New York, 1987; musical version, music by Jose Feliciano, produced Pasadena, California, 1990). Included in *The Wonderful Ice-Cream Suit and Other Plays,* 1972.
The Day It Rained Forever, music by Bill Whitefield (produced Edinburgh, 1988). New York, French, 1966.
The Pedestrian. New York, French, 1966.
Christus Apollo, music by Jerry Goldsmith (produced Los Angeles, 1969).
The Wonderful Ice-Cream Suit and Other Plays (includes *The Veldt* and *To the Chicago Abyss*). New York, Bantam, 1972; London, Hart Davis, 1973.
The Veldt (produced London, 1980). Included in *The Wonderful Ice-Cream Suit and Other Plays,* 1972.
Leviathan 99 (produced Los Angeles, 1972).
Pillar of Fire and Other Plays for Today, Tomorrow, and Beyond Tomorrow (includes *Kaleidoscope* and *The Foghorn*). New York, Bantam, 1975.
The Foghorn (produced New York, 1977). Included in *Pillar of Fire and Other Plays,* 1975.
That Ghost, That Bride of Time: Excerpts from a Play-in-Progress. Glendale, California, Squires, 1976.
The Martian Chronicles, adaptation of his own stories (produced Los Angeles, 1977).
Fahrenheit 451, adaptation of his own novel (produced Los Angeles, 1979).
Dandelion Wine, adaptation of his own story (produced Los Angeles, 1980).
Forever and the Earth (radio play). Athens, Ohio, Croissant, 1984.
On Stage: A Chrestomathy of His Plays. New York, Primus, 1991.

Screenplays: *It Came from Outer Space,* with David Schwartz, 1952; *Moby-Dick,* with John Huston, 1956; *Icarus Montgolfier Wright,* with George C. Johnston, 1961; *Picasso Summer* (as Douglas Spaulding), with Edwin Booth, 1972.

Television Plays: *Shopping for Death,* 1956, *Design for Loving,* 1958, *Special Delivery,* 1959, *The Faith of Aaron Menefee,* 1962, and *The Life Work of Juan Diaz,* 1963 (all *Alfred Hitchcock Presents* series); *The Marked Bullet* (*Jane Wyman's Fireside Theater* series), 1956; *The Gift* (*Steve Canyon* series), 1958; *The Tunnel to Yesterday* (*Trouble Shooters* series), 1960; *I Sing the Body Electric!* (*Twilight Zone* series), 1962; *The Jail* (*Alcoa Premier* series), 1962; *The Groom* (*Curiosity Shop* series), 1971; *The Coffin,* from his own short story, 1988 (U.K.).

Poetry

Old Ahab's Friend, and Friend to Noah, Speaks His Piece: A Celebration. Glendale, California, Squires, 1971.
When Elephants Last in the Dooryard Bloomed: Celebrations for Almost Any Day in the Year. New York, Knopf, 1973; London, Hart Davis MacGibbon, 1975.
That Son of Richard III: A Birth Announcement. Privately printed, 1974.
Where Robot Mice and Robot Men Run round in Robot Towns: New Poems, Both Light and Dark. New York, Knopf, 1977; London, Hart Davis MacGibbon, 1979.
Twin Hieroglyphs That Swim the River Dust. Northridge, California, Lord John Press, 1978.
The Bike Repairman. Northridge, California, Lord John Press, 1978.
The Author Considers His Resources. Northridge, California, Lord John Press, 1979.
The Aqueduct. Glendale, California, Squires, 1979.
The Attic Where the Meadow Greens. Northridge, California, Lord John Press, 1980.
Imagine. Northridge, California, Lord John Press, 1981.
The Haunted Computer and the Android Pope. New York, Knopf, and London, Granada, 1981.
The Complete Poems of Ray Bradbury. New York, Ballantine, 1982.
Two Poems. Northridge, California, Lord John Press, 1982.
The Love Affair. Northridge, California, Lord John Press, 1983.

Other

Switch on the Night (for children). New York, Pantheon, and London, Hart Davis, 1955.
R Is for Rocket (for children). New York, Doubleday, 1962; London, Hart Davis, 1968.
S Is for Space (for children). New York, Doubleday, 1966; London, Hart Davis, 1968.
Teacher's Guide: Science Fiction, with Lewy Olfson. New York, Bantam, 1968.
The Halloween Tree (for children). New York, Knopf, 1972; London, Hart Davis MacGibbon, 1973.
Mars and the Mind of Man. New York, Harper, 1973.
Zen and the Art of Writing, and The Joy of Writing. Santa Barbara, California, Capra Press, 1973.
The Mummies of Guanajuato, photographs by Archie Lieberman. New York, Abrams, 1978.
Beyond 1984: Remembrance of Things Future. New York, Targ, 1979.
About Norman Corwin. Northridge, California, Santa Susana Press, 1979.
The Ghosts of Forever, illustrated by Aldo Sessa. New York, Rizzoli, 1981.
Los Angeles, photographs by West Light. Port Washington, New York, Skyline Press, 1984.
Orange County, photographs by Bill Ross and others. Port Washington, New York, Skyline Press, 1985.
The Art of Playboy (text by Bradbury). New York, van der Marck Editions, 1985.
Zen in the Art of Writing (essays). Santa Barbara, California, Capra Press, 1990.
Yestermorrow: Obvious Answers to Impossible Futures (essays). Santa Barbara, California, Capra Press, 1991.
Editor, *Timeless Stories for Today and Tomorrow.* New York, Bantam, 1952.
Editor, *The Circus of Dr. Lao and Other Improbable Stories.* New York, Bantam, 1956.

*

Manuscript Collections: Bowling Green State University, Ohio.

Critical Studies: Interview in *Show* (New York), December 1964; introduction by Gilbert Highet to *The Vintage Bradbury,* 1965; "The Revival of Fantasy" by Russell Kirk, in *Triumph* (Washington, D.C.), May 1968; "Ray Bradbury's *Dandelion Wine:* Themes, Sources, and Style" by Marvin E. Mengeling, in *English Journal* (Champaign, Illinois), October 1971; *The Ray Bradbury Companion* (includes bibliography) by William F. Nolan, Detroit, Gale, 1975; *The Drama of Ray Bradbury* by Benjamin P. Indick, Baltimore, T-K Graphics, 1977; *The Bradbury Chronicles* by George Edgar Slusser, San Bernardino, California, Borgo Press, 1977; *Ray Bradbury* (includes bibliography) edited by Joseph D. Olander and Martin H. Greenberg, New York, Taplinger, and Edinburgh, Harris, 1980; *Ray Bradbury* by Wayne L. Johnson, New York, Ungar, 1980; *Ray Bradbury and the Poetics of Reverie: Fantasy, Science Fiction, and the Reader* by William F. Toupence, Ann Arbor, Michigan, UMI Research Press, 1984; *Ray Bradbury* by David Mogen, Boston, Twayne, 1986; *Ray Bradbury: An American Icon* (video cassette), Great Northern Productions, 1996; *Ray Bradbury and the Poetics of Reverie* by William F. Touponce, San Bernardino, California, Borgo Press, 1998; *American Science Fiction and Fantasy Writers* by Claire L. Datnow, Springfield, New Jersey, Enslow Publishers, 1999; *Ray Bradbury: A Critical Companion* by Robin Anne Reid, Westport, Connecticut, Greenwood Press, 2000; *Ray Bradbury,* edited by Harold Bloom, Philadelphia, Chelsea House, 2000.

Ray Bradbury comments:

I am not so much a science-fiction writer as I am a magician, an illusionist. From my beginnings as a boy conjurer I grew up frightening myself so as to frighten others so as to cure the midnight in our souls. I have grown into a writer of the History of Ideas, I guess you might say. Any idea, no matter how large or small, that is busy growing itself alive, starting from nowhere and at last dominating a town, a culture, or a world, is of interest. Man the problem solver is the writer of my tales. Science fiction becoming science fact. The machineries of our world putting away and keeping our facts for us so they can be used and learned from. Machines as humanist teachers. Ideas of men built into those machines in order to help us survive and survive well. That's my broad and fascinating field, in which I will wander for a lifetime, writing past science fictions one day, future ones another. And all of it a wonder and a lark and a great love. I can't imagine writing any other way.

* * *

Although he has written six novels, including the classics *Fahrenheit 451* (1953) and *Something Wicked This Way Comes* (1962), Ray Bradbury is best known as an author of short stories. His style is so economical, striking, and lyrical that it has been described as prose poetry, and he is as skillful at presenting horror and the grotesque as was Edgar Allan Poe (1809–1849), his primary influence. Bradbury is known as one of ''the big four'' of the genres of science fiction and fantasy, the others being Isaac Asimov, Arthur C. Clarke, and Robert Heinlein. He is deeply respected and beloved by genre fans and by students who study him in high school and college. His significance in fantasy and horror owe much to his background, his prose style, his recurrent themes, and the sense of wonder that pervades his work.

Bradbury's second story sale, ''The Candle'' (1941), marked the beginning of his association with *Weird Tales*, the legendary American pulp magazine that first appeared in 1923 and that, despite changes in editorial staff and many deaths and resurrections, keeps returning from the literary grave. This magazine published such enormously popular authors as H. P. Lovecraft, Robert Bloch of *Psycho* fame, and *Conan the Barbarian*'s creator Robert E. Howard. *Weird Tales* led supernatural fiction out of a poorly written Gothic and ghost tradition. It is essential to grasp the primacy of *Weird Tales* and its large fan base to recognize Bradbury's contemporary literary milieu and the adulation he earned during the years 1941 to 1948, when he became the most distinguished contributor to that magazine.

Bradbury began publishing collections of linked stories in the 1950s with *The Martian Chronicles* and *The Illustrated Man* (1951). *Fahrenheit 451* (1953) and *Dandelion Wine* (1957) are fix-ups, or novels constructed of previously published short stories. *Something Wicked This Way Comes* (1962), *Death Is a Lonely Business* (1985), and *A Graveyard for Lunatics* (1990) are stand-alone novels.

The Martian Chronicles and *The Illustrated Man* exemplify Bradbury's evolving style, motifs, and themes. Though his technique varies from the subtle to the ironic to the hair-raising, one can call *The Martian Chronicles* a fantasy based on science fiction motifs and *The Illustrated Man*, which is darker and more tainted by the supernatural, despite occasional nods to science fiction (futuristic machines, spaceships, aliens), overall a work of horror.

The Martian Chronicles tells of the emigration of humans to a Mars that is either peopled by or haunted by eerie, wistful, telepathic Martians. Humans gradually displace and replace the natives, and in 2003 (which, in the 1940s, seemed sufficiently distant to allow for terraforming technologies), the settlement of Tenth City has hardly any red dust blowing through it, so exactly is it like a small midwestern town. In 2005 Earth is destroyed by thermonuclear war (as recounted in the classic short story ''There Will Come Soft Rains'') and, not long after, human colonies and customs have erased all vestiges of the natives. The men now are the Martians.

This sounds like an allegory of the European colonization of the West, and read in one sitting the stories may be taken as a dirge for lost civilizations. The theme of loss runs like a sad tune throughout Bradbury's work: loss of loved ones, of friendships, of youth, of golden opportunities, of marvels trampled in a blind rush of capitalistic greed. The dictum that ''you can't stand in the way of progress'' is multivalent in Bradbury's fiction. Progress brings us to the stars, but dazzles us so that many other good things are left behind.

The stories in *The Illustrated Man* are united by a slight yet disturbing conceit: the narrator encounters a man whose skin is painted by ''living'' tattoos. One of these will show the death of the observer if watched long enough. After a night of viewing different tattoo stories as though films in miniature, the narrator is horrified to see his own destiny revealed—in the future, from some unimaginable need for revenge, the illustrated man will strangle him to death.

Both books testify to Bradbury's deceptively simple, sentimental, lyrical prose and to challenging themes such as revenge, insanity, loneliness, hope, and survival. Bradbury's short, straightforward sentences owe their delights and horrors to sensory descriptions (such as the aromas of cut grass or burning autumn leaves), to settings evocative of his fondly remembered hometown Waukegan, Illinois, and to pensive dialogues in which young children or old men express their sense of wonder when contemplating the star-filled night sky, the miracles of sunlight or the menace of shadows, the innocence of childhood, or the tragedies of missed meetings and lost loves.

Dandelion Wine is narrated by twelve-year-old Douglas (Bradbury's middle name) Spaulding, who is, like many of his young protagonists, loosely based on Bradbury himself. This work captures, as though in a glass of home-made wine, the recurring flavors and themes of his fiction. During the summer of 1928, Douglas gains maturity as the loss of a friend and the appearance of a murderer transform his perceptions of his world. The boy's powers of imagination, Bradbury emphasizes, both enrich and darken his life.

Something Wicked This Way Comes is again semi-autobiographical, but far darker—literally—than *Dandelion Wine*. Sunlight and sunset color *Dandelion Wine*, but much of *Something Wicked* occurs at night and in the dark places of the human psyche. Light and Dark are allegorized throughout the tale of Will Halloway and Jim Nightshade, who are seduced by the arrival in Green Town, Illinois, of a carnival called Cooger and Dark's Pandemonium Shadow Show. This evil carnival tempts the townsfolk with its supernatural powers to grant dreams—but also to steal souls. The merry-go-round, the Hall of Mirrors, the parade, and other carnivalesque trappings become truly creepy under Bradbury's skillful pen.

Fahrenheit 451 treats the themes of imagination and loss so powerfully that it is alluded to in discussions of governmental oppression and censorship almost as commonly as George Orwell's *1984*. The protagonist, Guy Montag, has happily labored as a ''fireman''—a burner of books—for ten years. As the novel opens, he meets seventeen-year-old Clarisse, who asks him unsettling questions: Does he ever think about his society instead of mouthing the socially acceptable phrases? Is he curious about the books he burns? Is he happy?

Their friendship changes his life. Montag begins to question his world, and finds fear and unhappiness everywhere. Eventually he meets a secret society of readers who preserve illegal books by memorizing them. A *New York Times* reviewer praised ''Bradbury's account of this insane world, which bears many alarming resemblances to our own.''

Bradbury's fiction developed into a more realistic (though still rhapsodic) mode during the 1960s and 1970s, and relied more on non-supernatural, if sometimes morbid, themes, such as dysfunctional marriages, the dangers of technology, fear of aging, and fear of death.

This development can be observed in the collections *The Machineries of Joy* (1964) and *I Sing the Body Electric* (1969). Bradbury contributed to his favorite genres by editing anthologies and writing children's stories; he also wrote nonfiction and plays.

Not until 1985 did a new Bradbury novel appear: *Death Is a Lonely Business*, which is based on his years as a pulp fiction writer. The protagonist's optimism and hope of success bizarrely preserve him from the deaths that are striking down many of his contemporaries. Like *Death, A Graveyard for Lunatics* is a detective novel about a writer, this one working in the Hollywood of the 1950s. Hired as a science fiction film writer at a big studio, he is led to the adjoining graveyard, where he discovers a body frozen in time. Though not as famous as his earlier work, both novels continue his theme of a past that cannot stop haunting the present.

Perhaps the greatest contribution Bradbury has made to fantasy and horror lies in his creating and ever re-creating a bona fide American romantic, melancholic tradition: a nostalgia for corn fields and small towns and suburbs, replacing the previously overwhelming European nostalgia for aristocracies and castles and cathedrals.

Bradbury began writing for television in 1951 for such programs as *Alfred Hitchcock* and *The Twilight Zone*, and the highly praised USA Network television series *The Bradbury Theatre* (1985–1992) is based on many of his short stories. Bradbury has also written plays and filmscripts, including the Gregory Peck-starring *Moby Dick* (1956) and the Academy Award-nominated *Icarus Montgolfier Wright* (1962). *Fahrenheit 451* was adapted for film (by François Truffaut) in 1966, *The Illustrated Man* in 1969, and *Something Wicked This Way Comes* in 1983, and *The Martian Chronicles* appeared as a television miniseries (1979). *Something Wicked* is the best of these adaptations.

In 1991 the extent of Bradbury's influence on later generations of writers was evidenced when William F. Nolan and Martin H. Greenberg commissioned twenty-two original stories (one by Bradbury) for *The Bradbury Chronicles*, published to honor his fiftieth year as a writer. The contributors included such noted names as Richard Matheson and his son Richard Christian Matheson, Charles L. Grant, F. Paul Wilson, Ed Gorman, and Chad Oliver. Horror authors Steven King and Clive Barker have also acknowledged his influence. Bradbury has earned the 1977 World Fantasy Award, the 1980 Grandmaster of Fantasy Gandalf Award, the 1989 Bram Stoker Award, and the 1988 Nebula Grand Master Award, and was inducted into the University of Kansas Center for the Study of Science Fiction's Science Fiction and Fantasy Hall of Fame (1999), all for Lifetime Achievement.

—Fiona Kelleghan

BRADLEY, David (Henry, Jr.)

Nationality: American. **Born:** Bedford, Pennsylvania, 7 September 1950. **Education:** Bedford Area High School, graduated 1968; University of Pennsylvania, Philadelphia (Franklin scholar, Presidential scholar), 1968–72, B.A. (summa cum laude) in creative writing 1972; King's College, University of London (Thouron scholar), 1972–74, M.A. in area studies 1974. **Career:** Reader and assistant editor, J.B. Lippincott, publishers, Philadelphia, 1974–76; visiting lecturer in English, University of Pennsylvania, 1975. Visiting instructor, 1976–77, assistant professor, 1977–82, associate professor of English, 1982–89, professor, 1989–96, Temple University, Philadelphia. Editorial consultant, Lippincott, 1977–78, and Ace Science Fiction, New York, 1979; visiting lecturer, San Diego State University, 1980–81. Member of the Executive Board, PEN American Center, 1982–84. **Awards:** American Academy award, 1982; PEN-Faulkner award, 1982. **Agent:** Wendy Weil, Julian Bach Literary Agency, 747 Third Avenue, New York, New York 10017. **Address:** P.O. Box 12681, La Jolla, California 92039–2681, U.S.A.

PUBLICATIONS

Novels

South Street. New York, Grossman, 1975.
The Chaneysville Incident. New York, Harper, 1981; London, Serpent's Tail, 1986.
The Lodestar Project. New York, Pocket Books, 1986.

Uncollected Short Story

"197903042100 (Sunday)," in *Our Roots Grow Deeper than We Know,* edited by Lee Gutkind. Pittsburgh, University of Pittsburgh Press, 1985.

Play

Sweet Sixteen (produced Louisville, Kentucky, 1983).

Other

From Text to Performance in the Elizabethan Theatre: Preparing the Play for the Stage. Cambridge, Cambridge University Press, 1991
Editor, with Shelley Fisher Fishkin, *The Encyclopedia of Civil Rights in America.* Armonk, New York, Sharpe Reference, 1998.

*

David Bradley comments:

(1996) I believe a work of fiction ought to more or less speak for itself—certainly the author ought to keep his mouth shut about it; he's *had* his chance. On the other hand, I have noticed a few things about my own attitudes that might bear mentioning. Nothing so deliberate as a "what I am trying to do with my writing" statement (which I find pretentious and usually wrong), but just observations about what I tend to think is good. I am, first of all, an Aristotelian writer. Meaning that I believe in the Gospel as laid down in *The Poetics.* Plot is paramount, and I do not like *any*thing that does not have one. Second, I do not believe in a sharp distinction between fiction and non-fiction. Most of my writing is grounded in real places and people. I always find myself "adapting" reality to the writing, as one might "adapt" a novel for a film. Third, I do not believe in art for art's sake. Art *has* no sake; people do. A work of art that cannot be understood is a voice crying in the wilderness. Fourth, I demand a lot from readers. I do not write "easy" things; they require effort and emotional commitment from me—and they require the same from readers. I hope only that readers feel their time and sweat are well spent.

* * *

For David Bradley, place matters, and history haunts. If the Stephen Dedalus of James Joyce's *A Portrait of the Artist as a Young*

Man tries desperately to fly over the nets of family, church, and state, Bradley speaks lyrically of those cords that bind him to his birthplace (the rural community of Bedford, Pennsylvania), to the black church in which he grew up, and to the family that nurtured his early interest in history, and in writing about that history. As put in ''A Personal View from the Third Generation'' (*New York Times Sunday Magazine*):

> For he [Bradley] realizes this is *his* church. Three generations of his family have occupied Mt. Pisgah's pulpit and worshipped in its pews. A plaque on the wall dedicates the 1960s redecoration to his grandmother. The Bible on the lectern was an offering by his father when his mother survived a dangerous illness. In the truest sense, he, not the denomination, owns Mt. Pisgah. And owes it.
>
> For, in a day when and a place where opportunities were restricted, Mt. Pisgah gave him the chance to speak, to lead, to learn the history of his people. When opportunities became available, it was the experience gained at Mt. Pisgah that equipped him to take advantage of them. But, after taking advantage of them, he abandoned the church that had nurtured him. He walked from Mt. Pisgah down into the Promised Land and never really looked back. Perhaps the time has come to turn around.

These are eloquent, confessional words. For Bradley has moved with astonishing speed from the raw, lusty talent that described the ''street people'' who hold forth on Philadelphia's *South Street* (published in 1975, when Bradley was only 24) to the sweep and ambition of *The Chaneysville Incident*, the novel that brought Bradley national recognition.

South Street is a novel anchored in the naturalism of ''elephantine cockroaches and rats the size of cannon shells,'' but it is also a novel that reaches well beyond the geography of urban despair. Bradley's South Street poises itself at the border of Philadelphia's black ghetto, where it ties ''the city's rivers like an iron bracelet or a wedding band, uniting the waters, sewer to sewer, before they meet at the city's edge.'' Place matters deeply, of course—in this case, the locus seems to be Lightnin' Ed's Bar—but it is the people, and Bradley's ear for their colorful language, that matters even more:

> Leo, the two-hundred-and-fifty-eight-pound owner-bartender-cashier-bouncer of Lightnin' Ed's Bar and Grill, looked up from the glass he was polishing to see a one-hundred-and-fifty-eight-pound white man walk into his bar. Leo's mouth fell open and he almost dropped the glass. One by one the faces along the bar turned to stare at the single pale face, shining in the dimness. ''Yes, sir, cap'n,'' Leo said uneasily, ''what can we be doin' for you?''
>
> George looked around nervously. ''I, ah, had a little accident. I, ah, ran over a cat in the street, and I, uh, don't know what to do about it.''
>
> ''Whad he say?'' a wino at the far end of the bar, who claimed to be hard of hearing, whispered loudly.
>
> The jukebox ran out and fell silent just as somebody yelled to him, ''Paddy says he run over some cat out in the street.'' The sound echoed throughout the bar. Conversation died.
>
> ''Goddamn!'' said the wino.
>
> Leo leaned over the bar, letting his gigantic belly rest on the polished wood. ''Yeah?'' he said to George. ''Didja kill him?''
>
> ''Oh yes,'' George assured him. ''I made certain of that.''

Bradley is at his best when he moves inside the set pieces, the extended anecdotes, that give *South Street* its resonance. What might well have become yet another unrelenting grim account of sordid conditions and despairing lives transmogrifies itself into a high, more humane key. It was, in short, a novel that prompted reviewers to say ''Keep your eye on Mr. Bradley.'' In this case, they were righter than they knew.

The Chaneysville Incident both widened and deepened the scope of Bradley's obvious talents. His postgraduate research in American history at the University of London sent him back, ironically enough, to a story he had heard in Bedford about 13 escaped slaves who asked to be killed rather than recaptured and about the 13 unmarked graves his mother once discovered.

The Chaneysville Incident tells this story from the perspective of John Washington, a black man who has bootstrapped himself from humble, rural origins to become a history professor at a Philadelphia university and who lives with Judith, a white psychologist. The question the book raises is simply, and perplexingly, how should a black man live in a world white men have made. The result is a thickly textured, multi-layered book, one that inextricably combines theory, historical research, and domestic tension. As Washington, the historian, puts it: ''The key to the understanding of any society lies in the observation and analysis of the insignificant and the mundane .... If you doubt it [i.e. that America is a classed society], consider the sanitary facilities employed in America's three modes of public long-distance transportation: airplanes, trains, and buses.''

Washington, however, not only discovers the historical truth of the ''Chaneysville incident,'' but also that the truth is more complex, more riddling than he had imagined. If part of his character serves as Bradley's mouthpiece, part of him must, finally, be rejected by Bradley, the novelist. Luckily, it is the latter part that matters most, when one has recovered from the racial anger that gives this important novel much of its initial energy.

—Sanford Pinsker

BRADLEY, John Ed

Nationality: American. **Born:** Opelousas, Louisiana, 12 August 1958. **Education:** Louisiana State University, B.A. 1980. **Career:** Staff writer, *Washington Post,* 1983–87; contributing writer, *Washington Post,* 1988–89. Since 1991 contributing editor, *Esquire;* since 1993 contributing writer, *Sports Illustrated.* **Agent:** Esther Newberg,

International Creative Management, 40 West 57th St., New York, New York 10019, U.S.A.

Publications

Novels

Tupelo Nights. New York, Atlantic Monthly Press, and London, Bloomsbury, 1988.
The Best There Ever Was. New York, Atlantic Monthly Press, and London, Bloomsbury, 1990.
Love and Obits. New York, Holt, and London, Bloomsbury, 1992.
Smoke. New York, Holt, 1994.
My Juliet. New York, Doubleday, 2000.

* * *

John Ed Bradley's first novel establishes his niche in the tradition of southern Gothic writers. Emphasis on the grotesque, the macabre, and the excessive pull of environment is predominant. Much of the setting in *Tupelo Nights* features the local cemetery, where the hero's best friend is a gravedigger and where he meets Emma Groves, the love of his life. Emma goes every night to pray at the grave of her infant son. The cemetery motif is constant. John Girlie, the novel's antihero, works the graveyard shift at a pipeline company, and images of death haunt the book.

Girlie had been an all-America football player at Louisiana State University and had a promising offer to play professional football. Under his domineering mother's influence, however, he returns to his hometown and cannot until late in the novel extricate himself from his oedipal situation.

At times Bradley's plot flirts with melodrama, but this is more than overcome by his keen gift for dialogue and vivid descriptions that are often poetically lyrical. Bradley captures the atmosphere of time and place with persuasive authenticity, totally immersing the reader in the stifling environment and grimness of Girlie's small Louisiana town.

Harold Gravely, the main figure in *The Best There Ever Was*, is a college football coach in his sixties. Almost thirty years ago his team won the national championship. Since then Gravely's teams have had mostly losing seasons, and the students, alumni, and college officials want him to resign. Learning that he has lung cancer, he decides to forego any treatment in the hope that the situation generated by his condition will force the college administration to renew his contract so that he can coach one final year.

The figure of Coach Gravely is drawn with believable and persuasive strokes perfectly conveying his loud, egotistical, and overbearing temperament. As the Old Man, a term he favors, he is a memorable if unpleasant character. Bradley also cleverly uses comedy to satirize the coach and emphasize the grotesque aspects of the situation. The novel's weakness is that often the descriptions of Gravely and many of the episodes he is involved in become essentially repetitive. The book at times becomes too wordy; too much material is presented. Even after the coach is murdered, many additional pages are devoted to his widow; this leads to a feeble anticlimax.

Joseph Burke, in *Love and Obits*, is a newspaper reporter who has been demoted to writing obituaries. Divorced, Burke lives with his wheelchair-bound father. Although he and his father are on good terms, Joseph is presented as one of the melancholy, lonely men who walk about the city at night looking for something they never had or for something they have lost and will never find again.

Burke's father, Woody, takes on more cheerfulness and hope when he falls in love with his day care nurse; Burke himself becomes more positive when he attracts the attention of widow Laura Vannoy. Burke had written the obituary article about her prominent husband, so even love is entwined with death. At the book's end, Woody, in an epiphany of love, performs a Christ-like action of feeding his fisherman's catch to the poor.

Smoke is both a continuation of previous characteristics of Bradley's work and a worrisome development, which was present on occasion in the earlier books. Smoke is a small town in Louisiana where Jay Carnihan's goal is to kidnap Monster Mart's founder, billionaire Rayford Holly, and require him to apologize for forcing so many downtown stores in America out of business. Kidnapped on one of his nationwide inspection trips, Holly proves to be an exceedingly lovable, down-to-earth individual who even pitches in as a short order cook at the lunch counter of Carnihan's small store.

Again, Bradley demonstrates his gifted talent for recording dialogue and lively characterization, but the narrative becomes too far-fetched. There comes a point when a tall tale can become too tall, when a novel can sprawl to an excessive degree, and when even an admirable talent can be overwhelmed by too many episodes, too many words, too drawn out a plot, and an unconvincing conclusion. As in *The Best There Ever Was*, Bradley does not seem to know when to stop, and melodrama and sentimentality predominate. Even the theme of love over death, which was so effectively presented in *Love and Obits*, becomes mawkish and cloying in *Smoke*.

Bradley is a considerable talent in handling dialogue and characterization, but he must temper plot excesses and a tendency to overelaborate a narrative.

—Paul A. Doyle

BRAGG, Melvyn

Nationality: British. **Born:** Carlisle, Cumberland, 6 October 1939. **Education:** Nelson-Thomlinson Grammar School, Wigton, Cumberland, 1950–58; Wadham College, Oxford, 1958–61, M.A. (honours) in modern history 1961. **Family:** Married 1) Marie-Elisabeth Roche in 1961 (died 1971), one daughter; 2) Catherine Mary Haste in 1973, one daughter and one son. **Career:** With BBC Television and Radio from 1961: general trainee, 1961–62; producer on *Monitor,* 1963; for BBC 2 editor on *New Release* (later *Review,* then *Arena*), *Writers World,* and *Take It or Leave It,* 1964–70; presenter, *In the Picture,* Tyne Tees Television, Newcastle-upon-Tyne, 1971, *Second House,* 1973–77, and *Read All About It,* 1976–77, BBC, London. Since 1978 editor and presenter, *South Bank Show;* Head of Arts, 1982–90, and since 1990 Controller of Arts, London Weekend Television; since 1988 presenter, *Start the Week,* BBC Radio 4. Chairman, Border Television, Carlisle. Since 1969 member, and chairman, 1977–80, Arts Council Literature Panel; president, Northern Arts, 1983–87, and National Campaign for the Arts since 1986. **Awards:** Writers Guild award, for screenplay, 1966; Rhys Memorial prize, 1968; Northern Arts Association prose award, 1970; Silver Pen award, 1970; Broadcasting Guild award, 1984; Ivor Novello award, for musical, 1985; BAFTA Dimbleby award, 1987; W. H. Smith Literary Award, 2000. D.Litt.: University of Liverpool, 1986; University of Lancaster, 1990; D.Univ.: Open University, Milton Keynes, Buckinghamshire, 1988. Fellow, Royal Society of Literature, 1970, and Royal Television Society; Honorary Fellow, Lancashire Polytechnic; Domus Fellow, St. Catherine's College, Oxford, 1990. Received the title of lord from Prime Minister Tony Blair, 1998. **Address:** 12 Hampstead Hill Gardens, London N.W.3., England.

PUBLICATIONS

Novels

For Want of a Nail. London, Secker and Warburg, and New York, Knopf, 1965.
The Second Inheritance. London, Secker and Warburg, 1966; New York, Knopf, 1967.
Without a City Wall. London, Secker and Warburg, 1968; New York, Knopf, 1969.
The Cumbrian Trilogy. London, Coronet, 1984.
The Hired Man. London, Secker and Warburg, 1969; New York, Knopf, 1970.
A Place in England. London, Secker and Warburg, 1970; New York, Knopf, 1971.
Kingdom Come. London, Secker and Warburg, 1980.
The Nerve. London, Secker and Warburg, 1971.
The Hunt. London, Secker and Warburg, 1972.
Josh Lawton. London, Secker and Warburg, and New York, Knopf, 1972.
The Silken Net. London, Secker and Warburg, and New York, Knopf, 1974.
Autumn Manoeuvres. London, Secker and Warburg, 1978.
Love and Glory. London, Secker and Warburg, 1983.
The Maid of Buttermere. London, Hodder and Stoughton, and New York, Putnam, 1987.
A Time to Dance. London, Hodder and Stoughton, 1990; Boston, Little Brown, 1991.
Crystal Rooms. London, Hodder and Stoughton, 1992.
Credo. London, Sceptre, 1996.
The Sword and the Miracle. New York, Random House, 1996.
The Soldier's Return. London, Sceptre, 1999.

Fiction (for children)

A Christmas Child. London, Secker and Warburg, 1976.

Uncollected Short Story

''The Initiation,'' in *Winter's Tales 18,* edited by A.D. Maclean. London, Macmillan, and New York, St. Martin's Press, 1972.

Plays

Mardi Gras, music by Alan Blaikley and Ken Howard (produced London, 1976).
The Hired Man, adaptation of his own novel, music and lyrics by Howard Goodall (produced Southampton and London, 1984). London, French, 1986.

Screenplays: *Play Dirty,* with Lotte Colin, 1968; *Isadora* with Clive Exton and Margaret Drabble, 1969; *The Music Lovers,* 1970; *Jesus Christ Superstar,* with Norman Jewison, 1973; *The Seventh Seal,* 1993.

Radio Play: *Robin Hood,* 1971.

Television Plays: *The Debussy File,* with Ken Russell, 1965; *Charity Begins at Home,* 1970; *Zinotchka,* 1972; *Orion,* music by Ken Howard and Alan Blaikley, 1977; *Clouds of Glory,* with Ken Russell, 1978.

Other

Speak for England: An Essay on England 1900–1975. London, Secker and Warburg, 1976; revised edition, London, Coronet, 1978; as *Speak for England: An Oral History of England 1900–1975,* New York, Knopf, 1977.
Land of the Lakes. London, Secker and Warburg, 1983; New York, Norton, 1984.
Laurence Olivier. London, Hutchinson, 1984; New York, St. Martin's Press, 1985.
Rich: The Life of Richard Burton. London, Hodder and Stoughton, 1988; as *Richard Burton: A Life,* Boston, Little Brown, 1989.
(With Ruth Gardiner). *On Giant's Shoulders: Great Scientists and Their Discoveries: From Archimedes to DNA.* New York, Wiley, 1998.
Editor, *My Favourite Stories of Lakeland.* Guildford, Surrey, Lutterworth Press, 1981.
Editor, *Cumbria in Verse.* London, Secker and Warburg, 1984.

*

Melvyn Bragg comments:

(1972) The ways in which I came to write are sketched in the last chapters of *A Place in England*: they are made the notions of a fictional self—Douglas Tallentire.

Present ideas on fiction are represented in the novel *The Nerve* and in an essay ''Class and the Novel'' in *Times Literary Supplement* (London), 15 October 1971.

* * *

Melvyn Bragg began his writing career with two good novels about wasted human potential, *For Want of a Nail* and *The Second Inheritance*. But it was *Without a City Wall* which secured for him a deserved reputation as one of the best contemporary novelists. Theme and structure reinforce each other as Bragg traces, first, the awakening of passion in Richard Godwin, a self-imposed exile from the chaos of London, for Janice Beattie, a Cumberland girl of unusual intelligence and powerful ambition; and then the challenges that the life of consummated passion entails for both of them. The drama develops principally from Janice whose ambition and fastidiousness prove stronger than sexual passion or her sense of responsibility to others. Her passion for Richard contracts, while his for her continues to expand. Richard is driven to the brink of self-destruction, but recoils in time to force Janice to some kind of modus vivendi between the claims of his passion and the claims of her individuality. *The*

Silken Net also develops the theme of sexual struggle. This book focuses on a restless intellectual, Rosemary Lewis, whose energy alienates her from life in the Cumberland village of Thurston. Her vigor is admirable but her egoism is destructive as she attempts to breed in her husband the same intensities that motivate her. The resulting conflict registers with less authority, however, than that developed in *Without a City Wall.*

The alternation of intensity and apathy in the passional life is again one subject explored in *The Hired Man.* Covering the years 1898 to 1920 in the life of John and Emily Tallentire, the novel articulates the nuances of their emotions. Communication between a man and a woman becomes a function of the body; and estrangement develops when perfect physical accord is broken. After Emily's death, at the age of 40, John is back where he was at the beginning, a man for casual hire on the great farms but now with all his zest gone. Bragg's artistry is at its best in his honest portrayal of the hard lives of agricultural laborers in the early 20th century. The protagonist of *A Place in England* is Joseph Tallentire, John's son. Bragg is less close to Joseph than to John; in fact, the most memorable pages of the novel feature the now patriarchal John. After much struggle Joseph is able to ''be his own man'' as owner of a public house; but his success is undercut by the disintegration of his marriage, a loss to him for which he cannot account.

Kingdom Come reveals much of the power found in *The Hired Man* and has much interest for the modern reader, as Bragg presents the contemporary generation of the Tallentire men. Lester, a con man and cousin, and Douglas, the son of Joseph and a writer of talent, lack the purposefulness and inner strength of their ancestors, though Harry, the adopted son who stays in Thurston, retains these qualities in large part. Douglas is the sympathetically presented protagonist who can neither be satisfied with the stern ancestral morality nor get clear of the claims of responsibility which derive from it. His divided nature defeats him because it leads him to betray the woman he loves and whose real worth he realizes too late.

In two other novels Bragg has again had recourse to Cumberland and its people. In *Josh Lawton,* a moving parable, Lawton has overtones of a Biblical patriarch and suffers the predictable fate of those who are too good for this world. In *Autumn Manoeuvres* Bragg traces the destructive and self-destructive career of Gareth Johnson. His violent loathing of his stepfather and his own violent self-loathing are linked to the violence of his begetting (his mother had been gang raped in World War I). Is he the victim of fatality or is he his own victim? (more the second than the first, Bragg implies).

London figures more than Cumberland in *The Nerve* and *Love and Glory.* In *The Nerve* Bragg traces, in a first-person narrative, the stages in the mental breakdown of his protagonist, Ted. Power accrues when Ted, the narrator, actualizes some of his experiences of physical and mental pain, but the breakdown which is a ''breakthrough'' is not precisely characterized. In *Love and Glory* Bragg explores the various forms of love from self-serving passion to selfless devotion. The conflict centers on the relationship between Ian Grant, an actor of genius, and Caroline, his Scottish mistress, who loves him with greater devotion than he can reciprocate. The central character is a writer for television, Willie Armstrong, who is Grant's best friend. He comes to love Caroline to distraction but gives her up when she fails to respond to his advances and when he realizes the claims of his wife, Joanna, upon him. Willie thus gains in insight and understanding while Ian Grant retrogresses spiritually and becomes even more submerged in his egotism.

The immediacy of Bragg's Cumberland milieu is, at least superficially, the quality that impresses most in his fiction. As in Thomas Hardy and D.H. Lawrence, milieu is integrally fused with the fortunes and development of the characters. Like Hardy he has in unusual degree insight into human beings who confront the elemental realities of nature, and like Hardy's his people encounter problems difficult to resolve when they lose rapport with nature. The protagonist of *The Soldier's Return,* coming home in 1946 from years spent fighting in the jungles of Burma, finds himself alienated from his wife and family. With *The Sword and the Miracle,* inspired by his discovery of a sign to St. Bega in Cumbria, the author went back some thirteen hundred years for a tale of seventh-century Ireland. Bragg's eye for detail, his compelling sense of drama, his penetration into the emotional and psychic life of his characters, his sense of the moral verities, and his supple and luminous prose have all contributed to his standing as a distinguished novelist.

—Frederick P.W. McDowell

BRATA, Sasthi

Nationality: British. **Born:** Sasthibrata Chakravarti in Calcutta, India, 16 July 1939. **Education:** Calcutta Boys School; Presidency College, Calcutta University. **Family:** Married Pamela Joyce Radcliffe (divorced). **Career:** Has worked in Europe as a lavatory attendant, kitchen porter, barman, air-conditioning engineer, and postman, and in New York as a freelance journalist; London columnist, *Statesman,* 1977–80. **Awards:** Arts Council grant, 1979. **Agent:** Barbara Lowenstein, 250 West 57th Street, Suite 701, New York, New York 10107, U.S.A. **Address:** 33 Savernake Road, London NW3 2JU, England.

PUBLICATIONS

Novels

Confessions of an Indian Woman Eater. London, Hutchinson, 1971; as *Confessions of an Indian Lover,* New Delhi, Sterling, 1973.
She and He. New Delhi, Orient, 1973.
The Sensuous Guru: The Making of a Mystic President. New Delhi, Sterling, 1980.

Short Stories

Encounter. New Delhi, Orient, 1978.

Poetry

Eleven Poems. New Delhi, Blue Moon, 1960.

Other

My God Died Young (autobiography). London, Hutchinson, and New York, Harper, 1968.
A Search for Home (autobiography). New Delhi, Orient, 1975.

Astride Two Worlds: Traitor to India. New Delhi, B.I. Publications, 1976; as *Traitor to India: A Search for Home,* London, Elek, 1976.
Labyrinths in the Lotus Land (on India). New York, Morrow, 1985.
India: The Perpetual Paradox. London, Tauris, 1986.

*

Sasthi Brata comments:

(1991) My first published book, *My God Died Young*, was a self-professed autobiography, written at the age of 28, before I had made any kind of a name for myself as a writer, or anything else. This led a good few publishers, readers, and finally critics to utter the exasperated cry: "What makes you think that the story of your life (woefully unlived-in up to that time) deserves to be told? Or that people will want to read it?" The answer to these questions was within the book itself, of course. But in a sense *all* of my writing, fiction, non-fiction, and journalism, has been an attempt to refute the assumptions lurking behind those superficially plausible and innocent-sounding queries. For they presume that only the heroic and the grand deserve artistic exploration and autobiographical treatment. While I believe, very firmly, that everyone, but everyone has *a* story to tell. The difference between the true artist and the pub bore is that the writer has a sure grasp over the instruments of his trade—words, sentences, paragraphs, syntax, metaphor, melody—and is then able to select, assemble, and present a somewhat more ordered and appetizing version of the world than the chaotic, often repetitive jumble of experiences from external reality which make up his raw material.

All my fiction has been supremely autobiographical. Even in those books which are listed as non-fiction on library shelves, I have used fictional devices, and equally freely introduced reportage techniques in books which profess to be novels. I should warn the prospective reader however not to deduce from this that every hero in every one of my novels is an exactly congruent picture of the man I am. In a review of the late Yukio Mishima's novels I wrote: "The obsessionally autobiographical writer may be an invisible man." For while he may not be telling lies, he is not necessarily telling the *truth* either, at least not of the kind the law courts would accept. Since he is an artist, he *has* used his imagination, but he has not necessarily let you into the secret of where the fictive imagination begins or where empirically verifiable reality ends.

There was a time when I used to be irked by attacks on the high sexual content in my writing. I am no longer. Few addicts of hardcore porn would find any of my books satisfactory. Prurient sensibilities, with a cavalier indifference to style and linguistic resonances, might equally be put off by their subject matter. Apologies to neither group.

I would call myself a "radical traditionalist" as a novelist, if only because to be a successful "experimental" writer, in the sense that Joyce and Borges are, requires a poetic sensibility I do not possess. It is easy to descend into the wholly bogus or deliberately pedantic in trying to achieve effects about which one is not totally sure. There are no rules in the use of language of course, but I would rather stick within certain wide but strictly defined limits, than stray into those unexplored territories where the arcane, obscure, or simply fraudulent vendors ply their wares. I believe that all my books can be read simply as good tales.

Labyrinths in the Lotus Land was my first commissioned work. I wrote it specifically for a Western audience. It was an ambitious attempt to inform a western reader, within the compass of a single book, everything that he or she might wish to know about the country, spanning the whole gamut of history, religion, art, politics, etc. Critics who complained about the apparent incongruity of introducing *personal* experiences into a book which purports to portray a picture of contemporary India were not aware of my long-held belief that by relating a particular incident or episode in a graphic and authentic manner, the universal is illuminated more poignantly than any amount of dry didactic scholarship can ever do.

* * *

Most of Sasthi Brata's books are written in the first person, and all his heroes seem to be modeled after the novelist himself. The hero is always a Bengali Brahmin, from a well-to-do family, who lives in Calcutta and studies physics at college. He leaves home in protest after the girl of his choice is married off to someone whom her parents have chosen. He drifts into a number of jobs, including journalism, and finally establishes himself comfortably in Hampstead. His chief hobby is haunting pubs. The narrator of his first novel, *Confessions of an Indian Woman Eater*, differs only in name from the narrator of the autobiographies *My God Died Young* and *Astride Two Worlds*. The physical characteristics remain the same, even if the hero is Zamir Ishmael of *She and He*: he is dark, of medium height, with dark eyes and an attractive smile; his success with women is unlimited. Brata's books are quite readable; his style is racy and adequate for his purpose, which is generally limited to describing the exploits of his hero in bed. The exception is *Astride Two Worlds*, the second part of his autobiography, which touches upon many serious topics like racial discrimination in Britain, the involvement of the Indian government in the guerrilla activities of the Mukti Bahini in Bangladesh in 1971, and the growing disillusionment of the young with established politicians in India. A couple of chapters, written in the third person, serve to give a proper perspective to this autobiography.

Brata's best selling novel, *Confessions of an Indian Woman Eater*, begins where his first book, *My God Died Young*, an autobiography, let off: Amit Ray, like Sasthi Brata, runs away from his Calcutta home. Amit recounts his varied sexual experiences in a number of capitals—New Delhi, Rome, London, Paris, Copenhagen. He finally ends up in Hampstead with a steady job, and becomes a successful writer. For a certain readership the chief attraction of the book would lie in the step-by-step accounts of copulation, found almost every ten pages. The next novel, *She and He*, has a hero born of an Arab father and a French mother; he is at home in England and lands a good job because he can speak the language with the proper accent. He always talks about writing the "Great English Novel," but does nothing about it until one of his ex-girlfriends sends him an unfinished novel, having written her side of the story, with blank pages for the hero to fill in. The first person account of Zamir alternating with the third person narrative of Sally is an interesting stylistic innovation, but the hero's mindless drifting from bed to bed is ultimately boring.

The Sensuous Guru: The Making of a Mystic President, perhaps the most imaginative of Brata's works, recounts the rise of Ram Chukker (short for Ram Chakravarti, just as Sasthi Brata is the shortened form of Sasthibrata Chakravarti). Chukker initially sets himself up as a Guru in New York, and makes a good living. He writes a short autobiographical novel, *The Making of a Guru,* which outdoes the worst that America can produce in pornography. Through high-pressure promotion with the help of an influential literary agent Chukker wins the Pulitzer Prize, is nominated for the Nobel Prize, manages one for Peace, and is ultimately elected President of the United States.

Brata has also published a collection of stories; most of them are like his novels (some have appeared, with modifications, as chapters in his novels). One very good story is ''Smiles among the Bric-a-Brac,'' about a young Oxford graduate from a rich English family, comfortably settling down to the girl and the job his parents have chosen for him, though he earlier loves the beautiful Nina Fernandez, of mixed parentage. The first person account, with the hero justifying the way he drops Nina, is a beautiful psychological study of the hero's lack of principles. It is significant that Robert Lomax, from an old English family, is very different from the usual Bengali hero. One feels that Brata could write better fiction, especially if he got rid of his autobiographical obsession.

—Shyamala A. Narayan

BRINK, André (Philippus)

Nationality: South African. **Born:** Vrede, Orange Free State, 29 May 1935. **Education:** Lydenburg High School; Potchefstroom University, Transvaal, B.A. 1955, M.A. in English 1958, M.A. in Afrikaans and Dutch 1959; the Sorbonne, Paris, 1959–61. **Family:** Married 1) Estelle Naudé in 1959 (divorced), one son; 2) Salomi Louw in 1965 (divorced), one son; 3) Alta Miller in 1970 (divorced), one son and one daughter; 4) Marésa de Beer in 1990. **Career:** Lecturer, 1963–73, senior lecturer, 1974–75, associate professor, 1976–79, and professor, 1980–90, Department of Afrikaans and Dutch Literature, Rhodes University, Grahamstown. Since 1991 professor of English, University of Cape Town. Editor, *Sestiger* magazine, Pretoria, 1963–65; *Standpunte* magazine, Cape Town, 1986–87. President, Afrikaans Writers Guild, 1978–80. **Awards:** Geerligs prize, 1964; CNA award, 1965, 1979, 1983; South African Academy award, for translation, 1970; Médicis étranger prize (France), 1980; Martin Luther King Memorial prize (UK), 1980. D.Litt.: Rhodes University, 1975; University of the Witwatersrand, Johannesburg, 1985. Chevalier, Legion of Honour (France), 1982; Commander, Order of Arts and Letters (France), 1992. **Agent:** Ruth Liepman, Maienburgweg 23, Zurich, Switzerland. **Address:** Department of English, University of Cape Town, Private Bag, Rondebosch 7700, South Africa.

Publications

Novels

Die gebondenes. Johannesburg, Afrikaanse Pers, 1959.
Die eindelose weë. Cape Town, Tafelberg, 1960.
Lobola vir die lewe (Dowry for Life). Cape Town, Human & Rousseau, 1962.
Die ambassadeur. Cape Town, Human & Rousseau, 1963; as *The Ambassador,* Johannesburg, CNA, 1964; London, Faber, 1985; New York, Summit, 1986; as *File on a Diplomat,* London, Longman, 1967.
Orgie (Orgy). Cape Town, Malherbe, 1965.
Miskien nooit: 'n Somerspel. Cape Town, Human & Rousseau, 1967.
Kennis van die aand. Cape Town, Buren, 1973; as *Looking on Darkness,* London, W.H. Allen, 1974; New York, Morrow, 1975.
An Instant in the Wind. London, W.H. Allen, 1976; New York, Morrow, 1977.
Rumours of Rain. London, W.H. Allen, and New York, Morrow, 1978.
A Dry White Season. London, W.H. Allen, 1979; New York, Morrow, 1980.
A Chain of Voices. London, Faber, and New York, Morrow, 1982.
The Wall of the Plague. London, Faber, 1984; New York, Summit, 1985.
States of Emergency. London, Faber, 1988; New York, Summit, 1989.
An Act of Terror. London, Secker and Warburg, 1991.
The First Life of Adamastor. London, Secker and Warburg, and New York, Summit, 1993.
On the Contrary. London, Secker and Warburg, 1993; New York, Little Brown, 1994.
Imaginings of Sand. New York, Harcourt Brace, 1996.
Devil's Valley. New York, Harcourt Brace, 1999.
The Rights of Desire. London, Secker & Warburg, 2000.

Short Stories and Novellas

Die meul teen die hang. Cape Town, Tafelberg, 1958.
Rooi, with others. Cape Town, Malherbe, 1965.
Oom Kootjie Emmer. Cape Town, Buren, 1973.
'n Emmertjie wyn: 'n versameling dopstories. Cape Town, Saayman & Weber, 1981.
Oom Kootjie Emmer en die nuwe bedeling: 'n stinkstorie. Johannesburg, Taurus, 1983.
Loopdoppies: Nog dopstories. Cape Town, Saayman & Weber, 1984.
Die Eerste lewe van Adamastor. Cape Town, Saayman & Weber, 1988.

Plays

Die band om ons harte (The Bond Around Our Hearts). Johannesburg, Afrikaanse Pers, 1959.
Caesar (in verse; produced Stellenbosch, Cape Province, 1965). Cape Town, Nasionale, 1961.
Die beskermengel en ander eenbedrywe (The Guardian Angel and Other One-Act Plays), with others. Cape Town, Tafelberg, 1962.
Bagasie (Baggage; includes *Die koffer, Die trommel, Die tas*; produced Pretoria, 1965). Cape Town, Tafelberg, 1965.
Elders mooiweer en warm (Elsewhere Fair and Warm; produced Bloemfontein, 1969). Cape Town, Malherbe, 1965.
Die verhoor (The Trial; produced Pretoria, 1975). Cape Town, Human & Rousseau, 1970.
Die rebelle (The Rebels). Cape Town, Human & Rousseau, 1970.
Kinkels innie kabel (Knots in the Cable), adaptation of *Much Ado About Nothing* by Shakespeare. Cape Town, Buren, 1971.
Afrikaners is plesierig (Afrikaners Make Merry). Cape Town, Human & Rousseau, 1973.
Pavane (produced Pretoria, 1980). Cape Town, Human & Rousseau, 1974.
Bobaas van die Boendoe, adapted from Synge's *Playboy of the Western World* (produced Bloemfontein, 1974). Cape Town, Human & Rousseau, 1974.

Die Hamer van die hekse (The Hammer of the Witches). Cape Town, Tafelberg, 1976.

Toiings op die langpad (Toiings on the Long Road). Pretoria, Van Schaik, 1979.

Other

Die bende (The Gang; for children). Johannesburg, Afrikaanse Pers, 1961.

Platsak (Broke; for children). Johannesburg, Afrikaanse Pers, 1962.

Orde en chaos: 'n Studie oor Germanicus en die tragedies van Shakespeare (Order and Chaos: A Study of *Germanicus* and the Tragedies of Shakespeare). Cape Town, Nasionale, 1962.

Pot-pourri: Sketse uit Parys (Pot-pourri: Sketches from Paris). Cape Town, Human & Rousseau, 1962.

Die verhaal van Julius Caesar (for children). Cape Town, Human & Rousseau, 1963.

Sempre diritto: Italiaanse reisjoernaal (Sempre diritto: Italian Travel Journal). Johannesburg, Afrikaanse Pers, 1963.

Olé: Reisboek oor Spanje (Olé: A Travel Book on Spain). Cape Town, Human & Rousseau, 1965.

Aspekte van die nuwe prosa (Aspects of the New Fiction). Pretoria, Academica, 1967; revised edition, 1969, 1972, 1975.

Parys-Parys: Retoer (Paris-Paris: Return). Cape Town, Human & Rousseau, 1969.

Midi: Op reis deur Suid-Frankryk (Midi: Travelling Through the South of France). Cape Town, Human & Rousseau, 1969.

Fado: 'n reis deur Noord-Portugal (Fado: A Journey Through Northern Portugal). Cape Town, Human & Rousseau, 1970.

Die poësie van Breyten Breytenbach (The Poetry of Breyten Breytenbach). Pretoria, Academica, 1971.

Portret van die vrou as 'n meisie (Portrait of Woman as a Young Girl). Cape Town, Buren, 1973.

Aspekte van die nuwe drama (Aspects of the New Drama). Pretoria, Academica, 1974.

Brandewyn in Suid-Afrika. Cape Town, Buren, 1974; as *Brandy in South Africa,* 1974.

Dessertwyn in Suid-Afrika. Cape Town, Buren, 1974; as *Dessert Wine in South Africa,* 1974.

Die Klap van die meul (A Stroke from the Mill). Cape Town, Buren, 1974.

Die Wyn van bowe (The Wine from Up There). Cape Town, Buren, 1974.

Ik ben er geweest: Gesprekken in Zuid-Afrika (I've Been There: Conversations in South Africa), with others. Kampen, Kok, 1974.

Voorlopige rapport: Beskouings oor die Afrikaanse literatuur van sewentig (Preliminary Report: Views on Afrikaans Literature in the 1970s). Cape Town, Human & Rousseau, 1976; *Tweede voorlopige rapport* (Second Preliminary Report), 1980.

Jan Rabie se 21. Cape Town, Academica, 1977.

Why Literature?/Waarom literatur? Grahamstown, Rhodes University, 1980.

Heildronk uit Wynboer saamgestel deur AB ter viering van die blad se 50ste bestaansjaar. Cape Town, Tafelberg, 1981.

Die fees van die malles. Cape Town, Saayman & Weber, 1981.

Mapmakers: Writing in a State of Siege. London, Faber, 1983; as *Writing in a State of Siege,* New York, Summit, 1984.

Literatuur in die strydperk (Literature in the Arena). Cape Town, Human & Rousseau, 1985.

Editor, *Oggendlied: 'n bundel vir Uys Krige op sy verjaardag 4 Februarie 1977.* Cape Town, Human & Rousseau, 1977.

Editor, *Klein avontuur,* by Top Naeff. Pretoria, Academica, 1979.

Editor, with J.M. Coetzee, *A Land Apart: A South African Reader.* London, Faber, 1986; New York, Viking, 1987.

Translator, *Die brug oor die rivier Kwaï,* by Pierre Boulle. Cape Town, Tafelberg, 1962.

Translator, *Reisigers na die Groot Land,* by André Dhôtel. Cape Town, Tafelberg, 1962.

Translator, *Die wonderhande,* by Joseph Kessel. Cape Town, HAUM, 1962.

Translator, *Nuno, die visserseun,* by L.N. Lavolle. Cape Town, HAUM, 1962.

Translator, *Verhale uit Limousin,* by Léonce Bourliaguet. Cape Town, Human & Rousseau, 1963.

Translator, *Die slapende berg,* by Léonce Bourliaguet. Cape Town, Human & Rousseau, 1963.

Translator, *Land van die Farao's,* by Leonard Cottrell. Cape Town, Malherbe, 1963.

Translator, *Die bos van Kokelunde,* by Michel Rouzé. Cape Town, Malherbe, 1963.

Translator, *Moderato Cantabile,* by Marguerite Duras. Cape Town, HAUM, 1963.

Translator, *Die goue kruis,* by Paul-Jacques Bonzon. Cape Town, Malherbe, 1963.

Translator, *Land van die Twee Riviere,* by Leonard Cottrell. Cape Town, Malherbe, 1964.

Translator, *Volke van Afrika,* by C.M. Turnbull. Cape Town, Malherbe, 1964.

Translator, *Alice se avonture in Wonderland,* by Lewis Carroll. Cape Town, Human & Rousseau, 1965.

Translator, *Die mooiste verhale uit die Arabiese Nagte.* Cape Town, Human & Rousseau, 1966.

Translator, *Die avonture van Don Quixote,* retold by James Reeves. Cape Town, HAUM, 1966.

Translator, *Ek was Cicero,* by Elyesa Bazna. Johannesburg, Afrikaanse Pers, 1966.

Translator, *Koning Babar,* by Jean de Brunhoff. Cape Town, Human & Rousseau, 1966.

Translator, *Die Swerfling,* by Colette. Johannesburg, Afrikaanse Pers, 1966.

Translator, *Die vindingryke ridder, Don Quijote de la Mancha,* by Cervantes. Cape Town, Human & Rousseau, 1966.

Translator, *Speuder Maigret, Maigret en sy dooie, Maigret en die Lang Derm,* and *Maigret en die Spook,* by Simenon. Johannesburg, Afrikaanse Pers, 4 vols., 1966–1969.

Translator, *Die mooiste sprokies van Moeder Gans,* by Charles Perrault. Cape Town, Human & Rousseau, 1967.

Translator, *Die eenspaaier,* by Ester Wier. Cape Town, Human & Rousseau, 1967.

Translator, *Die eendstert* (Brighton Rock), by Graham Greene. Johannesburg, Afrikaanse Pers, 1967.

Translator, *Mary Poppins in Kersieboomlaan,* by P.L. Travers. Cape Town, Malherbe, 1967.

Translator, *Die Leeu, die heks en die hangkas,* by C.S. Lewis. Cape Town, Human & Rousseau, 1967.

Translator, with others, *Die groot boek oor ons dieremaats.* Cape Town, Human & Rousseau, 1968.

Translator, with others, *Koning Arthur en sy ridders van die Ronde Tafel.* Cape Town, Human & Rousseau, 1968.

Translator, *Die Kinders van Groenkop,* by Lucy Boston. Cape Town, Human & Rousseau, 1968.

Translator, *Alice deur die spieël,* by Lewis Carroll. Cape Town, Human & Rousseau, 1968.

Translator, *Die Botsende rotse, Die Bul in die doolhoof, Die Horing van ivoor,* and *Die Kop van de gorgoon,* by Ian Serraillier. Cape Town, HAUM, 4 vols., 1968.

Translator, *Bontnek,* by Dhan Gopal Mukerji. Cape Town, HAUM, 1968.

Translator, *Die Draai van die skroef* (The Turn of the Screw), by Henry James. Johannesburg, Afrikaanse Pers, 1968.

Translator, *Die Gelukkige prins en ander sprokies,* by Oscar Wilde. Cape Town, Human & Rousseau, 1969.

Translator (into Afrikaans), *Richard III,* by Shakespeare. Cape Town, Human & Rousseau, 1969.

Translator, *Die Gestewelde kat,* by Charles Perrault. Cape Town, Human & Rousseau, 1969.

Translator, *Die groot golf,* by Pearl S. Buck. Cape Town, Human & Rousseau, 1969.

Translator, *Die Nagtegaal,* by H.C. Andersen. Cape Town, HAUM, 1969.

Translator, *Die Terroriste,* by Camus. Johannesburg, Dramatiese Artistieke en Letterkundige Organisasie, 1970.

Translator, *Eskoriaal,* by Michel De Ghelderode. Johannesburg, Dramatiese Artistieke en Letterkundige Organisasie, 1971.

Translator, *Ballerina,* by Nada Ćurčija-Prodanović. Cape Town, Malherbe, 1972.

Translator, *Die Seemeeu* (The Seagull), by Chekhov. Cape Town, Human & Rousseau, 1972.

Translator, *Die Bobaas van die Boendoe* (The Playboy of the Western World), by Synge. Cape Town, Human & Rousseau, 1973.

Translator, *Jonathan Livingston Seemeeu,* by Richard Bach. Cape Town, Malherbe, 1973.

Translator, *Hedda Gabler,* by Ibsen. Cape Town, Human & Rousseau, 1974.

Translator, *Die Wind in die wilgers,* by Kenneth Grahame. Cape Town, Human & Rousseau, 1974.

Translator, *Die Tragedie van Romeo en Juliet,* by Shakespeare. Cape Town, Human & Rousseau, 1975.

Translator, *Die Tierbrigade,* and *Nuwe avontuur van die Tierbrigade,* by Claude Desailly. Cape Town, Tafelberg, 2 vols., 1978–1979.

Translator, *Die Nagtegaal en die roos,* by Oscar Wilde. Cape Town, Human & Rousseau, 1980.

Translator, *Rot op reis,* by Kenneth Grahame. Cape Town, Human & Rousseau, 1981.

Translator, *Adam van die pad,* by Elizabeth Janet Gray. Cape Town, Human & Rousseau, 1981.

Translator, *Klein Duimpie,* by Charles Perrault. Cape Town, Human & Rousseau, 1983.

27 April: One Year Later/Een jaar later (editor). Pretoria, South Africa, Queillerie, 1995.

Destabilising Shakespeare. Grahamstown, South Africa, Shakespeare Society of Southern Africa, 1996.

The Novel: Language and Narrative from Cervantes to Calvino. New York, New York University Press, 1998.

Reinventing a Continent: Writing and Politics in South Africa. Cambridge, Massachusetts, Zoland Books, 1998.

*

Manuscript Collections: University of the Orange Free State, Bloemfontein; National English Literary Museum, Grahamstown.

Critical Studies: *Donker Weerlig: Literêre opstelle oor die werk van André P. Brink* edited by Jan Senekal, Cape Town, Jutalit, 1988; ''The Lives of Adamastor'' by Anthony J. Hassall, in *International Literature in English* edited by Pobert L. Ross, London and Chicago, St. James Press, 1991; *Colonization, Violence, and Narration in White South African Writing: André Brink, Breyten, Breytenbach, and J.M. Coetzee* by Rosemary Jane Jolly, Athens, Ohio University Press, 1996.

André Brink comments:

(1996) My early work revealed the influence of existentialism (notably of Camus) and was largely a matter of technical exploration. Ever since a year-long stay in Paris in 1968 a deep awareness of the responsibility of the novelist towards his society has shaped my work: not in the sense of ''using'' the novel for propaganda purposes, which degrades literature, but as a profound evaluation of social and interpersonal relationships as they affect the individual: the individual doomed to solitude and to more or less futile attempts to break out of this spiritual ''apartheid'' by trying to touch others—which means that the sexual experience is of primary importance to my characters.

With the dismantling of apartheid there is a new freedom to broaden the scope of my writing and to explore the possibilities of an African magic realism.

* * *

André Brink is an Afrikaner dissident who chose to remain inside the South African apartheid society which he regarded as morally insupportable. His powerful political and historical novels have been translated into 20 languages, while in South Africa he is regarded with a somewhat sceptical eye by writers and academics alike.

Brink is a prodigious, multi-talented literary figure. In addition to plays, travel writing, and critical work, he has written 16 novels and translated a great many works into Afrikaans. Formerly a professor of Afrikaans literature at Rhodes University, he now occupies a chair in English literature at the University of Cape Town. Despite three nominations for the Nobel Prize for literature, Brink is disliked by many Afrikaans writers and critics in South Africa, not so much (or not only) because of his outright moral opposition to apartheid, but for what is regarded as sentimentality and sensationalism in his writing. There is no doubt that Brink's writing is extremely uneven. His novels are almost always flawed in some respect, and they are often overwritten. Also, Brink has a singular penchant for placing gauche and inane statements in the mouths of his characters, while his rendition of sexual experience is often cliché-ridden and tasteless. Yet he has written some of the most powerful stories to emerge in recent South African writing, and he commands impressive narrative skills.

As an emerging Afrikaans novelist in the late 1950s and early 1960s, Brink almost singlehandedly modernised Afrikaans novel-writing. Arguably the most eclectic South African writer at the time, he knocked the conservative Afrikaans literary tradition out of complacency with themes and techniques drawn from writers like Camus, Beckett, Sartre, Nabokov, Henry Miller, Faulkner, Greene, and Durrell. In 1974, the Afrikaner establishment was hit by the sensational news that Brink's *Kennis van die aand*, later translated into English as *Looking on Darkness*, had been banned. The banning created a major division between the State and many of the country's Afrikaans writers, and introduced a new era of increasingly vocal dissidence from within the establishment. After a Supreme Court hearing and a further two appeals, the novel was finally unbanned in 1982, but given an age restriction which is impossible to enforce.

For Brink, expulsion from the laager was an important juncture. Capitalising on sudden international fame as South Africa's first Afrikaans writer to be banned under the country's comprehensive 1963 censorship legislation—usually reserved for girlie calendars, Communist publications, and morally and politically perverse writing in English—Brink translated *Kennis van die aand* into English and became, thenceforth, an international novelist writing in English. He has since produced nine weighty novels, roughly one every two years.

By his own admission Brink remains, in essence, an Afrikaner, but his recent novels are not "translated." Brink maintains that he produces the novels in both languages more or less simultaneously, starting out in Afrikaans, but completing the first "final" draft in English. However, Brink is far more idiomatic and comfortable in Afrikaans, and his English versions sometimes suffer from a certain rigidity of style.

Looking on Darkness is a compelling but uneven novel. As Nadine Gordimer has observed, it suffers from the "defiant exultation and relief" of Brink's first major cry of rebellion. The novel veers recklessly from profound historical reconstruction and metaphoric statement to the slushiest of sexual and emotional scenes. This book tells the story of Joseph Malan, a coloured man and a descendant of slaves who makes good as an actor after winning a grant to study at RADA in London, and who then comes home to launch a full-on cultural assault against apartheid. A passionate love affair with a white (British) woman develops, and Joseph is caught between the impossibility of love across the colour line, and the sinister manoeuvres of the Security Police against his theatre group. In a contrived and somewhat unconvincing denouement, Joseph murders his lover, whereupon the Security Police half kill him in unspeakably brutal fashion. He is sentenced to death, and the narrative is written from the death cell on sheets of paper which (we are asked to believe) Joseph daily flushes down the toilet, so determined is he to escape the scrutiny of his gaolers.

Looking on Darkness sets the pattern for Brink's later novels in several important respects. There is an uncompromising engagement with issues of race and politics, an insistence on exposing the sinister, vicious, and hypocritical elements at the heart of the apartheid system, an ability to rediscover the present in terms of a rich and violent frontier history, and a persistent fictional exploration of sexual love as a framework for a higher form of enquiry into the state of modern existence, subject to the peculiar restraints of apartheid society.

In *An Instant in the Wind*, Brink's first "English" novel following *Looking on Darkness*, a runaway slave escorts an eighteenth-century Cape lady back to civilisation after her husband and their party come to grief in an expedition into the interior. The story is a rich investigation into pertinent South African themes, and has a strong romantic appeal, but the love story between the erstwhile slave and the fallen lady constantly verges on a kind of sentiment more appropriate to popular romance fiction.

However, Brink's best talents come to the fore powerfully in his next—arguably his best—novel, *Rumours of Rain*. Like its successor, *A Dry White Season*, the novel examines the moral options of a contemporary Afrikaner who is rooted to a potent nationalistic history, but who is vulnerable to the short-comings and hypocrisy of Afrikaner nationalism. *Rumours of Rain* achieves remarkable depth and complexity, and contains some of Brink's best characterisation.

The narrative inventiveness of *Rumours of Rain* and *A Dry White Season* is taken further in Brink's other *tour de force, A Chain of Voices*. This is a major novel which fictionalises a slave revolt in the early 19th century in the Cape. Brink gives each of his several characters a narrating voice, and out of the overlapping narratives a story of great force and interlocking complexity emerges. Brink's exceptional ability to re-animate the past—especially that of slavery in South Africa—enables him to establish the recurrent motifs of a frontier history in which South Africa remains confined.

True to form, Brink followed up this success with a work which is thoroughly mediocre. *The Wall of the Plague* is a particularly clumsy attempt at metaphorically associating the Black Death plague of medieval Europe with modern apartheid. The novel degenerates into a lengthy implied debate between three South African expatriates about the merits of exile as opposed to active engagement in the country itself, expressed in terms of black versus white sexual potency (there is a coloured girl in the middle) with a great deal of melodrama and sheer inanity thrown in.

However, Brink's 1988 novel, *States of Emergency*, shows outstanding novelistic deftness. The "story" consists of "notes" towards a love story set in violence-torn South Africa during the State of Emergency in the 1980s. The story skillfully interweaves public and political emergency with the private emergency of conducting an illicit love affair in the midst of ceaseless violence and upheaval. Despite its brilliance, the novel uneasily mixes metafictional self-consciousness with a series of unexamined illusions—principally the illusion that the novel one reads is not a novel at all but incomplete notes for a novel. In a project where every fictional device is brought to the surface for debate, it seems a massive sleight-of-hand—and contrary to the deconstructive spirit in which the writing takes place—not to examine this, the biggest fictional strategy of all. *States of Emergency* is further complicated by the juxtaposition of Brink's actual divorce and his liaison with a young woman, and the metafictional "fabrication" of a similar story in the book: a love affair between a professor and a young colleague. As part of a divorce settlement, the novel was embargoed for distribution in South Africa after its publication.

In *Imaginings of Sand*, Brink tackled a particularly challenging problem for a male writer: portraying the world from a female point of view, in this case through two sisters, Anna and Kristien. Like their creator, they are Afrikaners, and underlying the narrative is a sense that in the "new," post-Apartheid South Africa, the only prevailing ethnic antipathy is toward the descendants of the old Dutch settlers. *Devil's Valley* offers an intriguing spin on the idea of those settlers by depicting a "lost colony" of sorts, an anti-Shangri-La, of unreconstructed Boers living in a mountain redoubt. They are like the Japanese soldier who struggled on in the jungles of the Philippines for three decades after World War II, only to be "captured" in 1975. Brink's Boers, seen through the eyes of reporter Flip Lochner, show little sign of surrendering to the outside world; yet elements of that world are nonetheless encroaching on their alternate version of reality.

—Leon de Kock

BRODBER, Erna (May)

Nationality: Jamaican. **Born:** Woodside, St. Mary, Jamaica, 21 April 1940. **Education:** University College of the West Indies, London, 1960–63, B.A. (honours) in history 1963; University of Washington, Seattle, (Ford Foundation fellowship), 1967; University College of the West Indies, Kingston, M.Sc. in sociology 1968, Ph.D. in history 1985; University of Sussex, (Commonwealth fellowship), 1979. **Family:** One son. **Career:** Lecturer in sociology, University of the West Indies for seven years, research fellow and staff member, Institute of Social and Economic Research, University of the West Indies, 1972–83; associate professor, Randolph-Macon College (DuPont scholar). Visiting scholar, University of Michigan, Ann Arbor, 1973; visiting fellow, University of Sussex, 1981; visiting professor, Gettysburg College, Pennsylvania, Clark-Atlanta University, Georgia, and University of California, Santa Cruz. **Awards:** University of the West Indies postgraduate award, 1964; National Festival award, Jamaica Festival Commission, 1975; Commomwealth Writers Prize for Canada and the Americas, 1989; Fulbright fellowship, 1990. **Address:** Woodside, Pear Tree Grove, P.O. St. Mary/St. Catherine, Jamaica, West Indies.

PUBLICATIONS

Novels

Jane and Louisa Will Soon Come Home. London, New Beacon, 1980.
Myal. London, New Beacon, 1988.
Louisiana. London, New Beacon, 1994; Jackson, University Press of Mississippi, 1997.

Plays

Jane and Louisa Will Soon Come Home, adaptation of her own novel (produced, 1990).

Other

Abandonment of Children in Jamaica. Mona, Jamaica, Institute of Social and Economic Research, University of the West Indies, 1974.
Yards in the City of Kingston. Mona, Jamaica, Institute of Social and Economic Research, University of the West Indies, 1975.
Perceptions of Caribbean Women: Towards a Documentation of Stereotypes. Mona, Jamaica, Institute of Social and Economic Research, University of the West Indies, 1982.
Rural-Urban Migration and the Jamaican Child. Santiago, Chile, UNESCO, Regional Office for Education in Latin America and the Caribbean, 1986.

*

Manuscript Collections: University of the West Indies, Kingston.

Critical Studies: *Healing Narratives: Women Writers Curing Cultural Disease* by Gay Wilent, New Brunswick, New Jersey, Rutgers University Press, 2000.

Theatrical Activities: Actor: **Radio**—*A Time to Remember,* for six years. **Play**—Role in *Eight O'Clock Jamaica Time.*

Erna Brobder comments:

My work, fiction and non-fiction, is devoted to helping Africans of the diaspora to understand themselves and hopefully to consequently undertake with more clarity the job of social (re)construction which we have to do. To better communicate with this target group, I use folk songs, etc., which are well known within the culture to make my points and to inform a group often far from archival data. I inject information which I think this group needs to have, and which I arrive at from my investigations, into my novels.

* * *

Trained as a sociologist, with a Ph.D. and several significant publications on Jamaican society, Erna Brodber has produced fiction that is anything but sociological regurgitation of mundane facts. Instead, in her powerful novels—including *Jane and Louisa Will Soon Come Home, Myal*, and *Louisiana*—Brodber weaves mythic and fantastical elements throughout, establishing non-rational events and happenings as just as crucially implicated in the psychology of her characters as their class, gender, education, or other more conventional factors. The central metaphor of *Jane and Louisa Will Soon Come Home* (1980) is the amorphous kumbla, a magical spell that can both protect and restrict. In *Myal* (1988), a community invokes myalism, the earliest documented Jamaican religion with African roots, to counteract the psychological damage inflicted on a young woman by the circumstances of her life. Finally, the premise of *Louisiana* (1994) is that a voice from the grave dictates into a recording device as a means of communicating with a young anthropologist.

This emphasis on non-Western forms and ways of understanding functions as a challenge to colonial practices and ways of ordering the world, while also valuing traditions that colonialism attempted to eradicate. Furthermore, these traditions are understood in Brodber's fiction to possess transformative potential to heal the psychic damage inflicted by slavery and colonialism, which both enforce erasures of subjectivity and specificity on their victims. In Brodber's novels her young female protagonists invariably must struggle with the variety of erasures and abuses enacted upon their bodies as colonized, racially ''othered'' females. Struggling to liberate themselves from colonial scripts and create new ways of self-(re)presentation, these women rely on their communities to assist them in recovering a past that has been alternately stolen, obscured, or misrepresented. Brodber's representation of historical recuperation as necessary for her characters' healing is in keeping with the project of de-colonization via the deconstructing of the historical methodologies and assumptions utilized in defining the colonial subject.

Brodber's first novel, *Jane and Louisa Will Soon Come Home*, is a coming-of-age story. A non-linear bildungsroman, the narrative shifts back and forth in both Nellie's personal history and that of her family, suggesting that both are crucial in her formation. Originally written as a case history for sociology students, Brodber's novel fails as such for its lack of simple didactic clarity—which is, of course, exactly why it is such a compelling novel. Nellie moves from an understand of herself as an outward construction, perceived, judged, defined by others, to an understanding of herself as an individual and a member of a community. Her previous conduct has been defined by this always-present external eye, resulting in her alienation from her body, her identity, and her people. Brodber's linguistic playfulness throughout the novel heightens this tension of alienation and acceptance, as cool, grammatically impeccable sentences that dislocate the subject must compete with the powers of vernacular speech to convey what is intimate and personal. As a linguistically shifting, heavily signifying, anti-linear work, the novel is a challenge to those accustomed to standard Western narratives, and as such provides a challenge to not only the reading practices of Western culture, but the discursive practices that inform them. Ordering this text, and the origin of the title, is a Jamaican children's song, the type often prematurely dismissed by uninformed listeners as the nonsensical production of those too young to understand meaning. Yet as Brodber demonstrates, that which is enacted upon the child is crucial to the formation of the adult, and children can therefore not be assumed to be uncritical repositories. *Jane and Louisa Will Soon Come Home* is a study of the ramifications of childhood colonial indoctrination and concomitant forms of resistance.

This concern with children as subjects of, and subjected to, colonial discourses is also evident in *Myal*. The novel opens at the beginning of the twentieth century, with a community gathering to heal the mysterious illness of a young woman who has returned to Jamaica after an unsuccessful marriage abroad. The Afro-Jamaican myal, which asserts that good has the power to conquer all, is invoked to heal Ella, who, like Nellie, has been alienated from herself by colonial practices. Ella, who is light skinned enough to pass for white, has suffered a complete breakdown after her white American husband has mounted a black face minstrel show based on the stories of her village and childhood that she has shared with him. This theft, or ''cultural appropriation,'' is just one of a series Ella has encountered in her life, and it parallels the ongoing theft of the labor and culture of colonized peoples for imperial gain and pleasure. In addition to this ongoing exploitation—particularly relevant in terms of U.S.-Jamaican relationships in the early pat of the century—is the attempt to cultivate an audience that is both worshipful of and submissive to British culture. In a series of flashbacks Brodber constructs a historical context for Ella's breakdown, from the sexual exploitation of her mother by an Irish police officer and the colorism present in her village, to her education and informal adoption by a local minister and his white English wife, for whom Ella becomes an anthropological subject. Ella is rewarded with her informal adoption because she has so successfully recited Kipling, and therefore distinguished herself. Yet an older Ella, recovering with the ongoing assistance of her community, becomes a teacher herself and begins to critique the local education system. Forced to teach a story in which the message of submission and resignation to higher authorities is implicit, Ella begins to develop alternative reading strategies, and to teach her students the necessity of always questioning the information with which they are presented, interrogating it for subversive possibilities. In rich, vivid language populated with vital characters, Brodber presents an anti-colonial road map for her own literary mission.

Brodber's third novel, *Louisiana*, continues her investigation of themes of colonial resistance, indigenous ways of knowing, female development, communal forces, and deconstructing colonial imperatives. Returning to the early twentieth-century United States, the novel concerns an anthropologist—again named Ella—of Jamaican extraction. Employed by the Works Progress Administration to record the narratives of elderly blacks, Ella connects with Anna, known as ''Mammy.'' The novel chronicles Ella's unraveling of Mammy's story over two decades, in part through the ghostly communications left by the deceased Mammy on Ella's tape recorder device, in part through research, and eventually through her own ability to hear the voices in her head. What Ella learns is that Mammy's tale is not hers alone: ''It was a tale of cooperative action; it was a community tale.'' The novel also assumes this communal form—the opening is dizzying in its multitude of voices, a transcription of a spirit conversation left behind on the recorder. Serving to disorient the reader and render them sympathetic to Ella's initial confusion, the opening also signals several of Brodber's thematic preoccupations, particularly the necessity of new reading practices, and attuned readers. Even as Ella's life becomes inextricable from Mammy's tale, Ella also re-evaluates her own training as a reader and thinker in addition to how her training as an anthropologist is culturally laden. A novel about preservation and retrieval, *Louisiana* also affirms the importance of transcending the presumptuous divide of investigator/subject, and articulates the desirability of human connection over the objective distance privileged by Western cultures.

—Jennifer Harris

BROOKE-ROSE, Christine

Nationality: British. **Born:** Geneva, Switzerland. **Education:** Somerville College, Oxford, 1946–49, B.A. in English, M.A. 1953; University College, London, 1950–54, B.A. in French, Ph.D. 1954. **Family:** Married Jerzy Peterkiewicz, *q.v.*, in 1948 (divorced 1975). **Career:** Freelance literary journalist, London, 1956–68; Maître de Conférences, 1969–75, and professeur, 1975–88, University of Paris VIII, Vincennes. **Awards:** Society of Authors traveling prize, 1965; James Tait Black Memorial prize, 1967; Arts Council translation prize, 1969. Litt.D.: University of East Anglia, Norwich, 1988. **Address:** c/o Cambridge University Press, P.O. Box 110, Cambridge CB2 3RL, England.

Publications

Novels

The Languages of Love. London, Secker and Warburg, 1957.
The Sycamore Tree. London, Secker and Warburg, 1958; New York, Norton, 1959.
The Dear Deceit. London, Secker and Warburg, 1960; New York, Doubleday, 1961.
The Middlemen: A Satire. London, Secker and Warburg, 1961.
Out. London, Joseph, 1964.
Such. London, Joseph, 1966.
Between. London, Joseph, 1968.
Thru. London, Hamish Hamilton, 1975.
Amalgamemnon. Manchester, Carcanet, 1984; Normal, Illinois, Dalkey Archive, 1994.
Xorandor. Manchester, Carcanet, 1986; New York, Avon, 1988.
Verbivore. Manchester, Carcanet, 1990.
Textermination. Manchester, Carcanet, and New York, New Directions, 1991.
Remake. Manchester, Carcanet, 1996.
Next. Manchester, Carcanet, 1998.
Subscript. Manchester, Carcanet, 1999.

Short Stories

Go When You See the Green Man Walking. London, Joseph, 1970.

Poetry

Gold. Aldington, Kent, Hand and Flower Press, 1955.

Other

A Grammar of Metaphor. London, Secker and Warburg, 1958.
A ZBC of Ezra Pound. London, Faber, 1971; Berkeley, University of California Press, 1976.
A Structural Analysis of Pound's Usura Canto: Jakobson's Method Extended and Applied to Free Verse. The Hague, Mouton, 1976.
A Rhetoric of the Unreal: Studies in Narrative and Structure, Especially of the Fantastic. Cambridge and New York, Cambridge University Press, 1981.
Stories, Theories and Things. Cambridge, Cambridge University Press, 1991.
With Umberto Eco, Richard Rorty, and Jonathan Culler, *Interpretation and Overinterpretation*, edited by Stefan Collini. New York, Cambridge University Press, 1992.
Translator, *Children of Chaos,* by Juan Goytisolo. London, MacGibbon and Kee, 1958.
Translator, *Fertility and Survival: Population Problems from Malthus to Mao Tse Tung,* by Alfred Sauvy. New York, Criterion, 1960; London, Chatto and Windus, 1961.
Translator, *In the Labyrinth,* by Alain Robbe-Grillet. London, Calder and Boyars, 1968.

*

Critical Studies: ''Christine Brooke-Rose'' by Sarah Birch, in *Contemporary Fiction* (Oxford), 1994; Christine Brooke-Rose issue of *Review of Contemporary Fiction* (Elmwood Park, Illinois),1994; *Christine Brooke-Rose and Contemporary Fiction* by Sarah Birch, New York, Oxford University Press, 1994; *Utterly Other Discourse: The Texts of Christine Brooke-Rose,* edited by Ellen J. Friedman and Richard Martin, Normal, Illinois, Dalkey Archive Press, 1995.

Christine Brooke-Rose comments:

(1996) From *Out* onwards, experiments with language and forms of fiction.

* * *

If one looks at the details of Christine Brooke-Rose's life, one is struck by the many displacements (both physical and linguistic) she has undergone. This feeling is magnified when one reads the novels she produced from 1964 on, where her lack of a strong national identity, coupled with her bilingualism, is reflected in the novels' unspecified settings. Because of the importance this borderline position has had in her career, any attempt to place her in a cultural/geographical tradition has failed. Paradoxically, whereas in Britain she is seen as responsible for introducing the French *nouveau roman* to this country, in France she is known principally as a teacher of British and American narrative, which she taught there from 1968 to 1988, before retiring to Provence in order to concentrate on novel-writing. We cannot deny the influence *nouveaux romanciers* such as Robbe-Grillet initially had on her work, but we also mustn't ignore the distance she soon put between herself and them, the fact that all her novels are written in English, that they share features common to those produced by various British and American authors such as Ann Quin, B. S. Johnson, and Thomas Pynchon, and that she was equally influenced by Ezra Pound, Samuel Beckett, and Mikhail Bakhtin among others.

Although she has often been labeled a ''difficult writer,'' the difficulties her novels pose have never been of a lexical or syntactical nature, but rather derive from the difficulty readers experience when trying to identify the various learned references in her texts. However, recognition of the source of these references is often irrelevant to an understanding of what the author is striving for, namely to shatter her readers' expectations and give these references fresh meanings, the discovery of which can be attained by readers only if they concentrate on how these elements work in the texts.

To this end, in her experimental novels Brooke-Rose replaces the narrator of Realist fiction with an impoverished narrator whose physical and psychological realities are never described, a perceiving consciousness who is ''hit'' by external phenomena and who simply registers what is happening around him/her. She creates worlds that cannot be placed in space or time; she produces texts that, by presenting different versions of the same events, prevent the reader from deciding which is the actual reality the novel depicts; she recognizes the poetic possibilities of specialized jargon and juxtaposes it to other discourses, in particular that of fiction.

Her Realist novels of the 1950s were essentially light and witty social satires, and although they already contained in embryonic form the thematics she would develop later—namely her concern with language (in particular the idea that there exist several, different languages interacting in the same person, and that language is all we have to apprehend reality)—it is only with *Out*, her first experimental novel, that she succeeded in adequately integrating them in her narrative. Here, she exploits for the first time the kind of discursive metaphor that would become fundamental in her work, and by positing a discursive system as her frame, she uses different discourses within that system as metaphors, making them interact with one another.

For instance, in *Out*—in which Brooke-Rose investigates what it means to be sick and to be made an outsider because of sickness—chemistry becomes a metaphor for illness and racial difference. Following a nuclear holocaust, referred to as the ''displacement,'' the previously dominant ''Colourless'' races suffer from a malady caused by the ensuing radiation. Since the ''Coloured'' are unaffected, they become the hegemonic race, and by invoking the discourse of chemistry as an arbitrary justification for racial discrimination, they turn it into the coercive language through which they impose a racial identity on the individual.

In *Such*—which describes the near-death experience and subsequent recovery of a psychiatrist working for the astrophysics department of an unspecified university—the language of astrophysics is used as a metaphor for human relations. Hence, the ''laws of communication'' investigated by the astrophysicists (who study the way in which light and radio waves bounce off astral bodies) are treated poetically by Brooke-Rose, and are applied to the signals between human beings; the theory of an expanding universe metaphorically indicates our society, in which everybody is becoming distanced from one another, and the theory of the Big Bang is used to construct a ''cosmic theory of identity'' in which the formation of the individual is equated with the event that began our universe.

In *Between*, which focuses on the idea of the loss of identity through language (also suggested by the total absence of the verb ''to be''), Brooke-Rose replaces the technical jargons of the previous novels with the languages of the specialized fields represented at the conferences attended by the narrator (a simultaneous translator), and the different national languages spoken in the countries she visits, thereby exploiting not only the metaphorical potential of different discourses, but also that of translation. Both aspects therefore function as agents of transition between different places, times, and contexts, and thanks to the novel's unique syntax, the reader can travel, within the same sentence, from one space/time to another.

Thru, which she wrote after moving to France, is an attempt to combine the disciplines of the critic and the writer, and pursues the discussion of gender issues she began in *Between*. The novel—in which Brooke-Rose urges the reader not to take the various theories the text plays with too seriously, since they are, after all, only words on a page—deals with the history of narratology, and is a maze of theories, linguistic games, typographical devices, verbal icons, and ambiguous settings. The book's myriad references are not always immediately recognizable, and all these ''textual blocks,'' combined with an essential ambiguity about the novel's world, make it impossible for the reader of this very demanding ''novel about the theory of the novel'' even to identify the narrators with any certainty.

Having realized that with *Thru* she had gone too far, Brooke-Rose decided to strive for more readability, and after a gap of nine years published *Amalgamemnon*, a novel focused on the opposition between the past and the future and on the notion of redundancy. The novel is characterized by the parodic tone she adopts while treating various preconceived notions derived from Western history (in particular the phallocratic approach of Herodotus in his *Histories*), by the singular rhythm created by the tenses used (predominantly future and conditional), and by the mythological and astronomical imagery the novel evokes. The narrator, a female professor of literature and history who fears redundancy, is clearly imagining all that is described, and the whole novel consists of a long interior monologue in which she projects her fears and expectations for her future. As a result, the narrative material consists of her thoughts, memories, and fragments of her classical knowledge ''amalgamated'' with situations, fairy-tales, and dialogues with students, friends, and relatives that she creates in her mind (who often desert the roles she assigns to them and actually begin to interact with her in her world), along with extracts from the news, advertisements, quiz-games, and talk-shows from the radio that often function as a trigger for her imagination, displacing the discourse to another time, space, and narrative situation.

Xorandor—and its sequel *Verbivore*—are much more straightforward novels that return to a defined plot and—if we disregard the presence of talking stones supposedly from outer space who feed on radioactivity and who can interrupt all terrestrial wave-communication—to fairly conventional characters. *Xorandor* is narrated by two children, and is a self-reflexive science-fiction focusing on the ontological problem of what makes a human being a human being, the undecidability of truth, and various other philosophical, linguistic, and ecological matters. In *Verbivore* the reader learns that *Xorandor* was in fact the creation of Mira, the narrator of *Amalgamemnon* who returns in both novels, and it is narrated from different points of view, appearing as a collage of short narratives that draw on different genres (mainly the epistolary novel and the personal journal, although we also find a radio-play script, newspapers cuttings, and so on), each set piece characterized by the idiolects of the various people writing.

Mira is also present in *Textermination*, in which Brooke-Rose exposes the ambiguities implied by the notion of a literary Canon and discusses the relationship between high and popular culture. Mira attends the Convention of Prayer for Being, at which the fictional characters from narratives written by authors of all nationalities and all times converge to pray to the Reader, their Almighty God, who can decide the life or death of each character by reading or not reading particular novels. Because the various characters retain the identity and personal qualities they were given in their narrative of origin, the novel is not simply a collage of different texts, but is an inter-national and inter-temporal meeting point where the fictional worlds the different texts construct (with their separate beliefs, religions, and systems of knowledge) meet, often provoking amusing incidents caused by the clash of different cultures and eras.

Having concluded her second experimental tetralogy, Brooke-Rose then published *Remake*, where her own personal experiences and memories give birth to a novel in which the problematic distinction between history (personal and otherwise) and fiction is investigated.

After this autobiographical novel, in which (except for one chapter) all personal pronouns are intriguingly absent, in *Next* Brooke-Rose imposes yet another grammatical constraint on her prose (one that, as happened in *Between* and *Amalgamemnon*, is justified on a thematic level). Since the novel deals with the homeless (who do not own anything), she completely eliminates from her narrative the verb ''to have.'' Twenty-six characters (one for each letter of the alphabet—a recurrent theme in this novel) appear in the text; all are loosely connected by the murder of one of the ten homeless characters whose initials, when taken together, form QWERTYUIOP, the first line of a typewriter. The murder remains unsolved, and by presenting no division into chapters or paragraphs, the novel—which denounces the responsibility that both the Government and the Media have for the creation of such a situation—emphasizes that the homeless are not only deprived of their homes, jobs, and social roles but of their identities as well, appearing alike to the outsider who hastily passes them by. Simultaneously, however, by transcribing phonetically the different levels of ''Estuarian'' language they speak, Brooke-Rose shows that they are, after all, different from one another, and by so doing not only does she render the changes of perspective that occur in the text very clearly, but she also enables her characters to oppose the attempted obliteration of their individuality enacted by their society.

Finally, in *Subscript* Broke-Rose exploits the discourse of paleontology and, beginning with a poetic description of a pre-biotic chemical reaction 4,500 million years ago, she deals with the history of evolution from unicellular organisms to the early human species, creating a ''pre-historic'' novel in which the genetic code almost becomes a character itself, steering various organisms through evolution. The novel is entirely told from these organisms' viewpoint: from a single cell, the story is passed from female organism to female organism, in ascending order of complexity, evolving into the creatures that will eventually become humanity. Throughout the novel the ''pack'' develops into a ''tribe'' of two-legged ''buntunaminu'' who slowly learn to create tools, make fire, cook food, rear animals, cover their nudity, and, above all, play the ''mouth-noise game'' that eventually evolves into different human languages, leading to the birth of story telling, medicine, simple mathematics, and the like. The tribes slowly develop the concept of a supreme being, thereby creating the rituals and paraphernalia of religion proper, and evolve into totemic clans. These communities consolidate the concept of politics and colonization, and in order to stipulate alliances among them, begin to use their females as tokens of exchange. Hence, although the novel is obviously focused on ontological issues, it also asks questions related to both gender (ironically likening the phallocratic clichés men still live by to those of ''cave-men'') and the notion of colonization, pointing, as Brooke-Rose had done in her previous novels, to an idiosyncrasy peculiar to human beings, namely that everyone has a latent disposition for oppression and coercion.

With her numerous novels, several major critical works, and a plethora of articles and essays (as well as poetry and a few extraordinary translations), Christine Brooke-Rose has earned her place among major British writers of the twentieth century, extending the scope of the novel and stretching the possibilities of language to its limit, offering an insightful representation of our society.

—Michela Canepari-Labib

BROOKNER, Anita

Nationality: British. **Born:** London, 16 July 1928. **Education:** James Allen's Girls' School; King's College, University of London; Courtauld Institute of Art, London, Ph.D. in art history. **Career:** Visiting lecturer, University of Reading, Berkshire, 1959–64; lecturer, 1964, and reader, 1977–88, Courtauld Institute of Art; Slade Professor, Cambridge University, 1967–68. Fellow, New Hall, Cambridge; fellow, King's College, 1990. **Awards:** Booker prize, 1984. C.B.E. (Commander, Order of the British Empire), 1990. **Address:** 68 Elm Park Gardens, London SW10 9PB, England.

PUBLICATIONS

Novels

A Start in Life. London, Cape, 1981; as *The Debut,* New York, Linden Press, 1981.
Providence. London, Cape, 1982; New York, Pantheon, 1984.
Look at Me. London, Cape, and New York, Pantheon, 1983.
Hotel du Lac. London, Cape, 1984; New York, Pantheon, 1985.
Family and Friends. London, Cape, and New York, Pantheon, 1985.
A Misalliance. London, Cape, 1986; as *The Misalliance,* New York, Pantheon, 1987.
A Friend from England. London, Cape, 1987; New York, Pantheon, 1988.
Latecomers. London, Cape, 1988; New York, Pantheon, 1989.
Lewis Percy. London, Cape, 1989; New York, Pantheon, 1990.
Brief Lives. London, Cape, 1990; New York, Random House, 1991.
A Closed Eye. London, Cape, 1991; New York, Random House, 1991.
Fraud. New York, Vintage Books, 1994.
Dolly. Thorndike, Maine, G.K. Hall, 1994.
A Private View. New York, Random House, 1994.
Incidents in the Rue Laugier. New York, Random House, 1996.
Altered States. New York, Random House, 1996.
Visitors. London, Jonathan Cape, 1997.
Falling Slowly. New York, Random House, 1999.
Undue Influence. New York, Random House, 2000.

Other

Watteau. London, Hamlyn, 1968.
The Genius of the Future: Studies in French Art Criticism: Diderot, Stendahl, Baudelaire, Zola, the Brothers Goncourt, Huysmans. London, Phaidon Press, 1971; Ithaca, New York, Cornell University Press, 1988.
Greuze: The Rise and Fall of an Eighteenth-Century Phenomenon. London, Elek, and Greenwich, Connecticut, New York Graphic Society, 1972.
Jacques-Louis David: A Personal Interpretation (lecture). London, Oxford University Press, 1974.
Jacques-Louis David. London, Chatto and Windus, 1980; New York, Harper, 1981; revised edition, Chatto and Windus, 1986; New York, Thames and Hudson, 1987.
Soundings (essays). London, Harvill Press, 1998.
Romanticism and its Discontents. New York, Farrar, Straus and Giroux, 2000.
Editor, *The Stories of Edith Wharton.* London, Simon and Schuster, 2 vols., 1988–89.
Translator, *Utrillo.* London, Oldbourne Press, 1960.
Translator, *The Fauves.* London, Oldbourne Press, 1962.
Translator, *Gauguin.* London, Oldbourne Press, 1963.

*

Critical Studies: *Four British Women Novelists: Anita Brookner, Margaret Drabble, Iris Murdoch, Barbara Pym: An Annotated and Critical Secondary Bibliography* by George Soule, Lanham, Maryland, Scarecrow Press, 1998.

* * *

Often compared to Jane Austen, Henry James, and Edith Wharton, sometimes simultaneously, Anita Brookner's brief, exquisitely wrought novels portray lonely, ordinary people, usually women, passively enduring somber ordinary lives in a bleak, gray London, skillfully delineated through reference to recognizable street names and shops. In her autobiographical first novel, *A Start in Life,* Brookner sets a characteristic theme and tone with another characteristic, references to literature and painting: '''About suffering they were never wrong, the Old Masters,' said Auden. But they were. Frequently. Death was usually heroic, old age serene and wise. And of course, the element of time, that was what was missing.'' In Brookner's novels, the present stretches on and on into an uncharted future, days need filling up, while the past only informs when it is too late. With little choice, Brookner's characters must bravely ''soldier on.''

Brookner's characters are immediately recognizable. As Brookner notes, she begins with an ''idea of the main character and how the story ends. Then, I work toward that end.'' Her typical protagonists, female or male, allow cultural and familial attitudes and pressures to shape their lives, like Dr. Ruth Weiss in *A Start in Life,* whose life has been ''ruined by literature.'' Brookner protagonists wear well-tailored clothes, live in well-furnished apartments, usually inherited from a parent dutifully nursed through a final illness, and vacation in France. Left to ''ponder the careers of Anna Karenina and Emma Bovary'' but ''emulate'' Little Dorrit, the women view life as offering limited choices, one being between marriage and spinsterhood. The unfulfilled young women of the early novels, crave the affection and love denied by their families, whose portraits are presented through the protagonists' memories and self-reflection. Yearning for the stuff of romantic novels, such as those written by Edith of the award-winning *Hotel du Lac,* the young women suffer in demeaning relationships, but although intelligent, lack the inner resources to take control of their lives. In sharp contrast, in *Lewis Percy,* the eponymous protagonist of Brookner's ninth novel and a student of 19th-century French fiction, escapes his dependency on his mother as well as a loveless marriage when he runs off to America with his best friend's eccentric sister.

The women in *Hotel du Lac* and *A Friend from England* also shed impossible relationships, from married men, but are not ''rewarded'' with happy endings. Edith analyzes the history of her predicament through letters never sent to her lover David; Rachel comes to understand that she will gamely ''plough on'' through middle age, her interior monologues never vocalized or shared.

Brookner's middle novels, *A Misalliance* and *Brief Lives* compound the meaninglessness of women's existence by exploring the present predicaments of older women through a retrospective on their past. This technique proves an excellent vehicle for Brookner's preoccupation with self-betrayal, the duplicity of others, and the betrayals of time. The defeats of time and the painful survival of destroyed illusions are portrayed in two novels best described as family chronicles: *Family and Friends* and *Latecomers.* The former brilliantly traces the contrasting stories of the members of the Dorn family by reading and projecting from a series of wedding photographs. *Latecomers,* a study of survivor-guilt, reviews the lives of the families of two Jewish friends—the melancholy Fibich and the epicurean Hartmann—through an emotional crisis in which Fibich comes to terms with his own history. These melancholy novels portray characters who barely survive, but with a modicum honor.

In both *A Closed Eye* and *Fraud,* however, Brookner suggests that people do not have to settle for a solitary, lonely life. In novels developed through similar structural techniques, dutiful daughters break the Brookner pattern. In *A Closed Eye,* although timid Harriet submits to an arranged marriage with well-to-do, divorced Freddie Lytton, she is partially fulfilled in motherhood, a new theme for Brookner, by the birth of her beautiful daughter Imogen, who, however, soon grows into an unspeakably selfish girl. Only when Harriet meets Jack, philanderer husband of Tessa, her best friend, does Harriet experience something of a sexual awakening, which, being a Brookner woman, she cannot act upon, despite their single shared kiss and her erotic dreams. Developed through retrospect, when the novel opens, Imogen is dead in an improbable car crash, Tessa is dead from cancer, and Harriet has dutifully accompanied Freddie to Swiss health spas. Liberated by his death, 53-year-old Harriet does not return home as would most defeated Brookner heroines. Instead she writes the letter which opens the novel and invites Lizzie, Tessa's daughter whom she partially raised, to her European villa to join her and her new male friend, thus opening the way to self understanding.

Brookner relies on the same circular technique in *Fraud,* which also develops the theme of mothers and daughters, but here from the daughter's point of view. Like a detective story, the novel opens with the report that 50-year-old Anna Durrant has gone missing; cleverly, the police inquiries spark the narrative. The reflections of Anna's few acquaintances introduce this obedient spinster daughter, who knows she lived in ''a pleasant collaboration of unrealities,'' dominated by her mother. Thus, we are prepared to learn of Anna's self-rescue after her mother's death; planning her disappearance, she ''refashions'' herself rather than allowing others to and begins a career designing clothing for ''women like myself.'' At novel's end, a chance encounter in Paris solves her mysterious disappearance and reveals a stronger Anna capable of inspiring another woman to resolutely follow an independent path and break from a married man.

Dolly, Brookner's thirteenth novel, brings the European to London in a vivacious aunt ''singing and dancing'' her way through life. Dolly collides with and, then, is eventually dependent upon, narrator Jane Manning, her young niece, whose keen observations delineate her parents' close, yet delicate, marriage and deaths, and, more importantly, reveal widowed Dolly's fraudulent gaiety. The power shifts when Jane reluctantly inherits the family money, but so does Jane's now benevolent understanding of her aunt's life. Young Jane finds contentment and success as a children's author while she installs her defeated, aging aunt in a much desired flat.

Despite these less melancholy endings, these new Brookner women still take long walks on melancholy Sunday evenings, drink bottomless cups of tea, and manage their days with little tricks of empty activity. Maud Gonthier in *Incidents in the Rue Langier* reads, sighs, and retires early; like Dolly, she too is a displaced French woman. Her daughter creates an unreliable, perhaps wishful, biography for her mother after she discovers a mysterious coded diary and silk kimono in Maud's belongings. The daughter's narrative spins a passionate romance-novel affair with the dashing, wealthy David Tyler in Paris. Almost in penance, Maud accepts marriage with Tyler's acquaintance, the staid, British used bookseller, Edward; thus an explanation for the marriage of the narrator's parents. Maud's male counterpart is Alan Sherwood, narrator of *Altered States* who also yearns for a former lover in Paris, sensual, heartless Sarah, while married to sexless Angela. Both novels examine the consequences of inopportune marriages from male and female points of view. Brookner also explores male-female relationships exacerbated this time by generational and cultural differences in her next paired novels which present the usual finely crafted portraits of the effects of loneliness.

Youth and age collide when young strangers interrupt the patterned, solitary well-to-do lives of retired bachelor George Bland in *A Private View* and widowed, 70-year-old Dorothea May in *Visitors.* Aware of their age, both meticulously prepare themselves for the day in front of the mirror and by novel's end both are forced to a new understanding of their futures. Bland, aptly named, succumbs to Katy Gibb (named for the American secretarial school?), a twenty-something intruder who sweet-talks her way into the neighboring apartment and eventually cons Bland into donating a large sum to help her set up a business based on New Age stress workshops; Katy talks about ''being in the moment'' or feeling ''a lot of negativity.'' Enthralled, George contemplates marriage seeing Katy as a chance to escape a life not lived; rejected and exhausted, after an ongoing interior monologue of self scrutiny, he settles for a shift in his years' long companionship with Louise. Over the telephone, he invites Louise on a vacation trip.

Coping with ill health and increasing anxiety attacks, Dorothea May's civilized world also shifts under self-scrutiny when she reluctantly responds to family duty by opening the room where her husband Henry died for Steven Best, who has accompanied her sister-in-law's granddaughter Ann, a homeopathic therapist, and David, a crusading evangelical sports teacher, to London for their sudden wedding. The novel becomes a comedy of contrasts—old, proper British versus young, brash American and family secrets keep tumbling out. Astonished at herself, Dorothea offers crucial assistance in dealing with the recalcitrant bride and succumbs to Steven's presence. She shops and busies herself with his comfort. Although Steven disappoints her with his thoughtlessness, she misses him when the trio leaves for Paris. Her revelation is that the unknown future must be "an enterprise in which help must be solicited and offered." Like George, she cautiously reaches out over the telephone to her overwrought sister-in-law.

Small items and techniques reappear in subsequent Brookner novels, each time usually more complete. In *Hotel du Lac,* Edith does not mail her letters; in *A Closed Eye,* Harriet's mailed letter leads to self-knowledge. A vague New Age business in *A Private View* is actually the bride Anna's occupation in *Visitors.* George Bland switches off the incomplete radio shipping forecast to take Louise's phone call, but *Falling Slowly* takes its title from the shipping bulletin's last words; Edith's romance novels also reappear or are inverted by Brookner's novels themselves. Brookner's eighteenth novel explores the now familiar marginalized lives of two sisters: Miriam, a translator of French, who spends half her day in the London library and the other half fretting over life's minutia and her evaporating love life; and Beatrice, an accompanist forced into retirement, who flutters about and reads romance novels. A typical Brookner figure, Miriam, once married for five years, slides into an affair with a married man for whom she yearns after he simply disappears. Unable to commit to the suitable Tom, Miriam retreats to care for her ailing sister Beatrice; at their deaths, Miriam, left alone in a self-inflicted, circumscribed emotionless life, tells her former husband when he accuses her of reading too much, "I'm better off alone ... there were no happy endings." Seeking early morning reassurance, she listens to the shipping forecast sipping a cup of tea knowing that the high moments of life she and Beatrice anticipated will never come.

Spinster sisters reappear in *Undue Influence* as Muriel and Harriet St. John, elderly owners of a secondhand bookshop inherited from their father. Dutifully devoted to his memory, they employ attractive, well-dressed, 29-year-old Claire Pitt to edit his numbingly dull writings. Claire, alone after caring for her mother, who, in turn, had tended Claire's ailing father, still spins elaborate fantasies and now fantasizes an unattainable marriage with handsome, shallow Martin Gibson, a bookstore patron. Her one friend, Wiggy, sits by the phone waiting for a phone call from her married lover. Although far more modern than the octogenarian St. John spinsters, Claire and Wiggy are destined to become them, for with this nineteenth novel, nothing has changed in Brookner territory. In an effort to occupy her time, Claire endlessly cleans her inherited apartment, takes long walks in London parks, reads, fantasizes, and has anonymous sexual encounters during vacations in France. Without any lasting relationships, Claire's future holds the same glum promise of a drab, controlled life. She will courageously slip into middle age as Brookner slowly closes yet another analysis of unfulfilled longing.

—Lyn Pykett, updated by Judith C. Kohl

BROWN, Rita Mae

Nationality: American. **Born:** Hanover, Pennsylvania, 28 November 1944. **Education:** University of Florida, Gainesville; New York University, B.A. 1968; New York School of Visual Arts, cinematography certificate 1968; Institute for Policy Studies, Washington, D.C., Ph.D. 1976. **Career:** Photo editor, Sterling Publishing Company, New York, 1969–70; lecturer in sociology, Federal City College, Washington, D.C., 1970–71. Since 1973 visiting member, faculty of feminist studies, Goddard College, Plainfield, Vermont. Founding member, Redstockings radical feminist group, New York, 1970s. **Awards:** Best Variety Show award (TV Writers Guild), 1982; New York Public Library Literary Lion award, 1986; Outstanding Alumni, American Association of Community Colleges, 1999; Outstanding Alumna, Broward Community College, 1999. **Agent:** Wendy Weil Agency, 232 Madison Avenue, New York, New York 10016–2901, U.S.A. **Address:** American Artists Inc., P.O. Box 4671, Charlottesville, Virginia 22905, U.S.A.

Publications

Novels

Rubyfruit Jungle. Plainfield, Vermont, Daughters, 1973; London, Corgi, 1978.
In Her Day. Plainfield, Vermont, Daughters, 1976.
Six of One. New York, Harper, 1978; London, W.H. Allen, 1979.
Southern Discomfort. New York, Harper, 1982; London, Severn House, 1983.
Sudden Death. New York, Bantam, 1983.
High Hearts. New York and London, Bantam, 1986.
Bingo. New York, Bantam, 1988.
Wish You Were Here, with Sneaky Pie Brown. New York, Bantam, 1990.
Rest in Pieces, with Sneaky Pie Brown. New York, Bantam, 1992.
Venus Envy. New York, Bantam, 1993.
Dolley: A Novel of Dolley Madison in Love and War. New York, Bantam, 1994.
Murder at Monticello; or, Old Sins, with Sneaky Pie Brown. New York, Bantam, 1994.
Pay Dirt, or, Adventures at Ash Lawn, with Sneaky Pie Brown. New York, Bantam Books, 1995.
Riding Shotgun. New York, Bantam Books, 1996.
Murder, She Meowed, with Sneaky Pie Brown. New York, Bantam Books, 1996.
Murder on the Prowl, with Sneaky Pie Brown. New York, Bantam Books, 1998.

Cat on the Scent, with Sneaky Pie Brown. New York, Bantam Books, 1999.

Loose Lips. New York, Bantam Books, 1999.

Outfoxed. New York, Ballantine Books, 2000.

Pawing through the Past, with Sneaky Pie Brown. New York, Bantam Books, 2000.

Plays

Television and film scripts: *I Love Liberty,* with others, 1982; *The Long Hot Summer,* 1985; *My Two Loves,* 1986; *The Alice Marble Story,* 1986; *Sweet Surrender,* 1986; *The Mists of Avalone,* 1987; *Table Dancing,* 1987; *The Girls of Summer,* 1989; *Selma, Lord, Selma,* 1989; *Rich Men, Single Women,* 1989; *The Thirty Nine Year Itch,* 1989.

Poetry

The Hand That Cradles the Rock. New York, New York University Press, 1971.

Songs to a Handsome Woman. Baltimore, Diana Press, 1973.

Poems. Freedom, California, Crossing Press, 1987.

Other

A Plain Brown Rapper (essays). Baltimore, Diana Press, 1976.

Starting from Scratch: A Different Kind of Writers Manual. New York, Bantam, 1988.

Rita Will: Memoir of a Literary Rabble-Rouser. New York, Bantam Books, 1997.

*

Critical Study: *Rita Mae Brown* by Carol M. Ward, New York, Twayne, 1993; *Ladies Laughing: Wit as Control in Contemporary American Women Writers* by Barbara Levy, Amsterdam, Netherlands, Gordon and Breach, 1997.

* * *

For a writer whose novels appear to be exclusively comic southern fiction, Rita Mae Brown has, in fact, produced a varied body of work. At the most basic level, her novels celebrate a particular image of the southern United States of America; they are funny, sassy, full of geographically specific language—expletives in particular seem to be strictly of the South rather than the North—and populated with hosts of astonishingly colorful characters.

Brown's writing is so particular to its location that her novels *Bingo* and especially *High Hearts* have led to her being accused of falling into the trap of depicting the South as ''wrong but romantic'' and the North as ''right but repulsive.'' This did not preclude her from being tipped seriously for the commission to write the sequel to *Gone with the Wind;* in fact, it was probably a main factor in the (ultimately unfounded) rumor that she *would* write it.

Considering the great success of her southern novels, it may be surprising to discover that her real claim to popular adulation is her parallel and entwined career as foremother of the modern lesbian novel. She is not an experimental writer in the style of Monique Wittig or Jeanette Winterson; she is not a stream of consciousness/ coming out writer like Verena Stefan or early Michelle Roberts; but her lasting fame among lesbian readers rests primarily on her first novel *Rubyfruit Jungle* which charted hilariously the coming-out process of a young Southerner called Molly Bolt—a joke untranslatable outside of American carpentry circles—and her consequent discovery and assertion that a) it was cool to be queer, b) the only problem is other people's reactions, and c) the rest of the world had better just get used to it.

In these heady days of (fairly) free expression of sexuality, it is difficult to realize just what a bombshell Brown dropped onto a world in which the most famous lesbian novel was *The Well of Loneliness* and lesbians in other fiction almost always recanted, threw themselves into a purifying orgy of self-sacrifice or—more frequently—committed suicide in despair. It is not stretching the point to say that for the overwhelming majority of lesbians, *Rubyfruit Jungle* was the first book we ever read which said it was OK.

After such a success with a first novel, it was hardly surprising that her second *In Her Day* was to many a disappointment. It tries to deal with the still thorny issues of lesbian-feminism versus ''political correctness,'' older and younger women, class, race and so on. All of this in a very slim volume. The book was published in one edition by a small US feminist press and disappeared without trace—except to obsessive collectors—until two years ago when it was republished. Interestingly, its long absence was the choice of the author who felt it was an inferior novel.

Brown's use of her own life for fiction is fascinating. While it is true that characters appear in *Rubyfruit Jungle, Six of One* and the latter's sequel *Bingo* who are clearly based on the same autobiographical raw material, the most obvious example is *Sudden Death.* With information clearly gathered during her highly public relationship with Martina Navratilova, Brown dissects the world of women's professional tennis with the satiric scalpel of an expert. A favorite game for some time after its publication was for the reader to try and identify the real-life models on which the characters were based.

Attentive readers, however, have found a shift in political values in Brown's novels; it appears to be towards the right whilst retaining an undying feminism. A seeming contradiction, but then the Women's Movement had always intended to be a broad church. This reading is suggested by some of the apparently pro-Confederate sentiments in *High Hearts* and less than liberal stances taken by her main characters in *Bingo.*

Her writer's manual *Starting from Scratch* is probably best explained by her own assertion that she was broke after her messy divorce from Martina and needed to write something quickly. It is most memorable for being probably the first writer's manual since the 19th century which suggests that a putative writer must do nothing until they have spent some years mastering both Latin and Ancient Greek.

Wish You Were Here, her 1990 novel, marks something of a progression. Her novels have always been jointly dedicated to her animals but this, a competent if not particularly spectacular thriller, claims to have been co-written by her cat. Brown has continued in this tradition and brought us a number of popular murder stories called ''Mrs. Murphy Mysteries.'' *Rest in Pieces, Murder at Monticello: Or Old Sins, Pay Dirt, Or Adventures at Ash Lawn, Murder, She Meowed, Cat on the Scent, Murder on the Prowl,* and *Pawing through the Past* have been all co-written by Rita Mae Brown and her cat, Sneaky Pie Brown. The protagonists of the murder stories, a tiger cat (Mrs. Murphy), a Welsh Corgi (Tucker), and a thirty-something postmistress (Mary Minor ''Harry'' Haristeen), live together in the small town of Crozet, Virginia, and attempt to solve the murders happening around them. In Brown's mysteries, animals, which make their witty comments and observations in italics, are always one step ahead of their human counterparts. Thus, Brown demonstrates her undying love for animals and respect for their natural wisdom. In 1999, Brown's prolific cat ''published'' (with Brown's co-authorship) its own cookbook, *Sneaky Pie's Cookbook for Mystery Lovers*, which introduces recipes for cats, dogs, and humans.

As stated before, however, Brown's scope includes much more than mysteries. As a lesbian author, Brown is to be celebrated alongside a writer such as Armistead Maupin for proving that queer life also has its hilarious side when the straight world lets it out. After the amusing as well as provocative *Rubyfruit Jungle*, Brown returned to the issue of lesbianism in *Venus Envy*. She lets her heroine, who is supposedly dying of lung cancer, come out with her sexual orientation as well as reveal her attitudes and opinions about others. When the 35-year-old gallery owner Frazier finds out that her diagnosis is a result of a computer mistake, she has to face the reality and the consequences of her disclosures. Once again, in *Venus Envy* Brown demonstrates her superb feel for satire, comicality, and nuances of the English language.

Rita Mae Brown does not forget her southern characters, though, and in *Loose Lips*, she brings back the Hunsenmeier sisters, whom she had already introduced in *Bingo* and *Six of One*. With the middle-aged Juts and Wheezie, Brown returns in an amusing manner to the atmosphere of a small southern town, touching on complex issues of adoption, friendship, and faithfulness. *Riding Shotgun* discusses similar issues in a story of the recently widowed Cig Blackwood, who, while fox hunting, travels back in time to the year 1699. Meeting her ancestors, Cig learns about love, betrayal, and, most importantly, herself. Brown also goes back in time in—for her atypical—a historical novel, *Dolley: A Novel of Dolley Madison in Love and War*. In this novel, Brown recreates a crucial year (1814) in the life of the fourth American president's wife during the conflict between America and Britain.

In her novel *Outfoxed*, Brown brings together the majority of her favorite subjects. Even though writing a murder story, this time Rita Mae Brown does not bring forth Mrs. Murphy to solve the mystery. Yet, the small Virginian town is full of speaking animals (hounds, foxes, birds, and horses), which become successful detectives in the murder case of Fontaine Buruss. Brown's passion for foxhunting is evident in the story, as she describes the sport and its elaborate rituals with precision and sometimes even exhausting detail. Again, this novel depicts, with a bit of nostalgia, the southern mentality, charm, and gallantry. Brown focuses her attention on the southern tradition, ancestry, land, and firm human ties, creating a charismatic and respected matriarchal character, Sister Jane Arnold, M.F.H. (Master of Fox Hunting).

In all her novels, Rita Mae Brown skillfully connects the autobiographical and the fictional. With its many specific details, Brown's autobiography, *Rita Will: Memoir of a Literary Rabble-Rouser*, becomes an invaluable source of information for readers interested in Brown's life and work. Brown does not shy away from any subject, discussing her poverty-stricken childhood with her adoptive parents, her struggle for public acceptance as a lesbian, and her love affairs with Martina Navratilova, Fannie Flagg, and Judy Nelson. With her typical sense of humor, she uncovers in front of the readers her life experiences, drawing together all that she loves and respects: southerners, close relationships between humans and animals, and meaningful, fulfilling work.

—Linda Semple, updated by Iva Korinkova

BROWN, Rosellen

Nationality: American. **Born:** 1939. **Career:** Instructor in American and English literature, Tougaloo College, Mississippi, 1965–67; instructor in creative writing, Goddard College, Plainfield, Vermont, 1976, and University of Houston, Texas, 1982–85. Since 1989 instructor in creative writing, University of Houston. Visiting professor of creative writing, Boston University, 1977–78. **Awards:** National Endowmment for the Arts fellowship, 1973, 1982; Guggenheim fellowship, 1976; Great Lake College Association best first novel award, 1976, for *The Autobiography of My Mother;* Janet Kafka best novel award, 1984, for *Civil Wars; Ms. Magazine* Woman of the Year, 1984; American Academy and Institute of Arts and Letters award, 1987, for literature; Ingram-Merrill grant, 1989–90. **Address:** 1401 Branard, Houston, Texas 77006, U.S.A.

Publications

Novels

The Autobiography of My Mother. Garden City, New York, Doubleday, 1976.
Tender Mercies. New York, Knopf, 1978; London, Hutchison, 1979.
Civil Wars: A Novel. New York, Knopf, and London, Joseph, 1984.
Before and After. New York, Farrar Straus, 1992; London, Hodder and Stoughton, 1993.
Half a Heart. New York, Farrar, Straus, and Giroux, 2000.

Short Stories

Street Games. Garden City, New York, Doubleday, 1974.

Plays

The Secret Garden, with Laurie MacGregor, adaptation of the novel by Frances Hodgson Burnett (produced, 1983).

Poetry

Some Deaths in the Delta, and Other Poems. Amherst, University of Massachusetts Press, 1970.
Cora Fry. New York, Norton, 1977.
Cora Fry's Pillow Book. New York, Farrar Straus, 1994.

Other

A Rosellen Brown Reader: Selected Poetry and Prose. Vermont, Middlebury College Press, 1992.
Editor, *The Whole World Catalog.* N.p., 1972.
Editor, *Men Portray Women, Women Portray Men.* N.p., 1978.

*

Critical Studies: *Conversations with American Novelists: The Best Interviews from The Missouri Review and the American Audio Prose Library,* edited by Kay Bonetti. Columbia, University of Missouri Press, 1997.

* * *

Rosellen Brown's characters—adults, teenagers, and children alike—are living on the edge, from the beginning to the end of her novels. These works start from the premise of lost innocence and move through the various permutations of damage that the condition wreaks upon the psyches of sensitive individuals. All of Brown's fictional marriages are in one stage or another of breakdown; most of her adolescents are experiencing extreme forms of alienation; all of her characters experience the cruel contingency of fate in the form of unhappy coincidence, accident, or death.

All of the novels use conditions of shock and horror to start off the narration. *Tender Mercies* begins with the boating accident of a young married couple. Through his macho bravado, the husband rams a motorboat, which he does not know how to steer, into his swimming wife, severing her spinal cord and rendering her a quadriplegic. *The Autobiography of My Mother* is narrated in part by a woman who, although she doesn't always take money for it, conducts her life somewhat like a prostitute. Meanwhile, her lawyer-mother encounters a series of clients whose conditions in poverty, jail, or the insane asylum are intended to horrify (though the mother herself is stoic as she submits to a forceful vaginal exam administered by black female convicts who want to demonstrate why they are angry). The civil-rights activist parents in *Civil Wars* are appointed legal guardians of children who have been raised by estranged relatives—estranged because they support the Ku Klux Klan. The orphaned daughter attempts suicide more than once. In *Before and After*, a middle-class, do-good family discovers that their son has murdered his girlfriend in a fit of rage at her name-calling.

As if these events were not enough, the narrations go on to describe how such crises, disasters, and shocks inevitably erode marriages. At the end of two of the three novels that are narrated by married partners, the spouses experience a qualified resolution of their relationship. In the third, the wife, after tolerating situations that would try the patience of Job, finally decides that she is through with her marriage. Working at the extremes of human experience, Brown analyzes the profound question of how much sadness the human mind is capable of absorbing without snapping. The human reader, however, may not be capable of absorbing all of Brown's plots, characters, and tone of sadness without losing interest. Although the plots are unique and different, the angst-ridden tone remains the same from one book to the next. Furthermore, the climaxes often arrive after too much delay. We may find ourselves reading on from morbid curiosity, simply to find out what happens: Did Jacob really kill his girlfriend, will Helen actually commit the suicide she obsesses about in her diary, will Renata's depression lead to insanity?

Brown's favored mode of narration contributes to this feeling of monotony: She switches back and forth between the interior monologues of her two main characters, usually spouses, whose private hatreds and sense of isolation become plots of their own, disconnected from the other half. These two subplots carry the narration without the necessary connection that makes for a coherent novel. Lacking are normal dramatic scenes that link characters: Caught between scenes of high-pitched crisis and interior monologues of despair, the scenes of quotidian family intercourse that do occur are laden with a sense of the ailing marriage and impending doom. Brown illustrates how such sadness permeates spouses' relations with their children, parents, and friends—as well as with each other.

Though all the novels rely heavily on plot, suspense, and character, they go lightly on place description and a kind of omniscience that one becomes accustomed to in the postmodern novel: an omniscience that contains a forgiving irony and mutes the pain of contemporary married life. Brown creates beautiful moments in characters' heads, but rarely are they communicated to other characters, especially spouses. Perhaps this is her own version of postmodern consciousness: She perceives life as a series of private, disconnected moments rather than a crescendo toward a good or bad ending. Postmodern or no, however, there is only so much blood, guts, and gore—of body or mind—that one can take and still have a good read.

The poetry volume, *Cora Fry*, contains some of the same sentiments and events as the novels, such as a serious accident. This suggests that the writing is closely autobiographical, which is no problem in itself. In general, however, I think that human beings either like the angst of specific other beings or they do not. There are certain kinds of angst, or expressions of it, that we relate to better than others. And some readers may not like angst at all. Reading Rosellen Brown is a highly personal experience; hers isn't the angst for everybody.

—Jill Franks

BROWN, Wesley

Nationality: American. **Born:** New York, New York, 23 May 1945. **Education:** Oswego State University, B.A. 1968.

Publications

Novels

Tragic Magic. New York, Random House, 1978.
Darktown Strutters. New York, Cane Hill Press, 1994.

Plays

Boogie Woogie and Booker T. New York, Theatre Communications Group, 1987.

Screenplays: *W.E.B. Du Bois, A Biography in Four Voices* (with others). 1996.

Other

The Teachers and Writers Guide to Frederick Douglass. New York, Teachers & Writers Collaborative, 1996.
Contributor, *Action: The Nuyorican Poets Cafe Theatre Festiva,* edited by Michael Algarin and Lois Griffith. New York, Simon & Schuster, 1997.
Editor, with Amy Ling, *Imagining America: Stories from the Promised Land.* New York, Persea Books, 1991.
Editor, with Amy Ling, *Visions of America: Personal Narratives from the Promised Land.* New York, Persea Books, 1992.

* * *

Though he may not be prolific, Wesley Brown is certainly a proficient author and his two novels *Tragic Magic* and *Darktown*

Strutters offer virtuoso proof of his talents. While both works explore issues of racial injustice roiling beneath the surface of white America, it is the seismic and shifting conscience of black America, of African-American men in particular, that invigorates Brown's work. Most compelling is his use of anxiety-laden themes such as masculinity in crisis, the double minoritization of black women, and the vexing conundrum of racial performativity: whether a socially constructed and thus ''mimicable'' blackness ever completely displaces a concept of black essentialism. And while nearly two decades span the publication of two vastly different novels (one recounts urban life in the 1970s while the other is set in the mid-nineteenth century) there is a binding aesthetic interweaving them—Brown's signature lyricism. Few novelists display such acumen for capturing the jazzy nuances of various types of black speech. With a crafty ear for a dialogue built upon generations of signifying, as well as the ribald ripostes of the dirty dozens and incantatory street poetics, Wesley Brown exemplifies the ''blues matrix'' which Houston Baker, Jr., and other literary critics have theorized as the central catalyzing framework through which all African-American art generates. This ''blues matrix'' is recognized as a central, shared component of a widely divergent body of late twentieth-century African-American writing loosely dubbed the ''New Black Aesthetic.''

Brown's first novel, *Tragic Magic* is the story of Melvin Ellington, a.k.a. Mouth, a black, twenty-something, ex-college radical who has just been released from a five-year prison stretch after being a conscientious objector to the Vietnam War. Brown structures this first-person tale around Ellington's first day on the outside. Although hungry for freedom and desperate for female companionship, Ellington is haunted by a past that drives him to make sense of those choices leading up to this day. Through a filmic series of flashbacks the novel revisits Ellington's prison experiences, where he is forced to play the unwilling patsy to the predatorial Chilly and the callow pupil of the not-so-predatorial Hardknocks; then dips further back to Ellington's college days where again he takes second stage to the hypnotic militarism of the Black Pantheresque Theo, whose antiwar politics incite the impressionable narrator to oppose his parents and to choose imprisonment over conscription; and finally back to his earliest high school days where we meet in Otis the presumed archetype of Ellington's ''tragic magic'' relationships with magnetic but dangerous avatars of black masculinity in crisis. But the effect of the novel cannot be conveyed through plot recapitulation alone, for its style is perhaps even more provoking than its subject.

Brown amplifies his hip coming-of-age story with a musical intonation making almost every paragraph ring with the cadences of jazz. Drawing from the trick chords of Thelonius Monk and the unresolving rhapsodies of Charlie ''Birdland'' Parker, Brown does more than simply quote music, he transcribes jazz into prose. Like inmate Shoobee Doobie who plays the ''lingo'' instrument and trades licks of street philosophy with his favorite records, Brown's narrative literally riffs on Ellington's past, building towards an epiphany of meaning which ultimately never really plays out as we, the listener-readers, or Ellington himself expect. After Otis is knifed while trying to restore his shattered manhood—whose disintegration he attributes more to the brainwashing bravado advertised in John Wayne movies than to the hand he lost in Vietnam—Ellington is also stabbed, but his wound results from a senseless act of selflessness as he attempts to stop a fight between two boys. The pain sends him into an aleatory fugue that begins with memories of Oedipal confusion, replays random moments of childhood, and crescendos into a psychological finale that mixes characters from each field of his past life and momentarily breaks the novel away from traditional narrative and temporal structures. In these last pages Brown evokes a postmodernist sense of what Frederic Jameson would call ''depthlessness,'' for Ellington finally learns after recovering from his near death experience that despite his constant modernist searching for an ultimate meaning in life, a Miles Davis tune called ''So What!'' has held the secret all along, that ''things really don't matter.'' But the novel does not terminate here. In a coda that dramatizes Ellington finally having sex with his new girlfriend, Brown provides a closure that is more erotic than emotional and redeems a hitherto problematic masculinity at the expense of the black woman, who is reduced to secondary status in the universe of the novel.

Darktown Strutters is a different sort of coming-of-age novel than *Tragic Magic*. This novel is not only set in the era of Jim Crow, its protagonist is Jim Crow, an antebellum slave whose dances are so incredible that they spawn a slave uprising, provide an avenue toward freedom in a white minstrelsy troupe, and even gain an interview with the renowned orator Frederick Douglass. As an example of what Linda Hutcheon calls ''historical metafiction,'' the novel reveals Brown's maturation in moving away from his own time and milieu in *Tragic Magic* and turning a backward glance to history—those harrowing years just leading up to and just beyond the Civil War, when Jim Crow embodied the color line that prohibited blacks from enjoying the same activities as whites such as riding in the same train cars—hence, the designation of Jim Crow cars reserved for African Americans. In the novel, Brown dramatizes the ''history'' of the Jim Crow car as Jim rides in isolation to cities where the troupe releases racial anxieties by making fun of them. This is not the first time, however, that Brown commingles historical celebrities with fictional characters. A look at the dramatis personae of his play *Boogie Woogie and Booker T* (Ida B. Wells, W.E.B. Du Bois, and Booker T. Washington) provides further evidence of this impulse to thematize black history. And yet, it is important to note that Brown's historical approach approximates the more traditional roman a clef, in that he does not disrupt either the history that he writes about nor the method used to write it, as does, for example, Ishmael Reed, a novelist to whom Brown is often compared.

If *Tragic Magic* is a novel that sings and scats, then *Darktown Strutters* is a book that dances and shuffles. But critics have been quick to point out moments where Brown stumbles in his performance. Remonstrances once again center on Brown's characterization of black women, in particular the Featherstone Sisters, with whom Jim and Jubilee (an unpredictably violent male who represents another variation on the ''tragic magic'' love-hate masculine friendship) travel and perform for audiences after the Civil War. Even though Brown goes against the grain of popular American history by making these women so unique—they own their own minstrel company, are outspoken proto-feminists, carry concealed knives, and ignore social as well as gender codes by pursuing bisexual relationships—the sisters still operate within the parameters of a patriarchal fantasy, becoming the focus of hetero-masculine love interests instead of the potentially oppositional figures that their initial description would seem to imply.

Notwithstanding a lackluster characterization of women and an unbalanced distribution of give-and-take dialogue, *Darktown Strutters* intervenes into a current academic debate over the historical significance of minstrelsy regarding not only black representationality, but also the construction of American whiteness. However, those moments where characters brood most profoundly over these issues (Jim explaining his refusal to blacken up, the homosexual minstrel leader who can only cope with life while blackened up) occur during the first part of the book set before the Civil War. Thereafter, the postbellum sections build towards an unexpected riotous ending that tragically leaves most of the characters dead. In this way, the plot trajectory of Brown's second novel mirrors that of his first: both seethe as moods turgidly push toward an explosive ending. But the tone of *Darktown Strutters* and the stakes of its tragedy give it a naturalistic quality that *Tragic Magic* does not possess.

—Michael A. Chaney

BUECHNER, (Carl) Frederick

Nationality: American. **Born:** New York City, 11 July 1926. **Education:** Lawrenceville School, New Jersey, graduated 1943; Princeton University, New Jersey, A.B. in English 1947; Union Theological Seminary, New York, B.D. 1958: ordained a Minister of the United Presbyterian Church, 1958. **Military Service:** Served in the United States Army, 1944–46. **Family:** Married Judith Friedrike Merck in 1956; three children. **Career:** English Master, Lawrenceville School, 1948–53; Instructor in Creative Writing, New York University, summers 1953–54; head of the employment clinic, East Harlem Protestant Parish, New York, 1954–58; chairman of the Religion Department, 1958–67, and School Minister, 1960–67, Phillips Exeter Academy, New Hampshire. William Belden Noble Lecturer, Harvard University, Cambridge, Massachusetts, 1969; Russell Lecturer, Tufts University, Medford, Massachusetts, 1971; Lyman Beecher Lecturer, Yale Divinity School, New Haven, Connecticut, 1976; Harris Lecturer, Bangor Seminary, Maine, 1979; Smyth Lecturer, Columbia Seminary, New York, 1981; Zabriskie Lecturer, Virginia Seminary, Lynchburg, 1982; lecturer, Trinity Institute, 1990. **Awards:** O. Henry prize, 1955; Rosenthal award, 1959; American Academy award, 1982. D.D.: Virginia Seminary, 1983; Lafayette College, Easton, Pennsylvania, 1984; Cornell College, Mt. Vernon, Iowa, 1988; Yale University, New Haven, Connecticut, 1990; D.Litt.: Lehigh University, Bethlehem, Pennsylvania, 1985. **Agent:** Harriet Wasserman, 137 East 36th Street, New York, New York 10016. **Address:** 3572 State Route 315, Pawlet, Vermont 05761–9753, U.S.A.

Publications

Novels

A Long Day's Dying. New York, Knopf, 1950; London, Chatto and Windus, 1951.

The Seasons' Difference. New York, Knopf, and London, Chatto and Windus, 1952.

The Return of Ansel Gibbs. New York, Knopf, and London, Chatto and Windus, 1958.

The Final Beast. New York, Atheneum, and London, Chatto and Windus, 1965.

The Entrance to Porlock. New York, Atheneum, and London, Chatto and Windus, 1970.

The Book of Bebb. New York, Atheneum, 1979.

Lion Country. New York, Atheneum, and London, Chatto and Windus, 1971.

Open Heart. New York, Atheneum, and London, Chatto and Windus, 1972.

Love Feast. New York, Atheneum, 1974; London, Chatto and Windus, 1975.

Treasure Hunt. New York, Atheneum, 1977; London, Chatto and Windus, 1978.

Godric. New York, Atheneum, 1980; London, Chatto and Windus, 1981.

Brendan. New York, Atheneum, 1987.

The Wizard's Tide. New York, Harper, 1990.

The Son of Laughter. San Francisco, HarperSanFrancisco, 1993.

On the Road with the Archangel. San Francisco, HarperSanFrancisco, 1997.

The Storm. San Francisco, HarperSanFrancisco, 1998.

Uncollected Short Stories

"The Tiger," in *Prize Stories 1955: The O. Henry Awards,* edited by Paul Engle and Hansford Martin. New York, Doubleday, 1955.

Other

The Magnificent Defeats (meditations). New York, Seabury Press, 1966; London, Chatto and Windus, 1967.

The Hungering Dark (meditations). New York, Seabury Press, 1969.

The Alphabet of Grace (autobiography). New York, Seabury Press, 1970.

Wishful Thinking: A Theological ABC. New York, Harper, and London, Collins, 1973.

The Faces of Jesus, photographs by Lee Boltin. Croton-on-Hudson, New York, Riverwood, 1974.

Telling the Truth: The Gospel as Tragedy, Comedy, and Fairy Tale. New York, Harper, 1977.

Peculiar Treasures: A Biblical Who's Who. New York, Harper, 1979.

The Sacred Journey (autobiography). New York, Harper, and London, Chatto and Windus, 1982.

Now and Then (autobiography). New York, Harper, 1983.

A Room Called Remember: Uncollected Pieces. New York, Harper, 1984.

Whistling in the Dark: An ABC Theologized. New York, Harper, 1988.

Telling Secrets (autobiography). New York, Harper, 1991.

The Clown in the Belfry: Writings on Faith and Fiction. San Francisco, HarperSanFrancisco, 1992.

Listening to Your Life: Daily Meditations with Frederick Buechner, compiled by George Connor. San Francisco, HarperSanFrancisco, 1992.

The Longing for Home: Recollections and Reflections. San Francisco, HarperSanFrancisco, 1996.

The Eyes of the Heart: A Memoir of the Lost and Found. San Francisco, HarperSanFrancisco, 1999.

*

Manuscript Collection: Wheaton College, Illinois.

Critical Studies: *Laughter in a Genevan Gown: The Works of Frederick Buechner 1970–1980* by Marie-Hélène Davies, Grand Rapids, Michigan, Eerdmans, 1983; *Frederick Buechner: Novelist* *and Theologian of the Lost and Found* by Marjorie McCoy, New York, Harper, 1988.

Frederick Buechner comments:

(1996) When I started out writing novels, my greatest difficulty was always in finding a plot. Since then I have come to believe that there is only one plot. It has to do with the way life or reality or God—the name is perhaps not so important—seeks to turn us into human beings, to make us whole, to make us Christs, to ''save'' us—again, call it what you will. In my fiction and non-fiction alike, this is what everything I have written is about.

* * *

The novels of Frederick Buechner represent a movement from a consideration of psychological textures to an assessment of the religious values that are expressed by those textures. The fact that Buechner is an ordained Presbyterian clergyman may not strike the reader of the earlier novels—*A Long Day's Dying*, *The Seasons' Difference*, and *The Return of Ansel Gibbs*—as particularly relevant to the interpretation of those novels. His early novels, indeed, may impress the casual reader as works that are in the tradition of Henry James, concerned as they are with the rather delicate and tenuously resolved relations among cultivated and privileged Americans. The characters in these novels are preoccupied with resolutions of their difficulties, but these resolutions go no farther than clarification of their identities in relation to each other. This clarification is conveyed in a style that was regarded, at the time of the novels' appearance, as oblique and over-worked. The actual course of events in the early novels issues, as indicated, in changes of orientation that can be spoken of as a clearing out of the psychological undergrowth that impedes the discovery of purpose and self-knowledge on the part of the chief characters. The course of the narratives is marked by a taste for ironic comedy—a comedy that records the experience of living in a world that, unlike the world of some older comedy, is bare of generally shared values. The values that are to be detached are values for a particular person and do not have much wider relevance.

It is in later novels—*The Final Beast*, *The Entrance to Porlock*, and *Lion Country*—that one can see Buechner moving, in an ironic and quite self-protective way, toward concerns that his ordination as a clergyman would suggest. He moves from concern with particular persons in special situations toward more inclusive concerns which announce that lives of individual characters are oblique annunciations of the general constraint and opportunity which all human beings can, if they are responsive, encounter. The psyche is also a soul—a focus of energy that achieves fulfillment by coming into relation with patterns that religion and mythology testify to. The style of the later work becomes simpler, and Buechner delights in reporting farcical aspects of American experience that found little place in his earlier work. And these farcical elements are organized by invocation of narrative patterns that are widely known. The narrative pattern that underpins *The Entrance to Porlock* is drawn from that item of popular culture, *The Wizard of Oz;* the motley company of his novel repeats and varies the quest that took Dorothy Gale and her companions along the Road of Yellow Bricks.

In *Lion Country* and the three novels that succeed it—*Open Heart*, *Love Feast*, and *Treasure Hunt*—the grotesque menagerie of characters has experiences that are organized by nothing less than the traditional patterns of the Christian religion itself. (The four novels are published together under the title of *The Book of Bebb*.) In this series, Christianity undergoes parody that on the surface is blasphemous. The reader is offered variation that is ironical rather than confirming, and yet—in the long run—achieves the only kind of validation that is possible at the present time. At the very least the series is a successful counter-weight to novels that confirm conventional piety by exercises in conventional piety. Yet beneath the adultery, farce, and sheer violence of the Bebb series is a set of insights that are very close to the assertions of conventional Christianity. The conventionality—and the sincerity—of Buechner's views can be sampled in the theological ABC contained in *Wishful Thinking* and other meditations.

On the Road with the Archangel draws on the Book of Tobit, dubbed apocryphal by Protestants but included in the Catholic Bible. In Nineveh, whence the Israelites (the future Lost Tribes) have been carried away, a wealthy and generous man named Tobit undergoes a Job-like series of trials. Tobit prays for death, while in the town of Ectabana, a beautiful girl named Sarah—plagued by a demon who has killed seven would-be husbands—makes the same request. The angel Raphael hears the prayers of both, and intervenes in their affairs, bringing the two together. The tale ends happily, with Sarah's marriage to Tobit's feckless son Tobias. *The Storm* likewise draws on a classic, though in this case one much more recent: Shakespeare's *The Tempest,* which Buechner places in a modern setting.

Buechner can, in summary, be seen as a novelist who at first was challenged by the sheer complexity of human behavior and who later finds that complexity comprehensible when linked with popular myth-work like the Oz books and, finally, with the self-mastery and self-discovery offered by the Christian religion.

—Harold H. Watts

BUJOLD, Lois McMaster

Nationality: American. **Born:** Lois McMaster in Columbus, Ohio, 2 November 1949. **Education:** Attended Ohio State University, 1968–72. **Family:** Married John Frederic Bujold in 1971 (divorced 1992); one son, one daughter. **Career:** Pharmacy technician, Ohio State University Hospitals, 1972–78. **Awards:** Nebula Award (Science Fiction Writers of America), best novel, 1988, best novella, 1989, best novel, 1995; Hugo Award (World Science Fiction Society), best novella, 1989, best novel, 1990, 1991, 1995; Locus Award (*Locus* magazine), 1991. **Agent:** Eleanor Wood, Spectrum Literary Agency, 111 Eighth Avenue, Suite 1501, New York, New York 10011, U.S.A.

Publications

Novels

Shards of Honor. Riverdale, New York, Baen Books, 1986; republished as *Cordelia's Honor.* New York, Simon & Schuster, 1996.
Ethan of Athos. Riverdale, New York, Baen Books, 1986.
The Warrior's Apprentice. Riverdale, New York, Baen Books, 1986.
Falling Free. Riverdale, New York, Baen Books, 1988.
Brothers in Arms. Riverdale, New York, Baen Books, 1989.
Borders of Infinity. Riverdale, New York, Baen Books, 1989.
The Vor Game. Riverdale, New York, Baen Books, 1990.

Vorkosigan's Game (contains *Borders of Infinity* and *The Vor Game*). Science Fiction Book Club, 1990.
Barrayar. Riverdale, New York, Baen Books, 1991.
The Spirit Ring. Riverdale, New York, Baen Books, 1992.
Mirror Dance. Riverdale, New York, Baen Books, 1993.
Cetaganda: A Vorkosigan Adventure. Riverdale, New York, Baen Books, 1996.
Memory. Riverdale, New York, Baen Books, 1996.
Young Miles. Riverdale, New York, Baen Books, 1997.
Komarr: A Miles Vorkosigan Adventure. Riverdale, New York, Baen Books, 1998.
A Civil Campaign: A Comedy of Biology and Manners. Riverdale, New York, Baen Books, 1999.

Short Stories

Dreamweaver's Dilemma: Stories and Essays, edited by Suford Lewis. Framingham, Massachusetts, NESFA Press, 1995.

Other

Editor, with Roland J. Green, *Women at War.* New York, Tor, 1995.

* * *

In 1986 Lois McMaster Bujold hit the science fiction reading world with the first installment of a remarkable space adventure series. What Bujold calls her ''serial novels'' center around the life of Miles Naismith Vorkosigan, a stunted, energetic, and charismatic character. Writing and publishing her saga, Bujold came to appreciate what she calls in her afterword to *Cordelia's Honor* the ''each-book-independent-format'' structure of serial novels: they have an almost hypertext-like freedom, as they are read in random order and can be written out of chronology as well. Her awareness of the form as well as her powerfully character-driven writing, have won Bujold Hugo and Nebula awards, as well as a devoted following of readers.

Although Bujold didn't begin writing science fiction until 1982, she traces that interest back to her early childhood and her father's influence on her. He was a professor of welding engineering who read science fiction on his travels as a consultant. Bujold's fourth novel, *Falling Free,* which she dedicated to her father and which won her her first Nebula award, has been praised for its depiction of the life of an engineer. One sequence in *Falling Free* involves the efforts of its central character to repair a broken mirror, a task that involves smelting and working molten materials. A similar focus on the material conditions of work also appears in *The Spirit Ring*, a novel not part of the Vorkosigan series, in which several characters cast a statue that comes to life and saves the day. Through such parallels as this, Bujold's 1992 departure from the Vorkosigan formula that has proved so popular offers an interesting insight into her central concerns.

The Spirit Ring shares with the Vorkosigan tales an interest in history and its implications, as well as an interest in marginalized people. It is a fantasy novel centering on a young woman who possesses magical powers. Despite its reliance on magic and supernatural creatures, the novel is grounded in historical research: it is set in Italy around the time of the Guelphs and Ghibellines, and much of the tension in the novel echoes historical events. Bujold details her sources in an authorial note, and outlines the connections several characters have to people from contemporaneous records. The lively heroine who must survive many pitfalls and find her true love is Bujold's invention.

To her many fans' delight, however, Bujold's desertion of the Vorkosigan universe was only temporary, and she continues to focus on detailing the many aspects of the multifaceted universe in which Miles lives. This fictional cosmos is made up of planets loosely linked by hubs of wormholes. Such a large and flexible structure allows Bujold to develop a range of cultures as well as a variety of interactions between them. For example, threats to different regions or to their access to a jump point, can cause shifting alliances. Bujold exploits these to vary the stresses and experiences of her characters. Although each novel in the series contains a time line indicating the chronology position of each work, Bujold does not limit herself to rehearsing the same plot—or even the same characters—in each novel or novella.

What does remain constant is that all Bujold's protagonists are in some way outsiders: a young woman with magical powers who must hide that skill or risk death (*The Spirit Ring*); a man with status in his home world who is reviled for his cultural practices and crippled by his beliefs when he must venture out of that safety (*Ethan of Athos*); a consulting engineer who must give up his identity as a downsider (planet dweller) and throw his lot in with genetically engineered people who can only live in freefall (*Falling Free*); Miles's own clone, who has been grown and deformed to subvert Barrayar (*Mirror Dance*).

Miles Naismith Vorkosigan also illustrates outsider status, even though he is the firstborn son of aristocratic parents in a militaristic, hierarchical culture on the planet Barrayar. Bujold has written that she first conceived of Miles as physically handicapped in a culture that valued physical strength and military might. Crippled by a chemical attack on his mother when he was in utero, Miles as a young man must struggle to find a role for himself other than pitied carbuncle.

This interest in underdogs may explain why Bujold is sometimes called a feminist writer. Certainly no overt ideological position arises in the Vorkosigan novels, unlike novels such as those by Sheri Tepper, who explicitly investigates environmentalist and feminist concerns. Bujold's novels are more swashbuckling space opera, usually centering on a male protagonist who outwits his superiors in brawn or authority. Some women feature as powerful assistants or, occasionally, a nemesis; but only *Cordelia's Honor*—the two-volume compilation of *Shards of Honor* and *Barrayar*—centers on a female protagonist.

Shards of Honor depicts the meeting of Miles's parents, Cordelia Naismith and Aral Vorkosigan. Both are persons of some position in their home cultures, but the two meet on territory alien to them both. Cordelia's team escapes, but she is captured, and therefore alone and friendless and facing alien values. Aral, who has captured her, is, ironically, equally on his own: his men have mutinied, and had the coup worked, he would be dead. In *Shards of Honor*, then, captor and captive must work together to save both their lives. This illustration of the power of cooperative action runs through many of the novels.

The follow-up novel, *Barrayar*—winner of a Hugo award—shows Bujold's strategy, as she has described it, of thinking of the worst thing to throw at her characters, and then watching them cope. Aral has become regent to the emperor; he and Cordelia are happily married and eagerly anticipating an offspring, when there is an attempted coup against the regency. Cordelia's outsider status is emphasized by the patriarchal structure of Aral's Barrayaran culture. When the fetal (yes, fetal—you have to read the book!) Miles is kidnapped, she mounts a rescue attempt that not only opposes her to the coup leaders, but to her own husband.

Bujold has written that she based Miles in part of T.E. Lawrence. At first a stronger parallel seems to be to Dick Francis's heroes, who can suffer torture without ever uttering a word or losing their machismo: Miles's bones snap at the least provocation, and the various dastardly forces he encounters don't hesitate to engage in brutality with their little victim (or with hapless females) when they can. Indeed, the early novels revel in evil, and too often place a dazed hero or heroine looking at the boots of some would be tormentor or rescuer.

The more properly Lawrentian quality becomes visible in the way Miles inspires near-fanatical loyalty and exertion in his followers. This effect leads to the almost accidental creation of the Dendarii mercenaries, the group that provides Miles with an identity outside Barrayar. The alienation of Admiral Naismith and Lord Vorkosigan—both Miles—gives Bujold a rich matrix in which to explore questions of personal and public identity.

But Bujold's interest in outsiders means that Miles cannot remain an accepted and powerful actor in the Dendarii fleet. As he approaches 30, Miles is killed and reconstituted with a flaw that prevents him from functioning properly under battle conditions. Shamed by hurting one of his crew, in *Memory* Miles returns home in disgrace. And once more Bujold studies the woes of an outsider. But likeable, self-deprecating, very wily Miles always turns defeat into victory. In the latest installments of his life, he has been appointed the youngest-ever imperial auditor. As in *Komarr* and *A Civil Campaign*, this structure promises a string of on-going adventures for Miles as he balances his aristocratic responsibilities with the challenges and excitement of exploring mysteries as an auditor exempt from the laws of each community he explores.

If not as philosophically inspiring as Octavia Butler's tales, Bujold's work is wholly—perhaps even wholesomely—enjoyable. From the earliest novels, which merged elements of romance and young adult fiction with sci fi, Bujold has shown an ability to weave elements of many genres together in her addictively engaging stories. As her main character matures, adventure gives way to detection, thus opening a wider scope for Bujold's ongoing interest in what her fictional universe reveals about the human condition.

—Victoria Carchidi

BURKE, James Lee

Nationality: American. **Born:** Houston, 5 December 1936. **Education:** University of Southwest Louisiana, Lake Charles, 1955–1957; University of Missouri, B.A. 1959, M.A. 1960. **Family:** Married Pear Pail; four children. **Career:** Social worker, Los Angeles, 1962–64; reporter, Lafayette, Louisiana, 1964; U.S. Forest Service, Kentucky, 1965–66; English instructor, University of Southern Louisiana, Lafayette, Louisiana; English instructor, University of Montana, Missoula; English instructor, Miami-Dade Community College, Florida. Currently English professor, Wichita State University, Kansas. **Awards:** Bread Loaf fellowship, 1970; Southern Federation of State Arts Agencies grant, 1977; Guggenheim fellowship, 1989; Mystery Writers of America Edgar Allan Poe award, 1989. **Agent:** Philip Spitzer, 788 Ninth Ave., New York, New York 10019, U.S.A. **Address:** 338 North Quentin, Wichita, Kansas 62708, U.S.A.

PUBLICATIONS

Novels (series: Dave Robicheaux, Billy Bob Holland)

To the Bright and Shining Sun. New York, Scribner, 1970; New York, Hyperion, 1995.
Lay Down My Sword and Shield. New York, Crewel, 1971.
The Lost Get-Back Boogie. Baton Rouge, Louisiana State University Press, 1986.
The Neon Rain (Robicheaux). New York, Holt, 1987; London, Mysterious Press, 1989.
Heaven's Prisoners (Robicheaux). New York, Holt, 1988; London, Mysterious Press, and London, Vintage, 1990.
Black Cherry Blues. Boston, Little Brown, 1989; London, Century, 1990.
A Morning for Flamingoes (Robicheaux). Boston, Little Brown, 1990; London, Arrow, 1993.
A Stained White Radiance (Robicheaux). New York, Hyperion, 1992; London, Arrow, 1993.
In the Electric Mist with Confederate Dead. New York, Hyperion, and London, Orion, 1993.
Dixie City Jam (Robicheaux). New York, Hyperion, and London, Orion, 1994.
Burning Angel. New York, Hyperion, 1995.
Half of Paradise. New York, Hyperion, 1995.
Two for Texas. New York, Hyperion, 1995.
The Convict: A Novel. New York, Hyperion, 1995.
Cadillac Jukebox. New York, Hyperion, 1996.
Cimarron Rose: A Novel. New York, Hyperion, 1997.
Sunset Limited. New York, Doubleday, 1998.
Heartwood. New York, Doubleday, 1999.
Purple Cane Road. New York, Random House, 2000.

Other

The Convict and Other Stories. Boston, Little, Brown, 1990.

* * *

In his thirteen novels, James Lee Burke sets up a basic confrontation between the beauties of the natural world and the stark, cruel, marginal existence of his characters. When he writes about the natural world of the Texas-Louisiana Gulf Coast with its swamps and bayous, or the blue mountains of Montana, he produces a poetic and lyrical prose, filled with affirmation and awe, based solidly on his descriptions and evocations of the weather, light, aromas, and colors. Such a world appears Edenic and, for the most part, unspoiled. Burke writes with a Thoreauvian attention to detail and a Whitmanic delight in the sheer boundlessness of nature, as in Burke's *To the Bright and Shining Sun.* Such a romantic sense of oneness and transcendence parallels his characters' often thwarted desire for escape, sex, occasional love, country music, and jazz. Titles such as *A Morning for Flamingos, A Stained White Radiance, Sunset Limited, Neon Rain,* and *Heaven's Prisoners* illustrate this core juxtaposition of nature's timeless beauty with the transient kitsch of the twentieth-century human struggle.

Burke's characters pollute the world they inhabit. The ex-cons, prostitutes, mobsters, drug dealers and runners, alcoholics, bad cops, psychopathic killers, and mindless thugs occupy a Darwinian combat zone of existence, of life at the edge. Burke's men are crude and violent, driven by their own testosterone tactics in a raunchy moral wasteland that portrays violent predators in a sprawling, sleazy underworld of society and the soul. His women often partake of the same characteristics, except for the few who manage to love and survive. Burke depicts this world in a hard-edged, Hemingway-style prose that is cryptic and often crude, a style that balances precariously between sadism and sentiment, terror and tenderness.

The hero of many of Burke's novels is Dave Robicheaux, a former cop on the New Orleans police force, who stakes his claim to New Iberia, a small town in southern Louisiana. He is a barely reformed alcoholic still suffering from the dark depressions and nightmares from his service in the Vietnam War and the murder of his first wife, Annie Ballard, a social worker. As one of the walking wounded, he continually examines his own existential doubts and uncertainties. In recent books he has married Bootsie, the widow of a mob boss who has lupus, and they have adopted Alafair, a Salvadoran orphan rescued from a plane crash. Robicheaux displays a tough Cajun code of honor and emerges as a kind of knight errant in the seedy underworld that is his life.

Burke's plots are sprawling and elaborate with their interlocking network of rednecks, racists, and raunchy hit men, served up in an intricate labyrinth of betrayals, double-dealings, frame-ups, and set-ups. In this grimly realistic and often nihilistic world, Robicheaux is usually able to find the connections beneath the murky mayhem, that touchstone of the mystery formula that assures us that some kind of rational order and moral victory can be achieved, however fitfully.

In *The Lost Get-Back Boogie* of 1986, an earlier novel that does not feature Robicheaux, Burke carefully lays out his landscape of prisons, dreary bars, holding cells, pickup trucks and gun racks, oil rigs and sleazy roadhouses, in which the ex-con, Iry Paret, tells the tale of his parole, released after having stabbed a man in a bar, and his journey to Montana from Louisiana to work on the ranch of his prison-buddy's father, Frank Riordan. In the course of the novel Paret, writing in the first-person, replaces Buddy Riordan, his friend from prison, by working well on the ranch and finally marrying Buddy's ex-wife Beth. In effect the story of this redneck's redemption is a complicated psychological process, for Iry's survival depends upon Buddy's death. Such Oedipal conflicts between "killer brothers" provide the novel with its terrible economy and vision: that personal triumph necessarily involves personal betrayal. That dark psychological subtext pervades all of Burke's subsequent novels.

An example of this kind of plot can be seen in one of the later books, *In the Electric Mist with Confederate Dead*, published in 1993. Here Burke mixes the Robicheaux milieu and mystery with gothic overtones that involve the apparition of a Confederate general, John Bell Hood, who appears in an eerie hallucinatory manner to become Robicheaux's advisor and conscience. The circuitous and labyrinthine plot involves the murder of a hooker, Robicheaux's memory of having witnessed the murder of a black man in the Atchafalaya Basin, and the return to New Iberia of the malignant mobster, Julie Balboni, to finance a Hollywood film there. Several murders and betrayals abound, Balboni is finally set afire in prison, and Robicheaux uncovers all the right solutions to the crimes.

James Lee Burke's novels build upon the "hard-boiled school" of American crime and detective fiction that was begun and carried on by Dashiell Hammett, Raymond Chandler, and Kenneth Millar writing as Ross Macdonald. Other contemporary writers continuing this tradition include Robert B. Parker, George V. Higgins, and Elmore Leonard. Such novels directly depict violent action in a world of total violence, corruption, and psychological mutants. Such writers create Dickensian characters who speak a tough, crude, naturalistic dialogue. Their vision of the world remains cruel, often heartless, relentlessly paranoid, and instinctually chaotic. Like Raymond Chandler, Burke emphasizes the thoughts and feelings of the main character, often in the foreground of the sizzling, danger-filled action.

In *Black Cherry Blues*, the winner of the 1990 Edgar Award for best mystery novel, Robicheaux is pursued by a professional killer and flees his home on the Bayou Teche to find a new life in Montana near the Blackfoot River Canyon. The ex-police officer's escape from the corrupt institutions of New Orleans crime into the anonymity of a fish and tackle business becomes another journey of self-reflection haunted by the memories of his wife's murder and father's death. His personal struggles are complicated by a surprise visit from an old Cajun friend, Dixie Lee Pughe, after which Robicheaux begins investigating an underworld scheme by the Mafia to take over Indian lands. Robicheaux is again involved with the violent world of Mafia thugs and federal agents. "The plot crackles with suspense," reported the *Los Angeles Times Book Review* about *Black Cherry Blues*, which is among the best of the Robicheaux series.

In novels such as *Purple Cane Road, The Lost Get-Back Boogie, Burning Angel, Cadillac Jukebox, Cimarron Rose, Dixie City Jam, Half of Paradise*, and *Lay Down My Sword and Shield*, Burke infuses his language with descriptive metaphors born of Louisiana's lush landscapes in combination with the "funky" music and myth unique to the culture of the state. He is not averse to exploiting the commercial potential of the genre, but infuses it with descriptive writing as lush as the settings he describes and as colorful as the denizens of the area. His is a genre writing grounded by a strong sense of place, one where the metaphysical and other-worldly events are commonplace and validated, as they are in Louisiana.

Burke brings to the hard-boiled school his own lyrical descriptions of the natural world, his own sense of loss for the Edenic world of his childhood in southern Louisiana, and his sounding of the psychological depths of guilt, obsession, and self-loathing that infect his characters. In using the mystery formula with its process of calculated revelation, he consistently exposes the darker, more frightening side of contemporary America, and even though the guilty may be captured and/or killed, that violent darker landscape remains brutally and masterfully intact.

From novels published earlier in his career during the 1980s with relatively nondescript titles such as *Sabine Spring* and *Two for Texas*, continuing to his 1999 novel, *Heartwood*, a Billy Bob Holland mystery, it is obvious that James Lee Burke is interested in commercial success. Choosing the mystery genre does not guarantee book sales, yet the simple and powerful eloquence that Burke brings to mystery writing elevates his novels toward comparisons with great literature while also increasing sales. He transforms an ordinary plot with a commercial edge into quality writing using metaphorical descriptions that ordinary writers of any genre can only envy.

—Samuel Coale, updated by Hedwig Gorski

BURNARD, Bonnie

Nationality: Canadian. **Born:** Stratford, Ontario, Canada, 1945. **Career:** Teacher, Sage Hill, Humber School of Writing; writer-in-residence, University of Western Ontario. Lives in London, Ontario, Canada. **Awards:** Commonwealth Best Book award, 1989;

Saskatchewan Book of the Year, 1994; Periodical Publishers award, 1994; Marian Engel award, 1995; Giller prize for Canadian Literature, 1999.

PUBLICATIONS

Novels

A Good House. Toronto, HarperFlamingoCanada, 1999.

Short Stories

Women of Influence. Regina, Canada, Coteau Books, 1988.
Casino and Other Stories. Toronto, HarperCollins, 1994.

Other

Editor, *The Old Dance: Love Stories of One Kind or Another.* Moose Jaw, Canada, Thunder Creek Publishing Co-operative, 1986.
Editor, *Stag Line: Stories by Men.* Regina, Canada, Coteau Books, 1995.

* * *

Establishing herself as a storyteller of the first rank through the considerable strengths of two books of short fiction—*Women of Influence* and *Casino and Other Stories*—Bonnie Burnard is recognized as a particularly sensitive chronicler of the extraordinary stories shaping seemingly ordinary lives. Her stories are thoughtful and intelligent meditations on the complex emotions attending the most powerful relationships in her character's lives (with siblings, parents, lovers, children) and with the tentative movements toward the defining moments of insight and self-awareness that accumulate slowly across years of experience. These are characters, as Burnard suggests in her first novel, *A Good House*, who come to understand that life, like love, is best lived with due respect for individual strength, common gentleness, absolute loyalty, and having a good ear with which to listen and learn.

Building on many of the themes and strategies that have drawn attention to her finest stories, Burnard proves herself an equally fine novelist in her management of this family saga that spans three generations of the Chambers family. Set mostly in a small town along the shores of Lake Huron, the novel begins with Bill Chamber's return from World War II, minus three fingers on his right hand, and builds slowly, tracing his readjustment to family life and to the subtle (and not so subtle) rhythms of the titular ''good house,'' the family home around which most of the ten dated sections that structure the novel eventually orbit. As in life, the parameters of Bill's experiences and stories expand gradually to include the events shaping the lives of his children and their families, the loss of his first wife and life with a second, and the deep disappoints and lasting joys.

Not surprising given the historical reach of the novel, characters gather into a kind of generational kaleidoscope that allows Burnard to shift effortlessly from a section dedicated primarily to the story of Bill's first wife, the wise and generous Sylvia, to one that privileges the struggles of Patrick, the eldest and hopeful son, to one in which free-spirited daughter Daphne holds center stage. Adding to this polyphony is the discovery of an old journal called, optimistically, ''Our New Life in Lambton County'' that Burnard positions as a kind of formalized genealogy, a stable record against and through which readers can begin to interpret and reinterpret the unrecordable and distinctly unstable nuances of lives lived to the fullest. It is these most resonant of shadings that Burnard captures most eloquently. In the final section of the book (''1997''), for instance, she narrativizes the thoughts of Margaret, Bill's second wife, while she reflects on a series of photographs, some of ''natural groupings'' (husbands and wives, sisters and brothers), others of a more random nature. As the novel concludes, Margaret contemplates her final gesture, one in which ''someone with a fine hand'' would label each picture. Such an inscription, she thinks to herself, would ''place'' the names in some sort of knowable and familiar arrangement, ''replicating the placement of the bodies'' in each image, organizing the chaos of so many people and so many stories into something akin to a key, ''or maybe it was more properly called a legend.'' In *A Good House* Burnard shows herself fully capable of remaining loyal to both the lives and the legends of people that she so clearly loves and respects.

—Klay Dyer

BURNS, Alan

Nationality: British. **Born:** London, 29 December 1929. **Education:** The Merchant Taylors' School, London; Middle Temple, London: called to the bar, 1956. **Military Service:** Served in the Royal Army Education Corps, 1949–51. **Family:** Married 1) Carol Lynn in 1954, one son and one daughter; 2) Jean Illien in 1980, one daughter. **Career:** Barrister in London, 1956–59; research assistant, London School of Economics, 1959; assistant legal manager, Beaverbrook Newspapers, London, 1959–62; Henfield fellow, University of East Anglia, Norwich, 1971; senior tutor in creative writing, Western Australian Institute of Technology, South Bentley, 1975; Arts Council writing fellow, City Literary Institute, London, 1976; associate professor and professor of English, University of Minnesota, Minneapolis, 1977–91. Since 1992, lecturer, Creative Writing Department, Lancaster University, England. **Awards:** Arts Council grant, 1967, 1969, and bursary, 1969, 1973; C. Day Lewis fellowship, 1973; Bush Foundation Arts fellowship, 1984. **Agent:** Diana Tyler, MBA Literary Agents Ltd., 45 Fitzroy St., London W1P 5HR, England. **Address:** Creative Writing Department, Lancaster University, Lancaster LA1 4YN, England.

PUBLICATIONS

Novels

Buster, in *New Writers One.* London, Calder, 1961; published separately, New York, Red Dust, 1972.
Europe after the Rain. London, Calder, 1965; New York, Day, 1970.
Celebrations. London, Calder and Boyars, 1967.
Babel. London, Calder and Boyars, 1969; New York, Day, 1970.
Dreamerika! A Surrealist Fantasy. London, Calder and Boyars, 1972.
The Angry Brigade: A Documentary Novel. London, Allison and Busby, 1973.
The Day Daddy Died. London, Allison and Busby, 1981.
Revolutions of the Night. London, Allison and Busby, 1986.

Uncollected Short Stories

''Wonderland,'' in *Beyond the Words.* London, Hutchinson, 1975.

Plays

Palach, with Charles Marowitz (produced London, 1970). Published in *Open Space Plays,* edited by Marowitz, London, Penguin, 1974.

Other

To Deprave and Corrupt: Technical Reports of the United States Commission on Obscenity and Pornography. London, Davis Poynter, 1972.

The Imagination on Trial: British and American Writers Discuss Their Working Methods, with Charles Sugnet. London, Allison and Busby, 1981.

*

Critical Study: Article by David W. Madden, in *British Novelists since 1960* edited by Jay L. Halio, Detroit, Gale, 1983.

* * *

Alan Burns's novels deserve the attention of serious readers. The first, *Europe after the Rain,* taking its title from a painting by Max Ernst, established him as a kind of infra-realist. Set in the unspecified future in a Europe devastated by internecine strife within ''the party,'' it deals with ruined figures in a ruined landscape, purposelessly dedicated to ''the work'' which is the only thing the party will reward with the food necessary to keep alive. The unnamed narrator alone possesses any genuine purpose. His quest to find and take care of the daughter of the Trotskyite leader of the rebel forces is inspired by something like love, doubtfully implicit in his actions, later developed into a statement of hope which comes as the one redeeming human fact in a world blasted beyond the usual trappings of humanity, but arrived at only after much violence: a woman is flogged, a dog stabbed and its legs dislocated, people fight over corpses for the gold fillings in the teeth, a leg is wrenched off a corpse and eaten by a woman, other women pursue and stone and half-crucify and eventually beat to death the commander of the forces who are in power at the book's beginning. To this nightmarish action Burns applies a style which may be described as burnt-out. His sentences are mostly short, or built up of short phrases resting on commas where one might have expected full-stops, the total effect being slipped, stripped, and abrupt.

Celebrations is similarly uncompromising, with six characters and seven funerals. Williams, boss of a factory, has two sons, Michael and Phillip, whom he dominates. A hero to himself, Williams is a most uncertain personality, inconstant in his psychological attributes, extravagant in behavior which is nevertheless always reported in the same flat and colorless prose. Phillip's death, following an accident which necessitates the amputation of his leg, leaves an even sharper taste of doubt in the reader's mind—for while it throws his father and his brother into grim rivalry for the attention of his widow, Jacqueline, these affairs are chronicled with such irony that they hardly seem to occur. All the time, it appears, we are meant to be reminded of Kierkegaard's dictum, ''The thought of death condenses and intensifies life,'' as Burns piles violence on violence, and funeral on funeral, abbreviating whole lives to a tapestry of gesture.

With *Babel* Burns seemed to have reached a dead end, though it confirms him in his role as infra-realist, anti-poet, steely perceiver of disconnections, writing as though he looks down on the rest of us from a private spaceship in unwilling orbit. Here he has assembled an ice-cold report on a world in chaos, stitching together clichés from the newspapers, fragments of misunderstood conversation, a babble of jokes and warnings. The cunningly fragmented styles owe too much to Burroughs and Ballard, and the comedy cannot quite conceal something merely self-disgusted in such furious insistence on unmeaning.

The Review of Contemporary Fiction devoted its Summer 1997 issue to Burns. Among the articles was a 1994 interview, conducted through the mail, with David Madden. The two discussed Burns's books, his influences, and his beliefs in a wide-ranging series of discussions that took in subjects ranging from James Joyce to the D-Day anniversary celebrations then taking place.

—Robert Nye

BURROWAY, Janet (Gay)

Nationality: American. **Born:** Tucson, Arizona, 21 September 1936. **Education:** The University of Arizona, Tucson, 1954–55; Barnard College, New York, B.A. (cum laude) in English, 1958; Cambridge University, B.A. (honours) in English 1960, M.A. 1965; Yale School of Drama, New Haven, Connecticut, 1960–61. **Family:** Married 1) Walter Eysselinck in 1961 (divorced 1973), two sons; 2) William Dean Humphries in 1978 (divorced 1981); 3) Peter Ruppert in 1993, one step-daughter. **Career:** Supply teacher and music director, Binghamton public schools, New York, 1961–63; costume designer, Belgian National Theatre, Ghent, 1965–70, and Gardner Centre for the Arts, University of Sussex, Brighton, 1965–71; lecturer in American Studies, University of Sussex, 1965–72; assistant to the Writing Program, University of Illinois, Urbana, 1972; associate professor, 1972–77, professor of English, 1977—; McKenzie Professor of English Literature and Writing, 1986–95, Florida State University, Tallahassee. Visiting lecturer, Writers Workshop, University of Iowa, Iowa City, 1980. Fiction reviewer, *New Statesman,* London, 1970–71, 1975, and since 1991, *New York Times Book Review.* Since 1994, columnist, *New Letters* (Kansas City). **Awards:** Amoco award, for teaching, 1974; National Endowment for the Arts grant, 1976; Florida Fine Arts Council grant, 1983; FSU Distinguished Teacher award, 1992; Lila Wallace-Reader's Digest fellowship, 1993. **Agent:** Gail Hochman, Brandt and Brandt Inc., 1501 Broadway, New York, New York 10036. **Address:** Florida State University, Department of English, Tallahassee, Florida 32306–1036.

PUBLICATIONS

Novels

Descend Again. London, Faber, 1960.

The Dancer from the Dance. London, Faber, 1965; Boston, Little Brown, 1968.

Eyes. London, Faber, and Boston, Little Brown, 1966.

The Buzzards. Boston, Little Brown, 1969; London, Faber, 1970.
Raw Silk. Boston, Little Brown, and London, Gollancz, 1977.
Opening Nights. New York, Atheneum, and London, Gollancz, 1985.
Cutting Stone. Boston, Houghton Mifflin, and London Gollancz, 1992.

Uncollected Short Stories

"Embalming Mom," in *Apalachee Quarterly* (Tallahassee, Florida), Spring 1985.
"Winn Dixie," in *New Letters* (Kansas City), January 1986.
"Growth," in *New Virginia Review* (Richmond), Spring 1990.
"I'toi," in *Prairie Schooner,* Spring 1991.
"Dad Scattered," in *The Day My Father Died.* New York, Running Press, 1994.

Plays

Garden Party (produced New York, 1958).
The Fantasy Level (produced New Haven, Connecticut, 1961; Brighton, Sussex, 1968).
The Beauty Operators (produced Brighton, Sussex, 1968).
Poenulus; or, The Little Carthaginian, adaptation of a play by Plautus, in *Five Roman Comedies,* edited by Palmer Boive. New York, Dutton, 1970.

Television Plays: *Hoddinott Veiling,* 1970; *Due Care and Attention,* 1973.

Poetry

But to the Season. Weston super Mare, Somerset, Universities' Poetry, 1961.
Material Goods. Tallahassee, University Presses of Florida, 1981.

Other

The Truck on the Track (for children). London, Cape, 1970; Indianapolis, Bobbs Merrill, 1971.
The Giant Ham Sandwich (verse only; for children), with John Vernon Lord. London, Cape, 1972; Boston, Houghton Mifflin, 1973.
Writing Fiction: A Guide to Narrative Craft. Boston, Little Brown, 1982; 3rd edition, New York, HarperCollins, 1991; 4th edition, HarperCollins, 1995; 5th edition, New York, Longman, 2000.

*

Manuscript Collection: Florida State University, Tallahassee.

Critical Studies: Article by Elisabeth Muhlenfeld, in *American Novelists since World War II,* 2nd series, edited by James E. Kibler, Jr., Detroit, Gale, 1980; "The Play in the Novel: *The Nuns* in *Opening Nights*" by Phyllis Zatlin, in *Modern Language Studies,* Summer 1993.

Janet Burroway comments:

(1996) I wrote my first novel, *Descend Again*, with the determination that it would be *fiction,* and not decorated autobiography. Therefore I set it in a town I knew only slightly, and in 1942, when I had been six years old. It was several years before I realized that it dealt with a heroine who, like myself, was driven by a desire to get out of Arizona and into a world of books.

I continued to choose subjects that seemed to me socially and politically "serious," eschewing concerns merely female, while certain themes chose me in spite of myself: the older-man-younger-woman relationship, near-suicide and the decision to live after all; the abandonment of children—even, recurrently, the image of proliferating garbage. I remember writing a scene in *The Buzzards*, when my children were toddlers, in which Eleanor walks out on her brood, myself thinking as I wrote: *I could never do this. Why do I keep writing about this?* Meanwhile my own boys pestered me to play and I kept sending them out of the room—"Can't you see mummy's working?"

After that novel I faced the fact that I had not considered women's lives sufficiently weighty for the content of fiction, and in the next book, *Raw Silk,* I faced my unchosen themes head on, beginning with the sentence, "This morning I abandoned my only child." The acknowledgement of gender as central to my identity has seemed to me a freeing and integrating change—freeing, even, to adopt a new breadth of attitude toward the global themes. I understand now why I kept fretting about all that garbage.

The greatest change in my work in the past five years has been in the process itself. I have paid deliberate attention to thwarting my linear, critical, perfectionist, left-brain proclivities, in favor of intuitive flow. It works; it makes for faster story, richer prose, more of the unexpected. The motto over my desk as altered, slightly but crucially, from "Don't Dread; Do" to "Writing is Easy. Not Writing is Hard." What's missing is mainly the imperative.

* * *

Janet Burroway depicts contemporary social issues through multiple points-of-view to convey strong, and sometimes nebulous, moral messages. Complicated relationships are neatly interconnected within sharply defined domestic and urban settings, as contrasting characters try to work out crises of conscience. The author's penchant for epigrams and symbols further unifies her narratives, but at the cost of excessive, self-conscious rhetoric. Likewise, while her abrupt and usually ambiguous endings avoid blatant didacticism, they also seriously mar the proportions of her careful structures. Stories do not seem to conclude so much as merely come to a halt. She also favors theatrical surprises which do not proceed necessarily from exigencies of plot but facilely exploit the sensational. These linguistic artifices and narrative ploys intrude more than they enlighten, weakening her otherwise admirable craftsmanship. Burroway's novels are well-paced, however, and she further enhances their popular appeal by providing plenty of practical information.

Eyes views the problems of race prejudice and of ethics in medicine and journalism through the individual perspectives of the four principal characters. Set in the South, the novel examines one day in the life of Dr. Rugg, an eye surgeon; his wife Maeve, who is pregnant at 40; their somewhat estranged son Hilary, a liberal reporter on a conservative paper; and Hilary's fiancée Jadeen, a junior high school teacher. Skillfully Burroway evokes the southern atmosphere and delineates the elaborate rituals of black-white relations as enacted by her sensitive protagonists. As a newly liberal and insecure daughter of an old Southern family, Jadeen's dilemma becomes acute: to refuse to teach an outrageously biased textbook and thus lose her job and alienate her genteel but bigotted mother, or to cave in and betray her recent convictions and lose her fiancée. Dr. Rugg, awkward in his charity and family relations and preoccupied in his profession, unwittingly destroys his career by casually mentioning his war-time experiments. Hilary, frustrated in his job and resentful of his famous father, carelessly misses the major scandal his father's seemingly innocuous lecture turns out to be—ironically, sent out on the national wires by Dodds, Rugg's soon-to-be-blind patient—which costs him and his mentor their positions. No totally satisfactory solution to these complications is possible. But Rugg heroically refuses to recant to save face for the State Department, and he serenely awaits his final heart-attack. Hilary, given a last chance, refuses to compromise his principles, or betray his father. Jadeen, however, is not strong enough for the sacrifice and buckles under to the "system;" she resigns herself (somewhat illogically) to being a subservient, dull teacher, without Hilary. Only Maeve, always understanding if inarticulate, and calm, maintains stability amid the domestic chaos. At the end, Jadeen points a moral of sorts: "Thoughts are complex. Actions are not. That is the subject of tragedy." Burroway's vignettes are telling, especially when she describes racial tension in a black bar or the techniques of surgery, reporting, teaching. But that's the rub: she prefers to tell more than to show. Dialogue is often wooden, and despite the neat plotting, the separate thematic strands don't quite mesh. The melodrama ends slightly out of focus.

The Dancer from the Dance is an ambitious and often subtle attempt at a novel of manners, in which the young, strangely innocent yet wise Prytania naively brings about the destruction and near-collapse of the older and more sophisticated people irresistibly drawn to her. 60-year-old Powers, the sensitive but detached narrator, gives the hapless girl a job in his UNICEF office in Paris and entrée into his elegant world. Soon Prytania holds all in thrall. Stoddard, a young and unimaginative medical student, she leads on but finally cannot marry. Old Riebenstahl, a primitive sculptor and curious sage, finally commits suicide, because he has acted as go-between for her illicit affair with the talented mime Jean-Claude. Even the worldly wise Mme. de Verbois, with whom she stays, and finally Powers himself are cruelly touched by her strange power. The nuances of social behavior, the curious transformations of character, and the complex emotional entanglements are deftly portrayed in several delicately drawn scenes. Yet, for all that, Prytania remains a shadowy figure, and the narrative barely escapes incredibility. Further, although the pages are cluttered with more witticisms and aphorisms than a Restoration comedy, the general tone is more that of a middling French film about yet another blighted romance. The several ironies and crises come off as contrived and formulaic, and ultimately the novel sadly disappoints: such an anticlimax after so much art.

In *The Buzzards* Burroway turns to the political realm, employing, yet again, several narrators. But as we follow the campaign trail of Alex, the conservative but likeable Senator from Arizona, the multiple perspectives—interior monologues, set speeches, newspaper articles, letters—soon become redundant and tedious. Especially so are the fatuous epigrams which clog the journal of the sententious and most implausible manager, Galcher (he calls them Axioms of God; e.g., "We are not subtle enough to contrive a machine in which disintegration contributes to maintenance and manufacture"). Alex's cold, brittle, and marvelously inept wife, his disaffected son, and neurotic daughter Eleanor (whose near-suicide and Mexican abortion pose serious threats to his chances), like the "allegorical" Galcher, are definite liabilities—not only for Alex but for the reader, who has little reason to be interested in them, let alone to like them. Younger daughter Evie, a vivacious, all-American, plastic pom-pom girl, is equally off-putting, though depicted as an asset in Alex's uphill struggle for re-election. Nonetheless, Burroway still has incisive power to reveal the moral ambiguities, contradictions, and rationalizations of her characters, especially the women. But beyond showing the hectic pace and many stratagems of modern politicking, the novel's rationale is not quite clear. And when Evie is precipitously assassinated in the last few pages, the event seems not tragic but merely expedient in terminating a journey that has no real destination. That a writer of Janet Burroway's obvious talents in use of detail and perspective should ultimately be defeated by a lack of control or malfunction of these very elements is an unfortunate irony of her otherwise impressive work.

—Joseph Parisi

BUSCH, Frederick (Matthew)

Nationality: American. **Born:** Brooklyn, New York, 1 August 1941. **Education:** Muhlenberg College, Allentown, Pennsylvania, 1958–62, A.B. 1962; Columbia University, New York (Woodrow Wilson fellow, 1962), 1962–63, M.A. 1967. **Family:** Married Judith Burroughs in 1963; two sons. **Career:** Writer and editor, North American Précis Syndicate, New York, 1964–65, and *School Management* magazine, Greenwich, Connecticut, 1965–66. Instructor, 1966–67, assistant professor, 1968–72, associate professor, 1973–76, professor of English, 1976–87, and since 1987 Fairchild Professor of Literature, Colgate University, Hamilton, New York. Acting director, Program in Creative Writing, University of Iowa, Iowa City, 1978–79; visiting lecturer in creative writing, Columbia University, New York, 1979. **Awards:** National Endowment for the Arts grant, 1976; Guggenheim fellowship, 1980; Ingram Merrill Foundation fellowship, 1981; National Jewish Book award, 1985; American Academy award, 1986; PEN/Malamud award, for short story, 1991. Litt.D.: Muhlenberg College, 1980. **Address:** Department of English, Colgate University, Hamilton, New York 13346, U.S.A.

Publications

Novels

I Wanted a Year Without Fall. London, Calder and Boyars, 1971.
Manual Labor. New York, New Directions, 1974.
The Mutual Friend. New York, Harper, and Hassocks, Sussex, Harvester Press, 1978.
Rounds. New York, Farrar Straus, and London, Hamish Hamilton, 1980.
Take This Man. New York, Farrar Straus, 1981.
Invisible Mending. Boston, Godine, 1984.
Sometimes I Live in the Country. Boston, Godine, 1986.
War Babies. New York, New Directions, 1988.
Harry and Catherine. New York, Knopf, 1990.
Closing Arguments. New York, Ticknor and Fields, 1991.
Long Way from Home. New York, Ticknor and Fields, 1993.
Girls. New York, Harmony Books, 1997.
The Night Inspector. New York, Harmony Books, 1999.
Don't Tell Anyone. New York, Norton, 2000.

Short Stories

Breathing Trouble and Other Stories. London, Calder and Boyars, 1974.
Domestic Particulars: A Family Chronicle. New York, New Directions, 1976.
Hardwater Country. New York, Knopf, 1979.
Too Late American Boyhood Blues. Boston, Godine, 1984.
Absent Friends. New York, Knopf, 1989.
The Children in the Woods: New and Selected Stories. New York, Ticknor and Fields, 1994.

Other

Hawkes: A Guide to His Fictions. Syracuse, New York, Syracuse University Press, 1973.
When People Publish (essays). Iowa City, University of Iowa Press, 1986.
A Dangerous Profession: A Book about the Writing Life. New York, St. Martin's Press, 1998.
Editor, *Letters to a Fiction Writer.* New York, Norton, 1999.

*

Manuscript Collection: Ohio State University, Columbus.

Frederick Busch comments:

I write about characters I want to matter more than my own theories and more than my own delights. The great problem is to face the fullest implications of one's insights and fears—and to sustain the energy to make a usable shape from them. No: the great problem is to sit and write something worthy of the people on the page, and the good reader.

* * *

Frederick Busch is a humanist with an eagle eye fixed on the family. Stricken rather than soothed by family ties, Busch's protagonists are kindred spirits with Ted Hughes's primal father: "Shot through the head with balled brains/ … Clubbed unconscious by his own heart/ … He managed to hear faint and far—'It's a boy!'"

Busch's concern with the vicissitudes of domestic life is shared by many of his peers—Richard Ford, Ray Carver, Andre Dubus—and is indeed a main preoccupation of post-World War II American fiction. What distinguishes Busch is his willingness to engage with history. Though *Closing Arguments* and *Girls* have contemporary settings, the protagonists, both Vietnam War veterans, cannot shake the burden of history in their own lives.

The Mutual Friend and *The Night Inspector* are actually set in the past. These novels are fictionalized accounts of the doings of nineteenth-century writers: Charles Dickens and Herman Melville, respectively. Though expertly rendered, the settings of these novels are obviously imagined; we cannot suspend disbelief here as easily as we might in the more familiar time and place of a book such as *Manual Labor.* This dynamic frees Busch to some extent from the demands of realism, giving him room to work figuratively and metafictionally. In both novels, he uses this space to explore the idea of disguise. Billy of *The Night Inspector* wears a papier-mâché mask to conceal his war-shattered face. In *The Mutual Friend*, the narrator looks back on his life as a series of "narratives I have perpetuated, in guises I have made." Busch here suggests parallels between the craft of fiction and the construction of personalities and "false fronts." Dickens and Melville are perfect protagonists, as writers preoccupied with the ways human beings trick each other.

Domestic Particulars is also set in the past. It blends more explicitly Busch's concern with history and the family. Set in New York City between 1919 and the 1970s, this family saga progresses amid the conditions of the great national social ambiance of these decades. Claire, Mac, and their son Harry strive to tap into the power of family affection. In the end, though, they achieve a less than expansive harmony. They are, after all, limited people of chary good will, to some extent outcharacterized by Busch's depictions of Brooklyn and Greenwich Village through the decades.

In both time and space, Busch is a true literary journeyman. He takes on a variety of settings and occupations, yet never feels like a tourist or an apprentice. He is equally alert to the countryside or the city, to the barn or the hospital. Natural settings save, as in "Trail of Possible Bones" (*Domestic Particulars*), or frighten, as in "What You Might as Well Call Love" (*Hardwater Country*). Either way, they are portrayed in minute detail. Likewise with work. Whether it's Prioleau making a television hook-up (*Take This Man*), or Silver and Hebner at their pediatrics (*Rounds; Domestic Particulars*), the enterprise is always vividly rendered. Work is often a small—though at times, illusory—grace in the fraught lives of his characters; thus Busch particularizes every type of labor with care.

I Wanted a Year Without Fall is legend passing from a father to his sleeping infant son. Its comic absurdity resides in parallels with *Pilgrim's Progress* and *Beowulf.* Ben recounts his adventures with Leo, who hits the road to escape urban destitution and a cuckold who wants his hide. For his part, Ben is fleeing a dead woman's voice. In a typical parody, Ben plays the Green Knight to an army of cockroaches. Here is the heroism of flight, not of the quest. Busch's anxious and ongoing preoccupation with the act of writing is central to the conclusion. Ben's last bardic utterance to his uncomprehending boy, "I will ask you to listen to an old time lay," is absurd indeed.

Another recurring concern in Busch's work is the death of children. In *The Mutual Friend*, the narrator reflects that "children die all the time, you know. It's 1900, and we ought to be learning why children die." Set decades later, *Manual Labor* makes it clear that modern medicine has not completely solved this "why," particularly in the existential sense. Anne and Phil Sorenson struggle to overcome the loss of their unborn child. Yet death pervades their lives. Abe, a vagrant whom they befriend in Maine, becomes the unhealthy focus of Anne's own suicidal attention, then kills himself. The novel esteems the victory of the couple over the nearly ubiquitous disintegration surrounding them. Their salvation is the manual labor of the two rebuilding an old house following the ruined labor of a childless mother. Phil's dictum, "You forget with your hands," is provided at the outset by the "child."

Rounds joins the Sorensons, Elizabeth Bean (a school psychologist), and Eli Silver, M.D. The Sorensons still need children. Elizabeth is pregnant, unmarried, and unwilling to abort the fetus. At the outset, Silver is all but ruined. His inadvertence has cost his son's life and, in the disastrous aftermath of the tragedy, his marriage. Busch separates and eventually intersects his characters' stories, a common strategy in his work. Silver intends to save himself from alcohol and emotional collapse by unflagging and expert attention to his pediatric practice, which is presented with surpassing realism. But only the

Sorensons' affectionate regard and Elizabeth's love for him finally achieve that. Silver's scrupulous decision to initiate the death of a little girl in her final agony is realized with superb ethical authenticity.

In *Take This Man*, Gus has two fathers. At ten he goes to Anthony Prioleau, the biological one. His mother follows suit. The three are a family, strangely but abidingly. Tony and Ellen never marry. The novel gradually sketches in backgrounds—why Tony was a conscientious objector during the war, why Ellen had a taste for leave-taking. The other father remains in emotional but not physical range, never betrayed by Gus, who nonetheless comes to love Ellen and Tony unreservedly. Gus's first meeting with Tony and Tony's passing are Busch at his emotional best. Two ministers, the Reverends Van Eyck and Billy Horsefall (a parody of Billy Joe Hargis), are Busch at his comic best.

Invisible Mending is equally hilarious and poignant. Though Zimmer, a ''Jew manqué,'' fears loneliness, his Gentile wife shows him the door. Her love isn't equal to his self absorption. For the first four pages it is 1980; it requires 214 pages to get back there. Meanwhile, Zimmer recollects his wondrous days with Rhona Glinksy, librarian and Nazi hunter, and his marriage with Lillian. Lil avers that Zimmer ''can make a secular mystery out of the holiest simplicity.'' Zimmer recollects himself as ''the treacherous amphibian who waddled on the Christian sands and swam in the blood of Jews.'' When Rhona reappears in 1980, times past and present merge. But Zimmer's young son provides a new and imperative focus. *Invisible Mending* brings Philip Roth to mind, both *Portnoy's Complaint* and *The Ghost Writer*. The novel is entirely up to the comparison.

War Babies, a novella, follows Pete Santore's ''mission of ignorant need'' from Illinois to Salisbury, England. Son of a now-dead father who was imprisoned for treason after his return from the Korean War, Santore seeks Hilary Pennel, daughter of a dead British officer with whom Santore's father had been held captive. Just below full consciousness, Santore needs to expiate his father's sin, which he fears pertained not only to America but to this hero. Thus the adult children meet, have a brief affair and discover the paradoxical likeness of their fathers' emotional bequests. Hilary has experienced her father's fatal resistance to his captors as abandonment, as Santore has his father's collaboration. Pennel's inadvertent gift to his daughter proved to be his vicious jingoist subaltern, aptly named Fox. After surviving the camp, Fox has held Hilary thrall to both his horrifying memories of the war and his sexual needs. This has cost Hilary an authentic life and a serious measure of sanity. This is a disturbing, morally insightful book.

Absent Friends is a strong collection of stories. Those in which the ''friends'' are family, either dead or at a distance, are especially compelling. ''From the New World,'' the first and longest, masterfully realizes a middle-aged son's relation to his dead father. But variety, both of absence and point of view about absence, gives the collection richness in subject and perspective.

Harry and Catherine tells us more than we need to know about the enduring relationship of an unmarried couple, separated over a decade and brought together again through Harry Miller's employment by a senator from New York. The boss wants to work out his political posture toward an upstate country mall being constructed over the bones of slaves who had died of the plague after finding their way north on the underground railway. Far too serendipitously, Catherine Hollander's current lover, Carter Kreuss, is the contractor. Harry is honorably disposed to the dead and Carter's case for free enterprise is not without merit, especially given that the town fathers had long since secretively moved the bones from their original locale, a fact not worth much to a presidential aspirant. The novel is principally shaped, however, by the bond between Harry and the independent, morally centered Catherine. Their endless, over-subtle exchanges strain patience. The novel's implausible integration of the characters' situations strains credulity.

In *Closing Arguments*, the burden of memory gives a menacing edge to family life in small-town America. Mark, a Vietnam vet, lives the ordered life of a Main Street attorney in upstate New York. His family life isn't so ordered, however. His marriage is on the rocks, his teenage son recalcitrant and troubled. Furthermore, these matters must compete with Mark's daily, horrific memories of the killing he did in Vietnam, some of it indiscriminate: ''once in a while I got to ride down howling and make popcorn out of people.'' So when Mark takes on the case of young Estella, accused of murdering her lover, his sense of recognition closes in. He becomes obsessed with her. The trembling hold he has on work and family life is ruined. He and Estella become comrades in destruction, the ruthless soldier-self finally uncovered.

In *Long Way From Home*, the protagonist, Sarah, also upturns the domestic order of her life. Suddenly seized with an ''emergency feeling,'' she abandons her husband and their six-year-old son to search for her biological mother. Cleverly, Busch explores the effects of Sarah's departure through shifting points of view. Her husband, Barrett, pursues her, at first heading in the wrong direction. His self-destructiveness along the way suggests that his journey is more about facing his own personal demons than finding his wife. Meanwhile, Sarah successfully finds her natural mother. But Gloria, an itinerant nurse-naturopath, is a dangerous discovery. The pull of ''blood ties'' that drove Sarah to find Gloria turns out to have a cruel kickback. Gloria kidnaps Sarah's son. The blood tie Sarah seeks becomes poisonous.

In *Girls*, Busch explores the most daunting aspect of ''why children die.'' In ''Ralph the Duck'' (Children in the Woods), the seed story for *Girls*, a young couple's daughter dies in infancy. This loss, mysterious and painful as it may be to Jack and Franny, is at least an ''innocent'' one. In *Girls*, the couple's grief is compounded first by the frivolous-seeming suicide attempt by a local college student—whom Jack saves—and then by the search for a missing 14-year-old girl. Jack's heroism, however impressive, can't erase the profound loss of his child. The awful twist of fate that took his daughter from him is compounded by the horrific will of the girl's murderer, who, like Camus' Caligula, grants no mercy in his quest to mimic and compound the cruelties of fate.

—David M. Heaton, updated by Lisa A. Phillips

BUTLER, Octavia Estelle

Nationality: American. **Born:** Pasadena, California, 22 June 1947. **Education:** Pasadena City College, A.A. 1968. **Awards:** Fifth prize, *Writer's Digest* Short Story Contest, 1967; Creative Arts Achievement award (Los Angeles YWCA), 1980; Hugo award (World Science Fiction Convention), 1984, 1985; Nebula award (Science Fiction Writers of America), 1985; Locus award (*Locus* magazine), 1985; Best novelette award (*Science Fiction Chronicle Reader*), 1985; MacArthur fellowship, 1995. **Address:** P.O. Box 6604, Los Angeles, CA 90055, U.S.A.

PUBLICATIONS

Novels

Patternmaster. New York, Doubleday, 1976.
Mind of My Mind. New York, Doubleday, 1977.
Survivor. New York, Doubleday, 1978.
Kindred. New York, Doubleday, 1979; second edition, Boston, Beacon Press, 1988.
Wild Seed. New York, Doubleday, 1980.
Clay's Ark. New York, St. Martin's Press, 1984.
Dawn: Xenogenesis. New York, Warner Books, 1987.
Adulthood Rites: Xenogenesis. New York, Warner Books, 1988.
Imago. New York, Warner Books, 1989.
The Evening and the Morning and the Night. Eugene, Oregon, Pulphouse, 1991.
Parable of the Sower. New York, Warner Books, 1995.
Parable of the Talents. New York, Seven Stories Press, 1998.
Lilith's Brood. New York, Warner Books, 2000.

Short Stories

Bloodchild and Other Stories. New York, Four Walls Eight Windows, 1995.

Other

Contributor, *Tales from Isaac Asimov's Science Fiction Magazine: Short Stories for Young Adults,* edited by Sheila Williams and Cynthia Manson. San Diego, Harcourt Brace Jovanovich, 1986.
Contributor, *Omni Visions One,* edited by Ellen Datlow. Greensboro, North Carolina, Omni Books, 1993.
Contributor, *Invaders,* edited by Jack Dann and Gardner Dozois. New York, Ace Books, 1993.
Contributor, *Women of Wonder: the Classic Years—Science Fiction by Women from the 1940s to the 1970s,* edited by Pamela Sargent. HBH/Harvest, 1995.
Contributor, *Virtually Now: Stories of Science, Technology and the Future,* edited by Jeanne Schinto. Persea, 1996.

*

Critical Studies: *Octavia Butler* by Marleen S. Barr, Mercer Island, Washington, Starmont House, 1986; *Across the Wounded Galaxies: Interviews with Contemporary American Science Fiction Writers,* edited by Larry McCaffery, Urbana, University of Illinois Press, 1990; *Ecofeminist Literary Criticism: Theory, Interpretation, Pedagogy,* edited by Greta Gaard and Patrick D. Murphy, Urbana, University of Illinois Press, 1990; *American Science Fiction and Fantasy Writers* by Clare L. Datnow, Springfield, New Jersey, Enslow Publishers, 1999; *A Companion Text for Kindred* by Janet Giannotti, Ann Arbor, University of Michigan Press, 1999.

* * *

The many efforts by literary critics to define the work of Octavia E. Butler speak to their challenge and the author's complexity. Among the categories Butler has fallen into: science fiction writer, African-American writer, feminist writer, and speculative fiction writer. But none seem to capture the eerie depth of Butler's work, which includes more than 10 works.

Butler has regularly garnered praise from literary critics, largely for her prose style and powerful female characters. The more Butler creates a character that is hard to pigeonhole, the more Butler herself displays a unique quality of writing. Her focus on issues of ethics, race, and gender are imbedded into her science fiction; but these issues do not consume the stories. Many critics have praised her for a social inquiry of sexual equality, and they have noted her intensely interesting focus on independent characters and the need for unity.

Four of her five earliest books have been dedicated to the Patternist series: *Patternmaster, Mind of My Mind, Survivor,* and *Wild Seed.* These books are about telepaths who are the central power figures on Earth. They are an integrated society, and central characters are often black women. This Patternist community started when Mary created a connection between mental abilities and actives who needed her help. There are many people needing help in these books, but they are often those struggling with latent mental abilities, or those who have been subsumed by diseases from travel. This new society based on mental acuity is also an imagined look at what the world would be like if men and women were truly equal. In *Patternmaster,* for example, a central female character becomes a man's mentor, has his baby, and saves him from evil forces without having any real desire to marry him. This is Butler's strong suit—imagining how a character would act in an equal society, how her decisions would be different, how real power would be an impetus to think individually and for others. Butler is certainly a proponent of love, but in this equal arrangement, her main characters are not about to simper around the parlor waiting for a man to take action.

In academic circles Butler is best known for her book *Kindred* about a contemporary African-American writer named Dana who is called back in time by her great-great-grandfather. He is a white plantation owner, and needs Dana to keep him from death. Without Dana's protection he will die, and consequently, Dana will not be born, either. This complex interconnection of races, and the mix of time periods, led to much praise for this book.

Parable of Talents, a more recent book, continues the story originated in *Parable of the Sower.* The story is set in 2032, when religious extremists have won government office. Lauren Olamina embraces another religious belief: Earthseed. Olamina sees herself as a future leader in this religion that focuses on mastering change, and sees truth in the stars. *Parable of Talents* shows the rift between Lauren and her daughter over this faith. The book has been highly praised for its eloquent writing and depth of character.

—Maureen Aitken

BUTLER, Robert Olen, Jr.

Nationality: American. **Born:** Granite City, Illinois, 20 January 1945. **Education:** Northwestern University, B.S. 1967; University of Iowa, M.A. 1969; postgraduate study at the New School for Social Research, 1979–81. **Military Service:** Military intelligence, U.S. Army, 1969–72: served in Vietnam, became sergeant. **Family:** Married 1) Carol Supplee in 1968 (divorced 1972); 2) Marilyn Geller in 1972 (divorced 1987), one son; 3) Maureen Donlan in 1987 (divorced 1995); 4) Elizabeth Dewberry in 1995. **Career:** Reporter/editor, *Electronic News,* New York, 1972–73; high school teacher, Granite

City, Illinois, 1973–74; reporter, Chicago, 1974–75; editor-in-chief, *Energy User News,* New York, 1975–85; assistant professor, McNeese State University, Lake Charles, Louisiana, 1985–93, professor of fiction writing, 1993—. **Awards:** TuDo Chinh Kien award for Outstanding Contributions to American Culture by a Vietnam Vet (Vietnam Veterans of America), 1987; Emily Clark Balch award, 1990; Pulitzer prize, 1993; Richard and Hilda Rosenthal Foundation award (American Academy of Arts and Letters), 1993; Notable Book award (American Library Association), 1993; Guggenheim fellow, 1993; National Endowment for the Arts fellow, 1994. L.H.D., McNeese State University, 1994. **Agent:** Kim Witherspoon, Witherspoon and Chernoff. **Address:** Department of English, McNeese State University, 4100 Ryan Street, Lake Charles, Louisiana 70609, U.S.A.

Publications

Novels

The Alleys of Eden. New York, Horizon Press, 1981.
Sun Dogs. New York, Horizon Press, 1982.
Countrymen of Bones. New York, Horizon Press, 1983.
On Distant Ground. New York, Knopf, 1985.
Wabash. New York, Holt, 1987.
The Deuce. New York, Holt, 1989.
They Whisper. New York, Holt, 1994.
The Deep Green Sea. New York, Holt, 1997.
Mr. Spaceman. New York, Grove Press, 2000.

Short Stories

A Good Scent from a Strange Mountain: Stories. New York, Viking Penguin, 1992.
Tabloid Dreams. New York, Holt, 1996.
Coffee, Cigarettes and A Run in the Park. Decantur, Georgia, Wisteria Press, 1996.

Other

Introduction, *Vietnam War Literature: A Catalog* by Ken Lopez, Francine Ness, and Tom Congalton. Hadley, Massachusetts, K. Lopez, 1990.
Foreword, *Fragments* by Jack Fuller. Chicago, University of Chicago Press, 1997.

*

Critical Studies: *Conversations with American Novelists: The Best Interviews from the Missouri Review and the American Audio Prose Library,* edited by Kay Bonetti, et al, Columbia, University of Missouri Press, 1997.

* * *

After writing six novels that received little attention, Robert Olen Butler won the Pulitzer Prize with his 1992 collection of short stories, *A Good Scent from a Strange Mountain.* What captured the attention of the Pulitzer judges—and of Butler's rapidly growing audience—is that these short stories are all narrated in first person by Vietnamese characters—businessmen, housewives, war veterans, all immigrants to the United States. This is a remarkable and unique achievement when compared with the ''Vietnam fiction'' of other authors such as Tim O'Brien and Elizabeth Scarborough. Butler speaks for the Vietnamese themselves, rather than about Americans affected by the war.

Butler's father taught theater in Illinois, so he earned a B.A. and M.A. in playwriting during the 1960s, assuming he would become an actor or dramatist. But after graduating in 1969, he anticipated conscription into military duty in Vietnam. He signed up for a position in counterintelligence, reckoning he could stay Stateside. He spent a year learning to speak Vietnamese fluently and in 1971 lived in Bien Ha and Saigon.

Returning to the States, Butler married, divorced, worked at journals and newspapers, remarried, and realized his calling was in fiction, not drama. He began writing novels on the commuter train from Long Island to Manhattan. When he flew to southern Louisiana in 1985 to accept a position as creative writing instructor at McNeese State University, the view from the plane of the wetlands and rice paddies reminded him so much of Vietnam that he moved there at once, and was please to find a thriving community of Vietnamese expatriates.

Because of these events, much of Butler's fiction is concerned with the search for a new home (or a lost one), the sadness of families separated by war and death, relationships between mothers and daughters, fathers and sons.

In Butler's first book, *The Alleys of Eden,* Clifford Wilkes, an American deserter in Vietnam, shares with lovely Lanh a blissful, passionate affair. The night the Viet Cong surround Saigon, Cliff must decide whether to run for the airlift, whether to bring Lanh with him, or whether to die now rather than risk capture and torture at the hands of the communists. During this night, which comprises the first half of the book, Cliff relives scenes from his past involving separation and loss: the death of his father, the disaffection of his mother, the flight of his best friend to Canada, his divorce. Cliff determines not to abandon Lanh, and they escape Saigon together. However, they cannot restore their happiness in America. With a culture shock too great, the two lovers drift into loneliness toward a hopeless conclusion.

When Cliff recalls his stint as a general infantryman in *Alleys,* Butler depicts the event that led him to desert. Two of his compatriots in the army were Wilson Hand and Captain David Fleming, the former of whom had been a prisoner of the Viet Cong and the latter his daring rescuer. Their stories comprise the next two novels, *Sun Dogs* and *On Distant Ground.*

In *Sun Dogs,* Wilson works for Royal Petroleum, which sends him from its New York office to Alaska to investigate theft of information. Wilson detests the city, where he feels ''dead and buried'' in its ''clutter.'' He yearns to stay in the Alaskan outback, with its purity of landscape and stark living conditions. However, like the ''sun dogs'' Wilson sees in the Alaskan sky—illusory suns formed by atmospheric ice crystals—two horrors dog him: the suicide of his ex-wife and the torture of imprisonment by the Viet Cong. Wilson has an affair with the beautiful, untrustworthy Marta, and becomes friends for life with Clyde, a loyal bush pilot. Butler peels away lies and red herrings, webs of deceit and murderous schemes, to reveal not merely a mystery about corporate greed and reserves of fuel, but an unexpected drama about the fuels that keep the body and spirit alive.

In *On Distant Ground,* David Fleming is court-martialed for having ''aided the enemy.'' An emotionally aloof man, he had been strangely affected by spying a graffito on a South Vietnamese prison wall: ''Hygiene is healthful.'' The irony and courage of these words speak to him as those written by a kindred soul. Finding the prisoner incarcerated there, a Viet Cong officer named Tuyen, whose name suggests ''twin,'' became an obsession. When at last he tracked Tuyen to a penal colony, he hijacked a helicopter and freed the prisoner. Years later, he is still unable to articulate even to his wife why he did this, and the jury sentences him to a dishonorable discharge.

Even as David and his wife see their first son born, circumstantial evidence convinces David that he also had a son by a Vietnamese woman while serving there. Remembering his own unkind father, he determines to find the boy. With his wife's reluctant compliance, he returns to Vietnam—during the very week that the communists overrun Saigon. While dodging various enemies, he learns the fate of his lover and finds a boy who may be their son. His desperate attempt to get them both out of the country alive culminates in a startling re-encounter with Tuyen, who tells David a truth that forces all of his experiences into new perspective.

Countrymen of Bones chronicles the rivalry of an archaeologist, Darrell Reeves, and a military physicist, Lloyd Coulter, against the backdrop of New Mexico on the eve of the first detonation of an atomic weapon at Los Alamos. The subplots involve the Manhattan Project, run by J. Robert Oppenheimer, who provides the theme of the novel with his famous, awestruck, grieving remark: ''I am become Death, the shatterer of worlds''; and a love affair between Reeves and Army private Anna Brown. Human failings such as opportunism and unrestrained anger become the shatterers of private worlds in this work.

At his new home in Louisiana, Butler drew upon autobiographical detail again for *Wabash.* Raised in Granite City, Illinois, Butler had as a teenager worked at a steel plant; his mother had lived there during the Depression years. This novel combines conflicts between the captains of profit (personified by the owner of the Wabash Steel foundry) and the budding communists, between Deborah Cole and her inarticulate, impotent husband Jeremy, and between Deborah's extended family of mother, aunts, and grandmother. As in so many of Butler's novels, the various conflicts parallel and play off each other in ingenious ways.

The Deuce marked a narrative breakthrough for Butler when he chose a first-person voice. The narrator is a teenager who seeks to understand his culture and identity as the son of a South Vietnamese bar girl and of a Vietnam vet who brings him to New Jersey. He used the technique again in *A Good Scent from a Strange Mountain.*

The fifteen stories therein are told by a war-time translator; an ex-spy in South Vietnam who goes to grotesque, Roald Dahl-esque measures to keep his gorgeous wife sexually faithful; a mother speaking to her unborn child; by Catholics and Buddhists; by the wealthy and the desperate; and in the title story by a saddened, dying old man who hallucinates a visitation by Ho Chi Minh. Some of these stories are slight, with a single, poignant point to make about the human condition. Most work on many levels to gather such themes as love, envy, loneliness, sensuality, miscommunication, hatred, vengefulness, and spiritual redemption into tales about ghosts, reincarnation, and cultural assimilation.

A Good Scent thrust Butler into the international spotlight. Besides the Pulitzer, it earned the Rosenthal Foundation Award from the American Academy of Arts and Letters, the *Southern Review*/Louisiana State University Prize for Short Fiction, a nomination for the PEN/Faulkner Award, and fellowships from the Guggenheim Foundation and the National Endowment for the Arts. Butler's earlier works were reissued, and he was commissioned by the Ixtlan film production company to write a screenplay for the collection. The literary world that had barely noticed Butler could now hardly get enough of him.

Butler next wrote a daring novel about sensuality and sexual relationships, *They Whisper.* The narrative technique is compelling and marvelous, consisting of a stream-of-consciousness recollection-cum-meditation by thirty-five-year-old Ira Holloway on the beauty and desirability of the women he has known, married, and lusted for. Imagining their thoughts and lives in his contemplation of and paean to the wonders of women, Ira seeks to solve the mystery of sexual yearning.

Two more collections followed: *Tabloid Dreams*, in which Butler takes inspiration from tabloid headlines, and *Coffee, Cigarettes, and A Run in the Park*, composed of three Vietnam stories. Butler's next foray into the stranger-in-a-strange-land mode came with *Mr. Spaceman*, superficially a science fiction novel. The stories of Desi, the humanoid extraterrestrial of the title, and of the twelve people who spend the last week of the twentieth century with him are explicitly modeled on the myths of the New Testament. Desi has been charged by his own race to reveal to humanity the existence of other sentient beings in the universe, and struggles with reluctance and fear when he is taken for the returning Messiah. Butler meditates upon language and its limitations, often to very funny effect, as Desi struggles in his precise and literal way to understand humans.

Butler has said in many interviews that he believes fiction can reveal human experience as universally understandable, that its power lies in connecting readers of all cultures through sensuality and emotion.

—Fiona Kelleghan

C

CALISHER, Hortense

Nationality: American. **Born:** New York City, 20 December 1911. **Education:** Hunter College High School, New York; Barnard College, New York, A.B. in philosophy 1932. **Family:** Married 1) H.B. Heffelfinger in 1935, one daughter and one son; 2) Curtis Harnack in 1959. **Career:** Adjunct professor of English, Barnard College, 1956–57; visiting professor, University of Iowa, Iowa City, 1957, 1959–60, Stanford University, California, 1958, Sarah Lawrence College, Bronxville, New York, 1962, and Brandeis University, Waltham, Massachusetts, 1963–64; writer-in-residence, 1965, and visiting lecturer, 1968, Univeristy of Pennsylvania, Philadelphia; adjunct professor of English, Columbia University, New York, 1968–70 and 1972–73; Clark Lecturer, Scripps College, Claremont, California, 1969; visiting professor, State University of New York, Purchase, 1971–72; Regents' Professor, University of California, Irvine, Spring 1976; visiting writer, Bennington College, Vermont, 1978; Hurst Professor, Washington University, St. Louis, 1979; National Endowment for the Arts Lecturer, Cooper Union, New York, 1983; visiting professor, Brown University, Providence, Rhode Island, 1986; guest lecturer, U.S.-China Arts Exchange, Republic of China, 1986. President, PEN, 1986–87; American Academy and Institute of Arts and Letters, 1987–90. Lives in New York City. **Awards:** Guggenheim fellowship, 1952, 1955; Department of State American Specialists grant, 1958; American Academy award, 1967; National Endowment for the Arts grant, 1967; Kafka prize, 1987; National Endowment for the Arts Lifetime Achievement award, 1989. Litt.D.: Skidmore College, Saratoga Springs, New York, 1980; Grinnell College, Iowa, 1986; Hofstra University, Hempstead, New York, 1988. **Member:** American Academy, 1977. **Agent:** Candida Donadio and Associates, 231 West 22nd Street, New York, New York 10011, U.S.A.

PUBLICATIONS

Novels

False Entry. Boston, Little Brown, 1961; London, Secker and Warburg, 1962.
Textures of Life. Boston, Little Brown, and London, Secker and Warburg, 1963.
Journal from Ellipsia. Boston, Little Brown, 1965; London, Secker and Warburg, 1966.
The Railway Police, and The Last Trolley Ride. Boston, Little Brown, 1966.
The New Yorkers. Boston, Little Brown, 1969; London, Cape, 1970.
Queenie. New York, Arbor House, 1971; London, W.H. Allen, 1973.
Standard Dreaming. New York, Arbor House, 1972.
Eagle Eye. New York, Arbor House, 1973.
On Keeping Women. New York, Arbor House, 1977.
Mysteries of Motion. New York, Doubleday, 1983.
The Bobby-Soxer. New York, Doubleday, 1986.
Age. New York, Weidenfeld and Nicolson, 1987.
The Small Bang (as Jack Fenno). New York, Random House, 1992.
In the Palace of the Movie King. New York, Random House, 1993.
In the Slammer with Carol Smith. New York, Marion Boyars, 1997.
The Novellas of Hortense Calisher. New York, Modern Library, 1997.

Short Stories

In the Absence of Angels. Boston, Little Brown, 1951; London, Heinemann, 1953.
Tale for the Mirror: A Novella and Other Stories. Boston, Little Brown, 1962; London, Secker and Warburg, 1963.
Extreme Magic: A Novella and Other Stories. Boston, Little Brown, and London, Secker and Warburg, 1964.
The Collected Stories of Hortense Calisher. New York, Arbor House, 1975.
Saratoga, Hot. New York, Doubleday, 1985.

Uncollected Short Stories

''The Gig,'' *Confrontation,* 1986.
''The Evershams' Willie,'' in *Southwest Review* (Dallas), Summer 1987.
''The Man Who Spat Silver,'' (novella) in *Confrontation* (41), Summer/Fall 1989.
''The Nature of the Madhouse,'' in *Story* (Cincinnati), Spring 1990.
''The Iron Butterflies,'' in *Southwest Review,* Winter 1992.
''Blind Eye, Wrong Foot,'' in *American Short Fiction* (10), Summer 1993.

Other

What Novels Are (lecture). Claremont, California, Scripps College, 1969.
Herself (memoir). New York, Arbor House, 1972.
Kissing Cousins: A Memory. New York, Weidenfeld and Nicolson, 1988.
Editor, with Shannon Ravenel, *The Best American Short Stories 1981.* Boston, Houghton Mifflin, 1981.

*

Critical Studies: In *Don't Never Forget* by Brigid Brophy, London, Cape, 1966, New York, Holt Rinehart, 1967; article by Cynthia Ozick in *Midstream* (New York), 1969; ''Ego Art: Notes on How I Came to It'' by Calisher, in *Works in Progress* (New York), 1971; article by Kathy Brown in *Current Biography* (New York), November 1973; interview in *Paris Review,* Winter 1987; ''Three Novels by Hortense Calisher'' by Kathleen Snodgrass, in *Texas Studies in Literature and Language* (Austin), Winter 1989, and *The Fiction of Hortense Calisher* by Snodgrass, University of Delaware Press, 1994.

Hortense Calisher comments:

(1972) *False Entry* and *The New Yorkers* are connected novels; either may be read first; together they are a chronicle perhaps peculiarly American, according to some critics, but with European scope, according to others. *Journal from Ellipsia* was perhaps one of the first or the first serious American novel to deal with ''verbal'' man's displacement in a world of the spatial sciences; because it dealt with the possibility of life on other planets it was classed as ''science fiction'' both in the USA and in England. The *Dublin Times* understood it; its review does well by it. It also satirizes male-female relationships, by postulating a planet on which things are otherwise. In category, according to some, it is less an ordinary novel than a social satire akin to *Erewhon, Gulliver's Travels, Candide,* etc. *The Railway Police* and *The Last Trollery Ride*—the first is really a long short story of an individual, the second a novella built around an environs, a chorale of persons really, with four main parts, told in the interchanging voice of two men.

I usually find myself alternating a ''larger'' work with a smaller one, a natural change of pace. *Textures of Life*, for instance, is an intimate novel, of a young marriage, very personal, as *Journal* is not. After the latter, as I said in an interview, I wanted to get back to people. *The New Yorkers* was a conscious return to a ''big'' novel, done on fairly conventional terms, descriptive, narrative, leisurely, and inclusive, from which the long monologue chapters of the two women are a conscious departure. Its earlier mate, *False Entry*, has been called the only ''metaphysical'' novel in the America of its period—I'm not sure what that means, except perhaps that the whole, despite such tangible scenes as the Ku Klux Klan and courtroom episodes, is carried in the ''mind'' of one man. It has been called Dickensian, and in its plethora of event I suppose it is; yet the use of memory symbols and of psyche might just as well be French (Proust and Gide)—by intent it does both, or joins both ways of narration. *The New Yorkers* is more tied to its environs in a localized way; part of its subject *is* the environs.

Queenie is a satire, a farce on our sexual mores, as seen through the eyes of a ''modern'' young girl. As it is not yet out at this writing, I shall wait to be told what it is about.

(1986) *Standard Dreaming*: short novel narrated through the consciousness of a surgeon who believes the human race may be in process of dying off. *Herself*: the autobiography of a writer, rather than of the total life. Included are portions of critical studies, articles, etc., as well as several in toto (including one on the novel and on sex in American literature), and commentary on the writer's role in war, as a feminist, critic and teacher. *Eagle Eye*: the story of a young American non-combatant during and after the Vietnam War. Just as Queenie, in the novel of that name, confided in her tape-recorder, Bronstein addresses his computer. In 1974 some critics were bemused at this; time has changed that. *The Collected Stories*: preface by author begins with the much-quoted ''A story is an apocalypse, served in a very small cup.'' *On Keeping Women: Herself* had broken ground in some of its aspects of what feminists were to term ''womanspeak.'' I was never to be a conventional feminist; conventional thought is not for writers. But I had always wanted to do a novel from within the female feelings I did have from youth, through motherhood and the wish for other creation. This is that book. *Mysteries of Motion*: as in *Journal from Ellipsia* I continue concern for the way we live daily with the vast efforts and fruits of the scientists, and the terrors, without much understanding. Begun in 1977, before shuttles had flown or manmade objects had fallen to earth from orbit, this story of the first civilians in space is I believe the first novel of character (rather than so-called ''science fiction'') to be set in space. Because of that intent, the lives of all six people before they embark are an essential part of the story. What may happen to people, personality—and nations—in the space race, is what I was after. Though I researched minimally—just enough to know the language, or some of it—one critic commented that its technical details could not be faulted. I imagined, rather than tried to be faithful to the momentary fact. And again, time has caught up with it, sadly so in the matter of ''star wars.'' *Saratoga, Hot*: short works, called ''little novels.'' Writing novels changes the short-story pen—the stories become novelistic, or mine do. The intent was ''to give as much background as you can get in a foreground.'' *The Bobby-Soxer*: the story of the erotic and professional maturing of a young girl of the 1950s, as narrated by the woman she has become, it is also a legend of American provincial life, akin to the early novellas.

I have just completed a short novel called *Age*, and am resuming work on a novel set in Central Europe and the United States.

(1991) The working title of the book I refer to above as ''a novel set in Central Europe and the United States'' is *In the Palace of the Movie King*. I've been at work on this longer book in the background behind the shorter works that have emerged since the last longer work (*Mysteries of Motion*). It is certainly a more overtly political novel than any of the others, although that concern has been present in my work since the first stories.

This time the scene is Central Europe versus the U.S., as seen through the eyes of a filmmaker, Russian in origin, who grew up in Japan. Part of my interest has also been to see the U.S. as the visually obsessed nation it has fast become—through the eyes of a man who sees the world visually, rather than verbally. I hope thereby to free the book from what I think of as the de Tocqueville syndrome.

I am currently working on a shorter novel, set in England, where I have lived from time to time.

(1995) The ''shorter work,'' set in England, is the novel, *The Small Bang*, published psuedonymously under the name Jack Fenno, to distinguish it from the other novel shortly to be published. As its title indicates, it poses the ''small'' bang that is human life against the ''big bang'' world views of the physicists. In the publisher's catalogue it is billed as a ''mystery;'' I wrote it as a novel purely, any novel being in a sense a ''mystery'' until its end.

On *In the Palace of the Movie King*: there comes a time for many of us when we feel seriously separated from the international intrigue that is happening all around us—and from the national picture also. Yet our domestic lives, urban or suburban or land-based, are always on that edge. I came to feel that I ought to be writing of what I thought of as ''the long adventure''—that panorama, with documents, which would move through what we've been too trained to think of as the ''thriller'' novel. At the same time I must unite this with the domestic scene.

That's a nineteenth-century ambition, from the books I cut my teeth on: Dickens, Victor Hugo, Mark Twain, and in my teens, the Russians. I miss their scope—if not necessarily their size. A sentence can embody the long view. But a novel so conceived will concentrate along that axis. What will the reader allow me to do for our twentieth century time? Meanwhile—my century feeding me what I ought to be seeing—in both the subtle and monumental. I was seeing the whole metaphor of ''the third world.'' Censorship, yes, torture for the dissident, death because one differs. But the crux of it: they—the citizens of that third world I happen to know best, Middle Europe—they were locked in. My country was not. Is not.

The Gonchevs, the couple I wrote about, emerged through those mists, along with a vision of the whole wide-screen planet we are now. The time is just before that savage Balkan conflict we are now witnessing. When Gonchev, an apolitical man entirely, is shipped to the U.S.A. and cast in the role of ''dissident,'' my own land emerges, as seen through his eyes. One strains like the devil not to be ''author,'' authoring. There the emigrants and transcontinentals I've known all my life surely helped.

At times Gonchev's story is taken to be satirical, even hilarious. That's a relief.

* * *

Many readers first encounter Hortense Calisher through her widely anthologized short stories, then anticipate her novels. After reading them, however, they may come away vaguely unsatisfied though seldom quite dissatisfied. She is too gifted a writer for that.

It seems impossible for Calisher to write poorly: she is a master of language. Precise, powerful verbs give scenes life and immediacy. In ''The Woman Who Was Everybody'' an overqualified department store employee reluctantly faces the day: ''She swung sideways out of bed, clamped her feet on the floor, rose and trundled to the bathroom, the kitchenette.'' Calisher's imagery is bountiful, original, and appropriate. In the same story, ''the mornings crept in like applicants for jobs.'' Equal to language, Calisher has evidently observed and experienced how truth is revealed in the course of living and can reconstruct these epiphanies readily in characters.

Then why, since hers are among the best American short stories of this century, are Calisher's novels less successful? At least two reasons are likely. One is that it is impossible to sustain in the long form the power she packs into the short form. The small cast, limited setting, single problem of the short story let her build the work to a final revelation which suggests that, for better or worse, a life will never be quite the same again. This is the classic short story.

Calisher novels often merely elongate the story format. Substituting for traditional plot and subplot, there are series of revelations related to the central situation. (A young couple disclose aspects of themselves as they cope with an ill child in *Textures of Life*. Another couple, from the novella *Saratoga, Hot* actually reveal more about their horsey social set than themselves.) Whether the reader can sustain interest in longer works whose internal logic is random and whose continuity needs occasional propulsion by fortuitous revelation is a question. Certainly that *does* work in *The New Yorkers* often called her most successful novel, an indulgent insight into family life. Ill-advised timing and treatment may have undercut Calisher's satirical novel, *Queenie*. The late 1960s were not laughing times and for many the new sexual freedom which Queenie fumbles toward was no laughing matter. What may be her least successful novel, *Mysteries of Motion*, distracts as much as discloses since six lives are revealed, and on a space journey at that. Better a bus ride in Brooklyn.

That more modest approach to setting is exactly what makes her short stories seem instantly relevant to our ordinary lives, that and the fact that each story—however brief—is also a life history of sorts. Calisher examines that life at a time of crisis and the reader comes away instructed in valuable experience. In the classic ''One of the Chosen'' a successful Jewish lawyer, Davy Spanner, always popular in his college days, has believed lifelong that he never needed the support of fraternity life and had comfortably rejected the early overtures of the campus societies. At a class reunion, a gentile classmate blurts out the unsettling truth that Spanner would *never* have been offered a serious membership bid.

Calisher's long interest in psychology and the supernatural is evident. Her life spans Freudianism and beyond, but psychology—eclectic and non-systematic—as it appears in her work at times is close to fantasy, at other times follows accepted dogma. ''Heartburn'' centers on the power of suggestion; ''The Scream on 57th Street'' treats fear. Both ''work'' just as her general grasp of family relationships seems valid, however it was acquired. On the other hand, *Standard Dreaming*, Calisher's unfortunate excursion into a dream world of searching characters, could be taken for a parody of surrealism.

Calisher's short stories and novellas may initially appear to be peopled by fully-rounded characters, but an overview of the stories reveals a high proportion of well-done types: the educated misfit, the eccentric family member, the young innocent, the at-odds mother-daughter (or husband-wife), the displaced southerner, the would-be radical. And type is all they need to be since hers are not primarily stories of character, but of complex situation, the result of long processes of cause and effect told in hints and subtleties. Where the Calisher protagonists have been, are now, and where they are probably going—or not going, depending on their revelations—*is* their story. Exactly *who* they are is incidental. Their external descriptions are often vivid, even witty, but their tastes and temperaments are revealed only to the degree that they serve the tale. If we flesh them out ourselves, it is a tribute to their creator's ability to write so that we *read* creatively.

The Collected Stories of Hortense Calisher, an enduring treasury of major works in her best genre, allows ready comparison of early and late works and reveals the consistency of Calisher's vision, even such traits as a vein of humor, a thread of the absurd, and a persistent interest in the power of the mind to direct fate. Similarly, *The Novellas of Hortense Calisher* gave readers an opportunity to savor some old treasures—*Tale for the Mirror*, *Extreme Magic*, *Saratoga, Hot*, *The Man Who Spat Silver*, *The Railway Police*, and *The Last Trolley Ride*—along with the previously unpublished *Women Men Don't Talk About*. Also in the late 1990s, Calisher published *Age*, an epistolary novel centering on Gemma, an architect, and Robert, four years her junior. She also produced *In the Slammer with Carol Smith*, whose title character has just been released from prison after a long sentence. Carol's imprisonment was not the result of a crime she actually committed, but rather the outcome of being at the wrong place at the wrong time—or more specifically, a poor black woman who fell in with wealthy white revolutionaries during the early 1970s.

Calisher is an eminently serious and concerned writer, despite the fatuous, the incompetents, the ditsy relatives, and the rattled authority figures who clamor for their share of attention in her works. Their truths are as true as anyone else's, Calisher suggests, and their numbers among us may be greater than we want to believe.

—Marian Pehowski

CALLOW, Philip (Kenneth)

Nationality: British. **Born:** Birmingham, 26 October 1924. **Education:** Coventry Technical College, 1937–39; St. Luke's College, Exeter, Devon, 1968–70, Teacher's Certificate 1970. **Family:** Married Anne Jennifer Golby in 1987 (third marriage); one daughter from previous marriage. **Career:** Engineering apprentice and toolmaker, Coventry Gauge and Tool Company, 1940–48; clerk, Ministry of Works and Minstry of Supply, 1949–51; clerical assistant, South West Electricity Board, Plymouth, 1951–66; Arts Council fellow, Falmouth School of Art, 1977–78; Creative Writing fellow, Open University, 1979; writer-in-residence, Sheffield City Polytechnic, 1980–82. **Awards:** Arts Council bursary, 1966, 1970, 1973, 1979;

Society of Authors traveling scholarship, 1973; C. Day Lewis fellowship, 1973; Southern Arts Association fellowship, 1974. **Agent:** John Johnson Ltd., 45–47 Clerkenwell Green, London EC1R 0HT, England.

PUBLICATIONS

Novels

The Hosanna Man. London, Cape, 1956.
Common People. London, Heinemann, 1958.
A Pledge for the Earth. London, Heinemann, 1960.
Clipped Wings. Douglas, Isle of Man, Times Press, 1964.
Another Flesh. London, Allison and Busby, 1989.
Going to the Moon. London, MacGibbon and Kee, 1968.
The Bliss Body. London, MacGibbon and Kee, 1969.
Flesh of Morning. London, Bodley Head, 1971.
Yours. London, Bodley Head, 1972.
The Story of My Desire. London, Bodley Head, 1976.
Janine. London, Bodley Head, 1977.
The Subway to New York. London, Martin Brian and O'Keeffe, 1979.
The Painter's Confessions. London, Allison and Busby, 1989.
Some Love. London, Allison and Busby, 1991.
The Magnolia. London, Allison and Busby, 1994.

Short Stories

Native Ground. London, Heinemann, 1959.
Woman with a Poet. Bradford, Yorkshire, Rivelin Press, 1983.

Uncollected Short Stories

"Merry Christmas," in *New Statesman* (London), 22 December 1961.

Plays

The Honeymooners (televised 1960). Published in *New Granada Plays,* London, Faber, 1961.

Radio Plays: *The Lamb,* 1971; *On Some Road,* 1979.

Television Play: *The Honeymooners,* 1960.

Poetry

Turning Point. London, Heinemann, 1964.
The Real Life: New Poems. Douglas, Isle of Man, Times Press, 1964.
Bare Wires. London, Chatto and Windus-Hogarth Press, 1972.
Cave Light. Bradford, Yorkshire, Rivelin Press, 1981.
New York Insomnia and Other Poems. Bradford, Yorkshire, Rivelin Grapheme Press, 1984.
Icons. Bradford, Yorkshire, Blue Bridge Press, 1987.
Soliloquies of an Eye. Todmorden, Lancashire, Littlewood Press, 1990.
Notes over a Chasm. Bradford, Yorkshire, Redbeck Press, 1991.
Fires in October. Bradford, Yorkshire, Redbeck Press, 1994.

Other

In My Own Land, photographs by James Bridgen. Douglas, Isle of Man, Times Press, 1965.
Son and Lover: The Young D.H. Lawrence. London, Bodley Head, and New York, Stein and Day, 1975.
Van Gogh: A Life. London, Allison and Busby, and Chicago, Dee, 1990.
From Noon to Starry Night: A Life of Walt Whitman. London, Allison and Busby, and Chicago, Dee, 1992.
Lost Earth: A Life of Cezanne. Chicago, Ivan R. Dee, 1995.
Chekhov: The Hidden Ground: A Biography. Chicago, Ivan R. Dee, 1998.

*

Manuscript Collection: University of Texas Library, Austin.

Critical Study: By Callow in *Vogue* (New York), 1 September 1969.

Philip Callow comments:

(1991) All my writing up to now has been autobiographical in style and content. My aim has simply been to tell the story of my life as truthfully as possible. In fact, this is impossible, and in the attempt to do so one discovers that another, spiritual, autobiography is taking shape. I now realize that by devising a narrative about total strangers based on events reported in a newspaper I reveal myself as nakedly as in a personal confession. Perhaps more so.

* * *

In all his earlier work Philip Callow is telling the same story—his life story. His "autobiography," *In My Own Land*, confirms a close approximation between himself and the "I" of the novels and the short stories in *Native Ground.* In his earliest novels he was seeking an idiom, which he found triumphantly in the freewheeling colloquialism of the trilogy *Going to the Moon*, *The Bliss Body*, and *Flesh of Morning*.

Callow's material is his working-class adolescence in the midlands, the experience of factory and clerical work there and in the west country, his artistic leanings and adult relationships. Louis Paul, Nicky Chapman, and Alan Lowry, the narrators respectively of *The Hosanna Man*, *Common People*, and *Clipped Wings*, and Martin Satchwell, the central character of *A Pledge for the Earth*, are prototypes for the Colin Patten of the trilogy, and its sequel *The Story of My Desire*, when Patten has qualified as a teacher. Parallels exist in the earliest books for the trilogy's other important characters, while in subsequent work the lecturer David Lowry, the central figure in *Janine*, and the poet and writer-in-residence Jacob Raby, the narrator of *The Subway to New York*, recall Patten.

Callow gives a full account of adolescence, describing the development of sexuality—more freely in the later books—as the boy grows up at the end of the war when "there was a ration even on questions." Then he has to adjust to life on the factory floor. Patten's painting and writing lead him into provincial artistic circles, amateur or bohemian and anarchic—the "city nomads." Callow's outstanding portrayal is Jack Kelvin, "the hosanna man" himself, a drop-out like Albert Dyer in *Clipped Wings*, who "sits up on a cliff like a dirty old monk;" in *Common People* there is the drunken Sunday painter,

Cecil Luce, leader of the "Birmingham Twelve." With the public poetry readings by the "Callow-figure" Jacob Raby in *The Subway to New York* (and the painter Breakwell's fame in *The Painter's Confessions*), the wheel has come full circle.

A Pledge for the Earth was the earliest of Callow's third-person novels. The most overtly structured of his novels, it describes two generations of Satchwells in a framework of natural imagery, and culminates in 20-odd pages in the first person written by Martin Satchwell. In *Clipped Wings* Callow returned to first-person narration: "I decided that the only way is to plant yourself down in the very center of things, and then set out. In the same railway carriage, with all the others." With its new forceful, colloquial idiom, *Clipped Wings* is the key book in Callow's stylistic development, and made possible the trilogy. At the same time, he had begun to publish a good deal of poetry, which perhaps cross-fertilized his prose.

In the trilogy Callow ranged over his experiences freely with only a rough chronological surge onward: "Going back is pure instinct with me." The rationale of his method is in a sense anti-art: "Who believes in a book cut away from its writer with surgical scissors? I don't, I never did. I don't believe in fact and fiction, I don't believe in autobiography, poetry, philosophy, I don't believe in chapters, in a story." Callow's refusal to categorize is also embodied in his non-fiction *In My Own Land*, differentiated from his novels only by the use of real names.

Yours is an extended letter written by a young girl to her ex-lover, recalling that first unhappy love affair. In *The Story of My Desire* Callow continued the trilogy, with Colin's affair with the married Lucy, both cause and effect of the breakdown of his own marriage, in turn inextricably linked in a nexus of guilt with his mental breakdown. *Janine* describes the middle-aged David Lowry's relationship with the mixed-up young girl of the title. It is written in the third person, and from the opening sentence, "His name was Lowry," the man is referred to throughout by surname. Until a key moment late in the novel, Janine never calls David by name, so that the third-person narration has an active structural role.

The structural rationale in *The Subway to New York* is circular: "always with a woman you go in circles." Thus Marjorie of *The Story of My Desire*, already resurrected as Kate in *Janine*, reappears as Carmel in *The Subway to New York*, and Lucy of *The Story of My Desire* is Nell in *Subway*.

Callow's return to fiction after a break of 10 years (apart from the small-press short story collection *Woman with a Poet*) seems less directly autobiographical, though the subject matter of *The Painter's Confessions* enables him to explore how an artist—in the broad sense—uses his experience. The painter Francis Breakwell's "confessions" begin "Even before my sister's violent death I had felt this urge to use words, to tell a story that would be my own, yet irradiated in some way by hers." The narrative moves forward to her drowning, through her love for the unbalanced Celia. The central figure in Breakwell's life is his former mistress and model, Maggie, with whom he remains tenuously in touch. His marriage disintegrates through the novel but his American wife seems peripheral beside Maggie's presence from the past. As a contemporary painter aged 50, Breakwell seems unrealistically successful given his predominant old-fashioned abstract expressionism. Inevitably, Patrick White's classic *The Vivisector* casts a long shadow over any novel about a painter but especially here given Breakwell's expressionism.

There are lacunae in *The Painter's Confessions* but the rambling reminiscence form could be held to justify loose ends. The structure is more problematic in *Some Love*, a moving third-person novel about the under-privileged Johnnie, who, after time in a children's home, gets involved as a minor in an affair with Tina, a younger friend of his mentally unstable mother. Initially, the viewpoint is mainly Johnnie's, but, with the emergence of Tina midway as a major character, the viewpoint switches predominantly to her, with no apparent rationale. Callow's often unstructured way of writing becomes more difficult when it is not applied to the solid corpus of autobiographical fact. However, Callow is too good a writer for that decade's silence not to be our loss.

In the 1990s, Callow published *Some Love* and *The Magnolia*, but he turned his attention increasingly to nonfiction, producing biographies of Van Gogh, Walt Whitman, Cezanne, and Chekhov.

—Val Warner

CALVIN, Henry

See HANLEY, Clifford (Leonard Clark)

CAMPBELL, Marion (May)

Nationality: Australian. **Born:** Sydney, 25 December 1948. **Address:** 45 Arkwell Street, Willagee, Western Australia 6156, Australia.

PUBLICATIONS

Novels

Lines of Flight. Fremantle, Western Australia, Fremantle Arts Centre Press, 1985.

Not Being Miriam. Fremantle, Western Australia, Fremantle Arts Centre Press, 1989.

Prowler. South Fremantle, Western Australia, Fremantle Arts Centre Press, 1999.

* * *

Marion Campbell is one of Australia's most powerful intellectual and postmodern writers and has an impressive reputation on the basis of three novels. Her first novel, *Lines of Flight*, is a work of luminous and startling intelligence, both elegant and playful. Through rival narrative modes, it is the story of Rita Finnerty, a young Australian artist in France, struggling to create a career, but struggling also to break free of the cloisters of other peoples' lives. Splinter scenes of her childhood and her early compositions emerge through the notion of cumulo-nimbus formations, but in France, amid emotional and artistic upheaval, the notion of *lignes de fuite* prevails, obedience to perspective and the lines of flight which taper to disappearance point.

Rita's involvement with Raymond, the entrepreneurial gay semiotician, and his two students, Gerard and Sebastien, becomes a locus of postmodern dissent and denial. Internal pressures in Rita's private world implode and the language too becomes implosive, yet the form of the novel remains precise, elegant, baroque. Campbell draws on spatial structures, such as framing and tripytch to cross the lines between art and self, between rival determinations of event, word, imagination, and vision. The development of Rita's painting in France and the sharp satire of the Australian art scene on her return to Australia, her disappearance even, are occasions of profound visual and spatial luminosity, her prose extraordinarily energetic and intellectually rich.

The novel is both witty and ludic, the scenes in France often droll, but beneath that surface there is a profound intellectual quest and a struggle to find in painting and in language areas of self-determination without confinement to the interstices of others' lives. Her writing is marked by the precision of elusive and complex notions and forms of trespass from the definitions and determinations of others. Campbell writes with

> ... wild vertigo, intoxication of turning on my own axis in freed space. In a long greedy scrutiny of space from that pinnacle, I would see that crazy queue of arbitrarily fused selves, oh yes, from moments past recede, I would pluralize and scatter on horizons ebbing into horizons ....

Narrative shifts and tilts with concentric planes, emanations, absences, default, space vacated, searching out the sacred, transgressing boundaries, as if the prose is on an inner spiral, measuring the space of self which defines and confines.

Prowler, published in 1999, has a similar spatial construct playing over reversals of perspective and the sides of mirror and glass, again with tense and intense pressures of trespass and self-determination.

Her second novel, 1989's *Not Being Miriam*, is about the ''danger of certainty.'' In its composition of shifting frames about the tendencies of things, the world is ''a tissue of complicated events only tending to occur.'' It is a fiercely celebratory vision, in which Campbell's remarkable energies and intelligence play across the intense inner dialogue of three women.

Through the interlocking stories of the three women, whose lives overlap, Campbell weaves a tapestry of lives compressed and defined by default. It is first the story of Bess, her childhood and her teaching life and her young son taken by the father to Italy, then her world as a middle-aged single woman. Through her sense of chaos and dissolution, of possibilities shrinking all around her, there is a quest for the center of gravity. When her own life palls and seems uninhabitable, she enters and enacts other lives, playing out putative selves, in her theater of masks.

Bess's story overlaps with that of Lydia from childhood in Nazi Germany to her adult life married to Harry; and the life of Elsie, Bess's working-class neighbor and the second wife of Roger, haunted by the presence of the first wife, the late Miriam, whose image is treasured openly by Roger. The women come together in the absence of Miriam, who stands as the figure of reference. Through Bess, Elsie and Lydia, Campbell conjures numerous images of woman. Each one is shadowed by antecedent figures: for Bess, Ariadne; for Elsie the second Mrs. de Winter from *Rebecca;* and for Lydia, Katerina Kepler, Johannes Kepler's mother, ''the last musician of the spheres.'' One of the most remarkable sequences is about Katerina Kepler, suspected of witchcraft and doomed. Her voice plays out many of the notions of women caught in the ellipses of male lives.

The novel has a series of interesting structures, with filigree lines of narrative, a labyrinth of voices and threads which lock together in one startling moment. In the climactic courtroom sequence, Bess is charged with manslaughter. Amid voices of gossip and condemnation, where every gesture of the self, past and present, is suspect, there are echoes of the charges against Lindy Chamberlain in the notorious Australian case which ran through the 1980s. As Bess feels the collapse of the past, the collapse of all her rival selves, the condemnation of Bess becomes a dark enclosure, as if she is trapped in the ellipses of the *other,* reduced to a figure of others' purposes, a player in a collective script.

Through themes of mechanistic and quantum physics, Campbell explores the causal links which *tended* towards this effect, seeking the rip, the breach in the fabric of things. Amid narrative modes of theater and script, of acting out roles and guises of the self, literary and mythological references abound, from the prophecies of Cassandra, to impassioned writing about Ariadne and Theseus, or to the sisters in Genet's *The Maids,* with Bess forever playing out ''this maid's revolt.'' *Not Being Miriam* is a bold and prismatic novel, in which voices spar in the deepest recesses of the self, while the narrative weaves in and out of the lives of women in a montage of voices. The prose is rich and crystalline, full of resonances and summonings of historical and mythological, literary and classical antecedents.

—Helen Daniel

CANNON, Curt

See HUNTER, Evan

CAREY, Peter (Philip)

Nationality: Australian. **Born:** Bacchus Marsh, Victoria, 7 May 1943. **Education:** Geelong Grammar School; Monash University, Clayton, Victoria, 1961. **Family:** Married 1) Leigh Weetman; 2) Alison Summers in 1985, one son. **Career:** Worked in advertising in Australia, 1962–68 and after 1970, and in London, 1968–70; partner, McSpedden Carey Advertising Consultants, Chippendale, New South Wales, until 1988. Currently teacher, New York University and Princeton University. Lives in New York. **Awards:** New South Wales Premier's award, 1980, 1982; Miles Franklin award, 1981; National Book Council award, 1982, 1986; Australian Film Institute award, for screenplay, 1985; *The Age* Book of the Year award, 1985, 1994; Booker prize, 1988; Commonwealth Prize for best novel, 1998. Fellow, Royal Society of Literature. **Agent:** International Creative Management, 40 W. 57th St., New York, New York 10019, U.S.A.

PUBLICATIONS

Novels

Bliss. St. Lucia, University of Queensland Press, London, Faber, and New York, Harper, 1981.

Illywhacker. London, Faber, and New York, Harper, 1985.

Oscar and Lucinda. London, Faber, and New York, Harper, 1988.

The Tax Inspector. London, Faber, and New York, Knopf, 1992.

The Unusual Life of Tristan Smith. London, Faber, and New York, Knopf, 1995.

The Big Bazoohley. New York, Henry Holt, 1995.

Jack Maggs. St. Lucia, Australia, University of Queensland Press, 1997; New York, Knopf, 1998.

Short Stories

The Fat Man in History. St. Lucia, University of Queensland Press, 1974; London, Faber, and New York, Random House, 1980; as *Exotic Pleasures,* London, Pan, 1981.
War Crimes. St. Lucia, University of Queensland Press, 1979.
Collected Stories. St. Lucia, Australia, University of Queensland Press, 1994.
A Letter to Our Son. St. Lucia, Australia, University of Queensland Press, 1994.

Plays

Screenplay: *Bliss: The Screenplay,* with Ray Lawrence, St. Lucia, University of Queensland Press, 1986; as *Bliss: The Film,* London, Faber, 1986.

* * *

Peter Carey's short story collections *The Fat Man in History* and *War Crimes* established his reputation as one of Australia's most skilled and innovative writers of short fiction. His stories break away from the Australian tradition of realism as he experiments with surrealism, fantasy, cartoon characterization, and the ''tall tale.'' In the often-anthologized story ''Peeling,'' for example, when an old man's fantasies about his neighbor begin to come to fruition, he realizes that the fantasy is more appealing than the woman herself. She is left, after he has undressed her of her layers of clothing, with her flesh unzipped and peeled away. Thereafter, ''with each touch she is dismembered, slowly, limb by limb.'' In ''American Dream,'' a less fantastic but no less disturbing story, a replica of a small town in miniature, complete with townspeople and their secrets, becomes the vehicle for a poignant criticism of both provincialism and tourism.

In his novels Carey never seems afraid to play with the kind of experimentation associated with postmodernist writing or to be scathing in his social criticism. While no two Peter Carey novels look alike, they all share his fascination with the juxtaposition of the disturbing, the nightmarish, and the unexpected with the mundane and the real. Readers frequently compare Carey's work with that of Gabriel Garcia Marquez, Salman Rushdie, Robert Kroetsch, and Murray Bail. Although Carey himself is ''wary'' of being labeled a magic realist, his work has often been cited as exemplary of the form in a postcolonial context.

Carey's tendency to write past the limits of expectation in his short stories is expanded in his novels. His stories and novels are thematically linked through a concern with contemporary social systems, the politics of everyday life, the oppressive remnants of colonialism, and consumer exploitation. Carey's first published novel, *Bliss*, displays a particularly sharp critique of the effects of capitalism. He relies on a combination of Juvenalian satire and metafiction to highlight both personal and corporate corruption. This is the sad-but-funny story of an advertising executive, Harry Joy, who suffers a near-fatal heart attack and revives with a radically different perception of reality. Upon recovery he believes that he is in Hell. It is through the theme of cancer (caused by the food additives in a product advertised by Harry's company) that Carey most forcefully links the capitalism represented by the advertising world and the deterioration of society into Hell. Harry's savior from this dystopian world is Honey Barbara, ''pantheist, healer, whore,'' with whom he escapes into a forest commune to spend his life planting trees and raising bees. The novel ends on a utopian note with the soul and blue essence of the dead Harry Joy being absorbed into a tree he planted 30 years earlier. Although the celebratory nature of the ending has been read by critics as providing too much of a cancellation of the sharp satiric criticism of the majority of the novel, Carey claims that it was not his intention to provide anything but a ''temporary escape from a terminal future.''

Such a ''terminal future'' is evident in *Illywhacker*, the story of the 139-year-old Herbert Badgery, the illywhacker or trickster/spieler hero-narrator of the title. Although Carey frequently plays with Australian myths in order to debunk them in his writing, such play reaches a crescendo in this novel. The stories of Badgery's life, and the lives of his son and grandson, provide a parallel history to the stories of Australia. The epigraph from Mark Twain points to the premise of the novel: ''Australian history ... does not read like history, but like the most beautiful lies; and all of a fresh sort, no moldy stale ones.'' The central lies of Australian history exposed in the novel are the notion of pre-colonial Australia as *terra nullis*, the denial of a reliance on American interests in the economy (illustrated in the form of General Motors' ''Australia's Own Car''), and the idea that Australians are free, proud, independent, and anti-authoritarian. The final third of the novel details the development of the Best Pet Shop in the World, which is clearly a metaphor for the increasing commercialization of Australian flora, fauna, and people. What begins as a celebration of ''pure Australiana'' ends as a grotesque exhibition of Australians themselves (including most of the surviving central characters). Again, Carey's exaggerated realism exposes the horrors of capitalism. *Illywhacker* celebrates the indomitable spirit of pioneers like Badgery, yet it also exposes flaws in the nation and culture they helped to create.

Carey's Booker Prize-winning third novel, *Oscar and Lucinda*, continues his fascination with the stories of Australian history. Set in the nineteenth century, the story follows the lives of Oscar, an ''Odd Bod'' English Anglican minister who chooses to emigrate to New South Wales as punishment for his gambling addiction, and Lucinda, an heiress who champions women's rights, owns a glass factory, and is a compulsive gambler herself. Narrated by Oscar's great-grandson in contemporary Australia, 1985, the novel is the story of how, 120 years earlier, Oscar and Lucinda come together in their addictions but not in their love. It is also a story that Woodcock notes ''reveals the brutal cultural expropriation'' of the land ''with disturbing violence.'' Carey weaves the love story into the commentary on aboriginal cultural genocide in the final sections of the novel as Oscar travels with a glass church through the Outback. In the style of historiographic metafiction, Kumbaingiri Billy, an aboriginal storyteller, tells an alternative version of history when he tells of Oscar's visit in the tale of how ''Jesus come to Belligen long time ago.'' Carey presents facts about the settling of Australia in a self-reflexive narrative structured around a series of seemingly unconnected episodes. *Oscar and Lucinda* is, therefore, both a story about storytelling and a story about the fictionality and arbitrariness of history. Carey's narrative rings with verisimilitudinous historical detail. It transports the reader to nineteenth-century Epsom Downs, Darling Harbour, and rural New South Wales. Oscar and Lucinda is thought by many readers to be Carey's most technically and narratively complete novel.

In a dramatic shift into the present, Carey's next novel, *The Tax Inspector*, is an unsettling portrait of urban social and moral decay in the 1990s. The novel follows the Catchprice family through the four days their family motor business is under investigation by a government tax inspector. In those four days we are witness, in an almost cinematic style, to the nightmarish lives of the caricatured members of the Catchprice clan. (The cinematic pace of the novel is perhaps because Carey was writing this novel at the same time as he was working on *Until the End of the World*, a film he co-wrote with Wim Wenders.) One of the most disturbing themes in the novel is that of incest and sexual abuse. This metaphor of moral degeneration is set beside the ideals of social reparation represented by the tax inspector.

While *The Tax Inspector* is a non-linear, hyper-realist novel relying on flashbacks and immediate narration, *The Unusual Life of Tristan Smith* signals a return to the fantastic nature of Carey's earlier short story writing. This futuristic, dystopian, picaresque novel, narrated by Tristan Smith, the physically deformed son of an actress and three fathers, is set in the small inconsequential nation of Efica (''so unimportant that you are already confusing the name with Ithaca or Africa'') and the overpowering and ruthless nation of Voorstand. The high-tech capitalist Voorstand Sirkus is juxtaposed with the morally and culturally idealist agit-prop theater group of Tristan's mother. Perhaps Carey's most overtly postcolonial novel, *The Unusual Life of Tristan Smith* is a complex allegory of colonialism. As a migrant narrator, Tristan can champion the culture and values of the colonized land even as he seeks salvation in the anonymity available to him in the overwhelming cultural imperialism of Voorstand.

In *Jack Maggs* Carey returns to early Victorian England, but it is a bleaker nation than in *Oscar and Lucinda*. The title character is a convict illegally returned to London from New South Wales in search of the young gentleman, Henry Phipps, he has made wealthy. As the novel ''writes back'' to Charles Dickens's *Great Expectations*, Carey compellingly recreates the gray, foggy, crowded nature of Dickensian London complete with devoted footmen, adulterous authors, and expert young silver thieves. Through the use of hypnosis, Tobias Oates, a young novelist-journalist whose sketches of London riffraff have made him a celebrity, unveils the secrets of Jack's past as he steals his story, the story of the Criminal Mind. *Jack Maggs* is the most overtly metafictional of Carey's novels. The biographic novel that Oates is writing about Jack Maggs is fittingly called *Jack Maggs*. In its use of postmodern hyperbole and untruths, this version of *Jack Maggs* contradicts the version that we are reading. As we see the unreliability of Oates's narrative, the unreliability of Carey's narrative is also, implicitly, called into question. In a sense, Carey is returning to the idea of questioning the lies of history he highlighted in both *Illywhacker* and *Oscar and Lucinda*.

Carey is one of the most important figures in recent Australian literature. He has consistently been at the forefront of literary experimentation in his use of form and at the forefront of cultural criticism in the themes he has chosen. Carey's work is certainly central in the growing canon of world literature written in English.

—Laura Moss

CASSILL, R(onald) V(erlin)

Nationality: American. **Born:** Cedar Falls, Iowa, 17 May 1919. **Education:** The University of Iowa, Iowa City, B.A. 1939 (Phi Beta Kappa), M.A. 1947; the Sorbonne, Paris (Fulbright fellow), 1952–53. **Military Service:** Served in the United States Army, 1942–46: Lieutenant. **Family:** Married Karilyn Kay Adams in 1956; three children. **Career:** Instructor, University of Iowa, 1948–52; editor, *Western Review,* Iowa City, 1951–52, *Colliers' Encyclopedia,* New York, 1953–54, and *Dude* and *Gent,* New York, 1958; lecturer, Columbia University and New School for Social Research, both New York, 1957–59, and University of Iowa, 1960–65; writer-in-residence, Purdue University, West Lafayette, Indiana, 1965–66. Associate professor, 1966–71, and professor of English, 1972–83, Brown University, Providence, Rhode Island; now emeritus. U.S. Information Service lecturer in Europe, 1975–76. Painter and lithographer: exhibitions—John Snowden Gallery, Chicago, 1946; Eleanor Smith Galleries, Chicago, 1948; Wickersham Gallery, New York, 1970. **Awards:** *Atlantic* ''Firsts'' prize, for short story, 1947; Rockefeller grant, 1954; Guggenheim grant, 1968. **Agent:** Candida Donadio and Associates, 231 West 22nd Street, New York, New York 10011. **Address:** 22 Boylston Avenue, Providence, Rhode Island 02906, U.S.A.

Publications

Novels

The Eagle on the Coin. New York, Random House, 1950.
Dormitory Women. New York, Lion, 1953.
The Left Bank of Desire, with Eric Protter. New York, Ace, 1955.
A Taste of Sin. New York, Ace, 1955; London, Digit, 1959.
The Hungering Shame. New York, Avon, 1956.
The Wound of Love. New York, Avon, 1956.
An Affair to Remember (novelization of screenplay; as Owen Aherne). New York, Avon, 1957.
Naked Morning. New York, Avon, 1957.
Man on Fire (novelization of screenplay; as Owen Aherne). New York, Avon, 1957.
The Buccaneer (novelization of screenplay). New York, Fawcett, 1958.
Lustful Summer. New York, Avon, 1958.
Nurses' Quarters. New York, Fawcett, 1958; London, Muller, 1962.
The Tempest (novelization of screenplay). New York, Fawcett, 1959.
The Wife Next Door. New York, Fawcett, 1959; London, Muller, 1960.
Clem Anderson. New York, Simon and Schuster, 1960.
My Sister's Keeper. New York, Avon, 1961.
Night School. New York, New American Library, 1961.
Pretty Leslie. New York, Simon and Schuster, 1963; London, Muller, 1964.
The President. New York, Simon and Schuster, 1964.
La Vie Passionée of Rodney Buckthorne: A Tale of the Great American's Last Rally and Curious Death. New York, Geis, 1968.
Doctor Cobb's Game. New York, Bantam, 1969.
The Goss Women. New York, Doubleday, 1974; London, Hodder and Stoughton, 1975.
Hoyt's Child. New York, Doubleday, 1976.
Labors of Love. New York, Arbor House, 1980.
Flame. New York, Arbor House, 1980.
After Goliath. New York, Ticknor and Fields, 1985.
The Unknown Soldier. Montrose, Alabama, Texas Center for Writers Press, 1991.

Short Stories

15 x 3, with Herbert Gold and James B. Hall. New York, New Directions, 1957.
The Father and Other Stories. New York, Simon and Schuster, 1965.

The Happy Marriage and Other Stories. West Lafayette, Indiana, Purdue University Press, 1967.
Three Stories. Oakland, California, Hermes House Press, 1982.
Patrimonies. Bristol, Rhode Island, Ampersand Press, 1988.
Collected Stories. Fayetteville, University of Arkansas Press, 1989.

Other

The General Said ''Nuts.'' New York, Birk, 1955.
Writing Fiction. New York, Pocket Books, 1963; revised edition, Englewood Cliffs, New Jersey, Prentice Hall, 1975.
In an Iron Time: Statements and Reiterations: Essays. West Lafayette, Indiana, Purdue University Press, 1967.
Editor, *Intro 1–3.* New York, Bantam, 3 vols., 1968–1970.
Editor, with Walton Beacham, *Intro 4.* Charlottesville, University Press of Virginia, 1972.
Editor, *Norton Anthology of Short Fiction.* New York, Norton, 1978; revised edition, 1981, 1985, 1989, 1994, 1995, 2000.
Editor, *Norton Anthology of Contemporary Fiction.* New York, Norton, 1988; (with Joyce Carol Oates), 1998.

*

Manuscript Collection: Mugar Memorial Library, Boston University.

Critical Studies: ''R.V. Cassill Issue'' of *December* (Chicago), vol. 23, nos. 1–2, 1981 (includes bibliography).

R.V. Cassill comments:

(1972) My most personal statement is probably to be found in my short stories. If few of them are reliably autobiographical at least they grew from the observations, moods, exultations, and agonies of early years. If there is constant pattern in them, it is probably that of a hopeful being who expects evil and finds worse.

From my first novel onward I have explored the correspondences between the interior world—of desire and anxiety—and the public world of power—extra-social violences and politics. In *The Eagle on the Coin* I wrote of the ill-fated attempt of some alienated liberals, including a compassionate homosexual, to elect a Negro to the schoolboard in a small midwestern city. In *Doctor Cobb's Game* I used the silhouette of a major British political scandal as the area within which I composed an elaborate pattern of occult-sexual-political forces weaving and unweaving. Between these two novels, almost 20 years apart, I have played with a variety of forms and subject matter, but the focus of concern has probably been the same, under the surface of appearances. In *Clem Anderson* I took the silhouette of Dylan Thomas's life and within that composed the story of an American poet's self-destructive triumph. It probably is and always will be my most embattled work, simply because in its considerable extent it replaces most of the comfortable or profitable clichés about an artist's life with tougher and more painful diagrams.

But then perhaps my whole productive life has been a swimming against the tide. A midwesterner by origin, and no doubt by temperament and experience, I worked through decades when first the southern and then the urban-Jewish novel held an almost monopolistic grip on the tastes and prejudices of American readers. In my extensive reviewing and lecturing I have tried more to examine the clichés, slogans, and rallying cries of the time than to oppose or espouse them—thus leaving myself without any visible partisan support from any quarter. To radicals I have appeared a conservative, to conservatives a radical—and to both a mystification or, I suppose, I would not have been tolerated as long as I have been. As I grow older I love the commonplace of traditional thought and expression with a growing fervor, especially as their rarity increases amid the indoctrinating forces that spoil our good lives.

* * *

From the first novel, *The Eagle on the Coin*, and the early stories, R.V. Cassill's art shows a steady development from the autobiographical and the imitative to the fully dramatic capabilities of the mature novelist and short story writer. The range of his talent is wide: from near-pastoral impressions of midwestern America, to urban life in Chicago and New York, to his most technically accomplished work, *Doctor Cobb's Game*, based on the Profumo scandals in London.

Cassill's most complex work relies on four broad kinds of material: stories and novels about the midwest, most notably Iowa as in *Pretty Leslie*; stories and novels concerning academic life, as in ''Larchmoor Is Not the World'' and *The President*; materials about art and the artist's life (*Clem Anderson*); and finally materials of a less regional nature which may be called the vision of modernity found in the short story ''Love? Squalor?'' and *Doctor Cobb*. A second lesser-known order of Cassill's work consists of a dozen novels, ''paperback originals'' so-called because of the contractual circumstances of their first publication. For the most part *The Wound of Love*, *Dormitory Women*, and others await sophisticated literary evaluation. These shorter, often more spontaneous novels also exploit the same kinds of material. It should be well understood that these categories are intended to be only suggestive; the most ambitious work, for example, displays all these materials.

Beyond the technical accomplishments of any professional novelist, Cassill's most noteworthy literary quality is the ''visual'' nature of his prose fiction. There is a steady exploitation of color, of the precise, telling, visual detail, a sensitivity to proportion, and to the architectonics of scene. In fact Cassill began his artistic career as a painter, a teacher of art; from time to time he still exhibits his work. His fiction shows some of the same qualities as the Impressionists, the Post-Impressionists, and the German Expressionistic painters.

The literary influences are wide-ranging and interestingly absorbed. In general these influences are evoked when necessary rather than being held steadily as ''models'' in any neoclassic sense. Specifically, Cassill values Flaubert, James, Joyce, and especially D.H. Lawrence. Of a different order of specific influence would be *Madam Bovary,* Gissing's *New Grub Street,* and Benjamin Constant's *Adolphe* (1815). It is interesting that Cassill has written the best extant appreciation of *Adolphe.* Thus Cassill is a highly literary writer, with a broad, useful knowledge of American and European literatures; for many years he has been a teacher of contemporary literature and a writer-in-residence at universities, a professional reviewer, essayist, a discerning cultural commentator and critic.

The governing themes of Cassill's work are less easy to identify. A recurring situation is the nature and the resultant fate of a human pair, the destiny of a man or woman in the throes of new love, old love, marriage, or adultery. Closely bound to these concerns is the nature of love and responsibility; the implications of choice, loyalty, and liberty. Often there are conflicts generated between rationality and a merely emotional yearning—real or imagined—genuine affection as against the implied necessity of sexual aggression or the ironies of ''modern love.'' At times these relationships are between teacher and pupil, lovers, man and wife; between artist and patron, mistress, or the world ''out there.''

A fascination with these and other difficult themes places a heavy obligation on the novelist, especially in the matter of plot-structures and the handling of sex scenes. Throughout Cassill's work there is the insistence of the centrality of the sexual aspect of all human relationships. If in real life such concerns are seldom finally resolved, so is it in many novelistic structures which tend to rely on sexual involvements as a central motivation. Often, therefore, a story or a novel will begin with a vivid, strong situation which in the end is obscured or vague rather than suggestive or resolved. The reliance on the sexual drive as a compelling motive becomes more insistent in the later work.

Although he is primarily a novelist, Cassill's most sustained work is often in the short fiction, of which he is a master. The best stories focus on domestic scenes, memories of youth, the pathos of age, the casual lost relationship, conversations of art, ideas, literature, and the meaning of life itself.

Taken together, the stories, novels, and criticism show a strongly unified sensibility, a dedicated, energetic artist, a man in a modern world imaginatively and at times romantically comprehended, a man whose powerful gifts are his best protection against his own vision of America and of the midwest where modernity is rampant and the end is nowhere in sight.

—James B. Hall

CASTRO, Brian

Nationality: Australian. **Born:** Kowloon, Hong Kong, 16 January 1950. **Education:** University of Sidney, M.A. 1976. **Family:** Married Josephine Mary Gardiner in 1976. **Career:** Teacher, Mt. Druitt High School, New South Wales, 1972–76; assistant in languages, Lycee Technique, Paris, 1976–77; French master, St. Joseph's College, Hunter's Hill, New South Wales, 1978–79; journalist, *Asiaweek* magazine, Hong Kong, 1983–87. Since 1989 tutor of literary studies, University of Western Sydney. Writer-in-residence, Mitchell College, New South Wales, 1985; visiting fellow, Nepean College, Kingswood, New South Wales,1988. Since 1989 writer for *All-Asia Review of Books,* Hong Kong. **Awards:** Vogel-Australian prize, 1982, for *Birds of Paradise;* Australian Council of Literature Board grant, 1983, 1988; Victorian Premier's Literary Award, for *Double-Wolf* and *After China.* **Address:** c/o Allen and Unwin, 8 Napier Street, North Sydney 2059, Australia.

Publications

Novels

Birds of Passage. Sydney and London, Allen and Unwin, 1983.
Double-Wolf. Sydney, Allen and Unwin, 1991.
Pomeroy. Sydney, Allen and Unwin, 1991.
After China. Sydney, Allen and Unwin, 1992.
Drift. Port Melbourne, Victoria, Australia, Heinemann, 1994.
Stepper. Milsons Point, New South Wales, Random House Australia, 1997.

Other

Writing Asia; and, Auto/biography: Two Lectures. Canberra, University College, Australian Defence Force Academy, 1995.

* * *

Of Portuguese and Chinese-American parents, Brian Castro has much to do in his fiction with questions of identity and place, with the influence of the past upon the present, and with the relationship between language and experience. His first novel, *Birds of Passage,* concerns the history of that very much persecuted race in Australia, the Chinese. It documents—with brief, dispassionate understatement—the persecution of Castro's ancestors on the goldfields one hundred years ago and points to the rejection of their descendants today, but the purpose of the work is far from polemical. *Birds of Passage* is a parable about and an inquiry into the nature of identity and the relationship between past and present.

Its method is to juxtapose the narrative of Seamus O'Young, an ABC (Australian-born Chinese), and his ancestor, Lo Yun Shan, who came to Australia from Kwangtung in 1856 in search of gold. Sensitive, intelligent, but an outsider in Sydney, O'Young discovers a manuscript that Shan had left behind and from that starting point begins to retell his ancestor's story and, in effect, to reinvent it. Events 120 years apart are strikingly paralleled. An old man on the boat to Australia shares his food with Shan; we cut to Seamus being offered bread by two old men in a Sydney park. Different characters with the same name appear in the two halves. Even individual images are replicated. As he ponders and recreates the past, Seamus becomes possessed by it. He begins to age physically and to feel the return of his Chinese consciousness. Physical and psychoanalytic reasons are offered for this but are unconvincing speculations only. The truth is that Seamus seems, by the power of his imagination, to *become* his ancestor until finally they meet. At the end of the novel Shan returns to Kwangtung, deserted by his lover Mary Young, never to see the son he has fathered with her but in a truer sense having established a sense of continuity with the future: ''He was on a different path now, in control of his destiny, and he brought with him something of the void he had experienced in Australia, the silence and the stillness that helped him to accept his microscopic role in the eternal recurrences of nature.''

Birds of Passage has some of the faults one might expect in a first novel. The prose tends to become abstract or showily sententious at times, and Castro is prone to gesture at significances, to throw in names for their own sake, as with Seamus's casual meeting with Roland Barthes. But most of the time it is a tenderly written work, immensely sad without being in the least sense depressing.

Castro's second novel, *Double-Wolf,* is as much a tour de force as his first. Based on the celebrated case of Sergei Wespe, Freud's Wolf-Man, who experienced a childhood nightmare of wolves appearing in a tree outside his window (Freud built much of his theory of infantile sexuality based on it). It proceeds to spin a complex web of surmise and speculation involving primarily the relationship between Wespe and a fraudulent Australian-born psychoanalyst who calls himself Artie Catacomb. Castro has said in interviews that after picking up a copy of the Wolf-Man's memoirs in a second-hand bookshop he was drawn to the case, first because the Wolf-Man had always wanted to be a writer and second because Freud many years later asked Wespe to testify that what he had told him was true, a curious and uncharacteristic gesture of lack of self-confidence on the great man's part. Equally unusual, Freud lent Wespe money during the 1920s when he was destitute.

Refusing to privilege any one narrator or narrative and meticulously listing date and place, Castro cuts between Catacomb, living out his last days in destitution at Katoomba in the Blue Mountains outside Sydney, and Wespe at various stages in his life—on his estate at Kherson, near Odessa, where he was born in 1887, in the Caucasus in 1906, Munich in 1910, and Vienna in 1972. Freud does not appear directly but is constantly a reported presence in the novel, and like much else in the novel he is often a comic one.

Strange things happened to Wespe when he was young. He watched his parents in the act of sex and saw his father crawl on all fours ''and [hide] behind sofas with a wolf-mask over his face, springing up and terrifying the children, who ran screaming into the garden.'' He had an ecstatic sexual relationship with his sister, Anna. Two years older than himself, Anna, like his father and later like his wife, commits suicide. Wespe's response to Freud when he goes to be treated by him is an ambivalent and shifting one. Freud, it is hinted, in effect expropriates his client's writings while in turn the Wolf-Man's position as one of Freud's most celebrated cases gives him a certain status in the psychoanalytic world. It is one he adds to by becoming a successful author: ''My book was a smash hit. Stayed on *The New York Times* best-seller list three months.''

Through all this, Castro insists on the importance of play. Wespe tells us, ''It was Freud who first taught me that parody comes before the paradigm, play before principle. The origin of man was a sort of partying without precedence.'' And again: ''People have forgotten that life's a game. Play is the essence of thinking.'' The novel is full of jokes, puns, and wordplay (''The ego has landed''). Freud speaks like a character from the lower East side. In one of Castro's best gags, Wespe tells us, ''When I got to Vienna I immediately visited Freud. He gave me an autographed copy of *From the History of an Infantile Neurosis.* I sold it for several hundred crowns to a fellow who came to see me. His name was Jung....'' In a neat reversal of Melville's famous opening the psychiatric entrepreneur Ishmael Liebmann says, ''Call me Doctor Liebmann.'' There is an almost promiscuous variety of allusion, from references to wolves to Little Red Riding Hood to a guesthouse in Katoomba called the Aeneas. Part of the point that Castro is making is the not vastly original one of the problematic nature of truth. Wespe says of Freud's demand by what authority he writes what he writes, ''I was dumbfounded. Did he believe that pornographers rendered something called the 'truth'? ... Did he really mean to say that sexuality had firmer narrations than narrative, than a patient construction of scenes?'' Similarly, he insists on the truth suggested in the title that reality is comprised of binary opposites. ''A wolf is always a double,'' says Freud. Wespe says, ''The Greeks understood how to be both true and false to themselves. Savagery and civilisation. Crudity and refinement.'' There are seven goats for seven wolves. *Double-Wolf* is an elegant and witty, if not always quite convincing, tour de force.

Given Castro's evident penchant for disconnectedness and fragmentation, the use of different narratorial personas and voices, the danger to his art lies in a heterogeneity of allusion so great that it makes finally for incoherence. This tends to happen in *Pomeroy*, his least typical and perhaps least successful novel. It is a novel of brilliant bits that finally do not make a whole. Pomeroy is a journalist cum detective cum aspiring writer who has been jilted by his cousin and former lover, Estrellita. He accepts a job in Hong Kong working for *I.D.* magazine, the initials standing variously for International Detective, Identity, Investigative Dialectics, and Indecent Disclosures. Pomeroy himself calls it Income for Destitutes. As the novel opens, however, he is living in Australia and has been summoned by Rory Halligan, the man whom Estrellita abandoned for him. In three sections, alternating first-person narration with third-person reportage, the novel crosses back and forth in time and space to tell the story of Pomeroy, one that leads finally to an anticipated end (''Give a man a chance to put off his own death'').

As always with Castro the novel is full of jokes (Pomeroy's esky is covered with words from *Finnegans Wake,* which he reads as he almost drowns; there is a also letter in gloriously mangled English from Pomeroy's aunt complaining of his sexual activities) and allusions (to Shakespeare, Forster, Barthes, Housman). The esky is full of Hunter Valley wine. The novel both pays tribute to postmodernism and parodies it. The characters speak with incongruous sophistication: ''That's why we're in the prison house of language. For us ... there is really nothing outside the incriminating text. Just think ... the mobster as reader.'' Castro is fond of repeating the injunction of E. M. Forster, the epitome of old-fashioned humanism, to ''only connect,'' but the connections here are hard to follow.

Double-Wolf won Castro the Victorian Premier's Literary Award and he followed it the next year with *After China*, which achieved him the same honor. Once again, he exhibits his liking for rapidly shifting perspectives. A short novel, *After China* has almost as many scenes, neatly spliced together, as there are pages. Characteristically, it cuts between past and present, China and Australia, and first and third person to tell the story of the relationship between a Chinese architect, You Bok Man, and an unnamed but distinguished Australian writer of short stories. We learn little about the woman, apart from one brief episode devoted to her adolescence, except that it slowly becomes apparent that she is dying of cancer. The architect, however, eventually gives us his life story, from his training in Paris, imprisonment, impotence through an accident, and final escape in Shanghai, to a brief life in New York, to his current empty existence in the hotel he himself designed on the eastern coast of Australia, which is tumbling down around him. Castro's novels are nothing if not cosmopolitan and he himself points repeatedly to the extraordinarily complex cultural and racial background from which he comes.

Graver and more personal in tone than Castro's other novels, *After China* is also structurally a little simpler and more straightforward; it is a meditation on writing and its relation to sexuality and the relationship of both to immortality. The tales with which the architect ''seduces'' the writer and that become the substance of her final book are both from his own life and from ancient Chinese history and concentrate on this notion of immortality and its connection with the will to self-annihilation. The buildings that You designs are made deliberately difficult for their occupants. ''When I built it,'' he says of his hotel, ''I wanted people to be lost in it. The guest was not to come round again with any recognition or familiarity. Movement is discovery.''

Similarly, we are told, ''The Bauhaus and the Aufbau had attracted him because they opposed the unification of history, nationalism, and racial identity. He broke these things down into parts. Rearranged them.'' Doubleness is, of course, a central motif of Castro's work and fracturing goes hand in hand with unification. Perhaps the most appropriate of the many metaphors of binding and division that Castro offers us in the novel is that of the 16th-century pornographic painter in one of his stories, Tang Yin, who devises a fan that when opened from left to right depicts a traditional Chinese landscape and from right to left discloses an erotic painting. Tang Yin becomes famous when an imperial concubine catches sight of the fan open on the illicit side and takes a fancy to it.

Drift takes now familiar themes and forms as far as they can go. It opens with a preface (reputedly written by one Thomas McGann in Tasmania in 1993) concerning the cult experimental author B. S. Johnson, who killed himself at the age of 40; it goes on to suggest that the novel itself is the last two thirds of Johnson's last projected work, a trilogy that he failed to complete. Based on a tiny passage in the only completed volume that McGann insists refers to Tasmania, McGann completes the trilogy, as Johnson had invited his readers to do, adopting the voice of the author. In addition, there are a number of other different narrative voices, including that of Johnson himself as well as Emma McGann, an aboriginal woman writing letters from Tasmania to Johnson that call him across the world.

In Castro's scenario, Bryan Stanley Johnson, or Byron Shelley Johnson, as he likes to dub himself (''he carried deep within a massive, debilitating romanticism''), journeys to Tasmania to meet the author of the letters. Slowly he becomes caught up in the predicament of the Aborigines, identifying with them, taking toxins that alter the color of his skin to the point where he becomes even blacker than the Aboriginals themselves: ''Extinction. No longer white, unquestioning, biblical. No more dreams of primogeniture and ownership. No longer an author. What a relief.''

Like Johnson, Castro is fond of wordplay, of allusions, and of arcane words; he loves puns, like his description of two sisters, ''one grave, one acute,'' or the sign on McGann's Volkswagen, ''-sabled driver.'' In everything he does he questions the simplistic notion that ''writing is writing, life is life ... and the former is always subordinate to the latter,'' which he quotes from an unsympathetic critic of Johnson. But like all of Castro's work the novel is fundamentally serious in its attempt to push his themes of estrangement and loss of identity as far as he can. From writing about being a person of Chinese origin in Australia he moves in this, his fifth novel, to the ultimate condition of exile, that of the aboriginal. The aim of the novel is best summed up in Johnson's final paradox: ''What I am really doing is challenging the reader to prove his own existence as palpably as I am proving mine by the action of writing.'' By a combination of sheer linguistic brilliance and fundamental integrity Castro has succeeded in breaking through conventional labels such as ''multicultural writer'' to demonstrate the truth of his own expressed conviction: ''Writing knows no boundaries. Its metaphors, its translations, are part of a migratory process, birds of passage, which wing from the subliminal to the page, leaving its signs for the reader.''

—Laurie Clancy

CAULDWELL, Frank

See KING, Francis (Henry)

CAUTE, (John) David

Nationality: British. **Born:** Alexandria, Egypt, 16 December 1936. **Education:** Edinburgh Academy; Wellington College, Crowthorne, Berkshire; Wadham College, Oxford, M.A. in modern history, D.Phil. 1963; Harvard University, Cambridge, Massachusetts (Henry fellow), 1960–61. **Military Service:** Served in the British Army, in Africa, 1955–56. **Family:** Married 1) Catherine Shuckburgh in 1961 (divorced 1970), two sons; 2) Martha Bates in 1973, two daughters. **Career:** Fellow, All Souls College, Oxford, 1959–65; visiting professor, New York University and Columbia University, New York, 1966–67; reader in social and political theory, Brunel University, Uxbridge, Middlesex, 1967–70; Regents' Lecturer, University of California, 1974; Benjamin Meaker Visiting Professor, University of Bristol, 1985. Literary and arts editor, *New Statesman,* London, 1979–80. Co-chair, Writers Guild of Great Britain, 1981–82. **Awards:** London Authors' Club award, 1960; Rhys Memorial prize, 1960. **Address:** 41 Westcroft Square, London W6 0TA, England.

Publications

Novels

At Fever Pitch. London, Deutsch, 1959; New York, Pantheon, 1961.
Comrade Jacob. London, Deutsch, 1961; New York, Pantheon, 1962.
The Decline of the West. London, Deutsch, and New York, Macmillan, 1966.
The Occupation. London, Deutsch, 1971; New York, McGraw Hill, 1972.
The Baby Sitters (as John Salisbury). London, Secker and Warburg, and New York, Atheneum, 1978.
Moscow Gold (as John Salisbury). London, Futura, 1980.
The K-Factor. London, Joseph, 1983.
News from Nowhere. London, Hamish Hamilton, 1986.
Veronica; or, The Two Nations. London, Hamish Hamilton, 1989; New York, Arcade, 1990.
The Women's Hour. London, Paladin, 1991.
Dr Orwell and Mr Blair. London, Weidenfeld and Nicolson, 1994.
Fatima's Scarf. London, Totterdown Books, 1998.

Plays

Songs for an Autumn Rifle (produced Edinburgh, 1961).
The Demonstration (produced Nottingham, 1969; London, 1970). London, Deutsch, 1970.
The Fourth World (produced London, 1973).

Radio Plays: *Fallout,* 1972; *The Zimbabwe Tapes,* 1983; *Henry and the Dogs,* 1986; *Sanctions,* 1988.

Television Documentaries: *Brecht & Co.,* 1979.

Other

Communism and the French Intellectuals 1914–1960. London, Deutsch, and New York, Macmillan, 1964.
The Left in Europe since 1789. London, Weidenfeld and Nicolson, and New York, McGraw Hill, 1966.
Fanon. London, Fontana, and New York, Viking Press, 1970.
The Illusion: An Essay on Politics, Theatre and the Novel. London, Deutsch, 1971; New York, Harper, 1972.
The Fellow-Travellers. London, Weidenfeld and Nicolson, and New York, Macmillan, 1973; revised edition, New Haven, Connecticut, Yale University Press, 1988.
Collisions: Essays and Reviews. London, Quartet, 1974.

Cuba, Yes? London, Secker and Warburg, and New York, McGraw Hill, 1974.
The Great Fear: The Anti-Communist Purge under Truman and Eisenhower. New York, Simon and Schuster, and London, Secker and Warburg, 1978.
Under the Skin: The Death of White Rhodesia. London, Allen Lane, and Evanston, Illinois, Northwestern University Press, 1983.
The Espionage of the Saints: Two Essays on Silence and the State. London, Hamish Hamilton, 1986.
Left Behind: Journeys into British Politics. London, Cape, 1987.
Sixty-Eight: The Year of the Barricades. London, Hamish Hamilton, 1988; as *The Year of the Barricades: A Journey Through 1968,* New York, Harper, 1988.
Joseph Losey: A Revenge on Life. London, Faber, 1994; New York, Oxford University Press, 1994.
Editor, *Essential Writings,* by Karl Marx. London, MacGibbon and Kee, 1967; New York, Macmillan, 1968.

*

Critical Studies: Article by Caute, in *Contemporary Authors Autobiography Series 4* edited by Adele Sarkissian, Detroit, Gale, 1986; *Caute's Confrontations: A Study of the Novels of David Caute* by Nicolas Tredell, West Bridgford, Paupers' Press, 1994.

David Caute comments:

(1996) My novels are (perhaps) about: how people interpret the world to make themselves better and larger than they are; the helpless guilt of the self-aware; and the strategies of fictional narrative itself. Every private life is touched, or seized, by a wider public life.

* * *

In his novels, David Caute has always been concerned to dramatize and explore the complex relations between political commitment, the urge for power, and sexual desire. His fiction vividly portrays characters caught up in a range of struggles: African decolonization in *At Fever Pitch, The Decline of the West, News from Nowhere*, and *The K-Factor*; the attempt by the seventeenth-century Diggers to establish a free community in the England of Oliver Cromwell, in *Comrade Jacob*; the campus revolts of the 1960s in *The Occupation*; the social conflicts of 1980s Britain in *Veronica*; feminism in *The Women's Hour*; anti-communism in *Dr Orwell and Mr Blair.* Caute's sympathies are with the left, but never, in his novels, in an uncritical or dogmatic way; indeed, he is sharply aware of the bad faith and vanity that may be bound up with left-wing commitment, and he can present a sympathetic portrait of a right-wing figure, as he does in *Veronica.*

Caute's first four novels were primarily realistic, but showed signs of strain, as if another kind of writer were trying to get out. In the context of English fiction in the 1950s, *At Fever Pitch* was notable for the variety of narrative techniques it employed, from interior monologues to attempts to imitate the style of African folktales. At moments, *Comrade Jacob* moved into caricature and deliberate anachronism. *The Decline of the West* went further in the direction of caricature, and its exuberant style, endlessly generating similes and metaphors, was a distraction from the narrative and from the impact of specific scenes. *The Occupation*, however, triumphantly resolved these strains: here Caute found a form and style well suited to his talents, and to his concerns at the time.

The protagonist of *The Occupation* is a radical English academic, Steven Bright, working in the USA at the height of the 1960s' student revolts. Roused by the tumults of the times, challenged by his students to live up to his radicalism, embroiled in fraught relationships with a range of women, Bright finds himself, and the novel he is in, falling apart. But this breakdown is a breakthrough for Caute: *The Occupation* mixes realism, fantasy, caricature, expressionism, and self-reflexive commentary in a way that vividly dramatizes its themes, but it also achieves aesthetic coherence through its skillful overall structure and the sustained pace, precision, and wit of its style. It is Caute's most frenetic but most assured achievement.

The Occupation was part of a trilogy that also included a play, *The Demonstration*, and a work of literary theory, *The Illusion*. This trilogy, which bore the overall title of *The Confrontation*, both advocated and sought to demonstrate a practice of politically committed writing that challenged and disrupted representation. Caute did not follow this up, however, and for the next thirteen years produced studies of modern history and politics. It was *Under the Skin*, his documentary account of the death of Ian Smith's Rhodesian regime, which heralded his return to fiction in *The K-Factor*; this short, fast-paced novel dramatized the identity crisis of Rhodesia in its last days, as definitions of reality were hotly disputed—were the black guerrillas, for example, to be seen as terrorists or freedom fighters? *The K-Factor* was followed by *News from Nowhere*, a long, serious, and absorbing chronicle of the fortunes of Richard Stern from his heady years as a Young Turk at the London School of Economics to his troubled existence as an ill-paid journalist in the twilight of white Rhodesia. *Veronica* explores the incestuous love of a Conservative Cabinet Minister for his half-sister, and *The Women's Hour* sharply and comically portrays the plight of an ageing, left-wing university lecturer who is accused of sexual harassment by a feminist colleague. *Dr Orwell and Mr Blair* offers a fictional memoir, supposedly written by a boy whom ''Mr Blair'' befriended, of George Orwell as he was developing the ideas for *Animal Farm.* All these novels are largely realistic, but they do sometimes highlight their own artifice, and call into question the veracity of representation in supposedly factual as well as fictional writing. They show neither the strain of Caute's early realist work nor the controlled frenzy of *The Occupation*; they are the work of a mature writer, skilled in his craft and balanced in his attitudes, who combines humour, scepticism, and clarity.

Caute's novels now comprise a significant body of work, but they have suffered some neglect. This is partly because they are difficult to classify. In their challenge to realism, they can be seen as postmodernist; in their political and ethical engagements, they subvert postmodernist playfulness. But it is precisely in this confrontation—between postmodernism and realism, politics and play, commitment and critical detachment—that their power and pleasure lies.

—Nicolas Tredell

CHARYN, Jerome

Nationality: American. **Born:** New York City, 13 May 1937. **Education:** Columbia University, New York, B.A. (cum laude) 1959 (Phi Beta Kappa). **Family:** Married Marlene Phillips in 1965 (divorced). **Career:** Recreation leader, New York City Department of Parks, early 1960s; English teacher, High School of Music and Art, and School of Performing Arts, both New York, 1962–64; Lecturer in

English, City College, New York, 1965; assistant professor of English, Stanford University, California, 1965–68; assistant professor, 1968–72, associate professor, 1972–78, and professor of English, 1978–80, Herbert Lehman College, City University of New York; Mellon Visiting Professor of English, Rice University, Houston, 1979; visiting professor, 1980, and lecturer in creative writing, 1981–86, Princeton University, New Jersey; Visiting Distinguished Professor of English, City College of New York, 1988–89. Founding editor, *Dutton Review,* New York, 1970–72; executive editor, *Fiction,* New York, 1970–75. Member of the Executive Board, PEN American Center, since 1984, International Association of Crime Writers, since 1988, and Mystery Writers of America, since 1989. Since 1986 member of Playwright/Director Unit, Actors Studio, New York. **Awards:** National Endowment for the Arts grant, 1979, 1984; Rosenthal Foundation award, 1981; Guggenheim grant, 1982. Chevalier, Order of Arts and Letters (France), 1989. **Agent:** Georges Borchardt Inc., 136 East 57th Street, New York, New York 10022, U.S.A.; or, Mic Cheetham, Anthony Sheil Associates, 43 Doughty Street, London WC1N 2LF, England. **Address:** 302 West 12th Street, Apartment 10-C, New York, New York 10014, U.S.A.; or, 1 rue Boulard, Paris 75014, France.

PUBLICATIONS

Novels

Once Upon a Droshky. New York, McGraw Hill, 1964.
On the Darkening Green. New York, McGraw Hill, 1965.
Going to Jerusalem. New York, Viking Press, 1967; London, Cape, 1968.
American Scrapbook. New York, Viking Press, 1969.
Eisenhower, My Eisenhower. New York, Holt Rinehart, 1971.
The Tar Baby. New York, Holt Rinehart, 1973.
The Isaac Quartet. London, Zomba, 1984.
  Blue Eyes. New York, Simon and Schuster, 1975.
  Marilyn the Wild. New York, Arbor House, 1976; London, Bloomsbury, 1990.
  The Education of Patrick Silver. New York, Arbor House, 1976.
  Secret Isaac. New York, Arbor House, 1978.
The Franklin Scare. New York, Arbor House, 1977.
The Seventh Babe. New York, Arbor House, 1979.
The Catfish Man: A Conjured Life. New York, Arbor House, 1980.
Darlin' Bill: A Love Story of the Wild West. New York, Arbor House, 1980.
Panna Maria. New York, Arbor House, 1982.
Pinocchio's Nose. New York, Arbor House, 1983.
War Cries over Avenue C. New York, Fine, 1985; London, Abacus, 1986.
The Magician's Wife. Tournai, Belgium, Casterman, 1986; New York, Catalan, 1987; London, Titan, 1988.
Paradise Man. New York, Fine, 1987; London, Joseph, 1988.
The Good Policeman. New York, Mysterious Press, 1990; London, Bloomsbury, 1991.
Elsinore. New York, Mysterious Press, and London, Bloomsbury, 1991.
Maria's Girls. New York, Mysterious Press, 1992; London, Serpent's Tail, 1994.
Montezuma's Man. New York, Mysterious Press, 1993.
Little Angel Street. New York, Mysterious Press, 1994.
El Bronx. New York, Mysterious Press, 1997.
Death of a Tango King. New York, New York University Press, 1998.
Citizen Sidel. New York, Mysterious Press, 1999.
Captain Kidd. New York, St. Martin's Press, 1999.

Short Stories

The Man Who Grew Younger and Other Stories. New York, Harper, 1967.
Family Man, art by Joe Staton, lettering by Ken Bruzenak. New York, Paradox Press, 1995.

Uncollected Short Stories

''The Blue Book of Crime,'' in *The New Black Mask.* San Diego, California, Harcourt Brace, 1986.
''Fantomas in New York,'' in *A Matter of Crime.* San Diego, California, Harcourt Brace, 1988.
''Young Isaac,'' in *The Armchair Detective* (New York), Summer 1990.

Other

Metropolis: New York as Myth, Marketplace, and Magical Land. New York, Putnam, 1986; London, Abacus, 1988.
Movieland: Hollywood and the Great American Dream Culture. New York, Putnam, 1989.
The Dark Lady from Belorusse: A Memoir. New York, St. Martin's Press, 1997.
The Black Swan: A Memoir. St. Martin's Press, 2000.
Editor, *The Single Voice: An Anthology of Contemporary Fiction.* New York, Collier, 1969.
Editor, *The Troubled Vision: An Anthology of Contemporary Short Novels and Passages.* New York, Collier, 1970.
Editor, *The New Mystery.* New York, Dutton, 1993.

*

Manuscript Collection: Fales Collection, Elmer Holmes Bobst Library, New York University.

Critical Studies: Introductions by Charyn to *The Single Voice,* 1969, and *The Troubled Vision,* 1970; ''Notes on the Rhetoric of Anti-Realist Fiction'' by Albert Guerard, in *Tri-Quarterly* (Evanston, Illinois), Spring 1974; ''Jerome Charyn: Artist as Mytholept'' by Robert L. Patten, in *Novel* (Providence, Rhode Island), Fall 1984; ''Exploding the Genre: The Crime Fiction of Jerome Charyn'' by Michael Woolf, in *American Crime Fiction,* London, Macmillan, 1988; Jerome Charyn issue of *The Review of Contemporary Fiction,* Summer 1992.

* * *

Jerome Charyn's work demonstrates a deep mistrust of the contemporary world, expressed frequently in alienation from mechanized or anti-humanistic institutions. At the same time, and in opposition to this perception, Charyn has celebrated humanity's heroic capacity for survival in the face of such alienation. A typical Charyn protagonist moves between worlds, between a landscape of urban decline and worlds of spiritual intensity and complexity where the capacity for magic and mayhem confronts the mundane and the menacing. Throughout his work he has imagined and re-imagined America (most commonly New York City) into forms that repeatedly challenge and subvert the reader's perception of contemporary reality. A dark comedy meets fragments of spiritual persistence that finally affirm the fragile survival of flawed but beautiful humanity in the rubble of our civilization. The fiction is formed and informed both by an awareness of contemporary literary practice and by a moral consciousness deeply influenced by Jewish experience and perception. Of all the novelists characterized as Jewish-American, Charyn is the most radical and inventive. There is in the body of his work a restless creativity which constantly surprises and repeatedly undermines the reader's expectation.

His first novel, *Once Upon a Droshky*, explored a recurrent conflict in Jewish-American writing, that between father and son. The narrative voice, however, is that of the father and the language is in an English that is shaped by Yiddish speech structures. This creates a powerful comic narrative but it also reveals a sense of continuity with, and nostalgia for, the lost world of Yiddish-American culture. The father reflects a sense of moral justice while the son represents a legalistic, inhumane America. He embodies a future against which the voices of the past have little power except that accrued by spiritual strength and the sense that reality is ambiguous, containing both the known and the transcendent. It is characteristic of Charyn's originality that his first novel, published when he was 26, should be told through the perception of the father.

The world as this kind of ambiguous landscape places Charyn's work, in one context, in relation to Isaac Bashevis Singer's. In one of Charyn's most important novels, *War Cries over Avenue C*, for example, he goes into the innermost heart of the desolate inner city to invent a world of heroes and grotesques, angels and demons. Avenue C is a world without God. The novel is not, though, a grim record of urban decline. A Jewish girl with bad skin becomes magically transformed into a mythic and heroic figure, Saigon Sarah, while her lover returns from Vietnam as ''The Magician'' picking shrapnel, like dandruff, from his skull. Vietnam is carried like a drug into the twisted heart of New York. Charyn is not, though, solely representing the familiar issues of violence and degeneration in the city but a complex synthesis of moral collapse and spirituality, degradation and salvation.

Charyn's prose precisely reflects his themes. It makes startling conjunctions, dramatically synthesizes the magical and the mundane. He thrusts the reader out of the known world and then back into it with a radically altered perception. The experience is comic, violent, and profoundly serious.

Another aspect of Charyn's writing is his awareness of contemporary literary issues; he is an editor and critic of considerable sophistication. His knowledge of this field is shown in his use of the notions of fictionality and fable-making that characterizes, in part, post-realist and postmodern writing. This aspect of his work is most clearly illustrated in the novels of the early 1970s: *Eisenhower, My Eisenhower* and *The Tar Baby*. In the first novel he creates a fictional gypsy tribe of Azazians who are essentially comic figures with tails and a belief in an anarchic God. The novel is told in the first person by an Azazian gypsy, and Charyn's achievement is to use that comic voice to record a tragic history. The voice reveals a condition of persecution that transforms the fable of Azazian history into one that reflects all histories of ethnic alienation and persecution. Non-realism paradoxically offers an incisive analysis into the real predicament of the ethnic stranger. A similar strategy is found in *The Tar Baby*. The novel is a parody of a literary periodical which ostensibly honors the life of one Anatole Waxman-Weissman. The form gives Charyn the opportunity to create a succession of literary jokes reminiscent of Nabokov's *Pale Fire,* but the formal issues co-exist with a sense of Anatole as an archetypal ethnic outsider in a society and institution hostile to the creative imagination.

Charyn's view of his own creativity is of a process that comes close to mystical experience in its transfer between real and quasi-surreal worlds: ''I start out each time to write a conventional story. All of a sudden, the story begins to shift. It's like a landslide—you're on one particular spot, and all of a sudden that spot disappears and you enter some other sort of crazy territory.'' These territories are rich indeed and they encompass many forms, from the Western landscape of *Darlin' Bill* to the immigrant history of America that informs *Panna Maria*. Of particular interest are two novels of quasi-mythical autobiography: *The Catfish Man* and *Pinocchio's Nose*. These frequently exuberant fables offer a kind of alternative history of Jewish America. This history counters the view of the Jews as an invariably upwardly mobile and successful immigrant group. Like the Azazians, Charyn's Jews remain on the edges of the world, occupying a territory that shifts and slides between alienation and magic. Charyn's Jews are in America but not always of it: a tribe apart.

Tribalism is, in fact, the mode in which he most frequently represents ethnicity. This is most clearly apparent in the crime novels that come close to offering an urban epic of major literary importance: *The Isaac Quartet* and *The Good Policeman*. In these five novels Charyn represents New York as a kind of tribal society populated by warring ethnic communities. The groups are intertwined in a system that blurs boundaries between good and evil, detective and criminal. In essence, the author uses the crime genre to complicate the nature of reality. He reverses a common objective of the form which frequently depends on a clear division between right and wrong, good and bad.

A writer of almost staggering energy, Charyn during the late 1990s seemingly turned out books as fast as his readers could read them. *El Bronx*, the ninth volume featuring New York mayor Isaac Sidel, is as much concerned with its preteen characters as with the fiftysomething mayor. Charyn followed this with a memoir about his mother, *The Dark Lady from Belorusse*, and a less successful work of fiction, *Death of a Tango King*. The latter, his 28th novel, was not part of the Sidel series, but with *Citizen Sidel* the writer returned full-force to his inimitable mayor. The book was a rollicking joyride, but the sprawling plot of *Captain Kidd*—ranging as it did from the invasion of Italy under Patton's Third Army to the internecine wars of dry-goods merchants in wartime Manhattan—proved confusing to some readers. *The Black Swan*, a sequel to the earlier memoir, recounts Charyn's childhood obsession with the movies.

Charyn's view of the world is inclusive and complex. He grafts onto the form of the detective novel a set of strategies which permit those mystical transformations that are characteristic of a view of reality in which nothing stays simple or still. He is not essentially concerned with the mechanics of crime but he exploits the genre to approach the profoundest of paradoxes: the persistence of love and redemption in an ostensibly doomed and damned world. Within the violent disorder of contemporary experience, Charyn perceives the heroic nature of flawed humanity as it crawls towards some bizarre version of spiritual salvation.

Charyn is one of a handful of living American novelists who combine prolific output with stylistic originality and imaginative zest.

Part of his claim to our attention is his unpredictability. He has taken hold of a vast range of American myths, locations, and dreams and reshaped these within his rich imagination. He melds that creativity with the fertile tradition of Jewish storytelling which traditionally envisages a spiritual potential within a mire of poverty and violence. The outcome is a deeply serious and profound vision of a world simultaneously half-catatonic at the edge of doom and heroically groping towards some version of God's grace.

—Michael Woolf

CHATTERJEE, Upamanyu

Nationality: Indian. **Born:** Bihar, India, 1959. **Career:** Currently, officer, Indian Administrative Service. **Address:** c/o Faber and Faber, Ltd., 3 Queen Square, London, WC1N 3AU, England.

Publications

Novels

English, August: An Indian Story. London, Faber, 1988.
The Last Burden. New Delhi, Viking, and London, Faber, 1993.

* * *

The corpus of Upamanyu Chatterjee is not vast but his is a powerful emergent voice in Indian postcolonial literature. Thus far he has published ''The Assassination of Indira Gandhi'' in 1986 and two novels, *English, August: An Indian Story* in 1988 and *The Last Burden* in 1993. Critics have found Chatterjee difficult to categorize in that the protagonists—August in *English, August* and Jamun in *The Last Burden*—just drift with no apparent purpose in life. Reviews of *English, August* liken August to Kingsley Amis's Lucky Jim as a portrayal of the angry young man. But such a comparison would thematically make August angrier, for this novel is focused on India's postcolonial condition and the necessity to decolonize.

English, August deals with August as a member of the Indian Administrative Service, a reincarnation of the Indian Civil Service, a behemoth left behind by the British to govern the country. A job in the IAS is highly sought after in postcolonial India; August, while appearing lackadaisical and self-centered and seeming to be its most inappropriate member, draws attention to a system which has become totally outmoded and out of touch with the needs of the Indian masses. Overtly, the novel attempts to do an expose of the IAS with its corruption and the tension which exists between the IAS officers representing the federal government and the state governments resulting in the victimization of the common people in the administrative nightmare in modern India.

Furthermore, there is a subtext of anger which is aimed not just at the IAS, but one which questions reality in India which is mediated by the English text or more particularly through Western eyes. For instance, watching Indian television, August makes references to *Peyton Place* and *Waiting for Godot,* which prompts his uncle to respond with ''the *first* thing you are reminded of by something that happens around you, is something obscure and foreign, totally unrelated to the life and language around you.'' This particular theme pervades the novel and all the characters agree that postcolonial India is unreal, ''a place of fantasy'' and ''confused metaphysics.'' To this extent, the IAS itself becomes a metaphor for India. Under the guise of decolonization, post-independence IAS once more reinscribes the colonial government as well as the profound sense of dislocation that a lot of Indians feel. Nationalism represented by the IAS can only be purchased by the homogenization of India and its people. The IAS and its policy of placing elite officers in locales and terrains they are unfamiliar with only goes further towards making it an inept administrative body, unable to cope with the intricacies of administering in a place and language alien to it. How can India/IAS decolonize then? August's only option is through taking a break from the IAS altogether.

If *English, August* is dark and bleak, *The Last Burden* comes to terms with and accepts such darkness. This novel of decolonization is truly ''indigenous'' in that its concern is not with India's relationship to the metropolitan centers but rather with middle-class life. It exposes the myth of the unity of the joint Hindu family (as opposed to the Western nuclear one) and its sense of duty, and dwells instead on the banality of urban life in India. The most striking aspect of this novel is the incredible language used by Chatterjee, which makes the reader oscillate between the beauty of the high serious prose and the ridiculous emotions that it covers. For instance, the novel is framed by the death of Jamun's mother. Upon being reprimanded at his demeanor and lack of sorrow at her impending death, Jamun retorts, ''She isn't Indira Gandhi, you know, that we've to hurtle out into the streets and thwack our tits to voice our grief.'' Thus the chaos in the aftermath of Indira Gandhi's assassination is contextualized as hyperbole. Again, when Urmila dies, the doctor advises them to cremate the body, for the mourners ''crack up, if after a few hours, the cadaver they're half-worshipping exudes the wispiest pong.'' Thus Chatterjee's use of language is effective on two counts. First, his code-switching and inscription of the banal and the slang defuses the hyperbole and exaggerated emotions associated with death. Death becomes real and a part of life and not a farce. In addition, his treatment of language forcibly inflects the Indian and indigenous within the language reserved for the English canon and its system of cultural assumptions.

With *The Last Burden* and the deliberate indigenization of English, Chatterjee finds a solution to the postcolonial anxiety articulated in *English, August.*

—Radhika Mohanram

CHEUSE, Alan

Nationality: American. **Born:** Perth Amboy, New Jersey, 23 January 1940. **Education:** Rutgers University, New Brunswick, New Jersey, B.A. 1961, Ph.D. in comparative literature 1974. **Family:** Married 1) Mary Ethel Agan in 1964 (divorced 1972), one son; 2) Marjorie Pryse in 1975 (divorced 1984), two daughters; 3) Kristin O'Shee in 1991. **Career:** Toll taker, New Jersey Turnpike, 1961–62; speechwriter, 1965; reporter, Fairchild Publications, 1966; instructor in literature, Bennington College, Vermont, 1970–78; visiting writer, University of the South, 1984, University of Michigan, Ann Arbor, 1984–86, University of Virginia, Charlottesville, and since 1987, George

Mason University. Book critic, National Public Radio, *All Things Considered,* since 1984, producer and host, *Sound of Writing,* since 1989. **Awards:** National Endowment for the Arts fellowship, 1979–80. **Member:** National Book Critics' Circle. **Agent:** Nat Sobel, 146 East 19th Street, New York, New York 10003, U.S.A.

PUBLICATIONS

Novels

The Bohemians: John Reed and His Friends. Cambridge, Massachusetts, n.p., 1982.
The Grandmothers' Club. Salt Lake City, Utah, Peregrine Smith, 1986.
The Light Possessed. Salt Lake City, Utah, Peregrine Smith, 1990.

Short Stories

Candace and Other Stories. Cambridge, Massachusetts, n.p., 1980.
The Tennessee Waltz and Other Stories. Salt Lake City, Utah, Peregrine Smith, 1990.
Lost and Old Rivers: Stories. Dallas, Texas, Southern Methodist University Press, 1998.

Other

Fall Out of Heaven: An Autobiographical Journey. Salt Lake City, Utah, Peregrine Smith, 1987.
Editor, with Caroline Marshall, *The Sound of Writing.* New York, Doubleday, 1991.
Editor, with Caroline Marshall, *Listening to Ourselves.* New York, Doubleday, 1993.
Editor, with Nicholas Delbanco, *Talking Horse: Bernard Malamud on Life and Work.* New York, Columbia University Press, 1996.

*

Manuscript Collection: Alderman Library, University Of Virginia, Charlottesville.

Alan Cheuse comments:

Two notes about my stories. I tend to see them as pieces as much in the lyric mode as straight narrative, in which I work the language as closely as a poet might. So my stories are as close to writing lyric poetry as I will probably ever get.

As far as grouping them, I can see a rough geographical configuration. There are southern stories, western stories, and some eastern stories. I suppose in another ten or twenty years I'll have boxed the compass in short fiction. But I doubt if this has much to do with their meaning—it's a category that helps me keep track of them, is all, I think.

With regard to *Fall Out of Heaven*, I have to say that I would like to do more nonfiction, but I haven't yet found a new subject. In the case of this memoir-travel book, the subject was as personal as my own skin, and I had done all the research just by living and suffering. The travel part was the reward, I suppose, for having gone through the hellish rest of it, the battles with my father, the awful separation from my son that came when his mother and I divorced.

As far as finding an overall pattern in my work, who knows? No writer wants to think that he's finished searching for that, not before he himself is finished with life and work. Hemingway noticed certain patterns and began to parody himself. Faulkner kept on reaching and though the work fell off a bit it never became uninteresting. On goes the quest.

* * *

Alan Cheuse is not only a prolific writer of fiction and nonfiction, but also a widely appearing commentator-critic-lecturer dealing with modern literature and—not least—a member of the writing faculty of George Mason University's MFA Program. Four of the topics he has addressed in his public-speaking engagements have a particular bearing on his concerns as an author. These are: ''Writing for the Ear,'' ''Imagining Ancestry,'' ''Fathers and Fictions,'' and ''The Elusive Matter of Form.'' In varying degrees these work together for Cheuse in his longer works, enabling him to be seen as an experimental, widely ranging littérateur of enormous power and troubling vision.

Cheuse's first novel, *The Bohemians: John Reed and His Friends*, is dedicated as follows: ''For Fathers and Sons—Phil and Josh.'' Phil, Cheuse's father, died shortly after *The Bohemians* was written; Josh is Cheuse's teenage son by his first wife. Considering its emotional impact and the way its historic characters are made to come alive for the reader, *The Bohemians* is perhaps Cheuse's most noteworthy work of fiction. It is an imaginative re-creation of the life of America's premier communist, wherein Cheuse blurs the line between documentary journalism and action-packed adventure fiction while making use of the personal memoir. Reed was a polemical journalist fiercely opposed to America's entering World War I, yet he was committed to overthrowing the capitalist system and replacing it with a radical redistribution of power such as that envisioned by the Bolshevik faction of the American Communist Party. Though Cheuse does not cite reference sources for his detailed ''life'' of this controversial figure, he seems to capture Reed's language, thereby enabling the reader to ''hear'' the fervent, irrepressible Reed in his comings and goings with associates on all levels of familiarity.

From childhood in Oregon to death from typhus in a Moscow hospital, Reed's life is played out in a largely first-person narrative pattern enriched through the inclusion of a postscript memoir by his wife, Louise Bryant, poetic inserts, a galaxy of important figures in Reed's life—each seeming to speak and act in propria persona—and a scattering of documentary details, real or imagined. Fascinating as are the occasional appearances of, among others, Lincoln Steffens, Max Eastman, Walter Lippmann, and Woodrow Wilson, Reed's stormy, sometimes tender, relationship with Louise Bryant makes an indelible impression on the reader. (Complicating their relationship was Reed's involvement with Edna St. Vincent Millay and Louise's with Eugene O' Neill.) Problematical as some of Cheuse's dramatic re-creations of Reed's personal history may appear, the live-voice dynamic of the supporting cast of *The Bohemians* lends plausibility to the book.

Hardly a novel in the literal sense, because it is not a fictional narrative, *Fall Out of Heaven: An Autobiographical Journey* integrates autobiographical episodes in Cheuse's life with an autobiographical manuscript left by his late father, a Russian immigrant and former captain and fighter pilot in the Soviet air force. The double-helix form of this experimental narrative, representing a heartfelt tribute to the parent with whom Cheuse had long had a tempestuous relationship, was foreshadowed in *The Bohemians*, written about six years before *Fall Out of Heaven*. Near the end of his life, John Reed tells his wife that he recently began "a novel in the form of a memoir" and then adds, "Or is it a memoir in the form of a novel? … Well, what the hell, to hell with form! Leave that to the bourgeois artistes!" The Alan Cheuse portion of *Fall Out of Heaven* is based on a sentimental journey Cheuse took with son Josh to the Far East in the mid-1980s. That journey in turn was based on a strange inner voice Alan felt he had heard at his father's funeral almost four years earlier. It seemed to come from his father, directing Alan to go to Khiva. "Take your own son and go to Khiva, that little desert outpost in Uzbekistan where I spent my best youth, and I'll meet you there, and we'll see what happens next." Another unnatural visitation is recorded in *Fall Out of Heaven*. The day after Cheuse's friend, John Gardner (fiction writer, medievalist, academic), died in a motorcycle accident in 1982, he appeared to Cheuse in a vision and told him plainly to keep on working. This occurrence took place on the following day as well.

Cheuse's next novel, *The Grandmothers' Club*, is more of an "imagined" work—though still a reconstruction from a real-life story—than *The Bohemians*. It grew, he explains in an author's note, out of a *New York Times* news item he had read in the late 1970s, when he was beginning to write *The Bohemians*. "The president and CEO of United Brands," which had started out early in the 1800s "trading New England ice for Central American fruit, had jumped from a window high atop the Pan-Am building in midtown Manhattan," because of a "financial scandal, involving, among other things, bribery of high Latin government officials." He had begun "as a rabbinical student;" his most recent position, before entering "the world of corporate finance, had been assistant rabbi" in a Long Island synagogue. However, the central feature of this demanding novel is not the tarnished career of Manny Bloch the self-destructing rabbi but grandmother Minnie Bloch's narrative voice, shaping and projecting more than a mere saga of her antihero son. Minnie is a kind of tribal storyteller, creating a world of cultural experience behind Manny and his troubled family: for example, now a song title ("Mood Indigo," "Light My Fire"), now a commercial-history note on the development of the banana trade. Although some of the dialogue in *The Bohemians* (Lou Bryant and John Reed before his death, discussing their love and his writing achievement) suggests a parody of Hemingway at his weakest, the vocalized brooding sensibility of Minnie Bloch now and then evokes the powerful sweep and commanding presence of the overseeing narrator of Joyce's *Ulysses*.

As in *Fall Out of Heaven*, in *The Grandmothers' Club* there are also secret messages from beyond the realm of ordinary human experience. Manny Bloch's life has been permanently affected by the tragedy, when he was eight years old, of his father's death in a street accident. From time to time he senses that his dead father is delivering messages to him through the beak of a mysterious bird. At a crucial point in his life, when he finds himself wondering why he is going to the Temple on the High Holy Days, the experience of the oracle-bird's arrival is overwhelming and he falls to the ground. Then Manny hears his father's mandate: He must do what he must do, he must go where he must go. His father adds, "Midway in this life, a point I never reached, you must take a new road." Manny thereupon leaves the rabbinate so that he can enter his wife's family's shipping business, and he later becomes a powerful commercial entrepreneur. Manny's suicide, as described poetically by his super-sensitive, unusually articulate mother, provides what is perhaps the most beautifully written passage in the entire novel. In the end it is Manny's long-dead father who dominates Manny's life course and who thereby also exercises an indirectly damaging influence on two other members of Manny's star-crossed family, his wife and daughter.

Cheuse's latest novel, *The Light Possessed*, reveals a particular artistic and visual trait that he shared with the poet Emily Dickinson, a sensitivity to light. For example, in *The Grandmothers' Club,* Minnie Bloch tells about one of Manny's bird-visitations. The bird calls Manny's name, "and if sound can have a light, it's a bright light in the middle of the darkness that surrounds him, like a burning bush in a dark meadow, or a star against a black field of velvet, like that, all of the sunlight that was present a moment before condensed into the sound." Light is of much greater importance in the subsequent novel, which deals with 20th-century American art and one of our greatest artists. Cheuse offers us a fictionalized career study of Georgia O'Keefe (here called Ava Boldin) against the background of her husband, Alfred Stieglitz (Albert Stigmar in the novel), numerous relatives, and fellow artists. One real-life character appears in propria persona: Stanley Edgar Hyman, Bennington College professor, literary critic, and free-living man-about-town.

Again in this novel there is the figure of the unnatural visitant. This time it is Eve, Ava's twin, who died at birth. When Ava was very young, she claimed that Eve appeared to her secretly, giving her information about future happenings. At the end of the book, it is this dead infant who has the last word, as she asks her sister (now so widely renowned for the use she has made of light in her scenes of the New Mexico desert) to clear up certain questions for her before she awakens from her dream. She wants to be shown, Eve pleads, "if color has a sound and how light creates music. And if the shape of things takes on a shade, visible near darkness … and … if light is the old metaphor for infinity, and … if color is light given in terms of the world." *The Light Possessed*, which contains a story line more difficult to follow than that of *The Grandmothers' Club*, exhibits to a fault three major features of the modernist mode in fiction: stream-of-consciousness narrative, jumbled plot sequences, and multi-vocal rendition, as in for example, William Faulkner's *The Sound and the Fury*.

A number of Cheuse's short stories, originally appearing in various literary and mass-market magazines, were collected in *Candace and Other Stories*; all but the title story were published again in a collection titled *The Tennessee Waltz and Other Stories*. Although Cheuse clearly prefers to write novel-length, biographically based fiction (currently [1995] he is at work on another historical/biographical novel), he appears to favor "short takes," i.e., thin slices of life, as alternative fiction forms. Here his writing suggests somewhat the minimalist mode of certain stories by the late Raymond Carver. There is an underlying sadness in these tales of unhappy families and family members, each unhappy in a different way. Nashville and country music feature prominently in this assortment. Cheuse's real power as a writer of fiction is most pronounced when he has long pondered, perhaps brooded, over a complicated individual caught up in a formidable struggle with self and ominous circumstances. And though Cheuse in his fiction reflects touches of various contemporaneous authors, he is also capable of producing passages of rare poetic beauty as well as narratives with memorable personal voices, which in a sense sets him apart from some of the better known commercial writers with literary aspirations.

—Samuel I. Bellman

CHILDRESS, Mark

Nationality: American. **Born:** Monroeville, Alabama, 1957. **Education:** Attended Louisiana State University, Shreveport, 1974–75; University of Alabama, 1974–78. **Career:** Writer, *Birmingham News,* Birmingham, Alabama, 1977–80; features editor, *Southern Living,* Birmingham, Alabama, 1980–84; regional editor, *Atlanta Journal-Constitution,* 1984–85. **Agent:** Frederick Hill Associates, 1842 Union Street, San Francisco, California 94123, U.S.A. **Address:** San Francisco, California.

Publications

Novels

A World Made of Fire. New York, Knopf, 1984.
V for Victor. New York, Knopf, 1984.
Tender. New York, Harmony Books, 1990.
Crazy in Alabama. New York, Putnam, 1993.
Gone for Good. New York, Knopf, 1998.

Fiction (for children)

Joshua and Bigtooth. Boston, Little, Brown, 1992.
Joshua and the Big Bad Blue Crabs. Boston, Little, Brown, 1996.
Henry Bobbity Is Missing and It Is All Billy Bobbity's Fault! Birmingham, Alabama, Crane Hill Publishers, 1996.

Plays

Screenplays: *Crazy in Alabama.* Columbia Pictures, 1999.

* * *

Mark Childress's five novels constitute one of the most interesting bodies of work by a contemporary Southern author. Born in Monroeville, Alabama, hometown of Harper Lee and childhood home of Truman Capote, Childress was positioned literally from birth within a specific literary tradition. However, his novels appear far more influenced by the magic realism of Gabriel Garcia Marquez and the compulsively readable narratives of Stephen King (who has enthusiastically endorsed Childress's work) than by William Faulkner or Eudora Welty. Although three of his five novels are set in his native Alabama, and all of his books demonstrate intimate knowledge of the Southern landscape and Southern mores, Childress seems most preoccupied with two basic themes: the perennial story of alienated youth coming to terms (or not) with their parents, and the more contemporary problem of such youths' desire for media stardom, and the public's willingness to provide it, often at a terrible cost.

Childress's first novel, *A World Made of Fire*, set in rural Alabama in the first two decades of the twentieth century, tells the story of Stella and her brother Jacko, survivors of a house fire that destroyed their home and family. While Stella struggles to raise her brother with the help of neighbors, Jacko, crippled by polio, begins to display an ability to influence supernaturally the world around him, an ability encouraged by a mysterious old African-American woman named Brown Mary. When Jacko is blamed for a polio epidemic and threatened by the townspeople, his powers save him and punish the guilty, but, by novel's end, it is unclear if his magical relationship with fire will be a force for good or evil. The fantastic elements of the book are convincingly integrated into the narrative, but the book as a whole falters under a melodramatic plot and an overly earnest lyricism. Published when the author was twenty-seven, *A World Made of Fire* is very much a first novel by a talented and ambitious young author not yet fully in control of his materials.

Childress's next novel, *V for Victor*, is an impressive leap forward to the spare and controlled narrative skills that mark his later novels. Victor is a teenager forced by a domineering father to care for his dying grandmother on a remote island in Mobile Bay during World War II. The first third of the novel promises a carefully considered coming-of-age story as Victor cares for his grandmother and deals with his brutally abusive father. However, once Victor escapes his father and hooks up with Butch, an outlaw island boy, the novel takes an abrupt turn into the territory of boys' adventure novels. Victor and Butch are very much Tom Sawyer and Huck Finn, with the former's romanticized notions of grand adventure and the latter's refusal to be "civilized," but they are also the Hardy Boys as they become embroiled in a dangerous escapade featuring Nazi spies, submarines, and a variety of explosions. However, *V for Victor* is not a simple adventure story. Victor and Butch operate within the shadow of dysfunctional families and an unforgiving landscape; by the end of the novel, Victor is cured of his romantic longings.

In a 1994 interview, Childress stated that his third novel, *Tender*, was written as a novel about Elvis Presley but then rewritten because of the publisher's lawyers' fears of legal challenges from the Presley estate. The result is a roman a clef whose protagonist, Leroy Kirby of Tupelo, Mississippi, rises to unprecedented fame as a rock and roll singer in the 1950s. Childress's longest novel to date is also his most tightly focused, as Kirby's life and career undergo their inevitable rise and fall. The very familiarity of the Presley story enables Childress to spend valuable time with his characters. Kirby's conflicted relationship with his overbearing mother and ineffectual father is memorably detailed, and his ongoing conversation with his dead twin brother yields additional insights into Kirby's character while effectively displaying Childress's tendency toward the fantastic. Additionally, Childress displays both great knowledge of the popular music scene of the 1950s and uncanny insight into the dynamics of fame and the overpowering need of the Leroy Kirbys of the world to not merely rise above their circumstances, but utterly transcend them.

Although quite different in terms of plot and tone from Childress's other novels, *Crazy in Alabama*, ties in closely to many aspects of the author's earlier books. Like Victor, young Peejoe suspects there must be something beyond the confines of south Alabama; like Leroy Kirby, Peejoe's aunt Lucille will settle for nothing less than show business stardom as an escape from the dismal life of a rural housewife. However, Peejoe's adventure of initiation occurs when he is caught up in the struggles and tragedies of the civil rights movement, while Lucille makes her escape by murdering her oppressive husband and hitting the road for Hollywood, where she realizes her dream of fame with an appearance on the television show *The Beverly Hillbillies.*

It is easy to see why *Crazy in Alabama* is Childress's most commercially successful novel to date. In Peejoe's story, Childress finally touches base with his townspeople Lee and Capote through a richly evocative portrait of a small Alabama town and an unflinching examination of racism within that town. In Lucille's story, Childress shows a genuine gift for black comedy as Lucille does whatever is necessary to get what she wants, and reaffirms his penchant for the fantastic as Lucille carries on an ongoing conversation with her husband's severed head, which she carries with her in a sealed Tupperware bowl. Childress makes his case for linking the two stories in a single comment from Lucille: ''Like them [African-Americans], she had done something radical to set herself free.'' Whether such a connection is reasonable or justified is open to debate.

In his most recent novel, *Gone for Good*, Childress continues his examination of the risk of celebrity while offering his most overt fantasy since *A World Made of Fire*. When 1970s folk-rock star Ben ''Superman'' Willis crashes his plane on an island off the coast of Central America, he finds himself in a paradise that is, on the one hand, a refuge for celebrities who have ''disappeared'' from the world (Marilyn Monroe, Jimmy Hoffa), and, on the other hand, a kind of prison run by a mysterious figure known as ''the Magician'' and from which there is no escape. As Willis acclimates to his life on the island and ponders his life's mistakes and his ambivalence about his own fame, he becomes privy to some of the island's magic (at one point, ''Superman'' literally flies) and leads the island's natives in a revolt against the Magician. Back in the ''real'' world, Willis's teenaged son makes a dangerous journey to find his lost father. The novel is almost a summary of Childress's ongoing concerns. Once again, a young man comes of age by placing himself in danger; once again, Childress conveys the glories and pitfalls of show business performance in extraordinarily convincing detail; once again, fantastic events suggest that, as Willis realizes, ''The things we think we know are just stories we have been told. They are not necessarily true.'' Like the earlier *V for Victor*, *Gone for Good* moves from introspection to violent action, in this case with somewhat mixed results; the frantic combat and confrontation in the last third of the novel is less satisfying than the novel's earlier, quieter surreal speculations.

From his second novel on, Mark Childress has proven to be one of the best pure storytellers of his generation. His books have sometimes displayed a problematic tendency toward trying to fit two dissimilar stories into a single novel; in this regard, *Tender* is arguably his most successfully realized work to date. However, Childress remains a tremendously talented writer who deserves great praise for his willingness to take chances and his insistence on challenging the expectations many readers bring to the work of Southern writers. We may hope that Childress, still in his early forties, will continue to entertain and challenge us for many books to come.

—F. Brett Cox

CHINODYA, Shimmer

Nationality: Zimbabwean. **Born:** Gweru, Zimbabwe, 30 May 1957. **Education:** University of Zimbabwe, B.A. (honors) in English 1979; University of Iowa, M.A. in creative writing 1985. **Family:** Married; two daughters and one son. **Career:** High school teacher, 1981–81; curriculum developer, 1983–87; editor, publisher and author, 1988–94; Dana Visiting Professor of creative writing, St. Lawrence University, 1995–96. **Awards:** Commonwealth Writers prize (African region), 1990, for *Harvest of Thorns;* Zimbabwe Writers award, 1990; Ragdale fellowship, Lake Forest, 1993. **Address:** 39 Lorraine Drive, Bluff Hill, P.O. Mabelreign, Harare, Zimbabwe.

Publications

Novels

Dew in the Morning. Gweru, Zimbabwe, Mambo Press, 1982.
Farai's Girls. Harare, Zimbabwe, College Press, 1984.
Child of War. Harare, Zimbabwe, College Press, n.d.
Harvest of Thorns. Harare, Zimbabwe, Baobab, 1989; Portsmouth, New Hampshire, Heinemann, 1991.

Short Stories

Can We Talk, and Other Stories. Harare, Zimbabwe, Baobab Books, 1998.

Other

Classroom Plays for Primary Schools. Harare, Longman Zimbabwe, 1986.
Traditional Tales of Zimbabwe, Books 1–6. Harare, Longman Zimbabwe, 1989.
Poems for Primary Schools. Harare, Longman Zimbabwe, 1990.

*

Shimmer Chinodya comments:

Read voraciously while still young!

* * *

> This was your initiation on a rock, in the forests of hoary mountains, with a girl who smelt of blue soap and beans and gunpowder, who wore denims and boots and carried a bazooka on her back; a girl who cut her hair short like a boy and whose fingers were stone-stiff from hauling crates of ammo. You were surprised when she said ''Thank you, I needed it,'' never having thought a woman could say that and you tried to say something nice back, wondering if she knew this was your first time.... You had left her there with your seed in her and would she have your child? ... And what if she had your child? Would she deliver here in the camp? Would she carry the child in a strap together with her bazooka? Would the child look like you?

Thus muses Benjamin Tichafa, a.k.a. Pasi NemaSellout, the central character of Shimmer Chinodya's *Harvest of Thorns,* after he loses his virginity to a female comrade in a guerrilla camp. The passage encapsulates the central markers of Chinodya's writing: his concern for children, also demonstrated by his children's works; his profound humanism; and his sharp awareness that the personal and specific make up the broad political picture, giving it both its tragedy and its hope.

Critics have referred to *Harvest of Thorns* as a ''coming-of-age'' story; others emphasize its politics, reading it as a tale of Zimbabwe's fight for independence. It is these, and more. Chinodya demonstrates that unless people die—as some do, here—they must come of age, inescapably. What that means will be determined by idiosyncratic politics, in conjunction with the oral communication and awareness of community that alone can, in this novel, preserve humanity. Those communal values shape the novel's structure and content, imbuing it with a revolutionary vision belied by its straightforward and engaging style. Postmodern fireworks of language do not interrupt the story here; no narrator self-importantly trumpets about the difficulties of writing. Instead, we are caught up in the story of a young man—but one told in a way not imagined by the traditional bildungsroman.

Harvest of Thorns opens with Benjamin's return to his mother and the brother he accidentally crippled in childhood. After a few days of welcome, tensions grow, and his mother tells Benjamin's young foreign wife, whom he has brought home, that she must know who Benjamin truly is. Intriguingly, however, to show who Benjamin is requires circling into the past—this young man, as all of us, does not come from a vacuum. So, Chinodya recounts the youth of Shamiso, Benjamin's mother. We watch her attract the intentions of Clopas Tichafa, we see their courtship and wedding, and we follow their difficulty conceiving a child—which leads them to consult a doctor and a witch doctor and to attribute their final success to the Church of the Holy Spirit.

This early sequence shows the range of options to which people will turn in their quests. Beliefs, whether gained accidentally or not, determine the family structures in which children are brought up and in turn shape their reactions and their future paths. Through a wholly unpredictable path, his fanatical religious upbringing leads Benjamin to become the guerrilla Pasi NemaSellout.

Chinodya's treatment of the struggle again subverts expectations; battles and atrocities occur but are not central. Rather than glorifying young people fighting for a cause, Chinodya's narrative voice becomes distanced, describing day-to-day concerns. The tedium of finding food, staying dry, and getting enough sleep interweaves with struggles against the group's leader and telling stories around fires to explain the struggle to villagers. But the cause, even death, attract less thought than another interest: sex. Flirtation ends in a sudden, deadly raid by the opposing troops; or in tribal custom and virginity; or in orders to decamp.

Benjamin does grow up: by returning home, reversing the blind movement outward that led him to fight. The struggle, won at a heavy cost, has changed little in everyday life. When Benjamin embraces his place as a son, a brother, a husband, and a father, the novel questions the obstacles he had to overcome. Perhaps, Chinodya suggests, fewer causes and greater human compassion—between men and women, parents and children, neighbors and outsiders—offers the only hope for true political change.

—Victoria Carchidi

CHUTE, Carolyn

Nationality: American. **Born:** Born Carolyn Penny in Portland, Maine, 14 June 1947. **Education:** Attended University of Southern Maine, 1972–78. **Family:** Married 1) James Hawkes in 1963 (divorced 1972); 2) Michael Chute in 1978; one daughter (one son, deceased). **Career:** Variously professions, including waitress, chicken factory worker, hospital floor scrubber, shoe factory worker, potato farm worker, tutor, canvasser, teacher, social worker, and school bus driver, 1970s–1980s; part-time suburban correspondent, *Portland Evening Express,* Portland, Maine, 1976–81; instructor in creative writing, University of Southern Maine, Portland, 1985. Lives in Parsonsfield, Maine. **Awards:** First prize for fiction, Green Mountain Workshop, Johnson, Vermont, 1977. **Agent:** Jane Gelfman, John Farquharson, Ltd., 250 West 57th Street, Suite 1914, New York, New York 10107, U.S.A.

Publications

Novels

The Beans of Egypt, Maine. New York, Ticknor & Fields, 1985; revised edition published as *The Beans of Egypt, Maine: The Finished Version,* San Diego, Harcourt Brace, 1995.
Letourneau's Used Auto Parts. New York, Ticknor & Fields, 1988.
Merry Men. New York, Harcourt Brace, 1994.
Snow Man. New York, Harcourt Brace, 1999.

Other

Up River: The Story of a Maine Fishing Community (nonfiction, with Olive Pierce). Hanover, New Hampshire, University Press of New England, 1996.
Contributor, *Inside Vacationland: New Fiction from the Real Maine,* edited by Mark Melnicove. South Harpswell, Maine, Dog Ear Press, 1985.
Contributor, *I Was Content and Not Content: The Story of Linda Lord and the Closing of Penobscot Poultry,* by Cedric N. Chatterley and Alicia J. Rouverol. Carbondale, Southern Illinois University Press, 2000.

* * *

With the publication of her 1985 breakthrough novel *The Beans of Egypt, Maine*, Carolyn Chute's literary voice was hailed as almost primeval, an immaculately conceived mouthpiece for Maine's rural white underclass. Chute's three subsequent novels have marked her as an uneven literary power—with *Snow Man* almost universally denounced—but as a major figure, nevertheless. Originality of both subject and tone is perhaps Chute's greatest strength. The Bean family and their literary brethren are landed white trash whose land may be a dump or a swamp, and their house a trailer, and yet they retain the kind of permanence and sustainability that we associate with New England's blue-blooded dynasties. This resilience is Chute's most optimistic message amidst her portraits of people whose lives provide a more obvious opportunity for despair.

Chute's fictional Egypt, Maine, the setting of *The Beans* and *Letourneau's Used Auto Parts* is not a consumer culture per se so much as it is a culture of worthless goods that seems all-consuming. Her novels are narratives of failure by middle-class standards, but her characters seem indifferent to their own cultural entrapment; they live their lives fervidly and giddily, for the most part disinterested in middle-class ''family values'' such as attentive parenting, education, privacy, cleanliness, and good nutrition. Chute depicts an immobile class system that contrasts vividly to the sprawling and rambunctious Beans and their neighbors. These are messy lives and the telling of them is messy too, sometimes hard to follow; characters ''gasp'' and ''choke'' and ''sputter'' their words but seldom simply talk, and the twists and gaps and abrupt narrative shifts structurally replicate Chute's characters' disordered lives.

Throughout her novels sex is a craven and unromantic aspect of everyday life, and sexual relations are foretold with the grim inevitability of Greek drama. Incest and rape are commonplaces, denoted without the accompanying moral assertion that conventionally accompany these acts as literary themes. In her early novels Chute recalls Dorothy Allison's probing of the imprisoning forces of poverty and pregnancy, but does not share Allison's political and feminist agenda. Instead, Chute's portrayal of impoverished families lacks the framing devices of anger, sympathy, or outrage.

The Beans of Egypt, Maine, published after Chute borrowed the money to send the manuscript to a New York editor, tells the story of Earlene Pomerleau. Earlene's childhood fascination with the neighboring Bean clan foretells her eventual marriage to the violent Beal Bean. This marriage is difficult not to interpret as the book's tragic turning point, even though Chute avoids framing this, and other abusive couplings, with a critical eye. Instead, Earlene's decision to marry Beal is represented as the inescapable destiny of a girl, even a smart girl, growing up in Egypt, Maine. But the absence of a judgmental voice does seem amiss when precocious Earlene joins the ranks of always pregnant and often abused Bean mothers, wives, and mistresses. Despite Chute's dispassionate treatment of such lives, it is hard not to see Earlene's fall from spunk and wit to toil and degradation as a tragedy, even if doing so is to be influenced by the very middle-class values that Chute so determinedly resists.

Chute's anger against the establishment, variously represented by government workers, the middle and upper classes in general, and politicians, becomes more distinct with each novel she writes. *Letourneau's Used Auto Parts* maintains the same buoyant spirit as *The Beans*, and the title's reference to devalued goods reflects the novel's characters. They are themselves cheerfully recycled goods, in and out of marriages, haphazardly begetting and raising children, living amongst rummage sale bargains, crumbling houses, and conversations disrupted by protests and mumbles. But the entrance into this novel of the ''code man,'' a census government worker who tries to regulate Lucien Letourneau's makeshift family (complete with illegitimate children, evicted neighbors, and a homeless old woman) establishes a theme even more overt in Chute's later novels: the disciplinary evil of the state.

Chute's most recent two novels are increasingly hostile in tone and her portrait of an unjust ruling class more reactionary than believable. In *Merry Men* Lloyd Barrington is a modern-day Robin Hood who has an affair with wealthy and hypocritical Gwen Curry Doyle, widow of a capitalist ''devil'' and Chute's scapegoat for the abuses and absurdities of capitalism. Lloyd is not one of Chute's typically down-and-out Maine workers—he's a poet and a college graduate, so his decision to be a gravedigger is exactly that—a decision that heroically marks his rejection of middle-class conventionality. Nothing and no one can make Lloyd anything but a kind of saint in gravedigger's clothing, and Chute's message is that ''real'' men can escape the pressures of corporate and soulless society and follow an independent, even consciously ignoble, path.

Snow Man, published in 1998, was almost routinely dismissed. Critics complained that the ''activist has silenced the novelist'' in this treatment of bourgeois hypocrisy. Robert Drummond, a construction-worker/militia man from Maine assassinates a U.S. senator and we are asked to condone this murder on the grounds that the senator was a corporate lackey. Following the murder, Drummond seduces the senator's daughter, a poorly drawn caricature of a Radcliffe-educated feminist/professor, and then he seduces her mother. What makes *Snow Man* disappointing is Chute's departure from what she does best: illustrate the lives of Maine's poor with humor, ingenuity, and a narrative voice largely indifferent to precedent.

Chute has said that it is not ''the place of fiction to make judgments—to prescribe changes,'' which confirms the dispassionate tone of *The Beans of Egypt, Maine* and *Letourneau's Used Auto Parts*. But in *Merry Men* and *Snow Man* Chute does appear to be writing prescriptively, demarcating characters as good and bad depending on their class association. At times the spiritedness of her characters compensates for the abuses they suffer. At other times, however, their own complicity in their damaged lives is troubling, and the placement of blame on a weakly drawn middle- and upper-class establishment is reductive.

What is so surprising about Chute's better novels is that the lives of her Egypt-dwellers manage to be messily unpredictable and overdetermined by the grim yoke of poverty at the same time. Chute's slight of hand, her ability to illustrate a culture paradoxically composed of vitality and defeat, is truly original. At her strongest Chute writes, or rather sounds, like no one else: her dialogue and descriptions are rendered with the nuances and rhythms of real conversations and all of their staccato incongruities. To Lucien Letourneau, the almost god-like patriarch of *Letourneau's Used Auto Parts*, ''everything is a miracle,'' and in Chute's improbable universe, we can begin to see his point. For despite its cruelty, even poverty is not without its own inchoate beauty.

—Tabitha Sparks

CISNEROS, Sandra

Nationality: American. **Born:** Chicago, Illinois, 20 December 1954. **Education:** Loyola University, B.A. 1976; University of Iowa, M.F.A. 1978. **Career:** Teacher, Latino Youth Alternative High School, Chicago, Illinois, 1978–80; college recruiter and counselor for minority students, Loyola University, Chicago, Illinois, 1981–82; artist-in-residence, Foundation Michael Karolyi, Vence, France, 1983; literature director, Guadalupe Cultural Arts Center, San Antonio, Texas, 1984–85; guest professor, California State University, Chico, 1987–88, University of California, Berkeley, 1988, University of California, Irvine, 1990, University of Michigan, Ann Arbor, 1990, University of New Mexico, Albuquerque, 1991. **Awards:** National Endowment for the Arts fellow, 1982, 1988; American Book Award (Before Columbus Foundation), 1985; Paisano Dobie fellowship, 1986; first and second proize, Segundo Concurso Nacional del Cuento Chicano (University of Arizona); Lannan Foundation Literary Award, 1991; H.D.L., State University of New York at Purchase, 1993; MacArthur fellow, 1995. **Agent:** Susan Bergholz Literary Services, 17 West 10th Street, Suite 5, New York, New York 10011, U.S.A. **Address:** Alfred A. Knopf Books, 201 East 50th Street, New York, New York 10022, U.S.A.

PUBLICATIONS

Novels

The House on Mango Street. Houston, Texas, Arte Publico Press, 1984.

Short Stories

Woman Hollering Creek and Other Stories. New York, Random House, 1991.

Poetry

Bad Boys. Mango Publications, 1980.
My Wicked, Wicked Ways. Bloomington, Indiana, Third Woman Press, 1987.
Loose Woman. New York, Knopf, 1994.

Other

Foreword, *Camellia Street* by Merco Rodoreda, translated by David H. Rosenthal. Saint Paul, Minnesota, Graywolf Press, 1993.
Hairs: Pelitos (juvenile, bilingual), translated from the English by Liliana Valenzuela, illustrated by Terry Ybanez, New York, Knopf, 1994.
Introduction, *My First Book of Proverbs/Mi primer libro de dichos* by Ralfka Gonzalez and Ana Ruiz. Emeryville, California, Children's Book Press, 1995.
Foreword, *Holler If You Hear Me: The Education of a Teacher and His Students* by Gregory Michie. New York, Teachers College Press, 1999.
Contributor, *Daughters of the Fifth Sun: A Collection of Latin Fiction and Poetry,* edited by Bryce Milligan, et al. New York, Riverhead, 1995.
Contributor, *Chicken Soup for the Teenage Soul: 101 Stories of Life, Love and Learning,* edited by Jack Canfield, et al. Health Communications, 1997.
Contributor, *Leaning into the Wind: Women Write from the Heart of the West,* edited by Linda M. Hasselstrom, et al. Boston, Houghton Mifflin, 1997.
Contributor, *A Book of Poems,* edited by Mark Warren. San Francisco, M. Warren, 1998.
Contributor, *Growing Up Ethnic in America: Contemporary Fiction about Learning to Be American,* edited by Maria Mazziotti Gillan and Jennifer Gillan. New York, Penguin, 1999.
Contributor, *Bearing Life: Women's Writings on Childlessness,* edited by Rochelle Ratner. Consortium, 2000.

*

Critical Studies: *Interviews with Writers of the Post-Colonial World,* conducted and edited by Feroza Jussawalla and Reed Way Dasenbrock, Jackson, University Press of Mississippi, 1992; *Having Our Way: Women Rewriting Tradition in Twentieth-Century America,* edited by Harriett Pollack, Lewisburg, Pennsylvania, Bucknell University Press, 1995; *Sandra Cisneros' The House on Mango Street* by Elizabeth L. Chesla, Piscataway, New Jersey, Research & Educational Association, 1996; *Sandra Cisneros: Latina Writer and Activist* by Caryn Mirriam-Goldberg, Springfield, New Jersey, Enslow, 1998.

* * *

Chicana feminist, poet, and novelist, Sandra Cisneros, has been described most recently as "frankly erotic" (*New York Daily News*) and as a writer "whose literary voice is a deluge of playfulness, naughtiness, heartbreak, and triumph" (*The Miami Herald*). On the cover of her latest volume of poetry, *Loose Woman, Time* magazine describes her as "a unique feminist voice that is at once frank, saucy, realistic, audacious." Cisneros would likely agree with her critics—for she, herself, rounds out this R-rated collection with a fierce and powerful self-assessment: "I'm Bitch. Beast. Macha." But to understand the resonating irony of such a statement—to hear at once the laughter and the rage in Cisneros's wanton self-stereotyping—we need to return to the innocent world of *Mango Street*, the fictional space where Cisneros first became a writer.

Her first novel, and perhaps most widely read work to date, *The House on Mango Street* tells the heartwarming story of Esperanza Cordero, the young Chicana heroine who, like Cisneros herself, "comes of age" in a Chicago barrio, despite obstacles imposed by racism, classism, and sexism. A collection of forty-four seemingly unrelated vignettes, the novel's style may appear simplistic and choppy, but Esperanza's character is the center of consciousness that provides both coherence and perspective from chapter to chapter. Because her interactions with relatives and friends help Esperanza to define her goals, critics are right to say she is at once dependent on and critical of the Chicano community; like Cisneros herself, Esperanza embraces her culture warmly, but criticizes gender injustices within it. In this sense, as Julian Olivares points out, Cisneros "breaks the paradigm of the traditional female bildungsroman"—where female characters, unlike their male counterparts, are typically portrayed as seeking solely marriage and motherhood, resulting in a restriction or loss of freedom. After observing her mother's lifetime of sacrifices and her friends' physical and sexual abuse at the hands of men, Esperanza instead desires to leave the barrio, have a house of her own, and become a writer. These goals are not intended merely for her own self-improvement, however, but to educate others—especially the women—in her community as well.

Many critics have drawn obvious parallels between Cisneros's life and that of Esperanza in *Mango Street*: both have a Mexican father and a Mexican-American mother, and thereby straddle two cultures; both desire to leave the barrio to become writers; both eventually find "a home in the heart"—which translates to the ability to succeed individually (to call her "home" her "self"), and collectively on behalf of the community (to reinvent certain cultural stereotypes for all Chicanos). In personal interviews, Cisneros confided that it was not until she took graduate-level writing workshops with predominantly white, wealthy classmates, that she began tapping into her "difference" in order to create unique writing material; thus, upon remembering and sketching characters and events from her impoverished childhood, Cisneros at last developed her own voice as a writer—one she had previously suppressed and sacrificed because there were no Chicano/a models in her classes to emulate. Similarly, this budding decisiveness applies to her character, Esperanza, as well. For example, Cisneros describes *Mango Street* as "a very political work ... about a woman in her twenties coming to her political consciousness as a feminist woman of color.'' Surely, this statement describes Cisneros's own experience, as well as Esperanza's.

One cultural stereotype that Cisneros attempts to reinvent is the portrayal of women in Chicano literature, which only reaffirms patriarchal values and the unrealistic, if not abusive, treatment of Chicanas. In an interview, Cisneros explains how the two role models in Mexican culture—la Virgen de Guadalupe y la Malinche—are difficult for women to negotiate. They signify the extremes of saint and traitor, respectively, and there are no ''in-betweens.'' Women are often sanctified or vilified, but rarely are they portrayed as ordinary or acceptable; therefore, their natural sexuality—and even their beauty—are often punished by protective fathers and brothers.

If *The House on Mango Street* paved the way for Cisneros's coming-into-feminist-consciousness, then her first volume of poetry, *My Wicked, Wicked Ways* took that new self-awareness one step further in its confrontation of a taboo subject in Chicano culture: a woman's (liberal) sexuality. The title of the collection, therefore, is simply ironic: while her culture may view her as ''wicked''—she writes about choosing not to marry, traveling abroad on her own, and sleeping with various men—for Cisneros, the term does not mean ''evil,'' but free; her poetry abounds in positive personal choices. The title thus pokes fun at the stereotypical notion that she is (wrongly) considered ''wicked'' by her culture for merely articulating her own story in her poems.

In her collection of short fiction *Woman Hollering Creek*, Cisneros returns to many of the same coming-of-age themes explored in *Mango Street*—pre-teen anxiety, sibling relationships in a culture where girls are less valued than boys, loss of virginity and its shameful consequences, and identity conflicts from living on both sides of the Mexican border. The stories represent a range of authorial voices—from young girls to housewives—who struggle with gender inequality in their culture and their lives. Perhaps the character that best bridges the adolescent Esperanza of *Mango Street* and the mature, confident macha of Cisneros's ''Loose Woman'' poem, is the young bride, Cleofilas, the protagonist of the eponymous story, ''Woman Hollering Creek.'' Based on the myth of the Llorona legend about a poor Mexican woman who drowned her children and died of grief after her husband abandoned her for another woman, Cisneros's story reinvents the tragic tale when Cleofilas is similarly victimized by an abusive husband and escapes a life of silent suffering in exchange for freedom across the border. At the end of the story, Cleofilas leaves her husband and crosses the arroyo to begin her own life, thus replacing the legendary wail of La Llorona with her own ''ribbon of laughter, like water.''

If we now return to the end of the 1994 collection *Loose Woman*, to Cisneros's brazen declaration, ''I'm a macha, hell on wheels,'' we understand that her tone is playful, but her message quite serious. Any writer who publicly implores publishers to print the work of younger Chicanas, as Cisneros does, is not truly ''bad'' as this poem implies. Once again, Cisneros is merely redefining stereotypical labels. In this collection, after supporting herself by her writing for ten years and living as ''nobody's wife and nobody's mother'' in a house of her own, Cisneros asserts her most confident identity—one that is comfortable with the contradictions of living in two cultures. In an interview, Cisneros claimed to be ''reinventing the word 'loose.''' It no longer need mean promiscuous, but rather, free. ''I really feel that I'm the loose,'' she said, ''and I've cut free from a lot of things that anchored me.'' While Cisneros has described her *Wicked Ways* (writing) days as ''wandering in the desert,'' she calls her recent collection, *Loose Woman*, a celebration of the home in her heart. Currently, Cisneros lives in San Antonio, Texas, and is working on another novel called ''Carmelito.''

—Susan E. Cushman

CLARKE, Arthur C(harles)

Nationality: British. **Born:** Minehead, Somerset, 16 December 1917. **Education:** Huish's Grammar School, Taunton, Somerset, 1927–36; King's College, London, 1946–48, B.Sc. (honours) in physics and mathematics 1948. **Military Service:** Flight Lieutenant in the Royal Air Force, 1941–46; served as Radar Instructor, and Technical Officer on the first Ground Controlled Approach radar; originated proposal for use of satellites for communications, 1945. **Family:** Married Marilyn Mayfield in 1954 (divorced 1964). **Career:** Assistant auditor, Exchequer and Audit Department, London, 1936–41; assistant editor, *Physics Abstracts,* London, 1949–50; since 1954, engaged in underwater exploration and photography of the Great Barrier Reef of Australia and the coast of Sri Lanka. Director, Rocket Publishing, London, Underwater Safaris, Colombo, and the Spaceward Corporation, New York. Has made numerous radio and television appearances (most recently as presenter of the television series *Arthur C. Clarke's Mysterious World,* 1980, and *World of Strange Powers,* 1985), and has lectured widely in Britain and the United States; commentator, for CBS-TV, on lunar flights of Apollo 11, 12 and 15; Vikram Sarabhai Professor, Physical Research Laboratory, Ahmedabad, India, 1980. **Awards:** International Fantasy award, 1952; Hugo award, 1956, 1969 (for screenplay), 1974, 1980; Unesco Kalinga prize, 1961; Boys' Clubs of America award, 1961; Franklin Institute Ballantine medal, 1963; Aviation-Space Writers Association Ball award, 1965; American Association for the Advancement of Science-Westinghouse Science Writing award, 1969; *Playboy* award, 1971; Nebula award, 1972, 1973, 1979; Jupiter award, 1973; John W. Campbell Memorial award, 1974; American Institute of Aeronautics and Astronautics award, 1974; Boston Museum of Science Washburn award, 1977; Marconi fellowship, 1982; Science Fiction Writers of America Grand Master award, 1986; Vidya Jyothi medal, 1986; International Science Policy Foundation medal, 1992; Lord Perry award, 1992; Presidential Award, University of Illinois, 1997. D.Sc.: Beaver College, Glenside, Pennsylvania, 1971. D.Litt.: University of Liverpool, 1995; University of Hong Kong, 1996. Chair, British Interplanetary Society, 1946–47, 1950–53. Guest of Honor, World Science Fiction Convention, 1956. Fellow, Royal Astronomical Society; Fellow, King's College, London, 1977; Chancellor, University of Moratuwa, Sri Lanka, since 1979. C.B.E. (Commander, Order of the British Empire), 1989; knighted, 1998. European satellite, launched in April 2000, named after Clarke in recognition of his contribution to the development of global communication networks.**Agent:** David Higham Associates Ltd., 5–8 Lower John Street, London W1R 4HA, England; or, Scouil, Chichak, Galen Literary Agency, 381 Park Avenue, New York, New York 10016, U.S.A. **Address:** 25 Barnes Place, Colombo 7, Sri Lanka; or, Dene Court, Bishop's Lydeard, Taunton, Somerset TA4 3LT, England.

Publications

Novels

Prelude to Space. New York, Galaxy, 1951; London, Sidgwick and Jackson, 1953; as *Master of Space,* New York, Lancer 1961; as *The Space Dreamers,* Lancer, 1969.

The Sands of Mars. London, Sidgwick and Jackson, 1951; New York, Gnome Press, 1952.

Against the Fall of Night. New York, Gnome Press, 1953; revised edition, as *The City and the Stars,* London, Muller, and New York, Harcourt Brace, 1956.

Childhood's End. New York, Ballantine, 1953; London, Sidgwick and Jackson, 1954.

Earthlight. London, Muller, and New York, Ballantine, 1955, 1998.

The Deep Range. New York, Harcourt Brace, and London, Muller, 1957.

Across the Sea of Stars (omnibus). New York, Harcourt Brace, 1959.

A Fall of Moondust. London, Gollancz, and New York, Harcourt Brace, 1961.

From the Oceans, From the Stars (omnibus). New York, Harcourt Brace, 1962.

Glide Path. New York, Harcourt Brace, 1963; London, Sidgwick and Jackson, 1969.

An Arthur C. Clarke Omnibus [and *Second Omnibus*]. London, Sidgwick and Jackson, 2 vols., 1965–68.

Prelude to Mars (omnibus). New York, Harcourt Brace, 1965.

2001: A Space Odyssey (novelization of screenplay), with Stanley Kubrick. New York, New American Library, and London, Hutchinson, 1968; with a new introduction, Thorndike, Maine, G. K. Hall, 1994.

The Lion of Comarre, and Against the Fall of Night. New York, Harcourt Brace, 1968; London, Gollancz, 1970.

Rendezvous with Rama. London, Gollancz, and New York, Harcourt Brace, 1973.

Imperial Earth. London, Gollancz, 1975; revised edition, New York, Harcourt Brace, 1976.

The Fountains of Paradise. London, Gollancz, and New York, Harcourt Brace, 1979.

2010: Odyssey Two. New York, Ballantine, and London, Granada, 1982.

The Songs of Distant Earth. London, Grafton, and New York, Ballantine, 1986.

2061: Odyssey Three. New York, Ballantine, and London, Grafton, 1988.

Cradle, with Gentry Lee. London, Gollancz, and New York, Warner, 1988.

Rama II, with Gentry Lee. London, Gollancz, and New York, Bantam, 1989.

Beyond the Fall of Night, with Gregory Benford. New York, Putnam, 1990; with *Against the Fall of Night,* London, Gollancz, 1991.

The Ghost from the Grand Banks. New York, Bantam, and London, Gollancz, 1990.

The Garden of Rama, with Gentry Lee. London, Gollancz, and New York, Bantam, 1991.

Rama Revealed, with Gentry Lee . London, Gollancz, and New York, Bantam, 1993.

The Hammer of God. London, Gollancz, and New York, Bantam, 1993.

Richter 10, with Mike McQuay. New York, Bantam Books, 1996.

3001: The Final Odyssey. New York, Ballantine Books, 1997.

The Trigger, with Michael Kube-McDowell. New York, Bantam Books, 1999.

The Light of Other Days, with Stephen Baxter. New York, Tor, 2000.

Short Stories

Expedition to Earth. New York, Ballantine, 1953; London, Sidgwick and Jackson, 1954; New York, Ballantine, 1998.

Reach for Tomorrow. New York, Ballantine, 1956; London, Gollancz, 1962; New York, Ballantine, 1998.

Tales from the White Hart. New York, Ballantine, 1957; London, Sidgwick and Jackson, 1972; New York, Ballantine, 1998.

The Other Side of the Sky. New York, Harcourt Brace, 1958; London, Gollancz, 1961.

Tales of Ten Worlds. New York, Harcourt Brace, 1962; London, Gollancz, 1963.

The Nine Billion Names of God: The Best Short Stories of Arthur C. Clarke. New York, Harcourt Brace, 1967.

The Wind from the Sun: Stories of the Space Age. New York, Harcourt Brace, and London, Gollancz, 1972.

Of Time and Stars: The Worlds of Arthur C. Clarke. London, Gollancz, 1972.

The Best of Arthur C. Clarke 1937–1971, edited by Angus Wells. London Sidgwick and Jackson, 1973.

The Sentinel. New York, Berkley, 1983; London, Panther, 1985.

A Meeting with Medusa, with *Green Mars,* by Kim Stanley Robinson. New York, Tor, 1988.

Tales from Planet Earth. London, Century, 1989; New York, Bantam, 1990.

Plays

Screenplay: *2001: A Space Odyssey,* with Stanley Kubrick, 1968.

Other

Interplanetary Flight: An Introduction to Astronautics. London, Temple Press, 1950; New York, Harper, 1951; revised edition, 1960.

The Exploration of Space. London, Temple Press, and New York, Harper, 1951; revised edition, 1959.

Islands in the Sky (for children). London, Sidgwick and Jackson, and Philadelphia, Winston, 1952.

The Young Traveller in Space (for children). London, Phoenix House, 1954; as *Going into Space,* New York, Harper, 1954; as *The Scottie Book of Space Travel,* London, Transworld, 1957; revised edition, with Robert Silverberg, as *Into Space,* New York, Harper, 1971.

The Exploration of the Moon. London, Muller, 1954; New York, Harper, 1955.

The Coast of Coral. London, Muller, and New York, Harper, 1956.

The Making of a Moon: The Story of the Earth Satellite Program. London, Muller, and New York, Harper, 1957; revised edition, Harper, 1958.

The Reefs of Taprobane: Underwater Adventures Around Ceylon. London, Muller, and New York, Harper, 1957.

Voice Across the Sea. London, Muller, 1958; New York, Harper, 1959; revised edition, London, Mitchell Beazley, and Harper, 1974.
Boy Beneath the Sea (for children). New York, Harper, 1958.
The Challenge of the Spaceship: Previews of Tomorrow's World. New York, Harper, 1959; London, Muller, 1960.
The First Five Fathoms: A Guide to Underwater Adventure. New York, Harper, 1960.
The Challenge of the Sea. New York, Holt Rinehart, 1960; London, Muller, 1961.
Indian Ocean Adventure. New York, Harper, 1961; London, Barker, 1962.
Profiles of the Future: An Enquiry into the Limits of the Possible. London, Gollancz, 1962; New York, Harper, 1963; revised edition, Harper, 1973; Gollancz, 1974, 1982; New York, Holt Rinehart, 1984.
Dolphin Island (for children). New York, Holt Rinehart, and London, Gollancz, 1963.
The Treasure of the Great Reef. London, Barker, and New York, Harper, 1964; revised edition, New York, Ballantine, 1974.
Indian Ocean Treasure, with Mike Wilson. New York, Harper, 1964; London, Sidgwick and Jackson, 1972.
Man and Space, with the editors of *Life.* New York, Time, 1964.
Voices from the Sky: Previews of the Coming Space Age. New York, Harper, 1965; London, Gollancz, 1966.
The Promise of Space. New York, Harper, and London, Hodder and Stoughton, 1968.
First on the Moon, with the astronauts. London, Joseph, and Boston, Little Brown, 1970.
Report on the Planet Three and Other Speculations. London, Gollancz, and New York, Harper, 1972.
The Lost Worlds of 2001. New York, New American Library, and London, Sidgwick and Jackson, 1972.
Beyond Jupiter: The Worlds of Tomorrow, with Chesley Bonestell. Boston, Little Brown, 1972.
Technology and the Frontiers of Knowledge (lectures), with others. New York, Doubleday, 1973.
The View from Serendip (on Sri Lanka). New York, Random House, 1977; London, Gollancz, 1978.
1984: Spring: A Choice of Futures. New York, Ballantine, and London, Granada, 1984.
Ascent to Orbit: A Scientific Autobiography: The Technical Writings of Arthur C. Clarke. New York and Chichester, Sussex, Wiley, 1984.
The Odyssey File, with Peter Hyams. New York, Ballantine, and London, Granada, 1985.
Astounding Days: A Science-Fictional Autobiography. London, Gollancz, 1989; New York, Bantam, 1990.
How the World Was One: Beyond the Global Village. London, Gollancz, and New York, Bantam, 1992.
By Space Possessed: Essays on the Exploration of Space. London, Gollancz, 1993.
The Snows of Olympus: A Garden on Mars. London, Gollancz, 1994.
Greetings, Carbon-Based Bipeds!: Collected Essays, 1934–1998, edited by Ian T. Macauley. New York, St. Martin's Press, 1999.
Editor, *Time Probe: Sciences in Science Fiction.* New York, Delacorte Press, 1966; London, Gollancz, 1967.
Editor, *The Coming of the Space Age: Famous Accounts of Man's Probing of the Universe.* London, Gollancz, and New York, Meredith, 1967.
Editor, with George Proctor, *The Science Fiction Hall of Fame 3: The Nebula Winners 1965–1969.* New York, Avon, 1982.
Editor, *July 20, 2019: A Day in the Life of the 21st Century.* New York, Macmillan, 1986; London, Grafton, 1987.

*

Bibliography: *Arthur C. Clarke: A Primary and Secondary Bibliography* by David N. Samuelson, Boston, Hall, 1984.

Manuscript Collection: Mugar Memorial Library, Boston University.

Critical Studies: ''Out of the Ego Chamber'' by Jeremy Bernstein, in *New Yorker,* 9 August 1969; *Arthur C. Clarke* edited by Joseph D. Olander and Martin H. Greenberg, New York, Taplinger, and Edinburgh, Harris, 1977; *The Space Odysseys of Arthur C. Clarke* by George Edgar Slusser, San Bernardino, California, Borgo Press, 1978; *Arthur C. Clarke* (includes bibliography) by Eric S. Rabkin, West Linn, Oregon, Starmont House, 1979, revised edition, 1980; *Against the Night, The Stars: The Science Fiction of Arthur C. Clarke* by John Hollow, New York, Harcourt Brace, 1983, revised edition, Athens, Ohio University Press-Swallow Press, 1987; *Odyssey: The Authorized Biography of Arthur C. Clarke* by Neil McAleer, Chicago, Contemporary Books, and London, Gollancz, 1992; *Arthur C. Clarke: A Critical Companion* by Robin Anne Reid. Westport, Connecticut, Greenwood Press, 1997; *Arthur C. Clarke and Lord Dunsany, a Correspondence,* edited by Keith Allen Daniels. San Francisco, Anamnesis Press, 1998.

Arthur C. Clarke comments:

I regard myself primarily as an entertainer and my ideals are Maugham, Kipling, Wells. My chief aim is the old SF cliché, ''The search for wonder.'' However, I am almost equally interested in style and rhythm, having been much influenced by Tennyson, Swinburne, Housman, and the Georgian poets.

My main themes are exploration (space, sea, time), the position of Man in the hierarchy of the universe, and the effect of contact with other intelligences. The writer who probably had most influence on me was W. Olaf Stapledon (*Last and First Men*).

* * *

Although Arthur C. Clarke's success in the literary field began in the 1950s, his early involvement in the 1930s with the British Interplanetary Society (BIS) heralded his intellectual devotion to outer space. Later, as an enlisted officer in the Royal Air Force, Clarke wrote ''Extra Terrestrial Relays'' (1945), a prescient article detailing a communications satellite system that predated by two decades the eventual launching of the Early Bird synchronous satellites. Finally, Clarke's first books, the nonfiction *Interplanetary Flight* and its successor, *The Exploration of Space*, promoted space travel. The ease with which he rendered complex scientific principles catapulted *The Exploration of Space* into a Book-of-the-Month selection.

Capitalizing on the relationships he fostered through his affiliation with BIS, Clarke wrote nineteen science fiction (sf) stories—some published under the pseudonyms Charles Willis and E.G. O'Brien—before his first two novels, *Prelude to Space* and *The Sands of Mars*, were published in 1951. While Peter Nicholls remarks in *The Encyclopedia of Science Fiction* that these early works are marred by wooden prose and a somewhat mechanical structure, the novels do prefigure the scientific optimism, technological sense of wonder, and sheer entertainment value that dominate Clarke's philosophy and define his sf writing.

A jewel in the wealth of Clarke's short stories, ''Sentinel of Eternity,'' reprinted in *Expedition to Earth* as ''The Sentinel,'' shines forth, as it is the inspiration for Stanley Kubrick's landmark movie *2001: A Space Odyssey* and Clarke's *2001* novel adaptation. *2001* tells the story of the *Discovery*, a spaceship operated by an intelligent computer, HAL 9000. The ship is sent into outer space to track a mysterious signal emanating from a black monolith on Earth's moon. HAL's secret agenda slowly eliminates *Discovery*'s human crew save Dave Bowman who, encountering a mirror monolith on a Saturn moon, evolves into the Star Child. This narrative of an enigmatic alien artifact, also shown four million years in the past helping encourage the dawn of Man, embodies the scientific and metaphysical qualities of Clarke's writings. Nicholls considers these qualities as Clarke's central paradox; namely, that a writer exploring scientific theories and detailing technological advances should be drawn to the metaphysical, mystical, even quasi-religious essence of space and the universe at large.

Never one to avoid the tensions between science and religion, Clarke's darkly comic ''The Nine Billion Names of God'' depicts Tibetan monks who, with the aid of Western computer salesmen and technicians, count all the names of God and, fulfilling the purpose of Man, trigger the end of the universe. In the Hugo-winning ''The Star,'' Clarke offers the reader a Jesuit astrophysicist questioning his faith after discovering evidence that the star of Bethlehem, which had announced the birth of Christ to the Three Wise Men, was a supernova that destroyed an entire alien race. ''Although the narrator's faith is troubled,'' writes David N. Samuelson in *Science Fiction Writers*, ''his trust in science—like Clarke's—is not.''

Childhood's End, Clarke's first successful sf novel, is replete with his thematic interests in its offering of humanity's transcendent evolution under the guidance and tutelage of the Overlords, a devil-shaped alien species steering Earth towards an admittedly ambiguous utopia. The true mission of the Overlords is revealed when Jeff Greggson—son of George and Jean Greggson, who, with others, have rejected the Overlords and established an independent New Athens—begins displaying extrasensory powers. Humanity's maturation, it seems, is available only to Earth's children whose mental evolution draws them into the Overmind, a galactic entity transcending physical form. Barred from achieving their own transcendence, the Overlords watch humanity's evolutionary leap while Jan Rodericks, returning from the Overlords' home planet, remains as the last human to record Earth's final destruction. The novel is bittersweet as it announces humanity's next step up the evolutionary ladder while, in the same breath, condemning a humanity left behind.

City and the Stars—an updated and expanded version of Clarke's earlier *Against the Fall of Night*—depicts the far-future city of Diaspar as an enclosed urban utopia mediated by a complex computerized system. The protagonist Alvin is a ''pure pattern'' born out of the Memory Banks matrix, the first human born on Earth in ten million years. With the help of Khedron, a jester designed to introduce randomness into the highly regulated cityscape, Alvin escapes Diaspar only to find a parallel race of mentally evolved agrarian humans living in the town of Lys. Joined by the Lys-born Hilvar, Alvin uncovers a long-buried spaceship and proceeds into outer space to encounter the Vanamonde, a body-less consciousness created to defend Earth from the destructive powers of the equally bodiless Shalmirance. *City and the Stars* narrates humanity's divergent evolution along mental and technical paths, its subsequent consequences and resultant retreat from outer space, and a resurgent humanity once again reaching out to the stars. With the closing sunset/sunrise imagery symbolizing the eclipse of one epoch and the dawn of another, the ''final passages blend a sense of loss and of transcendence with an almost mystical intensity,'' notes Nicholls.

While non-fiction books and articles—many of them dealing with undersea exploration— dominated Clarke's output in the 1960s, *Rendezvous with Rama* was the first of an unprecedented three-book deal Clarke signed following the immense success of *2001*. *Rama* follows a group of humans, led by Captain Bill Norton, who explore a derelict artifact (dubbed ''Rama'') hurtling through space towards the inner solar system. While exploration and adventure dominate a story full of surprises and technological wonders, transcendence and closure are denied in *Rama* as the ship's intentions are withheld, only to be explored further in a series of sequels—*Rama II, Garden of Rama*, and *Rama Revealed*—written in collaboration with Gentry Lee. Although Clarke's original *Rama* swept the awards circuit (winning the Hugo, Nebula, John W. Campbell Memorial Award and British Science Fiction Award), controversy swirled as to whether the book, due to its stylistic flaws and narrative structure, actually deserved the awards or whether the accolade stemmed from the return to fiction of a much beloved sf author.

Clarke's next two novels, *Imperial Earth: A Fantasy of Love and Discord* and *The Fountains of Paradise*, offer a treasure trove of technological wonders and scientific imagery. *Imperial Earth*, notable for descriptions of outer-planet mining, spaceship propulsion, and cloning, tells the story of Titan native Duncan Mackenzie's investigation of political and scientific intrigues on Earth and his bid, through cloning, to procure an heir to his empire. *The Fountains of Paradise* narrates Vannevar Morgan's attempts to construct a space elevator designed to escape Earth's gravity. Fleshing out the story are two revelations: first, a highly advanced galactic civilization has communicated with the human race through a robot probe; and, second, Prince Kalidasa had challenged the gods 2,000 years earlier by attempting to build a tower into heaven on Taprobane, the same island-site for Morgan's space elevator. While *The Fountains of Paradise* won the Hugo, some critics fault the novel for abruptly dropping the Kalidasa storyline and centering the action on a somewhat stereotyped Morgan. Nevertheless, both novels broach the topics of science, technological marvels, and the bid for a taste of immortality, if not godhood.

The 1980s saw Clarke attempt the impossible; namely, to catch lightning in a bottle and write two sequels to *2001*. *2010: Odyssey Two* and *2061: Odyssey Three* attempt to continue the magical weave of science, transcendence, and mystery embodied in the black monolith; unfortunately, the books fail to evoke the same narrative momentum as *2001*. *2010* is a proficient book offering a distinctly human story as American/Russian tensions threaten a joint rescue mission of Dave Bowman's *Discovery* and the reactivation of HAL 9000. *2061* follows Heywood Floyd's exploration of Halley's comet and his subsequent redirection to the Jovian moon of Europa—the one place the monoliths had expressively forbidden humans to visit. While Clarke attempts to sustain the mystery of the monolith through the course of these books, critics feel the monolith was adequately explained in *2001* or, on the other hand, disappointingly depicted in the subsequent sequels. Although the *2001* sequels offer high-caliber scientific ideas and wondrous descriptions of the universe, Clarke's success at plot advancement and narrative vision is questionable.

The lukewarm critical reception of the *2001* sequels is symptomatic of the response to Clarke's contemporary work; in fact, divergent opinions on Clarke's narrative execution has increasingly dogged the latter phase of his career. For example, popular and critical responses to *The Songs of Distant Earth*—an expansion of a 1958 short story about human survivors introducing conflict to the inhabited utopia of Thallassa—and *Richter 10* (with Mike McQuay)—a futuristic disaster novel—question the plausibility of Clarke's science, the privileging of scientific principles over plot development, and a pacing that is described alternately as taut and long-winded.

Quite possibly the most surprising novel of the 1990s was *3001: The Final Odyssey*, supposedly the last of the *Odyssey* series. In this story, Frank Poole, long believed dead, is revived from a frozen state and is surprised to find the Europa monolith has absorbed Dave Bowman and HAL. Once again, critical opinion varies, as some view the narrative as reasonably written with thoughtful explorations of technology and Freudian theory, while others consider the novel's contemporary rendition of the once-transcendent monolith as an alien threat to be a disappointing treatment with few surprises.

Despite increasingly ill health, Clarke has continued to produce a voluminous literary output, often writing in collaboration with contemporary sf authors who grew up reading his early work. Indeed, after more than 50 novels, 35 non-fiction texts, 600 articles and short stories, numerous television scripts, and stints as a commentator during the *Apollo* moon landings, the Science Fiction Writers of America acknowledged Clarke's extensive contributions and continuing output and bestowed upon him Grand Master status in 1986. Armed with a scientific optimism and a cosmic, even transcendent, perception of humanity's role in an infinitely larger universe, Arthur C. Clarke is credited with helping revolutionize the sf genre from the Golden Age of the 1940s and 1950s through six decades of sf writing and into a new millennium that begins, as Clarke impatiently reiterates, in 2001.

—Graham J. Murphy

CLARKE, Austin C(hesterfield)

Nationality: Barbadian. **Born:** Barbados, 26 July 1934. **Education:** Combermere Boys' School, Barbados; Harrison's College, Barbados; Trinity College, University of Toronto. **Family:** Married Betty Joyce Reynolds in 1957; three children. **Career:** Reporter in Timmins and Kirkland Lake, Ontario, 1959–60; since 1963, freelance producer and broadcaster, Canadian Broadcasting Corporation, Toronto; scriptwriter, Educational Television, Toronto; Ziskind Professor of Literature, Brandeis University, Waltham, Massachusetts, 1968–69; Hoyt Fellow, 1968, and visiting lecturer, 1969, 1970, Yale University, New Haven, Connecticut; fellow, Indiana University School of Letters, Bloomington, 1969; Margaret Bundy Scott Visiting Professor of Literature, Williams College, Williamstown, Massachusetts, 1971; lecturer, Duke University, Durham, North Carolina, 1971–72; visiting professor, University of Texas, Austin, 1973–74; cultural and press attaché, Embassy of Barbados, Washington, D.C., 1974–76; writer-in-residence, Concordia University, Montreal, 1977. General manager, Caribbean Broadcasting Corporation, St. Michael, Barbados, 1975–76. Member, Board of Trustees, Rhode Island School of Design, Providence, 1970–75; vice-chair, Ontario Board of Censors, 1983–85. Since 1988 member, Immigration and Refugee Board of Canada. **Awards:** Belmont Short Story award, 1965; University of Western Ontario President's medal, 1966; Canada Council senior arts fellowship, 1967, 1970, and grant, 1977; Casa de las Americas prize, 1980; Toronto Arts award, for writing, 1993; Toronto Pride Achievement award, for writing, 1995. **Agent:** Phyllis Westberg, Harold Ober Associates, 425 Madison Avenue, New York, New York 10017, U.S.A. **Address:** 62 McGill Street, Toronto, Ontario M5B 1H2, Canada.

Publications

Novels

The Survivors of the Crossing. Toronto, McClelland and Stewart, and London, Heinemann, 1964.
Amongst Thistles and Thorns. Toronto, McClelland and Stewart, and London, Heinemann, 1965.
The Meeting Point. Toronto, Macmillan, and London, Heinemann, 1967; Boston, Little Brown, 1972.
Storm of Fortune. Boston, Little Brown, 1973.
The Bigger Light. Boston, Little Brown, 1975.
The Prime Minister. Toronto, General, 1977; London, Routledge, 1978.
Proud Empires. London, Gollancz, 1986.
The Origin of Waves. Toronto, McClelland & Stewart, 1997.
The Question. Toronto, McClelland & Stewart, 1999.

Short Stories

When He Was Free and Young and He Used to Wear Silks. Toronto, Anansi, 1971; revised edition, Boston, Little Brown, 1973.
When Women Rule. Toronto, McClelland and Stewart, 1985.
Nine Men Who Laughed. Markham, Ontario, and New York, Penguin, 1986.
In This City. Toronto, Exile Editions, 1992.
There Are No Elders. Toronto, Exile Editions, 1994.

Other

The Confused Bewilderment of Martin Luther King and the Idea of Non-Violence as a Political Tactic. Burlington, Ontario, Watkins, 1968.
Growing Up Stupid under the Union Jack: A Memoir. Toronto, McClelland and Stewart, 1980.
A Passage Back Home: A Personal Reminiscence of Samuel Selvon. Toronto, Exile Editions, 1994.
The Austin Clarke Reader, edited by Barry Callaghan. Toronto, Exile Editions, 1996.
Pigtails 'n Breadfruit: The Rituals of Slave Food. Toronto, Random House Canada, 1999; New York, New Press, 2000.

*

Manuscript Collection: McMaster University, Hamilton, Ontario.

Critical Studies: "The West Indian Novel in North America: A Study of Austin Clarke," in *Journal of Commonwealth Literature* (Leeds), July 1970, and *El Dorado and Paradise: Canada and the Caribbean in Austin Clarke's Fiction,* Centre for Social and Humanistic Studies, University of Western Ontario, 1989, both by Lloyd W.

Brown; interview with Graeme Gibson, in *Eleven Canadian Novelists,* Toronto, Anansi, 1974; ''An Assessment of Austin Clarke, West Indian-Canadian Novelist'' by Keith Henry in *CLA Journal* (Atlanta), vol. 29, no. 1, 1985; *Austin C. Clarke: A Biography* by Stella Algoo-Baksh, University of West Indies Press, 1994.

Austin C. Clarke comments:

Whenever I am asked to give a statement about my work I find it difficult to do. All I can say in these situations is that I try to write about a group of people, West Indian immigrants (to Canada), whose life interests me because of the remarkable problems of readjustment, and the other problems of ordinary living. The psychological implications of this kind of life are what make my work interesting and I hope relevant to the larger condition of preservation. The themes are usually those of adjustment, as I have said, but this adjustment is artistically rendered in the inter-relationship of the two predominant groups of which I write: the host Jewish-Anglo Saxon group, and the black group (West Indian and expatriate black American).

* * *

As the West Indian population has surged in Canada over the past two decades, so too has West Indian writing in Canada flourished. On the whole, West Indian literature in Canada is dominated by the familiar themes of exile, return, colonialism, dislocation, and otherness. However, these themes are complicated by the West Indian's response to Canada's much-touted ideal of a cultural mosaic—the notion that the country is, or ought to be, a harmonious aggregation of distinctive cultures which maintain their distinctiveness while blending with each other to create a diversified cultural whole. But for West Indians the ideal of a cultural mosaic is not quite as simple as it sounds to those who espouse it. Given the usual disadvantages of being black in a predominantly white society, West Indians must choose between being integrated into a strange culture—at the cost of their cultural uniqueness and racial integrity—or being so dedicated to maintaining their black, West Indian identity that they risk being cultural and economic outsiders in their adopted homeland. As Rinaldo Walcott has observed in *Black Like Who,* ''To be black and 'at home' in Canada is to both belong and not belong,'' and it is from this ''in-between'' space that Canada's most enduring West Indian author, Austin Clarke, writes.

These Canadian issues are not the major concern in Clarke's earliest novels. Published a decade after Clarke's arrival in Canada, *The Survivors of the Crossing* and *Amongst Thistles and Thorns* are set in Barbados and explore the twin evils of colonial self-hatred and Caribbean poverty. *The Prime Minister* is centered on the experiences of a West Indian writer, John Moore, who has returned to Barbados, to a government appointment after 20 years in Canada, mirroring Clarke's own return to Barbados in 1975 as the manager of the Caribbean Broadcasting Company. Significantly, like Clarke, Moore does not stay in Barbados: he returns to his Canadian home after discovering to his mortification that he no longer has a real place in Barbados.

Moore's experiences can be viewed as paradigmatic of West Indians including Clarke himself, now living and writing in Canada. After almost half a century in Canada, it is logical enough that the Canadian presence dominates Clarke's fiction as a whole. His first collection of short stories includes works that take a close look at Canada as the West Indians' El Dorado. In ''They Heard a Ringing of Bells'' a group of West Indians discuss their experiences as immigrants—delighting in the sense of being released from Caribbean poverty while lambasting the hostility and indifference of white Canada to the West Indian presence. ''Waiting for the Postman to Knock'' is less ambivalent, more openly hostile to the adopted homeland. The heroine is one of the most typical and enduring symbols of West Indian life in Canada—the lonely and isolated West Indian domestic servant who feels equally exploited by her white employer and by her West Indian lover (if she is lucky enough to find a lover). For other West Indians in Clarke's short fiction, the problems of loneliness are compounded by racial self-hatred, especially in the lives of those who are achieving some degree of economic success at the cost of their racial pride or cultural integrity (''Four Stations in His Circle'' and ''The Motor Car'').

These related themes of loneliness, self-hatred, and cultural exclusion are the main concerns of Clarke's Canadian trilogy, *The Meeting Point, Storm of Fortune,* and *The Bigger Light.* The three works center on the lives of a group of West Indians in Toronto—especially Bernice Leach, her sister Estelle, Boysie Cumberbatch, his wife Dots, and Henry White. *The Meeting Point* concentrates on Bernice's experiences as a maid in the home of the wealthy Burrmann family, and emphasizes the usual themes of sexual loneliness, cultural isolation, and the sense of economic exploitation.

Storm of Fortune shifts the focus to Estelle and her somewhat uneven struggle to gain a toehold in Canada. The novel also traces the failures of Henry White and his subsequent death, and, most important of all, it depicts the gradual emergence of Boysie Cumberbatch, from shiftless bon vivant to ambitious small businessman with his own janitorial company. His success story is continued in *The Bigger Light,* which, despite some uneven writing, remains Clarke's most ambitious novel to date. Having devoted much of the preceding novels to the failures and half-successes in the West Indian community, Clarke concentrates here on a successful man, but one whose economic successes have not protected him from emotional failure (the gradual breakdown of his marriage and his increasing isolation from his less fortunate West Indian friends). And in fact his success as a Canadian businessman, in the Anglo-Saxon mould, has had the effect of encouraging a certain snobbery and a marked reserve towards matters of cultural and racial significance. In short he becomes increasingly hostile towards the issue of racial identity.

But in spite of his extreme and increasing isolation in the novel, Boysie is not an entire failure as a human being. His very isolation becomes a catalyst for a certain perceptiveness, which allows him to recognize the real nature of his choices, and the limitations of the world in which he has chosen to live. And as a consequence he remains the typical Clarke protagonist, one whose failures—economic and moral—are counterbalanced by a persistent ability to perceive their own lives, without self-deception or self-pity, as they really are. Given the persistent hostilities of the world in which they live, this kind of honest self-awareness is the most important quality of all—and Clarke invariably presents and invites judgments on his characters on the basis of their ability to achieve such an awareness.

These themes of isolation and self-conflict have increasingly been integrated with the issue of Canadian society and Canadian identity in Clarke's more recent writing. Canada is no longer a temporary (and deeply resented) resting-place for immigrants with a strong sense of transience. Clarke's fictional world, in his second collection of short stories, *When Women Rule,* is firmly located in the much-touted Canadian ideal of social mosaic. These are stories about immigrants from Europe (Italians, ''displaced'' Central and Eastern Europeans), as well as from the Caribbean. They are almost all about middle-aged men whose familiar anxieties about aging, sexual relationships, and socioeconomic success are interwoven with pervasive uncertainties about the directions of Canadian society: the disruptive and challenging presence of "newer" immigrants, urban changes in metropolitan Canada, and the unsettling implications of female equality. And in one story, "Give It a Shot," these fears are shared even by a born-and-bred "Anglo-Canadian." Indeed, it is the central irony of this collection that the very idea of a Canadian mosaic, with its implicit promise of social harmony and individual success, binds Clarke's diverse Canadians together by virtue of its failure, rather than its fulfillment, in their lives. Failure, however, as Clarke makes clear in his next short story collection *Nine Men Who Laughed,* not only stems from discrimination and displacement, but also is complicated by the selfish materialism, social alienation, and urban isolation increasingly common in modern life.

It is noteworthy that Clarke's Canadian themes actually reify the most central and universal of all his themes—alienation. In their alienation from society, family, and even from their once-youthful selves, his middle-aged protagonists are the familiar isolates of much 20th-century fiction, ranging—in Clarke's work—from the canefields of Barbados to the chic boutiques and working-class bars of modern Toronto. By way of emphasizing Clarke's insistence on the universality of alienation, it is only necessary to move from *When Women Rule* to his autobiography, *Growing Up Stupid under the Union Jack.* The title is no mere whimsy. The imperial reference sets the cultural theme—boyhood and adolescence in colonial Barbados. But the key word here is "stupid." It suggests the naiveté, the stunted self-consciousness of the (well educated) colonial, a culturally ingrained, institutionally enforced ignorance of one's history, society, and ethnicity. And, drawing on the Caribbean connotations of "stupid/tchupidness," it connotes absurdity as well as mental dullness. The colonial situation is the essence of the absurd because it both causes and symbolizes the condition of being isolated from one's self, one's cultural and personal roots. To be a colonial is therefore to be both the unique product of a concrete, specific process—colonial culture—and another archetype of 20th-century alienation. "Tchupidness" is simultaneously a Caribbean condition and a universal experience. Yet even as Clarke explores this "tchupidness," and the absurdity of the colonial condition, he personally refuses to accept these as immutable or fixed.

An albeit unsuccessful Conservative candidate in 1977's Ontario provincial election, Clarke nevertheless affirmed his status as full participant in Canadian society, solidified by his decision in 1981 to become a citizen. Between 1988 and 1993 Clarke served on the Immigration Board of Canada, and in 1992 published a political pamphlet, *Public Enemies: Police Violence and Black Youth,* which condemned the Toronto police force. A fierce social critic of preventable "tchupidness," Clarke has used both his writing and the public ear it has earned to call into question governmental policies that perpetuate certain inequalities in Canadian society.

After leaving the series of government appointments he fulfilled in the late 1980s and early 1990s, Clarke has returned to writing full-time, producing what many believe to be his strongest work to date. In 1997 *The Origin of Waves* gained national acclaim for its subtle, sophisticated treatment of the conversation two men, reunited in a Toronto snowstorm forty years after their childhood in the Caribbean. As the two attempt to "catch-up" on the lost years, they also must come to terms with certain events of their youth, and their own diverse personalities. The conversation is permeated by the spoken and the unspoken, and the lies, evasions, and contradictions that inevitably plague any attempt to explain and justify one's life to another. In a literary twist, Canada, while a source of alienation and betrayal, also becomes the space from which the two can reconsider the meaning of their childhood and the dynamic of their childhood friendship and experiences.

Clarke's latest novel, *The Question,* returns to the themes of friendship, betrayal, and imagining the other across the differences and distances that sometimes define our daily life. At its center is a judge at the immigration and refugee hearings whose own inability to distinguish between fact and fiction in his personal life must inevitably be reflected in his work, where he must determine the worthiness of applicants, based on what he perceives to be their need or veracity. In tandem with the publication of these increasingly introspective works on the nature of life in a transnational, fractured world, Clarke has also once more returned to the territory of his own youth, with *Pigtails 'n Breadfruit: The Rituals of Slave Food.* The process of remembering the recipes of his youth, and the roots, rituals, and familial activities associated with them leads Clarke into a complex but always compelling and readable analysis of the meaning of food in Barbadian culture. In 1998 Clarke's long time contributions to Canadian writing and culture at large were recognized as he was made a member of the Order of Canada, the highest form of recognition by the Canadian government.

—Lloyd W. Brown, updated by Jennifer Harris

COBB, William (Sledge)

Nationality: American. **Born:** Eutaw, Alabama, 20 October 1937. **Education:** Livingston State College, 1957–61, B.A. in English 1961; Vanderbilt University, 1961–63, M.A. in English 1963; Breadloaf School of English, Middlebury College, 1967–68. **Family:** Married Loretta Douglas in 1965; one daughter. **Career:** Professor of English, 1963–89, and since 1989, writer-in-residence, both University of Montevallo, Alabama. **Awards:** *Story Magazine*'s Story of the Year Award, 1964; National Endowment for the Arts fellowship, 1978, for creative writing; Atlantic Center for the Arts grant, 1985, for playwriting; Alabama State Council on the Arts grant, 1985, for playwriting, and 1995, for fiction writing. **Agent:** Albert Zuckerman, Writers House, 21 West 26th St., New York, New York 10011, U.S.A. **Address:** 200 Shady Hill Drive, Montevallo, Alabama 35115, U.S.A.

Publications

Novels

Coming of Age at the Y. Columbia, Maryland, Portals Press, 1984.
The Hermit King. Columbia, Maryland, Portals Press, 1987.
A Walk Through Fire. New York, Morrow, 1992.
The Fire Eaters. New York, Norton, 1994.
Harry Reunited. Montgomery, Alabama, Black Belt Press, 1995.
A Spring of Souls. Birmingham, Alabama, Crane Hill Publishers, 1999.

Uncollected Short Stories

"The Year of Judson's Carnival," in *The Sucarnochee Review,* 1961.
"A Single Precious Day," in *Livingston Life,* 1961.

''The Time of the Leaves,'' in *Granta,* 1963.
''The Stone Soldier,'' in *Story,* Spring 1964.
'''Suffer Little Children ... ,''' in *Comment,* Spring 1967.
''The Iron Gates,'' in *Comment,* Winter 1968.
''The Hunted,'' in *The Arlington Quarterly,* Summer 1968.
''A Very Proper Resting Place,'' in *Comment,* Autumn 1969.
''An Encounter with a Friend,'' in *Inlet,* Spring 1973.
''Walk the Fertile Fields of My Mind,'' in *Region,* November 1976.
''Somewhere in All This Green,'' in *Anthology of Bennington Writers,* edited by John Gardner. Delbanco, 1978.
''The Night of the Yellow Butterflies,'' in *Arete,* Spring 1984.
''Old Wars and New Sorrow,'' in *The Sucarnochee Review,* Spring 1984.
''Faithful Steward of Thy Bounty.'' N.p., n.d.
''The Queen of the Silver Dollar,'' in *Amaryllis,* Spring 1995.

Plays

The Vine and the Olive (produced Livingston, 1961).
Brighthope (produced Montevallo, 1985) .
Recovery Room (produced New Orleans, 1986).
Sunday's Child (produced Montevallo, 1986; New York, 1987).
A Place of Spring (produced New York, 1987).
Early Rains (produced New York, 1988).

*

Manuscript Collection: Vanderbilt University Library, Nashville, Tennessee.

William Cobb comments:

A strong influence, perhaps the strongest, on the structure of *Harry Reunited* is Robert Altman's wonderfully funny film *Nashville,* which I saw years ago when it was first released and have since watched countless times on video. I wanted to write a novel about a disparate group of people whose only real connection is something ephemeral—in this case a vague and distant past—whose lives touch others' lives in various ways as they pass through a sequence of events, and who are finally brought together and at the same time separated by one apocalyptic event. I did not, of course, want to retell *Nashville.* It had to be my own story.

Since I had not attended my own high school class's 25th reunion (I was somehow left off the invitation list; I'm still not sure what that says about me!), I was able to pose a hypothetical question to myself: What happens when a man goes back home, into an artificially created environment that attempts to mirror, even recreate, a period in his past, and he has to confront all the demons from that past? As I began to work on the novel all sorts of other nuances and themes began to appear, among them the inevitable facing of middle age, that middle passage in which we invariably begin to look both backward and forward with varying emotional consequences. And as a Southern writer, I've always been fascinated with the presence of the past, of our histories both individually and collectively, and with the notion of the abiding importance of ''place,'' and as I wrote I found those themes emerging as well.

And I quickly fell in love with Bud Squires. Even though it's Harry's book, it is Bud's book, too, because it is he who provides the counterpoint to Harry's semi-comfortable life. It is Bud who is the avenging angel, and I was able, in a way, through my creation of Bud, to exorcise some of the guilt I suspect I still carried around with me for the cruel things I must have done in my own adolescence and which I have conveniently forgotten or blacked out. Bud became a wonderful comic character for me, a man who awakens, in varying degrees and in various startling ways, all the people in the book—and gives a kind of new life to them.

Finally, it was the comic mode that most drove me as I created this book. I very consciously wished to return to the comedy of my first novel, *Coming of Age at the Y,* and I wanted to paint this story with broad strokes. It is full of the kind of humor that I love, subtle and sly and almost slapstick at the same time. A humor of character. I *love* all these characters—Bernie Crease, as ineffectual as he is; Marie, as innocently slutty as she is; the foul-mouthed adolescents in the Sacristy before the Sunday morning service; the little black kid in the fish-net shirt; the three women at the yard sale; Cholly Polly, poor, poor Cholly Polly; Vera Babbs, the ''message artist,'' and on and on; I love them all! That is the gift that comic writing like this gives back to the writer. I got the richest, warmest laughs of all. And I, too,—even though I was not invited—was finally reunited!

* * *

William Cobb studied with the last of the Fugitives at Vanderbilt, and his fiction is deeply rooted in the southern soil that the Agrarians revered; however, his political views have not always been in keeping with the conservative views of his mentors. Throughout his work there runs a deep respect for spirituality, the importance of family, and the necessity of maintaining a sense of place. Many readers feel that Cobb is at his best as a comic writer (his flair for the profane is certainly apparent); however, his more serious civil-rights novel, *A Walk Through Fire,* brought Cobb national acclaim. Cobb's body of work includes an impressive number of short stories, four novels, and three plays that were produced in New York.

Cobb's first national recognition came in 1964 when his story ''The Stone Soldier'' won the prestigious *Story Magazine*'s Story of the Year Award and was the title story in that year's collection. ''The Stone Soldier'' has since been anthologized a number of times. Cobb's flair for the vulgar was apparent in his vivid description of Lyman Sparks, a scalawag who preys on the families of Civil War soldiers. His ''sausage legs'' and ''squiggly eyes'' are indelibly printed in the reader's mind.

Another short piece of fiction was recognized as an outstanding contribution in the premier edition of *Arete: A Journal of Sport Literature,* published at San Diego State University. In ''The Night of the Yellow Butterflies'' the main characters are a minor league baseball coach and his star player, Luke Easter—who may or may not be an apparition. The theme of baseball, with its hopes and dreams—often lost ones—is recurrent in Cobb's work. This particular story weaves the real and the supernatural in a mysterious manner that is quite convincing.

There was some negative response to the bawdy nature of Cobb's satirical novel *Coming of Age at the Y.* Certainly, he took some chances writing a satirical coming-of-age story with a female protagonist (not always considered politically correct as early as the 1970s). However, it is hard to see how any reader could miss the tone of the book from its title. Though some readers felt that his heroine, Delores Lovelady, was a bit passive, most felt that it was a fine attack on sexism—loaded with irony. Lucille Weary, the ''worldly'' traveler on the Greyhound with Delores, is a wonderfully funny echo of

The Wife of Bath cramped in a century full of the New South and Shoney's Big Boys.

Cobb's second novel, *The Hermit King,* is a more traditional coming-of-age novel. The main story line here is between two runaway adolescents and an old black man who has lived a hermit's life much like Thoreau's a century earlier in quiet protest to the setting tradition offers him. Cobb's descriptive power is clear.

Cobb also has an ear for dialogue that seemed to lead him inevitably to write for the stage. Horton Foote, who admired his work, suggested that he send a trilogy to H. B. Playwright's Studio in New York. All three plays were done there over a two-year period. Herbert Berghoff said that Cobb's plays are like Foote's plays in that they are domestic plays that deal with quiet human conflicts.

Cobb's third novel, *A Walk Through Fire,* was well received. Both *Library Journal* and *Publisher's Weekly* gave the book a strong endorsement in 1992, its year of publication, and the *West Coast Review of Books* declared it one of the most important books of the year. Caught up in an interracial triangle, the three main characters spin a story filled with passion and strength. The reader can see clearly Cobb's firm sense of place in the following scene, where O. B. Brewster, a white farm implement dealer (and former baseball player), offers to help an old black farmer plow his field:

> The black earth turned smoothly on each side of the shiny blade. *I am not too far removed from this soil that I can't feel its message again, in my legs and in my heart.* The loamy earth was damp, and it smelled fecund and rich, fertile as life itself. Tears misted his eyes, one droplet spilling down his cheek, but he could not wipe his face because he held to the handles of the plow.

Reviewers have said that Cobb has undoubtedly had his turn at the plow in that soil. His description of the violence and pain of our collective history during those years is seared into the minds of his readers through the fire imagery that permeates the book. Most importantly, we are reminded that those with intense faith can walk through fire.

Many of Cobb's central characters have a quiet strength that comes from life lived close to the earth. The setting is almost always southern, but the struggles of the human heart transcend the regional boundaries and make valuable commentary on life in the last half of the 20th century in the United States.

—Chris Leigh

CODRESCU, Andrei

Nationality: Romanian-American. **Born:** Sibiu, Romania, 20 December 1946. **Family:** Married Alice Henderson in 1968; two sons. **Career:** Visiting assistant professor, Johns Hopkins University, Baltimore, 1979–80; visiting professor, Naropa Institute, Boulder, Colorado; professor of English, Louisiana State University, Baton Rouge, 1984—; regular commentator on National Public Radio's *All Things Considered.* **Awards:** Big Table Younger Poets Award, 1970; National Endowment for the Arts fellowships, 1973, 1983; Pushcart Prize, 1980, 1983; A. D. Emmart Humanities Award, 1982; National Public Radio fellowship, 1983; Towson University Prize for Literature, 1983; General Electric/CCLM Poetry Award, 1985; American Romanian Academy of Arts and Sciences Book Award, 1988; George Foster Peabody Award (San Francisco Film Festival), best documentary film, 1995; best documentary film award, Seattle Film Festival, 1995; Cine Award, 1995; Golden Eagle Award, 1995; ACLU Civil Liberties Award, 1995; Romanian National Foundation Literature Award, 1996. **Agent:** Jonathan Lazear, 930 First Avenue North, Suite 416, Minneapolis, Minnesota 55401, U.S.A.

Publications

Novels

The Repentance of Lorraine. New York, Pocket Books, 1976.
The Blood Countess. New York, Simon & Schuster, 1995.
Messiah. New York, Simon & Schuster, 1999.

Short Stories

Why I Can't Talk on the Telephone. San Francisco, Kingdom Kum Press, 1972.
Monsieur Teste in America and Other Instances of Realism. Minneapolis, Coffee House Press, 1987.

Poetry

License to Carry a Gun. Chicago, Big Table/Follett, 1970.
The Here What Where. San Francisco, Isthmus Press, 1972.
And Grammar and Money. Berkeley, California, Arif Press, 1973.
A Serious Morning. Santa Barbara, California, Capra Press, 1973.
The History of the Growth of Heaven. New York, George Braziller, 1973.
A Mote Suite for Jan and Anselm. San Francisco, Stone Pose Art, 1976.
For the Love of a Coat. Boston, Four Zoas Press, 1978.
The Lady Painter. Boston, Four Zoas Press, 1979.
Diapers on the Snow. Ann Arbor, Michigan, Crowfoot Press, 1981.
Necrocorrida. Los Angeles, Panjandrum, 1982.
Selected Poems: 1970–1980. New York, Sun Books, 1983.
Comrade Past and Mister Present: New Poems and a Journal. Minneapolis, Coffee House Press, 1986; second edition, 1991.
Belligerence: New Poems. Minneapolis, Coffee House Press, 1991.
Alien Candor: Selected Poems, 1970–1995. Santa Rosa, California, Black Sparrow Press, 1998.

Plays

Screenplays: *Road Scholar*, Metro-Goldwyn-Mayer, 1993.

Other

For Max Jacob. Berkeley, California, Tree Books, 1974.
The Life and Times of an Involuntary Genius (autobiography). New York, George Braziller, 1975.
In America's Shoes (autobiography). San Francisco, City Lights, 1975.

A Craving for Swan (essays). Columbus, Ohio State University Press, 1986.
Raised by Puppets Only to be Killed by Research (essays). Reading, Massachusetts, Addison-Wesley, 1988.
The Disappearance of the Outside: A Manifesto for Escape (essays). Reading, Massachusetts, Addison-Wesley, 1990.
The Hole in the Flag: A Romanian Exile's Story of Return and Revolution (reportage). New York, Morrow, 1991.
Acid Dreams: The Complete Social History of LSD: The CIA, the Sixties, and Beyond (introduction) by Martin A. Lee and Bruce Shlain. New York, Grove Weidenfeld, 1992.
The MUse is Always Half-Dressed in New Orleans and Other Essays. New York, St. Martin's Press, 1993.
Zombification: Stories from National Public Radio (essays). New York, St. Martin's Press, 1994.
Road Scholar: Coast to Coast Late in the Century (reportage), with photographs by David Graham. New York, Hyperion, 1994.
The Dog with the Chip in His Neck: Essays from NPR and Elsewhere. New York, St. Martin's Press, 1996.
Elysium: A Gathering of Souls: New Orleans Cemeteries (foreword), by Sandra Russell Clark. Baton Rouge, Louisiana State University Press, 1997.
Hail Babylon!: In Search of the American City at the end of the Millennium (essays). New York, St. Martin's Press, 1998.
Ay Cuba: A Socio-Erotic Journey to Castro's Last Stand (reportage), with photographs by David Graham. New York, St. Martin's Press, 1999.
A Bar in Brooklyn: Novellas & Stories 1970–1978. Santa Rosa, California, Black Sparrow, 1999.
Land of the Free: What Makes Americans Different (nonfiction, with David Graham, edited by Michael L. Sand). New York, Aperture, 1999.
The Devil Never Sleeps and Other Essays. New York, St. Martin's Press, 2000.
Contributor, *Walker Evans: Signs* (''with an essay by Andrei Codrescu''), by Walker Evans. Los Angeles, J. Paul Getty Museum, 1998.
Editor and Contributor, *American Poetry since 1970: Up Late.* New York, Four Walls Eight Windows, 1987.
Editor, *The Stiffest of the Corpse: An Exquisite Corpse Reader.* San Francisco, City Lights, 1988.
Editor, *Reframing America: Alexander Alland, Otto Hagel & Hansel Mieth, John Gutmann, Lisette Model, Marion Palfi, Robert Frank.* Albuquerque, University of New Mexico Press, 1995.
Editor, with Laura Rosenthal, *American Poets Say Goodbye to the Twentieth Century.* New York, Four Walls Eight Windows, 1996.
Editor, with Laura Rosenthal, *Thus Spake the Corpse: An Exquisite Corpse Reader, 1988–1998.* Santa Rosa, California, Black Sparrow Press, 1999.
Translator, *At the Court of Yearning: Poems by Lucian Blaga* by Lucian Blaga. Columbus, Ohio State University Press, 1989.

*

Critical Studies: *Nine Martinis* by Lita R. Hornick, New York, Kulchur Foundation, 1987.

Andrei Condrescu comments:

(2000) There were always so many things that didn't fit in my poems or essays: recipes, overheard conversations, intricate means of disposing of mean people, crushes on out-of-bounds women, and, above all, a sense of the passing of time. The capacious form of the novel could, it seemed to me, accommodate all those things and some. When I started writing one, I discovered that I was a good storyteller and that, in fact, the form was even more amazing, that it was a machine capable of activating myths and rituals and changing the status quo. After reading *Messiah*, a friend said, ''I can't look at New Orleans the same way anymore. It's been changed.'' I have also changed some peoples' memory cassettes: they now remember their novelistic representations better than the experiences they were based on. The novel is not exhausted, though the purveyors of the faux-memoir and psychological realism have done their best to run it into the ground. A squad of imaginative rescuers steeped in outrageous magic (such as the city of New Orleans) are getting it putt-putting again.

* * *

Andrei Codrescu is an artistic jack-of-all trades who mixes genres and juggles conventions, combining fact with fiction to produce hybrids: not exactly novels or novellas, not exactly histories or memoirs, but, like dragons in fairy tales, new conglomerations that share characteristics of many conventional beasts. Add political and social commentary, satiric portraits, a touch of the poet's life and thought, a little Cold War history, a mixed bag of poetic images, and comic and sexual romps, and the end result is a Codrescu short-story collection or novella.

A Romanian-born naturalized American, Codrescu draws on his experiences as a journalist, a weekly radio broadcaster and commentator on National Public Radio, and as an editor of the radical literary journal *Exquisite Corpse* to create witty and insightful essays, serio-comic memoirs, and autobiographical poetry and fiction. However, he prides himself more on his poetry than his short stories and novels, partly because, as he admits, he regards writing fiction as a relaxing vacation from his true vocation as a poet. Besides, it may be difficult for an English-as-a-second-language writer to sustain the consistently complex syntax required by novel-length performances, especially those duplicating speech and dialogue or an extended narrative voice. (Critics have been unenthusiastic about Codrescu's prose stylistics in his novels, a failing he cheerfully admitted to in his early works when he was still perfecting his self-taught English.) Rather, Codrescu plays to his strengths, contriving strikingly vivid poetic images and word play that capture a quirky and engaging sensibility. Language aside, Codrescu's Romanian-influenced take on the culture and foibles of his adopted country is his great strength as commentator and writer, for his childhood in a late-Soviet satellite shot through with collectivist distortion and socialist blather clearly gave him a sensitive ear and eye for sham and falsehood. Codrescu is at his best in satiric essays that unmask establishment hypocrisy, as in his exuberant *The Devil Never Sleeps and Other Essays*, with its discussions of William Burroughs, New Orleans' libertinism, and fundamentalist Christianity.

Although he calls his loosely structured memoirs *The Life and Times of an Involuntary Genius*, its sequel *In America's Shoes*, and *Road Scholar: Coast to Coast Late in the Century* fiction, their descriptions of why he left Romania, the culture shock he experienced in Italy and then in the United States, the experiences (particularly in the San Francisco Bay area) that helped Americanize him, and his coast-to-coast trek across the USA, marveling at American oddities (like crystal gazers in the Southwest and a drive-through wedding in Los Angeles), are too thinly disguised and too true to his biography to be pure fiction. Still, all his novels, like his poems and essays, explore autobiographical subjects based on his experiences as an expatriate *enfant terrible*. The third person narrative of *Involuntary Genius* does distance him somewhat from his personal story, but the other two narratives assertively assume the narrative ''I.'' Likewise, *The Muse Is Always Half-Dressed in New Orleans and Other Essays* has its inventive fictive moments but is more a collection of essays based on personal experience than of completely fictional short stories. In prose, Codrescu prefers a comically surreal mixture of philosophy, politics, science, and sex, bound together with attacks on oppression and repression, what Bruce Shlain of the *New York Times Book Review* sums up as ''lyrical intellectual gymnastics'' mixed with ''dime store philosophy'' (25 January 1987: 15). Again, Codrescu's upbringing in a rigid, corrupt system may in part explain his enthusiasm for bursting the constrictions of genre while indulging in (and often mocking) ideological and philosophical commentary, happily sampling an intellectual and stylistic freedom denied under the strictures of socialist realism.

The mix of poetry and short fiction in *Why I Can't Talk on the Telephone* is typically Codrescu in its defiance of genre conventions, as what has been called ''apocalyptic realism'' meets ''sentence-theatre,'' jumbling together vampires, reviews of imaginary books (à la Jorge Luis Borges), speeches given by hands or hairs, and thoughts on ''The Dada Council of World Revolution.'' The surreal *How I Became a Howard Johnson* provides early impressions of America in long conversations between stoned characters. Though published in 1999, *A Bar in Brooklyn: Novellas and Stories 1970–1978* is a collection of short stories from Codrescu's ''hip'' days as a self-proclaimed radical and mock revolutionist. In *Meat from the Goldrush*, a tale of cannibalism, Codrescu spoofs Gabriel Garcia Marquez's *One Hundred Years of Solitude* through a close-knit family of Eastern European butchers who contact their past (and that of their customers) directly: a time machine helps them transport bodies from the past, which they convert into prime cuts that are so popular they end up short-circuiting the present by killing off so many from the past—science fiction meets surrealism. A story of a quest for a mythic artifact, *The Repentance of Lorraine*, brings together a peculiar assortment of characters from past and present, including Roman harlots, modern Maoists, and university professors.

A horror story of sorts, *The Blood Countess: A Novel* is supposedly based on the life of a Codrescu ancestor. It interweaves in alternating chapters the true story of a sixteenth-century Hungarian countess, Elizabeth Bathory, and a fictive tale of her modern descendant, Drake Bathory-Kereshbur, a Hungarian-born American journalist. The cruel countess is a female version of Vlad the Impaler, having had 650 virgins killed so she could rejuvenate herself in their blood, and her life of debauchery and murder provides a disturbing study of tyranny, psychosis, superstition, and ruthless political machinations. Bathory-Kereshbur has returned to his homeland to cover Hungary's attempts to break away from the former Soviet Union and to move into the world of nations as a self-determined nation, so his position allows Codrescu to draw on his personal memories of life behind the Iron Curtain and the conflicts and hopes that ended the Cold War. However, even with Bathory-Kereshbur's confession to a dark family legacy that draws him into murder, modern events cannot compete with the nightmare images of past violence and violation that ultimately dominate this book.

As in *The Blood Countess*, the melodramatic *Messiah: A Novel*, a count-down to 2000 A.D. alternates chapters focusing on two heroines, New Orleanian Creole Felicity Odille LeJeune and Andrea Isbik, a Sarajevo refugee to Jerusalem, who together may save the world from Armageddon. LeJeune's prim and proper but senile 96-year-old grandmother hands over her $2 million-winning lottery ticket to a sleazy Baptist evangelical nicknamed ''Elvis'' and wishes for an orgasm just before she dies, and LeJeune's fight is a righteous one to bring the money back home. The teenaged Isbik, in turn, seduces an assortment of religious believers as a means to escape the hospice where she has been placed and finance a trip to ''New Jerusalem,'' a.k.a. New Orleans. Codrescu draws inspiration from everything from *Dr. Strangelove* to Terry Southern's *Candy* for his enmeshed plot of warring lunacies: fanatical religious fundamentalists who disagree over absurdities, tattooed nihilists and radical revolutionaries, millennial fears and extremist rhetoric, in a mordant social commentary on the hysteria attending the change in centuries.

Codrescu is an American success story, an immigrant finding fame and relative fortune not along the typical avenues to success traveled by newcomers—the fairly forgiving paths of entrepreneurship or business—but rather down the constricted alleyways of linguistic performance, cultural commentary, and literary creation in a new language. Making one's way in this enterprise means remaining alert to nuances that escape many native speakers, and to constructing a persona both appealing and critical with none of the foundations available to native speakers. Joseph Conrad showed that literary forms can be mastered in a second language as well as in a first, but few writers have duplicated his feat. Codrescu's achievement is quite different, but nonetheless remarkable, the creation of a distinct authorial voice, one heard in radio performance and fictional prose, which draws on a Romanian past, yet is distinctively, unequivocally, American.

—Andrew Macdonald

COE, Jonathan (Roger)

Nationality: British. **Born:** Birmingham, 19 August 1961. **Education:** Trinity College, Cambridge, 1980–83, B.A. (honours) in English literature; Warwick University, 1983–86, Ph.D in English literature. **Family:** Married Janine Maria McKeown in 1989. **Career:** Loan officer, Barclays Bank; poetry tutor, Warwick University; cabaret pianist; legal proofreader; arts journalist. **Agent:** Tony Peake, Peake Associates, 14 Grafton Crescent, London NW1 8SL, England.

PUBLICATIONS

Novels

The Accidental Woman. London, Buckworth, 1987.
A Touch of Love. London, Buckworth, 1989.
The Dwarves of Death. London, Fourth Estate, 1990.
What a Carve Up!. London, Viking, 1994; as *The Winshaw Legacy,* New York, Knopf, 1995.
The House of Sleep. New York, Knopf, 1998.

Other

Humphrey Bogart: Take It and Like It. London, Bloomsbury, and New York, Grove, 1991.

James Stewart: Leading Man. London, Bloomsbury, and New York, Autumn, 1994; published as *Jimmy Stewart: A Wonderful Life,* New York, Arcade, 1994.

*

Jonathan Coe comments:

My first impulse to write came from the films and television programmes I watched as a child: British film comedies such as *Kind Hearts and Coronets* and *I'm All Right, Jack,* and TV sitcoms like *Fawlty Towers.* At the same time I have a certain yearning towards the high European seriousness of great twentieth-century novelists such as Proust, Mann, and Musil, and my own novels have grown out of the tension between these two very different influences.

Another creative tension arises from my desire to reach a wide readership while remaining convinced that it is the novelist's job to innovate, to take formal risks and always attempt something new. I have never wanted to write historical or escapist fiction: contemporary Britain provides me with my source material.

An off-the-cuff list of all-time favourite writers would include Henry Fielding, Laurence Sterne, Charles Dickens, Dorothy Richardson, Rosamond Lehman, Bohumil Hrabal, Milorad Pavic, Flann O'Brien, and B.S. Johnson.

* * *

''Words are awkward sods, and very rarely say what you want them to say''—a thought expressed in Jonathan Coe's first novel, *The Accidental Woman.* The intractability of language seems to preoccupy the young novelist. This slight tale of a young woman, Maria, to whom things happen, rather than who makes things happen, is haunted by an authorial voice that is never far from intervention. ''Before the film they met for a drink, or at least they met at a place where drinks were served, and drank there.'' Such attention to detail is not uncommon in the first-time novelist; so keen to avoid cliché he is forever stopping the flow of the narrative to deconstruct the image: ''Her hand was being held with a strength which it would not be inappropriate to compare to that of a vice.''

The role of Maria reflects Coe's questing approach to narrative. Maria is the accidental woman; like one of Hardy's passive victims, things happen to her. Her actions never propel the narrative; the story is driven by her response to events. She marries Martin because she ate gammon.

In *A Touch of Love,* Coe eschews forthright authorial intrusion and tells a more direct story, although he does not completely forget his experimental roots. The story of Robin, a depressed postgraduate who is charged with indecency after a misunderstanding in a park, is seen from various viewpoints that allow the reader to build up a complete picture of his character. The clearest insight is allowed by the inclusion in the text of four of Robin's short stories. (The style of his work is reminiscent of *The Accidental Woman.*)

With *The Dwarves of Death,* Coe takes an enormous stride forward. The narrator, William, is a musician caught up in a murder case after being in the wrong place at the wrong time. Now, there is some heart (Maria and Robin had both been dealt their cards indifferently, even cruelly)—that is, William's frustrating relationship with the unreachable Madeline engenders the reader's sympathy. He gets us on his side early on, after all, by delivering blistering satirical salvos at Andrew Lloyd Webber's so-called music. Coe is experimenting. He constructs the novel like a popular song. It even has a middle eight—a hilarious account of waiting for a bus that never comes.

If Coe took a stride forward with *Dwarves,* he leaps to a higher plane with *What A Carve Up!* Societal satire, savage political attack, rip-roaring farce, in-depth character study, deeply moving love story. it's all here, and every aspect of it works like a dream. Especially the oneness of it, the masterful way in which the author brings it all together. Ostensibly, at least to begin with, it is the story of a rich and powerful Yorkshire family, the Winshaws, and writer Michael Owen, who is writing a book about the Winshaws for a vanity publisher. Tabitha Winshaw has been confined to an asylum, having overreacted to the death (she remains convinced it was no accident) of her brother, Godfrey. It is Tabitha who charges the Peacock Press with the task of finding someone to write the history of the Winshaws, and the more details that are revealed about the depths of greed and viciousness of her various relatives the more she emerges as the sanest of the bunch, despite being locked away.

Hilary Winshaw writes a vituperative, hawkish column for a right-wing tabloid; brother Roddy is a Cork Street gallerist sustaining the careers of talentless would-be artists. Henry becomes a Labour MP but veers sharply away from the party to become one of the powerful backroom thinkers and plotters behind the Conservatives' relentless drive to privatize everything they possibly can. Dorothy is a heartless factory farmer who becomes head of an insidious packaged-food business. Thomas is a merchant banker who involves himself in the film industry for the voyeuristic opportunities it will afford him. Mark sells arms to Saddam.

Exploiting this extraordinary cast of characters to the full, Coe tears apart the body politic of British society and lays bare its corrupt heart. Because the author handles his material so assuredly, the reader never gets lost in the richness of detail. The appalling political machinations remain fascinating throughout the book, but what really draws the reader in is the character of Michael Owen, who one senses may be only partly fictional. Though he is nine years older than the author, there's a strong temptation to read Coe into part of the part of Michael, and not only because of playful references to Michael's published novels, whose titles are reworkings of *The Accidental Woman* and *A Touch of Love.*

The passages taken from Michael's works seem deeply personal, as does the relationship between Michael and Fiona. It's an indication, however, of how absorbing the action is throughout the book, that 90 pages elapse after Michael and Fiona's first embrace before the narrative returns to them. And although the reader wants to get back to them because s/he cares for them now virtually as for real people, one remains captivated by all the many characters and narrative strands. This is partly due to ingenious plotting and a complicated structure that must have required the author constantly to go back and rework sections.

The scope of *What a Carve Up!* is dizzyingly ambitious, taking in the art world and factory farming; the depletion of the health service and the war against Saddam; the corruption of politicians and betrayal within the family; the philosophy that suggests that a course of events might be entirely accidental (harking back to Coe's first novel) set against elaborate and all-too-convincing conspiracy theories. It's a very brave novel and one that will have the reader laughing aloud and bursting into tears. The broad sweep and structure recall Michael Moorcock's *Mother London,* which was a masterpiece. In many respects, not least for the way in which the cinema metaphor is employed at the end of part one, that description would not be out of place here.

Coe continued his sly self-reference, once again using the device of a story within the story in *The House of Sleep*. This novel within the novel describes a series of ''midnight kidnappings'' committed by ''a notorious criminal called the Owl,'' and the book us just one of the spectres that haunt the characters in *The House of Sleep*. At the center of the story is Dr. Gregory Dudden, who operates a sleep clinic in a nineteenth-century mansion named Ashdown—which just happened to be his dormitory in college more than a decade earlier. Reminiscences arise, old loves and conflicts are resurrected, and all in all, Coe amply satisfies his readers' hopes for an entertaining experience.

—Nicholas Royle

COETZEE, J(ohn) M(ichael)

Nationality: South African. **Born:** Cape Town, 9 February 1940. **Education:** The University of Cape Town, B.A. 1960, M.A. 1963; University of Texas, Austin, Ph.D. 1969. **Family:** Married in 1963 (divorced 1980); one son and one daughter. **Career:** Applications programmer, IBM, London, 1962–63; systems programmer, International Computers, Bracknell, Berkshire, 1964–65; Assistant Professor, 1968–71, and Butler Professor of English, 1984, State University of New York, Buffalo. Lecturer, 1972–83, and since 1984 Professor of General Literature, University of Cape Town. Hinkley Professor of English, Johns Hopkins University, Baltimore, 1986, 1989. **Awards:** CNA award 1978, 1980, 1983; James Tait Black Memorial prize, 1980; Faber Memorial award, 1980; Booker prize, 1983; Fémina prize (France), 1985; Jerusalem prize, 1987; *Sunday Express* Book of the Year award, 1990; Mondello prize (Italy), 1994; *Irish Times* International Fiction prize, 1995; Booker prize, 1999; Commonwealth prize for best book, 2000. D.Litt.: University of Strathclyde, Glasgow, 1985; State University of New York, 1989. Life Fellow, University of Cape Town; Fellow, Royal Society of Literature, 1988; Honorary Fellow, Modern Language Association (U.S.A.), 1989. **Agent:** Murray Pollinger, 222 Old Brompton Road, London SW5 0BZ, England. **Address:** P.O. Box 92, Rondebosch, Cape Province 7701, South Africa.

PUBLICATIONS

Novels

Dusklands (two novellas). Johannesburg, Ravan Press, 1974; London, Secker and Warburg, 1982; New York, Viking, 1985.

In the Heart of the Country. Johannesburg, Ravan Press, and London, Secker and Warburg, 1977; as *From the Heart of the Country*, New York, Harper, 1977.

Waiting for the Barbarians. London, Secker and Warburg, 1980; New York, Penguin, 1982.

Life and Times of Michael K. London, Secker and Warburg, 1983; New York, Viking, 1984.

Foe. Johannesburg, Ravan Press, and London, Secker and Warburg, 1986; New York, Viking, 1987.

Age of Iron. London, Secker and Warburg, and New York, Random House, 1990.

The Master of Petersburg. London, Secker and Warburg, and New York, Viking, 1994.

Disgrace. New York, Viking, 2000.

Other

White Writing: On the Culture of Letters in South Africa. New Haven, Connecticut, Yale University Press, 1988.

Doubling the Point. Cambridge, Harvard University Press, 1992.

Giving Offense: Essays on Censorship. Chicago, University of Chicago Press, 1996.

Boyhood: Scenes from Provincial Life. New York, Viking, 1997.

Contributor, *Politics, Leadership, and Justice.*. Chicago, Great Books Foundation, 1998.

Editor, with André Brink, *A Land Apart: A South African Reader*. London, Faber, 1986; New York, Viking, 1987.

Translator, *A Posthumous Confession*, by Marcellus Emants. Boston, Twayne, 1976; London, Quartet, 1986.

Translator, *The Expedition to the Baobab Tree*, by Wilma Stockenström. Johannesburg, Ball, 1983; London, Faber, 1984.

*

Critical Studies: *The Novels of J.M. Coetzee* by Teresa Dovey, Johannesburg, Donker, 1988; *Countries of the Mind: The Fiction of J.M. Coetzee* by Dick Penner, Westport, Connecticut, Greenwood Press, 1989; *Critical Perspectives on J.M. Coetzee*, edited by Graham Huggan and Stephen Watson, preface by Nadine Gordimer. New York, St. Martin's Press, 1996; *Colonization, Violence, and Narration in White South African Writing: Andre Brink, Breyten Breytenbach, and J. M. Coetzee* by Rosemary Jane Jolly. Athens, Ohio University Press, 1996; *J.M. Coetzee* by Dominic Head. New York, Cambridge University Press, 1997; *Critical Essays on J.M. Coetzee*, edited by Sue Kossew. New York, G. K. Hall, 1998.

* * *

J. M. Coetzee is one of the most significant white South African novelists to emerge in the latter half of the twentieth century. His work engages powerfully, though not always directly, with apartheid and its aftermath; but he also brings into the South African novel a concern with the nature of narrative that is more often associated with European and North American postmodernism. It is this combination of textual and political preoccupations, allied to a spare prose style and an unsparingly bleak vision, that gives Coetzee's work its distinctive quality.

Coetzee's indirect approach to apartheid and his questioning of narrative modes is evident in his first novel, *Dusklands* (1974). This combines and challenges two kinds of imperialist discourse. The first section traces the descent into madness of Eugene Dawn, who is analyzing psychological warfare in Vietnam for the U.S. Defense Department; the second, ''The Narrative of Jacobus Coetzee,'' is supposedly a piece of travel writing by an early explorer of the African Cape. The founding moment of Afrikaner identity, and U.S. imperialism in Vietnam, are thus linked together and ironically subverted. Coetzee's second novel, *In the Heart of the Country*

(1977), addressed the South African situation more directly. Its narrator, Magda, a white South African spinster who lives with her father on an isolated farm, provides an account made up of 266 numbered sections in which she gives versions of events that are often contradictory—for example, she twice describes killing her father, once with an axe and once with a gun. She also describes an unsuccessful attempt, after her father's burial, to form a new relationship with the black servants, Hendrik and Anna; her rape by Hendrik and her desertion by both servants; and her final revival of her father. The novel can be read as an allegory of the whole South African position in the 1970s, as white South Africans made increasingly desperate attempts to alter or escape from a situation that was growing more and more violent; it also raises the question of how to write about South Africa in this moment of transition. To an extent, the novel invokes and subverts the tradition of the *plaasroman*, the lyrical, idealized Afrikaner novel of country life; it also invokes and implicitly interrogates the European literary and philosophical heritage—that of Hegel and Beckett, for instance—that sometimes speaks through Magda.

Waiting for the Barbarians (1980) is narrated by the long-serving, liberal-minded magistrate in a frontier settlement in a vaguely specified ''Empire'' where the ruthless Colonel Joll is torturing supposed barbarians. The magistrate, observing Joll's activities, is forced to conduct an agonizing analysis of his own unavoidable complicity in oppression and to undergo torture himself after rescuing a ''barbarian'' girl. Finally, Joll's forces, and many inhabitants, abandon the settlement, leaving a remnant ''waiting for the barbarians.'' The novel can certainly be interpreted as a powerful image of the painful position of the South African white liberal under a violent and paranoid apartheid regime; but it also takes on a more general significance, as a fictional dramatization of one of the ways in which imperial regimes—not only in South Africa—can end.

If *Waiting for the Barbarians* was, for some critics, too general in its significance, *The Life and Times of Michael K* (1983) was more specific, at least in its setting: modern South Africa in an era of armed struggle. Michael K is a non-white South African who apparently lives on the margins of politics and society. He leaves his post as a gardener in Cape Town to return his sick mother to the farm where she grew up. She dies on the way, but he continues the journey with her ashes. He finds what may be the farm of which his mother told him, now deserted by the white man, buries her ashes, and starts to cultivate the land. The grandson of the proprietor returns and drives K off, but, after a spell in hospital and in an internment camp, he escapes and goes back to the farm to grow pumpkins and melons. Arrested as a collaborator by South African soldiers who are pursuing guerrillas, K is interned in another camp, and the brief second section of the novel is supposedly by the camp doctor, who tries to understand K. But K escapes once more, and the last section of the novel rises to a powerfully lyrical close in which K imagines himself using a teaspoon on a long string to draw water from the shaft of a sabotaged pump. *The Life and Times of Michael K* is, characteristically for Coetzee, elusive in its explicit political stance. However, the novel's final affirmation of the possibility of survival and cultivation in the most difficult conditions can be seen as a symbol of a hope that will endure not only in the face of oppression but also beyond the immediate euphoria of liberation. *Michael K* won Coetzee the United Kingdom's most prestigious literary award, the Booker prize.

Foe (1986) is Coetzee's most sustained encounter with a founding text of imperialism and of the English novel, Daniel Defoe's *Robinson Crusoe* (1719). The story is supposedly told by Susan Barton, who is marooned on an island with ''Cruso'' and a Friday whose tongue has been cut out; in contrast to Defoe's Crusoe and Friday, Coetzee's duo focus simply on survival and build sterile stone terraces. Rescued and returned to England—Cruso dies on the voyage back—Susan and Friday seek out Daniel Foe—Defoe's original surname—to tell their story; Susan and Foe, however, become embroiled in a fight for control of the narrative of Cruso. Questions of authorship are shown not as abstract literary concerns but as bound up with questions of power, control, and empire; the kind of story that is told will have political implications and consequences.

Age of Iron (1990) returns to the contemporary South African situation. It takes the form of a long letter by Mrs. Curren to her daughter in the United States. Mrs. Curren is dying of bone cancer, and her physical disintegration is matched by her abandonment of her identification with the old South Africa as she registers the contrast between the country that the media portray and the violent reality of the ''age of iron'' around her that is exemplified, above all, by the deaths of the fifteen-year old son of her maid and his friend, shot by police. The novel is a kind of confession of complicity in apartheid with no one present to offer absolution—only the drunken down-and-out Vercueil, who does not even respond to Mrs. Curren's words. But this lack of response, Coetzee implies, may make her confession and renunciation less self-justifying, more complete.

The Master of Petersburg (1994) shifts to another site of political struggle, nineteenth-century Russia. In 1869 Coetzee's ''Dostoevsky'' returns from Europe to St. Petersburg to collect the papers of his dead stepson Pavel, who may have been murdered by the nihilist revolutionary Nechaev. Like *Foe, The Master of Petersburg* imagines the conflicts leading up to the emergence of a major novel—in this case, Dostoevsky's *The Devils* (1871–72; also translated as *The Possessed* and *The Demons*); and the issues of authorial control and responsibility are focused above all in the confrontation between Coetzee's ''Dostoevsky'' and Nechaev—and, as in *Foe*, there is a strong sense that such issues are not only literary but political.

Coetzee's memoir, *Boyhood* (1997), told in the third person and present tense, was followed by *Disgrace*, his seventh novel, and his first to be set in post-apartheid South Africa. Its protagonist is a fifty-two year old Professor of ''Communications'' who falls into disgrace and loses his university post as a result of a brief affair with a female student. He goes to the Eastern Cape to stay with his lesbian daughter, who is raped by three Africans who attack their home. His daughter does not report the rape and, finding herself pregnant as a result, decides to go ahead and have the child, despite the disgrace involved. *Disgrace* is a complex, compact, immensely resonant novel about coming to terms with disgrace—transgression, guilt, and punishment in radically changing times. It alludes to the ways in which white South Africans have to come to terms with their guilt at their complicity in the apartheid regime; at the same time it raises the issue of how black South Africans, in the post-apartheid world, will deal with their own transgressions; and it also poses the more global question of male culpability for the oppression of women. *Disgrace* once again gained Coetzee the Booker prize, making him the first novelist to win it twice. It also demonstrated his capacity, in his late fifties, to produce a fiction that could engage powerfully with the complexities and contradictions, not only of post-apartheid South Africa, but also of the postcolonial and postfeminist world.

—Nicolas Tredell

COLE, Barry

Nationality: British. **Born:** Woking, Surrey, 13 November 1936. **Education:** Balham Secondary School, London. **Military Service:** Served in the Royal Air Force, 1955–57. **Family:** Married Rita Linihan in 1958; three daughters. **Career:** Since 1958, staff member, Reuters news agency, London; reporter, 1965–70, and senior editor, 1974–94, Central Office of Information, London. Northern Arts Fellow, universities of Newcastle-upon-Tyne and Durham, 1970–72. **Address:** 68 Myddelton Square, London EC1R 1XP, England.

Publications

Novels

A Run Across the Island. London, Methuen, 1968.
Joseph Winter's Patronage. London, Methuen, 1969.
The Search for Rita. London, Methuen, 1970.
The Giver. London, Methuen, 1971.
Doctor Fielder's Common Sense. London, Methuen, 1972.

Poetry

Blood Ties. London, Turret, 1967.
Ulysses in the Town of Coloured Glass. London, Turret, 1968.
Moonsearch. London, Methuen, 1968.
The Visitors. London, Methuen, 1970.
Vanessa in the City. London, Trigram Press, 1971.
Pathetic Fallacies. London, Eyre Methuen, 1973.
The Rehousing of Scaffardi. Richmond, Surrey, Keepsake Press, 1976.
Dedications. Nottingham, Byron Press, 1977.

*

Barry Cole comments:

I have no general statement to make about my novels, but the epigraphs which precede *The Giver* may say more than any collected exegeses.

* * *

Barry Cole's novels have one striking thing in common: they are extremely well-written. It may, of course, be said that to write well is not so much a virtue in a novelist as a necessity. Yet the fact is that the majority of novelists lack Cole's gifts of verbal precision, wit, exact ear for conversation, and his feeling for the elastic possibilities of language, the way it can be stretched and twisted to provide unexpected meanings and insights. No doubt the fact that he is also a very fine poet accounts for much of his virtue as a writer of prose, but this should not be taken to mean that he writes poetic prose. On the contrary: his style is as free as possible from those encrustations of adjective and epithet that identify "fine" writing.

A Run Across the Island is a brilliant *tour de force* and for it Cole invented a form that he has used for all his subsequent novels. Although by far the larger part of the novel is seen through the eyes of its hero, Robert Haydon, there is no straightforward narrative or division into chapters. Instead, we move about in time, each remembered detail or incident given a section, small or large, that is juxtaposed against others. By the end of the novel, however, the different incidents have been worked out and together compose one man's life, and it has been so resourcefully done that we have a much more *real* sense of a man's identity than we would have through a straightforward narrative.

The major theme of *A Run Across the Island* is, perhaps, of loneliness, of the difficulties of establishing relationships, of the slippery impermanence of friendship and love, and this theme is also present in the next novel. *Joseph Winter's Patronage* is, however, very different from *A Run Across the Island* in that its characters are almost exclusively old people. Indeed, the novel is mostly set in a retirement home, and the novelist manages with great sensitiveness to create the feeling of the home itself and of its inhabitants. *Joseph Winter's Patronage* is the most touching and warmly sympathetic novel that Cole has so far written.

By contrast, *The Search for Rita* is the most glittering. It is an extremely elegant novel, but the elegance is not one that marks how far its author stands fastidiously aloof from life. It is rather that the mess of life is met by a keen-eyed wit that can be ironic, self-deprecatory, satiric, and bawdy by turns. Style means everything in a novel of this kind, and the novelist's style does not let him down.

—John Lucas

COLEGATE, Isabel (Diana)

Nationality: British. **Born:** Lincolnshire, 10 September 1931. **Education:** A boarding school in Shropshire and at Runton Hill School, Norfolk. **Family:** Married Michael Briggs in 1953; one daughter and two sons. **Career:** Literary agent, Anthony Blond Ltd., London, 1952–57. **Awards:** W.H. Smith Literary award, 1981. Hon. M.A.: University of Bath, 1988. Fellow, Royal Society of Literature, 1981. **Agent:** Peters Fraser and Dunlop, 503–504 The Chambers, Chelsea Harbour, Lots Road, London SW10 0XF, England. **Address:** Midford Castle, Bath BA1 7BU, England.

Publications

Novels

The Blackmailer. London, Blond, 1958.
A Man of Power. London, Blond, 1960.
The Great Occasion. London, Blond, 1962.
Statues in a Garden. London, Bodley Head, 1964; New York, Knopf, 1966.
The Orlando Trilogy. London, Penguin, 1984.
    Orlando King. London, Bodley Head, 1968; New York, Knopf, 1969.
    Orlando at the Brazen Threshold. London, Bodley Head, 1971.
    Agatha. London, Bodley Head, 1973.
News from the City of the Sun. London, Hamish Hamilton, 1979.
The Shooting Party. London, Hamish Hamilton, 1980; New York, Viking Press, 1981.
Deceits of Time. London, Hamish Hamilton, and New York, Viking, 1988.
The Summer of the Royal Visit. London, Hamish Hamilton, 1991; New York, Knopf, 1992.
Winter Journey. London, Hamish Hamilton, 1995.

Short Stories

A Glimpse of Sion's Glory. London, Hamish Hamilton, and New York, Viking, 1985.

* * *

> The English will never turn Communist, they're such snobs. An English Communist could have a duke at gunpoint; if he asked him to stay for the weekend he'd drop the gun and dash off to Moss Bros to hire a dinner-jacket.
>
> (*Agatha*)

Isabel Colegate's fiction dramatizes the English obsession with aristocracy and sensitivity to the nuances of class, even in the 20th century when traditional aristocratic power was declining. Against a backdrop of post-World War II global unrest, Colegate's first three novels, *The Blackmailer, A Man of Power,* and *The Great Occasion,* depict both the aristocrats' alliances with new sources of wealth and their inability to comprehend the welfare state: ''... a five-day week, holidays with pay, pensions, free this, free that ... There's no sense of values'' (*The Blackmailer*). Her later novels, *Statues in a Garden, The Orlando Trilogy,* and *The Shooting Party,* root these changes in the disintegrating world immediately before and after World War I. *The Blackmailer,* a ''self-making'' man of lower-middle-class origins, extorts money from the widow of a Korean War hero primarily to gain entry to the hero's ancestral home and family and complete his identification with the dead man. The thriller elements are not a sound basis for Colegate's social satire, though her comedy supports the anti-romantic ending triggered by the heroine's class loyalties. (Similarly the recent story ''Distant Cousins'' in *A Glimpse of Sion's Glory* uneasily mixes a science-fiction thriller plot with cold war satire in the service of a plea for world peace and tolerance.)

The protagonist of *A Man of Power,* a capitalist of lower-middle-class origins who has risen through wartime opportunities, plans to wed an impoverished aristocratic beauty because of her ''mystery'' and ability to reshape his image; his first wife and former secretary is inadequate to the role: ''It's always the wives that give them away.'' Upper-class characters respond as much to the protagonist's mystique as to his money: the aristocrat's daughter suffers a painful initiation into his chaotic world through her love for him. (Like the charismatic tycoon and the society beauty, the vulnerable young girl is a staple of Colegate's fiction.) Unfortunately, the novel's sentimentality undercuts the serious treatment of its themes.

The Great Occasion focuses on middle-class vulnerability by interweaving the lives of a magnate, whose success stemmed partly from his marriage to an upper-class wife, and his five daughters in a world that rejects his business integrity and their talents and idealism: ''... I expect she'll soon level down to the others.'' The tone wavers because of Colegate's mixing of Waughesque satire with family saga, but her skill at maintaining several story lines anticipates *Statues in a Garden* and *The Shooting Party.* Like these later works, *The Great Occasion* presents the natural world as both ironical commentary on human futility and a source of reconciliation to existence.

Developed cinematically in short scenes, *Statues in a Garden* portrays a group of aristocrats just before World War I and flashes forward to the futures implicit in their actions. A quasi-incestuous affair, one of many in Colegate's fiction, between a society beauty and her nephew, whom she has adopted, suggests the destructive narcissism of aristocratic lives. The nephew and aunt proceed to dubious futures, his business speculations undermining the stability of her settled world. Colegate controls detail and tone, the heroine's uncomprehending ''... not a very *close* sort of incest, surely?'' perfectly defining her shallowness and ability to survive. Though the nephew's schematic significance as disturber of both sexual and economic order seems obtrusive, the novel uses this type of symbolism more gracefully than *The Orlando Trilogy.*

The protagonist of *Orlando King,* raised on a remote island by his adoptive father to protect him from civilization, carries a heavy symbolic burden besides his name: his hammer toes and damaged eyesight link him with Oedipus, as do, more obviously, his partial responsibility for his father's death and marriage to his aristocratic stepmother. The participants learn the truth only after many years: '''I suppose you really think ... that I look old enough to be Orlando's mother.' 'Could be' he said.''' Though amusing, this dialogue puzzles; surely the stepmother's resultant breakdown and death and the consequences for the next generation make this stress on her superficiality misleading. Orlando's sense of guilt destroys his business and political careers in the England of the 1930s that is increasingly dominated by men like his father who capitalize on wartime connections and marriages to aristocrats. If such outsiders lust after class status, aristocrats display equal fascination with the challenge these newcomers represent. Orlando's initial success in emulating his father is presumably emblematic, but his other actions confuse the novel's political and social pattern. The incest motif seems especially intrusive: in *Orlando at the Brazen Threshold* he successfully pursues the mistress of his nephew, whom his daughter marries. Orlando's behavior seems motivated by a need to support the novel's symbolism and lacks the complexity that the interior monologues, letters, and searching dialogue initially promise. Similarly, the elliptical narration with flashwords and allusions to incidents as yet unknown to the reader creates an atmosphere of elusive reality puzzling to the characters through whose voices we perceive it; but then Colegate periodically destroys this rich ambiguity by over-explicit summary: ''Stephen and Paul were Orlando's half-brothers. Their father Leonard had in the far-off and scarcely imaginable days of his youth also been the father of Orlando ...'' Colegate's epigrams about the inevitable failure of Communism in a class-obsessed society clash with her serious treatment of radicals, who seem as futile and foolishly motivated as her capitalists: Graham, who dies on the Loyalist side in Spain (*Orlando King*); Paul, who sells secrets to Russia during the Burgess era because of family problems (*Agatha*). Set during the Suez crisis, *Agatha* focuses on the girl's Forsteresque commitment to Paul rather than to England, partly because of Orlando's earlier ruthlessness. (Raymond, who defects to Russia in the title story of *A Glimpse of Sion's Glory,* has more ambiguous, even more attractive, motives than these earlier characters.)

Negative aristocratic images abound in the trilogy, sometimes mocking the physical effects of reclusiveness: ''his little eyes directed their feeble gaze down the long organ through which his frail tones appeared to emerge (eugenically speaking, his breeding was a disaster).'' Another aristocrat embodies more damning inadequacies, from 1930s appeasement, through Suez arrogance to personal betrayal of Agatha in the name of patriotism. Though Colegate effectively dramatizes the peculiar fusion of charm, decency, egotism, and plaintive misunderstanding that characterizes such aristocrats, her trilogy fails to provide an adequate political context that explains the contribution of this class to the general malaise of English civilization.

Like other Colegate characters, Sir Randolph Nettleby, protagonist of *The Shooting Party,* set in 1913, prophesies, ''An age, perhaps a civilization, is coming to an end.'' The novel, Colegate's best, carefully places the Nettleby estate in its geographical and historical contexts and focuses on those details of dress and behavior that reveal the beauty and vulnerability of country life on the eve of destruction. Sir Randolph is at times over-generous in assessing his class: ''If you take away the proper functions of an aristocracy, what can it do but play games too seriously?'' But the novel's stress on the violence of these games redresses the balance: ''It was hard to remember that the keen concentration of their hunting instinct was not directed at their fellow man.'' The callousness of a visiting Hungarian count, however, helps define, by contrast, the English commitment to their tenants and to their land. The highflown language and sentiments that impress servants have real substance. The narrowness of the aristocratic code, the complacency with which aristocrats experience their rituals is offset by their willingness to limit their freedom for the sake of standards: Hartlib's agonizing headaches are the price his inbred nerves exact for his performance as a hunter. However foolish, the codes of this class give form and meaning to their lives, including the duty to sacrifice these lives in war. Restraining the epigrammatical tendencies that unbalanced earlier works, Colegate fuses an ironical view of society with a moving appreciation of its painful pleasures.

Colegate's story ''The Girl Who Had Lived Among Artists'' (*A Glimpse of Sion's Glory*) comes closest of all her work to the skill of *The Shooting Party.* Set in pre-World War II Bath, the story both illustrates and refutes the idea that ''The snobbery of England in the 1930s was the real thing,'' as it examines the complex attitudes of the classes toward each other, the even more painful situation among civil servants and merchants in India, where the English condescend to each other and unite against the Indians, the desperate anxieties of European refugees who stress the superiority of their own culture, the ambiguous social position of clerics, and the special relation between artists and the upper classes (''... there are three things that make people classless, talent, beauty, and something else I've forgotten''). What flaws this brilliantly conceived picture of the dangers of such a society is Colegate's attempt to pack so much rich material into a short story. Though the details are effective and the dialogue often chilling, the treatment is ultimately too truncated for such thematic wealth.

Colegate's 1988 novel, *Deceits of Time,* explores the mystery of a World War I hero's apparent pro-German activities before and during World War II and reveals the familiar milieu of social tensions and adjustments that *may* explain his actions. The middle-class biographer and Jewish holocaust survivor understandably learn much about themselves while investigating the hero's life, but the modest triumph of the novel is the gradual revelation of the character of the hero's aristocratic widow. Her values, however limited, are allowed their surprising victory. Despite the novel's occasionally fussy structure and tendency toward undramatic summary of other characters and their motives, this portrait is equal to the best in *The Shooting Party.* Colegate's fiction offers an impressive demonstration of genuine talent finding its strengths and continually refining its craft.

—Burton Kendle

COLLINS, Hunt

See HUNTER, Evan

COLVIN, James

See MOORCOCK, Michael

CONNAUGHTON, Shane

Nationality: Northern Irish. **Born:** County Cavan, Northern Ireland. **Career:** Screenwriter, actor, and producer for both film and television, 1980s—.

PUBLICATIONS

Novels

A Border Station. New York, St. Martin's Press, 1989.
The Run of the Country. New York, St. Martin's Press, 1992.

Plays

Screenplays: *My Left Foot* (with Jim Sheridan), Boston, Faber and Faber, 1989; Miramax Films, 1989; *The Playboys* (with Kerry Crabbe), Samuel Goldwyn Company, 1992; *O Mary This London,* produced 1994; *The Run of the Country,* Columbia Pictures, 1995.

Other

A Border Diary (nonfiction). London, Faber and Faber, 1995.

* * *

Much of Shane Connaughton's writing is concerned with the notion of boundaries or borders, and interest in these artificial constructs is reflected in the titles of two of his works, *A Border Station* and *A Border Diary.* Considering that Connaughton was born and raised in the county of Cavan, bordering Northern Ireland, this is not surprising. His novel *The Run of the Country* is a semi-autobiographical tale of adolescence that takes Cavan as its setting. It is an Irish coming-of-age story with all the obvious episodes included, but Connaughton imbues these moments with an original flair and unexpected twists. At times, he adopts or plays with cliches common to Irish literature—most particularly those of the hard domineering father and the saintly suffering wife.

Following the death of his mother, the unnamed protagonist attempts to live with his authoritative and headstrong father, a police sergeant who patrols the volatile borderland between Protestant and Catholic counties. He may be an authority figure, but he also expresses much of the rage and frustration that is a product of this seemingly unresolvable political-religious situation. While their love for each other is evident, the absence of a tempering female presence makes their living together impossible. The protagonist moves in with his friend, Prunty, and his mother, and begins an apprenticeship in which he learns about women, nature, fighting, smuggling, and the political realities of contemporary Ireland.

But a *bildungsroman* is incomplete without a love story. The protagonist is soon enamored of Annagh Lee, a young woman who lives in Fermanagh, across the border. This forbidden and doomed love affair serves to highlight some of the political realities that govern the country. Class and religion are the wedges that drive these young people apart. The world of the novel is a troubled place, and Connaughton emphasizes the arbitrariness of the border and the ways in which it influences the construction of identity. Death is everywhere, and the constant reminders of its presence serve to underline the absurdity of drawing lines in the sand: "It appears we destroy. And so we do. But the country remains long after we're gone. The land swallows us in the end." Connaughton's writing captures the volatility and unpredictability of border life. And the metaphor of crossing borders is extended throughout the novel to include other kinds of crossing—developmental, emotional, moral.

Despite its occasional doses of humor, the novel remains a bleak one. Annagh is sent away after she suffers a miscarriage and Prunty dies a painful death, crushed under a tractor. It is only later that the protagonist learns of Prunty's involvement with the IRA and the novel ends with a condemnation of the political situation. Resignation runs deep in Connaughton's writing. For individuals who have known nothing but tense and troubling circumstances the prospect of peace seems nothing more than an impossible dream. As the protagonist prepares to leave at the end of the novel, his father observes, "As long as that Border's there fools' blood is all you'll get in this country. If they wanted peace they wouldn't put a border up, would they? A border is a wall. Misguided fools will always smash their heads against it." This sentiment runs throughout most of the author's writing.

Published prior to *The Run of the Country*, *A Border Station* is a companion piece offering a series of seven loosely connected stories that focus on selected moments in the life of the same protagonist as a young boy, and can be read as a composite novel. We find the same characters and many of the same concerns. The innocence of the boy is used to good effect to highlight questions that have gone unasked, situations that have, for too long, been taken for granted. The answers provided by the adults are not always entirely satisfying. The conflictual relationship with his father and the Oedipal attraction to his mother are emphasized to a greater degree than they are in *The Run of the Country* (one of the stories, "Out," deals with the protagonist's struggle to remain sleeping in his mother's bed). Each story, in fact, describes some form of conflict between father and son, with the mother often acting as an ineffectual intermediary. In fact, mother and son often weather the storm by conspiring together. The events described are often simple everyday ones, but they are momentous in the life of the boy. In "Beatrice," for example, he witnesses his seemingly infallible father intentionally cut down a better tree for firewood than the one his benefactor had indicated, out of resentment. Connaughton resists the cliches and finally paints a realistic portrait of the relationship between a hard father and a son who wants nothing more than to please.

Like one of his contemporaries, Patrick McCabe, Connaughton returns to the 1950s of his childhood and adolescence as the setting for much of his work. Special attention is paid to the wit of dialogue, the quick turn of phrase, the play and the punning of words. And he uses narrative shifts, moving from present to past and back again, filling in plot details as they are needed, but also reflecting his protagonist's thought patterns.

In terms of popularity, Connaughton is perhaps best known for his screenplays, which highlight his strengths—his love of set pieces, and his play with dialogue. These screenplays also use the same setting and include a number of the same characters, including the police sergeant father (in *The Playboys*). In *My Left Foot* (co-written with director Jim Sheridan), the story of Irish painter and writer Christy Brown, Connaughton revisits the theme of the overbearing father and suffering mother. Born into a poor Catholic family and stricken with cerebral palsy, Christy must struggle to accomplish the most rudimentary activities. His eventual success and fame are an example of the triumph of the will over the most adverse circumstances, both physical and familial.

A Border Diary, a compilation of notes Connaughton kept during the making of the film *The Run of the Country*, serves to illuminate some of the themes and situations addressed in the novel. While witnessing the filming in his hometown of Redhills, Connaughton is forced to contend with the disparities among his imagination, the reality of Redhills, and the further discrepant interpretations of the filmmakers. The director and the actors interpret his screenplay in ways that differ from the scenes playing in his head. The Ireland of his youth is no longer, and the antagonisms dividing the land have only deepened. His attempts at reconciling the differences and, at times, raging against them are a powerful metaphor of Ireland's continuing struggle with the past and conflicting visions of its identity.

—Tim Gauthier

CONROY, (Donald) Pat(rick)

Nationality: American. **Born:** Atlanta, Georgia, 26 October 1945. **Education:** The Citadel, B.A. 1967. **Family:** Married 1) Barbara Bolling in 1969 (divorced 1977), one daughter and two stepdaughters; 2) Lenore Gurewitz in 1981, one daughter, one stepson and one stepdaughter. **Career:** High school teacher, Beaufort, South Carolina, 1967–69; elementary schoolteacher, Daufuskie, South Carolina, 1969. **Awards:** Anisfield-Wolf award (Cleveland Foundation), 1972; National Endowment for the Arts award for achievement in education, 1974; Georgia Governor's award for Arts, 1978; Lillian Smith award for fiction (Southern Regional Council), 1981; inducted into South Carolina Hall of Fame, Academy of Authors, 1988; Thomas Cooper Society Library award (Thomas Cooper Library, University of South Carolina), 1995; South Carolina Governor's award in the Humanities for Distinguished Achievement (South Carolina Humanities Council), 1996; Humanitarian award (Georgia Commission on the Holocaust), 1996; Lotos Medal of Merit in Recognition of Outstanding Literary Achievement, 1996. **Agent:** IMG-Bach Literary Agency, 22 East 71st Street, New York, New York 10021–4911, U.S.A.

Publications

Novels

The Boo. Verona, Virginia, McClure Press, 1970.
The Water is Wide. Boston, Houghton, 1972.
The Great Santini. Boston, Houghton, 1976.
The Lords of Discipline. Boston, Houghton, 1980.
The Prince of Tides. Boston, Houghton, 1986.
Beach Music. New York, Nan A. Talese/Doubleday, 1995.

Plays

Screenplays: *The Prince of Tides,* Columbia Pictures, 1991.

Other

Introduction, *Even White Boys Get the Blues: Kudzu's First Ten Years* by Doug Marlette. New York, Times Books, 1992.
Foreword, *Savannah Seasons: Food and Stories from Elizabeth on 37th* by Elizabeth Terry with Alexis Terry. New York, Doubleday, 1996.
Preface, *Gone with the Wind* by Margaret Mitchell. New York, Scribner, 1996.
Foreword, *Entertaining for Dummies* by Suzanne Williamson with Linda Smith. Foster City, California, IDG Books Worldwide, 1997.
Introduction, *Of Time and the River: A Legend of Man's Hunger in His Youth* by Thomas Wolfe. New York, Scribner, 1999.

*

Critical Studies: *Pat Conroy: A Critical Companion* by Landon C. Burns, Westport, Connecticut, Greenwood Press, 1996.

* * *

In a sense, once you've read one Conroy novel, you've read them all, for characters, themes, and setting remain fairly constant, regardless of any given novel's plot. As an ideological son of both William Faulkner and Thomas Wolfe, Conroy places his novels squarely in the South. He even writes about the perpetual themes of the Southern artist, such as family conflict, racism, a sense of place, and coming of age. As a result, each novel is like looking at oneself in the mirror only once every few years: the basic features remain the same with only slight variations as time passes.

So where lies the appeal of Pat Conroy? Why do his novels become instant bestsellers? Why do diehard fans return for more, knowing that each novel will be remarkably like the last? Answers to these questions must lie somewhere in Conroy's use of the language and his sense of his native South, both its geographical aspects and its struggles with timeless issues. Even if the story and characters are the same, Conroy entices the reading public every time.

Conroy's first two books were strictly autobiographical in nature. *The Boo*, a tribute to a respected teacher, was written and published by Conroy while he was still a student at the Citadel Military Academy in Charleston, South Carolina, a locale that recurs, both generally and specifically, in many of his novels. His second book, *The Water is Wide*, is somewhat of an exposé, chronicling his experiences teaching poor, disadvantaged children on Daufuskie Island, off the coast of South Carolina. Conroy began teaching at the height of idealism but realized quickly that fighting ''the system'' was more difficult than he expected. This personal experience engendered a frequent theme in his novels: seeking the approval of any authority, be it institutional or individual, is a vain pursuit. Instead, one must find intrinsic worth in standing for values held within. Because of his disrespect for the school's administration and his unconventional teaching style, Conroy was fired after only one year. He may have lost his job, but he gained material for more books than just one. He also garnered an award from the National Humanitarian Association for his work on Daufuskie Island.

While *The Boo* and *The Water is Wide* are strictly autobiographical, Conroy's subsequent ''novels'' are more correctly termed ''autobiographical fiction,'' for characters, places, and even plot often reflect his own life. Conroy's 1976 novel *The Great Santini* begins a common theme in both Conroy's work and his life: family conflict. Over and over again, we read of the father with a strong military connection, typically a Marine Corps pilot, who is physically and mentally abusive but elicits a mixture of love, loyalty, and fear from his son, who is usually the protagonist of the novel. Bull Meecham, the unchallengeable ''Great Santini,'' is a South Carolina Catholic, like all of Conroy's protagonists, and a Marine fighter pilot of 20-plus years. Ben Meecham, the son, is a young man coming of age—a son in conflict with his father. Though he initially tries to reach the stature of his father, he despises his father's authoritarianism and finally realizes that he is a worthwhile human being, with or without his father's approval. When Ben finally breaks away from his father's tyranny, he does so through a symbolic basketball game in which he becomes the first person to beat his father at anything. In some areas of the South, sports have become almost an institutionalized religion, and Conroy employs this arena as the archetypal battle between good and evil—a microcosm of life itself, full of rules yet pervaded by chaos. In fact, most of Ben's role models and father figures are coaches. After his victory, Ben seems to make a clean break from his father's authority, yet he puts on his father's fighter jacket when his father crashes his plane, seemingly illustrating Conroy's feelings toward his own father. Although Conroy's memories of his father have been overshadowed by ill will, Conroy admits that lurking beneath those negative feelings is a certain degree of affection and respect.

Conroy's 1980 novel *The Lords of Discipline* contains the same sort of father figure, only in the form of an institution rather than an individual. However, the novel does develop Conroy's archetypal mother with a depth not accomplished in *The Great Santini*. Similar to the fathers, the mothers in Conroy's novels are reflections of his own mother, whom he once described as ''a beautiful Southerner out of *Gone With the Wind*.'' Conroy's mothers are from the ''Old South'': typically aristocratic women (or women who aspire to social heights) who are refined, educated, lovers of art and literature. In *The Lords of Discipline* the character Abigail St. Croix epitomizes the Conroy mother, as she teaches Will McLean, the best friend of her son Tradd and the novel's protagonist, ''the difference between Hepplewhite and Regency, and between Chippendale and Queen Anne.'' The family's lineage goes so deeply into South Carolina's history that ''a passing knowledge of the Tradd-St. Croix mansion was a liberal education in itself.''

The Lords of Discipline is also the stage for new developments in Conroy's repertoire of themes: racism, betrayal, and tradition. Racism is a key issue as Will, a senior at the Carolina Military Institute (Conroy's fictional version of The Citadel), is called upon to protect the school's first black student during the Civil Rights/Vietnam era. The brutality of military life comes not from a father but from the institution itself and the elitism it transfers to its students. CMI is similar to the stereotypical, small, Southern town, with its closeness and sense of tradition and security. This close-knit setting operates much like the Southern barber shop or pool hall, where men gather to find comfort in orthodoxy or plot a lynching, should someone dare violate the customs of the community. This demand for conformity yields The Ten, a hate group on campus that operates much like a lynch mob. Even the stereotypical ''crooked sheriff'' is present in the character of General Durrell, who at first seems to only ignore the presence of The Ten but, as the reader learns, actually participates in its activities.

Will witnesses a great deal of cruelty at CMI toward any student viewed as different by The Ten, yet he feels a fierce love of the school and its traditions. Not only must he deal with his conflicting feelings toward the school, but he must also face betrayal by Tradd, who is not only a member of city's aristocratic elite but also of The Ten, after his roommates defy the school's code of honor. Through these circumstances, Will confronts the ultimate question: does he remain true to the traditions of the academy or to his personal sense of honor?

Although Conroy's books always take place in Beaufort, Savannah, Charleston or some variety of these cities, the importance of the South as a geographical locale is most obvious in his 1986 novel *Prince of Tides*. Though Conroy was born in Georgia and moved a great deal due to his father's military career, he bears deep connections to the southeast coast of South Carolina, especially Beaufort, where he graduated from high school. Some of his most lyrical passages are pastoral descriptions that make South Carolina sound like the Garden of Eden. Though Conroy's primary literary influences, Faulkner and Wolfe, rarely varied from their respective Yoknapatawpha County, Mississippi, and Altamont, North Carolina, Conroy does take his characters to distant places; however, they always make it ''home.''

In *Prince of Tides*, Tom Wingo's twin sister, successful but schizophrenic feminist poet Savannah, has moved to New York to escape the oppressions she feels in the South as a woman. Hoping to help Savannah, Tom goes to New York to open their childhoods to her therapist, Susan Lowenstein, and figuratively returns home through many anecdotal flashbacks, which are prime examples of Conroy's lyricism. Through Savannah and Tom's brother Luke, Conroy picks up the ''Lost Cause'' myth, which originated in the portrayal of Confederate soldiers as noble warriors protecting their beloved homeland from the rapacious, vile North. In this case, Luke sacrifices his life, not fighting off Yankees but battling the Atomic Energy Commission, which planned to build plutonium production plants on their beloved island. Conroy also utilizes the stereotypical ''good ol' boy,'' a phrase actually created by Thomas Wolfe that connotes a blue collar, outdoorsman who is deeply patriotic and unwaveringly honest. Wingo slips into this role as he comfortably teaches a ''Yankee'' youth to play football and plays the redneck at a party of elite New Yorkers given by Lowenstein, with whom he has an affair.

While *Prince of Tides* travels the country to some degree, *Beach Music* travels the world but still keeps South Carolina at the center of its vision. In *Beach Music*, Jack McCall takes his daughter from South Carolina to Rome after his wife Shyla commits suicide, but he is drawn back to Charleston by the mystery of her death and learns of her parents' roots in the Holocaust that so haunted Shyla's life. McCall's life in Rome takes up a great deal of the narrative, but Nazi Germany becomes as much a real part of the setting as any city because it has pervaded every moment of Shyla's life. As Conroy writes, ''The Foxes' house on the Point in Waterford was simply an annex of Bergen-Belsen, a rest stop on the way to the crematoriums.''

While Conroy's popularity has never been in question, the critical assessment of his novels has been mixed. Only one book devoted to his work exists. *Pat Conroy: A Critical Companion,* by Landon C. Burns, contains analyses of all of Conroy's books, plus chapters on biography and genre. Other criticism has been confined to reviews at the release of each book and scattered analyses in critical journals. While Burns's assessments are largely positive, many feel Conroy has ''sold out'' to Hollywood since all his books, except for *The Boo*, have been made into feature films. He has also been criticized for melodrama and sensationalism, and scenes like the tiger attack in *Prince of Tides* and the trial scene at the end of *The Lords of Discipline* give some credence to this criticism.

However, few challenge the emotional appeal of his novels, and his popularity remains steadfast. If a reader has experienced a Conroy novel before, he knows the book will be flawed, he knows the book is 500-plus pages, and he knows the characters are, in many ways, the same ones he knew in the last Conroy novel. But in ways, it's like returning to old friends and familiar places, and the lyricism of the prose is more than most readers can resist.

—Melissa Simpson

COOK, David

Nationality: British. **Born:** Preston, Lancashire, 21 September 1940. **Education:** The Royal Academy of Dramatic Art, London, 1959–61. **Career:** Since 1961 professional actor. Writer-in-residence, St. Martin's College, Lancaster, 1982–83. **Awards:** Writers Guild award, 1977; American Academy E.M. Forster award, 1977; Hawthornden prize, 1978; Arts Council bursary, 1979; Southern Arts prize, 1985; Arthur Welton scholarship, 1991.; Odd Fellow Concern Book award, 1992. **Agent:** Greene and Heaton Ltd., 37 Goldhawk Road, London W12 8QQ. **Address:** 7 Sydney Place, London SW7 3NL, England.

PUBLICATIONS

Novels

Albert's Memorial. London, Secker and Warburg, 1972.
Happy Endings. London, Secker and Warburg, 1974.
Walter. London, Secker and Warburg, 1978; Woodstock, New York, Overlook Press, 1985.
Winter Doves. London, Secker and Warburg, 1979; Woodstock, New York, Overlook Press, 1985.
Sunrising. London, Secker and Warburg, 1984; Woodstock, New York, Overlook Press, 1986.
Missing Persons. London, Secker and Warburg, 1986.
Crying Out Loud. London, Secker and Warburg, 1988.
Walter and June. London, Secker and Warburg, 1989.
Second Best. London, Faber, 1991.

Uncollected Short Stories

''Finding Out,'' in *Mae West Is Dead,* edited by Adam Mars-Jones. London, Faber, 1983.
''Growing Away,'' in *Daily Telegraph* (London), 1994.

Plays

Square Dance (produced London, 1968).
If Only (televised 1984). Published in *Scene Scripts 3,* edited by Roy Blatchford, London, Longman, 1982.

Radio Play: *Pity,* 1989.

Television Plays: *Willy,* 1973; *Jenny Can't Work Any Faster,* 1975; *Why Here?,* 1976; *Couples* series, 1976; *A Place Like Home* series, 1976; *Repent at Leisure,* 1978; *Mary's Wife,* 1980; *Walter,* from his own novel, 1982; *Walter and June,* from his own novel, 1982; *If Only,* 1984; *Singles Week-end,* 1984; *Love Match,* 1986; *Missing Persons,* from his own novel, 1990; *Closing Numbers,* 1994; also scripts for Schools Television.

Screenplay: *Second Best,* from his own novel, 1994.

*

Film Adaptation: *Second Best,* 1994.

David Cook comments:

I began writing because I was an out-of-work actor, and needed an occupation which would be creatively satisfying. From the beginning, therefore, I brought an actor's concern with character to the task of writing fiction, and all my work is based on the same sort of act of empathy by which any actor brings life to an invented person. My discovery was that I now had to make this empathetic act for all my characters, not just one, seeing through their eyes, thinking their thoughts, feeling their feelings, and to do it without the help of a text; creating the text was up to me.

So the questions for me always are ''Who are you?'' ''How do you live?'' ''How have you arrived at this condition?'', and from the answers, logic will make a narrative. My first novel was about an old bag-lady whom I used to see sitting in doorways near South Kensington Station. I did not write a story; I wrote little pieces of what the details of her life might be, and after a while they began to form themselves into a story. All my work since, both the novels and the TV plays, has been based on empathy and research, and with a strong bias to those who have been called ''the walking wounded.'' When I decided that my fifth novel, *Sunrising,* should be set in a time which was not my own, the research became different in kind. I could no longer walk to Fleetwood or work with autistic children, but had to find my material in books, and while it is not exactly easy for someone with no academic education whatever to gain access to Oxford's Bodleian Library, it was done. Now that I have the taste, for it, I shall write a sequel to *Sunrising* one day, but I do not anticipate that I shall abandon the walking wounded of the here and now; they press in too closely.

* * *

David Cook is a stage and television actor who began to write novels in the early 1970s. His first novel, *Albert's Memorial,* was acclaimed for its originality and its sharply detailed prose, and subsequent novels like *Happy Endings* and *Walter* won prestigious prizes. Finely and delicately crafted, Cook's novels build the interior perspectives of his characters with a meticulous sense of authenticity and convincing detail. Characteristically, Cook's characters are isolated, lonely, inward-dwelling creatures whose consciousness is limited by some form of impairment or crippling circumstance. Physical or emotional indigents, they wander through a world they perceive intensely, although never accurately, in only bits and pieces. The juxtaposition of their partial points of view, which Cook always sees sympathetically, with an assumed, seldom stated ''normal'' point of view provides the tension and the emotional energy of the novels. *Albert's Memorial,* for example, concentrates on two isolated creatures: Mary, who after her husband's death, tries to live in the cemetery where he is buried and later tramps to the seaside resort where they spent their honeymoon, interested only in the conversations she holds with him inside her head, and Paul, who establishes trivial routines in his more geographically circumscribed wanderings after his homosexual lover suddenly dies. In *Walter,* the world is seen through Walter's autistic point of view, tracing the origins and effects of the debility that has led to his being institutionalized. Cook's central characters are all dependent on others, or institutions, or fantasies, for a survival they cannot manage on their own.

Cook's characters welcome impingements on their isolation, respond to relationships that break through their defenses or their occluded and partial visions. In *Albert's Memorial,* Mary and Paul connect, finally living with each other and sharing the fantasy of Mary's phantom pregnancy (she has been raped while tramping, and mistakes symptoms because she and her husband had avoided having children by never fully consummating their love). The relationship exists in mutual dependency, as does that between Walter from the earlier novel and June, a more intellectually functioning although emotionally severely unstable resident of the mental institution, as they escape to wander England in *Winter Doves.*

Characters like Mary and Paul, Walter and June, are seen against the background of contemporary England. The reader is always aware of an ordinary England dimly seen through the distorted half-lens of the impaired, and Cook never explicitly and seldom even implicitly provides any significant social commentary. The understated conflict between the characters and the larger world is often effectively rendered as comedy, as in the scene in which Paul, consulting a doctor because he is worried that Mary's ''pregnancy'' may be endangered, is so haltingly unable to articulate his concern that the doctor tests him for gonorrhea and administers a preventive injection. Similarly, wandering characters, in *Winter Doves* and other novels, duplicate a muted version of the comic picaresque, as they clash with the society that they cannot understand. Cook frequently depicts representatives of the Welfare State who try to help or control the indigents. These representatives, nurses, social workers, custodians in mental hospitals, doctors, and bureaucrats, are generally benign and well-intentioned, although unable to touch or assuage the deeper disturbances of the central characters. England's postwar emphasis on the social services is seen as praiseworthy and humane, although never finally relevant, as if no social issue or characterization is ever as significant as is the tenuous establishment of the individual identity.

Much of that identity in Cook's fictional world is physical and direct. He concentrates on immediate experience, describing with acute sensitivity how his characters touch, feel, reason, and communicate. Long passages detail the tiring efforts necessary to establish oneself as a squatter in an uncompleted office building or the elaborate preparation for and physical progress of the homosexual love affair. In the emphasis on the physical and emotional, the detailed representation of how the impaired see and feel, Cook is attempting to shape his carefully developed prose to get at a primal quality within the human creature. Cook's versions of the primal are never aggressive or animalistic; rather, his novels are most frequently populated by birds, pigeons and doves, in both plot and metaphor. The birds suggest the delicacy, fragility, and tenuousness of identity, the only kind of precarious existence these impaired creatures can manage. Cook sees the bird-like fragility and tenacity of the creatures of limited consciousness with enormous sympathy that, because of his writing's directness, specificity, and lack of pretense, never descends to sentimentality.

—James Gindin

COOPER, William

Pseudonym: Harry Summerfield Hoff. **Nationality:** British. **Born:** Crewe, Cheshire, 4 August 1910. **Education:** Christ's College, Cambridge, M.A. in physics 1933. **Military Service:** Served in the Royal Air Force, 1940–45. **Family:** Married Joyce Barbara Harris in 1951 (died 1988); two daughters. **Career:** Schoolmaster, Leicester, 1933–40; assistant commissioner, Civil Service Commission, London, 1945–58. Part-time personnel consultant, United Kingdom Atomic Energy Authority, 1958–72, Central Electricity Generating Board, 1960–72, Commission of European Community, 1972–73; assistant director, Civil Service Selection Board, 1973–75; member of the Board, Crown Agents, 1975–77; adviser, Millbank Technical Services, 1975–77; personnel consultant, Ministry of Overseas Development, 1978. Adjunct professor of English, Syracuse University, London Center, 1977–90. Fellow, Royal Society of Literature. **Address:** 22 Kenilworth Court, Lower Richmond Road, London SW15 1EW, England.

Publications

Novels

Trina (as H.S. Hoff). London, Heinemann, 1934; as *It Happened in PRK,* New York, Coward McCann, 1934.
Rhéa (as H.S. Hoff). London, Heinemann, 1937.
Lisa (as H.S. Hoff). London, Heinemann, 1937.
Three Marriages (as H.S. Hoff). London, Heinemann, 1946.
Scenes from Provincial Life. London, Cape, 1950.
The Struggles of Albert Woods. London, Cape, 1952; New York, Doubleday, 1953.
The Ever-Interesting Topic. London, Cape, 1953.
Disquiet and Peace. London, Macmillan, 1956; Philadelphia, Lippincott, 1957.
Young People. London, Macmillan, 1958.
Scenes from Married Life. London, Macmillan, 1961.
Scenes from Life (includes *Scenes from Provincial Life* and *Scenes from Married Life*). New York, Scribner, 1961.
Memoirs of a New Man. London, Macmillan, 1966.
You Want the Right Frame of Reference. London, Macmillan, 1971.
Love on the Coast. London, Macmillan, 1973.
You're Not Alone: A Doctor's Diary. London, Macmillan, 1976.
Scenes from Metropolitan Life. London, Macmillan, 1982.
Scenes from Later Life. London, Macmillan, 1983.
Scenes from Provincial Life, and Scenes from Metropolitan Life. New York, Dutton, 1983.
Scenes from Married Life, and Scenes from Later Life. New York, Dutton, 1984.
Immortality at Any Price. London, Sinclair Stevenson, 1991.

Uncollected Short Stories

''Ball of Paper,'' in *Winter's Tales 1.* London, Macmillan, and New York, St. Martin's Press, 1955.
''A Moral Choice,'' in *Winter's Tales 4.* London, Macmillan, and New York, St. Martin's Press, 1958.

Plays

High Life (produced London, 1951).
Prince Genji (produced Oxford, 1968). London, Evans, 1959.

Other

C.P. Snow. London, Longman, 1959; revised edition, 1971.
Shall We Ever Know? The Trial of the Hosein Brothers for the Murder of Mrs. McKay. London, Hutchinson, 1971; as *Brothers,* New York, Harper, 1972.
From Early Life (memoirs). London, Macmillan, 1990.

*

Manuscript Collection: Humanities Research Center, University of Texas, Austin.

Critical Studies: *Tradition and Dream* by Walter Allen, London, Phoenix House, 1964, as *The Modern Novel in Britain and the United States,* New York, Dutton, 1964; introduction by Malcolm Bradbury to *Scenes from Provincial Life,* London, Macmillan, 1969; *William Cooper the Novelist* by Ashok Kumar Sinha, New Delhi, Jnanada, 1977.

William Cooper comments:

(1972) I don't know that I specially believe in artists making statements about their own work. An artist's *work* is *his* statement. And that's that. The rest is for other people to say. Perhaps a writer whose original statement has turned out obscure may feel it useful to present a second that's more comprehensible—in that case I wonder why he didn't make the second one first.

Speaking for myself, *Scenes from Provincial Life* seems to me so simple, lucid, attractive, and funny that anyone who finds he can't read it probably ought to ask himself: ''Should I be trying to read books at all? Wouldn't it be better to sit and watch television or something?'' I write about the real world and real people in it. And I stick pretty close to what I've had some experience of. That's why *Scenes from Metropolitan Life,* which is also simple, lucid, attractive and funny, was suppressed. *Scenes from Married Life,* makes the third of a trilogy. *Albert Woods* and *Memoirs of a New Man* are about goings-on in the world of science and technology; *You Want the Right Frame of Reference* in the world of arts—they have an added touch of wryness and malice. An unusual marriage is the core of *Young People* and of *Disquiet and Peace,* the former set in the provinces in the '30s, the latter in Edwardian upperclass London—its small group of admirers thinks it's a beautiful book. *The Ever-Interesting Topic* is about what happens when you give a course of lectures on sex to a boarding school full of boys: what you'd expect. *Shall We Ever Know?* is a day-by-day account of a most surprising and mystifying murder trial, a kidnapping for ransom in which no trace whatsoever of the body was ever found, and two men were found guilty of murder.

(1981) *Love on the Coast,* my only novel to be set outside England, is about some former ''flower children'' in San Francisco who are working their way back into society by running an ''experimental'' theater. And *You're Not Alone* is the diary of a London doctor, a retired GP of some distinction, to whom people come to confide their sexual quirks—as a start he tells them they are not alone.

(1986) In 1981 the 30-year suppression of *Scenes from Metropolitan Life* ended, allowing the trilogy to be published complete. The three novels fit together thus: *Provincial Life*—Boy won't marry Girl; *Metropolitan Life*—same Girl now won't marry Boy; *Married Life*—Boy meets another Girl and marries happily every after. In 1983 I published *Scenes from Later Life* as a companion volume to the trilogy, with the characters in their sixties and seventies, learning to cope with old age—in the final chapter I can make you laugh and make you cry within seven pages.

(1991) For my next novel I decided to make a change and embark on obvious satire. I completed a first draft which needed quite a lot of work, and two things happened which led me to put it aside. The first was a long drawn-out personal tragedy, on which I was persuaded to do a piece for *Granta* about the last stages—the most intimate thing I have ever written. The second was a friend's suggestion which caught my fancy, that I should try my hand at autobiography (from which I had previously had an aversion). I decided to write down things I could remember happening between the ages of 2 and 17 just as they came into my head—pure reminiscence unsullied by ''research,'' *From Early Life,* short and delightful. And then I came back to my new departure, the satirical novel called *Immortality at Any Price.* The jacket by Willie Rushton discloses its nature—my response to a most wounding comment once made by an American reviewer: ''Who wants to read a novel by a nice guy?'' Well! ...

* * *

William Cooper is the pen-name of a novelist who had already published four novels under his own name, H.S. Hoff, when in 1950 he emerged with a new literary identity, and won a new literary reputation, with *Scenes from Provincial Life*—a book which quickly became a classic of a new kind of postwar realism and undoubtedly had a very powerful influence on the development of the English novel in the 1950s and since. A delightful and tough-minded story set among young provincial intellectuals, in a British midland town that bears a close resemblance to Leicester, over the crucial months of change and crisis leading up to the outbreak of World War II, *Scenes from Provincial Life*—published at a time when new fictional directions were uncertain and no real postwar movement had shown itself—became the forerunner of a whole sequence of novels which, in the postwar years, were to treat local English life, and the familiar and ordinary experience of recognizable people, with a fresh, youthful, exploratory, and critical curiosity. There can be little doubt that the book did encourage, and often considerably influence, a number of younger writers like John Braine, David Storey, Stanley Middleton, and Stan Barstow, some of whom directly expressed their indebtedness; and it certainly helped writers thereafter to find a sense of direction in the period after the decline both of Modernism and the political fiction of the 1930s. Its force was strengthened by the fact that Cooper—along with C.P. Snow, Pamela Hansford Johnson, and some other younger writers like Kingsley Amis, Philip Larkin, and John Wain—was deliberately reacting against the Bloomsbury-dominated climate of ''cultured'' and cosmopolitan experimentalism, and was seeking out a form of fiction much more social, empirical, realistic, and humanly substantial in character, and concerned with a felt sense of texture and the issues of contemporary British life.

This spirit in writing has sometimes been characterized by critics as middlebrow, and it was self-defined as provincial. But it asserted a humanist vigor and a closeness to familiar life in the practice of serious British writing at a time when, in literary traditions in other countries, the break with the past was disquieting and the signs of literary strain were being felt. Joyce had seemed to bring the modern novel into a cul-de-sac, and Cooper and others pointed to the value of the native tradition, his argument clearly strengthened by the fact that his own novel was not just one of the first, but one of the best, of a kind. In time the tendency he represented was to come to seem a narrowed view of the direction of fiction, but Cooper represented this kind of novel in all its strength. *Scenes from Provincial Life* tells the story of Joe Lunn, the young science master at a provincial grammar school, and his friends, nonconforming emotional radicals who know they are distant witnesses to the world's great events, as a kind of conflict between the force of history and the force of the familiar. Fearful of a German occupation of Britain, they plan their exiles; but the day-to-day world of provincial life (especially their complex sexual relationships) seems all that matters, and they finally opt for it. The story was to go on through three more volumes, plotting the development of Joe's life as a scientific adviser to government, as a writer and a married man. *Scenes from Metropolitan Life,* written in the 1950s but not published for legal reasons until 1982, brings the story into the postwar world, the London scene, and the world of Whitehall, renewing Joe's relationship with his former mistress Myrtle in the context of urban sexual mores. *Scenes from Married Life,* which appeared in 1961, is, unusually in contemporary fiction, a celebration of marital life, reinforcing Cooper's gift for exploring the private underside of the public world in which Joe is now an important figure. *Scenes from Later Life* brings most of the characters forward into the world of the late 1970s, with Joe haunted by retirement and the ailments of his mother. But, despite a rising quota of pain, the characteristic Cooper good humor and the sense of celebration of the familiar prevails, and the sequence sustains the spirit with which it started. As in the novels of C.P. Snow, but without Snow's stoical and even tragic pessimism, we see the new bloods turn into the men of place and power in an age in which the scientist and technologist become important public figures. But Cooper's social history gives way to a history of the domestic and the familiar, a comedy of daily life done with great luminosity and delicacy.

Cooper's other novels are all marked by the same commitment to familiar life, and the same luminous good humor. One, *Disquiet and Peace,* is an historical novel, set in the high-society milieu of Edwardian political and drawing-room life as the strange death of Liberal England is taking place; another, *Love on the Coast,* takes radical Californian lifestyle as its subject. But most of his books are, in an approving sense of the term, ''banal'' novels—concerned, that is, with the world of everyday social and emotional experience, and capable of evoking a strong, strange sense of recognition. Set in the provinces, the suburbs, or the world of the urban middle-classes with its clubs and appropriate restaurants—the pieces of social experience Cooper knows and details very well—they describe with affection and understanding the way ordinary things happen to intelligent and skeptical people as they marry, breed families, have affairs, work at recognizable jobs, and worry about their sexual lives, their mortality, and their salaries. Many of them indeed belong to the world of the ''new men'' (one book is called *Memoirs of a New Man*) whose meritocratic ascent forms an important story in British social life.

Like that of his friend C.P. Snow (on whom he has written warmly), Cooper's fiction relates the life of ordinary origins to the commonsense decencies of public life, and, as with Snow, his realistic pleasure in the world seems to have to do with the fact that it is open to his mobility and talent. Like Snow's fiction, Cooper's achievement bears some relation to that desire for a better world that fed the postwar years, and also explores many of its ambiguities and disappointments.

But if one of Cooper's best qualities is his powerful realism, another is his comedy and wit. If he deals with familiar life, he lights it up with a striking sense of human oddity, and of the quirks and unexpected outrages that exist in his very recognizable characters. The outrage is often added to by the cool, undercutting tone of his narrators themselves. Like Muriel, who in *Disquiet and Peace* is provoked to stirring up disorder by donning an eyeglass and then dropping it in her soup, Cooper has a way of stirring up the surface of his world by his oblique vision. The struggles of the characters for sexual, social, or material success become matters for very cool irony. His plots often turn on conflicts between traditional and more liberal values, and he writes with a moral edge, but is also capable of moving lightly away from it all, leaving the chaos to itself, as in *The Ever-Interesting Topic,* about a headmaster who tries to bring lectures on sex education into his public school. All Cooper's books show a buoyant and vitalistic view of sexuality and an awareness of the way it undercuts so many of our social and moral pretensions. This comic vision is something he also handed on to his successors, and it makes his a realism of marvelous surprise, giving his books a sharp bite and clarity that distinguish them from Snow's sobered kind of realism. His Albert Woods and Joe Lunns may acquire influence, but they do not acquire sobriety. As a result they become attractive centers of vision, and that is especially true of Joe Lunn, who, in all the books where he is narrator, is both a performer in the chaotic and comic action and an artistic observer consciously knowing about fiction and busily interpreting, recalling, and shaping in a neat balance of sympathy and irony. Other narrative techniques are used in other novels, but they are usually distinguished by an adept mixture of sympathetic identification with lively characters and an ironic detachment from them.

With 17 novels over half a century to his credit, Cooper has contributed vitally to postwar British fiction. At times his committed support for realism and his distrust of writing in any way avant garde has been unfashionable and even inhibiting, though it has been an expression of his fierce literary individualism. Nonetheless his influence has been very considerable, and he did much to establish the "new realism" of British fiction from the 1950s onward. Though his own novels do vary somewhat in quality, they possess a very distinctive style, tone, and vision, and at their best a very cunning and powerful artistic control. Cooper's strengths are most apparent when—as in *Young People*—he is capturing the flavor of some distinctive period, milieu or generation, and then observing, with some cynicism, the characteristic, and comic, behavior of individuals within it. A strong admirer of the novelist H.G. Wells ("I loved it, enshrining Wells's message of optimism," Joe Lunn says of Wells's *The History of Mr. Polly* in *Scenes from Later Life*), and like him trained as a scientist, he can be compared with his master both for his concern with the way British society works and for his power to capture youthful, hopeful, buoyant pleasure from the stuff of ordinary life. At best, as in *Scenes from Provincial Life,* his balance of detail, reminiscence, sentiment, and irony comes together so exactly as to allow comparison with the great "artful realists," like Turgenev. Where many British novelists avoid the public world, of politics, government, law, and science, Cooper's books construct an important record of manners and moods, landscapes and cityscapes, social and historical changes, public operations and private and sexual emotions, in ways which are both morally and humanly illuminating and comically adept. Cooper has described his aim simply; it is "to tell the truth, laughing." These are the qualities that give the four novels of the *Scenes* series the classic status they now possess. Cooper has remained a vivid and influential writer, publishing in 1990 an autobiography of his midlands childhood, *From Early Life,* which captures his lower-middle-class social origins and ambitions with his familiar humane intelligence, and extends his chronicle of English life backwards to the years right after World War I. Meanwhile his late novel *Immortality at Any Price* deals in his sharp, cynical fashion with the raging competitiveness of the old, and turns on the principle that there is nothing like the animosity of old friends. Altogether, the long chronicle of his novels reminds us that the ability to see, illuminate, shape, and construct the experience of the ordinary and social world and to interpret the patterns of human behavior within it is something fundamental to the spirit of fiction.

—Malcolm Bradbury

COOVER, Robert (Lowell)

Nationality: American. **Born:** Charles City, Iowa, 4 February 1932. **Education:** Southern Illinois University, Carbondale, 1949–51; Indiana University, Bloomington, B.A. 1953; University of Chicago, 1958–61, M.A. 1965. **Military Service:** Served in the United States Naval Reserve, 1953–57: Lieutenant. **Family:** Married Maria del Sans-Mallafré in 1959; two daughters and one son. **Career:** Taught at Bard College, Annandale-on-Hudson, New York, 1966–67, University of Iowa, Iowa City, 1967–69, Columbia University, New York, 1972, Princeton University, New Jersey, 1972–73, Virginia Military Institute, Lexington, 1976, and Brandeis University, Waltham, Massachusetts, 1981. Since 1981 writer-in-residence, Brown University, Providence, Rhode Island. Fiction editor, *Iowa Review,* Iowa City, 1974–77. **Awards:** Faulkner award, 1966; Brandeis University Creative Arts award, 1969; Rockefeller fellowship, 1969; Guggenheim fellowship, 1971, 1974; American Academy award, 1976; National Endowment for the Arts grant, 1985; Rea award, for short story, 1987. **Agent:** Georges Borchardt Inc., 136 East 57th Street, New York, New York 10022, U.S.A.

PUBLICATIONS

Novels

The Origin of the Brunists. New York, Putnam, 1966; London, Barker, 1967; New York, Grove, 2000.

The Universal Baseball Association, Inc., J. Henry Waugh, Prop. New York, Random House, 1968; London, Hart Davis, 1970.

The Public Burning. New York, Viking Press, 1977; London, Allen Lane, 1978.

Spanking the Maid. New York, Grove Press, 1982; London, Heinemann, 1987.

Gerald's Party. New York, Linden Press, and London, Heinemann, 1986.

John's Wife. New York, Simon & Schuster, 1996.
Briar Rose. New York, Grove Press, 1996.
Ghost Town. New York, Henry Holt, 1998.

Short Stories

Pricksongs and Descants. New York, Dutton, 1969; London, Cape, 1971; New York, Grove Press, 2000.
The Water Pourer (unpublished chapter from *The Origin of the Brunists*). Bloomfield Hills, Michigan, Bruccoli Clark, 1972.
Hair o' the Chine. Bloomfield Hills, Michigan, Bruccoli Clark, 1979.
After Lazarus: A Filmscript. Bloomfield Hills, Michigan, Bruccoli Clark, 1980.
Charlie in the House of Rue. Lincoln, Massachusetts, Penmaen Press, 1980.
A Political Fable. New York, Viking Press, 1980.
The Convention. Northridge, California, Lord John Press, 1982.
In Bed One Night and Other Brief Encounters. Providence, Rhode Island, Burning Deck, 1983.
Aesop's Forest, with *The Plot of the Mice and Other Stories,* by Brian Swann. Santa Barbara, California, Capra Press, 1986.
A Night at the Movies; or, You Must Remember This. New York, Simon and Schuster, and London, Heinemann, 1987.
Whatever Happened to Gloomy Gus of the Chicago Bears? New York, Simon and Schuster, 1987; London, Heinemann, 1988.
Pinocchio in Venice. New York, Simon and Schuster, and London, Heinemann, 1991.

Plays

The Kid (produced New York, 1972; London, 1974). Included in *A Theological Position,* 1972.
A Theological Position (includes *A Theological Position, The Kid, Love Scene, Rip Awake*). New York, Dutton, 1972.
Love Scene (as *Scène d'amour,* produced Paris, 1973; as *Love Scene,* produced New York, 1974). Included in *A Theological Position,* 1972.
Rip Awake (produced Los Angeles, 1975). Included in *A Theological Position,* 1972.
A Theological Position (produced Los Angeles, 1977; New York, 1979). Included in *A Theological Position,* 1972.
Bridge Hand (produced Providence, Rhode Island, 1981).

Other

Editor, with Kent Dixon, *The Stone Wall Book of Short Fiction.* Iowa City, Stone Wall Press, 1973.
Editor, with Elliott Anderson, *Minute Stories.* New York, Braziller, 1976.

*

Critical Studies: *Fiction and the Figures of Life* by William H. Gass, New York, Knopf, 1970; *Black Humor Fiction of the Sixties* by Max Schulz, Athens, Ohio University Press, 1973; ''Robert Coover and the Hazards of Metafiction'' by Neil Schmitz, in *Novel 7* (Providence, Rhode Island), 1974; ''Humor and Balance in Coover's *The Universal Baseball Association, Inc.*'' by Frank W. Shelton, in *Critique 17* (Atlanta), 1975; ''Robert Coover, Metafictions, and Freedom'' by Margaret Heckard, in *Twentieth Century Literature 22* (Los Angeles), 1976; ''The Dice of God: Einstein, Heisenberg, and Robert Coover'' by Arlen J. Hansen, in *Novel 10* (Providence, Rhode Island), 1976; ''Structure as Revelation: Coover's *Pricksongs and Descants*'' by Jessie Gunn, in *Linguistics in Literature,* vol. 2, no. 1, 1977; *The Metafictional Muse: The Works of Robert Coover, Donald Barthelme, and William H. Gass* by Larry McCaffery, Pittsburgh, University of Pittsburgh Press, 1982; *Robert Coover: The Universal Fictionmaking Process* by Lois Gordon, Carbondale, Southern Illinois University Press, 1983; *Robert Coover's Fictions* by Jackson I. Cope, Baltimore, Johns Hopkins University Press, 1986; *Dissident Postmodernists: Barthelme, Coover, Pynchon* by Paul Maltby, Philadelphia, University of Pennsylvania Press, 1991; *Robert Coover: A Study of the Short Fiction* by Thomas E. Kennedy, New York, Twayne, 1992; *Comic Sense: Reading Robert Coover, Stanley Elkin, Philip Roth* by Thomas Pughe, Basel, Switzerland, Birkhäuser Verlag, 1994.

Robert Coover comments:

In reply to the question: ''Why Do You Write?'': Because art blows life into the lifeless, death into the deathless.

Because art's lie is preferable, in truth, to life's beautiful terror.

Because, as time does not pass (nothing, as Beckett tells us, passes), *it* passes the time.

Because death, our mirthless master, is somehow amused by epitaphs.

Because epitaphs, well-struck, give death, our voracious master, heartburn.

Because fiction imitates life's beauty, thereby inventing the beauty life lacks.

Because fiction is the best position, at once exotic and familiar, for fucking the world.

Because fiction, mediating paradox, celebrates it.

Because fiction, mothered by love, loves love as a mother might her unloving child.

Because fiction speaks, hopelessly, beautifully, as the world speaks.

Because God, created in the storyteller's image, can be destroyed only by His maker.

Because, in its perversity, art harmonizes the disharmonious.

Because, in its profanity, fiction sanctifies life.

Because, in its terrible isolation, writing is a path to brotherhood.

Because in the beginning was the gesture, and in the end to come as well: in between what we have are words.

Because, of all the arts, only fiction can unmake the myths that unman men.

Because of its endearing futility, its outrageous pretensions.

Because the pen, though short, casts a long shadow (upon, it must be said, no surface).

Because the world is re-invented every day and this is how it is done.

Because there is nothing new under the sun except its expression.

Because truth, that elusive joker, hides himself in fictions and must therefore be sought there.

Because writing, in all space's unimaginable vastness, is still the greatest adventure of all.

And because, alas, what else?

* * *

Robert Coover's fiction is built around his firm belief that realist modes of fiction are outworn and need to be revivified. He writes fictions that are highly self-conscious and that draw attention to their own artifice and invention. He rejects, too, the notion that there is a fixed, objective truth, pointing constantly to the highly subjective nature of different people's interpretations of reality. Although the reception of his books has varied considerably, Coover has remained ruthlessly loyal to his own artistic premises throughout his long career.

Pricksongs and Descants was the third book Coover published, but he actually wrote most of the stories before his first two novels and it contains many of his fundamental beliefs and practices. In ''The Magic Poker,'' for instance, he spells out the authority of the author over his creations: ''I have brought two sisters to this invented island, and shall, in time, send them home again. I have dressed them and may well choose to undress them.'' Rejecting any notion that fiction is an act of mimesis of the real world, Coover celebrates the delights of linguistic invention. Many of the stories are rewritings of well-known myths and fairy tales. ''J's Marriage,'' for instance, one of seven of what Coover calls ''Exemplary Fictions'' in homage to Cervantes, is a retelling of the story of Joseph and Mary. Other stories—most famously, ''The Babysitter''—offer a bewildering and ever-changing choice of narrative possibilities.

The Origin of the Brunists established an immediate reputation for Coover as one of America's most original writers. It concerns a cult of the millennium which is cynically promoted by the editor of a small town newspaper for his own complex ends. The Brunists are led by Giovanni Bruno, a miner who, because he alone has been spared in a disastrous explosion that killed 97 workers, believes he is a prophet who can announce the coming end of the world. Although written in a predominantly realist style (though it experiments with a whole smorgasbord of different approaches), the novel foreshadows Coover's preoccupation with fiction at the expense of reality in its ironic and sometimes even parodic treatment of the necessity—yet danger—of myth-making. The novel is satirical at the expense of the cult but reserves its most severe criticism for Justin Miller, the editor of the local newspaper, who manipulates the sect, with tragic consequences. *The Origin of the Brunists* is a novel crowded with characters, filled with many voices and different texts, from letters to songs to sermons. It is the work of a writer rich in ideas and talent.

The Universal Baseball Association Inc., J. Henry Waugh, Prop. once again shows Coover's interest in fantasy and invention. An accountant, bored and able to relate to few other human beings, Waugh invents his own baseball league and game, played with cards and dice and so comprehensive that it eventually comes to take up his whole life and sense of reality. He is particularly affected by the death of a young pitcher who is having a dream run until fatally struck by a wild pitch. Coover immerses the reader completely in the world of baseball, blurring the divisions between the real and the imaginary, just as they are blurred for Henry, who progressively cuts himself off from the few connections he has, his job and two friends.

The Public Burning is probably Coover's best know and certainly most ambitious novel, though as always it divided the critics. It is a lengthy account of the execution of Julius and Ethel Rosenberg for allegedly selling atomic secrets to Russia but it is far from a conventionally historical narrative. The case becomes the basis for a satirical account of American Cold War paranoia in which Uncle Sam, a fast-talking, double-dealing parody of American ideals, is pitted against the Phantom, the embodiment of the forces of atheistic, Communistic darkness. Coover employs a series of Brechtian devices to distance the reader from the action. The execution is set for the night of the Rosenbergs' fourteenth wedding anniversary and is to be a public celebration in New York's Times Square, the entertainment to be organized by Cecil B. de Mille. Though he satirizes many American public figures, Coover is hardest of all on Richard Nixon, who narrates considerable chunks of the novel. Nixon is portrayed as a sexually repressed, paranoid, ambition-obsessed egomaniac, whose drive for power is the product of his deep sense of inferiority. His narrative swings between self-extenuation and assertiveness, it is filled with contradictions, but topples finally into absurdity, as much of the novel does, when Nixon fantasize about visiting Ethel Rosenberg in jail just before her execution and having her fall in love with him. The novel seems informed by Coover's conviction that art cannot do justice to the absurdities of reality. It is as if he can contain and express his anger only in the form of demented parody, satire, and ridicule.

A Political Fable and *Gloomy Gus of the Chicago Bears* first appeared in the *New American Review* but were later published separately. *Fable* is a satirical account of the political process and especially the presidential election. The political heavies are outmaneuvered by the Cat in the Hat, a strange creature who proceeds to subvert the whole political contest, rendering it absurd by his antics. The story is scathingly contemptuous of the political system, or at least it would be if it were not clear that Coover derives a great deal of fun from its idiotic behavior. ''Gloomy Gus'' is set in the 1930s, in Chicago; Gus becomes the eleventh fatality in a confrontation between workers and Republic Steel. The political background involves Spain, Guernica, battles between unions and large companies. But is a kind of parody of the American dream: ''Winning was everything for him. Or at least scoring.'' One character says of him, ''If he's a bit demented . . . well, he's only a mirror image of the insane nation that created him,'' and it is clear that Coover agrees. But the book is much more interesting when it is simply being funny than when it is preaching lessons.

In his later work, Coover sticks resolutely to the set of aesthetic beliefs he had announced but the writing becomes less political, less engaged in criticism of American society, even while remaining as self-conscious, and the writing suffers a little as a result. *A Night at the Movies; or, You Must Remember This,* for instance, is arranged like a film program, with each story being given a subtitle: ''Previews of Coming Attractions,'' ''The Weekly Serial,'' and an intermission. It is simultaneously both a satire of American popular culture, which plays a large role in Coover's consciousness, and an act of homage to it. *Pinocchio in Venice* is one of Coover's strangest fictions. It opens with a distinguished professor stranded in Venice on a snowy night. He is attempting to complete his final, valedictory work, *Mamma,* and needs to come to Venice for purposes of research. The title refers to the Walt Disney figure who possessed an exceptionally long nose which in this novel assumes phallic properties. There are, as always, lots of jokes, puns (''the Immaculate Kunt''), aphorisms, and sayings—in short, an inventiveness with language that is one of Coover's trademarks.

Briar Rose reads like a fairy story, rather in the manner of Donald Barthelme's *Snow White.* As in *Spanking the Maid,* the same story is told over and over again. A knight sets out on an expedition: ''He has undertaken this great adventure, not for the supposed reward—what is another lonely bedridden princess?—but in order to provoke a confrontation with the awful powers of enchantment itself.'' Most of Coover's later fictions are to do with disenchantment, parody, the debunking of myths, especially of American dreams. We are told of the princess that ''Her longing for integrity is, in her spellbound innocence, all she knows of rage and lust.'' She is Briar Rose and she must rest easy: ''Your prince will come.'' But he must press valiantly through the thickening briar hedge. The parodic note is constant: "Her true prince has come at last, just as promised." The constant retellings, as always, indicate the problematic nature of truth—and myth. Even the dragon is bound by convention: "Well, nothing to do but eat the bony little thing, he supposed, compelled less by appetite than by the mythical proprieties." If there is one work which sums up Coover's fictional beliefs and practices it is probably the story "The Babysitter." No single interpretation of reality is possible, fiction is the exploration of a myriad of possibilities, and the author is both lord over and responsible for the construction of the worlds he makes.

—Laurie Clancy

COUPLAND, Douglas

Nationality: Canadian. **Born:** Baden-Soellingen, Germany, 30 December 1961. **Education:** Attended Emily Carr College of Art and Design, Vancouver, Canada; completed a two-year course in Japanese business science, Hawaii, 1986. **Career:** Writer, sculptor, and editor. Host of *The Search for Generation X* (documentary), PBS, 1991. Lives in Vancouver.

Publications

Novels

Generation X: Tales for an Accelerated Culture. New York, St. Martin's, 1991.
Shampoo Planet. New York, Pocket Books, 1992.
Microserfs. New York, ReganBooks, 1995.
Girlfriend in a Coma. New York, ReganBooks, 1998.
Miss Wyoming. New York, Pantheon, 1999.

Short Stories

Life after God. New York, Pocket Books, 1994.

Other

Polaroids from the Dead (essays and short fiction). New York, ReganBooks, 1996.
Lara's Book: Lara Croft and the Tomb Raider Phenomenon (with Kip Ward). Rocklin, California, Prima Publishers, 1998.

* * *

Douglas Coupland emerged in the 1990s as a novelist who seemed to capture the voice of a generation—the generation whose members were in their twenties by the last decade of the twentieth century and whose lives were rootless and marginal, caught between a desire to embrace and an urge to escape from the enticements of career success and consumer culture. Coupland's first book, *Generation X: Tales for an Accelerated Culture*, concerns Andy, Dag, and Claire, who live in Palm Springs, California, on the periphery of an affluent consumer culture, working at what Coupland calls "McJobs"—jobs with low pay, low status, low dignity, and no future. Each of the trio tell stories, some supposedly true, others obviously fictional, which all turn upon insecurity, dissatisfaction, exhaustion, and breakdown—the failure of youth, class, sex, and the future. Coupland wrote *Generation X* in a lively, up-to-the-minute style, incorporating or coining slang terms which were conveniently defined for the reader—for example, "emotional ketchup burst" means the sudden explosion of pent-up feelings—and the book was printed in bold typography with cartoon-style illustrations, rather like a graphic novel. *Generation X* immediately established Coupland as a writer to watch, but it was, in itself, an episodic, inconsequential, and possibly ephemeral work.

Coupland's second book, *Shampoo Planet*, was a more substantial novel. This time the story is told by 20-year-old Canadian Tyler Johnson who has returned to his home in a rundown Canadian town after a trip to Europe. With insight and good humor, the novel explores the complicated relationship between Tyler, whose memories began with Ronald Reagan and a little later encompassed the death of John Lennon, and his divorced ex-hippie mother, a 1960s survivor who was young in the era before the invention of conditioner, when people only used shampoo to wash their hair—shampoo and related hair products are the key symbol of postmodernity in the novel. Tyler's relationship with his girlfriend Anne-Louise is disrupted when a former girlfriend arrives from Paris, and he lights out to Los Angeles before finally returning for a reconciliation. The style of the novel combines much dropping of imaginary brand names with metaphysical reflections, for example on the nature of time. Although more focused than *Generation X*, *Shampoo Planet* remains rather ramshackle in its structure, and its postmodern surface does not conceal its conventional themes—the relationships between parents and grown-up children, and the complications of young love.

In 1994 Coupland published a collection of stories, *Life After God*, in which a variety of first person narrators, drifting around Canadian suburbia or setting out on the great roads of the U.S.A., try to find a purpose in their directionless postmodern lives. Here, Coupland was mining what had become a familiar vein, and critics began to wonder if he had anything new to say. With his third novel, however, he brought off a brilliant stroke by targeting the best-known phenomenon of the 1990s, the giant computer corporation Microsoft, and dissecting its corporate culture with graceful wit. *Microserfs* is set among the young programmers of the corporation who dwell in an intensely competitive, profit-driven world and have no real private life or profound relationships. Once more the story is told in the first person, this time by 26-year-old Daniel, who is writing a journal late at night, trying to make sense of his existence—increasingly, the protagonists of Coupland's novels become preoccupied with the quest for meaning in their lives. Daniel and a group of other microserfs desert the corporation to form their own software company, Oop!, but run into financial and other difficulties. As in *Shampoo Planet*, relations between parents and their young adult children are an important theme, and we are reminded that, in the postmodern world, job insecurity applies across the generations; there is an especially poignant portrait of the distress of Daniel's fifty-something father after he has been sacked by IBM. The novel consists largely of short paragraphs, rather in the manner of e-mail, combined with a range of typographical devices and an occasional excursion into binary code.

Coupland followed up a collection of short fiction and nonfiction pieces, *Polaroids from the Dead*, with the novel *Girlfriend in a Coma*. Ostensibly narrated by Jared, a ghost, it employs Coupland's favorite device of focusing on a group of friends, but this time their lives are haunted not so much by the dead Jared as by the inert presence of Karen, who fell into a coma in 1979 after taking Valium and a vodka cocktail at a party, and, though giving birth unconsciously to a baby, remained oblivious to the world for the next 17 years. The novel charts the fortunes of her friends through those years, and we find ourselves, to some extent, in familiar Coupland territory—travel, drink, drugs, money, drifting, disaffection. But the silent, enduring presence of Karen, which we are never allowed to forget, serves as a measure of seriousness by which to evaluate their lives. Then, like Rip Van Winkle, Karen wakes up, and the novel explores her responses to the world of the late 1990s, a world in which, she feels, all conviction seems to have been lost. *Girlfriend in a Coma* is written in a quieter, more serious style than Coupland's previous work, and has a complex narrative structure that enables him to achieve a deeper perspective on the last decade of the 20th century.

Coupland's latest novel, *Miss Wyoming*, is a more romantic work, which gives vent to a streak of sentimentality that has underlain his earlier fiction. In Los Angeles, John, a 37-year-old burnt-out star of action movies, meets Susan, an ex-television celebrity, whom he thinks he has seen in a near-death vision while in hospital—though in fact he saw her on a repeat of her TV show. He is promptly entranced with her, but she at once disappears, and he sets off on a quest across America for her with a group of oddball friends. The story skillfully combines the story of John's quest with flashbacks from his and Susan's past lives—both of them have tried to find a new meaning in their existence. It is evident in *Miss Wyoming* that Coupland's capacity to handle a sophisticated narrative has increased and that he is getting older: more insistently than in his previous work, the novel poses questions of the meaning and purpose of life.

There can be no doubt of Coupland's significant contribution to the fiction of the 1990s, his capacity to catch the tones and attitudes of a disaffected postmodern generation in a degraded consumer culture. But his earlier fiction, though very enjoyable, had evident weaknesses: it was episodic and its characterization was often perfunctory. *Girlfriend in a Coma* and *Miss Wyoming*, however, move beyond this to offer a more complex narrative technique, richer characterization, and an exploration of more serious concerns, and it will be interesting to see how far he develops these features of his fiction in the 21st century.

—Nicolas Tredell

COWAN, Peter (Walkinshaw)

Nationality: Australian. **Born:** Perth, Western Australia, 4 November 1914. **Education:** The University of Western Australia, Nedlands, B.A. in English 1940, Dip. Ed. 1946. **Military Service:** Served in the Royal Australian Air Force, 1943–45. **Family:** Married Edith Howard in 1941; one son. **Career:** Clerk, farm labourer, and casual worker, 1930–39; teacher, 1941–42; member of the faculty, University of Western Australia, 1946–50; Senior English Master, Scotch College, Swanbourne, Western Australia, 1950–62. Senior Tutor, 1964–79, and since 1979 Honorary Research Fellow in English, University of Western Australia. **Awards:** Commonwealth Literary Fund fellowship, 1963; Australian Council for the Arts fellowship, 1974, 1980; University of Western Australia fellowship, 1982; Patrick White prize, for literature, 1992. A.M. (Order of Australia), 1983. **Address:** Department of English, University of Western Australia, Nedlands, Western Australia 6009, Australia.

Publications

Novels

Summer. Sydney and London, Angus and Robertson, 1964.
Seed. Sydney and London, Angus and Robertson, and San Francisco, Tri-Ocean, 1966.
The Color of the Sky. Fremantle, Western Australia, Fremantle Arts Centre Press, 1986.
The Hills of Apollo Bay. Fremantle, Western Australia, Fremantle Arts Centre Press, 1989.
The Tenants. Fremantle, Western Australia, Fremantle Arts Centre Press, 1994.

Short Stories

Drift. Melbourne, Reed and Harris, 1944.
The Unploughed Land. Sydney, Angus and Robertson, 1958.
The Empty Street. Sydney and London, Angus and Robertson, and San Francisco, Tri-Ocean, 1965.
The Tins and Other Stories. St. Lucia, University of Queensland Press, 1973.
New Country, with others, edited by Bruce Bennett. Fremantle, Western Australia, Fremantle Arts Centre Press, 1976.
Mobiles. Fremantle, Western Australia, Fremantle Arts Centre Press, 1979.
A Window in Mrs. X's Place. Ringwood, Victoria, and New York, Penguin, 1986; London, Penguin, 1987.
Voices. Fremantle, Western Australia, Fremantle Arts Centre Press, 1988.

Other

A Unique Position: A Biography of Edith Dircksey Cowan 1861–1932. Nedlands, University of Western Australia Press, 1978.
A Colonial Experience: Swan River 1839–1888. Privately printed, 1979.
Maitland Brown: A View of Nineteenth-Century Western Australia. Fremantle, Western Australia, Fremantle Arts Centre Press, 1988.
Editor, *Short Story Landscape: The Modern Short Story.* Melbourne, Longman, 1964.
Editor, with Bruce Bennett and John Hay, *Spectrum 1–2.* Melbourne, Longman, 2 vols., 1970; London, Longman, 2 vols., 1971; *Spectrum 3,* Melbourne, Longman, 1979.
Editor, *Today: Short Stories of Our Time.* Melbourne, Longman, 1971.
Editor, *A Faithful Picture: The Letters of Eliza and Thomas Brown at York in the Swan River Country 1841–1852.* Fremantle, Western Australia, Fremantle Arts Centre Press, 1977.
Editor, with Bruce Bennett and John Hay, *Perspectives One* (short stories). Melbourne, Longman Cheshire, 1985.
Editor, *Impressions: West Coast Fiction 1829–1988.* Fremantle, Western Australia, Fremantle Arts Centre Press, 1989.

*

Critical Studies: ''The Short Stories of Peter Cowan,'' 1960, and ''New Tracks to Travel: The Stories of White, Porter and Cowan,'' 1966, both by John Barnes, in *Meanjin* (Melbourne); essay by Grahame Johnston in *Westerly* (Perth), 1967; ''Cowan Country'' by Margot Luke, in *Sandgropers* edited by Dorothy Hewett, Nedlands, University of Western Australia Press, 1973; ''Behind the Actual'' by Bruce Williams, in *Westerly* (Perth), no. 3, 1973; ''Regionalism in Peter Cowan's Short Fiction'' by Bruce Bennett, in *World Literature Written in English* (Guelph, Ontario), 1980; ''Practitioner of Silence'' by Wendy Jenkins, in *Fremantle Arts Review* (Fremantle, Western Australia), vol. 1, no. 3, 1986; ''Of Books and Covers: Peter Cowan'' by Bruce Bennett, in *Overland 114* (Melbourne), 1989, and *Peter Cowan: New Critical Essays* by Susan Miller and edited by Bennett, Nedlands, University of Western Australia with The Centre for Studies in Australian Literature, 1992.

Peter Cowan comments:

Up to the present time writing has been for me as much something I wanted to do to please myself as something aimed solely at publication and any kind of wide audience. Now, I don't think this kind of attitude is any longer possible, and the chances for this kind of fiction have greatly diminished.

My writing may have been concerned as much with place as with people, though I have tried to see people against a landscape, against a physical environment. If isolation is one of the themes that occur frequently, particularly in the short stories, this is perhaps enforced by the Australian landscape itself. I am deeply involved in everything to do with the physical Australia, the land, its shapes and seasons and colors, its trees and flowers, its birds and animals. And its coast and sea.

I have been more interested in the short story than the novel. The technical demands of a short story are high, and seldom met, and through the short story a writer has perhaps a better chance of trapping something of the fragmentary nature of today's living.

I am, however, interested in some present forms of the novel and an attempting to work within these forms. Novel and short story now perhaps seem closer to one another.

* * *

Peter Cowan is a quietly introspective writer, and consequently his intensity of vision and his scrupulous craftsmanship can easily be underrated. He has shown a particular talent for the short story or novella, in which he can focus on a single relationship and explore a single line of feeling. His stories, written in a spare, taut style, have as a recurring theme the relationship of a man and a woman seeking relief from their loneliness in sexual love. Cowan is intent upon an inner reality: his characters are seldom individualized very far; they seem almost anonymous, and the sensuous reality of the external world is only faintly felt. His imagination is compelled by a painful awareness of the feelings of loneliness and alienation that lie beneath the surface of commonplace lives; and in exploring this territory he has become, more than is generally recognized, a significant interpreter of Australian realities.

In Cowan's first collection of stories, *Drift,* the preoccupations of his mature work are merely sketched in. Uneven in quality and stylistically in debt to Hemingway, the book nevertheless has a coherence and a unity of impression unexpected in the work of a young writer. Cowan has known his subject right from the start. Most of these early stories are set in the poor farming country of southwestern West Australia before World War II, and they centre on the lives of people who are emotionally unfulfilled or unable to express themselves in normal relationships.

Over the next 14 years Cowan wrote little. In his second collection, *The Unploughed Land,* he reprinted seven of his stories from *Drift,* along with six new stories, which represent a distinct advance in technique. These new stories include the much-anthologized ''The Redbacked Spiders,'' a powerful story of a boy whose resentment at his brutal father leads to the man's death. The title story is an extended treatment of the pre-war country life about which he writes in his first volume. In its evocation of that life it is one of his finest pieces, and it marks the end of the first phase of his development.

From this point onward Cowan has been more prolific and more varied—though compared with most writers he has a small and narrow output. In his third collection, *The Empty Street,* there is a noticeable shift in setting. Cowan now writes of people in suburbia, for whom the country is a refuge. The sense of being caught in an irresistible and disastrous historical process is expressed in a story like ''The Tractor,'' which concerns the efforts of a hermit to stop the clearing of the land. Cowan's sympathies are with those who oppose ''progress,'' but he sees their dilemma truly. ''The Empty Street,'' a novella, is an impressive study of an unhappy middle-aged clerk, whose marriage is now a mere shell, and whose children are strangers to him: desperate to escape the pressures of a life that is meaningless to him, he collapses into schizophrenia and turns murderer. Cowan is especially responsive to the theme of the middle-aged, defeated, and desolate in marriage, groping for a way out. *The Tins and Other Stories* confirms the achievement of the earlier volumes, with stories like ''The Rock'' and ''The Tins,'' in which Cowan is seen at his characteristic best.

In recent years Cowan has spent a great deal of time researching the history of his family, which has been prominent in the public life of West Australia since colonial times. This turning to the past has the appearance of being a retreat from the present, of which he takes such a bleak view in his fiction. But the collection, *Mobiles,* and, even more strikingly, *The Color of the Sky,* show, rather, that the sense of the past has sharpened and enlarged his sense of the present. Four of the seven stories in *Mobiles* are set in the stony northwest, beyond the limits of settlement or where settlement has failed. In these starkly rendered episodes human beings are no more than transitory figures in an enduring and inhospitable landscape. The longest story in the volume, ''The Lake,'' reworks a favourite theme of 19th-century novelists—the ''hidden valley'' in the heart of the unexplored continent. In what is one of his most satisfying stories, the symbolic possibilities of the landscape—evoked here with more vividness than is usual in his writing—are subtly realized. This story points to a new strength in Cowan's writing which appears in his third and finest novel.

Peter Cowan's first two attempts at novels were not very successful. *Summer* is a short novel, more like two short stories that have been expanded and linked together. A businessman whose marriage has failed takes a job on the wheat bins, and in this lonely setting forms a relationship with the wife of the nearby storekeeper. The violent resolution is not well managed, and the central character tends to be a mouthpiece for Cowan's reflections on the spoiling of the natural environment. Yet there are some fine sequences establishing the relationship of the two lonely people in a solitary landscape.

In *Seed* Cowan set out to portray a group of middle-class families living in Perth. An Australian reader feels the force of his thesis about the boredom and frustration of suburban living, but it remains a thesis and seldom quickens into drama. It is a disappointing work, the result of Cowan's trying to write against the grain of his talent. He is not skilled at creating personalities or at suggesting the social facts of life, but in this rather old-fashioned, realistic novel the emphasis falls on just those aspects of his writing where he is weakest.

The Color of the Sky has the formal integrity and the imaginative vigour which the previous novels lacked. The narrator is a familiar enough Cowan creation—a man on his own, trying to make sense of his experience. In a visit to a place dimly remembered from a visit in childhood, the narrator is simultaneously exploring the past and the present, and much of the power of the narrative derives from the reader's realization of patterns only half-traced, elusive parallels, family likenesses, disturbing undercurrents and continuities. Both the past and the present contain events that could be sensationalized—drug-running, murder, illicit sexual liaisons—but Cowan's novel is a study of the consciousness of a man in search of himself. In the end, the narrator can no more complete the jigsaw puzzle of his family relationships than he can give shape to the incoherence of his own emotional and moral life, with its tangle of loose ends, evasions, and denials. This work is Cowan's most impressive treatment of (in his own words) ''the fragmentary nature of today's living.''

Cowan's output during the 1990s was slight, consisting primarily of the novel *The Tenants*.

—John Barnes

COX, William Trevor

See TREVOR, William

COYNE, P.J.

See MASTERS, Hilary

CRACE, Jim

Nationality: British. **Born:** Brocket Hall, Lemsford, Hertfordshire, 1 March 1946. **Education:** Enfield Grammar School, Middlesex, 1957–64; Birmingham College of Commerce, 1965–68; University of London (external), B.A. (honours) in English 1968. **Family:** Married Pamela Ann Turton in 1975; one son and one daughter. **Career:** Volunteer in educational television, Voluntary Service Overseas, Khartoum, Sudan, 1968–69; freelance journalist and writer, 1972–86; since 1986 full-time novelist. **Awards:** Arts Council bursary, 1986; West Midlands Arts Literature grant, 1980; David Higham award, 1986; Whitbread award, 1986; *Guardian* Fiction prize, 1986; Antico Fattore prize (Italy), 1988; International prize for literature, 1989. **Address:** c/o Viking/Penguin, 27 Wrights Lane, London W8 5TZ, England.

PUBLICATIONS

Novels

The Gift of Stones. London, Secker and Warburg, 1988; New York, Scribner, 1989.
Arcadia. London, Cape, and New York, Atheneum, 1992.
Signals of Distress. London, Viking, 1994; New York, Farrar Straus, 1995.
The Slow Digestions of the Night (novella). London, Penguin, 1995.
Quarantine. New York, Farrar, Straus and Giroux, 1997.
Being Dead. New York, Farrar, Straus and Giroux, 2000.

Short Stories

Continent. London, Heinemann, 1986; New York, Harper, 1987.

Uncollected Short Stories

''Refugees,'' in *Socialist Challenge,* December 1977.
''Annie, California Plates'' and ''Helter Skelter, Hang Sorrow, Care'll Kill a Cat,'' in *Introduction 6: Stories by New Writers.* London, Faber, 1977.
''Seven Ages,'' in *Quarto,* 1980.

Plays

Radio Plays: *The Bird Has Flown,* 1977; *A Coat of Many Colours,* 1979.

*

Critical Studies: *Jim Crace* by Judy Cooke, London, Book Trust and the British Council, 1992.

Jim Crace comments:

I count myself to be a traditional, old-fangled novelist rather than a conventional writer or a new-fangled modernist. I am more interested in the fate of communities than the catharsis of individuals. I owe more to the oral traditions of storytelling (rhythmic prose, moral satire, naked invention) than to the idiomatic, ironic, realist social comedies which typify post-war British fiction. My books are not an exploration of self. They are not autobiographically based. I do not write from experience. I focus on subjects—usually political or sociological, usually concerning the conflict between the old and new ways of humankind—which interest me, which seem worthy of exploration but of which I have no personal expertise. (I am surprised but not saddened to note that my novels are less progressive and more pessimistic than I am myself.) I shroud the offputting solemnity of my themes in metaphorical narratives which tease and subvert and flirt with the reader and which regard lies to be more eloquent than facts. Thus far, my novels seem to reach-and-preach the same conclusion: that everything new worth having, in both the private and public universes, is paid for by the loss of something old worth keeping. Those who do not like my novels consider them to be overwrought, passionless, schematic, and unEnglish.

* * *

The fiction of Jim Crace is an alchemical alloy of meticulous rationality wedded to a broadly inventive imagination and written in a seemingly arch style that belies its suppleness and tensile strength. While critics have noted his fondness for blank-verse iambic rhythms highlighted with occasional alliterative trills and rhetorical flourishes, this stylized writing has been used by Crace to construct narratives set in such exotic and varied places as the dawn of the Bronze Age, the deserts outside biblical Jerusalem, nineteenth-century rural England, and a present-day metropolis. But such scope should not imply that

Crace writes panoramic epic. Instead, Crace portrays characters who are anything but heroic in the Homeric sense, their very ordinariness precisely rendered with a focused attention on the minutiae of lives lived within their specific—and ever-changing—historical contexts. And Crace can easily shift gears from ornate to ordinary, often within the space of a few syllables, at one moment relating the rhetorical musings of an elderly magnate, then seamlessly morphing into a prosaic account of the old man's indigestion.

His first book, *Continent*, betrays the strong influence of Borges and other Latin-American fabulists. Considered by many to be a novel only in name, this narrative is a collection of interrelated stories set on a mythical continent where the main occupations are, according to the book's epigraph, ''trade and superstition.'' Far from being fanciful, however, these tales have the quality of parable, being both overtly fantastical as well as topically relevant to life on the real continents of our world. In the chapter entitled ''Sins and Virtues,'' an old calligrapher must stoop to an ingenious but ironic solution to meeting government demands for his suddenly lucrative artwork. In ''Electricity,'' the fate of a giant ceiling fan becomes emblematic of the promises and pitfalls of technological progress, and in ''Cross-Country,'' a visiting teacher from Canada, an aficionado of the alien sport of jogging, engages in a kind of tortoise-versus-hare footrace against a local horseman. For all its fabricated flora and fauna, the continent of *Continent* is a recognizable place where the tragicomedy of life is brought into sharp relief against a vivid backdrop. This book made a literary star of Crace, winning him three of Great Britain's most prestigious literary awards: the Whitbread prize, the Guardian Fiction prize, and the David Higham award.

His second novel, *The Gift of Stones*, is an evocative depiction of life at the moment in human prehistory when bronze supplanted stone. It is also a meditation on the art and purposes of storytelling in the life of a community, albeit a doomed one. In a village of stoneworkers, a maimed boy becomes the tribe's entertainer, wandering away from the village during the day only to return and relate, with embellishment, his travels to his fellows as a way of earning his keep. When the village's fortunes fade with the sudden appearance of traders in bronze, the storyteller, as the tribe's most imaginative member, becomes a guide to the outside world as remnants of the tribe begin to wander in search of a new home. Tellingly, Crace leaves open the question of whether the storyteller's guidance proves fruitful or not.

In *Arcadia*, Crace's third novel, he creates a contemporary fable of a self-made man that begins, ''No wonder Victor never fell in love.'' Now eighty, Victor, a produce magnate, decides to erase his dark and lowly past by erecting a huge, glass-enclosed mall over the open-air market where he spent his destitute childhood. But his aspiration is opposed by Rook, his former majordomo, and their conflict is further complicated by their involvement with Anna, Victor's assistant and Rook's mistress. But *Arcadia* is more than this triangle of competing motives; it's a meditation on life in and of cities, a novelistic aria on the theme of the city as an organism that thrives with the help of—and often in spite of—the efforts of its denizens, no matter their place in the socioeconomic strata. As befits a book about constructions, *Arcadia* is Crace's most overtly structured novel, and critics have praised this structure for its artfulness while berating it for creating a kind of clinical distance from his characters, blocking the reader from achieving any real sympathy.

Signals of Distress, Crace's fourth novel, has an even more specific historical setting: Wherry town, on the coast of England, during one week in November of 1836. An American sailing bark runs aground, stranding its Yankee crew, its cargo of cattle, and an African slave while the ship undergoes repairs. The townspeople, down-to-earthers who are mainly kelpers and fishermen, warily take in the sailors just as a priggishly moralistic abolitionist named Aymer Smith arrives to announce news of economic disaster for the Wherry. Like all of Crace's fiction, *Signals of Distress* is concerned with the clash of differing cultures in a time of historical upheaval, and this novel treats the ensuing conflicts with as much comedy as pathos. The slave escapes and becomes a local legend; Smith competes against a minister for the hand of a local girl only to lose his virginity unceremoniously to another woman; a local landmark is destroyed; and the sailing bark is repaired. The week passes, but nothing in Wherry—or the world—will ever be the same. Like *Arcadia, Signals of Distress* was both praised and condemned for Crace's contrivances of structure and theme at the expense of fully realized characterizations, a criticism Crace himself has repeatedly dismissed.

Quarantine is Crace's fifth and most provocative novel, being a reimagining of Christ's forty-day fast in the desert. However, Crace makes Christ a minor but pivotal character in the story of a group of pilgrims who have gone to the desert to seek spiritual renewal. Indeed, Crace's Christ is little more than a willfully deluded runaway who mistakes the proddings of his fellow fasters for the temptations of Satan. Beginning with the purely scientific premise that no mortal could survive forty days without food or water, *Quarantine* maintains a scrupulously realistic air that colors any mysticism with the patina of fever or madness. Jesus' prayers seem more like epileptic fits than communications with a Creator. But *Quarantine* is not just a literary debunking of the New Testament. Although Crace is a publicly avowed atheist who has admitted that the inspiration for this novel was in fact just such a debunking, the novel manages to rise above the level of anti-religious polemic by making its characters and setting come truly alive in ways his previous novels, at least according to reviewers, did not. Each of Christ's fellow pilgrims is a vivid character, from the beleaguered-yet-unflagging Miri to the proud-but-desperate Marta. Musa, the novel's true central character, is a deliberately coarse creation who nevertheless is the only one sensitive enough to realize that there is more to Christ and his story than the fate of a starving teenager who sees visions. In the end, Musa, though he is devious and even criminal, is the only one in the group to see a supposedly resurrected Christ following the pilgrims to Jerusalem after their fast, thence to start a movement that will sweep the globe. That Musa is able to envision the coming religion only in terms of its profit potential only deepens the questions raised by this book. *Quarantine* won Crace a second Whitbread prize, and it was a finalist for the Booker prize as well.

Throughout his first five novels, Crace again and again focuses his narratives on people living on the cusp of great historical change, be it the coming of electricity or Christianity. But setting his characters at such chronological crossroads allows Crace the freedom to sensationally dramatize the essential fact that life itself is flux, whether or not such flux is measurable along the timelines in history books. With his next novel, however, Crace eschewed such historically dramatic scene-setting; instead, he focused on the most dramatic change that any life can make.

Being Dead, Crace's sixth novel, is what one critic calls ''a secular meditation on death'' that, in vividly portraying the process of death in minute detail while recalling the lives previously lived by the corpses whose decay forms the structural spine of the novel, is also

Crace at his most convincing. The book begins with the murder of a middle-aged couple en flagrante delicto. From there, the narrative diverges into two major tributaries. The first concerns what happens to the corpses as they decay; the second concerns the life of the couple as it led up to death. By tracing these forking paths of story, Crace has fashioned a novel that unflinchingly fixes the human place in the physical universe while affirming—however briefly—the single human trait able to jump the chasm between life and death: love. Such a structure again raises criticisms of Crace's tendency to over-design his novels, but such a structure is perfectly suited to this one. Joseph and Celice, the married-then-murdered couple, are unlikable as characters, but their deaths and subsequent lives, when subjected to Crace's close study, render them automatically sympathetic in ways that enlarge the reader's capacities for compassion rather than merely affirming the reader's preconceptions. Life is made precious by mortality, while love is even more so.

—J. J. Wylie

CREWS, Harry (Eugene)

Nationality: American. **Born:** Alma, Georgia, 6 June 1935. **Education:** The University of Florida, Gainesville, B.A. 1960, M.S.Ed. 1962. **Military Service:** Served in the United States Marine Corps, 1953–56: Sergeant. **Family:** Married Sally Ellis in 1960 (divorced); two sons. **Career:** English teacher, Broward Junior College, Fort Lauderdale, Florida, 1962–68. Associate professor, 1968–74, and since 1974 professor of English, University of Florida. **Awards:** Bread Loaf Writers Conference Atherton fellowship, 1968; American Academy award, 1972; National Endowment for the Arts grant, 1974. **Address:** Department of English, University of Florida, Gainesville, Florida 32601, U.S.A.

PUBLICATIONS

Novels

The Gospel Singer. New York, Morrow, 1968.
Naked in Garden Hills. New York, Morrow, 1969.
This Thing Don't Lead to Heaven. New York, Morrow, 1970.
Karate Is a Thing of the Spirit. New York, Morrow, 1971; London, Secker and Warburg, 1972.
Car. New York, Morrow, 1972; London, Secker and Warburg, 1973.
The Hawk Is Dying. New York, Knopf, 1973; London, Secker and Warburg, 1974.
The Gypsy's Curse. New York, Knopf, 1974; London, Secker and Warburg, 1975.
A Feast of Snakes. New York, Atheneum, 1976; London, Secker and Warburg, 1977.
All We Need of Hell. New York, Harper, 1987.
The Knockout Artist. New York, Harper, 1988.
Body. New York, Poseidon Press, 1990.
Scar Lover. New York, Poseidon Press, 1992.
The Mulching of America. New York, Simon & Schuster, 1995.
Celebration. New York, Simon & Schuster, 1998.

Short Stories

The Enthusiast. Winston-Salem, North Carolina, Palaemon Press, 1981.
Two. Northridge, Lord John Press, 1984.

Uncollected Short Stories

''The Player Piano,'' in *Florida Quarterly* (Gainesville), Fall 1967.
''The Unattached Smile,'' in *Craft and Vision,* edited by Andrew Lytle. New York, Delacorte Press, 1971.
''A Long Wail,'' in *Necessary Fictions,* edited by Stanley W. Lindberg and Stephen Corey. Athens, University of Georgia Press, 1986.

Play

Blood Issue (produced Louisville, Kentucky, 1989).

Other

A Childhood: The Biography of a Place (on Bacon County, Georgia). New York, Harper, 1978; London, Secker and Warburg, 1979.
Blood and Grits. New York, Harper, 1979.
Florida Frenzy. Gainesville, University Presses of Florida, 1982.
Classic Crews (non-fiction pieces and previously published novels). New York, Poseidon Press, 1993; London, Gorse, 1994.

*

Critical Studies: *A Grit's Triumph: Essays on the Works of Harry Crews* edited by David K. Jeffrey, Port Washington, New York, Associated Faculty Press, 1983; *Getting Naked with Harry Crews: Interviews,* edited by Erik Bledsoe. Gainesville, University Press of Florida, 1999.

* * *

Harry Crews's novels establish him as the most astringent observer of contemporary good-old-boy culture, the grass roots of the South. An outrageous satirist of U.S. lies in general, Crews pits the empty materialism of our mainstream society against deep-South grotesques and misfits with results at once comic and horrific.

Beginning with *The Gospel Singer*, which probes the psychology of show-biz fundamentalism, Crews has inverted a gallery of social, sexual, and spiritual outcasts who seek salvation in a civilization that offers them only *things*. The theme is expanded in *Naked in Garden Hills*. Fat Man, the 600-pound protagonist, lives in an abandoned phosphorous mine, where the earth has been eaten away, and he tries to eat the world itself. This is echoed in *Car*, in which Herman Mack vows to eat an entire 1971 Ford Maverick. A refugee from a junkyard, Mack revenges himself on the world by trying to consume it and defecate it. *This Thing Don't Lead to Heaven* caricatures the old-folks industry, in which people are the used-up detritus of our society. In this novel, Jefferson Davis Munroe, a midget who works for a ''graveyard chain,'' competes with Axel's Senior Club for the bodies (if not the souls) of the dying.

In *Karate Is a Thing of Spirit*, Crews deals with the fads and obsessions of contemporary trendy culture. John Kaimon, its central character, wears a tee-shirt stenciled with William Faulkner's face and tries to find himself through a karate group. The story develops our sick fascination with sex and violence and the fear of love and belief that Crews sees as being the focus of our lives. *The Hawk Is Dying* portrays a more positive, even heroic, obsession, George Gattling's desire to ''man'' (train) a hawk in the prescribed medieval ritual. His attempt to fuse his soul with the raptor's is another way out of the stylized hell of a technologically focused world. George's need for belief is satisfied by the vitality of the hawk, its innate freedom and dignity.

The Gypsy's Curse returns to the world of physical violence and action with Marvin Molar, born with stunted legs, who walks on his hands and develops his upper body through exercise. In his upside-down world, he becomes sexually obsessed with Hester, a normal woman. The connection between possessiveness, ''normality,'' sexuality, and strength is a basic Crews theme. It appears also in the savage burlesque of *A Feast of Snakes*, in which high school football, baton-twirling, weight-lifting, moonshine selling and rattlesnake hunting are intermixed as American rituals. The story ends, like *The Gospel Singer*, in an explosion of mortal violence, as Joe Lon Mackey, ex-state-champ quarterback, loses his slender grip on his own life.

All We Need of Hell is a gentler satire examining the folkways of modern marriage. It is a lighter ''screwball comedy'' of marriage and divorce. *The Knockout Artist* and *Body* re-imagine the body-soul dichotomy that haunts Crews. *The Knockout Artist* centers on Eugene Talmadge Biggs, a failed glass-jaw boxer whose ''occupation'' is to fight himself in the ring and ultimately knock himself out. This caricatures phony ''sports'' like professional wrestling and boxing and defines guilt and masochism as motive forces in our culture. *Body* lampoons the already surreal world of bodybuilding and physical-culture narcissism. In the novel, Russell ''Muscle'' Morgan tries to re-live and better his bodybuilding success by transforming ''white trash'' Dorothy Turnipseed into hardbody and Ms. Cosmos-phenom ''Shereel Dupont.''

Crews's most recent work explores the effects of love and human kindness upon his typically afflicted characters. In *Scar Lover*, accident-survivor Pete Butcher is pulled from a life of mourning and solitude by cancer-stricken Sarah Leemer, who helps him locate moments of solace in an otherwise sad world. In *The Mulching of America*, company-man Hickurn Looney, who initially peddles ''cure-all'' soaps to the elderly and ill, re-discovers human honor (though not exactly happiness) through his relationship with a prostitute. *Celebration*, set in a retirement community, pits the deformed Stump, a man with one hand who owns the community, against a vivacious, youthful woman named Too Much; Stump callously rejects the individuality of his elderly (and dying) patrons while Too Much tries to revitalize them by providing meaning and joy in their waning years.

Crews's satire is directed toward the triviality and rootlessness of our culture, its lack of belief. His characters search frantically for salvation through money, sex, social status, physical strength, mystical rites—through sheer acquisitiveness. Crews shows how these are false paths, failures. John Kaimon, in *Karate Is a Thing of Spirit* thinks,

> … he also knew he did not believe. The breath of little children would leave his flesh only flesh. Belief could see through glass eyes, could turn flesh to stone or stone to flesh. But not for him. He could walk through the world naked. He would bruise and bleed. He saw it clearly.

Crews sees clearly, through his scathing satire, that the absence of faith leads to violence, madness, death. His creatures search through a world of junkyards and abandoned mines and prisons for their authenticity through belief, and our world fails and maims them in savage ways. Human kindness, *love*, provides some relief, but in Crews's fiction, such relief is contextualized within suffering.

—William J. Schafer, updated by Ryan Lankford

CRICHTON, (John) Michael

Pseudonyms: John Lange; Jeffery Hudson; Michael Douglas. **Nationality:** American. **Born:** 23 October 1942. **Education:** Harvard University, Cambridge, Massachusetts, A.B.(summa cum laude) 1964 (Phi Beta Kappa): Harvard Medical School, M.D. 1969: Salk Institute, La Jolla, California (postdoctoral fellow), 1969–70. **Family:** Married 1) Joan Radam in 1965 (divorced 1971); 2) Kathleen St. Johns in 1978 (divorced 1980); 3) Suzanne Childs (divorced); 4) Anne-Marie Martin in 1987, one daughter. **Career:** Visiting writer, Massachusetts Institute of Technology, Cambridge, 1988. **Awards:** Mystery Writers of America Edgar Allan Poe award, 1968, for *A Case of Need,* and 1980, for *The Great Train Robbery;* Association of American Medical Writers award, 1970, for *Five Patients: The Hospital Explained*; George Foster Peabody Award, for *ER,* 1995; Emmy Award, best dramatic series, for *ER,* 1996; Life Career Award, Academy of Science Fiction, Fantasy, and Horror Films, 1998. **Agent:** International Creative Management, 40 West 57th Street, New York, New York 10019, U.S.A.

PUBLICATIONS

Novels

A Case of Need (as Jeffery Hudson). Cleveland, World, and London, Heinemann, 1968.
The Andromeda Strain. New York, Knopf, and London, Cape, 1969.
Dealing; or, the Berkeley-to-Boston Forty-Brick Lost-Bag Blues (as Michael Douglas), with Douglas Crichton. New York, Knopf, 1971.
The Terminal Man. New York, Knopf, and London, Cape, 1972.
Westworld. New York, Bantam, 1974.
The Great Train Robbery. New York, Knopf, and London, Cape, 1975.
Eaters of the Dead: The Manuscript of Ibn Fadlan, Relating His Experiences with the Northmen in A.D. 922. New York, Knopf, and London, Cape, 1976.
Congo. New York, Knopf, 1980; London, Allen Lane, 1981.
Sphere. New York, Knopf, and London, Macmillan, 1987.
Jurassic Park. New York, Knopf, 1990; London, Century, 1991.
Rising Sun. New York, Knopf, and London, Century, 1992.
Disclosure. New York, Knopf, 1994.
The Lost World: A Novel. New York, Knopf, 1995.

Airframe. New York, Knopf, 1996.
Timeline. New York, Knopf, 1999.

Novels as John Lange

Odds On. New York, New American Library, 1966.
Scratch One. New York, New American Library, 1967.
Easy Go. New York, New American Library, 1968; London, Sphere, 1972; as *The Last Tomb* (as Michael Crichton), New York, Bantam, 1974.
The Venom Business. Cleveland, World, 1969.
Zero Cool. New York, New American Library, 1969; London, Sphere, 1972.
Drug of Choice. New York, New American Library, 1970; as *Overkill*, New York, Centesis, 1970.
Grave Descend. New York, New American Library, 1970.
Binary. New York, Knopf, and London, Heinemann, 1972.

Plays

Screenplays: *Westworld*, 1973; *Coma*, 1977; *The Great Train Robbery*, 1978; *Looker*, 1981; *Runaway*, 1984; *Jurassic Park*, with John Koepp, 1993; *Rising Sun*, with Philip Kaufman and Michael Backes, 1993; *Twister*, with Anne-Marie Martin, 1996

Other

Five Patients: The Hospital Explained. New York, Knopf, 1970; London, Cape, 1971.
Jasper Johns. New York, Abrams, and London, Thames and Hudson, 1977.
Electronic Life: How to Think about Computers. New York, Knopf, and London, Heinemann, 1983.
Travels. New York, Knopf, and London, Macmillan, 1988.
Twister: The Original Screenplay. New York, Ballantine Books, 1996.

*

Film Adaptations: *The Andromeda Strain*, 1971; *The Carey Treatment*, 1973, from the work *A Case of Need; Westworld*, 1973; *The Terminal Man*, 1974; *The Great Train Robbery*, 1978; *Jurassic Park*, 1993; *Rising Sun*, 1993; *Disclosure*, 1994; *Congo*, 1995; *The Lost World*, 1997; *Sphere*, 1998; *The 13th Warrior*, from the work *Eaters of the Dead*, 1999; *Jurassic Park 3*, from the works *Jurassic Park* and *The Lost World*.

Critical Studies: *Michael Crichton: A Critical Companion* by Elizabeth A. Trembley. Westport, Connecticut: Greenwood Press, 1996.

Theatrical Activities: Director: **Films**—*Westworld*, 1973; *Coma*, 1978; *The Great Train Robbery*, 1978; *Looker*, 1981; *Runaway*, 1984. **Television**—*Pursuit*, 1972; *ER* (executive producer), 1994.

* * *

Michael Crichton has an unerring instinct for the hot topic of the moment. His best-selling novels—most of them subsequently transformed into hit movies—tend to deal with the cutting edge of modern technology, the latest discoveries, the most exciting and terrifying innovations. Yet at their heart lies a far older theme evoked so memorably by Robert Louis Stevenson in his *Strange Case of Dr. Jekyll and Mr. Hyde*: the idea of the scientific discovery intended for the benefit of mankind that suddenly runs out of control to become a lethal threat. Whether the mutant plague virus of *The Andromeda Strain*, the homicidal android gunfighter of *Westworld*, or the dinosaurs recreated from prehistoric DNA who break out of Jurassic Park to spread death and devastation, all are testimony to the human pride that goes before a fall, the fumbling fingers that have released the imp from the bottle. This theme is at the core of his early works of the 1970s, a decade where disaster novels—and films—were the fashion. It's a point made to score more heavily by Crichton's skill in placing the latest technology within uneasy reach of mankind's basic instincts and the darker secrets of the mind. The pleasure electrodes of *The Terminal Man*, implanted in the brain of a potentially violent patient in order to render him manageable, end by driving him to greater violence as he becomes addicted to pleasurable sensations he can obtain only by assault and murder.

In *The Terminal Man* as elsewhere in his fiction, Crichton reminds us of the fragility of civilizing influences, our nobler impulses forever under threat from the atavistic animal brain beneath. "That cortex, which could feel love, and worry about ethical conduct, and write poetry, had to make an uneasy peace with the crocodile brain at its core. Sometimes, as in the case of Benson, the peace broke down, and the crocodile brain took over intermittently." The high-tech security of the dinosaur wonderland in *Jurassic Park* is undone by old-fashioned human greed and an electric storm that between them let the dinosaurs loose on an unprepared bunch of humans. In *Congo*, the state-of-the art computers used by the scientists of ERTS to pinpoint the lost African city with its rare industrial diamonds are thwarted by a group of hybrid killer apes trained centuries ago by long-dead "primitive" masters. Again and again technology breaks down or finds itself helpless in the face of man's worst instincts, or the world's wild places.

One factor often overlooked in Crichton's career is his erudition. His background reading takes in a mass of scientific literature and business reports and extends to Norse legends and Arab traveler's tales. Most of his novels contain substantial end-bibliographies and a text peppered with footnotes and references to the relevant scientific report, e.g. animal training and behavior in *Congo* and "mind control" in *The Terminal Man*. The latter novel also contains diagrams of brain sections and what appear to be Xeroxed police reports. This formidable amount of confirmatory material adds weight to whatever imaginative leap is being made by the writer, whether killer apes or recreated dinosaurs on the rampage. The extent of Crichton's reading is shown in what might be regarded as his two "historical" novels, *The Great Train Robbery* and *Eaters of the Dead* (later revamped as *The Thirteenth Warrior*). These have fairly un-Crichton-like themes in that neither deals with a current topic, but both reveal their author's impressive knowledge of his subject. In *The Great Train Robbery* Crichton displays a remarkably thorough awareness of Victorian England and its criminal underworld, commenting with apparent objectivity on the ruthless behavior of the robbers and their eventual escape from justice with a fortune in gold. This dispassionate narrative overview is found in his other novels, where his characters suffer or prosper in a life-like random fashion, rather than in accordance with their previous actions. *Eaters of the Dead/The Thirteenth Warrior* is presented in the form of a genuine travel narrative recounted in the first person by real-life Arab emissary Ibn Fadlan.

Using an understated style and the familiar corroborative footnotes, Crichton manages to work in his own version of the Beowulf legend and to suggest that some of the monsters the hero encountered may have been examples of Neanderthal Man.

Significant also is Crichton's mastery of technical jargon, which is heavily used both in dialogue and narrative. Evident in his earliest work, if anything this has increased to the extent that the reader may well feel he or she is being beaten over the head with techno-speak. The computerized location-finders of *Congo*, the minutiae of CD-Rom production in *Disclosure*, and the jargon of aircraft manufacture in *Airframe* are three examples of many. Sometimes Crichton goes too far in this direction—parts of *The Great Train Robbery* are virtually unintelligible through over-use of criminal slang—but while often baffling to the untrained reader there is no doubt that, like the constant footnotes, the jargon adds to verisimilitude. The author has a sure grasp of his subject, and narrative and speech have a convincing sound.

Recent Crichton novels have tended to forsake the wilder undiscovered regions of the world to bring the action closer to home. Granted in *The Lost World* the author returns to the island jungle of *Jurassic Park* to find more dinosaurs lurking in the foliage (this time infected by a B.S.E.-type disease from their sheep-offal feed) in a successful sequel to the original blockbuster, but more often the ''jungle'' is found in the workplace, the boardroom, or the factory floor. In *Rising Sun* competition over modern technology between Japanese and American corporations runs to outright murder, confirming the Oriental claim that ''business is war.'' Elsewhere the action stops short of killing, concerning itself with the threat of job loss or the stigma of business failure. The ruthless, predatory female executive who threatens to destroy Tom Sanders with a phoney sexual harassment claim in *Disclosure* (power, Crichton is careful to point out, is neither male nor female) may be seen as a modern variant on the flesh-eating velociraptors of *Jurassic Park*. The author avoids any obvious ''male-female'' confrontation by balancing the scary Meredith with defense lawyer Louise Hernandez and other sympathetic female characters. In *Airframe*, where a plane-making firm is wrongly accused of bad design following an in-flight ''incident,'' he has a female lead in executive Casey Singleton. Writing credible dialogue and constructing realistic backgrounds to his action, Crichton casts interesting light on the various shenanigans made use of by business organizations and the mass media to twist the facts to their own advantage. Reading his novels for this aspect alone can be a most informative experience! Accused of sexism by some readers of *Disclosure*, and (perhaps more justly) of chauvinism in *Rising Sun*, Crichton has also been criticized for writing books that are like embryo movie scripts, with a future film in mind. Given that Crichton is himself a film director and the creator of the successful TV series *ER*, he could scarcely be blamed if this was the case. In fact, there has been no obvious change in his style since the early 1970s, before his works made it to the screen. Brilliant descriptions and profound character studies are not his territory; Crichton doesn't need them. Rather, he writes to his strengths, hooking the reader immediately and carrying him or her along, pacing the action with great skill and constantly building tension to delay resolution to the last few pages. None too sure what's about to happen next and anxious to find out, the reader keeps turning those pages. The fact that his works translate so well to the cinema screen merely serves as a further tribute to the power of the novels and the ability of the man who has written them.

—Geoff Sadler

CUNNINGHAM, E.V.

See FAST, Howard (Melvin)

CUNNINGHAM, Michael

Nationality: American. **Born:** Ohio, 1952. **Education:** Attended Stanford University; University of Iowa, M.F.A. **Career:** Worked for Carnegie Corp., New York, beginning in 1986. **Awards:** Pulitzer prize, 1999.

Publications

Novels

Golden States. New York, Crown, 1984.

A Home at the End of the World. New York, Farrar Straus, and Giroux, 1990.

Flesh and Blood. New York, Farrar Straus, and Giroux, 1995.

The Hours. New York, Farrar Straus, and Giroux, 1998.

* * *

Recent critical praise for Michael Cunningham's novel *The Hours*, including the Pulitzer Prize in 1999, came as no surprise to those who followed his progression since the publication of *A Home at the End of the World* in 1990. *The Hours* addresses themes that have long been preoccupations of the author's: adopted social roles that end up owning us; the common desire to flee from our lives; the solution to that desire provided by suicide, but also by creativity; and the strained role of family in the late twentieth century. In addition, these universal issues are often explored within the further complicating frame of homosexuality. The manner in which Cunningham subtly inserts the many references to homosexuality has an effortless, natural quality. As some critics have noted, Cunningham's treatment of gay themes could only be a recent literary manifestation. This is no longer the ''fearful closet'' novel of the 1960s nor the ''defiant ghetto'' writing of the 1970s, rather it is fiction that treats homosexuality (and the looming shadow of AIDS) as just one subject among many.

Most of Cunningham's characters have a nagging suspicion that they are not living the lives they should be, that they are engaged in acts of ''impersonation'' that belittle their true selfhood. Despite depicting the occasional escape from role constraints, Cunningham's vision remains bleak with only flashes of hope shining through, often at the very conclusion of his texts. His novels focus on the shadow that falls between what is and what might have been, and the result is at best wistful and, at worst, despairing.

Told in four different voices, *A Home at the End of the World* presents the story of Jonathan and Bobby, boyhood friends in Cleveland during the 1970s. Each boy seeks to escape familial demands: Jonathan, his needy mother, Alice; Bobby the tragedy that slowly engulfs his family after the accidental death of his beloved older brother. Jonathan and Bobby's relationship becomes sexual, but, unlike openly homosexual Jonathan, Bobby's sexual identity remains ambiguous—the sex he has with both Jonathan and, later with Jonathan's roommate Clare, lacks any real desire on his part for either of them (''I'd had orgasms that passed through me like the spirits of people more devoted to the body than I was'').

The other voices in the novel belong to Alice, Jonathan's mother, and Clare, with whom he plans to have a child and begin a ''new'' family of his own. It is, in fact, Bobby, whom Clare ultimately chooses to conceive with. The three of them then attempt to live their version of utopia in a house in Woodstock, with both men playing father to the child. But this New Family splits at the seams, and Clare leaves with her child to begin her life anew. Jonathan and Bobby stay on to care for an old lover of Jonathan's who is dying of an unnamed virus and the novel ends in a mock baptism, as the three men stand in an icy pond in April. The new beginning implied leaves the reader with an unmistakable chill.

Actually creating a home at the end of the world may require that old models of family be trashed rather than revamped. After all, it is only when he finds himself with his ambivalent lover, Bobby, and his dying friend, Erich, that Jonathan finds some sort of epiphany: ''I was merely present, perhaps for the first time in my adult life. The moment was unextraordinary. But I had the moment, I had it completely. It inhabited me. I realized that if I died soon I would have known this, a connection with my life, its errors and cockeyed successes.'' Cunningham seems to be saying that life's imperfections, the mistakes, are the thing. Accepting them with integrity makes for happiness rather than engaging in a hapless quest to efface them.

Cunningham's next novel, *Flesh and Blood*, belongs to the family epic tradition, spanning a century in the lives of the Stassos family (beginning in 1935 and ending with a prophetic and imaginary chapter that takes place in 2035). The novel focuses on Greek-born Constantine, his wife, Mary, and their three children, Billy, Susan, and Zoe. But it is drag queen Cassandra who provides the psychic center of the novel. As best friend to Zoe, surrogate mother to Jamal, Zoe's son, and eventually confidante to Mary, Cassandra acts as the mouthpiece for Cunningham's particular blend of optimism and pessimism. Having tested HIV-positive, Cassandra still manages to dish out words of wisdom and find the true balance between the various absolutist philosophies presented in the novel.

Cunningham manages to involve us in the lives of his particular characters, despite the secondary emphasis on plotline. The novel once again reveals the author's predominant concerns. Family is not something to seek solace and security from, but rather to flee. The characters resort to aberrant behavior as a means of expression (physical abuse, kleptomania, promiscuity, adultery, substance abuse). In fact, deviancy is so commonplace in the novel that one begins to wonder whether Cunningham wishes us to reconsider our standards for determining what is indeed normal.

The various characters adopt roles that thwart any possibility of self-actualization: Susan's brush with incest propels her into an early marriage with her first boyfriend to play the devoted wife; Billy, a homosexual, reacts angrily to his father's physical abuse and becomes a fifth grade teacher instead of an architect, primarily to spite his father; Zoe rejects a well-defined role, but her aimlessness turns tragic as she contracts AIDS. They are all in some state of anguish. They watch their lives pass them by; it is not that their lives are unexamined, it is simply that they feel powerless to change them. Neither parenthood, nor homosexuality, nor an alternative lifestyle, are sufficient to ground their identities. The characters remain plagued by uncertainty, constantly wondering at the lives they might have lived. As one notes, ''We are adaptable creatures. It's the source of our earthly comfort and, I suppose, of our silent rage.'' This is an idea that Cunningham raises once more in his most balanced and accomplished work, *The Hours*.

Using Virginia Woolf's modernist techniques and *Mrs. Dalloway* as a springboard, *The Hours* consists of three concurrent narratives taking place at different times. The central narrative concerns Clarissa Vaughan, a present day book editor living in Greenwich Village, who is planning a party for her friend and former lover, Richard, a gay poet dying of AIDS. The second narrative tells a day in the life of Laura Brown, a housewife living in the suburbs of Los Angeles in 1949. To escape the monotony of her existence, she has given herself the task of reading all of Woolf's novels in order and has reached, of course, *Mrs. Dalloway*. The third narrative concerns Woolf herself as she sets out, in 1923, to write the novel that is the inspiration for Cunningham's text.

Cunningham subtly weaves a confluence of parallels to link the tales of these three women and revisit familiar themes: the notion of flight, restrictive roles, suicide as a means of escape, creativity as a means of momentarily eluding the grasp of that ''old devil'' that plagues us all (Woolf writing her novel, Laura making a cake, Clarissa hosting the party). Opening as the novel does with an evocative retelling of Woolf's suicide, the book is tinged with a longing for death. Death offers the ultimate escape, one that Woolf ponders for her protagonist, one that Laura Brown considers and attempts, and one that Richard actually accomplishes. Throughout Cunningham's oeuvre various characters become aware of the thin line that separates life from death, and that crossing that line is not the daunting experience they had always imagined it would be. Laura Brown sees that it would be, in fact, quite easy to end her own life; that the release suicide offers might compensate for whatever pain might be endured (''Think how wonderful it might be to no longer matter. Think how wonderful it might be to no longer worry, or struggle, or fail'').

Suicide is treated as a temptation—the ultimate expression of free will, proof that we are not trapped in our lives. This realization is both liberating and frightening for Cunningham's characters. As pawns of something they have set in motion (frequently without any thought or conscious decision), this realization offers a sense of relief that helps some live and some die. Cunningham's fiction explores the gaps between our (creative) expectations and the reality of our lives. The creative endeavors of the characters in *The Hours* are representative of the plights of the majority of the men and women who people his books—individuals who have difficulty living in that space between perceptions of utter perfection and dismal failure.

—Tim Gauthier

D

DABYDEEN, David

Nationality: Guyanian and British (immigrated to Britain, 1969). **Born:** Berbice, Guyana, 9 December 1956. **Education:** Cambridge University, 1974–78, B.A. (honours) in English 1978; London University, Ph.D. 1982. **Career:** Director, Centre for Caribbean Studies, University of Warwick. **Awards:** Cambridge University Quiller-Couch prize, 1978; Commonwealth Poetry prize, 1984; Guyana Literature prize, 1991. **Agent:** Curtis Brown, Ltd., Haymarket House, 28–29 Haymarket, London S.W.1 England. **Address:** c/o Centre for Caribbean Studies, University of Warwick, Coventry, England.

Publications

Novels

The Intended. London, Secker and Warburg, 1991.
Disappearance. London, Secker and Warburg, 1993.
The Counting House. London, J. Cape, 1996.
A Harlot's Progress. London, Cape, 1999.

Poetry

Slave Song. London, Dangaroo Press, 1984.
Coolie Odyssey. London, Hansib, 1988.
Turner. London, Cape, 1994.

Other

Hogarth, Walpole and Commercial Britain. London, Hansib, 1985.
Hogarth's Blacks: Images of Blacks in Eighteenth Century English Art. Manchester, Manchester University Press, 1987.
A Handbook for Teaching Caribbean Literature. London, Heinemann, 1988.
Editor, *The Black Presence in English Literature.* Manchester, Manchester University Press, 1985.
Editor, with Brinsley Samaroo, *India in the Caribbean.* N.p., Hansib Publishing Ltd., 1987.
Editor, with Paul Edwards, *Black Writers in Britain: An Anthology.* N.p., Columbia University Press, 1992.
Editor, *Cheddi Jagan: Selected Speeches 1992–1994.* London: Hansib, 1995.
Editor, with Brinsley Samaroo, *Across the Dark Waters: Ethnicity And Indian Identity In the Caribbean.* London, Macmillan Caribbean, 1996.

*

Critical Studies: *Configurations of Exile: South Asian Writers And Their World* By Chelva Kanaganayakam. Toronto: TSAR, 1995; *English Imaginaries: Six Studies In Anglo-British Modernity* By Kevin Davey. London: Lawrence & Wishart, 1999.

*   *   *

As a writer, editor, professor, and critic, David Dabydeen is remarkably committed to critically exploring the literary contributions of the Caribbean diaspora and the often conflicting polyglot identities that emerge from diasporic movements to and from homelands and *homeless lands* marked by racism, exploitation, and violence. Language—both the creolization of tongues and the overseer-institution of *standard* English—as an instrument of colonial bondage or the painful outcome of a brutal colonial past is also a central concern in Dabydeen's poetry and prose.

The Intended and *Disappearance* use Creole in ways that reveal a fascination with and resistance to *standard* English. First-person narrators in these bildungsroman-type novels start out by desiring assimilation and invisibility within white sociolinguistic norms. These norms are exemplified in an imagined purity and status associated with white bodies and *standard* English. Narrators in both novels are contrasted with characters and memories that recall them to the ''angry, crude, energetic'' (*Slave Song*) rawness associated with a Creole that has little patience for lyricism and cleanliness given the constantly intruding wounded history of its users. In *The Intended* and *Disappearance,* Dabydeen's focus shifts between England, Guyana, and Africa, playing with the intentions, memories, and desires of his fictional African and Asian diaspora in Britain. The writer juxtaposes his narrator's denial and shame with a series of narrative movements that double back on themselves, keeping the narrator both complicit and questioning as to the relationships between power and its consequences for race, gender, and empire.

The Intended presents a dilemma of diasporic writing. On the one hand, there is a pressure toward mimicry and the erasure of Black identity through the disciplinary projects of a seemingly apolitical aesthetics of reading practiced by some academic institutions. On the other hand, there is also a concentration on what Dabydeen called the ''*folking* up'' of Black literature that could lead to its being considered important only as an example of the ethnically exotic or aberrant (''On Not Being Milton: Nigger Talk in England Today''). *The Intended* problematizes these ambivalences by introducing the (ill) literate Joseph, who relentlessly questions the young student narrator and his friends in order to disrupt *the intended* narrative of mimicry. However, since Joseph sets fire to himself and dies, his influence on the narrator is mostly posthumous. It remains arguable, therefore, from the implications of Joseph's death, whether posing an alternate picture to colonial discourses can ever survive without tragic consequences. In *Disappearance,* the narrator is again compelled to move into the spaces between his present—as an engineer trained in Britain who resists cultivating a ''sense of the past''—and the African masks on the walls of his landlady's home in Britain. Ironically, this time it is the *English* Mrs. Rutherford who discomfits the narrator's sense of history. The novel also takes Ireland into consideration in its questioning of imperialism. The narrator and Mrs. Rutherford share a curious blend of friendship that at times approaches a romantic closeness, and there is a sense of mystery associated with her past that complements the *disappearance* that the narrator has practiced with regard to his own racial history. However, as with *The Intended,* the narrative moves toward distancing the past but constantly undercuts itself by advancing right into those areas, destabilizing any security that the narrative might *intend* to offer the reader.

Dabydeen's poetry and fiction also contains overtones of riposte, overtones that are sporadically marked in the form of intertextual interrogations of well-known pieces of English literature, such as William Shakespeare's *The Tempest,* Joseph Conrad's *Heart of Darkness,* and John Milton's poetry. Some of his poems in *Slave Song, Coolie Odyssey,* and *Turner* write back to English paintings depicting blacks, such as those by Francis Wheatley and J. M. W. Turner, among others. These rejoinders come alongside his extensive research into the depictions of blacks and Indians in English art and society and into the history of indentured labor in the Caribbean. This research can be seen in his books *Hogarth's Blacks: Images of Blacks in Eighteenth Century Art and Society* and *A Handbook for Teaching Caribbean Literature;* as well as in books he has edited, such as *The Black Presence in English Literature;* or in books he has coedited, such as *Black Writers in Britain 1760–1890* and *India in the Caribbean.* Dabydeen's poems, unlike his fiction, offer translations in *standard* English that accompany their creolized texts. The poetry collections also offer introductions and contexts (which the novels do not) for ways in which he uses Creole. These introductions also serve to emphasize some of his major poetic concerns, concerns that are present also in his fiction.

The Counting House begins in India, and takes protagonists Rohini and Vidia to Guiana as indentured servants in 1857. It is a novel of impotence, both literal (Vidia cannot father a child) and figurative. Mungo, the narrator of *A Harlot's Progress,* tells the story of a different but quite similar form of servitude: captured and sold into slavery, he has now been freed (as of ''22 April 17—''), but he refuses to tell his story on behalf of the abolitionists who freed him. Instead, he directly addresses the reader, who is forced—by virtue of his apparent ingratitude toward those who freed him, and by other aspects of his personality—to avoid a too-easy sense of sympathy for Mungo.

The critical reception to Dabydeen's novels has been largely positive, except for a sharp critique on narrative complicity by Benita Parry. However, the complex and often tense ways in which gender, race, and identity configure in his writings deserve further and closer scrutiny that existing scholarship has offered.

—Marian Gracias

D'AGUIAR, Fred

Nationality: English. **Born:** London, England, 2 February 1960. **Education:** University of Kent at Canterbury, B.A. 1985. **Career:** Trained and worked as a psychiatric nurse; visiting fellow, Cambridge University, Cambridge, England, 1989–90; visiting writer, Amherst College, Amherst, Massachusetts, 1992–94; assistant professor of English, Bates College, Lewiston, Maine, 1994–95; professor of English, University of Miami, Coral Gables, Florida, 1995. **Awards:** Minority Rights Group Award, 1983; University of Kent T. S. Eliot Prize, 1984; G.L.C. Literature Award, 1985; Guyana Prize for Poetry (Guyanese government), 1989; David Higham First Novel Award (The Book Trust), 1995; Whitbread Award (Booksellers Association of Great Britain and Ireland), 1995. **Agent:** Curtis Brown, Ltd., 10 Astor Place, New York, New York 10003, U.S.A.

Publications

Novels

The Longest Memory. New York, Pantheon, 1995.
Dear Future. New York, Pantheon, 1996.
Feeding the Ghosts. Hopewell, New Jersey, Ecco Press, 1999.

Plays

A Jamaican Airman Foresees His Death. London, Methuen, 1995; also appeared in *Black Plays,* edited by Yvonne Brewster. New York, Methuen, 1995.

Televisions Plays: *Sweet Thames.* BBC-TV 2, 1992; *Rain.* BBC-TV 2, 1994.

Radio Plays: *1492.* BBC Radio 3, 1992.

Poetry

Mama Dot. London, Chatto & Windus, 1985.
Airy Hall. London, Chatto & Windus, 1989.
British Subjects. Newcastle upon Tyne, England, Bloodaxe, 1993.
Bill of Rights. London, Chatto & Windus, 1998.

Other

Contributor, *New British Poetries: The Scope of the Possible,* edited by Robert Hampson and Peter Barry. New York, Manchester University Press, 1993.
Editor, with others, *The New British Poetry.* London, Paladin Grafton, 1988.

* * *

Fred D'Aguiar is part of a younger group of talented Black British writers and critics including David Dabydeen and Caryl Phillips who bring to their novels a multi-layered awareness of the aesthetic, cultural, literary, and political debates surrounding race and representation. All three novelists have experimented with the delivery of the novel, particularly in its manipulation of time, its use of metaphor and symbol as structuring devices that cut across the linear unfolding of the text, and its dialogic engagement with other narrative works as inter-texts. All three novelists have also tackled the history and legacy of slavery as a site for the imaginative interrogation of questions of history and memory, culture, power, and identity. As such, these novelists can be located within what Paul Gilroy has called a ''Black Atlantic'' web of diasporic connections and concerns.

D'Aguiar was known as a poet and had produced critically acclaimed collections such as *Mama Dot, Airy Hall,* and *British Subjects* long before he began to write novels. With the publication of *The Longest Memory*, a novel centered on the life of a slave set on an eighteenth-century Virginia plantation, *Dear Future*, a book about growing up in the political climate of Guyana in the 1960s and 1970s, and *Feeding the Ghosts*, based on the historic case of the Zong slave ship whose captain threw overboard ostensibly sick and dying slaves,

D'Aguiar's stature as a novelist is assured. All three texts show D'Aguiar's ability to create compelling characters and moods, but they also exhibit a willingness to experiment with the traditional form of the novel. In interviews, D'Aguiar himself has argued that the nineteenth-century realist novel, with its relatively straightforward unfolding of events, is not tenable in an age that has seen the innovations of writers like James Joyce and Wilson Harris. D'Aguiar's work is a good example of how the emotional strengths of the traditional novel need not be sacrificed for a more intellectual engagement with form.

The Longest Memory plays with voice and time. The book is narrated through different characters, all of whom are given their own voices: Whitechapel, the slave; his ''son'' Chapel; Chapel's mother, the cook; Whitechapel's granddaughter; Mr. Sanders senior, the overseer; Mr. Sanders junior, his son and Chapel's half brother; Mr. Whitechapel, the master of the plantation; his daughter Lydia; and the editor of the slavers' journal, *The Virginian.* These accounts function like dramatic monologues and offer very different emotional and intellectual responses to the same events, for example, the punishment and death of Chapel. There is no extra-diegetic narrator to mediate between his father, the Master, the overseer, the slavers' news report or the granddaughter's reconstruction of the event and its aftermath. Each are offered within the ideological context and are (at times) incommensurable: the overseer's need to assert his authority over runaway and rebellious slaves, the editor's belief in the righteousness of slavery, Whitechapel's conviction that resistance is futile, and his son's belief that freedom matters and that a different future exists where slavery will be outlawed. The book's abandonment of an overarching narrator in favor of a multiplicity of voice leads to a more fractured kind of narration. The use of dramatic monologues allows an event or a series of events to be told and returned to repeatedly in reconstruction and memory. Such a deliberate mixing up of chronology when assembling the novel's variety of stories and voices makes the reader's experience more disjointed; but this also has the effect of replicating how an event is experienced and remembered. Hence, as D'Aguiar himself acknowledges, the novel's circular structure. What results is that history behaves like trauma, a repetition that refuses to go away; as Whitechapel remarks, ''the future is just more of the past waiting to happen,'' ''memory is pain trying to resurrect itself.''

The representation of slavery as a trauma, the task of reconstructing the lives and stories of slaves from their relegation to the anonymity of history, are part of a modern and postcolonial ethical and archival project. The Black Atlantic preoccupation with slavery is often depicted as part of a process of reckoning that is required in order to move on (see, for example, Toni Morrison's *Beloved*). Coming to terms with the trauma of slavery enables one not to repeat the failures and mistakes of the past in new guises. But in an article, ''The Last Essay about Slavery,'' D'Aguiar argues that there is also a compulsive need to revisit slavery—in their own language and imagery—for every succeeding generation of black writers. Rather than the past being laid to rest when it is told, each imagining ''feeds the need for a further act of retrieval. In fiction as in song, the story continues both to bring to life a past that might otherwise remain lost or distorted into shame, and to convert that past from pain to cure.''

This awareness that cultural memory is in an important sense not simply about recovering the past but how the past is formed and performed in the present is an integral part of a postmodern critique of essentialist notions of identity. Cultural identity is not simply an unproblematic ethnic inheritance; it is created and produced. Such debates structure D'Aguiar's *Feeding the Ghosts*. The novel's central protagonist, the slave Mintah, is compelled to remember the deaths on the Zong, and her connection with her African homeland, and expresses such acts of memory through the crafting of wooden carvings of these murdered companions. D'Aguiar's choice of Mintah as a character that survives the seaboard murder of slaves is deliberate. It allows him to use her reproductive ability—her body—to explore slavery's severance of family and community; here, her black identity is based on filial and kinship connections. Yet D'Aguiar also characterizes Mintah as an artist, and depicts her woodwork as a kind of creative ''birthing.'' This allows D'Aguiar to capture a more complex articulation of black subjectivity as moving beyond the notion of the essential black subject that is based on a racialized culture; instead it is an affiliative connection that must be forged and renewed through creative and expressive forms.

If *Feeding the Ghosts* seems at first glance to be a more conventional novel than *The Longest Memory*, the novel's manipulation of metaphor and symbol cuts across the chronology of history and narrative and offers a more poetic meta-narrative. A body of metaphoric association, which accrues around the symbol of wood, land, and, especially, the sea (which owes much to Derek Walcott's poetry) forges a horizon of connections through the different spatial and temporal zones of the novel. D'Aguiar himself describes such a technique as abandoning the realism of the novel for the symbolism of poetry, but such a method of construction also performs the kind of diasporic aesthetics that Gilroy speaks about.

Dear Future looks not at slavery but at broader postcolonial issues such as the plight of former colonies, particularly Guyana, after independence. On the one hand, global capitalism makes nonsense of any form of political and economic autonomy, and on the other, the corruption of the indigenous elite undermines the future of the emerging nation. The black seamless bitumen road that replaces the red sand road of the village opens the rural heartland to a new form of colonial exploitation. Its huge articulated trucks ''never stopped for anyone or anything they hit'' as they convert the interior's raw materials to a stream of commodities for sale on the world's market. The indigenous politicians, with their hand in the country's till, collude with and profit from this traffic; they magic votes out of thin air in order to stay in power. The result is a betrayal of the promise of independence, to turn them into ''nightmare[s] from the republic of dreams.''

The political context of Guyana is not handled directly but is filtered through a child's eyes and the experiences of his family. The child's life stands in for the nation's future but D'Aguiar's portrait of Red Head (who has prophetic visions), his extended family, and their very full life together in rural Guyana is done lovingly—but economically—through episodes that depict the adventures of individual characters. (These are reminiscent of some of what appeared in D'Aguiar's first semi-autobiographic collection of poetry, *Mama Dot.*) The result is that Red Head's letters to the future, ''as a lost chance rather than an eager prospect,'' are all the more touching. As with D'Aguiar's other novel, there is a striking use of symbolism (notably the opposition between red and black in the child's view of things) and the manipulation of space (the spaces of the Guyanese village and that of London, where his mother resides). The chronology of the story is turned on its head, as episodes are not offered in their temporal sequence. Time becomes the ''ever present past'' of the future as Red Head asserts his memory of—and connection with—surviving family members. It goes without saying that such strategic use of kinship across and against time is also the basis of the notion of a black diaspora.

—Gail Low

d'ALPUGET, Blanche

Nationality: Australian. **Born:** Sydney, 3 January 1944. **Education:** Sydney Church of England Girls' Grammar School. **Family:** Married Anthony Ian Camden Pratt in 1965; one son. **Career:** Journalist, president of the Australian Capital Territory branch of the Oral History Association of Australia. **Awards:** PEN Sydney Centre Golden Jubilee award for literature, 1981; *Age* Book of the Year award, 1981, for *Turtle Beach;* South Australian Government award for literature, 1982; New South Wales Premier's award for non-fiction, 1983, for *Robert J. Hawke.* **Member:** Women's Electoral Body; Women's International League for Peace and Freedom; Australian Labor Party; Oral History Association of Australia; Australian Society of Authors. **Agent:** Robert Gottlieb, William Morris Agency, 1350 Avenue of the Americas, New York, New York 10019, U.S.A. **Address:** 18 Urambi Village, Kambah, Australian Capital Territory 2902, Australia.

Publications

Novels

Monkeys in the Dark. Sydney, Aurora Press, 1980.
Turtle Beach. New York, Simon and Schuster, 1981.
Winter in Jerusalem. New York, Simon and Schuster, and London, Secker and Warburg, 1986.
White Eye. New York, Simon and Schuster, 1994.

Other

Mediator: A Biography of Sir Richard Kirby. Melbourne, Melbourne University Press, 1977.
Robert J. Hawke: A Biography. East Melbourne, Schwarts in conjunction with Landsdowne Press, 1982.

* * *

If it is true, as novelist Tom Keneally has often complained, that Australia lacks middle-brow writers who can write intelligent, absorbing fiction that deals with serious issues in a mature way, then Blanche d'Alpuget is the exception that proves the rule. She writes comparatively conventional novels that nevertheless are highly competent and engaging, show a keen interest in contemporary affairs, and engage with moral dilemmas in an accessible way without being shallow. She was one of the first Australian novelists to realize the relevance of Asia to Australian life and more recently has turned her attention to such contemporary issues as environmental destruction (and extremism in its defense), genetic engineering, and human cruelty to animals.

Monkeys in the Dark is set in Indonesia at the time of the attempted communist uprising but a year or so later than Christopher J. Koch's better known *The Year of Living Dangerously.* The revolution has been suppressed, Sukarno is still president though his power is clearly declining, and there is uneasy speculation in the air as to whether the communists will attempt another coup. It deals with Alexandra Wheatfield, a rather naive young woman working with the Australian consulate, and her relations with her first cousin and former lover, Anthony Sinclaire, as well as those with the militant Indonesian poet Maruli, with whom she falls in love. Although he does have some feeling for her, Maruli takes advantage of her diplomatic immunity to carry on his revolutionary activities. More wickedly, Anthony tricks her into coming back to him at the end of the novel by blackening Maruli's name. It is a gripping and well-plotted novel that captures the atmosphere of Indonesia in the wake of the uprising, but its pessimistic, even fatalistic, mood is summed up in the extract from a speech by Sukarno that gives the novel its title: ''Oh, my people, if you abandon our history you will face a vaccuum… . Life for you will be no more than running amok. Running amok—like monkeys trapped in the dark!''

Turtle Beach is set in Malaysia, with the boat people arriving in the aftermath of the Vietnam War being greeted with hostility by local residents. When two hundred of them are drowned, the fish feed off their corpses and the livelihood of the fishermen is ruined, as people refuse to buy their produce. Ironies such as these abound in the novel. The heroine is again a reasonably attractive (not startlingly beautiful but with a seductively Monroe kind of voice) reporter in her late thirties, but unlike her predecessor, Judith Wilkes is a tough-minded careerist, determinedly carrying on with her work as she copes with a young family and a dying marriage to an ambitious political flunky back in Australia. Yet she has some of the same qualities as Alex: a tendency toward passivity, a weakness for sensual men, and a sense of idealism that renders her vulnerable to manipulation. Like Alex, she falls in love with one of the locals, Kanan, but is finally repelled by the fatalism of his Indian philosophy. Again the title of the novel embodies a metaphor to do with human helplessness in the face of larger historical movements. It comes from the turtles that battle against all odds to lay their eggs and bury them, only to have them dug up and sold or eaten by the local residents.

Winter in Jerusalem follows a relatively familiar format but with decreasing assurance. Its heroine is Danielle Green, a thirty-eight-year-old professional writer widowed after an unhappy marriage and with a teenage daughter in Sydney. She has arrived in Jerusalem to write the script for a film about an uprising of suicidal zealots in 73 A.D. and also to try and make contact with her father, whom she has not seen for many years. Although the novel has many of d'Alpuget's best qualities—her grasp of atmosphere, aphoristic wit, quick snapshots of characters—it is the least coherent and worse structured of her novels, heavily dependent on coincidence of an opportunistic kind. The theme of Danielle's relationship with her father is never explored in any depth and toward the end the action of the novel accelerates toward its upbeat resolution to a point that is almost laughable.

A gap of eight years followed before d'Alpuget published her fourth novel, *White Eye,* which again broke new ground for her. It is a kind of ecothriller, subsuming concerns the author has often spoken on in interviews in a popular format. Although written in a deliberately plain and simple style the novel has an extraordinarily intricate plot, involving illegal trafficking of chimpanzees between Thailand

and Australia, genetic engineering, and an attempt to destroy the world. It opens dramatically with the discovery of the naked body of a woman who has been tortured, then shot. It will be the first of at least eight murders in the novel, some of them quite horrific. The protagonist, Diana Pembridge, is a quintessential d'Alpuget heroine, thirty-two years old, beautiful and patrician in appearance, but vulnerable and unfulfilled in reality. She is a passionate lover of nature without being a fanatic, and some of the finest writing in the novel is devoted to accounts of her falconing and her struggle to heal and release a wounded wedgetail eagle.

Against her is pitted John Parker, a deeply misogynistic man whose disgust with a proliferating human race drives him to invent a vaccine that will prevent it breeding: ''He had succeeded in doing what every man, secretly, would like to do: he had created a vaccine that would sterilise all the other men on Earth.'' D'Alpuget has said that part of her aim was to preach against the excesses of environmentalists, but in Parker she has created not a zealot but a murderously pathological misanthrope with no redeeming qualities except a certain kind of mordant wit: Asked by a woman if he minds her smoking he replies amiably, ''Not at all. Smoking helps reduce the population.'' It comes as no surprise to the reader to discover eventually that he is also a covert homosexual; gays in general get a bad press in this novel. Like all of d'Alpuget's work, *White Eye* is a carefully and thoroughly researched novel that at times indeed wears its learning a little ostentatiously. It alternates scenes of lyrical evocation of landscape and the beauty of the colony of birds that Diana looks after with descriptions of violence and cruelty. Like *Winter in Jerusalem* it suffers from a rushed ending in which Diana and a charismatic photographer cum environmentalist meet and fall in love in what seems seconds. D'Alpuget has admitted that she has difficulty in writing scenes of sexual love and this is evident here. The effect of love on Diana seems to be to turn her into a kind of travelling light show: ''The colours around her body throbbed and flowed, rose-red, rose-pink, violet around her shoulders, orange around her and around her hands a bright, clear green.'' However, d'Alpuget does save a couple of ingenious twists in the plot till right near the end.

—Laurie Clancy

DANTICAT, Edwidge

Nationality: American. **Born:** Port-au-Prince, Haiti, 19 January 1969. **Education:** Barnard College, 1990; Brown University, M.F.A. 1993. **Career:** Freelance writer, 1994—. **Address:** c/o Soho Press, 853 Broadway, Number 1903, New York, New York 10003, U.S.A.

Publications

Novels

Breath, Eyes, Memory. New York, Soho Press, 1994.
The Farming of Bones. New York, Soho Press, 1998.

Short Stories

Krik? Krak! New York, Soho Press, 1995.

Other

Foreword, *The Magic Orange Tree, and Other Haitian Folktales,* edited by Diane Wolkstein. New York, Schocken Books, 1997.
Foreword, *A Community of Equals: The Constitutional Protection of New Americans* by Owen Fiss, edited by Joshua Cohen and Joel Rogers. Boston, Beacon Press, 1999.
Contributor, *Island on Fire: Passionate Visions of Haiti from the Collection of Jonathan Demme,* edited by Jonathan Demme. Nyack, New York: Kaliko Press, 1997.

*

Edwidge Danticat comments:

(2000) At the end of most readings and lectures, a writer is often asked, ''How much of your work is autobiographical?'' The writer's reaction to that question varies, depending on the subject of the work. I once heard a young, shy, soft-spoken, female novelist who had just published a thriller about a serial killer quickly answer, ''Not much.'' However, for most of us, the answer is not always so simple.

As novelist and short story writer Katherine Anne Porter once said, ''A story is something you wind out of yourself. Like a spider, it is a web you weave, and you love your story like a child.'' In an interview with Donna Perry for her book *Backtalk: Women Writers Speak Out,* British novelist and Booker Prize winner Pat Barker adds that the starting point of any work is ''inevitably always something in your life, just as the source of every single character you create has to be yourself.''

Is most writing on some level—large or small—autobiographical, whether it be emotional autobiography or straight out borrowing from our lives?

In order to create full-fledged, three dimensional characters, writers often draw on their encounters, observations, collages of images from the everyday world, both theirs and others'. We are like actors, filtering through our emotions what life must be like, or must have been like, for those we write about. Truly we imagine these lives, aggrandize, reduce, or embellish, however we often begin our journey with an emotion close to our gut, whether it be anger, curiosity, joy, or fear.

I always have trouble answering the ''How much of your work is autobiographical?'' question. Not so much because it feels like a curiosity probe or a violation of privacy, but simply because the question at times rings to me like an oxymoron. To ask a fiction writer how much truth is in her work seems like asking a jockey if his/her black horse is green. (Or maybe it's if his/her black horse is black?) I once heard a writer angrily answer that autobiographical question with ''If I wanted to write an autobiography, I would have written one.'' However, the question can be a valid one, for what about the little mannerisms of ourselves that show up in the main or minor characters in our stories? What of the characters that we plop fully formed on the page mimicking our friends and relatives? And what of the incidents from childhood that reappear over and over in different forms in our tales?

Still what do we answer? Is the work ten percent autobiographical, twenty percent? Fifty percent?

I was born in Haiti in 1969 and moved to the United States when I was twelve to be reunited with my mother and father who had left Haiti eight years before I did. My first novel, *Breath, Eyes, Memory,* is about a girl, Sophie Caco, who is born in Haiti as a result of a rape and comes to the United States to be reunited with her mother when she is twelve. Because of the obvious similarities between the character's and my childhood, many of my readers assume that I too was born as a result of a rape. I was not. However there are many other things that the main character in that novel, Sophie Caco, and I share.

In writing *Breath, Eyes, Memory*, I used the sadness and desolation I experienced as a child separated from my parents. When I invented Sophie Caco, I relived my wonder at seeing a new country for the first time and infused those moments into her first day in New York. Perhaps what I did was write an emotional autobiography, but not a factual one.

I have always split my memories into two realms: one of real memory and one of fictional memory. Fictional memory has a series of plot devices, ordered scenes, convenient settings, clever dialogue and revisions aimed at the ending of your choice. My fictional memories are what come up when I consider my real memories and ask myself ''What if?'' What if when Sophie Caco/Edwidge Danticat arrives in New York City for the first time she discovers a dark secret in her past, her mother's rape.

Real memory is fragmented, messy, disorganized, has no clever dialogue and you don't always get the ending of your choice. That's why I prefer to write fiction, though it is fiction that draws heavily from certain moments in my life. With my fictional memories, I can use lies to tell a greater truth, winding a different kind of tale out of myself, one in which the possibilities for tangents and digressions are boundless; I can also weave a more elaborate web, where everyone's life can serve as a thread, including my own.

* * *

American literature has produced more than its share of prodigies. From Stephen Crane to F. Scott Fitzgerald to Carson McCullers to Truman Capote, many American writers have achieved significant acclaim, and produced some of their most famous works, while still in their twenties. To this list may be added the name of Edwidge Dandicat. Her first novel, *Breath, Eyes, Memory*, appeared when the author was twenty-five and was guaranteed significant popular success as a selection of Oprah Winfrey's Book Club. Her next book, the short story collection *Krik? Krak!* was a finalist for the National Book award. Her second novel, *The Farming of Bones*, appeared in 1998.

Born in Haiti, Dandicat moved to the United States at the age of twelve, and all of her fiction to date has been devoted to an unflinching examination of her native culture, both on its own terms and in terms of its intersections with American culture. Dandicat's work emphasizes in particular the heroism and endurance of Haitian women as they cope with a patriarchal culture that, in its unswerving devotion to tradition and family, both oppresses and enriches them. When Sophie, the narrator of *Breath, Eyes, Memory*, is taken from Haiti to live with her mother in New York City, she adapts to American culture on the surface but is damaged by her mother's obsession with female ''purity'' and constant, degrading ''testing'' of Sophie's virginity—a procedure that was also done to Sophie's mother, and her mother before her. Sophie leaves her mother, marries an American, and has a daughter of her own, but she must make a return pilgrimage to Haiti before she can begin, if not to condone, then to come to terms with her mother's actions and begin to understand the history she and her mother share with all the other ''daughters of this land.''

While Dandicat's first novel and most of her short stories focus on the plight and legacy of ''those nine hundred and ninety-nine women who were boiling in your blood'' (to quote the author's ''Epilogue'' to *Krik? Krak!*), *The Farming of Bones* paints on an even broader canvas as we witness the horrors of dictator Rafael Trujillo's 1937 massacre of Haitians resident in the Dominican Republic. The narrator, Amabelle, Haitian servant to a prosperous Dominican family, at first is reluctant to believe the rumors of massacre but eventually has no choice as she and her lover Sebastien witness unspeakable brutalities during their attempt to flee to Haiti. The few who survive carry with them wounds beyond the physical; by the time Trujillo is finally assassinated almost a quarter-century later, Amabelle and the other survivors must cope not only with the enormity of their catastrophe but with ''the most unforgivable weaknesses of the dead: their absence and their silence.''

Dandicat's novels and stories are written with a passionate lyricism but also with a control of craft and seriousness of purpose that would be impressive in any writer and are astonishing in one so young. She is determined to bear imaginative witness to the history of her culture. In so doing, she offers no easy outs—*The Farming of Bones* in particular is a narrative of almost unrelieved suffering—but also never lets us forget that the people of her stories, no matter how wounded, are individuals of intelligence and dignity and irreducible worth. That is, of course, a message for all cultures, and we are fortunate that a writer as talented as Dandicat has made proclaiming it her life's work.

—F. Brett Cox

DAVIDSON, Lionel

Nationality: British. **Born:** Hull, Yorkshire, 31 March 1922. **Military Service:** Served in the Royal Naval Submarine Service, 1941–46. **Family:** Married 1) Fay Jacobs in 1949 (died 1988), two sons; 2) Frances Ullman in 1989. **Career:** Freelance magazine journalist and editor, 1946–59. **Awards:** Authors Club award, 1961; Crime Writers Association Gold Dagger, 1961, 1967, 1979. **Agent:** Curtis Brown, 28/29 Haymarket, London SW1Y 4SP, England.

PUBLICATIONS

Novels

The Night of Wenceslas. London, Gollancz, 1960; New York, Harper, 1961.

The Rose of Tibet. London, Gollancz, and New York, Harper, 1962.

A Long Way to Shiloh. London, Gollancz, 1966; as *The Menorah Men,* New York, Harper, 1966.

Making Good Again. London, Cape, and New York, Harper, 1968.

Smith's Gazelle. London, Cape, and New York, Knopf, 1971.

The Sun Chemist. London, Cape, and New York, Knopf, 1976.

The Chelsea Murders. London, Cape, 1978; as *Murder Games,* New York, Coward McCann, 1978.

Kolymsky Heights. London, Heinemann, and New York, St. Martin's, 1994.

Uncollected Short Stories

"Note to Survivors," in *Alfred Hitchcock's Mystery Magazine* (New York), May 1958.
"Where Am I Going? Nowhere!," in *Suspense* (London), February 1961.
"Indian Rope Trick," in *Winter's Crimes 13,* edited by George Hardinge. London, Macmillan, 1981.
"I Do Dwell," in *Winter's Crimes 16,* edited by Hilary Hale. London, Macmillan, 1984.

Fiction (for children) as David Line

Soldier and Me. New York, Harper, 1965.
Run for Your Life. London, Cape, 1966.
Mike and Me. London, Cape, 1974.
Under Plum Lake (as Lionel Davidson). London, Cape, and New York, Knopf, 1980.
Screaming High. London, Cape, and Boston, Little Brown, 1985.

* * *

A novelist in various genres, Lionel Davidson has become most widely known as a writer of mysteries, winning the Crime Writers Association Gold Dagger, an annual prize, three different times. His mystery stories are intricate and full of social and historical detail. *The Chelsea Murders* (published as *Murder Games* in the United States), for example, uses clues drawn from 19th-century literary and pre-Raphaelite figures. Each of the seven victims has the initials of one of the luminaries who lived in Chelsea, figures like Dante Gabriel Rossetti, Oscar Wilde, and Algernon Charles Swinburne; the mass killer, like one of the victims, has the initials of the satirist W.S. Gilbert. In addition, the clues, mailed to the police through different ingenious guises, are quotations from the writers, emphasizing the novel's resemblance to an intricate game. No clue is, in itself, more relevant than any of the others. *The Chelsea Murders* is also, like much of Davidson's fiction, socially referential, containing quick depictions of London porno clubs, film-making, language lessons for the acculturation of Arabs, a gay disco, and a jeans store on the King's Road. Within his quickly shifting and often comic scenes, Davidson pays deference to traditional elements in crime fiction, the establishment of time frame, the police procedure, and the use of disguise to confuse identity, although he allows himself little space for the treatment of motive, psychology, or any interior quality. His characterizations, like his characters themselves, are likely to operate in groups, and the most common theme in the mysteries is that of betrayal, the violation by one member of the ethos, the standards, or the lives of other members of the group.

Other of Davidson's novels shade the line dividing the mystery from the novel of espionage. One espionage novel is *Making Good Again* in which three lawyers in the 1960s, an Englishman, a German, and an Israeli, combine in an effort to find a long-missing German-Jewish banker or to decide what to do with the million Swiss francs still left in his name. Using various costumes and guises as they travel through the Bavarian forest and other parts of Europe, and shifting allegiances to various governments and national interests, they constantly confront echoes of Nazi feeling and raise questions about German guilt and possible reparations for crimes against the Jews and the rest of humanity. Again, the theme is betrayal; but the notion of a new international combination of responsibilities cannot sustain itself in a plot that involves a good deal of action and adventure. Another novel, published as *A Long Way to Shiloh* in England and *The Menorah Men* in the United States, combines adventure with a depiction of Israel in the 1960s. This novel places the search for a religious symbol originally lost or stolen from the Temple at Jerusalem against a background of contemporary Israel trying to develop a national identity through current forms of economic, social, sexual, and religious behavior.

Davidson manifests a considerable range among fictional genres, almost never writing the same kind of novel twice. *The Rose of Tibet* is pure adventure and travelogue, evoking that strange and isolated land held in by mountains. *Smith's Gazelle,* with considerable delicacy and sensitivity, deals with the excitements and problems of preserving a nearly extinct herd of deer, working its implicit argument for conservation into suggestions of a mythic statement about the origins of species. *Under Plum Lake* is a fantasy for children in which a young boy discovers a whole subterranean civilization underneath a familiar lake. Different as they are in genre and setting, all Davidson's novels depend on action and adventure, externalizing their themes and concerns into a constant involvement with a difficult, various, and morally confusing contemporary world.

Davidson's moral statements, however, never become obvious or heavy-handed. His humor and games are always visible, his social commentary more a matter of reference to or passing jabs at contemporary social phenomena than any sustained social criticism or analysis. His references, too, like those in *The Chelsea Murders,* are often literary, historical, or topical, references to other works or quick echoes of other styles that make the novels, especially those like *The Sun Chemist* (about the possible existence among Chaim Weitzmann's forgotten papers of a chemical formula that will free the world's industry from its dependence on Arab oil), sound derivative. *Kolymsky Heights,* Davidson's first thriller after a 16-year silence, plays on familiar themes—post-Cold War espionage involving the old superpower foes, a rough-and-tumble hero who must steal a secret from a remote base—but adds fresh details: for instance, the hero, Johnny Porter, is a Gitskan Indian from British Columbia.

Davidson has, as a novelist, not yet developed a strong or distinctive literary identity, but his protean skill, his deftness, his humor, and the excitement of the action and cleverness visible in all his novels, along with settings that always illustrate a responsiveness to the contemporary social and political world, have earned him a considerable and growing reputation.

—James Gindin

DAVISON, Liam

Nationality: Australian. **Born:** Melbourne, Victoria, 29 July 1957. **Education:** Melbourne State College, B.A. in education 1979. **Family:** Married Francesca White in 1983; one son and one daughter. **Career:** Taught creative writing, Peninsula College of Technical and Further Education. **Awards:** Australia Council/Literature Board fellowship, 1989, 1991; Marten Bequest Travelling Scholarship, 1992, for prose; National Book Council *Banjo* award, 1993, for fiction. **Address:** 1 Stephens Road, Mt. Eliza, Victoria 3930, Australia.

PUBLICATIONS

Novels

The Velodrome. Sydney, Allen and Unwin, 1988.
Soundings. St. Lucia, Australia, University of Queensland Press, 1993.
The White Woman. St. Lucia, University of Queensland Press, 1994.

Short Stories

The Shipwreck Party. St. Lucia, University of Queensland Press, 1989.

*

Manuscript Collection: University College, Australian Defence Force Academy, Campbell, Australia.

Liam Davison comments:

Much of my fiction is concerned with exploring the ways in which our knowledge of the past influences the way we perceive the world about us. Rather than writing historical fiction, I am interested in fiction that explores the notion of history itself and the relationship it bears with myth and story. Faulkner's notion of the past not being dead and not even being past yet, has had a strong influence on my work. I'm also interested in the idea of alternative and silenced histories which has a particular bearing on the post-colonial nature of Australian society and its attempts to redefine itself.

My third book *Soundings* integrates three narrative strands from different periods of Australian history, all set in the Westernport region of Victoria. While many have read it as a contemplation of the landscape of the region, it is also an exploration of the different cultural and historical perceptions and expectations imposed on a new land. *The White Woman* explores the notion of history in a quite different way. Operating largely as a re-working of a nineteenth century captivity myth about a virtuous white woman held captive by the Aborigines of Gippsland, it considers the power and consequences of story and the role it plays in shaping the way we live.

* * *

In four works of fiction, Liam Davison has made his mark among the younger generation of Australian novelists. He writes an elegant and cadenced yet earthly prose. Davison also has an individualistic preoccupation with humans' efforts to impose order on the world and to construct themselves by creating history, maps, roads, and canals. He is a landscape novelist, mapping the human psyche.

Davison's first novel, *The Velodrome,* is narrated by Leon, whose father, like his two friends Sam and Eric, is a passionate cyclist. Leon sees the three men constantly circle the cosmos on their biketrack, traveling eternally to the same spot and achieving ''order.''

In a cycling accident, Leon's father is killed and Eric is crippled. The two men and Leon's mother, now married to Eric, decide to find a new order by breaking the circle and making the long journey to the north of Australia. Traveling is a central theme in Davison's fiction, and most human interaction takes place on the road or on the water, shoulder-to-shoulder rather than face-to-face. There is a studied detachment in the prose, and dying is presented as an act of absent-mindedness. Being murdered is more thought-provoking. Characters do not turn to other people but to the stories they use to make themselves; to God as benign cartographer, to ''collecting the facts'' into a shoe box of index cards, to measuring out life with the wheels of a well-made bike. *The Velodrome* may at times seem a little too self-conscious in its emotional distancing, but its narrative line is strong, its images reverberate, and its spare, nuanced prose lingers tantalizingly.

The Shipwreck Party, Davison's collection of stories, furthers his preoccupation with landscape as a taken rather than a given. A party is held on a grounded ship. Water flows through most of the subsequent fiction. Davison does not write about people in the landscape. Rather he focuses on the landscape or the seascape within the people. At the shipwreck, characters see the same but different things. Seeing is creating.

A story about a famous Australian convict, Buckley, who escaped to live with the Aborigines, signals two interests that become central. Unpursued, Buckley experiences ''ironic disappointment.'' Characters are so busily creating a self in story that they are unable to read the stories of others. Each man is an island complete unto himself. And the causeway can offer drowning as well as welcome.

Also, in his two next novels, *Soundings* and *The White Woman,* Davison has moved from assiduous impersonality to a more emotionally energetic prose. His writing never risks death by flamboyance, but language has thawed and the grace of the prose takes on more force as both novels develop the interest in Australia's colonial past found earlier in Buckley.

If each person is an island, islands still have histories and changing shapes. *Soundings* is a deftly constructed novel covering three periods of Australian history. The first is the 1820s, predating the colony of Victoria. Wolfish sealers, French scientists, and the English explorer Hovell suspiciously track each other. Each sees a different country—and, in the indigenous people, a different species. Passionately calm, Davison stories a shame that even now is being only edgily owned by history.

Davison is not in any conventional sense ''an historical novelist,'' but he deeply probes the ways in which we talk ourselves into being. History becomes the present trying to run away from itself. His second era is the 1900s, when swamplands were reclaimed for ''progress.'' Canals are human bypass surgery on nature. Life might swamp them, but they leave scars of control. The natural world has signed no Geneva Convention for rules in war. There is a constant edge of absurdity in Davison's writing. The human animal is laughable but too busy making its story seriously important to notice. As one character remarks, ''history's a lot safer than boats.''

The third story is that of a contemporary landscape photographer who, with an old photo-finish camera, glimpses people long dead. Though sometimes a little contrived, this reinforces Davison's focus that seeing is inventing.

The White Woman, Davison's most powerful achievement yet, confirms that there are no absolutes in history, only ceremonial reunions or family squabbles of relatives. An old man looks back over half a century to 1847 when he took part in an expedition to rescue a white woman supposedly held captive by the Aborigines. As he relives his story, he makes clear ''how much we needed her.'' His narrative takes on religious dimensions—''It was love'' and ''I still had faith in her.'' She is the white Madonna, enslaved by ''savages, brutes, the very opposite of what we are ourselves.'' Such is history, official truth. The old man's truth is savagely different. Davison becomes a frontier novelist. The frontier is where civilization ends or behind which it has flourished for fifty thousand years.

Here Davison transcends fashionable political politeness. His most firmly modulated narrative brings into harmony his interest in history as the story we tell ourselves to make our dreams safe, his sense of landscape as invention, and his vision of the world as eternally elusive. All good stories are Revised Standard Versions and *The White Woman* has biblical rhythm and authority.

—John Hanrahan

DAWSON, Jennifer

Nationality: British. **Education:** Mary Datchelor School, London; St. Anne's College, Oxford, M.A. in history 1952. **Family:** Married Michael Hinton in 1964. **Career:** Has worked for Clarendon Press, Oxford, as a social worker in a mental hospital, and as a teacher. Lives in Charlbury, Oxfordshire. **Awards:** James Tait Black Memorial prize, 1962; Cheltenham Festival award, 1963; Fawcett prize, for *Judasland,* 1990. **Address:** c/o Virago Press, 20–23 Mandela Street, London NW1 0HQ, England.

Publications

Novels

The Ha-Ha. London, Blond, and Boston, Little Brown, 1961.
Fowler's Snare. London, Blond, 1962.
The Cold Country. London, Blond, 1965.
Strawberry Boy. London, Quartet, 1976.
A Field of Scarlet Poppies. London, Quartet, 1979.
The Upstairs People. London, Virago Press, 1988.
Judasland. London, Virago Press, 1989.

Short Stories

Penguin Modern Stories 10, with others. London, Penguin, 1972.
Hospital Wedding. London, Quartet, 1978.

*

Jennifer Dawson comments:

My greatest passion in life has always been music. I regard writing as a last resort, a *faute de mieux* for me. In a world where language has been eroded, gutted (''pre-emptive strike,'' ''take-out'' for the murder of eight million civilians, etc.) all art ''aspires to the condition of music,'' which cannot be exploited, interpreted, which explores the lost places of the heart, which makes all things new. Two of my novels have had musicians as their main characters—studies of the composer/musician who for social and political reasons experience dryness, aridity, and cannot play any more. Politics creep, burst inevitably into my novels. They then become shrill, rhetorical, routine, etc.

One feeling that has haunted me all my life is that life, social life as we know it, is a kind of game with correct moves, correct remarks and replies, correct procedures. I don't know the rules. I have struggled in vain for the real life as opposed to the game of men-and-women.

But the thing that obsesses me most, and which I feel I shall never put into language, is the strangeness of life, its accidentalness. Here we all are on a tiny, blue-green balloon in the midst of naked gases, chambers of violence. The planet as an accident that has produced music, literature, art, and the extraordinary theme-and-variations of religions. Here we are, with our fitted carpets and Mixmasters and spin-dryers, stilted above the world, talking about mock O-levels, who is to be next Master of St. Judas's, how all the cars in St. John's Street seemed badly parked today. Here we are in the midst of nothingness, in the midst of a mystery, accidental and yet behaving politically and socially as though the bizarre nature of our life on this planet has not hit us yet. To me this freak of life (like a purple flower growing out of the dumped tippings of a Hoover-bag) is the invitation to a new kind of freedom. Only art can introduce us to this. But my art? *No!* It must be someone else's. I shall never succeed in saying what I want to say.

* * *

Novels which explore madness have certain qualities in common. They describe a world which is enclosed, static and ruled by obsessions; they are vivid, fragmented, highly personal documents in which only one character can be fully realized. This intensity is double-edged. It can exclude, and ultimately bore, the reader or it can provide him with a vision of life which has a relevance beyond the barriers of mental illness. Kafka's metaphors have been readily accepted and understood. Jennifer Dawson's *The Ha-Ha* is one of the few contemporary novels significant enough to deserve the appellation ''Kafkaesque.''

The Ha-Ha is set in a mental hospital where the narrator, Jean, is slowly recovering from a breakdown. She has progressed from the ward and the company of the irretrievably mad; she is now allowed her own room and promised a suitable job, an eventual regrading. Even as the nurse explains these steps towards freedom, we see their sad irrelevance. Jean's private world is ready to obtrude at any moment; her existence is precarious, threatened by the anarchy in her own imagination. One of the most moving illustrations of her plight is given in the description of her work as a librarian. She happily catalogues books for an elderly couple in the nearby town but is nonplussed by their casual, friendly conversation. When fine weather is mentioned she remarks ''I wonder whether the monkeys would be better at the top or the bottoms of the trees.'' Her own company of animals, spotted, sleek, furred and quilled, wait relentlessly for the time when she will step back into their universe.

The inevitable relapse is brought about by her first real relationship, a love affair with another patient. Alastair is critical of doctors and routines; he alarms Jean by telling her the true nature of her illness, and she panics when he leaves the hospital. She runs away, is picked up by the police and brought back to face ''the black box crashing down around my head.'' It is at this point that the novel changes direction. Jean remembers Alastair for his anger; she begins to share his indignation, rejects the doctors and escapes for good, feeling that her own identity is worth more than any medical tag of health.

Schizophrenia is a disease that has received much attention from modern writers, particularly during the mid-twentieth century. It has been used to symbolize the artist's alienation from society and, by extension, presented as the condition of modern man— lost, lonely, unable to communicate. The schizophrenic is sometimes hailed as a prophet, whose view of life is not only as valid as that of his doctors but also morally superior to the standards they uphold. Dawson shares this fashionable, essentially romantic, attitude, but her writing is without the stridency of propaganda. The parallels with Sylvia Plath's *The Bell Jar* are many, and the prose is equally fine. Dawson has written further explorations of her subject, but has not yet matched the sustained brilliance of this first novel.

—Judy Cooke

de BERNIÈRES, Louis

Nationality: British. **Born:** London, 8 December 1954. **Education:** Manchester University, B.A. (honors) in philosophy; Leicester Polytechnic, P.G.C.E.; University of London, M.A. (with distinction) in English. **Career:** Has held jobs as landscape gardener, mechanic, and carpenter; teacher for ten years. **Awards:** Commonwealth Writers prize, 1991, 1992; Lannan Literary Award, 1995. **Agent:** Lavinia Trevor, 6 The Glasshouse, 49A Goldhawk Rd., London W12 8QP, England.

Publications

Novels

The War of Don Emmanuel's Nether Parts. London, Secker and Warburg, 1990; New York, Morrow, 1991.

Señor Vivo and the Coca Lord. London, Secker and Warburg, and New York, Morrow, 1991.

The Troublesome Offspring of Cardinal Guzman. London, Secker and Warburg, 1992; New York, Morrow, 1994.

Captain Corelli's Mandolin. London, Secker and Warburg, and New York, Pantheon, 1994.

*

Louis de Bernières comments:

I like to read and write books on a grand scale. I am interested in situations where ordinary people are caught up in abuses of power or historical crises and events. I disapprove of ''genre'' literature. I have hundreds of influences, but was moved to to want to become a writer by Nicholas Monsarratt's ''The Cruel Sea.'' I am much influence by the great Latin American writers, by Tolstoy and Cervantes, and by my studies in philosophy.

* * *

A novel by Louis de Bernières is like a series of brightly colored and boldly drawn murals that combine into an exotic epic of life, love, and struggle. His first three novels are set in an imaginary South American country and make full use of the stock resources of such a setting: political corruption and malpractice; murder, torture, and violence perpetrated by the military; revolutionary opposition, which sometimes also takes violent forms; drug trafficking and prostitution; *machismo* and exotic femininity; Roman Catholicism and native magic. These novels also spring large surprises; for example, a troop of *conquistadores,* frozen in a glacier for four centuries, who are brought back to life and have to adjust to the modern world. De Bernières's fourth novel, *Captain Corelli's Mandolin,* is set on an imaginary Greek island invaded by the Italians during World War II, and, allowing for the difference of place and time, it has many of the same elements as his earlier works.

De Bernières is perhaps best seen as a mythic populist, who celebrates people in all their variety and idiosyncrasy and in their covert and overt resistance to oppression. In *The War of Don Emmanuel's Nether Parts,* the struggle of a band of guerrillas and a group of villagers against the depredations of the army culminates in the discovery of a half-buried Inca city, which they reinhabit and which becomes an intimation of Utopia; *Señor Vivo and the Coca Lord* sees the people of the city battling against the biggest drug baron of their country; and *The Troublesome Offspring of Cardinal Guzman* shows them resisting the drive of a new Inquisition to impose religious orthodoxy. In *Captain Corelli's Mandolin,* the oppressor is not only the invading Italians but also war itself, and de Bernières dramatizes both the cruelties of the conflict and the possibilities of transcending them through love.

Memorable characters people de Bernières's pages. Figures who recur in the South American novels include General Carlo Maria Fuerte, a true patriot and lover of the people, who, after his kidnap by guerrillas, learns the truth about the brutality of some of his army colleagues and exacts condign punishment before retiring to private life to pursue his interests as a lepidopterist and ornithologist; Dona Constanza Evans, the plump, idle wife of a wealthy landowner, who is also kidnapped by the guerrillas, who becomes leaner, fitter, and more desirable through sharing their strenuous life, and who eventually throws in her lot with them, not out of any political conviction but because of her passionate affair with one of the young fighters; and Remedios, the courageous and capable woman guerrilla chief, who falls in love with the leader of the revived *conquistadores* and presents a troubling and sometimes comic challenge to his patriarchal and feudal assumptions. Among the notable characters in *Captain Corelli's Mandolin* are the Captain himself, a handsome, cultured, and amusing Italian officer with whom the daughter of the Greek house on which he is billeted becomes enamored (against her will); and Carlo Piero Guercio, a brave and strong Italian soldier tormented by his homosexuality and by having to oppress the people whose ancestors exalted love between men.

In all his novels, de Bernières employs a form of magic realism, moving between vividly rendered incidents that stay within the confines of credibility, pastiches of anthropological and travel writing, and evocations of preternatural events and entities, such as the resurrection of the frozen *conquistadores* or the haunting figure of Parlanchina, a beautiful 19-year-old girl killed by a land mine, who continues, after her death, to appear to, and speak with, her adoptive father. The novels are told from a variety of viewpoints and in a range of voices; the third person authorial narration is characterized by an impersonal quality that makes the novelist come across as the unflinching, but not uncompassionate, recorder of all that happens.

De Bernières's novels do tend to repeat the same formula, and the move in *Captain Corelli's Mandolin* from South America to Greece is more a shift of setting than of theme, structure, or style. Nonetheless, he has found a way of writing fiction that enables him to engage with major issues of modern times—in particular, political and religious corruption and oppression—while retaining a keen perception of the pleasures of life, a sense of humor, a tempered anger, and a graceful utopianism.

—Nicolas Tredell

de BOISSIÈRE, Ralph (Anthony Charles)

Nationality: Australian. **Born:** Port-of-Spain, Trinidad, 6 October 1907; moved to Australia, 1947; became citizen, 1970. **Education:** Queen's Royal College, Port-of-Spain, 1916–22. **Family:** Married Ivy Alcántara in 1935; two daughters. **Career:** Accounts clerk, 1927–28, and salesman, Standard Brands, 1929–39, both Trinidad; clerk, Trinidad Clay Products, 1940–47; auto assembler, General Motors-Holden, 1948, cost clerk in car repair shops, 1949–55, freelance writer, 1955–60, and statistical clerk, Gas and Fuel Corporation, 1960–80, all in Melbourne. **Agent:** Reinhard Sander, Department of Black Studies, Amherst College, Amherst, Massachusetts 01002, U.S.A. **Address:** 10 Vega Street, North Balwyn, Victoria 3104, Australia.

PUBLICATIONS

Novels

Crown Jewel. Melbourne, Australasian Book Society, 1952; London, Allison and Busby, 1981.

Rum and Coca-Cola. Melbourne, Australasian Book Society, 1956; London, Allison and Busby, 1984.

No Saddles for Kangaroos. Sydney, Australasian Book Society, 1964.

Uncollected Short Stories

"Booze and the Goberdaw" and "The Woman on the Pavement," in *From Trinidad,* edited by Reinhard Sander. New York, Africana, 1979.

Play

Calypso Isle, music by the author (produced Melbourne, 1955).

*

Manuscript Collection: The National Library of Australia.

Critical Study: *The Trinidad Awakening: West Indian Literature of the 1930s* by Reinhard Sander, Westport, Connecticut, Greenwood Press, 1988.

Ralph de Boissière comments:

I began writing *Crown Jewel* in 1935. As I am a slow writer who has rarely had much time to write I was still at it when the uprising took place in the oilfields of south Trinidad on 19 June 1937. I saw I was writing the wrong novel. The oil workers had lighted a torch to signal the breaking of the first bonds of colonialism, bonds which we novelists, short story writers, poets and artists who made up *The Beacon* group (after the name of the now-defunct magazine) had dared to dream would fall before our hatred of foreign masters and our urge to independence. A salesman at the time, I had come to know much of the oilfield area. From two of the important activists in the uprising I got important inside information on its origins, and I began again, discarding much of what I had already written.

I come from one of the best-known French-Creole families, families which, in days long gone, when cocoa was king, had been the real rulers of this British colonial outpost. But with 19 June 1937 my detestation of colonialism, simmering from childhood, and crudely expressed in a few short stories, now became clearly defined.

The second novel of the trilogy, *Rum and Coca-Cola,* deals with the war years when tens of thousands of American soldiers and civilians were building military bases on the island. The American military had in effect become our rulers. There is not the same tension as in *Crown Jewel* because everyone had a job and many had two. The conflicts were of a more subtle sort—the breaking down of British prestige, the mockery of former British might, under American occupation.

The third book of the trilogy, *Homeless in Paradise* (not yet published), covers the approach to Independence in 1962 and its immediate aftermath.

Readers sometimes want to know who was the real-life basis for such and such a character. It is both unwise and impossible to say because I am continually adding to and subtracting from people I have known and, what is more, putting myself into them as characters. The characters may have some resemblance to certain originals, that is all. It is in important crises that people truly reveal themselves: for the most part of our everyday lives we exhibit aspects of character that give only superficial insights into what we are made of. I chose a Black servant girl, Cassie, as one of the main figures in *Crown Jewel* because in Trinidad her class were the most oppressed, ill-paid, and despised among Blacks. In all of us there is potential of one kind or another, but I am thinking particularly of the potential of the human spirit to achieve greatness, something unsuspected by the individual until he or she is flung by events into a crucial situation which demands the utmost. Cassie has that potential. It made her a leader when the time came. There was no such woman as Cassie, but the point is, *there could have been.* In other more stable parts of the world there are fewer possibilities for the appearance of such characters because the social conflicts are not extreme or the time for their resolution is not ripe. This is evident in my third novel, *No Saddles for Kangaroos,* set largely in an automobile factory in Melbourne during the years of the Korean war; here I am dealing with different people at a different historical time.

In technology we have taken great leaps forward, but morally we lag far behind these attainments—which sometimes even threaten to destroy us. But under the surface of life there is always some urge, some movement to rise out of the mire, and it is this movement the writer should try to grasp, this spiritual strength that has to be encouraged. While a writer may profit greatly by displaying the potential for evil he fails if he does not also indicate the potential for creativity as well. The world does not need more hatred, gore, and contempt for life—especially now. It needs belief in the powers of ordinary people to achieve.

No Saddles for Kangaroos is based on experiences I and others had in the early 1950s. Those experiences, those times could produce a novel full of drama. But I find myself unable to write about other, quieter times in Australia because I wasn't born and schooled in that country. At the same time I am a West Indian who has become partly Australian without knowing it. Australia is in my blood, but home is still Trinidad, a home I intuitively, instinctively, emotionally understand as I do not understand Australia.

* * *

Ralph de Boissière's *Crown Jewel* and *Rum and Coca-Cola,* both published without much remark four decades ago in Australia, were rightly reissued in the 1980s and received with justified acclaim. They remain relevant because they give an unrivaled portrayal of two moments in Trinidad's recent past which are still very much alive in shaping its present. De Boissière's third novel, *No Saddles for Kangaroos,* deals with Cold-War politics in the Australian trade union movement, but it lacks the social inwardness and the shaping coherence that his own personal vantage point, as a white creole in a society moving towards black majority rule, gives his two Trinidadian novels.

Crown Jewel depicts Trinidadian society in the years between 1935 and 1937 when the black working class briefly threw aside the middle-class leaders who had diverted its power to their own ends and, through a series of bitter strikes and demonstrations began the process which led to universal suffrage, and political independence. *Rum and Coca-Cola* is set just before the end of World War II when the dollars from the American military presence changed Trinidad from a neglected and quasi-feudal British colony into a competitive market economy in which ''we is all sharks, the stronger feedin' on the weaker.'' Both forces remain alive in Trinidadian society, the unfinished revolts of 1937 and 1970, and the individualistic consumer materialism which was fueled by the oil boom. Now that the boom has gone and social tensions rise, de Boissière's novels seem more relevant than ever.

Both novels are, in a Caribbean context, rare and largely successful attempts to create fictional models which give a panoramic view of their society. They give not merely a static or descriptive background against which characters perform, but a dynamic image of society created by the actions and social relationships of the characters. And, particularly in *Crown Jewel,* de Boissière shows individuals who are aware that it is they who make history.

There are limitations, both social and fictional in origin, to de Boissière's portrayal of his society. His portrayal of the Indian role in the social conflicts is inadequate and stereotyped, a consequence perhaps both of ignorance and his concern with coming to terms with his own denied black ancestry, which leads to the exclusion of the more significant relationship between people of African and Indian origin. De Boissière also has a naturalistic concern with narrative plausibility which condemns him to providing each of the major characters with some link of blood, service, or mutual acquaintance. This gives an image of Trinidad as a much more comfortable though quarreling social family than is, I think, intended by the overt picture of class warfare.

However, while most critics have agreed that *Crown Jewel* gives a detailed and vigorous social and historical portrayal of Trinidad, some have felt that its attempts at the development of a coherent literary design are undermined by its commitment to documentary realism. In fact, its relationship to historical reality is of a different kind. If one compares the fictional character of Le Maitre, the black trade union leader, with the historical person of ''Buzz'' Butler on whom it is based, one sees not the pursuit of topical detail but the simplification of the character in response to the needs of the novel's shaping pattern. Thus Le Maitre becomes a character of massive moral certainty and clear historical consciousness as a touchstone against which to measure the confused and tentative leanings of the three central intermediary characters towards the black working class.

It is de Boissière's concern with the moral choices facing this group, in particular the character of André de Coudray, like the author an idealistic and socially concerned French Creole, which shapes the novel. And because de Boissière is refreshingly honest in his recognition that de Coudray's commitment involved the destruction of his comfortably privileged world without any guarantee of a place in the new, he is convincing in making de Coudray's journey towards self-knowledge, social responsibility, and cultural pride an image for that of the whole society.

As befitting his perception of the individualism that the power of the American dollar stimulated in Trinidadian society, *Rum and Coca-Cola* places much greater emphasis on the inner lives of its major characters. In this period moral commitment is not so much a question of social action but of the attempt to stay true to one's perceptions of what one is and to principles which are being swept aside in a society engaged in a competitive struggle for survival, money and power.

In this novel the issue of choice is focused on the triangular relationship of three characters confused about who they are and how they should act in a Trinidad which denies their ideals. Fred Collingwood, a principled black working-class socialist is doomed because of his ''moral strength in all its beauty'' and he destroys the relationship with Marie, the woman he most loves, because he displaces his desire to change society onto her and in the process destroys her sense of worth. Indra, the part-Indian girl from a lower-middle-class family, struggles against a ''terrible division of spirit'' which affects her social and racial sensibilities. Even though she makes a commitment to the working-class movement she still feels cut off, ''doomed at this time to a lonely pursuit of the dust they raised in their forward marching.'' But it is the character of Marie, trapped by the lightness of her color into believing that she can escape into whiteness, which provides the novel's tragic focus. Of the three main characters, she is the one to benefit most materially from the war-time boom, but her unremitting efforts to escape from her past of poverty and casual prostitution are made at the expense of her inner self. Her fate is tragic because she sees herself engaged in a battle for individual self-hood, but in the process becomes separated from what she most truly is and disintegrates as a personality.

Yet *Rum and Coca-Cola* does not succumb to pessimism. Indra's cry, ''O my God! But what am I capable of'' is agonized, but the possibilities of moral choice and the issues of human capacity remain central to de Boissière's vision. He sees Trinidad moving in a direction which he detests, but when he has Fred reflect on what has occurred, he shows him capable of taking something positive from it. He sees a society which is not yet free, but one in which old colonial illusions have been destroyed. ''Now that walls had falled, what lay exposed was a life of untrustworthy promises, treachery by those you trusted, servility …'' And in this process of laying bare, Fred sees the generation of a new disabused awareness and ''ideas which could be weapons.''

—Jeremy Poynting

DEIGHTON, Len

Nationality: British. **Born:** Leonard Cyril Deighton in London, 18 February 1929. **Education:** Marylebone Grammar School, St. Martin's School of Art, and Royal College of Art, 1952–55, all London. **Military Service:** Served in the Royal Air Force. **Family:** Married

Shirley Thompson in 1960. **Career:** Has worked as a railway lengthman, pastry cook, dress factory manager, waiter, illustrator, teacher, and photographer; art director of advertising agencies in London and New York; steward, British Overseas Airways Corporation, 1956–57; wrote weekly comic strip on cooking for the *Observer,* London, 1960s; founder, Continuum One literary agency, London. **Agent:** Jonathan Clowes Ltd., 10 Iron Bridge House, Bridge Approach, London NW1 8BD, England.

PUBLICATIONS

Novels

The Ipcress File. London, Hodder and Stoughton, 1962; New York, Simon and Schuster, 1963.
Horse under Water. London, Cape, 1963; New York, Putnam, 1968.
Funeral in Berlin. London, Cape, 1964; New York, Putnam, 1965.
Billion-Dollar Brain. London, Cape, 1966; as *The Billion-Dollar Brain,* New York, Putnam, 1966.
An Expensive Place to Die. London, Cape, and New York, Putnam, 1967.
Only When I Larf. London, Joseph, 1968; as *Only When I Laugh,* New York, Mysterious Press, 1987.
Bomber. London, Cape, and New York, Harper, 1970.
Close-Up. London, Cape, and New York, Atheneum, 1972.
Spy Story. London, Cape, and New York, Harcourt Brace, 1974.
Yesterday's Spy. London, Cape, and New York, Harcourt Brace, 1975.
Twinkle, Twinkle, Little Spy. London, Cape, 1976; as *Catch a Falling Spy,* New York, Harcourt Brace, 1976.
SS-GB: Nazi-Occupied Britain 1941. London, Cape, 1978; New York, Knopf, 1979.
XPD. London, Hutchinson, and New York, Knopf, 1981.
Goodbye Mickey Mouse. London, Hutchinson, and New York, Knopf, 1982.
Game, Set and Match. London, Hutchinson, 1985; New York, Knopf, 1989.
  Berlin Game. London, Hutchinson, 1983; New York, Knopf, 1984.
  Mexico Set. London, Hutchinson, 1984; New York, Knopf, 1985.
  London Match. London, Hutchinson, 1985; New York, Knopf, 1986.
Winter: A Berlin Family 1899–1945. London, Century Hutchinson, and New York, Knopf, 1987.
Spy Hook. London, Century Hutchinson, and New York, Knopf, 1988.
Spy Line. London, Century Hutchinson, and New York, Knopf, 1989.
Spy Sinker. London, Hutchinson, and New York, HarperCollins, 1990.
MAMista. New York, HarperCollins, 1991.
City of Gold. New York, HarperCollins, 1992.
Violent Ward. New York, HarperCollins, 1993.
Blood, Tears & Folly. London, Jonathan Cape, and New York, HarperCollins, 1993.
Faith. Bath, England, Chivers Press, and New York, HarperCollins, 1994.
Hope. New York, HarperCollins, 1995.
Charity. New York, HarperCollins, 1996.

Short Stories

Declarations of War. London, Cape, 1971; as *Eleven Declarations of War,* New York, Harcourt Brace, 1975.

Plays

Pests: A Play in Three Acts. Mansfield Woodhouse, England, C. Martin, 1994.

Screenplay: *Oh! What a Lovely War,* 1969.

Television Plays: *Long Past Glory,* 1963; *It Must Have Been Two Other Fellows,* 1977.

Other

Action Cook Book: Len Deighton's Guide to Eating. London, Cape, 1965; as *Cookstrip Cook Book,* New York, Geis, 1966.
Ou Est le Garlic; or, Len Deighton's French Cook Book. London, Penguin, 1965; New York, Harper, 1977; revised edition, as *Basic French Cooking,* London, Cape, 1979; Berkeley, California, Creative Arts, 1987; revised edition, as *Basic French Cookery,* London, Century, 1990.
Len Deighton's Continental Dossier: A Collection of Cultural, Culinary, Historical, Spooky, Grim and Preposterous Fact, compiled by Victor and Margaret Pettitt. London, Joseph, 1968.
Fighter: The True Story of the Battle of Britain. London, Cape, 1977; New York, Knopf, 1978.
Airshipwreck, with Arnold Schwartzman. London, Cape, 1978; New York, Holt Rinehart, 1979.
Blitzkrieg: From the Rise of Hitler to the Fall of Dunkirk. London, Cape, 1979; New York, Knopf, 1980.
Battle of Britain. London, Cape, and New York, Coward McCann, 1980; revised edition, with Max Hastings, London, Joseph, 1990.
The Orient Flight L.Z. 127-Graf Zeppelin (as Cyril Deighton), with Fred F. Blau. N.p., Germany Philatelic Society, 1980.
The Egypt Flight L.Z. 127-Graf Zeppelin (as Cyril Deighton), with Fred F. Blau. N.p., Germany Philatelic Society, 1981.
ABC of French Food. London, Century Hutchinson, 1989; New York, Bantam, 1990.
Editor, *Drinks-man-ship: Town's Album of Fine Wines and High Spirits.* London, Haymarket Press, 1964.
Editor, *London Dossier.* London, Cape, 1967.
Editor, with Michael Rund and Howard Loxton, *The Assassination of President Kennedy.* London, Cape, 1967.
Editor, *Tactical Genius in Battle,* by Simon Goodenough. Oxford, Phaidon Press, and New York, Dutton, 1979.

*

Bibliography: *Len Deighton: An Annotated Bibliography 1954–85* by Edward Milward-Oliver, Maidstone, Kent, Sammler, 1985.

Critical Studies: *Secret Agents in Fiction: Ian Fleming, John le Carré, and Len Deighton* by L.O. Sauerberg, London, Macmillan, 1984; *The Len Deighton Companion* by Edward Milward-Oliver, London, Grafton, 1987.

* * *

Partly as a result of the work of Len Deighton, the spy story has replaced the formal detective novel as the relevant thriller for its time. While continuing the tradition of literary excellence that has distinguished British espionage fiction since the days of Somerset Maugham, Eric Ambler, and Graham Greene, both Deighton and his gifted contemporary John le Carré have contributed new energy, intelligence, and meaning to the novel of espionage. Ever since his first novel, *The Ipcress File,* Deighton has instructed a large reading public in some of the factual and emotional realities of espionage and counterespionage. Writing with a lively wit, a keen eye for the surfaces of modern life, a convincing sense of authenticity, and a genuine intellectual concern for what the dark side of governmental practice can mean, Deighton has revealed, in all of his novels, some of the sham and self-delusion of contemporary politics.

The spy novels employ a nameless first-person narrator who owes something to Raymond Chandler's Philip Marlowe in his breezy wisecracks and sometimes strained metaphors; beneath the wiseguy surface, however, he possesses some of Marlowe's decency and compassion. Resolutely working-class in background, education, and point of view, Deighton's hero is a professional spy who must do constant battle with the forces of the British Establishment in their full and whinnying glory as well as with whatever is on the other side. Frequently, in fact, his spy never knows precisely which side he is on, and is so often betrayed by his colleagues and superiors that it sometimes doesn't matter. Professional and personal betrayal mesh perfectly in the two separate trilogies about Bernard Samson, whose wife and colleague, Fiona, turns out to be a defecting Soviet agent in the middle of an immensely complicated operation. The double trilogy—*Berlin Game, Mexico Set, London Match,* and *Spy Hook, Spy Line,* and *Spy Sinker*—initially appeared to signal a certain finality in Deighton's exploration of contemporary international politics, but he later resurrected the Samson saga in a third series: *Faith, Hope*, and *Charity.* Set in 1987—the backdrop includes the stock market crash of that year—*Hope* finds Samson in pursuit of his Polish brother-in-law, George Kosinski, who has returned to Poland in search of his wife. With *Charity,* the saga comes up to 1988, and while it would be difficult for someone new to the Samson trilogies to jump in with this ninth book in the series, the book offers plenty of satisfaction for Deighton's veteran fans.

As the ambitiousness of the three trilogies indicates, a complicated sense of novelistic architecture supports Deighton's energetic style and disillusioned outlook. His books frequently delay revelation of method and meaning until their conclusions. As the protagonist solves whatever mystery has been confounding him, or wraps up a long and tangled investigation, the book reaches the end of an often puzzling and complex narrative structure. The complications of its subject and of its fictional development appear to blend perfectly: the construction artfully becomes an emblem of the meaning of espionage, as much as the usual anonymity of the narrator suggests something about the problem of identity in this troubled world.

Deighton's fictional and nonfictional researches into the history of World War II and his knowledge of Germany reflect some of the same concerns and interests of his espionage fiction. Like his spy novels, his war novels, *Bomber* and *Goodbye Mickey Mouse,* demonstrate his passion for authenticity along with a bittersweet attitude toward a past that is both glorious and ignoble. His generally unsuccessful *Winter* deals with the history of a particular family through the turmoil of two wars, economic collapse, and the rise of Nazism; characters in that novel recur in his Samson books, as if his oeuvre, in effect, constituted a single work in many volumes about some of the central events of the 20th century. Deighton has also dabbled in such odd areas of the modern landscape as fantasies of German victory in World War II (*SS-GB*) and a Graham Greeneish exploration of South American revolution (*MAMista*), which indicate an almost heroic attempt to comprehend the violence and horror of political conflict in our age.

Like le Carré again, Deighton has done much to advance our knowledge of the way spies and spying work and what they really mean in our time. For both writers the novel of espionage serves an emblematic function. It shows, all too convincingly, the sad history of treason that marks the real battle in the shadows—a spy seems always to betray one cause, one country, one person or another in order to accomplish his task. The contemporary reality of the Western world provides the necessary historical context for Deighton's writing; daily headlines indicate the truth of his fictional perceptions, and the Kafkaesque quality of international politics and modern life itself reflects the deeper truth of his books.

Because Deighton's novels invariably show the folly, imbecility, and corruption of the wealthy and privileged classes in England, they suggest something of the satiric flavor of the Angry Young Men, and his hero is somewhat of a Lucky Jim of espionage. Because they present a labyrinthine picture of undeclared war, conflicting loyalties, multiple betrayals, misuse of power, and complicated national alignments, they provide a useful image of the world we all inhabit. Their dominant emotions are those of our time—puzzlement, anxiety, cynicism, and guilt. They recognize, further, one of the major lessons of the modern English spy novel, that an entire class, long protected by its own sense of unity and privilege, has sold its birthright, as the sordid history of Burgess, Maclean, Philby, and Blunt, among others, has proved.

In his own flip, entertaining, and exciting style, Deighton treats essentially the same problem that haunts a great deal of English fiction, the timeless question of who will inherit the virtue of the nation, who will save England from itself. His works thus show some connections with books like *Adam Bede, Tess of the d'Urbervilles,* and *Lady Chatterley's Lover,* continuing in a highly unlikely form the theme of a nation and a class that, ultimately, have betrayed themselves. His work at its best indicates that the continuing vitality of the English novel itself may very well depend upon the popular and subliterary genres. As a spy novelist and simply as an author of British fiction, he deserves sympathetic reading and consideration with some of the better writers of his time.

—George Grella

DELANY, Samuel R(ay)

Nationality: American. **Born:** New York City, 1 April 1942. **Education:** The Dalton School and Bronx High School of Science, both New York; City College of New York (poetry editor, *Promethean*), 1960, 1962–63. **Family:** Married the poet Marilyn Hacker in 1961 (divorced 1980); one daughter. **Career:** Butler Professor of English, State University of New York, Buffalo, 1975; Fellow, Center for Twentieth Century Studies, University of Wisconsin, Milwaukee, 1977; since 1988 professor of comparative literature, University of Massachusetts. **Awards:** Nebula award, 1966, 1967 (twice), 1969;

Hugo award, 1970. **Address:** Department of Comparative Literature, University of Massachusetts at Amherst, South College Bldg., Amherst, Massachusetts 01003, U.S.A.

Publications

Novels

The Jewels of Aptor. New York, Ace, 1962; revised edition, New York, Ace, and London, Gollancz, 1968; London, Sphere, 1971; Boston, Gregg Press, 1977.

The Fall of the Towers (revised texts). New York, Ace, 1970; London, Sphere, 1971.

Captives of the Flame. New York, Ace, 1963; revised edition, as *Out of the Dead City,* London, Sphere, 1968; New York, Ace, 1977.

The Towers of Toron. New York, Ace, 1964; revised edition, London, Sphere, 1968.

City of a Thousand Suns. New York, Ace, 1965; revised edition, London, Sphere, 1969.

The Ballad of Beta-2. New York, Ace, 1965.

Babel-17. New York, Ace, 1966; London, Gollancz, 1967; revised edition, London, Sphere, 1969; Boston, Gregg Press, 1976.

Empire Star. New York, Ace, 1966.

The Einstein Intersection. New York, Ace, 1967; London, Gollancz, 1968.

Nova. New York, Doubleday, 1968; London, Gollancz, 1969.

The Tides of Lust. New York, Lancer, 1973; Manchester, Savoy, 1979.

Dhalgren. New York, Bantam, 1975; revised edition, Boston, Gregg Press, 1977.

Triton. New York, Bantam, 1976; London, Corgi, 1977.

The Ballad of Beta-2, and Empire Star. London, Sphere, 1977.

Empire: A Visual Novel, illustrated by Howard V. Chaykin. New York, Berkley, 1978.

Nevèrÿona; or, The Tale of Signs and Cities. New York, Bantam, 1983; London, Grafton, 1989.

Stars in My Pocket Like Grains of Sand. New York, Bantam, 1984.

Flight from Nevèrÿon. New York, Bantam, 1985; London, Grafton, 1989.

The Bridge of Lost Desire. New York, Arbor House, 1987.

The Straits of Messina. Seattle, Serconia Press, 1989.

Return to Nevèrÿon. London, Grafton, 1989; Hanover, New Hampshire, Wesleyan University Press, 1994.

They Fly at Ciron. Seattle, Incunabula, 1993.

The Mad Man. New York, Masquerade Books, 1994.

Hogg. Normal, Illinois, FC2, 1998.

Short Stories

Driftglass: 10 Tales of Speculative Fiction. New York, Doubleday, 1971; London, Gollancz, 1978.

Tales of Nevèrÿon. New York, Bantam, 1979; London, Grafton, 1988.

Distant Stars. New York, Bantam, 1981.

The Complete Nebula-Award Winning Fiction. New York, Bantam, 1986.

Atlantis: Three Tales. Hanover, New Hampshire, University Press of New England, 1995.

Other

The Jewel-Hinged Jaw: Notes on the Language of Science Fiction. Elizabethtown, New York, Dragon Press, 1977.

The American Shore: Meditations on a Tale of Science Fiction by Thomas M. Disch—''Angouleme.'' Elizabethtown, New York, Dragon Press, 1978.

Heavenly Breakfast: An Essay on the Winter of Love (memoir). New York, Bantam, 1979.

Starboard Wine: More Notes on the Language of Science Fiction. Pleasantville, New York, Dragon Press, 1984.

The Motion of Light in Water: Sex and Science Fiction Writing in the East Village 1957–1965. New York, Arbor House, 1988; with *The Column at the Market's Edge,* London, Paladin, 1990.

Wagner-Artaud: A Play of 19th and 20th Century Critical Fictions. New York, Ansatz Press, 1988.

Silent Interviews: On Language, Race, Sex, Science Fiction, and Some Comics. Hanover, New Hampshire, Wesleyan University Press, 1994.

Longer Views: Extended Essays. Hanover, New Hampshire, University Press of New England, 1996.

Bread and Wine: an Erotic Tale of New York City: an Autobiographical Account, Illustrated by Mia Wolff with an introduction by Alan Moore. New York, Juno Books, 1998.

Times Square Red, Times Square Blue. New York, New York University Press, 1999.

Shorter Views: Queer Thoughts and the Politics of the Paraliterary. Hanover, New Hampshire, University Press of New England, 1999.

Editor, with Marilyn Hacker, *Quark 1–4.* New York, Paperback Library, 4 vols., 1970–71.

Editor, *Nebula Winners 13.* New York, Harper, 1980.

*

Manuscript Collection: Mugar Memorial Library, Boston University.

Critical Studies: *The Delany Intersection: Samuel R. Delany Considered as a Writer of Semi-Precious Words* by George Edgar Slusser, San Bernardino, California, Borgo Press, 1977; *Worlds Out of Words: The SF Novels of Samuel R. Delany* by Douglas Barbour, Frome, Somerset, Bran's Head, 1979; *Samuel R. Delany* by Jane Weedman, Mercer Island, Washington, Starmont House, 1982; *Samuel R. Delany* by Seth McEvoy, New York, Ungar, 1983; *Ash of Stars: On the Writing of Samuel R. Delany,* edited by James Sallis. Jackson, University Press of Mississippi, 1996.

* * *

Although Samuel R. Delany began his literary career at the age of 20 with *The Jewels of Aptor*, quickly followed by the *Fall of the Towers* trilogy and *The Ballad of Beta-2*, it wasn't until the prolific 1966–69 period—*Empire Star*, the Nebula-winning novels *Babel-17* and *The Einstein Intersection*, the Nebula-winning story ''Aye, and Gomorrah…'', *Nova*, and the Hugo/Nebula-winning ''Time Considered as a Helix of Semi-Precious Stones''—that Delany's literary power would reverberate throughout the science fiction (sf) community. It is in this early period that we can tease out the thematic threads Delany masterfully weaves throughout the corpus of his work.

Specifically, Delany is interested in the interactions among mythology, anthropology, linguistic theory, cultural history, psychology, poststructuralism, sociology, philosophy, and the quest/adventure story.

Quite often, Delany guides the reader through his complex worlds using figures of the socially outcast artist and/or criminal who, by their marginalized nature, pull at the underlying fabric of what constitutes reality. For example, *Babel-17*, a novel of galactic warfare, tells the story of poet Rydra Wong and her attempt to decipher communications intercepted from the Invaders by the Alliance. Wong soon discovers an unknown language and, in the process of deciphering these communications, both Wong and the reader are enlightened about the nature of language and its ability to structure reality. Of particular interest is the web, a symbol of interconnectedness and isolation suggesting that language can both constrain and structure reality.

The Einstein Intersection follows a race of aliens who, attempting to understand the post-apocalyptic Earth, take on corporeal form and immerse themselves in human myths, traditions, and archetypes. Unable to create their own culture out of the remnant world they occupy, the aliens encounter salvation in the form of ''difference,'' embodied in the Black musician Lobey. Playing music on his murderous machete, Lobey, who is both Orpheus and Theseus, cleaves through the old myths to create the order upon which the alien civilization can thrive. The novel is a treatise on difference and explores the patterns of interaction among myths, archetypes, imagination, and the conscious mind. *The Einstein Intersection* is further enhanced with Delany's own diaries providing part of the novel's text.

Nova is Delany's unique take on space opera, offering readers Prometheus and the Grail legend woven into a quest for the much-valued fuel illyrion, located in the heart of a nova star. The narrative follows the Mouse, a musician playing the sensory-syrnynx, and his role in the epic struggle between, on one side, Captain Lorq Von Ray and, on the other, Prince and Ruby Red. George Slusser notes in *The Delany Intersection* that Delany has inverted the traditional epic by offering us a narrative wherein men do not struggle *against* an inhuman system so much as *within* an unhuman one.

Following *Nova*, Delany released *The Tides of Lust*, a non-sf pornographic novel with traits of the fantastic. Peter Nicholls writes in *The Encyclopedia of Science Fiction* that the sadomasochism of the novel is reminiscent of a ''Baudelairean ritual of passage.'' This text occupies an important place in Delany's work as it was in the mid-1970s that his homosexuality became generally known; consequently, his work following *Tides of Lust* adds the cultural interplay of eroticism and love to his already extensive thematic interests.

From 1969 to 1973—a period that also saw Delany publish short stories, develop essays that would later appear in such studies as *The Jewel-Hinged Jaw: Notes on the Language of Science Fiction*, and edit four sf quarterlies—Delany put together his controversial 879-page opus *Dhalgren*. The narrative—which some critics do not consider sf proper—follows the anonymous Kid who embarks on a series of adventures in Bellona, an orderless city resting under the double-mooned sky of a familiar U.S. setting. The novel, according to Douglas Barbour's entry in *Science Fiction Writers*, is symbolized in the chain the Kid receives prior to entering Bellona; namely, ''it wraps in upon itself, a long, looped chain of mirrors, prisms, and lenses.'' Indeed, *Dhalgren*, like the earlier *Empire Star*, is both self-conscious and self-reflexive, evidenced in the novel the Kid writes which may be *Dhalgren* itself and, in Joycean style, the first sentence bringing an open-ended closure to the unfinished final sentence. Variously, the novel is about the tension between reality and reality models, the trials and tribulations of a writer's craft, and the representation of human lives with all their comedic, psychological, sociological, erotic, and emotional baggage.

Delany's next novel, *Triton*, is very much science fiction in its offering of a futuristic setting with technological advances and distinctly alien modes of relating to reality. In this novel, subtitled *An Ambiguous Heterotopia*, Delany explores future societies structured along sexual lines. The novel is particularly unique as the female protagonist, the former man Bron Helstrom, is an alienated character with whom the reader is *not* supposed to identify. Bron struggles through the course of the novel as her outdated twentieth-century misogyny rubs up against the sexual egalitarianism of Neptune's moon, Triton. In the end, Bron remains locked into herself, alienated and trapped ''in social and psychological stasis,'' as Barbour writes. One can't help but hear Delany speaking to the persecution of women, homosexuals, and multisexuals through Triton's narrative.

The 1980s saw Delany shift tactics, infusing his science fiction with the magical scenery of sword-and-sorcery fantasy. *The Nevèrÿon Series—Tales of Nevèrÿon, Nevèrÿona, Flight from Nevèrÿon*, and *The Bridge of Lost Desire*—continues to explore Delany's multiple interests, especially the issue of slavery as it appears in both economic and erotic economies. *The Nevèrÿon Series* demonstrates Delany's self-reflexivity—exemplified in the appendices wherein Delany reflects on the creative process and, in the later books, makes direct references to the contemporary AIDS epidemic—as well as his profound understanding of how lives are affected by cultural shifts in reality.

For many critics, *Stars in My Pocket Like Grains of Sand* revealed an increasingly complex, richly textured, and smoother Samuel Delany. The narrative, involving interstellar politics set in a galactic civilization, seeks to explore large social ethical expectations, all the while offering the reader a love story, an exploration of the variety of human relationships, and the mysterious magnetism of sexual attraction. At the time of its publication, *Stars in My Pocket Like Grains of Sand* was intended to be a diptych, but the long-awaited sequel, *The Splendor and Misery of Bodies, of Cities*, although slated for a mid-1990s release, has not yet appeared.

From Harlem of the 1970s, which inspired the city wreckage of *Dhalgren*, through the sexual interactions in *Stars in My Pocket Like Grains of Sand*, inspired by New York City's sexual variety, and culminating in the echoes of the Port Authority Bus Terminal in *The Nevèrÿon Series*, New York looms large in Delany's writings. In the 1990s, Delany's non-fiction focuses on weaving his sexuality into the fabric of New York (especially the former porn theatres of Eighth Avenue) and exploring the face of the homeless, embodied in his partner, Dennis Rickett, who spent six years living on the streets. Delany's autobiographical reflections on New York City are the lifeblood of *Bread & Wine: An Erotic Tale of New York; Heavenly Breakfast, an Essay on the Winter of Love; Atlantis: Three Tales; The Motion of Light in Water; Sex and Science Fiction Writing in the East Village, 1960–1965*; and *Times Square Red, Times Square Blue (Sexual Cultures)* .

The 1990s also saw Delany return to the fictive terrain of *The Tides of Lust* with a trio of novels—*Equinox* (a reprint of *The Tides of Lust*), *The Mad Man* and *Hogg*—that have been described as anti-pornographic. Through these texts, Delany engages both his own sexuality and depicts sexual escapades and violence in an unflinching manner, all the while calling for the valuation of sexual tolerance. As usual, Delany's theory and fiction intersect and intertwine into a complex exploration; specifically, Delany, as he notes in *Silent Interviews*, is interested in the relationship between eroticization and class relations and, consequently, in who benefits and loses in the act of eroticization.

Finally, the 1990s has seen a Delany renaissance, thanks in large part to Wesleyan University Press undertaking the task of reprinting *Dhalgren, Trouble on Triton*, and *The Einstein Intersection* as well as re-issuing *The Nevèrÿon Series*. With Delany's *1984*—a collection of 56 letters and documents—and *Shorter Views: Queer Thoughts & the Politics of the Paraliterary* both slated for a 2000 release, Samuel Delany's impact bodes well for a new millennium of science fiction, literary criticism, pornography, historical fiction, and autobiography.

—Graham J. Murphy

DELBANCO, Nicholas Franklin

Nationality: American. **Born:** London, England, 27 August 1942. **Education:** Harvard University, B.A. 1963; Columbia University, M.A. 1966. **Family:** Married Elena Greenhouse in 1970; two daughters. **Career:** Member of Department of Language and Literature, Bennington College, Bennington, Vermont, 1966–84, writing workshop director, 1977–84; professor of English, Skidmore College, Saratoga Springs, New York, 1984–85; Robert Frost Professor of English Language and Literature, University of Michigan, Ann Arbor, 1985—. **Awards:** National Endowment for the Arts creative writing award, 1973, 1982; National Endowment of Composers and Librettists fellowship, 1976; Guggenheim fellowship, 1980; Woodrow Wilson fellowship; Edward John Noble fellowship; New York State CAPS Award; Vermont Council of the Arts Award; Michigan Council of the Arts Award. **Agent:** Brandt & Brandt Literary Agents, Inc., 1501 Broadway, New York, New York 10036, U.S.A.

Publications

Novels

The Martlet's Tale. Philadelphia, Lippincott, 1966.
Grasse, 3/23/66. Philadelphia, Lippincott, 1968.
Consider Sappho Burning. New York, Morrow, 1969.
News. New York, Morrow, 1970.
In the Middle Distance. New York, Morrow, 1971.
Fathering. New York, Morrow, 1973.
Small Rain. New York, Morrow, 1975.
Possession. New York, Morrow, 1977.
Sherbrookes. New York, Morrow, 1978.
Stillness. New York, Morrow, 1980.
In the Name of Mercy. New York, Warner, 1995.
Old Scores. New York, Warner, 1997.
What Remains. New York, Warner, 2000.

Short Stories

About My Table, and Other Stories. New York, Morrow, 1983.
The Writer's Trade, and Other Stories. New York, Morrow, 1990.

Other

Group Portrait: Joseph Conrad, Stephen Crane, Ford Madox Ford, Henry James, and H. G. Wells (nonfiction). New York, Morrow, 1982.
The Beaux Arts Trio: A Portrait (nonfiction). New York, Morrow, 1985.
Running in Place: Scenes from the South of France (nonfiction). New York, Atlantic Monthly, 1989.
The Lost Suitcase: Reflections on the Literary Life (nonfiction). New York, Columbia University Press, 2000.
Contributor, *On the Vineyard* by Peter Simon. New York, Doubleday, 1980.
Editor and author of introduction, *Stillness and Shadows* by John Gardner. New York, Knopf, 1986.
Editor and author of introduction, *Speaking of Writing: Selected Hopwood Lectures.* Ann Arbor, University of Michigan Press, 1990.
Editor, with Laurence Goldstein, *Writers and Their Craft: Short Stories and Essays on the Narrative.* Detroit, Wayne State University Press, 1991.
Editor, with Alan Cheuse, *Talking Horse: Bernard Malamud on Life and Work* by Bernard Malamud. New York, Columbia University Press, 1996.
Editor and author of introduction, *The Writing Life: The Hopwood Lectures, Fifth Series.* Ann Arbor, University of Michigan Press, 2000.
Foreword, *Avery Hopwood: His Life and Plays* by Jack F. Sharrar. Ann Arbor, University of Michigan Press, 1998.

* * *

As a novelist, Nicholas Delbanco can be considered doubly fortunate in that he has always been able to draw inspiration and sustenance from two continents and two cultures.

Of Italian and German descent, he was born in London at the height of the German Blitz, and his family did not depart for America until he was six, and he was not naturalized as an American citizen until he was eleven. It is not surprising that, though later he would anchor himself firmly in New England and particularly in Vermont, and more recently in Michigan as the Robert Frost Professor of English Language and Literature, the influence of his European origins would play a consistent part in his fiction and non-fiction alike.

The cultural ambivalence, if such it may be called, manifested itself early. At Columbia, his B.A. thesis was devoted to a joint study of Rilke and Heredia, two noteworthy wanderers, and the subject of his M.A. thesis was that tragic outcast, Malcolm Lowry. Examining the numerous novels Delbanco has published to date, one finds that only five are set exclusively in the United States and that the majority are set, either in whole or part, in Provence, Tuscany, Greece, Switzerland, or as far afield as Barbados and Mexico. Several of his non-fiction books are concerned with Europe, one of them a study of that remarkable group of literary exiles, including Conrad, Crane, and James, who lived and worked together in a small corner of England at the turn of the last century. Indeed, one of the courses Delbanco has taught over the years is specifically entitled ''Exiles,'' and is devoted to Becket, Conrad, and Nabokov, while other courses have featured a gallery of roving and displaced novelists such as Joyce, Lawrence, Forster, Ford, Mann, Fitzgerald, and Hemingway, all of whom, like

Delbanco, shuttled between one country and continent and another and drew on the experience to add richness, variety and color to their work.

In Delbanco's case, these qualities have been enhanced by a cunning employment in his fiction of the kind of classical or Old World template that one encounters, for example, in *Ulysses* or in Eliot. These templates, or perhaps one might better call them armatures, none of them overtly stated, have included, to take random examples, the Theban Trilogy, the Orphic Mysteries, the Synoptic Gospels, and the stories of Eloise and Abelard, Tristan and Isolde, and the Prodigal Son. Delbanco, the supremely conscious craftsman, has always been a great one for what he would term his ''strategies,'' and the device has always lent a sense of depth and dimension to his otherwise contemporary plots. One must not, on the other hand, exaggerate the element of *dépaysement* in his work, or suggest that he is in any way a species of literary castaway. On the contrary, if in one sense he can be regarded in the honorable guise as an *homme de lettres* in the European mold, in another he must be regarded as an authentic if somewhat exotic performer—in the home-grown American manner. Since the age of eleven, after all, he has been domiciled in the United States, and therefore the cosmopolitan complexion of his work should be viewed as merely an addition to its natural elegance and polish.

We have mentioned Vermont as being one of the principal locations of his fiction. That state, where for two decades he was on the staff of Bennington College, has provided the setting for no less than five of his novels, including the magisterial Sherbrookes trilogy, which will possibly prove to be one of his greatest achievements. It was at Bennington, home to a close-knit company of writers, painters, and composers, that he conceived and brought into focus an idea that has been central to his career: the notion of the artistic community, and particularly the literary community, as a fellowship, a sodality, a guild almost in the sense of a craft guild in the mediaeval usage of the term. This conception was at the root of the notable series of Bennington Summer Writing Workshops that he founded in 1977 and presided over until 1985, when he left Vermont for Michigan. The aim of the Workshops (significant term) was to bind the band of mature writers who took part in them more closely together and to provide the students who would form the next generation of writers with an insight into the mysteries of technique. The preoccupation with technique has always been a prominent feature of Delbanco's fiction, as it was for Rilke, James, Ford, Conrad, Nabokov, and other writers who have influenced him, and as it was for John Gardner, Bernard Malamud, and other novelists who worked closely with him at Bennington and elsewhere, and for John Updike, his mentor and teacher at Columbia.

It was at Bennington that Delbanco wrote eleven books of fiction and three volumes of non-fiction, and where he developed his very personal style. How to describe this style? Delbanco's style is not at all the bald, slam-bang, in-your-face, go-for-the-jugular style common in American fiction. On the contrary, it is graceful, allusive, oblique, a cat's-cradle in which he artfully enfolds and enmeshes his characters and subjects. It is feline, the high style of the conscious craftsman. The prose is lyrical and inflected, and one may usefully indicate its general effect by noting its palpable affinities with painting and with music.

Delbanco's immediate family were intimately connected with the visual arts. His uncle Gustav was a founder of the firm of Roland, Browse and Delbanco, one of London's premier galleries. His father, a painter himself, and still exhibiting at the age of ninety, came to America to establish a branch of the gallery in New York. As a young man his son Nicholas, who had early tried his hand as a painter, recrossed the Atlantic to serve an apprenticeship in the original firm, and his wife Elena is herself an accomplished artist. Delbanco's stylistic methods have surely been affected by this lifelong link to the art of painting, both in the composition of the novels and in the meticulous laying on of color. He paints with a precise brush, not with a brash attack but with careful strokes. His characters and situations shape themselves with the subtle, suggestive, softly luminous half-light of a Chardin, say, or a Vuillard.

Similarly, the sister art of music has played a major role in Delbanco's evolution as individual and as writer. His wife is the daughter of the celebrated musician Bernard Greenhouse, for many years the cellist of the Beaux Arts Trio. Delbanco has not only devoted an entire book to an account of a European tour of the Beaux Arts Trio, but at this writing has in preparation a second book describing the fascinating history of his father-in-law's Stradivarius, the ''Countess Steinlen.'' And again, when one considers Delbanco's style in its relationship to the art of music, it is once more a French master who springs to mind, Debussy, in the intricate play of its motifs, its deft shifts of key, and the astute handling of its dynamics.

Delbanco, in short, over a long career, has not only paid scrupulous attention to the nurturing of his own talent, but has played an exemplary role in furthering the interests of his profession. It is for these reasons that he has earned his leading position in contemporary letters and the admiration of that literary fellowship to whose service he has been committed.

—Jon Manchip White

DeLILLO, Don

Nationality: American. **Born:** New York City, 20 November 1936. **Education:** Fordham University, Bronx, New York, 1954–58. **Awards:** Guggenheim fellowship, 1979; American Academy award, 1984; National Book award, 1985; *Irish Times*-Aer Lingus prize, 1989; PEN-Faulkner award for fiction, 1991; Jerusalem Prize, 1999. **Agent:** Wallace Literary Agency, 177 East 70th Street, New York, New York 10021, U.S.A.

Publications

Novels

Americana. Boston, Houghton Mifflin, 1971; London, Penguin, 1990.
End Zone. Boston, Houghton Mifflin, 1972; London, Deutsch, 1973.
Great Jones Street. Boston, Houghton Mifflin, 1973; London, Deutsch, 1974.
Ratner's Star. New York, Knopf, 1976; London, Vintage, 1991.
Players. New York, Knopf, 1977; London, Vintage, 1991.
Running Dog. New York, Knopf, 1978; London, Gollancz, 1979.
The Names. New York, Knopf, 1982; Brighton, Sussex, Harvester Press, 1983.

White Noise. New York, Viking, 1985; London, Pan, 1986; published as *White Noise: Text and Criticism,* edited by Mark Osteen, New York, Penguin, 1998.
Libra. New York and London, Viking, 1988.
Mao II. New York, Viking, and London, Jonathan Cape, 1991.
Underworld. New York, Scribner, 1997.

Uncollected Short Stories

''The River Jordan,'' in *Epoch* (Ithaca, New York), Winter 1960.
''Spaghetti and Meatballs,'' in *Epoch* (Ithaca, New York), Spring 1965.
''Take the 'A' Train,'' in *Stories from Epoch,* edited by Baxter Hathaway. Ithaca, New York, Cornell University Press, 1966.
''Coming Sun. Mon. Tues.,'' in *Kenyon Review* (Gambier, Ohio), June 1966.
''Baghdad Towers West,'' in *Epoch* (Ithaca, New York), Spring 1968.
''Game Plan,'' in *New Yorker,* 27 November 1971.
''In the Men's Room of the Sixteenth Century,'' in *The Secret Life of Our Times,* edited by Gordon Lish. New York, Doubleday, 1973.
''The Uniforms,'' in *Cutting Edges,* edited by Jack Hicks. New York, Holt Rinehart, 1973.
''Showdown at Great Hole,'' in *Esquire* (New York), June 1976.
''The Network,'' in *On the Job,* edited by William O'Rourke. New York, Random House, 1977.
''Creation,'' in *Antaeus* (New York), Spring 1979.
''Human Moments in World War III,'' in *Great Esquire Fiction,* edited by L. Rust Hills. New York, Viking Press, 1983.
''Walkmen,'' in *Vanity Fair* (New York), August 1984.
''Oswald in the Lone Star State,'' in *Esquire* (New York), July 1988.
''The Runner,'' in *Harper's* (New York), September 1988.
''Shooting Bill Gray,'' in *Esquire* (New York), January 1991.
''Pafko at the Wall,'' in *Harper's* (New York), October 1992.
''Videotape,'' in *Antaeus* (Hopewell, New Jersey), Autumn 1994.

Plays

The Engineer of Moonlight, in *Cornell Review* (Ithaca, New York), Winter 1979.
The Day Room (produced Cambridge, Massachusetts, 1986; New York, 1987). New York, Knopf, 1987.
Valparaiso: A Play in Two Acts. New York, Scribner, 1999.

*

Critical Studies: *In the Loop: Don DeLillo and the Systems Novel* by Thomas LeClair, Urbana, University of Illinois Press, 1988; *Introducing Don DeLillo* edited by Frank Lentricchia, Durham, North Carolina, and London, Duke University Press, 1991; *Don DeLillo* by Douglas Keesey, New York, Twayne, 1993; *American Literary Naturalism and Its Twentieth-Century Transformations: Frank Norris, Ernest Hemingway, Don DeLillo* by Paul Civello. Athens, University of Georgia Press, 1994; *Conspiracy and Paranoia in Contemporary American Fiction: The Works of Don DeLillo and Joseph McElroy* by Steffen Hantke. New York, P. Lang, 1994; *White Noise: Text and Criticism* by Don DeLillo, edited by Mark Osteen. New York, Penguin Books, 1998; *Critical Essays on Don DeLillo,* edited by Hugh Ruppersburg and Tim Engles. New York, G.K. Hall, 2000.

* * *

Don DeLillo's novels since 1985 have turned their attention to the paradoxes and contradictions of postmodern culture. DeLillo's is the terrain of shopping malls and supermarkets, the temples of the new consumerist creed, of a market organized entirely around consumer demand, of the detritus and waste of consumerism produced by that insatiable demand. His is a world in which the mode of production associated with modernism has given way to the postmodern mode of information in which television shapes perceptions and creates its own self-referential world. As he moved into the 1990s we see that his novels become concerned with what might be called the ''global postmodern,'' the point at which media spectacle itself becomes a world-wide phenomenon, the point at which every interstice of the international world is saturated in capital. His is a global landscape traversed by the indeterminate circulation of signs, by messages of resurgent nationalisms and religious fundamentalism, as well as the violence of international terrorism.

DeLillo is above all concerned with how the artist goes about representing this new world that, according to Frederic Jameson, exceeds the abilities of our ''cognitive mapping.'' What is the place for the artist in a world whose multifarious representations (electronic and otherwise) exceed, in both scale and inventiveness, those of the artist? DeLillo's own sensibility was shaped in the fifties, a time when art was cast in the heroic mould, a time when literature was conceived as oppositional, flouting the conventions of taste and defying the solicitations of the market. Yet as DeLillo understands, cultural forms are no longer confined to the enclave of high art and its oppositional impulses, but permeate all aspects of society. Rather than being oppositional, art is often complicit with the new market order. Thus postmodern culture challenges the assumptions of an older modernist aesthetic. Accordingly, DeLillo's artist figures (such as Bill Gray in *Mao II*) find themselves searching and groping for new ways to express their artistic concerns and formulate ''sneak attacks on the dominant culture'' (as DeLillo puts it in *Underworld*). DeLillo's novels both explore the conceptual horizons of modernism—and modernism's vanishing point—but enact and embody new ways of attempting to represent what seems unrepresentable.

Although he writes on this subject in many of his earlier novels, *White Noise* (1985) is his most sustained exploration of the media saturation that characterizes postmodern culture. The narrator, Jack Gladney (holding, like many of DeLillo's protagonists, to older modernist notions of culture), sifts through the layers of ''white noise'' of contemporary culture—electronic media, printed information, traffic sounds, computer read outs—listening for significance, for a grasp of essence in the flux. But clearly the impetus of the larger culture works against Gladney's attempts to find essences, fixities, and stable identities. For television, with its ''flow'' and its proliferating images, represents a ''peak experience'' of postmodern culture. As Murray Suskind, a visiting professor at Gladney's university, explains to Gladney, television ''welcomes us into the grid, the network of little buzzing dots that make up a picture patterns.... Look at the wealth of data concealed in the grid, the bright packaging, the jingles, the slice-of-life commercials, the products hurling out of darkness, the coded messages and endless repetitions, like chants, like mantras. 'Coke is it, Coke is it, Coke is it.''' Gladney may hold to notions of an authentic ground of being and authentic selfhood, but all about him the self is being saturated and colonized by media images, and the simulated environments of mall and mediascape are eclipsing the real.

Libra (1988) also reflects DeLillo's desire to explore postmodernity, with its televisional society of spectacle. For as DeLillo sees it the assassination of John F. Kennedy inaugurated the era of media spectacle, if not of a postmodern politics. For in a society increasingly filled with media representations (as was America by the early sixties), terrorism and assassination become one extreme in the logical extensions of spectacle. DeLillo depicts Lee Harvey Oswald as the first truly postmodern figure, desiring his ten minutes of media fame. Oswald is a protean figure engaged in a quest for self-fashioning in terms of what the culture offers—and what the culture offers is precisely the immortality of the image. Just before his attempt on General Walker's life, Oswald directs his wife, Marina, to take a picture of him with a black shirt on, a rifle in one hand and a revolutionary pamphlet in the other. Oswald's understanding of revolutionary ideology is at best vague; what he wants is for this picture to be printed on the cover of *Life* and *Time*.

If *Libra* is DeLillo's attempt to trace the originary moments of postmodernity in the 1960s, *Mao II* marks that moment when spectacle goes global in the 1990s. The novel depicts a world where televisional catastrophes, spectral fear, pseudo events, and spectacle are an integral part of daily life. This is a new ''geopolitical'' arena that defies spatial coordinates. A character sitting in a revolving ''designer'' bar atop a skyscraper— which could be in any urban center in the world— suddenly says to the person across the table ''Jesus. Where am I?'' Eerie ''nonplaces'' like embassies and airport transit lounges populate the narrative. Along with this disorienting globalization comes an ''everyday fear'' fuelled by perceived dangers that come from no single isolable place but rather lurk in some unspecifiable future. Terrorism is a ''x'' factor in this fear blur, and terrorism is as anonymous as a natural catastrophe: postmodern death comes not in the natural course of things but upon those who are in the wrong place at the wrong time.

Terrorism becomes part of a generalized ''everyday fear,'' however, because it is a media phenomenon. As part of the proliferation of image and spectacle, terrorism poses a ''crisis of representation'' insofar as its hyperreal character—and at the same time the totalizing logic of media spectacle— undermines the artist's traditional attempts at critical distance, analysis, and critical intervention. This is precisely the dilemma of Bill Gray, protagonist of the novel. As Bill Gray articulates this dilemma, terrorism presents the novelist with a ''zero-sum game.'' ''What terrorists gain, novelists, lose. The degree to which they influence mass consciousness is the extent of our decline as shapers of sensibility and thought. The danger they represent equals our own failure to be dangerous.''

Feeling that the contemporary writer can no longer be an oppositional force, Bill Gray decides to confront the real world and offer himself as a hostage in exchange for a French poet being held by a revolutionary group. Ironically, as hostage, Gray finds himself part of a media exhibition of signs, part of the larger phenomenon of the loss of referent, part of the semiotic flow and exchange of signifiers in late capitalism. The hostage's very identity is ultimately absorbed into the ''digital mosaic in the processing grid,'' the mutating set of signs of a technology of digitized global communication. Ultimately the novel asks, how can the artist be oppositional in a world where, like a Warhol silkscreen, simulations rule? How can the subversive imagination be effective when an image-saturated global network brings the single, universal story of prosperity and the global victory of the market? Even images of terrorism merge and mix with fashionable commodity images. An ad for a new soft drink, ''Coke II,'' becomes confused in the mind of one character with a placard announcing a Maoist group because in both cases the ''lettering is so intensely red.''

Underworld (1997) is DeLillo's summary statement of postmodernity and its discontents. The novel encompasses the period from the early 1950s to the present. The world of DeLillo's 1950s youth, the Italian neighborhood of the Bronx, intersects with the global postmodern in the trajectory of the novel's protagonist, Nick Shay. Shay is in effect the inheritor of the legacy of America's Cold War supremacy and prosperity. Living his middle years in suburbia in the Southwest, Shay is an executive in a company that specializes in waste management. One of the forms of waste the company ''manages'' is nuclear waste.

Thus while the novel recapitulates many of the themes of DeLillo's previous novels— consumer detritus, media saturation, and the decentered world of global capitalism—*Underworld* introduces an issue that remained in the shadows in his earlier novels: the bomb. For it is not just that nuclear waste goes ''underground'' in landfills and bunker systems under mountains in Nevada. Rather, the specter of nuclear disaster is part of the ''Underworld'' of the social unconscious. The bomb is the ''Other'' of the contemporary world, the real specter that haunts the ''floating zones of desire'' of postmodern culture. Nick Shay is so haunted by the bomb that in middle age, when he uses sun block, he remembers Dr. Edward Teller putting suntan lotion on his face just before observing the first nuclear explosion. Nick is also haunted by the trauma of the disappearance of his father when he was a youth, yet even these traumatic memories haunt him in images that suggest collective nuclear anxieties. As a middle-aged man Nick is obsessed by a particular image, the logotype on the package of Lucky Strike cigarettes—his father's brand. A series of concentric rings circling a void at the center, the image is an uncanny reminder of ground zero.

Ultimately, *Underworld* takes us into the postmodern terrain of the present, where nuclear power has triumphed. In the last section of the novel, Nick Shay is sent to Russia to investigate business prospects, specifically of investing in a Russian company that specializes in nuclear energy. The Russians have developed a new process for dealing with nuclear waste: ''we destroy contaminated nuclear waste by means of nuclear explosions.'' If waste is contamination, decay and death, it is also a ''remainder,'' something that cannot be assimilated by the system, something intractable, a reminder of the ''real.'' Yet here (in a way that parallels DeLillo's concern for the eclipse of the real by electronic representations and commodity signs), nuclear energy itself swallows all traces of the real. As such it is a form of postmodern production par excellence, part of a larger play of monetary entities and the total flow of financial speculation that circumscribes all aspects of culture.

DeLillo's novels have always been concerned with the limits of representation, how one represents the unrepresentable in a literary text. Indeed, one of the purposes of DeLillo's narrative in *Underworld* is to revisit historical anxiety and trauma, the ''unspeakable'' experience of the bomb, and to represent it in narrative form. DeLillo's narrative circles around the "unsayable" moments of nuclear trauma, but it also enables the unspeakable to be spoken by a narrative orchestration of events. This is, of course, part of the larger problem of the artist in the new world of the global postmodern, a problem that haunts, more than any of DeLillo's characters, Bill Gray in *Mao II*. To be sure the downward spiral of modernism and its subversive aesthetic DeLillo depicts in a novel like *Mao II* seems a truly grim topic for a writer who has aspirations, such as DeLillo clearly does, of critiquing society and interrogating culture. Yet DeLillo poses these problems precisely to indicate the need for new artistic strategies consonant with a new media age. His own novels go further than any other contemporary fiction to "cognitively map" the global postmodern. His works are comprised of "heteroglossic" narratives in which discourses clash and rebound, are decoded and recoded according to the logic of a society of information and spectacle. All this indicates an effort to understand—and thereby to critique— the semiotic and cultural dynamics of postmodernity. More than any other fiction of the contemporary period, DeLillo's novels probe the "limits of representation" of the novel and forge new ways of presenting the unpresentable.

—Leonard Wilcox

DESAI, Anita

Nationality: Indian. **Born:** Anita Mazumbar, Mussoorie, 24 June 1937. **Education:** Queen Mary's Higher Secondary School, New Delhi; Miranda House, University of Delhi, B.A. (honours) in English literature 1957. **Family:** Married Ashvin Desai in 1958; two sons and two daughters. **Career:** Since 1963 writer; Purington Professor of English, Mount Holyoke College, 1988–93; professor of writing, Massachusetts Institute of Technology, 1993—. Helen Cam Visiting Fellow, Girton College, Cambridge, 1986–87; Elizabeth Drew Professor, Smith College, 1987–88; Ashby Fellow, Clare Hall, Cambridge, 1989. Since 1972 member of the Sahitya Academy English Board. **Awards:** Royal Society of Literature Winifred Holtby prize, 1978; Sahitya Academy award, 1979; *Guardian* award, for children's book, 1982; *Hadassah Magazine* award, 1989; Tarak Nath Das award, 1989; Padma Sri award, 1989; Literary Lion Award, New York Public Library, 1993. Fellow, Royal Society of Literature, 1978; Girton College, Cambridge, 1988; Clare Hall, Cambridge, 1991. **Agent:** Deborah Rogers, Rogers Coleridge and White Ltd., 20 Powis Mews, London W11 1JN, England.

PUBLICATIONS

Novels

Cry, The Peacock. Calcutta, Rupa, n.d.; London, Owen, 1963.
Voices in the City. London, Owen, 1965.
Bye-Bye, Blackbird. New Delhi, Hind, and Thompson, Connecticut, InterCulture, 1971.
Where Shall We Go This Summer? New Delhi, Vikas, 1975.
Fire on the Mountain. New Delhi, Allied, London, Heinemann, and New York, Harper, 1977.
Clear Light of Day. New Delhi, Allied, London, Heinemann, and New York, Harper, 1980.
In Custody. London, Heinemann, 1984; New York, Harper, 1985.
Baumgartner's Bombay. London, Heinemann, 1988; New York, Knopf, 1989.
Journey to Ithaca. New York, Knopf, 1995.
Fasting, Feasting. London, Chatto & Windus, 1999; Boston, Houghton Mifflin, 2000.

Short Stories

Games at Twilight and Other Stories. New Delhi, Allied, and London, Heinemann, 1978; New York, Harper, 1980.
Diamond Dust: Stories. Boston, Houghton Mifflin, 2000.

Uncollected Short Stories

"Circus Cat, Alley Cat," in *Thought* (New Delhi), 1957.
"Tea with the Maharani," in *Envoy* (London), 1959.
"Grandmother," in *Writers Workshop* (Calcutta), 1960.
"Mr. Bose's Private Bliss," in *Envoy* (London), 1961.
"Ghost House," in *Quest* (Bombay), 1961.
"Descent from the Rooftop," in *Illustrated Weekly of India* (Bombay), 1970.
"Private Tuition by Mr. Bose," in *Literary Review* (Madison, New Jersey), Summer 1986.

Fiction (for children)

The Peacock Garden. Bombay, India Book House, 1974; London, Heinemann, 1979.
Cat on a Houseboat. Bombay, Orient Longman, 1976.
The Village by the Sea. London, Heinemann, 1982.

*

Critical Studies: *Anita Desai: A Study of Her Fiction* by Meena Belliappa, Calcutta, Writers Workshop, 1971; *The Twice-Born Fiction* by Meenakshi Mukherjee, New Delhi, Arnold-Heinemann, 1972; *The Novels of Mrs. Anita Desai* by B.R. Rao, New Delhi, Kalyani, 1977; *Anita Desai the Novelist* by Madhusudan Prasad, Allahabad, New Horizon, 1981; *Perspectives on Anita Desai* edited by Ramesh K. Srivastava, Ghaziabad, Vimal, 1984; *The Mind and Art of Anita Desai* by J.P. Tripathi, Bareilly, Prakash, 1986; *Stairs to the Attic: The Novels of Anita Desai* by Jasbir Jain, Jaipur, Printwell 1987; *The Novels of Anita Desai: A Study in Character and Conflict* by Usha Bande, New Delhi, Prestige, 1988; *Language and Theme in Anita Desai's Fiction* by Kunj Bala Goel, Jaipur, Classic, 1989; *Voice and Vision of Anita Desai* by Seema Jena, New Delhi, Ashish, 1989; *Virginia Woolf and Anita Desai: A Comparative Study* by Asha Kanwar, New Delhi, Prestige, 1989; *The Fiction of Anita Desai* edited by R.K. Dhawan, New Delhi, Bahri, 1989; *Symbolism in Anita Desai's Novels* by Kajali Sharma, New Delhi, Abhinav, 1991; *Anita Desai's Fiction: Patterns of Survival Strategies* by Mrinalini Solanki, Delhi, Kanishka, 1992; *Human Bonds and Bondages: The Fiction of Anita Desai and Kamala Markandaya* by Usha Pathania, Delhi, Kanishka, 1992; *Cultural Imperialism and the Indo-English Novel: Genre and Ideology in R.K. Narayan, Anita Desai, Kamala Markandaya, and Salman Rushdie* by Fawzia Afzal-Khan, University

Park, Pennsylvania State University Press, 1993; *The Novels of Margaret Atwood and Anita Desai: A Comparative Study in Feminist Perspectives* by Sunaina Singh. New Delhi, Creative Books, 1994; *Anita Desai As an Artist: A Study in Image and Symbol* by S. Indira. New Delhi, Creative Books, 1994; *A Critical Study of the Novels of Anita Desai* by N. R. Gopal. New Delhi, Atlantic Publishers and Distributors, 1995; *Women and Society in the Novels of Anita Desai* by Bidulata Choudhury. New Delhi, Creative Books, 1995; *The New Woman in Indian English Fiction: A Study of Kamala Markandaya, Anita Desai, Namita Gokhale & Shobha De* by Sharad Shrivastava. New Delhi, Creative Books, 1996; *Six Indian Novelists: Mulk Raj Anand, Raja Rao, R. K. Narayan, Balachandran Rajan, Kamala Markandaya, Anita Desai* by A. V. Suresh Kumar. New Delhi, Creative Books, 1996.

Anita Desai comments:

I have been writing, since the age of 7, as instinctively as I breathe. It is a necessity to me: I find it is in the process of writing that I am able to think, to feel, and to realize at the highest pitch. Writing is to me a proccess of discovering the truth—the truth that is nine-tenths of the iceberg that lies submerged beneath the one-tenth visible portion we call Reality. Writing is my way of plunging to the depths and exploring this underlying truth. All my writing is an effort to discover, to underline and convey the true significance of things. That is why, in my novels, small objects, passing moods and attitudes acquire a large importance. My novels are no reflection of Indian society, politics, or character. They are part of my private effort to seize upon the raw material of life—its shapelessness, its meaninglessness, that lack of design that drives one to despair—and to mould it and impose on it a design, a certain composition and order that pleases me as an artist and also as a human being who longs for order.

While writing my novels, I find I use certain images again and again and that, although real, they acquire the significance of symbols. I imagine each writer ends by thus revealing his own mythology, a mythology that symbolizes his private morality and philosophy. One hopes, at the end of one's career, to have made some significant statement on life—not necessarily a water-tight, hard-and-fast set of rules, but preferably an ambiguous, elastic, shifting, and kinetic one that remains always capable of further change and growth.

Next to this exploration of the underlying truth and the discovery of a private mythology and philosophy, it is style that interests me most—and by this I mean the conscious labour of uniting language and symbol, word and rhythm. Without it, language would remain a dull and pedestrian vehicle. I search for a style that will bring it to vivid, surging life. Story, action, and drama mean little to me except insofar as they emanate directly from the personalities I have chosen to write about, born of their dreams and wills. One must find a way to unite the inner and the outer rhythms, to obtain a certain integrity and to impose order on chaos.

* * *

If the male triumvirate—Mulk Raj Anand, Raja Rao, and R. K. Narayan—can be seen as the first generation of Indian writers in English, Anita Desai, who published her first novel in 1963, might usefully be described as in the vanguard of the second-generation of Indian writers in English, and—along with Kamala Markandaya and Ruth Prawer Jhabvala—among the first generation of Indian women writing in English. The daughter of a Bengali father and a German mother, her mixed background has enabled Desai to view India from something of an outsider's perspective, to see India both as Indians and as a non-Indians see it.

Desai has published novels, collections of stories, and books for young readers. In all these works, Desai has set about interpreting her country for outsiders.

The world of Desai's fiction is largely a domestic one. She is interested primarily in the lives of women in India since Independence, the lives of women in the modern Indian nation state, rather than the history or politics of the subcontinent on a more extensive scale.

Her early novels, to *Where Shall We Go This Summer?*, focus in various ways on the disharmony and alienation women frequently experience in marriage. And although novels like *Voices in the City* and *Bye-Bye Blackbird* in particular give the impression of being about the lives of their male characters, the focus inevitably shifts to the female characters and the limitations the patriarchal world places on them (as daughters, wives, or mothers).

Bye-Bye Blackbird, which moves out of India to look at wider postcolonial issues of displacement, is the most accomplished of Desai's early novels. Ostensibly a typical third-world immigrant novel focusing on the lives of Dev and Ajit, two Indians in Britain, and the racial discrimination with which they have to contend, it is ultimately more about the alienation Ajit's wife, Sarah, suffers in her own country following her marriage to an Indian and her changed position in relation to the (British) nation state.

Desai's exquisitely crafted fifth novel (and probably her most powerful work to date), *Fire on the Mountain*, brings a definite sense of politics to her hitherto essentially family-focused dramas. It is another female-centered narrative that portrays the lives of three women—the elderly Nanda Kaul, her great-granddaughter Raka, and Nanda Kaul's lifelong friend Ila Das—who one by one retreat to Carignano, a small villa in the Himalayan hill station of Kasauli, to escape the brutal patriarchal worlds in which they have each lived. Criticism of *Fire on the Mountain* has tended to focus on Desai's detailed study of her three female characters—particularly her presentation of Nanda Kaul—without paying sufficient attention to her attack on patriarchal oppression, which, Desai forcefully suggests in this novel, not only limits the opportunities given to women in India, but mentally and physically damages them.

In *Clear Light of Day*, although the fires of Partition riots burn in the background, Desai's interest is again firmly focused on the difficulties facing a woman who attempts to assert her identity within the family framework, on the relationships Bim, the central female character, has with the various members of her family. It is about the fragmentation of a family played out against the backdrop of a fracturing nation.

In Custody, in many respects a delightful and sad comedy in a Narayanish sort of vein, marks a broadening of Desai's oeuvre. The novel plots the disillusionment of Deven, a young Hindi lecturer at a college in the small town of Mirpore, and the various calamities that befall him after he is persuaded to go to Delhi to interview his hero, India's greatest living Urdu poet, Nur—only to find himself being dragged deeper and deeper into Nur's unsavory world. For all its comedy, there is a certain despair in this novel, which presents the decline of Muslim Urdu culture in the North of India in the years following Independence and Partition.

Despair of a different hue characterizes *Baumgartner's Bombay*. Here, through a series of flashbacks, Desai looks at the life of a now-elderly German Jew who fled to India fifty years earlier in the 1930s to escape the Nazis, and who stayed on after Independence only to be murdered in Bombay by a German youth he tried to help. It is another brilliant portrait of alienation.

Desai continues her interest in Europeans in India in *Journey to Ithaca*. The novel focuses on Matteo, a guru-seeking Westerner in India, his wife Sophie, and the charismatic Mother that Sophie desperately struggles to keep him from. This incursion into territory so definitively mapped by Ruth Prawer Jhabvala is Desai's least successful novel.

The various strands that can be traced through her previous nine novels are brought together in near perfect synthesis in *Fasting, Feasting*. In keeping with her earlier novels, there is a return to a focus on the family, and in particular the lot of women trapped in traditional family structures in a rapidly changing postcolonial world. At the same time Desai extends her interest in the West in this cleverly structured novel. *Fasting, Feasting* is an almost plotless novel that looks at the lives of two daughters and the son of a traditional Indian family in the modern world. The novel opens with Uma, the eldest daughter now in her forties, still at home and firmly under the authority of her parents. Through a series of flashbacks, the first part of the novel looks at how Uma came to be in this position. It is a view of a traditional Hindu family, including arranged marriages. The second part of the book shifts abruptly to the United States. If in the first part India is presented for Western eyes, in the second part the tables are effectively turned and America is viewed through Indian eyes when Arun, in the U.S. on a college scholarship, finds himself living with the Patton family during summer vacation. It is a carefully balanced novel of contrasts: between East and West; lack and excess; lack of ambition (for Uma and Melanie) and too much ambition (for Arun and Rod). It further explores the gendered condition of the nation state, both in Indian and the U.S.

Desai is undoubtedly one of the major Indian English writers of her generation. If her reputation was established on her early portraits of domestic disharmony in traditional Indian families and the suffering of women in a largely patriarchal world, her later novels demonstrate that she writes equally well about the world of men, about Indians abroad, and about Westerners in India. Above all, she demonstrates again and again how gender issues are central to politics and the nation as well as in the family.

—Ralph J. Crane

DESAI, Boman

Nationality: American. **Born:** Bombay, India, 4 March 1950. **Education:** Illinois Institute of Technology, 1969–71; Bloomsburg State College, 1971–72; University of Illinois at Chicago, B.A. 1977. **Family:** Married Marsha Lynne Dixon, 1972 (divorced 1976). **Career:** Has worked as telephone interviewer and demographics researcher. Currently, a secretary for Sears, Roebuck and Co., Chicago. **Award:** Illinois Arts Council award, 1990, for ''Under the Moon;'' *Stand Magazine* award, for ''A Fine Madness.'' **Address:** 567 West Stratford, No. 305, Chicago, Illinois 60657, U.S.A.

Publications

Novels

The Memory of Elephants. London, Deutsch, 1988.
David and Charles. N.p., 1990.

Uncollected Short Stories

''The Blond Difference,'' in *Debonair* (Bombay), February 1986.
''Beauty and the Beast,'' in *Debonair* (Bombay), April 1988.
''Baby Talk,'' in *Debonair* (Bombay), April 1988.
''A Fine Madness,'' in *Stand,* Fall 1989.
''Underneath the Bombay Moon,'' in *Another Chicago Magazine,* 1989.

* * *

Boman Desai, who grew up in Bombay and was educated in the United States, began writing in 1976. It follows that his debut novel, *The Memory of Elephants,* would shuttle back and forth between Anglo and Indian worlds, neither critical nor laudatory, but clearly giving credence to the efficacy of both. Grounded in history, both panoramic and intimate, *The Memory of Elephants* is a visually evocative story chiefly concerned with memory—collective, personal, and perceived.

The novel's protagonist, Homi Seervai, is a brilliant Parsi from Bombay attending school in the United States. Homi has been conducting experiments on himself with a memory machine—a memoscan—that allows him to rewind to any memory he wishes to retrieve. He becomes so enamored of one particular memory that he overplays it, threatening to sever his synapses forever. As a result, he is now in a semiconscious state, without a short-term memory, and totally at the whim of an unrelenting past. Slipping in and out of time and space, Homi's memory takes him as far back as the 7th century, when the Parsis were driven from what is now Iran by the conquering Arabs. But most of his memories concern the last three generations, transporting readers into 19th-century India, England, even Scotland, and into the lives of his family's matriarchs.

The intriguing device of the memoscan is fairly inconsequential to the novel itself, although it certainly enhances the omniscience of the omniscient narrator. Homi not only remembers the past from his own perspective, he peeks into and actually participates in the perspectives of others. In this way he meets the long-dead Bapaiji, the strong-minded tomboy spurned by Navsari's most eligible bachelor and who visits Homi's memory dressed as a man, and Granny, whose happiest years were the four she spent in Cambridge and who never got beyond the single betrayal of her youth that established a lifetime of paranoia. Homi's own father returns to him in Highland regalia and attempts to teach him to dance the Scottish fling.

With these and many other familial trysts as his backdrops, the author is able to explore far deeper issues: the definition of self in a colonialized culture or, as the author puts it, ''the pilgrimage to all things Anglo''; the strange contradiction of an India that is culturally chauvinistic yet submissive in its relation to England; and the freeing and fearsome aspects to being foreign, inside and outside of one's own culture.

Parsi words are interjected easily into the text without interrupting the narrative flow, and the author does a good job of explaining lingual distinctions, both quaint and exasperating. When presenting Indian perspectives on anything alien, the author is particularly adept, as when he describes a young American hippie having ''a nimbus of cauliflower hair.''

Especially persuasive are the passages describing Homi and his brother Rusi's struggles with cultural assimilation. Homi's observations of his host family—staid German farmers from Pennsylvania—are sympathetic and completely without condescension, even though he ultimately absorbs very little of their world.

Characters are drawn with warmth and penetrating satire. This is not a nostalgic memoir. We see these characters warts and all, and who they are is neither fixed nor immutable but changing and adaptive. Hence, the reader will often receive more than one perception of an event and, depending on the event itself, encounter different emphases and tones in much the same way that the memory functions, weeding out the things that are superfluous, selecting the things most strongly undergirded by emotion.

As the novel progresses, it becomes apparent that one memory has Homi held hostage. As he puts it, he could have ''learned the password of whales'' or ''probed the memory of elephants.'' Instead, he is a cerebral slave to a single recollection—the night he lost his virginity. It is a nice touch on the author's part to suggest that it is a peculiar propensity of humans to shun the profoundly wise in favor of the emotionally and egoistically persuasive.

—Lynda Schrecengost

DESHPANDE, Shashi

Nationality: Indian. **Born:** Dharwad, 19 August 1938. **Education:** The University of Bombay, B.A. (honors) in economics 1956, diploma in journalism 1970, M.A. in English 1970; University of Mysore, Karnataka, B.L. 1959. **Family:** Married D.H. Deshpande in 1962; two sons. **Awards:** Raugammal prize, 1984; Nanjangud Tirumalamba award, for *The Dark Holds No Terrors,* 1989; Sahitya Academy award, 1990. **Address:** 409 41st Cross, Jayanagae V Block, Bangalore 560041, India.

Publications

Novels

The Dark Holds No Terrors. New Delhi, Vikas, 1980.
If I Die Today. New Delhi, Vikas, 1982.
Roots and Shadows. Bombay, Sangam, 1983.
Come Up and Be Dead. New Delhi, Vikas, 1985.
That Long Silence. London, Virago Press, 1988.
The Binding Vine. London, Virago Press, 1994.
A Matter of Time. New Delhi, Penguin Books, 1996; afterword by Ritu Menon, New York, Feminist Press, 1999.
Small Remedies. New York, Viking, 2000.

Short Stories

The Legacy and Other Stories. Calcutta, Writers Workshop, 1978.
It Was Dark. Calcutta, Writers Workshop, 1986.
The Miracle and Other Stories. Calcutta, Writers Workshop, 1986.
It Was the Nightingale. Calcutta, Writers Workshop, 1986.
The Intrusion and Other Stories. New Delhi, Penguin India, 1994.

Play

Screenplay: *Drishte,* 1990.

Other (for children)

A Summer Adventure. Bombay, IBH, 1978.
The Hidden Treasure. Bombay, IBH, 1980.
The Only Witness. Bombay, IBH, 1980.
The Narayanpur Incident. Bombay, IBH, 1982.

*

Critical Studies: *Indian Women Novelists,* Vol. 5, Delhi, Prestige Books, 1991; *The Novels of Shashi Deshpande* by Sarabjit Sandhu, Delhi, Prestige Books, 1991; *Man-Woman Relationship in Indian Fiction, with a Focus on Shashi Deshpande, Rajendra Awasthy, and Syed Abdul Malik* by Seema Suneel. New Delhi, Prestige Books, 1995; *Shashi Deshpande: A Feminist Study of Her Fiction* by Mukta Atrey and Viney Kripal. New Delhi, D. K. Publishers, 1998; *The Fiction of Shashi Deshpande,* edited by R. S. Pathak. New Delhi, Creative Books, 1998.

Shashi Deshpande comments:

Though no writer in India can get away from the idea of social commitment or social responsibility, committed writing has always seemed to me to have dubious literary values. However, after 25 years of writing, I cannot close my eyes to the fact that my own writing comes out of a deep involvement with the society I live in, especially with women. My novels are about women trying to understand themselves, their history, their roles and their place in this society, and above all their relationships with others. To me, my novels are always explorations; each time in the process of writing, I find myself confronted by discoveries which make me rethink the ideas I started off with. In all my novels, from *Roots and Shadows* to *The Binding Vine,* I have rejected stereotypes and requestioned the myths which have so shaped the image of women, even the self-image of women, in this country. In a way, through my writing, I have tried to break the long silence of women in our country.

* * *

Shashi Deshpande's first book was *The Legacy,* a collection of short stories, and since then she has published dozens of stories. The authentic recreation of India, the outstanding feature of her stories, is a distinct feature of her novels also. There is nothing sensational or exotic about her India—no Maharajahs or snake charmers. She does not write about the grinding poverty of the Indian masses; she describes another kind of deprivation—emotional. The woman deprived of love, understanding, and companionship is the center of her work. She shows how traditional Indian society is biased against woman, but she recognizes that it is very often women who oppress their sisters, though their values are the result of centuries of indoctrination.

An early short story, ''A Liberated Woman,'' is about a young woman who falls in love with a man of a different caste, and marries him in spite of parental opposition. She is intelligent and hardworking, and becomes a successful doctor, but her marriage breaks up because of her success. *The Dark Holds No Terrors,* Deshpande's first novel, seems to have grown out of this story. Sarita, the heroine, defies her mother to become a doctor, and defies caste restrictions by marrying the man she loves. Her husband Manu is a failure, and resents the fact that his wife is the primary breadwinner. She uses Boozie to advance her career, and this further vitiates her relationship with Manu. Sarita goes to her parental home, but she cannot escape her past so easily. She realizes that her children and her patients need her, and finally reaches a certain clarity of thought: ''All right, so I'm alone. But so's everyone else.''

The next novel, *If I Die Today,* contains elements of detective fiction. The narrator, a young college lecturer, is married to a doctor, and they live on the campus of a big medical college and hospital. The arrival of Guru, a terminal cancer patient, disturbs the lives of the doctors and their families. Old secrets are revealed, two people murdered, but the tensions in the families is resolved after the culprit is unmasked. One of the memorable characters is Mriga, a 14-year-old girl. Her father, Dr. Kulkarni, appears modern and westernized, yet he is seized by the Hindu desire for a son and heir, and never forgives Mriga for not being a son; her mother, too, is a sad, suppressed creature, too weak to give Mriga the support and love a child needs to grow up into a well balanced adult.

Roots and Shadows describes the break-up of a joint family, held together by the money and authority of an old aunt, a childless widow. When she dies, she leaves her money to the heroine, Indu, a rebel. Indu left home as a teenager to study in the big city, and is now a journalist; she has married the man of her choice. But she realizes that her freedom is illusory; she has exchanged the orthodoxy of the village home for the conventions of the ''smart young set'' of the city, where material well-being has to be assured by sacrificing principles, if necessary. Indu returns to the house when her great-aunt dies after more than 12 years' absence. As she attempts to take charge of her legacy, she comes to realize the strength and the resilience of the village women she had previously dismissed as weak.

Perhaps Deshpande's best work is her fifth novel, *That Long Silence.* The narrator Jaya, an upper-middle-class housewife with two teenage children, is forced to take stock of her life when her husband is suspected of fraud. They move into a small flat in a poorer locality of Bombay, giving up their luxurious house. The novel reveals the hollowness of modern Indian life, where success is seen as a convenient arranged marriage to an upwardly mobile husband with the children studying in ''good'' schools. The repetitiveness and sheer drabness of the life of a woman with material comforts is vividly represented, ''the glassware that had to sparkle, the furniture and curios that had to be kept spotless and dust-free, and those clothes, God, all those never-ending piles of clothes that had to be washed and ironed, so that they could be worn and washed and ironed once again.'' Though she is a writer, Jaya has not achieved true self-expression. There is something almost suffocating about the narrowness of the narrator's life. The novel contains nothing outside the narrator's narrow ambit. India's tradition and philosophy (which occupy an important place in the work of novelists like Raja Rao) have no place here. We get a glimpse of Hinduism in the numerous fasts observed by women for the well being of husbands, sons or brothers. Jaya's irritation at such sexist rituals is palpable—it is clear that she feels strongly about the ill-treatment of the girl-child in India. The only reference to India's ''glorious'' past is in Jaya's comment that in Sanskrit drama, the women did not speak Sanskrit—they were confined to Prakrit, a less polished language, imposing a kind of silence on them. In spite of her English education, Jaya is like the other women in the novel, such as the half-crazed Kusum, a distant relative, or Jeeja, their poor maid-servant. They are all trapped in their own self-created silence, and are incapable of breaking away from the supportive yet stifling extended family. The narrow focus of the novel results in an intensity which is almost painful. All the characters, including Mohan, Jaya's husband, are fully realized, though none of them, including the narrator Jaya, are likable.

Deshpande usually has the heroine as the narrator, and employs a kind of stream-of-consciousness technique. The narrative goes back and forth in time, so the narrator can describe events with the benefit of hindsight. It would not be correct to term her a feminist, because there is nothing doctrinaire about her fiction; she simply portrays, in depth, the meaning of being a woman in modern India. Exemplary of her worldview is *A Matter of Time,* her first novel published in the United States: it is the tale of a woman abandoned by a man. The woman is Sumi, who has three daughters; the man is her husband, a professor named Gopal; and her abandonment forces her to return to the family's home in Bangalore. The issues Sumi faces are not Indian problems; they are universal ones—not just the difficulties in her marriage, but the conflicts within her family as well.

—Shyamala A. Narayan

DIDION, Joan

Nationality: American. **Born:** Sacramento, California, 5 December 1934. **Education:** California Junior High School and McClatchy Senior High School, both Sacramento; University of California, Berkeley, 1952–56, B.A. in English 1956. **Family:** Married John Gregory Dunne, *q.v.,* in 1964; one daughter. **Career:** Associate feature editor, *Vogue,* New York, 1956–63; moved to Los Angeles, 1964; columnist (''Points West''), with Dunne, *Saturday Evening Post,* Philadelphia, 1967–69, *Life,* New York, 1969–70, and ''The Coast,'' *Esquire,* New York, 1976–77. Visiting Regents' Lecturer, University of California, Berkeley, 1975. Lives in New York. **Awards:** *Vogue* Paris prize, 1956; Bread Loaf Writers Conference fellowship, 1963; American Academy Morton Dauwen Zabel award, 1979; Edward MacDowell medal, 1996. **Agent:** Lynn Nesbit, Janklow and Nesbit, 589 Madison Ave., New York, New York 10022, U.S.A.

Publications

Novels

Run River. New York, Obolensky, 1963; London, Cape, 1964; New York, Vintage, 1994.
Play It as It Lays. New York, Farrar Straus, 1970; London, Weidenfeld and Nicolson, 1971.
A Book of Common Prayer. New York, Simon and Schuster, and London, Weidenfeld and Nicolson, 1977.
Democracy. New York, Simon and Schuster, and London, Chatto and Windus, 1984.
The Last Thing He Wanted. New York, Knopf, 1996.

Uncollected Short Stories

''The Welfare Island Ferry,'' in *Harper's Bazaar* (New York), June 1965.
''When Did the Music Come This Way? Children Dear, Was It Yesterday?,'' in *Denver Quarterly,* Winter 1967.
''California Blue,'' in *Harper's* (New York), October 1976.

Plays

Screenplays: *Panic in Needle Park,* with John Gregory Dunne, 1971; *Play It as It Lays,* with John Gregory Dunne, 1972; *A Star Is Born,* with John Gregory Dunne and Frank Pierson, 1976; *True Confessions,* with John Gregory Dunne, 1981; *Hills Like White Elephants,* with John Gregory Dunne and Frank Pierson, 1992; *Broken Trust,* with John Gregory Dunne and Frank Pierson, 1995; *Up Close and Personal,* with John Gregory Dunne and Frank Pierson, 1995.

Other

Slouching Towards Bethlehem (essays). New York, Farrar Straus, 1968; London, Deutsch, 1969; New York, Modern Library, 2000.
Telling Stories. Berkeley, California, Bancroft Library, 1978.
The White Album. New York, Simon and Schuster, and London, Weidenfeld and Nicolson, 1979.
Salvador. New York, Simon and Schuster, and London, Chatto and Windus, 1983.
Essays and Conversations, edited by Ellen G. Friedman. Princeton, New Jersey, Ontario Review Press, 1984.
Miami. New York, Simon and Schuster, 1987; London, Weidenfeld and Nicolson, 1988.
After Henry. New York, Simon and Schuster, 1992; as *Sentimental Journeys,* London, Harper Collins, 1993.

*

Critical Studies: *Joan Didion* by Mark Royden Winchell, Boston, Twayne, 1980, revised edition, 1989; *Joan Didion* by Katherine Usher Henderson, New York, Ungar, 1981; *The Critical Response to Joan Didion,* edited By Sharon Felton. Westport, Connecticut, Greenwood Press, 1994.

* * *

Though very much a California writer, Joan Didion is not provincial. She uses her immediate milieu to envision, simultaneously, the last stand of America's frontier values pushed insupportably to their limits and the manifestations of craziness and malaise which have initiated their finale. And while her novels invite a feminist critique, her understanding of sexual politics is beyond ideology. Each of her major characters struggles with a demonic nihilism which is corroding the individual, the family, and the social organism. Affluent and glib, her people endure a relatively privileged despair which may initially suggest a narrow purview. But a considerable ability to render social and physical environment broadly is saving.

In addition to dialogue which rivals Albee's, Didion's finest gifts are her talents for keeping clean of self-indulgence and for realizing a moral dimension in lives veering *inevitably* out of control. Certain recurring features of her work constitute leitmotifs germane to their interpretation. These include newspaper headlines, phrases from popular ballads, cinematic jargon, snakes, and the genteel Christian educations of her females. All pertain to the disintegration of an orderly past into a chaotic present, perhaps Didion's most irreducible theme.

Run River follows the eroding marriage of Everett and Lily (Knight) McClellan through 20 years. Concomitantly it chronicles the collapse of a way of life and the betrayal of the land which had given an epoch its apparent order. Ryder Channing enters the McClellans' lives when he courts Everett's sister. Though Martha never misconceives his selfishness and venality, she kills herself when Channing quits her. Lily's many unfeeling liaisons express her isolation from her husband and fatally draw her into Channing's increasingly nihilistic orbit. In his futile attachment to their Northern California ranch, Everett lives at a tangent to Lily's very genuine crises. When Everett kills Channing, it is not simply because Channing and his sleazy economic machinations are the wave of California's future, the perverse energy which turns redwoods to taco stands. Everett's suicide ends an era. But Lily's justifiable conclusion that Channing is guiltless, because he is a ''papier-maché Mephistopholes,'' implies Didion's conviction that, however tawdry this interloper, he has only played upon a native tendency to ruin. Lily's survival implies her relatively greater, if tainted, adaptability and strength.

Play It as It Lays presents a culture beyond this metamorphosis. Consequently, it is set in Los Angeles where those tacky schemes of Ryder Channing are a *fait accompli* defining a whole state of being. Maria Wyeth's past is utterly disintegrated, her childhood home in Nevada having been detonated to oblivion by nuclear testing. Moribund, her marriage thins to extinction. With her brain-damaged daughter institutionalized and herself facing an abortion, Maria aimlessly drives the freeways to evade a ubiquitous dread.

Though Didion never politicizes abortion, she is morally obsessed with it. Lily and Maria endure the experience, but the treatment is fuller and more alarming here. A last straw, it pushes Maria closer to her counterpart and nemesis, BZ, another instance of modern demonic. Associated throughout with the serpent, this Hollywood Beelzebub tries with conscious nihilism to exploit Maria's drinking and sexual looseness. Maria's father, taking life as a crap game, had offered his case as a gambler and a cynic: ''it goes as it lays, don't do it the hard way;'' ''overturning a rock [is] apt to reveal a rattlesnake.'' For Maria, this worldview is an affliction of passivity and anxiety, until she finally manages the small victory of rejecting BZ's invitation to join him in his successful suicide.

With *A Book of Common Prayer,* Didion suggests that the country is in the throes of metastasized California. So she invents an archetypal banana republic devoid of history. Boca Grande (''big mouth'') yaps chamber of commerce propaganda and ingests North American residue. Charlotte Douglas, a San Francisco Pollyanna, weathers two difficult marriages: to a brilliant callous and cynical opportunist, and to a well-heeled radical lawyer. What she doesn't quite weather is the loss (à la Patty Hearst) of her daughter, Marin, ''to history.'' Marin's situation is really very simple. She suffers from severe cases of banality and political jargon. But her new way of life tests to the limit Charlotte's too selective memory of the girl in Easter dresses. With the FBI agents who litter her house and the futility of her marriages at her back, she makes it to Boca Grande and a marginal life of good works for the suffering masses. She continues to put the best light on dark matters: stateside things like her brother's miserable existence on the old homestead in Hollister; Grande things like the Army's confiscation, for profit, of the people's cholera serum. She becomes oddly Sisyphean but holds out for the idea that we all remember what we need. Charlotte dies in the crossfire between Army and revolutionary forces, the guerilleros having decided that for once their insurrection is not going to be a State-sponsored melodrama. We come to like her and to wonder about the future of such folks as the Simbianese Liberation Army.

Democracy concerns the long and amorous liaison between Inez Victor, a politician's wife, and Jack Lovett. The latter embodies personal and social values lacking in and inconceivable to the husband, a Congressman aspiring to the presidency. Southern California recollected and contemporary Southeast Asia, particularly Kuala Lumpur, provide settings in which the fabulous quality of Boca Grande yields to realism. The novel clearly depicts American and international political life in the very fast lane, and its ruinous effect on familiar relationships. But Inez Victor's moral tenacity and practical resolve to use the past ethically distinguish her from Didion's earlier protagonists. Technically the novel is fresh, if not unique, for cinematic effects which break linear narrative; and for including a narrator named Joan Didion, who remarks the discrete functions of journalism and fiction, both provinces of great success for the *real* author.

With *The Last Thing He Wanted,* Didion's first work of fiction after 12 years of silence following *Democracy,* she returned to her familiar Central American/Caribbean locales and the political intrigue she had woven so successfully in previous books. The year is 1984, and the protagonist, Elena McMahon, seeks to carry out her father's dying wish: to bring in weapons, covertly supplied by the U.S. government, to the Contras fighting the Soviet-aligned Sandinista government in Nicaragua. The narrator is an unnamed figure, piecing together the story after the fact, much like the reporter who uncovered the secret biography of Citizen Kane. Hence Elena's motivation remains shadowy, yet the prose is as distinct and crisp as Didion's best.

—David M. Heaton

DIVAKARUNI, Chitra Banerjee

Nationality: Indian-American. **Born:** Chitra Banerjee in Calcutta, India, 29 July 1956. **Education:** Calcutta University, B.A. 1976; Wright State University, M.A. 1978; University of California, Berkeley, Ph.D. 1985. **Family:** Married S. Murthy Divakaruni in 1979; two children. **Career:** Professor of creative writing, Diablo Valley College, 1987–89; Foothill College, Los Altos, California, 1989—. **Awards:** Memorial Award (Barbara Deming Foundation), 1989; Writing Award (Santa Clara County Arts Council), 1990; Writing Award (Gerbode Foundation), 1993; Before Columbus Foundation American Book Award; Bay Area Book Reviews Award for Fiction; PEN Oakland Josephine Miles Prize for Fiction; Allen Ginsberg Poetry Prize; Pushcart Prize. **Address:** Foothill College, English Department, 12345 El Monte Road, Los Altos, California 94022–4504, U.S.A.

Publications

Novels

The Mistress of Spices. New York, Anchor Books, 1997.
Sister of My Heart. New York, Doubleday, 1999.

Short Stories

Arranged Marriage: Stories. New York, Anchor Books, 1995.

Poetry

Dark Like the River. 1987.
The Reason for Nasturtiums. Berkeley Poets Press, 1990.
Black Candle: Poems about Women from India, Pakistan, and Bangladesh. Corvallis, Oregon, Calyx Books, 1991.
Leaving Yuba City: New and Selected Poems. New York, Anchor Books, 1997.

Other

Editor, *Multitude: Cross-Cultural Readings for Writers.* Boston, McGraw-Hill, 1993.
Editor, *We, Too, Sing America: A Reader for Writers.* Boston, McGraw-Hill, 1998.

* * *

Indian-American author Chitra Banerjee Divakaruni has recently published poems, short stories, and novels, all of which generally focus on similar themes: the roles of women in India and America; the struggle to adapt to new ways of life when one's cultural traditions are in conflict with new cultural expectations; and the complexities of love between family members, lovers, and spouses. Divakaruni's work is often considered to be quasi-autobiographical as most of her stories are set in California near where she lives, confront the immigrant experience—specifically, of Indians who settle in the U.S.—and evaluate the treatment of Indian-American women both in India and America. Divakaruni is also an editor of two anthologies, *Multitude: Cross-Cultural Readings for Writers* and *We, Too, Sing America: A Reader for Writers,* that include stories concerned with similar issues.

Divakaruni's volumes of poetry, *Dark Like the River*, *The Reason for Nasturtiums*, *Black Candle*, and *Leaving Yuba City*, each uniquely address images of India, the Indian-American experience, and the condition of children and women in a patriarchal society. Also exploring the relationship between art forms, Divakaruni writes poetry inspired by paintings, photographs, and films. And, as in her novels, she focuses intently in her poetry on the experiences of women pursuing identities for themselves.

Arranged Marriage, Divakaruni's collection of short stories that focus on Indian and Indian-American women caught between two conflicting cultures, seems to have developed from her poem ''Arranged Marriage'' in *Black Candle*. Both the poem and the stories are concerned with the emotions of women whose lives are affected by the Indian tradition of arranged marriages, though *Arranged Marriage* explores a broader scope of issues, including divorce, abortion, racism, and economic inequality. Relying heavily on techniques such as doubling and pairing, the stories expose the adverse conditions of women living in India, though the collection also suggests that life in America is as difficult as in India, and indeed perhaps more so because of the contradictory feelings immigrant women often experience as they are torn between Indian cultural expectations and American life. *Arranged Marriage* considers both cultures equally, critiquing and praising particular aspects of each.

The themes Divakaruni explores in her poems and short stories are developed in her novels, *The Mistress of Spices* and *Sister of My Heart*. Stylistically experimental, *The Mistress of Spices* combines poetic language with prose in order to, as Divakaruni suggests, ''collaps[e] the divisions between the realistic world of twentieth century America and the timeless one of myth and magic in [an] attempt to create a modern fable.'' Tilo, *Mistress*'s main character, is a young woman from a distant time and place whose training in the ancient craft of spices and initiation in the rite of fire allow her to become immortal and powerful. Traveling across time and space, Tilo comes to live in Oakland, California, in the form of an aged woman and establishes herself as a healer who prescribes spices as remedies for her customers. Although the novel appears to diverge thematically from the concerns in her poetry and short stories, *Mistress* does address similar issues, and as Tilo becomes involved in a romance that ultimately requires her to choose between two lifestyles—a supernatural immortal life and a more typical modern life—Divakaruni's themes of love, struggle, and opposing cultures become apparent.

Divakaruni's most recent novel, *Sister of My Heart*, is an expansion of and a variation on the short story ''The Ultrasound'' in *Arranged Marriage*. In the novel, two cousins, Anju and Sudah, who feel as though their lives are inextricably tied together, rely on each other for love, approval, and companionship. The women grow up together in the same house in Calcutta and have many similar experiences that bind them together, which leads them to feel as though they are sisters of the heart. However, when secrets regarding their births are revealed and the cousins are later physically separated because of arranged marriages, their unique relationship is tested, and the women struggle in the face of doubt and suspicion. Although one woman remains in India and the other moves to America, they experience similar traumas involving pregnancy and marriage and so come to rely on each other again for strength and support.

—Stephannie Gearhart

DIXON, Stephen

Nationality: American. **Born:** New York City, 6 June 1936. **Education:** City College, New York, 1953–58, B.A. in international relations 1958. **Family:** Married Anne Frydman in 1982; two daughters. **Career:** Worked in various jobs, including bartender, waiter, junior high school teacher, technical writer, journalist, news editor, store clerk, and tour leader, 1953–79; lecturer, New York University School of Continuing Education, 1979–80. Assistant professor, 1980–83, associate professor, 1984–88, and since 1989 professor of English, Johns Hopkins University, Baltimore. **Awards:** Stanford University Stegner fellowship, 1964; National Endowment for the Arts grant, 1975, 1990; American Academy award, 1983; Train prize (*Paris Review*), 1985; Guggenheim fellowship, 1985; O. Henry prize, 1993. **Address:** Writing Seminars, Gilman 135, Johns Hopkins University, Baltimore, Maryland 21218, U.S.A.

PUBLICATIONS

Novels

Work. Ann Arbor, Michigan, Street Fiction Press, 1977.
Too Late. New York, Harper, 1978.
Fall and Rise. Berkeley, California, North Point Press, 1985.
Garbage. New York, Cane Hill Press, 1988.
Interstate. New York, Henry Holt, 1995.
Gould: A Novel in Two Novels. New York, Henry Holt, 1997.
30: Pieces of a Novel. New York, Henry Holt, 1999.
Tisch. Los Angeles, California, Red Hen Press, 2000.

Short Stories

No Relief. Ann Arbor, Michigan, Street Fiction Press, 1976.
Quite Contrary: The Mary and Newt Story. New York, Harper, 1979.
14 Stories. Baltimore, Johns Hopkins University Press, 1980.
Movies. Berkeley, California, North Point Press, 1983.
Time to Go. Baltimore, Johns Hopkins University Press, 1984.
The Play and Other Stories. Minneapolis, Coffee House Press, 1988.
Love and Will: Twenty Stories. Latham, New York, Paris Review Editions-British American, 1989.
All Gone: 18 Short Stories. Baltimore, Johns Hopkins University Press, 1990.
Friends: More Will and Magna Stories. Santa Maria, California, Asylum Arts, 1990.
Frog. Latham, New York, British American, 1991.
Long Made Short. Baltimore, Maryland, Johns Hopkins University Press, 1993.
The Stories of Stephen Dixon. New York, Henry Holt, 1994.
Man on Stage: Play Stories, illustrations by the author. Davis, California, Hi Jinx Press, 1996.
Sleep: Stories. Minneapolis, Coffee House Press, 1999.

*

Manuscript Collection: Milton Eisenhower Library, Johns Hopkins University, Baltimore.

Critical Studies: ''Stephen Dixon: Experimental Realism,'' in *North American Review* (Cedar Falls, Iowa), March 1981, and *The Self-Apparent Word,* Carbondale, Southern Illinois University Press, 1984, both by Jerome Klinkowitz; ''Stephen Dixon Issue'' of *Ohio Journal* (Columbus), Fall-Winter 1983–84 (includes bibliography); *The Dramaturgy of Style* by Michael Stephens, Carbondale, Southern Illinois University Press, 1985.

Stephen Dixon comments:

(1991) I've just about nothing to say about my work, I only write fiction. I don't write book reviews or any nonfiction. In fact the only book review I've written is a story called "The Book Review," about a character writing one. The only non-fiction work I've written since 1963, when I stopped writing news, and 1968, when I stopped being a technical writer, is a piece called "Why I Don't Write Nonfiction," which proves its point and appeared in the *Ohio Journal* issue devoted to my work. I write novels and short stories only and I like writing both but for different reasons. Novels because they continue, stories because they end. All my novels but *Fall and Rise,* started off as short stories and just grew. I would rather the reader interpret what I write than I interpret it for the reader. I don't want to give my life away in a statement. Not only is my life not very interesting but sometime in the future I might use, in my own way, part of my life for my fiction and then a reader might say "That comes from his uninteresting life." Better the reader know next to nothing about my life and how I write, where I get my ideas, and so on.

Best for the reader to read my work and say for himself what to make of it. I have no way, nor do I have the means, nor do I have the inclination to simplify my work by explaining it, elucidating about it, or simply saying what I think about it. I work at one work at a time, story or novel, and when I'm done with it I begin another work. That's how I keep busy and also keep myself from thinking about my work once I finish with it.

(1995) I'm still pretty much the same. Dying to find more time to write, since I also teach fulltime and run a household. My ambition is to teach just half a year so I can devote eight months a year to my writing. I find it difficult to do all at once, but I still manage to complete 250 finished fiction pages a year. I don't know why but I still think I have something to write and a continually changing writing style to write it in.

* * *

Stephen Dixon is a master of self-generating fiction. While eschewing the flamboyantly anti-realistic experiments of authors such as Ronald Sukenick and Robert Coover, Dixon nevertheless refuses to propel his narratives on the energy of represented action. Instead, he contrives circumstances so that everything that happens within his novels grows from the initial elements of his fiction. Developing from itself, his narrative ultimately has no pertinent reference beyond itself; yet that growth is so organic that it offers all the delight expectable from a more realistically referential piece of storytelling.

Dixon's method can be traced to his way of writing sentences. Often his action will take place grammatically, as subjects have to battle their way past intransigent verbs in order to meet their objects, and as modifying phrases pop up to thwart syntactic progress. There are always modifications to everything, Dixon has learned, and his genius has been to apply this insight to the making of narratives.

His first novel, *Work,* finds this scheme in the workplace, as an image for both how hard it is to find employment and what a struggle it is to keep it. Hunting down a job takes his narrator fully one-third of the novel, and that turns out to be the easy part. Once he has signed on as a bartender in a New York City chain of restaurants, he has to cope with a prime ingredient of Dixon's fictionally generative world: in this case a self-contained universe of rules and relationships, which include how to mix drinks, charge for special orders, move customer traffic, scan the papers for conversation items, spot company spies, handle rush-hour jams, deal with the restaurant chain's union, thwart robberies, soothe tempers, counsel neurotics, and keep the whole mad dance of waiters, dishwashers, assistant managers, cashiers, and customers in step. And this is just three or four pages into the story. *Work* provides the ideal self-generating system for a Dixon novel.

Yet such a system also exists within the intimate relationship of a man and woman. *Too Late* borrows two favorite topics from Dixon's short stories—breaking off relationships and suffering through the endless complications of love—and rushes them through a breathless experience in the urban jungle, during which four days pass in an alternation of quick excitement and maniacal torture. The narrator's girlfriend has left him during a movie, the violence of which has sickened her. But she never arrives home, and tracing her disappearance becomes a full-time job. Not for the police, who want to brush it off as a jilting. Instead, the narrator's capabilities for worry (another self-generating machine for fiction) run through all the lurid possibilities, from abduction and rape to murder. The very worst fears are just what happen, as the ghouls who feed on sensational news rush into the narrator's life, and he himself experiences a Jekyll-and-Hyde transformation which costs him job, friends, and peace of mind. *Too Late* succeeds as a tangled web of disruptions and distractions, the very stuff of Dixon's fiction which is shown to be a built-in potential of city life.

Quite Contrary: The Mary and Newt Story assembles 11 related stories to form something less than a novel but much more than a story collection. Their unity, although established by subject and circumstance of action, comes from their address to the main concerns of Dixon's work: the fragility of human relationships and reality's dangerous tendency to run off into infinite digressions and qualifications. *Quite Contrary* treats the three-year off-and-on affair of a couple, familiar in Dixon's fiction, whose involvement breeds complications. Even their first meeting leads to a debate as to how they will leave to walk home. As their relationship develops, each finds fault: he is too demanding, she is noncommittal. Even breaking up becomes an endless complication, for if Newt tells a friend that he and Mary are "this time really through," a friend reverses his syntax to show that "Nah, you two are never really through. You're a pair: Tom and Jerry, Biff and Bang. You just tell yourselves you're through to make your sex better and your lives more mythic and poetic and to repeatedly renew those first two beatific weeks you went through." Here is Dixon's method established in the form of his sentences: the declaration that the pair (one *and* the other) are sundering their union leads directly to a restatement of that proposition in negative form, rebonding the relationship through a series of other conjunctions: mythic pairs, conjoined reasons, and most of all a grammatical structure which by virtue of more "ands" can string itself out indefinitely, just like their relationship which is commemorated in the final phrase.

Fall and Rise, a much longer and more ambitious novel, extends itself to its fullest fictional scope while requiring the least external circumstance. The affair which prompts it is the narrator's first sentence, "I meet her at a party." Its present tense is deliberate, for the narrator's voice moves through a constant set of possibilities to fill 245 closely-set pages with the action which devolves from just four or five hours of experience. Because so much of the narrator's action is made up of diffidence and fantasy, it has the character of fiction. In a Jamesian manner, Dixon examines every nuance, even of situations yet to transpire, and as a result the reader is caught up in the narrator's own imaginative experience. For one chapter, the narrative action is transferred to the object of these imaginative desires, and complications are amplified by having her point of view. The achievement of Dixon's work is that the smallest circumstance can expand to fill the space available, a reminder of fiction's infinite plenitude.

It is with *Frog* and *Interstate* that Dixon takes the novel form well past his standards for short stories, in both cases by contriving unique structural experiments. A massive work of 769 pages, *Frog* could be described as an initial collection of 14 stories followed by a novella, two additional stories, a second novella, a full-length novel, and a concluding story. All sections cover the life and times of a protagonist nicknamed ''Frog,'' though only in the closing piece do readers learn the meritorious nature of this name. In the meantime, Frog himself is put through variations of circumstance, history, and identity, making the larger work contradictory in a close sense but universal in its ability to encompass all fictive possibilities. In character, the protagonist is much like the figures appearing in typical Dixon stories: so conscientious that he becomes worried to distraction, so earnest as to be compulsive, so anxious for everything to be right that he makes almost all things turn out hilariously wrong. Yet even more so than in a thematically organized collection, *Frog* gives a complete sense of this style of being, not just in itself but because of the historically improbable but imaginatively apt connections the reader is invited to draw. These same readerly connections motivate *Interstate,* a novel whose eight chapters retell a highway tragedy in competing forms. In the first, a father suffers when his little girl is shot and killed by a gunman in a passing car. Five subsequent versions focus on the different aspects of the tragedy, each with the hope that its effects can be mitigated, if not fully escaped. In the seventh, the killing is avoided, but at the cost of something worse. Only in the eighth and final chapter does all end well, allowing the reader to savor scenes of quiet domestic bliss that without the preceding versions would never merit fictive treatment. The protagonist is the usual Dixon type, but here pushed into literal life-or-death circumstances.

As prolific as his work has been, Dixon always has a great range of stories from which to assemble a new collection. In *The Play* his focus rests on narratives generated by the dynamics of interpersonal relationships. The volume's initial stories deal with a narrator leaving a relationship, while later pieces find a similarly dispositioned character dealing with other problems, more material and external, which nevertheless follow the same pattern of involved disinvolvement. *Love and Will* sees his characteristic protagonist more involved in the outside world, with the addition of stories told from a shared perspective, such as ''Takes,'' in which a young woman's rape and attempted murder is considered (and worried about) by a range of bystanders who have varying amounts of information and differing degrees of involvement in her life. *All Gone* is Dixon's most thematically diverse yet technically unified collection in that almost every one of its 18 stories has its action derive from partial, confused, or incorrect information. Yet Dixon's writing habits often bring him back to familiar characters in typical predicaments; Will and Magna, the couple who appear in the title story of *Love and Will,* have a book to themselves in *Friends,* where their life yields a post-Beckettian sense of going on in narrative language within the very snares that language sets for us. Even though dialogue or other narrative situations threaten to trap these characters, Dixon's genius is, like Beckett, to write their way out of it with an energy which produces a sense of life in itself. The multiplicity of such life is celebrated in *Long Made Short,* a story collection focused on the idea of subtraction—specifically, how many elements can be withdrawn from the narrative and still let the story survive. ''Man, Woman, and Boy'' displays the elemental nature of this technique, as a scene that begins with a marital breakup is put through structural mechanisms of reversal, subtraction, and retraction until a more desired result is achieved—the method of *Interstate* in miniature.

Dixon's reputation is built on his short stories, over 300 of which have been published and 60 of which are collected in *The Stories of Stephen Dixon.* This large assemblage, drawing on the work of nearly four decades, shows his method in highest profile and establishes his talent for self-generative form. In ''Said'' he runs through the rise and fall of a relationship simply by dropping all content and running through the ''he said/she said'' rhythm of a fight. ''Time to Go'' uses fantasy to recapture the memory of a long-dead father, as an image of the old man accompanies his son and the young man's fiancee as they select wedding rings, the father forever hectoring about price and size in a voice only his son can hear. In all cases they are self-generating, perfectly made examples of fiction's ability to delight simply by its own working.

—Jerome Klinkowitz

DOCTOROW, E(dgar) L(awrence)

Nationality: American. **Born:** New York City, 6 January 1931. **Education:** The Bronx High School of Science; Kenyon College, Gambier, Ohio, A.B. (honors) in philosophy 1952; Columbia University, New York, 1952–53. **Military Service:** Served in the United States Army, 1953–55. **Family:** Married Helen Setzer in 1954; two daughters and one son. **Career:** Editor, New American Library, New York, 1960–64; editor-in-chief, 1964–69, and publisher, 1969, Dial Press, New York; member of the faculty, Sarah Lawrence College, Bronxville, New York, 1971–78. Adjunct professor of English, 1982–86, and since 1987 Glucksman Professor of American and English Letters, New York University. Writer-in-residence, University of California, Irvine, 1969–70; Creative Writing Fellow, Yale School of Drama, New Haven, Connecticut, 1974–75; visiting professor, University of Utah, Salt Lake City, 1975; Visiting Senior Fellow, Princeton University, New Jersey, 1980–81. Director, Authors Guild of America, and American PEN. Lives in New Rochelle, New York. **Awards:** Guggenheim fellowship, 1972; Creative Artists Public Service grant, 1973; National Book Critics Circle award, 1976, 1990; American Academy award, 1976; American Book award, 1986; Howells medal, 1990; PEN Faulkner award, 1990; National Humanities Medal, 1998; Commonwealth Medal, 2000. L.H.D.: Kenyon College, 1976; Brandeis University, Waltham, Massachusetts, 1989; Litt.D.: Hobart and William Smith Colleges, Geneva, New York, 1979. **Member:** American Academy, 1984. **Agent:** International Creative Management, 40 West 57th Street, New York, New York 10019, U.S.A. **Address:** c/o Random House Inc., 201 East 50th Street, New York, New York 10022, U.S.A.

Publications

Novels

Welcome to Hard Times. New York, Simon and Schuster, 1960; as *Bad Man from Bodie,* London, Deutsch, 1961; published under original title, New York, Plume, 1996.

Big as Life. New York, Simon and Schuster, 1966.

The Book of Daniel. New York, Random House, 1971; London, Macmillan, 1972; New York, Plume, 1996.
Ragtime. New York, Random House, and London, Macmillan, 1975.
Loon Lake. New York, Random House, and London, Macmillan, 1980.
World's Fair. New York, Random House, 1985; London, Joseph, 1986.
Billy Bathgate. New York, Random House, and London, Macmillan, 1989.
The Waterworks. London, Macmillan, 1994.
City of God. New York, Random House, 2000.

Short Stories

Lives of the Poets: Six Stories and a Novella. New York, Random House, 1984; London, Joseph, 1985.

Plays

Drinks Before Dinner (produced New York, 1978). New York, Random House, 1979; London, Macmillan, 1980.

Screenplay: *Daniel,* 1983.

Other

American Anthem, photographs by Jean-Claude Suarès. New York, Stewart Tabori and Chang, 1982.
Eric Fischl: Scenes and Sequences: Fifty-Eight Monotypes (text by Doctorow). New York, Abrams, 1990.
Jack London, Hemingway, and the Constitution: Selected Essays, 1977–1992. New York, HarperPerennial, 1994.

*

Film Adaptations: *Welcome to the Hard Times*, 1967; *Ragtime*, 1981; *Daniel* from the work *The Book of Daniel*, 1983; *Billy Bathgate*, 1991.

Bibliography: *E.L. Doctorow: An Annotated Bibliography* by Michelle M. Tokarczyk, New York, Garland, 1988.

Critical Studies: *E.L. Doctorow: Essays and Conversations* edited by Richard Trenner, Princeton, New Jersey, Ontario Review Press, 1983; *E.L. Doctorow* by Paul Levine, London, Methuen, 1985; *E.L. Doctorow* by Carol C. Harter and James R. Thompson, Boston, Twayne, 1990; *E.L. Doctorow* by John G. Parks, New York, Continuum Press, 1991; *Models of Misrepresentation: The Fiction of E.L. Doctorow* by Christopher D. Morris, Jackson, University Press of Mississippi, 1991; *Fiction as False Document: The Reception of E.L. Doctorow in the Postmodern Age* by John Williams. Columbia, South Carolina, Camden House, 1996; *Conversations with E.L. Doctorow,* edited by Christopher D. Morris. Jackson, University Press of Mississippi, 1999; *Critical Essays on E.L. Doctorow,* edited by Ben Siegel. New York, G.K. Hall, 2000.

* * *

Towards the end of E.L. Doctorow's novella *Lives of the Poets* his central character is discussing the art of writing with a fellow author. ''Each book,'' he believes, ''has taken me further and further out'' so that the place or idea he started out from is now no more than ''a weak distant signal from the home station.'' The same is only partly true of Doctorow himself. His novels for the most part revisit the same themes and places, in particular the America of the 1930s. What changes and excites is that the same themes and treatments when applied to different characters portray differing aspects of the America they are living through. Inevitably Doctorow's novels are considered very political.

Almost invariably (the exception being *Lives of the Poets*), Doctorow's central character is either a child or adolescent or else (*World's Fair*) an adult writing about his childhood. The central character is always a narrator. Again almost without exception, the child or adolescent becomes displaced from his roots, and the breakdown of family structure becomes a dominant ingredient in almost every novel. Doctorow himself may not have strayed ''further and further out'' as his novelist has, but his characters, seldom by choice, frequently do. In the more expressly political novel, especially *The Book of Daniel* and *Loon Lake,* this is a freedom granted to the character out of economic or political circumstances. Daniel's parents have been executed as Communists, while in *Loon Lake* the central character Joe is an economic migrant of the Depression, uprooted and adrift. In the less overtly political novels the circumstances behind the displacement become correspondingly less social. Billy Bathgate enjoys a freedom even Huckleberry Finn might envy due mainly to a mother who has little or no grasp either on him or on the world in general. Of the full-length novels, only *World's Fair* differs substantially, the displacement being one of time as the narrator looks back.

In each case Doctorow is drawing a parallel between the development of his central character and the development of America during the same period. *Ragtime* uses real historical figures as frequent landmarks in the narrator's childhood, intertwining his development and that of America. *The Book of Daniel* unfolds Daniel's discovery of the circumstances of his parents' execution alongside the portrayal of America's own discovery of Communism and the way the American government reacted to it. In *Loon Lake* the distorted, disjointed way Joe sees the world evokes the economic turmoil that has displaced him from his home. Similarly the World's Fair is both a forthcoming excitement for a small child and a symbol of hope for better times ahead. The displacement of the central figure in each case frees that figure to be a symbol of the wider environment, a product of the times. And, arguably, in each novel the child or adolescent learns whereas the world he has been thrown into does not: Billy Bathgate's era of childhood is ending as the era of gangsters is ending. He is a good luck charm who leaves the gangsters as the charm of childhood leaves him. By leaving, Billy is seen to have learned. He survives. The gang leader does neither.

As the central character in each novel develops and grows, the language with which that character expresses the narrative develops accordingly. *The Book of Daniel* begins in a confused manner, non-sequiturs exemplifying how Daniel takes in only exactly what he sees. He cannot yet put anything into context or draw conclusions. Similarly *Loon Lake* depicts the upheaval of the 1930s with sentences which lack formal structure, even verbs. It shows a time, historically, when established structure is shaken and falling. The effect of the language is like watching debris fall after an explosion. Slowly the language settles as in both novels the characters understand more of what has been happening. As with the history depicted, patterns emerge with time. In *World's Fair* time has elapsed, the language is therefore coherent, the patterns are clear. *Ragtime* uses both techniques side by side. Some parts are written in a style which would not be out of place in a straight historical narrative. Elsewhere Doctorow uses the pauseless—breathless—sentences of Billy Bathgate. And in *Billy Bathgate* itself Doctorow appears to be using this device to make a further point. As a young child Billy is comical in the way he expresses himself and the adult world he comes to inhabit sees him as such. As Billy begins to come of age, and just begins to become articulate, it is the world that has laughed at him which is shown up as comical. Billy has the last laugh. The characters in these novels, in their various ways, all offer what the wide-eyed Billy Bathgate at the end of his story calls ''this bazaar of life.''

Exemplary of Doctorow's wide-ranging interests is *City of God,* a novel so broadly based it is difficult to characterize at all. Written in the form of an author's notebook for a story to be written (this fact only emerges somewhere deep within the book), the novel is on one level the tale of a love triangle, and on another a deeply metaphysical series of questions about the meaning of religion at the end of the second millennium. One of the more understandable aspects of the plot is the relationship that develops between Fr. Thomas Pemberton and two Jewish rabbis, Joshua Gruen and Sarah Blumenthal. The two happen to be husband and wife, and ''Pem'' (as he is called) enters their lives after he gets caught up in the mystery of how a cross stolen from an Episcopal church in New York's East Village winds up on top of a synagogue across town.

—John Herbert

DONLEAVY, J(ames) P(atrick)

Nationality: Irish. **Born:** Brooklyn, New York, United States, 23 April 1926; became Irish citizen 1967. **Education:** A preparatory school, New York; Trinity College, Dublin. **Military Service:** Served in the United States Naval Reserve during World War II. **Family:** Married 1) Valerie Heron (divorced), one son and one daughter; 2) Mary Wilson Price in 1970 (divorced), one daughter and one son. **Awards:** London *Evening Standard* award, for drama, 1961; Brandeis University Creative Arts award, 1961; American Academy award, 1975; Gold award, Houston Worldfest, 1993; Cine Golden Eagle award. **Address:** Levington Park, Mullingar, County Westmeath, Ireland.

PUBLICATIONS

Novels

The Ginger Man. Paris, Olympia Press, and London, Spearman, 1955; New York, MacDowell Obolensky, 1958; complete edition, London, Corgi, 1963; New York, Delacorte Press, 1965.

A Singular Man. Boston, Little Brown, 1964; London, Bodley Head, 1964.

The Saddest Summer of Samuel S. New York, Delacorte Press, 1966; London, Eyre and Spottiswoode, 1967.

The Beastly Beatitudes of Balthazar B. New York, Delacorte Press, 1968; London, Eyre and Spottiswoode, 1969.

The Onion Eaters. New York, Delacorte Press, and London, Eyre and Spottiswoode, 1971.

A Fairy Tale of New York. New York, Delacorte Press, and London, Eyre Methuen, 1973.

The Destinies of Darcy Dancer, Gentleman. New York, Delacorte Press, 1977; London, Allen Lane, 1978.

Schultz. New York, Delacorte Press, 1979; London, Allen Lane, 1980.

Leila. New York, Delacorte Press, and London, Allen Lane, 1983.

DeAlfonce Tennis: The Superlative Game of Eccentric Champions: Its History, Accoutrements, Conduct, Rules and Regimen. London, Weidenfeld and Nicolson, 1984; New York, Dutton, 1985.

Are You Listening Rabbi Löw. London, Viking, 1987; New York, Atlantic Monthly Press, 1988.

That Darcy, That Dancer, That Gentleman. London, Viking, 1990; New York, Atlantic Monthly Press, 1991.

The History of the Ginger Man. Boston, Houghton Mifflin, 1994.

Short Stories

Meet My Maker the Mad Molecule. Boston, Little Brown, 1964; London, Bodley Head, 1965.

Uncollected Short Stories

''A Friend'' and ''In My Peach Shoes,'' in *Queen* (London), 7 April 1965.

''Rite of Love,'' in *Playboy* (Chicago), October 1968.

''A Fair Festivity,'' in *Playboy* (Chicago), November 1968.

''A Small Human Being,'' in *Saturday Evening Post* (Philadelphia), 16 November 1968.

Plays

The Ginger Man, adaptation of his own novel (produced London and Dublin, 1959; New York, 1963). New York, Random House, 1961; as *What They Did in Dublin, with The Ginger Man: A Play,* London, MacGibbon and Kee, 1962.

Fairy Tales of New York (produced Croydon, Surrey, 1960; London, 1961; New York, 1980). London, Penguin, and New York, Random House, 1961.

A Singular Man, adaptation of his own novel (produced Cambridge and London, 1964; Westport, Connecticut, 1967). London, Bodley Head, 1965.

The Plays of J.P. Donleavy (includes *The Ginger Man, Fairy Tales of New York, A Singular Man, The Saddest Summer of Samuel S).* New York, Delacorte Press, 1972; London, Penguin, 1974.

The Beastly Beatitudes of Balthazar B, adaptation of his own novel (produced London, 1981; Norfolk, Virginia, 1985).

Radio Play: *Helen,* 1956.

Other

The Unexpurgated Code: A Complete Manual of Survival and Manners, drawings by the author. New York, Delacorte Press, and London, Wildwood House, 1975.

Ireland: In All Her Sins and in Some of Her Graces. London, Joseph, and New York, Viking, 1986.

A Singular Country, illustrated by Patrick Prendergast. Peterborough, Ryan, 1989; New York, Norton, 1990.

The Lady Who Liked Clean Rest Rooms: The Chronicle of One of the Strangest Stories Ever to Be Rumored About Around New York. New York, St. Martins Press, 1997.

An Author and His Image: The Collected Shorter Pieces. New York, Viking, 1997.

Wrong Information Is Being Given Out at Princeton. New York, Thomas Dunne Books, 1998.

*

Bibliography: By David W. Madden, in *Bulletin of Bibliography* (Westport, Connecticut), September 1982.

Critical Studies: *J.P. Donleavy: The Style of His Sadness and Humor* by Charles G. Masinton, Bowling Green, Ohio, Popular Press, 1975; *Isolation and Protest: A Case Study of J.P. Donleavy's Fiction* by R.K. Sharma, New Delhi, Ajanta, 1983.

* * *

Perhaps because of his transatlantic and multinational character, J.P. Donleavy defies easy classification and suffers from a certain critical neglect. His books blend some of the special literary qualities of all three—American, English, Irish—of his national traditions. He has a typically American zaniness, an anarchic and sometimes lunatic comic sense, mingled with an undertone of despair. He possesses an English accuracy of eye and ear for the look and sound of things, for the subtle determinants of class in appearances and accents, a Jamesian grasp of density of specification. Finally, his novels display an Irish wit, energy, and vulgarity as well as a distinctly Irish sense of brooding and melancholy. Like any Irish writer, he is inevitably compared to Joyce, but in this case the comparison is apt—his tone echoes the comic brevity and particularity of many parts of *Ulysses,* and his prose style often wanders into Joycean patterns.

Ever since his great success with *The Ginger Man,* which sometimes seems the template for almost all the later works, Donleavy has followed a sometimes distressing sameness of pattern and subject in his books. Roughly speaking, they are serio-comic picaresques that mix a close attention to verifiable reality with an increasingly outrageous sense of fantasy. Although the fantasy is always strongly sexual—and Donleavy writes about sex with refreshingly carnal gusto—it also dwells on the sensuousness, perhaps even the eroticism of all materiality. When he sinks his teeth into the dense texture of life, Donleavy imparts an almost sexual appetite to his prose, glorying in the things of this world to the virtual exclusion of all else. He writes with the same zest about such matters as gentlemen's clothing, wines, liquor, food, tobacco, women's bodies, the interior and exterior decorations of luxurious homes, all the lovingly itemized concretions that represent the good life. In his most recent novels, like *Schultz* and its successor, *Are You Listening Rabbi Löw,* Donleavy records, with no diminution in his sense of awe, the dithyrambic praise of the appetitive view of life as fully, comically, and joyously as in *The Ginger Man.*

Because of the basic similarity of characters, events, style, and structure in his books, they often seem initially a mere continual rewriting of the first and most famous novel. They pile, often rather randomly, episode upon outrageous episode, repeat the scenes of sex, of comic violence, of pratfalls and ridicule in the same fragmented sentences, and often appear to run out of steam rather than end. Few of his books possess a real sense of closure: the protagonist most often is left, like the Ginger Man, suspended midway between triumph and ignominy, humor and sadness, still completely himself but also touched by defeat and despair. Their constant, most powerful note is elegiac—the protagonist may continue on his crazy way but he inevitably recognizes the most final and undeniable fact of all, the fact of death. The last perception of Sebastian Dangerfield in *The Ginger Man* is a vision of horses: ''And I said they are running out to death which is with some soul and their eyes are mad and teeth out.'' In *The Destinies of Darcy Dancer, Gentleman* and its sequels, *Leila* and *That Darcy, That Dancer, That Gentleman,* the fox hunt, which runs throughout the books, provides Dancer with the metaphors of mortality—''Till the Huntsman's blowing his long slow notes. Turn home. At end of day.''

Schultz and *Are Your Listening Rabbi Löw* mix the perception of death with a jaunty, life-loving energy in a broader comic style than most of Donleavy's other works, as if the only solution to the perception of mortality is the relentless pursuit of physical gratification. The Jewish theatrical producer Schultz, who tries to succeed among the aristocratic sharks of London, is Donleavy's version of the Jamesian innocent American abroad. The books make their protagonist the butt of dozens of jokes but also the lovable scoundrel whose lunatic schemes somehow rescue him from his own preposterous ambitions and land him, rather shakily, on his feet. Like Darcy Dancer, he concludes his second, though perhaps not final, appearance with the achievement of a sort of stasis—rich, successful, and loved, he cruises on a yacht with a beautiful, brilliant, and mad daughter of the British aristocracy.

His latest books suggest that Donleavy may be on the one hand simultaneously running out of energy and ideas, and on the other, attempting to bring his seemingly endless episodes to completion. In both *That Darcy, That Dancer, That Gentleman* and *Are You Listening Rabbi Löw* Darcy Dancer and Schultz ultimately achieve a state of apparent repose. With Donleavy, of course, one can never be fully sure; as his character Schultz realizes, ''if you can balance on top, you can not only scratch your fanny but touch the moon. But don't count on anything.''

Like all good comic writers, Donleavy grounds his vision in a dark view of the world; amid all his embracing vitality lurks a perception of the desperate need for comedy. His art derives from that perception—under the fully realized surfaces of life lie fear, guilt, and the dread of death. His books quite properly partake of the three national traditions with which he has associated himself; all three converge in his mixture of solemnity and humor and in the same mixture of resolution and disintegration that so often forms his conclusions. In his comic mode Donleavy is sometimes uproariously funny, sometimes brilliantly witty, sometimes just plain silly; often touched by a surprising melancholy, hedonistically devouring life but haunted by death, his novels end, at best, in a resounding ''if.'' You may touch the moon, but don't count on anything.

—George Grella

DOUGLAS, Ellen

Nationality: American. **Born:** Josephine Ayeres in Natchez, Mississippi, 7 December 1921. **Education:** The University of Mississippi, Jackson, B.A. 1942. **Family:** Married Kenneth Haxton in 1945 (divorced); three sons. **Career:** Writer-in-residence, Northeast Louisiana University, Monroe, 1978–82, and since 1982 University of Mississippi; visiting professor, University of Virginia, Charlottesville, 1984; Welty Professor, Millsaps College, Jackson, 1988. **Awards:** Houghton Mifflin fellowship, 1961; Mississippi Institute of Arts and Letters award, 1979; Fellowship of Southern Writers award, 1989. **Agent:** R.L.R. Associates, 7 West 51st Street, New York, New York 10020, U.S.A. **Address:** 1600 Pine Street, Jackson, Mississippi 39202, U.S.A.

PUBLICATIONS

Novels

A Family's Affairs. Boston, Houghton Mifflin, 1961; London, Cape, 1963; Baton Rouge, Louisiana State University Press, 1994.
Where the Dreams Cross. Boston, Houghton Mifflin, 1968.
Apostles of Light. Boston, Hougton Mifflin, 1973.
The Rock Cried Out. New York, Harcourt Brace, 1979; London, Virago Press, 1990; Baton Rouge, Louisiana State University Press, 1994.
A Lifetime Burning. New York, Random House, 1982; London, Bodley Head, 1983.
Can't Quit You, Baby. New York, Atheneum, 1988; London, Virago Press, 1990.

Short Stories

Black Cloud, White Cloud. Boston, Houghton Mifflin, 1963.
Truth: Four Stories I Am Finally Old Enough to Tell. Chapel Hill, North Carolina, Algonquin Books of Chapel Hill, 1998.

Uncollected Short Story

''On the Lake,'' in *Prize Stories 1963,* edited by Richard Poirier. New York, Doubleday, 1963.

Other

The Magic Carpet and Other Tales. Jackson, University Press of Mississippi, 1987.

*

Manuscript Collection: University of Mississippi Library, Jackson.

Critical Studies: *Conversations with Ellen Douglas,* edited by Panthea Reid. Jackson, University Press of Mississippi, 2000.

* * *

Ellen Douglas's novels, written over a period of 30 years, have consistently dealt with the South, with relationships between the individual and family, between men and women, and between blacks and whites. Never adopting a programmatic feminist stance, Douglas has nonetheless consistently made clear the difficulties faced by women in the world of Southern gentlemen and rednecks. Never adopting a stance of political activism, Douglas has also consistently stressed the close, complex, and ambiguous relationships between black and white Southern women. Throughout works notable for strong and sensitive characterizations, Douglas has created plots which test such humanistic values as love, responsibility, and respect for tradition against the impersonality, arrogant individualism, and materialism of the contemporary New South.

Her first novel, *A Family's Affairs,* won a Houghton Mifflin fellowship and was named one of the *New York Times* best novels of 1962. The novel focuses on the Anderson family during the years 1917–1948, when Kate, the family matriarch, dies at the age of 85. At the novel's center are five women: Kate, her three daughters, and a granddaughter. It is Anna through whose eyes we experience the family crises which make up the novel's plot—crises which usually result from the feckless behavior of the daughters' husbands and Kate's son. Their egocentric individualism contrasts with the women's sense of responsibility to the family and with what Anna calls at the end of the novel ''the habit of moral consciousness.''

Anna figures in one of the two novels and both of the short stories which form *Black Cloud, White Cloud,* Douglas's second book.

Here Douglas concentrates on the responsibilities of Southern whites to their black servants; the works attest to the complicated relationships between the races, acknowledging the guilt whites feel for their oppression of blacks and the difficulty of redeeming their relationships despite shared pasts.

Where the Dreams Cross is Douglas's weakest novel, attacking in obvious and easy ways the bigotry and greedy materialism of the New South's politicians and the empty-headed frivolity of Old and New Southern belles by contrasting those vices with the virtues of the beautiful but hard-drinking, scandalous but morally responsible heroine. *Apostles of Light,* however, deservedly won a nomination for the National Book award. Douglas here sensitively portrays the plight of the elderly, revealing the frustrations of her heroine, Martha, as, first, her mind and body begin to betray her, and as, eventually, her relatives begin to betray her as well. Torn between their sense of responsibility for Martha and their fear that she will become a financial burden to them, her relatives convert the old family mansion into a profitable nursing home, the ironically named Golden Age Acres. Douglas's powerful and contrasting characterizations of Martha with the home's villainous manager, who treated the elderly residents as prisoners, provide the novel's tension.

The Rock Cried Out won praise in the popular press for its portrayal of a young man's loss of innocence and for Douglas's original handling of elements of the Southern Gothic tradition. The novel chronicles the return of Alan McLaurin to Mississippi after years in Boston and his discovery that the car wreck which caused the death of his first love, Phoebe, was the result of a Ku Klux Klansman's bullet. The Klansman's confession of his crime during a 25-page monologue on the CB in his truck (which McLaurin overhears) marks a flaw in Douglas's narrative technique and strains the reader's credulity. However, McLaurin's maturation (his youthful idealism is gradually replaced by a worldly cynicism) is handled well, and Douglas portrays vividly the tensions in the South between both races and classes during the civil rights era. Here too Douglas reveals her angry sense that technology and materialism have replaced tradition values in the New South.

A Lifetime Burning takes the form of the diary of a 62-year-old English professor, Corinne, who discovers her husband George's infidelities and who writes in order to understand her own blindness, to make sense of what she had thought a ''good'' life with him, and to leave a record for their grown children. In the course of the six months during which Corinne keeps her diary, she first writes an absurdly comic (and perhaps false) account of George's affair with ''The Toad,'' worries that his distaste for her aging body has motivated that affair, and eventually writes of George's affair with ''The Musk-Rat,'' a male intern at the hospital where George practices. As critic Carol S. Minning has noted, Corinne's first diary entry makes it easier for her to accept the second, the comic anticipates the more shocking, the false anticipates the true. Throughout the novel invention anticipates confession; in dream begins reality. In Douglas's novel, as in the epistolary novels of the 18th century, Corinne writes so that she may find an order to the chaotic facts her life lacks; in her diary she seeks to illuminate the truth of human mystery, her own, her husband's, and her family's.

Douglas followed a collection of classic fairy tales, *The Magic Carpet and Other Tales,* with her best novel, *Can't Quit You, Baby.* It tells the stories of two middle-aged women, Cornelia—sheltered, privileged, white, and deaf—and her black servant, Julia or Tweet—experienced, vital, and enduring. As the women work at common household tasks in Cornelia's house, Julia's stories of her violent and poverty-ridden past awaken Cornelia's memories of crises in her own past. Julia's courage eventually helps Cornelia to survive the death of her husband, to endure her own grief, to live, and to help Julia sustain herself during a subsequent crisis. The novel also assesses the difficulties of story-telling; given the ''deafness'' of listeners such as Cornelia (or of the reader), how is a narrator such as Julia (or Douglas) to be heard? Intelligent, comic, and poignant, the novel validates the early claim of the New York Times Book Review that Douglas is ''one of the best ... American novelists.''

—David K. Jeffrey

DOUGLAS, Michael

See CRICHTON, (John) Michael

DOWSE, Dale Sara

Nationality: Australian. **Born:** Sara Fitch in Chicago, Illinois (immigrated to Australia in 1958, became naturalized citizen in 1972), 12 November 1938. **Education:** Attended University of California, Los Angeles, 1956–58; University of Sidney, B.A. 1968; attended Australian National University, 1968. **Family:** Married John Henry Dowse in 1958 (divorced 1977); four sons, one daughter. **Career:** Field editor, Thomas Nelson, Canberra, Australia, 1970–72; tutor in professional writing, Canberra College of Advanced Education; journalist, Australian Information Service, Canberra; press secretary, Federal Minister for Labor, Canberra, 1973; journalist, Australian Information Service, 1974; head of Office of Women's Affairs, Department of the Prime Minister and Cabinet, Canberra, 1974–78; tutor in women's studies, Australian National University, Canberra, 1978–80; freelance writer, 1980—. **Awards:** Women and Politics Prize (Australian Institute of Political Science), 1982. **Agent:** Rosemary Creswell, P.O. Box 161, Glebe, New South Wales 2037, Australia. **Address:** 43 Froggatt Street, Turner, Australian Capital Territory 2601, Australia.

Publications

Novels

West Block. Ringwood, Australia, Penguin, 1983.
Silver City. Ringwood, Australia, Penguin, 1984.
Schemetime. Melbourne, Australia, Penguin, 1990.
Amnesty. Port Melbourne, Australia, Minerva, 1993.
Sapphires. Ringwood, Australia, Penguin, 1994.
Digging. New York, Penguin, 1996.

Other

Contributor, *Decisions: Case Studies in Australian Public Policy,* edited by Sol Encel, Peter Wilenski, and Bernard Schaffer. Longman Cheshire, 1981.
Contributor, *Worth Her Salt: Women at Work in Australia,* edited by Margaret Bevege, Margaret James, and Carmel Shute. Hale & Iremonger, 1982.
Contributor, *Leaving School: It's Harder for Girls,* edited by Sue Dyson and Tricia Szirom. Young Women's Christian Association of Australia, 1983.
Contributor, *Women, Social Welfare, and the State,* edited by Cora Baldock and Bettina Cass. Allen & Unwin, 1983.
Contributor, *Unfinished Business: Social Justice for Women in Australia,* edited by Dorothy Broom. Allen & Unwin, 1984.
Contributor, *Sisterhood Is Global: The International Women's Movement Anthology,* edited by Robin Morgan. Anchor Press, 1984.
Contributor, *Canberra Tales* (anthology). Ringwood, Australia, Penguin, 1988; reprinted as *The Division of Love,* 1995

*

Critical Studies: *Rooms of Their Own* by Jennifer Ellison. Ringwood, Australia, Penguin, 1986.

* * *

Dale Sara Dowse was born in Chicago in 1938, lived as a child in New York and then Los Angeles, and came to Australia in 1956. She settled first in Sydney but ten years later moved to the Australian capital of Canberra, where she remained for a long time. Not surprisingly, her fiction reflects her diverse background. Her first book, *West Block,* is less a novel than five largely self-contained stories, each devoted to one character, though with others recurring in minor roles, and a brief introductory section that links up with the ending. Thematically, what they have in common is the presentation of power at work—or in some cases not at work. Part of what the book shows—very convincingly and no doubt intentionally—is the sheer tedium that is involved in much of the exercise of bureaucratic power. The compromises, the destruction of idealism, the constant jockeying for position, the formal thrusting and parrying, take up a good deal of the book. Although it does not come to the forefront until the last section, ''Cassie Down and Under,'' the continuing link among the stories is the concern with women's issues, with the relative helplessness of the women in a male-entrenched bureaucracy and specifically the cynical destruction of the Women's Equality Branch by a tough public servant appointed by the conservatives: Dowse was head of the Office of Women's Affairs during the early years of the conservative Fraser government in the late 1970s.

Dowse followed her first book with *Silver City*, a serious and ambitiously marketed attempt to translate Sophia Turkiewicz's film of that name into fiction. The title refers to a transit camp in which refugee Poles arrived to spend some time after the war. Though the story is fleshed out with a number of well-drawn characters, the protagonists are Nina Majowska, Julian Marcezewski, the man she falls in love with, and Julian's wife Anna. Although the writing is competent and holds the attention, there are some narrational problems arising from the attempt to translate film into literature. There is no central point of view, so that we are shifted quickly from the perspective of one character to another with no clear sense of a sustained and coherent position from which to view the action. This is accentuated by the rapid cutting; the cinematic cuts and ellipses work less successfully on paper than they do on screen. Apart from the personal relationships, the novel's interest lies mainly in its portrait of the reaction of ''reffos'' to their traumatic uprooting and relocation at the bottom of the world, and their unsympathetic treatment by Australians.

Schemetime is set in 1968 and continues to display Dowse's intense interest in political radicalism. The novel employs some of the same techniques as *West Block*, in particular moving from one to another of a set of characters without focusing on any one story, shifting constantly in time, and moving between first and third person. The part-time narrator, Frank Banner, is an Australian director who goes to Hollywood to try and make a film. His story is interwoven with a number of others: the Austrian director Mannheim Zuchter whom Frank tries to interest in his film; a lawyer and actor's agent Nathan Leventhal; a black singer named Paula Jackson; Nathan's wife Susan, who leaves him and who finally becomes the most important and interesting character. There are some fine scenes in *Schemetime* but the array of techniques that Dowse borrows from the cinema she writes about tends to be distracting and finally bewildering more than anything else.

Sapphires is one of Dowse's most interesting and attractive works. Again a loosely related collection of stories, it tells the story—or stories—of the Kozminsky family over four generations. Dowse has gone back deeply into her Jewish origins: ''Safar, to count, related to our word sapphire and the Kabalah's sephiroth, also derived from the Hebrew 'sappur,' said to be the substance of God's throne.'' The opening chapter offers a moral about the art of telling stories: '''A story is not only a story,' my grandmother said. 'A story that is only a story is, at best, a parable, with a moral that is easy to grasp. Everyone feels happy with a parable. But a story that is more than a story, my child, is a text.''' What follows is a number of ''texts,'' dealing with the successive generations of the family but especially the women. They range in place from Omaha, where Lev Kozminsky is finally joined by his reluctant wife Ruchel in 1898 as refugees from the Russian pogroms, to Chicago, where their granddaughter Bernice moves to work as an actress, to New York and finally to Sydney where Bernice's daughter Evelyn emigrates and marries a Rugby player named Paul Hazelwood. The women of the family are both its strength and length of continuity, symbolized in the Fibonacci sequence the novel refers to several times, which suggests the women are the sum of both themselves and the mothers who had preceded them. The loose structure allows Dowse to range widely in time and place to offer finally a kind of coherent and inclusive account of many kinds of Jewishry over the last one hundred years. It is a tender but unsentimental book, filled with unexpected insights and charity.

Digging begins with the appearance of the ghost of a dog named Carly, who had died twelve years ago. The first three chapters go back into the history of the dog, how she came to be with her owner and how she lost her. Carly gets lost and is eventually found again and then at the beginning of chapter 4 the author/narrator says, ''I suppose the time has come to tell you how the baby got sick and what may be of even greater interest, how the baby came to be.'' What follows is a fairly conventional account of a failed relationship with an academic archaeologist—another kind of ''digging,'' which is the central motif of the book. The novel deals with events that occurred twelve years before but is set even further back in the early 1970s. There are carefully unspecific but nevertheless unmistakable references to Canberra and to the decline of the Whitlam Labor government, which remains a crucial period in Dowse's life. There is a slowly growing sense of the narrator as embryonic writer; her notebooks become increasingly more important to her. The third part of the novel returns us to Carly and her eventual death, extremely painful to her, but the narrative of the dog is never quite integrated into those of the woman's relations with the child and with the child's coldly distant father. There is also a curious reticence about many things. The man is identified only as X, just as a female friend is L and a male friend from the narrator's workplace is H, perhaps a spurious attempt to convey some kind of universality.

Dowse, who now lives in Canada, also has one of seven stories in a collection originally titled *Canberra Tales*, reprinted in 1995 as *The Division of Love*. She has mastered a form which lies somewhere between the short story and the novel, what the Australian writer Frank Moorhouse calls ''discontinuous narratives.''

—Laurie Clancy

DOYLE, Roddy

Nationality: Irish. **Born:** Dublin, 1958. **Family:** Married; two sons. **Career:** Since 1980 teacher of English and geography, Greendale Community School, Kilbarrack, Dublin. **Award:** Booker prize, 1993, for *Paddy Clarke Ha Ha Ha.*

PUBLICATIONS

Novels

The Barrytown Trilogy. London, Secker and Warburg, 1992.

The Commitments, Dublin, King Farouk, 1987; London, Heinemann, 1988; New York, Vintage, 1989.

The Snapper. London, Secker and Warburg, 1990; New York, Penguin, 1992.

The Van. London, Secker and Warburg, 1991; New York, Viking, 1992.

Paddy Clarke Ha Ha Ha. London, Secker and Warburg, 1993.

The Woman Who Walked into Doors. New York, Viking, 1996.

Finbar's Hotel (serial novel, with others), devised and edited by Dermot Bolger. London, Picador, 1997.

A Star Called Henry. New York, Viking, 1999.

Not Just for Christmas (for children). Dublin, New Island Books, 1999.

The Giggler Treatment. New York, Arthur A. Levine Books, 2000.

Plays

War. Dublin, Passion Machine, 1989.

Brownbread. London, Secker and Warburg, 1992; published with *War* as *Brownbread and War*, New York, Penguin Books, 1994.

Screenplays: *The Commitments,* an adaptation of his own novel, 1991; *The Snapper,* an adaptation of his own novel, 1993; *The Van,* Fox Searchlight, 1996.

*

Film Adaptations: *The Commitments,* 1991; *The Snapper,* 1993; *The Van*, 1996.

* * *

Roddy Doyle's novels have fundamentally changed the possibilities open to any fictional representation of Ireland in the late twentieth century and early twenty first. Where Joyce had demolished the myth of rural Ireland as the only fit subject for ''high'' Irish literature by making Dublin the context for his fiction, Doyle has made Dublin the subject for a literature that questioningly straddles the boundaries between ''high'' and ''popular,'' even deliberately ''low,'' culture. Doyle's writing uses the urban in place of Joyce's sometimes-urbane Dublin. Doyle's novels are set outside the literary confines of central Dublin, among the post-war housing estates and the disenfranchised population; with his most recent novel he moves the style and simple assurance of his earlier work into the relatively surprising and unpopular genre of the Irish historical novel.

These two aspects of Doyle's work, his courting of the ''popular'' and the specific setting for his novels, have been apparent since his first work *The Commitments* (1987). Tracing the short lifespan of a soul group in ''Barrytown,'' *The Commitments* self-consciously makes an iconic use of popular cultures and watches their mutation, examines their applicability, in the context of contemporary urban Ireland. The early comments in the novel ''The Irish are the niggers of Europe ... An' the northside Dubliners are the niggers of Dublin'' need some sceptical scrutiny for their cultural resonance, but they undeniably enforce the continual assertion that Doyle's novels make: that Ireland cannot contemporarily be considered in a pre-1950s separatist mode. The terms of cultural reference in *The Commitments* are necessarily delimited by its subject matter (usually American soul music), but the hybrid ''Dublin soul'' that is briefly born in the narrative points the way forward in Doyle's fiction to a continual, and politicized, prioritization of all elements of lived culture over the strictures of readily available ''literary'' tropes. One influential model for the novel is the movie *The Blues Brothers*, which is referred to in the text, and which in turn became the model for Alan Parker's film version of *The Commitments* (1991)—that the novel was so readily convertible into cinematic media testifies to its cultural influences and how they have structured Doyle's writing, which certainly owes more to film and television than it does to a ''tradition'' of ''great'' Irish writing.

The progression of Doyle's novels through *The Commitments, The Snapper, The Van*, and *Paddy Clarke Ha Ha Ha* might almost represent a strategy that captivates an audience before delivering a message. If *The Commitments* contained populism as well as the popular, the succeeding novels have become increasingly hard-edged and interested in ever more troubling and difficult issues. *The Snapper* (1990) traces characters from the Rabbitte family (central to *The Commitments* and *The Van* also) through a teenage pregnancy—in Catholic Ireland; with contraception still having problematic connotations and abortion illegal, this is difficult enough in itself. But Doyle chooses to focus his text through Jimmy Rabbitte, Sr., thus filtering social issues with feminist/gender issues attached through an almost archetypal (but challenged) male ego. Doyle's dialogue-driven style, in his use of slang, dialect, and dialogue, remains relatively constant across *The Commitments* and *The Snapper*, and thus his readers feel themselves to be back in the groove of the first novel. However, where *The Commitments* narrates a temporary escape from pressing economic and social problems, *The Snapper* is able to confront those issues; the recognizable stylistics of humor and place retain their potentially comforting familiarity, but the subject matter increasingly politicizes what Doyle writes.

The Van (1991) moves on, in both accomplishment and content, from *The Snapper*. Like the novels of his Scottish contemporary James Kelman, Doyle's *The Van* is comfortable when almost narrativeless—indeed the same social context (unemployment) forces characters in the novels of both writers into periods of apparently unhealthy stasis. Doyle again makes Jimmy Sr., and his type of masculinity, central to his fiction, and traces the social and psychological effects of unemployment. The Van of the title is a chip van bought by Jimmy's similarly out-of-work friend, Bimbo, and in which Jimmy begins to work. The strains on male relationships and friendships become clear when the ownership of the business venture becomes an issue. The old structures of working-class male bonding are overthrown by economic circumstances that hint at the ''enterprise culture's'' intrusion into the Irish economy. And again Doyle uses popular culture, in this case Ireland's national soccer team, as a constant explanatory background for the sense of community and its breakdown that the novel hints at.

Paddy Clarke Ha Ha Ha (1993) is in many ways the most complex and rewarding of Doyle's novels. It steps back slightly from the overlapping but progressing narrative of what is now called the Barrytown Trilogy and looks to the formation of the communities on Dublin's housing estates in the 1950s and early 1960s. Paddy Clarke's childhood is concurrent with these social developments—their influence is mixed with his peculiar and carefully documented range of reading and the cruelties (inflicted and received) of childhood in a novel that builds with painstaking care towards an examination of the effects of marital breakdown on a child. *Paddy Clark* showed that Doyle was able to write novels that are political in the way that singing soul music in Dublin is, as Jimmy Jar says in *The Commitments*, ''real politics.'' With *The Woman Who Walked into Doors* (1996), Doyle put these ''politics'' to the test; having successfully narrated from the perspective of boyhood in *Paddy Clarke*, Doyle's narrator in *The Woman Who Walked into Doors*, Paula, presents an even greater challenge to the author's abilities and the reader's credulity. Paula's story tells of her experiences on the borders of poverty and of marital decline, including the constant experience of male domestic violence. Doyle's own voice is remarkably unobtrusive as Paula's story is told. The novel's focus is not on the sensational or the dramatic but on the heroic nature of everyday life under duress. Paula finally breaks out in her own way and finds her own voice, and Doyle's method and empathy are subtle enough to be able to register these changes too.

As if a process had reached its end with *The Woman Who Walked into Doors*, Doyle's *A Star Called Henry* (1999) sets out on a trilogy that explores Irish history, centering in this case around the Easter

Rising of 1916 and the events that eventually lead to Ireland's independence. While such formative national moments had been briefly referred to earlier in his work (most humorously perhaps in *Paddy Clarke*, in which the boy narrator fraudulently claims a lineage with Thomas Clarke, one of the rebellion's leaders), *A Star Called Henry* is a disjunctive move in the trajectory of Doyle's writing. Despite critical acclaim for the novel, it remains for the rest of the trilogy to prove the value of the new direction Doyle has taken.

—Colin Graham

DRABBLE, Margaret

Nationality: British. **Born:** Sheffield, Yorkshire, 5 June 1939; sister of A.S. Byatt, **Education:** Mount School, York; Newnham College, Cambridge, B.A. (honours) 1960. **Family:** Married 1) Clive Swift in 1960 (divorced 1975), two sons and one daughter; 2) the writer Michael Holroyd in 1982. **Career:** Deputy chair, 1978–80, and chair, 1980–82, National Book League. **Awards:** Rhys Memorial prize, 1966; James Tait Black Memorial prize, 1968; American Academy E.M. Forster award, 1973. D.Litt: University of Sheffield, 1976; University of Keele, Staffordshire, 1988; University of Bradford, Yorkshire, 1988; University of East Anglia, 1994; University of York, 1995. C.B.E. (Commander, Order of the British Empire), 1980. **Agent:** Peters Fraser and Dunlop, Drury House 34–43, Russell Street, London WC2B 5HA, England.

PUBLICATIONS

Novels

A Summer Bird-Cage. London, Weidenfeld and Nicolson, 1962; New York, Morrow, 1964.
The Garrick Year. London, Weidenfeld and Nicolson, 1964; New York, Morrow, 1965.
The Millstone. London, Weidenfeld and Nicolson, 1965; New York, Morrow, 1966; as *Thank You All Very Much,* New York, New American Library, 1969; published under original title, San Diego, Harcourt Brace, 1998.
Jerusalem the Golden. London, Weidenfeld and Nicolson, and New York, Morrow, 1967.
The Waterfall. London, Weidenfeld and Nicolson, and New York, Knopf, 1969.
The Needle's Eye. London, Weidenfeld and Nicolson, and New York, Knopf, 1972.
The Realms of Gold. London, Weidenfeld and Nicolson, and New York, Knopf, 1975.
The Ice Age. London, Weidenfeld and Nicolson, and New York, Knopf, 1977.
The Middle Ground. London, Weidenfeld and Nicolson, and New York, Knopf, 1980.
The Radiant Way. London, Weidenfeld and Nicolson, and New York, Knopf, 1987.
A Natural Curiosity. London and New York, Viking, 1989.
The Gates of Ivory. London and New York, Viking, 1991.
The Witch of Exmoor. London and New York, Viking, 1996.

Short Stories

Hassan's Tower. Los Angeles, Sylvester and Orphanos, 1980.

Uncollected Short Stories

''A Voyage to Cytherea,'' in *Mademoiselle* (New York), December 1967.
''The Reunion,'' in *Winter's Tales 14,* edited by Kevin Crossley-Holland. London, Macmillan, and New York, St. Martin's Press, 1968.
''The Gifts of War,'' in *Winter's Tales 16,* edited by A.D. Maclean. London, Macmillan, 1970; New York, St. Martin's Press, 1971.
''Crossing the Alps,'' in *Mademoiselle* (New York), February 1971.
''A Day in the Life of a Smiling Woman,'' in *In the Looking Glass,* edited by Nancy Dean and Myra Stark. New York, Putnam, 1977.
''A Success Story,'' in *Fine Lines,* edited by Ruth Sullivan. New York, Scribner, 1981.
''The Dying Year,'' in *Harper's* (New York), July 1987.

Plays

Bird of Paradise (produced London, 1969).

Screenplays: *Isadora,* with Melvyn Bragg and Clive Exton, 1969; *A Touch of Love (Thank You All Very Much),* 1969.

Television Play: *Laura,* 1964.

Other

Wadsworth. London, Evans, 1966; New York, Arco, 1969.
Virginia Woolf: A Personal Debt. New York, Aloe, 1973.
Arnold Bennett: A Biography. London, Weidenfeld and Nicolson, and New York, Knopf, 1974.
For Queen and Country: Britain in the Victorian Age (for children). London, Deutsch, 1978; New York, Seabury Press, 1979.
A Writer's Britain: Landscape in Literature. London, Thames and Hudson, and New York, Knopf, 1979.
Wordsworth's Butter Knife: An Essay. Northampton, Massachusetts, Catawba Press, 1980.
The Tradition of Women's Fiction: Lectures in Japan, edited by Yukako Suga. Tokyo, Oxford University Press, 1985.
Case for Equality. London, Fabian Society, 1988.
Stratford Revisited: A Legacy of the Sixties. Shipston-on-Stour, Warwickshire, Celandine Press, 1989.
Safe as Houses: An Examination of Home Ownership and Mortgage Tax Relief. London, Chatto and Windus, 1990.
Angus Wilson: A Biography. London, Secker and Warburg, 1995; New York, St. Martin's Press, 1996.
Editor, with B.S. Johnson, *London Consequences* (a group novel). London, Greater London Arts Association, 1972.
Editor, *Lady Susan, The Watsons, Sanditon,* by Jane Austen. London, Penguin, 1974.
Editor, *The Genius of Thomas Hardy.* London, Weidenfeld and Nicolson, and New York, Knopf, 1976.
Editor, with Charles Osborne, *New Stories 1.* London, Arts Council, 1976.
Editor, *The Oxford Companion to English Literature.* Oxford and New York, Oxford University Press, 1985; concise edition, edited

with Jenny Stringer, 1987; revised edition, 1995; revised edition, 1996; 5th edition, 1998.
Editor, *Twentieth Century Classics.* London, Book Trust, 1986.

*

Bibliography: *Margaret Drabble: An Annotated Bibliography* by Joan Garrett Packer, New York, Garland, 1988.

Manuscript Collections: Boston University; University of Tulsa, Oklahoma.

Critical Studies: *Margaret Drabble: Puritanism and Permissiveness* by Valerie Grosvenor Myer, London, Vision Press, 1974; *Boulder-Pushers: Women in the Fiction of Margaret Drabble, Doris Lessing, and Iris Murdoch* by Carol Seiler-Franklin, Bern, Switzerland, Lang, 1979; *The Novels of Margaret Drabble: Equivocal Figures* by Ellen Cronan Rose, London, Macmillan, 1980, and *Critical Essays on Margaret Drabble* (includes bibliography by J.S. Korenman) edited by Rose, Boston, Hall, 1985; *Margaret Drabble: Golden Realms* edited by Dorey Schmidt and Jan Seale, Edinburg, University of Texas-Pan American Press, 1982; *Margaret Drabble: Existing Within Structures* by Mary Hurley Moran, Carbondale, Southern Illinois University Press, 1983; *Guilt and Glory: Studies in Margaret Drabble's Novels 1963–1980* by Susanna Roxman, Stockholm, Almquist & Wiksell, 1984; *Margaret Drabble* by Joanne V. Creighton, London, Methuen, 1985; *The Intertextuality of Fate: A Study of Margaret Drabble* by John Hannay, 1986; *Margaret Drabble* by Lynn Veach Sadler, Boston, Twayne, 1986; *Margaret Drabble: Symbolic Moralist* by Nora Foster Stovel, San Bernardino, California, Borgo Press, 1989; *The In-Between of Writing, Experience and Experiment in Drabble, Duras, and Arendt* by Eleanor Honig Skoller. Ann Arbor, University of Michigan Press, 1993; *The Novels of Margaret Drabble: This Freudian Family Nexus* by Nicole Suzanne Bokat. New York, Peter Lang, 1998; *Woman's Space: The Mosaic World of Margaret Drabble and Nayantara Sahgal* by Sree Rashmi Talwar. New Delhi, India, Creative Books, 1997; *British Women Writing Fiction,* edited by Abby H. P. Werlock. Tuscaloosa, University of Alabama Press, 2000.

Margaret Drabble comments:

(1986) In this space I originally wrote that my books were mainly concerned with "privilege, justice and salvation," and that they were not directly concerned with feminism "because my belief in justice for women is so basic that I never think of using it as a subject. It is part of a whole." I stand by this, although the rising political consciousness of women has brought the subject more to the forefront in one or two of the later novels. I now see myself perhaps more as a social historian documenting social change and asking questions rather than providing answers about society: but my preoccupation with "equality and egalitarianism" remains equally obsessional and equally worrying to me, and if anything I am even less hopeful about the prospect of change.

* * *

With the appearance of her first novels in the early 1960s, Margaret Drabble gained a sizeable audience who felt their own discoveries and dilemmas in the contemporary world depicted with intelligence and immediacy. *A Summer Bird-Cage* presents a young woman, just after graduation from Oxford, alternately drawn to and repelled by her older sister, seen as brilliant and attractive, who marries a rich novelist. The marriage is ultimately hollow, and the young protagonist uses her recognition of this, as well as that of the marriage, affairs, and occupations of friends, to sort out her own approach to mature experience. The protagonist of *The Garrick Year* is more intimately involved. Married to an actor in a company playing in a provincial town, she falls in love with the producer and finally is able to draw away from the thickets of staged infidelities in her realization of her responsibility for her child. Moral issues, increasingly, become part of the protagonists' examinations of experience, as in *The Millstone,* in which a young academic, initially feeling "free" of the inhibitions of sexual morality and class, and, accidentally pregnant after a one-night stand, recognizes after the baby's birth that her concerns make her dependent on others, on community, and *Jerusalem the Golden,* in which a young graduate from the North, attracted to the cosmopolitan life represented by a London family, must sort out her own allegiances and responses to issues of love and class. Although *The Waterfall* is more internal, more exclusively concerned with the isolating emotions the protagonist feels in her affair with her cousin's husband, this novel, like the other early ones, reflects directly many of the problems concerning freedom, responsibility, sexual behavior, families, occupation, class, and geography confronted by young women in contemporary Britain.

Drabble's protagonists are invariably intelligent and literary, trying seriously (although not solemnly) to relate what they experience to what they've read. Often they define themselves, either positively or negatively, as characters within the fictions of the 19th-century middle classes, the heroines in George Eliot's world confronting moral dilemmas, or those in Hardy's measuring themselves in the metaphorical terms of landscape. *The Waterfall* rings changes on Jane Austen plots and attitudes: the protagonist in *The Millstone* superimposes Bunyan's allegorical geography on the dark streets of contemporary London. The frequency and the importance of the references indicate that Drabble has always seen herself as part of an English literary tradition, a consciousness of defining the self through fiction.

In Drabble's later novels, the consciousness and function of fiction change. Points of view are deliberately interrupted, fictionality is overtly proclaimed and manipulated, sometimes comically and sometimes not. Drabble relies on questions in literary criticism over the past 20 years as well as on the tradition of English literature. Library reference is likely to be more general and pervasive, as in the epigraph of *The Ice Age* which quotes Milton's *Areopagetica* about "the puissant Nation rousing herself like a strong man after sleep" to illustrate the possibility of British "recovery" from a debilitating period, or the literary party, explicitly connected to the one in Virginia Woolf's *Mrs. Dalloway,* which concludes *The Middle Ground.* The frame of moral reference in the later novels is much wider, more international or more a statement concerning the condition of England, and the novels are more amenable to metaphorical readings. *The Needle's Eye* establishes various gardens in unlikely places, the London slums, the North, and in Africa, gardens that are conscious devices to preserve and nourish the human spirit. *The Realms of Gold* depicts an archeologist who collects both the shards of a public past in excavations in Africa and those of the private past of her family amidst the local and class deprivations of East Anglia, trying to combine the implications of all the relics into a fuller public and private life. *The Ice Age* focuses on the depression, sterility, and violence of Britain in the mid-1970s, problems demonstrated as private in the particular characters and rendered public through the metaphors of property development and misuse that dominate the novel. National ''recovery'' is seen, perhaps equivocally, as possible. *The Middle Ground,* again combining the public and private, tries to collect representatives of various cultures and classes in a contemporary London reclaimed from the septic wastes of its origins, a metaphor like that in Dickens's *Our Mutual Friend. The Witch of Exmoor* approaches similar issues from the perspective of the late 1990s. The ''witch'' of the title, actually only an eccentric old woman named Frieda Haxby Palmer, sees her grown children as products of the new Britain, and her sudden disappearance sends them into a flurry of speculation as they try to understand the strange woman they thought they knew. Drabble's self-conscious play with fictional perspectives keeps these metaphors away from the potential solemnity of the grandiose, yet the moral implications of the metaphors, the statements judging both personal and public conditions in England, are serious and controlling.

—James Gindin

DREWE, Robert

Nationality: Australian. **Born:** Melbourne, Victoria, 9 January 1943. **Education:** Hale School, Perth, Western Australia, 1952–60. **Family:** Married to Candida Baker (third marriage); four sons and two daughters. **Career:** Cadet journalist, Perth *West Australian,* 1961–64; journalist, 1964–65, and head of Sydney bureau, 1965–70, the *Age,* Melbourne; daily columnist, 1970–73, features editor, 1971–72, and literary editor, 1972–74, the *Australian,* Sydney; special writer, 1975–76, and contributing editor, 1980–83, the *Bulletin,* Sydney; writer-in-residence, University of Western Australia, Nedlands, 1979, and La Trobe University, Bundoora, Victoria, 1986; columnist, *Mode,* Sydney, and Sydney *City Monthly,* 1981–83; visiting writer-in-residence, South Bank Centre, London, and Brixton Prison, 1994. **Awards:** Australia Council fellowship, 1974, 1976, 1978, 1983, 1988; Walkley award for journalism, 1976, 1981; U.S. Government Leader grant, 1978; Victorian Arts fellowship, 1987; National Book award, 1987; Commonwealth Literary prize, 1990; Australian Artists Creative fellowship, 1993–96. **Agent:** Hickson Associates, 128 Queen Street, Woollahra, New South Wales 2025, Australia.

PUBLICATIONS

Novels

The Savage Crows. Sydney and London, Collins, 1976.
A Cry in the Jungle Bar. Sydney, Collins, 1979; London, Fontana, 1981.
Fortune. Sydney, Pan, 1986; London, Pan, 1987.
Our Sunshine. Sydney, Pan, 1991.
The Drowner. Sydney, Macmillan, 1995; New York, St. Martin's Press, 1997.

Short Stories

The Bodysurfers. Sydney, Fraser, 1983; London, Faber, 1984.
The Bay of Contented Man. Sydney, Pan, 1989; London, Pan, 1991.

Plays

The Bodysurfers, adaptation of his own story (produced Lismore, New South Wales, 1989).
South American Barbecue (produced Sydney, 1991).

Other

The Shark Net (memoir). New York, Viking, 2000.
Editor, *The Picador Book of the Beach.* Sydney, Picador, 1993; London, Picador, 1994.

*

Manuscript Collection: University of Western Australia Library, Nedlands.

Critical Studies: ''Making Connections'' by Veronica Brady, in *Westerly* (Perth, Western Australia), June 1980; ''The Littoral Truth'' by Jim Crace, in *Times Literary Supplement* (London), 24 August 1984; ''Beaches and Bruised Loves'' by Jill Smolowe, in *Newsweek* (New York), 29 October 1984; ''Cartoons for the Lucky Country'' by J.D. Reed, in *Time* (New York), 15 December 1986; ''A New Angle on Our Uneasy Repose'' by Helen Daniel, in Sydney *Morning Herald,* 18 November 1989; ''Mining Dark Places'' by Don Anderson, in *Age Monthly Review* (Melbourne), May 1990.

* * *

Robert Drewe is an important, highly original voice in Australian fiction. Like other writers before him, Drewe deals with the plight of the Australian Aborigines, scrutinizes Australia's uneasy relationship with Asia, and shows an overriding concern with questions of Australian national identity (especially in regard to the role of urban life). But Drewe's approach to these issues is original and provocative.

Whereas a novel about the Australian Aborigines will usually be set among Aborigines, or at least involve white people who live in areas inhabited by Aborigines, *The Savage Crows* deals with a white youth whose contact with Aborigines is at first only theoretical. Stephen Crisp is researching the early 19th-century events which led to the extinction of the Aborigines living in the island state of Tasmania. His source material is a document titled ''The Savage Crows: My Adventures Among the Natives of Van Diemen's Land,'' which is the diary-journal of the clergyman G.A. Robinson, whose attempts to bring Christianity and civilization to the Tasmanian natives led to cultural misunderstanding, the spread of disease, and death.

Though Robinson was an actual historical figure, the Robinson journal is based upon a number of 19th-century documents and newspaper reports. *The Savage Crows* has been described as a ''documentary novel,'' but its concerns extend beyond the fictional recreation of history. Drewe presents a number of moral contrasts: Robinson's ''good intentions'' and their deplorable outcome; Crisp's clinical, academic approach and the dire human suffering to which it is directed; the petty ''problems'' of affluent 20th-century suburbia beside the plight of early colonists and Aborigines.

A Cry in the Jungle Bar explores Australia's relationship with Asia, once again with focus upon the experiences of a single individual. The Jungle Bar is an attraction of the Asian Eden Hotel, and the ''cry'' of the title is an utterance of helpless western frustration in the face of Asian complexities. Australian Dick Cullen is a tall, beefy, former football player who now works for the United Nations in Manila. Like Stephen Crisp, Cullen is a researcher; an expert on animal husbandry, he is writing a book about water buffalo titled ''The Poor Man's Tractor.'' More importantly, Cullen shares Crisp's desire to relate his own life to history (though Cullen is more interested in the future history of Australian-Asian relations), and he shares Crisp's struggle to come to terms with another race and culture.

Drewe presents a pessimistic, satirical view of the meeting of cultures. Cullen is marked indelibly a foreigner because of his massive physique, but also because of his inability to understand the subtle political divisions of Asia. (His Bangladeshi colleague, Z.M. Ali, is an enigma to him, and Cullen is bewildered when Ali's political activities lead to his expulsion.)

Fortune is written as a series of terse film-takes or cartoon-panels which tell the story of Don Spargo, a contemporary explorer who discovers a sunken treasure ship off the coast of Western Australia. This story has a ''factual'' basis (inasmuch as it is based upon a real-life character and posits the possible fate of a real-life 16th-century sailing ship, the *Fortuyn*) and in this sense it confirms the ''journalistic'' impulse in Drewe's writing. But the underlying themes are literary, for Spargo's story is a parable on contemporary issues, and the use of a young journalist as narrator raises postmodernist concerns about the nature of narrative: ''Officially the reporter was simply the recorder of events, the objective conduit, but events had a habit of including the messenger in the disorder.''

Drewe's novels feature an underlying concern with the malaise affecting suburban Australia. This is seen in the way in which Crisp, Cullen, and the journalist-narrator of *Fortune* are aloof and clinical about pressing human problems (each addressing social issues through reports and documentation, rather than experiencing the problems directly), and it is evident in the failed sexual relationships portrayed in each novel. The short stories in *The Bodysurfers* and *The Bay of Contented Man* develop these concerns in more detail, exploring the conflicts and contradictions in the national character. One of the epigraphs to *The Bodysurfers* is a statement from the polemical historian Manning Clark about the loss of national values: ''Just as Samson after being shorn of his hair was left eyeless in Gaza, was this generation, stripped bare of all faith, to be left comfortless on Bondi Beach?'' The stories contrast the carefree sensuality of Australian beach life (the nude sunbathers, the smell of suntan oil) with the characters' unconscious prurience and uneasiness about sexuality, and with the mundane anxieties and problems of urban life.

Drewe's portrayal of the beach culture is journalistically superb; to quote one reviewer: ''It's all here—the oiled bodies, the smell of the salt, the heat of the sun, the sensuality.'' But Drewe also offers a provocative analysis of Australian life, hinting at an inability to unite the ''masculine'' and ''feminine'' aspects of the national culture. In many stories the beach embodies the Australian myth of physical action and carefree hedonism, but these simplistic masculine values are often dispelled by the comments or actions of the female characters. And in the story called ''The Last Explorer'' an aged adventurer, slowly dying in hospital, symbolically turns his back on the sea (symbol of the young, feminine, new Australia) and faces the desert (symbol of the dead ''macho'' world of exploration and masculine deeds).

It is interesting, then, that the title of *The Drowner* seems to evoke the sea, but in fact its setting is the desert—where in the nineteenth century an irrigation engineer was known as a ''drowner.'' The novel is the story of Will Dance, who goes to England to learn his profession, falls in love there and marries, and brings his new bride Angelica back to the parched town he is determined to save. The characters of Will and Angelica are a bit too sparsely drawn, but the town itself comes alive in vivid detail.

—Van Ikin

DRIVER, C(harles) J(onathan)

Nationality: British. **Born:** Cape Town, South Africa, 19 August 1939. **Education:** St. Andrews College, Grahamstown; University of Cape Town, B.A. (honors) in English, B.Ed., and S.T.D. 1962; Trinity College, Oxford, M.Phil. 1967. **Family:** Married Ann Elizabeth Hoogewerf in 1967; two sons and one daughter. **Career:** President, National Union of South African Students, 1963–64; detained in 1964 under the ''90 Day Law;'' South African passport revoked, 1966. Assistant teacher, 1964–65 and 1967–68, and housemaster, International Sixth Form Center, 1968–73, Sevenoaks School, Kent; director of 6th Form Studies, Matthew Humberstone Comprehensive School, Humberside, 1973–78; principal, Island School, Hong Kong, 1978–83; headmaster, Berkhamsted School, Hertfordshire, 1983–89. Since 1989 master, Wellington College, Crowthorne, Berkshire. Research fellow, University of York, 1976. Fellow, Royal Society of Arts, 1984. **Agent:** John Johnson Ltd., 45–47 Clerkenwell Green, London EC1R 0HT. **Address:** Wellington College, Crowthorne, Berkshire RG11 7PU, England.

PUBLICATIONS

Novels

Elegy for a Revolutionary. London, Faber, 1969; New York, Morrow, 1970.
Send War in Our Time, O Lord. London, Faber, 1970.
Death of Fathers. London, Faber, 1972.
A Messiah of the Last Days. London, Faber, 1974.

Short Stories

Penquin Modern Stories 8, with others. London, Penquin, 1971.

Uncollected Short Story

''Impossible Cry,'' in *London Magazine,* February 1966.

Poetry

I Live Here Now. Lincoln, Lincolnshire and Humberside Arts, 1979.
Jack Copel/C.J. Driver. Cape Town, Philip, 1979.
Hong Kong Portraits. Oxford, Perpetua Press, 1986.
In the Water-Margins. Capetown, Snailpress, and London, Crane River Press, 1994.
Holiday Haiku, July-August 1996. Plumstead, England, Firfield Poetry Press, 1997.

Other

Patrick Duncan, South African and Pan-African. London, Heinemann, 1980.

Editor, with H.B. Joicey, *Landscape and Light:L Photographs and Poems of Lincolnshire and Humberside.* Lincoln, Lincolnshire and Humberside Arts, 1978.

*

C.J. Driver comments:

I am a writer and a teacher; the order depends on whether I am writing or teaching, but I am Master of a great national—and increasingly international—boarding school, so am kept busy in term. I write poems, though I do little about publishing them these days; I do much less reviewing than I used to, though I still read books; I spent two years writing the biography of Patrick Duncan, one of the tragic heroes of recent South African history; and I write novels. I believe profoundly that the novel is the ''great book of life,'' and I hope that all my concerns as a human being enter my work as a novelist—love, marriage, children, homes, money, food, work, leisure—though my predominant concerns are with politics—in the widest sense—the relation of self and society, and the relation of conscious and unconscious minds. I would, at the moment, regard myself more as a poet than a novelist; but I hope the picture may change before the final curtain.

* * *

C.J. Driver is a South African writer whose four novels have earned him a considerable reputation. Not exclusively South African in stetting or in theme, the novels concentrate on a sometimes challenging and always recognizable view of contemporary society.

Elegy for a Revolutionary, the first and least satisfactory of the novels, uses Driver's own experience of underground political action in South Africa during the early 1960s. Like Nadine Gordimer's *The Late Bourgeois World,* it is an attempt to examine the motives and the fate of a group of young white ''liberals'' who turned to violence as a means of opposing the repressive Nationalist Government. Driver's analysis centers on the personality of the student leader, Jeremy, whom he sees as both traitor and, paradoxically, hero. The Weakness of the novel lies in its excessively uncritical view of Jeremy. Unlike Nadine Gordimer, who presents her revolutionary as an integral part of a wider social setting, Driver fails to create a context in which Jeremy's actions can be understood. And, although he is much concerned with psychological motivation, the discussion of Jeremy's peculiar family relationships and obscure guilts remain too abstract to be really credible.

In *Send War in Our Time, O Lord* Driver's main theme is the examination of the liberal conscience under stress. His portrayal of Mrs. Allen, a middle-aged white widow, discovering the inadequacy of her life-long moral code based on decency and tolerance, demonstrates his ability to create a convincing character. The setting (an isolated missionary settlement on South Africa's northern border) is also well-presented. The major weakness of this novel lies in its melodramatic and somewhat far-fetched plot, which involves terrorist activity, much police brutality, madness and two or three suicides, all graphically described. In the welter of violent action, the central issues (the failure of liberal values, the need for dynamic leadership, the nature of political commitment) are almost submerged.

Death of Fathers and *A Messiah of the Last Days* are both set in England, and show a much surer grasp of technique and theme than the earlier books. Driver's interest in details of violence and suffering are still in evidence, but now become part of a general vision of modern life. *Death of Fathers* has a close affinity with *Elegy for a Revolutionary,* although it is set in the confines of an English public school. Its central character is a schoolmaster, and, as in the earlier novel, he is both ''heroic'' (larger in every way than his colleagues) and ''treacherous'' (he betrays the confidence of his most brilliant and difficult pupil, in an attempt to ''save'' him). Again, Driver explores the nature of guilt, and the concept of betrayal, which appears, in his view, to be an inherent part of human experience. Friendship between two different but complementary male characters forms another strand in the novel, and is more competently handled here than in the earlier book.

In *A Messiah of the Last Days* Driver returns to a contemplation of political action. This time he makes his anti-establishment figures a group of idealistic young anarchists, the Free People, who set up a commune in a disused warehouse in London. Their leader, charismatic John Buckleson, projects such a powerful and attractive vision of a new society that he wins the allegiance of a number of eminently respectable people, as well as exciting the younger members of society. The most ambitious of the four novels, *A Messiah of the Last Days* contrasts a number of different life styles, and presents a complex image of contemporary Britain. Through the fast-moving story runs what is clearly, by now, Driver's most persistent theme: the need society has for a ''leader'' with a compelling vision, and its equal need to destroy him. Buckleson, who ends his life as a ''vegetable'' in a psychiatric ward, having been shot at close range by a former follower of his, is the latest version of Jeremy, sentenced to death for sabotage; of the terrorist leader, gunned down by the police; and of Nigel, the schoolboy who hanged himself. Skilled as Driver undoubtedly is in contriving variations of his theme, one hopes that his interest in leadership and betrayal will not become obsessive.

—Ukrsula Edmands

DUCKWORTH, Marilyn

Nationality: New Zealander. **Born:** Marilyn Adcock, Auckland, New Zealand, 10 November 1935. **Education:** Victoria University of Wellington, 1953, 1956. **Family:** Married 1) Harry Duckworth 1955 (dissolved 1964); 2) Ian Macfarlane, 1964 (dissolved 1972); 3) Daniel Donovan, 1974 (died 1978); 4) John Batstone, 1985; four daughters. **Career:** Full-time writer. Has held positions in public relations, nurse aiding, factory work and library work. **Awards:** Scholarship in Letters, 1961, 1972, 1993; New Zealand award for achievement, 1963; Katherine Mansfield fellowship, 1980; New Zealand Book award, 1985, for fiction; Fulbright Visiting Writers fellowship, 1986; Australia New Zealand Exchange fellowship, 1989; Victoria University of Wellington Writers fellowship, 1990; Hawthornden Writers fellowship, Scotland, 1994; Sargeson Writers fellowship, Auckland, 1995. O.B.E. (Officer, Order of the British Empire), 1987. **Member:** New Zealand Society of Authors. **Agent:** Tim Curnow, Curtis Brown (Australia) Pty. Ltd., P.O. Box 19, Paddington, New South Wales 2021, Australia.

Publications

Novels

A Gap in the Spectrum. Auckland, Hutchinson, 1959.
The Matchbox House. London, Hutchinson, 1960; New York, Morrow, 1961.
A Barbarous Tongue. London, Hutchinson, 1963.
Over the Fence Is Out. London, Hutchinson, 1969.
Disorderly Conduct. Auckland, Hodder and Stoughton, 1984.
Married Alive. Auckland, Hodder and Stoughton, 1985.
Rest for the Wicked. Auckland, Hodder and Stoughton, 1986.
Pulling Faces. Auckland, Hodder and Stoughton, 1987.
A Message from Harpo. Auckland, Hodder and Stoughton, 1989.
Unlawful Entry. Auckland, Random Century, 1992.
Seeing Red. Auckland, Random House, 1993.
Leather Wings. Auckland, Random House, 1995.
Studmuffin. N.p. 2000.

Short Stories

Explosions on the Sun. Auckland, Hodder and Stoughton, 1989.
Fooling (novella). Auckland, Hazzard Press, 1994.

Poetry

Other Lovers' Children. Christchurch, New Zealand, Pegasus Press, 1975.

Other

Camping on the Faultline: A Memoir. Auckland, Random House New Zealand, 2000.
Editor, *Cherries on a Plate: New Zealand Writers Talk about Their Sisters.* Auckland, Random House New Zealand, 1996.

*

Marilyn Duckworth comments:

In my fiction I focus on the tension between individuals' need for each other and their need for independence. I'm fascinated by the words and the devices they use to conceal and reveal these needs.

Critic Heather Murray has said of my work that I espouse no ideology and that I refuse to dress my novels in the current colours of political correctness. My characters ''continue to search, perchance to make sense of the existential void in which they haplessly float.''

* * *

During a prolific 40-year career as the writer of 13 novels, short fiction, and poetry, Marilyn Duckworth has written about the plight of ordinary people, particularly women, in an indifferent universe. An early convert to Existentialism, Duckworth shows people adrift in free-falling mode amidst the trivia of daily life: nothing stays the same, the boundaries continually shift. Archetypal character Sophie in *Disorderly Conduct* realizes that her ''disorder'' is life itself:

> What she suffers from is the human condition, no less.... She can expect a succession of bizarre and distressing symptoms. Small disasters, small rejections, dripping like acid onto her nerves and burrowing into her sense of well being. Life is a sexually transmitted terminal disease.

In breaking away from the certainties of the great tradition of the English novel, with its underpinning faith in a benevolent God and an ordered universe, Duckworth was initially misunderstood by critics who believed her characters lacked morality and were impelled by nothing worthier than a shallow animal fortitude. But as she demonstrated in *A Message from Harpo*, once characters realize that there is ''No message,'' they are freed to pursue their own self-determination, a radical humanist and feminist message not often understood by her early readers. To Duckworth, the traditional English novel was male in themes, values, and modes of expression. She prefers to follow Virginia Woolf in seeking a female form of narrative, a code of values, which readers would accept as necessarily different but valid. Inspiration comes also from Muriel Spark's characters, who Duckworth said in a 1960 series of radio talks on women's writing, exude a sense of female normality and completeness: they are ''rarely martyrs, rarely self-pitying, and in spite of their eccentricities appear totally sane.'' Duckworth shows the influence also of Penelope Fitzgerald, who ''has a great deal to say and says it fast and quietly.''

A recent memoir, *Camping on the Faultline* (2000), reveals Duckworth to have experienced a domestic life as full of incident, upheaval, and uncertainty as that of any of her characters. As wife to four husbands, and lover of many others, amidst her role as mother to four and stepmother to three, Duckworth is well placed to write of the unheroic but fraught lives of women at home. The daily round of women barely coping, but searching for some personal vindication of their deep need to find love and independence (usually incompatible), is placed against, and affected by, the upheaval of contemporary societal events or issues, such as the Puritanism and maleness of New Zealand society, feminism, pedophilia, incest, homosexual law reform, gambling, female violence, and HIV/AIDS. Duckworth uses a bare minimum of description and explanation, relying on carefully drawn character and on crisp dialogue; her plots unwind at a brisk speed, usually offering at the end some hope of personal advancement, although not the happiness of knowing that everything is sorted and under control.

Duckworth has been a chronicler of women's lives since the 1950s. In *A Barbarous Tongue*, Frieda, a teenage unmarried mother, still hopes for happiness after a bleak start. Her break for freedom from her inadequate lovers on the final page suggests she will strike out alone with greater confidence, even though she knows that ''only children expect to be happy.'' As women have been engaged in redefining their status in society, claiming the right to a life of their own and to enjoy sex, so changing gender roles occupy a recurring place in Duckworth's novels. Children suddenly deprived of parents through death or desertion, the power games of siblings, incest, female refusal to mother and nurture, gender swapping and homosexuality, all provide tension and constitute traps for the unwary. In *Seeing Red*, Duckworth examines destructive family ties and female violence (not endearing herself to feminist readers). *Pulling Faces* transposes the traditional roles of man as leader and woman as dependent follower: in a tragi-comic love story that combines science fiction and social satire with the thriller genre, Stuart tries to bind elusive Gwyn in a conventional union. Towing her caravan wherever she likes, she eludes her mother and child, and Stuart; she alters her mind with drugs, and is ultra-secretive about her movements, playing childhood games of pulling faces to disguise self. Ironically she uses a machine to try to bind others to her by capturing their thoughts on videotape. Women are as prone to power complexes as the traditional male, and if communication exists only via computer, Utopia is a long way off.

Disorderly Conduct, Unlawful Entry, and *A Message from Harpo* are sophisticated studies of women as daughters, wives, and mothers. Duckworth is skilled at creating believable families and is particularly good at their intimate conversations. Aging mothers entrap and manipulate the young, but are often redeemed by some residual nobility. Children devour the strength of mothers with selfish demands, but are saved from monsterhood by honesty and disarming acts of kindness.

In the novella *Fooling*, Ros feels the strain of her independence (hard won by earlier generations of Duckworth women): ''A woman of the nineties is expected to want control of her life—but not necessarily self-control—to be centred and self-sufficient, but not, of course, self-centred. It isn't easy.'' Ros is honest in an age when everyone else is fooling. She wants to find love, but her hopes of finding lasting happiness are fading: ''Ros, you're going to have to grow up one day. You're 28 years old—aren't you?—and this is the real world. The freaky old real world.''

In *Leather Wings*, female independence has transmuted into selfishness. No one will put aside self to care for and love 6-year-old Jania, whose mother has recently died. Her father wallows in self-pity, sending Jania to her grandparents, but grandfather is preoccupied and introverted by decrepitude, and grandmother is too busy juggling her job, a lover, and the Mills & Boon novel she is writing. To fill the void, a pedophile door-to-door salesman steps in, providing threat, tension, and suspense. Duckworth shows feeling for the tragedy of pedophilia, as the simple Warren fails to understand the feelings that grip him so violently, and she is percipient in this complex study of hard-won female independence, showing that putting self first leads to failure to care for those who should be loved and cherished. What is the answer for women?

Studmuffin is a modern reworking of the Alice-in-Wonderland story, using magic realism, and looking to a future when humans lose the power of speech, either through destroying their brains by drugs, or through the power of a mad mind controller. Alice, a career girl, slips through the looking glass with her newly acquired ''white rabbit,'' an unhappily married albino accountant from her place of work, and they sail to a magic island that is in the grip of a nineties Mad Hatter who enslaves his community and destroys their power of speech and memory. Meanwhile in London, Alice's sister destroys her own speech and addles her mind with drugs. In the most optimistic end to a Duckworth novel yet, Alice and the albino escape after gothic adventures. Both find love: ''I love, therefore I am,'' says Alice as she rows back to the ''real world.''

—Heather Murray

DUFF, Alan

Nationality: New Zealander. **Born:** Rotorua, 26 October 1950. **Education:** Two years of high school. **Family:** Married Joanna Harper; two sons and three daughters. **Awards:** PEN Best First Book award, 1991; best screenplay, for *What Becomes of the Broken Hearted?*, New Zealand Film Awards, 1999. **Agent:** William Morris Agency, 1350 Avenue of the Americas, New York, New York 10019, U.S.A.

Publications

Novels

Once Were Warriors. Auckland, Tandem Press, 1990; Honolulu, University of Hawaii Press, 1994; London, Random House, 1995.
One Night Out Stealing. Auckland, Tandem Press, 1991; Honolulu, University of Hawaii Press, 1992.
State Ward. Auckland, Vintage, 1994.
What Becomes of the Broken Hearted? Auckland, Vintage, 1996.
Both Sides of the Moon. Auckland, Vintage, 1998.

Other

Maori: The Crisis and the Challenge. Auckland, HarperCollins, 1993.
Out of the Mist and Steam: A Memoir. Auckland, Tandem Press, 1999.

*

Film Adaptations: *Once Were Warriors*, 1994.

Critical Studies: *Writing along Broken Lines: Violence and Ethnicity in Contemporary Maori Fiction* by Otto Heim. Auckland, Auckland University Press, 1998.

Alan Duff comments:

Main influence: Contemporary American, Faulkner, Selby Jr., Doctorow, Gurganis, Styron.

* * *

Alan Duff is the enfant terrible of contemporary Maori writers. Like Witi Ihimaera and Patricia Grace, he focuses on the debilitating effect urban life has had on Maori. But the violent, drunken underworld of *Once Were Warriors* and *One Night Out Stealing* makes the cityscapes of Grace and Ihimaera look positively genteel.

Duff's formula for resolving the problems of the urban Maori likewise contrasts very sharply with the emphasis on traditional communal values in most Maori writing. In his syndicated newspaper articles, his autobiography (*Out of the Mist and Steam*), and his book-length survey of Maoridom (*Maori: The Crisis and the Challenge*), he has stressed the need for Maori to embrace orthodox Western education and an ethic of self-knowledge and self-help. Putting into practice the dreams of Beth Heke (in the opening pages of *Once Were Warriors*) and Tekapo (in the closing pages of *Both Sides of the Moon*), Duff has personally instigated a successful campaign to get books into every underprivileged Maori household. Conversely, he is wont to express contempt for many aspects of traditional Maori culture—though there have been signs recently of some softening in his attitudes.

In the early novels, Duff's politically incorrect views are implied by Grace Heke's excursions from her Pine Block ghetto to gaze on the plush Trambert house in *Once Were Warriors* and by Sonny's awed inspection of the Harland mansion in *One Night Out Stealing*. Typically Duff exaggerates the gap between these two worlds. The Harlands and the Tramberts, with their love of fine music, art, and furniture, are extreme examples of Pakeha patrician taste, and the account of the deep impression that their culture—especially their music—makes on the deprived Maori onlookers gets dangerously close to sentimentality.

Pakeha are not, however, depicted entirely uncritically in Duff's work. The men, in particular, have their shortcomings, ranging from Mr. Harland's penchant for pornographic pictures to the outright pedophilia of Mr. Dekka in *State Ward*. In *What Becomes of the Broken Hearted?* we learn of the moral and economic decay that underlies the splendid Trambert veneer. And in *One Night Out Stealing* the hardened recidivist, Jube McCall, is a Pakeha, while his softer sidekick, Sonny Mahia, is Maori.

In fact, *Once Were Warriors* does eventually grope towards a specifically Maori solution to the Maori problems that it illustrates so graphically—solutions that are ultimately much closer to the communal ethic proposed by Ihimaera, Grace, and others than Duff the journalist would probably care to admit. Towards the end of the book Beth reestablishes contact with her marae, in the countryside just outside Twin Lakes, the city where *Once Were Warriors*—like most of Duff's other novels—is set. (Twin Lakes is a fictional version not of Auckland—where the film of *Once Were Warriors* is set—but of Rotorua, the city where Duff himself grew up.) The funeral of Beth's daughter Grace takes place on this marae, presided over by ''the paramount chief of the tribe,'' Te Tupaea. And a little later, after Beth has succeeded in throwing her aggressive husband Jake out of the house, she brings to town ''a village committee,'' including Te Tupaea, to help her reestablish a sense of purpose among the Maori of the Pine Block ghetto.

On the one hand, Beth's ''project'' is a very practical one; she attempts to wean her people away from their reliance on state funding (notably the unemployment benefit) and to foster instead the spirit of ''self-help'' that Duff the journalist preaches. So, for example, she organizes the building of ''a changing room and shower block'' for a ''newly ploughed and sown rugby field'' conveniently donated by the benevolent Trambert family. On the other hand, all this practical ''self-help'' is underpinned by a strong dedication to traditional Maori culture, with the more aggressive aspects of that culture (the ''warrior''—or, as some historians term it, ''Red Maori''—heritage, particularly as exemplified in the haka) receiving special emphasis. So in the end the novel tentatively embraces a kind of primitivism, albeit a harder form of primitivism than the ''Green Maori'' version preferred by Ihimaera and Grace.

In fact it is not always easy to distinguish between the admirable aggression of the traditional ''warriors'' and the degenerate aggression of Jake Heke and his drunken mates. This confusion becomes particularly troubling in the final pages of the book, where scenes from Beth's ''project'' alternate with scenes from the last days in the life of Beth's son Nig, who has joined a Maori gang (the Brown Fists). The gang violence is presumably meant to act as a foil for the noble primitivism of the haka, but it is hard not to sense a kinship between the two. The film of *Once Were Warriors* actually seemed to some to present the gang in a positive light.

Meanwhile, in the background, the exiled Jake Heke, growing wiser as he lives rough and consorts with other down-and-outs, looks like a more realistic hope for the future. As a detached observer of Maori culture he actually occupies a position somewhat similar to Duff's own. Sure enough, in the sequel (*What Becomes of the Broken Hearted?*) Jake, guided by his new partner Rita, begins to adopt middle-class values: he finds work, takes up rugby and pig-shooting, and even becomes house-proud. Similarly, Beth's new partner, Charlie Bennett (a social worker), teaches her the importance of self-reliance. Even Mulla, a senior member of the Brown Fists gang, yearns for a better life.

One Night Out Stealing is less concerned with traditional Maori culture, but *State Ward* is built around the kind of liberating journey from city to country that features in the work of many Maori authors. George, a native Maori speaker, helps Charlie to escape from Riverton Boys' Home, where they have both been confined, and takes him back—not to Charlie's home in Twin Lakes, but to the Maori heartland of Ruapotiki (evidently a place not far away from the Waituhi of Ihimaera's fiction). Here George burns down the house haunted by the evil spirit (kehua) that has dogged his career hitherto, and celebrates the pair's ''freedom''—freedom to adopt Pakeha values perhaps?

In *Both Sides of the Moon* (the most autobiographical of the novels) Duff attempts—almost too explicitly—to clarify his view of the proper relationship between Maori and Pakeha values. The story of Jimmy, growing up half-Maori, half-Pakeha in present-day Twin Lakes runs parallel to a tale of his Maori ancestors around the beginning of the nineteenth century. While, in the present, Jimmy fumbles towards his father's Pakeha ethic of self-reliance, his ancestors' ''Red Maori'' culture (awful, in both senses of that word) splits, under the pressure of European colonialism, into two strands: a ''gang'' mentality intent on ''immediate satisfaction'' and a ''thinking'' approach to the new Pakeha ways that recognizes (among other things) the value of books. While *Once Were Warriors* hedged its bets on the issue, *Both Sides of the Moon* clearly argues that there is no longer—if indeed there ever was—any place for the old ''warrior'' culture.

To convey the tough concerns of his novels, Duff has developed a strikingly idiomatic and hard-hitting form of interior monologue that, at its best (in *One Night Out Stealing*, for example) is flexible enough to accommodate varying states of inebriation and drug use in the characters. His energy often leads to excess; critics have complained of his ''tendency to hector the reader'' and to use ''a vocabulary that would normally be out of the reach of his linguistically impoverished characters,'' and the purple prose of *Both Sides of the Moon* is sometimes almost indecipherable. *State Ward*, on the other hand, is generally regarded as Duff's weakest novel because of its departure from his customary in-your-face style. There are, however, two good reasons for this: the book deals with younger characters than its predecessors, and it was originally written to be read on radio, which requires a readily accessible idiom.

—Richard Corballis

DUFFY, Maureen (Patricia)

Nationality: British. **Born:** Worthing, Sussex, 21 October 1933. **Education:** Trowbridge High School for Girls, Wiltshire; Sarah Bonnell High School for Girls; King's College, London, 1953–56, B.A. (honours) in English 1956. **Career:** Schoolteacher for five years. Co-founder, Writers Action Group, 1972; joint chair, 1977–78, and president, 1985–89, Writers Guild of Great Britain; chair, Greater London Arts Literature Panel, 1979–81; vice-chair, 1981–86, and since 1989 chair, British Copyright Council; since 1982 chair, Authors Lending and Copyright Society; vice-president, Beauty Without Cruelty; fiction editor *Critical Quarterly,* Manchester, 1987; since 1992 vice-president, European Writers Congress. **Awards:** City of London Festival Playwright's prize, 1962; Arts Council bursary, 1963, 1966, 1975; Society of Authors travelling scholarship, 1976. Fellow, Royal Society of Literature, 1985. **Agent:** Jonathan Clowes Ltd., Ironbridge House, Bridge Approach, London NW1 8BD. **Address:** 18 Fabian Road, London SW6 7TZ, England.

Publications

Novels

That's How It Was. London, Hutchinson, 1962; New York, Dial Press, 1984.
The Single Eye. London, Hutchinson, 1964.
The Microcosm. London, Hutchinson, and New York, Simon and Schuster, 1966.
The Paradox Players. London, Hutchinson, 1967; New York, Simon and Schuster, 1968.
Wounds. London, Hutchinson, and New York, Knopf, 1969.
Love Child. London, Weidenfeld and Nicolson, and New York, Knopf, 1971.
I Want to Go to Moscow: A Lay. London, Hodder and Stoughton, 1973; as *All Heaven in a Rage,* New York, Knopf, 1973.
Capital. London, Cape, 1975; New York, Braziller, 1976.
Housespy. London, Hamish Hamilton, 1978.
Gor Saga. London, Eyre Methuen, 1981; New York, Viking Press, 1982.
Scarborough Fear (as D.M. Cayer). London, Macdonald, 1982.
Londoners: An Elegy. London, Methuen, 1983.
Change. London, Methuen, 1987.
Illuminations. London, Sinclair Stevenson, 1991.
Occam's Razor. London, Sinclair Stevenson, 1993.
Restitution. London, Fourth Estate, 1998.

Plays

The Lay-Off (produced London, 1962).
The Silk Room (produced Watford, Hertfordshire, 1966).
Rites (produced London, 1969). Published in *New Short Plays 2,* London, Methuen, 1969.
Solo, Old Thyme (produced Cambridge, 1970).
A Nightingale in Bloomsbury Square (produced London, 1973). Published in *Factions,* edited by Giles Gordon and Alex Hamilton, London, Joseph, 1974.

Radio Play: *Only Goodnight,* 1981.

Television Play: *Josie,* 1961.

Poetry

Lyrics for the Dog Hour. London, Hutchinson, 1968.
The Venus Touch. London, Weidenfeld and Nicolson, 1971.
Actaeon. Rushden, Northamptonshire, Sceptre Press, 1973.
Evesong. London, Sappho, 1975.
Memorials of the Quick and the Dead. London, Hamish Hamilton, 1979.
Collected Poems. London, Hamish Hamilton, 1985.

Other

The Erotic World of Faery. London, Hodder and Stoughton, 1972.
The Passionate Shepherdess: Aphra Behn 1640–1689. London, Cape, 1977; New York, Avon, 1979.
Inherit the Earth: A Social History. London, Hamish Hamilton, 1980.
Men and Beasts: An Animal Rights Handbook. London, Paladin, 1984.
A Thousand Capricious Chances: A History of the Methuen List 1889–1989. London, Methuen, 1989.
Henry Purcell. London, Fourth Estate, 1994.
Editor, with Alan Brownjohn, *New Poetry 3.* London, Arts Council, 1977.
Editor, *Oroonoko and Other Stories,* by Aphra Behn. London, Methuen, 1986.
Editor, *Love Letters Between a Nobleman and His Sister,* by Aphra Behn. London, Virago Press, 1987.
Editor, *Five Plays,* by Aphra Behn. London, Methuen, 1990.
Translator, *A Blush of Shame,* by Domenico Rea. London, Barrie and Rockliff, 1968.

*

Manuscript Collection: King's College, University of London.

Critical Study: *A Female Vision of the City* by Christine Sizemore, Knoxville, University of Tennessee Press, 1989.

* * *

Maureen Duffy is a prolific novelist, poet, and playwright whose work has consistently developed in range and importance. *That's How It Was* won her immediate acclaim for its simplicity and forcefulness. It is a moving account of the relationship between a mother and daughter; their existence is poor, insecure, even brutal, but transcended by mutual love. ''I grew six inches under the light touch of her hand,'' explains the narrator. The little girl has an acute sense of social isolation and a fierce loyalty to the one constant figure in her universe; her mother's death is thus cause for more than grief, it brings total despair. The loneliness, restlessness, and sexual hunger which spring from the situation are the dominating themes of each subsequent novel.

Realism is the touchstone of Duffy's style; like many other observers of working-class life, she is at her best when she relies on accurate, detailed reportage and at her weakest when tempted by sentiment. *The Paradox Players* is an example of her writing at its most compelling. It describes a man's retreat from society to live for some months in a boat moored on the Thames. The physical realities of cold, snow, rats, and flooding occupy him continually and the hardship brings him peace. He is a novelist, suffering from the hazards peculiar to that profession and has some pertinent comments to make about the vulnerability of the writer. ''When I saw the reviews I could have cut my throat. You see they're very kind to first novels for some mistaken reason but when the poor bastard follows it up with a second and they see he really means it they tear its guts out.'' The experience of winter on the river restores his faith in his own ability to survive.

Duffy's observations are acute, her use of dialogue witty and direct; this authenticity is complemented by an interest in the bizarre, the fantastic. Her best-known book uses these qualities to great effect in a study of lesbian society which is both informative and original. *The Microcosm* begins and ends in a club where the central characters meet to dance, dress up, and escape from the necessity of ''all the week wearing a false face.'' Their fantasies are played out in front of the juke box; then the narrative follows each woman back into her disguise, her social role. Steve is Miss Stephens, a schoolmistress; Cathy is a bus conductress; Matt works in a garage. Their predicament as individuals, the author suggests, extends beyond the interest of their own minority group. A plea is made for tolerance, understanding, and that respect without which the human spirit must perish. ''Society isn't a simple organism with one nucleus and a fringe of little feet, it's an infinitely complex structure and if you try to suppress any part … you diminish, you mutilate the whole.'' *Wounds* and *Love Child* reaffirm this belief.

In *Illuminations,* a retired professor journeys through post-Cold War Germany, and there finds not only a lesbian lover, but a counterpart of sorts in the person of Tetta, an eighth-century nun. Eventually she sees her own world as a reflection of Carolingian Europe. *Occam's Razor,* too, dwells on a historical parallel, but not one involving William of Ockham (sometimes rendered as Occam), the fourteenth-century philosopher who helped bring an end to medieval dogmatism; here, instead, Duffy draws a line between the old (c. 1916) and the latter-day IRA, and between these and the Mafia.

—Judy Cooke

DUNDY, Elaine

Nationality: American. **Born:** New York City, 1927. **Education:** Sweet Briar College, Virginia. **Family:** Married the writer Kenneth Tynan in 1951 (marriage dissolved 1964); one daughter. **Career:** Actress; worked for the BBC, London; directed the Winter Workshop of the Berkshire Festival; also journalist. **Agent:** Andrew Hewson, John Johnson Ltd., 45–47 Clerkenwell Green, London EC1R 0HT, England.

PUBLICATIONS

Novels

The Dud Avocado. London, Gollancz, and New York, Dutton, 1958.
The Old Man and Me. London, Gollancz, and New York, Dutton, 1964.
The Injured Party. London, Joseph, 1974.

Uncollected Short Stories

''The Sound of a Marriage,'' in *Queen* (London), 1965.
''Death in the Country,'' in *Vogue* (New York), 1974.

Plays

My Place (produced London, 1962). London, Gollancz, 1962; New York, French, 1963.
Death in the Country, and The Drowning (produced New York, 1976).

Screenplay: *Life Sign,* 1975.

Other

Finch, Bloody Finch. London, Joseph, and New York, Holt Rinehart, 1980.
Elvis and Gladys: The Genesis of the King. New York, Macmillan, and London, Weidenfeld and Nicolson, 1985.
Ferriday, Louisiana. New York, Fine, 1990.

* * *

In *The Dud Avocado* and *The Old Man and Me,* Elaine Dundy employs first-person, reflective narrators who self-consciously and self-indulgently record and evaluate their experiences in Paris and Soho. The narrators relate their stories in a candid, energetic, witty style, spiced with parenthetical revelations, word association games, and sensory impressions. Their language is often the jargon of the Beat-hipster; audacious, flippant, nervous, saucy. Their tone is the good-humored self-mockery of the cocktail party confession, the stage whisper, the open diary. The narrators are deliberate storytellers, replaying moments from their pasts, exposing their naivety and limitations, and benefiting from hindsight.

Sally Jay in *The Dud Avocado* is the contemporary American innocent abroad, superficially hip to the decadent Left Bank and ''running for her life.'' Caught in the ambiguity between naivety and sophistication, she is in pursuit of ''freedom'' and the ability ''to be so sharp that I'll always be able to guess right … on the wing.'' She expends her time and innocence in a disorganized, impulsive debauch with the avant-garde of Paris.

Through a series of wrong guesses, she eventually is schooled in the ways of the world. The glamorous, daring, free world of Paris is revealed as pretentious, opportunistic, grotesque. Her romantic vision of the rebellious life is destroyed when she understands that her would-be lover is a pimp and that her life in Paris has exposed her to ''too much prostitution.'' She declares herself a dud avocado—a seed without life potential.

In flight to Hollywood, the narrator confronts her runaway life strategy and determines that some ''unrunning'' is called for to ''[lay] the ghost once and for all.'' She seeks out the role of librarian and schools herself in cynicism until she recognizes the life which she wishes to embrace. Giddy with optimism, she accepts the love and marriage proposal of a famous photographer and embarks on a new life with ''an entirely new passport,'' the new self emerging from the old like the growth of an avocado seedling from the stone of the old fruit: ''It's zymotic!'' The narrator survives her initiation experience ready to ''Make voyages. Attempt them. That's all there is.''

Betsy Lou in *The Old Man and Me* is older and more experienced than Sally Jay, but like Sally Jay, she is on a quest which leads to greater self-knowledge. Motivated by puerile revenge, she journeys to London to recover her ''stolen'' inheritance from C.D. McKee. As his unknown heir, she plans to hasten the recovery of her money by any means necessary—lying, cheating, masquerading, or attempting murder. She partially achieves her declared end, and in the process realizes her injustice to those in her past, the reasons for the loss of her father's love, and her love for C.D. despite his age and possession of her money. Thus she corrects her mistaken view of her past and sees the futility of trying to salve emotional loss with money.

Betsy Lou's relationship to C.D. is never linear and controllable. The very complexity of the relationship betrays her ambiguity over her past, her present motives, and her unconscious needs. She loves/hates him, recognizes that he is/is not a father figure, accepts/rejects him as teacher, is repulsed/excited by his lust, and wishes him dead/fears for his life. This confusion drives her to abandonment in jazz, drink, dope, and sex, which results in C.D.'s collapse and her self-confrontation and confession.

Betsy Lou's declaration of her identity, her deceit, and her desire for C.D. comes too late. He rejects the contrite Betsy Lou, gives her fifty percent of her money, and leaves her with the advice that she ''use it. See its power to corrupt or save .... Learn from our stupidities.'' She is left with what she initially wanted ''only ... because it was mine.''

In both novels the narrators are left at the point of departure. For Sally Jay the future appears glorious with possibility. She sees her new life as ''the end. The end. The last word.'' However, the author implies that Sally Jay has ended one cycle of learning experiences and is beginning another with her marriage. One is reminded of Stefan's description of the Typical American Girl as the avocado, ''So green—so eternally green.'' She has experienced growth and is more worldly wise, but her final pronouncement indicates that her maturation is not complete. The process has just begun. Similarly, Betsy Lou is left facing her future. She hasn't Sally Jay's confidence of joy, but rather experiences a sense of unreality. She has no delusions about the future, and the past ''seems (to) never really (have) happened.'' She is no longer directed by spurious monetary goals; instead she suffers the bewilderment of a hollow victory. Thus, while both narrators experience an epiphany, that moment of awareness is tinged with irony.

Dundy is an entertaining novelist who rehearses the familiar theme of initiation with adeptness and flair. However, her craftsmanship and energy do not always compensate for her characters' lack of psychological depth nor for her rather formulaic situations. Her novels do not provoke new or refined insights, but they do provide moments of engaging and refreshing humor.

—Deborah Duckworth

DUNN, Nell (Mary)

Nationality: British. **Born:** London in 1936. **Education:** A convent school. **Family:** Married the writer Jeremy Sandford in 1956 (marriage dissolved); three sons. **Awards:** Rhys Memorial prize, 1964; Susan Smith Blackburn prize, for play, 1981; *Evening Standard* award, for play, 1982; Society of West End Theatre award, 1982. **Agent:** Curtis Brown, 162–168 Regent Street, London W1R 5TB.

PUBLICATIONS

Novels

Poor Cow. London, MacGibbon and Kee, and New York, Doubleday, 1967.
The Incurable. London, Cape, and New York, Doubleday, 1971.
I Want, with Adrian Henri. London, Cape, 1972.
Tear His Head Off His Shoulders. London, Cape, 1974; New York, Doubleday, 1975.
The Only Child: A Simple Story of Heaven and Hell. London, Cape, 1978.
My Silver Shoes. London, Bloomsbury, 1996.

Short Stories

Up the Junction. London, MacGibbon and Kee, 1963; Philadelphia, Lippincott, 1966; with drawings by Susan Benson, Washinton, D.C., Counterpoint, 2000.

Plays

Steaming (produced London, 1981; Stamford, Connecticut, and New York, 1982). Ambergate, Derbyshire, Amber Lane Press, 1981; New York, Limelight, 1984.
Sketches in *Variety Night* (produced London, 1982).
I Want, with Adrian Henri, adaptation of their own novel (produced Liverpool, 1983; London, 1986).
The Little Heroine (produced Southampton, 1988).

Screenplay: *Poor Cow,* with Ken Loach, 1967.

Television Plays: *Up the Junction,* from her own stories, 1965; *Every Breath You Take,* 1988.

Other

Talking to Women. London, MacGibbon and Kee, 1965.
Freddy Gets Married (for children). London, MacGibbon and Kee, 1969.
Grandmothers Talking to Nell Dunn. London, Chatto and Windus, 1991.
Editor, *Living Like I Do.* London, Futura, 1977; as *Different Drummers,* New York, Harcourt Brace, 1977.

* * *

Nell Dunn begins with vignettes or fragmental episodes to build a picture of British urban life. Much like Charles Dickens, with his newspaper sketches and small portraits of London street life, she began her career with a set of brilliant realistic snapshots of the mod world. In *Up the Junction* she collected these sketches, which in effect are much like the 17th-century Theophrastan ''character.'' They deal primarily with young working-class Britons in their milieu, incised in photographic reportage, built on their dialect, street signs, bits of popular music, the clichés and repetitious folk-wisdom of ghetto life. The feeling for the nagging, obstinate details of daily life is very strong—the sketches demonstrate how complex yet unrewarding most of these lives can be.

In *Poor Cow* Dunn develops the same method of terse, richly detailed sketches into a more unified form, a novel centering on the life of one young woman. Ironically named Joy, she becomes a ''poor cow'' through the constant erosion of her life. At 22 she has gone through one luckless marriage, and her life moves centrifugally around Jonny, her son. Joy drifts into casual prostitution, random affairs with anchorless men. She worries constantly about her looks, her body, her sexual responsiveness, the prospects of aging. Life is intractable, and wishes evaporate in the face of simple necessities. Joy's role as a mother is a transference of her egocentrism to Jonny, as an extension of her former hopes for herself. Her own life has run down a blind alley, but her son's life may be different. As she clings to Jonny, Joy invents a bitter epitaph for her youth: ''To think when I was a kid I planned to conquer the world and if anyone saw me now they'd say, 'She's had a rough night, poor cow.'''

A vision of the confusion and oppressiveness of modern life is extended in *The Incurable,* which deals with a middle-class woman, Maro, whose life collapses in crisis. Maro's husband develops multiple sclerosis, and her formerly orderly and manageable existence is destroyed. She falls into a state of anomie which, like her husband's progressive disease, eats up her life. She too is ''incurable,'' although her malaise is mental and spiritual. Her children's cannibalistic demands and the relentless pressure of everyday routine erode her will and energy: ''She felt like some country that had been oppressed for a long time and was slowly rising up and throwing over its oppressors. She was making a revolution but the bloodshed was horrifying and how many lives would be lost and when was it going to end and would she ever make the country of the free spirits?''

Tear His Head Off His Shoulders is another set of related vignettes and episodes in the lives of women. The narrative revolves around the sexual obsessions and conflicts of women, viewed in retrospect. The vernacular style and complex combination of nostalgia and revulsion give a bittersweet flavor to the work. A strong ''fascination of the abomination'' feeling makes the stories of sexual compulsion convincing.

In *The Only Child* Dunn constructs a novel again focused on sexual obsession and possessiveness—of a mother for her son. We follow Esther Lafonte through Dunn's careful sensual details as she drifts from her over-comfortable marriage to a search for her identity—sexual and spiritual—in her 19-year-old son, Piers. At one point she speaks for all of Dunn's lost women: ''I want to get in, I want to be somebody, I have a feeling that I could have done very much more with my life, that I could be doing more now, I want to be a part of things.''

Dunn's special province is the mind and spirit of the beleaguered woman—a view from the ''oppressed country'' of the woman trapped by circumstances. The vignettes she presents deal with developing sexuality, the allure of the pop world, the deadly immobility of domestic responsibilities. Her later fiction extends this vision to the perimeters of middle-class life.

—William J. Schafer

DUNNE, John Gregory

Nationality: American. **Born:** Hartford, Connecticut, 25 May 1932. **Education:** Princeton University, New Jersey, A.B. in English 1954. Married Joan Didion, *q.v.,* in 1964; one daughter. **Career:** Staff writer, *Time,* New York, 5 years; columnist (''Points West''), with Didion, *Saturday Evening Post,* Philadelphia, 1967–69; regular contributor, *Esquire* and the *New York Review of Books.* **Agent:** Janklow and Nesbit, 598 Madison Ave., New York, New York 10022, U.S.A.

Publications

Novels

Vegas: A Memoir of a Dark Season. New York, Random House, and London, Quartet, 1974.
True Confessions. New York, Dutton, 1977; London, Weidenfeld and Nicolson, 1978.
Dutch Shea, Jr. New York, Simon and Schuster, and London, Weidenfeld and Nicolson, 1982.
The Red, White and Blue. New York, Simon and Schuster, and London, Weidenfeld and Nicolson, 1987.
Playland. New York, Random House, 1994; London, Granta, 1995.

Plays

Screenplays (with Joan Didion): *Panic in Needle Park,* 1971; *Play It as It Lays,* 1972; *A Star Is Born,* also with Frank Pierson, 1976; *True Confessions,* 1981; *Hills Like White Elephants,* 1992; *Broken Trust,* 1995; *Up Close and Personal,* 1995.

Other

Delano: The Story of the California Grape Strike, photographs by Ted Streshinsky. New York, Farrar Straus, 1967; revised edition, 1971.
The Studio. New York, Farrar Straus, 1967; London, W.H. Allen, 1970; New York, Vintage Books, 1998.
Quintana and Friends (essays). New York, Dutton, 1978.
Harp. New York, Simon and Schuster, 1989.
Crooning. New York, Simon and Schuster, 1991.
L.A. Is It with John Gregory Dunne (television program). Kingfish Video Productions/WNET-13, New York, 1991.
Monster: Living off the Big Screen. New York, Random House, 1997.

* * *

His wife and sometime collaborator, Joan Didion, is undoubtedly better known than he, but John Gregory Dunne certainly deserves a measure of critical attention. Like his wife he has carved out a successful career as a versatile writer.

In addition to novels he has written essays, articles, columns, and books of contemporary journalism that combine objective observation with a generous quantity of personal display, confession, and self analysis. Whatever his subject, method, or venue of publication, he generally returns over and over again to his family history, financial standing, and ethnic and religious background: Hartford, Connecticut, apparently prosperous, middle-class, Irish Catholic.

The numerous essays, articles, and columns, (the early ones written with his wife), cover a large range of subjects that challenge the writer not only eager to speak his mind, but also desperate to meet deadlines and make an honest buck; many of them, nevertheless, are penetrating, intelligent, and informative. Luckily, Dunne has strong opinions on a great many subjects and can communicate those opinions clearly, forcefully, and often humorously; he has a keen eye for sham and hypocrisy and a constructive sense of rage and outrage. His early columns tend to reflect something of the sweet haze of the 1960s, but the later ones show a more characteristic tone of weary, cynical anger creeping into his voice.

In one of the most useful books about the business of making movies, *The Studio,* Dunne provides not only important information but also a valuable corrective to the highflown nonsense of film theorists and critics about the art of film.

Dunne's very personal confessional style surfaces most obviously in *Vegas,* the record of his recovery from a nervous breakdown, a subject roughly akin to Melville's Great White Whale for contemporary writers, and in *Harp,* an impressionistic memoir that begins with a brother's suicide, chronicles a number of deaths in his family, and culminates in his own cardio-vascular troubles. Because it also discusses other matters, including some of the fascinating processes of the author's own methods, it is actually somewhat more interesting than it sounds. For the son of a Hartford surgeon who attended private schools and graduated from Princeton, Dunne rather overdoes the Studs Lonigan role; for readers from the working class, he hardly seems the rough diamond of the tough, impoverished Irish ghetto. In *Harp* the generative narcissism of any writer finally gives way to the self pity of a poseur.

His novels clearly benefit from his journalism, since they also turn on the same subjects that engage his nonfiction, exploring with a good deal more energy and bite contemporary American politics and public behavior and the variousness of Irish American life. *True Confessions, Dutch Shea, Jr.,* and *The Red, White and Blue* reflect that variousness with some of the sensitivity and accuracy of a novelist of manners in the mold of John O'Hara. They constitute a contemporary trilogy that in this case perhaps really does deserve comparison with James T. Farrell's monumental *Studs Lonigan;* certainly Dunne seems to be the only American writer, except for Norman Mailer, still concerned with the Irish experience.

Dunne himself has stated that the three books attempt to show some of the history of the levels, from working class to upper class, that the Irish inhabit in America and how they have fared in this century. As a result, they concern themselves with historical events, from a famous murder case to national politics, in the public arena, while examining the lives and fortunes of some particular families. They also examine the traditional figures of Irish American life, literature, and cinema—policemen, priests, and politicians. In the process, his books touch on some of the major public events of the last 50 years.

True Confessions is based on the notorious unsolved Black Dahlia murder case of the 1940s, and uses one of those brother combinations of 1930s movies—Tom Spellacy, a detective, and Desmond, a priest. The fascinating murder investigation opens up a complicated tangle of religion, politics, and corruption in Los Angeles, a story told in the tough, cynical, funny, and wised-up manner of traditional American gangster and detective fiction. It is a brilliant, moving, and heartfelt performance, far superior to anything else Dunne has written. Less successful, *Dutch Shea, Jr.* revolves around the personal and public tragedy of a criminal lawyer's loss of his daughter, coyly hinting at but holding off the completion of its haunting and horrific background subject. Like *True Confessions,* however, the book handles its characters and especially its dialogue with considerable skill and confidence; it addresses, sometimes with defensive humor, the daily curse of criminality and the horrors of terrorism. The third volume of the trilogy, *The Red, White and Blue* reads at times like a *roman à clef* based on the history of some of the most successful Irish families in America, which of course means the Kellys and the Kennedys. With considerable ambition, the book takes aim at the all too familiar hypocrisy, horror, and tragedy of the waning decades of the 20th century—the culpability of politicians, the waste of war, the conspiracies of the media. This novel repeats the cynicism of the first two, but goes far beyond, to achieve a tone and a conclusion of utter despair, which though appropriate to its subject may signal the depths of the author's own reaction to contemporary American life.

Dunne's ethnicity, worn like a flag, seems somewhat anachronistic in a time when his fellow Irish Americans have practically become WASPs. At the same time, it has generated three good novels, some autobiographical writing, and numerous articles and essays, which means the concept remains useful to the writer, a notion that automatically endows it with meaning and value. The subject may no longer possess its former richness, however, and the author may have to look elsewhere. He may have now reached something of a crossroads in his career.

His bestselling novels and several screenplays have enabled him to enjoy some of the material rewards of the literary life that elude so many other writers, but like so many successful people in any field of endeavor, he has begun to question the importance and validity of his success. His new awareness of his own mortality, the serial losses of a number of loved ones, his own inherent cynicism, and perhaps even a certain Irish bitterness and melancholy have induced a gloom that his wisecracking cannot lighten.

The close relationship between fiction and fact in Dunne's work is amply illustrated by several of his offerings from the mid-1990s. In *Up Close and Personal,* cowriters Dunne and Didion set out to profile the tragic career of 1970s anchorwoman Jessica Savitch, but instead created a romance that provided an onscreen vehicle for stars Michelle Pfeiffer and Robert Redford. *Playland,* Dunne's sole novel from the period, is a satire that centers around child actress ''Baby Blue Tyler, Hollywood's number-one cinemoppet.'' *Monster: Living off the Big Screen* provides a behind-the-scenes look at how a story becomes a movie—and the story just happened to be *Up Close and Personal.*

—George Grella

DUNNETT, (Lady) Dorothy

Nationality: British. **Born:** Dorothy Halliday in Dunfermline, Fife, 25 August 1923. **Education:** James Gillespie's High School, Edinburgh; Edinburgh College of Art; Glasgow School of Art. **Family:** Married Alastair (later Sir Alastair) M. Dunnett in 1946; two sons. **Career:** Assistant press officer, Scottish government departments, Edinburgh, 1940–46; member of the Board of Trade Scottish Economics Department, Glasgow, 1946–55; non-executive director, Scottish Television plc, Glasgow, 1979–92. Since 1950 professional portrait painter; since 1986 trustee, National Library of Scotland; since 1990 a direcctor of the Edinburgh Book Festival. **Awards:** Scottish Arts Council award, 1976; St. Andrews Presbyterian College award, Laurinburg, North Carolina, 1993. Fellow, Royal Society of

Arts, 1986. **Agent:** Curtis Brown, 162–168 Regent Street, London W1R 5TB, England. **Address:** 87 Colinton Road, Edinburgh EH10 5DF, Scotland.

PUBLICATIONS

Novels (Dolly books prior to *Bird of Paradise* published as Dorothy Halliday in UK)

The Game of Kings. New York, Putnam, 1961; London, Cassell, 1962; New York, Vintage, 1997.
Queens' Play. London, Cassell, and New York, Putnam, 1964; New York, Vintage, 1997.
The Disorderly Knights. London, Cassell, and New York, Putnam, 1966; New York, Vintage, 1997.
Dolly and the Singing Bird. London, Cassell, 1968; as *The Photogenic Soprano,* Boston, Houghton Mifflin, 1968.
Pawn in Frankincense. London, Cassell, and New York, Putnam, 1969; New York, Vintage, 1997.
Dolly and the Cookie Bird. London, Cassell, 1970; as *Murder in the Round,* Boston, Houghton Mifflin, 1970.
The Ringed Castle. London, Cassell, 1971; New York, Putnam, 1972; New York, Vintage, 1997.
Dolly and the Doctor Bird. London, Cassell, 1971; as *Match for a Murderer,* Boston, Houghton Mifflin, 1971.
Dolly and the Starry Bird. London, Cassell, 1973; as *Murder in Focus,* Boston, Houghton Mifflin, 1973.
Checkmate. London, Cassell, and New York, Putnam, 1975; New York, Vintage, 1997.
Dolly and the Nanny Bird. London, Joseph, 1976; New York, Knopf, 1982.
King Hereafter. London, Joseph, and New York, Knopf, 1982.
Dolly and the Bird of Paradise. London, Joseph, 1983; New York, Knopf, 1984.
Niccolò Rising. London, Joseph, and New York, Knopf, 1986.
The Spring of the Ram. London, Joseph, 1987; New York, Knopf, 1988.
Race of Scorpions. London, Joseph, 1989; New York, Knopf, 1990.
Scales of Gold. London, Joseph, 1991; New York, Knopf, 1992.
Moroccan Traffic. London, Chatto and Windus, 1991; as *Take a Fax to the Kasbah,* New York, Harcourt Brace Jovanovich, 1992.
The Unicorn Hunt. London, Joseph, 1993; New York, Knopf, 1994.
To Lie with Lions. London, Joseph, 1995; New York, Knopf, 1996.
Caprice and Rondo. London, Michael Joseph, 1997; New York, Knopf, 1998.
Gemini. New York, Knopf, 2000.

Other

The Scottish Highlands, with Alastair M. Dunnett, photographs by David Paterson. Edinburgh, Mainstream, 1988.

*

Bibliography: In *Book and Magazine Collector 53* (London), August 1988.

Critical Study: *The Dorothy Dunnett Companion* by Elspeth Morrison, London, Joseph, 1994.

* * *

Dorothy Dunnett's fame as a best-selling novelist has been built on two major series of historical romances, a long novel on Macbeth which startled and impressed academic historians, and a series of modern thrillers apparently thrown off with ease as a diversion from her other work.

She came comparatively late to writing, having previously established a reputation as a portrait painter and sculptress. This artistic versatility in itself offers clues to her literary achievement. As a painter she has a remarkable ability to create instantly recognizable likenesses. Her sitters are portrayed with nicely calculated chiaroscuro, their faces and figures standing out against closely observed and romantically ordered backgrounds. As a sculptress she controls the modeling of her subjects with skill, shaping her material into volumes that satisfy from whatever angle they are viewed.

Dunnett's first major series, six novels known as the Lymond saga, opens in turbulent 16th-century Scotland, torn by war and intrigue both in its relations with England and in the domestic struggles of its noble families for power at court. This is the period of Henry VIII's rough dynastic wooing of the infant Mary, Queen of Scots, for his son Edward; it is the period also of the Reformation and the clash between the old Catholic order and Protestantism.

The hero of the saga, Francis Crawford of Lymond and later Comte de Sevigny, is condemned as a rebel and forced into exile. The six volumes of the saga recount his clandestine return to Scotland, his quest for the truth about his lineage and rightful inheritance, the adventures which take the wide-ranging story and its characters to France, Russia, Turkey and the Netherlands, and the final denouement of the intricate web of mystery surrounding Lymond's birth. As befits popular romances there is a happy ending; but a great deal goes on before it is delivered.

With each volume of this sprawling tale there is an extraordinary proliferation of sub-plots. The array of major and minor figures, both historical and fictitious, is so numerous that the reader might well get lost in the crowd had the author not prefaced each volume with lists of the leading characters, asterisked if they are her own inventions. Her research into historical events, places, people, their homes, dress and comportment, are so accurate and detailed that the reader can, like the author before starting to write, visit the scenes of the action and, book in hand, calculate the angle of a bow-shot or see where a duel or a lovers' meeting was arranged. Dunnett's stamina in historical and topographical research is indefatigable; and she seemingly cannot bear to throw anything away unused.

In many hands this accumulation of detail would make the story founder. But the author has such energy, such narrative pace, such inventiveness, wit and vitality, that the story is driven forward at breath-taking speed and the reader is kept easily afloat on the running tide of her prose. She has also a deft way with intelligent and witty women and their handling of intelligent, and not so intelligent, men. There is freshness and charm in the love scenes, muscle in the fights and swordplay.

The qualities of the Lymond saga were perceived and promoted by the publisher's editor who discovered *Gone with the Wind.* A suggestion that Dunnett's next novel should be about Mary, Queen of Scots, or Prince Charles Edward Stuart, ground tilled enough by others, was countered with a proposal to write a book about Macbeth. Hardly known to the public apart from the matter of Shakespeare's play, Macbeth and his world were pursued by the author through countless 11th-century sources, including those for Thorfinn, Earl of Orkney, who shared common ancestry with Macbeth and according to some accounts was his foster-brother. Eventually she became convinced that Macbeth and Thorfinn were possibly the same person, presented to the world for reasons of secret intrigue as two individuals. The coincidence of dates and common activities in extending and consolidating the kingdoms of the Northern Isles, Caithness, and Alba into the beginnings of a recognizable Scotland made the identification plausible if not proven beyond doubt. Armed with this historical thesis Dunnett wrote *King Hereafter,* a blockbuster of a novel whose claim to the popular title of saga is greater than that of the Lymond cycle.

Meantime she was also publishing a series of thrillers, revolving around the portrait painter, yachtsman and Secret Service agent Johnson Johnson and his yacht *Dolly.* An enterprising feature of these suspense stories is that each is narrated by the girl in the case—all of whom, it seems, are intimidated and repelled by Johnson's bifocal spectacles. The thrillers with their different narrators' voices are great fun, substituting for the classic car chase some hard sailing in foul weather in seas as far apart as the Caribbean and the Scottish Minches.

Dunnett's second long historical series, published under the generic title *The House of Niccolò,* takes us to the 15th century and the rise of the merchant class in Flanders, France, and Venice, financed by Florentine and Genoese bankers and trading throughout Europe and the Mediterranean. Again there has been a massive accumulation of source material for the detailed *mises-en-scène;* again the characters are highlighted in the foreground of the composition; again the author's sparkling style and swift pace make the work immensely readable. The sixth volume in the series, *To Lie with Lions,* involves an intensely complex, and strikingly modern-seeming conflict set in the Venice of 1471. In *Caprice and Rondo,* protagonist Nicholas de Fleury—a banker as resourceful as he is ruthless—recovers from the brink of ruin with a scheme to simultaneously protect Europe from Ottoman invasion and enrich his own purse.

—Stewart Sanderson

DYKEMAN, Wilma

Nationality: American. **Born:** Asheville, North Carolina, 1920. **Education:** Biltmore Junior College, Asheville, North Carolina; Northwestern University, Chicago, B.A. **Family:** Married James R. Stokely, Jr. (died 1977); two sons. **Career:** Writer and lecturer. **Awards:** Guggenheim fellowship, 1955; Thomas Wolfe Memorial Trophy, 1955; Hillman award, 1958; special Waukegan Club award (Chicago Friends of American Writers), 1963; National Endowment for the Humanities senior fellowship; named Tennessee Conservation Writer of the Year; honorary doctor of literature, Maryville College; named Tennessee Outstanding Speaker of the Year (State Association of Speech Arts Teachers and Professors); Distinguished Service award (University of North Carolina at Asheville). **Address:** 405 Clifton Heights, Newport, Tennessee, U.S.A.

Publications

Novels

The Tall Woman. New York, Holt, 1962.
The Far Family. New York, Holt, 1966.
Return the Innocent Earth. New York, Holt, 1973.
Explorations. Newport, Tennessee, Wakestone Books, 1984.

Other

The French Broad (nonfiction). New York, Rinehart, 1955.
Neither Black Nor White (nonfiction, with James R. Stokely). New York, Rinehart, 1957.
Seeds of Southern Change: The Life of Will Alexander (with James R. Stokely). University of Chicago Press, 1962.
Prophet of Plenty: The First Ninety Years of W.D. Weatherford. Knoxville, University of Tennessee Press, 1966.
Look to This Day (essays). New York, Holt, 1968.
The Border States (with James R. Stokely). New York, Time-Life Books, 1970.
Too Many People, Too Little Love (biography of Edna Rankin McKinnon). New York, Holt, 1974.
Tennessee: A Bicentennial History. New York, Norton, 1975.
Tennessee Women, Past and Present, edited by Carol Lyn Yellin. 1977.
Highland Homeland: The People of the Great Smokies (with son, Jim Stokely). Washington, D.C., National Park Service, 1978.
With Fire and Sword: The Battle of Kings Mountain, 1780, illustrated by Louis S. Glanzman. Washington, D.C., National Park Service, 1978.
Tennessee, photography by Edward Schell. Portland, Oregon, Graphic Arts Publishing Company, 1979.
Appalachian Mountains (with son, Dykeman Stokely), illustrated by Clyde H. Smith. Portland, Oregon, Graphic Arts Publishing Company, 1980.
Foreword, *Flowering of the Cumberland* by Harriette Simpson Arnow. Lexington, University Press of Kentucky, 1984.
Foreword, *Seedtime on the Cumberland* by Harriette Simpson Arnow. Lexington, University Press of Kentucky, 1984.
Tennessee: A History. New York, Norton, 1984.
At Home in the Smokies: A History Handbook for Great Smoky Mountains National Park, North Carolina and Tennessee. Washington, D.C., U.S. Department of the Interior, 1984.
Foreward, *The WPA Guide to Tennessee.* Knoxville, University of Tennessee Press, 1986.
Foreword, *Strangers in High Places: The Story of the Great Smoky Mountains* by Michael Frome. Knoxville, University of Tennessee Press, 1994.
Introduction, *Daughter of the Legend* by Jesse Stuart, edited by John H. Spurlock. Ashland, Kentucky, J. Stuart Foundation, 1994.
Haunting Memories: Echoes and Images of Tennessee's Past, photographs by Christine P. Patterson. Knoxville, University of Tennessee Press, 1996.
Foreword, *The Last Chivaree: The Hicks Family of Beech Mountain* by Robert Isbell. Chapel Hill, University of North Carolina Press, 1996.
Foreword, *Reverend Joseph Tarkington, Methodist Circuit Rider: From Frontier Evangelism to Refined Religion* by David L. Kimbrough. Knoxville, University of Tennessee Press, 1997.

Contributor, *We Dissent,* edited by Hoke Norris. New York, St. Martin's Press, 1962.

Contributor, *The Southern Appalachian Region: A Survey.* Lexington, University Press of Kentucky, 1962.

Contributor, *Nashville: The Faces of Two Centuries, 1780–1980* by John Egerton. Nashville, PlusMedia, 1979.

Contributor, *Tennessee, A Homecoming,* edited by John Netherton. Third National Corporation, 1985.

*

Critical Studies: *Tell It on the Mountain: Appalachian Women Writers* (sound recording, interviews by Nikki Giovanni), Whitesburg, Kentucky, WMMT-FM, 1995.

* * *

Wilma Dykeman was born in Asheville, North Carolina, in 1920, and she has lived most of her life near the French Broad River in the mountains of eastern Tennessee and western North Carolina. The river is the subject of her first book, *The French Broad*, a volume in the Rivers of America series and winner of the Thomas Wolfe Memorial Trophy, but it is also a recurring figure in Dykeman's work. A metaphor for generational continuity and the flow of history into the present, the river in many ways encapsulates Dykeman's concerns as a novelist, biographer, and historian: the importance of place, the connectedness of humanity, and the enduring relevance of the past.

Wilma Dykeman's first writings were short stories, radio scripts, and articles for *Harper's* and the *New York Times Magazine,* among other periodicals. Among her sixteen books, one finds a writerly fusion of social history, historical fiction, and memoir, all imbued with concerned engagement with contemporary sociopolitical issues. Dykeman's *Neither Black Nor White*, for instance, a collaboration with her husband, James Stokely, is a personal reflection on the Brown desegregation decision of 1954. The book won the Hillman Award for its contributions to world peace, civil liberties, and race relations.

Unfortunately, Dykeman's novels have too often been relegated to the minor category of regional fiction. Her fiction is decidedly rooted in Appalachia with the distinctive tenor of mountain dialect, but her themes are hardly unique to Southern life. Concerned especially with the changing roles of women and race relations, Dykeman in reality deals with some of the most universal issues of contemporary life. Her two most widely read works of fiction, *The Tall Woman* and its continuation *The Far Family*, both center around the lives of mountain women and challenge persisting stereotypes of Southern womanhood. Lydia McQueen, the protagonist of *The Tall Woman*, is especially antithetical to conventional portraits of the Southern lady. McQueen is committed to building a school for the mountain children of Thickety Creek in the years of Reconstruction, and she heroically stares down the man who would oppose her. But it is not only Dykeman's strong characters that offer an alternative view of femininity. The historical details that the author embeds in her novels—the realities of mountain midwifery, for example—also work to dispute female stereotypes by showing their basis in misinformation about the leading roles women have played throughout history.

In honor of the contributions her histories, biographies, and historical novels have made, the state of Tennessee named Dykeman State Historian in 1981. She is the recipient of numerous honorary doctoral degrees and an honorary Phi Beta Kappa. In addition, she has received a Guggenheim fellowship, a senior fellowship from the National Endowment for the Humanities, the Chicago Friends of American Writers Award, the Distinguished Southern Writer Award of the Southern Festival of Books, and the North Carolina Gold Medal for Contribution to American Letters. For over twenty years, she has served as a professor in the English department at the University of Tennessee, and she sits on numerous regional and national boards dealing with conservation, literature, history, and women's issues.

—Michele S. Shauf

E

EDGERTON, Clyde Carlyle

Nationality: American. **Born:** Durham, North Carolina, 20 May 1944. **Education:** University of North Carolina at Chapel Hill, B.A. 1966, M.A.T., 1972, Ph.D. 1977. **Military Service:** U.S. Air Force, 1967–71, piloted reconnaissance and forward air control missions in Southeast Asia during Vietnam War; received Distinguished Flying Cross. **Family:** Married Susan Ketchin in 1975; one daughter. **Career:** English teacher, Southern High School, Durham, North Carolina, 1972–73; codirector, English Teaching Institute, Chapel Hill, North Carolina, 1976; associate professor, Campbell University, Buies Creek, North Carolina, 1977–81, associate professor of education and psychology, 1981–85; associate professor of English and education, St. Andrews Presbyterian College, Laurinburg, North Carolina, 1985–89; full-time writer, 1989—. **Awards:** Guggenheim fellow, 1989; Lyndhurst fellow, 1991. **Agent:** Liz Darhansoff, 1220 Park Avenue, New York, New York 10128, U.S.A. **Address:** c/o Dusty's Air Taxi, 714 Ninth Street, G-7, Durham, North Carolina 27705, U.S.A.

PUBLICATIONS

Novels

Raney. Chapel Hill, North Carolina, Algonquin Books, 1985.

Walking Across Egypt. Chapel Hill, North Carolina, Algonquin Books, 1987.

The Floatplane Notebooks. Chapel Hill, North Carolina, Algonquin Books, 1988.

Killer Diller. Chapel Hill, North Carolina, Algonquin Books, 1991.

In Memory of Junior: A Novel. Chapel Hill, North Carolina, Algonquin Books, 1992.

Redeye: A Western. Chapel Hill, North Carolina, Algonquin Books, 1995.

Pete and Shirley: The Great Tar Heel Novel (serial novel, with others), edited by David Perkins. Asheboro, North Carolina, Down Home Press, 1995.

Where Trouble Sleeps: A Novel. Chapel Hill, North Carolina, Algonquin Books, 1997.

Poetry

Understanding the Floatplane (chapbook). Chapel Hill, North Carolina, Mud Puppy Press, 1987.

Cold Black Peas (chapbook). Chapel Hill, North Carolina, Mud Puppy Press, 1990.

Other

Contributor, *Weymouth: An Anthology of Poetry,* edited by Sam Ragan. Laurinburg, North Carolina, St. Andrews Press, 1987.

Contributor, *Family Portraits: Remembrances by Twenty Distinguished Writers,* edited by Carolyn Anthony. New York, Doubleday, 1989.

Contributor, *New Stories from the South: The Year's Best, 1990,* edited by Shannon Ravenel. Chapel Hill, North Carolina, Algonquin Books, 1990.

Contributor, *Books of Passage: 27 North Carolina Writers on the Books That Changed Their Lives,* edited by David Perkins, illustrated by David Terry. Asheboro, North Carolina, Down Home Press, 1997.

* * *

Clyde Edgerton burst on to the literary scene with his first work, *Raney*, in 1985. His subsequent works have been no less well-received, and Edgerton has continued to write equally interesting and controversial works such as *Walking Across Egypt*, *The Floatplane Notebooks*, *Killer Diller*, *In Memory of Junior*, *Redeye: A Western*, and his latest work, *Where Trouble Sleeps*. Edgerton's novels focus upon a variety of issues and present an array of intriguing characters, yet throughout his works, which are generally set in the South, the themes of hypocrisy, religion, and love emerge as pivotal elements.

Hypocrisy appears as a major theme in all of Edgerton's works. *Raney* illustrates the hypocrisy of the small, southern town, Listre, South Carolina, by relating the story through the perspective its naïve, female character, Raney. Her simplistic and often narrow view of the world forms the core of the novel. Because of the realism with which Edgerton imbues his characters, readers clearly understand, even if they do not always agree with, the perspective of such Southerners as Raney. Indeed, Raney's family's desperate desire to hide or to reform unacceptable relatives such as Uncle Nate demonstrates the hypocritical behavior of families such as Raney's. In *Where Trouble Sleeps*, Alease Toomey struggles to maintain the sobriety of her brother, Raleigh, who is an alcoholic veteran. She loves him, yet throughout the text, Alease agonizes over his state, not only for his health, but also for the bad reputation that he might bring to the family. This kind of double-edged, hypocritical simultaneous acceptance and condemnation of such characters becomes a mainstay of Edgerton's work.

Edgerton again explores hypocrisy in the image of the new Southerner. Raney's newlywed husband, Charles, who prides himself on enlightenment and progressiveness as a new Southern liberal, treats Raney's less-educated relatives in the same manner that he has seen whites treat blacks. He looks down on her family, viewing them as narrow-minded bumpkins, and he eagerly takes any opportunity to avoid spending extended amounts of time with them. Unfortunately, he never understands that he is guilty of the very kind of behavior that he so vociferously condemns in her relatives.

In *Killer Diller* Edgerton once again depicts characters mired in hypocrisy. The twin administrators of the small Baptist college in Listre, Ned and Ted Sears, cultivate devout and sincere public faces, yet all the while they work to enrich themselves by conducting shady business deals in the name of the college and the town.

Throughout his novels, characters such as those previously mentioned and those like Reverend Crenshaw in *Where Trouble Sleeps* and sisters Bette and Ansie in *In Memory of Junior* further illustrate Edgerton's attention to the hypocrisy apparent in Southern culture.

While hypocrisy is one of Edgerton's elemental themes, so too is religion. In all of Edgerton's works, a series of scenes convey his preoccupation with the Southern need to share what is right from what is wrong. These moral dictums often take the form of religious discussions. Such discussions generally occur between two to three characters who address a multitude of religious precepts from a conservative, southern Baptist view. To convey additional elements of the theme of religion, Edgerton employs the tempted or fallen pastor as an important character in his work.

In Memory of Junior contains a scene that illustrates the Southern preoccupation with God and religion. While hunting, Faison and Jimmy begin a discussion about killing animals. During the conversation, Jimmy begins to question the existence of God, and Faison shares his view of religious issues. This in-depth conversation lasts several pages until Faison shifts the conversation to a lighter subject.

In *Raney*, religion becomes a focal point of the text. Raney's insular view of what is and is not acceptable religious practice comes to light when Charles's mother, an Episcopalian, discusses her church traditions. To Raney, her mother-in-law's practices appear scandalous. Along with these discussions about the Episcopalians, she and Charles argue frequently about her views regarding sin and salvation. These religious discussions become a central part of many of Edgerton's works.

While religious discussions appear in Edgerton's novels, so too do characters who typify the fallen Christian. In *Where Trouble Sleeps* Reverend Crenshaw is tempted by Cheryl Daniels and almost falls prey to the blackmail scheme of the unscrupulous Jack Umstead, a.k.a. Delbert Jones. The Sears twins in *Killer Diller* further reflect this character of the fallen holy man when they plan university activities based not upon enhancing the lives of people within their community, but of selecting activities that provide good public relations opportunities. None of the author's fallen Christian characters appear to gain redemption by changing their behaviors. They remain corrupt throughout the works. Edgerton's novels depict religion as it is often actualized in the South—full of opinions and full of contradictions.

While hypocrisy and religion play significant roles in the Edgerton's work, the theme of love cannot be overlooked. Throughout his works, familial love, romantic love, and love of fellow humans transcends the pitfalls of the imperfect characters. Indeed, the love depicted may at times seem oddly termed as love, yet it is the kind of love reflective of reality. In *Where Trouble Sleeps* Mrs. Clark, the church receptionist, loves her husband, Claude T., yet she fears that he will go to hell because of his preoccupation with his Cadillac and diamond ring. In the same novel, Alease Harvey dotes on her son, Stephen, cares for her alcoholic brother, and pines for her overworked husband.

In *Raney* love again permeates the text. Raney, though married and living away from home, maintains strong ties to her younger siblings, her older relatives, and to her parents. She spends time with her younger sister and brother, and she would never dream of not being an integral part of their lives. Raney's family is large, loud, and expressive while her husband's family is small, quiet, and reserved. Both families, though, display deep love for their members, yet their different styles of communicating this love lead to many troubles within Charles's and Raney's relationship. Ultimately, however, during Raney and Charles's first year of married life, the couple embarks upon rough waters that are calmed by the love that they develop and the respect which they eventually gain for each other and for each one's family.

In Memory of Junior the character Faison holds such a great love for his wife's son that upon the child's death, Faison purchases a grave marker that has Faison's name with Jr. appended to replace the one that his wife, June Lee, has ordered with the child's legal name engraved upon it. Even though the child's paternity is uncertain, Faison loves this child tremendously. Toward the end of the text, June Lee and Faison read the child's journal from school in which he has written about the good times that he has shared with Faison. This touching scene reflects the love that the youngster possesses for his stepfather.

Edgerton's works vividly depict small town communities of the South without relying upon stereotypes or belittling the dignity of the characters. Edgerton shows the South as it is, warts and all. He creates realistic and well-developed characters who represent the contemporary every man. These characters display unceasing hypocrisy, a well-entrenched interest in religion, and many kinds of love which make Edgerton's characters realistic, interesting, and perplexing, all at the same time. Edgerton's works leave readers with the desire to always read more about these characters, who like many of our relatives, trouble, interest, and enlighten us.

—Lisa Abney

ELDRED-GRIGG, Stevan (Treleaven)

Nationality: New Zealander. **Born:** Grey Valley, New Zealand, 5 October 1952. **Education:** University of Canterbury, Christchurch, 1970–74, M.A. (honours) 1975; Australian National University, 1975–78, Ph.D. 1978. **Family:** Married in 1976 (marriage dissolved, 1994); three sons. **Career:** Postdoctoral fellow, University of Canterbury, 1981; writing fellow, 1986, scholar-in-letters, 1991, Victoria University; New Zealand writing fellow, University of Iowa, Iowa City. **Awards:** A.W. Reed memorial book award, 1984; Commonwealth Writers prize, 1988. **Agent:** Curtis Brown, P.O. Box 19, Paddington, New South Wales 2021, Australia.

Publications

Novels

Oracles and Miracles. Auckland and New York, Penguin, 1987.
The Siren Celia. Auckland, Penguin, 1989.
The Shining City. Auckland, Penguin, 1991.
Gardens of Fire. Auckland, Penguin, 1993.
Mum. Auckland, Penguin, 1995.
Blue Blood. Auckland and New York, Penguin, 1997.

Short Stories

Of Ivory Accents (novella). N.p., n.d.

Plays

Radio Play: *Oracles and Miracles,* from his own novel, 1989.

Other

A Southern Gentry: New Zealanders Who Inherited the Earth. Wellington, Reed, 1980.
A New History of Canterbury. Dunedin, McIndoe, 1982.

Pleasures of the Flesh: Sex and Drugs in Colonial New Zealand 1840–1915, 1984
New Zealand Working People, 1890–1990. Palmerston North, Dunmore Press, 1990.
My History, I Think. Auckland, Penguin, 1994.
The Rich: A New Zealand History. Auckland and New York, Penguin, 1996.

*

Manuscript Collection: Macmillan Brown Library, University of Canterbury, Christchurch, New Zealand.

Stevan Eldred-Grigg comments:

I'm a provincial writer, a writer of social comedy. My province is Canterbury, centred on the city of Christchurch. It's the comedy of a little white world, a small society, a very precise place. My novels resemble my province, a province whose history is as long or short as the history of the novel. A province civil, sociable, not unconcerned with style.

We write, though. We lie. We make meanings where there can be no meaning.

* * *

In the mid-1980s Stevan Eldred-Grigg switched his attention from history to fiction in order to challenge the customary ''literary portrait of working class life'' in New Zealand, which he saw as being ''very remote from working class reality.''

> I knew … that most of the people who had written serious history and fiction in New Zealand during the middle years of the twentieth century had been male and Pakeha. I also knew … that most had been middle class… . The worker who turned up in the pages of mid twentieth century literature was almost always a man… . And these working men were not only male, they were usually also itinerant, solitary and homeless. The working man was Man Alone. He lived in a world of ''casual workers and rouseabouts,'' ''station hands and street loungers.''

In a series of short stories and in his celebrated first novel, *Oracles and Miracles*—though not in a much earlier novella, *Of Ivory Accents,* which predates his socialist convictions—Eldred-Grigg set out to focus on the city rather than the country and on women rather than men. Rehabilitation of the Maori he has evidently left to New Zealand's rapidly expanding body of Maori writers.

Oracles and Miracles does not have a strong story line. Based on interviews with actual working-class women (and originally conceived as an oral history), it simply documents the lives of Ginnie and Fag from their births in 1929 through the Depression and World War II to their twenty-first birthdays. The method is akin to the realism of Arnold Bennett, but it must be said that Eldred-Grigg is not yet as adept as Bennett at suggesting human depth beneath the welter of surface detail.

Ginnie, who does not deviate from the working-class context of her birth, enables Eldred-Grigg to evoke what he calls the ''grit and texture'' of the times. Her working-class dialect is particularly well realized. Fag's voice is different since—like Eldred-Grigg's own mother, incidentally—she has realized the Cinderella myth by marrying out of her class and has cleaned up her idiom. Whereas Ginnie makes political statements unconsciously (as when she observes that ''the two words 'good' and 'work' didn't have anything to do with one another''), Fag can stand apart from her upbringing and comment on it quite explicitly. Thus when she shows her husband-to-be (who, incidentally, closely resembles Eldred-Grigg's own father) round the working-class suburb where she grew up, she tells us that she ''started to see it in a new way, thinking how strange it was that to him all this seemed interesting, important, this dreary old stamping ground of South Christchurch.'' Here she has become the mouthpiece for Eldred-Grigg's own concern about the destruction of working-class culture by the capitalist ideology of consumerism promulgated by the media of the day—including a popular magazine called *Miracles and Oracles.*

Ironically, at the very moment when she recognizes the authenticity of working-class culture, Fag is already in the process of deserting it for what turns out to be a sterile bourgeois existence. Ginnie, on the other hand, finds a partner from within the working class and seems happier at the end. The novel has been criticized for its naive implication that ''it's better to be working class and know it as long as you marry for love.'' The author himself insists that he did not intend this moral and that what he calls ''the tragedy'' of both sisters ''is not that they don't find love but that they do.''

These problems with the conclusion to *Oracles and Miracles* are not resolved by the disappointing sequel, *The Shining City.* Fag is still married—happily enough, it would seem, though she continues to live in a sterile middle-class suburb, where her behavior and idiom (now considerably closer to her working-class origins than they were in the earlier book) mark her out as an eccentric. But she is a minor character in the book, whereas Ginnie scarcely features. Instead the focus is on the formative years of two young men of the next generation: Fag's son, Ashley, and his cousin, Christopher, a scion of pure patrician stock.

The Shining City is in effect the obverse of *Oracles and Miracles* in that it focuses on the exploiting class rather than the exploited class. Eldred-Grigg the historian had already critiqued the Canterbury squattocracy mercilessly in his early works, *A Southern Gentry, A New History of Canterbury,* and *Pleasures of the Flesh.* In *The Shining City* and—more memorably—in *The Siren Celia* and *Gardens of Fire* he levels the same critique in fictional form. In all three novels an exploited working class is glimpsed from time to time, but the primary focus is on the foibles and corrupt practices of the landed gentry.

Gardens of Fire is closely based on fact. It is a compelling reconstruction of the disastrous fire of 1947 that destroyed Ballantynes—Christchurch's premier department store. Forty-one employees died in the blaze, and Eldred-Grigg's account rests the blame for their deaths squarely on the shoulders of their bosses.

The Siren Celia is based not on fact but on an earlier work of New Zealand fiction—George Chamier's *A South Sea Siren,* first published in 1895 and reprinted in 1970. Eldred-Grigg explains that he took from Chamier's novel ''all the bits that I thought worked really well and reinforced the themes I wanted to take up. I fed these chunks into my computer. Then I deconstructed them all and built them up again the way I wanted them.'' Other material is introduced from Chamier's earlier novel, *Philosopher Dick,* and from the writings of Sarah Amelia Courage.

His principal purpose in modifying Chamier was, he explains, to emphasize ''questions of gender and class.'' So the landed gentry of

Canterbury are effectively satirized, and the siren (who in Chamier's account was—according to one critic—''altogether too snaky and sinuous for modern belief'') is shown to be the victim of a series of boorish and incompetent men. It is in his depiction of one of these men, the protagonist, Richard Raleigh, that Eldred-Grigg departs most radically from his source. Chamier's ''philosopher Dick'' finally abjures the siren, takes up an honest profession, and seems set to marry the respectable Alice Seymour; Eldred-Grigg shows him degenerating into a corrupt entrepreneur with whom the siren is finally unfortunate enough to contract a marriage. Eldred-Grigg has done to Chamier precisely what Shaw's *Plays Unpleasant* did to the Victorian well-made play.

Eldred-Grigg also felt that Chamier ''didn't have the ability to dramatize''and tried to remedy this deficiency. He wisely cut the chapters in Chamier that amount to miniature Socratic dialogues led by ''philosopher Dick'' (Raleigh), but his version of the actual events of the story is really no more dramatic than Chamier's; as in *Oracles and Miracles* and *The Shining City,* the text conveys little sense of felt experience, even when Raleigh purports to be succumbing to the charms of the siren.

Mum continues the story, now with Ginnie as seen from the viewpoint of her children Jimmy and Viv. The alternating first-person voices work surprisingly well, as does the use of a real person—New Zealand writer Ngaio Marsh—in *Blue Blood.* The novel depicts Marsh in 1929, when her career was just beginning, and places her in the middle of a mystery that calls to mind her later writings.

—Dick Corballis

ELLIOTT, Janice

Nationality: British. **Born:** Derby, 14 October 1931. **Education:** Nottingham High School for Girls; Oxford University, 1950–53, B.A. (honours) 1953. **Family:** Married Robert Cooper in 1959; one son. **Career:** Journalist, *House and Garden, House Beautiful, Harper's Bazaar,* and *Sunday Times,* all London, 1954–62; since 1964 freelance reviewer, *Sunday Telegraph, Sunday Times, Times,* and *New Statesman,* all London. **Awards:** Southern Arts award, 1981. Fellow, Royal Society of Literature, 1989. **Agent:** Vivien Green, Richard Scott Simon Ltd., 43 Doughty Street, London WC1N 2LF, England. **Address:** Dolphin House, Trafalgar Square, Fowey, Cornwall PL23 1AX, England.

PUBLICATIONS

Novels

Cave with Echoes. London, Secker and Warburg, 1962.
The Somnambulists. London, Secker and Warburg, 1964.
The Godmother. London, Secker and Warburg, 1966; New York, Holt Rinehart, 1967.
The Buttercup Chain. London, Secker and Warburg, 1967.
The Singing Head. London, Secker and Warburg, 1968.
Angels Falling. London, Secker and Warburg, and New York, Knopf, 1969.
The Kindling. London, Secker and Warburg, and New York, Knopf, 1970.
England Trilogy:
A State of Peace. London, Hodder and Stoughton, and New York, Knopf, 1971.
Private Life. London, Hodder and Stoughton, 1972.
Heaven on Earth. London, Hodder and Stoughton, 1975.
A Loving Eye. London, Hodder and Stoughton, 1977.
The Honey Tree. London, Hodder and Stoughton, 1978.
Summer People. London, Hodder and Stoughton, 1980.
Secret Places. London, Hodder and Stoughton, 1981.
The Country of Her Dreams. London, Hodder and Stoughton, 1982.
Magic. London, Hodder and Stoughton, 1983.
The Italian Lesson. London, Hodder and Stoughton, 1985; New York, Beaufort, 1986.
Dr. Gruber's Daughter. London, Hodder and Stoughton, 1986.
The Sadness of Witches. London, Hodder and Stoughton, 1987.
Life on the Nile. London, Hodder and Stoughton, 1989.
Necessary Rites. London, Hodder and Stoughton, 1990.
City of Gates. London, Hodder and Stoughton, 1992.
Figures in the Sand. London, Sceptre, 1994.

Short Stories

The Noise from the Zoo. London, Hodder and Stoughton, 1991.

Other (for children)

The Birthday Unicorn. London, Gollancz, 1970.
Alexander in the Land of Mog. Leicester, Brockhampton Press, 1973.
The Incompetent Dragon. London, Blackie, 1982.
The King Awakes. London, Walker Books, 1987.
The Empty Throne. London, Walker Books, 1988.

*

Janice Elliott comments:

I have always tried to avoid writing in a way that might invite categorisation in either subject matter or treatment. The result is a body of work ranging from the bizarre and darkly magical (*Dr. Gruber's Daughter, Magic, The Sadness of Witches*) to the social realism of the England Trilogy and the poignancy of *Secret Places*—set in the war-time Midlands where I grew up.

I make frequent use of myth, which fascinates me (most overtly in *The Singing Head*). So does modern history (*Angels Falling* set in Britain 1901–68; *Life on the Nile,* Egypt today and in the 1920s). The domestic scene has interested me only when it is set in and interacts with, the larger, outer world (e.g. the menace of the authoritarian state in *Necessary Rites*). A sense of place is vital to me, even when I have invented a country (*The Country of Her Dreams*).

I have been consistent only in my aspiration, my attempt each time to try something that will set me a fresh challenge as a writer. I am consistent too, in my conviction that style is not the icing on the cake but an organic and essential element in a good novel. If there is one recurring theme it may be the fall from grace, the image of exile from the garden.

In the last decade I have felt an urge to get out of England (mentally, imaginatively, and physically), and so made use of a number of foreign settings (*The Italian Lesson, Life on the Nile*).

I have also been more drawn by humour, sometimes to the forefront, more often as a bright, sharp thread in the weave. I believe that as a result, my novels may become more accessible to a wider audience.

Given my inclination to dash off in different directions, I have been lucky in my critical reception. Not that I could have done otherwise. I am an entirely intuitive writer, often astonished to find myself where I am and in what company (e.g. with Hitler in an attic in North Oxford in *Dr. Gruber's Daughter*).

* * *

Most of Janice Elliott's carefully crafted novels share the same background (the affluent English middle-class), the same period of time, the same preoccupation with the menopausal crises of well-established marriages, and, to a surprising extent, the same characters under different names. The Farmers of *The Italian Lesson,* the Tylers of *Summer People,* the Contis of *Magic,* the Watermans of *The Sadness of Witches,* the Franklands of *Necessary Rites,* appear to be all in admired and envied perfect marriages, while in private they are becoming estranged, even hostile to one another. Infidelity in thought and deed is commonplace, but the real issue seems to be a questioning of the need to continue living together.

The stress is on women's strength and ability to survive while men crack up and break. When disaster strikes, women will instinctively carry on with the daily round, knowing its therapeutic value (''cooking being an orderly process, a gesture, in a small way, against chaos.'') Repeatedly Elliott emphasises the value of feminine friendships (''Friends ... are family nowadays, which is why there is so much kissing. For whatever reason, we seem to feel the need to touch''), in which there is unspoken understanding, the ''dolphin language, mind to mind communication.''

It is perhaps inevitable in these times when modish, half-understood cults and myths are elbowing out Christianity, that the bond between women should take the surprising form of a witches' coven, as in *Magic.*

Set against the praise of friendships between women is the recurrent theme of the absence of any such understanding between a mother and her daughter. Hinted at in *The Italian Lesson,* it is openly declared in *Summer People* (''she never cared for her mother because they were alike. And who can bear for long speaking to a mirror?''), and in *The Sadness of Witches* and *Necessary Rites.*

Conversely Elliott emphasizes the strength of the bond between a mother and her adolescent son (*Summer People, The Sadness of Witches, Necessary Rites*). There is a marked similarity both of physical appearance and of turn of mind between all these boys, as there is also between the young girls who float in and out of these people's houses and lives: long-haired, bare-foot flower children with little in the way of conversation and a terrifying egocentricity.

Some of the minor characters too bear an uncanny resemblance to one another (Felix Wanderman in *The Italian Lessons* and Max Stiller in *Life on the Nile* are both wise, elderly, Jewish, widowed, close to death—and sporting the same tufts of cottonwool after shaving).

Such similarities may perhaps be expected in a novelist who restricts herself largely to chronicle one small section of society. They are not due to a poverty of imagination; when she chooses Elliott can exercise her imagination with astonishing results: in *Dr. Gruber's Daughter* Adolf Hitler is hiding in a North Oxford attic, while his daughter, the offspring of an incestuous affair with his half-sister, roams leafy Oxford, a wraith from hell, in search of human and feline victims to devour. In *Magic* Sir Oliver and his housekeeper practise the skill of out-of-body experiences, and in *The Sadness of Witches* Martha, like the witches in *Macbeth,* can cause storms at sea and wreck or save boats.

The style is plain, straightforward; indeed in *The Italian Lesson* the short sentences seem to mimic those of the heroine's Italian phrase book. The form is usually that of a straight narrative; the horrors of bomb scares, car crashes, oil spills, murder, and suicide are all the more telling for this plainness. Only in *Life on the Nile* do we find a more complex form: the present-day story of Charlotte Hamp's experiences in Egypt is interwoven with extracts from the diary of her great-aunt who had lived in Egypt in the 1920s and was murdered there. This temporal crosscutting appears to even greater advantage in *Figures in the Sand,* which depicts the dying Roman Empire—only it is in the future, in a world of armored vehicles and cell phones. Christianity has been outlawed again, a fact that affects General Fidus Octavius's believing wife Livia, but not the agnostic general, who haunts a Syrian necropolis in hopes of finding proof that an afterlife truly exists.

Characteristic perhaps of most novels which present life through a woman's eyes are the descriptions of the small pleasures with which women shore up their lives. But always there is an undercurrent of unease beneath the calm surface (''a small daily terror''). In this respect particularly Elliott is a true chronicler of her chosen society.

—Hana Sambrook

ELLIS, Alice Thomas

Pseudonym for Anna Margaret Haycraft. **Nationality:** British. **Born:** Anna Margaret Lindholm in Liverpool, 9 September 1932; grew up in Penmaenmawr, Wales. **Education:** Bangor County Grammar School, Gwynedd; Liverpool School of Art; postulant, Convent of Notre Dame de Namur, Liverpool. **Family:** Married the publisher Colin Haycraft in 1956; four sons and one daughter (and one daughter and one son deceased). **Career:** Director, Duckworth, publishers, London. Columnist (''Home Life''), the *Spectator,* London, the *Universe,* London, 1989–91; and for *The Catholic Herald.* **Awards:** Welsh Arts Council award, 1977; *Yorkshire Post* award, 1986. **Address:** 22 Gloucester Crescent, London NW1 7DY, England.

Publications

Novels

The Sin Eater. London, Duckworth, 1977.

The Birds of the Air. London, Duckworth, 1980; New York, Viking Press, 1981.

The 27th Kingdom. London, Duckworth, 1982; Wakefield, Rhode Island, Moyer Bell, 1999.

The Other Side of the Fire. London, Duckworth, 1983.

Unexplained Laughter. London, Duckworth, 1985; New York, Harper, 1987.

The Inn at the Edge of the World. London, Viking, 1990.

The Summerhouse Trilogy. London, Penguin, 1991; New York, Penguin, 1994

The Clothes in the Wardrobe. London, Duckworth, 1987.

The Skeleton in the Cupboard. London, Duckworth, 1988.

The Fly in the Ointment. London, Duckworth, 1989.

Pillars of Gold. London, Viking, 1992; Wakefield, Rhode Island, Moyer Bell, 2000.
The Evening of Adam. Harmondsworth, England, Viking, 1994.
Fairy Tale. Wakefield, Rhode Island, Moyer Bell, 1998.

Uncollected Short Story

"Away in a Niche," in *Spectator* (London), 21–28 December 1985.

Other

Natural Baby Food: A Cookery Book (as Brenda O'Casey). London, Duckworth, 1977; as Anna Haycraft, London, Fontana, 1980.
Darling, You Shouldn't Have Gone to So Much Trouble (cookbook; as Anna Haycraft), with Caroline Blackwood. London, Cape, 1980.
Home Life. London, Duckworth, 1986; New York, Akadine Press, 1997.
Secrets of Strangers, with Tom Pitt-Aikens. London, Duckworth, 1986.
More Home Life. London, Duckworth, 1987.
Home Life 3. London, Duckworth, 1988.
Loss of the Good Authority: The Cause of Delinquency, with Tom Pitt-Aikens. London, Viking, 1989.
Home Life 4. London, Duckworth, 1989.
A Welsh Childhood, photographs by Patrick Sutherland. London, Joseph, 1990; Wakefield, Rhode Island, Moyer Bell, 1997.
Cat Among the Pigeons: A Catholic Miscellany. London, Flamingo, 1994.
Editor, *Mrs. Donald,* by Mary Keene. London, Chatto and Windus, 1983.
Editor, *Wales: An Anthology.* London, Collins, 1989.

* * *

In all her books Alice Thomas Ellis takes the form of the upper-class social comedy and turns it inside out, with mordant, often uncomfortable wit, satire (some of it quite savage), and a gift for dialogue which means much more than is apparent, in a background which alternates between the country (usually Wales) and London, patches of which must be regarded as the author's own territory.

Her first novel, *The Sin Eater,* is set in Wales, where the Welsh have given up farming and taken to preying on the holidaymaker. In a country house, near a small resort which has declined since its pre-war heyday, the Captain, patriarch of the family, lies dying, unable to speak or move. Only a matter of time, says the doctor, cheerfully. Not much grief is shown by the family assembling to say goodbye to him. Henry, the eldest son and heir, lives with his wife Rose and the twins in the family home. Visiting are younger brother Michael, his wife Angela, and Edward, a Fleet Street literary journalist, object of Angela's love (or lust). Ministering incompetently to the household is Phyllis, her son Jack ("Jack the Liar") and Gomer, Phyllis's adored but highly unpleasant grandson. The outsider is Ermyn, youngest daughter of the house, back from a secretarial course in London, regarded by the rest as half-witted (in fact she is slightly deaf, following measles in childhood, but no one has noticed). Rose (like Ellis) is a Roman Catholic, a brilliant organizer, one who arranges food, houses, and circumstances to disconcert others. Angela (who hates her) is disoriented by being put in a room newly arranged in 1930s style. A killing meal is eaten shortly before the cricket match of village versus Squire. When the village wins, for the first time, there follows a vengeful and dismaying Welsh saturnalia. Rose loves only the twins (absent from all but the first and last page of the novel) and the terrifying denouement is a fitting end to the outpouring of spite and malice so deftly observed.

Christmas is a family time, and in *The Birds of the Air,* Mrs. Marsh decides to invite all the family, to try to cheer Mary, whose grief will neither disappear, nor be assuaged. Mary's sister Barbara has just discovered her husband's infidelity by overhearing a sniggered comment that suddenly makes sense. She is on the way to a breakdown. Mary's grief is an indescribable agony, unhelped by her Catholicism, over the death of her illegitimate son, Robin. Everyone is embarrassed by Mary's grief. Barbara makes an exhibition of herself, getting drunk and pursuing Hunter, who rejects her. Social embarrassment to the last degree forms the basis for some hard, sharp things said about the nature of grief, love, and family life.

The 27th Kingdom (shortlisted for the Booker prize in 1982) is set in Chelsea in the 1950s, where Aunt Irene (of distant Russian descent) lives with her nephew Kyril in a pretty little house. Chelsea is still very socially mixed, and the cast includes the O'Connors, a large family of criminal Cockneys, and a passing parade of casual lodgers. The outsider and new lodger is Valentine, who wishes to be a nun, but has been sent out to see more of the world by Reverend Mother, who is Aunt Irene's sister. Valentine is, most inconveniently, a saint, as well as being very beautiful, and black. As in all the novels, the four last things of the Catholic Church—death and judgment, heaven and hell—loom in the background. Aunt Irene loves Kyril, but recognizes that he is evil and wicked. Both she and Mrs O'Connor, the Cockney matriarch, recognize the goodness of Valentine. Once again, it's very funny, and slightly more gentle in tone. Food plays its part, and so does Focus, a charming, beautiful, and amusing cat.

The Other Side of the Fire brings together a number of themes which can be claimed as standard ingredients in the Ellis novel. Claudia Bohannon is the second wife of Charles—they have two children of their own (absent at boarding school). Claudia finds herself inexplicably and shamingly in love with her stepson, Philip. Her confidante is Sylvie (living in the country, there are few congenial people around). Sylvie has given up love, and company, and has become a witch—or not, depending on how you view her. Certainly she has a familiar in the dog Gloria, evil-tempered and a perfect nuisance, rather like Sylvie's ex-husband, as one of the characters points out. Evvie, Sylvie's daughter, is writing a romantic novel along very predictable lines, containing stock characters like a Scottish vet with a dull fiancée, a housekeeper, a beautiful promiscuous girl, a mad Laird. Unfortunately and hilariously the characters from the novel invade life, and vice versa. Claudia is sweet but dim—it takes a brick dropped by Evvie before she realizes what everyone else knows—that Philip is a charming and unscrupulous homosexual. The book meditates on various forms of love—and its transitory nature—touching all but the maternal, which, as in *The Sin Eater,* is so important that it is never mentioned.

Unexplained Laughter is set in Wales, where Lydia, a tough London journalist, has retreated to get over a broken heart. With her is Betty, who is nice, but a bore. The only company (typically, a small group of characters at each other's throats) is a family. Hywel, a farmer, is married unhappily to Elizabeth; Angharad, his youngest sister, is speechless and considered mad but is not as mad as all that; Beuno, the younger brother, is studying for the ministry. There is also the doctor, formerly Elizabeth's lover. Lydia is witty and cruel. It is only when she starts hearing unexplained laughter in the air round the cottage, and she talks to Beuno about the existence of God and the devil that she begins to develop into a more human being and allows herself to become fond of others. The devil is at work; they are a nasty bunch, with exceptions. Beuno is some kind of saint, Betty is pleasant and dull, Angharad is a visionary, and Lydia is improving her soul. Beuno exorcises the laughter, and it disappears. Whatever it was, he considered it evil.

In *Fairy Tale,* young Simon and Eloise forsake the sinful pleasures of the city for a bucolic life of meditation, but Simon soon becomes alienated by his partner's mystic flights of fancy. She longs for a baby, which Simon refuses to provide her, so instead she goes wandering about the countryside, in hills haunted by a sexual predator, and eventually returns bearing a strange infant. *Pillars of Gold* almost seems to view the same situation from another angle: this time a young woman, an American named Barbs, has apparently succumbed to the clutches of a murderer, and is found dead in a canal. Her suburban London neighbors speculate as to the cause of the murder, and the outcome reveals facts about their community of which they would gladly have remained unaware.

These short novels are written with an uncanny ear for contemporary dialogue, the flash of steel beneath the apparently harmless words. There is a great deal said about the Catholic church, life, death, food, love, children, and the existence of evil, the devil in our midst (''Stan,'' Lydia calls him, a nickname for ''Satan''). Only in the short story, ''Away in a Niche,'' in which a tired housewife swaps places with the local saint for the three worst days of Christmas, do we get anything like a cheerful, happy conclusion.

—Philippa Toomey

ELLIS, Bret Easton

Nationality: American. **Born:** Los Angeles, 7 March 1964. **Education:** Bennington College, Vermont, B.A. 1986. **Agent:** International Creative Management, 40 West 57th Street, New York, New York 10019, U.S.A.

Publications

Novels

Less Than Zero. New York, Simon and Schuster, 1985; London, Pan, 1985.
The Rules of Attraction. New York, Simon and Schuster, 1987; London, Picador, 1988.
American Psycho. New York, Vintage, and London, Picador, 1991.
The Informers. New York, Knopf, and London, Picador, 1994.
Glamorama. New York, Knopf, 1999.

*

Film Adaptations: *Less Than Zero*, 1987; *American Psycho*, 2000.

* * *

Bret Easton Ellis's novels to date explore the apathy, boredom, and alienation of the ''brat pack'' or ''blank generation'' of affluent white youth in the United States in the 1980s. Whether set in Los Angeles (*Less Than Zero* and *The Informers*), a New England college (*The Rules of Attraction*), New York (*American Psycho*), or London and Paris (*Glamorama*), each of these novels represents the homogenizing and dehumanizing effect of late capitalist consumer culture. Through his cipher-like characters, who are mostly distinguished from each other only by the brand names of their designer clothes, Ellis traces the metonymies of desire in a culture where sex and the body are commodified and, like drugs, alcohol, and MTV, are addictively consumed.

The desire for excess that is underlain by ennui is recorded in an affectless and ''stunned'' prose style that is arguably mimetic of a ''depthless'' postmodern culture. Each of the novels has occasioned controversy as to whether this flat style merely reproduces the nihilistic lassitude of its characters or whether, through verisimilitude, Ellis is indeed offering a critique of the ethics of the society that he represents. This controversy culminated in the critical reception of *American Psycho,* Ellis's tale of serial killing and mass murder in yuppie Manhattan. This novel was variously perceived as a devastating indictment of the erosion of ethics by capitalism in the Reaganite 1980s, as a virulent brand of pornography thinly veiled as mainstream art for the middle classes, and as simply an aesthetic failure because it did not manage to create a metaphor for the violence that it repetitively detailed.

Arguably, each of Ellis's novels expresses a yearning for a meaningful reality that seems inaccessible through the inauthentic simulations of consumer culture. *Less Than Zero,* which begins with the observation that ''people are afraid to merge on the freeways in Los Angeles,'' a statement of disconnection that becomes a refrain in the novel, describes the spiraling loss of ethical bearings experienced by the narrator, Clay, as he spends a Christmas vacation in Los Angeles, away from his college in the East. The various forms of consumption—sex, shopping, drugs, alcohol—that dominate the lives of Clay and his peers fail to signify for Clay. He is haunted by the menacing extremity of the desert, by reports of random violence and disaster, and by childhood memories that disclose psychic violence within a family where, in the end, ''nobody's home.'' Passivity becomes voyeurism and consumption becomes pornographic spectacle as Clay is an unresisting witness to scenes of forced prostitution and gang rape. Nathaniel West's Hollywood of the 1930s is echoed by the broodingly apocalyptic vision of Los Angeles in the 1980s with which Ellis leaves us: ''The images I had were of people being driven mad by living in the city. Images of parents who were so hungry and unfulfilled that they ate their own children.''

The East Coast, an absent referent that would potentially signify in Ellis's first novel, fails to offer an authentic alternative to the artifice of Los Angeles in his second novel, *The Rules of Attraction.* The interior monologues of the three main characters and their somewhat indeterminate peers register the fluidity of desire that is sometimes shaped by romantic narratives but that ultimately is ''haphazard and random … episodic, broken … [showing] no sense of events unfolding from prior events,'' to quote from the epigraph by Tim O'Brien, which serves to interpret the ensuing trajectory of the novel.

Ellis's apparent withholding of explicit moral comment on the spiritual impoverishment of the culture that his novels represent was critically perceived as being more problematic in his detailed account of the activities of Patrick Bateman, the eponymous ''American

Psycho.'' In contrast to the classic realist novel, here no ''deep'' psychological exploration of or explanation for the protagonist's actions is offered. Instead, the reader is immediately introduced into the hermetic world of New York consumer culture with the opening words of the novel: ''Abandon all hope ye who enter here… .'' The randomness of desire that was the subject of *The Rules of Attraction* is now replaced by a deterministic consumerism whereby the serial killer is the parodic extremity of a cultural logic that reifies people and stimulates an addiction to excess that only violence can temporarily assuage.

If the relation between author, text, and reader is ambiguous in *American Psycho,* authorial comment seems foregrounded through the narrative strategies of *The Informers.* An impressionistic composite of narrative voices, this novel presents the estrangement between the generations and between the sexes in affluent Los Angeles. Images of anomie and personal and familial dissociation are interwoven with scenes of sexual violence that accelerate as the novel shifts into gothic fantasy, with vampires preying on their victims, and then moves toward a conclusion with the depiction of the sexual assault, torture, and murder of a child. The willfully blind romantic fantasy that concludes the novel would seem to draw attention to the cultural disavowal of what Ellis, speaking of the 1980s, has described as ''the absolute banality of a perverse decade.''

However, by the time of *Glamorama,* Ellis's stance as critic of a decade had lost most of the already modest moral punch it carried. There was the fact that Ellis himself, like many who criticized the 1980s, had done quite well in that decade, a period whose principal fault seemed to be that people made money during that time. In the 1990s, with the 1980s fading into memory—and with Wall Street generating far more millionaires than anyone in the ''greedy'' 1980s could ever have imagined—Ellis's posturing seemed all the more absurd, particularly given his origins among the nation's aristocracy. Plenty of critics still professed to find something new in the tired eighties-bashing of *American Psycho,* which found a new audience with its release as a motion picture, but *Glamorama* provided evidence that perhaps the author protested a bit too much. Set among the high-fashion upper echelons of London and Paris, the book was supposed to be another indictment of wealth and glamor, but Ellis's descriptions of the world inhabited by male models belie a certain fascination with that world—rather like a preacher who takes just a bit too much interest in condemning prostitution. The novel has a more traditional and discernible plot than its predecessors—a mysterious Mr. Palakon hires male model Victor Ward to save a film star in Paris from international terrorists—but is laden with threadbare postmodern narrative tricks. ''So you're telling me we can't believe in anything we're shown anymore,'' Victor tells Mr. Palakon at one point. ''I'm asking, 'That everything is altered? That everything's a lie? That everyone will believe this?''' Indeed.

—Joanna Price, updated by Judson Knight

ELLIS, Trey

Nationality: American. **Born:** Washington, D.C., 1962. **Education:** Attended Stanford University. **Agent:** c/o Publicity Department, Simon & Schuster, 1230 Avenue of the Americas, New York, New York 10020, U.S.A. **Address:** Santa Monica, California, U.S.A.

PUBLICATIONS

Novels

Platitudes. St. Paul, Minnesota, Vintage Books, 1988.
Home Repairs. New York, Simon & Schuster, 1993.
Right Here, Right Now. New York, Simon & Schuster, 1999.

Plays

Screenplays: *The Inkwell* (as Tom Ricostranza). Buena Vista Pictures, 1994.

Television Plays: *Cosmic Slop/Space Traders.* Home Box Office, 1994.

*

Critical Studies: *A Moveable Feast* (television documentary). South Carolina Educational Television/WETA-TV, 1991.

* * *

Among the vanguard of emerging African-American novelists, Trey Ellis is chiefly known for his highly celebrated first novel *Platitudes* and the multicultural, slightly apolitical ''New Black Aesthetic'' it cleverly demonstrates. Claiming to speak for other predominantly middle- to upper-class African-American males from filmmaker Spike Lee to hip-hop's Chuck D, Ellis describes the ''New Black Aesthetic,'' or NBA, as a ''post-liberated'' compilation of ''cultural mulattos'' whose members are shamelessly assimilative (if not assimilationist) of both white and black forms of cultural production. To the NBA tragic rock icon Jim Morrison is just as significant as novelist Toni Morrison. Thus, the NBA is much less skeptical of commodity culture, embracing the multicultural utopianism of commercialization, MTV, and brand name identification. However, this bold espousal of what Karl Marx might have referred to as ''false consciousness,'' comes at the expense of what W.E.B. Du Bois might call ''race consciousness.''

Ostensibly motivated by an urge to free the novelist from the limitations of ''race'' literature in which the African-American novelist must always address issues of race, Ellis refreshingly flouts the reader's expectation of ''authentic'' blackness. Instead of presenting familiar themes of racial misery and uplift, Ellis offers other kinds of African-American people, experiences, and lifestyles less visible in popular representations such as those of the black middle class, whose yuppies, preppies, and nerds have been routinely suppressed or villainized in traditional African American literary discourses. Set up as a panacea to internal fissures, Ellis's NBA attempts to mediate the aesthetic, social, racial, and even gender divisions of the black community that, in the universe of the novel *Platitudes*, polarizes into two recognizable factions: the masculine 1960s Black Arts Movement associated with Ishmael Reed and Amira Baraka, and the 1970–80s Womanist Movement as represented by Alice Walker and Toni Morrison. And although Ellis claims to satirize both traditions equally, his work has been charged with perpetuating sexism by returning obsessively to themes that glorify the adolescent male libido and mark the triumph of heterosexual attraction and patriarchal desire over political, racial, and class distinctions.

Like all works of metafiction, *Platitudes* is aware of its own writing. How to write the novel is precisely where the story begins.

Troubled by the vexed politics of race representation, Ellis's fictionalized experimentalist author Dewayne Wellington attempts to write a coming-of-age love story centering around the character of Earle, a chubby, adolescent geek more interested in computers, doing well on his PSATs, watching TV game shows, and getting laid than in the usual perilous activities found in typical narratives of black youth. After admitting failure, Dewayne pleads for assistance in plotting his quirky tale and invites readers to respond to an address under the title of ''Which Ones Do I Kill?'' He is answered by Isshee Ayam, Ellis's caricature of a Womanist or Black Feminist novelist who promptly inserts her own version of how the tale should begin. Her Earle inhabits a poor rural community sometime in the early 1900s and somewhere in Lowndes County, Georgia. He is suddenly the only male in a family of strong women held together by a frying pan wielding exaggeration of the self-sacrificing black matriarch. Thus, Isshee Ayam models the authentic mode of racially conscious storytelling, which not unhumorously parodies Alice Walker's *The Color Purple.* But Ellis makes it clear that neither is Isshee Ayam's illiterate Earle any more authentic than Wellington's portly genius. As an antidote to Ayam's inserted chapter re-writes, Wellington follows each of her revisions with a profusion of expansive stream-of-consciousness exposition full of movie dialogue, snatches of TV commercials, and other extraneous texts such as photos of Earle's apartment, portions of a ludicrous PSAT exam, and a similarly marked answer sheet to Earle's high school sex survey.

Out of the dialectic clash of gendered narrative techniques, Wellington's Earle emerges much changed from what he is at the beginning of the story, not least because his Jewish girlfriend is replaced, his mother quits her job working for a South African airline, and he finds himself promoting African American voting. And although this increase in Earle's politics seems directly the result of Wellington's association with Ayam, the parody of the Womanist position never quite disappears, especially at the end of the novel when the two authors meet only to consummate their relationship. By having Wellington write himself into a sexual mood that he cannot attain naturally, Ellis seems to be reasserting a connection between masculine sexuality and creativity once again at the expense of objectifying women as well as satirizing feminism. According to this patriarchal logic, hypermasculine and heteronormative sexuality trumps all differences. And if this sexuality is slightly sentimentalized as puppy love in *Platitudes*, it is brazen to the point of controversy in Ellis's next two novels.

Indeed, *Home Repairs* may be seen as a continuation of Earle's story, only now the plot focuses exclusively on its hero's sexual conquests. Intelligent, libidinous, and neurotic Austin McMillan sets out to keep a diary (ironically based on Puritan spiritual diary writing) of his sexual exploits but indirectly records his rites of passage through manhood. Spanning Austin's life from the early 1970s and his experiences as an exceedingly well-to-do African American at Andover school and Stanford to the late 1980s when he becomes the host of a TV fix-it show, the diary is comprised of sexual ''firsts'' often containing lengthy descriptions of women's body parts peppered with occasional moments of reflection. A similar angst infuses Austin as it does Earle. Both obsess over TV, pornography, and how they appear to women, yet both worry over exactly the type of racial issues that their narratives seem to downplay. Indeed, those moments in *Home Repairs* in which Austin considers such issues are few, as when he insists upon going to a black prostitute for his first time instead of a white one. Nevertheless, the novel has been read by many critics as less literary than *Platitudes*.

Although as an epistolary pastiche *Home Repairs* provides further evidence of Ellis's postmodern play with narrative form, many critics find its obsessive descriptions of sexual scenes more tedious than scintillating. Behind this sexual monotony Ellis may be intentionally drawing attention to our cultural thresholds for tolerating such characters, perhaps offering an insipid but relentless eroticism precisely in order to reveal the commercial constructedness of desire. But in the process, his revered aesthetic of ''cultural mulattoism'' is reduced to an offensive version of ''thirty-one flavors.'' Difference is redefined in the novel as a sexual smorgasbord of beautiful ethnic women for the Epicurean Austin to try.

In *Right Here, Right Now* Ellis offers yet another version of what we may call the typical Ellis protagonist in Ashton Robinson, an upper-class, globe-trotting genius. In the same way that Austin McMillan's story seems to be an extension of Earle's, so too does Ashton's tale seem to pick up exactly where Austin's television popularity leaves off. Completing the third installment of the Ellis hero's life, Ashton Robinson grows weary of the very same television fame that the hero of *Home Repairs* desired. Robinson turns his back on his infomercial celebrity to embark on a spiritual journey initiated by dream visions—the result of an evening's debauch of drugs and long expired cough syrup. He becomes the guru of his own religion called ''axe'' (aaa-shay). That axe is a Voo-dun spirit traceable to Africa mingles the novel's satiric jibes at America's ludicrous obsession with lucrative TV religions, New Age, Scientologists, psychics, and quack healers with a subtle endorsement of the genuine spirituality of traditional African-American folk traditions. Nevertheless, the hero's main objective is nothing so holy; he declares that the true path toward enlightenment involves orgiastic sex with his disciple's wives. And yet, Ashton undergoes a type of spiritual overhaul. His final insights diagnose the West in general as suffering from a ''chronic cold of the soul'' and, during a climactic interview for *60 Minutes,* he reveals his own complicity in perpetuating America's moral malaise.

There are also interesting metafictional scenes in the novel. Just as Austin McMillan reflects upon the function of diaries in *Home Repairs*, Ashton is able to comment on the process of orally telling one's story—the book itself is meant to be the transcribed recordings of Ashton speaking into a microphone. Although Ellis's stylistic refashionings and profound witticism have often been the object of critical praise, his objectification of women has also been the target of critical censure. That Ellis has been charged with participating in a black masculinist tradition is not surprising given his aesthetic affinities with Ishmael Reed. Ellis's experimental approach matches Reed's zealous incorporation of techniques widely thought of as postmodern—even though the novels of both Reed and Ellis tend to support arguments made by Henry Louis Gates, Jr., and Phillip Brian Harper that techniques such as pastiche and metafiction are not new to Afrocentric aesthetics, but have always been central to the parodic, tricksterish practices of African-American storytelling.

—Michael A. Chaney

ELLROY, James

Nationality: American. **Born:** 1948. **Family:** 1) married (divorced 1991); 2) Helen Knode. **Career:** Has held a variety of jobs, including country club caddy, 1965–84. Since 1984, full-time writer. **Agent:**

Nat Sobel, Sobel Weber Assc., 146 East 19th St., New York, New York 10003, U.S.A. **Address:** 84 Siwanoy Blvd., Eastchester, New York 10707, U.S.A.

PUBLICATIONS

Novels

Brown's Requiem. New York, Avon, 1981; London, Allison and Busby, 1984.
Clandestine. New York, Avon, 1982; London, Allison and Busby, 1984.
Blood on the Moon. New York, Mysterious Press, 1984; London, Allison and Busby, 1985.
Because the Night. New York, Mysterious Press, 1984; London, Century, 1987.
Suicide Hill. New York, Mysterious Press, 1986; London, Century, 1988.
Killer on the Road. New York, Mysterious Press, 1986.
Silent Terror. New York, Mysterious Press, 1986; London, Arrow, 1990.
L.A. Quartet:
The Black Dahlia. New York, Mysterious Press, 1987; London, Mysterious Press UK, 1988.
The Big Nowhere. New York, Mysterious Press, 1988; London, Mysterious Press UK, 1989.
L.A. Confidential. New York and London, Mysterious Press, 1990.
White Jazz. New York, Knopf, and London, Random House, 1992.
American Tabloid. New York, Knopf, and London, Century, 1995.
L.A. Noir. (contains *Blood on the Moon, Because the Night,* and *Suicide Hill*). New York, Mysterious Press, 1998.

Short Stories

Hollywood Nocturnes. New York, Knopf, 1994; as *Dick Contino's Blues and Other Stories.* London, Arrow, 1994.

Other

Murder and Mayhem: An A-Z of the World's Most Notorious Killers. London, Arrow, 1992.
My Dark Places: An L.A. Crime Memoir. New York, Knopf, 1996.
Crime Wave: Reportage and Fiction from the Underside of L.A. New York, Vintage, 1999.

*

Film Adaptations: *L.A. Confidential*, 1997.

Manuscript Collection: Thomas Cooper Library, University of South Carolina, Columbia, South Carolina.

* * *

Labeling James Ellroy a writer of hardboiled crime or *noir* fiction oversimplifies his contribution to American imaginative writing. Although his earliest novels belong to the generic crime mode perfected by masters like Chandler, Cain, and MacDonald, the originality of recent works like *Dick Contino's Blues* and *American Tabloid* compel a different critical attention. After ten successful works of a pulp fiction both unsentimental and romantic, this unorthodox author began to depict life in America at the end of the 20th century as a remembered story of comically exaggerated criminality.

Similar traits stamp Ellroy's first two novels, *Brown's Requiem* and *Clandestine,* as the work of a gifted but unpracticed author: disturbed cops corrupted by the crime world they are supposed to combat; redeeming women who are (or were) hookers; sprawling, ill-managed plots loaded with depravity and violence. The second book replicates the framework of the murder of Ellroy's mother (which occurred in 1958 and remains unsolved), and it includes a portrait of himself as the young boy he was at the time of her death. His next projects were a long saga of the caper-filled life of gangster Bugsy Siegel and an extended epic of the Los Angeles underworld that concluded with the city's burning down. Persuaded to abandon *The Confessions of Bugsy Siegel,* Ellroy reworked and published the L.A. epic as *Blood on the Moon* in 1984. With his next two novels, *Because the Night* and *Suicide Hill,* it formed a trilogy about the brilliant but tainted L.A. cop, Lloyd Hopkins, described by *New York* magazine contributor Martin Kihn as ''an evil-genius ... [who] becomes by the end of the series the archetypal Ellroy cop, indistinguishable from his prey and tortured by guilt.'' These were followed in 1986 by *Killer on the Road,* narrated by a serial killer named Martin Plunkett. Then Ellroy returned to the city and time of his own genesis—Los Angeles, from the late 1940s until 1958—to produce the four novels that constitute the ''L.A. Quartet'': *The Black Dahlia, The Big Nowhere, L.A. Confidential,* and *White Jazz.* Published between 1987 and 1992, they catapulted James Ellroy into the top rank of new, original crime fiction authors.

These progressively baroque stories of corruption, depravity, and violence turn Los Angeles into an emblematic urban inferno for our time. *The Black Dahlia*'s hero is the sensitive ex-boxer, Bucky Bleichert, who joins the LAPD after World War II and is soon plunged into the famous 1947 ''Black Dahlia'' murder case, a social storm whipped up by the discovery of a young woman's mutilated body in a Los Angeles vacant lot. Obsessively pursuing a solution to the case (in reality it went unsolved), the naive Bleichert is personally transformed through a violent plot that parallels both the course of the murder investigation and the path of his relationships with fellow cops, a kindred detective partner, their shared lover, and a sexually irresistible female in her twenties who perversely relives the sordid career of the mysterious ''Black Dahlia.'' Called by Harlan Ellison ''the shocker other writers would kill to have written,'' *The Black Dahlia* is dedicated to ''Geneva Hilliker Ellroy 1915–1958,'' and inscribed ''Mother: Twenty-nine Years Later, This Valediction in Blood.''

The heroes of the next three novels of the ''L.A. Quartet'' live, like Bucky Bleichert, in the region between morally unredeemable personal lives and the enveloping swamp of American urban corruption. Harboring terrible personal secrets, they are driven to accomplish something honest in their compromised lives, while also furiously compelled to identify the wellsprings of their spiritual torture. They move through plots that compound sensational incident and crazy complication at exponentially gathering paces, leading to tensilely wrought climaxes. Their adventures are narrated with a progressively condensed, high-energy expressiveness that mimics the several dictions of mainstream newspaper, sensational tabloid, gossip magazine, municipal bureaucracy, advertising agency, and police communication. Ellroy gives them speech and thought that convincingly captures the talk and intelligence of working cops, established gangsters, ethnic Los Angelenos, and most of the numerous types who populate the city's sprawling lowlife.

In *The Big Nowhere,* Ellroy employs a multiple point-of-view, his trio of compromised heroes carrying a three-strand plot that focuses on the early-1950s hunt for Communists in the movie business, the conspiracy between organized crime and the LAPD, and the growing phobia about homosexuality in American society. Young sheriff's deputy Danny Upshaw transforms his buried secret of unadmitted homosexuality into an obsessive zeal to prosecute the perpetrators of a string of revoltingly perverse sex murders. His counterparts, an ambitious police sergeant and an expulsed city cop turned private security guard, are similarly driven to compensate for self-perceived failures of character. The corrupt social system ultimately does them all in, leaving the Irish-born, diabolically conniving LAPD detective, Dudley Smith, to rule over the criminal infestation that defines American life more and more into the 1950s.

Dave Klein, the hero of *White Jazz,* is the most morally tortured cop-hero of the ''Quartet.'' A sublimated incestuous relationship with his sister not only prevents his finding pleasure in women, but also shackles him psychologically to every prurient vice assignment. Everything in his barely tolerable environment stimulates his murderous inclinations, and his history of quasi-official executions and betrayals allows his departmental superiors to expose him to deadly hazards. Klein nevertheless succeeds in enlisting our sympathy, both by wrestling with his inner torment and by regarding his repulsive world honestly. In the most extreme act of unlawfulness yet committed by an Ellroy cop-hero, he exacts a ferocious revenge on the plot's lead villains, as penalty for which he suffers a beating so thorough that his physiognomy requires rebuilding. Thus disguised, he escapes his avengers and finds the freedom to set down this supposed ''memoir'' of horrible events in Los Angeles of the mid-1950s which we are reading.

The theme of an archetypal villainy rooted in the police mentality itself may dominate the four novels of the ''L.A. Quartet,'' but Ellroy also injects them with an increasingly comic serum by portraying many of the secondary characters—especially the historically documentable gangsters and celebrities—as familiar caricatures. Although it seems clear that he means to suggest thereby the ludicrous influence wrought on the American imagination by these publicity-fashioned personalities, with their outlandish behavior and bizarrely demotic lingo, some critics have found it callously offensive of Ellroy to bestow such unacceptable views and articulateness upon both his demi-heroes and their low-life confreres. But this presumed political incorrectness is also quite authentic, both behaviorally and linguistically. Indeed, the characters' aggregate argot constitutes a colorfully ''hip'' language all its own, a kind of fictively vulgar tongue for late century. These figures may therefore be heard as speaking in the submerged ''voice of our time,'' uttering the unspoken views of a sickened national conscience. On this matter, Ellroy is quoted by Kihn as saying: ''I think that social revisionism and political correctness make for very, very bad crime novels.''

The 1994 collection of short pieces, *Hollywood Nocturnes,* offers an excellent sampling of Ellroy's developing dark-comic rendition of the world as a kaleidoscopic cartoon of corruption. The centerpiece of the compendium is the novella, *Dick Contino's Blues,* whose first-person narrator is the documentable Contino himself, a reasonably successful pop singer and accordionist of the 1950s. Ellroy has him tell a manic adventure story set in southern California, a tale of grade-Z Hollywood movies, sexual hustling, extortion, murder, and drug-dealing, enacted with a breathless brio by gangsters, politicians, moguls, detectives, and a gallery of L.A. citizenry—car salesmen, beat cops, real estate brokers, singers, hookers, waitresses, Disney artists, bureaucrats, small-time hoodlums, and every kind of proto-lounge lizard. In short, it is the usual Ellroy circus, but performing in a more than usually bizarre Ellroy plot.

Together with its introductory essay, ''Out of the Past,'' *Dick Contino's Blues* encapsulates all the energies and impetuses of Ellroy's literary quest for his own life's significance, a creative destiny he has been pursuing unwittingly (it turns out) since the age of 30, when, after almost dying from drug and alcohol abuse three years earlier, he finally decided to start writing. His impetus for the novelistic experiment came from a recalled image of the entertaining Contino in a 1958 television appearance, an image that coalesced with a photograph, sent to him years later by a friend, taken of the ten-year-old Ellroy on June 22, 1958, minutes after he was told that his mother had been found murdered. As he relates in ''Out of the Past:''

> The photo held me transfixed; its force transcended my many attempts to exploit my past for book sales. An underlying truth zapped me: my bereavement, even in that moment, as ambiguous. I'm already calculating potential advantages, regrouping as the officious men surrounding me defer to the perceived grief of a little boy.

After he had framed the photo and stared at it for ''a good deal of time,'' he writes, ''Spark point: late '50s memories re-ignited.'' In his sparked memory, the ''grade-Z movie'' *Daddy-O* that Contino made after his career had been torpedoed by a charge of draft-dodging merges with Ellroy's awakening perception that the ''L.A. Quartet'' novels contain the significant secrets still locked in his own memory; these secrets now promise an emergent clarity because they have been re-contextualized by the chance juxtaposition of shocked boy's photo and lounge entertainer's television image, both deriving from the late 1950s. ''Because I knew—instinctively—that he held important answers. I sensed that he could powerfully spritz narrative detail and fill up holes in my memory, bringing Los Angeles in the late '50s into some sort of hyper-focus.'' Memory, for Ellroy, is ''that place where personal recollections collide with history.''

Finding the 63-year-old Dick Contino in Las Vegas, the author of ten money-making crime novels confirmed the feeling that he was about to change direction in his writing. In two days of conversations—about how to adjust to shifting popular taste, what constitutes quality in popular entertainment, why the audience cannot be deprived of their easy entertainment—Ellroy solidified his sense that his ''world had tilted toward a new understanding of my past.'' After the accordionist had serenaded him for his forty-fifth birthday, Ellroy says: ''I asked Dick if he would consent to appear as the hero of a novella and my next novel.'' These would be books about ''fear, courage and heavily compromised redemptions.'' Contino agreed, saying: ''Good, I think I've been there.''

These insights and the narrative action of *Dick Contino's Blues* make it possible to appreciate Ellroy's earlier fiction for more than the raw, sensational, titillating effects of its plots and narrative energies. At a deeper level, the maniacal violence and cold-bloodedness in them manifest the author's passionate need to understand the fullness of his half-buried personal memory, which had both haunted and eluded him. As he says, quoting Jung: ''What is not brought to consciousness comes to us as fate.'' He refers both to his finding of

Dick Contino and to his fictive sallies into the period shared by Contino's mid-life and his own childhood, the American post-Korea 1950s.

In *American Tabloid,* the novel he was writing as he also plotted the Contino novella, Ellroy breaks away from Los Angeles as his main fictive venue. The crime chronicler's American version of the City of Dis now spreads out to encompass all the sites of the momentous events leading to the assassination of John F. Kennedy. And the plot, tapping the several modes of contemporary American fiction that have already engaged this modern mythic material, gleefully tangles up the high-fictional doings of the Mafia, the CIA, the Kennedys, J. Edgar Hoover, Jimmy Hoffa, and the sundry organizations involved in early 1960s civil rights, racket-busting, Kennedy electioneering, the Bay of Pigs, and anti-Communism, not to omit a menagerie of Hollywood and showbiz characters ranging from Marilyn Monroe to Howard Hughes.

Miami, Chicago, New York, Los Angeles, New Orleans, and several other purviews of the Mob, the CIA, and the FBI intertwine to form a plot terrain that could compete, in its sweep and detail, with the combined features of Dali, Brueghel, Villon, and Rabelais. This ground is traversed with extreme modern facility by the novel's three maculate heroes: Kemper Boyd, a stone-souled free agent of conspiracy and a genius at multiple role-playing; Ward Littell, a guilt-infected repository of self-destructiveness and Jesuit-schooled moral absolutism, deteriorating sympathetically into a helpless American amorality; and Pete Bondurant, the hired hitman and dope-runner carried over from his minor role in *White Jazz* to discharge the duties of an old-fashioned fictional heavy who turns out to be a romantic. An introductory note, presuming the would-be narrative authority to ''tell it like it is,'' declares that America, having long since lost its innocence, now needs to look at its recent traumatic history from the point of the view of the ''bad little men'' who have actually shaped it. These duly become the characters of Ellroy's most picaresque novel to date. *American Tabloid* presents the historic adventures of all the American rogues one can imagine participating in the early 1960s' *commedia* of Camelot, Cuba, and the CIA.

James Ellroy has declared that he wants to recreate the entire history of 20th-century America—''the story of bad white men''—through crime fiction, thereby becoming ''the Tolstoy of the crime novel.'' With the Contino novella and *American Tabloid,* he revealed a bold new direction to this design. He would not merely insert historical personages into his stories and rewrite their lives' facts, as docu-novelists like Norman Mailer and Don DeLillo were still doing; he would appropriate a still-living, modest entertainment figure from those ''bad old days'' like Dick Contino and make him the ''improved'' narrative hero of his memorial crime fictions. In this process, he would also refine the comic sensibility that has been growing through his years of holding off the demons of personal bitterness and egomania. As his friend Joseph Wambaugh told Martin Kihn: ''I always suspect that beneath [his anger and intensity] there's a performer there .... You sort of know you're being put on when you're with James Ellroy—maybe even when you read him, in a sense.'' Ellroy's fictional performances, inspired by their fiercely unsentimental vision of our times, do indeed disclose a Beckett-like comedian who, spawned in Los Angeles, California, in the middle of the century, seems destined to chronicle its absurd, criminal course ironically—as if it were his own life's perfect metaphor. In the memoir *My Dark Places,* Ellroy explores the relationship between his early influences—most of all the murder of his mother—and his eventual development as a writer. ''The 47-year-old man,'' he writes, ''had to interrogate the 10-year-old boy.''

—Peter W. Ferran

ELY, David

Nationality: American. **Born:** Chicago, Illinois, 19 November 1927. **Education:** The University of North Carolina, Chapel Hill, 1944–45; Harvard University, Cambridge, Massachusetts, 1947–49, B.A. 1949; St. Antony's College, Oxford (Fulbright scholar), 1954–55. **Military Service:** Served in the United States Navy, 1945–46, and the United States Army, 1950–52. **Family:** Married Margaret Jenkins in 1954; four children. **Career:** Reporter, St. Louis *Post-Dispatch,* 1949–50, 1952–54, 1955–56; administrative assistant, Development and Resources Corporation, New York, 1956–59. **Awards:** Mystery Writers of America Edgar Allan Poe award, for short story, 1962. **Address:** P.O. Box 1387, East Dennis, Massachusetts 02641, U.S.A.

PUBLICATIONS

Novels

Trot: A Novel of Suspense. New York, Pantheon, 1963; London, Secker and Warburg, 1964.
Seconds. New York, Pantheon, 1963; London, Deutsch, 1964.
The Tour. New York, Delacorte Press, and London, Secker and Warburg, 1967.
Poor Devils. Boston, Houghton Mifflin, 1970.
Walking Davis. New York, Charterhouse, 1972.
Mr. Nicholas. New York, Putnam, 1974; London, Macmillan, 1975.
A Journal of the Flood Year. New York, Fine, and London, Phoenix, 1992.

Short Stories

Time Out. New York, Delacorte Press, 1968; London, Secker and Warburg, 1969.
Always Home and Other Stories. New York, Fine, 1991.

Uncollected Short Stories

''The Wizard of Light,'' in *Amazing* (New York), March 1962.
''The Alumni March,'' in *Cosmopolitan* (New York), 1962.
''McDaniels' Flood,'' in *Elks Magazine* (Chicago), 1963.
''The Captain's Boarhunt,'' in *Saturday Evening Post* (Philadelphia), 21 March 1964.
''The Assault on Mount Rushmore,'' in *Cavalier* (New York), July 1969.
''The Carnival,'' in *Antaeus* (New York), 1971.
''The Light in the Cottage,'' in *Playboy* (Chicago), 1974.
''Starling's Circle,'' in *Ellery Queen's Mystery Magazine* (New York), July 1976.
''The Running Man,'' in *Ellery Queen's Mystery Magazine* (New York), December 1976.
''The Weed Killer,'' in *Ellery Queen's Mystery Magazine* (New York), May 1977.

''The Temporary Daughter,'' in *Seventeen* (New York), April 1978.
''The Rich Girl,'' in *Seventeen* (New York), July 1978.
''The Looting of the Tomb,'' in *Ellery Queen's Scenes of the Crime,* edited by Ellery Queen. New York, Davis, 1979; London, Hale, 1981.
''The Marked Man,'' in *Best Detective Stories of the Year 1980,* edited by Edward D. Hoch. New York, Dutton, 1980.
''Methuselah,'' in *Atlantic* (Boston), March 1980.

* * *

David Ely's fiction describes the cost and conditions of freedom—what an ordinary man must do to understand himself and his world. His novels are shaped like thrillers; in each a man is driven onto a quest (initially for the wrong motives) which ultimately leads him to himself, to his unconscious mind, his heart. The novels describe with remarkable sensitivity individuals coping with worlds that are alien, inimical and all-powerful. The triumph of the individual spirit in hostile modern milieu is accompanied by pain and sorrow, loss of innocence and simple comfort, but it brings both self-knowledge and peace.

Trot, Ely's first novel, is subtitled ''A Novel of Suspense'' and predicates the world of all of Ely's fiction: an alien, minatory and hostile environment, in this case the Paris underworld after World War II. An Army CID man, Sergeant Trot, abruptly becomes the victim in a case on which he is assigned. Suspected of corruption and murder, he hides with the criminals he has stalked. The inversion of his world causes him to reassess his concepts of justice and freedom. Finally he is able to reinstate himself by breaking an extortion-murder plot by escaped Nazis. But the significant victory is Trot's own self-revelation.

In *Seconds,* probably Ely's best-known novel, a Babbitt-like man, a cipher known only by the code name ''Wilson,'' abandons his comfortable but aimless upper-middle-class existence when a mysterious corporation offers him a new life, a second chance. He is surgically rehabilitated and supplied a total identity as a successful artist, but the new freedom proves too painful and challenging. Wilson disintegrates under the stress of his open and unfamiliar world of freedom and nonconformity. ''I never had a dream,'' he says when he returns to the corporation to be erased.

The Tour deals with the same theme in a more terrifying form. A parable of American imperialism and military-scientific manipulation of other cultures, it describes a ''tour'' designed to provide jaded bourgeois travelers with ultimate thrills in a mythical Central American banana republic. The tour includes episodes of sex, jungle survival and guerrilla fighting, carefully staged for the fuddled gringos. Behind the scenes a test is made on an automated counter-insurgency weapon, a robot tank which wipes out a starveling guerrilla band (and its builders) and nearly decimates the tour. The novel develops as an analogue for U.S. involvement in Southeast Asia and for other paramilitary ''tours'' of policy. It is similar in shape to Peter Matthiessen's important *At Play in the Fields of the Lord.*

Poor Devils attacks the sociological concepts of poverty and its alleviation. Another parable, it describes the slow education of a history professor, Aaron Bell, who stumbles onto a Project Nomad, a genocidal agency for a ''final solution'' to poverty, a technological bureau that fights poverty with coldly mechanical games theory and supertechnology. Bell's education leads him to discover the futility of his life and his career, the absurdity of history and ideals faced with amoral technology. The old man he has pursued, Lundquist, a ''picaresque saint,'' teaches him finally that he must discover (or invent) his values himself. Bell opts out of the system of research and manipulation to become a Whitmanesque wanderer, following the ''Lundquist heresy, the preamble written short for men in too big a hurry to read much: *Life, liberty, and the pursuit.*''

An allegorical study of personality in existentialist terms, *Walking Davis* describes Pierce Davis, who decides to walk around the world. Setting out from Spark, Iowa, Davis makes a Robinson Crusoe voyage of survival and self-discovery, finally plumbing all his human resources and learning that ''You can't build a monument to a hero. If a man's a hero, he builds his own.'' His walk leads him into a strange union with nature and himself, stripped of all pretense like Camus's Sisyphus, reduced to one essential human function—questing.

Mr. Nicholas describes the complete symptomology of paranoia, centering on an executive in the surveillance industry who becomes convinced that ''He was being watched everywhere and all the time.'' The protagonist, Henry Haddock, eventually adjusts to a life without privacy, wherein his public function subsumes his whole personality, and he becomes reconciled to a world without privacy, without self. The story develops allegorically in that it describes a whole world pressed and overcrowded, when personal rights are lost to the pressure of the many.

Ely's novels are all parables of the New Babbitt redeemed, the affluent and self-satisfied ''Executive Man'' freed to make real, life-or-death decisions, to direct his life and test the morality of his society. The transformations are costly, painful and sometimes tragic, but they are real and significant actions, leaps of faith which give meaning to the small existences Ely depicts.

—William J. Schafer

EMECHETA, (Florence Onye) Buchi

Nationality: British. **Born:** Lagos, Nigeria, 21 July 1944. **Education:** Methodist Girls' High School, Lagos; University of London, B.Sc. (honors) in sociology 1972. **Family:** Married Sylvester Onwordi in 1960 (separated 1969); two sons and three daughters. **Career:** Librarian, 1960–64; library officer, British Museum, London, 1965–69; youth worker and resident student, Race, 1974–76; community worker, Camden Council, London, 1976–78; visiting lecturer at 11 universities in the United States, 1979; senior research fellow and visiting professor of English, University of Calabar, Nigeria, 1980–81; lecturer, Yale University, New Haven, Connecticut, 1982. Since 1982, lecturer, University of London. Proprietor, Ogwugwu Afo Publishing Company, London; since 1979, member of the Home Secretary's Advisory Council on Race. **Address:** 7 Briston Grove, London N8 9EX, England.

Publications

Novels

In the Ditch. London, Barrie and Jenkins, 1972.
Second-Class Citizen. London, Allison and Busby, 1974; New York, Braziller, 1975.
The Bride Price. London, Allison and Busby, and New York, Braziller, 1976.

The Slave Girl. London, Allison and Busby, and New York, Braziller, 1977.
The Joys of Motherhood. London, Allison and Busby, and New York, Braziller, 1979.
Destination Biafra. London, Allison and Busby, 1982.
Double Yoke. London, Ogwugwu Afo, 1982; New York, Braziller, 1983.
Adah's Story. London, Allison and Busby, 1983.
The Rape of Shavi. London, Ogwugwu Afo, 1983; New York, Braziller, 1985.
A Kind of Marriage. London, Macmillan, 1986.
Gwendolen. London, Collins, 1989; as *The Family,* New York, Braziller, 1990.
Kehinde. Oxford, Heinemann, 1994.

Fiction (for children)

Titch the Cat. London, Allison and Busby, 1979.
Nowhere to Play. London, Allison and Busby, 1980.
The Moonlight Bride. Oxford, Oxford University Press, 1980.
The Wrestling Match. Oxford, Oxford University Press, 1981; New York, Braziller, 1983.
Naira Power. London, Macmillan, 1982.

Plays

Television Plays: *A Kind of Marriage,* 1976; *The Ju Ju Landlord,* 1976.

Other

Our Own Freedom, photographs by Maggie Murray. London, Sheba, 1981.
Head above Water (autobiography). London, Ogwugwu Afo, 1986.

*

Critical Studies: *Gender Voices and Choices: Redefining Women in Contemporary African Fiction* by Gloria Chineze Chukukere. Enugu, Nigeria, Fourth Dimension, 1995; *Emerging Perspectives on Buchi Emecheta,* edited by Marie Umeh. Trenton, New Jersey, Africa World Press, 1996; *A Teacher's Guide to African Narratives* by Sara Talis O'Brien. Portsmouth, New Hampshire, Heinemann, 1998; *This Is No Place for a Woman: Nadine Gordimer, Nayantara Sahgal, Buchi Emecheta, and the Politics of Gender* by Joya Uraizee. Trenton, New Jersey, Africa World Press, 1999.

* * *

The title *Second-Class Citizen* which Buchi Emecheta chose for one of her most successful novels constitutes a very fair summary of the major theme which she explores. She always feels for the oppressed and presents their plight in a way that engages the reader's sympathy. From childhood on she observed life in Nigeria, and since her early twenties she has looked at the ways of the west through the skeptical, appraising eyes of a trained sociologist. And what she has seen, whether in Africa or England, has been a bleak picture of antagonisms and tyranny. There are flashes of humor and moments of happiness, but generally she depicts the scouring of human relationships by the desire of the powerful to dominate and exploit those who are weaker.

Married life she depicts as a battle of the sexes, and if some white males are shown in a bad light, that is nothing compared with the portrayal of the Nigerian men. Francis, in *Second-Class Citizen,* is a Nigerian immigrant in London whose thoughtlessness is the ruin of his more gifted wife; lazy, egotistical, and feckless, he compounds every problem that confronts the pair in their struggle to make ends meet, and his sexual demands and irresponsibility about parenthood leave Adah a physical wreck, distraught and without a penny in her pocket. In *The Joys of Motherhood* we become aware of the mordant irony of the title as the novel chronicles the misfortunes of Nnu Ego, a simple Nigerian girl who comes to Lagos to marry and suffers every kind of humiliation as her husband proves himself incapable of overcoming the admittedly difficult circumstances of his wretched existence. Her agony reaches its peak when, in accord with custom, he takes as his second wife the widow of his brother and thoroughly enjoys the tensions this naturally creates.

Tyranny and heartlessness outside the domestic sphere also rouse Emecheta's ire. For many young people in Nigeria education seems to offer a route towards self-fulfillment, but *Double Yoke* shows what the price can be when a young girl tries to cope with the rival claims of tradition and modernity within a system which fundamentally has little to offer that is really valid. The cynicism of the whole enterprise is revealed when the heroine realizes she must trade sexual favors with her professor if she is to gain the examination results she covets. Once she has qualifications she will perhaps be able, like Adah in *Second-Class Citizen,* to go to the United Kingdom and enjoy what it has to offer. In fact, as *Second-Class Citizen* and its grim predecessor, *In the Ditch,* show, London is a hostile world where racialism is rife and housing is squalid. There is the welfare state, of course, yet it operates in such a way that a talented and qualified young woman is gradually but inexorably pauperized and deskilled. *Destination Biafra* is a chilling account of a different sort of horror, the disastrous civil war that ripped Nigeria apart in the difficult times immediately after the withdrawal of the inadequate colonial powers. No atrocity is too cruel for men in brief authority, and though Emecheta has sympathy for everyone, it is natural that the women are shown as those who suffer the most.

Gwendolen changes the focus to some degree, presenting the plight of Caribbean immigrants in London primarily through the perspective of the difficulties that a young girl has in finding any sort of fulfillment as a child and teenager in a culture which means very little to her at any time. A perfect symbol of this failure of integration lies in the fact that even her own family finds pronouncing her rather highfalutin name impossibly difficult. Emecheta is far from ascribing all her heroine's ills to the failure of the citizens of her adopted country to take her to their heart, though there are some criticisms, especially of the education service, that strike home. Gwendolen's misfortunes had, however, already begun before she ever left Jamaica, and in London tensions within the immigrant community are shown to be particularly damaging. Beneath the psychological problems of immigrants there runs, moreover, the deep current of protest at the exploitation of women by men whose sexual demands are never diminished by any sense of their only too apparent personal inadequacies and general fecklessness.

Few will seek to deny that Emecheta has grounds for the complaints she makes about marital relationships in particular and about the interplay of social and political forces in general. Yet she loads the dice a little too much. The girls and women she takes as her heroines always possess something which places them above the ordinary run of those with whom they mix. Birth or superior intelligence makes them outstanding. But it also has the unfortunate consequence of making them atypical of the group they represent. There is, too, some idealization of rural society in Nigeria in former times. It certainly had merits, which colonial powers were stupid not to recognize, yet by concentrating on the more advantaged members of such communities Emecheta distorts the picture. The problem becomes most acute in *The Rape of Shavi,* a somewhat mannered allegorical tale of Europeans who are fleeing from an impending cataclysm, and who have the privilege of insight into an almost Utopian Africa.

For the most part, however, Emecheta's mode is realistic. Indeed, *Kehinde* tackles the problem of idealization head-on, as the title character moves with her husband Albert from London—where she has lived for 18 years—back to Lagos. There she is overwhelmed by the appalling conditions of life, not least her expected role as virtual servant to Albert's every whim. And though *Destination Biafra* contains some devastating pictures of the pretentiousness and luxurious lifestyle of upper-class Nigerians, Emecheta generally concerns herself with the straightforward portrayal of the underprivileged. There is some description of locales, with Nigerian names for plants, foodstuffs, and fabrics adding a dash of local color which sometimes contrasts, especially in the earlier novels, a little too obviously with literary allusions in a dated English tradition. Dialogue is invariably crisp, highlighting important turns in the narrative or enhancing characterization. Above all, Emecheta is a storyteller. The titles of her novels, like the chapter headings, are direct and explicit, helping the reader to see the way forward through narratives that have the power to convince as well as the capacity to arouse sympathy with the misfortunes depicted.

—Christopher Smith

ERDRICH, (Karen) Louise

Nationality: American. **Born:** Little Falls, Minnesota, 7 June 1954. **Education:** Dartmouth College, Hanover, New Hampshire, B.A. 1976; Johns Hopkins University, Baltimore, M.A. 1977. **Family:** Married Michael Anthony Dorris in 1981 (separated; Dorris committed suicide in 1997); three sons and three daughters. **Career:** Visiting poetry teacher, North Dakota State Arts Council, 1977–78; creative writing teacher, Johns Hopkins University, 1978–79; visiting fellow, Dartmouth College, 1981. Member, Turtle Mountain Band of Ojibwa. **Awards:** MacDowell fellowship, 1980; Yaddo fellowship, 1981; Nelson Algren award, for story, 1982; National Book Critics Circle award, 1984; Virginia Sully prize, 1984; Sue Kaufman award, 1984; *Los Angeles Times* Book award, 1985; Guggenheim fellowship, 1985. **Address:** c/o Harper Collins, 10 East 53rd Street, New York, New York 10022, U.S.A.

PUBLICATIONS

Novels

Love Medicine. New York, Holt, 1984; London, Deutsch, 1985; revised and expanded edition, 1993.
The Beet Queen. New York, Holt, 1986; London, Hamish Hamilton, 1987.
Tracks. New York, Holt, and London, Hamish Hamilton, 1988.
Crown of Columbus, with Michael Dorris. New York and London, Harper Collins, 1991.
The Bingo Palace. New York and London, Harper Collins, 1994.
The Bluejay's Dance. New York and London, Harper Collins, 1995.
Grandmother's Pigeon, illustrated by Jim LaMarche. New York, Hyperion Books for Children, 1996.
Tales of Burning Love. New York, HarperCollins, 1996.
The Antelope Wife. New York, HarperFlamingo, 1998.
The Birchbark House, with illustrations by the author. New York, Hyperion Books for Children, 1999.

Uncollected Short Stories

''Scales,'' in *The Best American Short Stories 1983,* edited by Shannon Ravenel and Anne Tyler. Boston, Houghton Mifflin, 1983; as *The Year's Best American Short Stories,* London, Severn House, 1984.
''American Horse,'' in *Earth Power Coming,* edited by Simon J. Ortiz. Tsaile, Arizona, Navajo Community College Press, 1983.
''Destiny,'' in *Atlantic* (Boston), January 1985.
''Mister Argus,'' in *Georgia Review* (Athens), Summer 1985.
''Flesh and Blood,'' in *Buying Time,* edited by Scott Walker. St. Paul, Minnesota, Graywolf Press, 1985.
''Saint Marie,'' in *Prize Stories 1985,* edited by William Abrahams. New York, Doubleday, 1985.
''Fleur,'' in *Prize Stories 1987,* edited by William Abrahams. New York, Doubleday, 1987.
''Snares,'' in *The Best American Short Stories 1988,* edited by Shannon Ravenel and Mark Helprin. Boston, Houghton Mifflin, 1988.
''A Wedge of Shade,'' in *Louder than Words,* edited by William Shore. New York, Vintage, 1989.
''Crown of Thorns,'' in *The Invisible Enemy,* edited by Miriam Dow and Jennifer Regan. St. Paul, Minnesota, Graywolf Press, 1989.
''Matchimanito,'' in *The Best of the West 2,* edited by James Thomas and Denise Thomas. Layton, Utah, Peregrine Smith, 1989.
''The Bingo Van,'' in *New Yorker,* 19 February 1990.
''Happy Valentine's Day, Monsieur Ducharme,'' in *Ladies' Home Journal* (New York), February 1990.
''The Leap,'' in *Harper's* (New York), March 1990.
''Best Western,'' in *Vogue* (New York), May 1990.
''The Dress,'' in *Mother Jones* (San Francisco), July-August 1990.
''The Island,'' in *Ms.* (New York), January-February 1991.

Poetry

Jacklight. New York, Holt, and London, Sphere, 1990.
Baptism of Desire. New York, Harper Collins, 1991.

*

Critical Studies: *Conversations with Louise Erdrich and Michael Dorris,* edited by Allan Chavkin and Nancy Feyl Chavkin. Jackson, University Press of Mississippi, 1994; *The Broom Closet: Secret Meanings of Domesticity in Postfeminist Novels* by Louise Erdrich, Mary Gordon, Toni Morrison, Marge Piercy, Jane Smiley, and Amy Tan by Jeannette Batz Cooperman. New York, Peter Lang, 1999; *The Chippewa landscape of Louise Erdrich,* edited by Allan Chavkin. Tuscaloosa, University of Alabama Press, 1999; *A Reader's Guide to the Novels of Louise Erdrich* by Peter G. Beidler and Gay Barton. Columbia, University of Missouri Press, 1999; *Louise Erdrich: A Critical Companion* by Lorena L. Stookey. Westport, Connecticut, Greenwood Press, 1999; *The Gamefulness of American Postmodernism: John Barth and Louise Erdrich* by Steven D. Scott. New York, Peter Lang, 2000.

* * *

While it may seem that Americans might have recognized a Native American writer well before the end of the twentieth century, it was not until Louise Erdrich published her first novel, *Love Medicine* in 1984, to both critical and popular acclaim that a Native American writing about her heritage and the present condition of her people enjoyed so much notoriety and influence in that country's literature. Erdrich is a prolific writer, and from her novels more readers have begun to appreciate that contemporary Native Americans have important stories to tell that go beyond retelling their ancestors' rich creation myths and legends.

Most of Erdrich's novels have the same geographic center, a fictional Chippewa reservation in North Dakota. From this center characters appear and reappear in different books, and family lines cross and separate in deepening complexity much like an intricate braid or a beaded belt. Not only in the connected novels, but also in the totality of her *oeuvre* to date, Erdrich's accomplishment is that she is weaving a body of work that goes beyond portraying contemporary Native American life as descendants of a politically dominated people to explore the great universal questions—questions of identity, pattern versus randomness, and the meaning of life itself. As she writes at the end of *The Antelope Wife*, ''Who is beading us?...Who are you and who am I, the beader or the bit of colored glass sewn onto the fabric of this earth?''

The connected novels include *Love Medicine, The Beet Queen, Tracks, The Bingo Palace*, and *Tales of Burning Love*. In *Love Medicine*, which first appeared in 1984 but was revised, expanded, and reissued in 1993, the reader meets not only members of three interconnecting families that will populate the later novels, the Kashpaws, the Lazarres, and Lulu Nanapush's extended family, but also Erdrich's style of making a whole out of seemingly random parts. The novel is comprised of short stories that set up this premise both structurally and in content. Plotlines thread and interweave. Among others, plots and subplots include the rivalry between Lulu Nanapush and Marie Lazarre for Nector Kashpay's love; Gerry Nanapush's relationships with June and Dot Adare; and Lipsha Morrissey's giving the raw turkey heart to Nector as love medicine. While the events occur from around 1900 to 1984, they do not always happen chronologically, and the disappearance and reappearance of characters and their relationships to other characters in different time periods often confuse readers until they reach the end of the book.

Events in *The Beet Queen* occur from 1932 to 1972 and are set in the mostly European-American community of Argus, North Dakota. This novel is another gathering of stories into chapters, but this time the focus is turned away from the reservation to life off of it in characters such as Dot Adare, who is part Chippewa but has few on-reservation experiences. Families are separated and unhappy and there is a sense of betrayal, abandonment, and loneliness.

The time period for *Tracks*, the third book in the connected series of novels, is 1912 to 1924 and is told by two alternating narrators: Nanapush, who survived the 1912 consumption epidemic, and Pauline Puyat, a mixed European/Native American who is ashamed of the Indian side of her heritage. Relationships and claims of identity are at stake in this novel.

The Bingo Palace brings the storylines to around the time of 1994–95, shortly after the end of *Love Medicine* chronologically. The primary plot is Lipsha's love for Shawnee Ray, which is made problematic by Shawnee Ray's uncertainty and a rivalry with Lipsha's boss, Lyman. In *Tales of Burning Love*, the time period is from 1962–95, and many of the elements center around Jack Mauser and his five wives.

As her body of work grows, Erdrich's fictional Chippewa Reservation centered around Matchimanito Lake in North Dakota is increasingly compared to William Faulkner's Yoknapatawpha County in Mississippi. Both are imaginary regions of a real American landscape where mixing of the races has caused issues of identity and disconnection.

Some of the confusion readers experience in the connected books is supported by problems in consistency within the later novels. Using the revised *Love Medicine* as a reference point in studying the later novels, critics have since found discrepancies in facts, characterizations, geography, and time among the later books. Whether this is a sign that Erdrich's project became too ambitious and complex even for her to keep straight, or whether the discrepancies are intentional as an expression of randomness, or a signal by which to recognize unreliable narrators, or an echoing back to the lack of concern for facts in the oral tradition of storytelling, it should be noted that the inconsistencies are a facet of Erdrich's work in the connected novels that will undoubtedly be further studied and explored.

Erdrich appears to depart from the series with *The Antelope Wife*. This novel introduces a different set of families: the Roy family, the Shawango family, and the Whiteheart Beads. In this novel, Erdrich seems to be stretching the thread on which she has beaded her stories in the previous books. While in the previous books readers beheld animals that had human characteristics, in *The Antelope Wife* this connectedness is heightened to the point where people are actually descended from animals such as the deer and antelope. While genders cross in her earlier work, in this one a soldier suckles babies. One wonders if, perhaps, Erdrich is not attempting to explore the so-called circle of life from every possible direction.

With the publication of *Birch House*, a juvenile novel that is similar to Laura Ingalls Wilder's *Little House on the Prairie* but from a Native American perspective, Erdrich has embarked on yet another planned series of novels. This one promises to be an important, fruitful addition to the historical novel genre for children.

—Connie Ann Kirk

ERICSON, Walter

See FAST, Howard (Melvin)

ESSOP, Ahmed

Has also written as Ahmed Yousuf. **Nationality:** Indian. **Born:** Dabhel, Surat, 1 September 1931. **Education:** The University of South Africa, Pretoria, B.A. 1956, B.A. (honours) in English 1964. **Family:** Married Farida Karim in 1960; four children. **Career:** Teacher at a secondary school, Eldorado Park, Johannesburg, 1980–85. **Awards:** English Academy of Southern Africa Schreiner award, 1979. **Address:** Raven Press, P.O. Box 145, Randburg, Johannesburg 2125, South Africa.

PUBLICATIONS

Novels

The Visitation. Johannesburg, Ravan Press, 1980.
The Emperor. Johannesburg, Ravan Press, 1984.

Short Stories

The Hajji and Other Stories. Johannesburg, Ravan Press, 1978; as *Hajji Musa and the Hindu Fire-Walker,* Columbia, Louisiana, Readers International, 1988.
Noorjehan and Other Stories. Johannesburg, Ravan Press, 1990.

Poetry

The Dark Goddess (as Ahmed Yousuf). London, Mitre Press, 1959.

*

Manuscript Collection: National English Literary Museum, Grahamstown, South Africa.

Critical Studies: "Mr. Sufi Climbs the Stairs: The Quest and the Ideal in Ahmed Essop's *The Visitation*" by Eugenie Freed, in *Theoria* (Pietermaritzburg, Natal), May 1988; "Straightforward Politics and Ironic Playfulness: The Aesthetic Possibilities of Ahmed Essop's *The Emperor*" by Antje Hagena, in *English in Africa* (Grahamstown, Cape Province), October 1990.

* * *

Ahmed Essop's fiction displays a marvelously realized sense of place and the ability to regard human nature, even at its most absurdly self-centered or viciously craven, as still worthy of some pity. Fordsburg, within metropolitan Johannesburg, is in Essop's writing what Malgudi is in R.K. Narayan's. Both are Indian places; their inhabitants have Indian names, often speak with similar accents, and would not feel entirely lost culturally if translated to each others' towns. In Fordsburg the women wear saris and there are "the raucous voices of vendors … the spicy odors of Oriental foods, the bonhomie of communal life." Older Fordsburgians usually speak Gujarati or Urdu and try to preserve traditional customs like arranged marriages. Hindu and Muslim religious observances exist side by side, with both rivalry and some merging at the edges (as in the Caribbean) rather than as potential sources of communal violence. As in Trinidad and Guyana, the Indian proletariat and the educated alike speak a regional variety of English, illustrated by this passage of invective from "Hajji Musa and the Hindu Fire-Walker":

> "You liar! You come and tell me dat good-for-nutting Dendar boy, dat he good, dat he ejucated, dat he good prospect. My foot and boot he ejucated! He sleep most time wit bitches, he drink and beat my daughter. When you go Haj? You nutting but liar. You baster! You baster!"

The Afrikaans word "baster" (bastard) here signals the South African provenance of Essop's fiction about the largest population of Indian origin outside the sub-continent. Indeed Hindu and Muslim can taunt each other safely, in the knowledge that historically they have more in common than with members of other South African communities.

With its extension Newtown, Fordsburg seems to be based upon realities of Essop's childhood and youth before and during the 1950s campaign of passive resistance to apartheid, when there was a stronger sense of "Indianness," despite socializing and sexual encounters across racial boundaries. More secular and less traditional is Lenasia, beyond the Johannesburg perimeter, where *The Emperor* is set, a government-built township for the decanting of Fordsburg Indians, thus allowing white suburbs around Fordsburg to expand conveniently and cheaply.

It is in *The Hajji and Other Stories* that the life of Fordsburg/Newtown is most engagingly and unpretentiously set forth. Nearly half the stories are satirizations of human beings falling short of the high standards of personal and social behavior that they profess: Dr. Kamal's political cowardice in "The Betrayal"; Yogi Khrishnasiva's covert fornication in his pursuit of spiritual liberation in "The Yogi," the holy men forced to seek refuge in the cinema and watch a film on "The Prophet" so as to escape the public violence they have stirred up as a protest against the screening of that film, the irrepressible Hajii Musa, in hospital with badly burned feet, dismissing Hindu fire-walking as "showmanship" after his own unsuccessful attempt. At his best, Essop strips pretense, hypocrisy, untruth, and deviousness from his characters and shows the naked humanity beneath, but with an imaginative and delicate understanding of the humiliation that people suffer when thus exposed, as in "The Hajii," where obdurate refusal to condone a brother's past apostasy results only in self-inflicted hurt and spiritual aridity, or the 70-year-old father's pathetic defeat when his new young second wife divorces him, Muslim-fashion, in preference for his own son. Some of the stories are competent psychological studies, as of the victim-figure in "The Target," or of the self-important (unto insanity) high school headmaster in "Gladiators," of the ambivalently dedicated political characters eventually left utterly isolated in "Ten Years" and "In Two Worlds." A frequent theme is the loss of human dignity, whether of the genuine or the merely outward kind. Occasionally Essop unnecessarily resorts to melodrama and sensationalism, as in "Labyrinth" and "Mr. Moonreddy."

The novel, *The Visitation,* sparkles with lively ideas and flashes of invention that on the whole don't quite coalesce. Mr. Sufi, a wealthy, complacent property owner, married but with a satisfying concubine discreetly housed in each of his apartment buildings, conducts his life quietly and respectably, even turning his monthly payment of protection money to the racketeer Gool into a polite little social ceremony. By the simple expedient of delivering large quantities of obviously stolen electric lamps to Sufi's home, Gool gains the blackmailer's firm hold upon a timid victim. Ironically, the lamps usher Sufi into an existence of darkness, fear, panic, and hallucination. As Gool and his thugs take over Sufi's very life, including his rent-collecting, like a supernatural visitation, he gradually realizes that they are doing crudely and violently what he has always done urbanely but equally ruthlessly. Even his love-life is reduced, when he witnesses Gool's sexual contortions with one of his former concubines. Clearly Gool is a doppelgänger, revealing to Sufi his own true nature—selfish, sensual, and sadistic—which he'd tried to cloak respectably. The weakness is that Gool becomes a mere caricature of criminality. The narrative might have been even more persuasive had Gool's wilder actions been incorporated in Sufi's hallucinations.

Caricature as a substitute for characterization is a legitimate satirist's tool, though probably more successful within the narrower compass of a short story than in the fuller extent and more subtle shadings of a novel. The Lenasia headmaster, Mr. Dharama Ashoka, the central character in *The Emperor,* is a ''stooge'' Indian, a creature of the apartheid state with an unassuageable appetite for power. The ludicrous story of his rise and downfall is also the tragedy of his wrong-headedness. The author's ingenious schema isn't really credible—an analysis, in one persona, of both arrogance and its necessary pettinesses in exercising power, with Ashoka as a possible figuring of the apartheid state and his opponents as the resistance. But Essop's ultimate interest in human individuality undercuts such a reading, making Ashoka at the end (like Sufi in *The Visitation*), a man to be pitied in the hour of his humiliating self-knowledge.

—Arthur Ravenscroft

EVERETT, Percival L.

Nationality: American. **Born:** Fort Gordon, Georgia, 22 December 1956. **Education:** University of Miami, A.B. 1977; attended University of Oregon, 1978–80; Brown University, A.M. 1982. **Career:** Worked as jazz musician, ranch worker, and high school teacher; associate professor of English and director of graduate creative writing program, University of Kentucky, Lexington, 1985–89; associate professor of English, University of Notre Dame, Notre Dame, Indiana, 1989–92; professor of creative writing, University of California, Riverside, 1992—. **Awards:** D. H. Lawrence fellowship, University of New Mexico, 1984; Lila Wallace-Reader's Digest fellowship. **Agent:** Candida Donadio, 231 West 22nd Street, New York, New York 10011, U.S.A. **Address:** Department of Creative Writing, University of California, Riverside, CA 92521, U.S.A.

Publications

Novels

Suder. New York, Viking, 1983.
Walk Me to the Distance. New York, Ticknor & Fields, 1985.
Cutting Lisa. New York, Ticknor & Fields, 1986.
Zulus. Sag Harbor, New York, Permanent Press, 1989.
For Her Dark Skin. Owl Creek Press, 1989.
God's Country. Boston, Faber and Faber, 1994.
The Body of Martin Aguilera. Owl Creek Press, 1994.
Watershed. Saint Paul, Minnesota, Graywolf Press, 1996.
Frenzy. Saint Paul, Minnesota, Graywolf Press, 1997.
Glyph. Saint Paul, Minnesota, Graywolf Press, 1999.

Short Stories

The Weather and Women Treat Me Fair: Stories. Little Rock, Arkansas, August House, 1989.
Big Picture: Stories. Saint Paul, Minnesota, Graywolf Press, 1996.

Other

The One That Got Away (for children), illustrations by Dirk Zimmer. New York, Clarion Books, 1992.
Contributor, *From Timberline to Tidepool: Contemporary Fiction from the Northwest,* edited by Rich Ives. Owl Creek Press, 1989.

* * *

Born outside of August, Georgia, in 1956, Percival Everett grew up in Columbia, South Carolina, and seems to have the Southern penchant for storytelling in his bones. Averaging a new book about every 18 months, Everett is a prolific and ambitious writer with a fierce imagination.

Like other Southern writers, most notably William Faulkner and Flannery O'Connor, Everett is captivated by what literary criticism calls the grotesque, that sometimes absurd, other times enigmatic admixture of comedy and tragedy. His minor characters in particular are fantastical gargoyle creations that allow the author opportunities for surrealistic subterfuge in virtually all of his work.

Everett's first novel, *Suder,* appeared in 1983. Its African-American protagonist, Suder, is a third-baseman for the Seattle Mariners who is in a slump, both on the field and at home where relations with his wife and son are strained. Suder thus embarks on a journey of inner discovery paralleled by an outlandish series of external events, a thematic structure to be found again and again in Everett's fiction. Sharing an affinity with the eighteenth-century novel, *Suder* is a fast-paced, episodic narrative in which the reader is carried away in a swift stream of improbabilities. The protagonist runs into a drug deal, meets up with a 300-pound vending machine service man, adopts a pet elephant, and even tries his hand at flying. This last twist, however, is more than a fanciful plot device. It also points to Everett's deep interest in mythology and in particular to the myth of flying, a recurring figure in both African folklore and in African-American fiction—Toni Morrison's *Song of Solomon,* for instance. To date, Everett has written two book-length reworkings of ancient Greek mythology, *For Her Dark Skin* and *Frenzy,* about the half-man, half-god Dionysus.

In his latest novel, *Glyph,* Everett joins the tradition of academic satires by the likes of Nabokov or, more recently, Jane Smiley and Don DeLillo. The book is a send-up of academic jargon, especially deconstructionist ''language games,'' but it is also a meditation on language, the nature of genius, and the very real destructiveness of intellectual opportunism. Still, as is characteristic of Everett, *Glyph* is suffused with comedy. The protagonist and narrator is four-year-old Baby Ralph Townsend, a genius baby who reads the classics of Western philosophy and literature, and writes as well, but refuses to speak on aesthetic and philosophical grounds. Baby Ralph's father is a professor of literature and a scholar of the poststructuralist theories of Roland Barthes. At first believing his son retarded because of his refusal to speak, Baby Ralph's father soon realizes that in fact his son is a genius, capable even of blackmailing his father. Ralph's loving mother, by contrast, is a painter, who gives the child his first book, tellingly Wittgenstein's *Tractatus.* As one has come to expect, Everett steers the Townsend family through a veritable labyrinth of intrigue, meeting along the way a violently evil child psychologist, a top-secret military intelligence group, a delusional Catholic priest, and Ferdinand Marcos. Interspersed with the narrative, however, are Everett's pointed interrogations of postmodernism, semiotic analysis, and theoretical pretensions, all styled after the most esoteric discourses of French literary theory.

Everett is also the author of *The One That Got Away*, an imaginative children's book of wordplay about the numeral 1, as corralled by a comic trio of cowpokes.

—Michele S. Shauf

F

FAIRBAIRNS, Zoë (Ann)

Nationality: British. **Born:** Tunbridge Wells, Kent, 20 December 1948. **Education:** St. Catherine's School, Twickenham, Middlesex, 1954–67; University of St. Andrews, Fife, Scotland, 1967–72, M.A. in modern history 1972; College of William and Mary, Williamsburg, Virginia, 1969–70. **Career:** Editor, Campaign for Nuclear Disarmament newspaper *Sanity,* London, 1973–74; freelance journalist, 1975–82; poetry editor, *Spare Rib,* London, 1978–82; fiction reviewer, *Everywoman,* London, 1990–93. Since 1993 subtitler, Independent Television Facilities Centre, West London. C. Day Lewis Fellow, Rutherford School, London, 1977–78; creative writing tutor, City Literary Institute, 1978–82, Holloway Prison, 1978–82, Wandsworth Prison, 1987, Silver Moon Women's Bookshop, 1987 and 1989, and Morley College, 1988 and 1989, all London; writer-in-residence, Bromley schools, Kent, from 1981, and Deakin University, Geelong, Victoria, 1983, Sunderland Polytechnic, Tyne and Wear, 1983–85, and Surrey County Council, 1989. **Awards:** Fawcett prize, 1985; British Council travel grant 1990. Lives in London. **Agent:** A.M. Heath, 79 St. Martin's Lane, London WC2N 4AA, England.

PUBLICATIONS

Novels

Live as Family. London, Macmillan, 1968.
Down: An Explanation. London, Macmillan, 1969.
Benefits. London, Virago Press, 1979; New York, Avon, 1982.
Stand We at Last. London, Virago Press, and Boston, Houghton Mifflin, 1983.
Here Today. London, Methuen, and New York, Avon, 1984.
Closing. London, Methuen, 1987; New York, Dutton, 1988.
Daddy's Girls. London, Methuen, 1991.
Other Names. London and New York, Penguin, 1998.

Short Stories

Tales I Tell My Mother, with others. London, Journeyman Press, 1978; Boston, South End Press, 1980.
More Tales I Tell My Mother, with others. London, Journeyman Press, 1987.

Uncollected Short Stories

"Relics," in *Despatches from the Frontiers of the Female Mind,* edited by Jen Green and Sarah Lefanu. London, Women's Press, 1985.
"Spies for Peace: A Story of 1963," in *Voices from Arts for Labour,* edited by Nicki Jackowska. London, Pluto Press, 1985.
"Covetousness," in *The 7 Deadly Sins,* edited by Alison Fell. London, Serpent's Tail, 1989.
"By the Light of the Silvery Moon," in *By the Light of the Silvery Moon,* edited by Ruth Petrie. London, Virago, 1994.

Plays

Details of Wife (produced Richmond, Surrey, 1973).

Other

Study War No More. London, CND, 1974.
No Place to Grow Up, with Jim Wintour. London, Shelter, 1977.
Peace Moves: Nuclear Protest in the 1980s, with James Cameron, photographs by Ed Barber. London, Chatto and Windus, and Bridgeport, Connecticut, Merrimack, 1984.
Editor, *Women's Studies in the UK,* compiled by Oonagh Hartnett and Margherita Rendel. London, London Seminars, 1975.

*

Zoë Fairbairns comments:

I don't want to comment on my own work, but I'm always pleased and interested to receive comments from readers. (How will I know who you are or what you think, if you don't tell me?) Write to me c/o my agent—I will do my best to reply.

* * *

Zoë Fairbairns is, deservedly, one of the most popular feminist fiction writers working in Britain. Her pacey novels are very much a part of mainstream fiction, making their appeal much broader than that of many more overtly polemical books. At first glance her work seems straight genre fiction; science fiction in *Benefits;* the multi-generational family saga in *Stand We at Last;* the crime thriller in *Here Today.* However, what Fairbairns does is to take each genre and transform it for her own use.

The main theme underlying each of these works is the gradual, irresistible raising of feminist consciousness. Other themes are the complexity of relationships between the sexes; loneliness; the powerlessness of need; and the ever-changing yet somehow constant problems faced by women, whether they be women of the future, the past, or today. Fairbairns approaches all her characters with realism, sympathy, and a great deal of wit. Though her male characters tend to be lightly sketched, her women make up for this lack of depth; they are humorous, deep-thinking, and self-critical; and whenever a character seems to be slipping close to social stereotype, the author quickly steps in with a touch of irony.

Take, for example, the two main characters in *Here Today.* On the one hand there is Catherine, a 30-year-old virgin, feminist, and teacher who, having been made redundant, finds herself thrown into the world of temporary office employment. Shocked by the exploitation of her fellow temps by the employers and job agencies, she sets about undermining the temping system. On the other hand there is fashion-conscious Antonia, one-time self-satisfied "Temp of the Year," who is shaken out of her complacency both by the advent of word-processing which threatens her livelihood and by a bad case of genital herpes which brings about the end of her marriage. Drawn together in an uneasy alliance through their loneliness and their common need to earn a living, the two women embark on an adventurous road to self-fulfillment, fraught with contrasts between the traditional middle- and working-class attitudes to love and work.

The concept of romantic love, though not a central theme, plays a part in Fairbairns's novels. Men tend to be either saints or sinners—and, surprisingly, the saints predominate. In *Here Today,* Catherine forms a close relationship with Frank, a union leader who's extremely sympathetic to the women's movement. In *Benefits,* in many ways the most pessimistic of her books, we are presented with the enlightened, too-good-to-be-true Derek, who bends over backwards not to oppress his journalist wife, Lynn. However, the cold dictates of a superbureaucracy intent on controlling the reproductive rights of its women drives Lynn away from ''the women's pages of the *Guardian*'' towards a more radical feminism epitomized by Collindeane Tower, an abandoned block of council flats which has become home to a leaderless feminist community. As Lynn struggles with mixed feelings about her marriage and her own fertility, the women of Collindeane form ranks against Family, a political party dedicated to restoring so-called ''family values'' by methods of giving or holding back government benefits to those women who do or do not reproduce. The novel takes us from the late 1970s through to a twenty-first century where family planning has become government planning and the fabric of a once-prosperous society is, like Collindeane, crumbling away. Though *Benefits* is a science-fiction novel, the futuristic views of post-industrial Britain depicted in it are, at times, too close to aspects of then-present reality to be comfortable. Poverty and decay are rife in all aspects of society; the Family Party eventually brings about its own destruction; and leaderless feminism seems to lead nowhere. The result is a powerful, chilling, somewhat depressing book.

Despite her preoccupation with the present lot of women, Fairbairns seems more at home when writing about the future or the past. Nowhere is this more evident than in *Stand We at Last,* perhaps the most ambitious of her novels. In her own words ''a family saga with a feminist background,'' it traces the lives of a succession of women, starting in 1855 with the adventurous Sarah who emigrates to Australia hoping to make her fortune as a farmer, and ending with Jackie, a single parent living on a hippie commune in 1970s England. As in her other books, the writer remains true to the genre she has chosen: all of Life is present in this 600-page saga—births, suicides, miscarriages, abortions, raised hopes, dashed ambitions—not to mention love, passion, and sexual guilt. But this is no ordinary rags-to-riches saga; as in all Fairbairns's novels, ambitions are spiritual rather than material; children and men seem to be the rocks on which women's ambitions founder; and in order to break out of the cycle set up by her predecessors, the modern heroine must give up her man rather than get him in the end.

Though the themes in Fairbairns's writing are constant, each novel remains quite distinct in style. Her female characters, who are primarily ordinary people with ordinary problems, manage somehow to be extraordinarily interesting. Her plots are imaginative and gripping, yet as Fairbairns revealed in a 1998 interview with the *Independent,* after her initial success with *Benefits,* she struggled for many years to find her voice. Also in 1998, Fairbairns produced a new novel, *Other Names.*

—Judith Summers

FARAH, Nuruddin

Nationality: Somali. **Born:** Baidoa, 24 November 1945. **Education:** Istituto di Magistrale, Mogadiscio, Somalia, 1964; Panjab University, Chindigarh, India, 1966–70; University of London, 1974–75; University of Essex, Colchester, 1975–76. **Family:** Divorced, one son; remarried in 1992, one daughter. **Career:** Clerk-typist, Ministry of Education, and secondary school teacher, 1969–71, Mogadiscio; teacher, Wardhiigley Secondary School, 1970–71; lecturer, Somali National University, Mogadiscio, 1971–74; guest professor, Bayreuth University, Germany, 1981; associate professor, University of Jos, Nigeria, 1981–83; visiting professor, University of Minnesota, Minneapolis, Autumn 1988, State University of New York, Stony Brook, Spring 1989, and Brown University, Providence, Rhode Island, Autumn 1991. Since 1990 professor, Makerere University, Kampala, Uganda. **Awards:** Unesco fellowship, 1974; English-Speaking Union award, 1980; Corman Artists fellowship, 1990; Tucholsky award for literary exiles (Sweden), 1993; Cavour prize (Italy), 1993; Neustadt International Prize for Literature, 1998. **Agent:** Curtis Brown, 162–168 Regent Street, London W1R 5TB, England.

Publications

Novels

From a Crooked Rib. London, Heinemann, 1970.
A Naked Needle. London, Heinemann, 1976.
Variations in African Dictatorship:
Sweet and Sour Milk. London, Allison and Busby, 1979; St. Paul, Minnesota, Graywolf Press, 1992.
Sardines. London, Allison and Busby, 1981; St. Paul, Minnesota, Graywolf Press, 1992.
Close Sesame. London, Allison and Busby, 1983; St. Paul, Minnesota, Graywolf Press, 1992.
Maps. London, Pan, 1986; New York, Pantheon, 1987.
Gifts. London, Serif, 1992; New York, Arcade, 1999.
Secrets. New York, Arcade, 1998.

Uncollected Short Stories

''Why Dead So Soon?'' in *Somali News* (Mogadiscio), 1965.

Plays

A Dagger in Vacuum (produced Mogadiscio, 1970).
The Offering (produced Colchester, Essex, 1975).
Yussuf and His Brothers (produced Jos, Nigeria, 1982).

Radio Plays: *Tartar Delight,* 1980 (Germany); *A Spread of Butter.* n.d.

Other

Yesterday, Tomorrow: Voices from the Somali Diaspora. London and New York, Cassell, 2000.

*

Critical Studies: *The Novels of Nuruddin Farah* by Derek Wright. Bayreuth, Germany, Bayreuth University, 1994; *Nuruddin Farah* by Patricia Alden and Louis Tremaine. New York, Twayne, 1999.

* * *

When Nuruddin Farah's first novel in English, *From a Crooked Rib*, appeared in the Heinemann African Writers' Series (1970), the book was well received by critics, and Farah was immediately classified as a leading figure among the "second generation" of African writers. While *Sweet and Sour Milk* was about to appear, Farah stayed on a writer's fellowship in Italy and was warned not to return to Somalia, since the dictatorial regime of Siyad Barre had taken offense with his second novel, *A Naked Needle*. Farah decided "not to return home for the time being" and for more than thirty years now, he has been living in different African countries (Sudan, Gambia, Nigeria, Uganda) and has held a number of writer-in-residence positions in Europe and the United States. Since 1998 he has been living in Capetown, South Africa. Apart from his several published novels, Farah has written both stage and radio plays. He is also the author of a nonfiction book on the Somali refugee diaspora.

Since the publication of *From a Crooked Rib* with its first-person narration and simple diction, Farah's narrative style has become more complex. But he has remained faithful to Somalia as the space of his literary imagination and also to the predominant themes of the role of women, the psychology of power relations among men and women and between the generations, and the fragmentation of social structures from the family to the nation state in Africa.

From a Crooked Rib deals with the modern quest of Ebla, who escapes the supression of women in rural Somalia to achieve limited self-determination in the city, thus revolting against a male-dominated society. But Farah retains the structure and the idiom of an oral tale. We first meet Ebla in a community of camel nomads, where everything is determined by outside forces: the seasonal changes from drought to spring rains determine the annual life cycle, the needs of the camels determine the daily cycle of life, and the grandfather who heads the clan determines the social relations within his community. When he arranges a marriage with a husband 40 years her senior, Ebla escapes to a cousin in a small town, only to go through the same experience again, until she finally arrives in Mogadiscio. Ebla's quest unfolds in three stations—country, town, city. Following the typical structure of orality, she has to pass a test and prove herself at each of these stations. However, Ebla proves herself by rejecting female submission to social conformity, in clear contrast to oral morals. Parallel to Ebla's individual life cycle, Farah unfolds in exemplary fashion the life cycle of women from initiation to circumcision, marriage, and births. On the one hand Ebla accepts what seems to her the inescapable demands on women, on the other she learns to transform her traditional gender role into a source of empowerment in that she can exert control over men with her sexuality. She thus arrives at a delicate equilibrum between her individual sexual and moral responsibilties and her social conditioning. Ebla's quest leads her from a simplistic revolt against the domination by her grandfather to mature womanhood with an elaborate set of behavioral codes that allow her to evade male domination. *From a Crooked Rib* reveals two persistent features of Farah's writing: the ambigious tension between formal tradition and intended meaning—in this case the oral structure that carries an emancipatory message—and an ending that precludes unambigous moral conclusions.

After the publication of *A Naked Needle*, Farah designed a novel trilogy titled *Variations in African Dictatorship*. The first novel in this series, *Sweet and Sour Milk*, sets the tone for the following novels, *Sardines*—in which a journalist and her daughter, a national sports champion, decline popularity as puppets in the regime's propaganda machinery—and *Close Sesame*, which deals with the regimes tactics of whipping up clan rivalries to ensure the maintenance of power. As in *Crooked Rib* Farah uses an established literary form, the analytical detective novel, which he infuses with stylistic and structural elements of orality, thus achieving a complexity of form that subverts the simplicity of the "pure" form of the detective novel and the oral tale with contradictions and ambiguities. Loyaan, a dentist, is confronted with the mysterious death of his twin brother Soyaan, a journalist and top government official. Trying to unravel the deadly mysteries, Loyaan delves deeper and deeper into the life of his twin brother. He relives the same experiences as his brother. In a symbolic sequence of two cycles of seven days (death-wake-burial-final obsequities as prescribed in Somali tradition), Loyaan completes his double quest, at the end of which he practically becomes the double, the reincarnation of his own brother. His brother was appointed ambassador to Yugoslavia but died before assuming office. Now Loyaan is appointed to the very same position, and the novel ends with a government limousine picking him up. Just as with his brother, it is left open whether he is really taken to the airport, or rather to a prison cell or an execution chamber of the secret police. Farah bends the narrative form of the analytical detective novel, with its linear plot leading to a definite closure of demystification and the unravelling of the murder mystery, and brings it back in full circle to its beginning—as in an oral tale. Instead of unravelling the mysteries about Soyaan's death, he adds another mystery: whether Loyaan awaits the same fate as his double—his twin brother.

Farah essentially maintains a uniform narrative stance, but his narrator never seems to know more than his characters, and he never enters into complicity with his readers, as is common in detective novels. On the other hand, Farah arranges his characters in pairs, either as supportive doubles (Soyaan and Loyaan) or as Manichean opposites, e.g. the twins and their father, the twins and the regime—an oedipal conflict between the generations but also between modernism and fundamentalist dogmatism. This is exemplified when the twins play with a ball and run enthusiastically to their father, presenting him the ball as the globe. The father rudely denies this heretical idea, pronounces the earth to be flat, and strictly forbids any further games of that nature. He reveals himself as an unenlightened ideologue who acts as a third-rate informer for the secret police.

The trilogy *Variations of African Dictatorships* dealt with the relation of the individual to political power. Farah's second trilogy investigates the impact of international organizations and norms with *Maps* (on colonial boundaries), *Gifts* (on foreign aid), and *Secrets* (on ethical norms). *Maps* foregrounds Somalia's aspiration to true nation-statehood and the ensuing anxieties by neighboring states about Somali irredentism. The Somali people were divided among four different imperial powers, the British, the Italians, the French, and Imperial Ethiopia. At independence, only British and Italian Somali land were joined together as the Republic of Somalia. The five-pointed star in the national flag always reminds Somalis of the other three territories still under foreign domination: Northern Kenya, the Ogaden, and Djibuti.

Farah thematizes all these facets of national identity in *Maps* by focusing on the Ogaden war of 1977. He concentrates on the internal conflict, but the international involvement of the United States and the Soviet Union makes itself felt as an implied issue. The global conflict between capitalism and communism and the vicarious wars, together with the love of many African potentates for self-aggrandizement by playing the Russian-American rivalry card, constitutes the background to *Maps*.

Farah tells the life story of Askar, son of an Ogaden freedom fighter. Askar, an orphan and foundling, is brought up by Misra of mixed Oromo and Ethiopian/Amharic descent. Askar develops an intense relationship to his foster mother Misra, wavering between filial attachment, incestuous admiration, and machoistic urge for domination. For his future, Askar hovers between a career as an academic and poet and that of a freedom fighter. Eventually, he joins the West Somali Liberation Army. In the Ogaden war area, he meets Misra, who is accused of betraying the freedom fighters to the Ethiopian army. She falls victim to a gang rape and a nationalist-motivated ritual murder. Askar is arrested and accused of having participated in the crime.

This plot summary is misleading, since Farah no longer follows a linear narrative pattern. The time sequence and narrative perspective are disrupted—time and space, events and characters present themselves with a variety of contradictory associations. Meanings become ambiguous, multi-layered, inconclusive. Farah presents his reader with bits and pieces of a jigsaw puzzle that is deliberately left incomplete. The reader can never arrive at a complete reading of the novel, he can only formulate hypotheses or speculations; the author doesn't guide the reader, on the contrary he lures him into blind narrative alleys or traps him with deceiving images.

The plurality of meanings and voices manifest themselves through the three narrators: Askar appears as a first-person narrator, a self-centered egotistic chatter-box persona. His narrative stance is contrasted by a third-person authorial narrator with an uninvolved, condensed narrative voice. A dialogic narrative voice addresses his/her counterpart with a familial ''you.'' This could be Misra, the mother, addressing Askar and the children of the nation. The family, highlighted as the central institution in the socio-political fabric in the dictatorship novels, now falls victim to fragmentation: all the major characters are fatherless, motherless, or childless. Social organization is not based on the Somali extended family, nor the nuclear family, but on an amputated dual or triangular personal relationship. Farah even expands the image of amputation and fragmentation: Misra suffers amputation of one of her breasts due to cancer; Aw-Adan, teacher of the Quoran, loses one of his legs; Uncle Qorrax's fingers are hacked off. All these images are revealed as illustrations of different readings of the Somali national mythology, as it was passed on in the oral poetry of ''The Sayyid.'' Sayyid and Farah celebrate Somalia as a beautiful and liberal woman who has affairs with five suitors. Three of the affairs end in miscarriages—a parable for the aborted dreams of ''Great Somalia.'' When Farah retells this story from the oral tradition, he injects relativistic or divergent connotations on two levels. First, it is Misra, the Oromo-Amharic bastard who educates Askar about his national heritage. Secondly, he likens Misra to the mother Somalia of the oral tradition. Misra, too, has affairs with five different men, representing the various ethnic, social, and religious groups at the Horn of Africa. It is not Misra who betrays her suitors, but the suitors who betray her, enslave her, rape her, force her into abortion. Through Farah's retelling, the national epic acquires a new unheroic dimension. The moving story of the nation that has to forego the perfection of national unity is turned into a tale about intrigues, betrayal, and blackmail, where national pride is whipped up and strangers are prosecuted. Farah elaborates the metaphor of the nation as mother when he parallels the events and recurring cycles in Somalia's history with the pregnancies, miscarriages, and menstruation cycles of Misra. Farah even embarks on a gender-oriented interpretation of history.

With Askar's circumcision and initiation into adulthood, another set of images is imported into the narration that provided the title of the novel: maps. The prominent gift for his initiation is a globe, a map of the world. Maps are perceived as particularly reliable replicas of reality, and yet maps too are only reconstructions of reality. Farah emphasizes this aspect of maps as reconstructed reality. He shows us Askar and his freedom fighters plugging flags onto the map pretending to document the progress of the Ogaden war while they are really indulging in nationalist wishful thinking. Farah uses the one-dimensional medium of the map to inscribe broader dimensions by mapping out social, cultural, and mental spaces.

Farah's postmodern narrative stance leaves it to Askarto to unveil his naive enthusiasm for a national awakening of Somalia and ethno-fundamentalist attitudes. Farah also provides us with an insight into the rifts and cracks within Somalian society that resulted in the balcanization of the country and is the topic of *Secrets*.

Against the backdrop of the Ogaden war and the nationalist craze, Farah took up the issue of ethnic purity with Oromo-Amharic mongrel Misra and the pure-bred Somali Askar in *Maps*. With *Secrets* and the imminent clan wars of the rival warlords, Farah raises the issue of genealogical purity. *Secrets*, in spite of its title, is the only Farah novel where the major mystery is actually resolved, namely the parentage of Kalaman, a computer specialist and enterpreneur in Mogadiscio. What the very first line suggests, ''My name Kalaman conjures up memories of childhood,'' with its ambiguities about parentage inherent in the name, and what later continuously surfaces with the saying ''Mothers matter a lot, fathers matter not,'' points to the calamities of a Somali in Mogadiscio with its clan segregation. When he learns that he is the result of a gang rape committed by members of a rival clan, Kalaman has to accept that those people who were most influentual in his life—his grandfather Nonno, and his father Yaqut, who taught him everything—are in the terminology of the clan fanatics only strangers to him. And he also realizes that, contrary to the ideas of the clan fundamentalists, social and moral parenthood can matter more than biological parenthood. ''Certainty'' is a key word in *Secrets*, first as an opposite concept to secrets, but mainly as the biological certainty of motherhood. In the end, the social parenthoods of Nonno and Yaqut are the real certainties in Kalaman's life, while the biological certainty of motherhood loses in importance. Thus, the children's rhyme of ''Mothers matter a lot, Fathers matter not'' is a statement of social fact tranformed into a riddle, one that can be true or false. *Secrets* reflects the fragmentation, fluidity, and instability of life on the eve of the civil war through the multiple narrative voices and the fragmented flow of narrative continuity.

—Eckhard Breitinger

FARMER, Beverley

Nationality: Australian. **Born:** 1941. **Family:** Divorced, one son. **Address:** c/o University of Queensland Press, P.O. Box 42, St. Lucia, Queensland 4067, Australia.

Publications

Novels

Alone. Carlton South, Victoria, Sisters, 1980.
The Seal Woman. St. Lucia, University of Queensland Press, 1992.
The House in the Light. St. Lucia, University of Queensland Press, 1995; Portland, Oregon, International Specialized Book Services, 1995.

Short Stories

Milk. Fitzroy, Victoria, McPhee Gribble, and New York, Penguin, 1983.
Home Time. Fitzroy, Victoria, McPhee Gribble, and New York, Penguin, 1985.
A Body of Water: A Year's Notebook. St. Lucia, University of Queensland Press, 1990.
Place of Birth. London, Faber, 1990.
Collected Stories. St. Lucia, University of Queensland Press, 1996.

* * *

Beverley Farmer made an immediate impression with her first published work, the novella *Alone*. Published in 1980, it had been written ten years before and was set even earlier, in 1959. *Alone* concerns a student at Melbourne University who has been having an affair with another young woman. It ends when she becomes too importunate. In total despair, but quite rationally, she decides to end her life unless her estranged lover comes to see her before Sunday, the day of her eighteenth birthday. *Alone* describes exactly what the girl, Shirley Nunne, does during the last hours of her life, before she comes to the moment of her decision. Although Farmer's writing can sometimes be excessively sensuous to the point of over-ripeness, with a lavish use of color (golden, amber), more often it ranges from the poetic conjuring up of atmospheric detail—the beauty and ugliness of Melbourne at night—through to the meticulously objective rendition of harshly Australian idiomatic speech. It is a haunting and impressive debut.

Farmer confirmed the promise of this work with two fine collections of short stories, *Milk* and *Home Time*, in which the writing is noticeably sparer, more compressed. Nearly all the stories in the first collection concern the interaction between the cultures of Greece and Australia and the misunderstandings that occur between them, but their authenticity and almost elemental strength and intensity of feeling make them far more than merely sociological documents. Although frequently the protagonist is a young woman involved with a Greek man, the stories have a variety of voices and protagonists. Their most impressive quality is the author's ability to confront unflinchingly and immerse herself in the experience of her characters, no matter how distressing it is, without becoming self-pitying or maudlin. Violence—whether psychic or physical—is never far away; if it does not actually occur it hovers on the outskirts of the stories, constantly threatening as it does in ''Sally's Birthday.'' Frequently, especially when the victim is a woman as it most often is, it takes the form of a humiliation or violation of some kind. Estrangement—husband from wife, parent from child, Greek from Australian—is another pervasive element. Almost the sole source of comfort and consolation in this bleak world lies in the children who appear often in the collection, and whose joys and griefs—''the little tragedies of children''—are lovingly and tenderly evoked.

Many of the same themes recur in *Home Time*. Here again, few relationships are seen to be in any way harmonious; most are riddled with tension and often verge on violence. The sense of estrangement can be both emotional and geographical. In ''Place of Birth'' Bell (who appears in two stories) is pregnant and agonizing over whether to leave Greece and return to Australia. She receives little support from her husband. ''You're a stubborn, selfish, cold-blooded woman, Bell.'' Several of the stories are set in Greece, but the sense of isolation is not confined to place. Whether the character is called Bell or Anne or Barbara, the stories are enlivened by a sensuous awareness of landscape, especially in those set in Greece, and an extraordinarily acute ear for dialogue.

Farmer waited five years, a period of apparent sterility, to publish her first full-length novel, *A Body of Water*. Subtitled ''A Year's Notebook,'' it is in fact exactly that, her jottings from February 1987 to February 1988. It records her friendships, love affairs, conversations, thoughts, and above all her reading. Interspersed with the diary entries, which begin with the gloomy statement ''My forty-sixth birthday, and no end in sight to the long struggle to come to terms with this isolation, this sterility,'' are the five stories she managed to complete during the year. The reader is thus in the privileged and fascinating position of reading not only the fiction but the process of its writing, how it emerged from the writer's unconscious and finally took shape. Marking a determined attempt to break from the limits of realism, the novel is not about anything so much as itself. It is about the act and art of writing, not the result. In the end, however, the theme of artistic and emotional sterility threatens to invade the book like a virus, and there is a good deal of overblown writing that recalls the excesses of *Alone*, rather than the spareness and economy of the short stories: ''Tide coming in, a stiff wind. A black ship out, a white ship in. A flash out on the grey water—a pilot boat catching the sun. The dunes have grown fine long green hairs all over—their skin shows through.''

Bleakness and solitude are themes of Farmer's most recent fiction also. The protagonist of *The Seal Woman* is a Danish woman named Dagmar Mikkelsen, who has come to live in a seaside resort in Victoria for a few months at the invitation of two absent Australian friends whose house she is minding. She falls in love with a man named Martin, muses over her past and the husband she lost at sea and the child she was unable to have. Like *A Body of Water*, this is a highly self-conscious, literary novel that makes constant allusion to other forms of narrative including fiction, poetry, film, and above all myth. Dense with imagery and symbolism, the novel finally abandons itself completely to myth in the closing chapter, in the story of the tragic seal woman whose fate runs in counterpoint to Dagmar's own: at the end, having left her faithless lover to return home, she finds herself joyfully with his child.

In *The House in the Light*, Farmer turns her back on experimental and post-modern forms of narrative to return to the familiar country of the short stories and her alter ego Bell. Now fifty years old, divorced, with her son a student living his own independent life and her ex-husband's new wife about to give birth, Bell has returned to the Greek village in which she married, to celebrate Easter. Her former father-in-law has recently died but the family still welcomes her, if ambivalently, into their midst. The novel takes us through the week of Easter day by day. It is almost a dramatic meditation, an account of the private mental struggle in which Bell has to reconcile past affections and allegiances with the changed circumstances she finds herself in, to treat the line between respect for the hospitality and culture of her hosts, especially her aging former mother-in-law, and a fierce insistence on her own very different values, which she will neither abandon nor deny. Again, it becomes apparent that the most central fact in the universe of Farmer's fiction is solitude. Her characters are mostly physical and mental isolates, and Bell is no exception. At the end, however, in a beautifully written scene, Bell and the family come to some kind of tentative accommodation. *The House in the Light* is a profoundly desolate but moving novel. Farmer's *Collected Stories* include the stories from her two volumes, the five stories that appeared in a *Body of Water*, and five uncollected stories.

—Laurie Clancy

FAST, Howard (Melvin)

Pseudonyms: E.V. Cunningham; Walter Ericson. **Nationality:** American. **Born:** New York City, 11 November 1914. **Education:** George Washington High School, New York, graduated 1931; National Academy of Design, New York. **Military Service:** Served with the Office of War Information, 1942–43, and the Army Film Project, 1944. **Family:** Married Bette Cohen in 1937 (died 1994); one daughter and one son, the writer Jonathan Fast. **Career:** War correspondent in the Far East for *Esquire* and *Coronet* magazines, 1945. Taught at Indiana University, Bloomington, Summer 1947; imprisoned for contempt of Congress, 1947; owner, Blue Heron Press, New York, 1952–57. Since 1989 weekly columnist, New York *Observer.* Founder, World Peace Movement, and member, World Peace Council, 1950–55; currently, member of the Fellowship for Reconciliation. American-Labour Party candidate for Congress for the 23rd District of New York, 1952. Lives in Greenwich, Connecticut. **Awards:** Bread Loaf Writers Conference award, 1933; Schomburg Race Relations award, 1944; Newspaper Guild award, 1947; Jewish Book Council of America award, 1948; Stalin International Peace prize, 1954; Screenwriters award, 1960; National Association of Independent Schools, award, 1962; Emmy award, for television play, 1976. **Agent:** Sterling Lord Literistic Inc., 1 Madison Avenue, New York, New York 10010, U.S.A.

PUBLICATIONS

Novels

Two Valleys. New York, Dial Press, 1933; London, Dickson, 1934.
Strange Yesterday. New York, Dodd Mead, 1934.
Place in the City. New York, Harcourt Brace, 1937.
Conceived in Liberty: A Novel of Valley Forge. New York, Simon and Schuster, and London, Joseph, 1939.
The Last Frontier. New York, Duell, 1941; London, Lane, 1948.
The Unvanquished. New York, Duell, 1942; London, Lane, 1947.
The Tall Hunter. New York, Harper, 1942.
Citizen Tom Paine. New York, Duell, 1943; London, Lane, 1946.
Freedom Road. New York, Duell, 1944; London, Lane, 1946.
The American: A Middle Western Legend. New York, Duell, 1946; London, Lane, 1949.
The Children. New York, Duell, 1947.
Clarkton. New York, Duell, 1947.
My Glorious Brothers. Boston, Little Brown, 1948; London, Lane, 1950.
The Proud and the Free. Boston, Little Brown, 1950; London, Lane, 1952.
Spartacus. Privately printed, 1951; London, Lane, 1952.
Fallen Angel (as Walter Ericson). Boston, Little Brown, 1952; as *The Darkness Within,* New York, Ace, 1953; as *Mirage* (as Howard Fast), New York, Fawcett, 1965.
Silas Timberman. New York, Blue Heron Press, 1954; London, Lane, 1955.
The Story of Lola Gregg. New York, Blue Heron Press, 1956; London, Lane, 1957.
Moses, Prince of Egypt. New York, Crown, 1958; London, Methuen, 1959.
The Winston Affair. New York, Crown, 1959; London, Methuen, 1960.
The Golden River, in *The Howard Fast Reader.* New York, Crown, 1960.
April Morning. New York, Crown, and London, Methuen, 1961.
Power. New York, Doubleday, 1962; London, Methuen, 1963.
Agrippa's Daughter. New York, Doubleday, 1964; London, Methuen, 1965.
Torquemada. New York, Doubleday, 1966; London, Methuen, 1967.
The Hunter and the Trap. New York, Dial Press, 1967.
The Crossing. New York, Morrow, 1971; London, Eyre Methuen, 1972.
The Hessian. New York, Morrow, 1972; London, Hodder and Stoughton, 1973.
The Call of Fife and Drum: Three Novels of the Revolution. Secaucus, New Jersey, Citadel Press, 1987.
The Bridge Builder's Story. Armonk, New York, M. E. Sharpe, 1995.
An Independent Woman. New York, Harcourt Brace, 1997.
Redemption. New York, Harcourt Brace, 1999.
The Immigrants:
- *The Immigrants.* Boston, Houghton Mifflin, 1977; London, Hodder and Stoughton, 1978.
- *Second Generation.* Boston, Houghton Mifflin, and London, Hodder and Stoughton, 1978.
- *The Establishment.* Boston, Houghton Mifflin, 1979; London, Hodder and Stoughton, 1980.
- *The Legacy.* Boston, Houghton Mifflin, and London, Hodder and Stoughton, 1981.
- *Max.* Boston, Houghton Mifflin, 1982; London, Hodder and Stoughton, 1983.
- *The Outsider.* Boston, Houghton Mifflin, 1984; London, Hodder and Stoughton 1985.
- *The Immigrant's Daughter.* Boston, Houghton Mifflin, 1985; London, Hodder and Stoughton, 1986.

The Dinner Party. Boston, Houghton Mifflin, and London, Hodder and Stoughton, 1987.
The Pledge. Boston, Houghton Mifflin, 1988; London, Hodder and Stoughton, 1989.
The Confession of Joe Cullen. Boston, Houghton Mifflin 1989; London, Hodder and Stoughton, 1990.
The Trial of Abigail Goodman. New York, Crown, 1993.
Seven Days in June. New York, Crown, 1994.

Novels as E.V. Cunningham

Sylvia. New York, Doubleday, 1960; London, Deutsch, 1962.
Phyllis. New York, Doubleday, and London, Deutsch, 1962.
Alice. New York, Doubleday, 1963; London, Deutsch, 1965.
Lydia. New York, Doubleday, 1964; London, Deutsch, 1965.
Shirley. New York, Doubleday, and London, Deutsch, 1964.
Penelope. New York, Doubleday, 1965; London, Deutsch, 1966.
Helen. New York, Doubleday, 1966; London, Deutsch, 1967.
Margie. New York, Morrow, 1966; London, Deutsch, 1968.
Sally. New York, Morrow, and London, Deutsch, 1967.
Samantha. New York, Morrow, 1967; London, Deutsch, 1968; as *The Case of the Angry Actress,* New York, Dell, 1984.
Cynthia. New York, Morrow, 1968; London, Deutsch, 1969.
The Assassin Who Gave Up His Gun. New York, Morrow, 1969; London, Deutsch, 1970.
Millie. New York, Morrow, 1973; London, Deutsch, 1975.
The Case of the One-Penny Orange. New York, Holt Rinehart, 1977; London, Deutsch, 1978.
The Case of the Russian Diplomat. New York, Holt Rinehart, 1978; London, Deutsch, 1979.
The Case of the Poisoned Eclairs. New York, Holt Rinehart, 1979; London, Deutsch, 1980.
The Case of the Sliding Pool. New York, Delacorte Press, 1981; London, Gollancz, 1982.
The Case of the Kidnapped Angel. New York, Delacorte Press, 1982; London, Gollancz, 1983.
The Case of the Murdered Mackenzie. New York, Delacorte Press, 1984; London, Gollancz, 1985.
The Wabash Factor. New York, Delacorte Press, 1986; London, Gollancz, 1987.

Plays

The Hammer (produced New York, 1950).
Thirty Pieces of Silver (produced Melbourne, 1951). New York, Blue Heron Press, and London, Lane, 1954.
General Washington and the Water Witch. London, Lane, 1956.
The Crossing (produced Dallas, 1962).
The Hill (screenplay). New York, Doubleday, 1964.
David and Paula (produced New York, 1982).
Citizen Tom Paine, adaptation of his own novel (produced Williamstown, Massachusetts, 1985). Boston, Houghton Mifflin, 1986.
The Novelist (produced Williamstown, Massachusetts, 1987).
The Second Coming (produced Greenwich, Connecticut, 1991).

Screenplays: *The Hessian,* 1971.

Television Plays: *What's a Nice Girl Like You …?,* 1971; *The Ambassador* (*Benjamin Franklin* series), 1974; *21 Hours at Munich,* with Edward Hume, 1976.

Poetry

Never to Forget the Battle of the Warsaw Ghetto, with William Gropper. New York, Jewish Peoples Fraternal Order, 1946.
Korean Lullaby. New York, American Peace Crusade, n.d.

Other

The Romance of a People (for children). New York, Hebrew Publishing Company, 1941.
Lord Baden-Powell of the Boy Scouts. New York, Messner, 1941.
Haym Salomon, Son of Liberty. New York, Messner, 1941.
The Picture-Book History of the Jews, with Bette Fast. New York, Hebrew Publishing Company, 1942.
Goethals and the Panama Canal. New York, Messner, 1942.
The Incredible Tito. New York, Magazine House, 1944.
Intellectuals in the Fight for Peace. New York, Masses and Mainstream, 1949.
Tito and His People. Winnipeg, Contemporary Publishers, 1950.
Literature and Reality. New York, International Publishers, 1950.
Peekskill, U.S.A.: A Personal Experience. New York, Civil Rights Congress, and London, International Publishing Company, 1951.
Tony and the Wonderful Door (for children). New York, Blue Heron Press, 1952; as *The Magic Door,* Culver City, California, Peace Press, 1979.
Spain and Peace. New York, Joint Anti-Fascist Refugee Committee, 1952.
The Passion of Sacco and Vanzetti: A New England Legend. New York, Blue Heron Press, 1953; London, Lane, 1954.
The Naked God: The Writer and the Communist Party. New York, Praeger, 1957; London, Bodley Head, 1958.
The Howard Fast Reader. New York, Crown, 1960.
The Jews: Story of a People. New York, Dial Press, 1968; London, Cassell, 1970.
The Art of Zen Meditation. Culver City, California, Peace Press, 1977.
Time and the Riddle: Thirty Zen Stories. Boston, Houghton Mifflin, 1981.
Being Red: A Memoir. Boston, Houghton Mifflin, 1990.
War and Peace. Armonk, New York, Sharpe, 1992.
The Sculpture of Bette Fast. Armonk, New York, Sharpe, 1995.
Editor, *The Selected Work of Tom Paine.* New York, Modern Library, 1946; London, Lane, 1948.
Editor, *The Best Short Stories of Theodore Dreiser.* Cleveland, World, 1947.

*

Manuscript Collections: University of Pennsylvania, Philadelphia; University of Wisconsin, Madison.

Critical Studies: *History and Conscience: The Case of Howard Fast* by Hershel D. Meyer, Princeton, New Jersey, Anvil Atlas, 1958; *Counterpoint* by Roy Newquist, New York, Rand McNally, 1964; *Howard Fast: A Critical Companion* by Andrew Macdonald. Westport, Connecticut, Greenwood Press, 1996.

Howard Fast comments:

(1972) From the very beginning of my career as a writer, my outlook has been teleological. Since my first work was published at a very early age—my first novel at the age of eighteen—my philosophical position was naturally uncertain and in formation. Yet the seeds were there, and by the end of my first decade as a writer, I had clearly shaped my point of view. In the light of this, both my historical and modern novels (excepting the entertainments I have written under the name of Cunningham) were conceived as parables and executed as narratives of pace and, hopefully, excitement. I discovered that I had a gift for narrative in the story sense; but I tried never to serve the story, but rather to have it serve my own purpose—a purpose which I attempted in a transcendental sense.

In other words, I was—and am—intrigued by the apparent lunacy of man's experience on earth; but at the same time never accepted a pessimistic conclusion or a mechanical explanation. Thereby, my books were either examinations of moments or parables of my own view of history. As a deeply religious person who has always believed that human life is a meaningful part of a meaningful and incredibly wonderful universe, I found myself at every stage in my career a bit out of step with the current literary movement or fashion. I suppose that this could not have been otherwise, and I think I have been the most astounded of any at the vast audiences my work has reached.

Since I also believe that a person's philosophical point of view has little meaning if it is not matched by being and action, I found myself willingly wed to an endless series of unpopular causes, experiences which I feel enriched my writing as much as they depleted other aspects of my life. I might add that the more I have developed the parable as a form of literature, the more convinced I become that truth is better indicated than specified.

All of the above is of course not a critical evaluation of my work; and I feel that a writer is the last person on earth capable of judging his own work as literature with any objectivity. The moment I cease to feel that I am a good writer, I will have to stop writing. And while this may be no loss to literature, it would be a tragic blow to my income.

As for the books I have written under the name of E.V. Cunningham, they are entertainments, for myself primarily and for all others who care to read them. They are also my own small contribution to that wonderful cause of women's liberation. They are all about wise and brave and gallant women, and while they are suspense and mystery stories, they are also parables in their own way.

* * *

Howard Fast has written in virtually every genre—novels, plays, poems, filmscripts, critical essays and short stories—and in a number of subgenres of fiction, including science fiction, social satire, historical and contemporary novels, spy thrillers, and moral allegories. He began publishing novels at the age of eighteen and has kept up a brisk pace of production.

His strongest fictional gifts are a talent for swift, interesting narrative, the vivid portrayal of scenes of action, especially of violence, and an uncluttered style only occasionally marred by sentimental lapses. Although he became identified in the 1940s as a publicist for the Communist Party line, his novels reveal an intensely emotional and religious nature which eventually clashed with his left-wing allegiances. His ideals reflect a curious compound of slum-culture courage, Jewish concern for social justice, self-taught history, Cold-war Stalinism and, in his later years, Zen Buddhism. His entire literary career embodies his deepest beliefs: that life has moral significance, that the writer must be socially committed, that literature should take sides.

After two youthful blood-and-thunder romances, Fast found his métier in a series of class-conscious historical novels of the American Revolution. *Conceived in Liberty* heralded the loyalty of the common soldier; *The Unvanquished* celebrated the dogged persistence of George Washington (despite his aristocracy and wealth, Fast's favorite hero); and *Citizen Tom Paine* glorified our first professional revolutionary. Fast then championed anonymous heroes of other races: *The Last Frontier* is a spare but moving account of the heroic flight in 1878 of the Cheyenne Indians to their Powder River home in Wyoming; *Freedom Road* recounts the amazing social experiments of black Southern legislatures in the Reconstruction era. The best selling of the popular novels of the early 1940s, *Freedom Road* shows great power in its scenes of violent conflict but it is melodramatic and tendentious. By contrast, the poetically evocative *Last Frontier,* perhaps his best novel, enlists profound sympathy through great control and objectivity, and evades the pitfalls of ''noble redskin'' sentimentality.

In 1946 *The American* detailed the rise and fall of Illinois Governor John Peter Altgeld, who was politically defeated after he pardoned three anarchists convicted of bomb-throwing in Haymarket Square in 1886. Although Fast's novels had reflected Marxist thought since his youthful conversion to socialism, his propagandizing became too obtrusive with *Clarkton* in 1947. This proletarian strike novel of life in the Massachusetts textile mills revealed his inability to maintain the necessary distance to interpret contemporary events soundly. He returned in 1948 to the historical novel with *My Glorious Brothers,* a stirring account of the Maccabees and the thirty-year Jewish resistance to Greek-Syrian tyranny. This success was duplicated with *Spartacus,* the largely imagined story of the gladiatorial revolt against Rome in 71 BC. *Spartacus* was self-published in 1951 after the author was blacklisted for Communist activities and had spent three months in federal prison for contempt of Congress. But, predictably, Fast's other works of the early 1950s were failures in proportion to their nearness to the present day: *The Passion of Sacco and Vanzetti* recounted sentimentally the last hours of the doomed Italian anarchists; *Silas Timberman* depicted an academic victim of a McCarthyite witchhunt; and *The Story of Lola Gregg* described the FBI pursuit and capture of an heroic Communist labor leader. These self-published works of imprisoned martyrs, abounding in Christ-figures and symbolic Judases, reflect their author's bitter sense of entrapment and isolation, for he could neither publish with established houses nor leave the country.

In 1957 Fast publicly quit the Communist Party after the Hungarian revolution and then described his tortured apostasy in *The Naked God.* He soon revisited Jewish history as a favored novelistic subject with *Moses, Prince of Egypt; Agrippa's Daughter,* and *Torquemada.* He returned, with a more mature vision, thrice more to the American revolution in *April Morning, The Crossing,* and *The Hessian.* In other historical novels he continued to re-examine earlier themes: *The Winston Affair* deals with the court-martial of an American murderer, homosexual and anti-Semite who nevertheless deserves and wins justice in a military court, while *Power* shows the corruption by power by a John L. Lewis-type of labor leader: *Agrippa's Daugther* rejects the ''just-war'' theory of *My Glorious Brothers* in favor of Rabbi Hillel's pacifism.

Most readers saw Fast in two new guises (or disguises), as author of science-fiction stories and as a writer of ''entertainments'' in the manner of Graham Greene. These late science fiction or ''Zen stories'' include stories in *The Edge of Tomorrow, The Hunter and the Trap* and *The General Zapped an Angel* (late gathered into one volume, *Time and the Riddle*). The dozen or so ''entertainments'' are written under the pseudonym E.V. Cunningham, most built around the female title characters. Both the science fiction and the Cunningham novels criticize American institutions and values with wit and humor, and all show the deft hand of the professional storyteller at work. A newer series of Cunningham thrillers stars Masao Masuto, a Japanese-American detective of the Beverly Hills Police Department and a Zen Buddhist. In these, character holds the main appeal, especially that of family-man Masuto.

More recently, Fast has achieved repeated bestsellerdom with an immigrant-saga that has grown to several large novels, starting with *The Immigrants* and including, *The Immigrant's Daughter.* These volumes trace the Italian, Dan Lavette, and his family while newly arrived Italians, Jews, Orientals, and others struggle against the entrenched wealth and prejudice of old-line Americans. Beginning with the San Francisco earthquake of 1906, the series energetically sweeps across twentieth-century American history and recent world events. No longer ax-grinding, Fast uses well his own rich experiences for the first time, and he is at the top of his admirable narrative form.

—Frank Campenni

FAULKS, Sebastian

Nationality: British. **Born:** Newbury, 20 April 1953. **Education:** Wellington College; Emmanuel College, Cambridge, 1974, B.A. (honours). **Family:** Married Veronica Youlten in 1989; one son and one daughter. **Career:** Teacher of English and French, International School of London, 1975–79; journalist, *Daily Telegraph,* London, 1979–82; feature writer, *Sunday Telegraph,* 1983–86; literary editor, *Independent,* London, 1986–89. Since 1989 deputy editor, *Independent on Sunday.* Radio broadcaster, British Broadcasting Corp. Editor, *New Fiction Society,* 1978–81. **Address:** c/o *Independent,* 40 City Road, London E.C.1, England.

Publications

Novels

A Trick of the Light. London, Bodley Head, 1984.

The Girl at the Lion d'Or. London, Hutchinson, 1989; New York, Vintage, 1999.

A Fool's Alphabet. London, Hutchinson, and Boston, Little Brown, 1992.

Birdsong. London, Hutchinson, 1993.

Charlotte Gray. London, Hutchinson, 1998; New York, Random House, 1999.

Other

The Fatal Englishman: Three Short Lives. London, Hutchinson, 1996.

* * *

Although Sebastian Faulks had already published *A Trick of the Light* in 1984, it was his second novel, *The Girl at the Lion d'Or* (1989), that received attention. This novel is the first of a ''French trilogy'' that was published to critical acclaim. Faulks earned praise for his sensitive characterization of a love story set in 1930s France. The small town of Janvilliers is still haunted by the First World War and uneasy with rumors about fascism and communism. At the hotel Lion d'Or, young Anne Louvet becomes a waitress. Like so many heroines of romances set against the backdrop of war, she is an orphan with a dark past.

The opening of the novel, when Anne is driven from the train to the hotel, is detailed and sets the pace and style of the prose. Everything *en route* is observed with the fidelity of a camera, as are the appearances and nature of the characters. Anne falls for a middle-aged lawyer, Charles Hartmann, who with his wife Christine lives in a rambling country house. Hartmann hires her to work as domestic help, and soon they start an affair.

Faulks sympathetically conveys Anne's naïveté as her past gradually unfolds. She tells Hartmann how her father, a brave soldier in the Great War, refused an order from a bullying officer and was shot. The lies and gossip about her disgraced husband were too much for Anne's mother, who took her own life.

Hartmann, who cares little for his wife or indeed for others, loses his self-absorption. As his name suggests, he learns sympathy from listening and recalling his own experiences of the war. The dominant image is of Hartmann's brooding house, with its clutter of bric-a-brac and old books, metaphors for the general malaise of France. Shoddy repairs result in the collapse of part of it, presaging the unhappy conclusion of the romantic liaison. When a troublemaker reveals their affair to Christine, Hartmann ends the relationship very abruptly, although broken-hearted. Anne has no choice but to begin life again in Paris. After many thoughts on free will and the possible circularity of destiny, she now knows that love is possible and life enriching, which makes her new wound endurable.

A Fool's Alphabet (1992) is accomplished but perhaps too contrived and inadequately characterized to succeed as memorable fiction. Pietro Russell, of partial Italian descent, searches for influences on his own personality. He decides to pass a night in various Italian towns according to the letters of the alphabet. Twenty-six chapters in alphabetical order but random chronology reveal the shaping forces on Pietro's life, such as his mother's death and his ongoing quest for love. Pietro achieves his goal with the exception of X—Xianging in China, the symbolic dream city, representing the places he can never visit.

In 1993, Faulks produced a companion novel to *The Girl of Lion d'Or. Birdsong*, a chronicle of the lives of three generations of an English family, topped the bestseller charts in England for over a year. *Birdsong* opens with a callow Stephen Wraysford lodging with a family in Amiens. Faulks describes an erotic, passionate affair between young Stephen and Isabelle, the lady of the house—an affair that led romantic reviewers to write blurb-ready copy in their appreciation of ''heated passions and seething hatred,'' ''swollen emotion, in whose heat is forged an epic kind of love,'' ''a story so intense that at times the reader must put the book aside in order to catch her breath.''

Unfortunately, Isabelle becomes pregnant and deserts Wraysford. Shocked into an emotional stupor, he joins the army in 1916, only to find himself behind German lines. Faulks's depiction of the horrors of war is graphic. No detail of deprivation, lice, filthy food, or the aroma of rotting corpses is spared, because for Faulks there is no glory in war, only horror, which has to be experienced to be understood. As a soldier, Wraysford is considered cold-hearted, and his frigidity is contrasted with the other soldiers who each cope with the daily threat of death in their individual ways. The men who dig the trenches are significant in their representation of self-reliance. For Jack Firebrace, who digs the mine tunnels under enemy lines, the conditions of war are better than his life of poverty in London. His survival of every disaster with courage, including the death of his son, makes a deep impression on Wraysford, whose suppressed feelings are freed when he is wounded and left for dead in a tunnel.

From 1910 and 1916, the novel jumps to 1978 and the point of view of Elizabeth, the daughter of the child he had with Isabelle. Elizabeth desires to research her family, and after discovering her grandfather's coded diaries, she translates them and learns the truth of his scandalous affair, the torments of trench warfare, and the happiness he eventually finds. While decoding his story, she diagnoses her own life as lacking in the intensity that earlier generations had experienced.

Wraysford's conclusion that the meaning of life is the continuity of human love is metaphorically represented by the exuberant birdsong of the title, the twittering of birds that starts when the gunfire stops, and which echoes through to the epilogue. Faulks accentuates his belief in redeeming the past when Elizabeth's baby, the fourth generation, is born in a symphony of rapture as the living proof of goodness from past tragedy.

In 1995, Faulks was recognized as Author of the Year by the British Book Awards for *Birdsong*. The following year, the novel was nominated for the 1996 International IMPAC Dublin Literary Award; and in 1997, a television and bookshop poll among British readers placed it in their top fifty books of the century. A nonfiction work, *The Fatal Englishman: Three Short Lives* (1996), was another best-seller; it dealt with three young men, all heroic in their own ways, whose lives were tragically cut short.

Faulks returned to war-torn Europe—this time during World War II—with a third romantic best-seller, *Charlotte Gray* (1999). Again Faulks examines the insidious way that war affects individual lives. In 1942, Charlotte Gray, a young Scotswoman, has a brief love affair with a Royal Air Force fighter pilot, Peter Gregory. When his plane is lost on a mission to France, she arranges to go there herself as a British secret courier, sent over to help support the French Resistance against the invading Germans. Intensifying the suspense, Faulks shows that British intelligence is prepared to sacrifice her if necessary. Instead of returning to England when the undercover assignment is accomplished, Charlotte stays in France to search for Gregory.

In the small town of Lavaurette, Charlotte befriends some assimilated French Jews—the orphans André and Jacob, whose parents have been murdered in the death camps, and the Levades, father and son, who lead the local resistance. Once there, she witnesses the ugliness of French collusion with the Nazis, but also the tremendous courage of those who fought and died for the Resistance. Though unable to help the French in any serious way, Charlotte gains insights into herself and her family through living with them—and growing increasingly attracted to idealistic young Julien Levade. Faulks draws metaphorical links between the struggle for France and Charlotte's own struggles to take control of her life.

Reviewers complained that Faulks did not achieve the emotional impact in *Charlotte Gray* that he did in *Birdsong*, that the settings and physical props are more believable than the somewhat flat characters, that he too often dips into old-fashioned melodrama. However, his fans loved the book, and like the previous novel, it was nominated for the International IMPAC Dublin Literary Award in 1999.

Faulks's early career as a journalist provides his greatest strength, his masterful skill at detailed description and historical accuracy. To evoke each of the senses, his settings are gritty with the realism conveyed by the mind-shattering sights of war, the precious touch of a lover's skin, the stench of the decomposing dead, the taste of the carefully described meals eaten by the wealthy or the starving. Such verisimilitudinous detail enhances Faulks's power and credibility as a story-teller.

In Faulks's fiction, love and heroism are the two most important and valuable qualities of life, and each strengthens the other. Another recurring theme is the human capacity for hope beyond reason. Faulks calls himself a romantic writer and admits that his influences are ''old-fashioned.'' Among these influences he lists the French writers Gustave Flaubert, Marcel Proust, and Emile Zola. When it supports the physical and historical settings, he employs long sentences to convey a highly formal and stifling atmosphere. This elevated diction matches his grand themes about human experience, about the healing powers of love and the determination to survive despite tremendous pain and horror. Like William Faulkner's, the heroism of Faulks's characters is that they endure.

—Geoffrey Elborn, updated by Fiona Kelleghan

FAUST, Irvin

Nationality: American. **Born:** New York City, 11 June 1924. **Education:** City College of New York, B.S. 1949; Columbia University, New York, M.A. 1952, D.Ed. 1960. **Military Service:** Served in the United States Army, 1943–46. **Family:** Married Jean Satterthwaite in 1959. **Career:** Teacher, Manhattanville Junior High School, New York, 1949–53; guidance counselor, Lynbrook High School, Long Island, 1956–60. Since 1960 director of Guidance and Counselling, Garden City High School, Long Island. Taught at Columbia University, Summer 1963, New School for Social Research, New York, 1975, Swarthmore College, Pennsylvania, 1976, City College, 1977, and University of Rochester, New York, Summer 1978. **Awards:** O. Henry prize, 1983 and 1986; Charles Angoff award, for fiction, 1994. **Agent:** Gloria Loomis, Watkins Loomis Agency Inc., 150 East 35th Street, New York, New York 10016. **Address:** 417 Riverside Drive, New York, New York 10025, U.S.A.

Publications

Novels

The Steagle. New York, Random House, 1966.
The File on Stanley Patton Buchta. New York, Random House, 1970.
Willy Remembers. New York, Arbor House, 1971.
Foreign Devils. New York, Arbor House, 1973.
A Star in the Family. New York, Doubleday, 1975.
Newsreel. New York, Harcourt Brace, 1980.
Jim Dandy. New York, Carroll and Graf, 1994.

Short Stories

Roar Lion Roar and Other Stories. New York, Random House, and London, Gollancz, 1965.
The Year of the Hot Jock and Other Stories. New York, Dutton, 1985.

Uncollected Short Stories

''Action at Vicksburg,'' in *New Black Mask* (Orlando, Florida), Fall 1985.
''Artie and Benny,'' in *Michigan Quarterly Review* (Ann Arbor), Spring 1989.
''Let Me Off Uptown,'' in *Fiction* (New York), 1991.
''Black Auxiliaries,'' in *The Literary Review* (Madison, New Jersey), Summer 1994.

Other

Entering Angel's World: A Student-Centered Casebook. New York, Columbia Teachers College Press, 1963.

*

Critical Studies: By Richard Kostelanetz, in *The New American Arts,* New York, Horizon Press, 1965, in *Tri-Quarterly* (Evanston, Illinois), Winter 1967, and in *On Contemporary Literature,* New York, Avon, 1967; by R.V. Cassill, in *New York Times Book Review,* 29 August 1971; interview with Matthew Bruccoli, in *Conversations with Writers 2,* Detroit, Gale, 1978; by Martin Tucker in *Confrontation* (Brookville, New York), Fall 1994.

Irvin Faust comments:

(1972) It seems to me that thus far my work has dealt with the displacement and disorganization of Americans in urban life; with their attempt to find adjustments in the glossy attractions of the mass media—movies, radio, TV, advertising, etc.—and in the image-radiating seductions of our institutions—colleges, sports teams, etc. Very often this ''adjustment'' is to the ''normal'' perception a derangement, but perfectly satisfying to my subjects.

Recently my work has moved out to include suburban America and also back in historical directions. My characters to this date have been outside of the white anglo-saxon milieu, but have included Jews, Blacks, Puerto Ricans and the so-called Ethnic Americans.

Both *Roar Lion Roar* and *The Steagle* were published in France (Gallimard) and I feel the reviews were most perceptive, leading me to muse that perhaps, unbeknownst to me, I am quite close to the French literary sensibility.

(1995) *Jim Dandy* continues my exploration of the psychology and actuality of wars since 1898. This time I've dug into the Italo-Ethiopian conflict of 1936, which pre-figured World War II. We are still living with its ramifications, and fiction helps us to understand these relationships.

* * *

In his novels and short stories, Irvin Faust has attempted (as he said of one novel), ''to show the rise and fall of this nation over the last forty years.'' Were this all, he would be essentially a social historian disguised as fictional chronicler of our times. Faust, however, has managed to weave together a substantial number of additional themes, drawing upon his background as Jew, New Yorker, veteran, husband, and professional guidance counselor. The integration of these materials, when successful, produces a rich tapestry of life in contemporary urban America, especially when played off against the past, both mythicized and actual.

His first fictional book, *Roar Lion Roar,* treated with sensitive compassion the interior lives of disturbed adolescents of minority backgrounds. In the title story, Ishmael Ramos, a janitor at Columbia University, so identifies with the ''ivory leak'' school that he kills himself when the football team loses. Most of the protagonists of these stories are insane but even the sane have been mind-molded by the mass media or warped by the pressures of recent history. Indeed, Faust's major theme of the forming and deforming of personality by an empty culture in a violent, chaotic world may here have found its most solid embodiment.

The broader canvas of the novel form permitted Faust the breadth and depth needed to convey the specificity of a conflicted culture in its dizzying impact upon the individual. In Faust's first novel, *The Steagle,* English Professor Harold Weissburg develops a multiple personality while his sense of self disintegrates during the Cuban missile crisis. The title is a composite-name formed from two football teams, the Steelers and the Eagles. Thus, as the United States shifts from ''good neighbor'' to threatening nuclear power, Weissburg, in desperate flight across the country, becomes Bob Hardy (brother of Andy, of the wholesome movie family), gangster Rocco Salvato, a football hero, a flying ace, and, finally Humphrey Bogart. In *The File on Stanley Patton Buchta* his protagonist is an undercover policeman, Vietnam veteran, and college graduate who infiltrates both a paramilitary rightist group within the police department and a New Left organization. He is further divided in romantic loyalty to an all-American blonde beauty and a black militant on whom he is spying. Perhaps because the hero is not fully realized, or because the material lacks the historical density which the author prefers, this fairly conventional novel lacks impact.

Faust's next two novels, however, are probably his best to date. *Willy Remembers* features the redoubtable Willy Kleinhans, who at ninety-three is an embodiment and archive of America in the nineteenth century. The history he recalls is badly scrambled but curiously apt: Grover Cleveland is confused with baseball-pitcher Grover Cleveland Alexander; John F. Kennedy melds with McKinley, another assassinated President; Admiral and Governor Dewey, Franklin and Teddy Roosevelt likewise interchange. The Haymarket Riot, the frame-up of Tom Mooney, prohibition, and T.R. at San Juan hill all whiz by as kaleidoscopic snapshots. Despite Willy's anti-semitism, curmudgeonly judgments and angry confusion, he is a likable and likely representative of his time and place. Although R.V. Cassill rightly praised *Willy Remembers* for its ''overlapping stereotypes of urban and national memory'' and the novel's ''Joycean complexity,'' Faust does not always guide the reader adequately along these high-speed, involuted memory-trips. The novel does display, nevertheless, a marked advance in control of point-of-view and the blend of fantasy and realism. With *Foreign Devils* Faust achieves mastery in weaving together the items of popular culture, the myths by which many Americans live, and the disintegrating personality of a Jewish writer. His hero, Sidney Benson (born Birnbaum), is separated from his wife and living partly off his mother's earnings from a candy store. Inspired by President Nixon's trip to China, Benson, who has suffered from writer's block, begins a novel about the Boxer rebellion. This melodrama, or novel-within-the-novel, is an exquisite parody of the swashbuckling accounts of Richard Harding Davis, and is perhaps the chief attraction of *Foreign Devils.* The action in the present, except for Benson's reunion at the end with his father (who had deserted his family years ago), is cluttered with topical references, both a shortcoming and an attraction in Faust's fiction.

Faust's *A Star in the Family* and *Newsreel* show flashes of power as each book scans recent American history, but he is in danger of repeating himself. The tale of vaudevillian Bart Goldwine, protagonist of *A Star in the Family,* consists of interviews conducted by Goldwine's biographer, plus longer memoiristic accounts by Goldwine. The reproduction of showbusiness patter, street talk, fan magazine prose, courtship, and family discussions is flawless in evoking the cynicism and innocence of the last generation. Showman Goldwine's impression of John F. Kennedy is abruptly ended by the assassination; his long decline thereafter is symbolically entwined with the decline of American vitality and national will. In *Newsreel* former Army Captain Manny ''Speed'' Finestone is again the victim of his times. Linked spiritually with his wartime ''chief,'' Dwight Eisenhower, Speed cannot escape contrasting the purity of the great crusade against Hitler with the materialism of the affluent 1950s, the cold war mentality, and the slaying of President Kennedy (Chapter 29 is simply ''11/22/63''). Finestone's inability to write, his failed romances with two Jewish women and an Irish girl, his unraveling into psychosis are all played against national deterioration in a cultural wasteland. Other previous themes and motifs are also present: sex and sports, the abandoning father, the Jew fighting his ethnic identity, the writer supported by his mother, the use of dialogues with other selves or fantasy-heroes. Although their repeated use suggests personal concerns that are insufficiently integrated into fiction, Faust continues to portray both interior individual lives and cultural tension with skill and sincerity.

The protagonist of *Jim Dandy,* Faust's first novel after a silence of nine years, first appears in the book as a child in 1915, when he is employed as a member of a black minstrel show. In time ''Jim Dandy'' comes to be known as Hollis Cleveland, and gets into so much trouble as a small-time Harlem gangster that he has to leave the country. His travels take him first to Europe and eventually to an Ethiopia, caught up in war with Fascist Italy. All along the way, he is mistaken for other people—including ''Gallifa, the son of Ras Gugsa of Gondar... a Solomonic Prince'' of the African kingdom. Despite the fact that it sometimes groans under its magic realist weight—a by-product of the author's tampering with history—the novel is an enjoyable one, particularly in its first half.

—Frank Campenni

FEINSTEIN, Elaine

Nationality: British. **Born:** Bootle, Lancashire, 24 October 1930. **Education:** Wyggeston Grammar School, Leicester; Newnham College, Cambridge, B.A. in English 1952, M.A. 1955. **Family:** Married Arnold Feinstein in 1956; three sons. **Career:** Editorial staff member, Cambridge University Press, 1960–62; lecturer in English, Bishop's Stortford Training College, Hertfordshire, 1963–66; assistant lecturer in literature, University of Essex, Colchester, 1967–70. **Awards:** Arts Council grant, 1970, 1979, 1981; Daisy Miller award, for fiction, 1971; Kelus prize, 1978. Fellow, Royal Society of Literature, 1980. **Agent:** Rogers Coleridge and White, 20 Powis Mews, London W11 1JN; (plays and film) Lemon Unna and Durbridge, 24–32 Pottery Lane, London, W11 4LZ, England.

PUBLICATIONS

Novels

The Circle. London, Hutchinson, 1970.
The Amberstone Exit. London, Hutchinson, 1972.
The Glass Alembic. London, Hutchinson, 1973; as *The Crystal Garden,* New York, Dutton, 1974.
Children of the Rose. London, Hutchinson, 1975.
The Ecstasy of Dr. Miriam Garner. London, Hutchinson, 1976.
The Shadow Master. London, Hutchinson, 1978; New York, Simon and Schuster, 1979.
The Survivors. London, Hutchinson, 1982; New York, Penguin, 1991.
The Border. London, Hutchinson, 1984; New York, Boyars, 1989.
Mother's Girl. London, Century Hutchinson, and New York, Dutton, 1988.
All You Need. London, Century Hutchinson, 1989; New York, Viking, 1991.
Loving Brecht. London, Hutchinson, 1992.
Dreamers. London, Macmillan, 1994.
Lady Chatterley's Confession. London, Macmillan, 1995.
Daylight. Manchester, England, Carcanet, 1997.

Short Stories

Matters of Chance. London, Covent Garden Press, 1972.
The Silent Areas. London, Hutchinson, 1980.

Plays

Lear's Daughters (produced London, 1987).

Radio Plays: *Echoes,* 1980; *A Late Spring,* 1982; *A Captive Lion,* 1984; *Marina Tsvetayeva: A Life,* 1985; *A Day Off,* from the novel by Storm Jameson, 1986; *If I Ever Get on My Feet Again,* 1987; *The Man in Her Life,* 1989; *The Temptations of Dr. William Fosters,* 1991.

Television Plays: *Breath,* 1975; *Lunch,* 1982; *Country Diary of an Edwardian Lady* series, from work by Edith Holden, 1984; *A Brave Face,* 1985; *The Chase,* 1988; *A Passionate Woman* series, 1989.

Poetry

In a Green Eye. London, Goliard Press, 1966.
The Magic Apple Tree. London, Hutchinson, 1971.
At the Edge. Rushden, Northamptonshire, Sceptre Press, 1972.
The Celebrants and Other Poems. London, Hutchinson, 1973.
Some Unease and Angels: Selected Poems. London, Hutchinson, and University Center, Michigan, Green River Press, 1977.
The Feast of Euridice. London, Faber, 1980.
Badlands. London, Century Hutchinson, 1986.
City Music. London, Hutchinson, 1990.
Selected Poems. London, Carcanet, 1994.

Other

Bessie Smith. London, Penguin, 1985.
A Captive Lion: The Life of Marina Tsvetayeva. London, Century Hutchinson, and New York, Dutton, 1987.
Marina Tsvetayeva. London and New York, Penguin, 1989.
Lawrence's Women. London and New York, HarperCollins, 1993.
Pushkin. Hopewell, New Jersey, Ecco Press, 1999.
Editor, *Selected Poems of John Clare.* London, University Tutorial Press, 1968.
Editor, with Fay Weldon, *New Stories 4.* London, Hutchinson, 1979.
Editor, *PEN New Poetry.* London, Quartet, 1988.
Translator, *The Selected Poems of Marina Tsvetayeva.* London, Oxford University Press, 1971; revised edition, Oxford and New York, Oxford University Press, 1981.
Translator, *Three Russian Poets: Margarita Aliger, Yunna Moritz, Bella Akhmadulina.* Manchester, Carcanet, 1979.
Translator, with Antonia W. Bouis, *First Draft: Poems,* by Nika Turbina. London, Boyars, 1988.

*

Manuscript Collection: Cambridge University.

Critical Studies: Article by Peter Conradi, in *British Novelists since 1960* edited by Jay L. Halio, Detroit, Gale, 1983.

Elaine Feinstein comments:

My earliest fiction was very much an extension of my poetry, but as the novels have moved away from a single narrative voice to explore a wider territory, I have largely abandoned those rhythms and have come to prefer the traditional clarity of prose.

* * *

Lena, in Elaine Feinstein's first novel, *The Circle,* realizes *à propos* her husband "that she would have to take it up again. Her separate life. Her lonely life, the music of words to be played with, the books ... they would be her refuge; her private world. As his was this of the laboratory. And she must now move as securely into that ... and find magic." However, in the general context of Feinstein's work, which shows a progressive widening of focus, this is broader than a feminist prescription. Subsequent novels are dominated by men and women in search of "magic," partly via illegitimate means in *The Ecstasy of Dr. Miriam Garner,* and both actively and contemplatively through religion in *The Shadow Master.* "Magic" may be partially embodied in people, as in *The Amberstone Exit,* with Emily's fascination with the glamorous Tyrenes, the local rich family, and in *The Ecstasy of Dr. Miriam Garner,* with Miriam's fascination with the brilliant but brutal Stavros; in both novels there is a strong erotic element in the fascination, and Emily's youthful hunger for sexual experience, which comes to focus on Max Tyrene, anticipates Miriam's more sophisticated desire for Stavros. Similarly, in *Mother's Girl* Halina as a student is infatuated with the brilliant don Janos, while in *All You Need* middle-aged Nell falls for glamorous, powerful Theo.

The fundamental source of "magic" is inevitably "the music of words." For Lena and Emily it is joy in intoxicating language, and for Nell who aspires to writing poetry, and so it could be for the poet Hans in *The Border* were he not, as a part-Jew, persecuted by Hitler, while in the title story of *The Silent Areas* poetry must be "the words that ran in the blood of freezing men without food. Or the minds of the half-mad in lonely cells." In *The Shadow Master,* before the closing religious acceptance, the search for magic meant apocalyptic action. Thus, unfashionably, Feinstein is concerned with validation for people's lives outside as well as inside human relationships.

Perhaps drawing on her experience as a poet, in her first novel, *The Circle,* Feinstein used technical devices, notably spaces within paragraphs, intended for immediacy but in practice often distracting, and later abandoned. A staple technique throughout her work is the juxtaposition of different time-sequences. In *The Circle* this is unstructured, while *The Amberstone Exit* opens in a maternity ward where Emily is having her baby and swings back over the events bringing her there, with the two time-sequences running together toward the end.

The Glass Alembic is about a more mature woman, Brigid, and for the first time focuses on a group. Two passages from this novel are reworked with different names and alternative endings in the stories "Complicity" and "Strangers" (*The Silent Areas*). Brigid's arrival in Basel where her husband is a biochemist is a catalyst for various human reactions in the scientific community. The setting of Paracelsus-haunted Basel is merely coincidentally metaphoric of the action. By contrast, the settings are integral in *Children of the Rose,* which evokes Collaborationist tensions in present-day Provence and the reactions of Jews, once refugees, on revisiting Poland.

In *The Ecstasy of Dr. Miriam Garner* Feinstein plaits a strand of narrative from medieval Toledo with a glamorous female academic's life into a mystery story with spiritual side-lights. *The Shadow Master* is set mainly in Turkey, where an international religious and political apocalyptic movements begins, leading indirectly to the explosion of "a small nuclear device." In *The Survivors* Feinstein follows two Jewish émigré families in Liverpool, one rich and one poor, from 1914 to 1956, when Diana, the offspring of a surprising marriage linking the families, agonizes "So many had died in mud and fire for being Jewish. To give it up seemed a gross betrayal." This two-family saga not only describes the difficulties Jews found in Britain but also delineates both through the successor generations and within generations the characters' very different attitudes to their Jewishness. As the book ends, West Indians are moving into some of the old Jewish quarters.

The Border also draws on Feinstein's Jewish background. Through various narrative devices, notably the use of diaries kept by the scientist Inge and her husband the poet Hans, Feinstein highlights the personal and increasingly the political strains put upon the marriage. The book follows the part-Jewish couple's flight from Vienna to Paris and beyond, in 1983. In this powerful novella, where Walter Benjamin appears, "the border" is metaphoric as well as actual. The book is a technical *tour de force,* and a deeply moving human text.

Mother's Girl deals with the effect of the Holocaust on the next generation. As a child, Halina was sent to Britain in 1939 from Budapest. The novel is a story within a story, as Halina recounts her life to her much younger American half-sister before their father's funeral: this form brings out the continuing effects of a terrible and incompletely known past. The fate of Halina's mother, an unsung underground heroine, never emerges. Her debonair, womanizing father reappeared after the war though without revealing his wartime experience until dying, nursed by Halina. Meanwhile Halina was temporarily and unhappily married to Janos, who had known her father in wartime Budapest.

If through circumstances of history Halina cannot fully understand herself, neither can Nell in *All You Need,* through her own fault. Her husband's sudden arrest for fraud precipitates her into moving to London with her 12-year-old daughter and earning her own living. Some readers may feel less sympathy for her climb into the media world of the late 1980s than Feinstein does: middle-class Nell with a Cambridge degree was a privileged person who had chosen to become a housewife.

So far, *The Border* is Feinstein's major achievement, bringing together all her greatest strengths: the examination of a long-term relationship between a man and a woman, in which both are treated with equal sympathy; a poet's use of language; and a witnessing of history, however dark. A 1999 biography of Aleksandr Pushkin won high praise, overshadowing Feinstein's novels of the recently preceding years: *Lady Chatterley's Confession,* which continues D. H. Lawrence's erotic story, and *Daylight.*

—Val Warner

FIGES, Eva

Nationality: British. **Born:** Eva Unger in Berlin, Germany, 15 April 1932; came to England in 1939. **Education:** Kingsbury Grammar School, 1943–50; Queen Mary College, University of London, 1950–53, B.A. (honours) in English 1953. **Family:** Married John George Figes in 1954 (divorced 1963); one daughter and one son. **Career:** Editor, Longman, 1955–57, Weidenfeld and Nicolson, 1962–63, and Blackie, 1964–67, publishers, London. Since 1987 co-editor, Macmillan Women Writers series. **Awards:** *Guardian* Fiction prize, 1967; C. Day Lewis fellowship, 1973; Arts Council fellowship, 1977–79; Society of Authors traveling scholarship, 1988. Fellow, Queen Mary and Westfield College, 1990. **Agent:** Rogers Coleridge and White Ltd., 20 Powis Mews, London W11 1JN. **Address:** 24 Fitzjohn's Avenue, London N.W.3, England.

Publications

Novels

Equinox. London, Secker and Warburg, 1966.
Winter Journey. London, Faber, 1967; New York, Hill and Wang, 1968.
Konek Landing. London, Faber, 1969.
B. London, Faber, 1972.
Days. London, Faber, 1974.
Nelly's Version. London, Secker and Warburg, 1977; New York, Pantheon, 1988.
Waking. London, Hamish Hamilton, 1981; New York, Pantheon, 1982.
Light. London, Hamish Hamilton, and New York, Pantheon, 1983.
The Seven Ages. London, Hamish Hamilton, 1986; New York, Pantheon, 1987.
Ghosts. London, Hamish Hamilton, and New York, Pantheon, 1988.
The Tree of Knowledge. London, Sinclair Stevenson, 1990; New York, Pantheon, 1991.
The Tenancy. London, Sinclair Stevenson, 1993.
The Knot. London, Sinclair Stevenson, 1996.

Uncollected Short Stories

"Obbligato, Bedsitter," in *Signature Anthology.* London, Calder and Boyars, 1975.
"On the Edge," in *London Tales,* edited by Julian Evans. London, Hamish Hamilton, 1983.

Plays

Radio Plays: *Time Regained,* 1980; *Dialogue Between Friends,* 1982; *Punch-Flame and Pigeon-Breast,* 1983; *The True Tale of Margery Kempe,* 1985.

Television Plays: *Days,* from her own novel, 1981.

Other

The Banger (for children). London, Deutsch, and New York, Lion Press, 1968.
Patriarchal Attitudes: Women in Society. London, Faber, and New York, Stein and Day, 1970.
Scribble Sam (for children). London, Deutsch, and New York, McKay, 1971.
Tragedy and Social Evolution. London, Calder, 1976; New York, Persea, 1990.
Little Eden: A Child at War (autobiography). London, Faber, 1978; New York, Persea, 1987.
Sex and Subterfuge: Women Novelists to 1850. London, Macmillan, 1982; New York, Persea, 1988.
Editor, *Classic Choice 1.* London, Blackie, 1965.
Editor, *Modern Choice 1* and *2.* London, Blackie, 2 vols., 1965–66.
Editor, with Abigail Mozley and Dinah Livingstone, *Women Their World.* Gisburn, Lancashire, Platform Poets, 1980.
Editor, *Women's Letters in Wartime: 1450–1945.* London and San Francisco, Pandora, 1994.
Translator, *The Gadarene Club,* by Martin Walser. London, Longman, 1960.
Translator, *The Musicians of Bremen: Retold* (for children). London, Blackie, 1967.
Translator, *The Old Car,* by Elisabeth Borchers. London, Blackie, 1967.
Translator, *He and I and the Elephants,* by Bernhard Grzimek. London, Deutsch-Thames and Hudson, and New York, Hill and Wang, 1967.
Translator, *Little Fadette,* by George Sand. London, Blackie, 1967.
Translator, *A Family Failure,* by Renate Rasp. London, Calder and Boyars, 1970.
Translator, *The Deathbringer,* by Manfred von Conta. London, Calder and Boyars, 1971.

* * *

"I am using a different grid which I have first to construct by a painful process of trial and error," writes Eva Figes. In outright reaction against what she sees as the continuing conservative realist tradition of British fiction Figes resumes the modernist task of reshaping the novel and questioning the assumptions on which it is built. In her novels, as in those of Virginia Woolf (surely the greatest influence on her work), Figes seeks to bring together the properties of formal art and the intensities of the inner self. Here, life takes place between the acts, and we catch it unawares in the lives of ordinary people: Janus, the old man dying alone in his council house in *Winter Journey,* or Lily, the spinster sister and aunt who measures the subtly shifting relationships in *Light.* As Figes explores the self concealed behind the artifice of manners, the most elusive moments of existence are redefined in her novels as the prerequisite for creative vitality, and continuity is found in the lyric hoard of memories through which her characters resist the flux of time. In *Winter Journey* the presentation of a series of psychological states in place of a continuous narrative or plot results in an intense poetic lyricism. The same kind of unbroken texture, or openness and continuity, is found in *Light* (Figes's finest work to date), where Claude, artist and philosopher, explains: ''Everything is always in flux … it was both his overriding difficulty and essential to him.''

But there are darker realities here too. A sense of menace underlies the lyrical affirmation of the novels, and there is a corresponding sense that only a continuous style can soothe a narrative which is subject to unexpected disruptions and dislocations. ''My starting-point is inevitably Kafka,'' Figes claims, and there are echoes of Beckett too in her novels' unresolved ambivalence about their own representational activity. The negative energies of solipsism and angst are inseparable from the moments of heightened consciousness in the fragmented autobiography of Janus' winter journey. And in *Light,* Claude's fragile images of perfection are troubled by the motifs of transience and death. In the final analysis, perhaps the most fascinating and complex aspect of Figes's novels is that they do follow the Modernist tradition of showing art and memory as creative of a new order of reality. But they also remain firmly located in the destructive elements of historical time that many classic modernists would seek to bypass. The power and potency of the recurrent images of holocaust in her novels seem to reveal the author's deepest motivations for writing: ''I am a European wrestling with a different reality,'' she says. ''A piece of shrapnel lodges in my flesh, and when it moves, I write.''

Much of Figes's work, both in fiction and nonfiction, concerns the history, both internal and external, of women. One of many examples of the nonfiction treatment is *Women's Letters in Wartime;* more challenging, of course, is the fictional treatment, as when she portrays the seven ''ages'' of a woman's life in *Waking.* In *The Tree of Knowledge,* she turns a feminist light on the world of John Milton—a blind man who nonetheless ruled the women around him.

—Sandra Kemp

FINDLEY, Timothy

Nationality: Canadian. **Born:** Toronto, Ontario, 30 October 1930. **Education:** Rosedale Public School, Toronto; St. Andrews College, Aurora, Ontario; Jarvis Collegiate, Toronto; Royal Conservatory of Music, Toronto, 1950–53; Central School of Speech and Drama, London. **Career:** Stage, television, and radio actor, 1951–62; charter member, Stratford Shakespearean Festival, Ontario, 1953; contract player with H.M. Tennent, London, 1953–56; toured U.S. in *The Matchmaker,* 1956–57; studio writer, CBS, Hollywood, 1957–58; copywriter, CFGM Radio, Richmond Hill, Ontario. Playwright-in-residence, National Arts Centre, Ottawa, 1974–75; writer-in-residence, University of Toronto, 1979–80, Trent University, Peterborough, Ontario, 1984, and University of Winnipeg, 1985. Chair, Writers Union of Canada, 1977–78; president, English-Canadian Centre, International P.E.N., 1986–87. **Awards:** Canada Council award, 1968, 1978; Armstrong award, for radio writing, 1971; ACTRA award, for television documentary, 1975; Governor General's award, 1977; City of Toronto Book award, 1977, 1994; Anik award, for television writing, 1980; Canadian Authors Association prize, 1985, 1991, 1994; Western Magazine award, 1988; Government of Ontario Trillium award, 1989; Mystery Writers of America Edgar Allan Poe award, 1989; National Radio award, 1989, 1990; Gabriel award, 1990; Crime Writers of Canada award, for drama, 1994; Toronto Arts award, 1994; Gemini award, 1995; Knight of the Order of Arts and Letters (France), 1996. D.Litt.: Trent University, 1982; University of Guelph, Ontario, 1984; York University, Ontario, 1989; Lakehead University, Ontario, 1995; Memorial University, St. John's, Newfoundland, 1996. Officer, Order of Canada, 1986. **Agent:** Virginia Barber Literary Agency, 353 West 21st Street, New York, New York 10011, U.S.A. **Address:** Stone Orchard, Box 419, Cannington, Ontario L0E 1E0, Canada.

Publications

Novels

The Last of the Crazy People. New York, Meredith Press, and London, Macdonald, 1967.
The Butterfly Plague. New York, Viking Press, 1969; London, Deutsch, 1970.
The Wars. Toronto, Clarke Irwin, 1977; New York, Delacorte Press, and London, Macmillan, 1978.
Famous Last Words. Toronto, Clarke Irwin, and New York, Delacorte Press, 1981; London, Macmillan, 1987.
Not Wanted on the Voyage. Toronto, Viking, 1984; New York, Delacorte Press, and London, Macmillan, 1985.
The Telling of Lies. Toronto, Penguin, 1986; London, Macmillan, and New York, Dell, 1988.
Headhunter. Toronto, HarperCollins, 1993; New York, Crown, 1994.
The Piano Man's Daughter. Toronto, HarperCollins, and New York, Crown, 1995.
Pilgrim. New York, HarperCollins, 1999.

Short Stories

Dinner Along the Amazon. Toronto and London, Penguin, 1984; New York, Penguin, 1985.
Stones. Toronto, Penguin, 1988; New York, Delta, 1990.
Dust to Dust: Stories. Toronto, HarperCollins, 1997.

Uncollected Short Stories

''Island'' and ''The Long Walk'' in *The Newcomers,* edited by Charles E. Israel. Toronto, McClelland and Stewart, 1979.

Plays

The Paper People (televised 1968). Published in *Canadian Drama* (Toronto), vol. 9, no. 1, 1983.
The Journey (broadcast 1971). Published in *Canadian Drama* (Toronto), vol. 10, no. 1, 1984.

Can You See Me Yet? (produced Ottawa, 1976). Vancouver, Talonbooks, 1977.
John A. Himself music by Berthold Carriere (produced London, Ontario, 1979).
Strangers at the Door (radio script), in *Quarry* (Kingston, Ontario), 1982.
Daybreak at Pisa: 1945, in *Tamarack Review* (Toronto), Winter 1982.
The Stillborn Lover (produced London, 1993). Winnipeg, Blizzard, 1993.
The Trials of Ezra Pound. Winnipeg, Blizzard, 1994.

Screenplays: *Don't Let the Angels Fall,* 1970; *The Wars,* 1983.

Radio Plays and Documentaries: *The Learning Stage and Ideas* series, 1963–73; *Adrift,* 1968; *Matinee* series, 1970–71; *The Journey,* 1971; *Missionaries,* 1973; *The Trials of Ezra Pound,* 1990.

Television Plays and Documentaries: *Umbrella* series, 1964–66; *Who Crucified Christ?,* 1966; *The Paper People,* 1968; *The Whiteoaks of Jalna* (7 episodes), from books by Mazo de la Roche, 1971–72; *The National Dream* series (8 episodes), with William Whitehead, 1974; *The Garden and the Cage,* with William Whitehead, 1977; *1832* and *1911* (*The Newcomers* series), 1978–79; *Dieppe 1942,* with William Whitehead, 1979; *Other People's Children,* 1981; *Islands in the Sun* and *Turn the World Around (Belafonte Sings* series), with William Whitehead, 1983.

Other

Imaginings, with Janis Rapaport, illustrated by Heather Cooper. Toronto, Ethos, 1982.
Inside Memory: Pages from a Writer's Workbook. Toronto, Harper Collins, 1990.
From Stone Orchard: A Collection of Memories. Toronto, HarperFlamingo Canada, 1998.

*

Bibliography: *Timothy Findley: An Annotated Bibliography* by Carol Roberts and Lynne Macdonald, Downsview, Ontario, ECW Press, 1990.

Manuscript Collection: Historical Resources Branch, National Archives of Canada.

Critical Studies: *Eleven Canadian Novelists* by Graeme Gibson, Toronto, Anansi, 1973; *Conversations with Canadian Novelists* by Silver Donald Cameron, Toronto, Macmillan, 1973; ''An Interview with Timothy Findley,'' in *University of Toronto Review,* 1980; ''Timothy Findley Issue'' of *Canadian Literature* (Vancouver), Winter 1981; *Timothy Findley* by Wilfred Cude, Toronto, Dundurn Press, 1982; ''The Marvel of Reality'' (interview) with Bruce Meyer and Brian O'Riordan, in *Waves* (Toronto), vol. 10, no. 4, 1982; ''Prayers Against Despair'' by Gilbert Drolet, in *Journal of Canadian Fiction 33* (Montreal), 1982; ''Whispers of Chaos'' by Eugene Benson, in *World Literature Written in English* (Guelph, Ontario), Autumn 1982; *Second Words: Selected Critical Prose* by Margaret Atwood, Toronto, Anansi, 1982, Boston, Beacon Press, 1984; ''The Dubious Battle of Storytelling: Narrative Strategies in Timothy Findley's *The Wars*'' by Simone Vauthier, in *Gaining Ground: European Critics on Canadian Literature* edited by Robert Kroetsch and Reingard M. Nischik, Edmonton, Alberta, NeWest Press, 1985; *Timothy Findley's ''The Wars'': A Study Guide,* Toronto, ECW Press, 1990, and *''Front Lines'': The Fiction of Timothy Findley,* Toronto, ECW Press, 1991, both by Lorraine York; *Moral Metafiction: The Novels of Timothy Findley,* Toronto, ECW Press, 1991; *Praying for Rain: Timothy Findley's Not Wanted on the Voyage,* Toronto, ECW Press, 1992, both by Donna Pennee; *Timothy Findley: Stories from a Life* by Carol Roberts, Toronto, ECW Press, 1994; *Writing on Trial: Timothy Findley's Famous Last Words* by Diana Brydon, Toronto, ECW Press, 1995; *The Influence of Painting on Five Canadian Writers: Alice Munro, Hugh Hood, Timothy Findley, Margaret Atwood, and Michael Ondaatje* by John Cooke. Lewiston, New York, Edwin Mellen Press, 1996; *Timothy Findley* by Diana Brydon. New York, Twayne, 1998; *Paying Attention: Critical Essays on Timothy Findley,* edited by Anne Geddes Bailey and Karen Grandy. Toronto, ECW Press, 1998; Buffalo, New York, General Distribution Services, 1998.

Timothy Findley comments:

There are some who say you should only and always write about what you know. If I had taken this advise, then all my books would be about the theatre, rabbits and cats, a fairly standard version of family life and the road between the farm where I live and the City of Toronto. The fact is, only the rabbits and the cats have made it into my fiction—in one book as the companions of a man in World War I and in another as stowaways on Noah's Ark. Without apology, I must admit that I cannot imagine why I have written what I have. It does occur to me, however, that a thread runs through all my work that has to do with unlikely people being confronted with uncommon events.

* * *

It is an understatement to say that in his writing Timothy Findley engages with the history of the twentieth century. His novels span the Edwardian era, World War I, World War II, the Holocaust, and the end of the millennium. His emphasis on these central historical events is often highly critical. At the end of *The Butterfly Plague* the narrator paradoxically states ''We know that history repeats itself. We also know that it does not.'' Although reevaluating history is a preoccupation in his writing and although some of his writing has been labeled ''historiographic metafiction,'' Findley's style changes with each novel. He is a literary experimenter—with form, with setting, and with voice—experimenting in the service of social, historical, and political exposition. It is remarkable to think that the stylistically diverse novels *Pilgrim, The Piano Man's Daughter, The Wars* and *Not Wanted on the Voyage* are creations of the same author, yet it is less surprising if one considers the similarities in the novels' central thematic concerns.

Although the stories differ dramatically in plot and form, the symbolic content of Findley's work is often predictable. His writing proliferates with scenes of violence, loneliness, animal rights, abuses of power, madness, and apocalyptic visions. Indeed, Findley himself jokingly points to his own recurring images and themes: ''It came as something of a shock...to discover that for over thirty years of writing my attention has turned again and again to the same unvarying gamut of sounds and images.... I wish I hadn't noticed this. In fact, it became an embarrassment and I began to wonder if I should file A CATALOGUE OF PERSONAL OBSESSIONS. The sound of screen doors banging; evening lamplight; music held at a distance—always being played on a gramophone; letters written on blue-tinted note paper; robins making forays onto summer lawns to murder worms; photographs in cardboard boxes; Colt revolvers hidden in bureau drawers and a chair that is always falling over.'' Added to this list should be the butterfly—an image that proliferates in works ranging from the *Butterfly Plague* to *Pilgrim.* This catalogue also points to Findley's favorite technique of dramatically placing disturbing elements in an ordinary context (a gun in a drawer).

Findley began professional life as an actor touring Canada, the United States, and Britain but turned to writing in his early thirties with the encouragement of his mentor, the playwright, Thornton Wilder. Over the course of his career he has written several notable plays: *John A. Himself, The Stillborn Lover*, and *Can You See Me Yet?* Nevertheless, he is most well known for his fiction, which, indeed, retains a sense of drama in its evocation of startling visual images, its ear for dialogue, and most interestingly, the way in which characters momentarily step out of a scene to comment on their own actions within the scene. This is done with the use of ''voices'' that follow central characters throughout the narratives. In *Not Wanted on the Voyage*, the voices of Mottyl the Cat repeatedly come to her rescue, whereas in *Pilgrim*, the voices of Carl Gustav Jung are his conscience and are always in judgment of his actions. The use of the ''voices'' technique provides yet another layer of narration in what are already multi-voiced narratives. We know we are never to trust anything as the ''truth'' in Findley's works and, indeed, we are never really able to know what are ''the telling of lies.''

In his first novel, *The Last of the Crazy People*, Findley presents a child, obsessed by the futility of his family's existence in a post-war world, who eventually massacres his entire family as the logic of childhood and the logic of insanity blend together. In *The Butterfly Plague* Findley takes us into the late thirties in Hollywood, where the fate of a family threatened with an inherited disease parallels the rise of the Nazism and the breakdown of civilization in Europe.

In his next two novels, Findley revisits the horrors of the First and Second World Wars. In *The Wars*, the story of the breakdown of Robert Ross, a young Canadian soldier, is pieced together by a researcher searching through boxes of letters and photographs that provide only clues to Robert's life. Like his researcher in this novel, Findley's research is impeccable. He knows the periods of which he writes in depth, and in *The Wars*, he actually creates a deeper illusion of authenticity by presenting the story as the product of an intensive reconstruction of events, even to the extent of inventing taped interviews with survivors of the war who remember Robert and his quixotic attempt to rescue a troop of horses doomed to death.

Moving from the First to the second World War, *Famous Last Words* is a work of elaborate artifice in which fictional figures mingle with ''real'' famous people in history. *Famous Last Words* tells the story of a writer who relates his flirtation with fascism and with fascists such as the Duke and Duchess of Windsor and Ezra Pound by writing on the walls of the Grand Elyseum Hotel. For Diana Brydon, the novel is significant because it tries to understand the attraction of fascism (and other forms of intolerance) without trying to ''demonize'' it. The novel is narrated by Hugh Selwyn Mauberley, a minor character in the work of Ezra Pound made major by Findley. Mauberley has written his version of history on sixteen walls of the hotel. The story is only found by American soldiers along with Mauberley's frozen, mutilated corpse well after his death.

Not Wanted on the Voyage takes us far back from the world of war to Genesis. A retelling of the Noah's ark story from Genesis, the story features a decrepit lozenge-sucking Yaweh; a domineering, vivisecting, rapist patriarch, Noah Noyes; a marinated blue embittered Japeth; a gin-drinking and Edwardian song piano playing Mrs. Noyes; a largely benevolent androgynous Lucy/Lucifer figure; a blind cat named Mottyl; and a host of other talking animals (including sheep that sing hymns). This novel literally pits the marginalized figures of the lower orders on the lower decks of the ark (women, children, workers, animals) against the upper orders, or those with power. Findley bravely challenges the biblical story of Noah's ark from the opening line of the novel: ''Everyone knows it wasn't like that'' to the closing line when Mrs. Noyes prays: ''She prayed. But not to an absent God. Never, never again to the absent God, but to the absent clouds, she prayed. And to the empty sky. She prayed for rain.''

In *The Telling of Lies*, Findley takes another turn, this time towards mystery. It is the unraveling of the death of pharmaceutical industrialist Calder Maddox. Set in a seaside hotel in Maine, the novel intricately weaves together a story of personal loss and corporate greed. The mystery is complicated by the gradual emergence of the story of the narrator's time in a Japanese concentration camp in World War II.

While *The Telling of Lies* takes on the pharmaceutical companies, *Headhunter* addresses the structural problems of psychiatric institutions while delving deeply into intertextual worlds. The novel opens: ''On a winter's day, while a blizzard raged through the streets of Toronto, Lilah Kemp inadvertently set Kurtz free from page 92 of *Heart of Darkness*.'' The story follows both Kurtz and Lilah through the streets of Toronto as Lilah searches for a Marlow to help her capture Kurtz and return him to Conrad's novel. However, Kurtz has become the head of the fictional Parkin Institute of Psychiatric Research. He has become a modern day ''harbinger of darkness...horror-meister...headhunter.'' Writing about *Headhunter*, critic Marlene Goldman demonstrates Findley's incorporation and secularization of the apocalyptic paradigm through the recursive use of literary intertextuality; a visionary narrator with a transhistorical perspective; and a small group of ''the elect'' who battle the corrupt forces at work in their community. Yet, Goldman notes that while this narrative invokes the apocalyptic vision, Findley ''simultaneously counters this vision with a more earthly and historically oriented perspective.'' Even his futuristic vision is somewhat grounded in the problems of history.

If *Headhunter* is a horrific vision of the future, then *The Piano Man's Daughter* is a more optimistic vision of the past. Twenty-nine-year-old piano tuner Charlie Kilworth tells the story of his mother's life, death, schizophrenia, and pyromania and in the process reveals his own story and the story of past and future generations. The novel explores the inheritance of ''madness'' as a blessing and a curse. Two of Findley's most vividly painted tableaus are in this novel. The first is the act of giving birth in a field and the second is the act of performing emergency brain surgery on a kitchen table. The beauty and precision of each of these scenes remains with the reader well after the story has been read.

Pilgrim is another foray into the world of the insane (and another questioning of what it means to be labeled insane). The central character, Pilgrim, is ''a determined suicide who, by all appearances [is] unable to die.'' The novel shifts between a mental institution in Zurich in 1912 and Florence in 1497. It, too, unravels like a mystery as Carl Gustav Jung, the psychiatrist in charge of Pilgrim, reads the journals of a man who appears to have been as present in 1497 as he is in 1912. The elegance of this novel lies in the manner in which

Findley reveals 400 years of stories with such suspense that it is sometimes nearly impossible not to continue reading. The craftsmanship of *Pilgrim* surpasses Findley's other works, except perhaps *Not Wanted on the Voyage*, as he beautifully draws us into a world of deceit, betrayal, power, love, and death (again). Somehow, however, although Findley has returned to his favorite obsessions and we know that he repeats himself, we also know that he does not.

—Laura Moss

FISCHER, Tibor

Nationality: British. **Born:** Stockport, 15 November 1959. **Education:** Cambridge University. **Career:** Works as a freelance journalist. **Agent:** Nicholas Ellison Inc., 55 Fifth Ave., New York, New York 10003, U.S.A.

PUBLICATIONS

Novels

Under The Frog. Edinburgh, Polygon 1992; New York, New Press, 1994.
The Thought Gang. Edinburgh, Polygon, 1994; New York, New Press, 1995.
The Collector Collector. New York, Metropolitan Books, 1997.

Short Stories

I Like Being Killed: Stories. New York, Metropolitan Books, 2000.

* * *

That Tibor Fischer's first novel was shortlisted for Britain's most prestigious literary award, the Booker Prize, may have had something to do with its subject: Hungary from the end of World War II to the Uprising of 1956. But it is Fischer's treatment of his subject, his specific style as well as his overall approach, that sets the novel apart. Eschewing the elegiac quality of another Hungarian novel that covers much the same period, George Konrad's *Feast in the Garden,* the absurdist, blackly humorous *Under the Frog* is closer in tone to Czech novelist Milan Kundera's *The Joke* and Polish writers Tadeusz Borowski's *This Way to the Gas* and *Ladies and Gentlemen* and Tadeusz Konwicki's *A Minor Apocalypse.*

Fischer's odd title derives from a Hungarian saying meaning "nothing could be worse." For the novel's main character, Gyorgi Fischer, things in fact can be worse and usually become so. What this member of the Locomotive basketball team fears is that he may never be "given a future to lose." What he wants is to get out of the country; any place will do: if not Sweden, then Poland, and if not Poland, then Rumania or China or even Korea during the war, which, he believes, would be better than postwar Hungary. Pragmatic and apolitical, perhaps to a fault, he occupies the middle ground between idealists like his Polish girlfriend Jadwiga and opportunists like Farago, once a petty thief, then head of his district's "Nazi franchise," and now local secretary of the Communist Party. Gyorgi is an opportunist of a different stripe: too cynical to be an idealist, too moral to blow with the prevailing winds. The real horror in this novel is not that good people like Jadwiga who are committed to justice and freedom should die; nor is it that in the world Fischer describes even a little power seems to corrupt absolutely. Rather it is that so many people should find themselves in much the same position as the father of Gyorgi's friend, Tibor Pataki. Arrested in 1951, the elder Pataki must endure interrogation and torture before being released to face a different kind of humiliation, "having been judged too dull" to be a conspirator. In a world of opportunists and optimists, of a Catholic Church that "wasn't too topheavy with brilliance," and of a national infatuation with defeat born of centuries of invasions (from Mongol hordes to Soviet tanks), there is something understandable if not altogether noble in Gyorgi's choosing cynical detachment, self-interest, noncooperation, and, finally, escape. Getting what he wants does not bring relief, however. Once across the border, Gyorgi, like Lot's wife, looks back and turns not to a pillar of salt but to tears.

Fischer has described his second novel, *The Thought Gang,* as "a short book about all human knowledge and experience." The apparent flippancy of his remark matches the apparent flippancy of this playfully structured but nonetheless serious novel. Pushing his fondness for unfamiliar words and usages even further than he did in *Under the Frog* and employing a variety of mutually exclusive structural devices, Fischer creates a form that matches perfectly the character of its protagonist-narrator. Born on 9 May 1945 (the day after VE Day), Eddie Coffin has spent the last thirty years "in the thought trade," the philosophy "biz." On the run from the London police, he joins forces with the one-armed, one-eyed Hubert to form the Thought Gang, specializing in bank robberies with a philosophical twist. In a novel this fragmented having a plot this wayward dealing with the misadventures of a hero this antiheroic, the reader may well ask (as the novel does), "What's going on here?" and whether what is going on amounts to anything more than a "good deal of blagging" (nonsense-making). As in the art of Donald Barthelme, another writer fond of collage, blague, and cultural debris, the range of literary and subliterary reference is impressively diverse. The entire novel may be read as a weirdly angled takeoff on Boethius's *Consolation of Philosophy,* with opening gambit adapted from Kafka's *The Trial,* plot from *Bonnie and Clyde,* title from Orwell's *1984,* parts of the structure from Nietzsche's *The Will to Power,* and additional material from the Keystone Kops, Charlie Chaplin, and François Rabelais, among others. All this adds up to a great deal more than just another (and by now belated) example of postmodern plagiarism and randomness. *The Thought Gang* irreverently takes to task the entire Western philosophical tradition, from the earliest Ionians (Eddie's specialty) to the currently fashionable deconstructionists. In a world in which "brute force works," philosophy is either irrelevant or merely one kind of "biz" among others. Although it lacks *Under the Frog*'s sense of historical immediacy and prefers flights of cartoonish fantasy and intellectual slapstick to direct satire, *The Thought Gang* is nonetheless a deeply committed work, as the references to other failures of the postwar moral and political imagination—Vietnam, Afghanistan, and Sarajevo—clearly indicate. Near novel's end, Eddie makes his and Fischer's point clearer still. "It's embarrassing that the answer is so simple, so right in front of us. The sages have said so, but like most of the truths, we're bored with it. Change it round, say it backwards, make it foreign: evol, evol, evol. Unstealable money."

—Robert A. Morace

FLANAGAN, Thomas

Nationality: American. **Born:** Thomas James Bonner Flanagan in Greenwich, Connecticut, 5 November 1923. **Education:** Amherst College, Massachusetts, B.A. 1945; Columbia University, New York, M.A. 1948, Ph.D. in English 1958. **Military Service:** Served in the United States Naval Reserve, 1942–44. **Family:** Married Jean Parker in 1949; two daughters. **Career:** Instructor, 1949–52, and assistant professor, 1952–59, Columbia University; assistant professor, 1960–67, associate professor, 1967–73, professor, 1973–78, and chair of the Department of English, 1973–76, University of California, Los Angeles; professor of English, State University of New York, Stony Brook, 1978–92, distinguished professor, University of California, Berkeley, 1993—. **Awards:** American Council of Learned Societies grant, 1962; Guggenheim fellowship, 1962; National Book Critics Circle award, 1979. Named Literary Lion, New York Public Library, 1994. D.Litt.: National University, Ireland, 1994; Amherst College, 1995. **Agent:** Robin Straus Agency, Inc., 229 E. 79th St., New York, New York 10021, U.S.A. **Address:** Department of English, State University of New York, Stony Brook, New York 11794, U.S.A.

Publications

Novels

The Year of the French. New York, Holt Rinehart, and London, Macmillan, 1979.
The Tenants of Time. New York, Dutton, and London, Bantam, 1988.
The End of the Hunt. New York, Dutton, 1994.

Uncollected Short Stories

''The Cold Winds of Adesta'' April 1952, ''The Point of Honor'' December 1952, ''The Lion's Mane'' March 1953, ''This Will Do Nicely'' August 1955, ''The Customs of the Country'' July 1956, and ''Suppose You Were on the Jury'' March 1958, all in *Ellery Queen's Mystery Magazine* (New York).
''The Fine Italian Hand,'' in *Ellery Queen's Book of First Appearances,* edited by Ellery Queen and Eleanor Sullivan. New York, Dial Press, 1982.

Other

The Irish Novelists 1800–1850. New York, Columbia University Press, 1959.

* * *

Thomas Flanagan has written three novels of historical fiction that describe some of the most turbulent episodes in the history of Ireland. His first novel, *The Year of the French,* was based on an actual historical event in which a French military force landed at Killala, County Mayo, Ireland on 22 August 1798. The French, who came ostensibly to free Ireland from British rule, were apparently more interested in embarrassing and harassing the English than in actually aiding the Irish. The French troops were joined by many peasants and various Irish rebel organizations. After marching through much of western and central Eire and winning several battles, they were eventually badly defeated at Ballinamuk, near Longford, by a vastly superior army led by Lord Cornwallis, whose success redeemed his tarnished experience in America. One of the most fascinating aspects of Flanagan's novel, which gives it an epic quality, is his attempt to portray in depth all sides and viewpoints in the conflict: the high-born and the peasants, the Catholics and the Protestants, the French, Irish, and British military units, the clergy, the schoolmasters, the merchants—these and other groups are delineated with flesh and blood realization. At one point Flanagan even switches the scene to England and conveys a memorable portrait of an absentee landlord. Among the personages who beguile the reader are Arthur Broome, the local Anglican clergyman in Killala; Owen MacCarthy, the heavy-drinking itinerant poet and hedgerow schoolmaster; Jean-Joseph Humbert, the wily, pragmatic French general; Malcolm Elliott, an upper-class Protestant estate holder committed to a more equitable economic order; and Captain Ferdy O'Donnell, a courageous, sensitive rebel leader.

Fictional characters are interrelated with real-life figures such as Wolfe Tone, George and John Moore, Dennis Browne, and Maria Edgeworth. The social, political, economic, and historical background and climate are presented and examined in thorough detail. Flanagan effectively intersperses dialogue and description with numerous imaginary diaries and memoirs of the era, and this technique adds immeasurably to the verisimilitude.

The novel is also distinguished by capturing the scene with marvellously rendered poetic lyricism exemplified in both the written and spoken language of the period. The book is a mellifluous delight—many of the pages are sheer poetry glowing with beauty and picturesque phrasing. Further, *The Year of the French* possesses considerable narrative drive.

The book is not without flaws. Flanagan's portrayal of the Catholic clergy is virulently hostile, whereas the Protestant ministers are always presented as decent individuals. Flanagan also understates the suffering and oppression the common people had to endured. He takes a distastefully snobbish attitude toward them on several occasions. He also unduly fantasizes about a magical humanitarian union between Catholics and Protestants, which is certainly desirable but, as he presents it, totally unconvincing.

Flanagan's second novel, *The Tenants of Time,* deals with the Fenian Rising in Kilpeder in 1867, the Land Wars, the Phoenix Park killings, and the career of Charles Stewart Parnell. Although Flanagan still conveys vividly the beauty of the Irish countryside and the lilt of the language, this novel does not have the consistency of lyricism that distinguished his previous book. Flanagan's poetic sensibility is effective in portraying the old Fenian schoolmaster Hugh MacMahon; at other times the prose is frequently flat and uninspired. Flanagan tries also to present too many characters in too many different locations. As a consequence, the book frequently becomes sketchy and superficial.

The End of the Hunt, Flanagan's third novel, however, recaptures much of the force, lyricism, and convincing historical re-creation of his first book. He now focuses on the violent years after the 1916 Easter Rebellion when Irish rebel forces fought the English with guerrilla-style warfare and, then, after the British had granted the country Free State status, a civil war broke out between those Irish groups who wanted a Republic, completely independent of England, and their fellow countrymen who were willing to accept the Free State arrangement. Flanagan depicts with considerable force the conflicts, betrayals, terrorism, and treachery that marked this era. Numerous scenes are unforgettable, with Frank Lacy's ambush at Dawson

Crossings typical of the intensity of Flanagan's descriptions. Once again, historical personages, such as Eamon DeValera, Winston Churchill, and rebel leader Michael Collins, enter the narrative. Flanagan succeeds once more in conveying the musicality of the Irish language, whether spoken by uneducated farmers or by the intellectual leaders of the rebellion during battles, or in secret hideouts, or in the back rooms of public houses. The realism of speech and characterization is compelling, and the historical events in themselves provide a fast-paced, natural narrative movement.

The novel's only serious weakness is the love story between well-bred rebel Christopher Blake and the widowed Janice Nugent. It is obvious that this material has been superimposed on the narrative to add romantic interest. In general, throughout his writings, Flanagan is not as sure-handed in portraying female characters as he is in describing males.

After the relative failure of his second novel, several critics felt that Flanagan would not continue to write gripping fiction. His latest novel, however, disproves that notion and gives hope for more successful novels in the future.

—Paul A. Doyle

FOOTE, Shelby

Nationality: American. **Born:** Greenville, Mississippi, 17 November 1916. **Education:** The University of North Carolina, Chapel Hill, 1935–37. **Military Service:** Served in the United States Army, 1940–44: Captain, and Marine Corps, 1944–45. **Family:** Married Gwyn Rainer in 1956 (second marriage); two children. **Career:** Novelist-in-residence, University of Virginia, Charlottesville, November 1963; playwright-in-residence, Arena Stage, Washington, D.C., 1963–64; writer-in-residence, Hollins College, Virginia, 1968. **Awards:** Guggenheim fellowship, 1955, 1956, 1957; Ford fellowship, for drama, 1963; Fletcher Pratt award, for non-fiction, 1964, 1974; University of North Carolina award, 1975; Dos Passos prize for Literature, 1988; Charles Frankel award, 1992; St. Louis Literary award, 1992; Nevins-Freeman award, 1992; New York Public Library Literary Lion, 1994, 1998; Ingersoll-Weaver award, 1997; Richard Wright award, 1997. D.Litt.: University of the South, Sewanee, Tennessee, 1981; Southwestern University, Memphis, Tennessee, 1982; University of North Carolina, Chapel Hill, 1992; University of South Carolina, 1991; University of Notre Dame, South Bend, Indiana, 1994; College of William & Mary, 1999; Loyola University, 1999. **Member:** Society of American Historians, 1980; American Academy of Arts and Letters, 1994. **Address:** 542 East Parkway South, Memphis, Tennessee 38104, U.S.A.

Publications

Novels

Tournament. New York, Dial Press, 1949.
Follow Me Down. New York, Dial Press, 1950; London, Hamish Hamilton, 1951.
Love in a Dry Season. New York, Dial Press, 1951.
Shiloh. New York, Dial Press, 1952.
Jordan County: A Landscape in Narrative (includes stories). New York, Dial Press, 1954.
September September. New York, Random House, 1978.
Ride Out. New York, Modern Library, 1996.

Plays

Jordan County: A Landscape in the Round (produced Washington, D.C., 1964).

Other

The Civil War: A Narrative:
Fort Sumter to Perryville. New York, Random House, 1958; London, Bodley Head, 1991.
Fredericksburg to Meridian. New York, Random House, 1963; London, Bodley Head, 1991.
Red River to Appomattox. New York, Random House, 1974; London, Bodley Head, 1991.
The Novelist's View of History. Winston-Salem, North Carolina, Palaemon Press, 1981.
Conversations with Shelby Foote, edited by William C. Carter. Jackson, University Press of Mississippi, 1989.
Stars in Their Courses: The Gettysburg Campaign, June-July 1863. New York, Random House, 1994.
The Beleaguered City: The Vicksburg Campaign, December 1862-July 1863. New York, Random House, 1995.
The Correspondence of Shelby Foote and Walker Percy, edited by Jay Tolson. New York, Norton, 1997.
Editor, *Anton Chekhov: Later Short Stories, 1888–1903*, translated by Constance Garnett. New York, Modern Library, 1999.

*

Manuscript Collection: Southern Historical Collection, University of North Carolina, Chapel Hill, North Carolina.

Critical Studies: ''Shelby Foote Issue'' (includes bibliography) of *Mississippi Quarterly* (State College), October 1971, and *Delta* (Montpellier, France), 1977; *Shelby Foote* by Helen White and Redding Sugg, Boston, Twayne, 1982; *Shelby Foote: Novelist and Historian* by Robert L. Phillips, University of Mississippi Press, 1992.

* * *

Shelby Foote appears to succeed as a historian, not as a novelist; his multi-volume history *The Civil War: A Narrative* shows his ability to best advantage. However, one should remember that his entree into the literary world came as a promising novelist. His novels show a serious craftsman at work.

Foote experimented with technique. *Tournament* is a character study—approaching biography—with an objective omniscient point of view. *Follow Me Down* takes a single plot but incorporates a multiple point of view. This method is interesting because it allows eight characters—including protagonist and minor characters—to comment in a limited first person viewpoint on their reactions to a violent murder. *Love in a Dry Season* is a *tour de force* in which the author links two separate stories centered on the subject of money by a character who tries and fails to obtain a place in the financial elite of a small delta town. *Shiloh* enters the domain of historical fiction as the author recreates that Civil War battle through the eyes of six soldiers from both camps. Unlike the viewers in *Follow Me Down,* these narrators describe different aspects of the three-day confrontation, and only by adroit maneuvering does the author bring the respective narratives into contact. The battle, therefore becomes the hero of the novel. *Jordan County* is a collection of seven tales or episodes ranging from 1950 backwards to 1797. In each case the locale is Bristol, Jordan County, Mississippi. As his previous novel focused on a single battle, so this chronicles human drama of a fictional area, which becomes the only constant in a world of flux.

With the exception of his historical novel, all of Foote's novels are located in his microcosm, the delta country around Lake Jordan. This fictive locale includes two counties, Issawamba and Jordan, Solitaire Planatation, and the town of Bristol on the Mississippi River. Through a habit of cross reference, Foote links episodes from one novel to another. For instance, the novella ''Pillar of Fire'' (*Jordan County*) relates the story of Isaac Jameson, founder of Solitaire Plantation and a patriarch of the delta, while *Tournament* supplies information about the man, Hugh Bart, who brought Solitare back from devastation by war and reconstruction.

Foote's use of setting, as well as style, subject matter, themes, and characterization, invites comparison with his geographical neighbor, Faulkner, but Foote's accomplishments suffer thereby. Foote is competent, not great. Normally his style is simple, lean, and direct; it seldom takes on richly suggestive qualities. Most of his themes move in the negative, anti-social direction: violence instead of peace; lust rather than love; avarice, power, and pride instead of self-sacrifice; and loneliness rather than participation in community. At his best Foote deals effectively with dramatic situations and characterizations, for example, the concatenation of episodes in the life of Hugh Bart or Luther Eustis's murder (*Follow Me Down*); however, Harley Drew's career (*Love in a Dry Season*) of lust and avarice seems an exploitation of violence rather than art. Foote chronicles events in the realistic tradition without conveying a larger insight than the particular—an insight necessary for him to achieve a significant place in southern literature.

During the 1990s, Foote produced *Ride Out,* which attracted little critical attention— particularly when compared to his nonfiction efforts. The latter included, in addition to his writing on the Civil War, a book of correspondence with Walker Percy and a collection of Chekhov's stories, which Foote edited.

—Anderson Clark

FORD, Richard

Nationality: American. **Born:** Jackson, Mississippi, 16 February 1944. **Education:** Public schools in Jackson, 1950–62; Michigan State University, East Lansing, 1962–66, B.A. 1966; Washington University Law School, St. Louis, 1967–68; University of California, Berkeley, 1968–70, M.A. 1970. **Family:** Married Kristina Hensley in 1968. **Career:** Assistant professor of English, Williams College, Williamstown, Massachusetts, 1978–79; lecturer, Princeton University, New Jersey, 1980–81; teacher, Harvard University, 1994. **Awards:** Guggenheim fellowship, 1977; National Endowment for the Arts fellowship, 1978, 1983; New York Public Library Literary Lion award, 1989; American Academy award, 1989; Echoing Green Foundation award, 1991; Pulitzer Prize for fiction, 1997. **Agent:** Amanda Urban, International Creative Management, 40 West 57th Street, New York, New York 10023–2031, U.S.A.

Publications

Novels

A Piece of My Heart. New York, Harper, 1976; London, Collins, 1987.

The Ultimate Good Luck. Boston, Houghton Mifflin, 1981; London, Collins, 1989.

The Sportswriter. New York, Vintage, and London, Collins, 1986.

Wildlife. New York, Atlantic Monthly Press, and London, Collins, 1990.

Independence Day. New York, Knopf, 1995.

Short Stories

Rock Springs. New York, Atlantic Monthly Press, 1987; London, Collins, 1988.

Women with Men: Three Stories. New York, Knopf, 1997.

Play

Screenplay: *Bright Angel,* 1991.

Other

Editor, with Shannon Ravenel, *The Best American Short Stories 1990.* Boston, Houghton Mifflin, 1990.

Editor, *The Granta Book of the American Short Story.* London, Granta, 1991.

Editor, *The Essential Tales of Chekhov.* New York, Ecco Press, 2000.

*

Critical Studies: *Perspectives on Richard Ford,* edited by Huey Guagliardo. Jackson, University Press of Mississippi, 2000; *Richard Ford* by Elinor Walker. New York, Twayne, 2000.

Richard Ford comments:

I'm stymied in an attempt to introduce my work. I wish I could write something about it that would make it seem wonderful and irresistible. My belief is, though, that anybody's work ought to introduce itself from its first moment, and I would prefer to take my chances that way rather than to put on the critic's cap regarding my own efforts or risk confusing my later opinions about my book or my story or my essay with any of their actual effects. Writers, in my experience, often gain very lofty opinions of their *oeuvres* once their *oeuvres* are out of writerly control. Any number of wondrous intentions, structures, and philosophical underpinnings can be made to dress up a simple story after the fact. I've probably been guilty of it myself, though it's only human.

* * *

Near the end of *The Sportswriter*, Frank Bascombe tells a young woman in whom he's interested that he never lets himself feel sorry for anyone he writes about, ''since the next person you're liable to feel sorry for is you, and then you're in real trouble.'' While the settings of Richard Ford's fiction range from Montana to Arkansas to Mexico to New Jersey, his theme seems to remain constant. Emotional entanglements—with others, with the self—are to be avoided.

In *A Piece of My Heart*, after eight years of marriage to Jackie, Robard Hewes leaves their home in Bishop, California, and drives his truck to the Arkansas bank of the Mississippi River. There, in the sleepy town of Helena, he takes up again with Beuna, with whom he had a brief affair 12 years earlier. He has been led to do this because for a year Beuna, married to an obsessed minor-league pitcher, has been writing him letters persuading him to come see her and renew their affair. Robard, whose own marriage has lost some of its flavor, knows that fooling with another man's wife is risky business. But having made his decision to do it, he is bent on carrying out his mission.

In Arkansas, Robard encounters Sam Newel, just down from Chicago, where he was about to complete his education in the law. The two men end up sharing quarters on an island that is the destination of hunting parties from out of state. Sam has been urged to spend some time on the island by his girlfriend Beebe, who thinks Sam needs to raise his ''tolerance for ambiguity'' and to learn to keep going ''when nothing is very clearly defined,'' a notion that sounds very much like the poet John Keats's ''negative capability.''

Although it is obvious that Sam has a precarious hold on life, Robard does not like him or offer him anything resembling pity. Nor does Sam see anything in Robard worthy of his respect. Sam, burdened with intellect and guilt, thinks Robard is an impulsive fool. That Robard is not a reflective person clearly, in the view of the author, is very much to his credit; when called by his instincts, Robard acts. Sam's troubles are due to his willingness to dwell on the same old issues.

A Piece of My Heart is divided into seven parts. The first and last and two parts in the middle are Robard's; three alternate parts in the middle are Sam's. The effect of this path-crossing is that Sam is moved away from his Hamlet-like tendencies and Robard begins to reflect, in particular to realize his mistake in leaving Jackie. His realization, though, comes too late, for he is shot as a trespasser before he can start back to California.

Ford's second novel, *The Ultimate Good Luck*, is about 31-year-old Harry Quinn's adventures in Oaxaca, Mexico, where he is trying to gain the release from prison of a young American drug smuggler. Quinn is a more thoughtful Robard. Just as Robard left Jackie, Quinn too let a good woman get away from him. But he is given a chance to get Rae back when she writes and asks whether he would be interested in helping to get her brother out of a Mexican prison. As a former Marine helicopter pilot in Vietnam, Quinn has the skills and cast of mind needed for dealing with corrupt prison officials and the Mexican underworld.

Unlike Sam Newel, Quinn, despite the horrors of Vietnam, will not let the past take hold of him. He is determined to live in the present, free of anxiety. Quinn is convinced that the ultimate good luck comes only to those who live in the present. What Quinn learns, though, is that even living in the present is not sufficient for outrunning loneliness. Thus he is glad for the opportunity to win Rae back.

Quinn, whose language is spare and hardboiled, is a typical Ford protagonist. In language and temperament, Quinn is very much a descendent of Ernest Hemingway's heroes. Near the beginning of this novel is one of the best pieces of descriptive prose to be found in all of Ford's writing, and it too is reminiscent of Hemingway. It is a description of two teenage Mexican boys boxing. At first they haven't the heart to hit each other, but the bout ends with one boy poking the other's eyeball out of its socket.

The Sportswriter is Ford's best-known novel. His protagonist, Frank Bascombe, has a Hemingway-esque attraction to contests of strength and skill. But while Hemingway's characters enlist in wars and gather at bullfights, Bascombe is drawn to the safer, relatively antiseptic world of sports. After the death of his young son, Bascombe quits writing fiction (where clearly the more rigorous existential challenges lie) for sports writing because sports teach that there are ''no transcendent themes in life'': ''When a contest is over, it's over, finished. That's the way life is, and any other view is a lie. Athletes are completely happy living in the present.''

Though these thoughts echo Quinn's desires to live only in the present, Bascombe is more reminiscent of T. S. Eliot's Prufrock, or Mary McCarthy's Peter Levi, than a Hemingway protagonist. Bascombe thinks and observes but cannot act. When an acquaintance who clearly is suicidal reaches out to him after they have been on a fishing trip off the Jersey coast, Bascombe responds with anything but compassion. His only action is non-action: constant internal philosophizing that helps him maintain his emotional distance but accomplishes little else. He knows that ''for your life to be worth anything you must sooner or later face the possibility of terrible, searing regret. Though you must also manage to avoid it or your life will be ruined.''

Bascombe returns in *Independence Day*, the sequel to *The Sportswriter*. He has changed careers again—he's now a real estate agent—and moved into his ex-wife's house in the fictional town of Haddam, New Jersey. His investment in ''homes'' suggests a yearning for attachment. *Independence Day* indeed portrays Bascombe's shift from what he calls his ''Existence Period''—detached bachelorhood without crisis—to his consideration of ''The Permanent Period'' of marriage and a deeper commitment to fatherhood. ''Independence'' here represents the freedom to move toward such intimacy. But in the end, ''The Permanent Period'' remains a concept. Like Prufrock pondering the peach, Bascombe does not act. Watching the Fourth of July Parade in the closing scene of the book, he only *feels* ''the push, pull, the wave and sway of others'' from a distance.

In *Women with Men*, a collection of three novellas, Ford's protagonists continue to wallow in these cerebral epiphanies. They think themselves to the truth, or at least to deeper insight, but they either do not act at all, or their actions degenerate into aimlessness. The fruitlessness of his characters' contemplations begs the question: What is the value of epiphany without action?

In ''The Womanizer,'' Austin, a happily married man, leaves his wife to take up with a French divorcee. Certainly this is an action, a way of seizing control of one's romantic fate, of turning decisively away from commitment. Yet this pursuit fails terribly. On an outing, Austin loses sight of his lover's young son. The boy is molested, and Austin's affair ends bitterly as a result. Austin blames himself, then sinks into self-centered rumination: ''How could you regulate life, do little harm and still be attached to others?'' He might as well be asking, ''How do you get everything you want without consequences or mistakes?''—more a childish plaint than a serious existential query.

Ironically, his much younger teenage protagonist in ''Jealous'' seems more willing to accept limits of desire. He yearns for his flirty Aunt Doris, and even gets close enough to think ''she was going to kiss'' him. His heart-pounding panic when she doesn't, though, is short-lived. He tells himself: ''it's you who's causing it, and you who has to stop it.'' He lets himself revel in the closeness she does allow him, a moment of contentment before the selfish hungers of adulthood get a chance to overtake him.

Adult responsibility, in Ford's world, is usually up to female characters. Men leave their children for new lives. Women reject lovers who cannot protect their children. Even when children are not in the picture, women are able to take control in a way Ford's men can only sadly marvel at. Helen in ''Occidentals'' insists on being responsible for the terms of her life and her death. Matthews is awed by her actions, but, like so many of Ford's male characters, can only ponder what is missing in his own life: the ''spiritual component she'd wanted,'' the dignity and status of a man committed to something beyond himself.

—Paul Marx, updated by Lisa A. Phillips

FORSTER, Margaret

Nationality: British. **Born:** Carlisle, Cumberland, 25 May 1938. **Education:** Carlisle and County High School for Girls, 1949–56; Somerville College, Oxford (scholar), 1957–60, B.A. in modern history 1960. **Family:** Married the writer Hunter Davies in 1960; two daughters and one son. **Career:** Teacher, Barnsbury Girls' School, London, 1961–63; chief non-fiction reviewer, London *Evening Standard,* 1977–80. Fellow, Royal Society of Literature, 1975. **Agent:** Tessa Sayle Agency, 11 Jubilee Place, London SW3 3TE. **Address:** 11 Boscastle Road, London NW5 1EE, England.

Publications

Novels

Dames' Delight. London, Cape, 1964.
Georgy Girl. London, Secker and Warburg, 1965; New York, Berkley, 1966.
The Bogeyman. London, Secker and Warburg, 1965; New York, Putnam, 1966.
The Travels of Maudie Tipstaff. London, Secker and Warburg, and New York, Stein and Day, 1967.
The Park. London, Secker and Warburg, 1968.
Miss Owen-Owen Is at Home. London, Secker and Warburg, 1969; as *Miss Owen-Owen,* New York, Simon and Schuster, 1969.
Fenella Phizackerley. London, Secker and Warburg, 1970; New York, Simon and Schuster, 1971.
Mr. Bone's Retreat. London, Secker and Warburg, and New York, Simon and Schuster, 1971.
The Seduction of Mrs. Pendlebury. London, Secker and Warburg, 1974.
Mother Can You Hear Me? London, Secker and Warburg, 1979.
The Bride of Lowther Fell: A Romance. London, Secker and Warburg, 1980; New York, Atheneum, 1981.
Marital Rites. London, Secker and Warburg, 1981; New York, Atheneum, 1982.
Private Papers. London, Chatto and Windus, 1986.
Have the Men Had Enough? London, Chatto and Windus, 1989.
Lady's Maid. London, Chatto and Windus, 1990; New York, Doubleday, 1991.
The Battle for Christabel. London, Chatto and Windus, 1991.
Mothers' Boys. London, Chatto and Windus, 1994.
Shadow Baby. London, Chatto & Windus, 1996.

Play

Screenplay: *Georgy Girl,* with Peter Nichols, 1966.

Other

The Rash Adventurer: The Rise and Fall of Charles Edward Stuart. London, Secker and Warburg, 1973; New York, Stein and Day, 1974.
William Makespeace Thackeray: Memoirs of a Victorian Gentleman. London, Secker and Warburg, 1978; as *Memoirs of a Victorian Gentleman,* New York, Morrow, 1979.
Significant Sisters: The Grassroots of Active Feminism 1839–1939. London, Secker and Warburg, 1984; New York, Knopf, 1985.
Elizabeth Barrett Browning: A Biography. London, Chatto and Windus, 1988; New York, Doubleday, 1989.
Daphne du Maurier: A Biography. London, Chatto and Windus, and New York, Doubleday, 1993.
Hidden Lives: A Family Memoir. New York, Viking, 1995.
Rich Desserts and Captain's Thin: A Family and Their Times, 1831–1931. London, Chatto & Windus, 1997.
Precious Lives. Thorndike, Maine, Thorndike Press, 1999.
Editor, *Drawn from Life: The Journalism of William Makepeace Thackeray.* London, Folio, 1984.
Editor, *Selected Poems of Elizabeth Barrett Browning.* London, Chatto and Windus, and Baltimore, Johns Hopkins University Press, 1988.

* * *

Since the publication of her first novel, *Dames' Delight,* more than twenty-five years ago, Margaret Forster has written well over a dozen novels. In all of them she is preoccupied with human relationships or, to put it more precisely, with the impact of one person on another, with the possibility—or impossibility—of any real change in someone's character and outlook on life through emotional involvement with someone else. (She seems to declare her interest in character in the very choice of her titles; it is hardly an accident that so many of her novels carry someone's name, that badge of personal identity, in the title.)

Hers is a characteristically feminine preoccupation; even today love, whether within or outside marriage, or between those tied by the unbreakable blood knot, remains all-important to women, and Forster acknowledges this. Her perception of the impact of love seems to have changed somewhat, grown softer perhaps, over the years. In *Georgy Girl* behind all the clowning and laughter there hides a bleak, loveless little world, and George herself, so full of fierce, all-embracing love for children, has very little real lasting love to spare for her relationships with adults. In *The Travels of Maudie Tipstaff* Maudie, disappointed with her visits to her children, readily accepts the explanation of her disappointment offered in her son Robert's chilling words: ''Two people are always two people ... I'm on my own, and you, Mother, are on your own.'' In *Mr. Bone's Retreat,* however, we sense a change; Mr. Bone retreats indeed from his position of determined non-involvement, and slowly and with hesitation comes to accept the possibility of receiving graciously the love that is offered: ''Love had to be accepted. The quality of the gift was what mattered.''

The process of change does not, however, culminate in the happy ending of a romantic novel. In *The Seduction of Mrs. Pendlebury* Alice Oram nearly destroys Mrs. Pendelbury by demanding love and reassurance for her own doubts and insecurities which Rose Pendlebury cannot give. Her demands cannot be met because a personality cannot change totally without breaking in the violence of the change; the relationship between the two women sours into obsession and near madness. As in *Mr. Bone's Retreat* the young intruder acts as a catalyst, while remaining largely unchanged herself; her resilience and her strength in the possession of a future full of rich possibilities save her from disaster. For Mrs. Pendlebury salvation lies in flight to the isolation of a small seaside bungalow, set well back from its neighbors and screened so well by trees. However powerful human relationships are, they cannot radically alter a person's character, and tampering with people is a dangerous hobby.

In two more recent novels, *The Bride of Lowther Fell* and *Marital Rites,* the note of cautious acceptance of love is sounded more clearly. Alexandra, the liberated young woman in *The Bridge of Lowther Fell,* admits at the very end of her tale: ''The lessons are learned. No man is an island, and no woman either.'' In *Marital Rites,* though Robert and Anna Osgood come through their marriage crisis shattered and diminished, marriage itself, the conventional and convenient symbol of lasting love, survives triumphant; the value of giving and accepting love, and being altered by it, is tacitly acknowledged. The love between mother and daughter, crippling and even destructive, is the theme of *Private Papers* and *Have the Men Had Enough?* Though the emphasis in both novels is on the negative aspects of the relationship, yet affection and love are both there, implicit or openly declared.

There is always a touch of irony in a human relationship, in its misconceptions, its wishful attempts to make others see us as we see ourselves. Forster recognizes this irony and uses it, sometimes as part of the very structure of her novels. Not always as overtly as in *Mother Can You Hear Me?* where Angela's struggle against the emotional demands of her elderly mother is counterpointed by italicized passages recording her vain attempts to bring up her own daughter free of the crushing burden of filial guilt. A similar device is employed in *Private Papers* where Mrs. Butler's written record of her family's history is mocked and contradicted by her eldest daughter's interpolations, giving a radically different version of the same events. In *The Travels of Maudie Tipstaff,* too, Maudie's picture of herself and her children's perception of her behavior are offered with silent irony, the mutual miscomprehensions stressing the theme of human isolation. In *The Seduction of Mrs. Pendlebury* and in *Mr. Bone's Retreat* the same technique is used more subtly, and instead of the juxtaposition of two contrasting pictures there are oblique backward glances, slowly altering a remembered incident or conversation.

In all her novels Forster's style is plain, deliberately downbeat, letting the pathos and the irony speak for themselves. The impersonal third-person narrator tells the story in short sentences, except when—as in *The Seduction of Mrs. Pendelbury*—she is voicing the thoughts of her characters. Then the sentences stretch and curl, following the course of thought. In her more recent novels Forster dispenses with the impersonal narrator, using instead the diary form (in *Private Papers*) or two first-person narrators speaking in turn (in *Have the Men Had Enough?*). Though in *Lady's Maid* the impersonal authorial voice is heard again, it is interrupted by Elizabeth Wilson's letters, the plain, bleak style matching the drab existence of Elizabeth Barrett Browning's maid.

Like so many women novelists writing today, Forster has a sharp eye for domestic detail, for the social comedy of our times. She is very much a town dweller (except in *The Bride of Lowther Fell* where she clearly draws on her Cumbrian memories, as well as—nostalgically—on those of North London). She can sum up in a few telling phrases the gentrification process in Islington (''large removal van, stacked with pine tables and brass bedsteads''), a council house in Cornwall (''The cheap cotton, flowered curtains had never fitted and let in too much light''), middle-class life in Highgate (instant coffee always offered with apologies, a sluttish daily help tolerated as a sop to social conscience). All this has been done often, but is done here extremely well. (It should be added that in *Have the Men Had Enough?,* written from personal experience of the effect of senile dementia on a family, comedy turns to tragedy in the well-observed scenes in the geriatric ward of a mental hospital.)

She reproduces variants of speech with equal accuracy. Her characters come to us with full credentials of class and educational background. It is when she moves beyond the everyday that her skill fails her. Larger-than-life characters like the eponymous Miss Owen-Owen and Fenella Phizackerley may astonish us by their behavior, but they do not convince. Over Miss Owen-Owen the shadow of Miss Jean Brodie lies very heavily indeed; Fenella, the reader of popular women's magazines imprisoned inside a creature of breath-taking beauty, remains the impossible heroine of some extravagant fairy tale. The heroine of *The Bride of Lowther Fell* (a book subtitled ''a Romance,'' and boldly inviting by its very title a comparison with the Victorian novel) is no more convincing than the contrived plot. It is interesting to note here that in her recent novel *Lady's Maid* Forster turns from pastiche Victorian romance to a realistic, disturbing picture of that endlessly fascinating period.

Forster's skills as a biographer of William Makepeace Thackeray, Elizabeth Barrett Browning, and Daphne du Maurier inform her fiction, particularly in *Lady's Maid,* a novel centered on the relationship between the Victorian poet Elizabeth Barrett Browning and her maid, Elizabeth Wilson. Issues of character development and the centrality of a well-articulated point of view, especially for her female characters in the novel *Shadow Baby,* are important features of Forster's work. Experimentation with variations in point of view—a hallmark of her fictionalized autobiographical memoir of Thackeray—and a sympathetic treatment of the questions about sexuality in the non-fiction life of Daphne du Maurier influence the innovations and challenges Forster creates for herself as a writer of fiction. *Shadow Baby* is particularly intriguing in its manipulations of point of view and in its Gothic indebtedness to both du Maurier's example and to the novels of Dickens and Bronte that Forster read when she was growing up. In *Lady's Maid* Forster also foregrounds issues of class tensions and differences between the poor working class maid and the indulgently comfortable and cripplingly neurotic Victorian lady—concerns about class well-articulated in Dickens's novels.

In a family biography she wrote of her grandmother's life, *Hidden Lives,* Forster had tried to trace the life history of her grandmother's illegitimate daughter, and details of her inquiry found their way into *Shadow Baby*, a novel itself suffused with an air of mystery. Because of shifts in point of view between the nineteenth-century mother-daughter pair, Leah and Evie, and the twentieth-century daughter Shona and her mother, Hazel, and the narratives of why these abandoned daughters are, indeed, ''shadows,'' the reader is actively engaged in solving a mystery. The mystery goes to the dark heart of motherhood itself, the trauma of separation for a daughter, and the madness of obsession. In this respect, the concerns of *Shadow Baby* are the recurrent themes of Forster's earlier work in *Private Papers* and *Have the Men Had Enough?* In Forster's work motherhood is, at best, an ambivalently experienced phenomenon.

—Hana Sambrook, updated by Roberta Schreyer

FORSYTH, Frederick

Nationality: British. **Born:** Ashford, Kent, in 1938. **Education:** Tonbridge School, Kent. **Military Service:** Served in the Royal Air Force 1956–58. **Family:** Married Carrie Forsyth in 1973; two sons. **Career:** Journalist, *Eastern Daily Press,* Norwich, and in King's Lynn, Norfolk, 1958–61; reporter for Reuters, London, Paris, and East Berlin, 1961–65; reporter, BBC Radio and Television, London, 1965–67; assistant diplomatic correspondent, BBC, 1967–68; freelance journalist in Nigeria, 1968–70; television presenter, *Soldiers* series, 1985, and *Frederick Forsyth Presents* series, 1989–90. Lives in London. **Awards:** Mystery Writers of America Edgar Allan Poe award, 1971, 1983. **Address:** c/o Hutchinson Pub Group Ltd., 62–65 Chandos Pl, London WC2N 4NW, England.

PUBLICATIONS

Novels

The Day of the Jackal. London, Hutchinson, and New York, Viking Press, 1971.
The Odessa File. London, Hutchinson, and New York, Viking Press, 1972.
The Dogs of War. London, Hutchinson, and New York, Viking Press, 1974.
The Shepherd. London, Hutchinson, 1975; New York, Viking Press, 1976.
The Devil's Alternative. London, Hutchinson, 1979; New York, Viking Press, 1980.
The Fourth Protocol. London, Hutchinson, and New York, Viking Press, 1984.
The Negotiator. London and New York, Bantam, 1989.
The Deceiver. London, Corgi, and New York, Bantam, 1991.
The Fist of God. London and New York, Bantam, 1994.
Icon. New York, Bantam Books, 1996.
The Phantom of Manhattan. New York, St. Martin's Press, 1999.

Short Stories

No Comebacks: Collected Short Stories. London, Hutchinson, and New York, Viking Press, 1982.

Play

Screenplay: *The Fourth Protocol,* 1987.

Other

The Biafra Story. London, Penguin, 1969; as *The Making of an African Legend: The Biafra Story,* 1977.
Emeka (biography of Chukwuemeka Odumegwu-Ojukwu). Ibadan, Spectrum, 1982.
Editor, *Great Flying Stories.* Rockland, Massachusetts, Wheeler Publishing, 1996.

* * *

Although he is known exclusively as the author of political thrillers, Frederick Forsyth announced in 1999 that he was forsaking that genre and turning to other forms of fiction. In the twenty-five years between *The Day of the Jackal* and *Icon*, Forsyth published a series of novels following the same basic formula: start with a plausible international crisis; keep a number of narrative threads moving at all times; scatter violent and/or erotic incidents liberally through the story; explain in minute detail the techniques employed by criminals, terrorists, undercover agents, police; build toward an explosive climax; end with an unexpected but satisfying twist of plot. The formula has produced nine bestsellers, all a notch above standard popular fare, most made, or likely to be made, into popular films.

The Day of the Jackal, the first in the series and still widely regarded as the best, established the pattern Forsyth was to follow. A group of disgruntled veterans of the Algerian war hire a professional assassin from England, code-named the Jackal, to kill President De Gaulle for betraying the French cause in North Africa. Forsyth adds an abundance of peripheral plots and characters, many based on actual events of the time. We are jolted back and forth between two centers of intrigue: the solitary assassin meticulously planning each step of the murder and the special police unit trying to track him down. Forsyth's fascination with detail draws us into the story. We learn how to acquire false passports, how to obtain a custom-made rifle, how to travel around Europe under a variety of identities, and how, conversely, police forces of different nations coordinate efforts to prevent the assassination. Facing a complex plot and an overabundance of characters, we follow events without understanding the human motives behind them. But though we never get inside the main figure, the Jackal, we are willing to ascribe it to the nature of the character: a professional assassin keeping his own counsel, revealing nothing of himself to anyone. Thus a fundamental shortcoming in Forsyth's work, an unwillingness or inability to create convincing characters, works to his advantage in *The Day of the Jackal.*

The same flaw is more apparent, but less defensible, in the novels that followed. *The Odessa File* concerns a young German journalist's attempt to infiltrate an organization of influential former SS officers and to locate one war criminal in particular. The theme of hunter and hunted is repeated from the earlier book, but the absence of full characters seems glaring here. So too with *The Dogs of War*, a novel about mercenaries overthrowing an African dictator, and *The Devil's Alternative*, about a series of international events that brings the world to the brink of nuclear war. In *The Fourth Protocol*, however, as in *The Day of the Jackal*, the more shadowy the people, the more real they seem. The novel describes an ingeniously complex Soviet plot to undermine the British government, with intelligence experts from each side anticipating and thwarting each other's moves.

The Negotiator follows the Forsyth formula to a point, with the kidnapping and murder of a liberal American president's son serving as the entree into a more complicated story of right-wing conspiracies in both the Soviet Union and the United States to undermine stability in the Middle East. Atypically, Forsyth tries, without much success, to humanize his title character by creating a love interest for the otherwise solitary hero. Another solitary hero is Sam McCready, the unifying figure in *The Deceiver*, which contains four stories of counterespionage. McCready, a veteran agent of British Intelligence, personally outwits such enemies of freedom as the Soviets, Libyans, IRA, Castro, and Colombian drug lords. A recurring theme is the careerism or ineptitude of MIA and CIA bureaucrats whose rules McCready must violate to defeat an enemy who knows no rules.

Forsyth's plots have the short-term advantages and the long-term problems of dealing with topical world affairs. *The Fist of God*, set during the 1991 Gulf War, includes, in addition to its fictional characters, inside glimpses of the major players in that conflict: George Bush, Margaret Thatcher, Norman Schwarzkopf, and Saddam Hussein. Here Forsyth finds material to fit his strengths: international intrigue, behind-the-scenes manipulation of events, and weapons derived from high technology. The novel works well because the Gulf War event lends itself to the Forsyth formula.

The latest and, unless he changes his mind, last of Forsyth's thrillers, *Icon*, describes a right-wing plot to take over the Russian government. Published in 1996 but set in 1999, it describes the chaotic political and economic condition of post-Soviet Russia. The plot is thwarted by an American intelligence agent working with Chechneyans and the Patriarch of the Orthodox Church. Especially interesting is Forsyth's use of the Aldrich Ames case, which is woven into the story, and which provides factual details of the real-life CIA counterintelligence officer who betrayed agents to the KGB. It is interesting to note that Forsyth cites the dissolution of the USSR—the major opposing force in world affairs—as one of the reasons he decided to turn away from the genre that he had mastered.

All Forsyth thrillers include a wealth of detail on matters well beyond the experience of their readers, yet they convey a compelling atmosphere of verisimilitude. We learn how experts make and plant bombs, smuggle weapons, infiltrate secret agencies; we learn how terrorists operate, how world leaders confer and conspire, how spies attend to their daily chores, how politicians manipulate events and their reporting. But all of this detail does not produce convincing human beings. The events seem real, at least plausible, but not the people.

Forsyth's first effort in a different genre, *The Phantom of Manhattan*, has received neither the critical nor popular success of his earlier books. Conceived as a sequel to Gaston Leroux's *Phantom of the Opera* (1911) and inspired by Forsyth's friendship with composer Andrew Lloyd Webber, it deals with the Phantom's exile to America, where he emerges as a business tycoon and builds a new opera house. Not unexpectedly, his protégé, Christine de Chagny, arrives with their twelve-year-old son to sing at the premiere. In deliberate contrast to his typical work, this one is considerably shorter (less than a fourth the length of his earlier novels) and is told not by a disinterested narrative voice but by its various characters (most of whom sound alike). The story, despite its potential for plot detail, seems summarized rather than narrated, as if it were an outline for a longer book or a sketch for a new musical. The length and style imitate Leroux's novel, keeping the many flaws of the source but losing its originality.

Forsyth's sense that he had exhausted the potential of his earlier genre is understandable, but his first failed attempt to move in a new direction underscores a point made in all of his political thrillers—that mastering a skill, whether for crime or its detection—requires a lifetime of careful preparation and attention to detail.

—Robert E. Lynch

FOSTER, David (Manning)

Nationality: Australian. **Born:** Sydney, New South Wales, 15 May 1944. **Education:** The University of Sydney, B.Sc. in chemistry 1967; Australian National University, Canberra, Ph.D. 1970. **Family:** Married 1) Robin Ruth Bowers in 1965 (marriage ended); 2) Gerda Hageraats in 1975; has four daughters and two sons. **Career:** Research fellow, U.S. Public Health Service, Philadephia, 1970–71; senior research officer, University of Sydney Medical School, 1971–72. **Awards:** Australian Literature Board fellowships, 1973–91; *The Age* award, 1974; Marten Bequest award, 1978; Australian National Book Council award, 1981; New South Wales Premier's fellowship, 1986; Australian creative fellowship, 1992–95; Miles Franklin Award, 1997. **Address:** Ardara, Bundanoon, New South Wales 2578, Australia.

PUBLICATIONS

Novels

The Pure Land. Melbourne, Macmillan, 1974; New York, Penguin, 1985.

The Empathy Experiment, with D.K. Lyall. Sydney, Wild and Woolley, 1977.

Moonlite. Melbourne, Macmillan, 1981; London, Pan, 1982; New York, Penguin, 1987.

Plumbum. Ringwood, Victoria, Penguin, 1983.

Dog Rock: A Postal Pastoral. Ringwood, Victoria, and New York, Penguin, 1985.

The Adventures of Christian Rosy Cross. Ringwood, Victoria, London, and New York, Penguin, 1986.

Testostero. Ringwood, Victoria, and New York, Penguin, 1987.

The Pale Blue Crochet Coathanger Cover. Ringwood, Victoria, Penguin, 1988.

Mates of Mars. Ringwood, Victoria, Penguin, 1991.

The Glade within the Grove. Milsons Point, New South Wales, Australia, and New York, Vintage, 1996.

The Ballad of Erinungarah. Milsons Point, New South Wales, Australia, and New York, Vintage, 1997.

Short Stories

North South West: Three Novellas. Melbourne, Macmillan, 1973.

Escape to Reality. Melbourne, Macmillan, 1977.

Hitting the Wall: Two Novellas. Ringwood, Victoria, and London, Penguin, 1989.

Poetry

The Fleeing Atalanta. Adelaide, Maximus, 1975.

Other

Studs and Nogs: Essays 1987–98. Milsons Point, New South Wales, Australia, and New York, Vintage, 1999.
Editor, *Self Portraits.* Canberra, Australian National Library, 1991.

*

Manuscript Collection: Australian Defence Force Academy Library, Canberra.

* * *

David Foster's background as a scientist is very much in evidence in his fiction, in his interest in concepts such as entropy and in his vast and eclectic vocabulary, which is full of technical words. For instance, his first book, *North South West,* contains sentences such as ''We will fall before their arrows as before the nematocysts of a coelenterate.'' The stories foreshadow Foster's directions in other ways too, in their ambivalent dichotomy of country and city and in the writer's political conservatism: ''I functioned as the opponent of all liberalism,'' one of his characters says. In ''Mobil Medley,'' a kind of latterday *Canterbury Tales,* there is again a significant remark from the narrator which is applicable to Foster's fiction in general. ''His words never settled fully about the object, but created a diversion to themselves, leaving the naked.''

Foster's second book and first novel, *The Pure Land,* is an unusual and at times parodic example of that familiar Australian fictive stand-by, the generational novel. Divided into three parts, it tells the stories of three generations of a family, with only minor connecting links between the largely discrete sections. Beginning in Sydney it crosses to the United States before returning to its original base and finally petering out in a series of unanswered letters. *The Empathy Experiment* is set some time in the future and in a city something like Canberra, to judge from its obsessive bureaucracy. It concerns a scientist named FX and his experiments in harnessing the forces of empathic identification with his subjects. Although there are mad puns and various bizarrely comic incidents, the book is less playful than most of Foster's work. What emerges eventually from the novel's frantic improvisation is an angry satire of scientific experimentation which ignores the rights of its victims. *Escape to Reality* is Foster's only collection of short fiction to date. Like much of his work, it is concerned with outsiders or outlaws of some kind, and is written in a coolly objective, unjudging way, often in the first person. The collection is full of voices, the narrator's and other characters', in the many dialogues. In the longest and best story, ''The Job,'' the narrator Billie is a petty criminal who is picked up on his release by another petty criminal, Brian. The story follows a familiarly circular pattern, with Billie waiting outside the jail at the end to pick up another released man, just as Brian had waited for him.

By now Foster had made a mark as a writer but still gave the impression of a talent of considerable, if somewhat cerebral, intelligence, deeply uncertain as to the direction in which it wanted to go. It is with the novels of the 1980s and especially *Moonlite,* still probably the best work, that he seems to find that direction and that personal voice. It is a less coldly written but still ingenious narrative of the picaresque adventures of one Finbar (''Moonbar'') MacBuffie which amount to something like an allegorical account of the history of immigration to Australia. It is a wittily parodic novel, reminiscent in many ways of John Barth and especially of *The Sot-Weed Factor.* Foster displays his characteristic fascination with language, using arcane or self-invented words, punning vigorously, giving characters names like the Marquis of Moneymore and Grogstrife and employing a variety of dialects as well as a multitude of satiric targets, from academic scholarship and Christianity through advocates of temperance to Australian myths of heroism and identity.

Plumbum is written in a mode which Foster makes his own from *Moonlite* onwards, a self-conscious but also surreal, highly inventive but sometimes irritatingly cerebral comedy. It concerns a group of young musicians who form a heavy metal band, but the satiric targets are lost in the medley of competing voices and increasingly frantic pace. *Dog Rock* is a country town, population 776 of which the narrator D'Arcy D'Oliveres has been postman for ten years. A murderer known only as the Queen's Park Ripper is terrorising the town's citizens by progressively eliminating them. The novel is a parody of the detective genre, with an abundance of improbable clues and an impossibly complicated plot. Foster returned to Dog Rock and D'Arcy D'Oliveres later with the slight but genially witty *The Pale Blue Crochet Coathanger Cover.*

The Adventures of Christian Rosy Cross, which Foster has said he considers his magnum opus, is another picaresque novel, or parody of one. Its hero is born in 1378, the son of Comte de Rosencreutz who manages to finish off his own wife by immediately after the birth engaging in violent sexual intercourse with her. The novel recounts his adventures up until the age of twenty-three, after which, we are told at the end, ''By judicious speculation he acquires a modest income, and spends the remaining years of his life, till his death in 1483, keeping fit, playing the harpsichord, cultivating bulbs, arguing with his neighbour over who should build the new boundary fence, and striving to improve the local breed of dog.'' Foster speaks in his introduction of his conviction that our present age resembles that of Christian Rosy Cross but the connections he claims with modern parallels are tenuous and much of the humour is built on simple-minded juxtapositions between modern and medieval (''Would you care to see some filthy woodcuts?''). *Testostero* is sub-titled ''a comic novel'' but is in fact a laboured, tedious farce involving Noel Horniman, talented but ockerish Australian poet, and Leon Hunnybun, limp-wristed English aristocrat, who discover in the course of the novel that they are twins. *Hitting the Wall* is actually two novellas of which one, ''The Job,'' is reprinted from *Escape to Reality.*

Foster revived D'Arcy D'Oliveres for *The Glade within the Grove,* which chronicles the postman's tenure in the small town of Obligna Creek. There he discovers an intriguing manuscript, by a mysterious author named ''Orion''—and this later appeared as Foster's next novel, *The Ballad of Erinungarah.* Needless to say, the two books are meant to be read together.

On the face of it, Foster would seem to have an imagination as original and inventive as almost any contemporary Australian novelist, and he commands an astounding range of material. But that imagination seems difficult for him to harness, and like Barth and perhaps Thomas Pynchon, he reads better in bits and pieces than in toto. There are brilliantly original gags but no normative centre against which to place them. Perhaps he might do well to take note of one of his own witty scientific analogues from *Plumbum:* ''You will sometimes see a middle-aged man holding the jaws of his mind open with every intellectual prop and pole at his disposal. In such a state he resembles a bivalve mollusc, constrained to sup whatever shit floats by.''

—Laurie Clancy

FOWLES, John (Robert)

Nationality: British. **Born:** Leigh-on-Sea, Essex, 31 March 1926. **Education:** Bedford School, 1940–44; Edinburgh University, 1944; New College, Oxford, B.A. (honors) in French 1950. **Military Service:** Served in the Royal Marines, 1945–46. **Family:** Married Elizabeth Whitton in 1954 (deceased 1990); married Sarah Smith in 1998. **Career:** Lecturer in English, University of Poitiers, France, 1950–51; teacher at Anargyrios College, Spetsai, Greece, 1951–52, and in London, 1953–63. **Awards:** Silver Pen award, 1969; W.H. Smith Literary award, 1970; Christopher award, 1981. Honorary fellow, New College, Oxford, 1997. D.Litt., Exeter University, 1983; University of East Anglia, 1997. **Address:** c/o Jonathan Cape Ltd, 20 Vauxhall Bridge Road, London SW1V 2SA, England.

PUBLICATIONS

Novels

The Collector. London, Cape, and Boston, Little Brown, 1963.
The Magus. Boston, Little Brown, 1965; London, Cape, 1966; revised edition, Cape, 1977; Little Brown, 1978.
The French Lieutenant's Woman. London, Cape, and Boston, Little Brown, 1969.
Daniel Martin. Boston, Little Brown, and London, Cape, 1977.
Mantissa. London, Cape, and Boston, Little Brown, 1982.
A Maggot. London, Cape, and Boston, Little Brown 1985.

Short Stories

The Ebony Tower: Collected Novellas. London, Cape, and Boston, Little Brown, 1974.

Plays

Don Juan, adaptation of the play by Molière (produced London, 1981).
Lorenzaccio, adaptation of the play by Alfred de Musset (produced London, 1983).
Martine, adaptation of a play by Jean Jacques Bernard (produced London, 1985).

Screenplays: *The Magus,* 1968.

Poetry

Poems. New York, Ecco Press, 1973.
Conditional. Northridge, California, Lord John Press, 1979.

Other

The Aristos: A Self-Portrait in Ideas. Boston, Little Brown, 1964; London, Cape, 1965; revised edition, London, Pan, 1968; Little Brown, 1970.
Shipwreck, photographs by the Gibsons of Scilly. London, Cape, 1974; Boston, Little Brown, 1975.
Islands, photographs by Fay Godwin. London, Cape, 1978; Boston, Little Brown, 1979.
The Tree, photographs by Frank Horvat. London, Aurum Press, 1979; Boston, Little Brown, 1980; published as *The Tree; The Nature of Nature: Two Essays,* with woodcuts by Aaron Johnson. Covelo, California, Yolla Bolly Press, 1995.
The Enigma of Stonehenge, photographs by Barry Brukoff. London, Cape, and New York, Summit, 1980.
A Brief History of Lyme. Lyme Regis, Dorset, Friends of the Lyme Regis Museum, 1981.
A Short History of Lyme Regis. Wimborne, Dorset, Dovecote Press, 1982; Boston, Little Brown, 1983.
Land, photographs by Fay Godwin. London, Heinemann, and Boston, Little Brown, 1985.
Lyme Regis Camera. Stanbridge, Dorset, Dovecote Press, 1990; Boston, Little Brown, 1991.
The Man Who Died: A Story (commentary) by D. H. Lawrence. Hopewell, New Jersey, Ecco Press, 1994.
Wormholes: Essays and Occasional Writings, edited and introduced by Jan Relf. New York, H. Holt, 1998.
John Fowles and Nature: Fourteen Perspectives on Landscape, edited by James R. Aubrey. Madison, New Jersey, Fairleigh Dickinson University Press, 1999.
Editor, *Steep Holm: A Case History in the Study of Evolution.* Sherborne, Dorset, Allsop Memorial Trust, 1978.
Editor, with Rodney Legg, *Monumenta Britannica,* by John Aubrey. Sherborne, Dorset Publishing Company, 2 vols., 1981–82; vol. 1, Boston, Little Brown, 1981.
Editor, *Thomas Hardy's England,* by Jo Draper. London, Cape, and Boston, Little Brown, 1984.
Translator, *Cinderella,* by Perrault. London, Cape, 1974; Boston, Little Brown, 1975.
Translator, *Ourika,* by Claire de Durfort. Austin, Texas, Taylor, 1977.

*

Bibliography: ''John Fowles: An Annotated Bibliography 1963–76'' by Karen Magee Myers, in *Bulletin of Bibliography* (Boston), vol. 33, no. 4, 1976; *John Fowles: A Reference Guide* by Barry N. Olshen and Toni A. Olshen, Boston, Hall, 1980; ''John Fowles: A Bibliographical Checklist'' by Ray A. Roberts, in *American Book Collector* (New York), September-October, 1980; ''Criticism of John Fowles: A Selected Checklist'' by Ronald C. Dixon, in *Modern Fiction Studies* (Lafayette, Indiana), Spring 1985.

Manuscript Collection: University of Tulsa, Oklahoma.

Critical Studies: *Possibilities* by Malcolm Bradbury, London, Oxford University Press, 1973; *The Fiction of John Fowles: Tradition, Art, and the Loneliness of Selfhood* by William J. Palmer, Columbia, University of Missouri Press, 1974; *John Fowles: Magus and Moralist* by Peter Wolfe, Lewisburg, Pennsylvania, Bucknell University

Press, 1976, revised edition, 1979; *Etudes sur The French Lieutenant's Woman de John Fowles* edited by Jean Chevalier, Caen, University of Caen, 1977; *John Fowles* by Barry N. Olshen, New York, Ungar, 1978; *John Fowles, John Hawkes, Claude Simon: Problems of Self and Form in the Post-Modernist Novel* by Robert Burden, Würzburg, Königshausen & Neumann, and Atlantic Highlands, New Jersey, Humanities Press, 1980; *John Fowles* by Robert Huffaker, New York, Twayne, 1980; ''John Fowles Issue'' of *Journal of Modern Literature* (Philadelphia), vol. 8, no. 2, 1981; *Four Contemporary Novelists* by Kerry McSweeney, Montreal, McGill-Queen's University Press, 1982, London, Scolar Press, 1983; *John Fowles* by Peter J. Conradi, London, Methuen, 1982; *Fowles, Irving, Barthes: Canonical Variations on an Apocryphal Theme* by Randolph Runyon, Columbus, Ohio State University Press, 1982; *The Timescapes of John Fowles* by H.W. Fawkner, Rutherford, New Jersey, Fairleigh Dickinson University Press, 1983; *Male Mythologies: John Fowles and Masculinity* by Bruce Woodcock, Brighton, Harvester Press, 1984; *The Romances of John Fowles* by Simon Loveday, London, Macmillan, 1985; ''John Fowles Issue'' of *Modern Fiction Studies* (Lafayette, Indiana), Spring 1985; *The Fiction of John Fowles: A Myth for Our Time* by Carol M. Barnum, Greenwood, Florida, Penkevill, 1988; *The Art of John Fowles* by Katherine Tarbox, Athens, University of Georgia Press, 1988; *Form and Meaning in the Novels of John Fowles* by Susana Onega, Ann Arbor, Michigan, UMI Research Press, 1989; *John Fowles: A Reference Companion* by James R. Aubrey, New York, Greenwood Press, 1991; *Point of View in Fiction and Film: Focus on John Fowles* by Charles Garard, New York, P. Lang, 1991; *John Fowles's Fiction and the Poetics of Postmodernism* by Mahmoud Salami, Rutherford, Fairleigh Dickinson University Press, 1992; *Something and Nothingness: The Fiction of John Updike and John Fowles* by John Neary, Carbondale, Southern Illinois University Press, 1992; *Understanding John Fowles* by Thomas C. Foster, Columbia, University of South Carolina Press, 1994; *John Fowles* by James Acheson. New York, St. Martin's Press, 1998; *Conversations with John Fowles,* edited by Dianne L. Vipond. Jackson, University Press of Mississippi, 1999.

* * *

John Fowles is a highly allusive and descriptive novelist. In all his fictions, situations and settings are carefully and lavishly done: the French country landscape of ''The Cloud'' (*The Ebony Tower*); the blues and purples of the stark New Mexican mountains, the soft rainy contours of Devon in various greens and greys, the bleak and menacing deserts of Syria, all in *Daniel Martin.* Most frequently, Fowles's richly painted settings conceal a mystery, as in the title story of *The Ebony Tower,* in which an old English painter has created his ''forest'' in France, like that of Chrétien de Troyes, a ''mystery island'' to break away from the closed formal island into ''love and adventure and the magical.'' The lush Greek island of *The Magus* conceals mystery and magic, a stage for the complicated and elaborate series of theatricals that enchant, enslave, and instruct a young Englishman who has taken a teaching job there. The five eighteenth-century travellers in *A Maggot* go through the deep vales and caverns near Exmoor, which lead to death for one, to a vision of paradise that may have helped establish a new religion for another, and to unknowable disappearance for a third. Often, Fowles's characters, like Nicholas Urfe in *The Magus* or the interrogating magistrate in *A Maggot,* try to solve the mysteries, to make sense of what happens as they confront new worlds, but they are not entirely successful. Frequently, as in the short story ''The Enigma,'' in which a solid, stable, middle-aged Tory M.P. simply disappears, Fowles does not resolve the mystery and concentrates on the implications for others in living in terms of what is finally unknown.

In staging his mysteries, in choosing what to reveal and what to conceal, Fowles has often been seen by readers as manipulative. Such manipulation, however, is not merely a matter of tricks, ingenious switches, or ''the God-game.'' Rather, the sense of ''reality'' as something that has to be manipulated, rearranged, in order to be understood is central to Fowles's conception of both the nature and the function of fiction. When victimized by a mock trial in the culminating theatrical invented for him, Nicholas Urfe realizes that he is only getting what he has deserved, for ''all my life I had tried to turn life into fiction, to hold reality away.'' *Mantissa,* the title itself suggesting a trivial addition to literature, consists of a debate between the novelist and his erotic muse about the nature of fiction which satirizes simplistic solipsistic positions like ''Serious modern fiction has only one subject: the difficulty of writing serious modern fiction.'' The novelist's manipulation is more complex and immediately recognizable in *The French Lieutenant's Woman,* which is full of parodies of old novelistic devices, switches in time and history, and frequent interruptions of the Victorian narrative that acknowledge the author's deliberate arrangements. The reader is constantly led to question what ''Victorian'' means, to recognize the texture of anachronism, parody, research, quotations from Marx, Darwin, Victorian sociological reports, Tennyson, Arnold, and Hardy as various means of demonstrating the conditional nature of time and history, the necessity of locating oneself in the present before one can understand anything of the past. The novel also has three endings, not simply as a form of prestidigitation, but as a demonstration that three different possible resolutions, each characterizing a different possible perspective itself historically definable, are consistent with the issues and characters Fowles has set in motion. *A Maggot* deploys strategies of similar contemporary interruptions, like the child opening a gate for the travellers on horse-back who is thrown a farthing that falls ''over her bent crown of no doubt lice-ridden hair,'' or the actor playing a London merchant who changes from ''anachronistic skinhead'' to ''Buddhist monk,'' to present a conflict between legalistic dialogue and the origins of religion or art, later explained as a version of the universal conflict between the left-lobed brain and the right, in terms of its modern genesis in the socially static period of the 1730s. Only in *Mantissa* and in parts of *Daniel Martin* do Fowles's speculations about the nature of fiction become arid and modish.

The allusive references of Fowles's ingenious fictions have generally widened and deepened over the course of his development. In his first novel, *The Collector,* more sensational than those that followed, Fowles attempted to probe psychologically and sociologically on a single plane of experience, to demonstrate what in a young man of one class caused him to collect, imprison, and dissect the girl from another class he thought he loved. The fabrications of *The Magus* extend further into history, legend, and myth, exploring various kinds of Gods, of perspectives ''real'' and imaginary (one can never finally draw a line between the two) that negate human freedom. A number of the long stories of *The Ebony Tower,* like ''Eliduc,'' retell ancient myths or recreate them in contemporary terms. *The French Lieutenant's Woman,* with all its literary, historical, and artistic allusions, shows what of the story is of the past, what of the present, and what indeterminate, for history, for Fowles, invariably includes much of the time and perspective of the historian. Thematically, *Daniel Martin* is, in some ways, an expansion of *The*

French Lieutenant's Woman, an analysis of Fowles's own generation, the last in England that might still be characterized as Victorian, "brought up in some degree of the nineteenth century since the twentieth did not begin until 1945." *Daniel Martin* also makes explicit a theme implicit in Fowles's earlier fiction, the paralyzing and complicated effects of all the guilts originating in the Victorian past, what he calls a "pandemic of self-depreciation" that leads to emotional insularity and to the capacity to live gracefully with loss rather than expending effort to change. In this novel, which ranges geographically (America, Italy, and the Middle East, as well as England) and historically (past wars and cultural legends), the guilt and self-depreciation are also attached to attractions to lost civilizations, the American Indians, the Minoans, the Etruscans, and the contemporary English. *A Maggot,* following the metaphor of the "larval stage of a winged create," but also, according to Fowles, meaning in the eighteenth century a "whim or quirk ... an obsession," expands its terms historically into a vision of possible humanity, an "almost divine maggot" attempting social and religious change against "reason, convention, established belief."

Until the fictional focus on the mother and the creation of Ann Lee, the historical founder of the Shaker religion, in *A Maggot,* Fowles's central characters have been isolated, rational, self-punishing males who attempted to join with independent, passionate, and enigmatic women. As the voice of the author in *The French Lieutenant's Woman* claims, he may be simply transferring his own inabilities to understand the enigmatic female into the safety of his historically locatable Victorian story. The sexual focus, however, with its attendant guilts and metaphorical expansions, is characteristic, and the novels develop the rational and sometimes manipulative means the male uses to try to understand and control the amorphous and enigmatic female. The male is always limited, his formulations and understandings only partial. And, in his frustration, the necessity that he operate in a world where understanding is never complete, he acts so as to capture (*The Collector*), desert (*The Magus*), betray (*The French Lieutenant's Woman*), relate to through art (*Mantissa*), or both betray and finally recover (*Daniel Martin*) the female he can only partially comprehend. In *A Maggot,* the prestidigitating male finally disappears from the fiction entirely, leaving the woman, who incorporates both whore and saint, to bring forth significant life herself. Fowles has treated his constant metaphorical focus on relationships between the sexes with growing insight, sympathy, and intelligence, as well as with a fascinating complexity of sociological, historical, and psychological implications of the incessant human effort involved.

—James Gindin

FRAME, Janet (Paterson)

Nationality: New Zealander. **Born:** Dunedin, 28 August 1924. **Education:** Oamaru North School; Waitaki Girls' High School; University of Otago Teachers Training College, Dunedin. **Awards:** Hubert Church Prose award, 1952, 1964, 1974; New Zealand Literary Fund award, 1960; New Zealand Scholarship in Letters, 1964, and Award for Achievement, 1969; University of Otago Robert Burns fellowship, 1965; Buckland Literary award 1967; James Wattie award, 1983, 1985; Commonwealth Writers prize, 1989. D.Litt.: University of Otago, 1978. C.B.E. (Commander, Order of the British Empire), 1983. **Address:** P.O. Box 1118, Palmerston North, New Zealand.

PUBLICATIONS

Novels

Owls Do Cry. Christchurch, Pegasus Press, 1957; New York, Braziller, 1960; London, W.H. Allen, 1961.

Faces in the Water. Christchurch, Pegasus Press, and New York, Braziller, 1961; London, W.H. Allen, 1962.

The Edge of the Alphabet. Christchurch, Pegasus Press, New York, Braziller, and London, W.H. Allen, 1962.

Scented Gardens for the Blind. Christchurch, Pegasus Press, and London, W.H. Allen, 1963; New York, Braziller, 1964.

The Adaptable Man. Christchurch, Pegasus Press, New York, Braziller, and London, W.H. Allen, 1965.

A State of Siege. New York, Braziller, 1966; London, W.H. Allen, 1967.

The Rainbirds. London, W.H. Allen, 1968; as *Yellow Flowers in the Antipodean Room,* New York, Braziller, 1969.

Intensive Care. New York, Braziller, 1970; London, W.H. Allen, 1971.

Daughter Buffalo. New York, Braziller, 1972; London, W.H. Allen, 1973.

Living in the Maniototo. New York, Braziller, 1979; London, Women's Press, 1981.

The Carpathians. London, Bloomsbury, and New York, Braziller, 1988.

Short Stories

The Lagoon: Stories. Christchurch, Caxton Press, 1952; revised edition, as *The Lagoon and Other Stories,* 1961; London, Bloomsbury, 1991.

The Reservoir: Stories and Sketches. New York, Braziller, 1963.

Snowman, Snowman: Fables and Fantasies. New York, Braziller, 1963.

The Reservoir and Other Stories. Christchurch, Pegasus Press, and London, W.H. Allen, 1966.

You Are Now Entering the Human Heart. Wellington, Victoria University Press, 1983; London, Women's Press, 1984.

Poetry

The Pocket Mirror. New York, Braziller, and London, W.H. Allen, 1967.

Other

Mona Minim and the Smell of the Sun (for children). New York, Braziller, 1969.

An Autobiography. Auckland, Century Hutchinson, 1989; London, Women's Press, 1990; New York, Braziller, 1991.

- *To the Is-Land.* New York, Braziller, 1982; London, Women's Press, 1983.
- *An Angel at My Table.* Auckland, Hutchinson, New York, Braziller, and London, Women's Press, 1984.

The Envoy from Mirror City. Auckland, Hutchinson, New York, Braziller, and London, Women's Press, 1985.

The Inward Sun: Celebrating the Life and Work of Janet Frame, selected and edited by Elizabeth Alley. Wellington, New Zealand, Daphne Brasell Associates Press, 1994.

The Janet Frame Reader, edited by Carole Ferrier. London, Women's Press, 1995.

*

Film Adaptations: *An Angel at My Table,* 1991.

Bibliography: By John Beston, in *World Literature Written in English* (Arlington, Texas), November 1978.

Critical Studies: *An Inward Sun: The Novels of Janet Frame,* Wellington, New Zealand University Press, 1971, and *Janet Frame,* Boston, Twayne, 1977, both by Patrick Evans; *Bird, Hawk, Bogie: Essays on Janet Frame* edited by Jeanne Delbaere, Aarhus, Denmark, Dangaroo Press, 1978; *Janet Frame* by Margaret Dalziel, Wellington, Oxford University Press, 1981; *The Ring of Fire: Essays on Janet Frame* edited by Jeanne Delbaere, Sydney, Dangaroo Press, 1992; *I Have What I Gave: The Fiction of Janet Frame* by Judith Dell Panny, New York, Braziller, 1993; *Janet Frame: Subversive Fictions* by Gina Mercer. St. Lucia, Queensland, University of Queensland Press, 1994; *Critical Spaces: Margaret Laurence and Janet Frame* by Lorna M. Irvine. Columbia, South Carolina, Camden House, 1995; *Gendered Reistance: The Autobiographies of Simone De Beauvoir, Maya Angelou, Janet Frame and Marguerite Duras* by Valerie Baisnee. Atlanta, Rodopi, 1997; *Wrestling with the Angel: A Life of Janet Frame* by Michael King. Washington, D.C., Counterpoint, 2000.

* * *

''All dreams,'' Janet Frame writes in her 1970 novel *Intensive Care,* ''lead back to the nightmare garden.'' And all nightmares lead circuitously into truth. In all her novels, the looming threat of disorder, violent and disrupting, persistently attracts those that it frightens, for it proves more fertile, more imaginatively stimulating, more genuine, and more real than the too-familiar world of daily normality. The tension between safety and danger recurs as her characters—voyaging into strange geographies (like the epileptic Toby Withers in *The Edge of the Alphabet*), or madness (like Daphne in *Owls Do Cry,* or Istina Navet in *Faces in the Water*), or other people's identities (like Ed Glace in *Scented Gardens for the Blind*), or mirrors (like Vic in *The Adaptable Man*), or death (like Godfrey Rainbird in *The Rainbirds*)—discover both the mental deliberation that the safe state, in oxymoronic creativity, engenders, and the disembodying that danger contrives. The opening of *Faces in the Water* demonstrates the author's thematic density and sardonic touch:

> They have said that we owe allegiance to Safety, that he is our Red-Cross God who will provide us with ointment and ... remove the foreign ideas, the glass beads of fantasy, the bent hair-pins of unreason embedded in our minds. On all the doors which lead to and from the world they have posted warning notices and lists of safety measures to be taken in extreme emergency .... Never sleep in the snow. Hide the scissors. Beware of strangers .... But for the final day ... they have no slogan. The streets throng with people who panic, looking to the left and the right, covering the scissors, sucking poison from a wound they cannot find, judging their time from the sun's position in the sky when the sun itself has melted and trickles down the ridges of darkness into the hollows of evaporated seas. Nightmares and madness, the education in the nature of Apocalypse and survival, become not mere metaphors of sanity, but direct training in the reactivation of the mind's perceiving eyes.

By ''shipwrecking'' oneself in mad geographies, however (Frame speaks in one novel of ''an affliction of dream called Overseas''—as in another she observes that OUT is in man, is what he fears, ''like the sea''), one places oneself on ''the edge of the alphabet,'' in possession perhaps of insight, but no longer capable of communicating with the people who stay within regulated boundaries. Malfred Signal, in Frame's weakest novel, *A State of Siege,* for example, leaves her old self to live on an island and to find the perspectives of ''the room two inches behind the eyes.'' What she discovers, when the elements besiege her, is fear, but all she can do then is silently utter the strange new language that she clutches, alone, into seacalm and death. Like Ed Glace in *Scented Gardens,* who researches the history of the surname *Strang* and (discovering *strong, Strange,* and *Danger* along the way) wonders if people are merely anagrams, Malfred lives in a mad mirror world of intensely focused perception that anagrammatic Joycean punning-distorting day-to-day language—tries to render. As *Owls Do Cry* had earlier specified, in the shallow suburban character of Chicks, the ''safe'' world deals in language, too, as a defence against upset, hiding in the familiarity of conventional clichés and tired similes. What the brilliant punning passages of *The Rainbirds* show is what the title poem of *The Pocket Mirror* implies: that convention will not show ordinary men the ''bar of darkness'' that are optically contained within the ''facts of light''; ''To undeceive the sight a detached instrument like a mirror is necessary.'' Or will her narratives. But even that vantage point is fraught with deceit. Superstition, like convention, and Platonic forms, like safe order, can all interfere with true interpenetration with ''actuality.'' And to find the live language—the ''death-free zone'' of Thora Pattern, in *Edge of the Alphabet*—as a novelist inevitably dealing with day-to-day words becomes an increasingly difficult task the stronger the visionary sense of the individual mind on its own. Turnlung, the aging New Zealand writer in New York, in *Daughter Buffalo,* finds the challenge particularly acute; his exile to ''a country of death'' brings him into bizarrely creative contact with a young doctor, but in the epilogue to the story, he wonders if he has dreamed everything. What matters, as Turnlung puts it, is that ''I have what I gave.'' To conceive is to create some kind of reality, however unconventional the act, the result, and the language of rendering the experience may seem.

There are passages in France that are reminiscent of Doris Lessing—like the apocalyptic scenes of *Scented Gardens* and *Intensive Care,* the one anticipating the atomic destruction of Britain and the birth of a new language, the other observing the destruction of animals in Waipori City (the computerized enactment of the Human Delineation Act which will identify the strong normal law-abiding ''humans'' and methodically, prophylactically, eliminate the rest), and the ironic intensification of a vegetable human consciousness. In the earlier novel, particularly, the author emphasizes the relationship between the ''safety dance of speech'' and a kind of Coleridgean death-in-life, and that between winter (the gardenless season) and madness, life-in-death, ''Open Day in the factory of the mind.'' *The Rainbirds,* the writer's gentlest, most comic (however hauntingly, macabrely, relentlessly discommoding) book, takes up the metaphor in its story of a man *pronounced* dead after a car accident. Though Godfrey Rainbird lives, the official pronouncement, the conventional language, the public utterance, takes precedence over the individual spiritual actuality, depriving him of his job, his children, public acceptance, and so on. Indeed, he only becomes acceptable when he has ''died'' a second time, when his story is sufficiently distanced into legend and into the past to become a tourist attraction. But if you visit the grave in the winter, Frame adds, you must create the summer flowers within yourself. Summer gardens are openly available even to the spiritually blind; winter gardens are not. Her quiet acceptance, however, of that (mad, winter) power to change seasons within the mind expresses her most optimistic regard of humanity. And as *Living in the Maniototo* reaffirms, there is an ordering potentiality in the recognition of any person's several selves.

Intensive Care more broodingly evokes the same theme and provokingly points out the difference between the hospitalization of the body and the intensive care required to keep the mind truly alive. When the second world war is long over and the computer mentality takes over after the next impersonal War, all fructifying abnormality seems doomed; Deciding Day will destroy that which is not *named* human. Through the sharp memory of the supposedly dull Milly Galbraith, who is one of the few to appreciate an ancient surviving pear-tree, and the damningly conciliatory (and then expiatory) attitudes of Colin Monk, who goes along with the system, valuing Milly too late to save her, the apocalyptic days of Waipori City are told. Behind them both looms the mythical presence of Colin's twin Sandy, the Reconstructured Man, made of metal and transplanted part, who is also the Rekinstruckdead Man, a promise of technological finesse and an accompanying sacrifice of man's animal warmth and spiritual being. Milly is exterminated; Sandy is myth; Colin, declared human, breathes:

> I was safe, I had won.
>
> I had lost. I began losing the first day, when the news of the Act came to me and I signed the oath of agreement. Why of course, I said, I'll do anything you ask, naturally, it's the only way, the only solution, as I see it, to an impossible situation, as if situations needed solving, I mean, looked at objectively, as it must be seen to be ....
>
> The skimming words and phrases that need leave no footprints; one might never have been there, but one had spoken; and the black water lay undisturbed beneath the ice; and not a blade of grass quivered or a dead leaf whispered; a race of words had lived and died and left no relic of their civilization.
>
> As it must be seen to be, looked at objectively ....

The ironies multiply around each other. Language reasserts its fluid focus; the Society for the Prevention of Cruelty to Vegetation plants new pear trees on the Livingstone estate; the computer (not having been programmed for nostalgia) fails to account for the new enthusiasm for old abnormalities; and the Sleep Days cannot erase the time of the fires from the mind of Colin Monk. The mind survives. That her commitment to the spiritual independence of such perception is made so provocative is a tribute to Frame's arresting skill with images. She has an uncanny ability to arouse the diverse sensibilities of shifting moods and to entangle in language the wordless truths of her inner eye.

Language (always a motif in these works) is the central subject of the later novels *Living in the Maniototo,* with its artificial California setting, and the futuristic *The Carpathians.* The characters here contend not so much with a world outside themselves as with the kinds of world their imaginations create. Trained in words, they construct fantasies with the power of reality, often mistakenly accepting these ostensible ''realities'' as fixed truths. While most characters see only what they expect, some are given the gift of transcending their own verbal limitations. Understanding the *processes* of language is essential. Readers of the later novels are guided into limited insights: once the authoritarianism of their conventional expectations is exposed, they are offered a chance to glimpse alternative possibilities—within themselves, and consequently also in the ''ordinary'' world.

—W.H. New

FRAME, Ronald (William Sutherland)

Nationality: British. **Born:** Glasgow, 23 May 1953. **Education:** High School of Glasgow, 1962–71; University of Glasgow, 1971–75, M.A. 1975; Jesus College, Oxford, 1975–79, B.Litt. 1979. **Awards:** Betty Trask award, for first novel, 1984; Samuel Beckett award, 1986; Television Industries award, 1986; Scottish Arts Council award, 1987. **Address:** c/o Hodder and Stoughton Ltd, 47 Bedford Square, London WC1B 3DP, England.

PUBLICATIONS

Novels

Winter Journey. London, Bodley Head, 1984; New York, Beaufort, 1986.

A Long Weekend with Marcel Proust: Seven Stories and a Novel. London, Bodley Head, 1986.

Sandmouth People. London, Bodley Head, 1987; as *Sandmouth,* New York, Knopf, 1988.

A Woman of Judah: A Novel and Fifteen Stories. London, Bodley Head, 1987; New York, Norton, 1989.

Penelope's Hat. London, Hodder and Stoughton, 1989; New York, Simon and Schuster, 1991.

Bluette. London, Hodder and Stoughton, 1990.

Underwood and After. London, Hodder and Stoughton, 1991.

The Sun on the Wall: Three Novels. London, Hodder and Stoughton, 1994.

Short Stories

Watching Mrs. Gordon and Other Stories. London, Bodley Head, 1985.

Walking My Mistress in Deauville: A Novella and Nine Stories. London, Hodder and Stoughton, 1992.

Uncollected Short Stories

''Rowena Fletcher,'' in *Winter's Tales 3* (new series), edited by Robin Baird-Smith. London, Constable, and New York, St. Martin's Press, 1987.
''Trio-3 Stories,'' in *20 Under 35,* edited by Peter Straus. London, Sceptre, 1988.

Plays

Paris: A Television Play; with Privateers (includes story). London, Faber, 1987.

Radio Plays: *Winter Journey,* 1985; *Twister,* 1986; *Rendezvous,* 1987; *Cara,* 1988; *Marina Bray,* 1989.

Television Plays: *Paris,* 1985; *Out of Time,* 1987.

*

Ronald Frame comments:

My characters are caught between an imagined freedom to determine their lives and the machinations of fate. I write about the circular nature of time as we experience it, about repetitions and coincidences working through generations. About social ritual as a mental stabilizer.

''History'' to me is a kind of grand opera bouffe, scarcely believable sometimes. Social contact too is a complex game, perhaps a more serious one, of bluffs and evasions and all graduations of ''truth.''

I'm interested in the compelling power of imagination. My characters are inward, inhabiting a landscape of memory and desire, but are also ironically aware of how other people see them: I prefer my descriptions to come through, say, self-reflections in mirrors or window glass, or to be read in the facial reactions of others. I try to bring my third-person narratives as close to the first-person perspective as I can.

I hope I don't deal in heroes and villains. I write quite formally, but within that structure I mean to follow illogic where necessary; violence is implied, and it may appear the more desperate by contrast with this ambience of control.

While dissecting, I aim to preserve some essential mystery about my characters, so that not everything should be knowable, to themselves or to us. They partly live through received images—cinematic, for instance—and I appreciate that in writing about a period like the 1950s, as I frequently do, I'm approaching it through its own legend. I don't hold with research and verifiable realism; much more important to me is atmosphere, the evocation of a world—an approximately detailed but spiritually authentic world—which I can use to pit my individuals against the process of historical change. I hope the atmosphere will lure the reader, and induce for a short time a spell that might prove consistent and credible—and enjoyable.

* * *

Ronald Frame belongs to that select group of male novelists who write almost exclusively from the female point of view; indeed he has been described as the poet of *thé dansant,* obsessed with the minutiae of women's lives. Although in a novel like *Sandmouth People* he is capable of creating a whole range of characters reflecting different social strata and both sexes—in this case representative of a small English resort town during the 1950s—his preference is clearly for the female personality, and it is noticeable that the most memorable characters are women. In this record of a day in the life of a nondescript English town, Frame creates the milieu of a social comedy in which his characters reveal themselves through their past and present lives. Most notable among these is Nanny Filbert, whose hidden secrets are resurrected once more to haunt her. Other characters also remain in the memory: Lady Sybil de Castellet, representing the old monied aristocracy, who dreams only of death; or Penelope Prentice, middle-class and wealthy, who carries on a covert affair with Norman Pargiter, ''Sandmouth's own success story''; or Meredith Vane, the sub-Bloomsbury local author. All these, and a supporting cast of lesser lights, give the novel its knowing tone of a darker existence lying below the surface of a middle-class life so carefully depicted by Frame. It is indicative of the author's wit that he introduces a repertory company visiting Sandmouth to play Terence Rattigan's *Harlequinade,* a quintessential description of English middle-class life.

Although *Sandmouth People* is only his second novel—it was preceded by *Winter Journey* and by two collections of short stories—it is a good starting point for exploring Frame's fictional world. Similar to it in range of experience and in choice of background is *A Woman of Judah* which was published in a single volume with fifteen short stories. (Indeed, Frame is an excellent creator of shorter fiction.) Once again the time is the past, in this case England during one of the long hot summers of the 1930s, and the background is again peopled with a selection of suitably enigmatic characters. The story is told by Pendlebury, an elderly judge, reminiscing some fifty years after events which had a profound effect on him during his days as an articled clerk in rural Essex. While that is the starting point, Frame's main interest is the friendship Pendlebury strikes up with a couple called Davies: he is the local doctor and she appears to Pendlebury in all her ''glowing well-scrubbed voluptuousness.'' Slowly but surely the novel starts to revolve around her, and young Pendlebury is drawn ever more deeply into her life. Although he desires her, she remains curiously aloof and yet, following her husband's suspicious death, she continues to haunt Pendlebury, allowing him no peace in the years to come. It is a strange and diverting novel, and manages to seduce the reader into joining a claustrophobic and closed society inhabited by basically dishonest people.

In his next two novels, *Penelope's Hat* and *Bluette,* the themes Frame had been exploring in his earlier fiction come to fruition in a new and precocious way. *Penelope's Hat* is the story of an English novelist who disappeared in 1979, leaving only her straw hat as a clue to her fate. Seven years later she resurfaces in Australia, but this is not a literary whodunit; rather, it is a novel of layers which have to be drawn back to reveal the different stages of Penelope's life—her childhood in Borneo and the return to post-war Britain, Cornish summer holidays, her life as a young girl during World War II and the awakening of sexual desire. Different hats at various stages of her life punctuate the passing of the years and provide clues about Penelope, but the novel's real fascination is the central character herself. Here Frame displays an uncanny ability to unravel the strands of her past, to make sense of her obsessions with expensive clothes, silk stockings, even hats. Luxury is a key word in Penelope's life, and Frame revels in the goods that provide it—precious perfumes, fast cars, and designer-labelled clothes. Penelope might have hidden herself under several hats, but Frame has the measure of her personality, and the overall effect is of hearing whispered conversations behind half-closed doors.

It could be said that in *Bluette* Frame wrote a sequel; even the opening sentence is a promise of the exotic story that is about to unfold—''Follow the finger of Destiny.'' Like Penelope in the previous novel, protagonist Catherine Hammond occupies a world that is part reality and part make-believe, and shifts disconcertingly between the two. At different stages she works in a nightclub, as an actress and, later still, in an upper-class brothel, but throughout she manages to retain her integrity—ironically, through her ability to surround herself with the finer things of life. Vast, sprawling and eclectic, *Bluette* is both a saga and deeply touching story of a woman's search to find something approaching fulfillment and happiness. The book marks Frame as one of the most innovative writers of his generation.

—Trevor Royle

FRANCIS, Dick

Nationality: British. **Born:** Richard Stanley Francis in Tenby, Pembrokeshire, 31 October 1920. **Education:** Maidenhead County Boys' School, Berkshire. **Military Service:** Served as a Flying Officer in the Royal Air Force, 1940–45. **Family:** Married Mary Margaret Brenchley in 1947; two sons. **Career:** Amateur National Hunt (steeplechase) jockey, 1946–48; professional, 1948–57: National Hunt champion, 1953–54. Racing correspondent *Sunday Express,* London, 1957–73. Chairman, Crime Writers Association, 1973–74. **Awards:** Crime Writers Association Silver Dagger award, 1965, Gold Dagger award, 1980, Diamond Dagger award, 1989; Mystery Writers of America Edgar Allan Poe award, 1969, 1981, 1996; Nibbies award, 1998; Agatha Lifetime Achievement award, 2000. L.H.D.: Tufts University, Medford, Massachusetts, 1991. O.B.E. (Officer, Order of the British Empire), 1984. **Agent:** John Johnson, 45–47 Clerkenwell Green, London EC1R 0HT, England. **Address:** P.O. Box 30866 S.M.B., Grand Cayman, British West Indies.

PUBLICATIONS

Novels

Dead Cert. London, Joseph, and New York, Holt Rinehart, 1962.
Nerve. London, Joseph, and New York, Harper, 1964.
For Kicks. London, Joseph, and New York, Harper, 1965.
Odds Against. London, Joseph, 1965; New York, Harper, 1966.
Flying Finish. London, Joseph, 1966; New York, Harper, 1967.
Blood Sport. London, Joseph, 1967; New York, Harper, 1968.
Forfeit. London, Joseph, and New York, Harper, 1969.
Enquiry. London, Joseph, 1970; New York, Harper, 1971.
Rat Race. London, Joseph, 1970; New York, Harper, 1971.
Bonecrack. London, Joseph, 1971; New York, Harper, 1972.
Smokescreen. London, Joseph, and New York, Harper, 1972.
Slay-Ride. London, Joseph, and New York, Harper, 1973.
Knock-Down. London, Joseph, 1974; New York, Harper, 1975.
High Stakes. London, Joseph, 1975; New York, Harper, 1976.
In the Frame. London, Joseph, 1976; New York, Harper, 1978.
Trial Run. London, Joseph, 1978; New York, Harper, 1979.
Whip Hand. London, Joseph, 1979; New York, Harper, 1980.
Reflex. London, Joseph, 1980; New York, Putnam, 1981.
Twice Shy. London, Joseph, 1981; New York, Putnam, 1982.
Banker. London, Joseph, 1982; New York, Putnam, 1983.
The Danger. London, Joseph, 1983; New York, Putnam, 1984.
Proof. London, Joseph, 1984; New York, Putnam, 1985.
Break In. London, Joseph, and New York, Putnam, 1986.
Bolt. London, Joseph, 1986; New York, Putnam, 1987.
Hot Money. London, Joseph, 1987; New York, Putnam, 1988.
The Edge. London, Joseph, 1988; New York, Putnam, 1989.
Straight. London, Joseph, and New York, Putnam, 1989.
Longshot. London, Joseph and New York, Putnam, 1990.
Comeback. London, Joseph, and New York, Putnam, 1991.
Driving Force. London, Joseph, and New York, Putnam, 1992.
Decider. London, Joseph, and New York, Putnam, 1993.
Wild Horses. London, Joseph, and New York, Putnam, 1994.
Risk. Thorndike, Maine, G.K. Hall, 1994.
Come to Grief. London, Joseph, and New York, Putnam, 1995.
To the Hilt. New York, Putnam, 1996.
10 Lb. Penalty. New York, Putnam, 1997.
Second Wind. New York, Putnam, 1999.

Short Stories

Field of Thirteen. New York, Putnam, 1998.

Plays

Screenplays: *Dead Cert,* 1974.

Other

The Sport of Queens: The Autobiography of Dick Francis. London, Joseph, 1957; revised edition, 1968, 1974, 1982, 1988; New York, Harper, 1969.
Lester: The Official Biography. London, Joseph, 1986; as *A Jockey's Life: The Biography of Lester Piggott,* New York, Putnam, 1986.
Editor, with John Welcome, *Best Racing and Chasing Stories 1–2.* London, Faber, 2 vols., 1966–69.
Editor, with John Welcome, *The Racing Man's Bedside Book.* London, Faber, 1969.

*

Critical Studies: *Dick Francis* by Melvyn Barnes, New York, Ungar, 1986; *Dick Francis* by J. Madison Davis, Boston, Twayne, 1989; *Dick Francis: Steeplechase Jockey* by Bryony Fuller, London, Joseph, 1994.

* * *

''*Dying slowly of bone cancer the old man, shrivelled now, sat as ever in his great armchair, tears of lonely pain sliding down crepuscular cheeks.*'' Hardly the opening words one expects in a top-selling thriller. Yet they are what Dick Francis chose to write at the start of his 33rd novel, *Wild Horses,* and they tell us at once that the book will be more than a simple thriller—as, though in a less immediately obvious way, were each of its 32 predecessors.

There is perhaps a reason for this. Dick Francis did not come to fiction until he was approaching 40 and had already had a highly successful career in horse racing, ending as Champion jockey. Then, too, his life had not been without profound trouble. So it should be no surprise that his books, though designed first to entertain, each ask, with more pointedness or less, about one aspect of existence or another, the question, ''How should we live?''

His method is to write a first version and then to read it aloud on to tape. I suspect that it is this process that accounts for the first of his virtues, the extreme easiness of his style. But easy reading generally comes from hard work first, and Francis has said that producing a novel is ''just as tiring'' as race riding. Besides the style, there are solid plots underneath the whole; concluding events have reasonable and likely causes. There is the continuing pull of the story, so that you are all the time wanting to know what will happen next. You get told what you want to know, too, and not something just a little bit different, a mistake less skilled authors often make. And at the same time you are made to want to know some new thing.

Then there is the language. Francis chooses straightforward words and never wastes them. (Though in his later books he uses, where needed, something more resonant, such as the ''crepuscular'' in the passage quoted earlier.) This virtue comes perhaps from his sense of timing, a gift he brought with him from racing to writing. The art of judging at just what moment to put a new fact into the reader's head, whether the fact is as important as the discovery of a body (most adroitly done in *Slay-Ride*) or just some necessary detail, is one that Francis shares with the masters of his craft.

But more important than the pacing, or plot, or even skillful story-telling, are the people writers invent for their stories. It is through people that the storyteller affects an audience. The people in Francis's books are as real as real-life people. Perhaps the best example of the kind of human being in his pages is the girl the hero either loves or comes to love. There is not one in every book (Francis has succeeded in bringing considerable variety to thrillers that might, with their customary Turf settings or references, have become formula affairs), but she has featured often enough to be easily identifiable as a certain sort of person. She will have some grave handicap, such as needing to live in an iron lung, or simply being widowed, or, as in *The Danger,* having been the victim of a cruel kidnapping. Many thriller writers would not dare to use such people because the reality of their situation would show up the tinsel world around them. But Francis is tough enough, and compassionate enough, to be able to write about such things.

His knowledge of the effects of tragedy comes from his own experience. While his wife was expecting their first child she was struck down by poliomyelitis and confined to an iron lung. It is from personal experience, too, that the typically stoic Francis hero comes. One of the few complaints that have been made about the books is that the hero (usually a different one each time, a jockey, a horse-owner, a trainer, a painter, a film star, an accountant, a photographer, a merchant banker) is too tough to be credible. But the fact is that most critics are not used to taking actual physical hard knocks; Francis, the jumps jockey, was. So if you look carefully at what he says happens when one of his heroes gets beaten up (as almost invariably they do) you find that, unlike many a pseudo-Bond or carbon-copy private eye, he gets really hurt and recovers only as fast as a physically fit and resilient man would in real life.

A Francis hero will have another important characteristic: he will be a man not scared of judging. He weighs up the police he meets and sees them for what they are: tough men, good men, nasty men, weak men, tough women, greedy women, sensitive women. And, more than this, the Francis books make judgments on a wider scale. By its particular choice of hero each one addresses some particular human dilemma. *Slay-Ride,* for instance, though it might seem to be no more than a good story about dirty work on the Norwegian race-courses, is in fact a book about what it is like to be the parent of children, to give these hostages to fortune, to be taking part in the continuing pattern of human existence. Similarly *Reflex* is about the need to accept inevitable change, and *Twice Shy* is about the acquiring of maturity.

In *To the Hilt,* a wealthy artist is summoned to be with his stepfather at the latter's deathbed, and events soon hurl the protagonist into a melange of circumstances from which only Francis could untangle him. Less successful is *10-lb. Penalty* or its narrator, a 17-year-old naturally lacking in the voice that would compel adult readers to care fully about his work campaigning for his father's parliamentary election. Francis's 40th novel, *Second Wind,* likewise runs a little thin in spots. Perry Stuart, a TV weatherman, finds himself washed up on a Caribbean island where he discovers a safe containing a mysterious folder. Soon afterward he is rescued—by men in radiation-protection gear.

The Edge, though an exciting puzzle set on a Canadian train with a cargo of bloodstock and a posse of actors playing a ''murder mystery,'' is fundamentally about the need ''to retain order,'' and all its events reflect this. In *Straight* Francis takes the last yards of a jumps race course, ''the straight,'' as illustrating a man facing the end of a particular career (a jockey, once again), but he also goes deeper by saying something about that human ideal of being ''straight.'' It is such subtle themes that give the Francis books the weight that lifts them right out of the run of good but ordinary thrillers.

—H.R.F. Keating

FRAYN, Michael

Nationality: British. **Born:** Mill Hill, London, 8 September 1933. **Education:** Sutton High School for Boys; Kingston Grammar School, Surrey; Emmanuel College, Cambridge, B.A. 1957. **Military Service:** Served in the Royal Artillery and Intelligence Corps, 1952–54. **Family:** Married Gillian Palmer in 1960 (marriage dissolved 1990), married Claire Tomalin in 1993; three daughters. **Career:** Reporter, 1957–59, and columnist, 1959–62, the *Guardian,* Manchester and London; columnist, the *Observer,* London, 1962–68. Lives in London. **Awards:** Maugham award, 1966; Hawthornden prize, 1967; National Press award, 1970; *Evening Standard* award, for play, 1976, 1981, 1983, 1985; Society of West End Theatre award, 1977, 1982; British Theatre Association award, 1981, 1983; Olivier award, 1985; New York Drama Critics Circle award, 1986; Emmy award, 1990. Honorary Fellow, Emmanuel College, 1985. **Agent:** Elaine Greene Ltd., 37 Goldhawk Road, London W12 8QQ, England.

PUBLICATIONS

Novels

The Tin Men. London, Collins, 1965; Boston, Little Brown, 1966.

The Russian Interpreter. London, Collins, and New York, Viking Press, 1966.

Towards the End of the Morning. London, Collins, 1967; as *Against Entropy,* New York, Viking Press, 1967.

A Very Private Life. London, Collins, and New York, Viking Press, 1968.

Sweet Dreams. London, Collins, 1973; New York, Viking Press, 1974.
The Trick of It. London, Viking, 1989; New York, Viking, 1990.
A Landing on the Sun. London, Viking, 1991.
Now You Know. London, Viking, 1993.
Headlong. New York, Metropolitan Books, 1999.

Plays

Zounds!, with John Edwards, music by Keith Statham (produced Cambridge, 1957).
Jamie, On a Flying Visit (televised 1968). With *Birthday,* London, Methuen, 1990.
Birthday (televised 1969). With *Jamie, On a Flying Visit,* London, Methuen, 1990.
The Two of Us (includes *Black and Silver, The New Quixote, Mr. Foot, Chinamen*) (produced London, 1970; Ogunquit, Maine, 1975; *Chinamen* produced New York, 1979). London, Fontana, 1970; *Chinamen* published in *The Best Short Plays 1973,* edited by Stanley Richards, Radnor, Pennsylvania, Chilton, 1973; revised version of *The New Quixote* (produced Chichester, Sussex, and London, 1980).
The Sandboy (produced London, 1971).
Alphabetical Order (produced London, 1975; New Haven, Connecticut, 1976). With *Donkeys' Years,* London, Eyre Methuen, 1977.
Donkeys' Years (produced London, 1976). With *Alphabetical Order,* London, Eyre Methuen, 1977.
Clouds (produced London, 1976). London, Eyre Methuen, 1977.
The Cherry Orchard, adaptation of a play by Chekhov (produced London, 1978). London, Eyre Methuen, 1978.
Balmoral (produced Guildford, Surrey, 1978; revised version, as *Liberty Hall,* produced London, 1980; revised version, as *Balmoral,* produced Bristol, 1987). London, Methuen, 1987.
The Fruits of Enlightenment, adaptation of a play by Tolstoy (produced London, 1979). London, Eyre Methuen, 1979.
Make and Break (produced London, 1980; Washington, D.C., 1983). London, Eyre Methuen, 1980.
Noises Off (produced London, 1981; New York, 1983). London, Methuen, 1982; New York, French, 1985.
Three Sisters, adaptation of a play by Chekhov (produced Manchester and Los Angeles, 1985; London, 1987). London, Methuen, 1983.
Benefactors (produced London, 1984; New York, 1985). London, Methuen, 1984.
Wild Honey, adaptation of a play by Chekhov (produced London, 1984; New York, 1986). London, Methuen, 1984.
Number One, adaptation of a play by Jean Anouilh (produced London, 1984). London, French, 1985.
Plays I (includes *Alphabetical Order, Donkeys' Years, Clouds, Make and Break, Noises Off*). London, Methuen, 1986.
The Seagull, adaptation of a play by Chekhov (produced Watford, Hertfordshire, 1986). London, Methuen, 1986.
Clockwise (screenplay). London, Methuen, 1986.
Exchange, adaptation of a play by Trifonov (broadcast 1986; produced Southampton, Hampshire, 1989; London, 1990). London, Methuen, 1990.
Uncle Vanya, adaptation of a play by Chekhov (produced London, 1988). London, Methuen, 1987.
Chekhov: Plays (includes *The Seagull, Uncle Vanya, Three Sisters, The Cherry Orchard,* four vaudevilles). London, Methuen, 1988.
The Sneeze, adaptation of works by Chekhov (produced Newcastle-upon-Tyne and London, 1988). London, Methuen, and New York, French, 1989.
First and Last (televised 1989). London, Methuen, 1989.
Look Look (as *Spettattori,* produced Rome, 1989; as *Look Look,* produced London, 1990). London, Methuen, 1990.
Listen to This: 21 Short Plays and Sketches. London, Methuen, 1991.
Audience: A Play in One Act. London, French, 1991.
Here: A Play in Two Acts. London, French, 1994.
Now You Know: A Play in Two Acts (from the novel). London, Methuen Drama, 1995; New York, Samuel French, 1996.
Copenhagen. London, Methuen Drama, 1998.

Screenplays: *Clockwise,* 1986.

Radio Plays: *Exchange,* from a play by Trifonov, 1986.

Television Plays and Documentaries: *Second City Reports,* with John Bird, 1964; *Jamie, On a Flying Visit,* 1968; *One Pair of Eyes,* 1968; *Birthday,* 1969; *Beyond a Joke* series, with John Bird and Eleanor Bron, 1972; *Laurence Sterne Lived Here* (*Writers' Houses* series), 1973; *Imagine a City Called Berlin,* 1975; *Making Faces,* 1975; *Vienna: The Mask of Gold,* 1977; *Three Streets in the Country,* 1979; *The Long Straight* (*Great Railway Journeys of the World* series), 1980; *Jerusalem,* 1984; *First and Last,* 1989.

Other

The Day of the Dog (*Guardian* columns). London, Collins, 1962; New York, Doubleday, 1963.
The Book of Fub (*Guardian* columns). London, Collins, 1963; as *Never Put Off to Gomorrah,* New York, Pantheon, 1964.
On the Outskirts (*Observer* columns). London, Fontana, 1967.
At Bay in Gear Street (*Observer* columns). New York, Fontana, 1967.
Constructions (philosophy). London, Wildwood House, 1974.
Great Railway Journeys of the World, with others. London, BBC Publications, 1981; New York, Dutton, 1982.
The Original Michael Frayn: Satirical Essays, edited by James Fenton. Edinburgh, Salamander Press, 1983.
Speak After the Beep: Studies in the Art of Communicating with Inanimate and Semi-Inanimate Objects. London, Methuen, 1997.
Editor, *The Best of Beachcomber,* by J.B. Morton. London, Heinemann, 1963.

* * *

Three of Michael Frayn's novels, the first, fourth, and fifth, are highly original, a satire and fantasies; the second and third, on the other hand, are conventional. The second, *The Russian Interpreter,* concerns an English research student in Moscow who serves as interpreter for a mysterious businessman (he seeks ordinary Russians for exchange visits), and the pair become involved with a Russian girl. Though Moscow's streets and weather are described, soon the action is moving swiftly. Books are stolen and sought, somebody is tricking somebody, espionage or smuggling is occurring, and we read on eagerly, awaiting explanations. Even when the student is imprisoned, Frayn focuses on his comic efforts to obtain a towel, and the novel remains a good, cheerful read.

The American title of the third novel points to opposing inertia and conformity; the English one, only a little more relevantly, to the subject of being in the mid-thirties (the hero ''had spent his youth as one might spend an inheritance, and he had no idea of what he had bought with it''). Frayn's 37-year-old is a feature editor, worrying about repairs to his Victorian house with West Indian neighbors in S.W.23 and dreaming of escape, hopefully through appearances on a television panel. The plot is vehicle for comedy about a newspaper office, with a few shrewd observations, as when a girl reflects: ''She wasn't a girl at all, in any sense that the fashion magazines would recognize. She was just a young female human being, fit only to be someone's cousin or aunt.'' Some passages suggest Frayn intends more, a fuller study of his hero's marriage and serious focus on the future of newspapers (a cynical, pushy graduate challenges the office's ways), but these are not pursued.

The Tin Men, the first book, is about the William Morris Institute of Automation Research and its eccentric scientists. A thin plot-line turns on a new wing, the arrangements for the Queen to open it, and the TV company that plans to finance it. Most of the fun is about computers: the automating of football results because the Director believes ''the main object of organized sports and games is to produce a profusion of statistics,'' the programmed newspaper, which prints the core of familiar stories such as ''I Test New Car'' and ''Child Told Dress Unsuitable by Teacher,'' and Delphic I, the Ethical Decision Machine, which expresses its moral processes in units called pauls, calvins, and moses. Amid clever jokes, Frayn shows anxiety about the dangerous possibilities of computers and the limitations of the men responsible for them.

A Very Private Life begins ''Once upon a time there will be a little girl called Uncumber.'' In her world, ''inside people'' remain all their lives in windowless houses, supplied by tube and tap and using drugs—Pax, Hilarin and Orgasmin—for every experience. In very brief chapters, Frayn explains how life has grown more private, first physically, then through drugs to cope with anger and uncertainty. Dissatisfied Uncumber meets a man through a wrong number on ''holovision'' and goes to the other side of the world to visit him. The compelling story is part fairy tale, part fantasy, part morality, so that we ask ''Is it plausible?'' and ''What is the moral?'' Frayn's inspiration was contemporary America, where he noticed dark glasses used to hide feelings, and city people buying disused farmhouses to be alone in. He touches on penology, longevity, the treatment of personality, but concentrates on technology making possible a new kind of isolation which excludes uncomfortable realities. And Frayn the moralist never dominates Frayn the story-teller.

Even better is *Sweet Dreams*—clever, entertaining, dazzling. A typical middle-aged, middle-class Londoner is killed and finds himself in a Heaven where he can fly, speak any language, change his age, and retrieve long-lost possessions. He is set to invent the Matterhorn, returns to England and writes an official report on its condition, drops out to the simple country life and bounces back as right-hand man to God (who proves to be a blend of Freddie Ayer and A.J.P. Taylor, and says ''To get anything done at all one has to move in tremendously mysterious ways''). Slowly we realize the hero's Heavenly evolution is markedly similar to his earthly one. Frayn tells with wit and flourish his shrewd, sardonic and deceptively charming fable.

After sixteen years during which Frayn established a big reputation as a playwright, and also translated Chekhov's plays, he returned to the novel in 1989 with a highly original work which, however, was linked more closely with a real world than the fantasies. *The Trick of It* is told through the letters of a young lecturer in English to a friend in Australia. These describe how he first meets the successful woman novelist he studies (he refers to her as a ''MajWOOT,'' a major writer of our time) and marries her. He thinks that he can improve her next novel; is disturbed that the work which follows is about his mother and does not mention him; tries to write fiction himself, then discovers he has not ''the trick of it''; finally values his letters (which we are reading) only to learn that the recipient has lost them. The tone is playful, yet Frayn has insights into creativity and the relation of critic to creator.

A Landing on the Sun is less ingenious, although it cleverly unfolds as narrative and explores significant ideas. A civil servant investigates a mysterious death from seventeen years earlier, of a man involved with a ''policy unit'' on ''the quality of life,'' headed by an Oxford philosopher. Frayn writes of the bureaucratic world while pursuing the concept of ''happiness'' and the intriguing way in which the searcher becomes caught up with the object of his search.

Now You Know is about an elderly man with a varied past who runs an organization devoted to freedom of information. Gradually all the characters emerge as having something to hide and as misinterpreting the behaviour of others. Frayn's subject this time seems to be truth and when lying may be justified. Audaciously, the novel resembles a play, being told in a series of dramatic monologues.

These three novels have in common wit, elegance, page-turning storytelling, and a playful treatment of serious themes. *Headlong* is another witty comedy, but the intellectual details—e.g., information on the work of Peter Bruegel, and the world in which his paintings were conceived— threaten to weigh down the airy plot. This is a pity, since the story itself, of how art historian Martin Clay attempts to take a suspected Bruegel from its unsympathetic owner, is plenty enough to occupy readers' attentions.

—Malcolm Page, updated by Judson Knight

FREEMAN, Gillian

Nationality: British. **Born:** London, 5 December 1929. **Education:** The University of Reading, Berkshire, 1949–51, B.A. (honors) in English literature and philosophy, 1951. **Family:** Married Edward Thorpe in 1955; two daughters. **Career:** Copywriter, C.J. Lytle Ltd., London, 1951–52; schoolteacher in London, 1952–53; reporter, *North London Observer,* 1953; literary secretary to Louis Golding, 1953–55. Lives in London. **Agent:** Richard Scott Simon, Anthony Sheil Associates, 43 Doughty Street, London WC1N 2LF, England.

Publications

Novels

The Liberty Man. London, Longman, 1955.
Fall of Innocence. London, Longman, 1956.
Jack Would Be a Gentleman. London, Longman, 1959.
The Leather Boys (as Eliot George). London, Blond, 1961; New York, Guild Press, 1962.
The Campaign. London, Longman, 1963.
The Leader. London, Blond, 1965; Philadelphia, Lippincott, 1966.
The Alabaster Egg. London, Blond, 1970; New York, Viking Press, 1971.
The Marriage Machine. London, Hamish Hamilton, and New York, Stein and Day, 1975.

Nazi Lady: The Diaries of Elisabeth von Stahlenberg 1933–1948. London, Blond and Briggs, 1978; as *The Confessions of Elisabeth von S,* New York, Dutton, 1978; as *Diary of a Nazi Lady,* New York, Ace, 1979.
An Easter Egg Hunt. London, Hamish Hamilton, and New York, Congdon and Lattès, 1981.
Love Child (as Elaine Jackson). London, W.H. Allen, 1984.
Termination Rock. London, Unwin Hyman, 1989.
His Mistress's Voice. London, Arcadia, 1999.

Uncollected Short Stories

"The Soufflé" in *Courier* (London and New York), May 1955.
"Pen Friend," in *Woman's Own* (London), December 1957.
"The Changeling," in *London Magazine,* April 1959.
"The Polka (Come Dance with Me)," in *Woman's Own* (London), December 1962.
"Kicks," in *Axle Quarterly* (London), Summer 1963.
"Dear Fred," in *King* (London), June 1965.
"Venus Unobserved," in *Town* (London), July 1967.
"A Brave Young Woman," in *Storia 3,* edited by Kate Figes. London, Pandora Press, 1989.

Plays

Pursuit (produced London, 1969).

Screenplays: *The Leather Boys,* 1963; *That Cold Day in the Park,* 1969; *I Want What I Want,* with Gavin Lambert, 1972; *Day after the Fair,* 1986.

Radio Plays: *Santa Evita,* 1973; *Field Day,* 1974; *Commercial Break,* 1974.

Television Plays: *The Campaign,* 1965; *Man in a Fog,* 1984; *Hair Soup,* 1991.

Ballet Scenarios: *Mayerling,* 1978; *Intimate Letters,* 1978; *Isadora,* 1981.

Other

The Story of Albert Einstein (for children). London, Vallentine Mitchell, 1960.
The Undergrowth of Literature. London, Nelson, 1967; New York, Delacorte Press, 1969.
The Schoolgirl Ethic: The Life and Work of Angela Brazil. London, Allen Lane, 1976.
Ballet Genius: Twenty Great Dancers of the Twentieth Century, with Edward Thorpe. Wellingborough, Northamptonshire, Thorsons, 1988.

*

Manuscript Collection: University of Reading, Berkshire.

Critical Study: *Don't Never Forget* by Brigid Brophy, London, Cape, 1966, New York, Holt Rinehart, 1967; *Friends and Friendship* by Kay Dick, London, Sidgwick and Jackson, 1974.

Gillian Freeman comments:

I have always been concerned with the problems of the individual seen in relation to society and the personal pressures brought to bear because of moral, political or social conditions and the inability to conform. This is reflected in all my work to date, although I have never set out to propound themes, only to tell stories. After 12 novels I am able to make my own retrospective assessment, and I find recurring ideas and links of which I was unconscious at the time of writing.

My first six novels are in some way concerned with the class system in England, either as a main theme (*The Liberty Man, Jack Would Be a Gentleman*) or as part of the background (*The Leather Boys*). Although the rigid class patterns began to break up soon after the last war and have changed and shifted, they still remain subtle delineations that I find absorbing. In *The Liberty Man* there is the direct class confrontation in the love-affair between the middle-class school teacher and the cockney sailor. In *Fall of Innocence* I was writing about the sexual taboos of the middle class attacked by an outsider, a young American girl. This element, the planting of an alien into a tight social structure, reappears constantly in my novels—atheist Harry into the Church of England parish in *The Campaign;* the Prossers in *Jack Would Be a Gentleman* from one class area into an elevated one in the same town; the cross-visiting of Freda and Derek in *The Liberty Man;* strongest of all, Hannah in *The Alabaster Egg,* transplanted from Munich of the 1930s to postwar London. This is the theme pursued in *The Marriage Machine,* with Marion, from rural England, unable to adapt completely to life in the United States and battling against her-in-laws (also uprooted from Europe) for the mind of her young son. In *Jack Would Be a Gentleman* the theme is the sudden acquisition of money without the middle- or upper-class conditioning which makes it possible to deal with it. *The Campaign* has the background of a seedy seaside parish, against which the personal problems of a cross-section of individuals (all involved in a fund-raising campaign) are exacerbated; God and Mammon, the permissive society, the Christian ethics. *The Leather Boys* is the story of two working-class boys who have a homosexual affair; *The Leader* explores fascism in a modern democracy, which, on both sides of the Atlantic, throws up a sufficient number of people who are greedy, ruthless, intolerant, bigoted and perverted enough to gravitate towards the extreme right. In *Nazi Lady* the socially climbing heroine, Elisabeth, records in her diary her joy in meeting Hitler. in *The Alabaster Egg,* which I consider my best work to date, Hannah also meets Hitler and there is another fictitious diary, an historical memoir of a lover of Ludwig II. This earlier novel contains several of my recurring themes—fascism, homosexuality, the main characters all victims of the prevailing political scenes. There are parallels between Hitler's Germany and Bismarck's reflecting in two love affairs which end in betrayal. I used real as well as imaginary characters, linking fiction and reality closely, and did so, too, in *Nazi Lady. An Easter Egg Hunt* is concerned with the disappearance of a schoolgirl during Word War I—another character wrenched from her normal environment, a refugee from France now living in England's Lake District where the war harshly changes the lives of the four main protagonists. *Love Child,* in the psychological thriller genre, is about the problem of surrogate motherhood in both England and the United States. Once more, the heroine, feckless and easygoing Gwen, is thrust into a new society. In *Termination Rock* the narrator, Joanna, finds herself with an alter ego, Victorian Ann, the two stories paralleled as both of them travel to and in America. Whether Joanna's journey is into the paranormal or whether there is a psychological and logical explanation, is for the reader to decide. This novel, with its double time scale, has links with both *The Alabaster Egg* and *The Marriage Machine,* and also continues my fascination with the United States. *The Marriage Machine, Love Child,* and *Termination Rock,* in different ways and in different periods, deal with the adaptation to life in North America.

My choice of Einstein for a children's biography—a highly individual man whose life was spent in trying to eliminate the frontiers of prejudice—and the thesis of *The Undergrowth of Literature* (the need for fantasy in the sexually disturbed) illustrate my interest in and compassion for those unable to conform to the accepted social mores. To some extent my film writing has also dealt with social and sexual distress, as did my short play for The National Theatre, *Pursuit.* The ballet scenarios for Kenneth MacMillan, although the subjects were not selected by me, again present individuals who are ''outsiders''—Prince Rudolf in *Mayerling* and the strong, passionate and wayward Isadora Duncan.

* * *

Since her first novel, *The Liberty Man,* Gillian Freeman has shown an outstanding ability to get inside the skin of characters from very different social backgrounds. It should be remembered that *The Liberty Man* was considerably in advance of its time in its truly empathic conveyance of a working-class character (Derek, a naval rating) who becomes involved in an affair with an intellectual and middle-class woman. This book appeared when the prevailing literary method of portraying working-class people still tended to be by projecting the image of the well-intentioned but clumsy, scruffy, and inarticulate ''little man.'' The unusual power of *The Liberty Man,* however, does not rest only in its portrait of Derek, but in his relationship with Freda, the middle-class school teacher, through which Freeman analyses resonances between people from extremely diverse social groups, and between the inner experiences of the individual and the externals that he sees in operation around him.

Freeman is, in a sense, the writer of the archetypal anti-Cinderella story. She has acute honesty and a flair for precise, almost wickedly unerring observation of detail and motive. In her novels, despite changes of fortune (*Jack Would Be a Gentleman* is a good example) people's lives are *not* transformed, and their basic inadequacies remain. Her novels are preoccupied with frustration and fallibility; she frequently manages, however, by well-timed injections of compassion, to lift a book's mood of inadequacy and doubt into warmth and well-being that are almost physical in the strength of their expression.

Freeman observes and analyses the vagaries of human nature but rarely makes moral judgments. She highlights complexities in apparently ''ordinary'' or superficial characters, and makes her jaded sophisticates capable of sudden deep and challenging emotions. She explores conflicts between ambition and conscience, and the primitive feelings that underlie the veneer of our civilization. Permeating some of her narratives is a sense that the protective social structure we strive to perpetuate is deeply flawed. She is, in this context, extremely concerned with nonconformity—the healthily truculent attitudes of the working classes; the bewildered responses of the unconscious homosexual; the rootlessness of the young that can sometimes find expression only in violence (*The Leather Boys*).

Freeman's novels are synonymous with power and panache, though these qualities are often expressed in low-key and even throwaway language. She is in this respect quintessentially English, and until *The Alabaster Egg* her preoccupations were with issues particularly pertinent to English society. *The Alabaster Egg* is her most trenchant and telling work. It is about the pursuit of political power, and this is counterpointed by a probing of the exploitation of human beings at the personal level. Her setting is wider than in the earlier novels; it is no longer England but Europe—or the world—and the focus, significantly, is Germany—the vortex of 20th-century ''civilization,'' corruption, and decay.

Her earlier stories were concerned with displacement, in particular with the catalytic effect of an alien presence in a close-knit and apparently secure social structure (*Fall of Innocence, The Campaign*). *The Alabaster Egg* highlights an ironic reversal of this theme of dissociation; Hannah, the book's heroine, has the misfortune to be a Jew in Nazi Germany. She does not, however, see herself as an alien. In her own estimation she is as much a German as a Jew. Her situation, of course, stresses one of the most pernicious effects of Nazi racist policies—the enforced separation of certain people from their own communities, from the only group to which they had felt a sense of belonging. Hannah's tragic but resilient story has parallels with happenings in the time of Bismarck. Her love affair with a ''real'' German is illuminated by her readings from the diary of the homosexual lover of King Ludwig II. This affair—like Hannah's—ends in bewilderment and betrayal.

Having written compellingly from the viewpoint of a sensitive and intelligent Jewish woman caught up in the hideousness of fascism, Freeman goes on to write as if from the inside about a passionate supporter of Hitler's ideologies in *Nazi Lady.* This originally appeared as a factual diary; it was so convincing that one critic pronounced it ''unquestionably genuine.'' Genuineness, of course, does not have to be a matter of fact but of mood, and in this sense *Nazi Lady* is genuine, although it is a work of fiction. Freeman says that it was inspired by her publisher's observations on the extraordinary dichotomy between the anguishes of the battles of Stalingrad and the ''good life'' enjoyed at the same time by influential civilians in Germany.

In *Nazi Lady* the heroine's initial enthusiasm for Nazism is presented with subtlety and conviction. Elisabeth is German; to English readers she is possibly a slightly glamorized amalgam of Marlene Dietrich, Irma Greeser, and whatever the Nazi slogan ''Strength through Joy'' suggested. As well as being brittle she is beautiful, and her experiences are macabrely fascinating.

Freeman combines fact and fiction with aplomb. (For example, Elisabeth has to accept expert but distasteful seduction by Goebbels in order to save her husband from the rigors of the Russian Front.) In the end, all her convictions are reduced to ashes, as both her son and her husband become victims of Nazi ruthlessness and fanaticism. But she survives—and marries an American from the liberating forces.

An Easter Egg Hunt is set in a girls' school during Word War I, and it is not only an intriguing mystery story on its own account but memorable for its evocation of Angela Brazil's schoolgirl adventures. School was, of course, regarded by Angela Brazil as the (essentially neatly ordered) world in microcosm; but Freeman recognizes bizarre and eccentric elements even in the innately conservative and sheltered confines of school life. She adeptly creates and manipulates her adolescent characters without excesses or sentimentality, and they are in fact far removed from Brazil's colorful but artless embodiments of schoolgirlishness.

The narrative style of Freeman's novels is perfectly suited to her sensitive but down-to-earth approach. Her prose is robust and direct;

her plots are constructed with economy and excellence, and the stories seem to vibrate with energy and insight.

—Mary Cadogan

FRENCH, Marilyn

Nationality: American. **Born:** Marilyn Edwards in New York City, 21 November 1929. **Education:** Hofstra College (now University), Hempstead, Long Island, B.A. 1951, M.A. 1964; Harvard University, Cambridge, Massachusetts, Ph.D. 1972. **Family:** Married Robert M. French in 1950 (divorced 1967). **Career:** Instructor, Hofstra University, 1964–68; assistant professor of English, College of the Holy Cross, Worcester, Massachusetts, 1972–76; artist-in-residence, Aspen Institute for Humanistic Study, 1972; Mellon fellow, Harvard University, 1976. **Agent:** Sheedy Literary Agency, 41 King Street, New York, New York 10014, U.S.A.

PUBLICATIONS

Novels

The Women's Room. New York, Summit, 1977; London, Deutsch, 1978.
The Bleeding Heart. New York, Summit, and London, Deutsch, 1980.
Her Mother's Daughter. New York, Summit, and London, Heinemann, 1987.
Our Father. Boston, Little Brown, 1994; New York, Penguin, 1995.
My Summer with George. New York, Knopf, distributed by Random House, 1996.

Other

The Book as World: James Joyce's Ulysses. Cambridge, Massachusetts, Harvard University Press, 1976; London, Abacus, 1982.
Shakespeare's Division of Experience. New York, Summit, and, London, Cape, 1981.
Beyond Power: On Women, Men, and Morals. New York, Summit, and London, Cape, 1985.
The War against Women. New York, Summit, and London, Hamilton, 1992.
A Season in Hell: A Memoir. New York, Knopf, 1998.

* * *

The narrator of Marilyn French's phenomenally best-selling first novel, *The Women's Room,* leaves the subject of men's pain "to those who know and understand it, to Philip Roth and Saul Bellow and John Updike and poor wombless Norman Mailer." French's own most extensive treatment of male suffering appears not in her three long feminist fictions but in *The Book as World: James Joyce's Ulysses,* where she describes Stephen Dedalus's emotional paralysis and Leopold Bloom's moral heroism. By accepting his "participation in the human condition," Stephen can accept his own feelings and act in ways that will end his crippling numbness. "Such an end," says French, "is not equivalent to reaching some new Jerusalem where everything will become clear; it offers merely survival, the ability to live and grow." Stephen thus anticipates the shell-shocked female survivors of French's novels, who pass through their own nightmarish versions of Joyce's Nighttown.

French suggests that the endurance of Bloom and Stephen is "an affirmation of the human race;" the endurance of her protagonists—Mira, Dolores, and Anastasia—is a tribute to the "feminine principle" that offers the race's best hope for the future. In *Beyond Power,* French calls for a new synthesis of traditionally conflicting female and male values: "For women, as for society at large, it is necessary to reach out both to the dishonored body, discredited emotion, to blood and milk; and to self-control, power-to, assertive being in the world. Only by incorporating both can we attain integrity." French attributes much of the world's suffering to an obsession with patriarchal structures of power, a major concern too of her second novel, *The Bleeding Heart.* Pleasure, in the deep sense of felicity, must replace power as society's highest good. French's fictional women have several experiences of delight. Among the most memorable is the New Year's Eve dance in *The Women's Room,* where men and women, young and fortyish, join in a circle of "color and motion and love." Mira returns to the image as "a moment of grace vouchsafed them by something divine." Unfortunately, episodes of mutual nurturance are much less common than years of lonely anguish. French's central characters undergo agonies so severe that, as she says of Bloom and Stephen, "survival alone is a triumph."

Even as a girl, Mira Ward realizes that "Women are victims by nature." Almost raped by her boyfriend Lanny, she tearfully marries the gentle and intelligent Norm. Disinterested in sex and horrified at Mira's dreams of someday earning a doctoral degree, Norm makes her feel like "a child who had stumbled, bumbled into the wrong house." Almost two decades later, the divorced Mira still feels out of place even though she is finally working toward her long-deferred goal. French's novel opens in 1968 with Mira uneasily enrolled at Harvard. Supported by a women's group, which includes the outspoken Val, Mira gains a strong sense of woman's value that enables her to survive the rape of Val's daughter, Val's death in a confrontation between radical feminists and police, and even the break-up of her passionate affair with Ben, who asks her to delay her career by accompanying him to Africa and bearing his child. Only in the closing pages does it become clear that the somewhat cynical narrator—who considers her protagonist to be "a little ridiculous"—is actually Mira, now "unbearably alone" as she walks a Maine beach and waits for the fall semester to begin at the community college where she teaches English. Haunted by nightmares of a vacant-eyed man who pursues her with a phallic pipe and penknife, Mira nevertheless feels that it is "time to begin something new, if I can find the energy, if I can find the heart."

French's second novel lacks the narrative complexity, the large groups of characters, and the scope of *The Women's Room,* which traced Mira's growth from a naïve 1950s housewife to an independent woman of the 1970s against the cultural backdrop of the Eisenhower years, the assassinations of the Kennedys and Martin Luther King, Kent State, and My Lai. A tenured professor and author of two books, Dolores Durer—the bleeding heart of the title—seems to have achieved even greater success than Mira in recovering from an even worse marriage and divorce. Yet she feels like a "walking robot," and, celibate for years, her body is "dying of thirst." An affair with Victor Morrissey, an American businessman whom Dolores meets in England, relieves the sexual dryness but reconfirms her belief that "Women always end up paying" because the world follows "Men's rules, still, always." Victor does, however, encourage Dolores to share with him her most terrible memory, the suicide of her daughter

Elspeth, thus enabling her to feel again. Freed from her repeated identification with Lot's pillar-of-salt wife, Dolores refuses a potentially numbing marriage to Victor (as Mira refused Ben) and prepares to return to her students and good woman friends.

Her Mother's Daughter, French's most experimental novel, incorporates struggles of three generations: Anastasia Stevens, a world-famous photographer; Belle, her often silent mother, who has a symbolically ''defective heart;'' and her immigrant grandmother, Frances. Striving to avoid the misery of her mother and grandmother, the twice-divorced Anastasia comes closer than French's earlier women to achieving the freedoms more usually associated with a man's life, but in learning a masculine self-control she so thoroughly masters her feelings that she ''cannot find them myself.'' Anastasia's progress toward emotional recovery begins with the women's movement, a lesbian relationship with Clara Traumer, her reconciliation with the son and daughter who have grieved her, and—perhaps most significant—her mother's unprecedented words of praise: ''I will never forget how sweet you were to me.''

French's novels illuminate a distinction she makes between the ''feminine'' plots of comedy and the ''masculine'' plots of tragedy in ''Shakespeare's Division of Experience'': ''We lose, but we replace, we substitute: we go on. This is as profound a truth as that we lose and cannot replace, we die.'' Less profound are the ''truths'' explored in *My Summer with George,* the story of a sixtysomething romance author's infatuation with an overweight and altogether unromantic newspaper editor. The lesson we learn from the frustrating affair of Hermione Beldame (nee Elsa Schutz) and George Johnson is that notions of romantic love so cherished by women are a lie: as their bodies age, the possibility of achieving even a simulacrum—say, an emotionally clumsy dalliance with a man well past his prime—diminish as well.

—Joan Wylie Hall, updated by Judson Knight

FRIEDMAN, Bruce Jay

Nationality: American. **Born:** New York City, 26 April 1930. **Education:** De Witt Clinton High School, Bronx, New York; University of Missouri, Columbia, 1947–51, B.A. in journalism 1951. **Military Service:** United States Air Force, 1951–53: Lieutenant. **Family:** Married 1) Ginger Howard in 1954 (divorced 1977), three children; 2) Patricia J. O'Donohue in 1983, one daughter. **Career:** Editorial director, Magazine Management Company, publishers, New York, 1953–64. Visiting professor of literature, York College, City University, New York, 1974–76. **Address:** P.O. Box 746, Water Mill, New York 11976, U.S.A.

Publications

Novels

Stern. New York, Simon and Schuster, 1962; London, Deutsch, 1963.
A Mother's Kisses. New York, Simon and Schuster, 1964; London, Cape, 1965.
The Dick. New York, Knopf, 1970; London, Cape, 1971.
About Harry Towns. New York, Knopf, 1974; London, Cape, 1975.
Tokyo Woes. New York, Fine, 1985; London, Abacus, 1986.
The Current Climate. New York, Atlantic Monthly Press, 1989.
A Father's Kisses. New York, Fine, 1996.

Short Stories

Far from the City of Class and Other Stories. New York, Frommer-Pasmantier, 1963.
Black Angels. New York, Simon and Schuster, 1966; London, Cape, 1967.
Let's Hear It for a Beautiful Guy and Other Works of Short Fiction. New York, Fine, 1984.
Collected Short Fiction. New York, Fine, 1995.

Uncollected Short Stories

''Pitched Out,'' in *Esquire* (New York), July 1988.

Plays

23 Pat O'Brien Movies, adaptation of his own short story (produced New York, 1966).
Scuba Duba: A Tense Comedy (produced New York, 1967). New York, Simon and Schuster, 1968.
A Mother's Kisses, music by Richard Adler, adaptation of the novel by Friedman (produced New Haven, Connecticut, 1968).
Steambath (produced New York, 1970). New York, Knopf, 1971.
First Offenders, with Jacques Levy (also co-director: produced New York, 1973).
A Foot in the Door (produced New York, 1979).
Sardines (produced New York, 1994).
Have You Spoken to Any Jews Lately? (produced New York, 1995).

Screenplays: *Stir Crazy,* 1980; *Splash,* with others, 1984; *Dr. Detroit,* with others, 1988.

Other

The Lonely Guy's Book of Life. New York, McGraw Hill, 1978.
The Slightly Older Guy. New York, Simon and Schuster, 1995.
Even the Rhinos Were Nymphos: Best Nonfiction. Chicago, University of Chicago Press, 2000.
Editor, *Black Humor.* New York, Bantam, and London, Corgi, 1965.

*

Critical Study: *Bruce Jay Friedman* by Max F. Schulz, New York, Twayne, 1974.

Theatrical Activities: Director: **Play**—*First Offenders* (co-director, with Jacques Levy), New York, 1973.

* * *

For good or ill, Bruce Jay Friedman seems destined to be forever linked with the literary phenomenon of the 1960s known as ''black humor.'' In his foreword to *Black Humor,* an anthology he edited in 1965, Friedman ducks the business of rigid definition, insisting that each of the 13 writers represented is separate and unique, but he does suggest that ''if there is a despair in this work, it is a tough, resilient brand and might very well end up in a Faulknerian horselaugh.'' For

Friedman, style is a function, an extension, of the disorderly world that surrounds him. As he puts it, there is a ''fading line between fantasy and reality, a very fading line, a god-damned, almost invisible line.'' Friedman's slender fiction—as well as his drama and his screenplays—are pitched on this precarious edge. In such a world, the *New York Times* is ''the source and fountain and bible of black humor,'' while television news convinces Friedman, perhaps too easily, that ''there is a new mutative style of behavior afoot, one that can only be dealt with by a new, one-foot-in-the-asylum style of fiction.'' We are hardly surprised when a contemporary novelist declines rather than develops, when he or she adds increasingly smaller additions to the original house of fiction. For Friedman, *Stern* doubled as his debut and his most accomplished novel. It's all there in *Stern:* the uneasy Jewishness, the ulcers, the suburban situation. But the sense of terror it generates is actualized, altogether convincing, located in a compactness that never quite appears again in Friedman's fiction.

Stern is, in short, the angst-ridden apartment dweller, nose pressed against suburbia while visions of extra rooms dance in his head: ''As a child he had graded the wealth of people by the number of rooms in which they lived. He himself had been brought up in three in the city and he fancied people who lived in four were so much more splendid than himself.'' Alas, as Stern quickly discovers, he is not one of the Chosen People who can make the exodus from the bondage of crowded apartments to the Promised Land of suburban living. He is, at best, a reluctant pioneer, a man who misses the cop on the beat, the delicatessen at the corner.

Stern is a contemporary variation on the classical schlemiel, one victimized by darkly comic fantasies of his own making, rather than by accidents. Besieged by problems on all sides—caterpillars devour his garden, neighborhood dogs attack him on a nightly basis—Stern pictures the police as ''large, neutral-faced men with rimless glasses who would accuse him of being a newcomer making vague troublemaking charges.'' Especially if he complains about the threatening dogs: ''They would take him into a room and hit him in his large, white, soft stomach.'' And so he swallows his impulse to protest, only to imagine himself ''fighting silently in the night with the two gray dogs, lasting eight minutes and then being found a week later with open throat by small Negro children.'' Friedman's subsequent works confirmed two facts: that he is equally at home in the novel (*A Mother's Kisses*), the short story (*Far from the City of Class*), or the play (*Steambath*); and that he is a flashy writer of limited scope. For example, in *A Mother's Kisses,* the psychodynamics of black humor shrink to Momism and the difficulties of getting into college. As always, excess is the heart of Friedman's matter:

> He [Joseph] saw himself letting a year go by, then reapplying only to find himself regarded as a suspicious leftover fellow, his application tossed onto a pile labeled ''repeaters,'' not to be read until all the fresh new ones had been gone through. Year after year would slip away, until finally, at thirty-seven, he would enter night school along with a squad of newly naturalized Czechs, sponsored by labor unions and needing a great many remedial reading sessions.

Joseph's American-Jewish mother begins as a vulgar cliché, and Friedman's touch merely raises it to a second power. When Joseph went away to summer camp, mother struck a camp of her own just across the lake; when Joseph finally sets off for Kansas Land Grant Agricultural (where courses like ''the History and Principles of Agriculture'' and ''Feed Chemistry'' comprise the curriculum) Mom insists on coming too.

And yet, there are moments in *A Mother's Kisses* when the terrors of contemporary life are rendered with sharp, metaphysical precision:

> A long line had formed in the men's room, leading to a single urinal, which was perched atop a dais. When a fellow took too long, there were hoots and catcalls such as ''What's the matter, fella, can't you find it?'' As his turn came nearer, Joseph began to get nervous. He stepped before the urinal finally, feeling as though he had marched out onto a stage. He stood there a few seconds, then zipped himself up and walked off. The man in back of him caught his arm and said, ''You didn't go. I watched.''

Little of Kakfa's flavor is lost in the translation. And the hand that descends to unmask our smallest deception strikes us as real, all too real.

The problem, of course, is that Friedman throws off brilliantly comic moments without the inclination to turn them into sustained, comic fictions. He remains the perennial sophomore, chortling at what can only be called sophomoric jokes. In *The Dick,* for example, Friedman means to draw a parallel between sexuality and crime-fighting, as the title of the novel and the name of its beleaguered protagonist, LePeters, suggest. One bad joke begets another. When LePeters has his psychological interview, the conversation owes more to Hollywood than to Henry James:

> ''What do you think all these guns around her represent?'' he asked LePeters in a lightning change of subject.
>
> ''Oh, I don't know,'' said LePeters. ''Phalluses, I guess.'' Actually, he had dipped into a textbook or two and was taking a not-so-wild shot.
>
> ''Not bad,'' said Worthway, lifting one crafty finger in the Heidelberg style and making ready to leave. ''But some of them are pussies, too.''

About Harry Towns focuses on a moderately successful screenwriter, one given to verbal razzle-dazzle, urbane irony, and just enough innocence to be amazed about the money producers stuff into his pockets and the girls who fall into his bed. One shorthand way of putting it might be this: the Sexual Revolution caught Harry Towns with his pants up. The result is a man in his forties (formerly married, now anguishing through a permanent ''temporary separation'') trying too hard to be trendy and protesting too much about enjoying it. No doubt Friedman's biographer will, one day, point out just how ''biographical'' the stories in fact were.

In *Tokyo Woes,* Friedman introduces Mike Halsey, a more circumspect protagonist—at least in the sense that he is more routinized, more circumspect, than the likes of Harry Towns: ''Normally, Mike was a fellow who liked to stay close to his beat. Once he bought newspapers in one place, that's where he bought them.'' In short, Halsey ''was a fellow who kept to the center of the road, although he had to admit that every time he swerved off a bit it had worked out nicely.'' A short chapter later (indeed, all the chapters in *Tokyo Woes* run to fewer than ten pages), Halsey is on his way to Tokyo, where comic misadventures and sexual peccadilloes will follow him like the night the day. For Friedman followers, the highjinks are all to predictable, all too self-consciously offered up.

With *The Current Climate,* Friedman returns to Harry Towns, the Hollywood wordsmith he had invented as a comic projection of the writing business and himself. Harry is still crazy after all these years—still frisky, still foolish, and still likely to be found in a writers' bar where sex and drugs are the major attractions. Friedman relates Harry's escapades in short, choppy sentences and with appropriately coarse language, but if the result has its comic moments, they tell us precious little about the scriptwriting racket and even less about who the Harry Towns under the highjinks really is.

For nearly two decades, Friedman has been a steady worker in the vineyards of Hollywood. One learned to look quickly as his name, and the other credits, rolled over the silver screen. The heyday of the black humorist was over. Some, like Ken Kesey, dropped out. And some, like Bruce Jay Friedman, apparently found the medium their ''message'' had been looking for all along.

—Sanford Pinsker

FRIEDMAN, Kinky

Nationality: American. **Born:** Richard Friedman, near Kerrville, Texas, 1944. **Education:** University of Texas, B.A. **Career:** Peace Corps, Borneo, 1966–68; leader of the country-western band Kinky Friedman and the Texas Jewboys; actor. **Agent:** Esther Newburg, International Creative Management, 8942 Wilshire Boulevard, Los Angeles, California 90211, U.S.A.

PUBLICATIONS

Novels

Greenwich Killing Time. New York, Beech Tree Books, 1986.
A Case of Lone Star. New York, Beech Tree Books, 1987.
When the Cat's Away. New York, Beech Tree Books, 1988.
Frequent Flyer. New York, Morrow, 1989.
Musical Chairs. New York, Morrow, 1991.
The Kinky Friedman Crime Club (includes *Greenwich Killing Time, A Case of Lone Star*, and *When the Cat's Away*). London, Faber, 1992; published in the United States as *Three Complete Mysteries.* New York, Wings Books, 1993.
Elvis, Jesus, and Coca Cola. New York, Simon & Schuster, 1993.
Armadillos and Old Lace. New York, Simon & Schuster, 1994.
God Bless John Wayne. New York, Simon & Schuster, 1995.
The Love Song of J. Edgar Hoover. New York, Simon & Schuster, 1996.
Roadkill. New York, Simon & Schuster, 1997.
Blast from the Past. New York, Simon & Schuster, 1998.
Spanking Watson: A Novel. New York, Simon & Schuster, 1999.

Other

Sold American (musical recording). New York, Vanguard, 1973.
Lasso for El Paso (musical recording). New York, Epic, 1976.
Under the Double Ego (musical recording). Austin, Texas, Sunrise Records, 1984.
Afterword, *Daddy-O: Iguana Heads and Texas Tales* by Bob ''Daddy-O'' Wade with Keith and Kent Zimmerman, foreword by Linda Ellerbee. New York, St. Martin's Press, 1995.

*

Critical Studies: *Eat, Drink, and Be Kinky: A Feast of Wit and Fabulous Recipes for Fans of Kinky Friedman* by Mike McGovern, New York, Simon & Schuster, 1999.

* * *

Kinky Friedman is the author of a dozen mystery novels that star himself as a detective with a distinctive persona—a Texas Jew, a country singer and songwriter turned amateur detective, living in a converted New York loft with a lesbian dance class that practices in the room above, fond of cats, cigars and cracking jokes, and of parading his sometimes politically incorrect prejudices. Friedman's first-person narratives are fuelled by the force of their fast-moving, streetwise, hip style which hardly gives the reader time to draw breath as it moves from one scene and set of characters to another. His work is notable for its combination of comedy with casually-strung plots that are not always easy to follow; Friedman himself has said that he is not interested in intricate plotting and that the secret of a good mystery is that nothing is what it appears to be. He both employs and consciously sends up the conventions of the hardboiled thriller and the detective novel, of Raymond Chandler and Agatha Christie, but he updates Chandler and Christie to postmodern America and his gumshoe narrator has a sharp eye for the energy and oddity of the contemporary U.S.A.

Most of Friedman's novels are set in Manhattan and provide a kind of metropolitan picaresque as their hero follows complicated trails of crime across the city. His tone and manner were immediately established by his first book, *Greenwich Killing Time*, in 1986. Seeking to solve a murder in which the corpse is found holding eleven pink roses, Kinky takes a voyage into the lower depths of New York in pursuit of a strange group of suspects. In his second novel, *A Case of Lone Star*, he investigates a series of murders of performers at a country and western cafe in Manhattan, while in his third, *When the Cat's Away*, a friend's stolen cat leads him into a world of murders, gang warfare and illicit drugs trading.

With his fourth novel, *Frequent Flyer*, Friedman extends the reach of his work. Although Kinky is still largely based in New York, his visit to a friend's funeral in Cleveland, Ohio, where he seems to be the only person to notice that the body in the coffin is that of a total stranger, leads him into what he himself calls a grotesque puzzle that stretches back nearly fifty years to the Nazi era and spans three continents. In *Musical Chairs* the members of Kinky's own former band, the Texas Jewboys, are the murder targets, which understandably sharpens his investigative zeal, while in *Elvis, Jesus and Coca-Cola* the victim is a maker of documentary films about Elvis impersonators.

Armadillos and Old Lace sees Kinky, unusually, leaving New York for Texas, where he investigates a series of deaths of elderly ladies, while in *The Love Song of J. Edgar Hoover*, a wife—in what Kinky recognizes as one of the most stereotyped of thriller devices—asks him to find her missing husband and starts him off on a complex inquiry that takes him to New York and Chicago. In *Roadkill*, he sets out to save an old friend from a Native American curse, while *Blast from the Past*, as its title suggests, returns to his younger days in New York, recalling his transformation from country singer to detective and the origins of his ''Village Irregulars,'' McGovern, Rambam, and Ratso. *Spanking Watson* pursues the theme of the Village Irregulars when Kinky tries to find out which of the three would best serve as his Dr. Watson by asking each of them to find out who wrote a death threat to the teacher of the lesbian dance class that practices in the room above his loft; the writer of the threat is Kinky himself—but he then discovers that the teacher is really under threat from another, unknown source.

Friedman's fiction is not to everyone's taste. His novels are carried on his persona rather than on their plots, and the plots are not, in themselves, compelling—indeed, they can sometimes seem to be simply a pretext for the display of Kinky's personality. The other characters in his novels are very much refracted to us through that personality rather than emerging in their own right. Readers who find the personality engaging will enjoy the novels; others may find it oppressive or offensive. But there can be no doubt that Kinky Friedman has put an inimitable stamp upon the mystery thriller of the 1980s and 1990s and has acquired a devoted following. It remains to be seen whether his future work will continue to play variations on his well-established formulae or develop in new directions.

—Nicolas Tredell

FRUCHT, Abby

Nationality: American. **Born:** Huntington, New York, 27 April 1957. **Education:** Washington University, A.B. 1979. **Family:** Married Michael Zimmerman; one son. **Career:** Writer in residence, Cleveland State University, Cleveland, Ohio, 1988. **Awards:** Ohio Aid to Individual Artists fellowship, 1985; National Endowment for the Arts fellowship, 1987; short fiction award (University of Iowa Press), 1988. **Agent:** Tom Hart, 20 Kenwood Street, Boston, Massachusetts 02124, U.S.A. **Address:** 152 South Cedar Street, Oberlin, Ohio 44074, U.S.A.

Publications

Novels

Snap. New York, Ticknor & Fields, 1988.
Licorice: A Novel. St. Paul, Minnesota, Graywolf Press, 1990.
Are You Mine? New York, Grove Press, 1993.
Life Before Death. New York, Scribner, 1997.
Polly's Ghost: A Novel. New York, Scribner, 2000.

Short Stories

Fruit of the Month. Iowa City, University of Iowa Press, 1988.

* * *

Abby Frucht is a mistress of minutiae. In her novels and stories, love, lust, commitment, and betrayal are driven by detail. That oft-repeated dictum of fiction writing courses—''show not tell''—rules the roost in Frucht's work. She creates understated, highly visual worlds in the tradition of Anne Beattie: light on plot, heavy on tastes and smells and glimpses and the pondering of possibilities.

In her short story collection, *Fruit of the Month*, the character's epiphanies reside in sensual impression. In ''How to Live Alone,'' the newly-widowed Nancy is trailed by a sense of her late husband's egocentric presence until she discovers a hidden stash of marijuana. While high, she rubs lotion into her skin and ''watches as the cream disappears beneath her hands, into her skin, which has a reptilian look from the salt and sun.'' This moment of sensual indulgence allows her to keep her husband's ghost—and an eager male lover—at bay. She feels ''self-absorbed and private,'' able to dream of a future all her own. In ''Nuns in Love,'' Cynthia comes to accept the pretentious man who's courting her when she discovers they both appreciate pigeons, with their ''noble heads.'' In ''Fate and the Poet,'' the protagonist is so disappointed by her husband's gift, a tacky wilderness calendar—''the slick, bright images make her miserable''—that she's tempted to pursue a poet with whom she had an affair many years before. The question Frucht seems to pose is: are these sensually-inspired epiphanies frivolous, or born out of such deep existential angst that the sensual is the only way these characters can connect with the world?

In *Snap*, her first novel, Frucht lets Ida, one of her main characters, wise up to the potential emptiness of sensual impression. Her husband, Ruby, is so smitten with her that everything she does is a small miracle, including breaking an egg: ''Ruby had never considered that such an act … could be so moving.'' Ida is put off: ''I've turned my husband into a maniac. The way he touches me in bed, like a piece of Steuben glass.'' But this is also a woman who makes wedding cakes. When her husband engages in an affair she's practically wished upon him, she wants him back. Her desire to reunite with him is expressed through her gorging on a wedding cake, ''the most beautiful she has ever made.''

Much of Frucht's work is preoccupied with the shortcomings and triumphs of monogamy and the ways it satisfies the yearning for stability, yet cannot conquer the fundamental instability of desire. *Licorice* gives this theme a magical realism twist. Scores of people, initially women, are vanishing from a small midwestern town, driven by their desire for the sensual unknown. Liz, a temporary letter carrier, does not leave her husband and son, though she is drifting away from them emotionally. She sublimates her own lust for a local redneck by consuming unhealthy quantities of licorice. Here Frucht's juxtaposition of the serious with the frivolous raises the question: Is desire a primal force that mysteriously sucks us away from what we thought we were committed to? Or is it like candy—tempting, silly, unhealthy (but not very), all about sweet sensation and eroding tooth enamel?

In *Are You Mine?* Frucht takes her investigation of the nature of desire into new territory. In her earlier works, her characters are caught up in the offerings of their lovers. The poet in ''Fate and the Poet'' is imagined to offer a life of glamour and freedom; the redneck in *Licorice* represents ''something primitive.'' In *Are You Mine?* Frucht explores unintended pregnancy as the ultimate unknown possibility, the fetus a *tabula rasa* ready to be inscribed with Cara's love and dreams. Frucht reveals the many ways desire can, both literally and figuratively, determine an existence. As Cara considers whether to have an abortion, she can want or not want this baby, humanize or not humanize it. Isn't this what Frucht's earlier protagonists do with the lovers they take and abandon? To Ruby in *Snap*, Linelle fulfills him until he realizes he wants to return to his wife.

Then she is forgotten, her tears unheard, her importance in his life aborted.

In *Life Before Death*, the sensuousness of life takes on an existential importance for Isobel, who discovers she's dying of cancer. Herbal tea—the ultimate symbol of dilute sensation—is no longer enough for her. Where once ''she thought the steaming mug contained all that was required of the whole galaxy, a swirling hot eddy of subtle tart flavor,'' now it is the ''shard'' in her breast that determines her universe. The cancer is both destructive and sexy; as it kills her it serves her as a metaphor of her own untapped wildness. The lump in her breast, her ''surprise,'' ''spread(s) rapturously through me.'' Frucht's prose in *Life Before Death* is more startling and less understated than ever before. Frucht's investment in minutiae undergoes a radical transformation; by exploring the true minutiae of life, the cell-level ravages in a cancer victim, Frucht tackles the greatest of paradoxes: the will to live despite the certainty of death.

In *Polly's Ghost* Frucht further develops the suburban magical realism she first explored in *Licorice*. Polly is a ghost who longs to participate in the life of the son she died giving birth to. As the prospect of death emboldens *Life Before Death*'s Isobel, the ''real thing'' transforms the always-in-control living Polly with the over-eager, awkward dead one. She's the sort of ghost who, while attempting to entertain her son with a falling meteor, crashes a plane into a lake. Despite this ethereal clumsiness, Polly embodies our ultimate fantasy about the dead: that they are pure feeling, missing us and caring for us just as fiercely as we do them. In *Life Before Death*, Isobel describes a row of old-fashioned porcelain dolls, recently burned by a museum fire, as ''more alive dead than alive.'' It's a description Isobel herself will fit once the cancer slays her and all we're left with is the memory of her vibrant spirit. Polly, too, is at her best once she's a ghost, struggling to connect with the world in a way she never could while alive.

—Lisa A. Phillips

G

GAINES, Ernest J(ames)

Nationality: American. **Born:** Oscar, Louisiana, 15 January 1933. **Education:** Vallejo Junior College; San Francisco State College, 1955–57, B.A. 1957; Stanford University, California (Stegner fellow, 1958), 1958–59. **Military Service:** Served in the United States Army, 1953–55. **Career:** Writer-in-residence, Denison University, Granville, Ohio, 1971, Stanford University, Spring 1981, and Whittier College, California, 1982. Since 1983 professor of English and writer-in-residence, University of Southwestern Louisiana, Lafayette. **Awards:** San Francisco Foundation Joseph Henry Jackson award, 1959; National Endowment for the Arts grant, 1966; Rockefeller grant, 1970; Guggenheim grant, 1970; Black Academy of Arts and Letters award, 1972; San Francisco Art Commission award, 1983; American Academy award, 1987; National Book Critics Circle award, 1994, and Pulitzer prize, 1994, both for *A Lesson Before Dying.* D.Litt.: Denison University, 1980; Brown University, Providence, Rhode Island, 1985; Bard College, Annandale-on-Hudson, New York, 1985; Louisiana State University, Baton Rouge 1987; D.H.L.: Whittier College, 1986. **Agent:** JCA Literary Agency, 242 West 27th Street, New York, New York 10001. **Address:** 128 Buena Vista Boulevard, Lafayette, Louisiana 70503–2059, U.S.A.

PUBLICATIONS

Novels

Catherine Carmier. New York, Atheneum, 1964; London, Secker and Warburg, 1966.
Of Love and Dust. New York, Dial Press, 1967; London, Secker and Warburg, 1968.
The Autobiography of Miss Jane Pittman. New York, Dial Press, 1971; London, Joseph, 1973.
In My Father's House. New York, Knopf, 1978.
A Gathering of Old Men. New York, Knopf, 1983; London, Heinemann, 1984.
A Lesson Before Dying. New York, Knopf, 1993.

Short Stories

Bloodline. New York, Dial Press, 1968.

Uncollected Short Stories

''The Turtles,'' in *Transfer* (San Francisco), 1956.
''Boy in the Doublebreasted Suit,'' in *Transfer* (San Francisco), 1957.
''My Grandpa and the Haint,'' in *New Mexico Quarterly* (Albuquerque), Summer 1966.

Other

A Long Day in November (for children). New York, Dial Press, 1971.
Porch Talk with Ernest Gaines, with Marcia Gaudet and Carl Wooton. Baton Rouge, Louisiana State University Press, 1990.

*

Manuscript Collection: Dupree Library, University of Southwestern Louisiana, Lafayette.

Critical Studies: ''Human Dignity and Pride in the Novels of Ernest Gaines'' by Winifred L. Stoelting, in *CLA Journal* (Baltimore), March 1971; ''Ernest J. Gaines: Change, Growth, and History'' by Jerry H. Bryant, in *Southern Review* (Baton Rouge, Louisiana), October 1974; ''Bayonne ou le Yoknapatawpha d'Ernest Gaines'' by Michel Fabre in *Recherches Anglaises et Américaines 9* (Strasbourg), 1976; ''To Make These Bones Live: History and Community in Ernest Gaines's Fiction'' by Jack Hicks, in *Black American Literature Forum* (Terre Haute, Indiana), Spring 1977; ''Ernest Gaines: 'A Long Day in November''' by Nalenz Puschmann, in *The Black American Short Story in the 20th Century* edited by Peter Bruck, Amsterdam, Grüner, 1978; ''The Quarters: Ernest J. Gaines and the Sense of Place'' by Charles H. Rowell, in *Southern Review* (Baton Rouge, Louisiana), Summer 1985; *Critical Reflections on the Fiction of Ernest J. Gaines,* edited by David C. Estes. Athens, University of Georgia Press, 1994; *Wrestling Angels into Song: The Fictions of Ernest J. Gaines and James Alan McPherson* by Herman Beavers. Philadelphia, University of Pennsylvania Press, 1995; *Ernest J. Gaines: A Critical Companion* by Karen Carmean. Westport, Connecticut, Greenwood Press, 1998.

Ernest J. Gaines comments:

I have tried to show you a world of my people—the kind of world that I came from.

* * *

The fictive world of Ernest J. Gaines, as well as certain technical aspects of his works, might be compared to that of William Faulkner. But useful as such a comparison may be, it should not be pursued to the point of obscuring Gaines's considerable originality, which inheres mainly in the fact that he is Afro-American and very much a spiritual product, if no longer a resident, of the somewhat unique region about which he writes: south Louisiana, culturally distinguishable from the state's Anglo-Saxon north, thus from the nation as a whole, by its French legacy, no small part of which derives from the comparative ease with which its French settlers and their descendants formed sexual alliances with blacks.

Gaines's Afro-American perspective enables him to create, among other notable characters both black and white, a Jane Pittman (*The Autobiography of Miss Jane Pittman*) whose heroic perseverance we experience, rather than a housekeeping Dilsey (*The Sound and the Fury*) for whom we have little more than the narrator's somewhat ambiguous and irrelevant assurance that ''She endured.'' In general, Gaines's peculiar point of view generates a more complex social vision than Faulkner's, an advantage Gaines has sustained with dramatic force and artistic integrity. Gaines's fictive society consists of whites, blacks, and creoles, presumably a traditionally more favored socio-economic class of African American given to fantasies of racial superiority to those of darker skin, fantasies of the kind the Martinican psychiatrist Frantz Fanon explores in *Black Skin, White Masks.*

The Gainesian counterparts of the Sartorises and Snopeses (the moribund aristocracy and parvenu ''poor white trash'' respectively of Faulkner's mythical Mississippi county) are the south Louisiana plantation owners, mostly of French extraction, and the cajuns, of French extraction but of lesser ''quality.'' The cajuns are inheriting and spoiling the land and displacing the creoles and blacks, the former tragically though not irrevocably doomed by a persistent folly, the latter a people of promise who have never really betrayed their African heritage.

All Gaines's works reflect the inherent socio-economic intricacy of this quadruplex humanity, though we are never allowed to lose sight of its basic element of black and white. In his apprentice first novel *Catherine Carmier,* for instance, we see the sickly proscribed love of Jackson, who is black, and Catherine, daughter of an infernally proud creole farmer, as a perverted issue of the miscegenation that resulted from the white male's sexual exploitation of black people. This mode of victimization assumes metaphoric force in Gaines's works, figuring forth in historical perspective the oppression of black people generally. The fictive plantation world, then, is uniquely micro-cosmic. It is south Louisiana, the south, the nation as a whole. This aspect is explored, for example, in the title story of *Bloodline.* Copper, a character of mythopoeic proportion, the militant young son of a now deceased white plantation owner and a black woman field hand, stages a heroic return, presumably from his education in school and in the world at large, to claim his heritage: recognition of kinship by an aristocratic white uncle and his rightful share of the land. In *In My Father's House,* and for the first time, Gaines deals with the black father-son relationship, and explores a neglected aspect of African American life: the perplexities of the public vs. private person relative to individual responsibility. The Reverend Phillip Martin, a grass roots Civil Rights leader in the fictional south Louisiana town of St. Adrienne, is forced to confront his wayward past when his estranged son Etienne, reminiscent of Copper, comes to claim paternal recognition and redress of grievances.

In *A Gathering of Old Men* Gaines extends the thematic concerns of his earlier novels into a new South setting, employing a multiple first-person point of view in the manner of Faulkner's *As I Lay Dying.* The conflict between blacks and cajuns comes to a cinematically stylized, somewhat surrealistic climax and resolution as several old black men gather in mutual militant defense of one of their number who has been accused of killing Cajun farmer Beau Boutan, confronting the local sheriff as well as the slain man's avenging father, ''retired'' nightrider Fix Boutan. The result is a gripping allegorical tale of race relations in the new South resonant with the Gainesian theme of individual responsibility, this time for holding ground in the wake of the civil rights gains of the 1960s and 1970s.

In Gaines's 1993 novel *A Lesson Before Dying,* set in 1940, individual responsibility is highlighted again. Wiggins, the novel's narrator, is a young school teacher and one among a number of Gainesian tutelary figures. Wiggins is pressured by his elders into assuming the responsibility of mentor to Jefferson, a young black manchild who awaits execution for having taken part in the murder of a white storekeeper, a crime for which he is apparently unjustly convicted in a racist environment. A National Book Critics Circle award winner and recipient of the Pulitzer Prize for fiction in 1994, *A Lesson* chronicles the young Jefferson's gradual assumption of responsibility, under Wiggins's increasingly committed mentorship, for assimilating the attributes of manhood before he dies in the electric chair. In one of Gaines's characteristic ironies, Wiggins's mentorship of Jefferson contributes to his own edification as well.

—Alvin Aubert

GALLANT, Mavis

Nationality: Canadian. **Born:** Mavis de Trafford Young in Montreal, Quebec, 11 August 1922. **Education:** Schools in Montreal and New York. **Career:** Worked in Montreal, early 1940s; reporter, Montreal *Standard,* 1944–50; has lived in Europe since 1950, and in Paris from early 1960s. Writer-in-residence, University of Toronto, 1983–84. **Awards:** *Canadian Fiction* prize, 1978; Governor-General's award, 1982; Canada-Australia literary prize, 1984; Canada Council Molson Prize for the Arts, 1997; Medaille de la Ville de Paris, 1999. Honorary degrees: Université Sainte-Anne, Pointe-de-l'église, Nova Scotia, 1984; Queen's University, 1992; University of Montreal, 1995; Bishop's University, 1995. Officer, Order of Canada, 1981. **Agent:** Georges Borchardt Inc., 136 East 57th Street, New York, New York 10022, U.S.A. **Address:** 14 rue Jean Ferrandi, 75006 Paris, France.

PUBLICATIONS

Novels

Green Water, Green Sky. Boston, Houghton Mifflin, 1959; London, Deutsch, 1960.

A Fairly Good Time. New York, Random House, and London, Heinemann, 1970.

Short Stories

The Other Paris. Boston, Houghton Mifflin, 1956; London, Deutsch, 1957.

My Heart Is Broken: Eight Stories and a Short Novel. New York, Random House, 1964; as *An Unmarried Man's Summer,* London, Heinemann, 1965.

The Pegnitz Junction: A Novella and Five Short Stories. New York, Random House, 1973; London, Cape, 1974.

The End of the World and Other Stories. Toronto, McClelland and Stewart, 1974.

From the Fifteenth District: A Novella and Eight Short Stories. New York, Random House, and London, Cape, 1979.

Home Truths: Selected Canadian Stories. Toronto, Macmillan, 1981; New York, Random House, and London, Cape, 1985.

Overhead in a Balloon: Stories of Paris. Toronto, Macmillan, 1985; London, Cape, and New York, Random House, 1987.

In Transit: Twenty Stories. Markham, Ontario, Viking, 1988; New York, Random House, 1989; London, Faber, 1990.

Across the Bridge: Stories. New York, Random House, 1993.

The Collected Stories of Mavis Gallant. New York, Random House, 1996.

Plays

What Is to Be Done? (produced Toronto, 1982). Montreal, Quadrant, 1984.

Other

The Affair of Gabrielle Russier, with others. New York, Knopf, 1971; London, Gollancz, 1973.
Paris Notebooks: Essays and Reviews. London, Bloomsbury, and New York, Random House, 1988.

*

Bibliography: By Judith Skelton Grant and Douglas Malcolm, in *The Annotated Bibliography of Canada's Major Authors 5* edited by Robert Lecker and Jack David, Downsview, Ontario, ECW Press, 1984.

Manuscript Collection: Fisher Library, University of Toronto.

Critical Studies: ''Mavis Gallant Issue'' of *Canadian Fiction 28* (Prince George, British Columbia), 1978; *Mavis Gallant: Narrative Patterns and Devices* by Grazia Merler, Ottawa, Tecumseh Press, 1978; *The Light of Imagination: Mavis Gallant's Fiction* by Neil K. Besner, Vancouver, University of British Columbia Press, 1988; *Reading Mavis Gallant* by Janice Kulyk Keefer, Oxford, Oxford University Press, 1989; *Figuring Grief: Gallant, Munro, and the Poetics of Elegy* by Karen E. Smythe, Montreal, McGill Queens' University Press, 1992; *Mavis Gallant by Danielle Schaub.* New York, Twayne, 1998.

* * *

The characters who move through the fiction of Mavis Gallant are unwilling exiles and victims, born or made. Her first collection of short stories, *The Other Paris,* clearly sets the tone of her work: in a series of impersonal, almost clinical sketches the lonely and displaced struggle against an indifferent or hostile world. A naive American girl, engaged to a dull American in Paris, wonders why her colorless days have no connection with the legendary ''other Paris'' of light and civility; a pathetic American army wife in Germany faces her stale marriage and a rootless future; a bitter, unforgiving set of brothers and sisters gathers after the funeral of their mother, a dingy Romanian shopkeeper in Montreal; a cow-like Canadian girl with Shirley Temple curls is repeatedly deceived by seedy fiancés; a traveler staying in a Madrid tenement watches a petty bureaucrat trying to justify the new order ''to which he has devoted his life and in which he must continue to believe.'' These anti-romantic glimpses of dislocation and despair are rendered in deliberately hard, dry prose, reminiscent, like their subject matter, of Joyce's *Dubliners.* The narrative manner is flat, unadorned, without any relieving touches of wit—or, it seems, compassion (save for the best of the stories, ''Going Ashore,'' in which a sensitive child is dragged from port to port by a desperate, amoral mother). Although there is an admirable consistency of theme and feeling in these stories, and a high degree of professional skill, there is little here to suggest the brilliance of Gallant's later work and her gradual mastery of longer, more demanding fictional forms.

The title of the next collection, *My Heart Is Broken,* reveals a continuation of the same concerns. Yet there is a good deal more vigor here, and an indication as well that the author, if not her characters, may be taking some pleasure in the sharpness of her perceptions. There is also the first clear suggestion of a problem which is to become of major importance in Gallant's later work: the eccentricity and near-madness to which her losers may be driven by want or isolation. Gallant has an appallingly accurate eye for the desperation of the shabby genteel, the Englishwomen who live at the edge of poverty in unfashionable pensions out of season, and a shrewd eye as well for the vulgarities of those who try to keep up the pretense of well being. And there is at least one completely successful story, ''An Unmarried Man's Summer'' which manages to combine many of the earlier preoccupations with a degree of wit and energy not present before.

Gallant's first experiment with longer fiction, *Green Water, Green Sky,* despite a vivid central section, suffers from an uncertainty of focus. Three of the four parts of the novella offer peripheral views of the breakdown of a young American wife, raised abroad and now living in Paris. The reasons for her drift into madness are never fully explained, although the blame must in part rest with a vain and foolish mother. Florence remains an intriguing and pathetic puzzle; our questions are unanswered, our sympathies largely unresolved. A second short novel, ''Its Image on the Mirror'' (*My Heart Is Broken*), is an unqualified success, partly because the point of view is strictly limited to one character—a device which is the source of some ambiguity here as well as consistency. The faintly repressed family hostilities which have appeared in various guises in the earlier work are now given sustained treatment. The narrator, Jean, who has always suffered from a sense of drabness and compromise in contrast to her beautiful younger sister, tries to come to terms with her ambivalent feelings. After years of apparent freedom and romance the spoiled Isobel makes what seems to be an unhappy and confining marriage; looking back, Jean is able to move towards compassion and acceptance. But to what degree is she using the narrative as a kind of revenge for the years she was forced to take second place? Is her sympathy finally untainted by satisfaction? The reader has no means of deciding, precisely because the author makes no comments on Jean's reminiscences. The uncertainty we feel at the end of the work, however, is entirely appropriate: Jean herself is still divided between love, pity and jealousy.

A Fairly Good Time is a splendidly complex full-length novel. Again the plot is familiar and simple in outline: a well-off, still young Canadian woman passes over the borders of sanity as her second marriage, to a Parisian journalist, dissolves. The reasons for her collapse, again, are hinted at rather than developed: an eccentric, domineering mother, a happy first marriage cruelly ended by a freak accident, the frustrating sense of isolation in a foreign world of would-be intellectuals and amoral opportunists—all of these play a partial role. This time, however, Gallant operates directly inside the mind of her heroine, and the result is a spectacular *tour de force:* the writing is disconcertingly vivid, full of the unmediated poetry of near-hallucination, yet nothing is irrelevant or misplaced. Shirley's madness has a kind of honesty about it which attracts the users and manipulators around her. The sane world of her husband's family and the Maurel family, into whose civil wars she is thrust, seems finally to offer much less integrity than her own world of memories and fantasies. At the conclusion there is just a hint that Shirley may be returning to reality, as she learns to moderate her hopes: ''if you make up your mind not to be happy,'' runs the epigraph from Edith Wharton, ''there's no reason why you shouldn't have a fairly good time.''

There are no ideas in Gallant's work, no set of theses. The strong and willful may or may not succeed; the sensitive will almost certainly pay for their gifts. And if they endure, as Shirley may, or as Jean does in ''Its Image on the Mirror,'' the only wisdom is a kind of expensive stoicism:

> We woke from dreams of love remembered, a house recovered and lost, a climate imagined, a journey never made .... We would waken thinking the earth must stop now, so that we could be shed from it like snow. I knew, that night, we would not be shed, but would remain, because that is the way it was. We would survive, and waking—because there was no help for it—forget our dreams and return to life.

This is not exactly hopeful, but neither is it completely despairing: perhaps if we learned to moderate our hopes we might have a fairly good time. But Gallant's more recent collections *The Pegnitz Junction* and *From the Fifteenth District* seem to deny even this modest possibility. The mood here is that of *The Other Paris;* the effect is considerably more oppressive, however, since Gallant has extended the range of her style. The relatively dry, understated manner of the first books has now been replaced by a highly poetic technique in which feelings are conveyed by sudden, uncanny, and yet astonishingly precise images. Yet as before, her characters do not act, they are acted upon; they suffer, but in the end it hardly seems to matter. Life dwindles away and with it everything which gave pleasure, so perhaps nothing had much substance to begin with. The conclusion of ''An Autobiography'' (*The Pegnitz Junction*) is typical. A middle-aged woman thinks about her failure to hold onto the love of a shiftless young man called Peter (the cause of the failure is left undefined, these things just ''happen''):

> These are the indecisions that rot the fabric, if you let them. The shutter slams to in the wind and sways back; the rain begins to slant as the wind increases. This is the season for mountain storms. The wind rises, the season turns; no autumn is quite like another. The autumn children pour out of the train, and the clouds descend upon the mountain slopes, and there we are with walls and a ceiling to the village. Here is the pattern on the carpet where he walked, and the cup he drank from. I have learned to be provident. I do not waste a sheet of writing paper, or a postage stamp, or a tear. The stream outside the window, deep with rain, receives rolled in a pellet the letter to Peter. Actually, it is a blank sheet on which I intended to write a long letter about everything—about Véronique. I have wasted a sheet of paper. There has been such a waste of everything; such a waste.

''The only way to be free,'' reflects one of the battered characters in *From the Fifteenth District,* ''is not to love.'' This is the freedom of isolation, madness, and death, but perhaps any escape from being is preferable to the pain of living. Thus Piotr, for example, the central figure in the novella ''Potter,'' welcomes the imagined prospect of his death: ''Oh, to be told that there were only six weeks to live! To settle scores; leave nothing straggling, to go quietly.'' Yet even death may offer no release. In ''From the Fifteenth District,'' a truly harrowing prose-poem—it can hardly be called a story—the pathetic ghosts of the dead complain to the ''authorities'' that the memories of life and the intrusions of the still-living make any final rest impossible.

—Elmer Borklund

GALLOWAY, Janice

Nationality: Scottish. **Born:** Kilwinning, Scotland, 2 December 1956. **Education:** Glasgow University, M.A. 1978. **Family:** Has one son. **Career:** Welfare rights worker, 1976–77; teacher of English, Strathclyde Regional Council, Ayrshire, Scotland, 1980–89. **Awards:** Scottish Arts Council book award, 1990, and MIND book of the year/Allan Lane award, 1991, both for *The Trick Is to Keep Breathing; Cosmopolitan*/Perrier award, 1991, for short story writing; Scottish Arts Council book award, 1991, for *Blood*; E. M. Forster award in literature (American Academy of Arts and Letters), 1994; McVitie's prize for Scottish Writer of the Year, 1994; *Times Literary Supplement* research fellow, British Library, 1999. **Agent:** Cathie Thomson, 23 Hillhead Street, Hillhead, Glasgow G12 8PX, Scotland. **Address:** 25 Herriet Street, P.O. Hokshields, Glasgow G41 2NN, Scotland.

Publications

Novel

The Trick Is to Keep Breathing. Edinburgh, Polygon, 1989; Normal, Illinois, Dalkey Archive Press, 1994.

Foreign Parts. London, Vintage, 1995; Normal, Illinois, Dalkey Archive Press, 1995.

Where You Find It. London, Jonathan Cape, 1996.

Short Stories

Blood. London, Secker and Warburg, and New York, Random House, 1991.

Other

Editor, with Hamish Whyte, *New Writing Scotland 8.* Aberdeen, Aberdeen University Press, 1990.

Editor, with Hamish Whyte, *Scream, If You Want to Go Faster.* Aberdeen, Association for Scottich Literary Studies, 1991.

Editor, with Marion Sinclair, *Meantime.* N.p., 1991.

Editor, with Hamish Whyte, *Pig Squealing.* Aberdeen, Association for Scottich Literary Studies, 1992.

Editor, with Hamish Whyte, *New Writing Scotland 9.* Aberdeen, Aberdeen University Press, 1991.

Editor, with Hamish Whyte, *New Writing Scotland 10.* Aberdeen. Aberdeen University Press, 1992.

* * *

Hailed by novelist John Hawkes as ''a Scottish Poe of the lower middle class,'' Janice Galloway writes a grimly detached yet eerily familiar fiction that combines minimalist style, formal innovation, contemporary subject matter, and Gothic sensibility. In a bleak and sometimes blackly humorous manner, she chronicles various forms of social and psychological oppression, particularly as experienced by women.

The Trick Is to Keep Breathing creates an unnerving atmosphere of fragility and menace as it traces one woman's efforts over the course of several weeks to deal with the death of her married lover. ''This Is the Way Things Are'' in the post-Trollope world of the novel's ironically, indeed oxymoronically named narrator-protagonist, Joy Stone: straitened, empty, in-between in every sense, caught for the most part (as is the reader) in a perpetual, numbing present. On the one hand, Joy is too independent and intelligent to accept the bromides dispensed by the modern therapeutic community; on the other, she cannot entirely escape feeling that she is the problem: inadequate and therefore guilty, insufficiently persistent in her behavior or ''realistic'' in her attitude. Compounding her situation is the fact that she is a woman (depression and suicide run in the family on the female side) and a Scot. ''Love/Emotion = embarrassment: Scots equation. Exceptions are when roaring drunk or watching football. Men do rather better out of this loophole.'' Joy does rather worse in any and all of her roles: teacher, friend, patient, lover, Other Woman, ''harridan,'' and would-be princess awaiting the arrival of her prince.

Withdrawing further into herself, perhaps dangerously so, and out of necessity making do with the little that is financially and psychologically available to her, she fills in the blank that her life has become with writing that proves just as compelling as it is disturbing. At once highly fragmented and omnivorously, obsessively multifarious, her narrative includes the postcards she receives from her one (geographically distant) friend, the replies she writes, the lists she compiles, the pop-song lyrics she hears on the radio, the advice columns she reads in the tabloids, dramatized scenes depicting her brief encounters with others, painful memories, even marginalia. Surveying the contemporary wasteland from her bleak council housing estate on the outskirts of Glasgow, shoring the fragments against the ruin but without benefit of T. S. Eliot's ''mythic method'' and all it metaphysically implies, Joy seems less the latest version of the hysterical woman, the madwoman in the attic, than the female writer in a room not quite her own (it belongs to her dead lover) but able nonetheless to write in a voice at once entirely original yet filled with the echoes of Galloway's literary precursors, chief among them Plath, Kafka, Scheherazade, Stevie Smith, James Kelman, the Dickinson of ''After Great Pain,'' the Beckett of *The Unnamable,* and Krapp's *Last Tape.*

Where Galloway's novel takes something comparatively small and expands it, minutely and almost unbearably, the twenty-two stories that make up *Blood* move in the opposite direction toward an equally intense and unnerving compression. Long or short, Galloway's goal remains the same: giving voice to repressed narratives. In the novel Joy claims that she cannot actually scream; she can only write ''it'' down. In the collection, ''Things stick ... in her throat that she would never say,'' her ''voice full of splinters.'' The five ''Scenes from the Life'' take the form of little plays having little or no dialogue. In ''Two Fragments,'' a woman remembers her mother's macabre versions of how her father lost two fingers and her grandmother an eye—not during the war but while hungrily eating fish and chips, not while breaking a piece of coal but while trying to kill a cat by boiling it alive. ''Faire Ellen and the Wanderer Returned'' retells the Odysseus myth from a contemporary Penelope's point of view. Stories such as ''Love in a Changing Environment'' take literary minimalism to a chilly and chilling extreme, whereas the phantasmagoric ''Plastering the Cracks'' recalls the repressed protagonist of Roman Polanski's *Repulsion.* Throughout the collection there is the sense of trust and especially of innocence betrayed: The father who tricks his young son into falling from the fireplace mantle in order to teach him the lesson, ''Trust nae cunt,'' the woman who comes to the aid of an elderly man who has stumbled only to have him strike out at her. In the title story that opens the collection a young girl's having a tooth extracted becomes a horrific study in female shame, and in the haunting novella-length ''A Week with Uncle Felix'' at collection's end, speechlessness and sexuality come together in a particularly suspenseful and disturbing manner wholly characteristic of Galloway's larger aesthetic and unprogrammatically feminist concerns.

Foreign Parts is, for all its broad hints of comedy—two friends and opposites, Rona and Cassie, take to the French countryside on holiday—imbued with more than a wisp of tragedy. ''The knight on the white charger is never going to come, Rona,'' Cassie says. ''You know why? Because he's down the pub with the other knights, that's why.''

—Robert A. Morace

GANGEMI, Kenneth

Nationality: American. **Born:** Bronxville, New York, 23 November 1937. **Education:** Rensselaer Polytechnic Institute, Troy, New York, B.Mgt.E. 1959; San Francisco State College (now University), California. **Military Service:** Served in the United States Navy, 1960–61. **Family:** Married Jana Fisher in 1961. **Awards:** Stegner fellowship, 1968; PEN grant, 1975; Creative Artists Public Service fellowship, 1976. **Address:** 211 E. Fifth St., New York, New York 10003, U.S.A.

Publications

Novels

Olt. New York, Orion Press, and London, Calder and Boyars, 1969.
Corroboree: A Book of Nonsense. New York, Assembling Press, 1977.
The Volcanoes from Puebla. London, Boyars, 1979.
The Interceptor Pilot. London, Boyars, 1980.

Poetry

Lydia. Los Angeles, Black Sparrow Press, 1970.

* * *

A literary innovator whose works have often had their first appearance in French translation or in British editions, Kenneth Gangemi has distinguished himself as an uncompromising perfectionist whose fiction makes none of those gestures toward popularity that made similar developments part of mainstream American fiction in the later 1960s and 1970s. Without foregrounding techniques or dramatizing his pose as an anti-illusionistic writer, Gangemi has fashioned a style of narrative that at times questions itself comically and always highlights the pleasure of having referential materials from the world being transformed into the makings of literary art.

His short novel *Olt* remains the best introduction to Gangemi's fiction. Although it qualifies as anti-fiction (in the terms of refusing to capitalize on the effects of suspended disbelief), not a single convention of traditional fiction is violated. The characterization of Gangemi's protagonist, Olt, is coherent, and the narrative action of his adventures is linear. Gangemi's style is clear and concise. Yet none of these familiar aspects is used to accomplish the customary aim of narrative. There are no flashes of insight or moments ponderous with great meaning, and certainly no accumulation of wisdom that might add up to a conclusive point. Instead Gangemi fashions a narrative life in which his on-going language constitutes an experiential flow of life, as Olt's existence is generated by the fact that he lives within a sentence structure capable of accommodating an infinite series of actions. ''Olt knew he would never see a meteor striking an iceberg, a bat falling into snow, or a clown on a nun,'' for instance. ''He knew he would never go to a party and talk to thunderstorm experts, roller-coaster experts, vampire experts, sailplane experts, dinosaur experts, or volcano experts. He knew that he would never design bear grottos, furnish a time capsule, live in an orange grove, wade in a vat of mercury,'' and so forth. Even though all of these objects exist in the world, and even though syntax makes it possible to combine them, what readers know about the world confirms that seeing a bat fall into snow is among the unlikeliest of possibilities. Yet these sentences of Gangemi's have linked them linguistically, the word ''not'' preserving the narrative from utter nonsense. Readers can therefore delight in the combinatory action of language without having to suspend disbelief. Free of any obligation to add up to something, these fictive objects can be appreciated in and of themselves.

In *Corroboree*—like *Olt,* a short novel of about sixty pages—Gangemi uses similar found objects to constitute a style. These objects predominate over narrative, and where narrative exists it is often for the sake of a self-referential joke, such as the quickly summarized story of a man who makes a fortune in the shipping industry by realizing cargoes of ping-pong balls need not be insured against sinking. Gangemi's talent for construing off-base situations leads to such real-life observations as noting a woman at the Hong Kong Hilton suggesting a trip to Chinatown and considering the effect of filling a cello with jello. As a result, language is allowed to become its own subject without such artificial devices as concrete forms on the page or devices such as featuring a writer writing a story about a writer writing a story about a writer ....

Gangemi's most successful work is *The Volcanoes from Puebla.* As a transfictional narrative, it combines the most useful aspects of both the novel and the travel memoir by discarding those factors which prove overly determining for each form: in the case of fiction, the need for a developing story, and in the memoir a dedication to the chronology of time and integrity of space. In *The Volcanoes from Puebla,* the only true narrative results from the reader coming to an appreciation of Mexico as a sensual experience, while the autobiographical element of this experience is countered by the adventure being broken down by alphabetical points of reference. The references themselves are various, as idiosyncratic as a system devised by Jorge Luis Borges to show off its own infinite cleverness. While ''Calle Bolivar'' rates a description as a street in Mexico City, so do ''Helmets'' (as part of a motorcyclist's gear) and ''Mexican Day'' (as a reflection on typical daily rhythms). Read in this jigsaw-puzzle manner, the book stresses the materials of experience themselves, apart from any of the typical travelog conventions which by prioritizing such materials tend to falsify the experience. The test of Gangemi's effectiveness as a writer is how well he is able to hold this experience together, fragmented as it is by the alphabetical structure and antisystematics of its categories. Soon the reader sees how the author himself is experiencing Mexico free from traditional constraints—letting buses pass by while he appreciates the pleasure of waiting at the bus stop, seeing a beautiful girl walk by with a baby coati-mundi on her shoulder and not knowing whether to look at her or at the coati-mundi. *The Volcanoes from Puebla* is itself experienced by the reader just this way, free of both fictive narrative and biographical consequence.

The ultimate effect of Gangemi's art is seen in what is his most conventional narrative, a full-length novel titled *The Interceptor Pilot.* Its plot is traditional and has the interest of a politically pertinent action thriller: during the Vietnam War an American pilot volunteers his service in defense of the North against bombing by his own countrymen. The key to this novel is that it is told as simply and as sparely as possible; indeed, the form implied is that of the film treatment, a bare-bones, present-tense indication of how the camera is supposed to capture the action (''The scene is ... ,'' ''The time is ...''). Here Gangemi has taken just the element that his earlier fiction discarded, and now employs it to do the work that in other cases would be accomplished by detailed characterization, careful imagery, and complexly contrived action (all of which the movie treatment assumes will be displayed for the camera). Again like a film *The Interceptor Pilot* ignores every element except what can be seen; being so limited, it must rely on such cinematic devices as montage and quick cutting. What happens in the narrative becomes a dynamic collage in which each object remains itself just as much as it functions as an agent of action: kills stenciled beneath an airplane cockpit railing, a copy of *Le Monde* tossed on the seat of a French journalist's car, TOP SECRET stamped on an Air Force document. Just as the objects of *Olt, Corroboree,* and *The Volcanoes from Puebla* function as narrative and not just referential materials, the lightness and clarity of Gangemi's prose allows similar objects to take on similar artistic importance in *The Interceptor Pilot.*

—Jerome Klinkowitz

GARCIA, Cristina

Nationality: Cuban-American. **Born:** Havana, Cuba (immigrated to United States in 1960), 4 July 1958. **Education:** Barnard College, B.A. 1979. **Family:** Married Scott Brown in 1990; one daughter. **Career:** Reporter and researcher, *Time* magazine, 1983–85, correspondent, 1985–90, bureau chief in Miami, 1987–88. **Awards:** Hodder fellowship (Princeton University), 1992–93; Cintas fellowship, 1992–93; Whiting Writers Award, 1996. **Agent:** Ellen Levine, 15 East 26th Street, Number 1801, New York, New York 10010, U.S.A.

Publications

Novels

Dreaming in Cuban. New York, Knopf, 1992.
The Agüero Sisters. New York, Knopf, 1997.

Other

Cars of Cuba (essay), created by D.D. Allen, photographs by Joshua Greene. New York, Abrams, 1995.

* * *

Cristina Garcia's literary reputation is based on the publication of two novels in the 1990s, *Dreaming in Cuban* and *The Agüero Sisters.* In these two works, she explores similar themes—how the actions of different generations affect each, sibling differences, geographic displacement, political and personal deterioration, delusion, and the implausibility of emotional intimacy between the sexes—though the second work takes a stylistically more mature approach.

Born in Cuba in 1958, Garcia arrived in the United States in 1960 during the first wave of Cuban emigration. She was educated at Barnard College, studied at the School of International Affairs at Johns Hopkins, and worked as a reporter for *Time* magazine. Garcia was the first Cuban-America woman to publish a novel written in English; her work reflects the ongoing sensibility of those Cuban-Americans whose loyalties oscillate between Cuba and the United States.

Dreaming in Cuban focuses on three generations of Cuban and Cuban-American women whose ineffectual spouses and lovers often lead them to delusion and insanity. Women dominate the book, which is written in brief first and third person narratives. The inability of men to satisfy the basic desires of women—sexual and otherwise—leads them to unfulfilled fantasies and obsession. Matriarch Celia continues writing letters to an absent Spanish lover, despite her subsequent marriage and mental deterioration. One of her daughters fantasizes about having sex with ''El Líder,'' as Garcia dubs the phantom Fidel Castro. Madness has led this daughter to dispose of three spouses or lovers by violent means. A second daughter escapes Cuba for the United States after the revolution, grows grotesquely fat, makes unrealistic sexual demands on her husband—who in turn retreats from emotional intimacy—and is haunted by her father's ghost. The third generation is rootless, plagued by and rebelling against a sense of nonspecific loss and political and personal disinterest that perhaps will be overcome only by an exchange of Cuba for the United States or vice-versa, though Garcia ends the book ambiguously. Cuba's political situation comes under a critical microscope, though Garcia interweaves the political and the personal, blaming neither exclusively for the deterioration of the characters' lives. From the opening pages and throughout the book, Garcia undermines assumptions that *Dreaming in Cuban* is a political novel by leading the reader to that assumption and then abruptly switching focus onto the personal events of a character's life, which may take equal blame in the evolution of his or her situation.

The Agüero Sisters is a much more mature effort, focusing to a great extent on personal search and redemption. Though generational effects continue, as in *Dreaming in Cuban*, in *The Agüero Sisters* Garcia pares the story down to that of two sisters, one in the United States, the other in Cuba, and their parents. Men are again ineffectual, though the father, Ignacio, is permitted to speak for himself through diary entries that describe events leading up his wife's murder by his own hand. Madness, delusion, and an overwhelming desire to reach an uncharacterized essence of life through a direct relationship with the earth bring her to abandon her husband and child, humiliating the former. Her actions, his over-intellectualism, and the resulting inability to understand her or meet her needs drive him to murder and suicide. Garcia unfolds the story gradually through the intermittence of the diary entries. *The Agüero Sisters* also benefits from Garcia's linguistic maturity in choosing the appropriate rather than the significant word, as she had done in *Dreaming in Cuban*. Though *Dreaming in Cuban* had a few comic episodes, *The Agüero Sisters* has almost none. The Afro-Cuban religion of santería also plays a smaller role.

Critical reaction to Garcia's work has been limited by the small number of works to date, but has been exceptional. Thulani Davis, reviewing *Dreaming in Cuban* in the *New York Times,* compared Garcia's use of language to that of Louise Erdrich, writing that ''Ms. Garcia has distilled a new tongue from scraps salvaged through upheaval.'' Margarite Fernández Olmos, writing in *Bendíceme, America,* noted the powerful link between politics and Latina sexuality in Garcia's work.

—Harold Augenbraum

GARLAND, Alex

Nationality: English. **Born:** London, England, 1970. **Education:** Attended Manchester University. **Awards:** Betty Trask prize, 1998. **Address:** c/o Putnam Publishing Group, 200 Madison Avenue, New York, New York 10026, U.S.A.

Publications

Novels

The Beach. New York, Riverhead Books, 1997.
The Tesseract. New York, Riverhead Books, 1999.

* * *

Alex Garland creates exotic entertainments that have inspired comparisons to the work of Graham Greene and even Joseph Conrad with their mix of psychological exploration, moral conundrum, and suspenseful plotting. If these comparisons seem a bit generous, they can be seen as the natural consequence of Garland's phenomenal commercial success.

The Beach is a dystopian fantasy rooted in the very rootlessness of contemporary society. It is narrated by a young drifter whose affectless voice masks deep dissatisfactions and troubling, all-too-human drives. When he finds and joins other western culture refugees in a secret island commune off the coast of Thailand, this narrator proves to be the catalyst who ignites an emotional conflagration that destroys their idyll.

The Beach is a familiar tale of a perfected community raised by noble aspirations and felled by basic human failings, a tale whose most notable modern example is William Golding's *Lord of the Flies,* which has also been cited as a discernible precursor to Garland's work, although *The Beach*, for all its dead-on critiques of contemporary life, lacks Golding's primal resonance. Where *Lord of the Flies* plumbed the inherent barbarities of human nature, *The Beach* merely depicts humanity's pervasive pettiness. Indeed, one of the most telling and consequential conflicts in *The Beach* concerns two characters' claims over which of them is the discoverer of a wild mango orchard. Such a conflict might have serious import if starvation were at stake, as it is in *Lord of the Flies,* but *The Beach* is set in a geographic cornucopia of edible flora and fauna, so that the largest consequence of this argument is the loss of dessert and, of course, pride. Another misunderstanding stems from a chaste kiss given to a sick girl, a strangely immature dilemma given the ages of the commune-dwellers and the fact that they all came to this place to ostensibly escape the bounds of society. In fact, of all the appetites given free rein in the commune, the libidinous is hardly even mentioned. As *The Beach* concludes, the prevailing question is not so much how such a perfect place could be so terribly dismantled; it is how such a place ever got built at all.

In *The Tesseract* Garland creates a more complex and more ambitious narrative that still contains enough taut pacing to be packaged, like *The Beach*, as a thriller. Unlike its predecessor, however, *The Tesseract* eschews first-person, linear narration. Instead, Garland constructs and interweaves four separate narrative lines that come together in a violent and nihilistic climax. Set in the Philippines, *The Tesseract* involves a drugged-out English sailor, a Filipino mafioso and his henchmen, a doctor waiting for her husband to come home, a pair of street-urchins, and a grieving psychologist who studies dreams, all in a chase plot lifted right out of hard-boiled pulp.

In terms of craft, *The Tesseract* represents a more formal mode for Garland, as its narration jumps from character to character, often looping back in time to provide context and characterization. Where *The Beach* offered oblique commentary on contemporary life through its characters' use of pop-culture metaphors (the Vietnam War as a movie, death as the end of a video game), *The Tesseract* has a more overt message linked to its title, which refers to a type of shape that is the two-dimensional representation of something that exists in four dimensions, a mathematical construct called a hypercube. As Alfredo, the psychologist, tellingly muses about the shape's significance, Garland makes him an embedded critic of the novel itself, thinking, ''A hypercube is a thing you are not equipped to understand ... This means something ... We can see the thing unraveled but not the thing itself.'' In *The Tesseract*'s climax, this thought is meant to have a kind of prophetic resonance, but it comes off as a redundancy, given Garland's masterful construction itself.

—J.J. Wylie

GARNER, Helen

Nationality: Australian. **Born:** Helen Ford in Geelong, Victoria, 7 November 1942. **Education:** Manifold Heights State School; Ocean Grove State School; The Hermitage, Geelong; Melbourne University, 1961–65, B.A. (honors) 1965. **Family:** Married 1) William Garner in 1968, one daughter; 2) Jean-Jacques Portail in 1980. Teacher, Werribee High School, 1966–67, Upfield High School, 1968–69, and Fitzroy High School, 1971–72, all Victoria; journalist, *Digger,* 1973; lived in Paris, 1978–79. **Career:** Writer-in-residence, Griffith University, Nathan, Queensland, 1983, and University of Western Australia, Nedlands, 1984. Melbourne theater critic, *National Times,* Sydney, 1982–83. Since 1981 feature writer, *Age,* Melbourne. Since 1985 member of the Australia Council Literature Board. **Awards:** Australia Council fellowship, 1978, 1979, 1980, 1983; National Book Council award, 1978; New South Wales Premier's award, 1986. **Address:** 849 Drummond St., North Carlton, Victoria 3054, Australia.

PUBLICATIONS

Novels

Monkey Grip. Melbourne, McPhee Gribble, 1977; London, Penguin, 1978; New York, Seaview, 1981.
Moving Out (novelization of screenplay), with Jennifer Giles. Melbourne, Nelson, 1983.
The Children's Bach. Melbourne, McPhee Gribble, 1984.
Cosmo Cosmolino. Ringwood, Victoria, McPhee Gribble, 1992; London, Bloomsbury, 1993.

Short Stories

Honour, and Other People's Children: Two Stories. Melbourne, McPhee Gribble, 1980; New York, Seaview, 1982.
Postcards from Surfers. Melbourne, McPhee Gribble, 1985; New York, Penguin, 1986; London, Bloomsbury, 1989.
My Hard Heart: Selected Fiction. Ringwood, Victoria, Viking, 1998.

Plays

The Stranger in the House, adaptation of a play by Raymond Demarcy (produced Melbourne, 1982; London, 1986).

Other

La Mama: The Story of a Theatre. Melbourne, McPhee Gribble, 1988.
The First Stone: Some Questions About Sex and Power. Sydney, Pan Macmillan Australia, 1995; New York, Free Press, 1997.
True Stories: Selected Non-Fiction. Melbourne, Australia, Text Publishing, 1996.

*

Critical Study: ''On War and Needlework: The Fiction of Helen Garner'' by Peter Craven, in *Meanjin* (Melbourne), no. 2, 1985; *Helen Garner* by Kerryn Goldsworthy. New York, Oxford University Press, 1996.

* * *

Helen Garner's novels deal with the fractured relationships of ''alternative'' living in Melbourne. Against a background of communes and shared houses, the drug scene, rock bands, cooperative movies, suburb, and beach, her characters try to form relationships and cope with their inevitable failure. Her fiction explores the point at which freedom stops and irresponsibility begins. It is a world in which women with love to spare try to deal with men who have ''the attention span of a stick insect'' who monopolize them one minute and ignore them the next. There is a sympathetic, fatalistic cast to her writing. Most of her characters could be summed up by the line: ''Their mother was dead and they were making a mess of things.'' *Monkey Grip* is Nora's account of her obsessive love for Javo, a junkie. They belong to a subculture where drugs define the real and the tolerable, where there is no tomorrow only today, and therefore where commitments to another person are infinitely redefinable. ''I'm not all that worried about futures. I don't want to love anyone forever.'' Nora's love, her habit of ''giving it all away,'' is as addictive as Javo's heroin habit, and makes her as vulnerable. She supports and is supported by other women, sometimes finding herself consoling or being consoled by a sexual rival. The pain and the jealousy are intense but in the curiously reticent unreticence of this culture, protest about exploitation is limited to declarations as inadequate as, "That makes me feel bad." By the end of the novel Nora has achieved some degree of detachment from Javo, but there is no guarantee that the cycle will not be repeated with another exploitingly helpless male.

Honour, and Other People's Children is a pair of novellas which show characters similar to those in *Monkey Grip* at a later stage in their lives. Each involves separation. In "Honour" a woman who has been separated for five years from her husband is shocked by his asking for a divorce in order to remarry. Instead of the commune life he now wants "a *real* place to live, with a back yard where I can plant vegies, and a couple of walls to paint, and a dog—not a bloody room in a sort of railway station." Despite their five-year separation Elizabeth still feels a residual bonding which is now threatened. Relationships in this book are much more richly delineated than in the first novel. Here they are products of shared experience, shared jokes and personal rituals, family connections and mutual awareness. When Frank's father is about to die, it is Elizabeth who accompanies him on the visit. Their child stands in the middle of an awkward triangle wanting all to live together and not comprehending the nuances and difficulties of the situation. However her instinct is right, and ex-wife and future wife tentatively feel towards some sort of acquaintance, even friendship, symbolized by the balanced seesaw of the story's conclusion.

"Other People's Children" moves the focus away from heterosexual relationships to the declining friendship between two women who have been the nucleus of a shared house, and have gradually become abrasive towards each other. Over years in the same household Scotty has come to love Ruth's daughter, Laurel, and hers is the greatest loss when the house breaks up. Loving other people's children gives no rights, not even the limited access granted to the non-custodian parent by the divorce court. Ruth's relationship with the self-protective Dennis shows the same sort of male manipulation used by Javo in *Monkey Grip,* while Madigan, to whom Scotty turns for companionship, is so torn between misogyny and the need for acceptance that he ranks as the most destructive of Garner's male characters.

The Children's Bach extends Garner's range of characters, and puts them in a new arrangement. Whereas previous novels concentrated on the isolation of characters and on the failures of bonding, this novel offers at least one couple in a successful relationship: "She loved him. They loved each other. They were friends." Dexter and Athena embody an innocence which characters in the earlier novels seem never to have had. Their marriage is stable and caring despite the strains put on it by their retarded second son who has a musical sense but not speech. Set against them are Dexter's old friend from university days, Elizabeth, her lover Philip, and her younger sister, Vicky. There is a clash of values in this novel, and a sense that characters are redefining their perspectives instead of being depicted at a stage when they are already locked into a fixed way of seeing, and surviving in, the world.

Music has always been an important motif in Garner's books, and here it becomes dominant. In earlier works it offered, like sex or drugs, a way of immersion or escape. It is associated with most of the characters in this novel, and it generally suggests sanity and harmony. While Philip uses music to exploit people, it is a mark of Athena's unglamorous dedication to making life work, and of Dexter's uncomplicated gusto.

Postcards from Surfers is a collection of stories which offers vignettes on the ways people relate and report themselves to others. In the title story a woman holidaying with her parents who have retired to the seaside writes a series of postcards to a former lover which she does not post because it's "too late to change it now." Other stories tell of chance meetings, visits, trips in Europe and Australia. Males in this collection continue to be selfish, manipulative, and arrogant but Garner ends some of the stories more hopefully in the manner of *The Children's Bach.* Women trying to make something of their lives ("The Life of Art") are always going to find males unsatisfactory, but they can support each other. Women are always going to be racked by passion for men who want them less continuously and exclusively, but it is possible to "hang on until the spasm passes."

Cosmo Cosmolino, with its eponymous novella and two short stories—all three of which are interrelated—explores themes familiar to Garner's readers, but uses new motifs such as magic realism. Such developments may be an outgrowth of the author's deepened interest in spiritual matters.

—Chris Tiffin

GARRETT, George (Palmer, Jr.)

Nationality: American. **Born:** Orlando, Florida, 11 June 1929. **Education:** Sewanee Military Academy; The Hill School, graduated 1947; Princeton University, New Jersey, 1947–48, 1949–52, B.A. 1952, M.A. 1956, Ph.D. 1985; Columbia University, New York, 1948–49. **Military Service:** Served in the United States Army Field Artillery, 1952–55. **Family:** Married Susan Parrish Jackson in 1952; two sons and one daughter. **Career:** Assistant professor, Wesleyan University, Middletown, Connecticut, 1957–60; visiting lecturer, Rice University, Houston, 1961–62; associate professor, University of Virginia, Charlottesville, 1962–67; writer-in-residence, Princeton University, 1964–65; professor of English, Hollins College, Virginia, 1967–71; professor of English and writer-in-residence, University of South Carolina, Columbia, 1971–73; senior fellow, Council of the Humanities, Princeton University, 1974–77; adjunct professor, Columbia University, 1977–78; writer-in-residence, Bennington College, Vermont, 1979, and University of Michigan, Ann Arbor, 1979–84. Since 1984 Hoyns Professor of English, University of Virginia, Charlottesville. President of Associated Writing Programs, 1971–73. United States poetry editor, *Transatlantic Review,* Rome (later London), 1958–71; Contemporary Poetry Series editor, University of North Carolina Press, Chapel Hill, 1962–68; co-editor, *Hollins Critic,* Virginia, 1965–71; Short Story Series editor, Louisiana State University Press, Baton Rouge, 1966–69. Since 1970 contributing editor, *Contempora,* Atlanta; since 1971 assistant editor, *Film Journal,* Hollins College, Virginia; since 1972 co-editor, *Worksheet,* Columbia, South Carolina; since 1981 editor, with Brendan Galvin, *Poultry: A Magazine of Voice,* Truro, Massachusetts; since 1988 fiction editor, *The Texas Review;* contributing editor, *Chronicles,* Rockford, Illinois. Vice-chancellor, 1987–93, chancellor, 1993–97, Fellowship of Southern Writers. **Awards:** *Sewanee Review* fellowship, 1958; American Academy in Rome fellowship, 1958; Ford grant, for drama, 1960;

National Endowment for the Arts grant, 1967; *Contempora* award, 1971; Guggenheim fellowship, 1974; American Academy award, 1985; New York Public Library Literary Lion award, 1988; T. S. Eliot award, 1989; PEN/Malamud award for short fiction, 1990; Aiken-Taylor award, 1999. Cultural Laureate of Virginia, 1986; Hollins College medal, 1992; University of Virginia President's Report Award, 1992. D. Litt.: University of the South (Sewanee), 1994. **Agent:** Jane Gelfman, John Farquharson Ltd., 250 West 57th Street, New York, New York 10107, U.S.A. **Address:** 1845 Wayside Place, Charlottesville, Virginia 22903, U.S.A.

PUBLICATIONS

Novels

The Finished Man. New York, Scribner, 1959; London, Eyre and Spottiswoode, 1960.
Which Ones Are the Enemy? Boston, Little Brown, 1961; London, W. H. Allen, 1962.
Do, Lord, Remember Me. New York, Doubleday, and London, Chapman and Hall, 1965.
Death of the Fox. New York, Doubleday, 1971; London, Barrie and Jenkins, 1972.
The Succession: A Novel of Elizabeth and James. New York, Doubleday, 1983.
Poison Pen. Winston-Salem, North Carolina, Wright, 1986.
Entered from the Sun. New York, Doubleday, 1990.
The Old Army Game: A Novel and Stories. Dallas, Southern Methodist University Press, 1994.
The King of Babylon Shall Not Come Against You. New York, Harcourt Brace, 1996.
The Elizabethan Trilogy (includes *Death of the Fox, Entered from the Sun,* and *Succession*), edited by Brooke Horvath and Irving Malin. Huntsville, Texas, Texas Review Press, 1998.

Short Stories

King of the Mountain. New York, Scribner, 1958; London, Eyre and Spottiswoode, 1959.
In the Briar Patch. Austin, University of Texas Press, 1961.
Cold Ground Was My Bed Last Night. Columbia, University of Missouri Press, 1964.
A Wreath for Garibaldi and Other Stories. London, Hart Davis, 1969.
The Magic Striptease. New York, Doubleday, 1973.
To Recollect a Cloud of Ghosts: Christmas in England. Winston-Salem, North Carolina, Palaemon Press, 1979.
An Evening Performance: New and Selected Short Stories. New York, Doubleday, 1985.

Uncollected Short Stories

"The Other Side of the Coin," in *Four Quarters* (Philadelphia), (6), 1957.
"The Rare Unicorn," in *Approach* (Wallingford, Pennsylvania), (25), 1957.
"The Only Dragon on the Road," in *Approach* (Wallingford, Pennsylvania), (31), 1959.
"3 Fabliaux," in *Transatlantic Review* (London), (1), 1959.
"The Snowman," in *New Mexico Quarterly* (Albuquerque), (29), 1959.
"Two Exemplary Letters," in *Latitudes* (Houston), (1), 1967.
"Jane Amor, Space Nurse," in *Fly by Night,* 1970.
"There Are Lions Everywhere," "How Can You Tell What Somebody's Thinking on the Telephone," and "Moon Girl," all in *Mill Mountain Review* (Roanoke, Virginia), Summer 1971.
"Here Comes the Bride," in *Gone Soft* (Salem, Massachusetts), (1), 1973.
"Live Now and Pay Later," in *Nassau Literary Magazine* (Princeton, New Jersey), 1974.
"Little Tune for a Steel String Guitar," in *Sandlapper* (Columbia, South Carolina), (9), 1976.
"Soldiers," in *Texas Review* (Huntsville), (3), 1982.
"Wine Talking," in *Quarterly West* (Salt Lake City), (20), 1985.
"Ruthe-Ann," in *Texas Review* (Huntsville), (6), 1985.
"Genius Baby," in *Chattahoochie Review* (Dunwoody, Georgia), 1986.
"Dixie Dreamland," in *South Carolina Review* (Clemson), (19), 1986.
"The Confidence Man," in *Necessary Fictions,* edited by Stanley W. Lindberg and Stephen Corey. Athens, University of Georgia Press, 1986.
"Captain Barefoot Tells His Tale," in *Virginia Quarterly Review* (Charlottesville), Spring 1990.
"Velleities and Vicissitudes," in *Sewanee Review* (Tennessee), Fall 1990.

Plays

Sir Slob and the Princess: A Play for Children. New York, French, 1962.
Garden Spot, U.S.A. (produced Houston, 1962).
Enchanted Ground. York, Maine, Old Gaol Museum Press, 1981.

Screenplays: *The Young Lovers,* 1964; *The Playground,* 1965; *Frankenstein Meets the Space Monster,* with R.H.W. Dillard and John Rodenbeck, 1966.

Television Plays: *Suspense* series, 1958.

Poetry

The Reverend Ghost. New York, Scribner, 1957.
The Sleeping Gypsy and Other Poems. Austin, University of Texas Press, 1958.
Abraham's Knife and Other Poems. Chapel Hill, University of North Carolina Press, 1961.
For a Bitter Season: New and Selected Poems. Columbia, University of Missouri Press, 1967.
Welcome to the Medicine Show: Postcards, Flashcards, Snapshots. Winston-Salem, North Carolina, Palaemon Press, 1978.
Luck's Shining Child: A Miscellany of Poems and Verses. Winston-Salem, North Carolina, Palaemon Press, 1981.
The Collected Poems of George Garrett. Fayetteville, University of Arkansas Press, 1984.
Days of Our Lives Lie in Fragments: New and Old Poems, 1957–1997. Baton Rouge, Louisiana State University Press, 1998.

Other

James Jones (biography). New York, Harcourt Brace, 1984.
Understanding Mary Lee Settle. Columbia, University of South Carolina Press, 1988.
My Silk Purse and Yours: The Publishing Scene and American Literary Art. Columbia, University of Missouri Press, 1992.
The Sorrows of Fat City: A Selection of Literary Essays and Reviews. Columbia, University of South Carolina Press, 1992.
Whistling in the Dark: True Stories and Other Fables. New York, Harcourt Brace, 1992.
Bad Man Blues: A Portable George Garrett. Dallas, Southern Methodist University Press, 1998.
Editor, *New Writing from Virginia.* Charlottesville, Virginia, New Writing Associates, 1963.
Editor, *The Girl in the Black Raincoat.* New York, Duell, 1966.
Editor, with W.R. Robinson, *Man and the Movies.* Baton Rouge, Louisiana State University Press, 1967.
Editor, with R.H.W. Dillard and John Moore, *The Sounder Few: Essays from ''The Hollins Critic.''* Athens, University of Georgia Press, 1971.
Editor, with O.B. Hardison, Jr., and Jane Gelfman, *Film Scripts 1–4.* New York, Appleton Century Crofts, 4 vols., 1971–72.
Editor, with William Peden, *New Writing in South Carolina.* Columbia, University of South Carolina Press, 1971.
Editor, with John Graham, *Craft So Hard to Learn.* New York, Morrow, 1972.
Editor, with John Graham, *The Writer's Voice.* New York, Morrow, 1973.
Editor, with Walton Beacham, *Intro 5.* Charlottesville, University Press of Virginia, 1974.
Editor, with Katherine Garrison Biddle, *The Botteghe Oscure Reader.* Middletown, Connecticut, Wesleyan University Press, 1974.
Editor, *Intro 6: Life As We Know It.* New York, Doubleday, 1974.
Editor, *Intro 7: All of Us and None of You.* New York, Doubleday, 1975.
Editor, *Intro 8: The Liar's Craft.* New York, Doubleday, 1977.
Editor, with Michael Mewshaw, *Intro 9.* Austin, Texas, Hendel and Reinke, 1979.
Editor, with Sheila McMillen, *Eric Clapton's Lovers and Other Stories from the Virginia Quarterly Review.* Charlottesville, University Press of Virginia, 1990.
Editor, with Mary Flinn, *Elvis in Oz: New Stories and Poems from the Hollins Creative Writing Program.* Charlottesville, University Press of Virginia, n.d.
Editor, with Susan Stamberg, *The Wedding Cake in the Middle of the Road.* New York, Norton, 1992.
Editor, with Paul Ruffin, *That's What I Like (About the South).* Columbia, University of South Carolina Press, 1993.

*

Bibliography: In *Seven Princeton Poets,* Princeton University Library, 1963; ''George Garrett: A Checklist of His Writings'' by R.H.W. Dillard, in *Mill Mountain Review* (Roanoke, Virginia), Summer 1971; *George Garrett: A Bibliography 1947–1988* by Stuart Wright, Huntsville, Texas Review Press, 1989.

Manuscript Collection: Duke University, Durham, North Carolina.

Critical Studies: By James B. Meriwether, in *Princeton University Library Chronicle* (New Jersey), vol. 25, no. 1, 1963; ''George Garrett Issue'' of *Mill Mountain Review* (Roanoke, Virginia), Summer 1971; ''Imagining the Individual: George Garrett's *Death of the Fox*'' by W. R. Robinson, in *Hollins Critic* (Hollins College, Virginia), August 1971; ''The Reader Becomes Text: Methods of Experimentation in George Garrett's *The Succession*'' by Tom Whalen, in *Texas Review* (Huntsville), Summer 1983; ''George Garrett and the Historical Novel'' by Monroe K. Spears, in *Virginia Quarterly Review* (Charlottesville), Spring 1985; *To Come Up Grinning: A Tribute to George Garrett* edited by Paul Ruffin and Stuart Wright, Huntsville, Texas Review Press, 1989; *Understanding George Garrett* by R.H.W. Dillard, Columbia, University of South Carolina Press, 1989.

George Garrett comments:

(1972) I feel I am only just beginning, still learning my craft, trying my hand at as many things, as many ways and means of telling as many stories as I'm able to. I hope that this will always be the case, that somehow I'll avoid the slow horror of repeating myself or the blind rigor of an obsession. I can't look back, I'm not ashamed of the work I've done, but it is done. And I am (I hope) moving ahead, growing and changing. Once I've seen something into print I do not re-read it. I have tried always to write out of experience, but that includes imaginative experience which is quite as ''real'' to me and for me as any other and, indeed, in no way divorces from the outward and visible which we often (and inaccurately) call reality. I only hope to continue to learn and to grow. And to share experience with my imaginary reader. I use the singular because a book is a direct encounter, a conversation between one writer and one reader. Though I couldn't care less how many, in raw numbers, read my work, I have the greatest respect for that one imaginary reader. I hope to manage to please that reader before I'm done, to give as much delight, or some sense of it, as I have received from reading good books by good writers.

(1986) Years and scars, and various and sundry books, later, I would not change much in my earlier statement, innocent as it was. Now that I am in my mid-fifties I would not use the word *hope* so much. Naturally I have less hope for myself; though I insist on maintaining high hopes for the best of the young writers I teach. And I have every intention, with and without hope, to continue working, trying to learn my craft always (never to *master* it), still seeking, sometimes finding my imaginary reader. I know more than a decade's worth of darker, sadder things than I did in 1972. So does the world. So goes the world. Well, I have learned a full deck of new jokes, also, and never ceased to taste good laughter. If some hopes have faded and been abandoned, faith, which is altogether something else, has replaced them. And the old dog learns new tricks. One: to turn to the light and live on it until it's gone. Another: to be as open as I can until my book is closed.

(1991) In 1989 I was suddenly 60 years old, older than I had planned to be or ever imagined. Not that a whole lot has changed (I was and am still a viable candidate for the American Tomb of the Unknown Writer); but I did finish my Elizabethan trilogy; and now I have a new publisher and have embarked on three related American novels, coming out of our recent history. I am not planning to live forever, but I would like to finish telling these stories and some others on my mind. Meantime I'm a grandfather and have the pleasure of seeing a generation and a half of former students writing and publishing books on their own. And I am sometimes surprised by the kindness of strangers. The world is not (all claims to the contrary) a kinder or gentler place; but, somewhat to my cynical chagrin, I keep discovering worthy and amazing creatures in it.

(1995) Is there anything to add? Years-now I'm 65 and counting. And still working as hard as I can, hoping to get the work done, hoping, from here on, the work will simply speak for itself.

* * *

Directness, seriousness, a Chaucerian comic sense which in no way conflicts with that seriousness, imaginative vigor, sheer intelligence, and a rich variety of matter and manner—these qualities mark the fiction of George Garrett. An American, a southerner, Garrett has published seven novels, a collection of short novels, five collections of stories (including the major collection of new and selected stories, *An Evening Performance*), seven books of poems (including *The Collected Poems*), plays and screenplays, and a respectable body of critical work (including a biography of James Jones and a monograph on the fiction of Mary Lee Settle). This output reveals his energy and the scope of his interests, and they offer some indication of the seriousness with which he pursues his vocation as writer. Garrett approaches his world and his work with an Elizabethan forcefulness and range, directly and with all his strength.

Garrett is a Christian artist—not a pietist, but a writer whose very sense of the living world is infused with an Augustinian Christian understanding. He is a realist and not a fabulist, but, because of his Christian belief, his work is never far from parable, his direct reality always shaped by the enigmas of the spirit. His seven novels are very different each from each in subject and texture, but together they form a quest for a narrative structure sufficient to the expression of his increasingly more complex view of the ways of the world. *The Finished Man* is a novel of modern Florida politics; *Which Ones Are the Enemy?* takes place in Trieste during the American occupation following World War II; *Do, Lord, Remember Me* concerns the shattering visit of an evangelist to a small Southern town; *Death of the Fox* is an account of the events, exterior and interior, of the last two days of Sir Walter Raleigh's life; *The Succession* is a synoptic recreation of the events surrounding the succession of James I to the throne of Queen Elizabeth; *Poison Pen* (a new novel built upon the ruins of a larger, unfinished novel to have been called *Life with Kim Novak Is Hell*) is an acidly satirical examination of American public lives, illusion and reality, and the real and illusory nature of fiction itself; *Entered from the Sun* is an Elizabethan mystery novel which explores the illusion and impenetrable reality surrounding Christopher Marlowe's death. But they are all products of the same central concerns—a blessing of the dark and fallen world, a knowledge of the power of the imagination to enter that dark world and create and sustain values in it, a faith in the possibility of redemption and salvation even in the very process of the fall into sin and death, and a commitment to the individual moment as the sole window on eternity.

Garrett's major works thus far are the novels in his Elizabethan historical trilogy. In *Death of the Fox* all of his major thematic concerns come together in the person of Ralegh, the soldier, the politician, the sailor, the poet, and the morally creative man. In his imaginative union with Ralegh, Garrett fuses present and past into an artistic whole which is both truth and lie—the disappointing truth which nevertheless burns ideally in the imagination and dreams of the beholder (as in Garrett's earlier short story, ''An Evening Performance'') and the saving lie of love (as in his poem ''Fig Leaves'') which enables us ''to live together.'' *The Succession* both extends and fulfills the stylistic and formal advances of *Death of the Fox* by presenting a thoroughly researched and vividly written account of English and Scottish life in the years succeeding, following, and pivoting upon the succession in 1603, and at the same time developing an aesthetic meditation on the creation and revelation of meaning in the succession of moments that makes up the nexus of time. Set in 1597, *Entered from the Sun* brings the trilogy round full circle, allowing Ralegh to be viewed this time from the outside rather than from within, and commenting both upon the way time conceals truth and the way the fictive imagination attempts to penetrate those concealing veils—commenting, therefore, upon itself and upon the trilogy as a whole.

How he will develop as he moves beyond these major milestones of his career (the Elizabethan trilogy, the collected stories, and the collected poems) is fascinating to contemplate. Garrett has always continued to grow and change in his work while so many of his contemporaries have faltered or simply repeated themselves book after book. His importance becomes clearer year by year as the magnitude of his exploration of reality (outward and inward) reveals itself with each new and startlingly original book.

—R.H.W. Dillard

GASS, William H(oward)

Nationality: American. **Born:** Fargo, North Dakota, 30 July 1924. **Education:** Schools in Warren, Ohio; Kenyon College, Gambier, Ohio, 1942–43, 1946–47, A.B. 1947; Ohio Wesleyan University, Delaware, 1943; Cornell University, Ithaca, New York, 1947–50, Ph.D. 1954. **Military Service:** Served in the United States Navy, 1943–46: Ensign. **Family:** Married 1) Mary Pat O'Kelly in 1952, two sons and one daughter; 2) Mary Alice Henderson in 1969, two daughters. **Career:** Instructor in Philosophy, College of Wooster, Ohio, 1950–54; assistant professor, 1954–60, associate professor, 1960–65, and professor of philosophy, 1966–69, Purdue University, Lafayette, Indiana. Since 1969 professor of philosophy, now David May Distinguished University Professor in the Humanities and director, International Writers Center, both Washington University, St. Louis. Visiting lecturer in English and philosophy, University of Illinois, Urbana, 1958–59. **Awards:** Longview Foundation award, 1969; Rockefeller fellowship, 1965; Guggenheim fellowship, 1969; American Academy award, 1975; Award of Merit medal, 1979; National Book Critics Circle award, for criticism, 1986. L.H.D.: Kenyon College, 1973; George Washington University, Washington, D.C., 1982; Purdue University, 1985. **Member:** American Academy, 1983. **Agent:** International Creative Management, 40 West 57th Street, New York, New York 10019. **Address:** International Writers Center, Campus Box 1071, One Brookings Drive, Washington University, St. Louis, Missouri 63130–4899, U.S.A.

Publications

Novels

Omensetter's Luck. New York, New American Library, 1966; London, Collins, 1967.

Willie Masters' Lonesome Wife (essay-novella). New York, Knopf, 1971.

The Tunnel. New York, Knopf, 1995.
Cartesian Sonata and Other Novellas. New York, Knopf, 1998.

Short Stories

In the Heart of the Heart of the Country and Other Stories. New York, Harper, 1968; London, Cape, 1969.
The First Winter of My Married Life. Northridge, California, Lord John Press, 1979.
Culp. New York, Grenfell Press, 1985.

Uncollected Short Stories

''The Clairvoyant,'' in *Location 2* (New York), 1964.
''The Sugar Crock,'' in *Art and Literature 9* (Paris), 1966.
''We Have Not Lived the Right Life,'' in *New American Review 6,* edited by Theodore Solotaroff. New York, New American Library, 1969.
''The Cost of Everything,'' in *Fiction* (New York), vol. 1, no. 3, 1972.
''Mad Meg,'' in *Iowa Review* (Iowa City), Winter 1976.
''Koh Whistles Up a Wind,'' in *Tri-Quarterly 38* (Evanston, Illinois), 1977.
''Susu, I Approach You in My Dreams,'' in *Tri-Quarterly 42* (Evanston, Illinois), 1978.
''August Bees,'' in *Delta 8* (Montpellier, France), May 1979.
''The Old Folks,'' in *The Best American Short Stories 1980,* edited by Stanley Elkin and Shannon Ravenel. Boston, Houghton Mifflin, 1980.
''Why Windows Are Important to Me,'' in *The Best of Tri-Quarterly,* edited by Jonathan Brent. New York, Washington Square Press, 1982.
''Uncle Balt and the Nature of Being,'' in *The Pushcart Prize 7,* edited by Bill Henderson. Wainscott, New York, Pushcart Press, 1982.
''Family Album,'' in *River Styx.* St. Louis, Big River Association, 1986.

Other

Fiction and the Figures of Life. New York, Knopf, 1970.
On Being Blue. Boston, Godine, 1976; Manchester, Carcanet, 1979.
The World Within the Word: Essays. New York, Knopf, 1978.
The House VI Book, with Peter Eisenman. Boston, Godine, 1980.
Habitations of the Word: Essays. New York, Simon and Schuster, 1985.
Words about the Nature of Things. St. Louis, Washington University, 1985.
A Temple of Texts. St. Louis, Washington University, 1990.
Finding a Form: Essays. New York, Knopf, 1996.
Reading Rilke: Reflections on the Problems of Translation. New York, Knopf, 1999.
Editor, with Lorin Cuoco, *The Writer in Politics.* Carbondale, Southern Illinois University Press, 1996.
Editor, with Lorin Cuoco, *The Writer and Religion.* Carbondale, Southern Illinois University Press, 2000.

*

Bibliography: ''A William H. Gass Bibliography'' by Larry McCaffery, in *Critique* (Atlanta), August 1976.

Manuscript Collection: Washington University Library, St. Louis.

Critical Studies: ''Omensetter's Luck'' by Richard Gilman, in *New Republic* (Washington, D.C.), 7 May 1966; ''The Stone and the Sermon'' by Saun O'Connell, in *Nation* (New York), 9 May 1966; ''Nothing But the Truth'' by Richard Howard, in *New Republic* (Washington, D.C.), 18 May 1968; interview with Thomas Haas in the *Chicago Daily News,* 1 February 1969; *City of Words* by Tony Tanner, London, Cape, and New York, Harper, 1971; ''The Well Spoken Passions of William H. Gass'' by Earl Shorris, in *Harper's* (New York), May 1972; ''But This Is What It Is Like to Live in Hell,'' in *Modern Fiction Studies* (Lafayette, Indiana), Autumn 1974; ''Against the Grain: Theory and Practice in the Work of William H. Gass'' by Ned French, in *Iowa Review* (Iowa City), Winter 1976; *The Metafictional Muse: The Works of Robert Coover, Donald Barthelme, and William H. Gass* by Larry McCaffery, Pittsburgh, University of Pittsburgh Press, 1982.

William H. Gass comments:

I think of myself as a writer of prose rather than a novelist, critic, or storyteller, and I am principally interested in the problems of style. My fictions are, by and large, experimental constructions; that is, I try to make things out of words the way a sculptor might make a statue out of stone. Readers will therefore find very little in the way of character or story in my stories. Working in the tradition of the Symbolist poets, I regard the techniques of fiction (for the contemporary artist) as in no way distinct from the strategies of the long poem.

* * *

William H. Gass, a philosopher and literary critic as well as a fiction writer, derives from and is closely allied to the *symbolistes,* Gertrude Stein, Ortega y Gasset, John Crowe Ransom and the New Critics generally, Borges, Robbe-Grillet, Sarraute, and the structuralists. He believes that language is all in all; that words are not agents to instruct or direct us in fiction but that they exist there for their own sake; that the novelist must keep us imprisoned in his language, because there is nothing beyond it; and that the only events in novels are linguistic events. Metaphor is the means by which concepts are expressed in fiction. The writer, furthermore, does not simply render a world; he makes one out of language, creating imaginary objects and imaginary lives. He works toward the purity of prose fiction and the autonomy of art. He works against the concept of mimesis, that is the imitation of ''reality,'' partly because it is futile for the artist to strive for the illusion of life, and partly because he has no obligation to life. His commitment is to aesthetic satisfaction achieved through metaphorical language; it is to writing as process.

Omensetter's Luck, is accordingly, an exercise in the use of language, which in this instance is a prose that strives constantly to be like poetry or music. The words are better than experience, are, indeed, the experience, and the book is intended to be about language and writing. To give himself ample opportunity to exercise his writing capabilities, Gass designed the novel in three sections, each written in a different mode: the first in the narrative, the second in the lyric, and the third in the rhetorical and dramatic modes. The rhythms and images of the Bible, the baroque qualities of Sir Thomas Browne, the technical virtuosity of Flaubert, the stream of consciousness of Joyce all contribute to the writing of the novel in full freedom from the conventional principles of realism and the traditional values of humanism. Nevertheless, lurking behind this dedication to process are narrative and theme, those Gass-identified enemies to the purity of art. The novel dramatizes a conflict between Omensetter, a natural force who represents being-in-nature, and Jethro Furber, a man of religion and thought, obsessed with death and sex. Attractive as he is, Omensetter demonstrates the inadequacies of mindless and spiritless being, while Furber shows us the failure to fuse successfully word, belief, and action in such a way as to elevate the spirit. In short, Gass has drawn, perhaps despite himself, upon the mythological dimensions of Christianity.

While the title story in Gass's *In the Heart of the Heart of the Country* is confessedly modeled on reality, the collection as a whole is experimental. "The Pedersen Kid" is deliberately designed to call into question the nature of reality and the possibility of truth, matters that must live side by side with Gass's concern for the shape of his sentences and the relation of sentence to sentence in the paragraph. In the stories generally, the narrative voice struggles to get inside the characters and with words, magic words, steal their souls away and play with them.

But even more thoroughly committed to experimentalism is *Willie Masters' Lonesome Wife,* in which conventional narrative is largely discarded. The book offers instead a pastiche of various materials: reminiscences of the narrator, little essays on words and the imagination by the author, a variety of typographical play, authorial abuse of the reader, a parody of pornography, and footnotes. All this is designed to destroy the character and form of traditional fiction and to offer opportunities, once the old patterns of linear and logical thought, linear time, and linear print are broken up, for free-wheeling use of the imagination. The book is an experience in art, as Gass tells us at the end, where he inserts a motto: You have fallen into art—return to life. In *Willie Masters' Lonesome Wife* Gass gives himself to self-indulgent play, maximizing the freedom that the author, a god-like figure in Gass's view, justifiably claims in his dedication to the autonomy of art.

Cartesian Sonata, which contains four novellas written over the course of three decades, is, in typical Gassian form, long on style and short on emotion. To an even greater degree, this can be said for *The Tunnel,* promoted as a magnum opus that was, like *Cartesian Sonata,* three decades in coming. But whereas at least the earlier narratives possessed a recognizable shape, *The Tunnel* is so weighted by narrator William Kohler's world-weary observations that a plot is only barely discernible.

—Chester E. Eisinger

GAY, William

Nationality: American. **Born:** Hohenwald, Tennessee, 1943 or 1944 **Military Service:** U.S. Navy, 1960s. **Family:** Divorced; four children. **Career:** Worked variously as television tube assembly line worker, post-hole digger, roofer, painter, bricklayer, drywall hanger, and carpenter. Lives in Hohenwald, Tennessee. **Awards:** William Peden prize (*Missouri Review*). **Agent:** Amy Williams, New York, New York, U.S.A.

PUBLICATIONS

Novels

The Long Home. Denver, MacMurray & Beck, 1999.
Provinces of Night. New York, Doubleday, 2001.

* * *

After two novels and a handful of short stories, William Gay has emerged as one of the most important new Southern voices in American literature. However, the word "new" must be taken in context. Although *The Long Home* and *Provinces of Night* appeared recently in rapid succession, they are the mature works of a mature man who has spent a lifetime honing his craft.

Set in and around the small rural Tennessee town of Ackerman's Field during the early 1940s, *The Long Home* weaves in and out of a large cast of characters but centers on the relationships among four main figures: Nathan Weiner, a young carpenter still marked by the disappearance of his father; Dallas Hardin, the bootlegger who, unknown to Nathan, murdered Nathan's father; William Tell Oliver, an older man who befriends and mentors Nathan; and Amber Rose, the daughter of Hardin's mistress who is pursued by both Hardin and Weiner. *Provinces of Night* returns to Ackerman's Field in 1952 to tell the story of E.F. Bloodworth, a gifted but violent man who returns home late in life to make his peace with the town and the family he deserted twenty years earlier. Although he cannot mend his relationships with his three grown sons, he establishes a strong bond with his grandson Fleming, an aspiring young writer.

Such quick summaries do not, of course, begin to convey the richness and complexity of these novels. While Gay's work has been compared to such late twentieth-century Southern writers as Harry Crews, Barry Hannah, Larry Brown, and Cormac McCarthy (whose *Child of God* provides an epigraph and title for *Provinces of Night*), it is William Faulkner who most strongly informs these two novels, and both books bear up well under the burden of such a comparison. Through remarkable talent and, seemingly, sheer force of will, Gay has taken the potentially exhausted material of the Faulknerian South—the rhetorically dense narrative of the rural Southern poor—and reworked it into something immediately recognizable yet undeniably his own. Gay's characters are as timeless and elemental in their passions as Faulkner's; however, theirs is not an enduring world, but a landscape subject to cracks, ruptures, and nearly inexpressible changes. *The Long Home* begins with an earthquake that leaves both a literal and metaphorical crack in the world; *Provinces of Night* concludes with the Bloodworth land disappearing under the waters of a TVA project. As Fleming muses near the end of *Provinces of Night,* "the world had little of comfort or assurance .... there were no givens, no map through the maze .... Life blindsides you so hard you can taste the bright copper blood in your mouth then it beguiles you with a gift of profound and appalling beauty."

The residents of Ackerman's Field confront these changes with varying degrees of success, failure, bravery, cowardice, violence, and humor, and they do so within stories remarkable for their simultaneous density of detail, clarity of narrative, and seriousness of intent. As Tony Earley correctly observed in the *New York Times,* "Gay is unafraid to tackle the biggest of the big themes, nor does he shy away from the grand gesture that makes those themes manifest.'' His first two novels are grand gestures indeed.

—F. Brett Cox

GEE, Maggie (Mary)

Nationality: British. **Born:** Poole, Dorset, 2 November 1948. **Education:** Horsham High School for Girls; Somerville College, Oxford (open scholarship), B.A. 1969, M.Litt. 1972, Ph.D. in English 1980. **Family:** Married Nicholas Rankin in 1983; one daughter. **Career:** Editor, Elsevier International Press, Oxford, 1972–74; research assistant, Wolverhampton Polytechnic, 1975–79; Eastern Arts writing fellow, University of East Anglia, Norwich, 1982; since 1987 honorary visiting fellow, Sussex University, 1987. Lives in London. **Agent:** Anne McDermid, Curtis Brown, 3 Queens Square, London WC1, England.

PUBLICATIONS

Novels

Dying, In Other Words. Brighton, Harvester Press, 1981; Boston, Faber, 1984.
The Burning Book. London, Faber, 1983; New York, St. Martin's Press, 1984.
Light Years. London, Faber, 1985; New York, St. Martin's Press, 1986.
Grace. London, Heinemann, 1988; New York, Grove Weidenfeld, 1989.
Where Are the Snows. London, Heinemann, 1991; New York, Ticknor and Fields, 1992.
Lost Children. London, HarperCollins, 1994.
The Ice People. London, Richard Cohen Books, 1998.

Uncollected Short Stories

''Rose on the Broken,'' in *Granta 7* (Cambridge), 1982.
''Mornington Place,'' in *London Tales,* edited by Julian Evans. London, Hamish Hamilton, 1983.

Plays

Over and Out (broadcast, 1984). Published in *Literary Review* (London), February 1984.

Radio Plays: *Over and Out,* 1984.

Other

How May I Speak in My Own Voice?: Language and the Forbidden. London, Birkbeck College, 1996.
Editor, *For Life on Earth.* Norwich, University of East Anglia, 1982.

*

Maggie Gee comments:

My chief twentieth-century models are probably Woolf, Nabokov, and Beckett. But I was also raised on the great nineteenth-century writers like Dickens and Thackeray. And I loved *stories:* I read and re-read my mother's copy of Hans Christian Andersen. I wanted to write stories myself; and I always felt that the difficulty of much twentieth-century ''serious'' writing must be a problem, not a virtue. If I was difficult, it was despite myself. On the one hand I wanted to write new things, and tell the absolute truth according to my perception of it, which often seems to demand new ways of writing: on the other hand, I've become increasingly aware of the importance of an audience.

My first published novel, *Dying, In Other Words,* is probably the most difficult technically. It is a bizarre kind of thriller. Moira's body is found on the pavement one morning. The police assume it is suicide; yet the milkman who found the body turns out to be a mass-murderer, far too many of Moira's surviving acquaintances start to die in their turn, and increasingly often the sound of typing can be heard in Moira's ''empty'' room ... is she still alive, and writing the story? The novel is a circle; and when it returns inevitably to the point of Moira's death, we find it was neither suicide nor murder, after all... .

The Burning Book is a variation on the family saga. Two English working families, the Ships and the Lambs, shop-keepers and railway-workers, try to live their own lives, interrupted by two world wars and the threat of a third. One theme of the book is the stupidity of nuclear weapons, which endanger all stories and the continuity embodied in families. There are flashbacks to Hiroshima and Nagasaki. The family itself isn't perfect; violence and frustration inside it counterpoint violence and frustration outside. On a small scale, though, humans can learn to do better. The central couple, Henry and Lorna, finally learn to love each other by the last chapter of the book, when they go for a winter picnic in an earthly Eden, Kew Gardens. By a stupid irony, the public world of war-like headlines breaks in on their ''happy ending.'' *Light Years* is an inverted romance, set in 1984. The lovers, Lottie and Harold, split up on the first page of the novel, and are apart through the year (and 52 chapters) that the book lasts, though perhaps things change in the very last chapter .... The longer they are separated, the more they love each other. Meanwhile, the earth turns full circle, and the seasons, the stars, and the planets play their part in the very formal structure of this book. It is my ''easiest'' book I think—short chapters, short sections within the chapters, with much ''lighter'' looking pages: all of which was intended to help express a rather rare commodity in twentieth-century literature—happiness.

Retrospectively, I realized that each of these three books was an attempt to write a new version of a popular genre—thriller, family saga, romance—to appeal to basic emotions, and use basic narrative drives, but to re-work the genre in my own way, and to surprise my readers. All I am conscious of at the time of writing, though, is a desire to show the truth, in ways I never can in speech, and a desire to make structures as beautiful as I can.

(1995) *Grace* is an anti-nuclear thriller, whose form and themes both depend on ideas of splitting and one-ness—splitting of the atom, of the male and female sides of ourselves, of families, of society.

Where Are the Snows is a panoramic global love-story, the story of Christopher and Alexandria, a bourgeois couple who give up family and roots for love. They are both archetypal tourists—thinking they can buy the planet and use it as a backdrop for their personal drama—and embodiments of the ''transcendental homelessness'' that Georg Lukacs saw as central to the novel form. I was writing about a fantasy of eternal youth and romance that runs aground on the rocks of bodily aging, and about our human need for something wider than a couple bond; about the loneliness and greed of contemporary western society; about our selfish desire to have everything for ourselves, within our own individual life-spans, and a consequent contempt for the future and the past, most obviously shown in my central couple's abandonment of Christopher's teenage children, and Alexandra ''forgetting'' to have children of her own—until it is too late.

Lost Children is a British book, like *Grace.* It is about the process of dealing with loss—of a teenage daughter, Zoe, who runs away from home, in the first instance. But the bereaved mother, Alma, is driven back to her own lost childhood as she tries to understand what has happened; is it the working-through of an older pattern of unhappiness that has driven her daughter away in 1993? The 1990s London of the novel is full of poverty and literal lost, homeless children, a darker city than the already troubled London of *Light Years,* a decade earlier. The personal question the book asks is one that particularly concerns the middle-aged, like Alma—how can we understand our parents? How can we understand and forgive ourselves as parents?

The Keeper of the Gate (work in progress) is about the difficult transition between centuries, and that between life and death. One of London's last Park Keepers has a stroke and faces death. In his absence in the hospital, a racial murder takes place in a park which for a hundred years has never known a major crime. Meanwhile, the middle-class children of this working-class man jostle for position around his bed and try to understand their parents, themselves, and the frightening future. The sub-text of this book is the loss of public space, the breakdown of public order, the lost notion of truly shared society—and how black and white can live together.

* * *

In her as yet short career as a novelist Maggie Gee has gained the reputation of an experimentalist. Technically innovative would be the way I would prefer to describe her work, and this is certainly true of her first novel *Dying, In Other Words.* Beginning with the dramatic suicide of a young writer, Moira Penny, *Dying, In Other Words* could have been a brightly written but run-of-the mill suspense thriller, and in some ways it is. But it is considerably more than that, for Penny's suicide is dropped, as it were, into the pool of lives around her and the ripples spread and impinge on the lives of others and, what makes the novel remarkable, on the continuum of the past and present of those lives. *Dying, In Other Words* has been described as a ''Chinese box of a novel'' and that is well put. As the novel progresses the implications of Penny's suicide reach further and further into the lives of others. But while the past impinges, the future overshadows, and in *Dying, In Other Words* there are already dark hints of the Armageddon to come. What her characters are unaware of is as important as that of which they are aware: ''What Bill didn't know was that the girl he evoked, with her long brown limbs and her full yellow rose bud skirt and her underwear smelling of lemon perfume and seaweed died six months later in a car crash.'' Gee encourages an awareness that her characters exist in a fiction. She pushes beyond this and writes in her second novel *The Burning Book:* ''All of us live in a novel, and none of us do the writing. Just off the stage there are grim old men planning to cut the lighting.'' Thus Gee can be seen, in spite of (or perhaps because of) her experimentation, to be in the tradition of Fielding and Dickens where the author is ever-present, ready to comment or intervene.

If the ghost of the future is fleetingly glimpsed in *Dying, In Other Words,* it positively haunts *The Burning Book.* Indeed that is its theme and purpose as it explores the loves, joys, frustrations, quarrels, hates, degradations and pettinesses of Lorna and her family. ''In an ordinary novel,'' Gee interpolates, ''that would be the whole story,'' but the shadow cast on the future by Hiroshima and Nagasaki darkens the final episode in this everyday story of ordinary folk. It is to Gee's purpose that they are so ordinary, even petty, in their thoughts and relationships, and it is a tribute to her narrative skills that she carries us with them through their dull and messy lives. Because it is their very dullness and messiness that allow us to identify with them and make their final pointless agonizing destruction so telling and poignantly horrifying. As a nuclear warning the book certainly succeeds; and it succeeds as a work of literature as well.

Nevertheless, *The Burning Book* leaves two largish questions. One is that if Gee wishes her fears and anxieties for our future to be more universally understood, and the passion I sense behind her novels suggests she does, then she may well have to find less sophisticated means to her end. The other question is that having written the terminal novel where does she go? Where she went immediately was to her novel *Light Years.* ''An oddly simple and old fashioned love story'' one reviewer has described it. But all Gee's stories as such are simple and old fashioned: the story of a mysterious suicide in *Dying, In Other Words,* an everyday family saga in *The Burning Book.* It is what she makes of this material that leaves it far from simple and old fashioned. The narrative of Harold and Ottie in *Light Years* can be enjoyed on the story level alone, but Gee's intentions are more involved. She can entertain and does, but she has no wish to entertain alone: her narratives reflect a wider, less immediate, context. Sometimes, in order to do this, she has to rely on her author's interpolations and interventions and there is a danger that these can become digressive or intrusive and defeat their purpose. But there is no danger that Gee will cease to look with a compassionate but unblinking eye at a world in which there are no happy endings.

In her novel *Grace* there are signs that Gee is solving the problem posed by *The Burning Book. Grace* has the pace and structure of a superior thriller in the style of Ruth Rendell. The threads of the story and the lives they describe gradually and skillfully converge and intermesh. In addition *Grace* is finely written. Take this description of the seaside town where much of the action takes place:

> They do not have their grandeur, these white hotels, set square to the waves, with their flags streaming backwards, flying in splendor from the prevailing winds. Salt eats the paint every winter, and the wood and plaster underneath; each spring they repaint it, and if the walls have shrunk you would hardly detect it from one year to the next … in a few decades, the loss might show.
>
> Coming each year to the white hotels—The Empire, The Sandhurst, The Majestic, The Windsor—the regular guests never notice. Though may be the porter looks older, and that waitress is no longer here, retired, they suppose, to the country cottage she chatted about as she served the soup.

The description is graphic, but it is more than a visual description for there is something of the continuity of decay in it and in it something of the spirit of place. Though in this case we might call it the dispirit of place! Whatever we call it catches the place and its atmosphere beautifully. I quote this as an example of the quality of Gee's writing in *Grace*. But as her earlier novels have led us to expect the context of *Grace* and the lives of its characters is a much wider one. The context is of a world of fall-out from Chernobyl, of the trains running through our suburbs carrying nuclear waste, and of the murder of Hilda Murrell. The drama of *Grace* with its overlapping and interlocking lives and situations is played out against this background which impinges and is as fundamental to the story as Hardy's countryside is to his novels. *Grace* can be seen as an exciting and considerable advance in the art of Gee's novels.

—John Cotton

GEE, Maurice (Gough)

Nationality: New Zealander. **Born:** Whakatane, 22 August 1931. **Education:** Avondale College, Auckland, 1945–49; University of Auckland, 1950–53, M.A. in English 1953; Auckland Teachers College, 1954. **Family:** Married Margaretha Garden in 1970, two daughters; one son from previous relationship. **Career:** Schoolteacher, 1955–57; held various jobs, 1958–66; assistant librarian, Alexander Turnbull Library, Wellington, 1967–69; city librarian, Napier Public Library, 1970–72; deputy librarian, Teachers Colleges Library, Auckland, 1974–76. Since 1976 full-time writer; writing fellow, Victoria University of Wellington, 1989. **Awards:** New Zealand Literary Fund scholarship, 1962, 1976, 1986, 1987, and Award of Achievement, 1967, 1973; University of Otago Robert Burns fellowship, 1964; Hubert Church Prose award, 1973; New Zealand Book award, 1976, 1979, 1982, 1991; James Tait Black Memorial prize, 1979; Wattie award, 1979, 1993; New Zealand Children's Book of the Year award, 1984; New Zealand Library Association Esther Glen Medal, 1986. D.Litt.: Victoria University of Wellington, 1987. **Agent:** Richards Literary Agency, P.O. Box 31240, Milford, Auckland 9. **Address:** 41 Chelmsford Street, Ngaio, Wellington, New Zealand.

Publications

Novels

The Big Season. London, Hutchinson, 1962.
A Special Flower. London, Hutchinson, 1965.
In My Father's Den. London, Faber, 1972.
Games of Choice. London, Faber, 1976.
Prowlers. London, Faber, 1987.
The Burning Boy. London, Faber, 1990.
Going West. London, Faber, 1992.
Crime Story. Auckland, Viking, 1994; London, Faber, 1995.
Loving Ways. Auckland and New York, Penguin, 1996.
Live Bodies. Auckland, Penguin, 1998.
Orchard Street. Auckland, Viking, 1998.

Short Stories

A Glorious Morning, Comrade. Auckland, Auckland University Press-Oxford University Press, 1975.
Collected Short Stories. Auckland and London, Penguin, 1986; New York, Penguin, 1987.

Fiction (for children)

Plumb. London, Faber, 1978.
Under the Mountain. Wellington, London, and New York, Oxford University Press, 1979.
The World Around the Corner. Wellington, Oxford University Press, 1980; Oxford and New York, Oxford University Press, 1981.
Meg. London, Faber, 1981; New York, St. Martin's Press, 1982.
The Halfmen of O. Auckland and Oxford, Oxford University Press, 1982; New York, Oxford University Press, 1983.
Sole Survivor. London, Faber, and New York, St. Martin's Press, 1983.
The Priests of Ferris. Auckland and Oxford, Oxford University Press, 1984; New York, Oxford University Press, 1985.
Motherstone. Auckland and Oxford, Oxford University Press, 1985.
The Fire-Raiser. Auckland, Oxford University Press, 1986.
The Champion. Auckland, Oxford University Press, 1989.
The Fat Man. Auckland, Viking, 1994; New York, Simon & Schuster, 1997.

Plays

Television Series: *Mortimer's Patch,* 1980; *The Fire-Raiser,* from his own story, 1986; *The Champion,* from his own story, 1989.

Other

Nelson Central School: A History. Nelson, Nelson Central School Centennial Committee, 1978.

*

Bibliography: ''Maurice Gee: A Bibliography'' by Cathe Giffuni, in *Australian and New Zealand Studies in Canada* (London, Ontario), no. 3, Spring 1990.

Critical Studies: ''Beginnings'' by Gee, in *Islands* (Auckland), March 1977; *Introducing Maurice Gee* by David Hill, Auckland, Longman Paul, 1981; Trevor James, in *World Literature Written in English* (Guelph, Ontario), vol. 23, no. 1, 1984; Lawrence Jones, in *Landfall* (Christchurch), September 1984; *Maurice Gee* by Bill Manhire, Auckland, Oxford University Press, 1986; *Leaving the Highway: Six Contemporary New Zealand Novelists* by Mark Williams, Auckland, Auckland University Press, 1990.

* * *

Maurice Gee established himself as one of New Zealand's best writers with the trilogy of novels comprising *Plumb, Meg,* and *Sole Survivor*, published between 1978 and 1983. In his adult and juvenile fiction, he examines provincial and small-town mores, realistically evoking life in New Zealand. Favorite themes include isolation and loneliness framed in stories that discuss the effects of aging, the conflict between conformity and nonconformity, the emotional/spiritual claustrophobia of a middle-class society underscored by philistine aggression, and the moral wisdom of his youthful heroes. His style reverberates with subtle implications that transcend the surface realism and the immediate situations toward a universal symbolism.

Gee first attracted attention in the late 1950s with short stories published in New Zealand's major literary periodical, *Landfall*, and was highly praised by British reviewers for two stories, ''The Losers'' (1959) and the even more memorable ''Eleventh Holiday'' (1961). Gee's initial success with the publication of his short stories was followed by a bildungsroman, *The Big Season*, about protagonist Rob Andrews's search for identity in a stifling environment. A rebellious streak disturbs Rob's progress in rugby, his father's business, a future marriage, and his family's anticipation that he will become a pillar in their blinkered community. The short prologue, set in 1946 and 1947, describes Rob's voyeuristic interest as a child in a local boarding house, a den of iniquity and vice. Rob's involvement with ex-convict Bill Walters, a boarding-house resident, leads to the eventual rejection of his childhood values with a public act of defiance.

Structurally and technically Gee's second novel, *A Special Flower*, is more complex and adventurous than the straightforward prose of *The Big Season*. Gee uses shifting perspectives among characters from chapter to chapter in the overall third-person narration and an unconventional handling of time to tell the story of Donald Pinnock's failed marriage to Coralie Marsh, and her relationship with his family after his death. The ending optimistically reconciles the misunderstandings caused by Coralie's lower social status and lack of propriety as she awaits the birth of her baby in the inhibiting confines of New Zealand's middle-class with Donald's mother and sister.

The parent-child relationship plays a prominent part in Gee's third novel, *In My Father's Den*, which opens with a murder and ends with the identification of the killer, but is only incidentally a story of mystery and detection. After a prologue in the form of a newspaper cutting about the 1969 killing of Celia Inverarity, a schoolgirl at Wadesville College near Auckland, the novel intercuts two narrative strands as told by Paul Prior, an unmarried teacher at Celia's school, who is a prime suspect. One narration describes a few days during the time of the murder, while the other tells his life story in biographic slices such as ''1928–1937.'' The crime prompts Paul to review his entire life and the effects of returning to his small town as a literary intellectual and stranger. Even though the town suspects Paul because he has become an outsider, the killer is Paul's conventional brother, Andrew, stunted by his Oedipal relationship with his mother and by the pressures of New Zealand society.

Games of Choice is Gee's examination of a family as it disintegrates during a few days over Christmas, acquiring something of the intensity of Greek tragedy. The events are much less bloody and extreme than those tragedies, despite the brutal killing of a pet cat with a garden fork. The sham marriage of Kingsley Pratt, a provincial bookseller, and his wife, Alison, dissolves after their two children leave home. Kingsley's wife leaves him for another man, his student daughter has an affair with a much older lecturer, and his son chooses to join the army in defiance of the family's commitment to pacifism. Kingsley remains with his elderly father, Harry, whose memories describe his political activities as a youthful idealist and socialist.

Since the late 1970s, Gee has written a substantial body of fiction for adolescents. His principal imaginative undertaking has been the extremely ambitious trilogy of novels about the Plumb family, *Plumb, Meg*, and *Sole Survivor*. Many of the ingredients of the trilogy are present in his earlier novels: the emotional complexity of family life with its blend of loyalty and antagonism; the relationships between individual and community and between private and public life; and the relativity of viewpoint. Gee expands his scale to a saga that covers a century, from the late nineteenth century to the 1980s, and including six generations while concentrating on three. Because the trilogy incorporates so much of New Zealand's short history since British colonization and includes a number of real-life politicians and major events, it takes on the air of a national epic.

As in earlier novels, the narrators survey their lives from the vantage point of a fictional present, providing a framework to reconsider the past. Approximately twenty years separate the time lines of the three novels. *Plumb* covers the 1940s, while *Sole Survivor* brings the cycle to a conclusion in the early 1980s. Gee acknowledges that his family history was an important source of inspiration, especially for the first novel, in which the eponymous narrator, George Plumb, is partly based on Gee's maternal grandfather. In a trilogy containing a number of memorable characters, George Plumb is certainly the most extraordinary and interesting. He is a flawed hero, a failed saint, a dedicated idealist of religious and political vision whose moral integrity and over-active conscience blind him to the truth about himself and the world he inhabits. His quest for absolutes and his desire to build a New Jerusalem in New Zealand are undermined by the fanaticism that motivates him. Although not a tragic novel, Plumb is full of tragic irony.

After the spiritual and ideological crises of *Plumb*, *Meg* seems restrained, but, in its own way, is equally panoramic. The narrator, Meg Sole Plumb, is the youngest of George and Edith's twelve children and very much her father's favorite. A considerable part of her narrative overlaps chronologically with her father's in Plumb; however, Meg offers her own view of events previously mentioned while introducing a wide range of new material. The enormous size of the Plumb family does, of course, mean that there are many parallel strands, only a few of which can be given prominence in any one novel. By the end of her memoir, which Meg accurately calls ''a tale of deaths,'' the novel conveys a characteristically mid- and late twentieth-century sense of entropy in contrast to the passionate nineteenth-century romanticism and utopianism Plumb embodies in the earlier novel, although that too runs down as the century advances.

Just as George Plumb's death is reported in *Meg*, Meg's horrific death by fire in a domestic accident is described in *Sole Survivor* as narrated by one of her three children, the journalist Raymond Sole. This is another ''tale of deaths,'' triggered by the murder of Douglas Plumb, a cabinet minister and George's grandson, making him one of Raymond's numerous cousins. If *Plumb* is the most religious of the three novels and *Meg* the most domestic, *Sole Survivor* is the most political, occasioned by Douglas's membership in Muldoon's National Government.

In *Sole Survivor*, Raymond interweaves a selective account of his own life from childhood to middle age with a parallel account of Douglas's career. Raymond recalls his cousin's ruthless pursuit of advantage and power, from the sexual to the political. Douglas's opportunism perverts his grandfather's high-minded dedication, and the ascent to prominence, almost to the premiership, becomes, paradoxically, a story of decline—the collapse of George Plumb's unrealistic, yet noble, ideals. The ending of *Sole Survivor* and the trilogy as a whole is open-ended rather than pessimistic, but the emphasis is on the failure to realize the New Zealand dream, the slide from heroic vision to debased materialism. The trilogy's major arc may be the universal story of the twentieth century.

Two adult novels Gee has published since the trilogy, *Prowlers* and *The Burning Boy*, draw on his home town of Nelson. *Prowlers*, a family saga, spans much of the twentieth century and is narrated by a distinguished scientist and public servant, the octogenarian Sir Noel Papps. His grandniece Kate researches the past in order to write a biography about Noel's equally famous sister, Kitty, a leading figure in the Labor Party for many years. In their different ways Noel and Kate prowl through history and memory, focusing on aspects of their private lives. What emerges is a series of interrelated vignettes and episodes cohering into a panoramic tapestry of Jessop, the fictional town modeled on Nelson.

In both the trilogy and *Prowlers*, Gee offers a broad historical overview of his characters' lives. In *The Burning Boy*, he orchestrates his narrative around the four elements of fire, water, air, and earth in sections titled ''Spring Rain,'' ''Dry Times,'' and ''Fire.'' A devastating bush fire, which threatens the town of Saxton and kills one of the main characters, concludes the story, which begins with the burned boy of the title, a badly scarred victim of an accident in which another boy dies.

During the 1980s, Gee also wrote several works in the fantasy science-fiction genre for his juvenile readers, including the ''O'' trilogy. Most of his latest novels, including *Fat Man, The Champion*, and *The Fire-Raiser*, all published in the 1990s, are for young adults. *Fat Man*, set during the Great Depression, is a disturbing psychological thriller with its young hero, Colin Potter, rescuing his family and town from the revenge of a sadistic bully, the fat man, who returns from a life of crime in the United States. Gee's young characters prove themselves against the likes of cunning and unbalanced adults like Muskie, the fat man. Once Colin's disillusionment is replaced with a steely courage, he assists Muskie to his own doom by helping him fall into a gorge.

The Champion evaluates racism when an African-American soldier, Private Jackson Coop, recuperates in Kettle Creek during World War II. When twelve-year-old Rex compares Jackson's brand of heroic conduct with the racism the soldier's presence causes among the adults, he allies with New Zealand blacks to help Jack. Gee's juvenile fiction teaches impressionable readers about the superficiality of social status and the unjust evaluations of individuals created by such arbitrary designations of status as race.

The Fire-Raiser takes place during World War I and tells the story of four children who unravel the mystery of arson in their town. Kitty Wix, Irene, Noel, and Phil try to stop the arsonist after seeing him flee the scene of a fire at Dargie's stables. Gee's enthralling page-turner highlights the sick thoughts inside the arsonist's mind while shedding light on wartime attitudes in 1915 New Zealand. As with all of Gee's novels, whether written for adult or juvenile readers, the well-rounded characters are genuine and inhabit a vividly painted community.

Gee's novels offer the post-colonial world a gateway into New Zealand, a mysterious land to most because of its relatively brief history of independence from Britain. Cultural awareness about the network of islands that comprise New Zealand is often superceded by stereotypes based on Australian culture. Gee's fiction often presents cross-sections of the towns in which the stories take place through a variety of characters struggling with the contradictions inherited from the puritanical British and the realities of the ancient island life they claim. The complexity of the situation is reflected in the complexity of Gee's characters. Their inner conflicts and interpersonal tensions, which are analyzed in his fiction, illustrate New Zealand's specific culture while linking the country to the mainstream of the twentieth-century struggle typical in all Western societies.

—Peter Lewis, updated by Hedwig Gorski

GHOSE, Zulfikar

Nationality: British. **Born:** Sialkot, Pakistan, 13 March 1935. **Education:** Keele University, England, B.A. in English and philosophy 1959. **Family:** Married in 1964. **Career:** Cricket correspondent, the *Observer,* London, 1960–65; teacher in London, 1963–69. Since 1969 professor of English, University of Texas, Austin. **Awards:** Arts Council of Great Britain bursary, 1967. **Agent:** Aitken, Stone and Wylie, 29 Fernshaw Road, London SW10 0TG, England. **Address:** Department of English, University of Texas, Austin, Texas 78712, U.S.A.

PUBLICATIONS

Novels

The Contradictions. London, Macmillan, 1966.

The Murder of Aziz Khan. London, Macmillan, 1967; New York, Day, 1969.

The Incredible Brazilian:

The Native. London, Macmillan, and New York, Holt Rinehart, 1972.

The Beautiful Empire. London, Macmillan, 1975; Woodstock, New York, Overlook Press, 1984.

A Different World. London, Macmillan, 1978; Woodstock, New York, Overlook Press, 1985.

Crump's Terms. London, Macmillan, 1975.

The Texas Inheritance (as William Strang). London, Macmillan, 1980.

Hulme's Investigations into the Bogart Script. Austin, Texas, Curbstone Press, 1981.

A New History of Torments. New York, Holt Rinehart, and London, Hutchinson, 1982.

Don Bueno. London, Hutchinson, 1983; New York, Holt Rinehart, 1984.

Figures of Enchantment. London, Hutchinson, and New York, Harper, 1986.

The Triple Mirror of the Self. London, Bloomsbury, 1991.

Short Stories

Statement Against Corpses, with B.S. Johnson. London, Constable, 1964.

Veronica and the Gongora Passion. Toronto, Tsar, 1998.

Uncollected Short Stories

''The Absences,'' in *Winter's Tales 14,* edited by Kevin Crossley-Holland. London, Macmillan, and New York, St. Martin's Press, 1968.

''A Translator's Fiction,'' in *Winter's Tales 1* (new series), edited by David Hughes. London, Constable, and New York, St. Martin's Press, 1985.

Poetry

The Loss of India. London, Routledge, 1964.

Jets from Orange. London, Macmillan, 1967.

The Violent West. London, Macmillan, 1972.
Penguin Modern Poets 25, with Gavin Ewart and B.S. Johnson. London, Penguin, 1974.
A Memory of Asia. Austin, Texas, Curbstone Press, 1984.
Selected Poems. Karachi, Oxford University Press, 1991.

Other

Confessions of a Native-Alien (autobiography). London, Routledge, 1965.
Hamlet, Prufrock, and Language. London, Macmillan, and New York, St. Martin's Press, 1978.
The Fiction of Reality. London, Macmillan, 1983.
The Art of Creating Fiction. London, Macmillan, 1991.
Shakespeare's Mortal Knowledge. London, Macmillan, 1993.

*

Critical Studies: Zulfikar Ghose issue of *The Review of Contemporary Fiction,* 9 (2), Summer 1989; *Structures of Negation: The Writings of Zulfikar Ghose* by Chelva Kanaganayakam, Toronto, University of Toronto Press, 1993.

* * *

Zulfikar Ghose's five stories in *Statement Against Corpses* repeatedly concern the metaphysics that unites thought with action, life with death, success with failure, aspirations with accomplishment. ''The Zoo People'' is the best of these. Thematically complex, linguistically assured, subtle in its evocation of character, delicate in its responses to landscape, provocative in its approach to time, it probes the mind of the English émigré Emily Minns, as she comes to terms with physical and metaphysical perception in an India alien to her upbringing. Is an animal more beautiful in the wild than in a zoo, she asks—and what happens if, taking a cage away, one discovers ''primitive wildness'' *instead* of beauty? Her ultimate answer arises from her increased sensitivity to Indian paradoxes and her adaptation of them to her ''European Enlightenment'' patterns of thought:

> Absolute barrenness was a reality with which she now felt a sympathy. There were rocks and rocks: each, whether a pebble or a boulder, was a complete, homogeneous, self-sufficient mass of matter in itself; each stood or lay in the dust at perfect peace with the universe which did no more to it than round its edges; each was there in its established place, a defiant mass of creation, magnificently aloof, without ancestry and without progeny.

Order, in other words, is within her mind's eye.

The Contradictions not only continues the metaphor of barrenness, but also structures itself on East-West logical oppositions. The ''assertions'' that open the book explore an Englishman's inhibited barriers against India, and India's human fecundity nonetheless. The ''contradictions'' that close it are set in England and pick up each theme and symbol from the first half of the book—not in order to refute them, but to complete them. The English rationalist philosophers must be blended with India's atemporality; material welfare must be glimpsed concurrently with the nominal importance of the colour of silk squares; Sylvia's English miscarriage must encourage her to appreciate what her experience of India did not directly allow: that an ''area of nothingness'' might possess ''an odd attraction, and in this darkness, a disturbing power.''

Attached ambivalently to a landscape of heart as well as a landscape of mind, Sylvia spirals towards a point of balance between antitheses. For Ghose himself, as his autobiography clearly announces, the point of balance is represented by the tenuous hyphen in ''native-alien.'' Pakistan, India, British India, Britain, and the USA are all part of his experience, and all necessary to him, in conjunction. In another short story, ''Godbert,'' the antithesis is conveyed by a different metaphor: ''Donald ... looked at horizons whereas John examined the texture of cobblestones.'' Later in the story, in a similar tense vein, Ghose writes: ''One chooses a way of life. Or life imposes its own pattern upon one despite oneself.'' Such a dilemma lies at the core of Ghose's ambitious and moving novel *The Murder of Aziz Khan,* about a peasant farmer's futile effort to preserve his traditional land from industrial expansion, political roguery, blatant thuggery, and the power of money in other people's hands.

The metaphysics of perception and cultural tension continues to preoccupy Ghose in his later novels. Though *Crump's Terms,* the reflections of a London schoolteacher, is a weak foray into wry social comedy, the three volumes of *The Incredible Brazilian* show the author to be highly imaginative. Influenced by Márquez and others, these three books—*The Native, The Beautiful Empire,* and *A Different World*—tell the marvelous, almost picaresque narratives of a single character named Gregório, who in a series of reincarnations is variously native, explorer, soldier, planter, merchant, marketeer, writer, and revolutionary. In writing out the three ''lives'' of the three books, Gregório confronts various ethical, historical, and mythological claims to both the territory and the idea of Brazil: native land, European colony, and new nation. Beyond the claim to the land lies the claim to the future, he writes, and he asks if cultural contact must necessitate corruption, if power is really man's only motivation, and in a closing and magnificently eloquent irony, if efforts to prevent violence inevitably prove destructive. This knot of abstract ideas gives the work its breadth of vision; its success derives also from Ghose's skill in telling a vivid, concrete narrative.

Even more successful are Ghose's further forays into patterns of imaginative adventure. *A New History of Torments* and *Don Bueno* take prototypical quest cycles and turn them into contemporary adventures of the psyche. *A New History of Torments* follows the life of a young man from his rural South American home to a pleasure-palace island, only to watch him destroy himself after he becomes unwittingly entangled in an incestuous love. With a related setting, *Don Bueno* watches generations of young men grow up to inherit their fate: inevitably they pursue, kill off, and then replace their fathers—secure only in their blindness to the effects of time on their own ambition.

Figures of Enchantment, using metatextual and magic realist techniques, turns more consciously to analyze artifice, and probes the experience of exile in yet another way. Focusing on the *figures* of representation and imaginative understanding (each of the characters, or ''figures,'' for example, exists as a ''figure'' or ''type'' in other character's eyes), the novel draws the attention to its own syntax. It makes clear that ''figurative'' language both constructs versions of reality and removes people from any ''natural'' or ''unmediated'' relation with the external world.

The stories of *Veronica and the Gongora Passion* take place against a varied backdrop, both in time and space, that includes South America, the Indian subcontinent, and Spain during the Muslim period in the Middle Ages. By turns poetic, comic, and dramatic, Ghose's stories and novels are engaging narratives. They also constitute a continuing analysis of power: of its workings, and of its basis in the economics of ownership and desire.

—W.H. New

GHOSH, Amitav

Nationality: Indian. **Born:** 11 July 1956. **Education:** Delhi University, India, B.A. in history, M.A. in sociology; Oxford University, diploma in social anthropology, Ph.D.; Institut Bourguiba des Langues Vivants Tunis, diploma in Arabic. **Family:** Married Deborah Ann Baker in 1990. **Career:** Since 1986 lecturer in sociology, Delhi School of Economics, Delhi University. Contibutor to *Indian Express* (New Dehli), *Granta* (Cambridge), and *The New Republic* (Washington, D.C.). **Award:** Academy of Letters, India, annual prize, 1990. **Agent:** Wylie, Aitken and Stone, 250 West 57th Street, New York, New York 10107, U.S.A.

Publications

Novels

The Circle of Reason. London, Hamilton, and New York, Viking, 1986.

The Shadow Lines. New Delhi, Ravi Dayal, and London, Bloomsbury, 1988; New York, Viking, 1989.

The Calcutta Chromosome: A Novel of Fevers, Delirium and Discovery. New York, Avon Books, 1995.

Countdown. Delhi, Ravi Dayal Publisher, 1999.

The Glass Palace. New York, Random House, 2000.

Other

The Relations of Envy in an Egyptian Village. Trivandrum, Centre for Development Studies, 1982.

In an Antique Land. New Delhi, Ravi Dayal, 1992; New York, Knopf, 1993; London, Penguin, 1994.

Translator, *The Slave of Ms. H.* Calcutta, Centre for Studies in Social Sciences, 1990.

*

Critical Studies: *The Novels of Amitav Ghosh,* edited by R.K. Dhawan. New Delhi, Prestige Books, 1999.

* * *

Amitav Ghosh's fictional world is one of restless narrative motion. His central figures are travelers and diasporic exiles: exemplars of ''the migrant sensibility'' that Salman Rushdie calls ''one of the central themes of this century of displaced persons.'' If in Rushdie's metaphor ''the past is a country from which we have all emigrated,'' Ghosh's conflation of time and space—and of distinct times and distant places—is even more extreme. He treats national borders and conceptual boundaries as permeable fictions to be constantly transgressed. Through the multiple criss-crossings enabled by a free-ranging narrative, discrete binaries of order and category give way to a realm of mirror images and hybrid realities. Reason becomes passion, going away is also coming home, and the differences between us and them, now and then, here and there are disrupted by the itinerant maps of a roaming imagination.

The Circle of Reason follows Indian characters from a Bengali village to an Egyptian town to an outpost in the Algerian Sahara. This first novel begins as a comic tale of unlikely conjunctions. The scientific Reason with which Balaram is obsessed combines Hindu ideas of purity and Western notions of cleanliness with Louis Pasteur's microbiology; Balaram's vision of social progress through weaving suggests both Gandhi's nationalist self-sufficiency and a global multinational economy in which technology ''recognizes no continents and no countries.'' However, this eccentric version of Reason is almost wiped out in the novel by forces of unreason: ambition, paranoia, territoriality, and violence.

Balaram's last disciple, the mysterious Alu, is chased across oceans and continents as a narrative of shifting, spooling time within fixed village space gives way to a linear-time, picaresque story spread across the international space of diaspora. In al-Ghazira, Alu's charismatic socialism quixotically links the eradication of germs with the elimination of money. The final scenes in El Oued are more earnest and down-to-earth, favoring the migrant's adaptive ''making do'' and ''being human'' over the purist strictures of science and religious tradition. Nevertheless, Reason and the past both circle back in the form of Balaram's favorite book, the *Life of Pasteur*, which has also traveled from Bengal to Algeria, and which Alu can now ''reverently'' cremate.

Ghosh's second novel is more somber, less fanciful in its politics, and quite stunning in the power with which its formal experiments in sequence and location resonate thematically. *The Shadow Lines* traces nearly a half-century of interlocking relations among three generations of two families, one Indian and one British, giving perhaps the definitive fictional demonstration of Benedict Anderson's dictum that nations are ''imagined communities.'' When the same Hindu-Muslim conflict can take place simultaneously in Dhaka and Calcutta, the unnamed narrator must abandon his common-sense assumption ''that distance separates, that it is a corporeal substance,'' and his belief ''in the reality of nations and borders.'' The self, like the cosmopolitan cities it lives in, becomes a palimpsest, sedimented with history, memory, and others that the self has absorbed. The narrative mode echoes this intricate layering with its looping, Russian-doll-like nestling of story within story, place within place, memory within actuality.

The unnamed narrator, with his internationalized consciousness, wallows in an empowering sense of simultaneity and correspondence. Growing up with Tridib in Calcutta, he can ''know'' war-time London neighborhoods and see the English boy Nick Price as a spectral mirror image. His grandmother's confusion between her childhood Dhaka and the present-day foreign city becomes symptomatic of the violence done to people by artificial borders and partitions (poignantly allegorized in her family's divided house). If the novel valorizes the search for unbounded space and co-existing time, however, it refuses to endorse self-serving appropriations of ''other'' realities. When Ila compares her pleasure at bohemian living with that of war-time radicals, the narrator criticizes the ''easy arrogance'' by which she assumes ''that times and places are the same because they happen to look alike, like airport lounges.'' But after a futile argument about whether her London or his Calcutta is the site of real history and important politics, he realizes the shaky ground on which he too claims possession of people and places he has largely invented.

Ghosh thus recognizes the political stakes involved in drawing connecting lines, like airline routes, across the ''shadow lines'' of national boundaries and historical periods. His globe-shrinking project enables not only integration but also juxtaposition. The controlling metaphor of the airport lounge makes this point brilliantly: as replicated space (they all look alike) and individual place (each one is distinctive); as both attached to and detached from its national home; as a place where departures rub shoulders with arrivals, where everyone is always on the move. Full of complex cross-cultural encounters, *The Shadow Lines* makes a unique contribution to the debates over ''difference'' and ''otherness'' that have galvanized the contemporary post-colonial world.

Ghosh's astonishing third novel, *The Calcutta Chromosome*, plunges into the colorful medical history of European research into malaria a century ago. It begins with the unlikely discoveries of Ronald Ross, an imperial army doctor in India who, despite ignorance of microbiology and erroneous ideas about how malaria is transmitted, nonetheless managed to win a Nobel Prize for helping understand the disease. In an ingeniously plotted narrative, Ghosh unravels some mind-boggling alternative possibilities for where Ross's knowledge really came from and what it might—very radically—entail. Full of outrageous fantasy and ''decentering'' impulses that speculatively reroute European knowledges through Indian ones, the book imaginatively ventures into what Brian McHale, in *Postmodernist Fiction*, calls ''secret'' or ''apocryphal'' history. It does so through a genre—the mystery—that makes unlikely mental journeys, startling discoveries, and the revelation of secrets into its narrative life-blood.

Ghosh's protagonist, the Egyptian researcher Antar, works in a near-future New York on a highly advanced computer. The machine, Ava, outlandishly blends the visionary empowerment of recent Internet hype—it really can do anything, speak any dialect, find any document—with the oppressive scrutiny of Orwell's Big Brother—it won't let Antar stop work early, and its invasive hologram technology respects no bounds of privacy. Antar and Ava investigate the disappearance of the long-lost Murugan, a self-styled authority on Ronald Ross, who went to Calcutta in 1995 on the trail of some suspicious anomalies he'd found in Ross's work; he was last seen the day after his arrival. The narrative follows Murugan through two days of unsettling encounters and strange coincidences that augment and clarify his incipient theories; he also discovers an inextricable link between himself and one of Ross's research subjects.

The discovery process shared by Murugan, the reader, and Antar follows a narrative rollercoaster that at times resembles a fun-house, a ''laff in the dark'' ride with a carefully timed sequence of grotesque surprises popping out at every turn. In stylized prose emphasizing dialogue and description, Ghosh employs conventional devices of the mystery, the high-tech thriller, the ''hard-boiled'' detective novel, the science fiction adventure, and the Victorian ghost story—all with such boldness and panache that it can be hard to tell if he is parodying the genres or ''doing'' them in earnest.

But after the novel's controlling plot lays down the last bit of secret knowledge, it turns out to be very much *about* control, and about knowledge. And although Ghosh typically does not wear his politics on his sleeve, the implication of this novel's secret history is that control of medical knowledge is wrenched away from Europeans in the past and bestowed on Indians in the past, present, and future. Unhoused from the apparatus and methods of European science, malaria is repossessed by the locals—rightful owners, perhaps, since it is they and their ancestors who have most often been possessed by its malign fevers. Understanding of the disease is reclaimed and redefined on distinctly Indian terms; in Ghosh's version it has significance not just for science and bodily health, but also for spiritual health and worship, fate and predestination, reincarnation, time cycles and other notions more dear (by and large) to Indians than Westerners.

Ghosh is remarkable in his use of narrative structure to exemplify thematic interests. *The Circle of Reason*'s itinerant and wayward picaresque echoes the intellectual caprices of its characters, while *The Shadow Lines* makes impossible coexistences and disrupted metaphysical boundaries into real struggles both for its narrator and its readers. Similarly, *The Calcutta Chromosome* insists on a reading process that enacts its central ideas. It uses the controlled surprises and circuitous discoveries of the mystery-thriller to convey a story whose initial germ—malaria science—is all about circuitous routes to surprising discoveries. In Ghosh's exacting hands that story becomes a feverish literary journey into a possible world where to find that one is following someone else's agenda—indeed is totally trapped by it—can be paradoxically to achieve new mastery over the future agendas of oneself and others.

—John Clement Ball

GIBBONS, Kaye

Nationality: American. **Born:** Nash County, North Carolina, 1960. **Education:** Attended North Carolina State University and the University of North Carolina at Chapel Hill. **Family:** Married once (divorced); partner of Frank Ward; three daughters. **Awards:** Sue Kaufman prize for First Fiction (American Academy and Institute of Arts and Letters); National Endowment for the Arts fellowship; Nelson Algren Heartland award for Fiction (*Chicago Tribune*), 1991; PEN/Revson Foundation fellowship. **Address:** Raleigh, North Carolina, U.S.A.

PUBLICATIONS

Novels

Ellen Foster. Chapel Hill, North Carolina, Algonquin Books, 1987.

A Virtuous Woman. Chapel Hill, North Carolina, Algonquin Books, 1989.

A Cure for Dreams. Chapel Hill, North Carolina, Algonquin Books, 1991.

Charms for the Easy Life. New York, Putnam, 1993.

Sights Unseen. New York, Putnam, 1995.

On the Occasion of My Last Afternoon. New York, Putnam, 1998.

Other

Contributor, with others, *Pete and Shirley: The Great Tar Heel Novel* (serial novel). Asheboro, North Carolina, Down Home Press, 1995.

Contributor, *Southern Selves: From Mark Twain and Eudora Welty to Maya Angelou and Kaye Gibbons: A Collection of Autobiographical Writing,* edited by James H. Watkins. New York, Vintage Books, 1998.

*

Critical Studies: *Southern Selves: From Mark Twain and Eudora Welty to Maya Angelou and Kaye Gibbons: A Collection of Autobiographical Writing,* edited by James H. Watkins, New York, Vintage Books, 1998.

* * *

Kaye Gibbons is a prolific twentieth-century Southern writer whose fiction has garnered extensive praise from critics and gained national recognition through lengthy stints on the best-seller list. Much of her fiction derives from her experiences growing up in rural North Carolina, a locale which also provides the setting for her novels. She most often writes about women's efforts to become self-reliant despite the restrictive nature of Southern culture, and her use of this theme illustrates the importance of communal support in the development of female voices and independence. Gibbons's fiction also demonstrates the strength that women draw from their familial histories and from passing their oral histories on to generations of women that follow them.

Gibbons's novels examine the conflicts that women face in their marital relationships, as well as the strong bonds that develop between mothers and daughters when the marriages in question are less than satisfying. Gibbons tells her mother-daughter stories from a variety of perspectives and voices, consistently examining the consequences that await women who enter into marriages with the wrong men. Most of these men come from a lower social class than their wives and are emotionally closed, and accordingly, fail to provide the type of fulfilling relationships that their wives crave. Gibbons's novels do not degenerate into mere examinations of the pitiful state of these women's lives, however, but instead demonstrate the ways in which they find contentment after they have ''privately withdrawn their affections'' from their husbands. Instead, Gibbons's women find this contentment through their relationships with other women. Gibbons ultimately demonstrates the ways in which these women build the best lives that they can with the tools at hand: they do not bemoan the results of their poor choices, but simply learn to live with them and to take happiness where they find it.

Ellen Foster, Gibbons's first novel, is narrated from the perspective of a pre-teen girl who has suffered the suicide of her mother and who attempts to survive life with her sexually abusive, alcoholic father. Ellen finds herself in this predicament because her mother has married a man who is considered beneath her by her family, and because neither she nor her mother has an adequate support system to help her endure this man's abuse. Rather than descending into a pit of self-pity and loathing as a result of her mother's suicide, however, Ellen carves out a life for herself that is ultimately satisfactory, finding her place in a cheerful and loving foster home. She derives her last name, in fact, from the place that becomes her home, mistaking the term ''Foster family'' for the family's surname. Even in her most desperate state, Ellen manages to maintain a positive outlook, forging friendships with an African-American family that cares for her despite her initially racist attitudes which derive from her Southern heritage. As Ellen grows and finds a place, she develops a strong, independent voice, and comes to important realizations about the value of people—value that exists without regard to race.

A Virtuous Woman tells the story of an abiding love which develops between two unlikely partners, in spite of their widely divergent backgrounds. Ruby comes from a privileged family, which she does not fully appreciate until she runs away with migrant worker John Woodrow. To Woodrow, Ruby is a trophy who, having lost its newness very early on in their tempestuous marriage, becomes the recipient of abuse which results from Woodrow's frustration with his poverty-stricken existence. Following Woodrow's death, Ruby becomes involved with Jack, a tenant farmer who, although beneath her in rank in the Southern social hierarchy, treats her with respect, albeit the type of respect one would show to one's mother. The reader has a sense that Ruby has ''settled for'' her second husband in part because she is ashamed to return to her family after choosing the abusive Woodrow, but she builds a satisfactory life for herself that is only cut short by the lung cancer that she contracts as a result of a smoking habit that she develops during her first marriage as a means of stress relief.

A Cure for Dreams tells the story of three generations of women. The novel begins with the marriage of Lottie, to which she naively agrees, seeing it as a way to escape the desperate poverty of her Kentucky family. She rapidly learns that she has little in common with her husband, a man with an obsessive work ethic and a stunted ability to interact with other people. Unable to build a fulfilling relationship with her husband, Lottie showers all of her attention on her daughter, who, although devoted to Lottie, fails in her single attempt to thrive outside of the protection of her mother's wing. Lottie's story demonstrates the power of female solidarity through the growth of Lottie's weekly card-playing group. Not only do the members of the group meet expressly to engage in an activity traditionally reserved for men, but their meetings take place during a time when the men's work week would have generally been winding down, thus leaving them with free time. These women choose each other's company rather than that of their husbands, choosing female companionship over their duties to provide comfort for their inattentive husbands.

On the Occasion of My Last Afternoon is a series of flashbacks told from the perspective of an elderly woman who senses that her death is approaching. She relates tales of her childhood with a tyrannical, social-climbing father and a loving but beaten-down mother. Unlike Gibbons's other female protagonists, Emma Garnet finds true happiness in her marriage to a generous and kind-hearted Yankee doctor. Her marriage saves her from her father's evil actions—actions which include killing a slave in cold blood and terrorizing his wife, female children, and servants—but simultaneously dooms her mother to a dour and violent life. Emma Garnet ultimately stands up to her father, an event which is precipitated by his hand in her mother's death. Much like the protagonists of Gibbons's other novels, Emma Garnet is able to survive harsh realities: living in her father's home, serving as a Civil War nurse, and watching her beloved husband work himself into an early grave. She survives these devastating events because of a strong, supportive community of women. Clarice is a cherished African-American woman who first raised Emma Garnet's father, and then moved with Emma Garnet to her husband's home to help her set up housekeeping. Clarice provides a much-needed sense of stability which allows Emma Garnet to withstand the trials of war, to develop a relationship with the much-younger sister for whom she has no respect, and to bear the untimely loss of her husband. *On the Occasion of My Last Afternoon* once again illustrates the necessity of female community for women who would survive the trials of Southern womanhood.

Charms for an Easy Life again tells the story of mothers and daughters, beginning with Charlie Kate. Charlie Kate is a midwife who gains the respect of her community at an early age, and whose folk remedies are revered even above those that have been accepted for years. She raises her daughter alone, following her husband's desertion. The novel follows the developing relationships between three generations of women, illustrating their conflicts and the ways that they resolve them.

Sights Unseen deals with the impact of a mother's mental illness on her young family. Told from the perspective of the youngest child, this novel, much like the acclaimed *Ellen Foster,* tells the story of Hattie, a child cast adrift from a sense of place and belonging because of her mother's inability to bond with her. *Sights Unseen* focuses on Maggie's fight to regain her sanity and then to develop a meaningful relationship with her daughter. Gibbons's novel is founded on another long-standing Southern notion: that certain subjects aren't discussed by ''nice'' people, that odd behavior is accepted so long as it is not too outlandish, and that mental illness should be swept under the rug rather than being openly discussed or treated.

Kaye Gibbons is an important Southern writer in large part because of ways in which she represents Southern womanhood and the expectations placed upon it. Her characters are realistically drawn, demonstrating many of the difficulties that result from cultural mores governing women's behavior. The tightly-knit groups of women, whether familial or based in the larger community, illustrate the ways in which Gibbons's women attempt to control their own destinies within the confines of Southern social mores.

—Suzanne Disheroon Green

GIBSON, Graeme

Nationality: Canadian. **Born:** London, Ontario. **Education:** University of Western Ontario. **Family:** Married 1) Shirley Mann (divorced); 2) Margaret Atwood, *q.v.;* three sons. **Career:** Teacher of English, Ryerson Polytechnical Institute, Toronto, 1961–68; writer-in-residence, University of Waterloo, 1982–83. Founding member, Book and Periodical Development Council, 1975, chair, 1976, executive director, 1977. **Awards:** Scottish Canadian Exchange fellowship, 1978. **Member:** Amnesty International; Federation of Ontario Naturalists; Writers' Development Trust. **Address:** c/o Writers' Union of Canada, 24 Ryerson Ave., Toronto, Ontario M5T 2P3, Canada.

PUBLICATIONS

Novels

Five Legs. Toronto, Anansi, 1969.
Communion. Toronto, Anansi, 1971.
Perpetual Motion. New York, St. Martin's Press, 1982.
Gentleman Death. Toronto, McClelland and Stewart, 1993.

Other

Eleven Canadian Novelists Interviewed by Graeme Gibson. Toronto, Anansi, 1972.
St. Vincent and the Grenadines: Bequia, Mustique, Canouan, Mayreau, Tobago Cays, Palm, Union, PSV: A Plural Country, with Jill Bobrow, Margaret Atwood, and Raquel Welch; photographs by Dana Jinkins, Stockbridge, Massachusetts, Concepts, 1985.
How to Build a Clone Computer: The Clone Building Seminar. Independence, Missouri, Computer Training Corp., 1993.

* * *

Graeme Gibson has a solid reputation among Canadian novelists, based on both his fictional writings and his activities in cultural politics. His first two novels, *Five Legs* of 1969 and *Communion* two years later, are relatively short works, with decidedly modernist styles; *Perpetual Motion* of 1982 has a more clearly delineated narrative and narrator; and *Gentleman Death,* published in 1993, cuts between a writer's life and lives in his writings. In 1973 Gibson also contributed a collection of interviews titled *Eleven Canadian Novelists;* although not itself fiction, this work reveals something of Gibson's concerns about the professional pursuit of writing in questions repeated to different writers.

Five Legs, Gibson's first novel, tells the story of the gathering of several people for the funeral of a student acquaintance. Its first half consists of the perspective of Lucan Crackell, a university lecturer and mentor of the deceased, who has been commandeered into attending the funeral, as well as driving some others to it. The novel's modernist style blends objective dialogue between characters with verbalized thought in a manner that strongly recalls James Joyce. The opening of the novel might almost be a re-presentation of Bloom's breakfast in *Ulysses,* as Crackell prepares breakfast for his wife and assembles his clothes for the funeral. In the course of his thoughts, we find a realistic psychological portrayal of a petty and critical mind. Gibson uses Crackell's profession as an English lecturer to interweave motifs of literary death and rebirth with the conscious, social, ''real-world'' action of funeral preparations themselves. Allusions to Milton's ''Lycidas,'' among other elegies, lend texture to the novel. These notes are blended with an ironic tone introduced by Crackell himself, whose thoughts transform the traditional elegiac ''Who would not sing for Lycidas?'' to the blacker ''Who would not weep?'' when he thinks of Martin Baillie, nipped in his prime by a hit-and-run driver. Gibson skillfully interweaves hints of *Hamlet, Romeo and Juliet,* T. S. Eliot's characters in ''Prufrock'' and ''Gerontion,'' Browning's monologues, and other literary reflections on death. Some risk is taken that the text may become too self-consciously literary, however; readers may not feel like discerning between the literary mind of Crackell and the book itself.

The second half of the novel adopts the viewpoint of one of Crackell's passengers, the dead Baillie's friend Felix Oswald. He, like Crackell, muses about his life and dislikes. The novel leaves an impression of an anarchic despair, tempered with a glimmer of hope.

The brief sequel *Communion* traces Felix Oswald after his graduation from school, as he works for a veterinarian. In a slightly more coherent diction, Gibson moves toward a static closure that shows Felix breaking a dying epileptic husky from its cage and releasing it into the wild. Themes of abnormality and frustration are symbolically presented, often in analogy between Oswald and the dog.

Perpetual Motion diverges from *Five Legs* and *Communion* stylistically and fictionally, telling the story of Robert Fraser, a farmer in nineteenth-century Canada, whose plowing uncovers the skeleton of a mammoth in his field. His discovery brings him into contact with the world of Victorian pseudoscience, and he becomes seduced by the dream of building a perpetual motion machine in the form of an orrery, a working model of the solar system. His pursuit becomes obsessive and appears elusive as well, until he in a moment of inspiration makes the mammoth bone he discovered years earlier a part of his machine. It then starts to move, and gradually gains speed until it flies to pieces.

In *Perpetual Motion* Gibson investigates the implications of technology from a sophisticated perspective, mixing the dream of total human control over the machine with images of extinction, both of the mammoth and of the passenger pigeon. Gibson also introduces aspects of the tall tale and magic realism into *Perpetual Motion:* throughout the book, characters tell tales of the fabulous, and the creation of perpetual motion itself falls into this category, making the book itself a version of the fantastic epic. But Gibson's tale is one with a moral: the human costs of technological fixation are seen in Fraser's family, as they suffer under his monomania.

Gentleman Death is Gibson's return to the literary scene after eleven years. Ultimately, this novel reconciles its narrator with mortality, but his growth into this resolution is painful. Gibson essentially triangulates his book between the life of the Torontonian novelist Robert Fraser (coincidentally the great-grandson of the protagonist of *Perpetual Motion*) and the plot lives of two of his characters, travellers from Toronto to Britain and Germany. The interweaving of elements of Fraser's life with those of the characters he is laboring to bring to life is slightly disorienting, but gradually encircles the great unspoken in Fraser's soul: the source of his writing block and his greatest sadness, the death of his brother. In a conclusion that feels like the resolution of Woolf's *To the Lighthouse,* Gibson shows how love of people and place can bridge the life of the present and ghosts of the past.

—Ron Jenkins

GIBSON, William (Ford)

Nationality: American. **Born:** Conway, South Carolina, 17 March 1948. **Education:** University of British Columbia, B.A. 1977. **Family:** Married Deborah Jean Thompson in 1972; one daughter and one son. **Awards:** Hugo award, Philadelphia Science Fiction Society Philip K. Dick memorial award, Nebula award, Porgie award, all 1985, and Australian Science Fiction Convention Ditmar award, all for *Neuromancer.* **Agent:** Martha Millard Literary Agency, 293 Greenwood Avenue, Florham Park, New Jersey 07932–2335, U.S.A.

Publications

Novels

Neuromancer. New York, Ace, 1984, London, HarperCollins, 1994.
Count Zero. New York, Arbor House, 1986.
Mona Lisa Overdrive. New York, Bantam, 1988.
The Difference Engine, with Bruce Sterling. London, Gollancz, 1990; New York, Bantam, 1991.
Virtual Light. New York, Bantam, and London, Viking, 1993.
Johnny Mnemonic. New York, Ace Books, 1995.
Idoru. New York, Putnam, 1996.
All Tomorrow's Parties. New York, Putnam, 1999.

Play

Dream Jumbo (text to accompany performance art; produced, Los Angeles, 1989).

*

Film Adaptation: *Johnny Mnemonic,* 1995.

Critical Studies: *William Gibson* by Lance Olsen, San Bernardino, California, Borgo Press, 1992 (includes bibliography); *Cyberpunk and Cyberculture: Science Fiction and the Work of William Gibson* by Dani Cavallaro, New Brunswick, New Jersey, Athlone Press, 2000.

* * *

In 1922, T.S. Eliot published a review of Joyce's *Ulysses,* coining the now famous phrase ''mythical method'' to describe how Joyce created an effect of order in the chaos of modern fragmentation by invoking old stories and myths as compositional forms. William Gibson has demonstrated the continuing vitality of this ''method'' and come up with some new developments of his own in his ''cyberpunk'' trilogy that dominated science fiction of the 1980s, (*Neuromancer, Count Zero,* and *Mona Lisa Overdrive*), as well as in a second trilogy in the 1990s (*Virtual Light, Idoru,* and *All Tomorrow's Parties*).

There are strong plots in Gibson's novels, but they have little to do with the characters who inhabit them, who for the most part don't know much at all about the plot they are acting in. In *Neuromancer,* the ''cowboy'' computer-jockey Case—like the reader—only discovers at the end that he has been acting out a scheme composed by a seemingly omniscient and nearly omnipotent embodiment of artificial intelligence (AI) that merged with another AI to become the ''matrix.'' In the later two novels the AI/matrix chooses to manifest itself in the form of Voodoo beings called Loa. As the initiated Beauvoir explains to the novice Bobby, in *Count Zero,* we don't have to worry about ''whether it's a religion or not. It's just a structure. Lets you an' me discuss some things that are happening. … What it's about is getting things done.'' Gibson reports in an interview that all he knows about Voodoo he found by accident in an issue of *National Geographic* just when he needed to find a way to ''get things done'' in his second novel: ''That probably has a lot to do with the way I write—stitching together all the junk that's floating around in my head.'' This self-reflexivity in the writing, together with self-effacing creative modesty and tactics of conspicuously parodic pastiche, place Gibson's work within the discourse of postmodernism. Recycled cliches are the staple of his work, shared with the knowing reader who is hip to the ironic game being played with cultural artifacts.

Gibson's publishing career began the same year MTV hit the video market (1981), and his style reflects some of the same tactics and pace, where mundane music is transformed into a montage-collage of rapid-fire imagery in a placeless and timeless stream-of-consciousness continuum. Like the typical MTV presentation, his work seems designed to force a sensory overload onto a reader who can't keep up with the frantic pace. Oft-quoted lines from *Neuromancer* describe the effect nicely: ''Night City was like a deranged experiment in social Darwinism, designed by a bored researcher who kept one thumb permanently on the fast-forward button.'' The sensory overload is reflected in a stylistic saturation that has been aptly characterized as a ''neon epic style,'' a breathless linguistic texture that sweeps lyrically through mental states of stressed-out tension and drug highs, with an exhilaratingly desperate hallucinatory intensity, in a futuristic reenactment of the film noir cityscape of movies like *Blade Runner* (1982) or *The Terminator* (1984).

Things slow down a bit in the second and third novels of the trilogy, to allow for more complex character development and for a shift from major male characters to female ones. Things slow still more in *Virtual Light,* where we find a female main character who is a bicycle courier in San Francisco, physically transporting bits of information like a rider for the Pony Express. Both *Idoru* and *All Tomorrow's Parties* feature brisk capers as part of their plots: the former tells of the efforts of an adult data analyst and a teenage music fan to discover why a pop music performer has declared his intention to marry a virtual pop star, while the latter merges several plotlines at the point of discovery of a coming radical, worldwide change. However, they share with *Virtual Light* not only recurrent characters and settings, but also a more studied approach to their subject matter.

Gibson's work has an uneasy relationship to the genre of science fiction, comparable to what's called a ''crossover'' performance in the music world. In the early period of SF, the conventional goal was to expand human consciousness into outer space, under the secure control of scientist adventurers who combined the classical liberal virtues of morality with the forces of technological production. Gibson represents a strong turn away from this outward-bound surge, toward a more problematic contemporary frontier of science that is focused inwards, on an infinity of microcosms rather than the old-fashioned infinity of open space. Gibson's fiction follows the investments of current scientific research in the practical/theoretical fields of communication, data storage, miniaturization, artificial intelligence, bionic prosthetics, neurochemistry, genetics, and surgical interventions while continuing the exploration of paranoid subject positions inaugurated by the ''serious'' writers who inspired and influence him, like William S. Burroughs, J.G. Ballard, and Thomas Pynchon.

Paradoxically, the fact that Gibson himself knows no science (''I have no grasp of how computers really work,'' he admits in an interview), enables him to be all the more convincing to the millions of his readers who also know nothing about science. Like Edgar Rice Burroughs, who knew nothing of Africa, Gibson creates characters who glide mentally through cyberspace as effortlessly as Tarzan glided through the jungles of the Dark Continent. ''My ignorance had allowed me to romanticize them [computers],'' he admits, and our ignorance allows us to accept the romanticized exaggerations. Gibson's famous invention, ''cyberspace,'' is technically sheer nonsense, but since it exists as a form of belief, it also has a certain kind of reality, as ''a consensual hallucination experienced daily by billions of legitimate operators, in every nation.''

The cyberpunk movement leapt to prominence in the early 1980s, with Gibson at its helm, as an apparent manifestation of countercultural art. Ten years later, his fourth novel was on the *New York Times* bestseller list, raising an important question: can there be an authentic countercultural literature that achieves popularity and also resists becoming an imitation of itself suitable for mass consumption? Gibson himself has referred to the cyberpunk movement as ''mainly a marketing strategy—and one that I've come to feel trivializes what I do.'' His most recent work makes clear that he is no longer concerned by this ''marketing strategy,'' but instead is quite comfortable writing novels that show an increasingly mature concern for character, a confidently leisure approach to delineating those characters, and a calm acceptance of the fact that the startling innovations of *Neuromancer* are now simply part of the world—the characters', and the readers'.

—Thomas A. Vogler, updated by F. Brett Cox

GILCHRIST, Ellen (Louise)

Nationality: American. **Born:** Vicksburg, Mississippi, 20 February 1935. **Education:** Vanderbilt University, Nashville; Millsaps College, Jackson, Mississippi, B.A. in philosophy 1967; University of Arkansas, Fayetteville, 1976. Has three sons. **Career:** Broadcaster on National Public Radio 1984–85; also journalist. **Awards:** Mississippi Arts Festival poetry award, 1968; *New York Quarterly* award, for poetry, 1978; National Endowment for the Arts grant, 1979; *Prairie Schooner* award, 1981; Mississippi Academy award, 1982, 1985; Saxifrage award, 1983; American Book award, 1985; University of Arkansas Fulbright award, 1985; Mississippi Institute Arts and Letters award, for literature, 1985, 1990, 1991; O. Henry Short Story award, 1995. LHD, University of Southern Illinois, 1991. **Address:** c/o Little Brown, 34 Beacon St., Boston, Massachusetts 02108, U.S.A.

PUBLICATIONS

Novels

The Annunciation. Boston, Little Brown, 1983; London, Faber, 1984.
The Anna Papers. Boston, Little Brown, 1988; London, Faber, 1989.
Net of Jewels. Boston, Little Brown, and London, Faber, 1992.
Anabasis: A Journey to the Interior. Jackson, University of Mississippi, 1994.
Starcarbon: A Meditation on Love. Boston, Little Brown, and London, Faber, 1994.
Sarah Conley. Boston, Little, Brown, 1997.

Short Stories

In the Land of Dreamy Dreams: Short Fiction. Fayetteville, University of Arkansas Press, 1981; London, Faber, 1982.
Victory over Japan. Boston, Little Brown, 1984; London, Faber, 1985.
Drunk with Love. Boston, Little Brown, 1986; London, Faber, 1987.
Light Can Be Both Wave and Particle. Boston, Little Brown, 1989; London, Faber, 1990.
I Cannot Get You Close Enough: Three Novellas. Boston, Little Brown, 1990; London, Faber, 1991.
The Blue-Eyed Buddhist and Other Stories. London, Faber, 1990.
The Age of Miracles: Stories. Boston, Little, Brown, 1995.
Rhoda: A Life in Stories. Boston, Little Brown, 1995.
The Courts of Love: Stories. Boston, Little, Brown, 1996.
Flights of Angels: Stories. Boston, Little, Brown, 1998.
The Cabal and Other Stories. Boston, Little, Brown, 2000.
Collected Stories. Boston, Little, Brown, 2000.

Plays

Television Plays: *A Season of Dreams,* from stories by Eudora Welty, 1968.

Poetry

The Land Surveyor's Daughter. Fayetteville, Arkansas, Lost Road, 1979.

Riding Out the Tropical Depression: Selected Poems 1975–1985. New Orleans, Faust, 1986.

Other

Falling Through Space: The Journals of Ellen Gilchrist. Boston, Little Brown, 1987; London, Faber, 1988.

*

Critical Studies: *Ellen Gilchrist* by Mary A. McCay. New York, Twayne, 1997; *The Fiction of Ellen Gilchrist* by Margaret Donovan Bauer. Gainesville, University Press of Florida, 1999.

* * *

Ellen Gilchrist is one of America's best contemporary fiction writers. Throughout her work, some characteristics remain constant. Usually presented from a woman's point of view, the fiction includes convincing male figures. Gilchrist satirizes the foibles and arrogance of both sexes. Her women are not better than men, but their notably bad behavior is more often presented positively—as a sign of strength, a refusal to be victimized, or a daring determination to get pleasure through an outrageous act or verbal exchange. Most of her characters are self-centered, and their egoism can have both positive and negative effects. Gilchrist frequently employs an ironic juxtaposition of agony and comedy. Her stories usually present a series of scenes, with heavy use of dialogue and relatively little narrative comment. The stories generally close abruptly after a climactic episode. Narrators are either the main character, speaking in the first person, or an emotionally detached and critical observer. The settings, frequently in the South, include New Orleans, the rural Louisiana Delta, Oklahoma, North Carolina, Alabama, Mississippi, and Arkansas—although some stories in recent books take place in San Francisco, in Maine, and even in Istanbul.

In her first two volumes of stories, *In the Land of Dreamy Dreams* and *Victory over Japan,* Gilchrist includes a number of stories exploring the drug culture, alcoholism, diet faddism, and prescription drug abuse. The early stories include some of great violence. Among the early stories related to drugs are ''The President of the Louisiana Live Oak Society,'' which presents child-pushers; ''The Gauzy Edge of Paradise,'' which focuses on drug faddists (a topic pursued later in ''The Last Diet'' in *Drunk with Love*); and ''Defender of the Little Falaya.'' In some of these, Gilchrist skillfully contrasts the disorientation and hilarity induced by drugs with the dullness of the individuals' lives in their lucid states. *Victory over Japan* includes two sequences of compelling stories: one focusing on the engaging ninteen-year-old Nora Jane Whittington, introduced in *In the Land of Dreamy Dreams,* and the other on Crystal Weiss, who ''manages to have a good time'' while detesting her rich lawyer husband, Manny. ''Miss'' Crystal gains a sympathetic dimension, because in four of the stories she is seen through the eyes of her tolerant black maid, Traceleen, the only fully-developed black person in Gilchrist's work. Gilchrist's strengths throughout all of her collections of short stories lie in comic satire and the creation of highly memorable characters. Her satire sometimes misfires in its harshness or repetitiveness, as in her predictable sniping at religion, and she tends to overuse stereotypes—Jewish lawyers, sex-starved wives, black servants, Chinese-Americans, nuns, and tennis players at country clubs. Such stereotypical minor characters function effectively in many of the satiric stories but lessen the impact of the two novels. In *The Annunciation* Amanda sustains the novel well in her childhood and early adolescence as she innocently enjoys incest and as she suffers a nightmarish and life-changing cesarean at the age of 14. In the final chapters, Amanda also responds with a moving and dramatic range of emotion to the challenge of bearing a child in her forties after more than twenty-five years of infertility. But Amanda is unconvincing both in her conversion to scholarly research at the University of Arkansas and her affair with the working-class student who makes love as beautifully as he plays the guitar. This novel possesses many of the strengths of the stories: forceful scenes, aggressive, stubborn, reckless characters, interesting eccentrics, and abundance of dialogue. In two stories in *Light Can Be Both Wave and Particle* (''The Song of Songs'' and ''Life on Earth'') Gilchrist has recently provided alternative endings for *The Annunciation,* which should revive interest in the novel. Gilchrist's second novel, *The Anna Papers,* lacks the orderly structure of the first. It breaks into several episodic narratives, punctuated by letters, journal notes, and other fragments that comprise the papers of the author Anna Hand. Anna discovers she has cancer, returns home to Charlotte, North Carolina for a final year, and then drowns herself. Her dutiful sister, Helen Abadie, with reluctance and resentment, is sorting through Anna's papers as Anna's literary co-executor. The informing presence of Anna, the pointed statements and questions she left behind in her papers, the re-creation of her life by the friends who gather for a memorable six-day wake, the appearance of the New England poet, Mike Carmichael (literary co-executor with Helen) and—most of all—the surprising and refreshing renewal of the deadened life and spirit of Helen Abadie blend sorrow, anger, and comedy in *The Anna Papers.*

Anna Hand is central in Gilchrist's other recent fiction: in ''Anna, Part I'' in *Drunk with Love* and in all three novellas (*Winter, De Haviland Hand, Summer in Maine*) collected in *I Cannot Get You Close Enough.* She appears also in many references in the other recent publications, especially in *Light Can Be Both Wave and Particle.* The titles of these last two books by Gilchrist are provided by Anna in her papers, and both refer to the conflict between individualism and connection with others. The words, quoted near the end of *A Summer in Maine,* are Anna's last words and were addressed to her lover, the ''married physician'': ''I cannot get you close enough .... We never can get from anyone else the things we need to fill the endless terrible need, not to be dissolved, not to sink back into sand, heat, broom, air, thinnest air. And so we revolve around each other.'' The words imply not only her recognition of the failure of this love affair and of her year's efforts to forge strong bonds within her family before her death, but also her recognition of universal human inability to fully relate to others. Similarly, she chooses *Light Can Be Both Wave and Particle* to be the title of her ''one last book.'' The title implies again that one is a separate and inconsequential particle in the universe, but it also suggests that one can tenuously or temporarily identify the self with the great waves of nature and of human history. The first two novellas in *I Cannot Get You Close Enough* chronicle Anna's two major efforts to establish solidity in her unstable family. *Winter* recounts her journey to the slums of Istanbul to expose the irresponsibility of Daniel Hand's wife, Sheila, in order to assure Anna that custody of her niece, Jessica, now 15, will remain with the Hand family. Jessica, a beautiful and talented pianist and dancer, is a slow learner and despises school. The second novella, *De Haviland Hand,* describes Anna's efforts, including a trip to a Cherokee community in rural Tahlequah, Oklahoma, to prepare the way for Daniel's other 15-year-old daughter, Olivia de Haviland Hand, to join the Hand enclave. (Spring Deer, Olivia's mother, died during childbirth, after her brief marriage to Daniel. Daniel was never notified of Olivia's existence.) Olivia has grown up fearing sex and childbirth as precursors of death, and consequently shuns the attention of boys. Achievement in horseback riding and getting high grades in school have become obsessions. She decides eventually to follow Anna by choosing a career as a writer and also to become a famed research scientist. At the close of *A Summer in Maine,* Jessica is pregnant and enters an ill-advised marriage. Olivia cries out that, if she is not accepted by Harvard, she will, like Anna, drown herself. This novella allows Gilchrist to gather at the rented house in Maine several figures from New Orleans who appeared memorably in her earlier books. They include the Weiss family (Miss Crystal, her husband, Manny, their children, King and Crystal Anne, their maid Traceleen and her niece, Andria); Lydia, a painter; Noel, an aging actress, who fears possible publication of her intimate correspondence with Anna Hand; and Alan Dalton, a handsome tennis player who causes estrangement between Lydia and Miss Crystal. The formerly inhibited and unimaginative Helen Abadie and the poet/literary co-executor arrive (as lovers), adding to the gossip and excitement in this novella. In other recent books, Gilchrist rewards faithful readers by returning to still more familiar figures. For example, in *Drunk with Love* Rhoda Manning appears at different ages—childhood, puberty, adolescence, and early marriage—in ''Nineteen Forty-one,'' ''The Expansion of the Universe,'' and ''Adoration.'' Traceleen returns in a monologue, ''Traceleen at Dawn,'' comically recalling Miss Crystal's attempt to quit drinking. In *The Anna Papers* Miss Crystal and Phelan Manning and other longtime companions enliven a six-day wake. In *Light Can Be Both Wave and Particle* Rhoda Manning again dominates three stories: as a child in ''The Time Capsule,'' an adult in ''Blue Hills at Sundown,'' and as a 53-year-old woman, ''having run out of men'' in the very long story, ''Mexico.'' Rhoda, her brother, Dudley, and cousin Saint John attempt to prove in several days in Mexico that they can still have as wild a time as in their youth. The story, however, includes three sobering events: their attendance at a bull-fight, Rhoda's reckless arranging of a liaison with the champion matador, and a disastrous visit to Dudley's insecurely fenced compound, where wild animals are procured by thrill-seeking hunters. In the end, Rhoda finds herself, as in childhood, angry and dependent on her brother, but always willing to take risks for pleasure and excitement. Nora Jane Whittington, the anarchist, bandit, and lover of Sandy in *In the Land of Dreamy Dreams* and *Victory over Japan,* also returns in the title story of *Drunk with Love*—pregnant and with two lovers. She gives birth to twins in ''The Starlight Express'' in *Light Can Be Both Wave and Particle,* a story in which Gilchrist also introduces her most intriguing new character, a Chinese geneticist, Lin Tan Sing, who will surely reappear in another volume.

In just five years, from 1995 to 2000, Gilchrist produced no less than six story collections. Not only *Rhoda: A Life in Stories* but *The Courts of Love,* half of which consisted of a novella, drew on previously established characters and situations, offering the reader a satisfyingly tactile experience of Gilchrist's fictional world. The tales in *Flights of Angels,* too, primarily concerned the Manning family and touched on familiar themes and locales. The title story of *The Cabal* concerns a tightly knit group that controls the social life of Jackson, Mississippi, and it introduces characters that reappear throughout the book. Thus these collections function, essentially, as novels; but Gilchrist also produced a novel in the traditional sense, *Sarah Conley.* In this, the story of a 52-year-old journalist and National Book Award winner torn by competing relationships and loyalties, she made a refreshing break from the well-worn circles of her earlier work.

—Margaret B. McDowell

GLANVILLE, Brian (Lester)

Nationality: British. **Born:** London, 24 September 1931. **Education:** Newlands School; Charterhouse School, Surrey, 1945–49. **Family:** Married Elizabeth Pamela De Boer in 1959; two sons and two daughters. **Career:** Literary adviser, Bodley Head, publishers, London, 1958–62. Since 1958 sportswriter for the *Sunday Times,* London. **Awards:** Berlin Film Festival award, for documentary, 1963; British Film Academy award, for documentary, 1967; Thomas Coward Memorial award, 1969; Sports Council Reporter of the Year award, 1982. **Agent:** John Farquharson, 162–168 Regent Street, London W1R 5TB. **Address:** 160 Holland Park Avenue, London W.11, England.

Publications

Novels

The Reluctant Dictator. London, Laurie, 1952.

Henry Sows the Wind. London, Secker and Warburg, 1954.

Along the Arno. London, Secker and Warburg, 1956; New York, Crowell, 1957.

The Bankrupts. London, Secker and Warburg, and New York, Doubleday, 1958.

After Rome, Africa. London, Secker and Warburg, 1959.

Diamond. London, Secker and Warburg, and New York, Farrar Straus, 1962.

The Rise of Gerry Logan. London, Secker and Warburg, 1963; New York, Delacorte Press, 1965.

A Second Home. London, Secker and Warburg, 1965; New York, Delacorte Press, 1966.

A Roman Marriage. London, Joseph, 1966; New York, Coward McCann, 1967.

The Artist Type. London, Cape, 1967; New York, Coward McCann, 1968.

The Olympian. New York, Coward McCann, and London, Secker and Warburg, 1969.

A Cry of Crickets. London, Secker and Warburg, and New York, Coward McCann, 1970.

The Financiers. London, Secker and Warburg, 1972; as *Money Is Love,* New York, Doubleday, 1972.

The Comic. London, Secker and Warburg, 1974; New York, Stein and Day, 1975.

The Dying of the Light. London, Secker and Warburg, 1976.
Never Look Back. London, Joseph, 1980.
Kissing America. London, Blond, 1985.
The Catacomb. London, Hodder and Stoughton, 1988.

Short Stories

A Bad Streak and Other Stories. London, Secker and Warburg, 1961.
The Director's Wife and Other Stories. London, Secker and Warburg, 1963.
Goalkeepers Are Crazy: A Collection of Football Stories. London, Secker and Warburg, 1964.
The King of Hackney Marshes and Other Stories. London, Secker and Warburg, 1965.
A Betting Man. New York, Coward McCann, 1969.
Penguin Modern Stories 10, with others. London, Penguin, 1972.
The Thing He Loves and Other Stories. London, Secker and Warburg, 1973.
A Bad Lot and Other Stories. London, Penguin, 1977.
Love Is Not Love and Other Stories. London, Blond, 1985.

Plays

A Visit to the Villa (produced Chichester, Sussex, 1981).
Underneath the Arches, with Patrick Garland and Roy Hudd (produced Chichester, Sussex, 1981; London, 1982).

Screenplays (documentary): *Goal!,* 1967.

Radio Plays: *The Diary,* 1987; *I Could Have Been King,* 1988.

Television Documentaries: *European Centre Forward,* 1963.

Other

Cliff Bastin Remembers, with Cliff Bastin. London, Ettrick Press, 1950.
Arsenal Football Club. London, Convoy, 1952.
Soccer Nemesis. London, Secker and Warburg, 1955.
World Cup, with Jerry Weinstein. London, Hale, 1958.
Over the Bar, with Jack Kelsey. London, Paul, 1958.
Soccer round the Globe. London, Abelard Schuman, 1959.
Know about Football (for children). London, Blackie, 1963.
World Football Handbook (annual). London, Hodder and Stoughton, 1964; London, Mayflower, 1966–72; London, Queen Anne Press, 1974.
People in Sport. London, Secker and Warburg, 1967.
Soccer: A History of the Game, Its Players, and Its Strategy. New York, Crown, 1968; as *Soccer: A Panorama,* London, Eyre and Spottiswoode, 1969.
The Puffin Book of Football (for children). London, Penguin, 1970; revised edition, 1984.
Goalkeepers Are Different (for children). London, Hamish Hamilton, 1971; New York, Crown, 1972.
Brian Glanville's Book of World Football. London, Dragon, 1972.
The Sunday Times History of the World Cup. London, Times Newspapers, 1973; as *History of the Soccer World Cup,* New York, Macmillan, 1974; revised edition, as *The History of the World Cup,* London, Faber, 1980, 1984; revised edition, as *The Story of the World Cup,* London, Faber, 1997.
Soccer 76. London, Queen Anne Press, 1975.
Target Man (for children). London, Macdonald and Jane's, 1978.
The Puffin Book of Footballers. London, Penguin, 1978; revised edition, as *Brian Glanville's Book of Footballers,* 1982.
A Book of Soccer. New York, Oxford University Press, 1979.
Kevin Keegan (for children). London, Hamish Hamilton, 1981.
The Puffin Book of Tennis (for children). London, Penguin, 1981.
The Puffin Book of the World Cup (for children). London, Penguin, 1984.
The British Challenge (on the Los Angeles Olympics team), with Kevin Whitney. London, Muller, 1984.
Footballers Don't Cry: Selected Writings. London, Virgin, 1999.
Football Memories. London, Virgin, 1999.
Editor, *Footballer's Who's Who.* London, Ettrick Press, 1951.
Editor, *The Footballer's Companion.* London, Eyre and Spottiswoode, 1962.
Editor, *The Joy of Football.* London, Hodder and Stoughton, 1986.

*

Critical Study: "Khaki and God the Father" in *A Human Idiom* by William Walsh, London, Chatto and Windus, 1965.

Brian Glanville comments:

(1972) There has, I suppose, been some tendency to categorize my work under three headings; that which deals with Italy (*Along the Arno, A Cry of Crickets, A Roman Marriage*), that which deals with Jewish life (*The Bankrupts, Diamond*), and that which deals with professional football (*The Rise of Gerry Logan* and many of the short stories). I think I might accept the categorization of the two Jewish novels, but it scarcely places *The Olympian,* which uses an athlete as its figure, athletics as its theme, or rather as its metaphor; or *A Second Home,* which is narrated in the first person by a Jewish actress—and has been bracketed with *A Roman Marriage,* itself narrated by a young girl. Again, one can, and does, use similar material for widely different purposes.

A large disenchantment with the conventional novel and its possibilities has, I think, led one gradually away from it, to more experimental methods. Like many novelists of serious intentions, one lives uneasily from one novel to the elusive next, always questioning and trying to establish the validity of the form.

* * *

Brian Glanville has written of his novels that "large disenchantment with the conventional novel … has, I think, led one gradually away from it, to more experimental methods." Each novel from this prolific writer has demonstrated that impatience; his need to break away from the manners of the traditional novel and from its central narrative line to a more fluid exposition of his thought has meant that the action frequently unfolds through his characterization instead of through the plot. In *A Roman Marriage* the story is told by the young English girl who has allowed herself to be trapped into a futile, claustrophobic marriage to a handsome young Italian; and through her outraged consciousness we experience, too, the suffocation of her husband's clinging, over-protective mother as the tentacles of family life cut the girl off from reality and draw her in to a nightmare. Similarly the tensions and cabalistic integrity of the family are strikingly unfolded in his Jewish novels such as *The Bankrupts, Diamond,* and *A Second Home.*

A further strength of the novels in this latter group is Glanville's sure ear for the cadences of everyday speech. The Jewish patois is never forced to gain its effect through comic music-hall over-indulgence but is allowed to expose itself through Glanville's feeling for the poetic possibilities of the spoken language. Although the unforced ease of his dialogue gives it a down-to-earth integrity, Glanville never allows it to become mundane or demeaning, and the simplicity of effect is a structural strength of all his writing.

As a commentator on professional sport Glanville has also written several novels about the stamina and passion that make up the modern athlete. In *The Olympian* a young miler, Ike Low, is torn between his passion for his wife Jill and the almost sexual release that he finds in winning races. Against their uneasy relationship stands the ambiguous figure of Sam Dee, Ike's trainer, who acts as both *agent provocateur* and chorus over their slowly disintegrating marriage. The narrative is broken up with journalese and taut, film-like dialogue as the drama of Ike's racing career draws to an unexpected climax. *The Dying of the Light* is perhaps Glanville's most profound and satisfying sporting novel to date. Although it is described as ''a football novel,'' it is in effect a parable of contemporary life. Len Rawlings, a footballing hero in the post-war years, slumps gradually to the bottom of the ladder in a world where the aged and the losers are quickly forgotten. In desperation he turns to petty crime but finds salvation in the love of his daughter, so unlike him in character, but the only one to understand the terrifying loneliness of his personal predicament. As in all Glanville's novels, the moralizing is made manifest by its absence—Rawlings may have broken the law but it is the law of the jungle that is at fault, the ''sporting'' code that allows a talented man to be driven to despair through no fault of his own.

Contemporary obsessions of another kind are examined in *Never Look Back,* a novel that explores the world of rock and roll bands and the attitudes of its denizens: the stars, their managers and hangers-on, the agents and the crooks. The documentary detail is impressive but Glanville's mastery of language and skillful handling of dialogue convey subtle shifts of feeling, and they also constantly change his and the reader's focus on this kaleidoscopic world. Above all, Glanville shows that he is one of the few contemporary novelists capable of tackling and expressing the values, or lack of them, in our rapidly changing society.

After *Never Look Back,* Glanville produced two more novels in the 1980s, *Kissing America* and *The Catacomb.* Later years saw an increased production of nonfiction writing on sport, but no additional novels—which, given the outstanding ability shown in his earlier works, must certainly be counted a shame.

—Trevor Royle

GLOVER, Douglas (Herschel)

Nationality: Canadian. **Born:** Simloe, Ontario, 14 November 1948. **Education:** York University, Toronto, 1966–69, B.A. in philosophy; University of Edinburgh, 1969–71, M.Litt. in philosophy; University of Iowa, Iowa City, 1980–82, M.F.A. in creative writing. **Family:** Married Helen Edelman in 1990; two sons. **Career:** Lecturer in philosophy, University of New Brunswick, Saint John, 1971; reporter, *The Evening Times-Globe,* Saint John, New Brunswick, 1972; reporter, *The Examiner,* Peterborough, Ontario, 1973–75; copy editor, *The Montreal Star,* 1975; copy editor, *The Star-Phoenix,* Saskatoon, Saskatchewan, 1979. Since 1991 lecturer in English, Skidmore College, Saratoga Springs, New York, and since 1994 faculty, Norwich University, Montpelier, Vermont. Writer-in residence, University of New Brunswick, Fredericton, 1987, State University of New York, Albany, 1992–94. Fiction editor, *The Iowa Review,* 1980–81. Since 1991 editor, with Maggie Helwig, *Coming Attractions,* Oberon Press, Ottawa. Since 1994 host, *The Book Show,* National Public Radio, Albany. **Awards:** Canadian Fiction Magazine annual prize, 1984, and Literary Press Group award, 1986, both for ''Dog Attempts to Drown Man in Saskatoon''; Canadian National Magazine awards gold medal, 1990, for ''Story Carved in Stone''; New York Foundation for the Arts Artists' fellowship, 1994. **Address:** R.R. 1, Waterford, Ontario, Canada N0E 1Y0.

PUBLICATIONS

Novels

Precious. Toronto, Seal, 1984.
The South Will Rise at Noon. Toronto. Viking, 1988; New York, Viking, 1989.
The Life and Times of Captain N. Toronto, McClelland and Stewart, and New York, Knopf, 1993.

Short Stories

The Mad River and Other Stories. Windsor, Black Moss Press, 1981.
Dog Attempts to Drown Man in Saskatoon. Vancouver, Talonbooks, 1985.
A Guide to Animal Behaviour. Fredericton, Goose Lane, 1991.

Other

Notes Home from a Prodigal Son. Ottawa, Oberon Press, 1999.
Editor, with Maggie Helwig, *Coming Attractions 91–94,* 4 vols. Ottawa, Oberon Press, 1991–94.
Editor, with Diane Schoemperlen, *Coming Attractions 95.* Ottawa, Oberon Press, 1995.

*

Critical Studies: In *Canadian Fiction Magazine,* 65, 1989; in *Paragraph,* 13 (1), 1991; in *The New Story Writers* edited by John Metcalf, Quarry Press, 1992; in *Matrix,* 40, Summer 1993.

Douglas Glover comments:

Most of what I write comes from a place so personal, so intimate, and so painful that I cannot write about it except as fiction. Elements of my style—the obsessive repetitions, the phantasmagoria of images, allusions and comparisons, the mix of comedy and violence, the grotesquerie which is the joke of horror—were always present, but have been reinforced by reading the novels of the late great

French Canadian writer Hubert Aquin, especially *Blackout* and *The Antiphonary*. Nabokov lurks somewhere. And back of Nabokov the ghost of Viktor Shklovsky telling us to make things ''strange.''

I like to write stories that touch the mind and the heart at once, stories that don't necessarily mean but which nonetheless refer to the world's miraculous complexity, its unexpectedness, its divine playfulness. I write about love and memory, the weight of memory and history and the multifarious messages of culture and the past which run through us and, briefly, use us before passing on. What is the self that's being used and what is using it? I ask. And how do lovers love? Why are people cruel? And whither the words, when the wind blows … ?

As an individual I find it difficult to separate the rhetorical from the personal. I am a nomad, an expatriate, a wandering Canadian (which is worse than just being a Canadian, I am doubly displaced, a Canadian squared), and I can no longer tell whether that's because I am a writer or why I am a writer. Some mornings I wake up and it's a problem. Some mornings I wake up and it's a dance.

* * *

Since 1981, Douglas Glover has yoked highly cerebral concerns with a witty and passionate style, a steadily growing array of techniques serving an increasingly complex vision. ''Life has a way of complicating itself,'' the narrator says in ''The Obituary Writer'' (from *A Guide to Animal Behavior*). In many Glover stories, as in ''Pender's Visions'' (*The Mad River and Other Stories*) and in the title story of *Dog Attempts to Drown Man in Saskatoon,* the writer embraces that complexity in a flexible style that has steadily grown in power and resource. A further example is ''A Man in a Box'' (*A Guide to Animal Behavior*) in which a pandemonic, logorrheic universe swirls within the confines of an obsessed derelict's cardboard shelter.

The same growth can be traced in his novels. *Precious* is a rococo play on mystery-novel conventions, whose antihero is a much-married newspaper reporter in a small Lake Ontario shoreline community (''It seemed to me that I had spent a lifetime, more or less, in towns just like Ockenden, changing buses to get to other towns''). *The South Will Rise at Noon,* after a start somewhat straining suspension of disbelief, builds to brilliant comedy in telling of one Tully Stamper's misadventures in Gomez Gap, Florida, scene of a preposterous cinematic re-creation of a Civil War battle.

To some extent *Precious* and *The South Will Rise at Noon* amount to a novelist's accomplished apprenticeship. But *The Life and Times of Captain N.,* a story of violent border transactions set in the Niagara frontier, 1779–81, marks a breakthrough, the first thirty pages or so of it among the most engaged and involving Canadian prose in recent years. The novel bodies forth a startlingly vivid historical imagination (in a favorable notice *The New Yorker* said the book belongs to the ''Apocalypse The'' school of historical fiction), previously only hinted at in a few stories like ''Swain Corliss, Hero of Malcolm's Mills (Now Oakland, Ontario), November 6, 1814'' in *A Guide to Animal Behavior.* (''The Indians skinned and butchered Edwin Barton's body, Ned having no further use for it.'') Amid a treacherous landscape of shattered alliances, psychological as much as political, Glover tells of Captain Hendrick Nellis, Tory guerrilla and ''redeemer'' of Indian-abducted whites; his son, Oskar, whom Hendrick kidnaps to fight the Yankee rebels; and Mary Hunsacker, a German immigrant girl captured and culturally assimilated by the Mississauga tribe. Then there are the Mohawk, Oneida, Cayuga, Onondaga, and Seneca—Iroquoian shape-shifters viciously caught in a no-holds-barred conflict between Loyalists and ''Bostonians.'' The narrative language, especially that of the psychically riven Oskar, is a virtuoso mix of period-sensitive verisimilitude and the shifting premises of the postmodern.

Glover has thought and written extensively about the art of fiction; more importantly, his stories and novels are not just five-finger exercises on the theme of extreme situations but work out a deeply felt, still-evolving vision. Complexity is never achieved at the expense of clarity.

—Fraser Sutherland

GODWIN, Gail (Kathleen)

Nationality: American. **Born:** Birmingham, Alabama, 18 June 1937. **Education:** Peace Junior College, Raleigh, North Carolina, 1955–57; University of North Carolina, Chapel Hill, 1957–59, B.A. in journalism 1959; University of Iowa, Iowa City, 1967–71, M.A. 1968, Ph.D. in English 1971. **Family:** Married 1) Douglas Kennedy in 1960 (divorced); 2) Ian Marshall in 1965 (divorced 1966). **Career:** Reporter, Miami *Herald,* 1959–60; consultant, U.S. Travel Service, United States Embassy, London, 1962–65; researcher, *Saturday Evening Post,* New York, 1966; Instructor in English, 1967–70, and lecturer at the Writers Workshop, 1972–73, University of Iowa; instructor and fellow, Center for Advanced Studies, University of Illinois, Urbana, 1971–72; American specialist, United States Information Service, Brazil, 1976; lecturer, Vassar College, Poughkeepsie, New York, 1977, and Columbia University, New York, 1978, 1981. **Awards:** National Endowment for the Arts grant, 1974, and fellowship, for libretto, 1978; Guggenheim fellowship, 1975; St. Lawrence award, 1976; American Academy award, 1981; Thomas Wolfe Memorial award, 1988; Janet Kafka award, 1988. **Agent:** John Hawkins and Associates, 71 West 23rd Street, Suite 1600, New York, New York 10010. **Address:** P.O. Box 946, Woodstock, New York 12498–0946, U.S.A.

Publications

Novels

The Perfectionists. New York, Harper, 1970; London, Cape, 1971.
Glass People. New York, Knopf, 1972.
The Odd Woman. New York, Knopf, 1974; London, Cape, 1975.
Violet Clay. New York, Knopf, and London, Gollancz, 1978.
A Mother and Two Daughters. New York, Viking Press, and London, Heinemann, 1982.
The Finishing School. New York, Viking, and London, Heinemann, 1985.
A Southern Family. New York, Morrow, and London, Heinemann, 1987.
Father Melancholy's Daughter. New York, Morrow, and London, Deutsch, 1991.
The Good Husband. New York, Ballantine, and London, Deutsch, 1994.
Evensong. New York, Ballantine Books, 1999.

Short Stories

Dream Children. New York, Knopf, 1976; London, Gollancz, 1977.
Mr. Bedford and the Muses. New York, Viking Press, 1983; London, Heinemann, 1984.

Uncollected Short Stories

''Fate of Fleeing Maidens,'' in *Mademoiselle* (New York), May 1978.
''The Unlikely Family,'' in *Redbook* (New York), August 1979.
''Over the Mountain,'' in *Antaeus* (New York), 1983.

Plays

The Last Lover, music by Robert Starer (produced Katonah, New York, 1975).
Journals of a Songmaker, music by Robert Starer (produced Philadelphia, 1976).
Apollonia, music by Robert Starer (produced Minneapolis, 1979).

Recordings: *Anna Margarita's Will* (song cycle), music by Robert Starer, C.R.I., 1980; *Remembering Felix,* music by Robert Starer, Spectrum, 1987.

Other

Woodstock Landscapes: Photographs by John Kleinhans (text). Woodstock, New York, Golden Notebook Press, 2000.
Editor, with Shannon Ravenel, *The Best American Short Stories 1985.* Boston, Houghton Mifflin, 1985.

*

Manuscript Collection: Southern Collection, University of Northern Carolina Library, Chapel Hill.

Critical Studies: ''*The Odd Woman:* Literature and the Retreat from Life'' by Susan E. Lorsch, in *Critique* (Atlanta), vol. 20, no. 2, 1978; ''Reaching Out: Sensitivity and Order,'' in *Recent American Fiction by Women* by Anne Z. Mickelson, Metuchen, New Jersey, Scarecrow Press, 1979; interview and ''Gail Godwin and Southern Womanhood'' by Carolyn Rhodes, both in *Women Writers of the Contemporary South* edited by Peggy Whitman Prenshaw, Jackson, University Press of Mississippi, 1984; *Gail Godwin* by Jane Hill, New York, Twayne, 1992; *The Evolving Self in the Novels of Gail Godwin* by Lihong Xie. Baton Rouge, Louisiana State University Press, 1995; *Moving On: The Heroines of Shirley Ann Grau, Anne Tyler, and Gail Godwin* by Susan S. Kissel. Bowling Green, Ohio, Bowling Green State University Popular Press, 1996.

Gail Godwin comments:

Since I began writing fiction I have been most interested in creating characters who operate at a high level of intelligence and feeling as they go about trying to make sense of the world in which they find themselves, and as they make decisions about how to live their lives.

* * *

In her fiction Gail Godwin depicts the choices that modern women make. Whether within marriage or the single life, motherhood or career, these choices necessitate compromise, and none brings complete happiness. Godwin's characters often explore their options through art as they create or analyze images that may reveal or even change reality. A common crisis that precipitates this artistic endeavor or self-exploration is a death in the family, and within renewed family relationships, either nuclear or extended, Godwin's characters defend, dismiss, or display their choices.

Godwin demonstrates the effects of lack of choice in her first two novels, both violent and oppressive tales. In *The Perfectionists* Dane Empson's rage against her stifling marriage erupts when she beats her husband's illegitimate son. Obsessed with sexual acts in which she is either completely powerless or powerful, Dane views any relationship as invasive. Francesca Bolt, a passive princess in *Glass People,* makes not even basic decisions about food and clothes. She may ''open out'' like a beautiful flower but only if husband Cameron provides the container. Like Dane Empson, Francesca longs for a dark angel to transport her to her ''true but unknown destiny.'' Neither Dane nor Francesca finds the strength to leave her marriage.

In her most insightful novel to date, *The Odd Woman,* Godwin creates Jane Clifford, an academic who researches life in order to control it. Unlike Dane Empson and Francesca Bolt, Jane believes in relationships, in perfect unions, like that of Marian Evans (George Eliot) and George Henry Lewes, in which men and women can communicate but retain separate identities. If she can analyze her married lover's words, Jane believes she can discover his feelings. And to some extent she succeeds, for in a rare moment Jane experiences Gabriel completely. However, she cannot sustain her moment, and her analyses usually lead her away from reality toward melodramas with faceless villains.

The fictive present in *The Odd Woman* begins with Jane's grandmother's death, an event that forces Jane's rediscovery of family relationships. Within her family and in George Gissing's *The Odd Women,* a novel for her next teaching assignment, Jane explores women's choices. Although she hates her aggressive stepfather, the man with whom her mother makes an apparent compromise, Jane still cheers for women who strive for marriage. She destroys the family myth about great-aunt Cleva who ran away with a villain actor in the melodrama *The Fatal Wedding.* Caught between the world of literature in which every plot seems probable and reality in which married lovers seldom leave their wives, Jane struggles with her own possibilities. She rejects total withdrawal into literature after living in isolation the winter she writes her dissertation. Gerda, her radical feminist *doppelgänger,* cannot convince her to give up on men, but neither will Jane continue to play the role of Understanding Mistress. Jane's insomnia functions as her muse, and keeping herself open to relationships may free the ending of the Jane Clifford Story, with all its Aristotelian requirements. At the end of the novel, back in her apartment, Jane may not have found an Eliot-Lewes union, but she clings to her belief that one can ''organize the loneliness and the weather and the long night into something of abiding shape and beauty.''

Moving the reader closer to the main character through first-person point of view and less reliance on interior monologue than in *The Old Woman,* Godwin nevertheless continues her reflections on the thin line between reality and imagination, between art and life in *Violet Clay.* The title character in *Violet Clay* searches idly for her options in ''the book of Old Plots'' while she projects herself into the romance novels she illustrates for a living. The death of Violet's Uncle Ambrose serves as catalyst for change when he commits suicide in his Adirondack cabin. Ambrose's note to Violet reads: ''I'm sorry, there's nothing left.'' Violet sketches his face and interprets the punctuation in the note until she realizes that the ''nothing'' is artistic inspiration. When Violet realizes the meaning of Ambrose's note, she takes up serious art again, and the goal in the fictive present becomes the proper artistic subject. Violet finally remembers Ambrose's advice: write about (or create) something you want to happen. Art is a way of seeing life rather than postponing it, Violet learns. In her portrait of her neighbor Samantha De Vere, a woman who survives incest and rape, Violet captures the human spirit and earns artistic recognition. Exploring relationships and testing possibilities through artistic expression contribute to Violet's growth; as she states, ''Sam put me into proportion, as Ambrose put me into perspective.'' Godwin continues to explore this connection between art and life in her two short story collections, *Dream Children* and *Mr. Bedford and the Muses.*

Each female character in *A Mother and Two Daughters* represents one choice for women. Cate, the academic who chooses abortion, Lydia, the divorcée who returns to school and career, and Nell, the widow who finds contentment in a second husband, all receive narrative attention in Godwin's longest novel to date. Although Godwin reduces her focus on art to a few comments on *The Scarlet Letter,* the theme of that novel is clearly relevant: ''Can the individual spirit survive the society in which it has to live?'' The society in *A Mother and Two Daughters* is that of the family, which Cate and Lydia's sibling rivalry threatens to pull apart after their father's death. Although blinded by misunderstanding, Lydia and Cate experience much the same anxiety and desire, as Lydia writes a research paper on Eros, a ''striving for what one lacks,'' and Cate defines hope as ''keeping a space ready for what you did want, even though you didn't know what it would be until it came.'' Neither daughter wants to close off her possibilities, whatever her destiny might bring.

In the most intense scene in the novel, Cate and Lydia explode at each other in anger. They express their resentment of their childhood roles: Cate as rebel, Lydia as dutiful daughter. After the fight, their neglect causes their father's cabin to burn, the fire taking with it not only childhood possessions but much of the sisters' anger. In the peace that follows, Lydia and Cate incorporate each other into their lives, and the connections between Lydia's real family and Cate's extended one allow each to survive as individual spirits: ''Do you remember? ... Does it still hurt here? ... Oh, it all passes, but that's the beauty of it, too.'' Music written by Lydia's son Dickie unites the family in the final scene.

''Your soul craves that constant heightening of reality only art can give you,'' Ursula DeVane tells Justine Stokes in *The Finishing School* and thus continues Godwin's theme of art affecting life. Fourteen-year-old Justine, grieving for her dead father and grandparents, turns to forty-four-year-old Ursula for friendship. Twenty-six years later Justine still struggles to understand that tragic summer. Curiosity about that tragedy, Godwin's portrayal of eccentric Ursula, and her sensitive depiction of adolescent Justine propel the reader through *The Finishing School.* Much like Muriel Spark's Jean Brodie, Ursula DeVane serves as muse to the innocent. Always ''keep moving forward and making new trysts with life,'' Ursula advises Justine, and you'll never grow old. However, the time comes when the student becomes independent and sees her teacher as flawed rather than ideal. This inevitability forms the essential part of Ursula's definition of tragedy: the ''something terrible'' that happens when a person lives out her own ''destiny.'' The intensity of their relationship causes Justine to betray Ursula much as Ursula betrayed her own mother. The adult Justine realizes that now she must use ''all the fate'' that has happened to her and ''make possible what still may happen.'' Her yearnings and torments strengthen her acting talent: ''As long as you can go on creating new roles for yourself, you are not vanquished,'' Justine concludes, much as Ursula would. In Godwin's fictional world, roles for women are artistically created and recreated until they become real.

One senses, reading *Evensong,* that Godwin did a great deal of research to create a believable account of protagonist Margaret Bonner's daily routines as an Episcopalian priest. The title is apt in more ways than one, since the book is set in the final weeks of 1999, when many fear that the world is on the brink of some sort of cataclysm. (Godwin published the novel about a year before that time.) These fears can even penetrate a seemingly idyllic community in the Smoky Mountains of western North Carolina, but equally endangering of Margaret's peace are circumstances from her past, as well as figures from the present who intrude on her life with husband Adrian, a struggling teacher. Throughout the story, Godwin displays her characteristic grace and nimble talent.

—Mary M. Lay

GOLD, Herbert

Nationality: American. **Born:** Cleveland, Ohio, 9 March 1924. **Education:** Columbia University, New York, B.A. 1946, M.A. 1948; the Sorbonne, Paris (Fulbright scholar), 1949–51. **Military Service:** Served in the United States Army, 1943–46. **Family:** Married 1) Edith Zubrin in 1948 (divorced 1956), two daughters; 2) Melissa Dilworth in 1968 (divorced 1975), one daughter and two sons. **Career:** lecturer in philosophy and literature, Western Reserve University, Cleveland, 1951–53; lecturer in English, Wayne State University, Detroit, 1954–56. Visiting professor, Cornell University, Ithaca, New York, 1958, University of California, Berkeley, 1963, Harvard University, Cambridge, Massachusetts, 1964, Stanford University, California, 1967, and University of California, Davis, 1973–79. **Awards:** Inter-American Cultural grant, to Haiti, 1950; *Hudson Review* fellowship, 1956; Guggenheim fellowship, 1957; American Academy grant, 1958; Longview Foundation award, 1959; Ford fellowship, for drama, 1960; Sherwood Anderson prize, 1989. L.H.D.: Baruch College, City University, New York, 1988. **Address:** 1051-A Broadway, San Francisco, California 94133–4205, U.S.A.

PUBLICATIONS

Novels

Birth of a Hero. New York, Viking Press, 1951.

The Prospect Before Us. Cleveland, World, 1954; as *Room Clerk,* New York, New American Library, 1955.

The Man Who Was Not With It. Boston, Little Brown, 1956; London, Secker and Warburg, 1965; as *The Wild Life,* New York, Permabooks, 1957.

The Optimist. Boston, Little Brown, 1959.
Therefore Be Bold. New York, Dial Press, 1960; London, Deutsch, 1962.
Salt. New York, Dial Press, 1963; London, Secker and Warburg, 1964.
Fathers: A Novel in the Form of a Memoir. New York, Random House, and London, Secker and Warburg, 1967.
The Great American Jackpot. New York, Random House, 1970; London, Weidenfeld and Nicolson, 1971.
Swiftie the Magician. New York, McGraw Hill, 1974; London, Hutchinson, 1975.
Waiting for Cordelia. New York, Arbor House, 1977; London, Hutchinson, 1978.
Slave Trade. New York, Arbor House, 1979.
He/She. New York, Arbor House, 1980; London, Severn House, 1982.
Family: A Novel in the Form of a Memoir. New York, Arbor House, 1981; London, Severn House, 1983.
True Love. New York, Arbor House, 1982; London, Severn House, 1984.
Mister White Eyes. New York, Arbor House, 1984; London, Severn House, 1985.
A Girl of Forty. New York, Fine, 1986.
Dreaming. New York, Fine, 1988.
She Took My Arm As If She Loved Me. New York, St. Martin's Press, 1997.

Short Stories

15 x 3, with R.V. Cassill and James B. Hall. New York, New Directions, 1957.
Love and Like. New York, Dial Press, 1960; London, Deutsch, 1961.
The Magic Will: Stories and Essays of a Decade. New York, Random House, 1971.
Stories of Misbegotten Love. Santa Barbara, California, Capra Press, 1985.
Lovers and Cohorts: Twenty-Seven Stories. New York, Fine, 1986.

Other

The Age of Happy Problems (essays). New York, Dial Press, 1962.
Biafra Goodbye. San Francisco, Twowindows Press, 1970.
My Last Two Thousand Years (autobiography). New York, Random House, 1972; London, Hutchinson, 1973.
The Young Prince and the Magic Cone (for children). New York, Doubleday, 1973.
A Walk on the West Side: California on the Brink (stories and essays). New York, Arbor House, 1981.
Travels in San Francisco. New York, Arcade, 1990.
The Best Nightmare on Earth: A Life in Haiti. New York, Prentice Hall Press, and London, Grafton, 1991.
Bohemia. New York, Simon and Schuster, 1993.
Editor, *Fiction of the Fifties: A Decade of American Writing.* New York, Doubleday, 1959.
Editor, with David L. Stevenson, *Stories of Modern America.* New York, St. Martin's Press, 1961; revised edition, 1963.
Editor, *First Person Singular: Essays for the Sixties.* New York, Dial Press, 1963.

*

Herbert Gold comments:

Subjects: Power, money, sex and love, intention in America.
Themes: The same.
Moral: Coming next time.

* * *

In Herbert Gold's introduction to *Fiction of the Fifties,* he makes a distinction between fiction which *avows* and fiction which *controls.* The fiction which avows is a rather faithful transcription of the immediate and personal experience of the writer; such fiction makes use of the writer's own experience of his past and the section of social life where that experience took place. The other sort of fiction makes an attempt to present the experiences of persons who indeed are not the writer; these experiences are given clarity by an effort of the imagination which takes the writer outside himself and immerses him in circumstances that are not his own. All this is done by the exercise of *control.*

These interesting categories can be used to classify Gold's own fiction. A great deal of that fiction falls into the first category, that of avowal, as one can see from an inspection of his autobiographical *My Last Two Thousand Years.* This book is a narrative of Gold's own life, a life that finds its way into several of his novels. It was a life in which, as the son of a Jewish immigrant who settled in Cleveland, Gold experienced a difficult youth in the shadow of a strong father who had found a place for himself in an alien society. Gold's narrative relates his own struggles to detach himself from his father's ambitions for him, and to achieve his own goals, in New York and elsewhere, as student, critic, and novelist. All this was a process of self-discovery that demanded acts of will and personal heroism. This self-discovery, as Gold relates it, also involved a succession of painful relationships: marriage, parenthood, divorce, and a second marriage, with various temporary relationships along the way.

These are all matters that various other novelists would regard as private. So are they for Gold. But they are also the stuff of much of his fiction. These are the novels which *avow* (or assert) the essentials of the writer's own life. Such fiction contrasts with other novels in which Gold borrows and reshapes elements of other lives; it is in these latter novels that Gold *controls* the experiences of other persons and also depicts social patterns which the writer does not know directly and immediately.

Gold's frequent adherence to the dictum of Sir Philip Sidney's muse—''Fool ... look in thy heart and write''—is illustrated by an excellent novel, *Fathers,* which is subtitled ''A Novel in the Form of a Memoir.'' The novel tells of the relation between an immigrant father and his son; it is a vivid recollection of matters that Gold also puts down in *My Last Two Thousand Years. Fathers* offers homage to a courageous father and to the equally courageous son who chooses to turn aside from his father. The novel offers a convincing texture of loyalty and enmity. The same section of Gold's life appears in *Therefore Be Bold* which, however, centers attention on ''Daniel Berman's'' adolescent years in Cleveland: his encounters with poetry and sex and his bitter first experience of anti-Semitism.

Other novels, one can judge, are transcriptions of Gold's own experience of self-assertion and self-discovery in the New York literary world. Thus, *Swiftie the Magician* displays Gold's creative imagination moving onwards from his youth and assessing a man's attempts to find his own way through the jungles of professional and emotional life that surround a person in the second half of the twentieth century. The novel relates the involvement of a writer with three women: an East Coast innocent, a West Coast ''experienced'' young woman, and the hard-bitten Swiftie, a ''magician'' who knows what the score is in a rough world. *Salt* gives the reader a more complex version of such pursuits of identity. Two men—one a complacent Wasp and the other once more an alter ego for Gold—move from woman to woman, the Wasp learning little and the young Jew from Cleveland a great deal.

Such are the novels in which Gold reworks the stuff of his own life. But there are other novels in which Gold is exercising *control*—is, in more conventional literary language, inventing persons not himself and following the courses of their experiences. *Birth of a Hero* follows the attempts of a middle-aged business man, Reuben Flair, a faceless cipher, to become a man fully aware of what he has done, in marriage and beyond marriage. As in other novels by Gold, the outlines of Reuben's achievement are cloudy, but a sense of travel and change is conveyed. In *The Prospect Before Us* Gold moves still farther afield. In this novel the chief person is Harry Bowers, manager of a run-down motel in Cleveland. A level of life—low, raunchy, and cruel, and quite different from the world of the novels of avowal—is presented in colors that convince. And there is no touch of the frequent father-son situation; Harry Bowers allows a black woman to rent a room in his motel and is hounded for what he has done. *The Man Who Was Not With It* allows us to inhabit the awareness of a carnival worker. Here, however, there is an approach to the themes of the novels of avowal. Bud, the carnie, is saddled with two fathers: one, his real one in Pittsburgh, and the other a carnival barker. The barker delivers Bud from his drug habit (and falls foul of it himself) and hovers like a threatening cloud over the early weeks of Bud's marriage: a relation that links this novel with other work of Gold. In *The Great American Jackpot* the persona is also not Gold's own (the hero is a Berkeley student of the 1960s), but the student's preoccupations are not unfamiliar. Al Dooley loves and hates his teacher, a black sociologist; Dooley tries to find out who he is in the arms of two girls; and, finally, he asserts his identity by breaking out: in this instance, by robbing a bank and experiencing the farce of American justice. Dooley reappears in *Waiting for Cordelia* where he is doing a thesis on prostitution in the San Francisco area. A madam (Cordelia) and Marietta, a woman eager to become a reforming mayor of San Francisco, enrich Dooley's research. In the course of writing his study, Dooley faces Gold's usual questions about the nature of love and the sadness and the loneliness which hamper its realization. Similar preoccupations mark the early novel, *The Optimist,* in which Burr Fuller makes his way through a failed marriage and achieves some mastery of the mysteries of love and career. And similar struggles mark *True Love* where the subject is the uneasiness of middle age; a ''respectable'' man is harassed by the dreams of his youth and by his fears about his later life. Will the late discovery of ''true love'' allay these discontents? In all, a considerable variety. It is a variety bound together by a style that is generally pervasive save for variations that reflect the different social levels reproduced.

In *She Took My Arm As If She Loved Me,* private eye Dan Kasdan gets a lead on the location of Priscilla, the wife he loved and lost many years before. That lead comes from a sleazy pornographer—yet the real story centers around Dan's enduring love for Priscilla. A certain vigor results from the determined contemporary quality of Gold's references, including commercial products and public diversions, and even turns of speech. What usually holds this variety together is Gold's own sense of the worth of what he is doing. The language of the novels is a considerable support to the portions of wisdom that appear in the novels.

—Harold H. Watts

GOLDMAN, William

Nationality: American. **Born:** Chicago, Illinois, 12 August 1931; brother of the writer James Goldman. **Education:** Highland Park High School; Oberlin College, Ohio, 1948–52, B.A. in English 1952; Columbia University, New York, 1954–56, M.A. in English 1956. **Military Service:** Served in the United States Army, 1952–54: Corporal. **Family:** Married Ilene Jones in 1961 (divorced); two daughters. **Awards:** Oscar, for screenplay, 1970, 1977. **Address:** 50 East 77th Street, New York, New York 10021, U.S.A.

Publications

Novels

The Temple of Gold. New York, Knopf, 1957.
Your Turn to Curtsy, My Turn to Bow. New York, Doubleday, 1958.
Soldier in the Rain. New York, Atheneum, and London, Eyre and Spottiswoode, 1960.
Boys and Girls Together. New York, Atheneum, 1964; London, Joseph, 1965.
No Way To Treat a Lady (as Harry Longbaugh). New York, Fawcett, and London, Muller, 1964; as William Goldman, New York, Harcourt Brace, and London, Coronet, 1968.
The Thing of It Is. . . . New York, Harcourt Brace, and London, Joseph, 1967.
Father's Day. New York, Harcourt Brace, and London, Joseph, 1971.
The Princess Bride: S. Morgenstern's Classic Tale of True Love and High Adventure: The ''Good Parts'' Version, Abridged. New York, Harcourt Brace, 1973; London, Macmillan, 1975.
Marathon Man. New York, Delacorte Press, 1974; London, Macmillan, 1975.
Magic. New York, Delacorte Press, and London, Macmillan, 1976.
Tinsel. New York, Delacorte Press, and London, Macmillan, 1979.
Control. New York, Delacorte Press, and London, Hodder and Stoughton, 1982.
The Color of Light. New York, Warner, and London, Granada, 1984.
The Silent Gondoliers (as S. Morgenstern). New York, Ballantine, 1984.
Heat. New York, Warner, 1985; as *Edged Weapons,* London, Granada, 1985.
Brothers. New York, Warner, and London, Grafton, 1986.

Uncollected Short Stories

''Something Blue,'' in *Rogue* (New York), 1958.
''Da Vinci,'' in *New World Writing 17.* Philadelphia, Lippincott, 1960.
''Till the Right Girls Come Along,'' in *Transatlantic Review 8* (London), Winter 1961.
''The Ice Cream Eat,'' in *Stories from the Transatlantic Review,* edited by Joseph F. McCrindle. New York, Holt Rinehart, 1970.

Plays

Blood, Sweat and Stanley Poole, with James Goldman (produced New York, 1961). New York, Dramatists Play Service, 1962.
A Family Affair, with James Goldman, music by John Kander (produced New York, 1962).
Butch Cassidy and the Sundance Kid (screenplay). New York, Bantam, and London, Corgi, 1969.
The Great Waldo Pepper (screenplay). New York, Dell, 1975.
Memoirs of an Invisible Man, with Robert Collector and Dana Bodner, 1992.
William Goldman: Four Screenplays with Essays. New York, Applause Books, 1995.
William Goldman: Five Screenplays. New York, Applause, 1996.
The Ghost and the Darkness: The Book of the Film. New York, Applause, 1996.
Absolute Power: The Screenplay. New York, Applause, 1997.

Screenplays: *Masquerade,* with Michael Relph, 1964; *Harare* (*The Moving Target*), 1966; *Butch Cassidy and the Sundance Kid,* 1969; *The Hot Rock* (*How to Steal a Diamond in Four Uneasy Lessons*), 1972; *The Stepford Wives,* 1974; *The Great Waldo Pepper,* 1975; *All the President's Men,* 1976; *Marathon Man,* 1976; *A Bridge Too Far,* 1977; *Magic,* 1978; *The Princess Bride,* 1987; *Heat,* 1987; *Misery,* 1990; *The Chamber*, Universal, 1997.; *Absolute Power*, Columbia Pictures, 1997; *The General's Daughter.* Paramount Pictures, 1999.

Television Films: *Mr. Horn,* 1979.

Other

The Season: A Candid Look at Broadway. New York, Harcourt Brace, 1969; revised edition, New York, Limelight, 1984.
Wigger (for children). New York, Harcourt Brace, 1974.
The Story of ''A Bridge Too Far.'' New York, Dell, 1977.
Adventures in the Screen Trade: A Personal View of Hollywood and Screenwriting. New York, Warner, 1983; London, Macdonald, 1984.
Wait Till Next Year: The Story of a Season When What Should've Happened Didn't and What Could've Gone Wrong Did, with Mike Lupica. New York, Bantam, 1988.
Hype and Glory. New York, Villard, and London, Macdonald, 1990.
The Big Picture: Who Killed Hollywood? and Other Essays. New York, New York, Applause Books, 1999.
Which Lie Did I Tell?, or, More Adventures in the Screen Trade. New York, Pantheon Books, 2000.

*

Critical Studies: *William Goldman* by Richard Andersen, Boston, Twayne, 1979.

* * *

William Goldman is a successful novelist, film scenarist, playwright, critic, and children's book author who focuses much of his attention on the illusions by which men and women live. These illusions often make existence more miserable than it need be and provide a core from which all of Goldman's protagonists seek to escape. Ironically, what they escape to is more often than not other illusions, which, because of the artificial distinctions society attaches to them, rarely satisfy their human needs.

When Raymond Trevitt's desperate attempts to protect the ideals of his childhood from adult realities in *The Temple of Gold* inadvertently cause the deaths of his closest friends, he leaves his home, but discovers only frustration and intolerance elsewhere. In *Your Turn to Curtsy, My Turn to Bow,* Chad Kimberly is driven by his ambitious illusions into believing he is a new Messiah, whose schizophrenic demands frighten the novel's protagonist, Peter Bell, into a life of escapist day-dreaming. Ambition is not the only illusion that drives the characters of *Boys and Girls Together* to New York; most of them are escaping from the unbearable circumstances of their home lives. Nevertheless, their hopes for self-improvement are dashed by unsuccessful love affairs, domineering parents, professional failures, embarrassing social exposures, and suicide. In *Soldier in the Rain,* Eustis Clay and Maxwell Slaughter cannot free themselves from the military-economic complex of which they are so much a part.

The great American illusions about success are the central concerns of *The Thing of It Is …* and *Father's Day,* in which the talented, rich, but quirky Amos McCracken spends a tremendous amount of money trying to save his marriage and then his relationship with his daughter. In the end, his guilt-ridden personal failures lead him to create fantasies that enable him to fulfill the images he has of himself but that also pose a serious threat to the safety and well-being of others.

Unlike Amos McCracken or Kit Gil of *No Way to Treat a Lady,* Westley and Buttercup of *The Princess Bride,* Babe Levy of *Marathon Man,* and Corky Withers of *Magic* cannot retreat to a fabulous land to try to make themselves whole; they already live in fabulous land, where they are constantly assaulted by its empirical and psychological facts. Forced to encounter a vast confusion of fact and fiction, to deal with pain and death, and to seek power against forces that are difficult to pinpoint and consequently understand, the protagonists of these three novels must stay rooted in social systems that attempt to deny their vitality while creating illusions that life is what it should be.

Combining the everyday reality of Goldman's early novels with the fabulous reality of his later works, *Tinsel* tells the story of three women who desperately try to escape from the boredom of their daily lives to the fame and fortune of movie stardom, which, like all illusions, eludes them. As he did in *Marathon Man* and *Magic,* Goldman divides this into many chapters, so short and so different from any other in terms of setting and action that they flash by the reader like scenes in a movie. Because of their length, Goldman can keep simultaneously occurring stories running vividly in the reader's imagination without making any significant connections between them. When the individual stories eventually come together, Goldman continues flashing different scenes containing markedly different actions at such a pace that reading Goldman's story about the film industry becomes as close to a cinematic experience as literature can provide.

With *The Color of Light* Goldman returned to the themes of innocence and loss that concerned him in his early novels, only this time around he discusses them as subjects for writing. Unfortunately, this serious book, like some of his early serious novels, wasn't as well received as it should have been, and Goldman returned to the fabulist landscape of *Marathon Man* and *Magic* in *Control* and *Heat.* But he passed through fantasyland on the way just as he did in 1973 with *The Princess Bride. The Silent Gondoliers* tells us why the gondoliers in

Venice no longer sing. Even they have lost their innocence in a world from which there is no escape.

Perhaps because of his popularity or the reputation he has established in Hollywood (many of his novels have been adapted to the screen), many critics have misunderstood or underrated Goldman's works. Perhaps these critics have been confused by Goldman's use of multiple modes—novel of manners, confessional journal, psychological novel, social satire, romantic parody, black humor novel, detective story, spy novel, radical protest novel, soap opera, absurdist novel, and more—within a wide frame of genres. Whatever the reason, Goldman is an extraordinarily talented and prolific writer whose incorporation of cinematic techniques with conventional narrative forms mark a significant contribution to the novel tradition. His success in the screen trade has perhaps influenced a move away from fiction, with a growing number of successful screenplays, along with memoirs of his work in Hollywood, to his credit.

—Richard Andersen

GORDIMER, Nadine

Nationality: South African. **Born:** Springs, Transvaal, 20 November 1923. **Education:** A convent school, and the University of the Witwatersrand, Johannesburg. **Family:** Married 1) G. Gavron in 1949; 2) Reinhold Cassirer in 1954; one son and one daughter. **Career:** Visiting lecturer, Institute of Contemporary Arts, Washington, D.C., 1961, Harvard University, Cambridge, Massachusetts, 1969, Princeton University, New Jersey, 1969, Northwestern University, Evanston, Illinois 1969, and University of Michigan, Ann Arbor, 1970; Adjunct Professor of Writing, Columbia University, New York, 1971; presenter, *Frontiers* television series, 1990. **Awards:** W.H. Smith Literary award, 1961; Thomas Pringle award, 1969; James Tait Black Memorial prize, 1972; Booker prize, 1974; Grand Aigle d'Or prize (France), 1975; CNA award, 1975; Scottish Arts Council Neil Gunn fellowship, 1981; Common Wealth award, 1981; Modern Language Association award (U.S.A.), 1981; Malaparte prize (Italy), 1985; Nelly Sachs prize (Germany), 1985; Bennett award (U.S.A.), 1986; Royal Society of Literature Benson medal, 1990; Nobel prize, 1991, for literature. D.Lit.: University of Leuven, Belgium, 1980; D.Litt.: Smith College, Northampton, Massachusetts, 1985; City College, New York, 1985; Mount Holyoke College, South Hadley, Massachusetts, 1985; Harvard University, 1986; Yale University, New Haven, Connecticut, 1986; Columbia University, 1987; New School for Social Research, New York, 1987; University of York, 1987. Honorary Member, American Academy of Arts and Sciences, 1980; Honorary Fellow, Modern Language Association (U.S.A.), 1985. **Agent:** A.P. Watt Ltd., 20 John Street, London WC1N 2DR, England; or, Russell and Volkening Inc., 50 West 29th Street, New York, New York 10001, U.S.A.

Publications

Novels

The Lying Days. London, Gollancz, and New York, Simon and Schuster, 1953.

A World of Strangers. London, Gollancz, and New York, Simon and Schuster, 1958.

Occasion for Loving. London, Gollancz, and New York, Viking Press, 1963.

The Late Bourgeois World. London, Gollancz, and New York, Viking Press, 1966.

A Guest of Honour. New York, Viking Press, 1970; London, Cape, 1971.

The Conservationist. London, Cape, 1974; New York, Viking Press, 1975.

Burger's Daughter. London, Cape, and New York, Viking Press, 1979.

July's People. London, Cape, and New York, Viking Press, 1981.

A Sport of Nature. London, Cape, and New York, Knopf, 1987.

My Son's Story. London, Bloomsbury, and New York, Farrar Straus, 1990.

None to Accompany Me. London, Bloomsbury, and New York, Farrar Straus, 1994.

Harald, Claudia, and Their Son Duncan. London, Bloomsbury, 1996.

The House Gun. New York, Farrar, Straus and Giroux, 1998.

Short Stories

Face to Face. Johannesburg, Silver Leaf, 1949.

The Soft Voice of the Serpent and Other Stories. New York, Simon and Schuster, 1952; London, Gollancz, 1953.

Six Feet of the Country. London, Gollancz, and New York, Simon and Schuster, 1956.

Friday's Footprint and Other Stories. London, Gollancz, and New York, Viking Press, 1960.

Not for Publication and Other Stories. London, Gollancz, and New York, Viking Press, 1965.

Penguin Modern Stories 4, with others. London, Penguin, 1970.

Livingstone's Companions. New York, Viking Press, 1971; London, Cape, 1972.

Selected Stories. London, Cape, 1975; New York, Viking Press, 1976; as *No Place Like,* London, Penguin, 1978.

Some Monday for Sure. London, Heinemann, 1976.

A Soldier's Embrace. London, Cape, and New York, Viking Press, 1980.

Town and Country Lovers. Los Angeles, Sylvester and Orphanos, 1980.

Something Out There. London, Cape, and New York, Viking, 1984.

Crimes of Conscience. London, Heinemann, 1991.

Plays

Television Plays and Documentaries: *A Terrible Chemistry* (*Writers and Places* series), 1981 (UK); *Choosing for Justice: Allan Boesak,* with Hugo Cassirer, 1985 (USA and UK); *Country Lovers, A Chip of Glass Ruby, Praise,* and *Oral History* (all in *The Gordimer Stories* series), 1985 (USA); *Frontiers* series, 1990 (UK).

Other

African Lit. (lectures). Cape Town, University of Cape Town, 1972.

On the Mines, photographs by David Goldblatt. Cape Town, Struik, 1973.

The Black Interpreters: Notes on African Writing. Johannesburg, Spro-Cas Ravan, 1973.

What Happened to Burger's Daughter; or, How South African Censorship Works, with others. Johannesburg, Taurus, 1980.

Lifetimes: Under Apartheid, photographs by David Goldblatt. London, Cape, and New York, Knopf, 1986.

Reflections of South Africa, edited by Kirsten Egebjerg and Gillian Stead Eilersen. Herning, Denmark, Systime, 1986.

The Essential Gesture: Writing, Politics, and Places, edited by Stephen Clingman. London, Cape, and New York, Knopf, 1988.

Conversations with Nadine Gordimer, edited by Nancy Topping Bazin and Marilyn Dallman Seymour. Jackson, University Press of Mississippi, 1990.

Writing and Being. Cambridge, Harvard University Press, 1995.

Living in Hope and History: Notes from Our Century. New York, Farrar, Straus and Giroux, 1999.

Editor, with Lionel Abrahams, *South African Writing Today.* London, Penguin, 1967.

*

Bibliography: *Nadine Gordimer, Novelist and Short Story Writer: A Bibliography of Her Works* by Racilia Jilian Neil, Johannesburg, University of the Witwatersrand, 1964.

Critical Studies: *Nadine Gordimer* by Robert F. Haugh, New York, Twayne, 1974; *Nadine Gordimer* by Michael Wade, London, Evans, 1978; *Nadine Gordimer* by Christopher Heywood, Windsor, Berkshire, Profile, 1983; *The Novels of Nadine Gordimer: Private Lives/Public Landscapes* by John Cooke, Baton Rouge, Louisiana State University Press, 1985; *The Novels of Nadine Gordimer: History from the Inside* by Stephen Clingman, London, Allen and Unwin, 1986; *Nadine Gordimer* by Judie Newman, London, Macmillan, 1988; *Critical Essays on Nadine Gordimer* edited by Rowland Smith, Boston, Hall, 1990; *Rereading Nadine Gordimer* by Kathrin Wagner. Bloomington, Indiana University Press, 1994; *Nadine Gordimer* by Dominic Head. New York, Cambridge University Press, 1994; *From the Margins of Empire: Christina Stead, Doris Lessing, Nadine Gordimer* by Louise Yelin. Ithaca, New York, Cornell University Press, 1998; *A Writing Life: Celebrating Nadine Gordimer,* edited by Andries Walter Oliphant. London and New York, Viking, 1998; *Nadine Gordimer Revisited* by Barbara Temple-Thurston. New York, Twayne Publishers, 1999; *This Is No Place for a Woman: Nadine Gordimer, Nayantara Sahgal, Buchi Emecheta, and the Politics of Gender* by Joya Uraizee. Trenton, New Jersey, Africa World Press, 1999.

Theatrical Activities: Director: **Television**—*Choosing for Justice: Allan Boesak,* with Hugo Cassirer, 1985.

* * *

Nadine Gordimer, through her courageous and probing search for understanding and insight, has achieved international status as one of the finest living writers in English. Despite this international status, her work has been firmly rooted in her native country, South Africa, where she has remained throughout her career. Her position within the tumultuous social structure of this diverse and divided country—confined within the white, liberal, English, middle class—has been a source of both strength and weakness in her writing. On the one hand, she has been able to effectively make sense of the inextricably intertwined factors of South African social existence—political, sociological, and sexual—focusing on the apartheid regime's excessive intrusion into the realm of the individual. On the other hand, many of her characters, while exposing the limitations of Western, liberal humanism as a way of life, have been unable to escape these very limitations.

Most of Gordimer's main characters are involved in the very serious business of finding suitable moral apparatus to cope with the excruciating mental difficulties of living white—with a conscience—in a minority within a greater South African minority. Viewed as a group, Gordimer's male and female protagonists show a parallel development of consciousness towards a point at which most moral options appear to be exhausted (two of her later heroes end up running away, blindly, to nowhere).

In Helen Shaw, Jessie Stilwell, and Liz van den Sandt, the heroines of *The Lying Days, Occasion for Loving*, and *The Late Bourgeois World*, respectively, Gordimer charts the development from the racially exclusive confines of a white childhood in South Africa, to the discovery of—and disillusion with—the ''freedom'' of adult liberal thinking, and from there to the point where personal sacrifice becomes necessary for the sake of political integrity. In *The Lying Days*, Helen Shaw triumphs against the provincial narrowness and racial bigotry of her parents' mining village existence, yet she discovers that she, too, is sealed within her social limitations when she watches, from behind the windscreen of a car, a riot in a black township in which a man is shot dead by the police. As is the case with a number of Gordimer's characters, Helen Shaw's sense of moral failure is realized within and suggested by the failure of a love relationship in which certain moral suppositions function as a way of life. She goes away, to Europe, aware of a need for new sustenance, but essentially disillusioned. She is succeeded by Jessie Stilwell, an older version of Helen, back from Europe, now married and running a family, and committed to a makeshift liberal ideology, because the general (white) South African way of life is unacceptable. Yet the action of the novel shows this ideology to be vulnerable and in danger of hypocrisy—Jessie's world is ''invaded'' by an illicit love affair between a black artist and a young woman from England who, with her white musicologist husband, is a guest in the Stilwell home. The liberal idea of openness is belied by Jessie's wish to be left to her own kind of semi-romantic isolation, and all legitimate human reactions to the situation are bedeviled by a factor the Stilwells profess not to take undue account of—skin color. In *The Late Bourgeois World*, the developments in *The Lying Days* and *Occasion for Loving* find a conclusion. For Liz van den Sandt, the old liberal ''way of life'' is already dead when the book opens—her liberal-activist former husband has just committed suicide—while her present existence is nothing more than a kind of helpless withdrawal, reflected by a particularly pallid love affair she is conducting. She faces her moment of truth when a black friend, and activist, challenges her to step outside the sealed area of sensibility and conscience, and *do* something to help, at considerable personal risk. Thirteen years later, in *Burger's Daughter*, Rosa Burger appears: she is the daughter of the generation that did in fact take the struggle further from where Liz van den Sandt was poised at the end of *The Late Bourgeois World*. But now the process is inverted: Rosa's father dies while in prison for Marxist ''subversion,'' and Rosa finds herself unable simply to go on from where her father and his kind were stopped by politically repressive authority. She is heir to the failure of left-wing activism among whites in South Africa, and she settles for an occupation as a physiotherapist at a black hospital (treating Soweto riot victims), before she too is detained and committed to trial, merely on the basis of her connections with the nether-world of political dissent.

Gordimer's other major female protagonist, Hillela in *A Sport of Nature*, encapsulates and transcends all her predecessors. Hillela's story, told in a dingy factual and documentary manner, encompasses an upbringing in a liberal South African household, political activity in exile, and marriages to an ANC activist as well as to the leader of an African State. But the novel awkwardly mixes documentary style with picaresque form (Hillela's travels and adventures). Although Hillela completely breaks free of the barriers that had constrained her predecessors, the novel comes across as stodgy and contrived.

Gordimer's male heroes differ in that they either come in from the outside, or they represent a significantly non-liberal approach to life in South Africa. *A World of Strangers*, in which the new post-1948 apartheid is anatomized with great clarity, shows the rapid disillusionment of a young Englishman, Toby Hood, who comes to South Africa, determined to live a ''private life.'' An altogether different kind of disillusionment faces the more mature and intellectually well-equipped figure of Colonel Evelyn James Bray, hero of *A Guest of Honour*. He returns to the newly independent African state to witness the realization of ideals of freedom for which, as a colonial civil servant, he was deported. The political situation gradually slips out of control, and Bray is killed as a result of a misunderstanding that underscores the ambiguity of any European's role in Africa.

It is as though all illusions of a meaningful political existence for whites have been stripped bare when Mehring the technologist appears in Gordimer's Booker prize-winning masterpiece, *The Conservationist*. This is a novel of immense symbolic power and great descriptive beauty. For once, Gordimer's main protagonist is representative of far more than just the white English liberal: he is simply white, South African, of ambiguous European heritage, rich, and politically conservative. His symbolic struggle in the book is a struggle for possession of the land against its black inheritors. Mehring (and by implication the whole of white South Africa) loses the struggle. It is thus not surprising that the protagonists of *July's People* find themselves being run off the land. They escape revolution by running away with, and becoming captives of, their lifelong black servant, July.

One of Gordimer's most recent male creations, Sonny in *My Son's Story*, is a ''coloured'' activist whose extramarital love affair with a white woman is reconstructed by his writer-son, Will. This is a highly readable and unusual novel for Gordimer, although the parameters of love and politics, of public commitment and personal betrayal, are shown to invade each other tellingly, as often happens in Gordimer's fiction.

Gordimer's novel *The House Gun* is unique in that it is her first novelistic attempt to delve into the issues—social, political, and emotional—of post-apartheid South Africa. In this work, Gordimer moves beyond the intense political engagement found in her earlier novels to the earnest attempt to expand the cultural interchange in this ''new'' South Africa. Through the struggles of Duncan Lindgard—on trial for murdering a gay ex-lover—and his parents, Gordimer both interrogates the persistent violence in modern society and offers a careful observation of the potential oppression that may occur as South Africa asserts its new nationhood. Gordimer's fiction may seem to be shifting its focus here, but the message it conveys is essentially unchanged: interrogate the ills and prejudices of society in an attempt to create a hybrid social blend of cultures and goodwill.

—Leon de Kock, updated by Rima Abunasser

GORDON, Giles (Alexander Esme)

Nationality: British. **Born:** Edinburgh, 23 May 1940. **Education:** Edinburgh Academy, 1948–57. **Family:** Married 1) Margaret Anna Eastoe in 1964 (died 1989); two sons (one deceased, 1994) and one daughter; 2) Margaret Anne McKernan in 1990, two daughters. **Career:** Advertising executive, Secker and Warburg, publishers, London, 1962–63; editor, Hutchinson Publishing Group, London, 1963–64, and Penguin Books, London, 1964–66; editorial director, Victor Gollancz, publishers, London, 1967–72. Since 1972 partner, Anthony Sheil Associates, literary agents, London. Lecturer in Creative Writing, in London, for Tufts University, Medford, Massachusetts, 1971–76; C. Day Lewis Fellow in Writing, King's College, London, 1974–75; lecturer in drama, in London, for Hollins College, Virginia, 1984–85. Editor, *Drama* magazine, London, 1982–84; theater critic, *Spectator,* London, 1983–84, *Punch* and *House Magazine,* both London 1985–87, and *London Daily News,* 1988. Since 1993 books' columnist, London *Times.* **Member:** Arts Council of Great Britain Literature Panel, 1966–69, and Society of Authors Committee of Management, 1973–75. **Awards:** *Transatlantic Review* prize, 1966; Scottish Arts Council grant, 1976, Fellow. Royal Society of Literature, 1990. **Agent:** Sheil Land Associates Ltd., 43 Doughty Street, London WC1N 2LF, England. **Address:** 6 Ann St., Edinburgh EH4 1PG, Scotland.

PUBLICATIONS

Novels

The Umbrella Man. London, Allison and Busby, 1971.
About a Marriage. London, Allison and Busby, and New York, Stein and Day, 1972.
Girl with Red Hair. London, Hutchinson, 1974.
100 Scenes from Married Life: A Selection. London, Hutchinson, 1976.
Enemies: A Novel about Friendship. Hassocks, Sussex, Harvester Press, 1977.
Ambrose's Vision: Sketches Towards the Creation of a Cathedral. Brighton, Harvester Press, 1980.

Short Stories

Pictures from an Exhibition. London, Allison and Busby, and New York, Dial Press, 1970.
Penguin Modern Stories 3, with others. London, Penguin, 1970.
Farewell, Fond Dreams. London, Hutchinson, 1975.
The Illusionist and Other Fictions. Hassocks, Sussex, Harvester Press, 1978.
Couple. Knotting, Bedfordshire, Sceptre Press, 1978.

Uncollected Short Stories

''The Line-up on the Shore,'' in *Mind in Chains,* edited by Christopher Evans. London, Panther, 1970.
''The Partition,'' in *Triangles,* edited by Alex Hamilton. London, Hutchinson, 1973.
''Crampton Manor,'' in *The Ninth Ghost Book,* edited by Rosemary Timperley. London, Barrie and Jenkins, 1973.

''Peake,'' in *The Eleventh Ghost Book,* edited by Aidan Chambers. London, Barrie and Jenkins, 1975.
''Morning Echo,'' in *The Sixteenth Pan Book of Horror Stories,* edited by Herbert Van Thal. London, Pan, 1975.
''In Spite of Himself,'' in *The Twelfth Ghost Book.* London, Barrie and Jenkins, 1976.
''Horses of Venice,'' in *The Thirteenth Ghost Book,* edited by James Hale. London, Barrie and Jenkins, 1977.
''The Necessary Authority,'' in *The Midnight Ghost Book,* edited by James Hale. London, Barrie and Jenkins, 1978.
''Room, With Woman and Man,'' in *New Stories 3,* edited by Francis King and Ronald Harwood. London, Hutchinson, 1978.
''Liberated People,'' in *Modern Scottish Short Stories,* edited by Fred Urquhart and Gordon. London, Hamish Hamilton, 1978.
''The Red-Headed Milkman,'' in *The Punch Book of Short Stories,* edited by Alan Coren. London, Robson, 1979.
''Screens,'' in *Labrys 4* (Hayes, Middlesex), 1979.
''Mask,'' in *The After Midnight Ghost Book,* edited by James Hale. London, Hutchinson, 1980; New York, Watts, 1981.
''Drama in Five Acts,'' in *New Terrors 2,* edited by Ramsey Campbell. London, Pan, 1980.
''Madame Durand,'' in *Punch* (London), 19 November 1980.
''The Indian Girl,'' in *Winter's Tales 27,* edited by Edward Leeson. London, Macmillan, 1981; New York, St. Martin's Press, 1982.
''Three Resolutions to One Kashmiri Encounter,'' in *Scottish Short Stories 1981.* London, Collins, 1981.
''Your Bedouin,'' in *Logos* (London), 1982.
''The South African Couple,'' in *Scottish Short Stories 1983.* London, Collins, 1983.
''A Bloomsbury Kidnapping,'' in *London Tales,* edited by Julian Evans. London, Hamish Hamilton, 1983.
''Father Christmas, Father Christmases,'' in *A Christmas Feast,* edited by James Hale. London, Macmillan, 1983.
''The Wheelchair,'' in *New Edinburgh Review 61,* 1983.
''The Battle of the Blind,'' in *New Edinburgh Review 65,* 1984.
''Hans Pfeifer,'' in *Winter's Tales 1* (new series), edited by David Hughes. London, Constable, and New York, St. Martin's Press, 1985.
''Mutual of Omaha,'' in *Critical Quarterly* (Manchester), Winter 1988.

Plays

Radio Plays: *Nineteen Policemen Searching the Sedway Shore,* 1976; *The Jealous One,* 1979; *Birdy,* from the novel by William Wharton, 1980.

Poetry

Landscape Any Date. Edinburgh, M. Macdonald, 1963.
Two and Two Make One. Preston, Lancashire, Akros, 1966.
Two Elegies. London, Turret, 1968.
Eight Poems for Gareth. Frensham, Surrey, Sceptre Press, 1970.
Between Appointments. Frensham, Surrey, Sceptre Press, 1971.
Twelve Poems for Callum. Preston, Lancashire, Akros, 1972.
One Man Two Women. London, Sheep Press, 1974.
Egyptian Room, Metropolitan Museum of Art. Rushden, Northamptonshire, Sceptre Press, 1974.
The Oban Poems. Knotting, Bedfordshire, Sceptre Press, 1977.

Other

Book 2000: Some Likely Trends in Publishing. London, Association of Assistant Librarians, 1969.
Walter and the Balloon (for children). London, Heinemann, 1973.
The Twentieth-Century Short Story in English: A Bibliography. London, British Council, 1990.
Aren't We Due a Royalty Statement?: A Stern Account of Literary, Publishing and Theatrical Folk. London, Chatto and Windus, 1993.
Editor, with Alex Hamilton, *Factions: Eleven Original Stories.* London, Joseph, 1974.
Editor, with Michael Bakewell and B.S. Johnson, *You Always Remember the First Time.* London, Quartet, 1975.
Editor, *Beyond the Words: Eleven Writers in Search of a New Fiction.* London, Hutchinson, 1975.
Editor, with Dulan Barber, ''*Members of the Jury —*'': *The Jury Experience.* London, Wildwood House, 1976.
Editor, *Prevailing Spirits: A Book of Scottish Ghost Stories.* London, Hamish Hamilton, 1976.
Editor, *A Book of Contemporary Nightmares.* London, Joseph, 1977.
Editor, with Fred Urquhart, *Modern Scottish Short Stories.* London, Hamish Hamilton, 1978; revised edition, London, Faber, 1982.
Editor, *Shakespeare Stories.* London, Hamish Hamilton, 1982.
Editor, *Modern Short Stories 2: 1940–1980.* London, Dent, 1982.
Editor, with David Hughes, *Best Short Stories 1986 [-1995].* London, Heinemann, 10 vols., 1986–95; vols. 4–6 as *The Best English Short Stories 1989–1991.* New York, Norton, 3 vols., 1989–91.
Editor, *English Short Stories: 1900 to the Present.* London, Dent, 1988.
Editor, with David Hughes, *The Minerva Book of Short Stories 1–6.* London, Minerva, 6 vols., 1990–95.
Editor, *Cocktails at Doney's and Other Stories*, by William Trevor. London, 1996.
Editor, *The Fisherman and His Soul and Other Fairy Tales*, by Oscar Wilde. New York, St. Martin's Press, 1998.

* * *

Relationships lie at the root of Giles Gordon's novels and short stories, relationships between man and woman, woman and woman, man and man, husband and wife, lover and lover—and also the relationship between the writer and the reader. In his first novel, *The Umbrella Man,* Gordon was content to view the burgeoning affair between Felix and Delia from the outside, using the technique that a film director might bring to bear in building up a scene from different camera angles. This is a device of which Gordon is particularly fond, and its exposition is seen to good effect in his story ''Nineteen Policemen Searching the Solent Shore.''

About a Marriage is a more straightforward narrative in which the seeming detritus of modern married life assumes a form that the protagonists, the husband and wife, can understand. A reasonably well-off couple Edward and Ann, move from a bland acceptance of their marriage to a blazing revelation of the strengths of their relationship and of the bond that exists between them. Their love is based not so much on a romantic attachment, although that is also present, as on the many-sided passions and frustrations that ultimately give each partner a vivid insight into their own strengths and weaknesses. Of growing importance in this novel is Gordon's mastery of dialogue and his relaxed ability to enter the minds of his characters who cease to exist as mere ciphers and have grown into stark, living creatures.

Enemies (''A Novel about Friendship'') is in the now-familiar Gordon mold of a terse examination of how people relate to each other in familiar and not so familiar circumstances, but its stylistic achievement lies in his ability to strip the central narrative line to a series of scenes which embody sharp dialogue with an internalization of the characters' thoughts and emotions. The Hiltons live in an unspecified European country, and the action centers on the events of a few days while they are being visited by their parents and friends from England. Events outside their house, which at the beginning of the novel seems to be so secure against outside interference, threaten the fabric of their cozy world as it becomes a microcosm of a beleaguered society with all its concomitant stresses. Faced with the center falling away, the adults find their relationships shifting uneasily before they reach the triumphant conclusion of the salving power of their own friendships.

100 Scenes from Married Life picks up again the story of Edward and Ann. The intensity of their love for each other is still apparent, but growing self-doubt and encroaching middle age, with its sense of the loss of youth and vitality, gnaw at Edward's vitals. Interestingly, as if to prove the security of their marriage, Gordon disconcertingly opens the first scene with Edward returning from a week in Venice with his mistress. The novel's title reflects Gordon's debt to Ingmar Bergman's *Scenes from a Marriage,* and in a series of eighteen scenes he has captured the warm, womblike, yet claustrophobic story of a close relationship. The inscription is from Philip Roth's *My Life as a Man:* ''You want subtlety, then read *The Golden Bowl.* This is life, bozo, not high art.'' And there are many echoes from Roth's and John Updike's style in Gordon's low-key examination of the matter of middle-class life.

With those two American writers he also shares an interest in language and the economy of its use. At his best he is able to strip his sentences to an almost surreal invisibility which is allied disconcertingly to a lively, sparkling wit. His first collection of what Gordon calls ''short fictions,'' *Pictures from an Exhibition,* was stylistically naive but there was a sense of innovatory excitement as he adopted the attitude of the detached observer in his frequently startling revelations. *Farewell, Fond Dreams* continued many of the same conventions but it showed a surer touch as Gordon risked some breathtaking conceits in his mixture of fact and fantasy, as in the sequence ''An attempt to make entertainment out of the war in Vietnam.'' *The Illusionist and Other Fictions* showed a return to calmer waters, with Gordon seeming to take a fresh interest in the traditional structure of the short story, although he can never lose sight completely of their liquid, three-dimensional possibilities. Critics have been frequently exasperated by the audacious verve of much of Gordon's writing, but he remains one of the few British writers interested in pushing the possibilities of the novel to their outer limits.

—Trevor Royle

GORDON, Mary (Catherine)

Nationality: American. **Born:** Long Island, New York, 8 December 1949. **Education:** Holy Name of Mary School, Valley Stream, New York; Mary Louis Academy; Barnard College, New York, B.A. 1971; Syracuse University, New York, M.A. 1973. **Family:** Married 1) James Brain in 1974 (marriage dissolved); 2) Arthur Cash in 1979, one daughter and one son. **Career:** English teacher, Dutchess Community College, Poughkeepsie, New York, 1974–78; lecturer, Amherst College, Massachusetts, 1979. **Awards:** Janet Kafka prize, 1979, 1982. **Address:** c/o Viking Penguin, 375 Hudson Street, New York, New York 10014–3658, U.S.A.

Publications

Novels

Final Payments. New York, Random House, and London, Hamish Hamilton, 1978.
The Company of Women. New York, Random House, and London, Cape, 1981.
Men and Angels. New York, Random House, and London, Cape, 1985.
The Other Side. New York, Viking, 1989; London, Bloomsbury, 1990.
Spending: A Utopian Divertimento. New York, Scribner, 1998.

Short Stories

Temporary Shelter. London, Bloomsbury, and New York, Random House, 1987.
The Rest of Life: Three Novellas. New York, Viking, 1993.

Uncollected Short Stories

''Vision,'' in *Antaeus* (New York), Spring 1989.
''Separation,'' in *Antaeus* (New York), Spring-Autumn, 1990.
''At the Kirks',' ' in *Grand Street* (New York), Winter 1990.

Other

Good Boys and Dead Girls and Other Essays. New York, Viking, and London, Bloomsbury, 1991.
The Shadow Man. New York, Random House, 1996.
Seeing through Places: Reflections on Geography and Identity. New York, Scribner, 2000.
Joan of Arc: A Penguin Life. New York, Lipper/Viking, 2000.

* * *

For Mary Gordon, *tout comprendre* is emphatically not *tout pardonner.* Guilt rages through her fiction like a prairie fire, sweeping her heroines to and fro between the poles of autonomy and dependence, religious faith and neurosis, greed for life and masochistic self sacrifice. Although reviewers have celebrated her nineteenth-century virtues—irony, intellect, powerful moral themes, and such classically realist skills as an eye for detail, an ear for dialogue, and a gift for the creation of memorable characters—Gordon's overarching concerns are recognizably modern: the exploration of the female psyche, the relations between parents and children, and between feminism and patriarchal religion.

In her first novel, *Final Payments,* the seductive securities of dependence are explored through the relationship of Isabel Moore to her bedridden father, a Catholic intellectual whom she nurses for eleven years. Trapped by sexual guilt, Isabel is effectively cut off in a time warp, until his death. Set free, she makes a venture into the world of the 1970s, only to recoil again into renunciation, sacrificing her life anew to the odious Margaret Casey as a penance for a second sexual transgression. Although Isabel is ultimately rescued (an embryonic feminist moral) by two close female friends, she has only just begun to learn how to put paid to the obligations imposed by both father and faith. Gordon's heroines tend to rebel against a dominant father figure, adopt a surrogate father, and reconcile themselves in some fashion, learning the deficiencies of patriarchal institutions in the process. Felicitas, the heroine of *The Company of Women,* is no exception. As the daughter of one of five women (the company of the title) each devoted to Father Cyprian, a conservative Catholic intellectual, Felicitas gets away only temporarily, is impregnated, and returns, to bequeath to her daughter her mixed heritage of Catholicism and liberation. Unfathered (by careful plotting) Linda shares the same group of good and bad fairy-godmothers as Felicitas, but without the patriarch's overriding authority. Catholic values have been feminized and ''macho clericalism'' crippled and humanized. (The novel's intertextual allusions to *Jane Eyre* are no accident).

With *Men and Angels,* however, Gordon leaves behind the subculture of Catholicism, in favor of a broader exploration of women's relation to artistic and social structures. When Anne Foster, dismissed as merely a college wife, has the chance to investigate the life of a (fictional) neglected American painter, Caroline Watson, she faces a dilemma: how to tell a woman's story as fully and as realistically as possible. As biographer Anne sets out to rescue Caroline from obscurity, so her childminder, Laura, in the grip of religious obsession, sets out to save Anne from the lusts of the flesh. The feminist rescue mission is therefore attended with tragic ironies. Just as Anne seeks a nurturing foremother and role model in Caroline, so Laura pursues Anne. The dead female artist is lovingly investigated and re-created at the price of a living girl. Laura's scorn for the ''Religion of Art'' indicates her potentially strong affiliations with Gordon's father, and makes her a splendid vehicle for an exploration of the tragic consequences of the phallocentric appropriation of religious experience. Dividing its narration between third-person, realist Anne and Laura's fantastic stream of consciousness, the novel sets up a series of mirrorings and doublings, both in terms of character and narrative mode, in order to investigate the utility to women of models and precedents, the means by which a woman's story may best be told, and the benefits of realist modes of representation in dealing with women's issues. Anne's representation of Caroline is re-presented by Laura, with major events twice told, in realism and in fantasy, to ironic effect. Though Laura's chapters are shorter (as befits the Pyrrhic psychomachia, the body of the text is Anne's) they are technically and psychologically compelling. Laura's experiences are organized according to the fantasies of male culture, and a quality of fascinated horror accrues to them. Gordon often uses fairy tale and melodrama to sharpen the menace of her plots. Domestic horror stalks her characters, whether in the shape of witch-housekeepers (Laura, Margaret), bad fairies, terrible mothers or passive, masochistic victims.

Gordon's own essay on the difference between writing a story as a fairy tale or as realist fiction is memorably embodied in ''A Writing Lesson,'' one of the twenty stories collected in *Temporary Shelter.* Two others, a five-voiced story ''Now I Am Married,'' and ''Delia'' anticipate in theme and structure Gordon's latest novel, *The Other Side,* which marries an Irish family saga with a popularization and updating of two founder figures of Modernism. Ulysses-like, 88-year-old Vincent MacNamara returns after an absence to his wife Ellen, a demented Penelope, now dying. Through the events of one day, 14th August 1985, the Woolfian narrative recounts their lives, together with those of their children, grandchildren and great-grandchildren, moving through the individual consciousnesses of some dozen family members. Gordon's psychological themes now expand to the national stage. Mother Ireland, rather than mothers, is rejected—America is no longer ''the other side'' but home—yet the dying matriarch remains a brooding presence. Although religion has largely evaporated on the moving staircase of American immigrant striving, Ellen's granddaughter Cam displays a recognizable mixture of idealism, self-sacrifice, dutifulness and self-love and her awareness that unhappiness is ''the sickle-cell anemia of the Irish'' pervades the book. Slowly the ''other side'' to each story comes into focus, as the jigsaw of memories from different individuals finally coheres into a three-dimensional pattern, revealing the inner significance of each apparently contingent event.

Gordon more explicitly explored the question of father-identity in two books from the late 1990s, *The Shadow Man* and *Spending: A Utopian Divertimento.* The former sounds like the title of a novel, and the latter vaguely like nonfiction, but exactly the opposite is true: the first book chronicles the ugly truths Gordon discovered about her father. Research into his past revealed that David Gordon, the man who had inspired her to be a writer, was nothing he had claimed to be, and Gordon uncovered many unsavory truths as well: that he had operated a sleazy porn magazine, for instance, and supported Mussolini, radical right-wing priest Father Coughlin, and anti-Semitic causes—despite the fact that he had come from a Jewish family. He had even hidden the fact of an earlier marriage from her. *Spending* suggests that these discoveries had unleashed an almost angry eroticism: protagonist Monica Szabo engages in a dizzying array of sexual encounters on the beach, in an armchair, in the shower, and even in a role-playing game in which her lover pretends to be a wounded soldier and she a nurse.

Although critical attention has centered upon her feminist response to Catholicism, Gordon would be a first-rate novelist if she were an atheist. Fiercely intellectual, unafraid to unite modernist irony with popular plot and pace, clearly non-androcentric, Gordon will clearly remain a figure to watch.

—Judie Newman

GOTLIEB, Phyllis Fay

Nationality: Canadian. **Born:** Phyllis Fay Bloom in Toronto, Canada, 25 May 1926. **Education:** University of Toronto, B.A. 1948, M.A. 1950. **Family:** Married Calvin Gotlieb in 1949; one son, two daughters. **Address:** 29 Ridgevale Drive, Toronto, Ontario M6A 1K9, Canada.

Publications

Novels

Sunburst. Greenwich, Connecticut, Fawcett Publications, 1964; with a new introduction by Elizabeth A. Lynn, Boston, Gregg Press, 1978.

Why Should I Have All the Grief? Toronto, Macmillan, 1969.

O Master Caliban! New York, Harper, 1976.

A Judgment of Dragons. New York, Berkley Publishing, 1980.

Emperor, Swords, Pentacles. New York, Ace Books, 1981.
The Kingdom of the Cats. New York, Ace, 1983.
Heart of Red Iron. New York, St. Martin's Press, 1989.
Blue Apes. Edmonton, Alberta, Canada, Tesseract Books, 1995.
Flesh and Gold. New York, Tor, 1998.
Violent Stars. New York, Tor, 1999.

Short Stories

Son of the Morning and Other Stories. New York, Ace, 1983.

Poetry

Within the Zodiac. Toronto, McClelland & Stewart, 1964.
Ordinary, Moving. Oxford University Press, 1969.
Doctor Umlaut's Earthly Kingdom. Toronto, Calliope Press, 1978.
The Works: Collected Poems. Toronto, Calliope Press, 1978.

Plays

Radio plays: *Dr. Umlaut's Earthly Kingdom, Anthology,* Canadian Broadcasting Corporation, 1970; *The Military Hospital,* Canadian Broadcasting Corporation, 1971; *Silent Movie Days,* Canadian Broadcasting Corporation, 1971; *The Contract,* Canadian Broadcasting Corporation, 1972; *Garden Varieties, Tuesday Night,* Canadian Broadcasting Corporation, 1973; *God on Trial before Rabbi Ovadia, Best Seat in the House,* Canadian Broadcasting Corporation, 1976.

Other

Contributor, *Poems for Voices,* edited by Robert Weaver. Toronto, Canadian Broadcasting Corporation, 1970.
Contributor, *Visions 2020,* edited by Stephen Clarkson. Edmonton, Canada, Hurtig, 1970.
Contributor, *To the Stars: Eight Stories of Science Fiction,* edited by Robert Silverberg. New York, Hawthorn Books, 1971.
Contributor, *The A.M. Klein Symposium,* edited by Seymour Mayne. Ottawa, Canada, University of Ottawa Press, 1975.
Contributor (*The King's Dogs*), *The Edge of Space: Three Original Novellas of Science Fiction,* edited by Robert Silverberg. New York, Elsevier/Nelson Books, 1979.
Editor, with Douglas Barbour, *Tesseracts²*. Victoria, British Columbia, Canada, Press Porcépic, 1987.

* * *

When most of us approach a text, we expect that it will give us something concrete and that we will be able to uncover that offering through a process that has a distinct beginning and end, as well as a logical progression between the two. In the work of Toronto-born author Phyllis Gotlieb, however, we find an incessant refusal to conform to this established hierarchical structure of discourse. She is a writer who does not depend on binary logic, but instead, spreads out, crisscrosses, makes connections, not just between things that we expect should be connected, but between anything and everything. Her writing, like her career, which spans several decades and numerous genres, is a spinning spiral of juxtaposed pieces that can be layered, stacked, and/or joined in an infinite number of ways.

Gotlieb, the science fiction genre's universally recognized grande dame, has been a significant figure in Canadian science fiction for more than forty years and has been, in more recent years, ranked among the best science fiction writers of the century. Her best known science fiction novels include *Sunburst, O Master Caliban!, Emperor, Sword, Pentacles, A Judgment of Dragons, Heart of Red Iron, Flesh and Gold,* and *Violent Stars*. Gotlieb won the Canadian Science Fiction Award for *Judgment of Dragons* in 1981. In 1987 she co-edited *Tesseracts²* with Douglas Barbour.

Her novel *Sunburst* takes place entirely on Earth, but it hints at what is to come in future works through its whisperings of space travel and introduction to Impers—beings whose minds cannot be penetrated by telepathy. Although there are critics who speak of this novel as unrelated to those that follow, most agree that there are traces of it throughout Gotlieb's work, and her most recent novel, *Violent Stars*, brings the reader full circle as it traces the beginnings of a galaxy-wide gambling and prostitution ring to Sol-Three—our Earth. From beginning to end, it is obvious that this author has continually centered her work around the idea of planets constantly in turmoil and of the characters of those planets who are set into motion as much to probe the future's potential as to chart the past.

Her poetry, short stories, and novels all look at beings struggling through situations in which the powers that surround them are constantly beating them down, where the hostile environment often wins, an environment in which the reader finds not a happy ending but an ending where the major characters are no better off, and sometimes worse off, at the end of the story than at the beginning. Her work seeks astonishment, terror, ecstasy, speed, power, and dread—all of the elements of real, complex social and metaphysical problems—in a rich, gritty, poetic style.

Her novel *Flesh and Gold*, considered one of her best, contains a bewildering array of these characters and situations. In this non-linear text, where words such as center, repeat, bubble, curl, swarm, encircle, loop, and cluster resurface continually, the author uses lyrical images, beautifully written, to create various human hybrids and clones that are variations and combinations of things that have existed or do exist in our world and in the world of this author's writings. Here, genres are intertwined, seamlessly weaving the perceived notions of undisciplined, popular science fiction with those of polished, highbrow poetry and thought. Past characters are brought back to life, in a realm where there is no such thing as closure—only circular movement, and prehistoric/futuristic/cyborg beings dip into the minds of those around them in a world of centuries-old mines and ore refineries, guarded ESP, and galactic federation security.

The "streamlined baby allosauruses" known as Khagodi, and the Lyhhrt, fleshy beings, wanting nothing more than to be "lying in a layer with pseudopods entwined under the wet and grey-green skies," were born many worlds (and stories) before we meet them in *Flesh and Gold*, and again in her latest novel, *Violent Stars*. They are born and begin their evolutionary process in *A Judgment of Dragons*, a "novel" comprised of short stories where the later sections, although they each contain a set up, conflict, and denouement, could not coherently stand alone. And they continue to evolve across time and genre because of this author's desire to explore meaning, not in respect to things in a mimetic system of one-to-one correspondence, but relational meaning—meaning built and dissolved through the similarities and differences from other people and worlds.

The Lyhhrt are alive and well in Gotlieb's latest novel as well. *Violent Stars* is, as all that has come from Gotlieb before, a novel fluid in style, frank in depictions, and adroit in social observations; it is a textual realm where personal and political are symbolically intertwined, where people and worlds continue to be both the same and ever-changing, where we are all always winning and loosing, exploiting and being exploited. It is a novel of intellectually sophisticated interweaving of unresolved stories, stories that are an intricate examination of fate and free will, where past, present, and future all exist simultaneously.

The Lyhhrt, here, as before, stand as an example of Gotlieb's need to slip in and out of time, space, bodies, and scenes, to explore and examine the effects of the past on the future and the future on the past. Her sensitive attention to dialogue, attitude, and poignant realizations in this and all of her work, pulls Gotlieb's readers further and further into a world where themes are subtly drawn, vast technological resources are mobilized to satisfy age-old urges, and science and social problems collide. Her circular movements of the words within the texts, as well as from text to text, lead us through pasts and futures that are palpably real, with continuing concerns, continuing conflicts, and continuing, evolving civilizations. These texts lead us to endings without closure in a vividly imagined universe that we don't want to know but have to work our way through just the same.

—Tammy Bird

GOVER, (John) Robert

Nationality: American. **Born:** Philadelphia, Pennsylvania, 2 November 1929. **Education:** Girard College, Philadelphia; University of Pittsburgh, B.A. in economics 1953. **Family:** Married 1) Mildred Vitkovich in 1955 (divorced 1966); 2) Jeanne-Nell Gement in 1968; two sons. **Career:** Held a variety of jobs, including reporter on various newspapers, in Pennsylvania and Maryland, until 1961. **Address:** K8 River's Bend, Carney's Point, New Jersey 08069, U.S.A.

PUBLICATIONS

Novels

J.C. Kitten Trilogy. Berkeley, California, Reed, 1982.
One Hundred Dollar Misunderstanding. London, Spearman, 1961; New York, Grove Press, 1962.
Here Goes Kitten. New York, Grove Press, 1964; London, Mayflower, 1965.
J.C. Saves. New York, Simon and Schuster, 1968; London, Arrow, 1979.
The Maniac Responsible. New York, Grove Press, 1963; London, MacGibbon and Kee, 1964.
Poorboy at the Party. New York, Simon and Schuster, 1966.
Going for Mr. Big. New York, Bantam, 1973; London, Arrow, 1979.
To Morrow Now Occurs Again (as O. Govi). Santa Barbara, California, Ross Erikson, 1975.
Getting Pretty on the Table (as O. Govi). Santa Barbara, California, Capra Press, 1975.

Short Stories

Bring Me the Head of Rona Barrett. San Francisco, Hargreaves, 1981.

Other

Voodoo Contra. York Beach, Maine, Weiser, 1985.
Editor, *The Portable Walter: From the Prose and Poetry of Walter Lowenfels.* New York, International Publishers, 1968.

*

Bibliographies: *Robert Gover: A Descriptive Bibliography* by Michael Hargreaves, Westport, Connecticut, Meckler, 1988.

Manuscript Collection: Boston University.

Robert Gover comments:

His trilogy, *One Hundred Dollar Misunderstanding, Here Goes Kitten,* and *J.C. Saves,* captures in two characters relations between Black and White in America, especially as it evolved during the 1960s.

J.C. Holland first meets Kitten while he is a university sophomore and she a thirteen-year-old prostitute. In the second book, J.C. is public relations director of the local political party in power and encounters Kitten as a nightclub singer, or ''B-girl.'' In the third, he finds her ducking police gunfire during a ''race riot.'' *The Maniac Responsible* examines the *why* of a rape-murder case. The protagonist, Dean, becomes so involved in the invisible mental process that led to the brutal slaying that he becomes ''possessed.'' Gover uses Joycean techniques to vivify his character's mental world.

Poorboy at the Party mythologizes the split between rich and poor in America. Randy, the main character, goes with his wealthy friend to a party in a large mansion containing art treasures. Conflicting emotions and values plant seeds of frustration and the party erupts into a violent orgy of destruction.

Going for Mr. Big is the tale of a pimp and his two ladies and a millionaire and his wife. Luke Small is a self-styled revolutionary with a lust to pull down the rich and powerful, but his ''campaign'' to conquer Malcolm McMasters first backfires, then resolves itself in a meaningful togetherness that is outside the prevailing economic system.

To Morrow Now Occurs Again, published under Gover's penname O. Govi, is a surrealist romp through a mythical land called all Damnation, which is one big Plantation where Big Money is the Holy Spirit. The protagonist, Big I and little me, soul and ego of one entity, is baffled by the situation he finds himself in. The Rat Doctor, whose experimental maze of millions of rats is periodically studied to show the workings of society and shed light on the religion of Big Money, does not deter Big I from asserting that his currency is eternal.

Victor Versus Mort, a novella published only in Portuguese, pits two archetypal forces against each other in an American social setting. In the end, the main character's worldly successes are eclipsed by death.

Getting Pretty on the Table, also a novella, carries into a suburban orgy a game played by pimps and prostitutes. The game combines psychic therapy and spiritual cleansing.

* * *

In the ''After Words'' to *J.C. Saves* (the last volume of the trilogy begun with *One Hundred Dollar Misunderstanding* and *Here Goes Kitten*), Robert Gover tell us that at the beginning ''I had no preconceived idea where these two characters would lead me, their author.'' Unfortunately, the reader's sharing of that aimlessness is such that he arrives at the last page of the last volume with the sense that the trilogy is completed only because the author has told him so. There is no reason why the characters might not go on in book after book, *ad infinitum,* like the Rover Boys. When J.C. Holland, the white middle-class protagonist, and Kitten, his black prostitute love, achieve their partial understanding at the end of *J.C. Saves,* it is clear that the slightest alteration provided by another time and other circumstances will be enough to set another story in motion. For the fact is that this is formula fiction: shake up the characters, move them to a new starting point, put them in motion, follow the formula, and you have another book. The other works, from *Poorboy at the Party* through *Getting Pretty on the Table,* play variations on the same basic themes.

Yet there is an honesty in Gover, a vision of the life about him and a quality of writing that raises him above the level of either the pulp pornographer or the slick composer of bestsellers. However much he taxes the reader's impatience with shallow characterizations, absurd plot manipulations, gratuitous sex, and moral implications that are occasionally downright silly, he is at times an accomplished satirist. One must only imagine his books in the form of Classic Comics, illustrated by cartoonists for *Mad Magazine,* to be made aware how sure is his touch of the particular grotesque exaggeration that comically, or cruelly, reveals a specific truth. His are not realistic novels, but verbal comic strips, sharing a good many of the virtues and faults of such a paradigm of the genre as Norman Mailer's *An American Dream.*

In large measure he is a moralist—disgusted at times, bitter and angry at others, but always subordinating the matter to the message. And the message is always the same: the Anglo-Saxon American power structure has created a society in which sex and violence are so perversely twisted together that there is no place for honest respect and affection between individuals, classes, or races. Never showing what society might be, he concentrates his attention on the extremes of actuality that he sees as emblematic of the whole. In some respects his most memorable statement is *The Maniac Responsible,* where he parallels the movements of a reporter covering a brutal sex murder with the man's movements while attempting to seduce his teasingly voluptuous neighbor. Finally driven by circumstances (the natural circumstances, the author suggests, of the American way of life) and his own sensitivity, he becomes a suspect in the murder and breaks down into an admission that he, himself, is the maniac responsible (as we all are) for the rape and murder of the girl.

Sex is in the forefront of all Gover's novels. However, the human failures he depicts are not to be blamed on sex, but rather on the failure of its right use, the tendency to treat the other human beings as a means rather than an end. Significantly, in the twisted world of Gover's vision the individual who seems best to know how to use her sex is Kitten, the African-American prostitute. Significantly, too, the Kitten trilogy, *Poorboy at the Party,* and *The Maniac Responsible* all end in rejections of the middle-class societies they have portrayed.

—George Perkins

GRACE, Patricia (Frances)

Nationality: New Zealander. **Born:** Wellington in 1937. **Education:** Green Street Convent, Newtown, Wellington; St. Mary's College; Wellington Teachers' College. **Family:** Married; seven children. **Career:** Has taught in primary and secondary schools in King Country, Northland, and Porirua. **Awards:** Maori Purposes Fund Board grant, 1974; New Zealand Literature Fund grant, 1975, 1983; Hubert Church Prose award, 1976; Children's Picture Book of the Year award, 1982; Victoria University Writing fellowship, 1985; Wattie award, 1986; New Zealand Fiction award, 1987; New Zealand Maori Scholarship in Letters, 1988, 1992–93; Literary Fund grant, 1990; Victoria University Archive Project grant, 1993; LiBeraturepreis (Germany), 1994. D.H.L.: Victoria University, 1989. **Address:** Box 54111, Plimmerton, New Zealand.

Publications

Novels

Mutuwhenua: The Moon Sleeps. Auckland, Longman Paul, 1978; London, Women's Press, 1988.
Potiki. Auckland, Penguin, 1986; London, Women's Press, 1987; Honolulu, University of Hawaii Press, 1995.
Cousins. Auckland, Penguin, 1992.
Baby No-Eyes. Honolulu, Hawaii, University of Hawaii Press, 1998.

Short Stories

Waiariki. Auckland, Longman Paul, 1975.
The Dream Sleepers and Other Stories. Auckland, Longman Paul, 1980.
Electric City and Other Stories. Auckland, Penguin, 1987.
Selected Stories. Auckland, Penguin, 1991.
The Sky People. Auckland, Penguin, 1994.
Collected Stories. Auckland, Penguin, 1995.

Other (for children)

The Kuia and the Spider. Auckland, Longman Paul, 1981; London, Penguin, 1982.
Watercress Tuna and the Children of Champion Street. Auckland, Longman Paul, 1984; London, Penguin, 1986.
He aha te mea nui?, Ma wai?, Ko au tenei, Ahakoa he iti (Maori readers). Auckland, Longman Paul, 4 vols., 1985.
The Trolley. Auckland, Penguin, 1993.
Areta and the Kahawai. Auckland, Penguin, 1994.

Other

Wahine Toa: Women of Maori Myth, paintings by Robyn Kahukiwa. Auckland, Collins, 1984.

*

Critical Studies: *Writing Along Broken Lines: Violence and Ethnicity in Contemporary Maori Fiction* by Otto Heim. Auckland, Auckland University Press, 1998.

* * *

Perhaps it is inevitable that, as a New Zealand writer of short stories whose subject matter is the intimate, self-sufficient world of the family, Patricia Grace should suggest certain similarities with Katherine Mansfield. Both deal with themes such as the passing of innocence, the constraints of daily routine and close relationships, and the elusiveness of answers to life's meaning and purpose. Both seek to retrieve the past through a receptive and finely tuned consciousness, and cultivate a narrative style whose modulations extend from childish excitement to crisp exposition.

Yet when a reference to Katherine Mansfield actually occurs in one of Grace's short stories, ''Letters from Whetu,'' it signals not their affinity only, but their separateness as well. For Mansfield (as for the little girl in her ''How Pearl Button Was Kidnapped''), Maori life could only be, at best, a momentary escape from the *Pakeha* values of time, money, and respectability. For Grace, writing seventy-odd years later and from an insider's point of view, the life is binding and vital, qualities that are figured in the recurring images of the extended family (*whanau*) gathered within the home or at some other spot of cherished ground often located by the sea. The shared activities—feast-making, or gardening, or collecting mussels, or diving for *kina*—combine the dual aspects of work and play, and participate in the rhythm of the tides, the seasons, growth, and decay.

Even so, the life Grace celebrates bears the ineradicable marks of *Pakeha* encroachments and *Pakeha* progress. Old ways and old names are often put aside for the sake of seeming modern; land is abandoned for work in the cities; roads and buildings appear in places that were once held to be *tapu*. In a number of the short stories (''Transition,'' ''And So I Go,'' ''Letters from Whetu''), an awareness that the world is large and that new ways must be learned is explicitly stated. But running against this, and through all of Grace's writing, is the stronger and more insistent feeling of displacement and loss, and of an obligation to keep alive what remains of the old inheritance. The objective correlative of this burden of consciousness is the land, and in her best work—notably the short story ''Journey'' and her second novel *Potiki*—the complexity of this emblem, and therefore of the Maori experience, is fully and imaginatively developed.

At the basis of ''Journey'' is the very real issue of land ownership, dramatized here as a confrontation between the old Maori who claims the right to leave his land sub-divided among his heirs according to Maori custom, and the government department that has appropriated his land and the entire locality for development. Between the two parties no communication is possible, a situation underlined by the differences in their language. One argues for people and their need for houses, the other enumerates the engineering problems; one speaks from first-hand experience of the nature of the soil and the vegetables it will produce, the other resorts to maps and plans and the abstractions of ''aesthetic aspects.''

''Journey'' is characteristic of Grace's stories in that the action is sited in the consciousness of the main character. Virtually all her early work accesses this consciousness by way of first-person narration. In the first of her novels, *Mutuwhenua*, the ''I'' is a young Maori woman who—like the sisters in another celebrated story, ''A Way of Talking''—moves between the worlds of Maori and *Pakeha*, using a different idiom and even a different name in each. In the *Pakeha* world she is Linda, and she says things like ''I happen to like Graeme''—a remark that prompts her grandmother to scold, ''Happen to like, happen to like, what's that talk? You talk like them already.'' But it is Linda's alter ego Ngaio who dominates the story, bringing to it not just a Maori idiom but—for the first half anyway—a distinctively oral structure. The story begins on the eve of Ngaio's marriage to Graeme but continually flashes back as Ngaio recalls episodes from her childhood, so that the marriage does not take place until the book is more than half-way through. Then, disappointingly, the format changes; the traumatic events that follow the marriage are set down in chronological order, with only a few contrived questions and premonitions to suggest the oral mode.

In her subsequent work Grace's narrative technique has become increasingly adventurous and assured. The early reliance on the first person gives place to third and even (in one section of *Cousins*) second person narratives, the former (e.g. in ''Journey'') using a species of free indirect discourse that enables her still to suggest oral Maori usage. And the subtle use of Maori myth as an undercurrent (e.g. the Rangi and Papa creation myth in ''Between Earth and Sky'' and ''Sun's Marbles'' and the Tawhaki myth in *Baby No-Eyes*) reinforces this effect.

All these threads come together in her second and most-celebrated novel, *Potiki*. Grace explains that she ''modelled *Potiki* on the way an orator would structure an oration—which would begin with a chant, go on to greetings, then the main body of the speech, then conclude with *awai-ata*.'' Within this overriding structure Grace presents the viewpoints of several members of one family in distinct but overlapping chapters—or (as they are constantly called in *Potiki*) ''stories.'' The effect is of unity in diversity—the ideal of the Maori *whanau*. Some of the stories are told in third-person free indirect discourse, but the two principal characters, Roimata and Toko, tell theirs in the first person. Toko is a crippled child with a ''special knowing'' who epitomizes the state of Maori culture—physically broken but spiritually profound. Given that his death saves his endangered people, that his mother's name is Mary and that his father is either an itinerant called Joseph or a carved figure of great spiritual significance in the *wharenui*, Toko has obvious affinities with Christ. In other ways—not least his success in catching a huge eel while out fishing with his brothers—he is akin to the mythical Maori trickster Maui.

This blend of Maori and Christian myths may suggest that Grace wants to preach an accommodation between Maori and *Pakeha* ways. She certainly does so in *Mutuwhenua*, where Ngaio's mission is evidently to marry the *Pakeha* Graeme and make him accept traditional Maori customs. She succeeds, and the book can be seen as an allegory that recommends that New Zealand society become a bicultural melting-pot, though the force of the allegory is compromised by the insipid depiction of Graeme, who never challenges Maori ways but simply accepts what he cannot understand. The plot of *Potiki*, on the other hand, comes to a less comfortable conclusion. The Maori community must adopt aggressive tactics to preserve their integrity and their land from the threat of *Pakeha* capitalism, and the book ends with an uneasy truce between the two races. The blend of Maori and *Pakeha* in Toko may be seen as a muted counterpoint to this stand-off, or it may be simply an indication that—like most contemporary Maori authors—Grace takes Christianity to be a traditional feature of Maori culture.

Though Grace claimed in a recent interview that she has ''never thought about the political element'' in her work, she would seem to have become an angrier, more committed writer between *Mutuwhenua* and *Potiki*. And a subsequent novel, *Baby No-Eyes*, focuses on a series of *Pakeha* infringements against Maori culture. The ownership and use of land is once again an issue, but there is also a poignant flash-back to the days when the Maori language was banned in schools, and the book's title alludes to a more contemporary problem:

the way in which scientific—especially medical—research can ride rough-shod over cherished Maori beliefs and protocols.

Stories like ''Journey,'' ''Going for the Bread,'' and ''House of the Fish'' are similarly polemical. But other recent stories (e.g. ''Ngati Kangaru'') bring a note of levity to the treatment of Maori grievances, while still others (e.g. ''Flower Girls'' and ''My Leanne'') show that Grace is not impervious to the darker side of contemporary Maori society to which authors like Alan Duff have recently drawn attention. She is—as a recent critic has observed—''far too good and various a writer to allow herself only one side of any story,'' and her third novel *Cousins* bears out this point. Makareta, the most articulate of the three protagonists, becomes a Maori activist, but only after she has escaped the stifling atmosphere of the *whanau* where she was born and the arranged marriage that its formidable old matriarch sought to impose on her. (She marries instead a *Pakeha* who is even less substantial than *Mutuwhenua*'s Graeme.) The *whanau* is not entirely discredited, however; Missy steps happily into Makareta's role (including the arranged marriage), and the return of the book's third protagonist, Mata, after a desolate life in the city, reinforces the enduring value of the communal existence that characterizes the *whanau* at its best.

—Shirley Chew, updated by Richard Corballis

GRAHAM, Winston (Mawdsley)

Nationality: British. **Born:** Victoria Park, Manchester, 30 June 1910. **Family:** Married Jean Mary Williamson in 1939 (died 1992); one son and one daughter. **Career:** Chair, Society of Authors, London, 1967–69. **Awards:** Crime Writers Association prize, 1956. Fellow, Royal Society of Literature, 1968. O.B.E. (Officer, Order of the British Empire), 1983. **Agent:** A.M. Heath, 79 St. Martin's Lane, London WC2N 4AA. **Address:** Abbotswood House, Buxted, East Sussex TN22 4PB, England.

PUBLICATIONS

Novels

The House with the Stained-Glass Windows. London, Ward Lock, 1934.
Into the Fog. London, Ward Lock, 1935.
The Riddle of John Rowe. London, Ward Lock, 1935.
Without Motive. London, Ward Lock, 1936.
The Dangerous Pawn. London, Ward Lock, 1937.
The Giant's Chair. London, Ward Lock, 1938.
Strangers Meeting. London, Ward Lock, 1939.
Keys of Chance. London, Ward Lock, 1939.
No Exit: An Adventure. London, Ward Lock, 1940.
Night Journey. London, Ward Lock, 1941; New York, Doubleday, 1968.
My Turn Next. London, Ward Lock, 1942.
The Merciless Ladies. London, Ward Lock, 1944; revised edition, London, Bodley Head, 1979; New York, Doubleday, 1980.
The Forgotten Story. London, Ward Lock, 1945; as *The Wreck of the Grey Cat,* New York, Doubleday, 1958.
Ross Poldark: A Novel of Cornwall 1783–1787. London, Ward Lock, 1945; as *The Renegade,* New York, Doubleday, 1951.
Demelza: A Novel of Cornwall 1788–1790. London, Ward Lock, 1946; New York, Doubleday, 1953.
Take My Life. London, Ward Lock, 1947; New York, Doubleday, 1967.
Cordelia. London, Ward Lock, 1949; New York, Doubleday, 1950.
Night Without Stars. London, Hodder and Stoughton, and New York, Doubleday, 1950.
Jeremy Poldark: A Novel of Cornwall 1790–1791. London, Ward Lock, 1950; as *Venture Once More,* New York, Doubleday, 1954.
Warleggan: A Novel of Cornwall 1792–1793. London, Ward Lock, 1953; as *The Last Gamble,* New York, Doubleday, 1955.
Fortune Is a Woman. London, Hodder and Stoughton, and New York, Doubleday, 1953.
The Little Walls. London, Hodder and Stoughton, and New York, Doubleday, 1955; abridged edition, as *Bridge to Vengeance,* New York, Spivak, 1957.
The Sleeping Partner. London, Hodder and Stoughton, and New York, Doubleday, 1956.
Greek Fire. London, Hodder and Stoughton, and New York, Doubleday, 1958.
The Tumbled House. London, Hodder and Stoughton, 1959; New York, Doubleday, 1960.
Marnie. London, Hodder and Stoughton, and New York, Doubleday, 1961.
The Grove of Eagles. London, Hodder and Stoughton, 1963; New York, Doubleday, 1964.
After the Act. London, Hodder and Stoughton, 1965; New York, Doubleday, 1966.
The Walking Stick. London, Collins, and New York, Doubleday, 1967.
Angell, Pearl and Little God. London, Collins, and New York, Doubleday, 1970.
The Black Moon: A Novel of Cornwall 1794–1795. London, Collins, 1973; New York, Doubleday, 1974.
Woman in the Mirror. London, Bodley Head, and New York, Doubleday, 1975.
The Four Swans: A Novel of Cornwall 1795–1797. London, Collins, 1976; New York, Doubleday, 1977.
The Angry Tide: A Novel of Cornwall 1798–1799. London, Collins, 1977; New York, Doubleday, 1978.
The Stranger from the Sea: A Novel of Cornwall 1810–1811. London, Collins, 1981; New York, Doubleday, 1982.
The Miller's Dance: A Novel of Cornwall 1812–1813. London, Collins, 1982; New York, Doubleday, 1983.
The Loving Cup: A Novel of Cornwall 1813–1815. London, Collins, 1984; New York, Doubleday, 1985.
The Green Flash. London, Collins, 1986; New York, Random House, 1987.
Cameo. London, Collins, 1988.
The Twisted Sword: A Novel of Cornwall 1815–1816. London, Chapmans, 1990; New York, Carroll and Graf, 1991.
Stephanie. London, Chapmans, 1992; New York, Carroll and Graf, 1993.
Tremor. London, Macmillan, 1995; New York, St. Martin's Press, 1995.

Short Stories

The Japanese Girl and Other Stories. London, Collins, 1971; New York, Doubleday, 1972; selection, as *The Cornish Farm,* Bath, Chivers, 1982.

Uncollected Short Stories

''The Circus,'' in *Winter's Crimes 6,* edited by George Hardinge. London, Macmillan, and New York, St. Martin's Press, 1974.

''Nothing in the Library,'' in *Winter's Crimes 19,* edited by Hilary Hale. London, Macmillan, 1987.

Plays

Shadow Play (produced Salisbury, 1978).

Circumstantial Evidence (produced Guildford, Surrey, 1979).

Screenplays: *Take My Life,* with Valerie Taylor and Margaret Kennedy, 1948; *Night Without Stars,* 1951.

Television Plays: *Sleeping Partner,* 1967.

Other

The Spanish Armadas. London, Collins, and New York, Doubleday, 1972.

Poldark's Cornwall, photographs by Simon McBride. London, Bodley Head, 1983.

*

Winston Graham comments:

I look on myself simply as a novelist. I have written—always—what I wanted to write and not what I thought people might want me to write. Reading for me has always been in the first place a matter of enjoyment—otherwise I don't read—and therefore I would expect other people to read my books for the enjoyment they found in them—or not at all. Profit from reading a novel should always be a by-product. The essence to me of style is simplicity, and while I admit there are depths of thought too complex for easy expression, I would despise myself for using complexity of expression where simplicity will do.

If there has been a certain dichotomy in my work, it is simply due to a dichotomy in my own interests. I am deeply interested in history and deeply interested in the present; and I find a stimulus and a refreshment in turning from one subject and one form to another.

I like books of suspense at whatever level they may be written, whether on that of Jane Austen or of Raymond Chandler; so I think all my books of whatever kind contain some of that element which makes a reader want to turn the page—the ''and then and then'' of which E.M. Forster speaks. This can be a liability if over-indulged in; but so of course can any other preference or attribute.

Although I have always had more to say in a novel than the telling of a story, the story itself has always been the framework on which the rest has depended for its form and shape. I have never been clever enough—or sufficiently self-concerned—to spend 300 pages dipping experimental buckets into the sludge of my own subconscious. I have always been more interested in other people than in myself—though there has to be something of myself in every character created, or he or she will not come to life. I have always been more interested in people than in events, but it is only through events that I have ever been able to illuminate people.

* * *

Of the forty-odd novels Winston Graham has published over more than sixty years, many of the modern ones are in some way concerned with crime. But they are not, in the usual sense of the term, ''crime stories.'' In them, crime is a kind of catalyst speeding and provoking action, rather than an end in itself or a sufficient reason for the story, as it is in thrillers. It is seen as an aberration in otherwise normal lives, something non-criminal people, generally respectable and middle-class, may slip into or become involved with, gradually, almost imperceptibly, for all kinds of reasons—greed, love, loyalty, even a sudden impulse, but not through a ''professional'' criminal background. It is not surprising that his novel *Marnie* became one of Hitchcock's most successful films—since Hitchcock too is interested in the way ordinary people may become entangled in the bizarre.

Graham has written straightforward thrillers, and what Michael Gilbert wrote in choosing *The Little Walls* for his ''classics of detection and adventure'' series applies to the other novels equally well. It was, he says, ''the very best of those adventure stories which introduce what has come to be known in critical jargon as the anti-hero … a useful portmanteau expression to describe someone who undertakes the hero's role, without the hero's normal equipment.'' The characters in all Graham's novels are, in fact, floundering and all-too-human amateurs, realistically placed in a present-day life that includes jobs and domesticity well observed, and with a normal proneness to fear, indiscretion, and lack of nerve; caught in the end by their moral attitudes, by those who love them, by grief, conscience, and the realistic eye of their creator, who knows that their amateur status fails to give them the professional's coolness, his moral indifference.

Graham's sinners are nearly all racked by their sins, and he is fascinated both by the ''congenital'' liars and outsiders (Marnie, or the crook-lover in *The Walking Stick*), who are conditioned by their past yet devotedly loved in the present, and by their victims, or the victims of circumstances, mistakes, impulses, devotions: the narrator of *After the Act,* for instance, who pushes his ailing wife off a balcony, then finds he cannot face the mistress he ostensibly did it for. Graham values suspense; and, for his own fiction, at least, believes in action rather than analysis as the means to bring his characters to life.

His novels can roughly be divided into two, the modern and the historical. To the historical novels he brings the same *kind* of realism that he does to the present day. Through *Cordelia,* the Poldark novels set in eighteenth-century Cornwall, or *The Forgotten Story,* another tale about ordinary people involved in murder, this time at the turn of the last century, one walks familiarly. Graham has the good historical novelist's ability to suggest, rather than describe, the physical surroundings; above all to avoid gadzookery and picturesqueness. As he can get the feel of an insurance office, a printing works, or an auctioneer's, so he can walk into the past, giving the sense and atmosphere of it rather than the physical detail, making one breathe its air.

Tremor recounts the story of a 1960 earthquake in Agadir, a Moroccan resort town, that killed some 12,000 people. On the surface it is a disaster epic, but in Graham's hands it becomes much more: a penetrating examination of diverse lives brought together by disaster.

—Isabel Quigly

GRAU, Shirley Ann

Nationality: American. **Born:** New Orleans, Louisiana, 8 July 1930. **Education:** Booth School, Montgomery, Alabama, 1938–45; Ursuline Academy, New Orleans, 1945–46; Sophie Newcomb College, Tulane University, New Orleans (associate editor, *Carnival;* Lazarus Memorial medal, 1949), 1946–50, B.A. 1950 (Phi Beta Kappa); graduate study, Tulane University, 1950–51. **Family:** Married James Kern Feibleman in 1955; two sons and two daughters. **Career:** Creative writing teacher, University of New Orleans, 1966–67. **Awards:** Pulitzer prize, 1965. LL.D.: Rider College, New Jersey; D.Litt.: Spring Hill College, Alabama. **Agent:** Brandt and Brandt, 1501 Broadway, New York, New York 10036. **Address:** 210 Baranne Street, Suite 1120, New Orleans, Louisiana 70112–4179, U.S.A.

PUBLICATIONS

Novels

The Hard Blue Sky. New York, Knopf, 1958; London, Heinemann, 1959.
The House on Coliseum Street. New York, Knopf, and London, Heinemann, 1961.
The Keepers of the House. New York, Knopf, and London, Longman, 1964.
The Condor Passes. New York, Knopf, 1971; London, Longman, 1972.
Evidence of Love. New York, Knopf, and London, Hamish Hamilton, 1977.
Roadwalkers. New York, Knopf, 1994.

Short Stories

The Black Prince and Other Stories. New York, Knopf, 1955; London, Heinemann, 1956.
The Wind Shifting West. New York, Knopf, 1973; London, Chatto and Windus, 1974.
Nine Women. New York, Knopf, 1986.

Uncollected Short Stories

"The Things You Keep," in *Carnival* (New Orleans), December 1950.
"The Fragile Age," in *Carnival* (New Orleans), October 1951.
"The First Day of School," in *Saturday Evening Post* (Philadelphia), 30 September 1961.
"The Beginning of Summer," in *Story* (New York), November 1961.
"The Empty Night," in *Atlantic* (Boston), May 1962.
"The Loveliest Day," in *Saturday Evening Post* (Philadelphia), 5 May 1962.
"One Night," in *Gentlemen's Quarterly* (New York), February 1966.
"The Young Men," in *Redbook* (New York), April 1968.

*

Critical Studies: *Shirley Ann Grau* by Paul Schlueter, Boston, Twayne, 1981; *Moving On: The Heroines of Shirley Ann Grau, Anne Tyler, and Gail Godwin* by Susan S. Kissel. Bowling Green, Ohio, Bowling Green State University Popular Press, 1996.

* * *

Shirley Ann Grau may be described as a Southern writer, whose range is sometimes narrowly regional. She may also, therefore, be described as a local colorist whose observations of custom and character suggest an anthropologist at work in a fictional mode. She is a white author who deals with blacks and the black sub-culture, which makes her an anomaly in a period of black militancy. And she is finally a novelist of manners who is sharply aware of the collapse of conventional behavior patterns in modern life. The pervasive style and mood of her work may be summed up best in the terms tough, cold, and realistic. The toughness and the apparent realism seem to reveal a debt to Hemingway. She is never sentimental, and almost always she maintains sufficient distance from her characters to depict them with an objectivity that is sometimes little short of chilling. At her best she displays a kind of cold power. But she is, in general, a limited writer. She lacks originality, especially in her treatment of African-Americans and of the South. More seriously, she lacks the complex vision that enables her both to see around and to penetrate deeply into her subject. She is a competent writer who stands at some distance from the center of the Southern Renaissance.

Her best work to date is *The Keepers of the House,* a novel about a southern family. The story concerns Will Howland who inherits a great deal of land and acquires more. After the death of his wife, he brings a black girl into his house and has by her three children who survive. Late in the book, it is revealed that Will had secretly married the girl. He is portrayed as a good, compassionate man whose miscegenation arose out of love. His white granddaughter marries a man who enters politics, joins the Klan, runs for governor, and makes racist speeches. One of Will's children by the black woman reveals that his father is related to a racist politician. As a result of the revelation, the latter is ruined and the Howland family estate attacked. The estate endures, and the daughter revenges herself upon the town.

Grau is fully aware that the glamorous past may be a trap, as one of her short stories reveals. But she also knows that family traditions which are rooted in the past may endow life in the present with an illuminating sense of time and a stabilizing sense of place; in these ways the past provides a sense of continuity which enriches life in the present. This novel centers on these conceptions of life, which are characteristically Southern and which mark the work of other contemporary Southern writers as different as Robert Penn Warren and Eudora Welty. The treatment of inter-racial love here, made acceptable by marriage, appears to be an apologia for Southern miscegenation, which is, of course, usually conceived in much harsher terms.

The same is true of the manipulation of racial animosities in politics, which in itself is authentic enough in the novel. But in depicting the defeat of the racist, Grau seems to depart from her characteristically objective stance.

That stance she had maintained in *The Hard Blue Sky,* which reveals her talent for local color. The scene is an island in the Gulf of Mexico inhabited by characters of French and Spanish descent. The principal conflict is between them and the inhabitants of another island who are Slavic in descent. A boy from one island marries a girl from another; the marriage precipitates a feud. Added to the violence of men is the violence of nature, displayed when a hurricane sweeps through the Gulf. Grau does not dwell on the quaintness of character or place in her novel, and she does not patronize her characters, although the temptation to do so must have been quite real, since she conceives them as primitives. She looks at them coldly and clearly, dramatizing their attitudes toward life but passing no judgment on their behavior. These are people who recognize no canons of respectability, who admit of no restraints on their passions, and who recognize no guilt. Their sexual attitudes are thus quite free, sex being simply in the natural order of things, and their tendency towards violence is always close to the surface, since they believe that a good fight is healthy. Their life is hard and the hazards of nature, whether snakes or wind, make it harder.

Her treatment of the characters in this novel is the same, generally speaking, as her treatment of African-Americans throughout her fiction. Her composite African-American lives an unstructured life in which he obeys appetite and impulse in a naturally selfish movement toward gratification. His morality is virtually non-existent, but casual if apparent at all. His capacity for violence is like that of the islanders. This black does not rise to the level of self-consciousness. Ralph Ellison might say that he is a stereotype, perceived because the white writer suffers from a psychic-social blindness caused by the construction of the inner eye; that is, either Grau is blind or the real African-American is invisible.

Grau's chief contribution to the novel of manners is *The House on Coliseum Street.* Although it is an inferior work, it demonstrates, as some of her short stories have, that she understands the various kinds of moral corruption that mark modern life. She knows that the contemporary world is without values, and she makes divorce and sexual promiscuity the obvious signs, in this novel, of the disintegration of well-to-do society.

The Condor Passes is another family novel, melodramatic in plot but of interest for its method: much of the story is told from the five points of view of the five major characters. *Evidence of Love,* like James Gould Cozzen's *By Love Possessed,* concerns the varieties of love, some a burdensome chore, as Grau shows in the sensitive and effective section on the old mother who, content in her loneliness, awaits the coming of death. The title story of her collection *The Wind Shifting West* displays Grau's feel of water and sky, but only occasionally do the other stories reveal the detachment and power which distinguish her fictional voice at its best. *Roadwalkers* offers a powerful dual story, on the one hand of a black child named Baby, and on the other of her daughter Nanda, growing up years later. What we learn about Baby's youth among a group of homeless "Roadwalkers" in 1934 inevitably fuels our understanding of Nanda's first-person account of her own quite different experience.

—Chester E. Eisinger

GRAY, Alasdair (James)

Nationality: Scottish. **Born:** Glasgow, 28 December 1934. **Education:** Whitehill Senior Secondary School, 1946–52; Glasgow Art School (Bellahouston traveling scholarship, 1957), 1952–57, diploma in mural painting and design 1957. **Family:** Married 1) Inge Sorensen in 1962 (divorced 1970); one son; 2) Morag McAlpine in 1991. **Career:** Art teacher, Lanarkshire and Glasgow, 1958–61; scene painter, Pavilion and Citizens' theaters, Glasgow, 1961–63; freelance painter and writer, Glasgow, 1963–76; artist recorder, People's Palace Local History Museum, Glasgow, 1976–77; writer-in-residence, Glasgow University, 1977–79. Since 1979 freelance writer and painter. **Address:** Dog and Bone Books, 175 Queen Victoria Drive, Glasgow G14 9BP, Scotland.

Publications

Novels

Lanark: A Life in Four Books. Edinburgh, Canongate, and New York, Harper, 1981.

1982, Janine. London, Cape, and New York, Viking, 1984.

The Fall of Kelvin Walker: A Fable of the Sixties. Edinburgh, Canongate, 1985; New York, Braziller, 1986.

Something Leather. London, Cape, 1990; New York, Random House, 1991.

McGrotty and Ludmilla; or, The Harbinger Report. Glasgow, Dog and Bone, 1990.

Poor Things. London, Bloomsbury, 1992; New York, Harcourt Brace, 1993.

A History Maker. Edinburgh, Canongate, 1994; New York, Harcourt Brace, 1995.

Mavis Belfrage: A Romantic Tale, with Five Shorter Tales. London, Bloomsbury, 1996.

Short Stories

The Comedy of the White Dog. Glasgow, Print Studio Press, 1979.

Unlikely Stories, Mostly. Edinburgh, Canongate, 1983; New York, Penguin, 1984.

Lean Tales, with Agnes Owens and James Kelman. London, Cape, 1985.

Ten Tales Tall and True. London, Bloomsbury, 1993; New York, Harcourt Brace, 1994.

Plays

Jonah (puppet play; produced Glasgow, 1956).

The Fall of Kelvin Walker (televised 1968; produced on tour, 1972).

Dialogue (produced on tour, 1971).

The Loss of the Golden Silence (produced Edinburgh, 1973).

Homeward Bound (produced Edinburgh, 1973).

Tickly Mince (revue), with Tom Leonard and Liz Lochhead (produced Glasgow, 1982).

The Pie of Damocles (revue), with others (produced Glasgow, 1983).

Radio Plays: *Quiet People,* 1968; *The Night Off,* 1969; *Thomas Muir of Huntershill* (documentary), 1970; *The Loss of the Golden Silence,* 1974; *The Harbinger Report,* 1975; *McGrotty and Ludmilla,* 1976; *The Vital Witness* (on Joan Ure), 1979.

Television Plays and Documentaries: *Under the Helmet,* 1965; *The Fall of Kelvin Walker,* 1968; *Triangles,* 1972; *The Man Who Knew about Electricity,* 1973; *Honesty* (for children), 1974; *Today and Yesterday* (3 plays; for children), 1975; *Beloved,* 1976; *The Gadfly,* 1977; *The Story of a Recluse,* 1986.

Poetry

Old Negatives: Four Verse Sequences. London, Cape, 1989.
The Artist in His World: Prints, 1986–1997 (descriptive poems), by Iam McCulloch. Glendaruel, Argyll, Scotland, Argyll Publishing, 1998.

Other

Self-Portrait (autobiography). Edinburgh, Saltire Society, 1988.
Why Scots Should Rule Scotland. Edinburgh, Canongate, 1992.
Editor, *Poor Things: Episodes from the Early Life of Archibald McCandless M.D., Scottish Public Health Officer.* San Diego, Harcourt Brace, 1994.

*

Manuscript Collections: Scottish National Library, Edinburgh; Hunterian Museum, Glasgow University.

Critical Studies: *The Arts of Alasdair Gray* edited by Crawford and Naion, Edinburgh, Edinburgh University Press, 1991; *Alasdair Gray* by Stephen Bernstein. Lewisburg, Pennsylvania, Bucknell University Press, 1999.

Theatrical Activities: Actor: **Television**—*The Story of a Recluse,* 1986.

Alasdair Gray comments:

Lanark was planned as a whale, *1982, Janine* as an electric eel, *The Fall of Kelvin Walker* as a tasty sprat. Of the short stories I think ''A Report to the Trustees'' has the most honestly sober prose, ''Five Letters from an Eastern Empire'' the most inventive fancy, ''Prometheus'' the greatest scope.

(1995) My stories try to seduce the reader by disguising themselves as sensational entertainment, but are propaganda for democratic welfare—state Socialism and an independent Scottish parliament. My jacket designs and illustrations—especially the erotic ones—are designed with the same high purpose.

* * *

Alasdair Gray came late to the novel and was in middle life when *Lanark* his first and most successful novel was published. Prior to that he had been a painter and a scriptwriter and visual influences bear heavily on all his work: even his book jackets are designed by him. His eye for detail and his taste for color combine especially well in his short stories which were published together under the title *Unlikely Stories, Mostly.* Some stories in this collection are long, such as ''Logopandocy'' a pastiche in the writings of Sir Thomas Urquhart of Cromartie whom Gray much admires; others short, and two, ''A Likely Story in a Non-Marital Setting'' and ''A Like Story in a Domestic Setting,'' only five lines long. Some are set in modern everyday life, others in a fantastic other world; above all, they are rich in imaginative background detail. His story ''Five Letters from the Eastern Empire'' is set in the time of Marco Polo and the letters are supposedly written by Bohum the Chinese emperor's tragic poet, to his parents and they describe the court—''the evergreen garden''—in all its magnificence and all its cruelty. On the other hand it is an evocative description of the lives led by the divinely justified and the sharp, cinematic cuts and finely observed detail make it seem an exercise in scriptwriting. On another level it is a parable of power that oppresses, of a backsliding emperor whom Bohu discovers to be an ''evil little puppet, and all the cunning, straightfaced, pompous men who use him.''

Although Gray makes considerable use of myth and parable in his fiction and delights in creating imaginative worlds and societies, the matter of Scotland is never far away from the heart of his fiction. In *1982, Janine,* the hero, an aging, divorced alcoholic, insomniac supervisor of security installations tells his story while sitting in the dingy bedroom of a small Scottish hotel: to him, his native country and his fellow countrymen are subjects of disgust. ''The truth is that we are a nation of arselickers, though we disguise it with surfaces: a surface of generous, openhanded manliness, a surface of dour practical integrity, a surface of futile, maudlin defiance like when we break goalposts and windows after football matches on foreign soil and commit suicide on Hogmanay by leaping from fountains in Trafalgar.'' Although this novel is only loosely connected to the reality of present-day Scotland, and more concerned with the general human condition as experienced in the narrator's drunken reverie, *1982, Janine* is rich in Scottish literary allusions. In one section the narrator meets a pantheon of Scottish poets in an Edinburgh pub; in another Gray's richly lyrical exploration of time, space, and inebriation is reminiscent of Hugh MacDiarmid's long poem, ''A Drunk Man Looks at the Thistle.'' That Gray should be so concerned with Scotland and yet repelled by it—a classic theme in Scottish cultural life—should come as little surprise to readers of *Lanark.* In this phantasmagoric exploration of modern city life Gray has an index of plagiarisms, a recurring literary device in his fiction, and this includes an entry on the Scottish novelist George Douglas Brown (1869–1902): ''Books 1 and 2 owe much to the novel *The House with the Green Shutters* in which heavy paternalism forces a weak-minded youth into dread of existence, hallucination and crime.'' In Brown's novel, Gourlay, a wealthy self-made man is ruined by his monstrous self-willed nature and his son is castrated both by his malignancy and by the squalid ethics of Barbie, the mean town in which the Gourlays live. Although Duncan Thaw, the narrator of *Lanark* is not subjected to similar pressures he has to cope with a loveless family and the dreary drudgery of growing to maturity in a far-from-idealized version of the city of Glasgow. To escape from the numbing mindlessness of his life Thaw finds himself in a world which might yet be; this is the afterlife to which he is condemned after a death which is half accidental and half suicidal. Called Unthank it contains echoes of his life on earth in Scotland but is peopled by creatures which have the power of transmogrification.

For all the brilliance of his imaginative inventiveness, Gray showed himself to be on less secure ground in these fantasy sections and was at his best in dealing with the realities of modern life; indeed his descriptions of life in post-war Scotland have a sure and naturalistic touch. This virtue resurfaces in *Something Leather,* a quirky meandering novel which examines the nature of female sexuality as experienced by three different women, Senga, Donalda and June. As has become *de rigueur* in Gray's novels there is also a full cast of supporting characters, including the self-deluding and destructive Tom who bears a close resemblance to Duncan Thaw. Gray has spiced the narrative with a number of erotic cameos—the effect is of reading a number of short stories—but the end result is curiously asexual.

Most of Gray's writing leaves an impression of linguistic inventiveness and artistic energy but his later fiction, including the bizarre *McGrotty and Ludmilla,* has revealed a growing impatience with the confines of the novel's form. In ''Critic-Fuel,'' an epilogue to *Something Leather* he made the surprising admission that he had run out of interest in his writing, hence the change to female central characters. ''Having discovered how my talent worked it was almost certainly defunct. Imagination will not employ whom it cannot surprise.'' His Mavis, central figure in the title piece of *Mavis Belfrage: A Romantic Tale, with Five Shorter Tales,* is an undeniably strong figure who manipulates the men around her. Much the same is true of the other women in the volume—suggesting that they are pushing their creator forward to explore new frontiers in his own literary consciousness.

—Trevor Royle

GRAY, Stephen

Nationality: South African. **Born:** Cape Town, South Africa, 1941. **Education:** St. Andrew's College, Grahamstown; University of Cape Town; Cambridge University, B.A. in English, M.A. in English; University of Iowa, M.F.A. in creative writing; Rand Afrikaans University, Johannesburg, D.Litt and d.Phil., 1978. **Career:** Lecturer in English, Aix-en-Provence, two years; professor of English, Rand Afrikaans University, Johannesburg, until 1991. Since 1991 full-time writer. Editor, *Granta,* and director, Cambridge Shakespeare Group, both while a student at Cambridge; writer-in-residence, 1982, University of Queensland, Australia. **Address:** P.O. Box 86, Crown Mines, South Africa, 2025.

PUBLICATIONS

Novels

Local Colour. Johannesburg, Ravan Press, 1975.
Visible People. Cape Town, Philip, and London, Collings, 1977.
Caltrop's Desire. Cape Town, Philip, and London, Collings, 1980.
John Ross: The True Story. Johannesburg, Penguin, 1987.
Time of Our Darkness. Johannesburg and London, Muller, 1988.
Born of Man. Johannesburg, Justified Press, and London, GMP, 1989.
War Child. Johannesburg, Justified Press, 1991; London, Serif, 1993.
Drakenstein. Johannesburg, Justified Press, 1994.

Plays

Schreiner: A One-Woman Play. Cape Town, Philip, 1983.

Poetry

It's About Time,. Cape Town, Philip, 1974.
The Assassination of Shaka, with woodcuts by Cecil Skotnes. Johannesburg, McGraw-Hill, 1974.
Hottentot Venus and Other Poems. Cape Town, Philip, and London, Collings, 1979.
Season of Violence. Aarhus, Dangaroo Press, 1992.
Selected Poems, 1960–92. Cape Town, David Philip, 1994.
Gabriel's Exhibition: New Poems. Bellville, South Africa, Mayibuye Books-UWC, 1998.

Other

Southern African Literature: An Introduction. Cape Town, Philip, London, Collings, and New York, Barnes and Noble, 1979.
Douglas Blackburn. Boston, Twayne, 1984.
Human Interest and Other Pieces. Johannesburg, Justified Press, 1993.
Accident of Birth. Johannesburg, COSAW, 1993.
Editor, *Writers' Territory.* Cape Town, Longman Southern Africa, 1973.
Editor, *Mhudi,* by Solomon T. Plaatje. London, Heinemann, 1978.
Editor, *Theatre One: New South African Drama.* Johannesburg, Donker, 1978.
Editor, *Modern South African Stories.* Johannesburg, Donker, 1980.
Editor, *Stormwrack,* by C. Louis Leipoldt. Cape Town, Philip, 1980.
Editor, *Turbott Wolfe,* by William Plomer. Johannesburg, Donker, 1980.
Editor, *Theatre Two: New South African Drama.* Johannesburg, Donker, 1981.
Editor, *Athol Fugard.* Johannesburg, McGraw-Hill, 1982.
Editor, *Modern South African Poetry.* Johannesburg, Donker, 1984.
Editor, with David Schalkwyk, *Modern Stage Directions: A Collection of Short Dramatic Scripts.*Cape Town, Maskew Miller Longman, 1984.
Editor, *Three Plays,* by Stephen Black. Johannesburg, Donker, 1984.
Editor, *The Penguin Book of Southern African Stories.* Harmondsworth, Middlesex, Penguin, 1985.
Editor, *Selected Poems,* by William Plomer. Johannesburg, Donker, 1985.
Editor, *Bosman's Johannesburg.* Cape Town, Human and Rousseau, 1986.
Editor, *Herman Charles Bosman.* Johannesburg, McGraw-Hill, 1986.
Editor, *Market Plays.* Johannesburg, Donker, 1986.
Editor, *The Penguin Book of Southern African Verse.* London, Penguin, 1989.
Editor, *My Children! My Africa! and Selected Shorter Plays,* by Athol Fugard. Johannesburg, Witwatersrand University Press, 1990.
Editor, *The Natal Papers of ''John Ross'',* by Charles Rawden Maclean. Pietermaritzburg, University of Natal Press, 1992.
Editor, *South Africa Plays.* London, Hern, 1993.
Editor, *Willemsdorp,* by Herman Charles Bosman. Cape Town, Human & Rousseau, 1998.

* * *

In addition to his significant work as a poet, playwright, editor, and novelist, Stephen Gray is a prominent literary critic in his native South Africa. Always one to blur the boundaries between categories (be they generic or sociopolitical), Gray frequently combines these writerly personae, revisiting and reassessing his own fiction in his essays. As he has noted on more than one occasion, the legacy of apartheid has forced the South African writer into a position of negotiating between cultural extremes, into crossing multiple and manifold borders. This ''hybrid'' aesthetic, this ''translational'' ethic, is well represented in Gray's eight published novels, which regularly transgress the margins of race, class, and sexuality.

Gray's first novel, *Local Colour,* displays many of the central preoccupations that recur throughout his entire oeuvre: experimentation with form; a facility with the finer details of setting; a penchant for exploring the limits of racial and sexual taboos, in this case so-called miscegenation. A five-part satirical allegory set in Saldanha Bay, a remote outpost near the Cape, the narrative is a fragmentary and complex amalgam of Western literary conventions (interior monologue, epistolary romance) and African modes of oral storytelling (fable, myth). In the main section of the novel, while an American oil tanker burns and lists offshore, Beattie, Chris, and Alex hatch a plot to swindle Beattie's dying Aunt Miriam out of her property. What begins as a mere act of greed soon turns into an epic quest for the truth about Miriam's relationships with the legendary Captain McBlade and Elsabie, her colored maid. This quest motif, which is given even more satirical treatment in Gray's next novel, *Visible People,* juxtaposes the prejudices inherent in a dominant white mode of perception against the historical contingencies of the indigenous landscape, with decidedly ambivalent results.

The dialectic between past, present, and future operates at some level in all of Gray's novels, but two in particular are concerned with specific watershed moments in South African history. In *Caltrop's Desire,* on the eve of the 1948 national elections, a dying war correspondent records the waning moments of white liberalism in South Africa and anticipates an even bloodier future for the country under apartheid. In *John Ross,* Gray writes against the grain of both early-ninteenth-century historical documentation and late-twentieth-century popular mythmaking (Gray's ''novel'' was meant as a companion volume to the 1987 South African television serial, *John Ross: An African Adventure*), offering readers ''the true story'' of the young, redheaded Scottish lad who was shipwrecked at Port Natal in 1825 and subsequently became a member of King Shaka's Zulu court. Drawing attention to both the factual authenticity and the fictionality of his texts, Gray illuminates the often contradictory ways in which history gets written and stories get told.

The bond between dispossessed child and powerful adult is examined further in *Time of Our Darkness.* Here, however, Gray reverses the races of his central characters; he also complicates their relationship by introducing homosexual desire into the admixture of competing social differences. Nine years after the 1976 Soweto uprising, Disley Mashinini, a young black boy from the townships, transfers into Saint Paul's, an all-white private school. He is soon receiving more than just extracurricular instruction from his teacher, Pete Walker. Gray maps this potentially explosive territory forthrightly and candidly, underscoring South Africa's erotic investments in the more visible markers of identity, such as race. In this regard, Disley proves to be the wiser of the two protagonists. '''You know, but you don't want to know,''' Pete quotes him as saying at the outset of the novel. ''That was the theme of our relationship.''

Gay subcultural affiliation receives an altogether more vernacular treatment in *Born of Man.* Adopting a narrator with a distinctively camp idiom and filling his text with all manner of playful posturing by members of the extended community of Bairnsford Nursery, Gray reinscribes homosexual difference in ways that signify strength, attitude, and ironic pride.

Although most of Gray's novels are highly metafictional (in *Born of Man,* for example, Gray revisits the epistolary genre via the word processor), *Drakenstein* is by far Gray's most self-reflexive work to date. Clearly having fun with some of the basic tenets of postmodern theory, he uses the generic codes of the horror story—fictional *and* cinematic—precisely in order to undermine and subvert them. In confronting the horrific crimes of the past and the present in order to imagine a future for postapartheid South Africa at its time of transition, the narrator, John Raeburn, like the monster in *Frankenstein,* must also confront the horrors of his own fragmented subjectivity. ''Who is this I,'' he asks at the end of the novel, ''impatient but regretful, spitting out his flesh? Which I—I—I—half these sentences begin with I.'' This referentially unstable first-person pronoun, which surfaces throughout Gray's fiction, has gradually grown more introspective over the course of his career. The autobiographical experiments of *Accident of Birth* and some of the short pieces in *Human Interest* are, in many ways, a natural progression from the childhood reminiscences that make up *War Child.* In the opening sketch of *Human Interest,* Gray notes that even before he had ''grown to any consciousness of how morally *wrong* apartheid was,'' he nevertheless understood ''that I must become someone who would write about those aspects of life that were not recorded, were never mentioned, not even imagined to exist.'' Four decades later, decades that comprise a ''time of darkness'' from which South Africa is only now emerging, Gray has clearly made good on his teenaged vow.

—Peter Dickinson

GREENBERG, Joanne

Pseudonym: Hannah Green. **Nationality:** American. **Born:** Brooklyn, New York, 24 September 1932. **Education:** American University, Washington, D.C., B.A. **Family:** Married Albert Greenberg in 1955; two sons. **Career:** Medical officer, Lookout Mountain Fire Department; certified emergency medical technican. Since 1983, adjunct professor of anthropology, Colorado School of Mines, Golden. **Awards:** Frieda Fromm-Reichman memorial award, 1967; National Jewish Welfare Board Harry and Ethel Daroff award, 1963, and William and Janice Epstein award, 1964, both for *The King's Persons;* New York Association of the Deaf Marcus L. Kenner award, 1971; Christopher book award, 1971, for *In This Sign;* Rocky Mountain Women's Institute award, 1983; Denver Public Library Bookplate award, 1990; Colorado Author of the Year award, 1991. D.L.: Western Maryland College, 1977. D.H.L.: Gallaudet College, 1979. J.H.L.: University of Colorado, 1987. **Agent:** Wallace Literary Agency, 1977 East 70th Street, New York, New York 10021, U.S.A. **Address:** 29221 Rainbow Hill Road, Golden, Colorado 80401–9708, U.S.A.

PUBLICATIONS

Novels

The King's Persons. New York, Holt, and London, Gollancz, 1963.
The Monday Voices. New York, Holt, and London, Gollancz, 1965.
In This Sign. New York, Holt, 1968; London, Gollancz, 1970.

The Dead of the House. Garden City, New York, Doubleday, 1972.
Founder's Praise. New York, Holt, 1976.
A Season of Delight. New York, Holt, 1981.
The Far Side of Victory. New York, Holt, and London, Gollancz, 1983.
Simple Gifts. New York, Holt, and London, Gollancz, 1986.
Age of Consent. New York, Holt, and London, Gollancz, 1987.
Of Such Small Differences. New York, Holt, and London, Gollancz, 1988.
No Reck'ning Made. New York, Holt, 1993.
Where the Road Goes. New York, Henry Holt, 1998.

Short Stories

Summering: A Book of Short Stories. New York, Holt, and London, Gollancz, 1966.
Rite of Passage. New York, Holt, 1971; London, Gollancz, 1972.
High Crimes and Misdemeanors. New York, Holt, 1979; London, Gollancz, 1980.
With the Snow Queen and Other Stories. New York, Arcade, 1991.

Other

I Never Promised You a Rose Garden (as Hannah Green). New York, Holt, and London, Pan, 1964.
In the City of Paris (as Hannah Green; for children). Garden City, New York, Doubleday, 1985.

*

Film Adaptations: *I Never Promised You a Rose Garden,* 1977.

* * *

Joanne Greenberg, also known as Hannah Green, is a writer whose style lends itself to the mature reader yet simultaneously presents themes suitable for all ages. Greenberg addresses the persistent doubts that plague all of us by relating stories of others in need. Though the scenarios in which her characters find themselves may be unfamiliar to the average reader, the emotions they feel while enmeshed in the plotlines are universal in appeal and scope. Her works include magazine publications, short stories, novels, and a movie adaptation of her book, *I Never Promised You a Rose Garden.*

Greenberg wrote *I Never Promised You a Rose Garden* under the pseudonym Hannah Green. In this book, she details the struggle of a 16-year-old girl fighting for her sanity. The descriptive and, at times, poetic uses of language bring the reader inside the character's world of fantasy. The depiction of the brilliant psychiatrist grappling with the reality of her own life while immersed in the treatment of her patient is explicitly detailed and well written. As Greenberg's personal encounter with mental problems was a basis for the character's ordeal with psychosis and schizophrenia, her empathy for her character is clearly evident.

Another popular book, *In This Sign,* was heralded by those both within and outside of the deaf community. The themes of loneliness, isolation, and of being different are dramatically brought to life by the experiences of Greenberg's characters. She transforms the occurrences within the realm of her deaf character into common circumstances with which we can all identify. Readers can gain an affinity for the handicapped through edification and education that is expertly interwoven into the story line.

In another book, *Of Such Small Differences,* Greenberg expands the reader's mind to encompass the daily trials and tribulations of a character who is not only deaf but also blind. The leading character's experiences and ensuing love affair are portrayed as one might relate a story told by one friend to another. The primary difficulties handled by the protagonist are those of anyone involved in a growing relationship. It is a love story. The physical disabilities are secondary in the development of the characters' union.

In *Simple Gifts,* we also see people somewhat "out of sync" with the world around them. Their lives are complicated by secrets long thought buried. Love, for them, usually comes after much turmoil, when it is least expected.

One of Greenberg's sadder stories is *The Far Side of Victory.* This book examines such themes as crime and punishment of the human soul. One's guilt or innocence is primarily determined by the ability to cope with life's adversities. In the search for truth and meaning, there lies the experience of love and loss.

In *Age of Consent,* Greenberg strongly portrays the mysterious loner no one ever really knew. By examining a character's life following untimely death at the hands of murderers, Greenberg cleverly utilizes the technique of flashback. The investigators are forced to look at their own lives as the impact of both the life and death of the main character is revealed. Once again we see a study in solitude; of being alone in the company of many.

A book that includes references to actual historical events is *Founder's Praise.* This book details the climb of a family through hard times during the history of the United States. Their belief in the goodness of people through religion and morality guides them into their future. *Where the Road Goes* has the air of, in the words of one character, a "sixties parody." Sixty-two-year old Tig has been involved in every cause of that decade, and three decades later, as she embarks on a walk across the United States to raise consciousness concerning environmental issues, she is unchanged. At home, however, both her daughters are in need, and the book—written in the form of letters and diary entries—reveals that, in Tig's words, "Were I home, I would be less a part of the family's lives. Our distance has brought us closer to one another."

Greenberg has also written several collections of short stories. In one book, *Summering,* her tales again reflect the themes of love and misunderstanding, loneliness and friendship. We are subsequently captivated by her imaginative characterizations and narratives that uniquely embody her freshness and innovation. In another book of short stories, *With the Snow Queen and Other Stories,* she writes of people we know. We can relate to people with basic human needs, even in peculiar situations. In one story, she employs the unconventional tact of having a character break through the "third wall" to "speak" directly to the reader. Her range of unusual topics runs the gamut from time travel to the solemnity of the life of a monk. Another collection, *High Crimes and Misdemeanors,* utilizes much humor and fantasy. Yet Greenberg is still able to embroil the readers in the particulars of her characters that most closely link us all to the hopes, fears, and dreams of life. Additionally, this book contains several stories that derive from Greenberg's religious background.

Greenberg's popularity lies in both her creativity and her originality. Her ability to incorporate common themes into uncommon situations makes her a most readable author.

—Laurie Schwartz Guttenberg

GRENVILLE, Kate

Nationality: Australian. **Born:** Kate Gee in Sydney, Australia, 14 October 1950. **Education:** University of Sydney, B.A. 1972; University of Colorado, M.A. 1982. **Family:** Married Bruce Petty; one son, one daughter. **Career:** Arts administrator, Australia Council, Sydney, 1973–74; documentary film production assistant, Film Australia, Sydney; freelance film editor and writer, London, 1974–80; subtitle editor, Multicultural TV, Sydney, 1983–85; instructor in writing, University of Sydney. **Awards:** Fellowship (International Association of University Women), 1981; Australian/Vogel award, 1984; writer's fellowship (Australia Council), 1985. **Agent:** C. Lurie, 26 Yarraford Avenue, Alphington, Victoria 3067, Australia.

PUBLICATIONS

Novels

Lilian's Story. North Sydney, Australia, Allen & Unwin, 1984; New York, Viking, 1986.

Dreamhouse. University of Queensland Press, 1986; New York, Viking, 1987.

Joan Makes History. Latham, New York, British American Publishers, 1988.

Dark Places. London, Picador, 1994; published as *Albion's Story.* New York, Harcourt, 1994.

The Idea of Perfection. South Melbourne, Picador, 1999.

Short Stories

Bearded Ladies. St. Lucia, Queensland, Australia, University of Queensland Press, 1984.

Other

The Writing Book: A Workbook for Fiction Writers. North Sydney, Australia, Allen & Unwin (Australia), 1990.

Making Stories: How Ten Australian Novels Were Written (with Sue Woolfe). North Sydney, Australia, Allen & Unwin, 1993.

* * *

Kate Grenville first came to prominence when her novel *Lilian's Story* won the 1984 Australian/Vogel award for the best manuscript by an unpublished writer under the age of thirty-five. By the time it appeared, however, she was already the author of a collection of short stories, *Bearded Ladies.* The title of the collection is ambiguous. The suggestion of sexual ambiguity is present in some of the stories. In another sense, though, the various but similar young protagonists of these stories are "bearded" by men, subjected to male demands, deprived of the opportunity to grow into selfhood; strongly feminist themes run through all Grenville's work. Many of them have difficulty establishing worthwhile relationships with men or breaking with failed ones. The writing is carefully flat and laconic, the point of view almost always that of a dispassionate observer, even when the observer is also the protagonist.

The eponymous Lilian in Grenville's very well-received first novel goes further than the collection of bearded ladies and breaks free entirely from the conventional demands of society. Based loosely on the life of an eccentric, well-known Sydney woman named Bea Miles (it was originally called Bea's Story) the novel tells the story of Lilian Singer, a grossly fat, engagingly individualistic woman who decides that she will follow her own path wherever it takes her and will not be bound by the conventions of society. She struggles early to escape the two constrictions that bind her—being ugly and, worse still, being a girl, a misfortune that has dogged her literally since the day of her birth. After a period in an asylum, her eccentricity blossoms; she harasses strangers with long recitations of Shakespeare for which she demands payment, boards trains and refuses to buy a ticket, steps into taxis with strangers and exuberantly embarrasses them. But for all its racy energy and strikingly original characterization, the claims Grenville makes for her protagonist—that she has been forced into eccentricity by a patriarchal society and that her eccentricity is in any case a form of greatness—remain arguable.

Dreamhouse sprang from the final, novella-length story "Country Pleasures" in *Bearded Ladies* and is a blackly satiric comedy about an English couple in Italy and a series of people they encounter who all turn out to be having unorthodox or unnatural affairs. As the novel opens, "Rennie" Dufrey and his beautiful ex-secretary wife Louise are driving towards a house in Tuscany that has been lent to him by his academic mentor Daniel. The house proves to be derelict, with mice, spiders, and even a snake in occupancy. Daniel's children, Hugo and Viola, are unfriendly and behave strangely, and before long Louise begins to uncover a number of curious sexual liaisons. The novel is narrated by Louise in a style that is peculiarly factual, dispassionate, written almost like a report. She herself is an almost disembodied presence, reacting to events in only a muted way. Nevertheless, Grenville piles on the horrors lavishly. Spiders hang over the uncomfortable beds the characters sleep in. Hugo collects and stuffs birds; his cruelties are documented in detail. Loads of revulsion are invested in even the most banal of actions. At the end, Louise's decision to leave her husband seems common-sensed and far from being as momentous as the author seems to think.

Joan Makes History was written in response to a commission from the Bicentennial Authority to write a book that was relevant to the celebration of the white occupation of Australia. It is quite ingeniously conceived. A dozen scenes headed "JOAN" describe the life of a very ordinary woman, Joan Radulesco. Although fiercely conscious of her aspirations to greatness she lives an uneventful life except for leaving her husband and later returning. She accomplishes nothing but eventually realizes that in simply living her own life she is part of history. Against this banal, contemporary Joan there is juxtaposed another historical Joan who is seen in eleven key episodes of Australian history. This Joan can be anyone, go anywhere, she wants to. When Captain Cook claims Australia for the British in the *Endeavour* in 1770 she is on board as his wife, contemptuous of the passes the foppish Joseph Banks is making at her. She is present at the opening of Parliament in 1901; as an Aboriginal girl she meets the explorer Flinders when he encounters Aborigines for the first time.

Each episode stands in some kind of relationship to the life of the contemporary Joan. For instance, the historical Joan is Mrs. Cook; the contemporary one goes with her husband and child to visit Cook's Cottage. Joan's leaving her husband Duncan and wandering over Australia is paralleled by a black Joan leaving her similarly stolid Warra, and so on. One of Grenville's keenest ambitions is to speak for the silent in Australian history, especially women and Aboriginal people.

Dark Places takes us back to the territory of *Lilian's Story* and includes many of the same incidents, but this time presented from the viewpoint of Lilian's father, Albion Gidley Singer, whose first person narrative guides the novel. This is both its strength and limitation. To sustain the narrative voice of Singer is an impressive feat but also a somewhat wearying one. Long before the end of the novel we have come to know as much as we need to about his real evil, and although Grenville offers occasional glimpses of the possibility of self-knowledge, it is clear that he will not change radically. He is, in his own words, ''an embattled and lonely atom'' whose traditional incapacities are established early, though in sparklingly incisive prose. His love of facts, the extinction of feeling and the reduction of all human complexity to things measurable and quantifiable become a prevailing and blackly comic theme in the novel. Added to this is an extraordinarily intense misogyny. Albion is a man brought up to hate and fear women as the mysterious Other. All the sexual encounters in the novel are filled with a sense of abhorrence of the female body and reduced to financial transactions, or else become violent fantasies in which women's protests at his mistreatment of them are totally disbelieved. The pattern emerges in his frequent rapings of his wife and finally in the rape of his daughter. It comes as no surprise that Albion displays traits of a covert homosexual as well. The problem is not one of making Singer believable but of making him dramatically interesting. He is an essentially static character. The only changes that take place in him are cosmetic; they relate only to the appearance of the self that he constructs and then presents to the world.

Kate Grenville's most recent novel, *The Idea of Perfection*, is a patient, affectionate study of an unlikely romance between a bridge engineer and a quilt maker. Both of them are, on the surface, dysfunctional people. Douglas Cheeseman is the son of a man who died winning the VC. Harley Savage is the only apparently untalented member of a family of gifted artists. Cheeseman's wife left him out of boredom. Harley has been married unsuccessfully three times. He suffers from vertigo; she has had a heart attack. Both are physically unattractive. The couple meet when Cheeseman is assigned to the tiny town of Karakarook to decide whether a scenic bridge needs replacing. Although he soon works out a win-win situation he is too uncomfortable to actually put it to his boss. But the ending of the novel has them getting together as Cheeseman finally asserts himself and wins the hand of his lover. Juxtaposed against these are Felicity Porcelline and her banker husband. Felicity spends a lifetime denying her own needs and desires, including the lust she feels for the local Chinese butcher Freddy Chang. She is obsessed with her appearance and every gesture, every pose, is designed to enhance her skin. Even smiling has to be rationed.

Grenville takes a perhaps excessive time to tease these themes out. The lack of composure, the diffident uncertainty of Harley and especially Cheeseman, are stressed repeatedly, as are Felicity's prurience and superficiality. So are the contrasts between the two women. Harley is the embodiment of unpretentious naturalness. In contrast, Felicity rations her feelings and expression of them. The portrait of her borders on caricature if it hasn't already gone past it, though Grenville does offer her one momentary insight into her own phoniness—''Just for one puncturing moment she saw herself: a cruel smiling child''—before she draws the curtain on her feelings again.

Grenville's *The Writing Book,* subtitled ''A Workbook for Fiction Writers,'' is exceptionally useful and interesting, not least because it illuminates many of her own practices as a writer.

—Laurie Clancy

GRISHAM, John

Nationality: American. **Born:** Jonesboro, Arkansas, 8 February 1955. **Education:** Mississippi State University, B.S. in accounting 1977; University of Mississippi, LL.D in 1981. **Family:** Married Renee Jones; three children. **Career:** Practiced law, Southaven, Mississippi, 1981–91; member Mississippi House of Representatives, 1984–90. **Address:** c/o Doubleday, 1540 Broadway, New York, New York 10036–4039, U.S.A.

Publications

Novels

A Time to Kill. New York, Wynwood Press, 1989; London, Century, 1993.
The Firm. New York, Doubleday, and London, Century, 1991.
The Pelican Brief. New York, Doubleday, and London, Century, 1992.
The Client. New York, Doubleday, and London, Century, 1993.
The Chamber. New York, Doubleday, and London, Century, 1994.
The Rainmaker. New York, Doubleday, and London, Century, 1995.
The Runaway Jury. New York, Doubleday, 1996.
The Partner. New York, Doubleday, 1997.
The Street Lawyer. New York, Doubleday, 1998.
The Testament. New York, Doubleday, 1999.
The Brethren. New York, Doubleday, 2000.

*

Film Adaptations: *The Firm,* 1993; *The Pelican Brief,* 1993; *The Client,* 1994; *The Chamber,* 1996; *The Rainmaker,* 1998.

Critical Studies: *John Grisham: A Critical Companion* by Mary Beth Pringle. Westport, Connecticut, Greenwood Press, 1997.

* * *

John Grisham hit the best-seller lists as a kind of publishing phenomenon, a blockbuster novelist whose books are instant hits and are snapped up by Hollywood even before they hit the bookstores. Grisham writes a type of novel that might best be described as a ''legal procedural.'' His books deal with the law and those who practice it. If, as surveys indicate, Americans are antilawyer, they are certainly not antilaw novel. Grisham and others have made the legal novel vastly popular with the American reading public.

There are probably two main reasons for Grisham's popularity among contemporary readers. First, Grisham invites his reader into the often confusing and arcane world of legal practice. He cuts through the ''heretofores'' and ''whereases'' to simplify law for the reader. He shows how the law works, how lawyers work, why the law sometimes doesn't work, and what's going on when we can't see legal workings. Furthermore, he does this with a page-turning style that is hard to resist for those curious about the legal system in this country.

Second, Grisham suggests to his readers that the law can be made to work for all of us, even neophytes, even in the face of huge companies with high-priced representation, even against overwhelming odds, even against government oppression. Grisham's protagonists are always underdogs. They may be law students (*The Pelican*

Brief), brand new lawyers (*The Firm, The Chamber, The Rainmaker*), or practicing lawyers fighting against great odds (*A Time to Kill, The Client*). Whatever the situation, the message is powerful and seductive. Americans hold strongly and dearly the belief that we are all equal under the law and that all of us have a chance to win if our cause is right, never mind the reality of expensive attorneys.

One of Grisham's gifts is that he is able to make sympathetic to the reader even those characters who might ordinarily have no claim to those sympathies. In *The Chamber,* for instance, Grisham presents his readers with a character who deserves the death penalty, if indeed anyone ever has. He is a multiple murderer, an unrepentant racist—a virtual compendium of all that could possibly be wrong with a character facing capital punishment. Still, it would be the hard-hearted reader who could reach the end of this book and not feel sorry for the death of an old man who glories in a last gift of Eskimo Pies.

Grisham's first book, *A Time to Kill,* is probably his weakest, although that could be said of most first novels. He introduces plot lines and characters that he fails to develop sufficiently or to tie up neatly at the end. By his second book, *The Firm,* he has overcome those problems quite thoroughly. Grisham likes introducing involved plot lines and twists and weaving them into a fast-paced whole. One almost suspects that he considers complexity a personal challenge, taking it on in the way one might consider constructing a puzzle.

Although his novels are generally well edited and fairly seamless, *The Chamber* showed signs of a syndrome unfortunately common to blockbuster writers, one that sometimes appears after their first few novels. When writers become so valuable to their publishers that publishers are afraid to edit them, sloppiness in the minor aspects of editing may begin to pop out, and that is the case with *The Chamber.* Yet no such problems surface in *The Rainmaker,* the novel following *The Chamber;* perhaps the writer had been made aware of the editing lapses.

The Runaway Jury, with its plot concerning a tobacco-liability lawsuit, could not have been more well-timed when it appeared in 1996, as states sued tobacco companies for billions of dollars. *The Testament* focuses on a much more localized concern, and as with many another Grisham novel, the premise—a wealthy man sidesteps his greedy children and wives in his will to reward a stranger of good character—is hardly original; but, as is also characteristic of Grisham, his execution of the story is engaging. The book is also the most overtly spiritual work by Grisham, a devout Christian. By contrast, *The Brethren* offers the first Grisham anti-heroes, with hardly a major character that an audience is likely to cheer for. Absent are the typical underdog heroes, and in their place is a trio of crooked judges serving prison time, a ruthless presidential candidate, and a conniving CIA chief.

Overall, Grisham's work is well constructed, tightly plotted, fast paced, and, if undemanding, certainly exciting for the reader looking for a hard-to-put-down novel.

—June Harris

GROOM, Winston

Nationality: American. **Born:** Washington, D.C., 23 March 1943. **Education:** University of Alabama, A.B. 1965. **Military Service:** U.S. Army, 1965–67: served in Vietnam, became captain. **Family:** Married Ruth Noble in 1969 (divorced 1974), married Anne Clinton Bridges in 1987. **Career:** Reporter and later columnist, *Washington Star,* Washington, D.C., 1967–76; full-time novelist, 1976—. **Awards:** Best fiction award (Southern Library Association), 1980. **Agent:** Theron Raines, Raines & Raines, 71 Park Avenue, New York, New York 10016, U.S.A.

Publications

Novels

Better Times Than These. New York, Summit Books, 1978.
As Summers Die. New York, Summit Books, 1980.
Only. New York, Putnam, 1984.
Forrest Gump. New York, Doubleday, 1986.
Gone the Sun. New York, Doubleday, 1988.
Gump & Co. New York, Pocket Books, 1995.
Such a Pretty, Pretty Girl. New York, Random House, 1999.

Other

Conversations with the Enemy: The Story of PFC Robert Garwood (with Duncan Spencer). New York, Putnam, 1983.
Shrouds of Glory: From Atlanta to Nashville—The Last Great Campaign of the Civil War. Boston, Atlantic Monthly Press, 1994.
Gumpisms: The Wit and Wisdom of Forrest Gump. New York, Pocket Books, 1994.
The Bubba Gump Shrimp Co. Cookbook. Birmingham, Alabama, Oxmoor House, 1994.
Forrest Gump: My Favorite Chocolate Recipes: Mama's Fudge, Cookies, Cakes, and Candies. Leisure Arts, 1995.
The Crimson Tide: An Illustrated History of Football at the University of Alabama. Tuscaloosa, University of Alabama Press, 2000.
Foreword, *James Jones: A Friendship* by Willie Morris. Urbana, University of Illinois Press, 1999.

*

Film Adaptations: *Forrest Gump*, 1994.

* * *

Winston Groom is a Southern novelist in the truest sense of the word. His Southernness permeates both his novels and his non-fiction. His characters speak with Southern voices, and life in his novels moves according to a distinctly Southern timeline. Following the tradition of other Southern writers like William Faulkner, Carson McCullers, and Pat Conroy, Groom lovingly peoples his books with quirky characters who pay homage to Southern history and the modern-day South in a single breath. While the South is more evident in his novels, Groom's non-fiction also echoes his Southern roots.

Groom was born in Washington, D.C., but grew up in Mobile, Alabama, on the Gulf Coast. After a stint in the Army, Groom returned to Washington, D.C., where he worked as a reporter on the now defunct *Washington Star,* covering the political and court beat. Willie Morris, the newspaper's writer-in-residence believed that young Groom had the potential to become a writer and encouraged him to go to New York. In the Big Apple, the newly single Groom spent little time writing. Most of the time, he hung out with literary cronies like James Jones, George Plimpton, Kurt Vonnegut, Joseph

Heller, Irwin Shaw, and Truman Capote. It was an essential learning experience for Groom, but to him New York was alien territory.

Returning to Alabama, Groom settled down to writing and enjoying life with his second wife and his dogs. The return to his native South was beneficial to Groom. His strong sense of place thrived on the day-to-day replenishment of Southern life and Southern people. Groom believes that Southerners make good storytellers because they are surrounded by families and friends who like to relate life's experiences. Sometimes the writer embellishes the story, but the strength of the narrative is found in the absorption of the story into his/her own conscious memory. This interweaving of past and present is an essential ingredient of Southern novels.

The name of Winston Groom will forever be associated with the award-winning movie *Forrest Gump*. Groom wrote *Forrest Gump* in 1986, and the novel about an amiable slow-witted Southern man who achieved success and adventure sold a respectable 40,000 copies. When Paramount bought the right to his fourth novel in 1994, Groom's life changed forever. The re-release of *Forrest Gump* in 1994 sold more than 1.7 million copies. The movie grossed over $657 million worldwide, garnering six Academy Awards, including best picture, best director, and best actor. The immensely popular Tom Hanks brought Forrest Gump to endearing life, and Forrest's assertion that, according to his mama, ''life is like a bowl of chocolates'' became part of the American language.

The Forrest Gump phenomenon so intrigued the American public that Groom wrote *Gumpisms: The Wit and Wisdom of Forrest Gump* and two Forrest Gump cookbooks. Forrest Gump hats and T-shirts appeared around the country. In the furor over the movie and Hank's almost unheard of back-to-back Oscars, the fact that Groom was a respected author of both fiction and non-fiction works was somewhat overshadowed.

Forrest Gump chronicles the life of the title character, a slow-thinking individual with an I.Q. of 75. Despite what many would see as drawbacks, Forrest becomes an All-American football hero with a knack for being in the right place at the right time. It is obvious that Groom *likes* Forrest Gump. The author insists that the novel is about dignity. He argues that Forrest was not a symbol of conservatism and had no political agenda. Not everyone liked *Forrest Gump*. He was perceived by some critics as too simplistic, too unrealistic, and too predictable. It has been said that Southerners celebrate their eccentrics rather than hiding them. It follows, then, that *Forrest Gump* is a celebration of Southern eccentricities.

Groom's Forrest Gump sequel in 1995, *Gump & Co.* tied up loose ends in Forrest's life and reportedly made a good deal of money for Groom, but it never achieved the wide appeal of the original. Groom knew that critics would be gunning for him. By the time that Groom wrote *Gump & Co.*, Forrest Gump belonged to America as much as to the author who created him. Forrest, like his creator, had learned a lesson from the success of the movie about his life; and in *Gump & Co.*, he cautions readers ''don't *never* let nobody make a movie of your life's story.''

As a result of the years before Forrest Gump became a household name, Groom became a writer who wrote simply to tell a story. His novels published before and after *Forrest Gump* reveal that he is a master storyteller. Groom determined that he would continue to write whatever he wished. Admittedly an eclectic anachronism, Groom asserted that he would stop writing and practice law when he stopped having fun.

Better Times Than These, Groom's first novel, explored his firsthand experience of the Vietnam conflict where he served 1966–67. He wrote with heartbreaking reality of the Bravo Company facing a world and a situation that was unlike anything they had ever known. Critics hailed *Better Times Than These* as a landmark treatment of the American experience in Vietnam. It is from the perspective of a Southern writer who lives daily with the specter of Vietnam that *Better Times Than These* is written. With the horrors of Vietnam behind him, Billy Kahn realizes that those who survived had inherited a legacy from the dead, a charge to go back to being ''bankers or salesmen, or service-station attendants, or farmers, or forklift operators or geologists.'' He understands that the important thing is ''to have a place to go and be with people like themselves, since anyone who hadn't been there probably wouldn't know what in hell you were talking about.''

Groom's second novel is set in 1950s Louisiana. *As Summers Die* tells the story of Willie Croft, a small town lawyer who has settled into an unexciting life where each day follows the next with predictable regularity. Willie's placidity is shaken up when black sharecroppers discover oil. Groom handles the resulting upheaval with a master's touch, presenting a segregated South with a stranglehold on the last vestiges of its glory days faced with a second great battle that will change the fabric of their lives forever. Critics complained that the novel's characters were all either good or bad, which resulted in an overly moralistic novel. However, this is one of the strengths of the novel because the period of desegregation was a time when right and wrong were clearly drawn lines in the sand.

Gone the Sun allowed Groom to explore the experiences of Beau Gunn, a Vietnam veteran who returns home to Alabama to take over a failing newspaper. In the course of his work, Groom finds that the people of Bienville are hiding many secrets. Gunn's determination to see justice done starts him on a journey of self-discovery, where he must deal with unresolved relationships and lost ideals. Groom reveals in *Gone the Sun* that he can go beyond telling a story to unraveling complex relationships and experiences. With a sure touch, he peoples the town of Bienville with characters that are shaped both by the world around them and a past they can never escape.

Such A Pretty, Pretty Girl signaled Groom's first foray into the thriller genre. Critics saw *Such A Pretty, Pretty Girl* as Groom's homage to 1940s Hollywood. Groom's protagonist is Johnny Lightfoot, a well-known screenwriter who is obsessed with his former girlfriend Delia Jamison, a Los Angeles news anchor. The lovely Delia has a past strewn with broken hearts and rejected lovers. Johnny Lightfoot is flawed by his inability to redeem himself. He believes that his redemption can be achieved by saving Delia from herself and her pursuers because the success of his quest will prove to both Johnny and Delia that he is worthy of being loved.

A respectable body of non-fiction works by Groom attests to his credibility as a chronicler of fact as well as of fiction. *Conversations with the Enemy: The Story of PFC Robert Garwood*, written with Duncan Spencer, was nominated for a Pulitzer Prize. PFC Robert Garwood is taken prisoner in Vietnam. Initially, Garwood is placed in a cage by himself with no one to talk to and nothing to relieve the boredom of prison life. Over a period of time, other prisoners appear, and life takes on a survival-of-the-fittest mentality as each of the Americans attempts to survive whatever the cost to his compatriots. *Conversations with the Enemy* is more indicative of Groom's journalistic career than of his experience as a respected novelist.

Groom's *Shrouds of Glory* was a labor of love in which he told the Civil War narrative of beleaguered John Bell Hood, a Southern general convinced that his efforts could turn the tide of the war. Reviews of the book were mixed. Some critics claimed that the book was boring in its attention to details, while others argued that Groom made the battles come alive. Groom's own great-grandfather participated in the defense of Atlanta, and his personal interest in the Southern campaign is evident.

The praise for Groom's non-fiction is well deserved, but it is as a chronicler of tales that Groom is at his best. He has a natural gift for well-written dialogue, and his strong sense of place draws the reader into his fictional world. Groom brings the Old South and the New South together in a seamless whole. His writing represents the best of Southern fiction in the latter half of the twentieth century. As Jenny's ghost takes leave of Forrest Gump in *Gump & Co.*, she leaves him with her philosophy of life: ''Memories are what count in life, Forrest, when there's nothing else left, it'll be the memories that mean everything.'' Jenny's parting words sum up Groom's success as a writer. He builds on memories that are the product of his own experiences and that of his beloved South, and he leaves his readers with the memory of well-crafted characters who live on in individual memories.

—Elizabeth Purdy

GRUMBACH, Doris (Isaac)

Nationality: American. **Born:** New York City, 12 July 1918. **Education:** Washington Square College, A.B. 1939; Cornell University, M.A. 1940. **Military Service:** U.S. Navy WAVES. **Family:** 1) married Leonard Grumbach, 1941 (divorced 1972), four children; 2) companion of Sybil Pike. **Career:** Title writer for Metro-Goldwyn-Mayer, New York City, 1940–41; proofreader and copyeditor, Time, Inc., 1941–42; associate editor of *Architectural Forum,* 1942–43; English teacher at Albany Academy for Girls, Rochester, New York, 1952–55; held a variety of positions from instructor to professor of English at College of St. Rose, Albany, New York, 1952–73; literary editor for *The New Republic,* 1973–75; professor of American literature, American University, Washington, D.C., 1975–85. Columnist for *Critic,* 1960–64; *National Catholic Reporter,* 1968–76; *New York Times Books Review,* 1976–83; *Saturday Review,* 1977–78; and *Chronicle of Higher Education,* 1979–84. Contributor of reviews and criticism to *New York Times Books Review, Chicago Tribune, Commonweal, Los Angeles Times, Nation, Washington Post, New Republic,* National Public Radio, and the *MacNeil-Lehrer Newshour.* Board of directors, 1984–89, and executive board, 1985–91, PEN/Faulkner. **Awards:** Lifetime Achievement Award (New England Booksellers Association), 1996. **Member:** American Association of University Professors, Phi Beta Kappa. **Agent:** Maxine Groffsky, 2 Fifth Avenue, New York, New York 10011, U.S.A.

PUBLICATIONS

Novels

The Spoils of Flowers. Garden City, New York, Doubleday, 1962.
The Short Throat, the Tender Mouth. Garden City, New York, Doubleday, 1964.
Chamber Music. New York, Dutton, and London, Hamish Hamilton, 1979.
The Missing Person. New York, Putnam, and London, Hamish Hamilton, 1981.
The Ladies. New York, Dutton, and London, Hamish Hamilton, 1984.
The Magician's Girl. New York, MacMillan, 1987.
The Book of Knowledge. New York, Norton, 1995.

Other

The Company She Kept (biography). New York, Coward, 1967.
Coming into the End Zone (autobiography). New York and London, Norton, 1991.
Extra Innings: A Memoir. New York, Norton, 1993.
Fifty Days of Solitude. Boston, Beacon Press, 1994.
Life in a Day. Boston, Beacon Press, 1996.
The Presence of Absence: On Prayers and an Epiphany. Boston, Beacon Press, 1998.
The Pleasure of Their Company. Boston, Beacon Press, 2000.

Recordings: *The Craft of My Fiction,* Archive of Recorded Poetry and Literature, 1985.

*

Doris Grumbach comments:

(2000) I write fiction to make sense of the world I have known in my eighty-two years of life. I use the people I have known, the ones I have thought might have existed, and myself, as I imagine myself to have been or to be, as characters. They live in real places, or places I remember as real, and what happens to them is what seems reasonable or likely to me. The prose I utilize is plain song to suit the reduction I have made of the poetry of existence. There is no lesson in any of these seven novels, unless it is the lesson that life is infinitely varied, that characters (persons) are never typical, and that place/setting is always filtered through the vagaries of memory.

* * *

Immediately apparent in Doris Grumbach's fiction is its decency. She prefaces some of her novels without resorting to the usual disclaimer, ''no relationship to anyone living or dead,'' but declares her characters as typifying numerous individuals: ''This novel is a portrait, not of a single life but of many lives melded into one.'' However, her stereotypes attracted the most pejorative criticism of her work and are likely to be the reason that her most widely acclaimed books are recent nonfictional memoirs.

Her novels' inflammatory scenes and subjects are treated delicately, with an unfashionable sense of niceness. *The Ladies* is a polite narrative of an eighteenth-century lesbian relationship between Eleanor, who at seven decides to ''be a boy, and then a man,'' and Sarah, whose ''steps were prim and careful.'' Leaving behind authoritarian fathers and hand-wringing mothers, the women spend their first night together in a cold barn where ''they put their arms about each other, ignoring the wet discomforts of their clothes, seeking to dry themselves in the heat of their creature love.'' Later, free and established in Wales, ''they lay close together,'' which does not explain the trouble to which they have gone. More warmth has already occurred in a scene from Eleanor's childhood, masturbating on a stone lion and ''never allowing herself to believe that in her ecstasy it was she who dampened his granite back.''

Nor are we given more than an implication of a physical relationship between *Chamber Music*'s Caroline and Anna: ''the way we moved together at the start of sleep to lie close, often in each other's arms, the sense of creature warmth and security we kindled between our two bodies as we touched.'' Grumbach relies upon the imagination of her audience to equate ''creature love'' or ''creature warmth and security'' with passion.

Lovemaking is more vividly portrayed in *The Magician's Girl* through Minna's reverie after Lowell has left her bed: ''Enlivened by the pressure of his young presence, she greeted his entry with moisture long absent from the unused region of her sex.'' Readers spoiled by the power of a D.H. Lawrence novel or desensitized by pulp fiction may have jaded tastes, but also Grumbach seems to be writing to an easily offended, past generation. She sacrifices credibility by making scant distinction between friendship, love, and sex.

She is much less ambiguous about other themes, such as the lonely survivor, the wasted lives of those who wait for excitement to come to them. *Chamber Music*'s heroine Caroline is ''raised by a lovely, heartbroken mother,'' and the book concludes with Caroline's observation that, ''Conceived in the age of the Centennial's bentwood sofa, I lived an almost empty life into an overcrowded and hectic century.'' *The Ladies*' Sarah barely sustains herself with memories, indeed the ghost, of Eleanor. *The Magician's Girl* leaves the ineffectual Liz musing that she is ''the one left. Odd woman out. Or in. Still afloat, still kicking,'' but without direction.

Sarah alone finds peace with herself: ''After a time of crying at her fears and her life's small tragedies, she never shed a tear again.'' Likewise, in *Magician's Girl,* Minna loses the fear taught by her mother, and although ''Minna Grant's first memory, at five, was of terror,'' she leaves ''fearless.'' By contrast, Caroline's worst fear is realized as she is ''deserted by the single point of light, the one glowing coal, in a long, cold, dark life.'' Franny has no personality, only her stage persona: ''Eddie Puritan, the agent of her real self, the slate man for all her inner takes, was the only one … who thought Fanny Marker was a person. And then, of course, he died.'' As a homosexual (''nance''), he was the only man who had not been a sexual threat.

The four principal characters in *The Book of Knowledge,* which begins in the resort town of Far Rockaway, New York, are unable to overcome the circumstances of their lives, some of which come from outside—the story opens around the time of the 1929 stock market crash—and some of which are internally motivated. Caleb and Kate Flowers are driven by their ''twinned sensibility'' to become furtive sexual partners, and Kate retains her affection for her brother while Caleb discovers longings that in that time were almost as taboo as incest. Later, at Cornell, he rediscovers childhood friend Lionel Schwartz—the book takes place over a fifteen-year period—and the two embark on a doomed gay relationship. Roslyn Hellman, the fourth friend, discovers that she is a lesbian, but like Caleb she suppresses her desires. Though America recovers from the Great Depression to fight a good war in the 1940s, the characters never recover from their own personal crashes.

Despite all of the unusual, improbable, or unexpected situations that actually happen to people and which Grumbach employs in her novels, she nonetheless maintains a detachment from her characters, unlike Charles Dickens's or John Irving's emotive qualities. Grumbach readers feel little sympathy for those who will cry no more, little arousal from those who snuggle faithfully rather than intimately, little compassion for those who never really lived. What then engages us so deeply about these characters who reveal their worst flaws and banalities, their deepest fears, and self-knowledge, but realism? What Grumbach's critics fault her for is intermixing realism and romanticism. Her books are not intended for readers who need to identify with hyperbolic characters, rather for those with enough sense of self to know that they too are at times ordinary, prudish, or in need of a cuddle.

—Maril Nowak

GUERARD, Albert (Joseph)

Nationality: American. **Born:** Houston, Texas, 2 November 1914. **Education:** Stanford University, California, B.A. 1934, Ph.D. 1938; Harvard University, Cambridge, Massachusetts, M.A. 1936. **Military Service:** Served in the Psychological Warfare Branch of the United States Army, 1943–45: Technical Sergeant. **Family:** Married Mary Maclin Bocock in 1941; three daughters. **Career:** Instructor in English, Amherst College, Massachusetts, 1935–36; instructor, assistant professor, and associate professor of English, 1938–54, and professor of English, 1954–61, Harvard University; professor of literature, Stanford University, 1961–85, now emeritus. **Awards:** Rockefeller fellowship, 1946; Fulbright fellowship, 1950; Guggenheim fellowship, 1956; Ford fellowship, 1959; *Paris Review* prize, 1963; National Endowment for the Arts grant, 1967, 1974; literature award, American Academy of Arts and Letters, 1998. **Member:** American Academy of Arts and Sciences. **Agent:** Clyde Taylor, Curtis Brown, 10 Astor Place, New York, New York 10003. **Address:** 635 Gerona Road, Stanford, California 94305, U.S.A.

PUBLICATIONS

Novels

The Past Must Alter. London, Longman, 1937; New York, Holt, 1938.

The Hunted. New York, Knopf, 1944; London, Longman, 1947.

Maquisard: A Christmas Tale. New York, Knopf, 1945; London, Longman, 1946.

Night Journey. New York, Knopf, 1950; London, Longman, 1951.

The Bystander. Boston, Little Brown, 1958; London, Faber, 1959.

The Exiles. London, Faber, 1962; New York, Macmillan, 1963.

Christine/Annette. New York, Dutton, 1985.

Gabrielle: An Entertainment. New York, Fine, 1992.

The Hotel in the Jungle. Stanford, California, CSLI, 1995.

Maquisard: A Christmas Tale. Novato, California, Lyford Books, 1995.

Short Stories

Suspended Sentences. Santa Barbara, California, John Daniel, 1999.

Uncollected Short Stories

''Davos in Winter,'' in *Hound and Horn* (Cambridge, Massachusetts), October-December 1933.

''Tragic Autumn,'' in *The Magazine* (Beverly Hills, California), December 1933.

''Miss Prindle's Lover,'' in *The Magazine* (Beverly Hills, California), February 1934; revised edition, in *Wake* (Cambridge, Massachusetts), Spring 1948.

''Turista,'' in *The Best American Short Stories of 1947,* edited by Martha Foley. Boston, Houghton Mifflin, 1947.
''The Incubus,'' in *The Dial* (New York), vol. 1, no. 2, 1960.
''The Lusts and Gratifications of Andrada,'' in *Paris Review,* Summer-Fall 1962.
''On the Operating Table,'' in *Denver Quarterly,* Autumn 1966.
''The Journey,'' in *Partisan Review* (New Brunswick, New Jersey), Winter 1967.
''The Rabbit and the Tapes,'' in *Sewanee Review* (Tennessee), Spring 1972.
''The Pillars of Hercules,'' in *Fiction* (New York), December 1973.
''Bon Papa Reviendra,'' in *Tri-Quarterly* (Evanston, Illinois), Spring 1975.
''Post Mortem: The Garcia Incident,'' in *Southern Review* (Baton Rouge, Louisiana), Spring 1978.
''Diplomatic Immunity,'' in *Sequoia* (Stanford, California), Autumn-Winter, 1978.
''The Poetry of Flight,'' in *Northwest Magazine* (Portland, Oregon), 22 January 1984.
''The Mongol Orbit,'' in *Sequoia* (Stanford, California), Centennial Issue, 1989.

Other

Robert Bridges: A Study of Traditionalism in Poetry. Cambridge, Massachusetts, Harvard University Press, and London, Oxford University Press, 1942.
Joseph Conrad. New York, New Directions, 1947.
Thomas Hardy: The Novels and Stories. Cambridge, Massachusetts, Harvard University Press, 1949; London, Oxford University Press, 1950; revised edition, 1964.
André Gide. Cambridge, Massachusetts, Harvard University Press, and London, Oxford University Press, 1951; revised edition, 1969.
Conrad the Novelist. Cambridge, Massachusetts, Harvard University Press, 1958; London, Oxford University Press, 1959.
The Triumph of the Novel: Dickens, Dostoevsky, Faulkner. New York, Oxford University Press, 1976; London, Oxford University Press, 1977.
The Touch of Time: Myth, Memory, and the Self. Stanford, California, Stanford Alumni Association, 1980.
Editor, *Prosateurs Américains de XXe Siécle.* Paris, Laffont, 1947.
Editor, *The Return of the Native,* by Thomas Hardy. New York, Holt Rinehart, 1961.
Editor, *Hardy: A Collection of Critical Essays.* Englewood Cliffs, New Jersey, Prentice Hall, 1963.
Editor, *Perspective on the Novel,* special issue of *Daedalus* (Boston), Spring 1963.
Co-Editor, *The Personal Voice: A Contemporary Prose Reader.* Philadelphia, Lippincott, 1964.
Editor, *Stories of the Double.* Philadelphia, Lippincott, 1967.
Editor, *Mirror and Mirage.* Stanford, California, Stanford Alumni Association, 1980.

*

Manuscript Collection: Stanford University Library, California.

Critical Studies: *The Modern Novel in America* by Frederick Hoffman, Chicago, Regnery, 1951; *The Hero with the Private Parts* by Andrew Lytle, Baton Rouge, Louisiana State University Press, 1966; ''The Eskimo Motor in the Detection Cell'' by Paul West, in *Southern Review* (Baton Rouge, Louisiana), Winter 1979; *The Touch of Time,* 1980, ''The Past Unrecaptured: The Two Lives of Lya de Putti,'' in *Southern Review* (Baton Rouge, Louisiana), Winter 1983, and ''Divided Selves,'' in *Contemporary Authors Autobiography Series 2* edited by Adele Sarkissian, Detroit, Gale, 1985, all by Guerard; ''The New Historical Romance'' by David Levin, in *Virginia Quarterly Review* (Charlottesville), Spring 1986.

Albert Guerard comments:

My work has been notably affected by wartime experience (political intelligence work in France) and by the pressures and ambiguities of the subsequent cold war. I have tried without success to put the political subject aside; thousands of unpublished pages, many of them angry, testify to inescapable contemporary pressures.

Maquisard, written immediately after the 1944 events it describes, is an affectionate record of wartime comradeships among men who had been in the underground. Apologetically subtitled *A Christmas Tale,* it is the slightest of my novels and was the most warmly received. *Night Journey,* my most complex and most substantial novel, is more truthful in its picture of the political and moral devastation caused by American-Soviet rivalries in a world as deceptive, and as self-deceptive, as that of *1984.* It was, on publication, repeatedly compared to Orwell's book. The confession of Paul Haldan (wandering and evasive, with his final crime left undescribed, and indeed undetected by most readers) is that of a liberal ''innocent'' who can accept neither his mother's sexual betrayals nor his country's systematic abuse of power and liberal ideology, nor its threatened use of germ warfare. Haldan's night journey into temporary regression takes him into the middle European city of his childhood, disrupted by the two great powers and betrayed by both. The ambiguities of an undeclared war are internalized by Paul Haldan, and his psychosexual anxieties projected onto the screen of public conflict. *The Exiles* (based on a journey to Cuba, Haiti, and Santo Domingo during the turmoil of 1959) explores deception and self-deception in the tragi-comic context of Caribbean propaganda and political intrigue. It dramatizes the conflict of a quixotic Trujillo assassin incorrigibly drawn to the exiled statesmen he is supposed to destroy. Manuel Andrada appears to be the most winning of my fictional creations.

In *The Hunted,* an earlier novel and conventionally realistic in technique, psycho-sexual anxieties and monumental vanities reflect public disorders in a small New England college just before World War II. Oedipal conflicts and fantasies, dramatized fairly unconsciously in *The Past Must Alter,* are central to *Night Journey* and to *The Bystander,* another story of romantic love vitiated by immaturity and regression. The technique of *The Bystander* is that of the French *récit,* with the motives either concealed or distorted by the narrator-protagonist. But the story is also of a collision between American ''innocence'' and European compromise. One of my central aims has been to avoid, while writing fairly complex psychological novels, the deadening burden of explicit and accurate analysis. *The Bystander*—very easy to read, perhaps too easy to read—requires, to be truly understood, the closest attention to hint, to image, to nuance of voice and style.

In *Christine/Annette* I wanted to bring a number of perspectives and narrative methods to bear on the ambiguous case of an actress who changes her name and even her personality several times. We see her through fragments of her own journal, her son's reconstructive memoir, a former lover's screen play, brief oral histories by old friends, a few letters. No two versions entirely agree. A good young writer urged me to simplify my novel in accord with contemporary taste by making it more ''linear,'' with a clear story line and third-person narration. But I kept to my ambiguities and contradictory witnesses, knowing they were true to a past that was irrecoverable and had become mythical. I was much pleased by a reviewer who found in this novel a combination of Proust's impressionism and the post-modern qualities of Italo Calvino.

I was bemused by the turbulent self-destructive life of Louise Brooks, but even more by that of Lya de Putti, a Hungarian star of silent films whom I met when I was ten years old. She left husband and infant daughters to become an actress, and the children were led to believe she was dead. More than fifty years later I met the daughters, and was struck by their loyalty to the lost mother and to the father who had kept them in ignorance. I knew none of this family history when I brought a remembered ''Lia'' briefly into my first novel of 1937. But the loyalty of the daughters, as well as Lya de Putti's turbulent life, is reflected in *Christine/Annette*.

Gabrielle was subtitled ''An Entertainment'' after the model of Graham Greene, who thus labeled his less complex novels. The subtitle may have been a mistake. Although structured as a psychological thriller, *Gabrielle* is a serious political satire. More than ever before I was conscious, as I wrote, of an earlier work as an ideal model: Voltaire's *Candide.* The immediate provocation for the novel was the misguided and complacent attitude of the State Department toward Latin America.

The Hotel in the Jungle is laid in 1870, 1922, and 1982, with two characters appearing in both 1870 and 1922 and two appearing in both 1922 and 1982. The setting is a resort hotel located in Santa Rosalia, an isolated Indian village in southern Mexico. The novel is based on the premise that the filibuster William Walker might not have been executed after his loss of Nicaragua and on the hypothesis that the poet Mina Loy, looking for her disappeared husband the poet-boxer Arthur Cravan, might have come to Santa Rosalia at the same time as the former heavyweight champion Jack Johnson. Cravan had fought Johnson in Barcelona and hoped to enlist Johnson in a boxing academy in Mexico. In 1982 a woman scholar, bemused by the disappearance of one major character in 1922 and another in 1982, comes to Santa Rosalia to investigate the ambiguous past. The final owner of the hotel was Cyrus Cranfield, an entrepreneur who resembles in some ways Howard Hughes.

* * *

Albert Guerard's seven novels, published over a period of nearly fifty years, have shown a steady progression in technique and a constant reconsideration of theme. Nearly all his novels represent a controlled madness, a largely successful attempt to valorize political/psychological issues in a modern world where the center cannot hold. Guerard concentrates on intense moments of introspective terror and possibility for brooding protagonists trapped in futile or apocalyptic situations. The subjects of his major works of literary criticism—Hardy, Conrad, Gide, Dickens, Dostoevsky, Faulkner—and his admiration for the macabre humor and sexual fantasies of anti-realists liked Joyce, Kafka, Nabokov, Hawkes, Pynchon, Barthelme lead Guerard to a kind of fiction that refuses linear narration and embraces time distortion, untrustworthy observers, and ambiguous relationships. Dangerously close to the critical praise gained by the academic novelist, with its ensuing commercial failure, Guerard has never wavered from his commitment to the novel as complex experiment. As he states in *The Triumph of the Novel,* the effects he seeks are inventive fantasy, intuitive psychology, solitary obsessions, and political trauma.

Guerard's first novel, *The Past Must Alter,* deals with his major theme, a young man fascinated by his abortive desire for a beautiful older woman and bothered by an implausible relationship with a shadowy father. Drives to gamble and to test himself obsess and threaten the youth. *The Hunted* takes a more traditional fictional approach—the story of a waitress who marries an arrogant college instructor, of her increasing disillusion with his weakness and growing awareness of her own strength. *The Hunted* has a special quality that comes not from this anti-love story, nor from the New England rural college setting, but from a near-Faulknerian treatment of a violent flood and of a hunt for a doomed mythomaniac, the Bomber, who awakens the aggressions of the truly lost ''normal'' inhabitants and releases the female protagonist. Equally familiar in form is *Maquisard.* Subtitled, deliberately, ''A Christmas Tale''—and Guerard's most commercial novel—the short book deals with a group of maquis and an American officer during the last months of World War II. Brilliantly compressed, coming close to but ultimately avoiding sentimentality, the novel is Guerard's most positive statement: the personal comradeship, solidarity, and dedication to a cause formed in combat allow the characters to act out their loyalties and sacrifices as well as to discover emotional and political possibilities that can sustain them in the postwar world. The book is warm, dramatic, lyrical.

In *Night Journey* Guerard creates this postwar world as a surreal one that joins varieties of betrayals. Paul Haldan (even the name echoes Conrad) betrays—deserts, literally—his superior officer in a move that re-enacts Haldan's guilt towards his father's death. Even darker themes of sexual betrayals by a form of projected rape and political betrayal by a military maneuver that alternately liberates and abandons a city qualify *Night Journey* as a work of inward and outer deception and destruction. Certainly Guerard's most imaginative and ambitious book, this novel is intelligent, probing, and yet, like many works of the psycho-political genre, ultimately lacking in human vitality. The madness is too controlled; the passion is too spent.

The Bystander concentrates on personal relations. Anthony, a young man in France, pursues the actress subject of his adolescent dreams. Poor and self-destructive, Anthony does attain his erotic desires, only to discover in Christiane a fundamental pragmatist who can reject passion for financial support from an older man. The book circles back on itself and is as much about loss as about gain. Tormented, sensual, self-lacerating, this anti-hero remains one of Guerard's most fascinating psychological portraits. *The Exiles* returns to the Conrad-Greene political arena that Guerard is drawn to as powerfully as to the psychological realm. (Indeed, sections of two unpublished political novels have appeared during the past decade in magazines; *Suspended Sentence,* which concerns an aging middle-European political exile, and *Still Talking,* a post-holocaust vision of wandering armies across a destroyed landscape.) Guerard's most comic effort, *The Exiles* satirizes Central American political refugees and their hangers-on and sympathetically presents a comic/tragic secret agent who combines absolute loyalty to a dictator and emotional commitment to a dissident, quasi-revolutionary poet. The comedy of Manuel Andrada's maneuverings in Boston is effective; the tragedy of his self-immolation in his beloved homeland is moving. Guerard's use of an objective, rather colorless narrator, however, mutes both the laughter and terror.

Constantly dedicated to the writing of fiction despite his careers as professor and critic. Guerard finally achieves his aim of definitively catching his fascination with his earliest subject—the love of an innocent young man for a more experienced lovely actress ... only for Charles Strickland the actress is in reality his lost mother, and the novel *Christine/Annette* is at once a rewriting of the past and an acceptance of the present. The book is indeed a triumph, easily Guerard's finest. He is lyrical and humorous, wistful and historical, tough-minded and sensitive. Part detective story, part family romance, part *bildungsroman,* part American and European social history, *Christine/Annette* is largely about the mystery of identity. The search for the mother, in all its Freudian and Jungian potentials, takes place in the real, richly evoked worlds of Paris and Berlin, Houston and Los Angeles. The narration is equally sure and varied—autobiography, movie script, objective frame, letters—and the film trope superbly sustained. The novel displays a confidence that comes from years of successful writing, certainly, but the special quality of this 1985 work is its freshness, its variety, its flexibility, its combination of an open, experimental structure, an authentic voice, and a traditional theme of loss, search, and discovery. Like Shakespeare's *The Tempest* or Faulkner's *The Reivers,* Guerard's novel of his mature years recapitulates his earlier concepts and techniques. The book provides as well a sparkle and energy, an argument with himself rather than with others that in Yeats's formulation leads not to political rhetoric but to lyrical achievement.

—Eric Solomon

GUNESEKERA, Romesh

Nationality: British (originally Sri Lankan, immigrated to England). **Awards:** Rathbone prize for philosophy, University of Liverpool, 1976; Writers' Bursary, Arts Council, London, 1991; Yorkshire Post Best First Work award, 1995.

Publications

Novels

Reef. London, Granta, 1994; New York, New Press, 1995.
The Sandglass. New Delhi, Viking, 1998; New York, Riverhead Books, 1999.

Short Stories

Monkfish Moon. New Delhi, Penguin, London, Granta, and New York, New Press, 1992.

* * *

On a photo depicting ''India's leading novelists'' that was printed in a 1997 special issue of the *New Yorker* on the occasion of the fiftieth anniversary of India's independence, Romesh Gunesekera is half concealed by another writer. Never has the young Sri Lankan received a mass audience's attention like, say, a flamboyant personality such as Arundhati Roy, nor has his work provoked a literary sensation of any sorts. Salman Rushdie's quipping identification of Sri Lanka with a drop of goo dangling from India's nose in *Midnight's Children* shows well enough how the notoriously problem-ridden island is regarded by ''Mother India.'' Nonetheless, Gunesekera's quiet and elegant, yet sharp and precise prose deserves without any doubt to be counted among the best writing from the literary flourishing subcontinent, and—as he has made a second home in London—in the same measure among the best young writers in the British literary landscape.

The immigrant experience informs all of Gunesekera's writing, but in a decidedly different vein than Rushdie's comic grotesquerie, V.S. Naipaul's venom, or Bharati Mukherjee's uncompromising disdain. If a comparison had to be suggested, probably Amitav Ghosh comes most closely, especially with regard to Gunesekera's *The Sandglass* (1998)—which is strongly reminiscent of Ghosh's *The Shadow Lines*—a fascinatingly controlled novel whose narrator's mind continuously shuttles between home and away, building a kind of uneasy bridge between Sri Lanka and England.

Gunesekera's first volume, the short-story collection *Monkfish Moon*, received much acclaim. The nine stories revolving around the turmoil of Sri Lanka's civil war are haunted with the striking violence introduced to the Edenic island by the fighting groups. It is only obliquely, however, that the violence enters the stories. Gunesekera focuses on personal misunderstanding and the breakdown of communication, on the parting and fracture of human relationships. So in ''A House in the Country,'' the developing comradeship between master and servant is sundered as the trace of destruction comes closer and closer; ''Batik'' sees the split between Tamil husband and Sinhala wife (though the story ends on a more optimistic note); the protagonist in ''Ranvali'' visits her father's beach bungalow after many years and cherishes nostalgic reminiscences of a time before her father turned to political activism and estranged himself from his family; the final story, ''Monkfish Moon,'' elaborates on the whole collection's title. As we learn from the fat, aging business magnate Peter, who always wanted to live like a monk in complete detachment, for good meat you need a good moon. An introductory note informs us that ''There are no monkfish in the ocean around Sri Lanka.'' While there is no political hiding place in the now spoilt paradise, Gunesekera tries to capture and maybe thereby aesthetically to salvage his home country.

Gunesekera's powerful first novel, *Reef,* shortlisted for the prestigious Booker Prize in 1994, puts even more emphasis on the domestic space while the grim violence of the war looms large in the background. *Reef* is the story of young Triton, who works as cook and factotum for the marine biologist Mr. Salgado. Throughout the novel the first-person narrator emphasizes an ahistorical perspective, focusing on the different household chores, rather than on the serious political problems of the island. More than anything else, *Reef* is a culinary novel, a mouthwatering tour through the joys and virtues of the country's cuisine. The reader learns the right temperature for a perfect string-hopper dough, how to prepare coconut *kavum*, a love cake or a curry in a hurry, and how to disguise the dubious taste of a parrot fish with a sauce rich with chilli *sambol.* The exoticism that arguably accrues from this gastronomic reduction of Sri Lanka has evoked rather polarized responses. While the novel received high critical acclaim in Britain where it was published, critics from Sri Lanka often took short shrift with Gunesekera's ''blinkered attitude'' to his country of birth. Gunesekera was accused of merely restating western stereotypes about Sri Lanka. This critique, however, seems overstated, misreading Gunesekera's fine chisel for a broad brush. In fact, Triton, who uncompromisingly idolizes his master, plots against the brute servant Joseph, and eventually leaves Sri Lanka for England where he opens a restaurant ''to show the world something really fabulous,'' is a character whom Gunesekera has quite consciously drafted problematic. Like *Monkfish Moon*, the novel is powerful in its treatment of personal relations, especially after Miss Nili—with whom Mr. Salgado falls in love—enters the household. The novel, which gets its title from the vanishing coral reef in the south that points to the threat of the encroaching sea, has most convincingly confirmed Gunesekera's promise as a fine writer.

In his second novel *The Sandglass*, Gunesekera's style seems even more refined, his language even more tactile. The narrative is set in London, on a February day when Prins Ducal arrives from Colombo to attend his mother Pearl's funeral. Again, the story's events are complexly filtered, this time with a strong emphasis on time, as Prins unravels his memories in the company of the narrator, who adds his own flashbacks on the seventeen years he has known the Ducal family. These bits and pieces form a chronicle of four generations of the Ducals, a family that is intricately related to another clan, the Vatunases. The hatred between the neighbouring families, which started after Prins's father Jason had bought a house on Vatunase ground (ironically called Arcadia), reflects the situation on the war-torn island. Once more Gunesekera abstains from depicting ''the inferno back home'' in terms of bloodshed, but focuses on family warfare, comprador corruption, and political power struggle. The mysterious death of his immensely successful father troubles Prins even forty years later, while the curiously evasive narrator who lives vicariously the Ducals' fate wants to read Pearl's life, ''hoping to find something that would make sense out of the nonsense of my life.''

—Tobias Wachinger

GUPTA, Sunetra

Nationality: Indian. **Born:** Calcutta, India, 15 March 1965. **Education:** Princeton University, A.B. 1987; London University, Ph.D. 1992. **Family:** Married Adrian Vivian Sinton Hill in 1994; two daughters. **Career:** Research assistant, Department of Biology, Imperial College, London, 1988–89, principal investigator for grant, 1989–92; Wellcome Training Fellow in mathematical biology, Department of Zoology, University of Oxford, England, 1992–95; junior research fellow, Merton College, Oxford, England, 1993–96; researcher, Wellcome Trust Centre for the Epidemiology of Infectious Disease, Department of Zoology, University of Oxford, England, 1995–99, reader in epidemiology of infectious disease, 1999—. **Agent:** David Higham Associates, Ltd., 5–8 Lower John Street, London W1R 4HA, England. **Address:** Department of Zoology, University of Oxford, Oxford OX1 3PS, England.

PUBLICATIONS

Novels

Memories of Rain. New York, Weidenfeld, 1992.
The Glassblower's Breath. New York, Grove Press, 1993.
Moonlight into Marzipan. London, Phoenix House, 1995.
A Sin of Colour. London, Phoenix House, 1999.

* * *

Sunetra Gupta belongs to that Rushdie and post-Rushdie generation of ''Indian English'' writers whose members are essentially cosmopolitan in their cultural and linguistic affinities—though they are often read and marketed as predominantly ''Indian'' writers in the West. Gupta, born in 1965, spent her childhood in Bengal and Africa, studied biology at Princeton University, and obtained her Ph.D. from London's Imperial College. She now lives in Oxford with her husband and daughter and divides her time between writing and researching infectious diseases. Sunetra Gupta is the author of four novels: *Memories of Rain*, *The Glassblower's Breath*, *Moonlight into Marzipan*, and *A Sin of Colour*. She has been described as ''a prodigious talent'' by the *Independent on Sunday* and her work has been pronounced ''brilliant'' by *The Times.*

Being a resident in the famous university town, it is not surprising that Oxford provides some of the backdrop for Sunetra Gupta's fourth and latest novel, *A Sin of Colour*. This is a book, written in consciously literary English, that sets out to tell the story of three generations with their roots in a house called Mandalay in Calcutta. Bought from a British officer by a wealthy Bengali family, it is to Mandalay that Indranath Roy brings his clever and innocent bride. It is to Mandalay that Indranath's eldest son brings his own brilliant wife, the beautiful, collected and successful woman with whom the younger brother, Debendranath Roy, falls in love. Fleeing the house, his family and his apparently futile love, Debendranath moves to Oxford and marries an English woman, whom he largely neglects. Debendranath is later presumed drowned. It is left to his niece, Niharika, another of those brilliant, successful women who stock Gupta's narratives and share many similarities with the author, to provide the finishing touches. It turns out that Debendranath had fled back to India where he had lived incognito. His growing blindness drives him back to the family and to his writer-niece Niharika, who is almost the only family member living in Mandalay, now in ruins and abandoned by the next generation.

The thinness of the plot evident from the above summary of *A Sin of Colour* is also noticeable in Gupta's first novel, *Memories of Rain*—but in both these novels this thinness is brilliantly obscured by Gupta's virtuosity with *literary* language. Again, in both the novels, Gupta's extremely literary—even canonical—sensibility is revealed in the centrality and profusion of the references to Euripedes's *Medea.* In *Memories of Rain*, the entire plot is concentrated within the span of a single day. On that day, Moni, an Indian woman who had come to England after having married the English Anthony, decides to leave her unfaithful husband and returns to India with her daughter. The relationship between Moni and Anthony presents the usual paraphernalia of cross-cultural differences and racism, with the onus of ''primitivity'' reversed and applied implicitly to ''cold'' England rather than the Bengal of *Rabindra Sangeet.*

In between these two novels with relatively simple narrative and thematic structures, Gupta wrote two other novels that were somewhat more experimental. *The Glassblower's Breath* is the story of a brilliant young Indian woman and her relationships with a variety of people, such as the tragic Jon Sparrow (''poet and mathematician, child prodigy''), and places (''the inadequacy of your relationship with the city''). Against the backdrop of Calcutta, New York, and London, replete with echoes of the modernist big city experience, the second-person protagonist—always referred to as ''you''—tries to satisfy the demands of individuality, family, and society. She fails, but in the process provides a narrative of a brilliant young woman's capacity for experience and the desire of men and society to control and define her. From the stylistic perspective, *The Glassblower's*

Breath is interesting because it is one of those rare novels with a second-person protagonist—an experiment that necessarily induces Gupta to employ the stream-of-consciousness technique, or something very similar to it.

Moonlight into Marzipan is also interesting from a stylistic perspective, as it mixes up first person narration (''I'') with second person address (''you''). Moreover, it does not follow a chronological order of events, leaving the reader to assemble the parts of an open-ended story. In effect, *Moonlight into Marzipan* is not one text: it consists of various overlapping and at times incomplete texts. As in the other novels, we have an assemblage of brilliant characters, with the world of science leading to the experience of creative writing.

At its simplest, *Moonlight into Marzipan* is about two promising scientists, Promothesh and Esha, who marry each other and set up house in Calcutta. Marriage turns Esha into the typical housewife and obstructs her career. However, by accident, she enables Promothesh to achieve international renown for a major scientific discovery, a discovery that is clearly meant by the narrator to carry redemptive significance for the so-called Third World. Newly achieved celebrity enables the couple to move to London. However, this move leads to Promothesh's infidelity and Esha's ultimate suicide.

The above story line is tied up with Promothesh writing his autobiography, which provides us with the axis around which the novel turns. The novel is in many ways the autobiography. Later it is revealed that the autobiography was to be written for Promothesh by the expatriate Russian writer, Alexandra Vorobyova. As the Italian critic Sandra Ponzanesi has noted, ''when Alexandra Vorobyova goes away and abandons the text, Promothesh is left with pieces of his life scribbled in notes; the result of his long conversations and confessions with the dismissive narrator.''

As is obvious from the summaries given above, Sunetra Gupta's novels share many stylistic, narrative and thematic characteristics: a dexterity with *literary* language, a profusion of *canonical* references (ranging from Euripedes to Tagore), a tendency towards versions of the stream-of-consciousness technique, a concentration on brilliant protagonists straddling the worlds of science and literature, and thin plots resolved by or revolving around momentous events (deaths, disappearances, drowning, suicides).

What is perhaps less evident is the position that Gupta occupies between the two dominant trends in contemporary Indian English fiction—that of magic realism (Salman Rushdie and Vikram Chandra) and that of ''domestic realism'' (Vikram Seth and Anita Desai). At first glance, Gupta seems to belong to the first group, as she usually writes about individuals defined by their family relationships in an ostensibly realistic manner. But much of Gupta's oeuvre is also sustained by the evocative, non-metaphorical language of magic realism in extracts like this one: ''From North Bengal, Indranath Roy had journeyed into the foothills of the Himalayas, to seek out the Japanese Cedars, with which they would line their new make of wardrobes—one of these they later had in their bedroom, and whenever she opened it, the room would fill with the fragrance of his shapeless desire to know and possess her'' (*A Sin of Colour*). Gupta is not the only Indian English writer to use the language of magic realism in a narrative that is not really magic realist: Arundhati Roy has done it at a more complex level in *The God of Small Things.*

Given Gupta's concentration on female protagonists, her limited textual experiments, and her language, it is predictable that critics in the West would compare her to Virginia Woolf. *Kirkus Reviews,* for example, has called Gupta ''a young, true heir to Virginia Woolf.'' This comparison is both justified and exaggerated. Above all, it is a comparison that reveals more about Gupta than it seems to.

Like Woolf, Gupta is a literary stylist. But unlike Woolf, her stylistic experiments are not at the cutting edge of the contemporary literary scene. Again like Woolf, Gupta is a highly *literary* writer—after all, Gupta's social background is no less privileged, brilliant, and ''arty'' than Woolf's Bloomsbury circle. But, unlike Woolf, Gupta seldom—if ever—critiques and subverts the literary canon in a significant manner. It is in this context that one should be wary of providing a typically post-colonial (''subversive mimicry,'' ''subaltern agency,'' etc.) reading of Gupta's—and, for that matter, many other so-called post-colonial writers'—texts. The situation is much more complex: there are both elements of cultural subversion and linguistic hegemony in Gupta's and other Indian English writers' texts.

Finally, like Woolf, Gupta provides a gendered reading of society while not making a militant political statement. However, while Woolf might have had a poor opinion of female suffragettes, her writings adopted feminist perspectives that were often far ahead of contemporary opinion even in literary circles. Something similar cannot be said of Gupta. In fact, women writing in other Indian languages (such as Ismat Chughtai and Mahasweta Devi) as well as some Indian English writers (Githa Hariharan and Shashi Deshpande) have taken the gendering of novelistic discourse to far more radical levels than anything that may be encountered in Gupta's novels. Gupta's novels remain interesting, though more for what they promise than what they actually achieve.

—Tabish Khair

GURGANIS, Allan

Nationality: American. **Born:** Rocky Mount, North Carolina, 11 June 1947. **Education:** Rocky Mount Senior High, 1965; Philadelphia Academy of Fine Arts, 1965–66; Sarah Lawrence College, Bronxville, New York, 1970–72. **Military Service:** United States Navy, 1966–70. **Career:** Desk clerk and salesperson of art reproductions, 1969–70; night watchman in a vitamin factory, 1970–72; professor of fiction writing, University of Iowa, Iowa City, 1972–74, Stanford University, Stanford, California, 1974–76, Duke University, Durham, North Carolina, 1976–78, Sarah Lawrence College, Bronxville, New York, 1978–86, and University of Iowa Writers' Workshop, 1989–90. Artist, with paintings in many private and public collections. Member of board, Corporation of Yaddo; cofounder, ''Writers for Harvey Gantt.'' **Awards:** Jones lecturer, Stanford University; PEN prizes for fiction; National Endowment for the Arts grants; Ingram Merrill award; Wallace Stegner fellowship; National Magazine prize, National Magazine Association, 1994. **Agent:** c/o International Creative Management, 40 West 57th Street, New York, New York 10019, U.S.A.

PUBLICATIONS

Novel

Oldest Living Confederate Widow Tells All. New York, Knopf, and London, Faber, 1989.
Plays Well with Others. New York, Knopf, 1997.

Short Stories

Good Help, with illustrations by the author. Rocky Mount, North Carolina Wesleyan College Press, 1988.

Blessed Assurance: A Moral Tale (novella). Rocky Mount, North Carolina Wesleyan College Press, 1990.

White People: Stories and Novellas. New York, Knopf, and London, Faber, 1991.

The Practical Heart. Rocky Mount, North Carolina Wesleyan College Press, 1993.

*

Critical Studies: ''Black and Blue and Gray: An Interview with Allan Gurganis'' by Jeffrey Scheuer, in *Poets and Writers,* November-December 1990.

* * *

Allan Gurganus is an old-fashioned storyteller. The stories he tells are multi-layered and contain strong, varied voices. While both his novel, *Oldest Living Confederate Widow Tells All,* and his short story collection, *White People,* are set primarily in the South, he should not be considered a ''Southern Writer'' solely. In American literature, the oral tradition that feeds his ability with voice and character is strongly associated with that region, but Gurganus covers territory that is all-American by bringing uniquely American questions to light, all somehow having to do with how Americans perceive themselves.

In *Oldest Living Confederate Widow Tells All,* a 99-year-old woman named Lucy Marsden relates stories that take place during more than a century of time, from the beginnings of the Civil War to the 1980s. At the time of its publication, some critics were happy to see, in light of recent literary trends toward the abstract, the minimal, and the eccentric, the emergence of such a ''big'' story; others considered the premise unequal to the task of carrying such a sizeable narrative. Lucy tells stories of her life and the life of her Civil War veteran husband, whom she had married when she was fifteen. She regales us with tales of his experiences before she was even born, becoming her husband's voice. Indeed, she even takes on the voice of his one-time slave, Castalia, as well as many others. This multiple-narrator role makes her at once story and storyteller, participant and omniscient observer. While this raises interesting questions about narrative authority, it also presents a fascinating experience for the perceptive reader, for there is also the author to consider. Through Lucy, he has entered and presented male and female lives, historical lives, young and old lives, warrior lives—American lives that embrace and reflect more than one American epoch, more than one American region.

In addition to all of this, there is more than the Civil War being fought here, although many issues from the other battles contained in the book are related to that war between the states. Sex, race, class, age—all those words which so efficiently assume the -ism suffix—are concepts in conflict within the novel. Gurganus has much to say about it all. However, at the core of the novel's resolution is forgiveness and the hope it can bring. Because of this, the comparison to at least one other Southern writer may come quickly to mind, for Flannery O'Connor's famous ''Moment of Grace'' resembles the theme closely. There is also Gurganus's sense of humor to tempt us into such a comparison. But it is his use of voice which makes the humor effective, the theme accessible. The author has quite an ear and quite an imagination, and it is his accuracy with the female voice that is most impressive.

Gurganus has said that he chose Lucy as narrator for this novel because he wanted a new version/vision of history that had not before been solicited: that of a female who was neither rich nor beautiful. He is successful in this; but in Castalia, the former Marsden slave, he is successful in giving us the vision of a female who was neither rich nor beautiful (in a white man's world) nor white. The Captain himself is not a particularly likeable character; still, he too has his sympathetic side and his own particularly strong voice. But again—we hear this voice only through Lucy and, thus, must be cautious about what we conclude from it.

It is a long book; and the plot, although guided by chronology, is not strictly linear in its construction. There are many side roads taken, even to Africa during the slave trade. Although necessary to the theme of his/her-story that the author is illuminating, this technique is often cited as the weakness of the book. But for those who enjoy an old-fashioned story treated with respect in the telling, *Oldest Living Confederate Widow Tells All* lives up to the promise of its title. It is rather like sitting around the kitchen table listening to previous generations tell what they know about family members and small town denizens in anecdotal but wise and witty tones. What could be more American?

In *White People,* Gurganus's collection of short stories and novellas, we are given just such an image in the opening passages of ''A Hog Loves Its Life.'' The boy Willie and his grandfather, ''hiding'' from the other relatives, are forced into a ''story-hour'' by Willie's ignorance of local lore. The story of this novella, and the story within the story, are fine examples of what a writer can do with a talent for voice. The ritual engaged in by these two characters is related in tones of solemnity balanced by humor. It is important to the participants, and to the reader, that each understands the significance of what is being told at both levels—that of the grandfather telling the tale and the boy/man retelling it. As with *Oldest Living Confederate Widow Tells All,* the narrator is both story and storyteller. Gurganus's narrative constructions resemble the double helix of DNA: simultaneously, and deceptively, simple and complex.

Embedded in the themes weaving through the various tales of the collection is a penetrating look at what the passage of time and the losses it naturally brings, can mean to our individual sense of hope and forgiveness. One of the most often mentioned and poignant of the stories is ''Blessed Assurance,'' the final novella of the collection. In telling the story of an aging, Southern, white man looking back on his days as a college student who sold funeral insurance to poor blacks in the late 1940s, Gurganus requires that the reader look carefully at the loss of youthful innocence and naiveté, the use of exploitation in race relations, the burden of guilt—and the absurdity of all these things. For that sense of humor is here, too, at the base of this and the other tales.

The author seems to possess a core belief in the terrible beauty of daily survival; and this belief transcends geography, gender, age, race, and sexual orientation. In this way, Gurganus contributes to contemporary American literature while retaining an old-fashioned faith in, and a sizeable talent for, the telling of the tale.

—Maggi R. Sullivan

GURNAH, Abdulrazak S.

Nationality: English. **Born:** Zanzibar (now part of Tanzania), 1948. **Education:** Earned a Ph.D. **Career:** Worked as a hospital orderly; lecturer in English and American literature, Rutherford College, University of Kent, Canterbury, Kent, England. **Address:** School of English, Rutherford College, University of Kent, Canterbury, Kent CT2 7NX, England.

PUBLICATIONS

Novels

Memory of Departure. London, Jonathan Cape, 1987.
Pilgrim's Way. London, Jonathan Cape, 1988.
Dottie. London, Jonathan Cape, 1990.
Paradise. New York, New Press, 1994.
Admiring Silence. New York, New Press, 1996.

Other

Editor and contributor, *Essays on African Writing 1: A Re-evaluation.* Oxford, England, Heinemann, 1994.
Editor and contributor, *Essays on African Writing 2: Contemporary Literature.* Oxford, England, Heinemann, 1996.

*

Critical Studies: ''Abdulrazak Gurnah's *Paradise* and *Admiring Silence:* History, Stories, and the Figure of the Uncle'' by Jacqueline Bardolphin, in *Contemporary African Fiction*, edited by Derek Wright, 1997.

* * *

Abdulrazak Gurnah, born in Zanzibar, had already acquired a reputation as a scholar and critic of African literature and published three novels set in the immigrant community in England when in 1994 *Paradise* was short-listed for the Booker Prize. This was followed in 1996 by *Admiring Silence*, partly set in the UK and Tanzania. Critics wondered how to classify Gurnah—as a Black British author, African writer, or simply a modern writer of the English language.

Paradise certainly deserves a place in East-African prose fiction, because the language policies in Tanzania had for a long time discouraged the use of English and gave preference to Kiswahili, while the coastal Swahili and Zansibari writers such as Said Khamis would never think of writing in English. The only other English novels of comparable caliber are those written by the African-Indian author M.G. Vassanji, *The Gunny Sack* (1989) or *Uhuru Street* (1991). Just like Vassanji, whose attention focuses on the East-African Indian community and their interaction with the ''others,'' Gurnah's novel deploys multi-ethnicity and multiculturalism on the shores of the Indian Ocean from the perspective of the Swahili elite. *Paradise* spans the period from 1900–14, the time when the German colonial presence began to interfere drastically with the lives of the different communities in Tanganyika until the end of the short-lived episode of German colonialism. The dominant topic of the novel being an inland journey into the ''heart of Africa,'' other colonial texts interfere intertextually: First of all, Joseph Conrad's *Heart of Darkness* about Kurtz's boat trip up the Congo river, but also the famous narrative of Tippu Tip, who reached the central lake area with his slave-hunting expeditions. Gurnah's text also relates to the imperial grand tales of exploration—Speke's *Discovery of the Sources of the Nile* (1863) and Richard Burton's *The Lake Regions of Central Africa* (1860).

The novel begins in Kawa, a small inland trading town that came into existence through the construction of the Tanganyika railway. Kawa, in the eyes of the novel's characters, is the liminal town between savagery and heathenism or the coastal civilization of the Arab-Swahili Muslim elite. From Kawa, Uncle Aziz, a rich Arab trader, sets out for his trading safaris into the hinterland, shipping his goods from the coast to Kawa by rail. Twelve-year-old Yusuf, through whose eyes and voice we follow the story, is the son of a petty trader who runs a hotel-plus-shop for Uncle Aziz. He pawns his son into the services of the Seeyid/Master to serve his debts. Thus, Yusuf comes to the coastal city to work as the shop assistant together with Khalil, five years his senior and also pawned to Aziz by his impoverished parents. The shop is situated at the edge of Aziz's compound, facing the city and the harbor. Inside his palace, Aziz had a beautiful ''walled garden,'' modeled according to the Quoranic description of paradise, where Yusuf can sneak in occasionally to assist Mzee Hamdani, the gardener and guardian. At one time, Aziz hires out Yusuf to Hamid Suleiman, another shop owner in a nameless town at the foothills of Mount Kilimanjaro. But the most dramatic part of the plot is the journey into the hinterland across the Great Lake (Victoria?) to the capital of the powerful African king Chatu, renowned for his savagery, treachery, and being a bloodthirsty ruler. Uncle Aziz's safari does reach the goal of its quest, but instead of doing profitable business, buying ivory from Chatu, Chatu attacks Aziz's camp in the night, kills many men, and robs all the provisions and trade goods. Aziz, Yusuf, and a few others are lucky to escape with their lives.

Abdulrazak Gurnah thus created three distinct spaces in which the novel unfolds: the cultured and civilized coastal city, unquestionably controlled by the Arab traders and the Swahili elite; the inland trading town with their liminal position between civilization and the wilderness; and thirdly, the indefinite open space of lands, stretching from those outposts of civilization to the power center of ''savagery.'' Lastly, there are the German colonialists who don't care about the Swahili elite's niceties of distinguishing between coastal sophistication and inland barbarism, because for them all non-whites are savages.

The concept of paradise is of paramount importance throughout the novel; once as a crucial issue of debate about religious concepts between the Hindu Kalasinga and the Muslim Hamid. But Paradise is also visualized and concretized in the gardens, first Aziz's garden in the city: ''...the garden was divided into quarters, with a pool in the center and water channels running off it in the four direction. The quadrants were planted with trees and bushes, some of them in flower: lavender, henna, rosemary and aloe ... clovers and grass, and scattered clumps of lilies and irises''; and second, the poor replica of the paradisiacal garden behind Hamil's shop at the foot of the mountain: ''... scrubs and thickets full of snakes and wild animals .... Instead of the shade and flowers which Mzee Hamdani had created ... here there was only the bush beyond their backyard which was used for rubbish. It shuddered with secret life, and out of it rose fumes of putrefaction and pestilence.'' Scenic vistas and landscape descriptions during the disastrous trading expedition underline the contrast between the uncultured natural scenery and the sophistication of the pleasure garden. Gurnah develops the garden on the coast and the roughly-hewn makeshift residence of the inland king Chatu as symbolic spaces, representing the Swahili perspective of civilization against barbarism. Aziz's garden however is paradisiacal only in appearance, in reality it reflects social and racial oppression: Mzee Hamdani, who tends the garden lovingly, has the status of a mere chattel slave. Aziz's senior wife, who haunts the garden, is facially disfigured and morally degenerated. Her walks in the garden resemble prison yard exercises, her lusting for young Yusuf approaches a pedophilic perversion while her open sore, which she tries to hide under her shaddor, can only be read as an image for the sickening quality of Aziz's home. And Aziz's youngest child-wife Amina, with whom Yusuf is enamoured, is another pawn given by Aziz's tenants. What might look like paradise and is designed according to the Quoranic scriptures, proves to be pure hell for the members of Aziz's household. The ending of the novel reveals the falsity of another idealization, that of the paradisiacal harmony of pre-colonial Africa. Yusuf runs after the German recruiting officer, although he has just witnessed the brutality with which forced recruitment is practiced in the wake of World War I. Yusuf as the young African obviously came to the conclusion that the brutality of German colonialism is still preferable to the ruthless exploitation by the Arabs. As Achebe does in *Things Fall Apart,* Gurnah draws a picture of East-African society that is on the verge of drastic change. Colonialism only accelerated this process, but did not initiate it. Gurnah narrates his story with two parallel but contrastive plot lines: Yusuf's is a story of growing up and gaining stature—a *bildungsroman*—while the historical plotline is one of decay and degeneration of pre-colonial African society.

With *Admiring Silence*, Gurnah returns to postcolonial Tanzania. *Admiring Silence*, like *Paradise*, has storytelling as one of its main subjects. His protagonist is a leftish dissident intellectual who left the country and settled in England, precariously but permanently, with his partner Emma. He tries to pacify Emma's father, a diehard imperialist, with idealized and idyllic stories about his youth, about the gallant courtship of his father and mother, inventing ever new fabrications about ''home'' as the demands of his British audience seems to require. When he returns home, he is frustrated by the discrepancy between the stories he invented—and started to half believe—and the dreary realities. The house of his parents is close to decay; essential services like water, electricity, and garbage disposal fail regularly. In addition, his schoolmates have become corrupt, self-seeking bureaucrats, and his mother was not gallantly courted but given as a pawn to his father. And yet, he never found the courage to inform his parents that he has been living together with a white infidel—a ''kafir woman.'' When he is introduced to the child-wife who his relatives chose for him, he panics and flees ''home,'' which is now England, only to find that Emma left and that he is condemned to be ''on the edges of everything,'' on his own island in England. The hero despairs of establishing communication between the two worlds.

—Eckhard Breitinger

GUTERSON, David

Nationality: American. **Born:** Seattle, Washington, 4 May 1956. **Education:** University of Washington, B.A. 1978, M.A. 1982. **Family:** Married Robin Ann Radwick in 1979; three children. **Career:** High school English teacher, Bainbridge Island, Washington, 1984—. **Agent:** Georges Borchardt, Inc., 136 East 57th Street, New York, New York 10020, U.S.A.

Publications

Novels

Snow Falling on Cedars. San Diego, Harcourt Brace, 1994.
East of the Mountains. New York, Harcourt Brace, 1999.

Short Stories

The Country Ahead of Us, the Country Behind. New York, Harper, 1989.

Other

Family Matters: Why Homeschooling Makes Sense. New York, Harcourt Brace, 1992.

* * *

David Guterson acknowledges that a few of his early short stories owe a debt to the basic, naturalistic style of Raymond Carver; however, he continues, ''You mature, your sensibilities become refined, you find your own voice.'' Nevertheless, Guterson established several characteristic techniques in his early pieces which carry over into his novels, suggested by the collection's metaphoric title, *The Country Ahead of Us, the Country Behind.* The ''country'' is the Pacific Northwest, the setting for most of his stories and his subsequent novels, *Snow Falling on Cedars* and *East of the Mountains*, while ''ahead'' and ''behind'' refer to the very lives of his protagonists, who recall salient events in their past through Guterson's use of flashback. In the stark, tough short stories about fathers and sons, brothers and buddies, a nostalgic adult recalls a boyhood adventure, usually involving hunting or fishing or some other self-test against nature, but leading to personal discovery. In the novels, Guterson's detailed descriptions of vast landscapes or intimate interiors achieve a atmospheric sense of place, and the single flashback of the short story deepens to complicated time strata; both enhanced by Guterson's now characteristic extended, meticulous research, acknowledged by lengthy lists in the novels. These techniques partially account for the phenomenal runaway success of *Snow Falling on Cedars*, which sold over three million copies, followed by a movie directed by Scott Hicks and starring Max Von Sydow and Ethan Hawke.

Set in December 1954 on a fictionalized San Piedro Island in Puget Sound, the novel seems, at first, a classic courtroom drama compounded by a long ago forbidden interracial romance which hints at a present-day love triangle. But, beneath the serene snow-muffled island and within its inhabitants simmers a matter-of-fact racial bigotry now exacerbated by the trial of Japanese-American Kabuo Miyamoto, accused of murdering fellow islander and salmon fisherman Carl Heine, found tangled in his boat's gill net. Kabuo and local newspaper reporter Ishmael Chambers were childhood playmates, but Ishmael and Kabuo's wife, Hatsue Imada were playmates and, then, teenage lovers before World War II and before Ishmael lost his arm in battle and she suffered internment with other Japanese-Americans at Manzanar in 1942.

Not surprisingly, Guterson acknowledges Harper Lee's *To Kill a Mockingbird* as a thematic influence, but in *Snow Falling on Cedars*, he uses his characters' courtroom testimonies to create a complex multileveled narrative evolving through serial flashbacks from the courtroom of the present to the retold incident pertinent to the trial to an evoked personal memory and often to a retelling of an historical event, such as Ishmael as participant in and witness to the Allied invasion against the Japanese on the South Pacific island of Betio. Alongside this intricate technique, Guterson increases the novel's suspense by withholding Kabuo's version of events, a standard detective novel ploy. Although some label the omniscient narrative voice as ''leaden,'' Guterson's skillful use of these personal histories enlarges the novel, for it allows him to relate the history of the island while taking the reader beyond the three-day courtroom trial into the lush, yet often harsh, environment of the Pacific Northwest, which comes alive as if a character in both the novels.

Outside Amity Harbor's overheated courtroom, a severe blizzard wraps itself around the island eventually knocking down power lines and testing everyone's resolve as heat dissipates and cars run off iced roads. Guterson is at his best as he captures a warm, languid excursion of Kabuo's family or the ripe, sweet strawberry fields during picking time. The sensual encounters of Ishmael and Hatsue in their secret hollowed-out cedar tree contrast sharply with those of the married Hatsue and Kabuo in her family's sheet-divided room in Manzanar before he goes off to kill Germans, an act for which his guilt will have repercussions during the trial. Although some argue that the sex scenes achieve little, particularly because they replace dialogue and narrative, for the reader, they resonate years later as reminders of the characters' and the island's loss of innocence during World War II. Throughout Guterson's evocative descriptions, the reader is aware of the treacherous immediacy of the sea, the unwritten code of the men who man the fishing boats and their animosity towards the island's Japanese-Americans, especially Kabuo who turned to salmon fishing in lieu of farming the land he believes Heine's mother has cheated him of; his obsession with the lost land provides the motive for the alleged murder.

At one point, Guterson set aside writing this novel to complete *Family Matters: Why Homeschooling Makes Sense*. Hailed as an honest evaluation of the educational method Guterson himself, then a high school teacher, chose for his children, he describes a classroom visit by his father, a criminal lawyer, clearly the model for Nels Gudmundsson, the aging, ailing defense attorney in *Snow Falling on Cedars*. In his trial summation, Gudmundsson calls for the jurors to overcome the human frailties of hate and irrational fears; he urges them to try Kabuo as an American, to use reason, not prejudices left over from the war. Any flaws in the novel lie in the swift ending to trial and book. Ishmael, heretofore emotionally numb, heeds Gudmundsson's exhortation and provides the court with newly discovered evidence.

In his second novel, *East of the Mountains*, Guterson uses the same techniques of flashback and precise descriptions to create a philosophical novel; however, his own analysis identifies a leaner, more understated style. His protagonist is Seattle cardiac surgeon Dr. Ben Givens, a seventy-three-year-old, recent widower diagnosed with terminal colon cancer. As the title suggests, the ''country'' is east of Puget Sound into the desert and apple regions of the Columbia Basin, an area Guterson hunted and hiked as a youngster as did his protagonist. As in *Snow Falling on Cedars*, a front map guides the reader through the unknown territory which Guterson describes in beautiful, lyric detail. Notwithstanding a loving daughter and family, Givens has devised, what some critics have called inexplicable, a plan to commit suicide making it look like a hunting accident; thus, he meticulously creates a home scene suggesting his return and sets off from Seattle in his 1969 International Scout with his Winchester and his two Brittanies during a torrential downpour. As expected, Givens's plan goes awry, for the novel is, as Guterson says, ''squarely in the genre of the mythic journey.''

As a writer, Guterson believes that his role is to create fiction which addresses human needs and sustains the culture's themes and central myths. He likens *East of the Mountains* to *Don Quixote* since, in both, older men undertake quests which follow the conventions of the mythic journey. Ben Givens travels, Guterson continues, beyond his ordinary life ''into some strange place . . . [where] he can ultimately resolve whatever question drove him to leave in the first place.'' Along the way Givens encounters strangers and incidents which test him physically and emotionally and which prompt memories, developed through lengthy flashbacks, that humanize any of his character's mythic traits. The flashbacks bear the mark of Guterson's research, including a trip to Italy's Dolomites for the recounting of young Givens's World War II experiences.

After the blockbuster success of *Snow Falling on Cedars*, apprehension increased Guterson's ''sense of being challenged'' as he prepared to write *East of the Mountains*. As a result, his style matured through his individualized voice and refined sensibilities, thus verifying his earlier identification by critics as a talent to watch.

—Judith C. Kohl

H

HAILEY, Arthur

Nationality: British and Canadian. **Born:** Luton, Bedfordshire, 5 April 1920; emigrated to Canada in 1947: became citizen, 1952. **Education:** Elementary schools in England. **Military Service:** Served as a pilot in the Royal Air Force, 1939–47: Flight Lieutenant. **Family:** Married 1) Joan Fishwick in 1944 (divorced 1950), three sons; 2) Sheila Dunlop in 1951, one son and two daughters. **Career:** Office boy and clerk, London, 1934–39; assistant editor, 1947–49, and editor, 1949–53, *Bus and Truck Transport,* Toronto; sales promotion manager, Trailmobile Canada, Toronto, 1953–56. Since 1956 freelance writer. **Awards:** Canadian Council of Authors and Artists award, 1956; Best Canadian TV Playwright award, 1957, 1958; Doubleday Prize Novel award, 1962. **Address:** Lyford Cay, P.O. Box N. 7776, Nassau, Bahamas.

PUBLICATIONS

Novels

Flight into Danger, with John Castle. London, Souvenir Press, 1958; as *Runway Zero-Eight,* New York, Doubleday, 1959.
The Final Diagnosis. New York, Doubleday, 1959; London, Joseph-Souvenir Press, 1960; as *The Young Doctors,* London, Corgi, 1962.
In High Places. New York, Doubleday, and London, Joseph-Souvenir Press, 1962.
Hotel. New York, Doubleday, and London, Joseph-Souvenir Press, 1965.
Airport. New York, Doubleday, and London, Joseph-Souvenir Press, 1968.
Wheels. New York, Doubleday, and London, Joseph-Souvenir Press, 1971.
The Moneychangers. New York, Doubleday, and London, Joseph-Souvenir Press, 1975.
Overload. New York, Doubleday, and London, Joseph-Souvenir Press, 1979.
Strong Medicine. New York, Doubleday, and London Joseph-Souvenir Press, 1984.
The Evening News. New York, Doubleday, and London, Doubleday-Souvenir Press, 1990.
Detective. New York, Crown Publishers, 1997.

Plays

Flight into Danger (televised 1956). Published in *Four Plays of Our Time,* London, Macmillan, 1960.
Close-up on Writing for Television. New York, Doubleday, 1960.

Screenplays: *Zero Hour,* with Hall Bartlett and John Champion, 1958; *The Moneychangers,* 1976; *Wheels,* 1978.

Television Plays: *Flight into Danger,* 1956 (USA); *Time Lock* 1962 (UK); *Course for Collision,* 1962 (UK); and plays for *Westinghouse Studio One, Playhouse 90, U.S. Steel Hour, Goodyear-Philco Playhouse,* and *Kraft Theatre* (USA).

*

Critical Studies: *I Married a Best Seller* by Sheila Hailey, New York, Doubleday, and London, Joseph-Souvenir Press, 1978.

Arthur Hailey comments:

My novels are the end product of my work and are widely available. Therefore I see no reason to be analytical about them.

Each novel takes me, usually, three years: a year of continuous research, six months of detailed planning, then a year and a half of steady writing, with many revisions.

My only other comment is that my novels are the work of one who seeks principally to be a storyteller but reflect also, I hope, the excitement of living here and now.

* * *

Arthur Hailey has developed and virtually perfected a highly efficient and extremely successful (and profitable) process of novel writing. Whether he is writing about doctors (*The Final Diagnosis, Strong Medicine*) or airline pilots (*Flight into Danger*), hotels (*Hotel*) or airports (*Airport*), government (*In High Places*) or industry (*Wheels*), he follows the same formula. Each of his novels is filled with enough information about the subject of his exhaustive research to satisfy the most curious reader; there are enough character types to appeal to the widest possible audience; everything is interwoven into a complex web of plots and sub-plots to satisfy every reader's desire for a good, suspenseful story.

Hailey writes documentary fiction, or what has been called ''faction,'' that is, a mixture of the real and the fictitious. After spending a year of research for each novel, Hailey is prepared to give his reader as much factual information as he can work into the novel. Consequently, only his characters and situations are imaginary, and they are sometimes only slightly fictitious.

To speak of any Hailey novel is to speak of every Hailey novel for there is little to distinguish one from the rest except subject matter. Each novel shares the same characteristic strengths and weaknesses. *Airport* is a typical example. The action of the novel is centered at a fictitious Chicago airport during one of the worst blizzards in the city's history. To give his reader an inside look at the operations of a major airport and into the lives of the people responsible for its existence, Hailey devises several plots; an airliner is stuck in the snow, blocking a runway and causing emergency situations in the air; an air-traffic controller is planning suicide; a trans-Atlantic airliner is about to take off with a bomb aboard; a stewardess has discovered she is pregnant; a group of local citizens is demonstrating against the excessive noise of the airport. The novel follows each plot to its conclusion, but not before the reader's intellectual curiosity about airports and his emotional curiosity about the characters are satisfied.

The narrative is slick and fast-moving, the information is interesting, the prose is readable, but the seams in Hailey's fabric too often show through. In order to introduce all his researched information into the novel, he is frequently forced to construct irrelevant sub-plots or to break the flow of the narrative for a lecture on such things as the safety records of commercial airlines or the pressures suffered by air-traffic controllers. To manage all his characters, he is forced into a ''holding pattern'' of his own. The focus of the novel shifts from one character to another as Hailey abandons characters temporarily only to return to them later when their number in the rotation comes up again. Consequently what unity there is in the book is provided only by the subject matter. The characters themselves are paper thin, reduced to simple dimensions; they are so typical that they could be interchanged from one novel to the next with little difficulty.

Wheels is much like *Airport* in its intention and its execution. The main difference is its lack of dramatic suspense; there is less drama to be derived from the introduction of a new car, the primary plot device in the novel, than from the naturally more exciting subjects of the earlier novels.

With *Detective,* Hailey made it clear that he still possessed the skills that had made him a bestselling author in preceding decades. The novel also showed that Hailey had changed with the times, departing from aspects of his established formula to delve into a serial-killer story of the type popularized by Thomas Harris and many others. Like Harris, Hailey purports to take readers into the mind of a killer, in this case Elroy ''Animal'' Doil, convicted of killing numerous elderly couples in south Florida. The true protagonist is a considerably more sympathetic figure, former priest Malcolm Ainsley, now serving as a homicide investigator with the Miami police. Ainsley's quest is personal as well as professional, since he is certain that Doil's victims include the parents of his former lover Cynthia Ernst—but Doil, with no apparent reason to lie, insists that this is not true. Revealing himself as a master of suspense, Hailey manages to reveal the true killer's identity long before the novel's denouement, yet still keeps readers engaged.

—David Geherin

HALEY, Russell

Nationality: New Zealander (originally English: immigrated to Australia, 1961, then to New Zealand, 1966). **Born:** Dewsbury, England, 1934. **Education:** University of Auckland, M.A. in English, 1970. **Address:** c/o Viking Penguin, 375 Hudson St., New York, New York 10014, U.S.A.

Publications

Novels

The Settlement. Auckland and London, Hodder and Stoughton, 1986.
Beside Myself. Auckland and New York, Penguin, 1990.
All Done with Mirrors. Christchurch, New Zealand, Hazard Press Publishers, 1999.

Short Stories

The Sauna Bath Mysteries and Other Stories. Auckland, Mandrake Root, 1978.
Real Illusions: A Selection of Family Lies and Biographical Fictions in Which the Ancestral Dead Also Play Their Part. Wellington, Victoria University Press, 1984; New York, New Directions, 1985.
The Transfer Station. N.p., 1989.

Poetry

The Walled Garden. Auckland, Mandrake Root, 1972.
On the Fault Line and Other Poems. Paraparaumu, New Zealand, Hawk Press, 1977.

Other

Haley: A New Zealand Artist. Auckland, Hodder and Stoughton, 1989.
Editor, with Susan Davis, *The Penguin Book of Contemporary New Zealand Short Stories.* Auckland and New York, Penguin, 1989.

* * *

The Sauna Bath Mysteries and Other Stories established Russell Haley's reputation as a pioneering writer of postmodernist experimental fiction with affinities with writers such as Nabakov, Beckett, John Barth, Robert Coover, and Thomas Pynchon. This has been confirmed in the achievement of his two novels, *The Settlement* and *Beside Myself,* and the series of interlinked stories that are collected in *The Transfer Station.* These extend the narrative strategies of his short stories, such as the classic ''Barbados—A Love Story,'' into ambitious performances in which he collapses the boundaries between fiction and reality, overlapping dream, memory, and experience and undermining epistemological certainties. Such metafictional constructions do more than challenge the reader's ingenuity. Haley, who came to New Zealand from England in the 1960s, has masterminded the characteristic dilemmas of the hero who is displaced due to ''migratio'' and whose extreme self-consciousness as subject and paranoid distrust of the world transforms a condition of existential disease into an absurdist vision of life.

The Settlement, partly inspired by public conflict over the Springbok tour of New Zealand in 1981, leaves the reader with minimalized certainties. In The Settlement at Moorfields, identified first as a convalescent home and later as a mental asylum, in which the middle-aged hero, Walter Lemanby, finds himself after falling from his roof, images of menacing control abound—mysterious installations, searchlights, helicopters, curfews, nameless uniformed assailants. They point either to civil unrest or to the existence of a centralized, totalitarian state that represses the individual; they are reinforced in the plot in the sinister, masked figure of Dr. Grimshaw. Yet Haley draws attention to the fictionality of his omniscient hero by creating a narrative break after 50 pages in an italicized passage, implying that he is the ''secret collaborator within this text'' who ''threw the stone'' by creating its circumstances, and then he starts over again. This authorial self-consciousness is reminiscent of the challenge issued to the reader in ''Barbados—A Love Story'' as to who should throw the first stone, call the narrator's bluff, and so undermine the fictionality of his creation.

Haley's foregrounding of the process of writing through metafictional games that stress the artifice of illusion and the fictional nature of subjectivity, however, rarely lapses into linguistic solipsism. His narratorial self-consciousness is both artful and endearing. Walter's struggles to familiarize himself with an alien world, to reorder experience by labeling his landscape, are intensely personal if not moving. In *Beside Myself,* a sequence of unsettling experiences destabilize the hero's attempts to impose order on his life: A heady sexual encounter with a woman he meets at a party, followed by the revelation of his best friend's death, lead to comical yet painful struggles to understand himself. In these works lyrical moments appear sporadically, creating sudden shifts of tone.

In his more recent writing Haley gestures nostalgically toward values of longing, loss, and love. The nine linked stories in *The Transfer Station,* an extended meditation on the meaning of death, represent the aging protagonist's bereavement at the death of his wife. The nearby Transfer Station, a rubbish dump on the outskirts of Auckland that chews up detritus and waste, has a unifying function as a symbol of death in its most dehumanized form as a sought-after memorable extinction of life. This is articulated by the two teenage girls whom the narrator befriends briefly and whose memory becomes a preoccupation until he is able to reaffirm the value of his own life. Cumulatively these stories convey the impression of a mind in a state of psychological dislocation recovering its mental balance. The customary zaniness and humor of Haley's heroes, although functioning near the surface of the text, are partly displaced into the girls' vision of life as brief, juvenile, yet imaginatively enduring.

Just as patterns of displacement characterize Haley's fiction, so too does the antilinear, multidirectional narrative and an insistence on the fragmented and uncertainly known nature of reality as conveyed through language. In his novels and in stories such as ''Looping the Loop,'' ''Barbados—A Love Story,'' or ''The Balkan Transformer,'' he uses fantasy, dream transformations, and the uncertainties of memory to present events as occurring in the context of the multiple possibilities of the narrator's mind. Yet he insists equally on the physical presence of the body—its inevitable habits of defecation, erection, eating, and sleeping—as a point of entry into the often comical collusion between his narrators' self-conscious subjectivity and the constraints imposed by physical existence.

Haley's innovative humor is most immediately accessible in his short stories, whereas his two novels explore more fully the tragicomic conditions of existential angst leading to an absurdist worldview; at his best he has produced some of the liveliest, most engaging postmodern fiction yet to have been written in New Zealand.

—Janet Wilson

HALL, James B(yron)

Nationality: American. **Born:** Midland, Ohio, 21 July 1918. **Education:** Miami University, Oxford, Ohio, 1938–39; University of Hawaii, Honolulu, 1938–40; University of Iowa, Iowa City, B.A. 1947, M.A. 1948, Ph.D. 1953; Kenyon College, Gambier, Ohio, 1949. **Military Service:** United States Army, 1941–46. **Family:** Married Elizabeth Cushman in 1946; five children. **Career:** Writer-in-residence, Miami University, 1948–49; instructor, Cornell University, Ithaca, New York, 1952–53; writer-in-residence, University of North Carolina, Greensville, 1954; assistant professor, 1954–57, associate professor, 1958–60, and professor of English, 1960–65, University of Oregon, Eugene; director of the Writing Center, and professor of English, University of California, Irvine, 1965–68. Since 1968, professor of literature, and Provost of College V. University of California, Santa Cruz. Writer-in-residence, University of British Columbia, Vancouver, Summer 1956; guest artist, Pacific Coast Festival of Art, Reed College, Portland, 1958; writer-in-residence, University of Colorado, Boulder, 1963. Co-founding editor, *Northwest Review,* Eugene, Oregon, 1957–60; founder and director, University of Oregon Summer Academy of Contemporary Arts, Eugene, 1959–64. Editorial consultant, Doubleday and Company, publishers (West Coast staff), 1960; cultural specialist, United States Department of State, Washington, 1964. **Awards:** Octave Thanet prize, 1950; Yaddo grant, 1952; Oregon Poetry prize, 1958; Chapelbrook fellowship, 1967; Institute of Creative Arts fellowship, 1967; Balch Fiction prize, 1967. **Address:** 1080 Patterson #901; Eugene, Oregon 97401, U.S.A.

PUBLICATIONS

Novels

Not by the Door. New York, Random House, 1954.
TNT for Two. New York, Ace, 1956.
Racers to the Sun. New York, Obolensky, 1960; London, Corgi, 1962.
Mayo Sergeant. New York, New American Library, 1967.

Short Stories

15 x 3, with Herbert Gold and R.V. Cassill. New York, New Directions, 1957.
Us He Devours. New York, New Directions, 1964.
The Short Hall: New and Collected Stories. Athens, Ohio University Press, 1980.
I Like It Better Now. Fayetteville, University of Arkansas Press, 1992.

Poetry

The Hunt Within. Baton Rouge, Louisiana State University Press, 1973.
Bereavements. Brownsville, Oregon, Story Line Press, 1991.

Other

The Art and Craft of the Short Story. Murphy, Oregon, Castle Peak Editions, 1994.
Editor, with Joseph Langland, *The Short Story.* New York, Macmillan, 1956.
Editor, *The Realm of Fiction: 61 Short Stories.* New York, McGraw Hill, 1965; revised edition, 1970, 1977.
Editor, with Barry Ulanov, *Modern Culture and the Arts.* New York, McGraw Hill, 1967; revised edition, 1972.
Editor, *John Barleycorn: Alcoholic Memoirs,* by Jack London. Santa Cruz, California, Western Tanager Press, 1981.
Editor, with Hotchkiss and Shears, *Perspectives on William Everson.* Blackfoot, Idaho, Castle Peak Editions, 1992.

*

James B. Hall comments:

Although the novels are interesting, the central significance of the work resides largely in the short stories; the poetry is various, and by intention ancillary to the prose.

The novels, short stories, and poetry are thematically interrelated. The reccurring motifs are the effects of competition on individuals in a system of modified capitalism such as obtains in the United States. Thus acquisitive, frustrated, evasive protagonists reccur, some of them mad or nearly so. Extreme conduct in a hostile world is not infrequent; the adjustments which protagonists make vary from callous acceptance or the exploitation of others to withdrawal, revenge, and self-destruction. In general, the work shows the difficulty of remaining human in a competitive, non-Darwinian world fashioned in large part by a democratic society. Specifically, *Racers to the Sun* traces the ''rise'' and fall of a motorcycle racer who builds his own machine; the hero is injured (used up), and then is dropped by those who exploited his talent for machinery and speed. Likewise, in the typical short stories, ''Us He Devours'' and ''The Claims Artist,'' the protagonists are in some ways laudable, but in the end are victims of their own and of society's demands. A typical poem, ''Pay Day Night,'' treats the counterproductive nature of experience in another bureaucracy, the Army.

The short stories are experimental, highly compressed, and exploit language poetically for artistic effect. They are condensed statements that very often extend the possibilities of the genre. Many of the stories are anthologized; because they are complex they apparently ''teach well'' in classrooms.

(1995) Increasingly the short forms of imaginative writing claim most of my attention: the short story, poetry, nonfiction articles. This comes as no surprise for increasingly the literary artist under (finance) capitalism has the obligation to justify corporate investment, and the long forms, such as the novel, presently require greater sponsorship by the publisher and more author-time dedicated to promotion(s) of the work. This drift has evident impact on modernist (and postmodernist) work and is suggested merely as ways the writer's ''work place'' has changed in the past twenty years. No practicing writer may claim exemption therefrom; nevertheless, work of high literary quality does get written, published, and read. The new writer, I think, faces the greatest challenges for, among other things, the institutions which once offered some order of literary apprenticeship now offer too early specialization from which there seems no rise and no return.

*   *   *

James B. Hall is of that generation of writers who hit the beaches of American literature following World War II. Like Mailer and Vonnegut, Hall is a veteran. Unlike them, however, he did not write a war novel and get a literary Purple Heart. His medals are yet in the drawer. Along with having grown up on a farm, his military experiences are significant to an understanding of his social vision, and to the imagery and tropes in many of the short stories, especially ''The Snow Hunter,'' ''The Rumor of Metal,'' and ''The War in the Forest,'' (in *I Like It Better Now*).

The three stories mentioned above are also typical of the way Hall works. They are compressed and complex, very close to poetry. The imagery is both precise and evocative; scenic and narrative paragraphs are modulated; the swift and brief dialogue often in counterpoint to the description elements. Character in Hall's stories and novels develops within a particular phenomenological environment. In other words, character is what character does in the world.

Here is a passage from Hall's second novel, *Racers to the Sun.* Though of course he doesn't know it, Harold ''Speedy'' Hill is about to enter his last race. The way that Speedy sees the arriving motorcycles is at the same time beautiful and threatening:

> Delicate, the red, black, and sun-burst orange racing machines reared imperceptibly as their trailers stopped. They were vicious and lovely, imperious and chaste in orange or bone-white paint, the waspish handle bars curved downward over the front wheels, the magnetoes humped, fetal-like, in the coarse belly of the engine.

In *Not by the Door,* Hall has already discovered how to use scene to flesh out character. The Reverend Howard Marcham, an Episcopal minister in his first pastorate, has gotten himself into somewhat of a moral pickle. He decides to take a drive in the country, parks his car and goes for a walk. He comes upon a water moccasin sleeping on a willow branch. The snake has recently shed its skin. Hall makes the most of the biblical and mythological reference to sin, evil and rebirth. But he does it subtly, by scenic description. As a reader one ''gets it'' as an after-image. By this method of writing, Hall is very much a poet. The prose fiction is as burnished as a Spenserian stanza. In Hall's case, the genre boundaries among lyric, short story, and novel dissolve, and this in particular makes him a singular voice in contemporary fiction.

The Reverend Marcham is also typical of many of Hall's male characters. Very often the personae suggest some aspect of the author as self-critical. Unlike Hall, brought up Methodist, Howard Marcham is already a notch up, because he is an Episcopalian. Hall's protagonists fight to get ahead in the social world: fight for control of a motorcycle, a race, a yacht, a woman, real estate, or money; attempt to put a rein on personal anarchy but often end up in self-destruction. Howard Marcham is a pastor without spiritual depth, and he lacks a feeling for community. The reverend also prefigures *Mayo Sergeant,* an even emptier and more venal person.

We get to the last novel, with its much darker and sardonic social canvas, by way of *Racers to the Sun.* It is in the second novel that Hall begins to strike the note of class conflict and of the brutal nature of capitalism. Harold ''Speedy'' Hill and his boss, Jeffcoat, at the novel's beginning, are two of Hall's most sympathetic male characters. The author's rural upbringing, and his stint as a labor officer on the German docks during the occupation, are obviously influences on his social point of view. Hall favors the rural and urban working classes, those who try to make an honest living with their hands. No other prose writer writes so lovingly of tools and machinery as Hall in *Racers to the Sun.*

Generally, the female characters in his fiction come off better than the males. Lucern ''Gunner'' Greener in the racing novel is an exception. The daughter of a motorcycle agency owner, she gives herself to the winners. As soon as Hill is injured, she leaves him flat out. Gunner is a sexual metaphor for a system that uses people for its own needs and then dumps them. The motorcycle agency and the racing track owners drop the hero, too, when they can no longer profit from his status as a winner.

Whereas the system uses Speedy Hill, Mayo Sergeant uses women and the sleight-of-hand world of real estate as he glad-hands and charms and screws his way up the social ladder in Cutlass Bay, until he moves into the Moorish house on the hill and takes part possession of the racing yacht, *Indus.* The novel is narrated by

Roberte "Bombie" Glouster, who lost his foot in World War II. Glouster represents "old money" in Cutlass Bay, and is in love with the very wealthy Hildy Moorish himself. At first Roberte befriends Mayo, who arrives from nowhere; but then he is taken in by Mayo and cuckolded as well. There is something of both Gatsby and Willy Loman in Mayo Sergeant, but Hall's novel perhaps surpasses the other two works in its savage judgment of the way we live. Hall's vision is indeed Dantean here, Hall's own version of Hell. There is not one likeable character in *Mayo Sergeant,* either male or female. But the novel should be reissued, for it contains some of the finest prose in American fiction today. And if the portrait of America is an unlikeable one, that is Hall's very point.

—Bill Witherup

HALL, Rodney

Nationality: Australian. **Born:** Solihull, Warwickshire, England, 18 November 1935; immigrated to Australia during his childhood. **Education:** City of Bath Boys' School; Brisbane Boys' College; University of Queensland, Brisbane, B.A. 1971. **Family:** Married Maureen Elizabeth MacPhail in 1962; three daughters. **Career:** Freelance scriptwriter and actor, 1957–67, and film critic, 1966–67, Australian Broadcasting Corporation, Brisbane. Tutor, New England University School of Music, Armidale, New South Wales, summers 1967–71 and 1977–80; youth officer, Australian Council for the Arts, 1971–73; lecturer in recorder, Canberra School of Music, 1979–83. Since 1962 advisory editor, *Overland* magazine, Melbourne; since 1967 poetry editor, *The Australian* daily newspaper, Sydney. Traveled in Europe, 1958–60, 1963–64, 1965, and the United States, 1974. Australian Department of Foreign Affairs Lecturer in India, 1970, 1981, Malaysia, 1972, 1980, and Europe, 1981, 1983, 1984. **Awards:** Australian National University Creative Arts fellowship, Canberra, 1968; Commonwealth Literary Fund fellowship, 1970; Literature Board fellowship, 1973, 1976, 1982, 1986, 1990; Grace Leven prize, 1974; Miles Franklin award, Australian Natives Association award, and Barbara Ramsden award, all 1982, all for *Just Relations;* Victorian Premier's literary award, 1989, for *Captivity Captive.* **Address:** c/o Penguin Books, P.O. Box 257, Ringwood, Victoria 3134, Australia.

PUBLICATIONS

Novels

The Ship on the Coin: A Fable of the Bourgeoisie. St. Lucia, University of Queensland Press, 1972.

A Place Among People. St. Lucia, University of Queensland Press, 1975.

Just Relations. Ringwood, Victoria, Penguin, 1982; London, Allen Lane, and New York, Viking Press, 1983.

Kisses of the Enemy. Ringwood, Victoria, Penguin, 1987; New York, Farrar Straus, 1988; London, Faber, 1989.

Captivity Captive. Melbourne, McPhee Gribble, New York, Farrar Straus, and London, Faber, 1988.

The Second Bridegroom. Ringwood, Victoria, McPhee Gribble, and London, Faber, 1991.

The Grisly Wife. Sydney, Macmillan, and London, Faber, 1993.

A Dream More Luminous than Love: The Yandilli Trilogy. Sydney, Picador Australia, 1994; New York, Noonday Press, 1995.

Poetry

Penniless till Doomsday. London, Outposts, 1962.

Four Poets, with others. Melbourne, Cheshire, 1962.

Forty Beads on a Hangman's Rope: Fragments of Memory. Newnham, Tasmania, Wattle Grove Press, 1963.

Eyewitness. Sydney, South Head Press, 1967.

The Autobiography of a Gorgon. Melbourne, Cheshire, 1968.

The Law of Karma: A Progression of Poems. Canberra, Australian National University Press, 1968.

Heaven, In a Way. St. Lucia, University of Queensland Press, 1970.

A Soapbox Omnibus. St. Lucia, University of Queensland Press, 1973.

Selected Poems. St. Lucia, University of Queensland Press, 1975.

Black Bagatelles. St. Lucia, University of Queensland Press, 1978.

The Most Beautiful World: Fictions and Sermons. St. Lucia, University of Queensland Press, 1981.

Recordings: *Romulus and Remus,* University of Queensland Press, 1971

Other

Social Services and the Aborigines, with Shirley Andrews. Canberra, Federal Council for Aboriginal Advancement, 1963.

Focus on Andrew Sibley. Brisbane, University of Queensland Press, 1968.

J.S. Manifold: An Introduction to the Man and His Work. Brisbane, University of Queensland Press, 1978.

Australia, Image of a Nation, 1850–1950, with David Moore. Sydney, Collins, 1983.

Journey Through Australia. Richmond, Victoria, Heinemann, and London, Murray, 1989; as *Home, A Journey through Australia.* Port Melbourne, Minerva, 1990.

The Writer and the World of the Imagination. Armidale, New South Wales, Faculty of Arts, University of New England, 1995.

Editor, with Thomas W. Shapcott, *New Impulses in Australian Poetry.* Brisbane, University of Queensland Press, 1968.

Editor, *Australian Poetry 1970.* Sydney, Angus and Robertson, 1970.

Editor, *Poems from Prison.* Brisbane, University of Queensland Press, 1973.

Editor, *Australians Aware: Poems and Paintings.* Sydney, Ure Smith, 1975.

Editor, *Voyage into Solitude,* by Michael Dransfield. Brisbane, University of Queensland Press, 1978.

Editor, *The Second Month of Spring,* by Michael Dransfield. Brisbane, University of Queensland Press, 1980.

Editor, *The Collins Book of Australian Poetry.* Sydney, Collins, 1981; London, Collins, 1983.

Editor, *Collected Poems* by Michael Dransfield. St. Lucia, University of Queensland Press, 1987.

* * *

One of Australia's most prolific writers, Rodney Hall established his reputation first as a poet before turning to fiction. His early novelistic ventures were less than successful. *The Ship on the Coin* is a rather heavy-handed satire based on the ''Creosus'' travel agency, which rebuilds a quinquereme and invites customers to row their own ship for a holiday. The scheme is wildly successful but the allegory concerning voluntary subservience to the United States (''Buy your way into slavery now'') seems somewhat dated today and the comedy is very broad. *A Place Among People* is a more sensitively written novel about a small town just out of Brisbane called Battery Spit. Set in the 1950s, a period where bigotries and conformist attitudes are skillfully conveyed, it concerns the nonconformist (intellectual, aboriginal) Collocott who is persecuted by the townspeople. The central incident involves the town's attempt to drive a black woman, Daisy Daisy, out of their midst and onto a reservation the blacks call Prison Island and Collocott's stubborn defiance of them in defense of her. However, it is relatively benign and even optimistic in many of its views. When it finally comes to the crunch only eleven of the townspeople actually turn up outside Collocott's house to force him to release Daisy, and others among them come unexpectedly to his aid. Many of the characters achieve minor victories over their own lesser instincts, and of the unorthodox hero Collocott the novel concludes, ''He wavered on the brink of life.'' Occasional obscurities aside, *A Place Among People* is an intelligent and graceful novel.

Hall established his reputation, however, with his third novel, *Just Relations.* A long, complex, and sometimes overwritten book, it is set in the ironically named Whitey's Fall, a declining former gold town peopled by a set of aging eccentrics, whose only religion is ''Remembering.'' There is Felicia Brinsmead, a seventy-three-year-old spinster who has never had her hair cut so that it hangs over her like a huge, dirty web and who believes that she is the mother of a twelve-year-old boy, Fido. There is the narcissistic Mr. Ping, who willfully destroys his fading beauty. There is the spirit of Kel McAlon, who has killed himself. In the local pub a group of people are sitting around drinking; they are aged between eighty and 114. Into this community comes beautiful thirty-four-year-old Vivien Lang, with whom the teenager Billy Swan falls in love, to the scandal of some of the town. To it also comes Senator Frank Halloran to inform the community that a highway is being built through to bring the town to life. All but one of the forty-nine residents are outraged. Their creed is summed up by Uncle, Billy's grandfather, who proudly lists the examples of ''progress'' that he has opposed—hospital, old people's home, police station, jail, school, highways, and the draft. Hall seems to intend the community to be a paradigm of a dying Australia that he sees as infinitely superior to the current one. The book is unnecessarily long and the writing often clumsy, particularly in any of the scenes to do with sex: ''Her fingers fluttered round him, giant butterflies afraid to alight but fatally attracted by the honey hidden in him.'' The presence of Patrick White is felt at times in the deliberately dissonant rhythms of the prose, and there is a positive smorgasbord of techniques brought to bear as the novel moves between past and present, employing all kinds of texts—diaries, newspaper reports, letters—to illuminate the theme. Nevertheless, the conception is original and eventually the novel gains conviction, particularly through the beautifully realized figures of the women and its fine treatment of landscape.

In *Kisses of the Enemy,* Hall returns to political satire with a novel set in the near future. Australia has become a republic under the leadership of Bernard Buchanan, who represents the multinational Interim Freeholdings Incorporated of Delaware; Buchanan, in fact, is really the front man for the company's Luigi Squarcia and Australia is rapidly becoming the puppet state of the United States. Hall manages to draw this parable out to over 600 pages, but though the object of the satire is legitimate enough, the novel rarely comes to life and the jokes are even more labored than in *The Ship on the Coin.* For instance, Buchanan is very fat at the start of the novel, with two men carrying him around; at the height of his power the retinue has grown to eight and still later, when his power begins to decline, he simultaneously begins to lose weight. The very topicality of the satire ensures that the jokes become dated.

Just Relations apart, Hall's major novelistic achievement to date is found in his three most recent novels, *Captivity Captive* (published in 1988 but set in 1888), *The Second Bridegroom* (1991, 1836), and *The Grisly Wife* (1993, 1898). Hall has finally drawn these together as a trilogy under the title *A Dream More Luminous than Love,* or the Yandilli trilogy. According to the author, the first volume grew out of the Gatton murders, the macabre killing of three siblings in New South Wales in 1898. Then, according to an interview he gave, ''Hall began working on an earlier setting and then realized that, ideally, there should be an even earlier novel, introducing the theme of the white presence and—almost immutably—that of the Aborigines.'' *The Grisly Wife* is the middle novel in terms of chronology and the only one to have a woman as its narrator, though all three are monologues. Hall explained, ''In the two outside books I had two male voices, a pagan outcast from the Isle of Man and a working-class Catholic. Symmetry required me to have the voice of a Protestant middle-class woman.'' All three books have the same setting, the backwoods of south coastal New South Wales, where Hall himself now lives and which critics frequently compare to William Faulkner's Yoknapatawpha County as an example of a novelist creating his own fictive territory. All three are monologues spoke in an almost unnaturally eloquent, even poetic voice, though Hall has gone out of his way to anticipate this objection by giving each of his narrators a background of literacy. The convict forger in *The Second Bridegroom* learned about words from his mother and how to use them from his trade as a printer. Catherine Byrne, the eponymous wife, is the daughter of an Anglican clergyman. And Patrick Malone was the one child (of ten) chosen by his brutal father to be educated outside the closed family by a learned old Catholic priest.

The Second Bridegroom is the story of an unnamed youth told (we eventually learn) to the widow of his master with whom he has fallen blindly in love and who he wrongly believes to have at least some sympathy for him. Transported to Australia in the ''Fraternity'' for the forgery of a fifteenth-century document, he is manacled to Gabriel Dean, whose mistreatment of him drives him to strangle the man. He then escapes into the bush and joins a tribe of Aborigines who make him their king. When the tribe attack a settlement, killing a young woman and then most of the rest of the settlers and setting fire to their property, the narrator takes the guilt upon himself as having somehow willed it: ''The truth was this, that while the Men knew no word of my language they must have known my thoughts. So, they had felt my fury and sensed my need. They had obeyed. I had given orders as sure as if I spoke them.''

Although the Aborigines are not individualized and the narrator never learns even a single word of their language, their mode of life is shown to be inherently superior to that of the whites. The narrator quickly adjusts to their ways of thinking. When he comes upon a white settlement after a few months in the wilderness he speaks of their efforts to ''tame'' and fence the land in horrified terms of ''the sheer scale of violence.'' He notes the Aborigines' generosity and selflessness toward himself, their patience with his clumsiness, and their refusal to steal more food than they need. The theme of the novel is perhaps best summed up in one of the narrator's many bouts of sententiousness: "I want you to understand that there is something to be understood out there, something free of the law, free of any comforting faith in a God whose motives may be explained through our own, something that has to become the map of my heart."

The Grisly Wife is a monologue delivered by Catherine Byrne before a silent audience, which we discover only at the end to be a sergeant who has come to inquire about the murder of the three Malone siblings, her neighbors and the subject of *Captivity Captive.* We learn also that Catherine believes he is inquiring about a different murder, that of the unnamed narrator of *The Second Bridegroom.* The year is 1898 and not the least of Hall's concerns is the intrusion of the secular and scientific world upon the kind of messianic faith inspired in Catherine and her female friends by the charismatic preacher Muley Moloch. There is mention of Charles Darwin, for instance, of Richard Wagner as some kind of herald of a new age, and of new scientific phenomena such as cameras, lawnmowers, and steam trains. Muley marries Catherine after she has been impressed by his apparent feat of levitation and then persuades a group of eight women to sail with him to Australia and found a new community on the south coast of New South Wales, christening them the Household of Hidden Stars. One by one the women die of consumption at the mission they establish, as the prophet's hold on them diminishes. Eventually the survivors kick him out after he shoots and kills a wild white man (the escaped convict).

This is an almost ostentatiously feminist novel, as *The Second Bridegroom* concerns itself conspicuously with environmental issues. A sense of close camaraderie grows among the women, especially after they dismiss Muley, and extends eventually to a close friendship between Catherine and Louisa Theuerkauf, the woman she had once hated. Protests against male authority keep emerging in the text, particularly in Catherine's constant reproaches of Sergeant Arrell, her silent audience. "Tenderness grows among us," we are told of the women, and they embrace frequently.

In *Captivity Captive,* Barney Barnett, the unsuccessful suitor of one of the girls shot and clubbed to death on a remote New South Wales farm, has confessed to the crime on his deathbed, but it soon becomes clear that his claim is merely a piece of retrospective self-aggrandizement. One of the surviving siblings sets out to tell the story of what actually happened. It does not take the reader too long to find out who the actual killer is, but the question of why remains almost as much of an enigma at the end as at the beginning. In a prose that is in turn poetic, highly self-conscious, rhetorical, and obsessive, Hall explores the relationship between guilt and innocence, captive and tyrant.

For all its occasional stylistic excesses, the trilogy is an impressive attempt to reexplore and rewrite white Australian history. One of the key themes in all three novels is the sense that the land was not empty but was seized by white people; hence the constant presence of the Aborigines, seen as ghosts or demons by the whites, hovering constantly around the outskirts of the narratives, their presence both a threat and an admonishment to the whites: "They were briefly there and soon gone but it was evident to me that they knew more than we had ever believed possible," Catherine says in *The Grisly Wife.* One critic has gone so far as to suggest that "Each of these characters attempts to live and reenact a myth, to take on some self-imposed mantle of immortality: the Second Bridegroom, the Second Coming or the Second Fall from Grace. Each fails."

—Laurie Clancy

HALLIGAN, Marion

Nationality: Australian. **Born:** Marion Mildred Crothall, Newcastle, New South Wales, 16 April 1940. **Education:** University College, 1957–62, B.A.(honours) in education 1962. **Family:** Married Graham James Halligan in 1963; one daughter and one son. **Career:** Teacher, Canberra High School, Australian Capital Territory, 1963–65, Canberra Church of England Girls' Grammar School, 1974–86. Since 1993, chair of literature, Board of Australia Council. Writer-in-residence, Charles Stuart University, Riverina, 1990. **Awards:** Patricia Hackett prize for best creative contribution to *Westerly,* 1985; Butterly/Earla Hooper award, for short story; Steele Rudd award, 1989, and Braille book of the year, 1989, for *The Living Hothouse;* Geraldine Pascall award, 1990, for critical writing; Australia/New Zealand Exchange, 1991; Keesing Studio Cite Internationale des Arts, Paris, 1991; Award for Gastronomic writing, 1991, for *Eat My Words; Age* book of the year, 1992, ACT book of the year, 1993, 3M talking book of the year, 1993, and Nita B. Kibble award, 1994, for *Lovers' Knots;* The Newton-John award, 1994. **Agent:** Margaret Connolly, 37 Ormond Street, Paddington, New South Wales 2021, Australia. **Address:** 6 Caldwell Street, Hackett, Australian Capital Territory 2602, Australia.

Publications

Novels

Self Possession. Brisbane, University of Queensland Press, 1987.
The Hanged Man in the Garden. Melbourne, Penguin, 1989.
Spider Cup. Melbourne, Penguin, 1990.
Lovers' Knots. Melbourne, Heinemann, 1992; London, Minerva, 1995.
Wishbone. Melbourne, Heinemann, 1994.
Cockles of the Heart. Port Melbourne, Australia, Minerva, 1996.
The Golden Dress. Ringwood, Victoria, Penguin, 1999.

Short Stories

The Living Hothouse. Brisbane, University of Queensland Press, 1988.
The Worry Box. Melbourne, Heinemann, 1993.
Collected Stories. St. Lucia, Queensland, University of Queensland Press, 1997.

Plays

Gastronomica (produced Melbourne Festival, 1994).

Other

Out of the Picture. Canberra, National Library of Australia, 1990.
Eat My Words. Sydney, Angus and Robertson, 1990.
Editor, with Rosanne Fitzgibbon, *The Gift of Story: Three Decades of UQP Short Stories.* St. Lucia, Queensland, University of Queensland Press, 1998; Portland, Oregon, International Specialized Book Services, 1998.

*

Manuscript Collections: National Library of Australia, Canberra.

Marion Halligan comments:

I am interested in words and stories. I think that when you find the words you find out what it is you want to say. Stories are what people are good at, both telling them and listening to them. In both fiction and non-fiction story-telling is important, though it may not always be simple; sometimes narratives are hidden.

Looking back over my writing I realise it is often about choice and chance, though I don't start with these notions. And I write about ordinary lives, and how amazing they are.

* * *

Marion Halligan's fiction moves through daily life to its structuring fantasies, personal and cultural. Her narratives of ''what if'' interrupt routine: Beyond the ordinary, other worlds beckon. At the beginning of ''The Orangery,'' found in her third collection of short stories, *The Worry Box,* a woman sits on a train reading. From the seat opposite a stranger breaks into her containment. Lift your eyes, he admonishes her. The world is there to see. Get off at the next stop and visit the stationmaster's orangery. When the train halts, she looks out the window at orange trees covered with flower and fruit and, yielding to a sudden desire to breathe the sharp scented air of orange blossom, she puts down her book and follows the man. Suddenly the narrative, moving along a trajectory of erotic seduction, veers off into death. Anticipating elegance and artifice, the woman encounters explosion, a bomb blast, bodies in bits. What was she doing there? Did she choose, or was she lured? Where were the meanings for this violent intrusion?

Questions like these have disturbed Halligan's writing since she began publishing seriously in 1981. She is a writer of unease and yet a celebrator of story and the senses. In less than ten years she has become one of Australia's best-known writers, highly regarded for her work across an unusual range of forms. Her short stories, which have won many prizes, appear in literary and mainstream magazines, are read on national radio, and are frequently anthologized. The first collection, *The Living Hothouse,* with its stories set in Australia, New Zealand, and France, won the Steele Rudd Award and the Braille Book of the Year Award. Since that initial book, she has published over six years two more collections of short fiction, four novels, and a work of nonfiction. Her most ambitious novel to date, *Lovers' Knots,* won the *Age* Book of the Year Award. Set in the coastal town of Newcastle, where Halligan grew up and went to university, the novel begins as if it were a family saga covering the century 1911–2011, but its narrative denies the conventional chronology evoked and shatters into the fragments caught by photographs.

Halligan is fascinated by story and, refusing as she does the borders of telling, her narratives surface in unexpected places. She has written the libretto for a children's opera, a trilogy of plays for the Melbourne Theater Company, and the narratives to accompany photographs in *Out of the Picture,* commissioned by the National Library of Australia. Above all, however, she is admired for writing food. Food and story, she has said, are the most important things in life. Together they are irresistibly seductive. We cannot live without them. Probably her work of widest appeal is *Eat My Words* (winner of the Prize for Gastronomic Writing), a book of food and story set largely in France and loosely structured as autobiography. Its sequel, *A Second Helping* (forthcoming) will within a framework of travel through France offer readers another helping of words. Metaphor and reality took a new twist in Halligan's œuvre during 1994 when the patrons dining in five opulent 19th-century restaurants in Melbourne ate their way through menus specially devised as accompaniments for theater pieces performed between courses. Each of Halligan's five ''Gastronomicas,'' commissioned by the Melbourne International Festival, was created for the particular eating space and drew for its stories on writers like Dickens and Wilde selected as fitting that restaurant. Diners ate the highest of cuisine amid the best of story.

Such pampering of desire takes strange twists in Halligan's most recent novel, *Wishbone.* Like the fairy tales where wishes come true to the considerable consternation of those careless with words, the wealthy characters in this fable of contemporary Australia find themselves swept up in narratives of murder, sex, and intrigue they never anticipated in their wishing. In the materialistic culture imagined, the opportunities for pleasures and indulgence abound, but no narrative of desire is genuinely to be wished. This novel has received little of the critical praise accorded *Lovers' Knots.* Perhaps those who delighted in the humor, warmth, and poignancy of the preceding novel are uncomfortable with the wicked wit and uncompromising satire of *Wishbone.* Gender may play its part. Although women writers in Australia have incorporated the satiric moment into their fiction, the sustained narratives of satire have belonged predominantly to men (such as Patrick White, Frank Moorhouse, and Morris Lurie). Marion Halligan is praised for writing the meals set on Australian tables; making a meal of Australia may be another matter, may be unbecoming in a woman writer. If the cultural cringe is gone from Australian readers, the gender cringe still seems to linger.

—Lucy Frost

HAMILTON, Hugo

Nationality: Irish. **Born:** Hugo O'Urmoltaigh in Dublin, Ireland, 28 January 1953. **Career:** Worked in the music business; freelance journalist, Dublin. Lives in County Dublin, Ireland. **Awards:** Rooney prize for Irish Literature, 1992. **Agent:** Derek Johns, 20 John Street, London WC1N 2DR, England.

PUBLICATIONS

Novels

Surrogate City. London, Faber and Faber, 1990.

The Last Shot. London, Faber and Faber, 1991; New York, Farrar, Straus, and Giroux, 1992.

The Love Test. London, Faber and Faber, 1995; Boston, Faber and Faber, 1995.

Dublin Where the Palm Trees Grow. London, Faber and Faber, 1996.

Headbanger. London, Secker & Warburg, 1996.

Sad Bastard. London, Secker & Warburg, 1998.

Other

Finbar's Hotel (serial novel, with others), devised and edited by Dermot Bolger. London, Picador, 1997.

* * *

Hugo Hamilton was born in 1953 of Irish-German parentage. He grew up with three languages—Irish, English, and German—and his fiction often works to suture these cultures into points of intersection. In particular, Hamilton is concerned both to make sense of the collapse of Communism in Eastern Europe, as epitomized by the fall of the Berlin Wall, and to understand the ''New Ireland'' and the cultural meanings of its trading outsider status for inclusion in the global marketplace.

In his novel *The Last Shot*, Hamilton takes on the final days of the Nazi regime and interweaves their chaos with a parallel narrative of the collapse of the Berlin Wall in 1989 and the promise of German reunification. The first narrative thread, set in 1945, centers around Franz Kern, a radio technician for the Wehrmacht, and Bertha Sommer, a civil secretary, who had been stationed in Laun, Czechoslovakia, and are fleeing after the surrender to return to Germany. The second plot line is related in the first person by an unnamed American who finds himself inexplicably drawn to Germany. Foregoing matriculation at an American university, he opts to study in Dusseldorf, where he begins an affair with a young German woman, which continues after she marries another man and bears a child with Down's syndrome. In an act eerily reminiscent of Nazi eliminations, the narrator, his mistress, and her husband eventually collaborate, ''in an act of mercy,'' to cut short the child's agony when he develops leukemia. Hamilton braids these two narratives together with an oedipal quest, as it becomes plain that the American narrator is in fact the son of Bertha Sommer and that his obsession is to locate the precise day, indeed hour, of the Wehrmacht's withdrawal from Czechoslovakia. Like so much contemporary German fiction, Hamilton's novel takes care to complexify each character, refusing to give anyone a free and clear conscience and to suggest that, as a moral figure, Germany signifies ''something that everybody secretly wants and openly denies.''

Hamilton also explores the years immediately following the fall of the Wall in *The Love Test*, but here he adds a specifically Irish contrast, as a cynical West German woman takes as her lover a hapless Irishman onto whom she projects the seductive scent of Otherness. By juxtaposing Continental affluence, jadedness, and spiritual emptiness with this Irish Otherness, Hamilton suggests that cultural identity is a play of signifiers that both glamorizes and subjugates the subaltern.

In his more recent novels, Hamilton ventures into detective fiction and, at the same time, undertakes close, if sarcastic, scrutiny of modern Ireland, whose biggest growth industry is crime. In *Sad Bastard*, the sequel to Hamilton's *Headbanger*, Dublin Garda (that is, policeman) Pat Coyne enters psychotherapy and therein encounters what he calls ''cartoon psychology,'' familiar to critics of self-help culture as platitudes masquerading as wisdom. In the tradition of hard-boiled detectives, as crafted by writers like Raymond Chandler, Coyne is full of pithy one-liners, and the Coyne novels succeed most as black comedy.

—Michele S. Shauf

HAMILTON, Jane

Nationality: American. **Born:** Oak Park, Illinois, 13 July 1957. **Education:** Carleton College, B.A. 1979. **Family:** Married Robert Willard in 1982; two children. **Career:** Apple farmer, 1979—; freelance writer, 1982—. Lives in Rochester, Wisconsin. **Awards:** Ernest Hemingway Foundation award (PEN American Center), 1989. **Agent:** c/o Doubleday Publishers, 1540 Broadway, New York, New York 10036, U.S.A.

PUBLICATIONS

Novels

The Book of Ruth. New York, Ticknor & Fields, 1988; published in England as *The Frogs Are Still Singing,* London, Collins, 1989.
A Map of the World. New York, Doubleday, 1994.
The Short History of a Prince: A Novel. New York, Random House, 1998.
Disobedience: A Novel. New York, Doubleday, 2000.

* * *

Jane Hamilton is a best-selling author whose novels deal primarily with the varieties of pain. She gives voice to exceptionally dimensional characters, and renders ordinary and extreme hardship alike with a moving and wholesome realism.

In 1982, on her way to the promise of a job in the New York publishing industry, Hamilton stopped off in rural Wisconsin where she has remained. Her plots grow out of this environment—unremarkable and yet, like every place with human entanglements, extraordinary in every way. Hamilton has described herself as ''an anthropologist in a foreign country,'' and her novels are studies of emotional territory.

In her first novel, *The Book of Ruth*, Hamilton maps the dreary life of the emotionally abused Ruth Grey, who, like all of her protagonists, searches for meaning in an apparently irrational universe. What distinguishes Hamilton's fiction from other novelists who examine this kind of existential pain, however, is the fact that her characters nonetheless manage to find meaning and grace—even eking out pleasure and a measure of pride. Ruth recounts her life in rural Illinois as a story about dignity, and Hamilton's attention to detail vivifies both Ruth's hardship and resilience. The novel received the 1989 PEN/Hemingway Foundation award for best new novel, and it was selected by Oprah Winfrey for her TV book club in 1996.

Hamilton's next book, *A Map of the World*, is also a domestic narrative set in the Midwest. Inspired by a drowning accident at her son's day-care center, Hamilton tells the story of Howard and Alice Goodheart who, the author suggests, are victims of the provincial prejudice that prevents people from embracing difference. The farming Goodhearts are received with a chill by their suburban neighbors, except for one friendly couple, Dan and Theresa Collins. When the youngest Collins child drowns in the Goodheart pond, Alice blames herself for the death. Then, later, she is accused by a boy of sexual abuse in her capacity as a part-time school nurse. The book has been praised for Hamilton's characterization of a broad range of characters—from women locked in jail to little children, each with a history—and for its belief that ''a map of the world'' is indeed possessable.

Hamilton continues this biographical approach to fiction in her third novel, *The Short History of a Prince*, which recounts the history of Walter McCloud, first as a young boy who loves Tchaikovsky and dreams of being a dancer, then as a homosexual teenager growing up in 1970s, and finally as a man returning home and confronting his memories of pain and loss. Once again, Hamilton's themes are family and friendship, cruelty and redemption, and yet in this novel she also considers the contours of artistic ambition and failure, as Walter must acknowledge the limits of his talent.

—Michele S. Shauf

HANLEY, Clifford (Leonard Clark)

Pseudonym: Henry Calvin. **Nationality:** British. **Born:** Glasgow, Scotland, 28 October 1922. **Education:** Eastbank School, Glasgow. Conscientious objector in World War II. **Family:** Married Anna E. Clark in 1948 (died 1990); one son and two daughters. **Career:** Reporter, Scottish Newspaper Services, Glasgow, 1940–45; sub-editor, *Scottish Daily Record,* Glasgow, 1945–57; feature writer, *TV Guide,* Glasgow, 1957–58; director, Glasgow Films Ltd., 1957–63; columnist, Glasgow *Evening Citizen,* 1958–60; television critic, *Spectator,* London, 1963. Visiting professor, Glendon College, York University, Toronto, 1979–80. **Awards:** Oscar award, 1960, for *Seawards the Great Ships.* **Member:** Close Theatre Management Committee, Glasgow, 1965–71, Inland Waterways Council, 1967–71, and Scottish Arts Council, 1967–74; vice-president, 1966–73, and president, 1974–77, Scottish PEN; Scottish chairman, Writers Guild of Great Britain, 1968–73. **Agent:** Curtis Brown, 162–168 Regent Street, London W1R 5TB, England. **Address:** 35 Hamilton Drive, Glasgow G12 8DW, Scotland.

PUBLICATIONS

Novels

Love from Everybody. London, Hutchinson, 1959; as *Don't Bother to Knock,* London, Digit, 1961.
The Taste of Too Much. London, Hutchinson, 1960.
Nothing But the Best. London, Hutchinson, 1964; as *Second Time Round,* Boston, Houghton Mifflin, 1964.
The Hot Month. London, Hutchinson, and Boston, Houghton Mifflin, 1967.
The Red-Haired Bitch. London, Hutchinson, and Boston, Houghton Mifflin, 1969.
Prissy. London, Collins, 1978.
Another Street, Another Dance. Edinburgh, Mainstream, 1983; New York, St. Martin's Press, 1984.

Novels as Henry Calvin

The System. London, Hutchinson, 1962.
It's Different Abroad. London, Hutchinson, and New York, Harper, 1963.
The Italian Gadget. London, Hutchinson, 1966.
The DNA Business. London, Hutchinson, 1967.
A Nice Friendly Town. London, Hutchinson, 1967.
Miranda Must Die. London, Hutchinson, 1968; as *Boka Lives,* New York, Harper 1969.
The Chosen Instrument. London, Hutchinson, 1969.
The Poison Chasers. London, Hutchinson, 1971.
Take Two Popes. London, Hutchinson, 1972.

Plays

The Durable Element (produced Dundee, Scotland, 1961).
Saturmacnalia, music by Ian Gourlay (produced Glasgow, 1965).
Oh for an Island, music by Ian Gourlay (produced Glasgow, 1966).
Dick McWhittie, music by Ian Gourlay (produced Glasgow, 1967).
Jack o'the Cudgel (produced Perth, 1969).
Oh Glorious Jubilee, music by Ian Gourlay (produced Leeds, 1970).
The Clyde Moralities (produced Glasgow, 1972).

Screenplays: *Seawards the Great Ships,* 1960; *The Duna Bull,* 1972.

Television Plays: *Dear Boss,* 1962; *Down Memory Lane,* 1971; *Alas, Poor Derek,* 1976.

Poetry

Rab Ha': The Glasgow Glutton. Glasgow, General District Libraries, 1989.

Other

Dancing in the Streets (autobiography). London, Hutchinson, 1958.
A Skinful of Scotch (travel). London, Hutchinson, and Boston, Houghton Mifflin, 1965.
Burns Country: The Travels of Robert Burns. Newport, Isle of Wight, Dixon, 1975.
The Unspeakable Scot. Edinburgh, Blackwood, 1977.
Poems of Ebenezer McIlwham. Edinburgh, Gordon Wright, 1978.
The Biggest Fish in the World (for children). Edinburgh, Chambers, 1979.
A Hypnotic Trance. Edinburgh, BBC Scotland, 1980.
The Scots. Newton Abbot, Devon, David and Charles, and New York, Times, 1980.
Another Street, Another Dance. Edinburgh, Mainstream, 1983.
Glasgow: A Celebration. Edinburgh, Mainstream, 1984.
The History of Scotland. London, Hamlyn, and New York, Gallery, 1986.
The Sheer Gall, with Willie Gall. Edinburgh, Mainstream, 1989.
Gall in a Day's Work, with Willie Gall. Edinburgh, Mainstream, 1989.

*

Clifford Hanley comments:

(1972) *Dancing in the Streets,* my first published book, was written at the suggestion of my publisher, who wanted a book about the city of Glasgow. At the time I thought it a rather pedestrian recital of childhood memories and was taken aback by its critical and commercial success (it is still used as background reading in schools of social studies and urbanology). My first novel, *Love from Everybody,* written previously but published later, was frankly intended as a light entertainment, to make money, and was later filmed as *Don't Bother to Knock.* Having then retired from journalism, I wrote what I considered my first serious work, *The Taste of Too Much,* as a study of ''ordinary'' adolescence, without crime and adventitious excitement, and it may well be my most successful book in the sense of fully achieving the author's original conception. In the subsequent novels under my own name, I think my intention was to look at some areas of life—a businessman's troubles, the family situation, the agonies of work in the theater—simply in my own way, without reference to fashionable literary conceptions. I have often been surprised when people found the novels "funny" because their intention was serious; but an author can't help being what he is. I do see the human condition as tragic (since decay and death are the inevitable end), but I don't distinguish between comedy and tragedy. Funerals can be funny too, and life is noble and absurd at the same time. I also insist on distinguishing between seriousness and solemnity, which are opposite rather than similar. On looking back, I realize that the tone of the novels tends to be affirmation rather than despair. This may be a virtue or a fault, or an irrelevance—a novelist should probably leave such judgments to critics and simply get on with what he must do. Maybe they also betray some kind of moral standpoint of which I was unconscious. This was explicit, in fact, in my first professionally produced play, *The Durable Element,* which was a study of the recurrent urge to crucify prophets. It was also deliberate in *The Chosen Instrument,* a pseudonymous Henry Calvin ten years later, in which a contemporary thriller mode was used to do a sort of feasibility study on the New Testament mythology. (The intention was so well disguised that no critic noticed it).

But I suppose cheerfulness keeps breaking through. I am an entertainer as well as novelist, and the two may be compatible. My first commandment as a writer is not at all highfalutin. It is Thou Shalt Not Bore. *A Skinful of Scotch* is an irreverent guide to one man's Scotland and was written for fun. So, originally, were the Henry Calvin thrillers. I enjoy reading thrillers and I adopted the pen-name simply to feel uninhibited. The thriller too is a morality, but the morality is acceptable only if it has character and pace. These are not intellectual mysteries but tales of conflict between good and evil. My later work for the theater was exclusively devoted to calculated entertainment and I am glad that people were actually entertained. I find now that I see life in more somber terms, but whether this will show in future novels is hard to tell. It may even be a temporary condition.

(1991) Self-assessment has always struck me as a futile exercise, in the sense that we can study a bug through a microscope, but we can't study the microscope through itself. I wrote my novels for fun or from internal compulsion (the two are the same, maybe) but have always seen myself as an entertainer, so they were intended for the reader's fun, which could include laughter, fear, enlightenment, puzzlement, and any other response.

They are not bad, probably. I did feel I hit the target with *The Taste of Too Much* (a committee title I don't like too much) in picturing the pangs of teenage love. School pupils agreed, especially girls, and it seems nothing has changed in 30 years. *Nothing But the Best* was partly stolen from life, and when I myself was widowed in 1990 I was interested in how my own responses followed those of the hero. *Another Street, Another Dance* was compulsive. The heroine, Meg, came into my mind fully formed, I was back in the time and place of my autobiographical first book *Dancing in the Streets.* It went onto the typewriter at the rate of 4,000 to 7,000 words a day with no hesitation because Meg was in the room with me. A very strange experience.

The Henry Calvin thrillers were entirely for fun, and I can only hope readers have shared it. (Odd, how many Scottish writers have hidden under pseudonyms). Henry was my father's name, and I picked Calvin because in these light tales virtue would triumph over vice, and to hell with some of the grim realities.

Not sure if I'll produce any more. I am now lazy, and comfortably fixed—a serious disincentive to work. But I am being nagged by an idealistic young New Yorker on a voyage of discovery through working-class and academic Glasgow, and I fear I shall have to let him right into the brain to dictate his misadventures and revelations. He is taking over, and I mildly resent that, but life is real and life is earnest, and the gravy is our goal, still.

* * *

Humor is never far away from the prose writings of Clifford Hanley. Although it is not officially a work of fiction and is based largely on his childhood experiences, his autobiographical study *Dancing in the Streets* gives the best clue to his literary technique. Partly, its success was due to Hanley's ability to realize the sharp and witty cadences of Glasgow patois; partly, too, it was his by no means dispassionate discovery of objective gaiety in a city in which it is not a common commodity. But the main reason for the book's place as Hanley's seminal work was his ability to work himself and his own comic experiences into a punchy and furiously paced narrative. Thus, when he came to write his first novel, *Love from Everybody,* he not only confirmed his competence to write with wit and humor about people and places, but he also gave notice that in his future fiction his persona was never going to be far absent from his writing.

This gift is seen to good advantage in *The Taste of Too Much,* a sensitive study of adolescence clearly based not only on his own experiences in Glasgow but also on his observations of the lives of young people in the city during the late 1950s. (Hanley was then working as a journalist for a Glasgow newspaper). Once again, as in *Dancing in the Streets,* the central theme is of a clever boy who is about to make good in the world, but in this instance, Peter Haddow, the intelligent and sensitive teenager, has to come face-to-face with a reality that is not always comic. The pinpricks of parental coexistence, an exasperating older sister, a ghoulish younger one, and an outrageous Aunt Sarah make young Peter's life miserable at times, yet shining like a candle in a wicked world is the gleam of his first love for the fabulous Jean Pynne. Although lightly written, *The Taste of Too Much* perceptively records Peter Haddow's adolescent feelings, and its modern council-estate setting marks it as a precursor of the later Scottish school of proletarian romanticism.

In his subsequent novels it became obvious that although Hanley had not lost his comic touch he was striving too hard to achieve his humorous effects. *The Red-Haired Bitch,* with its promising plot combining historical romance and modern reality, is superficially treated, Hanley being unable to sustain the historical motif of Mary Queen of Scots and the *realpolitik* of Glasgow's gangland. An earlier novel, *The Hot Month,* suffered from similar flaws with Hanley treating the Scots Calvinist ethos in comic fashion before plunging on to an attempt at analysis.

Hanley found his touch again in *Another Street, Another Dance* which takes a panoramic view of Glasgow from the troubled years of the Depression and Red Clydeside to the events of World War II and the beginning of the end of the city's great industrial supremacy. Much of the action is seen through the eyes of the family of Meg Macrae, a young girl from the western islands of Scotland who has come to terms with the big city and all its associated problems. Through her we come face to face with the reality of spiritual and physical poverty, drunkenness, wretched housing conditions, bad schooling, and furtive sex. Her triumphant ability to rise above those problems and to overcome a series of harrowing domestic disasters without ever losing grasp of her essential femininity gives the book its main theme and provides the backbone to Hanley's narrative, yet it is his sure ear for Glasgow dialogue and his compassion for all of the characters—good and bad—which finally beguile the reader.

Hanley has also written several modest detective novels under the mischievous pseudonym of Henry Calvin; but he is at his most successful when he remains in Glasgow, a city which nourishes his fiction and provides him with a realistic backdrop, and whose people offer unfailingly witty patterns of speech.

—Trevor Royle

HANNAH, Barry

Nationality: American. **Born:** Meridian, Mississippi, 23 April 1942. **Education:** Mississippi College, Clinton, B.A. 1964; University of Arkansas, Fayetteville, M.A. 1966, M.F.A. 1967. **Family:** Divorced; three children. **Career:** Member of the Department of English, Clemson University, South Carolina, 1967–73; writer-in-residence, Middlebury College, Vermont, 1974–75; member of the Department of English, University of Alabama, University, 1975–80; writer for the director Robert Altman, Hollywood, 1980; writer-in-residence, University of Iowa, Iowa City, 1981, University of Mississippi, Oxford, 1982, 1984, 1985, and University of Montana, Missoula, 1982–83. **Awards:** Bellaman Foundation award, 1970; Bread Loaf Writers Conference Atherton fellowship, 1971; Gingrich award (*Esquire*), 1978; American Academy award, 1979; Award in Fiction, Mississippi Institute of Arts and Letters, 1994. **Address:** c/o Houghton Mifflin Company, 2 Park St., Boston, Massachusetts 02108, U.S.A.

PUBLICATIONS

Novels

Geronimo Rex. New York, Viking Press, 1972.
Nightwatchmen. New York, Viking Press, 1973.
Ray. New York, Knopf, 1980; London, Penguin, 1981.
The Tennis Handsome. New York, Knopf, 1983.
Power and Light. Winston-Salem, North Carolina, Palaemon Press, 1983.
Hey Jack! New York, Dutton, 1987.
Boomerang. Boston, Houghton Mifflin, 1989.
Never Die. Boston, Houghton Mifflin, 1991.
High Lonesome. New York, Atlantic Monthly Press, 1996.

Short Stories

Airships. New York, Knopf, 1978; London, Vintage, 1991.
Two Stories. Jackson, Mississippi, Nouveau Press, 1982.
Black Butterfly. Winston-Salem, North Carolina, Palaemon Press, 1982.
Captain Maximus. New York, Knopf, 1985.
Bats Out of Hell. Boston, Houghton Mifflin/Seymour Lawrence, 1993.

Uncollected Short Stories

''Sources Agree Rock Swoon Has No Past,'' in *Harper's* (New York), June 1986.

Other

In Honor of Oxford at One Hundred and Fifty. Grenada, Mississippi, Salt-works, 1987.

*

Critical Studies: *Barry Hannah* by Mark J. Charney, New York, Twayne, 1992; *Barry Hannah: Postmodern Romantic.* Baton Rouge, Louisiana State University Press, 1998.

* * *

Barry Hannah's favored form is the monologue, his subject matter the grotesqueries of American life. Hannah's work includes incidents of beheading, a car wreck in the upper branches of an oak tree, a man who saves himself from drowning by balancing on the tip of a car aerial, a walrus's sexual attack on a woman who is having an affair with her nephew, and a drowned man who jump starts himself using a bus battery. ''But that's farfetched, and worse than that, poetic, requiring a willing suspension of disbelief along with a willing desire to eat piles of air sausage,'' complains a character in *Nightwatchmen* while trying to make sense of a senseless death. A reader must bring along this willingness when reading Hannah.

Geronimo Rex, Hannah's first novel, is a long song of remembrance, an ode to southern adolescence, his discoveries of music and women and firearms and, perhaps most importantly, the extra spark style can give to life. Style is very important to Hannah's characters; this and endurance are the virtues they admire and aspire to. Style is also a large element in Hannah's writing: in *Geronimo Rex* impressionistic sentences that at first seem a beginning writer's excesses grate against the coming-of-age context, stylize the bar-stool braggart tone of voice: ''I felt very precise in the oily seat; I was a pistol leaking music out of its holster.'' Far from being excesses the mature Hannah would weed out, sentences such as these (what Thomas McGuane admiringly referred to as Hannah's ''moon-landing English'') come to dominate the later works, from *Airships* on.

In the stories collected in *Airships* much of the traditional connective tissue of setting and exterior atmosphere is absent, leaving us with thick, nervous monologues by emotionally damaged men and women with a lot of style. Even the Civil War stories (which are enough alike to suggest Hannah may once have planned a Civil War novel) are narrated by characters with a jaded, violent sensibility identical with that of Hannah's characters from a hundred years later—particularly those with some involvement in the Vietnam War in their past. (Vietnam and the Civil War thread through much of Hannah's work.) Sentences such as ''Levaster did not dream about himself and French Edward, although the dreams lay on him like the bricks of an hysterical mansion,'' mix southern gothic with an updated ''hardboiled dick'' tone, sometimes moving past intelligibility into a private impressionistic flow. At other times this same mix produces beautiful straight-to-the-heart images: ''There is a poison in Tuscaloosa that draws souls toward the low middle.'' Plots are sketchy here, short portraits or sketches of fragmented lives. Characters, as in much of the work that follows, tend to stand or sit around listlessly, or to strike poses that accentuate their stylized speeches.

The title character in the short novel *Ray* is hardly a character at all, serving for the most part as a kind of tuning fork adjusted to the pitches of certain kinds of misery, those that reflect his own. Dr. Ray is a drinker, an adulterer, and perhaps a little too free with his drug prescriptions. Dr. Ray was a pilot during the Vietnam War, and has begun confusing this experience with what he knows of the Civil War. Others living the low middle life around Dr. Ray get ahead or fall, but his yearnings are too huge or too vague, too subject to change, and he remains stalled in a stasis of half-hearted healing, sex, and war memories.

The Tennis Handsome was expanded from a story in *Airships*. The title character, French Edward, sustains brain damage when he is nearly drowned trying either to save or to kill his mother's lover, who is also his old tennis coach. French Edward is still able to continue his career as a tennis pro through the Svengali-like attentions of Levaster, an unsavory old friend who likes to shoot people with a gun loaded with popcorn. The story version ends with everyone admiring, even taking solace in, French Edward's mindless grace and endurance, his perfect second of ''blazing'' serve. In the novel French Edward phases in and out, sometimes shocking himself into lucidity, writing poetry, finding religion, and generally frustrating everyone around him. Despite its brevity *The Tennis Handsome* seems to sprawl.

Captain Maximus, Hannah's second story collection, is even more spare, more knife-edged than *Airships*. Again these vignettes are filled with people consumed by yearning, but devoid of hope. Only in ''Idaho,'' an ode to the late poet Richard Hugo which captures some of the poet's own style, and in ''Power and Light,'' a reflection on the travails of working women, does Hannah's tone lighten at all, and only marginally.

Standing apart from his other works is Hannah's second novel, *Nightwatchmen.* While the novel's grotesqueries outnumber those of the other novels, it is a much more emotional, caring work. The writing here is much less stylized, and conflicts are not kept at a callous distance. Hannah's other works are plotted concentrically or in parallel lines, with groups of characters having some experience in common rather than sharing some common experience; only in *Nightwatchmen* do lives truly intersect in any significant way. The primary narrator, Thorpe Trove, is open and vulnerable, concerned for the people around him. He spends two years solving the mysteries of who knocked a half dozen people unconscious, and who then beheaded two nightwatchmen. When Thorpe records the stories of the ''innocent'' parties involved it becomes clear that they care only for their own fears and defenses. In the end the whodunit aspect is overshadowed by the realization of how much the other characters have in common with The Knocker and The Killer.

Mississippi State Press published *Boomerang* and *Never Die* in 1991, which was quickly followed by *Bats out of Hell,* a collection of stories that brings with it the same flair for the grotesque as *Airships.* Reviews of the collection were mixed, but given that the reader agrees to bring along a generous willingness to suspend disbelief, there is much to enjoy. Again, the Civil War provides the setting when the Confederate soldiers win the Union troops by playing Tchaikovsky in the title story, ''Bats out of Hell Division.''

The War in Vietnam also recurs as a shaping force in Hannah's short pieces. For example, in ''I Taste Like a Sword,'' which appeared in *The Oxford American,* a character named Fagmost pukes at football games ''but smiling.'' When he is dragged off by policeman, we see a glimpse of him that calls to mind the 1960s in the United States: ''... him all wet in his lumpy flowered shirt and dirty beard.'' The narrator tells us that the veteran ''... had a good four year war behind [him] and was carried down the street by a flock of children on Memorial Day.''

The usual monologue is delivered by a waiter whose sense of humor saves him from the start. He speaks of his father: ''... now I realize he might have been interesting although something about my devoted apathy in my teens wouldn't let me like him.'' By the end of the story, we have seen through his eyes and find him endearing, worthy of the same compassion as Flannery O'Connor's flawed characters. His father, a helicopter technology expert who was exposed to poisonous gas during the war, cries out on his deathbed, ''God bless war otherwise the pestilent hordes rising up to level us. There you'd really have your flat plains.'' Hannah's work continues to be ''farfetched and worse than that, poetic,'' yet the vision seems more tender.

—William C. Bamberger, updated by Loretta Cobb

HANNON, Ezra

See HUNTER, Evan

HARRIS, Mark

Nationality: American. **Born:** Mark Harris Finkelstein in Mount Vernon, New York, 19 November 1922. **Education:** The University of Denver, B.A. in English 1950, M.A. in English 1951; University of Minnesota, Minneapolis, Ph.D. in American Studies 1956. **Military Service:** Served in the United States Army, 1943–44. **Family:** Married Josephine Horen in 1946; one daughter and two sons. **Career:** Reporter, *Daily Item,* Port Chester, New York, 1944–45, *PM,* New York, 1945, and International News Service, St. Louis, 1945–46; writer for *Negro Digest* and *Ebony,* Chicago, 1946–51. Member of the English Department, San Francisco State College, 1954–68, Purdue University, Lafayette, Indiana, 1967–70, California Institute of the Arts, Valencia, 1970–73, Immaculate Heart College, Los Angeles, 1973–74, and University of Southern California, Los Angeles, 1973–75; professor of English, University of Pittsburgh, 1975–80. Since 1983 professor of English, Arizona State University, Tempe. Fulbright Professor, University of Hiroshima, 1957–58; visiting professor, Brandeis University, Waltham, Massachusetts, 1963. **Awards:** Ford grant, for theater, 1960; American Academy grant, 1961; Guggenheim fellowship, 1965, 1974; National Endowment for the Arts grant, 1966. D.H.L.: Illinois Wesleyan University, Bloomington, 1974. **Member:** San Francisco Art Commission, 1961–64; U.S. Delegate, Dartmouth Conference, Kurashiki, Japan, 1974. **Address:** Department of English, Arizona State University, Tempe, Arizona 85287, U.S.A.

Publications

Novels

Trumpet to the World. New York, Reynal, 1946.

City of Discontent: An Interpretive Biography of Vachel Lindsay, Being Also the Story of Springfield, Illinois, USA, and of the Love of the Poet for That City, That State, and That Nation, by Henry W. Wiggen. Indianapolis, Bobbs Merrill, 1952.

The Southpaw: by Henry W. Wiggen: Punctuation Inserted and Spelling Greatly Improved. Indianapolis, Bobbs Merrill, 1953.
Bang the Drum Slowly, by Henry W. Wiggen: Certain of His Enthusiasms Restrained. New York, Knopf, 1956.
A Ticket for a Seamstitch, by Henry W. Wiggen: But Polished for the Printer. New York, Knopf, 1957.
Something about a Soldier. New York, Macmillan, 1957; London, Deutsch, 1958.
Wake Up, Stupid. New York, Knopf, 1959; London, Deutsch, 1960.
The Goy. New York, Dial Press, 1970.
Killing Everybody. New York, Dial Press, 1973.
It Looked Like For Ever. New York, McGraw Hill, 1979.
Lying in Bed. New York, McGraw Hill, 1984.
Speed. New York, Fine, 1990.
The Tale Maker. New York, Fine, 1994.

Short Stories

The Self-Made Brain Surgeon, and Other Stories. Lincoln, University of Nebraska Press, 1999.

Uncollected Short Stories

''Carmelita's Education for Living,'' in *Esquire* (New York), October 1957.
''Conversation on Southern Honshu,'' in *North Dakota Quarterly* (Grand Forks), Summer 1959.
''Hi, Bob!,'' in *Arizona Quarterly* (Tuscon), Summer 1986.
''Titwillow,'' in *Michigan Quarterly Review* (Ann Arbor), Summer 1986.
''Flattery,'' in *Sequoia* (Stanford, California), Winter 1988.

Plays

Friedman & Son (produced San Francisco, 1962). New York, Macmillan, 1963.
The Man That Corrupted Hadleyburg, adaptation of the story by Mark Twain (televised, 1980). Published in *The American Short Story 2,* edited by Calvin Skaggs, New York, Dell, 1980.

Screenplays: *Bang the Drum Slowly,* 1973.

Television Plays: *The Man That Corrupted Hadleyburg,* 1980; *Boswell for the Defence,* 1983 (UK); *Boswell's London Journal,* 1984 (UK).

Other

Mark the Glove Boy; or, The Last Days of Richard Nixon (autobiography). New York, Macmillan, 1964.
Twentyone Twice: A Journal (autobiography). Boston, Little Brown, 1966.
Public Television: A Program for Action, with others. New York, Harper, 1967.
Best Father Ever Invented: The Autobiography of Mark Harris. New York, Dial Press, 1976.
Short Work of It: Selected Writing. Pittsburgh, University of Pittsburgh Press, 1979.
Saul Bellow, Drumlin Woodchuck. Athens, University of Georgia Press, 1980.
Diamond: Baseball Writings of Mark Harris. New York, Fine, 1994.
Editor, *Selected Poems,* by Vachel Lindsay. New York, Macmillan, 1963; London, Collier Macmillan, 1965.
Editor, with Josephine and Hester Harris, *The Design of Fiction.* New York, Crowell, 1976.
Editor, *The Heart of Boswell.* New York, McGraw Hill, 1981.

*

Manuscript Collection: University of Delaware Library, Newark.

Critical Studies: *Mark Harris* by Norman Lavers, Boston, Twayne, 1978.

Mark Harris comments:

(1972) I have written eight novels. I think that a constant line travels through them. I didn't know this was happening while it was happening, but I can see it now, looking back after a quarter of a century since my first novel was published.

They are about the writer. That is, if you will, they are about the artist. Which is to say, if you will, they are about the one man against his society and trying to come to terms with his society, and trying to succeed within it without losing his own identity or integrity.

My novels are always very carefully written. Since hard work makes the writing look easy, there exist stupid reviewers and critics who think I (and others) just slam these writings out. My books are all constructed with great care. Nothing is missing from any of them in the way of plot. I forget nothing.

Of course, although I am spiritually at the center of my novels (every novel is mainly about one man), I am disguised as poet or baseball player or professor or historian. I am always a minority person in some sense, either because I am fictionally left-handed or, most recently, gentile in a Jewish milieu. (My first book was about a black man in a white milieu). I don't know why this is so. I believe that it is most deeply the result of being a Jew, but it may be attributable to other things I am not fully aware of. Maybe I was just born that way. It is a mystery.

Subject and theme: sometimes these aren't really stated in the works, and people feel disappointed. They want to know what they shouldn't: where does the author stand? In my heart, if not always dogmatically in my books, I stand for human equality and peace and justice.

I also stand for writing well: I don't believe that good ends can come of false or shoddy or hasty means. Books must be beautiful so that the world is put into a mood of beauty. Books mustn't merely *say* but must, on the other hand, *exist* as beauty.

I am opposed to the reduction or paraphrase of works of art. Thus I feel that I may on this page already have written more than I should.

* * *

Mark Harris's fiction and autobiography share several themes: the problems of racism and racial justice, the dilemma of violence and pacifism, the price of individualism and the forms of democracy and social justice. His work is dominated by genial comedy, a gentle optimistic view of man's possibilities and capacities, and Harris has pursued his own life through his fiction. His journal-autobiographies *Mark the Glove Boy* and *Twentyone Twice* complement fictionalized self-portraits like pitcher-author Henry Wiggen (*The Southpaw, Bang the Drum Slowly, A Ticket for a Seamstitch*), boxer-novelist-teacher

Lee Youngdahl (*Wake Up, Stupid*), soldier-pacifist Jacob Epstein (*Something about a Soldier*) and historian-diarist Westrum (*The Goy*).

Harris's novels depict individuals in pursuit of themselves, discovering through self-analysis, experience, and observation who they are and what their lives mean. His first novel, *Trumpet to the World,* follows a black man through self-discovery and self-education to his rejection of war and violence and his attempts to reach the world through writing. He suffers poverty, hatred, and violence but also discovers friendship and love. Through determination and courage, he overcomes dehumanizing conditions to become fully alive, a fully functioning man. The baseball tetralogy (*The Southpaw, Bang the Drum Slowly, A Ticket for a Seamstitch, It Looked Like For Ever*) describes the career of Henry W. Wiggen, a young man who succeeds in big-league baseball. In a Lardneresque style, Wiggen writes the journal of his maturity as an athlete and a man. Wiggen grapples with the mysteries of love, the problem of hatred and violence, becomes reconciled with the finality of death. Each story shows Wiggen's growth, mentally and spiritually, and his progress down a road to self-understanding and reconciliation. Overtly a comedy of athletics and folk-hero rambunctiousness, the four books also form a study of pacifism, love and justice.

Something about a Soldier turns explicitly to the problems of violence and nonviolence which appear in the earlier novels. In it Jacob Epp (Epstein) discovers the importance of his identity, the meaning of love and loyalty, and the relationship between violence and justice. A young, very bright, but naive recruit, Jacob rejects the Army and the war (World War II), militantly works for justice and equality for black people and begins to understand love and friendship. He rejects death for life, war for peace, goes AWOL, and through meditation in prison comes to self-reconciliation.

In *Wake Up, Stupid* Harris uses the epistolary form to follow a crisis of insecurity in the life of a man who is successful as an athlete, teacher, and writer. Lee Youngdahl, during a lull in artistic creativity, takes up letter-writing to occupy his imagination. Comic crises of his fantasy life involve all his friends and enemies and lead him to a final understanding of his needs and desires, the sources of his imagination. *Lying in Bed* continues Harris's exploration of marital comedy through the viewpoint of Lee Youngdahl. Older and wiser in the ways of love and literature, Youngdahl extends his imaginative self-analysis and reviews his love affairs, real and fictive, as he tries to defend his virtuous monogamy and his need for varied romance.

The Goy continues the theme of self-discovery. In it, Westrum, a midwestern gentile who has married an eastern Jew, pursues his identity through a massive, life-long journal. He comes to understand, through the journal, his relationship with the Jews in his life, his father's virulent anti-semitism, his own obsession with history, his relationship with his son, his wife, and his mistress. The past, through his journal and his study of history, ultimately explains his present.

In *Killing Everybody* Harris explores opposing passions of love and rage, life-giving and death. The novel deals with the madness of the world and of individuals caught up in its madness. It studies revenge and charity, physical love and sexual fantasy, a dialectic skillfully developed as a complex dance between four central minds. The story moves more deeply into the roots of modern psychic life than Harris's earlier fiction, and he confronts a massive theme—civilization and its discontents.

All of Mark Harris's fiction is comic in conception, and sports and games are at the center of the work, especially the social games which are the substance of comedy of manners. Lee Youngdahl, in *Wake Up, Stupid,* analyzes American literature in a statement epitomizing Harris's own work:

> What is it that thrusts Mark Twain and Sherwood Anderson into one stream, and Henry James into another? ... It has so much to do with a man's early relationship to the society of boys and games—that miniature of our larger society of men and business, with its codes and rules, its provision for imagination within these rules, with winning, losing, timing, bluffing, feinting, jockeying, with directness of aim and speech and with coming back off the floor again.

Harris's fiction is solidly within this tradition, which translates social games into comedy, a comedy which explains our secret lives more clearly than any social or psychological theory. *Speed* shows his talents to less advantage: the story is a confusing tale of two brothers, one of whom (nicknamed ''Speed'') has a painful stammer. The other, the narrator, suggests that he may have pushed Speed off of a table when he was baby, thus perhaps causing his lifelong stutter. Eventually these and other misfortunes visited on Speed by his brother lead to his disappearance, and the narrator ends up wondering what happened to him. Much stronger are the tales in *The Self-Made Brain Surgeon.* The title story, for instance, concerns a grocer who fancies himself a psychologist, and dispenses harebrained advice to the unwary. Throughout the volume, readers will find many of the ingredients most appreciated in Harris's work, from baseball to comedy to criticism of social injustice.

—William J. Schafer

HARRIS, (Theodore) Wilson

Nationality: British. **Born:** New Amsterdam, British Guiana, now Guyana, 24 March 1921. **Education:** Queen's College, Georgetown. **Family:** Married 1) Cecily Carew in 1945; 2) Margaret Whitaker in 1959. **Career:** Government surveyor in the 1940s, and senior surveyor, 1955–58, Government of British Guiana; moved to London in 1959. Visiting lecturer, State University of New York, Buffalo, 1970; writer-in-residence, University of the West Indies, Kingston, Jamaica, and Scarborough College, University of Toronto, 1970; Commonwealth Fellow in Caribbean Literature, Leeds University, Yorkshire, 1971; visiting professor, University of Texas, Austin, 1972, and 1981–82, University of Mysore, 1978, Yale University, New Haven, Connecticut, 1979, University of Newcastle, New South Wales, 1979, and University of Queensland, St. Lucia, 1986; Regents' Lecturer, University of California, Santa Cruz, 1983. Delegate, National Identity Conference, Brisbane, and Unesco Symposium on Caribbean Literature, Cuba, both 1968. **Awards:** Arts Council grant, 1968, 1970; Guggenheim fellowship, 1973; Henfield fellowship, 1974; Southern Arts fellowship, 1976; Guyana fiction prize, 1987; Premio Mondello International award, 1992. D.Litt.: University of the West Indies, 1984; University of Kent, Canterbury, 1988. **Address:** c/o Faber and Faber Ltd., 3 Queen Square, London WC1N 3AU, England.

PUBLICATIONS

Novels

Palace of the Peacock. London, Faber, 1960.
The Far Journey of Oudin. London, Faber, 1961.
The Whole Armour. London, Faber, 1962.
The Secret Ladder. London, Faber, 1963.
Heartland. London, Faber, 1964.
The Eye of the Scarecrow. London, Faber, 1965.
The Waiting Room. London, Faber, 1967.
Tumatumari. London, Faber, 1968.
Ascent to Omai. London, Faber, 1970.
Black Marsden: A Tabula Rasa Comedy. London, Faber, 1972.
Companions of the Day and Night. London, Faber, 1975.
Da Silva da Silva's Cultivated Wilderness, and Genesis of the Clowns. London, Faber, 1977.
The Tree of the Sun. London, Faber, 1978.
The Angel at the Gate. London, Faber, 1982.
Carnival. London, Faber, 1985.
The Guyana Quartet. London, Faber, 1985.
The Infinite Rehearsal. London, Faber, 1987.
The Four Banks of the River of Space. London, Faber, 1990.
Resurrection at Sorrow Hill. London and Boston, Faber, 1993.
The Carnival Trilogy. London, Faber, 1993.

Short Stories

The Sleepers of Roraima. London, Faber, 1970.
The Age of the Rainmakers. London, Faber, 1971.

Poetry

Fetish. Privately printed, 1951.
The Well and the Land. Georgetown, Magnet, 1952.
Eternity to Season. Privately printed, 1954; revised edition, London, New Beacon, 1979.

Other

Tradition, The Writer, and Society: Critical Essays. London, New Beacon, 1967.
History, Fable, and Myth in the Caribbean and Guianas. Georgetown, National History and Arts Council, 1970; Wellesley, Massachusetts, Calaloux Publications, 1995.
Fossil and Psyche (lecture on Patrick White). Austin, University of Texas, 1974.
Explorations: A Selection of Talks and Articles, edited by Hena Maes-Jelinek. Aarhus, Denmark, Dangaroo Press, 1981.
The Womb of Space: The Cross-Cultural Imagination. Westport, Connecticut, Greenwood Press, 1983.
The Radical Imagination: Lectures and Talks, edited by A. Riach and M. Williams. Liège, Belgium, Université de Liège, 1992.
Selected Essays of Wilson Harris, the Unfinished Genesis of the Imagination, introduced and edited by A.J.M. Bundy. New York, Routledge, 1999.

*

Manuscript Collections: University of the West Indies, Mona, Kingston, Jamaica; University of Texas, Austin; University of Indiana, Bloomington; University of Guyana, Georgetown.

Critical Studies: *Wilson Harris: A Philosophical Approach* by C.L.R. James, Port of Spain, University of the West Indies, 1965; *The Novel Now* by Anthony Burgess, London, Faber, and New York, Norton, 1967, revised edition, Faber, 1971; essay by John Hearne, in *The Islands in Between* edited by Louis James, London, Oxford University Press, 1968; *Wilson Harris and the Caribbean Novel* by Michael Gilkes, Trinidad and London, Longman, 1975; *Enigma of Values* edited by Kirsten Holst Petersen and Anna Rutherford, Aarhus, Denmark, Dangaroo Press, 1975; *The Naked Design: A Reading of Palace of the Peacock,* Aarhus, Denmark, Dangaroo Press, 1976, and *Wilson Harris,* Boston, Twayne, 1982, both by Hena Maes-Jelinek; *West Indian Literature* edited by Bruce King, London, Macmillan, 1979; ''The Eternal Present in Wilson Harris's *The Sleepers of Roraima* and *The Age of the Rainmakers*'' by Gary Crew, in *World Literature Written in English* (Arlington, Texas), Autumn 1980; ''Limbo, Dislocation, Phantom Limb'' by Nathaniel Mackey, in *Criticism* (Detroit), Winter 1980; *Wilson Harris and the Modern Imagination: A New Architecture of the World* by Sandra E. Drake, Westport, Connecticut, and London, Greenwood Press, 1986; *The Literate Imagination: Essays on the Novels of Wilson Harris* edited by Michael Gilkes, London, Macmillan, 1989; *Wilson Harris: The Uncompromising Imagination* edited by Hena Maes-Jelinek, Aarhus, Kangaroo Press, 1991.

Theatrical Activities: Actor: **Television**—*Da Silva da Silva,* 1987.

Wilson Harris comments:

(1972) *Palace of the Peacock* through *The Guyana Quartet* and successive novels up to *The Sleepers of Roraima* and *The Age of the Rainmakers* are related to a symbolic landscape-in-depth—the shock of great rapids, vast forests and savannahs—playing through memory to involve perspectives of imperiled community and creativity reaching back into the Pre-Columbian mists of time.

I believe that the revolution of sensibility of defining community towards which we may now be moving is an extension of the frontiers of the alchemical imagination beyond an *opus contra naturam* into an *opus contra ritual.* This does not mean the jettisoning of ritual (since ritual belongs in the great ambivalent chain of memory; and the past, in a peculiar sense, as an omen of proportions, shrinking or expanding, never dies); but it means the utilization of ritual as an ironic bias—the utilization of ritual, not as something in which we situate ourselves absolutely, but as an unraveling of self-deception with self-revelation as we see through the various dogmatic proprietors of the globe within a play of contrasting structures and anti-structures: a profound drama of consciousness invoking contrasting tones is the variable phenomenon of creativity within which we are prone, nevertheless, to idolize logical continuity or structure and commit ourselves to a conservative bias, or to idolize logical continuity or anti-structure and commit ourselves to a revolutionary bias. Thus we are prone to monumentalize our own biases and to indict as well as misconceive creativity. A capacity to digest as well as liberate contrasting figures is essential to the paradox of community and to the life of the imagination.

* * *

With the publication in 1990 of *The Four Banks of the River of Space,* Wilson Harris completed a trilogy of novels which began with *Carnival* and continued through *The Infinite Rehearsal.* Although each book involves different characters and locations, when taken together, they form a complex revision of three crucial texts of Western Culture: *The Odyssey, The Divine Comedy,* and *Faust.* This is the culmination of a process which began with Harris's first novel, *Palace of the Peacock,* published thirty years earlier, and has continued through twenty-six volumes of fictional prose, criticism and verse.

Like Blake, Harris is a visionary, and his work is the complex literary expression of a vision which offers redemptive hope. For Harris, creativity is an intrinsic value in all the forms taken by the expressions of the intuitive imagination. Harris's prose is not seductively mimetic, like that of a realist novel. Rather, it demands concentrated attention as it works through continual disclosures of its own ambivalence. For example, the opening of *Palace of the Peacock* seems to describe a character on horseback ''approaching at breakneck speed.'' A shot rings out, the man falls dead and a second man approaches (an unnamed ''I''). The narrative seems straightforward, but close scrutiny of Harris's language reveals ambivalent meanings. The word ''breakneck'' suddenly suggests that the man has been hanged, not shot, and the noise of the gunshot may be the sound of the trapdoor dropping. Harris puns repeatedly on ''I''/''eye'' and brings together ''one dead seeing eye'' and ''one living closed eye'' to suggest that the contemplative man of vision and the unimaginative man of action are not absolute types but only aspects of a complex wholeness, wherein no individual has absolute authority. Harris extends this notion radically in the *Carnival* trilogy, where cultural archetypes like Ulysses are seen to be no longer viable as the property of any single culture, but demand to be shared among cultures globally.

Thus the journey upriver into the rainforests of Guyana which forms the narrative ''line'' of *Palace* is better understood as a prismatic perspective which reveals the ''characters'' as parts of a vast, interrelated family. They are the representatives of numerous cultures, scattered from pole to pole by the processes of imperialism and colonialism. Though they are symbolic, the symbolism is unreliable and inconstant.

The strategy of Harris's novels is therefore to draw hope from a narrative which would seem to be linear and closed by opening it up to historical and geographical dimensional senses and formal experimentation. Although ostensibly ''set'' in South America, *Palace* is as much an inquiry into the nature of language and literary form as it is a story of conquistadors striking out for El Dorado. Indeed, the forbidding opacities and dazzling visions of the Guyanese rainforests seem sometimes to act metaphorically for Harris's written English, its adamantine immediacy and allusive depths. The name of the principal character, Donne, echoes that of the late Renaissance poet who stands at the end of the medieval world and at the beginning of the modern, at the point where colonial expansion began. Harris is hopefully signaling an equally transitional period. He addresses the questions of the dissolution of personal identity and ''the open wound of human history'' in ways which are significant not only in terms of ''Caribbean literature'' or ''post-colonial literature,'' but rather in terms of modern literature in English.

The three novels which follow *Palace* are thematically distinct as they deal with slavery and indenture on the rice plantations, the imposition of law on frontier society and finally the rise of the modern state. But throughout *The Guyana Quartet,* themes and characters from past and present meet and mingle with each other. The space between the hinterland of forest and the cultivated coastal areas is shifting, just as language is a vast repository of unarticulated expression, an ''enabling'' or ''womb-like space.'' As Harris has said, ''The human person has very deep resources. We tend to live our lives on the surface and eclipse those deep and incredible resources. It happens on the individual as well as on the cultural level.''

After the *Quartet,* Harris embarked upon a further cycle of novels beginning with *Heartland,* whose main character vanishes into the jungle (as Harris's own stepfather did), leaving only fragments of letters and notes. *The Eye of the Scarecrow, The Waiting Room, Tumatumari,* and *Ascent to Omai,* delve further into questions about the condition of irretrievable absence and loss. Yet for Harris, even the most dreadful conditions are intricately and indissolubly linked to processes of change which might reveal a further regeneration of possibility. Such regeneration is never glib or easy. But it is this motivating and empowering sense which Harris works through, as catastrophe and deprivation is understood to be in a difficult but actual relationship with emergent reality. Two volumes of short stories were followed by *Black Marsden,* subtitled ''A Tabula Rasa Comedy,'' and set mainly in Scotland. Harris recognized in Scotland and in Scottish literature an implicit quality of diverse cultural and linguistic layers which corresponded with his understanding of the Caribbean, a country whose people were both exploiters and exploited, both a tributary and a backwater of empire. In *Black Marsden,* he takes a recognizable motif from Scottish fiction (the Devil as familiar tempter) and loads it with the unfamiliar depths of his vision. The following novels continued this process in Mexico, London, and later through the *Carnival* trilogy, in which the philosophical understanding of the relations between absence and presence, possession and loss, paradise, purgatory, and hell, is presented in fictional terms with diamond clarity and refractive depth.

With *Resurrection at Sorrow Hill,* Harris returned to motifs first used in the *Quartet,* grafting a highly complex set of observations and poetic myths onto the framework of a story with at least some roots in realism. Because the tale is set in an insane asylum located in the hinterlands of Guyana, it becomes possible to include all kinds of historical figures, using characters who believe themselves to *be* those people: Socrates, Montezuma, Leonardo, Karl Marx. The people outside the asylum are hardly more stable than the ones within, and Harris throws them together in a web of conflicting relationships.

Harris's peculiar distinction among modern novelists is threefold. He imagines in a complex dynamic and changing condition aspects of that condition which are normally held to be separate and static. He understands that imaginative act to be a radical departure from normal imaginative procedures, which are frequently run along familiar lines. And he embodies this in a major and invigorating sequence of novels which break down the rigidities of the form as drastically as they reconfirm potential in the protean forms of humanity.

—Alan Riach

HARRISON, Jim

Nationality: American. **Born:** James Thomas Harrison in Grayling, Michigan, 11 December 1937. **Education:** Michigan State University, East Lansing, B.A. in comparative literature 1960, M.A. in comparative literature 1964. **Family:** Married Linda King in 1959;

two daughters. **Career:** Assistant professor of English, State University of New York, Stony Brook, 1965–66. Lives in Michigan. **Awards:** National Endowment for the Arts grant, 1967, 1968, 1969; Guggenheim fellowship, 1969. **Agent:** Robert Datilla, 233 East 8th Street, New York, New York 10028. **Address:** Box 135, Lake Leelanau, Michigan 49653–0135, U.S.A.

Publications

Novels

Wolf. New York, Simon and Schuster, 1971; London, Flamingo, 1993.
A Good Day to Die. New York, Simon and Schuster, 1973; London, Flamingo, 1993.
Farmer. New York, Viking Press, 1976; London, Flamingo, 1993.
Legends of the Fall (novellas). New York, Delacorte Press, 1979; London, Collins, 1980.
Warlock. New York, Delacorte Press, and London, Collins, 1981.
Sundog: The story of an American foreman, Robert Corvus Strang, as told to Jim Harrison. New York, Dutton, 1984; London, Heinemann, 1985.
Dalva. New York, Dutton, 1988; London, Cape, 1989.
The Woman Lit by Fireflies (three novellas). Boston, Houghton Mifflin, 1990; London, Weidenfeld and Nicolson, 1991.
Julip. Boston, Houghton Mifflin/Seymour Lawrence, and London, Flamingo, 1994.
The Road Home. New York, Atlantic Monthly Press, 1998.
The Beast God Forgot to Invent: Novellas. New York, Atlantic Monthly Press, 2000.

Uncollected Short Stories

''Dalva: How It Happened to Me,'' in *Esquire* (New York), April 1988.

Poetry

Plain Song. New York, Norton, 1965.
Locations. New York, Norton, 1968.
Walking. Cambridge, Massachusetts, Pym Randall Press, 1969.
Outlyer and Ghazals. New York, Simon and Schuster, 1971.
Letters to Yesenin. Fremont, Michigan, Sumac Press, 1973.
Returning to Earth. Ithaca, New York, Ithaca House, 1977.
Selected and New Poems 1961–1981. New York, Delacorte Press, 1982.
The Theory and Practice of Rivers. Seattle, Winn, 1986.
The Theory and Practice of Rivers and New Poems. Livingston, Montana, Clark City Press, 1989.
After Ikky'u and Other Poems. Boston, Shambhala, 1996.
The Shape of the Journey: New and Collected Poems. Port Townsend, Washington, Copper Canyon Press, 1998.

Other

Natural World, with Diana Guest. Barrytown, New York, Open Book, 1983.
Just Before Dark: Collected Nonfiction. Livingston, Montana, Clark City Press, 1991.
Wolf (screenplay, with Wesley Strick). Columbia Pictures, 1994.
The Boy Who Ran into the Woods. New York, Atlantic Monthly Press, 2000.

*

Film Adaptations: *Legends of the Fall,* 1994.

Critical Studies: *Jim Harrison* by Edward C. Reilly. New York, Twayne Publishers, London, Prentice Hall, 1996.

* * *

A reviewer for the *Times* observed that Jim Harrison is ''a writer with immortality in him.'' Archivist Bernard Fontana, of the University of Arizona, has expressed his belief in the quality of Harrison's work in another way: ''To read Jim Harrison is to be tattooed.'' Harrison's early reputation was founded on four volumes of poetry. In 1971, his first novel, *Wolf,* was published. *Wolf* is the story of one man's quest for identity and freedom through the primal levels of nature and sex. The novel's themes and northern Michigan location drew critical comparisons to Ernest Hemingway's Nick Adams stories.

Two years after *Wolf, A Good Day to Die* appeared as a statement about the decline of America's ecological systems. In a blending of Edward Abbey's *The Monkey Wrench Gang* and Hemingway's *The Sun Also Rises,* readers are presented with three characters who are launched on a cross-country trek to blow up a dam and rescue the Grand Canyon. A modern day Tom Sawyer and Huck Finn and an earthy Becky Thatcher are faced with the bankruptcy of the American dream. The novel also illustrates the author's fascination with Native Americans and begins a thematic interest that is found in other novels.

Farmer is a *Lolita*-like account of a country school teacher coming to grips with middle age while caught between two love affairs—one with a nymphet student and the other with a widowed co-worker who was his childhood sweetheart.

Harrison's first three novels resulted in many attacks by critics who saw him as a stereotype of the Hemingway myth: a writer obsessed with the macho male activities of hunting, drinking, and manly sex. In later novels Harrison would confront these criticisms head-on.

After *Farmer,* Harrison entered into an unusual contract with the actor Jack Nicolson. For $15,000 in advance of writing and publication, Nicholson purchased half the film rights to Harrison's yet-to-be-written project. Harrison produced three novellas which were published in book form under the title of *Legends of the Fall.* The first novella, ''Revenge,'' is the story of a love affair between Cochran; an ex-fighter pilot; and Miryea, the wife of a Mexican gangster. ''The Man Who Gave Up His Name'' chronicles Nordstrom's divorce, his run-ins with the New York underworld and his attempt to form a new life built around a new identity. *Legends of the Fall* is an epic story that spans fifty years and tells the tale of William Ludlow and his three sons. The story is filled with beautiful characterizations and with great action from its beginning, when the brothers ride out to Calgary to join the Canadian army and fight in World War I; to its end, when Ludlow confronts Irish bootleggers who have come to kill one of his sons.

Published in 1981, *Warlock* parodies nearly everything for which critics had taken Harrison to task. Johnny Lundgren, a.k.a. Warlock, becomes a private detective after he loses his job as a foundation executive. Unable to handle women, earn the devotion of his dog or remember to load his pistol, he bumbles through a series of adventures on the behalf of a deranged physician. *Sundog,* subtitled ''The story of an American foreman, Robert Corvus Strang, as told to Jim Harrison,'' is a piece of fiction presented as a true tale. Strang recounts the story of his life, his several marriages and children, dozens of lovers, and his work on giant construction projects around the world.

Dalva, which was published in 1988, contains two stories: a tale of a middle-aged women's search for her out-of-wedlock child as well as her tribulations with her almost-boyfriend professor; and a story of her pioneer ancestor, an Andersonville survivor and naturalist whose diaries vividly tell of the destruction of the Plains Indian way of life by Anglo invasion.

The Woman Lit by Fireflies is a collection of three novellas. The first, ''Brown Dog'' is the comic memoir of an ex-Bible college student who loves to eat, drink, and chase women and his discovery of an Indian chief submerged in Lake Superior. ''Sunset Limited'' concerns a group of 1960s radicals who reunite to rescue an old friend held in a Mexican jail. ''The Woman Lit by Fireflies'' is the story of a woman who walks away from her husband at an Interstate Welcome Center near Davenport, Iowa and is a tale of transfiguration and discovery.

A complex work that recalls aspects of *Dalva*—not least by bringing in characters related to those in the earlier novel—*The Road Home* uses several narrators, takes place over wide stretches of time, and emphasizes the interdependent quality of all life. One of the central figures is John Wesley Northridge II, Dalva's grandfather, who is told by his granddaughter, ''When you tell me stories about your life, why do you always pretend you were such a nice person? … Everyone in town says you were the scariest man in the county …. So I wish you wouldn't just tell the good parts about yourself.'' The novel, as it unfolds, reveals much more than just the ''good parts,'' and does so with Harrison's usual masterful touch.

—Tom Colonnese

HARROWER, Elizabeth

Nationality: Australian. **Born:** Sydney, New South Wales, 8 February 1928. **Career:** Lived in London 1951–58; worked for the Australian Broadcasting Commission, Sydney, 1959–60; reviewer, Sydney *Morning Herald,* 1960; worked for Macmillan and Company Ltd., publishers, Sydney, 1961–67. **Awards:** Commonwealth Literary Fund fellowship, 1968; Australian Council for the Arts fellowship, 1974. **Address:** 5 Stanley Avenue, Mosman, New South Wales 2088, Australia.

Publications

Novels

Down in the City. London, Cassell, 1957.
The Long Prospect. London, Cassell, 1958.
The Catherine Wheel. London, Cassell, 1960.
The Watch Tower. London, Macmillan, 1966.

Uncollected Short Stories

''The Cost of Things,'' in *Summer's Tales 1,* edited by Kylie Tennant. Melbourne and London, Macmillan, and New York, St. Martin's Press, 1964.
''English Lesson,'' in *Summer's Tales 2,* edited by Kylie Tennant. Melbourne and London, Macmillan, and New York, St. Martin's Press, 1965.
''The Beautiful Climate,'' in *Modern Australian Writing,* edited by Geoffrey Dutton. London, Fontana, 1966.
''Lance Harper, His Story,'' in *The Vital Decade,* edited by Geoffrey Dutton and Max Harris. Melbourne, Sun, 1968.
''The Retrospective Grandmother,'' in *The Herald* (Melbourne), 1976.
''A Few Days in the Country,'' in *Overland* (Melbourne), 1977.

*

Critical Studies: ''The Novels of Elizabeth Harrower'' by Max Harris, in *Australian Letters* (Adelaide), December 1961; *Forty-Two Faces* by John Hetherington, Melbourne, Cheshire, 1962; ''Elizabeth Harrower's Novels: A Survey,'' in *Southerly* (Sydney), no. 2, 1970, and *Recent Fiction,* Melbourne, Oxford University Press, 1974, both by R.G. Geering; *The Directions of Australian Fiction 1920–1974* by D.R. Burns, Melbourne, Cassell, 1975; ''The Novels of Elizabeth Harrower'' by Robyn Claremont, in *Quadrant* (Sydney), November 1979; Nola Adams, in *Westerly* (Nedlands, Western Australia), September 1980; ''Deep into the Destructive Core'' by Frances McInherny, in *Hecate* (St. Lucia, Queensland), vol. 9, nos. 1–2, 1983; ''Down in the City: Elizabeth Harrower's Lost Novel'' by Rosie Yeo, in *Southerly* (Sydney), no. 4, 1990; ''The Watch Tower: Bluebeard's Castle'' by Deirdre Coleman, in *(Un)common Ground* edited by A. Taylor and R. McDougall, Bedford Park, South Australia, CRNLE, 1990.

* * *

An ideal introduction to Elizabeth Harrower's work is the short story ''The Beautiful Climate,'' since it provides a paradigm of her fictional universe. It is a world in which selfish men manipulate their women and material possessions in a vain attempt to achieve happiness; frustrated by their blind male egotism, they become subject to fits of smoldering violence and frequent relapses into bouts of alcoholism and morbid self-pity. The woman's role is to suffer, to pity, and to provide the innocent seeing eye for the narrative. In ''The Beautiful Climate'' the paranoiac male is Mr. Shaw, who secretly buys a holiday island, reduces his wife and daughter to domestic slavery there, then sells the place behind their backs. The consciousness that develops from innocent passivity to partial sad wisdom is the daughter's, who reflects her creator in turning from psychology to literature as a guide to truth. The same basic situations and characters recur throughout the novels; and the tormented relationship between father and daughter in this short story might seem to offer a psychological clue to the novelist's preoccupation with male domination.

In *Down in the City,* a very remarkable first novel, Harrower traces the disenchantment that follows when the heroine exchanges the empty security of her wealthy bay-side suburb in Sydney for the puzzling ups and downs of her husband's shady business world. In describing the characteristic claustrophobia of the flat-dwelling city wife, she succeeds wonderfully well in evoking the typical sights and sounds of Sydney and in establishing a connection between climate and states of mind. And the hero, who oscillates between his classy wife and his obliging mistress, reflects the conflicting drives and split personality of many an Australian business man.

What distinguishes Harrower's second novel, *The Long Prospect,* from all her others is that the malevolent main character is a woman not a man. But once again the viewpoint is through an innocent seeing eye; in this case, it is a child's. By the end of the novel, she has plumbed the seedy adult world to its depths. The scene in which four irredeemably corrupt adults spy on the 12-year-old and her middle-aged friend, transferring their own ''atmosphere of stealth'' onto the innocent pair, is only one of many pieces of superb psychological drama in this accomplished novel.

While the third novel, *The Catherine Wheel,* laudably attempts to extend the range of the fictional world by having its setting in London bed-sitter-land, it is a somewhat disappointing work that hardly prepares the reader for the splendid fourth novel, *The Watch Tower.* The conspicuous success in *The Watch Tower* lies in the creation of Felix Shaw, the Australian business man, who climaxes a series of similar portraits and shares the surname of the father in ''The Beautiful Climate.'' But equally subtle is the analysis of pity, through the contrasted characters of Shaw's two victims, who show that pity may enslave as well as ennoble (this a continuous preoccupation in the novels). Shaw's capriciousness, his bursts of petty pique and rage, his resentment at others' success, his dark nihilism, brutal aggression, unrecognized homosexuality and alcoholism, all point to a profound psychic disorder. But it is the novelist's triumph to suggest that this disorder is at least partly the product of a society that worships materialism and masculinity.

In most of her work, Harrower combines sharp observation of individual life with a searching critique of Australian society. Although she lacks the resilient vitality of such English novelists as Margaret Drabble, her vision of a male-dominated society is depressingly authentic. She has been highly praised and compared favorably with Patrick White, but her unflattering, somewhat drab and disenchanted view of Australian life is now winning her the wide local readership her work certainly deserves.

—John Colmer

HART, Veronica

See KELLEHER, Victor

HASLUCK, Nicholas (Paul)

Nationality: Australian. **Born:** Canberra, 17 October 1942; son of the politician and diplomat Sir Paul Hasluck. **Education:** The University of Western Australia, Nedlands, 1960–63, LL.B. 1963; Oxford University, 1964–66, B.C.L. 1966. **Family:** Married Sally Anne Bolton in 1966; two sons. **Career:** Lawyer, admitted to Supreme Court of Western Australia as barrister and solicitor, 1968. Deputy Chairman, Australia Council, 1978–82. **Awards:** *The Age* Book of the Year award, 1984. **Member:** A.M. (Order of Australia), 1986. **Agent:** Murray Pollinger, 222 Old Brompton Road, London SW5 0B2, England. **Address:** 14 Reserve Street, Claremont, Western Australia 6010, Australia.

Publications

Novels

Quarantine. Melbourne and London, Macmillan, 1978; New York, Holt Rinehart, 1979.

The Blue Guitar. Melbourne and London, Macmillan, and New York, Holt Rinehart, 1980.

The Hand That Feeds You: A Satiric Nightmare, photographs by the author. Fremantle, Western Australia, Fremantle Arts Centre Press, 1982.

The Bellarmine Jug. Ringwood, Victoria, Penguin, 1984.

Truant State. Ringwood, Victoria, Penguin, 1987; New York, Penguin, 1988.

The Country Without Music. Ringwood, Victoria, Viking, 1990.

The Blosseville File. Ringwood, Victoria, Penguin, 1992.

A Grain of Truth. Ringwood, Victoria, Penguin, 1994.

Short Stories

The Hat on the Letter O and Other Stories. Fremantle, Western Australia, Fremantle Arts Centre Press, 1978.

Poetry

Anchor and Other Poems. Fremantle, Western Australia, Fremantle Arts Centre Press, 1976.

On the Edge, with William Grono. Claremont, Western Australia, Freshwater Bay Press, 1980.

Chinese Journey, with C.J. Koch. Fremantle, Western Australia, Fremantle Arts Centre Press, 1985.

Other

Collage: Recollections and Images of the University of Western Australia, photographs by Tania Young. Fremantle, Western Australia, Fremantle Arts Centre Press, 1987.

Offcuts from a Legal Literary Life. Nedlands, University of Western Australia Press, 1993.

Editor, *The Chance of Politics*, by Paul Hasluck. Melbourne, Text Publishing, 1997.

*

Critical Studies: Review by Martin Seymour-Smith, in *Financial Times* (London), 15 June 1978; article by Helen Daniel, in *The Age Monthly Review* (Melbourne), December 1984; *Liars* by Helen Daniel, Ringwood, Victoria, Penguin, 1988.

* * *

Nicholas Hasluck's first novel, *Quarantine,* introduced the combination of intrigue, dark humour, and fable that have become characteristic of Hasluck's style. In an ominous, rundown hotel on the bank of the Suez canal, the passengers of a cruise ship are unaccountably held in isolation under the sinister charge of the proprietor Shewfik Arud and the dipsomaniac Dr. Magro. The exiles themselves are caught between the menacing Burgess and the moral hero of the story, David Shears, who loses his life through the moral cowardice of the narrator. Parallels with Camus's *La Peste* do not deny the individuality of Hasluck's brand of mordant absurdism.

The more restrained *The Blue Guitar,* unusually for an Australian novel, is concerned with commerce, and is set in a vividly-evoked urban jungle (recognisably Sydney). As a speculator, Dyson Garrick attempts to promote the inventor Herman's ''blue guitar'' that automatically creates music. His quest is idealistic (the title directs us to Wallace Steven's poem ''Things as they are are changed by the blue guitar'') but also tangled in the temptations of commercial exploitation, and this conflict leads to Garrick's own moral disintegration as he finally betrays his friend.

The Hand That Feeds You subtitled ''A Satiric Nightmare,'' turns to a science-fiction framework for its satirical fantasy of an Australia controlled by the trade unions and the mass media, where paid work has become taboo, tax evasion and social handouts the ideal. A product of New Right thinking of the early 1980s, the novel lacks the universality of *The Bellarmine Jug,* his most complex and assured novel to date.

The Bellarmine Jug explores the roots of Australian identity on both personal and social levels, using techniques from the spy thriller and a legal examination that probes each layer of truth to reveal alternative realities. In 1948, student unrest in the Grotius Institute, Den Haag, is linked to an attempt by the authorities to suppress evidence that the 1629 mutiny of the *Batavia* off Western Australia was led by the son of Grotius, codifier of international law and founder of the institute. The evidence has implications for the status of Grotius, the institute, and the relationship between authority and rebellion. As the mutiny is envisaged as leading to atrocities surrounding a Rosicrucian settlement of the Abrolhos islands, it is also conjecturally linked to the first white settlement of Australia. The plot moves between Holland, London, and Australia, implicating issues such as the British atomic tests in the Monte Bellow islands, and Australian involvement in Sukarno's independence movement, to question the nature of international law, human rights, and individual morality. Exploring these through a taut and compelling narrative, the novel rates amongst the finest Australian novels of the 1980s.

Truant State is set in Western Australia in the heady days of the 1920s and the depression of the 1930s. It is narrated by the young Jack Taverne, an immigrant from England, whose father becomes caught in the illusory hopes of the era. There is a vivid recreation of the conflict between the trades unions, and the reactionary West Guard secret society which sought seccession for Western Australia (the ''truant state'' of the title). A subtext involves D.H. Lawrence's *Kangaroo* which also draws on the Fremantle riots and the right-wing secret organisations. The novel, which shows Hasluck's characteristic interweaving of personal, social, and metaphysical issues, with detective intrigue, is remarkable for its regional evocation of the fictional Butler's Swamp and Western Australia between the wars. The short stories of *The Hat on the Letter O* show Hasluck's technical versatility, and they are interesting as background to the novels.

In his most recent fiction, *The Country Without Music, The Blosseville File,* and *A Grain of Truth,* Hasluck, like John O'Hara and William Faulkner, has created an imaginary territory through which to explore contemporary actuality. Blosseville and the Baie de Baudin, and the off-shore islands of Depuis and Gournay, provide a subtle and complex milieu through which to explore historical and political issues of Western Australia. *The Country Without Music* is set on the island of Gournay, the site of a penal colony founded by French Revolutionaries. The ruins of the ''panopticon'' prison—Jeremy Bentham's model of penal reform—and the preserved guillotine stand as the ambivalent ideals of rational justice on which the island's administrator tries to build a modern capitalist society. But it is ''without music'' (or soul), and at the climax the island folk interact violently with authority in the rituals of Carnival.

If that novel explores political justice within the role of history, Hasluck's most recent work, *A Grain of Truth* turns directly to issues of contemporary law, and the novel is set on the mainland in Blosseville. The central character, the lawyer Michael Cheyne, finds himself standing for human rights against the weight of apparent justice within the legal system. The novel, which has an optimistic ending, underlines Hasluck's conviction that life is a conflict between the structures of social order—exemplified by the law—and the anarchy that lies at the core of human experience. Hasluck has declared that it is the ''kind of quirky unpredictable exotic side of things'' beneath the rational surface that is the task of literature to explore. Hasluck continues to develop his highly individual vein of intelligent and inventive fiction.

—Louis James

HASSLER, Jon

Nationality: American. **Born:** Minneapolis, Minnesota, 30 March 1933. **Education:** St. John's University, B.A. 1955; University of North Dakota, M.A. 1961. **Family:** Married (divorced), two sons and one daughter; remarried. **Career:** High school teacher of English for ten years; faculty member, Bemidji State University and Brainerd Community College. Since 1980 writer-in-residence, St. John's University. **Awards:** Friends of American Writers Novel of the Year, 1978, for *Staggerford;* Guggenheim grant, 1980; Society of Midland Authors Best Fiction award, 1987, for *Grand Opening.* D.Litt.: Assumption College, Massachusetts, 1993; University of North Dakota, 1994; University of Notre Dame, 1996. **Address:** St. John's University, Collegeville, Minnesota 56321, U.S.A.

Publications

Novels

Staggerford. New York, Atheneum, and London, Deutsch, 1977.
Simon's Night. New York, Atheneum, and London, Deutsch, 1979.
The Love Hunter. New York, Morrow, and London, Weidenfeld and Nicolson, 1981.
A Green Journey. New York, Morrow, 1985; London, Allen, 1986.
Grand Opening. New York, Morrow, 1987.
North of Hope. New York, Ballantine, 1990.
Dear James. New York, Ballantine, 1993.
Rookery Blues. New York, Ballantine, 1995.
The Dean's List. New York, Ballantine Books, 1997.
Underground Christmas. Afton, Minnesota, Afton Historical Society Press, 1999.

Poetry

The Red Oak and Other Poems. Privately printed, 1968.

Short Stories

Keepsakes and Other Stories. Afton, Minnesota, Afton Historical Society Press, 1999.
Rufus at the Door and Other Stories. Afton, Minnesota, Afton Historical Society Press, 2000.

Other

Four Miles to Pinecone (for children). New York, Warne, 1977.
Jemmy (for children). New York, Atheneum, 1980.
My Staggerford Journal. New York, Ballantine Books, 1999.

*

Manuscript Collections: St. Cloud State University, St. Cloud, Minnesota.

Critical Studies: *An Interview with Jon Hassler* (includes bibliography), Minneapolis, Dinkytown Antiquarian Bookstore, 1990.

* * *

Until very recently, only one comprehensive essay had ever been published about Jon Hassler—by Andrew Greeley in a Catholic journal. Why this should be so is not greatly surprising. Hassler is a very traditional writer with exciting, real, complex, and intriguing subject matter. But his strengths are quiet and (on the surface) unremarkable. And he is not bold and audacious like so many of our writing personalities—like, say, Norman Mailer or Camille Paglia—and takes no overt political position. He is always present in his novels but he never identifies wholly with any of his major characters like Agatha McGee in *Staggerford* (his first novel) or Peggy Benoit in *Rookery Blues* (his most recent one). In fact, I would go so far as to say that although he is strongly attracted to characters like Agatha, Peggy, and Simon Shea, they don't much resemble him and often do things or take positions that he would probably not take himself. The only character he has created that is even remotely autobiographical is the young protagonist/observer of *Grand Opening,* Brendan Foster, whose father, like Hassler's, owns a grocery store in a small, rural Minnesota town called Plum.

Hassler's presence is subtle, quiet, and apparently unobtrusive. He is absorbed in what he is writing about and as indifferent to public recognition (as a persona) as Andrew Wyeth the painter. He does not take bold political positions, even though he sometimes seems obsessed with Church politics and the behaviors of the priests, sisters, and laypersons who people many of his novels. In some cases, he defuses potentially explosive conflicts by turning them into high comedy, as he does in *Staggerford,* with the confrontation between whites (or Anglos) and Native Americans, or in the strike action that takes place in *Rookery Blues.*

His four predominantly ''Catholic'' novels (*Simon's Night, A Green Journey, North of Hope,* and *Dear James*) more closely resemble the Barchester and distinctly Anglican novels of Anthony Trollope than they do the Catholic novels of Graham Greene (to whom he is sometimes compared). Like Trollope he is more fascinated with the political infighting and machinations of a huge and powerful Church that is in a state of transition than he is in the spiritual or mystical character of its clergy and laypeople. He is intrigued by the fact that laypeople like Agatha McGee and Simon Shea, both highly traditional Catholics, take vows and commitments more seriously than many of the clergy and are, in fact, ''better Catholics.'' Shea, for instance, in one of Hassler's very best novels, *Simon's Night,* remains faithful for twenty years, not so much to the woman whom he marries early and who runs off with one of his colleagues as to their marriage vows. He gives up a warm and passionate relationship with one of his students who has seduced him not because he doesn't love this young woman but because he regards his vows to his unfaithful wife, Barbara, as binding. And Agatha McGee, who, at sixty-seven and on the verge of retirement from her teaching position in a religious elementary school, is startled nearly out of her mind when she discovers that an older Irishman named James O'Hannon—with whom she has engaged in a long and deeply personal correspondence—is in fact a priest. This violates her whole conception of herself as a Catholic and her conception also of what it is proper—and sacred—for a priest to do and not do. Yet the power of that friendship and its personal if not sexual intimacy fuels the action of two novels, *A Green Journey* and *Dear James.*

In a radio interview, Hassler once said that he likes to challenge his protagonists. This means, first of all, that his characters are fully alive to him, as if they were actors in a repertoire company or simply real, breathing human beings. Sometimes, as with Agatha McGee and her friend, James O'Hannon, they are central to more than one novel, larger than that one canvas. They are fully alive to him but also creatures of his own imagination and in the end they challenge him—his creative ability to make them work convincingly in new contexts and sometimes highly complex plots.

As a mark of his traditional practice, Hassler never uses stream of consciousness and other techniques perfected by such early modernists as James Joyce, Virginia Woolf, and Dorothy Richardson, even though he regularly enters the minds and sensibilities of his protagonists. Nor does he use first person singular narrative as perfected by Mark Twain in *The Adventures of Huckleberry Finn* or the soliloquy familiar to readers of Melville's *Moby-Dick.*

What Hassler does use with increasing mastery and fluidity are three other mnemonic techniques: flashbacks, journal entries, and letters. He does this because he knows all too well that what a particular character does in the present is strongly conditioned by what he or she has done or believed in the past. In his most recent novel, *Rookery Blues,* he inserts five two- or three-page flashbacks (set in italics) at various and appropriate points in the novel to tell us crucial things—in a very funny way—about each of the five members of the Icejam Quintet, the jazz group that forms the heart and soul of the book from beginning to end. In *Staggerford,* he uses the sometimes extensive journal entries written by protagonist Miles Pruitt about his early love life, especially his attraction to Carla Carpenter, the high school girl whom his brother seduces. In *Dear James* (as the title suggests), he makes extensive and highly dramatic use of some of the letters that Agatha McGee writes to James O'Hannon (but only mails to him much later) and the letters that she has saved from him.

Traditionally, plot is character in action or, in Hassler's case, many characters in action. For a novel to succeed, the protagonist and other major characters must first of all be rich and interesting in themselves; second, the actions they are involved in should be at least worthy of that depth and flow from it. Thus Simon Shea, in *Simon's Night,* is both an excellent college professor and a strong, believing Catholic. As the novel opens, he has retired from his college position and commits himself to a weirdly comic nursing home because he feels he is losing his ability to remember anything significant and is thus ready to cash in his chips. The young female doctor who regularly visits that home immediately decides that Simon is too interesting and has too much to live for to give up and in essence put himself to sleep or to death. She engineers his reunion with his wife, Barbara, and the novel ends with their beginning life together anew.

That Hassler is fascinated by richly compelling individuals who have sacrificed themselves to principle of one sort or another is equally manifest in his two later Agatha McGee-James O'Hannon novels, *A Green Journey* and *Dear James,* both of which test Agatha's rigidly held Catholic principles; she, like Simon Shea, is forced by the external circumstances of her life and her age to compromise that rigidity. This compromise grows out of the depth and richness of Agatha's character, her resilience, and the fact that she acts finally out of a character that those rigidly held principles don't explain.

In *Rookery Blues,* his most complex, funniest, and most satisfying novel to date, he manages to control in every respect the five protagonists—each radically different from one another—who make up the Icejam Quintet: Victor Dash is a hotheaded labor organizer, who happens also to be an aptly hotheaded drummer in the quintet; Neil Novotny is a poor teacher and an obsessed but dreadful novelist, who thinks he is in love with Peggy Benoit; Leland Edwards is a conservative, mother-bound professor and opponent of the teachers' strike Dash foments, who is a superb jazz pianist; Connor is a good portrait painter obsessed with doing paintings of mothers and daughters, who is a bass player and in a dreadfully unhappy marriage; and Peggy Benoit herself is a beautiful music professor and blues singer, who falls in love with Connor and eventually succeeds in wresting Connor away from his marriage. Any one or two of these characters might well have been the subject of a novel because each is fully, comically, ironically developed, but their interreactions and their roles in the external tensions of Rookery State University together form a complex, comic, and believable series of actions.

What makes Hassler such an interesting and engaging novelist—and what will probably make him outlast all or almost all of his flashier contemporaries—is not just that he is unashamedly a traditional novelist but that he does so well what he does, that he involves the reader so deeply in his characters that no matter who we might be we really care about them, talk about them as if they were very real and interesting people. Limited, sometimes myopic, often obsessive, they work their slow and ironic ways through recognizable and familiar situations or even rather unlikely ones (like the relationship between Agatha McGee and James O'Hannon) as if they were familiar. We come to know many of his characters better than we know most people and even ourselves (sometimes). I suspect that Jon Hassler will come to be recognized as a major 20th-century novelist.

—C.W. Truesdale

HAUSER, Marianne

Nationality: American (originally French; granted U.S. citizenship, 1944). **Born:** Sreasbourg, Alsace, France, 11 December 1910. **Education:** University of Berlin; Sorbonne. **Family:** Married Frederic Kirshberger (divorced); one son. **Career:** Journalist, French and Swiss newspapers and periodicals; lecturer, Department of English, Queens College, New York, 1962–79; held various teaching positions, including positions at New York University and New School until 1988. **Awards:** Rockefeller grant; National Endowment for the Arts grant. **Agent:** Perry Knowlton, Curtis Brown, 1 Astor Pl., New York, New York, U.S.A. **Address:** 2 Washington Square Village, apt. 13-M, New York, New York 10012, U.S.A.

Publications

Novels

Monique. Zurich, n.p., 1934.
Shadow Play in India. Vienna, n.p., 1937.
Dark Dominion. New York, Random House, 1947.
The Choir Invisible. London, Gollancz, 1958; New York, McDowell Obolensky, 1959.
Prince Ishmael. New York, Stein and Day, 1963; London, Michael Joseph, 1964.
The Talking Room. New York, Fiction Collective, 1976.
The Memoirs of the Late Mr. Ashley: An American Comedy. N.p., Sun and Moon Press, 1986.
Me and My Mom. N.p., Sun and Moon Classics, 1993.

Short Stories

A Lesson in Music. N.p., 1964.

Uncollected Short Stories

"The Colonel's Daughter," in *Tiger's Eye,* March 1948.
"The Rubber Doll," in *Mademoiselle,* 1951.
"Mimoun of the Mellah," in *Harper's Bazaar,* 1966.
"The Seersucker Suit," in *Carleton Miscellany,* 1968.
"O-To-Le-Do," in *Parnassus,* 14(1).
"Weeds," in *Denver Quarterly,* 1983.
"It Isn't So Bad That It Couldn't Be Worse," in *City,* 9, 1984.
"Blatant Artifice," in *Hallwalls,* 1986.
"Heartlands Beat," in *Fiction International,* 1988.
"The Missing Page," in *Witness,* 1989.
"No Name on the Bullet," in *Fiction International,* 1991.
"Scandal at the Bide-a-Wee Nursing Home for Mature Seniors," in *Fiction International,* 1992.

*

Manuscript Collections: Florida University, Gainsville.

Marianne Hauser comments:
To write without compromise or an eye on the market.

* * *

Early on in Marianne Hauser's first major work, *Prince Ishmael*—an historical novel based on the legend of Caspar Hauser—the narrator observes, "I wasn't ready for reality black or white." This same inability to relate to a world of dizzying complexity and ambiguity through linguistic systems that reduce experience to simple binary categories is evident in all of Hauser's fiction; it also expresses Hauser's personal conviction that "reality" is a dynamic, multilayered process for which the conventions of traditional realism—with its empirical biases and emphasis on causal relationships and logic—are ill-equipped to represent. This conviction has resulted in a series of novels and stories that weave together dream and waking reality, the known and unknown, the perverse and banal, and the poetic and idiomatic into darkly humorous fables of great emotional power, uniqueness, and universal relevancy. Yet ironically enough it has been precisely the uniqueness and poetic intensity of Hauser's fiction that has thus far relegated her work to relative popular and critical obscurity—a situation that is almost certain to change as feminist and postmodern critics discover her works.

In a career that now spans some six decades, Marianne Hauser has published a total of eight books of fiction; these include an early novel written in German, *Shadow Play in India,* and seven subsequent English-language works: a story collection, *A Lesson in Music,* and five novels—*Dark Dominion, The Choir Invisible, Prince Ishmael, The Talking Room, Memoirs of the Late Mr. Ashley: An American Comedy,* and *Me and My Mom.* In the most extended and perceptive analysis of Hauser's work to date, Ewa Ziarek, writing in the Fall 1992 issue of *Contemporary Literature,* noted: "Marianne Hauser's fiction represents an interesting intersection between experimentation challenging literary conventions and feminist concerns. Significantly, both interests converge on the issue of articulating specifically feminine desires—sexual, reproductive, and linguistic." Yet, despite such recurrent themes—which have found their expression in remarkably rich, subtle, and evocative prose mannerisms—it would be a mistake to view her works solely or even primarily as feminist documents. Although several of her major novels—for example, *Me and My Mom* and *The Talking Room*—have been narrated by women and have focused on psychological issues peculiar to women's experiences, others have male narrators and can't be said to be specifically feminist in orientation. This isn't to deny the importance of Hauser's work from feminist perspectives—indeed, *The Talking Room* ranks with Marilynne Robinson's *Housekeeping* and Toni Morrison's *Beloved* as among the most significant and original feminist novels of the past 20 years; rather what needs to be stressed is that although Hauser's work has naturally always expressed viewpoints and concerns central to her own experiences as a woman, it has also consistently been concerned with expressing larger, more universal issues. Central to all her works, for example, has been an emphasis on human loneliness and the need for people to escape from isolation, understand their origins, and find erotic fulfillment. There is also a persistent fascination with epistemological and metaphysical issues—the role of dreams, fantasy, and language in constructing memory and our sense of the waking world; a suspicion of empiricism and linguistic categories and a corresponding appreciation of storytelling and personal reverie in making sense of our lives.

Despite such thematic commonalties, the language, style, and tone of her work has undergone significant transformations over the last five decades. The precise, almost classical prose of *Dark Dominion*—which depicts a strange, haunting relationship between a nondreaming New York psychiatrist, his wife (whom he wins when he analyzes her dreams), her obsessively devoted brother, and her lover—has loosened; and Hauser has increasing incorporated American idioms, slapstick, and absurdist humor. She has also been increasingly adventurous in devising experimental formal strategies suited for portraying her sense of the permeability of dream and waking reality. The obsessions explored in *Dark Dominion*—the role of the imagination in shaping one's response to life, the search for and discovery in the "dark dominion" of the unconscious as a multilayered space in which phantom and reality coexist to create the drama of the self, and the difficulty in inhabiting a coherent "self"— continue through her next two books, *The Choir Invisible,* which is set in a small town in the Midwest, and *Prince Ishmael,* a fictional account of the Caspar Hauser legend.

Her most recent novels, *The Talking Room, The Memoirs of the Late Mr. Ashley: An American Comedy,* and *Me and My Mom* all display a command of American lingoes and cultural references that range effortlessly from urban to rural, straight to gay, highbrow to lowbrow—all the voices a chorus of pathos, absurdity, lyricism, and beauty that sing the bittersweet song of the America Hauser found herself living when she took up permanent residency there beginning in 1937. From her earliest work, Hauser has explored how dreams, the unconscious, and the irrational affect our perception of the "real"; but with her last three novels (as well as her more recent short stories), this notion is no longer so much an element of "theme" but finds its expression as a fully integrated aspect of her style. Thus, to enter her recent fiction is to find oneself in a unsettling landscape where the strange becomes familiar and the familiar strange—a realm where people, events, and associations ebb and flow with the logic of dreams. Partly this effect comes from connections that make no rational sense but which are brought together by Hauser's ability to ground her fiction in details that are vivid and sensual; it arises too from the playfulness of her language and her willingness to let go of the linear in favor of something wilder and less predictable.

It was Hauser's 1976 novel, *The Talking Room,* where she first found a voice and a method uniquely her own. The plot of *The Talking Room* is as simple as it is outrageous. The book is narrated by B, a pregnant thirteen-year-old girl who is the daughter of a lesbian couple (her mother, V, and her lover J) who are living in a deserted neighborhood of New York City. Fearful of being forced by her "Aunt" J to have an abortion, B hides her pregnancy under the pretense of being fat and stays in her room. There she attempts to uncover the mystery of her origins (was she perhaps a test-tube baby?) by sifting through the many voices that drift up into her "talking room." These voices—which include those of her own imagination, the turbulent sounds of V and J arguing and reminiscing from downstairs, the funny and surrealistic chitchat of their eccentric friends, and the radio (which provides political and pop culture references)—combine to form what Ewa Ziarek described as a "polyphonic composition" that "makes it impossible to uncover the simplicity of origin in the maternal body." Ziarek goes on to note the ways that B's search for a matrilineal genealogy reinforces a metafictional critique of the "traditional idea of authorship as a conscious begetting, grounded in the intentionality of the author." This critique, in turn, links up to Hauser's ongoing presentation of the limitations of rationality and the ways that the search for one's self and one's origins are ultimately limited by the fact that the self is never a discrete entity but a plurality of different selves whose "essences" are themselves shifting perpetually in a state of transformation.

—Sinda Gregory

HAZZARD, Shirley

Nationality: American. **Born:** Sydney, New South Wales, Australia, 30 January 1931; became U.S. citizen. **Education:** Queenwood School, Sydney. **Family:** Married the writer Francis Steegmuller in

1963 (deceased 1994). **Career:** Staff member, Combined Services Intelligence, Hong Kong, 1947–48, United Kingdom High Commissioner's Office, Wellington, New Zealand, 1949–50, and United Nations Headquarters, New York (General Service Category), 1951–61. **Awards:** American Academy award, 1966; Guggenheim fellowship, 1974; O. Henry award, 1977; National Book Critics Circle award, 1981. **Address:** 200 East 66th Street, New York, New York 10021, U.S.A.

PUBLICATIONS

Novels

The Evening of the Holiday. New York, Knopf, and London, Macmillan, 1966.
People in Glass Houses: Portraits from Organization Life. New York, Knopf, and London, Macmillan, 1967.
The Bay of Noon. Boston, Little Brown, and London, Macmillan, 1970.
The Transit of Venus. New York, Viking Press, and London, Macmillan, 1980.

Short Stories

Cliffs of Fall and Other Stories. New York, Knopf, and London, Macmillan, 1963.

Uncollected Short Stories

''The Flowers of Sorrow,'' in *Winter's Tales 10,* edited by A.D. Maclean. London, Macmillan, and New York, St. Martin's Press, 1964.
''Forgiving,'' in *Ladies' Home Journal* (New York), August 1964.
''Comfort,'' in *New Yorker,* 24 October 1964.
''The Evening of the Holiday,'' in *New Yorker,* 17 April 1965.
''Out of Itea,'' in *New Yorker,* 1 May 1965.
''Nothing in Excess,'' in *New Yorker,* 26 March 1966.
''A Sense of Mission,'' in *New Yorker,* 4 March 1967.
''Swoboda's Tragedy,'' in *New Yorker,* 20 May 1967.
''Story of Miss Sadie Graine,'' in *New Yorker,* 10 June 1967.
''Official Life,'' in *New Yorker,* 24 June 1967.
''The Separation of Dinah Delbanco,'' in *New Yorker,* 22 July 1967.
''The Everlasting Delight,'' in *New Yorker,* 19 August 1967.
''Statue and the Bust,'' in *McCall's* (New York), August 1971.
''Sir Cecil's Ride,'' in *Winter's Tales 21,* edited by A.D. Maclean. London, Macmillan, 1975; New York, St. Martin's Press, 1976.
''A Long Story Short,'' in *Prize Stories 1977: The O. Henry Awards,* edited by William Abrahams. New York, Doubleday, 1977.
''A Crush on Doctor Dance,'' in *Winter's Tales 24,* edited by A.D. Maclean. London, Macmillan, 1978; New York, St. Martin's Press, 1979.
''Something You'll Remember Always,'' in *New Yorker,* 17 September 1979.
''She Will Make You Very Happy,'' in *New Yorker,* 26 November 1979.
''Forgiving,'' in *Ladies' Home Journal* (New York), January 1984.
''The Meeting,'' in *The Faber Book of Contemporary Australian Short Stories,* edited by Murray Bail. London, Faber, 1988.
''The Place to Be,'' in *Prize Stories 1988,* edited by William Abrahams. New York, Doubleday, 1988.
''In These Islands,'' in *New Yorker,* 18 June 1990.

Other

Defeat of an Ideal: A Study of the Self-Destruction of the United Nations. Boston, Little Brown, 1972; London, Macmillan, 1973.
Coming of Age in Australia (lectures). Sydney, Australian Broadcasting Corporation, 1985.
Countenance the Truth: The United Nations and the Waldheim Case. New York, Viking, 1990; London, Chatto and Windus, 1991.
Greene on Capri: A Memoir. New York, Farrar, Straus, Giroux, 2000.

*

Critical Studies: ''Patterns and Preoccupations of Love: The Novels of Shirley Hazzard'' by John Colmer, in *Meanjin* (Melbourne), December 1970; *Recent Fiction* by R.G. Geering, Melbourne, Oxford University Press, 1974; ''Shirley Hazzard: Dislocation and Continuity'' by Robert Sellick, in *Australian Literary Studies* (Hobart), October 1979; ''Shirley Hazzard Issue'' of *Texas Studies in Literature and Language* (Austin), vol. 25, no. 2, 1983.

* * *

Shirley Hazzard is a slow, painstaking writer who seems to have known where she was going in her art right from the beginning. Her first published work, the 10 stories in *Cliffs of Fall and Other Stories,* is like the rest of her fiction with the exception of *People in Glass Houses* in that it is concerned with the tensions, complications, and disappointments of adult sexual love. The stories involve doubles, triangles, and sometimes quadrilaterals of people caught up with one another in complex webs of relationships, the trails of which are traced out in the subtle, witty, biting prose that is Hazzard's trademark. Usually the stories are told from the perspective of the female protagonist and often, as is the case with much of Hazzard's fiction, they are set in a fairly recent past. The scenes range from England to the United States and in one case Switzerland. Sometimes they consist simply of observation of manners at some occasion or gathering—''The Party,'' ''The Weekend,'' ''The Picnic''—but almost invariably they are chronicles of pain and betrayal.

The Evening of the Holiday is a short novel, a simple and rather inconclusive account of a love affair between a woman named Sophie and an Italian, Tancredi, who is separated from his wife but cannot gain a divorce under Italian law, a situation that occurs in several of these stories. It is a tender, elegantly written book with a strong but rather cryptic sense of fatalism hanging over it. *People in Glass Houses* is a brilliantly funny and scathing collection of eight interrelated stories concerning an unnamed ''Organization'' which is transparently the United Nations, where Hazzard worked for a time. The stories are linked, not merely by the reappearance of several characters such as Mr. Bekkus, Clelia Kinglake, Swoboda, Rodriguez-O'Hearn, and others but by the repetition of the savage criticisms that the author offers in each story. In her view, the U.N. is characterized by petty and insensitive bureaucracy, a determination to squeeze out the individual and the gifted, an absence of personal feeling and a refusal to promote loyal and efficient, if limited, employees such as Swoboda and Dinah Delbanco. It is especially unfair in the last respect to women. Hazzard's interest in language itself, always strong in her fiction, has never been livelier or more intense than in this book and she constantly points to bureaucratic inertia, insensitivity, and finally lack of human feeling by concentrating on the way people use language. The interest surfaces early in the figure of Algie Wyatta, rebel, iconoclast, and therefore doomed, who collects contradictions in terms such as ''military intelligence,'' ''competent authorities'' and ''easy virtue.'' The egregious Mr. Bekkus is characterized in terms of his employment of jargon. The story ''The Flowers of Sorrow'' hinges around an important personage intruding a personal note into his speech— ''In my country ... we have a song that asks, Will the flowers of joy ever equal the flowers of sorrow''—and the diverse but almost always disparaging reaction to this on the part of his staff.

The Bay of Noon is again a short novel, set in Naples and dealing with the complex relationships worked out among four people from a perspective of some twelve or fifteen years later. The story is told in the first person by Jenny, an English girl sent to Italy as a translator, who becomes involved with Gioconda, her lover Gianni and a Scot named J.P. (Justin) Tulloch. Hazzard brings to her treatment of the familiar theme of love and its entanglements all the sophisticated techniques she has been steadily developing in her fiction and which culminate in her finest and most ambitious novel, *The Transit of Venus.* The language is packed with literary allusion. There are aggressively bracketed interpolations, such as a violent attack on the military. There is a flash forward to Tulloch's eventual death in a plane crash, a recurring event in Hazzard's fiction. It is an enjoyable but finally rather lightweight novel that has an uncharacteristic look of improvisation about its plot.

But Hazzard's masterpiece and the basis of her reputation is undoubtedly *The Transit of Venus.* A young Australian woman travels to England with her sister, has a relationship with a worthless man, is reduced to material poverty and emotional impoverishment, out of which she is rescued by a rich, liberal-minded, middle-aged American. However, the novel moves on to the deeply melancholy ending of the death of its heroine Caroline (Caro) Bell in an air crash and the post-fictive suicide of Ted Tice, the man she has finally realized she loved and was on the way to meet. The novel is about love and about truth, about the difference between those who love truly and those who exploit emotions for selfish ends. It is also about chance and the contingent, specifically the accident referred to in the title by which Australia came to be discovered by Captain Cook.

The motif of Venus itself becomes an important one in the novel, along with a number of others of which perhaps the most important is that of the shipwreck. Caro is indeed a child of Venus in that for her, love is a total commitment; it is part of her complete emotional honesty, her belief in the possibility of an excellence and distinction that are not necessarily related to any demonstrable achievement or worldly success but may consist solely in a life of constant personal integrity: ''the truth has a life of its own,'' she says. *The Transit of Venus* is an unfashionably romantic novel. Coupled with this, however, is the fact that in terms of structure and technique it is also ruthlessly calculating, even cold-blooded. This paradoxical combination has upset many of its critics. The novel is structured around an inferential method that makes heavy demands on the reader's ability to connect different events and personages, and demonstrates the author's almost lordly superiority over and distance from her material. Of these demands, the most important is the suicide of Ted Tice which, though mentioned explicitly early in the novel, takes place after its close and can be worked out by the reader only by carefully following a number of clues scattered carefully throughout its pages. However, the meticulous—sometimes almost too meticulous—craftsmanship of the novel and the elegance and subtle wit of the style are a delight and almost unique among contemporary Australian fiction writers.

—Laurie Clancy

HEALY, Dermot

Nationality: Irish. **Born:** Finea, County Westmeath, Ireland, 9 November 1947. **Family:** Married Anne Mari Cusack in 1974; two children. **Career:** Worked as laborer and insurance underwriter in England and Ireland; owner and editor, *Drumlin* magazine, 1978–79; director, Hacklers Drama group, 1980–81. **Awards:** Hennessy Literary Awards, 1974, 1976; Tom Gallan Award (Society of Authors), 1983; All-Ireland Athlone Award. **Agent:** c/o Allison & Busby Ltd., 6A Noel Street, London W1V 3RB, England.

Publications

Novels

Fighting with Shadows; or, Sciamachy. London and New York, Allison & Busby, 1984.
A Goat's Song. London, HarperCollins, 1993; New York, Viking, 1995.
Sudden Times. New York, Harcourt, 2000.

Short Stories

Banished Misfortune. London and New York, Allison & Busby, 1982.

Plays

Screenplays: *Our Boys,* 1979; *Interrogations* (also radio play), 1980.

Poetry

The Ballyconnell Colours. Loughcrew, Ireland, Gallery Press, 1992.
What the Hammer. Oldcastle, Ireland, Gallery Press, 1998.

Other

The Bend for Home (autobiography). New York, Harcourt Brace, 1987.
Contributor, *Soft Day,* edited by Sean Golden and Peter Fallon. Dublin, Wolfhound, 1977.
Contributor, *Paddy No More,* edited by William Vorm. Dublin, Wolfhound, 1978.
Contributor, *Firebird.* Harmondsworth, England, Penguin, 1982.
Contributor, *A Feast of Christmas Stories.* London, Macmillan, 1983.

* * *

Dermot Healy's first novel, *Fighting with Shadows*, is set in the rural border village of Fanacross, the midlands country between Northern Ireland and the Republic, during the renewal of the Troubles and the civil rights movements for Catholics in the 1960s and 1970s. No one else talks or thinks like the characters of this novel. If Healy's singular representation of human behavior wins belief, then every other novelist is wrong, or centuries of conflict in Ireland have produced a tribe for whom a different psychology and sociology is needed.

It is possible to evoke a story from this novel of forty-two chapters in eight parts. The extended family of Allens suffer. Joseph Allen's aunt was run down by a car, a murder more likely than an accident. His uncle George futilely searches with a gun for the car. Joseph's father was shot opening the door of their home, perhaps mistaken for his twin brother George; George disappeared into the South, returning only to clear his dead brother's name so that his widow can be compensated by the State.

Perhaps to get him clear of trouble, Joseph is sent to another uncle in the South. He works in their hotel which eventually fails because the Troubles ruin the easier atmosphere that it requires. When Joseph and his friend the hotel chef try to break up a fight, the chef is arrested; Joseph asks to accompany him to jail where he is beaten savagely, and made to confess to a misdemeanor to get rid of their attention. The novel closes on Joseph's mother receiving compensation by ignoring the advice of her lawyer to settle the case against the State (Frank Allen's killer was a part-time member of the UDR, in company with the Royal Ulster Constabulary [RUC]). They buy a house and move what is left of the family out of Fanacross.

No plot summary does justice to a novel, of course. The tone and sequence of narrative is skewed, lost. What happens in *Fighting with Shadows* violates no laws of probability. But Healy offers characters who think differently. There is some explanation at the beginning, perhaps to accommodate our customary psychological understanding. Fanacross is between North and South; there is a severe drought; even an improving economy in the South is named as cause of a greater questioning, and a greater consciousness.

In a chapter given over to letters, we read one that Joseph receives from Margaret, his cousin, describing his mother's distress. ''It was not your mother's sanity went but her memory. She sees things isolated, as they are, connected to nothing in the past, irreversibly severed from their fellows and therefore offered up obscene.'' Her perspicacity is in no way unusual among fellow characters. If it were not for their troubles, the book would read like *Nightwood:* a set-piece for poetic prose.

A Goat's Song is Healy's second novel, after ten years (he also writes short stories and poetry). Thirty-four chapters are distributed over four sections. ''Christmas Day in the Workhouse'' is the first section, which sees the way Jack Ferris's drinking frustrates his career as a playwright and his love for Catherine. He works off a fishing boat in the west of Ireland. His time on land is devoted to drink, not his plays or Catherine, except for making things between them worse. As the novel begins, Jack comes back to his cottage with a letter from Catherine, which says that she loves him and will rejoin him.

Their promise to each other is that they will grow old and sober together, but Jack can't keep the promise. Because Catherine knows he has broken it, she doesn't return. Jack embarrasses himself by repeatedly phoning her at the Dublin theatre which is rehearsing the play he wrote for her. At the end of this section Jack has finally taken himself to the hospital to dry out. He knows that his relationship is over, that once he writes about her, they can never get back together.

The novel offers no gimmick to prove it is Jack's own work, but the following sections tell the story he intends to write. We blame Jack in the first section, but that is not tragedy, which is what the novel's title seems to mean. The following sections begin by telling the story of Catherine and her family as Protestants from the North. Her father trained for the clergy, but couldn't preach. He joined the RUC to answer his sense of duty. His life provides an effective incentive to the reader to leave blaming behind. He is a serious family man, thoughtful, even scholarly. Yet when he is caught up in the early stages of the civil rights in Belfast (he is one of the constables imported into Belfast to increase security), he is surprised to see himself on television beating an old man with his truncheon.

We follow Catherine's early life in the North, and her family's gradual shift to the South. We learn more about her life than Jack's life. When it comes to her time with him, we get a different view from our first one. They are both drinkers, both unable to be constant to each other's love. When the novel closes in the present time of their difficult relationship breaking up, at a moment of unreasoning hope, blaming or accusing either of them is behind us now, replaced by our sorrow for them.

Sudden Times begins in Sligo. Oliver Ewing (Ollie) is a damaged narrator and central character, reminding an American audience of Faulkner's Benjy, but an Irish readership will think of McCabe's ''butcher boy.'' The source of Ollie's trouble is reflected in a series of flashbacks that gradually fill in, taking us back to London. He first shared a portakabin with his friend Marty Kilgallan, night-watching a construction area. Their life is an idyllic late (male) adolescence, drinking, partying, staying ''home'' to listen to music. But Marty is worried about having angered some toughs who run a protection racket in the construction industry. Eventually Ollie finds Marty's corpse in the back of his truck, disfigured with acid.

Ollie's brother Redmond arrives after Ollie has confronted Silver John, an employer of day laborers, with Marty's death. The first-person narration helps the reader to understand how Ollie allows himself to suspect Silver John yet find it necessary to work for him. Silver John's bodyguard gets into a fight with Redmond at a party. He returns to torch Redmond, burning himself as well. The novel closes on the trial, where the judicial system makes a fool of Ollie through cross-examination, turning what we have read as understandable decisions against him. One example: after Redmond is taken to the hospital, Ollie cleans up the flat, sickened by the traces of the violence. Yet the defense for Redmond's killer accuses Ollie of destroying evidence. All that we have to balance against Ollie's diminished being at the end of the book is the reconciliation with his father, narrated to us by Ollie early on before we understand the basis of their estrangement.

Although three novels in twenty years is less than his immediate peers in Irish fiction, Healy has so far produced original work without repeating himself. The prose style of his autobiographical *The Bend for Home* most closely resembles his first novel, which suggests that originality requires that he move further away from himself as subject.

—William A. Johnsen

HEATH, Roy A(ubrey) K(elvin)

Nationality: Guyanese. **Born:** British Guiana, now Guyana, 13 August 1926. **Education:** Central High School, Georgetown; University of London, 1952–56, B.A. (honours) in French 1956; called to the bar, Lincoln's Inn, 1964. **Family:** Married Aemilia Oberli; three children. **Career:** Treasury clerk, Georgetown, 1944–51; clerical worker, London, 1951–58; primary school teacher, Inner London Education Authority, 1959–68. Since 1968 French and German teacher, Barnet Borough Council, London. **Awards:** Guyana Theatre Guild award, 1972; *Guardian* Fiction prize, 1978; Guyana Literature prize, 1989. **Agent:** Bill Hamilton, A.M. Heath, 79 St. Martin's Lane, London WC2N 4AA. **Address:** c/o Allison and Busby Ltd, 44 Hill St, London W1X8LB, England.

Publications

Novels

A Man Come Home. London, Longman, 1974.
The Murderer. London, Allison and Busby, 1978; New York, Persea, 1992.
Kwaku; or, The Man Who Could Not Keep His Mouth Shut. London, Allison and Busby, 1982.
Orealla. London, Allison and Busby, 1984.
The Shadow Bride. London, Collins, 1988.
The Armstrong Trilogy. New York, Persea, 1994.
From the Heat of the Day. London, Allison and Busby, 1979.
One Generation. London, Allison and Busby, 1981.
Genetha. London, Allison and Busby, 1981.
The Ministry of Hope. London and New York, Marion Boyars, 1997.

Uncollected Short Stories

''Miss Mabel's Burial,'' in *Kaie* (Georgetown, Guyana), 1972.
''The Wind and the Sun,'' in *Savacou* (Kingston, Jamaica), 1974.
''The Writer of Anonymous Letters,'' in *Firebird 2,* edited by T.J. Binding. London, Penguin, 1983.
''Sisters,'' in *London Magazine,* September 1988.
''The Master Tailor and the Lady's Skirt,'' in *Colours of a New Day: New Writing for South Africa,* edited by Sarah Lefanu and Stephen Hayward. London, Lawrence and Wishart, and New York, Pantheon, 1990.
''According to Marx,'' in *So Very English,* edited by Marsha Rowe. London, Serpent's Tail, 1991.

Plays

Inez Combray (produced Georgetown, Guyana, 1972).

Other

Art and History (lectures). Georgetown, Guyana, Ministry of Education, 1984.
Shadows Round the Moon: Caribbean Memoirs. London, Collins, 1990.

*

Roy A.K. Heath comments:

A Man Come Home relates the story of a large working-class Guyanese family whose mores provide a striking contrast to those of their middle-class brethren. *From the Heat of the Day* and *One Generation* are the first two parts of a trilogy treating the condition of the middle classes in Guyana in the 20th century. *Genetha* completes the trilogy and shows the heroine faced with the choice of joining the Catholic church, returning to a life of prostitution, or living with her aunts in a stifling middle-class atmosphere. *Kwaku* is the tale of a trickster figure. Orealla, the unseen haven for the main character in the novel of that title, is real, yet imagined.

I see myself as a chronicler of Guyanese life in this century.

* * *

Roy A.K. Heath's eight novels, beginning with *A Man Come Home* and concluding with the most recent, *The Shadow Bride,* represent a distinctive body of fictive insights into contemporary Guyanese society. It blends traditional social realism with local folklore and myths to dramatize the everyday lives of the poor and the lower middle class in the capital, Georgetown, and, occasionally, in the rural hinterlands. Indeed, it is this kind of blending, or interweaving, that makes for one of Heath's distinctive strengths as a novelist. The folk myths of ''obeah'' or voudun (''voodoo''), the strict orthodoxies of biblical morality, local legends drawn from Amerindian or East Indian sources—these all co-exist with the empirical ''realities'' of everyday village life, the familiar routine of middle-class home life, or the rough-and-tumble of the streets and slumyards of Georgetown's impoverished districts. Heath's is a world of popular beliefs and customs which determine the perceptions and choices of his characters; and the very diversity of values and viewpoints, not only within the community but also within any single individual, dramatizes the discrete complexities of the social milieu, complicates the very notion of moral judgment or social choices in the recurrent tensions between classes, religious traditions, and cultural backgrounds, and, finally, challenges conventional assumptions about ''social realism'' in prose fiction.

This discreteness also goes hand in hand with Heath's other strength—his ability to evoke a given environment and its social milieu (urban slum, middle-class neighborhood, rural village, and so forth), bringing to life the sights and sounds of a family dining room or a Georgetown whorehouse in vivid, richly suggestive vignettes. In his more recent fiction, especially in the impressively crafted *Kwaku,* he has shown signs of developing a flair for a lively, effective prose style as well as for credible characterization; but even in the previous novels where thinness of characterization and of style is often a problem, Heath's reader is always aware of a provocative intelligence perpetually raising questions about the nature of social reality and of moral judgments in a vividly realized world. These questions are integrated with recurrent themes which typify all of Heath's fiction: the inevitable obsession with material success in a society dominated by poverty, and the price of success as well as of failure; the conflict between the needs and desires of the private self and the restrictive conventions of a world in which ideals of family responsibility, social respectability, and moral conventions are paramount; and that unending war between the sexes in which mutual exploitiveness and shared dependency, hostility and desire all seem to mirror tensions and contradictions in human society as a whole. In turn all of these conflicts center on a fundamental dilemma which links all the novels, the dilemma of freedom: for whether the quest be freedom from poverty or from some intolerable marriage, Heath's rebel-protagonists must always wrestle, usually inconclusively, with certain unresolved contradictions—it seems all but impossible to flee from poverty without losing a part of one's basic humanity in the process of amassing wealth; the despised spouse (Heath's marriages are invariably wretched) is also an integral, indispensable part of one's self; and the young rebels against family and conventional morality soon discover that the target of their rebellion is also an ineradicable part of themselves.

In *A Man Come Home* the chief rebel is Archie ''Bird'' Foster who tries to escape from the poverty of Georgetown's slum-yards by entering into a liaison with one of the legendary ''Water People'' of Guyanese folklore, a ''Fair Maid,'' or witch. She gives him unlimited wealth on condition that he returns regularly to her bed at her bidding. Now wealthy, he quickly collects the usual trappings of middle-class affluence—an ostentatious house in the suburbs, expensive habits, and a wife (in the person of his long-suffering girlfriend from the slum-yard). The legendary materials provide Heath with a rather obvious and ready-made allegory on the middle-class aspirations of the poor, and the moral cost of acquiring wealth in exchange for one's humanity—for the contract with the Fair Maid is, in effect, a Faustian pact. His marriage, his ties with the rest of his family and with his old friends all conflict with that pact, and when he reneges on his agreement with the Fair Maid in order to re-establish the ''normal'' relationships and ''respectable'' conventions of his society, she exacts the inevitable price: he dies in a car accident which also claims the life of his sister's children.

Bird's tragedy is not isolated, for even the most isolated of Heath's characters are bound up with their families and the rest of society. The deaths of the children therefore emphasize that Bird's tragedy has become a family disaster. His sister never recovers from her loss, and her marriage eventually collapses. At the same time his father's household continues the steady decline which actually started before Bird's misadventures. Egbert Foster, the father, tries, unsuccessfully, to establish peace in a home in which his mistress envies the social life and sexual activity of her young daughter Melda. She administers a savage beating from which Melda never recovers fully, spending the rest of her life as an idiot. In the meanwhile the older woman enters upon an affair with one of Bird's slum-yard friends (who is also Melda's lover), then betrays him to her husband's inevitable violence. Viewed in the context of the Foster family as a whole, then, it becomes clear that Bird's liaison with the Fair Maid is not only an allegory on the moral dilemmas of poverty and materialism; it is also a mythological re-enactment of sexual conflicts and contradictions. The weakness and domination, the mutual exploitation, the futile obsession with escape and freedom—these are not only the patterns of Bird's ill-fated liaison with the Fair Maid, but also the familiar, repetitive patterns in his family and among his friends.

This grim vision of sexual relationships dominates *The Murderer,* where the waste and mutual destructiveness of many conventional relationships are explored through the experiences of abnormal psychology—a narrative strategy which allows Heath to juxtapose images of the ''normal'' or ''conventional'' with patterns of ''abnormality'' in order to challenge settled assumptions about these terms. The murderer is an archetypal psychotic: Galton Flood has been scarred by a wretched childhood in which his sexuality and social instincts were repressed or warped by the ridicule and harshness of a domineering mother who also made life miserable for her husband. His parents' marriage is a model of the shared resentment and contempt which characterize sexual unions in Galton's world, and when he becomes an adult he is deeply suspicious of women, a suspiciousness that is aggravated by his general inability to socialize. When he does marry, he chooses a wife whose prior experience (with an older lover and a dependent but unloving father) has convinced her that men are unreliable and weak beneath the usual male bravado. The marriage quickly fails because of Galton's jealousy and because of the unsociability which prevents him from developing a stable career. His jealousy is the first symptom of criminal insanity. He kills his wife, and although he confesses the murder to both her family and to his own, he is never brought to justice. He ends up, instead, as a street derelict, a relatively harmless idiot who is supported by his kind-hearted brother. Galton's inability to function as part of the family unit or in society at large is partly counteracted by the generosity and family loyalties of his older brother; but Heath's main achievement is to evoke ironic parallels between Galton's ''abnormal'' obsessions and those familiar habits of possessiveness and abusiveness which characterize the sexual relationships of ''normal'' people. ''Abnormal'' psychology is as much an allegory of the ''real'' world here, as ''supernatural'' events are in *A Man Come Home.*

Heath's other family tragedy, the tragedy of the Armstrong family, is the subject of his Georgetown trilogy, *From the Heat of the Day, One Generation,* and *Genetha.* The first work traces the history of the parents' marriage (Sonny Armstrong, from a poor, relatively uneducated background, resents his wife's middle-class family even before he marries her). It is a history of failing affections and growing isolation on both sides, a growing misery which inevitably affects the two children, Genetha and Rohan, and which concludes with the death of Mrs. Armstrong. *Her* misery, at least, ends with her death. He drowns his in drink, until he dies as a derelict pensioner, early in *One Generation.* The second novel describes Rohan's flight from the Georgetown family home, away from the possessive caring of his sister, to a Civil Service job in rural Guyana where he falls in love with a married woman while living with her sister. He is killed by his impoverished East Indian assistant who envies him his social standing and relative prosperity. His murderer is never discovered, and his impunity reinforces the grim realities which lend an air of inevitability and repetition to the trilogy as a whole: Rohan's personal life has been as wasted as his parents'; his sexual relationships have been equally fraught with betrayals and exploitation; and he, too, leaves behind him a legacy of hurt. The inheritors of that legacy are Dada, the mother of his unborn child, who has been victimized by his duplicity with her sister, and his own sister, Genetha, whom he has abandoned to face life alone as a single, inexperienced girl in Georgetown. Finally, in the third part of the trilogy, Genetha recalls her late mother by virtue of her loneliness and isolation, her inability to develop satisfactory relationships with men, and the perpetual tension between her need for the middle-class respectability of her mother's family and her dislike of the family's suffocating propriety. She ends as a total dependent on the family's former maid, now a very successful ''madam'' of a Georgetown whorehouse (another ''success'' acquired at the cost of one's humanity). Esther, like Mr. Armstrong before her, despises the middle-class attitudes of Genetha and the late Mrs. Armstrong, but the eventual bond between Genetha and Esther transcends the barriers, for it has been strengthened by their common experiences as women in a world of weak, bullying men.

Kwaku, the hero of the novel of the same name, is no bully, but he is another weak, insecure male whose dependency on his wife (Gwendoline) and his close, lifelong friend (Blossom) has been intensified by the fact that as a social misfit he has never made friends among the villagers with whom he has grown up. Like the other figures of poverty in Heath's fiction, he tries to make money, succeeding for a while as a ''healer'' in the small town of New Amsterdam. But his insecurity, his need to brag and command respect, leads to his downfall: he runs afoul of the village fisherman when he fails to ''cure'' the latter's family problems. The fisherman retaliates by resorting to obeah: Gwendoline becomes blind and the family sinks into utter destitution. Kwaku's children rebel or are forced to leave home for sheer survival, and both Kwaku and Gwendoline end up as a drunken pair of derelicts in New Amsterdam. It is worth noting that, to his credit, Kwaku never deserts his family in order to resuscitate his business as ''healer''—despite the fact that the expenses of supporting a blind wife and eight children make it impossible for him to start up his business again. But the familiar irony with which Heath handles family and love remains the final judgment here. Kwaku is loyal to his family because he needs them. As he himself recognizes, his love for his wife is a kind of possessiveness—a possessiveness which we can easily recognize, in some of its most repulsive forms, in Gwendoline. Unlike Gwendoline, Blossom is fiercely independent—but her own marriage survives, after a fashion, because she has bullied her own husband into his (accepting) place, even manipulating him into ''accepting'' a child which, he himself knows, he never fathered. In the uncompromising realism of Heath's 20th-century vision, Wilfred's marital happiness with Blossom is the happiness of the Swiftian fool in *A Tale of a Tub*—a state of being well deceived. It is the kind of ''happiness'' which exemplifies the solid achievements and rich possibilities of Heath's narrative irony.

—Lloyd W. Brown

HEGI, Ursula

Nationality: German-American. **Born:** Ursula Koch in West Germany (emigrated to United States, 1965; naturalized citizen, 1970), 23 May 1946. **Education:** University of New Hampshire, B.A. 1978, M.A. 1979. **Family:** Married Ernest Hegi in 1967; two sons. **Career:** Lecturer in English, University of New Hampshire, Durham, 1978—. **Agent:** Gail Hochman, Paul R. Reynolds, Inc., 12 East 41st Street, New York, New York 10017, U.S.A. **Address:** Department of English, University of New Hampshire, Durham, New Hampshire 03824, U.S.A.

Publications

Novels

Intrusions. New York, Viking Press, 1981.
Floating in My Mother's Palm. New York, Poseidon Press, 1990.
Stones from the River. New York, Poseidon Press, 1994.
Salt Dancers. New York, Simon & Schuster, 1995.
The Vision of Emma Blau. New York, Simon & Schuster, 2000.

Short Stories

Unearned Pleasures and Other Stories. Moscow, Idaho, University of Idaho Press, 1988.

Other

Tearing the Silence: Being German in America. New York, Simon & Schuster, 1997.

* * *

There are three dominant subjects in the fiction of Ursula Hegi: the twentieth-century experience of being German in Germany and in America, the pain and complexity of the private lives of families and individuals, and the flow of experience in communities. Her method is a fine tapestry of prose of great subtlety and humanity, a naturalism often enriched by luminous images that telescope or expand time, linking generations or events in a gossamer pattern.

Hegi's *Intrusions* differs from her later fiction as it is an experimental metafictional novel in the style of John Barth and Robert Coover. The intrusions are those of the author and the characters, who get into rows about how the novel is going. The author frequently breaks off to complain about intrusions from her husband and children, and then her characters begin to attack her for misusing them. ''The characters have moved in. They follow me around, even crowd my family at the dinner table.'' Both her heroine Megan Stone and she herself are trying to get peace and isolation and the stories of their lives converge without actually meeting towards the end of the book. There are brilliantly funny sections, such as the intrusions of a Norman Mailer supporter who vividly outlines the gross chauvinist style he thinks should be used for the sex scenes or the moment when Megan finds out what childbirth labor really feels like. While Hegi's later novels move away from this intellectual play, the concern with the management of the story remains one of her central concerns.

Although Hegi's *Floating in My Mother's Palm* is described as a novel, it is closer to a series of linked sketches of the girlhood of Hanna Malter and her perceptions of the fictional town of Burgdorf, a central construction in much of Hegi's writing. Hanna has complex memories of her mother, an artist and an unusual person in a small town, who dies in a car accident when Hanna is fourteen. The title chapter/story is about her mother's love of swimming and how she taught her young daughter to swim, supporting her in the water with safe hands as they swam in thunderstorms and rain in the nearby quarry. The final chapter/story ''Saving a Life'' occurs shortly after Hanna's mother's death when Hanna, wanting to save a life, goes swimming in the Rhein and is trapped by a barge's cables underwater. After escaping she realizes that she has saved a life—her own—and the reader sees in this her mother's loving care in teaching her to swim as well as her model to Hanna of daring and independence. The sections of *Floating in My Mother's Palm* are all from Hanna's point of view, so her experience shapes the events. In ''The Woman Who Would Not Speak,'' for example, a drunken husband hangs himself by accidentally kicking away the chair while trying to get his wife to accept his apology. His wife sits clutching the kitchen table while he dies. When Hanna relates this horrifying tale she wishes to freeze the moment,

> Fixed in my mind, they have stayed like this—in that instant when everything is still possible, when luck lies suspended and wants to mold itself into a new beginning.

The moving *Floating in My Mother's Palm* is a set of finger exercises for *Stones from the River*. This sweeping panoramic novel begins during World War I and follows the flow of the lives of the citizens of Burgdorf to 1952, through the horrors of Hitler's regime, through deaths and births and murders and romances and humor and madness and all the profound and absurd possibilities of human experience. Its central figure is Trudi Montag, a *Zwerg* or dwarf who grows up in the love of her father after her mother's early insanity and death. She and her father keep the town pay-library and she becomes the town center for gossip and information. While on the one hand this novel is a vast chronicle of a culture in turmoil, on another it is an intimate study of how Trudi comes to accept and understand herself and the lives of those around her. Although comparison with Günter Grass's Oskar in *The Tin Drum* is inevitable, Trudi is far less acerbic and surreal a character, a *Zwerg* rather than a boy frozen in miniature as a result of the horrors of Nazi Germany. Moreover, in Trudi Hegi is pursuing a more elusive and poetic goal—the implications of the storymaker as a maker and interpreter of reality.

The central metaphor of *Stones from the River* is the idea of the river of experience which is defined by the ''stones'' of persons and events. In her childhood pain Trudi piles a cairn of stones at the river for her painful memories of individuals, a cairn beside which she and her wartime lover later make love. But those stones are also the pebbles embedded in her mother's knee, which she later realizes are the evidence of her mother's adultery with a motorcyclist while her father fought in World War I. Slowly Trudi becomes aware that she shapes stories through her intuition, and that stories give her power over people. She saves her own life in this way by making up the exact story that captures the cynical nihilism of a Gestapo interrogator who waives his power to send her to a camp because she reads him so well. This novel, Hegi's masterpiece to date, has both scope and a lyrical richness of detail and sensitivity. It in no way defends Nazi horrors except in the Latin sense of the word apology: being an explanation of a people, a history, and a time. But through Trudi and those delineated around her it is also an intense document of the poetry of lives lived.

Salt Dancers tells of the struggle of 41-year-old Julia Ives to resolve her relationship with her father before she has a first child. She has not seen him for twenty-three years and carries memories of his drinking and his beating and mistreating her after her mother mysteriously left the family. In an increasingly painful and complex unraveling that leaps through time to childhood from the present, Julia realizes the degree to which she has confused the past, a revelation that tempers her vision of events. As with Trudi's revelations in *Stones from the River* Julia's truth opens an understanding of the meanings of the interlocked lives so richly depicted. The salt dance of the title refers to a family tradition that walking over a line of salt will mean leaving cares behind. The novel clarifies that this is not so simply possible, but it also indicates that a new beginning is possible.

Next Hegi produced *Unearned Pleasures*, a collection of short stories set in the United States, and *Tearing the Silence: Being German in America*, a brilliant shaped collection of interviews that reveal the struggles, the denials, the forms of acceptance and the struggle against prejudice for German Americans. This latter collection undoubtedly influenced Hegi's most recent novel, *The Vision of Emma Blau*. It follows Stefan Blau, who runs away from his home in Burgdorf at the age of thirteen in 1894, as he comes to America and becomes wealthy by a lake in New Hampshire as a restaurateur and as the owner of a large apartment building, the *Wasserburg,* or water fortress. It follows Stefan through two brief American marriages, the first of which ends at childbirth and the second one week afterward. He then brings Helene Montag, Trudi's aunt, from Burgdorf to be his third wife but his fear of losing her blunts his passion and blights their marriage, although they do have one child, Robert, who in turn has Emma, Stefan's granddaughter. Stefan had had a vision of the six-year-old Emma dancing before *Wasserburg* was even built, a vision he lives to see. After his death the property becomes the subject of complex struggles as it gradually declines, and in the closing passages Emma frees herself from the legacy she has tried to preserve.

Once again Hegi constructs a rich vision of a community, this time in New Hampshire, passing through the generations. In this novel she deals with the German heritage and American attitudes to it. But the true power of Hegi's writing lies in the detail, in the wealth of vision of human struggles within the frame of societies. Her characters are their fathers' and mothers' children, but they grow, struggle, and change, always in a natural world as powerfully depicted as the worlds of families and communities. That she has given Germans of the twentieth century a voice is no doubt a product of her own circumstances, but that is not the limit of her powers. Like the water that figures so prominently in the images in her novels she sees the unending flow of the human scene, rich with love and sometimes diverted by hate. Always there is the flow, and those who tell stories about both ripples and waves.

—Peter Brigg

HELPRIN, Mark

Nationality: American. **Born:** New York, New York, 28 June 1947. **Education:** Harvard University, A.B. 1969, A.M. 1972; postgraduate study at Magdalen College, University of Oxford, 1976–77. **Military Service:** British Merchant Navy; infantrymen, Israeli Army, and field security officer, Israeli Air Force, 1972–73; British Merchant Navy. **Family:** Married Lisa Kennedy in 1980; two daughters. **Career:** Instructor, Harvard University; senior fellow, Hudson Institute; advisor, Bob Dole presidential campaign, 1996; journalist and contributing editor, *Wall Street Journal.* **Awards:** PEN/Faulkner award, 1982; National Jewish Book award, 1982; Prix de Rome (American Academy and Institute of Arts and Letters), 1982; Guggenheim fellow, 1984. **Address:** c/o Harcourt Brace Jovanovich, Inc., 15 East 26th Street, New York, New York 10010, U.S.A.

PUBLICATIONS

Novels

Refiner's Fire: The Life and Adventures of Marshall Pearl, a Foundling. New York, Knopf, 1977.
Winter's Tale. San Diego, California, Harcourt, 1983.
A Soldier of the Great War. San Diego, California, Harcourt, 1991.
Memoir from Antproof Case. New York, Harcourt, 1995.

Fiction (for children)

Swan Lake, illustrated by Chris Van Allsburg. Boston, Houghton, 1989.
A City in Winter: The Queen's Tale, illustrated by Chris Van Allsburg. New York, Viking, 1996.
The Veil of Snows, illustrated by Chris Van Allsburg. New York, Viking, 1997.

Short Stories

A Dove of the East, and Other Stories. New York, Knopf, 1975.
Ellis Island and Other Stories. New York, Seymour Lawrence/Delacorte, 1981.

Other

Introduction, *Manhattan Lightscape,* photographs by Nathaniel Liebe. New York, Abbeville Press, 1990.

Preface, *Moby Dick, or, The Whale* by Herman Melville. New York, Barnes & Noble Books, 1994.

Foreword, *Only Spring: On Mourning the Death of My Son* by Gordon Livingston. San Francisco, HarperSanFrancisco, 1995.

Contributor, *In the Name of the Father: Stories About Priests,* edited by Michael F. McCauley. Chicago, T. More Press, 1983.

Contributor, *Reinventing the American People: Unity and Diversity Today,* edited by Robert Royal. Grand Rapids, Michigan, William B. Eerdmans Publishing Company, 1995.

Editor, with Shannon Ravenel, *The Best American Short Stories, 1988,*1989.

* * *

Mark Helprin is a Jewish-American novelist, essayist, and short story writer. His stories and essays have appeared in *The New Yorker, The Atlantic Monthly, The New Criterion, The Wall Street Journal,* and the *New York Times.* His fiction blends flights of fantasy with realism, so that he has been often compared with Colombian magical realist author Gabriel García Marquéz. Helprin writes thick, ambitious novels full of bizarre and mystical complications. His characters have a larger-than-life fairy-tale quality; they are fervent believers in the richly lived life and the conviction that love and beauty will prevail. Though his plotting and characterization are occasionally fantastical, his settings and dialogue are in the realist tradition.

Tradition is a key word to use when describing Helprin. Politically and literarily conservative, Helprin is a senior fellow of the Hudson Institute, where he writes on foreign policy and defense issues, his specialty being Middle East Studies.

Yet Helprin's life has been so full of adventure that many commentators have accused him of flat-out falsehood. Helprin grew up in the British West Indies, attended Harvard and the University of Oxford, and balanced this apparently bookish side of his nature by serving in the British Merchant Navy, the Israeli infantry, and the Israeli Air Force, and is an avid mountain-climber.

During the late 1970s, he became an Israeli citizen and went on dozens of counter-infiltration patrols at the Lebanese border. The experiences he gained there became materials for his short fiction, much of which was gathered into two early collections, *A Dove of the East and Other Stories*, which contains some fantastic elements, and *Ellis Island and Other Stories.* The latter won the 1982 National Jewish Book Award in America, was awarded a Guggenheim Fellowship and the Prix de Rome, and was nominated for the P.E.N. Faulkner Award and the National Book Award.

Helprin's short fiction foreshadowed what was to come. These stories deal with children, old reminiscing men, travelers in many exotic lands, rabbis, war, love, beauty, guilt, and death. Some recurrent images that symbolize life and love are Helprin's use of light, color, and music.

Like the short fiction, *Refiner's Fire: The Life and Adventures of Marshall Pearl, a Foundling* contains many autobiographical incidents. It is a rollicking *bildungsroman* about an orphan born on an illegal immigrant ship attempting to fight its way through the British naval cordon around Palestine during a sea battle in 1947 (the year of Helprin's birth). Adopted by a wealthy couple of the Hudson River Valley, Marshall leaves the United States for Israel and joins the army to fight in the 1973 Israeli-Arab war, as Helprin did. The novel is episodic, jumping from one continent to another, from one extravagant adventure to another. Marshal swims through a hurricane, romances various women, endures epileptic fits, and finds glory in a climactic battle on the Golan Heights. The novel was both praised and condemned for its ''old-fashioned'' writing style; some critics faulted Helprin for its romanticism, its shallow characterization of women, its length. However, most agree that *Refiner's Fire* has moments of dazzling lyrical prose and transcendent perception.

Helprin's greatest novel is *Winter's Tale*, an epic fable set in an imaginary New York, potentially the site for the establishment of the New Jerusalem. The century-long story begins with a talking horse and an itinerant mechanic/thief named Peter Lake and concludes with an ambiguously redemptive apocalypse. A fairy tale that includes science-fictional conventions such as extraordinary machines and time travel, *Winter's Tale* possesses an intricate plot with a huge cast of characters.

One winter night at the turn of the twentieth century, Peter attempts to burgle a mansion on the Upper West Side. He unexpectedly meets beautiful heiress, Beverly Penn, and they fall in love. However, Beverly is dying of consumption, and when tragedy befalls them, Peter makes up his mind to ''stop time and bring back the dead.'' He and his magical horse vanish into a mysterious ''cloud wall,'' and the narrative jumps seventy years ahead. The reader now journeys with a young man from San Francisco to New York in search of a transcendent city. He endures several humorous adventures before witnessing an inferno that rages across Manhattan and heralds the millennium. In the year 2000, New York becomes a golden city, kingdom of heaven on earth.

The novel is remarkable in its sweep of wondrous and mysterious detail—such as a house in the middle of a lake, an impossible bridge, and a nineteenth-century village lost in winter somewhere beyond the city and the bounds of time—with broad strokes of comedy, villainy, tragedy, and exaltation. The treasures of the earth, Peter Lake says, are movement, courage, laughter, and love. Helprin provides these in generous abundance. The novel was critically acclaimed and became a national best-seller.

His next book, *A Soldier of the Great War*, also received warm attention. In August 1964, Alessandro Giuliani, an elderly Italian, unexpectedly finds himself walking the road to a town seventy kilometers away with an illiterate seventeen-year-old factory worker. To pass the time on their two-day journey, Alessandro tells the boy the story of his life. As a young man, he had ridden horses, climbed mountains, studied painting and aesthetics, and fell in love. Then World War I interrupts his life and he loses the girl of his dreams. Passionate, romantic, Alessandro becomes a soldier and hero while learning the horror and brutality of war, fighting in northern Italy, fighting with Sicilian bandits against the Italian army, fighting the Germans. He is imprisoned by the Austrian emperor's Hussars, then becomes a deserter. The hell of war and the insanity of the bureaucratic world are embodied in the person of Orfeo Quatta, a grotesque figure laboring in a dusty government office.

Alessandro enthralls his companion with stories about religion, politics, and morality, about the family he built and loved and lost. Through narrating his life of adventure, horror, absurdity, and loneliness, Alessandro finally understands the meaning of his retreat into his memories and realizes that in death he will join those he loved. Helprin told an interviewer that what he really meant by ''The Great War'' is the war which we fight against conditions of mortality—in other words, life. Critical response to *A Soldier of the Great War* was almost unanimously positive, with many calling it Helprin's ''masterpiece.''

Helprin's next novel was a brilliant work of dark comedy. *Memoir from Antproof Case* is narrated by an ancient American hiding out in Brazil from real or imagined assassins. The old man writes his life story and carefully secretes the pages in an ant-proof case for his beloved ten-year-old stepson to read when he is older. Why must these adventures be hidden? Perhaps the boy will be able to find the tens of millions in gold bullion that his father stole years earlier.

The narrator, who comically refuses to give his real name but introduces himself as ''Oscar Progresso,'' claims to have been a murderer, a patient in a Swiss insane asylum, a lover to rival Don Juan, a billionaire, a World War II fighter pilot who was shot down twice, the greatest bank robber of the century, a protector of the innocent, a banker who met with popes and presidents, and a constant crusader against ''the greatest enslaver of mankind: coffee.'' Progresso may be eccentric, to put it mildly, but he is also a man who possesses good and evil in large portions, a man who dizzies with the sheer joy of life.

Helprin has also written stories for children with the noted author and illustrator Chris Van Allsburg. *Swan Lake* is a popular and acclaimed reworking of Tchaikovsky's ballet about Odette, an orphaned princess. *A City in Winter* is narrated by a young queen whose parents were slaughtered by the evil Usurper, so that she was raised deep in the forest until, at the age of ten, she journeyed to reclaim her kingdom. Helprin's storytelling is still both comical and fantastical, though some reviewers complained that the tale is too violent and wordy for children. *The Veil of Snows* takes up the story some years later, when the Queen has ruled in peace but worries because her husband and his army have vanished in the wilderness. A battle with the vile Duke of Tookisheim foreshadows her greatest fear—the return of the cruel Usurper. Her faithful tale-singer joins forces with her to overthrow the invaders against enormous odds.

In both his juvenile and adult fiction, Helprin's themes of loyalty and courage in the face of danger, the heartless efficiency of evil, and the power of love to endure and prevail burn like a steady flame. Helprin credits Dante Alighieri as his greatest literary influence, an influence evident in his fables of redemption and revelation gained by surviving the terrible and beautiful vicissitudes that life has to offer. His fiction is sublime in its portrayal of great suffering and great joy. His novels present lionhearted, if occasionally foolhardy, quests for truth and love. What his fans cherish most is Helprin's certitude that life is worth living to the fullest, and that even in the face of death, the world is still full of hope.

—Fiona Kelleghan

HIGGINS, Aidan

Nationality: Irish. **Born:** Celbridge, County Kildare, 3 March 1927. **Education:** Celbridge Convent; Killashee Preparatory School; Clongowes Wood College, County Kildare. **Family:** Married Jill Damaris Anders in 1955; three sons. **Career:** Copywriter, Domas Advertising, Dublin, early 1950s; factory hand, extrusion moulder, and storeman, London, mid-1950s; puppet-operator, John Wright's marionettes, in Europe, South Africa, and Rhodesia, 1958–60; scriptwriter, Filmlets (advertising films), Johannesburg, 1960–61. British Arts Council grants; James Tait Black Memorial prize, 1967; DAAD grant (Berlin), 1969; Irish Academy of Letters award, 1970; American-Irish Foundation grant, 1977. Lives in Kinsale, County Cork. **Address:** c/o Secker and Warburg, Michelin House, 81 Fulham Road, London SW3 6RB, England.

Publications

Novels

Langrishe, Go Down. London, Calder and Boyars, and New York, Grove Press, 1966.
Balcony of Europe. London, Calder and Boyars, and New York, Delacorte Press, 1972.
Scenes from a Receding Past. London, Calder, and New York, Riverrun Press, 1977.
Bornholm Night-Ferry. Dingle, County Kerry, Brandon, and London, Allison and Busby, 1983.
Lions of the Grunewald. London, Secker and Warburg, 1993.

Short Stories

Felo de Se. London, Calder, 1960; as *Killachter Meadow,* New York, Grove Press, 1961; revised edition, as *Asylum and Other Stories,* Calder, 1978; New York, Riverrun Press, 1979.
Helsingør Station and Other Departures: Fictions and Autobiographies 1956–1989. London, Secker and Warburg, 1989.

Plays

Radio Plays (UK): *Assassination,* 1973; *Imperfect Sympathies,* 1977; *Discords of Good Humour,* 1982; *Vanishing Heroes,* 1983; *Texts for the Air,* 1983; *Winter Is Coming,* 1983; *Tomb of Dreams,* 1984 (Ireland); *Zoo Station,* 1985; *Boomtown,* 1990.

Other

Images of Africa: Diary 1956–60. London, Calder and Boyars, 1971.
Ronda Gorge and Other Precipices: Travel Writings 1959–1989. London, Secker and Warburg, 1989.
Donkey's Years: Memories of a Life as Story Told. London, Secker and Warburg, 1995.
Samuel Beckett. London, Secker and Warburg, 1995.
Flotsam and Jetsam. London, Minerva, 1997.
Dog Days. N.p., 1999.
Editor, *A Century of Short Stories.* London, Cape, 1977.
Editor, *Colossal Gongorr and the Turkes of Mars,* by Carl, Julien, and Elwin Higgins. London, Cape, 1979.

*

Manuscript Collection: University of Victoria, British Columbia.

Critical Studies: By David Holloway, in *The Bookman* (London), December 1965; ''Maker's Language'' by Vernon Scannell, in

Spectator (London), 11 February 1966; in *New Leader* (London), 25 September 1967; Morris Beja, in *Irish University Review* (Dublin), Autumn 1973; ''Aidan Higgins Issue'' of *Review of Contemporary Fiction* (Elmwood Park, Illinois), Spring 1983.

* * *

Aidan Higgins was born in 1927 to a rich legacy in Irish fiction dominated by the experimentations of James Joyce. Higgins makes full use of Joyce's innovative techniques in his novels and collections of short fiction, but with a broader world sensibility based on his extensive travels. In addition to his novels and short stories, Higgins documents his international experiences in non-fiction travel books based on his travel diaries and assorted memoirs, which constitute the primary resource for his fictional works. His recent autobiography, *Dog Days* (1999), confirms how much his personal experiences have informed the picaresque elements in his fiction.

Higgins's first major novel, *Langrishe, Go Down*, which received the James Tait Black Memorial Prize and the Irish Academy of Letters Award in 1966, is the story of Imogen Langrishe, the youngest of four spinster sisters. As the Langrishe sisters live their dried-up lives in the gentle landscapes of Ireland, Germany is rising to war and the Spanish Civil War is in full swing. Framed by these historical events, Imogen's only love affair with the German Otto Beck carries symbolically political undertones. Otto poaches on the sisters' estate, invading their lives while stealing their game. His invasion of Springfield and Imogen ends with his indifferent departure as Germany invades Austria.

Balcony of Europe, Higgins's second major novel, was shortlisted for the 1972 Booker Prize. The author's interest in phenomenology shapes the disjointed narrative, which is Dan Ruttle's first-person account of his adulterous affair with an American Jewess, Charlotte Bayless. Dan, a passionate Irish artist, is oblivious to the external reality of war as bombers fly over them in Andalusia. The experiences of the senses predominate in the sun-drenched area of southern Spain, which contrasts with the dreary gray weather of Ireland, where the story begins and ends. Higgins tries to coalesce the moment of experience and expression. Plot is largely sacrificed for a number of cognitive tableaux, held together by cross-references and an idiosyncratic authorial voice.

Balcony of Europe exercises the Joycean interior monologue technique with emphasis on rhetorical and grammatical distortions, such as repetitions and ellipses. The interior monologue focuses less attention on Dan's point of view than on the author's labored and insistent symbolism, often in homage to Joyce and Yeats. The planes that fly overhead, for example, alternately turn into the ghost of Dan's mother or a football that is kicked in the air on the Spanish beach.

Scenes from a Receding Past adds further scraps to the memory of Dan Ruttle from his early childhood and adolescence to his early maturity. The book is set in Sligo, which represents Celbridge, the author's birthplace and the parish near the big house in Langrishe. Young Ruttle's bildung is quite similar to young Stephen's in Joyce's bildungsroman, *Portrait of the Artist as a Young Man*. The pangs of growing up are projected onto Dan's brother, the inflexible and intransigent Wally, who ends up in a lunatic asylum. Interleaved are records, and records of records, including a—faulty—Dutch Mass Card, a clothes list for La Sainte Union Convent, and two pages from the score book for the Fifth Oval, August 20–23, 1938. Dan meets and woos Olivia Orr, a girl from New Zealand who hovers in the background of *Balcony of Europe* as his unhappy wife. The present and glimpses of their pasts are woven with mawkish poetry and casual prose disrupted, in one instance, by a page-long list of names for the baby that Olivia loses in her fifth month.

The epistolary form of *Bornholm Night-Ferry* is a logical follow-up to the snap-shot technique of *Scenes from a Receding Past*. It enables Higgins to combine his modernist techniques with a crafted attention to detail. The novel is as full of linguistic distortions, chronological jumps, and occasional lyricism as any of his works, but it is more organized by the epistolary form. The plot is again grounded by a love affair, this time between a Danish girl, Elin Marstrander, with poor English language skills, and an Irish writer, Finn Fitzgerald, with little commonsense. Higgins introduces an implied narrator-as-archivist who identifies letters and diaries as they come to him.

Lions of the Grunewald, published in 1995, is set in Europe and Berlin just before the Berlin Wall came down. It is a picaresque novel of frenzy that jaunts around postwar Europe with giddy abandon and inebriated characters engaged with each other's lusty mannerisms and surrealistic pranks. The novel's publication is surrounded by the publication of numerous collections of memoirs, including *Images of Africa: Diary 1956–60* and *Donkey's Years: Memories of a Life as a Story Told* (1996), the prequel to *Dog Days*, supporting Higgins's admission that most of his books follow his life ''like slug-trails.''

In addition to Higgins's novels, several collections of shorter fiction works, such as *Helsingør Station and Other Departures*, *Asylum and Other Stories*, as well as his travel writing, such as *Ronda Gorge and Other Precipices* (1989), have earned Aidan Higgins a reputation as one of modern Ireland's greatest writers. The influence of the great Irish modernists, Yeats and Joyce, is unshakeable in all of the genres he has mastered, to which he adds a pantheistic verve and hedonism not uncommon in the lives and literature of twentieth-century writers following World War II. He does not shy away from rattling family skeletons or dissecting the follies of Irish Catholics as he sheds light on Ireland just before, during, and after the pivotal Second World War.

—Hedwig Gorski

HIGHWAY, Tomson

Nationality: Canadian. **Born:** Northwestern Manitoba, Canada, 6 December 1951. **Education:** Attended University of Manitoba; University of Western Ontario, B.Mus. 1975, B.A. 1977. **Career:** Member, De-ba-jeh-mu-jig Theatre Group, West Bay, Ontario; artistic director, Native Earth Performing Arts, Inc., Toronto, Ontario, until 1992; associated with numerous Native support groups; playwright. **Awards:** Chalmers Award, 1986; Dora Mavor Moore Award, 1987–88; *The Rez Sisters* was selected to represent Canada at Edinburgh Festival, 1988; four Dora Mavor Moore Awards, including one for best play, 1989–90; Wang Festival Award, 1989. **Address:** Playwrights Canada, 54 Wolseley Street, 2nd Floor, Toronto, Ontario M5C 1A5, Canada.

PUBLICATIONS

Novels

Kiss of the Fur Queen. Toronto, Doubleday Canada, 1998

Plays

The Rez Sisters: A Play in Two Acts. Toronto, Native Canadian Centre, 1986; Saskatoon, Saskatchewan, Fifth House, 1988.
Aria (monologues). Toronto, Makka Kleist Annex Theatre, 1987.
New Song ... New Dance (multimedia dance production, with Rene Highway), 1987.
Dry Lips Oughta Move to Kapuskasing (also known as *The Red Brothers*). Toronto, Theatre Passe Muraille, 1989; Saskatoon, Saskachewan, Fifth House, 1989; also appeared in *Modern Canadian Plays,* edited by Jerry Wasserman, Vancouver, British Columbia, Talon Books, 1993.
The Sage, the Dancer, and the Fool (with Rene Highway and Bill Merasty). Toronto, Native Canadian Centre, 1989.

*

Critical Studies: *Aboriginal Voices: Amerindian, Inuit, and Sami Theatre* by William Morgan. Baltimore, Johns Hopkins University Press, 1992.

* * *

Tomson Highway is best known as the author of two award-winning plays. *The Rez Sisters* and *Dry Lips Oughta Move to Kapuskasing* focus, respectively, on the lives of seven Native-Canadian women and seven Native-Canadian men from the fictional Wasaychigan Hill Reservation in northern Ontario. The plays, part of a projected seven-play cycle that has prompted comparisons with the work of Michel Tremblay (whom Highway counts as a major influence) and James Reaney (with whom Highway studied at the University of Western Ontario), announce most of the major themes and aesthetic practices that Highway has pursued in all of his writing: the sexual and racial apartheid wrought upon First Nations communities in North America as a result of the colonial encounter with white Europeans; the attendant clash between Native and Christian mythologies; a preoccupation with the shape-shifting, gender-bending figure of the trickster Nanabush; and a wickedly irreverent humor that is as much scatological as it is eschatological.

Highway has said that he only seriously turned to novel writing (having already published several shorter fictional pieces) when he couldn't get the third installment of his ''Rez cycle'' produced. The musical *Rose* brings together both the Wasy Hill men and women from the first two plays; but major Canadian producers balked at the cast size and logistical constraints of the staging. (The play, workshopped across the country, has since received a full-scale amateur staging at the University of Toronto.) This setback for theater-goers has, however, been a boon for readers of fiction. For out of his frustration at failing to get his play produced, Highway composed his first novel, *Kiss of the Fur Queen* (in which the Wasy Hill Reserve makes a brief but pivotal appearance).

The novel recounts the story of the Okimasis brothers, Jeremiah and Gabriel, from their births in a tent on their parents' trapline in northern Manitoba, through their forced relocation to a Catholic residential school in the south (where both boys are physically and sexually abused), and on to their respective sexual awakenings and initial artistic successes (Jeremiah as a pianist and Gabriel as a dancer). Along the way, the brothers, who had always been extremely close, become estranged, in part because of their differing responses to the pressures of cultural assimilation, and in part because of Jeremiah's uneasiness with Gabriel's emerging homosexuality. With Gabriel's death from AIDS-related complications imminent, the brothers are reunited at the end of the novel, collaborating artistically on a play that Jeremiah has written, *Ulysses Thunderchild*, a Joycean exploration of one day in the life of a Cree man in Toronto.

The reference to Joyce is telling, for it is an indication of how successfully Highway has fused in *Kiss of the Fur Queen* modernist narrative techniques with traditional Native oratory and storytelling practices. While the novel can certainly be read as a dual *Küntslerroman*, progressing linearly from their idyllic childhood in a seeming arctic paradise on to the later painful lessons of life and art learned by Jeremiah and Gabriel in the urban centres of Winnipeg and Toronto, Highway's is nevertheless very much a Cree ''Portrait of the Artist.'' The novel constantly circles back upon itself, employing repetition, embedded narrative, much dialogue, unglossed Cree phrases, and other stylistic features in order to bind together speaker/writer and listener/reader in a negotiated performance of both a *literate* narrative and an *oral* storytelling event. Central to this endeavor is, once again, the figure of Nanabush, who for Highway is not simply a magical gender-transgressive character (here incarnated variously as the spirit of the Fur Queen herself and as a breathy, cigarette-smoking, torch song-singing arctic fox named Maggie Sees) who knows all, but also a discursive trope or textual device that allows him to manipulate, rearrange, and reorder his story. Unlike the dispassionate God paring his fingernails in James Joyce's *Portrait*, Highway's Fur Queen and Miss Maggie actively interrupt and interfere with Jeremiah, encouraging him to mix things up even further. Linked to this is a larger concern that runs throughout the novel, namely Highway's conscious construction of Native mythology as matrilineal. As Maggie puts it to Jeremiah, ''Show me the bastard who come up with this notion that who's running the goddamn show is some grumpy, embittered, sexually frustrated old fart with a long white beard hiding like a gutless coward behind some puffed-up cloud and I'll slice his goddamn balls off.''

Kiss of the Fur Queen is very much an autobiographical novel. One must, of course, be wary of conflating the fictional Jeremiah with his author, but it is nevertheless worth pointing out that Highway began his artistic career as a pianist, and that his younger brother, René, was also a dancer, collaborating with Tomson on his plays (he danced the role of Nanabush in *The Rez Sisters* and choreographed *Dry Lips*) before succumbing to AIDS in 1990. And yet, while there is undoubtedly a very personal story that Highway is telling in this novel, he is also concerned with addressing and redressing a larger political issue, recovering the lost stories of a lost generation of Native children in Canada who, during the 1940s, 1950s, and 1960s, were forcibly removed from their families, denied the right to communicate in their own language, and compelled to undergo a frequently violent process of acculturation to dominant white society. *Kiss of the Fur Queen* speaks eloquently and powerfully to the decades-old silence surrounding this dark chapter in Canadian history.

—Peter Dickinson

HIJUELOS, Oscar

Nationality: American. **Born:** New York, New York, 24 August 1951. **Education:** City College of the City University of New York, B.A. 1975, M.A. 1976. **Family:** Divorced. **Career:** Advertising media traffic manager, Transportation Display, Inc., Winston Network, New York, 1977–84; writer, 1984—; professor of English, Hofstra University, Hempstead, New York, 1989—. **Awards:** ''Outstanding writer'' citation (Pushcart Press), 1978; Fellowship for Creative Writers award (National Endowment for the Arts), 1985; American Academy in Rome fellowship in Literature (American Academy and Institute of Arts and Letters), 1985; Pulitzer prize for fiction, 1990. **Address:** Hofstra University, English Department, 1000 Fulton Avenue, Hempstead, New York 11550, U.S.A.

Publications

Novels

Our House in the Last World. New York, Persea Books, 1983.
The Mambo Kings Play Songs of Love. New York, Farrar, Straus, 1989.
The Fourteen Sisters of Emilio Montez O'Brien. New York, Farrar, Straus, 1993.
Mr. Ives' Christmas. New York, HarperCollins, 1995.
Empress of the Splendid Season. New York, HarperCollins, 1999.

Other

Preface, *Iguana Dreams: New Latino Fiction,* edited by Delia Poey and Virgil Suarez. New York, HarperPerennial, 1992.
Introduction, *Cool Salsa: Bilingual Poems on Growing up Latino in the United States,* edited by Lori M. Carlson. New York, Holt, 1994.
Introduction, *The Cuban American Family Album* by Dorothy and Thomas Hoobler. New York, Oxford University Press, 1996.
Contributor, *Best of Pushcart Press III.* Pushcart, 1978.
Contributor, *You're On!: Seven Plans in English and Spanish,* edited by Lori M. Carlson. New York, Morrow Junior Books, 1999.

*

Critical Studies: *Life on the Hyphen: The Cuban-American Way,* Gustavo Pérez Firmat, Austin, University of Texas Press, 1994; *Dance Between Two Cultures: Latino Caribbean Literature Written in the United States* by William Luis, Nashville, Vanderbilt University Press, 1997; *U.S. Latino Literature: A Critical Guide for Students and Teachers* edited by Harold Augenbraum and Margarite Fernández Olmos, Westport, Connecticut, Greenwood Press, 2000.

* * *

Oscar Hijuelos is the only Latino to have been awarded the Pulitzer Prize in fiction, which he won in 1990 for *The Mambo Kings Play Songs of Love*, a bittersweet exploration of the lives of two Cuban-born musicians and their families in the 1950s. His work is characterized by a beautiful literary style through which he captures and explores individual character.

Hijuelos was born in New York City and spent a very small part of his early years in Cuba. He graduated from the City College of New York, and has acknowledged an early debt to Henry Roth and his ultimate novel of Jewish adaptation, *Call It Sleep.* At the age of three, during a trip to the island, Hijuelos fell ill and subsequently lived for a period of time in a Connecticut children's sanitorium, which he chronicled in his first novel, the Bildungsroman *Our House in the Last World.*

Our House sets out many of the themes with which Hijuelos has grappled during his career: a search for spiritual meaning, memory and loss, the difficulty of maintaining a stable family life, poverty in immigrant communities, the implausibility of certainty in self-definition—especially among men, an extraordinary appreciation of both the physical and emotional presence of women, and the plasticity of national culture. An autobiographical novel, *Our House* is the story of the Santinios, father Alejo, mother Mercedes, brothers Horacio and Hector, who is the writer's Kunstlerroman alter ego. Alejo is an ineffectual husband and father—a theme to which Hijeulos returned in subsequent works. He is a womanizer and heavy drinker whose inability to pull the family out of its dire poverty in Spanish Harlem, lack of intimacy with his sons, and emotional abuse of his wife angers and embarrasses his family. Hector, the younger son, fair and sickly, develops a conflicted relationship with his own culture. Battered by what his mother calls Cuban microbios, one of the few Spanish words in the book that is not set in italics, and American culture's rejection of his ''Cuban-ness,'' Hector cannot separate the personal and the political (''But he continued to pack up his junk … he was thinking about sex with that blond girl [sic] … He thought he would leave all the bad feelings behind … he wouldn't … think about microbios …). *Our House* is a solid entry in the tradition of the American immigrant Bildungsroman, highly focused on the ideas of loss versus gain, adaptation versus assimilation.

In *The Mambo Kings Play Songs of Love* Hijuelos took a significant step forward in his career. He spent a great deal of time researching the Cuban music culture of 1950s America, setting the opening of the novel in the quintessential situation comedy of the period, *I Love Lucy,* which featured the only Hispanic professional on television, Desi Arnaz, who has since become a cultural icon. The eponymous brothers César and Nestor Castillo, man of action and man of contemplation, develop their musical careers to the point that they appear on television. César is a charming womanizer, lover of the American goddess, the large-breasted blonde Vanna Vane. Nestor settles into family life, though he is haunted by memories of María, who had rejected him back in Cuba. With the backdrop of the fast-moving, bygone world of mambo, in *Mambo Kings* Hijuelos explores the world of sex, music, and fame, creating a highly charged world of carpe diem sensuality, sensational and forbidding, contraposing it to anchors of the past, neither of which are fulfilling. *Mambo Kings* was made into a film starring Armand Assante.

The Fourteen Sisters of Emilio Montez O'Brien, Hijuelos's third novel, represents his most successful stylistic achievement, though it has serious structural problems. Gustavo Pérez Firmat has noted that *The Fourteen Sisters* continues Hijuelos's movement in his fiction away from a direct relationship with Cuba, but this evaluation was written before Hijuelos's most recent book, *Empress of the Splendid Season* and omits Hijuelos's preoccupation with memory as an important factor in the search for meaning. The latter is especially important in *The Fourteen Sisters.* The main characters, an Irish husband and Cuban wife, live a seemingly idyllic existence in rural Pennsylvania in the early part of the twentieth century. As one would imagine by the book's title, family dynamics are dominated by femininity, and the maternal and sexual presence of femaleness overwhelms the household. Various views of memory and their effects on the present and the future dominate the work, often in a gauzy pastorality and through discussions of the father's photography. Though *The Fourteen Sisters* contains Hijuelos's most beautiful prose, the sylvan world removes him from the urban landscape Hijuelos knows best, and the novel's structure suffers. With seventeen important fictional persons, his character explorations make the cast into a landscape in itself. There is too much there, and the lack of focus becomes detrimental to Hijuelos's seeming desire to home in on one character. In the end, he loses control and the ending falls apart, an admirable, ambitious, ultimately flawed effort.

In his fourth novel, Hijuelos returns to New York, and the fictional backdrop that allows him to focus on the search for meaning. *Mr. Ives' Christmas* is Hijuelos most spiritual work to date. The title character was adopted as a young child and has few cultural roots, though Hijuelos implies that Ives is Hispanic, as he is drawn time and again to New York's Hispanic community. Ives's successful marriage and professional life are thrown into disarray when his son is killed in a random act of violence. The book focuses on Ives's coming to terms with this death, re-learning identity and transforming himself as a man.

In his most recent work, *Empress of the Splendid Season*, Hijuelos returns to Spanish Harlem through the intimate portrait of a cleaning lady, cultural adaptation and assimilation (''Rico, with all his studies and for the way he was striving to become something in the English-speaking world ... felt as if he were on the outside looking in ... at the very source of his own emotionality ...''), ephemerality, male ineffectuality, and the search for meaning in an individual life (''After so much work and effort, what on earth am I doing here?''), especially among those who have suffered loss or rejection. As so often happens in Hijuelos's work, courtship and nuptials represent the high point of relationships between men and women (though the marriage in *Mr. Ives' Christmas* is an exception).

Because he won the Pulitzer Prize and is the most prolific Cuban-American author, Hijuelos has drawn a great deal of critical interest. His books are reviewed in all major newspapers and magazines, and have received discussion in several critical studies. Hijuelos has also been interviewed for various publications, including Ilan Stavans's ''Habla Oscar Hijuelos'' (Linden Lane, 1989).

—Harold Augenbraum

HILL, Carol

Nationality: American. **Born:** Carol DeChellis, New Jersey, 20 January 1942. **Education:** At Chatham College, Pittsburgh, 1957–61, B.A. in history 1961. **Career:** Publicist, Crown Publishers, 1965–67, and Bernard Geis Associates, 1967–69, both New York; publicist, 1969–71, and editor, 1971–73, Pantheon Books, New York; publicity manager, Random House, New York, 1973–74; senior editor, William Morrow, publishers, New York, 1974–76; senior editor, editor-in-chief, vice-president, and publisher, Harcourt Brace Jovanovich, New York, 1976–79. Since 1980 full-time writer. Formerly, actress at Judson Poets Theatre, New York, and in summer stock, Gateway Playhouse, New Jersey. **Agent:** Lynn Nesbit, Janklow and Nesbit Associates, 598 Madison Avenue, New York, New York 10022. **Address:** 2 Fifth Avenue, Apartment 19-U, New York, New York 10011, U.S.A.

PUBLICATIONS

Novels

Jeremiah 8:20. New York, Random House, 1970.

Let's Fall in Love. New York, Random House, 1974; London, Quartet, 1975.

An Unmarried Woman (novelization of screenplay). New York, Avon, and London, Coronet, 1978.

The Eleven Million Mile High Dancer. New York, Holt Rinehart, 1985; as *Amanda and the Eleven Million Mile High Dancer,* London, Bloomsbury, 1988.

Henry James' Midnight Song. New York, Poseidon Press, 1993.

Uncollected Short Stories

''The Shameless Shiksa,'' in *Playboy* (Chicago), September 1969.

''Gone,'' in *Viva* (New York), November 1974.

''Lovers,'' in *Viva* (New York), April 1975.

Plays

Mother Loves (produced New York, 1967).

Other

Subsistence U.S.A., photographs by Bruce Davidson, edited by Jamie Shalleck. New York, Holt Rinehart, 1973.

*

Manuscript Collections: Mugar Memorial Library, Boston University.

* * *

Carol Hill writes with a wit and sense of the absurd that some critics have likened to the bizarre humor found in the novels of Tom Robbins. Her characters are varied, genuine, and somewhat offbeat. The protagonists usually find themselves in absurd situations sometimes of their own making, but often coming as a surprise. Contemporary issues are interwoven in the plots, although they are not necessarily central to the stories.

In her first novel, *Jeremiah 8:20,* peace marchers protesting the war in Vietnam and problems of racial integration affect the rather unusual hero of this novel. Jeremiah Francis Scanlon, fat, balding, and 39, is a bookkeeper of mediocre abilities who has worked for the same company for almost 20 years. After years of living in the protective environment of his parents' suburban home he has taken the plunge and moved to New York City, not far from his place of employment. He rents a room in a boarding house that comes complete with a cast of strange and unusual characters. Hill's talent for delineating a varied array of individuals is evident in her description of Jeremiah, the social misfit; Miles, a part-time actor who specializes in female roles and is often seen prancing around the house in full costume and makeup; his friend Jocko, a pseudo-revolutionary and a cynic who excels in debate and delights in flustering his opponent. There are also two ladies: a prim old maid, and a wasp-tongued librarian who secretly yearns for Jocko. Although Jeremiah seems the most unlikely sort of protagonist to carry a novel, Hill makes us care for this pathetic, befuddled man who suffers great loneliness and despair. He does not, however, give up on life, but in a strangely courageous way keeps seeking an answer to his misery. Admittedly the answer he comes up with—that there is a secret held by Negroes that will end all his problems—seems absurd, but we have come to know Jeremiah so well that we can believe he would believe such nonsense.

The humor in *Jeremiah* is dark, though not oppressive. In Hill's next two novels the tone is lighter. *Let's Fall in Love* has a $10,000-a-shot hooker caught up in a web of murder and intrigue. This book has plenty of sex, including some very strange forms of coupling, a considerable departure from her first novel (about which, she says, people complained because there was not enough sex). *Let's Fall in Love* offers Hill's usual humor, and satire that some readers may find shocking, others erotic. Although this novel sold well, in the author's own estimation it lacked the power of her first. With *The Eleven Million Mile High Dancer* Hill is back on form although writing in a very different vein from *Jeremiah.* She combines her flare for the comic with a layman's knowledge of physics, a concern for the environment, and a natural penchant for fantasy. And here again is a multitude of characters.

The heroine is Amanda Jaworski, pilot, particle physicist, ardent feminist (most of the time), America's leading lady astronaut, and free spirit who roller skates through the NASA complex in red and white striped non-regulation shorts. She lives with a cat named Schrodinger who spends 23 out of 24 hours in a catatonic state that Amanda believes must be a form of narcolepsy. Meanwhile Amanda, a champion of female rights, finds herself wildly in love with the ultimate macho man, Bronco McCloud. He was ''devastating in the most literal sense of the word. It was quite exciting to be devastated by McCloud, and he knew it. His business was devastation not love. And this was why women adored him.'' Fortunately for Amanda there is another man in her life, Donald Hotchkiss, who is as masculine as Bronco, but capable of loving Amanda in a way she deserves to be loved. Love is an important theme in Hill's works: Jeremiah spent an entire novel in a desperate, futile search for it, while Amanda not only receives love in its many guises but returns it in abundance.

Bringing everything together is an intricate plot in which Amanda is selected to make an 18-month journey to Mars, but is diverted from this mission by the Great Cosmic Brain who kidnaps Schrodinger. The GCB is a disgustingly huge, bloated snake-like creature that discharges a foul odor with every exhalation. He is earth's creator and he is angry that humankind seems so ready to destroy itself either with nuclear weapons or pollution of the air and water. Amanda is helped in her search for Schrodinger by a tough-talking subatomic particle named Oozie. Their adventure in another dimension brings all Hill's imaginative skills to the fore. She amazes the reader with ever more exotic creatures and situations, culminating in a starry spin through space with the Dancer of the title. Throughout the story she intersperses quotes from scientists writing on the new physics which show how strange our world of reality can be (Paul Davies: ''One of the more bizarre consequences of quantum uncertainty is that matter can appear more or less out of nowhere''). So perhaps the wild imaginings of Hill are not so farfetched after all.

Not only the writer named in the title of *Henry James's Midnight Song,* but Sigmund Freud, Carl Jung, Edith Wharton, Emperor Franz Josef, and a host of other real people appear in the story, a murder mystery set in Vienna in the early twentieth century. At one point Hill has playwright Arthur Schnitzler observe, in a comment that sums up much of the narrative, ''Vienna lies like a dream, singing songs to us of our daylight selves. All masks and deception. Beautiful masks, but masks . . . . No one believes either in himself or in anything else, and in my opinion, they are quite right not to do so.''

Hill's literary style is often blunt, filled with contemporary jargon, and always to the point. She demonstrates the feelings of her characters by letting the reader eavesdrop on internal conversations. In this way she shows the desperate unhappiness and bewilderment suffered by Jeremiah as well as the gutsy determination and deeply felt love that drive Amanda to the ends of the universe to save Schrodinger. Although the themes of her books have varied greatly, there is one element that permeates them all—her ability to portray the human condition in all of its terrible and wonderful ways, and to portray even the darkest moments with plenty of wit.

—Patricia Altner

HILL, Susan (Elizabeth)

Nationality: British. **Born:** Scarborough, Yorkshire, 5 February 1942. **Education:** Grammar schools in Scarborough and Coventry; King's College, University of London, B.A. (honours) in English 1963. **Family:** Married the writer and editor Stanley Wells in 1975; three daughters (one deceased). **Career:** Since 1963 full-time writer: since 1977 monthly columnist, *Daily Telegraph,* London. Presenter, *Bookshelf* radio program, 1986–87. **Awards:** Maugham award, 1971; Whitbread award, 1972; Rhys Memorial prize, 1972. Fellow, Royal Society of Literature, 1972, and King's College, 1978. **Address:** Longmoor Farmhouse, Ebrington, Chipping Campden, Glos GL55 6NW England.

Publications

Novels

The Enclosure. London, Hutchinson, 1961.
Do Me a Favour. London, Hutchinson, 1963.
Gentleman and Ladies. London, Hamish Hamilton, 1968; New York, Walker, 1969.
A Change for the Better. London, Hamish Hamilton, 1969.
I'm the King of the Castle. London, Hamish Hamilton, and New York, Viking Press, 1970.
Strange Meeting. London, Hamish Hamilton, 1971; New York, Saturday Review Press, 1972.
The Bird of Night. London, Hamish Hamilton, 1972; New York, Saturday Review Press, 1973.
In the Springtime of the Year. London, Hamish Hamilton, and New York, Saturday Review Press, 1974.
The Woman in Black: A Ghost Story. London, Hamish Hamilton, 1983; Boston, Godine, 1986.
Air and Angels. London, Sinclair Stevenson, 1991.
The Mist in the Mirror. London, Mandarin, 1993.
Mrs. de Winter. London, Sinclair Stevenson, and Thorndike, Maine, Thorndike Press, 1993.
The Service of Clouds. London, Vintage, 1999.

Short Stories

The Albatross and Other Stories. London, Hamish Hamilton, 1971; New York, Saturday Review Press, 1975.
The Custodian. London, Covent Garden Press, 1972.
A Bit of Singing and Dancing. London, Hamish Hamilton, 1973.
Lanterns Across the Snow (novella). London, Joseph, 1987; New York, Potter, 1988.

Uncollected Short Stories

''Kielty's,'' in *Winter's Tales 20,* edited by A.D. Maclean. London, Macmillan, 1974; New York, St. Martin's Press, 1975.

Plays

Lizard in the Grass (broadcast 1971; produced Edinburgh, 1988). Included in *The Cold Country and Other Plays for Radio,* 1975.
The Cold Country and Other Plays for Radio (includes *The End of Summer, Lizard in the Grass, Consider the Lilies, Strip Jack Naked*). London, BBC Publications, 1975.
On the Face of It (broadcast 1975). Published in *Act 1,* edited by David Self and Ray Speakman, London, Hutchinson, 1979.
The Ramshackle Company (for children; produced London, 1981).
Chances (broadcast 1981; produced London, 1983).

Radio Plays: *Taking Leave,* 1971; *The End of Summer,* 1971; *Lizard in the Grass,* 1971; *The Cold Country,* 1972; *Winter Elegy,* 1973; *Consider the Lilies,* 1973; *A Window on the World,* 1974; *Strip Jack Naked,* 1974; *Mr. Proudham and Mr. Sleight,* 1974; *On the Face of It,* 1975; *The Summer of the Giant Sunflower,* 1977; *The Sound That Time Makes,* 1980; *Here Comes the Bride,* 1980; *Chances,* 1981; *Out in the Cold,* 1982; *Autumn,* 1985; *Winter,* 1985; *I am the King of the Castle, Susan Hill,* London, Longman, 1990.

Television Plays: *Last Summer's Child,* from her story ''The Badness Within Him,'' 1981.

Other (for children)

One Night at a Time. London, Hamish Hamilton, 1984; as *Go Away, Bad Dreams!,* New York, Random House, 1985.
Mother's Magic. London, Hamish Hamilton, 1986.
Suzy's Shoes. London, Hamish Hamilton, 1989.
I Won't Go There Again. London, Walker Books, 1990.
Septimus Honeydew. London, Walker Books, 1990.
Stories from Codling Village. London, Walker Books, 1990.
The Collaborative Classroom. with Tim Hill. Portsmouth, New Hampshire, Heinemann, 1990.
Beware, Beware, with illustrations by Angela Barrett. Cambridge, Massachusetts, Candlewick Press, and London, Walker, 1993.
The Christmas Collection, with illustrations by John Lawrence. Cambridge, Massachusetts, Candlewick Press, and London, Walker, 1994.
The Glass Angels. London, Walker, 1991. Cambridge, Massachusetts, Candlewick, 1992.
White Christmas. London, Walker, and Cambridge, Massachusetts, Candlewick, 1994.
King of Kings. Cambridge, Massachusetts, Candlewick, 1993; London, Walker Books, 1994.
Can It Be True? A Christmas Story. London, Hamish Hamilton, and New York, Viking Kestrel, 1988.
A Very Special Birthday. London, Walker, 1992.

Other

The Magic Apple Tree: A Country Year. London, Hamish Hamilton, 1982; New York, Holt Rinehart, 1983.
Through the Kitchen Window. London, Hamish Hamilton, 1984.
Through the Garden Gate. London, Hamish Hamilton, 1986.
Shakespeare Country, photographs by Rob Talbot. London, Joseph, 1987.
The Lighting of the Lamps. London, Hamish Hamilton, 1987.
The Spirit of the Cotswolds, photographs by Nick Meers. London, Joseph, 1988.
Family. London, Joseph, 1989; New York, Viking, 1990.
Crown Devon: The History of S. Fielding and Co. Stratford Upon Avon, Jazz, 1993.
Diana: The Secret Years, with Simone Simmons. New York, Ballantine Books, 1998.
Editor, *The Distracted Preacher and Other Tales,* by Thomas Hardy. London, Penguin, 1979.
Editor, with Isabel Quigly, *New Stories 5.* London, Hutchinson, 1980.
Editor, *People: Essays and Poems.* London, Chatto and Windus, 1983.
Editor, *Ghost Stories.* London, Hamish Hamilton, 1983.
Editor, *The Parchment Moon: An Anthology of Modern Women's Short Stories.* London, Joseph, 1990; as *The Penguin Book of Modern Women's Short Stories,* 1991.
Editor, *The Walker Book of Ghost Stories.* London, Walker Books, 1990; as *The Random House Book of Ghost Stores,* New York, Random House, 1991.
Editor, *Contemporary Women's Short Stories.* London, Joseph, 1995.

*

Manuscript Collections: Eton College Library, Windsor, Berkshire.

Critical Studies: *Susan Hill: I'm the King of the Castle* by Hana Sambrook, London, Longman, 1992.

* * *

One striking feature of Susan Hill's novels is the wide-ranging diversity of the experience they depict; and another, a maturity of understanding remarkable in a writer who began publishing her work at the age of only 19.

From the first she has shown a painful awareness of the dark abysses of the spirit—fear, grief, loneliness, and loss. A recurring early theme is that of lives warped and ruined by the selfishness of maternal domination. In *A Change for the Better* Deirdre Fount struggles in vain to break the shackles of dependence forged by her overbearing mother. The boy Duncan in the short story ''The Albatross'' is the impotent victim of a similar situation, dogged by the mother-created image of his own inadequacy. Driven finally over the brink of desperation, he does achieve his desired freedom, however brief, through a climactic act of violence.

Hill has always been especially perceptive in her portrayal of children. One of her most memorable novels, *I'm the King of the Castle,* is a penetrating study of mounting tensions in a bitter conflict between two eleven-year-old boys. This arises when a widower engages a new housekeeper, who brings with her a son the same age as his own. The peevish weakling already in possession is outraged at this invasion of his cherished territory, and in a subtle campaign of persecution, relentlessly hounds the hapless intruder towards an inevitably tragic denouement.

Hill's sensitive insight into the behavior and motivations of the young is matched by equal acuteness in delineating the problems and attitudes of those at the opposite end of the human life-span. *Gentleman and Ladies,* a novel simultaneously funny and sad, observes with a shrewdly amused yet compassionate eye the daily life and personalities of the inmates of an old people's home. The same intuitive sympathy informs the short story called ''Missy.'' Through a dying woman's fragmentary memories—frustratingly interrupted by the ministrations of brisk nurse and single visitor—the author intimately identifies with the thought-processes of extreme age.

Hill's gift of imaginative projection into worlds of experience far removed from her own is nowhere more apparent than in *Strange Meeting.* Probably her most notable *tour de force,* this is set in the trenches of Flanders during the 1914–18 war, and depicts with power, and at times almost intolerable poignancy, the doomed friendship of two young officers drawn together by their mutual daily contact with destruction and imminent death. There is also an irresistible attraction between opposite temperaments and family backgrounds: the reserved, introspective Hilliard finding inhibition magically thawed in the warmth of his companion Barton's easy, outgoing generosity.

The impact of actuality in this novel, both in its factual detail and the immediacy of involvement in the responses of combatants, is an astonishing achievement for a young woman. *Strange Meeting* also exemplifies Hill's capacity—comparatively rare among women novelists either past or present—for the convincing depiction of life from a male viewpoint. *The Bird of Night* is another highly original novel of great intensity which surveys a close relationship between two men. The central character is a poet, Francis Croft, whose tormented struggle against intermittent but increasing insanity is chronicled by the withdrawn scholar Lawson, whose life becomes devoted to care of his friend. The first-person masculine narrative of *The Woman in Black,* published after a silence of some years in her career as a novelist, provides a further instance of this aspect of Hill's talent. An atmospherically charged ghost story, it is related in a formal, rather stately past idiom, although carefully unlocated in any particular time. Full of Jamesian echoes and undercurrents, it traces with chilling compulsiveness the progress of a mysterious and sinister haunting.

Her adventurous charting of such varied areas of experience—childhood and old age, loyalties between men, the horrors of war and of insanity—demonstrates this versatile writer's ability to participate truthfully in many states of mind and conditions of life. But this does not preclude her treatment of the more conventionally ''feminine'' subject. Perhaps more than any of her books, *In the Springtime of the Year* has a direct appeal for a readership of women. Its heroine is a young widow cruelly bereaved after a short and happy marriage; and it movingly explores the successive stages of her grief, from initial angry refusal to accept the fact of loss through a gradual coming to terms and adjustment to her changed situation. The surrounding countryside, evoked with poetic precision, plays a key role in Ruth's final renewal of hope. This echoes the author's own belief in the restoring influence of rural rhythms and simplicities, reflected in her volumes of essays, such as *The Magic Apple Tree, Through the Kitchen Window,* and *Through the Garden Gate.*

Mrs. De Winter constitutes a sequel to Daphne du Maurier's 1938 classic *Rebecca,* but adds little to the original. With *The Service of Clouds,* Hill offers a tale of a woman's journey from girlhood, through triumphs and misfortunes to the time when she seemingly sees her hopes fulfilled in her son. But the story of Florence Hennessey is executed in the manner of an archetype, with few specific details, as though Hill intended to make it an Ur-version of a distinctly female *Bildungsroman.* The results are uneven; still, as with her effort to sequelize Daphne du Maurier, one lauds Hill for the courage of her attempt.

—Margaret Willy

HINDE, Thomas

Pseudonym for Sir Thomas Willes Chitty, Baronet. **Nationality:** British. **Born:** Thomas Willes Chitty in Felixstowe, Suffolk, 2 March 1926; succeeded to the baronetcy, 1955. **Education:** Winchester School, Hampshire; University College, Oxford. **Military Service:** Served in the Royal Navy, 1944–47. **Family:** Married Susan Elspeth Glossop (i.e., the writer Susan Chitty) in 1951; one son and three daughters. **Career:** Worked for Inland Revenue, London, 1951–53; staff member, Shell Petroleum Company, in England, 1953–58, and in Nairobi, Kenya, 1958–60. Granada Arts Fellow, University of York, 1964–65; visiting lecturer, University of Illinois, Urbana, 1965–67; visiting professor, Boston University, 1969–70. Fellow, Royal Society of Literature. **Address:** Bow Cottage, West Hoathly, near East Grinstead, Sussex RH19 4QF, England.

PUBLICATIONS

Novels

Mr. Nicholas. London, MacGibbon and Kee, 1952; New York, Farrar Straus, 1953.

Happy as Larry. London, MacGibbon and Kee, 1957; New York, Criterion, 1958.

For the Good of the Company. London, Hutchinson, 1961.

A Place Like Home. London, Hodder and Stoughton, 1962.

The Cage. London, Hodder and Stoughton, 1962.

Ninety Double Martinis. London, Hodder and Stoughton, 1963.

The Day the Call Came. London, Hodder and Stoughton, 1964; New York, Vanguard Press, 1965.

Games of Chance: The Interviewer, The Investigator. London, Hodder and Stoughton, 1965; New York, Vanguard Press, 1967.

The Village. London, Hodder and Stoughton, 1966.

High. London, Hodder and Stoughton, 1968; New York, Walker, 1969.

Bird. London, Hodder and Stoughton, 1970.

Generally a Virgin. London, Hodder and Stoughton, 1972.

Agent. London, Hodder and Stoughton, 1974.

Our Father. London, Hodder and Stoughton, 1975; New York, Braziller, 1976.

Daymare. London, Macmillan, 1980.

Other

Do Next to Nothing: A Guide to Survival Today, with Susan Chitty. London, Weidenfeld and Nicolson, 1976.
The Great Donkey Walk, with Susan Chitty. London, Hodder and Stoughton, 1977.
The Cottage Book: A Manual of Maintenance, Repair, and Construction. London, Davis, 1979.
Sir Henry and Sons: A Memoir. London, Macmillan, 1980.
A Field Guide to the English Country Parson. London, Heinemann, 1983.
Stately Gardens of Britain, photographs by Dmitri Kasterine. London, Ebury Press, and New York, Norton, 1983.
Forests of Britain. London, Gollancz, 1985.
Just Chicken, with Cordelia Chitty. Woodbury, New York, Barron's, 1985; London, Bantam Press, 1986.
Capability Brown: The Story of a Master Gardener. London, Hutchinson, 1986; New York, Norton, 1987.
Courtiers: 900 Years of English Court Life. London, Gollancz, 1986.
Tales from the Pump Room: Nine Hundred Years of Bath: The Place, Its People, and Its Gossip. London, Gollancz, 1988.
Imps of Promise: A History of the King's School, Canterbury. London, James and James, 1990.
Paths of Progress: A History of Marlborough College. London, James and James, 1992.
Highgate School: A History. London, James and James, 1993.
Editor, *Spain: A Personal Anthology.* London, Newnes, 1963.
Editor, *The Domesday Book: England's Heritage, Then and Now.* London, Hutchinson, and New York, Crown, 1985.
Editor, *Looking-Glass Letters,* by Lewis Carroll. New York, Rizzoli, 1992.

*

Manuscript Collections: University of Texas, Austin.

Critical Studies: In *New York Herald Tribune,* 24 May 1953; *The Angry Decade* by Kenneth Allsop, London, Owen, 1958; *Times Literary Supplement* (London), 26 May 1961, 27 October 1966, 7 November 1968, 11 September 1970; *Observer* (London), 7 June 1964; *New York Times,* 9 August 1967; *Books and Bookmen* (London), September 1974.

Thomas Hinde comments:

I write novels because I like novels and I like trying to make my own. These aim to be—but unfortunately hardly ever succeed in being—the novels I will like best of all. Just as my taste in novels changes, so the sort of novel I try to write changes. I also believe in the importance of the novel—one of the few places where individual art as opposed to script-conference art can still flourish. I believe that it can and will change and develop, however fully explored it seems at present. I believe that people will go on wanting to read novels. But however much I am convinced by these logical arguments of the vitality, value, and survival of the form, the real reason why I go on writing novels remains personal: despite its anxiety and difficulties, I like the process, and, despite disappointments, I am still excited by the results which I aim for.

* * *

When in 1957, American popular journalism first discovered the ''Angry Young Men,'' Thomas Hinde was listed, in articles in *Time* and *Life,* along with Kingsley Amis, John Wain, and John Braine, as one of the principal progenitors of the ''Movement.'' *Happy as Larry,* Hinde's second novel, had just been published and the novel's protagonist was a rather feckless young man who lost menial jobs, was vaguely trying to write, and irresponsibly drifted away from his wife. Yet the designation of ''Angry Young Men,'' over-generalized and inappropriate as it was for all the writers to whom it was applied, was particularly inappropriate for Hinde. Far from ''angry'' or defiantly rebellious, Hinde's protagonist wanders about apologetically, full of guilt, trying to help a friend recover a lost photograph that might be used for blackmail. His indecision, inhibitions, and constant self-punishment characterize him far more consistently than do any articulate attitudes toward society. In addition, Hinde's point of view in the novel is far from an unqualified endorsement of his protagonist's actions and attitudes. The ending, like the endings of most of Hinde's novels, is left open, without any definitive or summarizable statement. And the kind of judgment frequently assumed in popular accounts of novelists, the clarion call for a new way of life or the castigation of depraved contemporary morality, is entirely absent.

At the same time, however, in other terms, *Happy as Larry* is a novel of the 1950s. The protagonist's wandering, his lack of certainty, his allegiance only to close personal friends, his inhibitions and apologies, his insistence on self as a starting point for value, are all characteristic of much of the serious fiction of the decade. London, too, shrouded in rain, and gloom, spotted with crowded pubs that provide the only refuge, is also made the grim postwar city. In addition, Hinde uses a frequent symbol in fiction, the photograph, as central to the plot of his novel. In a world in which identity was regarded as shifting, unreliable, unknowable, only the photograph, the fixed and permanent image, could give identity any meaning, although that meaning, far more often than not, was itself a distortion, an over-simplification, occasion for blackmail. In fact, Hinde's novels most characteristically begin with categories definable in terms of other novels and novelists, with genres to which the reader is accustomed.

His first novel, *Mr. Nicholas,* chronicles the struggles of a young Oxonian, home on holidays, to define himself against his domineering and insensitive father. Another novel, *For the Good of the Company,* deals with the struggles for definition and power within the business combine, the complex organization that seemed a microcosm to depict human efforts to maintain a sense of rational control. *The Cage* and *A Place Like Home* are Hinde's African novels, *The Cage* a particularly sensitive and effective treatment of a young British colonial girl in Kenya attempting to retain her ties to the world of her parents while simultaneously understanding sympathetically the emerging black society. *The Village* establishes, without sentimentality or nostalgia, the world of the small English village about to be leveled by bulldozers and flooded for a new reservoir. *High* is Hinde's American visit novel, an account of the 40-year-old British writer teaching at an American university, including the familiar device of a novelist character writing a novel which is itself partly reproduced within the novel. In other words, the themes, techniques, concerns, and atmosphere of Hinde's novels are all familiar, all representative of their time and place—the heroine of *The Cage* often sounds like a more restrained Doris Lessing heroine, the protagonist of *High* is well established in a lineage that stretches back to Eric

Linklater—yet Hinde is also an individual novelist of great skill with an individual sense of texture and intelligence.

Hinde is frequently at his best in describing the sensitivities of his young characters—their introspections, their naivety, their commitments to attitudes and to people they cannot entirely understand. The heroine of *The Cage,* unable to untangle the racial antagonisms she does not entirely understand, thinks her young colonial boyfriend will kill the black man he thinks she's been sleeping with, overdramatizing a conflict she cannot solve. The young budding capitalist in *For the Good of the Company* makes love to the boss's daughter but cannot really fathom all the perplexities of her emotions. He is loyal to the enigma he has partially observed and partially constructed, always wondering how much he has made up himself. A similarly intelligent sensitivity characterizes the love affair in *The Village* between the harassed local doctor and the opportunistic young stockbroker's wife, an affair in which love is created out of mutual desperation. Hinde's sensitivity is applied not only to personal relationships, but to exterior atmospheres as well. Each novel contains many descriptions of weather, rich and subtle evocations of different climates and seasons—equally acute whether England, America or Africa—that are shaped carefully to suit the emotions or the problems of the characters. Weather is both the material for physical description and a principal means of controlling the atmosphere of the novel.

Hinde's novels are also full of action, concerned with plot. Yet the plots never reach definitive conclusions, never entirely resolve the issues they present. The protagonist of *Happy as Larry* finally finds the photograph, but may or may not become a solid citizen and create a home for his faithful wife. The young capitalist in *For the Good of the Company* is enmeshed in the system and, at the end, like his boss, is about to live his past over again. But whether or not he will be any wiser is an open question. *The Village* ends with the feeling that the old English village is probably doomed, as much from its own hypocrisies and inadequacies as from an insensitive ''urban bureaucracy,'' but the fight to save the village is not completely finished. Hinde's novels are, in a way, slices of recognizable contemporary life, a life in which people live and react, in which things happen although those things are not irremediably conclusive, and in which judgment is superficial or irrelevant. And these slices, communicated with a rich sense of personal and historical atmosphere, are never distorted by conversion into an object lesson or part of a message. In fact, Hinde, as author, keeps his distance. He can use familiar themes effectively because he treats them from a distance, stands far enough away to demonstrate a compassionate irony or an intelligent sympathy with his fictional world, a world effectively communicated because, like our larger world, it is one not easily reduced to understandable principles or judgments.

—James Gindin

HINES, (Melvin) Barry

Nationality: British. **Born:** Barnsley, South Yorkshire, 30 June 1939. **Education:** Ecclesfield Grammar School, 1950–57; Loughborough College of Education, Leicestershire, 1958–60, 1962–63, teaching certificate. **Family:** Divorced; one daughter and one son. **Career:** Teacher of physical education in secondary schools in London, 1960–62, Barnsley, 1963–68, and South Yorkshire, 1968–72; Yorkshire Arts Fellow in Creative Writing, University of Sheffield, 1972–74; East Midlands Arts Fellow in Creative Writing, Matlock College of Further Education, Derbyshire, 1975–77; Fellow in Creative Writing, University of Wollongong, New South Wales, 1979; Arts Council Fellow, Sheffield City Polytechnic, 1982–84. **Awards:** Writers Guild award, for screenplay, 1970; Society of Authors traveling scholarship, 1989. Fellow, Royal Society of Literature, 1977; Honorary Fellow, Sheffield City Polytechnic, 1985. **Agent:** Lemon Unna and Durbridge Ltd., 24 Pottery Lane, London W11 4LZ. **Address:** 323 Fulwood Road, Sheffield, Yorkshire S10 3BJ, England.

Publications

Novels

The Blinder. London, Joseph, 1966.
A Kestrel for a Knave. London, Joseph, 1968; as *Kes,* 1974.
First Signs. London, Joseph, 1972.
The Gamekeeper. London, Joseph, 1975.
The Price of Coal. London, Joseph, 1979.
Looks and Smiles. London, Joseph, 1981.
Unfinished Business. London, Joseph, 1983.
The Heart of It. London, Joseph, 1994.
Elvis over England. London and New York, Penguin Putnam, 1999.

Uncollected Short Stories

''First Reserve,'' in *Argosy,* 1967.
''Another Jimmy Dance,'' in *Dandelion Clocks,* edited by Alfred Bradley and Kay Jamieson. London, Joseph, 1978.
''Christmas Afternoon,'' in *The Northern Drift,* edited by Alfred Bradley. London, Blackie, 1980.

Plays

Billy's Last Stand (televised 1970; produced Doncaster, Yorkshire, 1984; London, 1985).
Two Men from Derby (televised 1976; produced London, 1989). Published in *Act Two,* edited by David Self and Ray Speakman, London, Hutchinson, 1979.
Kes, with Allan Stronach, adaptation of the novel by Hines (produced Oldham, Lancashire, 1979). London, Heinemann, 1976.
The Price of Coal (includes *Meet the People* and *Back to Reality*) (televised 1977; produced Nottingham 1984). London, Hutchinson, 1979.

Screenplays: *Kes,* with Ken Loach, 1969; *Looks and Smiles,* 1981.

Television Plays: *Billy's Last Stand,* 1970; *Speech Day,* 1973; *Two Men from Derby,* 1976

*

Critical Studies: *The Silent Majority: A Study of the Working Class in Post-War British Fiction* by Nigel Gray, London, Vision Press, and New York, Barnes and Noble, 1973; *Fire in Our Hearts* by Ronald Paul, Gothenburg, Sweden, Gothenburg Studies in English, 1982;

''Miners and the Novel'' by Graham Holderness, in *The British Working-Class Novel in the Twentieth Century* edited by Jeremy Hawthorn, London, Arnold, 1984.

Barry Hines comments:

My novels are mainly about working-class life. They are about people who live on council estates or in small terraced houses. The men work in mines and steelworks, the women in underpaid menial jobs—or, increasingly, are on the dole. I feel a strong sense of social injustice on behalf of these people which stems from my own mining background. The hardness and danger of that life (my grandfather was killed down the pit, my father was injured several times) formed my attitudes and made me a socialist.

My political viewpoint is the mainspring of my work. It fuels my energy; which is fine, as long as the characters remain believable and do not degenerate into dummies merely mouthing my own beliefs. However, I would rather risk being didactic than lapsing into blandness—or end up writing novels about writers writing novels. If that happens it will be time to hang up the biro.

My books are all conventional in form. They have a beginning, a middle, and a sort of ending (mainly in that order), with the occasional flashback thrown in. I think, after seven novels, I've now probably exhausted this form and need to explore different ways of telling a story, using some of the more fractured techniques I employ in writing film scripts.

* * *

The setting of all Barry Hines's novels is the working-class community of his native West Riding of Yorkshire. But every new work has dealt with another section or facet of this community, a new experience or dilemma as encountered by a representative, if highly individualized, figure from this class.

The author began his writing career in the wake of the late 1950s and 1960s movement in which a whole generation of northern working-class novelists had come to the fore, imprinting themselves on the map of English literary history through an unblinking representation of their native milieu and its language. Like Alan Sillitoe, Keith Waterhouse, Brendan Behan, or Sid Chaplin, Hines is initially concerned with the problems of young people. Like David Storey's *This Sporting Life,* Hines's first novel *The Blinder* considers professional football as an escape route from the working class, and Lenny Hawk is clearly akin to Arthur Seaton or Arthur Machin in his unbounded confidence, ready wit, and aggressiveness, though his gifts—intellectual as well as physical—reach far beyond the football pitch.

However, almost from the outset, certainly from *A Kestrel for a Knave* onward, Hines has found his own voice. It is not only an angry voice denouncing class prejudice and class privilege, and attacking the shortcomings of the once celebrated affluent society. It has also a cautiously hopeful ring emanating from the creative, defiant, and ultimately invincible qualities which his working-class characters display, often against overwhelming opposition. Thus *The Blinder* ends with Lenny publicly throwing torn-up sterling notes in the face of the powerful mill owner and football club director Leary who has sought to take revenge on the young soccer star by aiming to destroy his brilliant career through ugly intrigue. And even Billy Casper, despite being more isolated than ever after the violent death of the hawk which he has reared and looked after with the care and devotion that he has never himself received from any human being, will, we feel, somehow carry on unsubdued, a victim but also an Artful Dodger of the ways of the adults.

A Kestrel for a Knave, better known by the title of the acclaimed film adaptation *Kes,* remains Hines's best-know and bestselling novel to date. It is technically an accomplished work, breaking up the story of a day in the life of an undersized lad from a one-parent family through a series of skillfully interwoven flashbacks. It has a number of memorable scenes (e.g., Billy before the careers officer), some of which have entered textbooks. What they convey is not only a sense of the complete breakdown of communication between adults and the adolescent but also his consequent negative perception of social relations and institutions—the family, school, law, work. Significantly, his one point of succor and fulfillment in an otherwise hostile and crippling environment lies outside society—the hawk, trained but not tamed, embodying strength, pride, and independence.

The author pursues this theme in *The Gamekeeper* just as the previous novel had developed the school subject from *The Blinder.* If *A Kestrel for a Knave* could be read as an affirmation of the Lawrentian opposition between an alienating and degrading urban-industrial world and a fuller, more aware natural life, *The Gamekeeper* demonstrates that the author has either emancipated himself from this view or has never fully endorsed it. For the life of George Purse, who works on a ducal estate rearing and protecting pheasants from predators and poachers alike, is unspectacular and bare of romanticism. It is true that he has chosen this ill-paid job precisely in order to get away from the heat and dust of shiftwork in a steel mill. But the contentment and pride that he finds in his occupation are questioned and subverted by its inherent contradictions: the game is preserved for no other reason than to provide the Duke and his shooting party with the maximum bag; the gamekeeper's family suffers from the isolation imposed by living in a far-off cottage; chasing the poachers implies turning against members of his own class. Gamekeeping may thus be a personal alternative to industrial labor, but this form of living in direct contact with natural processes cannot shed capitalist relations of property and domination.

With *The Price of Coal* Hines returns to the industrial working class, this time confronting squarely such central issues as the nature of the work underground, the relationship between management and workforce, and the exigencies of an industrial policy to which, despite nationalization, the interests of the men remain firmly subordinated. The miners of this novel—the author has here visibly widened his cast even though he retains a central working-class family—are a singularly class-conscious and humorous breed; the way they poke fun at the absurdly exaggerated preparations for the impending Royal Visit to the colliery shows them drawing upon unfailing sources of resilience.

The militant spirit and satirical perspective of *The Price of Coal* clearly owe something to the 1972 and 1974 strikes in the industry, which goes to show how close to the thoughts and feelings of ordinary working people Hines has remained over the years, how loyal to his roots and faithful to his socialist humanist creed. The episodic structure of this terse narrative, its revealing juxtaposition of contrasting scenes and parts, and the dominance of dialogue derive in part from cinematographic techniques. The film version of *The Price of Coal* did, in fact, precede the novel by two years, and it is important to remember that Hines is a television playwright and filmscript writer as well as a novelist. He has been lucky to find a congenial interpreter of his material in the film director Ken Loach, whose documentary realist approach successfully transposed *Kes, The Gamekeeper, The Price of Coal,* and *Looks and Smiles* onto the screen, and has thus enabled the author to reach new audiences at home and abroad. In the

1990s, Hines published *The Heart of It* in Britain, and *Elvis over England* in both Britain and the United States.

—H. Gustav Klaus

HOAGLAND, Edward (Morley)

Nationality: American. **Born:** New York City, 21 December 1932. **Education:** Deerfield Academy; Harvard University, Cambridge, Massachusetts, 1950–54, A.B. 1954. **Military Service:** Served in the United States Army, 1955–57. **Family:** Married 1) Amy Ferrara in 1960 (divorced 1964); 2) Marion Magid in 1968 (deceased 1993); one daughter. **Career:** Taught at the New School for Social Research, New York, 1963–64, Rutgers University, New Brunswick, New Jersey, 1966, Sarah Lawrence College, Bronxville, New York, 1967 and 1971, City College, New York, 1967–68, University of Iowa, Iowa City, 1978 and 1982, Columbia University, New York, 1980–81, Bennington College, Vermont, 1987–95, and University of California, Davis, 1990 and 1992. Editorial writer, *New York Times,* 1979–89. Since 1985 general editor, Penguin Nature Library, New York. **Awards:** Houghton Mifflin fellowship, 1956; Longview Foundation award, 1961; Guggenheim fellowship, 1964, 1975; American Academy traveling fellowship, 1964, and Vursell Memorial award, 1981; O. Henry award, 1971; New York State Council on the Arts fellowship, 1972; Brandeis University citation, 1972; National Endowment for the Arts grant, 1982; New York Public Library Literary Lion award, 1988, 1996; National Magazine award, 1989; Lannan fellowship, 1993; Literary Lights Award, Boston Public Library, 1995. **Member:** American Academy, 1982. **Address:** P.O. Box 51, Barton, Vermont 05822, U.S.A.

Publications

Novels

Cat Man. Boston, Houghton Mifflin, 1956.
The Circle Home. New York, Crowell, 1960.
The Peacock's Tail. New York, McGraw Hill, 1965.
Seven Rivers West. New York, Summit, 1986.

Short Stories

City Tales, with *Wyoming Stories,* by Gretel Ehrlich. Santa Barbara, California, Capra Press, 1986.
The Final Fate of the Alligators. Santa Barbara, California, Capra Press, 1992.

Other

Notes from the Century Before: A Journal from British Columbia. New York, Random House, 1969.
The Courage of Turtles: Fifteen Essays about Compassion, Pain, and Love. New York, Random House, 1971.
Walking the Dead Diamond River (essays). New York, Random House, 1973.
The Moose on the Wall: Field Notes from the Vermont Wilderness. London, Barrie and Jenkins, 1974.
Red Wolves and Black Bears (essays). New York, Random House, 1976.
African Calliope: A Journey to the Sudan. New York, Random House, 1979; London, Penguin, 1981; with a new afterword by the author, New York, Lyons & Burford, 1995.
The Edward Hoagland Reader, edited by Geoffrey Wolff. New York, Random House, 1979.
The Tugman's Passage (essays). New York, Random House, 1982.
Heart's Desire: The Best of Edward Hoagland. New York, Summit, 1988; London, Collins, 1990.
Balancing Acts (essays). New York, Simon and Schuster, 1992.
Balancing Acts: Essays. New York, Lyons Press, 1999.
Tigers & Ice: Reflections on Nature and Life. New York, Lyons Press, 1999.
Editor, *The Circus of Dr. Lao,* by Charles Finney. New York, Vintage, 1983.
Editor, *The Mountains of California,* by John Muir. New York and London, Penguin, 1985.
Editor, *The Maine Woods,* by Henry David Thoreau. New York, Penguin, 1988.
Editor, *Walden,* by Henry David Thoreau. New York, Vintage, 1991.
Editor, *Steep Trails,* by John Muir. Sierra Club, 1994.

* * *

In the years since he published his first novel, *Cat Man* (1956), Edward Hoagland has gradually developed a reputation as one of America's leading essayists and a distinctive creator of fiction about both city life and the wilderness. His circus and boxing novels have been labeled required reading for those interested in these activities. In all his novels and many of his short stories, he shows a detailed, often first-hand knowledge of occupations where brawn or physical skills are more important than intellect. His essay, ''Big Cats,'' is a deft description of the cat family; *Cat Man* is a novel of circus life that contains sordid but not unrealistic detail about the human struggles unseen by the spectators; and *The Circle Home* is a novel full of information about the training of boxers and life among the destitute. In his third but not best novel, *The Peacock's Tail,* he still shows an interest in the lower classes, for the protagonist is a young white man who gradually loses cultural and racial prejudice as he works among the urban poor. In his most recent novel, *Seven Rivers West,* a small group of white men and two women make an arduous journey through the Canadian west.

His prose style, though varied, is often unembellished, staccato, and unpretentious; yet since his narrators and central characters are usually lower class people, relatively uneducated and inarticulate, the straightforward colloquial prose is appropriate. In its direct, deflationary tone, the beginning of his short story, ''The Final Fate of the Alligators,'' is a succinct introduction to most of his main characters: ''In such a crowded, busy world the service each man performs is necessarily a small one. Arnie Bush's was no exception.'' Yet the lack of subtle, intellectual prose does not mean that the author offers no insights. A description of leopards in motion ends, for example, with a deft comment: ''Really, leopards are like machines. They move in a sort of perpetual motion. Their faces don't change; they eat the same way, sleep the same way, pace much the same as each other. Their bodies are constructed as ideally as a fish's for moving and doing, for action, and not much room is left for personality.'' Regrettably, the final clause may aptly be applied to his characters, for many of them are so busy learning survival techniques in an uncaring world that their personalities are never fully developed. We may believe in them, but we are not always interested in them. The lack of interest sometimes results from the brevity of a character's role or the analysis devoted to it. Thus when characters fall back into self-destructive habits such as self-pity or alcoholism, we feel little sympathy. We impatiently dismiss them as born losers. On reflection, however, we may realize that we lack the compassion that Hoagland has for the urban poor or the uneducated easterner following his dream.

An accurate and just sense of Hoagland's strengths and weaknesses in prose style, narrative technique, characterization, and thought may be obtained from *The Circle Home,* the story of Denny Kelly, an irresponsible 29-year-old who has failed and continues to fail as a prize fighter and husband. In prose direct and at times colorful, the author demonstrates a close knowledge of the world of third-rate boxers.

> A lively fight: One-hand found occasion to maneuver into every foot the ring provided. He'd be close, mining in the belly, and spring back with a lithe light antelope-type movement. Often when his left returned from thrusts his arms dropped by his sides to balance him. Those leaps, narrow body straight upright and turning in the air to face the way he wanted, were the essence of his style… .

The author seems intent, not upon muckraking, but upon having readers understand the world of boxers and boxing. The reader comes to know Denny through the straight chronological flow of his attempted comeback, and through a series of flashbacks that chronicle his irresponsible and immature behavior as a husband and father. In re-creating the flow of events Hoagland shows a keen ear for dialogue. The end of the novel, however, is weak: Denny, contrite yet once more, phones to inform his wife that he is determined (because of *his* miseries) to return and to be henceforth a good family man. The title, *The Circle Home,* suggests that at last he will be truly home, but because he has failed so often before and has shown no true deep reformation, the reader may prophesy further backsliding. If we are meant to view Denny's future optimistically, the author's compassion for the dwellers in the ''lower depths'' has led him to a sentimental conclusion.

Seven Rivers West contains some of Hoagland's best fictional writing. Set in the Canadian west of the 1880s, not yet settled by Europeans, though it has been touched by them, it gives a vivid and detailed look at the white men pressing on with their railroad and seeking their future in the territory of the Indians, some of whom are still defiant, others already tainted by an alien civilization. Hoagland makes us appreciate both the energy and activities of the native people, and the magnificent challenge of the landscape. John Updike rightly praised it for being ''wonder-ful.'' The conclusion of the novel, however, is somewhat disappointing in its treatment of Cecil Roop's capture of a bear he has long sought and the depiction of the mythic Bigfoot.

From his works as a whole, Hoagland appears as a careful writer who, steeped in firsthand knowledge of his material, attempts with some humor and considerable compassion to show us men and women struggling first to survive and then to improve themselves or the world. There is, indeed, a definite sense of the author's feelings and involvement in the fiction and essays. (One reviewer objected to Hoagland exposing his neuroses in his travel essays.) But Hoagland does not hesitate to acknowledge the autobiographical aspects of his fiction. In the foreword to *City Tales,* he says:

> I found at the end of the 1960s that what I wanted to do most was to tell my own story; and by the agency of my first book of nonfiction, *Notes From the Century Before*—which began as a diary intended only to fuel my next novel—I discovered that the easiest way to do so was by writing directly to the reader without filtering myself through the artifices of fiction. By the time another decade had passed, however, I was sick of telling my own story and went back to inventing other people's, in a novel I hope will be finished before this book you are holding comes out.

Because Hoagland has the skill to make vivid the plight of the unprivileged, whether in the city or in the wilderness, he deserves the esteem that has gradually gained during his writing career.

—James A. Hart

HOBAN, Russell (Conwell)

Nationality: American. **Born:** Lansdale, Pennsylvania, 4 February 1925. **Education:** Lansdale High School; Philadelphia Museum School of Industrial Art, 1941–43. **Military Service:** Served in the United States Army Infantry, 1943–45: Bronze Star. **Family:** Married 1) Lillian Aberman (i.e., the illustrator Lillian Hoban) in 1944 (divorced 1975, deceased 1998), one son and three daughters; 2) Gundula Ahl in 1975, three sons. **Career:** Magazine and advertising agency artist and illustrator; story board artist, Fletcher Smith Film Studio, New York, 1951; television art director, Batten Barton Durstine and Osborn, 1951–56, and J. Walter Thompson, 1956, both in New York; freelance illustrator, 1956–65; advertising copywriter, Doyle Dane Bernbach, New York, 1965–67. Since 1967 full-time writer; since 1969 has lived in London. **Awards:** Christopher award, 1972; Whitbread award, 1974; Ditmar award (Australia), 1982; John W. Campbell Memorial award, 1982. Fellow, Royal Society of Literature, 1988. **Agent:** David Higham Associates Ltd., Golden Square, 5–8 Lower John Street, London W1R 4HA, England.

PUBLICATIONS

Novels

The Lion of Boaz-Jachin and Jachin-Boaz. London, Cape, and New York, Stein and Day, 1973.
Kleinzeit. London, Cape, and New York, Viking Press, 1974.
Turtle Diary. London, Cape, 1975; New York, Random House, 1976.
Riddley Walker. London, Cape, and New York, Summit, 1980; expanded edition, with afterword, notes, and glossary by the author, Bloomington, Indiana University Press, 1998.
Pilgermann. London, Cape, and New York, Summit, 1983.
The Medusa Frequency. London, Cape, and New York, Atlantic Monthly Press, 1987.

The Moment under the Moment. London, Cape, 1992.
Fremder. London, Jonathan Cape, 1996.
Angelica's Grotto. London, Bloomsbury, 1999.

Uncollected Short Stories

"Schwartz," in *Encounter* (London), March 1990.

Fiction (for children)

Bedtime for Frances. New York, Harper, 1960; London, Faber, 1963.
Herman the Loser. New York, Harper, 1961; Kingswood, Surrey, World's Work, 1972.
The Song in My Drum. New York, Harper, 1962.
London Men and English Men. New York, Harper, 1962.
Some Snow Said Hello. New York, Harper, 1963.
The Sorely Trying Day. New York, Harper, 1964; Kingswood, Surrey, World's Work, 1965.
A Baby Sister for Frances. New York, Harper, 1964; London, Faber, 1965.
Bread and Jam for Frances. New York, Harper, 1964; London, Faber, 1966.
Nothing to Do. New York, Harper, 1964.
Tom and the Two Handles. New York, Harper, 1965; Kingswood, Surrey, World's Work, 1969.
The Story of Hester Mouse Who Became a Writer. New York, Norton, 1965; Kingswood, Surrey, World's Work, 1969.
What Happened When Jack and Daisy Tried to Fool the Tooth Fairies. New York, Four Winds Press, 1965.
Henry and the Monstrous Din. New York, Harper, 1966; Kingswood, Surrey, World's Work, 1967.
The Little Brute Family. New York, Macmillan, 1966.
Save My Place, with Lillian Hoban. New York, Norton, 1967.
Charlie the Tramp. New York, Four Winds Press, 1967.
The Mouse and His Child. New York, Harper, 1967; London, Faber, 1969.
A Birthday for Frances. New York, Harper, 1968; London, Faber, 1970.
The Stone Doll of Sister Brute. New York, Macmillan, and London, Collier Macmillan, 1968.
Harvey's Hideout. New York, Parents' Magazine Press, 1969; London, Cape, 1973.
Best Friends for Frances. New York, Harper, 1969; London, Faber, 1971.
The Mole Family's Christmas. New York, Parents' Magazine Press, 1969; London, Cape, 1973.
Ugly Bird. New York, Macmillan, 1969.
A Bargain for Frances. New York, Harper, 1970; Kingswood, Surrey, World's Work, 1971.
Emmet Otter's Jug-Band Christmas. New York, Parents' Magazine Press, and Kingswood, Surrey, World's Work, 1971.
The Sea-Thing Child. New York, Harper, and London, Gollancz, 1972.
Letitia Rabbit's String Song. New York, Coward McCann, 1973.
How Tom Beat Captain Najork and His Hired Sportsmen. New York, Atheneum, and London, Cape, 1974.
Ten What? A Mystery Counting Book. London, Cape, 1974; New York, Scribner, 1975.
Dinner at Alberta's. New York, Crowell, 1975; London, Cape, 1977.
Crocodile and Pierrot, with Sylvie Selig. London, Cape, 1975; New York, Scribner, 1977.
A Near Thing for Captain Najork. London, Cape, 1975; New York, Atheneum, 1976.
Arthur's New Power. New York, Crowell, 1978; London, Gollancz, 1980.
The Twenty-Elephant Restaurant. New York, Atheneum, 1978; London, Cape, 1980.
The Dancing Tigers. London, Cape, 1979.
La Corona and the Tin Frog. London, Cape, 1979.
Flat Cat. London, Methuen, and New York, Philomel, 1980.
Ace Dragon Ltd. London, Cape, 1980.
The Serpent Tower. London, Methuen, 1981.
The Great Fruit Gum Robbery. London, Methuen, 1981; as *The Great Gumdrop Robbery,* New York, Philomel, 1982.
They Came from Aargh! London, Methuen, and New York, Philomel, 1981.
The Battle of Zormla. London, Methuen, and New York, Philomel, 1982.
The Flight of Bembel Rudzuk. London, Methuen, and New York, Philomel, 1982.
Ponders (*Jim Frog, Big John Turkle, Charlie Meadows, Lavinia Bat*). London, Walker, and New York, Holt Rinehart, 4 vols., 1983–84; 1 vol. edition, London, Walker Books, 1988.
The Rain Door. London, Gollancz, 1986; New York, Crowell, 1987.
The Marzipan Pig. London, Cape, 1986; New York, Farrar Straus, 1987.
Monsters. London, Gollancz, and New York, Scholastic, 1989.
Jim Hedgehog's Supernatural Christmas. London, Hamish Hamilton, 1989; New York, Clarion, 1992.
Jim Hedgehog and the Lonesome Tower. London, Hamish Hamilton, 1990; New York, Clarion, 1992.
M.O.L.E. Much Overworked Little Earthmover, with Jan Pienkowski. London, Cape, 1993.
The Court of the Winged Serpent. London, Cape, 1994.
The Trokeville Way. New York, Knopf, 1996.
Trouble on Thunder Mountain. New York, Orchard Books, 1999.

Plays

The Carrier Frequency, with Impact Theatre Co-operative (produced London, 1984).
Riddley Walker, adaptation of his own novel (produced Manchester, 1986).
Some Episodes in the History of Miranda and Caliban (opera libretto), music by Helen Roe (produced London, 1990).

Television Plays: *Come and Find Me,* 1980.

Poetry (for children)

Goodnight. New York, Norton, 1966; Kingswood, Surrey, World's Work, 1969.
The Pedalling Man and Other Poems. New York, Norton, 1968; Kingswood, Surrey, World's Work, 1969.
Egg Thoughts and Other Frances Songs. New York, Harper, 1972; London, Faber, 1973.

Other

The Second Mrs. Kong: An Opera in 2 Acts (libretto), music by Harrison Birtwistle. London, Universal Edition, 1994.
A Russell Hoban Omnibus. Bloomington, Indiana University Press, 1999.
Russell Hoban: Forty Years: Essays on His Writings for Children, edited by Alida Allison. New York, Garland, 2000.

Other (for children)

What Does It Do and How Does It Work? Power Shovel, Dump Truck, and Other Heavy Machines. New York, Harper, 1959.
The Atomic Submarine: A Practice Combat Patrol under the Sea. New York, Harper, 1960.

*

Critical Studies: *Through the Narrow Gate: The Mythological Consciousness of Russell Hoban* by Christine Wilkie, Rutherford, New Jersey, Fairleigh Dickinson University Press, and London, Associated University Presses, 1989.

* * *

Russell Hoban's novels for adults have a compelling strangeness made up of the most elusive aspects of myth, riddle, history, fantasy, philosophy, and humor. For many readers this is a deeply intriguing mixture which has made him something of a cult author. Drop the title of his most-discussed book, *Riddley Walker,* into any literary conversation and it will divide the group into three parties: the excited supporters who believe it to be one of the great underestimated novels of the 20th century, the bored opposition who didn't get past page six because it was ''odd,'' and the remainder who've never heard of Russell Hoban. This last group is smaller since the success of the film *Turtle Diary,* which follows the bare plot of Hoban's third novel, but with scarcely a shadow of the book's power.

Turtle Diary is the most approachable of Hoban's works for readers familiar with the ''realist'' novel, although its structure is unusual. The first chapter is a kind of journal note by William G. who works in a London bookshop and whose deliberately limited life is metaphorically connected to the lives of the giant turtles he visits in the London Zoo. Chapter 2 is an apparently unrelated narration by Neaera H., an author of children's books, but now in a state of block about a water-beetle she had hoped would become a new character. As William and Neaera meet and join forces to free the turtles the parallel narration continues, creating two characters of powerful immediacy, and allowing the reader to know far more about them than either is willing to reveal to the other. Like all Hoban's major characters these two are seekers, looking for answers, or even the right questions, about the meaning of life. The starting point is often a sudden perception of the extraordinariness of the ordinary, whether it's the daily human routine or the world of landscape and natural objects.

Animals are often used by Hoban as metaphors, or totems, or familiars. Through them he questions reality and identity, Thing-in-Itself. What a turtle is to itself remains a riddle for Neaera and William. The lion in *The Lion of Boaz-Jachin and Jachin-Boaz,* Hoban's first novel for adults, begins as a figure in a lion-hunt Boaz-Jachin sees carved in relief upon a tomb. It develops as a richly ambiguous image during his search for his father and the map of life his father has promised him. Like many other objects in the internal worlds of Hoban's narrators, the lion becomes increasingly ''real,'' and moves into the external world with farcical, sad, moving, results. Although some of the black comedy, like the outrageously funny scene in the asylum, is similar to the surrealism of Samuel Beckett, the bleakness is always moderated in Hoban's work by a far more benign, optimistic view of the world than Beckett's. Love is possible, even probable, in Hoban's world, though it is always love with toughness, risk, and no certainties. Like life, it requires courage, hope, and a sense of humour.

Kleinzeit and *The Medusa Frequency* have hints of Beckett too, but also of Charlie Chaplin, Woody Allen, and ''magic realism.'' Kleinzeit tells Ward Sister that his name means ''hero'' in German, but his rival explains that it really means ''smalltime,'' and the unheroic hero, struggling with inner states which have become inseparable from outer, is often at the center of Hoban's novels. Gifts are given to Kleinzeit as he leaves the hospital with Ward Sister, ''cured'' of his ''dismemberment,'' if not of the pains in his hypotenuse, diapason, and stretto. God gives the lovers a week free of electricity-strikes to start them off on their joint life, Hospital gives a week's postponement of Kleinzeit catching the flu, and Death gives Kleinzeit the power to draw with a calligraphy brush in ''one fat sweep'' of black ink, a perfect circle, symbol of harmony and completion. But although the symbols in Hoban's novels are often universal ones, and frequently have a classical source, like the recurrent Orpheus and Eurydice myth, their particular appearances are always full of wit and unexpected application. The Orpheus and Eurydice myth allows scope to some of Hoban's strongest interests, the need to love which has as its dark side the possibility of loss and death, the power of memory and history, and the urge to make sense of experience by remaking it in song, story, and art.

Hoban has fun with names and words in all his books, but *Riddley Walker* is, among other things, an extended examination of the connections between language and the world. The action is narrated by Riddley Walker himself in an extraordinary dialect, a cross between phonetic Cockney, mixed regional, and corrupted remnants of computer-speak, which succeeds brilliantly in suggesting the language of England over two thousand years after the ''1 Big 1,'' a nuclear explosion around 1997 A.D. With no words for half the abstractions we take for granted, Riddley expresses ideas of religion, science, and art in terms of the practical things he knows, and the resulting metaphors are exhilarating. (In 1998—the *real* 1998—Hoban published an expanded edition of the book, including a glossary and explanatory notes.) The two parts of Riddley's name hint at the two aspects of his adventures, mental and physical, during the ten days after he earns manhood in his tribe. ''Walker is my name and I am the same. Riddley Walker. Walking my riddles where ever they've took me and walking them now on this paper the same.'' One of the great pleasures of Hoban's novels lies in the participation demanded from the reader. In this novel the distant past of Riddley's society, known to him only from scraps of myth, song, and game, is the reader's twentieth-century present. There are continual shocks in the collision between our own and Riddley's view of events. A very funny scene satirizes ''expert'' interpretation of the past when Goodparley explains the meaning of a manuscript dating from the twentieth century.

Pilgermann, Hoban's most violent and disturbing novel, is an equally startling use of history to ask philosophical questions, but this time with a complexity of biblical and Islamic allusions. The pilgrim-hero is a Jew in the eleventh century, another of Hoban's seekers on whom the riddles of life suddenly force an imperative physical journey and metaphysical quest. Any answers come through connections demonstrated, not merely told.

Nick Hartley, the hero of *The Trokeville Way,* a novel for children, has a grown-up mind: he compares the object of his affection (an older girl, naturally) to a pre-Raphaelite painting, and has trouble fitting in with the world of children. Harold Klein of *Angelica's Grotto* also has problems adjusting, but his difficulties are much more serious, since he is seventy-two. Whereas Nick may be an art historian in the making, Harold is the genuine article. Obsessed by Gustav Klimt's nudes, he stumbles onto a titillating Web site called Angelica's Grotto, and enters into a complex relationship—first in cyberspace, then in real life— with the site's mistress, a feminist intellectual. ''I'm on the edge of madness,'' Klein confesses. ''On the other hand ... I've got a lot of company.''

—Jennifer Livett

HODGINS, Jack

Nationality: Canadian. **Born:** John Stanley Hodgins in Comox Valley, Vancouver Island, British Columbia, 3 October 1938. **Education:** Tsolum School, Courtenay, British Columbia; University of British Columbia, Vancouver, 1956–61, B.Ed. 1961. **Family:** Married Dianne Child in 1960; one daughter and two sons. **Career:** Teacher, Nanaimo District Senior Secondary School, British Columbia, 1961–80; visiting professor, University of Ottawa, 1981–83; visiting professor, 1983–85, and currently professor of creative writing, University of Victoria, British Columbia. Writer-in-residence, Simon Fraser University, Burnaby, British Columbia, 1977, and University of Ottawa, 1979; Canadian Department of External Affairs lecturer, Japan, 1979. **Awards:** University of Western Ontario President's medal, for short story, 1973; Canada Council award, 1980; Governor-General's award, 1980; Canada-Australia award, 1986. D.Litt., University of British Columbia, 1995. **Agent:** Bella Pomer Agency, 22 Shallmar Boulevard, Toronto, Ontario M5N 2Z8. **Address:** Creative Writing Dept., University of Victoria, Box 1700, Victoria, British Columbia, Canada V8W 2Y2.

PUBLICATIONS

Novels

The Invention of the World. Toronto, Macmillan, 1977; New York, Harcourt Brace, 1978.
The Resurrection of Joseph Bourne; or, A Word or Two on Those Port Annie Miracles. Toronto, Macmillan, 1979.
The Honorary Patron. Toronto, McClelland and Stewart, 1987.
Innocent Cities. Toronto, McClelland and Stewart, 1990.
The Macken Charm. Toronto, McClelland & Stewart, 1995.
Broken Ground. Toronto, McClelland & Stewart, 1998.

Short Stories

Spit Delaney's Island: Selected Stories. Toronto, Macmillan, 1976.
The Barclay Family Theatre. Toronto, Macmillan, 1981.
Beginnings: Samplings from a Long Apprenticeship: Novels Which Were Imagined, Written, Re-Written, Submitted, Rejected, Abandoned, and Supplanted. Toronto, Grand Union, 1983.

Uncollected Short Stories

''The God of Happiness,'' in *Westerly,* (Nedlands, Australia) 4, 1968.
''Promise of Peace,'' in *The North American Review,* New Ser. 6(4), 1969.
''A Matter of Necessity,'' in *The Canadian Forum,* January 1970.
''The Graveyard Man,'' in *Descant* (Fort Worth, Texas) 15(4), 1971.
''Witness,'' in *Alphabet* 18–19, 1971.
''Edna Pike, on the Day of the Prime Minister's Wedding,'' in *Event: Journal of the Contemporary Arts,* 2(1), 1972.
''Open Line,'' in *The Antigonish Review* 9, 1972.
''Passing by the Dragon,'' in *Island: Vancouver Island's Quarterly Review of Poetry and Fiction,* (Nanaimo, British Columbia), 2, 1972.
''The Importance of Patsy McLean,'' in *Journal of Canadian Fiction,* 2(1), 1973.
''In the Museum of Evil,'' in *Journal of Canadian Fiction,* 3(1), 1974.
''Silverthorn,'' in *Forum* (Houston) 12(1), 1974.
''Great Blue Heron,'' in *Prism International,* 14(2), 1975.
''A Conversation in the Kick-and-Kill: July,'' in *Sound Heritage,* (Victoria, British Columbia), 6(3), 1977.
''The Invention of the World,'' in *Viva,* February 1978.
''Spit Delaney's Nightmare,'' in *Toronto Life,* January 1978.
''Miss Schussnigg's First Spring,'' in *Peter Gzowski's Spring Tonic,* edited by Peter Gzowski. Edmonton, Alberta, Hurtig, 1979.
''Victims of the Masquerade,'' in *Interface,* 4(8), 1981.
''Change of Scenery,'' in *Small Wonders: New Stories by Twelve Distinguished Canadian Writers,* edited by Robert Weaver. Toronto, CBC, 1982.
''The Day of the Stranger,'' in *Chatelaine,* December 1982.
''Faller Topolski's Arrival,'' in *True North/Down Under* (Lantzville, British Columbia), 1, 1983.
''The Crossing,'' in *Vancouver Magazine,* February 1985.
''Earthquake,'' in *The Canadian Forum,* March 1986.
''Loved Forever,'' in *Books in Canada,* August-September 1988.
''Balance,'' in *Paris Transcontinental: A Magazine of Short Stories* 7, 1993.
''Galleries,'' in *O Canada 2,* edited by Cassandra Pybus, *Meanjin* (Parkville, Victoria), 54, 1995.
''In the Forest of Discarded Pasts,'' in *Paris Transcontinental: A Magazine of Short Stories,* 11, c. 1995.
''Over Here,'' in *Prism International,* 33(3), 1995.

Other

Teachers' Resource Book to Transition II: Short Fiction, with Bruce Nesbitt. Vancouver, CommCept, 1978.
Teaching Short Fiction, with Bruce Nesbitt. Vancouver, CommCept, 1981.
Left Behind in Squabble Bay (for children), illustrated by Victor Gad. Toronto, McClelland and Stewart, 1988.

Over Forty in Broken Hill: Unusual Encounters Outback and Beyond. St. Lucia, University of Queensland Press, 1992.
A Passion for Narrative: A Guide for Writing Fiction. Toronto, McClelland & Stewart, 1993; New York, St. Martin's Press, 1994.
Editor, with W.H. New, *Voice and Vision.* Toronto, McClelland and Stewart, 1972.
Editor, *The Frontier Experience.* Toronto, Macmillan, 1975.
Editor, *The West Coast Experience.* Toronto, Macmillan, 1976.
Editor, with Bruce Nesbitt, *Teaching Short Fiction; A Resource Book to ''Transitions II: Short Fiction.''* Vancouver, CommCept, 1978.

*

Bibliography: ''Jack Hodgins,'' in *The Writers' Union of Canada: A Directory of Members,* edited by Ted Whittaker, Toronto, The Writers' Union of Canada, 1981; ''Hodgins, Jack (1938–)'' by Helen Hoy, in her *Modern English-Canadian Prose: A Guide to Information Sources,* Detroit, Gale Research, 1983; ''Hodgins, Jack (1938–)'' by Allan Weiss, in his *A Comprehensive Bibliography of English-Canadian Short Stories, 1950–1983,* Toronto, ECW Press, 1988; ''Selected Bibliography'' by David [L.] Jeffrey, in his *Jack Hodgins and His Works,* Toronto, ECW Press, 1989.

Manuscript Collection: The National Library of Canada, Ottawa, Ontario.

Critical Studies: ''The Mind of the Artist: The Soul of the Place,'' in *Essays on Canadian Writing,* 5, 1976, ''Fantasy in a Mythless Age'' in *Essays on Canadian Writing,* 9, 1977–78, ''Thinking about Eternity,'' in *Essays on Canadian Writing,* 20, 1980–81, all by J.R. (Tim) Struthers; ''An Interview with Jack Hodgins'' by Jack David, in *Essays on Canadian Writing,* 11, 1978; ''Jack Hodgins and the Island Mind,'' in *Canada Emergent: Literature/Art,* edited by James Carley, *Book Forum,* 4, 1978, ''A Crust for the Critics,'' in *Canadian Literature,* 84, 1980, ''It Out-Hodgins Hodgins: Burlesque and the Freedoms of Fiction,'' in *Essays on Canadian Writing,* 26, 1983, and *Jack Hodgins and His Works,* Toronto, ECW Press, 1989, all by David L. Jeffrey; ''Jack Hodgins'' by Geoff Hancock, in his *Canadian Writers at Work: Interviews with Geoff Hancock,* Toronto, Oxford University Press, 1987; ''Haunted by a Glut of Ghosts: Jack Hodgins' *The Invention of the World*'' by Robert Lecker, in *Essays on Canadian Writing,* 20, 1980–81; ''Canadian Burlesque: Jack Hodgins' *The Invention of the World*'' by Susan Beckmann, in *Essays on Canadian Writing,* 20, 1980–81; ''Western Horizon: Jack Hodgins'' by Alan Twigg, in his *For Openers: Conversations with 24 Canadian Writers,* Madeira Park, British Columbia, Harbour, 1981; ''*The Barclay Family Theatre*'' by Ann Mandel, in *The Fiddlehead,* 134, 1982; ''An Interview with Jack Hodgins'' by Peter O'Brien, in *Rubicon* (Montreal), 1, 1983; ''Irish and Biblical Myth in Jack Hodgins' *The Invention of the World*'' by Jan C. Horner, in *Canadian Literature,* 99, 1983; ''Isolation and Community in Jack Hodgins's Short Stories,'' in *Recherches Anglaises et Américaines,* 16, 1983, ''Jack Hodgins: Interview,'' in *Kunapipi* 9(2), 1987, and ''Magic Realism in Jack Hodgins's Short Stories,'' in *Recherches Anglaises et Nord-Américaines* 20, 1987, all by Jeanne Delbaere-Garant; ''Jack Hodgins' *The Invention of the World* and Robert Browning's 'Abt Vogler''' by Laurence Steven, in *Canadian Literature,* 99, 1983; ''Brother XII and *The Invention of the World,*'' in *Essays on Canadian Writing,* 28, 1984, and ''Lines and Circles: Structure in *The Honorary Patron*'' in *Canadian Literature,* 128, 1991, both by JoAnn McCaig; ''Disbelieving Story: A Reading of *The Invention of the World*'' by Frank Davey, in *Present Tense, The Canadian Novel,* edited by John Moss, vol. 4, Toronto, NC Press, 1985; '''If Words Won't Do, and Symbols Fail': Hodgins' Magic Reality'' by Cecilia Coulas Fink, in *Journal of Canadian Studies,* 20(2), 1985; ''The Invention of a Region: The Art of Fiction in Jack Hodgins' Stories'' by Waldemar Zacharasiewicz, in *Gaining Ground: European Critics on Canadian Literature,* edited by Robert Kroetsch and Reingard M. Nischik, Edmonton, NeWest, 1985; ''Jack Hodgins's Island: A Big Enough Country'' by Allan Pritchard, in *University of Toronto Quarterly,* 55, 1985; ''Jack Hodgins and the Sources of Invention,'' in *Essays on Canadian Writing* 34, 1987, ''Jack Hodgins,'' in *A Sense of Style: Studies in the Art of Fiction in English-Speaking Canada,* Toronto, ECW Press, 1989, ''Hodgins's 'Pack of Crazies': *The Resurrection of Joseph Bourne*'' and ''On the Edge of Something Else: Jack Hodgins's Island World,'' both in *An Independent Stance: Essays on English-Canadian Criticism and Fiction,* Erin, Ontario, Porcupine's Quill, 1991, all by W.J. Keith; ''Out on the Verandah: A Conversation with Jack Hodgins'' by Alan Lawson and Stephen Slemon, in *Australian-Canadian Studies* 5(1), 1987; ''Jack Hodgins: Interview'' by Russell McDougall, in *Kunapipi,* 12(1), 1990; ''Reader's Squint: An Approach to Jack Hodgins' *The Barclay Family Theatre*'' by Simone Vauthier, in *Modes of Narrative: Approaches to American, Canadian, and British Fiction,* edited by Reingard M. Nischik and Barbara Korte, Würzburg, Germany, Königshausen and Neumann, 1990; *The Counterfeit and the Real in Jack Hodgins' ''The Invention of the World''* by Carol Langhelle, Lund, Sweden, Nordic Association for Canadian Studies—L'Association Nordique d'études Canadiennes, 1992; *How Stories Mean* edited by John Metcalf and J.R. (Tim) Struthers, Erin, Ontario, Porcupine's Quill, 1993.

Jack Hodgins comments:

(1981) I write fiction in order to free myself of those shadowy creatures that walk briefly across the back of my mind and then return to grow into living breathing people who aren't satisfied to live in my skull: Spit Delaney, the engineer who falls apart when his steam locomotive is sold to a museum; Maggie Kyle, the gorgeous ''loggers' whore'' who sets herself up a new life in the ruins of a failed utopian colony; Joseph Bourne, the famous poet who dies and returns to life in a tiny town on the edge of the world; Jacob Weins, the small-town mayor never seen without a different costume on, who after his town has slid off the mountain and into the sea has to search for a new role for himself, and a new costume. Writing them down is a way of getting rid of them. It is also, I hope, a way of sharing them—of allowing other people to love them too, as I must do myself before I'm through with them. I write fiction in order to explain their mysteries to myself—what makes them tick?—but always in the process of writing uncover more mystery than I solve. I write fiction in order to nail down a place before it disappears. If much has been made of the fact that most of my stories are set on Vancouver Island, it is not just that there is some excitement in introducing a part of the world seldom represented before in fiction. The place is changing while I look at it and I want to get the trees, the rocks, the beaches down right before they disappear. I also feel that if I nail the place down right, the people who walk around in it will be just that much more convincing to the reader, wherever he is in the world. I write fiction, finally, for the same reason the magician creates *his* illusions—in order to start something magical happening in the audience's (reader's) mind. If the critics insist on calling me a ''magic realist'' it isn't because I distort reality or indulge in fantasy but because I see the magic that's already there.

* * *

Jack Hodgins is a strongly regional writer who has never significantly departed in his fiction from the setting of Vancouver Island, the fairly circumscribed region where he was born and spent his childhood and young manhood. As Canada's westernmost edge of settlement, the rural north of Vancouver Island is a region that runs to excess. Until recently it still counted as a frontier area, attracting with its fine scenery and good winters a rich variety of eccentrics who populated its fishing villages, stump farms, and logging camps. Yet, in common with the best of regional writers, Hodgins portrays the local as a staging point for the universal, and his novels and stories owe their appeal largely to his ability to realize the fact that ''imagination can redeem or transcend the physical,'' as Frank Davey observed in the *Oxford Companion to Canadian Literature*. Hodgins's imagination is indeed prodigious, and its inventions, while often seemingly improbable in their carnivalesque scope or burlesque nature, nevertheless reveal a commitment to humanity at large, as well as the dignity of the individual. Until recently Hodgins's fiction was overflowing with humor, and suggested a temperamental inability on the author's part to see life as other than good, prospects as other than expansive, and human nature as other than extravagant in its potentialities. However, his 1998 novel, *Broken Ground*, suggests that a darker side of Hodgins's imagination has emerged, and with it brought a new complexity to his work without sacrificing the outrageous and sometimes magical visions that have to date defined his writing.

Hodgins's first book was a group of loosely linked stories, *Spit Delaney's Island*; Spit Delaney himself, wild and often shocking in the unconventionality of his behavior, is the first of Hodgins's roguish and exuberant heroes who live by their dreams and in the process expose the futility of the limited lives of the literal-minded. Hodgins in fact practices a latter-day picaresque fiction. His central characters are often variants on the classical picaro, the ultimately redeemable rogue. His novels take on the loose structure of the picaresque romance, and in the process he constantly intertwines parables with the deceptions of verisimilitude. *The Invention of the World* is still to date the best known of Hodgins's longer fictions and the most representative of his writing. It is a mingling of the eccentrically regional and the extravagantly parabolical. A larger-than-life evangelist (based on an actual confidence trickster who once operated in the same area under the name Brother Twelve) persuades a whole Irish village to follow him to Vancouver Island and form a community subservient to his wishes. In a way the evangelist invents a world, but it is a false one; the real heroine and creative spirit of the book is the exuberant and promiscuous Maggie Kyle, eventual bride in an epic and Brueghelesque wedding at which the island loggers break into ferocious battle. Maggie is not only a splendidly complex personality; she also spans literary genres and approaches, from Joycean interior monologue to vitalist action.

Winner of the Gibson Literary Award as best first novel of the year, *The Invention of the World* was followed by *The Resurrection of Joseph Bourne*, for which Hodgins received Canada's most prestigious literary award, the Governor General's. *The Resurrection of Joseph Bourne* is even more emphatically vitalist than its predecessor in its insistence on the power of the human imagination to make its own terms with existence. The once internationally renowned, now reclusive poet, Joseph Bourne, is revitalized by the appearance of a mysterious woman whose mystical powers endow Bourne with the ability to regenerate his isolated community through a succession of comical yet genuine encounters.

The occasional problem of sustaining exaggerative fantasy surfaced in Hodgins's 1981 collection, *The Barclay Family Theatre*. While it more explicitly treats Hodgins's interest in the figure of the artist than in his previous work, this series of stories concerning the daughters of a single backwoods family and their disconcerting impact on the world is somewhat shallow in parts and occasionally artificial in its construction. The Barclay daughters, in a reprise of their appearance in *Spit Delaney's Island*, do not capture the reader's sympathy or interest in the manner of their original vehicle. Some wondered whether Hodgins had come to the point where the possibilities of his existing material and his current methods were almost exhausted. Instead, Hodgins has expanded as a writer, producing a striking number and variety of new works that range widely in both a geographical and a generic sense. These include a children's book, *Left Behind in Squabble Bay*, a travel book, *Over 40 in Broken Hill*, based on an expedition with Australian writer Roger McDonald, and a creative writing text, *A Passion for Narrative*. Several novels have also since appeared, demonstrating his versatility and ability to learn from exploring different literary forms, and inject his novels with new energy.

Hodgins's literal exploration of different geographic territory led to his fictional explorations in *The Honorary Patron*, divided between Europe and Vancouver Island, and *Innocent Cities*, divided between Australia and Vancouver Island. While *The Honorary Patron* presents an unprecedented central figure in Hodgins's oeuvre, the older, cautious, and chronically pensive Jeffrey Crane, it is in *Innocent Cities* that Hodgins departs most radically from his earlier work. It is, in its own way, a historical novel, set in Victoria during the 1880s, the period of lull between the Cariboo and the Klondike gold rushes. Yet this ''Victorian'' novel is anything but Victorian in form. Inspired by the actual letters of a woman who invited her sister to join her in Canada, so as to assume certain ''wifely'' duties for her husband, the novel defies Victorian convention and notions of decorum from the onset. In a frontier society where names and identities are easily exchanged, masquerades are revealed to be common, even necessary for the society's belief in itself to prosper. Hodgins uses these deceptions as the basis of a post-modern investigation of history, meaning, language, and narrative. *Innocent Cities* is a work of parody and palimpsest, an imitation Victorian novel presented through an ironic modern sensibility.

Comfortable in his departure from form, Hodgins's was just as comfortable in his return in 1995's *The Macken Charm*, a bildungsroman covering the 1956 summer before Rusty Macken's departure from Vancouver Island for university on the mainland. The novel possesses the semi-autobiographical elements that an author usually mines earlier in his career. Coming as it does, however, mid-career, *The Macken Charm* avoids the romantic rememberings or sentimental meanderings that sometimes characterize the genre. Instead Hodgins navigates the young Macken's sensitive recognition of his family's peculiarities and strengths, as framed by the events of a cousin's anything but funereal funeral and just as outlandish wake. Combining the magical realism and extravagant humor of his earlier works with the sensitive perception of an isolated narrator, Hodgins's proved himself and his subject matter inexhaustible.

Nevertheless, he challenged himself again in his critically acclaimed novel *Broken Ground*. Set in 1922 in Portuguese Creek, a ''soldiers' settlement'' on Vancouver Island, the novel is permeated by the horror of war and the ethos of settlement, as the characters who populate the novel struggle with love and loss in their lives, the complexities of truth, and the difficulties of assigning coherent meaning to events. A forest fire looms throughout the first one-third of the novel, paralleling the war in its random destructiveness and forcing the issues many would rather suppress to the fore. Nature is a cataclysmic force not welcoming to the inhabitants of the settlement; the land they have been rewarded with by the government is unsuitable for farming, ultimately causing numerous deaths and disasters. Just as the fire erupts and the settlers are evacuated, Hodgins moves his novel to 1919 and the letters of one couple separated by the war, providing a few answers to the novel's many mysteries, and an insightful portrait of one soldier's experience of war. Part three is set in 1996 as Rusty Macken—of *The Macken Charm*—returns to Vancouver Island with a cinematic version of the events of the now legendary fire, causing one elderly survivor to recall the aftermath with devastating clarity, and wonder how quiet personal lives are reinterpreted over time as staunch purposefully heroic archetypes. Hodgins, always interested in the process of mythmaking, has raised the stakes in *Broken Ground*, his self-reflexive playfulness traded in for thoughtful introspection and exceptionally sensitive characterization. *Broken Ground* was nominated for the 2000 International Impac Dublin Literary Award.

—George Woodcock, updated by J.R. (Tim) Struthers and Jennifer Harris

HOFF, Harry Summerfield

See COOPER, William

HOFFMAN, Alice

Nationality: American. **Born:** New York City, 16 March 1952. **Education:** Adelphi University, Garden City, New York, B.A. 1973; Stanford University, California (Mirelles fellow), M.A. 1975. **Family:** Married to Tom Martin; two sons. Lives in Boston, Massachusetts. **Awards:** Bread Loaf Writers Conference Atherton scholarship, 1976. **Address:** c/o Putnam, 200 Madison Avenue, New York, New York 10016, U.S.A.

Publications

Novels

Property Of. New York, Farrar Straus, 1977; London, Hutchinson, 1978.
The Drowning Season. New York, Dutton, and London, Hutchinson, 1979.
Angel Landing. New York, Putnam, 1980; London, Severn House, 1982.
White Horses. New York, Putnam, 1982; London, Collins, 1983.
Fortune's Daughter. New York, Putnam, and London, Collins, 1985.
Illumination Night. New York, Putnam, and London, Macmillan, 1987.
At Risk. New York, Putnam, and London, Macmillan, 1988.
Seventh Heaven. New York, Putnam, and London, Virago Press, 1991.
Turtle Moon. New York, Putnam, and London, Macmillan, 1992.
Second Nature. New York, Putnam, and London, Macmillan, 1994.
Practical Magic. New York, Putnam, and London, Macmillan, 1995.
Fireflies. New York, Hyperion Books for Children, 1997.
Here on Earth. New York, Putnam, 1997.
Local Girls. New York, G.P. Putnam's Sons, 1999.
Horsefly. New York, Hyperion Books for Children, 2000.
The River King. New York, G.P. Putnam's Sons, 2000.

Uncollected Short Stories

''Blue Tea,'' in *Redbook* (New York), June 1982.
''Sweet Young Things,'' in *Mademoiselle* (New York), June 1983.
''Sleep Tight,'' in *Ploughshares* (Cambridge, Massachusetts), vol. 15, no. 2–3, 1989.

*

Film Adaptations: *Practical Magic,* 1998.

* * *

Alice Hoffman's female protagonists have much in common. They are all drawn to dangerous men: a saboteur, a gang leader, a drug-dealing older brother, a nihilistic singer. They are all estranged from their parents, though most have strong relationships with their grandparents or someone of their grandparents' age. These older people are often fortunetellers of some kind. There is a strong undercurrent of magic in Hoffman's work.

In Hoffman's first novel, *Property Of,* the unnamed narrator attaches herself to McKay, a gang leader whose life is dedicated to the notion of honor as the gang had adapted it to the violent world of The Avenue, gang territory on the edge of New York City. When she leaves McKay it is because his glittering image and his honor have both crumbled. Hoffman brings almost nothing new to this old-hat situation, and only in the scattered passages where the narrator meditates on deeper things does her language come alive. The neo-hardboiled style dialogue is undermined by an unrealistic candor between characters who hardly know one another. Hoffman tries to pass this off as cool detachment, but it is clearly narrative strategy; a way to delineate character without much development. Hoffman's interest in ceremonial or ritual behavior, and in personal myth-making that will continue to be a part of all her work is present here, though muffled by the screen of toughness. There is also the first of many magic charms and talismans: a locket with a human tooth inside given to the narrator by Monty, an older man who tries to look out for her.

Property Of's narrator, like many of Hoffman's women, seeks a life of magic. She contrasts the ''little magic'' of herbs and that nature that fights its way up through the concrete with the ''big magic'' of alcohol and drugs. ''Difficult to categorize, until, of course, the consequences are seen. The little magic only causes a smile, but the big magic always seems to end up in the slammer or at a wake.'' In the last sentence of the novel she smiles.

The Drowning Season is the story of Esther the White and her granddaughter Esther the Black. The generation between these two women, Esther the Black's parents, are both lost: her father to his compulsion to drown himself every summer, and her mother to drink and dream of escape to the desert. Esther the White and the caretaker who loves her try to help the younger Esther come to grips with the emptiness of her life.

Like *The Drowning Season, Angel Landing* is set on the shore of a large cove. Two women live in a nearly empty boarding house across the bay from a nuclear plant under construction. When the plant is sabotaged the younger of the women, Natalie, discovers who ''the bomber'' is and finds herself falling in love with him. This ''dangerous'' man works his way through his feelings of alienation through his commitment to Natalie. Aunt Minnie, the older woman and owner of the boarding house, encourages Natalie in the relationship, even when she knows the man is ''the bomber.'' As in *Property Of* the parts of this novel that are timely—the protesting over the nuclear plant, the struggle for better conditions in an old age home—clutter the story and add little. And again there is the unbelievable openness: Finn, the ''bomber,'' who had been completely closed up, speaks his first emotionally committed words to Natalie in front of five strangers at a Thanksgiving dinner. After a *deus ex machina* helps Finn escape prosecution, he and Natalie run off to Florida, ending the novel on a hopeful but vague note.

White Horses is a difficult novel. The writing is as emotional and poetic as Hoffman's best work, but there is no character with which a reader might comfortably identify, or even sympathize. Aversion or pity are the likely responses. Young Teresa spends her life waiting for an ''Aria,'' a mythical kind of outlaw lover, whose image has been passed down to her from her mother. The mother passes up real love while she waits, surrendering the myth only as she is dying. Both Teresa and her mother believe Teresa's brother Silver is an Aria, and Teresa enters into an incestuous relationship with him. Mother and daughter are both caught between the romance of the wild outlaw lover and the harsh life of attachment to the self-centered cruel Silver. Teresa breaks away from this destructive love only in the last pages.

Fortune's Daughter is a story of nurturing, and of ''female mythology'' as the jacket copy reads. Rae Perry is pregnant by a cruel and dangerous man, Jessup. Here the older woman Rae (who has cut herself off from her parents) turns to is Lila, a fortune-telling woman whose illegitimate daughter was given up at birth. She helps Rae, though her tea-leaf reading turns up the image of a dead baby. The dead child, however, turns out to be Lila's daughter, and Lila has to choose between isolating herself with the (''actual'') ghost of her dead child, or giving it up and accepting her childless life with her supportive husband—who had a dangerous reputation when she met him. (In all Hoffman's novels women are the real movers, the instigators. The men run in circles raising dust, but accomplish little.) Lila chooses the living. Rae does not cut herself off completely from Jessup, and their relationship is left an open question at the novel's end.

Turtle Moon again invokes the theme of magic and mysticism, this time in a community of divorcees, Verity, Florida, a place where sea turtles migrate during the month of May. When the sea turtles mistake ''the glow of streetlights for the moon, people go a little bit crazy;'' marriages crumble and affairs begin. The story of Verity is the story of Lucy Rosen and her twelve-year-old son Keith, who find out just how bad life can be when the turtles migrate. A woman in Lucy's apartment building, also a runaway wife from New York, is murdered and Lucy's son rescues the victim's baby daughter and runs off, making him suspect in the murder. When Verity native Julian Cash investigates the murder and the missing children, he becomes romantically involved with Lucy, and another of Hoffman's female protagonists is drawn to a reckless man.

In *Second Nature,* there's a primal blend of the mysterious and the commonplace as compelling as the moon-besotted turtles found in *Turtle Moon.* Stephen and Robin are a modern-day Beauty and the Beast; Stephen, now an attractive man, was a feral child raised by wolves and Robin the woman who falls under his spell. It is when Robin tries to hide Stephen away in the small island community where she lives that the love story unfolds. By the end of the story the astute reader has taken Hoffman's foreshadowing as the inevitable ending of a good fairy tale, and the magic has worked again.

In Hoffman's eleventh novel, *Practical Magic,* another tale of love, the magic is not so much practical as predictable. As in earlier novels, Hoffman's older generation of characters are seers. Sally and Gillian are two orphaned sisters who live with their two aunts, women who grow strange herbs to make their magical brews and who are visited by lovesick women seeking their love potions and charms. Shunned by superstitious classmates, Sally and Gillian finally flee the small New England town in an attempt to flee the mysteries of love, which is always one step behind them. They cannot escape the magic of love and of life, even when it takes a malevolent form. Unlike earlier Hoffman stories, by the end of the story the overwhelming dose of magic becomes as hard to swallow as the aunts' mysterious love potions.

Hoffman seems content to rework her favored themes and ideas again and again, but usually manages to keep them fresh. Of the several tellings of the Hoffman story, *Fortune's Daughter* is surely the finest, with *The Drowning Season* not far behind. In attempting to keep her ideas always fresh, Hoffman's strengths at times seem to verge on self parody, seen occasionally in *At Risk* and *Seventh Heaven.*

—William C. Bamberger, updated by Sandra Ray

HOGAN, Desmond

Nationality: Irish. **Born:** Ballinasloe, County Galway, 10 December 1950. **Education:** Garbally College, Ballinasloe, 1964–69; University College, Dublin, 1969–73, B.A. in English and philosophy 1972, M.A. 1973. **Career:** Writer and actor with Children's T. Company theatre group, Dublin, 1975–77; moved to London, 1977: teacher, 1978–79; writer-in-residence, University of Glasgow, 1989. **Awards:** Hennessy award, 1971; Irish Arts Council grant, 1977; Rooney prize (USA), 1977; Rhys Memorial prize, 1980; *Irish Post* award, 1985. **Agent:** Rogers Coleridge and White Ltd., 20 Powis Mews, London W11 1JN, England.

PUBLICATIONS

Novels

The Ikon Maker. Dublin, Co-op, 1976; London, Writers and Readers, and New York, Braziller, 1979.

The Leaves on Grey. London, Hamish Hamilton, and New York, Braziller, 1980.

A Curious Street. London, Hamish Hamilton, and New York, Braziller, 1984.

A New Shirt. London, Hamish Hamilton, 1986.

The Edge of the City. London, Faber, 1993; Boston, Faber, 1994.

A Farewell to Prague. London and Boston, Faber, 1995.

Short Stories

The Diamonds at the Bottom of the Sea and Other Stories. London, Hamish Hamilton, 1979.
Children of Lir: Stories from Ireland. London, Hamish Hamilton, and New York, Braziller, 1981.
Stories. London, Pan, 1982.
The Mourning Thief and Other Stories. London, Faber, 1987; as *A Link with the River,* New York, Farrar Straus, 1989.

Plays

A Short Walk to the Sea (produced Dublin, 1975). Dublin, Co-op, 1979.
Sanctified Distances (produced Dublin, 1976).
The Ikon Maker, adaptation of his own novel (produced Bracknell, Berkshire, 1980).

Radio Plays: *Jimmy,* 1978 (UK).

Television Plays: *The Mourning Thief,* 1984 (UK).

* * *

The writings of Desmond Hogan testify to the strength of the creative impulse, and the fragility of those who carry it within them. In his novels and stories he depicts the struggles of isolated individuals to assert and define themselves in the face of social pressures. The tragedies he explores—whether set in rural Ireland or urban Britain—present a vision of human frailty, with characters unable to withstand the force of their own destructive passions and the smothering proprieties of the world. They are rendered vulnerable to attack by their fellows, succumbing to a collective psychological violence whose inevitable outcome is madness and suicide. The mental hospital and the dark depths of the river are images that recur constantly in Hogan's fiction. Equally common to his work are other images, the ikon objects used by his characters to give meaning to their lives.

The Ikon Maker, Hogan's first novel, describes the close, obsessional relationship between a mother and son in a remote part of Galway. Charting its growth from the boy's childhood, through the trauma of a friend's early death, and later through his travels among hippies, homosexuals, and IRA activists in England, Hogan portrays compellingly the son's desire for freedom and the fierce, all-consuming need of the mother who pursues him in a doomed effort to re-establish the original bond between them. Building up his narrative from a pattern of terse, fragmented sentences, the author draws the threads of plot neatly together, his style at once jagged and poetic. Diarmaid, the quiet, self-contained youth creating his own inner world through ''ikons'' of collage, and the mother struggling to suppress her rampant life-force, are both memorable. Here too, as elsewhere in his works, Hogan reveals the bleak, stultifying nature of life in rural Ireland, and its gradual change under the impact of the modern world with its television and terrorism.

The Leaves on Grey has as its central point the friendship ripening into love, of three privileged youngsters in 1950s Dublin. Growing up in a world where the ideals of the Easter Rising have already been betrayed, forming an elite distinct from their fellows, the three friends see themselves as being chosen for a noble destiny, prospective arbiters of their country's regeneration. Liam the mystic intellectual, Sarah with her religiously charged sexuality, and the narrator Sean together experience the varieties of love and loss, pursuing in their different ways the search for fulfillment. The suicide of Liam's mother, a beautiful Russian émigré, binds them closer, and shadows the course of their future lives. Hogan evokes with subtlety the characters and their shifting perceptions, and once more employs his ''splintered'' technique of short, sharp sentences to good effect. He also uses a device not unlike Joyce's epiphany, fixing on moments of revelation and insight which bridge chronological time and emphasize the continuity of human experience. (This device, as well as the fragmented style, is used later in the more ambitious *A Curious Street*). *The Leaves on Grey* contains the symbol which most appropriately sums up the nature of Hogan's art: the stained glass window, here the last act of creation by a dying artist, in which broken shards are fitted together and transformed by light into a vision of beauty, perfectly encapsulates the method—and the achievement—of this writer.

A Curious Street is arguably the most impressive of Hogan's novels. Taking as its beginning the suicide of Alan Mulvanney, a teacher and unpublished writer, in Athlone in 1977, the story is presented in the form of a memoir by its half-English narrator, son of the woman with whom Mulvanney enjoyed a brief, frustrating affair. Scanning these two lives and the lives of those closest to them, the narrative glides freely in and out of time, going back to explore previous generations, returning to touch on an intense threefold friendship involving the narrator himself. The novel appears to expand outward, branching through families and friends, delving by way of Mulvanney's unpublished writings into the traumas of the past—the Cromwellian invasion, the devastating famine of the 1840s, the 1916 revolution. Hogan's treatment of his subject is nothing less than inspired. As ever, he constructs from broken splinters of sentences, adroitly marshalling his devices—potted ''biographies'' of his numerous characters, spreading outward from the novel's core, dream-vision passages from history and legend that still strike echoes in the modern Irish consciousness, the transcendent moment linking the experience of successive generations. *A Curious Street* probes at the purity and the loss of innocence, the brutal violence that lurks in family relationships, the destructive power of creativity. Images of the quest, of constant journeyings in search of peace through a wartorn land, and of the ever-present threat of death and madness haunt the pages. Recent writings yield fresh explorations of those themes central to the author's fiction, touching once more on vulnerability, alienation and exile, the struggle for self-assertion in the face of tribal disapproval. *The Mourning Thief and Other Stories* is perhaps the most accessible, childhood memories resurfacing in the flawed hero-figures of ''Teddyboys'' and ''The Man from Korea.'' ''Afternoon'' gives a moving account of an ancient tinker queen's adventures, while the title story examines the conflict between a young pacifist and his dying father, a former I.R.A. activist now troubled by the bombings in the North. The stories of Lebanon Lodge provide further variations on the theme—the Irish-Jewish actor of the title-story recalling the birth and death of love from exile in England, the murderous response of a rural village to illicit love in ''The Players,'' the fraught marriage of a Catholic beauty queen and her violent clergyman husband in ''The Vicar's Wife.'' By turns gentle and savage, Hogan's vision challenges with undeniable conviction.

A Farewell to Prague shows the author at his least accessible and most complex. The novel follows its narrator, Des, in his wanderings through Europe and the United States, his dream-visions and reminiscences. Des recounts his bisexual love affairs, his bond with the unattainable Eleanor and the doomed Marek, who later dies of

AIDS. Nightmare memories pervade the text, of World War II concentration camps and racial hatred, a scenario viewed as beginning again in wartorn Croatia. As always, Hogan builds his work from disparate visual images, bringing alive the wastelands and high-rise blocks of Prague, the desolation of rural Ireland, the dirt roads of Georgia. At the heart of his narrative is the quest for love, the fight to maintain the self against the tribal will. His distrust of the herd and its values is given perhaps its most ferocious expression to date: ''Community leads to fascism, the swastikas in the churches, the lilies of the valley under Hitler.'' His positive images are of artistic creation, the familiar talismans of the stained glass window, the ancient Russian religious ikons. In these later works, as in all his writings, Hogan assembles the shards of experience to produce a literary ikon of his own, light shining through a sequence of moments seized from the passage of time.

—Geoff Sadler

HOLLINGHURST, Alan

Nationality: British. **Born:** Stroud, Gloucestershire, 26 May 1954. **Education:** Magdalen College, Oxford, B.A. in English 1975, M.Litt. 1979. **Career:** Lecturer of English, Magdalen College, 1977–78; Somerville College, 1979–80, and Corpus Christi College, 1981, all Oxford University, and University of London, 1982; assistant editor, 1982–90, and since 1990 poetry editor, *Times Literary Supplement,* London, 1982–90. **Address:** c/o Times Literary Supplement, Priory House, St. John's Lane, London EC1M 4BX, England.

PUBLICATIONS

Novel

The Swimming-Pool Library. London, Chatto and Windus, 1988; New York, Vintage, 1989.
The Folding Star. London, Chatto and Windus, and New York, Pantheon, 1994.
The Spell. London, Chatto & Windus, 1998; New York, Viking, 1999.

Poetry

Confidential Chats with Boys. Oxford, Sycamore Press, 1982.

Other

Editor, with A. S. Byatt, *New Writing 4.* London, Vintage, 1995.
Translator, *Bajazet,* by Jean Racine. London, Chatto and Windus, 1991.

* * *

With the publication of *The Swimming-Pool Library* in 1988, British writer Alan Hollinghurst emerged as one of the most articulate voices in the expanding field of contemporary gay fiction. The success of Hollinghurst's novel arose from its erotically charged depiction of contemporary gay life in London, as well as from its attempt to articulate that ever-elusive ''gay sensibility'' that so many gay writers claim to understand but can never, it seems, adequately describe.

Stylistically and thematically, Hollinghurst places his novel within a richly intertextual framework of other gay texts, characters, events, and literary traditions. The novel is peopled with various gay historical characters, such as E.M. Forster and Ronald Firbank, and it draws eclectically upon various alternative forms of expression that have historically served the clandestine needs of the gay community, such as camp, pink prose, and classical mythology. Throughout *The Swimming-Pool Library* echoes of other homosexual writers can be heard. These include, for example, the Genet-like encounter with a gang of skinheads, or the Firbank-like thematics found in the novel's racist commodification of the black male body. The novel's proliferation of witty aphorisms and anecdotes reminds one of Wilde, while its meditative moments and search for sexual identity are reminiscent of Proust.

The novel's narrative revolves around two historically separate, yet thematically comparable, events that expose the continuity and insidiousness of oppression used by British authorities against homosexuals throughout the last two centuries. When, for example, the novel's modern-day protagonist is naively told that sexual oppression is no longer an issue and that it belongs to another time, to ''another world,'' he responds with what is surely the most important utterance of the novel: ''it isn't another world ... it's going on in London almost every day.'' Oppression and bigotry, as Hollinghurst's novel reveals, continued as frequently in Thatcher's Britain as they did during any other place or time.

The central narrative takes place in London during the summer of 1983, ''the last summer of its kind,'' and describes, with tragicomic flourish, the amorous adventures of 25-year-old Will Beckwith, whose primary concern, he writes, is ''making passes at anything in trousers.'' Hollinghurst's Will Beckwith, like White's unnamed narrator and Andrew Holleran's Malone, is one of the most memorable characters of recent gay fiction. That summer, Will writers, ''I was riding high on sex and self-esteem—it was my time, my *belle époque.*'' Egotistical and unreflective, Will lives a privileged life of luxury, supported by his wealthy grandfather. During the course of the summer, Will meets an elderly and eccentric homosexual, Lord Charles Nantwich, and their unlikely alliance forms the cornerstone of the novel's detective-like narrative. Will is commissioned by the older man to write his biography because, as a character tells Will, ''he thinks you will understand.'' In the process of reading through Charles's journal entries Will discovers that in 1954 his own grandfather, as the former Director of Public Prosecutions, was responsible for entrapping and imprisoning Charles, along with many other homosexual men, for the sin of ''male vice.'' When a similar event happens to James, Will's best friend, he is outraged and takes action to prevent history from cruelly repeating itself: ''I decided that if necessary, and if it might save James, I would testify in court ... and so perhaps do something, though distant and symbolic, for Charles, and for Lord B's other victims.'' In this act of defiance against his own grandfather, and, in turn, against the whole legal system which suppresses homosexual expression, Will puts aside his over-developed ego for the first time and becomes aware of his communal identity with other homosexuals. These ''experiences,'' declares Will, ''gave me an urge to solidarity with my kind.'' The suffering of

Charles and James ultimately serves as a catalyst for Will's own developing sense of responsibility and underscores the central theme of Hollinghurst's novel: the journey toward liberation can only begin when one acknowledges a political responsibility to a community under siege.

Although *A Swimming-Pool Library* brilliantly achieved what the author intended, it can never be granted the status of a ''classic'' in general fiction. To achieve that universality, such a novel would have to embody a world where gay and heterosexual characters, including women, are integrated equally. Sexual description would have to be balanced against the rather obvious, deliberate purpose of much of *A Swimming-Pool Library,* and also his next novel, *A Folding Star,* where one feels that Hollinghurst is aware of the market demands of readers whose main concern is the enjoyment of gay erotic description. *A Swimming-Pool Library* partly delineated a gay world where frequency of sex on demand was easily achieved and nearly all the sexual partners were unrealistically physically perfect—it was amongst the last fiction of its kind that could do so. Since the advent of AIDS, the moral responsibility in writing of safe sex became obligatory, something Hollinghurst is conscious of in *A Folding Star.*

A Folding Star, with its exceptionally clear prose, is more impressive than Hollinghurst's first novel, for the charmed world of the 1980s is replaced by a broader range of personalities as well as more introspection. Hollinghurst also gives a welcome unblinkered handling of his main character, Edward Manners: gay, physically unattractive in his early thirties, and fond of a drink. The unrelenting ugliness of the Belgium town where Manners has arrived to teach English to two boys corresponds to Manners' hopeless and obsessional love for one of his pupils, the attractive and seventeen-year-old Luc Altidore. Hollinghurst's vivid account of the semi-underworld of gay life, represented here by a bar called ''The Casette'' and its inhabitants, is far less self-conscious than that of *A Swimming-Pool Library,* with more engaging and likeable characters. He also makes Manners a rounded portrait by relating flashbacks of his childhood experiences, often with comic humour and a strong awareness of the ridiculous. The circumstances of Edward Manners' love force him into repeated self-examination, as he knows he cannot yet escape the grip of this temporary insanity. He does have sex with Luc, an experience that has physical satisfaction but ridicules any hopes of love. The theme of loyalty and betrayal, traitors and victims, connects the main topic with the sub-plots. Although *A Folding* Star makes a significant contribution towards lifting gay fiction out of a narrow gay ghetto, it is not quite broad enough to escape limitations of the label of ''genre writing.''

—Thomas Hastings, updated by Geoffrey Elborn

HOOD, Hugh

Nationality: Canadian. **Born:** Hugh John Blagdon Hood in Toronto, Ontario, 30 April 1928. **Education:** De La Salle College, Toronto; St. Michael's College, University of Toronto, 1947–55, B.A. 1950, M.A. 1952, Ph.D. 1955. **Family:** Married Ruth Noreen Mallory in 1957; two sons and two daughters. **Career:** Teaching fellow, University of Toronto, 1951–55; associate professor, St. Joseph College, West Hartford, Connecticut, 1955–61; professor titulaire, Department of English Studies, University of Montreal, 1961–95. **Awards:** University of Western Ontario President's medal, for story, 1963, for article, 1968; Women's Canadian Club of Toronto Literary award, 1963; Beta Sigma Phi prize, 1965; Canada Council grant, 1968, award, 1971, 1974, and Senior Arts grant, 1977; Province of Ontario award, 1974; City of Toronto award, 1976; Queen's Jubliee medal, 1977; QSPELL award, 1988; 125th anniversary of Canadian Confederation medal, 1992; University of Montreal medal for distinguished service, 1995. Officer, Order of Canada, 1988. **Address:** 4242 Hampton Avenue, Montreal, Quebec H4A 2K9, Canada.

Publications

Novels

White Figure, White Ground. Toronto, Ryerson Press, and New York, Dutton, 1964.
The Camera Always Lies. New York, Harcourt Brace, 1967.
A Game of Touch. Don Mills, Ontario, Longman, 1970.
You Can't Get There from Here. Ottawa, Oberon Press, 1972; New York, Beaufort, 1984.
Great Realizations. Concord, Ontario, Anansi Press, 1997; Buffalo, New York, General Distribution Services, 1997.
The New Age/Le nouveau siècle:
The Swing in the Garden. Ottawa, Oberon Press, 1975.
A New Athens. Ottawa, Oberon Press, 1977.
Reservoir Ravine. Ottawa, Oberon Press, 1979.
Black and White Keys. Downsview, Ontario, ECW Press, 1982.
The Scenic Art. Toronto, Stoddart, 1984.
The Motor Boys in Ottawa. Toronto, Stoddart, 1986.
Tony's Book. Toronto, Stoddart, 1988.
Property and Value. Toronto, Anansi, 1990.
Be Sure to Close Your Eyes. Toronto, Anansi, 1993.
Dead Men's Watches. Toronto, Anansi, 1995.
Five New Facts about Giorgione (novella). Windsor, Ontario, Black Moss Press, 1987.

Short Stories

Flying a Red Kite. Toronto, Ryerson Press, 1962.
Around the Mountain: Scenes from Montreal Life (sketches). Toronto, Peter Martin, 1967.
The Fruit Man, the Meat Man, and the Manager. Ottawa, Oberon Press, 1971.
Dark Glasses. Ottawa, Oberon Press, 1976.
Selected Stories. Ottawa, Oberon Press, 1978.
None Genuine Without This Signature. Downsview, Ontario, ECW Press, 1980.
August Nights. Toronto, Stoddart, 1985.
A Short Walk in the Rain. Erin, Ontario, Porcupine's Quill, 1989.
The Isolation Booth. Erin, Ontario, Porcupine's Quill, 1991.
You'll Catch Your Death. Erin, Ontario, Porcupine's Quill, 1992.

Plays

Friends and Relations, in *The Play's the Thing: Four Original Television Dramas,* edited by Tony Gifford. Toronto, Macmillan, 1976.

Other

Strength Down Centre: The Jean Béliveau Story. Toronto, Prentice Hall, 1970.
The Governor's Bridge Is Closed: Twelve Essays on the Canadian Scene. Ottawa, Oberon Press, 1973.
Scoring: The Art of Hockey, illustrated by Seymour Segal. Ottawa, Oberon Press, 1979.
Trusting the Tale (essays). Downsview, Ontario, ECW Press, 1983.
Unsupported Assertions (essays). Concord, Ontario, Anansi, 1991.
Editor, with Peter O'Brien, *Fatal Recurrences: New Fiction in English from Montréal.* Montreal, Véhicule Press, 1984.

*

Bibliographies: ''A Bibliography of Works by and on Hugh Hood,'' in *Before the Flood: Our Examination round His Factification for Incamination of Hugh Hood's Work in Progress,* edited by J.R. (Tim) Struthers, Downsview, Ontario, ECW Press, 1979, and ''Hugh Hood: An Annotated Bibliography'' also by Struthers, in *The Annotated Bibliography of Canada's Major Authors: Volume Five,* edited by Robert Lecker and Jack David, Downsview, Ontario, ECW Press, 1984; ''Hood, Hugh (1928-)'' by Allan Weiss, in his *A Comprehensive Bibliography of English-Canadian Short Stories, 1950–1983,* Toronto, ECW Press, 1988.

Manuscript Collections: The University of Calgary Libraries, Alberta.

Critical Studies: ''Grace: The Novels of Hugh Hood'' by Dennis Duffy, in *Canadian Literature* 47, 1971; ''An Interview with Hugh Hood,'' in *World Literature Written in English,* (11)1, 1972, and ''An Interview with Hugh Hood,'' in *Le Chien d'or/The Golden Dog,* 3, 1974, both by Victoria G. Hale; ''An Interview with Hugh Hood,'' in *Journal of Canadian Fiction* (2)1, 1973, and ''Space, Time and the Creative Imagination'' in *Journal of Canadian Fiction,* 3(1), 1974, both by Pierre Cloutier; ''Hugh Hood and His Expanding Universe,'' in *Journal of Canadian Fiction,* 3(1), 1974, and ''Formal Coherence in the Art of Hugh Hood'' in *Studies in Canadian Literature,* 2, 1977, both by Kent Thompson; ''An Interview with Hugh Hood'' by Robert Fulford, in *The Tamarack Review,* 66, 1975; ''Near Proust and Yonge: That's Where Hugh Hood Grew Up and Why He's Making a 12-Novel Bid for Immortality'' by Linda Sandler, in *Books in Canada,* December 1975; *The Comedians: Hugh Hood and Rudy Wiebe* by Patricia A. Morley, Toronto, Clarke Irwin, 1977; ''Hugh Hood and John Mills in Epistolary Conversation'' by Hugh Hood and John Mills, in *The Fiddlehead,* 116, 1978; *Before the Flood: Our Examination round His Factification for Incamination of Hugh Hood's Work in Progress,* Downsview, Ontario, ECW Press, 1979, and *The Montreal Story Tellers: Memoirs, Photographs, Critical Essays,* Montreal, Véhicule Press, 1985, both edited by J.R. (Tim) Struthers; ''Hugh Hood'' in *Profiles in Canadian Literature,* edited by Jeffrey M. Heath, vol. 2, Toronto, Dundurn Press, 1980, and ''A Secular Liturgy: Hugh Hood's Aesthetics and *Around the Mountain,*'' in *Studies in Canadian Literature,* 10, 1985, both by Struthers; ''The Case for Hugh Hood,'' in *An Independent Stance: Essays on English-Canadian Criticism and Fiction,* Erin, Ontario, Porcupine's Quill, 1991, and ''The Atmosphere of Deception: Hugh Hood's 'Going Out as a Ghost','' in *Writers in Aspic,* edited by John Metcalf, Montreal, Véhicule Press, 1988, and ''Hugh Hood,'' in *A Sense of Style: Studies in the Art of Fiction in English-Speaking Canada,* Toronto, ECW Press, 1989, all by W.J. Keith; ''Hugh Hood's Celebration of the Millenium's End'' by Geoff Hancock, in *Quill and Quire,* November 1980; ''Field of Vision: Hugh Hood and the Tradition of Wordsworth'' by Anthony John Harding, in *Canadian Literature,* 94, 1982; '''Incarnational Art': Typology and Analogy in Hugh Hood's Fiction'' by Barry Cameron, in *The Fiddlehead,* 133, 1982; *On the Line: Readings in the Short Fiction of Clark Blaise, John Metcalf and Hugh Hood* by Robert Lecker, Downsview, Ontario, ECW Press, 1982; ''Tradition and Post-Colonialism: Hugh Hood and Martin Boyd'' by Diana Brydon, in *Mosaic: A Journal for the Interdisciplinary Study of Literature,* 15(3), 1982; ''Faith and Fiction: The Novels of Callaghan and Hood'' by Barbara Helen Pell, in *Journal of Canadian Studies,* 18(2), 1983; *Hugh Hood* by Keith Garebian, Boston, Twayne, 1983; ''Hugh Hood's Edenic Garden: Psychoanalysis Among the Flowerbeds'' by Patrick J. Mahony with a reply by Hugh Hood, in *Canadian Literature,* 96, 1983; *Hugh Hood and His Works,* Toronto, ECW Press, 1985, and ''Onward to the New Age,'' in *Books in Canada* October 1990, both by Keith Garebian; *Pilgrim's Progress: A Study of the Short Stories of Hugh Hood* by Susan Copoloff-Mechanic, Toronto, ECW Press, 1988; ''On the Trail of Hugh Hood: History and the Holocaust in *Black and White Keys*'' by Dave Little, in *Essays on Canadian Writing,* 44, 1991; ''Changing Metropolis and *Urbs Eterna:* Hugh Hood's 'The Village Inside''' by Simone Vauthier, in her *Reverberations: Explorations in the Canadian Short Story,* Concord, Ontario, House of Anansi Press, 1993; *Canadian Classics: An Anthology of Short Stories,* Toronto, McGraw-Hill Ryerson, 1993, and *How Stories Mean,* Erin, Ontario, Porcupine's Quill, 1993, both edited by John Metcalf and J.R. (Tim) Struthers; ''A *Scriptible* Text'' by John Mills, in *Essays on Canadian Writing* 50, 1993; ''The History of Art and the Art of History: Hugh Hood's *Five New Facts About Giorgione*'' by Alex Knoenagel, in *Mosaic:* 27(1), 1994; *The Influence of Painting on Five Canadian Writers: Alice Munro, Hugh Hood, Timothy Findley, Margaret Atwood, and Michael Ondaatje* by John Cooke, Lewiston, New York, Edwin Mellen Press, 1996.

Hugh Hood comments:

(1971) My interest in the sound of sentences, in the use of colour words and the names of places, in practical stylistics, showed me that prose fiction might have an abstract element, a purely formal element, even though it continued to be strictly, morally realistic. It might be possible to think of prose fiction the way one thinks of abstract elements in representational painting, or of highly formal music… . It's the seeing-into-things, the capacity for meditative abstraction, that interests me about philosophy, the arts and religious practice. I love most in painting an art that exhibits the transcendental element dwelling in living things. I think of this as true super-realism. And I think of Vermeer, or among American artists of Edward Hopper, whose paintings of ordinary places, seaside cottages, a roadside snack bar and gasoline station, have touched some level of my own imagination which I can only express in fictional images… . Like Vermeer or Hopper or that great creator of musical form, Joseph Haydn, I'm trying to concentrate on knowable form as it lives in the physical world. These forms are abstract, not in the sense of being inhumanly non-physical but in the sense of communicating the perfection of the essences of things—the formal realities that create things as they are in themselves. A transcendentalist must first study the things of this world, and get as far inside them as possible… . That is where I come out: the spirit is totally *in* the flesh. If you pay close enough attention to things, stare at them, concentrate on them as hard as you can, not just with your intelligence, but with your feelings and instincts, you will begin to apprehend the forms in them... . The illuminations in things are there, really and truly *there,* in those things. They are not run over then by the projective intelligence, and yet there is a sense in which the mind, in uniting itself to things, creates illumination in them... . The poetry of Wordsworth supplies us again and again with examples of this imaginative colouring spread over incidents and situations from everyday life... . Like Wordsworth, I have at all times endeavoured to look steadily at my subjects. I hope my gaze has helped to light them up.

(1978) I am trying to assimilate the mode of the novel to the mode of fully-developed Christian allegory, in ways that I don't fully understand. I want to be more ''real'' than the realists, yet more transcendent than the most vaporous allegorist. In short, I am following what I conceive the method of Dante... . Now let me put it to you that since I am *both* a realist and a *transcendentalist allegorist* that I cannot be bound by the forms of ordinary realism.

(1979) I think it would be marvellous for Canada if we had one artist who could move easily and in a familiar converse with Joyce, and Tolstoy, and Proust; and I intend to be that artist if I possibly can; and I am willing to give the rest of my life to it. I don't say that to put down Margaret Atwood or to make Margaret Laurence seem insignificant. That isn't my point at all. I want simply—and I think every artist does—to do what I think I can do as fully, and as powerfully, and as many-modally, and as exhaustively, as I can... . I really want to endow the country with a great imperishable work of art. If I do, it will be the first one that we have. I think it would make an enormous difference to the confidence of this country if we did have one thing like the plays of Shakespeare or *War and Peace* or *A la recherche du temps perdu,* and we knew it, and were sure of it. *Jalna,* ha, ha, won't do. It isn't good enough. I think that *The New Age* and the works of mine which go with it and around it *will* be good enough, and I think it will do a lot for the country.

(1995) I am now, February 1995, at work on the eleventh volume (of twelve) in the novel sequence *The New Age/Le nouveau siècle,* which I've been working on since I began to make notes for the project in late 1966. The first volume actually appeared, as *The Swing in the Garden,* in 1975, and the final book in the series is scheduled for publication at the end of 1999 when the ''new age'' will really be directly in front of us as new century and new millenium. At this moment I can feel myself beginning to wonder how it will feel to write the closing page. Now I can suspect what Gibbon, Proust, and Joyce of *Finnegans Wake* (seventeen years in the making) must have gone through towards the end, an end that Proust unfortunately never saw. Temptations and distractions of a long work!

* * *

Hugh Hood is a writer in whom pedantry wars with creative gifts of a high order. His best work so far occurs in his short stories which demonstrate his mastery at revealing what is immense through what is small. He is an indefatigable explorer of human aspiration, conveying much of its mystery, heroism, and comedy. An impassioned drive towards some symbolic victory is celebrated seriously or gaily in such stories as ''Silver Bugles, Cymbals, Golden Silks'' (*Flying a Red Kite*), ''The Pitcher'' (*Dark Glasses*), and ''Le Grand Déménagement'' (*Around the Mountain*). His art is at its finest in ''Looking Down from Above'' (*Around the Mountain*), where separate characters connect in a visionary moment of great beauty, crowded like a medieval tapestry with life: ''inscrutable but undeniable.''

Hood's earlier novels have something of this imaginative intensity, as in the burning warehouse scene (*A Game of Touch*), an incident pivotal to the hero's fate and a keystone in the novel's structure. However, Hood is unable to control the tone of his prose over the long course of a novel. When the painter in *White Figure, White Ground* retreats to the safety of his old manner and family life, Hood's point of view is unclear. Although the hard urbanity and narrow sympathies of the wife offend, it is uncertain whether the artist's glorification of her is to be received with irony or approval. In *The Camera Always Lies,* a romance, Hood's continuing problem with creating likeable characters re-emerges. A romance requires archetypal figures on whom fantasies can be projected: yet ''virtuous'' Rose Leclair, suffering through near-death and rebirth, is a bore, the hero who saves her an overbearing prig. Precise detail of film financing, production, and costume design merely throws into relief Hood's difficulty with his characters. *You Can't Get There from Here,* set in an imaginary African nation, is both a study of struggle in a new society and ''Christological [except] ... that the Christ figure does not rise again... .'' Because he is writing satire and allegory, Hood must be excused for missing opportunities of further defining the two tribes, and of describing the personal history of his sketchy hero; but his Cabinet villains need sharper outlines to succeed either as allegory or satire.

When Hood attempts in *The New Age,* a serial novel in twelve volumes of which eight have been completed, to work on the scale of ''Coleridge, Joyce, Tolstoy, and Proust,'' his inadequacies become obvious. He is striving for ''a very wide range of reference without apparent connection on the surface which nonetheless will yield connections and networks and links and unities if you wait and allow them to appear.'' Moving back and forth through time, the huge project includes passages of philosophy, social history, topography, and lectures on a broad variety of topics, as well as the fictionalized incidents of his own life.

As a simultaneous ''realist and transcendental allegorist'' (his admitted aim), Hood falls short in these novels, for although characters and events have a formal importance, they rarely achieve emotive significance. The marriage in *A New Athens,* for instance, is never felt as the redemptive force intended, because Edie is no more than a shadow, and Matt Goderich remains, as one character observes, ''a pompous ass.'' Too often Hood offers neither psychological nor pictorial realism, but the factuality of an encyclopedia or a catalogue. Obsessive lists of, for example, baseball players (*The Swing in the Garden*) suggest an inability to select. Local history and neighborhood cartography too often supply the substance rather than the raw material of these fictions. Pedantic tenacity in description cannot of itself invest places or objects with meaning, nor is Hood's style sufficiently adept, usually, to produce this result by its own power. He even slips into bathos with the showpiece engagement scenes in *A New Athens* and *Reservoir Ravine.* His uninspired prose has created a bland, provincial world where values do not develop organically, but are imposed from without. Only when he writes of marvels does the reader's interest freshen, as with the appearance of the visionary painter (*A New Athens*). Striving to write a masterpiece, Hood is so concerned with large patterns and themes that he fails to breathe life into the material of which these patterns are composed. Heterogeneity can succeed only for the writer gifted enough to consume disparate materials in the unifying fire of his art; but, with one third of the sequence still to come, Hood may yet produce work on a level comparable to that of the short stories.

Of course critical assessments may vary strikingly from one person to another; indeed, judgments frequently say as much about readers' assumptions as they do about writers' achievements. Perhaps genius needs to create—that is, to educate—its own audience, an audience that appreciates and quite possibly revels in the idiosyncrasies that some readers find disconcerting. A number of volumes so far in Hood's sequence, including *The Swing in the Garden, A New Athens, Black and White Keys, Property and Value,* and *Dead Men's Watches,* have been received with considerable enthusiasm by individual reviewers and critics. With time—and with the altered understanding that further attention, different assumptions, and a broader perspective can bring—*The New Age* may win the distinguished audience that its advocates believe it deserves. With the completion of the last two of twelve volumes as we reach a new millenium, the overall design and the inner workings of the sequence will certainly become clearer. Perhaps then *The New Age* will stand as Hood envisioned it twenty-five years earlier: "I hope it will be an enormous image, an enormous social mythology, an enormous prism to rotate, to see yourself and your neighbors and friends and your grandparents."

—Margaret Keith, updated by J.R. (Tim) Struthers

HOPE, Christopher

Nationality: South African. **Born:** Christopher David Tully Hope in Johannesburg, 26 February 1944; moved to Europe in 1975. **Education:** Christian Brothers College, Pretoria, 1952–60; University of the Witwatersrand, Johannesburg, 1963–65, B.A. 1965, M.A. in English 1970; University of Natal, Durban, 1968–69, B.A. (honours) 1969. **Military Service:** Served in the South African Navy, 1962. **Family:** Married Eleanor Marilyn Klein in 1967; two sons. **Career:** English teacher, Halesowen Secondary Modern School, 1972; editor, *Bolt,* Durban, 1972–73; writer-in-residence, Gordonstoun School, Elgin, Morayshire, 1978. Lives in London. **Awards:** English Academy of Southern Africa Pringle award, 1974; Cholmondeley award, for poetry, 1978; David Higham prize, 1981; Natal University Petrie Arts award, 1981; Silver Pen award, 1982; Arts Council bursary, 1982; Whitbread award, 1985; CNA award, 1989. Fellow, Royal Society of Literature. **Agent:** Deborah Rogers, Rogers Coleridge and White Ltd., 20 Powis Mews, London W11 1JN, England.

Publications

Novels

A Separate Development. Johannesburg, Ravan Press, 1980; London, Routledge, and New York, Scribner, 1981.
Kruger's Alp. London, Heinemann, 1984; New York, Viking, 1985.
The Hottentot Room. London, Heinemann, 1986; New York, Farrar Straus, 1987.
My Chocolate Redeemer. London, Heinemann, 1989.
Serenity House. London, Macmillan, 1992.
Darkest England. New York, W.W. Norton, 1996.
Me, the Moon, and Elvis Presley. London, Macmillan, 1997.

Short Stories

Private Parts and Other Tales. Johannesburg, Bateleur Press, 1981; London, Routledge, 1982; as *Learning to Fly,* London, Minerva, 1990.
Black Swan (novella). London, Hutchinson, and New York, Harper, 1987.
The Love Songs of Nathan J. Swirsky. London, Macmillan, 1993.

Uncollected Short Stories

"Carnation Butterfly," in *London Magazine,* April-May 1985.
"Strydom's Leper," in *Colours of a New Day: Writing for South Africa,* edited by Sarah Lefanu and Stephen Hayward. London, Lawrence and Wishart, and New York, Pantheon, 1990.

Plays

Radio Plays: *Box on the Ear,* 1987; *Better Halves,* 1988.

Television Plays: *Ducktails,* 1976; *Bye-Bye Booysens,* 1979; *An Entirely New Concept in Packaging,* 1983.

Poetry

Whitewashes, with Mike Kirkwood. Privately printed, 1971.
Cape Drives. London, London Magazine Editions, 1974.
In the Country of the Black Pig and Other Poems. Johannesburg, Ravan Press, and London, London Magazine Editions, 1981.
Englishmen. London, Heinemann, 1985.

Other

The King, the Cat, and the Fiddle (for children), with Yehudi Menuhin. Tonbridge, Kent, Benn, and New York, Holt Rinehart, 1983.
The Dragon Wore Pink (for children). London, A. and C. Black, and New York, Atheneum, 1985.
White Boy Running: A Book about South Africa. London, Secker and Warburg, and New York, Farrar Straus, 1988.
Moscow! Moscow! London, Heinemann, 1990.
Signs of the Heart, London, Picador, 2000.
Editor, *Life Class: Thoughts, Exercises, Reflections of an Itinerant Violinist,* by Yehudi Menuhin. London, Heinemann, 1986.

*

Christopher Hope comments:

Writing has always seemed to me to be a rather mischievous occupation. I write not to change the world but to undermine it, since the models on offer seem pretty dull most of the time. Much of life is odd and disorganized. Many people who pretend to be sure about things are either ingenuous or wicked. They are also often charlatans. One wants to record their utterances as a warning to others.

I was lucky enough to grow up in South Africa, a place where the lethal folly of what everyone assured me was ''normal'' life outstripped even the most audacious imaginations. For a writer, this was wonderful training. It taught me about the sheer inventiveness of life. And it gave me a subject—the triumph of power and the terminal comedy provided by those who wield it.

* * *

Christopher Hope is a leading example of an important new group of white South African writers who have broken free of the traditional mold of liberal realism in South African fiction. These writers have cast off the predictable and often sterile tones of superior intellectual humanism or impassioned but helpless outrage against apartheid. Seen against the seriousness and moral sanctimony of the liberal idiom, Hope's writing is positively liberating. His vision is black, wicked, and surreal, and his satire and humor have a measure of viciousness that seems peculiarly appropriate to South Africa. In the case of two of his novels, *A Separate Development*, winner of the 1981 David Higham Prize for Fiction, and *Kruger's Alp*, winner of the 1985 Whitbread Prize for Fiction, one feels that here is a writer who has found a language of fiction that matches the system for ruthlessness, power, subtlety, and the ability to knock down targets.

Hope, who had been living in voluntary exile in London since 1976, recently moved to a remote village in rural France. *Signs of the Heart* is a non-fiction account of life in the village over the past few years of his residence there. It is populated with the types of characters his readers expect to find in his fiction. Two additional non-fiction works, *White Boy Running*, winner of the 1988 CNA Literary Award in South Africa, and *Moscow! Moscow!*, clarify his sentiments and political understandings about the new democratic South African government from his international perspective.

He also published several volumes of poetry and a collection of short stories, *Private Parts*. In the stories, as in the novels, Hope's unusual blend of familiar reality and bizarre, surreal inventiveness is apparent. Increasingly in his fiction, Hope has created a special space for himself halfway between the real and the bizarre while establishing newly capacious and flexible fictional conventions.

Like Herman Charles Bosman and Tom Sharpe before him, Hope demonstrates how endlessly funny South African life is when seen from a great and merciless distance. In *A Separate Development* the notions of mixed blood and miscegenation, so tragically dealt with by such South African heavyweights as Sarah Gertrude Millin and Alan Paton, become a mainspring for blackish and farce-filled comedy. The young first-person narrator, Harry Moto, thrives on irony and absurdity, having grown up as a white South African and then being forced to take refuge as a ''black'' denizen of Johannesburg. Moto scrambles the categories: his darkish skin and somewhat frizzy hair suggest certain irregularities in his ancestry, and through no fault of his own, he becomes a comic victim. In Harry, Hope achieves what has always remained impossible for South African writers in their more serious efforts, which is to combine or unify black and white experience. By discarding the heavy mantle of serious liberalism, Hope permits his character, Harry, who has grown up spending idle hours around swimming pools and ruminating about sex, to finally go ''black.''

Because of Harry's hue of skin, his sexual liaison with a wealthy white girl is humiliatingly close to sexual impropriety. Harry faces absolute disapproval from his parents, who see in him tangible evidence of their deep psychological fears about mixed blood. Harry disappears to become a black, working first as a runner for an Indian clothing merchant, and later as a ''living proof'' assistant to a man who sells skin-lightening creams to infinitely deluded blacks. He ends up as the invisible ''boy'' collecting trays from cars at a roadhouse, and finally as a detainee writing his story to stay alive.

If *A Separate Development* is an unusually deft first novel, then *Kruger's Alp* is a truly remarkable effort for a second novel. More ''serious'' in effect, the novel demonstrates literary artifice and fictional inventiveness of masterful proportions. Hope combines modern political mystery with historical myth, revelatory allegorical structure with acid-strength satire. This amalgam is based on a wide vision of present and past South African experience, in which social and historical myth is reformulated and given new meaning. As in Bunyan's Puritan allegory, *A Pilgrim's Progress*, the story begins with a dream of revelation leading to a physical journey of discovery to a mythic destination. Hope's main protagonist, Blanchaille (whitebait), is obsessed with the notion of escaping acute anxiety due to being part of a ''despised sub-group within a detested minority [waiting] for the long-expected wrath to fall on them and destroy them.'' Blanchaille's anxiety is fueled by the news that a former friend of his, a top fiscal official, has been murdered, apparently by his own government for political reasons.

As boys, Blanchaille and the murdered official, Tony Ferreira, both served under a prophesying and idiosyncratic Irish priest, Father Lynch. Lynch preaches the truth about a great hoard of gold gone missing. The president of the Transvaal republic during the Boer War, Paul Kruger, is reputed to have taken the gold away with him into exile in Switzerland. As interpreted in this novel, Kruger is supposed to have established a ''shining city,'' like the ''celestial city'' in The Pilgrim's Progress, for white South Africans seeking an ultimate haven after lifetimes of trekking. Ferreira is killed because he uncovers massive irregular spending on huge projects to buy world opinion (the situation is closely modeled on the Information Scandal that rocked South Africa in the late 1970s). Blanchaille undertakes an allegorical journey of revelation to Kruger's ''white location in the sky'' in Switzerland, traveling even deeper into the heart of the mythic secrets of white South African existence.

In *The Hottentot Room* a group of South African exiles find a fellow sufferer in Frau Katie, a German Jew and refugee from Nazi Germany. Frau Katie presides over the Hottentot Room, a London club for South African expatriates. The novel's protagonist, Caleb Looper, is an expatriate who joins the club, but he is a spy for the South African regime, while the regulars of the club are enslaved to illusions about themselves and their former homeland. These illusions, as well as the secret of betrayal in their midst, all find a correlative, or mythical resonance, in Frau Katie's story. But there is self-deception at the heart of her sustaining myth, and a complementary self-deception in all the ''Hottentots'' who use her story for their own ends. The novel is an intricately patterned fable that says much about the condition of exile.

Hope's next work, *Black Swan* (a novella), exhibits his satirical and ironic skill at its pared-down best. The story of an idiosyncratic black township boy who wants to be a ballet dancer but is eventually executed exhibits Hope's ability to create fictions that reveal the victory of the cruel over the poignant in South African life.

My Chocolate Redeemer tells the story of a friendship between a French-English girl and the deposed head of a black African state. It is set in France and a fictional African country called Zanj, and relies heavily on principles borrowed from the New Physics about truth being a function of observation. It would appear as though Hope may be trying to move away from South Africa as subject matter, but *My Chocolate Redeemer* lacks Hope's usual ironic punch, and survives merely as an odd but forgettable novel by an excellent writer. It is followed by the redemptive *Serenity House*, which was shortlisted for the 1992 Booker Prize, about Old Max, the giant of Serenity House, North London's "Premier Eventide Refuge," who might have been left to die in peace. Old Max's son-in-law Albert, an MP with an interest in the new War Crimes Bill, has other ideas.

Darkest England deals with South African and British racism and hatred shortly after the South African democratization. The story begins with the narration of a UN observer during the first free election in South Africa; nevertheless, it presents the point of view of a Bushman tribe. The tribe challenges modern Britain to uphold a nineteenth-century promise to protect them from the Boer, consequently mounting an expedition in the 1990s to Britain. The bulk of the novel is therefore set in Britain and is written from the perspective of the bushman. After arriving in Britain, he passes through detention centers and immigration procedures. The bushman interprets the harsh treatment he receives as hospitality, even, ironically, as special consideration, because of his faith in the British promise of aid.

Me, the Moon and Elvis Presley begins during 1949 in Karoo, a remote village of Lutherburg. Old Aunt Betsy acquires a little servant girl at a bargain price of six bars of soap. Forty-five years later, when Lutherburg becomes Buckingham, its new deputy-mayor, Mimi de Bruyn, is disturbed by identity problems. In a typical Hope paradox about South Africa, the protagonist is plagued by the past as well as haunted by the future. Mimi suspects she was the lost child sold into semi-slavery, but no one will speak to her of the old days. Mimi also seeks proof that new Buckingham is an improvement over old Lutherburg, when Pascal Le Gros, dressed entirely in white, becomes her love interest. He is a dreamer, disgraced lawyer, and presents a stout lunar image representative of Elvis Presley. Elvis is an apt figurehead for the new Buckingham as the novel moves between past and present while humorously surmising the future.

Christopher Hope states that politically pivotal nations, such as South Africa, Poland, and Russia, have a nostalgia for the future while they overcome the haunting of the past. He is keen to observe how quickly the white populations have adapted to the new policies in South Africa, despite their deepest objections during that time of "racial lunacy." People in the outside world, he points out, approvingly pray that nothing disturbs the optimistic change of governments. He views the change in South Africa from Europe and quotes the French symbolist poet Paul Valéry to describe his forebodings about the future of South Africa's new democracy: "the future is not what it used to be." Those governments that don't change, like North Korea or Cuba, become quaint outposts of an outdated past and political system. Perhaps South Africa was the final cause for outrage by international liberalism, and Hope's sarcastic fictional commentaries may illustrate this "disturbing" state of world calm.

—Leon de Kock, updated by Hedwig Gorski

HORNBY, Nick

Nationality: English. **Born:** c. 1957. **Agent:** c/o Victor Gollancz Ltd., Villiers House, 41–47 Strand, London WC2N 5JE, England.

PUBLICATIONS

Novels

High Fidelity. New York, Riverhead Books, 1995.
About a Boy. New York, Riverhead Books, 1998.

Other

Contemporary American Fiction (essays). London, Vision Press and New York, St. Martin's Press, 1992.
Fever Pitch (memoir). London, Gollancz, 1992; New York, Penguin Books, 1994.
Editor, *My Favourite Year: A Collection of New Football Writing.* London, Gollancz/Witherby, 1993.

*

Film Adaptation: *High Fidelity*, 2000.

* * *

With just two novels and one memoir of his life as a soccer fan to his credit, Nick Hornby has become one of the defining voices of the past decade. He is a keenly observant recorder of, and self-deprecating commentator on, the changing nature of masculine identity in the late twentieth century. His men—whether the autobiographical Arsenal fan of *Fever Pitch* or the fictionalized protagonists of the no less punningly titled novels, *High Fidelity* and *About a Boy*—would have been minor cads in any earlier period, but in Hornby's narratives of "the way we live now," they strike a surprisingly sympathetic chord. Their plights, however self-created, make them seem strangely poignant and therefore more deserving of the reader's compassion than of his, or her, disdain.

Hornby's phenomenal success (all three books have been bestsellers and *High Fidelity* turned into a critically acclaimed and commercially successful film) derives in large measure from his being a generational writer—spokesman for the thirty-somethings, mainly but not exclusively English (the film version of *High Fidelity* is set in Chicago) and male (Hornby is suprisingly popular with female readers as well). In his work, the New Laddism so evident in British culture as something of a backlash against women's gains, appears, but in gentler form, at its most benign and self-examining: not the lowlifes of Irvine Welsh's fiction, but the male equivalent of the protagonist of Helen Fielding's similarly successful *Bridget Jones' Diary.* In seemingly effortless but hardly artless prose, as deliberately scaled back as his anti-heroes' psyches, Hornby examines his male characters' obsessions (soccer, popular music—often of a slightly dated kind—and being cool) as well as the double-bind in which they find themselves: on the one hand, wanting to belong, while on the other, fearing commitment of any kind to anyone. It is a fear that both stems from and contributes to a low-grade awareness of their own inadequacy, one that they further worry will be all too obvious to others, women in particular, and that helps account for lives of quiet desperation marked by stasis and drift. Although English to their nearly hollow core, his young men seem in many ways latter-day versions of those quintessentially American characters, Huck Finn, Holden Caulfield, and Sal Paradise, or a younger, hipper version of J. Alfred Prufrock.

Rob, *High Fidelity*'s narrator-protagonist, is thirty-six and the owner of Championship Vinyl, a moribund, North London record shop he opened ten years earlier and that he now runs with the help of Dick and Barry, two lesser versions of himself. Rob's twin obsessions are Laura, the lawyer-lover who has recently left him, and the records that not only give voice to his own ideas about love and life but shape those ideas as well. One way Rob tries to shape his life is by making lists of everything from favorite songs to old girlfriends. However, because these lists are little more than a comic reflex, they provide no lasting relief from the constant fear of not being able to measure up, along with the complementary but more insidious fear of losing what little he has. Even as he deliberately cultivates the superficial life and a defensive, self-ironized stance in relation to it (''Is it so wrong to want to be at home with your record collection?''), he is nonetheless made somewhat bitter by feeling out of his depth. When Rob and Laura first meet, she works as a legal aide lawyer, poorly paid and dressed accordingly. By the time they split up, she is working for a City law firm, well paid and dressing the part. (It is a part she did not choose; in what passes for political consciousness in Hornby's novel, Laura is the victim of Tory economics, which cut funding for her earlier position and left her no choice but highly paid City work.) Feeling that he is alternately stuck in a groove and ''falling off the edge,'' Rob fears both stasis and change, which are just what Hornby gives him when the emasculating lawyer is transformed into a sexy fairy godmother. Although Rob fears that he is nothing more than the music he collects, Laura contends he has some vaguely defined ''potential'' which she will use some of her money to bring out in a happy ending that turns novel into fairy tale. The sentimentality allows Hornby and his admiring readers to evade the serious psychological and political issues raised, however jokingly, in *Fever Pitch*, where the fan is clearly a case of arrested development and where the nervous humor masks a very real sense of political compromise (''Yes the terrible truth is that I was willing to accept a Conservative government if it guaranteed an Arsenal Cup Final win'').

About a Boy plays a variation on the Rob theme. Although similarly unattached, thirty-six, and lacking ambition, Will Freeman is more financially secure and self-confident (or at least self-consciously cool) than Rob. His sole patrimony—royalties from a popular Christmas song that his father wrote in 1938 and that Will despises—provides Will with the money and therefore the time to indulge his only real passion: sex. Pretending to be a single father, he finds a ready supply of young as well as vulnerable women at a meeting of SPAT (Single Parents—Alone Together). The existence of Marcus, a needy preteen newly arrived in London with his suicidal mother, complicates Will's life and Hornby's novel, which moves back and forth between the two characters (as centers of consciousness) in alternating chapters. Although even more self-centered than Rob, and more willing to use others (including children, both real or imagined) to serve his purpose (making him more attractive to women), Will has something Marcus needs. Will knows things about popular culture—about clothes and Kurt Cobain and Manchester United—that can help Marcus as this consummate outsider tries to find his way in the unknown territories of London and early adolescence. Despite his misgivings, Will does help Marcus, offering him the only kind of advice he can: not on how to grow up but on how to be a kid. Marcus too has some advice to give that addresses the somewhat larger social context of Hornby's second novel. Where *High Fidelity* portrays a representative weak male, *About a Boy* offers an epidemic of dysfunctional adults. It also offers an ending that, although no less sentimental than Laura's rescuing Rob, seems more convincing: '''those human pyramids,''' as Marcus explains at novel's end, '''that's the sort of model for living I'm looking at now .... You're safer as a kid if everyone's just friends. When people pair off ... it's more insecure.''' And insecurity is the name of Hornby's finely tuned, or attuned, writing.

—Robert Morace

HOSPITAL, Janette Turner

Nationality: Australian. **Born:** Melbourne, Victoria, 12 November 1942. **Education:** The University of Queensland, St. Lucia, Brisbane, B.A. in English 1965; Queen's University, Kingston, Ontario, M.A. 1973. **Family:** Married Clifford G. Hospital in 1965; one son and one daughter. **Career:** Teacher, Queensland, 1963–66; librarian, Harvard University, Cambridge, Massachusetts, 1967–71; lecturer in English, Queen's University, and St. Lawrence College, Kingston, Ontario, 1971–82. Since 1982 full-time writer. Writer-in-residence, Massachusetts Institute of Technology, Cambridge, 1985–86, 1987, 1989; University of Ottawa, Ontario, 1987; University of Sydney, New South Wales, 1989; Boston University, 1991; La Trobe University, Melbourne, Australia, 1992–93; University of East Anglia, Norwich, England, 1996; adjunct professor of English, La Trobe University, 1990–93. Lived in the United States, 1967–71, and India, 1977, and 1990. Currently divides year between Australia, Boston, and Paris. **Awards:** Seal award (Canada), 1982; Atlantic First citation from Atlantic Monthly, 1978; CDC Literary Prize, for short story, 1986; Fellowship of Australian Writers Fiction award, 1988; Torgi award, Canadian Association for the Blind, 1988; Australian National Book Council award, 1989. **Agent:** Jill Hickson Associates, P.O. Box 271, Woollahra, New South Wales 2025, Australia; or, Molly Friedrich,, Literary Agent, 708 Third Ave., 23rd Floor, New York, New York 10017, U.S.A.

PUBLICATIONS

Novels

The Ivory Swing. Toronto, McClelland and Stewart, 1982; New York, Dutton, and London, Hodder and Stoughton, 1983.

The Tiger in the Tiger Pit. Toronto, McClelland and Stewart, 1983; New York, Dutton, and London, Hodder and Stoughton, 1984.

Borderline. Toronto, McClelland and Stewart, New York, Dutton, and London, Hodder and Stoughton, 1985.

Charades. St. Lucia, University of Queensland Press, 1988; New York and London, Bantam, 1988.

A Very Proper Death (as Alex Juniper). Melbourne, Penguin, 1990; New York, Scribner, 1991.

The Last Magician. London, Virago, and New York, Holt, 1992.

Oyster. London, Virago Press, 1996; New York, W.W. Norton, 1998.

Short Stories

Dislocations. Toronto, McClelland and Stewart, 1986; Baton Rouge, Louisiana State University Press, 1988.
Isobars. St. Lucia, University of Queensland Press, 1990; Baton Rouge, Louisiana State University Press, 1991; London, Virago, 1992.
Collected Stories: 1970–1995. St. Lucia, Queensland, University of Queensland Press, 1995.

*

Critical Studies: ''Recent Australian Writing: Janette Turner Hospital's Borderline'' by Michael Wilding, in *Working Papers in Australian Studies,* Australian Studies Center, University of London, 1988; ''The Commonplace of Foreignness: the Fictions of Janette Turner Hospital'' by Sabrina Achilles, in *Editions,* (Sydney), 1989; Introduction by Helen Daniel to *Virago Modern Classics* edition of *Borderline,* 1990; Janette Turner Hospital issue of LINQ Magazine, (Queensland, Australia), 17(1) 1990; ''Charades: Searching for Father Time: Memory and the Uncertainty Principle'' by Sue Gilett, in *New Literature's Review* (Australia), 21, Summer 1991; ''Janette Turner Hospital'' by Elspeth Cameron in *Profiles in Canadian Literature, No. 8,* edited by Jeffrey M. Heath, Toronto, Dundum Press, 1991; *Janette Turner Hospital,* edited by Selina Samuels. London, British Australian Studies Association, 1998.

Janette Turner Hospital comments:

In childhood, I felt like a space voyager, traveling daily between two alien worlds, daily mediating between them, decoding mutually unintelligible sign systems, an instinctive semiotician from the age of six. This was the result of growing up within a subculture of evangelical fundamentalist Pentecostalism (in which almost everything was forbidden to me) within the wider culture (encountered at school each day) of boisterous working-class anti-religious subtropical Australia. The incantatory rhythms of the King James version of the bible (especially the Psalms), read aloud at the family dinner-table every night for the first twenty years of my life until I left home, are a dominant influence on my prose, as are the jagged, irreverent, piquant, slangy bush-ballad rhythms of working-class Australia. My weirdly cross-cultural childhood turned out to be a good rehearsal for the rest of my life, which, by happenstance (economic, academic, and marital) rather than by deliberate choice, has been culturally nomadic. I have lived for extended periods of time in the U.S.A., Canada, India, and England, although for some time I have been spending an increasing portion of each year back in Australia, and the drift of things is toward a permanent return.

All my writing, in a sense, revolves around the mediation of one culture (or subculture) to another. Wherever I am, I live about equally (in terms of company kept and haunts frequented) in the rarefied academic/literary/cultural worlds and the netherworlds of working-class pubs/cops/street people/gutter people (with, I must confess, an instinctive preference for the latter). I mix easily in both worlds, I switch accent and idiom easily. I have, in general, (there are always individual exceptions on both sides), a higher moral opinion of the denizens of the netherworld than of pillars of the community.

My first novel *The Ivory Swing,* was written after a period of living in a village in South India and explored the fact that, regardless of the degree to which educated and enlightened individuals of western and Asian cultures bend over backwards to understand and appreciate one another, there are certain basic and intractable differences that, given a particular course of events, will result in insoluble dilemmas and cataclysms. Since then, all my novels and short stories have explored the same basic situation of clashing perspectives (particularly the clash between the socially favored and the disempowered) but have stayed within a western framework.

The themes of dislocation and connection are constant in my work. So are the themes of moral choice and moral courage. I am always putting my characters into situations of acute moral dilemma (this encompasses the political), to find out what they will do. This is, it seems to me, the question of maximum interest about the human species: what will she, or he, do under extreme pressure? The attempt to find a fictional form which will bridge the disparate worlds I explore has meant that I have often seen myself categorized as ''postmodernist.'' I don't object to this, except that I am disturbed when I read Terry Eagleton, a critic whom I esteem, extolling modernism but finding postmodernism morally nihilistic. I object. (His definition of the term is too narrow). I have passionate moral and political commitments (though I like to feel that these can be surmised but cannot be precisely located in my work. I would like to think that my writing forces the reader to make inner moral and political choices and alignments, but does not tell the reader what such alignments should be).

Stylistically, I probably have more in common with poets and formalists than with other politically *engagé* writers and postmodernists. Words, images, rhythms are of major sensual importance to me. I have an erotic relationship with language. (Ironically, this goes back to those family bible readings. The stern prophets of the Old Testament were voluptuous with words.) I am a feminist who has frequently been trashed by literary ''career feminists.'' I am, it seems, ''ideologically unsound.'' Apparently I'm much too exuberant about female sexuality, seeking, for example, to redeem and reclaim words like ''slut;'' and much too fond of male characters.

All labels, in fact, are a bad fit. I'm a maverick and a guerrilla.

* * *

Janette Turner Hospital was born in Melbourne, moved to Brisbane at the age of seven, and then to the United States in 1967. She spent a number of years in Canada and accompanied her husband to India on his study leave. More recently she has divided her time between Australia, Boston, and Canada. It is hardly surprising, then, that her fiction should be deeply concerned with clashes between cultures, beliefs, nationalities, as even the titles of some of her works suggest: *Borderline, Dislocations, Isobars.* In one of the stories in *Isobars*, the narrator could well be speaking of the author when she says, ''I live at the desiccating edge of things, or the dividing line between two countries, nowhere.''

The Ivory Swing is a study of the faltering marriage of a Canadian academic on leave and his wife and family, focusing on the wife as she struggles to decide when it is legitimate to interfere in the lives of others and when it is not. At the end her well-meant intrusion has disastrous effects, and she is left pondering the ensuing tragedy she might or might not have caused, or prevented, had she acted differently. Early in the novel we are told that ''There was a blurred borderline crossed by accident at certain times,'' and this question of where to draw the line recurs often in Hospital's fiction. At the end the novel intimates the precarious but perhaps hopeful condition of the couple's marriage.

Though the title of *The Tiger in the Tiger Pit* refers to the irascible, dying old man Edward Carpenter, the most important character is really his wife, Bessie, who on the occasion of their golden anniversary manipulates the various members of the family in order to bring them together. The novel slowly builds up composite sense of the myriad dramas that have unfolded among the members in the past and that will lead towards a climax. Hospital cuts skillfully among them, shifting point of view and focus, enacting her belief in the people's subjective perceptions of reality. It is Bessie who ''arranges'' the various lives. Having given up a promising career for her husband, she is now working on a composition of her own, ''a family symphony,'' that is both actual and metaphorical; she ''conducts'' the members of the family as if they were players in an orchestra.

Borderline is one of Hospital's most accomplished novels, working well simultaneously on the levels of narrative thriller and moral speculation and inquiry, especially of where to draw the ''borderline'' between intrusion into others' lives and responsibility for them that she raised in *The Ivory Swing*. A meat truck is stopped at the border between the U.S. and Canada and found to be carrying a number of refugees inside with the frozen carcasses. One of them, however, escapes by hiding inside a beef carcass and is rescued on the spur of the moment by the occupants of two following cars. Gus Kelly is a Catholic, guilt-ridden, alcoholic philanderer and Felicity one of those very beautiful, slightly unworldly young woman who are the characteristic heroines in Hospital's novels. They assist the woman, and out of that impulsive action a complicated, ambiguous web of mystery develops, within which they are both eventually embroiled. Though the themes raised are almost too many for the novel to handle with complete authority, *Borderline* is a highly intelligent and gripping novel.

Hospital's later novels have grown increasingly speculative and even in parts apocalyptic. *Charades*, for instance, opens: ''The grand unified theories, Koenig writes, are difficult to verify experimentally.'' Koenig is an American scientist, tipped for the Nobel Prize, who is accosted late at night by an Australian named Charade Ryan. Charade is engaged on a quest for her father, which proves in the end to be a quest for her mother; only much later do we learn why she has sought out Koenig. He is working on Heisenberg's Uncertainty Principle, and the novel is itself a dramatization of the principle, of the ''necessity of uncertainty,'' as Charade puts it. Hospital announces the theme repeatedly, and the novel is filled, too, with images of dissolution, change, uncertainty. *Charades* is the account of a wanderer and a search, a psychological study in guilt, an intellectual thriller, a rewriting of *A Thousand and One Nights*, but above all a narrative that simply hums and crackles with tension. If there is a criticism it is again that at times the author appears to have taken on too much: the quest for the father, the Holocaust, Heisenberg, allusions to other scientists and writers, Scheherazade, the logbooks of early Australian explorers. What tends to result is a kind of intellectual promiscuity, with the author struggling to do justice to the richness of her material.

The Last Magician begins in startling fashion, with a woman fainting in a London cinema as she unexpectedly sees herself on screen. Still in a state of shock, she takes a flight home to Australia, where she begins her agonizing reappraisal of the lives of four people born in Queensland who grew up together and whom she has come to know later in Sydney. Slowly sifting through the rubble of memories and photographs, the narrator Lucy Barclay eventually arrives as nearly as she can at the truth of their entangled relationships, though the author, in self-mocking anticipation of critical objections, points out, ''Late twentieth century social realism cannot always provide definitive and enclosed endings to novels.'' Speaking in an energetic, often self-contradictory voice, addressing the non-existent reader, breaking off to indulge in long parentheses, Lucy patiently follows the trail right back to its beginnings, trying to ''salvage the future and to predict the past.'' But *The Last Magician* is also a philosophical inquiry into what the novel postulates as the overground and the underground, into the contingent and uncertain nature of the self, and into the concept of ''triage,'' by which the powerless are sacrificed to those in power.

Hospital's writing is as usual dizzyingly energetic, full of allusions, sudden shifts in time and place and above all packed with images, the most important of which is that of the quarry. Here, she proposes a giant system of caves, tunnels, and canals beginning under Sydney's suburbs and reaching as far perhaps as Brisbane. In the novel's most pervasive motif they are a kind of Inferno, the eighth circle of hell, and ''the last magician,'' the photographer Charlie Chang, becomes an antipodean Dante. Hospital's sympathies are clearly with the undergrounders and outsiders of this world, rather than with characters like the complacent judge Robinson Gray. Worldly society, she seems to be arguing, can only exist at the expense of those it drives out, or under: ''The quarry props up a lot of walled gardens.''

Oyster picks up and foregrounds the apocalyptic elements in parts of *The Last Magician*. Written with an eye on the millennium, it tells the story of a cult in the tiny town of Outer Maroo in outback Queensland, so remote that it does not appear on any map. Mail occasionally gets into the town but never leaves it; the postmistress makes sure of that. This doesn't stop its citizens from behaving violently, especially towards ''foreigners.'' Oyster attracts young people to his fabulous underground opal site and then exploits and enslaves them. This is a novel crowded with metaphysics, rollicking in ideas, rendered in a prose that borders on the riotously portentous if it does not cross over into it, and ending in a long-heralded and spectacular apocalypse. As often, Hospital highlights the problematic nature of truth by employing a partial narrator who is close to but never a central part of the story and whose search for the truth enacts the sense of indeterminacy that is central to the author's vision. Much of her narrative is to do with the difficulty of creating coherent narratives. But it is hard to find any coherence at all in this one, with its gallery of characters whose evil is so relentless that finally they lack not merely plausibility but even interest.

Although best known as a novelist, Hospital is also an accomplished and productive short story writer, as her *Collected Stories* attest. These bring together the stories from her two collections, as well as a further seven more recent ones, gathered together under the title ''North of Nowhere.'' They amount to some thirty-nine stories in all. They are cosmopolitan, ranging widely over the various countries in which Hospital has lived, and the variety of her protagonists is equally impressive. Again though, a common theme is displacement; the characters are often at odds with their environment. Most of the protagonists are estranged or solitary in some form or other, outside the mainstream of humanity. Sometimes the estrangement is by choice, as in ''Port After Port, the Same Baggage,'' in which, in defiance of the young members of her own family, an aging widow makes the decision to embark on a world voyage. At others times, as in ''After the Fall,'' estrangement is thrust upon the protagonist; the artist figure in the story has become unhinged after her husband abandoned her. The later stories tend to be set more often in Australia and especially Queensland, which the author has acknowledged to be her real home, and are often autobiographical in nature.

—Laurie Clancy

HOWARD, Elizabeth Jane

Nationality: British. **Born:** London, 26 March 1923. Educated privately; trained as an actress at the London Mask Theatre School and with the Scott Thorndike Student Repertory; acted in Stratford-on-Avon, and in repertory theatre in Devon. **Military Service:** Served as an air raid warden in London during World War II. **Family:** Married 1) Peter M. Scott in 1942 (divorced 1951), one daughter; 2) James Douglas-Henry in 1959 (divorced); 3) Kingsley Amis, *q.v.*, in 1965 (divorced 1983). **Career:** Worked as a model, and in radio and television broadcasting, 1939–46; secretary, Inland Waterways Association, London, 1947–50; editor, Chatto and Windus Ltd., London, 1953–56, and Weidenfeld and Nicolson Ltd., London, 1957; book critic, *Queen* magazine, London, 1957–60. Honorary artistic director, Cheltenham Literary Festival, 1962; co-artistic director, Salisbury Festival, 1973. Fellow, Royal Society of Literature. Lives in Suffolk. **Awards:** Rhys Memorial prize, 1951; *Yorkshire Post* award, 1983. **Agent:** Jonathan Clowes Ltd., Iron Bridge House, Bridge Approach, London NW1 8BD, England.

PUBLICATIONS

Novels

The Beautiful Visit. London, Cape, and New York, Random House, 1950.
The Long View. London, Cape, and New York, Reynal, 1956.
The Sea Change. London, Cape, 1959; New York, Harper, 1960.
After Julius. London, Cape, 1965; New York, Viking Press, 1966.
Something in Disguise. London, Cape, 1969; New York, Viking Press, 1970.
Odd Girl Out. London, Cape, and New York, Viking Press, 1972.
Getting It Right. London, Hamish Hamilton, and New York, Viking Press, 1982.
The Light Years. London, Macmillan, and New York, Pocket Books, 1990.
Making Time. London, Macmillan, and New York, Pocket Books, 1991.
Confusion. London, Macmillan, and New York, Pocket Books, 1993.
Anemones. Memphis, Tennessee, Grandmother Earth Creations, 1998.

Short Stories

We Are for the Dark: Six Ghost Stories with Robert Aickman. London, Cape, 1951.
Mr. Wrong. London, Cape, 1975; New York, Viking Press, 1976.

Plays

Screenplays: *The Very Edge,* 1963; *Getting It Right,* 1989.

Television Plays: *The Glorious Dead* (*Upstairs, Downstairs* series), 1974; *Skittles* (*Victorian Scandals* series), 1976; *Sight Unseen* (*She* series), 1977; *After Julius,* from her own novel, 1979; *Something in Disguise,* from her own novel, 1980.

Other

Bettina: A Portrait, with Arthur Helps. London, Chatto and Windus, and New York, Reynal, 1957.
Howard and Maschler on Food, with Fay Maschler. London, Joseph, 1987.
Cooking for Occasion, with Fay Macshler. London, Macmillan, 1994.
Editor, *The Lover's Companion: The Pleasure, Joys, and Anguish of Love.* Newton Abbot, Devon, David and Charles, 1978.
Editor, *Green Shades: An Anthology of Plants, Gardens, and Gardeners.* London, Aurum Press, 1990.

*

Elizabeth Jane Howard comments:

I consider myself to be in the straight tradition of English novelists. I do not write about ''social issues or values''—I write simply about people, by themselves and in relation to one another. The first aim of a novel should be readability. I do not write (consciously, at least) about people whom I know or have met.

My methods are to be able to write in one sentence what my novel is to be about, to test this idea for several months, and then to invent situations that will fit the theme. I make the people last—to suit the situations. I write only one draught and rarely make any alterations to it. Occasional cutting has sometimes seemed necessary. I write about 300 words a day with luck and when I am free to do so. I do it chiefly because it is the most difficult thing that I have ever tried to do.

I began by writing plays when I was 14. Before that I wrote 400 immensely dull pages (since destroyed) about a horse. I have also written a film script of *The Sea Change* with Peter Yates, but this has not yet been produced. I would very much like to write a good play, and, indeed, come to that, a first rate novel.

* * *

Elizabeth Jane Howard's novels are distinguished by sharp and sensitive perceptions about people—their loves, their guilts, the damage they wittingly or unwittingly do to others. Sometimes, the perceptions are worked into satirical set pieces, like the treatment of a group of feckless post-Oxford young people sponging in London in *Something in Disguise.* Often the satire is more gentle and generous, like that of the patriotic major in *After Julius* who combines long, boring speeches about the past with silent sensitivity to the human dramas around him. Howard's protagonists, often simple, gentle young girls from a variety of backgrounds, are treated with a great deal of sympathy, with respect for their quiet intelligence and their capacity to feel for others. Any tendency toward the mawkish or sentimental is carefully controlled by a prose that works on sharp and often comic juxtapositions of images: the heavy-handed Colonel, trying to appear sympathetic to others in *Something in Disguise,* is ''about as jocular and useless as the Metro-Goldwyn-Mayer Lion,'' in *The Sea Change* a young actress tries desperately to impress a playwright by showing a knowledge of his plays, ''broadcasting her innocuous opinions like weed killer on a well kept lawn,'' the repressed and deferential hairdresser who is the central character in *Getting It Right* begins by noticing a wealthy and demanding client whose face has the ''apoplectic bloom of unpeeled beetroot'' and eyes ''the shade of well-used washing-up water,'' and then proceeds, in a moment of personal conflict, to discover his mind like a ''partially disused branch railway line.''

The careful control visible in Howard's prose is also apparent in the structure of her novels. Sometimes, as in all of *The Sea Change* and most of *After Julius,* the novel consists of alternate narrations from the point of view of a small number of closely connected characters. Each episode is seen from at least two points of view, started by one character, taken up by the next who then moves the narrative on a little further until a third character takes it up. In *After Julius* the action of the novel is confined to a three-day week-end, although most of the characters are engaged in sorting out casual connections of current problems to the heroic death of Julius at Dunkerque twenty years earlier. *Something in Disguise* compresses action into three segments: April, August, and December of a single year. *The Long View* begins with a marriage breaking up in 1950 and its consequences for the couple's children, then traces the marriage back, through several precisely dated stages of problem and uneasy reconciliation, to its desperate origin in 1926. The past invariably leads to the present in Howard's fictional world, and the structural control often indicates both a working out of causation in human affairs and a kind of moral control, an insistence on a combination of awareness, responsibility, and refusal to hurt others in order to end the painful isolation of contemporary dilemmas.

More tightly controlled, and showing characters able to resolve their dilemmas more positively than do some other novels, *After Julius* depends, to some extent, on a rather striking coincidence. A young woman, visiting her mother for the week-end, finds her London lover, whom she had thought in Rome, arriving, with his wife, for dinner, and the affair explodes in a scene where fireworks are literal as well as symbolic. The structured plot shapes a novel in which moral or immoral actions eventually reveal themselves, in which moral judgment insists that characters take publicly visible responsibility for their actions. Similarly, in *Odd Girl Out* the young girl, amoral from a conventional point of view, who visits a young couple who have established a self-sufficient ''island'' in ten years of marriage and, in turn, sleeps with each of the partners, refuses to lie and insists on confronting both together to try to establish the ''truth'' of a three-way love that could nourish a child. Although the *ménage à trois,* full of ironic parallels and other forms of structural compression, cannot work for these three characters, the young girl who proposes it is seen as more moral, more willing to face the consequences of her actions and her emotions, than is the superficially more respectable couple. Virtue, in Howard's world, is not fragmented or buried, never the private gesture of an alienated sensibility; rather, actions have consequences, visible and direct, on the people closest to one.

Knowing and facing the past allows all three of the central women in *After Julius* some kind of resolution of their current dilemmas, but Howard's endings are not always so positive. In *The Sea Change* an aging playwright, who has longed for a renewal of youth in loving a young girl brought up in a village parsonage, and his wife, who has lost her only child, can understand and forgive each other in an acknowledgment of mutual pain and loss. The acknowledgment, the assumption of responsibility, allows them to survive, although it is far from a triumphant resolution. In *Something in Disguise* the resolution is melodramatic. The mother, a war widow who has raised her children alone, finally marries a retired army colonel to whom both her children object. Underneath the colonel's blunt, dull, insensitive exterior, the author slowly reveals, is the criminal heart of a man who tries gradually to poison his wife for her money, as he has poisoned two previous wives. And the daughter, who unpredictably marries a man who is both exciting and considerate, both a successful man of the world and a paragon of simple understanding and virtue, is desolate when the man is killed in an auto accident, having been sent on a fool's errand by one of the inconsiderate. Although moral judgment on each of the characters is clear enough, the plot punishes with an intensity that seems, somewhat sensationally, to detract from the emphasis on moral choice in some of the other novels. In *Getting it Right* melodrama and sensationalism recede into the background, useful for the hairdresser's discovery of sex, but not finally relevant to his moral choices that require the careful adjustment of both his concern for others' pain and his need to establish a satisfying life for himself.

Howard's carefully shaped moral tales are also dense with descriptions and references that convey the social texture of the times. *The Long View* is skillful in recreating both the sense of the wealthy English in southern France between the wars and the austerely genteel dinner party of 1950. *The Sea Change* contrasts the conventional life in the village parsonage with that of the 1950s playwright conveying a young girl to London, New York, and a Greek island. *After Julius* is brilliant with settings: the tiny attic office of the editorial staff of an old, respectable publishing firm; the spacious, chintzy Tudor of the mother's house in Sussex; the cheerful chaos of a young doctor's and his family's crowded flat. *Something in Disguise* contains a terrifying portrait of daily life in the pseudo-Spanish surroundings of the ''distinguished'' house on a new suburban housing estate. Within these tartly observed and wholly recognizable environments, certain types appear in novel after novel. The apparently dull retired Army officer, either basically sensitive and kindly or basically cruel and criminal, represents an older England, an irrelevant survival. The confident man of the world, playwright in *The Sea Change,* doctor in *After Julius,* international businessman in *Something in Disguise* (though quickly parodied in *Getting It Right*), generally has not allowed charm, success, or the modern world to distort his basically simple sense of responsibility. But all these men are seen from the point of view of women, and the novels reiterate a constant sense that women are more responsible, more affectionate, more genuinely concerned with others than men are. After the dinner party that opens *The Long View,* the men rejoin the women ''having discussed the fundamentals as superficially as the women in the drawing room discussed the superficialities fundamentally.'' *Getting It Right* switches the emphasis to the young lower-middle class male hairdresser discovering his need for risking conflict and responsibility, his recognition that one ''can't take out a kind of emotional insurance policy with people.'' The three principal women in the novel have known this all along.

Howard's intelligent and sensitive heroines are, however, far from independent. They often regret or seek to rediscover the wise father lost. The benign and revered village parson father in *The Sea*

Change is killed in a bicycle accident; fathers in other novels are killed in World War II; still other fathers, like the one in *The Long View,* are remote and indifferent or, like the actor who deserts his family in a melodramatic sub-plot in *Odd Girl Out,* completely irresponsible. The heroines seek protection, look for the man who might replace the absent father and make smoothly decisive all the hard and complex edges of a difficult world. They want to be safe and cosseted, a desire that can lead to the aridity of *The Long View,* the self-discovery of *After Julius,* or the impossible fantasies of *Something in Disguise* and *Odd Girl Out.* The complexities of the search for protection are stated explicitly near the end of *Odd Girl Out,* when the couple turns the amoral young girl who proposed it into a scapegoat who can be exorcised. Yet they cannot return to their ''island'': ''Each thought of what he had to do to sustain life for the other; each considered his efforts and translated them into nobility and unselfish determination.'' The roles are not equivalent, for, a few pages later, at the very end of the novel, the wife realizes that she, who had thought herself protected originally, must now become the principal protector. And they will not have a child.

Howard's *Cazalet Chronicle,* published in the 1990s, begins with *The Light Years.* The latter is set in 1937 and 1938, and depicts three generations of a wealthy Sussex family as they become entangled in problems of class, sexuality, and politics—each of them experienced on a deeply personal level. *Marking Time* takes up their saga in 1939, with the outbreak of the war, and provides a particularly compelling portrait of the three young Cazalet girls, Louise, Polly, and Clary. The series concludes with *Confusion,* which carries the three into adulthood amid the mayhem of wartime. Polly suffers from the loss of her mother, but even more painful is Clare's longing for her father, missing since the Normandy invasion of 1944. In Howard's fictional world sympathetic and competent mothers, who abound, are not enough. Heroines need the wisdom, the control, and the safety of the responsible and caring father, a safety dimly seen, always lost, and invariably over-compensated for. Looking for safety, always precarious in a world of airplanes and betrayals, requires a great deal of risk, sensitivity, and control. Howard's great distinction is that the search for safety is presented with such rare and intelligent discrimination.

—James Gindin

HOWARD, Maureen

Nationality: American. **Born:** Maureen Keans in Bridgeport, Connecticut, 28 June 1930. **Education:** Smith College, Northampton, Massachusetts, B.A. 1952. **Family:** Married 1) Daniel F. Howard in 1954 (divorced 1967), one daughter; 2) David J. Gordon in 1968; 3) Mark Probst, 1981. **Career:** Worked in publishing and advertising, 1952–54; lecturer in English, New School for Social Research, New York, 1967–68, 1970–71, and since 1974, and at University of California, Santa Barbara, 1968–69, Amherst College, Massachusetts, Brooklyn College, and Royale University. Currently, Member of the School of the Arts, Columbia University, New York. **Awards:** Guggenheim fellowship, 1967; Radcliffe Institute fellowship, 1967; National Book Critics Circle award, 1979; Merrill fellowship, 1982. **Address:** c/o Penguin, 375 Hudson Street, New York, New York 10014, U.S.A.

PUBLICATIONS

Novels

Not a Word about Nightingales. London, Secker and Warburg, 1960; New York, Atheneum, 1962.
Bridgeport Bus. New York, Harcourt Brace, 1965.
Before My Time. Boston, Little Brown, 1975.
Grace Abounding. Boston, Little Brown, 1982; London, Abacus, 1984.
Expensive Habits. New York, Summit, and London, Viking, 1986.
Natural History. New York, Norton, 1992.
A Lover's Almanac. New York, Viking, 1998.

Uncollected Short Stories

''Bed and Breakfast,'' in *Yale Review* (New Haven, Connecticut), March 1961.
''Sherry,'' in *The Best American Short Stories 1965,* edited by Martha Foley and David Burnett. Boston, Houghton Mifflin, 1965.
''Three Pigs of Krishna Nura,'' in *Partisan Review* (New Brunswick, New Jersey), Winter 1971–72.
''Sweet Memories,'' in *Statements,* edited by Jonathan Baumbach. New York, Braziller, 1975.

Other

Facts of Life (autobiography). Boston, Little Brown, 1978; with a new afterword by the author, New York, Penguin, 1999.
Editor, *Seven American Women Writers of the Twentieth Century.* Minneapolis, University of Minnesota Press, 1977.
Editor, *The Penguin Book of Contemporary American Essays.* New York, Viking, 1984.

* * *

In her award-winning autobiography, *Facts of Life,* Maureen Howard explains the conflict between her goals and her father's hopes for her: ''I think because I loved him, coarse and unlettered as he pretended to be, that he would have known from experience that our lives do not admit the fictional luxury of alternate endings.'' Howard's fiction reflects this view that alternate endings are illusive. As her characters attempt to recreate their stories, they discover that the past has predetermined their lives. One cannot alter personality; one can only understand, accept, and grow within the frame of individual talent. At the end of *Facts of Life,* Howard describes herself at twenty-three: ''I am beginning. My life is beginning which cannot be true.'' Her life began long ago, her character determined years before that moment. That the majority of Howard's fictional characters are female seems coincidental; in her introduction to *Seven American Women Writers of the Twentieth Century,* Howard asserts her preference for universal concerns: ''To my mind this is the most egalitarian manner in which to study women's literature—to presume that these women are artists first and do not have to be unduly praised or their reputations justified on grounds of sex.'' In Howard's novels, discovery and acceptance of one's own character challenge both genders.

When Professor Albert Sedgely, in *Not a Word about Nightingales,* prolongs his sabbatical in Italy, he wants ''to take his life as it was and alter its limits as though he lived in a theatrical set, movable flats—and having created a new scene, then he could shift his tastes, his emotions, even his appearance.'' To create this illusive possibility, Howard emphasizes Albert's daughter Rosemary's reaction. As with Henry James's Strether in *The Ambassadors,* Rosemary, sent to bring Albert back, is so charmed by his new personality and environment that she ignores her pledge until she discovers Albert's affair with Carlotta Manzini. Sexual awakening so threatens Rosemary, her mother Anne, and even Albert that all three retreat to narrow and confined lives. Is this the novel that Howard alludes to in *Facts of Life* as her ''mannered academic novel,'' that displays a ''sense of order as I knew it in the late fifties and early sixties with all the forms that I accepted and even enjoyed: that was the enormous joke about life—that our passion must be contained if we were not to be fools?'' If so, at least Albert's final decision rests on acknowledgment of his own character; that his love for Carlotta is ''incomplete'' and his business with Anne ''unfinished'' brings Albert home.

With humor Howard tackles the same questions in *Bridgeport Bus.* Although Howard shifts point of view frequently between her protagonist Mary Agnes Keely and other characters, the central question belongs to Mary Agnes: is ''the mutually destructive love of mother and daughter more substantial than tidy freedom?'' Howard's readers view Mary Agnes's attempts as recorded in her journals. When Mary Agnes begins her affair with Stanley Sarnicki, she records the event twice: first as ''a thirty-five-year-old virgin would write it—the easy dodge and genteel fade-out,'' and then ''done by a thirty-five-year-old lady *writer* who fancies herself a woman of experience when really there will always be something too delicate about her sensibility.'' Mary Agnes cannot escape her own nature, despite the different journal entries. As in her play, ''The Cheese Stands Alone,'' one of several creative interludes in her journal, Mary Agnes recognizes that her fate is ''inextricably woven'' to her mother's. She returns, pregnant and unmarried, to help her mother die. Truth and fiction are not always discernible in Mary Agnes's journal, but as her friend Lydia comments, ''she has in fact got at us in every meaningful respect.'' Mary Agnes's ''triumph'' is that she knows that ''it was not a great sin to be, at last, alone.'' She has grown within her limits.

By sharing personal histories, Laura Quinn in *Before My Time* exchanges spirits with her cousin's son, Jim Cogan. At the end of the novel, a more responsible Jim returns to face drug charges while Laura writes of personal rather than public feelings. However, Howard states clearly, ''Whoever compares the present and the past will soon perceive that there prevail and always have prevailed the same desires and passions.'' Although beneficial, this ending reflects an awakening, not a creation, of character. To develop the pedagogy to instruct young Jim, Laura resees her brother Robert's failed relationship with their father; silently to Jim, Laura urges, ''Think that this story is your answer: Robert and all my honesty and self-knowledge are here for you at last. Think before you run.'' Howard also offers histories of other family members. The most successful story, that of Jim's twin siblings Cormac and Siobhan, parallels Jim and Laura's as the twins have similar desires but are out of step with each other. Mary Agnes Keely may have had ''triumph'' in *Bridgeport Bus,* but at the end of *Before My Time,* Laura Quinn's new doubt is as ''sweet''; the confines of her personality contain newly tapped emotion.

Because Howard's characters in *Grace Abounding* remain isolated from each other, the reader senses little more than ongoing struggle at the end of this novel. Within shifts of point of view and time frame, each character attempts to discern what in the past enlightens the present. The reader first meets Maude and Elizabeth Dowd in shock after Frank Dowd's death; widow Maude and daughter Elizabeth, ''unable to speak of their abandonment,'' ''have drawn off into private desolation.'' Maude's mother, lost in the world of senility, and her nurse die soon after. Years later, neither Maude's nor Elizabeth's husbands know their wives' true natures. In a disturbing scene, three-year-old Warren, a victim of child abuse who is locked within himself, dies before Maude, now a psychologist, can reach him. Only the mad poet Mattie appears to have a whole life, but, after her death, her heir inadvertently burns all her poems. After the first two sections of the novel, ''Sin'' and ''Sorrow,'' the reader expects in the final ''Grace Note'' some resolution but encounters instead Theodore Lasser, Maude's husband's son, a priest more concerned with public relations than spiritual needs. Where then is that ''grace abounding''? The last line holds some answer: ''The young priest stumbles back and forth from bush to lemon tree, brushing and brushing at cold cobwebs that will fade with the morning dew.'' The reader knows that Theodore's ghostly cobwebs stem from unresolved conflicts with his father. *Grace Abounding* may well serve as Howard's warning rather than model: to accept limits, one must discover, know, and then share one's nature.

The starting point of *A Lover's Almanac* is a party to welcome in the year 2000 (Howard published the book two years earlier). Events at the party place her protagonists, Louise or Lou Moffett and Artie Freeman, at odds with one another after a besotted Artie attacks two of the guests. Though much of the ensuing plot involves Artie's attempts to reconcile with Lou, the most compelling aspect of the story involves Artie's grandfather Cyril. The latter, who raised his grandson, finds himself face to face with Sylvie, a lover he has not seen in half a century. His tale unfolds in a series of flashbacks, and throughout the story, Howard brings to bear her considerable talents with the use of numerous motifs, ranging from biographical sketches of Sir Isaac Newton and Benjamin Franklin to tidbits of folk wisdom.

—Mary M. Lay

HUDSON, Jeffrey

See CRICHTON, (John) Michael

HUGHES, David (John)

Nationality: British. **Born:** Alton, Hampshire, 27 July 1930. **Education:** Eggar's Grammar School, Alton; King's College School, Wimbledon; Christ Church, Oxford (editor, *Isis*), B.A. in English 1953, M.A. 1965. **Military Service:** Served in the Royal Air Force, 1949–50. **Family:** Married 1) the actress and director Mai Zetterling in 1958 (divorced 1976); 2) Elizabeth Westoll in 1980; one daughter and one son. **Career:** Assistant editor, *London Magazine,* 1953–54; editor, *Town* magazine, London, 1960–61; documentary and feature film writer in Sweden, 1961–68; lived in France, 1970–74; editor, New Fiction Society, 1975–77, 1981–82; film critic, *Sunday Times,* London, 1982–83. Since 1982 film critic, *Mail on Sunday,* London. Assistant visiting professor, University of Iowa, Iowa City, 1978–79 and 1987, and University of Alabama, University, 1979; visiting associate professor, University of Houston, 1986. **Awards:** W.H.

Smith Literary award, 1985; Welsh Arts Council prize, 1985. Fellow, Royal Society of Literature, 1986. **Agent:** Anthony Sheil Associates, 43 Doughty Street, London WC1N 2LF, England.

PUBLICATIONS

Novels

A Feeling in the Air. London, Deutsch, 1957; as *Man Off Beat,* New York, Reynal, 1957.
Sealed with a Loving Kiss. London, Hart Davis, 1959.
The Horsehair Sofa. London, Hart Davis, 1961.
The Major. London, Blond, 1964; New York, Coward McCann, 1965.
The Man Who Invented Tomorrow. London, Constable, 1968.
Memories of Dying. London, Constable, 1976.
A Genoese Fancy. London, Constable, 1979.
The Imperial German Dinner Service. London, Constable, 1983.
The Pork Butcher. London, Constable, 1984; New York, Schocken, 1985.
But for Bunter. London, Heinemann, 1985; as *The Joke of the Century,* New York, Taplinger, 1986.
The Little Book. London, Hutchinson, 1996.

Uncollected Short Stories

"The Coloured Cliffs," in *Transatlantic Review* (London), Spring 1961.
"Rough Magic," in *Shakespeare Stories,* edited by Giles Gordon. London, Hamish Hamilton, 1982.

Plays

Flickorna (screenplay). Stockholm, PAN/Norstedt, 1968.

Screenplays (with Mai Zetterling): *Loving Couples,* 1964; *Night Games,* 1966; *Dr. Glas,* 1967; *The Girls,* 1968.

Television Plays: *The Stuff of Madness,* with Mai Zetterling, from story by Patricia Highsmith, 1990.

Other

J.B. Priestley: An Informal Study of His Work. London, Hart Davis, 1958; Freeport, New York, Books for Libraries, 1970.
The Road to Stockholm and Lapland. London, Eyre and Spottiswoode, 1964.
The Cat's Tale (for children), with Mai Zetterling. London, Cape, 1965.
The Seven Ages of England. Stockholm, Swedish Radio, 1966.
The Rosewater Revolution: Notes on a Change of Attitude. London, Constable, 1971.
Himself and Other Animals: A Portrait of Gerald Durrell. London, Hutchinson, 1997.
Editor, *Memoirs of the Comte de Gramont,* translated by Horace Walpole. London, Folio Society, 1965.
Editor, *Sound of Protest, Sound of Love: Protest-Songs from America and England.* Stockholm, Swedish Radio, 1968.
Editor, *Evergreens.* Stockholm, Swedish Radio, 1977.
Editor, *Winter's Tales 1* (new series). London, Constable, and New York, St. Martin's Press, 1985.
Editor, *The Stories of Ernest Hemingway.* London, Folio Society, 1986.
Editor, with Giles Gordon, *Best Short Stories 1986 [1988].* London, Heinemann, 3 vols., 1986–88.
Editor, with Giles Gordon, *Best Short Stories 1989 [1991].* London, Heinemann, 3 vols., 1989–91; as *The Best English Short Stories 1989 [1991].* New York, Norton, 3 vols., 1989–91.
Editor, with Giles Gordon, *The Minerva Book of Short Stories 1–6.* London, Minerva, 6 vols., 1990–94.

* * *

David Hughes takes war for his subject, but he is certainly not concerned to make stirring adventures out of the sordid tragedies, mass killings, and crowd emotions of armed conflict, nor to contrive intellectual puzzles out of the intrigues of international enmity. His business is with individuals and the way that their lives have been shaped (and frequently grossly distorted) by the wars of this century.

His skillful control of his subject matter, his ingenuity as a story teller, and his subtle and powerful delineation of character enable him to create unforgettable novels out of his chosen material. He seldom makes overt judgments. His characters may condemn themselves out of their obsessions and stored guilt, but their creator insists that, whatever they may have done to other people, they are themselves frail and vulnerable, and therefore, in some respects at least, lovable. However much the readers are kept at a distance by the way Hughes structures his novels, they are never allowed to forget that he is dealing with people not ciphers.

The history of the war-torn first half of this century is epitomized in *Memories of Dying* in which Flaxman, a prosperous business man on the brink of a nervous breakdown is suddenly caught up into the consciousness of his old history teacher, Hunter. As Flaxman flies to the south of France, in a vain attempt to escape from the pressures of work and family, he finds his mind invaded by thoughts of his home town and the aged lonely man who once taught him, now engaged in the impossible task of writing a history of the world that will present the facts honestly to future generations of schoolchildren. It is an act of penitence, for in the first world war Hunter through accident and panic shot one of his fellow officers. For years thereafter he carried the man's wallet around with him, vowing that he would marry the widow whose photograph it contained. He achieved his aim. He located the woman, who had turned into a lonely alcoholic, married her, and had one son. At the outbreak of World War II he insisted that she should leave their home for a more remote cottage. In that place, of his choosing, she was killed by a random air raid. History had not finished with Hunter. Sometime in the years of unsteady peace, his son was found dead of drugs and alcohol in an Oxford college.

Like Hunter, the narrator of *The Imperial German Dinner Service* tries to make some reparative and creative response to the war-torn century into which he has been born. In his case, his task takes the symbolic form of collecting the scattered pieces of a dinner service made in Edwardian England as a gift for the Kaiser. Many threads are drawn into his search, for Hughes is determined to show, yet again, how individual needs are woven into public events. As his obsessed narrator journeys to meet his unlikely contacts in the countries of western Europe and Scandinavia, and ultimately reaches the precarious geology of Iceland in his search for the fragile pieces of china, he is reconstructing his own life as well as searching for the innocence of an impossible golden age. Each bit of the dinner service is adorned with an English scene, which he has visited at some time with his estranged wife. So, as Europe is torn, so is he, both by the torments of his marriage to an ambitious Sunday columnist (who discovered the first plate of the dinner service and so set him off on his quest) and the futility of his own work as a freelance journalist.

Ernst Kestner, the protagonist of *The Pork Butcher,* Hughes's most important and serious novel so far, is also on a quest. A widower from Thomas Mann's town of Lubeck, he is dying of lung cancer and determined that his final act shall be a confrontation with the guilt of his wartime past. So he goes to Paris to take his coldly neurotic, self-obsessed daughter (who has married a Frenchman) on a weekend trip to the village where he had been stationed in the 1940s. In that village, Kestner had met Jannie and become so infatuated with her that he wrote home to his German fiancée breaking off the engagement. The letter never arrived, for the day he posted it, the order came that the village was to be "punished," the inhabitants were to be lured to the central square and shot, and the whole place was to be abandoned. In the numbed brutality of that act, Kestner killed the girl he loved. Now, like Hunter, he is determined to make some amends, even if all he can do is to give himself up to the mayor of the restored village. Beating the usual intransigence of local bureaucracy, he manages to talk to the mayor and gradually realizes that the man is Jannie's brother. When the mayor also recognizes to whom he is talking, he drives the car in which he is conveying Kestner with such wild fury that it is involved in a fatal accident. The mayor is killed; and Kestner, now badly injured, has to end his life with a double guilt on his shoulders. This irony underlines the impossibility of making amends either internationally or personally for the obscenities of war.

But for Bunter takes up the same theme in a strangely light-hearted vein. Hughes imagines that Billy Bunter (the fat boy of Greyfriars, who entertained generations of schoolboys) has survived into the 1980s, and is now ready to confess his own responsibility for the horrors of the century he has lived through. Once again Hughes makes his point: none of us, not even the most unlikely, can shelve responsibility for the times we live in.

—Shirley Toulson

HULME, Keri

Nationality: New Zealander. **Born:** Christchurch, 9 March 1947. **Education:** North Beach primary school; Aranui High School; Canterbury University, Christchurch. **Career:** Formerly, senior postwoman, Greymouth, and director for New Zealand television; writer-in-residence, Canterbury University, 1985. **Awards:** New Zealand Literary Fund grant, 1975, 1977, 1979, and scholarship in letters, 1990; Katherine Mansfield Memorial award, for short story, 1975; Maori Trust Fund prize, 1978; East-West Centre award, 1979; ICI bursary, 1982; New Zealand writing bursary, 1984; Book of the Year award, 1984; Mobil Pegasus prize, 1985; Booker prize, 1985; Chianti Ruffino Antico Fattor award, 1987. **Address:** Okarito, Private Bag, Hokitika Post Office, Westland, New Zealand.

PUBLICATIONS

Novels

The Bone People. Wellington, Spiral, 1983; London, Hodder and Stoughton, and Baton Rouge, Louisiana State University Press, 1985.

Lost Possessions (novella). Wellington, Victoria University Press, 1985.

Short Stories

The Windeater/Te Kaihau. Wellington, Victoria University Press, 1986; London, Hodder and Stoughton, and New York, Braziller, 1987.

Uncollected Short Stories

"See Me, I Am Kei," in *Spiral 5* (Wellington), 1982.

"Floating Words," in *Prize Writing,* edited by Martyn Goff. London, Hodder and Stoughton, 1989.

"The Plu-perfect Pawa," in *Sport 1* (Wellington), 1989.

"Hinekaro Goes on a Picnic and Blows Up Another Obelisk," in *Subversive Acts,* edited by Cathie Dunsford. Auckland, New Women's Press, 1991.

Poetry

The Silences Between (Moeraki Conversations). Auckland, Auckland University Press-Oxford University Press, 1982.

Strands. Auckland, Auckland University Press, 1991.

Other

Homeplaces: Three Coasts of the South Island of New Zealand, with photographs by Robin Morrison. Auckland, Hodder and Stoughton, 1989; London, Hodder and Stoughton, 1990.

*

Critical Studies: "In My Spiral Fashion" by Peter Simpson, in *Australian Book Review* (Kensington Park), August 1984; "Spiraling to Success" by Elizabeth Webby, in *Meanjin* (Melbourne), January 1985; "Keri Hulme: Breaking Ground" by Shona Smith, in *Untold 2* (Christchurch); *Leaving the Highway: Six Contemporary New Zealand Novelists* by Mark Williams, Auckland, Auckland University Press, 1990; *Writing Along Broken Lines: Violence and Ethnicity in Contemporary Maori Fiction* by Otto Heim. Auckland, New Zealand, Auckland University Press, 1998.

Keri Hulme comments:

I have a grave suspicion that Life is a vast joke: we are unwitting elements of the joke.

It is not a nice or kind joke, either.

I write about people who are in pain because they can't see the joke, see the point of the joke.

What I write is fantasy-solidly-based-in-reality, everyday myths.

I rarely write out of a New Zealand context and, because I am lucky enough to be a mongrel, draw extensively from my ancestral cultural heritages—Maori (Kai Tahu, the South Island tribe), Scots (the Orkneys), and English (Lancashire). (Remember that the Pakeha elements of my ancestry predominate, but they have been well-sieved by Aotearoa.) I want to touch the raw nerves in NZ—the violence we largely cover up; the racism we don't acknowledge; the spoliation of land & sea that has been smiled at for the past 150 years—and explore *why* we (Maori & Pakeha) have developed a very curious type of humor which not many other people in the world understand, like, or appreciate and which is a steel-sheathed nerve I want to hide inside.

I'm not particularly serious about anything except whitebaiting. (Whitebait are the fry of NZ galaxids: they are a greatly relished and *very* expensive-about $75NZ a kilo—delicacy. I whitebait every season.)

* * *

Keri Hulme comes from the heartland of New Zealand—the South Island's west coast—and, perhaps as a consequence, she has developed an idiom which remains distinctively New Zealand even when it is feeding on the great traditions of English, Irish, American, and other (notably sufic) literature. This New Zealandness is the most immediately striking feature of the work for which she is best know, *The Bone People.*

The Maori phrases which permeate the text immediately proclaim its provenance. But the texture of the English which she writes is also unmistakably New Zealand. Many writers before her have managed a passable imitation of Kiwi pub argot, but Hulme is one of the first to have succeeded in giving a characteristic account of the speech and thoughts of New Zealanders as educated and intelligent as her protagonist, Kerewin Holmes. In passages like the following one can sense the typical rhythms and accents (''thunk''), the half-suppressed obscenities (''whateffers''), the gentle ironies and not-so-gentle prejudices (''Poms'' are Englishmen) of New Zealand's more articulate denizens. (Kerewin has just discovered that her young protégé, Simon Gillayley, may have aristocratic Irish blood):

> Ah hell, urchin, it doesn't matter, you can't help who your forbears were, and I realized as I thunk it, that I was reveling in the knowledge of my whakapapa and solid Lancashire and Hebridean ancestry. Stout commoners on the left side, and real rangatira on the right distaff side. A New Zealander through and through. Moanawhenua bones and heart and blood and brain. None of your (retch) import Poms or whateffers.

The uncovering of Simon's background constitutes one strand of the plot of *The Bone People,* but ultimately—like the plots of many of Hulme's short stories—it turns out to be an inconclusive strand. All we can be sure of is that he comes from a background of violence and drug-dealing. The more detailed clues lead nowhere, and it seems that Hulme intended merely to tease her readers with these elements of a ''well-made'' plot, and that her real interest lay elsewhere. As Kerewin begins to check out Simon's Irish background she apologizes for ''dragging'' the reader ''out of the cobweb pile, self-odyssey.'' The phrase highlights not only the book's principal concern (Kerewin's mental and spiritual progress) but also one of its dominant images (the spider's web, which at different times represents entanglement and intricate harmony).

Even more prominent than the spider and its web is the traditional Maori (and sufic) motif of the spiral. Kerewin lives in a tower full of spirals, notably a spiral staircase and a double spiral engraved on the floor: ''one of the kind that wound your eyes round and round into the center where surprise you found the beginning of another spiral that led your eyes out again to the nothingness of the outside … it was an old symbol of rebirth, and the outward-inward nature of things….'' At the beginning of the book Kerewin has clearly begun a downward spiral into ''nothingness.'' Her Tower, conceived as a ''hermitage,'' ''a glimmering retreat,'' has become an ''abyss,'' a ''prison,'' She is entangled in a web of self-absorption and materialism.

Into her life walks Simon, who is her opposite in almost every respect. She is dark (though only one-eighth Maori); he is fair. She is ''heavy shouldered, heavy-hammed, heavy-haired''; he is lithe, almost skeletal. She is wonderfully articulate; he is a mute. (Again Hulme teases our expectations of a ''well-made'' plot by holding out the promise that he will eventually learn to speak. He does not.) She is obsessed by her possessions, and fears as a consequence that she has ''lost the main part'' of life; he is ''rough on possessions,'' but has a sense of the deeper aura of things. She shrinks from touching others; he and his adoptive father (Joe) are, as Hulme has subsequently put it, ''huggers and kissers deluxe.'' She is clever; he is trusting—two terms which are juxtaposed in the book. She is associated with the moon; he is a ''sunchild.'' She is an introvert; he and Joe are extroverts.

Symbol-hunters have been quick to latch on to Simon's character, but they have so far been baffled by the diffuseness of the portrait. Hulme herself claims that she writes ''from a visual base and a gut base rather than sieving it through the mind,'' and so it is probably futile to search for any conscious allegorical design in the book. A psycho-analytical approach offers greater rewards. Many aspects of *The Bone People*—notably the dreams (which often foretell the future), the paintings, the search for ''wholeness'' (and the dance imagery which accompanies it), the emphasis on myth, the eclectic attitude to religion, the disdainful attitude towards sex, and the mandala-like tricephalos which anticipates the asexual harmony (''commensalism'') achieved by the principal characters at the end—suggest the influence of Jung. Jung also provides as good an explanation as any of Simon's relationship with Kerewin.

The book is full of projections and personifications of deviant aspects of the characters' personalities. Kerewin's more cynical thoughts are attributed to an inner voice labeled ''the snark''; her violent tendencies turn at length into a palpable cancer; and the mysterious character who helps her to grapple with this cancer (''a thin wiry person of indeterminate age. Of indeterminate sex. Of indeterminate race'') appears to be a projection of her own enfeebled self. Similarly Simon (who was originally conceived as a figment of Kerewin's dreams and not as an independent character) may be seen as her ''shadow''—the embodiment of everything she has lost by withdrawing from society. This includes not only positive factors like trust and responsiveness to touch but also negative ones, especially violence.

Simon brings with him a long history of violence, culminating in the savage beatings inflicted on him by Joe. Kerewin's spiraling descent is accompanied and to a large extent occasioned by her recognition of this violence, and the nadir of her ''self-odyssey'' comes when she gives way to violence herself. At the same time an orgy of violence (effectively amplified by the recurrent images of knives and splintered glass) erupts among the other characters, so that at the end of the third part of the novel Simon is hospitalized, Joe (wounded) is in jail, one minor character is dead, another seriously ill, and Kerewin's Tower has been reduced to a single story.

Many readers feel that Hulme should have left the book there—that, as in much of her other fiction (of which the fine story "Hooks and Feelers" and the novella *Lost Possessions* are the most accessible examples) it is the violence, and especially the violence that wells out of love, which is the most compelling element. But Hulme added a fourth section and an epilogue in which the principals, aided by a set of unorthodox assistants and (except in Simon's case) by a deep draught of Maori culture, spiral back towards "rebirth," "wholeness," and harmony.

In a recent interview Hulme has acknowledged that the ending owes something to Jung, which encourages the notion advanced here that the whole novel is susceptible to a Jungian interpretation. Just who is really the focus of this interpretation—Kerewin Holmes or her virtual namesake, Keri Hulme—is a question difficult to resolve. Hulme concedes that the three protagonists emerged from her dreams. (She keeps a dream diary, and at least one of the dreams in *The Bone People*—Kerewin's at Moerangi—is lifted straight from it.) Much of the material also seems quasi-autobiographical. Time will tell if she can write effectively on less personal subjects.

—Richard Corballis

HUMPHREYS, Emyr (Owen)

Nationality: British. **Born:** Prestatyn, Clwyd, Wales, 15 April 1919. **Education:** University College of Wales, Aberystwyth, 1937–39; University College of North Wales, Bangor, 1946–47. **Military Service:** Served as a relief worker in the Middle East and the Mediterranean during World War II. **Family:** Married Elinor Myfanwy Jones in 1946; three sons and one daughter. **Career:** Teacher, Wimbledon Technical College, London, 1948–50, and Pwllheli Grammar School, North Wales, 1951–54; producer, BBC Radio, Cardiff, 1955–58; drama producer, BBC Television, 1958–62; freelance writer and director, 1962–65; lecturer in drama, 1965–72, and Honorary Professor, 1988, University College of North Wales. Since 1972 freelance writer. **Awards:** Maugham award, 1953; Hawthornden prize, 1959; Welsh Arts Council award, 1972, 1975, 1979, for non-fiction, 1984; Gregynog fellowship, 1974; Society of Authors traveling scholarship, 1979; Welsh Arts Council Book of the Year, 1992, for *Bonds of Attachment.* D.Litt.: University of Wales, Cardiff, 1990. Honorary Fellow, University of Wales, 1987. **Agent**: Anthony Sheil Associates, 43 Doughty Street, London WC1N 2LF, England. **Address:** Llinon, Pen-y-berth, Llanfairpwll, Pnys Môn, Gwynedd LL61 5YT, Wales.

PUBLICATIONS

Novels

The Little Kingdom. London, Eyre and Spottiswoode, 1946.
The Voice of a Stranger. London, Eyre and Spottiswoode, 1949.
A Change of Heart. London, Eyre and Spottiswoode, 1951.
Hear and Forgive. London, Gollancz, 1952; New York, Putnam, 1953.
A Man's Estate. London, Eyre and Spottiswoode, 1955; New York, McGraw Hill, 1956.
The Italian Wife. London, Eyre and Spottiswoode, 1957; New York, McGraw Hill, 1958.
Y Tri Llais (in Welsh). Llandybie, Dyfed, Llyfrau'r Dryw, 1958.
A Toy Epic. London, Eyre and Spottiswoode, 1958.
The Gift. London, Eyre and Spottiswoode, 1963.
Outside the House of Baal. London, Eyre and Spottiswoode, 1965.
National Winner. London, Macdonald, 1971.
Flesh and Blood. London, Hodder and Stoughton, 1974.
The Best of Friends. London, Hodder and Stoughton, 1978.
The Anchor Tree. London, Hodder and Stoughton, 1980.
Jones. London, Dent, 1984.
Salt of the Earth. London, Dent, 1985.
An Absolute Hero. London, Dent, 1986.
Open Secrets. London, Dent, 1988.
Bonds of Attachment. London, Macdonald, 1991.
Unconditional Surrender. Chester Springs, Pennsylvania, Dufour Springs, 1996.
The Gift of a Daughter. Bridgend, Wales, Seren, 1998.

Short Stories

Natives. London, Secker and Warburg, 1968.
Miscellany Two. Bridgend, Glamorgan, Poetry Wales Press, 1981.

Uncollected Short Stories

"Down in the Heel on Duty," in *New English Review* (London), 1947.
"Michael," in *Wales* (London), vol. 7, nos. 26–27, 1947.
"A Girl in the Ice" and "The Obstinate Bottle," in *New Statesman* (London), 1953.
"Mrs. Armitage," in *Welsh Short Stories.* London, Faber, 1959.
"The Arrest," in *Madog 3* (Barry), 1977.

Plays

King's Daughter, adaptation of a play by Saunders Lewis (produced London, 1959; as *Siwan,* televised, 1960). Published, as *Siwan,* in *Plays of the Year 1959–60,* London, Elek, 1960.
Dinas, with W.S. Jones. Llandybie, Dyfed, Llyfrau'r Dryw, 1970.

Radio Plays: *A Girl in a Garden,* 1963; *Reg,* 1964; *The Manipulator,* 1970; *Etifedd y Glyn,* 1984; *The Arrest,* 1985.

Television Plays and Documentaries: *Siwan,* 1960; *The Shining Pyramid,* from a story by Arthur Machen, 1979; *Y Gosb* (The Penalty), 1983; *Wyn ir Lladdfa* (Lambs to the Slaughter), 1984; *Hualau* (Fetters), 1984; *Bwy yn Rhydd* (Living Free), 1984; *Angel o'r Nef* (An Angel from Heaven), 1985; *Teulu Helga* (Helga's Family), 1985; *Cwlwm Cariad* (A Love Knot), 1986; *Twll Ole* (A Hole), 1987; *Yr Alwad* (The Call), 1988; *The Triple Net,* 1988; *Yr Alltud* (The Exile), 1989; *Dyn Perig* (A Dangerous Fellow), 1990; *Outside Time,* 1991; *Dwr Athân* (Fire and Water), 1991.

Poetry

Roman Dream, music by Alun Hoddinott. London, Oxford University Press, 1968.
An Apple Tree and a Pig, music by Alun Hoddinott. London, Oxford University Press, 1969.

Ancestor Worship: A Cycle of 18 Poems. Denbigh, Gee, 1970.
Landscapes, music by Alun Hoddinott. London, Oxford University Press, 1975.
Penguin Modern Poets 27, with John Ormond and John Tripp. London, Penguin, 1979.
The Kingdom of Bran. London, Holmes, 1979.
Pwyll a Riannon. London, Holmes, 1979.

Other

The Taliesin Tradition: A Quest for the Welsh Identity. London, Black Raven Press, 1983; revised edition, Chester Springs, Pennsylvania, Dufour, 1990.
The Triple Net: A Portrait of the Writer Kate Roberts 1891–1985. London, Channel 4 Television, 1988.
The Crucible of Myth. Swansea, University of Swansea, 1990.

*

Bibliographies: *A Bibliography of Anglo-Welsh Literature 1900–1965* by Brynmor Jones, Swansea, Library Association, 1970.

Manuscript Collections: National Library of Wales, Aberystwyth.

Critical Studies: *The Novel* 1945–1950 by P.H. Newby, London, Longman, 1951; *Y llenor a'i Gymdeithas* by A. Llewelyn Williams, London, BBC, 1966; *The Dragon Has Two Tongues* by Glyn Jones, London, Dent, 1968; *Ysgrifau Beirniadol VII* by Derec Llwyd Morgan, Denbigh, Gee, 1972; Jeremy Hooker and Andre Morgan, in *Planet 39* (Llangeitho Tregaron, Dyfed), 1977; *Emyr Humphreys,* Cardiff, University of Wales Press, 1980, and "Land of the Living," in *Planet 52* (Llangeitho Tregaron, Dyfed), 1985, both by Ioan Williams; "Channels of Grace: A View of the Earlier Novels of Emyr Humphreys," in *Anglo-Welsh Review 70* (Tenby, Dyfed), 1982, and article in *British Novelists 1930–1959* edited by Bernard Oldsey, Detroit, Gale, 1983, both by Roland Mathias; *Emyr Humphreys* by M. Wynn Thomas, Caernarvon, Pantycelyn, 1989.

* * *

The preoccupations of Emyr Humphreys are peculiarly Welsh, and since there are very few Welsh novelists writing in English who spring from or have assimilated the Welsh Nonconformist religious heritage, his work has few parallels in that of his contemporaries. Humphreys manifests in his novels a Puritan seriousness about the purpose of living, about the need for tradition and the understanding of it, and about the future of the community (usually seen as Wales) as well as the good of the individual. Welsh Nationalist as well as Christian, he re-emphasised in 1953 that "personal responsibility is a Protestant principle" and saw himself as engaged in writing the Protestant novel. His interest in the non-realist novel is minimal and his technical experimentation is limited to the use, in *A Man's Estate,* of a number of narrators and, in *Outside the House of Baal,* to an interleaving of narratives in which the past rapidly catches up with the present.

His first two novels, *The Little Kingdom* and *The Voice of a Stranger,* are concerned respectively with idealism betrayed by false leadership and idealism bludgeoned by Knavery. Their conclusions are pessimistic. The earlier of those themes appears again in *A Toy Epic.* But with *A Change of Heart* begins Humphreys's concern with the Christian belief in the gradual progress of society towards *the good* and the means by which *good* is transmitted from generation to generation. Heredity is soon discarded in favour of answers more complex. Perhaps the finest of the earlier novels which pursue this theme is *Hear and Forgive,* and of the later, *Outside the House of Baal.* In this book Humphreys faces the apparently total defeat of his Calvinistic Methodist minister, leaving the reader only with the silence which might make room for faith.

The Anchor Tree is a digression—with the same preoccupations—into his Welsh-American experience; but Humphreys devoted much of his time in the 1970s and 1980s to a series in which he intended *National Winner* to occupy the fourth position. *Flesh and Blood, The Best of Friends,* and *Salt of the Earth* are part of this sequence, while *Jones* is a single-volume study of the refusal of responsibility. Set during the final days of World War II, *Unconditional Surrender* recalls Anthony Trollope's *The Warden* with its complex tale of conflicting loyalties.

—Roland Mathias

HUNTER, Evan

Pseudonyms: Curt Cannon; Hunt Collins; Ezra Hannon; Richard Marsten; and Ed McBain. **Nationality:** American. **Born:** Salvatore A. Lombino, New York City, 15 October 1926. **Education:** Evander Childs High School, New York; Cooper Union, New York, 1943–44; Hunter College, New York, B.A. 1950 (Phi Beta Kappa). **Military Service:** United States Navy, 1944–46. **Family:** Married 1) Anita Melnick in 1949 (divorced), three sons; 2) Mary Vann Finley in 1973, one step-daughter. **Career:** In the early 1950s taught in vocational high schools and worked for Scott Meredith Literary Agency, New York. Lives in Norwalk, Connecticut. **Awards:** Mystery Writers of America Edgar Allan Poe award, 1957, and Grand Master award, 1985. **Agent:** John Farquharson Ltd., 250 West 57th Street, New York, New York 10107, U.S.A.; or, 162–168 Regent Street, London, W1R 5TB, England.

PUBLICATIONS

Novels

The Big Fix. N.p., Falcon, 1952; as *So Nude, So Dead* (as Richard Marsten), New York, Fawcett, 1956.
The Evil Sleep! N.p., Falcon, 1952
Don't Crowd Me. New York, Popular Library, 1953; London, Consul, 1960; as *The Paradise Party,* London, New English Library, 1968.
Cut Me In (as Hunt Collins). New York, Abelard Schuman, 1954; London, Boardman, 1960; as *The Proposition,* New York, Pyramid, 1955.
The Blackboard Jungle. New York, Simon and Schuster, 1954; London, Constable, 1955.
Second Ending. New York, Simon and Schuster, and London, Constable, 1956; as *Quartet in H,* New York, Pocket Books, 1957.
Tomorrow's World (as Hunt Collins). New York, Avalon, 1956; as *Tomorrow and Tomorrow,* New York, Pyramid, 1956; as Ed McBain, London, Sphere, 1979.

Strangers When We Meet. New York, Simon and Schuster, and London, Constable, 1958.
I'm Cannon—For Hire (as Curt Cannon). New York, Fawcett, 1958; London, Fawcett, 1959.
A Matter of Conviction. New York, Simon and Schuster, and London, Constable, 1959; as *The Young Savages,* New York, Pocket Books, 1966.
Mothers and Daughters. New York, Simon and Schuster, and London, Constable, 1961.
Buddwing. New York, Simon and Schuster, and London, Constable, 1964.
The Paper Dragon. New York, Delacorte Press, 1966; London, Constable, 1967.
A Horse's Head. New York, Delacorte Press, 1967; London, Constable, 1968.
Last Summer, New York, Doubleday, 1968; London, Constable, 1969.
Sons. New York, Doubleday, 1969; London, Constable, 1970.
Nobody Knew They Were There. New York, Doubleday, and London, Constable, 1972.
Every Little Crook and Nanny. New York, Doubleday, and London, Constable, 1972.
Come Winter. New York, Doubleday, and London, Constable, 1973.
Streets of Gold. New York, Harper, 1974; London, Macmillan, 1975.
Doors (as Ezra Hannon). New York, Stein and Day, 1975; London, Macmillan, 1976
The Chisholms: A Novel of the Journey West. New York, Harper, and London, Hamish Hamilton, 1976.
Walk Proud. New York, Bantam, 1979.
Love, Dad. New York, Crown, and London, Joseph, 1981.
Far from the Sea. New York, Atheneum, and London, Hamish Hamilton, 1983.
Lizzie. New York, Arbor House, and London, Hamish Hamilton, 1984.
Criminal Conversation. New York, Warner, 1994.
Privileged Conversation. New York, Warner Books, 1996.
Me and Hitch. London and Boston, Faber and Faber, 1997.

Novels as Richard Marsten

Runaway Black. New York, Fawcett, 1954; London, Red Seal, 1957.
Murder in the Navy. New York, Fawcett, 1955; as *Death of a Nurse* (as Ed McBain), New York, Pocket Books, 1968; London, Hodder and Stoughton, 1972.
The Spiked Heel. New York, Holt, 1956; London, Constable, 1957.
Vanishing Ladies. New York, Permabooks, 1957; London, Boardman, 1961.
Even the Wicked. New York, Permabooks, 1958; as Ed McBain, London, Severn House, 1979.
Big Man. New York, Pocket Books, 1959; as Ed McBain. London, Penguin, 1978.

Novels as Ed McBain

Cop Hater. New York, Permabooks, 1956; London, Boardman, 1958.
The Mugger. New York, Simon and Schuster, 1956: London, Boardman, 1959.
The Pusher. New York, Simon and Schuster, 1956; London, Boardman, 1959.
The Con Man. New York, Permabooks, 1957; London, Boardman, 1960.
Killer's Choice. New York, Simon and Schuster, 1958; London, Boardman, 1960.
Killer's Payoff. New York, Simon and Schuster, 1958; London, Boardman, 1960.
April Robin Murders, with Craig Rice (completed by McBain). New York, Random House, 1958; London, Hammond, 1959.
Lady Killer. New York, Simon and Schuster, 1958; London, Boardman, 1961.
Killer's Wedge. New York, Simon and Schuster, 1959; London Boardman, 1961.
'Til Death. New York, Simon and Schuster, 1959; London, Boardman, 1961.
King's Ransom. New York, Simon and Schuster, 1959; London, Boardman, 1961.
Give the Boys a Great Big Hand. New York, Simon and Schuster, 1960; London, Boardman, 1962.
The Heckler. New York, Simon and Schuster, 1960; London, Boardman, 1962.
See Them Die. New York, Simon and Schuster, 1960; London, Boardman, 1963.
Lady, Lady, I Did It! New York, Simon and Schuster, 1961; London, Boardman, 1963.
Like Love. New York, Simon and Schuster, 1962; London, Hamish Hamilton, 1964.
Ten Plus One. New York, Simon and Schuster, 1963; London, Hamish Hamilton, 1964.
Ax. New York, Simon and Schuster, and London, Hamish Hamilton, 1964.
The Sentries. New York, Simon and Schuster, and London, Hamish Hamilton, 1965.
He Who Hesitates. New York, Delacorte Press, and London, Hamish Hamilton, 1965.
Doll. New York, Delacorte Press, 1965; London, Hamish Hamilton, 1966.
Eighty Million Eyes. New York, Delacorte Press, and London, Hamish Hamilton, 1966.
Fuzz. New York, Doubleday, and London, Hamish Hamilton, 1968.
Shotgun. New York, Doubleday, and London, Hamish Hamilton, 1969.
Jigsaw. New York, Doubleday, and London, Hamish Hamilton, 1970.
Hail, Hail, The Gang's All Here! New York, Doubleday, and London, Hamish Hamilton, 1971.
Sadie When She Died. New York, Doubleday, and London, Hamish Hamilton, 1972.
Let's Hear It for the Deaf Man. New York, Doubleday, and London, Hamish Hamilton, 1973.
Hail to the Chief. New York, Random House, and London, Hamish Hamilton, 1973.
Bread. New York, Random House, and London, Hamish Hamilton, 1974.
Where There's Smoke. New York, Random House, and London, Hamish Hamilton, 1975.
Blood Relatives. New York, Random House, 1975; London, Hamish Hamilton, 1976.
Guns. New York, Random House, 1976; London, Hamish Hamilton, 1977.

So Long as You Both Shall Live. New York, Random House, and London, Hamish Hamilton, 1976.
Long Time No See. New York, Random House, and London, Hamish Hamilton, 1977.
Goldilocks. New York, Arbor House, 1977; London, Hamish Hamilton, 1978.
Calypso. New York, Viking Press, and London, Hamish Hamilton, 1979.
Ghosts. New York, Viking Press, and London, Hamish Hamilton, 1980.
Rumpelstiltskin. New York, Viking Press, and London, Hamish Hamilton, 1981.
Beauty and the Beast. London, Hamish Hamilton, 1982; New York, Holt Rinehart, 1983.
Ice. New York, Arbor House, and London, Hamish Hamilton, 1983
Jack and the Beanstalk. New York, Holt Rinehart, and London, Hamish Hamilton, 1984.
Lightning. New York, Arbor House, and London, Hamish Hamilton, 1984.
Snow White and Rose Red. New York, Holt Rinehart, and London, Hamish Hamilton, 1985.
Eight Black Horses. New York, Arbor House, and London, Hamish Hamilton, 1985.
Another Part of the City. New York, Mysterious Press, 1985; London, Hamish Hamilton, 1986.
Cinderella. New York, Holt, and London, Hamish Hamilton, 1986.
Poison. New York, Arbor House, and London, Hamish Hamilton, 1987.
Puss in Boots. New York, Holt, and London, Hamish Hamilton, 1987.
Lullaby. New York, Morrow, and London, Hamish Hamilton, 1987.
The House That Jack Built. New York, Holt, and London, Hamish Hamilton, 1988.
Downtown. New York, Morrow, and London, Heinemann, 1989.
Three Blind Mice. New York, Arcade, 1990.
Vespers. New York, Morrow, and London, Heinemann, 1990.
Widows. London, Heinemann, 1991.
Kiss. London, Heinemann, 1992.
Mary, Mary. London, Heinemann, 1992.
Mischief. London, Hodder and Stoughton, 1993.
The Last Dance. New York, Simon & Schuster, 1999.

Short Stories

The Jungle Kids. New York, Pocket Books, 1956.
I Like 'em Tough (as Curt Cannon). New York, Fawcett, 1958
The Last Spin and Other Stories. London, Constable, 1960.
The Empty Hours (as Ed McBain). New York, Simon and Schuster, 1962; London, Boardman, 1963.
Happy New Year, Herbie, and Other Stories. New York, Simon and Schuster, 1963; London, Constable, 1965.
The Beheading and Other Stories. London, Constable, 1971.
The Easter Man (a Play) and Six Stories. New York, Doubleday, 1972; as *Seven,* London, Constable, 1972.
The McBain Brief. London, Hamish Hamilton, 1982; New York, Arbor House, 1983.
McBain's Ladies: The Women of the 87th Precinct. New York, Mysterious Press, and London, Hamish Hamilton, 1988.
McBain's Ladies Too. New York, Mysterious Press, 1989; London, Hamish Hamilton, 1990.
Barking at Butterflies, and Other Stories. Unity, Maine, Five Star, 2000.
Running from Legs and Other Stories. Unity, Maine, Five Star, 2000.

Uncollected Short Stories

"Ticket to Death," in *Best Detective Stories of the Year 1955,* edited by David Coxe Cooke. New York, Dutton, 1955.
"Classification: Dead" (as Richard Marsten), in *Dames, Danger, and Death,* edited by Leo Margulies. New York, Pyramid, 1960.
"Easy Money," in *Ellery Queen's Mystery Magazine* (New York), September 1960.
"Nightshade" (as Ed McBain) in *Ellery Queen's Mystery Magazine* (New York), August 1970.
"Someone at the Door," in *Ellery Queen's Mystery Magazine* (New York), October 1971.
"Sympathy for the Devil," in *Seventeen* (New York), July 1972.
"Weeping for Dustin," in *Seventeen* (New York), July 1973.
"The Analyst," in *Playboy* (Chicago), December 1974.
"Dangerous Affair," in *Good Housekeeping* (New York), March 1975.
"Eighty Million Eyes" (as Ed McBain), in *Ellery Queen's Giants of Mystery.* New York, Davis, 1976.
"Stepfather," in *Ladies' Home Journal* (New York), June 1976.
"What Happened to Annie Barnes?," in *Ellery Queen's Mystery Magazine* (New York), June 1976.

Plays

The Easter Man (produced Birmingham and London, 1964; as *A Race of Hairy Men,* produced New York, 1965). Included in *The Easter Man (a Play) and Six Stories,* 1972.
The Conjuror (produced Ann Arbor, Michigan, 1969).

Screenplays: *Strangers When We Meet,* 1960; *The Birds,* 1963; *Fuzz,* 1972; *Walk Proud,* 1979.

Television Plays: *Appointment at Eleven* (Alfred Hitchcock Presents series), 1955–61; *The Chisholms* series, from his own novel, 1978–79; *The Legend of Walks Far Woman,* 1982.

Other (for children)

Find the Feathered Serpent. Philadelphia, Winston, 1952.
Rocket to Luna (as Richard Marsten). Philadelphia, Winston, 1952; London, Hutchinson, 1954.
Danger: Dinosaurs! (as Richard Marsten). Philadelphia, Winston, 1953.
The Remarkable Harry. New York and London, Abelard Schuman, 1961.
The Wonderful Button. New York, Abelard Schuman, 1961; London, Abelard Schuman, 1962.
Me and Mr. Stenner. Philadelphia, Lippincott, 1976; London, Hamish Hamilton, 1977.

Other (as Ed McBain)

Editor, *Crime Squad.* London, New English Library, 1968.
Editor, *Homicide Department.* London, New English Library, 1968.

Editor, *Downpour.* London, New English Library, 1969.
Editor, *Ticket to Death.* London, New English Library, 1969.

*

Manuscript Collections: Mugar Memorial Library, Boston University.

Critical Studies: *Neither Seen the Picture Nor Read the Book: Literary References in Ed McBain's 87th Precinct Series: Homage to Ed McBain/Evan Hunter on His Seventieth Anniversary, October 15, 1996* by Ted Bergman. Grover Park, 1996.

Evan Hunter comments:

(1972) The novels I write under my own name are concerned mostly with identity, or at least they have been until the most recent book. (I cannot now predict what will interest or concern me most in the future.) I change my style with each novel, to fit the tone, the mood, and the narrative voice. I have always considered a strong story to be the foundation of any good novel, and I also apply this rule to the mysteries I write under the Ed McBain pseudonym. Unlike my ''serious'' novels, however, the style here is unvaried. The series characters are essentially the same throughout (although new detectives appear or old ones disappear from time to time, and each new case involves a new criminal or criminals). The setting is the same (the precinct and the city), and the theme is the same—crime and punishment. (I look upon these mysteries, in fact, as one *long* novel about crime and punishment, with each separate book in the series serving as a chapter.) I enjoy writing both types of novels, and consider each equally representative of my work.

* * *

The vividness and immediacy of the author's prose, coupled with the timeliness of his subject, drew considerable attention to Evan Hunter's novel *The Blackboard Jungle.* This story of a young teacher confronting the brutal realities of a big city vocational high school was praised for its realism and for opening to fiction an area of public concern that had begun to attract national attention in the United States. *Second Ending* was an even more aggressively topical novel, tracing the effects of drugs on four young New Yorkers. The central character, a young trumpet player who has been addicted for two years, draws the other characters together, and they are all altered in some way by his descent toward death. Some of the novel's episodes, which were termed ''sensational'' at the time of publication, now no longer seem so unique, and despite the awkwardness with which portions of the novel are narrated. Hunter's power as a storyteller moved his characters unerringly toward the slough of mutual desperation.

In *Strangers When We Meet* Hunter elected to describe a more muted kind of action in which a young architect, happily married and the father of two children, drifts into an affair with a suburban neighbor. Hunter showed a keen eye for the minute details that slowly gather round the illicit relationship, creating a highly realistic impression of a young man unable to cope with conflicting loyalties. Nonetheless, his characters finally seem insignificant—certainly not sufficiently strong to carry the philosophical baggage that the author gives them in an improbable conclusion.

A Matter of Conviction was a return to the mode of social protest that Hunter had developed so successfully in his two earlier novels. A polemic against the forces in society that make young men into killers, it was too contrived to offer more than passing interest. *Mothers and Daughters,* which chronicles the youth and maturity of four middle-class women—their dreams and their loves—is a more substantial work, despite its occasional melodrama.

Much of Hunter's fiction is over-written: striving for a realistic thickness, it bogs down in minutiae, and while the author writes with a high and consistent degree of professionalism, his vision rarely penetrates beneath the elaborate surfaces that his prose projects. *Last Summer* is a major exception to this adroit verbosity. It is told with an unforgettable simplicity and directness, which nonetheless conveys the author's own highly sophisticated point of view. During a summer holiday two teenage boys and a girl explore an Atlantic island, tell each other the ''truth,'' and dominate a shy young girl. Their experiences end in violence, which vividly symbolizes the moral degeneracy of their society.

Few contemporary writers can match the versatility and consummate professionalism of Evan Hunter. His work includes a highly successful series of detective novels published under the pseudonym of Ed McBain; a science-fiction novel for children; a comic cops-and-robbers novel, *A Horse's Head,* written with great inventiveness and wit; and a spirited children's book in verse, illustrated by his own sons. *Sons* tells the story of three generations of a Wisconsin family, powerfully challenging some of the basic presumptions of the American Dream; *The Paper Dragon* is a densely plotted intriguing story of a five-day plagiarism trial; and *Buddwing* plunges its amnesiac hero into the heart of a Washington Square riot, a hold-up, and a crap game. *Nobody Knew They Were There* takes a futuristic look at the innate forces of violence that assail man's attempt to achieve world peace.

In *Privileged Conversation,* Hunter somewhat sketchily tells the tale of a New York stalker who invades the furtive affair of a married psychiatrist and a woman he has met in Central Park. *The Last Dance* marks the 50th novel of the 87th Precinct in Isola, his (that is, McBain's) fictional New York. Throughout a varied and highly prolific career, Hunter has produced a body of work distinguished for its sound craftsmanship, although only one of his novels, *Last Summer,* clearly demonstrates the art which such craft should sustain.

—David Galloway

HUNTER, Kristin (Elaine)

Nationality: American. **Born:** Kristin Elaine Eggleston, Philadelphia, Pennsylvania, 12 September 1931. **Education:** Charles Sumner School and Magnolia Public School, both Philadelphia; Haddon Heights High School, New Jersey, graduated 1947; University of Pennsylvania, Philadelphia, 1947–51, B.S. in education 1951. **Family:** Married 1) Joseph Hunter in 1952 (divorced 1962); 2) John I. Lattany in 1968. **Career:** Philadelphia columnist and feature writer, Pittsburgh Courier, 1946–52; teacher, Camden, New Jersey, 1951; copywriter, Lavenson Bureau of Advertising, Philadelphia, 1952–59; research assistant, School of Social Work, University of Pennsylvania, 1961–62; copywriter, Wermen and Schorr, Philadelphia, 1962–63; information officer, City of Philadelphia, 1963–64, 1965–66; director of health services, Temple University, Philadelphia, 1971–72; director, Walt Whitman Poetry Center, Camden, 1978–79. Lecturer in creative writing. 1972–79, adjunct professor of English, 1980–83, and since 1983 senior lecturer in English, University of Pennsylvania. Writer-in-residence, Emory University, Atlanta, 1979. **Awards:** Fund for the Republic prize, for television documentary, 1955; Whitney fellowship, 1959; Bread Loaf Writers Conference De Voto fellowship 1965; Sigma Delta Chi award, for reporting, 1968; National Council on Interracial Books for Children award, 1968; National Conference of Christians and Jews Brotherhood award, 1969; Christopher award, 1974; Drexel citation, 1981; New Jersey Council on the Arts fellowship, 1982, 1985; Pennsylvania Council on the Arts fellowship, 1983. **Agent**: Don Congdon Associates, 156 Fifth Avenue, Suite 625, New York, New York 10010. **Address:** 721 Warwick Road, Magnolia, New Jersey 08049, U.S.A.

Publications

Novels

God Bless the Child. New York, Scribner, 1964; London. Muller, 1965.
The Landlord. New York, Scribner, 1966; London, Pan, 1970.
The Survivors. New York, Scribner, 1975.
The Lakestown Rebellion. New York, Scribner, 1978.
Kinfolks. New York, Ballantine Books, 1996.
Do Unto Others. New York, One World, 2000.

Uncollected Short Stories

"To Walk in Beauty," in *Sub-Deb Scoop* (Philadelphia), 1953.
"Supersonic," in *Mandala* (Philadelphia), vol. 1, no. 1, 1956.
"There Was a Little Girl," in *Rogue* (New York), 1959.
"An Interesting Social Study," in *The Best Short Stories by Negro Writers,* edited by Langston Hughes. Boston, Little Brown, 1967.
"Debut," in *Negro Digest* (Chicago), June 1968.
"Honor among Thieves," in *Essence* (New York), April 1971.
"The Tenant," in *Pennsylvania Gazette* (Philadelphia).
"Bleeding Berries," in *Callaloo* (Lexington, Kentucky), vol. 2, no. 2, 1979.
"The Jewel in the Lotus," in *Quilt 1* (Berkeley, California), 1981.
"Bleeding Heart," in *Hambone* (Santa Cruz, California), 1983.
"Perennial Daisy," in *Nightsun* (Frostburg, Maryland), 1984.
"Brown Gardenias," in *Shooting Star Review* (Pittsburgh), Fall, 1989.

Fiction (for children)

The Soul-Brothers and Sister Lou. New York, Scribner, 1968; London, Macdonald, 1971.
Boss Cat. New York, Scribner, 1971.
The Pool Table War. Boston, Houghton Mifflin, 1972
Uncle Daniel and the Raccoon. Boston, Houghton Mifflin, 1972.
Guests in the Promised Land: Stories. New York, Scribner, 1973.
Lou in the Limelight. New York, Scribner, 1981.

Plays

The Double Edge (Produced Philadelphia, 1965).

Television Plays: *Appointment at Eleven* (Alfred Hitchcock Presents series), 1955–61; *The Chisholms* series, from his own novel, 1978–79; *The Legend of Walks Far Woman,* 1982.

*

Critical Studies: *From Mammies to Militants: Domestics in Black American Literature* by Trudier Harris, Philadelphia, Temple University Press, 1982, and article by Sondra O'Neale, in *Afro-American Fiction Writers after 1955* edited by Harris and Thadious M. Davis, Detroit, Gale, 1984.

Kristin Hunter comments:

The bulk of my work has dealt—imaginatively, I hope—with relations between the white and black races in America. My early work was "objective," that is, sympathetic to both whites and blacks, and seeing members of both groups from a perspective of irony and humor against the wider backdrop of human experience as a whole. Since about 1968 my subjective anger has been emerging, along with my grasp of the real situation in this society, though my sense of humor and my basic optimism keep cropping up like uncontrollable weeds.

* * *

In her first two novels, Kristin Hunter plays upon the contradictions between reality as it is experienced by the black urban poor and the false optimism of popular story. *God Bless the Child* parodies the tale of the enterprising but low-born youngster who, since the origins of middle-class fiction, has set out to achieve a place in society by the application of nerve and energy. In the case of Rosie Fleming, however, vitality leads to failure, for by setting herself up as a small entrepreneur, she earns the animosity of the white men who manage the poor people's version of finance capitalism. Despite her portrayal of the relentless power that destroys Rosie, Hunter is not resigned to a sense of human powerlessness. A sympathetic and complex portrayal of three generations of black women conveys an intensely humanistic conception of character, which in her second novel, *The Landlord*, becomes the basis for an optimistic theme. Its main character, determined to "become a man" by exercising mastery over his tenants, is frustrated and tricked at every turn as they purge him of the mythology of white male dominance. Against his will, and contrary to the assumptions of middle-class convention, the landlord forms an admiration and appreciation for the diverse styles by which blacks cope with life's troubles.

Following the publication of *The Landlord*, Hunter occupied herself with stories of ghetto life directed toward younger readers. Like the adult novels that preceded them, these children's books reject the idealizations of popular genres while preserving a belief in the capacity of the black underclass to transform their lives by the power of their spirit. In both the adult and children's books, the message has been that society's "victims" refuse the dehumanization that either social relations or a literature of pity would assign them. *The Soul Brothers and Sister Lou*, one of the earliest attempts to realistically depict the black urban experience, is Hunter's most famous example of young adult fiction. This novel gained her recognition as a gifted author of young adult literature. In this work, Hunter tells the story of a juvenile gang that forms a music group in order to escape the violence within their community. In her next work of children's literature, *Boss Cat*, Hunter explores the same theme of underprivileged youths. Her third example of young adult fiction, *Guests in the Promised Land*, which is a collection of short stories, describes the experiences of black children as they struggle with racial adversity. It was in 1981 that Hunter returned to *The Soul Brothers and Sister Lou* to compose its sequel, *Lou in the Limelight*. In this work, Hunter examines the ramifications of success.

Committed to the verve and quality of black life, Hunter wrote four additional adult novels that must be termed celebrations. The first, *The Survivors*, signifies by its title its author's devotion to the rendition of character traits that enable a middle-aged dressmaker and a street kid to form an emotional and practical alliance that enables them both to overcome the predacious circumstances of the neighborhood.

In *The Lakestown Rebellion*, Hunter tells the story of a small black township that was originally settled by fugitive slaves. As the community battles against plans to build a highway that will destroy their homes, the tradition of the folk trickster is renewed. The novel's wit perfectly suits Hunter's optimistic humanism. The book is so enjoyable one is almost unaware that it is also a symbolic reenactment of cultural history.

Hunter's next novel, *Kinfolks*, is the story of Cherry and Patrice. These two former political radicals and lifelong friends learn to accept their past mistakes. While this text probes serious questions about family, sexual freedom, and responsibility, it has also been recognized for its humor. In *Do Unto Others*, Hunter once again shows an ability to take the reader through a broad range of emotions. The text deals with the gap between Africans and African-Americans, while acknowledging the bridge that links the two cultures. The main character, Zena, an African-American woman, struggles with her own ancestry, while housing a twenty-year old Nigerian girl. This text follows Hunter's tradition of examining important emotional and social problems. Hunter combines humor with her social criticism, and her works provide an optimistic look at African-American culture.

—John M. Reilly, updated by Marta Krogh

I

IGNATIEFF, Michael

Nationality: Canadian. **Born:** Toronto, Ontario, 12 May 1947. **Education:** Upper Canada College, Toronto; University of Toronto, B.A., 1969; Harvard University, Boston, (teaching fellow in social studies), 1971–74, Ph.D., 1975; Cambridge University (research fellow, King's College), 1978–84, M.A., 1978. **Family:** Married Susan Barrowclough in 1977; one son and one daughter. **Career:** Reporter, *The Globe and Mail,* 1966–67; assistant professor of history, University of British Columbia, 1976–78; broadcaster, Channel 4, London, 1986. Since 1987, broadcaster, British Broadcasting Corp, London. Visiting fellow, École des Hautes Études, Paris, 1985; Alistair Horne Fellow, St. Anthony's College, Oxford, 1993–95. Editorial columnist, *The Observer,* 1990–93. **Awards:** Canadian Governor General's award, 1988, Heinemann prize, 1988, both for *The Russian Album.* **Agent:** Sheil Land Associates, 43 Doughty Street, London WC1N 2LF, England. **Address:** 37 Baalbec Road, London N5 1QN, England.

Publications

Novels

Asya. London, Chatto and Windus, and New York, Knopf, 1991.
Scar Tissue. London, Chatto and Windus, 1993; New York, Farrar Straus, 1994.

Plays

1919 (screenplay), with Hugh Brody. London, Faber, 1985.

Other

A Just Measure of Pain: The Penitentiary in the Industrial Revolution, 1750–1850. London, Macmillan, 1978.
The Needs of Strangers. London, Chatto and Windus, and New York, Viking, 1984.
The Russian Album. London, Chatto and Windus, and New York, Viking, 1987.
Blood and Belonging. London, BBC, 1993; New York, Farrar Straus, 1994.
The Warrior's Honor: Ethnic War and the Modern Conscience. New York, Metropolitan Books, 1998.
Isaiah Berlin: A Life. New York, Metropolitan Books, 1998.
Virtual War: Kosovo and Beyond. New York, Henry Holt, 2000.
Editor, with Jeffrey Rose, *Religion and International Affairs.* Toronto, Anansi, 1968.
Editor, with Istvan Hont, *Wealth and Virtue: The Shaping of Political Economy in the Scottish Enlightenment.* Cambridge, Cambridge University Press, 1983.

* * *

Michael Ignatieff arrived at fiction by the route of introspection, through sensitive and intelligent effort to understand both his personal and historical moment. He has produced two novels, *Aysa* and *Scar Tissue,* but his arrival as a fiction writer emerges organically from earlier prose works.

Trained as an historian, Ignatieff gravitated to social philosophy in *The Needs of Strangers,* a study of the issue of social responsibility in the modern state that focuses on the relationship between material and emotional needs, the question of rights to the fulfillment of needs, and a history of the concept of needs. He then produced *Blood and Belonging,* an intense, personal, and philosophical study of the pain-filled nationalisms in the Balkans, Northern Ireland, Germany, Ukraine, Quebec, and Kurdistan. In these volumes he demonstrates a rare balance between analysis and personal involvement, commitment conditioned by historical perspective.

Ignatieff won the 1988 Governor General's Award for Non-Fiction (the Canadian Pulitzer Prize) for *The Russian Album,* his account of his family's White Russian history and emigration to England and, later, Canada. In it he dramatizes life under the tsars in terms of the personal lives of his ancestors, including his grandfather, who was minister of education under Nicholas II, the last tsar.

From his knowledge of the Russian past comes *Aysa,* the life of a Russian princess who escapes to France and, much later, to England. The novel is enriched both by historical accuracy of detail and by the development of Aysa herself from a self-willed rich child to a suffering and perceptive woman. It is patently not stereotyped, for many of its emigres are prosperous and able, aware that the Russia they have left is gone yet constantly orbiting around things Russian, such as the struggle between the motherland and Hitler. It has a fatalism to its shape, coming to a conclusion when the ninety-year-old Aysa finds the grave of her first husband in Moscow's Novodevichy cemetery. Although it owes structural debts to the sweeping historical epic novel, *Aysa* is anchored to the intimate life of a woman whose stature grows gently in the reader's eyes until she stands as a marker of strength of will mixed with keen self-knowledge drawn from the century of pain.

Scar Tissue is a book dominated by such a searing immediacy of anguish that it is, simply, hard to read. Yet it is so powerful and its subject matter so central to human experience that it exerts a grip on the imagination matched only by other unrelentingly direct fictions, like those of Samuel Beckett. It is the retrospective story of a man experiencing the degeneration and death of his mother from neurological disease and its effects on family, on love, on loyalty. Beyond that it subtly places the situation of one death and one family in medical and philosophical frameworks that go to the heart of human experience.

When, Ignatieff asks, does selfhood disappear when the mind is breaking apart—when memory goes, when recognition goes, when the plague overtakes the pathways in the brain? Is there always a self inside? And, if so, how horribly chaotic must be the terrible collage of the unlinked present and past, the life always lived among strangers because even loved ones are not remembered?

What makes these questions truly excruciating is the intense emotional and intellectual perspective of the middle-aged professor whose mother is dying. In an immense leap from the conventional omniscient chronological narration of Aysa, Ignatieff has mastered a style that mixes time and allows for the flows of feeling and language. The narrator looks backward for the first signs of his mother's change and charts the slow decline as it drags her loving husband to self-sacrifice and death and then immerses the narrator himself in a struggle of responsibility that ruins his marriage, damages his relationship with his brother, and nearly ruins his life.

Towering above all this affliction is his growing knowledge that he is seeing his own destiny, for his brother, who has become a neuroscience researcher, makes clear the condition is genetic. The narrator sees the scans of his mother's brain, strangely beautiful abstract colored designs, and he sees the patterns of the damaged chromosomes that mark the start of the cascade of tiny events of disease. As he struggles to continue to see his once vital, gifted mother as a person, she loses her personhood before his eyes, and he comes face to face with protracted living death.

The narrator's voice is so intense that criticism has been leveled at the autobiographical elements of the text. But that is to mistake its real achievement. *Scar Tissue* marks the emergence of a fully disciplined and original writer who communicates the deepest and most painful of human questions through the lives it portrays.

—Peter Brigg

IHIMAERA, Witi (Tame)

Nationality: New Zealander. **Born:** Gisborne, 7 February 1944. **Education:** Te Karaka District High School, 1957–59; Church College of New Zealand, 1960–61; Gisborne Boys High School, 1962; University of Auckland, 1963–66; Victoria University, Wellington, 1968–72, B.A. 1972. **Family:** Married Jane Cleghorn in 1970. **Career:** Cadet reporter, Gisborne *Herald,* 1967; journalist, Post Office Headquarters, Wellington, 1968–72; information officer, 1973–74, Third Secretary, Wellington, 1975–78, Second Secretary, Canberra, 1978, and First Secretary, Wellington, 1979–85, Ministry of Foreign Affairs; New Zealand Consul, New York, 1986–88; Counsellor on Public Affairs, New Zealand Embassy, Washington, D.C., 1989; lecturer, University of Auckland, 1990–95. **Awards:** Freda Buckland Literary award, 1973; James Wattie award, 1974, 1986; University of Otago Robert Burns fellowship, 1974; Scholarship in Letters, 1990; Katherine Mansfield fellowship, 1993. **Address:** 2 Bella Vista Road, Herne Bay, Auckland, New Zealand.

PUBLICATIONS

Novels

Tangi. Auckland and London, Heinemann, 1973.
Whanau. Auckland, Heinemann, 1974; London, Heinemann, 1975.
The Matriarch. Auckland and London, Heinemann, 1986.
The Whale Rider. Auckland, Heinemann, 1987; London, Heinemann, 1988.
Bulibasha. Auckland, Penguin, 1994.
Nights in the Gardens of Spain. Auckland, Secker and Warburg, 1995.
The Dream Swimmer. Auckland and New York, Penguin, 1997.

Short Stories

Pounamu, Pounamu. Auckland, Heinemann, 1972; London, Heinemann, 1973.
The New Net Goes Fishing. Auckland, Heinemann, 1977; London, Heinemann, 1978.
Dear Miss Mansfield: A Tribute to Kathleen Mansfield Beauchamp. Auckland, Viking, 1989; New York, Viking, 1990.
Kingfisher Come Home: The Complete Maori Stories. Auckland, Secker & Warburg, 1995.

Other

Maori. Wellington, Government Printers, 1975.
New Zealand Through the Arts: Past and Present, with Sir Tosswill Woollaston and Allen Curnow. Wellington, Friends of the Turnbull Library, 1982.
Land, Sea and Sky (text), photographs by Holger Leue. Auckland, Reed, 1994.
Editor, with D.S. Long, *Into the World of Light: An Anthology of Maori Writing.* Auckland, Heinemann, 1982.
Editor, *Te Ao Marama: Maori Writing Since the 1980s, Vols. 1–4.* Auckland, Reeds, 1992–94.
Editor, *Te Ao Marama: Contemporary Maori Writing.* Auckland, Reed Books, 1993–96.
Editor, *Vision Aotearoa: Kaupapa New Zealand.* Wellington, Bridget Williams Books, 1994.
Editor, *Mataora, the Living Face: Contemporary Maori Art.* Auckland, D. Bateman, 1996.

*

Critical Studies: ''Participating'' by Ray Grover, in *Islands* (Auckland), Winter 1973; ''Tangi'' by H. Winston Rhodes, in *Landfall* (Christchurch), December 1973; ''Maori Writers,'' in *Fretful Sleepers and Other Essays* by Bill Pearson, Auckland, Heinemann, 1974; *The Maoris of New Zealand* by Joan Metge, London, Routledge, 1977; *Introducing Witi Ihimaera* by Richard Corballis and Simon Garrett, Auckland, Longman Paul, 1984; *Writing Along Broken Lines: Violence and Ethnicity in Contemporary Maori Fiction* by Otto Heim. Auckland, Auckland University Press, 1998.

Witi Ihimaera comments:

There are two cultural landscapes in my country, the Maori and the Pakeha (European), and although all people, including Maori, inhabit the Pakeha landscape, very few know the Maori one. It is important to both Maori and Pakeha that they realize their dual cultural heritage, and that is why I began to write. Not to become the first Maori novelist but to render my people into words as honestly and as candidly as I could; to present a picture of Maoritanga which is our word for the way we feel and are, in the hope that our values will be maintained. I like to think that I write with both love—aroha—and anger in the hope that the values of Maori life will never be lost. So far I have written about exclusively Maori people within an exclusively Maori framework, using our own oral tradition of Maori literature, our own mythology, as my inspiration. Cultural difference is not a bad thing, it can be very exciting, and it can offer a different view of the world, value system, and interpretation of events. This is what I would like to offer: a personal vision of Maori life as I see it, the Maori side of New Zealand's dual heritage of culture.

* * *

Witi Ihimaera writes with a keen awareness of his cultural heritage, and a profound commitment to the values and traditions of his people. A central feature of his imaginative landscape is the *whanau*, or extended family community, an emotional and cultural bastion eroded by urbanization and social fragmentation. Writing with ''both love and anger,'' Ihimaera documents the traditional Maori way of life and the changes it has undergone since the coming of the Pakeha. Although his early works can be seen as pastoral and elegiac, Ihimaera does not idealize his subjects; rather, he renders their trials and conflicts, joys and sorrows, shortcomings and strengths, with remarkable honesty and clarity. Drawing upon the rich resources of Maori myth and legend, he blends the past with the present, evoking the ancestral framework of historical continuity that is an essential part of Maoritanga. His work proclaims the vitality and significance of New Zealand's ''other culture,'' one that Ihimaera suggests enriches the lives of Maori and Pakeha alike.

Many of the stories in Ihimaera's first collection, *Pounamu, Pounamu*, are set in the village of Waituhi, the geographical and cultural hearth—and heart—of the *Whanau A Kai* to which much of his subsequent fiction returns. Both celebration and lamentation, they are lyrical evocations of a rural, communal way of life that is rapidly becoming a thing of the past. Pounamu, or greenstone-semi-precious jade traditionally used to make weaponry and jewelry, is Ihimaera's symbol of Maoritanga, and he contrasts it with the cold, glittering attractions of Pakeha culture in ''the emerald city.'' One story in particular, ''The Whale,'' dramatizes the conflicting claims of tradition and change, as an old man sits in the meeting house mourning the decay of the world that he knew and the loss of the young to the city's siren call. It is his granddaughter who articulates the dilemma that the young people face: ''The world isn't Maori any more. But it's the world I have to live in. You dream too much. Your world is gone. I can't live it for you. Can't you see?''

Ihimaera's first novel, *Tangi*, is an extended meditation on the subject of *Pounamu, Pounamu*'s concluding story: Tama Mahana's return from Wellington (the emerald city) to attend the burial of his father. Structured by the ceremonial patterns of the funeral itself, *Tangi* is a work that mines the emotional intensity of loss and the communal rituals surrounding death. It is at once a mourning of the dead and an affirmation of the living, for Tama's personal grief and memories are tempered by the spirit of love and kinship that draws the community together on such occasions. Past, present, and future interconnect as Tama's individual response to his father's death is framed by the history of his *whanau*, and the mythic history of Maori legend: the separation of Rangitane, the sky father, from Papatuanuku, the earth mother, so that their children could dwell in the light. Coming to terms with his loss is, for Tama, a voyage of self-discovery and a recognition of his responsibility to uphold the tradition that is his father's legacy. Thus, Tama's journey into the future is focused through the myth of creation that underpins the novel, the separation of earth and sky that allowed ''the dawning of the first day.''

If, through the single consciousness of an individual, Ihimaera introduced his readers to the communal basis of Maoridom, then *Whanau* gives that extended grouping full fictional rein. Since the *whanau* is the combination of the land and its people, Ihimaera's approach is utterly in keeping with his title and theme. In an interrelated series of vignettes spanning a single day, he captures the lives of the individuals who comprise the *Whanau A Kai*. Although deftly drawn, no one character in this novel could be said to be central; rather, it is the *whanau* itself that is the subject and focus. Through the reflections of sorrowing elders, disillusioned adults, and rebellious adolescents, *Whanau* records the slow disintegration of the traditional way of life as Pakeha culture encroaches and many of the young people willingly embrace its values at the expense of their Maoritanga. But it also symbolically affirms the strength of the cultural ties that bind this community as the *whanau* come together to search for their missing *kaumatua*, the revered patriarch who is their living link with the past.

The New Net Goes Fishing heralded a new streak of anger in Ihimaera's writing that would find its most clear expression in *The Matriarch* and its sequel, *The Dream Swimmer*. Framed by two stories that allude to *The Wonderful Wizard of Oz, The New Net Goes Fishing* examines Maori in the urban setting of the emerald city. Although a few of the stories register success or acceptance in the Pakeha world, many focus on the conflicts arising from an impersonal, alien environment and the clash of two different value systems. While this collection often proffers a bleak view of race relations, it does conclude on a note of hope. Returning to Waituhi after twenty years in Oz, an old man stresses the need for his people to experience the best of both worlds. The complexities of Maori/Pakeha concourse, however, and Ihimaera's need to find a new means with which to express it, prompted a self-imposed hiatus. Nearly ten years later, Ihimaera broke his silence with a novel of epic historical proportions, *The Matriarch*.

Unabashedly aggressive, *The Matriarch* constitutes Ihimaera's battle cry. Mixing fact and fiction, biography and autobiography, myth and ''reality,'' Ihimaera imaginatively reconstructs New Zealand colonial history from a Maori perspective. The novel challenges the claims of official history even as it declares its own contingency, and the inadequacy of any history to enclose and explain its subject. The woman warrior of the novel's title is Artemis Riripeti Mahana, the enigmatic figure who dominated the narrator's youth and who now dominates his memories as he struggles to understand her. Tama Mahana's recollective investigation of his grandmother leads him further back to two significant ancestors, the warrior prophet, Te Kooti, and the politician, Wi Pere Halbert. All three are linked by a common cause: the fight to retain Maori land under Maori control, and this theme is the driving force behind the various histories and narrative styles that compose the novel. Maori myth-history and spirituality feature prominently in *The Matriarch*, but Ihimaera also draws freely upon European history and culture: the trials of his people are likened to those of the Israelites in Egypt, and the matriarch's instruction of her grandson is liberally interspersed with snatches of Verdi (in a symbolic paralleling of nationalist struggles). Although the matriarch herself remains shadowed by historical controversy, her political legacy is clear: ''to fight the Pakeha you must learn to be like him. You must become a Pakeha, think like him, act like him and, when you know that you are in his image then turn your knowledge to his destruction.'' Critics are divided over the success of Ihimaera's unwieldy epic; what cannot be denied, however, is the scope and power of this ambitious work.

Ihimaera's next two works can be termed ''occasional'': *The Whale Rider* was written in anticipation of a visit by his teenage daughters, and the collection *Dear Miss Mansfield* marks the centenary celebrations of New Zealand's most famous writer. While *The Whale Rider* returns to the mythic territory of Ihimaera's ancestry in a lyric and positive revisioning of *Pounamu, Pounamu*'s ''The Whale,'' *Dear Miss Mansfield* is a response to the work of an equally important literary ancestor, Katherine Mansfield. The titular letter that opens the collection is a song of homage to the divine Miss M., but the stories themselves evoke the subversive notion of ''writing back'' that characterizes *The Matriarch* and *The Dream Swimmer*. Playing Maori variations on Mansfield's themes, or retelling some of her most famous short stories from a Maori perspective, Ihimaera presents the other side of Mansfield's New Zealand in a self-conscious, intertextual refashioning. Ihimaera interprets his world through the lens of Maori culture, but he is also aware that that culture is not a static entity. Although *The Matriarch* and *Dear Miss Mansfield* proclaim that the Maori cannot be subsumed under the banner of Pakeha history, they also demonstrate that the latter has become a part of an ongoing Maori genealogy. Like the old man of ''Return from Oz,'' Ihimaera incorporates the best of both worlds.

Bulibasha: King of the Gypsies continues the exploration of New Zealand's dual cultural heritage in Ihimaera's typical blend of fiction and autobiography. In some ways, *Bulibasha* is the paternal complement to *The Matriarch*, since the central relationship of the narrator with his grandparent is intermingled with the history of the tribe. With this novel, however, Ihimaera eschews metafictional bricolage in favor of a straightforward Bildungsroman concerning the anxiety of influence. The king of the novel's title is the Mahana family patriarch, a powerful economic and religious leader who rules the familial shearing gangs with an iron fist. Set against Bulibasha is the rival Poata clan, and his grandson, Simeon, whose verbal audacity and intellectual pursuits label him as *whakahihi*: too big for his boots. It is from Simeon's precocious perspective that the twin rivalries are related, and, like the matriarch, it is he who both challenges and upholds the traditions of his people. Set in the era of Ihimaera's youth, *Bulibasha* examines generational conflict and social change, offering an often-humorous insight to the oral histories of which family legends are made. Simeon's perceptions testify to the intermingling of cultural landscapes: family dramas are often recounted and comically illuminated by the formulaic plots of the American movies that Simeon watches so avidly; the ritualized conflicts between the two clans are the rivalries of Montagues and Capulets, and his heretical challenges to Bulibasha's authority are construed as those of a mortal intent on toppling Olympus. The novel concludes with a resounding deconstruction of Bulibasha's mythic status, but Simeon's assumption of responsibility prompts a recognition of his grandfather's guiding principle: the family always comes first.

For Ihimaera, *Bulibasha* concerns the challenge of surviving familial influence and establishing one's separate identity. *Nights in the Gardens of Spain* explores the conflict between family and sexual identity. Equally as autobiographical as his earlier work, *Nights in the Gardens of Spain* nevertheless represents a radical new departure in Ihimaera's writing. The central character is a Pakeha, a university lecturer torn between the love of his wife and two daughters, and his sexuality as a gay man. A coming out novel, *Nights* traces David's exploration of his sexual identity and the social and emotional complexities of being married and being gay. Many of the minor characters in the novel are satiric caricatures, and the narrator's characterization is an odd blend of cardboard gay Everyman and particularized individuality. While *Nights* presents a provocative foray into the steamroom gardens of gay culture, the emotional center of the book—and of its web of Peter Pan allusions—lies in the narrator's powerful and often-anguished relationship with his young daughters. *Nights in the Gardens of Spain* is Ihimaera's novelistic declaration that his writing need not necessarily be restricted to exclusively Maori issues. It also indicates, as one commentator has noted, that the category ''Maori writer'' is not one in which Ihimaera can be expected to stay.

In interviews, Ihimaera has often mentioned an unfinished companion-piece to his award-winning historical epic. His most recent novel, *The Dream Swimmer*, is the long-awaited sequel to *The Matriarch*, one that continues Tama Mahana's odyssey as he assumes the mantle of power that is his grandmother's legacy. Less a sequel than a completion of the earlier work, *The Dream Swimmer* fills in some of the historical gaps in *The Matriarch*, most particularly in the narrator's relationship with his mother, Tiana, the mythically charged dream traveler of the novel's title. Although as monumental in scope as its predecessor, *The Dream Swimmer* is a much more coherent narrative, interweaving the history of twentieth-century struggle for Maori land rights with a dramatic tale of family conflict. With his characteristic cross-cultural blend of literary and mythological allusions, Ihimaera presents his epic tale in six operatic acts, and accords the fraught history of the Mahana clan the dimensions of Greek tragedy, likening their conflicts to those that divided the House of Atreus. If this novel is as politically passionate as *The Matriarch*, critics also comment that this intensity leads occasionally to the hyperbolic and the melodramatic. And, while *The Dream Swimmer* is compelling reading, it is also characterized by the autobiographical self-indulgence—even self-mythologization—that has tinged Ihimaera's work since *The Matriarch*. Nevertheless, the very breadth of its ambitious vision demonstrates that Ihimaera's is a powerful and important voice in New Zealand literature.

—Jackie Buxton

IRELAND, David

Nationality: Australian. **Born:** Lakemba, New South Wales, 24 August 1927. **Family:** Married 1) Elizabeth Ruth Morris in 1955 (divorced 1976), two sons and two daughters; 2) Christine Hayhoe in 1984. **Career:** Worked as a greenskeeper, in factories, and at an oil refinery. **Awards:** *Adelaide Advertiser* award, 1966; Miles Franklin award, 1972, 1977, 1980; *The Age* Book of the Year award, 1980. **Member:** Order of Australia, 1981.

Publications

Novels

The Chantic Bird. London, Heinemann, and New York, Scribner, 1968.

The Unknown Industrial Prisoner. Sydney and London, Angus and Robertson, 1971.

The Flesheaters. Sydney and London, Angus and Robertson, 1972.

Burn. Sydney and London, Angus and Robertson, 1975.

The Glass Canoe. Melbourne and London, Macmillan, 1976.

A Woman of the Future. Ringwood, Victoria, Allen Lane, and New York, Braziller, 1979; London, Penguin, 1980.

City of Women. Ringwood, Victoria, Allen Lane, 1981.

Archimedes and the Seagle. Ringwood, Victoria, Viking, 1984; London, Viking, 1985; New York, Penguin, 1987.
Bloodfather. Ringwood, Victoria, Penguin, 1987; London, Hamish Hamilton, 1988.

Uncollected Short Stories

"The Wild Colonial Boy," in *Winter's Tales 25,* edited by Caroline Hobhouse. London, Macmillan, 1979; New York, St. Martin's Press, 1980.

Plays

Image in the Clay (produced Sydney, 1962). Brisbane, University of Queensland Press, 1964.

*

Critical Studies: *Double Agent: David Ireland and His Work* by Helen Daniel, Ringwood, Victoria, Penguin, 1982; *Atomic Fiction: The Novels of David Ireland* by Ken Gelder, Brisbane, University of Queensland Press, 1993.

* * *

David Ireland is one of Australia's most innovative prose stylists. His first three novels depict a world that is in its "industrial adolescence," obsessed with profit and production to the point where those who do not contribute to industry (the poor, the aged, the unemployed) are treated as failures and misfits—as social lepers. *The Chantic Bird* offers this view in semi-comic fashion, its alienated teenage narrator providing a jaded running commentary on existence: "If there is no other life, why is this one so lousy?" Written in the absurdist-surrealist mode, but viewing its subject matter more somberly, *The Flesheaters* is set in a boarding-house for the poor and unemployed.

To counter the pervasive "functional" mentality (which insists that all human activity must have a public and profit-making purpose), Ireland's fictions insist upon the psychic value to the individual of such "useless" (but natural) activities as day-dreaming, fantasizing, and self-expression. Realistic treatments merge with fantasy sequences, and oblique viewpoints reveal familiar behavior from unusual angles. (Some of these effects verge on magical-realism, and Ireland has acknowledged his interest in South American writers of this school.) Ireland structures his works as scattered fragments, like elaborate mosaics constructed from tiny pieces, and this presentation clearly reflects not only his sense of the fragmentation of experience but also a celebration of its gloriously frustrating diversity.

Arguably the best of Ireland's early novels, *The Unknown Industrial Prisoner* portrays the life of workers in a foreign-owned Sydney oil refinery, examining their plight piece by piece and layer by layer until the fragmented mosaic builds into a microcosm of Australian industrial society. Ireland himself worked for a time in such a refinery, and the novel provides an absurdist (but acutely authentic) record of the dehumanization of the workforce, the emasculation of management, and the laziness and inefficiency of both employer and employee.

The Unknown Industrial Prisoner is an angry and rigorous account of the absurdities of industrialism. But Ireland is Australia's most intensely *analytical* writer, and it should therefore come as no surprise that he is prepared to question the assumptions behind his own angry sense of injustice. This analytic quality is seen in frequent bitter references to the workers as "the soil" in which the "money tree" of industry is growing. This is primarily an image of protest at exploitation and degradation, but it can also be seen as a wholly natural organic image (for if there is to be a "money tree" there must be "soil" to sustain it). Instead of accepting social realities at face value, Ireland digs for underlying assumptions and implications.

Monotonous conformity is the keynote of Ireland's vision of Australian society. He sees Australians as tame and insipid, bowed in philistine worship to the god of materialism. *The Chantic Bird* portrays the people of Sydney sitting at home at night, "filling in insurance policies on their fowls, their wrought-iron railings, concrete paths, light globes, their health, funeral expenses, borers, carpets," and so on; *The Glass Canoe* deals with characters who escape this monotony by drowning their woes in "amber fluid" (beer). A bawdy and violent celebration of life in a Sydney pub, *The Glass Canoe* portrays the urban drinkers as the last of a colorful "tribe" which preserves values (such as mateship and "macho" brawniness) from Australia's mythic past.

Though the writer of this essay would defend Ireland's earlier novels, most critical opinion favors the works of his "second phase." These recent novels have moved more clearly in the direction of fable, the prose style has become remarkably agile and witty, and the author's earlier concern with specific political issues has broadened into a preoccupation with the inner world of the imagination. The later novels are more mellowed and sensuous without having lost any of their radical analytical edge.

A Woman of the Future is Ireland's first attempt to create a full-scale female character, but—more importantly—it is an attempt to confront Australia's dauntingly masculine national self-image. It deals with the outlook and adventures of an intellectually gifted young female about to take crucial end-of-school exams before venturing upon life in the larger world. By setting the novel some years in the future, Ireland allows himself to extrapolate the effects of current social problems (especially unemployment), but the novel's chief concern is to draw a parallel between the young heroine stepping out into life, and her country—Australia—stepping out into nationhood. Ireland has argued in an interview that "women seem more open [than men] to experience and to new things," and *A Woman of the Future* attempts to redefine the national consciousness in these terms. But the book is also concerned with female sexuality, and many of its sexual episodes proved controversial (some because they were explicit, some because they addressed female sexuality in allegedly male language).

City of Women pursues these preoccupations, but often by questioning them. Ostensibly, the novel is set in the city of Sydney after all males have been expelled, and tells the story of an aging mother's loneliness after her daughter has joined an engineering project in the heart of the continent. Challenging the premise that women have an outlook different to that of men, Ireland portrays the city of women as being no different from the former city of men. The functions of bully or criminal or whinger are still fulfilled—but by women, not men (which suggests that the basic humanity of the sexes is more important than their differences). However, this judgment in turn is questioned when the novel's ending reveals that the City of Women exists only in the mind of the eccentric central character. Though frequently criticized as a "cop out," this unexpected denouement is an effective means of insisting upon the value of individual viewpoint and perception.

As if having had enough of women, Ireland's most optimistic novel takes a dog as its central character. *Archimedes and the Seagle* is the memoir of a dog in the city of Sydney ... but it is also a deliberately (and successfully) ''upbeat'' novel, celebrating the joys of life and the beauties of nature even in the midst of a huge city's urban sprawl. The novel asserts Ireland's optimism about the world, re-affirming his preoccupation with fantasy and individual perception. It is a slight work, but successfully exuberant.

Bloodfather is generally considered to be Ireland's best work to date. A *Bildungsroman,* presented in the by now familiar fragmentary ''mosaic'' pattern, it clearly draws deeply upon aspects of Ireland's own experience. The life of young David Blood is traced from infancy to his teenage years, recording the child's evolving perception of his environment, his growing awareness that he needs a God (and that this God will provide him with his life's work). But the book's richness lies not in *what* it is about but the *way* it deals with that material; in the words of reviewer Mary Rose Liverani, ''The sources of pleasure in *Bloodfather* are too many to explore in a very brief review: enjoyment of characters who are portrayed with uninhibited affection, exploration of religious, moral and social issues in language that is genuinely fresh and unexpected, and the affirmation of the god-like in mankind and the universe.''

—Van Ikin

IRVING, John (Winslow)

Nationality: American. **Born:** Exeter, New Hampshire, 2 March 1942. **Education:** Phillips Exeter Academy, Exeter, graduated 1962; University of Pittsburgh 1961–62; University of Vienna, 1963–64; University of New Hampshire, Durham, B.A. (cum laude), 1965; University of Iowa, Iowa City, M.F.A. 1967. **Family:** Married 1) Shyla Leary in 1964 (divorced 1981), two sons; 2) Janet Turnbull in 1987. **Career:** Taught at Windham College, Putney, Vermont, 1967–69; lived in Vienna, 1969–71; writer-in-residence, University of Iowa, 1972–75; assistant professor of English, Mount Holyoke College, South Hadley, Massachusetts, 1975–78. **Awards:** Rockefeller grant, 1972; National Endowment for the Arts grant, 1974; Guggenheim grant, 1976; American Book Award, for paperback, 1980; Academy Award, Best Adapted Screenplay (*Cider House Rules*), 2000. **Agent:** Sterling Lord Literistic, 1 Madison Avenue, New York, New York 10010. **Address:** c/o Random House, Inc., 201 E. 50th Street, New York, New York 10022–7703, U.S.A.

PUBLICATIONS

Novels

Setting Free the Bears. New York, Random House, 1969; London, Corgi, 1979.
The Water-Method Man. New York, Random House, 1972; London, Corgi, 1980.
The 158-Pound Marriage. New York, Random House, 1974; London, Corgi, 1980.
The World According to Garp. New York, Dutton, and London, Gollancz, 1978.
The Hotel New Hampshire. New York, Dutton, and London, Cape, 1981.
The Cider House Rules. New York, Morrow, and London, Cape, 1985.
A Prayer for Owen Meany. New York, Morrow, and London, Bloomsbury, 1989.
A Son of the Circus. New York, Random House, and London, Bloomsbury, 1994.
John Irving: Three Complete Novels (contains *Setting Free the Bears*; *The Water-Method Man*; and *The 158-Pound Marriage*). New York, Wings Books, 1995.
A Widow for One Year. New York, Random House, 1998.

Short Stories

Trying to Save Piggy Snead. London, Bloomsbury, 1993.

Uncollected Short Stories

''A Winter Branch,'' in *Redbook* (New York), November 1965.
''Weary Kingdom,'' in *Boston Review,* Spring-Summer 1968.
''Almost in Iowa,'' in *The Secret Life of Our Times,* edited by Gordon Lish. New York, Doubleday, 1973.
''Lost in New York,'' in *Esquire* (New York), March 1973.
''Brennbar's Rant,'' in *Playboy* (Chicago), December 1974.
''Students: These Are Your Teachers!,'' in *Esquire* (New York), September 1975.
''Vigilance,'' in *Ploughshares* (Cambridge, Massachusetts), no. 4, 1977.
''Dog in the Alley, Child in the Sky,'' in *Esquire* (New York), June 1977.
''Interior Space,'' in *Fiction* (New York), no. 6, 1980.

Plays

Screenplays: *The Cider House Rules: A Screenplay.* New York, Hyperion, 1999.

Other

My Movie Business: A Memoir. New York, Random House, 1999.

*

Film Adaptations: *The World According to Garp*, 1982; *The Hotel New Hampshire*, 1984; *Simon Birch*, based on the work *A Prayer for Owen Meany*, 1998; *The Cider House Rules*, 1999.

Manuscript Collections: Phillips Exeter Academy, Exeter, New Hampshire.

Critical Studies: Introduction by Terrence DuPres to *3 by Irving* (omnibus), New York, Random House, 1980; *Fowles, Irving, Barthes: Canonical Variations on an Apocryphal Theme* by Randolph Runyon, Columbus, Ohio State University Press, 1982; *John Irving* by Gabriel Miller, New York, Ungar, 1982; *Understanding John Irving* by Edward C. Reilly, Columbia, South Carolina, University of South Carolina Press, 1991.

Theatrical Activities: Actor: **Film**—*The World According to Garp,* 1982.

* * *

The publication of *The World According to Garp* was an important event in contemporary American literature. For John Irving himself, of course, the novel's reception must have been extremely gratifying: the book neatly divided his career forever into the pre- and post-*Garp* periods. Initially a little-known academic novelist whose first three books—*Setting Free the Bears, The Water-Method Man,* and *The 158-Pound Marriage*—rapidly sought the remainder lists, he suddenly found himself inundated by critical superlatives and, no doubt, positively drenched in money. He achieved that rare combination of literary acclaim and wide readership that every writer dreams of. The success of *Garp,* following the previous achievement of E.L. Doctorow's *Ragtime,* indicated that after many years of stifling academicism, fiction may have finally graduated from college and ventured out into the arena of ordinary life. Because many professors seem to believe that literature was written exclusively to be studied in their courses and because far too many writers receive their training in those courses, a great deal of American writing has been marked by a sterile obsession with technique for its own sake, a conscious avoidance of traditional subjects, a fatal attraction to critical theory, and a perverse desire to appeal only to a coterie of initiates.

Irving's works in general, and *Garp* most spectacularly, signal the return of fiction to its proper and honorable concerns—a close engagement with the stuff of real life, a profound compassion for humanity, and—inextricably and possibly even causally connected to these qualities—great dedication to the narrative process, to storytelling itself. Irving cares deeply for his characters and their stories and makes his readers care for them as well; in doing so he places his work in the great lineage of the novel. Only a bold and innovative writer could venture so daringly backward into the literary past. His three most significant books at this point in his career—*The World According to Garp, The Cider House Rules,* and *A Prayer for Owen Meany*—indicate that this late twentieth-century American novelist also participates in the traditions of the nineteenth-century English novel. Long, leisurely narratives, densely populated with eccentrics, attentive to the whole lives of virtually all the characters, replete with coincidence and foreshadowing, full of allusions to specific writers and works, his novels combine a Dickensian richness of character and emotion with a Hardyesque sense of gloom and doom.

In addition to his refreshingly old-fashioned qualities, Irving also demonstrates his appropriateness to his own time and place. His novels are in many ways as contemporary as those of any of his peers. In addition to a growing sense of topicality, most fully realized in *A Prayer for Owen Meany,* they display all the familiar landmarks of the American literary countryside: violence, grotesquerie, a certain craziness, a racy, energetic style, and a powerful interest in the fiction-making process. They differ from one another in manner, matter, and merit—*The 158-Pound Marriage* seems his weakest performance—but they also share certain peculiarly Irvingesque subjects that create their special zany charm. Until *The Cider House Rules,* his books all dealt with such matters as academia, art, children, marital triangles and quadrangles, wrestlers, writers, sexual mutilation, Vienna, and bears. Bears creep through his first book and also show up in the long story ''The Pension Grillparzer,'' that appears in *The World According to Garp* as well as *The Hotel New Hampshire.*

The pre-*Garp* Irving is lively, comic, whimsical, a writer whose works display immense confidence, a kind of assured easiness rare in a young beginner, far beyond the usual condescending cliches about promise. *Setting Free the Bears* is a revitalized American picaresque improbably set in Austria; the goal of its protagonist's lunatic quest is suggested in its title and works out to be as improbable as its location. *The Water-Method Man* deals with the sexual escapades, personal failures, and professional problems of a more or less lovable rogue wonderfully named Bogus Trumper; it explores, with rich glee, some fascinating notions about the creation of art from the chaos of Trumper's life, through the medium of avant-garde filmmaking and Trumper's absurd doctoral dissertation.

Whatever the value of his earlier work, however, in retrospect it seems a preliminary for *The World According to Garp,* which entirely altered Irving's career. The novel is written with enormous energy and strength, clearly the work of writer in full command of his material and his method. Although its style presents no particular problems and its plot moves in a leisurely, straightforward manner, the novel seems radically experimental for its complicated narrative progress. Its ostensibly simple story of the life of T.S. Garp from conception to death is interrupted by a number of other fictions from ''The Pension Grillparzer'' to a horribly violent account of rape, murder, and despair, Garp's own novel, *The World According to Bensenhaver;* the book also includes bits from Garp's mother's autobiography, *A Sexual Suspect,* other short stories, and parts of the biography of Garp that will only be written after his life and the book are over. In an action that must have called for some courage, Irving even includes an epilogue, detailing the lives of his characters after the main events of his major fiction have concluded: once again, in reverting to the methods of the past the author seems daringly innovative.

The actual subjects and events of *Garp,* just as unusual as its narrative archaism, come to dominate all of Irving's works. Although the novel itself was almost universally regarded as comic and, in Irving's words, ''life affirming,'' it is an immensely sad and troubling book, haunted by violence, savagery, fear, horror, and despair. From beginning to end a bleeding wound gapes across the book: Garp's mother slashes a soldier in a theater; his father dies of a terrible war wound; his wife bites her lover's penis off in the same automobile accident that kills one of Garp's sons and half-blinds the other; and Garp's own novel, *The World According to Bensenhaver,* employs one of the most vivid rape scenes in all of literature. The relationship between sexuality and mutilation is emphasized through virtually every character—from Roberta Muldoon, the transsexual former football player to the man-hating feminists who cut out their own tongues to commemorate the maiming of a rape victim; Garp himself is assassinated by a cult member, the sister of the girl who was responsible for his sexual initiation.

Irving's fascination with sex-related violence and sexual mutilation winds disturbingly through most of his works, from the gang rapes of *The Cider House Rules* through the *hijras*—transvestite eunuchs—of India and the transsexual serial murderer Rahul in *A Son of the Circus.* Along with the bizarre and horrific narratives and the close attention to the character and life of the artist, the theme of sexual mutilation suggests something about the creative act itself. Throughout his works, art is generated out of sex, fear, pain, blood, and guilt; experiencing all these, Irving's artists create their fictions, which also make up a large part of the books about them, sometimes even as in *A Son of the Circus,* attempting to ''write'' life as if it were their own narrative. Sex, art, life, and the interpretation of both provide his rich and often puzzling structures, sometimes leading away from their initially simple, comic narrative lines into a region of horror, grotesquerie, insanity, and myth.

The post-*Garp* Irving, no longer the obscure academic writer, was rapidly transformed into the celebrity author, attentive to sales, publicity, and movie rights. He soon began to appear on the television talk shows, demonstrating his recipe for breaded veal cutlet; dressed in wrestler's togs and flexing his wrestler's muscles, he brooded handsomely in full color for readers of slick magazines. His good looks, his popularity, and his willingness to publicize his books and films earned him a more than literary fame and no doubt a more than literary fortune—his post-*Garp* works are copyrighted by something called Garp Enterprises Ltd. *The Hotel New Hampshire* and *The Cider House Rules* demonstrate the pernicious influence of success. The former continues some of the subjects of its predecessor, boiling over with violence and whimsy—a gang rape, a plane crash, suicide, terrorism, a lesbian in a bear suit, and a flatulent dog named Sorrow. Although the obsessions remain intact, they seem mechanical and perfunctory in style and substance; the laborious drollery and the easy cynicism, along with the specious profundities of the repeated catch phrases and verbal tags, read like warmed-over Vonnegut.

The Cider House Rules, on the other hand, shows that the author can move away from a possibly fatal self-imitation in new directions. Irving discovers for the first time the depths and possibilities of his natural penchant for Dickensian storytelling by inventing a truly Irvingesque place, an orphanage where abortions are performed. Though heavily dependent on the kind of research that hinders so many academic authors, *The Cider House Rules* recaptures some of the original Garpian compassion. The quirkiness of style and the fascination with genital wounds and sexual pain remain, but they are mixed with less labored touches of lightness and a good deal of love.

The Dickens and the Hardy influences flourish in *A Prayer for Owen Meany,* his finest work after *Garp,* which shows the author once again in full command of his considerable gifts and more fully aware of the tradition in which he works. Returning to the autobiographical mode that fuels the energy of *Garp,* Irving once again reports terrible events in a straightforward, even comic style, invents some remarkable people—especially the title character—and explores some of his favorite subjects. In addition, he more explicitly confronts his repeated theme of problematic paternity and this time attempts to provide reason and causality for what he had previously presented as the horrible mischancing of coincidence and fate; in *A Prayer for Owen Meany* Irving has found religion, specifically Christianity. He employs a nicely orchestrated set of typically unusual symbols and a variety of people and events to express the religious dimension, which encompasses the primitive and mythic as well as the various Protestant orthodoxies. As a result the book suggests a more energetic but less lapidary and learned John Updike.

The novel, along with the long, rather disordered exploration of India in *A Son of the Circus,* demonstrates that Irving has challenged himself in new ways: instead of settling for the sort of repetition that pleases far too many readers, he has chosen to break new ground. By contrast, *A Widow for One Year* marked a return to somewhat familiar territory, constituting a sort of female Garp saga with novelist Ruth Cole as its protagonist.

In a relatively brief time and at a relatively young age, John Irving has become a major contemporary novelist. His considerable body of work displays originality, development, and richness of subject and theme. His startling mixture of humor and sorrow, accessibility and complexity, clarity and confusion, of strong narrative with humane vision, of horrified despair with life-affirming comedy seems perfectly suited to end-of-century culture and literature. The chord he struck in a large and varied public with *Garp* continues to resonate; his works still appeal to a readership that encompasses many levels of literacy, an indication of their timeliness and power.

—George Grella

ISHIGURO, Kazuo

Nationality: British. **Born:** Nagasaki, Japan, 8 November 1954. **Education:** Woking County Grammar School for Boys, Surrey, 1966–73; University of Kent, Canterbury, B.A. (honors) in English and Philosophy 1978; University of East Anglia, Norwich, M.A. in creative writing 1980. **Career:** Community worker, Renfrew Social Works Department, 1976; social worker, 1979–80, and resettlement worker, West London Cyrenians Ltd., 1979–80. **Awards:** Winifred Holtby prize, 1983; Whitbread award, 1986; Booker prize 1989; Premio Scanno for Literature (Italy), 1995; Order of the British Empire (O.B.E.), 1995. D.Litt.: University of Kent, 1990; University of East Anglia, 1995. Fellow, Royal Society of Literature. **Agent:** Deborah Rogers, Rogers Coleridge and White Ltd., 20 Powis Mews, London W11 1JN, England. **Address:** c/o Faber and Faber, 3 Queen Square, London WC1N 3AU, England.

Publications

Novels

A Pale View of Hills. London, Faber, and New York, Putnam, 1982.
An Artist of the Floating World. London, Faber, and New York, Putnam, 1986.
The Remains of the Day. London, Faber, and New York, Knopf, 1989.
The Unconsoled. New York, Knopf, 1995.
When We Were Orphans. New York, Knopf, 2000.

Uncollected Short Story

''A Family Supper,'' in *The Penguin Book of Modern British Short Stories,* edited by Malcolm Bradbury. London, Viking, 1987; New York, Viking, 1988.

Plays

Television Plays: *A Profile of Arthur J. Mason,* 1984; *The Gourmet,* 1986.

*

Film Adaptations : *Remains of the Day,* 1993.

Critical Studies: *Understanding Kazuo Ishiguro* by Brian W. Shaffer. Columbia, South Carolina, University of South Carolina Press, 1998;

Narratives of Memory and Identity: The Novels of Kazuo Ishiguro by Mike Petry. New York, Peter Lang, 1999.

* * *

Kazuo Ishiguro is the author of five novels, and he was awarded the Booker prize in 1989 for his third, *The Remains of the Day*. It is not surprising that Ishiguro was given this literary accolade so early on in his writing career, as each of these novels is powerfully crafted in the inimitable, meticulously observed manner that has brought much critical and popular acclaim to their author. His more recent novels have been characterized by a formal adventurousness and willingness to experiment that have brought him further acclaim as a stylist and explorer of the possibilities of the novel.

Ishiguro's novels are characterized by the way that the calm expository style and seemingly unimportant concerns of the narrators disguise a world fraught by regrets, unresolved emotional conflicts, and a deep yearning to recapture (and make sense of) the past. In the case of *A Pale View of Hills* and *An Artist of the Floating World*, the central figures are, like Ishiguro, Japanese by birth, and their personal desires to excavate the past suggest not only their troubled personal history, but also broader issues concerned with post-war Japanese society.

Ishiguro's first full-length work, *A Pale View of Hills*, is set in present-day rural England, where Etsuko, a Japanese widow, comes to terms with her elder daughter's recent suicide. The sad event of the present precipitates memories of the past and leads the mother to recall certain aspects of her life in Nagasaki just after the war. In particular, she remembers her friendship with the displaced, independent, and rather cruel Sachiko, a woman once of high rank now living in poverty with her neglected, willful daughter, Mariko. An elegant, elliptical composition, this novel (or perhaps more precisely novella) hints at connections between Etsuko's Nagasaki days and her present-day English existence. Her half-understood relationship with the enigmatic Sachiko and Mariko prefigures her problematic one with her own daughters, while Sachiko's displacement from her class, and eventually her turning away from her race as well, anticipate Etsuko's future anomie.

A striking feature of this confident first novel is the underlying sense of the macabre that pervades Etsuko's memories, particularly in her recollection of the strange, perhaps not entirely imaginary, woman whom young Mariko claims to know, and who appears like a character from a Japanese folk tale. This hinting at sinister possibilities, coupled with the way that Ishiguro with the skill of a miniaturist delicately shapes the story around shifting perspectives and selective memories, marks out *A Pale View of Hills* as a compelling and intriguing debut work.

While Etsuko's narrative betrays hesitation and uncertainty from the beginning, the narrator of *An Artist of the Floating World* is a much more robust creation. It is 1948 and Masuji Ono, a painter who has received great renown for his work, some of it decidedly nationalistic in its objectives, reconsiders his past achievements in the light of the present. As with the previous novel, little of consequence seems to happen. Over a number of months, Ono is visited by his two daughters, is involved in marriage negotiations on the part of one of them, re-visits old artist colleagues, drinks in the ''Migi-Hidari,'' and, in a beautifully evoked scene, attends a monster movie with his grandson. However, these seemingly mundane domestic occurrences gradually force the elderly painter to review his past to reveal a complex personal history of public and private duties, professional debts and ambitions, and possible culpability in Japan's recent military past. More obviously than in *A Pale View of Hills*, the central character is both an individual and a representative figure. Through Ono's re-visiting of his past life, Ishiguro very skillfully describes an artist's training and work conditions before the war, raising much broader questions about artistic and personal responsibility during this contested period in Japan's history.

Ono's ''floating world'' is ''the night-time world of pleasure, entertainment and drink,'' frequented by fellow artists. The narrators of all Ishiguro's novels seem to inhabit ''floating worlds'' distinct from the much visited, and joyfully described, pleasure-quarter. For them the old assumptions they held about their lives are under scrutiny, leaving them to try to make sense of the brave new ''floating worlds'' they inhabit. In *The Remains of the Day*, Ishiguro examines the changed cultural climate of post-war England through the attempts by Stevens, a ''genuine old-fashioned English butler'' (in the words of his American employer), to make sense not only of the present but, more acutely, of the past as well. As with the other novels, this tale of self and national discovery is precisely dated. In July 1956 the butler of the late Lord Darlington sets forth on a motoring holiday, accompanied by Volume III of Mrs. Jane Symons's *The Wonders of England*, to meet Miss Kenton, housekeeper at Darlington Hall during the inter-war years.

In the previous novels, Ishiguro raises questions about the relationship between personal and public morality. In the figure of Stevens, he presents public and domestic behavior as indivisible. Stevens has renounced family ties in order to serve his masters, having given up many years of his life to Darlington. As he sojourns in the West Country, Stevens reconsiders his time in service to the English aristocracy. *The Remains of the Day*, like the novels with Japanese settings, is distinguished by the skilled use of first-person narration. Here the stiff formality and prim snobbery of the butler's voice are maintained throughout, demonstrating the way that Stevens has renounced his individuality in order to serve well, and creating also some splendid moments of comedy when the events narrated are inappropriately described in such dignified and constrained tones.

In Ishiguro fashion, the ''truth'' is gradually hinted at through summoning up memories of things passed, and Stevens has to admit that his former master to whom he has devoted a good part of his life was possibly an incompetent amateur diplomat who was manipulated by National Socialists in the 1930s. However, as with the previous novels, the confrontation with an earlier, at times misguided, self offers hope for the future, and the endings of these precisely composed books are gently optimistic, rather than painfully elegiac, celebrating people's capacity for adaptation, understanding, and change.

Ishiguro's 1995 novel *The Unconsoled*, revisits much of the terrain of memory, regret, and aesthetic culpability that have been the hallmarks of his style. In this stylistically ambitious novel, however, Ishiguro inflects those concerns through a nightmarish dream-space where a Kafka-esque circularity results in a relentlessly anxiety-provoking narrative. The central character, a concert pianist of some renown named Ryder, arrives at an unnamed, vaguely central European town to give a recital. He then proceeds, in a time-frame that is stubbornly indeterminate, to pursue a bewildering number of delays, deferrals, and wild goose-chases, all of which may or may not be related to his own personal history.

The town that Ryder encounters has several fault lines in its social fabric. The most significant involves the civic implications of his performance, which differing factions within the town see as either a vindication or discrediting of an aesthetic conflict that is mapped along vaguely conservative and progressive lines. Ryder's unawareness of the broader ramifications of this performance, along with the continual emergence of new factional strife, produces a vertiginous plot, where encounter after encounter fail to resolve the issue at hand, and instead follow a bewildering line of deferral. Adding to the confusion is the fact that the characters themselves are frequently realized through what Ishiguro calls ''appropriation,'' a technique by which, as in a dream, they appear as refracted manifestations of the narrator or his submerged fears and desires: the child Boris, whom Ryder frequently consoles with an insight that seems unnaturally empathetic; Stephan, an anxiety-ridden young pianist who looks to Ryder for advice on how to please his parents; and the elderly porter Gustav, who has ceased to speak to his daughter Sophie (Boris's mother) as an act of will. Ryder finds himself responsible for the suturing of these various social wounds, which are replayed through the many fractured parent-child relationships whose suffering permeates the novel, and his success or failure is to be measured by some nameless epiphany to be revealed through his endlessly deferred recital.

As in the earlier novels, there is a brooding sense of intergenerational trauma with which the narrator must somehow come to terms. In *The Unconsoled*, however, that trauma remains disturbingly unresolved. Ryder is unable to reconcile the various splintered relationships—too many to recount—that the narrative mourns throughout. Unlike *The Remains of the Day*, in which Stevens manages to recover the illusion of redeeming insight by the novel's close, *The Unconsoled* ends only with Ryder's tortured realization that resolution of the conflicts that have beset him throughout the novel—both personal and social—will evade him as surely as the recital that is the ostensible reason for his presence in the town. Ultimately, the hallucinatory style of the plot colludes so insidiously with Ryder's personal dream-world that the consolation of an ending where fragments are resolved in some measure is denied the reader as well.

When We Were Orphans proves a fitting stylistic continuance to *The Unconsoled*. Again, the territory is that of memory and nostalgia, and the failure of generational inheritance to relieve a painfully revisited nostalgia. Christopher Banks, the narrator and protagonist of the novel, is a well-known detective in pre-war England who is haunted by the disappearance of his parents in Shanghai years earlier. In 1937 he sets off to Shanghai to solve the mystery of their vanishing, and in so doing is forced to come to terms with the shady business practices not only of his father but of the colonial community as a whole. While the denouement may clarify some of the mystery, as in all of Ishiguro's novels there is much going on beneath the limpid prose of the narrative.

The undercurrents in the novel are again history—personal and public—as well as the troubling instability of memory in the face of trauma. Banks's failed relationship with fellow orphan Sarah Hemmings, as well as his childhood friendship with the Japanese boy Akira, emerge as part of a doubled time-line that triggers his recollections. While Banks as a narrator seems disarmingly disingenuous, upon closer reflection significant discrepancies begin to appear between his memories and the reported reactions of those around him. The resulting instability is a familiar one to the attentive reader of Ishiguro's fiction: the truth, as usual, is not the sole province of the narrator or memory, and resides instead in a more nebulous space where history and memory—trauma and wound—are indivisible from their informants.

—Anna-Marie Taylor, updated by Tom Penner

IYAYI, Festus

Nationality: Nigerian. **Born:** 1947. Educated in Nigeria; University of Bradford, Yorkshire, Ph.D. 1980. **Career:** Economic correspondent for several newspapers in Bendel; industrial training officer, Bendel State University, Ekpoma. Currently lecturer in business administration, University of Benin, Benin City. **Awards:** Association of Nigerian Authors prize, 1987; Commonwealth Writers prize, 1988. **Address:** Department of Business Administration, University of Benin, PMB 1154, Ugbowo Campus, Benin City, Nigeria.

Publications

Novels

Violence. London, Longman, 1979.
The Contract. London, Longman, 1982.
Heroes. London, Longman, 1986.

Short Stories

Awaiting Court Martial. Lagos, Malthouse Press, 1996.

* * *

> ''... those who carry the cross for society always get crucified in the end ...''
>
> *Heroes*

Festus Iyayi's three novels, *Violence, The Contract*, and *Heroes*, as well as his collection of short stories, *Awaiting Court Martial*, expose the abject penury and disenfranchisement that constitute the social reality of the majority of Nigerians. In language that is often vitriolic and stinging, Iyayi's protagonists potently display his contempt for the rampant corruption that strangles contemporary Nigeria. Businesspersons, politicians, generals, and other officials hoard the country's wealth and power at the expense of the working class. This base depravity of the ruling class manifests itself in various forms and ultimately trickles down to the ruled class. In each of Iyayi's novels the real tragedy is that those of the ruled class are either forced or coerced to absorb their oppressor's abuse. They in turn release their anger and frustration not upon the deserving ruling class, but amongst themselves. Iyayi, however, does weave threads of hope within each of his narratives via truculent calls by the main characters to defy their oppressors en masse and fight for their civil rights as well as for the future of their country. Also driving Iyayi's political critique is a profound acceptance of humanity's fragility and frailty. Especially in *Awaiting Court Martial*, Iyayi displays an uncanny ability for capturing the details of his character's troubled psyches through crisp metaphors and often naturalistic imagery.

Violence usually connotes physical abuse, but in his first novel, *Violence*, Iyayi redefines it as a continual, demoralizing structure that eliminates hope, pride, self-esteem, health, and the ability to live independently. Having to always rely on borrowed *naira* from those who are more fortunate leaves deep scars of shame and guilt. Iyayi's violence creeps into the corners of the *pneuma* of the lower classes, the have-nots, and renders them helpless against the socio-political machine powered solely by money, corruption, and privilege.

Obofun and Queen exemplify Nigeria's corrupt, monied class. Obofun makes his millions by winning coveted building contracts through his connections in the government and through the relinquishing of percentages of the contracts' total worth to those who award them. His wife, Queen, sleeps with other men to get what she wants—namely, supplies, which are otherwise expensive and scarce, for her hotels. When Idemudia, a typical, destitute laborer, is fortunate enough to find work, the conditions at the site are deplorable. If he wants to keep his job and be able to feed himself and his wife, Adisa, then he has to swallow the maltreatment. If he chooses to fight the system, to organize the workers against his boss, Queen, and to ask for higher wages and better conditions, then he risks being fired and subsequent starvation.

One of the most effective passages in *Violence* is a series of lines from a play performed at a local hospital. Iyayi utilizes this poignant and very effective device to convey his definition of violence. Idemudia witnesses this play is educated and inspired by the actor who denounces violence and advocates resistance, and then leads his co-workers in threatening to strike for better wages and conditions.

Iyayi's writing continues to be mordacious and gripping in his second novel, *The Contract*. The main character, Ogie, returns to Benin after an absence of four years and is amazed and disgusted at how quickly and completely the city has decayed. There is filth and chaos everywhere. He learns that the government awards contracts for building hospitals, roads, and low-cost housing, then demands percentages for awarding the contract. This practice leaves little or no money for building the structures the contract was for—resulting in inferior and often-abandoned projects. The people of Benin live in squalor while a few wealthy, corrupt officials get fatter. Anything can be bought or sold. Men will even offer their wives for a favored chance at winning a contract, or lie, cheat, and even kill for fortunes. Like Idemudia in *Violence*, Ogie's abomination of the stark contrasts of wealth and poverty in his hometown is potently conveyed. He swears he will fight the system of which even his father is a part. He takes a job at the council and soon finds himself tortuously torn and confused over right and wrong. He continues to reaffirm decent convictions, but eventually compromises his values to become ''corruption with a human face.'' He decides he cannot beat the system entirely, but can take the money he receives from the contract percentages and invest it in Benin and local businesses, rather than hoard it in a Swiss bank account.

Heroes, Iyayi's third novel, is set against the background of Nigeria's civil war in the late 1960s. As in his previous work, Iyayi's style is forceful and bold. Once again, he cries out against the injustices in Nigeria through well-crafted characters and electrifying writing.

Osime is a journalist who supports the vociferous calls for a united Nigeria and those denouncing the Biafran soldiers and exalting the Federal troops. He sees the Federal troops as the saving force for Nigeria. But when the Federal troops shoot and kill his girlfriend's father without cause in cold blood, he begins to realize that there is more to the war than he had originally thought. Osime quickly sees that even though the Biafran and Federal troops commit wretched crimes, the generals and the officers are the real enemies of the people of Nigeria. The soldiers have learned to become murderers from the military's officers—they are merely instruments of destruction under the orders of officers who seek power, territory, and fortune. In its critique of the generals and military power, therefore, the novel offers a useful analogy for unveiling the hypocrisy and self-interest that lie hidden behind bourgeoisie ideology. Osime's solution is the formation of a third army—one that fights the greedy politicians, businesspersons, and generals. A total revolution, powered by the third army, could eliminate the corrupt officials reigning at the top of all sectors of Nigerian society and replace it with rule by those who love the land, work the land, and therefore respect it and its inhabitants.

Iyayi's criticism of Nigerian society is relentless in all three novels, but even among the dire revelations and depressing reality of the polarities of privation and opulence in Nigeria, he offers an encouraging creed for social change: ''A people are never conquered. Defeated, yes, but never conquered.'' And some of the more striking moments of defeat are explored in *Awaiting Court Martial*.

The collection's fifteen stories create a gallery of tortured souls, poignantly imagined and rendered visibly luminous by Iyayi's piercing psychological descriptions. As in the novels, the main character's crisis, no matter how unique or personal, often reflects the political chaos and social disintegration of the nation at large. For example, the opening story, ''Jeged's Madness,'' is about a mutually destructive marriage that ruinously ends when a rich bureaucrat, Mr. Throttle Cheat-Away, offers the husband advancements only so that he can rape the wife. The title story, ''Awaiting Court Martial,'' is a dream-like, first-person confession made by a once-efficient executioner of the state. The doomed soldier did not give the order to shoot his latest victim, his brother, who came boisterously laughing to his own execution. The brother's laughter disarms and ridicules the effectiveness of the mass execution, transforming the marksmen into boys simply ''spitting at the sun.'' Uniting the stories are themes also prevalent in Iyayi's novels: political corruption, interpersonal cruelty, the nightmarish threats of kidnapping, murder, home invasion, or robberies, psychological obsessions, the power of dreams and folk values, and the political responsibility of the artist-intellectual—a few of the narrators seem to be Iyayi himself.

Current literary criticism of Iyayi's works has focused on the validity of postcolonial theories when applied to Iyayi and other non-exile writers (Femi Osofisan), and the aesthetic intertwining of radical narrative techniques with radical politics (Fírinne Nì Chréachàin); but perhaps the most popular treatment of Iyayi deals mainly with his exemplification of characteristics commonly associated with Chinua Achebe and other renowned authors of the Nigerian canon as it is articulated by and for Western readers (John Bolland).

—Susie deVille, updated by Michael A. Chaney

J

JACKSON, Mick

Nationality: English. **Born:** Great Harwood, Lancashire, England, 1959 or 1960. **Education:** Graduated in Theatre Studies from Dartington College of Arts; University of East Anglia, M.A. 1992. **Career:** Founder and singer-songwriter for band, variously called The Screaming Abdabs and The Dinner Ladies, 1980s. **Agent:** Derek Johns, 20 John Street, London WC1N 2DR, England.

PUBLICATIONS

Novels

The Underground Man. New York, William Morrow, 1997.

Other

Rock the World (muscial recording, with others). New York, Select Records, 1985.

* * *

In 1997 Mick Jackson's debut novel, *The Underground Man*, was short-listed for both the popular Whitbread Best First Novel award, and the internationally coveted Booker McConnell prize. While it won neither, it nevertheless garnered much praise for the inventive treatment of its subject, the real life fifth Duke of Portland, William John Cavendish-Bentinck-Scott. The Duke, a reclusive eccentric, is as much remembered for the extensive network of tunnels he constructed under his estate as for the popular myths his peculiarities inspired. Combining the factual record with the public and authorial imagination, Jackson created a narrative that weaves through the mind and journals of the Duke and the thoughts of those who encounter him. The tunnels themselves serve as the unifying motif of the novel, providing a parallel to the internal burrowing of the Duke as he retreats further into himself, finally severing his already tenuous connection with the outside world and the human contact that governs it. In the character of the elderly Duke, Jackson explores a mind unsuited for the everyday world, lacking the ability to discriminate between ideas, and betrayed by the aging body that contains it. Even in the face of this betrayal, the Duke attempts to maintain control over both the physical property of the body, and the physical property of the estate—the logical extension of the self for a titled property owner—and it is his failure to recognize his own limitations in both that brings the novel to its startling conclusion.

Not merely imaginative historical fiction, *The Underground Man* signals a contemporary tendency to mine the past for the purposes of considering contemporary preoccupations with the individual, the relationship between the self and other, and the possibilities and limits of both humanity and the human intellect. That Jackson bestows upon the Duke a childlike innocence, curiosity, and enthusiasm, however, provides both humor and pathos to the novel, and ensures that its theoretical preoccupations never alienate the reader or disrupt the trajectory of the story itself.

Ultimately, the narrative of *The Underground Man* is very much an act of story telling, and Jackson himself is not unqualified as a storyteller. Trained as an actor at the Dartington College of Arts (1983), Jackson has written and directed several short films. Previously he also wrote lyrics for a number of bands with which he performed at the Glastonbury and Reading rock festivals: Dancing with the Dog, The Screaming Abdabs, and The Dinner Ladies. When his bandmates complained that his lyrics were becoming unwieldy, Jackson moved to poetry, and then short story writing. In 1991, with only a few short stories to his credit, Jackson was accepted into the prestigious University of East Anglia (Norwich) Creative Writing M.A. program. The program's literary pedigree is impeccable, and it boasts an impressive list of alumni, including Andrew Cowan, Kazuo Ishiguro, Deirdre Madden, Ian McEwan, and Rose Tremain. Today Jackson has joined UEA's list of successful and recognized graduates.

—Jennifer Harris

JACOBSON, Dan

Nationality: British. **Born:** Johannesburg, South Africa, 7 March 1929. **Education:** The University of the Witwatersrand, Johannesburg, 1946–49, B.A. 1949. **Family:** Married Margaret Pye in 1954; three sons and one daughter. **Career:** Public relations assistant, South African Jewish Board of Deputies, Johannesburg, 1951–52; correspondence secretary, Mills and Feeds Ltd., Kimberley, South Africa, 1952–54. Fellow in Creative Writing, Stanford University, California, 1956–57; visiting professor, Syracuse University, New York, 1965–66; visiting fellow, State University of New York, Buffalo, 1971, and Australian National University, Canberra, 1980; lecturer, 1976–80, reader, 1980–88, professor of English, 1988–94, University College, London. Since 1994, professor emeritus, University College, London. Vice-chair of the Literature Panel, Arts Council of Great Britain, 1974–76. **Awards:** Rhys Memorial prize, 1959; Maugham award, 1964; H.H. Wingate award (*Jewish Chronicle*, London), 1978; Society of Authors traveling scholarship, 1986; J.R. Ackerley award, for autobiography, 1986. Fellow, Royal Society of Literature, 1974. D.Litt., University of Witwatersrand, 1997. **Agent:** A.M. Heath, 79 St. Martin's Lane, London WC2N 4AA, England; or, Russell and Volkening Inc., 50 West 29th Street, New York, New York 10001, U.S.A.

PUBLICATIONS

Novels

The Trap. London, Weidenfeld and Nicolson, and New York, Harcourt Brace, 1955.

A Dance in the Sun. London, Weidenfeld and Nicolson, and New York, Harcourt Brace, 1956.

The Price of Diamonds. London, Weidenfeld and Nicolson, 1957; New York, Knopf, 1958.

The Evidence of Love. London, Weidenfeld and Nicolson, and Boston, Little Brown, 1960.
The Beginners. London, Weidenfeld and Nicolson, and New York, Macmillan, 1966.
The Rape of Tamar. London, Weidenfeld and Nicolson, and New York, Macmillan, 1970.
The Wonder-Worker. London, Weidenfeld and Nicolson, 1973; Boston, Little Brown, 1974.
The Confessions of Josef Baisz. London, Secker and Warburg, 1977; New York, Harper, 1979.
Her Story. London, Deutsch, 1987.
Hidden in the Heart. London, Bloomsbury, 1991.
The God-Fearer. London, Bloomsbury, 1992; New York, Scribner, 1993.

Short Stories

A Long Way from London. London, Weidenfeld and Nicolson, 1958.
The Zulu and the Zeide. Boston, Little Brown, 1959.
Beggar My Neighbour. London, Weidenfeld and Nicolson, 1964.
Through the Wilderness. New York, Macmillan, 1968.
Penguin Modern Stories 6, with others. London, Penguin, 1970.
A Way of Life and Other Stories, edited by Alix Pirani. London, Longman, 1971.
Inklings: Selected Stories. London, Weidenfeld and Nicolson, 1973; as *Through the Wilderness,* London, Penguin, 1977.

Plays

Radio Plays: *The Caves of Adullan,* 1972.

Other

No Further West: California Visited. London, Weidenfeld and Nicolson, 1959; New York, Macmillan, 1961.
Time of Arrival and Other Essays. London, Weidenfeld and Nicolson, and New York, Macmillan, 1963.
The Story of the Stories: The Chosen People and Its God. London, Secker and Warburg, and New York, Harper, 1982.
Time and Time Again: Autobiographies. London, Deutsch, and Boston, Atlantic Monthly Press, 1985.
Adult Pleasures: Essays on Writers and Readers. London, Deutsch, 1988.
The Electronic Elephant: A Southern Africa Journey. London, Hamilton, 1994.
Heshel's Kingdom (memoir). Evanston, Illinois, Northwestern University Press, 1999.
Editor, with Daniel Bar-Tal and Aharon Klieman, *Security Concerns: Insights from the Israeli Experience.* Stamford, Connecticut, JAI Press, 1998.

*

Bibliographies: *Dan Jacobson: A Bibliography* by Myra Yudelman, Johannesburg, University of the Witwatersrand, 1967.

Manuscript Collections: National English Literary Museum, Grahamstown, South Africa; University of Texas, Austin.

Critical Studies: ''The Novels of Dan Jacobson'' by Renee Winegarten, in *Midstream* (New York), May 1966; ''Novelist of South Africa,'' in *The Liberated Woman and Other Americans* by Midge Decter, New York, Coward McCann, 1971; ''The Gift of Metamorphosis'' by Pearl K. Bell, in *New Leader* (New York), April 1974; ''Apollo, Dionysus, and Other Performers in Dan Jacobson's Circus,'' in *World Literature Written in English* (Arlington, Texas), April 1974, and ''Jacobson's Realism Revisited,'' in *Southern African Review of Books,* October 1988, both by Michael Wade; ''A Somewhere Place'' by C.J. Driver, in *New Review* (London), October 1977; *Dan Jacobson* by Sheila Roberts, Boston, Twayne, 1984; ''Stories'' by John Bayley, in *London Review of Books,* October 1987; ''Intolerance'' by Julian Symons, in *London Review of Books,* October 1992; ''The Mother's Space'' by Sheila Roberts, in *Current Writing* (South Africa) 5(1), 1993; ''Weapons of Vicissitude'' by Richard Lansdown, in *The Critical Review* (Australia) 34, 1994.

Dan Jacobson comments:

My novels and stories up to and including *The Beginners* were naturalistic in manner and were written almost entirely about life in South Africa. This is not true of the novels I have written subsequently.

* * *

Dan Jacobson's first two novels, *The Trap* and *A Dance in the Sun,* marked him as a writer of considerable ability, with an interest in typically South African ''problems.'' Since then, he has developed rapidly to become one of South Africa's best known and most interesting novelists.

The two early novels are both concerned with the tensions inherent in the extremely close, almost familial, relationships between white employer and black employee, which tend to develop in the particular kind of farm community Jacobson describes. Both embody what might be described as allegorical statements about the South African situation. Jacobson implies that the inhabitants of the country are trapped in their own environment and condemned to perform a ritualistic ''dance in the sun.'' To an outsider this can only appear to be a form of insanity. This vision of South Africa leaves out of account, or, at best, finds irrelevant, the group (English speaking, liberal, white) to which Jacobson himself belongs, and it is, therefore, not surprising that he should have chosen to live and work abroad.

For some years, however, his novels continued to deal with South African subjects. *The Evidence of Love* tells the story of a black man and a white woman who fall in love and attempt to defy South African law and custom by living together. The novel treats the theme of interracial love in a more relaxed and naturalistic way than is usual in South African fiction, and also highlights aspects of the individual struggle for freedom and the achievement of self-identity. *The Price of Diamonds* focuses on shady dealings and financial corruption in a small town in South Africa, and reveals Jacobson's quite considerable gift for comedy.

The Beginners, which, together with the collection of stories *A Long Way from London,* established Jacobson's position as a writer of stature, is an ambitious and substantial novel. The story of three generations of an immigrant Jewish family, it offers a penetrating, subtle, and complex analysis of what it means to be a ''demi-European at the foot of Africa'' and a ''demi-Jew'' in the modern world. The novels which follow *The Beginners* are not concerned with South Africa directly, nor are they naturalistic in manner. But two of the three later novels deal with political tensions and power struggles, and in so doing appear to have deliberate parallels with the contemporary situation in South Africa. Jacobson's continuing interest in South Africa is also reflected in his collection of autobiographical pieces, *Time and Time Again,* in which he reflects, among other things, on the way in which his perceptions of the country have changed since the days when he could see it only as a place from which he had to escape.

The Rape of Tamar is a witty and sophisticated reconstruction of an episode at the court of the biblical King David, focusing on a power struggle between the aging king and his politically ambitious sons. *The Wonder-Worker,* set in contemporary London, explores the world of a sensitive and lonely character whose inability to establish meaningful relationships leads inevitably to his complete alienation from the world around him, but, paradoxically, also to his ability to understand people completely. Jacobson's novel, *The Confessions of Joseph Baisz,* is a brilliantly inventive and deeply disturbing fantasy: the ''extraordinary autobiography'' of an emotionally stunted individual who discovers very early in his bleak life that he is capable of loving only those people whom he has first betrayed. Set in an imaginary country with a nightmarish but distinctly recognizable resemblance to South Africa, the novel is wholly convincing in its portrayal of a society whose members illustrate what Baisz calls ''the iron law: the wider their horizons, the narrower their minds.''

Like other contemporary South African novelists, Jacobson has written some excellent short stories. Many of them probe the guilts and fears of white South Africans living in the midst of what they regard as an alien and hostile black culture. Two stories that are among the best things he has done are ''The Zulu and the Zeide'' and ''Beggar My Neighbour.'' The former contrasts the small-minded meanness of a wealthy Jewish businessman with the unaffected humanity of the black servant he employs to care for his ailing father; while ''Beggar My Neighbour'' movingly evokes the world of a young white boy forced to come to terms with the cruel realities of a racist society through his chance meeting with two black children. In these stories, as in all his work, Jacobson's special skills are displayed: detailed observation, economic presentation, and a compassionate but objective analysis of the varieties of human behavior.

Jacobson showed his imaginative talent to good advantage in *The God-Fearer,* a novel that takes place in a sort of alternate reality. Set in an indeterminate period that might well be medieval times, the novel gradually unfolds its secret: in this world, Jews are the culturally dominant group in Western civilization, and the ''Christers'' are a persecuted minority. It is a challenging vision, deftly executed.

—Ursula Edmands

JACOBSON, Howard

Nationality: British. **Born:** Manchester, 25 August 1942. **Education:** Stand Grammar School, 1953–60; Downing College, Cambridge, 1961–64, B.A. in English 1964. **Family:** Married Rosalin Sadler in 1978; one son from a previous marriage. **Career:** Lecturer, University of Sydney, New South Wales, 1965–68; supervisor, Selwyn College, Cambridge, 1969–72; senior lecturer, Wolverhampton Polytechnic, West Midlands, 1974–80. Presenter, *Traveller's Tales* television series, 1991; currently freelance book reviewer, the *Independent,* London. **Agent:** Peters Fraser and Dunlop, 503–504 The Chambers, Chelsea Harbour, Lots Road, London SW10 0XF, England.

PUBLICATIONS

Novels

Coming from Behind. London, Chatto and Windus, 1983; New York, St. Martin's Press, 1984.
Peeping Tom. London, Chatto and Windus, 1984; New York, Ticknor and Fields, 1985.
Redback. London, Bantam Press, 1986; New York, Viking, 1987.
The Very Model of a Man. London, Viking, 1992; New York, Overlook Press, 1994.
No More Mister Nice Guy. London, Jonathan Cape, 1998.
The Mighty Walzer. London, Jonathan Cape, 1999.

Uncollected Short Stories

''Travelling Elsewhere,'' in *Best Short Stories 1989,* edited by Giles Gordon and David Hughes. London, Heinemann, 1989; as *The Best English Short Stories 1989,* New York, Norton, 1989.

Other

Shakespeare's Magnanimity: Four Tragic Heroes, Their Friends and Families, with Wilbur Sanders. London, Chatto and Windus, and New York, Oxford University Press, 1978.
In the Land of Oz (travel). London, Hamish Hamilton, 1987.
Roots Schmoots: Journeys Among Jews. London, Viking, 1993; New York, Overlook, 1994.

*

Howard Jacobson comments:

It is an irony not lost on novelists that though they inveigh against all characterizations of their work in reviews, in profiles, and even on the covers of their own books, the moment they are invited to describe themselves, they say they would rather not.

I too, would rather not. Except to say that an argument about the nature of comedy—an argument I go on having largely with myself—is at the back of everything I write. The familiar formula, that comedy stops where tragedy begins, is unsatisfactory to me. The best comedy, I maintain, deals in truths which tragedy, with its consoling glimpses of human greatness, cannot bear to face. Comedy begins where tragedy loses its nerve. That's the sort of comedy I try to write, anyway.

* * *

''You know what novelists are like—they spill their guts on every page and claim it's plot.'' So Barney Fugelman is told by his second wife Camilla in Howard Jacobson's second novel, *Peeping Tom.* That fiction writers must draw on their own experience in order to give their work a ring of truth is something of a truism, but Jacobson's easy familiarity with Lancashire, Wolverhampton, Cambridge, Cornwall, and Australia, and his sharply observed portrayals of academic life and the urban Jewish psyche give his bawdy, scatological books a piquant verisimilitude. The themes that pervade his novels—ideological duplicity, cultural self-consciousness, sexual ambivalence, and gnawing self-doubt—could make some readers uncomfortable as they recognize themselves within his glass, were it not for the verve and aplomb of the humor with which they are relayed. And although Jacobson's protagonists often share the same individual afflictions and obsessions—identity crises, failed relationships, self-conscious Judaism, robustly masculine sexual preoccupations—and inhabit similar *milieux* (characters occasionally put in appearances in one another's novels), the underlying issues have universal appeal and are dealt with in a way which is simultaneously reassuring and thought-provoking.

Sefton Goldberg, the subject of Jacobson's first novel and only third-person narrative, *Coming from Behind,* is a man with a great future behind him. Manchester born, Cambridge educated and now doomed to ignominy in his post at a Midlands polytechnic which is in the throes of merging with the local football club, he spends his days applying unsuccessfully for every available academic post and skirmishing with colleagues. He is jealously obsessed with the success of these colleagues' publications while he himself, as yet unpublished, plans to write a tome on failure, which trait in himself is another obsession. Doggedly leading the lifestyle of a transient visitor, his condition is aggravated by his refusal to make the best of his situation and environment. He is finally granted an interview for a post in Cambridge, only to discover that he is to be in competition with, and interviewed by, his former students. The result is a success which is so thoroughly compromised on all sides that it is practically a Pyrrhic victory: a success achieved through a failure to fail consummately.

In Jacobson's most ribald book, *Peeping Tom,* Barney Fugelman discovers under hypnosis that he is somehow reincarnated from (or possibly related to) Thomas Hardy and, it transpires, the Marquis de Sade. Incest, voyeurism, troilism, and autoerotic hanging all feature in the plot as the sexual predilections of the narrator's alteregos manifest themselves through him, helping to precipitate his downfall and the ruin of his two marriages. What is being examined is the confusion of sexual and personal identities: Barney has two unwanted guests in his psyche and cannot tell if he is loved for himself, for Hardy, or for de Sade. Nor is it made easy for him to get a purchase on his real self in terms of his psychological make-up or his personal history. His parents swap spouses with their neighbors and so, compounded by his mother's intimations and revelations, Barney is never sure of his true relationship to Rabika Flatman, his father's paramour and the object of his own erstwhile voyeuristic fantasies. The discovery that Mr. Flatman is in fact his real father merely completes the symmetry, it is the resolution of the comic mechanism.

Redback is remarkable not least of all because the logistics of the plot neatly mirror Clive James's semi-autobiographical trilogy, *Unreliable Memoirs.* But James—himself namechecked within—tells a vastly different story to that of Leon Forelock, who leaves Cambridge with a degree in Moral Decencies and is assigned by the CIA to purge Australia of its non-conformist elements. Castigating homosexuals, drug-takers, and anyone voicing an opinion remotely left of the far-right, he censors and bans his way through university campuses and bookstalls. But Leon practices much of what he preaches against and relishes the privileges of the Englishman abroad while setting obscure questions on Langland's *Piers Plowman* as a test for prospective immigrants. The narrative is informed, however, by Forelock's epiphanic conversion, the occasion of which is a bite inflicted by the venomous redback spider of the title. Given a new outlook on humanity, doomed to suffer a myriad of recurring symptoms which include priapism, and kept under surveillance by his former employers, Leon overtly embraces all that is radical and bohemian in the world. His priapism is a metaphor for the contradictions of his moral condition: the rampant impotence of his own self.

The protagonist of *The Very Model of a Man* is no less than Cain himself, who bemoans a series of misfortunes that pepper his long life, from his parents' unfortunate decision in the Garden to the Tower of Babel. Jacobson's work has been compared to that of Kingsley Amis, Malcolm Bradbury, and David Lodge and rightly so, for he exhibits many themes, nuances, and preoccupations in common with them. Certain elements of his work do lack finesse: tendencies toward stereotypical characters and meandering narrative are apparent on occasions, as is what some might claim to be an unhealthy dwelling on all things phallic. Nonetheless, his characters evoke pathos even in their more grotesque or puerile moments, his plots are thoughtful and rounded, and his wit is dry and infectious. After less than a decade spent writing in his chosen genre, Jacobson seems set to become a major force in English comic fiction.

—Liam O'Brien

JAMES, Kelvin Christopher

Nationality: Trinidadian (immigrated to United States, U.S. citizenship pending). **Born:** Port of Spain, Trinidad. **Education:** University of West Indies (St. Augustine), B.S. (honors) in zoology and chemistry 1967; Columbia University, New York, M.A. in 1975, M.Sc. in education 1976, and doctorate in science education, 1978. **Career:** Science researcher, Department of Agriculture, Trinidad, 1961–64; high school science teacher, Trinidad, 1968–70; technologist in chemistry lab, Harlem Hospital, 1970–76. Since 1980, full-time writer. **Awards:** New York Foundation for the Arts award, 1989. **Agent:** Joy Harris, 156 Fifth Ave., Suite 617, New York, New York 10010, U.S.A. **Address:** 1295 Fifth Ave., New York, New York 10029, U.S.A.

Publications

Novels

Secrets. New York, Random House, 1993.
A Fling with a Demon Lover. New York, HarperCollins, 1996.

Short Stories

Jumping Ship and Other Stories. New York, Random House, 1992.

* * *

Trinidadian writer Kelvin Christopher James began writing full-time in 1980. Prior to that he taught high school science in Sangre Grande before emigrating to New York, where he worked as a lab technician at Harlem Hospital Center and eventually earned a Ph.D. in science education from Teachers College, Columbia University. His background in zoology contributes richly to the lush, sensual landscapes in both of his works.

In his debut collection of short stories—*Jumping Ship and Other Stories*—James paints a bold canvas of savage sexuality, physical and mental incarceration, and bloody revenge. The first five stories are set in the Caribbean, followed by two transitional tales of immigrants making the difficult adjustment to a new country. The remaining stories take place in a hard-edged, gritty Harlem. At a first glance, the collection appears desultory in theme. But a closer look reveals an intriguing evocation of ritual that is a unifying thread through most of the stories—in the intense games of sibling rivalry in ''Littleness''; in the rote cruelties of the street in ''Guppies''; in the inscrutable circumstances of an Obeah voodoo ceremony in ''Tripping.'' These rituals, both terrifying and essential, bring into sharp relief the visceral quality of life for many of the characters.

The descriptive language of the stories is potent and visual, if occasionally self-conscious. At times, the violence of the Harlem tales seems to be gratuitous, and one wishes for a little more narrative cohesion to lend them some purposefulness. Still, the author is quite effective with a story like ''Home Is the Heart,'' in which a father severs the bonds of his youth in order to form a stronger alliance with his son.

In James's second work, the novel *Secrets,* he seems more at ease and in his natural element. Here the author uses idiomatic language and natural description to good effect: The fecund earth—the ripening fruit and buzzing flies of island life—mirror a young girl's sexual coming-of-age. And as with most mythopoeic tales, the prosaic becomes profound. An expedition in search of *balata,* an elusive, pulpy fruit that nests high in the trees, transcends the commonplace to become a virtual odyssey.

The story is told from the viewpoint of Uxann, a plump, bookish Catholic schoolgirl, who steals mangoes from her neighbor, cooks mouthwatering meals for her Paps, and gossips mercilessly with best friend Keah. The author captures convincingly the easy rhythms and musings of a typically self-absorbed adolescent, and from the opening sentences he thrusts the reader into her almost excessively sensual, dangerously naive world. But soon the novel and Uxann's life take on the character of a folktale, with the discovery of a snake in her island's Garden of Eden. Uxann's journey becomes at once universal and disturbingly out of the ordinary. The author is commended for retelling an age-old story in such an imaginative way and for capturing a young girl's sexual odyssey with candor and insight.

In both these works, James unearths the darker forces that lie in wait beneath the surface, whether they be in a tropical jungle or an asphalt one.

—Lynda Schrecengost

JAMES, P(hyllis) D(orothy)

Nationality: British. **Born:** Oxford, 3 August 1920. **Education:** Cambridge Girls' High School, 1931–37. During World War II worked as a Red Cross nurse and at the Ministry of Food. **Family:** Married Ernest Connor Bantry White in 1941 (died 1964); two daughters. **Career:** Prior to World War II, assistant stage manager, Festival Theatre, Cambridge; principal administrative assistant, North West Regional Hospital Board, London, 1949–68; principal, Home Office, in police department, 1968–72, and criminal policy department, 1972–79. Justice of the Peace, Willesden, London, 1979–82, and Inner London, 1984. Chair, Society of Authors, 1984–86; governor, BBC, and board of the British Council, 1988–93; chair, Arts Council Literature Advisory Panel, 1989–92. Lives in London. **Awards:** Crime Writers Association award, 1967, Silver Dagger award, 1971, 1975, 1986, Diamond Dagger award, 1987; Grand Master, Edgar Allan Poe Awards, 1999. D.Litt.: Buckingham, 1992; London, 1993; Hertfordshire, 1994; Glasgow, 1995; Essex, 1996; Durham, 1998; Portsmouth, 1999. Associate Fellow, Downing College, Cambridge, 1986; Fellow, Institute of Hospital Administrators, Royal Society of Literature, 1987, and Royal Society of Arts; honorary fellow, St. Hilda's College, Oxford, 1996. O.B.E. (Order of the British Empire), 1983. Baroness, 1991. **Agent:** Greene & Heaton, Ltd., 37 Goldhawk Road, London W12 8QQ, England.

PUBLICATIONS

Novels

Cover Her Face. London, Faber, 1962; New York, Scribner, 1966.
A Mind to Murder. London, Faber, 1963; New York, Scribner, 1967.
Unnatural Causes. London, Faber, and New York, Scribner, 1967.
Shroud for a Nightingale. London, Faber, and New York, Scribner, 1971.
An Unsuitable Job for a Woman. London, Faber, 1972; New York, Scribner, 1973.
The Black Tower. London, Faber, and New York, Scribner, 1975.
Death of an Expert Witness. London, Faber, and New York, Scribner, 1977.
Innocent Blood. London, Faber, and New York, Scribner, 1980.
The Skull Beneath the Skin. London, Faber, and New York, Scribner, 1982.
A Taste for Death. London, Faber, and New York, Knopf, 1986.
Devices and Desires. London, Faber, 1989; New York, Knopf, 1990.
The Children of Men. London, Faber, 1992; New York, Knopf, 1993.
Original Sin. London, Faber, 1994; New York, Knopf, 1995.
A Certain Justice. New York, Knopf, 1997.

Uncollected Short Stories

''Moment of Power,'' in *Ellery Queen's Murder Menu.* Cleveland, World, 1969.
''The Victim,'' in *Winter's Crimes 5,* edited by Virginia Whitaker. London, Macmillan, 1973.
''Murder, 1986,'' in *Ellery Queen's Masters of Mystery.* New York, Davis, 1975.
''A Very Desirable Residence,'' in *Winter's Crimes 8,* edited by Hilary Watson. London, Macmillan, 1976.
''Great-Aunt Ellie's Flypapers,'' in *Verdict of Thirteen,* edited by Julian Symons. London, Faber, and New York, Harper, 1979.
''The Girl Who Loved Graveyards,'' in *Winter's Crimes 15,* edited by George Hardinge. London, Macmillan, and New York, St. Martin's Press, 1983.
''Memories Don't Die,'' in *Redbook* (New York), July 1984.
''The Murder of Santa Claus,'' in *Great Detectives,* edited by D.W. McCullough. New York, Pantheon, 1984.
''The Mistletoe Murder,'' in *The Spectator* (London), 1991.
''The Man Who Was 80,'' in *The Man Who.* London, Macmillan, 1992.

Plays

A Private Treason (produced Watford, Hertfordshire, 1985).

Other

The Maul and the Pear Tree: The Ratcliffe Highway Murders, 1811, with Thomas A. Critchley. London, Constable, 1971; New York, Mysterious Press, 1986.

Time to Be in Earnest: A Fragment of Autobiography. New York, Knopf, 2000.

*

Critical Studies: *P.D. James* by Norma Siebenheller, New York, Ungar, 1981; *P.D. James* by Richard B. Gidez, Boston, Hall, 1986.

* * *

Starting from a conventional first detective story, *Cover Her Face,* P.D. James has moved toward fiction in which criminal investigation provides merely a loose structure for characterization, atmosphere, and theme, which now seem most important to her. In this assault on generic boundaries, she resembles, but is more determined than, Dorothy L. Sayers, Josephine Tey, and Ngaio Marsh. Consequently, James's detectives—Cordelia Gray (private and young) and Adam Dalgliesh (professional and middle-aging)—have been absent from or muted in recent works.

Commander Dalgliesh resembles other detectives created by women writers: tall, dark, attractive, and frangible (he is ill, bashed, or burned in half his novels). ''When the Met … want to show that the police know … what bottle to order with the *canard à l'orange* … , they wheel out Dalgliesh,'' a hostile chief inspector says. Sensitive under seeming coldness, he has published several volumes of poetry. Before his first appearance, Dalgliesh's wife has died in childbirth, but in successive novels her presence dies away. At one time readers hoped that Cordelia Gray would take her place, but romantic notes have ceased to be struck; Cordelia has disappeared, and Inspector Kate Miskin, introduced in *A Taste of Death,* has not replaced her. In fact, few James characters are happily married, and there are no juvenile leads to assert the normality of love. There are, however, close, psychologically incestuous brother-sister relationships.

James once told an interviewer that she believes detective fiction can lessen our fear of death. Yet her details of what happens after death—the doctor's fingers penetrating the orifices of the female body, the first long opening cut of an autopsy—are scarcely reassuring. Other shocks of mortality include the skulls of plague victims packed cheekbone to cheekbone in the crypt of Courcy Castle in *The Skull Beneath the Skin,* James's most gothic novel, and boatloads of the elderly sailing out to die in *The Children of Men.*

Although few of James's settings are as conventional as the house party in *Skull,* her action generally takes place in closed, often bureaucratic communities: e.g., a teaching hospital, a psychiatric clinic, a forensic laboratory, or a nuclear power station, organizations which draw, no doubt, upon the author's own administrative experiences.

In terms of plot, James is most successful when dealing with the processes of investigation and is weakest in motivation. She has said she thinks in terms of film sequences; her latest novels contain variants of the ''chase,'' and the long ''panning'' shots and close-ups in which she relentlessly describes interiors have become at times an intrusive mannerism. Perhaps her best, most controlled use of domestic detail occurs in *Innocent Blood,* where Phillipa furnishes a flat to greet her just-released murderess mother. Indeed, this violent *Lehrjahr* with its slower discoveries, its ambiguities, and its psychological images in ''the wasteland between imagination and reality'' is James's best claim to consideration as a ''serious'' novelist.

James's characters have always thought and talked about truth, faith, responsibility, and justice, even if not profoundly. But in the books that follow *Innocent Blood,* plot is almost lost amid talkiness and theme. The nature of Sir Paul Berowne's religious experience in *A Taste for Death,* for instance, is more important and less explicable than the identity of his blood-happy killer. In *Devices and Desires* (title drawn from the Book of Common Prayer), a nuclear power station and a ruined abbey confront each other, perhaps adversarially, in one of James's bleak coastal landscapes. They are surrounded by serial murder, terrorism, anti-nuclear and pro-animal protesters, cancer, drowning, anti-racism, a libel suit—all pretexts and conveniences for a plot which the novel is not about. Dalgliesh is present, but almost a bystander, although he finds a corpse and almost dies in the fire that consumes the killer. Since then he has appeared in *Original Sin,* heading the investigation into the deaths of a young publisher and his sister, but is even more detached, except for brief bravura scenes, which demonstrate his sureness of touch and of technique. Instead, Kate Miskin is to the fore, with a Jewish detective who tries to be an atheist. The ''original sin'' is presumably the Nazi murder long ago of a woman and her two children, whom her husband finally avenges by murdering the two children of the man responsible. Ironically, however, they had merely been adopted to satisfy a childless wife, whose infertile husband is not particularly fond of his ''offspring.''

In *The Children of Men,* a futurist thriller, published between *Devises and Desires* and *Original Sin,* James opts for brutality. The year is 2021; mankind has lost the power to reproduce, and Xan is Warden of England. The narrator, Xan's cousin and once his advisor, is attracted to a tiny protest group, ''The Five Fishes,'' and particularly to Julian, who is almost miraculously pregnant. To escape Xan's protective care, they embark on a wild drive, during which the religious Luke is bludgeoned to death by a band of ''Painted Faces.'' Julian bears a son, but her midwife is murdered. When Xan appears, the narrator shoots him and becomes Warden in his stead. He signs a cross on the newborn's head. But, the reader wonders, will the state of the world really improve? In a 1985 interview, James described herself as born with a sense ''that every moment is lived, really, not under the shadow of death but in the knowledge that this is how it's going to end.'' This sense now dominates her fiction.

—Jane W. Stedman

JANOWITZ, Tama

Nationality: American. **Born:** San Francisco, California, 12 April 1957. **Education:** Barnard College, New York, B.A. 1977; Hollins College, Virginia, M.A. 1979; Yale University, New Haven, Connecticut, 1980–81. **Career:** Model, Vidal Sassoon, London and New York, 1975–77; assistant art director, Kenyon and Eckhardt, Boston, Massachusetts, 1977–78; writer-in-residence, Fine Arts Works Center, Provincetown, Massachusetts, 1981–82; since 1985 freelance writer. **Awards:** Bread Loaf Writers fellowship, 1975; Janoway Fiction prize, 1976, 1977; National Endowment award, 1982. **Agent:** Jonathan Dolger, 49 East 96th Street, New York, New York 10028. **Address:** c/o Crown Publishers, 201 E. 50th St., New York, New York 10022, U.S.A.

PUBLICATIONS

Novels

American Dad. New York, Putnam, 1981; London, Picador, 1988.
A Cannibal in Manhattan. New York, Crown, 1987; London, Pan, 1988.
The Male Cross-Dresser Support Group. New York, Crown, and London, Picador, 1992.
By the Shores of Gitchee Gumee. New York, Crown Publishers, 1996.
A Certain Age. New York, Doubleday, 1999.

Short Stories

Slaves of New York. New York, Crown, 1986; London, Picador, 1987.

Uncollected Short Stories

''Conviction,'' in *The New Generation,* edited by Alan Kaufman. New York, Doubleday, 1987.
''Case History No.179: Tina,'' in *Between C and D,* edited by Joel Rose and Catherine Texier. New York, Penguin, 1988.

* * *

Few can match Tama Janowitz's commentaries on the race of fakes, freaks, and flakes who inhabit the sprawling metropolis of social non-achievement. By her own admission, satiric observations designed for humorous entertainment limit an author's appeal to those readers who share a similar sense of humor with the author. In addition, sharp-tongued social critics like Janowitz seem to invite harsher criticism of their writing, easily falling prey to the reactionary statement that their attempts at humor are not funny. Janowitz matches wits—and takes the resulting jabs—with writers such as Ring Lardner and Mark Twain, situating her novels in the tradition of ''comic American misanthropy.'' Other favorable reviews compare her witty observations to those of Lewis Carroll and Kurt Vonnegut. *The San Francisco Chronicle* relegates her ''adventurous narratives'' to a category of classics like *Tom Jones* and *Tristram Shandy*, albeit feminist versions of them. It is clear that Janowitz's six books, beginning with the debut of *American Dad* in 1981, have established her reputation as a successful woman among male satirists.

American Dad is a tale of familial disaffection centering on Earl Przepasniak and his mother Mavis, a neglected poet, with the awe-inspiring shadow of father and husband, Robert, falling over them both. Robert's reputation rests less on his skills as a psychiatrist than on his social achievements with the opposite sex. ''Can you imagine what it is for me, five-foot-six-inches,'' asks Earl ''to live up to a six-foot-tall Dad whose sexual prowess is mythical in the northwestern corner of a certain New England state?'' Following the inevitable divorce of his parents, Earl cultivates misanthropy in his mother's house with the aim of escaping his father's admonishing glare. After Mavis dies, Earl slips back into society with a highly developed feminine side, lacking overtly masculine merit in a seemingly male-oriented meritocracy.

Slaves of New York elevated Janowitz to literary stardom in 1986 and was made into a movie shortly after. It is an assortment of loosely connected short stories about an array of aspiring Greenwich Village artists, gallery owners, and their associates. Janowitz casts her gaze around the sparse crowd of her fellow disaster addicts and is rewarded with a splendid display of self-delusion, clashing colors, and reckless hope. Eleanor, an extension of Earl Przepasniak's female aspects, appears in several stories linking them together. The theme that coheres the separate stories, which were previously printed in magazines such as *Spin, The New Yorker, Paris Review*, and *Interview*, is how an insecure woman becomes a social being in the world's most significant bohemian society. It is a society of egos shackled by their own modish attitudes and the self-promoting opinions of others in a highly artificial environment about which they can only barely make sense.

Taken in isolation, the stories in *Slaves of New York* lack the epigrammatic sparkle that enlivened *American Dad* and, as a whole, lack the dynamism of the earlier work. Neither of these problems is apparent in Janowitz's second novel, *A Cannibal in Manhattan*, which was published in 1987. It received mixed reviews: enough negative press to dampen the excitement that followed her best-seller of 1986.

A Cannibal in Manhattan tells the story of Mgungu Yabba Mgungu, who is transplanted from his native island of New Burnt Norton to even more fierce surroundings. The eponymous ''cannibal'' relates the history of his intended journey toward greater civilization, which is Manhattan. Mgungu, nominal leader of the withered and disenfranchised Lesser Pimbas, possesses the recipe for a narcotic that has made his tribal life bearable during sixty-five years of indolence. We soon discern that he has been brought to America solely to be exploited. That this only becomes explicit through the knowing use of extra-narrative devices deployed by Janowitz is testimony to the sophistication of her wit and the profundity of Mgungu's gullibility.

Duped at every turn, unwittingly implicated in a horrendous crime, and abandoned by his erstwhile sponsors, this distinctly unmythical savage slides towards vagrancy and is eventually apprehended in typically ridiculous circumstances. Yet his mind-numbing naivete, a fondness for drink, his unenviable record as a chief, and his occasionally incongruous use of language serve to alert readers to the possibility that he may be an unreliable narrator. Manipulating her characters with a barely concealed Nabokovian glee, Janowitz draws a world of drug-dealing, treachery, and self-aggrandizement, while underpinning it with an alternate landscape of itinerancy, drunken camaraderie, and self-destruction.

Mgungu's passage through the first sphere of the drug business is a journey of missed connections and plans gone awry, allowing the reader plenty of space to fill in the details; his trawl through the second sphere of self-destruction leaves less to the imagination. Guilty or innocent, Mgungu is a thoroughly engrossing guide to his own misfortune. The richly inventive tale of a decline into contemporary civilization is both stunningly funny and damningly true.

The Male Cross-Dresser Support Group, published in 1992, followed *A Cannibal in Manhattan* with similar mixed reviews, prompting some critics to refer to the author as a one-book phenomenon. *The Male Cross-Dresser Support Group* suggests a metaphorical connection to the notion that being a male member of society affords greater privilege than being female. Protagonist Pamela Trowell works for a hunting magazine while living in a grotesque basement apartment. Pamela, who considers herself ''ponderous and dumpy and unpleasant,'' concludes that her sole disadvantage in the hierarchy of her love life and employment by equally disadvantaged men is her gender. After a journey to Maine with her adopted son, Abdul, a stray adolescent who follows her home from a pizza parlor one night, she tests her premise by returning to Manhattan dressed as a man.

Despite mixed reactions from critics and readers, the novel was selected as Notable Book of the Year by *The New York Times*, which did commend the satirical humor in the abnormalities that constitute Pamela's normal life as a single woman in Manhattan. The exaggerations that constitute her hysterically funny observations about the curiosities of gender identity, family values, and motherhood in the 1990s de-politicize the universal truth of gender discrimination. The redeeming relationship between Pamela and Abdul, who are the least perverted in the array of family members and associates surrounding Pamela, offers a foothold of genuine affection in a seriously defective system of values.

By the Shores of Gitchee Gumee again covers this uncomfortable territory of modern values from the perspective of Maud Slivenowicz, the 19-year-old narrator who lives with her mother and four siblings in a trailer on the outskirts of a small city in upstate New York. Like the stereotype of white trailer trash, each child is fathered by different absent men. Maud schemes against her sister in a race to see who will marry into a life of wealth and privilege, as if that were a realistic option. She is distracted from this by her brother, Pierce, who is as dense as ''Neanderthal man'' but handsome enough to move to Los Angeles and become a movie star. This humorous look at sibling rivalry received the usual contradictory critical reviews, especially that the novel's satirical elements conflict with the human moments, creating a sense of incompleteness in the novel as a whole.

Janowitz's skills as a novelist found redemption in *A Certain Age*, published in 1999. In this parody of a consuming theme in Jane Austen's parlor dramas, a well-educated Sarah Lawrence graduate, Florence Collins, is desperate to find a husband. Whereas Austen's single women worry about being past it when they reach twenty, Florence is concerned about being thirty-two. She travels to the Hamptons, the equivalent of Austen's British country estates, displays her charms, clothing, and beauty, and is exploited or rejected by the coterie of men who might be marriageable suitors. Unlike an Austen novel, where suitable men and women happily marry into love and agreeable financial circumstances, nothing Florence does saves her from her damaging, graceless superficiality. Like an Edith Wharton novel, the ending for this most recent of Janowitz's insecure women protagonists is at the bottom of a downward spiral.

Janowitz states that the difficulty of finding a publisher for humorous novels by women equals the limitations of satisfying a mass audience's sense of humor. Her unique farcical voice speaks in a brilliant and biting prose while trying to balance insight with social criticism. Although seeming to avoid overtly political statements in her fiction, Janowitz addresses the issues of feminism, racism, capitalism, and cultural imperialism in a genuinely original and surprising manner, containing equal parts of humor, seriousness, and warmth. She accomplishes this in a wonderfully light and fanciful style that is often outrageously funny.

—Ian McMechan, updated by Hedwig Gorski

JEN, Gish

Nationality: American. **Born:** Lillian Jen, c. 1956. **Education:** Harvard University, B.A. 1977; attended Stanford University, 1979–80; University of Iowa, M.F.A. 1983. **Career:** Lecturer in fiction writing, 1986, Tufts University; visiting writer, University of Massachusetts, 1990–91. **Awards:** *Transatlantic Review* award (Henfield Foundation), 1983; resident, MacDowell Colony, 1985 and 1987; fellow, Radcliffe Bunting Institute and James A. Michener Foundation/Copernicus Society, 1986; fellow, Massachusetts Artists Foundation, 1988; fellow, National Endowment for the Arts, 1988; Katherine Anne Porter Contest prize, 1987; Urban Arts Project prize (Boston MBTA), 1988. **Agent:** Maxine Groffsky, Maxine Groffsky Literary Agency, 25th Avenue, New York, New York 10011, U.S.A.

Publications

Novels

Typical American. Boston, Houghton Mifflin, 1991.
Mona in the Promised Land. New York, Knopf, 1996.

Short Stories

Who's Irish?: Stories. New York, Knopf, 1999.

Other

Contributor, *Best American Short Stories of 1988.* Boston, Houghton Mifflin, 1988.
Contributor, *New Worlds of Literature.* New York, Norton, 1989.
Contributor, *Home to Stay: Asian American Women's Fiction.* Greenfield Review Press, 1990.

* * *

For someone whose first novel was just published in 1991, Gish Jen has already made quite a mark on the literary scene. Her first novel, *Typical American,* was a finalist for the National Book Critics' Circle award, and her second novel, *Mona in the Promised Land,* was listed as one of the ten best books of the year by the *Los Angeles Times.* In addition, both novels made the *New York Times* ''Notable Books of the Year'' list. Jen's latest work, a collection of short stories entitled *Who's Irish,* has also been largely acclaimed, putting Jen's name once again on the *New York Times* ''Notable Books of the Year'' list, while one of the short stories in the collection, ''Birthmates,'' was chosen for inclusion in *The Best American Short Stories of the Century.* Jen's work has been canonized via inclusion in the *Heath Anthology of American Literature,* discussions of her work appear in various studies of American—and particularly Asian-American—literature, and her writing is well-represented in college literature courses.

All of Jen's work to date centers around similar themes, each set within a distinctly American context: identity, home, family, and community. This fictional ground is clearly claimed in *Typical American*, which announces itself from the beginning as ''an American story.'' It is the story of Ralph Chang and his family—from his life in China (quickly covered) to his arrival in the U.S. in 1947, to his education, marriage, children, and career as a scholar and entrepreneur in America. The novel chronicles Ralph's rise and fall in business (somewhat like a latter-day Chinese American Silas Lapham), as well as the Chang family's immersion in American culture. Ralph dubs his family the ''Chang-kees'' (Chinese Yankees), they celebrate Christmas, they go to shows at Radio City Music Hall, Ralph buys a Davy Crockett hat, Helen (Ralph's wife) learns the words to popular musicals, Theresa (Ralph's sister) gets her M.D., Ralph gets his Ph.D. and a tenured job. But Ralph is unhappy; he is convinced that in America you need money to be somebody, to be something other than ''Chinaman.'' It is only after Ralph makes and loses his money—and tears apart his family—that he realizes that the real freedom offered in America is not the freedom to get rich, to become a self-made man, but the freedom to be yourself, to float in a pool, to wear an orange bathing suit—to define your own identity.

While Jen's novels—and particularly *Typical American*—have been classified as ''immigrant novels,'' it is essential to recognize the ways in which her novels stand apart from traditional immigrant novels of the early twentieth century. *Typical American*'s departure from earlier immigrant novels, for example, is immediately apparent upon Ralph's arrival in America: rather than being greeted by the glorious Golden Gate Bridge (symbol of ''freedom, and hope, and relief for the seasick'' in Ralph's mind), Ralph is greeted by fog so thick that he can't see a thing. While earlier immigrant novels focused largely on the goal of assimilation and their characters (usually white European immigrants) achieved this goal, Jen's *Typical American*—like other contemporary immigrant novels such as Mei Ng's *Eating Chinese Food Naked,* Chang-rae Lee's *Native Speaker,* Amy Tan's *The Joy Luck Club* and *The Kitchen God's Wife,* Gus Lee's *China Boy,* Fae Myenne Ng's *Bone,* and Maxine Hong Kingston's *Woman Warrior* and *Tripmaster Monkey*—focuses on a different generation of (''nonwhite'') immigrants with substantially different problems and goals. In this contemporary generation of immigrant novels, the ''American dream'' is shrouded, like the Golden Gate Bridge upon Ralph's arrival, in fog—and underneath the dream is old, tarnished, and not quite what the characters thought it would be. Their effort is not to assimilate and become ''American'' but—recognizing that they lack the ''whiteness'' that leads to full assimilation as unhyphenated ''Americans''—they work to negotiate the space occupied by the hyphen and stake out their own uniquely American territory. As *Typical American* illustrates, in this generation of immigrant novels there really is no ''typical American''—Ralph Chang, as much as anyone, can stake claim to that title.

As part of this new generation of novelists focusing on the immigrant experience in America, Jen then reconstructs and recasts the ways in which we see both the ''American dream'' and American identity. At least since Crevecoeur posed the question in 1782, ''What is an American?'' has echoed throughout American literature. The answer to this question, of course, has never been easy or stable—American identity is fluid, shifting, unstable, and never more so than now. Nothing illustrates this better, perhaps, than Jen's second novel, *Mona in the Promised Land.* In many ways a sequel to *Typical American, Mona in the Promised Land* moves the Changs to a larger house in the suburbs, to the late 1960s/early 1970s, and to a focus on Ralph's and Helen's American-born children, Callie and Mona. Americans, this novel suggests, are constantly reinventing themselves, and no one more so than Mona, who in the course of the novel ''switches'' to Jewish (after entertaining thoughts of ''becoming'' Japanese) and becomes, to her friends, ''the Changowitz.'' Callie likewise reinvents herself during her years at Radcliffe, where she ''becomes'' Chinese (she was ''sick of being Chinese—but there is being Chinese and being Chinese''); she takes a Chinese name, she wears Chinese clothes, cooks Chinese food, chants Chinese prayers—all under the influence and tutelage of Naomi, her African-American roommate. It is also through Naomi that both Callie and Mona decide that they are ''colored.'' While the contemporary theorist Judith Butler has argued that gender identity is performative, Jen's works suggest that ethnic identity is also performative—at least to an extent. The ''promised land'' in *Mona in the Promised Land* is one in which the characters have the freedom to be or become whatever they want—within, of course, the limitations placed upon them by American culture and society.

Mona in the Promised Land, like *Typical American,* is narrated in a straightforward, realistic fashion, without the self-conscious narrative stance or vast intertextual references of writers such as Maxine Hong Kingston (there is no winking at the reader or formal pyrogenics here). While Jen's writing is poignant and beautiful—as well as often hilariously funny—she clearly puts her characters, rather than her narrative, center stage. It is the characters, with wonderful dialogue that catches all the idiosyncrasies of American speech (regardless of ethnicity or gender of the character), who stand out in Jen's novels. Jen's later work is also distinguished by her use of tense; *Mona in the Promised Land* is narrated rather unconventionally in the present tense, giving the reader a sense of immediacy and placing us right there with Mona as she navigates through her adolescence. (*Who's Irish* continues Jen's experimentation with tense, with some stories told in the first person—including the voice of a young, presumably white, boy—and one even told partially in the second person.)

While Jen has been most often compared to other Asian-American authors such as Kingston and Amy Tan, she has stated that the largest influence on her writing has been Jewish-American writers—partly as a result of her upbringing in a largely Jewish community in Scarsdale, New York, but also partly as a result of a commonality she finds between Jewish and Chinese cultures. Other authors Jen has noted as influential on her work include diverse contemporary writers such as Grace Paley, Cynthia Ozick, and Jamaica Kincaid, as well as realistic nineteenth-century women writers such as Jane Austen. Jen has also been paired with Ursula K. LeGuin on an audiocassette, with both authors reading stories about a female protagonist struggling to make sense of the sometimes culturally foreign world in which she finds herself. In terms of literary associations and influences, one might also observe that Jen's focus on suburban family life invites comparisons to well-known chroniclers of the American suburbs such as John Cheever. Although the suburbs and the marital malaise that Cheever depicts in them have been cast as overwhelmingly white in the American imagination, Jen shows us that those ''nonwhite'' immigrants newly ''making it'' to the suburbs have their own problems, secrets, skeletons—all of which are complicated by the strange rituals and ways that govern the American suburban landscape, right down to its neatly trimmed lawns.

There is no doubt that Jen is here to stay. She is a writer of great insight and power. While her writing evokes the alienation and pain of the immigrant experience, it also shows us the possibility and hope embodied in new versions of the ''American dream.'' As her characters continually reinvent themselves and seek to define their place within America, Jen encourages her readers to see the ways in which ''identity'' in America is a complex, multifaceted, constantly shifting thing. Overall, Jen shows us that the Chinese-American story, like her first novel, is truly and simply ''an American story.''

—Patricia Keefe Durso

JENKINS, (John) Robin

Nationality: British. **Born:** Cambuslang, Lanarkshire, Scotland, 11 September 1912. **Education:** Hamilton Academy; Glasgow University, 1931–35, B.A. (honors) in English 1935, M.A. 1936. **Family:** Married Mary McIntyre Wyllie in 1937; one son and two daughters. **Career:** Teacher at Dunoon Grammar School; Ghazi College, Kabul, Afghanistan, 1957–59; British Institute, Barcelona, 1959–61; and Gaya School, Sabah, Malaysia, 1963–68. **Awards:** Frederick Niven award, 1956. **Address:** Fairhaven, Toward, by Dunoon, Argyll PA23 7UE, Scotland.

Publications

Novels

So Gaily Sings the Lark. Glasgow, Maclellan, 1951.
Happy for the Child. London, Lehmann, 1953.
The Thistle and the Grail. London, Macdonald, 1954.
The Cone-Gatherers. London, Macdonald, 1955; New York, Taplinger, 1981.
Guests of War. London, Macdonald, 1956.
The Missionaries. London, Macdonald, 1957.
The Changeling. London, Macdonald, 1958.
Love Is a Fervent Fire. London, Macdonald, 1959.
Some Kind of Grace. London, Macdonald, 1960.
Dust on the Paw. London, Macdonald, and New York, Putnam, 1961.
The Tiger of Gold. London, Macdonald, 1962.
A Love of Innocence. London, Cape, 1963.
The Sardana Dancers. London, Cape, 1964.
A Very Scotch Affair. London, Gollancz, 1968.
The Holy Tree. London, Gollancz, 1969.
The Expatriates. London, Gollancz, 1971.
A Toast to the Lord. London, Gollancz, 1972.
A Figure of Fun. London, Gollancz, 1974.
A Would-Be Saint. London, Gollancz, 1978; New York, Taplinger, 1980.
Fergus Lamont. Edinburgh, Canongate, and New York, Taplinger, 1979.
The Awakening of George Darroch. Edinburgh, Harris, 1985.
Just Duffy. Edinburgh, Canongate, 1988.
Poverty Castle. Nairn, Balnain, 1991.
Leila. Edinburgh, Polygon, 1995.
Matthew and Sheila. Edinburgh, Polygon, 1999.

Short Stories

A Far Cry from Bowmore and Other Stories. London, Gollancz, 1973.
Lunderston Tales. Edinburgh, Polygon, 1996.

Uncollected Short Stories

"Exile," in *Modern Scottish Short Stories,* edited by Fred Urquhart and Giles Gordon. London, Hamish Hamilton, 1978.

* * *

Scotland, Spain, Afghanistan— the countries in which he has lived—have provided the backdrops for much of Robin Jenkins's writing, and it is his uncanny ability to realize those settings and the people who inhabit them which has given so much immediate strength to his fictional output. ''You must write about people you know best,'' Jenkins has written, ''and they are the ones you were born and brought up with.'' His Scottish novels— *So Gaily Sings the Lark, Happy for the Child, The Thistle and the Grail, The Cone-Gatherers, Guests of War, The Missionaries, The Changeling, Love Is a Fervent Fire, A Love of Innocence, The Sardana Dancers, A Toast to the Lord, A Would-Be Saint, Fergus Lamont, The Awakening of George Darroch,* and *Just Duffy*— tend to focus on the sterner aspects of Calvinism. The best of the early novels, *The Cone-Gatherers,* set on the patrician country estate of Lady Runcie-Campbell, follows to its bitter conclusion the enmity between Duror the gamekeeper and Calum, a simple-minded hunchback who gathers pine cones for their seeds. Loss of innocence is also a central theme of *The Changeling* and *Guests of War,* and is transformed in Jenkins's later novels to a yearning for the level of grace that transcends human frailty.

In all his work Jenkins's writing is characterized by his probing insights into the paradox that makes human relationships both loving and self-destructive, and by his skillful delineation of character and psychological make-up. Poverty, too, is a central issue, whether it be the spiritual poverty which disfigures men like Mungo Niven, the self-deluding hero of *A Very Scotch Affair,* or the physical poverty of the slums of Drumsagart in *The Thistle and the Grail.* Yet, despite his moral stance and his round condemnation of a society which breeds those twin evils, Jenkins is not without mercy. The reader is invited to examine the reasons which make Niven such an unattractive character and to understand how other factors, such as religion, upbringing, and heredity have helped to warp his life. Even when Niven commits adultery, sympathy for his stupidity is never far away from Jenkins's narrative. Similarly, the citizens of the mean town of Drumsagart experience a moment of grace when their football team wins a cup competition. Irony is never far away from Jenkins's literary style.

Nowhere is this virtue seen to better advantage than in *The Awakening of George Darroch.* Set in 1843, the year of the Disruption (the schism in the Church of Scotland over livings and privileges which led to the foundation of the Free Church of Scotland), it follows the crisis of conscience which affects George Darroch, a minister of the church whose parish is in a typically grim and Jenkinsian small Scottish town. On one level Darroch's dilemma is political in origin. Should he follow the dictates of his conscience and side with the Free Church reformers, or should he allow himself to be tempted into staying with the established church? At that level the arguments for following the first option are his engrained beliefs in the necessity for change, beliefs which he wishes to make manifest; balanced against these is his brother-in-law's promise of a rich living in a decent country area. On another level, Darroch is besieged by a moral problem. To throw in his lot with the reformers means that he will have to sacrifice his family and their well-being.

As time passes and the day of the ''Disruption'' meeting comes closer, Darroch sways from one direction to the other, much to the dismay of his family who expect him not only to remain constant to the established church but also to have the good sense to accept the offer of a new and more agreeable parish. When he eventually makes the fateful decision to join the reformers it seems, superficially, that Darroch is doing so to expiate past sins, in the full knowledge that he is of the Elect. But Jenkins is too clever a writer and too committed a critic of the effects of extreme Calvinism to allow Darroch such a simple exit. It is not religious faith that carries Darroch forward but simple hypocrisy: the important motive for him is not the action itself but the view which others will have of his part in it.

Despite the maturity of the writing and the sense of culmination which suggested that he had little more to say on the subject, Jenkins returned once more to the matter of sin and betrayal in *Just Duffy*. This is set in contemporary small-town Scotland, a world which the author obviously detests: Duffy lives in a bleak, urban, and uncaring environment in which achievement and greed are preferred to the more ordinary values of respect and friendship. Never addressed by his Christian name of Thomas—hence the title—Duffy is the only child of an unmarried mother and, considered stupid, he occupies a never-never land between leaving school as a simpleton and entering a world dominated by despair and poverty. Instead of accepting meekly what is offered to him, Duffy declares war on society, indulging in a growing number of meaningless actions until he commits the ultimate crime of murder. Although Jenkins reserves much sympathy for his central character, he also makes clear that Duffy's crimes are born of a frightful innocence which allows him to imagine that he can act with impunity. Eventually, Duffy retreats into the silence of madness, the only justification he can discover for what he has done.

Although Jenkins is capable of ranging easily and fluently over a wide range of social backgrounds, his vision of the demonic state of the world and the salving balm of love remain the central motifs. Anger, sexual disappointments, the betrayal of innocence are emotions never far from the surface, and like Edwin Muir (1887–1959) Jenkins is aware of the fall from grace and the widening gulf between man and Eden.

—Trevor Royle

JHABVALA, Ruth Prawer

Nationality: American. **Born:** Ruth Prawer in Cologne, Germany, of Polish parents, 7 May 1927; sister of the writer S.S. Prawer; moved to England as a refugee, 1939; became British citizen, 1948; now U.S. citizen. **Education:** Hendon County School, London; Queen Mary College, University of London, 1945–51, M.A. in English literature 1951. **Family:** Married C.S.H. Jhabvala in 1951; three daughters. Lived in India, 1951–75, and in New York City from 1975. **Awards:** Booker prize, 1975; Guggenheim Fellowship, 1976; Neil Gunn International fellowship, 1978; MacArthur fellowship, 1984; Academy of Motion Picture Arts and Sciences award for screenplay (Oscar), 1987, 1992. LHD., London University, 1995; D.Arts, London University, 1996. **Agent:** Harriet Wasserman, 137 East 36th Street, New York, New York 10016. **Address:** 400 East 52nd Street, New York, New York 10022, U.S.A.

Publications

Novels

To Whom She Will. London, Allen and Unwin, 1955; as *Amrita,* New York, Norton, 1956.
The Nature of Passion. London, Allen and Unwin, 1956; New York, Norton, 1957.
Esmond in India. London, Allen and Unwin, and New York, Norton, 1958.
The Householder. London, Murray, and New York, Norton, 1960.
Get Ready for Battle. London, Murray, 1962; New York, Norton, 1963.
A Backward Place. London, Murray, and New York, Norton, 1965.
A New Dominion. London, Murray, 1972; as *Travelers,* New York, Harper, 1973.
Heat and Dust. London, Murray, 1975; New York, Harper, 1976.
In Search of Love and Beauty. London, Murray, and New York, Morrow, 1983.
Three Continents. London, Murray, and New York, Morrow, 1987.
Poet and Dancer. London, Murray, and New York, Doubleday, 1993.
Shards of Memory. New York, Doubleday, 1995.

Short Stories

Like Birds, Like Fishes and Other Stories. London, Murray, 1963; New York, Norton, 1964.
A Stronger Climate: Nine Stories. London, Murray, 1968; New York, Norton, 1969.
An Experience of India. London, Murray, 1971; New York, Norton, 1972.
Penguin Modern Stories 11, with others. London, Penguin, 1972.
How I Became a Holy Mother and Other Stories. London, Murray, and New York, Harper, 1976.
Out of India: Selected Stories. New York, Morrow, 1986; London, Murray, 1987.
East into Upper East: Plain Tales from New York and New Delhi. Washington, D.C., Counterpoint, 1998.

Uncollected Short Stories

''Parasites,'' in *New Yorker,* 13 March 1978.
''A Summer by the Sea,'' in *New Yorker,* 7 August 1978.
''Commensurate Happiness,'' in *Encounter* (London), January 1980.
''Grandmother,'' in *New Yorker,* 17 November 1980.
''Expiation,'' in *New Yorker,* 11 October 1982.
''Farid and Farida,'' in *New Yorker,* 15 October 1984.
''The Aliens,'' in *Literary Review* (Madison, New Jersey), Summer 1986.

Plays

A Call from the East (produced New York, 1981).

Screenplays: *The Householder,* 1963; *Shakespeare Wallah,* with James Ivory, 1965; *The Guru,* 1968; *Bombay Talkie,* 1970; *Autobiography of a Princess,* 1975; *Roseland,* 1976; *Hullabaloo over Georgie and Bonnie's Pictures,* 1978; *The Europeans,* 1979; *Jane Austen in Manhattan,* 1980; *Quartet,* 1981; *Heat and Dust,* 1983; *The Bostonians,* 1984; *A Room with a View,* 1986; *Madame Sousatzka,* with John Schlesinger, 1988; *Mr. and Mrs. Bridge,* 1990; *Howard's End,* 1992; *The Remains of the Day,* 1993; *Jefferson in Paris,* 1995.; *Surviving Picasso.* Warner Brothers, 1996.; *A Soldier's Daughter Never Cries,* 1998.; *The Golden Bowl,* 2000.

Television Plays: *The Place of Peace,* 1975.

Other

Meet Yourself at the Doctor (published anonymously). London, Naldrett Press, 1949.
Shakespeare Wallah: A Film, with James Ivory, with *Savages,* by James Ivory. London, Plexus, and New York, Grove Press, 1973.
Autobiography of a Princess, Also Being the Adventures of an American Film Director in the Land of the Maharajas, with James Ivory and John Swope. London, Murray, and New York, Harper, 1975.

*

Film Adaptations: *The Householder,* 1963; *Heat and Dust,* 1983.

Critical Studies: *The Fiction of Ruth Prawer Jhabvala* by H.M. Williams, Calcutta, Writer's Workshop, 1973; ''A Jewish Passage to India'' by Renee Winegarten, in *Midstream* (New York), March 1974; *Ruth Prawer Jhabvala* by Vasant A. Shahane, New Delhi, Arnold-Heinemann, 1976; *Silence, Exile and Cunning: The Fiction of Ruth Prawer Jhabvala* by Yasmine Gooneratne, New Delhi, Orient Longman, and London, Sangam, 1983; *Cross-Cultural Interaction in Indian English Fiction: An Analysis of the Novels of Ruth Prawer Jhabvala and Kamala Markandaya* by Ramesh Chadha, New Delhi, National Book Organisation, 1988; *The Fiction of Ruth Prawer Jhabvala* by Laurie Sucher, London, Macmillan, 1989; *The Novels of Kamala Markandaya and Ruth Prawer Jhabvala* by Rekha Jha, New Delhi, Prestige, 1990; *Passages to Ruth Prawer Jhabvala* edited by Ralph J. Crane, New Delhi, Sterling, 1991, and *Ruth Prawer Jhabvala* by Crane, New York, Twayne, 1992; *Ruth Prawer Jhabvala in India: The Jewish Connection* by Ronald Shepherd, Delhi, Chanakya Publications, 1994; *The Challenge of Cross-Cultural Interpretation in the Anglo-Indian Novel: The Raj Revisted, a Comparative Study of Three Booker Prize Authors: Paul Scott, the Raj Quartet, J.G.Farrell, the Siege of Krishnapur, Ruth Prawer Jhabvala, Heat and Dust* by Gerwin Strobl, Lewiston, New York, E. Mellen Press, 1995; *Ruth Prawer Jhabvala: A Study in Empathy and Exile* by Aruna Chakravarti, Delhi, B.R. Publishing, 1998.

Ruth Prawer Jhabvala comments:

(1972) The central fact of all my work, as I see it, is that I am a European living permanently in India. I have lived here for most of my adult life and have an Indian family. This makes me not quite an insider but it does not leave me entirely an outsider either. I feel my position to be at a point in space where I have quite a good view of both sides but am myself left stranded in the middle. My work is an attempt to charter this unchartered territory for myself. Sometimes I write about Europeans in India, sometimes about Indians in India, sometimes about both, but always attempting to present India to myself in the hope of giving myself some kind of foothold. My books may appear objective but really I think they are the opposite: for I describe the Indian scene not for its own sake but for mine. This excludes me from all interest in all those Indian problems one is supposed to be interested in (the extent of Westernisation, modernity vs. tradition, etc! etc!). My work can never claim to be a balanced or authoritative view of India but is only one individual European's attempt to compound the puzzling process of living in it.

(1981) In 1975 I left India, and am now living in and writing about America—but not for long enough to be able to make any kind of comment about either of these activities.

(1986) I have now lived in the U.S. for ten years and have written one novel, several stories, and several film scripts about the experience. I cannot claim that India has disappeared out of—synonymously—myself and my work; even when not overtly figuring there, its influence is always present. But influence is too weak a word—it is more like a restructuring process: of one's ways of thinking and being. So I would say that, while I never became Indian, I didn't stay totally European either.

* * *

In a writing career that now spans five decades, Ruth Prawer Jhabvala has successfully combined the writing of novels, short stories, and screenplays. She is perhaps still best known as a novelist of India, even as a novelist who interprets India for the Western reader; yet for almost twenty years now her novels have focused less on India than on America and England, revealing the author's desire to combine her own triple European, Indian, and American background in her fiction.

Jhabvala's life of exile and expatriation has placed her in an unusual position among novelists who write about India, and has enabled her to write about that country from the ambiguous position of an outsider who is also an intimate insider. All of Jhabvala's fiction up to *Heat and Dust* (with the exception of two short stories) is set in India. For the most part Jhabvala has avoided the harsher problems of post-Independence India (the communal violence, the political unrest, etc.) in these novels, and, except in *Heat and Dust*, she has also avoided the subject of the British Raj. In her early work Jhabvala focuses on the domestic and social problems of predominantly middle-class urban Indians living in Delhi in the years following Independence. Her first two novels, *To Whom She Will* and *The Nature of Passion*, both deft comedies of manners in an Austenish vein, treat the subjects of arranged marriage and romantic love and explore the conflicts that arise as the modern, Western views of characters like Amrita (in *To Whom She Will*) or Viddi and Nimmi (in *The Nature of Passion*) clash with the traditional values of their families. Both novels express the author's obvious delight in all she found in the West. But she was never blind to the overwhelming social problems facing India. In *Get Ready for Battle*, those problems are confronted as far as the limits of her domestic drama will allow; this is Jhabvala's darkest portrait of modern India, and the last of her novels to deal primarily with Indian characters.

In her next three novels, *A Backward Place, A New Dominion*, and *Heat and Dust*, Jhabvala moves away from the presentation of India to a portrayal of the Westerner in India, a subject she had previously broached in *Esmond in India*, and an interest in the effect of India on her Western characters. She explores the problems faced by expatriate Westerners (mostly women) and the world of often-fraudulent gurus encountered by the young Western seekers who flocked to India in the 1960s and 1970s. This shift in emphasis is also reflected in her short stories—all nine stories in *A Stronger Climate* are concerned with Westerners in India—and in her screenplays—in such films as *Shakespeare Wallah, The Guru*, and *Autobiography of a Princess*.

In *A Backward Place* Jhabvala considers whether or not it is possible for some Europeans to live in India and survive, and through the character of Judy she shows that it is possible if one is willing to adopt Indian values, to accept India on its own terms. In *A New Dominion* and *Heat and Dust* Jhabvala again shows that Westerners can remain in India and survive, as Miss Charlotte does, and as both Olivia and the unnamed narrator of *Heat and Dust* do, but the question of whether this is desirable remains largely unanswered in her fiction. For the first time, these two novels move out of Delhi and beyond the confines of the largely domestic, interior settings of her earlier novels. The landscape, the heat and the dust, become increasingly important metaphors that show how unsuitable India is for most of the Westerners who populate Jhabvala's fiction. Quite different narrative techniques are employed, too—the straightforward realist narrative method of the earlier novels gives way to a more experimental form in which the reader is addressed directly, through monologues, letters, and journal entries, both by characters and the author herself. Jhabvala attributes these innovations to the influence of her writing for the cinema.

Heat and Dust contains two parallel stories, skillfully interwoven to contrast two time periods fifty years apart. The earlier of the two stories, Olivia's story, set in 1923, invites comparison with E. M Forster's *A Passage to India*. The later story, that of the unnamed narrator, which began in response to her reading of Olivia's letters, updates the 1923 story, and reveals Jhabvala's postmodernist interest in the effect of text on life.

Since moving to America, Jhabvala's interest has moved away from Indian subjects and settings. In *In Search of Love and Beauty*, which focuses on a group of German and Austrian refugees in New York, Jhabvala writes for the first time on a sustained level about the German-Jewish background she knew as a child. At the center of this novel and her subsequent novel, *Three Continents*, is a concern with the search for identity and heritage—and an attempt to explain and understand the sense of alienation and expatriation that has been her own experience as well as that of many of her Western characters. While these novels mark a new phase in Jhabvala's writing career, it is clear to the reader familiar with her oeuvre that the concerns of her Indian fiction have not been entirely left behind; both novels share much in common with her later Indian fiction. The guru figures, Leo of *In Search of Love and Beauty* and the Rawul of *Three Continents*, recall, among others, the unprincipled Swami of *A New Dominion*, while the seekers of these novels are variations on the young questing figures like Lee of *A New Dominion* and Katie of ''How I Became a Holy Mother,'' for example. An interesting development is that for the first time in her fiction Jhabvala explores the backgrounds of the Western characters who populate her Indian fiction.

In her 1993 novel *Poet and Dancer*, India as a locale is altogether absent, and the presence of an Indian mother and son is too peripheral to the main narrative to bring the spirit of the place into the work. And so in some ways *Poet and Dancer* marks the greatest single shift in Jhabvala's career as a novelist. In other ways, though, there is still common ground between this work and her earlier fiction. At the heart of this novel is an exploration of the dichotomy between good and evil—played out through the destructive relationship between Angel and her cousin Lara, whose love Angel obsessively pursues—that is reminiscent of the destructive relationships between the many seekers and bogus gurus found in her earlier work.

Maintaining the shift away from India begun with *In Search of Love and Beauty*, India as a literal landscape exists only in the recollections of a few characters in 1995 novel, *Shards of Memory*, where the principal settings are again New York and London (specifically the limited geographical locations of Manhattan and Hampstead). Yet in other ways, India, like continental Europe, pervades the very core of this novel, and is literally in the blood of the Kopf family. *Shards of Memory* is intrinsically a family saga, concerned with four generations of the Kopf and Keller families and their involvement with ''the Master''—the latest in a long line of such spiritual leaders to appear in Jhabvala's fiction. Here, though, the question of whether or not the Master is a charlatan is of less consequence than it is in earlier novels and stories. Instead, Jhabvala's focus is entirely on the bonds of family.

The oriental and occidental locations that characterize the two major phases of her novel writing career are effectively juxtaposed in her 1998 collection of short stories, *East into Upper East*, which carries the Kiplingesque subtitle, *Plain Tales from New York and New Delhi*. Six of the stories in this robust collection are set in New Delhi, a further seven in New York's Upper East Side. The final story, ''Two Muses,'' the only exception to the two-town pattern promulgated in the title, deals with the German-Jewish community in North-West London between 1939 and 1951. Its only companion in Jhabvala's writing is ''A Birthday in London,'' included in her first collection of short stories, *Like Birds, Like Fishes*, almost 40 years ago.

Ruth Prawer Jhabvala's reputation as a writer of fiction has been built around her Indian novels, particularly the Booker prize-winning *Heat and Dust*. Her later novels show that she can write equally well about America and Europe, and suggest that she is an international writer who deserves to be numbered amongst the best novelists writing in English today.

—Ralph J. Crane

JOHNSON, Charles (Richard)

Nationality: American. **Born:** Evanston, Illinois, 23 April 1948. **Education:** Southern Illinois University, Carbondale, B.A. in journalism 1971, M.A. in philosophy 1973; State University of New York, Stony Brook, 1973–76. **Family:** Married Joan New in 1970; two children. **Career:** Reporter and cartoonist, Chicago *Tribune,* 1969–70; member of art staff, St. Louis *Proud,* Missouri, 1971–72; assistant professor, 1976–79, associate professor, 1979–82, and since 1982 professor, University of Washington, Seattle. Since 1978 fiction editor, *Seattle Review.* **Awards:** Governor's award for literature, 1983; *Callaloo* creative writing award, 1985; National Book award, 1991. **Address:** c/o Antheneum Publishers, Macmillian Publishing Company, 866 3rd Avenue, New York, New York 10022; c/o University of Washington, Department of English, Seattle, WA 98105 U.S.A.

PUBLICATIONS

Novels

Faith and the Good Thing. New York, Viking, 1974.
Oxherding Tale. Bloomington, Indiana University Press, 1982; London, Blond and Briggs, 1983; with a new introduction by the author, New York, Plume, 1995.
Middle Passage. New York, Atheneum, 1990; London, Picador, 1991.
Dreamer. New York, Scribner, 1998.

Short Stories

The Sorcerer's Apprentice: Tales and Conjuration. New York, Atheneum, 1986; London, Serpent's Tail, 1988.

Plays

Olly Olly Oxen Free. New York, French, 1988.

Television Writing: *Charlie's Pad* series, 1971; *Charlie Smith and the Fritter Tree,* 1978; *For Me Myself,* 1982; *A Place for Myself,* 1982; *Booker,* with John Allmann, 1984.

Other

Black Humor (cartoons). Chicago, Johnson, 1970.
Half-Past Nation Time (cartoons). Westlake Village, California, Aware Press, 1972.
Being and Race: Black Writing since 1970. Bloomington, Indiana Press, and London, Serpent's Tail, 1988.
I Call Myself an Artist: Writings by and about Charles Johnson, edited by Rudolph P. Byrd. Bloomington, Indiana University Press, 1999.
King: The Photobiography of Martin Luther King, Jr. (with Bob Adelman). New York, Viking Studio, 2000.
Editor, with John McCluskey, Jr., *Black Men Speaking*. Bloomington, Indiana University Press, 1997.

*

Critical Studies: *I Call Myself an Artist: Writings by and about Charles Johnson,* edited by Rudolph P. Byrd. Bloomington, Indiana University Press, 1999.

* * *

Like many contemporary writers, Charles Johnson has a particular interest in the historical novel, and he uses this form to question the nature of the self and its relation to society and history. Two of his novels, *Oxherding Tale* and *Middle Passage*, are neo-slave narratives (novels that use the first person form to recount a story of slavery), and another, *Dreamer*, follows the end of Martin Luther King, Jr.'s campaign for racial equality. Each of these novels presents a highly educated and deeply philosophical first-person narrator who undergoes a spiritual transformation as he participates in and comes to understand his connection to African-American history.

Johnson's critically acclaimed *Middle Passage* won the 1990 National Book award, and has been favorably compared to Melville's *Moby Dick.* In *Middle Passage,* Rutherford Calhoun, a newly freed slave and petty thief, seeks to avoid his personal responsibilities by working on board a slave clipper bound for Africa. During his time on ship, Calhoun becomes familiar with both the slave ship captain, Ebenezer Falcon, and the slaves, and his interaction with them forces him to revise his worldview. Falcon, an embittered dwarf wedded to the doctrine of Manifest Destiny, spouts the philosophy of dualism, of the split between mind and body, knower and known, as the natural (and just) cause of slavery. Calhoun recognizes and begins to fear his own resemblance to Captain Falcon's quest for "experience" and willingness to appropriate the possessions of others. In contrast, the slaves, from Johnson's mythical Allmuseri tribe, believe in the unity of Being, and the worst feature of slavery, in their view, is the fact that they learn the philosophy of dualism as they learn the English language. Caught in the middle when the slaves take over the ship (named *The Republic*), Calhoun increasingly learns to view life through the Allmuseri's beliefs, experiencing a death to his former self when the ship breaks apart and he is thrown into the sea, and a resurrection as the embodiment of the Allmuseri philosophy when he is rescued.

As this summary suggests, Johnson's novels work as allegories as much as they work as historical fiction. In fact, his novels are a pastiche of forms, including spiritual autobiography, tall tale, adventure story, philosophical treatise, and comedy of manners. Part of Johnson's literary goal is to draw on multiple genres and traditions in order to create novels capable of conveying the richness of African-American history. Johnson's first novel, *Faith and the Good Thing*, embeds a naturalist story within an oral tale, combining myth, fantasy, and realism. The embedded story has many similarities to Richard Wright's *Native Son*, but Faith Cross, the main character, is able to transcend the limitations placed on her by racism and socioeconomic oppression by becoming a conjurer. The philosophical traditions that Johnson's narrators share are as rich as the literary forms they narrate. Johnson's novels are filled with allusions to Buddhist and Hindu texts, Enlightenment philosophers, and Thomist theologians. But the central philosophy that underpins all of Johnson's writing is phenomenology, which he presents as the philosophy of the Allmuseri.

Thus in *Oxherding Tale*, the extensively educated, mixed-race slave Andrew Hawkins, who has met Karl Marx and can quote from Lao Tze, still has a great deal to learn from his fellow slave Reb, an Allmuseri tribesman. Without the belief in the interconnectedness of all beings, which leads to the conclusion that the "self" is a fiction, Hawkins cannot understand his relationship to either the black or the white worlds. Hawkins must first reject the beliefs of his Black Nationalist father, whose violent revolt against slavery leads to his death and the dispersal of the other plantation slaves. He must also reject his own too-easy assimilation, when his flight from the slave catcher leads him to assume a white identity. Reb releases both himself and Hawkins from the slave catcher by having no essential identity, no static self that allows the slave catcher to identify, and thus entrap, him. Neither black nor white yet both, Hawkins finally becomes free only when he can both acknowledge his slave past and imagine a future beyond the restrictions of imposed racial identity. Dividing his novel into "House and Field" and "The White World," Johnson signifies upon and updates both the fugitive slave narrative and the classic novel of passing.

Although Johnson's novels are philosophical and sometimes difficult, they are also immensely comic. Johnson's comedy permeates his entire work from character depictions to a style of dialogue that is often Wodehousian in its wit: ''Peggy Undercliff gave me what I have often read described in popular fiction as the 'eye,' though I'll not swear on it, never having seen the 'eye' at such close range before'' (*Oxherding Tale*). Much of Johnson's comedy works by inverting expectations and by throwing his characters into highly improbable situations. The story of Hawkins's conception, for instance, is a masterpiece of social satire. Because he has stayed up too late drinking with his slave, Jonathan Polkinghorne is afraid to face his wife and thus sends his slave (Hawkins's father) to spend the night with her. After enjoying herself with the slave, Anna Polkinghorne screams, locks herself in a separate wing for the rest of her life, and refuses to acknowledge Hawkins as her son.

In his most recent novel, *Dreamer*, Johnson explores the nature of the self by creating a doppelganger for Martin Luther King, Jr., and imagining how the circumstances of their lives determine their different identities. Chaym Smith, who looks so much like King that he becomes a stand-in, and who is equally well educated in philosophy and religious theory as King, nonetheless has lived an entirely different life. Where King was raised in a middle-class household, Smith was abandoned by his father. This juxtaposition allows Johnson to meditate upon the way in which social and historical forces shape identity, and conversely, how individual identity shapes history. The reception of *Dreamer* is more mixed than was the response to the neo-slave narratives, with some critics praising the empathetic portrayal of King and others criticizing what they perceive to be the lack of coherence, as Smith simply disappears partway through the novel, picked up by the FBI.

Other critical controversy surrounds Johnson's use of the supernatural. He has been criticized for overuse of the supernatural purely for reasons of effect, but this is to misunderstand both the author and his intentions. The fantastic and uncanny play an important role in disrupting the reader's ability to read Johnson's fiction according to standard generic conventions, and this in turn meshes with Johnson's goal of dismantling our conceptions of essentialist identities.

—Harry Bucknall, updated by Suzanne Lane

JOHNSON, Colin

See MUDROOROO

JOHNSON, Denis

Nationality: American. **Born:** Munich, Germany, in 1949. **Awards:** American Academy Kaufman prize, 1984; Whiting Foundation award, 1986; literature award, American Academy of Arts and Letters, 1993. **Address:** c/o Robert Cornfield, 145 W. 79th Street, New York, New York 10024–6407, U.S.A.

PUBLICATIONS

Novels

Angels. New York, Knopf, 1983; London, Chatto and Windus, 1984.
Fiskadoro. New York, Knopf, and London, Chatto and Windus, 1985.
The Stars at Noon. New York, Knopf, 1986; London, Faber, 1987.
Resuscitation of a Hanged Man. New York, Farrar Straus, 1991.
Already Dead: A California Gothic. New York, HarperCollins, 1997.
The Name of the World. New York, HarperCollins, 2000.

Short Stories

Jesus' Son. New York, Farrar, Straus, 1992.

Uncollected Short Stories

''The Taking of Our Own Lives,'' in *Three Stances of Modern Fiction,* edited by Stephen Minot and Robley Wilson, Jr. Cambridge, Massachusetts, Winthrop, 1972.
''There Comes after Here,'' in *Atlantic* (Boston), April 1972.
''Tattoos and Music,'' in *North American Review* (Cedar Falls, Iowa), Spring 1977.
''Two Men,'' in *New Yorker,* 19 September 1988.
''Work,'' in *New Yorker,* 14 November 1988.
''The Bullet's Flight,'' in *Esquire* (New York), March 1989.
''Car-Crash While Hitchhiking,'' in *Paris Review,* Spring 1989.
''Dirty Wedding,'' in *New Yorker,* 5 November 1990.

Poetry

The Man among the Seals. Iowa City, Stone Wall Press, 1969.
Inner Weather. Port Townsend, Washington, Graywolf Press, 1976.
The Incognito Lounge and Other Poems. New York, Random House, 1982.
The Veil. New York, Knopf, 1987.
The Throne of the Third Heaven of the Nations Millennium General Assembly: Poems, Collected and New. New York, HarperCollins, 1995.

*

Film Adaptations: *Jesus' Son,* 1999.

* * *

Denis Johnson's first two novels, *Angels* and *Fiskadoro,* delineate the lives of outcasts on the fringes of their societies. The first is a contemporary urban novel whose characters drift into tragedy and moral and physical decline; still, it is a novel of hope. In the second, though the landscape is bleaker, an even deeper, more elemental hope for human survival is posited. Johnson brings his considerable gifts as a poet to help explore the possibilities of persistence and redemption in two separate worlds, one in decline, the other struggling to be born.

The surface of *Angels* is sensational, melodramatic, and even savage at times. Occasionally the characters are presented as cartoon-like as Johnson depicts the contemporary world in ways that bring this work close to the absurdist novel; however, *Angels* is finally a novel more in the realistic mode, and the self-conscious gothicism is meant as a comment on the irrationalism and hysteria that have become commonplace in descriptions of contemporary urban life in the United States.

The two lower-class characters, Jamie Mays and Bill Houston, an ex-sailor and ex-convict, are losers who travel across America in a state of radical drift. What we see is a society spiritually blighted by vacuous radio, movies, and TV, and superstitious cults that function as ersatz religions; all these derive from the human need for moral purpose and personal transcendence that have everywhere been lost and which only serve to disguise the destructive forces that lay just beneath the surface, often represented in images of self-immolation: ''Scarlet light and white heat awoke her. She was in flames… . It was not her clothing, but her flesh itself that was burning.'' The setting of this hallucination is a mental ward where Jamie is taken after a psychotic break precipitated by a rape that is motivated by an almost indifferent sadism, itself the amoral outcome of a society spiritually lost, one in which self-identity is always at risk: ''For a second standing in line behind a half dozen people, she felt as if no one part of herself was connected to any other.'' Bill Houston becomes involved in a bank robbery during which he kills a bank guard, but given the circumstances of his life, it is difficult to determine moral culpability. Mainly for political reasons, he is sentenced to die in the gas chamber, but the angel of light finally prevails and Bill's life is at the end given moral dimension in his epiphany at the moment of death: ''He got it right in the dark between heartbeats, and rested there. And then he saw that another one wasn't going to come. That's it. That's the last. He looked at the dark. I would like to take this opportunity, he said, to pray for another human being.'' This is the angel of light, corresponding to Jamie's return to sanity and wholeness, and is the hope that infuses the end of the novel. However, no such hope is held out for a social healing.

Fiskadoro, Johnson's second novel, set in the Florida Keys two generations after the nuclear holocaust, is also a novel about survival, this time removed from an urban environment and put in the larger social context of the entirety of human society.

The question posed at the center of the novel is ''What must be done to ensure the rebirth of civilization?'' Several alternate societies coexist, and it is their clash and intermingling that provide the answer. Mr. Cheung represents the old pre-nuclear society built on art and rationalism; members of his group meet to try and reconstruct the Western (and to some extent, the Eastern) tradition from the bits and pieces of it that have survived: various artifacts, a book on nuclear war, a clarinet, spent radiation-sensitive buttons that declare the wearers believers in reason and science. The anti-culture, represented by Fiskadoro, a young teen, clashes with the defunct culture when Fiskadoro comes to Mr. Cheung (who is manager of the bedraggled Miami Symphony Orchestra) for clarinet lessons, as if asking Cheung to integrate him into the old cultural tradition. However, Fiskadoro has no talent for music and fails to master the instrument until at the end of the novel when he is transformed.

Fiskadoro becomes the leader of the new order, but only after he spends days among the jungle savages who destroy his memory through drugs and primitive ritual, which includes self-inflicted circumcision. This memory loss fits Fiskadoro as the harbinger, and perhaps founder, of the new world struggling to be born because, Johnson says, memory is the faculty through which history lives and culture is transmitted; memory severed makes rebirth possible. After the cleansing, the historical cycle will again be put in motion: ''Everything we have, all we are, will meet its end, will be overcome, taken up, washed away. But everything came to an end before. Now it will happen again. Many times. Again and again.'' Alternating action at the end of the novel juxtaposes Fiskadoro's rebirth with that of Cheung's grandmother, a ship-wrecked Vietnamese refugee who is the offspring of a Western father and Asian mother. She spends twenty hours in the sea awaiting rescue: ''The shock of finding herself here where she'd always been was like a birth.'' She has obvious parallels with Fiskadoro: ''… saved not because she hadn't given up, because she had, and in fact she possessed no memory of the second night… .'' Thus Johnson integrates within this complex poetic novel the themes of social and individual regeneration. The novel at times strains to keep these and other elements in balance, but manages to do so often enough to make this ambitious work succeed.

With *Already Dead,* Johnson uses biting humor in a tale that is—on the surface at least—as light as Fiskadoro's is ponderous. Though a marijuana farmer, protagonist Nelson Fairchild, Jr., is a highly sympathetic figure, and when he gets himself between a rock and a hard place, the reader is compelled to care. In the midst of this, he saves the enigmatic Carl Van Ness from a suicide attempt, and the two hatch a scheme to rescue Fairchild's fortunes. As the book progresses, however, Nelson begins to wonder if Carl is not really his worst problem. Particularly compelling is Johnson's portrayal of the northern California setting: ''hills above them massed with redwoods and the waves beating themselves to pieces in the mist below.''

—Peter Desy

JOHNSON, Diane

Nationality: American. **Born:** Diane Lain in Moline, Illinois, 28 April 1934. **Education:** Stephens College, Columbia, Missouri, 1951–53, A.A. 1953; University of Utah, Salt Lake City, B.A. 1957; University of California, Los Angeles (Woodrow Wilson fellow), M.A. 1966, Ph.D. 1968. **Family:** Married 1) B. Lamar Johnson, Jr., in 1953, two sons and two daughters; 2) John Frederic Murray in 1968. **Career:** Member of the Department of English, University of California, Davis, 1968–87. **Awards:** American Association of University Women fellowship, 1968; Guggenheim fellowship, 1977; American Academy Rosenthal award, 1979; Strauss Living award, 1987. **Agent:** Lynn Nesbit, New York, New York. **Address:** 24 Edith Street, San Francisco, California 94133, U.S.A.

Publications

Novels

Fair Game. New York, Harcourt Brace, 1965.

Loving Hands at Home. New York, Harcourt Brace, 1968; London, Heinemann, 1969.

Burning. New York, Harcourt Brace, and London, Heinemann, 1971.

The Shadow Knows. New York, Knopf, 1974; London, Bodley Head, 1975.

Lying Low. New York, Knopf, 1978; London, Bodley Head, 1979.

Persian Nights. New York, Knopf, and London, Chatto and Windus, 1987.

Health and Happiness. New York, Knopf, 1990; London, Chatto and Windus, 1991.

Le Divorce. New York, Dutton, 1997.

Le Mariage. New York, Dutton, 2000.

Uncollected Short Stories

''An Apple, An Orange,'' in *Prize Stories 1973,* edited by William Abrahams. New York, Doubleday, 1973.

Plays

Screenplays: *The Shining,* with Stanley Kubrick, 1980.

Other

The True History of the First Mrs. Meredith and Other Lesser Lives. New York, Knopf, 1972; London, Heinemann, 1973.
Terrorists and Novelists. New York, Knopf, 1982.
Dashiell Hammett: A Life. New York, Random House, 1983; as *The Life of Dashiell Hammett,* London, Chatto and Windus, 1984.
Natural Opium. New York, Knopf, and London, Chatto and Windus, 1993.

*

Critical Studies: Article by Judith S. Baughman, in *Dictionary of Literary Biography Yearbook 1980,* edited by Karen L. Rood, Jean W. Ross, and Richard Ziegfeld, Detroit, Gale, 1981; *Women Writers of the West Coast: Speaking of Their Lives and Careers,* edited by Marilyn Yalom, Santa Barbara, California, Capra Press, 1983.

Diane Johnson comments:

(1986) I try not to think about my novels in sum too directly; but I guess I think of them as serious comic novels on subjects of contemporary concern. At the moment I'm writing a novel (set in Iran) about being American, and about political meddling, being a woman, relationships and ideas. I think these are pretty much the subjects of my other novels too. This is the first one not set in California.

* * *

In *Fair Game,* Diane Johnson's first novel, the characters' movement is toward pairing off and finding stability, despite some outward denials that this is what they want. The characters here are ''types'': the frustrated virgin, the ambitious executive, the frustrated executive, the ambitious writer, and the libidinous eccentric writer (clearly modeled on Henry Miller). Only in some of the matchmaking and in making the woman writer the author of a children's book taken up by intellectuals, does Johnson show much originality in dealing with the clichéd material.

Beginning with *Loving Hands at Home* the momentum of the characters' lives tends toward the splitting of bonds between people; man-woman love relationships in particular require heroic efforts to sustain them. In Johnson's later novels the women characters stand almost completely alone.

On the first page of *Fair Game* a man is said to have a knack for finding ''moments of truth'' in the course of any experience. Most of Johnson's protagonists are sensitized—at times to an obsessive degree—to this search for epiphanies. In *The Shadow Knows* N. Hexam is haunted by her premonition of evil and probes every occurrence for significance; Ouida in *Lying Low* believes in ''old'' magic, and watches for signs. And, as Karen Fry says in *Loving Hands at Home,* ''It is odd how events follow suspicions, as if, by wondering about things, you cause them to happen.'' This is often the case in Johnson's work, though the characters are never prepared for the form these conjured-up events ultimately take. Despite this hunger for signs (and, in the early novels, a glut of psychiatrists) Johnson's characters are not particularly inward-looking; the outside world has to nudge or shake them. Karen Fry, for example, discovers she is unhappy with her life only after she impulsively accepts a motorcycle ride from a stranger and falls off: ''A pratfall in the middle of Santa Monica Boulevard is too large a symbol to be overlooked.'' Karen, married into a tradition-bound Mormon family, longs to be like a shiftless girl she knew when she was younger; a girl who, in Karen's mind, directed her own fate in defiance of convention. Karen finally does free herself, becomes ''shiftless,'' and takes up residence on the sand at the Pacific beach. There she creates her own symbol: a huge baroque sandcastle she contentedly lets the waves destroy because she knows she has done her work on it well.

In *Burning* the jolt that forces Barney and Bingo Edwards to look at themselves is the removal of a high hedge that kept out the sight of the disturbing, passionate lives of their psychiatrist neighbor and his patients. Bingo is a perfect wife, ''infinitely erudite ... witty when she wasn't depressed,'' and the mother of two. But when she stands in for a junkie mother whose children are about to be taken by the state, her truthful answers to a bank of psychological tests classify her as an unfit mother. Here, as in all Johnson's novels except *Fair Game,* the main female character encounters women who personify hidden aspects of her own makeup: in Bingo's case, the unfit mother and promiscuous women. With their protective hedge gone, Bingo and Barney are infected with the neighbor's passions and the neighborhood burns—literally.

If the problem in these first three novels is how to attain and manage a passion-filled, self-determinate life, the problem in *Lying Low* and *The Shadow Knows* is not one of escaping the clichéd life, but how to be protected from slipping out of such a life into something truly horrible. In *Lying Low* Marybeth lives ''underground,'' in fear of imprisonment for her part in a political bombing that took a life. Her life of passionate commitment has led her to a decade of the most mundane, restricted kind of life. Marybeth's landlady, Theo, is a dancer who chose the unsung life rather than risk failure trying to become a prima ballerina. Marybeth and Ouida, a Brazilian girl who is hiding from officials who want to have her deported, hide and live in fear of discovery, but when tragedy comes it comes not to them but to Theo while she is trying to move out of her mundane life and do something worthwhile for others.

The Shadow Knows is Johnson's most complex novel, partly because its subject is the indeterminate, lurking nature of evil. N. Hexam begins the new year with a prophetic dread she interprets as a premonition that she will be murdered. As in *Loving Hands at Home,* the root of her fear is ''the realization that life can change on you, can darken like a rainy day; wretchedness and dread can overtake the lightest heart.'' It is this dread that is N. Hexam's worst enemy. For her evil is a closing circle with its center nowhere and its circumference all around her. (Johnson has said that *The Shadow Knows* was in part intended to show how race relations stood at the time of its writing, 1974, but the blackness of the two women that figure most prominently in N. Hexam's life is not their most important attribute; what is important about these women is that they live out two of N. Hexam's own possible fates: life drives one mad, while the other is killed by a violent man.)

All through *The Shadow Knows* N. Hexam tries to solve the puzzle of how and from where the anticipated evil will strike. The method she uses is to conceive an ideal Famous Inspector, someone part lover and part Sherlock Holmes, to whom she compares her own efforts at finding the answers she seeks. (Still, she knows such a Famous Inspector would be unable to understand her fears, because he would be male. Here, more clearly than in her other novels,

Johnson insists there is a basic irreconcilable difference between women and men based in their different fears.) When a real life counterpart of this Famous Inspector appears, his name is Dyce, ''suggesting the tincture of chance.'' He tells her many mysteries are insoluble, and so is the voice not of reason but of reality. As in *Lying Low* the anticipated evil does manifest itself, though in a form N. Hexam never anticipates. Her reaction is one of relief: now that she truly knows evil (''I ... have taken on the thinness and the lightness of a shadow ...'') she can live with it.

One might expect *Le Mariage* to precede *Le Divorce,* but exactly the opposite is the case. In the latter book, Isabel Walker, a high-spirited but disorganized drop-out from Berkeley film school, goes to Paris to rally round her stepsister Roxy. Roxy has one child and is pregnant with another; meanwhile, her French husband has left her for another woman. In the aftermath, much of which centers around a valuable painting disputed in the divorce settlement, Isabel gets an education in the conflicts of men and women, French and American. *Le Mariage* is not a sequel, though it is set in Paris and one of the characters from the earlier book, the faithless husband Antoine de Persand, joins the ensemble cast in a rollicking tale of misunderstanding, misadventure, and romance.

—William C. Bamberger

JOHNSON, Stephanie

Nationality: New Zealander. **Born:** Auckland, New Zealand, 1961. **Family:** Married Tim Woodhouse; three children. **Career:** Actress, temporary secretary, 1980s; writer and homemaker, 1990s—. Lives in Auckland, New Zealand. **Awards:** Bruce Mason Memorial Playwright's Award.

PUBLICATIONS

Novels

Crimes of Neglect. Auckland, New Zealand, New Women's Press, 1992.
The Heart's Wild Surf. London, Vintage, 1996.
The Whistler. Auckland, New Zealand, Vintage, 1998.

Short Stories

The Glass Whittler: And Other Stories. New York, Penguin, 1989.
All the Tenderness Left in the World: Short Stories. Dunedin, New Zealand, University of Otago Press, 1993.

Other

Editor, with Graham Beattie, *Penguin 25 New Fiction.* Auckland, New Zealand, Penguin, 1998.

* * *

For a young writer, Stephanie Johnson is surprisingly well published in the genres of the novel, short fiction, and poetry, and her dramatic works have been extensively produced on stage, over radio, in film, and on television. She is a reviewer and commentator on the arts, as well as being a drawing card at literary festivals, where she performs with flair and vigor. Johnson spent much of the 1980s living in Australia, a setting for her first and third novels. The second novel, *The Heart's Wild Surf,* explores the Pacific and Fijian antecedents of Johnson's New Zealand family.

Johnson, university-educated in history and drama, has a sharp satiric eye and a mordant wit, yet she shows sympathy for the human condition, in particular for derelicts, misfits, and for the innocence of youth, soon to meet the corruption of adult life. Basing her two historical novels on thorough research, she uses realism with post-modern touches, and a leavening of magic realism to create present and—in *The Whistler*—imaginative evocations of future dystopias.

In *Crimes of Neglect,* Johnson creates an anti-heroine, Bea, aged forty-two, failed wife, mother, and erstwhile failed cellist, ''huge and ugly with open pores and dull red hair,'' often drunk and dirty, whose crimes have been to avoid all responsibility and to neglect traditional female duties. She is a ''complete hedonist and selfish to the last,'' someone who has avoided responsibility by adhering blindly to her ''Driftwood Theory,'' that she merely drifts at the mercy of the currents of life. When her daughter, who cares and is anxious for her, tells her that she must now stand on her own two feet, Bea is probably beyond redemption: ''What an impossible idea, to look after myself.... How could I? I don't know how.'' Johnson plays with conventional notions of female beauty and novel heroines, of the efficacy of the nuclear family in a disintegrating society, and she reverses the normal child-parent roles. Bea is somehow made worthy by having a daughter who loves her. Some enlightenment comes to Bea in the last chapter as she prepares to latch onto a new man to take responsibility for her: ''I would like to believe that my involvement [in the death and destruction that has followed her] was coincidental .... But I can't, of course.'' Terrible as Bea is, she is treated with sympathy by Johnson. Bea's conventional sisters are treated more harshly, as their more conforming female paths lead also to disaster. They lack the redeeming feature of Bea: her subversive and anarchic spirit. A cellist herself, Johnson cannot reject totally another cellist, Bea, however badly she plays.

The Heart's Wild Surf is a colonial novel, set in Fiji in 1918 during the British administration and the influenza epidemic, written from hindsight with all the post-modern tricks of a satiric post-colonial writer. Based on Johnson's own family history, the novel features the McNabs, chandlers and sailmakers working out of Suva. Being in trade, and connected only too recently with the stage and its elastic morals, the family is considered not respectable by fellow Englishmen, striving to keep up appearances before the natives. The McNabs are not coping with the epidemic, nor with the farce of colonial overlordship and increasingly restless natives; the First World War has left its toll on a son. Life is unpredictable and threatening, symbolized by a rampant tropical vine that destroys the Church and entwines almost unto death the innocent Olive, perhaps the only innocent person in the narrative. Johnson awards colonialism the full Technicolor satiric treatment: the stiff Brits, unable to forsake rubber corsets, flannel petticoats, fur stoles, trying to live out a raj of their own with support from Indian servants and a boost from gin-laced teapots. Romantic notions of a Pacific paradise, personified by an earlier visit from Rupert Brooke, who conducted an affair with the mad Elvira McNab (Gothic elements abound), are stubbed out by the present realities of British failure to adapt to that paradisiacal life. Being there, they have learned nothing from it, and have corrupted Paradise as well.

The story is narrated through the eyes of young Olive, who has second sight (elements of magic realism), and of her mother, dying of influenza. It is through the new generation of Olive that some accommodation with Fiji might be achieved: she does things her own instinctive way, not bound by the idiocies of British colonial heritage.

Johnson's novel *The Whistler* is her most difficult to fathom, and has been liked least by critics who point to its disjointed and episodic nature. Johnson admits to working in short infrequent bursts to accommodate bringing up her young family, and offers that this might lead to the work lacking clear narrative drive and cohesion. The book is set in dystopic Sydney in 2318, after collapse of the environment through exploitation and nuclear accident, when democracy is sacrificed to the corporate principle (rule by autocratic Tower Kings), when genetic modification has led to weird mutations of people and animals, and life itself seems in its terminal stage. Johnson calls this novel her protest, an angry book prompted by what she sees as the dumbing down of knowledge, the deletion of historical memory (which gives cohesion to society), the shrinkage of communality, and the elevation of economic agendas above human needs. She believes, and works out through the novel, the idea that only a sense of history may rescue the world from such an ignominious fate. Clinging still to a knowledge of the past in the novel is an underground group (inhabiting a sewer) who, as Record Keepers, keep hope alive. Hope exists also with the severely mutated boy, Vernon, and his mother, who maintain an old library of outlawed books. The story is narrated mostly through the "voice" of a mutant legless dog, the Whistler, who as well as narrating the story via his brain linkage to a computer, acts as the link between past and present, in that he has experienced many incarnations and deaths, from his presence at the birth of Christ, until now, possibly his last incarnation. The episodic nature of his narrative comes from his retelling of each incarnation as a complete episode. He puts his story on record, but the question is whether anyone will read it and learn from it.

The novel abounds in black humor, filth reminiscent of Gulliver among the Yahoos—in all Johnson's novel she dwells on human filth and detritus as symptom of inner lack of health and right thinking. There are gothic elements, mystery, and adventure (will dog and boy find out who Vernon's father is? Will they reach Grandfather and the Record Keepers before all remaining memory is erased?), science fiction and the nightmare of laboratory experiment, as well the traditional simple joys of telling a good story: the dog has plenty of them from former lives. In her novels Johnson reveals a diverse and genuinely creative mind, drawing on widely disparate material and methods of telling.

—Heather Murray

JOHNSTON, Jennifer (Prudence)

Nationality: Irish. **Born:** Ireland, 12 January 1930; daughter of the dramatist Denis Johnston. **Education:** Park House School, Dublin; Trinity College, Dublin. **Family:** Married 1) Ian Smyth in 1951, two sons and two daughters; 2) David Gilliland in 1976. **Awards:** Pitman award, 1972; *Yorkshire Post* award, 1973, 1980; Whitbread award, 1979. Fellow, Royal Society of Literature, 1979; member, Aosdana. D.Litt.: University of Ulster, Coleraine, 1984. **Address:** Brook Hall, Culmore Road, Derry BT48 8JE, Northern Ireland.

PUBLICATIONS

Novels

The Captains and the Kings. London, Hamish Hamilton, 1972.
The Gates. London, Hamish Hamilton, 1973.
How Many Miles to Babylon? London, Hamish Hamilton, and New York, Doubleday, 1974.
Shadows on Our Skin. London, Hamish Hamilton, 1977; New York, Doubleday, 1978.
The Old Jest. London, Hamish Hamilton, 1979; New York, Doubleday, 1980.
The Christmas Tree. London, Hamish Hamilton, 1981; New York, Morrow, 1982.
The Railway Station Man. London, Hamish Hamilton, 1984; New York, Viking, 1985.
Fool's Sanctuary. London, Hamish Hamilton, 1987; New York, Viking, 1988.
The Invisible Worm. London, Sinclair-Stevenson, 1991; New York, Carroll and Graf, 1993.
The Illusionist. London, Sinclair-Stevenson, 1995.
Finbar's Hotel (serial novel, with others), edited by Dermot Bolger. London, Picador, 1997; Dublin, New Island Books, 1997; San Diego, California, Harcourt Brace, 1999.
Two Moons. London, Review, 1998.

Uncollected Short Stories

"Trio," in *Best Irish Short Stories 2,* edited by David Marcus. London, Elek, 1977.
"The Theft," in *Irish Ghost Stories,* edited by Joseph Hone. London, Hamish Hamilton, 1977.

Plays

The Nightingale and Not the Lark (produced Dublin, 1979). London, French, 1981.
Indian Summer (produced Belfast, 1983).
Andante un Poco Mosso, in *The Best Short Plays 1983,* edited by Ramon Delgado. Radnor, Pennsylvania, Chilton, 1983.
The Porch (produced Dublin, 1986).
Three Monologues: Twinkletoes, Mustn't Forget High Noon, and Christine. Belfast, Lagan Press, 1995.
The Desert Lullaby: A Play in Two Acts. Belfast, Lagan Press, 1996.

*

Critical Studies: "Three Writers of the Big House: Elizabeth Bowen, Molly Keane and Jennifer Johnston" by Bridget O'Toole, in *Across a Roaring Hill: The Protestant Imagination in Modern Ireland* edited by Gerald Dawe and Edna Longley, Belfast, Blackstaff Press, 1985; *Studies in the Fiction of Jennifer Johnston and Mary Lavin* by Eileen Fauset. Ft. Lauderdale, Florida, Nova Southeastern University, 1998.

* * *

Jennifer Johnston is often described as a Big House novelist, writing in the tradition (beginning with Maria Edgeworth and continuing to William Trevor) of those who delineate the plight of the

Anglo-Irish, strangers alike in Ireland and England, living an attenuated half-life of divided loyalties and allegiances in crumbling houses filled with the ghostly remains of better days and a broader culture, more and more alienated from the world of the native Irish around them, treated by their former inferiors with, at best, indifference, at worst, open hostility.

There are, of course, reasons for grounding Johnston in this tradition. All her novels focus on a situation in which a member of the Anglo-Irish is led to try to overcome their political and personal isolation by creating a relationship, across the barriers of national identity, class, religion, and political allegiance, with a member of the native Irish. This attempt is doomed to failure from the start; the barriers to be surmounted being too well entrenched in time and history.

Yet, in spite of the apparent familiarity of the setting and subject matter, and even the depiction of family relationships in her novels, it is far too limiting to regard Johnston merely as a Big House novelist. In a 1987 article she said:

> What the characters in my books are trying to do ... is to keep for a few moments their heads above the waters of inexorable history. ''I know that in the end I will drown,'' they shout. ''But at this moment I am waving.''

This statement encapsulates a central aspect of Johnston's parable-like novels. The personal and the historical are so intertwined, with metaphors and allusions resonating from one sphere to the other, that it is impossible to say whether what is paramount is a portrait of class at a crucial historical juncture, modulated through the experiences of particular characters or the examination of personal situations of alienation, loneliness, choice, and the necessity for and function of art against the determining and limiting background of time, history, and tradition.

Most of Johnston's characters are would-be artists, musicians, or writers. They are concerned with the relationship between art and life; the formality and perfection of art and the shapelessness and failure of life. Many of them look for subjects for their art and, because she has a fondness for first-person, retrospective narratives, that subject is often their own lives and the crucial moments when the choices that determined the shape of those lives were made. To this extent, many of her novels are *Bildungsroman*—portraits of the artist as a young man or woman, even if recollected from age or at the point of death. The themes that are crucial in this, essentially personal, focus are the forces of family, society, and tradition that entrap the writer. As Alex Moore shapes his life before his execution (*How Many Miles to Babylon?*) he makes it clear that it is his rejection by his cold, manipulative mother and the social pressures that compel him, against his own inclination, to be ''an Officer and a Gentleman'' that have led directly to his impending death. The focus seems to be less on the background of World War I or the 1916 rising than on Alex's sense of silence and isolation in the murderous battle between his parents. However, it is also clear that Alex's parents represent different allegiances, different senses of history. He is caught in more than a personal impasse. He is torn between conflicting roles, identities, allegiances. His attempt to escape in his companionship with Jerry Crowe, cannot succeed. The ''inexorable'' force of ''history'' is against it. That history conditions Jerry Crowe, too. One of the achievements of Johnston's novels is her capacity to suggest levels of complexity beneath the apparent simplicity and lyricism of her prose. Jerry is not presented as the stereotyped ''peasant'' living in harmony with the land and his own senses, the opposite to Alex's repressed intellectualism. Jerry too is sent to his death by his mother and is, in his way, as alienated from his home and class as is Alex. In the presentation of these destructive mothers (and in the naming of the horse which the two young men train for the Morrigan, the Celtic Goddess of war), Johnston is extending the scope of her themes from conflicted nationalisms to a consideration of the human capacity for violence.

It is noticeable that all of her novels deal with war in one form or another. Two are set against the background of World War I. *The Old Jest* and *Fool's Sanctuary* deal with the period of the Black and Tans. *Shadows on Our Skin* and *The Railway Station Man* are concerned with the modern IRA. *The Christmas Tree* is centrally concerned with the holocaust. In one sense, Johnston's novels represent an answer to the question of whether it is possible to deal with the reality of contemporary violence in the north without being programmatic or strident. She is able to do this because the violence is seen as both almost unimportant and as a permanent part of human experience. The essential question about war and death is how the experience is used, and in this aspect, there has been a notable development in the novels. The early ones concentrate on defeat. The wave before the drowning is very subdued; the characters are in retreat from life, insulating themselves behind writing, drinking, or accepting that there is no possibility of a relationship with the world or with another individual. In the later novels, however, the outlook is more hopeful. Even though Constance Keating dies (*The Christmas Tree*) she has left behind her a child who will provide hope for Jacob's future, and she has got young Bridie May to arrange her papers into a, finally, publishable book. The latest novel, *The Invisible Worm,* is the most ambitious to date, providing in its story of incest and abuse of a daughter by her successful politician father, a chilling metaphor of the state of modern Ireland, and a new variation of Johnston's old reworking of the stereotype of ''Mother Ireland.'' It also continues to suggest that moments of personal happiness can be snatched in spite of violence and madness and that the ghosts of the past which haunt all Johnson's characters, can be appeased.

—Anne Clune

JOLLEY, (Monica) Elizabeth

Nationality: Australian. **Born:** Monica Elizabeth Knight in Birmingham, England, 4 June 1923; moved to Australia, 1959; became citizen, 1978. **Education:** Friends' School, Sibford, Oxfordshire, 1934–40; St. Thomas' Hospital, London (orthopaedic nursing training), 1940–43; Queen Elizabeth Hospital, Birmingham (general training), 1943–46. **Family:** Married Leonard Jolley; two daughters and one son. **Career:** Salesperson, nurse, and domestic, 1960s. Part-time tutor in creative writing, Fremantle Arts Centre, Western Australia, from 1974; part-time tutor in English from 1978, writer-in-residence, 1982, and since 1984 half-time tutor in English, Western Australian Institute of Technology, Bentley; half-time lecturer and writer-in-residence from 1986, and since 1989 honorary writer-in-residence, Curtin University of Technology, Perth, Western Australia. Writer-in-residence, Scarborough Senior High School, Winter 1980, and Western Australian College of Advanced Education, Nedlands, 1983. President, Australian Society of Authors, 1985–86. **Awards:** State of

Victoria prize, for short story, 1966, 1981, 1982; Sound Stage prize, for radio play, 1975; Wieckhard prize, 1975; Australian Writers Guild prize, for radio play, 1982; *Western Australia Week* prize, 1983; *The Age* Book of the Year award, 1983, 1989; Australia Council Literature Board senior fellowship, 1984; New South Wales Premier's award, 1985; Australian Bicentennial National Literary award, 1986; Miles Franklin award, 1987; Fellowship of Australian Writers Ramsden plaque, 1988; Australian Literary Society Gold Medal award, 1991, for *Cabin Fever;* The France-Australia award, 1993, for translation of *The Sugar Mother;* The Premier of West Australia's prize, 1993, for *Central Mischief;* National Book Connail Banjo award, 1994, for *The Georges' Wife.* D.Tech.: Western Australian Institute of Technology, 1986. Officer, Order of Australia, 1988. **Agent:** Caroline Lurie, Australian Literary Management, 2-A Armstrong Street, Middle Park, Victoria 3206. **Address:** 28 Agett Road, Claremont, Western Australia 6010, Australia.

PUBLICATIONS

Novels

Palomino. Collingwood, Victoria, Outback Press, and London, Melbourne House, 1980; New York, Persea, 1987.
The Newspaper of Claremont Street. Fremantle, Western Australia, Fremantle Arts Centre Press, 1981; New York, Viking, 1987; London, Penguin, 1988.
Mr. Scobie's Riddle. Ringwood, Victoria, Penguin, 1983; New York, Penguin, 1984; London, Penguin, 1985.
Miss Peabody's Inheritance. St. Lucia, University of Queensland Press, 1983; New York, Viking, 1984; London, Viking, 1985.
Milk and Honey. Fremantle, Western Australia, Fremantle Arts Centre Press, 1984; New York, Persea, 1986; London, Viking, 1987.
Foxybaby. St. Lucia, University of Queensland Press, and New York, Viking, 1985; London, Viking, 1986.
The Well. Ringwood, Victoria, London, and New York, Viking, 1986.
The Sugar Mother. Fremantle, Western Australia, Fremantle Arts Centre Press, and New York, Harper, 1988; London, Viking, 1989.
My Father's Moon. Ringwood, Victoria, and London, Viking, and New York, Harper, 1989.
Cabin Fever. Ringwood, Victoria, Viking, 1990; London, Sinclair-Stevenson, and New York, Harper Collins, 1991.
The Georges' Wife. Ringwood, Victoria, Viking, 1993.
The Orchard Thieves. Ringwood, Victoria, Viking, 1995.
Lovesong. Victoria, Australia, and New York, Viking, 1997.

Short Stories

Five Acre Virgin and Other Stories. Fremantle, Western Australia, Fremantle Arts Centre Press, 1976.
The Travelling Entertainer and Other Stories. Fremantle, Western Australia, Fremantle Arts Centre Press, 1979.
Woman in a Lampshade. Ringwood, Victoria, Penguin, 1983; New York and London, Penguin, 1986.
Stories. Fremantle, Western Australia, Fremantle Arts Centre Press, 1984; New York, Viking, 1988; London, Penguin, 1989.
Fellow Passengers: Collected Stories, edited by Barbara Milech. Ringwood, Victoria, New York, Penguin Books, 1997.

Uncollected Short Stories

''The Talking Bricks,'' in *Summer's Tales 2,* edited by Kylie Tennant. Melbourne and London, Macmillan, and New York, St. Martin's Press, 1965.
''The Rhyme,'' in *Westerly* (Nedlands, Western Australia), no. 4, 1967.
''The Sick Vote,'' in *Quadrant* (Sydney), vol. 12, no. 5, 1968.
''The Well-Bred Thief,'' in *South Pacific Stories,* edited by Chris and Helen Tiffin. St. Lucia, Queensland, SPACLALS, 1980.
''Mark F,'' in *The True Life Story of ... ,* edited by Jan Craney and Esther Caldwell. St. Lucia, University of Queensland Press, 1981.
''Night Report,'' ''It's about Your Daughter Mrs. Page,'' and ''Poppy Seed and Sesame Rings,'' in *Frictions,* edited by Anna Gibbs and Alison Tilson. Fitzroy, Victoria, Sybylla, 1982.
''Night Runner,'' in *Room to Move,* edited by Suzanne Falkiner. Sydney, Allen and Unwin, 1985.
''Bathroom Dance,'' in *Transgressions,* edited by Don Anderson. Ringwood, Victoria, Penguin, 1986.
''Frederick the Great Returns to Fairfields,'' in *Portrait: A West Coast Collection,* edited by B.R. Coffey and Wendy Jenkins. Fremantle, Western Australia, Fremantle Arts Centre Press, 1986.
''This Flickering, Foxy Man, My Father,'' in *Vogue Australia* (Sydney), October 1986.
''Mr. Berrington,'' in *Australian Literary Quarterly,* April 1987.
''Melon Jam,'' in *The Crankworth Bequest and Other Stories,* edited by Jennifer Haynes and Barry Carozzi. Adelaide, Australian Association for the Teaching of English, 1987.
''A Miracle of Confluence,'' in *Landfall* (Christchurch), no. 2, 1988.
''727 Chester Road,'' in *Southern Review* (Adelaide), vol. 21, no. 3, 1988.
''The Fellmonger,'' in *Eight Voices of the Eighties,* edited by Gillian Whitlock. St. Lucia, University of Queensland Press, 1989.
''My Mother's Visit,'' in *Westerly* (Nedlands, Western Australia), vol. 34, no. 4, 1989.
''The Widow's House,'' in *Expressway,* edited by Helen Daniel. Ringwood, Victoria, Penguin, 1989.
''The Goose Path,'' in *Best Short Stories 1990,* edited by Giles Gordon and David Hughes. London, Heinemann, 1990; as *The Best English Short Stories 1990,* New York, Norton, 1990.
''The Widder Tree Shadder Murder,'' in *Crimes for a Summer Christmas,* edited by Stephen Knight. Sydney, Allen and Unwin, 1990.

Plays

Woman in a Lampshade (broadcast 1979). Published in *Radio Quartet,* Fremantle, Western Australia, Fremantle Arts Centre Press, 1980.

Radio Plays: *Night Report,* 1975; *The Performance,* 1976; *The Shepherd on the Roof,* 1977; *The Well-Bred Thief,* 1977; *Woman in a Lampshade,* 1979; *Two Men Running,* 1981; *Paper Children,* 1988; *Little Lewis Has Had a Lovely Sleep,* 1990.; *Off the Air: Nine Plays for Radio.* Ringwood, Victoria, Penguin Books, 1995.

Poetry

Diary of a Weekend Farmer. Fremantle, Western Australia, Fremantle Arts Centre Press, 1993.

Other

Travelling Notebook: Literature Notes. Fremantle, Western Australia, Arts Access, 1978.
Central Mischief. Ringwood, Victoria, Viking, 1992.

*

Manuscript Collections: Mitchell Library, Sydney.

Critical Studies: Articles by Jolley and by Laurie Clancy, in *Australian Book Review* (Melbourne), November 1983; Helen Garner, in *Meanjin* (Melbourne), no. 2, 1983; ''Between Two Worlds'' by A.P. Riemer, in *Southerly* (Sydney), 1983; ''The Goddess, the Artist, and the Spinster'' by Dorothy Jones, in *Westerly* (Nedlands, Western Australia), no. 4, 1984; Joan Kirkby, in *Meanjin* (Melbourne), no. 4, 1984; Martin Harrison, in *The Age Monthly Review* (Melbourne), May 1985; *Elizabeth Jolley: New Critical Essays* edited by Delys Bird and Brenda Walker, Sydney, Angus and Robertson, 1991; *Bio-Fictions: Brian Matthews, Drusilla Modjeska, and Elizabeth Jolley* by Helen Thomson. Townsville, Queensland, Foundation for Australian Literary Studies, 1994.

Elizabeth Jolley comments:

(1991) In my writing I try to explore and celebrate the small things in human life. I am interested in people and their needs and feelings. I work with imagination from moments of truth and awareness. Characters stay with me for years.

* * *

Elizabeth Jolley has had perhaps the most meteoric rise to fame of any Australian writer during the last quarter of the twentieth century. Apart from stories in anthologies and journals Jolley had had no work published until 1976 when, at the age of fifty-three, her collection *Five Acre Virgin and Other Stories* appeared under the aegis of the newly formed Fremantle Arts Centre Press. Since then her rate of publication has been as phenomenal as the rise in critical acclaim of her work. The stories were written over a period of sixteen years prior to publication in book form and show already her peculiar combination of unsentimental realism and original, often bizarre humor. The title itself suggests one of the most pervasive themes in her early work. ''There's nothing like having a piece of land,'' a protagonist in several of the stories says. ''Having a piece of land'' is crucial to the characters in these works, many of whom are dispossessed or migrants or both. They have come from Vienna, where the author's father grew up, or the Black Country of England where she herself lived, or Holland from where the recurring figure of Uncle Bernard migrated. They struggle all their lives to buy the talismanic five acres only to find out that they cannot live off them. They lie and blackmail in order to stay on other people's land. Adam, in ''Adam's Wife,'' one of the most powerful and somber stories that Jolley has written, even marries a retarded woman in order to gain possession of her miserable shack and few acres.

Jolley's second collection, *The Travelling Entertainer,* contains her longer stories from much the same period and shows her going back and revising and reworking the same material—themes, characters, landscapes, situations and motifs, even names. As well as the preoccupation with land again, the stories contain many elements that appear throughout her work: allusions to music (especially Beethoven), to literature (especially Tolstoy), the interest in nursing homes and hospitals, the figure of the defeated salesman, the migrants from Holland and the Black Country including Uncle Bernard again, and the first of Jolley's many treatments of lesbian relationships and of women offering themselves to other women as a form of comfort or consolation or even occasionally as a means of achieving power. A lesbian relationship is at the center of her first and least typical novel, *Palomina,* which was written partly in the late 1950s, partly in 1962, and then rewritten over 1970, 1973, and 1974 before finally appearing in 1980. It is a lyrical, even reverential account of a love affair between a sixty-year-old deregistered doctor and another woman barely half her age. It is totally devoid of her usual humor and sense of the incongruous and despite the then controversial subject the two women behave with such relentless nobility towards each other that they threaten to become merely boring. *The Newspaper of Claremont Street* is vintage Jolley, not her most profound book but a delightfully amusing and at times quite poignant one. The heroine of this novella is a cleaning woman known as Newspaper, or Weekly, because she gathers gossip from her rich clients and passes it on to the rest of the community.

Mr. Scobie's Riddle placed Jolley instantly in the forefront of Australian novelists. Set in the appalling nursing home of St. Christopher and St. Jude, the novel gives full vent to her penchant for mordant and grotesque humor; it is both hilarious and horrifying and yet its triumph is that it avoids the extremes of seeing the aged people of the home as either the victims of society's cruelty and indifference on the one hand, or merely comic eccentrics on the other. *Woman in a Lampshade* is an assured collection of stories, though there is little in it to surprise readers of the author's earlier work, while *Miss Peabody's Inheritance* is an earlier novella, rewritten, which cuts back and forth between two separate and interrelated stories. At the end of the book, the two stories, set in England and Australia, converge in an unexpected way to make a comment on a theme that increasingly concerns Jolley in her later work: the relationship between life and art, and between reality and fantasy.

Throughout the 1980s Jolley continued her prolific output, confirming her reputation and winning all major Australian literary awards at some stage or other. The short novel *Milk and Honey* is a strange parable and a darkly disturbing, somber book. *Foxybaby,* on the other hand, returns more to the bizarrely comic and almost surreal mode of *Mr. Scobie's Riddle. The Well* is a fusion of Grimm fairytale (there are many images and motifs to do with fairytales) and psychological thriller, about two women who lower a man down into a well after they believe they have killed him in a car accident. The significance of the well itself, as both fact and symbol, steadily expands as disturbing ripples swell out from the initial action. The title of *The Sugar Mother* refers to the surrogate mother used by one of the characters in this strange but delicate novel in which most of the meanings are both subterranean and suggestive, the comedy present but muted and somber.

But perhaps Jolley's finest achievements came later, with the publication of *My Father's Moon* and *Cabin Fever.* Here Jolley has returned to her roots, to what Yeats called ''the foul rag and bone shop of the heart,'' in order to reassess her life and work. What the critic Helen Daniel said of *My Father's Moon*—that it is ''the novel at the heart of all her work''—is equally true of its successor and the two books read in fact like the first two parts of a closely autobiographical and linked trilogy. Their protagonist is Vera or Veronica Wright and the setting is England in all the misery of its immediate postwar austerity. *My Father's Moon* depicts Vera as a young girl, growing up to become a student nurse during the war and becoming pregnant by a worthless doctor. By the time of *Cabin Fever* her lover is dead, she has given birth to a daughter and become a qualified nurse. Vera speculates at one point on ''Whether things are written down or they dwell somewhere within and surface unbidden at anytime.'' The two novels are a record of that unbidden surfacing, a confrontation with the events of the past and all their shaping of the novelist's subsequent art.

—Laurie Clancy

JONES, Gayl

Nationality: American. **Born:** Lexington, Kentucky, 23 November 1949. **Education:** Connecticut College, New London, B.A. in English 1971; Brown University, Providence, Rhode Island, M.A. 1973, D.A. 1975. **Career:** Member of the Department of English, University of Michigan, Ann Arbor, 1975–83. **Awards:** Howard Foundation award, 1975; National Endowment for the Arts grant, 1976. **Address:** c/o Lotus Press, P.O. Box 21607, Detroit, Michigan 48221, U.S.A.

Publications

Novels

Corregidora. New York, Random House, 1975; London, Camden, 1988.
Eva's Man. New York, Random House, 1976.
The Healing. Boston, Beacon Press, 1998.
Mosquito. Boston, Beacon Press, 1999.

Short Stories

White Rat. New York, Random House, 1977.

Uncollected Short Stories

''Almeyda,'' in *Massachusetts Review* (Amherst), Winter 1977.
''Ensinança,'' in *Confirmation,* edited by Amiri and Amina Baraka. New York, Morrow, 1983.

Plays

Chile Woman. New York, Shubert Foundation, 1975.

Poetry

Song for Anninho. Detroit, Lotus Press, 1981.
The Hermit-Woman. Detroit, Lotus Press, 1983.
Xarque. Detroit, Lotus Press, 1985.

Other

Liberating Voices: Oral Tradition in African American Literature. Cambridge and London, Harvard University Press, 1991.

*

Critical Studies: *Engendering the Subject: Gender and Self-Representation in Contemporary Women's Fiction* by Sally Robinson, Albany, State University of New York Press, 1991; *Bridging the Americas: The Literature of Paula Marshall, Toni Morrison and Gayl Jones* by Stelamaris Coser, Philadelphia, Temple University Press, 1994.

* * *

Gayl Jones's first novel, *Corregidora,* focuses on the lingering effects of slavery in black America—specifically on its sexual and psychological manifestations in the life of Ursa Corregidora, a Kentucky blues singer. The great granddaughter of a Portuguese plantation owner who fathered not only her grandmother but also her mother, and who used his progeny both in the fields and in his own whorehouse, Ursa is unable to free herself of painful and obsessive family memories. In each personal relationship she finds yet again the sickness of the master-slave dynamic. Her short-lived first marriage is convulsive with desire, possessiveness, humiliation, and violence; her second, safer, marriage fails as she cannot forget the first. In relating Ursa's story, Jones shows the difficulty of loving when abusive relationships have been naturalized by cultural continuity, when so much has been taken that one's only dignity is in withholding. Her taut and explicit idiom, sometimes plainly narrative, sometimes wildly stream-of-consciousness, captures the nuances of a tormented sexuality that is both specific to black experience and symptomatic of our troubled gender system. ''I knew what I still felt. I knew that I still hated him. Not as bad as then, not with the first feeling, but an after feeling, an aftertaste, or like an odor still in a room when you come back to it, and it's your own.'' The book's ending, almost unbearably intense but strangely hopeful, suggests that we may begin to heal ourselves only as we confront the deep sexual hatred that pervades our lives.

Whereas *Corregidora* allows us to perceive the construction of personality as historical process, *Eva's Man* offers a very different kind of experience, one that many readers have found profoundly disturbing. Eva Canada, the main character of the novel, tells her tale from an institution for the criminally insane, where she has been imprisoned for a hideous sexual crime of murder and dental castration. Like Ursa, Eva has been damaged by abuse and by a legacy of violence; unlike the protagonist of *Corregidora,* she has no sense of how her past motivates her present. As she speaks her disjointed narrative, an ugly story disrupted by flashes of recalled nastiness, she remains alien to us, a personality beyond promise or repair.

> I put my hand on his hand. I kissed his hand, his neck. I put my fingers in the space above his eyes, but didn't close them. They'd come and put copper coins over them. That's why they told you not to suck pennies. I put my forehead under his chin. He was warm. The glass had spilled from his hand. I put my tongue between his parted lips. I kissed his teeth.

In *Eva's Man*, Jones takes us into the pathological mind, and we do not find ourselves there. As the tidy reader-protagonist identification is denied us, we are left with the horror of what we can't sympathetically imagine. Jones's unflinching violation of our strongest taboos—made all the more chilling by her starkly controlled prose—raises a number of questions about the roles of writers, readers, and cultural conventions. Beyond shock value, what does a writer achieve in presenting the truly sordid? Is our understanding necessarily dependent upon the protagonist's understanding? What do disturbing books demand of us that comforting ones do not? How must we see the world in order to change it? The stories that make up *White Rat* suggest that Jones is intent on keeping those questions before us. The majority of these pieces (''Legend,'' ''Asylum,'' ''The Coke Factory,'' ''The Return,'' ''Version 2,'' ''Your Poems Have Very Little Color in Them'') are about madness or extreme psychic alienation. Some (''The Women,'' ''Jevata'') address the painful complications of desperate sexual arrangements. The most attractive, of course, are those few (''White Rat,'' ''Persona,'' ''The Roundhouse'') that hint at successful human connection despite overwhelming odds. Like *Eva's Man*, most of the stories in *White Rat* challenge our notions of what fiction should do.

Jones's later novels, *The Healing* and *Mosquito*, press the limits of the novel in an entirely different direction, by evoking the sound and form of oral storytelling. The narration in both novels is idiomatic and non-linear, following the syntax and associative logic of the spoken word. And though both novels are written in the first-person, they incorporate multiple voices through free indirect discourse, and through a technique in which the narrator responds to the implied questions of her audience, creating a dialogic, multi-voiced narrative. In *Mosquito*, the narrator expressly comments on this form, suggesting that she's creating a jazz narrative in which the readers can join in and improvise as they will.

This new dialogic narrative form corresponds to a greater emphasis on the beneficial possibilities in human interaction. The narrator of *The Healing* is a faith healer who can cure afflictions of both the body and mind; the narrator of *Mosquito* is an African-American woman truck driver in south Texas who becomes involved in the new Underground Railroad, transporting illegal immigrants and providing sanctuary. Both of these narrators experience transformation and a change of consciousness, yet the narratives' non-linear forms suggest that these changes are neither sudden nor isolated, but instead interconnected with the narrators' histories.

Harlan Jane Eagleton, the narrator of *The Healing*, for instance, tells her tale backwards. She moves from her experience as a faith healer to her previous career as the manager of the rock star, Joan ''the bitch'' Savage, her affairs with Joan's husband and with an African-German horse breeder, her brief marriage to a medical anthropologist, and her first career, as a beautician. As a faith healer, Harlan continues to promote natural beauty products and to listen to Joan's music. The bodyguard of her horse-breeder lover is her ''witness,'' so that all of the experiences of Harlan's life inform her contemporary identity as a healer. Harlan's ability to heal is never explained; instead, the retrospective narrative stands in for the explanation, suggesting that Harlan's increasing independence and ability to ''manage herself'' eventually leads to her ability to heal herself, and then to heal others.

African-American women's independence is a major theme in *Mosquito* as well. Mosquito herself (aka Sojourner Jane Nadine Johnson) is an independent truck driver who refuses to join the union and who eventually forms the worker-owned Mosquito Trucking Company. Her childhood friend, Monkey Bread, joins the ''Daughters of Nzingha,'' an African-American women's group that pursues womanist philosophy and advocates economic independence for its members. This emphasis on independence complements rather than contradicts the novel's other main theme, of interdependence. It is because Mosquito remains independent from the union that she can carry immigrants in the back of her truck and thereby discharge her social obligations to the immigrants that she understands to be the contemporary versions of fugitive slaves. Thus in this novel as well, history (both personal and cultural) informs the main character's change of consciousness.

Jones's skillful control of African-American idiom, use of parody, and ability to subtly signify on everything from the CIA's illegal activities to movie stars' hair color in *Mosquito* has led reviewers to compare Jones's work to that of Zora Neale Hurston, Ralph Ellison, and Ishmael Reed. In fact, Jones's more recent work draws on both the traditions of the African-American vernacular and on the forms of postmodern literature, creating novels that layer many forms and provide commentary on the state of the novel. Both *Mosquito* and *The Healing* are replete with references to, and analysis of, other novels from *Invisible Man* to *Huckleberry Finn*. Much of Jones's brilliance lies in her ability to use the colloquial voice of working-class African-American women to provide not only extensive social commentary but also intriguing metafictional discourse on the nature of narrative, or, in the words of *The Healing*'s narrator, ''confabulatory truth.''

—Janis Butler Holm, updated by Suzanne Lane

JONES, (Morgan) Glyn

Nationality: British. **Born:** Merthyr Tydfil, Glamorgan, 28 February 1905. **Education:** Castle Grammar School, Merthyr Tydfil; St. Paul's College, Cheltenham, Gloucestershire. Married Phyllis Doreen Jones in 1935. **Career:** Formerly a schoolmaster in Glamorgan; now retired. First chair, Yr Academi Gymreig (English Section). **Awards:** Welsh Arts Council prize, for non-fiction, 1969, and Premier award, 1972. D.Litt.: University of Wales, Cardiff, 1974. **Agent:** Laurence Pollinger Ltd., 18 Maddox Street, London W1R 0EU, England. **Address:** 158 Manor Way, Whitchurch, Cardiff CF4 1RN, Wales.

Publications

Novels

The Valley, The City, The Village. London, Dent, 1956.
The Learning Lark. London, Dent, 1960.
The Island of Apples. London, Dent, and New York, Day, 1965; revised edition, Cardiff, University of Wales Press, 1992.

Short Stories

The Blue Bed. London, Cape, 1937; New York, Dutton, 1938.
The Water Music. London, Routledge, 1944.
Selected Short Stories. London, Dent, 1971.
Welsh Heirs. Llandysul, Dyfed, Gomer, 1977.

Plays

The Beach of Falesá (verse libretto), music by Alun Hoddinott (produced Cardiff, 1974). London, Oxford University Press, 1974.

Poetry

Poems. London, Fortune Press, 1939.
The Dream of Jake Hopkins. London, Fortune Press, 1954.
Selected Poems. Llandysul, Dyfed, Gomer, 1975.
The Meaning of Fuchsias. Newtown, Gregynog Press, 1987.
Selected Poems, Fragments, and Fictions. Bridgend, Glamorgan, Poetry Wales Press, 1988.
The Story of Heledd, with T.J. Morgan; edited by Jenny Rowland and engravings by Harry Brockway. Newtown, Powys, Gwasg Grefynog, 1994.
The Collected Poems of Glyn Jones, edited by Meic Stephens. Cardiff, University of Wales Press, 1996.

Other

The Dragon Has Two Tongues: Essays on Anglo-Welsh Writers and Writing. London, Dent, 1968.
Profiles: A Visitor's Guide to Writing in Twentieth Century Wales, with John Rowlands. Llandysul, Dyfed, Gomer, 1980.
Setting Out: A Memoir of Literary Life in Wales. Cardiff, University College Department of Extra Mural Studies, 1982.
Random Entrances to Gwyn Thomas. Cardiff, University College Press, 1982.
Editor, *Poems '76.* Llandysul, Dyfed, Gomer, 1976.
Translator, with T.J. Morgan, *The Saga of Llywarch the Old.* London, Golden Cockerel Press, 1955.
Translator, *What Is Worship?,* by E. Stanley John. Swansea, Wales for Christ Movement, 1978.
Translator, *When the Rose-bush Brings Forth Apples* (Welsh folk poetry). Gregynog, Powys, Gregynog Press, 1980.
Translator, *Honeydew on the Wormwood* (Welsh folk poetry). Gregynog, Powys, Gregynog Press, 1984.
Translator, *A People's Poetry: Hen Benillion.* Bridgend, Wales, Seren, 1997.

*

Bibliographies: By John and Sylvia Harris, in *Poetry Wales 19* (Bridgend, Glamorgan), 3–4, 1984.

Manuscript Collections: National Library of Wales, Aberystwyth.

Critical Studies: Article by Iolo Llwyd, in *South Wales Magazine* (Cardiff), Autumn 1970; *Glyn Jones* by Leslie Norris, Cardiff, University of Wales Press, 1973, and article by Norris in *British Novelists 1930–1959* edited by Bernard Oldsey, Detroit, Gale, 1983; Harri Pritchard-Jones, in *Welsh Books and Writers* (Cardiff), Autumn 1981; David Smith, in *Arcade* (Cardiff), February 1982.

Glyn Jones comments:

I began my literary life as a poet. In 1934 I first became friendly with Dylan Thomas, who suggested I should write short stories, as he himself was doing then. My first published book was a volume of short stories, *The Blue Bed.* This was written when the great industrial depression was at its most intense in South Wales and the longest story in the book takes this for its subject. South Wales, industrial and agricultural—this is the theme in all the stories in *The Blue Bed.* Indeed, all my prose, and much of my poetry, is concerned with this region. The novel *The Valley, The City, The Village,* which is partly autobiographical, tries to convey what it was like to grow up in South Wales; *The Learning Lark* deals with learning and teaching in the area; *The Island of Apples* describes childhood and its fantasies in a closely knit community in the Welsh valleys.

The Water Music has stories about both the industrial east of South Wales (Glamorgan) and the agricultural west (Carmarthen, Pembroke, Cardigan). To quote my publisher—I have "carried the medium [i.e., the imaginative short story] to an unexcelled synthesis of realism and fantasy, magic and humor. From the regional contrasts of industrialism and pastoralism, modernity and tradition, he builds up a world of convincing beauty, and expresses himself in a prose style of unusual poetic vitality." I would accept this as a statement of what I have *tried* to do in my short stories. Whether I've done it is of course quite another question.

* * *

"While using cheerfully enough the English language, I have never written in it a word about any country other than Wales, or any people other than Welsh people," wrote Glyn Jones in *The Dragon Has Two Tongues.* This deliberate limitation of his material is the only reason I can suggest for any kind of restriction to the general recognition his gifts deserve.

Certainly his stories and novels, although they share a Welsh background, are set in widely separate countries of the mind, pose different problems, and offer to us recognizable human situations. His prose, too, is very much more than the "cheerful use" of the English language. Always exuberant and seemingly spendthrift ("I fancy words," he says in his poem, "Merthyr"), it is also exact, muscular, very energetic. He can range from elegant and mannered writing—and the use of a vocabulary so exotic that it upset some reviewers of his first novel, *The Valley, The City, The Village*—to the direct, racy, almost physical style, the true, idiosyncratic speaking voice we find in some of the stories and in the two later novels.

His Wales commonly has two contrasting faces, that of the idyllic land of country happiness opposing the suppurating mining towns where the ugly, comical people are unfailingly kindly. But it also exists as a metaphysical universe, and the young people who are to be found in almost everything Jones writes are given early experience of both Heaven and Hell. To some extent this duality reflects Jones's own early life; during his impressionable boyhood he lived in the grimy steel and coal town of Merthyr Tydfil, but spent significant periods in Llanstephan, a beautiful Carmarthenshire village.

His identification with the scenes and characters of his imagination is absolutely complete, and it is noticeable that many of these stories and all three of his novels are told in the first person. Many critics, indeed, thought *The Valley, The City, The Village* largely autobiographical, although this story of a young painter, aware of his vocation but forced by the obstinate love of his grandmother to go to university to train as a preacher, has only tenuous links with Jones's own life. It is the quality of Jones's visual imagination and the unjudging tolerance that lies behind his observation that make his young artist credible.

For in the end Jones's love of his people is the illuminating quality of his work. He has created a whole gallery of memorable characters, some of them fully realized, some of whom enter his pages but once. He sees their blemishes, particularly their physical shortcomings, as clearly as their virtues, but to him they are lovable because their faults are the faults of human beings. Even in *The Learning Lark,* that picaresque send-up of the state of education in a corrupt mining valley where teachers have to bribe their way to headships, there is no scalding satire. Both bribed and bribers are seen as only too human and the book is full of gargantuan laughter.

The world of childhood and adolescence, that magical period when the real and the imagined are hardly to be distinguished, has been a particularly fertile area of Jones's concern. *The Water Music,* for example, is a collection of stories about young people: of his three novels only one is set entirely in the world of adults, and even that one has some very realistic schoolboys in it.

The Island of Apples is a full-scale exploration of the world of adolescence, seen through the eyes of the boy Dewi. It is a remarkable novel, using a prose which is obviously the boy's voice, yet flexible and powerful enough to describe an enormous range of events and emotions. Its sensitivity, its combination of dreamlike confusion and the clear, unsentimental observation which is the adolescent state of mind, the excitement with which the boy invests the commonplace with the exotic, are perfectly balanced attributes of a work which is as individual and complete as *Le Grand Meaulnes,* that other evocation of vanishing youth.

Perhaps the greatest of Jones's qualities is that of delight in the created world and the people who inhabit it. If he writes of a small and often shabby corner of that world—the first story in *The Blue Bed* is called "I Was Born in the Ystrad Valley" and it is to Ystrad that he returns for *The Island of Apples*—yet his writing is a celebration, an act of praise. To this end he has shaped his craftsmanship and inspiration, and his achievement is permanent and real.

—Leslie Norris

JONES, Gwyneth A(nn)

Also writes as Ann Halam. **Nationality:** English. **Born:** Manchester, England, 14 February 1952. **Education:** University of Sussex, B.A. 1973. **Family:** Married Peter Wilson Gwilliam in 1972; one son. **Career:** Executive officer, Manpower Services Commission, Hove, England, 1975–77; author of books for young people and adults, 1977—. **Awards:** First prize, children's story competition (*Manchester Evening News*), 1967; James Tiptree, Jr., award, 1991; Children of the Night Award (Dracula Society), 1996; World Fantasy Award, 1996. **Agent:** Anthony Goff, David Higham Associates, Ltd., 5–8 Lower John Street, Golden Square, London W1R 4HA, England. **Address:** 30 Roundhill Crescent, Brighton, East Sussex BN2 3FR, England.

PUBLICATIONS

Novels

Ally Ally Aster (as Ann Halam). London, Allen and Unwin, 1981.
The Alder Tree (as Ann Halam). London, Allen and Unwin, 1982.
Divine Endurance. Boston, Allen and Unwin, 1984.
Escape Plans. London, Allen and Unwin, 1986.
King Death's Garden (as Ann Halam). London, Orchard, 1986.
The Daymaker ("Inland" trilogy; as Ann Halam). London, Orchard, 1987.
Transformations ("Inland" trilogy; as Ann Halam). London, Orchard, 1988.
Kairos. London, Unwin Hyman, 1988.
The Hidden Ones. London, Women's Press, 1988.
The Skybreaker ("Inland" trilogy; as Ann Halam). London, Orchard, 1990.
White Queen. London, Gollancz, 1991; New York, Tor, 1993.
Dinosaur Junction (as Ann Halam). London, Orchard, 1992.
Flowerdust. London, Headline, 1993; New York, Tor, 1995.
North Wind. London, Gollancz, 1994; New York, Tor, 1996.
The Haunting of Jessica Raven (as Ann Halam). London, Orion, 1994.
The Fear Man (as Ann Halam). London, Orion, 1995.
Phoenix Café. London, Gollancz, 1996; New York, Tor, 1998.
The Powerhouse (as Ann Halam). London, Orion, 1997.
Crying in the Dark. (as Ann Halam). N.p., n.d.
The Shadow on the Stairs. (as Ann Halam). N.p., n.d.
The NIMROD Conspiracy. (as Ann Halam). N.p. 1999.

Fiction for Children

Water in the Air. New York, Macmillan, 1977.
The Influence of Ironwood. London, Macmillan, 1978.
The Exchange. London, Macmillan, 1979.
Dear Hill. London, Macmillan, 1980.

Short Stories

Identifying the Object. Austin, Texas, Swan Press, 1993.
Seven Tales and a Fable. Cambridge, Massachusetts, Edgewood Press, 1995.

Other

Editor, *Deconstructing the Starships: Science, Fiction and Reality.* Liverpool, England, Liverpool University Press, 1998.

* * *

Gwyneth Jones is a British author of science fiction and fantasy and a feminist critic who has earned many literary awards and nominations. Her fiction is famous for its feminist approach and its recurring themes of the importance of community and of respect for the Earth. Her fantasy novels are unconventional, primarily for showing that happy endings are difficult to achieve.

Jones began with juvenile fiction. Her first novels were *Water in the Air, The Influence of Ironwood, The Exchange,* and *Dear Hill.* These follow the not unusual pattern of an adolescent girl who must come to grips with her changing attitudes and world.

To escape this formula, Jones began writing as Ann Halam with the Nordic myth-based *Ally Ally Aster,* which tells of an ice spirit who conjures up a terrible winter. *The Alder Tree* is a Gothic fantasy featuring a dragon. *King Death's Garden* and *The Haunting of Jessica Raven* are ghost stories. *The Hidden Ones,* published as Gwyneth

Jones, concerns a rebellious teenager struggling against a Sussex farmer who plans to industrialize a magic piece of wilderness. *The Fear Man* earned the Children of the Night Award given by The Dracula Society. Further Halam thrillers include *Dinosaur Junction*, *The Powerhouse*, *Crying in the Dark*, *The Shadow on the Stairs*, and *The NIMROD Conspiracy*.

Jones's ''Inland'' series, composed of *The Daymaker*, *Transformations*, and *The Skybreaker*, are her best juvenile novels. Jones designed this far-future England (''Inland'') as a humorous take on the quantum mechanics hypothesis that reality holds together simply because people observe it. In Inland, magic has replaced technology, and observable reality is held together by people's consensus. If the characters disagree, their world literally begins falling apart. Zanne's community, a matriarchal utopia, has renounced technology for the ''Covenant,'' which lets people use the magic of nature to build and heal. However, Zanne is attracted to the ''Daymakers,'' ancient power plants. She wishes to restore the wonders of the machine era, but learns that the powers of technology and magic cannot be balanced.

If sorrow for lost things weaves a thread of tragedy through *Daymaker*, the tone of *Transformations* is much darker. Zanne finds a Daymaker in a remote region whose inhabitants lead harsh, puritanical lives. Zanne tries to restore happiness to these mining folk, but gradually realizes something is very wrong in the community. Here and in *Skybreaker*, she discovers that her healing powers are suited to shutting down the evil machines, dramatizing a philosophy of balance between people and their land and between people's desires and fears.

Jones gained attention in the United States with the publication of *Divine Endurance*. This remarkable novel is flavored by the years she lived in Singapore and Southeast Asia (1977–80). In the far future, an undescribed apocalypse has wasted the Earth and destroyed the wisdom of past civilizations. Her richly imagined Malay Peninsula, though, is a matriarchal society, bound by traditions of ''hearth magic'' and strict gender roles. The Peninsulans are governed by the mysterious Rulers, who reserve what little technology remains to themselves and rule by martial law. The arrival of Cho—an innocent girl who is not what she seems and who can grant the heart's desire—and a cat called Divine Endurance catalyzes a civil war between rebels and matriarchs. Jones paints a melancholy landscape of a dying Earth in this meditation on utopia and the results of getting what you wish for.

Escape Plans uses a dystopian setting and the computer jargon typical of cyberpunk, a fast-paced computer-savvy subgenre of science fiction. A spacewoman from an orbital station is unaware of the dismal lives of a dehumanized worker class until she journeys through their underground world and uncovers a secret history. The novel was nominated for the Arthur C. Clarke Award, given annually to the best science fiction novel published in the British Commonwealth.

With *Kairos*, Jones began dealing seriously with gender issues. In post-apocalyptic London, two pairs of homosexual lovers endure a repressive government, brutal poverty, social anarchy, and the experiments of BREAKTHRU Ltd., which intends to end the world for its own gain. This company has developed a drug, ''kairos,'' so powerful it can change the nature of physical reality. Jane, called ''Otto,'' a political and sexual radical, sets up shop with Sandy, the first victim of kairos. Their friends James and Gordon (''Luci'') discover the evil of the BREAKTHRU representatives called ''angels,'' and when the surviving protagonists flee London, they find different worlds outside. A lesbian druidic cult challenges BREAKTHRU, but reality metamorphoses so drastically that time and causality unravel. Apocalypse is eventually prevented, but the ''happy'' ending cannot overcome the mood of futility and despair.

White Queen was another Clarke Award nominee and a co-winner of the James Tiptree, Jr., Memorial Award, given to science fiction that explores sex and gender roles. It is the first of the ''Aleutian'' series, the others being *North Wind* and *The Phoenix Café*. Mysterious humanoids arrive on Earth in 2038; apparently telepathic hermaphrodites, they are called Aleutians, a name suggesting ''aliens.'' The relationship between aliens and humans becomes a metaphor for the relationship between men and women. Johnny Guglioli, exiled as a ''petrovirus'' victim from the United States, befriends journalist Braemar Wilson and the ''woman'' Clavel. From Clavel's behaviors, they deduce the insidious invasion, but cannot unriddle what the aliens want. Are they superbeings, candidly offering assistance to a world shaken up by geological and political catastrophes? Similar to humans, they differ in important details—such as their attitudes towards sex, death, and personal identity.

White Queen, a ''preemptive resistance movement'' that works to undermine trust in the aliens's promises, sees the Aleutians as technologically superior conquerors. Played out among conflicts arising from miscommunication, gender, and identity, the plot accelerates when a White Queen agent attempts to take an alien tissue sample. The Aleutians kill her and disrupt technologies across the world, nearly causing global war. Braemar and Johnny attempt to infiltrate the aliens' starship, precipitating a showdown. The novel has been praised for its well-rounded characterization, exotic settings, convincing technology, and eroticism.

In *Flowerdust*, Jones returned to the Southeast Asia of *Divine Endurance*. The first book had introduced Derveet Garuda, a rebel against the matriarchal government, who now prepares to undertake a full-scale revolution. Derveet journeys to the refugee camps on the island of Ranganar to learn the source of their unrest, which might explode prematurely into an easily suppressed rebellion. Uncovering a Ruler conspiracy to distribute flowerdust, a bliss-generating drug, Derveet must stop its spread and venture into enemy territory. The book is a satisfying adventure novel, full of political intrigue and intercultural conflict in a colorful setting.

North Wind, the Clarke Award-nominated sequel to *White Queen*, takes place a century later. Bella, a crippled Aleutian, and ''her'' human caretaker, Sydney Carton, share an unusual relationship in a world riven by gender war. Men want to violently eradicate the Aleutians and human collaborators, while the women desire a return to power through a more nurturing society. ''Halfcastes,'' such as Carton, admire the Aleutians. The Aleutians' proposal to level the Himalayas generates violent anti-alien sentiment. While sheltering Bella, Sydney seeks an instantaneous travel device that the legendary Johnny Guglioli used to reach the Aleutians' starship. Unknown to him, Bella's importance to the Aleutians signals her critical role in finding the device. Evoking the courage of Charles Dickens's Sydney Carton in *A Tale of Two Cities*, Carton helps Bella on a journey across the war-ravaged remains of Europe, gradually falling in love with her.

Where *White Queen* presented first contact, and *North Wind* showed the conquerors at the height of their empire, *Phoenix Café* is about their disengagement from Earth. Jones considers the trilogy a version of the European invasion of Africa and India in the nineteenth century, dramatizing different aspects of a dominating culture with attractively powerful technology. Jones blames the Europeans for having looted those continents, establishing ''democracies,'' and finally leaving town because everything was still a mess. What do natives do when the invaders depart? How can they discard the practices that have been imposed and assimilated?

After 300 years, the Aleutians have decided to go home. The problem is getting there; they must perfect their instantaneous-transfer drive. At this point, bodily transformation is so evolved that humans have dropped the old distinctions and now come in all varieties. Catherine, the protagonist, is an experiment, an Aleutian in human form. Engaging in increasingly deeper involvement with humans, Catherine enters a sexually perverse relationship that brings him/her among the planet's elite, who plot a conspiracy that might mean the end of the Aleutian Expedition or all life on Earth.

Jones pushes ever harder against our notions of identity, sex, and gender assumptions. Not only are the Aleutians impossible to classify in male/female terms, but almost no one's appearance in *Phoenix Café* can be trusted because of virtual reality and designer sex drugs. Jones upsets reader expectations in depicting alien/human sex, same-gender sex, clone sex, and even computer sex. The reader is left to ponder the possibility of lasting peace between humans and aliens, men and women, Self and Other.

Deconstructing the Starships: Science, Fiction and Reality gathers critical essays and reviews on various subjects, from genre limitations to creating aliens, from the need for more incisive feminist commentary to a biology textbook on sexual differentiation. The collection earned applause from science fiction scholars and belongs in major academic libraries.

Jones is one of the most important feminist science fiction authors, a growing group that includes award winners Joanna Russ, Suzy Charnas, and Sheri Tepper. From her young adult novels that emphasized the importance of moderation and balance, Jones has developed into a writer of disturbing, destabilizing novels concerned with the human preoccupation with arbitrary divisions by gender, race, politics, and other discriminations that lead to conflict.

—Fiona Kelleghan

JONES, Madison (Percy, Jr.)

Nationality: American. **Born:** Nashville, Tennessee, 21 March 1925. **Education:** Vanderbilt University, Nashville, A.B. 1949; University of Florida, Gainesville, 1950–53, A.M. 1951. **Military Service:** Served in the United States Army in the Corps of Military Police, Korea, 1945–46. **Family:** Married Shailah McEvilley in 1951; two daughters and three sons. **Career:** Farmer in Cheatham County, Tennessee, 1940s; instructor in English, Miami University, Oxford, Ohio, 1953–54, and University of Tennessee, Knoxville, 1955–56. Member of the Department of English from 1956, writer-in-residence, 1967–87, and professor of English, 1968–87, Auburn University, Alabama; now emeritus. **Member:** Alabama Academy of Distiguished Authors; Fellowship of Southern Writers. **Awards:** *Sewanee Review* fellowship, 1954; Alabama Library Association Book award, 1968; Rockefeller fellowship, 1968; Guggenheim fellowship, 1973; Lytle prize, for short fiction, 1992. **Agent:** Harold Matson Company, Inc., 276 Fifth Avenue, New York, New York 10001. **Address:** 500 Brook Stone Way, Louisville, Kentucky, U.S.A. 40202.

PUBLICATIONS

Novels

The Innocent. New York, Harcourt Brace, and London, Secker and Warburg, 1957.
Forest of the Night. New York, Harcourt Brace, 1960; London, Eyre and Spottiswoode, 1961.
A Buried Land. New York, Viking Press, and London, Bodley Head, 1963.
An Exile. New York, Viking Press, 1967; London, Deutsch, 1970; as *I Walk the Line,* New York, Popular Library, 1970.
A Cry of Absence. New York, Crown, 1971; London, Deutsch, 1972.
Passage through Gehenna. Baton Rouge, Louisiana State University Press, 1978.
Season of the Strangler. New York, Doubleday, 1982.
Last Things. Baton Rouge, Louisiana State University Press, 1989.
To the Winds. Atlanta, Georgia, Longstreet Press, 1996.
Nashville 1864: The Dying of the Light: A Novel. Nashville, J.S. Sanders, 1997.

Uncollected Short Stories

"The Homecoming," in *Perspective* (St. Louis), Spring 1952.
"Dog Days," in *Perspective* (St. Louis), Fall 1952.
"The Cave," in *Perspective* (St. Louis), Winter 1955.
"Home Is Where the Heart Is," in *Arlington Quarterly* (Texas), Spring 1968.
"A Modern Case," in *Delta Review* (Memphis, Tennessee), August 1969.
"The Fugitives," in *Craft and Vision,* edited by Andrew Lytle. New York, Delacorte Press, 1971.
"The Family That Prays Together Stays Together," in *Chattahoochee Review* (Dunwoody, Georgia), Winter 1983.
"A Beginning," in *Homewords,* edited by Douglas Paschall. Knoxville, University of Tennessee Press, 1986.
"Zoo," in *Sewanee Review,* Summer 1992.
"Before the Winds Came," in *Oxford American* (Oxford, Mississippi), Winter 1994.

Other

History of the Tennessee State Dental Association. Nashville, Tennessee Dental Association, 1958.

*

Film Adaptations: *I Walk the Line,* 1970, from the novel *An Exile.*

Manuscript Collections: Emory University, Atlanta; Auburn University, Alabama.

Critical Studies: By Ovid Pierce, in *New York Times Book Review,* 4 July 1971; Joseph Cantinella, in *Saturday Review* (New York), 9 July 1971; Reed Whittemore, in *New Republic* (Washington, D.C.), July 1971; *Separate Country* by Paul Binding, London and New York, Paddington Press, 1979; interview, in *Southern Quarterly* (Hattiesburg,

Mississippi), Spring 1983; in *The History of Southern Literature* edited by Louis Rubin, Louisiana State University Press, 1986.

Madison Jones comments:

Generally, on a more obvious level, my fiction is concerned with the drama of collision between past and present, with emphasis upon the destructive elements involved. More deeply, it deals with the failure, or refusal, of individuals to recognize and submit themselves to inevitable limits of the human condition.

* * *

There is a homogeneity of theme that links together into a coherent body the published fiction of Madison Jones. The setting of these books is invariably Jones's native south. But whether their time be late eighteenth-century settlement days or the region's more recent past, his unvarying song is abstraction, ideology, and its consequences. *The Innocent,* his first novel, set in rural Tennessee immediately after the coming of modernity, treats of the attempts by a young southerner, Duncan Welsh, to repent of earlier impiety and reestablish himself upon inherited lands in inherited ways. The enterprise is a failure because of Duncan's deracinated preconception of it. Welsh ''sets up a grave in his house.'' Soon he and his hopes are buried in another.

A Cry of Absence again focuses on a fatal archaist, a middle-aged gentlewoman of the 1960s who is anything but innocent. Hester Glenn finds an excuse for her failures as wife, mother, and person in a self-protective devotion to the tradition of her family. But when her example proves, in part, responsible for her son's sadistic murder of a black agitator, Hester is driven to know herself and, after confession, to pay for her sins with suicide.

A kind of Puritanism distorts Mrs. Glenn. In *The Innocent* the error is a perversion of the Agrarianism of Jones's mentors (Lytle, Davidson). But in his other novels the informing abstractions are not so identifiably southern. Jones's best, *A Buried Land,* is set in the valley of the Tennessee River during the season of its transformation. Percy Youngblood, the heir of a stern hill farmer (and a central character who could be any young person of our century), embraces all of the nostrums we associate with the futurist dispensation. He attempts to bury the old world (represented by a girl who dies aborting his child) under the waters of the TVA; but its truths (and their symbol) rise to haunt him back into abandoned modes of thought and feeling. In *An Exile* Hank Tawes, a rural sheriff, is unmanned by a belated explosion of passion for a bootlegger's daughter. His error has no date or nationality, but almost acquires the force of ideology once Tawes recognizes that, because he followed an impulse to recover his youth, his ''occupation's gone.'' *Forest of the Night* tests out an assumption almost as generic, the notion that man is inherently good. An interval in the Tennessee ''outback'' is sufficient to the disabusement of Jonathan Cannon. There is no more telling exposé of the New Eden mythology.

In all of Jones's fiction there operates an allusive envelope embodied in a concrete action and supported by an evocative texture. That action is as spare as it is archetypal; and in every case its objective is to render consciousness. Jones is among the most gifted of contemporary American novelists, a craftsman of tragedy in the great tradition of his art.

—M.E. Bradford

JONES, Marion Patrick

Nationality: Citizen of Trinidad and Tobago. **Born:** Trinidad. **Family:** Married. **Career:** Librarian and social anthropologist. A founder of Campaign Against Racial Discrimination, London. **Address:** c/o Columbus Publishers, 64 Independence Square, Port of Spain, Trinidad.

PUBLICATIONS

Novels

Pan Beat. Port of Spain, Columbus, 1973.
J'Ouvert Morning. Port of Spain, Columbus, 1976.

* * *

The relatively limited contributions of women writers to Caribbean literature has been one of the long-standing curiosities about the region. In the area of prose fiction there has been a small handful of women novelists, and from the English-language Caribbean in particular there have only been Sylvia Wynter of Jamaica, the Barbados-born Paule Marshall of the United States, and Merle Hodges and Marion Patrick Jones of Trinidad. Jones therefore belongs to a rather small circle in Caribbean literature, one that has unfortunately been slow—with the exception of Paule Marshall—to attract significant attention from students and teachers of the literature. And on the basis of her published works it is clear that Jones has carved out a distinctive niche for herself within that small circle.

Thus far, at any rate, she has chosen to concentrate on domestic drama as the main staple of her novels. For example, both *Pan Beat* and *J'Ouvert Morning* center on middle-class marriages in Port of Spain, Trinidad, each work concentrating on not one but several couples, on the quality of the marriages (invariably bad and getting worse), on the circle within which the couples move (usually since their childhood), and on a social background that is experiencing the growing pains of new nationhood. And in the case of *J'Ouvert Morning* this all spans three generations. As this synopsis is intended to imply, Jones's fiction usually borders on soap opera. Her plots are endless strands of unrelieved misery that are interwoven in a pattern of endless conflicts and unmitigated wretchedness.

In *Pan Beat,* for example, the narrative events are sparked by Earline MacCardie's return home to Trinidad for a holiday visit. As a high-schooler she was associated with the Flamingoes steel band. After high school she and David Chow, a member of the band, emigrated to England. He committed suicide after their estrangement, and she promptly turned to prostitution to assuage her grief—and to express her resentment at his suicide. Then she had subsequently married a British homosexual in New York (where she has been ''passing'' as a white Brazilian). Now that she is in Trinidad her husband breaks off the marriage, and she discovers that her former friends have been just as unhappy as she has been abroad: another old boyfriend, Louis Jenkins, is a futile, left-wing radical who is eventually killed in a gang war during Earline's visit; Louis's wife, Denise, enjoys some success, but merely as an insipid, commercially popular artist; Alan Hastings is a highly paid oil refinery worker who divides his time between a disastrous marriage and an affair with Earline herself. Of the two persons who have managed to avoid the endemic miseries of marriage, Tony Joseph is a desperately lonely prude of a civil servant, while Leslie Oliver, a Roman Catholic priest, is tormented by his sexual passion for Denise Jenkins.

The middle-class miseries of *J'Ouvert Morning* are less convoluted, largely because Jones mercifully concentrates on a smaller, more tightly knit group of sufferers in this novel—the Grant family. But their collective wretchedness is no less acute. Helen and Mervyn Grant have worked hard to secure a good education and middle-class affluence for their children. But one daughter, Elizabeth, is a well-known city drunk whom everyone knows as "Stinking Fur Liz." Their son, John, is a wealthy Port of Spain doctor with an unhappy marriage and a rebellious son, John Jr. Eventually John Jr.'s rebelliousness leads to an anti-government, left-wing plot that ends in his death at the hands of the police. The novel itself ends with the abortive suicide attempt by John Jr.'s distraught mother.

In spite of the soap operatic quality of her narrative materials, Jones's novels succeed as riveting documents of a troubled society in a state of transition. Jones's Trinidad has left official colonialism behind, but it has not yet discovered a vital sense of its own direction and purpose. It is soulless, without a driving motive, except the predictable trappings of neo-colonial values and the second-hand middle-class aspirations that have been handed down from Europe and the United States. The present tragedies and failures of her characters therefore reflect the unfulfilled promise of a generation that grew up in the years before independence. The empty successes of her achievers demonstrate the limitations of the neocolonial imitativeness that too often thwarts the growth of a healthy national consciousness. The radical dissidents like Louis Jenkins or John Jr. are equally failures in their own way: their radicalism is too often a self-destructive aimlessness that merely underscores their irrelevance in a society which is completely indifferent to them and their revolutionary messages.

Moreover, all of this remains convincing in the long run, because, despite Jones's melodramatic tendencies, the characters are vividly drawn and the language—especially in *J'Ouvert Morning*—is original and invigorating. Thus far she has demonstrated considerable promise, one that should be fulfilled to a significant degree if she continues to integrate an engaging narrative language with both disturbing social insights and a formidable grasp of the human personality.

—Lloyd W. Brown

JONES, Mervyn

Nationality: British. **Born:** London, 27 February 1922. **Education:** Abbotsholme School, Derbyshire; New York University, 1939–41. **Military Service:** Served in the British Army, 1942–47: Captain. **Family:** Married Jeanne Urquhart in 1948; one son and two daughters. **Career:** Assistant editor, 1955–60, and dramatic critic, 1958–66, *Tribune*, London; assistant editor, *New Statesman*, London, 1966–68. **Awards:** Society of Authors traveling scholarship, 1982. **Agent:** Scott Ferris Associates, 15 Gledhow Gardens, London S.W.5. **Address:** 1 Evelyn Mansions, Carlisle Place, London SW1P 1NH, England.

Publications

Novels

No Time to Be Young. London, Cape, 1952.
The New Town. London, Cape, 1953.
The Last Barricade. London, Cape, 1953.
Helen Blake. London, Cape, 1955.
On the Last Day. London, Cape, 1958.
A Set of Wives. London, Cape, 1965.
John and Mary. London, Cape, 1966; New York, Atheneum, 1967.
A Survivor. London, Cape, and New York, Atheneum, 1968.
Joseph. London, Cape, and New York, Atheneum, 1970.
Mr. Armitage Isn't Back Yet. London, Cape, 1971.
Holding On. London, Quartet, 1973; as *Twilight of the Day*, New York, Simon and Schuster, 1974.
The Revolving Door. London, Quartet, 1973.
Strangers. London, Quartet, 1974.
Lord Richard's Passion. London, Quartet, and New York, Knopf, 1974.
The Pursuit of Happiness. London, Quartet, 1975; New York, Mason Charter, 1976.
Nobody's Fault. London, Quartet, and New York, Mason Charter, 1977.
Today the Struggle. London, Quartet, 1978.
The Beautiful Words. London, Deutsch, 1979.
A Short Time to Live. London, Deutsch, 1980; New York, St. Martin's Press, 1981.
Two Women and Their Man. London, Deutsch, and New York, St. Martin's Press, 1982.
Joanna's Luck. London, Piatkus, 1984.
Coming Home. London, Piatkus, 1986.
That Year in Paris. London, Piatkus, 1988.

Short Stories

Scenes from Bourgeois Life. London, Quartet, 1976.

Uncollected Short Stories

"The Foot," in *English Story 8*, edited by Woodrow Wyatt. London, Collins, 1948.
"The Bee-Keeper," in *English Story 10*, edited by Woodrow Wyatt. London, Collins, 1950.
"Discrete Lives," in *Bananas* (London), 1978.
"Five Days by Moonlight," in *Encounter* (London), November 1978.
"Living Together," in *Woman* (London), 1979.

Plays

The Shelter (produced London, 1982).

Radio Plays: *Anna,* 1982; *Taking Over,* 1984; *Lisa,* 1984; *Generations,* 1986.

Other

Guilty Men, 1957: Suez and Cyprus, with Michael Foot. London, Gollancz, and New York, Rinehart, 1957.
Potbank (documentary). London, Secker and Warburg, 1961.
Big Two: Life in America and Russia. London, Cape, 1962; as *The Antagonists,* New York, Potter, 1962.
Two Ears of Corn: Oxfam in Action. London, Hodder and Stoughton, 1965; as *In Famine's Shadow: A Private War on Hunger,* Boston, Beacon Press, 1967.
Life on the Dole. London, Davis Poynter, 1972.
Rhodesia: The White Judge's Burden. London, Christian Action, 1972.
The Oil Rush, photographs by Fay Godwin. London, Quartet, 1976.
The Sami of Lapland. London, Minority Rights Group, 1982.
Chances: An Autobiography. London, Verso, 1987.
A Radical Life: The Biography of Megan Lloyd George. London, Hutchinson, 1991.
Michael Foot. London, Gollancz, 1994.
Editor, *Kingsley Martin: Portrait and Self-Portrait.* London, Barrie and Rockliff, and New York, Humanities Press, 1969.
Editor, *Privacy.* Newton Abbot, Devon, David and Charles, 1974.
Translator, *The Second Chinese Revolution,* by K.S. Karol. New York, Hill and Wang, 1974.

*

Critical Studies: Chapter by Kiernan Ryan, in *The Socialist Novel in Britain* edited by H. Gustav Klaus, Brighton, Harvester Press, 1982.

Mervyn Jones comments:

(1981) I have become known as a political novelist, although only two of my books—*Joseph* and *Today the Struggle*—could be defined strictly as political novels, and some others are deliberately limited to the study of personal relationships. Probably, this reveals how rarely most British novelists concern themselves with the political framework of life. Taking account of that framework does, I think, extend the novel's range. But I also think, decidedly, that a novel ceases to be a novel when it does not have human character and human experience at its center. Those interested in my views on the matter are referred to a *Guardian* interview, 9 July 1979.

I have never planned a recurrent theme in my writing, but when I consider it I believe that there is one: the nobility and irony of idealism. I take both the nobility and the irony to be realities. This is the subject of *Strangers,* the novel with which I am least dissatisfied and by which I should wish to be judged.

* * *

Mervyn Jones is a fine storyteller whose skill has continued to improve over a career that spans half a century. While some of his novels are about a broad variety of characters, and tend to be built on his journalistic experience, his specialty seems to be the problems of those people who have enough time and money to enable them to reflect on life. The conflicts between their ideals and their experiences, or between values related to ideals, are the themes of *The New Town, Mr. Armitage Isn't Back Yet, Strangers, Joanna's Luck,* and the short stories ''The Syndrome'' and ''Happiness Is ...'' How these people reconcile themselves to reality while retaining their ideals or, more often, how they retain ideals that have less and less to do with their actions and decisions is of primary interest to Jones. He has said that the theme of the nobility and irony of idealism is a recurrent one in his writing, and crucial to his depiction of this theme is his calculated distance from his characters. They are intellectual rather than emotional; their thoughts are clear, their emotions suppressed; and if they seem to lack depth, it may be because this lack is an aspect of the modern middle-class idealist.

Strangers, the novel by which Jones has said he would like to be judged, is the best example of his study of the problems of idealism. Andrew Stanton is a pacifist who refuses to live in his native South Africa, and whose refusal to fight in the Second World War has alienated him from his conservative family. He has devoted himself to the ideal of fighting the pure evil in the world with the pure good of compensatory charitable actions. His first wife was a frail survivor of a concentration camp, who was killed by a sniper in Israel. His young second wife, Val, marries him out of her own idealism and faith in him. When Andrew leaves to work with refugees in Uganda, Val is left with a house full of charity cases: a pregnant teenager on the run from her parents, an American on the run from the draft, and a foreign student who runs off with a local schoolgirl. As Andrew and Val struggle in their separate situations, both are confronted with the futility of charity, but while Val sheds specific failures to become more hopeful, Andrew, after a major success, is cruelly struck by the failure of his ideals.

A Short Time to Live is a more cynical view of the idealist. A charismatic journalist with a conscience, Michael Kellet, dies mysteriously on a Pacific island. Each of the old school-friends, teacher, ex-wife, and widow who attend his funeral is carefully examined, as the solution to the mystery gradually becomes apparent. None of them cherishes much of any ideal, except the old teacher, secure in his faith in education, and each is laid bare with a cold, journalistic precision that could have been that of the dead Kellet.

Joanna's Luck is a study of one of the children of the idealists of the 1960s. Joanna's mother and father are ex-hippies, described with the snide acceptance of a disillusioned young woman of the 1980s: the one is still smoking dope and wearing beads at forty-eight, the other has shed it all to become a prosperous businessman. Locked in the thoughts of their era, they cannot comprehend why Joanna cares so much about finding a rewarding job or about wanting to feel close to a man before she goes to bed with him. Joanna is bright, but muddled in her emotions, lonely and drifting. It is not until she drifts into situations that force decisions that she begins to analyze her own emotions and beliefs with the same clarity that she had applied to her work in social research. Jones has always written sympathetically about women, but here he extends that to a deeper, fuller portrayal of a character.

The Beautiful Words is probably Jones's finest book, combining his excellent storytelling with interesting characterization. Here he contrasts a sensitive, full description of his main character, Tommy, with flatter, colder perceptions of the many people Tommy encounters but cannot understand. Tommy is a handsome boy of seventeen with the mind of a very small child. After a life of being shunted among relatives, he becomes a homeless drifter. All that his confused mind can offer for consolation in times of loneliness, fear, and despair are the ''beautiful words'' his one kind aunt taught him to memorize.

He wanders into the home of a prostitute, who cares for him and has him do her cleaning, but her pimp uses him for a robbery and he gets beat up by the police. Lost, he lives with the dossers and drunks on London's Embankment until he finds an empty house and becomes a squatter. Others move in and care for him in a haphazard way, finally dumping him on Belle, a rich and greedy old woman who uses him as a watchdog. The story is about how all of these people deal with the responsibility of innocence as much as what it is like for poor Tommy to be an innocent, and Jones tells the sad story with compassion.

Because of their topical nature, some of Jones's novels date quickly, but not those which delve deeply into the effort of modern people trying to find something to believe and to live by it. For the craft of his storytelling alone, Jones continues to be well worth reading.

—Anne Morddel

JONG, Erica

Nationality: American. **Born:** Erica Mann in New York City, 26 March 1942. **Education:** The High School of Music and Art, New York; Barnard College, New York (George Weldwood Murray fellow, 1963), 1959–63, B.A. 1963 (Phi Beta Kappa); Columbia University, New York (Woodrow Wilson fellow, 1964), M.A. 1965; Columbia School of Fine Arts, 1969–70. **Family:** Married 1) Michael Werthman in 1963 (divorced 1965); 2) Allan Jong in 1966 (divorced 1975); 3) the writer Jonathan Fast in 1977 (divorced 1983), one daughter; 4) Kenneth David Burrows in 1989. **Career:** Lecturer in English, City College, New York, 1964–66, 1969–70, and University of Maryland European Division, Heidelberg, Germany, 1967–68; instructor in English, Manhattan Community College, New York, 1969–70. Since 1971 instructor in poetry, YM-YWHA Poetry Center, New York. Member of the literary panel, New York State Council on the Arts, 1972–74. Since 1991 president of Author's Guild. **Awards:** Academy of American Poets award, 1963; Bess Hokin prize (*Poetry,* Chicago), 1971; New York State Council on the Arts grant, 1971; Madeline Sadin award (*New York Quarterly*), 1972; Alice Fay di Castagnola award, 1972; National Endowment for the Arts grant, 1973; Creative Artists Public Service grant, 1973; International Sigmund Freud prize, 1979. **Agent:** Ed Victor Ltd., 162 Wardour Street, London W1V 3AT, England.

PUBLICATIONS

Novels

Fear of Flying. New York, Holt Rinehart, 1973; London, Secker and Warburg, 1974.

How to Save Your Own Life. New York, Holt Rinehart, and London, Secker and Warburg, 1977.

Fanny, Being the True History of the Adventures of Fanny Hackabout-Jones. New York, New American Library, and London, Granada, 1980.

Parachutes and Kisses. New York, New American Library, and London, Granada, 1984.

Serenissima: A Novel of Venice. Boston, Houghton Mifflin, and London, Bantam, 1987.

Any Woman's Blues. New York, Harper, and London, Chatto and Windus, 1990.

Megan's Two Houses: A Story of Adjustment. West Hollywood, California, Dove Kids, 1996.

Inventing Memory: A Novel of Mothers and Daughters. New York, HarperCollins, 1997.

Uncollected Short Stories

''From the Country of Regrets,'' in *Paris Review,* Spring 1973.

''Take a Lover,'' in *Vogue,* April 1977.

Poetry

Fruits and Vegetables. New York, Holt Rinehart, 1971; London, Secker and Warburg, 1973.

Half-Lives. New York, Holt Rinehart, 1973; London, Secker and Warburg, 1974.

Here Comes and Other Poems. New York, New American Library, 1975.

Loveroot. New York, Holt Rinehart, 1975; London, Secker and Warburg, 1977.

The Poetry of Erica Jong. New York, Holt Rinehart, 1976.

Selected Poems 1–2. London, Panther, 2 vols., 1977–80.

At the Edge of the Body. New York, Holt Rinehart, 1979; London, Granada, 1981.

Ordinary Miracles: New Poems. New York, New American Library, 1983; London, Granada, 1984.

Becoming Light: Poems: New and Selected. New York, HarperCollins, 1991.

Other

Four Visions of America, with others. Santa Barbara, California, Capra Press, 1977.

Witches (miscellany). New York, Abrams, 1981; London, Granada, 1982.

Megan's Book of Divorce: A Kid's Book for Adults. New York, New American Library, 1984; London, Granada, 1985.

The Devil at Large: Erica Jong on Henry Miller. New York, Turtle Bay, and London, Chatto and Windus, 1993.

Fear of Fifty: A Midlife Memoir. New York, HarperCollins, 1994.

What Do Women Want?: Bread, Roses, Sex, Power. New York, HarperCollins, 1998.

*

Critical Studies: Interviews in *New York Quarterly 16,* 1974, *Playboy* (Chicago), September 1975, and *Viva* (New York), September 1977; article by Emily Toth, in *Twentieth-Century American-Jewish Fiction Writers* edited by Daniel Walden, Detroit, Gale, 1984; ''Isadora and Fanny, Jessica and Erica: The Feminist Discourse of Erica Jong'' by Julie Anne Ruth, in *Australian Women's Book Review* (Melbourne), September 1990; *Feminism and the Politics of Literary Reputation: the Example of Erica Jong* by Charlotte Templin. Lawrence, Kansas, University Press of Kansas, 1995; *Writing Mothers,*

Writing Daughters: Tracing the Maternal in Stories by American Jewish Women by Janet Handler Burstein. Urbana, University of Illinois Press, 1996.

* * *

Erica Jong is an impressive poet who writes in the confessional vein of Anne Sexton, Robert Lowell, Sylvia Plath, and John Berryman. She also creates an energetic, garrulous, witty, and tender verse, both erudite and earthy, about the conflict between sexuality and inhibiting intelligence, about death (and one's impulse both toward and away from suicide), the problems of sexual and creative energy (both consuming and propelling), and the hunger for love, knowledge, and connecting. Although she has aligned herself with the feminist movement, her poetry goes beyond the dilemma of being a woman in a male-dominated world, or for that matter, a Jew in an urban culture, to the ubiquitous need for human completeness in a fiercely hostile social and cosmic world.

Jong distinguishes her poetic and fictional forms: ''In poetry I could be pared down, honed, minimal. In the novel what I wanted was excess, digression, rollicking language, energy, and poetry.'' Her stated preference was always for the novel that made one believe ''it was all spilled truth.'' To be sure, ''excess,'' ''energy,'' and ''rollicking language'' are terms that well describe her fiction, along with its absolute quest for truth.

Fear of Flying, still Jong's most influential work, is a funny, moving, and deeply serious book. ''Nothing human was worth denying,'' her heroine, Isadora Wing, says, ''and even if it was unspeakably ugly, we could learn from it, couldn't we?'' Isadora, a picaresque heroine, is a bright, pretty, Jewish, guilt-ridden writer, who accompanies her Chinese-American, child psychiatrist husband, Bennett Wing, to a psychoanalytic congress in Vienna. Torn between the stability of marriage and her sexual fantasies for the ''zipless fuck,'' she abandons Bennett for Adrian Goodlove, an illiterate, sadistic, but very sexy London psychiatrist. Adrian is a selfish and pompous bully, whose words arouse her as much as his sexual promise. (Bennett, though ''often wordless,'' is a far better lover.) Her excursions into the past, where we meet her family and childhood world, her brilliant but sad and mad first husband, and her various sexual partners, are drawn in an earthy and ebullient fashion. But beneath all the bravura is Isadora's basic lack of fulfillment. Sex is only the apparent means toward connecting and feeling alive, an outlet that confounds desperation and freedom. It is only a temporary departure from guilt, an illusory means of flying. Isadora's life remains tortured. The end of the book only half-heartedly suggests some sort of insight and the half-believed: ''People don't complete us. We complete ourselves.'' Isadora has struggled to write as a means of self-discovery and as a sublimated but illusory fulfillment for the frustrations of the real world. She retains an unremitting sense of guilt, vulnerability, childish impulsiveness, and romanticism.

The less successful sequel, *How to Save Your Own Life*, focuses on Isadora's literary success, her divorce from Bennett, and her subsequent move to Hollywood with its virtually limitless number of disappointments, sexual and otherwise. As Jong again portrays it, the plight of the woman is to be torn between her own restlessness and the bourgeois virtues of marriage. She illustrates poignantly and powerfully how a woman's greatest fear is of being alone, and yet her deepest wish is to break free as ''hostage'' to her own ''fantasies,'' her ''fears,'' and ''false definitions.''

Fanny, Being the True History of the Adventures of Fanny Hackabout-Jones is an extraordinary tour de force. In the style and spirit of the eighteenth century, it tells of the tragic and comic fortunes of the beautiful and brilliant young Fanny, whose picaresque adventures en route to becoming a writer and member of the gentry include everything from membership in a witches' coven—really a modern sisterhood—a brothel, and a pirate ship to a series of sexual adventures with the likes of Alexander Pope, Jonathan Swift, and Theophilus Cibber. It is a rich, racy, and enormously funny and serious book—moving, at times to the extreme, in its focus on love, friendship, motherhood, and courage. It is filled with serious, playful, and frequently ironic references to an enormous body of literature. Fanny is conversant with Homer, Virgil, Horace, Boileau, La Rochefoucauld, Voltaire, Locke, and Pascal. Although as a character, Fanny speaks with a 1980s consciousness, the kind of woman she represents might have lived during any age for, to quote Jong's stated intention in creating her, Fanny transcends her own time. Fanny, as a character and novel, embodies, above all, an unflagging and uncompromising search for truth.

''A Woman is made of Sweets and Bitters.... She is both Reason and Rump, both Wit and Wantonness,'' Fanny remarks, in an observation that is applicable to all of Jong's females, including her Isadora Wing character in *Parachutes and Kisses*. Here Jong portrays the famous, rich, brilliant, and beautiful writer, now nearly forty and separated from her husband. Isadora once again possesses a prodigious sexuality, but it is now accompanied by a purposive loneliness. Although she would seem to have reconciled her sexuality with her personal and professional responsibilities—mainly as mother and writer—it is the quest for love that remains her driving force. Isadora relates her experiences with a series of lovers—including a real estate developer, rabbi, antiques dealer, plastic surgeon, and medical student—but the need for love and security remains insatiable. Isadora may long ago have given up the fear of flying, but she remains, in many ways, the woman she described herself as in the earlier works: ''My life had been a constant struggle to get attention, not to be ignored, to be the favored child, the brightest, the best, the most precocious, the most outrageous, the most adored.'' Such is her relationship with parents, lovers, and not least of all, the world.

Serenissima, another historical novel and tour de force of the order of the Rabelaisian Fanny, is set in the Venice of Shakespeare's *The Merchant of Venice*. It is filled not only with details and characters from Shakespeare's life and plays but also with echoes from any number of other Elizabethan writers, as well as often hilarious reminders of numerous more modern authors—from Byron and Ruskin to Dylan Thomas, Henry James to James Joyce. Jessica Pruitt, a middle-aged, jet-setting movie star, has come to Venice as a judge for the Film Festival. Although she plans to play Jessica in a ''filmic fantasy'' of *The Merchant of Venice*, she is forced to remain in Italy, since she has become ill. She takes this as the occasion to embark upon a trip back in time to sixteenth-century Venice. The city, with its grand history, labyrinthine canals, and reflexive surfaces, permits not just her thorough investigation of the Bard himself—in all his natural (i.e., sexual), as well as social and literary capabilities—but it provides the means for a personal journey into her own female identity, in fact and fantasy. It is a pagan rite de passage in preparation for her future. She is, after all, forty-three—an aging woman who must survive within a professional and everyday world that adulates youth; even Shakespeare's heroine, Jessica, is a celebration of youth.

Once back in time, in Shakespeare's Venice, she is a reborn Jessica. She cavorts with an enormous retinue of suitors and even fancies herself as Shakespeare's Dark Lady, among any number of other real and fantasized roles. Amid all the disguises, ruses, and exposes, however, Jong casts a number of tasteless scenes, such as the incredible romping of the Bard with his own creations (like Juliet), or with specifically important people who lived during his lifetime, like his patron, the Earl of Southampton. Jong portrays, for example, Shakespeare and Southampton with a courtesan posing as a boy. They were, she writes, ''a three-backed beast that pants and screams and begs for mercy.'' The reader may be similarly offended by Jessica's numerous attempts to describe ''Will's stiff staff.'' Jong remains at her best linguistically, in her use of quotes and puns. When Jessica first meets Shakespeare, for example, in the Ghetto Vecchio, he says to her: ''Who ever loved, who loved not at first sight?'' and ''What's in a name? A rose by any other name would smell as sweet.''

Any Woman's Blues portrays yet another ''sexaholic,'' as Jong's newest sexual Wonderwoman, Leila Sand, describes herself. Presumably authored by Isadora Wing (which we learn in a foreword and afterword), the novel deals with an artist in her mid-forties. Leila's (midlife) crisis, as the epigraph announces, is that ''the blues ain't nothing/but the facts of life.'' Despite all her celebrity, Leila fears that her talent is waning; she must also come to terms with drugs and alcohol; most importantly, she must confront her masochistic relationship with a young, blond WASP named Darton Veneble Donegal IV. (When she first sees him he is ''helmeted like Darth Vader.'') On the one hand, Leila says, in the typical poor prose of the novel: ''He rarely said anything that wasn't loving, sweet, and dear. He spoke, in fact, like a Hallmark greeting card.'' But she adds: ''It was just that his actions belied his words.'' Dart, her ''great primitive god,'' is also, a ''con man, a hustler, a cowboy, a cocksman, an addict.'' He is also well celebrated for being ''born with an erection.'' As Leila tries, still like Isadora in *Fear of Flying*, to ''get free'' and be her own person, she utters the cloying: ''Life ... is a feast. It is there for the taking. You have only to ... love one another, thank God, and rejoice. At its most simple, it is a prayer.'' Leila's words ring hollow: ''Give, give, give! is the cry of the gods. It rhymes with: ''Live, live, live! Why else are we passing through this sublunary sphere?'' Such a conclusion—and the language in which it is couched—is unworthy of the lusty, witty, and utterly unrepentant Jong persona, whose wild and wicked adventures we have otherwise enjoyed in her previous novels.

Having coined the term ''zipless fuck'' in *Fear of Flying*, virtually a classic in its portrayal of female libido, Jong now uses the word ''whiplash'' in *Fear of Fifty* to describe what she calls the ''women of her generation.'' Once more, in her autobiographical novel form, Jong focuses on many women who grew up during the respectable 1950s and feminist 1960s—women who burned their bras but subsequently had children and discovered the joys of simple motherhood. The book rings painfully true for many women torn between career and motherhood, sexuality and traditional reserve, and even feminism as opposed to femininity. Subtitled ''A Midlife Memoir,'' *Fear of Fifty* more importantly deals with the ''terror'' women experience when they realize they are no longer young and beautiful. Although Jong appears less concerned with her body (while still capable of great sexual prowess), her words ring true in such statements as: ''I wander around,'' wondering if ''I have the right to my immortal soul.'' Perhaps she laments her earlier *romans a clef* and the devastating impact they must have had on her barely disguised characters; now she says: ''Writing matters only if it ... ripens your humanity.''

Jong's most recent offering is strikingly reminiscent of the rash of multi-narrator, mother-daughter novels that have become popular in the past decade—novels such as Amy Tan's *The Joy Luck Club* and Rebecca Wells's *Divine Secrets of the YaYa Sisterhood* and *Little Altars Everywhere*. Sadly, Jong's *Inventing Memory* does not live up to the high standards set by other novels of this genre. Telling the story of four generations of women, in this case of Jewish heritage, she demonstrates their growth as they are ''shaped by the challenges of Jewish history and the misery created by the deeply flawed men they choose.'' The novel was greeted with highly critical reviews, suggesting that the greatest value in Jong's fiction may be found in her early work.

—Lois Gordon, updated by Suzanne Disheroon Green

JORDAN, Neil

Nationality: Irish. **Born:** Sligo in 1950. **Education:** University College, Dublin. **Career:** Co-founder, Irish Writers Co-operative, 1974. Lives in Bray, County Wicklow. **Awards:** Arts Council bursary, 1976; *Guardian* Fiction prize, 1979; Cannes Film Festival Palme d'Or, 1986; Sorrento Film Festival De Sica award, 1986; New York Film Critics Circle award, Best Screenplay, 1992; Alexander Korda award, Best British Film, Best Direction, 1993; Writers Guild American Screen award, Best Screenplay Written Directly for Screen, 1993; Academy Award, Best Writing, Screenplay Written Directly for Screen 1993; Golden Lion award, Venice Film Festival, 1996; Crystal Isis award, Brussels International Film Festival, 1998; Silver Raven award, Brussels International Festival of Fantasy Film, 1999. **Address:** c/o Faber and Faber, 3 Queen Square, London WC1N 3AU, England.

Publications

Novels

The Past. London, Cape, and New York, Braziller, 1980.

The Dream of a Beast. London, Chatto and Windus, 1983; New York, Random House, 1989.

Sunrise with Sea Monster. London, Chatto and Windus, 1994; New York, Random House, 1995.

Nightlines. New York, Random House, 1995.

Short Stories

Night in Tunisia and Other Stories. Dublin, Co-op, 1976; London, Writers and Readers, 1979.

Collected Fiction. London, Vintage, 1997.

Uncollected Short Stories

''A Bus, a Bridge, a Beach'' and ''The Old-Fashioned Lift,'' in *Paddy No More.* Nantucket, Massachusetts, Longship Press, 1978.

''The Artist'' and ''The Photographer,'' in *New Writing and Writers 16.* Atlantic Highlands, New Jersey, Humanities Press, 1979.

Plays

Screenplays: *Angel (Danny Boy)*, 1982; London, Faber, 1989; *The Company of Wolves,* with Angela Carter, 1984; *Mona Lisa,* with David Leland, 1986; London, Faber, 1986; *High Spirits,* 1988; London, Faber, 1989; *We're No Angels,* 1989; *The Miracle,* 1991; *The Crying Game,* 1992; *Interview with the Vampire,* 1994; *Michael Collins,* Geffen Pictures, 1996; published as *Michael Collins: Screenplay and Film Diary,* New York, Plume, 1996; (With Patrick McCabe), *The Butcher Boy,* Warner Brothers, 1997; (With Bruce Robinson), *In Dreams,* DreamWorks, 1999; *The End of the Affair,* 1999.

*

Theatrical Activities: Assistant director: **Film**—*Excalibur* (John Boorman), 1981; Director: **Films**—*Angel (Danny Boy)*, 1982; *The Company of Wolves,* 1984; *Mona Lisa,* 1986; *High Spirits,* 1988; *We're No Angels,* 1990; *The Miracle,* 1991; *The Crying Game,* 1992; *Interview with the Vampire,* 1994.

* * *

Irish-born Neil Jordan first came into prominence in 1976 with his publication of *Night in Tunisia and Other Stories*, which won the Somerset Maugham award and the Guardian Fiction prize. These perceptive stories, often about lonely or displaced people, seem strongly influenced by James Joyce's *Dubliners*, but to Joyce's crisp realism Jordan characteristically adds a poetic quality.

He followed this with *The Past*, a similarly well-received novel about a man searching for the truth about his parentage. But Jordan treats this apparently straightforward theme in a highly complex way. The novel takes us over various places in England and (mainly) Ireland over the years from 1912 to 1934. Una, a mediocre but successful actress, has a child, Rene, by Michael O'Shaughnessy, a lawyer, and marries him. There is little love, merely resignation, between them. Many years later, when the unnamed narrator comes looking for his past, Rene's close friend Lili becomes a major source of information. She tells much of the story in her own words and the narrator often addresses her. But the main narrative voice is that of the unnamed man who is rediscovering—even, he constantly insists, reinventing and remaking—the past in order to discover the truth about his own origins. The novel is an act of imaginative reconstruction, with the past often having to be guessed at, conjured up, in the absence of information. The narrator frequently directs his speculations, hypotheses, and deductions directly to Lili and by implication the reader. Jordan's writing is deeply sensuous, lyrical, almost painterly at times and saturated with visual imagery. As often in his work, both fictional and cinematic, the political and the romantic are deeply entwined, and the novel is deeply aware of what it calls ''the slow irony of history.'' The story of the novel is to a certain extent the story of Ireland in those years. Eamonn de Valera makes frequent guest appearances, Roger Casement is arrested off-stage, and Michael O'Shaughnessy, an active Free Stater, is assassinated.

Jordan's next work of fiction, a novella titled *The Dream of a Beast*, could hardly be more different. Set in a mysteriously dystopian Dublin, it is the nightmarish story of a man who slowly turns into some kind of animal. He becomes estranged from his wife and young daughter, increasingly cut off from an urban world that is subtly intimated as undergoing its own dark metamorphoses. At the same time, there are strange epiphanies occurring constantly, such as a young woman who visits him in his advertising office and falls in love with him, or a young boy who also feels love for him. In the ambiguous ending it is possible even that his family returns to him. The Dream of a Beast is a deeply imagistic novel about a man who has lost touch with feelings and perhaps learns to recover them. Jordan himself has said of it that it is less Kafka than *Creature from the Black Lagoon.*

Given his highly visual imagination, it is not so surprising in retrospect that since this novella Jordan has turned away from fiction in favor of film, although he himself denies any conflict. He says, ''I don't know any novelists, particularly the younger ones, who aren't working in film. In the fifties, people used to talk about the death of the novel and saw television as a threat to writing. Now the writers have pushed their way in.'' He has become a world-famous director and scriptwriter, with hits like *Mona Lisa* , *The Crying Game*, and *Michael Collins.* He co-wrote the original screenplay of *Mona Lisa*, of which he said, ''The attraction of it was that it could become a love story, a contemporary moral tale with two characters so far apart, but so inherently likeable that an audience might empathize, understand each point of view, feel the depth of their misplaced passion, and yet know from the start how impossible it was.''

—Judy Cooke, updated by Laurie Clancy

JORGENSON, Ivar

See SILVERBERG, Robert

JOSHI, Arun

Nationality: Indian. **Born:** 1939. **Education:** Attended schools in India and the United States. **Career:** Director, Shri Ram Centre for Industrial Relations.

PUBLICATIONS

Novels

The Foreigner. Bombay and London, Asia Publishing House, 1968.
The Strange Case of Billy Biswas. Bombay, London, and New York, Asia Publishing House, 1971.
The Apprentice. Bombay and New York, Asia Publishing House, 1974; London, Asia Publishing House, 1975.
The Last Labyrinth. New Delhi, Vision, 1981.
The City and the River. New Delhi, Vision, 1990.

Short Stories

The Survivor: A Selection of Stories. New Delhi, Sterling, 1975.

Other

Shri Ram: A Biography, with Khushwant Singh. London and New York, Asia Publishing House, 1968.
Laia Shri Ram: A Study in Entrepreneurship and Industrial Management. New Delhi, Orient Longman, 1975.

*

Critical Studies: *Arun Joshi: A Study of His Fiction* edited by N. Radhakrishnan, Gandhigram, Tamilnadu, Gandhigram Rural Institute, 1984; *The Fictional World of Arun Joshi,* New Delhi, Classical, 1986, and *The Novels of Arun Joshi,* New Delhi, Prestige, 1992, both edited by R.K. Dhawan; *The Novels of Kamala Markandaya and Arun Joshi* by A.A. Sinha. Jalandhar, India, ABS Publications, 1998; *Arun Joshi: The Existentialist Element in His Novels by Mukteshwar Pandey.* Delhi, B.R. Publishing, 1998.

* * *

Arun Joshi is a novelist who, more strongly than most, has brought to his work that detachment from the everyday, while still acknowledging its existence, which is perhaps India's particular gift to the literature of the world. The rising up into the transcendental is a trait that has increasingly marked out his novels from his first, *The Foreigner*—where the young hero, after experiencing life and love in America, is, back in Delhi, at last persuaded by a humble office worker that sometimes detachment lies in actually getting involved—on up to *The City and the River,* which takes place wholly in an imaginary land.

To venture as a writer into such territory it is necessary to be equipped with the means to make the everyday credible and sharply present. This Joshi was from the start well able to do, as his early short stories, subsequently collected in *The Survivor,* clearly show. "The Gherao" tells simply and effectively of how a young college teacher arrives at maturity when his aged Principal is subjected to that peculiar Indian form of protest action, the *gherao,* the preventing of a target figure from moving anywhere or receiving any succor.

The Strange Case of Billy Biswas is the story of a young, rich, American-educated Indian who ends up in the wilderness of central India living as a semi-naked "tribal" seeking a meaning to things above and beyond all that everyday civilization can provide. A key to Joshi's whole intent can be found in the words he puts into the mouth of his narrator; as he grows old he realizes that the most futile cry of man is his impossible wish to be understood.

The Apprentice, Joshi's third novel, takes his search for understanding man's predicament one step further toward the transcendental. Its central figure is a man essentially docile and uncourageous whose life more or less parallels the coming into being of postcolonial India. Eventually gaining a post in the civil service, he ends, as many real-life civil servants did, by taking a huge bribe. But in the final pages he comes to see that at least corrupt man can strive to do just a little good—he cleans shoes at a temple—and that while there are in the world young people still untainted, there is a spark of hope.

In *The Last Labyrinth,* the hero, if that always is not too strong a term for the men Joshi puts at the center, is a man crying always "I want! I want!" and not knowing what it is he desires, in some ways a parallel figure to Saul Bellow's Henderson, the rain king. His search takes him, however, to infinitely old Benares, a city seen as altogether intangible, at once holy and repellent, and to an end lost in a miasma of nonunderstanding. But the way there is gripping. Joshi writes with a persuasive ease and illuminates the outward scene with telling phrase after telling phrase.

Then there is *The City and the River,* where the city is not the Delhi or the Bombay Joshi has elsewhere described so concretely but a wholly intangible place, removed from time, where nonetheless a man can be seen wearing jeans. Joshi, in his search for a way to describe the meaning of things, has now come to a world akin to those of science fiction or perhaps to the mystical poetry of Blake writing of "Golgonooza the spiritual Fourfold London eternal." But all the while there are digs or sly hints at the current ills of Indian society and, by implication, of all societies everywhere. And in the final pages, where the wild river sweeps over the whole complex city, there is, again, sounded that faint note of hope. The question is not of success or failure, an old yogi tells his disciple; the question is of trying.

—H.R.F. Keating

JOSIPOVICI, Gabriel (David)

Nationality: British. **Born:** Nice, France, 8 October 1940. **Education:** Victoria College, Cairo, 1950–56; Cheltenham College, Gloucesteshire, 1956–57; St. Edmund Hall, Oxford, 1958–61, B.A. in English 1961. **Family:** Married in 1963. **Career:** Lecturer, 1963–74, reader, 1974–80, part-time reader, 1981–84, and since 1984 professor of English, University of Sussex, Brighton. Northcliffe Lecturer, University College, London, 1981. **Awards:** *Sunday Times* award, for play, 1970; South East Arts prize, 1978. **Agent:** John Johnson, 45–47 Clerkenwell Green, London EC1R 0HT. **Address:** Department of English, University of Sussex, Falmer, Brighton, Sussex BN1 9RH, England.

Publications

Novels

The Inventory. London, Joseph, 1968.
Words. London, Gollancz, 1971.
The Present. London, Gollancz, 1975.
Migrations. Hassocks, Sussex, Harvester Press, 1977.
The Echo Chamber. Brighton, Harvester Press, 1980.
The Air We Breathe. Brighton, Harvester Press, 1981.
Conversations in Another Room. London, Methuen, 1984.
Contre-Jour: A Triptych after Pierre Bonnard. Manchester, Carcanet, 1986.
The Big Glass. Manchester, Carcanet, 1991.
In a Hotel Garden. Manchester, Carcanet, 1994; New York, New Directions, 1995.
Moo Pak. Manchester, Carcanet, 1995.
Now. Manchester, England, Carcanet, 1998.

Short Stories

Mobius the Stripper: Stories and Short Plays (includes the plays *One, Dreams of Mrs. Fraser, Flow*). London, Gollancz, 1974.
Four Stories. London, Menard Press, 1977.
In the Fertile Land. Manchester, Carcanet, 1987.

Plays

Dreams of Mrs. Fraser (produced London, 1972). Included in *Mobius the Stripper,* 1974.
Evidence of Intimacy (produced London, 1972).
Flow (produced Edinburgh and London, 1973). Included in *Mobius the Stripper,* 1974.
Echo (produced London, 1975). Published in *Proteus 3,* 1978.
Marathon (produced London, 1977). Published in *Adam* (London), 1980.
A Moment (produced London, 1979).
Vergil Dying (broadcast 1979). Windsor, SPAN, 1981.

Radio Plays: *Playback,* 1973; *A Life,* 1974; *Ag,* 1976; *Vergil Dying,* 1979; *Majorana: Disappearance of a Physicist,* with Sacha Rabinovitch, 1981; *The Seven,* with Jonathan Harvey, 1983; *Metamorphosis,* from the story by Kafka, 1985; *Ode for St. Cecilia,* 1986; *Mr. Vee,* 1988; *A Little Personal Pocket Requiem,* 1990.

Other

The World and the Book: A Study of Modern Fiction. London, Macmillan, and Stanford, California, Stanford University Press, 1971; revised edition, Macmillan, 1979.
The Lessons of Modernism and Other Essays. London, Macmillan, and Totowa, New Jersey, Rowman and Littlefield, 1977.
Writing and the Body: The Northcliffe Lectures 1981. Brighton, Harvester Press, 1982; Princeton, New Jersey, Princeton University Press, 1983.
The Mirror of Criticism: Selected Reviews 1977–1982. Brighton, Harvester Press, and New York, Barnes and Noble, 1983.
The Book of God: A Response to the Bible. New Haven, Connecticut, Yale University Press, 1988.
Steps: Selected Fiction and Drama. Manchester, Carcanet Press, 1990.
Text and Voice. Manchester, Carcanet, 1992.
Touch. New Haven, Connecticut, Yale University Press, 1996.
On Trust: Art and the Temptations of Suspicion. New Haven, Connecticut, Yale University Press, 1999.
Editor, *The Modern English Novel: The Reader, The Writer, and the Work.* London, Open Books, and New York, Barnes and Noble, 1976.
Editor, *The Sirens' Song: Selected Essays,* by Maurice Blanchot. Brighton, Harvester Press, and Bloomington, Indiana University Press, 1982.

*

Critical Studies: Interview with Bernard Sharratt, in *Orbit* (Tunbridge Wells, Kent), December 1975; ''True Confessions of an Experimentalist'' by Josipovici, and interview with Maurice Kapitanchik, in *Books and Bookmen* (London), 1982; article by Linda Canon and Jay L. Halio, in *British Novelists since 1960* edited by Halio, Detroit, Gale, 1983; interview with Timothy Hyman, in *Jewish Quarterly* (London), 1985; James Hansford, in *Prospice* (Portree, Isle of Skye), 1985; essay by Josipovici, in *Contemporary Authors Autobiography Series 8* edited by Mark Zadrozny, Detroit, Gale, 1988; ''Bonnard and Josipovici'' by Jean Duffy, in *Word and Image,* 9(4), October-December 1993.

* * *

''Modern art,'' says Gabriel Josipovici in *The Lessons of Modernism,* ''moves between two poles, silence and game.'' In his own novels the game is that of verbal art; the silence is that of unanswered questions. Conversations abound, explanations are sought, inquiries are pursued, but answers are always lacking. Characters experience an overwhelming pressure to speak, like a weight on the chest. But there is no narrator with authority to pronounce on the truth. The reader is drawn into puzzled involvement, impotent attentiveness, and pleasure in the play of the text.

In *The Inventory* a young man is constructing a list of the contents of a flat in which an old man and his son Sam used to live. They are both now dead. The precision of the inventory contrasts with the uncertainty of what he hears about their lives from Susan who tells him stories about her experiences of the two men. Why did Sam suddenly leave? Was he in love with Susan? Did she love him? Are her stories based on memory or invention? The novel is almost entirely in dialogue form and its effect depends on the author's precise control of rhythm, pace, and tone. It demonstrates his fascination with the musical, kinesthetic, and dramatic aspects of speech which he has explored equally in his work for radio and theater.

In *Words* Louis and his wife Helen are visited by Jo, who was once Louis's girlfriend and who may or may not also have had an affair with his brother Peter. The reader learns about the characters only through what they say to each other. Conversations return again and again to certain nagging questions. What happened years ago when Louis and Jo separated? Are either of them in earnest now when they talk about going away together? Are they serious or are they playing games? We only have their words to go on and words always leave open a variety of possible interpretations: cheerful banter or wounding aggression, flirtation or contempt, honesty or evasion? *The Present* represents a change in fictional technique, for in this novel even the basic narrative situation is left undecided. The narrative, in the present tense, simultaneously develops stories in a number of different possible directions. The present leaves the future open. Reg and Minna share a flat with Alex; Minna is in hospital after a breakdown and dreams or imagines her life with Reg; Minna is married to Alex and they live with their two daughters in the country; Alex is dead having thrown himself from the window of Reg and Minna's flat. The stories interweave, each compelling but inconclusive.

Since 1977 Josipovici has written his most ambitious and accomplished work, including the major radio play *Vergil Dying* and the novels *Migrations* and *The Air We Breathe.* In these novels he moves further away from the conventions of realist narrative. Whereas the early novels (and *The Echo Chamber*) are constructed around inconclusive stories and are primarily in dialogue form the later novels are constructed around multiple repetitions of fragmentary scenes and haunting images.

In *Migrations* a man lies on a bed in an empty room; a man collapses in an urban street; an autistic child fails to communicate with uncomprehending adults; a man talks in an over-furnished room with an unsympathetic woman, and so on. The text migrates restlessly from scene to scene: ''You try to find a place to stop, roots ... attempt to find a resting place for the imagination.'' ''A series of places. Each must be visited. In turn. Then it will be finished. Then they will disappear.'' Temporary stillness and a disturbing sense of the physicality of speech, of words in the mouth, are achieved as the narrative voice repeats certain rhythms, images, and sound patterns and occasionally settles on certain sensuous sentences: ''The black sky presses on his face like a blanket.'' ''The sun streams in through the closed panes.'' ''Silence drains away from him in dark streams.'' There is a poetic preoccupation with certain elemental forces, water and light, motion and rest, air and breath, which are to become an explicit theme of inquiry in *The Air We Breathe.*

In *Conversations in Another Room* an old woman, Phoebe, lies in bed. She shares her flat with a companion and is visited regularly by her niece. The narration is in the present tense and is mostly dialogue, at times very funny. The conversations circle around unanswered questions about Phoebe's husband who vanished without trace, and her son David whose marriage has broken up. In the hall the niece's boyfriend sits under a convex mirror, occasionally jotting in a notebook. To the reader's surprise, towards the end of the book there is suddenly a section in an unfamiliar and unidentified voice, in the first person. We do not know what the relationship is between this voice and the characters in Phoebe's flat. The voice says: ''Perhaps we cannot write about our real selves, our real lives, the lives we have really lived. They are not there to be written about. The conversation always goes on in another room.'' *Contre-Jour* derives from a fascination with the French painter Pierre Bonnard. The first half of the novel is in the voice of his daughter, who has left home. The second half is in the voice of his wife. She compulsively bathes as her husband sits and sketches her. She voices her complaints and her unhappiness about her daughter's behavior. She writes odd notes and pins them around the house. We begin to realize that she is seriously disturbed. Perhaps the daughter does not exist at all but is made up as a consolation or a demented irritant by the painter's wife. We hear only short fragments of the painter's own speech as they are quoted by the women. Through all of his wife's miseries he continues, apparently serenely, to paint. Is his absorption in his work immensely cruel or is it that he has extraordinary patience? At the end we read a short, formal letter from the painter to a friend announcing the death of his wife. It has come to seem that the main subject of the work is the painter himself even though we scarcely hear his own voice directly. We view him only in the negative shapes he makes against the background of those who surround him, against the light.

The plot of *In a Hotel Garden* takes place as much in flashback as in forward motion, with the glum protagonist Ben attempting to sort out the problems of his past. All in all, the book offers little to hold a reader's attention. One central image from *Migrations* can serve as an index of Josipovici's concerns as a novelist. The friends and relations of Lazarus wait outside the tomb, excited, anticipating a miracle. Lazarus emerges and slowly unwinds the linen cloth. He unwinds and unwinds and when he is finished there is nothing there, nothing but a little mound of dust. There is nothing in the center. There is no central meaning. As Josipovici says in *The Lessons of Modernism* the modern writer, like Eliot's Prufrock, rejects the role of Lazarus, ''come back from the dead, come back to tell you all.''

—John Mepham

JUST, Ward

Nationality: American. **Born:** Michigan City, Indiana, 5 September 1935. **Education:** Trinity College, Hartford, Connecticut, 1953–57. **Family:** Has two daughters, one son; married Sarah Catchpole, 1983. **Career:** Reporter, *Newsweek,* Chicago and Washington, 1959–62; *The Reporter Magazine,* Washington, 1962–63; *Newsweek,* London and Washington, 1963–65; *The Washington Post,* Washington and Saigon. **Awards:** Overseas Press Club award, 1968; National Magazine award, 1970, for non-fiction, and 1980, for fiction; Chicago *Tribune* Heartland award for fiction, 1989, for ''Jack Gance''; O. Henry Award, 1985, 1986, 1993. **Address:** RFD 342, Vineyard Haven, Massachusetts 02568, U.S.A.

Publications

Novels

A Soldier of the Revolution. New York, Knopf, and London, Weidenfeld and Nicolson, 1970.
Stringer. Boston, Atlantic, 1974.
Nicholson at Large. Boston, Atlantic, 1975.
A Family Trust. Boston, Atlantic, and London, Secker, 1978.
Honor, Power, Riches, Fame and the Love of Women. New York, Dutton, 1979.
In the City of Fear. New York, Viking, 1982.
The American Blues. New York, Viking, 1984.
American Ambassador. Boston, Houghton Mifflin, and London, Serpent's Tail, 1987.
Jack Gance. Boston, Houghton Mifflin, and London, Hale, 1989.
The Translator. Boston, Houghton Mifflin, 1991.
Ambition and Love. Boston, Houghton Mifflin, 1994.
Echo House. Boston, Houghton Mifflin, 1997.
A Dangerous Friend. Boston, Houghton Mifflin, 1999.

Short Stories

The Congressman Who Loved Flaubert: 21 Stories and Novellas. Boston, Atlantic, and London, Little Brown, 1973.
Twenty-One: Selected Stories. Boston, Houghton Mifflin, 1990.

Other

To What End: Report from Vietnam. New York, Knopf, 1968; New York, Public Affairs, 1968.
Military Men. New York, Knopf, 1970.

*

Manuscript Collection: Cranbrook School Archives, Bloomfield Hills, Michigan.

Critical Studies: ''Just Deserts'' by Tad Friend, *GQ,* June 1990; ''Just So: The Odyssey of a Quintessentially American Novelist'' by Dinitia Smith, *New York Magazine,* 19 August 1991.

* * *

Though Ward Just has distinguished himself as a journalist, he has also produced an impressive body of fiction. As a novelist, he has been compared favorably with Ernest Hemingway and Henry James. Much of his work centers around war—portrayed by the keen eye of a newsman—as is often true of Hemingway; however, his characters and their settings seem more Jamesian in their affluence and jaded sophistication. It is as if Just has felt the pulse of America for the past fifty years and produced ''our story,'' one that is frighteningly familiar. The primary criticism of Just's work is that his action is slow and plodding. Although his characters are articulate and witty, they often do just sit and talk, especially in his fine piece on Washington during Vietnam, *In the City of Fear.*

Stringer, published in 1974 during the era of disillusion that followed Watergate, received mixed reviews. The general response was that this was a small book with flaws but a powerful look at the Vietnam War and the society that lived through it. In the opening scene, when Stringer savors the taste of chocolate and limeade through a high that captures his readers with the physical surroundings, he might well be a Hemingway character discovering watercress except that this war is different for the individual soldier who feels more alienated than heroic. The main character does not feel connected to the war anymore than he does to his education, his career as a journalist, or to his family.

In his next novel, *Nicholson at Large,* Just captures the spirit of Washington as it reflects whatever else is going on in the nation. Many readers, however, felt that the work revealed flaws of an early novelist who, nonetheless, showed promise. Other reviewers insisted that this novel was more than promising—that it had, in fact, established Just as a serious writer to be watched. In 1978, *A Family Trust* was widely praised for its insightful treatment of family conflict. The word ''promising'' was less audible but still heard in response to Ward Just.

With *In the City of Fear,* the promise came to fruition almost without dispute. Just was praised for the convincing character of Colonel Sam Joyce and for his satirical look at some of Washington's key figures, including the presidents (even if he does not name them). One of the most stirring scenes in the book helps to illustrate the realization of Just's ability to portray strong female characters. Sheila has disrupted the chatter of a Washington dinner party (attended by military men, politicians, newspaper men, and their wives) by producing a poignant photo of her young son, who is in Vietnam. The photo quiets even the most enthusiastic war conversationalists, and Marina muses:

> Watching Sheila now, Marina was surprised at her—forbearance. At the general forbearance of women—Sheila's, Jo's, her own. It would not last, they concealed so much. She knew the tempo of the dance was increasing. … They would all go to pieces, men would leave their wives and women their families. Children would disappear. There would be heart attacks and suicides and breakdowns and no one would be as he or she had been. The thin would grow fat, and the fat would grow fatter. They were all fighting the same war, in this murderous twilight of the American century. Now she was drawn to Sheila, tired and distraught, her grief worn like a black badge of courage.

She goes on to say they were all beguiled in the way that Henry James once described ''women traveling in exotic Italy.'' The echo of James is significant in the middle of this musing, but even more so is the echo of Stephen Crane's badge of courage. No wonder this book brought Just praise as a sensitive, distinguished writer of our time.

The American Blues, a first-person narrative, is disarming, given the close relationship of journalism and fiction that readers of Just already grapple with. His work often reads more like a factual account than a novel, particularly here.

The theme of father and son pitted against one another recurs in *The American Ambassador,* when William and Bill Jr., a diplomat and a terrorist respectively, struggle in the exciting backdrop of international intrigue. Not surprisingly, *The Translator,* which appeared in 1991, covers the historic lifting of the Iron Curtain. An American woman in Paris marries a refugee who has become a linguist—a skill that leads to international intrigue again. Critics found this a gloomy portrayal of humanity as it nears the twenty-first century, but none of them were arguing that a more hopeful picture is deserved.

With *Ambition and Love* Just moved away from the political scene and gives the reader a delightful ''tour'' of Paris through the eyes of an artist, who may well be Just's strongest female character, and her lover, who is a writer. *Echo House,* the name for the Washington, D.C., mansion occupied by the prestigious Behl family, offers a sort of family history of postwar America, and presents insights into the intelligence community and the operations of government. In *A Dangerous Friend,* Just pictured America on the brink of full commitment to the Vietnam War in 1965. Through the eyes of a misguided civil servant, the book compellingly depicts the nation's descent down the slippery slope to folly.

—Loretta Cobb

K

KAPLAN, Johanna

Nationality: American. **Born:** New York City, 29 December 1942. **Education:** The High School of Music and Art, New York; University of Wisconsin, Madison; New York University, B.A. 1964; Columbia University Teachers College, M.A. in special education 1965. **Career:** Since 1966 teacher of emotionally disturbed children in New York public schools at Mount Sinai Hospital, New York. **Awards:** Creative Artists Public Service grant, 1973; National Endowment for the Arts grant, 1973; Jewish Book Council Epstein award, 1976; Wallant award, 1981; Jewish Book award, 1981; Smilen-*Present Tense* award, 1981. **Agent:** Georges Borchardt Inc., 136 East 57th Street, New York, New York 10022. **Address:** 411 West End Avenue, New York, New York 10024, U.S.A.

PUBLICATIONS

Novel

O My America! New York, Harper, 1980.

Short Stories

Other People's Lives. New York, Knopf, 1975.

Uncollected Short Stories

''Not All Jewish Families Are Alike,'' in *Commentary* (New York), January 1976.
''Family Obligations,'' in *Forthcoming* (New York), March 1983.
''Close Calls,'' in *Commentary* (New York), May 1986.
''Christmas Party,'' in *City Journal* (New York), Winter 1995.

*

Johanna Kaplan comments:

(2000) What I aim for in my work, both for my readers and for myself, is that self-transcendent state we all remember from the ecstasy of reading in childhood. In other words, a deep plunge into the world of otherness—not at all surreal or magical otherness, but rather an intense imaginative joining with lives going on about us which we might otherwise only guess at: a face glimpsed from a bus window, a transaction overheard in a store. Who *are* these people is what I want to know; what are their lives really like? Such (gossipy) wonderings instigate my fiction. I think it's also fair to say that I am concerned with the ways in which the past, specifically Jewish history, has a way of peeking and poking through to the everyday present.

* * *

By all the laws of literary logic, Johanna Kaplan should not have a career at all, much less an increasingly successful one. She began publishing short fiction about American-Jewish life in the early 1970s, at a time when the tapestry of American-Jewish life seemed threadbare, when sheer exhaustion had taken its toll on imaginative transformations of American-Jewish material, when critics and reviewers alike outraced themselves to say ''Enough already!'' *Other People's Lives* proved how wrong the nay-sayers had been. In this collection of five short stories and a novella, Kaplan made us aware, once again, of how vital, how dynamically alive, renderings of the American-Jewish milieu could be—especially if one had Kaplan's ear for speech rhythms and an instinctive grasp of our time, our place. Here, for example, is a snippet from the title story:

> When your mother wrote that book [a character hectors a disaffected daughter], it was the Age of Conformity. And I'm not just talking about gray flannel suits! What I'm talking about is all those people who got caught up—they couldn't help themselves—in the whole trend and sway and spirit of the times. Not that I got trapped into it even then. Because it always seemed escapist and reactionary to me. And that's all that was going on—the flight to the suburbs! Your own *lawn.* Your own *house.* Your own *psyche.* Your own little *garden*—and for some people, not so little! And *that,* Julia darling, was what your mother was up against! Forget the city and live in the trees! And these were genuinely progressive people, not just ordinary *shtunks!*

Kaplan's congenial turf is the ordinariness of ordinary New York Jewish life. You walk into her stories as if through a crowded living room—never as an invited, ''formal'' guest, but, rather, as some distant cousin catching up on family gossip. It is a world where one's childhood is fixed forever in the mind of an aunt, even when that ''child'' is now an adult, and a psychiatrist to boot:

> ''Naomi!'' the aunt said, jumping up from a green plastic chair that could easily have come from the office of a dentist with no eye for the future.
>
> ''I know,'' Naomi said. ''My panti-hose are crooked. I'll go to the ladies' room and fix them.''
>
> ''*When* did I—''
>
> ''All right, then, I'll go to the *men's* room and fix them …''

But that much said about the comic ironies, the delicately shaded satire of Kaplan's stories, what *lasts* in these fictions are the complex privacies that simmer just beneath the surface. In ''Sour or Suntanned, It Makes No Difference,'' for example, a ten-year-old protagonist who hates, absolutely *hates,* the regimen and artificiality of a summer camp (''at flag lowering you joined hands and swayed … in swimming you had to jump for someone else's dripping hand… . There was no reason to spend a whole summer hugging them''), is confused, and frightened, by the part she must play in a camp production directed by a visiting Hebrew playwright. The story's concluding sentence, brilliantly written and hauntingly evocative, might stand for many of the stories in *Other People's Lives:* ''standing there on the stage, a little girl in braids and a too-long dress who would end up not dead, Miriam promised herself that never again in her life would anyone look at her face and see in it what Amnon did, but just like the girl who could fake being dead, she would keep all her aliveness a secret.''

O My America! extended the range and depth of Kaplan's fiction. It is, on one level, the story of Ezra Slavin, a crusty, unremitting social critic who dies at an anti-war rally in 1972. As an obituary puts it:

> From very early in his career, Mr. Slavin was harshly critical of the anomic trends of urban, mechanized American life, yet his vision of the city as a place of ''limitless, tumultuous possibility'' was a lyrical, even celebratory one. ''I have had a lifelong affair with the idea of America,'' Mr. Slavin once said. ''And when people find that difficult to believe, I remind them of that flintier vision which is bound to result when love is unrequited.''

That, one might say, is the ''official,'' the pundit's, version of Ezra Slavin and what he stood for. *O My America!,* on the other hand, is that life told in flashback by his daughter Merry, one of his six children and part of what can only be called a complicated, free-form and exasperatingly extended ''family.''

The result is a canvas large enough for Kaplan to pour in a satiric history of immigrant Jewish life, to sketch minor characters by the dozen and to deepen the connections between American Jews and contemporary versions of the American Dream. Even more impressive, *O My America!* opened new possibilities for American-Jewish fiction, at a time when its dimensions seemed limited to pale retellings of Borsht Belt jokes or to pale imitations of major writers like Bernard Malamud, Saul Bellow, and Philip Roth. Even the most skeptical reviewers admitted that if Kaplan's fiction were the norm, there would be plenty of American-Jewish novels to kick around, for some time to come.

—Sanford Pinsker

KATZ, Steve

Nationality: American. **Born:** New York City, 14 May 1935. **Education:** Cornell University, Ithaca, New York, 1952–56, A.B. (honors) 1956; University of Oregon, Eugene, M.A. in English 1959. **Family:** Married Patricia Bell in 1956 (divorced 1979); three sons. **Career:** Staff member, English Language Institute, 1960, and faculty member, University of Maryland Overseas, 1961–62, both Lecce, Italy; Assistant Professor of English, Cornell University, 1962–67; Lecturer in Fiction, University of Iowa, Iowa City, 1969–70; writer-in-residence, Brooklyn College, New York, 1970–71; Assistant Professor of English, Queens College, New York, 1971–75; Associate Professor of English, Notre Dame University, Indiana, 1976–78. Since 1978 Associate Professor of English, and Director of Creative Writing, 1978–81, University of Colorado, Boulder. Has also worked for the Forest Service in Idaho, in a quicksilver mine in Nevada, and on dairy farms in New York State; since 1971 teacher of Tai Chi Chuan. **Awards:** National Endowment for the Arts grant, 1976, 1981; Creative Artists Public Service grant, 1976. **Agent:** Georges Borchardt Inc., 136 East 57th Street, New York, New York 10022. **Address:** 3060 8th Street, Boulder, Colorado 80302, U.S.A.

PUBLICATIONS

Novels

The Lestriad. Lecce, Italy, Milella, 1962; Flint, Michigan, Bamberger, 1987.
The Exagggerations of Peter Prince. New York, Holt Rinehart, 1968.
Posh (as Stephanie Gatos). New York, Grove Press, 1971.
Saw. New York, Knopf, 1972.
Moving Parts. New York, Fiction Collective, 1977.
Wier and Pouce. College Park, Maryland, Sun and Moon, 1984.
Florry of Washington Heights. Los Angeles, Sun and Moon, 1988; London, Serpent's Tail, 1989.
Swanny's Ways. Los Angeles, Sun & Moon Press, 1995.

Short Stories

Creamy and Delicious: Eat My Words (in Other Words). New York, Random House, 1970.
Stolen Stories. New York, Fiction Collective, 1984.
43 Fictions. Los Angeles, Sun and Moon, 1991.

Plays

Screenplays: *Grassland* (*Hex*), with Leo Garen, 1972.

Poetry

The Weight of Antony. Ithaca, New York, Eibe Press, 1964.
Cheyenne River Wild Track. Ithaca, New York, Ithaca House, 1973.
Journalism. Flint, Michigan, Bamberger, 1990.

*

Critical Studies: *The Life of Fiction* by Jerome Klinkowitz, Urbana, University of Illinois Press, 1977; ''Fiction and the Facts of Life'' by J.K. Grant, in *Critique* (Atlanta), Summer 1983; article by Sinda J. Gregory and Larry McCaffery, in *Dictionary of Literary Biography Yearbook 1983* edited by Mary Bruccoli and Jean W. Ross, Detroit, Gale, 1984.

Steve Katz comments:

(1991) The nature of our work is determined by our peculiar collaborative procedures. There are nine Steve Katz and each of us makes a contribution to each piece. Three of the Steve Katz are women, putting them in a minority, but allowing, at least, for some female input into all of the work, which sometimes invokes misogyny, but because of the female component in its composition transcends that inference. We break down into three groups of three, each one with a woman at its pivot most of the time, though sometimes the women collaborate as a separate cadre. Three of us live in New York City, three travel all over North America, and sometimes to South

America, and are stationed in Boulder, Colorado, and the third three never rest as travelers of the remaining world. Sometimes for variety one Steve Katz from the New York triumvirate will replace one Steve Katz from the world travelers and etc., generally without disruption or conflict. Some of the works can be written by only five of us (this blurb, for instance), and some by seven. In these instances we arbitrarily eliminate the four Steve Katz, or the two, by a process we call "blistering." For more information about this process please contact our agent. We have never before revealed our method of composition because we had expected great financial gain from this unique procedure. Since this has not been forthcoming, voilà!

* * *

Steve Katz's fictions are woven from two distinct strands: from playful fable-like tales, often of serious intent, and from disruptive watch-the-writer-writing materials. The proportions in which these two narrative impulses are mixed vary from book to book, and give each its individual character.

Experiments in textual disruption dominate and shape *The Exagggerations of Peter Prince.* Devices used include crossed-out pages, notices of deleted passages, partially whited-out ads, and authorial injunctions to the characters and to the author himself. Despite the emphasis on technical manipulations, the emotional contour of a caring young man's struggles to do the right thing comes through—both from Peter Prince and from Katz. Katz's hope here, as in most of his quasi-autobiographical fiction, is that by writing *Peter Prince* he will invent for himself a better life. It is an admission of uncertainty about the future that the novel has no ending, that the planned ending is lost in the "archives of the unwritten." (The ending was to have been "America, with a rock and roll band at the castle, and all the new dances, formal and primitive ..." This scene does appear, sixteen years later, as "The Death of Bobby Kennedy" in *Wier and Pouce.*) Between disruptive passages Katz also shows himself to be a visually oriented writer, with a gift for evoking realistic detail: "... trees like candelabra, holding vultures, their gray and carmine heads flickering, and the small dark kites circling the umbrella crowned acacias." With the stories in *Creamy and Delicious* Katz's neo-fable style hits its stride. This book collects the "Mythologies," satirical reworkings and defacings of the stories and images of Wonder Woman, Nancy and Sluggo, Dickens, and Greek mythology. The writing here shares with *Peter Prince* a tense feel, and a need to discomfit or shock the reader: "Wonder Woman was a dike, but she was nice." The plain speech style is in places extended and stylized, with results not unlike some of Gertrude Stein's work: "A man there was called Thomas who in the aged long ago time before I was a boy was the man of many creatures, a many-creatured man in the hills before my youth... ." Katz's disruptive side is here confined to two short, comparatively unsuccessful pieces, and some short poems. Katz followed this collection with the erotic novel *Posh,* which he wrote in six weeks.

With *Saw* Katz finds his mature voice. The disruptive and the fabulous are blended in a much more confident and relaxed, even whimsical, way. Characters in the novel include Eileen, who feeds a puppy to a hawk; a sphere from the center of the earth; a cylinder; a talking fly; and an astronaut from a distant galaxy—who, as Katz confesses midway through the book, is really the author. The Astronaut has come to Earth seeking a substance which can revitalize his world, a substance which is an amalgam of "ambition, greed, bullshit, pride, envy, bourbon, and smut." If we can credit the authorial interruptions in *Saw,* this is identical with Katz's idea of the substance of fiction. So in some ways *Saw* is about, not the process, but the experience of creating fiction. The final chapter (titled "The First Chapter") is a detailed account of a long hot day filled with poets and worries, and concludes with Katz getting away from it all in the more genial company of The Astronaut; leaving his everyday life behind and going off to explore his fictional world.

Beginning with "Female Skin" in *Moving Parts* Katz's fables move into new territory, become more deeply reflective of modern life and concerns than was possible through the more conventionally satirical characters of the earlier "Mythologies." "Female Skin" takes literally the metaphorical idea of getting inside another's skin. Called a novel, *Moving Parts* contains stories, diary entries, photographs, and a log of encounters with the number forty-three. Katz's playful side is evident everywhere: a photograph of Katz with a beard is followed by one of a barber shop, then one of a clean-shaven Katz. The author's face is one more "moving part" employed in the process of creating his fiction.

In *Stolen Stories* the literary experimentalist and the fable-wright once again speak separately. Half the pieces here are disembodied monologues, which are disruptive not in the sense of any authorial intrusion, but through their staccato, Burroughs-like use of language ("come in: this is my tent: you carry the sickness:"). These monologues succeed only in evoking the sounds of the experiences and states Katz deals with, with little of the emotional depth of his best work. The fabulous stories here are Katz's best. "Friendship" makes a convincing case for cannibalism being the logical and loving end toward which all friendships should move. "Death of the Band" crosses John Cage-style compositional ideas with psychotic urban violence to prophesy a new musical form.

Wier and Pouce is Katz's masterpiece, an encapsulation of the spiritual/ideological crisis in America since the 1950s. (*Wier and Pouce* is a very American novel: it begins and ends with ball games.) The writing style varies to mirror the temper of the times, from the Horatio Algerish first chapter, through anagramic and alphabetical sections (covering roughly the years of Katz's early literary experiments), before settling into the mature Katz voice.

Dusty Wier is clearly Katz's stand-in here, but he is also representative of everyone who grew up in those times hoping for a better American Way to manifest itself. E. Pouce embodies the arrogance and ambition of the dark side of that Way: among his other deeds he drops napalm on his own party—this in the wake of "The Death of Bobby Kennedy," that is, of the death of 1960s idealism. Episodes and images subtly mirror one another from scene to scene and country to country, reinforcing the universal feel Katz is striving to establish. Fiction's role here is spelled out for the reader: "When the day gets short people must make up stories just to get through the nights." As at the end of *Peter Prince,* Katz here is uncertain about what is to come: an impossibly high fly ball is falling toward a long-dormant giant's glove as the novel closes.

—William C. Bamberger

KAVANAGH, Dan

See BARNES, Julian (Patrick)

KAY, Jackie

Nationality: Scottish. **Born:** Jacqueline Margaret Kay in Edinburgh, Scotland, 9 November 1961. **Education:** University of Stirling, B.A. 1983. **Family:** One son. **Career:** Writer-in-residence, Hammersmith, London, 1989–91. **Awards:** Eric Gregory award, 1991; Scottish Arts Council Book award, 1991; Saltire First Book of the Year award, 1991; Forward prize, 1992; Signal Poetry award, 1993; Somerset Maugham award. **Agent:** Pat Kavanagh, Peters Fraser & Dunlop, 503/4 The Chambers, Chelsea Harbour, London SW10 0XF, England. **Address:** 20 Townsend Road, London N15 4NT, England.

PUBLICATIONS

Novels

Trumpet. New York, Pantheon, 1998.

Poetry

That Distance Apart (chapbook). London, Turret, 1991.
The Adoption Papers. Newcastle upon Tyne, England, Bloodaxe, 1991.
Two's Company (for children). London, Puffin, 1992.
Other Lovers. Newcastle upon Tyne, England, Bloodaxe, 1993.
Three Has Gone (for children). London, Blackie Children's, 1994.

Other

Bessie Smith (biography). New York, Absolute, 1997.
Contributor, *Stepping Out: Short Stories on Friendships Between Women.* New York, Pandora Press, 1986.
Contributor, *Lesbian Plays,* edited by Jill Davis. New York, Methuen, 1987.
Contributor, *Gay Sweatshop: Four Plays and a Company,* edited by Philip Osment. Portsmouth, New Hampshire, Methuen Drama, 1989.

* * *

Jackie Kay is part of a vibrant literary scene of black British writers who among others include Grace Nichols, Bernadine Evaristo, and David Dabydeen. Unlike most black British writers she has grown up in Scotland and is therefore in the position to craft a new literary language that bears both a ''Scottish'' and a ''black'' inflection. Kay published her first novel after establishing herself with three collections of poetry, and her lyrical tone and mature control of language reveal the poet behind the novelist. Kay's novel also connects with her interest in trans-racial adoption, and specifically with her first collection of poetry, *The Adoption Papers.*

The Trumpet is love story and lament, full of tension and pain. It is loosely influenced by the life of Jazz musician Billy Tipton, whose story is transposed from 1930s America to 1950s Scotland. The black Scottish trumpeter Joss Moody has led life as a man—but in the body of a woman. Only his wife Millie shared this secret, while their adopted son Colman finds out when he sees Moody's body in the funeral parlour. The novel opens with Millie not only having to deal with her personal loss but also fending off the press, which relishes the potential sensationalism of Joss Moody's double life. As the book unfolds, several characters relate their own version of Moody, including his mother, a former school friend, and his drummer ''Big Red.'' Puzzled by the Jazz musician's gender bending, Dr. Krishnamurty reluctantly signs the death certificate. The novel's characters find it difficult to reconcile their former knowledge of Moody with the revelation made upon his death. Indeed, Moody himself could not speak to his wife about his life as a young girl until shortly before his death. Resembling short riffs and solo instruments, these and many other voices are variations of a theme, Moody's life, which is rendered as a piece of jazz.

The stories of those who knew Moody compete with each other for validity—they are not disinterested accounts. Presenting conflicting stories of Moody's life, the novel questions the notion of authenticity. Moody had been a trespasser between reality and performance; by remaining in control of his story for most of his life, he deliberately divided private and public, thereby creating his own identity and effectively inventing himself. The price paid is the exclusion of his son Colman. The novel thereby also addresses the issue of investment into stories. What are they used for, whom do they serve, what is their cost? Colman's case drastically shows that the threat to the recollection of his father is profoundly unsettling: ''I don't know any of us any more. He has made us all unreal.''

While Millie retreats to a remote coastal village in an attempt to protect her own privacy and her husband's memory, her son's incomprehension and hurt lead him to bond with tabloid journalist Sophie Stone, whose investment in Moody's story is purely commercial. She becomes Colman's ghost-writer, and they travel through England and Scotland together, looking for Moody's acquaintances and family for their bare-all biography. But their research becomes a quest for Colman himself. He traces not his unknown biological parents but his adoptive father, thereby pursuing a partly illusory figure. His father's trumpet resounded with a yearning for the past, with displacement. Colman quests his fantasy father and authors his own memory, his own story, putting himself into his father's lineage.

—Mark Stein

KELLEHER, Victor

Pseudonym: Veronica Hart. **Nationality:** British (also a citizen of Australia). **Born:** Victor Michael Kitchener Kelleher in London, 19 July 1939. **Education:** The University of Natal, Pietermaritzburg, South Africa, B.A. in English 1962; University of St. Andrews, Fife, Dip. Ed. 1963; University of the Witwatersrand, Johannesburg, B.A. (honors) 1969; University of South Africa, Pretoria, M.A. 1970, D.Litt. et Phil. 1973. **Family:** Married Alison Lyle in 1962; one son and one daughter. **Career:** Junior lecturer in English, University of the Witwatersrand, 1969; lecturer, then senior lecturer, in English, University of South Africa, 1970–73; lecturer in English, Massey University, Palmerston North, New Zealand, 1973–76; senior lecturer, 1976–84, and associate professor of English, 1984–87, University of New England, Armidale, New South Wales. **Awards:** Patricia Hackett prize, for short story, 1978; West Australian Young Readers' Book award, 1982, 1983, 1993; Australia Council fellowship, 1982, 1989–91, 1995–98; Australian Children's Book of the Year award, 1983, 1987; Australian Science Fiction Achievement award, 1984; Australian Children's Book Council Honour award, 1987, 1991; Australian Peace prize, 1989; Koala award, 1991; Hoffman award,

1992, 1993; Cool award, 1993. **Address:** 1 Avenue Rd., Clebe, New South Wales 2037, Australia.

Publications

Novels

Voices from the River. London, Heinemann, 1979; St. Lucia, University of Queensland Press, 1991.
The Beast of Heaven. St. Lucia, University of Queensland Press, 1984.
Em's Story. St. Lucia, University of Queensland Press, 1988.
Wintering. St. Lucia, University of Queensland Press, 1990.
Micky Darlin'. St. Lucia, University of Queensland Press, 1992.
Double God (as Veronica Hart). Melbourne and London, Mandarin, 1994.
The House That Jack Built (as Veronica Hart). Melbourne and London, Mandarin, 1994.
Fire Dancer. Ringwood, Victoria and New York, Viking, 1996.
Storyman. Milsons Point, New South Wales, Random House Australia, 1996.
Earthsong. Ringwood, Victoria, Puffin Books, 1997.
Into the Dark. Ringwood, Victoria, Viking, 1999.

Short Stories

Africa and After. St. Lucia, University of Queensland Press, 1983; as *The Traveller,* 1987.

Other (for young adults)

Forbidden Paths of Thual. London, Kestrel, 1979.
The Hunting of Shadroth. London, Kestrel, 1981.
Master of the Grove. London, Kestrel, 1982.
Papio. London, Kestrel, 1984; as *Rescue,* New York, Dial Books, 1992.
The Green Piper. Melbourne, Viking Kestrel, 1984; London, Viking Kestrel, 1985.
Taronga. Melbourne, Viking Kestrel, 1986; London, Hamish Hamilton, 1987.
The Makers. Melbourne, Viking Kestrel, 1987.
Baily's Bones. Melbourne, Viking Kestrel, 1988; New York, Dial Press, 1989.
The Red King. Melbourne, Viking Kestrel, 1989; New York, Dial Press, 1990.
Brother Night. London, MacRae, 1990; New York, Walker, 1991.
Del-Del. London, MacRae/Random House, 1991; New York, Walker, 1992.
To the Dark Tower. London, MacRae/Random House, 1992.
Where the Whales Sing. Melbourne and London, Viking, 1994; published as *Riding the Whales,* New York, Dial, 1995.
Parkland. Melbourne and New York, Viking, 1994.

* * *

Although he has spent considerable periods of time in several countries, it is his experiences in Africa that dominate Kelleher's fiction. He says of himself, ''Central Africa, where I was to spend a good portion of the next twenty years [after leaving England], did more to alter my attitudes and prospects than anything before or since,'' and he speaks also of his immense grief at being compelled to leave it. His first novel, *Voices from the River* is, like most of his work, a study of the many forms that racism and also racial interaction generally can take, and of the necessity of finding what is universal in human nature that can overcome the superficialities of differences in the color of skin. The voices belong to five different people: two brothers, Davy and Jonno, their father Cole (whom one or both of them murder), and two policemen, Samuels and Priestly, who are temperamentally and philosophically poles apart. In its complex structure and deliberate, even willful creation of uncertainty about motive and even fact, the novel seems influenced by Faulkner. Kelleher's view of Africa and Africans is far from misty-eyed. In many ways the novel could be read as a critique of the philanthropic liberalism of Samuels, who returns after retirement to England. But the fact that he is killed because, as Priestly had predicted, he is too trusting and sentimental, is offset by the large numbers of Africans at his funeral.

Africa and After contains fifteen stories: seven set in Africa, one bridging story which looks back upon Africa from self-imposed exile, and seven set in Australia, where Kelleher finally settled. The first half of the book is far better than the second. The material itself is richer, and Kelleher's imagery seems engaged by it in a way that is not true of the later stories where the view of human behavior is often reductive and even cynical, the observations of an uninvolved outsider.

Kelleher has spoken of his wish to write in a diverse variety of modes. He is a very successful writer of young adult fiction and has published two bloodthirsty novels of terror under the pseudonym of Veronica Hart. Even his third book of adult fiction under his own name, *The Beast of Heaven,* represents another radical departure from anything he had written previously. The novel is set 100,000 years after a nuclear holocaust that has taken place in the year 2027, and is a moral fable about the merit of continuing the human race. Two computers, the survivors of a war which destroyed the ''Ancients'' who created them, debate the issue while the only survivors, the peaceful Gatherers, struggle amid the desolate landscape to eke out a living and to evade the predatory Houdin, the Beast of Heaven. It is an ingeniously constructed and often lyrically written novel which leads ineluctably to an apocalyptic ending of dreadful irony. Reviewers have mentioned Dylan Thomas in connection with it but a more appropriate analogy would be with Yeats' ''The Second Coming.''

Em's Story returns us to Africa and the question of race. A young woman named Eva is asked by her grandmother Emma Wilhelm to write the story of an heroic trek she undertook sixty years before. Rebelling against her German ancestors and their virtual extinction of the Hereros, she offers shelter to a Herero tribesman and then makes love to him. After he is murdered by her father, she sets out on her journey north to rejoin the remnants of the tribe she has come to accept as her own people. Sixty years later, her granddaughter undertakes the same journey in circumstances which, as she observes, are markedly different, bent on a similar mission of reconciliation and recovery of her personal identity. Kelleher cuts frequently between past and present, and the similarity of Eva's circumstances to those of Em are pointedly stressed, but the novel's emphasis is on the healing and hopeful qualities of Eva's journey across the bridge between white and black Africa.

Wintering is set in Australia in 1988, the year of the bicentennial, but returns to many of the same themes as Kelleher's earlier fiction. The narrator, a young man named Jack Rudd, writes out his story in between visiting his friend Benny, who lies comatose in hospital. The novel cuts rapidly between the present—Benny's condition and Jack's struggle to revive his relationship with his Aboriginal former girlfriend Bridget—the past of a year before, and the events that led to Benny's destruction and the end of the relationship. Once again, Kelleher finds the soil of Australia a little too arid to write the kind of novel he had in mind: his 1960s white radicals are hardly more complex or interesting than his Redfern Aboriginals, and the upbeat ending of the novel is both startling and unconvincing. Nevertheless, the pleasures to be found in this work are those in all of his fiction—a fine ear for dialogue, a command of narrative, an ability to evoke landscape, and more importantly and less definably, a fundamental integrity in the way he approaches the issues that concern him.

The same qualities are evident in *Micky Darlin',* in which the author has returned to the first of his three countries for his material. The book consists of a number of interrelated stories which together comprise a history of the sprawling Donoghue family of Irish expatriates, spread over many years and narrated by the eponymous Micky. Beginning in the early 1940s in wartime London when Micky is of preschool age, the tales take us through the following decade when Micky has grown to be a young adult, the witness and recorder of the family's progressive disintegration over the different generations. More or less abandoned by his weak mother and alcoholic father, Micky has been brought up by his grandparents, Nan and Gramps, but when Gramps dies in a foolish accident, the family falls apart and the embittered Micky feels forsaken yet again. In the hands of a lesser writer the Donoghues would be almost Irish stereotypes—constantly drinking, brawling, angrily divided from another over questions of religion—but Kelleher's unsentimental, sharply observant prose brings them alive.

—Laurie Clancy

KELLEY, William Melvin

Nationality: American. **Born:** Bronx, New York, 1 November 1937. **Education:** Fieldston School, New York; Harvard University, Cambridge, Massachusetts (Read prize, 1960), 1957–61. **Family:** Married Karen Gibson in 1962; two children. **Career:** Writer-in-residence, State University College, Geneseo, New York, Spring 1965; teacher, New School for Social Research, New York, 1965–67, and University of the West Indies, Mona, Jamaica, 1969–70. **Awards:** Dana Reed Literary prize, Harvard University, 1960; Bread Loaf Writers Conference grant, 1962; Whitney Foundation award, 1963; Rosenthal Foundation award, 1963; *Transatlantic Review* award, 1964; Black Academy of Arts and Letters award, 1970. **Address:** The Wisdom Shop, P.O. Box 2658, New York, New York 10027, U.S.A.

PUBLICATIONS

Novels

A Different Drummer. New York, Doubleday, 1962; London, Hutchinson, 1963.

A Drop of Patience. New York, Doubleday, 1965; London, Hutchinson, 1966.

Dem. New York, Doubleday, 1967.

Dunfords Travels Everywheres. New York, Doubleday, 1970.

Short Stories

Dancers on the Shore. New York, Doubleday, 1964; London, Hutchinson, 1965.

Uncollected Short Stories

''Jest, Like Sam,'' in *Negro Digest* (Chicago), October 1969.

''The Dentist's Wife,'' in *Women and Men, Men and Women,* edited by William Smart. New York, St. Martin's Press, 1975.

* * *

William Melvin Kelley's novels to date have dealt with interracial conflict, but the emphasis has been on the examination of characters, black and white, and the myths with which they delude themselves. His novels pose no ''solutions'' to the conflict but the solution of self-understanding, and his depiction of the relationships—loving and competitive—between men and women and blacks and whites combines compassion, objectivity, and humor.

His first novel, *A Different Drummer,* set realistically rendered characters in a fantasy plot. From multiple points of view he displayed the reactions of the whites of a fictional Southern state to the spontaneous grass-roots emigration of the state's blacks. A minor incident in *A Different Drummer* concerns Wallace Bedlow, who is waiting for a bus to take him to New York City, where he plans to live with his brother, Carlyle. Bedlow appears only that one time, but he surfaces again in ''Cry for Me,'' probably the best short story in *Dancers on the Shore,* in which he becomes a famous folk singer. In that story the themes of one's public image versus the true self and commercialism versus art are explored.

These themes are developed further in Kelley's second novel, *A Drop of Patience.* The protagonist is a blind, black jazz musician, whose intuitive experimentation is contrasted to the intellectualization of critics, and whose love of music comes into conflict with the commercialization of music. More important than these themes, however, is the development of the character himself, who passes through various rites of passage as he learns to deal with sex, love, racism, and fame.

Carlyle Bedlow, who appeared in several of the stories in *Dancers on the Shore,* reappears in *Dem,* Kelley's third novel. ''Lemme tellya how dem folks live,'' the novel begins. It goes on to show dem white folks living out their myths of white superiority, masculine prerogative, and soap-opera escapism. They are such victims of the pernicious myths of their culture that they are no longer even a threat to black people.

Racial conflict nearly disappears amidst the experimentation and fantasy of *Dunfords Travels Everywheres,* Kelley's own clever and original permutation of *Finnegans Wake.* A triptych in plot, style, and character, *Dunfords Travels Everywheres* is an ambitious short novel; it succeeds in being clever, but as an exploration into character it's less satisfying than his earlier novels.

Kelley has shown himself a skillful craftsman in a variety of styles and approaches. In his stories and in his first three novels his exploration of character develops as the character seeks—or refuses to seek—a unity between the person he feels he is and the personality he or society thinks he should be. This is true also in one of the three interwoven stories of *Dunfords Travels Everywheres.* In the other two stories a playful fantasy dominates. If Kelley's fiction has a direction, it's one that moves from seriousness and psychological probing to fantasy, playfulness, and comedy.

—William Borden

KELLY, Maeve

Nationality: Irish. **Born:** Ennis, County Clare, Ireland, 1930. **Education:** Studied nursing at St. Andrew's Hospital, London. **Family:** Married Gerard O'Brien-Kelly; two sons. **Career:** Founder and administrator of Adapt, shelter for victims of domestic violence, 1978—. **Awards:** Hennessey Award, 1972. **Agent:** Mic Cheetham, Sheil Land Associates, 43 Doughty Street, London, England. **Address:** Adapt House, Rosbrien, County Limerick, Ireland.

PUBLICATIONS

Novels

Necessary Treasons. London, M. Joseph, 1985.
Florrie's Girls. London, M. Joseph, 1989.
Alice in Thunderland: A Feminist Fairytale. Dublin, Attic Press, 1993.

Short Stories

A Life of Her Own, and Other Stories. Dublin, Poolbeg Press, 1976.
Ms Muffet and Others: A Funny, Sassy, Heretical Collection of Feminist Fairytales (contributor). Dublin, Attic Press, 1986.
Mad and Bad Fairies (contributor). Dublin, Attic Press, 1987.
Orange Horses. London, M. Joseph, 1990.

Poetry

Resolution. Dover, New Hampshire, Blackstaff Press, 1986.

* * *

Maeve Kelly writes in several genres, and all of her work is informed by clear feminist principles. Born in 1930, Kelly has lived through significant changes in Irish society's attitudes toward women, but her literary works suggest some of the ways in which the changes have been insufficient. Her fictional representation of what life is like for Irish women is both emotionally and intellectually convincing.

A Life of Her Own, her first published collection of short stories, introduces the themes that recur throughout her oeuvre. Most of these stories have a clear feminist voice, and Kelly creates sympathetic characters whose ordinary lives embody the barriers women face. The title story, ''A Life of Her Own,'' is told by a young female narrator who recounts the attempts of her aunt to achieve a measure of independence after spending many years as housekeeper for her bachelor brother. Her brother ridicules her for marrying and literally starves himself to death in a display of self-pity; Aunt Brigid herself dies in childbirth, for she was not young and the risks were greater in those days.

Kelly's first novel, *Necessary Treasons*, draws on her own experiences establishing and directing a Limerick-area shelter for battered women. Young Eve Gleeson is pulled in two directions: she becomes engaged to a middle-aged doctor, Hugh Creagh, at the same time as she grows steadily more involved in the women's movement. Her fiancé's relatives are living proof of the tenacity of sexism and the vilification of independent women. His sisters participate enthusiastically in denigrating Eve's political involvement and mistreat their former sister-in-law, Eleanor; Eleanor was physically abused by their brother, Donogh, who absconded to England with their child while Eleanor was being treated for the injuries he inflicted. Eleanor's search for her daughter was fruitless, but at novel's end it is revealed that she has been spending a month at the Creagh home, with the four sisters, every year since her father spirited her away. Eve's work with the women's shelter, in its infancy, brings her into contact with many kinds of concrete wrongs that women all around her suffer daily. As she leaves behind her sheltered, middle-class existence, Hugh becomes increasingly resentful; he is fascinated by the sufferings of the past, as manifested in old family papers he is studying, but refuses to grant any credibility to the present-day sufferings Eve brings to his attention. As the novel progresses, Eve becomes more outspoken about women's rights, and the others pull away from her. Even Eleanor, an outspoken feminist, fears that Eve will become an ''earnest, humourless missionary.'' Finally, Eve breaks off her engagement and goes to California for six months to learn from women's activists there. The novel's representation of women's issues is compelling; Kelly shows the political, legal, religious, medical, and social forces arrayed against Irish women. It is sometimes unclear, however, whether readers are to see Eve's changes as maturity or if Eleanor and the others are right to criticize her for being ''obsessive.''

After a volume of poetry, *Resolution*, Kelly published her next novel, *Florrie's Girls. Florrie's Girls* draws on Kelly's experiences as a student nurse in London. Caitlin Cosgrave leaves the family farm in County Clare at age eighteen to train as a nurse in London. The farm cannot support more than one family member, and it is to go to Caitlin's brother. The narrative is written in journal form; there are no dates given, though sometimes days of the weeks or months are named. The journal begins with Caitlin's journey on the train taking her away from home, and continues throughout her four-year training course. It shows her growth as a person and includes often-scathing commentary on the medical profession. The novel underscores the rigid male hierarchies of medicine; while the nurses perform virtually all of the practical care of patients and become quite skilled at diagnosis, they have to bow before the male doctors who come in and make pronouncements, often dictating procedures with little consideration for the dignity and humanity of the patients. A brief stint with a gynecologist underscores for Caitlin how the medical community treats women's health as abnormal and somehow grotesque. Another significant theme in the novel is relations between English and Irish, but here again the rhetoric and the example of the novel seem to be in conflict. For example, Caitlin complains often of stereotypical English views of the Irish, but she herself is full of anti-English stereotypes. She contrasts English ''bossiness'' and craving for order with Irish virtues, but as a character she often embodies those supposedly English traits. She loves her uniform and notes repeatedly that she enjoys opportunities to manage things and believes herself to be better at it than others.

After another collection of short stories, *Orange Horses*, Kelly published a satirical novel, *Alice in Thunderland.* Subtitled *A Feminist Fairytale*, the satire takes on the social codes that continue to denigrate and limit women. *Alice in Thunderland* examines contemporary society by creating a fictional world of ''memblies'' and ''fremblies'' whose interactions reveal very strange codes of conduct; Alice comes from Harmony Isle and is baffled by what she sees in Thunderland. Kelly's satire is in the tradition of Swift's *Gulliver's Travels* (notably, the embittered brother in ''A Life of Her Own'' reads Swift's condemnation of the female Yahoos) but takes on its own targets. Kelly's satire is insightful; hilarious and provocative by turns, no summary could do it justice. The book includes cartoon-style illustrations (drawn by Trina Mahon), showing Alice as a very large figure, looming over the inhabitants of Thunderland with her big hair and Doc Martens-style boots.

Kelly is a notable figure in contemporary Irish literature, disproving the critical commonplace that there were no serious Irish women writers until the 1990s. Hers is an important feminist voice, and her fiction creates a realistic and compelling portrait of the everyday lives of Irish women.

—Rosemary Johnsen

KELMAN, James

Nationality: Scottish. **Born:** Glasgow, 9 June 1946. **Education:** Greenfield School, Stonedyke School, and Hyndland School, all Glasgow, 1951–61. University of Strathclyde, Glasgow, 1975–78, 1981–82. **Family:** Married Marie Connors in 1969; two daughters. **Career:** Has worked at a variety of semi-skilled and labouring jobs. Scottish Arts Council Writing fellowship, 1978–80, 1982–85. **Awards:** Scottish Arts Council bursary, 1973, 1980, and book award, 1983, 1987, 1989; Cheltenham prize, 1987; James Tait Black Memorial prize, 1990; Booker McConnell Prize, 1994. **Agent:** Cathie Thomson, 23 Hillhead Street, Glasgow G12. **Address:** 244 West Princess Street, Glasgow G4 9DP, Scotland.

PUBLICATIONS

Novels

The Busconductor Hines. Edinburgh, Polygon Press, 1984.
A Chancer. Edinburgh, Polygon Press, 1985.
A Disaffection. London, Secker and Warburg, and New York, Farrar Straus, 1989.
How Late It Was, How Late. London, Secker and Warburg, 1994.

Short Stories

An Old Pub Near the Angel. Orono, Maine, Puckerbrush Press, 1973.
Three Glasgow Writers, with Tom Leonard and Alex Hamilton. Glasgow, Molendinar Press, 1976.
Short Tales from the Nightshift. Glasgow, Print Studio Press, 1978.
Not Not While the Giro and Other Stories. Edinburgh, Polygon Press, 1983.
Lean Tales, with Alasdair Gray and Agnes Owens. London, Cape, 1985.
Greyhound for Breakfast. London, Secker and Warburg, and New York, Farrar Straus, 1987.
The Burn. London, Secker and Warburg, 1991.
Busted Scotch: Selected Stories. New York, Norton, 1997.
The Good Times. London, Secker & Warburg, 1998; New York, Anchor Books, 1999.

Plays

The Busker (produced Edinburgh, 1985).
Le Rodeur, adaptation of the play by Enzo Cormann (produced Edinburgh, 1987).
In the Night (produced Stirling, 1988).
Hardie and Baird: The Last Days (produced Edinburgh, 1990). London, Secker and Warburg, 1991.

Radio Plays: *Hardie and Baird: The Last Days,* 1978.

Screenplays: *The Return,* 1990.

Other

Some Recent Attacks: Essays Cultural and Political. Stirling, Scotland, AK Press, 1992.
Editor, *An East End Anthology.* Glasgow, Clydeside Press, 1988.

*

Manuscript Collections: Mitchell Library, Glasgow.

Critical Studies: ''Patter Merchants and Chancers: Recent Glasgow Writing'' in *Planet* (Aberystwyth), no. 60, 1986–87, and article in *New Welsh Review,* (Aberystwyth), no. 10, 1990, both by Ian A. Bell.

James Kelman comments:

Glasgow is a post-industrial city; its culture comprises many different cultural traditions: I work within this.

* * *

James Kelman has established himself as one of the most compelling new voices in British fiction. Combining intense local affiliation with the west of Scotland and great stylistic inventiveness, he represents commitment and integrity, frankness and exuberance, and has been compared with Kafka and Beckett. His first novel, *The Busconductor Hines* takes a sombre subject, but articulates its central character through a mixture of impersonal reports and stream-of-consciousness imaginings. Kelman ignores the conventions of orthodox ''realist'' fiction in favour of a kaleidoscopic juxtaposition of fact and fantasy, in tribute to the imaginative capacities of ''ordinary people.'' Here is a sample:

> Life is too serious.
>
> Hunch the shoulders and march. The furtively fast figure. One fine morning Hines R. was arrested. Crackle crackle crackle. We have this fantasy coming through on the line sir should we tape it and hold it against him or what. Naw but honest sir he's just a lowly member of the transport experience; he slept in a little and perforce is obliged to walk it to work, having missed the bastarn omnibus. A certain irony granted but nothing more, no significance of any insurrectionary nature.

It may be tempting to read this as a purely formal experiment, and relax into appreciating the multivocal texture of the writing. However, the stylistic extravaganza is always at the service of a purposive exploration of Hines's world, and the book retains its human centre in moving descriptions of Hines at work and at home.

Kelman's second novel, *A Chancer,* adopts a different approach. It portrays a young man without qualities, with no attempt to investigate what goes on inside his head. Instead, it narrates his day-to-day existence as he drifts and gambles—a perennial interest of Kelman's—without overt or coercive authorial intrusion. The novel is interspersed with brief scenes where Kelman scrupulously describes events, and just as scrupulously keeps his distance. Such reluctance to invade his character's privacy is yet another way of resisting the pseudo-omniscience of more conventional third person narrative. It challenges us to make sense of events, without allowing us any special privileges. The formal features are not decorative, but are ways of identifying the limits of knowledge. What we eventually see through the sombre narrative is a life of purposelessness and indecision, lived within day-to-day privations, invigorated by the austerity of its unadorned, skeletal telling.

In his collections of short fictions, *Greyhound for Breakfast* and *The Burn,* Kelman shows more of his range. Some stories are brief vignettes, less than a page long, an anecdotal form he has experimented with from his earliest full collection—*Not Not While the Giro*—onwards. Others are more elaborately developed, in alternating moods of wit, exhilaration, exasperation, and despair. They are certainly the most diverse and exuberant collections of recent years, with the power and intensity and wit of the prose encapsulating very large social and political concerns within miniaturist sketches.

''Greyhound for Breakfast'' is an exceptional piece, showing the author at his best. Without ornament, it recounts a couple of hours in the life of a character and his newly-acquired greyhound. It sounds comic, a not-very-shaggy dog story, but it is not. Ronnie has bought the dog for more money than he really has, and as the day goes on he can find no good reason for having done so. He had a half-formed idea of entering it in races, but this soon seems ridiculous. As he wanders, more and more of his life begins to look absurd. He has no job, no proper communication with his wife, his son has just left home, and the whole business of living seems meaningless. As the story ends, the narrative drifts into a wonderfully controlled and frightening stream-of-consciousness reverie. The nihilism is deeply unsettling, representing the inarticulate yearnings and unsatisfied desires of an ordinary man undergoing the alienations of contemporary urban life. Kelman's language is of necessity frank, but never gratuitously so, dramatising the painful struggle towards articulacy of the most complex emotions. The dog is used as a symbol, but to call it that suggests a cruder, more schematic technique than Kelman offers. The story is typically suggestive, enigmatic, and nuanced. Without overly directive authorial intervention, the connections between individual lives and the circumstances which prescribe them are made. Although Kelman's work is insistently angry, it is angry on behalf of his subjects, rather than exasperated with them.

The same intensity and the same humanity can be found in Kelman's 1989 novel, *A Disaffection,* which returns to the fabric of interior and exterior description. This book puts on display a Glasgow school teacher at the moment when he sees the paucity of his own life. It offers an engagement with the traditional concerns of the social realist novel, but also a more tense mixture of moods than in comparable work by David Storey or Alan Sillitoe. Kelman uses his very flexible style to move inside and outside Doyle's head, to maintain scrupulous attention to him and his fantasies. The novel becomes an unsentimental education, taking us through Doyle's crisis of confidence. Although it is an attack on the constraints and hypocrisies of the State educational system, it is a much more broadly-based revelation of a culture clinging onto the vestiges of its self-esteem.

Doyle's yearnings for something better, represented by the strange pair of pipes he finds and his unsatisfied fancy for a fellow-teacher, become a way of intensifying and demonstrating not only Doyle's own malaise, but also broader national circumstances. At times, the political leanings are explicit. Kelman uses the book to insinuate a disturbing critique of those who believe in the possibilities of change from within. Doyle struggles all the way through under the pressures to effect change, pressures which are much greater than he fully realises. In very powerful scenes with his parents and his unemployed brother, he enacts his alienation from the conditions of their lives, yet he has found nothing to replace their dignity. In the classroom and the staffroom, the futility of trying to educate people genuinely in circumstances so adverse is made very clear.

Yet the book is neither a simple diatribe, nor a purely personal vision. Kelman introduces complex framing devices through Doyle's interests in Hölderlin and Pythagorean philosophy. As in *The Busconductor Hines* the author seems very close to his character, but these references, like the frequent allusions to Hamlet, are ways of introducing new perspectives, and encouraging distance. At times, Kelman shows a Swiftian taste for irony, using that form as the only possible way of coping with the revealed awfulness of the world. We are not allowed to hold Doyle in contempt, and the sharp oscillations in the narrative between wit and horror are both compulsive and disturbing.

In 1994 Kelman's novel *How Late It Was, How Late* won the Booker McConnell Prize, a highly prestigious award. Yet this harrowing tale of blindness and affliction provoked an extraordinary controversy in Britain. Unable to see the book's deep humanity, many critics castigated its harsh language and its intense concentration on the lives of the dispossessed. *How Late It Was, How Late* is Kelman's toughest book yet, his most clearly focussed and uncompromising. His fascinating style, combining the darkest humour with glimpses of the horror of everyday life, allows him to produce narratives capable of the caustic and the tender, the intimate and the aloof. Moving in and out of the central figure's consciousness makes possible a fully human realisation of an individual's plight, and a recognition of the material circumstances that impose such pressure. More recently, Kelman has written plays (notably *Hardie and Baird*) and numerous political pamphlets, and his development is clearly continuing.

—Ian A. Bell

KENAN, Randall (G.)

Nationality: American. **Born:** Brooklyn, New York, 12 March 1963. **Education:** University of North Carolina, B.A. 1985. **Career:** Editor, Alfred A. Knopf, New York, 1985–89; lecturer, Sarah Lawrence College, 1989—, Vassar College, Poughkeepsie, New York, 1989—, and Columbia University, New York, New York, 1990—. **Awards:** MacDowell Colony fellowship, 1990. **Address:** Lecturer in Writing, Sarah Lawrence College, Bronxville, New York 10708, U.S.A.

Publications

Novels

A Visitation of Spirits. New York, Grove Press, 1989.

Short Stories

Let the Dead Bury Their Dead and Other Stories. San Francisco, Harcourt, 1992.

Other

James Baldwin. New York, Chelsea House, 1994.
Walking on Water: Black American Lives at the Turn of the Twenty-First Century. New York, Knopf, 1999.
Contributor, *Crossing the Color Line: Readings in Black and White,* edited by Suzanne W. Jones. Columbia, University of South Carolina Press, 2000.

*

Critical Studies: *The Power of the Porch: The Storyteller's Craft in Zora Neale Hurston, Gloria Naylor, and Randall Kenan* by Trudier Harris, Athens, University of Georgia Press, 1996.

* * *

James Baldwin, about whom Randall Kenan has written eloquently, used to say with characteristic irony that by being both black and gay in America, he had ''hit the jackpot.'' If so, then Kenan is a Powerball winner; he is black, gay, and southern—and rural southern, too, as Kenan's hometown of Chinquapin, North Carolina, in contrast to Baldwin's native New York City, is a community so small and obscure that most people even in Raleigh and Chapel Hill have never heard of it. Chinquapin is transmogrified into Tims Creek in Kenan's two books of fiction to date, the novel *A Visitation of Spirits* and the story collection *Let the Dead Bury Their Dead*, an output slim but nevertheless sufficient to establish Kenan as one of the most distinctive voices in contemporary American fiction.

In alternating chapters, *A Visitation of Spirits* tells two related Tims Creek stories, separated in time by more than a year. on April 29 and 30, 1984, brilliant but troubled teenager Horace Thomas Cross, plagued by his community's high expectations and by his shame at his secret homosexuality, puts into effect a strange plan drawn from folklore, an attempt to escape his circumstances by turning himself into a bird. Horace's clumsy ritual succeeds only in summoning evil spirits who may or may not exist outside Horace's fevered imagination but who force poor Horace to re-live the most tormenting episodes of his young life. The reader gradually realizes that these are the last hours of that life, as Horace descends into a suicidal phantasmagoria akin to that experienced by Quentin Compson in another snall-town southern novel of fractured April chronology, William Faulkner's *The Sound and the Fury.*

In the alternating chapters of Kenan's novel, which take place on December 8 of the following year, Horace's older cousin, the Rev. Jimmy Green, grudgingly drives his aged aunt and uncle to visit a sick relation. The shadow of Horace's death still lies over the family, and tensions in the car run high as Jimmy ponders his troubled marriage and as the decades-long bickering between the aunt and uncle reaches a frightening new pitch of intensity and revelation.

Much of the commentary on *A Visitation of Spirits* focused on its gay themes and its Toni Morrison-like use of magic realism to convey the African-American experience. Yet the novel is remarkable, too, for its closely observed and compassionate depiction of the bickering old-timers, and for its witty and insightful examination of pop-culture appropriation on the margins of society. Certainly Horace derives more inspiration from his white-bread comic-book collection than from any more authentically African-American influence.

Though *Let the Dead Bury Their Dead* is a collection of stories rather than a novel per se, most of it is set in Tims Creek or among its expatriates, and characters from *A Visitation of Spirits* reappear—Horace being a notable exception. Moreover, consecutive stories within the book give the reader different perspectives on the same characters. For example, the Right Reverend Hezekiah Barden, the fire-breathing homophobe who so terrifies Horace in the novel, reappears in one story in a comic supporting role, as an unwelcome dinner guest who pries into everyone's business. In another story, however, the reader shares Barden's point of view as he preaches a platitudinous eulogy over the casket of a parishioner who was his secret lover; Barden's simultaneous private eulogy for the woman is quite different from the public one.

The collection thus has the feel of an episodic novel, if not a sequel then certainly a continuation of the Tims Creek story begun in *A Visitation of Spirits.* Again Kenan displays a flair for dialogue, for the rhythms of country speech. Again his senior citizens are his most fully realized characters. Again he makes Tims Creek a magical place: In one story, a hog apparently bestows the gift of clairvoyance; in another, a very out-of-place Asian man falls from the sky. More often in the stories than in the novel, however, Kenan allows himself to be funny, culminating in the title story, which is partially a parody of the academic folkloric study and partially a fond homage to our funniest folklorist, Zora Neale Hurston.

Having placed Tims Creek and himself on the landscape of American fiction, at an age when many young writers are just beginning to put stamps onto their self-addressed envelopes, Kenan then turned to non-fiction, most notably to the seven-year odyssey of cross-country interviewing that resulted in the nearly 700 pages of the impressive *Walking on Water: Black American Lives at the Turn of the Twenty-First Century.* Confronted with the many faces of black American culture, Kenan concludes that it was always postmodern, because ''folks made it up as they went along.'' One hopes that Kenan, having shaken the road dust from his feet, now feels like making up some new stories of his own. Tims Creek, like Faulkner's Jefferson, is a locale too rich in possibilities to leave unvisited for long.

—Andy Duncan

KENEALLY, Thomas (Michael)

Nationality: Australian. **Born:** Sydney, New South Wales, 7 October 1935. **Education:** St. Patrick's College, Strathfield, New South Wales; studied for the priesthood 1953–60, and studied law. **Military Service:** Australian Citizens Military Forces. **Family:** Married Judith

Mary Martin in 1965; two daughters. **Career:** High school teacher in Sydney, 1960–64; lecturer in drama, University of New England, Armidale, New South Wales, 1968–69; lived in the U.S., 1975–77; visiting professor of English, University of California, Irvine, 1985; Berg Professor of English, New York University, 1988. **Member:** Australia-China Council, 1978–83; member of the advisory panel, Australian Constitutional Commission, 1985–88; member, Australian Literary Arts Board, 1985–88; president, National Book Council of Australia, 1985–89; chairman, Australian Society of Authors, 1987. **Awards:** Commonwealth Literary Fund fellowship, 1966, 1968, 1972; Miles Franklin award, 1968, 1969; Captain Cook Bicentenary prize, 1970; Royal Society of Literature Heinemann award, 1973; Booker prize, 1982; Los Angeles *Times* award, 1983;. Fellow, Royal Society of Literature, 1973, American Academy of Arts and Sciences, 1993; Officer, Order of Australia, 1983. **Agent:** Deborah Rogers, Rogers, Colleridge and White, 20 Powis Mews, London W11 1JN, England.

PUBLICATIONS

Novels

The Place at Whitton. Melbourne and London, Cassell, 1964; New York, Walker, 1965.
The Fear. Melbourne and London, Cassell, 1965; as *By the Line,* St. Lucia, University of Queensland Press, 1989.
Bring Larks and Heroes. Melbourne, Cassell, 1967; London, Cassell, and New York, Viking Press, 1968.
Three Cheers for the Paraclete. Sydney, Angus and Robertson, 1968; London, Angus and Robertson, and New York, Viking Press, 1969.
The Survivor. Sydney, Angus and Robertson, 1969; London, Angus and Robertson, and New York, Viking Press, 1970.
A Dutiful Daughter. Sydney and London, Angus and Robertson, and New York, Viking Press, 1971.
The Chant of Jimmie Blacksmith. Sydney and London, Angus and Robertson, and New York, Viking Press, 1972.
Blood Red, Sister Rose. London, Collins, and New York, Viking Press, 1974.
Moses the Lawgiver (novelization of television play). London, Collins-ATV, and New York, Harper, 1975.
Gossip from the Forest. London, Collins, 1975; New York, Harcourt Brace, 1976.
Season in Purgatory. London, Collins, 1976; New York, Harcourt Brace, 1977.
A Victim of the Aurora. London, Collins, 1977; New York, Harcourt Brace, 1978.
Passenger. London, Collins, and New York, Harcourt Brace, 1979.
Confederates. London, Collins, 1979; New York, Harper, 1980.
The Cut-Rate Kingdom. Sydney, Wildcat Press, 1980; London, Allen Lane, 1984.
Schindler's Ark. London, Hodder and Stoughton, 1982; as *Schindler's List,* New York, Simon and Schuster, 1982.
A Family Madness. London, Hodder and Stoughton, 1985; New York, Simon and Schuster, 1986.
The Playmaker. London, Hodder and Stoughton, and New York, Simon and Schuster, 1987.
Towards Asmara. London, Hodder and Stoughton, 1989; as *To Asmara,* New York, Warner, 1989.
Flying Hero Class. London, Hodder and Stoughton, and New York, Warner, 1991.
Woman of the Inner Sea. N.p., Doubleday and Hodder, 1992; New York, Plume, 1993.
Jacko. N.p., Heinemann, 1993.
A River Town. London, Reed Books, 1995; New York, N. A. Talese, 1995.
Bettany's Book. New York, Bantam, 1999.

Uncollected Short Stories

''The Performing Blind Boy,'' in *Festival and Other Stories,* edited by Brian Buckley and Jim Hamilton. Melbourne, Wren, 1974; Newton Abbot, Devon, David and Charles, 1975.

Plays

Halloran's Little Boat, adaptation of his novel *Bring Larks and Heroes* (produced Sydney, 1966). Published in *Penguin Australian Drama 2,* Melbourne, Penguin, 1975.
Childermass (produced Sydney, 1968).
An Awful Rose (produced Sydney, 1972).
Bullie's House (produced Sydney, 1980; New Haven, Connecticut, 1985). Sydney, Currency Press, 1981.
Gossip from the Forest, adaptation of his own novel (produced 1983).

Screenplays: *The Priest* (episode in *Libido*), 1973; *Silver City,* with Sophia Turkiewicz, 1985.

Television Writing (UK): *Essington,* 1974; *The World's Wrong End* (documentary; *Writers and Places* series), 1981; *Australia* series, 1987.

Other

Ned Kelly and the City of Bees (for children). London, Cape, 1978; Boston, Godine, 1981.
Outback, photographs by Gary Hansen and Mark Lang. Sydney and London, Hodder and Stoughton, 1983.
Australia: Beyond the Dreamtime, with Patsy Adam-Smith and Robyn Davidson. London, BBC Publications, 1987; New York, Facts on File, 1989.
Child of Australia (song), music by Peter Sculthorpe. London, Faber Music, 1987.
Now and in Time to Be: Ireland and the Irish, photographs by Patrick Prendergast. N.p., Panmacmillan, n.p., Ryan, and n.p., Norton, 1992.
The Great Shame: A Story of the Irish in the Old World and the New. Milsons Point, New South Wales, Random House, 1998; published as *The Great Shame, and the Triumph of the Irish in the English-speaking World,* New York, Nan A. Talese, 1999.

*

Manuscript Collections: Mitchell Library, Sydney; Australian National Library, Canberra.

Critical Studies: *Thomas Keneally* by Peter Quartermaine, London, Arnold, 1991.

Theatrical Activities: Actor: **Films**—*The Devil's Playground,* 1976; *The Chant of Jimmie Blacksmith,* 1978.

Thomas Keneally comments:

(1972) I would like to be able to disown my first two novels, the second of which was the obligatory account of one's childhood—the book then that all novelists think seriously of writing.

I see my third novel as an attempt to follow out an epic theme in terms of a young soldier's exile to Australia.

The fourth and fifth were attempts at urbane writing in the traditional mode of the English novel: confrontations between characters whose behaviour shows layers of irony and humour, in which all that is epic is rather played down.

For *A Dutiful Daughter,* the best novel I have written (not that I claim that matters much), I have turned to myth and fable, as many a novelist is doing, for the simple reason that other media have moved into the traditional areas of the novel.

(1986) I can see now that a great deal of my work has been concerned with the contrast between the new world—in particular Australia—and the old; the counterpoint between the fairly innocent politics of the new world and the fatal politics of Europe. One of the most remarkable phenomena of my lifetime has been the decline of both the British Empire and the European dominance in the world. As a colonial, I was just getting used to these two phenomena and adjusting my soul to them when they vanished, throwing into doubt the idea that artists from the remote antipodes must go into the northern hemisphere to find their spiritual source and forcing me to reassess my place in the world as an Australian.

Blood Red, Sister Rose, for example, concerned a European aboriginal, a potent maker of magic, Joan of Arc. *Gossip from the Forest* concerned the war, World War I, by which Europe began its own self destruction. These books are characteristic of my middle period, the historical phase, when in a way, coming from a fairly innocent and unbloodied society, I was trying to work Europe out. There was some of this too in *Schindler's Ark.* In my last book, *A Family Madness,* you have Australian ingenuousness and the ancient, complicated and malicious politics of Eastern Europe standing cheek by jowl.

I feel it is significant that *A Family Madness* is set in 1985. I believe the historic phase is nearly over for me and was merely a preparation for the understanding of the present. Time—and future work—will tell.

* * *

Within the past two decades, Thomas Keneally has evolved from one of Australia's best-known and most prolific writers to a novelist with a worldwide following. Even before *The Great Shame*, his recent historical work, Keneally had worked extensively with material from Australia's past. But his body of work is noteworthy for its range of material. He has written on subjects as varied as Joan of Arc, the American Civil War, the Holocaust, and contemporary Africa. However diverse the material, Keneally brings a consistently humanistic point of view, an eye for accuracy of detail, and a knack for engaging storytelling, all of which account both for his wide readership and critical acclaim.

The novels set in colonial Australia are built around cultural conflict. *The Chant of Jimmie Blacksmith*, a fictional meditation on a real event in Australian history, is about the ritualistic murder of a white woman by the title character, an aborigine desperately trying to resist the imposition of European ways. Keneally resists the temptation to make Jimmy and his rage understandable to his readers; instead he takes pains to distance reader and character, an effect that is discomforting but true to the material. Australia's relation to Britain provides the setting for *The Playmaker* (adapted by Timberlake Wertenbaker for the stage as *Our Country's Good*). Keneally uses a seemingly insignificant detail from the history of the Sydney Cove prison and converts it into a compelling metaphor for his country's birth. When an idealistic British officer is asked to stage Farquhar's restoration comedy *The Recruiting Office* with a cast of convicts, he, they, and we come to a new understanding of the meaning of human dignity and freedom. The Australian setting is also dominant in *Woman of the Inner Sea*, whose sophisticated heroine, having lost her two children in a fire, finds in the basic values of the Outback the strength to confront her grief and throw off her unwarranted guilt. Again in *A River Town*, Keneally uses the origin of a rural settlement to convey the essential identity of Australia: outcasts coming together to form a community and, through their diversity, to define a national character.

When it is not his primary setting, Australia is often involved indirectly in Keneally's novels, as in *Passenger*, in which the story of an Irish girl's pregnancy is narrated by her unborn child. While living in London, she is writing a historical novel about a group of Irish prisoners being transported to Australia for their part in the Rebellion of 1798. The determination of the fetal narrator to survive parallels that of the Irish rebels, and, in fact, the birth eventually does take place in Australia. The influence of history is also apparent in *A Family Madness*, in which an Australian worker falls in love with his boss's daughter and becomes involved with their haunted past in Byelorussia during World War II. Keneally uses the double plot structure again in *To Asmara*, in which the Eritrean guerrilla war against Ethiopia mirrors the prior struggles of the main character, the journalist Darcy, to reconcile his European heritage with his determination to help the Australian tribes. In all these novels Keneally's native Australia is a vital presence regardless of where the story takes his characters.

When Keneally chooses historical material from foreign sources, the effect is usually less engaging. *Blood Red, Sister Rose*, his version of the Joan of Arc legend, and *Confederates*, set in Northern Virginia during the summer of 1862, both feature typical Keneally heroes—realistically earthy characters caught up in the historical moment—but despite a wealth of historical detail, neither the Maid of Orleans nor the Virginian farmer-turned-soldier really seem to live in their respective worlds. Even Stonewall Jackson, who figures prominently in *Confederates*, has more Australian pluck than Southern grit in him.

Two novels dealing with twentieth century world wars, on the other hand, display considerable insight and power. The diplomats in *Gossip from the Forest*, gathered at Compiegne in the fall of 1918 to negotiate an armistice, are compelling characters. The cultured German delegate, Matthias Erzbergen, finds himself in an impossible political bind as he tries to deal with the imperious Marshall Foch, who takes full advantage of his superior position. The tenuous political alliances of the period are reflected in the negotiations at Compiegne, with the tragic realization that an opportunity for lasting peace is lost and another war becomes inevitable. Of greater scope is *Schindler's List*, the story of a Catholic industrialist who ran an arms factory using Jewish workers from concentration camps. The Oskar Schindler of Keneally's novel is as enigmatic as the man seems to have been in life, conveying no sense of high moral principle even though he was saving hundreds of Polish Jews by convincing the gullible Nazis that his factory's productivity depended on their labor.

The narrative voice in *Schindler's List*, like that of *Jimmie Blacksmith*, is detached and distant, as if Keneally is determined to allow Schindler to maintain his privacy, a hero we need not like or even understand. This fascinating ambiguity of character was lost in Stephen Spielberg's popular film based on Keneally's book.

The clash of cultures, a recurring theme in Keneally's work, dominates *Flying Hero Class*, in which an airplane carrying Barramatjara tribal dancers from New York to Frankfurt is hijacked by a group of Palestinians. The hijackers try to convince the aborigines that theirs is a common cause, but without much success. The danger is averted by the courage of the troupe's Australian manager and supposed exploiter. Although contrived, the novel summarizes Keneally's ambivalence toward cultural assimilation. Rejecting the comforting liberal assumption that cultural diversity is to be cherished and celebrated, he more often shows the inevitability of misunderstanding and conflict when cultures collide, whether it be as direct as the murderous outburst of a Jimmie Blacksmith or as subtle as the Australian journalist's inability to express his emotions to an Eritrean woman in *To Asmara*.

With *The Great Shame*, his exhaustively researched treatise on the plight of the Irish exiled to Australia's penal colonies for petty crimes or political resistance to British rule, Keneally crosses from historical fiction into history, but the epic scope of the material relies on the human stories he finds hidden in the official documents. With hundreds of characters, some of historical significance, others not (including his own and his wife's ancestors), Keneally conveys through multiple narratives the same virtues of determination, redemption, and survival as in his novels. The material he had used for background in the earlier works, especially *Passenger, The Playmaker*, and *A River Town*, emerges again in a seemingly different form. In reality, despite its extensive index, notes, and bibliography, *The Great Shame* reads like Keneally's best fiction.

Given his steady output and his often-risky choices of material, Keneally has maintained a remarkable level of quality in his work, a testament to the power of the historical imagination and to the novelist's craft.

—Robert E. Lynch

KENNEDY, A. L.

Nationality: Scottish.

Publications

Novels

Looking for the Possible Dance. London, Secker and Warburg, 1993.
So I Am Glad. London, Cape, 1995.
Original Bliss. London, Jonathan Cape, 1997.
Everything You Need. London, Jonathan Cape, 1999.

Short Stories

Night Geometry and the Garscadden Trains. London, Secker and Warburg, 1990.
Now That You're Back. London, Cape, 1994.

Other

The Life and Death of Colonel Blimp (screenplay). London, British Film Institute, 1997.
Editor, with Hamish Whyte. *The Ghost of Liberace.* Aberdeen: Association for Scottish Literary Studies, 1993.
Editor, with James McGonigal. *A Sort of Hot Scotland.* Aberdeen: Association for Scottish Literary Studies, 1994.

* * *

Throughout her work, Scottish writer A.L. Kennedy has explored the potentially infinite spaces within "ordinary" people's minds. Kennedy's novels and short stories focus on the mental and emotional confinement that is caused by isolation, psychic and physical violence in personal relationships, and enclosure within the ritualized routines of "the average shape of the day." These conditions are frequently met with an obsessive striving for control and the repetition of violence. Yet Kennedy's works also express a yearning for connection and an almost religious sense of the expansiveness of human life as glimpses are gained of a potentiality that exceeds the trammels of the quotidian. Her characters frequently represent a desire to perceive a larger, more harmonious pattern beyond both their own psychic turmoil and the apparent political and social chaos of the late twentieth century.

These concerns are introduced in Kennedy's first collection of short stories, *Night Geometry and the Garscadden Trains.* Here, in her already notably economic style, Kennedy writes of "small people" who, "withered by lack of belief," "live their lives in the best way they can with generally good intentions and still leave absolutely nothing behind." In her second collection of short stories, *Now That You're Back,* Kennedy, returning to the minds of "small people," explores the fine distinctions between normality and perversity as she probes the points at which isolation and estrangement produce what is perceived as obsession and deviance. As Kennedy ventriloquizes her characters' voices, several of the stories being written in the form of dramatic monologues, she confers upon them an impression of bodilessness, a fitting signifier of their disconnection from the world. Yet her characters seek that correspondence through which "a spasm of what I might call completeness" may be attained.

Kennedy retains her focus on subtle gradations of psychic spaces in her first novel, *Looking for the Possible Dance,* where she explores the way in which her protagonist's relationship with her father inscribes that with her lover. Here, as in her other works, Kennedy's exploration of parental legacy is allusive rather than diagnostic as she displays the proximity between pleasure and pain, particularly the pleasure that is sought through self-denial. Through one of the novel's central structural metaphors, that of the dance, Kennedy weaves together several of the novel's main concerns. Margaret's father's words at a Methodist ceilidh are echoed in her reflection that the search for meaningful political opposition in Britain in the 1980s was "looking for the possible dance, the step, the move to beat them all." The possibility that the discrete spaces that individuals occupy may be choreographed into an overarching pattern is adumbrated by the novel's concluding image: "Margaret walks to one door and sinks into brilliant air, becoming first a moving shadow, then a curve, a dancing line."

The concerns of Kennedy's earlier works are strikingly elaborated in her novel, *So I Am Glad.* Like the characters of her short stories, Kennedy's narrator, Jennifer Wilson, has learned "to enjoy a small, still life,'' achieving a ''calmness'' that is ''empty space ... a pause.'' Having been made a voyeur, as a child, of her parents' violent sexual practices, she now pathologizes other people's emotions as ''moles ... violent, tunnelling mammals.'' Jennifer's desire to free herself from her body and its emotional history is facilitated by her work as a radio commentator, a ''professional enunciator.'' The novel recounts her attempt to discover the identity of her lover who, it transpires, is Cyrano de Bergerac, reincarnated in late-twentieth-century Scotland. This fantastic device enables Kennedy to explore further a number of the concerns of her earlier works. De Bergerac becomes a vehicle for metaphysical speculation that is the more poignant as it is incorporated into Jennifer's mourning for his inevitable loss and her search for the words to articulate this. Through de Bergerac's estranged perspective, he is able to comment on the ''madness'' of the late twentieth century, defamiliarizing horrors to which, it is implied, the reader may have become acculturated. De Bergerac's history of dueling is extended through his verbal parrying with Jennifer as he explains, ''The point is that single moment when you truly touch another person. You reach to them with a word, a thought, a gesture.'' The duel codifies the desire for violence that is elsewhere in the narrative less successfully contained, whether in scenes of sadomasochistic sex or the political atrocities that are the subject of Jennifer's news broadcasts.

In *So I Am Glad,* as in Kennedy's earlier works, the movement between the personal and the political, between the poetic and the polemic, is uneven, the power of Kennedy's work lying in her painterly detailing of psychic spaces rather than in the large brush strokes with which she comments on the political turbulence of the late twentieth century. Her work is, however, already notable for its combination of wit, precision, and restraint with bold imaginative gestures.

Original Bliss, Kennedy's next novel, is a tale of abuse, lust, and longing as Helen Brindle, a middle-aged Glaswegian caught in a painful marital relationship, turns from her cruel husband to a German sex guru for fulfillment. Gradually, however, she becomes repelled by both men, and discovers that she can depend only on herself and on God. This quest for redemption amid spiritual squalor also plays itself out in *Everything You Need,* in which young Mary Lamb comes to the writers' colony of Foal Island on a fellowship. The island's inhabitants are all writers, a depressed lot given to rather disgusting fantasies. This is particularly true of Nathan Staples, who will be Mary's advisor for the period of her fellowship—and who, as we learn early in the book, is also her father.

—Joanna Price

KENNEDY, William (Joseph)

Nationality: American. **Born:** Albany, New York, 16 January 1928. **Education:** Siena College, Loudonville, New York, B.A. 1949. **Military Service:** Served in the United States Army, 1950–52: sports editor and columnist for Army newspapers. **Family:** Married Ana Daisy Dana Segarra in 1957; two daughters and one son. **Career:** Assistant sports editor and columnist, Glens Falls *Post Star,* New York, 1949–50; reporter, Albany *Times-Union,* 1952–56; assistant managing editor and columnist, *Puerto Rico World Journal,* San Juan, 1956; reporter, Miami *Herald,* 1957; Puerto Rico correspondent for Time-Life publications, and reporter for Dorvillier business newsletter and Knight newspapers, 1957–59; founding managing editor, San Juan *Star,* 1959–61; full-time writer, 1961–63; special writer, 1963–70, and film critic, 1968–70, Albany *Times-Union;* book editor, *Look,* New York, 1971. Lecturer, 1974–82, and since 1983 professor of English, State University of New York, Albany; visiting professor of English, Cornell University, Ithaca, New York, 1982–83. Since 1957 freelance magazine writer and critic; brochure and special project writer for New York State Department of Education and State University system, New York Governor's Conference on Libraries, and other organizations; director, New York State Writers Institute. **Awards:** Puerto Rican Civic Association of Miami award, 1957, NAACP award, 1965, Newspaper Guild Page One award, 1965, and New York State Publishers award, 1965, all for reporting; National Endowment for the Arts fellowship, 1981; Siena College Career Achievement award, 1983; MacArthur Foundation fellowship, 1983; National Book Critics Circle award, 1984; Celtic Foundation Frank O'Connor award, 1984; Before Columbus Foundation award, 1984; New York Public Library award, 1984; Pulitzer prize, 1984; Governor's Arts award, 1984; Brandeis University Creative Arts award, 1986. L.H.D.: Russell Sage College, Troy, New York, 1980; Siena College, 1984; Rensselaer Polytechnic Institute, Troy, New York, 1987; Long Island University, Greenvale, New York, 1989; D.Litt.: College of St. Rose, Albany, 1985. D.H.L.: Skidmore College, 1991; Fordham University, 1992; Trinity College, 1992. Commander, Order of Arts and Letters, France, 1993. **Agent:** Liz Darhansoff Literary Agency, 1220 Park Avenue, New York, New York 10128. **Address:** R.D. 3, Box 508, Averill Park, New York 12018, U.S.A.

Publications

Novels

The Ink Truck. New York, Dial Press, 1969; London, Macdonald, 1970.

Legs. New York, Coward McCann, 1975; London, Cape, 1976.

Billy Phelan's Greatest Game. New York, Viking Press, 1978; London, Penguin, 1983.

Ironweed. New York, Viking Press, 1983; London, Penguin, 1984.

Quinn's Book. New York, Viking, and London, Cape, 1988.

Very Old Bones. New York, Viking, 1992.

The Flaming Corsage. New York, Viking, 1996.

An Albany Trio: Three Novels from the Albany Cycle. New York, Penguin Books, 1996.

Uncollected Short Stories

''The Secrets of Creative Love,'' in *Harper's* (New York), July 1983.

''An Exchange of Gifts,'' in *Glens Falls Review* (Glens Falls, New York), no. 3, 1985–86.

''The Hills and the Creeks (Albany 1850),'' in *Harper's* (New York), March 1988.

Plays

Screenplays: *The Cotton Club,* with Francis Ford Coppola, 1984; *Ironweed,* 1987.

Other

Getting It All, Saving It All: Some Notes by an Extremist. Albany, New York State Governor's Conference on Libraries, 1978.

O Albany! Improbable City of Political Wizards, Fearless Ethnics, Spectacular Aristocrats, Splendid Nobodies, and Underrated Scoundrels. Albany and New York, Washington Park Press-Viking Press, 1983.

The Capitol in Albany (photographs). New York, Aperture, 1986; as *Albany and the Capitol,* London, Phaidon, 1986.

Charlie Malarkey and the Belly Button Machine (for children), with Brendan Kennedy. Boston, Atlantic Monthly Press, 1986; London, Cape, 1987.

Riding the Yellow Trolley Car. New York, Viking, 1993.

Charlie Malarkey and the Singing Moose (for children), with Brendan Kennedy. Viking Children's Books, 1994.

*

Bibliographies: ''A William Kennedy Bibliography'' by Edward C. Reilly, in *Bulletin of Bibliography* 48(2), June 1991.

Critical Studies: ''The Sudden Fame of William Kennedy'' by Margaret Croyden, in *New York Times Magazine,* 26 August 1984; *Understanding William Kennedy* by J.K. Van Dover, Columbia, University of South Carolina Press, 1991; *William Kennedy* by Edward C. Reilly, Boston, Twayne, 1991; *Conversations with William Kennedy,* edited by Neila C. Seshachari, Jackson, University Press of Mississippi, 1997.

* * *

In *O Albany!,* William Kennedy's ''urban biography'' of Albany, New York, he describes himself as ''a person whose imagination has become fused with a single place.'' This fusion has proved an impressive resource and theme in his novels which present an expansive yet intimate fictional and historical tableau of Albany life. While there is a humanist breadth of vision in Kennedy's writings—he views Albany as a city ''centered squarely in the American and human continuum''—his treatment of the city is closely focused on the lives and histories of Irish-Americans. His novels pay detailed attention to the culture and politics of this ethnic group, exploring both the local historical conditions and the internal mechanisms of ethnic identity, and illuminating the rich interplay of history, myth, and memory as these give meaning to the lives of Irish-Americans.

Kennedy offers his readers a richly detailed world where language is always inventive. The interactions of realism and romance, and of historical and mythical vision in his novels have led many critics to describe them as ''magic realist.'' The lyrical treatment of larger-than-life characters and use of vernacular humor also suggest the influences of American strains of imaginative journalism and oral storytelling. If there is a ''magic'' in the narratives it is the sense of intimacy they convey. The sounding of a common past and shared memories is an important element in Kennedy's writings and in having places, characters, and everyday objects animated by reminiscence and anecdote he shows how the past may be kept alive in ''memory and hearsay.'' Kennedy's first novel, *The Ink Truck,* is a black comedy which details the pathetic attempts of a small group of strikers to keep alive a failed strike against their newspaper employers. The true center of the novel is Bailey, a garrulous loner who invents crazy plots to challenge the newspaper company. Like the other strikers, Bailey is caught in the paradoxes of ideal and action which emerge from supporting a lost cause, but Kennedy draws his protagonist with an irrepressible energy and wit which mark his repeated failures with curious heroism. Although there is clearly a satirical intention to illuminate the way American society can both foster and thwart idealism, the narrative relies a little too heavily on the egotistical rhetoric and surreal imaginings of Bailey. If he is a failed hero there is little to draw the reader into his predicament.

Legs deals with a form of hero in the character of Jack ''Legs'' Diamond, the prohibition gangster-cum-celebrity whose life story is narrated by Marcus Gorman, a lawyer who is simultaneously attracted to and perturbed by this ''venal man of integrity.'' Diamond is an entertainer who is able to act out his fantasies and appetites in public, only to find that he is ''created anew'' by the media who draw on, add to, and manipulate his glamour. Kennedy interweaves history and myth in his characterization of Diamond as a powerful public figure who finds that fame is not a force he can control: ''Jack had imagined his fame all his life and now it was imagining him.'' Kennedy uses Gorman to mediate the multiple and conflicting documents, stories and cultural references surrounding Diamond's life. *Legs* is less a close study of what motivated this particular criminal than an examination of how he became a product of America's ''collective imagination.'' In *Billy Phelan's Greatest Game* Kennedy shows a more localized interest in how memory and myth circulate in the everyday actions and discourses of Albany's Irish-Americans in the 1930s. Billy Phelan, a young Irish-American hustler, has his world turned upside down when he is caught up in the kidnapping of Charlie McCall, son of the city's political boss. While Kennedy keeps the kidnap plot moving steadily along it is clear that his real interest is in exploring how an ethnic past is absorbed into the present day lives of his characters. Billy's encounters with the McCalls reveal a political network which maintains its power by endorsing and exploiting a rhetoric of family, morality, and loyalty that draws heavily on mythicized immigrant experiences. Kennedy also identifies rich seams of a common or collective memory which establishes a knowledge of the past in stories and anecdotes engendered by commonplace stimuli. In detailing and juxtaposing multiple rememorisations of the Irish-American past he shows how all members of the ethnic group, not only the politically powerful, are engaged in reconstructing the past to meet the demands of the present.

Ironweed, a Pulitzer prize-winner, is widely viewed as Kennedy's finest novel to date. The novel is closely connected to *Billy Phelan's Greatest Game* in terms of character, event, theme, and temporal setting. Francis Phelan, father of Billy and the ''Ironweed'' of the title, is a vagrant who returns to Albany after twenty-two years ''on the bum,'' a partly self-induced exile sustained by the guilt he feels about the deaths of a scab he felled during a strike and of his thirteen-day-old son Gerald whom he accidentally dropped and killed. On his return to Albany he confronts voices and images of ghosts which press him to re-examine his past. Returning to a community which has projected him into myth Francis reaches no clear resolution of his need to locate himself ''in time and place,'' but he does discover that in releasing memories and sharing them with others he is able tentatively to embrace much that he has repressed. Kennedy brilliantly meshes fantasy and realism in this narrative, examining both the inner confusions of his protagonist's ethnic identity and the powerful cultural and social forces which willfully idealize or obscure aspects of the ethnic past.

Set in mid-nineteenth-century Albany, *Quinn's Book* is the narrative of Daniel Quinn, an orphaned boy who witnesses such major historical events as the Underground Railroad, the Civil War and the New York draft riots. While there is a wealth of historical detail in this novel it is the apocalyptic opening—as Albany experiences freak disasters of fire and flood—and the surreal tinge to the events which imaginatively fire the narrative. Kennedy evokes a spirit world which shadows the lives of his characters providing sometimes comic, sometimes frightening perspectives on the past, present, and future. A sense of prescience grips the narration as Daniel grows to become the journalist-writer who views his life as a ''great canvas of the imagination.'' As in his earlier novels Kennedy intermingles fact and fantasy, but is perhaps more ambitious with his historical sweep, constructing a phantasmagoria of human actions and desires that denies any simple patternings or resolutions.

In Kennedy's novels the Irish-American past is always under construction, its reinvention important to the patterning of social relations in the present. Kennedy is a speculative historian of this ethnic past, self-consciously aware that he is himself playing a part in its reinvention. He skillfully dissolves distinctions between the real and the fictional as his writings explore how memory and fantasy can influence historical understanding. In *Billy Phelan's Greatest Game* he offers an ironical authorial note: ''Any reality attaching to any character is the result of the author's creation, or of his own interpretation of history. This applies not only to Martin Daugherty and Billy Phelan, to Albany politicians, newsmen, and gamblers, but also to Franklin D. Roosevelt, Thomas E. Dewey, Henry James, Damon Runyon, William Randolph Hearst, and any number of other creatures of the American imagination.''

—Liam Kennedy

KESEY, Ken (Elton)

Nationality: American. **Born:** La Junta, Colorado, 17 September 1935. **Education:** A high school in Springfield, Oregon; University of Oregon, Eugene, B.A. 1957; Stanford University, California (Woodrow Wilson fellow), 1958–59. **Family:** Married Faye Haxby in 1956; four children (one deceased). **Career:** Ward attendant in mental hospital, Menlo Park, California; president, Intrepid Trips film company, 1964. Since 1974 publisher, *Spit in the Ocean* magazine, Pleasant Hill, Oregon. Served prison term for marijuana possession, 1967. **Awards:** Saxton Memorial Trust award, 1959. **Address:** 85829 Ridgeway Road, Pleasant Hill, Oregon 97455, U.S.A.

PUBLICATIONS

Novels

One Flew over the Cuckoo's Nest. New York, Viking Press, 1962; London, Methuen, 1963.
Sometimes a Great Notion. New York, Viking Press, 1964; London, Methuen, 1966.
Demon Box. New York, Viking, and London, Methuen, 1986.
Caverns, with others. New York, Viking, 1990.
The Further Inquiry. New York, Viking, 1990.
Sailor Song. New York, Viking, 1992; London, Black Swan, 1993.
Last Go Round, with Ken Babbs. New York, Viking, 1994.

Short Stories

The Day Superman Died. Northridge, California, Lord John Press, 1980.

Uncollected Short Stories

''The First Sunday in October,'' in *Northwest Review* (Seattle), Fall 1957.
''McMurphy and the Machine,'' in *Stanford Short Stories 1962,* edited by Wallace Stegner and Richard Scowcroft. Stanford, California, Stanford University Press, 1962.
''Letters from Mexico,'' in *Ararat* (New York), Autumn 1967.
''Excerpts from Kesey's Jail Diary,'' in *Ramparts* (Berkeley, California), November 1967.
''Correspondence,'' in *Tri-Quarterly* (Evanston, Illinois), Spring 1970.
''Once a Great Nation,'' in *Argus* (College Park, Maryland), April 1970.
''Dear Good Dr. Timothy,'' in *Augur* (Eugene, Oregon), 19 November 1970.
''Cut the Motherfuckers Loose,'' in *The Last Whole Earth Catalog.* San Francisco, Straight Arrow, 1971.
''The Bible,'' ''Dawgs,'' ''The I Ching,'' ''Mantras,'' ''Tools from My Chest,'' in *The Last Supplement to the Whole Earth Catalog-The Realist* (New York), March-April 1971.
''Over the Border,'' in *Oui* (Chicago), April 1973.
'''Seven Prayers' by Grandma Whittier,'' in *Spit in the Ocean 1–5* (Pleasant Hill, Oregon), 1974–79.

Other

Kesey's Garage Sale (miscellany; includes screenplay *Over the Border*). New York, Viking Press, 1973.
Little Tricker the Squirrel Meets Big Double the Bear (for children). New York, Viking, 1990.
The Sea Lion: A Story of the Sea Cliff People (for children). New York, Viking, 1991.

*

Manuscript Collections: University of Oregon, Eugene.

Critical Studies: *The Electric Kool-Aid Acid Test* by Tom Wolfe, New York, Farrar Straus, 1968, London, Weidenfeld and Nicolson, 1969; *Ken Kesey* by Bruce Carnes, Boise, Idaho, Boise State College, 1974; ''Ken Kesey Issue'' of *Northwest Review* (Eugene, Oregon), vol. 16, nos. 1–2, 1977; *Ken Kesey* by Barry H. Leeds, New York, Ungar, 1981; *The Art of Grit: Ken Kesey's Fiction,* Columbia, University of Missouri Press, 1982, and *One Flew over the Cuckoo's Nest: Rising to Heroism,* Boston, Twayne, 1989, both by M. Gilbert Porter; *Ken Kesey* by Stephen L. Tanner, Boston, Twayne, 1983; *On the Bus: The Legendary Trip of Ken Kesey and the Merry Pranksters* by Ken Babbs, photographs by Rob Bivert, New York, Thunder's Mouth Press, 1989, London, Plexus, 1991.

* * *

Ken Kesey's celebrity and critical reputation were instantly established with the publication of his first two novels. *One Flew Over the Cuckoo's Nest* was a widely popular commercial success as a novel and was also successful in its adaptations for stage and screen. *Sometimes a Great Notion* was initially received with some critical reservations. Seen as an ambitious but not altogether satisfying attempt to enter the rank of great American novels, it has since received more favorable attention from the academic critics, though it has not found a secure place in the established canon of contemporary American literature. After finishing it, Kesey announced a shift from ''literature'' to ''life,'' and achieved a great deal of public notoriety in the process of making the change. He was frequently public news during the late 1960s, forming a band of ''Merry Pranksters'' (reported on at length in Tom Wolfe's *The Electric Kool-Aid Acid Test*) who attempted to live life as a work of comic fiction. His arrest and conviction for marijuana possession made still more news and provided experiences that he would frequently exploit in his writing. Stray and often occasional pieces of a miscellaneous nature were published in countercultural venues during the late 1960s and early 1970s, suggesting that perhaps a new project was in the works, and some of these were assembled in *Kesey's Garage Sale,* an apt title for a collection of miscellaneous items. In 1986 a more ambitious collection was assembled for *Demon Box,* a series of largely autobiographical pieces that continued to look back in time to the historical period of Kesey's public notoriety. The volume is loosely united by a first-person narrator whose name, Devlin Deboree (pronounced *debris*), hints at a devil-may-care attitude towards social and artistic conventions, and at the disorganized, self-consciously problematic value of his observations.

Both of Kesey's early novels are richly northwestern and regional in setting and atmosphere, with a strong sense of the incursion of the white man on the Indian's land and way of life. The emphasis is a bit one-sided in *Cuckoo's Nest,* which is set in a mental institution and has for its stream-of-consciousness narrator a ''dumb'' (thought to be deaf, but in fact choosing not to speak) Indian nick-named Chief, whose father was the last chief of his tribe. The novel can be read as an allegory of how the invaders have been driven to subjugate the Native Americans because they are a reminder of what must be sacrificed in the process of western civilization and its discontents, and an exploration of the power struggle between a desire to be free and the fearful consequences of that freedom. Most of the characters confined in the institution could leave if they wished; but their fear of the outside is more intense than their hatred of the inside, until the raucous protagonist McMurphy comes along to inspire their lapsed self-confidence and zest for life. Recognizable as a tragicomic parodic microcosm of the world we all live in, the book captures and reflects the reality of a Walt Disney world, as perceived through the eyes of the ''Big Chief'' who used to be on the bright red covers of the writing tablets of children all over the United States, but who is now pretending to be a vegetable in a nut house. What he sees is ''Like a cartoon world, where the figures are flat and outlined in black, jerking through some kind of goofy story that might be real funny if it weren't for the cartoon figures being real guys …'' The comic-book quality has lent itself nicely to dramatic production, as have the compactness and wild humor of the novel. These qualities also tempt one to allegorize, but at the same time mock the attempt as absurd, for the work is not itself allegorical. It is a report on the way people choose to see themselves and their world in allegorical or comic-book fashion. The reality of the villain, ''Big Nurse,'' is as exaggerated by the characters who fear and hate her as it is by the novelist. It is their insecurity and weakness that feed her power and make her ''big,'' while the institution, with its equipment and routines, becomes the pretext for sociological and cultural myths pushed to an exaggerated but all-too-plausible extreme. The prefrontal lobotomy performed on McMurphy at the end is any operation on or treatment of or way of seeing a man designed to limit him for his own sake, to protect him from his own human nature. The Big Nurse is that spirit which loves the ''idea'' of man so much it can't allow individual men to exist.

Sometimes a Great Notion was Kesey's stab at writing the great American novel in a Faulknerian mode, and it deserves more attention than can be given it here. Like an *Absalom, Absalom!* set in Oregon, intensely regional, with elaborate and intricately complex narrative structure (flashbacks, shifts of point of view), the work demands several readings. With such attention, what at first seem like gratuitous confusions and exploitations of narrative technique begin to emerge as the necessary supports for a novelistic structure which commands respect even though it fails in the end to achieve its full potential. In this novel Kesey aimed high, and he came impressively close to his target. The publication two decades later of *Demon Box* produces the effect of a long-deferred anti-climax. Lingering colloquially and nostalgically over his acquaintances and escapades in the 1960s and 1970s, in a deliberately naive reportage style, this work often succeeds in capturing the colloquial idiom of prison life or Hell's Angels banter, but it does little to enhance Kesey's reputation as an innovative writer of the first rank. As if aware of this critical judgment, Kesey deliberately prefaced the book with a poem called ''TARNISHED GALAHAD—*what the judge called him at his trial,*'' two lines of which ask and answer the significant question:

> Tarnished Galahad—did your sword get rusted?
>
> Tarnished Galahad—there's no better name!

—Thomas A. Vogler

KIDMAN, Fiona

Nationality: New Zealander. **Born:** Fiona Judith Eakin, Hawera, 2 March 1940. **Family:** Married Ian Kidman in 1960; one daughter, one son. **Career:** Librarian, Rotorua Boys High 1961–62; wrote and produced radio plays in the 1970s, has taught creative writing, and has been a weekly columnist for *The Listener;* President of the New Zealand Book Council, since 1992. **Awards:** New Zealand Scholarship in Letters, 1981, 1985, 1995; Mobil Short Story award, 1987; Arts Council award for achievement, 1988; New Zealand Book award, 1988, for fiction; Writers Fellow, Victoria University, 1988; OBE (Officer, Order of the British Empire); DNZM (Dame Commander of the New Zealand Order of Merit). **Member:** New Zealand Writers' Guild; New Zealand Book Council. **Agent:** Ray Richards, Richards Literary Agency, P.O. Box 31–240, Milford, Auckland 9, New Zealand. **Address:** 28 Rakan Rd., Hataitai, Wellington 3, New Zealand.

PUBLICATIONS

Novels

A Breed of Women. Ringwood, Victoria, Harper and Row, 1979; New York, Penguin, 1988.
Mandarin Summer. Auckland, Heinemann, 1981.
Paddy's Puzzle. Auckland, Heinemann, 1983; London, Penguin, 1985; as *In the Clear Light,* New York, Norton.
The Book of Secrets. Auckland, Heinemann, 1987.
True Stars. Auckland, Random Century, 1990.
Ricochet Baby. Auckland, Vintage, 1996.

Short Stories

Mrs Dixon and Friend. Auckland, Heinemann, 1982.
Unsuitable Friends. Auckland, Century Hutchinson, 1988.
The Foreign Woman. Auckland, Vintage, 1993.
The Best of Fiona Kidman's Short Stories. New York, Vintage, 1998.

Plays

Search for Sister Blue. Wellington, New Zealand, Reed, 1975.

Poetry

Honey and Bitters. Christchurch, New Zealand, Pegasus Press, 1975.
On the Tightrope. Christchurch, New Zealand, Pegasus Press, 1978.
Going to the Chathams, Poems 1977–84. Auckland, Heinemann, 1985.
Wakeful Nights, Poems Selected and New. Auckland, Vintage, 1991.

Other

Gone North, with Jane Ussher. Auckland, Heinemann, 1984.
Wellington, with Grant Sheehan. Auckland, Random House, 1989.
Palm Prints. Auckland, Vintage, 1994.
Editor, *New Zealand Love Stories: An Oxford Anthology.* Oxford, Oxford University Press, 1999.

*

Manuscript Collection: Alexander Turnbull Library, Wellington, New Zealand.

Fiona Kidman comments:

I was brought up in the northern part of New Zealand in isolated country areas, an only child whose family moved a lot, and was hard-up. Perhaps because of this, I have often examined the situation of people who live at "the edge" and find it difficult to communicate. My work has been identified to some extent with the feminist movement in New Zealand, particularly my historical novel, *The Book of Secrets,* (winner of the New Zealand Book award, 1988) which examined the life of migrant Scottish women on their journeys from Scotland to Nova Scotia, and ultimately New Zealand. My most recent short story collection *The Foreign Woman,* (runner-up to New Zealand Book award, 1994) has been likened to the work of Alice Munro—a great, but probably undeserved, compliment.

* * *

Fiona Kidman is one of a generation of New Zealand's women writers born during World War II whose works espouse the sub-texts of feminist self-discovery and social validation. Her efforts on behalf of New Zealand's writers, however, are not restricted to gender-based advocacy. As president of PEN and the New Zealand Book Council, she used her influence to establish Women's Book Week in conjunction with her involvement in the United Women's Conventions in the 1970s and the 1975 International Women's Year, which profoundly affected her. She has stated that any account of women's writing in New Zealand during the past two decades is incomplete without reviewing 1975. In a socialist realist style, her fiction depicts New Zealand women, both contemporary and historical, as rebellious heroines who resist the social values that threaten to engulf them.

She brilliantly describes the atmosphere of small towns like Waipu in her first novel, *A Breed of Women*, which created something of a sensation in New Zealand as it broke social taboos. Kidman believes that she is not wholly responsible for her characters' choices, which originate in the subtle underpinnings that construct her psyche and history. That reaction of New Zealand society to frankly feminist estimations of it was repeated around the globe during the crucial 1970s when women began to speak and write about such matters. Kidman exposes the narrow-minded, conformist mentality of bourgeois New Zealand and the limited choices open to her heroine. Harriet, a bright but unsophisticated farm girl, falls into the hands of milkbar cowboys, and ends up in a shotgun marriage to a Maori. Harriet and her friend Leonie present contrasting pictures of unfulfilled women driven to take risks and seek alternative sources of happiness outside marriage, providing a near-perfect paradigm for middle-class New Zealand women of the late 1970s.

Her second novel, *Mandarin Summer*, owes more to the genre of Gothic horror, for it tells a disturbing story by evoking a macabre atmosphere. Set in 1946 in a small Northland community, it narrates the encounter between a wealthy, decadent European family and their hangers-on and a New Zealand family, the Freemans, who have been duped into buying unsuitable land from the Europeans. In a tidy reversal of colonial history, the Machiavellian Brigadier Barnsley coerces the Freemans into a servitude that embroils them in his disputes and passions. Although the scenes concerning his opium-addicted, incarcerated wife, his Jewish mistress, and the final conflagration that destroys the homestead are inspired by *Jane Eyre*, the novel exerts a weird fascination while exploring a new twist on the theme of incest. Emily, the eleven-year-old narrator, sees more than is good for her, even though at times her retrospective child's point of view slips into adult reportage. Kidman distorts the lens of romantic fiction by telling an implausible tale with compelling directness.

Although the second half of *Paddy's Puzzle* is also set at the end of World War II, the novel opens in the small town of Hamilton during the 1930s depression. The traumas caused by Winnie's pregnancy, poverty, and her husband's abandonment of the family to seek work anticipate the abortive, juvenile love affair of her heroine Clara, whom Winnie has also raised. But her early life does not entirely explain Clara's subsequent fate—a life of abandonment in prostitution, and then tuberculosis—outlined in a grim account of her dying days in Paddy's Puzzle, the name of a tenement slum for prostitutes on Karangahape Road. Through this cityscape Kidman explores the seedy side of life during the war with pathos and dramatic flair. Although Clara's death may convey a message about the afflictions women suffered at a time of limited social support, it reveals Kidman's fascination with forms of self-entrapment and marginal states of existence. Paddy's Puzzle was re-issued in the United States under the title *In the Clear Light*.

In *The Book of Secrets* Kidman returns to historical fiction, telling the lives of three women through letters, journals, and dreams. The novel is an exploration of the isolated, strangely un-emancipated figure of Maria, who lives in solitude as a witch. Her story has its roots in fact: the account of the charismatic figure of Reverend McLeod who led his followers from poverty-stricken Scotland to Nova Scotia and New Zealand is true. The plot's main focus is the three generations of women who enact some pattern of retribution through their association with McLeod. Isabella defies him, is raped, and goes mad; her daughter, Annie, submits to his order; and Maria eventually achieves some kind of spiritual victory. The theme of hidden lives once more demands negotiation with religious and social values, which reflect an irrational patriarchal power structure. But Kidman lets her story take its path rather than imposing a determinedly feminist pattern on her historical sources.

Kidman's *True Stars* tells a contemporary story of love, betrayal, politics, and death in the last days of Lange's Labour government. Her subjects are the citizens of Weyville: the left-wing yuppies who rose to prominence at the time of the 1981 Springbok tour. They gained a political voice through their freshly elected Labour MP, Kit Kendall, and the Maori activists, along with the drop-out generation. Together they represent a range of topical issues in New Zealand during the 1980s, including the need to confront a collapsing dream with the reality of a nearly defunct government. The victimization of Kit's wife, Rose, and her conflicting family and social loyalties signal the full extent of those confused times. Kidman shows her strengths as a journalist, capturing with immediacy the class and social divisions of the times, the tensions of small-town politics as played out against a national context, and the personal dilemmas faced by the middle-aged Rose. In a tightly organized plot, she ties together these different strands in such a way that each interacts with the other to create a thrilling denouement.

Kidman has been called an ''ordinary woman'' who dares to challenge, and she takes on a common effect of provincial and lower middle-class life with *Ricochet Baby*. Lower economic classes are often forced to ignore the serious effects of the so-called mysterious women's illnesses, such as post-natal depression. Kidman's examination of one woman's bout with the hormonal imbalance reveals how devastating the postpartum syndrome can be on the family as well as the individual. The novel *The House Within* delves even further into an ordinary woman's psyche as Bethany Dixon negotiates her complex network of relationships, the numerous roles to which women often devote themselves in an irrationally generous manner. She plays mother and step-mother, wife and ex-wife, daughter-in-law, sister, and lover in fragments and snapshots that span twenty-five years. Despite her devotion to the woman's roles she plays, Bethany has yet to establish her own identity separate from those she serves, and her own place in the world. In compensation for this, she is addicted to food, children, and Peter, a departed ex-husband who Bethany continues to regard as her emotional focal point.

Fiona Kidman is one of New Zealand's most honored novelists, as well as the author of numerous critically acclaimed collections of short stories, poetry, and non-fiction, as well as dramatic works including radio plays. She has won a number of awards and scholarships: the Ngaio Marsh Award for Television Writing; the 1988 New Zealand Book Award for Fiction for *The Book of Secrets*; the Literary Fund Award for Achievement. As a writing fellow at Victoria University in 1988, she was awarded the OBE, and in 1998 was made a Dame Commander of the New Zealand Order of Merit for her ceaseless, all-encompassing service to literature.

Like her predecessor, Katherine Mansfield, she may be remembered best for her short stories, which discuss marital infidelity, marital break-up, and failed relationships. However, her talent for weaving together stories as easily as many women juggle the bits and pieces of their families' lives is evident in the novel *The House Within*, which takes the form of interwoven stories, each narrated by the central character. Kidman's prose is economical, yet often sensual. Her women characters become the outsiders in a narrowly conformist society, and this status is dramatized by sexual transgression and punishment. She has been called a ''raider of the real'' because of her unerring look and prolonged gaze at women's lives written in the social-realism style.

—Janet Wilson, updated by Hedwig Gorski

KIELY, Benedict

Nationality: Irish. **Born:** Dromore, County Tyrone, 15 August 1919. **Education:** Christian Brothers' schools, Omagh; National University of Ireland, Dublin, B.A. (honours) 1943. **Family:** Married Maureen O'Connell in 1944; three daughters and one son. **Career:** Journalist in Dublin, 1939–64. Writer-in-residence, Hollins College, Virginia, 1964–65; visiting professor, University of Oregon, Eugene, 1965–66; writer-in-residence, Emory University, Atlanta, 1966–68. Since 1970 visiting lecturer, University College, Dublin. **Awards:** American-Irish Foundation award, 1980; Irish Academy of Letters award, 1980. **Member:** Of the Council, and President, Irish Academy of Letters. **Address:** c/o The Irish Times, Westmoreland Street, Dublin, Ireland.

Publications

Novels

Land Without Stars. London, Johnson, 1946.
In a Harbour Green. London, Cape, 1949; New York, Dutton, 1950.
Call for a Miracle. London, Cape, 1950; New York, Dutton, 1951.
Honey Seems Bitter. New York, Dutton, 1952; London, Methuen, 1954.
The Cards of the Gambler: A Folktale. London, Methuen, 1953.
There Was an Ancient House. London, Methuen, 1955.
The Captain with the Whiskers. London, Methuen, 1960; New York, Criterion, 1961.
Dogs Enjoy the Morning. London, Gollancz, 1968.
Proxopera. London, Gollancz, 1977; Boston, Godine, 1987.

Nothing Happens in Carmincross. London, Gollancz, and Boston, Godine, 1985.

The Trout in the Turnhole. Dublin, Wolfhound Press, 1995.

Short Stories

A Journey to the Seven Streams: Seventeen Stories. London, Methuen, 1963.

Penguin Modern Stories 5, with others. London, Penguin, 1970.

A Ball of Malt and Madame Butterfly: A Dozen Stories. London, Gollancz, 1973.

A Cow in the House and Nine Other Stories. London, Gollancz, 1978.

The State of Ireland: A Novella and Seventeen Stories. Boston, Godine, 1980; London, Penguin, 1982.

A Letter to Peachtree and Nine Other Stories. London, Gollancz, 1987; Boston, Godine, 1988.

God's Own Country. London, Minerva, 1993.

Other

Counties of Contention: A Study of the Origins and Implication of the Partition of Ireland. Cork, Mercier Press, 1945.

Poor Scholar: A Study of the Works and Days of William Carleton 1794–1869. London, Sheed and Ward, 1947; New York, Sheed and Ward, 1948.

Modern Irish Fiction: A Critique. Dublin, Golden Eagle, 1950.

All the Way to Bantry Bay and Other Irish Journeys. London, Gollancz, 1978.

Ireland from the Air. London, Weidenfeld and Nicolson, and New York, Crown, 1985.

Yeats' Ireland: An Illustrated Anthology. London, Aurum Press, and New York, Crown, 1989.

Drink to the Bird: A Memoir. London, Methuen, 1991.

25 Views of Dublin (commentary), photographs by James Horan. Dublin, Town House in Association with the Office of Public Works, 1994.

The Waves Behind Us: A Memoir. London, Methuen, 1999.

Editor, *The Various Lives of Keats and Chapman and The Brother,* by Flann O'Brien. London, Hart Davis MacGibbon, 1976.

Editor, *The Penguin Book of Irish Short Stories.* London, Penguin, 1981.

Editor, *Dublin.* Oxford and New York, Oxford University Press, 1983.

Editor, *And As I Rode by Granard Moat.* Dublin, Lilliput Press, 1996.

*

Critical Studies: *Benedict Kiely* by Daniel J. Casey, Lewisburg, Pennsylvania, Bucknell University Press, 1974; *Benedict Kiely* by Grace Eckley, New York, Twayne, 1974.

* * *

Myth and legend, the heroic and the mock-heroic, form the central strands to the short stories of Benedict Kiely. He relies heavily on the Irish genius for creating epic myths about man, his heroic deeds and his human frailties. Although his fiction is largely set in the County Tyrone of his boyhood, a landscape that he knows intimately and with a sense of delight, it is transformed in a story like "A Journey to the Seven Streams" to a land of eternal and universal childhood. The trip to the stone-fiddle beside Lough Erne in Hookey Baxter's whimsical motor car takes on the aspect of a pilgrimage to a shrine or the tale of travellers in a magic, dreamlike land who have to face numerous adventures and dangers.

In a second collection, *A Ball of Malt and Madame Butterfly,* Kiely confirmed that although his work continues to be rooted in the Ireland that he knows so well, it has a breadth of vision and humanity in its subject matter and literary style that raises it above the merely provincial. The Tyrone of his childhood and the Dublin of his formative years are favorite backdrops for his novels where the mood changes from the mock-epic to the mock-gothic romance in a work like *The Captain with the Whiskers* with its memorable scene of the mad captain drilling his three sons in Boer War uniforms in the doomed big house; and in *Dogs Enjoy the Morning* with its satirical mixture of pub gossip and idle anecdote in the grotesque, but finely drawn, village of Cosmona where a newspaper reporter remarks, aptly enough, that "all human life is here." Kiely is at his best when he is writing short stories in which fantasy, satire, anecdote, and comic inventiveness play vital parts. The stories in *A Letter to Peachtree* are all told from a narrator's point of view, often as rambling comic monologues, and the end result is similar to listening to saloon bar badinage or half-heard eclectic conversations. Much of it is very funny and in each story the voice of the narrator is of paramount importance. A countryman reminisces about the past in a Dublin pub, attempting to put faces to half-remembered acquaintances in long-forgotten incidents; a writer attends a curious re-enactment of the events of 1690; a "secret poltroon" desires the girls at the dancing class and in the title story an American is caught up in other people's lives as he attempts to write about an Irish writer. It is not stretching a point to compare Kiely's later short stories to the great classical short fiction written by his fellow countrymen Frank O'Connor and Sean O'Faolain.

A new note in Kiely's work was struck with the publication of *Proxopera* in 1977, a savagely indignant novel with its anger directed against all men of violence in Ireland. The title comes from an "operation proxy" when an elderly grandfather, Binchey, is forced by three terrorists holding his family ransom to take a bomb into the neighboring town. The background is again Tyrone, but the mood is at once savage in Binchey's outrage at the terrorism that Ireland has helped to spawn, and at once an elegy for the non-sectarian, chivalrous past of his own childhood. Everything is seen through the enraged consciousness of Binchey and his sense of loss that nothing, his past, his family, the countryside and his relationship to them, will ever be the same again.

The same theme is continued—although this time on a larger canvas—in *Nothing Happens in Carmincross,* a novel which is constructed with enormous skill, layer upon layer, until its final and devastating act of violence. Mervyn Kavanagh, the central character, has a career as an academic in America, but has retained a great love for his native Ireland. Unlike many Irish-Americans, though, he has no love for terrorism; this cannot save him from the reality he has to confront when, on a visit to Ireland, he is brought face to face with the violence of his country's past and present history.

At the novel's end the reader is left with the certainty that another meaningless act of horror is about to become just another memory, part of the historical process: in that sense Kiely has faced up courageously to the peculiar tragedy of the Irish situation. In contrast to his morbid theme Kiely writes with zest and grace, humor and irony, in a style which is totally individual, the cadences of his language pointing and counterpointing feelings and ideas.

—Trevor Royle

KINCAID, Jamaica

Nationality: American. **Born:** Elaine Potter Richardson in St. John's, Antigua, 25 May 1949. **Education:** Princess Margaret girls' school, Antigua; New School for Social Research, New York; Franconia College, New Hampshire, **Family:** Married Allen Evan Shawn; one daughter and one son. **Career:** Since 1974 contributor, and currently staff writer, *The New Yorker.* **Awards:** American Academy Morton Dauwen Zabel award, 1984. Honorary doctorate: Williams College, 1991; Long Island College, 1991; Amherst College, 1995; Bard College, 1997; Middlebury College, 1998. **Address:** The New Yorker, 25 West 43rd Street, New York, New York 10036, U.S.A.

PUBLICATIONS

Novels

Annie John. New York, Farrar Straus, and London, Pan, 1985.
Lucy. New York, Farrar Straus, 1990; London, Cape, 1991.
The Autobiography of My Mother. New York, Farrar, Straus, Giroux, 1996.

Short Stories

At the Bottom of the River. New York, Farrar Straus, 1983; London, Pan, 1984.
Annie, Gwen, Lily, Pam, and Tulip, illustrated by Eric Fischl. New York, Library Fellows of the Whitney Museum of American Art, 1986.
Talk Stories. New York, Farrar, Straus and Giroux, 2000.

Uncollected Short Stories

''Autobiograph of a Dress,'' in *Grand Street Magazine.*

Other

A Small Place. New York, Farrar Straus, and London, Virago Press, 1988.
My Brother. New York, Farrar, Straus and Giroux, 1997.
Poetics of Place (essay), photographs by Lynn Geesaman. New York, Umbrage Editions, 1998.
My Garden Book, illustrations by Jill Fox. New York, Farrar Straus Giroux, 1999.
Editor, with Robert Atwan, *The Best American Essays 1995.* Boston, Houghton Mifflin, 1995.
Editor, *My Favorite Plant: Writers and Gardeners on the Plants They Love.* New York, Farrar Straus Giroux, 1998.

*

Critical Studies: *Jamaica Kincaid: Where the Land Meets the Body* by Moira Ferguson, Charlottesville, University Press of Virginia, 1994; *Jamaica Kincaid* by Diane Simmons, New York, Twayne Publishers, 1994; *Jamaica Kincaid,* edited by Harold Bloom, Philadelphia, Chelsea House, 1998; *Jamaica Kincaid: A Critical Companion* by Lizabeth Paravisini-Gebert, Westport, Connecticut, Greenwood Press, 1999.

* * *

Jamaica Kincaid is a talented writer, who has so far published five arresting books of fiction: *At the Bottom of the River; Annie John; Lucy; Annie, Gwen, Lily, Pam, and Tulip;* and *The Autobiography of My Mother.* Her nonfiction work includes an extended essay on her homeland, *A Small Place;* a meditation on her brother's 1996 death from AIDS, *My Brother;* and *My Garden Book,* which considers her particular relationship to gardening and the history of horticulture. Kincaid's work has been described variously as elegant, beguiling, gentle, graceful, dazzling, poetic, and lyrical.

Her fiction is sensuous, evocative, and sometimes erotic. The meanings are elusive in her first, second, and fourth books, and they emerge gradually from an almost hypnotic litany marked by repetition, echoes, and refrains as well as by brilliant descriptions of people, objects, and geography. The third book, *Lucy,* and Kincaid's most recent novel, *The Autobiography of My Mother,* depart from this style with their more direct prose. In the first two books Kincaid uses the narrative voice of a girl preoccupied with love and hate for a mother who caresses her only child one moment and then berates her as ''the slut you are about to become.'' The child's father, thirty-five years older than her mother, is seldom with his wife and daughter and has had more than thirty children by various women, who jealously seek his wife's death through *obeah* rites. In the ten meditative sections of *At the Bottom of the River,* neither the child nor her homeland, Antigua, have names; in *Annie John* both do. In *Annie John,* Annie ages from ten to seventeen, giving the second book greater continuity and a more specific chronology. In both books the narrator describes her experiences and reflects upon them in monologues that complement one another but could stand separately. In both of these episodic works Kincaid achieves a degree of aesthetic unity through her careful and sparse selection of characters, an emphasis on the relative isolation of the child, a preoccupation with the mother/daughter relationship, and the use of a distinctive narrative voice. Kincaid reflects the childlike simplicity and apparent naiveté of the speaker, even while she conveys Annie John's sophisticated vision of her cultural milieu, her sexual awakening, her responses to nature, and her sensitivity to events, persons, and influences possessing symbolic overtones. Hypnotically talking to herself, Annie John uses parallel phrases reminiscent of biblical poetry. She is keenly receptive to sense impressions—sounds, scents, and colors. These two books offer insight into the nature of a typical girl's growth to maturity, but they also offer analysis of an atypical and highly sensitive child as she moves inevitably toward psychological breakdown, which occurs when she is fifteen.

Annie John lives in constant conflict with her unpredictable mother. She must choose always to submit or to resort to lies, trickery, and even open rebellion. In both books, transitions from everyday school and home life into the psychic are lacking as Kincaid shifts abruptly from realistic depiction of the Caribbean milieu to disclosure of the child's dreams and fantasies. At the most intense crisis of her protagonist's experiences Kincaid approaches the mythic and archetypal. She projects the unusual and timeless aspects of the mother/daughter relationship as an alternate merging and separating of two spirits. Annie John also views the strength of a mature woman symbolically—as the shedding of the skin, so that a woman stands up naked, vulnerable, and courageous before the world and leaves her protective covering rolled into a ball in the corner. The child in both books recites rules dictated by her mother, defining the female role in household routines and in social behavior. Some of these chants are ominous: "This is how to make a good medicine for a cold; this is how to make a good medicine to throw away a child before it even becomes a child ... this is how to bully a man; this is how a man bullies you." The narrator in *At the Bottom of the River* parodies the commandments as she mischievously recites, "this is how to spit up in the air if you feel like it, and this is how to move quick so that it doesn't fall on you."

The protagonist in both books moves into the disordered and the surreal as in dreams she walks with her mother through caves, empty houses, and along the shores of the sea. She dreams of happy marriage to a "red woman," who seems to be her mother (or an idealized mother-substitute), who wears skirts "big enough to bury your head in," and who will make her happy by telling stories that begin with "Before you were born."

In *At the Bottom of the River* the most notable explorations of the visionary and contemplative mind of the child occur in the sections entitled "Wingless" and "My Mother" and most disturbingly in "Blackness." In *Annie John* the girl's narrative of her mental and physical breakdown, marked by hallucinations, appears in "The Long Rain," and her illness is concurrent with rain that continues for ten weeks. Annie John's mother and maternal grandmother treat her with medications supplied by a British physician, but they also use—in spite of her father's objections—various *obeah* potions and rituals. In her fantasy the child never loses all contact with reality. At the bottom of the river of her mind, trust exists as cold, hard, and uncompromising as rocks embedded below moving water. Moving into the surreal or unconscious, she does not quite abandon her world of household routine, the rigors of her life at school, or her sensitivity to the details of external nature. In the midst of a visionary passage, she startles the reader with a meditative statement based upon her observations of concrete realities: "I covet the rocks and the mountains their silence." On the closing page of *At the Bottom of the River,* the girl finds direction and substance, not so much in her visionary flights as in familiar objects: books, a chair, a table, a bowl of fruit, a bottle of milk, a flute made of wood. As she names these objects, she finds them to be reminders of human endeavor, past and present, though in themselves they are transient. She identifies herself as part of this endeavor as it betokens a never-ending flow of aspiration and creativity. She declares: "I claim these things then—mine—and now feel myself grow solid and complete, my name filling up my mouth." Annie John admires the courage and wildness of an imaginary "red girl," whom her mother denounces. Near the close of *Annie John,* the girl moves away, implying that Annie John no longer needs this double. Such kinship—even with an imagined role model—determines her positive self-identity in the last analysis as a human being and as a part of nature. As she leaves at seventeen to study nursing in England, she stands quietly and stoically on the ship, watching her mother become a mere dot in the distance.

The protagonist of *Lucy* similarly leaves Antigua at nineteen to become an au pair, caring for the children of a rich white couple in New York, and studying in night school, with nursing as a possible goal. Lucy Josephine Potter's mother is considered to be saintly, although Lucy suspects she angrily named her Lucifer at birth. Her father, like Annie John's, is a philanderer, with mistresses who have borne his many children and who jealously threaten his wife through *obeah* schemes. But Lucy, except for occasional moments in this novel, presents herself as a relatively unemotional, detached, and self-centered woman, far different from Annie John. Her tough cynicism may arise primarily from resentment of her parents and from her anger at what she perceives as an oppressive island background. She despises the negative impact on her education of historic British imperialism, the exploitation of the island's beauty by Antiguan promoters of tourism, and the corruption of Antiguan politicians. At home she was punished for her healthy refusal to regard Columbus as a hero for his part in the "discovery" of West Indies, and she suffered silently the failure of books and teachers to recognize black African heritage in Antiguan students.

In general, however, Lucy's emotional repression is so great that she is a far less vibrant character than Annie John, whose imagination, passion, amusing impudence, and open laughter and grief make her unforgettable. Annie John's sensitive response to surroundings transformed the most mundane and familiar objects into art, but Lucy in her new surroundings allows herself to notice and remember only a few selected scenes. Protectively, she closes her mind and heart to new people and events, as if to cut herself off from the future and the present. She has already cut herself off from the past in her refusal even to open any letters from home. Only for a moment does she feel guilt upon learning a month late of her father's death. She sends her penniless mother a little money, but no message, and then burns all the unread letters from home. Yet when Peggy, her Irish apartment-mate, speaks of having "outgrown" her parents, Lucy is startled. She thinks she has never known anyone who could think of parents as pests, rather than as people "whose presence you are reminded of with each breath you take." At such rare moments, Lucy reveals the difficulty with which she maintains her cold isolation from emotion and intimacy. In all of her relationships, she seeks to appear detached. When her employer, Mariah, who is forty confides that her marriage is breaking up, Lucy simply wants to declare, "Your situation is an everyday thing. Men behave in this way all the time... . Men have no morals." Lucy contends she and Peggy have nothing in common except that they feel at ease when together. She manages to learn to love only one of the four children she cares for. Her companionship with Peggy and Peggy's sister lessens; her evenings with young men she meets at night school provide welcome and exciting sexual experience but no warmth and love. She remains always critical in evaluating their skill in arousing her but never viewing them as people worthy of love. On the last page we glimpse Lucy without her protective mask. She lies alone in her bed and on the first white page of a book Mariah has given her, she writes: ''I wish I could love someone so much that I would die from it.'' Her tears fall on the page and blur the words. Kincaid's writing style—a plain prose lacking the imagery, cadence, and brilliant descriptions of the earlier books—reinforces the rigidity of the mask that Lucy hides behind throughout most of the novel.

Kincaid's fourth book of fiction, *Annie, Gwen, Lily, Pam, and Tulip,* blends literature with visual art in the evocative meditations of five young women in this collaboration with the artist Eric Fischl. Kincaid's text and Fischl's full-page lithographs of the women—nude, loosely draped, or shadowed—appear on alternate pages in this beautifully designed fine-press book. Kincaid's interest in photography flourished in university night classes in New York before she began publishing stories, and in her effort to blend her writing with visual art, she feels kinship with Virginia Woolf, James Joyce, and other modernists. The speeches of the five women resemble the style of *At the Bottom of the River,* and bear close resemblance also to the Song of Solomon in their relating of the beauty of women's bodies to nature imagery—animals, birds, mountains, and valleys. The influence of Woolf, particularly in *The Waves,* may also be evident. Though usually idyllic, the tone becomes ominous at times. As their thoughts dip into the unconscious, one senses their loving concern for one another, but the meanings are elusive and the abstraction of the poetic monologues seems to demand the abstraction of the visual artistry of Fischl's lithographs.

The Autobiography of My Mother continues Kincaid's charting of the interior lives of intelligent yet stifled women and their ambivalences about the choices they make. Via the now familiar form of a first-person monologue, seventy-year-old Xuela Claudette Richardson engages in an extended retrospective meditation on the direction of her life, and the choices she has made. While the title might suggest a narrative return to the conflicted mother/daughter relationships common in Kincaid's work, in fact in this novel the exploration of mothering is fundamentally different, in its complete absence of mothers as characters. The novel opens with Kincaid ''killing off'' the narrator's mother: ''My mother died at the moment I was born, and so for my whole life there was nothing standing between myself and eternity.'' Furthermore, Xuela refuses to bear children, recognizing that: ''I would bear children, but I would never be a mother to them ... I would destroy them with the carelessness of a god.'' Her aborting of her pregnancy then, is not a refusal of the unborn child, but an acknowledgement of her inability to engage in the act of mothering. Like all of Kincaid's fiction there is an element of the autobiographical at the center of her fictional plot; in this instance it is her belief that her mother should not have had children. However, *The Autobiography of My Mother* should not be dismissed as a mere therapeutic exercise—it is far more compelling. Like Lucy, Xuela longs for love, but the only person to whom she extends her love is her mother. Others she is unable to sustain connections with, and in old age she admits: ''All the people I knew intimately from the beginning of my life died. I should have missed their presence but I did not.'' Emotionally distant, Xuela admits growing ''to love not loving my father'' and in another instance admits to the reader that this act of withholding is not passive: ''He did not look like anyone I could love, and he did not look like anyone I should love, and so I determined then that I could not love him and I determined that I should not love him.'' Whether Xuela's inability to love anyone who exhibits the imperfections of humanity is a response to her childhood is almost irrelevant; the novel is about how Xuela asserts herself and her independence in the face of her inherited lot. Vivid characterization and mesmerizing lyrical prose chart her development from an observant child to an introspective adult, her relationships with others entering, but never defining, her life story. If, as some observe, Kincaid is continually rewriting the story of the difficulties of moving from childhood to womanhood—negotiating sexuality, power, colonialism, patriarchy, and other forces—then in the elderly Xuela she brings that story to a close for the first time. Yet as the novel ends, and Xuela is alone contemplating her life, there is no sense of an unqualified resolution in her life. Instead the novel reproduces the ambivalence common to all of Kincaid's endings, as Xuela asserts ''Since I do not matter, I do not long to matter, but I matter anyway.''

All the definitive themes of Kincaid's fiction are reworked in her nonfiction, which assumes the musing circular style of her novels. Her fierce criticism of colonialism and its legacy assumes full force in *A Small Place,* where she takes aim at the legacy of colonialism, as well as the continuing imperial exploitation of Antigua via tourism, and the failure of Independence to take seriously the needs of the people. Cultural exchange, Kincaid argues, must be measured and weighed, bringing the nation to task for adopting Europe's emphasis on capitalism instead of that on education. Likewise, *My Garden Book,* examines the cultural exchange of gardening via colonialism, and the history of attempts at cultivation in, or exportation from, foreign climes. Exceptionally perceptive, Kincaid examines the function of gardens as sites of luxury, and as repositories of history and memory, sometimes oppressive. While Kincaid favors hollyhocks, for instance, as a cousin of the cotton plant they elicit memories of childhood labor, and the institution of slavery. However, for Kincaid, memory is inescapable, and any event can generate an opportunity for exploration of the past and both its personal and larger meanings. Nowhere is this more apparent than in Kincaid's *My Brother,* where the dying of her brother becomes an opportunity to revisit the fraught familial relations that haunt much of her writing. A return not only to the past, the moving memoir is also a return to the ''what might have been'' had she not found greater opportunities elsewhere, or perhaps if her brother had. While Kincaid's nonfiction prose is powerful enough to stand as such, these personal meditations also read as powerful companions to her works of fiction.

—Margaret B. McDowell, updated by Jennifer Harris

KING, Francis (Henry)

Pseudonym: Frank Cauldwell. **Nationality:** British. **Born:** Adelboden, Switzerland, 4 March 1923. **Education:** Shrewsbury School; Balliol College, Oxford, B.A. in English, 1949, M.A. 1951. **Career:** Poetry reviewer, the *Listener,* London, 1945–50; worked for the British Council, 1949–63: lecturer in Florence, 1949–50, Salonika, 1950–52, and Athens 1953–57; assistant representative, Helsinki, 1957–58; regional director, Kyoto, 1959–63. Literary reviewer, 1964–78, and theatre reviewer, 1978–89, *Sunday Telegraph,* London. Since 1978 fiction reviewer, *Spectator,* London. Member of the Executive Committee, 1969–73, vice-president, 1977, and president, 1978–85, English PEN; International President, PEN, 1986–89; chair, Society of

Authors, 1975–77; member of the Royal Literary Fund Committee, 1977–89; member of the Executive Committee, National Book League, 1980–81. **Awards:** Maugham award, 1952; Katherine Mansfield-Menton prize, 1965; Arts Council bursary, 1966; *Yorkshire Post* award, 1983. Fellow, Royal Society of Literature, 1952; resigned, then re-elected, 1967. O.B.E. (Officer, Order of the British Empire), 1979; C.B.E. (Commander, Order of the British Empire), 1985. **Agent:** A.M. Heath, 79 St. Martin's Lane, London WC2N 4AA. **Address:** 19 Gordon Place, London W8 4JE, England.

PUBLICATIONS

Novels

To the Dark Tower. London, Home and Van Thal, 1946.
Never Again. London, Home and Van Thal, 1948.
An Air That Kills. London, Home and Van Thal, 1948.
The Dividing Stream. London, Longman, and New York, Morrow, 1951.
The Dark Glasses. London, Longman, 1954; New York, Pantheon, 1956.
The Firewalkers: A Memoir (as Frank Cauldwell). London, Murray, 1956.
The Widow. London, Longman, 1957.
The Man on the Rock. London, Longman, and New York, Pantheon, 1958.
The Custom House. London, Longman, 1961; New York, Doubleday, 1962.
The Last of the Pleasure Gardens. London, Longman, 1965.
The Waves Behind the Boat. London, Longman, 1967.
A Domestic Animal. London, Longman, 1970.
A Game of Patience. London, Hutchinson, 1974.
The Needle. London, Hutchinson, 1975; New York, Mason Charter, 1976.
Danny Hill: Memoirs of a Prominent Gentleman. London, Hutchinson, 1977.
The Action. London, Hutchinson, 1978.
Act of Darkness. London, Hutchinson, and Boston, Little Brown, 1983.
Voices in an Empty Room. London, Hutchinson, and Boston, Little Brown, 1984.
The Woman Who Was God. London, Hutchinson, and New York, Weidenfeld and Nicolson, 1988.
Punishments. London, Hamish Hamilton, 1989; New York, Viking, 1990.
Visiting Cards. London, Constable, 1990.
The Ant Colony. London, Constable, 1991.
The One and Only. London, Constable, 1994.
Ash on an Old Man's Sleeve. London, Constable, 1996.

Short Stories

So Hurt and Humiliated and Other Stories. London, Longman, 1959.
The Japanese Umbrella and Other Stories. London, Longman, 1964.
The Brighton Belle and Other Stories. London, Longman, 1968.
Penguin Modern Stories 12, with others. London, Penguin, 1972.
Flights (2 novellas). London, Hutchinson, 1973.
Hard Feelings and Other Stories. London, Hutchinson, 1976.
Indirect Method and Other Stories. London, Hutchinson, 1980.
One Is a Wanderer: Selected Stories. London, Hutchinson, 1985; Boston, Little Brown, 1986.
Frozen Music (novella). London, Hutchinson, 1987; New York, Harper, 1988.
Secret Lives (novella). London, Constable, 1991.
A Hand at the Shutter. London, Constable, 1996.

Plays

Far East (produced Coventry, 1980).

Radio Plays: *The Prisoner,* 1967; *Corner of a Foreign Field,* 1969; *A Short Walk in Williams Park,* from a story by C.H.B. Kitchin, 1972; *Death of My Aunt,* from the novel by C.H.B. Kitchin, 1973; *Desperate Cases,* 1975.

Poetry

Rod of Incantation. London, Longman, 1952.

Other

Japan, photographs by Martin Hürlimann. London, Thames and Hudson, and New York, Viking Press, 1970.
Christopher Isherwood. London, Longman, 1976.
E.M. Forster and His World. London, Thames and Hudson, and New York, Scribner, 1978.
Florence, photographs by Nicolas Sapieha. New York, Newsweek, 1982.
Florence: A Literary Companion. London, Murray, 1991.
Yesterday Came Suddenly. London, Constable, 1993.
Editor, *Introducing Greece.* London, Methuen, 1956; revised edition, 1968.
Editor, *Collected Short Stories,* by Osbert Sitwell. London, Duckworth, 1974.
Editor, with Ronald Harwood, *New Stories 3.* London, Hutchinson, 1978.
Editor, *Prokofiev by Prokofiev: A Composer's Memoir,* translated by Guy Daniels. London, Macdonald and Jane's, 1979.
Editor, *My Sister and Myself: The Diaries of J.R. Ackerley.* London, Hutchinson, 1982.
Editor, *Writings from Japan,* by Lafcadio Hearn. London, Penguin, 1984.
Editor, *Twenty Stories: A South East Arts Collection.* London, Secker and Warburg, 1985.

*

Manuscript Collections: Humanities Research Center, University of Texas, Austin.

Critical Studies: Essay by King, in *Leaving School,* London, Phoenix House, 1957; ''Waves and Echoes: The Novels of Francis King'' by John Mellors, in *London Magazine,* December 1975-January 1976; ''Francis King's Obscured Passions'' by Barbara Hardy, in *European Gay Review,* vols. 6–7, 1991; ''Francis King'' by Val Warner, in *Dictionary of Literary Biography,* Detroit, Gale Research; *Privileged Moments: Encounters with Writers* by Jeffrey Meyers. Madison, University of Wisconsin Press, 2000.

Francis King comments:

(1972) Except for the period of my schooling and the war, mine has, until the last decade, always been an itinerant life. As a child, I was brought up alternately in India and Switzerland (the country of my birth); subsequently I worked for the British Council in Italy, Greece, Egypt, Finland and Japan. This desire always to set off for another destination is reflected in my novels. Of course, certain themes in them are constant; but I have never wished to be identified with only one type of fiction. Perhaps this has harmed me in popular esteem; the public tends to like its novelists to write the same novel over and over again.

Foreign places have always provided me with imaginative stimulation and the majority of my books have foreign settings. Most English novelists, like the society from which they derive, seem to me to be too much preoccupied with differences of class, which obscure for them differences more profound between human beings. In choosing so often to write about ''abroad,'' I have, perhaps subconsciously, attempted to avoid this class-obsession.

I believe strongly in national character, and a recurrent theme of my books is the way in which people struggle to break out of the patterns of national behavior in which they have been imprisoned since birth.

Critics sometimes say that they find my work ''depressing'' and my readers sometimes ask why I never write about ''nice'' people or ''normal'' people—not surprisingly perhaps, since mine is an attitude of profound, if resigned, pessimism about the world. I do not expect people to behave consistently well, and my observation is that few of them do. But I should like to think that the tolerance and compassion that I genuinely feel are also reflected in my writing.

I have always been preoccupied with style and form. I feel that I am most successful in achieving both if the reader is unconscious of any straining for them.

In my early books, written at a period of loneliness in my own life, isolation is a recurrent theme; in my later books I see now that envy and jealousy—to my mind the least attractive of human traits—have taken over.

My biggest and most successful novels were *The Custom House* and *Act of Darkness.* The novel that comes nearest to saying what I wanted to say—and that cost me most—was *A Domestic Animal.*

* * *

Francis King's first novel, *To the Dark Tower,* is his most experimental. In some of the stories in *The Japanese Umbrella* he adopts Isherwood's trick of using a narrator to whom he gives his own name, and *The Firewalkers,* subtitled ''a memoir,'' was first published under the pseudonym of Frank Cauldwell, who is also the narrator, and who first appeared as a novelist in *To the Dark Tower.* King's stress on the plurality of truth, as formulated in the early story ''A True Story'' (*So Hurt and Humiliated*), led him to write from both first- and third-person angles in *The Custom House* and *The Last of the Pleasure Gardens. The Action,* actually about a novel, seems redolent with echoes from King's previous work. The bawdy *Danny Hill,* with much linguistic humor, purports to be an eighteenth-century text by John Cleland and is written by King in that idiom, modernized. The very structure of *Voices in an Empty Room,* linking three separate stories of attempts at communication with the dead, mirrors death's arbitrary cut-off and residual loose ends.

The themes of separation and loss recurring throughout King's work may be traced to his second novel, *Never Again,* a moving evocation of childhood and adolescence in India and at an English prep school. In his third novel, *An Air That Kills,* there is a lyricism, often negated, in the spirit of Housman's poem whence the title comes. *The Dividing Stream,* a complex novel set in Florence, is imbued with a sense of decay and the melancholy that pervades much of King's world. These moods are articulated in the stark ending of *The Dark Glasses,* as Patrick recognizes ''the terrible, morbid beauty of this world.'' Yet the Greek setting seems to make for an easier sensuous acceptance: in *The Dark Glasses* King evokes the natural beauty of Corfu, while *The Firewalkers* is a mainly happy reminiscence of a group of friends in Athens centered on the dilettante and metaphorical firewalker, Colonel Grecos. In *The Man on the Rock* King succeeds in impersonating as narrator the parasitic Spiro, a character utterly removed from the self-effacing King/Cauldwell persona. King is as skillful with the short story form as the novel, with some of the stories in his first collection, *So Hurt and Humiliated,* set in Greece. So is the second novella in *Flights,* ''The Cure,'' which like the other, ''The Infection,'' set in Hungary, has political overtones.

King's most ambitious book to date, *The Custom House,* also has political implications. In this long, complex novel he focuses on a cross-section of Japanese society, both from within and through western eyes. King's writing is always rich in ambivalence; he found congenial material in Japanese formalism, recording ''the echoes which surround events, not merely after they have taken place but also before them.'' Yet the novel has his characteristic intense sensuousness hedged with negatives. Like the collection of short stories, *The Japanese Umbrella, The Waves Behind the Boat* is set in Japan, though its theme of incest and dishonesty concerns expatriates, including the woman narrator.

Christine Cornwell in *The Widow* is outstanding among King's female portraits. The novel's opening illustrates his skill in manipulating the reader's sympathy in a few pages as he highlights alternately her unlikeable and likeable traits. His evocation of wartime London in part 2 of *The Widow* is complemented by his account of civilian rural experience, chiefly through the eyes of a seventeen-year-old land-girl, in *A Game of Patience.* In *The Last of the Pleasure Gardens* King shows how a severely retarded child exacerbates beyond endurance the weaknesses in a marriage. Most of the short stories in *The Brighton Belle* are studies in decay, symbolized in the town itself. *A Domestic Animal,* about unreciprocated homosexual love, is a poignant and powerful study of sexual jealousy; the narrator's attitude to Pam recalls the narrator's attitude to Anne in *An Air That Kills,* although the novels are different in tone.

The darkness of *The Needle,* about a doctor's love for her weak brother, is expressed too in some of the stories in *Hard Feelings.* The stories in *Indirect Method* are either set abroad or involve foreigners in Britain. *The Action,* about the libel action threatened against Hazel's novel on the eve of publication, incidentally reveals much about King's understanding of the novel form; the ending, as Hazel begins a new story, is something of a writer's credo. *Act of Darkness,* set mainly in 1930's India, focuses on a child's murder apparently by someone in his family circle; it is a major novel of suspense with powerful psychological depths. *Voices in an Empty Room* shows para-normal communication as mainly fraudulent, though the only certainty is doubt.

The affirmative novella *Frozen Music,* set in contemporary India, shows an elderly Englishman ''giving'' his young Finnish wife to his son, her lover, in an extraordinary act of love. In *The Woman Who Was God* Ruth, unable to accept that her son's death in an African commune was accidental, travels there and confronts its charismatic leader, "Mother." Through King's skillful sleight-of-hand narrative, Ruth not "Mother" emerges as playing God—with a destructiveness stemming from inability to understand her son. The moving *Punishments* opens in 1981 with Michael dreaming about his trip to Germany in 1948 in a party of students including the woman he married. The novel then describes that visit among Germans forced to see themselves as punished and guilty, the setting for Michael's seduction by a male German student: "And no future experience of my whole life was ever to be so thrilling." *Visiting Cards* is a brilliant comic novel set at a World Association of Authors conference, presided over by the undistinguished Amos Kingsley, mistakenly elected as Kingsley Amis. The serious underlying issue is whether public agitation is necessarily in the interests of imprisoned writers if it further alienates their governments.

Though always a skillful storyteller, King's outstanding quality through all his work is his understanding of a wide range of characters' emotions. He is a master of implication, and writes with unnerving precision, strength, and sensitivity.

—Val Warner

KING, Stephen (Edwin)

Also writes as Richard Bachman. **Nationality:** American. **Born:** Portland, Maine, 21 September 1947. **Education:** University of Maine at Orono, B.Sc. 1970. **Family:** Married Tabitha Jane Spruce in 1971; two sons, one daughter. **Career:** Worked as a janitor, a laborer in an industrial laundry, and in a knitting mill; English teacher, Hampden Academy (high school), Hampden, Maine, 1971–73; University of Maine, Orono, writer-in-residence, 1978–79; owner, Philtrum Press (publishing house), and WZON-AM (rock 'n' roll radio station), Bangor, Maine; actor in films, television, and commercials, 1981—; reviewer, *New York Times Book Review.* **Awards:** Balrog Awards, second place in best novel category and second place in best story collection category, 1979; American Library Association's list of best books for young adults, 1979, 1981; World Fantasy Award, 1980, 1982; Career Alumni Award (University of Maine at Orono), 1981; special British Fantasy Award (British Fantasy Society), 1982; Hugo Award (World Science Fiction Convention), 1982; Best Fiction Writer of the Year (*Us* Magazine), 1982; Locus Award for best collection (Locus Publications), 1986; World Fantasy award for short story, 1995; Tommy Award, 2000. **Agent:** Arthur Greene, 101 Park Avenue, New York, New York 10178, U.S.A.

PUBLICATIONS

Novels

Carrie: A Novel of a Girl with a Frightening Power. New York, Doubleday, 1974; with an introduction by Tabitha King, New York, Plume, 1991.

Salem's Lot. New York, Doubleday, 1975; with an introduction by Clive Barker, New York, Plume, 1991.

The Dark Tower: The Gunslinger. Amereon Ltd., 1976; published as *The Gunslinger,* illustrated by Michael Whelan. New York, New American Library, 1988.

The Shining. New York, Doubleday, 1977; with an introduction by Ken Follett, New York, Plume, 1991.

Rage (as Richard Bachman). New York, New American Library/Signet, 1977.

The Stand. New York, Doubleday, 1978; enlarged and expanded edition published as *The Stand: The Complete and Uncut Edition.* New York, Doubleday, 1990.

The Long Walk (as Richard Bachman). New York, New American Library/Signet, 1979.

The Dead Zone. New York, Viking, 1979; movie edition published as *The Dead Zone: Movie Tie-In.* New York, New American Library, 1980; *The Dead Zone,* introduction by Anne Rivers Siddons, New York, Plume, 1994.

Firestarter. New York, Viking, 1980.

Cujo. New York, Viking, 1981.

Roadwork: A Novel of the First Energy Crisis (as Richard Bachman). New York, New American Library/Signet, 1981.

The Running Man (as Richard Bachman). New York, New American Library/Signet, 1982.

Different Seasons. (novellas; contains *Rita Hayworth and Shawshank Redemption: Hope Springs Eternal, Apt Pupil: Summer of Corruption, The Body: Fall from Innocence,* and *The Breathing Method: A Winter's Tale*). New York, Viking, 1982.

Pet Sematary. New York, Doubleday, 1983.

Christine. New York, Viking, 1983.

Cycle of the Werewolf (novella), illustrated by Berni Wrightson. Westland, Michigan, 1983.

The Talisman (with Peter Straub). New York, Viking Press/Putnam, 1984.

The Eyes of the Dragon (young adult), illustrated by Kenneth R. Linkhauser, Philtrum Press, 1984; illustrated by David Palladini, New York, Viking, 1987.

Thinner (as Richard Bachman). New York, New American Library, 1984.

It. New York, Viking, 1986.

Misery. New York, Viking, 1987.

The Tommyknockers. New York, Putnam, 1987.

The Dark Half. New York, Viking, 1989.

The Dark Tower II: The Drawing of the Three, illustrated by Phil Hale. New York, New American Library, 1989.

Needful Things. New York, Viking, 1991.

The Dark Tower III: The Waste Lands, illustrated by Ned Dameron. New York, New American Library, 1991.

Gerald's Game. New York, Viking, 1992.

Dolores Claiborne. New York, Viking, 1993.

Insomnia. New York, Viking, 1994.

Rose Madder. New York, Viking, 1995.

The Green Mile (serialized in six chapters). New York, Signet, 1996; published as *The Green Mile: A Novel in Six Parts.* New York, Plume, 1997.

Desperation. New York, Viking, 1996.

The Regulators (as Richard Bachman). New York, Dutton, 1996.

The Two Dead Girls (with a foreword by the author), New York, Signet, 1996.

The Bachman Books: Four Early Novels (all previously published, with a new introduction by the author). New York, Plume, 1996.

The Dark Tower IV: Wizard and Glass. New York, Plume, 1997; published as *Wizard and Glass,* illustrated by Dave McKean. Hampton Falls, New Hampshire, D. H. Grant, 1997.

Bag of Bones. New York, Scribner, 1998.
The Girl Who Loved Tom Gordon. New York, Scribner, 1999.
Hearts in Atlantis. New York, Scribner, 1999.
Riding the Bullet (e-book novella). New York, Scribner, 2000.

Short Stories

The Star Invaders. Durham, Maine, Gaslight Books, 1964.
Night Shift New York, Doubleday, 1978; published as *Night Shift: Excursions into Horror*. New York, New American Library/Signet, 1979.
Stephen King's Skeleton Crew, illustrated by J. K. Potter. New York, Viking, 1985.
Dark Visions. London, Gollancz, 1989.
My Pretty Pony (with Barbara Kruger). New York, Knopf, 1989.
Four Past Midnight. New York, Viking, 1990.
Nightmares & Dreamscapes. New York, Viking, 1993.

Plays

Screenplays: *Creepshow*. Warner Brothers, 1982; published as *Stephen King's Creep Show: A George A. Romero Film*, illustrated by Berni Wrightson and Michele Wrightson, New York, New American Library, 1982.; *Cat's Eye*, Metro Goldwyn-Mayer/United Artists, 1984; *Silver Bullet*, Paramount Pictures/Dino de Laurentiis's North Carolina Film Corp., 1985, illustrated by Berni Wrightson, New York, New American Library/Signet, 1985; *Maximum Overdrive* (and director), Dino de Laurentiis's North Carolina Film Corp., 1986, New York, New American Library, 1986; *Pet Sematary*, Paramount Pictures, 1989; *Stephen King's Sleepwalkers*. Columbia, 1992.

Television Plays: *Battleground*, Martin Poll Productions/NBC-TV), 1987; *Tales from the Dark Side* (teleplay of episode, ''Sorry, Right Number''), 1987; *Stephen King's Golden Years*, CBS-TV, 1991; *Stephen King's The Stand* (also executive producer), ABC-TV, 1994; *The X-Files* (teleplay of episode, ''Chinga,'' with Chris Carter), Fox-TV, 1998; *Storm of the Century*, ABC-TV, 1999, New York, Pocket Books, 1999.

Poetry

Another Quarter Mile: Poetry. Dorrance, 1979.

Other

Stephen King's Danse Macabre (nonfiction). Everest House, 1981.
The Plant (privately published episodes of a comic horror novel in progress). Bangor, Maine, Philtrum Press, 1982.
Black Magic and Music: A Novelist's Perspective on Bangor (pamphlet). Bangor, Maine, Bangor Historical Society, 1983.
The Mist (sound recording). Fort Edward, New York, ZBS Foundation, 1984.
Nightmares in the Sky: Gargoyles and Grotesques, photographs by F. Stop FitzGerald. New York, Viking, 1988.
Dolan's Cadillac. Northridge, California, Lord John Press, 1989.
On Writing: A Memoir of the Craft. New York, Scribner, 2000.

Contributor, *The Year's Finest Fantasy*, edited by Terry Carr. New York, Putnam, 1978.
Contributor, *Shadows, Volume 1*, edited by Charles L. Grant. New York, Doubleday, 1978.
Contributor, *Shadows, Volume 4*, edited by Charles L. Grant. New York, Doubleday, 1981.
Contributor, *New Terrors*, edited by Ramsey Campbell. New York, Pocket Books, 1982.
Contributor, *World Fantasy Convention 1983*, edited by Robert Weinberg. Weird Tales Ltd., 1983.
Contributor, *The Writer's Handbook*, edited by Sylvia K. Burack, Boston, Writer, Inc., 1984.
Contributor, *The Dark Descent*, edited by David G. Hartwell. Doherty Associates, 1987.
Contributor, *Prime Evil: New Stories by the Masters of Modern Horror*, edited by Douglas E. Winter. New York, New American Library, 1988.
Contributor, *The Complete Masters of Darkness*, edited by Dennis Etchison. Novato, California, Underwood-Miller, 1990.
Contributor, *Shock Rock*, edited by Jeff Gelb. New York, Pocket Books, 1992.
Contributor, *Death Walks Tonight: Horrifying Stories*, edited by Anthony Horowitz. New York, Puffin, 1996.
Contributor, *Twists of the Tale: Cat Horror Stories*, edited by Ellen Datlow. New York, Dell, 1996.
Contributor, *Screamplays*, edited by Richard Chizmar. New York, Ballantine, 1997.
Contributor, *The Best of the Best: 18 New Stories by America's Leading Authors*, edited by Elaine Koster and Joseph Pittman. New York, Signet, 1998.
Foreword, *Tales from the Nightside: Dark Fantasy* by Charles L. Grant. Sauk City, Wisconsin, Arkham House, 1981.
Foreword, *Scars and Other Distinguishing Marks* by Richard Christian Matheson. Los Angeles, Scream/Press, 1987.
Foreword, *Archie Americana Series: Best of the Forties*, created by John L. Goldwater. Mamaroneck, New York, Archie Comic Publications, 1991.
Foreword, *Fear Itself: The Early Works of Stephen King*, edited by Tim Underwood and Chuck Miller. San Francisco, Underwood-Miller, 1993.
Introduction, *The Arbor House Treasury of Horror and the Supernatural*, edited by Bill Pronzini, Barry M. Malzberg, and Martin H. Greenberg. New York, Arbor House, 1981.
Introduction, *Grande Illusions: A Learn-by-Example Guide to the Art and Technique of Special Make-up Effects from the Films of Tom Savini* by Tom Savini. Pittsburgh, Pennsylvania, Imagine, 1983.
Introduction, *The Blackboard Jungle* by Evan Hunter. New York, Arbor House, 1984.
Introduction, *Fear Itself: The Horror Fiction of Stephen King*, edited by Tim Underwood and Chuck Miller. New York, New American Library, 1984.
Introduction, *Joe Bob Goes to the Drive-In* by Joe Bob Briggs. New York, Delacorte Press, 1987.
Introduction, *Classic Tales of Horror and the Supernatural*, edited by Bill Pronzini, Barry N. Malzberg, and Martin H. Greenberg. New York, Quill, 1991.
Introduction, *Graven Images: The Best of Horror, Fantasy, and Science Fiction Film Art from the Collection of Ronald V. Borst*, edited by Ronald V. Borst and Margaret A. Borst. New York, Grove Press, 1992.

Introduction, *The Fugitive Recaptured: The 30th Anniversary Companion to a Television Classic* by Ed Robertson. Los Angeles, Pomegranate Press, 1993.

Introduction, *Heading Home: Growing Up in Baseball*, photographs by Harry Connolly. New York, Rizzoli, 1995.

Introduction, *Horripilations: The Art of J. K. Potter*, text by Nigel Suckling. Woodstock, New York, Overlook Press, 1995.

Introduction, *The Shawshank Redemption: The Shooting Script* by Frank Darabont. New York, Newmarket Press, 1996.

Introduction, *Saturday Night at Moody's Diner: Even More Stories* by Tim Sample. Camden, Maine, Down East Books, 1996.

Introduction, *The Green Mile: The Screenplay* by Frank Darabont. New York, Scribner Paperback Fiction, 1999.

*

Manuscript Collection: Folger Library, University of Maine at Orono.

Critical Studies: *Fear Itself: The Horror Fiction of Stephen King,* edited by Tim Underwood and Chuck Miller, San Francisco, Underwood-Miller, 1982, new edition, with introduction by King and afterword by George Romero, New York, New American Library, 1984; *Stephen King* by Douglas E. Winter, Mercer Island, Washington, Starmont House, 1982; *Dream Makers: The Uncommon Men and Women Who Write Science Fiction* by Charles Platt, New York, Berkley, 1983; *Stephen King: The Art of Darkness* by Douglas E. Winter, New York, New American Library, 1984; *Stephen King as Richard Bachman* by Michael R. Collings, Mercer Island, Washington, Starmont House, 1985; *The Many Facets of Stephen King* by Michael R. Collings, Mercer Island, Washington, Starmont House, 1985; *The Shorter Works of Stephen King* by Michael R. Collings and David Engebretson, Mercer Island, Washington, Starmont House, 1985; *Discovering Stephen King,* edited by Darrell Schweitzer, Mercer Island, Washington, Starmont House, 1985; *The Annotated Guide to Stephen King: A Primary and Secondary Bibliography of the Works of America's Premier Horror Writer* by Michael R. Collings, Mercer Island, Washington, Starmont House, 1986; *The Films of Stephen King* by Michael R. Collings, Mercer Island, Washington, Starmont House, 1986; *Kingdom of Fear: The World of Stephen King,* edited by Tim Underwood and Chuck Miller, San Francisco, Underwood-Miller, 1986; *The Stephen King Phenomenon* by Michael R. Collings, Mercer Island, Washington, Starmont House, 1987; *Stephen King Goes to Hollywood: A Lavishly Illustrated Guide to All the Films Based on Stephen King's Fiction* by Jeff Conner, New York, New American Library, 1987; *The Gothic World of Stephen King: Landscape of Nightmares,* edited by Gary Hoppenstand and Ray B. Browne, Bowling Green, Ohio, Bowling Green State University Popular Press, 1987; *The Author Talks* by Stephen King (sound recording), Charlotte Hall, Maryland, Recorded Books, 1987; *Reign of Fear: Fiction and Film of Stephen King,* edited by Don Herron, Los Angeles, Underwood-Miller, 1988; *Landscape of Fear: Stephen King's American Gothic* by Tony Magistrale, Bowling Green, Ohio, Bowling Green State University Popular Press, 1988; *Stephen King: The First Decade, Carrie to Pet Sematary* by Joseph Reino, Boston, Twayne, 1988; *Bare Bones: Conversations on Terror with Stephen King,* edited by Tim Underwood and Chuck Miller, New York, McGraw-Hill, Warner Books, 1988; *The Stephen King Companion,* edited by George W. Beahm, Kansas City, Missouri, Andrews & McMeel, 1989; *The Moral Voyages of Stephen King* by Anthony Magistrale, Mercer Island, Washington, Starmont House, 1989; *American Horror Fiction: From Brockden Brown to Stephen King,* edited by Brian Docherty, New York, St. Martin's Press, 1990; *The Shape Under the Sheet: The Compete Stephen King Encyclopedia,* Ann Arbor, Michigan, Popular Culture, 1991; *The Stephen King Story* by George W. Beahm, Kansas City, Missouri, Andrews & McMeel, 1991, revised and updated edition, 1992; *The Dark Descent: Essays Defining Stephen King's Horrorscape,* edited by Tony Magistrale, Westport, Connecticut, Greenwood Press, 1992; *A Casebook on ''The Stand'',* edited by Tony Magistrale, Mercer Island, Washington, Starmont House, 1992; *Stephen King: The Second Decade—''Danse Macabre'' to ''The Dark Half''* by Tony Magistrale, New York, Twayne, 1992; *Stephen King, Master of Horror* by Anne Saidman, Minneapolis, Minnesota, Lerner Publications, 1992; *Feast of Fear: Conversations with Stephen King,* edited by Tim Underwood and Chuck Miller, New York, Carroll & Graf, 1992; *The Works of Stephen King: An Annotated Bibliography and Guide* by Michael R. Collings and edited by Boden Clarke, San Bernardino, California, Borgo Press, 1993; *The Films of Stephen King* by Ann Lloyd, New York, St. Martin's Press, 1993; *Fear Itself: The Early Works of Stephen King,* edited by Tim Underwood and Chuck Miller (foreword by King, introduction by Peter Straub, afterword by George A. Romero), San Francisco, Underwood-Miller, 1993; *Stephen King's America* by Jonathan P. Davis, Bowling Green, Ohio, Bowling Green State University Popular Press, 1994; *More Things That Are Dreamt Of: Masterpieces of Supernatural Horror, from Mary Shelley to Stephen King, in Literature and Film* by James Ursini and Alain Silver, New York, Limelight Editions, 1994; *Observations from the Terminator: Thoughts on Stephen King and Other Modern Masters of Horror Fiction* by Tyson Blue, San Bernardino, California, Borgo Press, 1995; *Susie Bright's Sexwise: America's Favorite X-Rated Intellectual Does Dan Quayle, Catherine MacKinnon, Stephen King, Camille Paglia, Nicholson Baker, Madonna, the Black Panthers, and the GOP—* by Susie Bright, Pittsburgh, Pennsylvania, Cleis Press, 1995; *Scaring Us to Death: The Impact of Stephen King on Popular Culture* by Michael R. Collings, San Bernardino, California, Borgo Press, 1995; *Stephen King* by Amy Keyishian and Marjorie Keyishian, New York, Chelsea House, 1995; *Writing Horror and the Body: The Fiction of Stephen King, Clive Barker and Anne Rice.* by Linda Badley, Westport, Connecticut, Greenwood Press, 1996; *The Work of Stephen King: An Annotated Bibliography and Guide* by Michael R. Collings and edited by Boden Clarke, San Bernardino, California, Borgo Press, 1996; *Maps of Heaven, Maps of Hell: Religious Terror as Memory from the Puritans to Stephen King* by Edward J. Ingebretsen, Armonk, New York, M. E. Sharpe, 1996; *Stephen King: A Critical Companion* by Sharon A. Russell. Westport, Connecticut, Greenwood Press, 1996; *Reading Stephen King: Issues of Censorship, Student Choice, and Popular Literature,* edited by Brenda Miller Power, Jeffrey D. Wilhelm, and Kelly Chandler, Urbana, Illinois, National Council of Teachers of English, 1997; *Fangoria Masters of the Dark,* edited by Anthony Timpone, New York, HarperPrism, 1997; *Stephen King: America's Best-Loved Boogeyman* by George Beahm, Kansas City, Missouri, Andrews & McMeel, 1998; *Stephen King from A to Z: An Encyclopedia of His Life and Work* by George Beahm, Kansas City, Missouri, Andrews & McMeel, 1998; *Stephen King,* edited and with an introduction by Harold Bloom, Philadelphia, Chelsea House, 1998; *Treks Not Taken: What If Stephen King, Anne Rice, Kurt Vonnegut, and Other Literary Greats Had Written Episodes of Star Trek, The Next Generation?*, New York, HarperPerennial, 1998; *Imagining the Worst: Stephen King and the Representation of*

Women, edited by Kathleen Margaret Lant and Theresa Thompson, Westport, Connecticut, Greenwood Press, 1998; *The Lost Work of Stephen King: A Guide to Unpublished Manuscripts, Story Fragments, Alternative Versions, and Oddities,* Secaucus, New Jersey, Birch Lane Press, 1998; *Stephen King Country: The Illustrated Guide to the Sites and Sights That Inspired the Modern Master of Horror* by George Beahm, Philadelphia, Running Press, 1999; *Stephen King* by John F. Wukovits, San Diego, Lucent Books, 1999; *On Writing: A Memoir of the Craft* by Stephen King, New York, Scribner, 2000; *American Horror Writers* by Bob Madison, Berkeley Heights, New Jersey, Enslow Publishers, 2000; *Stephen King: King of Thrillers and Horror* by Suzan Wilson, Berkeley Heights, New Jersey, Enslow Publishers, 2000.

* * *

Stephen King is a prolific, best-selling, internationally famous author who is known primarily as a writer of horror fiction but who has also worked extensively in other genres, particularly fantasy. In his horror stories, King draws on a range of classic motifs, such as vampirism and evil spirits, and masterfully employs a variety of techniques drawn from popular fiction, for example in the way he creates narrative suspense by skilful concealment and timely revelation. But he is not only interested in sensational effects; his novels also provide him with canvases—usually large ones—on which he can explore communities, especially those of small New England towns, and evoke the workings of the human mind, particularly when it is subject to terror and fear.

King's first novel, *Carrie*, was a powerful debut that introduced a number of his key themes. Carrie, bullied by her fanatically religious mother and shunned by her schoolfriends, finds the psychokinetic power she possessed as an infant reviving with her first period. Humiliated at the high school prom night, she takes a terrible revenge, unleashing her psychic wrath to set the town ablaze and bring about many deaths. *Carrie* combines King's skills as a horror writer with his insights into the feelings of the vulnerable and the abused, and the combination of these two elements recurs in many subsequent novels, giving them a human interest that deepens their horrific aspects. But *Carrie* is an uncharacteristically short novel; its success allowed King to work on a larger scale with his next book, *Salem's Lot*. This novel deals with a vampire takeover of a small New England town, and a significant element of its strength comes from the way in which King carefully, almost affectionately, builds up his portrayal of the life of the community. Most of King's later books are long, and while he has been criticized for this, it does enable him to enrich the complexity of his characterization and narrative. *Salem's Lot* is also significant in that the key protagonist is a writer—and writers, though rather less successful ones than King himself, will feature in a number of his later novels. Indeed his third book, *The Shining*, is a powerful story of an unsuccessful author spending the winter as a caretaker with his wife and child in an isolated, haunted hotel; he is prone to drunkenness and violence in a way that terrifies his precognitive son, through whose mind some of the most disturbing scenes of the novel are evoked.

A batch of novels followed that moved away from horror and employed more of a mixture of popular genres. *The Stand* shows the human beings who have survived the ravages of an escaped germ warfare virus setting out to rebuild civilization. Starting as science fiction, it develops into a powerful fantasy that dramatizes the contest between good and evil. *The Dead Zone* focuses on a young man with precognitive and telepathic powers who determines to kill a politician whom he foresees will begin a nuclear war if he becomes President. *Firestarter* echoes Carrie in that its protagonist, a little girl called Charlie, has the power to set off fires and is hunted by a mysterious government agency that wants to use her for malign ends, while *Cujo* features a monstrously transformed St. Bernard dog that menaces a small New England town.

In 1982 King brought out four suspense novellas under the title *Different Seasons*, the best-known of which is *The Shawshank Redemption*, where a prisoner unjustly convicted of his wife's murder spends years digging his way out of his cell. 1982 also saw the first novel of the still unfinished ''Dark Tower'' series, *The Gunslinger*. Subsequent novels in the series are *The Drawing of the Three*, *The Waste Lands*, and *Wizard and Glass*, and there are perhaps three more novels to come. The series takes its title and some of its symbolism from Robert Browning's complex, sinister Victorian poem ''Childe Roland to the Dark Tower Came'' (1855). Its central character, Roland of Gilead, a gunslinger in a strange, bleak fantasy future with some echoes of our own civilization, is engaged on a quest for the Dark Tower, where he hopes to arrest and possibly to reverse the accelerating destruction of Mid-World. King himself regards this series as a very important work that encompasses the elements of all the other fictional worlds that he has created.

King's horror fiction continued in the 1980s with *Pet Sematary*, in which pets and people buried in an old Indian burial ground return to life in distorted, savage form, and in which a doctor's attempt to resurrect his dead son has horrific consequences. *Christine* is about a possessed car, a 1958 Plymouth Fury, that takes over its owners. King collaborated with Peter Straub on the novel *The Talisman*, which follows a twelve-year old boy on a quest for the Talisman that will save his dying mother, but the styles and narrative techniques of the two writers did not quite gel. In 1986 King returned to his own work with *It*, which deals once more with a New England town under threat, this time by an evil spirit that lives in its storm-drains and sewers and that a band of children finally destroy. This was followed by the highly praised *Misery*, in which a writer, badly injured in a car crash, is brought back to life by a woman who insists that he write another book about her favorite character, whom he has previously killed off. A longer, more diffuse novel, *The Tommyknockers* concerns the finding of a spaceship that sends out vibrations that change the behavior of the citizens of a small town in destructive ways. *The Dark Half*, like *Misery*, features a writer who is unable to dispose of a character he has created; Thad Beaumont has written a number of best-selling thrillers under the pseudonym of George Stark, and endowed Stark with a sinister character. But when he tries to kill Stark off, Stark, the ''dark half'' of his imagination, enters his actual life and starts to murder his friends.

King's books in the 1990s included *Four Past Midnight*, a collection of novels, of which the most chilling is *The Library Policeman*, in which a monster that takes the shape of a librarian needs to regenerate itself by feeding off the fears of children and incarnating itself in adult bodies. In *Needful Things*, a devilish shopkeeper creates conflict among the townsfolk of Castle Rock by offering to gratify their most private desires. *Gerald's Game* is a tormented, claustrophobic novel in which a wife left handcuffed to a bed in a bondage game, after her husband has died of a heart attack, has to relive an experience of being abused by her father in order to survive. In *Dolores Claiborne*, a companion housekeeper tells the story of her troubled relationship with an almost insane crippled widow whom she looked after, while *Rose Madder* follows the trail of a woman who flees from a murderous husband, enters a picture to discover her own powers of resistance, and later persuades her husband to get into the picture, where he effectively murders himself—a remarkable combination of thriller and fantasy elements. *Desperation*, like *The Stand*, dramatizes the battle between good and evil, this time in a desolate Nevada town. The protagonist of *Bag of Bones* is again an author, suffering from writer's block after his wife's death, who returns to their lakeside retreat and starts to uncover dark secrets, while *The Green Mile* focuses on a strange prisoner awaiting execution for two brutal murders. *Hearts in Atlantis* comprises five interlinked stories that run from 1960 to 1999 and explore the continuing impact of the 1960s and the Vietnam War. King's greatest achievement of the 1990s, however, is *Insomnia*, with its harrowing descriptions of an acute form of sleeplessness that produces the power of transcendent vision in an elderly man who, in a town riven by battles over abortion, has to restore the balance between the ''Purpose,'' which ends human lives at the appropriate time, and the ''Random,'' which can cut the thread of life at whim.

King was struck by a car and seriously injured in June 1999, and for a time it seemed that he might be unable to go on writing. However, he has recently enjoyed success with the publication, in electronic form, of the novella *Riding the Bullet*. Many of his books have been filmed, though the results have rarely met with his approval. His huge output and immense popularity have proved barriers to sustained critical consideration of his work in the past, but now that literary and cultural criticism has broadened its scope to take in popular writing, there is a growing volume of analysis of King as a cultural phenomenon and of the structural and stylistic qualities of his fiction. While the standard of his work is variable, and he can sometimes fall back on the stock devices and images of the horror or fantasy writer, his writing at its best demonstrates a vivid style and a capacity for imaginative penetration into dark and disturbing areas of human psychology that place him in a tradition of American novelists that includes Charles Brockden Brown, Nathaniel Hawthorne, and Edgar Allan Poe.

—Nicolas Tredell

KING, Thomas

Nationality: Canadian citizen. **Born:** Sacramento, California, 24 April 1943. **Career:** Currently Chair of American Indian Studies, University of Minnesota.

PUBLICATIONS

Novels

Medicine River. Toronto, Penguin, 1989.

A Coyote Columbus Story. Toronto, Douglas and McIntyre, 1992.

Green Grass, Running Water. Toronto, HarperPerennial, and Boston, Houghton Mifflin, 1993.

Truth and Bright Water. New York, Atlantic Monthly Press, 2000.

Short Stories

One Good Story, That One. Toronto, HarperPerennial, 1993.

* * *

In Canada, Thomas King is well known as an author of fiction; as the straightman side kick in a weekly radio show he also writes called ''The Dead Dog Café Comedy Hour'' on national public radio; and as an associate professor of English literature at the University of Guelph. The three sides of Thomas King are not as far apart as they might seem: King addresses native issues through satire and humor in his novels, his radio show, and classes. Introduced in his second novel, *Green Grass, Running Water*, The Dead Dog Café, with a neon sign of a dog in a stewpot, is a tourist trap that capitalizes on the appetite of non-native tourists for consumption of stereotypes about indigenous peoples. In his first two novels, *Medicine River* and *Green Grass, Running Water*, particularly, King relies on the humor generated by the subversion of expectation to combat stereotypes and normalize the quotidian elements of life of the Native Canadian. Blanca Chester argues that ultimately, ''King's novel shows how First Nations storytelling continues to theorize the world through a Native literature written in English.'' King retells the stories of history (through non-linear, overlapping versions of stories) from new perspectives as he attacks the cultural icons of patriarchal settler society by obliquely critiquing materialism, capitalism, and neo-imperialism. He does all this through an almost lighthearted circular storytelling style. King's writing often seems to contain a dialogue between storyteller and audience, between theories of postcoloniality and native modes of narration, and between traditional stories and popular culture. As King says of Harry Robinson's work, the stories resist being read silently. They recreate the sense of an oral storytelling in a written form.

King's fiction explores what it means to be native in a predominantly white culture. However, his writing does not simply separate native elements from a corrupt white influence or mythologize native life, strategies that tend to create dehumanizing stereotypes of indigenous peoples as members of a ''vanishing race'' or as ''noble savages.'' Rather, King sees the native experience as hybrid. King himself is of Greek and Cherokee descent, and he appears to understand ethnicity as an inherently unstable set of self-created fictions, to be treated ironically rather than merely accepted. His writing is playfully satiric; with broad humor he debunks both white and native misconceptions of native life. King's native person plays a dual role, at once participant and critic, a member of mainstream society and social misfit. His satire hinges on this duality, with its troubling, comic contradictions.

In *Green Grass, Running Water*, more than his other novels, King engages with the myth of Canada as an empty wilderness, and the subsequent myths of the ''Indians'' (the term King uses so he can ''talk about Native people in general'') in a ''Cowboy and Indian''-dominated Western landscape. One of the pivotal moments in the novel is when the ending of a popular Western film is revised so that the Indians win and kill John Wayne. The novel highlights the fact that First Nations people have often been constructed in Hollywood movies and Western books as artifacts and commodities or have been romanticized. King's satire is perhaps sharpest in the novel in the depiction of Portland, a Native man who goes to Hollywood to become an actor in Westerns but who must don a fake nose because he does not look ''Indian enough.'' Through Portland, King tackles the notions of falsely constructed identity and performative ethnicity. Before he can act in the movies he must go through an initiation into Hollywood culture by dancing in a strip show. He dances an almost pornographic dance with Pocahontas, during which a cowboy dancer comes on stage and defeats him, the Indian. In the end, however, Portland has a moment of triumph, after several moments of humiliation, when he is transformed into the Chief who leads the Indians into victory over the cowboys in the revised film.

While King has been criticized for glossing over, or sentimentalizing, the ''real'' issues of native life in America and Canada instead of creating a realistic portrait of the everyday problems of alcoholism, suicide, and poverty, he argues that he is simply presenting a positive portrait of those often depicted as oppressed and down-trodden. In a sense, his work acts as a normalizing corrective to both the representation of negative stereotypes of native people and to the ''issue''-dominated genre of fiction by several other Native North American writers. His characters are not drawn according to type, nor as political mouthpieces, and, indeed, they often defy both stereotype and polemics. In *Medicine River*, for instance, one of the central characters, Louise Heavyman, is an accountant and a single mother by choice—not by accident and not as a feminist maneuver. In the naming of Louise's daughter ''South Wing,'' after the area in the hospital in which the child is born, we can see the humor with which King combines ''Indian'' and white symbolism. South Wing is a hybrid character. Like Will, the internationally acclaimed photographer and mediocre basketball player, South Wing defies categorization and expectation. The native person in King's work often acts as a detached observer, pointing with amazement and disbelief to the self-interested behavior within North American culture. Lionel James, one of many storytellers who inhabit *Medicine River*, is mystified by what he calls this ''crazy world.'' He can not understand why people want to fly him to Japan to recite, and he worries about his audiences ''living in the past like that,'' listening to other people's ''old'' stories instead of making up their own.

While *Green Grass, Running Water* is written as a story cycle in the vein of an Aboriginal oral tradition cloaked in satire, and *Medicine River* is a more linear satirical novel, King's subsequent novel, *Truth and Bright Water*, is a simpler coming-of-age tragedy. Unlike *Medicine River* and *Green Grass, Running Water*, in this novel the fact that the characters are native is almost incidental to the story. Set in the American border town of Truth and the Canadian town across the river, Bright Water, the novel is the story of two cousins, a dog, and an artist returning home. The boys search for the identity of a human skull found in the river between the two towns. In the process they come to terms with their own positions in the community. Perhaps the most engaging element of the novel concerns the return of Monroe Swimmer, ''famous Indian artist,'' to Truth. He paints a church into the prairie landscape to such an extent that not even he can find its door. He also (re)populates the prairie with iron statues of buffalo. In the end, we learn that Monroe is responsible for the skull in the river as he repatriates ''Indians'' to the land from which they were taken. *Truth and Bright Water* may not have the lyricism or the magic of *Green Grass, Running Water*, but it does have a cast of characters who illicit strong readerly responses in their acts of betrayal and reconciliation, love and death, and an ending that will draw even skeptics to tears.

—Kevin McNeilly, updated by Laura Moss

KINGSLEY, Johanna

See PERUTZ, Kathrin

KINGSOLVER, Barbara

Nationality: American. **Born:** Annapolis, Maryland, 8 April 1955. **Education:** DePauw University, B.A. 1977; University of Arizona, M.S. 1981; additional graduate study. **Family:** Married Joseph Hoffmann in 1985 (divorced); one daughter. **Career:** Research assistant in department of physiology, University of Arizona, Tucson, 1977–79, technical writer in office of arid lands studies, 1981–85; freelance journalist, 1985–87; full-time writer, 1987—; book reviewer, 1988—. **Awards:** Feature-writing award (Arizona Press Club), 1986; American Library Association award, 1988, 1990; citation of accomplishment from United Nations National Council of Women, 1989; PEN fiction prize, 1991; Edward Abbey Ecofiction Award, 1991; Woodrow Wilson Foundation/Lila Wallace fellow, 1992–93; D.Litt., DePauw University, 1994. **Agent:** Frances Goldin, 305 East 11th Street, New York, New York 10003, U.S.A.

Publications

Novels

The Bean Trees. New York, Harper, 1988.
Animal Dreams. New York, Harper, 1990.
Pigs in Heaven. New York, HarperCollins, 1993.
The Poisonwood Bible. New York, HarperFlamingo, 1998.

Short Stories

Homeland and Other Stories. New York, Harper, 1989.

Poetry

Another America/Otra America (with Spanish translations by Rebeca Cartes). Seal Beach, California, Seal Press, 1992.

Other

Holding the Line: Women in the Great Arizona Mine Strike of 1983 (nonfiction). Ithaca, New York, ILR Press, 1989; with new introduction, 1996.

High Tide in Tucson: Essays from Now or Never. New York, HarperCollins, 1995.

Contributor, *Rebirth of Power*, edited by P. Portwood, M. Gorcey, and P. Sanders. Mother Courage Press, 1987.

Contributor, *Florilegia, an Anthology of Art and Literature by Women*, edited by M. Donnelly. Calyx Books, 1987.

Contributor, *New Stories from the South: The Year's Best, 1988*, edited by Shannon Ravenel. Chapel Hill, North Carolina, Algonquin Books, 1988.

Contributor, *I've Always Meant to Tell You: Letters to Our Mothers, An Anthology of Contemporary Women Writers*, edited by Constance Warlow. Pocket Books, 1997.

Contributor, *The Eloquent Essay: An Anthology of Classic and Creative Nonfiction from the Twentieth Century*, edited by John Loughery. New York, Persea Books, 1999.

Introduction, *Off the Beaten Path: Stories of Place*, edited by Joseph Barbato and Lisa Weinerman Horak. New York, North Point Press, 1998.

*

Critical Studies: *Tell It on the Mountain: Appalachian Women Writers* (sound recording), Whitesburg, Kentucky, WMMT-FM, 1995; *Barbara Kingsolver: A Critical Companion* by Mary Jean DeMarr, Westport, Connecticut, Greenwood Press, 1999.

* * *

Barbara Kingsolver's novels emerge as answers to implicitly embedded ''very big'' questions that she devises in hopes that she might ''shift the world a little bit on its axis.'' Rising from her unwavering commitments to social justice, her novels, as well as her nonfiction, address political issues such as Western colonialism, cultural imperialism; disappearing cultures, particularly of Africans and Native Americans; class and economics; nature and ecology; along with race and gender issues. Not a preacher, Kingsolver skillfully weaves her political ideologies into the fabric of her fiction, often subtly enlightening her reader through educating a character. She first creates a detailed world right down to the appropriate flowers, and then invents characters who, through interaction with one another and the setting, answer her devised question.

In *The Bean Trees*, Kingsolver's question probes how friendship and community sustain and assist people through periods of great difficulty. Spurning a predictable life of early pregnancy, spunky Marietta Greer flees Pittman, Kentucky, renames herself Taylor in Illinois, ironically has thrust upon her a Native American infant in Oklahoma, and halts in Tucson. In this *bildungsroman*, reworked from a woman's point of view, Taylor's rich Kentucky voice introduces the new community and family she fashions for herself. With its ''instant motherhood'' and multitude of problems, Taylor's new life collides with social injustices. Forced to seek medical treatment and then social services for the withdrawn, abused infant Turtle, so named for her tenacious clinging, Taylor learns of the physical and emotional aftermath of child abuse. Through her activist employer Mattie, she meets and grows to love Estevan and Esperanza, illegal aliens, and thus learns of political unrest, torture, and disappeared ones in Guatemala. With her housemate Lou Ann Ruiz, a new mother whose husband has left her, Taylor redefines family. Through Kingsolver's gradual revelations, Taylor matures to greater self-assurance and political sophistication; thus without hesitation she aids her Guatemalan friends to safely relocate and secures fraudulent adoption papers for Turtle.

The prize-winning sequel *Pigs in Heaven*, Kingsolver's third novel, catches up with Taylor and Turtle several years later. Here Kingsolver's motivation is to explore the complications created when the beliefs and needs of an individual and a community clash, in this instance the illegally adopted child Turtle and the Cherokee Indian Nation, represented by lawyer Annawake Fourkiller of Heaven, Oklahoma. At issue is the removal, through adoption by white families, of Native American children from their people and culture. Dedicated to multiple points of view, Kingsolver uses the novel's title to illustrate different ways of seeing and telling things. Annawake relates her tribal myth of the ''Six Bad Boys'' who are changed into ''The Six Pigs in Heaven.'' She interprets this Cherokee variation of the Pleiades or Seven Sisters as meaning ''Do right by your people.'' A white man's credo might be ''Do right by yourself.'' These incompatible value systems of individualism versus community and tradition provide the conflict for the plot, which some have criticized as too coincidental and manipulated with too many settings.

One of the glaring manipulations brings together Taylor's mother Alice Stamper Greer, who appeared in the previous novel only in phone conversations, and Turtle's Cherokee Grandfather, Cash Stillwater. In an effort to help Taylor, Alice travels to Heaven where she joins her cousin, Sugar Boss, who introduces Alice to the Cherokee community and explains its traditions and history, such as the Trail of Tears, the stomp dance, and the Indian Child Welfare Act. Not surprisingly, the affection between Alice and Cash helps resolve the conflict and by novel's end, a matured Taylor returns to Tucson committed to a family with Jax, her rock musician boyfriend, and Turtle, for whom she now shares custody with Pop-Pop Stillwater, her new stepfather.

Kingsolver's fiction is not autobiographical. Her characters are what she calls ''complex conglomerates'' based on features that she has carefully observed or experienced. Her second novel, *Animal Dreams*, illustrates this point. The strong Mexican-American women she interviewed while researching the nonfiction *Holding the Line* provided the models for the novel's Emelina Domingos and the elder women of the Stitch and Bitch Club; in addition, their remote southern Arizona villages outlined the novel's Grace, Arizona, a fictionalized town set in a nurturing yet dying landscape. Intrigued by why individuals either engage or detach themselves from life, to dramatize the answer Kingsolver creates undirected, passive Codi Noline and her idealistic younger sister Hallie, who has gone to Nicaragua to teach crop management. Codi returns to Grace to teach high school and care for her Alzheimer's-stricken father, Homer, the respected town doctor. His short narrations brilliantly capture his wandering mind's inability to determine present from past. Through his confused flashbacks and Codi's incomplete memories, eventually filled in by women in the community, Kingsolver provides partial answers to her fundamental question about engagement.

Citing Doris Lessing's ''Children of Violence'' series as an influence, Kingsolver believes that writing is a form of political activism; thus, she readily accepts the classification of ''political novelist''; however, author Jane Smiley criticizes Kingsolver for packing *Animal Dreams* with too many issues—Native Americans, U.S. involvement in Nicaragua, parental relationships, acculturation, environmental issues, loss and grief, anti-violence, women taking charge. And again, although integral to the character development and plot, some of the political issues lead to predictable outcomes. Hallie is kidnapped, tortured, and murdered in Nicaragua; numbed by this loss, Codi mounts a national campaign to first rescue and, then, memorialize her sister. Loyd Peregrina, the father of teenaged Codi's miscarried child and now her adult, supportive lover, proves to be unmarred emotionally from the death of his twin brother, perhaps because of his loving matriarchal family. After Codi succeeds as an offbeat teacher whose students discover the silent environmental catastrophe of the town's ''dead'' river, her lecture to the Stitch and Bitch Club sparks the women to fight the mining company's plan to build a dam and, thus, flood the town and cover up their culpability. Raising money through selling piñatas as folk art, they succeed.

All of Kingsolver's novels portray women taking charge, many narrating their own success stories of personal growth through political involvement. In fact, her novels are often labeled ''chick books,'' implying that they are written for women and, hence, seemingly about unimportant issues. *The Poisonwood Bible* put this unfortunate assumption to rest.

This long-awaited novel grew from Kingsolver's brief childhood experience in Africa as well as the 1991 short story ''My Father's Africa,'' but was developed through extensive research (the novel contains a bibliography) and a careful reading of the King James Bible. Within the Bible, Kingsolver found the novel's structure, leitmotif, cadences, and vocabulary for the vivid voices who narrate their missionary family's experiences in Kilanga, Belgian Congo. Set on the eve of Zaire's independence, Africa, as the catalyst in irrevocably shaping and changing lives, becomes a character in the novel, reminiscent of Joseph Conrad's *Heart of Darkness*. Historical incidents, such as Patrice Lumumba's assassination and Mobutu's betrayal through complicity with the CIA, play out as background to the Price family's destruction by a land that they completely misunderstand in a village where they are not trusted. The novel's brilliance originates in Kingsolver's stunning development of characters through language. Through first-person narration, five female voices provide the shifting points of view that develop the complex portrait of their family, headed by an evangelical Baptist Reverend, the smugly superior, abusive Nathan Price. Although never a narrator in his own story, Nathan is nevertheless fully developed by narratives of his wife and four daughters.

One of Kingsolver's constant reference books was K. E. Laman's *Dictionnaire Kikongo-Français*, a Kikongo-French dictionary that she read daily to grasp the ''music and subtlety of this amazing African language, with its infinite capacity for being misunderstood and mistranslated.'' Characteristically, as with *Pigs in Heaven*, she uses her accumulated knowledge of another culture to enrich the novel's title as well as reveal Nathan's character. In Kikongo, ''bangala,'' pronounced one way, describes something very precious; pronounced slightly differently it refers to the deadly poisonwood tree, whose woodsmoke can kill. Stubborn Nathan Price insists on preaching ''Tata Jesus is 'bangala,''' complete with mispronunciation so that he insists, ''Jesus is poisonwood.'' Ironically, his fierce, strict interpretation of the Bible coupled with his arrogant superiority poisons his very mission in Africa.

Another research tool was a pile of popular magazines. Kingsolver used them to attune her ear to the language of the Price teenagers. Rachel, a shallow, self-centered fifteen year old, walks right out of the beauty advertisements in *Look* and *Life* of the late 1950s. Her voice provides some comic relief to the family's nightmarish situation. A second playful voice is that of Adah, a mute twin suffering from hemiplegia but who thinks in palindromes and quotes Emily Dickinson. Readers are amused by Rachel, but they gravitate to the other twin, Leah, as she struggles to understand Africa; eventually Leah becomes a part of the continent by marrying her father's interpreter, the revolutionary Anatole, and living in Angola with their four sons. The childish voice of Ruth May, who parrots overheard discussions, is stilled by her death, then seen as senseless, in Africa in 1961; that tragedy provides the impetus for the girls' mother, Orleanna, to gather her three remaining daughters and flee the village, leaving Nathan to his own increasingly insane devices.

Kingsolver moves the novel into the mid-1980s in the introspective sixth section, titled ''Song of the Three Children,'' from the Apocrypha, which exposes the adult sisters' views of one another at a reunion and as they discuss their father's awful death in Africa and update their mother's new life in Georgia. Orleanna's voice opens the novel, reconstructing an African picnic. By partially addressing the reader with an invitation to become the conscience and the eyes in the trees of the African forest and partially addressing Ruth May, long buried in African soil, Orleanna seeks some insight into her responsibility for the destruction of her family as well the international issue of the West's destruction of Africa. By the novel's epilogue, ''The Eyes in the Trees,'' a symbolic Ruth May eerily speaks of forgiveness and understanding as muntu Africa—''all that is here.''

Appearing on best-seller lists for months and hailed for its rich style and language, fully fleshed out, believable characters and complex plot woven through with political issues such as social injustice, colonial occupation, and genocide, *The Poisonwood Bible* drew inevitable comparisons with novels by Lessing and Nadine Gordimer. Following their lead, Kingsolver will no doubt continue to speak out to contemporary issues through her fiction. By establishing the Bellwether prize, awarded for literature that supports social responsibility, Kingsolver guarantees that others will follow her lead.

—Judy Kohl

KINGSTON, Maxine Hong

Nationality: American. **Born:** Maxine Ting Ting Hong, Stockton, California, 27 October 1940. **Education:** University of California, Berkeley, A.B. 1962, teaching certificate, 1965. **Family:** Married Earll Kingston in 1962; one son. **Career:** Teacher of English and mathmatics, Sunset High School, Hayward, California, 1965–67; teacher of English, Kahuku High School, Hawaii, 1967; teacher, Kahaluu Drop-In School, 1968; teacher of English as a second language, Honolulu Business College, Hawaii, 1969; teacher of language arts, Kailua High School, Hawaii, 1969, and Mid-Pacific Institute, Honolulu, 1970–77. Since 1977 visiting associate professor of English, Univeristy of Hawaii, Honolulu. **Awards:** National Book Critics Circle award, 1976, for nonfiction; *Mademoiselle* award, 1977; Anisfiel-Wolf Race Relations award, 1978; National Education Association writing fellowship, 1980; American Book award, 1981, for nonfiction; Arts Commission award, 1981; Hawaii Award for Literature, 1982; California Governor's Award, 1989; Major Book Collection Award, Brandeis University, 1990; Award for Literature, American Academy & Institute for Arts & Letters, 1990; Lila Wallace Reader's Digest Writing Award, 1992; Special Achievement, Oakland Business Arts award, 1994; Cyril Magnin Award for Outstanding Achievement in the Arts, 1996; Distinguished Artists Award, the Music Center of L.A. County, 1996; National Humanities Medal, NEH, 1997; Fred Cody Lifetime Achievement Award, 1998; John Dos Passos Prize for Literature, 1998; Ka Palapola Po'okela Award, 1999; Profiles of Courage Honor, Swords to Plowshares, 1999. Honorary doctorate, Eastern Michigan University, 1988; Colby College, 1990; Brandeis University, 1991; University of Massachusetts, 1991. Named Living Treasure Hawaii, 1980; Woman of the Year, Asian Pacific Women's Network, 1981. **Address:** University of California, Department of English, 322 Wheeler Hall, Berkeley, California 94720–1030, U.S.A.

PUBLICATIONS

Novels

Tripmaster Monkey, His Fake Book. New York, Knopf, and London, Pan, 1989.
Hawaii One Summer. Honolulu, University of Hawaii Press, 1998.

Other

The Woman Warrior: Memoirs of a Girlhood Among Ghosts. New York, Knopf, 1976; London, Allen Lane, 1977.
China Men. New York, Knopf, 1980; London, Pan, 1981.
The Making of More Americans. Honolulu, Hawaii, InterArts, 1980.
Through the Black Curtain. Berkeley, University of California Press, 1987.
Conversations with Maxine Hong Kingston, edited by Paul Skenazy and Tera Martin. Jackson, University Press of Mississippi, 1998.

*

Critical Studies: *Approaches to Teaching Kingston's 'The Woman Warrior'* edited by Shirley Geok-Lim, New York, Modern Language Association of America, 1991; *Articulate Silences: Hisaye Yamamoto, Maxine Hong Kingston, Joy Kogawa* by King-Kok Chueng, Ithaca, Cornell University Press, 1993; *Stories of Resilience in Childhood: The Narratives of Maya Angelou, Maxine Hong Kingston, Richard Rodrigues, John Edgar Wideman, and Tobias Wolff* by Daniel D. Challener, New York, Garland, 1997; *The Female Bildungsroman by Toni Morrison and Maxine Hong Kingston: A Postmodern Reading* by Pin-chia Feng, New York, P. Lang, 1998; *Critical Essays on Maxine Hong Kingston* edited by Laura E. Skandera-Trombley, New York, G.K. Hall, 1998; *In Her Mother's House: the Politics of Asian American Mother-Daughter Writing* by Wendy Ho, Walnut Creek, AltaMira Press, 1999; *Maxine Hong Kingston* by Diane Simmons, New York, Twayne Publishers, 1999; *Asian-American Authors* by Kathy Ishizuka, Berkeley Heights, New Jersey, Enslow Publishers, 2000; *Maxine Hong Kingston: A Critical Companion* by E.D. Huntley, Westport, Connecticut, Greenwood Press, 2000.

* * *

Myth, legend, history, and biography are so seamlessly blended in Maxine Hong Kingston's books that it is often difficult to know how to categorize them. Are *The Woman Warrior: Memoirs of a Girlhood Among Ghosts* and *China Men* works of non-fiction? Officially, they are cataloged as such, but in the deepest sense of reader's experience they seem more akin to fairy tales, folkloric stories, even epic poems. Based on the history and myth passed on to Kingston by members of her immediate family, as well by ''story-talkers'' in the Stockton, California, community where she grew up, the result is a species of magical realism, one that continually hovers between fact and the imagination, between what was and what might have been.

Kingston regards *The Woman Warrior* and *China Men* as a single large book, despite the fact that they were published separately. Moreover, she often confuses, willfully or no, family members who actually lived with those she invents. This penchant for blurring the distinctions between the actual and the invented has occasioned some criticism, especially among those who feel that Kingston plays fast and loose with history, but most reviewer-critics showered her with praise.

No doubt categories matter when one is handing out literary prizes (both *The Woman Warrior* and *China Men* received awards for general excellence in non-fiction), and the confusion of actuality and invention may be worth quarreling about, but what matters finally are the stories themselves—and they are quite good. Indeed, one would be hard-pressed to think of books that detail the joys and pains of growing up within a strictly defined ethnic community that could match Kingston's sentence for sentence, paragraph for paragraph, page for page. She is, quite simply, a marvelous writer.

Moreover, Kingston so experiments with form that the result is a species of algebra: stories that interlock or comment on each other; life lessons that creep inextricably out of mythic depths; and perhaps most of all, an eerie sense of that the burdens of the past rest securely on the shoulders of those in the present. Kingston herself straddles two vibrant worlds, each as menacing as it is mysterious.

The Woman Warrior is dominated by Kingston's mother (Brave Orchid, in the book) and the other women of China—ghosts of the heart, all—who formed her sensibility and willed her strength. By contrast, *China Men* focuses on the man who labored for fifteen years in a laundry to pay for Brave Orchid's passage. The books beg to be read as a inseparable pair, as yin and yang are seen as opposite sides of a unified principle.

In Kingston's culture, it is the women who use story as a means to understanding and survival. By contrast, Chinese men tend toward silence, which forces Kingston to invent multiple versions of what may have happened in her father's past. No doubt some must have wondered if Kingston could write as penetratingly about men as she clearly did about women, especially given the restricted circumstances under which Chinese women traditionally functioned. The worries, however, were unfounded, for the effect of *China Men* is as riveting as it is daring.

As for Wittman Ah Sing, the male protagonist of *Tripmaster Monkey: His Fake Book,* one can hardly get him to shut up. A typical rant has him complaining frenetically about ''F.O.B.'' or ''fresh off the boat'' immigrants from Asia, and at various places in the book, he jumps around and chatters and generally moves so fast it is hard to follow him. Named—perhaps—after Walt Whitman, Wittman represents an ancient archetype not only of Chinese but of world literature, best known to Western readers through personae such as Loki, the Norse god of mischief. In Kingston's skillful hands, myth is not only a source of refuge and inspiration, but also of power. Thus she works not as a professional Sinologist—one factor that contributes to the antipathy toward her on the part of ethnic stalwarts such as Frank Chin, who insists on calling himself a ''Chinaman'' rather than Chinese—but as a creative writer operating in a world tradition. The result is the construction of a deeper truth than facts normally allow. Kingston's extraordinary books remind us that what James Joyce, an Irishman on the other side of the world, set out to accomplish when his protagonist set off to forge on the smithy of his soul ''the uncreated conscience of my race'' can also happen when a young Chinese-American writer sets out to discover who she is amid the rich tapestry of memory and the imagination.

—Sanford Pinsker

KINSELLA, W(illiam) P(atrick)

Nationality: Canadian. **Born:** Edmonton, Alberta, 25 May 1935. **Education:** Eastwood High School, Edmonton, graduated 1953; University of Victoria, British Columbia, B.A. in creative writing 1974; University of Iowa, Iowa City, 1976–78, M.F.A. 1978. **Family:** Married 1) Myrna Salls in 1957, two children; 2) Mildred Clay in 1965 (divorced 1978); 3) Ann Knight in 1978 (divorced 1997). **Career:** Clerk, Government of Alberta, 1954–56, and manager, Retail Credit Co., 1956–61, both Edmonton; account executive, City of Edmonton, 1961–67; owner, Caesar's Italian Village restaurant, 1967–72, editor, *Martlet,* 1973–74, and cab driver, 1974–76, all Victoria, British Columbia; assistant professor of English, University of Calgary, Alberta, 1978–83. Since 1983 full-time writer. **Awards:** *Edmonton Journal* prize, 1966; *Canadian Fiction* award, 1976; Alberta Achievement award, 1982; Houghton Mifflin Literary fellowship, 1982; *Books in Canada* prize, 1982; Canadian Authors Association prize, 1983; Leacock medal, for humor, 1987; Vancouver Writing award, 1987, Order of Canada, 1994. Named Author of Year, Canadian Library Association, 1987. D.Litt., Laurentian University, Sudbury, 1990; University of Victoria, 1991. **Address:** 9442 Nowell, Chilliwack, British Columbia, Canada, V2P 4X7.

Publications

Novels

Shoeless Joe. Boston, Houghton Mifflin, 1982; London, Allison and Busby, 1988.
The Iowa Baseball Confederacy. Boston, Houghton Mifflin, 1986.
Box Socials. Toronto, HarperCollins, 1991; New York, Ballantine, 1992.
The Winter Helen Dropped By. Toronto, HarperCollins, 1995.
If Wishes Were Horses. Toronto, HarperCollins, 1996.
Magic Time. Toronto, Doubleday Canada, 1998.

Short Stories

Dance Me Outside. Ottawa, Oberon Press, 1977; Boston, Godine, 1986.
Scars. Ottawa, Oberon Press, 1978.
Shoeless Joe Jackson Comes to Iowa. Ottawa, Oberon Press, 1980; Dallas, Southern Methodist University Press, 1993.
Born Indian. Ottawa, Oberon Press, 1981.
The Ballad of the Public Trustee. Vancouver, Standard, 1982.
The Moccasin Telegraph and Other Indian Tales. Toronto, Penguin, 1983; Boston, Godine, 1984; London, Arrow, 1985.
The Thrill of the Grass. Toronto and London, Penguin, 1984; New York, Viking, 1985.
The Alligator Report. Minneapolis, Coffee House Press, 1985.
The Fencepost Chronicles. Toronto, Collins, 1986; Boston, Houghton Mifflin, 1987.
Red Wolf, Red Wolf. Toronto, Collins, 1987; Dallas, Southern Methodist University Press, 1990.
Five Stories. Vancouver, Hoffer, 1987.
The Further Adventures of Slugger McBatt. Toronto, Collins, and Boston, Houghton Mifflin, 1988.
The Miss Hobbema Pageant. Toronto, Harper Collins, 1989.
The Dixon Cornbelt League and Other Baseball Stories. Toronto, HarperCollins, 1993.
Brother Frank's Gospel Hour, and Other Stories. Toronto, HarperCollins, 1994; Dallas, Southern Methodist University Press, 1996.
Go the Distance: Baseball Stories. Dallas, Southern Methodist University Press, 1995.
The Secret of the Northern Lights. Saskatoon, Saskatchewan, Thistledown Press, 1998.

Uncollected Short Stories

''These Changing Times'' (as Felicien Belzile), in *Civil Service Bulletin* (Edmonton), vol. 35, no. 9, October 1955.
''I Walk Through the Valley'' (as Felicien Belzile), in *Civil Service Bulletin* (Edmonton), vol. 36, no. 1, January 1956.
''I Was a Teen-age Slumlord,'' in *Edmonton Journal,* 27 May 1966.
''Hofstadt's Cabin,'' in *Edmonton Journal,* 14 June 1966.
''The Jackhammer,'' in *Edmonton Journal,* 24 June 1966.
''Something Evil This Way Comes,'' in *Edmonton Journal,* September 1966.
''Night People Never Come Back,'' in *Martlet* (Victoria, British Columbia), 10 February 1972.
''White Running Shoes,'' in *View from the Silver Bridge,* vol. 2, no. 1, May 1972.
''Children of the Cartomancy,'' in *Martlet* (Victoria, British Columbia), November 1972.
''Does Anyone Know How They Make Campaign Buttons?,'' in *Karaki* (Victoria, British Columbia), January 1973.
''Broken Dolls'' (as Leslie Smith), in *Martlet* (Victoria, British Columbia), Fall 1973.
''The Snow Leprechaun,'' in *This Week* (Coquitlam, British Columbia), 9 March 1974.
''Famines'' (as Angie Jean Jerome), in *Martlet* (Victoria, British Columbia), Spring 1974.
''A Literary Passage at Arms; or, TX vs. BK,'' in *Iowa City Creative Reading Series Magazine,* Spring-Summer 1977.
''The Elevator,'' in *Canadian Fiction* (Vancouver), nos. 40–41, 1981.
''Intermediaries,'' in *Scrivener* (Montreal), Spring 1982.

Poetry

Rainbow Warehouse, with Ann Knight. Lawrencetown Beach, Nova Scotia, Potterfield Press, 1989.

Other

Two Spirits Soaring: The Art of Allen Sapp, The Inspiration of Allan Ganor. Toronto, Stoddart, 1990.
The First and Last Annual Six Towns Area Old Timers' Baseball Game, with wood engravings by Gaylord Schanilec. Minneapolis, Coffee House Press, 1991.
Even at This Distance (with Ann Knight). Lawrencetown Beach, Nova Scotia, Pottersfield Press, 1994.

*

Bibliographies: *W.P. Kinsella: A Partially-Annotated Bibliographic Checklist (1953–1983)* by Ann Knight, Iowa City, Across, 1983.

Manuscript Collections: National Library of Canada, Ottawa.

Critical Studies: ''Down and Out in Montreal, Windsor, and Wetaskiwin'' by Anthony Brennan, in *Fiddlehead* (Fredericton, New Brunswick), Fall 1977; ''Don't Freeze Off Your Leg'' Spring 1979, and ''Say It Ain't So, Joe'' Spring-Summer 1981, both by Frances W. Kaye, in *Prairie Schooner* (Lincoln, Nebraska); article by Brian E. Burtch, in *Canadian Journal of Sociology* (Edmonton), Winter 1980; essay by Anne Blott, in *Fiddlehead* (Fredericton, New Brunswick), July 1982; Marjorie Retzleff, in *NeWest Review* (Edmonton), October 1984; ''Search for the Unflawed Diamond'' by Don Murray, in *NeWest Review* (Edmonton), January 1985; *The Fiction of W.P. Kinsella: Tall Tales in Various Voices* by Don Murray, Fredericton, New Brunswick, York Press, 1987.

* * *

Before the publication of his best-known novel, W.P. Kinsella had already written extensively about baseball in four short story collections. *Shoeless Joe* (filmed as *Field of Dreams*) is preeminently a paean to baseball as it was once played when it was the national pastime, before inflated salaries, players' disputes, and artificial turf. The novel is almost studiously old-fashioned in its unabashed lyricism and unmitigated affirmation of life and love. *Shoeless Joe* has nothing in common with either the modernist or postmodernist traditions, and very little with the realist tradition. It posits the possibility of achieving the Whitmanesque dream, but denies that *Democratic Vistas* had ever been written. Its antecedent is J.D. Salinger's *The Catcher in the Rye,* but only Holden Caulfield's vision of a world redeemed through his sister Phoebe's innocence. *Shoeless Joe* is, in many ways, a plea for a return to the Edenic dream in which the serpent appears only to be crushed. Although Kinsella's novel often seems to be all surface, it can be read on the levels of love story, tall tale, and myth.

Shoeless Joe affirms the absolute redemptive power of human love. Ray Kinsella, the narrator and main character, makes love to his wife Annie who ''sings to me, love songs in tongues, bird songs thrilling and brilliant as morning,'' and he marvels that he ''can love her so much ... that [their] love puts other things in perspective.'' (The reader may suspect that Kinsella owes more to E.E. Cummings's views of love and his detestation of technology than he does to any novelist.) Above all, baseball has the power to unite in love those estranged by time and emotional distance. Eddie Scissons, an old player, advised Ray that to be reconciled with his dead father he must realize that they ''both love the game. Make that your common ground, and nothing else will matter.''

But it is baseball mythologized and raised to the levels of magic and religion that has the transcendent power. As a Moses of the midwest, Ray hears a voice tell him ''If you build it, he will come;'' the ''he'' is Shoeless Joe Jackson, a member of the infamous 1919 Black Sox team that fixed the World Series. So bidden, Ray erects a baseball stadium, replete with bleachers and lights, on his Iowa farm, which is soon peopled with the entire Chicago team that nightly play their opponents on a field of planted grass, undefiled by the artificial turf of modern playing fields. But only those who firmly believe in magic and love the game can see the players or the action, when ''all the cosmic tumblers have clicked into place and the universe appears for a few seconds, or hours, and shows you what is possible.'' Ray's twin brother, Richard, is not privy to the shades because his ''eyes are blind to the magic,'' and he must ask Ray to ''teach me how to see.''

At times Kinsella puts too great a burden on baseball's redemptive power by giving it too many of the trappings of religion and myth. J.D. Salinger (whom Ray, obeying the voice, has kidnapped from his home in New Hampshire, and who soon becomes Ray's mythic accomplice) eulogizes that people will ''watch the game, and it will be as if they have knelt in front of a faith healer, or dipped themselves in magic waters where a saint once rose like a serpent and cast benedictions to the wind like peach petals.'' Playing baseball is like being ''engaged in a pagan ceremony,'' and as Eddie ''Kid'' Scissons says, ''I know there are many who are troubled, anxious, worried, insecure. What is the cure? ... The answer is in the word, and baseball is the word,'' and those who heed the message ''will be changed by the power of the living word.'' The game becomes too freighted with symbolism to survive the attributions. Then there is the question of evil, which in this Garden takes two forms. One is Ray's wife's brother who contrives to buy Ray's land and plans to turn it into part of a vast computerized farm, destroying the stadium and playing field. Needless to say, his brother-in-law is foiled; technology cannot prevail against the pastoral ideal. The second is Eddie Scissons who has lied about his baseball triumphs and is punished by striking out in a game he is allowed to play as a returned youth; the serpent head cane he fondles is too intrusive and obvious a symbol.

But *Shoeless Joe* has a great many strengths, in particular its sustained lyricism and Kinsella's love for the literal game and its authentic rituals. It is worth noting that in his recent short story collection *The Thrill of the Grass* Kinsella continues to write about baseball; his lyricism is unabated, but he usually avoids the excesses that mar *Shoeless Joe.*

In *The Iowa Baseball Confederacy,* much of the same imagery of magic and religion recurs. Gideon Clarke finds himself inspired by the presence of his absent father to carry the family tradition forward and prove to the historians and to the Chicago Cubs that the Confederacy did exist. Matthew, the father, dreams a wife named Maudie who steps out of a carnival side show and into his life at least long enough to produce Gideon, whose shoulder-length white hair and strange blue eyes set him apart in the same way that his father was set apart even before the lightning bolt struck him during his first contact with Maudie. These characters continue the tradition of ''being dipped in magic waters'' that offer healing to a modern world through the ritual of baseball. The stakes of the game are high here: the losers will be consigned to everlasting oblivion. Of course, there is the suggestion that baseball is eternal, and the winners will bask in it forever.

Box Socials, a strong affirmation of love, is set in rural Canada, outside Edmonton. The central hero is one who does not quite make it in the big leagues, but he is admired in his community. All the families take box lunches to church socials, and their social lives are centered around the activity. Kinsella offers a generous portrait of rural Alberta, some touching pictures of life out on the plains.

Throughout Kinsella's work, there is a refreshing belief that love is possible and that life is good. He lifts us to the level of myth where we, too, can walk taller.

—Peter Desy, updated by Loretta Cobb

KNOWLES, John

Nationality: American. **Born:** Fairmont, West Virginia, 16 September 1926. **Education:** Phillips Exeter Academy, Exeter, New Hampshire, graduated 1945; Yale University, New Haven, Connecticut, B.A. 1949. **Career:** Reporter, Hartford *Courant,* Connecticut, 1950–52; freelance writer, 1952–56; associate editor, *Holiday* magazine, Philadelphia, 1956–60. Writer-in-residence, University of North Carolina, Chapel Hill, 1963–64, and Princeton University, New Jersey, 1968–69. **Awards:** Rosenthal Foundation award, 1961; Faulkner Foundation award, 1961; National Association of Independent Schools award, 1961. **Address:** c/o Penguin Putnam, 405 Murray Hill Parkway, East Rutherford, New Jersey 07073–2136, U.S.A.

Publications

Novels

A Separate Peace. London, Secker and Warburg, 1959; New York, Macmillan, 1960; edited and with an introduction by Harold Bloom, Philadelphia, Chelsea House, 1999.
Morning in Antibes. New York, Macmillan, and London, Secker and Warburg, 1962.
Indian Summer. New York, Random House, and London, Secker and Warburg, 1966.
The Paragon. New York, Random House, 1971.
Spreading Fires. New York, Random House, 1974.
Vein of Riches. Boston, Little Brown, 1978.
Peace Breaks Out. New York, Holt Rinehart, 1981.
A Stolen Past. New York, Holt Rinehart, 1983; London, Constable, 1984.
The Private Life of Axie Reed. New York, Dutton, 1986.

Short Stories

Phineas: Six Stories. New York, Random House, 1968.

Other

Double Vision: American Thoughts Abroad. New York, Macmillan, and London, Secker and Warburg, 1964.
Backcasts: Memories and Recollections of Seventy Years as a Sportsman. Fowlerville, Michigan, Wilderness Adventure, 1993.

*

Manuscript Collections: Beinecke Library, Yale University, New Haven, Connecticut.

*   *   *

John Knowles writes, in general, not about his home turf but about New England or Europe. Only one novel, *Vein of Riches,* and that not his best, is about West Virginia, his childhood home. His fictional world is a cultivated, cosmopolitan, somewhat jaded world. He is a fine craftsman, a fine stylist, alert to the infinite resources and nuances of language. Yet, as he says, he is one of the live-around-the-world people, rootless, nomadic, and making a virtue of that rootlessness. He is a connoisseur of different cultures but master of none—or perhaps of one only, the sub-culture of the New England prep school. One defect of this very cosmopolitanism is the feeling of alienation that Knowles feels from his fictional world. As a veteran of many cultures he finds this trait an advantage when he writes graceful travel essays for *Holiday* magazine. He finds it a disadvantage when he wishes to create for *Vein of Riches* a thoroughly credible fictional character.

A Separate Peace, his first novel, is also by far his most important. It is a prep school novel about Gene Forrester and his close friend, Finney, and the studied set of ambiguities and ambivalences arising from the intense and complex relationship between the two. Gene, beset by a love-hate attitude toward Finney, causes Finney to suffer a serious injury and still later is the putative cause of his death from a second injury. But Finney's death is preceded by Gene's reconciliation with him, a redemptive act which to some degree assuages his feeling of guilt. Thus, the novel recounts Gene's initiation into manhood and into both worldly and moral maturity. Fifteen years after Finney's death, Gene returns to Devon to conclude the novel by thinking—''Nothing endures, not a tree, not love, not even a death by violence.'' What does endure is the extraordinary popularity of this novel with prep school and college students.

Knowles's later books display his writing grace but not the inner strength of *A Separate Peace.* His second novel, *Morning in Antibes,* has a pot-pourri of comatose characters revolving about the deracinated Nicolas Petrovich Bodine in a kind of latter day *The Sun Also Rises;* it lacks, however, the Hemingway tone, atmosphere, and taut dialogue. The people are phony and maybe the novel is too. The long passivity of Nick makes him seem to move under water. The novel fails in characterization.

Indian Summer follows Cleet Kinsolving, World War II vet, in his jousting with his friend, Neil Reardon, Irish Catholic and heir to multi-millions (seemingly modeled on John Kennedy). Cleet's conviction, which he shares with T.S. Eliot's Sweeney, is that each man needs to do someone in. A good deal of cultural primitivism is spread about, but again the characters are unconvincing. *The Paragon* describes Lou Colfax, a brilliant, handsome sophomore in love with a beautiful actress four years older than he. In spite of the Yale ambiance and a plethora of cocktail parties and beautiful people the intended ''Gatsby glamour'' never comes to this novel. Perhaps because we miss the ''yellow cocktail music'' of *Gatsby,* perhaps because the characters remain partially developed. *Spreading Fires,* a brief novel of decadence and homosexual vagaries set in the south of France, deals with madness, potential madness, and the low life of the upper class.

Vein of Riches is a study of the great coal boom of 1910–1924 in a West Virginia town. Knowles shows a house, a family, and an industry, and the interactions of the three; he employs one of the central themes of American fiction, money versus land. It is a pleasant novel but the characters again are given perfunctory treatment. We do not have the empathy and zest that bubbled up from *A Separate Peace.* Coal does not interest Knowles the way New England prep school life did.

Peace Breaks Out is set in Devon School, New Hampshire, and is an attempt by Knowles to revisit the scene of his greatest fictional success, *A Separate Peace.* The parallels between the two novels are very strong: the place is the same school, the time is five years later and the crux of the plot is the wrongful death of a disliked schoolmate,

Hochschwender, who dies of heart failure after being tortured by four of his classmates. Again, as in *A Separate Peace,* there is a legacy of guilt suffered by the four survivors. Knowles is much at home in the world of the private school and depicts it with grace and clarity. But it has all been done before in his earlier and better novel and thus lacks freshness and spontaneity. Many readers will find the excessive hypocrisy of Wexford, the ringleader of the torturers, a little unrealistic. This novel will not achieve the status of *A Separate Peace,* although it is well crafted and knowledgeably written.

In summary, Knowles is intelligent, highly literate, a skilled and sensitive craftsman and stylist. He is knowledgeable of the world, tolerant, a connoisseur of many cultures. He possesses in his own person that bifocal vision which he praises in *Double Vision.* He has created one extraordinary novel, *A Separate Peace,* which for many young people has truly caught the *zeitgeist.* There is also a negative side. Every novel but his first suffers from one fundamental defect—the characters are not plausible. There is not a single memorable woman character in his fiction and only two male characters—Gene Forrester and Phineas—that stay in our memory. The result is an imperfect empathy and a resultant lack of reader interest. In general his male protagonists are inert, deracinated, ambivalent, depersonalized, dehumanized. Why does Knowles create such types? Only he can answer this definitively, but perhaps he gives us the answer in his book *Double Vision* where he argues against roots and for rootlessness, the new form of nomadism. ''We need to be nomadic and uprooted today,'' he maintains. As he says, he is not regional, does not come from a town or a city. He is one of the live-around-the-world people. So he is and so are the characters in his books. This is his fundamental failure and it is a major one. He may yet overcome this and give us again a convincing, brilliant novel as was *A Separate Peace.*

—Ruel E. Foster

KNOX, Calvin M.

See SILVERBERG, Robert

KNOX, Elizabeth (Fiona)

Nationality: New Zealander. **Born:** Wellington, 15 February 1959. **Education:** Tawa College, 1972–76; Victoria University, Wellington, 1983–86, B.A. in English 1986. **Family:** Married Fergus Barrowman in 1989, one son. **Career:** Clerk, Department of Inland Revenue, 1977–78; printer, Butterworths, and PPTA, 1980–81; insurance underwriter, 1981; publicity officer, National Museum, 1983–84; assistant editor of *Sport,* 1988–93; tutor in film studies, Victoria University, 1989–95. **Awards:** PEN award, 1988, and fellowship, 1991; New Zealand Book award, 1993. **Address:** 74 Glen Rd., Kelburn, Wellington, New Zealand.

PUBLICATIONS

Novels

After Z-Hour. Wellington, Victoria University Press, 1987.
Paremata. Wellington, Victoria University Press, 1989.
Treasure. Wellington, Victoria University Press, 1992.
Pomare. Wellington, Victoria University Press, 1994.
Glamour and the Sea. Wellington, Victoria University Press, 1996.
Tawa. Wellington, Victoria University Press, 1998.
The Vintner's Luck. New York, Farrar, Straus, and Giroux, 1998.

Uncollected Short Stories

''From the Treasury,'' in *Sport* (Wellington), April 1989.
''After Images,'' in *New Zealand Listener* (Wellington), March 1990.
''Post Mortem,'' in *Landfall* (Christchurch), March 1990.
''The Sword,'' in *Sport* (Wellington), October 1990.
''Sex of Metals,'' in *Now See Hear!* edited by Ian Wedde and Gregory Burke. Wellington, Victorian University Press, 1990.
''Afraid,'' in *Sport* (Wellington), April 1991.
''Take as Prescribed,'' in *Soho Square 4.,* edited by Bill Manhire. London, Bloomsbury, 1991.
''Fiona Pardington,'' in *Pleasures and Dangers,* edited by Wystan Curnow and Trish Clark. Auckland, Moet and Chandon/Longman Paul, 1992.
''Going to the Gym,'' in *Into the Field of Play,* edited by Lloyd Jones. N.p., Tandem, 1992.
''A Doubtful Guest,'' in *Stout Centre Review,* February 1992.
''The Black Disc (*Treasure 2.2),*'' in *Metro,* May 1992.

Plays

Screenplays: *The Dig* (*Un Certain Regard*), 1994.

* * *

As early as her award-winning first novel, *After Z-Hour*, New Zealand author Elizabeth Knox has displayed a fascination with place. In each of her works since, the characters are impelled through their experiences due to the locations in which they find themselves. This concentration on place then bleeds into the narratives themselves, turning childhood or grief or love into places the characters inhabit, places whose geographies must be discovered and navigated in order to learn to live within them and ultimately to move beyond them into newer realms. Into each of these experiential states, Knox adds a layer of mystery or the supernatural, as if to say that since all of life is a strange environment needing to be explored, nothing is beyond the realm of the possible. The improbable elements of the stories would seem to contradict the simple or mundane aspects of life, which are ultimately the indicators of the beauty of the human landscape, from a child's halting move into adolescence to an old man's life and eventual death.

Each of the novels engages in new ways with Knox's concerns: the human groping for understanding in a world that often defies comprehension; how thinking, feeling creatures come to know and interact with one another; and the eventual connections between people that ultimately give meaning to life despite the distances between them. What the novels share is a tendency to inhabit various points of view in order to tell a story that moves through time and the psychological journeys of the characters. They are, however, never simply constrained by chronology. Knox's narratives often incorporate the experiences and voices of people dead before the figures of the main plot-line were ever born. The result of this layering of time and psychology is that emotional salvation, even if imperfect, can be effected in a past to which those dwelling in the present have no immediate access. This device allows all of time to interact, and the mythic, extra-ordinary element of Knox's works becomes fully apparent.

Her first novel, *After Z-Hour*, perfectly illustrates all of the trends that have become signatures of Knox's novelistic style. Set in an abandoned house during a freak spring storm, the novel brings together six strangers to try to cope with the possible haunting of the house and their own personal hauntings, from the recent death of one character's stepdaughter, to the feelings of perpetual alienation felt by another, and finally the communication between a third character and a dead World War I veteran, both of whom also provide narrative episodes. The inclusion of the dead man's story acutely draws attention to memory, the novel's main focus, and how the horrors of the past, whether personal or national, both inform and allow passage into the future.

Her second novel, *Paremata*, relies least on the paranormal to tell its tale. Instead, the novel enters the world of children, who supply their own mystery through the power of imagination and curiosity. *Paremata*, like the other novels, is concerned with place, in this case the landscape of childhood set within the shifting cultural scene of late 1960s New Zealand. Knox is interested in the ways in which children make sense of the world, the acuteness of their observations. She uses the make-believe world that the children of *Paremata* create to delineate their fumbling towards an understanding of loyalty, belief, and their own eventual adulthood. Though the novel stays focused on the children's experience, they bring the mysterious past into play with their evocations of a shamanistic religion replete with ritual, curses, and tribal allegiances. Through this game, the children are able to safely explore their feelings and filter the bewildering adult ideas that surround them.

Treasure, Knox's third novel, sets up an ambitious scheme, alternating between an exterior plot, set in New Zealand, and an interior story that takes place in the southern United States. As opposed to the earlier novels, the two main plot lines converge at the end, bringing together all of the major themes that the novel explores. Once again, Knox inserts the supernatural and mysterious to help explain the growth of the characters involved. Here, religion, specifically the enthusiastic expression of fundamental Christian belief and its reliance on extraordinary powers, plays a central role. The ability to heal with the human touch becomes associated with the psychological healing that is afforded to the characters. Once again, Knox evokes the physical worlds in which these stories occur with careful and illustrative detail.

In *The Vintner's Luck*, Knox moves the setting to France during the nineteenth century. The novel is structured chronologically, each chapter recounting the events of a single year in the relationship between a vintner and the immortal angel who becomes the most important figure in his life. Knox's control over narrative and structure are fully apparent in this novel, in which the landscape in which the vintner lives and the landscape of his life as it unfolds intertwine and inform one another. Here, too, salvation becomes a reciprocal gift, the angel enriching and giving meaning to the man's short life, and the man sustaining the angel long after his human life has ended. This chronicle of a complex relationship that develops in human time despite the eternal youth of one of its participants once again highlights Knox's tendency to see the mundane and incredible as intersecting states that not only inform one another but have the ability to directly interact and influence each other and the world.

—Michal Lemberger

KOCH, C(hristopher) J(ohn)

Nationality: Australian. **Born:** Hobart, Tasmania, 16 July 1932. **Education:** Clemes College; St. Virgil's Christian Brothers College; Hobart State High School, 1946–50; University of Tasmania, Hobart, 1951–54, B.A. 1954. Has one son. **Career:** Until 1972, radio producer, Australian Broadcasting Commission, Sydney. **Awards:** *The Age* Book of the Year award, 1978; Australian National Book award, 1979; Miles Franklin award, 1986. **Agent:** Curtis Brown, 27 Union Street, Paddington, New South Wales 2021, Australia.

Publications

Novels

The Boys in the Island. London, Hamish Hamilton, 1958; revised edition, Sydney, Angus and Robertson, 1974.
Across the Sea Wall. London, Heinemann, 1965; revised edition, Sydney and London, Angus and Robertson, 1982.
The Year of Living Dangerously. Melbourne, Nelson, and London, Joseph, 1978; New York, St. Martin's Press, 1979.
The Doubleman. London, Chatto and Windus, 1985; New York, McGraw Hill, 1986.
Highways to a War. New York, Viking, 1995.
Out of Ireland. London, Heinemann, 1999.

Plays

Screenplay: *The Year of Living Dangerously,* with Peter Weir and David Williamson, 1983.

Other

Chinese Journey, with Nicholas Hasluck. Fremantle, Western Australia, Fremantle Arts Centre Press, 1985.
Crossing the Gap: A Novelist's Essays. London, Chatto and Windus, 1987.

*

Manuscript Collections: Australian National Library, Canberra.

Critical Studies: "In the Shadow of Patrick White" by Vincent Buckley, in *Meanjin* (Melbourne), no. 2, 1961; "The Novels of C.J. Koch" by Robyn Claremont, in *Quadrant* (Sydney), 1980; "Asia, Europe and Australian Identity: The Novels of Christopher Koch," May 1982, and "Asia and the Contemporary Australian Novel," October 1984, both by Helen Tiffin, in *Australian Literary Studies* (St. Lucia, Queensland); "*Pour mieux sauter:* Christopher Koch's Novels in Relation to White, Stow and the Quest for a Post-colonial Fiction," in *World Literature Written in English* (Guelph, Ontario), 1983, and "Living Dangerously: Christopher Koch and Cultural Tradition," in *Quadrant* (Sydney), September 1985, both by Paul Sharrad; "Oedipus in the Tropics: A Psychoanalytical Interpretation of C.J. Koch's *The Year of Living Dangerously*" by Xavier Pons, in *Colonisations* (Toulouse), 1985; "Expanding Other-world: The Achievement of C.J. Koch" by Andrew Sant, in *The Age Monthly*

Review (Melbourne), June 1985; ''The Envenomed Dreams of C.J. Koch'' by Laurie Clancy, in *Island* (Hobart, Tasmania), Winter 1985.

C.J. Koch comments:

(1991) I began by writing verse, but gave my main attention to the novel from the age of 19. I believe that the novel can be a poetic vehicle, and that it has taken over the function of narrative poetry in this century. By this I do not mean that it uses the techniques of verse; nor do I mean that it can replace the lyric.

My first two novels were youthful and over-written. I have cut and revised both, and am now more satisfied with them. I don't expect to do this again, since I feel that I reached the stage of mastering my craft with *The Year of Living Dangerously.*

Two things preoccupy me as a novelist: the way in which many people search for a world just outside normal reality; and dualities: the dualities that run through both the human spirit and the world itself. It is the effort to reconcile these contradictions that makes for the pathos and drama I am interested in. Perhaps an Australian is attuned to duality more than some other writers, since he comes from a country born of Europe, but lying below Asia.

* * *

C. J. Koch (who originally signed himself Christopher Koch) had his first poem accepted when he was seventeen and began writing fiction in his teens. He wrote two novels but became silent until, at the age of forty, he left his senior position at the Australian Broadcasting Commission to devote himself full-time to writing. Since then he has established himself as one of Australia's leading novelists. Koch substantially revised his first two novels and published a fine book of essays, *Crossing the Gap*, which does much to illuminate his own art, but most importantly has produced several outstanding novels. His concerns in all his books remain remarkably consistent, as do the imagery and symbolism through which he explores them. He is preoccupied with the nature of reality and illusion and the relationship between them, and with the related question of whether it is not, after all, necessary to live by illusion if one is to live at all. Waking up and growing up are, for Koch's earlier and younger characters especially, conditions to be feared. Koch's concern also is with the flaws in his male protagonists that lead to their betrayal or near betrayal of the women with whom they become involved.

The Boys in the Island tells the story of a sensitive young boy through his school days and adolescence to his final, reluctant initiation into early manhood. Francis falls in love with a young girl who suddenly, heartbreakingly, abandons him. He fails his exams and travels from Tasmania to Melbourne, where he becomes involved in a meaningless life of petty crime. Then the suicide of a friend and his own near death in a car crash send him back to his home to reassess his life and accept unprotestingly ''the iron bonds of his imminent adulthood.'' Despite the familiarity of the material, Koch's keen ear for colloquial speech, sensuous command of natural detail, and understated prose give the novel a fresh and poignant flavor.

Across the Sea Wall opens with journalist Robert O'Brien looking back over an affair he had six years ago. Fleeing from marriage and the life of a staid suburbanite working for his future father-in-law, O'Brien and a childhood friend take a boat to Naples, Italy. En route he falls in love with Ilsa Kalnins, and they skip the boat at Ceylon. But eventually O'Brien discovers that he cannot accept the challenge of Ilsa's love or believe in its sincerity when confronted with the accusations that his friends bring against her, and he returns to Australia. Two years later she appears in Sydney and they make plans to marry, but once again O'Brien abandons her. The novel has many shrewd touches of characterization and the same sensitivity in dealing with the impact of love on the uninitiated, the failure of the males to respond adequately to its demands, that is a recurring them in Koch's work.

The Year of Living Dangerously is set in Indonesia in the last year of Sukarno's regime. The Sukarno of this novel is a man who seemed originally to embody the hopes and dreams of his people (including those of an Australian-Chinese dwarf named Billy Kwan who is in the country as a press photographer) but who has now lost himself in grandiose schemes and the pursuit of private gratification. A coup is being prepared against him, and it is this that provides the spectacular climax to the novel. Slowly, as Billy begins to see through Sukarno, his idealistic allegiance to and hope in a savior begin to switch towards Guy Hamilton, the journalist who has been sent out to replace Billy's previous boss. The novel is narrated by someone identified only as ''Cookie'' or by the initials he supplies to his occasional footnotes, R.J.C. Through the use of diaries, speaking through the voices of various characters, using purloined documents from Billy Kwan's private files, speculating and inventing when he cannot know for certain, the narrator builds up layer after layer of texture upon the basic structure of the narrative. At the end, Koch tries, unfashionably and audaciously, to suggest Hamilton's final redemption and capacity to love as he ascends into insight via partial blindness.

The central character in *The Doubleman* is Richard Miller, a thoughtful, complex man but an observer rather than a participant in life and a man who has developed a heavy psychological dependence on worlds of fantasy and illusion. Although barred from an active physical life, he is drawn towards his athletic cousin Brian Brady, who is both simpler and more adventurous than himself; such relationships are common in Koch's fiction. Miller leaves Tasmania and follows Brady and his friend Darcy Burr to the mainland, where he pursues a career as a radio actor and the other two form a musical group. When the three men come together again in Sydney, Miller is now a successful media producer; Burr, Brady, and eventually Miller's emigre wife Katrin form a folk group called Thomas and the Rymers; and it is inevitable that he will become entangled in the complex moral and ethical choices that confront Koch's protagonists sooner or later. As with the previous novel, comparisons with Graham Greene come to mind—the superb sense of place and atmosphere, the conviction of the ambiguous and double-edged nature of innocence—and in fact Greene expressed his admiration for it.

The locale of *Highways to a War* is Vietnam and then Cambodia (after a beautifully written section on Tasmania), but the period is the 1960s and 70s; again the confrontation is between an Australian innocent and a world of Asian complexity that leaves him vulnerable and bewildered. As presented by his friend Ray Barton, the protagonist Langford is a deeply romanticized character; he is even, if we are to believe the ending, a Christ figure who attracts his own Judas in the person of the secret operative Aubrey Hardwick. But he is also a man fatally in love with the past, and although it is not primarily his own fault, his relations with women are all doomed ones that he spends his life, unsuccessfully and in the end fatally, trying to keep alive.

As he did in *The Year of Living Dangerously*, Koch tells the story by adding layer upon layer, voice upon voice, so that the effect is of a kind of palimpsest that has been painted over repeatedly, with each portrait of the main character adding to or contradicting the ones previously offered. The effect is of a rich and multi-faceted tapestry of meanings that involve not just Langford himself but the history of the Vietnam War and of Asia during the bloody decade that the novel covers. The history of Langford being slowly sucked into the vortex of the war becomes a history of that decade and what Koch sees, even though he is careful not to take sides, as its betrayals.

There is a scene in *Highways to a War* in which two young boys break into a locked room and discover a portrait, a cache of letters, and two calfskin-covered notebooks. The portrait is of Irish patriot Robert Devereux, who was tried before a rigged jury and sentenced to exile for inciting rebellion against the English occupiers of Ireland in 1848. *Out of Ireland* purports to be a record of the contents of those diaries—Devereux's account of his three years in exile before escaping to America, as edited again by Ray Barton. In *Highways to a War* different people wrote the text that is put together by Barton. In *Out of Ireland*, however, the whole long novel is written in the voice of Devereux himself. That it succeeds is mainly because Koch is able to capture that voice—grave, measured, beautifully lucid—so well; he makes it consistent and plausible while varying it sufficiently to maintain interest.

Devereux is the charismatic head of the Young Irish movement, a brilliant writer and orator and potentially a leader of Ireland's rebellion against its oppressors. Barton says of Devereux that he ''stood on the brink of the modern world,'' and Koch seems to want to make him an avatar of historical change, the kind of change, he seems to imply, that is not always for good. The novel is set in 1848, that quintessentially revolutionary year in Europe, and yet for his fervor Devereux is at heart a conservative, even aristocratic, figure. He praises France as the capital of freedom and the new order yet at the same time argues that ''Socialism and feudalism are brothers under the skin.'' One suspects that Koch agrees. It was the French intellectual tradition , after all, that gave birth to and nurtured the terrible ideology of the Khmer Rouge.

At the same time Devereux is Prometheus—potential savior of mankind but now bound to a rock. And in one of Koch's favorite tropes he speaks of himself as a ''man of double nature.'' For all his genuine qualities there is something stiff-necked about him. As with many of Koch's protagonists, his insistence on standing on his dignity carries disastrous consequences for the woman he loves and very nearly for himself. *Out of Ireland* brings to its conclusion an impressive and formidable achievement. Although both *Out of Ireland* and *Highways to a War* are self-sufficient, when read together they illuminate one another more fully as commentaries on two crucial and interrelated periods of history.

—Laurie Clancy

KOGAWA, Joy

Nationality: Canadian. **Born:** Toronto, 6 June 1935. **Family:** Has one son and one daughter. **Awards:** Books in Canada First Novel award, 1981, Canadian Authors Association Book of the Year award, 1981, Before Columbus Foundation's American Book award, 1982, and American Library Association Notable Book award, 1982, all for *Obasan;* Ryerson Polytechnical Institute fellowship, 1991; Urban Alliance Race Relations award, 1994; Grace MacInnis Visiting Scholar award, 1995. D.L.: University of Lethbridge, 1991; Simon Fraser University, 1993. D.Litt: University of Guelph, 1992. **Member:** Officer, Order of Canada, 1986. **Address:** 447 Montrose Ave., Toronto, Ontario M6G 3H2, Canada; and 845 Semlin Dr., Vancouver, British Columbia V5l 4J6, Canada.

PUBLICATIONS

Novels

Obasan. Toronto, Dennys, 1981; New York, Anchor, 1994.
Itsuka. New York, Viking, 1992; revised edition, New York, Penguin, 1993.
The Rain Ascends. Toronto, Knopf Canada, 1995.

Poetry

The Splintered Moon. St. John, University of New Brunswick, 1967.
A Choice of Dreams. Toronto, McClelland and Stewart, 1974.
Jericho Road. Toronto, McClelland and Stewart, 1977.
Woman in the Woods. Oakville, Ontario, Mosiac Press, 1985.

Other

Naomi's Road (for children). Toronto, Oxford University Press, 1986.

*

Critical Studies: *Articulate Silences: Hisaye Yamamoto, Maxine Hong Kingston, Joy Kogawa* by King-Kok Chueng, Ithaca, Cornell University Press, 1993.

* * *

Joy Kogawa, after several collections of poetry, published her first novel, *Obasan,* in 1981. It and its sequel, *Itsuka,* written eleven years later, show Kogawa's poetic origins, as they are extremely lyrically written books. *Obasan* is the story of the internment of Japanese Canadians and Canadians of Japanese descent during World War II. In so doing, it is one of few fictional accounts of the North American treatment of ethnic Japanese during this period, others being Carlos Bulosan's *America is in the Heart* of 1943, John Okada's *No-No Boy,* written in 1957, Jean Wakatsuki Houston and Jones Houston's *Farewell to Manzanar* of 1974, and Maxine Hong Kingston's 1980 novel, *China Men.*

Obasan (''aunt'') is a unique and successful blending of the literary, the historical, and the autobiographical. Kogawa's novel is the account of two families' experiences told primarily from the point of view of Naomi Nakane, a schoolteacher in Alberta in 1972. The occasion of her uncle's death brings her brother (Stephen), her widowed aunt (Aya Obasan), and another aunt (Emily) together for the first time in years and precipitates a series of recollections and revelations about the war that begin when Naomi was about six (and Kogawa herself about seven). The war leads to the dissolution of Naomi's parents' families, the Nakanes and the Katos, and the seizure of their property. Naomi, her brother, father, aunt, and uncle are shunted progressively further east as the internment proceeds through and after the war, ending in Canada in 1949.

Obasan's narrative is essentially retrospective, a backward movement into Naomi's childhood seeded by a packet of materials given to her by her Aunt Emily. They lead to a series of memories of childhood as seen through the consciousness of the young Naomi, and shaped by the literary consciousness of Kogawa, who delineates a texture of symbols that become the personal metaphoric language of this book. Thus, a loaf of ''stone bread'' baked by her uncle just before his death becomes a symbol of a Eucharistic sort as it is eaten by his grieving relatives. It also serves as a symbol of the Japanese exile to the prairies as it is connected to the manna of Moses' people in Egypt in *Obasan*'s epigraph. Kogawa develops a rich texture of personal and biblical symbolism throughout to reinforce her themes.

The novel moves into the present gradually, and the past and present are linked in the import of some documentary materials which have been kept from Naomi and Stephen until their adulthood. Naomi, who has grown up with a mixture of puzzlement and misplaced guilt about the failure of her mother to return from Japan, is eventually initiated into the horrors of her death in the atomic bombing at Nagasaki through a letter from the distant past.

This news breaks the silence of the past in *Obasan,* and begins the process of final healing. Aunt Emily, a fully Canadianized ''word warrior'' who crusades for publicity or compensation in the Japanese cause, and Aya Obasan, Naomi's ancient aunt who still has only rudimentary English after spending most of her life in Canada, seem diametrically opposed in their cultural adaptations. Secretiveness about the fate of Naomi and Stephen's mother is perhaps the only thing they have in common. Yet this novel does not attempt to dichotomize attitudes to silence into ''good'' or ''bad,'' and itself negotiates the fine line between telling the past and giving the present room to grow. *Obasan* explores language, euphemism, and silence; traces the ties of the self to family and place; and initiates the process of healing.

Itsuka (''someday'') resumes Naomi's story in Toronto in 1983, and traces her involvement in the Japanese-Canadian fight for redress for the internment, as Joy Kogawa was herself involved. The novel, like *Obasan,* is simultaneously mixed-up in both the personal and the political, but in *Itsuka* the sharp line that Naomi has tried to maintain between the two in her life becomes blurred. *Itsuka* also shows Naomi's personal development in her tentative romance with Cedric, a priest involved in her political world.

In *Itsuka,* Kogawa tells a story well worth telling, but perhaps not so successfully fictionalized. At many points the narrative verges on the didactic, and the psychology of Naomi remains static and somewhat tangential to the politics of the tale she narrates.

—Ron Jenkins

KOPS, Bernard

Nationality: British. **Born:** London, 28 November 1926. **Education:** Attended London elementary schools to age 13. **Family:** Married Erica Gordon in 1956; four children. **Career:** Has worked as a docker, chef, salesman, waiter, lift man, and barrow boy; writer-in-residence, London Borough of Hounslow, 1980–82; lecturer in Drama, Spiro Institute, 1985–86, Surrey, Ealing, and Inner London education authorities, 1989–90, and City Literary Institute, London, 1991. **Awards:** Arts Council bursary, 1957, 1979, 1985, 1990, 1991; C. Day Lewis fellowship, 1981–83. **Agent:** John Rush, Sheil Land Associates, 43 Doughty St., London WC1N 2LF, England. **Address:** 35 Canfield Gardens, Flat 1, London N.W.6, England.

Publications

Novels

Awake for Mourning. London, MacGibbon and Kee, 1958.
Motorbike. London, New English Library, 1962.
Yes from No-Man's Land. London, MacGibbon and Kee, 1965; New York, Coward McCann, 1966.
The Dissent of Dominick Shapiro. London, MacGibbon and Kee, 1966; New York, Coward McCann, 1967.
By the Waters of Whitechapel. London, Bodley Head, 1969; New York, Norton, 1970.
The Passionate Past of Gloria Gaye. London, Secker and Warburg, 1971; New York, Norton, 1972.
Settle Down Simon Katz. London, Secker and Warburg, 1973.
Partners. London, Secker and Warburg, 1975.
On Margate Sands. London, Secker and Warburg, 1978.

Plays

The Hamlet of Stepney Green (produced Oxford, London, and New York, 1958). London, Evans, 1959.
Goodbye World (produced Guildford, Surrey, 1959).
Change for the Angel (produced London, 1960).
The Dream of Peter Mann (produced Edinburgh, 1960). London, Penguin, 1960.
Stray Cats and Empty Bottles (produced Cambridge, 1961; London, 1967).
Enter Solly Gold, music by Stanley Myers (produced Wellingborough, Northamptonshire, and Los Angeles, 1962; London, 1970). Published in *Satan, Socialites, and Solly Gold: Three New Plays from England,* New York, Coward McCann, 1961; in *Four Plays,* 1964.
Home Sweet Honeycomb (broadcast 1962). Included in *Four Plays,* 1964.
The Lemmings (broadcast 1963). Included in *Four Plays,* 1964.
Four Plays (includes *The Hamlet of Stepney Green, Enter Solly Gold, Home Sweet Honeycomb, The Lemmings*). London, MacGibbon and Kee, 1964.
The Boy Who Wouldn't Play Jesus (for children; produced London, 1965). Published in *Eight Plays: Book 1,* edited by Malcolm Stuart Fellows, London, Cassell, 1965.
David, It Is Getting Dark (produced Rennes, France, 1970). Paris, Gallimard, 1970.
It's a Lovely Day Tomorrow, with John Goldschmidt (televised 1975; produced London, 1976).
More Out Than In (produced on tour and London, 1980).
Ezra (produced London, 1981).
Simon at Midnight (broadcast 1982; produced London, 1985).
Some of These Days (produced London, 1990).
Sophie! Last of the Red Hot Mamas (produced London, 1990).
Dreams of Anne Frank (produced London, 1993).
Who Shall I Be Tomorrow (produced London, 1993).
Playing Sinatra (produced London, 1993).
Call in the Night (produced West Yorkshire, 1995).
Golem (produced London, 1995).

Radio Plays: *Home Sweet Honeycomb,* 1962; *The Lemmings,* 1963; *Born in Israel,* 1963; *The Dark Ages,* 1964; *Israel: The Immigrant,* 1964; *Bournemouth Nights,* 1979; *I Grow Old, I Grow Old,* 1979; *Over the Rainbow,* 1980; *Simon at Midnight,* 1982; *Trotsky Was My Father,* 1984; *Kafe Kropotkin,* 1988; *Colour Blind,* 1989; *Congress in Manchester,* 1990; *The Ghost Child,* 1991; *Soho Nights,* 1991; *Sailing with Homer,* 1994; *Protocols of Fire,* 1995.

Television Plays: *I Want to Go Home,* 1963; *The Lost Years of Brian Hooper,* 1967; *Alexander the Greatest,* 1971; *Just One Kid,* 1974; *Why the Geese Shrieked* and *The Boy Philosopher,* from stories by Isaac Bashevis Singer, 1974; *It's a Lovely Day Tomorrow,* with John Goldschmidt, 1975; *Moss,* 1975; *Rocky Marciano Is Dead,* 1976; *Night Kids,* 1983; *The Survivor,* serial, 1991–92.

Poetry

Poems. London, Bell and Baker Press, 1955.
Poems and Songs. Northwood, Middlesex, Scorpion Press, 1958.
An Anemone for Antigone. Lowestoft, Suffolk, Scorpion Press, 1959.
Erica, I Want to Read You Something. Lowestoft, Suffolk, Scorpion Press, and New York, Walker, 1967.
For the Record. London, Secker and Warburg, 1971.
Barricades in West Hampstead. London, Hearing Eye, 1988.

Other

The World Is a Wedding (autobiography). London, MacGibbon and Kee, 1963; New York, Coward McCann, 1964.
Neither Your Honey nor Your Sting: An Offbeat History of the Jews. London, Robson, 1985.
Editor, *Poetry Hounslow.* London, Hounslow Civic Centre, 1981.

*

Manuscript Collections: University of Texas, Austin; Indiana University, Bloomington.

Critical Studies: By Colin MacInnes, in *Encounter* (London), May 1960; ''The Kitchen Sink'' by G. Wilson Knight, in *Encounter* (London), December 1963; ''Deep Waters of Whitechapel'' by Nina Sutton, in *The Guardian* (London), 6 September 1969.

* * *

The novels of Bernard Kops are an extension of his work as poet and playwright. His prose is rhythmic, almost ritualistic, and his plots unfold through dialogue. He is concerned with Jewishness, with the Jew as outsider to the world at large, and as a trapped insider in the claustrophobic atmosphere of the tightly knit Jewish family in which a child can find it almost impossible to grow up. So sixteen-year-old Dominick in *The Dissent of Dominick Shapiro* is driven to run away from home and join a collection of drop-outs protesting against established society; and in *By the Waters of Whitechapel* Aubrey, at thirty-five, can only free himself from his financial and emotional dependency on his mother by indulging in far-fetched fantasies of a prospective career which will bring him wealth and fame.

These goals have indeed been realized by the successful Jewish businessman, Daniel Klayman, in *Partners,* but his achievement leads him to madness. At the very height of his powers, while the house-warming celebrations for his new St. John's Wood home are in progress, he goes crazy. Lionel is his partner in lunacy, a projected *doppelgänger,* who pushes him into killing his new neighbor's dog, and which eventually engineers the situation which makes him responsible for the death of his beloved son, Zachary. Until that moment, despite the disastrous party, Daniel manages to disguise his madness by running away from his wife and family, and by pretending that Lionel is a real person, who is going to become a partner in his business and so relieve him of the stress and strain which has caused his strange behavior.

The lengths that the mad will go to in attempts to hide their condition is the theme of Kops's most mature novel, *On Margate Sands.* Here he abandons his Jewish concern for one which affects the whole of society, and which is even more urgent in Britain now than it was when this novel was published. He wrote his study of five former patients of a psychiatric hospital in the light of the 1975 Parliamentary White Paper on the revised services to the mentally ill as a result of new drug treatments. Because their sickness can be more or less controlled by ''Happy tabs'' as their warden landlady calls them, Brian, Larry, Dolores, Buzz, and Michelle can exist in sheltered accommodation outside the hospital.

On Margate Sands should be compulsory reading for any planners concerned with the present widespread closure of psychiatric hospitals, who still believe that ''Community care'' is anything more than a socially acceptable phrase. Kops's confused characters experience the reality of being ''post-mad'' in a society that is both fearful and uncaring. The owners of the run-down seaside hotel in which they are housed are clearly on to a money-making enterprise, squeezing their sick lodgers into cramped rooms, and kicking them out of the house during the daylight hours. The five of them walk the streets and lounge on the beach, and the ''pre-mad'' citizens of Margate and the frenzied holidaymakers do their best to ignore them.

Yet this is not simply a novel of social concern. It is one which could only have been written by a poet, for it demands that the reader experience the simultaneous levels of rational thought and irrational emotional response that lead to the bizarre and anti-social behavior of the insane. Like most of Kops's characters, Brian, the most integrated of the quintet, is a middle-aged man still in thrall to his parents, even though they are long dead. His emotional life stopped at the age of seven; and although he is both intellectually aware and well read (the novel's title comes from a quotation from T.S. Eliot with which he is familiar—''On Margate Sands/I can connect/Nothing with nothing'') he is incapable of controlling the violent impulses that push him back into his past. Yet he is capable of a real, non-sexual affection for the adolescent boy, Buzz, and is seriously concerned when the lad runs off with a group of drop-outs, who can be compared with the hippies that Dominick linked up with in the previous novel. In Brian's estimation, and in that of his creator, the Alternative Society offers its ''ragged and self-indulgent'' adherents a life that is no better than the killing waste of time experienced by former psychiatric patients at the mercy of the community.

Despite his wretched and crazy behavior, Brian has courage, determination and an ability to appreciate reality and the cruelty of the machine age. In a lyrical, rural passage, the old man Larry recalls family holidays in the Kent hop fields; so all five go off in search of the farm where he spent those childhood, summer days. Of course it has been mechanized, and this abrupt encounter with present reality is the fulcrum of the novel. His companions return to Margate, but Brian goes off on his own, tablet-less, on a quest for his lost sister and a sane and normal life. It cannot be achieved. In a state far worse than the one in which he set out he returns to Margate beach. His story of tragic waste is repeated in thousands of case studies, but it takes a poet to enable the ''pre-mad'' to enter the turbulent, sad world of the ''post-mad.''

—Shirley Toulson

KOTZWINKLE, William

Nationality: American. **Born:** Scranton, Pennsylvania, 22 November 1938. **Education:** Attended Rider College and Pennsylvania State University. **Family:** Married Elizabeth Gundy in 1970. **Career:** Worked as a short order cook and editor/writer in the 1960s; full time writer, 1960s—. **Awards:** National Magazine awards for fiction, 1972, 1975; O'Henry prize, 1975; World Fantasy Award for best novel, 1977; North Dakota Children's Choice Award, 1983; Buckeye Award, 1984. **Address:** c/o David R. Godine, Inc., Horticultural Hall, 300 Massachusetts Avenue, Boston, Massachusetts 02115, U.S.A.

Publications

Novels

Hermes 3000 (science fiction). New York, Pantheon, 1972.
The Fan Man, drawings by Keith Bendis. New York, Avon, 1974.
Night-Book. New York, Avon, 1974.
Swimmer in the Secret Sea. New York, Avon, 1975.
Doctor Rat (science fiction). New York, Knopf, 1976.
Fata Morgana. New York, Knopf, 1977.
Herr Nightingale and the Satin Woman. New York, Knopf, 1978.
Jack in the Box. New York, Putnam, 1980; published as *Book of Love.* Boston, Houghton Mifflin, 1990.
Christmas at Fontaine's, illustrations by Joe Servello. New York, Putnam, 1982.
E.T., the Extra-Terrestrial Storybook (juvenile, novelization of screenplay by Melissa Mathison). New York, Putnam, 1982.
Superman III (novelization of screenplay by David and Leslie Newman). New York, Warner, 1983.
Queen of Swords, illustrations by Joe Servello. New York, Putnam, 1983.
E.T., the Storybook of the Green Planet: A New Storybook (juvenile, based on story by Steven Spielberg), illustrations by David Wiesner. New York, Putnam, 1985.
The Exile. New York, Dutton/Lawrence, 1987.
The Midnight Examiner. Boston, Houghton Mifflin, 1989.
Hot Jazz Trio, illustrations by Joe Servello. Boston, Houghton Mifflin, 1989.
The Game of Thirty. Boston, Houghton Mifflin, 1994.
The Bear Went over the Mountain. New York, Doubleday, 1996.

Fiction (for children)

The Fireman. New York, Pantheon, 1969.
The Ship That Came Down the Gutter. New York, Pantheon, 1970.
Elephant Boy: A Story of the Stone Age. New York, Farrar, Straus, 1970.
The Day the Gang Got Rich. New York, Viking, 1970.
The Return of Crazy Horse. New York, Farrar, Straus, 1971.
The Supreme, Superb, Exalted, and Delightful, One and Only Magic Building. New York, Farrar, Straus, 1973.
Up the Alley with Jack and Joe. New York, Macmillan, 1974.
The Leopard's Tooth. New York, Seabury Press, 1976.
The Ants Who Took Away Time. New York, Doubleday, 1978.
Dream of Dark Harbor. New York, Doubleday, 1979.
The Nap Master. New York, Harcourt, 1979.
The World Is Big and I'm So Small, illustrations by Joe Servello. Crown, 1986.
The Empty Notebook, illustrations by Joe Servello. Boston, Godine, 1990.
The Million Dollar Bear, illustrations by David Catrow. New York, Random House, 1994.

Short Stories

Elephant Bangs Train. New York, Pantheon, 1971.
The Oldest Man, and Other Timeless Stories (juvenile). New York, Pantheon, 1971.
Trouble in Bugland: A Collection of Inspector Mantis Mysteries (juvenile), illustrations by Joe Servello. Boston, Godine, 1983.
Jewel of the Moon. New York, Putnam, 1985.
Hearts of Wood, and Other Timeless Tales (juvenile), illustrations by Joe Servello. Boston, Godine, 1986.
Tales from the Empty Notebook (juvenile), illustrations by Joe Servello. New York, Marlow, 1996.

Poetry

Great World Circus (juvenile), illustrations by Joe Servello. New York, Putnam, 1983.
Seduction in Berlin, illustrations by Joe Servello. New York, Putnam, 1985.

Other

The Dream Master (with Brian Helgeland), based on characters created by Wes Craven, adapted by Bob Italia. Edina, Minnesota, Abdo & Daughters, 1992.

* * *

William Kotzwinkle is an accomplished author who is best known for his book of the film *E.T.: The Extra-Terrestrial*, but who has produced a range of work for both adults and children that often transgresses genre boundaries and the distinction between serious and popular fiction. His key theme is the conflict between materialism and spiritual awareness, a conflict that he sometimes explores through fantasy and sometimes through satire. Beginning as a children's writer with *The Fireman*, he then published novels for adults such as *Hermes 3000*, *The Fan Man*, and *Queen of Swords*, which began to establish him as an original and distinctive novelist and won him praise from, for example, Kurt Vonnegut. But it was *Doctor Rat* that made his reputation as a powerful fantasy writer with a sharp satirical edge. The novel focuses upon laboratory rats whose spokesman, the Doctor Rat of the title, eventually escapes from the vast laboratory where experiments on his fellow-creatures are taking place, and whose adventures are interwoven with shorter tales told by animals of different kinds who finally try to form a whole that will make humans more peaceful and benign. But they are all killed.

Parallel, intersecting worlds are a favorite theme of Kotzwinkle's, and his most remarkable novel in this respect is *Fata Morgana*. Starting in Paris in 1861, and structured around three Tarot cards—The Fool, the Valet of Coins, and the Magician—it combines elements of fantasy and of the detective story. The tale traces the quest of a case-hardened French detective, Inspector Picard, to expose the truth about Ric Lazare, a dazzling magician whom Picard believes to be a fake and a killer. Picard's journey across Europe to probe the magician's past takes him into the beds of beautiful women and into strange worlds in which reality and illusion merge. He finally reaches the powerful and threatening Fata Morgana, but the difference between illusion and reality remains uncertain at the end of the novel. Further novels of Kotzwinkle's that combine detection with fantasy and the supernatural include *Herr Nightingale and the Satin Woman* and *The Midnight Examiner*.

Among Kotzwinkle's other notable novels are *The Exile*, in which a movie star is trapped in the body of a World War II German gangster who is eventually tortured by the Gestapo, and *The Game of Thirty*, in which a game that survives from ancient Egypt is played out again on the streets of modern New York. New York is also the setting for much of *The Bear Went over the Mountain*, an engaging animal fantasy for adults and a hilarious satire on literary and media success in the modern world. A large black bear, finding a manuscript written and abandoned by a literary academic under a tree, reads it because he cannot eat it, and, styling himself Hal Jam—his favorite food—he goes to New York and is taken up as a writer who might possibly be the next Hemingway. When the literary academic sues him for stealing his novel, the bear wins the case and his literary standing is assured.

Kotzwinkle's ability to write in a variety of genres and to combine elements of those genres in specific works has made him difficult to classify, while his willingness to produce film tie-ins in the 1980s has sometimes given the impression that he is solely a commercial writer. But in his best work, such as *Fata Morgana* and *The Bear Went over the Mountain*, there can be no doubt of his narrative skills and his capacity to produce both suggestive fantasy and shrewd satire that is engaging and penetrating. This has won him a devoted following, but his most substantial fiction merits a wider readership and a more detailed critical examination than it has so far received.

—Nicolas Tredell

KROETSCH, Robert (Paul)

Nationality: Canadian. **Born:** Heisler, Alberta, 26 June 1927. **Education:** Schools in Heisler and Red Deer, Alberta; University of Alberta, Edmonton, B.A. 1948; McGill University, Montreal, 1954–55; Middlebury College, Vermont, M.A. 1956; University of Iowa, Iowa City, Ph.D. 1961. **Family:** Married 1) Mary Jane Lewis in 1956 (divorced 1979), two daughters; 2) Smaro Kamboureli in 1982. **Career:** Laborer and purser, Yellowknife Transportation Company, Northwest Territories, 1948–50; information specialist (civilian), United States Air Force Base, Goose Bay, Labrador, 1951–54; assistant professor, 1961–65, associate professor, 1965–68, and professor of English, 1968–78, State University of New York, Binghamton. Professor of English, 1978–85, and since 1985 Distinguished Professor, University of Manitoba, Winnipeg. Artist-in-residence, Calgary University, Alberta, Fall 1975, University of Lethbridge, Alberta, Spring 1976, and University of Manitoba, 1976–78. Co-founder, *Boundary 2* magazine, Binghamton, 1972. **Awards:** Bread Loaf Writers Conference grant, 1966; Governor-General's award, 1970; Killam award, 1986. Fellow, Royal Society of Canada, 1986. **Agent:** Sterling Lord, 10 St. Mary Street, Suite 510, Toronto M4Y 1P9. **Address:** Department of English, University of Manitoba, Winnipeg, Manitoba R3T 2N2, Canada.

Publications

Novels

But We Are Exiles. Toronto, Macmillan, 1965; London, Macmillan, and New York, St. Martin's Press, 1966.
The Words of My Roaring. Toronto and London, Macmillan, and New York, St. Martin's Press, 1966.
The Studhorse Man. Toronto, Macmillan, and London, Macdonald, 1969; New York, Simon and Schuster, 1970.
Gone Indian. Toronto, New Press, 1973.
Badlands. Toronto, New Press, 1975; New York, Beaufort, 1983.
What the Crow Said. Toronto, General, 1978.
Alibi. Toronto, Stoddart, and New York, Beaufort, 1983.
The Puppeteer. Toronto, Random House, 1993.
The Man from the Creeks. Toronto, Random House of Canada, 1998.

Plays

The Studhorse Man, adaptation of his own novel (produced Toronto, 1981).

Poetry

The Stone Hammer: Poems 1960–1975. Nanaimo, British Columbia, Oolichan, 1975.
The Ledger. London, Ontario, Applegarth Follies, 1975.
Seed Catalogue. Winnipeg, Turnstone Press, 1977.
The Sad Phoenician. Toronto, Coach House Press, 1979.
The Criminal Intensities of Love as Paradise. Lantzville, British Columbia, Oolichan, 1981.
Field Notes: Collected Poems. Toronto, General, and New York, Beaufort, 1981.
Advice to My Friends. Toronto, Stoddart, 1985.
Excerpts from the Real World: A Prose Poem in Ten Parts. Lantzville, British Columbia, Oolichan, 1986.
Completed Field Notes: The Long Poems of Robert Kroetsch. Toronto, McClelland and Stewart, 1989.

Other

Alberta. Toronto, Macmillan, and New York, St. Martin's Press, 1968.
The Crow Journals. Edmonton, Alberta, NeWest Press, 1980.
Labyrinths of Voice: Conversations with Robert Kroetsch, with Shirley Neuman and Robert Wilson. Edmonton, Alberta, NeWest Press, 1982.

Letter to Salonika. Toronto, Grand Union, 1983.
The Lovely Treachery of Words: Essays Selected and New. Toronto, Oxford University Press, 1989.
A Likely Story: The Writing Life. Red Deer, Alberta, Red Deer College Press, 1995.
Editor, with James Bacque and Pierre Gravel, *Creation* (interviews). Toronto, New Press, 1970.
Editor, *Sundogs: Stories from Saskatchewan.* Moose Jaw, Saskatchewan, Thunder Creek, 1980.
Editor, with Smaro Kamboureli, *Visible Visions: The Selected Poems of Douglas Barbour.* Edmonton, Alberta, NeWest Press, 1984.
Editor, with Reingard M. Nischik, *Gaining Ground: European Critics on Canadian Literature.* Edmonton, Alberta, NeWest Press, 1985.

*

Bibliographies: ''An Annotated Bibliography of Works by and about Robert Kroetsch'' by Robert Lecker, in *Essays on Canadian Writing* (Toronto), Fall 1977.

Manuscript Collections: University of Calgary Library, Alberta.

Critical Studies: *Robert Kroetsch* by Peter Thomas, Vancouver, Douglas and McIntyre, 1980; ''Robert Kroetsch Issue'' of *Open Letter* (Toronto), Spring 1983 and Summer-Fall 1984; *Robert Kroetsch* by Robert Lecker, Boston, Twayne, 1986; *The Old Dualities: Deconstructing Robert Kroetsch and His Critics* by Dianne Tiefensee. Montreal and Buffalo, New York, McGill-Queen's University Press, 1994; *Ledger Domain: An Anthology for Robert Kroetsch,* edited by Charlene Diehl-Jones and Gary Draper. Stratford, Ontario, Trout Lily Press, 1997.

Robert Kroetsch comments:

(1991) My novels, often set on the open plains and in the new cities of the Canadian West, border on the comic and hint of the bawdy. The critic Linda Hutcheon has called me the champion of postmodern in Canada because of the experimental nature of my work. I think of myself as a storyteller trying to tell stories amidst the radical discontinuities of contemporary life.

* * *

Robert Kroetsch has been viewed as the father of Canadian postmodernism, and the novels that he has published over a period of more than thirty years explore issues of Canadian identity in a range of non-realistic modes. They have been accompanied by several volumes of self-reflexive poetic and prose autobiography and numerous theoretical essays, which, like his fiction, address ways in which notions of self, region, gender, genre, and nation are constructed. Kroetsch's work is centrally concerned with ''the anxiety of influence,'' and he has habitually avoided historiographical accounts of the traditions that have shaped writers and cultures in favour of a Foucault-like archaeological mode of investigation, which suggests that texts contain multiple layers from earlier texts and that, however deeply one digs, it is finally impossible to arrive at an original source-narrative.

Throughout his career Kroetsch has drawn on a broad range of cultural intertexts ranging from Greek myths and eighteenth-century English novels to western Canadian oral tales and the mythologies of the Blackfoot and Cree nations. Oral elements are prominent in all his fiction, particularly in his magic-realist version of an Albertan tall tale, *What the Crow Said*, and his 1998 novel, *The Man from the Creeks*, which takes its initial inspiration from Robert Service's gold rush ballad, ''The Shooting of Dan McGrew.'' Kroetsch's sceptical, postmodernist approach to his influences characteristically leads to their being reworked as pastiche or even parody. Nevertheless, his fiction engages with the politics of particular regional and cultural issues to a greater extent than that of many of his American postmodernist contemporaries.

Kroetsch was born in Alberta and is first and foremost a prairie writer, committed to realizing a sense of the distinctiveness of western Canadian experience, while turning away from the primarily realistic narrative modes of such precursors in the Canadian prairie novel as Sinclair Ross and W. O. Mitchell. He has written of the problem of establishing ''any sort of close relationship in a landscape ... whose primary characteristic is distance,'' and his fictional practice is similarly concerned with the difficulties of encapsulating a sense of prairie experience within the closed form of the book. For the most part he has confronted this difficulty through the use of quest narratives. *The Studhorse Man* employs a comic analogy with *The Odyssey*, as the eponymous hero, Hazard Lepage, tramps the prairies in search of a mare for his stallion to ''cover,'' so that the breed and his occupation may be preserved. Meanwhile, the narrator of the novel, Demeter Proudfoot, a Swiftian ''madman'' writing naked in a bathtub, embarks on his own abortive quest, as he struggles to write the definitive biography of Hazard, only to find his Boswellian endeavours culminating in a story that has more affinity with Sterne's *Tristram Shandy*. In *Gone Indian*, an American graduate student, attempting to write a thesis on the origins of the archetypal westward journey exemplified by Columbus's voyages, travels to Alberta and finds himself caught up in a carnivalesque, northwestern version of the quest for new beginnings. *Badlands* moves between two, interlocking quest narratives: a third-person tale about a 1916 archaeological expedition hunting for dinosaur bones, symbolic on one level of the search for a prehistoric source, and a first-person account of the expedition leader's daughter's attempt to retrace her father's footsteps, and through so doing liberate herself from paternal influence, in 1972. The protagonist in *Alibi* is initiated into a similar quest for an originary source, when, at the outset of the novel, his mysterious employer instructs him to find a spa.

In Kroetsch's first two novels, *But We Are Exiles* and *The Words of My Roaring*, the quest patterns demonstrate the influence of the myth criticism that was highly influential in academic circles in the 1950s and 1960s. Both novels are focused on conflicts between an older and a younger man, Freudian struggles that reflect Kroetsch's belief that the storyteller has to find ways of rejecting the authority of the previous generation. They also employ classic mythic elements, such as the doppelgänger motif, the scapegoat figure, and the cyclic continuity of death and rebirth. They foreshadow Kroetsch's subsequent attempts to evolve a distinctive Canadian fictional practice, but provide little indication of the formal innovation that would characterize his subsequent fiction.

With *The Studhorse Man*, Kroetsch discovered the fictional terrain for which he is best known. Built around lacunae, digressions, and narrative unreliability, it is his first major statement, written in a postmodernist mode, on the problematics of writing about the Canadian West. Demeter's attempt to record the life of Hazard, a latter-day Odysseus whose comic misadventures mainly take the form of being lured into sexual liaisons with a series of women, may initially seem to celebrate western macho values—and it *is* possible to read the novel as an elegy for the passing away of older male myths—but it becomes increasingly clear that Hazard's biography, as narrated by the ambivalently named Demeter (the cult of Demeter and Persephone is a myth of seasonal rebirth centered on *female* genealogies), interrogates popular western male mythologies. The novel moves towards an androgynous conclusion, having along the way also redefined relationships between the Canadian West and East and the western vernacular and literary discourse. In *Gone Indian* the American narrator, Jeremy Sadness, travels to Edmonton for an academic interview, only to find himself confronted by the possibility of transforming his identity when he discovers that he has someone else's suitcase. Prior to his journey he has had frontier fantasies, centered on Grey Owl, the English-born fake Indian, Archie Belaney. Now he is able to effect a similar transformation in his own identity in the ambience of a rural winter carnival. In this novel Kroetsch's absorption with theory manifests itself in an obvious indebtedness to Bakhtin's writing on the carnivalesque, but once again this is translated into a vividly realized comic fable that is firmly located within the Canadian West.

Badlands also initially appears to be a male quest novel. The members of the archaeological expedition undertake a quest for origins that draws on Conrad's *Heart of Darkness* and various classical accounts of descents into the underworld. However, the male story is framed and punctuated by the comments of the contemporary female narrator, who suggests the futility of male adventuring. In the text's present, she journeys west, as her father has done before her, refusing to play the role of a waiting Penelope in the settled eastern environment of Georgian Bay. On one level, the novel belongs very obviously to the feminist climate of the period in which it was published, the 1970s, and its account of a journey into "prehistory" is reminiscent of Margaret Atwood's *Surfacing*. On another level, through the use of its two narrative voices, it engages in a more dialectical debate about gender mythologies.

What the Crow Said is in many ways the strangest of all Kroetsch's western fables. It begins with a scene in which a young Albertan woman is impregnated by a swarm of bees, and the tall tale continues in this vein, relating a series of interconnected events that have more in common with Greek myth than the kind of action normally associated with the novel form. The story proceeds at breakneck pace, so that this comparatively short novel contains as much action as an epic. At the same time it demonstrates an obvious indebtedness to Gabriel Garcia Marquez, once again implicitly suggesting the need to explore and develop new conventions in order to evolve a fictional practice that can respond to the problematics of prairie "realities," seen here to be every bit as fantastic as those of Latin American "marvelous realism."

Kroetsch's quest for new forms takes a different turn again in *Alibi* and its companion-piece, *The Puppeteer*, in both of which notions of identity are radically unsettled, with Kroetsch exploring Lacanian themes of desire and concealment in elliptical texts that, despite their theoretical density, move with the swiftness and economy of a Hitchcock thriller. In *The Man from the Creeks*, Kroetsch tells a tale of the gold rush that once again sees the North as the last frontier. Ostensibly the narrative mode is more realistic than that of most of Kroetsch's fiction, and the ingenuous first-person narrator employs an oral register that has more in common with Kroetsch's first novels than his other more recent fiction. However, the Robert Service intertext is a highly self-conscious use of a literary source and foregrounds the extent to which the novel is mediating between a literary construction of an experience and other possible versions. While it can be seen to mark a partial retreat from fabulation and postmodernism, it is nevertheless typical of all Kroetsch's fiction in that its metaliterary elements emanate from a compelling narrative that makes extensive use of oral idioms.

—John Thieme

KUREISHI, Hanif

Nationality: British. **Born:** Bromley, England, 5 December 1954. **Education:** King's College, London, B.A. **Career:** Film director, playwright, screenwriter, novelist; writer-in-residence, 1981 and 1985–86, Royal Court Theatre, London. **Awards:** Themes Television Playwright award, 1980, for *The Mother Country;* George Devine award, 1981; *Evening Standard* award, 1985, for screenplay; Rotterdam Festival's Most Popular Film award, New York Film Critics' Circle Best Screenplay award, and National Society of Film Critics' Best Screenplay award, all 1986, all for *My Beautiful Launderette;* Whitbread book of the Year award, and Booksellers Association of Great Britain and Ireland first novel category, both 1990, both for *The Buddha of Suburbia.* **Agent:** Sheila Lemon, Lemon and Durbridge Ltd., 24 Pottery Lane, London W11 4 LZ, England.

Publications

Novels

The Buddha of Suburbia. London, Faber, and New York, Viking, 1990.
The Black Album. London, Faber, 1995.
Love in a Blue Time. New York, Scribner, 1997.
Intimacy. New York, Scribner, 1999.

Short Stories

Midnight All Day. London, Faber, 1999.

Plays

Soaking Up the Heat (produced London, 1976).
The Mother Country (produced London, 1980).
The King and Me (produced London, 1980).
Borderline (produced London, 1981). London, Metheun, 1981.
Cinders, adaptation of a play by Janusz Glowacki (produced London, 1981).
Tomorrow—Today! (produced London, 1981).
Birds of Passage (produced London, 1983). London, Amber Lane, 1983.
Outskirts, The King and Me, Tomorrow—Today! London, River Run Press, 1983.
Mother Courage, adaptation of a play by Bertold Brecht (produced London, 1984).
Sleep with Me. London and New York, Faber, 1999.

Screenplays: *My Beautiful Launderette,* 1985; published with other works as *My Beautiful Laundrette and Other Writings,* London, Faber and Faber, 1996; *Sammy and Rosie Get Laid,* 1987.

Radio Plays: *You Can't Go Home,* 1980; *The Trial,* adaptation the novel by Franz Kafka, 1982.

Other

Editor, with Jon Savage, *The Faber Book of Pop*. London and Boston, Faber and Faber, 1995.

*

Critical Studies: *Hanif Kureishi: Postcolonial Storyteller* by Kenneth C. Kaleta. Austin, University of Texas Press, 1998.

* * *

Hanif Kureishi's fiction is a conglomeration of influences; youth culture, the British Asian experience, sexuality and experimentation, politics and resistance. *The Buddha of Suburbia* and *The Black Album*, in including these influences, make a political aesthetic of their interaction. The ironies of adolescence explored in *The Buddha of Suburbia* depend on the ability of the reader to see wry and sly humour in the meeting of unstable cultural entities; but more significantly Kureishi's version of British Asian identity insists on critiquing the reification of that identity, and implies a necessary and layered complexity in the politics of identity in general. For this reason, Kureishi's novels make him an extraordinarily perceptive commentator on the complexities of post-coloniality and immigrant experiences, a perception that he has applied to the status of Asian identity in the widest contexts of post-1960s Britain.

The Buddha of Suburbia, Kureishi's first novel, opens with an uncovering of the ''Indianness'' and Englishness of the adolescent Karim. Karim asserts his right to describe himself as an ''Englishman,'' but this soon becomes qualified (''a funny sort of Englishman'') and then shifts to a discussion of ''the odd mixture of continents and blood, of here and there, of belonging and not belonging, that makes me so restless and easily bored.'' Already established then is the assumption that the novel will examine this movement from cultural fixity to flux and that the ability to recognize the constituent parts of the result of these changes is a vital outcome in itself. *The Buddha of Suburbia* begins from a similar position to that described autobiographically by Kureishi in ''The Rainbow Sign'' (published with the script of *My Beautiful Laundrette* in 1986): ''From the start I tried to deny my Pakistani self. I was ashamed. It was a curse and I wanted to be rid of it. I wanted to be like everyone else.'' *The Buddha* has a narrative starting point in which Karim and his father Haroon are archetypally ''like everyone else''—Haroon is the perfect civil servant, Karim behaves like the typical adolescent. Yet the novel is spurred by the events that begin to transform both characters, as Haroon adopts a comically (but never entirely ridiculed) Buddhist personality while Karim develops along the unpredictable cultural and sexual trajectories of teenage life.

The Buddha of Suburbia opens up these moments of stasis. Its narrative progresses almost without the participation of its main characters; their lives are affected by perceptions of their identity constructed by those around them, and Kureishi continually emphasizes the importance of particular versions of being Indian/Muslim that resurface. *The Buddha*, for example, is scathing in its satire of the apparently well-intentioned liberal/left in Britain and its over-indulgence in the ''East'' as a site of mysticism and spirituality. Indeed most of the humor associated with Haroon in the novel depends on the discrepancy between his Islamic roots and his newfound Buddhism. Edward Said's notion that the West constructs a monolithic East for its own purposes is neatly played out through Haroon, yet with an irony at the expense of the ''West'' that is in some ways lacking in Said. Thus a fixed ''Indian'' cultural identity, desired and projected by those liberal spiritualists who come to Haroon's meditations, is never allowed to settle; it is undermined by their own inability to see Haroon's ''inauthenticity'' because of their preconceptions.

While liberal Western mysticism is under scrutiny in *The Buddha of Suburbia*, Kureishi uses his second novel to examine a more serious ''usage'' of marginalized racial groups in the metropolis. *The Black Album* is set during the Rushdie affair (when a fatwa was imposed by Iran's spiritual leader upon Salman Rushdie, author of *The Satanic Verses*) and takes the brave step (considering Kureishi's credentials during the Rushdie affair as someone outspoken in his defense of Rushdie) of attempting to enter the thought processes involved in the anger caused by *The Satanic Verses*. Shahid, the novel's central character, is placed between the familiar poles of an essentialist Asian identity (in this case anti-Rushdie fundamentalism) and Western liberalism. But *The Black Album* (and this is part of its comparative seriousness) produces other options within these polarities. The apparently insupportable monolithic ideology of cultural essentialism represented by Chad and Riaz is given an attraction through its ability to produce a sense of cultural cohesion, community, and comfort. From the liberal Western pole splinters Brownlow, who is used as an example of the Western leftist tendency to over-prioritize the marginality of marginal groups—this becomes a drama playing out a guilt that is apparently purged if reversed. *The Black Album* is then more complex than *The Buddha of Suburbia* in the delineation of race in British society; it is also a more serious and intense piece of writing, dealing with the same issues in a more threatening, highly charged context. Kureishi's fiction has thus moved along the trajectories of the experience of post-colonial immigration in Britain with an intelligence and irony, while developing a more complex attitude to political issues and continually using narrative and writing stylistics to place that experience in its political and (popular) cultural context.

Intimacy, Kureishi's 1999 novel (at a time when his short story and screenplay writing continue to be prolific), moves away from cultural-identity politics and brings out a strand that has always been part of his writing—the loneliness, cruelty and disconnectedness of human relations. The narrator, Jay, is on the point of leaving his partner and their two children and, at times viciously and egotistically, he assesses his soon-to-be past relationship. Jay's self-justification hovers always between alienating and challenging the reader, as Kureishi dares to deploy a central character whose apparently objectionable sense of himself and disregard for others seems to be posited as necessary and universal. *Intimacy*'s title is its key; deeply ironic at the expense of the text, the novel takes the reader to the boundaries of his own moral judgement and then asks if he can be sure of the ground he stands on. In this it shares with Kureishi's earlier two novels a belief that writing and reading should not be processes of comfort.

—Colin Graham

L

LAMMING, George (Eric)

Nationality: Barbadian. **Born:** Carrington Village, 8 June 1927. **Education:** Roebuck Boys' School; Combermere School. **Career:** Teacher in Trinidad, 1946–50; moved to England, 1950; host of book review programme, BBC West Indian Service, London, 1951. Writer-in-residence, University of the West Indies, Kingston, 1967–68. Co-editor of Barbados and Guyana independence issues of *New World Quarterly,* Kingston, 1965 and 1967. **Awards:** Guggenheim fellowship, 1954; *Kenyon Review* fellowship, 1954; Maugham award, 1957; Canada Council fellowship, 1962. D.Litt.: University of the West Indies, Cave Hill, Barbados, 1980. **Address:** 14-A Highbury Place, London N.5., England.

PUBLICATIONS

Novels

In the Castle of My Skin. London, Joseph, and New York, McGraw Hill, 1953.
The Emigrants. London, Joseph, 1954: New York, McGraw Hill, 1955.
Of Age and Innocence. London, Joseph, 1958; New York, Schocken, 1981.
Season of Adventure. London, Joseph, 1960; Ann Arbor, University of Michigan Press, 1999.
Water with Berries. London, Longman, 1971; New York, Holt Rinehart, 1972.
Natives of My Person. London, Longman, and New York, Holt Rinehart, 1972.

Uncollected Short Stories

''David's Walk,'' in *Life and Letters* (London), November 1948.
''Of Thorns and Thistles'' and ''A Wedding in Spring,'' in *West Indian Stories,* edited by Andrew Salkey. London, Faber, 1960.
''Birds of a Feather,'' in *Stories from the Caribbean,* edited by Andrew Salkey. London, Elek, 1965; as *Island Voices,* New York, Liveright, 1970.
''Birthday Weather,'' in *Caribbean Literature,* edited by G.R. Coulthard. London, University of London Press, 1966.

Other

The Pleasures of Exile. London, Joseph, 1960; Ann Arbor, University of Michigan Press, 1992.
Influencia del Africa en las literaturas antillanas, with Henry Bangou and René Depestre. Montevideo, Uruguay, I.L.A.C., 1972.
The Most Important People, with Kathleen Drayton. Bridgetown, Barbados, Drayton, 1981.
Western Education and the Caribbean Intellectual: Coming, Coming, Coming Home. New York, House of Nehesi, 1995.
Coming, Coming Home: Conversations II: Monographs. Philipsburg, St. Martin, House of Nehesi, 1995.
Editor, *Cannon Shot and Glass Beads: Modern Black Writing.* London, Pan, 1974.
Editor, *On the Canvas of the World.* Port of Spain, Trinidad and Tobago Institute of the West Indies, 1999.

*

Bibliographies: *George Lamming: A Select Bibliography,* Cave Hill, Barbados, University of the West Indies Main Library, 1980.

Critical Studies: *The Novels of George Lamming* by Sandra Pouchet Paquet, London, Heinemann, 1982; *Anancy in the Great House: Ways of Reading West Indian Fiction* by Joyce Jonas, New York and London, Greenwood Press, 1990; *Caliban in Exile: The Outsider in Caribbean Fiction* by Margaret Paul Joseph, New York and London, Greenwood Press, 1992; *Caliban's Curse: George Lamming and the Revisioning of History* by Supriya Nair. Ann Arbor, University of Michigan Press, 1996.

Theatrical Activities: Director: **Play**—*Meet Me at Golden Hill,* Barbados,1974.

* * *

The critical reception of George Lamming's first four novels fell short of their real merits and originality. It is often said that Lamming demands too much of the reader; it might be truer to say that the reader demands too little of Lamming. West Indian fiction has often been distinguished by a certain energy and rhetorical glow but not, except in the work of Lamming and Wilson Harris, by much complexity of form or texture. Right from his first book, *In the Castle of My Skin,* Lamming made it clear that the real complexity of West Indian experience demanded some adequate response of its writers. He has since elaborated this view in an important essay called ''The Negro Writer and His World,'' where he wrote: ''To speak of his [the Negro Writer's] situation is to speak of a general need to find a center as well as a circumference which embraces some reality whose meaning satisfies his intellect and may prove pleasing to his senses. But a man's life assumes meaning first in relation to other men …'' *In the Castle of My Skin* may at first appear to be an autobiography of childhood, but it soon becomes apparent that the book is also the collective autobiography of a Barbadian village moving through the break-up of the old plantation system dominated by the Great House and into the new age of nationalism, industrial unrest and colonial repression. The four boys who stand at the center of the book are given a more or less equal importance though it is ''George'' who ultimately registers the meaning of their disparate experiences as they are driven asunder by education, travel, and emerging social distinctions.

The collective quality already evident in this, the most personal of all Lamming's books, is more strongly present in *The Emigrants.* Here the portrait is of one boatload of the black emigrants (the title is significant, for it stresses what they leave as well as what they find) who flocked from the Caribbean to Britain between 1950 and 1962. On the boat the emigrants discover a new identity as ''West Indians,'' only to lose it again as they fly centrifugally apart under the stresses of life in an alien culture.

The Emigrants is the saddest of all Lamming's books, because there is almost no focus of hope amid so much disillusionment and despair. By contrast both *Of Age and Innocence* and *Season of Adventure* are powerfully positive books in which what is shed is a set of values adhering to the older generation, those who are unable to match the pace and tendency of the times. *Of Age and Innocence* is set in San Cristobal, a fictional Caribbean island colony rapidly approaching independence. The dominant generation of islanders is unable to break away from its class and racial identities to work together for a new society which will redeem the past of slavery and colonialism, but it is throughout juxtaposed to the generation of its children, who struggle towards that meaning which the nationalist leader Shepherd has glimpsed and then lost again.

> I had always lived in the shadow of a meaning which others had placed on my presence in the world, and I had played no part at all in making that meaning, like a chair which is wholly at the mercy of the idea guiding the hand of the man who builds it.... But like the chair, I have played no part at all in making that meaning which others use to define me completely.

Shepherd is destroyed by the forces of the past, but the children look out through the flames of destruction which end the novel towards a future they have already presaged in their games. At the center of *Season of Adventure* stands another unawakened character, the ''big-shot coloured'' girl Fola, whose father is a West Indian police officer imbued with all the old ideas of order, dominance, and segregation. A visit to a Voduñ ceremony awakens her to the real capacity of her nature for self-discovery and self-renewal. This awakening by ancestral drums is in itself a cliché of Caribbean literature, but here it escapes banality by the intensity of Lamming's lyrical style and the bizarre violence of much of the action. *Season of Adventure* is in some ways the finest of his novels, just as *The Emigrants* is certainly the weakest. Yet the hesitancy which overtakes the drums at the end of the novel, in the very moment of their triumph as the expression of popular values, is analogous to the problem of language Lamming faces in projecting a West Indian culture which will be truly united, consistent and free: ''But remember the order of the drums ... for it is the language which every nation needs if its promises and its myths are to become a fact.''

After a silence of more than ten years, Lamming published two new novels within a year. These were powerfully contrasted in style and theme. *Water with Berries* is superficially a naturalistic novel about three West Indian artists living difficult and ever more lonely lives in modern London. Gradually, however (and the quotation of Caliban in the title gives a clue), the reader becomes aware that this is a study of what happens when Caliban comes to Prospero's original home. The revenges of history work themselves out through characters who are helpless to prevent completing the bizarre and violent patterns of the past. Each of the friends is an aspect of Caliban and each passes through an extreme personal crisis at the novel's end. But Derek, erect upon the stage before a howling audience, having completed the rape of Miranda at last, or Teeton, erect upon a northern island after destroying his last links with the racial past, have at least sketched the possibilities of freedom from these tyrannies of history.

Natives of My Person is more of an extended reverie upon certain dominant themes in Atlantic mythology—the demonic captain, the slave-ship, the imprisoned Amerindian prince, the crew variously haunted by tragedy and terror—which are treated like themes in music. The style is deliberately wrought from the timbers of seventeenth-century maritime prose, in which this mythology finds its roots. Hence the novel voyages freely in the dimension of space-time, deriving its structure simply from the musical resolution of its dominant themes. This is a work of great beauty, originality, and difficulty, which may finally prove to be Lamming's most important achievement.

—Gerald Moore

LANGE, John

See CRICHTON, (John) Michael

Le CARRÉ, John

Pseudonym for David John Moore Cornwell. **Nationality:** British. **Born:** Poole, Dorset, 19 October 1931. **Education:** Sherborne School, Dorset; St. Andrew's Preparatory School; Bern University, Switzerland, 1948–49; Lincoln College, Oxford, B.A. (honours) in modern languages 1956. **Family:** Married 1) Alison Ann Veronica Sharp in 1954 (divorced 1971), three sons; 2) Valerie Jane Eustace in 1972, one son. **Career:** Tutor, Eton College, Berkshire, 1956–58; member of the British Foreign Service, 1959–64: second secretary, Bonn Embassy, 1961–64; consul, Hamburg, 1963–64. **Awards:** British Crime Novel award, 1963; Maugham award, 1964; Mystery Writers of America Edgar Allan Poe award, 1965, and Grand Master award, 1984; Crime Writers Association Gold Dagger, 1978, 1980, and Diamond Dagger, 1988; James Tait Black Memorial prize, 1978; Nikos Kasanzakis prize, 1991. Honorary doctorate: University of Exeter 1990; St. Andrews University, 1996; University of Southampton; University of Bath. Honorary fellow, Lincoln College, 1984. **Agent:** David Higham Associates, 5–8 Lower John Street, London W1R 4HA, England.

PUBLICATIONS

Novels

Call for the Dead. London, Gollancz, 1961; New York, Walker, 1962; as *The Deadly Affair,* London, Penguin, 1966.

A Murder of Quality. London, Gollancz, 1962; New York, Walker, 1963.

The Spy Who Came In from the Cold. London, Gollancz, 1963; New York, Coward McCann, 1964.

The Looking-Glass War. London, Heinemann, and New York, Coward McCann, 1965.

A Small Town in Germany. London, Heinemann, and New York, Coward McCann, 1968.

The Naive and Sentimental Lover. London, Hodder and Stoughton, 1971; New York, Knopf, 1972.

The Quest for Karla. London, Hodder and Stoughton, and New York, Knopf, 1982.

Tinker, Tailor, Soldier, Spy. London, Hodder and Stoughton, and New York, Knopf, 1974.

The Honourable Schoolboy. London, Hodder and Stoughton, and New York, Knopf, 1977.

Smiley's People. London, Hodder and Stoughton, and New York, Knopf, 1980.
The Little Drummer Girl. London, Hodder and Stoughton, and New York, Knopf, 1983.
A Perfect Spy. London, Hodder and Stoughton, and New York, Knopf, 1986.
The Russia House. London, Hodder and Stoughton, and New York, Knopf, 1989.
The Secret Pilgrim. London, Hodder and Stoughton, and New York, Knopf, 1991.
The Night Manager. London, Hodder and Stoughton, and New York, Knopf, 1993.
Our Game. London, Hodder and Stoughton, and New York, Knopf, 1995.
John Le Carré: Three Complete Novels (contains *Tinker, Tailor, Soldier, Spy, The Honourable Schoolboy,* and *Smiley's People*). New York, Wings Books, 1995.
The Tailor of Panama. New York, Knopf, 1996.
Single & Single. New York, Scribner, 1999.

Uncollected Short Stories

''Dare I Weep, Dare I Mourn,'' in *Saturday Evening Post* (Philadelphia), 28 January 1967.
''What Ritual Is Being Observed Tonight?,'' in *Saturday Evening Post* (Philadelphia), 2 November 1968.

Play

Television Play: *Smiley's People,* with John Hopkins, from the novel by le Carré, 1982.

Other

The Clandestine Muse. Portland, Oregon, Seluzicki, 1986.
Vanishing England, with Gareth H. Davies. Topsfield, Massachusetts, Salem House, 1987.

*

Film Adaptations: *The Spy Who Came In from the Cold*, 1965; *The Deadly Affair*, from the work *Call for the Dead*, 1967; *The Looking Glass War*, 1970; *Tinker, Tailor, Soldier, Spy* (for television), 1980; *Smiley's People* (for television), 1982; *The Little Drummer Girl*, 1984; *The Russia House*, 1990; *A Murder of Quality* (for television), 1991; *The Tailor of Panama*, 2000.

Critical Studies: *John le Carré* by Peter Lewis, New York, Ungar, 1985, London, Lorrimer, 1986; *The Novels of John le Carré: The Art of Survival,* Oxford, Blackwell, 1985, and *Smiley's Circus: A Guide to the Secret World of John le Carré,* London, Orbis, 1986, both by David Monaghan; *John le Carré* by Eric Homberger, London, Methuen, 1986; *Taking Sides: The Fiction of John le Carré* by Tony Barley, Milton Keynes, Buckinghamshire, Open University Press, 1986; *Corridors of Deceit: The World of John le Carré* by Peter Wolfe, Bowling Green, Ohio, Popular Press, 1987; *The Quest for John le Carré* edited by Alan Bold, London, Vision Press, and New York, St. Martin's Press, 1988; *Understanding John Le Carré* by John L. Cobbs, Columbia, South Carolina, University of South Carolina Press, 1998; *The Spy Novels of John Le Carré: Balancing Ethics and Politics* by Myron J. Aronoff, New York, St. Martin's Press, 1998.

* * *

Though John le Carré had written two thrillers, *Call for the Dead* and *A Murder of Quality,* it was when *The Spy Who Came In from the Cold* was published that it became obvious that a new talent for writing a different kind of spy story had emerged. Le Carré caught a new mood of chilling horror in this picture of the beastliness underlying the espionage of the cold war, for this is a novel which shows how man's capacity for inhumanity to man and woman is heightened through the process of espionage. The style matches the material. The moods evoked are of gray despair. The tone is cold, almost clinical. The conversations convince; they have the authentic texture of contemporary speech. And the details of the British, Dutch and German background are painted in with a casual assurance. The story is unfolded, given fresh twists, until the reality of life itself becomes warped. Leamas, the British agent, is created convincingly; he carries out his role of defector only to find that his own people have framed him, in order to frame Fiedler, an East German who has discovered the truth about Mundt, his chief.

This is a world of intellectual skills applied arbitrarily, of brilliance without scruple, of brutality without restraint. The inexorable march of the story continues: its destiny is disaster, the same kind of disaster which opens its account of the effects of treason and betrayal. And yet in the final moment Leamas returns for Liz, the English communist party member who befriended him in London, who has been brought to East Germany to testify against him. Before their final moments, before they attempt to cross the Berlin wall, he makes his apology to her. To him it seems the world has gone mad. His life and hers, their dignity, are a tiny price to pay. They are, ultimately, the victims of a temporary alliance of expediency. His people save Mundt because they need him, ''so that,'' he says to her, ''the great moronic mass that you admire can sleep soundly in their beds at night. They need him for the safety of ordinary crummy people like you and me.'' He sees the loss of Fiedler's life as part of the small-scale war which is being waged, with a wastage of innocent life sometimes, though it is still smaller than other wars. Leamas doesn't believe in anything, but he sees people cheated, misled, lives thrown away, ''people shot and in prison, whole groups and classes of men written off for nothing.'' Her party, he remarks, was built on the bodies of ordinary people, and she remembers the German prison wardress describing the prison as one for those who slow down the march, ''for those who think they have the right to err.''

Le Carré's next book, *The Looking-Glass War,* carries his exploration of the work of intelligence services further. This story opens impressively, with the death of a courier who has gone to Finland to pick up films made by the pilot of a commercial flight apparently off course over Eastern Germany. An unconfirmed report indicates the likelihood of a rocket site there. Then a small intelligence unit is authorized to put an agent into the area. The preparations are described in detail: the recruiting and training of the agent, the ineptitude involved, and the rivalry among the different agencies—and ultimately the schooled indifference with which the older professionals see their scheme fail abysmally. They are already planning the future, disowning the agent whose slow broadcasting on single frequencies on an obsolete radio has doomed him to capture. The story is well told; it explores the stresses and the vanities, the dangerous risks, even delusions, which beset the world of intelligence; it has a curious pathos, accentuated by the naivety and decency of the young man Avery which is opposed in fury by Haldane, who has become a technician: ''We sent him because we needed to; we abandon him because we must.''

In *A Small Town in Germany* there is an enlarging of scope. Here is a story of the British embassy in Bonn, from which secret files—and Leo Harting—have vanished. Turner comes from London to investigate. His interrogations of some of the embassy staff are brilliant. The pattern of thieving, of treachery, of insinuation, of making himself indispensable, of using others, emerges slowly as Turner tries to build up his picture of Leo Harting. The contrasts of personalities as Turner painstakingly pursues his inquiries give this picture depth, and yet the nature of the vanished man remains elusive. The complications of the British negotiations in Brussels where German support is necessary, the student riots, and the ugly neo-nazism give the man-hunt an extreme urgency. The attitude of the German authorities, and that of the Head of Chancery, surprise Turner. And the events he unravels surprise the reader.

The novel has a continuous tension; the discoveries of the investigator are cumulative, and finally his aggressive desire to hunt out the missing man turns to a sympathetic understanding of just what Harting has been doing. At this point his attitude differs markedly from that of the Head of Chancery. To a certain extent his reactions are parallel to those of Avery in *The Looking-Glass War.* Both are younger men, outside the orthodoxies of their elders, possessed ultimately of more humanity, though they have no capacity to influence the final stages of the story. The difference lies between the character who professes to control the processes of his own mind and the character who believes we are born free, we are not automatons and cannot control the processes of our minds. The novel is, in fact, about the problems of forgetting, and about the problems of idealism, innocence, and practical politics; and the incidental picture it gives of the complex working life of an embassy provides a very suitable background against which political issues can be spotlit.

The Naive and Sentimental Lover lacks the punch and energy of his earlier works. In them the tendency of the characters to be warped, maimed, frustrated men and women mattered little because the action backed by skillful description carried the plot forward at such headlong speed that analysis of character *per se* was less important than the actions taken by the participants. In this novel there is a need for a deeper analysis of character, and this does not seem to have been fully achieved, while the story does not move with the same sureness. However, it is likely that le Carré was experimenting with a new genre, and just as *The Spy Who Came In from the Cold* needed preliminary studies this may herald a development in character depiction similar to his earlier advances in technique and architectonic power in *The Spy Who Came In from the Cold,* which will remain as a chilling exposé of the continuous underground battle of intelligence services.

Tinker, Tailor, Soldier, Spy and *The Honourable Schoolboy* are both surpassed by *Smiley's People,* the narrative art of which is combined with a sympathetic compassion for its characters. Here le Carré shows Smiley torn by loyalties, uncovering instead of covering up the murder of an ex-agent, and in the process peeling layer after layer from the mystery of betrayal, getting steadily closer to his old enemy the Russian Karla. The story moves deliberately, the details are amassed, but the tension is maintained right to the climax. This is a *tour de force* because its present action demands an understanding of the past, and that past is revealed so skillfully that its actions live as a pressing part of the present. The reader is involved in the characters' memories, their evasions and searchings.

In *The Little Drummer Girl* le Carré portrays the violent conflicts of Arab and Israeli, moving his characters freely about Europe as he tightens the tense atmosphere created by terrorism. His characters are meticulous in their attention to detail; he conveys the concentration, the ruthlessness, the tyranny of abstract concepts made utterly inhuman. This is a story in which several ways of looking at life—and the deaths of victims—are juxtaposed convincingly; the effect is achieved through le Carré's capacity to create confidence in his readers through an inside knowledge of how terrorists and counter-terrorists operate.

A Perfect Spy and *The Russia House* both show le Carré's maturity, his established mastery of his medium. In *The Russia House* he moves to the new situation in the Soviet Union and brings alive the nature of its strange society. Deftly he indicates the effect of *glasnost,* the shift from suppression of public debate to new speculation, new credulity, new idealism, all balanced by old shortages, old skepticism, old inertias. The analysis is effective, the shifting pattern of change suggested with subtlety, the tension maintained. Bailey, the blundering British publisher, and Katya, the unselfish Russian woman with whom he falls in love, hold our attention, watched over by the British and American intelligence agents. It is convincing, at times moving, always exciting; it blends irony with a sense of the absurdity of suspicion, while at the same time suggesting the need for political caution in reacting to the unpredictable turmoil of the then-contemporary Soviet scene.

The Secret Pilgrim is a collection of short stories that functions as a novel, or a novel broken into a series of stories. In this context, the method of disjointed chapters serves well to tell the story of a spy's education, and of the sometimes pathetic characters he has encountered in his career. *The Tailor of Panama* illustrates how le Carré can reduce a story of global proportions to one on a very personal scale, and moreover how he has effectively moved beyond the lines of the Cold War—not to mention his penchant for humor both dry and black. Under false pretenses, protagonist Harry Prendel operates a tailor shop in Panama, and when he is called down by an agent of British intelligence named Andrew Osnard, he has to come up with ''evidence'' of a conspiracy involving the transfer of the Panama Canal from U.S. to Panamanian hands. The title of le Carré's next novel, *Single & Single,* refers to the name of a shady British bank that assists Russian black marketeers with money laundering. When the Russians shoot a bank employee and company president Tiger Single has to go into hiding, his son Oliver sets out—rather like Telemachus in the *Odyssey*—to avenge his father. What ensues is indeed an odyssey of sorts, one that shows le Carré at his intriguing best.

—A. Norman Jeffares

LEE, Chang-rae

Nationality: American. **Born:** Seoul, South Korea, 29 July 1965. **Education:** Yale University, B.A. 1987; University of Oregon, M.F.A. 1993. **Family:** Married Michelle Branca in 1993. **Career:** Assistant professor of creative writing, University of Oregon, Eugene, 1993—. **Agent:** Amanda Urban, International Creative Management, 40 West 57th Street, New York, New York 10019, U.S.A. **Address:**

Creative Writing Program, University of Oregon, Eugene, Oregon 97403, U.S.A.

Publications

Novels

Native Speaker. New York, Riverhead Books, 1995.
A Gesture Life. New York, Riverhead Books, 1999.

* * *

Chang-rae Lee, the first Korean-American novelist to be published by a major press, focuses on the experiences of first- and second-generation immigrants. His novels explore the nuances of intergenerational relations, the problems of assimilation, and the relationship of culture and memory to identity. While these concerns link him to other contemporary Asian-American writers, Lee's fiction also draws heavily on other influences. Lee experiments with form in his first novel, *Native Speaker*, which is part detective story, part minimalist chronicle of a failing marriage, reminiscent of John Updike. His prose style has been compared to that of both John Cheever and Kazuo Ishiguro.

In *Native Speaker*, Korean-American Henry Park must negotiate the dual forces of alienation and assimilation to establish a coherent ethnic identity. Park, an undercover investigator for a private firm whose specialty is infiltrating ethnic enclaves, describes his work as creating "a string of serial identity." Lee presents Park's skill at intelligence gathering and impersonation as an extension of his bicultural childhood, in which his Korean identity of home differed widely from his American identity at school. But Park's ability to assimilate, to portray American-ness, veils his persistent inability to establish a workable ethnic identity. We meet Park in the midst of a separation from his Caucasian wife, Lelia, who has left Park a list of traits that define him, including "stranger," "emotional alien," and "false speaker of language." Park's desire to reunite with Lelia leads him to confront this habit of presenting facades; to restore his life, Park must find and then "speak" a self that is his own. In this tightly woven narrative, Lee integrates Park's memories of childhood, his quest to regain Lelia, and his increasingly dangerous undercover assignment as an aid to the Korean-American politician, John Kwang, in order to explore the complex process of identity formation.

Lee's second novel, *A Gesture Life*, revisits the themes of alienation and displacement developed in *Native Speaker*. The narrator, "Doc" Hata, is doubly displaced, as an ethnic Korean raised in Japan who immigrates to America after serving in the Japanese Army during World War II. Hata runs a successful medical supply business and becomes a leading civic figure and prototypical private, suburban resident in Bedley Run, a rich community in upstate New York. From the outside, his life, like his impeccable Tudor home, seems complete, but from the inside, both are sterile and isolated. Hata's adopted daughter, Sunny, a Japanese orphan, remains distant and aloof, and Hata himself never fully connects to his new community or to the woman who becomes his lover; instead, Hata remains a marginal character in his own life. His commanding officer in Japan is the first to suggest that he leads the "gesture life" of the title, following the form but missing the essential meaning of any activity, but his daughter too finds this emphasis on gesture to be the central fact of Hata's life. In this novel, Lee emphasizes Hata's personal history and the displacement itself more than Korean cultural background as the cause of Hata's reserve.

For the narrators of both of these novels, form often substitutes for essence, as they assimilate by learning in detail the language, gestures, and attitudes of Americans but have difficulty expressing their selves through these gestures. But the brilliance of Lee's novels lies precisely in his focus on these minute details of daily life, and in his ability to convey emotional depth through these detached narrators.

—Suzanne Lane

LEE, Sky

Nationality: Canadian. **Born:** Port Alberni, British Columbia, 1952. **Education:** University of British Columbia, B.A.; Douglas College, diploma in nursing. **Family:** Has one son. **Career:** Nurse and writer.

Publications

Novels

Disappearing Moon Cafe. Vancouver, Douglas and McIntyre, 1990; Seattle, Washington, Seal Press, 1991.
Bellydancer. Vancouver, Press Gang, 1994.

Short Stories

Teach Me to Fly, Skyfighter! and Other Stories, with Paul Yee. Toronto, Lorimer, 1983.

* * *

In "All Spikes but the Last" (1957), F. R. Scott rebukes E. J. Pratt for failing in his epic, *Towards the Last Spike* (1952), to acknowledge the contribution Chinese laborers made in finishing the transnational Canadian Pacific Railway. "Where are the coolies in your poem, Ned? / Where are the thousands from China who swung their picks with bare hands at forty below?" Who, Scott asks, "has sung their story?"

A revisionist narrative returning presence to historical absence, defying silence with song and story, *Disappearing Moon Cafe* tells the story of Vancouver's Chinese community, whose role in British Columbia's development has, until recently, been disregarded. Sky Lee's novel is a formidable addition to the growing, though relatively small, body of Chinese-Canadian literature. Epic in scope and intent, spanning four generations and nearly a century (1892 to 1986), *Disappearing Moon Cafe* weighs the cultural cost of survival, particularly for generations of Chinese-Canadian women, and charts the tangled connections between Wong Gwei Chang, who is entrusted by the Chinese community with the responsibility of collecting the bones of laborers who died building the railway and returning them to China for burial, and his descendants. Great-granddaughter Kae Ying Woo, inspired by her pregnancy, narrates the story and exposes murky familial secrets. Like her ancestor, Kae searches for her family's bones. Powerful vignettes, flashbacks, multiple perspectives, and temporal juxtapositions are features of her narrative as she wrestles with the problems of knowing and representing the past. At times, though, the sameness of Lee's narration and its occasional inchoateness restrain the promising elasticity of her invention.

Lee's family saga deals with repatriation and assimilation, the tug between cultures. The young migrants maintain connections with China to protect themselves from the Canadian wilderness and nativism. But as they settle down and have families, as the Canadian government restricts passage between China and Canada, and as China is politically transformed and then isolated, their Canadian-born children forge new identities, negotiating the conflicting demands of the old world, where customs and laws are clear, and the new, where values are less certain. For some, such as relocated village teenager Wong Choy Fuk, this is easy. He proves "amazingly quick to shed his bumpkin ways in favour of a more cocky western style." Indeed, the cafe of the title is symbolically divided in two. One section, "a nostalgic replica of an old-fashioned Chinese teahouse," is very popular with "homesick Chinese clientele;" the other, a "more modern counter-and-booth section," enchants Choy Fuk: "He loved the highly polished chrome and brightly lit glass, the checkerboard tiles on the floor, the marble countertop. And except for the customers, his mother, and perhaps the cacti, there was nothing Chinese about it."

The family plays an important role offsetting the dislocations of immigration. Mui Lan, Gwei Chang's Chinese wife, expends considerable malicious energy ensuring that the Wong name does not evaporate. Although her obsession with her daughter-in-law's fertility may appear to be a traditional Chinese concern, conditions in Canada—the Canadian government imposed an expensive head tax and then prohibited Chinese immigration for many years, thus obstructing the possibility of family reunion—helped shape and exacerbate this concern also.

The genealogy of the Wong family, a potential dynasty, structures *Disappearing Moon Cafe.* Maintaining a pure lineage is impossible, as Kae discovers when she probes the secrets, allegiances, demands, and contradictions of family. Anything is permissible, so long as a son is born and the Wong name perpetuated. Security, honor, and prestige, for example, will be Fong Mei's reward on the condition that she let her husband, Choy Fuk, who we later learn is impotent, sleep with Song An, a waitress at Disappearing Moon Cafe. The Wong family tree prefaces the story; primarily Chinese, it includes aboriginal Shi'atko and an anonymous French-Canadian woman, although both are nominal figures. Positioning the family tree at the start of the narrative and thus disclosing the infidelities and incest that motivate various characters does, however, drain the narrative of much of its tension.

Lee's 1994 short story collection, *Bellydancer,* augments her range of characters, if not her colloquial prose, which favors explanation and exclamation over ellipsis. Some stories focus on Chinese-Canadian experience and expand upon themes addressed in *Disappearing Moon Cafe*—"Broken Teeth" is about conflict between a mother born in China and her Canadian-born daughter, and the marvelous "The Soong Sisters" revolves around a genealogy only slightly less complicated than the Wong family's. Others consider relationships: heterosexual, lesbian, and, in "Safe Sex," something mysterious that transcends gender altogether.

—Stephen Milnes

LE GUIN, Ursula K(roeber)

Nationality: American. **Born:** Berkeley, California, 21 October 1929; daughter of the anthropologist Alfred L. Kroeber. **Education:** Radcliffe College, Cambridge, Massachusetts, AB in French 1951 (Phi Beta Kappa); Columbia University, New York (Faculty fellow; Fulbright fellow, 1953), MA in romance languages 1952. **Family:** Married Charles A. Le Guin in 1953; two daughters and one son **Career:** Instructor in French, Mercer University, Macon, Georgia, 1954, and University of Idaho, Moscow, 1956; department secretary, Emory University, Atlanta, 1955; taught writing workshops at Pacific University, Forest Grove, Oregon, 1971, University of Washington, Seattle, 1971–73, Portland State University, Oregon, 1974, 1977, 1979, 1995, in Melbourne, Australia, 1975, at the University of Reading, England, 1976, Indiana Writers Conference, Bloomington, 1978 and 1983, and University of California, San Diego, 1979. **Awards:** Boston *Globe-Horn Book* award, 1968; Nebula award, 1969, 1975, 1990, 1996; Hugo award, 1970, 1973, 1974, 1975, 1988; National Book award, 1972; Newbery Silver Medal award, 1972; *Locus* award, 1973, 1984, 1995, 1996; Jupiter award, 1975 (twice), 1976; Gandalf award, 1979; Lewis Carroll Shelf award, 1979; University of Oregon Distinguished Service award, 1981; Janet Kafka award, 1986; Prix Lectures-Jeunesse (France), 1987; Pushcart prize, 1991; Harold Vursell award, 1991; Oregon Institute of Literary Arts HL Davis award, 1992; *Hubbub* Annual Poetry award, 1995; *Asimov's* Reader's award, 1995; James Tiptree, Jr. Award, 1995; Theodore Sturgeon Award, 1995; Retrospective Award, 1996, 1997. Guest of Honor, World Science Fiction Convention, 1975. DLitt: Bucknell University, Lewisburg, Pennsylvania, 1978; Lawrence University, Appleton, Wisconsin, 1979; DHL: Lewis and Clark College, Portland, 1983; Occidental College, Los Angeles, 1985. Lives in Portland, Oregon. **Agent:** Virginia Kidd, 538 East Harford Street, Milford, Pennsylvania 18337, USA

PUBLICATIONS

Novels

Rocannon's World. New York, Ace, 1966; London, Tandem, 1972.
Planet of Exile. New York, Ace, 1966; London, Tandem, 1972.
City of Illusions. New York, Ace, 1967; London, Gollancz, 1971.
A Wizard of Earthsea. Berkeley, California, Parnassus Press, 1968; London, Gollancz, 1971
The Left Hand of Darkness. New York, Ace, and London, Macdonald, 1969; 25th anniversary edition, with a new afterword and appendices by the author, New York, Walker, 1994.
The Lathe of Heaven. New York, Scribner, 1971; London, Gollancz, 1972.
The Tombs of Atuan. New York, Atheneum, 1971; London, Gollancz, 1972.
The Farthest Shore. New York, Atheneum, 1972; London, Gollancz, 1973.
The Dispossessed: An Ambiguous Utopia. New York, Harper, and London, Gollancz, 1974.
The Word for World Is Forest. New York, Putnam, 1976; London, Gollancz, 1977.
Earthsea. London, Gollancz, 1977; as *The Earthsea Trilogy,* London, Penguin, 1979.

Malafrena. New York, Putnam, 1979; London, Gollancz, 1980.
The Eye of the Heron. New York, Harper, and London, Gollancz, 1983.
Always Coming Home. New York, Harper, 1985; London, Gollancz, 1986.
Tehanu: The Last Book of Earthsea. New York, Atheneum, and London, Gollancz, 1990.
Buffalo Gals, Won't You Come Out Tonight, illustrated by Susan Seddon Boulet, San Francisco, Pomegranate Artbooks, 1994.
Four Ways to Forgiveness. New York, HarperPrism, 1995.

Short Stories

The Wind's Twelve Quarters. New York, Harper, 1975; London, Gollancz, 1976.
The Water Is Wide. Portland, Oregon, Pendragon Press, 1976.
Orsinian Tales. New York, Harper, 1976; London, Gollancz, 1977.
The Compass Rose. New York, Harper, 1982; London, Gollancz, 1983.
The Visionary: The Life Story of Flicker of the Serpentine, with *Wonders Hidden,* by Scott Russell Sanders Santa Barbara, California, Capra Press, 1984.
Buffalo Gals and Other Animal Presences. (includes verse) Santa Barbara, California, Capra Press, 1987; as *Buffalo Gals,* London, Gollancz, 1990.
Searoad. New York, HarperCollins, 1991; London, Gollancz, 1992.
A Fisherman of the Inland Sea: Science Fiction Stories, New York, HarperPerennial, 1994.
Worlds of Exile and Illusion. New York, Orb, 1996.

Fiction (for children)

Very Far Away from Anywhere Else. New York, Atheneun, 1976; as *A Very Long Way from Anywhere Else,* London, Gollancz, 1976.
Leese Webster. New York, Atheneum, 1979; London, Gollancz, 1981.
The Beginning Place. New York, Harper, 1980; as *Threshold,*London, Gollancz, 1980
The Adventure of Cobbler's Rune. New York, Virginia, Cheap Street, 1982.
Solomon Leviathan's Nine Hundred and Thirty-First Trip Around the World. New Castle, Virginia, Cheap Street, 1983.
A Visit from Dr Katz. New York, Atheneum, 1988; as *Dr Katz,* London, Collins, 1988.
Catwings. New York, Orchard, 1988.
Catwings Return. New York, Orchard, 1989.
Fire and Stone. New York, Atheneum, 1989.
A Ride on the Red Mare's Back. New York, Orchard, 1992.
Fish Soup. New York, Atheneum, 1992.
Wonderful Alexander and the Catwings. New York, Orchard, 1994.
Tom Mouse, illustrated by Julie Downing, New York, DK, 1998.
Jane on Her Own: A Catwings Tale, illustrations by S.D. Schindler. New York, Orchard Books, 1999.

Plays

No Use to Talk to Me, in *The Altered Eye,* edited by Lee Harding Melbourne, Norstrilia Press, 1976; New York, Berkley, 1980.
King Dog(screenplay), with *Dorstoevsky,* by Raymond Carver and Tess Gallagher Santa Barbara, California, Capra Press, 1985.

Poetry

Wild Angels. Santa Barbara, California, Capra Press, 1975.
Tillai and Tylissos, with Theodora K. Quinn. Np, Red Bull Press, 1979.
Torrey Pines Reserve. Northridge, California, Lord John Press, 1980.
Gwilan's Harp. Northridge, California, Lord John Press, 1981.
Hard Words and Other Poems. New York, Harper, 1981.
In the Red Zone. Northridge, California, Lord John Press, 1983.
Wild Oats and Fireweed. New York, Harper, 1988.
Blue Moon over Thurman Street. Portland, Oregon, NewSage Press, 1993.
Going Out with Peacocks and Other Poems New York, HarperPerennial, 1994
Sixty Odd: New Poems. Boston, Shambhala, 1999.

Other

From Elfland to Poughkeepsie (lecture). Portland, Oregon, Pendragon Press, 1973.
Dreams Must Explain Themselves. New York, Algol Press, 1975.
The Language of the Night: Essays on Fantasy and Science Fiction, edited by Susan Wood. New York, Putnam, 1979; revised edition, London, Women's Press, 1989.
The Seasons of Oling: For Narrator, Viola, Cello, Piano, Percussion (words), music by Elinor Armer. Albany, California, Overland Music Distributors, 1987.
Dancing at the Edge of the World: Thoughts on Words, Women, Places. New York, Grove Press, and London, Gollancz, 1989.
The Way the Water's Going: Images of the Northern California Coastal Range, photographs by Ernest Waugh and Alan Nicolson. New York, Harper, 1989.
Tao Te Ching: A Book about the Way and the Power of the Way (Paraphraser, with J.P. Seaton), by Lao Tzu. Boston, Shambhala, 1997.
Steering the Craft: Exercises and Discussions on Story Writing for the Lone Navigator or the Mutinous Crew. Portland, Oregon, Eighth Mountain Press, 1998.
Editor, *Nebula Award Stories 11.* London, Gollancz, 1976; New York, Harper, 1977.
Editor, with Virginia Kidd, *Interfaces.* New York, Ace, 1980.
Editor, with Virginia Kidd, *Edges.* New York, Pocket Books, 1980.
Editor, with Brian Attebery, *The Norton Book of Science Fiction: North American Science Fiction, 1960–1990.* New York, Norton, 1993.

Recordings: *The Ones Who Walk Away from Omelas,* Alternate World, 1976; *Gwilan's Harp and Intracom,* Caedmon, 1977; *The Earthsea Triology,* Colophone, 1981; *Music and Poetry of the Kesh,* Valley Productions, 1985

*

Bibliography: *Ursula K Le Guin: A Primary and Secondary Bibliography* by Elizabeth Cummins Cogell, Boston, Hall, 1983.

Manuscript Collection: University of Oregon Library, Eugene.

Critical Studies: *The Farthest Shores of Ursula K. Le Guin* by George Edgar Slusser, San Bernardino, California, Borgo Press, 1976; ''Ursula Le Guin Issue'' of *Science-Fiction Studies* (Terre

Haute, Indiana), March 1976; *Ursula Le Guin* by Joseph D. Olander and Martin H. Greenberg, New York, Taplinger, and Edinburgh, Harris, 1979; *Ursula K. Le Guin: Voyage to Inner Lands and to Outer Space* edited by Joseph W. De Bolt, Port Washington, New York, Kennikat Press, 1979; *Ursula K. Le Guin* by Barbara J. Bucknall, New York, Ungar, 1981; *Ursula K. Le Guin* by Charlotte Spivack, Boston, Twayne, 1984; *Approaches to the Fiction of Ursula K. Le Guin* by James Bittner, Ann Arbor, Michigan, UMI Research Press, and Epping, Essex, Bowker, 1984; *Understanding Ursula K. Le Guin* by Elizabeth Cummins Cogell, Columbia, University of South Carolina Press, 1990; *Zephyr and Boreas: Winds of Change in the Fiction of Ursula K. Le Guin: A Festschrift in Memory of Pilgrim Award Winner, Marjorie Hope Nicolson (1894–1981),* edited by Robert Reginald and George Edgar Slusser, San Bernardino, California, Borgo Press, 1996; *Between Two Worlds: The Literary Dilemma of Ursula K. Le Guin* by George Edgar Slusser, San Bernardino, Calif., Borgo Press, 1996; *Presenting Ursula K. Le Guin* by Suzanne Elizabeth Reid, New York, Twayne Publishers and London, Prentice Hall International, 1997.

* * *

Ursula K. Le Guin's earliest works attracted, almost exclusively, the devoted audience of science-fiction readers. *Rocannon's World, Planet of Exile,* and *City of Illusions* are interconnected novels which depict a situation entirely familiar to such readers. Earth and other planets of a far-future ''League of All Worlds'' are peopled by ''Human'' races which must struggle to recognize one another as such. The League prepares to meet a rather vaguely defined invasion from afar. Heroes out of touch with lost civilization undertake quests of self-discovery, or get the enemy's location through to headquarters just in time to repel the invasion. In short, Le Guin offers us space opera, although the delicate tone, the theme of communication, and the imagery of light and darkness suggest her future development.

With *The Left Hand of Darkness, The Word for World Is Forest,* the *Earthsea* fantasy trilogy, and *The Dispossessed,* Le Guin moved to another level, and began, deservedly, to attract an audience outside the science-fiction ghetto. The treatment of androgyny in *The Left Hand of Darkness* has made the book into a minor classic. The League of All Worlds has been succeeded by a non-imperialistic ''Ekumen,'' which sends a lone envoy, Genly Ai, to make an alliance with the isolated planet Winter (Gethen). The Ekumen has no wish to subdue Winter but to extend ''the evolutionary tendency inherent in Being; one manifestation of which is exploration.'' Subverting the stock situation of civilization brought to the savages, Le Guin has Ai learn at least as much from the relatively primitive Gethenians as they from him. Gethenians mate only once a month, and they may adopt alternatively male and females roles. We learn at one point that ''the King is pregnant.'' Ai, a male chauvinist, learns how difficult it is to think of our fellow humans as people rather than as men and women. When he forms an alliance with a Gethenian called Estraven, Ai learns how close together the words ''patriot'' and ''traitor'' can be. Ai's loyalty begins to shift from the Ekumen to Gethen, but this shift is a precondition of his mission's success. Conversely, Estraven's loyalty shifts to Ai, but only because he loves his country well enough to want Ai to succeed.

Although Ai and Estraven grow closer to one another, a vast distance also remains between them. Humans are alienated from one another in a wintry universe. But hope springs from the melancholy. The universe is dark but young, and spring will follow winter. The book reverberates with a non-theistic prayer: ''Praise then darkness and Creation unfinished.''

Although they meet as equal individuals, Ai and Estraven are members of differing societies. Le Guin would insist on Aristotle's definition of people as social animals. In her ambivalent utopia *The Dispossessed,* Le Guin preserves this insistence—while making it equally clear that anarchism is one of her centers of value. The book is an important break in science fiction's anti-utopian trend. A scientist, Shevek, moves to and fro between an anarchist utopia which is becoming middle-aged, and a world—obviously analogous to our own—that is divided between propertarian (capitalist) and statist (communist) countries. Nowhere does he find full self-expression; conversely, full self-expression requires one's participation in a society. In alternating chapters which disrupt sequential chronology, Shevek moves both away from the anarchist utopia and back toward it. Le Guin identifies herself both as a stylistic artist and as a thinker. Her stark, wintry worlds are philosophically rich with dialectical Taoism, and the co-reality of such opposites as light and darkness, religion and politics, and language and power. In *A Wizard of Earthsea* the magician has power over things when he knows their true names, so that his power is the artist's power. Le Guin plays with the notion, in ''The Author of the Acacia Seeds and Other Extracts from *The Journal of the Association of Therolinguistics,*'' that ants, penguins, and even plants might be producing what could be called language and art.

Since writing *The Dispossessed,* Le Guin has been turning in the direction of fantasy. *Malafrena* is a compelling mixture of fantasy and historical fiction. Le Guin sets the imaginary country of Orsinia into central Europe in the 19th century. It is Itale Sorde's story: he rejects the ease of an inherited landed estate (Malafrena) to work for revolution against Orsinia's domination by the Austrian Empire. After being jailed for several years and after a failed insurrection in 1830, he returns to Malafrena, but there are hints that he will leave again. True voyage is return, and structure and theme coalesce, as in *The Dispossessed.*

In subsequent works Le Guin often presents us with the ambiguity of revolution, once again the theme of a long short story, ''The Eye of the Heron.'' A colony of young counter-culturalists attempts to break away from their elders, with typically ambiguous results. A central paradox in Le Guin's fiction is her simultaneous recognition of the need for harmony and the need for revolt .

Praise for Le Guin has been high—too uniformly high. Her style is unexceptional and her desire for peace and harmony borders on sentimentality at times. But she has taken important steps toward blending politics and art in her novels, and she is still experimenting with both form and content. Thus *Always Coming Home* both returns to the anthropological format of *The Left Hand of Darkness* and greatly expands that format. Le Guin has gathered together stories, folklore, histories, and other materials into what she calls ''an archaeology'' of primitive people living in a far-future northern California. The central story (occupying only a small part of the book) is of the coming of age of the woman ''Stone Telling,'' whose mother lives in the peaceful Valley, which is integrated with nature, and whose father is of the war-like Condor people. Stone Telling leaves her valley to join her father for a while, but she becomes ''woman always coming home'' when she returns, her to-and-fro motion reminding us of *The Dispossessed.* When we discover that the Condor can build bridges and that they have electric lights, we may wonder how their traditional culture is supposed to have survived. But Le

Guin's ability to capture the language, culture, and thought of primitive people is, despite some lapses, generally remarkable.

Harmony with nature is more than just a greeting card sentiment in Le Guin's short story collection *Buffalo Gals and Other Animal Presences* and the novel *Buffalo Gals, Won't You Come out Tonight.* In *Animal Presences,* the gap between the natural world and the human has become a virtual chasm. Shifting points of view allow even a lab rat his voice of protest. But voice alone is not sufficient to narrow the gap: one must set fire to complacency and open oneself up to hearing voices other than one's own, as in the story ''May's Lion,'' about a woman who transcends her fears to help a mountain lion to die. The intriguing novella *Buffalo Gals, Won't You Come out Tonight,* which first appeared in the *Magazine of Fantasy and Science Fiction,* is a parable of the disintegrating relationship between humankind and the natural world. A remarkably resilient girl-child survives a plane crash only to find herself in different plane of reality, a desert world not unlike pre-settlement America, where the line between animals and man is less clearly drawn. As the girl becomes increasingly aware of the sour smell of humanity and its encroachments, she becomes more and more uprooted and unsure of her place. She eventually returns to her own people, but with an eye, both figuratively and literally, to seeing the world differently. Although occasionally heavy-handed, the story is compelling and visually rich. The girl protagonist speaks with the recognizable and sympathetic voice of a child.

The short story collection, *Searoad,* reveals how definitions of mainstream fiction and science fiction are not mutually exclusive. Though clearly a work of realistic fiction, the novel contains aspects of myth and ritual that fall into the realm of fantasy. Each story can be read as a separate entity, yet each contributes to one unified vision. This vision is unabashedly feminist, and as such is chiefly and somewhat exclusively concerned with the lives of women. Set in the small resort town of Klatsand, located on the Oregon coast, the stories contrast the different ways in which males and females communicate, the first being authoritative and unyielding, the other conversational and communal. This rigid polarity marks one of the problems with the novel, especially in terms of its persuasiveness. Male characters are impotent, if not downright evil; female characters are still waters running effortlessly deep. This seems to diminish rather than enhance believability. In addition, one questions the validity of rejecting outright the male world as a means of acquiring personal freedom. Nonetheless, characterization is compelling enough to sustain interest. One admires the resiliency of women who have also recognized the incontrovertibility of choice, or as the character Jilly in the story ''In and Out'' realizes, ''doing something wasn't just a kind of practice for something that would keep happening .... You didn't get to practice''.

In *A Fisherman of the Inland Sea,* Le Guin returns to science fiction, with a disparate collection of tales, both humorous and serious, that asserts many of the recurrent themes in her work: the responsibility we have to nature; cultural diversity and ethnic tolerance; the importance of communication in spite of the inadequacies of language; and the interdependency of peoples. Among the most compelling stories in the collection is ''Newton's Sleep,'' which casts a circumspect eye on the elitism of technology and suggests the need for the irrational, for the unknown and unseen in our lives. As with all of the author's work, this collection seeks to expand and challenge the reader's ideas as to what it means to be human. In *Four Ways to Forgiveness,* a quartet of novellas, Le Guin returned to the Hainish culture first examined in *The Left Hand of Darkness.* This time, however, the setting runs as far afield as the planets Werel and Yeowe, explained by the author in copious footnotes; and the roles of men and women are treated with much greater complexity and reality.

—Curtis C. Smith, updated by Lynda Schrecengost

LELCHUK, Alan

Nationality: American. **Born:** Brooklyn, New York, 15 September 1938. **Education:** Brooklyn College, B.A. 1960; University College, London, 1962–63; Stanford University, California, M.A. 1963, Ph.D. in English 1965. **Family:** Married Barbara Kreiger in 1979; two sons. **Career:** Assistant professor of English, 1966–75, and writer-in-residence, 1975–81, Brandeis University, Waltham, Massachusetts. Since 1985 professor of English, Dartmouth College, Hanover, New Hampshire. Visiting writer, Amherst College, Massachusetts, 1982–84; writer-in-residence, Haifa University, Israel, 1986–87. Associate editor, *Modern Occasions* quarterly, Cambridge, Massachusetts, 1970–72. Guest, Mishkenot Sha'Ananim, Jerusalem, 1976–77. **Awards:** Yaddo Foundation grant, 1968, 1971, 1973; MacDowell Colony fellowship, 1969; Guggenheim fellowship, 1976; Fulbright grant, 1986. **Agent:** Georges Borchardt, 136 East 57th Street, New York, New York 10022. **Address:** RFD 2, Canaan, New Hampshire 03741, U.S.A.

PUBLICATIONS

Novels

American Mischief. New York, Farrar Straus, and London, Cape, 1973.

Miriam at Thirty-four. New York, Farrar Straus, 1974; London, Cape, 1975.

Shrinking: The Beginning of My Own Ending. Boston, Little Brown, 1978.

Miriam in Her Forties. Boston, Houghton Mifflin, 1985.

Brooklyn Boy. New York, McGraw Hill, 1989.

Playing the Game. Dallas, Baskerville, 1995.

Uncollected Short Stories

''Sundays,'' in *Transatlantic Review 21* (London), Summer 1966.

''Of Our Time,'' in *New American Review 4,* edited by Theodore Solotaroff. New York, New American Library, 1968.

''Winter Image,'' in *Transatlantic Review 32* (London), Summer 1969.

''Cambridge Talk,'' in *Modern Occasions 1* (Cambridge, Massachusetts), Fall 1970.

''Hallie of the Sixties,'' in *Works in Progress 6* (New York), 1972.

''Doctor's Holiday,'' in *Atlantic* (Boston), March 1981.

''New Man in the House,'' in *Boston Globe Magazine,* 29 March 1987.

''Adventures of a Fiction Boy,'' in *Partisan Review* (Boston), Fall 1989.

Plays

Screenplays: *Tippy,* with Jiri Weiss, 1978; *What Ashley Wants,* with Isaac Yeshurun, 1987.

Other

On Home Ground (for children). New York, Harcourt Brace, 1987.
Editor, with Gerson Shaked, *Eight Great Hebrew Short Stories.* New York, New American Library, 1983.

*

Manuscript Collections: Mugar Memorial Library, Boston University.

Critical Studies: By Philip Roth in *Esquire* (New York), September 1972; ''Lelchuk's Inferno'' by Wilfrid Sheed, in *Book-of-the-Month Club News* (New York), March 1973; ''The Significant Self'' by Benjamin DeMott, in *Atlantic* (Boston), October 1974; ''Faculty in Fiction: Images of the Professor in Recent Novels'' by Frances Barasch, in *Clarion* (New York), June 1982; ''Aaron's Rod'' by Sven Birkerts, in *New Republic* (Washington, D.C.), 5 February 1990.

Alan Lelchuk comments:

Some points about my fiction: A realism of extreme sensibilities and modernism of content ... the intensity and ambiguity of the sensual life ... a blurring of the line between the comic and the serious ... vibrating the odd strings of obsession ... character through sexuality, and sexuality as (native) social gesture ... a mingling of lofty thought and contemporary vulgarity ... playing out the deep comic disorders of our culture ... some unnerving fables and comic myths of our time camouflaged by realistic garb and inhabited by real souls ...

* * *

Alan Lelchuk's first four novels recreate that rich Jewish-American intellectual life which synthesizes John Garfield with Bakunin. These cautionary tales dramatize the self-destructiveness inherent in political, artistic, and sexual revolt, the three frequently fused, as an academician (*American Mischief*), a woman photographer (*Miriam at Thirty-four, Miriam in Her Forties*), and a novelist (*Shrinking*) painfully test the boundaries of contemporary experience. *American Mischief,* Lelchuk's variation on *The Possessed,* explores 1960s campus upheaval through the contrapuntal voices of a radical student, Lenny Pincus (''Not the son of Harry and Rose Pincus of Brooklyn, but a boy with fathers like Reston and Cronkite, mothers such as Mary McCarthy and Diana Trilling''), and a liberal dean, Bernard Kovell (''a kind of Americanized version of Romanov-Quixote, a European Liberal-Idealist turned Massachusetts sensualist, tilting simultaneously at foolish theories and female bodies''). A wealth of political and literary allusions threatens to overwhelm the novel, as the protagonists share both their private agonies and extensive bibliographies with the reader. But the novel impresses with its vivid style, ultimately sane perspective, and brilliant bursts of imagination: the notorious episode detailing Norman Mailer's symbolically appropriate bloody end manages to outdo an already bizarre reality. Like Lelchuk's other novels, *American Mischief* attempts narrative complexity by telling its story through a variety of ''documents'': Lenny's preface; Kovell's journal focusing on his six mistresses; his lengthy speech during a campus uprising, interlarded with Lenny's comments; Lenny's ''Gorilla Talk,'' an account of radical activities that occupies more than half the book. This stylistic attempt to heighten the dialectical tension between the two men fails because their voices sound so alike from the beginning that the fusion of their ideologies into a statement of concern for man's ultimate victimization seems predictable.

Victimization goes even further in *Miriam at Thirty-four.* The heroine's sexual experimentation (three lovers with a variety of backgrounds and tastes) parallels her exploration of the Cambridge setting, which is ''a male with secrets ... one whom she could arouse by uncovering different parts of his anatomy and photographing them.'' This obsession with exposing truth leads Miriam to take sexually revealing pictures of herself and exhibit them at a prestigious gallery to the sounds of ''early Dylan, trio sonatas (Tartini? Bach?), the Beatles.'' Her final breakdown results from the uncomprehending responses of her audience: ''they were cannibals who had just feasted on human flesh with no time yet for digestion. And the flesh was herself, Miriam.'' To provide multiple views of Miriam, Lelchuk supplements the narrative with her letters and notebook (''her self-therapy kit, her doctor between covers, her book of reason, reflection, questions ...'') Shorter and less ambitious than *American Mischief,* the novel primarily conveys Miriam's pathos and leaves the sources of her disaster uncertain: a society that simultaneously seeks and savages the new, or the self-destructive urges that are implicit in Miriam's authentic artistry? A similar uncertainty pervades *Shrinking,* which chronicles the breakdown of novelist/academician Lionel Solomon, victimized by both inner doubts and a hostile world epitomized by Tippy, a predatory young woman who humiliates him sexually, reveals his inadequacies in an *Esquire* exposé, and leads him on a strange journey into Hopi country. Elaborately narrated, *Shrinking* includes a foreword and afterword by Solomon's psychiatrist, letters from other characters, and the text of Tippy's article with Solomon's comments. The article forces a comparison of Tippy's version with the ''real'' experience, a contrast that underscores the novel's obsession with truth: ''what happens in life, when put into fiction, can sound 'in poor taste' and be near impossible to write about.'' This apologia and Lelchuk's witty parodies of reviewers almost disarm criticism, but cannot obscure the catch-all quality of the book: essays on Hopi culture and Melville, however they reflect the workings of Solomon's mind, are too long for the effects they achieve, and Lelchuk's wit seems more forced, less outrageous than in *American Mischief.*

Miriam in Her Forties lacks much of the excitement and the sense of discovery of *Miriam at Thirty-four,* despite the weaknesses of the original. The sequel provides Miriam with an overly facile ability to analyze and resolve the types of problems that threatened to destroy her ten years earlier. The rape by a black man that triggered her breakdown in the original seems to have strengthened her to the extent that she now responds to a renewed threat from the rapist by using gangster-government ties to imprison him on trumped-up charges. She then helps arrange his release and rehabilitation, though the outcome of these efforts is left ambiguous. Like the teenage Aaron of Lelchuk's latest novel, *Brooklyn Boy,* who is seduced by a Jamaican librarian, Miriam must investigate the meaning of black-white sexuality. She may reject such a relationship for herself, as she does the lesbian overtures of a feminist artist, but she certainly considers the possibilities. Besides, she already has commitments to an emblematic Israeli, and WASP surgeon, with whom she experiences Maileresque sex in an almost deserted medical school lecture hall, and she has recently come to accept the validity of masturbation (in an implicit tribute to Roth). These teasing echoes of slightly older contemporaries seem appropriate in a writer very conscious of his place in the pantheon of American-Jewish authors and give the book some leavening wit. Significantly, despite her anxieties and occasional bouts of dangerous sex, Miriam sometimes echoes Bellow's Sammler in her sense of being the one sane person in a lunatic world: "In short, one is ready at last for the higher stage—wisdom, contemporary-style. So, wisdom, where do you reside?" The novel's chief weakness, in addition to the sentimentalized treatment of Miriam's son and some easy anti-Cambridge satire, is the third-person narrative voice which often unconvincingly infuses Miriam's experiences with an instant analysis that sounds more like the author's notes than a transcript of Miriam's mind. This technique threatens to stifle her distinctiveness and to parody her responses to serious issues.

Brooklyn Boy and *Playing the Game* are Lelchuk's most conventional work thus far, though both novels introduce material that almost unbalances their narrative flow. *Brooklyn Boy* is an expansion of the slightly earlier *On Home Ground* (designed "for young readers"). The novel develops Aaron's obsession with the Brooklyn Dodgers and the resultant conflict with his European-born father, who has a different set of priorities for his son, but then the novel seems to abandon this theme to trace Aaron's interest in writing and his job as a deckhand on a freighter that in the final scene heads up the Congo so that Aaron can complete his education with blacks begun in his affair with the Jamaican librarian. Unfortunately, the most lively sections of *Brooklyn Boy* are the excerpts from Aaron's school reports on local history. Though the novel shifts, early on, to a first-person narrative, it fails to provide Aaron with a plausible voice, and the reader has met variants of the character in other coming-of-age works (*On Home Ground,* which focuses on the father-son relation, is on its own terms the stronger of the two narratives).

Sidney Berger, the protagonist of *Playing the Game,* a fifty-one-year-old assistant coach with a Ph.D. in history, is given the opportunity to coach basketball at an ivy-league college and manages to produce a Cinderella team that attracts international media coverage. The team members suggest a World War II bomber crew film—black, Hispanic, native American, white ethnic, and even a Soviet Jew. Some of the boys have problems that hint at serious tensions later on, but these problems, like Berger's with the college and the NCAA, get easily resolved, primarily through Berger's commitment to coaching and basic decency. What inspires the team to victorious exploits is Berger's practice of half-time reading from key American writers like Parkman and Thoreau, whose prose apparently awes the players into an almost mystical awareness of the meaning of America, a prose that stimulates them to a better game than elaborate discussions of strategy or the personal humiliations inflicted by some coaches would have accomplished. One problem with these long excerpts, aside from their breaking the tension of the novel, is that the prose and its ideas are more exciting than anything in the framework narrative and leave the reader reluctant to return to the main story, a reluctance stemming partly from the stereotyped portraits of the players and various college and sports officials. Berger's voice, which narrates the story, seems at times a surrogate for the author's views on sports, education, and current American values, and only rarely conveys the idiosyncratic flavor of Lelchuk's earlier protagonists.

Lelchuk's shift to the relatively conventional material of these last two novels perhaps provides a breathing space from the bravura performances of earlier works. Admirers of Lelchuk's talent anticipate a return to his distinctive voice, often brilliant, often charmingly irrelevant to the apparent themes of the books, and often suggesting an underlying despair that the writing can only imperfectly capture.

—Burton Kendle

LEONARD, Elmore

Nationality: American. **Born:** New Orleans, Louisiana, 11 October 1925. **Education:** The University of Detroit, 1946–50, Ph.B. in English 1950. **Military Service:** Served in the United States Naval Reserve, 1943–46. **Family:** Married 1) Beverly Cline in 1949 (divorced 1977); 2) Joan Shepard in 1979 (died 1993), two daughters and three sons; 3) Christine Kent in 1993. **Career:** Copywriter, Campbell Ewald advertising agency, Detroit, 1950–61; writer of industrial and educational films, 1961–63; director, Elmore Leonard Advertising Company, 1963–66. Since 1967 full-time writer. **Awards:** Western Writers of America award, 1977; Mystery Writers of America Edgar Allan Poe award, 1984; Michigan Foundation for the Arts award, 1985; Mystery Writers of America Grand Master Award, 1992. **Agent:** Michael Siegel and Associates, 502 Tenth St., Santa Monica, California 90402, U.S.A.

PUBLICATIONS

Novels

The Bounty Hunters. Boston, Houghton Mifflin, 1953; London, Hale, 1956.

The Law at Randado. Boston, Houghton Mifflin, 1955; London, Hale, 1957.

Escape from Five Shadows. Boston, Houghton Mifflin, 1956; London, Hale, 1957.

Last Stand at Saber River. New York, Dell, 1959; as *Lawless River,* London, Hale, 1959; as *Stand on the Saber,* London, Corgi, 1960.

Hombre. New York, Ballantine, and London, Hale, 1961.

Valdez Is Coming. London, Hale, 1969; New York, Fawcett, 1970.

The Big Bounce. New York, Fawcett, and London, Hale, 1969.

The Moonshine War. New York, Doubleday, 1969; London, Hale, 1970.

Forty Lashes Less One. New York, Bantam, 1972.

Mr. Majestyk (novelization of screenplay). New York, Dell, 1974; London, Penguin, 1986.

Fifty-Two Pickup. New York, Delacorte Press, and London, Secker and Warburg, 1974.

Swag. New York, Delacorte Press, 1976; London, Penguin, 1986; as *Ryan's Rules,* New York, Dell, 1976.

The Hunted. New York, Delacorte Press, 1977; London, Secker and Warburg, 1978.

Unknown Man No. 89. New York, Delacorte Press, and London, Secker and Warburg, 1977.

The Switch. New York, Bantam, 1978; London, Secker and Warburg, 1979.

Gunsights. New York, Bantam, 1979.

City Primeval: High Noon in Detroit. New York, Arbor House, 1980; London, W.H. Allen, 1981.

Gold Coast. New York, Bantam, 1980; London, W.H. Allen, 1982.

Split Images. New York, Arbor House, 1982; London, W.H. Allen, 1983.

Cat Chaser. New York, Arbor House, 1982; London, Viking, 1986.
Stick. New York, Arbor House, 1983; London, Allen Lane, 1984.
LaBrava. New York, Arbor House, 1983; London, Viking Press, 1984.
Glitz. New York, Arbor House, and London, Viking, 1985.
Bandits. New York, Arbor House, and London, Viking, 1987.
Touch. New York, Arbor House, 1987; London, Viking, 1988.
Freaky Deaky. New York, Arbor House, and London, Viking, 1988.
Killshot. New York, Arbor House, and London, Viking, 1989.
Get Shorty. New York, Delacorte Press, and London, Viking, 1990.
Maximum Bob. New York, Delacorte Press, and London, Viking, 1991.
Rum Punch. New York, Delacorte Press, and London, Viking, 1992.
Pronto. New York, Delacorte Press, and London, Viking, 1993.
Riding the Rap. New York, Delacorte Press, and London, Viking, 1995.
Out of Sight. New York, Delacorte Press, 1996.
Cuba Libre. New York, Delacorte Press, 1998.
Be Cool. New York, Delacorte Press, 1999.
Pagan Babies. New York, Delacorte Press, 2000.

Uncollected Short Stories

''Trail of the Apache,'' in *Argosy* (New York), December 1951.
''Red Hell Hits Canyon Diablo,'' in *Ten Story Western,* 1952.
''Apache Medicine,'' in *Dime Western,* May 1952.
''You Never See Apaches,'' in *Dime Western,* September 1952.
''Cavalry Boots,'' in *Zane Grey's Western* (New York), December 1952.
''Long Night,'' in *Zane Grey's Western 18* (London).
''The Rustlers,'' in *Zane Grey's Western 29* (London), 1953.
''Under the Friar's Ledge,'' in *Dime Western,* January 1953.
''The Last Shot,'' in *Fifteen Western Tales,* September 1953.
''Trouble at Rindo's Station,'' in *Argosy* (New York), October 1953.
''Blood Money'' in *Western Story* (London), February 1954.
''Saint with a Six-Gun,'' in *Frontier,* edited by Luke Short. New York, Bantam, 1955.
''3:10 to Yuma,'' in *The Killers,* edited by Peter Dawson. New York, Bantam, 1955.
''The Hard Way,'' in *Branded West,* edited by Don Ward. Boston, Houghton Mifflin, 1956.
''No Man's Gun,'' in *Western Story* (London), May 1956.
''Moment of Vengeance,'' in *Colt's Law,* edited by Luke Short. New York, Bantam, 1957.
''The Tall T,'' in *The Tall T and Other Western Adventures.* New York, Avon, 1957.
''The Rancher's Lady,'' in *Wild Streets,* edited by Don Ward. New York, Doubleday, 1958.
''Only Good Ones,'' in *Western Roundup,* edited by Nelson Nye. New York, Macmillan, 1961.
''The Boy Who Smiled,'' in *The Arbor House Treasury of Great Western Stories,* edited by Bill Pronzini and Martin H. Greenberg. New York, Arbor House, 1982.
''The Nagual,'' in *The Cowboys,* edited by Bill Pronzini and Martin H. Greenberg. New York, Fawcett, 1985.
''The Captive,'' in *The Second Reel West,* edited by Bill Pronzini and Martin H. Greenberg. New York, Doubleday, 1985.
''Law of the Hunted Ones,'' in *Wild Westerns,* edited by Bill Pronzini and Martin H. Greenberg. New York, Walker, 1986.
''The Colonel's Lady,'' in *The Horse Soldiers,* edited by Bill Pronzini and Martin H. Greenberg. New York, Fawcett, 1987.
''Jugged'' in *The Gunfighters,* edited by Bill Pronzini and Martin H. Greenberg. New York, Fawcett, 1987.
''The Big Hunt,'' in *More Wild Westerns,* edited by Bill Pronzini. New York, Walker, 1989.

Plays

Screenplays: *The Moonshine War,* 1970; *Joe Kidd,* 1972; *Mr. Majestyk* (with Joseph Stinson), 1974; *Stick* (with John Steppling), 1985.

Television Plays: *High Noon, Part II: The Return of Will Kane,* 1980.

*

Film Adaptations: *Get Shorty,* 1995; *Jackie Brown*, 1997; *Last Stand at Saber River*, 1997; *Out of Sight*, 1998.

Manuscript Collections: University of Detroit Library.

Critical Studies: *Elmore Leonard* by David Geherin, New York, Ungar-Continuum, 1989; *Elmore Leonard* by James E. Devlin, New York, Twayne Publishers, 1999.

* * *

Elmore Leonard is one of those rare authors who began as a pulp writer and ended top of the bestseller lists. More impressive, however, is his feat of moving from being considered a mere genre novelist to being credited with elevating the crime novel to new levels of artistic achievement.

Leonard began as a writer of Westerns, turning out stories for the pulps that still flourished in the 1950s. One of his early novels, *Hombre,* the story of a white man raised by Indians whose bravery saves the lives of his fellow stagecoach passengers, was selected by the Western Writers of America as one of the twenty-five best Westerns of all time.

With *The Big Bounce* in 1969, Leonard switched to writing about the contemporary scene. Set in the author's home state of Michigan, the novel describes the dangerous encounter between Jack Ryan, an ex-convict, and Nancy Hayes, a restless 19-year-old with a thirst for thrills. *The Big Bounce* highlights the two kinds of characters that would become trademarks of Leonard's fiction: those who run afoul of the law, and those who become involved with those who do.

In 1972, after reading George V. Higgins's *The Friends of Eddie Coyle,* a comic novel about the activities of a small-time Boston hoodlum narrated through colorful dialogue and extended monologues, Leonard began to experiment with new ways of telling his stories. He found that by relying more on dialogue he could effectively shift the burden of storytelling to his characters. The result was *Fifty-Two Pickup,* his first major success as a crime novelist.

Fifty-Two Pickup is the story of a Michigan businessman named Harry Mitchell who is being framed by a trio of low-life characters for the murder of his mistress. Like many of Leonard's protagonists, Mitchell is an easygoing guy until pushed. Then he takes control of the situation and single-handedly extricates himself from his predicament.

In 1978, Leonard was commissioned by a local newspaper to write a non-fiction profile of the Detroit police. Though he planned to spend only a few days hanging around police headquarters, he ended up staying for two and a half months, soaking up atmosphere, listening to the cops and criminals, lawyers and witnesses who passed through the squad room. This rich assortment of colorful characters provided a new source for the distinctive sounds and speech rhythms that would heighten the realism of his fiction.

The first novel that resulted from this experience was *City Primeval,* also his first book to feature a policeman as protagonist. Raymond Cruz, a Detroit Police Homicide Lieutenant, crosses paths with Clement Mansell, a killer known (with ample reason) as the ''Oklahoma Wildman.'' Their final showdown reads like the climax to one of Leonard's early Westerns. (Appropriately, the novel is subtitled *High Noon in Detroit.*) Besides exciting action, the novel also owes its success to its authentic characters and unflinching realism.

Convinced of the benefits of research on his fiction, Leonard now began employing a part-time researcher to assist him in his efforts. No amount of background research can guarantee a novel's success. However, combined with Leonard's gift for creating fresh and believable characters and dialogue that unerringly rings true, research provides a factual grounding that enhances an already solid core of believability. Such a combination resulted in some of the most notable crime novels in recent American fiction.

Glitz is a good example. Vincent Mora is an off-duty Miami policeman who is recuperating from a bullet wound in sunny Puerto Rico. There he meets and takes a liking to a young woman named Iris Ruiz. When she plunges to her death from a hotel room in Atlantic City, where she has gone to work as a hostess, Mora heads north to investigate. Soon he is engaged in a deadly cat-and-mouse game with Teddy Magyk, a sociopathic ex-convict who seeks revenge on Mora for having sent him to prison.

Thanks to Leonard's extensive research, the reader enjoys an insider's peek behind the scenes at the Atlantic City casinos and gets to meet the distinctive inhabitants of that world. Vincent Mora and Teddy Magyk give life to *Glitz,* while the setting and colorful supporting cast flesh it out in vivid detail.

Leonard employs a similar recipe with equal success in novels like *Stick, LaBrava, Bandits, Freaky Deaky, Get Shorty, Rum Punch,* and *Be Cool.* However, he is careful never to repeat a stale formula. The settings vary from Miami Beach to New Orleans to Hollywood and back to Detroit, and each novel introduces a fresh cast of memorable characters and plots filled with unpredictable twists.

Though his novels are about serious—often deadly—matters, they also reveal Leonard's gift for comedy, especially comic dialogue. Leonard has a talent for mimicking voices that capture the distinctive personality of the speaker. Once these characters open their mouths, they open their minds, and the result is fiction filled with amusingly offbeat points of view.

In several of his recent novels, Leonard has introduced a fresh new element—smart, independent women—to his usual colorful mix of offbeat characters. *Rum Punch*, for example, centers around Jackie Burke (re-named Jackie Brown in the Quentin Tarentino film version of the novel), a forty-four-year old flight attendant who is arrested when the police find cocaine someone has hidden in the money she has been hired to transport from the Bahamas to the U.S. on her flights. Taking matters into her own hands, she concocts an elaborate shell game that outfoxes both the feds and the killer whose money she was carrying. *Out of Sight* features Karen Sisco, a deputy U.S. marshal who deftly manages to balance her attraction to an escaped convict into whose path she stumbles with her sworn duties as a law enforcement officer.

Leonard is sometimes mistakenly categorized as a mystery writer. Though suspenseful, his novels contain little mystery. Instead, they are novels about character and, because many of those characters are either criminals or policemen, novels about crime. The best of them are rich in texture, authentic in detail, and colorful in the richness and variety of character and voice. Over the past three decades, Leonard has produced an impressive body of fiction that sets the standard for what the crime novel in the hands of a talented artist is capable of achieving.

—David Geherin

LESSING, Doris (May)

Pseudonym: Jane Somers. **Nationality:** British. **Born:** Doris May Tayler in Kermanshah, Persia, 22 October 1919; moved with her family to England, then to Banket, Southern Rhodesia, 1924. **Education:** Dominican Convent School, Salisbury, Southern Rhodesia, 1926–34. **Family:** Married 1) Frank Charles Wisdom in 1939 (divorced 1943), one son and one daughter; 2) Gottfried Lessing in 1945 (divorced 1949), one son. **Career:** Au pair, Salisbury, 1934–35; telephone operator and clerk, Salisbury, 1937–39; typist, 1946–48; journalist, Cape Town *Guardian,* 1949; moved to London, 1950; secretary, 1950; member of the Editorial Board, *New Reasoner* (later *New Left Review*), 1956. **Awards:** Maugham award, for fiction, 1954; Médicis prize (France), 1976; Austrian State prize, 1981; Shakespeare prize (Hamburg), 1982; W.H. Smith Literary award, 1986; Palermo prize (Italy), 1987; Mondello prize (Italy), 1987; Cavour award (Italy), 1989; Premi Internacional Catalunya, 1999. Honorary doctorate: Princeton University, New Jersey, 1989; Durham, 1990; Warwick, 1994; Bard College, New York, 1994; Harvard, 1995. Named Woman of the Year, Norway, 1995. Associate member, American Academy, 1974; Honorary Fellow, Modern Language Association (U.S.A.), 1974. **Agent:** Jonathan Clowes Ltd., Iron Bridge House, Bridge Approach, London, NW1 8BD, England.

Publications

Novels

The Grass Is Singing. London, Joseph, and New York, Crowell, 1950.
Children of Violence:
Martha Quest. London, Joseph, 1952; with *A Proper Marriage,* New York, Simon and Schuster, 1964.
A Proper Marriage. London, Joseph, 1954; with *Martha Quest,* New York, Simon and Schuster, 1964.
A Ripple From the Storm. London, Joseph, 1958; with *Landlocked,* New York, Simon and Schuster, 1966; published under original title, 1995.
Landlocked. London, MacGibbon and Kee, 1965; with *A Ripple From the Storm.* New York, Simon and Schuster, 1966.
The Four-Grated City. London, MacGibbon and Kee, and New York, Knopf, 1969.

Retreat to Innocence. London, Joesph, 1956; New York, Prometheus, 1959.
The Golden Notebook. London, Joseph, and New York, Simon and Schuster, 1962.
Briefing for a Decent into Hell. London, Cape, and New York, Knopf, 1971.
The Summer Before the Dark. London, Cape, and New York, Knopf, 1973.
The Memoirs of a Survivor. London, Octagon Press, 1974; New York, Knopf, 1975.
Canopus in Argos: Archives:
Shikasta. London, Cape, and New York, Knopf, 1979.
The Marriages Between Zones Three, Four, and Five. London, Cape, and New York, Knopf, 1980.
The Sirian Experiments. London, Cape, and New York, Knopf, 1980.
The Making of the Representative for Planet 8. London, Cape, and New York, Knopf, 1982.
The Sentimental Agents. London, Cape, and New York, Knopf, 1983.
The Diaries of Jane Somers. New York, Vintage, and London, Joseph, 1984.
The Diary of a Good Neighbour (as Jane Somers). London, Joseph, and New York, Knopf, 1983.
If the Old Could— (as Jane Somers). London, Joseph, and New York, Knopf, 1984.
The Good Terrorist. London, Cape, and New York, Knopf, 1985.
The Fifth Child. London, Cape, and New York, Knopf, 1988.
Love, Again: A Novel. New York, HarperCollins Publishers, 1996.
Mara and Dann: An Adventure by Doris Lessing. New York, HarperFlamingo, 1999.
Ben, in the World: The Sequel to the Fifth Child. New York, HarperCollins, 2000.

Short Stories

This Was the Old Chief's Country. London, Joseph, 1951; New York, Crowell, 1952.
Five: Short Novels. London, Joseph, 1953.
No Witchcraft for Sale: Stories and Short Novels. Moscow, Foreign Language Publishing House, 1956.
The Habit of Loving. London, MacGibbon and Kee, and New York, Crowell, 1957.
A Man and Two Women. London, MacGibbon and Kee, and New York, Simon and Schuster, 1963.
African Stories. London, Joseph, 1964; New York, Simon and Schuster, 1965.
Winter in July. London, Panther, 1966.
The Black Madonna. London, Panther, 1966.
Nine African Stories, edited by Michael Marland. London, Longman, 1968.
The Story of a Non-Marrying Man and Other Stories. London, Cape, 1972; as *The Temptation of Jack Orfkney and Other Stories,* New York, Knopf, 1972.
Collected African Stories. New York, Simon and Schuster, 1981.
This Was the Old Chief's Country. London, Joseph, 1973.
The Sun Between Their Feet. London, Joseph, 1973.
(Stories), edited by Alan Cattell. London, Harrap, 1976.
Jack Orkney. London, Cape, 2 vols., 1978; as *Stories,* New York, Knopf, 1 vol., 1978.
London Observed: Stories and Sketches. London, and New York, HarperCollins, 1992.

Uncollected Short Stories

''The Case of the Foolish Minister'' (as Doris M. Wisdom), in *Rafters* (Salisbury, Rhodesia), November 1943.
''A Sense of Humour'' (as D.M. Wisdom), in *Rafters* (Salisbury, Rhodesia), December 1943.
''Esperanto and Others'' (as D.M. Wisdom), in *Rafters* (Salisbury, Rhodesia), April 1944.
''Politics and Alister Warren,'' in *Labour Front* (Salisbury, Rhodesia), September 1948.
''The Twitching Dog,'' in *N.B.* (Salisbury, Rhodesia), January 1949.
''Fruit from the Ashes,'' in *Trek* (Johannesburg), October 1949.
''Pretty Puss,'' in *Trek* (Johannesburg), March 1950.
''Womb Ward,'' in *New Yorker,* 7 December 1987.
''The Real Thing,'' in *Partisan Review* (Boston), Fall 1988.
''Debbie and Julie,'' in *Antaeus* (New York), Spring 1989.
''Among the Roses,'' in *Ladies' Home Journal* (New York), April 1989.

Plays

Before the Deluge (produced London, 1953).
Mr. Dollinger (produced Oxford, 1958).
Each His Own Wilderness (produced London, 1958). Published in *New English Dramatists,* London, Penguin, 1959.
The Truth about Billy Newton (produced Salisbury, Wiltshire, 1960).
Play with a Tiger (produced Brighton and London, 1962; New York, 1964). London, Joseph, 1962; in *Plays by and about Women,* edited by Victoria Sullivan and James V. Hatch, New York, Random House, 1973.
The Storm, adaptation of a play by Alexander Ostrovsky (produced London, 1966).
The Singing Door (for children), in *Second Playbill 2,* edited by Alan Durband. London, Hutchinson, 1973.
The Making of the Representative for Plant 8 (opera libretto), music by Philipo Glass, adaptation of the novel by Lessing (produced London, 1988).

Television Plays: *The Grass Is Singing,* from her own novel, 1962; *Care and Protection* and *Do Not Disturb* (both in *Blackmail* series), 1966; *Between Men,* 1967.

Poetry

Fourteen Poems. Northwood, Middlesex, Scorpion Press, 1959.

Other

Going Home. London, Joseph, 1957; revised edition, London, Panther, and New York, Ballantine, 1968.
In Pursuit of the English: A Documentary. London, MacGibbon and Kee, 1960; New York, Simon and Schuster, 1961.
Particularly Cats. London, Joseph, and New York, Simon and Schuster, 1967.
A Small Personal Voice: Essays, Reviews, Interview, edited by Paul Schlueter. New York, Knopf, 1974.
Prisons We Choose to Live Inside. Montreal, CBC, 1986; London, Cape, and New York, Harper, 1987.
The Wind Blows Away Our Words, and Other Documents Relating to Afghanistan. London, Pan, and New York, Vintage, 1987.

Particularly Cats and More Cats. London, 1989; as *Particularly Cats ... and Rufus,* illustrated by James McMullen, New York, Knopf, 1991.
The Doris Lessing Reader. London, Cape, and New York, Knopf, 1990.
African Laughter: Four Visits to Zimbabwe. London, and New York, HarperCollins, 1992.
Under My Skin. London, and New York, HarperCollins, 1994.
Doris Lessing: Conversations, edited by Earl G. Ingersoll. Princeton, New Jersey, Ontario Review Press, 1994.
Putting the Questions Differently: Interviews with Doris Lessing, 1964–1994, edited by Earl G. Ingersoll. London, Flamingo, 1996.
Walking in the Shade: Volume Two of My Autobiography, 1949–1962. New York, HarperCollins, 1997.
On Women Turning 70: Honoring the Voices of Wisdom, interviews and photography by Cathleen Rountree. San Francisco, Jossey-Bass Publishers, 1999.

*

Bibliography: *Doris Lessing: A Bibliography* by Catharina Ipp, Johannesburg, University of the Witwatersrand Department of Bibliography, 1967; *Doris Lessing: A Checklist of Primary and Secondary Sources* by Selma R. Burkom and Margaret Williams, Troy, New York, Whiston, 1973; *Doris Lessing: An Annotated Bibliography of Criticisim* by Dee Seligman, Westport, Connecticut, Greenwood Press, 1981; *Doris Lessing: A Descriptive Bibliography of Her First Editions* by Eric T. Brueck, London, Metropolis, 1984.

Critical Studies (selection): *Doris Lessing* by Dorothy Brewster, New York, Twayne, 1965; *The Novels of Doris Lessing* by Paul Schlueter, Carbondale, Southern Illinois University Press, 1973; *Doris Lessing,* London, Longman, 1973, and *Doris Lessing: Critical Studies* edited by Annis Pratt and L.S. Dembo, Madison, University of Wisconsin Press, 1974; *The Tree Outside the Window: Doris Lessing's Children of Violence* by Ellen Cronan Rose, Hanover, New Hampshire, University Press of New England, 1976; *The City and the Veld: The Fiction of Doris Lessing* by Mary Ann Singleton, Lewisburg, Pennsylvania, Bucknell University Press, 1977; *The Novelistic Vision of Doris Lessing: Breaking the Forms of Consciousness* by Roberta Rubenstein, Urbana, University of Illinois Press, 1979; *Doris Lessing: The Problem of Alienation and the Form of the Novel* by Rotraut Spiegel, Frankfurt, Germany, Lang, 1980; *From Society to Nature: A Study of Doris Lessing's Children of Violence* By Ingrid Holmquist, Gothenburg, Studies in English, and Atlantic Highlands, New Jersey, Humanities Press, 1980; *Notebooks/Memoirs/Archives: Reading and Re-reading Doris Lessing* edited by Jenny Taylor, London and Boston, Routledge, 1982; *Substance under Pressure: Artistic Coherence and Evolving Form in the Novels of Doris Lessing* by Betsy Draine, Madison, University of Wisconsin Press, 1983; *Doris Lessing* by Lorna Sage, London, Methuen, 1983; *Transforming the World: The Art of Doris Lessing's Science Fiction,* Westport, Connecticut, Greenwood Press, 1983; and *The Unexpected Universe of Doris Lessing: A Study of Narrative Technique,* Greenwood Press, 1985, both by Katherine Fishburn; *The Implicit Feminism of Doris Lessing's The Four-Gated City* by Lisa Maria Hogeland, Stanford, California, Stanford University Press, 1983; *Doris Lessing* by Mona Knapp, New York, Ungar, 1984; *Doris Lessing and Women's Appropriation of Science Fiction* by Mariette Clare, Birmingham, University of Birmingham Centre for Contemporary Cultural Studies, 1984; *Doris Lessing* edited by Eve Bertelsen, Johannesburg, McGraw Hill, 1985; *Critical Essays on Doris Lessing* edited by Claire Sprague and Virginia Tiger, Boston, Hall, 1986; *Rereading Doris Lessing: Narrative Patterns of Doubling and Repetition* by Claire Sprague, Chapel Hill, University of North Carolina Press, 1987, and *In Pursuit of Doris Lessing: Nine Nations Reading* edited by Sprague, London, Macmillan, 1990; *The Theme of Enclosure in Selected Works of Doris Lessing* by Shirley Budhos, Troy, New York, Whitston, 1987; *Doris Lessing: The Alchemy of Survival* edited by Carey Kaplan and Ellen Cronan Rose, Athens, Ohio University Press, 1988; *Doris Lessing* by Ruth Whittaker, London, Macmillan, 1988; *Doris Lessing* by Jeannette King, London, Arnold, 1989; *Understanding Doris Lessing* by Jean Pickering, Columbia, University of South Carolina Press, 1990; *Doris Lessing: Sufi Equilibrium and the Form of the Novel* by Shadia S. Fahim. New York, St. Martin's Press, 1994; *Doris Lessing* by Margaret Moan Rowe, New York, St. Martin's Press, 1994; *Doris Lessing: The Poetics of Change* by Gayle Greene, Ann Arbor, University of Michigan Press, 1994; *Text/Countertext: Postmodern Paranoia in Samuel Beckett, Doris Lessing, and Philip Roth* by Marie A. Danziger, New York, P. Lang, 1996; *From the Margins of Empire: Christina Stead, Doris Lessing, Nadine Gordimer* by Louise Yelin, Ithaca, Cornell University Press, 1998; *Doris Lessing—In This World But Not of It* by Carole Klein, Boston, Little, Brown, 1999; *Spiritual Exploration in the Works of Doris Lessing,* edited by Phyllis Sternberg Perrakis, Westport, Connecticut, Greenwood Press, 1999.

* * *

Doris Lessing's writings extend the boundaries of fiction, experiment with different genres, explore the worlds of Africa, Britain, and Space, and offer a socio-political and cultural commentary upon the postmodern world. She is a descendant of those nineteenth-century women writers who made poverty, class conflict, women's suffrage, and slavery the subjects of their novels. She is a writer of epic scope and startling surprises. Her novels range from social realism to science fiction, with brief forays into speculative mysticism and fables of horror. After completing five books in her science-fiction sequence, *Canopus in Argos,* in 1983, Lessing startled her public by turning away from the Antarctic cold of two of her planetary realms and returning to novels of postwar London with its welfare state, terrorists, and aging population. Two of these books, *The Diary of a Good Neighbour* and *If the Old Could—,* were originally published under the pseudonym of Jane Somers; the third, *The Good Terrorist,* offers a detailed psychological and political portrait of a group of radicals-turned-terrorists living in London in a dilapidated council flat. Her novella *The Fifth Child,* tells the chilling tale of a changeling, a goblin-child, and questions whether this child is actually the incarnation of evil, a bad seed, a genetic freak—or is it the mother who is deeply disturbed, projecting her own fears and ambivalence regarding the child onto a child who might, in fact, be nearly normal, or minimally retarded, had he not been so cruelly treated by his family and relatives who thought they had an evil ''alien'' in their midst?

The Antartic expeditions of Britain's once revered, now tarnished hero, Robert Falcon Scott, profoundly influenced Lessing's *The Sirian Experiments* and *The Making of the Representative for Plant 8,* not only by providing her with an understanding of the landscape of paralyzing ice and snow, but by offering her insights into the social processes of Scott's time—the Edwardian era of fierce nationalistic pride and Imperial longings—and of ours. Subsequent books, departing completely from her science-fiction vein, nonetheless continue her preoccupation with human behavior and social processes. Two depict, with graphic psychological realism and rich naturalistic detail, the ordinary day-to-day life of an unmarried, middle-aged career woman living in London and tending society's outcast aged, and belatedly trying to love and give—something she was always too busy to do. Another recounts the life of a group of squatters whose radical spirits transform them into revolutionaries.

Many greeted *The Golden Notebook,* written in 1962, as Lessing's feminist manifesto, underestimating its critique of the twin gods, Communism and Freud. Later in life, Lessing was a pioneer in writing novels of aging and dying, confronting the pressing social problems these entail and depicting the grim reality we so often ignore or repress. Her fierce reformist spirit pervades her writing; her anger very much with her, she nonetheless tempers her disillusionment with a wisdom learned through living. Her uncanny gift for knowing characters deeply is very much in evidence.

Lessing's books have always articulated her ideas, whether they be about women's orgasms, Armageddon, or utopia. More often than one would expect from so prolific a writer, she is sufficiently imaginative to integrate smoothly her ideas into her narrative. Even more to her credit is that her writing is continually evolving and is unusual in its breadth. Her plunge into science fiction seemed entirely unexpected. In its incipient stages, in *Briefing for a Descent into Hell,* it was startling and seemed to mark a change as radical as Picasso's when he moved from the Blue Period to Abstract Cubism. With more reflection, one can discover the thread that connects *The Golden Notebook* to her science-fiction sequence, *Canopus in Argos;* but it is hard to think of a writer of her stature in the past half-century who has demonstrated such range.

Her career began with *The Grass Is Singing,* a gem of a book. Set in Rhodesia, it charts with an economy rare in Lessing's works the dissolution of a couple's relationship. After Lessing left Africa in 1949, she devoted ten years to the *Children of Violence* series which explored exhaustively the theme of the "free Woman" long before it was fashionable. It also displayed Lessing's preoccupation with politics, which many have criticized as tedious. *The Golden Notebook* is the best of her works from this period despite its obvious flaws. It is as much a book about writing as it is an exploration of women's relationships with each other and men. In many ways it ought to be compared to Gide's *The Counterfeiters*—the writer's quest to capture the self intended in fiction, not a different, diminished, or enhanced self; the journey through madness that this task requires—the visions of violence it calls up are integral to both books. Both descend from Joyce; both require a sophisticated audience who enjoys unraveling puzzles; both mirror an age when the Heisenberg Uncertainty Principle threatens the reliability of all narrators and estranges the artist from world and self.

In the 1970s came the unexpected turn to science fiction. Lessing's interest in extra-sensory perception first emerged in *Landlocked.* Madness had been seen as a state offering Anna Wulf a respite from the obsessional insistence upon the self that Saul Green spattered out like machine-gun bullets in *The Golden Notebook.* In *Briefing for a Descent into Hell* Lessing took her interest in madness a step further. Calling the book a work of "inner space fiction," she built a story around Charles Watkins, a fifty-year-old classics professor who is found wandering on Waterloo Bridge and is confined for a stay in a psychiatric hospital. Two doctors, of conflicting views, struggle to bring back his memory while he follows a visionary journey in which he enjoys a different, higher identity—one conferred upon him by the Crystal—and one that ordained that he enter earth, hell, as part of a Descent Team whose mission is to show the mad, ego-obsessed humans that they are part of a larger harmony. Lessing, following R.D. Laing, explores the possibility that only the mad are sane. But much more intriguing than this idea is Lessing's decision to fashion the language and metaphors of madness from the idiom of science fiction and the visions experienced through ESP. The inner journey of this modern Odysseus is traveled on the space-time warp of science fiction. The regions he visits are vividly depicted. The language which attempts to capture the visions Watkins is experiencing is one where words are understood by their sounds, not their connotative meanings. "I" glides into "aye" and "eye" as Watkins's mind seems to float in limbo, carrying his body through an unfamiliar medium, revealing images from the visionary realm. Lessing sustains this style, interrupted by only the curt notations of the two psychiatrists, for over a hundred pages. The effect is startling. At times one almost drowns in verbiage, but the flow of the vision is interrupted with the banal observations of the doctors or the staccato questioning of the patient. Undoubtedly, Lessing's style will cost her some readers, but those who bear with her will find themselves caught up in this bizarre account and caring very much whether this amnesiac will tenaciously hang on to his visionary self or succumb to the pressures of the doctors and society and return to the ordinary realm where he is merely a slightly eccentric don. Watkins's hold on the link between the two ways of seeing is most precarious. The reader must try to decide whether Felicity, Constancia, and Nancy, creatures in his visions, correspond with his wife, Felicity, his mistress, Constance, and the wife of a friend. We are also left puzzling whether Miles and Watkins are at some level identical, and whether it matters at all since others in the Descent Team seem still to be around. Also, of course, there is the possibility that Watkins is nothing more than temporarily schizophrenic, though the weight of the story seems to negate this alternative. This book introduces all the ideas and the paraphernalia of science fiction that dominate the *Canopus in Argos* sequence. In its ambiguous treatment of Watkins's identity, it anticipates questions raised in *The Fifth Child.*

Shikasta and *The Marriages Between Zones Three, Four, and Five* are the first works in the sequence. In the first a compilation of reports, historical documents, letters, and psychiatric diagnoses is used to unfold the story of Johor's three visits to Shikasta (Earth), the last taking place in the final phase just following the Third World War. Johor is an emissary from the galactic Empire of Canopus, sent to Shikasta to report on the colony. It is Johor's task to educate those who survive the Third World War to their true place in a larger planetary System, where cosmological accidents have heavily contributed to the blighted human condition, and where Shammat, the criminal planet of another galactic empire, has temporarily obstructed the lock that will connect Shikasta to Canopus. A Chronicler from zone Three is the narrator of the second book. He tells one of the myths that accounts for man's fallen state and reveals the will of the Powers that the potentates of three hitherto separate zones are to marry and so hasten the evolutionary design that governs the six zones encircling Earth. The myth he tells is of the marriage of Al-Ith, Queen of Zone Three, to Ben Ata, ruler of Zone Four, and, later, the marriage of Ben Ata to Vahshi, ruler of Zone Five. Two births follow. The marriages alter the Zones, estrange their monarchs from the old dispensation, and bring about alterations which enable all the peoples to move between the Zones to explore again, in new metaphors, the human qualities responsible for the catastrophic happenings in this century, and the nature of the kinds of relationships men and women must make and the kinds of societies that must be constructed to move humans to a higher consciousness. *The Marriage Between Zones Three, Four, and Five* is far more lyrical than *Shikasta.* The Chronicler uses songs and pictures to capture the mythic dimension of the story he tells. *The Sirian Experiments* recounts the colonial experiments practiced upon Shikasta, leading its people into their 20th century of Destruction. *The Making of the Representative for Planet 8* tells of Johor's journeys to the planet and the ordeal that he and Doeg, the narrator of the novel, along with other representatives, encounter when the planet begins to freeze to death. Doeg comes to understand his part in the Canopean grand design and recognizes finally the mystical transformation which makes him both many and one and enables him to transcend time and space, entering the realm of all possibility under the tutelage of the Canopean Agents. The last book in the series, *The Sentimental Agents,* is the most disappointing. The history of invasions and conquests of the Volyen Empire enables Lessing to reflect on Klorathy's educational process and his attempts to free the Volyens from the power of words and rhetoric, and teach them the power of thought. The book aspires to place itself in the tradition of Plato, Rousseau, Mill, and Orwell as a novel about an educational project, but it is over-written and the ideas seem tedious. Her old concerns abound—how a revolutionary is made; why man has created a world he cannot manage; that history is a repetition of invasion and conquest with the oppressors of one age the oppressed of the next—but the narrative frame is predictable and the ideas simplistic.

Lessing's next four books return to the kind of fiction she was writing before she tackled science fiction. *The Summer Before the Dark, The Memoirs of a Survivor,* and the ambitious *The Golden Notebook* are of a piece with her later writing. *The Summer Before the Dark* is one of Lessing's most perfectly crafted novels. Compact, tightly constructed, it tells the moving story of a woman's coming to terms with aging. Kate Brown, the forty-five-year-old mother of four children, all grown, and the wife of a neurologist of some standing, is a woman who has lived her married years making accommodations, to her husband's choices and to the needs of her children. In the summer of the story, events unexpectedly leave Kate Brown without family responsibilities and alone in London for the first time since her marriage. She holds a job briefly, depending again on the talents that the sympathetic understanding of mothering taught her. Then she has a brief affair with a young man on the continent. Both fall sick; Kate returns to London where she lies ill, preoccupied with the recurring dream of a seal which she must complete. She loses weight; her brightly tinted red hair becomes brassy, then banded in gray. In the last phase of the story, she shares quarters with a young woman who is struggling with her own coming of age. The two women work upon each other; Kate's dream is completed; both separate to enter another stage of their lives—the young woman choosing marriage, children, even responsibility; Kate, returning to her husband, with her hair gray, as a woman who acts for her own reasons, not merely to please others.

The Memoirs of a Survivor is an even more remarkable book, and equally as mature. It is the memoirs of a nameless woman who has survived "it," a nameless war that has left the cities of England empty shells, with conclaves of people living barricaded in their apartments while the gangs of youths roam the streets and the air is so polluted that hand-driven machines are necessary to purify it. The narrator retells how she lived through this period; how she came by a child, Emily, who was entrusted to her care; how she entered a space behind the white walls of her living-room, and inhabited others rooms, from earlier times, and witnessed the traumatic moments of Emily's youth spent with her real parents. She struggles to tell in words how the two worlds, at first so different, began to impinge upon one another. She contrasts what she calls "personal" moments of experience with others that she labels "impersonal." Both reside in the world behind the wall. The story blends the dreamy, prophetic, timeless moments behind the wall where some heightened consciousness, some visionary powers, exist, with a dispassionate, often chilling, realistic account of "ordinary" life in a ravaged London apartment. Always, when the narrator goes behind the wall, she seeks, with a sense of urgency, the inhabitant of the other house, those other gardens. The protagonist's memoirs end with her account of how they somehow came through the darkest times, and realized that the worst was over, that something new would be built. The final paragraphs describe the moment when the walls opened again, and she saw the face she had sought so long, the inhabitant of that hidden world. And that presence takes the hands of Emily, her boyfriend, and the evil child who had terrorized the London streets and leads them into the garden. It is a mystical moment, transfiguring, mysterious, and a consummate end for this exquisitely crafted book.

In *The Diary of a Good Neighbour* Jane Somers, like Kate Brown, is a middle-aged, seemingly successful woman, but, unlike Kate, she is childless and recently widowed with only a career to give her definition. To compensate for her lack of relationships and to try to come to terms with cancer and dying—she had faced neither when her husband was terminally ill—she befriends an elderly woman, Maudie, whom she has met in a corner store. The book offers an extraordinarily moving, also frightening, story of this stubborn old woman's final years, living in a council flat, tended to by Meals on Wheels, day nursing, a cadre of Home Helpers, and the volunteer Good Neighbours. Lessing diligently details the life of the ninety-year-old woman, alone in London, too ill to care for herself, too proud to let others help her, and too angry to let friendship or death come easily to her. Soiled in her own clothing, almost too weak and brittle to walk to the unheated lavatory in the hall outside her flat, or to light her meager fire, far beyond any ability to clean her rooms or even dress or bathe. Maudie fiercely clings to her independence, refusing to be put in a home or a hospital which she knows will only mark her end. This is a novel about our time, aging, and society's refusal to differentiate between growing old and dying. It calls forth Lessing's gifts—a precise eye for detail, an absorption in the quotidian, a psychological understanding of people, and the ability to tell a story. The book is full of stories—Maudie's, the elderly Anne's, another of the women Jane comes to help, and, of course Jane's. The second book in the series is less successful. *If the Old Could*—tells a triter story of Jane's affair with a married man whose unhappy daughter shadows them and whose son baffles her with his unexpected declaration of love. The portions that deal with the elderly, however, are again excellent. Lessing, in both these books, forces the reader to see the elderly. After reading the books, I found myself looking searchingly at the solitary old people sitting on benches, or queuing in the grocery store, or shuffling to a bus, and more important, I looked forward and within.

The Good Terrorist is absorbing, so apt is its portrait of Alice Mellings, a 36-year-old over-aged adolescent, and her "family" of squatters. Alice's instincts are motherly; her zeal to save council flats from being condemned makes her a valuable friend for other, younger, motley members of the Communist Centre Union who join her as a squatter. Her rages are instantaneous and inexplicable to her. Immersed in her day-to-day life, we witness her transformation into a terrorist.

The Fifth Child again demonstrates Lessing's ability to defy labels and forge in new directions. Although its world relates back to a world she revealed in both *Briefing for a Descent into Hell* and *Memoirs of a Survivor,* the tale is told in a new and disquieting form. It begins with a too idyllic account of a pair of young Londoners and their old-fashioned dream of a large family, housed in a mammoth Victorian mansion, comfortably away from the strife of the city. After recounting a cycle of yearly house parties and the arrival of four healthy children, it moves to the birth of the fifth child and the disastrous consequences. Folk ingredients, elements of *Frankenstein,* and images of gnomes and trolls and distant ancestors of the Nebelung haunt the imagination of the mother as her child grows. Mysterious stranglings of animals, and, later, a beating of a classmate, and then thefts and worse crimes occur. All seem the work of the demon child and the idyll of a happy family disintegrates. Throughout the book, we are conscious not only of the desperate plight of the mother of this hapless child, but also of deeper societal unrest. As in many of her other novels, Lessing questions whether there is a higher dimension, or whether mankind has reverted to some darker, primitive age where troll-like creatures dominate the land.

Mara and Dann, Lessing's twenty-first novel, is set during an ice age some 15,000 years in the future, and takes place on the continent of Ifrik, formerly known as Africa, one of the few habitable regions on Earth. Throughout the book are references to the past, and how the world got to be the way it had become—primarily because of an asteroid that hit the Mediterranean. The territory of *Love, Again,* is much more familiar, and the contrast between the two books mirrors Lessing's wide-ranging talent. This time the protagonist is a sixty-five-year-old widow, Sarah, who takes part in the production of a play based on the life of Julie Vairon. The latter, a feminist writer who committed suicide in 1912, is as much a character as any in the story, and throughout the novel's panorama of failed relationships (between Sarah and a daughter-like niece, and Sarah and a son-like lover), she forms an abiding presence.

It is too early to assess Lessing's place in literary history. Her imagination is too rich. What can be said is that she is deeply concerned with the human condition, and hungry to explore new dimensions, to redefine relationships. Her writings reflect a nearly obsessive effort to find a way through the historical ravages of the twentieth century to a condition beyond the one of personal unhappiness that plagues so many human relationships. Her novels expose a world out of control, and attempt to teach us how better to manage our world.

—Carol Simpson Stern

LETHEM, Jonathan (Allen)

Nationality: American. **Born:** New York, New York, 19 February 1964. **Education:** Attended Bennington College, 1982–84. **Career:** Bookseller, Brazen Head Books, New York, 1977–80, Gryphon Books, New York, 1982–84, Pegasus Books, Berkeley, California, 1985–90, Moe's Books, Berkeley, California, 1990–94; writer. **Awards:** Best first novel of the year (*Locus* magazine), 1994; Crawford Award for best first fantasy novel, 1995; Nebula award finalist, 1995; National Book Critics' Circle award, 1999. **Agent:** Richard Parks Agency, 138 East 16th Street, Number 5B, New York, New York 10003, U.S.A.

Publications

Novels

Gun, With Occasional Music. San Diego, Harcourt, 1994.
Amnesia Moon. San Diego, Harcourt, 1995.
As She Climbed Across the Table. New York, Doubleday, 1997.
Girl in Landscape. New York, Doubleday, 1998.
Motherless Brooklyn. New York, Doubleday, 1999.

Short Stories

The Wall of the Sky, the Wall of the Eye: Stories. San Diego, Harcourt, 1996.

Other

The Vintage Book of Amnesia: An Anthology. New York, Vintage Books, 2000.
Contributor, *In Dreams,* edited by Paul J. McAuley and Kim Newman. London, Gollancz, 1992.

* * *

Jonathan Lethem is unquestionably one of the most interesting writers of the late twentieth and early-twenty-first centuries. He began writing science fiction, publishing forty or so short stories before selling his first novel, *Gun, With Occasional Music*, in 1994. Fans and scholars of his work, however, speculate about Lethem's goals in fiction, because he has achieved crossover success, garnering praise among reviewers outside of the science fiction field.

Gun, With Occasional Music arrived with all the fanfare a beginning novelist could wish for. In this dark, funny, highly imaginative mystery, ''Private Inquisitor'' Conrad Metcalf is hired by a man who has been framed for murder. The corpse is that of wealthy Maynard Stanhunt, who had once hired Metcalf to follow Stanhunt's wife Celeste. Metcalf interviews various acquaintances of the Stanhunts and exchanges wise-aleck banter with gangster Danny Phoneblum and gunsel Joey Castle, who threaten him to drop the matter if he knows what's good for him.

So far we are in familiar Raymond Chandler territory, and Lethem imitates Chandler's voice with astonishing fidelity. The novel's premises, however, require much faith in the author, who proves himself capable of establishing his bizarre, dystopian setting as both science-fictional and admirably original. For one thing, only Inquisitors are socially permitted to ask any kind of question. For another, everyone is addicted to government-issued drugs such as Acceptol, Avoidol, and Forgettol. Stranger elements of this society include a judicial system based on ''karma points'' and a disturbing proliferation of bio-engineered animals and infants, the former developed for use as servants, the latter a delinquent class known as ''babyheads.'' Joey Castle is a kangaroo—and he's a mean one.

Metcalf seeks the truth, making enemies of the decadent Bay Area residents and the Public Inquisitors alike, but is finally jailed in cryonic suspension as punishment for his inquisitiveness. Nevertheless, when he awakens he succeeds in solving the crime, a bleak triumph in a rapidly deteriorating society.

Gun won the 1995 Crawford Award for Best First Fantasy Novel (given by the International Association for the Fantastic in the Arts) and was a finalist for the 1995 Nebula Award (bestowed by the Science Fiction and Fantasy Writers of America).

Lethem's second novel, *Amnesia Moon*, was a departure, but allowed recurrent themes to emerge. It is a road novel set in a fragmented future America; if one called it a quest novel, the quest would be for a definitive shared sense of reality. In an interview, Lethem described it as ''a collage of disaster and dystopia scenarios, where I tried to dispose of all my impulses to destroy the world in one book.'' Where Chandler's voice haunted *Gun, With Occasional Music*, science fiction author Philip K. Dick's hovers throughout *Amnesia Moon*, with mystery novelist Cornell Woolrich and *The Wizard of Oz* as added shaping influences. An amnesiac loner called Chaos journeys from Wyoming to San Francisco through various communities, each of which is blind or obsessed in its own distressed way. What has happened to his world? Nuclear holocaust? Alien invasion? As Chaos uncovers pieces of his own past and self, the truth retreats into ever deeper obscurity, because he is one of the survivors who can change reality with his dreams.

These novels established Lethem as a brilliant pasticheur, as well as a master ironist and fabulist of the difficult themes of entropy and epistemology. With *The Wall of the Sky, The Wall of the Eye*, his World Fantasy Award-winning collection of short stories, Lethem proved that his narrative materials were not solely derivative. While alluding to classics and contemporary pop culture, he could also create nightmarish compositions in his own voice. ''The Happy Man,'' his first Nebula winner, ''Light and the Sufferer,'' '''Forever,' Said the Duck,'' ''Five Fucks,'' ''The Hardened Criminals,'' and ''Sleepy People'' are dreamlike, edgy, funny, and painful. They emulsify various themes including dysfunctional family, social, and sexual relationships with nightmarish images of journeys into hell, virtual reality parties whose guests' conversations and character assassinations are as superficial as their presences, prison walls formed of living human criminals, and devolution of humans into creatures scuttling across the ocean floor.

Lethem's next novel, the tour-de-force campus comedy *As She Climbed Across the Table*, homages American Book Award-winning author Don DeLillo's 1985 novel *White Noise* as well as Lewis Carroll's *Alice's Adventures in Wonderland.* Physicist Alice Coombs and her colleagues have created a void on their laboratory table, a hole of nothingness that may be a portal to another universe, which she and her colleagues name ''Lack.'' Narrator Philip Engstrand, a professor who studies other professors, loves Alice, but Alice has fallen in love with her physics experiment.

Alice anthropomorphizes the void, calling it ''him'' and feeding it various objects in an obsessive need to satisfy Lack. While campus professors debate the nature of Lack and the absurdities of each other's theories—in one funny scene, two blind men are brought in to solve the quantum-mechanical ''problem of the observer''—Philip strives to regain Alice's affections. Lethem expertly blends DeLillo's cool, wry narrative tone with the futility-burdened voice and plot of John Barth's 1958 novel *End of the Road.*

Girl in Landscape is not nearly as playful. The book is based on John Ford's 1956 film *The Searchers,* which starred John Wayne as the hard, Indian-hating Ethan Edwards who for years pursues the band of Comanches who abducted his niece. Ford's most sophisticated film challenges Western genre conventions and shows the dark side of the popular cowboy hero.

Lethem's frontier is a newly colonized planet, its despised natives a race known as ''Archbuilders.'' A rich and lyrical portrayal of an adolescent girl, Pella Marsh, growing into adulthood while coping with the death of her mother, her emotionally alienated father, and her strange new home, *Girl in Landscape* pits Pella against Efram Nugent, the Ethan Edwards figure.

The central mystery is complex, involving the Archbuilders' strange quiescence and wistful glorification of the majority of their race, who left the planet long ago for unknown parts; the role of the tiny ''household deer'' in the ecosystem; and Efram's hatred for both. Though a loner, Efram rules the town by the force of his ugly charisma. He clashes horns with the Marshes when learning that they decline to take a drug that everyone else swallows religiously. These pills counteract a contagious Archbuilder virus that psychologically transforms humans in a disturbing way: ''It's called becoming a witness.'' The settlers are secretive about the matter, displaying the obliquities, the alarums and excursions, the displacements and inarticulations of normative values that distort the fabric of a guilt-wracked society. So Pella decides to act on her own. She ''becomes a witness,'' and learns the appalling truth about Efram's reclusivity and hatred of the natives.

Following the climax, which, in ironized Western fashion, features a shoot-out and a major character fleeing Dodge, Pella learns from an Archbuilder a truth hidden within herself. After grappling with racism, complicity, pathological secrecy, and alien mysteries, in a gentle moment of revelation the novel discloses an underlying theme that was never really concealed, survivor's guilt.

Lethem's fans remained loyal, but grumblings from other readers began to appear and echo. He was forgetting his roots. Lethem's fiction was too alloyed, die-hard science fiction readers accused, with the materials of other genres. He was getting too much attention from the highbrow list-makers of New York. The dogs growling in the manger were especially discomfited by an essay Lethem published in the *Village Voice,* ''The Squandered Promise of Science Fiction'' (June 1998).

Lethem took the high road. He politely insists in interviews that he must follow his muse. His next novel showed this determination: *Motherless Brooklyn*, a National Book Critics' Circle Award winner, was yet another radical departure from earlier works.

Motherless Brooklyn is narrated by Tourette's syndrome victim Lionel Essrog, who pursues the killer of the man who saved him from orphanage and life as an outcast. Frank Minna had selected Lionel and three other hapless youths from the St. Vincent's Home for Boys in Brooklyn, New York, and given them a job, a sense of self-worth, and even a family of sorts. They deride Lionel as a ''Human Freakshow'' because of his physical tics and uncontrollable linguistic syncopations, but he is smart enough to realize that their gopher jobs for Minna run the shady side of the street. Their primary front is a car service, their secondary front an alleged detective agency, and their real business is delivering packages for mobsters. When Lionel finds Minna stabbed to death in a dumpster, he decides with goofy but lovable determination to become a real detective.

The book can fit perfectly well onto bookstore mystery shelves, though it has been classified as that cryptomorphic creature, ''Literature.'' Indeed, *Motherless Brooklyn* cries out for a new genus, one that would include novelists such as Vladimir Nabokov, Jorge Luis Borges, and David R. Slavitt. The whimsical richness of the twisting linguistic world in Lionel's mind is nothing short of genius. Every word or phrase that Lionel locks onto produces birth pangs of anagrammatizing and spoonerizing logogenesis.

Many critics have described Lethem's fiction as postmodern, as it suggests that the disappearance of a stable, universal context is the context for contemporary culture. Lethem's divided impulses and resistance to easy categorization are certainly postmodern. His unpredictable novels become unstable whenever the slightest perturbation in plotting is introduced. Every narrative factor is potentially unreal and negotiable.

One does not have to be a card-carrying postmodernist to see paradox and flux as symptomatic of twentieth-century modes of thinking. Lethem's irony focuses on disorder in the human condition itself, his novels comedies of ignorance and interpretation. He analyzes human nature with compassion, rejecting Barth's dictum that the truth is that nothing makes any difference, including that truth. For Lethem, meaning matters, values matter, human happiness matters. As *Newsweek* announced in its April 21, 1998, issue, Lethem is an artist to watch in the twenty-first century.

—Fiona Kelleghan

LEVIN, Ira

Nationality: American. **Born:** New York City, 27 August 1929. **Education:** Drake University, Des Moines, Iowa, 1946–48; New York University; 1948–50, A.B. 1950. **Military Service:** Served in the United States Army Signal Corps, 1953–55. **Family:** Married 1) Gabrielle Aronsohn in 1960 (divorced 1968), three sons; 2) Phyllis Finkel in 1979 (divorced 1982). **Awards:** Mystery Writers of America Edgar Allan Poe award, 1954, 1980; Bram Stoker award, 1997. **Agent:** Harold Ober Associates, 425 Madison Avenue, New York, New York 10017, U.S.A.

PUBLICATIONS

Novels

A Kiss Before Dying. New York, Simon and Schuster, 1953; London, Joseph, 1954.

Rosemary's Baby. New York, Random House, and London, Joseph, 1967.

This Perfect Day. New York, Random House, and London, Joseph, 1970.

The Stepford Wives. New York, Random House, and London, Joseph, 1972.

The Boys from Brazil. New York, Random House, and London, Joseph, 1976.

Sliver. New York, Bantam, and London, Joseph, 1991.

Son of Rosemary: The Sequel to Rosemary's Baby. Thorndike, Maine, Thorndike Press, 1998.

Plays

No Time for Sergeants, Adaptation of the novel by Mac Hyman (produced New York, 1955; London, 1956). New York, Random House, 1956.

Interlock (produced New York, 1958). New York, Dramatists Play Service, 1958.

Critic's Choice (produced New York, 1960; London, 1961). New York, Random House, 1961; London, Evans, 1963.

General Seeger (produced New York, 1962). New York, Dramatists Play Service, 1962.

Drat! That Cat!, music by Milton Schafer (produced New York, 1965).

Dr. Cook's Garden (also director: produced New York, 1967). New York, Dramatists Play Service, 1968.

Veronica's Room (produced New York, 1973; Watford, Hertfordshire, 1982). New York, Random House, 1974; London, Joseph, 1975.

Deathtrap (produced New York and London, 1978). New York, Random House, 1979; London, French, 1980.

Break a Leg (produced New York, 1979). New York, French, 1981.

Cantorial (produced Stamford, Connecticut, 1984; New York, 1989). New York and London, French, 1990.

*

Film Adaptations: *A Kiss Before Dying,* 1956, 1991; *Critic's Choice,* 1963; *Rosemary's Baby,* 1968; *Dr. Cook's Garden* (TV), 1970; *The Stepford Wives,* 1975 (also *Revenge of the Stepford Wives,* TV, 1980; *The Stepford Children,* TV, 1987; *The Stepford Husbands,* TV, 1996); *The Boys from Brazil,* 1978; *Deathtrap,* 1982; *Sliver,* 1993.

Critical Study: *Ira Levin* by Douglas Fowler, Mercer Island, Washington, Starmont, 1988.

Theatrical Activities: Director: **Play**—*Dr. Cook's Garden,* New York, 1967.

* * *

The heroine of *Rosemary's Baby* is overwhelmed by the ''elaborate ... evil'' of the witches' coven through whose agency she has unknowingly borne Satan's child, which now lies in a black bassinet with an inverted crucifix for a crib toy. Elaborateness is, indeed, the chief characteristic of both evil and good in Ira Levin's novels. Bud Corless of *A Kiss Before Dying* makes neat lists of ways to arrange his pregnant girlfriend's ''suicide'' and to win her eldest sister's love. In *This Perfect Day* all human actions are ostensibly directed by a world computer and everyone must touch his identification bracelet to scanners before he can do anything, go anywhere, or receive any supplies. The novel's hero, Chip (or Li RM35M4419, to give him his ''nameber'') fights system with system in a complicated expedition to disable UniComp's memory banks. The first dozen pages of *The Boys for Brazil* describe, course by course, Dr. Mengele's dinner party-*cum*-briefing for the assassination of ninety-four retired civil servants, each of whom has unwittingly adopted a clone of Hitler, produced by the Doctor, who now intends to recreate Hitler's family environment.

Such procedures provide the sustaining interest and suspense of Levin's novels, combining neatness and system with Satanism, secrets, universal surveillance, violence, and death. Rosemary uses a Scrabble set to work out the anagram which identifies her friendly neighbor Roman Castevet as devil-worshipping Steven Marcato. In *A Kiss Before Dying* Dorothy's provision of ''Something old, Something new, Something borrowed, And something blue'' enables her sister to deduce that Dorothy intended marriage, not suicide. The husbands of *The Stepford Wives* make speaking, moving replicas of their spouses. They begin with seemingly innocuous sketches of each real wife and tape recordings of her voice; they end by killing her offstage. Levin increases the ''reality'' of such sinister processes by mingling them with ordinary routines of eating, pregnancy, moving to a new house, etc.

Both good and bad characters must, at times, revise their elaborate plans on the spur of the crisis. Their expedients are ingenious, often complex, and the pleasure of following Levin's details is enough to make some of his novels re-readable when their surprise is over.

The forward movement and acceleration of the plots are further complicated by sudden reversals, single or double, overt or psychological, in which characters (and often readers) are temporarily disoriented. For example, Rosemary, arriving at the logical conclusion that her husband had joined the coven, ''didn't know if she was going mad or going sane.'' Joanna cannot tell if her best friend is still a person or has become an automaton. (She *is* an automaton, and stabs Joanna). Although the reader is sometimes prepared for these discoveries, there are also unexpected shocks, such as when Rosemary, thinking herself safe, sees her witch-obstetrician enter, or when Chip, suddenly taken prisoner by a trusted team-member, discovers that betrayal is really recruitment by the elite subterranean programmers. The effect on the reader of such continual reversals and realignments is a constant uneasiness as to his personal safety and moral identity, which produces horror very successfully in *Rosemary's Baby,* but rather mechanically in *This Perfect Day* and *The Stepford Wives.* No doubt Levin's constant readers now anticipate his surprises, which may account for his increasing detail of violence as excitement in *The Boys from Brazil.*

Occasionally and chiefly in *This Perfect Day,* Levin's literary antecedents are apparent. His shock techniques are essentially those of Ambrose Bierce and Villiers de l'Isle Adam. Bud's slow plunge into a vat of molten copper recalls H.G. Wells's ''The Cone'' with its archetypal death by blast furnace. The world of UniComp is essentially a Brave New World with a Big Brother mentality, but controlled by a mad scientist out of Edgar Rice Burroughs, who rejuvenates through body transference. In short, Levin has drawn upon the almost inescapable traditional materials of his genre, but he uses them intelligently and individually.

Increasingly, Levin's novels imply larger significances. Looking at the copper smelter, the murderer says seriously, ''It makes you realize what a great country this is.'' Rosemary's subtly evil apartment house is owned by the church next door, and there are seemingly casual references to the Death of God. An ideal universe of ''the gentle, the helpful, the loving, the unselfish'' is the vision of a power-joyful egoist. Even the intelligent Stepford husbands in a strange feminist fable want only big-breasted, floor-waxing, mindless wives. A wise old Nazi-hunter, clashing with a radical rabbi, refuses to let ninety-four teenage Hitlers be exterminated for the sake of future Jewish safety, saying, ''This was *Mengele's* business, killing children. Should it be ours?'' These moral paradoxes, undeveloped though they are, both extend and intensify the disquieting uncertainty which had been Levin's chief characteristic.

Sliver, which came fifteen years after *The Boys from Brazil,* seems almost a parody of earlier motifs. There is the sinister apartment house of *Rosemary's Baby,* now dominated by the corrupting power of television. Its owner, Peter Henderson, a hi-tech Peeping Tom, has bugged every room for closed circuit TV and watches the most intimate lives of his tenants—the soap operas God sees. Like God, Peter rewards and punishes, while manipulating a plot to avenge his actress-mother's death. There is also the violent fall of *A Kiss Before Dying* as Peter pushes Kay (less innocent and sympathetic than Rosemary) backward through a window—although she manages to hold on while her cat claws out his eyes. Levin's processes in this novel have become pedestrian, and there is no real shock of reversal since Kay has known of and participated in Peter's surveillance. Nor is a reader likely to be much disquieted by learning that three other New York buildings have been similarly wired. Instead, *Sliver* is basically a melodramatic parable about television, for which Levin himself wrote in its golden age. Then, a character says, it was more real because shows were live. Now it corrupts, and Sam Yale, Peter's intended victim, points out that ''TV madness'' was bound to come. He and Kate give in quickly to the lure of Peter's multiple screens, even while disapproving.

There is promise in the premise of *Son of Rosemary,* sequel to the book that shocked the world thirty years earlier. But the world has changed a great deal since then, as Rosemary learns when she awakens from a coma on November 9, 1999, to discover that her son Andy has since become a guru revered and loved throughout the world. She finds herself surrounded by similar adoration as a sort of latter-day Virgin Mary—only the ''savior'' she has spawned is an anti-Christ who has managed to hide his past from a spiritually hungry world. Despite the intriguing idea behind the story, it lacks the impact of the earlier book—yet another sign that times have changed.

—Jane W. Stedman

LEVINE, (Albert) Norman

Nationality: Canadian. **Born:** Ottawa, Ontario, 22 October 1923. **Education:** York Street School and High School of Commerce, Ottawa; Carleton College, Ottawa, 1945; McGill University, Montreal, 1946–49, B.A. 1948, M.A. 1949; King's College, London, 1949–50. **Military Service:** Served in the Royal Canadian Air Force, 1942–45: Flying Officer. **Family:** Married 1) Margaret Payne in 1952 (died 1978), three daughters; 2) Anne Sarginson in 1983. **Career:** Employed by the Department of National Defence, Ottawa, 1940–42; lived mainly in England, 1949–80; head of the English Department, Barnstaple Boys Grammar School, Devon, 1953–54; resident writer, University of New Brunswick, Fredericton, 1965–66. **Awards:** Canada Council fellowship, 1959, and Arts award, 1969, 1971, 1974. **Address:** Penguin Books, 10 Alcorn Avenue, Toronto, Ontario M4V 3B2, Canada.

PUBLICATIONS

Novels

The Angled Road. London, Laurie, 1952.
From a Seaside Town. London, Macmillan, 1970.

Short Stories

One Way Ticket. London, Secker and Warburg, 1961.
I Don't Want to Know Anyone Too Well: 15 Stories. London, Macmillan, 1971.
Selected Stories. Ottawa, Oberon Press, 1975.
In Lower Town, photographs by Johanne McDuff. Ottawa, Commoners', 1977.
Thin Ice. Ottawa, Deneau, and London, Wildwood House, 1980.
Why Do You Live So Far Away? A Novella and Six Stories. Ottawa, Deneau, 1984.

Champagne Barn. Toronto and London, Penguin, 1984; New York, Penguin, 1985.
Something Happened Here. Toronto and London, Viking, 1991.

Poetry

Myssium. Toronto, Ryerson Press, 1948.
The Tight-Rope Walker. London, Totem Press, 1950.
I Walk by the Harbour. Fredericton, New Brunswick, Fiddlehead, 1976.

Other

Canada Made Me. London, Putnam, 1958.
The Beat & the Still. Toronto, North Edition, 1990.
Editor, *Canadian Winter's Tales.* Toronto and London, Macmillan, 1968.

*

Manuscript Collections: University of Texas, Austin; York University, Toronto.

Critical Studies: ''The Girl in the Drugstore'' by Levin, in *Canadian Literature 41* (Vancouver), 1969; interview in *Canadian Literature 45* (Vancouver), 1970; Philip Oakes, in *Sunday Times* (London), 19 July 1970; Alan Heuser, in *Montreal Star,* 26 September 1970; *Times Literary Supplement* (London), 3 December 1971; Maurice Capitanchik, in *Books and Bookmen* (London), September 1972; Frederick Sweet, in *Profiles in Canadian Literature 4* edited by Jeffrey M. Heath, Toronto, Dundurn, 1982; George Galt, in *Saturday Night* (Toronto), June 1984; ''A Small Piece of Norman Levine'' (interview) by Michael Winter, in *TickleAce 26* (St. John's, Newfoundland), Winter 1993.

Norman Levine comments:

For anyone who wants to know where to begin, I suggest that the start would be *Canada Made Me, From a Seaside Town,* then *Champagne Barn.*

I wrote in the *Atlantic Advocate:* ''When you go to a writer's work—it is into his personal world that you enter. What he is doing is paying, in his own way, an elaborate tribute to people and places he has known.''

* * *

Norman Levine has always been remarkable for the reserve of his writing; but it took him some years to learn what best to withhold and what to reveal. In his early autobiographical stories and novel, *The Angled Road,* he was ''trying to cut out [his] past, to cover … up'' his origins as the Canadian-bred son of a Jewish street-peddler. As if to compensate for this leaching of color from his material, he was also experimenting with patches of vulgar prose-poetry. While teaching himself to write simply and directly, he came to terms with his personal history. Now, in *Thin Ice,* although his range is narrow, he shapes his stories with the unmistakable authority of a writer who has found his subject and style.

Speaking for the most part in the first person, Levine relates in neutral prose incidents from his Canadian upbringing and his years in England. Certain worlds are revealed which he leaves and is drawn back to: Jewish society, life at McGill University summer cottages by the Richelieu, the tourist villages of Cornwall, poverty in a small town. He has achieved the outsider's vantage point from which he turns a telephoto lens on ordinary people and events. The danger of his method is that when it miscarries, as sometimes it does, the reader is left with a commonplace, colorless anecdote that adds up to nothing. His later stories and novel do not differ greatly from his travel narrative, *Canada Made Me,* except in being increasingly crafted, concise, and superficially detached. Although he has escaped the heavy cold of Montreal and the intimate squalor of lower Ottawa, he takes with him wherever he goes his Canadian melancholy and taste for failure.

In drawing on his personal past, Levine often returns to the same scenes, characters, and even fragments of conversation, as if he were unable to invent afresh or to leave behind any of his life. An Englishman awaiting the flowering of a large cactus, a woman without a nose, a prowling man whom a couple nicknames ''the house detective,'' are only a few of many recurrent elements in the work of this man who mines his own writings, word for word, as well as his past. The friction of repeated use has polished his memories until all that is inessential has worn away, leaving a smooth pebble of experience.

Levine consistently avoids evocative vocabulary, choosing instead to make a plain statement of fact in language so empty of implication that it becomes mysterious. It is as if he is trying to create prose as objective as the reality he perceives. Yet, in his best work, when everything possible has been jettisoned, a core of emotion remains. He writes in short, often broken, sentences that correspond to the fragmentary moments of human contact in his tales. Sometimes an ugly expression such as ''less worse'' (*Canada Made Me*) has been selected as the only way of expressing what he means, but at other times a sentence muddles into ambiguity that adds nothing, or an angularity almost illiterate. Except for brief periods, Levine lived in England from 1949 until 1980, so it is not surprising that he somewhat lost his grasp of Canadian idiom and fact. His use of such expressions as ''the School of Seven,'' ''motorways,'' ''left luggage,'' and ''do some walks'' is evidence of the distance he traveled from his native speech. Even his distinguished German translator, Heinrich Böll, the Nobel prize-winner, must have felt it a hopeless task to convey in all its aspects Levine's continual shuttling between England and Canada.

Although Levine says little about his feelings, one cannot miss the passion that concentrates his prose and sends him back to places and people he cannot forget. His journeys are the counterpart of the sexual hunger that runs through *From a Seaside Town.* His appetite for experience and his enjoyment of the grotesque have so far saved him from the sterility that threatens autobiographical writers in middle age. In his low-keyed world even tiny incidents stand out like figures against a landscape of snow. They may mean nothing or anything, but to him they have an importance which the reader feels, but never entirely understands.

—Margaret Keith

LIM, Catherine

Nationality: Singaporean (naturalized). **Born:** Kedah, Malaysia, 23 March 1942. **Education:** University of Malaya, B.A. (honours) in English 1963; National University of Singapore, M.A. in applied linguistics 1979, Ph.D. 1987. **Family:** Married in 1964 (divorced 1980); one daughter and one son. **Career:** Education officer, 1965–78; deputy director of curriculum development, Institute of Singapore, 1979–85; lecturer in sociolinguistics, Seameo Regional Centre, Singapore, 1989–90. **Address:** 18 Leedon Heights, #07–05, Farrer Road, Singapore 1026.

PUBLICATIONS

Novel

The Serpent's Tooth. Singapore, Times Books International, 1982.
The Bondmaid. Singapore, Catherine Lim Publishing, 1995; New York, Overlook Press, 1997.
The Teardrop Story Woman. Woodstock, New York, Overlook Press, 1998.

Short Stories

Little Ironies: Stories of Singapore. Singapore and Portsmouth, New Hampshire, Heinemann, 1978.
Or Else, the Lightning God and Other Stories. Singapore and Portsmouth, New Hampshire, Heinemann, 1980.
They Do Return. Singapore, Times Books International, 1983.
The Shadow of a Shadow of a Dream: Love Stories of Singapore. Singapore, Times Books International, 1987.
O Singapore!: Stories in Celebration. Singapore, Times Books International, 1989.
Deadline for Love and Other Stories. Singapore, Heinemann, 1992.
The Woman's Book of Superlatives. Singapore, Times Books International, 1993.
The Best of Catherine Lim. Singapore, Heinemann, 1993.

Poetry

Love's Lonely Impulses. Singapore, Heinemann, 1992.

*

Critical Studies: ''Catherine Lim and the Singapore Short Story in English'' by Robert Yeo, in *Commentary,* 2, 1981; ''An Interview with Catherine Lim'' by Siti Rohaini Kassim, in *Southeast Asian Review of English,* December 1989; in *Literary Perspectives on Southeast Asia: Collected Essays* by Peter Wicks, 1991; *Women in Bondage: The Stories of Catherine Lim* by Lim Yi-En, Singapore, Times Books International, 1999.

Catherine Lim comments:

Absorbing, enduring interest in the Chinese culture of my childhood; aware of my unusual position as an English-educated Chinese writing in English, with a perspective inevitably coloured by the fact of straddling two worlds.

* * *

Catherine Lim's writing is fuelled by the energies of incongruities, incongruities that power themes including clashes between generations and cultures, the disparity of attitudes and lifestyles found amongst various income-groups, and the discrepancy between the society's ever-improving economic profile and its state of moral poverty. While the themes are large ones, they are expressed within a context of the mundane, in terms of the bric-a-brac of everyday life which lend these themes concreteness and believability. The authorial voice is generally ironic though not uncompassionate, the irony exploiting the territory between differing levels of awareness (e.g., between author, reader, and characters) and pointing sharply to the complacence and the unthinking selfishness displayed by individuals that must be remedied. Lim, however, seldom intrudes judgement; action is allowed to serve as its own comment, and the discrepancies, blandly presented, (e.g., Angela in *The Serpent's Tooth* spends 5,000 dollars on a birthday dinner whereas 17 dollars and 25 cents is undreamed-of wealth to Ah Bah in ''Ah Bah's Money'') insist on the reader's attention, engendering social/moral awareness even if none should have existed before.

The Serpent's Tooth brings together many of the concerns treated of separately in the short stories. As its reference to *King Lear* makes clear, it is on one level about ingratitude and thankless children. But more importantly, it is about the tensions born of the different assumptions and perspectives brought to bear upon things and events, by the main character, Angela and her mother-in-law, (and to a lesser extent, by other members of the extended family). The one stands for the modern, English-speaking Singaporean, for whom money stands in place of culture, the other is an adherent of traditional Chinese beliefs and practices, impervious to change in the world around. They are each other's serpents, each seeing the other as the cause of separation from her child, each making life intolerable for the other, yet ironically unaware of her own shortcomings and insensitivity. What emerges here, and in the short stories, is a sketch of a culture/society comprising morally indifferent and solipsistic individuals. Neither set of values (modern or traditional) is seen as being above reproach. The antique bed belonging to the mother-in-law serves as a vehicle by which both the callousness of the older generation: a bondmaid (who subsequently bled to death) has been raped on it, and also the mercenary tendencies of the younger generation, concerned only with the value of the antique, are exposed.

Certain of the short stories (e.g. ''Gold Dust,'' ''Miss Pereira,'' and ''Deadline for Love'') examine the disparity between economic plenty and emotional/spiritual starvation, and the groping of the individual for meaning un-indexed by the ownership of material things. However, genuine piety or spirituality is seldom encountered in Lim's stories; instead, what is made to substitute for this is a shallow and formal worship of supernatural forces. These forces must be propitiated, not out of devotion, but from a desire to avert ill-fortune (''Or Else the Lightening God'') or to increase wealth. Kindness goes ill-repaid (''A.P. Velloo'') and hopes are, more often than not, thwarted. Thus, while as a body of work, Lim's stories stand as testimony to culture in transit, the older traditions particular to race becoming slowly eradicated or homogenized, they also stand as an indictment of materialism on the increase which threatens to destroy things of intangible value.

Lim was forced to self-publish *The Bondmaid,* due to censorship of the work in Singapore. It is a novel of modern slavery, as four-year-old Han is sold into slavery during the 1950s. Raised in the wealthy House of Wu, she falls in love with her young master, who had been her playmate as a child; yet she can never be his equal, and she reaps a harvest of bitterness and betrayal. The 1950s also provides the setting for *The Teardrop Story Woman,* which takes place in Malaya during the latter years of the British occupation. The title refers to a teardrop-shaped mole beside the eye of protagonist Mei Kwei, a defect that the Chinese associate with a destiny of suffering. Much of her life fulfills that destiny, but the indomitable Mei rises above all challenges to find fulfillment in the forbidden love of a young French priest.

—Susan Ang

LIVELY, Penelope (Margaret)

Nationality: British. **Born:** Penelope Margaret Low in Cairo, Egypt, 17 March 1933; came to England, 1945. **Education:** Boarding school in Sussex, 1945–51; St. Anne's College, Oxford, B.A. (honors) in modern history 1956. **Family:** Married Jack Lively in 1957; one daughter and one son. **Career:** Has been presenter for BBC Radio program on children's literature; regular reviewer for newspapers and magazines in England. **Awards:** Library Association Carnegie Medal, 1974; Whitbread award, 1976; Southern Arts Association prize, 1979; Arts Council National Book award, 1980; Booker prize, 1987. Fellow, Royal Society of Literature, 1985. **Agent:** Murray Pollinger, 222 Old Brompton Road, London SW5 OB2, England.

Publications

Novels

The Road to Lichfield. London, Heinemann, 1977; New York, Grove Weidenfeld, 1991.
Treasures of Time. London, Heinemann, and New York, Doubleday, 1979.
Judgement Day. London, Heinemann, 1980; New York, Doubleday, 1981.
Next to Nature, Art. London, Heinemann, 1982.
Perfect Happiness. London, Heinemann, 1983; New York, Dial Press, 1984.
According to Mark. London, Heinemann, 1984; New York, Beaufort, 1985.
Moon Tiger. London, Deutsch, 1987; New York, Grove Press, 1988.
Passing On. London, Deutsch, 1989; New York, Grove Weidenfeld, 1990.
City of the Mind. London, Deutsch, 1991.
Cleopatra's Sister. London, Viking, and New York, HarperCollins, 1993.
Heat Wave. New York, HarperCollins, 1996.
Beyond the Blue Mountains. London and New York, Viking, 1997.
Spiderweb. New York, HarperFlamingo, 1999.

Short Stories

Nothing Missing But the Samovar and Other Stories. London, Heinemann, 1978.
Corruption and Other Stories. London, Heinemann, 1984.
Pack of Cards: Stories 1978–86. London, Heinemann, 1986; New York, Grove Press, 1989.
The Five Thousand and One Nights. Seattle, Washington, Fjord Press, 1997.

Plays

Television Plays: *Boy Dominic* series (3 episodes), 1974; *Time Out of Mind,* 1976.

Other (for children)

Astercote. London, Heinemann, 1970; New York, Dutton, 1971.
The Whispering Knights. London, Heinemann, 1971; New York, Dutton, 1976.
The Wild Hunt of Hagworthy. London, Heinemann, 1971; as *The Wild Hunt of the Ghost Hounds,* New York, Dutton, 1972.
The Driftway. London, Heinemann, 1972; New York, Dutton, 1973.
The Ghost of Thomas Kempe. London, Heinemann, and New York, Dutton, 1973.
The House in Norham Gardens. London, Heinemann, and New York, Dutton, 1974.
Going Back. London, Heinemann, and New York, Dutton, 1975.
Boy Without a Name. London, Heinemann, and Berkeley, California, Parnassus Press, 1975.
A Stitch in Time. London, Heinemann, and New York, Dutton, 1976.
The Stained Glass Window. London, Abelard Schuman, 1976.
Fanny's Sister. London, Heinemann, 1976; New York, Dutton, 1980.
The Voyage of QV66. London, Heinemann, 1978; New York, Dutton, 1979.
Fanny and the Monsters. London, Heinemann, 1979.
Fanny and the Battle of Potter's Piece. London, Heinemann, 1980.
The Revenge of Samuel Stokes. London, Heinemann, and New York, Dutton, 1981.
Uninvited Ghosts and Other Stories. London, Heinemann, 1984; New York, Dutton, 1985.
Dragon Trouble. London, Heinemann, 1984; New York, Baron, 1989.
Debbie and the Little Devil. London, Heinemann, 1987.
A House Inside Out. London, Deutsch, 1987; New York, Dutton, 1988.
The Cat, the Crow, and the Banyan Tree, illustrated by Terry Milne. Cambridge, Massachusetts, Candlewick Press, 1994.
Good Night, Sleep Tight, illustrated by Adriano Gon. Cambridge, Massachusetts, Candlewick Press, 1995.
One, Two, Three, Jump!, illustrated by Jan Ormerod. New York, McElderry Books, 1999.

Other

The Presence of the Past: An Introduction to Landscape History. London, Collins, 1976.
Oleander, Jalaranda: A Childhood Perceived. London, Viking, 1994.
Egypt: Antiquities from Above (essay), photographs by Marilyn Bridges. Boston, Little, Brown, 1996.

*

Critical Studies: *Penelope Lively* by Mary H. Moran, New York, Twayne, 1993.

* * *

In addition to a mass of children's novels, short story collections, and historical works, British writer Penelope Lively has to her credit numerous adult novels. The main intellectual preoccupation of these novels has been contingency. In other words, she asks what do we do with the facts that don't get explained by the myths of the family and self-expressive authorship that guide us. Lively has answered her query differently at different times. During the first period of her career, Lively faithfully held that the dominant myth of family must be deconstructed. Even the idea of a dominant myth proved restricting to Lively during her middle period: the narratives of her novels grew exponentially with no narrative dominating. After watching the narratives proliferate, in her most recent period, Lively feared cultural fragmentation, and her most recent three novels have reinstated the realist narrative.

Lively's realist period lasted from *The Road to Lichfield* (1977) to *Next to Nature, Art* (1982). Housewife, mother, and history teacher Anne Linton regularly drives the road to Lichfield, where her father is slowly dying in a nursing home. Her father had been a traditional man: an educator; a husband and father of two; a fisherman and outdoorsman. Linton's discovery of her father's extra-marital affair comes as a shock: Was her father a hypocrite? Had she never known her father? Linton deconstructs the myth of the family man to show the irrationality of the ideal, which had led her father to an affair no happier than was his home life. Learning from the past, Anne happily reunites with her estranged husband. What happens when the myth of the family man is not deconstructed? is the question asked in Lively's next book, *Treasures of Time* (1979). In contrast to Anne Linton, who faces the unpleasant truth about her parents' marriage, the young Kate Paxton is so immersed in the myth of the family that she is blind to her parents' mutual loathing. So completely has the myth of the happy family structured Kate's view of the world that she has repressed a memory of her mother kissing a boy, who wasn't her husband. So completely has the myth of the happy family structured her mother's view of herself that she has repressed the fact that her sister and her husband had truly loved one another. The repressed memories of both women return, however: for Kate Paxton, the repressed returns as irrational jealousy of her fiancé; for Laura Paxton, the repressed returns as uncontrollable grief at her sister's death. The contrast between Lively's representations of Anne Linton and Kate Paxton's responses suggests that the myths of the family must be deconstructed, or else they will lead to senseless violence. What is the artist's responsibility when it comes to myths? asks Lively in her fourth novel, *Next to Nature, Art* (1982). ''The artist's responsibility, so far as I'm concerned, is to himself,'' says Toby Standish, a central character. As the artists of the Framleigh Creative Study Centre withdraw entirely from the demands of reconstructing a viable narrative, the result is a bunch of casual affairs, superficial production by both students and teachers, and the Centre's relentless pursuit of the Big Buck.

The novels from *According to Mark* (1984) through *City of the Mind* (1991) make up Lively's romantic period. All of the deconstruction of her previous period has led her to believe that no myth—realist or romantic—is dominant. Like Linton, Mark Lamming makes a surprising discovery at odds with the public construct of the subject of his current biography. Whereas Linton manages to reconstruct the narrative of her traditional father, Lamming abandons an agreed-upon Gilbert Strong for multiple *Gilbert Strongs*: Bloomsbury aesthete Strong; Georgian Strong; moralist Strong; plagiarist Strong; jaded husband Strong; earnest lover Strong. ''The producer interrupts once to say the balance is good but that the programme is perhaps too fragmentary now, are we skipping about too much, what do you think? And Mark, not really paying attention, shakes his head and says no, he thinks it will work like this.'' In *Moon Tiger*, Lively begins to critique her realist preoccupations of prior novels. She locates the novel's center of consciousness in the iconoclastic historical novelist, Claudia Tate, who proves too big for the world around her. Her first love is killed during the War. Her brother marries for convenience. Her conventional daughter proves a disappointment. Now resigned to a nursing home, the elderly Claudia can only remember the joyous episodes of her life as she drifts closer towards death. Rather than succumbing to the disorder that threatens her at the end of her life, Claudia remains driven to narrativize events in her life: as she lies dying, she begins to write a ''History of the World.'' *Passing On* (1989) chronicles the lives of Helen and Edward, who are coping with the recent death of their domineering mother. Beginning with *City of the Mind*, the center has failed to hold: there is not London, but *Londons*. Multiple narratives interweave without unifying into a single vision. One London is that of Matthew Halland, a father, whose divorce has left him without direction, until he falls in love with a woman at first sight. Another London is that of Richard Owen, a Victorian paleontologist. Another London is that of Martin Frobisher, an Elizabethan Arctic explorer; another is that of Rose, a street urchin; yet another is that of Jim, a World War II fire warden. If the drive to discover uncharted territory spurred on the Victorians, Matthew's journey is interior: to find love. None of these Londons is dominant, so there is no agreement on what London is.

After relativizing myths in *According to Mark, Moon Tiger*, and, especially, *City of the Mind*, Lively felt it was time to reinstate a realist myth. *Cleopatra's Sister* (1993), *Heat Wave* (1996), and *Spiderweb* (1999) return to the agreed-upon reality of the family—a reality that Lively now worried was under excessive attack by skeptical deconstructionists. In *Cleopatra's Sister*, Omar Sharif, president of Callimbia, is of mixed cultural parentage: a Callimbian father and a British mother. Sharif's feelings of cultural alienation lead him to commit violent acts, such as overthrowing the Callimbian government, that threaten the lives of Howard Beamish and Lucy Faulkner. One of the least likeable of these deconstructionists is Maurice, the cultural critic of *Heat Wave*. '''My task is the deconstruction of a myth,' says Maurice.'' In contrast, his wife, Teresa, is completely absorbed by the demands of her family. Their disagreement over what is meant by ''family'' leads Teresa's mother, Pauline, to wonder, ''Is this the original Eden of the senses or is it a harsh imprisonment?'' In contrast to earlier novels in which the characters' absorption in the myth of the family required their repression of alternative feelings, here it is Maurice's casual subversion of his marriage that escalates the violence. His bland acceptance of his extra-marital affair—reviving Pauline's repressed fury at her own philandering husband—provokes Pauline to murder Maurice: ''Later, much later, when she tries to recover each moment, she knows that she moved towards him, powered by anger. She has never felt such rage—it came roaring up from somewhere deep within.'' In *Spiderweb*, Stella Brentwood is an anthropologist whose task also ''is the deconstruction of a myth.'' Her deconstruction of kinship systems illustrates her skepticism of such institutions, as also later illustrated in her refusal of three marriage proposals. Like Maurice's rude handling of his wife, Brentwood's rejection pains her suitors. Her casual handling of her manic neighbors has even more dire consequences. By giving the boys a place to vent their rage, their repressed fury returns in their murder of her dog—a symbol of her lone attempt to establish bonds. In these most recent works, Lively has warned that the senseless violence of the uncommitted threatens the fragile bonds of civilization.

—Cynthia Cameros

LODGE, David (John)

Nationality: British. **Born:** London, 28 January 1935. **Education:** St. Joseph's Academy, London; University College, London, 1952–55, 1957–59, B.A. (honors) in English 1955; M.A. 1959; University of Birmingham, Ph.D. 1967. Military Service: served in the Royal Armoured Corps, 1955–57. **Family:** Married Mary Frances Jacob in 1959; two sons and one daughter. **Career:** Assistant, British Council, London, 1959–60. Assistant lecturer, 1960–62, lecturer, 1963–71, senior lecturer, 1971–73, reader, 1973–76, and professor of modern English literature, 1976–87, University of Birmingham; now honorary professor. Since 1987 full-time writer. Visiting associate professor, University of California, Berkeley, 1969; Henfield Writing Fellow, University of East Anglia, Norwich, 1977. Chairman of the Booker prize judges, 1989. **Awards:** Harkness Commonwealth fellowship, 1964; *Yorkshire Post* award, 1975; Hawthornden prize, 1976; Whitbread award, for fiction and for book of the year, 1980; *Sunday Express* Book-of-the-Year award, 1988. Fellow, Royal Society of Literature, 1976, University College, London, 1982, and Goldsmiths' College, London, (honorary), 1992. **Address:** English Department, University of Birmingham, Birmingham B15 2TT, England.

PUBLICATIONS

Novels

The Picturegoers. London, MacGibbon and Kee, 1960.
Ginger, You're Barmy. London, MacGibbon and Kee, 1962; New York, Doubleday, 1965.
The British Museum Is Falling Down. London, MacGibbon and Kee, 1965; New York, Holt Rinehart, 1967.
Out of the Shelter. London, Macmillan, 1970; revised edition, London, Secker and Warburg, 1985; New York, Penguin, 1989.
Changing Places: A Tale of Two Campuses. London, Secker and Warburg, 1975; New York, Penguin, 1979.
How Far Can You Go? London, Secker and Warburg, 1980; as *Souls and Bodies,* New York, Morrow, 1982.
Small World: An Academic Romance. London, Secker and Warburg, 1984; New York, Macmillan, 1985.
Nice Work. London, Secker and Warburg, 1988; New York, Viking, 1989.
Paradise News. London, Secker and Warburg, 1991.
Therapy. New York, Viking, and London, Secker, 1995.

Uncollected Short Stories

''The Man Who Couldn't Get Up,'' in *Weekend Telegraph* (London), 6 May 1966.
''My First Job,'' *London Review of Books,* 4 September 1980.
''Hotel des Boobs,'' in *The Penguin Book of Modern British Short Stories,* edited by Malcolm Bradbury. London, Viking, 1987; New York, Viking, 1988.
''Pastoral,'' in *Telling Stories,* edited by D. Minshull. London, Hodder and Stoughton, 1992.

Plays

Between These Four Walls (revue), with Malcolm Bradbury and James Duckett (produced Birmingham, 1963).
Slap in the Middle (revue), with others (produced Birmingham, 1965).
The Writing Game (produced Birmingham, 1990). London, Secker and Warburg, 1991.

Television Writing: *Big Words ... Small Worlds* (also presenter), 1987; *Nice Work,* from his own novel, 1989; *The Way of St. James* (also presenter), 1993; and *Martin Chuzzlewit* (adapted from Charles Dickens), 1994.

Other

About Catholic Authors (for teenagers). London, St. Paul Publications, 1958.
Language of Fiction. London, Routledge, and New York, Columbia University Press, 1966; revised edition, Routledge, 1984.
Graham Greene. New York, Columbia University Press, 1966.
The Novelist at the Crossroads and Other Essays on Fiction and Criticism. London, Routledge, and Ithaca, New York, Cornell University Press, 1971.
Evelyn Waugh. New York, Columbia University Press, 1971.
The Modes of Modern Writing: Metaphor, Metonymy, and the Typology of Modern Literature. London, Arnold, and Ithaca, New York, Cornell University Press, 1977.
Working with Structuralism: Essays and Reviews on Nineteenth- and Twentieth-Century Literature. London, Routledge, 1981.
Write On: Occasional Essays 1965–1985. London, Secker and Warburg, 1986.
After Bakhtin: Essays on Fiction and Criticism. London and New York, Routledge, 1990.
The Art of Fiction. New York, Viking, and London, Secker and Penguin, 1992.
Editor, *Jane Austen: ''Emma'': A Casebook.* London, Macmillan, 1968; Nashville, Aurora, 1970(?).
Editor, with James Kinsley, *Emma,* by Jane Austen. London, Oxford University Press, 1971.
Editor, *Twentieth-Century Literary Criticism: A Reader.* London, Longman, 1972.
Editor, *Scenes of Clerical Life,* by George Eliot. London, Penguin, 1973.
Editor, *The Woodlanders,* by Thomas Hardy. London, Macmillan, 1974.
Editor, *The Best of Ring Lardner.* London, Dent, 1984.
Editor, *The Spoils of Poynton,* by Henry James. London, Penguin, 1987.
Editor, *Modern Criticism and Theory: A Reader.* London, Longman, 1988; revised edition, 1999.
Editor, *Lucky Jim,* by Kingsley Amis. London, Penguin, 1992.

*

Manuscript Collections: University of Birmingham Library.

Critical Studies: Interview with Bernard Bergonzi, in *Month* (London), February 1970, ''The Decline and Fall of the Catholic Novel,'' in *The Myth of Modernism and Twentieth-Century Literature* by Bergonzi, Brighton, England, Harvester Press, 1986, *Exploding English: Criticism, Theory, Culture* by Bergonzi, Oxford, England, n.p., 1990; ''The Novels of David Lodge'' by Michael Parnell, in *Madog* (Barry, Wales), Summer 1979; article by Dennis Jackson, in *British Novelists since 1960* edited by Jay L. Halio, Detroit, Gale, 1983; *Novelists in Interview* by John Haffenden, London and New York, Methuen, 1985; *The Dialogic Novels of Malcolm Bradbury and David Lodge* by Robert A. Morace, Carbondale, Southern Illinois University Press, 1989; *Modern Critics in Practice: Critical Portraits of British Literary Critics* by P. Smallwood, London, n.p., 1990; *David Lodge: How Far Can You Go?* by M. Moseley, San Bernardino, California, n.p., 1991; *Faithful Functions: The Catholic Novel in British Literature* by T. Woodman, n.p., Milton Keynes, 1991; *David Lodge: An Annotated Primary and Secondary Bibliography* by Norbert Schurer. Frankfurt am Main and New York, P. Lang, 1995; *David Lodge* by Bergonzi, Plymouth, England, Northcote House, 1995; *David Lodge* by Bruce K. Martin, New York, Twayne, 1999.

David Lodge comments:

(1972) My novels belong to a tradition of realistic fiction (especially associated with England) that tries to find an appropriate form for, and a public significance in, what the writer has himself experienced and observed. In my case this experience and observation include such things as: lower-middle-class life in the inner suburbs of South East London; a wartime childhood and a postwar ''austerity'' adolescence; Catholicism; education and the social and physical mobility it brings; military service, marriage, travel, etc. My first, second, and fourth novels are ''serious'' realistic novels about such themes, the last of them, *Out of the Shelter,* which is a kind of Bildungsroman, being, as far as I am concerned, the most inclusive and most fully achieved.

My third novel, *The British Museum Is Falling Down,* was something of a departure in being a comic novel, incorporating elements of farce and a good deal of parody. I plan to write more fiction in the comic mode, as I enjoy the freedom for invention and stylistic effect it affords. On the other hand, I have not (like many contemporary writers) lost faith in traditional realism as a vehicle for serious fiction. The writer I admire above all others, I suppose, is James Joyce, and the combination one finds in his early work of realistic truthtelling and poetic intensity seems to me an aim still worth pursuing.

As an academic critic and teacher of literature with a special interest in prose fiction, I am inevitably self-conscious about matters of narrative technique, and I believe this is a help rather than a hindrance. I certainly think that my criticism of fiction gains from my experience of writing it.

(1981) Since writing the above I have come to have less faith in the viability of the traditional realistic novel of the kind that seeks, by suppressing the signs that it is written and narrated, to give the illusion of being a transparent window upon the real. This shift of attitude does not entail abandoning the novel's traditional function of engaging with, organizing and interpreting social-historical experience—merely being open about the necessarily conventional and artificial ways in which it does so. My last two works of fiction, therefore, have a prominent ''metafictional'' thread running through them through which the self-consciousness about fictional technique referred to above is allowed some play in the texts themselves—licenced by comedy in *Changing Places,* but with more serious thematic intent in *How Far Can You Go?*

(2000) The comic-carnivalseque-metafictional strain in my fiction that started with *The British Museum Is Falling Down* perhaps reached its fullest development in *Small World: An Academic Romance* (1974). After that book I began to move back towards a more realistic, and perhaps more ''serious,'' engagement with my material, though still aiming to amuse, and still experimenting with narrative technique. *Nice Work* (1988), for instance, has a playful intertextual relationship with certain Victorian Industrial Novels, but it also attempts to give a faithful account of what it was like to work in industry and academia in England in the 1980s, the Thatcher years. *Nice Work* was also the most ''researched'' of my books to date, since the industrial side of the story was unknown territory to me when I first got the idea. This set the pattern for subsequent work. The basic story of *Paradise News* (1991)—the hero's visit to his dying aunt in Honolulu—was based on personal experience, but I made two research trips to Hawaii and did a great deal of reading in modern theology and about tourism before beginning the novel. *Therapy* (1995) drew on personal experience of depression and knee surgery, but involved extensive reading of Kierkegaard. In these two novels I made extensive use of first-person narrative for the first time in my work since *Ginger You're Barmy,* but with more variation and conscious artifice than in that early novel. This will also be a feature of my next full-length novel, to be published in 2001. I try to write novels that tell more than one story, that have several levels of meaning and many voices, that will entertain but also provoke thought, that reflect contemporary social reality, but at the same time acknowledge their debt to literary tradition.

* * *

David Lodge's novels use and stay close to material that he knows well. Without being overtly autobiographical, they often draw on personal experience: a lower-middle-class South London childhood and adolescence in *The Picturegoers* and *Out of the Shelter,* military service in *Ginger, You're Barmy,* and academic life in his ''campus'' novels. Lodge was brought up as a Catholic and some of his novels examine the culture and customs of English Catholic life. His emphasis is sociological rather than theological, providing sharp but affectionate observations of the lives of a minority group. In *The British Museum Is Falling Down* he gives brisk comic treatment to the human problems arising from the Catholic ban on contraception. In *How Far Can You Go?,* a longer and more serious-minded novel (though none of his fiction is without comic elements), Lodge traces the lives of a group of middle-class English Catholics from the early 1950s when they are students at London University, to the late 1970s when they are approaching middle age and have lived through the transformations of Catholicism which followed the Vatican Council.

Though he is an entertaining and sharp-eyed recorder of personal and social embarrassment, Lodge is a good-humored writer, and rather too genial to be a thoroughgoing satirist. These qualities are apparent in the three novels set wholly or partly in the city of Rummidge and its university, which form a sequence with recurring characters, covering the years from 1969 to 1986. Lodge describes their settings as imaginary places which for the purposes of fiction occupy ''the space where Birmingham is to be found on maps of the so-called real world.'' They draw on Lodge's long career as a university teacher of English between 1960 and 1987, during which time he published several academic critical books in addition to his fiction. *Changing Places* is subtitled ''A Tale of Two Campuses'': Rummidge is contrasted with Plotinus, a celebrated Californian university which bears much the same relation to Berkeley as Rummidge does to Birmingham. Philip Swallow, a mild, amiable, unsophisticated lecturer in English at Rummidge, goes to Plotinus as an exchange professor; in return Rummidge gets one of the biggest guns at Plotinus, the high-powered Professor Morris Zapp, who comes to England to escape his marital problems. The story moves, with a wealth of inventiveness, back and forth between Swallow in Plotinus and Zapp in Rummidge, each coping with different kinds of culture shock. They end up having exchanged not only jobs but wives; the reader is left uncertain whether the exchange will be permanent. *Changing Places* exploits polarities to splendid comic effect: Britain and America, the Midlands and San Francisco Bay, English academic life and American. Zapp and Swallow are representative types, well observed and culturally placed: the ruthless professional Zapp wants to be the greatest expert on Jane Austen in the world, even though he dislikes her novels; the dithering Swallow likes the whole of English literature so much that he can never find a "field" to specialize in, to the amused incredulity of the Americans.

In *Small World,* set ten years on, Zapp is divorced and even more famous; Swallow and his wife are together again, though he is now more worldly and has achieved some modest academic success. It is a formally elaborate novel, making use of the conventions of the epic romances of the Italian Renaissance, where narratives are interwoven, the characters have frequent and surprising adventures, and a beautiful maiden flits elusively in and out of the narrative. It opens in Rummidge but moves over the globe, as the academic participants fly from one conference or lecturing engagement to another. There is a rich mixture of comedy, sex, and scholarship, sometimes all on the same plate. *Small World* is learned and allusive—among other things, it offers an ordinary reader's guide to structuralism—but at the same time farcical, fast-moving, and highly entertaining.

Nice Work is set wholly in Rummidge, when the university is suffering from the financial cuts of the 1980s. Zapp and Swallow put in appearances, but the principal characters are new, a man and woman who are completely different types but whose lives become fascinatingly entwined. Vic Wilcox runs a local engineering works; he is tough, energetic, and good at his job but socially and emotionally insecure. Robyn Penrose teaches English and Women's Studies at the university. She is a recognizable figure of the age: attractive, intellectual, and self-assured, an articulate feminist and supporter of left-wing causes, at home in the abstruse reaches of critical theory. But she is also narcissistic and naive, and entirely ignorant of the industrial world (represented by Wilcox, the factory, and its workers) into which she finds herself thrown. She is an expert on the Victorian "Condition of England" novel, and *Nice Work* is Lodge's own essay in the genre, surveying Margaret Thatcher's England. The unfashionably happy ending has what looks like a deliberately Victorian air. In this novel, Lodge, like Robyn, takes a good look at the world outside the academy—*Nice Work* appeared soon after he had taken early retirement from teaching—with rewarding results.

His next novel, *Paradise News,* returns to the Catholic topics of *How Far Can You Go?* and takes them further still. The central character, Bernard Walsh, is an ex-priest in his forties, from the South London Irish milieu of Lodge's first novel. He is a sad, lonely figure who has lost not only faith but hope; he makes a meagre living as a part-time, unbelieving lecturer in theology at a non-denominational college. His life picks up when he and his cantankerous widower father travel to Hawaii, where Bernard's expatriate aunt has lived for many years and where she is now dying of cancer. Hawaii, the self-styled island paradise, is contrasted in Bernard's thoughts with the Christian heaven which he used to preach about and can no longer believe in. But in Hawaii he unexpectedly finds love, and, if not faith, a renewed sense of hope. In this gentle, quietly moving novel Lodge takes another look at the themes and some of the settings of his earlier work; but it is a little lacking in the ingenuity and wit that readers have come to expect in his fiction.

Those qualities, though, are triumphantly present in *Therapy,* which Lodge published soon after his sixtieth birthday. It is the story, told in the first person, of Tubby Passmore, a successful and prosperous television scriptwriter. He has most things he could want in life, including, he believes, a stable and happy marriage. He wonders, therefore, why he is consumed by anxiety and dread, neuroses which have sent him to a variety of therapists, and which make him an avid reader of Kierkegaard, the Danish philosopher who wrote books with titles that Tubby finds irresistible: *Fear and Trembling, The Concept of Dread,* and *Sickness Unto Death.* Tubby's world falls apart when his wife suddenly leaves him after thirty years, not for anyone else but because she finds him too moody and boring to live with any longer. Tubby is shattered but he survives and fights back in ways which involve him in farcical humiliations, especially when he tries, in late middle age, to get some sexual variety into his life. He resembles the heroes of many American novels, who undergo all kinds of personal, professional, and sexual disasters, but who remain fiercely articulate and opinionated in the midst of everything—an English cousin of Saul Bellow's Herzog, perhaps. *Therapy* shows Lodge at the top of his form, comic, thoughtful, and continually surprising.

—Bernard Bergonzi

LOVELACE, Earl

Nationality: Trinidadian. **Born:** Taco, Trinidad, 13 July 1935. **Family:** Married; two sons, one daughter. **Career:** Proofreader, *Trinidad Guardian,* 1953–54; civil servant: agricultural assistant in Jamaica, 1956–66; journalist, *Trinidad and Tobago Express,* 1967; lecturer in English, University of the District of Columbia, 1971–73; writer-in-residence, Hartwick College, Oneonta, New York, 1986. Since 1977 teacher, University of the West Indies, Saint Augustine, Trinidad. **Awards:** B.P. Independence award, 1965; Pegasus Literary award, 1966; Guggenheim fellowship, 1980; National Endowment for the Humanities grant, 1986; Commonwealth Writers' prize, 1997. **Address:** c/o Andre Deutsch, 105 Great Russell St., London WC1B 3LJ, England.

PUBLICATIONS

Novels

While Gods Are Falling. London, Collins, 1965; Chicago, Regnery, 1966.

The Schoolmaster. London, Collins, and Chicago, Regnery, 1968.

The Dragon Can't Dance. London, Deutsch, 1979; Washington, D.C., Three Continents Press, 1981.

The Wine of Astonishment. London, Deutsch, 1982; New York, Vintage, 1984.

Salt. New York, Persea Books, 1997.

Short Stories

A Brief Conversation and Other Stories. London, Heinemann, 1988.

Plays

The New Hardware Store (produced London, 1985). Included in *Jestina's Calypso and Other Plays,* 1984.

Jestina's Calypso and Other Plays (includes *The New Hardware Store* and *My Name Is Village*). London, Heinemann, 1984.

The Dragon Can't Dance, adaptation of his own novel (produced London, 1990).

*

Bibliography: "Earl Lovelace: A Bibliography" by Chezia Thompson-Cager, in *Contributions in Black Studies,* 8, 1986–87.

Manuscript Collection: The Lovelace Archives, Port of Spain, Trinidad.

Critical Studies: "In Search of the West Indian Hero: A Study of Earl Lovelace's Fiction" by Marjorie Thorpe, in *Critical Issues in West Indian Literature,* edited by Erika Sollish Smilowitz and Roberta Quarles Knowles, Parkersburg, Iowa, Caribbean, 1984; "Salvation, Self, and Solidarity in the Work of Earl Lovelace" by Norman Reed Cary, *World Literature Written in English,* Spring 1988; "Earl Lovelace's Bad Johns, Street Princes and the Masters of Schools" by Chezia Thompson-Cager, in *Imagination, Emblems, and Expressions,* edited by Helen Ryan, Bowling Green, Ohio, Bowling Green University Popular Press, 1992.

* * *

Earl Lovelace has established himself as one of Trinidad's most well known literary talents. As a writer and storyteller his novels, short stories, and plays explore the effects the significant social, economic, and political change of late twentieth-century Trinidad have had on the lives of individuals and communities. Lovelace has witnessed this change first hand: born into a large family in Toco, Trinidad, in 1935, Lovelace spent his early life in part with his grandparents in Tobago, and in different districts on the outskirts of Port of Spain. This travelling attuned Lovelace to the nuances of local dialects, whether mitigated by class, region, ethnicity, or mood. These linguistic subtleties are utilized in his exceptionally vivid writing, as dialect functions to convey the cultural particularities of his subjects, while also contributing to his distinct brand of lyrical realism. A storyteller at heart, the prevalence of dialect in Lovelace's writing, and the ease with which he uses it, foregrounds the importance of the Caribbean's oral traditions to his writing and narrative structure.

At the thematic center of Lovelace's narratives is an exploration of the ambiguous relationship between change and progress. His characters often must weigh the merits of tradition and cultural continuity against financial gain and upward mobility. In his first novel, *While Gods Are Falling,* Lovelace considers the dilemma of Walter, whose frustration with the urban congestion, cacophony, and confusion of Port of Spain results in a nostalgia for the imagined opportunities of the rural environment for independence and self-assertion. However, Lovelace reveals Walter's construction of the rural environment to be flawed, influenced more by his dissatisfaction with the present than any long-standing romance with the past. Nevertheless, in his measured representation of both rural and urban environments, Lovelace asserts the reality of the limited opportunities for self-realization available to those politically and economically disempowered in—and by—a colonial society. Continuing this investigation of progress and its inextricable connection to colonialism and power in his second novel, *The Schoolmaster,* Lovelace presents the small community of Kumaca, whose longing for economic advancement makes them vulnerable to the manipulations of others. The black teacher who arrives to educate the isolated townspeople is a product of colonial schooling, and reproduces the dynamics of domination in his relationship to the illiterate villagers. Even as the local villagers recognize the inevitable intrusion of the ever-expanding Port of Spain into their lives, and desire the skills that will permit them to access the opportunities the nation's capital will provide, they are not prepared for the ways in which the teacher will use his knowledge to exploit them. The novel ends with an uneasy resolution, suggesting that while the residents of Kumaca will adapt, this adaptation does is not a mark of superiority or triumph.

It is the changing nature of Trinidad's annual Carnival, and how these changes are indicative of larger shifts in communities and the nation at large, that is the subject of Lovelace's third novel, *The Dragon Can't Dance.* Here, the members of a small community define themselves through their participation in the pageantry of Carnival and the roles they assume in it. While the festival itself has remained consistent in many of its practices, the characters must confront how the meaning of enacting the Carnival has changed. For example, those participants previously valorized as warriors have no place in the contemporary city except as "Bad Johns" who cause trouble, while their stick fighting battles have been displaced in popularity and importance by competitions between calypso bands. The nature and rhythms of calypso are central to Lovelace's text. Just as calypso's consistent rhythm overlaid by improvisation results in a repetition-with-difference, new nuances and beats, the changes in Trinidadian culture have caused new forms and meanings to emerge with which its citizens must learn to live.

Music as a repository of cultural and communal practices is also thematically significant in *The Wine of Astonishment.* As the practice of the Spiritual Baptist religion and its raucous musical style of worship is legally outlawed in the early part of the twentieth century, one small community attempts to maintain faith. This faith, however, receives constant challenges from colonial society and its policies, including the corruption that they engender. Lovelace's ongoing fascination with the dynamics of individual communities, as well as the relationships of individuals within those communities, is at the core of *The Wine of Astonishment.* While the decriminalization of Spiritual Baptism comes too late for many of its practitioners, who have lost the spirit required for its form of worship, one woman who has maintained her faith recognizes its cultural continuance in the energetic music of the steel bands. Recognized as a form of cultural persistence, this continuity functions as a spiritual affirmation of the people in the face of racial discrimination, economic disadvantages, and other trials. Lovelace does not end this story on an uncritically uplifting note, however. The novel, like his others, is woven through with tragedies and disappointments. Even as characters assert "God will not put on a people more than they can bear," it is clear that what is "bearable" is not by definition necessarily desirable or sustaining.

Lovelace's collections published in the 1980s—*Jestina's Calypso and Other Plays* and *A Brief Conversion and Other Stories*—are further investigations of the thematic preoccupations established in his previous work. However, in his latest novel, *Salt* published in 1997, Lovelace's recurring themes—change, colonialism, community, culture, desire, materialism, belonging, self-definition, etc.—are all reworked via the historical framework provided by Guinea John, resulting in Lovelace's most pointed social critique to date. Guinea John is a mythic figure is said to have fled the death sentence imposed for his part in an unsuccessful slave rebellion by placing two corncobs under his arms and flying back to Africa. His descendents who remain behind in Trinidad alternately struggle to establish a place for themselves or to escape overseas. In this epic tale, Lovelace weaves together narrators from various centuries and the multiple ethnicities that make up Trinidad's multi-ethnic, culturally creolized society, to create a stunning literary portrait of Trinidad's history and its people. Implicit in this tale is the moral and ethical necessity for reparations to those populations displaced and dehumanized by slavery, disenfranchised by colonialism, and continually dislocated by the inheritance of both. Guinea John's rejection of slavery and its ''authority'' is echoed in his great-grandson's disdain for the façade of Emancipation, which provided financial compensation for those who lost their slave property, but none for those formerly enslaved who had endured generations of stolen labor and other heinous abuses. Lovelace's primary twentieth-century protagonist is the schoolteacher Alford George, whose realization that he spent nineteen years preparing his students to ''escape'' overseas causes him to reevaluate his relationship to Trinidad. An ''Everyman,'' George struggles to overcome the psychological legacy of slavery in order to teach his people about the necessity of investing one's self in Trinidad. Here the acceptance characterizing the refrain of his previous book, ''God will not put on a people more than they can bear,'' is reworked into an aggressive political manifesto, as characters prove their strength not by endurance, but by action. As always, Lovelace's characters are masterfully drawn, captivating and convincing in their struggles and the resolutions they reach. *Salt* marks Lovelace's move from writing of the ramifications of what Langston Hughes identifies as ''the dream deferred'' (by the failure of Emancipation), to asserting the necessity of facing that deferral and demanding the right to realize the dream, the first step being the right to demand reparations. *Salt* was awarded the 1997 Commonwealth Writers' Prize.

—Jennifer Harris

LURIE, Alison

Nationality: American. **Born:** Chicago, Illinois, 3 September 1926. **Education:** Radcliffe College, Cambridge, Massachusetts, A.B. in history and English 1947. **Family:** Married Jonathan Peale Bishop, Jr., in 1948 (divorced 1985); three sons. **Career:** Lecturer, 1968–73, adjunct associate professor, 1973–76, associate professor, 1976–79, and since 1979 professor of English, Cornell University, Ithaca, New York. **Awards:** Yaddo Foundation fellowship, 1963, 1964, 1966; Guggenheim fellowship, 1965; Rockefeller grant, 1968; New York State Council on the Arts grant, 1972; American Academy award, 1979; Pulitzer prize, 1985; Prix Femina Etranger (France), 1989. **Address:** Department of English, Cornell University, Ithaca, New York 14853, U.S.A.

PUBLICATIONS

Novels

Love and Friendship. London, Heinemann, and New York, Macmillan, 1962.

The Nowhere City. London, Heinemann, 1965; New York, Coward McCann, 1966.

Imaginary Friends. London, Heinemann, and New York, Coward McCann, 1967.

Real People. New York, Random House, 1969; London, Heinemann, 1970.

The War Between the Tates. New York, Random House, and London, Heinemann, 1974.

Only Children. New York, Random House, and London, Heinemann, 1979.

Foreign Affairs. New York, Random House, 1984; London, Joseph, 1985.

The Truth about Lorin Jones. Boston, Little Brown, and London, Joseph, 1988.

The Last Resort. New York, Henry Holt, 1998.

Short Stories

Women and Ghosts. New York, Doubleday, and London, Heinemann, 1994.

Uncollected Short Stories

''Hansel and Gretel,'' in *New Story 2* (New York), 1951.

''Fat People,'' in *Vogue* (New York), October 1989.

Other (for children)

The Heavenly Zoo: Legends and Tales of the Stars. London, Eel Pie, 1979; New York, Farrar Straus, 1980.

Clever Gretchen and Other Forgotten Folktales. New York, Crowell, and London, Heinemann, 1980.

Fabulous Beasts. New York, Farrar Straus, and London, Cape, 1981.

Don't Tell the Grown-ups: Subversive Children's Literature. Boston, Little Brown, and London, Bloomsbury, 1990; as *Not in Front of the Grown-ups: Subversive Children's Literature,* London, Cardinal, 1991.

Cap o'Rushes. London, BBC, 1991.

The Black Geese: A Baba Yaga Story From Russia (reteller), illustrated by Jessica Souhami. New York, DK, 1999.

Other

V.R. Lang: A Memoir. Privately printed, 1959; in *Poems and Plays,* by V.R. Lang, New York, Random House, 1975.

The Language of Clothes. New York, Random House, 1981; London, Heinemann, 1982.

Steve Poleskie, Artflyer, with Stephen Foster. Southampton, Hampshire, John Hansard Gallery, 1989.

Editor, *The Oxford Book of Modern Fairy Tales.* Oxford and New York, Oxford University Press, 1993.
Editor, *The Secret Garden*, by Frances Hodgson Burnett. New York, Penguin Books, 1999.

*

Manuscript Collections: Cornell University Library, Ithaca, New York.

Critical Studies: *Alison Lurie* by Richard Hauer Costa, New York, Twayne, 1992.

* * *

It is difficult to think of any other North American writer who has held up the mirror to the nature of the professional middle classes as exactly and as wittily as Alison Lurie. From *Love and Friendship* (1962) all the way through to *The Truth about Lorin Jones* (1988), the customs and usages, fancies and foibles, of comfortable (usually East Coast) America are carefully scrutinized with Lurie's wryly amused, detached, yet not unsympathetic gaze.

Events that could have become the stuff of American tragedy in another writer's hands—marital breakdown, illicit sexual passion, madness, problems of artistic creation, loss of innocence, crisis in personal identity, emotional neglect—are transformed deftly and sharp-wittedly by Lurie into a compelling comedy of affluent U.S. life. The reader's pleasure is further enhanced by the meticulously composed and poised nature of Lurie's prose, and her ability to create vigorous characters and to spin an engaging tale.

In particular, Lurie is skilled at describing North American campus life and the idiosyncratic behavior of U.S. academics. Her novels are self-referential, employing recurrent characters usually connected with the successful, confident and combative Zimmern family. The Lurie reader looks forward to further acquaintanceship with the aggressive and influential critic Leonard D. Zimmern, for example, and the Zimmern brood are used to represent the fortunes of artistic and intellectual life in postwar East Coast America.

All her novels depict characters who are subject to rapid, and often unexpected, changes which precipitate crises in previous and usually smoothly organized existences. Rational academics join crazy religious sects, careful WASP wives have affairs with unsuitable musicians and artists, besuited historians turn beatnik, while refined East Coast ladies on vacation in London have passionate flings with waste-disposal engineers from Tulsa. Like fellow campus chroniclers David Lodge and Malcolm Bradbury, Lurie obviously enjoys the narrative strategy of placing her characters in unfamiliar surroundings, testing their previous relationships and assumptions to the limit.

Thus in *Love and Friendship* upper-class metropolitan Emily Turner finds her relationship with her rather insensitive academic husband tried by her new life as college wife in an inward-looking rural community. *The Nowhere City,* set in Los Angeles, shows how Californian attitudes gradually reshape the social presumptions of historian Paul Cattleman and his New England wife, Katherine. *Imaginary Friends* explores how two sociologists, much given to behavior models, are forced into serious reconsideration of their own identities and actions by their fieldwork among the religious group, the Truth Seekers, in a small town in rural New York State. This questioning of self and motive results in Lurie's possibly most hilarious episode when the two rationalists cast off their professional clothing in preparation for a supreme being's arrival in Sophis.

In *Real People,* an intimate novel about the act of writing, successful novelist Janet Belle Smith finds her principles tested and her status as happily married woman threatened during her transposition from well-run home to the less rule-bound atmosphere of the writer's retreat, Illyria. *The War Between the Tates* sees Erica's orderly home and long-established marriage completely transformed by the presence of her ''nasty, brutish and tall'' teenage offspring and husband Brian's absence due to fluffy-headed and hippyish Wendee, while the adults in *Only Children* (the only novel without a contemporary setting) shed their adult social apparel and behave in an often childish manner, when weekending on a rural retreat in the Catskill Mountains during the Depression.

The search for self-knowledge when an accepted life is disrupted becomes even more pronounced in Lurie's later novels. *Foreign Affairs,* played out in London, is the only novel set abroad, and, here in a Jamesian fashion, a group of North American exiles are challenged by the people and customs of the Old World. But it is *The Truth about Lorin Jones* that tries most ambitiously and strenuously to combine the novel of social displacement with the quest for self-knowledge. Here art historian Polly Alter, in her attempt to write a biography of a prematurely deceased artist, discovers an ''alter ego'' in her subject, and, on her visit to Key West to search for Lorin's past, finds her own life under question, as it becomes increasingly entwined with that of the dead painter.

Lorin Jones (born Lolly Zimmern) is seen as a young girl in *Only Children,* in which novel, as might be expected from Lurie's own academic research into children's literature and authorship of books for children, the child's view of adult behavior is portrayed very sensitively and winningly. Also present in this novel, and indeed discernible throughout her work, is the sense that Lurie's adults themselves crave the release from responsibility, decision-making, and conventional behavior that is present in a happy childhood. Many of her central figures are products of less than contented childhoods (a point not labored in any way by Lurie), and the topsy-turvy, fantastic ways they choose to change their lives reflect such a desire for liberation as an adult.

Lurie's work is intelligent, entertaining and consistently well crafted, and, like that of an earlier novelist with a superior talent for social portraiture, Jane Austen, the American writer's books provide us with a very keen and real understanding of the everyday life and aspirations of a particular group of people.

—Anna-Marie Taylor

LURIE, Morris

Nationality: Australian. **Born:** Melbourne, Victoria, 30 October 1938. **Education:** Melbourne High School; Royal Melbourne Institute of Technology. Divorced; one son and one daughter. **Career:** Worked in advertising, early 1960s; lived in Europe and Morocco, 1965–72, then in Melbourne. **Address:** c/o Penguin Books, P.O. Box 257, Ringwood, Victoria 3134, Australia.

PUBLICATIONS

Novels

Rappaport. London, Hodder and Stoughton, 1966; New York, Morrow, 1967.
The London Jungle Adventures of Charlie Hope. London, Hodder and Stoughton, 1968.
Rappaport's Revenge. London, Angus and Robertson, 1973.
Flying Home. Collingwood, Victoria, Outback Press, 1978; London, Penguin, 1982.
Seven Books for Grossman. Ringwood, Victoria, Penguin, 1983.
Madness. Sydney, Angus and Robertson, 1991.
The String. Ringwood, Victoria, McPhee Gribble Publishers, 1995.
Welcome to Tangier. Ringwood, Victoria and New York, Penguin, 1997.

Short Stories

Happy Times. London, Hodder and Stoughton, 1969.
Inside the Wardrobe: 20 Stories. Fitzroy, Victoria, Outback Press, 1975; New York, Horizon Press, 1978.
Running Nicely. Melbourne, Nelson, and London, Hamish Hamilton, 1979.
Dirty Friends. Ringwood, Victoria, Penguin, 1981; New York, Penguin, 1983.
Outrageous Behaviour: Best Stories. Ringwood, Victoria, Penguin, 1984; London and New York, Penguin, 1985.
The Night We Ate the Sparrow: A Memoir and Fourteen Stories. Ringwood, Victoria, and New York, Penguin, 1985.
Three Stories. Melbourne, Grossman Press, 1987.
Two Brothers, Running: Seventeen Stories and a Movie. Ringwood, Victoria, Penguin, 1990.

Plays

Waterman: Three Plays (includes *Jangle, Jangle; A Visit to the Uncle; Waterman*). Collingwood, Victoria, Outback Press, 1979.

Other (for children)

The Twenty-Seventh Annual African Hippopotamus Race. London, Collins, and New York, Simon and Schuster, 1969.
Arlo the Dandy Lion. London, Collins, and New York, McGraw Hill, 1971.
Toby's Millions. Ringwood, Victoria, Kestrel, 1982; London, Penguin, 1983.
The Story of Imelda, Who Was Small. Melbourne, Oxford University Press, 1984; Oxford, Oxford University Press, 1985; Boston, Houghton Mifflin, 1988.
Night-Night! Seven Going-to-Bed Stories. Melbourne, Oxford University Press, 1986.
Heroes. North Ryde, New South Wales, Methuen, 1987.
Alison Gets Told. Crows Nest, New South Wales, ABC Enterprises, 1990.
What's That Noise? What's That Sound? Milsons Point, New South Wales, Random Century, 1991.

Other

The English in Heat. Sydney and London, Angus and Robertson, 1972.
Hack Work. Collingwood, Victoria, Outback Press, 1977.
Public Secrets. Melbourne, Sun, 1981.
Snow Jobs. Carlton, Victoria, Pascoe, 1985.
Whole Life: An Autobiography. Fitzroy, Victoria, McPhee Gribble, 1987.
My Life as a Movie and Other Gross Conceits: 24 Essays Sportifs. Fitzroy, Victoria, McPhee Gribble-Penguin, 1988.
Editor, *John Hepworth, His Book.* Sydney, Angus and Robertson, 1978.

* * *

Morris Lurie is one of Australia's most prolific writers, centering himself firmly in the fabulist tradition, or, more colloquially, as a spinner of yarns. The son of Jewish immigrant parents, Lurie shares the call of ancient European traditions, practiced and firmly clung to by the older migrant group among whom he grew up, and about whom he writes so well, with the irresistible sense of freedom from such tradition which Australian life produced for the boy and young man in the 1950s and early 1960s.

Lurie, like Judah Waten before him, explores this conflict between the New World and the Old in compassionate, yet humorous, terms, finding a voice for hundreds of thousands of people caught up in the postwar migration and refugee flood which brought so much to Australian life and culture. Here was a different tradition, neither English nor Celtic, but firmly Euro-centered, and just as firmly Jewish, transported to a country which neither understood nor appreciated what that tradition would eventually offer.

Little wonder, then, that four of Lurie's novels, *Rappaport, The London Jungle Adventures of Charlie Hope, Rappaport's Revenge,* and *Flying Home,* as well as many of his short stories, focus on the theme of the young Australian attempting to cope with cultural traditions learned first from books and the memories of his parents and their friends, yet having to be confronted firsthand and experienced personally before any of their richness or folly can be assessed. It is not for nothing that Charlie Hope finds London a jungle and capers about with shrewd simian nimbleness, or that Rappaport, having received something of a drubbing when he first arrived in London, nevertheless manages to exact his revenge, financially and culturally, when he is safe and sound back in Australia.

Lurie's major work is the novel *Flying Home.* It is both a love story, as Leo Axelrod seeks to understand the mystery of his lover Marianne, and a novel which seeks to explore the confused and confusing tangle of roots and origins which migrant families carry within their displaced baggage. Leo comes to realize that he will never exorcise, much less comprehend, his demons until he visits Israel, for somewhere in that promised land lies the secret to his own self and the ambiguities which enclose his relationship with his parents and grandparents. As he reflects:

> It was the way I was brought up, it was what *they* felt. They didn't like Australia. Well, it wasn't even a matter of like. They ignored it. They pretended it wasn't there. Australia was an unfortunate thing that had happened to them; that Hitler had done, that's all it was to them. An accident. A terrible accident. It wasn't the real

> world. The real world was Bialystock, Poland, Europe. . . .
> So that's where I was born, that's where I grew up, that's
> where I lived. Nowhere. In a black cage.

The conflict between the "nowhere" of Australia and the "real world" of Europe is exigent and drives Leo to explore that "real world" in search of his self and his true home. This exploration of the mystery of family relationships—their tortuous and often painful ambiguities—and the search for a locus, a spiritual natal place, are the predominant themes of Lurie's work until the early 1980s.

During the 1970s his trips to the U.S.A. provided him with a rich source of material for exploring the Jewish community in that country of immigrants, and allowed him to see how a more established and larger community handled the translocation from Europe to a new country of considerable freedom and material progress. Several of his books of reportage, *Hack Work* and *Public Secrets,* for example, contained witty and ebullient pieces on the Jewish community in America, particularly in New York. His novella *Seven Books for Grossman* explores the mad and funny world of the Jewish fantasist, coping with sexual anarchy, a maddening intelligence, and a material culture at war with ancient demons which demand guilt and obeisance to vestigial traditions. As book tumbles after book (*Dirty Friends, Outrageous Behaviour, The Night We Ate the Sparrow* and *Two Brothers, Running* are recent story collections), Lurie shows himself not only as an acute and funny social observer, but as something of a transcultural anthropologist. His interest in the quirky, the outrageous, the madcap, in no way diminishes his exploration of the roots of human behavior and ideals.

Despite, or perhaps because of, the steady and voluminous flow of his work, Lurie remains a professional craftsman. His style is colloquial and confessional, brimming with witty aphorisms and incisive dialogue. His humor teeters on the brink of the absurd, often the anarchistic, and his later works show a considerable freedom of imagination, particularly when he, or his fictive creations, explore sexual situations, as though, by having confronted a range of taboos in his earlier work, he has earned for himself the freedom to move unselfconsciously wherever his keen nose for the funny, the eccentric, or the absurd, might lead him.

One aspect of his work often overlooked by critics as though it were secondary to his short stories, essays, and novels is his attention to and success in children's fiction. His first foray into this field was as far back as 1969 with *The Twenty-Seventh Annual African Hippopotamus Race,* followed by *Arlo the Dandy Lion, The Story of Imelda, Who Was Small,* and several other stories. These simple, homespun yarns have proved immensely popular with young children, partly because Lurie manages the difficult feat of containing his narrative within the perspective of a child's eye and allowing his fictive heroes moderate, but not overwhelming, success in a world seen as competitive, but not threatening.

When one looks at the range and volume of Lurie's work, one can only admire his dedication to the creative tasks and his skill as a craftsman. Where some have found a certain sameness about his earlier works and their concentration on the young Jewish male, squirming his way to maturity through the mess of memory, tradition, and lore imposed upon him, others have seen in his humor and aphoristic style, his sharp eye for the idiosyncratic, and his keen sense of human folly a writer deeply concerned for the constant rediscovery of human values and human freedom. Behind the sophisticated wit, the mock-heroic style of so much of his works, lies a writer making sense of the modern world, noting its curiosities and failures of sensibility, but realizing, through his imaginative creations, the human capacity to survive with sadness, but also with humor.

—D.J. O'Hearn

M

MacDONALD, Ann-Marie

Nationality: Canadian. **Born:** 1958. **Education:** National Theatre School. **Career:** Actress; playwright and novelist; host, *Life and Times* (CBC- TV), Toronto. Lives in Toronto, Canada. **Awards:** Gemini Award; Governor General's award; Chalmers award; Canadian Authors Association award; Commonwealth prize; Best First Book award.

PUBLICATIONS

Novels

Fall on Your Knees. New York, Simon & Schuster, 1996.

Short Stories

The Day the Men Went to Town: 16 Stories by Women from Cape Breton (contributor), selected by Ronald Caplan. Wreck Cove, Nova Scotia, Cape Breton Books, 1999.

Plays

Goodnight Desdemona (Good Night Juliet). Toronto, Nightwood Theatre, 1988; Toronto, Coach House Press, 1990; New York, Grove Press, 1998.

The Arab's Mouth. Toronto, Factory Theatre, 1990; Winnipeg, Manitoba, Blizzard Publishing, 1995.

Negredo Hotel. Toronto, Tarragon Theatre, 1992.

Anything That Moves. Toronto, Canadian Stage, 2000.

* * *

Ann-Marie MacDonald has worked as an actor, director, producer, playwright, and novelist. It is in the last role, however, that she has garnered the most critical and popular acclaim. When her debut novel, *Fall on Your Knees*, was published it received such flattering praise as: "so assured is the style, so intricate the plotting, and so accomplished the portrait of the four unforgettable Piper sisters, one would expect that the author was a seasoned novelist" and "Not since Newfoundland poet E.J. Pratt's epic poem, 'Brebuff and his Brethen,' have we seen Canadian Literature writ so large and wide, and with such energy, passion, and nerve." While the merit of Pratt's poem has been called into question, the elegance of MacDonald's first novel is not often in debate. Perhaps what makes the novel stand out is its curious mixture of dramatic tableaux, detailed characterization, and musical language. In fact, her training in the theater is perhaps most evident in MacDonald's use of language and dialogue. The naturalness of the conversations between lovers, neighbors, and sisters creates a believable backdrop for the sometimes horrific events in the novel. For all its theatricality, the novel is anything but a lightweight romp through the Canadian maritimes. The story of four sisters growing up in industrial Cape Breton, Nova Scotia, swirls through incidents of racism, incest, social exploitation, class conflict, and religious intolerance. These are balanced with moments of intense love, humor, and sacrifice.

Fall on Your Knees exemplifies what Njabulo Ndebele has called, in another context, the need for the "rediscovery of the ordinary." His point is that spectacular events have lost their shock value, because they have become accepted as ordinary. In order to reject the spectacular and show it as extraordinary, it is necessary to reinscribe the ordinary. MacDonald's novel progresses through a series of ordinary events in order to highlight the horrors and passions of the spectacular events with which they are juxtaposed. In this manner she shows the prejudices of the Catholic church, the seediness of nightclubs, the anger of fathers, the excitement of music, and the love of sisters.

The novel differs sharply from her first solo-written play, *Good Night Desdemona (Good Morning Juliet)*, which is a comedy about a mousy lecturer in Renaissance drama who is trying to decipher a coded manuscript for what she believes to be the lost manuscripts for *Romeo and Juliet* and *Othello*. She travels through a time warp into both plays in order to search for a Fool/Author to give her the key to the plays. Instead, however, she meets Desdemona and Juliet and discovers that Desdemona is violent and bloodthirsty, and Juliet is in love with the romance of love and death, rather than with Romeo. MacDonald cleverly weaves dialogue from Shakespeare's plays into her own play's dialogue, with a few key substitutions, for comic results. The first director of the play notes in her introduction that the story is a journey into the "zone of the unconscious mind" where Desdemona and Juliet represent elements of the lecturer's psyche. While the sardonic use of humor links the play to MacDonald's first novel, the novel goes far beyond the play in interrogating the depths of the individual characters' minds and relationships with others. That said, the novel does not read as a Jungian exploration of the sisters' collective unconscious. Indeed, one of the characters, Frances, is described as a "sealed letter. It doesn't matter where she's been or who's pawed her, no one gets to handle the contents no matter how grimy the envelope. And it's for sure no one's going to be able to steam her open" (293). The reader's role in *Fall on Your Knees* is to follow the narrative's developments as if putting an envelope up to a light. We can't be certain what the letter inside says, but we can see the writing inside, at first opaquely and then gradually with increased clarity, as scrutiny is increased. By the end of the investigation we are certainly rewarded for our persistence.

—Laura Moss

MacLAVERTY, Bernard

Nationality: Irish. **Born:** Belfast, Northern Ireland, 14 September 1942. **Education:** Queen's University, Belfast, B.A. (honors) in English 1974, diploma in education 1975. **Family:** Married Madeline McGuckin in 1967; three daughters and one son. **Career:** Medical laboratory technician, Belfast, 1960–70; teacher of English, St. Augustine's High School, Edinburgh, 1975–78, and Islay High School, 1978–81; writer-in-residence, University of Aberdeen, 1983–85. Since 1981 full-time writer. **Awards:** Northern Ireland Arts

Council award, 1975; Scottish Arts Council award, 1978, 1981, 1982; Pharic McLaren award, for radio play, 1981; Jacobs award, for television play, 1982; Irish *Sunday Independent* award, 1983; London *Evening Standard* award, for screenplay, 1984. **Address:** 26 Roxburgh Street, Hillhead, Glasgow G12 9AP, Scotland.

Publications

Novels

Lamb. London, Cape, and New York, Braziller, 1980.
Cal. London, Cape, and New York, Braziller, 1983.
Grace Notes. New York, W.W. Norton, 1997.

Short Stories

Secrets and Other Stories. Belfast, Blackstaff Press, 1977; New York, Viking, 1984.
A Time to Dance and Other Stories. London, Cape, and New York, Braziller, 1982.
The Great Profundo and Other Stories. London, Cape, 1987; New York, Grove Press, 1988.
Walking the Dog and Other Stories. London, Cape, 1994; New York, Norton, 1995.

Uncollected Short Stories

''For My Wife's Eyes Only,'' in *Redbook* (New York), February 1985.
''A Foreign Dignitary,'' in *Best Short Stories 1989,* edited by Giles Gordon and David Hughes. London, Heinemann, 1989; as *The Best English Short Stories 1989,* New York, Norton, 1989.
''Life Drawing,'' in *The Oxford Book of Irish Short Stories,* edited by William Trevor. Oxford and New York, Oxford University Press, 1989.

Plays

Screenplays: *Cal,* 1984; *Lamb,* 1986.

Radio Plays: *My Dear Palestrina,* from his own story, 1980.

Television Plays: *My Dear Palestrina,* from his own story, 1980; *The Real Charlotte,* from the novel by Somerville and Ross, 1991.

Other (for children)

A Man in Search of a Pet. Belfast, Blackstaff Press, 1978.
Andrew McAndrew. London, Walker, 1989.

*

Critical Studies: ''An Introduction to the Stories of Bernard MacLaverty'' by Arnold Saxon, in *Journal of the Short Story in English,* Spring 1987.

* * *

Vivid imagery and emotional dialogue distinguish much of Bernard MacLaverty's writing, and combined with his use of such compelling themes as isolation and dissociation, the reader quickly becomes engrossed in MacLaverty's art. A concern with the artist and his relationship to the audience occasionally emerges and blends with the major thematic concerns found in MacLaverty's pages, and he skillfully shapes his writing with the proficiency of an experienced craftsman, all the while giving time and attention to the Irish culture and people. MacLaverty's first major literary work, *Secrets and Other Stories*, introduces the reader to an intriguing array of characters who regularly face a myriad of conflicts including loneliness, isolation, and the frustration associated with human relationships. The title story features a young man who grapples with the guilt he feels over past violations of secrecy and trust. ''Hugo,'' along with ''Secrets,'' introduces the strong, recurring theme of the relationship between the artist and audience. This theme of aesthetics runs throughout the entire canon of MacLaverty, and he adeptly mingles his observations on art with the main narrative, yet the reader never loses interest in the characters or their struggles.

Shortly after publishing *Secrets and Other Stories*, MacLaverty produced his first novel, *Lamb*, which tells the story of Brother Sebastian, an Irish priest who runs away with Owen, an unwanted, sickly young boy. Brother Sebastian attempts to rekindle the love he remembers from his youth, but problems arise when he learns that nurturing a child (especially a sick and rebellious child such as Owen) involves much more than simply being called ''Dad.'' Brother Sebastian fails to reach Owen in any significant way, and his failure demonstrates MacLaverty's fascination with the intricacies involving human relationships. Society rejects and abuses Owen through the course of his short life; his despair is such that he states at one point, ''I don't care if I live or die.'' The novel ends with the death of Owen and the bewilderment of Brother Sebastian. The ending encourages the reader to ponder the thematic hints at the ''troubles'' of Ireland; hints that suggest that while people may possess the basic components for a successful relationship, Ireland's social ills so dominate her citizens that survival becomes at best a whimsical fantasy.

MacLaverty's fascination with human relationships continued with the publication of *A Time to Dance*, a collection of short stories that offers the reader a fascinating look at a myriad of relationships and how they succeed, fail, or maintain a level of impartiality. In the title story, Nelson rebels by refusing to wear his protective eyepatch in school, thus speeding up his chances of going blind via eyestrain. Nelson's rebellion exemplifies the attitudes of many protagonists in this work, and while many of the characters wind up facing isolation, anger, and despair, Norman in ''Language, Truth, and Lockjaw'' finds some success by going against the grain and attempting a reconciliation with his family. This optimistic ending suggests that, at least for some, hope may be found if one puts forth the necessary effort.

MacLaverty's next novel, *Cal*, features a young man who makes a valiant effort to exist in a perplexing world, but fails due to the violence perpetuated by the Catholics and Protestants. *Cal*'s powerful narrative and gripping story line illuminate the socially pervasive ''troubles'' of Ireland and bring the reader, natives and aliens alike, into a world where warring religious factions dictate almost every citizen's action. Cal (a Roman Catholic) abhors the terrorist tactics of his friends in the IRA. He only wants to live in peace, but if Cal refuses to aid the ''Catholic Cause,'' he will become an adversary to both sides. Cal further complicates matters when he falls in love with

Marcella, a widow who lost her husband to a violent death orchestrated by Cal's friends. Cal feels guilt over his role in the death of Marcella's husband and his ''abandoning'' the ''Catholic Cause,'' and his guilt forces him to avoid making a decisive choice, either for or against the Catholics. Cal chooses neither, but he does not get to enjoy his neutrality very long; he falls victim to a divided Ireland when violence and hatred overcome his best efforts at peace. MacLaverty's powerful dialogue (a trademark of many of his works) helps make *Cal* a moving tale that admirably depicts the ''troubles'' that plague Ireland.

MacLaverty's *The Great Profundo* continues to explore and develop the themes of isolation and despair he introduced in *Secrets and Other Stories*. Many of the protagonists in this collection of short stories experience isolation and despair due to their failed attempts to reconcile a medley of deep emotional scars firmly embedded in past atrocities. A motif concerning aesthetics subtly traces the relationship between artist and audience, especially in ''Words the Happy Say'' and ''The Drapery Man.'' The title story deals with a magician whose skills break down and fail him in front of an unsympathetic audience. The Great Profundo derives its strength from an energetic and compassionate narrative that binds universal themes with Irish concerns and exciting characters with their struggles. At times, MacLaverty feels the weight of his literary forefathers, but he also feels the tension created by the Catholics and Protestants. Consequently, the author's skillful narrative and vivid imagery not only allow readers to share the character's concerns and cares, they also force us to confront the everyday horrors felt by many Irish citizens.

In MacLaverty's next collection of short stories, entitled *Walking the Dog*, many of the protagonists grapple with the problems usually held to the confines of close personal friends and family. The title story examines the fears of a man who tries to avoid the violence associated with the Catholics and Protestants. John insists he ''believes in nothing,'' but to no avail: two members of the IRA kidnap, interrogate, and beat him, then eventually leave him to ponder his neutral position. Like Cal, John learns that a neutral position does not exempt him from the emotional and physical duress associated with living in a divided country. Perhaps the most compelling feature of *Walking the Dog* is the brief italicized stories that occur at odd intervals. These brief stories examine the private concerns of a writer as well as the problems some artists experience while creating art. With this ingenious structuring device, MacLaverty shrewdly voices his concerns about the relationship between artist and audience and between art and connoisseur, all the while maintaining the delicate balance dictated by the short story's literary form.

MacLaverty's critically acclaimed *Grace Notes* observes Catherine McKenna's struggle to balance her music career with her home life. The narrative fluctuates back and forth between Catherine's musical career, her childhood history, and her adult years, thus giving the reader a wealth of information. Like Cal, Catherine faces serious dilemmas and paradoxes and no matter what choice she makes, it does not turn out to be the right choice. As a single woman, Catherine gives birth to a baby girl, but her fears of being rejected by her parents and ostracized by society force her to give up her daughter. As the novel progresses, Catherine's music career stagnates and her relationship with her live-in lover deteriorates. She has hopes of making a fresh start, so she returns to visit her daughter, but her plans for reconciliation fail. Catherine finally returns to Ireland, and the novel ends with an enthusiastic performance of one of her musical compositions. All of Catherine's relationships fail, but her efforts at music succeed; the audience gives her a standing ovation at the end. Once again, MacLaverty provides an intriguing look behind the scenes of creative art. Beauty may indeed be produced, but there is always a price to pay for such accomplishments, and in the end, willing or not, Catherine learns this truth.

MacLaverty's ingenious use of spatial imagery combined with color and sound resonates throughout *Grace Notes*, and even though the novel's primary concern lies with the artist and the demands of her art, MacLaverty still introduces and sustains thematic references to the troubles of the Irish. As an Irish novelist, MacLaverty remains true to his culture and the plight of his people, but his writing talents and skills invite readers of all nationalities to explore his literary works. MacLaverty's literature in general and *Grace Notes* in particular delivers something for everyone, and his art whets the reader's appetite for future literary efforts.

—James Ortego

MADDEN, (Jerry) David

Nationality: American. **Born:** Knoxville, Tennessee, 25 July 1933. **Education:** Knox High School, Knoxville; Iowa State Teachers College (now University of Northern Iowa), Cedar Falls, 1956; University of Tennessee, Knoxville, B.S. 1957; San Francisco State College, M.A. 1958; Yale Drama School (John Golden fellow), New Haven, Connecticut, 1959–60. **Military Service:** Served in the United States Army, 1955–56. **Family:** Married Roberta Margaret Young in 1956; one son. **Career:** Instructor in English, Appalachian State Teachers College, Boone, North Carolina, 1958–59, and Centre College, Danville, Kentucky, 1960–62; lecturer in creative writing, University of Louisville, Kentucky, 1962–64; member of the Department of English, Kenyon College, Gambier, Ohio, and assistant editor, *Kenyon Review,* 1964–66; lecturer in creative writing, Ohio University, Athens, 1966–68. Writer-in-residence, 1968–92; director, Creative Writing Program, 1992–94; founding director, United States Civil War Center, 1992–99; Donald and Velvia Crumbley professor of creative writing, 1999—, all Louisiana State University, Baton Rouge. **Awards:** Rockefeller grant, 1969; National Endowment for the Arts prize, 1970; Bread Loaf Writers Conference William Raney fellowship, 1972. **Address:** 614 Park Boulevard, Baton Rouge, Louisiana 70806, U.S.A.

PUBLICATIONS

Novels

The Beautiful Greed. New York, Random House, 1961.
Cassandra Singing. New York, Crown, 1969.
Brothers in Confidence. New York, Avon, 1972.
Bijou. New York, Crown, 1974.
The Suicide's Wife. Indianapolis, Bobbs Merrill, 1978.
Pleasure-Dome. Indianapolis, Bobbs Merrill, 1979.
On the Big Wind. New York, Holt Rinehart, 1980.
Sharpshooter: A Novel of the Civil War. Knoxville, University of Tennessee Press, 1996.

Short Stories

The Shadow Knows. Baton Rouge, Louisiana State University Press, 1970.

The New Orleans of Possibilities. Baton Rouge, Louisiana State University Press, 1982.

Uncollected Short Stories

"My Name Is Not Antonio," in *Yale Literary Magazine* (New Haven, Connecticut), March 1960.

"Hair of the Dog," in *Adam* (Los Angeles), April-November 1967.

"The Master's Thesis," in *Fantasy and Science Fiction* (New York), July 1967.

"Nothing Dies But Something Mourns," in *Carleton Miscellany* (Northfield, Minnesota), Fall 1968.

"The Day the Flowers Came," in *The Best American Short Stories 1969,* edited by Martha Foley and David Burnett. Boston, Houghton Mifflin, 1969.

"A Voice in the Garden," in *English Record* (Oneonta, New York), October 1969.

"Traven," in *Short Stories from the Little Magazines,* edited by Jarvis Thurston and Curt Johnson. Chicago, Scott Foresman, 1970.

"Home Comfort," in *Jeopardy* (Bellingham, Washington), March 1970.

"No Trace," in *The Best American Short Stories 1971,* edited by Martha Foley and David Burnett. Boston, Houghton Mifflin, 1971.

"Night Shift," in *Playboy's Ribald Classics 3.* Chicago, Playboy Press, 1971.

"A Secondary Character," in *Cimarron Review* (Stillwater, Oklahoma), July 1972.

"The Spread-Legged Girl" (as Jack Travis), in *Knight* (Los Angeles), October 1972.

"The Singer," in *Scenes from American Life: Contemporary Short Fiction,* edited by Joyce Carol Oates. New York, Vanguard Press, 1973.

"Here He Comes! There He Goes!," in *Contempora* (Atlanta, Georgia), Summer 1973.

"Wanted: Ghost Writer," in *Epoch* (Ithaca, New York), Fall 1973.

"The World's One Breathing," in *Appalachian Heritage* (Pippa Passes, Kentucky), Winter 1973.

"Hurry Up Please, It's Time," in *The Botteghe Oscure Reader,* edited by George Garrett and Katherine Garrison Biddle. Middletown, Connecticut, Wesleyan University Press, 1974.

"The Hero and the Witness," in *New Orleans Review,* vol. 4, no. 3, 1974.

"On the Big Wind," in *The Pushcart Prize 5,* edited by Bill Henderson. Yonkers, New York, Pushcart Press, 1980.

"Putting an Act Together," in *Southern Review* (Baton Rouge, Louisiana), Winter 1980.

"Code-a-Phone," in *Crescent Review* (Winston-Salem, North Carolina), vol. 1, no. 1, 1983.

"Lights," in *New Letters* (Kansas City), Winter 1984–85.

"Rosanna," in *South Dakota Review* (Vermillion), Summer 1985.

"Was Jesse James at Rising Fawn?," in *South Dakota Review* (Vermillion), Autumn 1985.

"Willis Carr at Bleak House," in *The Bread Loaf Anthology of Contemporary American Short Stories,* edited by Robert Pack and Jay Parini. Hanover, New Hampshire, University Press of New England, 1987.

"Gristle," in *Appalachian Heritage* (Berea, Kentucky), Spring-Summer 1988.

"Children of the Sun," in *New Letters* (Kansas City), Summer 1988.

"The Invisible Girl," in *The Southern California Anthology 7.* Los Angeles, University of Southern California Master of Professional Writing Program, 1989.

"The Demon in My View," in *Southern Review* (Baton Rouge, Louisiana), Spring 1989.

"Crossing the Lost and Found River," in *Chattahoochie Review* (Dunwoody, Georgia), Winter 1989.

"James Agee Never Lived in This House," in *Southern Review* (Baton Rouge, Louisiana), Spring 1990.

"A Forgotten Nightmare," in *The Southern Californian Anthology* (Los Angeles), 1991.

"The Last Bizarre Tale," in *Southern Short Stories.* Huntsville, Texas, Huntsville Texas Review Press, 1991.

A Survivor of the Sinking of the Sultana," in *Appalachian Heritage* (Berea, Kentucky), 1992.

"If the Ash Heap Begins to Glow Again ... " in *Louisiana English Journal* (Eunice, Louisiana), October 1993.

"Fragments Found on the Field," in *Gulf Coast Collection* (Montrose, Alabama), 1994.

"Hairtrigger Pencil Lines," in *Louisiana Cultural Vistas Magazine* (New Orleans), Spring 1994.

Plays

Call Herman in to Supper (produced Knoxville, Tennessee, 1949).

They Shall Endure (produced Knoxville, Tennessee, 1953).

Cassandra Singing (produced Knoxville, Tennessee, 1955). Published in *New Campus Writing 2,* edited by Nolan Miller, New York, Putnam, 1957; (expanded version, produced Albuquerque, New Mexico, 1964).

From Rome to Damascus (produced Chapel Hill, North Carolina, 1959).

Casina, music by Robert Rogers, lyrics by Joseph Matthewson (produced New Haven, Connecticut, 1960).

In My Father's House, in *First Stage* (Lafayette, Indiana), Summer 1966.

Fugitive Masks (produced Abingdon, Virginia, 1966).

The Day the Flowers Came (produced Baton Rouge, Louisiana, 1974). Chicago, Dramatic Publishing Company, 1975.

Other

Wright Morris. New York, Twayne, 1965.

The Poetic Image in Six Genres. Carbondale, Southern Illinois University Press, 1969.

James M. Cain. New York, Twayne, 1970.

Harlequin's Stick, Charlie's Cane: A Comparative Study of Commedia dell'Arte and Silent Slapstick Comedy. Bowling Green, Ohio, Popular Press, 1975.

A Primer of the Novel, For Readers and Writers. Metuchen, New Jersey, Scarecrow Press, 1980.

Writers' Revisions: An Annotated Bibliography of Articles and Books about Writers' Revisions and Their Comments on the Creative Process, with Richard Powers. Metuchen, New Jersey, Scarecrow Press, 1981.

Cain's Craft. Metuchen, New Jersey, Scarecrow Press, 1985.
Revising Fiction: A Handbook for Writers. New York, New American Library, 1988.
The Fiction Tutor. Fort Worth, Texas, Harcourt Brace, 1990.
A Pocketful of Essays: Thematically Arranged. Fort Worth, Texas, Harcourt College Publishers, 2001.
Editor, *Tough Guy Writers of the Thirties.* Carbondale, Southern Illinois University Press, 1968.
Editor, *Proletarian Writers of the Thirties.* Carbondale, Southern Illinois University Press, 1968.
Editor, *American Dreams, American Nightmares.* Carbondale, Southern Illinois University Press, 1970.
Editor, *Rediscoveries: Informal Essays in Which Well-Known Novelists Rediscover Neglected Works of Fiction by One of Their Favorite Authors.* New York, Crown, 1971.
Editor, with Ray B. Browne, *The Popular Cultural Explosion: Experiencing Mass Media.* Dubuque, Iowa, William Brown, 2 vols., 1972.
Editor, *Nathanael West: The Cheaters and the Cheated.* Deland, Florida, Everett Edwards, 1973.
Editor, with Jeffrey J. Folks, *Remembering James Agee.* Baton Rouge, Louisiana State University Press, 1974.
Editor, *Creative Choices: A Spectrum of Quality and Technique in Fiction.* Chicago, Scott Foresman, 1975.
Editor, with Virgil Scott, *Studies in the Short Story.* New York, Holt Rinehart, 1975; 6th edition, 1984.
Editor, with Peggy Bach, *Rediscoveries II.* New York, Carroll and Graf, 1988.
Editor, *8 Classic American Novels.* San Diego, Harcourt Brace, 1990.
Editor, *The World of Fiction* (short stories). Fort Worth, Texas, Holt Rinehart, 1990.
Editor, with Peggy Bach, *Classics of Civil War Fiction.* Jackson, University of Mississippi, 1991.
Editor, *A Pocketful of Prose: Contemporary Short Fiction.* Fort Worth, Texas, Harcourt Brace, 1992.
Editor, *A Pocketful of Plays: Vintage Drama.* Fort Worth, Texas, Harcourt Brace, 1996.
Editor, *A Pocketful of Poems: Vintage Verse.* Fort Worth, Texas, Harcourt Brace, 1996.
Editor, *Beyond the Battlefield: The Ordinary Life and Extraordinary Times of the Civil War Soldier.* New York, Touchstone, 2000.
Editor, *The Legacy of Robert Penn Warren.* Baton Rouge, Louisiana State University Press, 2000.
Editor, with Kimberly J. Allison, *A Pocketful of Essays.* Fort Worth, Texas, Harcourt Brace, 2001.

*

Bibliographies: ''A David Madden Bibliography 1952–1981'' by Anna H. Perrault, in *Bulletin of Bibliography* (Westport, Connecticut), September 1982.

Manuscript Collections: University of Tennessee Library, Knoxville.

Critical Studies: ''A Conversation with David Madden,'' and ''The Mixed Chords of David Madden's *Cassandra Singing*'' by Sanford Pinsker, in *Critique* (Atlanta), vol. 15, no. 2, 1973; ''An Interview with David Madden,'' in *The Penny Dreadful* (Bowling Green, Ohio), vol. 3, no. 3, 1974; ''The Story Teller as Benevolent Con Man'' by Madden, in *Appalachian Heritage* (Pippa Passes, Kentucky), Summer 1974; interviews in *Southern Review* (Baton Rouge, Louisiana), vol. 11, no. 1, 1975, *New Orleans Review,* Spring 1982, and *Louisiana Literature* (Hammond), Fall 1984; by Jeffrey Richards in *Contemporary Poets, Dramatists, Essayists, and Novelists of the South,* edited by Robert Bain and Joseph M. Flora, Westport, Connecticut, Greenwood Press, 1994.

David Madden comments:

I've been trying all my life to pass the test F. Scott Fitzgerald set for himself. ''The test of a first-rate intelligence is the ability to hold two opposed ideas in the mind at the same time and still retain the ability to function.'' Camus's concept of the absurd helped clarify Fitzgerald's: one's life should be a self-created contradiction of the fact that life is basically absurd. A similar polarity has given some form to my art as well as my life. It was not books but my grandmother's storytelling and the movies' charged images that inspired me to write. My first literary hero was the Dionysian Thomas Wolfe; then came the Apollonian James Joyce. In the tensions between those two extremes I have tried to shape my own work. I have practiced for a long time now the concept that it is between the limitations externally imposed by the form I'm working in and limitations I imposed on myself in the writing of a specific work that I experience genuine and productive freedom. Two metaphors of the artist (and the teacher) are useful for me: the magician and the con man. As with the magician's techniques of illusion, art works by a phantom circuit; and the relationship between writer and reader is like that between the con man and his mark, except that the climax (the sting) is beneficial for both. For me, the function of fiction is to create imaginary words; discipline and technique enable me to cause that to happen. And in that process I consider my reader as an active collaborator.

(1995) Because it is on the crest of a single great wave of creative energy that I enter up all the activities in my life and in my writing, I reject the perception that the fact that I have not published a novel in fifteen years is evidence of diminished capacity. In all that time, I have researched and revised *Sharpshooter,* a Civil War novel, and published fourteen chapters from it. I have also created the United States Civil War Center. I have the first draft of a book that provides a unique perspective on ancient London Bridge (1110 to 1828). I have always worked simultaneously on five major projects, while taking up dozens of other life and literary projects. Surfing on the one great, never-ending wave of creative force is the life-work for me.

(2000) Recently, in my mid-sixties, as a matter of cold fact, I came to see that most of my fiction, and the best of it, reaches into unique characters or predicaments and unique other places, and unique other selves—unique in both life and literature, as I have lived, read, and imagined them.

From childhood, my fiction was written in a specific place and out of the specific oral traditions of the southern Appalachian Mountains, and out of radio drama and the movies, more than out of classic and modern literature. But the lure has always been nonspecific, extraordinary other places where my ordinary characters could explore and create unique other selves. For some characters, that uniqueness lasts only for the time duration of the fiction, for others, it is permanent. My characters cross the border between the ordinary and the extraordinary very rapidly.

Reading my contemporaries, I seldom see inclinations toward the kind of stories and novels I have just described as my own. I feel very little affinity for them or their work, except for Steven Millhauser. Although my masters in the art of fiction are Hemingway, Joyce, Fitzgerald, Faulkner, Conrad, and Mansfield, I see now, looking back at the age of 67, more kinship in the creation of character and situation with Poe, Borges, Marquez, Michel Tournier, Jules Romains, Kafka, John Collier, A. E. Coppard, E. M. Forster. ''Tales of Mystery and Imagination,'' title of a Poe collection, fits my own corpus.

In my childhood, I viewed every specific place (my bedroom) and every general place (my hometown) as *other,* and even as I moved from place to place, my imagination was stimulated to create other places, other selves (for my characters, more than myself). Sometimes the more specific the place and time, in the conventional sense (San Francisco in 1957, for instance), the more my imagination reached for possibilities beyond. In my novel in progress (since Christmas 1991), *London Bridge Is Falling Down,* nothing could be more specific than a bridge, even one with almost 200 houses and shops built on it. The first version reaches back and forth in time over the 800-year history of the ancient bridge and draws on times, places, people, real and imagined, and events up to the 365 nights I took nocturnal walks on London Bridge. For instance, Harpo Marx shows up on the bridge in the year 1342. Fragments of a story and facts about the building, maintenance, and final demolition of the bridge are scattered throughout those walks in words. My recent conversion to Christianity may affect the way I revise that first draft, but it won't be less *other* in time, place, and character, nor less exotic, bizarre, and demonic.

''When I am writing, I am far away and when I return I have already left.'' Neruda, *Muchos Somos.*

* * *

Much of David Madden's fiction is autobiographical. Like Lucius Hutchfield in *Bijou,* Madden goes over his personal history again and again, remolding details. Incidents appear in more than one work; short stories are absorbed into novels; the short novel *Brothers in Confidence* becomes the first half of the longer novel *Pleasure-Dome,* as Madden works at perfecting the tale of his life. Arranged in chronological order Madden's fictional autobiography would begin with two stories from *The Shadow Knows,* ''The Pale Horse of Fear'' and the title story, then continue on through *Bijou, The Beautiful Greed, Pleasure-Dome,* to the elegiac story ''The World's One Breathing.''

Madden's goal is to transport his readers into ''the Pleasure-Dome.'' As Lucius says in the novel of that name, ''Everyday life is an effort to disentangle facts and illusions. There are rare moments in our lives when we transcend captivity in fact-and-illusion through pure imagination and dwell in the Pleasure-Dome, a luminous limbo between everyday experience and a work of art.'' Lucius knows well the value of a good story. He is an aspiring writer, and his older brother is a con man—which for Madden is nearly the same thing: ''The relationship between the storyteller and the listener is like that between the con man and his mark,'' Madden has said. Madden himself is at his best when emulating the oral storytelling style he learned from his grandmother when he was growing up in the Tennessee hills, the setting of much of his fiction.

In the stories collected in *The Shadow Knows* the characters are caught between the knowledge that their old lives—in many cases rural or small town lives—are disappearing, and that the new lives available to them are spiritually unsatisfying. Madden's world here is primarily one of moonshiners and county fairs, motorcycles and coalmines, but a few of these stories are set outside the mountains. ''Love Makes Nothing Happen,'' set in Alaska, is the best of these, while ''The Day the Flowers Came,'' set in some faceless suburb, is maudlin and unbelievable. Two of the mountain stories here turn up as Lucius's memories in *Bijou.*

Bijou picks up Lucius's story in early adolescence, when he becomes an usher in a movie theater. Lucius tries to reinvent his life in the image of the films he sees. The Bijou itself is a symbol of the exotic mysteries of adulthood: ''... the Bijou ... seemed foreign, beyond his life, as if he were entering a special Bijou experience prematurely. The Bijou was somehow for other people, people who were superior to him because they'd had Bijou experiences he hadn't had.'' The promising framework of the theater as Lucius's doorway into adulthood is unfortunately overloaded with page after page of movie synopses, and undercut by the repetitive nature of his experiences with the other characters. We last see Lucius lurking about Thomas Wolfe's house, ready to give up films for the idea of the writer's life.

The Beautiful Greed relates the adventures of a young man named Alvin (who is just a little older than Lucius at the end of *Bijou*) on a merchant marine voyage to South America. This novel was Madden's first, and it seems thin in almost all regards when compared to his later works, though the plot here is unusually straight for Madden.

Pleasure-Dome is perhaps Madden's finest novel to date, despite a structure of two clumsily hinged together story lines. Lucius Hutchfield is once again the main character. He has been in the merchant marine and has become a writer since the events of *Bijou.* Lucius spends the first half of the novel trying to free his younger brother from jail by using his storytelling gifts. But it is the eldest brother, the con man, who succeeds in this—by telling taller tales than those Lucius tells. The second half is a cautionary tale about the responsibilities of being a storyteller. A boy's outlaw side lies dormant until Lucius awakens it with a story about Jesse James. The boy tries to emulate the outlaw's success with a young woman, with disastrous results. Though the boy goes to prison he is happy: he has on some small scale entered the world of legendary figures.

Cassandra Singing, the story of a wild boy and his invalid sister, is generally considered one of Madden's least autobiographical works, but it would be more accurate to say that Madden's character is here split between Lone and his sister Cassie. Lone is the motorcycle rider, the one with the need to escape the small world of the hills, while bedridden Cassie's life is in touch with the country's oral tradition, through the songs and stories she knows. That these two lie down together as the novel's end may be more of a self-portrait than a suggestion of incest. *On the Big Wind* is a loose string of satiric sketches with obvious targets, tied together by the voice of Big Bob Travis, nomadic radio announcer. The most telling thing here is ''The World's One Breathing,'' spliced in from *The Shadow Knows.*

The Suicide's Wife stands apart from the rest of Madden's work. It is the story of a woman, and a story of the city. The language and plot are very spare and straightforward. Ann Harrington's husband kills himself, leaving ''a vacuum into which *things* rushed.'' The novel is the story of Ann's struggle to gain a command over these ''things,'' which is also the struggle to open herself to possibilities: ''Before, I had never really imagined possibilities. Since she never caused events, they just happened, and she took them as they came.'' Ann's triumph over the foreboding world of ''things'' is symbolized by her successful quest to earn a driver's license, an official recognition of her right to take herself where she wants to go.

—William C. Bamberger

MADDEN, Deirdre

Nationality: Northern Irish. **Born:** Belfast, Northern Ireland, 20 August 1960. **Education:** Trinity College, Dublin, B.A. 1983; University of East Anglia, M.A. 1985. **Awards:** Hennessy literary award, 1980; Rooney Prize for Irish Literature, 1987; Somerset Maugham award (Society of Authors), 1989. **Agent:** A. P. Watt Ltd., 20 John Street, London WC1N 2DR, England. **Address:** County Antrim, Northern Ireland.

PUBLICATIONS

Novels

Hidden Symptoms. Boston, Atlantic Monthly Press, 1986.
The Birds of the Innocent Wood. London, Faber and Faber, 1988.
Remembering Light and Stone. Boston, Faber and Faber, 1992.
Nothing Is Black. London, Faber and Faber, 1994.
One by One in the Darkness. London, Faber and Faber, 1996.

Other

Afterword, *The Ante-Room* by Kate O'Brien. New York, Penguin Books, 1990.
Contributor, *First Fictions: Introduction 9.* London, Faber and Faber, 1986.

* * *

Deirdre Madden, born in 1960, is an important voice in Northern Irish writing. The winner of several literary awards, Madden in her novels examines the state of individual consciousness in the fragmented and confusing late-twentieth-century world. Her interest in how individuals discern their place in the world leads her to examine institutions that affect people's lives: religion, geography, politics (particularly in Northern Ireland), violence, and women's rights. All of her novels rely heavily on conversation; in the tradition of Elizabeth Bowen's fiction, Madden's work uses in-depth conversations to advance characters' understanding of themselves and each other while developing her themes for the reader.

Her first novel, *Hidden Symptoms*, offers an excellent introduction to life in Belfast. The title refers to Ulster before the renewal of violence broke out; it has always been "sick," but the symptoms only became visible with the violence. The main character, Theresa Cassidy, lost her twin brother Francis to sectarian violence. In her first exposition of an injustice she will return to in *One by One in the Darkness*, Madden makes clear that Francis was not politically active, but was singled out as a representative of his "tribe." The other main character is Robert McConville, a lapsed Catholic. Although he makes regular visits to his working-class sister and her family, he thinks that he has left behind his past to embrace an artistic and intellectual life; the novel (and Theresa) proclaim the impossibility of that goal. Conversations between Theresa and Robert develop most of the book's themes, and the principal importance of events is often the conversations they inspire. The baptism of Robert's niece prompts a long discussion of Theresa's religious faith. That faith is examined as a source of anguish to her, as she struggles to maintain her belief in a benevolent God and forgive those who killed her twin. Tellingly, Theresa uses "Christian" to mean Roman Catholic; she despises the Presbyterians and seems unaware of other Christian denominations. Madden's novel examines the inner lives of Theresa and Robert, but always reminds readers of how their options are limited by Belfast political/religious realities. Theresa explains to Robert why his agnosticism is a worthless evasion: "'there's a big difference between faith and tribal loyalty, and if you think that you can escape tribal loyalty in Belfast today you're betraying your people and fooling yourself.'"

Madden's next novel, *The Birds of the Innocent Wood*, focuses on family relationships and sets aside much of the national context by refusing to name places: there is simply an unnamed "city" and a countryside with "farm" and "lough." While in some ways this decision universalizes the characters and their inner lives, at times it also makes them seem two-dimensional. Chapters represent varying characters' points of view, and the narrative is not structured in traditional chronological order. *The Birds of the Innocent Wood* is a very dark book about families and their secrets (the father has an unacknowledged illegitimate half-sister living next door, for example, and news of a twin's terminal illness is kept from her by her sister). Communication is fraught with difficulty; in contrast to the probing conversations found in other Madden novels, here the characters seem intent on deception, dishonesty, and concealment. This attitude is perhaps best summed up by one sister's perception that the diary of the other is "not by necessity honest" simply because it is written solely for herself. The novel's events include suicide, stillbirth, terminal illness, an affair that is revealed to be incestuous, and many instances of small cruelties.

Remembering Light and Stone focuses on a young Irish woman, Aisling, who has spent most of her adult life in Europe, first France and then Italy. She struggles to find her place in society. As an individual, she knows herself to be a solitary person but finds that all societies expect her to prefer family life; as an Irish woman, she ponders her and her country's place in Europe. This novel is very rooted in its time, incorporating references to contemporary political events (e.g., the destruction of the Berlin Wall) as a way of recording those significant historical moments but also to contextualize Aisling's exploration of her European identity. Although the novel appears to endorse derogatory stereotypes about Americans, it is an exchange between Aisling and her American lover, Ted, that best suggests the novel's picture of the interconnected fragments that make up contemporary culture: as they walk to a café for breakfast, Aisling decides not to point out a historical marker on the house where Dostoyevsky finished writing *The Idiot* in 1868 because it is "precious" to her and she is sure that Ted will not "share [her] appreciation." At breakfast, they talk about their grandmothers; on the way back to his flat, Ted points out the marker to her, exclaiming over its significance. This moment of accord represents a tapestry woven of diverse threads: an Irish woman and an American man viewing a plaque, in a country not their own, that commemorates a nineteenth-century novel written in

Italy by a Russian. At novel's end, what Aisling has learned about herself allows her to return home to Ireland. On a visit there with Ted, she is overwhelmed by her response to the family home in Clare, now used only for holidays by her brother's family, and she decides to move back home.

Madden's next novel, *Nothing Is Black*, is set entirely in Ireland. Claire is an artist living in a cottage in rural Donegal; as a favor to her father, she consents to a summer-long visit from her cousin Nuala, who is having troubles following the death of her mother and the birth of her first child. Nuala and her husband Kevin run a very successful restaurant in Dublin; the concept—good Irish food—and the management are Nuala's but, ironically, she is indifferent to food. Another important character is Anna, a Dutch woman who summers in her Donegal cottage. All three of these women analyze their places in life; men appear briefly, or are remembered, but remain strictly minor players. Nuala is baffled by her own behavior, stealing things she does not want from restaurants, while Anna cannot understand her estrangement from her adult daughter. The women help each other in various ways and have long, searching conversations about life, but finally all must accept what Claire has been first to acknowledge: ''the severe limits of one's understanding and abilities, the power of love and forgiveness; and that life was nothing if not mysterious.''

One by One in the Darkness was shortlisted for the 1997 Orange prize for fiction. This novel is set in Belfast and the Northern Irish countryside, and its main characters are three sisters, Cate, Sally, and Helen Quinn. Cate is a glamorous journalist in London, unmarried and pregnant, home to tell her family the news; Sally lives at home with their mother and teaches at the primary school the sisters themselves attended; Helen is a lawyer in Belfast, where part of her practice is representing Catholics being tried for political crimes. The sisters grew up in the country, and were children when the Troubles began. Their father, Charlie, was a victim of its violence, murdered in their uncle's kitchen in full view of their aunt. His is the most obvious example of a phenomenon examined closely in the novel: how innocents are murdered but deemed guilty by association, assumed to be terrorists and thus deserving of their fate. The retrospective portions of the novel look at the early days of the Troubles and record important political events such as the early civil rights marches and the arrival and reception of the British troops. The main theme of the novel concerns the aftermath of the brutal sectarian violence: how can the survivors come to terms with what has happened? The Quinns' aunt and uncle remodel their kitchen, but they can never reclaim it from the murder that took place there; further, Cate finds that the new kitchen has erased some of her happy memories of earlier times. Other themes include the importance of the growing Catholic middle class (lawyers, doctors, teachers) and the role of women in Northern Irish society.

This novel, like *Hidden Symptoms*, argues that the parades of the marching season express openly the hatred everyone feels towards Catholics, but it expresses a broader verdict on the Northern violence. In the very early days of the Troubles, the family attends a funeral for a boy they all knew. He was blown up by his own bomb as he attempted to destroy an electricity pylon, and some IRA members make a militaristic display by the side of the grave. Leaving the funeral, Charlie Quinn tells his daughters: '''Never forget what you saw today; and never let anybody try to tell you that it was anything other than a life wasted, and lives destroyed.''' Madden is at her best in *One by One in the Darkness*, examining the struggles of individuals to achieve their identity while at the same time appraising particular Northern Irish obstacles to a full and confident life. No less an authority than Seamus Heaney has said that Madden's ''work always rings true,'' and readers can look forward to more Madden novels in the future.

—Rosemary Johnsen

MAHJOUB, Jamal

Nationality: English-Sudanese. **Born:** London (raised in Sudan), 1960. **Education:** Comboni College, Sudan; Atlantic College, Wales; University of Sheffield, England. **Career:** Translator and writer. Lives in Aarhus, Denmark. **Awards:** Guardian/Heinemann African Short Story prize.

Publications

Novels

Navigation of a Rainmaker: An Apocalyptic Vision of War-Torn Africa. Oxford, England, Heinemann International, 1989.

Wings of Dust. Portsmouth, New Hampshire, Heinemann Educational Publishers, 1994.

In the Hour of Signs. Portsmouth, New Hampshire, Heinemann Educational Publishers, 1996.

The Carrier. London, Phoenix House, 1998.

* * *

According to Abiola Irele, modern African fiction by writers such as Chinua Achebe and Wole Soyinka predominantly explores issues of tradition. While tradition in a central African sense incorporates both the vision of a collective future shaped by the past and also the recognition of a brutal dislocation from the past because of slavery and colonialism, Sudanese-British writer Jamal Mahjoub engages in an ironically ''High Modernist'' reinterpretation of tradition. In Mahjoub's fiction, conceptions of the post-colonial tradition are rooted in a history of colonial collision, hearkening back to the British occupation of the Sudan (1898–1955), which resulted in the intensification of differences of an already disparate Sudanese population, the gentrification of an educated elite in the north, and the alienation of a nomadic agrarian poor in the south.

Born in the Sudan but educated in England and now living in Denmark, Mahjoub straddles many zones of identification and uses High Modernist novel techniques to produce narratives that poignantly critique colonialism. Although focussing on Ghanaian and Nigerian novelists, David I. Kier in *The African Novel and the Modernist Tradition* offers perhaps the best critical lens through which Mahjoub's novels may be illuminated. According to Kier, Modernism supplies the postcolonial novelist with an art able to express a particular view of history that emphasizes disorder, despair, and anarchy. Modernism thus becomes the perfect medium for the African novelist for conveying nostalgia for the African past while issuing bitterly ironic indictments of the present. In *Navigation of a Rainmaker*, *Wings of Dust*, and *In the Hour of Signs*, Jamal Mahjoub maps the psychological, political, and historical geographies of postcolonial consciousness in all of its opposing manifestations and from a myriad of perspectives.

Through the main character of Tanner, *Navigation of a Rainmaker* personifies the ideological complexities arising from the geographical splitting of the Sudan into the Westernized North and the aboriginal South. The structure and thematics of the novel echo this polarization. In ''North,'' the first section of the book, Tanner broods listlessly over the social decay that wells up all around him. Like the angst-ridden heroes of James Joyce or Jean Paul Sartre, Tanner suffers from a profound alienation. However, unlike the typical Modernist hero, the cause of Tanner's anomie is made clear as Mahjoub explicitly links it to colonialism's forced separation of Northerners—a mix of wild, begging children, ex-colonial bureaucrats, and white-color service workers—from the nomadic Southerners, whose proximity to the desert and nativist lifestyle offer a pathway toward a pre-colonial origin. The novel charts Tanner's journey to this mythological, originary South, which is both a physical place and a state of unified being, where he may repair the psychic trauma inflicted upon him by diasporic separation and national disintegration. Written at a time when many Northern Sudanese people were fleeing a newly installed military government, Tanner's jeremiadic quest for a purer homeland thus reflects the country's larger crisis of self-definition.

On his mission South, Tanner accompanies a mysterious African-American surveyor who turns out to be a secret agent representing international parties with a vested interest in the country's political turmoil. The scenes of espionage only confirm Tanner's suspicions that his search for a pre-colonial space untouched by corruption and colonial power is futile, even in the heart of the sacred desert. And yet, this futility is part of the motivational paradox that drives many of Mahjoub's protagonists: behind the surface of the postcolonial's moribund cynicism lies a fierce optimism that cannot be extinguished even in the face of growing instability.

Just as *Navigation of a Rainmaker* juxtaposes two, distinct places in space, *Wings of Dust* is a semi-autobiographical novel that relays between two periods of time in the life of Sharif, another first-person narrator haunted by the colonial past and tragically doomed to seek in the postcolonial present some semblance of meaning, coherence, or reunion. From his present life in exile, where he inhabits a dilapidated hotel owned by an aimless, insane woman, Sharif struggles to tell the story of his past. In the style of the bildungsroman, Sharif's early life and London education unfold to reveal the ephemeral idealisms of a motley band of Sudanese students, who, in the 1950s, dream of rebuilding their home country only to find years later that their Western experiences only alienate them from their families and native communities. When Sharif finally does return to the Sudan and attains a position of political leadership, corruption at all levels flouts his idealistic efforts and forces him into his present state of paranoid, death-obsessed insularity. In addition to exposing the vexed psychology of the postcolonial, the novel plays lyrically with themes of time and temporality. Even the most trivial characters from the past are introduced in a manner that suddenly leaps forward in time to capture them in their eventual decay.

Wings of Dust also provides a clear expression of Mahjoub's postcolonial literary aesthetic. While defending his Western appropriations, Sharif describes a form of literary defiance that helps define Mahjoub's use of Modernism: Sharif advises that postcolonial artists must ignite a ''cultural rebellion'' by openly borrowing from Western language, turning its inflections against the West, and metaphorically assassinating the sacred poets of the West. And although the novel performs precisely this method of artistic resistance, the metaphysical loneliness of its cryptic narrator sheds light on the price that such cultural warfare exacts—by blurring the line between what constitutes the authentic native and the culturally British writer, Sharif also may be assassinating himself in his narrative seizure of Western aesthetics.

Mahjoub's third novel, *In the Hour of Signs*, turns to the last two decades of the nineteenth century to recount the divergent political, religious, and military movements that led up to the British victory over the Islamic followers of the messianic Mahdi at El Obeid Town. This pivotal victory set in motion all of the psychological rupture, boundary disputes, and internal polarization of the Sudan which Mahjoub's first two novels explore. The structure of the novel reflects a mature style as it expands Mahjoub's signature cross-cutting technique between places and times to include panoply of characters, each representing a particular national interest in the ensuing conflict. Indeed, with the role of narrator shared among four or more characters, the novel exercises a vigorous cinematic point of view that forces the reader to constantly move between points of identification, to appropriate the very same sense of historical confusion and contradictory sympathies that perhaps Mahjoub and other present-day British-Sudanese feel towards the historic battle.

Premiere among the novel's oscillating narrators is Hawi, a questing ex-hermit who seeks to validate the religious legitimacy of the Mahdi—the Expected One prophesied by Islam, whose military repulsion of British forces also entails a zealous purification of traditional Islamic practices. Other narrators include Hamilton Ellesworth, an ambivalent British officer coming to terms with the crude justifications for empire building; Kodoro, a young Turkish boy and an innocent slave in the Pasha's Ottoman empire; and Nejumi, an idealistic general in the Mhadi's army, the ansar, who is committed to defending the town of Khartoum. The novel thus reprises the postcolonial condition by imagining a constellation of histories converging around a single event. But despite its historical focus, the novel may also be read as a commentary on the way that current issues specific to North Africa and the Middle East (civil wars, jihads, the Gulf War) are constantly processed in the Western media, always from only one point of view.

Working within British, central African, and Arabic traditions, Mahjoub's diverse literary affiliations on the one hand reflect the specific radical multiculturalism of the Sudan's various classes, ethnic groups, and religions, and on the other, provide another instance of what Anthony Appiah terms a ''shifting of canonical territories.'' Mahjoub's fissure is part of a larger disruption in the modern British canon recently infused with an exciting roster of expatriate postcolonial writers. In a 1997 speech ''The Writer and Globalism'' Mahjoub aligns himself with Fred D'Aguiar, Meera Syal, Andrea Levy, Bidisha, and Corttia Newland as the inheritors of an English literary renaissance begun by the group collectively known as the ''Empire Writes Back'' writers—Kazuo Ishiguro, Salman Rushdie, Timothy Mo, and Michael Ondaatje. In the same speech Mahjoub argues that postcolonial subjects naturally develop an ironic attitude towards history and globalism, and suggests that the same conditions which forced subaltern subjects to accept hybridity also led to an increased literary ability, an acumen for interweaving past and present in order to reinvent a culture never yet permitted to define itself on a global scale.

—Michael A. Chaney

MAILER, Norman (Kingsley)

Nationality: American. **Born:** Long Branch, New Jersey, 31 January 1923. **Education:** Boys' High School, Brooklyn, New York, graduated 1939; Harvard University, Cambridge, Massachusetts (associate editor, *Harvard Advocate*), 1939–43, S.B. (cum laude) in aeronautical engineering 1943; the Sorbonne, Paris, 1947. **Military Service:** Served in the United States Army, 1944–46: Sergeant. **Family:** Married 1) Beatrice Silverman in 1944 (divorced 1951), one daughter; 2) Adele Morales in 1954 (divorced 1961), two daughters; 3) Lady Jeanne Campbell in 1962 (divorced 1963), one daughter; 4) Beverly Bentley in 1963 (divorced 1979), two sons; 5) Carol Stevens in 1980 (divorced 1980); 6) Norris Church in 1980, one son. **Career:** Co-founder, 1955, and columnist, 1956, *Village Voice,* New York; columnist (''Big Bite''), *Esquire,* New York, 1962–63, and *Commentary,* New York, 1962–63. Member of the Executive Board, 1968–73, and president, 1984–86, PEN American Center; Independent Candidate for Mayor of New York City, 1969. Lives in Brooklyn, New York. **Awards:** *Story* prize, 1941; American Academy grant, 1960; National Book award, for non-fiction, 1969; Pulitzer prize, for non-fiction, 1969, 1980; MacDowell medal, 1973; National Arts Club gold medal, 1976. D.Litt.: Rutgers University, New Brunswick, New Jersey, 1969. **Member:** American Academy, 1985. **Agent:** Scott Meredith Literary Agency, 845 Third Avenue, New York, New York 10022. **Address:** c/o Rembar, 19 West 44th Street, New York, New York 10036, U.S.A.

PUBLICATIONS

Novels

The Naked and the Dead. New York, Rinehart, 1948; London, Wingate, 1949; 50th anniversary edition, with a new introduction by the author, New York, Holt, 1998.
Barbary Shore. New York, Rinehart, 1951; London, Cape, 1952.
The Deer Park. New York, Putnam, 1955; London, Wingate, 1957.
An American Dream. New York, Dial Press, and London, Deutsch, 1965.
Why Are We in Vietnam? New York, Putnam, 1967; London, Weidenfeld and Nicolson, 1969.
A Transit to Narcissus: A Facsimile of the Original Typescript, edited by Howard Fertig. New York, Fertig, 1978.
Ancient Evenings. Boston, Little Brown, and London, Macmillan, 1983.
Tough Guys Don't Dance. New York, Random House, and London, Joseph, 1984.
Harlot's Ghost. New York, Random House, and London, Joseph, 1991.
The Gospel According to the Son. New York, Random House, 1997.
The Time of Our Time. New York, Random House, 1998.

Short Stories

New Short Novels 2, with others. New York, Ballantine, 1956.
Advertisements for Myself (includes essays and verse). New York, Putnam, 1959; London, Deutsch, 1961.
The Short Fiction of Norman Mailer. New York, Dell, 1967.
The Short Fiction of Norman Mailer (not same as 1967 book). New York, Pinnacle, 1981; London, New English Library, 1982.

Plays

The Deer Park, adaptation of his own novel (produced New York, 1960; revised version, produced New York, 1967). New York, Dial Press, 1967; London, Weidenfeld and Nicolson, 1970.
A Fragment from Vietnam (as *D.J.,* produced Provincetown, Massachusetts, 1967). Included in *Existential Errands,* 1972.
Maidstone: A Mystery (screenplay and essay). New York, New American Library, 1971.

Screenplays: *Wild 90,* 1968; *Beyond the Law,* 1968; *Maidstone,* 1971; *The Executioner's Song,* 1982; *Tough Guys Don't Dance,* 1987.

Poetry

Deaths for the Ladies and Other Disasters. New York, Putnam, and London, Deutsch, 1962.

Other

The White Negro. San Francisco, City Lights, 1957.
The Presidential Papers. New York, Putnam, 1963; London, Deutsch, 1964.
Cannibals and Christians. New York, Dial Press, 1966; London, Deutsch, 1967.
The Bullfight. New York, Macmillan, 1967.
The Armies of the Night: The Novel as History, History as a Novel. New York, New American Library, and London, Weidenfeld and Nicolson, 1968.
Miami and the Siege of Chicago: An Informal History of the Republican and Democratic Conventions of 1968. New York, New American Library, and London, Weidenfeld and Nicolson, 1968.
The Idol and the Octopus: Political Writings on the Kennedy and Johnson Administrations. New York, Dell, 1968.
Of a Fire on the Moon. Boston, Little Brown, 1971; as *A Fire on the Moon,* London, Weidenfeld and Nicolson, 1971.
The Prisoner of Sex. Boston, Little Brown, and London, Weidenfeld and Nicolson, 1971.
The Long Patrol: 25 Years of Writing from the Works of Norman Mailer, edited by Robert F. Lucid. Cleveland, World, 1971.
King of the Hill: On the Fight of the Century. New York, New American Library, 1971.
Existential Errands. Boston, Little Brown, 1972; included in *The Essential Mailer,* 1982.
St. George and the Godfather. New York, New American Library, 1972.
Marilyn: A Novel Biography. New York, Grosset and Dunlap, and London, Hodder and Stoughton, 1973.
The Faith of Graffiti, with Mervyn Kurlansky and John Naar. New York, Praeger 1974; as *Watching My Name Go By,* London, Mathews Miller Dunbar, 1975.
The Fight. Boston, Little Brown, 1975; London, Hart Davis MacGibbon, 1976.
Some Honorable Men: Political Conventions 1960–1972. Boston, Little Brown, 1976.
Genius and Lust: A Journey Through the Major Writings of Henry Miller, with Henry Miller. New York, Grove Press, 1976.
The Executioner's Song: A True Life Novel (on Gary Gilmore). Boston, Little Brown, and London, Hutchinson, 1979.

Of Women and Their Elegance, photographs by Milton H. Greene. New York, Simon and Schuster, and London, Hodder and Stoughton, 1980.
The Essential Mailer. London, New English Library, 1982.
Pieces and Pontifications (essays and interviews). Boston, Little Brown, 1982; London, New English Library, 1983.
Huckleberry Finn: Alive at 100. Montclair, New Jersey, Caliban Press, 1985.
Conversations with Norman Mailer, edited by J. Michael Lennon. Jackson, University Press of Mississippi, 1988.
Pablo and Fernande: Portrait of Picasso as a Young Man. New York, Talese, 1994; published as *Portrait of Picasso as a Young Man: An Interpretive Biography,* New York, Atlantic Monthly Press, 1995.
Oswald's Tale: An American Mystery. New York, Random House, 1995.

*

Bibliography: *Norman Mailer: A Comprehensive Bibliography* by Laura Adams, Metuchen, New Jersey, Scarecrow Press, 1974.

Critical Studies (selection): *Norman Mailer* by Richard Foster, Minneapolis, University of Minnesota Press, 1968; *The Structured Vision of Norman Mailer* by Barry H. Leeds, New York, New York University Press, 1969; *Sexual Politics* by Kate Millett, New York, Doubleday, 1970, London, Hart Davis, 1971; *Norman Mailer: The Man and His Work* edited by Robert F. Lucid, Boston, Little Brown, 1971; *Norman Mailer* by Richard Poirier, London, Collins, and New York, Viking Press, 1972; *Norman Mailer: A Collection of Critical Essays* edited by Leo Braudy, Englewood Cliffs, New Jersey, Prentice Hall, 1972; *Down Mailer's Way* by Robert Solotaroff, Urbana, University of Illinois Press, 1974; *Norman Mailer: A Critical Study* by Jean Radford, London, Macmillan, and New York, Barnes and Noble, 1975; *Existential Battles: The Growth of Norman Mailer* by Laura Adams, Athens, Ohio University Press, 1976; *Mankind in Barbary: The Individual and Society in the Novels of Norman Mailer* by Stanley T. Gutman, Hanover, New Hampshire, University Press of New England, 1976; *Norman Mailer* by Philip Bufithis, New York, Ungar, 1978; *Norman Mailer,* Boston, Twayne, 1978, and *Norman Mailer Revisited,* New York, Twayne, 1992, both by Robert Merrill; *Norman Mailer: The Radical as Hipster* by Robert Ehrlich, Metuchen, New Jersey, Scarecrow Press, 1978; *Norman Mailer's Novels* by Sandy Cohen, Amsterdam, Rodopi, 1979; *Norman Mailer, Quick-Change Artist* by Jennifer Bailey, London, Macmillan, 1979, New York, Barnes and Noble, 1980; *Acts of Regeneration: Allegory and Archetype in the Work of Norman Mailer* by Robert J. Begiebing, Columbia, University of Missouri Press, 1980; *An American Dreamer: A Psychoanalytic Study of the Fiction of Norman Mailer* by Andrew M. Gordon, Rutherford, New Jersey, Fairleigh Dickinson University Press, 1980; *Mailer: A Biography* by Hilary Mills, New York, Empire, 1982, London, New English Library, 1983; *Mailer: His Life and Times* by Peter Manso, New York, Simon and Schuster, and London, Viking, 1985; *Mailer's America* by Joseph Wenke, Hanover, New Hampshire, University Press of New England, 1987; *Radical Fictions and the Novels of Norman Mailer* by Nigel Leigh, London, Macmillan, 1990; *The Lives of Norman Mailer* by Carl Rollyson, New York, Paragon House, 1991; *Norman Mailer* by Brian Morton, London, Arnold, 1991; *Norman Mailer* by Michael K. Glenday, New York, St. Martin's Press, 1995; *The Last Party: Scenes from My Life with Norman Mailer* by Adele Mailer, New York, Barricade Books, 1997; *Ex-Friends: Falling out with Allen Ginsberg, Lionel and Diana Trilling, Lillian Hellman, Hannah Arendt, and Norman Mailer* by Norman Podhoretz, New York, Free Press, 1999.

Theatrical Activities: Director: **Films**—*Wild 90,* 1968; *Beyond the Law,* 1968; *Maidstone,* 1971; *Tough Guys Don't Dance,* 1987. Actor: **Films**—his own films, and *Ragtime,* 1981.

* * *

A formal distinction between fiction and non-fiction, or between fiction and journalism, is not the most helpful way to approach either the direction or the value of Norman Mailer's work. Involving himself directly with public events as well as private concerns, reporting on activities as diverse as protest marches, prizefights, the moon landing, political conventions, and the life of the first man executed for murder in America in more than ten years, Mailer characteristically blurs, argues about, and plays with the conventional categories of fiction and non-fiction. The public events he reports become metaphors that clarify and demonstrate the issues he sees as significant, apocalyptic, or destructive about contemporary America. This combination of reporting with a personal fictive vision underlies some of Mailer's best and most searching prose, particularly *The Armies of the Night* or much of *The Executioner's Song.* Mailer began his career with a much more conventional idea of the difference between fiction and non-fiction, for, in the early novel *The Deer Park,* he had Sergius O'Shaugnessy, the young Air Force veteran trying to become a writer in the "new" Hollywood off-shoot of Desert D'Or, smugly certain that "a newspaperman is obsessed with finding the facts in order to tell a lie, and a novelist is a galley-slave to his imagination so he can look for the truth." More central to Mailer's later, more complicated, fiction and reporting is another statement from the same novel, the remark by Charles Eitel, the failed and (in the 1950s) politically suspect Hollywood writer and director, musing that "the artist was always divided between his desire for power in the world and his desire for power over his work." This emphasis on power, on the capacity to change both public and private circumstances, is never far from the center of Mailer's consciousness.

Rather than using any formal means of distinguishing one example of Mailer from another, the reader recognizes that a problem of selectivity, of what to include and what to exclude, is always visible. At times, Mailer seems to concentrate too repetitiously for too long on the relatively trivial or excessively personal, as in the rather stereotyped and remote satire of Hollywood in *The Deer Park,* all the legalisms of the last third or so of *The Executioner's Song,* or the defense of his own part in literary squabbles at the beginning of *The Prisoner of Sex.* Frequently, as he recognized himself in *The Presidential Papers,* he lacks a sense of proportion, is not sure about "how to handicap the odds."

Mailer's considerable literary ambition and the popular success of his first novel, *The Naked and the Dead,* published when he was just twenty-five, placed his own development as a writer in a highly public focus. In spite of all the claims (many of them not from Mailer himself) about the "new" voice of his generation, his first three novels were somewhat literary and derivative. *The Naked and the Dead,* the novel about the platoon fighting both the Japanese and its own army on a Pacific island during World War II, shows considerable allegiance to the fiction of Hemingway and Dos Passos, as well as deference to the ethnic mix visible in Hollywood films made during the war. *Barbary Shore,* probably the best of the three novels, taking place in a Brooklyn rooming house after the war, using characters to debate all the various perspectives of radical politics in the 1930s, and ending with no resolution for the young alienated writer, is reminiscent of James T. Farrell. And *The Deer Park,* depicting the Hollywood world of drugs, pimps, mate-swapping, and politics, contains echoes of Fitzgerald and Nathanael West without the force of originality of either, all seen at a great distance, as if the chronicle of events could shock with nothing of the feelings rendered. Although interesting, often competent, and (particularly *Barbary Shore*) full of excellent description, this fiction was more distinctive in aim than in achievement. Mailer's perspective, however, changed considerably in the middle and late 1950s, a change first visible in the 1957 essay *The White Negro,* a recognition of the clash of cultures and the violence endemic in American life. In that essay, as well as in the work that followed, Mailer began to associate imagination and creativity with the position of a sociological minority, a potentially healthy underside of American life. As he later, in *The Presidential Papers,* explained, he had not earlier acknowledged his own secret admiration for his violent characters in *The Naked and the Dead,* his own obsession with violence. From *The White Negro* on, although still disapproving strongly of the ''inhuman'' or abstract violence of technology, Mailer recognized the possibilities of creative change through violence, both in himself and in others. He also began to probe himself more consciously as a metaphor for the larger world he described.

Mailer regards his central characters, whether in the persona of himself in works like *The Armies of the Night* or *Miami and the Siege of Chicago* or through fictional personae in the novels *An American Dream, Why Are We in Vietnam?,* or *Ancient Evenings,* as ''existential'' heroes who constantly test the possible edges of human experience. Always in conflict, within themselves and with others, they dare, like Rojack walking around the parapet of the terrace high above New York, possible destruction in order to live all the possibilities of the self. Through action, they create the self, as Rojack does through murder, varieties of sexual experience, escape, criminality, and understanding. The self-creation involves a good deal of fear, as well as overcoming fear, for the hero must break away from the safe and familiar, acknowledging violence and destruction within himself. In *Why Are We in Vietnam?,* the novel of Texans on a bear hunt in Alaska, a metaphor that coalesces all those attitudes, tests, totems, and taboos that explain the American presence in Vietnam, the young voice, D.J., must create himself by recognizing and overcoming his own fear of the bear. The most frequent action in Mailer's work, which overcomes stasis and safety, is sex, the direct relationship with another being. In *Ancient Evenings* sexuality extends to procreation and lineage, speculations about new means of explaining human continuity and change. Each sexual encounter is a victory over isolation and abstraction, and, as Mailer explains in *The Prisoner of Sex,* he objects to masturbation and contraception because, in different ways, they prevent the fullest exploration of direct physical relationship. Mailer has always implicitly thought of sex in these terms, ending *The Deer Park* with a God-like voice intoning ''think of Sex as Time, and time as the connection of new circuits.'' Yet the full development of self-creation through sexual experience, the sense of the orgasm as ''the inescapable existential moment,'' detailed variously and explicitly, is in the work that follows *The White Negro.*

Mailer's ''existentialism'' is not simply private self-definition. In the first place, he frequently argues that existentialism is rootless unless one hypothesizes death as an ''existential continuation of life,'' so that how one dies, how one faces destruction, matters. In addition, and emphasized much more frequently, Mailer's ''existential'' values are also social, the public consequences of definitions at the edges of experience. Social conflict is always visible, men defining themselves through the active public and social metaphors of parties, prize-fights, and wars. War (and Mailer frequently distinguishes ''good'' wars from ''bad'') has the possibility, seldom actually achieved, of changing the consciousness of a sufficient number of people to alter the whole society. Mailer began his definition of ''existential politics'' in 1960, with his essay called ''Superman Comes to the Supermarket,'' on the nomination of John Kennedy for president at the convention in Los Angeles. He called Kennedy an ''existential'' leader because he displayed the capacity to commit himself to the ''new'' when ''the end is unknown,'' a contrast to the safety and the public predictability of the Eisenhower years, although Mailer doubted that Kennedy had the ''imagination'' to create a wholly beneficial revolution. Yet, for Mailer, the potentiality for change and revolution, for self-creation on a public scale, is always there, a human impulse that if repressed or thwarted causes ''cancer'' on either the individual or social level. In these terms, Mailer, through subsequent ''reports'' on protests, political conventions, and public events, propounds both a vision and an analysis of contemporary American society.

In rather undiscerning popular terms, Mailer is often accused of a monstrous ego. Yet, the persona of ''Norman Mailer,'' as it develops through many of the ''journalistic'' works, is highly complicated and self-critical, a metaphor for all the possibilities in contemporary man that the author can visualize and understand. As he explains in *The Armies of the Night,* he can accept the ambivalences of all the personae he adopts, ''warrior, presumptive general, ex-political candidate, embattled aging enfant terrible of the literary world, wise father of six children, radical intellectual, existential philosopher, hard-working author, champion of obscenity, husband of four battling sweet wives, amiable bar drinker, and much exaggerated street fighter, party giver, hostess insulter.'' But the one persona he finds ''insupportable'' is that of ''the nice Jewish boy from Brooklyn,'' the one with which he began, which would deny his possibility to change and create himself. The personae of his later fiction are also complicated and carefully structured voices: the violent explosions, sensitivities, challenges, and social concerns of Rojack in *An American Dream* (still, to some extent, literary, as one critic, Richard Poirier, has explained, ''both a throwback to Christopher Marlowe and … a figure out of Dashiell Hammett''); the scatology, sensitivity, fear, bravery, and self-recognition of D.J. in *Why Are We in Vietnam?* These voices, rhetorical and linguistic creations of a point of view, effectively express much of Mailer's complexity, although they lack something of the arch self-criticism (though not the humor) and the multiplicity of the persona of Norman Mailer who enriches *The Armies of the Night* and *Of a Fire on the Moon,* and whose implicit and more self-abnegating presence created *The Executioner's Song.* As personae, creative and capacious as they are, Rojack and D.J. can sound slightly more insistent, missing something of the ''Norman Mailer'' acknowledged incapacity to represent immediately all of America.

More recent examples of Mailer's fiction extend the personae into different forms. *Ancient Evenings,* an ambitious novel on which he worked for more than a decade, magnifies Mailer's scope as cultural historian. Set in Egypt over two centuries more than a thousand years before Christ, the novel locates the historical genesis and implications of many of Mailer's ideas concerning sexuality, lineage, violence, public power, society, and religion. Critically regarded as either the most probing or most pretentious of Mailer's fictions, *Ancient Evenings* manifests the enormous intellectual risks which the persona confronts. A much more limited and comic side to Mailer is visible in *Tough Guys Don't Dance,* his contemporary extension of Dashiell Hammett's world. The form, the multiple killings and suicides, as well as their discovery by the ''macho'' narrator who could have but, in fact, did not commit them, leaves room for many characteristic digressions. In addition to the central charting of the ''tough guy'' lineage, Mailer includes pages on topics such as the geological and historical topography of Provincetown, the implications of different uses of adjectives in the prose of Hemingway and Updike, the horrors for an addict of giving up smoking, and the inverse relationship between cancer and schizophrenia—all done with a sharp infusion of the comic that fits both the style and substance of Mailer's personae.

Both *Harlot's Ghost* and *Oswald's Tale* are massive books that mythologize the not-so-distant American past—CIA shenanigans in the case of the former, the Kennedy assassination in the case of the latter—and both met with mixed receptions. To some, the two volumes constituted a virtual poetry of espionage, Melville meets John le Carré; to others, they were yawning door-stoppers full of digressions, unbelievable dialogue, and bad grammar. One can hardly doubt the lengths to which Mailer went in his research, however: for *Oswald's Tale,* he and business partner Lawrence Schiller travelled to the former Soviet Union and studied old files kept on Oswald during Oswald's two-and-a-half-year stay in the country. For *The Gospel According to the Son,* the author tackled no less a story than that of Jesus, which he tells in first person: thus the protagonist confesses that during his famous verbal battle with Satan in the wilderness, he felt ineffective, and it seemed that ''my words were like straw.''

As a writer, Mailer is variously talented. He is a superb journalist, always aware of the differences between what an observer sees directly and what he creates. He is an excellent literary critic, as in his attack on Kate Millett and his defenses of Henry Miller and D.H. Lawrence in *The Prisoner of Sex.* He can describe pictorially and movingly, as in *Of a Fire on the Moon,* or select brilliantly to chronicle American life, as in most of *The Executioner's Song.* More than any of these, he is consciously, seriously, humorously, and often convincingly the heir to a tradition of American visionaries, the writer who can create, in terms of the imagination, a new consciousness for his time and his country. In spite of his prolixity, his repetition, his occasional tendency to simplify polarities (his arguments against ''technology'' can become a rant that denies his own understanding of science), and his occasional insistence on the literal applications of his own metaphors (as in parts of *The Prisoner of Sex*), Mailer has achieved something of his own revolutionary form in transforming the consciousness of others.

—James Gindin

MAJOR, Clarence

Nationality: American. **Born:** Atlanta, Georgia, 31 December 1936. **Education:** The Art Institute, Chicago (James Nelson Raymond scholar), 1952–54; Armed Forces Institute, 1955–56; New School for Social Research, New York, 1972; Norwalk College, Connecticut; State University of New York, Albany, B.S. 1976; Union Graduate School, Yellow Springs and Cincinnati, Ohio, Ph.D. 1978. **Military Service:** Served in the United States Air Force, 1955–57. **Family:** Married 1) Joyce Sparrow in 1958 (divorced 1964); 2) Pamela Ritter in 1980. **Career:** Research analyst, Simulmatics, New York, 1966–67; director of creative writing program, Harlem Education Program, New Lincoln School, New York, 1967–68; writer-in-residence, Center for Urban Education, 1967–68, and Teachers and Writers Collaborative, Columbia University Teachers College, 1967–71, both New York; lecturer, Brooklyn College, City University of New York, 1968–69, Spring 1973, 1974–75, Cazenovia College, New York, Summer 1969, Wisconsin State University, Eau Claire, Fall 1969, Queens College, City University of New York, springs 1972, 1973, and 1975, and Fall 1973, Sarah Lawrence College, Bronxville, New York, 1972–75, and School for Continuing Education, New York University, Spring 1975; writer-in-residence, Aurora College, Illinois, Spring 1974; assistant professor, Howard University, Washington, D.C., 1974–76, and University of Washington, Seattle, 1976–77; visiting assistant professor, University of Maryland, College Park, Spring 1976, and State University of New York, Buffalo, Summer 1976; associate professor, 1977–81, and professor, 1981–89, University of Colorado, Boulder. Director of Creative Writing, 1991–93, and since 1989 professor, University of California, Davis. Visiting professor, University of Nice, France, 1981–82, Fall 1983, University of California, San Diego, Spring 1984, and State University of New York, Binghamton, Spring 1988; writer-in-residence, Albany State College, Georgia, 1984, and Clayton College, Denver, Colorado, 1986, 1987; distinguished visiting writer, Temple University, Philadelphia, Fall 1988; guest writer, Warren Wilson College, 1988. Editor, *Coercion Review,* Chicago, 1958–66; staff writer, *Proof* and *Anagogic and Paideumic Review,* Chicago, 1960–61; associate editor, *Caw,* New York, 1967–70, and *Journal of Black Poetry,* San Francisco, 1967–70; reviewer, *Essence* magazine, 1970–73; columnist 1973–76, and contributing editor, 1976–86, *American Poetry Review,* Philadelphia; editor, 1977–78, and since 1978 associate editor, *American Book Review,* New York; associate editor, *Bopp,* Providence, Rhode Island, 1977–78, *Gumbo,* 1978, *Departures,* 1979, and *par rapport,* 1979–82; member of the editorial board, *Umojo,* Boulder, Colorado, 1979–80; editorial consultant, Wesleyan University Press, Middletown, Connecticut, 1984, and University of Georgia Press, Athens, 1987; since 1986 fiction editor, *High Plains Literary Review,* Denver. Also artist: individual shows—Sarah Lawrence College, 1974; First National Bank Gallery, Boulder, Colorado, 1986. **Awards:** National Council on the Arts award, 1970; National Endowment for the Arts grant, 1970, 1975, 1979; Creative Artists Public Service grant, 1971; Fulbright-Hays Exchange award, 1981; Western States Book award, for fiction, 1986; Pushcart prize, for short story, 1989. **Agent:** Susan Bergholtz, 340 West 72nd Street, New York, New York 10023. **Address:** Department of English, 281 Voorhies Hall, University of California, Davis, California 95616, U.S.A.

PUBLICATIONS

Novels

All-Night Visitors. New York, Olympia Press, 1969.
NO. New York, Emerson Hall, 1973.
Reflex and Bone Structure. New York, Fiction Collective, 1975.

Emergency Exit. New York, Fiction Collective, 1979.
My Amputations. New York, Fiction Collective, 1986.
Such Was the Season. San Francisco, Mercury House, 1987.
Painted Turtle: Woman with Guitar. Los Angeles, Sun and Moon Press, 1988.
Dirty Bird Blues. San Francisco, Mercury House, 1996.

Short Stories

Fun & Games. Duluth, Minnesota, Holy Cow! Press, 1990.

Uncollected Short Stories

''Church Girl,'' in *Human Voices 3* (Homestead, Florida), Summer-Fall 1967.
''An Area in the Cerebral Hemisphere,'' in *Statements,* edited by Jonathan Baumbach. New York, Braziller, 1975.
''Dossy O,'' in *Writing under Fire,* edited by Jerome Klinkowitz and John Somer. New York, Dell, 1978.
''Tattoo,'' in *American Made,* edited by Mark Leyner, Curtis White, and Thomas Glynn. New York, Fiction Collective, 1987.

Poetry

The Fires That Burn in Heaven. Privately printed, 1954.
Love Poems of a Black Man. Omaha, Nebraska, Coercion Press, 1965.
Human Juices. Omaha, Nebraska, Coercion Press, 1965.
Swallow and Lake. Middletown, Connecticut, Wesleyan University Press, 1970.
Symptoms and Madness. New York, Corinth, 1971.
Private Line. London, Paul Breman, 1971.
The Cotton Club: New Poems. Detroit, Broadside Press, 1972.
The Syncopated Cakewalk. New York, Barlenmir House, 1974.
Inside Diameter: The France Poems. Sag Harbor, New York, and London, Permanent Press, 1985.
Surfaces and Masks. Minneapolis, Coffee House Press, 1988.
Some Observations of a Stranger at Zuni in the Latter Part of the Century. Los Angeles, Sun and Moon Press, 1989.
Parking Lots. Mount Horeb, Wisconsin, Perishable Press, 1992.
Configurations: New and Selected Poems, 1958–1998. Port Townsend, Washington, Copper Canyon Press, 1998.

Other

Dictionary of Afro-American Slang. New York, International, 1970; as *Black Slang: A Dictionary of Afro-American Talk,* London, Routledge, 1971.
The Dark and Feeling: Black American Writers and Their Work. New York, Third Press, 1974.
Juba to Jive: A Dictionary of African-American Slang. New York, Viking, 1994.
Editor, *Writers Workshop Anthology.* New York, Harlem Education Project, 1967.
Editor, *Man Is Like a Child: An Anthology of Creative Writing by Students.* New York, Macomb's Junior High School, 1968.
Editor, *The New Black Poetry.* New York, International, 1969.
Editor, *Calling the Wind: Twentieth Century African-American Short Stories.* New York, Harper Collins, 1993.
Editor, *The Garden Thrives: Twentieth Century African-American Poetry.* New York, Harper Collins, 1995.

*

Bibliographies: ''Clarence Major: A Checklist of Criticism'' by Joe Weixlmann, in *Obsidian* (Fredonia, New York), vol. 4, no. 2, 1978; ''Toward a Primary Bibliography of Clarence Major'' by Joe Weixlmann and Clarence Major, in *Black American Lierature Forum* (Terre Haute, Indiana), Summer 1979.

Critical Studies: In *Interviews with Black Writers* edited by John O'Brien, New York, Liveright, 1973; ''La Problematique de la communication'' by Muriel Lacotte, unpublished dissertation, University of Nice, 1984; *Clarence Major and His Art: Portraits of an African American Postmodernist,* edited by Bernard W. Bell, Chapel Hill, North Carolina, University of North Carolina Press, 2001.

* * *

''In a novel, the only thing you have is words,'' Clarence Major told the interviewer John O'Brien. ''You begin with words and you end with words. The content exists in our minds. I don't think it has to be a reflection of anything. It is a reality that has been created inside of a book.'' Major's fiction exists as a rebellion against the stereotype of mimetic fiction—that telling a story, one of the things fiction can do, is the only thing fiction can do.

His first novel, *All-Night Visitors,* is an exercise in the imaginative powers of male sexuality. Major takes the most physical theme—the pleasure of the orgasm—and lyricizes it, working his imagination upon the bedrock and world of sense not customarily indulged by poetry. The pre-eminence of the imagination is shown by blending Chicago street scenes with fighting in Vietnam—in terms of the writing itself, Major claims that there is no difference. His second novel, *NO,* alternates narrative scenes of rural Georgia life with a more disembodied voice of fiction, and the action advances as it is passed back and forth, almost conversationally, between these two fictive voices. In both books, language itself is the true locus of action, as even the most random and routine development is seized as the occasion for raptures of prose (a fellatio scene, for example, soon outstrips itself as pornography and turns into an excuse for twelve pages of exuberant prose).

Major's best work is represented in his third and fourth novels, *Reflex and Bone Structure* and *Emergency Exit.* In the former, he describes an action which takes place legitimately within the characters' minds, as formed by images from television and film. ''We're in bed watching the late movie. It's 1938. *A Slight Case of Murder.* Edward G. Robinson and Jane Bryan. I go into the bathroom to pee. Finished, I look at my aging face. Little Caesar. I wink at him in the mirror. He winks back./I'm back in bed. The late show comes on. It's 1923. *The Bright Shawl.* Dorothy Gish. Mary Astor. I'm taking Mary Astor home in a yellow taxi. Dorothy Gish is jealous.'' Throughout this novel, which treats stimuli from social life and the output of a television set as equally informative, Major insists that the realm of all these happenings is in language itself. ''I am standing behind Cora,'' he writes. ''She is wearing a thin black nightgown. The backs of her legs are lovely. I love her. The word standing allows me to watch like this. The word nightgown is what she is wearing. The nightgown itself is in her drawer with her panties. The word Cora is wearing the word nightgown. I watch the sentence: the backs of her legs are lovely.''

As a result, the action of this novel takes place not simply in the characters' behavior but in the arrangements of words on the page. Here Major makes a significant advance over the techniques of his innovative fiction contemporaries. Many of them, including Ronald Sukenick (in *Up*) and John Barth (in the stories of *Lost in the Funhouse*), took a metafictive approach, establishing fiction's self-apparency and anti-illusionism by self-consciously portraying the writer writing his story. In *Reflex and Bone Structure,* however, Major accomplishes the task of making the words function not as references to things in the outside world but as entities themselves; the action is syntactic rather than dramatic, although once that syntactic function is served the action, as in the paragraph cited, can return for full human relevance. Indeed, because the activity is first located within the act of composition itself, the reader can empathize even more with the intensity of feeling behind it.

Emergency Exit is Major's most emphatic gesture toward pure writing, accomplished by making the words of his story refer inward to his own creative act, rather than outward toward the panoramic landscape of the socially real. The novel's structure makes this strategy possible. *Emergency Exit* consists of elementary units of discourse; words, sentences, paragraphs, vignettes, and serial narratives. The novel is composed of equal blocks of each, spread out and mixed with the others. At first, simple sentences are presented to the reader. Then elements from these same sentences (which have stood in reference-free isolation) recur in paragraphs, but still free of narrative meaning. The plan is to fix a word, as word, in the reader's mind, apart from any personal conceptual reference—just as an abstract expressionist painter will present a line, or a swirl of color, without any reference to figure. Then come a number of narratives, coalescing into a story of lovers and family. When enough sections of the serial narrative have accumulated to form a recognizable story, we find that the independent and fragmentary scenes of the sentences and paragraphs have been animated by characters with whom we can now empathize. Forestalling any attempt to rush off the page into incidental gossip is the memory and further repetition of these words—whether they be of black mythology, snatches of popular song, or simply brilliant writing—all within Major's arresting sentences and paragraphs. A word, an image, or scene which occurs within the narrative leads the reader directly back to the substance of Major's writing. All attention is confined within the pages of the book.

Silent as a writer for the better part of a decade, though actively engaged in teaching, speaking, and world travel, Major takes the occasion of his fifth novel, *My Amputations,* to comment on his own identity as a writer and person. His protagonist, named Mason Ellis, has a biography which matches Major's own, and his responsiveness to black music and folklore recalls the techniques of *Emergency Exit.* Mason's writing is like a closet he steps into in a recurring dream: a ''door to darkness, closed-off mystery'' through which his muse leads him in search of his personal and literary identities, both of which have been assumed by an ''Impostor'' nearly a decade ago (when Major's last novel was written). Mason's personal struggle has been with ''the unmistakable separation of Church and State,'' which for him produces an unbearable polarity between spirit and body, mentality and sexuality, and eventually a contradiction between ''clean'' and ''dirty'' which he refuses to accept. His muse must guide him away from this middle ground of separation where he languishes; imprisoned in various forms of life (which correspond to Major's background growing up in Chicago and serving in the Air Force), he must literally ''write his way out'' by constructing a different paradigm for God's interests and Caesar's. Falsely jailed while ''the Impostor'' continues his career, Mason joins a group of urban terrorists who rob a bank to finance their dreams—in his case, the recovery of his role as novelist. To do this, Mason adopts the pose of the black American writer abroad, living in Nice and speaking at various universities across Europe. But at every stage the concerns of State intervene, as each country's particular style of political insurgency disrupts his visit. Even his idealistic goal of Africa is torn by conflicts of body and spirit, and he finds himself either caught in the crossfire of terrorists or imprisoned as a political suspect. These circumstances, while being complications in the narrative, prompt some of the novel's finest writing, as Major couches Mason's behavior in a linguistic responsiveness to the terroristic nature of our times. The achievement of *My Amputations* is its conception of Mason Ellis as a creature of the world's signs and symbols. He moves in a world of poetic constructions, where even crossing the street is an artistic adventure: ''Mason Ellis sang 'Diddie Wa Diddie' like Blind Blake, crossed the street at Fifth Avenue and Forty-Second like the Beatles on the cover of *Abbey Road* and reaching the curb leaped into the air and coming down did a couple of steps of the Flat Foot Floogie.'' Not surprisingly, Major points his character toward a tribal sense of unity in Africa, pre-colonial and hence pre-political, where the separations of ''Church'' and ''State'' do not exist.

With his novels *Such Was the Season* and *Painted Turtle: Woman with Guitar* Major makes his closest approach to narrative realism, yet in each case the mimesis is simply a technical device that serves an equally abstract purpose. *Such Was the Season* is ostensibly a gesture toward that most commercially conventional of formats, the family saga, as a nephew from Chicago returns to the Atlanta home of an old aunt who helped raise him. His visit, however, entails not just the usual thematics of family history and a touch of matriarchy but rather a spectrum study of African-American culture in its many forms, from bourgeois society to political power-playing. Because the narrator is Aunt Eliza herself, the novel becomes much more a study in language than social action, however, for the emphasis remains not on the events themselves but upon her blending them into an interpretive narrative. That Major is ultimately interested in these aesthetic dimensions rather than in the simply social is evident from *Painted Turtle,* in which the story of a native American folksinger's career is told only superficially by the episodic adventures surrounding her work; at the heart of her story is the nature of her poetic expression, passages of which are reproduced as transcriptions of her songs—which are unlike any folksongs the reader may have heard, but much like the linguistic constructions Aunt Eliza fashions in the previous novel as a way of making the emerging reality of her family meaningful to her.

The 1990s saw Clarence Major's position in the American literary canon strengthened, as he edited a major text anthology for HarperCollins, expanded his original lexicological work into *Juba to Jive: A Dictionary of African American Slang* for Penguin Books, and had his own fiction included in *The Norton Anthology of American Literature*. Solidifying his own canon were three key volumes: his stories, *Fun & Games*; his novel, *Dirty Bird Blues*; and the unexpurgated version of his first novel, *All-Night Visitors*, published in a university press edition introduced by the distinguished scholar Bernard W. Bell. The short story collection displays the full range of Major's talents, from the language-based lyricism of his early work to the autobiographical reminiscences that also motivate *Such Was the Season*. As in *All-Night Visitors*, a sexual energy runs through the collection. But as the restored text of the first novel shows, Clarence Major was as far as possible from being a pornographer; indeed, Bell's edition is probably the first in literary history that had to restore nonsexual material that the original publisher had cut in order to make the book appear salacious (which it isn't). Instead, the restored novel and stories such as "Fun and Games" and "My Mother and Mitch" reveal sexuality as innocent as a child's quest for self-discovery (where the passion is his mother's) and as complex as a Vietnam veteran's attempt to reintegrate himself into a society more violent than the world in which he waged war. In each case, sex may be the stimulus to thought, but language is its resolution, as in the novel's scene where the protagonist is assaulted by a rival in love: "He dashes over—picks me up as though I'm a feather. One becomes the word, the name very quickly. Like a cunt or a flirt."

Dirty Bird Blues becomes Major's most accessible work by virtue of locating this same dynamic in the world not of words but of music. As tools of literary realism, words inevitably point to their references, things in the outside world. Notes of music and even blues lyrics themselves are more easily considered in their artistic dimension, and in letting the life of musician Manfred Banks parallel his own writer's experience, Clarence Major constructs a narrative that needs no metafictive devices to remind readers that the essence of his story is imaginative. As Banks's music struggles against the hard reality of blue-collar employment, the author's narrative wends its way through the complexities and challenges of being a man to one's self but also a husband to one's wife and a father to one's daughter. Accomplishing the task lets readers appreciate how doing so is a masterpiece for both character and writer.

—Jerome Klinkowitz

MALOUF, David

Nationality: Australian. **Born:** David George Joseph Malouf in Brisbane, Queensland, 20 March 1934. **Education:** Brisbane Grammar School, 1947–50; University of Queensland, Brisbane, 1951–54, B.A. (honours) in English 1954. **Career:** Lecturer, University of Queensland, 1955–57; teacher, St. Anselm's College, England, 1962–68; lecturer, University of Sydney, 1968–77. **Awards:** Australian Literature Society gold medal, 1974, 1983; Grace Leven prize, 1975; James Cook award, 1975; Australia Council fellowship, 1978; New South Wales Premier's prize, for fiction, 1979; *The Age* Book of the Year award, 1982; Commonwealth prize for fiction, 1991; Prix Femina Étranger, 1991; Miles Franklin award, 1991; New South Wales award for fiction, 1991; Los Angeles *Times* Fiction prize, 1993; International IMPAC Dublin Literary award, 1993. **Address:** 53 Myrtle St., Chippendale, New South Wales 2008, Australia.

Publications

Novels

Johnno. St. Lucia, University of Queensland Press, 1975; New York, Braziller, 1978.

An Imaginary Life. New York, Braziller, and London, Chatto and Windus, 1978.

Child's Play, with Eustace and the Prowler. London, Chatto and Windus, 1982; as *Child's Play, The Bread of Time to Come: Two Novellas,* New York, Braziller, 1982.

Fly Away Peter. London, Chatto and Windus, 1982.

Harland's Half Acre. London, Chatto and Windus, and New York, Knopf, 1984.

The Great World. London, Chatto and Windus, 1990; New York, Pantheon, 1991.

Remembering Babylon. London, Chatto and Windus, and New York, Knopf, 1993.

The Conversations at Curlow Creek. New York, Pantheon Books, 1996.

Short Stories

Antipodes. London, Chatto and Windus, 1985.

Dream Stuff: Stories. New York, Pantheon Books, 2000.

Plays

Voss (opera libretto), music by Richard Meale, adaptation of the novel by Patrick White (produced Sydney, 1986).

Blood Relations. Sydney, Currency Press, 1988.

Baa Baa Black Sheep (opera libretto). London, Chatto and Windus, 1993.

Poetry

Four Poets, and others. Melbourne, Cheshire, 1962.

Bicycle and Other Poems. St. Lucia, University of Queensland Press, 1970; as *The Year of the Foxes and Other Poems,* New York, Braziller, 1979.

Neighbours in a Thicket. St. Lucia, University of Queensland Press, 1974.

Poems 1975–76. Sydney, Prism, 1976.

Selected Poems. Sydney, Angus and Robertson, 1980.

Wild Lemons. Sydney, Angus and Robertson, 1980.

First Things Last. St. Lucia, University of Queensland Press, 1980; London, Chatto and Windus, 1981.

Poems, 1959–89. St. Lucia, University of Queensland Press, 1992.

Selected Poems, 1959–1989. London, Chatto & Windus, 1994.

Other

New Currents in Australian Writing, with Katharine Brisbane and R.F. Brissenden. Sydney and London, Angus and Robertson, 1978.

12 Edmondstone Street (essays). London, Chatto and Windus, 1985.

Johnno, Short Stories, Poems, Essays, and Interview, edited by James Tulip. St. Lucia, University of Queensland Press, 1990.

A Spirit of Play: The Making of Australian Consciousness. Sydney, ABC Books for the Australian Broadcasting Corporation, 1998.

The Fox and the Magpie: A Divertissement for 2 Voices (lyrics), music by Kurt Schwertsik. London, Boosey & Hawkes, 1998.

Editor, with others, *We Took Their Orders and Are Dead: An Anti-War Anthology.* Sydney, Ure Smith, 1971.

Editor, *Gesture of a Hand* (anthology of Australian poetry). Artarmon, New South Wales, Holt Rinehart, 1975.

*

Manuscript Collections: University of Queensland, St. Lucia; Australian National University Library, Canberra.

Critical Studies: Interviews in *Commonwealth 4* (Rodez, France), 1979–80, *Meanjin 39* (Melbourne), and *Australian Literary Studies* (Hobart, Tasmania), October 1982; ''David Malouf as Humane Allegorist'' by James Tulip, in *Southerly* (Sydney), 1981; ''David Malouf and the Language of Exile'' by Peter Bishop, in *Australian Literary Studies* (Hobart, Tasmania), October 1982; ''David Malouf's Fiction'' by P. Pierce, in *Meanjin* (Melbourne), vol. 41, no. 4, 1982; ''Discoveries and Transformations: Aspects of David Malouf's Work'' by L.T. Hergenhan, in *Australian Literary Studies* (Hobart, Tasmania), May 1984; ''Secret Companions: The Continuity of David Malouf's Fiction'' by M. Dever, in *World Literature Written in English* (Guelph, Ontario), vol. 26, no. 1, 1986; ''David Malouf's *Child's Play* and 'The Death of the Author''' by S. Woods, in *Australian Literary Studies* (Hobart, Tasmania), May 1988; ''Body Talk: The Prose of David Malouf'' by N. Mansfield, in *Southerly* (Sydney), vol. 49, no. 2, 1989; *Australia in Mind: Thirteen Influential Australian Thinkers* by M. Thomas, Sydney, Hale and Iremonger, 1989; ''Mapping the Local in the Unreal City'' by E. Ferrier, in *Island* (Sandy Bay, Tasmania), no. 41, 1989; *Imagined Lives: A Study of David Malouf* by P. Neilsen, St. Lucia, University of Queensland Press, 1990; *Sheer Edge: Aspects of Identity in David Malouf's Writing* by Karin Hansson, Lund, Lund University Press, 1991; *David Malouf* by Ivor Indyk, Melbourne and Oxford, Oxford University Press, 1993; *Provisional Maps: Critical Essays on David Malouf,* edited by Amanda Nettelbeck. Nedlands, University of Western Australia, 1994; *Reading David Malouf* by Amanda Nettelbeck, South Melbourne, Oxford University Press, 1995; *Imagined Lives: A Study of David Malouf* by Philip Neilsen, St Lucia, Queensland, University of Queensland Press and Portland, Oregon, International Specialized Book Services, 1996.

* * *

David Malouf is never slow to point, in interviews, to his own interest in what he calls the ''matter of Australia,'' and each of his novels can be seen as an exploration of a range of experience perceived to have been crucial to the making of Australians today. This determination to circumscribe Australian experience and identity responds to an impulse that is at base a nationalistic and a post-colonial one. Indeed, the longstanding obsession in his country with the question of national identity probably conceals the felt necessity to inscribe distance, or to affirm cultural independence, from England, seen as a point of origin. It can even be argued that, in the case of Australia, the post-colonial desire to differentiate oneself from England (apparent in the perennial theme of exile) in fact springs from a perception of embarrassing proximity to that very place and cultural model.

On the other hand, some critics have noted a deep tension in Malouf's work between this post-colonial radicalism and what has been called his profound nostalgia for a prelapsarian state of absolute unity. This kind of theme actually goes back to the earliest phase of his career as a writer, when Malouf made a name for himself as a lyrical poet on the look-out for alternative ontologies. Many of the poems collected in *Bicycle and Other Poems* (1970) and *Neighbours in a Thicket* (1974) pursue the theme of metamorphosis as providing intellectual entry into the animal, the vegetal, and the mineral states. For example, in the poem entitled ''The Crab Feast,'' the persona finally reaches a level of awareness at which it becomes possible to claim: ''We are one at last. Assembled here / out of earth, water, air / to a love feast.'' This moment of communion with a crab is ironically achieved at the dinner table in the act of consumption; but it also involves an imaginative descent into the crab's life and habitat, conducted so that the eater experiences ''the taste of so much air, so much water,'' until he/it actually becomes the landscape. Malouf's poetry can perhaps be called post-lyrical in that it registers the dissolution of the self's limits, acknowledging in the process the erotic possibilities offered by this breach of boundaries, but resulting always in a surrender of identity equivalent to dying: ''You were / myself in another species, brute / blue, a bolt of lightning, maybe God.''

It seems clear that this desire for totality beyond speech runs counter to the wish to create or consolidate a sense of national identity for Australia. It is then a paradox that Malouf's post-lyrical impulses should carry over into his fiction, which is avowedly post-colonial in purpose. *Johnno* (1975), his first novel, is a largely autobiographical account of difficult adolescence in Brisbane. The protagonist Johnno's sense of the vanity of all experience has been called existentialist; but it is an existentialism with a political edge to it, as Brisbane is resented for its lack of potentialities, so that the ''entirely unnecessary fate'' of being born there implies the need to travel overseas with a view to embracing a more ''authentic'' life-style. Eventually, after years of travelling in the Congo, in Paris, and Athens, Johnno returns to Queensland, only to die in the Condamine River in a drowning accident that is possibly a disguised suicide. Johnno's death can thus be seen as his final quizzical message, one that can be interpreted (as it is by Dante, the novel's puzzled narrator) as a gesture of ambiguous reconciliation with the place—into which the protagonist is literally absorbed.

This sets the pattern for a good deal of Malouf's subsequent fiction. Although *An Imaginary Life* (1978), the invented story of Ovid's life of exile on the outskirts of the Roman Empire, seems resolutely un-Australian in terms of setting and subject matter, it traces a process of cultural attunement to an austere and alien environment, which is especially resonant in an Australian context. It is also significant that this story of gradual acclimatization should play itself out in terms of a search for linguistic fit. Malouf has been known to remark that, in Australia, the plight of the first settlers may have consisted in lacking a language to adequately describe and relate to an inscrutable environment. Similarly, in *An Imaginary Life*, Ovid's Latin is found too articulate to come to grips with a place that, in its rudimentary bleakness, remains close to ''the first principle of creation.'' It is apt, therefore, that the poet should relinquish his native tongue and take steps towards learning the language of the natives, which he finds more expressive of ''the raw life and unity of things.'' Thus far, the novel could pass muster as an allegory of the post-colonial condition; but Malouf characteristically pushes matters ahead by having Ovid meet the Child, a wolf-boy discovered living wild in the forest. Attempts to bring the Child within the compass of human civilization will strangely backfire, as the roles are reversed and it is finally Ovid who takes lessons in the ways of nature. As a wild boy in perfect tune with the natural world, the Child commands a mimetic ''language'' of sounds and cries that allows him to commune with the creatures peopling the bush. In his own attempts to imitate animal sounds, Ovid, too, becomes aware that the creatures ''will settle in us, re-entering their old lives deep in our consciousness. And after them, the plants...'' However, he only achieves perfect wholeness when settling ''deep into the earth,'' at the end of a life-long quest, when his body dissolves into the landscape in a way that seems finally de-creative.

After the (post-)lyrical experiments of *An Imaginary Life*, Malouf's work has tended to gesture more and more towards the quality of epic, as the author rehearsed a succession of major episodes in Australian history. In novel after novel, he strived to imaginatively assess the extent to which these events, which have in the meantime acquired the status of myth, actually served to shape up a sense of national consciousness. Throughout, though, this positive (celebratory) historian's approach is pursued alongside the usual morbid interest in the more entropic dimensions of human experience.

Fly Away Peter (1982) thus engages with the issue of Australia's participation in the Great War, while *The Great World* (1990) evokes, among other things, the Malaysian campaign and the anti-heroic sufferings and degradations endured by ANZAC troops kept prisoners in Southeast Asia during the Second World War. *The Great World* is like its predecessor, *Harland's Half Acre* (1984), in that it also ranges over several decades of Australian life, so that, taken together, these two books probe Australians' experience of the First World War (again), the Great Depression, the Second World War and the Holocaust, the post-war mining and property boom, and finally the financial crash of 1987. Also, these books include a variety of representative characters and types from all walks of life, so that they can be said to aspire to the quality of national realist epics, indeed just like Tolstoy's *War and Peace* (with which *The Great World* has been compared).

In each of his novels from *Fly Away Peteré* onwards, Malouf also addresses a stereotype of national identity with a view to apprehending it imaginatively from within. The first of these superficial clichs of national character is the myth of the ''digger,'' as Australian soldiers in World War I were commonly nicknamed. In *Fly Away Peter*, the myth (with its connotations of self-indulgent pride in physical prowess and undisciplined ''mateyness'') is pitted against the horrific reality of large-scale massacres in the trenches of Flanders. The image is further redressed and expanded in *The Great World* in which one of the main characters, precisely called Digger, is endowed with an encyclopaedic memory allowing him to record ''the little sacraments of daily existence,'' those that constitute ''our *other* history, the one that goes on under the noise and chatter of events and is the major part of what happens each day in the life of the planet.'' Malouf's portrait of Digger thus foregrounds qualities like contemplativeness (rather than physical prowess), as well as a fossicking urge to lay bare new strata of experience. The point is clearly that the writer approaches national identity not as fixed, a matter of given characteristics, but as an ongoing process of inclusion and change, susceptible to being revisited and transformed.

A similar approach is perceptible in *Remembering Babylon* (1993) and *The Conversations at Curlow Creek* (1996), in which Malouf challenges traditional representations of the settler and of the bushranger, respectively. *Remembering Babylon* recreates the lives of the Scottish settlers of a small Queensland township in the middle of the nineteenth century, and so reveals a continuing interest in revisiting history. The villagers' peacefulness is disturbed by the intrusion of Gemmy, a young British castaway who was rescued and raised by the Aborigines. Gemmy's appearance compels the white settlers to address the fact of native presence in new, unbiased ways; in this respect, he emerges as a catalyst of cultural change, which is in keeping with his status as a ''forerunner'' of the time in the future when Australian culture can be considered as equitably hybrid or ''geminate.'' *The Conversations at Curlow Creek* can be seen to extend this kind of reflection since, starting from an evocation of bushranging (itself partly inspired by the story of Ned Kelly, the most famous of Australian outlaws), Malouf embarks on a meditation upon the restrictions of official law, in the context of which legal truth is implicitly contrasted with the cosmic laws of the land, or else with the putative laws (and narratives) potentially released by the imagination.

One way of reconciling Malouf's constructive (post-colonial) endeavour with his more de-creative leanings would consist in stating that the death of his protagonists on Australian soil amounts to claiming that territory as an authentic source of cultural roots. In a sense, then, his writing can be seen to conceal colonialist attitudes, or at least a spirit of competition with the natives for possession of the continent as a *locus* of valid experience. But perhaps this must be qualified, with the recognition that Malouf is acutely aware of the political and epistemological limitations imposed upon him by his own subject matter. For example, in *Remembering Babylon*, Aboriginal culture is only envisioned through the authorising prism of Gemmy's hybrid consciousness. If it were not for this kind of subterfuge, indigenous experience would of course remain strictly out of bounds for the white writer, who has therefore no other option than to keep exploring his own side of the culture. In the last analysis, it is probably fair to say that Malouf gives literary expression to the profound dilemmas and traumas lying at the very foundation of Australian settler culture; or that, conversely, this kind of issue entered the domain of literature thanks to the consummate skills of a writer who will remain known as one of the most beautiful stylists in the English language.

—Marc Delrez

MANTEL, Hilary (Mary)

Nationality: British. **Born:** Glossop, Derbyshire, 6 July 1952. **Education:** The London School of Economics, 1970; Sheffield University, Yorkshire, B. Jurisprudence 1973. **Family:** Married Gerald McEwen in 1972. **Career:** Social worker in a geriatric hospital, 1974–75; teacher of English, Botswana, 1977–80; lived in Saudi Arabia, 1981–86. **Awards:** Naipaul Memorial prize, for travel writing, 1987; Winifred Holtby prize, 1990; Cheltenham fiction prize, 1991; Soultrem Arts Literary prize, 1991; Sunday Express Book of the Year prize, 1992. Fellow, Royal Society of Literature, 1990. **Agent:** Bill Hamilton, A.M. Heath, 79 St. Martin's Lane, London WC2N 4AA, England.

PUBLICATIONS

Novels

Every Day Is Mother's Day. London, Chatto and Windus, 1985; New York, Owl Books, 2000.

Vacant Possession. London, Chatto and Windus, 1986; New York, Holt, 2000.

Eight Months on Ghazzah Street. London, Viking, 1988; New York, Holt, 1997.

Fludd. London, Viking, 1989.

A Place of Greater Safety. London, Viking, 1992; New York, Athenaeum, 1993.

A Change of Climate. London, Viking, 1994; New York, Atheneum, 1994.
An Experiment in Love. London, Viking, 1995; New York, Holt, 1996.
The Giant, O'Brien. New York, Holt, 1998.

Uncollected Short Stories

"Poor Children" (as Hilary McEwen), in *Punch* (London), 21 February 1979.
"Something for Sweet," in *Literary Review* (London), December 1986.
"Alas for the Egg," in *Best Short Stories 1987,* edited by Giles Gordon and David Hughes. London, Heinemann, 1987.
"A Dying Breed," in *London Magazine,* April-May 1987.
"Dog Days," in *Encounter* (London), May 1987.

*

Hilary Mantel comments:

My first two novels are set in the north of England, in 1974 and 1984 respectively. *Every Day Is Mother's Day* tells the story of Muriel Axon and her mother Evelyn, two reclusive women who live together in mutual disgust, united only by their fear of the outside world. Their peculiar lives touch the lives of their neighbors at many points, but true contact is never made. Muriel Axon becomes mysteriously pregnant, and at the end of the story there are two violent deaths.

The mood of this book is comic and satirical, with excursions into the fantastic; at times it has the flavor of a ghost story. Some of the ideas come from a short period I spent as a hospital social worker. At a deeper level, I was interested by different theories of mental health and illness, and especially by Bruno Bettelheim's writings on autism. Muriel's internal world consists of a series of terrifying misapprehensions about the nature of cause and effect; but her major problem is that there is a gap where her imagination should be. Because of this gap, she cannot put herself in anyone else's place, or guess what their feelings might be. So she is equipped to evolve from a pathetic person into a wicked one.

Vacant Possession takes up Muriel's story ten years later. Released from a long-stay mental hospital, which is closing as a result of government policy, Muriel returns to her old haunts and begins to wreak havoc in the lives of the new owners of her mother's house.

Here I wanted to make some topical points about the hospital closures and the kinds of problems they might create; sadly, the points remain topical several years on. I also wanted to expand the character of Muriel to its logical limits. Since she had no center—no soul, really—it is possible for her to assume other identities at will. In one incarnation she is a cleaning woman called Lizzie Blank; in another, she is a depressive hospital orderly called Poor Mrs. Wilmot. She has the knack of finding out the fears and vulnerabilities of the people around her, and dealing with them accordingly.

Vacant Possession is superficially less serious than *Every Day Is Mother's Day.* It has a faster pace, more jokes per page, and a more farcical plot-line. As epigraph to the first book I used a quotation from Pascal: "Two errors: one, to take everything literally; two, to take everything spiritually." When reading anything I have written, my *ideal* reader would hear that warning in mind.

My third novel *Eight Months on Ghazzah Street* is a psychological thriller set in Saudi Arabia, where I lived for some years. My fourth novel, *Fludd* is a comedy set in the north of England in the 1950s in a fictitious moorland village. The main characters are nuns and priests. Here I used motifs, mishaps and miseries from my own Catholic childhood; but the book is not a satire on the Church. Its central device is the notion of alchemy. I wanted to explore what alchemy meant, as a liberating and creative process, and to see what form my own earliest memories would take if I worked to transform them into fiction.

* * *

British writer Hilary Mantel's oeuvre is distinguished by both its versatility and its singular fascination with the relationship between social and international politics. Mantel's eight novels offer an intriguing graph of a novelist's preoccupations and of her development.

Mantel's first two novels, *Every Day Is Mother's Day* and *Vacant Possession,* are unusual in that they deal with the same people and, up to a point, with the same events. In *Every Day Is Mother's Day* the madness, infanticide, and matricide in the Axon household are described mostly through Mrs. Axon's eyes (giving us some idea of her marriage to the horrible Mr. Axon, now mercifully dead), and in *Vacant Possession* the same events are recalled by her daughter Muriel in a flashback that asserts her hate for her mother, yet tells us nothing of the cunning ways in which Muriel reinforced her mother's belief in the evil spirits possessing the house (it is left to the reader to guess at these from Mrs. Axon's terrors in the first book). The action in *Vacant Possession* then moves forward to two more murders committed by Muriel and two by her mad landlord. There is a terrible neatness about the second book: multiple links never thought of in the first book are now established and explored. Coincidences abound, all part of a carefully worked out pattern, and what happens has the inevitability of a fairy tale. Mantel's preoccupation is with evil, with human wickedness that pursues its ends rigorously and appears to triumph, at least in the first novel. At the end of *Vacant Possession,* however, Muriel Axon is back in her old house: like a dreadful sorcerer's apprentice she has called up spirits that will destroy her—retribution at last.

Mantel's third book, *Eight Months on Ghazzah Street,* is a very different kind of novel. Presumably based on personal experiences, and written out of the shock and outrage of living in a society that has little time for Western liberal ideals and none for Western women, it is a mixture of a thriller (with no clear-cut solution of the mystery) and a record (some of it in diary form) of the heroine's progress, or disintegration. Frances Shore comes to Saudi Arabia to join her husband, a civil engineer. A cartographer, she is not permitted to work in the Kingdom, finds the expatriate society uncongenial, and tries to make friends with two young women neighbors, one a Pakistani, one a Saudi. An Englishman is murdered and there are hints of Fundamentalist plots and gunrunning. The end of the novel finds Frances and her husband silent, defeated, waiting to leave for good. There are no real villains, just a clash of two worlds, two cultures, two moralities, and, ultimately, a deep dislike of the hot, dusty city and its ways.

In *Fludd,* Mantel once again focuses on the vagaries of good and evil. Fludd, who seems to be a reincarnation of the 16th-century mystical theosophist and alchemist Robert Fludd, comes to the northern village of Fetherhoughton as curate to the Roman Catholic priest, Father Angwin. Like a catalyst in a chemical process he brings change to the village: the traditional old faith is reinforced; the cruel Mother Perpetua of the local convent apparently meets the devil and is burnt; a young nun, Sister Philomena, escapes with Fludd, spends the night with him and is left to face the unknown world with confidence born out of love. There is perhaps a devil in the shape of the local tobacconist, and there is a miracle: the priest's housekeeper is cured of a disfiguring wart. There is some unexpected kindness, another miracle perhaps (the old nuns help Philomena to run away), and in the end the message is reassuring: ''the ways of the wicked shall perish.''

The political paradigm of *Eight Months on Ghazzah Street*—a clashing of two distinct cultures—serves once again as the model for Mantel's 1994 novel, *A Change of Climate.* Truly a work obsessed with memory and secrets, and with how these private concerns interact with the larger political environment, the story involves the domestic trials of a modern Norfolk family. Ralph and Anna Eldred are former missionaries to Africa and people who have not only spent time in a South African prison but, in Bechuanaland, have had their two babies abducted. Their story is obviously novel-ready but Mantel avoids pandering by inflecting the Eldred's terrible ''secrets'' with descriptions of the equally terrible realities of an apartheid South Africa, and, as the Eldreds return to England, with a portrait of socially torn 1980s Britain. What makes Mantel's novel so fascinating is her bold grafting of the everyday with the international—*A Change of Climate,* like Nadine Gordimer's finest work, concerns itself with the nature of faith and social commitment in the face of hostile, predictably bigoted forces. While the Eldred family leans towards chaos, they also come to terms with their past and the novel is resolved on a constructive, if precarious, note of reconciliation.

Even in her lengthier novels there is a trademark quality of concentration in Mantel's prose that affords many of her works the tight power of fine short stories. Unmannered, lucid, and always realist, Mantel's fiction-writing perhaps owes much of its style to her background as a literary, political, and cultural studies essayist. She captivates, in both her fiction and criticism, and then often startles a reader with a no-fuss, vivid journalism. Consider the opening line in *A Change of Climate:* ''One day when Kit was ten years old, a visitor cut her wrists in the kitchen.'' The same kind of ominous, seemingly ho-hum descriptions of suffering are also notable in *An Experiment in Love,* Mantel's seventh novel. This first-person fiction is essentially a coming-of-age story about Carmel McBain, the daughter of a rather disinterested working class English family. Carmel eventually escapes her unsupportive household and attends London University. Mantel broadens a typical college novel to explore the political territories of gender and class. *An Experiment in Love,* set in the 1960s, is a knowingly feminist work—contrasting Carmel's goals (and sometimes self-destructive frustrations) with the frustrated desires of her mother and her mother's generation.

The fascination with ''the wicked'' that is a clear preoccupation in Mantel's novels explicitly marks her historical fictions, *A Place of Greater Safety* and *The Giant, O'Brien. A Place of Greater Safety* is an ambitious re-telling of the French Revolution, and Mantel's principal characters are historical figures now associated directly with the Terror—Camille Desmoulins, George-Jacques Danton, and Maxmilien Robespierre. This is a massive novel that, like so much of Mantel's fiction, is obsessed with the origins and then the necessary unions of social and political power. We follow the three characters from their prosaic provincial beginnings to their ultimate destruction at the hands of a world-changing, anarchic force that they were directly responsible for inspiring. Mantel is able to infiltrate the consciousnesses of her subjects and so, in the best possible way, she renders these historical lives immediate and palpable. But if *A Place of Greater Safety* is a sprawling and rather grand study of the workings of power, Mantel's most recent novel *The Giant, O'Brien* manages the same investigation in a much more compact frame. An at times rollicking tale of an actual 18th-century Irish giant, Charles Byrne, the novel is distinguished by brilliant dialogue and by effortless transitions between the first and third person narrative voice. Mantel has created a first-rate adventure tale—Byrne travels from Ireland to London, with a group of good fellows, to make his fortune as the tallest man on Earth—but she's also crafted a macabre meditation on nationhood and social justice. Byrne's counterpoint is the Scottish experimental doctor John Hunter, who must resort to grave-robbing to ensure the subjects necessary for his radical biological experiments. As Mantel develops the two protagonists, what we are offered is two distinct but complimentary portraits of marginalized geniuses—men who struggle to ''make it'' to the center only to be, in the end, consumed by their own originality.

It should be stressed that there is much to amuse the reader in Mantel's novels, surprisingly so given the grim events that take place. She has a wicked sense of the absurd and a sharp eye for detail. This latter quality she shares of course with most present-day novelists, but in her descriptions of the present-day world, evil, banal but powerful, is caught and held for the reader to inspect and recognize.

—Hana Sambrook, updated by Jake Kennedy

MARKANDAYA, Kamala

Pseudonym for Kamala Purnaiya Taylor. **Nationality:** Indian. **Born:** 1924. **Education:** Madras University. **Family:** Married; one daughter. **Career:** Journalist; now full-time writer. Lives in London. **Awards:** National Association of Independent Schools award (U.S.A.), 1967; English-Speaking Union award, 1974. **Address:** c/o Chatto and Windus, 20 Vauxhall Bridge Road, London SW1V 2SA, England.

Publications

Novels

Nectar in a Sieve. London, Putnam, 1954; New York, Day, 1955.

Some Inner Fury. London, Putnam, 1955; New York, Day, 1956.

A Silence of Desire. London, Putnam, and New York, Day, 1960.

Possession. Bombay, Jaico, London, Putnam, and New York, Day, 1963.

A Handful of Rice. London, Hamish Hamilton, and New York, Day, 1966.

The Coffer Dams. London, Hamish Hamilton, and New York, Day, 1969.

The Nowhere Man. New York, Day, 1972; London, Allen Lane, 1973.

Two Virgins. New York, Day, 1973; London, Chatto and Windus, 1974.

The Golden Honeycomb. London, Chatto and Windus, and New York, Crowell, 1977.

Pleasure City. London, Chatto and Windus, 1982; as *Shalimar,* New York, Harper, 1983.

*

Critical Studies: *Kamala Markandaya* by Margaret P. Joseph, New Delhi, Arnold-Heinemann, 1980; *Cross-Cultural Interaction in Indian English Fiction: An Analysis of the Novels of Ruth Prawer Jhabvala and Kamala Markandaya* by Ramesh Chadha, New Delhi, National Book Organisation, 1988; *The Novels of Kamala Markandaya and Ruth Prawer Jhabvala* by Rekha Jha, New Delhi, Prestige, 1990; *Cultural Imperialism and the Indo-English Novel: Genre and Ideology in R.K. Narayan, Anita Desai, Kamala Markandaya, and Salman Rushdie* by Fawzia Afzal-Khan; *Human Bonds and Bondages: The Fiction of Anita Desai and Kamala Markandaya* by Usha Pathania, Delhi, Kanishka, 1992; *Kamala Markandaya: A Thematic Study* by Anil Kumar Bhatnagar, New Delhi, Sarup & Sons, 1995; *The New Woman in Indian English Fiction: A Study of Kamala Markandaya, Anita Desai, Namita Gokhale and Shobha De* by Sharad Shrivastava, New Delhi, Creative Books, 1996; *Six Indian Novelists: Mulk Raj Anand, Raja Rao, R.K. Narayan, Balachandran Rajan, Kamala Markandaya, Anita Desai* by A.V. Suresh Kumar, New Delhi, Creative Books, 1996; *Kamala Markandaya: A Critical Study of Her Novels, 1954–1982* by A.V. Krishna Rao and K. Madhavi Menon, Delhi, B.R. Publishing Corporation, 1997; *The Novels of Kamala Markandaya and Arun Joshi* by A.A. Sinha, Jalandhar, India, ABS Publications, 1998; *The Novels of Kamala Markandaya: A Critical Study* by Ramesh K. Srivastava, Amritsar, India, Guru Nanak Dev University, 1998; *Kamala Markandaya* by Uma Parameswaran, Jaipur, India, Rawat Publications, 2000.

* * *

Kamala Markandaya is one of the best of contemporary Indian novelists. Her novels are remarkable for their range of experience. *Nectar in a Sieve* is set in a village and examines the hard agricultural life of the Indian peasant; *Some Inner Fury,* which includes a highly educated woman and her English lover who are torn apart by the Quit India campaign of the time, has to do with the quarrel between Western and Indian influences, as they are focussed in a marriage; *A Silence of Desire* deals with the middle class, and *A Handful of Rice* with the city poor; *Possession* moves from the West End of London to a South Indian village, and is centred on the conflict of Eastern spirituality with Western materialism; *The Coffer Dams* is a highly contemporary examination of the activities of a British engineering firm which is invited to build a dam in India. Markandaya has not the same intimacy and familiarity with all these areas of life, and she has indeed been criticised by Indian critics for a certain lack of inwardness with the life of the Indian poor. Her particular strength lies in the delicate analysis of the relationships of persons, particularly when these have a more developed consciousness of their problems, and particularly when they are attempting to grope towards some more independent existence. She has, too, the genuine novelist's gift for fixing the exact individuality of the character, even if she is less successful at establishing it in a reasonably convincing social context. She has been most successful and at her best, an impressive best, in dealing with the problems of the educated middle class, and she has a gift in particular for delineating the self-imposed laceration of the dissatisfied.

Perhaps Markandaya's most achieved and characteristic work is *A Silence of Desire.* It is a delicate, precise study of husband and wife, although the wife has less actuality than the husband, Dandekar, a nervy, conscientious, petty government clerk. He is rocked off his age-old balance by his wife's strange absences, excuses, and lies. It turns out that she has a growth and is attending a Faith Healer. The husband is by no means a Westernised person, but he is to some degree secular and modern, and the situation enables the author to reflect on the tensions, the strength and the inadequacies and aspirations of middle-class Indian life. The book is gentle in tone but sharp in perception, and the mixture of moods, the friction of faith and reason, the quarrel of old and young, are beautifully pointed. There are conventional, perfunctory patches in the novel, but Markandaya shows a very high skill in unravelling sympathetically but unflinchingly the structure of the protagonist's motives and the bumbling and stumbling progress of his anxieties.

Towards the end of *A Silence of Desire* there occurs a suggestion in an encounter between Sarojini and Dandekar, the husband and wife, of a theme which clearly much engages Markandaya. The wife reverences the tulasi tree as embodying the divine spirit, whereas the husband understands its purely symbolic function. ''You with your Western notions, your superior talk of ignorance and superstition … you don't know what lies beyond reason and you prefer not to find out. To you the tulasi is a plant that grows in earth like the rest—an ordinary common plant… .'' She is preoccupied with the opposition between a cerebral, Western—and, she seems to be suggesting, a narrowly Benthamite—habit of mind and the more inclusive, the more ancient and ritualistic Indian sensibility. This is a theme which works its way in and out of *Possession,* in which the artist Valmiki is discovered and taken over by Lady Caroline Bell, a relationship which appears to offer itself as a tiny image of India's being taken over by Britain. Neither Valmiki nor Lady Caroline is irresistibly convincing. There is a certain put-up, slightly expected, air about them. The novel's merit lies in the clarity and point of the prose, in an unusual metaphorical capacity and in a gift for the nice discrimination of human motives.

Markandaya's failure as yet is to establish a context as impressively real and as sympathetically grasped as her central characters. She is very much more conscious in *A Handful of Rice* of the context, in this case an urban one, which nevertheless still suffers from a lack of solidity. Ravi, on the other hand, the central character, an educated peasant, is seen with the coolest and most accurate eye and realised with a very considerable creative skill. Nor does this novel offer any easy solution or any obvious superiority of one side of a spiritual dilemma over the other. The novel ends flatly and hopelessly but rightly in a way which suggests the achievement by the author of a bleaker and more necessary kind of wisdom.

—William Walsh

MARKFIELD, Wallace (Arthur)

Nationality: American. **Born:** Brooklyn, New York, 12 August 1926. **Education:** Abraham Lincoln High School, New York; Brooklyn College, B.A. 1947; New York University, 1948–50. **Family:** Married Anna May Goodman in 1949; one daughter. **Career:** Film critic, *New Leader,* New York, 1954–55; worked as a publicist and in public relations for several years. **Awards:** Guggenheim fellowship, 1965; National Endowment for the Arts grant, 1966. **Address:** c/o Bruccoli Clark, 2006 Sumter Street, Columbia, South Carolina 29201, U.S.A.

PUBLICATIONS

Novels

To an Early Grave. New York, Simon and Schuster, 1964; London, Cape, 1965.
Teitlebaum's Window. New York, Knopf, 1970; London, Cape, 1971.
You Could Live If They Let You. New York, Knopf, 1974.
Radical Surgery. New York, Bantam, 1991.

Short Stories

Multiple Orgasms. Bloomfield Hills, Michigan, Bruccoli Clark, 1977.

Uncollected Short Stories

''Notes on the Working Day,'' in *Partisan Review* (New Brunswick, New Jersey), September-October 1946.
''Ph.D.,'' in *These Your Children,* edited by Harold U. Ribalow. New York, Beechhurst Press, 1952.
''The Patron,'' in *Partisan Review* (New Brunswick, New Jersey), January 1954.
''The Country of the Crazy Horse,'' in *Commentary* (New York), March 1958.
''The Big Giver,'' in *Midstream* (New York), Summer 1958.
''A Season of Change,'' in *Midstream* (New York), Autumn 1958.
''Eulogy for an American Boy,'' in *Commentary* (New York), June 1962.
''The Decline of Sholem Waldman,'' in *My Name Aloud,* edited by Harold U. Ribalow. New York, Yoseloff, 1969.
''Under the Marquee,'' in *Jewish-American Stories,* edited by Irving Howe. New York, New American Library, 1977.

*

Critical Studies: ''Wallace Markfield Issue'' of *Review of Contemporary Fiction* (Elmwood, Illinois), vol. 2, no. 1, 1982.

* * *

Philip Roth helped enormously, if inadvertently, to make people conscious of Wallace Markfield by referring to him in *Portnoy's Complaint.* ''The novelist, what's his name, Markfield, has written in a story somewhere that until he was fourteen he believed 'aggravation' to be a Jewish word.'' Roth is referring to ''The Country of the Crazy Horse,'' which sets the tone and milieu of New York Jewish life that carries through all of Markfield's work: the story begins in this way, ''As the train began the long crawl under the tunnel to Brooklyn... .'' Markfield's characters travel by subway or Volkswagen as they negotiate the impossible distances separating the boroughs of New York City and encounter the unique kind of aggravation which is part of their Jewish vantage point.

Stanley Edgar Hyman spoke of Markfield's first novel, *To an Early Grave,* as a more modest *Ulysses* and as ''Mr. Bloom's Day in Brooklyn.'' The part of *Ulysses* it most nearly resembles is the sixth episode, ''Hades.'' Joyce's ''creaking carriage'' has been replaced by a Volkswagen; Paddy Dignam has turned into a young writer named Leslie Braverman; and the four mourners who attend the Dignam funeral, Martin Cunningham, Leopold Bloom, John Power, and Simon Dedalus, give way to the more literary foursome of Morroe Rieff, Holly Levine, Felix Ottensteen, and Barnet Weiner. The Jew, Leopold Bloom, feels uncomfortable and unwanted among his Christian companions during the ride to the cemetery. Braverman and his mourners are Jews, as are the other characters who figure prominently in *To an Early Grave.* Their conversation on the way to the cemetery reflects the urban chic of New York City, with its literary quarterlies, its literary critical conscience (''And he hissed softly, 'Trilling ... Leavis ... Ransom ... Tate ... Kazin ... Chase ...' and saw them, The Fathers, as though from a vast amphitheater, smiling at him, and he smiled at them''), its intellectual's obsession with popular culture, its carefully placed Yiddishisms.

Markfield has been fascinated by Joyce since his early story ''Notes on the Working Day''; there are nods here toward the Joyce of *Finnegan's Wake* (''There Goes Everyman, Here Comes Everybody, the H.C.E. of our culture-lag'') and toward the Joyce of *Ulysses* (''Leopold Bloom of the garment center'' and ''Leopold fat-belly Bloom''). When the Volkswagen of *To an Early Grave* arrives at a chapel, Braverman's four friends are treated to an elaborate funeral oration by a rabbi, which seems indeed to be the Jewish equivalent of the terrifying sermons which dominate chapter three of Joyce's *A Portrait of the Artist as a Young Man.* Here is a sample of the rabbi's language: ''*That* on the Day of Judgment *in* the Valley of Jehoshaphat you'll be called up. *Either* to everlasting life *or* to such a shaming there's no imagining *how* terrible.'' Markfield manages to turn this into a wonderfully comic scene when the four mourners discover on examining the corpse that they have attended the wrong funeral. The novel ends with the most sympathetic of the four mourners, Morroe Rieff, finally breaking into tears—the only genuine tears shed in all of *To an Early Grave*—but the humorous and satirical effects in character and situation linger on; the comic survives the fleeting attempts at tragedy.

Teitlebaum's Window is the Brighton Beach-Coney Island version of the *Bildungsroman,* the Jewish boy, Simon Sloan, coming of age between the Depression years and the beginnings of World War II. *To an Early Grave* takes place during a single day, a Sunday, while *Teitlebaum's Window* covers a ten-year period. Joyce continues to be very much on Markfield's mind in this novel, especially in the use of certain impressionistic techniques and symbolic patterns. The narrative proceeds in a vastly complicated way, with traditional storytelling methods giving way frequently to diary notations, letters, classroom notes, and snatches of monologue. Many of the chapters begin with a single convoluted sentence which may go on for several pages: dating the events, reintroducing characters, referring to celebrities in the political, film and comic book worlds, and quoting the signs in Teitlebaum's store window (for example, ''There will always be an England but there will not always be such a low low price on belly lox''). These long sentences act rather like the interchapters in Virginia Woolf's *The Waves.* The references to Teitlebaum's window offer the novel a symbolic design and supply the reader with a useful *point de repère.*

Teitlebaum's Window is a vintage American-Jewish novel. Here the mother-son confrontation is quite as convincingly realized as it was in *Portnoy's Complaint.* Markfield's Jewish mother, with her ''dropped stomach,'' gargantuan stutter, constant aggravation, and dislocated syntax, is quite as believable in her own way as Sophie Portnoy.

You Could Live If They Let You continues Markfield's concern with Jewish subjects, but is less closely plotted than either of the previous novels. It offers what is probably, according to reviewers, another version of the Lenny Bruce saga, following closely on the heels of Albert Goldman's book *Ladies and Gentlemen, Lenny Bruce!!* and Bob Fosse's film *Lenny*. The Lenny Bruce character appears under the name Jules Farber and he has a Boswell in the person of Chandler Van Horton (whom one is tempted to think of as a non-Jewish Albert Goldman). The novel is dedicated to "the wisest men of our time—the stand-up comics" and indeed its narrative procedures often remind us of the staccato verbal habits of a Lenny Bruce or a Woody Allen.

Farber's stand-up comic delivery favors the incongruous, the unexpected: 'Plehnt hah treee in Eretz Yisroel for Norman Vincent Peale"; "Readings from Kierkegaard, Kafka and Julia Child"; "it's Bobby Fischer's end game and Thomas Aquinas quoting from William Buckley and Bella Abzug buying two-and-a-half pounds of the best flanken... ." It is consistently irreverent as it takes on such formidable adversaries as the Anti-Defamation League, American rabbis, the Modern Language Association of America, and the world of popular culture. There is seemingly no end to the literary echoes and allusions: "cold, iron-hard epiphany which Farber favored"; "because every carhop and every checkout girl and every chippy and every cellar-club thumper is Molly Boom and Madeline *[sic]* Herzog." (Joyce is unmistakably a presence here as he was in Markfield's earlier fiction!)

We not only hear the voice of Farber, the "vertical monologist," but also that of Chandler Van Horton and that of Farber's sister, Lillian Federman. Farber's life story is eventually fleshed out in bits and pieces as we find out about his autistic son, Mitchell, and his Christ Therapist estranged wife, Marlene. We find Markfield's latest hero to have the same Jewish awareness and identity as the characters in *To an Early Grave* and *Teitlebaum's Window*. He shares with them the assurance that "there are certain things only a Jewish person can understand" and that "when you're in love the whole world is Jewish; and perhaps, in fact, even when you're not in love." We recognize the Markfield touch most emphatically when Farber proclaims: "I got a terminal case of aggravation."

—Melvin J. Friedman

MARLATT, Daphne

Nationality: Canadian (originally Maylasian, immigrated to Canada in 1951). **Born:** Daphne Shirley Buckle, Melbourne, Australia, 11 July 1942. **Education:** University of British Columbia, Vancouver, 1960–64, B.A.; University of Indiana, Bloomington, 1964–67, M.A. 1968. **Family:** Married G. Alan Marlatt in 1963 (divorced 1971), one son; companion of 1) Roy Kinooka, 1975–82; 2) Betsy Warland, 1982–94; 3) Bridget MacKenzie, since 1994. **Career:** Has taught at University of British Columbia, University of Victoria, University of Saskatchewan, University of Western Ontario, Simon Fraser University, University of Calgary, Mount Royal College, University of Alberta, McMaster University, University of Manitoba; second vice chair of the Writers' Union of Canada, 1987–88. **Awards:** MacMillan and Brissenden award for creative writing; Canada Council award. **Member:** Founding member of West Coast Women and Words Society. **Address:** c/o The Writers' Union of Canada, 24 Ryerson Avenue, Toronto, Ontario M5T 2P3, Canada.

PUBLICATIONS

Novels

Ana Historic. Toronto, Coach House, 1988; London, Women's Press, 1990.
Taken. Concord, Ontario, Anansi, 1996.

Poetry

Frames of a Story. Toronto, Ryerson, 1968.
leaf leaf/s. Los Angeles, Black Sparrow, 1969.
Rings. Vancouver, Vancouver Community Press, 1971.
Vancouver Poems. Toronto, Coach House, 1972.
Steveston, photographs by Robert Minden. Vancouver, Talonbooks, 1974.
Our Lives. Carrboro, North Carolina, Truck Press, 1975.
The Story, She Said. Vancouver, Monthly Press, 1977.
What Matters: Writing 1968–70. Toronto, Coach House, 1980.
Net Work: Selected Writing, edited by Fred Wah. Vancouver, Talonbooks, 1980.
here & there. Lantzville, Island Press, 1981.
How to Hug a Stone. Winnipeg, Turnstone, 1983.
Touch to My Tongue. Edmonton, Longspoon, 1984.
Double Negative, with Betsy Warland. Charlottetown, Gynergy Books, 1988.
Salvage. Red Deer, Red Deer College Press, 1991.
Ghost Works. Edmonton, NeWest Press, 1993.
Two Women in a Birth, with Betsy Warland. Toronto and New York, Guernica, 1994.

Plays

Radio Plays: *Steveston*, 1976.

Other

Zócalo. Toronto, Coach House, 1977.
Readings from the Labyrinth. Edmonton, Alberta, NeWest Press, 1998.
Editor, *Lost Language: Selected Poems of Maxine Gadd*. Toronto, Coach House Press, 1982.
Editor, *Telling It: Women and Language Across Cultures*. Vancouver, Press Gang, 1990.
Editor, *Mothertalk: Life Stories of Mary Kiyoshi Kiyooka*. Edmonton, Alberta, NeWest Press, 1997.
Translator, *Mauve*, by Nicole Brossard. Montreal, Nouvelle Barre du Jour/Writing, 1985.

*

Manuscript Collections: The National Library of Canada, Ottawa, Ontario.

Critical Studies: *Translation A to Z: Notes on Daphne Marlatt's "Ana Historic"* by Pamela Banting, Edmonton, NeWest Press, 1991; *"I Quote Myself"; or, A Map of Mrs. Reading: Re-siting "Women's*

Place'' in ''Anna Historic'' by Manina Jones, Toronto, University of Toronto Press, 1993; *The Country of Her Own Body: Ana Historic,* by Frank Davey, Toronto, University of Toronto Press, 1993.

Daphne Marlatt comments:

Although I think of myself as a poet first, I began writing both fiction and lyric poems in the early 1960s. My collections of poetry have usually had a loose narrative shape as I tend to write in sequences, or ''books.'' As an immigrant, I'd long held the ambition to write an historical novel about Vancouver, but *Ana Historic* actually critiqued and broke open the genre, as it also increased my fascination with the potential for openness in the novel form. Influenced by the development of ''fiction/theory'' in Quebec by feminist writers there, I see open structures combined with a folding or echoing of women's experiences in different time periods as a way to convey more of the unwritten or culturally overwritten aspects of what it means to be alive as a woman today.

* * *

With the arguable exception of *Zócalo,* a Mexican travel memoir she wrote in 1977, *Ana Historic* of 1988 is Daphne Marlatt's first novel. Heavily influenced by the French feminism filtering through Quebec women's writing at the time she wrote it, *Ana Historic* continues to excite attention from feminist critics interested in the politics of language, history, colonialism, gender, race, and sexuality.

Ana Historic is really two novels in one. In the course of doing historical research in the Vancouver City Archives for her professor husband, Richard, protagonist Annie Anderson discovers two short references to a Mrs. Richards, who comes to Vancouver in 1873 to teach school. Obsessed by the way official history erases Mrs. Richards's life, Annie begins writing a novel that imagines the life Ana Richards (Annie supplies a first name for her) might have had. This novel becomes *Ana Historic*'s embedded narrative. Annie's writing of this novel continually interrupts itself with reminiscences of her mother, Ina, now dead, and metacritical reflections on the process of writing itself. Underneath all of this reflective activity, in the narrative present, Annie moves slowly but steadily away from her relationship with her husband toward a sexual relationship with a woman named Zoe.

Only recently have critics focused on the lesbian aspects of Marlatt's work. Initial criticism of *Ana Historic* emphasized formal continuities with Marlatt's earlier writing. Certainly the etymological play in the text shows the same careful attention to language that one finds in her poetry. This poetic wordplay reaches its height in *Touch To My Tongue,* a book of prose poems, and the critical essay published along with it, ''musing with mothertongue.'' In ''musing,'' Marlatt follows Julia Kristeva in theorizing language as a living, maternal body of expressive potential that has been bastardized by patriarchy's insistence on singularity, hierarchy, and mastery. In *Ana Historic,* Marlatt demonstrates how patriarchal language excludes women from the dominant narrative of official history, but through both Annie's embedded narrative and the novel's etymological wordplay, she also shows a way in which women might be written back into history.

Feminist critics were swift to pick up on *Ana Historic* as an empowering story for women. But just as the term ''woman'' grew increasingly complicated by vectors of race, class, and sexuality at the end of the 1980s, so did readings of Marlatt's fiction gain in complexity. Rather than focusing on Annie as a literary Everywoman, critics have begun to examine the relationships among all the characters in the novel. Particularly important to this inquiry is the status of the Native Canadian characters in the embedded narrative, because it is against their silence that Ana Richards—and, by extension, white Canadian women generally—understand their particular subject positions. In turn, the examination of native figures in the novel has opened up the possibility for considering Ina's colonial background and Annie's uneasy Canadian identity.

This recognition of specific subject positions contextualizes the lesbian ending of the story. Although *Ana Historic* is perhaps most easily read as a lesbian-feminist utopia that ultimately abandons history in favor of imagination, a critical reader can see in the novel an argument for rethinking gender, historically and imaginatively, in conjunction with race, sexuality, colonialism, and post-colonialism. It is such scope that makes Marlatt's fiction significant.

—Heather Zwicker

MARSHALL, Owen

Nationality: New Zealander. **Born:** Owen Marshall Jones in Te Kuiti, 17 August 1941. **Education:** Timaru Boy's High School; University of Canterbury, Christchurch, 1960–63, M.A. (honours) in history 1963; Christchurch Teachers College, teaching diploma, 1964. **Family:** Married Jacqueline Hill in 1965; two daughters. **Career:** Deputy rector, Waitaki Boys High School, Oamaru, 1983–85; deputy principal, Craighead Diocesan School, Timaru, 1986–91. Since 1993, tutor, Aoraki Polytechnic, Timaru. Literary fellow, University of Canterbury, 1981. **Awards:** Lillian Ida Smith award, 1986, 1988; Queen Elizabeth II Arts Council scholarship, 1987; *Evening Standard* award, for short story, 1987; American Express award, for short story, 1987; New Zealand Literary Fund scholarship in letters, 1988, and Distinction award, 1989; University of Otago's Robert Burns fellowship, 1992. **Agent:** Glenys Bean, 15 Elizabeth Street, Freeman's Bay, Auckland. **Address:** 10 Morgan's Road, Glenwood, Timaru, New Zealand.

PUBLICATIONS

Novel

A Many Coated Man. Dunedin, Longacre, 1995.
Coming Home in the Dark. Auckland, Vintage, 1995.

Short Stories

Supper Waltz Wilson and Other New Zealand Stories. Christchurch, Pegasus Press, 1979.
The Master of Big Jingles and Other Stories. Dunedin, McIndoe, 1982.
The Day Hemingway Died. Dunedin, McIndoe, 1984.
The Lynx Hunter and Other Stories. Dunedin, McIndoe, 1987.
The Divided World: Selected Stories. Dunedin, McIndoe, 1989.
Tomorrow We Save the Orphans. Dunedin, McIndoe, 1992.
The Ace of Diamonds Gang. Dunedin, McIndoe, 1993.

Plays

Radio Plays: *An Indirect Geography,* 1989.

Other

Editor, *Letter from Heaven.* Auckland, L. Paul, 1995.

*

Critical Studies: *Barbed Wire and Mirrors: Essays on New Zealand Prose* by Lawrence Jones, Dunedin, University of Otago Press, 1987; "The Naming of Parts: Owen Marshall" by Vincent O'Sullivan, in *Sport 3* (Wellington), 1989; *In the Same Room* edited by Alley and Williams, Auckland, Auckland University Press, 1992.

* * *

In an essay in *Sport* Owen Marshall has written of his growing interest in books during his childhood and of his early attempts at writing, including two unpublished novels. He turned to the short story form in the mid-1970s and published his first piece in the New Zealand *Listener* in 1977. It was the beginning of a success which has been sustained since then, and which has gained him recognition as one of the most substantial short story writers in present-day New Zealand.

By 1979 he was able to present a collection of fourteen stories to the Christchurch publisher Pegasus Press. *Supper Waltz Wilson and Other New Zealand Stories* was financed by the author in a venture well-justified by the publication's success and by its favourable reviews. Frank Sargeson's praise helped confirm Marshall's reputation as an important new writer, and from then on his stories began to appear regularly in New Zealand periodicals and anthologies of contemporary fiction as well as being broadcast by Radio New Zealand. Three further books made Marshall's work widely available over these years: *The Master of the Big Jingles, The Day Hemingway Died,* and *The Lynx Hunter.* These were followed by *The Divided World,* a retrospective selection of his work in 1989, and more recently a new collection, *Tomorrow We Save the Orphans,* and a further selection, *The Ace of Diamonds Gang and Other Stories.*

Marshall's stories fit easily into a tradition of realism that has long been one of the strengths of the New Zealand short story; they serve, moreover, to extend and enhance that tradition. The narratives frequently describe a middle or lower-middle class New Zealand world, with its Anglo Saxon parameters of conventionality. It is a world that is frequently small town or rural in its perspectives, and masculine in its point of view, though Marshall treats his female characters with more subtlety and sensitivity than has traditionally been associated with male New Zealand writers. In some of his most successful stories—the title stories of his first two volumes, for example, or in "Kenneth's Friend," "Valley Day," and "The Paper Parcel"—his characters recall childhood and adolescence, the rites of passage, and the awareness of an impinging world that the young have to take into account. There are similar cool recognitions in his stories that tell of young adults who perceive the realities of an older generation's experiences of life, as in "The Day Hemingway Died," "A Poet's Dream of Amazons," and the superb study of a son's vision of his dying father—"The Seed Merchant." In Marshall's fictional world the sense of loss or of poignancy that habitually accompanies such awareness is not allowed to deteriorate into sentimentality. Indeed, Marshall is distinctive among the New Zealand writers who have treated such themes for his quiet ironic detachment, and for the clear-eyed recognitions (akin to those of his literary predecessor Maurice Duggan) of inevitability and common culpability in his little scenes from the human comedy.

Characterisation, perhaps even more than plot, is of principal importance to Marshall, and his proclivity for first person narration allows him both the opportunities for narrative insights, and the possibilities of unconscious ironic self-revelation on the part of his protagonists. He handles dialogue fluently and has a sharp ear for the cadences and nuances of the local idiom, but it is perhaps in his settings, of places and people alike, that New Zealand readers most clearly recognise an indigenous writer of considerable ability. Sargeson very early saw that Marshall could move us to "experience an environment which has mysteriously become a character in its own right"; the idea is as valid in Marshall's latest work as in his earliest.

Marshall's reputation still rests on his work as a short story writer at the present time, though his first novel, *A Many Coated Man,* written when he held the Robert Burns fellowship at the University of Otago in 1992, was published in 1995. A novel that is both wry and tragicomic, it looks at the politics and society of a New Zealand some years into the future from our own time when immense social and economic changes are reconstructing the nation and its sense of identity. It reveals many of the skills that have made Marshall's stories so popular, though tonal unevennness and a sense that the writer is possibly less assured in writing fiction on this scale, have meant a muted critical response to the book thus far.

A literary tradition of strength and vitality in the field of the short story has distinguished New Zealand writing since the late 1930s, and Marshall is clearly one of the most important contemporary exponents of the form. The last ten years have seen an increasing interest in the postmodern ludic invention in prose; some of New Zealand's best new writers have pursued this interest, but Marshall has to a considerable extent chosen to remain within an older tradition of realism that gives priority to characterisation and plot narration. Though some of the stories in *The Lynx Hunter* and the title story of *The Divided World* show an increasing preparedness to work experimentally with new forms and with nonrealist modes of presentation, Marshall is still primarily a teller of tales. His writings seek to remind us of the known and the forgotten alike; their narrative vision suggest the wish to reveal sympathies that are never sentimental, seldom other than compassionate, and always couched in the language of one who is thoroughly sensitive to the power of words.

—W.S. Broughton

MARSHALL, Paule

Nationality: American. **Born:** Paule Burke, Brooklyn, New York, 9 April 1929. **Education:** Brooklyn College, B.A. (cum laude) 1953 (Phi Beta Kappa); Hunter College, New York, 1955. **Family:** Married 1) Kenneth E. Marshall in 1950 (divorced 1963), one son; 2) Nourry Menard in 1970. **Career:** Librarian, New York Public Library; staff writer, *Our World,* New York, 1953–56; taught creative writing at Yale University, New Haven, Connecticut, Columbia University, New York, University of Iowa, Iowa City, and University of California, Berkeley, 1984. **Awards:** Guggenheim fellowship, 1961; Rosenthal award, 1962; Ford grant, for drama, 1964; National Endowment for the Arts grant, 1966, 1977; Creative Artists Public Service fellowship, 1974; Before Columbus Foundation award, 1984. **Address:** Virginia Commonwealth University, 910 West Franklin Street, Richmond, Virginia, U.S.A. 23284–9004.

PUBLICATIONS

Novels

Brown Girl, Brownstones. New York, Random House, 1959; London, W.H. Allen, 1960.
The Chosen Place, The Timeless People. New York, Harcourt Brace, 1969; London, Longman, 1970.
Praisesong for the Widow. New York, Putnam, and London, Virago Press, 1983.
Daughters. New York, Atheneum, 1991; London, Serpent's Tail, 1992.
The Fisher King. New York, Scribner, 2000.

Short Stories

Soul Clap Hands and Sing. New York, Atheneum, 1961; London, W.H. Allen, 1962.
Reena and Other Stories. Old Westbury, New York, Feminist Press, 1983; as *Merle and Other Stories,* London, Virago Press, 1985.

Uncollected Short Stories

"To Da-duh, in Memoriam," in *Afro-American Writing 2,* edited by Richard Long and Eugenia Collier. New York, New York University Press, 1972.

Other

Language Is the Only Homeland: Bajan Poets Abroad. Bridgetown, Central Bank of Barbados, 1995.

*

Critical Studies: *Bridging the Americas: The Literature of Paule Marshall, Toni Morrison, and Gayl Jones* by Stelamaris Coser, Philadelphia, Temple University Press, 1994; *The Fiction of Paule Marshall: Reconstructions of History, Culture, and Gender* by Dorothy Hamer Denniston, Knoxville, University of Tennessee Press, 1995; *Places of Silence, Journeys of Freedom: The Fiction of Paule Marshall* by Eugenia C. DeLamotte, Philadelphia, University of Pennsylvania Press, 1998; *"Re/Visioning" the Self Away from Home: Autobiographical and Cross-cultural Dimensions in the Works of Paule Marshall* by Bernhard Melchior, Frankfurt am Main, Germany, and New York, P. Lang, 1998; *Caribbean Waves: Relocating Claude McKay and Paule Marshall* by Heather Hathaway, Bloomington, Indiana University Press, 1999.

* * *

In "From the Poets in the Kitchen," her contribution to "The Making of a Writer" series in the *New York Times Book Review* (9 January 1983), Paule Marshall declares the sources of her art to be the expressive talk she heard as a young girl among her mother's friends as they sat around a table in the basement kitchen of her Brooklyn brownstone home. For these immigrants from Barbados, language was therapy for the tribulations they endured as invisible citizens of a new land—invisible because black, female, and foreign. But talk was more than that, too, for the West Indian dialect, syntactically unique and metaphorically inventive, sustained these women whom Marshall characterizes, in the words of James Weldon Johnson's famous poem, as "unknown bards" in the nurturing culture of home while in exile. In their native everyday speech Marshall's forebears, mothers, and kin in Marshall's mind and imagination, affirmed themselves in the world through spontaneously creative use of the idiom, which bears in its forms and sound the conception of life, the philosophy, that embodies an Afro-Caribbean heritage. Finding the means for later generations to emulate the kitchen poets she knew in her childhood is the burden of Marshall's fiction.

Marshall's "unknown bards" of reminiscence experienced their place in an affirmative culture naturally, because after all one hardly needs to reflect upon the significance involved in the intimate possession of language, but the protagonists of her fiction must struggle with necessities that either sever their connection to an affirmative culture or encourage them to find identity in the values of individualism. Her first published story, "The Valley Between" (1954), relates the contest between a wife's wish to return to school to prepare for a career and her husband's resentment of the apparent departure from a conventional woman's role. The conflict encodes Marshall's own experience in an early marriage while also restricting its significance through the fact that the fictional characters are white. *Brown Girl, Brownstones,* her first novel, can also be read as partly autobiographical, but in this case the author's story is inserted into a typified set of circumstances. The book traces the maturation of young Selina Boyce beyond a loving father, whose incapacity for the get-ahead life of New York City issues in romantic dreams of a big-paying job or self-sufficiency on two acres of inherited land home in Barbados, and beyond, as well, the equally deadening illusions of her mother who sacrifices her being to the successful Bajan's goal of property ownership. Selina's autonomy is welcome, except that Marshall's pleasing rendition of Barbados English and folk-say, definitely a version of the kitchen talk of the instinctive poets she knew in her childhood, makes it clear that Selina's necessary sacrifice of community tragically likens her to the mass of other rootless Americans.

Each of the four stories in *Soul Clap Hands and Sing,* Marshall's second published volume of fiction, shows the ways individual animation is replaced in modern life by a protective but deadening routine. Whether in "Barbados," "Brooklyn," "British Guiana," or "Brazil" an aged man discovers that in seeking ease he has in fact lost the surety of selfhood. Yet, despite these protagonists it is not entirely correct to present the accomplishment of *Soul Clap Hands and Sing* as solely the tales of wasted men, since in the construction of the plot for each narrative Marshall sets up a relationship with a woman more vital than the man to develop the point of the Yeatsian epigraph, that the older man has become "a paltry thing." Thus the geographic breadth given to the condition of modern rootlessness by the range of settings is accompanied in each story by evidence of Marshall's continuing interest in the distinctive roles women can assume in society. A later story, "Reena" (1962), returns the theme of the unique concerns of female identity to the center of the narrative, where it remains for all of Marshall's later work. "Reena" investigates the matrimonial and political choices made by an educated black woman, using the occasion of a wake for Reena's aunt as opportunity to frame the matter of self-definition within consideration of the continuities and differences between two generations of women. ''Reena'' together with ''To Da-duh, in Memoriam,'' the story of a nine-year-old girl exchanging boasts about the size and energy of New York City for an introduction to the flora and fauna of Barbados from her grandmother, establish the focus for Marshall's mature fiction: the importance of lineage in the lives of women on the cusp of historical change.

Her first major novel, *The Chosen Place, The Timeless People,* reveals that focus to be profoundly political as well as intensely personal. The book records the encounter of an American research team with the ''backward'' people inhabiting Bournehills, the wasted corner of an island resembling perhaps Barbados but signifying the entire Caribbean. Marshall sympathetically portrays both aliens and natives in terms of the motives of guilt and frustration by which they characterize their own lives. As Merle Kinbona, a woman of Bournehills whose residence in England included schooling in painfully exploitive relationships along with professional training, assumes predominance in the narrative personal drama is translated into general social meaning. A native of the island despite her ''modernization,'' Merle shares the timelessness of the people to whom the experience of slavery and particularly the momentary success of the rebellion of Cuffee Ned remain palpably present. On a level as deep as culture and as unavailable to measurement as the subconscious, they know that technological change is nothing compared to the redemption presaged in Cuffee's rebellion, and in their integrity they will settle for nothing less. The politics of the novel are conservative in a way that is unknown in parliaments or organized parties. This conservative politics grows from knowledge that the configurations of character and the complex relationships of love or resentment gain their shape from historical cultures.

With *Praisesong for the Widow* Marshall tentatively completes the exploration of black women's relationship to their history. Having begun with Selina Boyce, a young adult intent on gaining personal independence before all else, and then continuing with the narrative of Merle Kinbona, who seeks a viable cause beyond herself in middle age, Marshall carries her study forward with Avey Johnson, the sixty-four-year-old widow who leaves her friends on a cruise ship for reasons she cannot articulate though they are as compelling as a subconscious drive. Juxtaposing memory of the past with present setting, the narrative recalls Avey's relationship to her great aunt who brought alive the tale of slaves who had left Ibo Landing, South Carolina, to walk home across the sea to Africa, and traces the course of Avey's marriage to Jay, who with respectability assumed the proper name of Jerome and the distant manner of a man mistaking status for integrity. Avey understood the value of middle-class security, but the loss of joy and spontaneity subsequent to its attainment has left her bereft in age. The sense of loss originates as an individual's trouble, its remedy lies in regaining a sense of collectivity; therefore, the later sections of the novel are structured around the symbolic rituals of a journey to Carriacou and the ceremonies of the blacks who annually return to the island to ''beg pardon'' of their ancestors and to dance the ''nation dances'' that survive from their African origins. By these means *Praisesong for the Widow* leads Avey through her crisis of integrity so that she can re-experience the connection to collective history she once felt as a child, reclaim her original name of Avatara (for which Avey is the diminutive), and join the movements of traditional dance that link her in body and spirit to her heritage.

Unquestionably more deliberate in its aesthetic form than the talk of the West Indian women in her childhood kitchen, Paule Marshall's stories share qualities with that speech while also distinguishing itself as markedly literary. Full of rich detail, the best of her writing brings character and incident alive in the vivid manner of popular tale telling. Informed, however, by a reflexivity that is absent from the creations of ''unknown bards,'' the tales Marshall makes into novels reach beyond simulation of folk art, beyond the surface realism, nostalgia, or elementary denunciations of modernization that would constitute the easy and simple responses to historical transformation of traditional culture. Instead Marshall makes complex literature of the proposition that every woman needs to gain the power to speak the language of her elder kinswomen.

—John M. Reilly

MARS-JONES, Adam

Nationality: British. **Born:** London, 26 October 1954. **Education:** Cambridge University, B.A. 1976, M.A. 1978. **Career:** Film critic and reviewer, the *Independent,* London. **Awards:** Maugham award, 1982. **Agent:** Peters Fraser and Dunlop, 503–504 The Chambers, Chelsea Harbour, Lots Road, London SW10 0XF. **Address:** 42B Calabria Road, Highburn, London N5 1HU, England.

PUBLICATIONS

Novels

The Waters of Thirst. London, Faber, 1993; New York, Knopf, 1994.

Short Stories

Lantern Lecture and Other Stories. London, Faber, 1981; as *Fabrications,* New York, Knopf, 1981.
The Darker Proof: Stories from a Crisis, with Edmund White. London, Faber, 1987.
Monopolies of Loss. London, Faber, 1992; New York, Knopf, 1993.

Other

Venus Envy. London, Chatto and Windus, 1990.
Editor, *Mae West Is Dead: Recent Lesbian and Gay Fiction.* London, Faber, 1983.

* * *

Few writers have established a reputation on as slight an output as Adam Mars-Jones. In the decade since *Lantern Lecture* (comprising three prose pieces totaling under 200 pages), Mars-Jones, though active as an arts journalist, has published only half a book of short stories, *The Darker Proof* with Edmund White, where he abandoned the experimentalism that had distinguished his first collection.

The opening and title piece of *Lantern Lecture* outlines the life of eccentric landowner Philip Yorke. The story is told in the present tense in a series of two-paragraph sections. In the opening section, Philip's christening is described in the first paragraph and his Memorial Service in the second: ''The fame of his house and of his own appearances on television attracts a large crowd. The overflow is awkwardly accommodated in the adjoining Church Hall, by chance the site of Philip's last magic-lantern lecture only weeks before his death.'' In fact, Mars-Jones's prose sections are the linguistic equivalent of lantern-slides. About halfway through, the reader becomes aware that the order of the pair of paragraphs in each section has been reversed with the first paragraph about his later life and the second about his earlier life, so that the second paragraph of the final section reproduces the first paragraph of the opening section—with the odd significant change.

The second prose piece is entitled ''Hoosh-Mi,'' which we later learn ''is a nonsense word coined by Princess Margaret as a child, and means (as a noun) mixed food of any sort, or by extension ... 'disorderly jumble . . .' small'' The piece opens with an off-course rabies-infected American hoary bat infecting a dog, who turns out to be no less than a royal corgi and who infects Queen Elizabeth II. Her condition becomes apparent on ''walkabout'' in Australia when she attacks a sightseer's hat; decline through hydrophobia follows until Prince Philip authorizes euthanasia. A key element in this *tour de force* is the interpolation in the narrative of a speech by Dr. John Bull on ''Royalty and the Unreal'' at the Annual Dinner of the Republican Society. Thus the absurdity of royalty is shown both in theory and practice in this subversive tale.

The third prose piece, ''Bathpool Park,'' focuses on the trial of Donald Neilson, the so-called ''Black Panther,'' who after a series of post office robberies involving three murders kidnapped seventeen-year-old Lesley Whittle of whose murder he was also convicted. (Mars-Jones acknowledges indebtedness to Harry Hawkes's *The Capture of the Black Panther.*) Mars-Jones intercuts his description of the behavior in court of all those concerned, including the insignificant marshal-cum-judge's-social-secretary, with reconstructions of Neilson's crimes. In invented dialogue between the two barristers, after Neilson's sentencing, Mars-Jones suggests possibilities that could not emerge in court through the inevitably flawed working of both legal procedure and the preceding police investigation, in turn handicapped by the press. This is the most ambitious of the three pieces in *Lantern Lecture:* while maintaining the witty, dissecting style of the two previous pieces, Mars-Jones must encompass the suffering caused by Neilson, which indeed he achieves.

It's all the more disappointing, therefore, that when Mars-Jones wrote four stories about AIDS sufferers and those involved with them—lovers, friends, ''buddies,'' families etc.—in *The Darker Proof,* he jettisoned his experimentalism. Possibly, he opted here for conventional techniques to write as vividly as possible about a few individuals, whereas in ''Bathpool Park'' the focus was not on individuals but the judicial machine.

The opening story ''Slim'' is a 10-page interior monologue by a man with AIDS about his ''buddy,'' that is his helper from ''the Trust,'' presumably the Terrence Higgins Trust. In his state of permanent exhaustion, he imagines a World War II ration-book ''only instead of an allowance for the week of butter or cheese or sugar, my coupons say One Hour of Social Life, One Shopping Expedition, One Short Walk. I hoard them, and I spend them wisely.''

The other three stories are all in the third person, longer and plotted. ''An Executor'' follows the ''buddy'' Gareth's attempts to fulfill the charge laid on him by the dying Charles—whose moment of death in hospital we witness—to find a suitable recipient for his leather clothes. ''A Small Spade'' describes a weekend spent in Brighton by schoolteacher Bernard and his lover Neil, the young HIV-positive hairdresser from New Zealand. Because a bad splinter in Neil's fingernail ''like a small spade'' takes them to out-patients, Bernard fully comprehends ''A tiled corridor filled with doctors and nurses opened off every room he would ever share with Neil.''

All the main characters in these three stories are deeply sympathetic, unlike architect Roger in ''The Brake,'' who ranges across America as well as London fully exploiting his sex-appeal in search of his perfect lover, while smoking heavily, taking drugs and overeating. The unfortunate Larry ''became very attached.'' Though warned by a doctor to ''put the brake on,'' Roger carries on until a faulty heart-valve forces a change of life-style, roughly coinciding with the beginning of the AIDS crisis: ''he made his accommodation. In the end, he found it easier to give up men than to give up the taste, even the smell, of fried bacon.''

It's ironic, given Mars-Jones's fully justified attack on the tabloid press in ''An Executor,'' that in his stories AIDS appears to be exclusively confined to Western gay men. And Western gay men with a certain level of income. This is not the world of the terminally ill struggling along on inadequate Social Security benefits. Given that the book is subtitled ''Stories from a Crisis,'' it seems fair to harbor these worries—though the subtitle may have been the publisher's rather than the author's choice.

Albeit devoid of the exciting experimental structures of *Lantern Lecture,* the same basic strengths of Mars-Jones's writing come through in *The Darker Proof.* The humor, fully retained in the later stories, springs from an awareness of the maximum possible motivations and interpretations of any action, and his subject matter of whatever kind, is imbued with absolute precision.

—Val Warner

MARSTEN, Richard

See HUNTER, Evan

MASO, Carole

Nationality: American. **Born:** New Jersey. **Education:** Vassar College, B.A. 1977. **Family:** Companion of Helen Lange. **Career:** Worked as a waitress, an artist's model, and a fencing instructor; writer-in-residence, Illinois State University, Normal, 1991–92; writer-in-residence, George Washington University, Washington, D.C., 1992–93; associate professor, Columbia University, New York, 1993; professor and director of creative writing, Brown University, Providence, Rhode Island, 1995—. **Agent:** Georges Borchardt Inc., 136 East 57th Street, New York, New York 10022, U.S.A. **Address:** Brown University, Box 1852, Providence, Rhode Island 02912, U.S.A.

Publications

Novels

Ghost Dance. New York, Perennial Library, 1987.
The Art Lover. San Francisco, North Point Press, 1990.
Ava. Normal, Illinois, Dalkey Archive Press, 1993.
The American Woman in the Chinese Hat. Normal, Illinois, Dalkey Archive Press, 1994.

Aureole. Hopewell, New Jersey, Ecco, 1996.
Defiance. New York, Dutton, 1998.

Short Stories

Contributor, *Tasting Life Twice: Literary Lesbian Fiction by New American Writers*, edited by E. J. Levy. New York, Avon Books, 1995.

Other

Break Every Rule: Essays on Language, Longing, and Moments of Desire. Washington, D.C., Counterpoint, 2000.
The Room Lit by Roses: A Journal of Pregnancy and Birth. Washington, D.C., Counterpoint, 2000.
Contributor, *Tolstoy's Dictaphone: Technology and the Muse*, edited by Sven Birkerts. St. Paul, Minnesota, Graywolf Press, 1996.

* * *

The author of six novels (only the first and last of which have been issued by commercial publishers) and director of the writing program at Brown University (where the master postmodernist fiction-writers John Hawkes and Robert Coover preceded her), Carole Maso is very much a writer's writer. Although she makes few concessions to the ordinary reader, her work, for all its nearly high-modernist aestheticism, proves intensely emotional and engaging. Conventional plot and character development—two of ''the enemies of the novel,'' as Hawkes once called them—hardly figure in Maso's fiction. At once erudite and lyrical, her work does not so much develop as deepen and is built upon the principles of recurrence and obsession, yearning and loss. Believing that conventional narrative ''reassures no one,'' Maso pushes beyond the conventions ''so that form takes as many risks as the content.'' Maso's preoccupation with form—with finding a form both enabling and provisional, appropriate to her subject yet self-consciously subjective and therefore provisional—is matched by her interest in, or obsession with, language. Rejecting both realism's self-effacing transparency and metafiction's self-regarding gamesmanship, she conceives language in sensuous terms and as an evocative rather than merely descriptive medium. Like Helene Cixous, she believes that language should serve to ''extend'' possibility rather than limit it and should ''heal'' as much as ''separate.'' Consequently, her published fiction possesses the openness of a work-in-progress in which the connections are tenuous, lyrical, and erotically charged.

In *Ghost Dance* Vanessa Wing struggles with the deaths of her parents—one a Princeton philosopher, the other a famous poet—and with the disappearance of her brother. Torn between her dual paternity, seeking to reconcile order and freedom, the Jamesian house of fiction and the Romantics' bird of imagination, she attempts to weave scraps of memory and imagination into a protective ghost shirt as she searches for the missing piece/peace that will give shape and meaning to her troublingly disjunctive but deeply elegiac ghost dance. The elegiac quality is underscored by the novel's title, which alludes to the massacre of Native Americans at Wounded Knee.

The Art Lover tells a similar story but in a much more complex manner. The recent death of her father, a painter and art historian, leads Caroline Chrysler back to her mother's suicide and from there to assembling the pieces of so many shattered lives drawn from a multitude of sources into a coherent narrative. The effort is further complicated by the novel's *mise-en-abime* effect. The life-story Caroline tries to construct mirrors the novel she is writing, a novel that mirrors the one Maso herself has written and in which she appears, grieving for her dead lover. In this complex rendering, writing itself is a necessary but ambivalent act. It is a way of remembering and of keeping the world at bay and of savoring the details that refuse to shape themselves into something final and whole.

The savoring is especially strong in *Ava*, Maso's best and riskiest novel. In this ''living text'' about a dying woman, Maso narrates the story of Ava Klein, thirty-nine-year-old professor of comparative literature, a ''rare bird'' (*rara ava*) dying of a rare blood disease. Dismayingly disjointed at first, the novel becomes increasingly lyrical as it progresses ahead (''Morning,'' ''Afternoon,'' ''Night'') through Ava's last day while simultaneously and erratically back over her life. The brief, seemingly random sections—the bits and pieces of Ava's richly lived and cultured life—flash before her eyes and the reader's. As this ingeniously crafted novel ''throbs'' and ''pulses,'' it takes on a coherence apart from the simple continuity that ''reassures no one'' to reveal a woman who was, and is, even in her dying, intensely alive, erotically, culturally, and intellectually.

After the immense if understated power of this ''story without a message,'' in which the joyousness of Ava's life plays itself out against the backdrop of her dying and Maso's awareness that things ''can go terribly wrong,'' Maso's next two books—*The American Woman in the Chinese Hat* (written before *Ava*, though published after) and *Aureole*—seem less intense and somewhat less effective. There are the ''stories of love and love taken away'' in the former and the more desperate erotics ''of the woman who wants'' in the latter. *Defiance*, however, even as it repeats Maso's most characteristic thematic and stylistic concerns, represents something of a new direction in her work. Its overall form and sensational subject help explain its having been published by a large commercial house and reissued as a trade paperback despite the novel's fierce language and dense interweaving of past and present. *Defiance* takes the form of a woman awaiting execution for murder. This is Bernadette O'Brien, the precocious misfit from a variously abusive Irish-Catholic, working-class background who became the youngest-ever professor of physics at Harvard before killing two of her undergraduate students/sex-partners. Neither the platitudes of the therapeutic society nor the mathematical equations of her profession help Bernadette understand and explain her difficult life. And so she becomes a latter-day Scherherazade, or Molly Bloom, desperately and determinedly longing for the ideal reader, the art lover, the dead or otherwise missing brother, in a world in which, for Bernadette, ''the obsessive fear of our own erotic power has done us in.''

—Robert Morace

MASON, Bobbie Ann

Nationality: American. **Born:** Mayfield, Kentucky, 1 May 1940. **Education:** The University of Kentucky, Lexington, 1958–62, B.A. 1962; State University of New York, Binghamton, M.A. 1966; University of Connecticut, Storrs, 1972. **Family:** Married Roger B. Rawlings in 1969. **Career:** Writer, Mayfield *Messenger,* 1960, and Ideal Publishers, New York; contributor to numerous magazines including *Movie Star, Movie Life,* and *T.V. Star Parade,* 1962–63;

assistant professor of English, Mansfield State College, Pennsylvania, 1972–79. Since 1980, contributor to *The New Yorker.* **Awards:** Hemingway award, 1983; National Endowment award, 1983; Pennsylvania Arts Council grant, 1983, 1989; Guggenheim fellowship, 1984. **Agent:** Amanda Urban, International Creative Management, 40 West 57th Street, New York, New York 10019.

Publications

Novels

In Country. New York, Harper, 1985; London, Chatto and Windus, 1986.
Spence + Lila. New York, Harper, 1988; London, Chatto and Windus, 1989.
Feather Crowns. New York, Harper, and London, Chatto and Windus, 1993.

Short Stories

Shiloh and Other Stories. New York, Harper, 1982; London, Chatto and Windus, 1985.
Love Life. New York, Harper, and London, Chatto and Windus, 1989.
Midnight Magic: Selected Stories of Bobbie Ann Mason. Hopewell, New Jersey, Ecco Press, 1998.

Uncollected Short Story

''With Jazz,'' in *New Yorker,* 26 February 1990.

Other

The Girl Sleuth: A Feminist Guide to the Bobbsey Twins, Nancy Drew, and Their Sisters. New York, Feminist Press, 1975.
Nabokov's Garden: A Nature Guide to Ada. Ann Arbor, Michigan, Ardis, 1976.
Clear Springs: A Memoir. New York, Random House, 1999.

*

Film Adaptations: *In Country,* 1989.

Manuscript Collection: University of Kentucky, Lexington.

Critical Studies: ''Making Over or Making Off: The Problem of Identity in Bobbie Ann Mason's Short Fiction'' in *Southern Literary Journal* (Chapel Hill, North Carolina), Spring 1986, and ''Private Rituals: Coping with Changes in the Fiction of Bobbie Ann Mason'' in *Midwest Quarterly* (Pittsburg, Kansas), Winter 1987, both by Albert E. Wilhelm; ''Finding One's History: Bobbie Ann Mason and Contemporary Southern Literature'' in *Southern Literary Journal* (Chapel Hill, North Carolina), Spring 1987, and ''Never Stop Rocking: Bobbie Ann Mason and Rock-and-Roll'' in *Mississippi Quarterly* (Jackson), Winter 1988–89, both by Robert H. Brinkmeyer, Jr; ''The Function of Popular Culture in Bobbie Anne Mason's *Shiloh and Other Stories* and *In Country*'' by Leslie White, in *Southern Quarterly* (Hattiesburg, Mississippi), Summer 1988; ''Bobbie Ann Mason: Artist and Rebel'' by Michael Smith, in *Kentucky Review* (Lexington), Autumn 1988; ''Downhome Feminists in *Shiloh and Other Stories*'' by G.O. Morphew, in *Southern Literary Journal* (Chapel Hill, North Carolina), Spring 1989; *Bobbie Ann Mason: A Study of the Short Fiction* by Albert Wilhelm, New York, Twayne, 1998.

* * *

Bobbie Ann Mason is known for her portrayal of everyday Americans who perhaps read the newspapers and the tabloids and a favorite ladies or hobby magazine each week rather than pick up a book but who are, nonetheless, people whose stories deserve to be told. Mason's characters are farmers and truckers and waitresses and hairdressers as well as the unemployed. They are usually people working, or attempting to work, without college degrees, though some may be taking a course or two at their local community college. Like the late short story writer Raymond Carver, Mason gives voice to the working class in American life who labor long and hard, often without being taken seriously by those who are educated and who consequently may have some kind of power over decisions that affect these people's lives. Mason's contribution to American literature is important because, as she has often noted in interviews, there are more people living in the working classes in America than there are in the professions, and to ignore their stories is to ignore the fertile heartland of what makes that large nation tick.

Most of Mason's characters are European-Americans from, or around, her native state of Kentucky. Her award-winning short story collection, *Shiloh and Other Stories,* is a good introduction to Mason's interests and concerns. Ironically, it is this work that most of the people she writes about will least likely read themselves. Several of the stories first appeared in *The New Yorker* magazine, which is geared toward an audience of urban professionals. ''Shiloh'' and other stories from the collection are often now anthologized in college textbooks. Exploitation of the working class might be a fair charge to level at Mason in this context, were not the stories themselves told with such dignity toward the characters' hopes and dreams as well as the everyday problems and deeper tragedies of despair that are universal. The book portrays a phenomenon called the ''new South'' of the 1970s and 80s, when suburban icons such as shopping malls, fast food and discount store chains, and cable television first moved to the more remote rural areas of the Southern states.

Oddly enough it was probably Mason's first novel, *In Country,* that made her work more known by the people of western Kentucky. This was probably more due to the film version that was shot in Paducah a few years later. Mason says that it gave her particular pleasure to see area residents used as extras in the filming of the story, which is primarily about the aftermath of the Vietnam War on a family and a community. Sam is a teenager whose father died in Vietnam and whose Uncle Emmett returned home infected with Agent Orange. The novel explores Sam's quest for her father, her desire to know him through his diary and letters, and her attempt to unlock long-kept secrets from her uncle who, like may vets who came back, does not want to talk about the war. In many ways, Sam represents the next generation of American youth, as well as those of the same generation as the war who have unanswered questions about a history that is being kept silent and locked away by those who came home to a national ambivalence about the conflict. By the end of the novel, Sam comes to some measure of knowledge and understanding about the conflict, and many vets have heralded Mason's novel and the subsequent film for helping start a long overdue national dialogue about the Vietnam war and its aftermath.

What may be unfortunate about Mason's choice of details, such as the use of the television show *M*A*S*H,* which fuels Sam's imagination about war and begins her discussions with Emmett, is that the ''new South'' will not stay new forever. She is often criticized for her heavy use of allusions to popular culture, which are trendy and transient, at best. It will be an interesting facet of Mason's work in the years ahead to examine whether the pop culture allusions to television shows and commercials, for example, which are so familiar to her contemporary readers, will interfere with future readers' understanding and enjoyment of the novel.

Spence + Lila is, on the surface, a simple love story between a man and a woman who have been married for forty years. They are a farm couple who suddenly come face to face with a much more technical world when Lila is diagnosed with breast cancer. This is a couple for which love has been enacted on a daily basis, but perhaps not spoken about much. Spence struggles with words to express to Lila how he feels about her and his fear of losing her, and much of the novel is about the value of the verbal expression of love in a relationship that has every other sign of it intact.

Feather Crowns is perhaps Mason's weakest novel to date. In this novel, she veers away from the people and times she knows so well and attempts to put some of the same themes to work back at the turn of the century with a family that bore North America's first set of quintuplets. The couple tours with them like a sideshow act. The carnival-like atmosphere surrounding the couple echoes the artificiality of today's celebrities in popular culture, but so far Mason is on sounder ground writing about contemporary people and issues.

Perhaps Mason herself felt the need to regain her footing on familiar soil as well. In *Clear Springs: A Memoir,* her next book after *Midnight Magic,* a remix of previously published stories, Mason literally brings her writing back home to western Kentucky, describing her own experience coming of age in the middle of the twentieth century.

—Connie Ann Kirk

MASSIE, Allan

Nationality: British. **Born:** Singapore in 1938. **Education:** Glenalmond College, Perthshire; Trinity College, Cambridge. **Family:** Married; three children. **Awards:** Niven award, 1981; Scottish Arts Council award, 1982, 1987; Society of Authors travelling scholarship, 1988. Fellow, Royal Society of Literature. **Address:** Thirladean House, Selkirk TD7 5LU, England.

Publications

Novels

Change and Decay in All Around I See. London, Bodley Head, 1978.
The Last Peacock. London, Bodley Head, 1980.
The Death of Men. London, Bodley Head, 1981; Boston, Houghton Mifflin, 1982.
One Night in Winter. London, Bodley Head, 1984.
Augustus: The Memoirs of the Emperor. London, Bodley Head, 1986; as *Let the Emperor Speak,* New York, Doubleday, 1987.
A Question of Loyalties. London, Hutchinson, 1989.
Tiberius. London, Hodder and Stoughton, 1990.
The Hanging Tree. London, Heinemann, 1990.
The Sins of the Father. London, Hutchinson, 1991.
Caesar. London, Hodder and Stoughton, 1993; New York, Carroll & Graf, 1994.
These Enchanted Woods. London, Hutchinson, 1993.
The Ragged Lion. London, Hutchinson, 1994.
King David. London, Sceptre, 1995.

Uncollected Short Stories

''In the Bare Lands,'' in *Modern Scottish Short Stories,* edited by Fred Urquhart and Giles Gordon. London, Hamish Hamilton, 1978.

Other

Muriel Spark. Edinburgh, Ramsay Head Press, 1979.
Ill Met by Gaslight: Five Edinburgh Murders. Edinburgh, Harris, 1980.
The Caesars. London, Secker and Warburg, 1983; New York, Watts, 1984.
A Portrait of Scottish Rugby. Edinburgh, Polygon, 1984.
Colette. London, Viking, and New York, Penguin, 1986.
101 Great Scots. Edinburgh, Chambers, 1987.
Byron's Travels. London, Sidgwick and Jackson, 1988.
The Novelist's View of the Market Economy. Edinburgh, David Hume Institute, 1988.
Glasgow: Portrait of a City. London, Barrie and Jenkins, 1989.
The Novel Today: A Critical Guide to the British Novel 1970–1989. London, Longman, 1990.
Editor, *Edinburgh and the Borders: In Verse.* London, Secker and Warburg, 1983.
Editor, *PEN New Fiction 2.* London, Quartet, 1987.

* * *

Allan Massie occupies a curious place in Scottish letters. As a journalist and political commentator he embraces the politics of the conservative new right; in newspaper columns and elsewhere he has espoused the economic dogma of Margaret Thatcher (the British prime minister between 1979 and 1990), yet he is also a novelist of rare talent whose sympathies belong to the corrupted and the downtrodden, whatever their rank in society. All too often his critics are confused by the apparent contradictions between his public and his private face. In fact, a key to his thinking can be found in his novels about the emperors Augustus and Tiberius. Like Robert Graves before him, Massie uses the Roman world as suitable material with which to reconstruct the lives of these two very different men but then he goes a step further. In both he finds something of the loneliness of power and the constant battle between a temptation to use it for good or as a diabolic agency which can only corrupt and destroy. A recurring theme in both novels—parts of a planned trilogy—is the realisation that for rulers to do nothing is an evasion of responsibility yet action itself creates the possibility of doing wrong.

The idea is taken a stage further in *A Question of Loyalties* which takes a sympathetic view of the confusion of political ideologies in the establishment of Vichy France in 1940. Although this novel is rich in historical detail and contains real-life characters like Petain and de Gaulle, Massie's real concern is with the moral corruption of Lucien, the main character and a force behind the creation of a Vichy government. His life is recalled by Etienne his son and the action swings across Europe and between the modern world and the events of World War II as the moral ambiguities in both men's lives become ever apparent. It is an inventive and intellectually satisfying novel.

When Massie's first novel, *Change and Decay in All Around I See,* was first published, comparisons were made with the young Evelyn Waugh. The analogy was not fanciful. Atwater, the central character would feel equally at home in the flawed world of *Decline and Fall,* and the wasteland of 1950s London created by Massie is a timeless city in which social and spiritual life has slumped to a new ebb. The theme of things falling apart is explored further in *The Last Peacock,* a sensitive comedy of manners set among the Scottish landed gentry. Massie returned to Scotland in his fourth novel, *One Night in Winter,* but it is a very different country from the place he previously portrayed. Whereas his earlier preoccupations had been social, Massie plunged into the world of Scottish nationalist politics. Dallas Graham looks back from his middle-class London middle age to the years of his young manhood in Scotland when he found himself drawn into a bizarre coterie of nationalists and their fanatical camp followers. A murder lies at the heart of the novel, but Massie's theme is the tragedy of overweening ambition and flawed motives. Fraser Donnelly, a self-made man who espouses political nationalism, has his career ruined when fantasy overcomes his sense of reality, but Massie's concern seems to be less with the murder which Donnelly commits than with the effect it has on young Graham. In that sense, Donnelly's rise and fall seem to mirror the imperfect political ambitions of those who take up the cause of nationalism.

Political nationalism of a different kind also informs Massie's best novel to date, *The Death of Men.* In this modern parable of terrorism and politics, the scene is set in Rome in the summer of 1978, a period of political instability in Italy. Corrado Dusa, senior minister in the ruling Christian Democratic Party and a leading proponent of resolving the crisis of dissent and violence permeating his country, is mysteriously kidnapped, and a tangled series of political trails leads to the involvement of his son in the kidnap. At this point in the novel there are echoes of the uneasy relationship between Lucien and Etienne in *A Question of Loyalties.*

The action is based loosely in the events surrounding the real-life kidnap and murder of the Italian politician Aldo Moro in 1978, but it would be misleading to draw too many parallels between *The Death of Men* and those real events; neither would it be accurate to describe Massie's novel as a *roman à clef.* Writing with great assurance, Massie transforms the style into a fast-moving thriller, building up to a conclusion which, however expected it might be, is still cleverly handled. His gallery of characters all play expected roles and the Italian background is expertly and lovingly described: there are few better pictures of life in the inner city of modern Rome. And in the near distance Massie keeps open his moral options. Terrorism is roundly condemned, but he never loses sight of the question which is central to its occurrence: what are the political conditions which bring it into existence?

—Trevor Royle

MASTERS, Hilary

Pseudonym: P.J. Coyne. **Nationality:** American. **Born:** Kansas City, Missouri, 3 February 1928. **Education:** Davidson College, 1944–46; Brown University, 1948–52, B.A. **Military Service:** United States Navy (naval correspondent), 1946–47. **Family:** Married 1) Robin Owett Watt in 1953 (divorced 1954); 2) Polly Jo McCulloch in 1955 (divorced 1985); 3) Kathleen E. George in 1994; one son, two daughters (from first marriage). **Career:** Theatrical press agent, New York, 1952–56; journalist and founder, *The Hyde Park Record,* Hyde Park, New York. Since 1983 professor of English, Carnegie Mellon University, Pittsburgh, Pennsylvania. **Awards:** Yaddo fellowship, 1980, 1982; Fulbright Lecturer, Finland, 1983. **Member:** Authors Guild. **Agent:** Christina Ward, Box 515, North Scituate, Massachusetts 02060, U.S.A. **Address:** Department of English, Carnegie Mellon University, Pittsburgh, Pennsylvania 15213, U.S.A.

PUBLICATIONS

Novels

The Common Pasture. New York, Macmillan, 1967.
An American Marriage. New York, Macmillan, 1969.
Palace of Strangers. New York, World, 1971.
Clemmons. New York, Godine, 1985.
Cooper. New York, St. Martin's Press, 1987.
Manuscript for Murder (as P.J. Coyne). New York, Dodd, Mead, 1987.
Strickland: A Romance. New York, St. Martin's Press, 1990.
Home Is the Exile. Sag Harbor, New York, Permanent Press, 1996.

Short Stories

Hammertown Tales. N.p., Stuart Wright, 1987.
Success. New York, St. Martin's Press, 1992.

Other

Last Stands: Notes from Memory. New York, Godine, 1982.
In Montaigne's Tower: Essays. Columbia, University of Missouri Press, 2000.

*

Hilary Masters comments:

My approach to my work is to sit down and try to do a little bit of it every morning. Earliest influence at age eight was Robinson Crusoe. Since then everyone I read has been an ''influence.'' Most particularly H. James, Faulkner, Wright Morris, J. Conrad, etc.

* * *

Critics often see similarities between the writings of Hilary Masters and his father, poet Edgar Lee Masters. Thus, Hilary Masters's fictional characters, created with bold strokes, are ordinary people caught up in ordinary events that reshape their lives. Increasingly, Masters sharpens his use of locale often, placing a character in a detailed building or neighborhood. His most characteristic technique is filtering the past through memory to inform a character's present.

Often a shift in time occurs without warning as a present event replays an earlier one in a character's consciousness. Deftly done, these shifts demonstrate Master's control of plot and character.

His early novels, *The Common Pasture* and *An American Marriage,* reveal the roots of these characteristics. The former elaborates on the tensions between folks in a small town over twenty-four hours as they prepare for a community-day celebration. Masters economically draws stock characters as he develops his theme of corrupting power. The latter novel places an American college professor and one of his students, now his wife, in Ireland. Masters wittily sends up the Irish, visiting professorships, newlyweds, and the CIA as he moves the story line back and forth between Ireland and America. *Palace of Strangers,* set in upstate New York, follows a congressional primary as it progresses through smoke-filled rooms and done-deal politics. Cynically told through the newcomer's campaign manager, the novel was faulted for this narrator's keener interest in his own sexual prowess. Masters himself ran for political office in New York; thus the novel's noted credibility.

The memoir, *Last Stands: Notes from Memory,* transcends pure autobiography as it lovingly portrays the author's maternal grandparents, Molly and Thomas Coyne, who raised him, and his poet father and mother, Ellen, who he joined during the summers. Placing in the foreground his own memories of these four people most important in his childhood, Masters uses their memories to create an historical portrait of America that includes the 1983 Columbia Exposition; immigrants moving across America; American myths of the American West, as feisty Grandpa Gee Gee relives on-site Custer's battle at the Little Big Horn; and Edgar Lee Masters's success and waning as a poet while living in the Chelsea Hotel and being visited by other 1930s poets. All these are set against the organization and determination of his mother as she earns a master's degree in teaching and supports her family, even in widowhood. Masters's skillful mixture of three generations highlights the importance of family in one's life. Stylistically, his stream-of-consciousness technique allows him to use his father's and grandfather's letters to him, poems, allusions to music, remembered conversations, and events, particularly his grandfather's suicide, his father's near-penniless demise, and their somber funerals.

His later novels, *Clemmons, Cooper,* and *Strickland,* form a "Harlem Valley Trilogy." Masters's wit and humor come through best in these novels, where family and understanding the past play crucial roles in self-understanding. The first two portray men who have fled Manhattan, seeking organized lives in the solitude of lazy country towns; their memories or imaginations contrast the quotidian. In *Clemmons,* the eponymous protagonist's reveries move between his past and current relationships with his mother, his Southern wife, and mistresses as he frets over the complications created by the upcoming marriage of an estranged daughter. Rich comedy results when his New York mistress, his daughters, and his almost divorced wife converge on the family farm as he attempts simultaneously to paint the house and flee the festivities. As in other works, small incidents have enormous consequences; for instance, a reconciling family squabble erupts when Clemmons corrects the spelling of the son-in-law's rock album, *Find Stanley Livingston.*

Cooper continues Masters's use of upstate New York as a peaceful background for family turmoil; in this instance, Jack Cooper sells old magazines in Hammertown while he churns out World War I adventure tales and, in an echo of Grandpa Gee Gee, corresponds with a veteran flying ace whose wartime memories result in Cooper/Masters writing an exciting, lively, detailed story of World War I dogfights, which is in sharp contrast to the boring life from which Ruth, his promiscuous wife, seeks escape. Additional, somber, and melancholy echoes of *Last Stands* appear in both novels in the form of failed poets, infidelities, and suicides. And neither protagonist escapes life's confounding complications.

This darker vein continues in *Strickland: A Romance* as Masters alternates Vietnam War experiences with events in the life of former war correspondent Carrol Strickland, now a sixty-year-old widower living in upstate New York with his fifteen-year-old daughter. Fantasizing his war experiences, Strickland tries to recapture lost emotions through their pathetic simulation.

Masters's short stories continue his vivid sketches of place and the use of a present incident to spark a memory that infuses understanding into the now. The melancholy stories of *Hammertown Tales* portray a small, dying town in upstate New York; the sixteen stories of *Success* show Masters's sensitivity to ordinary people who long for the unretrievable past.

—Judith C. Kohl

MATHERS, Peter

Nationality: Australian. **Born:** Fulham, London, England, in 1931; brought to Australia as an infant. **Education:** Sydney Technical College. **Family:** Married in 1961 (divorced); two daughters. **Career:** Worked as a farmer, laborer, in wool-classing, in a brewery, and for the public service in Victoria, 1950s-early 1960s; lived in Europe, mainly in London, 1964–67, and worked as a researcher; theater adviser, University of Pittsburgh, 1968. **Awards:** Miles Franklin award, 1967. **Address:** c/o The Almost Managing Company, 83 Faraday St., Carlton, Victoria 3053, Australia.

PUBLICATIONS

Novels

Trap. Melbourne, Cassell, 1966; London, Sphere, 1970.
The Wort Papers. Melbourne, Cassell, 1972; London, Penguin, 1973.

Short Stories

A Change for the Better. Adelaide, Wav, 1984.

* * *

Peter Mathers is the author of only a few books of fiction, yet he is undoubtedly one of the best of the generation of Australian fiction writers that followed in the wake of White, Stead, and Xavier Herbert. Though he was born in England, his work is marked by a deep strain of Australian nationalism, a conscious attempt at mythologizing Australian experience.

His first novel, for instance, begins as the story of the eponymous Jack Trap, part-Aboriginal, but as it continues its concerns steadily widen until finally it takes in, with the discussion of Trap's forebears, the whole savage history of the Aboriginal race over the last 200 years: its shooting down and poisoning by white settlers, exploitation by businessmen and missionaries, abuse and mistreatment by foremen and fellow workers, and, finally, assaults by police and jailing by magistrates. If the novel is dominated by the angry, ebullient presence of its central character, the author makes it clear nevertheless that Jack is in part the product of a whole history of exploitation, cruelty, and contemptuous indifference on the part of white people. Trap is a misfit—neither craven nor surly, neither in society nor wholly out of it. Although he schools himself to patience, he is prone to violent eruptions at periodic intervals, and the result is always ''six months from an understanding magistrate.'' He is resentful of his Aboriginal features and hopes they will not be recognized but at the same time he ''marries'' an Aboriginal woman and his final scheme is to lead a party of followers across the continent to the Narakis Mission.

Despite its subject matter, *Trap* is essentially a comic novel with its author much given to word play, puns, and episodes of slap-stick. In *The Wort Papers* Mathers takes both his concerns and his experiments with language a good deal further, virtually out of the realm of social realism altogether. Style in *The Wort Papers* is not merely the means of recording the rebellious and independent freedom to which the protagonist aspires; it is also the means of achieving it. The last word in the novel is MATTERS, the name of the protagonist's alter ego and the mysterious writer who has hovered on its outskirts throughout the narrative.

Although it is concerned with a smaller period of time than *Trap*—roughly from the 1930s onward—*The Wort Papers* is similarly involved with questions of identity and mythic journeys inland; there are two series of journeys which are described in comic and even parodic terms. The first third of the novel is taken up with the various expeditions of William Wort, and his attempt to define himself in terms of a sense of Englishness. Like his son later, William is constantly ''In Flight.'' Mathers's awareness that William's peregrinations carry him over territory already covered by other Australian writers such as Patrick White is shown by the heading of one section: ''Journey and Employers (& obligatory bushfire).''

William's son Percy is an explorer, but whereas earlier explorers and even his father had traveled on foot or on horseback, Percy mounts a 500 cc Norton motorbike. Whereas they had traveled into the heart of the inland, he sticks mostly to the cities, and his predicaments are urban ones, often taking a farcical form. Where their enemies were droughts or hostile natives, Percy's are figures of bureaucratic authority—policemen, mysterious representatives of the A.S.I.O. (the Australian equivalent of the C.I.A.), and recalcitrant bosses and bar-keepers.

Percy's acts of insurrection are embodied in the language of the novel itself. Wort's words are exuberant, very funny, and finally surreal weapons fired by his ''sturdy, 350 shot Remington.'' At the end of the novel Percy dies but his doppelgänger Matters is still around. It is the artist, the word-maker, who in Mathers's view survives.

A gap of twelve years separates *The Wort Papers* from Mathers's third book of fiction, a collection of short stories titled *A Change for the Better,* and when it did appear it was greeted by sympathetic reviewers with no more than respectful disappointment. The distinguishing elements of Mathers's writing—the compression, density, and self-conscious linguistic play—have been taken as far as they can possibly go, to the point where the style is cryptic, rather than merely compressed, not so much self-conscious as hermetic. The title story is both witty and accessible. It tells of a young boy with homosexual inclinations who is therefore the scandal of his country district. Eventually he is discovered peering through the bathroom at a girl bathing. The outraged parents send for his father but are deeply chagrined at his reaction of delight: at least his sexual proclivities indicate ''a change for the better.'' Another story that works well is ''Like a Maori Prince,'' which returns the reader to the territory of the novels: a black man poses as a Maori Prince in order to escape the tag of ''Lairy Boong'' and is treated with fawning respect by the whites of the town. For the most part, though, the stories are marked by long exchanges of almost indecipherable puns and one-liners. One of the characters in ''Like a Maori Prince'' comments on the pun that ''People have been run out of town for better jokes.'' There are enough bad ones in this collection to cause a mass exodus.

Mathers continues to write constantly but like Malcolm Lowry is never able to consider a work finished, and is deeply reluctant to relinquish it to a publisher. Like Lowry, also, it is probable that much of his writing will be published posthumously, a suggestion that delights the author when it is put to him.

—Laurie Clancy

MATHEWS, Harry (Burchell)

Nationality: American. **Born:** New York City, 14 February 1930. **Education:** Harvard University, Cambridge, Massachusetts, B.A. 1952. **Military Service:** Served in the United States Navy, 1949–50. **Family:** Married 1) Niki de Saint Phalle in 1949 (divorced 1964), one son and one daughter; 2) Marie Chaix in 1992. **Career:** Publisher and editor with John Ashbery, Kenneth Koch, and James Schuyler, *Locus Solus,* New York, 1960–62; part-time teacher, Bennington College, Vermont, 1978, 1979–80; Hamilton College, New York, 1979; Columbia University, New York, 1982–83; Brown University, Providence, Rhode Island, 1988; Temple University, Philadelphia, 1990. Since 1989 Paris editor, *Paris Review,* Paris and New York. **Awards:** National Endowment grant, 1982; Award for Fiction Writing, American Academic Institute of Arts and Letters, 1991; American Award for Literature, 1994. **Agent:** Maxine Groffsky, 2 Fifth Avenue, New York, New York 10011, U.S.A. **Address:** 67 Rue de Grenelle, 75007 Paris, France.

PUBLICATIONS

Novels

The Conversions. New York, Random House, and London, Weidenfeld and Nicolson, 1962.

Tlooth. New York, Doubleday, 1966; Manchester, Carcanet, 1987.

The Sinking of the Odradek Stadium and Other Novels (includes *The Conversions* and *Tlooth*). New York, Harper, 1975; Manchester, Carcanet, 1985.

Cigarettes. New York, Weidenfeld and Nicolson, 1987; Manchester, Carcanet, 1988.

The Journalist. Boston, Godine, 1994.

Short Stories

Selected Declarations of Dependence (includes verse). Calais, Vermont, Z Press, 1977.

Country Cooking and Other Stories. Providence, Rhode Island, Burning Deck Press, 1980.

Singular Pleasures. New York, Grenfell Press, 1988.

The American Experience. London, Atlas Press, 1991.

Poetry

The Ring: Poems 1956–1969. Leeds, Juilliard, 1970.
The Planisphere. Providence, Rhode Island, Burning Deck Press, 1974.
Trial Impressions. Providence, Rhode Island, Burning Deck Press, 1977.
Armenian Papers: Poems 1954–1984. Princeton, New Jersey, Princeton University Press, 1987.
Out of Bounds. Providence, Rhode Island, Burning Deck Press, 1989.
A Mid-Season Sky: Poems 1954–1989. Manchester, Carcanet, 1991.

Other

20 Lines a Day (journal). Elmwood Park, Illinois, Dalkey Archive Press, 1988.
The Orchard (on Georges Perec). Flint, Michigan, Bamberger, 1988.
The Way Home: Collected Longer Prose. London, Atlas Press, 1989.
L'oeil. Paris, L'Oulipo, 1994.
Translator, *The Laurels of Lake Constance,* by Marie Chaix. New York, Viking Press, 1977.
Translator, *The Life: Memoirs of a French Hooker,* by Jeanne Cordelier. New York, Viking Press, 1978.
Translator, *Blue of Noon,* by Georges Bataille. New York, Urizen, 1978; London, Boyars, 1979.
Translator, *Ellis Island,* by Georges Perec with Robert Bober. New York, New Press, 1995.

*

Critical Studies: Harry Mathews issue of *Review of Contemporary Fiction* (Elmwood Park, Illinois), Fall 1987 (includes checklist by William McPheron); ''Locus Solu et Socii: Harry Mathews and John Ashbery'' by Christopher Sawyer-Lauçanno, in *The Continual Pilgrimage: American Writers in Paris, 1944–1960,* New York, Grove Weidenfeld, 1992; *Harry Mathews* by Warren Leamon, New York, Twayne, 1993.

Harry Mathews comments:

(2000) A constant that has inspired my writing through many years of varied efforts is my original passion for reading. From late childhood on, poetry and imaginary narrative seemed to me to give access to compelling realities that could be communicated in no other way; and of these two, poetry has always had a primordial supremacy. So I think I have tried to bring to my prose writing poetry's intensity and authority, which depend essentially on abstract as opposed to representational elements. This had led some readers to consider me a writer who plays games, an attitude apparently justified by my membership in the Oulipo. To the extent that this may be so, I would like to say that the games are played in dead earnest and that their only purpose is to lure onto the page my obsessive and otherwise indecipherable sense of what is true.

* * *

Harry Mathews takes semiotics out of the seminar and makes it live as fiction. Language is anything but transparent for him. He is not a self-centered performer, or a member of the Look Ma, I'm Writing! school. Nor does he make us uncomfortably aware of ourselves as readers. But (although he ridicules McLuhan) Mathews does treat his medium as his message; language, in its multimeaning, ambiguous, tragicomic potential, is itself his subject matter. His first three novels are in fact intricate allegories of the reader or listener caught in the act of interpretation.

The distinctive appeal of Mathews's novels lies in their extraordinarily rich and playful linguistic texture, rather than in the plot structures that are relatively straightforward and easy to recount. *The Conversions* begins when its anonymous narrator is given a golden ceremonial adze by a wealthy eccentric named Grent Wayl. The adze is engraved with a series of seven mysterious scenes which the narrator attempts, tentatively, to explain. When Wayl dies, a provision in his will turns the narrator's mild curiosity into exegetical zeal, by conferring immense wealth on the person who can answer three riddles: 1) When was a stone not a king?; 2) What was *La Messe de Sire Fadevant?*; and 3) Who shaved the Old Man's beard?

The riddles all have to do with the engravings on the adze, and all seem to depend upon puns. Along with the narrator, the reader gradually learns of a secret society that has persisted through the centuries despite repeated persecution, a society that, in a ceremony involving the golden adze, crowns its leader King and calls him Sylvius. An impostor named Johnstone once claimed falsely to be Sylvius—hence the ''stone'' that was ''not a king.'' *La Messe de Sire Fadevant* devolves upon musical and translingual puns: *Sire* denotes not a noble title but two musical notes, while *Fadevant* places a third note in front: *fa-si-re.* Tracking down a Mass that begins with these notes, the narrator finds that its words shed further light upon the followers of Sylvius. The third riddle stumps him, however, and he abandons the quest, seemingly inconclusively, at the end of the novel.

Mathews' second novel, *Tlooth* achieved some renown when Martin Gardner described it glowingly in *Scientific American.* Its narrator and protagonist (whose name and even gender are concealed until close to the end) spends the novel pursuing a fellow ex-convict, for reasons that are tucked away as an aside to a footnote on the first page. (It appears that the object of pursuit, a criminally perverse surgeon, unnecessarily amputated two fingers from the left hand of the narrator, who until then had been a violinist.)

''Texts True and False'' (one of *Tlooth's* chapter titles) litter the trail of vengeance, as do documents in a dozen lingos, clashing symbols, and uncracked codes. ''Tlooth'' itself, the sound uttered by a bizarre oracle, is, when properly construed, a prophecy that comes true: the narrator, now turned dentist, succeeds in strapping the object of her pursuit into her own dentist's chair. Mercifully for both reader and quarry, no painful drilling takes place, for reasons not to be divulged here.

An epistolary novel, *The Sinking of the Odradek Stadium* presents the letters of two correspondents, Zachary McCaltex, an American treasure-hunter from Miami, and Twang, his obscurely Asian wife, answering in comically bad but meliorative English from various spots in Italy. The two of them are pursuing, by diverse machinations, a fortune in gold hidden in a chest and then lost by the Medici family. Again much of the action consists of the perusal, translation, interpretation, and verification of a host of documents, maps, clues, and false leads. In the very last letter of the book we learn that Twang has actually gotten her hands on the gold, and is about to ship it to Zachary via the freighter *Odradek Stadium.* Only the novel's title hints at what happens next.

In *Cigarettes,* his fourth novel, Mathews makes a fresh departure, overlaying his earlier artificial principles of construction with a richly textured family chronicle set among a certain privileged set of New Yorkers in the late 1930s and the early 1960s. The narrative proceeds nonlinearly, by focusing in turn on pairs of characters, at moments of considerable drama in their lives. We have fraud among friends in the insurance business; painters, critics, gallery owners; homosexual couples in scenes of bondage and domination. Schemes and betrayals, illnesses and disappointments make of the novel a quick-paced tumult of emotional highs and lows. Filial guilt and obligation play prominent roles.

One passage in *Cigarettes* offers a capsule summary of Mathews's esthetic program; ostensibly it describes an art-history essay:

> Morris was showing him what writing could do. He advanced the notion that creation begins by annihilating typical forms and procedures, especially the illusory ''naturalness'' of sequence and coherence. Morris did more than state this, he demonstrated it. He made of his essay a minefield that blew itself up as you crossed it. You found yourself again and again on ground not of your choosing, propelled from semantics into psycho-analysis into epistemology into politics. These displacements seemed, rather than willful, grounded in some hidden and persuasive law that had as its purpose to keep bringing the reader back fresh to the subject.

The intentional fallacy notwithstanding, this passage offers the clearest exposition of Mathews's practice now in print. It is deepened by Lewis's paraphrase: ''one can't really *describe* anything. So you pretend to describe—you use words to make a false replica. Then we're absorbed by the words, not by the illusion of a description. You also defuse reactions that might get in our way.''

The characters of *Cigarettes,* like their namesake, are consumed by a certain self-destructive yet elegant passion. More than their predecessors in Mathews's fiction, they are defined not by their arbitrary utility to a quest pattern, but by their relations of loyalty, betrayal, and abuse. By the novel's end, several mysteries—including the forging of new links between love and language—are illuminated as if by the striking of a match in a darkened room.

—Brian Stonehill

MATTHEWS, Jack

Nationality: American. **Born:** John Harold Matthews in Columbus, Ohio, 22 July 1925. **Education:** Ohio State University, Columbus, 1945–49, 1952–54, B.A. in classics and English 1949, M.A. in English 1954. **Military Service:** Served in the United States Coast Guard, 1943–45. **Family:** Married Barbara Jane Reese in 1947; two daughters and one son. **Career:** Post office clerk, Columbus, 1950–59; associate professor, 1959–62, and professor of English, 1962–64, Urbana College, Ohio; associate professor, 1964–70, professor of English, 1971–77, and since 1978 Distinguished Professor, Ohio University, Athens. Distinguished Writer-in-Residence, Wichita State University, Kansas, 1970–71. **Awards:** Florence Roberts Head award, 1967; Quill award (*Massachusetts Review,* Amherst), 1967; Guggenheim grant, 1974; Ohio Arts Council award, 1989. **Agent:** Ann Elmo Agency, 60 East 42nd Street, New York, New York 10165. **Address:** 24 Briarwood Drive, Athens, Ohio 45701, U.S.A.

Publications

Novels

Hanger Stout, Awake! New York, Harcourt Brace, 1967.
Beyond the Bridge. New York, Harcourt Brace, 1970.
The Tale of Asa Bean. New York, Harcourt Brace, 1971.
The Charisma Campaigns. New York, Harcourt Brace, 1972.
Pictures of the Journey Back. New York, Harcourt Brace, 1973.
Sassafras. Boston, Houghton Mifflin, 1983.

Short Stories

Bitter Knowledge. New York, Scribner, 1964.
Tales of the Ohio Land. Columbus, Ohio Historical Society, 1978.
Dubious Persuasions. Baltimore, Johns Hopkins University Press, 1981.
Crazy Women. Baltimore, Johns Hopkins University Press, 1985.
Ghostly Populations. Baltimore, Johns Hopkins University Press, 1987.
Dirty Tricks. Baltimore, Johns Hopkins University Press, 1990.
Storyhood as We Know It and Other Tales. Baltimore and London, Johns Hopkins University Press, 1993.

Poetry

An Almanac for Twilight. Chapel Hill, University of North Carolina Press, 1966.
In a Theater of Buildings. Marshall, Minnesota, Ox Head Press, 1970.

Other

Collecting Rare Books for Pleasure and Profit. New York, Putnam, 1977.
Booking in the Heartland. Baltimore, Johns Hopkins University Press, 1986.
Memoirs of a Bookman. Athens, Ohio University Press, 1990.
Booking Pleasures. Athens, Ohio University Press, 1996.
Reading Matter: Rhetorical Muses of a Rabid Bibliophile. New Castle, Delaware, Oak Knoll Press, 2000.
Editor, with Elaine Gottlieb Hemley, *The Writer's Signature: Idea in Story and Essay.* Chicago, Scott Foresman, 1972.
Editor, *Archetypal Themes in the Modern Story* (anthology). New York, St. Martin's Press, 1973.
Editor, *Rare Book Lore: Selections from the Letters of Ernest J. Wessen.* Athens, Ohio University Press, 1992.

*

Manuscript Collections: Ohioana Library, Ohio Departments Building, Columbus; Alden Library, Ohio University, Athens.

Critical Studies: ''That Appetite for Life So Ravenous'' by Dave Smith, in *Shenandoah* (Lexington, Virginia), Summer 1974; ''One Alternative to Black Humor: The Satire of Jack Matthews'' by Stanley W. Lindberg, in *Studies in Contemporary Satire* (Cambridge Springs, Pennsylvania), vol. 1, no. 1, 1977; ''Jack Matthews and the Shape of Human Feelings'' by Elmer F. Suderman, in *Critique* (Atlanta), vol. 21, no. 1, 1979.

Jack Matthews comments:

I think of every literary work as a place where three classes of people come together: the author, the reader, and the characters. The work is importantly, if not solely, definable in terms of these three classes and their relationships to one another and to the story (or poem) which is the arena of their convention. Thus, every story can be viewed as, in varying degrees, an occasion and ceremony of passionate learning.

All stories are philosophical probes, hypotheses, heuristic journeys, maps of powerful and conceivable realities, speculations, ceremonies of discovery. All these, every one. Some attempts to write a good story work beautifully; others prove sadly unworthy, false, flat, silly. Nevertheless, an author should have the courage and energy to experiment constantly and knowledgeably (i.e., remembering and adding to his craft), even in his awareness that he will often miss whatever mark is there, and knowing also that whatever can conceivably happen to him and come out of him will ultimately be found to have taken place within his signature.

Man's character is his fate, but he should never let this fact inhibit his real freedom of the real moment. I celebrate this truth in my stories, as well as in the act of writing them.

* * *

Many contemporary fiction writers—especially in America—are displaced persons: they don't really live *in* any particular location, they merely reside there. But Jack Matthews's mature imagination lives in the American heartland where it was shaped. In fact, Matthews is at his best when he is taking the pulse of Middle America (not merely a geographical area, of course, but a state of consciousness extending far beyond Matthews's native Ohio). In his six novels (and in many of his remarkable short stories) the reader can sense the wide-open spaces of the Midwest, the often-closed minds of its inhabitants, the limitless possibilities of success and failure, the comic and the tragic in ironic balance. Like Sinclair Lewis, Matthews captures the essence of Middle America. He does so, however, without the didacticism of Lewis and with more of the comic and a surer control of the dramatic.

Matthews's early novels are all rather short, though they are richly developed and populated with memorable characters—originals with much more than just literary validity, ranging from gas-station attendants and warehouse laborers to used-car salesmen and battered cowboys. Most of them are essentially innocents, viewed with unsentimental compassion as they try to cope with what they see of the confusion around them; but they carry their innocence in interestingly differing ways.

The most openly naive of his characters is "Hanger" Stout, the narrator of Matthews's first novel, who relates a poignant but truly funny account of how he was tricked into competing for the championship of a nonexistent sport ("free-hanging" by one's hands). Genuinely unaware of how much others are using him, and often unaware of the refreshing comedy in his tale, "Hanger" emerges from his experiences relatively untouched, still kind and trusting, a most convincing original.

Less convincing is the self-conscious narrator of *Beyond the Bridge,* a middle-aged man who narrowly escapes death when the Silver Bridge collapses, plunging a number of people into the Ohio River. Knowing that his family expects him to be crossing the bridge at that hour, he seizes this unique chance to shed all his responsibilities, to disappear and begin a new life elsewhere. Such a break with one's past is not that easy, Matthews demonstrates, and the novel offers some nicely detailed moments in the mind of the neurotic narrator. When compared to Matthews's other fiction, however, the action here seems excessively internalized, and the symbolism often too overt.

Matthews's ironic sense of humor surfaces as witty sexual satire in *The Tale of Asa Bean,* where the innocent is a former Ph.D. candidate in philosophy now working in an A & P grocery warehouse. Asa, burdened with an IQ of more than 170 and an over-active libido, is a compulsive verbalist with a tendency to drop recondite phrases (often in Latin) at inappropriate moments—a habit that regularly scares off the women he so desperately wants. "What ironic man can make love?" Asa agonizes, "And yet, how can man achieve truth, understanding, humor, manhood, without irony?" But Asa's hilarious misadventures end triumphantly—despite himself—in a brilliant demonstration of wit and verbal precision, a winning performance.

In *The Charisma Campaigns* Matthews takes a calculated risk in creating a character who is announced as possessing magnetic charisma—and, indeed, convincingly projects it on the page. A used-car dealer in a small Ohio town, Rex McCoy plays with a full deck of corny sales slogans and gimmicks, but like nearly all of Matthews's characters, he moves far beyond any stereotyped model. His cunning machinations and energetic naivety, his success in selling cars and his failures in other aspects of life, all blend into a fascinating portrait. It is easy to agree with Anthony Burgess, who proclaimed it "an American classic." This is a superb novel—Matthews's finest accomplishment to date.

In *Pictures of the Journey Back,* set in the early 1970s, Matthews portrays a trip from Kansas to Colorado by three disparate characters: a weathered ex-rodeo hand, a confused college girl estranged from her mother, and the girl's hippie lover, an aspiring filmmaker. The cowboy insists upon returning the girl to her dying mother because, he argues, it is "only right," and the boyfriend accompanies them to make a film of the total experience. Here is the vehicle for the unending dialectics of youth *vs.* age, freedom *vs.* tradition, appearance *vs.* reality, etc. More ambitious technically than his earlier work, *Pictures* employs a shifting point of view to examine a concern that occupies much of Matthews's fiction—a sense that something is slowly being lost: "the sacred ideals of one's family and culture," as Matthews sees it, "what the Romans termed *Pietas.*"

In his most recent (and longest) novel, Matthews sets the action in 1840 on the American frontier. The protagonist/narrator of *Sassafras* is Thad Burke, a young phrenologist who takes his show from village to village, lecturing and "reading" the heads of a wild assortment of soldiers, Indians, settlers, and whores. Thad's Candide-like journey is not without its moving and painful lessons, but Matthews infuses a marvelous comic energy into this picaresque novel, and the dominant tone is that of a boisterous tall tale. Like Huck Finn, Thad is a splendid innocent—despite his natural "sass" and the sophistication he thinks he has acquired.

All of Matthews's novels have distinct merit, inviting and convincingly sustaining subsequent readings, but it would be a serious mistake to measure his achievement solely by these longer works. During the past four decades, well over 200 of his stories have appeared in major American quarterlies and magazines (with a number of them reprinted in prize anthologies), and significantly, this is the genre that has been receiving most of his energies in recent years.

Of the six splendid collections of Matthews's stories that have been published, perhaps the best is the thematically integrated *Tales of the Ohio Land,* which is particularly rich in its blend of history and myth. Unfortunately, neither this nor his first collection, *Bitter Knowledge,* is easily available, but his last four volumes are all in print, thanks to Johns Hopkins University Press. These include *Dubious Persuasions, Crazy Women* (''dedicated to all those who will understand how negotiable and variously ironic the title is''), *Ghostly Populations,* and *Dirty Tricks.* Together they provide solid evidence of Matthews's range and versatility, his sure powers of observation, and his compassionate understanding of the human comedy.

Engaging wit and irony have been characteristic of Matthews's writing from the start, and both are strongly present in his latest gatherings of stories. His irony is increasingly darker, however, and his characters' obsession with memory and its distortions plays a more dominant role in this later work, much of which deals with death. For the most part, these are stories with deceptively simple and ordinary surfaces, but they are driven by powerful and ominous undercurrents, which often fuse the local and regional with the archetypal. Few can do it better. Without question, Matthews has established himself as one of America's finest storytellers.

—Stanley W. Lindberg

MATTHIESSEN, Peter

Nationality: American. **Born:** New York City, 22 May 1927. **Education:** Hotchkiss School, Connecticut; Yale University, New Haven, Connecticut, B.A. in English 1950; the Sorbonne, Paris, 1948–49. **Family:** Married 1) Patricia Southgate in 1951 (divorced); 2) Deborah Love in 1963 (died 1972), two children; 3) Maria Eckhart in 1980. **Career:** Commercial fisherman, 1954–56. Has made anthropological and natural history expeditions to Alaska, the Canadian Northwest Territories, Peru, New Guinea (Harvard-Peabody expedition, 1961), Africa, Nicaragua, and Nepal. Co-founder, 1952, and editor, *Paris Review.* Trustee, New York Zoological Society, 1965–79. **Awards:** *Atlantic* Firsts award, 1951; American Academy award, 1963; National Book award, for nonfiction, 1979; Brandeis University Creative Arts award, 1979; American Book award, for nonfiction, 1980; John Burroughs medal, 1982; Philadelphia Academy of Sciences gold medal, 1984; Heinz Award, Arts and Humanities, 1999. **Member:** American Academy of Arts and Letters, 1974. **Address:** Bridge Lane, Sagaponack, Long Island, New York 11962, U.S.A.

PUBLICATIONS

Novels

Race Rock. New York, Harper, 1954; London, Secker and Warburg, 1955; as *The Year of the Tempest,* New York, Bantam, 1957.

Partisans. New York, Viking Press, 1955; London, Secker and Warburg, 1956; as *The Passionate Seekers,* New York, Avon, 1957.

Raditzer. New York, Viking Press, 1961; London, Heinemann, 1962.

At Play in the Fields of the Lord. New York, Random House, 1965; London, Heinemann, 1966.

Far Tortuga. New York, Random House, 1975; London, Collins, 1989.

Killing Mister Watson. New York, Random House, and London, Collins, 1990.

Lost Man's River. New York, Random House, 1997.

Bone by Bone. New York, Random House, 1999.

Short Stories

Midnight Turning Gray. Bristol, Rhode Island, Ampersand Press, 1984.

On the River Styx and Other Stories. New York, Random House, and London, Collins, 1989.

Uncollected Short Stories

''Fifth Day,'' in *Atlantic* (Boston), September 1951.

''A Replacement,'' in *Paris Review 1,* Spring 1953.

''Lina,'' in *Cornhill* (London), Fall 1956.

Other

Wildlife in America. New York, Viking Press, 1959; London, Deutsch, 1960; revised edition, Viking, 1987.

The Cloud Forest: A Chronicle of the South American Wilderness. New York, Viking Press, 1961; London, Deutsch, 1962.

Under the Mountain Wall: A Chronicle of Two Seasons in the Stone Age. New York, Viking Press, 1962; London, Heinemann, 1963.

The Shorebirds of North America. New York, Viking Press, 1967; as *The Wind Birds,* 1973.

Oomingmak: The Expedition to the Musk Ox Island in the Bering Sea. New York, Hastings House, 1967.

Sal Si Puedes: Cesar Chavez and the New American Revolution. New York, Random House, 1970.

Blue Meridian: The Search for the Great White Shark. New York, Random House, 1971.

Everglades: Selections from the Writings of Peter Matthiessen, edited by Patricia Caulfield. New York, Ballantine, 1971.

Seal Pool (for children). New York, Doubleday, 1972; as *The Great Auk Escape,* London, Angus and Robertson, 1974.

The Tree Where Man Was Born, with *The African Experience,* photographs by Eliot Porter. New York, Dutton, and London, Collins, 1972.

The Snow Leopard. New York, Viking Press, 1978; London, Chatto and Windus, 1979.

Sand Rivers (on the Selous Game Reserve), photographs by Hugo van Lawick. New York, Viking Press, and London, Aurum Press, 1981.

In the Spirit of Crazy Horse. New York, Viking Press, 1983; revised edition, Viking, and London, Harper Collins, 1991.

Indian Country. New York, Viking, 1984; London, Collins, 1985.

Nine-Headed Dragon River: Zen Journals 1969–1982. Boston, Shambhala, and London, Collins, 1986.

Men's Lives: The Surfmen and Baymen of the South Fork. New York, Random House, 1986; London, Collins, 1988.

African Silences. New York, Random House, 1991.

African Shadows. New York, Harry Abrams, 1993.

East of Lo Monthang: In the Land of Mustang, photography by Thomas Laird. Boston, Shambhala Publications, 1995.

The Peter Matthiessen Reader, edited by McKay Jenkins. New York, Vintage Books, 2000.

Tigers in the Snow, photographs by Maurice Hornocker. New York, North Point Press/Farrar, Straus and Giroux, 2000.

*

Bibliography: *Peter Matthiessen: A Bibliography 1952–1979* by D. Nicholas, Canoga Park, California, Orirama Press, 1980.

* * *

Peter Matthiessen has a dream of mankind living gracefully in the world, one species of many in an organic relationship. Unlike earlier American authors given to a version of this dream, Matthiessen can have no illusions. He writes with our contemporary knowledge that the ''natural man,'' whose free application of energy to the environment was for earlier Americans to be the means of achieving a paradise, has wrought ecological disaster. Materially that disaster derives from the rapacious application of technology to the subjugation of nature, and Matthiessen's works of nonfiction are its historical record reporting the extinction and threatened destruction of animal species, the fateful meetings of representatives of industrial society with people yet to experience even the agricultural revolution, and the desperate resistance of American farm workers to the culminating stage of exploitation. Philosophically, the disastrous consequences of the traditional American dream result from the theoretical separation of society, usually conceived of as oppressive, and the individual, always assumed to be noble; thus, people celebrating individualism but nonetheless required to construct a social system find that their rejection of the claims of fraternity does not foster sturdy independence but merely produces anomie. The counterpart of his historical record of the destruction of the natural environment, Matthiessen's first novels are a representation of this disabled American character.

Writing evocatively of his own generation and social class in *Race Rock,* he links four young Americans in exploring the directions their lives have taken since their adolescence in the same seacoast setting. The shifting viewpoint and intermingling of recollection and present event provide the sense of movement we associate with growth, but it is ironic since there has been no growth. Two of the male characters—George and Sam—are the ineffectual products of middle-class culture: uncertain of vocation, implausible in deeds, in short unable to complete the arc between thought and action because they doubt the efficacy of their thought. Providing the apex of a triangle is a woman who, though female and, therefore, less intensively drawn by the romance of achievement, is herself ungratified. Her fulfillment must come through the ineffectual males to one of whom she has been married and with the second of whom she is involved in a love affair. The point of reference for all three is Cady, a man whose natural capacity to act let him bully them in childhood. As adults these four are bound as they were in adolescence into personally destructive relationships. Cady's irresponsible brutishness has merely become more lethal. He still seeks to get what he wants according to a base code of individual force, while George, Sam, and Eve ambivalently resent and admire his dominance. For Matthiessen the behavior of the characters has explanation, but no excuse. Carefully avoiding extenuating circumstances that would lift their personal responsibility, he shows that they have neither the direction nor the will to exist in other than an unjustifiably predatory arrangement.

In *Partisans* Matthiessen again focuses upon an ineffectual son of the American bourgeoisie. Barney Sand, alienated from family and culture, proceeds on a search for a revolutionary who had befriended him as a child. By means of a descent into Parisian working class life on which Barney is led by a Stalinist Party functionary named Marat, Matthiessen parallels the physical search with an inquiry into the motives for revolutionary action. The Brechtian portrayal of proletarian conditions denies Barney the clarity available to those who think in the abstract. The bestial lives of the poor make sympathy, or even the belief in their natural rectitude, impossible for Barney, and a politics without idealism is beneath his consideration. All that Matthiessen permits Barney to grasp is that revolutionaries have strong convictions for which they will sacrifice—the man for whom he searches gives life and reputation. But since there can be no doubt that revolutionary forces are in motion, the failure to comprehend must lie in Barney. Matthiessen seems to be suggesting that so long as thought and action are held to be categorically separate, as they are in Barney's mind, no motive will be sufficient for action and no action entirely justifiable. It is integration of both in practice that makes a revolutionary, and comprehension of that fact is necessary for modern men to make their lives adequately human.

Technically Matthiessen's neatest explication of character occurs in *Raditzer.* The figure who gives his name to the book is a passive-aggressive, physically weak and socially a parasite, yet able to strike through the mask of civilized respectability and mastery to reveal in those he victimizes a deep-seated guilt and bewildering remorse. The kinship Raditzer insists he shares with the respectable Navy men whose tenuous security he undermines conveys, as in *Race Rock,* Matthiessen's perception of the split between thought and action that manifests itself in the indecisiveness of American men. The tight narrative construction enforcing psychological parallels goes beyond the earlier novel, however, making it evident in *Raditzer* through the substance of style that the leading characters of the book amalgamate into a general type.

Successful though he has been in the manner of psychological realism, Matthiessen's developing vision has required that he exceed the form of his first three novels, and in *At Play in the Fields of the Lord* he introduces to fiction the comprehensiveness of philosophical anthropology. Carrying the ineffectual civilized types he has previously described into the jungle of South America, Matthiessen strips away the protective coloration they gain from their native culture; thus, they are as exposed as the jungle Indians to the test of survival. As the narrative increasingly centers upon the grand attempt of a reservation-trained North American Indian to reclaim his past by immersing himself in the natural and cultural world of the primitive South American Indians, three levels of meaning emerge. The first concerns the historical conflict between modern technological civilization and the less developed societies whose destruction is only a matter of time. Through imaginative sympathy with both Indians and whites Matthiessen, then, establishes a second theme of the unity of desire to humanize the world. For the Indians this involves a balanced relationship to nature that yet allows a sense of transcendence. For the North Americans sharing the same impulse the desire is domination. Certainly their technology will eventually dominate but for the time being they are alone with only personal resources inadequate to sustain their sanity. Finally, on a third level of meaning he reveals both Indians and whites to be lonely beings who must find salvation through development of community that embraces the total material and social world.

Thematically more spare than the previous novels, *Far Tortuga* embodies in literary technique itself the forces of the natural and human world that might make a community. The crew of a Grand Cayman fishing boat going about the business of sailing to the turtle banks off Nicaragua communicates in dialogue detached from expository context. Their speech, afloat as they are, concerns the specifics of job and personality but is imbued with the sense that fishing has come upon hard times. Tales of past voyages, former captains, and historical events imply the decline their way of life has suffered because excessive fishing has depleted marine life. Impressionistic description of sea and weather and time dominates the narrative just as natural forces dominate the watery world. There is no significant plot to the narrative, for at sea the men cannot be a cause of their destiny, and, for the same reason, narrative movement is simply temporal. Human purpose appears in the novel's title, which refers to a legendary bay where fishing is eternally good, but that very purpose has sustained material nature as the ultimate force in human life.

Matthiessen's fiction and nonfiction are one. As he writes in *Sal Si Puedes:* ''In a damaged human habitat, all problems merge.'' The good life will be achieved, if at all, only when man and society and nature are equally nurtured and cherished.

—John M. Reilly

MAVOR, Elizabeth (Osborne)

Nationality: British. **Born:** Glasgow, 17 December 1927. **Education:** St. Leonard's School, St. Andrews, Scotland; St. Anne's College, Oxford (editor, *Cherwell*), 1947–50, B.A. in history, M.A. **Family:** Married Haro Hodson in 1953; two sons. **Address:** c/o Hutchinson, 20 Vauxhall Bridge Road, London SW1V 2SA, England.

PUBLICATIONS

Novels

Summer in the Greenhouse. London, Hutchinson, 1959; New York, Morrow, 1960.
The Temple of Flora. London, Hutchinson, 1961.
The Redoubt. London, Hutchinson, 1967.
A Green Equinox. London, Joseph, 1973.
The White Solitaire. London, Hutchinson, 1988.

Other

The Virgin Mistress, A Study in Survival: The Life of the Duchess of Kingston. London, Chatto and Windus, and New York, Doubleday, 1964.
The Ladies of Llangollen: A Study in Romantic Friendship. London, Joseph, 1971; New York, Penguin, 1984.
Editor, *Life with the Ladies of Llangollen.* London, Viking, 1984.
Editor, *The Grand Tour of William Beckford: Selections from Dreams, Waking Thoughts, and Incidents.* London, Penguin, 1986.
Editor, *Fanny Kemble: The American Journals.* London, Weidenfeld and Nicolson, 1990.
Editor, *The Grand Tours of Katherine Wilmot: France 1801–3 and Russia 1805–7.* London, Weidenfeld and Nicolson, 1992.
Editor, *The Captain's Wife: The South American Journals of Maria Graham 1821–23.* London, Weidenfeld and Nicolson, 1993.

* * *

The strength of Elizabeth Mavor's writing is her sensuous evocation of nature, gardens, art, and sex. The quirky interest in the past apparent in her earlier novels flowered in *The White Solitaire* into a full-scale historical novel. Each of her four earlier novels centres on a woman in love, around whom revolve questions of the justification of adultery, and who pits herself against time, past or future.

In Mavor's first novel, *Summer in the Greenhouse,* the predominant mood of lyrical reminiscence contrasts with the stylized and fantastic plotting on which it is hinged. The middle-aged Claire Peachey recounts the sad love affair of her youth to a child and a young man who see ''not so much Mrs. Peachey's house and the walks and flower-beds about it as the buildings and monuments of Florence beneath an identical burning sky in that June of 1895.'' Mrs. Peachey is observed through the granddaughter of her old admirer; the child's quest for the Fra Angelico painting of ''the face,'' which she has seen reproduced, brings the adults together after forty-five years. Though anticipated throughout the book, this encounter remains a *tour de force,* upstaged by the radio announcement of Britain's entry into World War II.

Mavor extends the range of broad comedy in *The Temple of Flora,* which switches from rural fun reminiscent of *Cold Comfort Farm* to sometimes serious theology. Dinah Gage's aspirations to reform the semipagan village of Thrussel are complicated by her tangling with a local youth. In a heavily symbolic but hilarious climax, a bull disrupts the harvest festival, which has already transformed the church into the temple of the title. The novel shifts to a consideration of the eternal triangle in which Dinah now involves herself. In the closing farewell scenes, as she decides to renounce her married lover, Mavor successfully treads a dizzy tightrope between poignance and ridicule, with Dinah's wish for ''a sacramental relationship between him and me so that I could live apart from him with courage and a belief that I was doing something true and creative.''

In *The Redoubt* Mavor broke away from the third-person narration of her two previous novels for a mixture of first-and third-person narration which she retained in *A Green Equinox* and *The White Solitaire,* though in all three books the potentialities of this freedom are left unexplored. In *The Redoubt,* too, she extended her range of characterization with the publican Lil, who is her only full-scale lower-class portrait before the eighteenth-century figures of *The White Solitaire.* The novel is set over the weekend of the 1953 East Coast floods, as Eve gives birth to a child. Through flashbacks grafted on to the chaos of the floods and the proverbial reliving of the past before drowning, the flickering validity of a childhood friendship comes across, ''a kind of marriage in that childhood moment.'' Mavor's most experimental writing in any of her novels shows Eve's mind, in labour, ranging across history in hysterical metaphors for her life and predicament now. But the novel's ending is facile as Eve, who wishes that the father of her child were not her abandoned husband, but Faber, her rediscovered—married—and now drowned childhood friend and recent lover, resolves that ''it is out of his death that my own life must be remade somehow.''

A Green Equinox ends on a similar note after a death: '''Now,' she had said, 'do without me!''' Earlier, it had ranged even wider than

The Temple of Flora, and fuses its diverse material better in an ironical circular structure. It follows Hero Kinoull's search for ''Heaven now'' in her successive loves for Hugh Shafto, the rococo expert, his wife and his mother, in Beaudesert—to be found on the same allegorical map as Thrussel. The novel partially resolves itself into a meditation on age, as Hero's third love is seen as the most lyrical; old Mrs. Shafto's gardens and model boats— ''a love for the miniature'' —recall Faber's in *The Redoubt. A Green Equinox* combines the bathetic comedy of saving the Bunyan Elm with a plethora of dramatic disasters—car accident, typhoid epidemic, near-drowning, drowning, and fire. Complete with metaphysical overtones, all this is crammed into six months which culminate in Hero's defiance of time; the reader has been initially forewarned of her ''love affair, sexual almost, with the lost past.'' The rococo, ''the worst and most provocative of all styles,'' subsumes all the ramifications of this tale under its imagery.

In *The Virgin Mistress,* the earlier of her historical biographies, Mavor affirmed that ''a human personality is not mewed up in its own life-span.'' She has an antiquarian fascination with objects, just as Imogen in *Summer in the Greenhouse* listening to Mrs. Peachey's story was spellbound by ''all the props of the play that had been.'' In *A Green Equinox,* the extended metaphor of rococo frivolity permitted her even greater licence for lyricism and satire.

The White Solitaire relates the life of the pirate Mary Read (1693–1715). This book tellingly musters a huge amount of historical and geographical detail as context for Read, whose roles included trooper in Marlborough's army as well as innkeeper in Holland with her husband. At the beginning, Mavor prints ''the only known biography'' of Read from Johnson's *A General History of the Robberies and Murders of the Most Notorious Pirates* (probably written by Defoe), though as there seems no structural rationale for outlining Read's drift into piracy in advance, it might have been better printed as an appendix at the end. If the rationale for Mavor's use of extended extracts supposedly from Read's journal is to point to the contrast between Read as seen by others and by herself—most of his/her life disguised as a man with consequent sexual complications—this technique isn't fully developed. Mary Read seems a less vivid presence in the novel than Eve or Hero in their contexts. In fact, Eve's and Hero's motivations don't bear very close scrutiny, and *The White Solitaire* albeit using ''given'' historical material parallels this interesting author's weakness elsewhere—over-reliance on exciting plot.

—Val Warner

MAXWELL, William (Keepers)

Nationality: American. **Born:** Lincoln, Illinois, 16 August 1908. **Education:** The University of Illinois, Urbana, B.A. 1930; Harvard University, Cambridge, Massachusetts, M.A. 1931. **Family:** Married Emily Gilman Noyes in 1945; two daughters. **Career:** Member of the Department of English, University of Illinois, 1931–33. From 1936, in the art department, then fiction editor, *New Yorker;* retired 1976. **Awards:** Friends of American Writers award, 1938; American Academy award, 1958; William Dean Howells medal, 1980; American Book Award, for paperback, 1982; Brandeis University Creative Arts Medal for Fiction, 1984; Ivan Sandrof award, National Book Critics Circle, 1994; Gold Medal for Fiction, American Academy of Arts and Letters, 1995. D.Litt.: University of Illinois, 1973. **Member:** President, National Institute of Arts and Letters, 1969–72. **Address:** 544 East 86th Street, New York, New York 10028, U.S.A.

Publications

Novels

Bright Center of Heaven. New York, Harper, 1934.
They Came like Swallows. New York, Harper, and London, Joseph, 1937.
The Folded Leaf. New York, Harper, 1945; London, Faber, 1946.
Time Will Darken It. New York, Harper, 1948; London, Faber, 1949.
The Chateau. New York, Knopf, 1961.
So Long, See You Tomorrow. New York, Knopf, 1980; London, Secker and Warburg, 1989.

Short Stories

Stories, with others. New York, Farrar Straus, 1956; as *A Book of Stories,* London, Gollancz, 1957.
The Old Man at the Railroad Crossing and Other Tales. New York, Knopf, 1966.
Over by the River and Other Stories. New York, Knopf, 1977.
Five Tales. Omaha, Nebraska, Cummington Press, 1988.
Billie Dyer and Other Stories. N.p., 1992.
All the Days and Nights: The Collected Stories of William Maxwell. New York, Knopf, 1995.

Uncollected Short Stories

''Billie Dyer,'' in *New Yorker,* 15 May 1989.
''Fable Begotten of an Echo of a Line of Verse by W.B. Yeats,'' in *Antaeus* (New York), Spring-Autumn 1990.

Other

The Heavenly Tenants (for children). New York, Harper, 1946.
The Writer as Illusionist (lecture). New York, Unitelum Press, 1955.
Ancestors. New York, Knopf, 1971.
The Outermost Dream: Essays and Reviews. New York, Knopf, 1989.
Mrs. Donald's Dog Bun and His Home Away from Home (for children), illustrated by James Stevenson. New York, Knopf, 1995.
The Happiness of Getting It Down Right: Letters of Frank O'Connor and William Maxwell, 1945–1966, edited by Michael Steinman. New York, Knopf, 1996.
Editor, *The Garden and the Wilderness,* by Charles Pratt. New York, Horizon Press, 1980.
Editor, *The Letters of Sylvia Townsend Warner.* London, Chatto and Windus, 1982; New York, Viking Press, 1983.
Editor, with Susanna Pinney, *Selected Stories,* by Sylvia Townsend Warner. London, Chatto and Windus, 1988.

* * *

The subjects of William Maxwell's major novels vary, but the sensibility that informs them is a Midwestern one. In both *They Came like Swallows* and *The Folded Leaf,* for example, the novelist is reworking and focusing his recollections of an Illinois boyhood and college experience. The materials he draws on in these novels he thus shares with somewhat older writers like Sinclair Lewis and Sherwood Anderson. But these novelists were involved in labors of repudiation; their work was marked by what has been called the ''revolt from the village,'' by a keen sense that the Midwestern setting was a stultifying one from which the writer, by a satirical and unflattering report, had to separate himself. This accent of mockery and dismissal is absent from Maxwell's novels, which render the texture of Midwestern life in the early decades of this century. It is an accent which is absent from Maxwell's *Ancestors,* a work of nonfiction which gives an attentive account of the writer's forebears.

In general, then, there is a cherishing of the provincial limitations that other writers have found galling. There is, in most of the novels, a precise if not loving recollection of the diversions and the limited esthetic taste that created upper-class, prosperous sensibility in ''downstate'' Illinois towns. *They Came like Swallows,* for example, tells of the impact of a mother's death on a decent and conventional Illinois household. *Time Will Darken It* is an account of a protracted visit which Southern relatives pay and the disruption that the visitors bring to what was a moderately happy family. *The Folded Leaf,* which the French critic Maurice Coindreau has referred to as the best novel about college experience, tells of the adolescent and college experiences of two young Midwestern men; it leaves them on the threshold of an uneasy maturity, a maturity far short of ideal, but the only maturity that is open to them under Midwestern conditions.

The clearest indications of Maxwell's attitude toward his American materials appears in two novels: *The Folded Leaf* and *So Long, See You Tomorrow. The Folded Leaf* is about the ''coming of age'' of two boys; the author draws explicit parallels between the boys' rather casual passage from youth to maturity and the ''rites of passage'' that anthropologists and students of comparative religion describe in the tradition-oriented societies they study. *So Long, See You Tomorrow* also deals with the friendship of two boys. It is friendship terminated by the sensational crime and death of the father of one of the boys. Here also Maxwell deals with studious attention to matters that other writers handle sensationally or ironically. Maxwell even allows us to see how he has collected his materials—old newspapers—as a first step to his imaginative reconstruction. Both novels contain controlled attention, free of animus.

The same sort of attention is offered adult experience in *The Chateau.* The American travelers at the center of this novel undergo contacts with an enigmatic culture—that of the French—which are a series of challenges that are neither mockingly presented, as in Sinclair Lewis's *Dodsworth,* nor offered as proof of American superiority, as in Booth Tarkington's *The Plutocrat.* Rather is Maxwell's prevailing note that of detached comprehension, the same sort of comprehension that the anthropologist offers the alien culture that he wishes to grasp. The anthropologist does not question the values of his ''informants''; he reports those values. Such is also the attitude of Maxwell toward the aspirations of the characters he creates.

—Harold H. Watts

McBAIN, Ed

See HUNTER, Evan

McCABE, Patrick

Nationality: Irish. **Born:** Clones, County Monaghan, Ireland, 27 March 1955. **Education:** St. Patrick's Training College, Dublin. **Family:** Married Margot Quinn in 1981, two daughters. **Career:** Since 1980 teacher, Kingsbury Day Special School, London. **Awards:** *Irish Press* Hennessy award, 1979, for *The Call*; Aer Lingus prize, for *The Butcher Boy,* 1992. **Address:** Kingsbury Day Special School, Kingsbury, London N.W.9, England.

Publications

Novels

Music on Clinton Street. Dublin, Raven Arts Press, 1986.
Carn. N.p., Aidan Ellis, 1989; New York, Delta, 1997.
The Butcher Boy. London, Picador, 1992; New York, Fromm International, 1993.
The Dead School. London, Picador, and New York, Dial Press, 1995.
Breakfast on Pluto. New York, HarperFlamingo, 1998.
Mondo Desperado: A Serial Novel. New York, HarperCollins, 1999.

Plays

Radio Plays: *Ulster Final,* 1984; *Frontiers,* 1984; *The Adventures of Shay Mouse,* 1983; *Belfast Days,* n.d.; *The Outing,* n.d.; *The Butcher Boy,* n.d.

Radio Plays: *The Butcher Boy* (with Neil Jordan). Warner Brothers, 1998.

Other

The Adventures of Shay Mouse: The Mouse from Longford (for children). Dublin, New Island, 1994.

* * *

Patrick McCabe's first two novels, *Music on Clinton Street* and *Carn,* garnered him little attention outside his native Ireland, but his third novel, *The Butcher Boy,* earned him international acclaim, not only making him a celebrity, but also marking him as a representative voice for a new generation of Irish writers. Like the work of Roddy Doyle and Dermot Bolger, McCabe's books express a break with what is normally perceived as the Irish literary tradition. His novels resist both the romantic nationalism of Yeats and the modernist mythologizing of Joyce, and, while they share Doyle's focus on the everyday lives of ordinary Irish citizens, McCabe's characterizations are anything but warmly sentimental. Indeed, McCabe's portrayals have more in common with the grotesques of Sherwood Anderson's *Winesburg, Ohio* than they have with the comic vignettes of Doyle's Barrytown trilogy.

Also, McCabe's characters, like those of Doyle, exhibit a fascination with American and British popular culture, being more familiar with comic books and television shows than they are with Irish history. In *Carn,* the title town's boom era is accompanied by a gradual assimilation of American culture, culminating in the opening of the ''tavern-cum-roadhouse,'' the Turnpike Inn, which is decorated with American flags and portraits of Davy Crockett and John F. Kennedy. But the establishment does not survive when age-old troubles violently resurface in the town. Francie Brady, the eponymous narrator of *The Butcher Boy,* peppers his story with pop references, often affecting lampoonish accents and phraseologies that accrete into a palpable—but never opaque—barrier between Francie and his stifling environment. Malachy Dudgeon of *The Dead School* woos his lover by impersonating Jack Nicholson and later chooses the Tubes' hit ''White Punks on Dope'' as his personal anthem, a telling choice for an effort at self-actualization that ends in addled dissipation. And *Breakfast on Pluto*'s Patrick ''Pussy'' Braden has a fascination with pop diva Dusty Springfield, but his dead-on impersonations do nothing to keep British authorities from arresting him as a terrorist. Thus, while McCabe's characters may often be ignorant or at least dismissive of history, they are nevertheless still at its cruel mercy. Their personal fantasies and delusions do not exempt them from history's nightmare.

Critics have sometimes taken McCabe's antic and darkly comic portrayals to be wallowings in absurd futility. And, while it is true that many of his characters make ineffective attempts to rebel against the seemingly predetermined failure of their lives, McCabe's explorations of the interplay of aspiration and circumstance make the final dispositions of his creations almost tragic, instead of being merely pathetic. Francie Brady's dogged innocence and irrepressible humor make him a compelling, even appealing narrator, and the early parts of *The Butcher Boy,* which portray his relationship with his buddy Joe Purcell, his mother's suicide, and his father's sense of angry hopelessness, evoke much empathy for a boy who seems only to be trying to make the best of an impossible situation. However, as the novel progresses, this empathy finds itself conflicting with an increasing awareness of Francie's violent madness. Despite his clearly psychotic actions, Francie's desperate quest for affection, intimacy, and recognition obviate reactions of complete revulsion. In *Breakfast on Pluto,* Pussy Braden's seemingly amoral opportunism, which culminates in his becoming a prostitute, and his insistent attention to frivolities amidst the violent political upheaval of London in the 1970s, are both made poignant by his desperate and pervasive longing for simple familial belonging. His transvestite lifestyle may be outlandish, but his dream, which is vividly depicted throughout the novel, is to be accepted by a family with open arms, saying to him, ''He's one of ours!''

McCabe's later novels share the structural ploy of being framed by narrators who tell of events in the distant past, often beginning their narrations by foreshadowing the violent climaxes which characterize his books. And it is these foreshadowings which lend an air of inexorability to McCabe's novels, despite their humor. But such inexorability does not make mere victims of McCabe's characters. What dooms them to failure is more than the force of historical circumstance; it is their own failure to truly connect. In *The Dead School,* two teachers from different generations grow to hate each other over what each perceives is the other's culpability in the destruction of their dreams. Yet their conflict involves much more than a generation gap. Their superficial differences only belie deeper correspondences in the two men, most notably a failure to successfully love a mate. Instead of allowing a connection, however, Malachy Dudgeon and Raphael Bell act out the truism that like repels like, with cataclysmic consequences for both. These deeper correspondences—the failures of love and aspiration—link all of McCabe's characters into a universe of lost souls, and it is a testament to McCabe's aesthetic achievement that he is able to wring both sympathy and laughter from such dark matter.

—Victoria A. Smallman, updated by J.J. Wylie

McCARTHY, Cormac

Nationality: American. **Born:** Charles McCarthy, Providence, Rhode Island, 20 July 1933. **Education:** University of Tennessee. **Military Service:** United States Air Force, 1953–56. **Family:** Married 1) Lee Holman in 1961 (divorced), one child; 2) Anne de Lisle, 1967 (divorced). **Awards:** Ingram-Merrill Foundation grant for creative writing, 1960; William Faulkner Foundation award, 1965, for *The Orchard Keeper;* Rockefeller Foundation grant, 1966; MacArthur Foundation grant, 1981; Jean Stein Award, American Academy and Institute for Arts and Letters, 1991; National Book award, 1992, for *All the Pretty Horses;* Lyndhurst Foundation grant; National Book Critics Circle award for Fiction, 1993; Institute of Arts and Letters award. American Academy of Arts and Letters traveling fellowship to Europe, 1965–66; Guggenheim fellowship, 1976. **Agent:** Amanda Urban, International Creative Management, 40 West 57th Street, New York, New York 10019, U.S.A.

PUBLICATIONS

Novels

The Orchard Keeper. New York, Random House, 1965; London, Picador, 1994.

Outer Dark. New York, Random House, 1968; London, Picador, 1994.

Child of God. New York, Random House, 1974; London, Chatto and Windus, 1975.

Suttree. New York, Random House, 1979; London, Chatto and Windus, 1980.

Blood Meridian; or, The Evening Redness in the West. New York, Random House, 1985; London, Picador, 1989.

All the Pretty Horses. New York, Knopf, 1992; London, Picador, 1993.

The Crossing. New York, Knopf, and London, Picador, 1994.

Cities of the Plain. New York, Knopf, 1998.

The Border Trilogy. New York, Everyman's Library, 1999.

Plays

The Stonemason: A Play in Five Acts. Hopewell, New Jersey, Ecco Press, 1994.

Television Play: *The Gardener's Son,* 1977; published as *The Gardener's Son: A Screenplay,* Hopewell, New Jersey, Ecco Press, 1996.

*

Film Adaptations: *All the Pretty Horses,* 2000.

Critical Studies: *The Achievement of Cormac McCarthy* by Vereen M. Bell, Baton Rouge, Louisiana State University Press, 1988; *Perspectives on Cormac McCarthy* edited by Edwin T. Arnold and Dianne C. Luce, Jackson, University Press of Mississippi, 1993; *Notes on 'Blood Meridian'* by John Sepich, Louisville, Kentucky, Bellarmine College Press, 1993; *Sacred Violence: A Reader's Companion to Cormac McCarthy: Selected Essays from the First McCarthy Conference, Bellarmine College, Louisville, Kentucky, October 15–17, 1993,* edited by Wade Hall and Rick Wallach, El Paso, University of Texas at El Paso, 1995; *Cormac McCarthy* by Robert L. Jarrett, New York, Twayne Publishers, 1997; *Perspectives on Cormac McCarthy,* edited by Edwin T. Arnold and Dianne C. Luce, Jackson, University Press of Mississippi, 1999; *Myth, Legend, Dust: Critical Responses to Cormac McCarthy,* edited by Rick Wallach, New York, Manchester University Press, 2000.

* * *

Many contemporary writers who enjoy an academic following are themselves academics, or are at least willing to address academic audiences through public readings or interviews. However, along with other notorious hermits like J.D. Salinger and Thomas Pynchon, Cormac McCarthy is unusual in that he evades the spotlight. Unlike Salinger and Pynchon, McCarthy's reputation in the academic world and with a widespread general audience has come about only in the late 1980s, even though the first of his seven novels was published in 1965. The delay in recognition for McCarthy is perhaps due to the fact that he doesn't fit comfortably among his contemporaries; his writing seems to connect best with an older tradition, one which explores the often tragic implications of the rugged individual trying to survive the hostile North American frontier. While narrating the lives of his rough-hewn outsiders, McCarthy subtly reveals a profound awareness of literary tradition; he is frequently compared to William Faulkner and Herman Melville. Yet McCarthy's ability to tell stories, notably his command of descriptive language and his unfailing ear for dialogue, ultimately supersedes the allusive aspects of his work.

The critical connection to Faulkner is most apparent in McCarthy's first four novels which take place in and around his native Tennessee, and which are characterized by Faulknerian prose style and themes. From the opening page of his first novel *The Orchard Keeper,* which describes how a piece of barbed-wire fence has grown and tangled itself throughout an elm tree, we are conscious of being in a world where something human and malignant has tainted the landscape. *The Orchard Keeper* is less concerned with detailing the life of its protagonist, John Wesley Rattner, than with showing the deterioration of the social order of Rattner's community. The characters in this community struggle in vain for some sense of cultural value; the implication is that revenge and survival instincts will prevail over any sense of community, or even common respect for others. The novel's ending involves one character's feverish search for a platinum plate rumored to be in the head of the corpse of Kenneth Rattner, John Wesley's father. This profiteering disrespect for the traditional sanctity of human life and the rights of others is evident to a greater degree in *Outer Dark,* McCarthy's second novel, which examines the result of incest between a brother and sister. The child borne of their incest, initially abandoned, becomes the object of the individual searches of Culla and Rinthy Holme. On their journeys, they meet with characters who exploit, mistreat, or abuse them to various degrees. The social order that was deteriorating in McCarthy's first novel seems entirely dissolved in his second. His third novel, *Child of God,* puts no more faith in the future of humanity. Lester Ballard, the protagonist, metamorphoses from a potentially dangerous outsider to a necrophilic sociopath, hunted by his fellow townspeople in a labyrinth of caves under Sevier County, Tennessee. Taken together, these first three novels provide a bleak vision of the rural South and its tragic history; they are also the source of some of McCarthy's most experimental prose, revealing his masterful command of idiom and gift for description, the beauty of which provides a stark contrast to the subject matter.

Suttree, McCarthy's fourth novel, stands apart from his first three novels in more than one way. Though it is also about an outsider drifting through eastern Tennessee, the tone is somewhat more affirmative. *Suttree* is considerably longer than its predecessors, and McCarthy uses the space to make the protagonist, Cornelius Suttree, human in a way that his other characters are not. Suttree, a fisherman, seems to have some regard for the future; his objective is not merely to survive the circumstances of his social condition, but also to embody some version of grace, in contrast to the band of misfits who surround him. His life continues even after incarceration, a period of mental illness, repeated nights of drunken brawling, and two failed attempts at love. *Suttree* is more humorous than McCarthy's other work, and notably less violent, especially when placed next to *Blood Meridian,* his fifth novel, which may be one of the most violent novels in recent literary history. It focuses on a group of mid-nineteenth century bounty hunters who roam the Texas-Mexico border murdering Indians for their scalps. Moving away from the type of a unified single character he created in *Suttree,* McCarthy depicts his band of marauders as archetypes—three are known as the judge, the ex-priest, and the kid. Amidst all the bloodshed—the same disregard for the sanctity of human life evident in McCarthy's first three novels—one can sense something intensely philosophical in *Blood Meridian;* these killers, so alien to the reader's world, represent a more fundamental element of human nature than we would care to admit.

McCarthy updates the landscape from *Blood Meridian* to the twentieth century in order to confront some element of human experience again in his most recent novels, *All the Pretty Horses, The Crossing,* and *Cities of The Plain,* which constitute the three volumes of ''The Border Trilogy.'' *All the Pretty Horses* contains McCarthy's familiar convention of characters bent on surviving unfavorable circumstances. John Grady Cole, without hope for a future in his hometown, sets forth on horseback with his friend Lacey Rawlins into Mexico, where they attempt to make a living breaking horses on a farm. The romance of this journey vanishes abruptly when they find themselves in a Mexican prison, where their survival is threatened by hostile prisoners. Billy Parham faces similar hostility in *The Crossing.* His journeys into Mexico, sometimes accompanied by his brother, Boyd, are necessitated by revenge and a sense of duty to family and to nature. The necessity that the youthful protagonist grow up quickly in the face of harsh external circumstances gives his journeys into Mexico mythical import. *Cities of the Plain* finds the protagonists of the first two volumes of the trilogy united. John Grady Cole and Billy Parham are friends and work together on a ranch in New Mexico. John Grady falls in love with a young, epileptic Mexican whore early in the novel, and the novel focuses on his attempts to unite with her. John Grady is reminiscent of the nameless archetypes of *Blood Meridian* in that he seems to represent ''the cowboy.'' The novel is a tale of the destruction of the cowboy way of life. The ranch is about to be taken over by the military, and the ranch hands spend much of their time reminiscing about the past. Additionally, the action is in this novel is subdued. Sparks of excitement are displayed, but for the most part, the painful death is being detailed. Seen in this light, even John Grady's love for the whore becomes a metaphor for this extinction and thus is doomed to end badly.

All three of these novels are concerned with borders; crossing the line between Mexico and the U.S. signals a change. This physical border is more than symbolic as the disparity of the two countries is often responsible for changes, but subtler borders are at play. McCarthy relies more on his ear for dialogue in these novels than on his gift for description; consequently, his recent prose reads more like Hemingway than Faulkner. Getting the story out also seems more important to McCarthy in the Border Trilogy, and consequently may be less obscure to a general readership than his earlier novels. But whether one chooses to read the denser, earlier novels, or the more accessible Border Trilogy, McCarthy is indisputably worth reading as heir-apparent to various American literary traditions and as a storyteller with a gift for both description and dialogue.

—D. Quentin Miller, updated by Josh Dwelle

McCAULEY, Sue (Montgomery)

Nationality: New Zealander. **Born:** Dannevirre, 1 December 1941. **Family:** Married 1) Denis McCauley in 1962, one son and one daughter; 2) Pat Hammond in 1979. **Career:** copywriter, New Zealand Broadcasting Corporation, Napier, 1959–61; journalist, *New Zealand Listener,* Wellington, 1961–62, Taranaki *Herald,* New Plymouth, 1963–64, and Christchurch *Press,* 1964–65; writer-in-residence, University of Auckland, 1986. **Awards:** New Zealand Book award, 1983; Mobil award, for radio play, 1982; New Zealand Literary Fund grants. **Agent:** Glenys Bean, 15 Elizabeth Street, Freeman's Bay, Auckland. **Address:** 59 Laurence Street, Christchurch 1, New Zealand.

PUBLICATIONS

Novels

Other Halves. Auckland, Hodder and Stoughton, 1982; London, Hodder and Stoughton, 1983; New York, Penguin, 1985.
Then Again. Auckland, Hodder and Stoughton, 1986; London, Hodder and Stoughton, 1987.
Bad Music. Auckland, Hodder and Stoughton, 1990.
A Fancy Man. Auckland, Vintage, 1996.
It Could Be You. Auckland, Random House New Zealand, 1997.

Uncollected Short Stories

"The Alternative Life," in *New Zealand Listener* (Wellington), 1976.
"Mothers Day," "John Harrison Is a Drip," "The Puzzle," and "Pansy," all in *Thursday Magazine* (Auckland), 1970s.
Waiting for Heathcliff (produced Christchurch, 1988).

Screenplay: *Other Halves,* adaptation of her own novel, 1984.

Radio Plays: *The Obituary,* 1967; *The Evening Out,* 1968; *ABC,* 1970; *Robbie,* 1972; *Crutch,* 1975; *Minor Adjustment,* 1975; *Some Without a Sigh,* 1975; *Letters to May,* 1977; *The Ordinary Girl,* 1978; *When Did He Last Buy You Flowers?,* 1980; *The Voice Despised,* 1980; *The Missionaries,* 1981; *Isobel, God and the Cowboy,* 1981; *The Ezra File,* 1982; *Thank You Buzz Aldrin,* 1982; *The Man Who Sleeps with His Mother,* 1983; *Family Ties,* 1986; *Waiting for Heathcliff,* adaptation of her own play.

Television Plays: *As Old as the World,* 1968; *Friends and Neighbours,* 1973; *The Shadow Trader* series, 1989; *Shark in the Park* (episodic), 1991; *Married,* 1993; *Matrons of Honour,* 1993; *Marlin Bay,* with Greg McGee, 1993.

Other

Escape from Bosnia, Aza's Story. Christchurch, New Zealand, Shoal Bay Press, 1996.
Editor, *Erotic Writing.* New York, Penguin, 1992.

*

Sue McCauley comments:

Writers for screen and radio are never asked to provide an introduction to their work. That may be why I feel more comfortable in the role of script writer—being taken seriously is a terrifying thing. Another plus about writing for screen is that, providing you have an IQ over fifty, you can sample the genre and feel needed. But (and I say this after many years in journalism) prose fiction is still the only medium I know where a writer is allowed to tell the truth (at least as s/he perceives it). And every so often that freedom feels hard to resist.

All three of my novels have been about modern social attitudes and personal relationships. They have focused on people of low-to-average education and limited financial means—not by way of a political statement but because, as a person of low-to-average education and limited financial means, these have been the kind of people I know best.

However, in style all the novels are, I believe, unalike. I was attempting different things and driven by different motivations. *Other Halves* grew out of personal anger and *Then Again* out of generalized fear. *Bad Music,* my third novel was, I suspect, something of a reaction to the cultural circles that had been prepared (somewhat diffidently) to embrace me on account of my having written two novels. *Bad Music* I wrote just to please myself and other people with bad attitudes.

I've been writing for a living for thirty years and I don't think I've yet got the hang of it. But I do have one simple philosophy—the reader is a friend and should not be subjected to boredom, posturings or … I would say lies, but lies are a kind of fiction. I'm afraid the only word that suits it is … bullshit.

* * *

Sue McCauley is from a younger generation of New Zealand writers who are influenced as much by popular culture as by the classics. On the other hand, post-colonial culture must rethink the stereotypic images that abound in the pop dimension, so McCauley's fiction takes on the dual role of bypassing academic chauvinism in literature and the pop chauvinism of mainstream culture's portrayals of minorities. In New Zealand, the Maori are the primary focus of the political correctness McCauley's generation has been applying to revise old attitudes toward oppressed groups that fall to disadvantage within the outdated hierarchies of contemporary society. In her debut novel, *Other Halves,* which received the 1983 New Zealand Book Award, McCauley draws parallels between the oppression of women and that of the colonized, indigenous people.

The protagonist in *Other Halves,* Liz Harvey, admits herself into a psychiatric hospital after her husband, Ken, convinces her that he has been busy growing while she has been, unfortunately, regressing. The clear-headed husband progresses at the expense of the supportive wife whose subservience to his goals becomes deafening. In time, the wife loses her sense of self and, ironically, even loses her usefulness in the one-sided partnership. The downward spiral of the disenfranchised begins. Liz leaving behind her marriage and acquaintances is due to the lack of respect shown for her remaining, burned-out shell. Liz's story can serve as an appropriate allegory for the effect of colonial rule on indigenous culture. McCauley implies this comparison when Liz befriends a sixteen-year-old Maori boy, Tug, who is also dislocated from his previous associations when forced into treatment at the same psychiatric facility.

Liz and Tug's problematic relationship encapsulates the rising challenge to the dominant discourse by both women and Maori. The discomfiture that results from the increasing awareness of social injustice indicates the push out of complacent official policies that result in privilege for some, and lack of education, and job opportunities, poverty and homelessness for the rest. In *Other Halves,* McCauley's characters are less comfortable with the process of improvement than the privileged in society are by the major political movements Liz and Tug's personal stories represent. One of the institutionalized women tells Liz, ''I dunno how the fuck I'm gonna manage here. It's not really my chosen environment.''

Reform and progress for the disenfranchised requires suffering by both ''halves,'' which, in *Other Halves,* takes on a multitude of double entendre implications. More than a novel of suburban neurosis or of women and madness resulting from the exploitation by her ''other half,'' the husband, and more than the revelatory friendship of a white, middle-class woman with a streetwise but illiterate Maori boy, McCauley's first novel indicts the institutions that render both powerless. The prescriptive story is not couched in the elegant, academic language of feminist Betty Friedan, instead, it demonstrates an acute ear for the vernacular while offering a clear understanding of the social issues which inform her fiction.

In *Then Again,* McCauley's second novel, her use of the Maori word ''Motuwairua'' is indicative of McCauley's corrosive wit. One literal translation for ''Motuwairua'' is Island of the Spirit/Soul, a place where the characters from a motley cross-section of society choose to live in order to escape from the pressures and demands of a materialistic, self-absorbed, corrupt and corrupting ''civilization.'' Despite the name's meaning, the novel's location is less utopic than representative of the underbelly in a microcosm of the larger society.

The protagonist, Maureen, is a single mother who escapes a sadistic marriage with her three small children to a tumbledown shanty only to find herself under the scrutiny of an impersonal welfare system and an anonymous, vindictive neighbor. She is worn down by economic and emotional uncertainties in addition to the demands made upon her by her children. Her response to her younger son's query about a beautiful artifact of nature describes her complete exhaustion: ''a large, perfect, transparent shell of which once may have been a cicada or a cricket,'' which she cruelly names for her son as ''a mother'' because, she tells him, ''See how her children have eaten her all away.''

In contrast to the faceless Maureen, the seismic, ebullient Josie, who is ''fair, fat and forty-six,'' refuses to marry her lover of seven years because she doubts that marriage is a guarantee against unhappy endings. Josie keeps her relationship alive with occasional partner swapping and frequent fantasy. Despite her amorous nature, Josie is well aware of the negative effects of patriarchal power in the henhouse, so to speak. McCauley describes a procreative rooster ramming the hens against the netting or trapping them in corners while duty to ''Mother England'' is served. Josie's rejection of male exploitation supported by the system makes a stronger political statement than Maureen's, the victim who is forced into rejecting it.

McCauley is careful to give her characters credible inner lives which provide suitable motivations to explore a variety of emotional concerns. The characters rage, hurt, long for empathy and friendship, are embittered and sensitive or outwardly secure in fringe communities, such as the stroppy group of lesbian feminist separatists found in *Then Again.* She eliminates the stereotypical by rarely allowing her characters to become pompous or didactic, and avoids overkill by diffusing statements with varying doses of self-knowledge, wit, and humor.

McCauley's third novel, *Bad Music,* has a deceptively simple premise, the expression of yearning for the Golden Age of innocence. It's selective reminiscence for a time when Elvis Presley ruled the air waves and would-be pop stars acted out rebellion in fantasy shoot-outs at the local cinema or played at the Town Hall reflects a clouded nostalgia. *Bad Music* is an investigation of the power of myth and the mechanism of popular culture when it persuades our perception to accept broadly drawn stereotypic images. This novel speaks, as do McCauley's previous two novels, for the inarticulate, and dissects with skill and elegance a society renowned for its taciturnity.

Hal, a musician, admits to becoming an ''old codger'' because time has wrought his creative expertise. He no longer plays with a band that sounds ''like a pack of uncoordinated roosters.'' Age and experience, however, come with a price and older musicians lack the verve that youth experiences as ''hearing'' music with the heart, when everything seems bigger, faster, and freer. The protagonist, Kath, supplies an appropriate metaphor for the phenomenon of recycled dreams with her business of selling used clothing. In the end, nostalgia produces tatty and unfashionable garments to cover reality. In *Bad Music,* the reality of the popular music business comes with rag-tag groupies, the drug subculture where a ''muso'' will inform on his mate in order to avoid a bust. Because her reality deals with fringe societies, her realism is often unfamiliar ground for most readers.

McCauley has been called ''a boundary writer'' because of *Other Halves,* which was made into a movie in 1985, and her more recent book, *A Fancy Man* (1996). In another 1996 book, *Escape from Bosnia,* she writes about the power of transcendent love in war-torn Bosnia based on a true story told to her by Aza King. The nonfiction account of the Serbian-Moslem betrayal in Bosnia and the love that blossomed in that setting benefits from McCauley's appreciation of social concerns and social change, and her general irreverence toward sacred cows. In addition, her ear for the vernacular and understanding of human nature provide verity and texture in the fictional explorations of her characters' inner lives. McCauley's writing discusses a politically correct revision of society with a characteristic wit and humor from the entertaining perspective of unlikely but real worlds.

—Caroline Steemson, updated by Hedwig Gorski

McDERMOTT, Alice

Nationality: American. **Born:** Brooklyn, New York, 27 June 1953. **Education:** State University of New York, B.A. 1975; University of New Hampshire, M.A. 1978. **Family:** Married David M. Armstrong in 1979. **Career:** Lecturer in English, University of New Hampshire, Durham, 1978–79; fiction reader for *Redbook* and *Esquire,* 1979–80; lecturer in writing, University of California, San Diego. **Awards:** Whiting Writers award, 1987. **Agent:** Harriet Wasserman Literary Agency, 137 East 36th Street, New York, New York 10016, U.S.A. **Address:** 8674–3 Villa La Jolla Drive, La Jolla, California 92037, U.S.A.

Publications

Novels

A Bigamist's Daughter. New York, Random House, 1982.
That Night. New York, Farrar, Straus, 1987.
At Weddings and Wakes. New York, Farrar, Straus, 1991.
Charming Billy. New York, Farrar, Straus, 1998.

* * *

Alice McDermott approaches each novel as if she were a novice writer since each, she says, is ''a new story and you have to find a new way to tell it and it makes its own demands.'' Nevertheless, her first novel, *A Bigamist's Daughter*, hints at topics and nascent stories which spill into future novels as well as introduces her characteristic style which critics describe as ''prismatic.'' Interested in seeing ''ordinary things, ordinary moments, in a variety of ways,'' McDermott achieves this variety by manipulating time and chronology. Her fiction aims not just to narrate the events, but to validate what one says about events. Thus, her characters tell or embellish their stories using hindsight refracted through new experiences. Their storytelling, and by extension ours, closely imitates the way memory works; one event spinning off another, not necessarily chronologically, but revealing much about the characters' inner lives.

In writing her first novel, McDermott's approach was ''to learn to write a novel.'' Storytelling, therefore, is the basis of *A Bigamist's Daughter*. Elizabeth Connelly, a twenty-something, cynical vanity press editor in New York meets Tupper, a wealthy southern writer with an unfinished novel about a bigamist. Caught in an attempt to help Tupper, now her lover, find an ending to his novel, Elizabeth tells Tupper personal stories while inevitably meditating upon others. Through these interwoven flashbacks, we learn about Elizabeth's mysterious father whose frequent disappearances were ''explained'' by stories—he was on secret government business. Elizabeth remembers her mother Dolores telling her yet one more time how she met her father, or Elizabeth remembers discovering how Dolores refashioned herself after widowhood and her death and funeral. In exchange, Tupper relates a family tradition of birth and death. Together, they finish her father's story, which Tupper appropriates, in front of an aunt's newly discovered tombstone. Finally, Elizabeth narrates her love for Bill, with whom she lived for two years, but provides multiple answers only for herself as to why, despite his charm, she left him.

McDermott continues the theme of separated couples and the technique of time manipulation in her second novel as well as a movie, the highly acclaimed *That Night*, a rite of passage story which, McDermott knew, demanded a strong voice. Here, through layer upon layer of memory, a first person narrator looks back trying to make sense of events she witnessed as a ten-year-old child. Through the prism of adulthood, she remembers a hot summer night in a 1960s Long Island suburbia not unlike those of John Cheever or John Updike, according to the *Los Angeles Times.* Teenager Rick attempts to find his sweetheart, Sheryl, who is pregnant and, unknown to him, has been sent away by her mother. When he and his neighborhood buddies pull her mother from the house, neighborhood men rescue her and Rick is jailed. The familiar bittersweet tale of lost young love introduces the narrator to the adult world; her narration captures the raw, wild emotions of the neighborhood upheaval achieved through McDermott's strong words and rich, complex sentence structure, described as baroque by critic David Leavitt.

When McDermott began *At Weddings and Wakes*, she was most interested in the family theme of ''what goes on between and among generations,'' especially what does not get passed on, what invents a family's heritage. First, she created a world she knows well, Irish Americans in Brooklyn during the 1950s; then the three spinster sisters who live with ''Momma'' and married sister Lucy grew organically to populate her narrative, for, McDermott says, ''the writing itself generates stories for me.'' McDermott excels at spotlighting individuals within large gatherings, such as the festive wedding of sister May, an ex-nun who is marrying Fred, the mailman, or the tragedy of May's wake quickly following. McDermott allows the stock characters to play out their roles so that gradually they coalesce to form a picture of the Townes family, a prototypical dysfunctional Catholic clan. Simultaneously, the novel's theme of familial love, despite all the quarrels and closed doors, strengthens amidst heartbreak and emerges through the observations of Lucy's three children. Compared to the Anglo-Irish writer William Trevor in *Kirkus Reviews,* McDermott also dignifies, to use her word, ''ordinary'' people whose ''ordinary'' lives are infused with an elegiac eloquence, the tone which dominates her next novel.

Charming Billy, McDermott's fourth novel, opens at a wake; nearly fifty Irish-American Catholic friends and relatives have gathered at a musty Bronx bar to eulogize the eponymous title character Billy Lynch. McDermott describes him as ''that stereotypical, lovable Irishman, drinks too much, talks too much, puts his arm around you at 3 AM, when everybody else has gone home and with tears in his eyes tells you how much he loves you.'' But no one could stop Billy from drinking himself to death. The novel exists because McDermott found this easily recognizable character appealing.

Everyone at the wake has been affected by Billy's alcoholism, especially Maeve, his long-suffering wife, and Dennis, his cousin and best friend. Using her prismatic approach, McDermott actually resurrects Billy through the stories each lovingly offers and which she filters through the unsentimental memory of Dennis's daughter, thereby adroitly avoiding Billy as cliché and again making each of the group essential. The story involves three generations of this tightly knit group and through their stories McDermott moves back and forth between present and past going as far back as World War II. Almost all their stories refer to ''the Irish girl,'' Eva, the love of Billy's life whom he met the summer after military duty at Dennis's small East

Hampton cottage. Eva returns to Ireland, accepts Billy's hard earned money for her eventual return, yet marries another. In order to protect Billy, just one among many such efforts, Dennis tells him Eva has died of pneumonia, and so commences the ''Big Lie'' which perhaps ruins Billy's life.

In her own evaluation of *Charming Billy*, McDermott, a practicing Catholic, believes that faith as well as storytelling play key roles in the novel. As her Irish-American characters tell their stories about Billy they believe they can make his wasted life important. But their stories are also about themselves, for they believe they can make all their lives meaningful.

—Judith C. Kohl

McDONALD, Roger

Nationality: Australian. **Born:** Young, New South Wales, Australia, 23 June 1941. **Education:** University of Sydney, B.A. 1962. **Family:** Married Rhyll McMaster in 1967; two daughters. **Career:** High school teacher, Murrumburrah and Wellington, Australia, 1963–64; producer, Educational Radio and Television, Brisbane, Australia, 1964–67, Hobart, Australia, 1967–69; editor, University of Queensland Press, St. Lucia, Australia, 1969–76; full-time writer, 1977—. **Awards:** Book of the Year award (*The Age*), 1979; Biennial Prize for Literature from South Australian Government, 1980; Canada-Australia Literary Prize, 1981; Banjo Award for Nonfiction, 1993. **Address:** P.O. Box 338, Dickson, Australian Capital Territory, Australia 2602.

PUBLICATIONS

Novels

1915: A Novel. St. Lucia, University of Queensland Press, 1979; New York, Braziller, 1980.
Slipstream. Boston, Little Brown, 1982.
Flynn: A Novelisation. New York, Penguin, 1992.
Water Man. Sydney, Picador, 1993.
Rough Wallaby. Sydney, Picador, 1995.
The Slap. Sydney, Picador, 1996.
Mr. Darwin's Shooter. New York, Atlantic Monthly Press, 1998.

Poetry

Citizens of Mist. St. Lucia, University of Queensland Press, 1968.
Airship. St. Lucia, University of Queensland Press, 1975.

Other

Australia's Flying Doctors: The Royal Flying Doctor Service of Australia (text), photographs by Richard Woldendorp. Sydney, Pan McMillan, 1994.
Editor, *The First Paperback Poets Anthology.* St. Lucia, University of Queensland Press, 1974.

* * *

Roger McDonald established a considerable reputation within Australia as a poet and editor before turning to fiction with *1915*, a novel which was an immediate commercial and critical success. The title is a reference to Australia's entry into World War I at the battle of Gallipoli, now seen as a watershed in the country's history and the origin of many of its myths of nationalism. The two central characters, Billy McKenzie and Walter Gilchrist, enlist; within a few months both of them are out of action but terminally scarred. Walter is a prisoner of the Turks; Billy has returned to Australia with a head wound that confines him to a lunatic asylum.

McDonald seems to be setting out quite consciously to question the mythic status of Gallipoli, pondering as to why the country's young men signed up so eagerly in the war though without coming to any definite answers. England is thought by some to be the Mother Country, inherently superior, though no one (including the novel's heroine Frances) is quite sure why; both she and her best friend Diana, plump for the un-English sides of their ancestry when pressed. War relieves the young men of the difficult business of dealing with women and sexuality. The two young men go, a socialist school teacher Tom Larsen suggests, because they are simply bored and attracted by the prospect of adventure.

Walter and Billy are carefully conceived as opposites. Billy is the larrikin, successful if sometimes brutal with women, unintellectual, a lethal sniper in the war but basically unsure as to what he is doing there. Walter plans to become a writer: ''If it came to a fight,'' McDonald tells us, ''Walter's only weapon, words, would be next to useless. Billy's weapons, sharpened on rough experience, could do their work swiftly.'' McDonald's background as a poet emerges in the nature of his highly mannered, self-conscious prose. Highly elaborate similes alternate with bland generalizations about the characters. There are frequent foreshadowings: ''Later Walter was to recall nearly everything Hurst said.'' The artful mannerism of the writing is often at odds with the brutality of its subject matter.

McDonald's second novel, *Slipstream*, seems to be based loosely on the life of a well-known Australian aviator, Charles Kingsford-Smith, but again McDonald is most interested in exploring and perhaps challenging Australian myths. His protagonist is Roy Hilman, superb flyer, World War I hero, stunt aviator in Hollywood but a man so taciturn that one of the more intelligent characters, the politician Leonard Baxter, claims that ''there was nothing inside him,'' and that he was ''a brave youth but had never arrived at manhood.'' It is impossible to judge the truth of Baxter's assessment because the novel offers a number of enigmatic portraits of Hilman without privileging any one of them. Hilman seems to exists mainly as an idea in the minds of a number of other characters who themselves are kept at a distance from the reader. Abandoning the poetic lyricism of his first novel, McDonald writes often in the tone of a dispassionate observer/reporter.

Rough Wallaby is the least demanding of McDonald's novels. It is an almost burlesque work about a group of knockabout characters and a racing scam involving the substitution of one horse for another. As is sometimes the case with McDonald there are almost too many characters to keep track of. McDonald defines the title as ''what you get when your dreams come true. Only nobody said you were going to like it.'' Or in the novel, ''what everyone got at the end, when they were forced down to living out their dreams.'' *Rough Wallaby* is a raucously Australian novel in a self-conscious kind of way. The characters are constantly cracking ''tinnies,'' talking in ostentatious slang.

Water Man is divided into two sections—''Departure,'' which starts off in 1939, and ''Return,'' set in 1993. The first half is associated with Gunner Fitch, a water diviner, married to Rosan who has fallen in love with one of Fitch's clients. William D'Inglis commissions Gunner to find water on his property but before he is able to confirm his discovery he has enlisted in the army and is blown to pieces at the siege of Tobruk. McDonald is, as ever, not averse to the poetic phrase, speaking for instance of ''thoroughbreds with hooves like lacquered half-coconuts.'' The tension between Gunner Fitch and William D'Inglis does not end with the former's death but is replayed half a century later with Mal Fitch and Ida D'Inglis, with a city locale this time, rather than a country one. McDonald makes his novel as complicated as possible by frequent cuts between past and present and from one character and scene to another, crowding his novel with a plethora of minor characters, and writing at times in a quasi-poetic style that strains for clarity and leans heavily on mysteriously recurring motifs such as the torch, the snake ring.

The critic Katharine England has noted the use of the four elements in McDonald's work—air (*Slipstream*), earth (*Rough Wallaby*), water (*Water Man*) and, in *The Slap*, fire. The ''hero'' of the novel, the weakly Tanner Hatton Finch, is a fire bug and again an intricate narrative tells his history. Disabled to the point where he is not expected to live beyond twenty-five, his annealed body is miraculously cured when he is accidentally stabbed with a knife he himself has stolen. The first half of the novel is set in 1954, though there are frequently italicized flash forwards to what we eventually discover is Tanner's (now Ted's) situation: he blew up the police station occupied by the sergeant who had tormented him but without knowing that it was occupied by a young constable, his wife and baby. Finch is sentenced to life imprisonment, never to be released, but eventually friends secure his freedom and the second half of the novel picks up Ted's life after twenty-five years in prison. McDonald strains for an ironically redemptive ending but the highly self-conscious nature of both the structure and the writing mitigate against it.

Mr. Darwin's Shooter is McDonald's biggest success since *1915*, winning the Premier's Awards in both Victoria and New South Wales. The eponymous shooter is Syms Covington, a man who rates only brief mentions in most biographies of Charles Darwin but who is elevated to the status of protagonist in the novel, dwarfing the great man himself. Adopted by Darwin on board the *Beagle* as a youth, Covington becomes his assistant, responsible for the gathering of many of Darwin's specimens, as well as the treatment and dispatch of them to England. He is also copyist and general factotum. McDonald cuts between the periods of 1828 and the twelve-year-old Covington, and 1858–1861, with the middle-aged Covington in New South Wales, worrying about, among other things the implications of Darwin's forthcoming book. The novel works by binary oppositions like these: Bunyan's *The Pilgrim's Progress* with its pious certainty versus the revolutionary skepticism of *On Origin of the Species;* Covington's own simple faith versus Darwin's growing distance from it; the death of a young boy Joey and the later death in Australia, in similar circumstances, of another lad, Charley Pickastick; Covington's tense youthful relationship with Darwin in contrast to Doctor MacCracken's similar problematic relationship in turn with him. McDonald throughout the novel constantly, if delicately, suggests homoerotic elements in the relationships between many of the male figures in the novel: ''You have been lying in brother Phipps's arms, and he has been a-whispering in your ear, and lo he has made a slave of you to his affections,'' Covington tells Joey.

McDonald's prose is again mannered. We get many jocular passages like this: ''She startled him, pulling at his clothes. 'Now we play hunt the dummy,' he thought to himself. Out flipped his Nimrod from his trousers, and she took it in her fingers, trilling 'Olay.' She favoured him, then, in such a surprising movimiento that he forthwith spilled his milk.'' It is also full of knowing anticipations—''When in later years MacCracken got through to a settled plan of life … .'' But the story is a fascinating one, researched with all the assiduousness that is a trademark of his work. Covington is an impressive creation in his complex mixture of animal appetite and piety, submissiveness and ambition, in contrast to the Gent, as Darwin is called in the novel, who is a less realized and less sympathetic figure.

McDonald has also written fictionalized biographies of two famous Australian identities, Nellie Melba and Errol Flynn, and has written for television.

—Laurie Clancy

McELROY, Joseph (Prince)

Nationality: American. **Born:** Brooklyn, New York, 21 August 1930. **Education:** Williams College, Williamstown, Massachusetts, 1947–51, B.A. 1951; Columbia University, New York, 1951–52, 1954–56, M.A. 1952, Ph.D. in English 1961. **Military Service:** Served in the United States Coast Guard 1952–54. **Family:** Married 1) Joan Leftwich in 1961, one daughter; 2) Barbara Ellmann in 1988, one son. **Career:** Instructor and assistant professor of English, University of New Hampshire, Durham, 1956–62. Since 1964 professor of English, Queens College, City University of New York. Visiting professor, Johns Hopkins University, Baltimore, 1976, Columbia University, 1978, University of Paris, 1981, and New York University, 1984; Visiting Scholar, Temple University, Philadelphia, 1991. Writer-in-residence, Northwestern University, Evanston, Illinois, 1977; Hurst Professor, Washington University, St. Louis, 1979. Lives in New York City. **Awards:** Rockefeller grant, 1968; Ingram-Merrill Foundation grant, 1970, 1985; Creative Artists Public Service grant, 1973; National Endowment for the Arts fellowship, 1973, 1986; Guggenheim fellowship, 1976; American Academy award, 1977; D.H. Lawrence fellowship, 1979. **Agent:** Melanie Jackson Agency, 250 West 57th Street, New York, New York 10107, U.S.A.

Publications

Novels

A Smuggler's Bible. New York, Harcourt Brace, 1966; London, Deutsch, 1968.

Hind's Kidnap: A Pastoral on Familiar Airs. New York, Harper, 1969; London, Blond, 1970.

Ancient History. New York, Knopf, 1971.

Lookout Cartridge. New York, Knopf, 1974.

Plus. New York, Knopf, 1977.

Ship Rock, A Place: From Women and Men, A Novel in Progress. Concord, New Hampshire, Ewert, 1980.

Women and Men. New York, Knopf, 1987.

The Letter Left to Me. New York, Knopf, 1988.

Uncollected Short Stories

"The Accident," in *New American Review 2,* edited by Theodore Solotaroff. New York, New American Library, 1968.
"The Future," in *The Best American Short Stories 1981,* edited by Hortense Calisher and Shannon Ravenel. Boston, Houghton Mifflin, 1981.
"The King's Reforms," in *New York Journal of the Arts,* Spring 1981.
"The Departed Tenant," in *New Yorker,* 23 November 1981.
"The Man with the Bag Full of Boomerangs in the Bois de Boulogne," in *Partisan Review* (Boston), vol. 51, no. 1, 1984.
"Preparations for Search," in *Formations* (Wilmette, Illinois), Spring 1984.
"Daughter of the Revolution," in *Prize Stories 1985,* edited by William Abrahams. New York, Doubleday, 1985.
"Canoe Repair," in *Review of Contemporary Fiction* (Elmwood Park, Illinois), Spring 1990.

*

Manuscript Collection: Middlebury College, Vermont.

Critical Studies: "Joseph McElroy Issue" of *Review of Contemporary Fiction* (Elmwood Park, Illinois), Spring 1990 (includes bibliography by Steven Moore); *Conspiracy and Paranoia in Contemporary American Fiction: The Works of Don DeLillo and Joseph McElroy* by Steffen Hantke, Frankfurt am Main and New York, P. Lang, 1994.

* * *

Joseph McElroy explores the many implications of symmetries between the behavior of electrons and the behavior of humans. The flow of traffic in our cities, the pulse of blood through one's aorta, the dash of information through a computer from keyboard to printout: McElroy adumbrates these analogies, and assesses their intent. This is, of course, in addition to the imaginative depth and human scope that we have a right to expect from one of the major writers of the period.

A Smuggler's Bible introduced McElroy's first readers to a new world of narrative discontinuities, multiple viewpoints, and a heightened modernist sense that the telling is inseparable from the tale. Eight numbered chapters are divided from each other by discursive intrusions from a witty if disembodied narrator. David Brooke, on board ship from New York to London, is determined to bring coherence to seven autobiographical manuscripts he has written himself. Formally, then, we are in a universe parallel to that of Doris Lessing's *The Golden Notebook,* but the narrative mentality is considerably wider-ranging and more freely associative in McElroy. The novel's title refers to a hollowed-out copy of a Bible used for purposes of contraband; McElroy fills it with a trove of metaphoric readings for the ways in which we smuggle meanings beneath a host of impostures in daily life.

In *Hind's Kidnap: A Pastoral on Familiar Airs* Jack Hind, a six-foot-seven New Yorker, is obsessed with the kidnapping, seven years earlier, of a four-year-old boy named Hershey Laurel. Hind spends the novel accumulating clues—some of them imagined, some apparently real—in an effort to solve the crime. It emerges that sleuthing means to dislodge information from its context—that the very act of perception qualifies as a kind of kidnapping. McElroy uses such master metaphors as smuggling, in the first novel, and kidnapping here, to cast a polarized light over the action which revolves prismatically for the reader's surprise, recognition, and delight.

Ancient History, as McElroy has described in a remarkable self-study ("Neural Neighborhoods and Other Concrete Abstracts," *TriQuarterly,* Fall 1975), extrapolates certain concepts of time and narrative form that he learned from Michel Butor's novel *Degrees.* "Concrete abstracts" may define the characters as well as the plot, since the principals are named, alphabetically, Al, Bob, Cy, and Dom. Upon Dom's death, Cy begins to examine the lives of Bob, a city dweller, and Al, a country boy. The novel explores spatial relationships analogous to field theory in physics; its subtitle, accordingly, denotes "a new time, or state like time, or state of being outside or beside time."

Lookout Cartridge may well be McElroy's masterpiece; of his seven novels to date, it is the one most often compared to William Gaddis's *The Recognitions* and Thomas Pynchon's *Gravity's Rainbow.* It concerns the efforts by one Cartwright to track down the thief of several rolls of film from a clandestinely shot movie which may or may not have captured scenes of political crime. The locations shift speedily and often between New York, London, and Stonehenge, where part of the film was shot, as the narrative, following Cartwright's thoughts closely, veers from the comically pedantic to the cosmically profound. Analog and digital models of computing are presented as analogies of human fate and freedom, and the concept of human divinity itself glimmers behind much of the action. In the opinion of many, *Lookout Cartridge* is one of the most unjustly overlooked novels in the American canon. Amid much else it offers a knowledgeable survey of the mindsets of London and New York. The novel suspends itself, figuratively speaking, on an airplane's flightpath between the English and the American, much as *A Smuggler's Bible* had done by ship. McElroy's Anglo-American binocularity recalls that of Henry James.

Plus, offering in its title to negate the negators, is the most abstract of McElroy's already challenging fiction. The main character is called IMP PLUS where IMP stands for "Interplanetary Monitoring Platform." "He" has been distilled from a disembodied human brain, a conceit reminiscent of Isaac Asimov's "positronic brain."

The novel's strangely unnerving conclusion mentions "a power raised to wholeness by camouflage," adding camouflage to smuggling and kidnapping as master metaphors for the dishonesty of consciousness. *Plus* suggests an artificial angel—a high-tech, human artifact that manages a plausible mimesis of something divine. Lessing, in other ways entirely different, neighbors McElroy in "intellectual science fiction" too.

Women and Men (another way, *inter alia,* of saying "plus") comprises 1192 pages, and not for that reason alone McElroy's sixth novel, upon its publication in 1987, invited comparisons both to Joyce's major work and to that of Tolstoy. The electron model suggests polarity, so McElroy slips over his lens the polarizing filter of sex. How women behave, how men behave, a "division of labor" susceptible to extensive and minute study. Grace Kimball and Jim Mayn share overlapping orbits—they inhabit the same New York apartment house—but they never meet. Around and about and through them pass a large cast of relations both distinctive and familiar. Binary rhythms—such as the links and contrasts of knowledge, or the inhaling and exhaling at every level of life—animate a novel that itself claims to breathe. A chorus-like collective voice speaks in occasional interstitial chapters, called ''breathers.'' As before, McElroy eschews continuity, and seems to follow André Gide's dictum, ''*Ne jamais profiter de l'élan acquis*'' (roughly, never to take advantage of the narrative's momentum). The demands upon the reader, and the corresponding rewards, are strong.

A much briefer novel, and perhaps the most accessible introduction to McElroy's work, *The Letter Left to Me* tells of a late father's letter of advice delivered to the fifteen-year-old narrator by his mother. The narrator observes, with some particularity, his own reactions to the letter, the response of his family, and, when he gets to college, that of everyone around him—for his mother sends a copy of the letter to the Dean, who has it distributed to the college community. The novel offers a placid and nearly affectless surface, quite *à la nouveau roman,* beneath which ripples a potent pathos, the loss of father and the loss of missed opportunities.

McElroy's career attests to his refusal to confuse language with life, conjoined to a refusal to let life pass unwitnessed by words. His intelligence and achievement are unique in American letters.

—Brian Stonehill

McEWAN, Ian (Russell)

Nationality: British. **Born:** Aldershot, Hampshire, 21 June 1948. **Education:** Woolverstone Hall School; University of Sussex, Brighton, B.A. (honours) in English 1970; University of East Anglia, Norwich, M.A. in English 1971. **Family:** Married Penny Allen in 1982 (divorced 1995); two stepdaughters and two sons. Lives in Oxford. **Awards:** Maugham award, 1976; *Evening Standard* award, for screenplay, 1983; Booker prize, 1998. D.Litt.: University of Sussex, 1989; University of East Anglia, 1993. Fellow, Royal Society of Literature, 1984. **Address:** c/o Jonathan Cape Ltd., 20 Vauxhall Bridge Road, London SW1V 2SA, England.

Publications

Novels

The Cement Garden. London, Cape, and New York, Simon and Schuster, 1978.
The Comfort of Strangers. London, Cape, and New York, Simon and Schuster, 1981.
The Child in Time. London, Cape, and Boston, Houghton Mifflin, 1987.
The Innocent. London, Cape, and New York, Doubleday, 1990.
Black Dogs. London, Cape, and New York, Doubleday, 1992.
Enduring Love. New York, Nan A. Talese, 1998.
Amsterdam. New York, N.A. Talese, 1999.

Short Stories

First Love, Last Rites. New York, Random House, and London, Cape, 1975.
In Between the Sheets. London, Cape, 1978; New York, Simon and Schuster, 1979.

Uncollected Short Stories

''Intersection,'' in *Tri-Quarterly* (Evanston, Illinois), Fall 1975.
''Untitled,'' in *Tri-Quarterly* (Evanston, Illinois), Winter 1976.
''Deep Sleep, Light Sleeper,'' in *Harpers and Queen* (London), 1978.

Plays

The Imitation Game: Three Plays for Television (includes *Solid Geometry* and *Jack Flea's Birthday Celebration*). London, Cape, 1981; Boston, Houghton Mifflin, 1982.
Or Shall We Die? (oratorio), music by Michael Berkeley (produced London, 1983; New York, 1985). London, Cape, 1983.
The Ploughman's Lunch (screenplay). London, Methuen, 1985.
Soursweet (screenplay). London, Faber, 1988.
A Move Abroad: Or Shall We Die? and *The Ploughman's Lunch.* London, Pan, 1989.

Screenplays: *The Ploughman's Lunch,* 1983; *Soursweet,* 1989; *The Good Son,* 1994.

Radio Play: *Conversation with a Cupboardman,* 1975.

Television Plays and Films: *Jack Flea's Birthday Celebration,* 1976; *The Imitation Game,* 1980; *The Last Day of Summer,* from his own short story, 1983.

Other (for children)

Rose Blanche. London, Cape, 1985.
The Daydreamer. London, Cape, and New York, HarperCollins, 1994.

*

Critical Studies: ''*The Cement Garden* d'Ian McEwan'' by Max Duperray, in *Études Anglaises* (Paris), vol. 35, no. 4, 1982; ''McEwan/Barthes'' by David Sampson, in *Southern Review* (Adelaide), March 1984; *Ian McEwan* by Kiernan Ryan, Plymouth, Northcote House, 1994; *Ian McEwan* by Jack Slay, Jr., New York, Twayne Publishers, 1996.

* * *

Ian McEwan gained notoriety early in his career for his shocking and often disquieting subject matter. Child sexuality, murder, and bizarre characters became even more disturbing because of the unemotional, matter-of-fact manner in which they were described. While his work has matured, McEwan has not lost his ability to shock his readers and the loss of innocence that motivated much of his early work is still a prominent theme. McEwan, a stunningly diverse writer, has written short stories, plays, an oratorio, television and radio scripts, screenplays, and even a children's book, but the novel has long been the central focus of his efforts.

With the publication of his first book, a collection of short stories entitled *First Love, Last Rites,* McEwan was hailed as a new and exciting British voice. The disturbing and often surreal tales deal with a range of subjects, but child sexuality is a primary concern. One story tells of a group of orphans and their sexual initiation ritual, and another tells of a teenage boy's seduction of his younger sister. Though the content is sexual, the description is not erotic, but instead deeply disturbing. *In Between the Sheets,* another collection of short stories, was published next. Though it dealt with a wider variety of material, this book continues McEwan's use of shocking material.

The Cement Garden was McEwan's first novel and contains many elements familiar to readers of his short stories. Jack, the fourteen-year-old narrator, feels partially responsible for his father's heart attack, which took place while he masturbated instead of helping his father. When their mother dies, Jack and his siblings, two girls and a boy, bury her without reporting the death. They continue to live together, but their freedom and guilt send them into a descending spiral of bizarre behavior. This hedonism culminates in the arrival of the police while Jack and his oldest sister fulfill their incestuous desires in, of all places, a baby bed. The obvious symbolism here is present throughout the novel; children are being placed in adult situations. How McEwan shows them to react is frightening.

McEwan's next novel, *The Comfort of Strangers,* presents the readers with Colin and Mary, an English couple on holiday, who fall in with a local couple that they meet while lost. Though it appears so at first, their meeting was no accident. Robert, the husband of the Italian couple, is a brutish and abusive man. Though the couple disapproves of Robert's violent behavior, his influence improves their sex life. The situation soon descends into nightmare, concluding in murder. The novel, like all of McEwan's works, is beautifully written, thereby enhancing the disturbing aspects of the fiction. This novel's exploration of male chauvinism presents the reader with a new aspect to this troubling writer, but his obsession with the loss of innocence continues.

After *The Comfort of Strangers,* McEwan took a break from novels and short stories in order to pursue some of his other writing interests. McEwan returned to the novel with *The Child in Time,* set in the near-future. Stephen Lewis, a writer of children's books and a member of the Prime Minister's Official Commission on Childcare, experiences the loss of a daughter when she is abducted and never returned. He and his wife struggle to come to terms with the pain which soon forces them apart. The sexual imagery of McEwan's early work is notably absent from this novel. Even more surprising is the ending of the novel, which concludes on a hopeful note. Though their pain is not over, Stephen and his wife appear to be reconciling their differences. The focus of the novel continues a trend which began with *The Comfort of Strangers.* The characters still experience a loss of innocence, but the novel concentrates, not on the loss itself, but rather on the attempts of the characters to recover from that loss.

Another change for the author took place with the publication of *The Innocent.* Though on the surface the novel appears to be an espionage thriller, the espionage is more of a setting than a central concern of the novel. Based on an actual 1955–56 British-U.S. operation to tap the communications system located near the wall in Berlin, McEwan even uses real characters to flesh out his tale. The story, however, is more concerned with Leonard Marnham, a British technician at work on the project, and his relationship with Maria, a local woman with whom he is having an affair. Their love is complicated by Maria's abusive and usually absent husband, Otto. Predictably this complication culminates in the impulsive murder of Otto. In the ensuing attempt to cover up the killing, the two dismember the corpse and stuff it into two suitcases which they plan to dispose of. The grisly mutilation of the corpse is sure to convince any reader that McEwan continues to be aware of shock value. The subsequent, darkly comic attempts to dispose of the corpse are disastrous, and Leonard and Maria are forced to separate. This novel, like the last, ends on a hopeful note. Though McEwan seems unwilling to give his readers a simple happy ending, the two appear to be reconciled.

Separation continues to be a focus of McEwan's in his next novel, *Black Dogs.* Jeremy, the narrator, has formed a friendship with the parents of his wife. June and Bernard were once a young couple in love with much in common and a lifetime ahead of them, but a bizarre experience with the black dogs, who give the book its title, forces them apart. The incident deeply affected June and gave her an appreciation for mysticism and religion. Her husband, the rationalist, was unable to accept this change. The destruction of the Berlin Wall forms the backdrop to Jeremy's attempts to trace his way back and discover the truth about the incident which forced this couple apart. The novel concludes with June and Bernard's black dog story, and McEwan's trademark disturbing surprise appears.

One novel that stands apart from the rest is *The Daydreamer,* a book for children. This tale about transformations is centered around Peter, a ten-year-old boy who has a number of sensational adventures. That McEwan would write such a book is surprising considering his early works; however, *The Daydreamer* clearly demonstrates McEwan's remarkable versatility.

Enduring Love begins with the death of a man in a freak ballooning accident. The narrator, Joe, was involved and feels partially responsible. While dealing with his own feelings about the incident, he must also fend off the advances of Jed Parry, another participant in the incident, who begins stalking Joe. No one believes Joe's stories about a love-crazed pursuer, and even the reader may doubt Joe's sanity. The combination of experiences comes between Joe and his wife. The novel deals with a number of themes including the impossibility of objective knowledge, normalcy and lunacy, and love. A secondary plotline is even introduced involving the dead man and his family. McEwan skillfully juggles all of these themes and plots to create a powerful work. Once again, the novel ends on a hopeful note as the couple seems to be heading towards reconciliation.

McEwan's latest work is a dark comedy dealing with friendship, ethics, loyalty, artistry, morality, and even revenge. *Amsterdam* begins with a funeral. Molly Lane has died, and her friends and former lovers are together at her funeral. Two of the latter, Clive Linley and Vernon Halliday, are friends. Molly's long and painful illness preceding her death encourages the pair to make a mutual suicide pact should either succumb to a similar illness. As the two attempt to get back to their lives, Vernon acquires compromising pictures of Julian Garmony, another of Molly's former lovers and major political figure, and must decide whether to publish the pictures in the newspaper of which he is the editor. Clive, meanwhile, is struggling to compose a millennial symphony commissioned by the British government. The symphony has not been going well, and while in the grip of inspiration, Clive must make a difficult moral decision. Both characters' decisions end badly, and each character ends up despising the other for his choice. McEwan beautifully details each painful moment of their downfall. The ending is no surprise, but still manages to shock the reader. The novel winds up as an indictment of human nature.

McEwan's skill lies in his ability to get inside his characters and describe their thoughts and emotions. His skill at narration, description, dialogue, characterization, and suspense makes his novels difficult to ignore, and the sharp contrast between his beautiful writing and his often disturbing and shocking subject matter only serves to emphasize his skill. Issues of guilt, love, and fear are all involved with McEwan's primary concern with lost innocence. For

McEwan that loss brings self-consciousness, and his large body of work explores this theme in a wide variety of situations.

—Josh Dwelle

McGAHERN, John

Nationality: Irish. **Born:** Leitrim, 12 November 1934. **Education:** Presentation College, Carrick-on-Shannon, County Leitrim; St. Patrick's Training College, Dublin; University College, Dublin. **Family:** Married 1) Annikki McGahern; 2) Madeline Green in 1973. **Career:** Primary school teacher, St. John the Baptist Boys School, Clontarf, 1956–64; research fellow, University of Reading, Berkshire, 1968–71; Visiting O'Connor Professor of Literature, Colgate University, Hamilton, New York, 1969, 1972, 1978, 1980; Northern Arts Fellow, University of Newcastle, 1974–76. Lives near Mohill, County Leitrim. **Awards:** [AE] Memorial award, 1962; Macauley fellowship, 1964; Society of Authors Award, 1967; British Arts Council award, 1968, 1970, 1973, 1981; Society of Authors travelling scholarship, 1975; American Irish Foundation award, 1985; Galway Festival Tenth Anniversary award, 1987; Chevalier Ordre des Arts et des Lettres (France), 1989; *Irish Times*-Aer Lingus Literature prize, 1990; GPA Literature award, 1992; Prix de Literature Etrangere Ecureuil, 1994. D.Litt., Dublin University, 1991; Galway University, 1993. Fellow, Royal Society of Literature; member, Aosdana. **Address:** c/o Faber and Faber Ltd., 3 Queen Square, London WC1N 3AU, England.

Publications

Novels

The Barracks. London, Faber, 1963; New York, Macmillan, 1964.
The Dark. London, Faber, 1965; New York, Knopf, 1966.
The Leavetaking. London, Faber, 1974; Boston, Little Brown, 1975; revised edition, Faber, 1984.
The Pornographer. London, Faber, and New York, Harper, 1979.
Amongst Women. London, Faber, and New York, Viking, 1990.
The Power of Darkness. London, Faber, 1991.

Short Stories

Nightlines. London, Faber, 1970; Boston, Little Brown, 1971.
Getting Through. London, Faber, 1978; New York, Harper, 1980.
High Ground and Other Stories. London, Faber, 1985; New York, Viking, 1987.
The Collected Stories. New York, Knopf, and London, Faber, 1993.

Plays

Sinclair (broadcast, 1971; produced London, 1972).

Radio Play: *Sinclair,* 1971.

Television Plays: *Swallows,* 1975; *The Rockingham Shoot,* 1987.

*

Bibliography: *Brian Moore, Alasdair Gray, John McGahern: A Bibliography of Their First Editions* by David Rees, London, Colophon Press, 1991.

Critical Studies: *Outstaring Nature's Eye: The Fiction of John McGahern* by Denis Sampson, Washington, D.C., Catholic University of America Press, and Dublin, Lilliput Press, 1993; *Feminine Nation: Performance, Gender, and Resistance in the Works of John McGahern and Neil Jordan* by Lori Rogers, Lanham, Maryland, University Press of America, 1998.

* * *

John McGahern's novels create a world where domesticity is dramatic and the mundane is important, and where the most bland conversation is underlain with tension and emotion. McGahern's writing has an obsession with the home (both domestic and national) and the family; taken as a whole, his work is a revealing insight into the relationships between family, the individual, the state, religion, and education, especially in Ireland, where most of his novels are set.

It is in the style which he has found, or forged, for himself that McGahern's success lies. The language of his novels is terse, unflamboyant and pared down to the essentials. But, as the protagonist of *The Pornographer* says, "The words had to be mixed with my own blood." The superficial flatness of his prose manages to create a tension suited to the themes with which the novels deal, so that descriptions of everyday tasks, washing or working in the fields, can suggest melancholy or simmering fury. What initially seems a restrictive narrative technique carries with it emotion and commitment, and opens the way for a piercing and studied observation of domestic life.

McGahern's first novel, *The Barracks,* which centered on the story of a policeman's wife dying of breast cancer, was widely acclaimed for its sensitive handling both of the homelife of the barracks and, especially, of the suffering of Elizabeth, the main character. It was, however, McGahern's second novel, *The Dark,* which earned him a "reputation" (in a pejorative sense). The novel was seized by Irish Customs and banned in Ireland because it was considered indecent. *The Dark,* appropriately named, certainly goes further than *The Barracks* did in its portrayal of the violence and intense claustrophobia of family life. The father of the family, who is seen beating his son in the first chapter of the novel, is at other times sullen or contrite, while remaining at all times the center holding together the family. His stifling egoism, which gains its strength from the ethos of "family," is at once repulsive and compelling, and is seen best in his maudlin but pathetic sentimentality when he sleeps in the same bed as his son. This part of the novel is narrated, unusually, in the second person ("What right had he to come and lie with you in bed …"), effectively stressing the horrified distance between the son, as narrator, and his father, and putting a safer distance between the narrator and his past "self," to whom these events have happened.

The Leavetaking takes further McGahern's interest in "home" as an idea, and focuses more directly on Ireland and Irish institutions as a "home." An Irish schoolteacher, taking a year's leave (one of the variants on the title), finds himself in London and married to a divorced woman. The story is told within the framework of the teacher's last day at the school when he faces the inevitability of being sacked because he has married outside the laws of the Catholic church. But even here the magnetism of home is stressed; the teacher, when in London, sees a return to Ireland, despite knowing the consequences, as the only course of action, and he prolongs his stay until the last possible moment, not taking his last ''leave'' of the job (and the country) until he is forced to. Indeed the bulk of the novel is taken up with the long ''leavetaking'' (the death) of the teacher's mother, stressing the formative importance of his home and childhood. The novel ends with the teacher and his wife on the verge of leaving for England again, with the incantatory words, reminiscent of the end of Joyce's ''The Dead,'' that stress a final ''leavetaking'': ''I would pray for the boat of our sleep to reach its morning, and see that morning lengthen to an evening of calm weather that comes through night and sleep again to morning after morning, until we meet the first death.'' What *The Leavetaking* suggests is the beginning, in McGahern's novels, of a sharper sense of detachment from, of less unquestioning commitment to, the home and childhood than has previously been the case. England offers a potentially new perspective for both the characters of the novels and McGahern as author, though it remains a perspective very much defined by being not-Ireland/home, and leads to reflection on ''home'' in a new way, so that Ireland, Irish childhood and family remain the central concern of the novels and short stories after *The Leavetaking*.

Evidence of this is *Amongst Women,* which came at the end of a ten year period in which McGahern had published no novels. Again it is the family that provides the locus of the novel, a center around which McGahern is able to explore the male-female relationships within a household. Moran, the ''daddy'' of the novel, an old and disillusioned Republican, places ultimate faith in the importance of his family. As the novel moves towards the death of Moran, carefully, and with exacting detail, it studies the increasingly tense father-daughter and father-son relationships, showing the various degrees of detachment attained by the children. For its understated drama, its controlled prose, and its carefully drawn central character, *Amongst Women* is the most solidly crafted of McGahern's novels.

—Colin Graham

McGRATH, Patrick

Nationality: British. **Born:** London in 1950. **Education:** The University of London, B.A. in English. **Career:** Orderly, Ontario State Mental Hospital, Oakridge, from 1971, then teacher in Vancouver. **Agent:** Jane Gregory Agency, Riverside Studios, Crisp Road, London NW6 9RL, England.

PUBLICATIONS

Novels

The Grotesque. London, Viking, and New York, Poseidon Press, 1989.

Spider. New York, Simon and Schuster, 1990; London, Viking, 1991.

Dr. Haggard's Disease. London, Viking, and New York, Poseidon Press, 1993.

Asylum. New York, Random House, 1997.

Martha Peake: A Novel of the Revolution. New York, Random House, 2000.

Short Stories

Blood and Water and Other Tales. London, Penguin, and New York, Poseidon Press, 1989.

Other

Editor, with Bradford Morrow, *The New Gothic: A Collection of Contemporary Gothic Fiction.* New York, Random House, 1991; London, Picador, 1992.

* * *

The grotesque and macabre dominate Patrick McGrath's work, as his writing seeks to explore the dimensions of the bizarre, the pathological and the neurotic. In *The Grotesque,* the main protagonist observes ''that in the absence of sensory information, *the imagination always tends to the grotesque* ... I mean when I speak of the grotesque—the fanciful, the bizarre, the absurdly incongruous.'' The struggle to control hypothesis by incontrovertible fact, to restrain the imagination by empirical data, structures *The Grotesque,* as well as many of the short stories in *Blood and Water.* The reader is frequently faced with the problems arising from a collapse of the distinctions between reality and illusion. McGrath's most recent novel *Spider,* a riveting suspense narrative, also explores the motives of the murderer, the insane, and the causes of psychological trauma.

McGrath's collection *Blood and Water* is a fresh approach to the Gothic genre, the deft combination of horror and comedy striving after what he terms an ''elegant weirdness.'' With speaking boots, talking flies, blood-drinking humans, severed hands, putrefying angels, psychopathic killers, and such classic horror-story locations as the lonely country inn, the isolated mansion, the prison, and the remote English public school, these stories construct a fiction which is both compulsive and intriguing. While there are aspects of these stories which suggest a consciously stylized treatment of the supernatural, this does not detract from their originality of conception.

The Grotesque continues this fascination with murder and mystery. It is part suspense thriller, part horror story, part detective story. The narrative is related retrospectively (if somewhat improbably) by a severely physically and mentally disabled country gentleman bound to a wheelchair, Sir Hugo Crook, who reflects upon the series of bizarre events that followed the employment of Fledge the new butler. The murder of Sidney Giblet, Sir Hugo's prospective son-in-law, emerges as the first step in a devious strategy of a *coup d'état* in the Crook household, during which Fledge seduces Sir Hugo's wife, causes Sir Hugo to be severely paralysed and ultimately manages to supplant Sir Hugo as lord of the manor. Sir Hugo's gardener and longtime friend, George Lecky, is framed and wrongly convicted of the murder, despite the efforts of various characters to save him from execution.

The Grotesque frequently involves itself in philosophical speculation, pondering the nature and materiality of the ''self,'' particularly as Sir Hugo is pronounced ''ontologically dead'' in the wheelchair. These existential speculations occur as the result of the attempt to establish the events to which Sir Hugo is witness, as a form of order: ''Retrospection does yield order, no doubt about that, but I wonder if this order isn't perhaps achieved solely as a function of the remembering mind, which of its very nature tends to yield order.'' For challenge to social order and hierarchy are at the heart of the narrative. As a paleontologist, the predominant interest in Sir Hugo's life is the ''birdlike'' dinosaur that he discovered in Africa—*Phlegmosaurus Carbonensis*—and the prehistoric predatory behaviour of this animal increasingly becomes an analogy for the manner in which Sir Hugo is attacked and savaged by Fledge, ''in this case, calculated opportunism on the part of an innately devious inferior with inflated social aspirations.'' The novel presents the dinosaur world of hunter and hunted, transplanted into the modern peaceful rural scenes of the ''civilized'' home county of Berkshire. Thus, the novel is not merely a mystery-suspense thriller, but also a sustained, wry critique and analysis of the values of the landed gentry and the relationship between master and servant, where the traditional relationship is comically, but subtly and calculatingly undermined.

Spider, also continues McGrath's preoccupation with murder and mystery, but achieves a complexity and intensity missing from his earlier work. As with *The Grotesque,* one is again presented with the perspective of a passive observer, Denis Cleg (alias Spider), who is recording in a journal, his lonely, isolated childhood in the East End of London, seeking to piece together his life by the means of narrative, ''like a shattered window, in the quiet years that followed, fragment by fragment until the picture was whole.'' Spider's father murders his wife to make way for his new relationship with the prostitute Hilda Wilkinson, who proceeds to take over the household, and which leads to Spider's own breakdown and incarceration in a hospital for the mentally insane. The unexpected twist in the conclusion is well disguised by a complex narrative which throws out proleptic hints about its future direction, and traces the threads back to Spider's early life, as the narrative becomes a web that Spider weaves about his childhood: ''And oddly, as my childhood took shape, so did I, Spider, become more coherent, firmer, stronger—I began to have substance.''

The book is a study of both mental and physical cruelty, mapping the development of a schizophrenia resulting from the psychological trauma that Spider undergoes. Spider increasingly has a sense of doubleness, and erects barriers against the people he meets: ''I would speak and eat and move and *to their eyes* be me, and only I knew that 'I' wasn't there ...'' The crisis of identity becomes increasingly more forceful as Spider's journal progresses, since the difficulties of language and representation become part of the preoccupation with ordering the past and protecting a self-identity, ''for I am conscious always of the danger of shattering, which in turn makes me crave *control,* which is why the sensation of being formed, framed, *written* makes me so desperately afraid. For that which can write me can also destroy me.''

McGrath is a novelist whose fiction interestingly explores a wide range of ideas in a condensed space, and he has breathed new and vigorous life into the well-trodden paths of the Gothic and mystery genres.

—Tim Woods

McGUANE, Thomas (Francis), III

Nationality: American. **Born:** Wyandotte, Michigan, 11 December 1939. **Education:** The University of Michigan, Ann Arbor; Olivet College, Michigan; Michigan State University, East Lansing, 1958–62, B.A. 1962; Yale University School of Drama, New Haven, Connecticut, 1962–65, M.F.A. 1965; Stanford University, California (Stegner fellow), 1966–67. **Family:** Married 1) Portia Rebecca Crockett in 1962 (divorced 1975), one son and one daughter; 2) the actress Margot Kidder in 1976 (divorced 1977), one daughter; 3) Laurie Buffett in 1977, two daughters. **Career:** Since 1968 freelance writer and film director. **Awards:** Rosenthal Foundation award, 1972; Montana Governor's award, 1988; Northwest Bookseller's Award, 1992; Golden Plate Award, American Academic Achievement, 1993. Honorary Ph.D., Montana State University, 1993. **Agent:** Amanda Urban, International Creative Management, 40 West 57th Street, New York, New York 10019. **Address:** P.O. Box 25, McLeod, Montana 59052, U.S.A.

PUBLICATIONS

Novels

The Sporting Club. New York, Simon and Schuster, 1968; London, Deutsch, 1969.

The Bushwhacked Piano. New York, Simon and Schuster, 1971; London, Minerva, 1989.

Ninety-Two in the Shade. New York, Farrar Straus, 1973; London, Collins, 1974.

Panama. New York, Farrar Straus, 1978.

Nobody's Angel. New York, Random House, 1982.

Something to Be Desired. New York, Random House, 1984; London, Secker and Warburg, 1985.

Keep the Change. Boston, Houghton Mifflin, 1989; London, Secker and Warburg, 1990.

Nothing But Blue Skies. Boston, Houghton Mifflin, and London, Secker and Warburg, 1992.

Short Stories

To Skin a Cat. New York, Dutton, 1986; London, Secker and Warburg, 1987.

Uncollected Short Stories

''Another Horse,'' in *Atlantic* (Boston), October 1974.

''The El Western,'' in *Writers of the Purple Sage,* edited by Russell Martin and Marc Barasch. New York, Viking, 1984.

Plays

The Missouri Breaks (screenplay). New York, Ballantine, 1976.

Screenplays: *The Bushwhacked Piano,* 1970; *Rancho Deluxe,* 1973; *The Missouri Breaks,* 1975; *Ninety-Two in the Shade,* 1975; *Tom Horn,* with Bud Shrake, 1980.

Other

An Outside Chance: Essays on Sport. New York, Farrar Straus, 1980; revised edition, Boston, Houghton Mifflin, 1990.

Live Water. Stone Harbor, New Jersey, Meadow Run Press, 1996.

Some Horses. New York, Lyons Press, 1999.

The Longest Silence: A Life in Fishing. New York, Knopf, 1999.

*

Manuscript Collections: University of Rochester, New York; Brigham Young University, Provo, Utah; Michigan State University, East Lansing.

Critical Study: *The New American Novel of Manners: The Fiction of Richard Yates, Dan Wakefield, and Thomas McGuane* by Jerome Klinkowitz, Athens, University of Georgia Press, 1986; *Thomas McGuane* by Dexter Westrum, New York, Twayne.

Theatrical Activities: Director: **Film**—*Ninety-Two in the Shade,* 1975.

Thomas McGuane comments:

I write fiction in the hope of astounding myself. I am seldom successful, and have long ago lost interest in the rest of my audience.

* * *

Thomas McGuane writes a new style novel of manners, crafted for an age in which the signs of behavior have become a self-conscious medium with the name of *semiotics.* We cannot know characters until we understand the codes by which they function—Henry James established that truth in his own mastery of the novel of manners. But in McGuane's world manners have become a topic themselves, and as his characters posture in a display of cultural signs the novelist is challenged to sort out the active from the reflexive. It is the drama between these two poles which creates the energy of McGuane's fiction.

His first novel, *The Sporting Chance,* adapts the Hemingway code of sportsmanship and grace under pressure to contemporary times. There has been an apparent generational decline, as the descendants of a 100-year-old sporting club destroy themselves and the camp in an atavistic fury. Two main characters, Stanton and Quinn, emerge as the contrary tendencies within the club's tribal framework: the spokesman for order, and the shamanistic ''fiend'' who by exaggerating all tendencies to disorder provides the tension which holds the group intact even as it threatens to fly apart. As in all of McGuane's novels, there is ''a readiness for calamity … in the air,'' and expressing this sense allows the author scope for his best writing. Stanton ''thrusts'' rather than ''steps,'' and transforms the club's civil practice of sport into a primeval combat. When Quinn himself reverts to Stanton's beliefs, the cycle is nearly complete, and is rounded off when a time capsule reveals that the founders' genteel standards have been a sham all this time.

From the northern Michigan woods McGuane moves the action of his next three novels to the Florida Keys, ''America's land's end'' as he calls it, and within this context of intermingled exoticness and shabbiness he conducts his most thorough survey of manners. In *The Bushwhacked Piano* it is the region to which young Nicholas Payne flees with his girlfriend (who has decided to adopt ''floozihood'' with the ambition other girls her age would look forward to a prestigious woman's college). Payne has rejected the bland ''Waring blender'' world of his parents' suburbia, choosing instead to embrace the raw aspects of his country and its people with a sensuosity that infuses his prose. A motorcycle ride through a valley and out onto a beach is described with a heady sense of smell and sound; even an inventory of his girlfriend's room becomes a riot of unconnected materiality celebrated for its sense of being. ''I am at large'' is Payne's testimony to his role in life, and in his vision the extremes of America are created.

Ninety-Two in the Shade finds another dropout, Thomas Skelton, leaving college for a life of guide-fishing in the Keys. Here he finds two alternative models of conduct, and even though he knows one is a sure road to destruction, he embraces it with a sense of destiny. ''He had long since learned that the general view was tragic, but he had simultaneously learned that the trick was to become interested in something else. Look askance and it all shines on,'' which is Skelton's method for feasting on the manners of Key West while his own life rushes toward its destructive end. *Panama* transforms the typical McGuane hero into a rock star whose career and sanity are on the skids. Because of his inability to control his own poetic vision, he has destroyed everything of value around him. As a performer he is ''paid to sum up civilization or to act it out in a glimmer,'' and as his rock theatrics become more bizarre the culture rushes ahead of him. One of contemporary fiction's best insights into drug use, *Panama* shows its central character walking a tightrope between life and death. In lucid moments between the effect of drugs one can appreciate ''memory,'' which is ''the only thing which keeps us from being murderers.'' Yet destruction predominates. ''Something about our republic makes it go armed,'' the narrator confesses. ''I myself am happier having a piece within reach, knowing that if some goblin humps into the path, it's away with him.'' In this subtle rhythm of cultural malevolence lies the novel's fascination.

Key West proved to be a burnout for McGuane himself as well as for his characters, and his recent novels have been set in the harsher country of Montana, where nature conspires to enforce an isolated sense of stability and self-reliance on the characters McGuane now considers. *Nobody's Angel* finds an Army officer returning to his family's ranch, where he serves as the reflector of a narrative action whose language expresses his feelings of change and loss—from an empty water sluice which cooled milkcans before the supermarket days to a friend's Cadillac which is parked nose-up to the straw outside the barn. A devotee of lost causes, McGuane's protagonist invites danger and failure by falling in love with a married woman, largely because she is as unobtainable as the fantasy girlfriend he used to keep life at bay as a teenager. But as his barren West is peopled, he must flee it for a more pure legend of himself, living alone in Seville, Spain, from whence his old friends can concoct their own off-base fantasies of what his life is like.

With *Something to Be Desired* McGuane shows the ability to synthesize his work, using a Montana setting for the enactment of a carnival equal to any of the excesses of his previous novels. His protagonists have always gravitated toward living at the edge, and in this case Lucien Taylor withdraws from a conventional career and marriage in order to tempt fate by romancing the much wilder woman timidity kept him from years before. Yet even on the edge in Montana, where he begins an outlandish tourist resort attracting all types of crazies, he still finds that life is shrouded in a protective textuality. People relate via lines of dialogue instead of with meaningful statements, and roles are played more often than lives are lived. Yet Lucien is also a painter, and his artistic eye relates to nature better than to the thin, superficial social types around him, which gives him a higher goal.

Returning to ranch life from a life of painting motivates the plot of *Keep the Change* as well. Here protagonist Joe Starling faces several issues: the decline of his father's once grand ambitions of ranching and the consequent economic and moral decay attendant upon such lost hopes, and Joe's own attempt to recapture a style of perception from his youth which prompted his career as a painter. The key events for each center on the image of an abandoned mansion constructed in the last century by a would-be silver-rush baron and now fallen into ruin. Joe remembers how one of the few scraps of ambition and success remaining in the ruins is a picture still hanging on the wall, a painting that captures the purest essence of white. Having pursued a painter's career and now returning to save his ranch and place it in hands that will assure its future, Joe ventures back to the crumbling mansion to find that its painting, his ideal of perfect art, is not a painted canvas at all, but only an empty frame designating a blank expanse of wall. Thus even though Joe has recovered his ranch only to lose it again, it is the act of framing that remains important.

Frank Copenhaver, the protagonist of *Nothing But Blue Skies,* is a more sociologically representative Montanan. As a successful rancher and real estate developer he finds himself positioned to enjoy the fishing that is such an important element in McGuane's fiction, perhaps the most important in a major American novelist's work since Ernest Hemingway. Like the Hemingway hero, McGuane's has woman trouble, too, and having his wife leave him coincided with financial ruin and personal disarray. McGuane's genius is to play this familiar crisis against the backdrop of American popular culture (some of which is a response to Hemingway himself in equal parts adulation and parody), such as the scene where Frank and his equally distraught friend Phil listen to a radio interview with Dolly Parton where ''country'' equated with ''family'' and ''You could feel her dimples come over the airways.... As though each man were assigned one of Dolly's big breasts, the room grew calm. They gazed off in comfortable friendship, the ghastly weeping now subsided into tolerable ungainliness. They sucked down the bourbon.''

Since 1981 McGuane has published short fiction in a wide range of magazines. Collected in *To Skin a Cat,* these stories employ the same styles of quirky dialogue, behavior exquisitely mannered yet idiosyncratic to the modern American West, and metaphorical expression that have characterized his novels. Like his friend Richard Brautigan, McGuane delights at stretching the distance between tenor and vehicle as he draws similes from the most surprising places, as when a story's protagonist suffers ''a spell of dullness like the two weeks that make the difference between a bad and a good haircut.'' Such devices remind McGuane's readers that one of his primary interests remains in language, and how the subtle turn of it can reawaken attention to matters that might otherwise remain deadeningly familiar.

McGuane's progress has been to celebrate the materiality of his fiction—the lilting song of his characters' language, especially the minor ones; the mad fandango of their behavior, especially when it counterpoints the narrator's more inquisitive action; and the special atmospheres of the regions about which he writes. Like his protagonists, these regions are always on the edge: in the northernmost woods of Michigan, at the extreme tip of Florida, and at America's virtual disappearance into perspective in the foothills of the Rocky Mountains. Finding the right words for each makes his fiction a success of language and image, providing readers with an aural picture of life in these places and times.

—Jerome Klinkowitz

McINERNEY, Jay

Nationality: American. **Born:** Hartford, Connecticut, 13 January 1955. **Education:** Williams College, Williamstown, Massachusetts, B.A. 1976; Syracuse University, New York. **Family:** Married 1) Merry Reymond in 1984 (deceased); 2) married Helen Bransford in 1991. **Career:** Reporter, Hunterdon *Country Democrat,* Flemington, New Jersey, 1977; editor, *Time-Life,* Osaka, Japan, 1978–79; fact checker, *New Yorker,* 1980; reader, Random House, publishers, New York, 1980–81; Instructor in English, Syracuse University, 1983. Since 1983 full-time writer. Lives in New York. **Agent:** Amanda Urban, International Creative Management, 40 West 57th Street, New York, New York 10019, U.S.A.; or Deborah Rogers, Rogers Coleridge and White Ltd., 20 Powis Mews, London W11 1JN, England.

PUBLICATIONS

Novels

Bright Lights, Big City. New York, Vintage, 1984; London, Cape, 1985.
Ransom. New York, Vintage, 1985; London, Cape, 1986.
Story of My Life. London, Bloomsbury, and New York, Atlantic Monthly Press, 1988.
Brightness Falls. New York, Knopf, 1992; London, Penguin, 1993.
The Last of the Savages. New York, Knopf, 1996.
Model Behavior: A Novel and 7 Stories. New York, Knopf, 1998.

Uncollected Short Stories

''The Real Tad Allagash,'' in *Ms.* (New York), August 1985.
''It's Six a.m. Do You Know Where You Are?,'' in *Look Who's Talking,* edited by Bruce Weber. New York, Washington Square Press, 1986.
''Reunion,'' in *Esquire* (New York), March 1987.
''Smoke,'' in *Atlantic* (Boston), March 1987.
''She Dreams of Johnny,'' in *Gentlemen's Quarterly* (New York), March 1988.
''Lost and Found,'' in *Esquire* (New York), July 1988.

Plays

Screenplays: *Bright Lights, Big City,* 1988; *Gia,* with Michael Cristofer, Home Box Office, 1998.

Other

Introduction, *New Japanese Voices: The Best Contemporary Fiction from Japan,* edited by Helen Mitsios. New York, Atlantic Monthly Press, 1991.
Dressed to Kill: James Bond, the Suited Hero (with others). New York, Flammarion, 1996.
Editor, *Cowboys, Indians and Commuters: The Penguin Book of New American Voices.* London, Viking, 1994.

*

Critical Studies: ''You Will Have to Learn Everything All Over Again'' by Richard Sisk, in *Pacific Review,* Spring 1988.

* * *

Jay McInerney has been heralded as the ''J.D. Salinger of the 1980s,'' and his first novel, *Bright Lights, Big City,* has been called ''a *Catcher in the Rye* for MBA's.'' It might also be accurate to call McInerney the ''Fitzgerald of current fiction.'' In the same way that *This Side of Paradise* captured the spirit of the ''Jazz Age,'' *Bright Lights, Big City* earned McInerney almost instant fame for its timely chronicling of New York City's club scene in the 1980s, a scene that could be found in recognizable form in almost any big city in America.

Bright Lights, Big City is the story of a disillusioned young man who is trying to deal with the impending death of his mother from cancer, the breakup of his marriage to a fashion model, his addiction to cocaine, and his pointless job in the ''Department of Factual Verification'' for a large magazine. (The last is McInerney's sarcastic exposure of the *New Yorker*'s fact-checking department where he worked for a time). In the novel, the narrator travels from club to club in search of women and cocaine. McInerney illustrates how pointless life is for those addicted to the pursuit of sensation and the forgetfulness that accompanies that pursuit. In the end, the narrator has lost mother, wife, and job; but he has gained a sense of direction: ''I was thinking that we have a responsibility to the dead—the living, I mean.'' The novel's final scene places the narrator on his knees, eating bread. ''You will have to learn everything all over again,'' he says. The narrator must learn that life's true value rests in a place where hedonism is not the central altar.

McInerney's next novel follows the theme of searching for direction and meaning in life. *Ransom* is the tale of Chris Ransom, an American expatriate in Japan who is studying Goju karate and trying to come to terms with the death of his friends in Pakistan when a dope deal turns deadly. For Ransom, ''the dojo, with its strange incantations and white uniforms seemed a sacramental place, an intersection of body and spirit, where power and danger were ritualized in such a way that a man could learn to understand them.'' This is especially important to the narrator because, ''Ransom had lost his bearings spiritually, and he wanted to reclaim himself.''

Ransom is also the story of the protagonists' manipulation by his Hollywood-director father and his conflict with DeVito, a fellow American and ''karate-ka'' (Japanese for ''karate artist'') who is dangerous because he is ''the sort who made a personal contest out of a coin toss'' and who would ''stake everything on nothing.'' The novel moves to a climax on ''a wide stretch half way between the Kitaoji and Imadegawa bridges'' in Japan's ancient capital where Ransom and DeVito face off with Samurai swords.

Although Ransom's search for meaning in life ultimately is not successful, the disillusionment that motivates him continues to be McInerney's primary concern as one can see in his next novel.

Story of My Life is the hip narrative of Allison Poole who is caught in the sexual hedonism and committed shallowness of the 1980s. As Allison says, ''The first year I was in New York I didn't do anything but guys and blow. Staying out all night at the Surf Club and the Zulu, waking up at five in the afternoon with plugged sinuses and sticky hair. Some kind of white stuff in every opening. Story of my life.''

Story of My Life is an all-talk novel like Brett Easton Ellis's *The Rules of Attraction* or Norman Mailer's *Why Are We in Vietnam?* The novel depends upon pop idiom catchphrases. Throughout the novel, Allison asks her friends what the three biggest lies are. She remembers that one is, the check is in the mail and that two is, I won't come in your mouth. But she can't remember the third biggest lie until the book's final pages when she says, ''The third lie is, I love you.''

Allison is more than a representative character, ''a postmodern girl,'' as she calls herself. She is representative of a demographic entity. She, like Jamie Conway in *Bright Lights, Big City* and like Chris Ransom, is representative of a portion of a generation that wealth and privilege cannot protect from disillusionment and pain.

McInerney's next novel, *Brightness Falls,* is the story of Corrine and Russell Calloway, a Manhattan couple envied for their success by their friends. Corrine is a stockbroker who also works in a soup kitchen. Russell is an editor for a major publisher. Like the characters of his other novels, characters in *Brightness Falls* suffer from alcoholism, drug addiction, anorexia, and depression. *Brightness Falls,* like its predecessors, is a satire of the excess and materialism that are considered the hallmarks of the 1980s. Specifically, the novel satirizes 1980s big business a la Wall Street through Russell's failed attempt at a hostile takeover of his publishing house when an unscrupulous co-conspirator wrests power from Russell.

Three years after *Brightness Falls* McInerney wrote *Last of the Savages.* The novel's narrator, Patrick Keane, relates the adventures of his prep school friend Will Savage over a thirty-year period. Savage, the last of his family, is a rebel who seems bent on doing precisely the opposite of what is expected of him. Against his bigoted family's wishes, he marries a black woman and later begins a record label for black blues musicians. However, his actions are not strictly reactionary but driven by an underlying integrity, as Keane comes to realize.

In February 2000, McInerney published his sixth novel, titled *Model Behavior,* about a man named Connor McKnight who suffers from pre-millennial boredom and obsession with celebrity. Connor is McInerney's Jamie Conway/Alison Poole for the 1990s: while Jamie and Alison have too much time and too much cocaine on their hands, Connor has seen it all.

After *Bright Lights, Big City,* McInerney became something of a critical darling: the distinctive narrative voice of Jamie and Alison illustrated the way that the urban WASPs of the 1980s constructed their reality. Today, that narrative voice (found in *Brightness Falls* and *Model Behavior*) is seen as hackneyed, dated, or just old hat.

In addition to the three novels he produced during the 1990s, McInerney has edited an anthology (*Cowboys, Indians and Commuters*) and collaborated on a James Bond novel (*Dressed to Kill*).

—Tom Colonnese, updated by Drew Tidwell

McMILLAN, Terry

Nationality: American. **Born:** Port Huron, Michigan, 18 October 1951. **Education:** University of California, Berkeley, B.A. 1979; Columbia University, M.F.A. 1979. **Family:** Married Jonathan Plummer in 1998; one son (with Leonard Welch). **Career:** Visiting professor of creative writing, University of Wyoming, Laramie, 1987–90; associate professor of English, University of Arizona, Tucson, 1990–92; teacher of writer's workshop, Stanford University, Stanford, California; columnist and book reviewer for newspapers, including the *New York Times, Atlanta Constitution,* and the *Philadelphia Inquirer.* **Awards:** Award for fiction (New York Foundations for the Arts), 1986; National Book award (Before Columbus Foundation), 1987; Matrix Award for Career Achievement in Books (Women in Communication), 1993. **Agent:** c/o Viking Penguin, 375 Hudson Street, New York, New York 10014, U.S.A.

Publications

Novels

Mama. Boston, Houghton, 1987.
Disappearing Acts. New York, Viking, 1989.
Waiting to Exhale. New York, Viking, 1992.
How Stella Got Her Groove Back. New York, Viking, 1996.

Plays

Screenplays: *Waiting to Exhale* (with Ronald Bass). Twentieth-Century Fox, 1995.

Other

Editor, *Breaking Ice: An Anthology of Contemporary African-American Fiction.* New York, Viking, 1990.
Contributor, *Five for Five: The Films of Spike Lee.* New York, Stewart, Tabori, and Chang, 1991.
Introduction, *By Any Means Necessary: The Trials and Tribulations of the Making of Malcolm X ... Including the Screenplay* by Spike Lee with Ralph Wiley. New York, Hyperion, 1992.

*

Critical Studies: *Lauren Hutton and ... Terry McMillan* (video recording), directed by Luca Babini, Turner Program Services, 1995; *Terry McMillan: The Unauthorized Biography* by Diane Patrick, New York, St. Martin's Press, 1999; *Terry McMillan: A Critical Companion* by Paulette Richards, Westport, Connecticut, Greenwood Press, 1999; *African American Women Writers* by Brenda Wilkinson, New York, J. Wiley, 2000.

* * *

Enormously successful, increasingly over-imitated, Terry McMillan became a literary superstar during the 1990s. *Waiting to Exhale* and *How Stella Got Her Groove Back* cemented her status as the decade's preeminent chronicler of contemporary middle-class African American women's lives. Both books achieved tremendous financial and popular success and were transformed into Hollywood films, demonstrating her appeal with a multitude of audiences. McMillan is not an overnight success, however. Her first novel, *Mama*, was the culmination of years of preparation. Her training in journalism at UC Berkley in the 1970s no doubt influenced the realism common to her novels; certainly it was during her time there that she began to write creatively, publishing her first short story. Likewise, McMillan's ability to create compelling visual scenes that are so well suited to cinematic treatment has been similarly attributed to her graduate studies in film at Columbia University.

McMillan's first novel, *Mama*, is the story of Mildred Peacock, who throws out her alcoholic husband and struggles to raise five children alone. The story is a familiar one: a feisty woman attempts to retain her sense of self while struggling for economic survival and negotiating the demands of family. However, McMillan's novel is complicated by the historical specificity of black women's lives. *Mama* is at once a response to the myth of the black welfare queen that gained significant cultural currency in the 1980s, and the earlier image of a castrating black woman popularized by the now infamous Moynihan Report. The character of Mildred provides a counter-image to these stereotypes: she is complex, dignified, and committed to raising her children to be capable, responsible adults. In asserting Mildred's dedication to her children and their future as inextricable from her personal success, both the book and its protagonist are revealed to have roots in the racial uplift ideology that has historically characterized much of African American women's literature. While the novel occasionally succumbs to the lack of focus common to first novels, one cannot fault its intervention in existing popular representations of black women, or resist the appeal of its energetic protagonist. Not surprisingly, *Mama* received an award for fiction from the Before Columbus Foundation.

With the publication of *Mama* McMillan asserted herself as a force with which to be reckoned. In the face of indifference from her publishers, McMillan launched an aggressive one-woman marketing campaign, sending out thousands of letters, primarily to black organizations, colleges, universities, and bookstores, urging them to promote her novel. Her persistence paid off, and with the publication of her second novel, *Disappearing Acts*, McMillan proved to have an established base of enthusiastic fans.

Disappearing Acts returns to McMillan's thematic imperative of creating counter-narratives to mainstream images of African American women—and men. The novel alternates between the voices of Zora Banks, a music teacher, and Franklin Swift, the construction worker with whom she falls in love. While McMillan has been accused of relying on unsympathetic male characters to prop up her female characters' dilemmas, Franklin is a fully realized three-dimensional individual whose humanity—like Zora's—the reader connects with through extended introspective passages. The alternating narrative results in a novel that is not just a study of two individuals, but is also a consideration of relationships and romance in the modern world. An antidote to the glut of popular novels featuring white women and their quest for love, *Disappearing Acts* is a consideration of the dynamics of heterosexual relationships for African American men and women. The novel furthermore functions as a corrective to the lack of solidly middle-class African American heroines within this genre, empowering black female readers by allowing them to see their own reality reflected.

Throughout her exploration of the lives of African American middle-class women, McMillan has refused to create characters who are victims, instead preferring to concentrate on women who assert their agency and are willing to tackle adversity with determination and spunk. Her third novel, *Waiting to Exhale*, focuses on four such women. It is not the plot that carries this novel, but rather the portrait of female friendships that is so compelling. The relationship between the four women who sustain and nurture each other through heartbreak and loneliness may not be as dramatic as their relationships with men, but it is ultimately more convincing and, the novel suggests, more enduring. With over four million copies sold, the novel clearly struck a chord with American readers who identified with the frustrated desires, betrayals, and personal triumphs experienced by its protagonists.

Embraced by the popular press and the mainstream reading public, McMillan has yet to achieve widespread critical recognition, whether from the literary academy or known African American intellectual women like Alice Walker and Toni Morrison. However, the instant success of *How Stella Got Her Groove Back* attests to the fact that while this kind of recognition may not be forthcoming, it is not really relevant to her fans. Like all of McMillan's fiction to date, the work had as its seed an element of the autobiographical, expanded and reworked via the author's imagination. Like the protagonist, Stella, an emotionally depleted McMillan also took a vacation to Jamaica to recharge and unexpectedly fell in love with a young man nearly half her age. The experience led to her writing an intense stream-of-conscious narrative that charts the ennui and rebirth of one woman. Despite her assertive independence and financial empowerment—she is *very* wealthy—Stella has lost her sense of self. Through the restorative power of love—and sex—Stella is able to reassert herself and her desires as being more important than the vision of success that she previously embodied. A reversal of her second novel, where McMillan charted how love can make one lose one's self, this novel is nevertheless not so uncritical as to ignore the difficulties posed by its primary relationship and the differences between the characters and their situations in life. This does not mean, however, that the representation of the Caribbean as an imperialist outpost for Western consumption receives sustained consideration, unlike *Praisesong for the Widow*, by fellow African American author Paule Marshall. While she most definitely critiques white American racism and its impact on her heroines, McMillan also endows her African American heroines with many of white middle-class America's values, asserting their right to hold them without apologizing.

Currently McMillan devotees are awaiting the publication of her much anticipated fifth novel, *A Day Late & A Dollar Short*, which returns to the themes of family and community through a family headed by a loving mother, and populated by siblings who must work out their own fraught relationships, rivalries, and jealousies. *A Day Late & A Dollar Short* promises to once again assert McMillan's recurring theme: that personal relationships are the foundation of African American individual and communal success.

—Jennifer Harris

McMURTRY, Larry (Jeff)

Nationality: American. **Born:** Wichita Falls, Texas, 3 June 1936. **Education:** Archer City High School, Texas, graduated 1954; North Texas State College, Denton, B.A. 1958; Rice University, Houston, 1954, 1958–60, M.A. 1960; Stanford University, California (Stegner fellow), 1960–61. **Family:** Married Josephine Scott in 1959 (divorced 1966); one son. **Career:** Taught at Texas Christian University, Fort Worth, 1961–62, Rice University, 1963–64 and 1965, George Mason College, Fairfax, Virginia, 1970, and American University, Washington, D.C., 1970–71. Since 1971 owner, Booked Up Inc., antiquarian booksellers, Washington, D.C., Archer City, Texas, and Tucson, Arizona. Regular reviewer, Houston *Post,* 1960s, and Washington *Post,* 1970s; contributing editor, *American Film,* New York, 1975. President, PEN American Center, 1989. **Awards:** Guggenheim grant, 1964; Pulitzer prize, 1986. **Address:** Booked Up Inc., 2509 North Campbell Avenue, No. 95, Tucson, Arizona 85719, U.S.A.

Publications

Novels

Horseman, Pass By. New York, Harper, 1961; as *Hud,* New York, Popular Library, 1963; London, Sphere, 1971.
Leaving Cheyenne. New York, Harper, 1963; London, Sphere, 1972.
The Last Picture Show. New York, Dial Press, 1966; London, Sphere, 1972.
Moving On. New York, Simon and Schuster, 1970; London, Weidenfeld and Nicolson, 1971.
All My Friends Are Going to Be Strangers. New York, Simon and Schuster, 1972; London, Secker and Warburg, 1973.
Terms of Endearment. New York, Simon and Schuster, 1975; London, W.H. Allen, 1977; with a new preface, New York, Scribner, 1999.
Somebody's Darling. New York, Simon and Schuster, 1978.
Cadillac Jack. New York, Simon and Schuster, 1982.
The Desert Rose. New York, Simon and Schuster, 1983; London, W.H. Allen, 1985.
Lonesome Dove. New York, Simon and Schuster, 1985; London, Pan, 1986.
Texasville. New York, Simon and Schuster, and London, Sidgwick and Jackson, 1987.
Anything for Billy. New York, Simon and Schuster, 1988; London, Collins, 1989.
Some Can Whistle. New York, Simon and Schuster, 1989; London, Century, 1990.
Buffalo Girls. New York, Simon and Schuster, 1990; London, Century, 1991.
Pretty Boy Floyd, with Diana Ossana. New York, Simon and Schuster, 1994; London, Orion, 1995.
Three Bestselling Novels. New York, Wings Books, 1994.
Streets of Laredo. Thorndike, Maine, G. K. Hall, 1994.
Dead Man's Walk. New York, Simon & Schuster, 1995.
The Late Child. New York, Simon and Schuster, and London, Orion, 1995.
Zeke and Ned, with Diana Ossana. New York, Simon & Schuster, 1997.
Comanche Moon. New York, Simon & Schuster, 1997.
Crazy Horse. New York, Viking, 1999.
Duane's Depressed. New York, Simon & Schuster, 1999.
Roads. New York, Simon & Schuster, 2000.

Uncollected Short Stories

''The Best Day Since,'' in *Avesta* (Denton, Texas), Fall 1956.
''Cowman,'' in *Avesta* (Denton, Texas), Spring 1957.
''Roll, Jordan, Roll,'' in *Avesta* (Denton, Texas), Fall 1957.
''A Fragment from Scarlet Ribbons,'' in *Coexistence Review* (Denton, Texas), vol. 1, no. 2, 1958(?).
''There Will Be Peace in Korea,'' in *Texas Quarterly* (Austin), Winter 1964.
''Dunlop Crashes In,'' in *Playboy* (Chicago), July 1975.

Plays

Screenplays: *The Last Picture Show,* with Peter Bogdanovich, 1971.; *Streets of Laredo,* with Diana Ossana. CBS, 1995.

Other

In a Narrow Grave: Essays on Texas. Austin, Texas, Encino Press, 1968.
It's Always We Rambled: An Essay on Rodeo. New York, Hallman, 1974.

Larry McMurtry: Unredeemed Dreams, edited by Dorey Schmidt. Edinburg, Texas, Pan American University, 1980.
Film Flam: Essays on Hollywood. New York, Simon and Schuster, 1987.
Rodeo: No Guts No Glory (notes), photographs and text by Louise L. Serpa. New York, Aperture, 1994.
Irving Paul Lazat: 1907–1993. Tucson, Arizona, Flood Plain Press, 1994.
Walter Benjamin at the Dairy Queen: Reflections at Sixty and Beyond. New York, Simon & Schuster, 1999.
Editor, *Still Wild: Short Fiction of the American West: 1950 to the Present.* New York, Simon & Schuster, 2000.

*

Manuscript Collection: University of Houston Library.

Critical Studies: *Larry McMurtry* by Thomas Landess, Austin, Texas, Steck Vaughn, 1969; *The Ghost Country: A Study of the Novels of Larry McMurtry* by Raymond L. Neinstein, Berkeley, California, Creative Arts, 1976; *Larry McMurtry* by Charles D. Peavy, Boston, Twayne, 1977; *Larry McMurtry's Texas: Evolution of a Myth* by Lera Patrick Tyler Lich, Austin, Texas, Eakin Press, 1987; *Taking Stock: A Larry McMurtry Casebook* edited by Clay Reynolds, Dallas, Southern Methodist University Press, 1989; *Larry McMurtry and the Victorian Novel* by Roger Walton Jones, College Station, Texas, A & M University Press, 1994; *Larry McMurtry and the West: An Ambivalent Relationship* by Mark Busby, Denton, Texas, University of North Texas Press, 1995; *Telling Western Stories: From Buffalo Bill to Larry McMurtry* by Richard W. Etulain, Albuquerque, University of New Mexico Press, 1999; *Larry McMurtry: A Critical Companion* by John M. Reilly, Westport, Connecticut, Greenwood Press, 2000.

* * *

In the 1880s if a cowhand woke up one day with blood on his knife and shirt, or if an Ohio bank teller made off with the receipts, or if a woman stared at her husband as he snored and decided she had enough, escape required moving to the Territories. In the vast rugged western portion of the United States, a person's name could be invented and unverified, and one could ride a horse for three or four days without seeing another human being. The West took its toll, however, on those who tried to live there.

In an October 1990 *New Republic* article, "How the West Was Won or Lost," Larry McMurtry writes about the Old West and reminds his readers that in the Real West "it was too hot or too cold, too wet or too dry, the animals wouldn't behave, the Indians were scary, the distances interminable, and the pioneers were starving, sick, injured and often defeated." But despite this reality, the West was and remains a place of freedom, individuality, and opportunity. McMurtry's accomplishment as an author has been to restructure the western myth by harnessing its vitality in memorable characters. They populate the vast spaces of almost two dozen novels since the first one published in 1961.

In his first two novels McMurtry weaves tales that link the past with the present. *Horseman, Pass By* is the story of three generations of cowboys and is told from the point of view of a seventeen-year-old boy. The boy's grandfather, Homer Bannon, seeks to protect a neighbor's cattle from the disease infecting his own herd, even though it means financial destruction. Hud, Homer's amoral stepson, desires to defy the government, sell the cattle and take control of the ranch. The novel's young narrator witnesses two Wests collide: the West of cowboys and old-time values and the New West where nothing matters except making money.

McMurtry's second novel, *Leaving Cheyenne,* is the story of two cowboys, Johnny and Gid, who compete from boyhood to old age for the love of Molly. Written in three sections with each character taking a turn as narrator, the novel illustrates that Molly loves both male characters and that this love is due, in part, to what each man represents. Each represents a historical type—the rancher who loves the land but has to convert to big ranching in order to save that land, and the cowboy who will never own much of anything but his individualism, which is as misplaced as his dying craft. This heart-warming story of a love triangle typically illustrates McMurtry's faith in the nobility of enduring friendship through changing circumstances.

The Last Picture Show begins a trilogy which includes *Texasville* and *Duane's Depressed.* The metaphor of the last picture show to be shown in a shrinking, oil-patch Texas town's only movie theater frames the stories of Duane Moore, his buddy Sonny, and his girlfriend Jacy, who discover love and sex as they enter adulthood. Duane wants to marry Jacy, whose main ambition is to find a way into a better life than the isolation a small town like Thalia offers. Their romantic ideals are dashed in that crucial transitional period after leaving high school when the demands of adult society also apply to them. *Texasville* follows the lives of the three twenty years later through boom-time and bust. *Duane's Depressed* takes the colorful trio into their twilight years focusing on Duane, a sixty-two-year-old oil-man married to Karla, his unfaithful wife, and saddled with the four children and nine grandchildren, who ruminates about his past.

Moving On introduces characters who take central stage in later novels. Pete and Patsy Carpenter, the primary characters of the novel, are involved in the seemingly unconnected worlds of rodeo and graduate school. Pete and Patsy wish to move from their affluent Texan backgrounds to some form of individual achievement. Pete wishes to capture ritualized cowboy skills in a photography book on rodeo. The failure of this ambition is indicated early on when one of the rodeo stars accidentally introduces himself to Patsy by urinating on the side of her car while she waits for her husband at the darkened rodeo grounds. Pete drops his rodeo book project and takes up the study of literature, becoming absorbed in collecting first editions of old works. Another McMurtry theme, the relevancy of the past in the present, overlays his characters' sense of purpose during the aimless sixties.

Danny Deck, who is briefly introduced in *Moving On,* becomes the main figure in *All My Friends Are Going to Be Strangers.* Autobiographical elements from McMurtry's life inform Deck's reactions to instant fame and wealth as his first novel is produced as a movie. When Deck, who represents the rootless young people of the 1970s, loses his wife and newborn daughter, his final sense of security is obliterated. It is a tradeoff Deck rejects, wading into a river to destroy his second novel and, possibly, himself. Despite the tragic circumstances his stories describe, McMurtry's style relies on humor to relay tender human emotions.

Emma Horton is also introduced in *Moving On.* She and her mother, Aurora Greenway, are the primary characters in *Terms of Endearment.* The novel traces the relationship between mother and daughter and explores their relationships with men. Jill Peel is a girlfriend of Danny Deck in *All My Friends Are Going to Be Strangers. Somebody's Darling* deals with her advancement as a film artist. *Moving On, All My Friends Are Going to Be Strangers, Terms of Endearment* with its sequel *Evening Star,* and *Somebody's Darling* are loosely tied by characters who keep reappearing in one another's lives. McMurtry's next two novels introduce new characters and explore new issues.

Cadillac Jack is the story of a former rodeo cowboy whose job is to scout for antiques at yard sales and farm sales in the Texas flatlands. The author has stated that he was introduced to the yard sale scene by an actress friend. In the novel, Jack discovers a plot to sell off priceless treasures from the Smithsonian Institution and readers are treated to a humorous portrayal of life in Washington, D.C.

The Desert Rose is the story of a Las Vegas showgirl who maintains her optimism in the commercialized world of casinos and second-rate hustlers. Harmony was once known as the most beautiful showgirl in the city, but at age thirty-nine she is being replaced by her own daughter. McMurtry deals well with the issues of exploitation of women, creating a testament to female strength and resilience. *The Late Child,* a sequel to *The Desert Rose,* follows Harmony in her travels with her son after the loss of her daughter before she returns to her family in Oklahoma.

McMurtry's next novel received a Pulitzer Prize in 1986 and made him one of the most popular novelists in America. *Lonesome Dove* started out as a screen offering in 1971 for John Wayne, James Stewart, and Henry Fonda as a bittersweet end-of-the-West western in which no victories were won. The three actors were horrified at the thought of the West ending and with the thought of a western with no triumph, no white man holding up the scalp at the movie's end. *Lonesome Dove* is a western divested of myth and is built around the true hardships of life in the West. The novel is about a trail drive from Texas to Montana and is set in 1876, the year of the first national centennial, the battle of the Little Big Horn, and the beginning of the cowboy's heyday. However, as the characters travel north, readers are struck by how hard the journey is and even the young characters who initially see the trip as a grand adventure learn quickly how fast the fun can run out. One is struck finally with this point: the winning of the West was in large measure an imaginative act and the spirit of the West, a place of freedom, opportunity, and imagination, is still a big part of the framework of contemporary America.

Dead Man's Walk and *Comanche Moon* form a trilogy with *Lonesome Dove* by providing the events that shape the personalities and friendship of the aging Texas Rangers, Augustus McCrae and Woodrow F. Call, in the masterpiece *Lonesome Dove.* They begin their careers as Texas Rangers with the youthful energy and egotism that supports their heroic invincibility against the terrain, weather, and vicious Comanche attacks of the wild West in the nineteenth century. Struggling with the harsh frontier, Gus and Call share life-changing adventures and romance as they protect the flow of settlers into west Texas. McMurtry explores the foundations of the unbreakable bond between the lifelong friends, his most compelling and proud heroes. *Streets of Laredo* is almost an epilogue to the first three books as it follows Captain Call's life after Gus's death.

Anything for Billy continues McMurtry's fascination with the historical old West. The narrator of the novel is Ben Sippy, a writer of dime novels and a cultured Easterner who travels west to compare the real West to the West he has portrayed in fiction. He falls in with Billy the Kid, but the Billy of this novel is a runt and a terrible shot who ''never killed a man who stood more than 20 feet from him. Billy was a blaster, not a marksman.'' McMurtry reworks the myth by having Billy die at the hands of a jealous woman and seems to be emphasizing a point he makes in the novel: ''Gunfighters spent their lives in ugly towns, ate terrible food and drank a vile grade of whisky, and few managed to die gloriously in a shoot-out with a peer.'' Like Calamity Jane in *Buffalo Girls,* the biography *Crazy Horse,* and *Zeke and Ned,* which dramatizes the stories of Ezekiel Proctor and Ned Christie, the last Cherokee warriors, a scarcity of factual documentation gives McMurtry license to recreate historic personages with breathtaking excitement.

In what would seem to be a pattern, McMurtry alternates the western genre with family sagas in multiple volumes that bring his readers up to date on earlier characters. In *Some Can Whistle,* readers learn that Danny Deck did not drown himself. Instead, he walks out of the river and creates a TV sitcom called *Al and Sal* which earns him three-hundred million dollars. Deck is retired in an isolated mansion near Thalia, Texas, and his life is fairly simple until his daughter shows up. Deck is happy at the thought of a reunion, but his daughter turns out to be a foul-mouthed, dope-smoking mother of two who wins his love.

McMurtry's novels, whether they are set in the past or the present, illustrate the power of the West in the American imagination. He masterfully places human hearts inside the mythic characters who represent the pioneer spirit of a nation's trek into its unknown wilderness. In addition, he translates human folly into a universal humanity by the love in his characters and his authorial affection for the characters who live in his stories. A combination of humor, Texan charm, heartwarming characters, and authentic plots in epic proportions mark his style of writing, one that has rewarded McMurtry with unforgettable film adaptations of his novels.

—Tom Colonnese, updated by Hedwig Gorski

McNEISH, James

Nationality: New Zealander. **Born:** Auckland, New Zealand, 23 October 1931. **Education:** University of Auckland, B.A. 1952. **Military Service:** Territorial Service Army of New Zealand, World War II. **Family:** Married 1) Felicity Wily in 1960 (divorced 1964), one daughter; 2) Helen Schnitzer in 1968. **Career:** Journalist and arts editor, *New Zealand Herald,* Auckland, New Zealand, 1950–58; teacher, London, England, 1960–62; freelance radio broadcaster and radio documentary producer, 1962—. Lives in New Zealand. **Agent:** Vivienne Schuster, John Farquharson Ltd., 162 Regent Street, London W1R 5TB, England.

PUBLICATIONS

Novels

Mackenzie. Auckland, New Zealand, Hodder & Stoughton, 1970.
The Mackenzie Affair. Auckland, New Zealand, Hodder & Stoughton, 1972.
The Glass Zoo. New York, St. Martin's, 1976.
Joy. Auckland, New Zealand, Hodder & Stoughton, 1982.
Lovelock. Auckland, New Zealand, Hodder & Stoughton, 1986.
Penelope's Island. London, Hodder & Stoughton, 1990.
My Name Is Paradiso. Auckland, New Zealand, David Ling, 1995.
Mr. Halliday and the Circus Master. N.p. 1996.

Other

Tavern in the Town. Wellington, New Zealand, A.H. and A.W. Reed, 1957.

Fire under the Ashes (biography of Danilo Dolci). Auckland, New Zealand, Hodder & Stoughton,1965.

Larks in a Paradise: New Zealand Portraits (text), photographs by Marti Friedlander. Auckland, New Zealand, Collins, 1974.

As for the Godwits (autobiographical diary), with photographs by James and Helen McNeish. Auckland, New Zealand, Hodder & Stoughton, 1977.

Art of the Pacific (text), photos by Brian Brake, commentary by David Simmons. New York, H. N. Abrams/Queen Elizabeth II Arts Council of New Zealand, 1979.

Belonging: Conversations in Israel (with research by Helen McNeish). New York, Holt, 1980.

Walking on My Feet (biography, with wife, Helen McNeish). Collins & World, 1983.

Ahnungslos in Berlin (diary). Berlin, Literarisches Colloquium, 1986.

Contributor, *Salute to New Zealand*, edited by Michael King. Lansdowne Press, 1990.

The Man from Nowhere and Other Prose (with photographs by Helen McNeish, James McNeish, and Marti Friedlander). Auckland, New Zealand, Godwit, 1991.

The Mask of Sanity: The Bain Murders (Helen McNeish, photographic editor). Auckland, New Zealand, David Ling, 1997.

An Albatross Too Many: A Sequel to As for the Godwits. Auckland, New Zealand, David Ling, 1998.

*

Critical Studies: *As for the Godwits* by James McNeish, with photographs by James and Helen McNeish, Auckland, New Zealand, Hodder & Stoughton, 1977; *An Albatross Too Many: A Sequel to As for the Godwits* by James McNeish, Auckland, New Zealand, David Ling, 1998.

* * *

New Zealand author James McNeish is nothing if not prolific. Since the publication of his first book, *Tavern in the Town*, McNeish has gone on to publish over a dozen more works, countless articles, and has been translated into seven languages. Nominated in 1986 for the Booker-McConnell Prize for Literature for *Lovelock*, McNeish has twice been awarded the New Zealand Scholarship in Letters. In 1999 McNeish won the prestigious British National Library Research Fellowship, allowing him to research the lives and friendships of five prominent New Zealanders who attended Oxford University in the 1930s—four as Rhodes scholars—and who, minus one, chose not to return to their birthplace. This project—currently titled *Wandering Scholars*—and its concern with how the limitations or opportunities of a given historical moment shape the individual and define their choices, is indicative of much of McNeish's writing.

McNeish began as a writer of non-fiction, progressing to novels, then plays. This transition seems natural when one considers the subject of his second book, *Fire under the Ashes*, an account of the Sicilian former architect turned anti-Mafia reformer and outspoken social critic, Danilo Dolci. McNeish's factual account of this activist intellectual and his reform activities segues neatly into his imagining of the nineteenth-century New Zealand figure, James Mackenzie. In *Mackenzie* McNeish creates a vibrant figure that embodies both the emerging nation's desire for expansion and success, as well as the possibility for spiritual reform and equity as imagined by an individual. In James Mackenzie, McNeish realized the potential for a creative treatment of a mythologized man not available to him with the living Dolci. Furthermore, through Mackenzie, McNeish was able to explore a theme close to him: the mythic power and specificity of the New Zealand landscape, and the cultures that inhabit it. First documented in *Tavern in the Town* through the assembling of legends, myths, and anecdotes, in *Mackenzie* McNeish considers the dark, less picturesque side of the nation and the experiences of its settlers as they battle the inhospitable weather and attempt to colonize and displace indigenous Maori peoples. This sensitive rendering of New Zealand's mercurial landscape was no doubt influenced by McNeish's own 1967 inhabitation of a sandspit in the Tasman Sea, something he chronicles in *As for the Godwits*.

In all of his writing McNeish has continued to be fascinated by the image of an individual negotiating or even battling the elements, whether environmental, social, or cultural, while seeking some greater meaning or truth. In his acclaimed fictional ''autobiography'' of Dr. Jack Lovelock, a Rhodes scholar considered the ''first modern athlete'' and noted for his achievements in the 1936 Olympics, McNeish takes as his subject a man battling his own limits, and challenging the possibilities of the human body. As the world celebrates Lovelock's numerous accomplishments, however, his interior life is shrouded in mystery, culminating in his bizarre death at the age of thirty-nine. That McNeish imagines Lovelock as ultimately engaged in a quest that can only be properly understood by the individual himself, is central to his preoccupation with exceptional individuals. It is apparent in his factual and fictional treatment of Dolci, Lovelock, and Mackenzie. Equally apparent is McNeish's fascination with the exceptional individual's search as a moral measure of the politics of his time and place. In *My Name Is Paradiso* the son of a New Zealand British officer who was ''lost'' in World War II visits 1960s Sicily in an attempt to discover the truth of his father's death. Instead, he is shocked by his experience of a violent and immoral 1960s Sicily, the same Sicily condemned by Dolci. Likewise, in the novels *Joy*, *Penelope's Island*, and *Mr. Halliday and the Circus Master*, oppressive political forces are explored through individuals whose own beliefs are often at odds with governmental agendas.

McNeish's thematic preoccupations have remained consistent over the last forty-odd years, as has his desire to revisit specific events in a variety of forms. Just as *Lovelock* led to the *Wandering Scholars*, and *Fire under the Ashes* to *My Name Is Paradiso*, so too did McNeish return to *Mackenzie* in *The Mackenzie Affair*, and *As for the Godwits* in *An Albatross Too Many*, where he questions the government's proposals for the remote Te Kuaka. Recently he expanded his quest to understand the individual with a book on the high profile New Zealand Bain family murders. *The Mask of Sanity: The Bain Murders* draws on McNeish's skill as a creator of psychologically complex fictional or historical figures to contemplate the actions of convicted killer David Bain. In *The Mask of Sanity*, however, the quest is not Bain's but McNeish's, as he struggles to imagine and reconcile possible motives for the five-person murder. A departure from his other works, where the protagonists generally confront the moral implications of their acts and those of the world around them, McNeish's consideration of an exceptional figure with no apparent rationale for his acts signals a new thematic preoccupation to be watched for in future works.

—Jennifer Harris

McWILLIAM, Candia

Nationality: British. **Born:** Candia Francis Juliet McWilliam in Edinburgh, Scotland, 1 July 1955. **Education:** Cambridge University, 1973–76, B.A. **Family:** Married 1) Q.G.C. Wallop in 1981 (divorced 1985), one son and one daughter; 2) F.E. Dinshaw in 1986, one son. **Career:** *Vogue* Magazine, 1976–79; Slade, Bluffix, and Bigg, 1979–81. **Awards:** *Vogue* talent contest, 1970; Betty Trask prize, 1988, Scottish Arts Council prize, 1989; *Guardian* prize for fiction, 1994. **Member:** Society of Authors, Royal Society of Literature. **Agent:** Janklow and Nesbit, 598 Madison Avenue, New York, New York 10022, U.S.A.

PUBLICATIONS

Novels

A Case of Knives. London, Bloomsbury, and New York, Beech Tree, 1988.

A Little Stranger. London, Bloomsbury, and New York, Doubleday, 1989.

Debatable Land. London, Bloomsbury, and New York, Nan A. Talese, 1994.

Short Stories

Wait Till I Tell You. London, Bloomsbury, 1997.

Other

Editor, *The Macallan: Scotland on Sunday Short Story Collection.* Edinburgh, Polygon, 1999.

* * *

Candia McWilliam's three novels have established her as one of a trio of exceptionally talented young Scottish writers (Janice Galloway and A. L. Kennedy being the other two). In her fiction style is just as seductive as the story. Her language is spare and exact, yet elegant and strangely mysterious, though not without a touch of mordant humor. Descriptions are precise but less important for what they reveal about the external world than about inner reality; quotidian facts serve as the raw material for intricate psychological musings on social, sexual, and national identity.

A Case of Knives is her highly accomplished first novel. Divided into four parts, each told by a different character and in a different style, the novel is a study in English class structure and the ways people ''experiment with human flesh,'' both physically and psychologically. Lucas Salik, the son of Polish Jews, has transformed himself into a proper Englishman, a respected pediatric cardiologist. He is also a homosexual (a fact known only to his very closest friends) who, as the novel's ominous opening line puts it, ''needs a woman,'' for his lover, Hal, who has decided to lead a more respectable and conventional life as a married man. The girl Lucas selects proves, however, less the helpless prey than hungry predator in need of a husband to play the part of father of her unborn child. Indeed no character is quite what he or she appears. Neither is any character nearly as much in control of his or her respective plot as he or she assumes, except for the novel's most manipulative, and therefore most monstrous character, the ''vegan carnivore'' Angelica Coney, whose evil nature is the by-product of upper-class privilege. Pulling a series of skeletons out of her characters' figurative closets, McWilliam crafts a story that both seduces and shocks with its succession of narratively compelling and at times morally appalling surprises.

The capacity for self-delusion and the negative, potentially tragic consequences of English class structure reappear in *A Little Stranger,* a shorter and still more intense (and more intensely secretive) novel. Rendered with all the precision of a seventeenth-century still life and reminiscent of Jane Austen, *Jane Eyre,* and Henry James (*The Turn of the Screw, What Maisie Knew*), this study in repression is narrated by another of McWilliam's culturally and psychologically divided characters. Raised by her Dutch father after her English mother ''waltzed off to Vienna, bored by Amsterdam,'' the self-effacing narrator does not even mention her name until novel's end. Daisy only slowly realizes that she has lived at the very margin of her own life, ''the useless but essential'' wife of a wealthy landowner. She has little to do as wife and even less as mother—-other than write letters to people she does not know and closely observe (though not quite understand) the latest nanny, Margaret Pride. At first the novel seems to be about Margaret, who is not the pearl of great price Daisy believes her to be. Margaret's lower-class background has led her to create a fantasy in which she patiently awaits the coming of her prince, Daisy's emotionally and often geographically distant husband. More interesting than the revelations concerning Margaret are those having to do with Daisy's failure to apprehend something amiss earlier, as the reader does (though not altogether correctly). As in *A Case of Knives,* the sudden introduction of a topical issue (AIDS then, anorexia now) seems at once relevant and intrusive. More successful is McWilliam's appending to her novels—which seem about to end so disastrously—tentatively happy endings that do not so much resolve matters as remind readers of the precariousness of the characters' lives.

The claustrophobic intensity of the first two novels is not so much lacking as differently figured in *Debatable Land,* McWilliam's third and most ambitious work, in which her interest in the shaping effects of childhood is most pronounced. Following the last leg of a sailing voyage from Tahiti to New Zealand, this modern-day *Odyssey* brings six characters together on the *Ardent Spirit.* Playing the vastness of the ocean against the confinement of the sailboat, the sense of freedom and adventure against the sense of commitment and community, the novel creates a debatable land of its own. As the *Ardent Spirit* navigates well-charted but at times treacherous seas and reef-rimmed coastal waters, *Debatable Land* narratively tacks back and forth between characters, between a variously idealized past and a disappointing present, between a postparadisiacal (and postcolonial) Pacific and a Scotland that seems less a specific place than a multiplicity of psychological meanings resulting from her Scots having been raised in quite diverse geographical and socioeconomic settings. Although more intricately structured and broad-ranging than her two earlier novels, *Debatable Land* renders the complex inner lives of its characters with the same combination of intelligence, precision, and sympathetic understanding.

All the time she was writing her novels, McWilliam was also writing short fiction. *Wait Till I Tell You* comprises twenty-four stories: twenty-two that originally appeared 1988–1997 and two others that had not been previously published. The stories display the same eye for detail, the similarly precise, refined style, and the understated, mordant wit found in the novels and more than make up for what they necessarily lack in development with an unnerving, even claustrophobic compression well-suited to McWilliam's thematic purpose. For these are stories of terribly, if quietly constrained lives—mainly the lonely, powerless lives of women—set in ''a country so rich in emptiness.'' Whether they take place in tearooms or nursing homes, at the seaside, on islands, or in a department store, the stories deal with displacements and disappointments, futility and frustration, of aging and merely holding on as best one can to the very little one has. They are stories in which lives do not so much progress as they are prolonged and in which even averting disaster (as in ''The Only Only'') deepens rather than relieves the foreboding.

McWilliam's restrained style is the perfect match for her characters' constrained lives; it also provides the reader, if not the characters, with a measure of aesthetic relief, the fineness of the writing contrasting with the smallness and drabness of those lives. All the stories are good, but at least three are much more than that. ''A Revolution in China'' is a sad comedy dealing with the last days (retirement and death) of Miss Montanari at age sixty-two, after forty-two uneventful years working in the same department store. The other two, ''The Shredding of Icebergs'' and ''White Goods,'' are in effect versions of the same story, this time of wives whose marriages have become matters of deadening routine. ''And so the days go on, chopped into finer and finer shreds of lightness that I think at last I can feel, each one, just before it goes.'' Lines such as this one demonstrate the combination of repressed emotional feeling and restrained yet elegant, even lyrical style that has become the hallmark of McWilliam's writing.

—Robert A. Morace

MEHTA, Gita

Nationality: Indian. **Born:** Gita Patnaik in Delhi, India, 1944. **Education:** Cambridge University. **Family:** Married Ajai Singh (''Sonny'') Mehta; one son. **Career:** Writer, journalist, and filmmaker. Lives in New York, London, and Delhi.

Publications

Novels

Raj. New York, Simon & Schuster, 1989.

A River Sutra. New York, N. A. Talese, 1993; excerpt included in *Happiness and Discontent.* Chicago, Great Books Foundation, 1998.

Other

Karma Cola: Marketing the Mystic East. New York, Simon & Schuster, 1979.

Snakes and Ladders: Glimpses of India. New York, N. A. Talese, 1997.

* * *

Gita Mehta is a writer known, perhaps, more for her essays than her novels. She is also a documentary filmmaker and a journalist. These activities all share a focus on India, the country of her birth—its history, politics, and cultures. The same concerns inform her novels: *Raj*, a historical novel set during the early stages of India's struggle for independence from Britain, and *A River Sutra*, a modern revisitation of prevalent traditions of Indian aesthetic and philosophical thought.

Mehta has made a number of documentary films about India, covering the Bangladesh war, the Indo-Pakistan war, and the elections in the former Indian princely states. Her essays, as represented by two collections, *Karma Cola: Marketing the Mystic East* and *Snakes and Ladders: Glimpses of Modern India*, muse on things Indian, from politics and social unrest, the endless clash of religions and cultures, spirituality, and the Indian textile industry to Indian literature and film, and so on. The style of the essays is personal and lucid, often bitingly clear and always honest. This same lucid immediacy and intimacy marks *A River Sutra. Raj*, lacking this intimate voice, is a more distanced work, valuable rather for its meticulous and even-handed grasp of a complex and important period in history.

Raj, Mehta's first novel, begins during the last years of the nineteenth century. The novel's protagonist, Jaya Singh, is the daughter of the Maharaja and Maharani of Balmer, one of the kingdoms of Royal India. Mehta paints Jaya's childhood, the traditions and rituals, political pressures and duties that inform her life, with evocative detail. She deals even-handedly with the political and social issues, conveying the immense pain and demoralizing powerlessness with which the Indian people had to deal, while still managing to portray the British with some objectivity. The novel achieves historical sweep, following Jaya from childhood through adolescence to her betrothal and then through her marriage to a Prince of Royal India who has no interest in Indian women, but who, as a Westernized playboy, prefers European women, airplanes, and polo to the duties of a protector of the people. Mehta uses Jaya as a lens through which to view these turbulent years of India's struggle for independence. She does an admirable job of portraying Jaya's world—a woman with resources and education raised half in and half out of the traditions of purdah and Hindu ritual that reigned unchanging for generations before her. The novel is rich in detail and complexity. But much of the action, like Gandhi's salt march or the violent struggles between Hindus and Muslims, is experienced from a distance, through those to whom Jaya is connected rather than through Jaya herself. The novel has been criticized for a lack of character development and depth. Rather than drawing the reader deeply into the unfolding of history, the evenness and limited scope of Mehta's handling present a somewhat flat aspect, as of great events viewed through the wrong end of a telescope. The novel is most valuable as an account of a lost way of life as it was vanishing within the complex political realities that gave birth, ultimately, to the modern nations of India and Pakistan.

Mehta's second novel, *A River Sutra*, is a more intimate and deeply focused work. The narrative centers on India's holiest river, the Narmada, in the form of a series of tales, or modified *sutras* of

Indian literature. The tales—of various pilgrims to the river—tap the deep veins of Indian mythology and artistic traditions while also forming a prose meditation on the country's secular-humanist tradition. The character of an unnamed civil servant who has retired from the world to run a government rest house on the river is the thread loosely weaving the stories together—along with the Narmada itself. Mehta's subject matter here is as rich as the tradition she taps. Classical Sanskrit drama, Hindu mythology, and Sufi poetry all find reflection and reiteration in the novel. One recurring motif playing through the book is that of the raga of Indian classical music. Another is that of Kama, god of love, and the passions and mysteries of the human heart. For all its substance of ancient Indian tradition and thought, *A River Sutra* is a modern work that acknowledges the difficulties facing modern India at the same time as it takes the reader on a skillfully realized journey into a resonant culture.

Mehta occupies a unique position as a writer who elucidates uniquely Indian experience in a clear and intelligent voice. She relates a rich and ongoing history—its nuance, complexity, and contradiction—opening doors and windows into Indian life in ways few other writers do. While her first novel may be seen as thinly characterized and lacking in depth, the balance of her work, including her second novel, constitutes a unique and valuable contribution to the literature of the world.

—Jessica Reisman

MELVILLE, Pauline

Nationality: Guyanese. **Born:** Guyana, 1948. **Awards:** Whitbread First Novel Award, 1997. **Agent:** c/o St. Martin's Press, 175 Fifth Avenue, New York, New York 10010, U.S.A. **Address:** London, England.

Publications

Novels

The Ventriloquist's Tale. London, Bloomsbury, 1997.

Short Stories

Shape Shifter: Stories. New York, Pantheon, 1990.
The Migration of Ghosts. London, Bloomsbury, 1998.

Other

Contributor, *In Our Nature: Stories of Wilderness*, edited by Donna Seaman. New York, DK Publishing, 2000.

* * *

A Guyanese author of mixed European and Amerindian ancestry, Pauline Melville has emerged in the last few years as a leading Caribbean writer, and one of the most accomplished talents on the modern literary scene. *Shape-shifter*, her first collection of stories, revealed the impressive extent of her abilities, and subsequent works have confirmed her previous achievement. A professional actress in Europe before making it as a published writer, Melville has a cosmopolitan knowledge of both the Old and the New Worlds, and her fiction informs her experiences with her own mixed cultural heritage, Western philosophy nudging shoulders with Amerindian creation myths and the resulting blend touched with a sardonic, iconoclastic wit.

Shape-shifter, her award-winning debut collection of stories, displays the variety and range of her writing. Moving from her native Guyana to Europe and the United States, Melville's stories describe the experiences of her various exiles and misfits in a highly individual way. Her title reflects not only the metamorphoses of her characters, but the constant switching of time frames, narrative styles, and devices by which they are presented. As so often in Melville's fiction, the real and surreal blend seamlessly into one, the everyday world of Western notional "reality" overtaken by an eerie dream (or nightmare) universe in which the limbs and souls of her creations take on new and disturbing life. Throughout the collection, Melville impresses with her wry, detached humor and her impatience with the sacred cows of literature and philosophy.

Her novel *The Ventriloquist's Tale* returns to Guyana and concerns itself with the mixed-race Mackinnon family, offspring of Scottish and Wapisiana Amerindian parents, who live in tribal fashion in a remote area of the country. Chofoye Mackinnon's journey to the city, his love affair with Western literary researcher Rosa Mendelson, and his eventual return to wife and family is intercut with flashbacks describing the incestuous relationship of Sonny Mackinnon and his sister, and the collision of the Wapisiana culture with that of various intruding whites. This, at least, is the most obvious aspect of the novel. But what the West considers to be real is regarded by the Amerindian as no more than a mask, a waking dream. Behind the screen of everyday life lies the true reality of the spirit-world, of dream and myth and magic. *The Ventriloquist's Tale* reflects this other reality in its many layers, the incest of Sonny and Violet mirrored in the cosmic Wapisiana myth that sets a pattern for the stars. This is the essence of an Amerindian world that eludes all efforts of the invading whites and their constant obsession to enclose, measure, and evaluate. Just as the Mackinnon patriarch was overtaken by the Wapisiana lifestyle now accepted by his descendants, so the efforts of those other cultural colonizers—the Catholic priest; the anthropologist; the novelist Evelyn Waugh, who appears in a cameo role—are doomed to failure. The Mackinnons and the Wapisiana people absorb these incursions and shrug them off, holding to their own way of life. In a single novel Melville manages to condense a portrayal of Guyana with its incredibly rich blend of cultures and lifestyles, a memorable picture of the Wapisiana people and their beliefs, the interplay of striking individual characters, and a view of Amerindian cosmology and the spirit-world. This she achieves with a narrative style that avoids solemn stereotypes and finds room at every stage for humor, self-mockery, and irreverence. All the same, there is no doubting the seriousness of her insights, and *The Ventriloquist's Tale* shows Melville to be as formidable a novelist as she is a writer of shorter fiction.

Her latest collection of stories, *The Migration of Ghosts*, follows on from *Shape-shifter* in having a thematic base to its stories. This time the central thread is death and afterlife, and like the earlier collection the action switches from Guyana to London and various parts of Europe. Melville's mastery of narrative and dialogue is little short of breath-taking; she presents with equal conviction the risqué conversation of workers in a London pub and the somber thoughts of a financier in "The Sparkling Bitch." Once again the daylight world is indissolubly blended with the world beyond. A ghostly President visits scenes of his triumph and humiliation, finally falling asleep on his (apparently riderless) horse. An aging Spanish widow, recalling her dead husband, breaks into dance in the *duende*, the moment "when a ghost suddenly appears and vanishes and the world is reborn." An escaped Guyanese murderess (reincarnated as a goddess?) drowns a crooked businessman in the river his chemicals have polluted. Melville moves easily from the deadpan humor of "The Parrot and Descartes," where Western philosophy is ridiculed alongside Guyanese creation myths, to the harrowing account of a friend's death from cancer in "Lucifer's Shank," where she comments on the Amerindian belief that "the real self is revealed only in death." The title story follows an Englishman and his Guyanese Indian wife on their travels through Europe, and presents the many connections and differences between their own cultures and those they meet. An infinitely varied and skilful collection, *The Migration of Ghosts* confirms Melville as a leading writer of the new millennium, and gives the promise of future achievement.

—Geoff Sadler

MERTZ, Barbara

Pseudonyms: Barbara Michaels; Elizabeth Peters. **Nationality:** American. **Born:** Barbara Louise Gross Mertz in Canton, Illinois, 29 September 1927. **Education:** University of Chicago Oriental Institute, Ph.B. 1947, M.S. 1950, Ph.D. 1952. **Family:** Married Richard R. Mertz in 1950 (divorced 1968); one daughter and one son. **Career:** Egyptologist. **Awards:** Grandmaster award, Bouchercon, 1986; Agatha award for best mystery novel, 1989, and Malice Domestic Convention, 1989, both for *Naked Once More;* Grand Master, Mystery Writers of America Edgar Awards, 1998. D.H.L.: Hood College, 1989. **Member:** American Crime Writers League, Egypt Exploration Society, American Research Council in Egypt, Society for the Study of Egyptian Antiquities, National Organization for Women. **Agent:** Dominick Abel Literary Agency, 146 West 82nd St., Suite 1B, New York, New York 10024, U.S.A.

Publications

Novels as Elizabeth Peters (series: Vicky Bliss; Amelia Peabody Emerson; Jacqueline Kirby)

The Jackal's Head. New York, Meredith, 1968; London, Jenkins 1969.
The Camelot Caper. New York, Meredith, 1969; London, 1976.
The Dead Sea Cipher. New York, Dodd Mead, 1970; London, Cassell, 1975.
The Night of Four Hundred Rabbits. New York, Dodd Mead, 1971; *as Shadows in the Moonlight,* London, Coronet, 1975.
The Seventh Sinner (Kirby). New York, Dodd Mead, 1972; London, Coronet, 1975.
Borrower of the Night (Bliss). New York, Dodd Mead, 1973; London, Cassell, 1974.
The Murders of Richard III (Kirby). New York, Dodd Mead, 1974; London, Piatkus, 1989.
Crocodile on the Sandbank (Emerson). New York, Dodd Mead, 1975; London, Cassell, 1976.
Legend in Green Velvet. New York, Dodd Mead, 1976; as *Ghost in Green Velvet,* London, Cassell, 1977.
Devil-May-Care. New York, Dodd Mead, 1977; London, Cassell, 1978.
Street of the Five Moons (Bliss). New York, Dodd Mead, 1978; London, Piatkus, 1988.
Summer of the Dragon. New York, Dodd Mead, 1979; London, Souvenir Press, 1980.
The Love Talker. New York, Dodd Mead, 1980; London, Souvenir Press, 1981.
The Curse of the Pharaohs (Emerson). New York, Dodd Mead, 1981; London, Souvenir Press, 1982.
The Copenhagen Connection. New York, Congdon and Lattes, 1982; London, Souvenir Press, 1983.
Silhouette in Scarlet (Bliss). New York, Congdon and Weed, 1983; London, Souvenir Press, 1984.
Die for Love (Kirby). New York, Congdon and Weed, 1984; London, Souvenir Press, 1985.
The Mummy Case (Emerson). New York, Congdon and Weed, 1985; London, Souvenir Press, 1986.
Lion in the Valley (Emerson) . New York, Atheneum, 1986; London, Piatkus, 1987.
Trojan Gold (Bliss). New York, Atheneum, and London, Piatkus, 1987.
The Deeds of the Disturber (Emerson). New York, Atheneum, and London, Piatkus, 1988.
Naked Once More (Kirby). New York, Warner, 1989; London, Piatkus, 1990.

Novels as Barbara Michaels

The Master of Blacktower. New York, Appleton Century Crofts, 1966; London, Jenkins, 1967.
Sons of the Wolf. New York, Meredith, 1967; London, Jenkins, 1968.
Ammie, Come Home. New York, Meredith, 1968; London, Jenkins, 1969.
Prince of Darkness. New York, Meredith, 1969; London, Hodder and Stoughton, 1971.
The Dark on the Other Side. New York, Dodd Mead, 1970; London, Souvenir Press, 1973.
Greygallows. New York, Dodd Mead, 1972; London, Souvenir Press, 1973.
The Crying Child. New York, Dodd Mead, and London, Souvenir Press, 1973.
Witch. New York, Dodd Mead, 1973; London, Souvenir Press, 1975.
House of Many Shadows. New York, Dodd Mead, 1974; London, Souvenir Press, 1975.
The Sea King's Daughter. New York, Dodd Mead, 1975; London, Souvenir Press, 1977.
Patriot's Dream. New York, Dodd Mead, 1976; London, Souvenir Press, 1978.
Wings of the Falcon. New York, Dodd Mead, 1977; London, Souvenir Press, 1979.
Wait for What Will Come. New York, Dodd Mead, 1978; London, Souvenir Press, 1980.
The Walker in Shadows. New York, Dodd Mead, 1979; London, Souvenir Press, 1981.

The Wizard's Daughter. New York, Dodd Mead, 1980; London, Souvenir Press, 1982.
Someone in the House. New York, Dodd Mead, 1981; London, Souvenir Press, 1983.
Black Rainbow. New York, Congdon and Weed, 1982; London, Souvenir Press, 1983.
Here I Stay. New York, Congdon and Weed, 1983; London, Souvenir Press, 1985.
Dark Duet. New York, Congdon and Weed, 1983.
The Grey Beginning. New York, Congdon and Weed, 1984; London, Souvenir Press, 1986.
Be Buried in the Rain. New York, Atheneum, 1985; London, Piatkus, 1986.
Shattered Silk. New York, Atheneum, 1986; London, Piatkus, 1987.
Search the Shadows. New York, Atheneum, 1987; London, Piatkus, 1988.
Smoke and Mirrors. New York, Simon and Schuster, and London, Piatkus, 1989.
Into the Darkness. New York, Simon and Schuster, 1990.
Vanish with the Rose. New York, Simon and Schuster, 1992.
Houses of Stone. New York, Simon and Schuster, 1993.

Uncollected Short Stories

''The Locked Tomb Mystery'' (as Elizabeth Peters) in *Sisters in Crime,* edited by Marilyn Wallace. New York, Berkley, 1989; London, Robinson, 1990.
''The Runaway'' (as Barbara Michaels) in *Sisters in Crime,* edited by Marilyn Wallace. New York, Berkley, 1989; London, Robinson, 1990.

Other

Temples, Tombs, and Hieroglyphs: The Story of Egyptology. New York, Coward McCann, and London, Gollancz, 1964; revised edition, New York, Dodd Mead, 1978; revised edition, New York, Bedrick, 1990.
Red Land, Black Land: The World of the Ancient Egyptians. New York, Coward McCann, 1966; London, Hodder and Stoughton, 1967; revised edition, New York, Dodd Mead, 1978; revised edition, New York, Bedrick, 1990.
Two Thousand Years in Rome, with Richard Mertz. New York, Coward McCann, 1968; London, Dent, 1969.

*

Manuscript Collections: Mugar Memorial Library, Boston University; University of Wyoming, Laramie.

* * *

Barbara Mertz is a prolific writer using several pseudonyms for her forays into different types of novels. As Barbara Michaels, Mertz writes gothic romances about human and supernatural terrors. An Elizabeth Peters mystery relies on history, mythology, and archaeology to provide an erudite foundation for modern romantic suspense: a Yuma turquoise mine (*Summer of the Dragon*), the sacred Scottish Stone of Scone (*Legend in Green Velvet*), Nefertiti's lost tomb (*The Jackal's Head*), King Arthur's crown (*The Camelot Caper*), Mexico City's Walk of the Dead (*The Night of Four Hundred Rabbits*), the Schliemann treasure (*Trojan Gold*), Richard the Third (*The Murders of Richard III*), the subterranean Temple of Mithra (*The Seventh Sinner*), and so on. Typical of the genre is *The Dead Sea Cipher* wherein the American heroine searches exotic cities (Beirut, Sidon, Tyre, Damascus) to explain odd marks on torn paper from a doomed stranger; her search leads to treasure and two compelling men, an enemy and a future lover. Mertz's academic heroines (anthropologists, librarians, antiquarians, and students) become enmeshed in criminal pursuits related to historical concerns, but eventually find themselves forcibly assisted by a strong, practical, intellectually challenging male, like the irritatingly handsome, gruff, down-to-earth, unromantic young Scottish laird Jamey Erskine in *Legend in Green Velvet.*

Mertz revels in parody and satire, as in *Die for Love,* set at a convention for the Historical Romance Writers of the World, or in *Naked Once More,* in which series character Jacqueline Kirby, a middle-aged, copper-haired librarian who regularly abandons her academic boyfriends for a smart cop, is chosen to write the sequel to a blockbuster novel, a cross between *The Clan of the Cave Bear* and *Gone with the Wind.* Wry, cynical, witty, and courageous, Mertz's heroines challenge men with spirited confrontations, antagonistic love-hate responses, and sometimes role-reversals, as when series character Vicky Bliss, a tall, blonde, good-humored art historian at a Munich museum, must regularly rescue her wandering lover, Sir John Smythe, an art thief of distinction.

Mertz's finest creation in her Peters mode is Amelia Peabody-Emerson, a highly unconventional, independently wealthy Victorian bluestocking, deeply interested in Egyptology and in the hot-blooded, hot-tempered, irascible Egyptologist she eventually marries, Radcliffe Emerson. Her keen intellect, sharp tongue, curiosity, and competitiveness repeatedly place her in awkward and threatening situations. An amateur sleuth, she trusts logic, good sense, and reason but then leaps intuitively to sometimes quite erroneous conclusions. However, her resilient inductive method allows her to discard the untenable and to readily formulate new theories. The Peabody-Emerson series incorporates delightful satire of Victorian types, comic romping, tongue-in-cheek high romance, and the excitement of archaeological discovery (with all the attendant rivalries, mummy's curses, haunted pyramids, flooded tombs, dangerous pitfalls, and outrageous hoaxes); at the same time readers learn much about scholarly research and archaeological methods. Always the Emersons find rational explanations to debunk the supernatural.

Ms. Peabody-Emerson records her judiciously edited memoirs (to the ''Gentle Reader'') in elevated, convoluted, euphemistic Victorian prose, prides herself on her nursing skills (she must frequently deal with dagger wounds, poisons, and murderous attacks) and repeatedly effects rescues with a wickedly deft use of her umbrella. She is a sensible woman, continually frustrated by encumbering clothing decreed by fashion; in later novels she creates her own practical wardrobe, a compromise between Victorian propriety and archaeological necessity. She never meant to marry, but in Emerson she finds her match and defines marriage with him as ''a balanced stalemate between equal adversaries.''

Peabody-Emerson becomes a highly competent Egyptologist, finding in that field clues to modern mysteries. The romance begun in *Crocodile on the Sandbank* produces an imperious, precocious son

Ramses, who, with his Egyptian cat Bastet, evokes biting, unsentimental commentaries on the tribulations of parenthood and domesticity. In *The Curse of the Pharaohs,* a mysterious death and inexplicable accidents at a ''cursed'' tomb point to a modern perpetrator, in *Lion in the Valley* a master criminal dealing in illegal antiquities pursues Amelia romantically, and in *The Last Camel Died at Noon* the Emersons face death on sun-scorched Nubian desert sands while pursuing a cryptic map and an enigmatic papyrus message. Mertz as Peters merges the gothic romance and the romance thriller with satiric comedy and detailed Egyptology to create a winning combination that intrigues, teaches, and delights.

Mertz's Barbara Michaels incognita is more overtly ''thrilling,'' dealing as it does with gothic romance and the spiritually questionable. Some of these, like *Here I Stay* and *Shattered Silk,* are very convincing ghost stories, lent strength by practical, no-nonsense heroines. They draw on historical events (*Wings of the Falcon, Search the Shadows, Patriot's Dream*) and legend (*Ammie, Come Home*), involve psychic powers (*Wizard's Daughter*) and psychological trauma (*The Crying Child*), include werewolves (*Mystery on the Moors*), haunted castles (Greygallows) and demonic possession (*The Dark on the Other Side*), or provide interesting background on an assortment of oddities (like old roses in *Vanish with the Rose*).

Mertz's battles of the sexes are equal contests, and the verbal repartee of her main characters is lively, witty, and literate. She is a skillful storyteller, who thrills, chills, and amuses.

—Gina Macdonald

METCALF, John (Wesley)

Nationality: Canadian. **Born:** Carlisle, Cumberland, England, 12 November 1938. **Education:** Bristol University, 1957–61, B.A. (honors) in English 1960, Cert. Ed. 1961. **Family:** Married 1) Gail Courey in 1965 (marriage dissolved 1972), one daughter; 2) Myrna Teitelbaum in 1975, one stepson and two adopted children. **Career:** Taught at a secondary school and a boys' borstal, Bristol, 1961; Rosemount High School, Montreal, 1962–63; Royal Canadian Air Force Base, Cold Lake, Alberta, 1964–65; at a Catholic comprehensive school in England, 1965; and at schools and universities in Montreal, part-time, 1966–71. Writer-in-residence, University of New Brunswick, Fredericton, 1972–73, Loyola College, Montreal, 1976, University of Ottawa, 1977, Concordia University, Montreal, 1980–81, and University of Bologna, Italy, 1985. **Awards:** Canada Council award, 1968, 1969, 1971, 1974, 1976, 1978, 1980, 1983, 1986; University of Western Ontario President's medal, for short story, 1969. **Agent:** Denise Bukowski, The Bukowski Agency, 125B Dupont St., Toronto, Ontario M5R 1V4. **Address:** P.O. Box 2700, Station D, Ottawa, Ontario K1P 5W7, Canada.

Publications

Novels

Going Down Slow. Toronto, McClelland and Stewart, 1972.
Girl in Gingham. Ottawa, Oberon Press, 1978; as *Private Parts: A Memoir,* Scarborough, Ontario, Macmillan-New American Library of Canada, 1980.
General Ludd. Downsview, Ontario, ECW Press, 1980.
Kayhut: A Warrior's Odyssey. Minneapolis, Minnesota, Four Directions, 1998.

Short Stories

New Canadian Writing 1969, with C.J. Newman and D.O. Spettigue. Toronto, Clarke Irwin, 1969.
The Lady Who Sold Furniture. Toronto, Clarke Irwin, 1970.
The Teeth of My Father. Ottawa, Oberon Press, 1975.
Dreams Surround Us: Fiction and Poetry, with John Newlove. Delta, Ontario, Bastard Press, 1977.
Selected Stories. Toronto, McClelland and Stewart, 1982.
Adult Entertainment. Toronto, Macmillan, 1986; New York, St. Martin's Press, 1989.
Shooting the Stars (novellas). Erin, Ontario, Porcupine's Quill, 1993.

Other

Kicking Against the Pricks (essays). Downsview, Ontario, ECW Press, 1982.
Freedom from Culture. Vancouver, Tanks, 1987; revised edition published as *Freedom from Culture: Selected Essays 1982–1992.* Toronto, ECW Press, 1994.
What Is Canadian Literature? Guelph, Ontario, Red Kite Press, 1988.
Acts of Kindness and of Love. Oakville, Ontario, Presswerk Editions, 1995.
An Aesthetic Underground. Guelph, Ontario, Red Kite Press, 1999.
Editor, with others, *Wordcraft 1–5* (textbooks). Toronto, Dent, 5 vols., 1967–77.
Editor, *Razor's Edge,* by Somerset Maugham. Richmond Hill, Ontario, Irwin, 1967.
Editor, *The Flight of the Phoenix,* by Elleston Trevor. Scarborough, Ontario, Bellhaven House, 1968.
Editor, *Daughter of Time,* by Josephine Tey. Richmond Hill, Ontario, Irwin, 1968.
Editor, with Gordon Callaghan, *Rhyme and Reason.* Toronto, Ryerson Press, 1969.
Editor, with Gordon Callaghan, *Salutation.* Toronto, Ryerson Press, 1970.
Editor, *Sixteen by Twelve: Short Stories by Canadian Writers.* Toronto, Ryerson Press, and New York, McGraw Hill, 1970.
Editor, *The Narrative Voice: Short Stories and Reflections by Canadian Authors.* Toronto, McGraw Hill Ryerson, 1972.
Editor, *Kaleidoscope: Canadian Stories.* Toronto, Van Nostrand, 1972.
Editor, *The Speaking Earth: Canadian Poetry.* Toronto, Van Nostrand, 1973.
Editor, with Joan Harcourt, *76 [77]: Best Canadian Stories.* Ottawa, Oberon Press, 2 vols., 1976–77.
Editor, with Clark Blaise, *Here and Now.* Ottawa, Oberon Press, 1977.
Editor, with Clark Blaise, *78 [79, 80]: Best Canadian Stories.* Ottawa, Oberon Press, 3 vols., 1978–80.
Editor, *Stories Plus: Canadian Stories with Authors' Commentaries.* Toronto, McGraw Hill Ryerson, 1979.

Editor, *New Worlds: A Canadian Collection of Stories.* Toronto, McGraw Hill Ryerson, 1980.
Editor, *First [Second, Third] Impressions.* Ottawa, Oberon Press, 3 vols., 1980–82.
Editor, with Leon Rooke, *81 [82]: Best Canadian Stories.* Ottawa, Oberon Press, 2 vols., 1981–82.
Editor, *Making It New: Contemporary Canadian Stories.* Toronto, Methuen, 1982.
Editor, with Leon Rooke, *The New Press Anthology 1–2: Best Canadian Short Fiction.* Toronto, General, 2 vols., 1984–85.
Editor, *The Bumper Book.* Toronto, ECW Press, 1986.
Editor, with Leon Rooke, *The Macmillan Anthology 1–2.* Toronto, Macmillan, 2 vols., 1988–89.
Editor, *Carry On Bumping.* Toronto, ECW Press, 1988.
Editor, *Writers in Aspic.* Montreal, Véhicule Press, 1988.
Editor, with Kent Thompson, *The Macmillan Anthology 3.* Toronto, Macmillan, 1990.
Editor, with Sam Solecki and W.J. Keith, *Volleys* (critical essays). Erin, Ontario, Porcupine's Quill, 1990.
Editor, *The New Story Writers.* Kingston, Ontario, Quarry Press, 1992.
Editor, with J.R. Struthers, *Canadian Classics.* Toronto, Ryerson, 1993.
Editor, with J.R. Struthers, *How Stories Mean.* Erin, Ontario, Porcupine's Quill, 1993.

*

Manuscript Collections: Special Collections, University of Calgary, Alberta; University of Maine, Orono.

Critical Studies: *On the Line* by Robert Lecker, Downsview, Ontario, ECW Press, 1982; article by Douglas Rollins, in *Canadian Writers and Their Works 7* edited by Lecker, Jack David, and Ellen Quigley, ECW Press, 1985; ''John Metcalf Issue'' of *Malahat Review 70* (Victoria, British Columbia); *John Metcalf* by Barry Cameron, Boston, Twayne, 1986; two essays in *Feat of the Open Heart* by Constance Rooke, Toronto, Coach House, 1989.

* * *

When one realizes why so little commentary has been devoted to John Metcalf's fiction, one also understands the unique quality of his work: his prose is so chaste, so uncompromisingly direct, that exegesis often seems to be redundant. But to be seduced by this directness is to ignore the extraordinary narrative compression which multiplies the weight of Metcalf's words, and thus to miss the ideas he develops through his concentration on things. As a mature writer, Metcalf advises the novice to ''avoid literary criticism which moves away from the word on the printed page'' and to ''stick to the study of the placement of commas.'' Only through this study, and by knowing ''the weight, color, and texture of *things*'' will the writer create ''the distillation of experience'' that makes fiction valid.

The terminology here suggests that Metcalf is a traditionalist, and he is. He believes that a plot should be interesting, mysterious, and constructed in such a way that it will endure. He is concerned with the morality of his characters and their culture. His stories are generally realistic in their emphasis on the details of time and place. Above all, he is preoccupied with a traditional theme: the relationship between art and human experience. Consequently his stories explore the nature of the aesthetic process and the ingredients from which his own art is composed.

The Lady Who Sold Furniture contains several stories in which the nature of art and the nature of learning about art are explored through a central character who is sensitive, intelligent, and in the process of learning about himself as he learns about his world. In the title novella, Peter's encounter with Jeanne forces him to examine his own values and his responsibility as a teacher. ''The Tide Line'' presents a younger protagonist, but one who must also define his future—here explicitly connected with art—against the influence of his parents and the various forms of tradition their presence implies. ''Keys and Watercress,'' one of Metcalf's most anthologized stories (along with ''Early Morning Rabbits'' from the same collection), again focuses on the initiation of a young boy into a world of symbols, and, by extension, into a new world that can be transformed through imagination. If the stories seem self-conscious it is because they are actually self-critical. Here, as in his later fiction, Metcalf uses the story to explore the value of storytelling itself.

This self-critical stance is certainly revealed in his first novel, *Going Down Slow,* through the character of David Appelby, a teacher who is obviously involved with the conflict between his ideals—both aesthetic and political—and those held by a provincial social order that would stifle all forms of personal expression, be they social, sexual, or cerebral. The novel's episodic form suggests that it is the first long work of a writer who really feels most at home in the short story mode. Nevertheless, it provides a strong sense of Metcalf's finicky attention to detail, and to the linguistic precision that is the hallmark of all his writing.

The Teeth of My Father, a second short story collection, revealed a much more mature writer than the earlier works. Metcalf's language is tighter than before; his attention to structure is more sophisticated and complex; and the stories are increasingly autobiographical and overtly concerned with the implications of storytelling. Five of the stories focus explicitly on art and artists, often in allegorical terms. Metcalf is most successful in ''Gentle As Flowers Make the Stones,'' a bitter, complex, and ultimately poignant record of one day in the life of the poet Jim Haine; in ''The Years in Exile,'' a moving record of a senescent, displaced writer's thoughts; and in the title story, in which the antiphonal structure suggests an implicit exchange between writer and critic, significant because it allows Metcalf to assume the role of self-commentator, the role his fiction seems to seek from its inception.

In *Girl in Gingham* his commentary is expressed through Peter Thornton, whom we meet after the divorce that isolates him, shakes his sense of identity, and forces him to attempt some form of personal recovery by finding a new, ideal woman. The juxtaposition of Peter's educated sensibility with the tastelessness and frequently grotesque lifestyles of successive CompuMate dates invests the novella with a sustained level of comedy that tends to mask Peter's tragic desperation. Peter's encounters with the CompuMate women provide a fertile ground for Metcalf to satirize the debased values of contemporary society. But Peter's failure in those encounters, and Anna's fate, are connected with a death of taste that Metcalf increasingly mourns. As the story develops it becomes clear that for Peter the pursuit of true art is inseparable from the pursuit of true love. Because the search for an ideal girl in gingham is part of Peter's quest for aesthetic fulfillment, he becomes more and more preoccupied with art as his relationship with Anna takes form.

This preoccupation is even more obvious in *Private Parts,* Metcalf's third published novella. Here the narrator is all-too-conscious of the aesthetic implications arising from the autobiographical fragments he presents. ''Life,'' as T.D. Moore sees it, is ''mainly lies.'' In short, life in *Private Parts* is private art. It comes as no surprise to discover that Moore is himself a writer dedicated to mythologizing those autobiographical fragments which constitute the private parts of memory. In him we find the qualities and frustrations that define all of Metcalf's highly articulate first-person narrators: an ability to fashion life through meaning; a rejection of contemporary taste and the threat it poses to genuine creativity; an involvement in others' art; and a consciousness of being involved in the narrative structure of his tale.

Metcalf's second novel makes his criticism of contemporary society hard to ignore. *General Ludd* takes its name from the nineteenth-century Luddite movement's radical opposition to so-called ''progress'' through technology and mechanization. Metcalf's Jim Wells is a contemporary Luddite, and a poet, who takes exception to the debased forms of communication—be they audiovisual, sartorial, or verbal—that seem ever-present in his world. No summary of this kind can do justice to the range of Metcalf's ferocious satire, his exposition of a host of characters through powerful vignettes, or the continual purity of his language. Similarly, the title *Adult Entertainment* hardly describes the lives one meets in the book's two novellas and three short stories. These are images of failure, men who would love to experience the fulfillment of lust, but who are instead surrounded by frustration. The collection serves to further confirm not only Metcalf's dedication to his craft, but also his reputation as one of Canada's most accomplished fiction writers.

—Robert Lecker

MICHAELS, Anne

Nationality: Canadian. **Born:** Toronto, 15 April 1958. **Education:** University of Toronto, B.A. 1980. **Awards:** Epstein Award, 1980; Commonwealth Prize for the Americas, 1986; Canadian Authors' Association Award for Poetry, 1991; National Magazine Award (Gold) for Poetry, 1991; Martin and Beatrice Fisher Award, 1997; Trillium Award, 1997; Orange Prize, 1997. **Agent:** c/o McLelland & Stewart, 481 University Avenue, Suite 900, Toronto, Ontario M5G 2E9, Canada. **Address:** Toronto, Ontario, Canada.

PUBLICATIONS

Novels

Fugitive Pieces. Toronto, McClelland & Stewart, 1996; New York, Knopf, 1997.

Poetry

The Weight of Oranges. Toronto, Coach House, 1985.
Miner's Pond: Poems. Toronto, McClelland & Stewart, 1991.
Skin Divers. Toronto, McClelland & Stewart, 1999.
Poems: The Weight of Oranges, Miner's Pond, Skin Divers. New York, Knopf, 2000.

Other

Contributor, *Poets 88*, edited by Ken Norris and Bob Hilderley. Kingston, Ontario, Quarry, 1988.
Contributor, *Poetry by Canadian Women*, edited by Rosemary Sullivan. Don Mills, Ontario, Oxford, 1989.
Contributor, *Sudden Miracles: Eight Women Poets*, edited by Rhead Tregebov. Toronto, Second Story Press, 1991.

* * *

Three award-winning books of poetry, now published in one volume as *Poems*, and one novel, *Fugitive Pieces*, are hardly a writer's career, but a more auspicious beginning would be difficult to imagine. *Fugitive Pieces* was a New York Times Notable Book of the Year and was Winner of the Lannan Literary Fiction award, the Guardian Fiction award, the Trillium prize, the Chapters/Books in Canada First Novel award, The Beatrice and Martin Fischer award (the main prize in the Jewish Book Awards), and England's prestigious Orange prize. It is at once one of the most poetic, harrowing, and complex considerations of the Holocaust, seeing it through the interlocked lives of a string of survivors, and a revelation of how people construct their selves, using not only personal events but knowledge of the natural world and history. Michaels is a poet writing a novel—in the tradition of Canadian novelist-poets Margaret Atwood, Michael Ondaatje, and Jane Urquhart—so every event, sight, and concept are held up to revelation through the miracle of language.

The central figures of *Fugitive Pieces* are Jacob Beer, who rises from the mud of Polish farm fields where he has hidden his seven-year-old self after the Nazis murdered his family; Athanasios Roussos, or Athos, the Greek geologist-polymath who smuggles Jacob from Poland to the island of Zakynthos and raises him after the War; and Ben, whose Holocaust-survivor parents immigrate to Toronto, where he becomes immersed in Jacob's heritage after the latter's death. Athos is a geologist, fascinated by limestone and the decay/preservation of wood, Jacob a Holocaust poet and writer on how the Nazis perverted archaeology to further the Aryan myth, and Ben a student of the relationship between weather and literature. These fascinations become the rich fields of metaphor for the Holocaust. Images of mud and burying, of Scott's ill-fated Antarctic expedition, and of Dostoyevsky's exile in the Siberian winter become testing places for human suffering and meaning.

In her poem ''Miner's Pond'' Michaels says, ''Even now, I wrap whatever's most fragile / in the long gauze of science. / The more elusive the truth, / the more carefully it must be carried.'' ''The long gauze of science'' signals one source of Michael's poetic inspiration in *Fugitive Pieces.* Archaeology, geography, and meteorology, the sciences of man exposed in and on the hostile land, are the sciences of Michaels's narrators. The 1942 discovery of the caves at Lascaux is placed against the ''Jews crammed into the earth then covered with a dusting of soil,'' and the discovery of the bog-preserved men is seen beside the Moorsoldaten, the ''Peat Bog Soldiers'' of Borgermoor Concentration Camp.

Fugitive Pieces has a frame of the lives of its characters, men for whom the varied loves of women provide surcease, yet who always return to the anguish of the Holocaust and its correlatives in all of human suffering. But the book's vitality is in its powerful, evocative weaving of images of past, present, and environment, a twisting relationship between the unnatural disaster of the Holocaust and the natural disasters man is heir to.

Truth emerges from Michaels's language like Jacob Beer rising from the mud of Poland. Of the Holocaust's relation to carbon dating she writes:

> Grief requires time. If a chip of stone radiates its self, its breath, so long, how stubborn might be the soul. If sound waves carry on to infinity, where are their screams now? I imagine them somewhere in the galaxy, moving forever towards the psalms.

Michaels, like many of the later characters in the novel, is not herself a Holocaust survivor but depicts a world forever changed for the children of the survivors and those drawn in by the pain of the survivors and their dead. The struggle is complex—a recognition of horror and pain beyond belief in nightmare and daily thought and behavior set into the shattered multifaceted gestures of caring and sacrificial love both in the Holocaust and by the living afterwards. This novel slowly extracts the sheer human will to understand and to give love to both the living and the dead. It is a remarkable achievement.

—Peter Brigg

MICHAELS, Barbara

See MERTZ, Barbara

MICHAELS, Leonard

Nationality: American. **Born:** New York City, 2 January 1933. **Education:** The High School for Music and Art, New York, graduated 1949; New York University, 1949–53, B.A. 1953; University of Michigan, Ann Arbor, M.A. 1956, Ph.D. in English 1967. **Family:** Married 1) Priscilla Older in 1966 (divorced), two sons; 2) Brenda Hillman in 1976, one daughter. **Career:** Teacher, Paterson State College, New Jersey, 1961–62; assistant professor of English, University of California, Davis, 1967–69. Since 1970 professor of English, University of California, Berkeley. Visiting professor at many universities, including Johns Hopkins University and the University of Alabama. Since 1977 editor, *University Publishing* review, Berkeley. Corresponding editor, *Partisan Review;* contributing editor, *Threepenny Review,* 1980. Contributor of short stories to numerous literary journals and popular magazines, including *Esquire, Paris Review, Evergreen Review, Partisan Review,* and *Tri-Quarterly.* **Awards:** Quill award, *Massachusetts Review,* 1964, 1966; National Endowment for the Arts grant, 1967; *Massachusetts Review* award, 1969, 1970; Guggenheim fellowship, 1969; National Endowment for the Humanities fellow, 1970; American Academy award in Literature, National Institute of Arts and Letters, 1971; *New York Times Book Review* Editor's Choice award, 1975. **Agent:** Lynn Nesbit, Janklow and Nesbit, 598 Madison Avenue, New York, New York 10022. **Address:** Department of English, University of California, Berkeley, California 94720, U.S.A.

PUBLICATIONS

Novel

The Men's Club. New York, Farrar Straus, and London, Cape, 1981.
Sylvia: A Fictional Memoir, illustrated by Sylvia Block. San Francisco, Mercury House, 1992.

Short Stories

Going Places. New York, Farrar Straus, 1969; London, Weidenfeld and Nicolson, 1970.
I Would Have Saved Them If I Could. New York, Farrar Straus, 1975.
A Girl with a Monkey: New and Selected Stories. San Francisco, Mercury House, 2000.

Play

City Boy (produced in New York City, 1985).

Screenplay: *The Men's Club,* 1986.

Other

Shuffle. New York, Farrar Straus, 1990; London, Cape, 1991.
To Feel These Things: Essays. San Francisco, Mercury House, 1993.
A Cat, illustrated by Frances Lerner. New York, Riverhead Books, 1995.
Time out of Mind: The Diaries of Leonard Michaels, 1961–1995. New York, Riverhead Books, 1999.
Contributor, *American Review 26,* edited by Theodore Solotaroff. New York, Bantam, 1977.
Contributor, *Prize Stories, 1980: The O. Henry Awards,* edited by William Abrahams. New York, Doubleday, 1980.
Editor, with Christopher Ricks, *The State of the Language.* Berkeley, University of California Press, 1980; University of California Press, and London, Faber, 1990.
Editor, with Raquel Scherr and David Reid, *West of the West: Imagining California.* Berkeley, California, North Point Press, 1990.

*

Critical Studies: *Passion and Craft: Conversations with Notable Writers,* edited by Bonnie Lyons and Bill Oliver, Urbana, University of Illinois Press, 1998.

Leonard Michaels comments:

My writing tends to be terse and quick, usually about urban types and the kinds of psychological violence they inflict upon one another. I have no philosophical or political messages. My work depends on traditional beliefs.

* * *

The fiction of Leonard Michaels is not easily described—it resists categories. It is realistic, but its dominant feature is irrationality of plot, sometimes comic, sometimes tragic, sometimes both at once. It is symbolic in its depiction of urban life, but its meanings are never reducible to messages, never allegorical. It is surreal and fragmented, but there is a consistency of viewpoint which can tie stories together and make for an overall coherence not to be found in the individual pieces. It reflects, sometimes self-consciously, the influence of such writers as Kafka, Roth, Malamud, Barthelme, and Borges, but it is nevertheless distinctive and compelling. At their best, Michaels's stories are intense, active, and imaginative; they can also be incomplete, vague, even incomprehensible.

Michaels's fiction has been published in three volumes of stories, *Going Places, I Would Have Saved Them If I Could,* and *A Girl With a Monkey,* and one short novel, *The Men's Club.* He has published a book of essays on various subjects, *To Feel These Things;* a mix of essays and autobiographical vignettes, *Shuffle;* and a selection of entries from his diaries, *Time Out of Mind.* With most writers, the distinction between their fiction and their autobiographical writing is reasonably clear. With Michaels, there is little to distinguish, in form or content, his diary entries, for example, made during his ill-fated marriage to Sylvia Bloch from his ''fictional memoir,'' entitled *Sylvia.*

The earlier pieces provide brief glimpses of contemporary urban existence, bizarre incidents suggesting the unnatural condition of city life: a naked boy is denied entrance to the subway for lack of a token; a couple maim each other in a fight and then decide to marry; a Talmudic scholar slips on an icy street and is assumed to be a drunken derelict; a professor of philosophy, by never speaking in class, wins a reputation for profundity; an honors graduate preferring to make a living by driving a cab is beaten gratuitously; a boy spying on his rabbi making love to his wife falls to his death; a telephone caller trying to reach a friend speaks instead to the burglar ransacking the friend's apartment. Some form of intense, though often anonymous, sexual encounter begins or ends many of the stories. In all of this there is the recognition of the craziness of things and yet of their plausibility—especially the stories set in New York City during the 1960s.

The element that provides continuity in Michaels's stories is the ''central intelligence'' of Phillip Liebowitz. Identified in many stories, present as unnamed narrator in others, he is a self-proclaimed, street-smart ''city boy.'' Phillip emerges as a character not in any particular story but only in the collection as a whole. His contact with others is almost entirely in a sexual context: the women in the stories are merely objects of lust, the other men his rivals for their favors. Through sexual conquest, Phillip asserts his existence and a degree of control over the hostile urban environment.

The one novel Michaels has published, *The Men's Club,* is strongly reminiscent of his story collections. A group of men get together to form what might be called a consciousness-raising group. They decide that each will tell the story of his life, but what we get instead are fragments of stories, not biographical data but moments of intense self-awareness. As in Chaucer's ''marriage group'' of tales (one of the characters is named Canterbury), there is a recurring theme: the fascinating power of women over men. These husbands who come together one evening specifically to be free of women can speak of nothing but their wives and lovers, some women whom they have lived with for many years, others they spent a few moments with many years ago. These anecdotes, like most of Michaels's stories, lack endings. When one character complains that he did not get the point of another's story, the narrator expresses views which apply to all Michaels's fiction:

> Doesn't matter ... I don't get it either. I could tell other stories that have no point. This often happens to me. I start to talk, thinking there is a point, and then it never arrives. What is it, anyhow, this point? Things happen. You remember. That's all. If you take a large perspective, you'll realize there never is a point.

Sylvia, ''a fictional memoir,'' is the story of the stormy relationship between a young writer and the troubled woman he marries. Interspersed within the narrative are passages labeled as ''journal'' entries dated between 1960, the year the narrator meets Sylvia Bloch, and 1963, the year of her suicide. As in his stories, Michaels has his narrator recount anecdotes of his life with Sylvia without any attempt to convey why the characters behave as they do. Throughout his narrative, the writer refuses to explain: ''My life, after all, wasn't a story. It was just moments, what happens from day to day, and it didn't mean anything, and there was no moral.''

Things happen in Michaels's fiction, often strange things, but there are no explanations, no point, no moral. The same traits which have drawn a cult following to Michaels alienates others. Readers who choose to enter the world of Leonard Michaels world do so on his terms.

—Robert E. Lynch

MIDDLETON, Stanley

Nationality: British. **Born:** Bulwell, Nottingham, 1 August 1919. **Education:** High Pavement School, Nottingham; University College of Nottingham (now Nottingham University), 1938–40, 1946–47, B.A. (London) 1940; M.Ed. (Nottingham) 1952. **Military Service:** Served in the Royal Artillery and the Army Education Corps, 1940–46. **Family:** Married Margaret Shirley Welch in 1951; two daughters. **Career:** English Master, 1947–81, and head of the English Department, 1958–81, High Pavement College, Nottingham. Judith E. Wilson Visiting Fellow, Emmanuel College, Cambridge, 1982–83. **Awards:** Booker prize, 1974. Honorary M.A., Nottingham University, 1975; M.Univ., Open University, 1995. **Address:** 42 Caledon Road, Sherwood, Nottingham NG5 2NG, England.

PUBLICATIONS

Novels

A Short Answer. London, Hutchinson, 1958.
Harris's Requiem. London, Hutchinson, 1960.
A Serious Woman. London, Hutchinson, 1961.
The Just Exchange. London, Hutchinson, 1962.
Two's Company. London, Hutchinson, 1963.
Him They Compelled. London, Hutchinson, 1964.
Terms of Reference. London, Hutchinson, 1966.
The Golden Evening. London, Hutchinson, 1968.
Wages of Virtue. London, Hutchinson, 1969.
Apple of the Eye. London, Hutchinson, 1970.
Brazen Prison. London, Hutchinson, 1971.
Cold Gradations. London, Hutchinson, 1972.
A Man Made of Smoke. London, Hutchinson, 1973.
Holiday. London, Hutchinson, 1974.
Distractions. London, Hutchinson, 1975.
Still Waters. London, Hutchinson, 1976.
Ends and Means. London, Hutchinson, 1977.

Two Brothers. London, Hutchinson, 1978.
In a Strange Land. London, Hutchinson, 1979.
The Other Side. London, Hutchinson, 1980.
Blind Understanding. London, Hutchinson, 1982.
Entry into Jerusalem. London, Hutchinson, 1983; New York, New Amsterdam, 1989.
The Daysman. London, Hutchinson, 1984.
Valley of Decision. London, Hutchinson, 1985; New York, New Amsterdam, 1987.
An After-Dinner's Sleep. London, Hutchinson, 1986.
After a Fashion. London, Hutchinson, 1987.
Recovery. London, Hutchinson, 1988.
Vacant Places. London, Hutchinson, 1989; New York, New Amsterdam, 1990.
Changes and Chances. London, Hutchinson, 1990.
Beginning to End. London, Hutchinson, 1991.
A Place to Stand. London, Hutchinson, 1992.
Married Past Redemption. London, Hutchinson, 1993.
Catalysts. London, Hutchinson, 1994.
Toward the Sea. London, Hutchinson, 1995.
Live and Learn. London, Hutchinson, 1996.
Brief Hours. London, Hutchinson, 1997.
Against the Dark. London, Hutchinson, 1998.

Uncollected Short Story

''The Noise,'' in *Critical Quarterly* (Manchester), Winter 1987.

Plays

Radio Plays: *The Captain from Nottingham,* 1972; *Harris's Requiem,* 1972; *A Little Music at Night,* 1972; *Cold Gradations,* from his own novel, 1973.

*

Manuscript Collection: Central Library, Nottingham.

Critical Studies: ''Stanley Middleton and the Provincial Novel'' by John Lucas, in *Nottingham Quarterly,* 1978; article by June Sturrock, in *British Novelists Since 1960* edited by Jay L. Halio, Detroit Gale, 1983; ''The Art of Stanley Middleton'' by A.S. Byatt, in *Fiction Magazine* (London), 1985; ''A Roaring Whisper,'' in *Stand* (Newcastle upon Tyne), Autumn 1988, and ''Einstein in the Patent Office,'' in *Encounter* (London), July-August 1989, both by Philip Davis; ''Master of the Unspectacular'' by John Mellors, in *London Magazine,* August-September 1990; *Stanley Middleton at Eighty,* edited by David Belbin and John Lucas, Nottingham, Five Leaves Publications, 1999.

Stanley Middleton comments:

(1972) I put down a few obvious points about my novels.

They are set mainly in the English midlands with characters drawn from the professional middle-classes (students, teachers, actors, writers, musicians, lawyers, painters, architects), though one will find laborers and factory workers as well as businessmen of real affluence.

The action usually occupies a short period of some months only (*Wages of Virtue* is an exception), and the plot deals with people in a state of crisis or perplexity caused by illness and death, or a breakdown of personal relationships, or the difficulties of creating a work of art (which may be music, *Harris's Requiem,* or poetry, *Him They Compelled,* or a novel in *Brazen Prison*). At this time of dilemmas, friends or relatives intervene, and thus learn their own inadequacies and, sometimes, strengths. No perfect characters or solutions exist; all is difficult, compromising, but a bonus of success or joy is occasionally found.

My idea is not only to tell an interesting story but to demonstrate the complexity of human character and motive. One must not only describe what has happened to people, or what they are like; one must make the characters live out what they are said to be, and this must include deviations from normality and actions ''out of character.'' I find this most difficult, but when I am charged, sometimes, with ''mere reportage,'' I can see no sense at all in the accusation. My novels are imaginative attempts to write down illuminating actions and talk from the lives of fictional people, and not transcriptions of tape recordings of real conversations or blow-by-blow commentaries on events which have really taken place. I am sometimes praised for the ''realism'' of my dialogue, and this makes me wonder if these critics, who may of course be using a ''shorthand'' dictated by the small space at their disposal, know how different my sort of dialogue is from that of real life.

This preoccupation leads to a choice of different levels of writing. A novel cannot always be intense; both by the shape of my work and my use of language I try constantly to interfere with the reader, to rest him as well as violently assault him. Therefore it is galling when I find critics who apparently subscribe to the notion that contemporary novels are either ''well-written'' (i.e. in ''mandarin'') or dashed down without care. Mine are usually dumped by such people in the second category. Shifts on my part from the point of view of one character to that of another also seem to pass unnoticed. I enjoy putting obstacles in my own way to find out if I can surmount them.

I am often asked if my novels are didactic. I wouldn't object to that word since the greatest work of art I know—Bach's *St. Matthew Passion*—could be so described. But unless a novel is complex, memorable, capable of holding a reader and moving him deeply, I've not much time for it.

I can't think these notes very helpful. General exegesis as opposed to critical discussion of precise points in specific books has little attraction for me as a writer. A novel should be its own defense; if it does not speak for itself to a well-equipped reader, call out echoes in him, it's not properly written.

* * *

Middle-class, middle-aged, midland dwellers provide most of the material for Stanley Middleton's novels from 1960 to the 1990s. His remarkable achievement in producing such lively work from such an unpromising source lies in his ability to make most of his characters both unlikeable and interesting at the same time. His women for the most part are tormented frigid tormentors, while his affluent men are generally mediocrities in their professions and indecisive shamblers in their personal lives, if they are not driven by an ugly and ruthless streak of ambition or obsessed by the demands of art.

He makes his readers understand that people at the end of their tether do not become heroic and loveable through their suffering, and that emotional snarl-ups render the participants selfish, irritable, and dull. The skill of Middleton's handling of dialogue is that although the first two qualities are caught, the third is avoided. The reader is held by the way the seemingly pointless remarks of the speakers can grate against each other. This is especially true when there is any attempt to bridge gaps of generation, social class, or economic status. In *Terms of Reference* the two late-middle-aged couples are perplexed and powerless when confronted by the failure of the marriage between the son of the very wealthy pair and the daughter of the academics. Yet although they can do nothing to hold their wayward children together, and are by no means certain that it would be a good thing to do so, all four are too fascinated by the situation to leave it alone.

Edward Tenby, the architect hero of *Apple of the Eye,* is not only the sole moderately creative and productive character in the novel, he is also the only man. He becomes involved with three neurotic women, each young enough to be his daughter. One of them has enough money to indulge her sickness to its limit, while the other two are poor enough to be flattered and astounded at making any contact so high in the social scale. In *Brazen Prison* Charles Stead, the ex-grammar school novelist, has to cope with the social nuances of relating to his wealthy socialite wife and the company she keeps, while at the same time involving himself with the husband and family of the local girl he had picked up in the dance hall as a youth.

Many novelists use the device of seeing their created world through the eyes of a fellow writer, and it is one that Middleton is fond of. As well as Charles Stead, there is the bestselling novelist Eric Chamberlain in *Ends and Means.* His obsession with success makes him almost insensitive to the fatal distress of his son and mistress, who both kill themselves. His detachment is matched by that of Frank, the modest, doomed, and isolated poet in *Two Brothers.*

Middleton is at his best, however, when he uses music or the visual arts to convey the excitement and compulsion of creation, and to give an added dimension to the construction of a novel. There are marvelous passages of musical analysis in *In a Strange Land,* which is an unusual Middleton novel in that the protagonist, James Murren, organist and composer, leaves the midlands to further his career in London. In *Valley of Decision,* which concerns a young music teacher married to an ambitious singer, the stages of the novel almost correspond to musical movements which are heightened by the analysis of the performances of an amateur quartet with whom the husband is invited to play.

Entry into Jerusalem explores the way a man can be driven to create a visual image. Like Middleton's novelists and musicians, John Worth, the thirty-year-old painter of this novel, successfully harnesses his imagination by living a life somewhat detached from his fellows, however many disasters take place around him. His work is barely touched when his former teaching colleague has a breakdown and kills himself.

Suicides of minor characters are frequent in Middleton's later novels, throwing the main events into a sharper focus. Death is ever-present, lurking in the background of everyday life, or accepted as a concomitant of age as it is in *Blind Understanding.* That novel follows the ruminations of a retired small-town solicitor as he lives out a day between attending a funeral in the morning and hearing of the heart attack suffered by a member of his wife's bridge party in the evening.

In these later novels, Middleton makes little use of his experience as a school teacher, the main exception being his sensitive exploration in *The Daysman* of the character of John Richardson, headmaster of a comprehensive school in a middle-class area and general friend and counselor to pupils and staff alike. He is a man who lets ambition and the lure of the media gradually rot his integrity and understanding. In this he is contrasted with his practical, capable wife, and the working out of their marriage is the main point of that novel. Indeed Middleton's preoccupation with the shifting adjustment of marriages enables him to make full use of his remarkable gift for describing the minute nuances of human interaction from the merest twitchings of ''body language'' to full-scale emotional and physical outbursts.

The most recent novels, however, tackle a different problem: the adjustment to reality that has to be made by anyone living on their own. This is often, but not always, linked to the circumstance of aging. So, in *An After-Dinner's Sleep,* the widower Alaistair Murray, a recently retired Director of Education, struggled with his need to fill his days in a meaningful way, and with an intermittent relationship with a woman friend from a long distant past.

Job Turner in *Recovery* is also widowed, but although he is coming towards the end of his career as a headmaster, he has yet to face the empty days of retirement. Both men are influenced by their grown children, and these connections make a natural web of time into which their married years are absorbed.

Joe Harrington in *After a Fashion* and Henry Fairfax in *Vacant Places* come into a different category. They are both young and successful enough to envisage promotion in their different careers; Harrington is an academic, Fairfax a business executive. They both live alone because their marriages have failed. Yet they both still have a relationship with their ex-wives, and the reader is left feeling that they are both the sort of men who will eventually remarry.

The theme of old age comes up as a subplot in both these novels. In *After a Fashion,* Joe Harrington is confronted with the declining powers of the professor of English in the university where he lectures, as well as the more extreme senility of one of his former schoolmasters and a neighbor's father, whose reminiscences he has reluctantly agreed to read. These three characters form a constant, if shadowy, chorus to the main action. In *Vacant Places,* the reminder of old age comes in the form of a garrulous Welshman, met in a pub. It is a brief but haunting portrait.

In *Changes and Chances* the novel pivots on a really disagreeable character, and that is a rare feature in Middleton's work. Adrian Hillier is a rich dilettante in his forties, who likes to dabble in the arts. His halfhearted attempt at marriage was doomed to failure, and the course of the novel finds him enlivening his pampered and solitary existence with bouts of sensual but loveless womanizing, embarked on from the maternal and sexual comforts provided by his housekeeper, Elsie. In this novel old age is presented in its most positive aspects in the person of the poet, Stephen Youlgrave; and the chorus is provided by an astutely observant child, Peter Fowler, who takes a Saturday job helping with the chores in Adrian's household.

In all these novels, the disciplines of music and poetry provide solace for the challenges of loneliness and the passage of time; and give meaning to the apparently trivial events through which Middleton displays and shapes his characters.

—Shirley Toulson

MILLER, Alex

Nationality: Australian (originally British, immigrated to Australia c.1952). **Born:** 1936. **Career:** Has held a variety of jobs, including cattle ranching, horse breaking, art brokering, and teaching. Currently a full-time writer. **Awards:** Miles Franklin award, 1993, and Commonwealth Writers prize, 1993, both for *The Ancestor Game.*

PUBLICATIONS

Novels

Watching the Climbers on the Mountain. Sydney, Pan, 1988.
The Tivington Nott. Ringwood, Victoria, Penguin, 1989.
The Ancestor Game. Ringwood, Victoria, Penguin, 1992; St. Paul, Minnesota, Graywolf Press, 1994.
The Sitters. Ringwood, Victoria, Viking, 1995.
Conditions of Faith. New York, Scribner, 2000.

Plays

Exiles. Melbourne, Australian Nouveau Theatre, 1981.

* * *

Migration is a recurrent theme in Alex Miller's writing, which vividly reveals the pressures of alienation and the need to belong. Miller's first novel, *Watching the Climbers on the Mountain* of 1988, is set in the Central Highlands of Queensland. The novel's intensity of passion in isolated situations is reminiscent of D.H. Lawrence, of Molly Skinner's *The Boy in the Bush*, and of Randolph Stow's first novel *A Haunted Land.* Miller's landscape and climate are, however, those of north Queensland with its heat, tropical storms, and mosquitoes. When the eighteen-year-old English stockman Robert Crofts arrives at a remote cattle station to work, he is drawn into a series of physical and psychological struggles. Initiation occurs when he becomes the focus of the simmering discontents and desires of the family on whose station he works. His sexual relationship with the station owner's wife leads to tragedy. Anger, jealousy, madness, and revenge drive the plot, but these are counterpointed by the woman's sense of belonging to the mountainous landscape into which she was born. As in later novels, sexual ambivalence is evident and the psychological relationships of parents with children, and brothers with sisters are important elements.

Miller's second novel *The Tivington Nott,* written in 1989, returns to the English West Country setting of Somerset on the edges of Exmoor. The novel's youthful first-person narrator, a Londoner, is a newcomer to the strict class barriers of provincial England. He is perhaps incipiently Australian in refusing to call his employer ''master'' but settling for ''boss.'' But his main access to power is through retreat to a private inner world: he thus identifies with the elusive wild stag (the ''nott'') on Exmoor, which has eluded the local hunters for years by retreating to its secret soiling pit in the woods. The novel's major action is a hunt which celebrates the call of the wild in defiance of the forces of ''civilization.''

The Ancestor Game of 1992 is a more finely wrought, ambitious novel than the previous two, bringing to a point of subtle imaginative development Miller's preoccupations with home, homeland, and alienation. The sentient center of this novel is an English immigrant, Steven Muir, who lives and teaches in Melbourne. Muir's struggles with his sense of identity as an English-born Australian find their imaginative correlatives in a Chinese-Australian friend, Lang Tzu, and an artist friend of German and Asian extraction, Gertrude Spiess. The Chinese-born Lang Tzu's name is made up of two characters in Mandarin signifying ''the son who goes away.'' But Lang's ancestry is complicated by the fact that his great-grandfather Feng had come to Australia in 1848, and made his fortune on the Victorian goldfields before returning to China. Thus the ''son who goes away'' paradoxically returns to an ancestral dwelling-place when he migrates to Australia.

The action in *The Ancestor Game,* carried on in a series of parallel or interwoven histories, moves principally between the cities of Melbourne, Shanghai, and Hangzhou (Marco Polo's ''City of Heaven''). At a thematic level, much is made of the notion of ''extraterritoriality,'' a state of being beyond history, place, and circumstance, promoted principally by the German-born Dr. Spiess, father of Gertrude. For Dr. Spiess, life in the International Settlement in prewar Shanghai had seemed ideally ''extraterritorial,'' but he too is drawn inexorably towards a recognition of his involvement in history. When Lang Tzu burns his maternal grandfather's book of ancestors he recognizes himself, like other protagonists in Miller's work, as ''a stranger on this earth.'' But Dr. Spiess offers the young Lang an antidote: ''Long for something you can't name … and call it Australia.'' One of the novel's chief sources of appeal is that it reappraises Australia as a country of postcolonial possibility where ancestry, allegiance, and identity coalesce in an uncertain process of becoming.

Miller's fourth novel, *The Sitters,* develops a leitmotif from earlier work, namely the power of art to release human emotions and to transcend local conditions. The first-person narrator in this short novel is a late-middle-aged English-born painter living in Canberra. He lives alone, having been left some years previously by his wife and son. When he meets an Australian-born woman academic who works in England but has returned on a visiting appointment to a university in Australia, the two lives and lineages intersect. The narrator is attracted to the woman as a person and as a potential subject of his paintings. As the relationship develops, so too does his renewed desire to paint, which releases him in turn to cope with the psychological effects of his unresolved and truncated past in England. While postcolonial theory informs aspects of *The Ancestor Game, The Sitters* draws to some extent on Roland Barthes's speculative essays on words and images. A feature of *The Sitters* is its interweaving of present circumstances with vignettes of memory. A crisis occurs when the narrator returns with his new friend to her childhood home in the Araluen Valley in New South Wales. Here, in a finely evoked poetry of place the artist achieves a consummation through art, and imagines himself for the first time in a place of belonging. Through a deft use of parallel images and intersecting motifs, Miller's fourth novel explores afresh his preoccupations with place, community, and individual identity.

Very much the same could be said of *Conditions of Faith,* for which Miller drew part of his inspiration from a journal of his mother's that he discovered after her death. In it, she described a sojourn in Paris during the 1920s, and this Miller translated into the tale of Emily, an Australian who marries a Franco-Scottish engineer named Georges. Emily has the sensibilities of a Madame Bovary, and when she discovers just how dull and conventional a life Georges (who is ten years her senior) leads in Paris, she determines to find adventure. The result is an affair and an unwanted child, and Emily pushes herself beyond the frontiers of all emotional comfort to satisfy her longings. Her journey takes her as far as the ruins of Carthage, a fitting symbol for frustrated ambition.

—Bruce Bennett

MILLHAUSER, Steven (Lewis)

Nationality: American. **Born:** New York, 3 August 1943. **Education:** Columbia College, New York, 1961–65, B.A., Brown University, Providence, Rhode Island, 1968–1971 and 1976–77. **Family:** Married Cathy Allis in 1984, one son and one daughter. **Career:** Visiting associate professor of English, Williams College, 1986–88; associate professor of English, Skidmore College, 1988–1992. Since 1992 professor of English, Skidmore College. **Awards:** Prix Medicis Étranger, 1975; American Academy and Institute of Arts and Letters award, 1987, for literature; Lannan literary award, 1994, for fiction; Pulitzer prize for fiction, 1997. **Agent:** Amanda Urban, International Creative Management, 40 West 57th St., New York, New York 10019, U.S.A.

PUBLICATIONS

Novels

Edwin Mullhouse: The Life and Death of an American Writer. New York, Knopf, 1972.
Portrait of a Romantic. New York, Knopf, 1977.
From the Realm of Morpheus. New York, Morrow, 1986.
Martin Dressler: The Tale of an American Dreamer. New York, Crown, 1996.
Enchanted Night: A Novella. New York, Crown, 1999.

Short Stories

In the Penny Arcade. New York, Knopf, 1986.
Little Kingdoms: Three Novellas. New York, Simon and Schuster, 1993.
The Barnum Museum: Stories. Normal, Illinois, Dalkey Archive Press, 1997.
The Knife Thrower and Other Stories. New York, Crown Publishers, 1998.

* * *

Steven Millhauser is an explorer of the uneasy relationship between imagination and experience, portraying their various effects and conflicts on the personalities of his characters. He is also a stylistic virtuoso, adept at creating precise and allusive prose that both mirrors and perfects literary tradition. All of his protagonists are disappointed dreamers who long to see their fantasies realized, though each meets with varying degrees of success.

In his first novel, *Edwin Mullhouse: The Life and Death of an American Writer,* Millhauser creates the mock biography of an eleven-year-old novelist, ostensibly written by a twelve-year-old scholar, that is both a shrewd literary parody and a convincing portrayal of the emotional vicissitudes of childhood. With discernible influences from Nabokov's *Pale Fire* and Mann's *Doctor Faustus,* this novel explores the murky border between history and fiction, suggesting a kind of culpability in the biographer's efforts to shape the life of his subject into a narrative whole, at one point even having the biographer Jeffrey Cartwright assert that his chosen mission is even greater than Mullhouse's vocation as an artist, ''for the artist creates the work of art, but the biographer, so to speak, creates the artist.'' It is an erudite arrogance made all the more absurd for being the musings of a proud little boy. Paradoxically, this assertion also emphasizes the very artifice of history. By condensing all the conventions of literary biography into a single though prodigious lifetime of a dozen years, Millhauser manages to combine a meticulous observation of the minutiae of childhood with a critical satire in an alchemical mix that many critics consider to be his finest novel.

In *Portrait of a Romantic,* Millhauser again creates a novel that is both a pitch-perfect critique, this time of romanticism, as well as a harrowingly vivid account of the turmoils of adolescence. Arthur Grumm, the narrator, tells the story of his formative years, when he was an American Werther, a being of passionate urges, emotional idealism, and painful sensitivity. Grumm and his friends divert themselves decadently as each struggles to reconcile their yearnings with their circumstances. Like Goethe's character, Grumm contemplates suicide as an escape from the dreariness of existence. The book climaxes with a particularly fateful game of Russian roulette between these two boys, but not before examining, in seventy-five chapters of highly-charged language that evokes comparisons to writers such as Goethe and Poe, the emotional upheavals of adolescence in a way that equates that nether region between childhood and adulthood with an artistic temperament characterized by excessive passions and egoism.

After the publication of these two novels, critics focused on Millhauser's fictional evocations of children, noting that his main characters are both recognizable children as well as extremely precocious geniuses. But Millhauser depicts genius as the ability to sustain obsessions—and children, with their wild emotions coupled to a naive worldview, are naturally obsessive. And, while it is true that Millhauser depicts growing up as the loss of some essential power of imagination that is the province of childhood, this is part and parcel of his more basic exploration of the conflict between imagination and experience. Millhauser's later work would be concerned less with children than with the dreams and disappointments of adults.

Millhauser's third novel, *From the Realm of Morpheus,* is a monumental travelogue of the imagination, its plot being more impressionistically thematic than dramatic, lending the book both the vividness and insubstantiality of a dream. But no mere dream is as encyclopedic as Millhauser's novel, which both borrows and steals from dozens of works of fabulist literature, from Ovid to Kafka, from Spenser's *The Faerie Queene* to Homer's *Odyssey.* Carl Hausman, a young man who could be Arthur Grumm's grown and disaffected avatar, literally falls down a hole to enter a dreamland ruled by Morpheus, the god of sleep, who takes Hausman on a comprehensive tour of his kingdom, where such fantastical things as libraries of unwritten books, halls of talking mirrors, and living paintings abound. By far the longest of Millhauser's novels, *From the Realm of Morpheus* is also his most complex, being more an aria of fantasies than a dramatically structured tale that conforms to the Aristotelian unities. This may explain why the book has such an arduous publishing history as well as, at best, an ambiguous critical reputation.

Martin Dressler: The Tale of an American Dreamer is Millhauser's marriage of a rags-to-riches Horatio Alger tale to his oft-adopted motif and modus operandi of depicting and delineating the imagination as an endless labyrinth that, at its farthest remove from the workaday world, approaches the rarefied and static nature of death itself. On the other hand, this novel breaks Millhauser's pattern of constructing a narrative in which a first-person narrator tells of his

Boswell-to-Johnson relationship with a generally more brilliant central character. Instead, Millhauser conforms to the American tradition of third-person narrations of the rise and fall of men attempting to achieve that golden fleece of American mythology: the American Dream. Echoing the novels of Theodore Dreiser, though without Dreiser's pessimistic sense of naturalistic fate, Millhauser depicts the life of the eponymous character, at the same time evoking a turn-of-the-century portrait of New York City that is both realistic and romanticized. Dressler rises from cigar-shop success to hotel-chain magnate, building ever more grandiose creations that culminate in the Grand Cosmo, a hotel that is nothing less than the universe contained in a single building. The failure of this final construct is a telling indictment of the often corrosive relationship between idealism and pragmatism, between dream and reality. It is Dressler's failure to reconcile his dreams with a clear-eyed view of the real world that causes him to fail; his fantasies have been allowed to run amok in the Grand Cosmo, but even this most substantial of dreams is too ethereal to survive in the bustling world of the city. Because it eschews the linguistic pyrotechnics of *Edwin Mullhouse* while telling a recognizably unified and dramatic story, *Martin Dressler* has become Millhauser's most commercially successful novel.

The novella, *Enchanted Night,* which was published as a book in 1999, is the story of a single night in a small town in the state of Connecticut, a night of the full moon in which the dreams of the town's inhabitants begin to merge with their real lives. In short episodes, sometimes only a sentence in length, Millhauser weaves several strands of story into a unified text that explores the relationship between dreaming and living, questioning whether one type of experience is more authentic than the other. A mannequin comes to life for a date with a lonely mechanic, while the moon itself descends in bodily form to seduce a young man. The Pied Piper arrives to summon the children of the town with his flute, while a gang of young female prowlers breaks into the house of a spinster. However, as dawn breaks, each of these encounters ends and reality is restored. But the townspeople remember, if unconsciously, what has happened. Indeed, as this night ends and as the various dreams depicted begin to fade, their effects on the townspeople are no less profound than actual memory.

If *From the Realm of Morpheus* is Millhauser's creativity at its grandest realization, then *Enchanted Night* is his imaginative vision at its most focused, while his Pulitzer prize-winning *Martin Dressler* is Millhauser's most realistic creation. *Edwin Mullhouse,* his auspicious debut, is also his most insightful exploration of character, but all of these novels are instances of Millhauser's aesthetic at work, best summarized at the beginning of chapter nine in *Portrait of a Romantic:*

> A work of fiction is a radical act of the imagination whose sole purpose is to supplant the world. In order to achieve this purpose, a work of fiction is willing to use all the means at its disposal, including the very world it is plotting to annihilate. Art imitates Nature as Judas imitates Christ.

Since the publication of *Edwin Mullhouse,* Millhauser has created such radical works of fiction, whose very authenticity lies in their ability to supplant reality with an equal, even insidious vivacity. Critics may fault Millhauser's fiction for being fantastically unrealistic, but Millhauser would himself argue that such unreality is precisely his point.

—J.J. Wylie

MINOT, Susan (Anderson)

Nationality: American. **Born:** Boston, Massachusetts, 1956. **Education:** Brown University, Providence, Rhode Island, B.A.; Columbia University, New York, M.F.A. **Career:** Associate editor, Grand Street, New York, 1982–86; adjunct professor, Graduate Writing Program, New York University, 1987, and Columbia University, New York, 1989. **Awards:** Prix Femina Étranger, 1987. **Address:** c/o Georges Borchardt, 136 East 57th St., New York, New York 10022, U.S.A.

Publications

Novels

Monkeys. New York, Dutton, 1986.
Folly. Boston, Houghton Mifflin, 1992.
Evening. New York, Knopf, 1998.

Short Stories

Lust and Other Stories. Boston, Houghton Mifflin, 1989.

Plays

Screenplays: *Stealing Beauty.* Fox Searchlight, 1996; published as *Stealing Beauty: Screenplay,* New York, Grove Press, 1996.

* * *

A loving detailer of her region—Boston and the North Shore—and a detailed critic of love, Susan Minot weaves stories whose sadness bespeak a piercing intelligence and courageous honesty. Her contribution to the genres of short story and novel is a feminized minimalist style. Although minimalism is more often associated with male writers such as the late Raymond Carver, Minot gives us a hybridized version. She incorporates minimalism's narrow brush strokes, while at the same time painting the emotions clearly.

Minot's protagonists, mostly women, are searching for love. The theme remains constant in different milieus: *Monkeys* is set in 1970s North Shore; *Lust* takes place in yuppie 1980s New York City; *Folly* is set on Beacon Hill from the 1920s to the 1950s. Although the language and mores of each time and place are different, the sentiments expressed by the characters are similar: in the space where love should be, there is emptiness, lack, "an overwhelming sadness, an elusive gaping worry."

Family love is the primary concern in her first two novels, whereas romantic love is the aim in the short story collection, *Lust.* Although romance is harder to achieve and more transitory, family love is also elusive, unexpected, sometimes even a great surprise. In *Monkeys,* Minot creates a whole family, including seven kids, with a degree of particularity that one would expect for a smaller cast. Her portraits of troubled adolescent males are as sensitive as those of their sisters. In the chapter, "Accident," teenaged Sherman is introduced by a typically minimalist *reductio ad absurdum,* which succeeds in conveying a sufficient amount of information: "Sherman has the cat in his lap, not thinking much, sixteen years old." As if being a sixteen-year-old male means, *prima facie,* that you don't think too much, but you do like to feel living creatures in your lap. This story climaxes in a scene that any of us would like to have written: Sherman, dead drunk and talking like a thug, confronts his alcoholic dad with the question: ''Are you my faddah? Then why don't you act like a faddah?'' Predictably, Dad scurries away, leaving Sherman in an uncharacteristically expressive state. One wail escapes him; it sets his siblings in motion. Chicky, the younger brother, knows that this is not like the grief when their mother died: *that* was like seeing the Devil for a flash; *this* was the Devil swooping down, hulking in the middle of the kitchen table, and settling down to stay. In this family, as in many real-life ones, the children have been forced to take responsibility for their alcoholic father. Minot creates a recognizable family dynamic, evoking pathos without melodrama.

In *Lust,* the characters are wistful; they can't quite understand what it is they stand to gain from their sexual relationships, even though they need them like bodies need water. Women pursue and are pursued by men in a fast-whirling social environment that includes cocaine-snorting and glamorous careers in film and journalism. Minot's sure rhythms capture the hard-boiled verities of this party life. In short paragraphs, she begins with short, simple sentences, building gradually to longer ones to create the inevitable conclusion: men don't love like women do. Her logic appears in simple two- or three-liners that capture a sense of futility. After sex, boys are like this: ''Their blank look tells you that the girl they were fucking is not there anymore. You seem to have disappeared.'' Before sex, things are much better: ''He pressed close. She felt as if she were setting off for a place she'd only vaguely heard about. Her heart was going madly, knowing nothing, feeling no pain.'' During the affair, you learn that you can't take it: ''Slowly it dawned on me this was one of those loose and easy things. Maybe I'll learn something, I thought. I did. I learned things. I learned I didn't have the stomach for it. You need an iron stomach, and nerves of steel.'' Do not look for a happy, mutual, heterosexual relationship in Minot. You will not find it.

Folly's title warns us that it is about another inadequate relationship, this time a marriage that begins in the 1920s. Because Lilian is more sheltered than the protagonists of *Monkey* and *Lust,* her loss of innocence is more gradual. Her life is measured by three encounters with Walter Vail that take place every dozen years. He is the kind of cad who first appears in *Lust,* but whose looks and actions are even more deceiving to a 1920s Boston girl who is not exactly a flapper. The story is a realistic account of changed feelings over time. After Walter leaves her the first time, Lilian eventually finds a man, Gilbert Finch, who is Walter's opposite in temperament: deeply sensitive, introverted, and conservative. She convinces herself that *this* is true love, not that heart-flapping sensation she had felt with Walter. She marries Gilbert and has children. But when Gilbert's sensitivity develops into clinical depression, Lilian decides that Walter is her type of man, after all. Walter haunts her Bostonian scene at decade-intervals, always aware that Lilian is still infatuated with him, and always neglectful of the consequence of his actions. In the last scene, Lilian is finally able to name his indifference for what it is: ''Caring was beneath him. He could not have done a better job if someone had dared him not to care.'' Minot dramatizes his condition in an absurd, yet realistic gesture: he doesn't care enough to finish his sentence. He reaches for a drink instead.

Minot's titles, *Monkeys, Lust,* and *Folly,* tell us what she thinks about people seeking or running from love. Yet she is not a pessimist; rather, she accepts that life contains greater mystery than words can say. This quality is borne out in *Evening,* a novel in which the title serves as a metaphor for the end of one's days: dying of cancer at age sixty-five, Ann Grant remembers her life, in particular a torrid weekend four decades in the past.

—Jill Franks

MIRSKY, Mark (Jay)

Nationality: American. **Born:** Boston, Massachusetts, 11 August 1939. **Education:** Harvard University, Cambridge, Massachusetts, B.A. (magna cum laude) 1961 (Phi Beta Kappa); Stanford University, California (Woodrow Wilson fellow), M.A. 1962. **Military Service:** Served in the United States Air Force Reserve, 1962–68. **Family:** Married Kinger Channah Grytting in 1980; two children. **Career:** Schoolteacher, Boston, 1962; staff writer, *American Heritage,* New York, 1964; lecturer in English, Stanford University, 1966. Lecturer, 1967–70, assistant professor, 1970–74, associate professor, 1975–80, director of the M.A. program, 1978–84, and since 1980 professor of English, City College, New York. Founding member of the Board, Teachers-Writers Collaborative, 1967, and Fiction Collective, 1974, both New York; editor, *Fiction,* New York, 1972–91. **Awards:** Bread Loaf Writers Conference grant; National Endowment for the Arts award, for editing, 1980, and senior fellowship, 1981; Creative Artists Public Service grant, 1982. **Address:** 513 E. 13th St., New York, New York 10009, U.S.A.

Publications

Novels

Thou Worm, Jacob. New York, Macmillan, and London, Collier Macmillan, 1967.

Proceedings of the Rabble. Indianapolis, Bobbs Merrill, 1970.

Blue Hill Avenue. Indianapolis, Bobbs Merrill, 1972.

The Red Adam. Los Angeles, Sun and Moon Press, 1989.

Short Stories

The Secret Table. New York, Fiction Collective, 1975.

Uncollected Short Stories

''Swapping,'' in *Statements 1,* edited by Jonathan Baumbach. New York, Braziller, 1975.

''The Last Lecture,'' in *Tri-Quarterly* (Evanston, Illinois), Spring 1976.

''Last Boat to America,'' in *Massachusetts Review* (Amherst), Summer 1981.

''Child's Alphabet,'' in *Literary Review* (Madison, New Jersey), Summer 1982.

Other

My Search for the Messiah: Studies and Wanderings in Israel and America. New York, Macmillan, 1977.

The Absent Shakespeare. Rutherford, New Jersey, Fairleigh Dickinson University Press, 1994.

Editor, with David Stern, *Rabbinic Fantasies: Imaginative Narratives from Classic Hebrew Literature*. Philadelphia, Jewish Publication Society of America, 1990.
Editor, *Diaries, 1899–1941* by Robert Musil, translated by Philip Payne. New York, Basic Books, 1998.

* * *

A catalogue of Mark Mirsky's fictional liabilities in his early work is short and bittersweet: he reworks worn material; he cannot resist dreamworld and fantasyland scenes; he is too delighted with royal-purple prose and ''experimentalism''; finally he breaks himself up with broad ethnic humor that often offends. Yet he has such large talent that he skillfully turns each of these faults to advantage even when he does not transcend them.

His first volume of fiction seemed partly to be a parodic mélange of Aleichem, Singer, and Malamud. The inversions of Yiddish, the barrage of exclamation and interrogation points, the spread-finger resignation of the Jewish immigrant, all knotted and clotted the young writer's style and suggested the bar mitzvah school of cheap Catskill entertainment. Thus, the ''Introduction'' begins:

> ''I've got the whole state of Jewish affairs right between my fingers! What? You don't understand? Take a seat. Don't worry, it won't break. A bit cracked but it's had a rest. Watch out! Watch out for that pile of books. Knock one over, my whole place is on your head. Pages, dust, dirty yarmulkes. Eh! Let it fall.''

In spite of such false starts, Mirsky knows and loves his ''material'' and manages to move us to both laughter and pity in this collection of tales about East European immigrants struggling to remain Jews in their new homeland. The familiar figure of the schlemiel hero is brilliantly renewed in the collection's finest story, ''The Shammos from Aroostook County.'' Five years later, Mirsky returned to the struggling Jews of the old towns near Boston with *Blue Hill Avenue.* Although he labeled his tale ''vaudeville,'' he writes here with more control, except for an inappropriate slapstick ending. Four of the characters are superbly drawn: Rabbi Lux, who is ''a little too good, too pious for much of Dorchester''; the rabbi's wife, once timid and passionate, now a loving, lunatic protectress; Simcha Tanzenn, a canny, lisping politician who collects on favors rarely delivered; and a demented Jewish mother, who uses the telephone like a mortar and wills her war-lost (and worthless) son back to safety. Mirsky's latest treatment of Jewish traditions, *The Secret Table,* is more serious in tone and, despite some obscurity of form, marks another fictional advance for the author in portraying his fierce bookish forebears. The first novella depicts the search through memory of thirty-year-old Maishe for the womb-security now lacking in the decayed streets of Blue Hill Avenue: the companion novella, ''Onan's Child,'' builds upon Genesis to explore, through Jacob, Isaac, Joseph, and Onan, the terrible contradictions of man's nature and Jewish history. In both stories, past and present, subjective and objective worlds, the Jew and the universal man, are blended into a believable, densely-textured reality.

Mirsky's second novel, *Proceedings of the Rabble,* may be his most ambitious. Anticipating Robert Altman's film, *Nashville,* in an urban locale, Mirsky uses the evangelical right-wing political crusade of William Starr to portray the murderous impotence moving American democracy toward rage, outrage, and self-destruction. Despite the straining interior-cinema technique employed, Mirsky's apocalyptic ending matches the final upheaval of West's *The Day of the Locust.*

The first clue that *The Red Adam* is a modern fable lies in its title; a close second is the name of its narrator, Job. But this Job goes much further than his biblical counterpart, who tried to understand the mind of Job: Job Schwartz attempts to *become* God by creating a man in his own image. In his novels, Mirsky renews such staple items of contemporary American fiction as megalomania, violence, sexual sickness, and the Jew as representative sufferer, so that they still serve to tell us about ourselves.

—Frank Campenni

MISTRY, Rohinton

Nationality: Canadian (originally Indian; immigrated to Canada, 1975; naturalized Canadian citizen). **Born:** Bombay, India, 1952. **Education:** University of Bombay, B.S. 1975; University of Toronto, B.A. 1984. **Family:** Married Freny Elavia; two daughters. **Career:** Has worked in a bank in Toronto. Since 1985 full-time writer. **Awards:** *Canadian Fiction* annual contributor's award, 1985; Governor General's award for best fiction, 1991, Smith Books/*Books in Canada* first novels award, and Commonwealth Writers prize, 1992, all for *Such a Long Journey.* **Agent:** Lucina Vardey Agency, 297 Seaton St., Toronto, Ontario M5A 2T6, Canada.

Publications

Novels

Such a Long Journey. Toronto, McClelland, New York, Knopf, and London, Faber, 1991.
A Fine Balance. New York, Knopf, 1996.

Short Stories

Tales from Firozsha Baag. Toronto, Penguin, 1987; London, Faber, 1992; as *Swimming Lessons, and Other Stories from Firozsha Baag,* Boston, Houghton Mifflin, 1989.

*

Critical Studies: *The Fiction of Rohinton Mistry: Critical Studies,* edited by Jaydipsinh Dodiya, New Delhi, India, Prestige Books, 1998.

* * *

Rohinton Mistry's small body of fiction has received high praise, numerous honors, and been favorably, if inevitably, compared to the work of the best known and most respected contemporary Indian writers. Much of his achievement derives from the seamless way in which he has fashioned a decidedly personal style from a variety of literary precursors (Euro-American as well as Indian: Joyce, Cheever, Malamud, and Bellow most notably) perfectly suited to his Indian subject matter. Although his style lacks Rushdie's postmodern brilliance, it deftly avoids Mukherjee's melodramatic excesses and Naipaul's air of critical detachment while successfully adapting Narayan's studied naivete to more modern urban as well as immigrant experience. Mistry's achievement also derives from his willingness to devote himself to those aspects of his subject that he knows best and that most of his Western readers know not at all: the small Parsi community, both in Bombay and in Toronto.

Mistry's is an art of the bittersweet about a world more sad than tragic, where frustrations rather than defeats are the general rule. It is an art gently ironic in its depiction of the everyday lives of mainly middle-class Parsi characters either living in apartment complexes in Bombay or struggling to adapt to immigrant life in Canada. The religious strife that figures prominently in much writing about India serves as backdrop for the more pressing quotidian problems faced by Mistry's characters: straitened finances, the effect of modern ways on cultural traditions (particularly as manifested in generational conflict), ambivalence regarding immigration, and the consequences of sexual repression—all compounded by life's little inconveniences: shoddy goods, petty neighbors, government corruption, and the like. The eleven stories included in *Swimming Lessons* concern the interconnected lives of the residents of Forozsha Baag, with its ''surfeit of bank clerks and bookkeepers'' leavened by the occasional professor, lawyer, or chartered accountant. In these stories spanning about a decade, people grow old, spouses die, and children emigrate only to exchange the constrictiveness of home life for a new set of anxieties. The title story brings together the two worlds and generations in an especially effective manner, shuttling between two cities, two typefaces, and two sensibilities. In writing a book of stories not unlike *Swimming Lessons,* the son comes to understand the world he has left behind; in reading that book his parents come in turn to understand the son whom they feared was growing not just geographically distant but culturally distant as well.

Such a Long Journey is at once a more narrowly focused fiction (having a single protagonist and center of consciousness) and, in its depiction of life in modern India, more wide-ranging (even if temporally more circumscribed). The novel is set in 1971, during the time of Pakistan's brutal but (as the result of Indian intervention) unsuccessful attempt to suppress the uprising in its eastern wing, the future Bangladesh, and against the backdrop of India's 1965 war with Pakistan over Kashmir and the 1962 defeat by the Chinese army. It deals more specifically with Gustad Noble in his various roles: husband, father, bank clerk, resident in the block of flats called the Khodadad Building. At once petty and heroic (in a decidedly minor, middle-class key), Noble struggles on various fronts: with the threat of war, his youngest daughter's persistent illness, his wife's superstitious beliefs, his son's preferring to pursue a worthless liberal arts degree rather than study engineering, and the decline of the family's fortunes (from the bankruptcy of his grandfather's furniture business to his father's ''despoiled'' bookstore to Gustad's ignoble position at the bank). There are the surly bus conductors, rising prices resulting from the Refugee Relief Tax, and passersby who relieve themselves on the wall surrounding his apartment block, a wall the municipal government wants to raze in order to widen the road, and thus deprive Gustad of the little space he has to breathe the already fetid air. And there are the deaths of the building's retarded caretaker whom Gustad must himself take care of, a coworker whose antics both amuse and irritate, and the former friend and neighbor, Major Jimmy Bilimoria, whose mysterious letter makes Gustad an accomplice in crime even as it exposes him to corruption in government that leads all the way to the prime minister herself. Caught between resignation and resistance, Gustad is an essentially good man doing the best he can in troubling times and under difficult circumstances. Within his unassuming public self, one finds a depth of quiet heroism that corresponds to those moments of elegiac lyricism that arise from Mistry's artfully artless prose.

Like *Such a Long Journey,* Mistry's second novel, *A Fine Balance,* was short-listed for Britain's most prestigious literary award, the Booker Prize. It is by far the author's most ambitious work to date. Rushdie-like in scope, Dickensian in approach, the novel is set chiefly in an unnamed city by the sea (Bombay) in 1975–76, in the period leading up to and during the state of Emergency that Prime Minister Indira Gandhi declared to avoid being cast out of office and to crack down on her political opponents under cover of protecting the nation. Against that backdrop, Mistry tells the three intertwined stories of his four main characters, weaving them together with numerous others. Dina Dalal is a widow struggling to make ends meet (by making clothes on consignment) while avoiding being evicted from her home by her greedy landlord. Maneck Kohlah, who illegally rents a room from her, is a student unwilling to resign himself to taking over his father's shop. Ishvan and his nephew Omprakash work in Dina's home as tailors, having left the confines of a village ruled by the caste system (they belonged to the cobbler caste) and wealthy landlords. The city they find ''so huge and so confusing'' is for Mistry ''a story factory,'' ''a modern Mahabharat.'' His novel is in effect an epic of physical violence and economic exploitation, in which the desire to succeed is reduced to the struggle merely to survive and in which individual, random destruction is the reflection of, and is dwarfed by, the violence of a corrupt government promoting sterilization programs and euphemistic Beautification Projects that sweep beggars off the streets and into labor camps. It is a world in which even good intentions (the Rent Act) quickly go awry, leaving those it was designed to protect no better off than before. In such a world, and such a novel, Mistry invariably sides with ''the ones who are weak and without influence,'' which is to say with everyone of narrative importance in a novel that wears its sympathies on its sleeve yet manages to avoid becoming unconvincingly sentimental. Although not one of these characters will succeed, some not even survive, Mistry nonetheless strikes in the novel and in his readers ''a fine balance between hope and despair'' that is characteristic of his work in general.

—Robert A. Morace

MITCHELL, (Charles) Julian (Humphrey)

Nationality: British. **Born:** Epping, Essex, 1 May 1935. **Education:** Winchester College, Hampshire, 1948–53; Wadham College, Oxford, B.A. 1958; St. Antony's College, Oxford, M.A. 1962. **Military**

Service: Served in the Royal Naval Volunteer Reserve, 1953–55: Midshipman. **Career:** Member, Arts Council Literature Panel, 1966–69; formerly, Governor, Chelsea School of Art, London; chair, Welsh Arts Council Drama Committee, 1988–92. Lives in Gwent, Wales. **Awards:** Harkness fellowship, 1959; Rhys Memorial prize, 1965; Maugham award, 1966; International Critics prize, for television play, 1977; Christopher award, for television play, 1977 (U.S.A.); Florio prize, for translation, 1980; Society of West End Theatre award, 1982. **Agent:** Peters Fraser and Dunlop Group, 503–504 The Chambers, Chelsea Harbour, Lots Road, London SW10 0XF, England.

PUBLICATIONS

Novels

Imaginary Toys. London, Hutchinson, 1961.
A Disturbing Influence. London, Hutchinson, 1962.
As Far as You Can Go. London, Constable, 1963.
The White Father. London, Constable, 1964; New York, Farrar Straus, 1965.
A Circle of Friends. London, Constable, 1966; New York, McGraw Hill, 1967.
The Undiscovered Country. London, Constable, 1968; New York, Grove Press, 1970.

Short Stories

Introduction, with others. London, Faber, 1960.

Plays

A Heritage and Its History, adaptation of the novel by Ivy Compton-Burnett (produced London, 1965). London, Evans, 1966.
A Family and a Fortune, adaptation of the novel by Ivy Compton-Burnett (produced Guildford, Surrey, 1966; Seattle, 1974; London, 1975). London, French, 1976.
Shadow in the Sun (televised 1971). Published in *Elizabeth R,* edited by J.C. Trewin, London, Elek, 1972.
Half-Life (produced London, 1977; New York, 1981). London, Heinemann, 1977.
Henry IV, adaptation of the play by Pirandello. London, Eyre Methuen, 1979.
The Enemy Within (produced Leatherhead, Surrey, 1980).
Another Country (produced London, 1981; New Haven, Connecticut, 1983). Ambergate, Derbyshire, Amber Lane Press, 1982; New York, Limelight, 1984.
Francis (produced London, 1983). Oxford, Amber Lane Press, 1984.
After Aida; or, Verdi's Messiah (produced London, 1986). Oxford, Amber Lane Press, 1986.
Adelina Patti, Queen of Song (produced Swansea, 1987).
The Evils of Tobacco, adaptation of a work by Chekhov, translated by Ronald Hingley (produced London, 1987).
August, adaptation of Chekhov's *Uncle Vanya* (produced Mold, 1994). Oxford, Amber Lane Press, 1993.
Falling Over England (produced London, 1994). Oxford, Amber Lane Press, 1994.

Screenplays: *Arabesque,* with Stanley Price and Pierre Marton, 1966; *Another Country,* 1984; *Vincent and Theo,* 1990; *Wilde,* London, Orion Media, 1997.

Radio Documentary: *Life and Deaths of Dr. John Donne,* 1972.

Television Plays: *Persuasion,* from the novel by Jane Austen, 1971; *Shadow in the Sun,* 1971; *The Man Who Never Was,* 1972; *A Perfect Day,* 1972; *Fly in the Ointment,* 1972; *A Question of Degree,* 1972; *The Alien Corn,* from a story by W. Somerset Maugham, 1972; *Rust,* 1973; *Jennie,* 1974; *Abide with Me,* from the book *A Child in the Forest,* by Winifred Foley, 1976; *Staying On,* from the novel by Paul Scott, 1980; *The Good Solider,* from the novel by Ford Madox Ford, 1981; *The Weather in the Streets,* from the novel by Rosamond Lehmann, 1984; episodes for *Inspector Morse* series, 1986–93; *All the Waters of Wye* (documentary), 1990; *Survival of the Fittest,* 1990.

Other

Truth and Fiction (lecture). London, Covent Garden Press, 1972.
Jennie, Lady Randolph Churchill: A Portrait with Letters, with Peregrine Churchill. London, Collins, 1974; New York, St. Martin's Press, 1975.
Editor, with others, *Light Blue, Dark Blue: An Anthology of Recent Writing from Oxford and Cambridge Universities.* London, Macdonald, 1960.

*

Film Adaptations: *August,* 1995.

* * *

Julian Mitchell's books reveal a remarkably talented writer, whose work is consistently fluent, witty and ingenious. But they do leave a doubt in the mind whether his literary gifts are, in the last analysis, those of a natural novelist. He began his career precociously early, and published four novels before he was thirty. The first of them, *Imaginary Toys,* is, like many other first novels, a partly sentimental, partly satirical recreation of university life. It covers a small group of young people during a few days in one summer term at Oxford; the story is of the slightest, but Mitchell uses it as the vehicle for some serious disquisitions on sexual and social problems. The novel is at its most engaging, though, in its fanciful, essay-like speculations, which make it a little reminiscent of the early Aldous Huxley. Mitchell is like Huxley, too, in his acute sense of period; *Imaginary Toys* effectively catches the feel of the late 1950s, though this responsiveness to contemporary atmosphere inevitably made the book seem dated after a few years. His next novel, *A Disturbing Influence,* was not a particularly exciting development, though it was a smoothly written narrative. It described the impact on a complacent, even sleepy Berkshire village of a strange, destructive, amoral young man, the ''disturbing influence'' of the title. Such types evidently have a particular fascination for Mitchell, for they tend to recur in his fiction. This book was followed by a more substantial and interesting work, *As Far as You Can Go,* in which Mitchell drew on some of his own recent experience to write the kind of novel that was to become increasingly common in England in the 1960s—the account of a peripatetic Englishman's adventures in America. Harold Barlow, the central character, is a typical Mitchell hero—intelligent, amiable, rather inept—and he conveys a tourist's eye view of life in the hipster subculture of California.

The White Father, which won Mitchell the Somerset Maugham award, was a more determinedly ambitious novel than its predecessors. The narrative is divided between London and a remote African territory, and Mitchell shows much of the action through the eyes of Hugh Shrieve, a district officer in Africa who has come to London to plead for his tribe at a conference to arrange independence for the territory. Shrieve has been out of England for years, and he is unprepared for what he finds when he arrives: the frenetic beginnings of the ''Swinging London'' cult. Mitchell looks satirically though tolerantly at the world of pop music, and there is a powerful imaginative touch in his portrayal of the megalomaniac Mr. Brachs, head of a vast commercial empire catering to the youth cult, who is going steadily mad in his inaccessible penthouse on top of the London skyscraper that houses all his many enterprises. *The White Father* is one of Mitchell's best novels, which makes some sharp observations about life in a high-consumption society, as well as telling an entertaining story. The novelist and the essayist are more closely fused than is usual in his fiction. Two years later Mitchell published an extremely thin novel, *A Circle of Friends,* which moves between New York and the English Home Counties, showing how one of his characteristically weak young men gets unhappily entangled with a wealthy Anglo-American family, culminating in a wholly undeserved position as co-respondent in a divorce action.

All these novels present, at varying levels of literary achievement, some recurring characteristics: a tendency to draw fairly directly on personal experience and to use the novel as a vehicle for airing ideas, a taste for likable but weak central characters, and a generally relaxed and good-humored tone. In *The Undiscovered Country,* Mitchell's most striking fiction, all these qualities are present in a new combination. Unlike his previous novels, it is a deliberately experimental work, which plays with the conventions of fiction writing, and the relations between art and reality, in the manner of Nabokov or Borges. The first part is, on the face of it, undisguised autobiography, where Mitchell writes in his own person about his friendship with an enigmatically attractive young man, Charles Humphries, who dies at an early age. He leaves behind the fragmentary manuscript of a novel called ''The New Satyricon,'' which Mitchell edits with introduction and commentary, and presents as the second part of *The Undiscovered Country.* Undoubtedly ''Humphries'' is an alter ego for ''Mitchell'' (whose full Christian names are Charles Julian Humphrey), though the relation between them remains teasing. *The Undiscovered Country* is a generally entertaining novel, and the second part is full of pleasant literary jokes, where Mitchell engages to the full his essayistic tendencies. It also marks his dissatisfaction with his more conventional earlier novels. Indeed, at the end of part one, before he introduces ''The New Satyricon,'' Mitchell observes, ''I think it unlikely that I shall write another book of my own for a long time, with the fact of this one before me. Charles said that all art comes from an inner need. He said that I began to write because I wanted to be a writer, and that was the wrong kind of need.'' Mitchell continued to write, but as a dramatist rather than a novelist. He has not published a novel since *The Undiscovered Country,* which is a pity, given the wit and liveliness of his fiction at its best. But the course of his later career suggests that for Mitchell novel-writing was a temporary early phase, where he learned how to be a writer but was never entirely at home.

—Bernard Bergonzi

MO, Timothy

Nationality: British. **Born:** Hong Kong in 1950; brought to London in 1960. **Education:** Mill Hill School, London; St. John's College, Oxford. **Career:** Journalist, *Times Educational Supplement, New Statesman,* and *Boxing News,* all London. **Awards:** Geoffrey Faber Memorial prize, 1978; Hawthornden prize, 1982; James Tait Black Memorial prize, 1999. **Address:** c/o Chatto and Windus, 20 Vauxhall Bridge Road, London SW1V 2SA, England.

Publications

Novels

The Monkey King. London, Deutsch, 1980; New York, Doubleday, 1980.
Sour Sweet. London, Deutsch, 1982; New York, Vintage, 1985.
An Insular Possession. New York, Chatto and Windus, 1986; New York, Random House, 1987.
The Redundancy of Courage. London, Chatto and Windus, 1991.
Brownout on Breadfruit Boulevard. London, Paddleless, 1995.
Renegade or Halo2. London, Paddleless, 1999.

* * *

Hong Kong-born Timothy Mo, the son of a Cantonese father and an English mother who moved to England in the early 1960s (when Mo was ten years old), is one of the head figures in British immigrant writing of the last two decades. Often compared to Salman Rushdie or Kazuo Ishiguro because of his double cultural background, Mo's naturalist eye for human weakness and his sardonic amusement with the desperate state of the modern world nonetheless guarantee him recognition as a very individual writer. His novels have won different awards like the Geoffrey Faber Memorial Prize or the Hawthornden Prize, and with *Sour Sweet, An Insular Possession,* and *The Redundancy of Courage,* Mo was a Booker contender three times within ten years, a record not easily matched by any other contemporary writer.

Already with his first novel, *The Monkey King,* published when Mo was still in his twenties, the note was struck that determines his work to the present day: the exploration of cultural outsiders and their development in the worlds they enter. Wallace Nolesco, the half-Portuguese protagonist of *The Monkey King,* marries into the Chinese Poon family where he step by step assumes his father-in-law's—the King Monkey's—position as head of family. Moving between 1950s' Hong Kong and the New Territories, the plot shows the in-betweener Wallace maturing into a wiser individual, surviving in the midst of various cultures' incomprehension for each other: the Hong Kong finance business world and the traditional Chinese hinterland society, the Portuguese and the English. On the other hand, the parallels between these different cultures are also foregrounded at times, for example when Mr. Nolasco, Wallace's father, advises his son: ''Understand the English, and you will understand the Chinese, too.'' *The Monkey King* is a funny but cruel novel, already showing Mo on his way to become the detached satirist and meticulous observer he is now.

If *The Monkey King* gave evidence of the young writer's great ingenuity and ambition, his second novel *Sour Sweet* is widely reputed to be Mo's masterpiece. Published in 1982, right after Salman Rushdie's *Midnight's Children* had flung the doors wide open for a new reading interest in literatures from a culturally different background, the novel immediately caught a large audience's attention and received much critical acclaim. *Sour Sweet* is Mo's only novel to deal with the immigrant situation in Britain. The Chen family, described as a jelly-like amoeba adapting to the new environment, opens a take-away restaurant in suburban London. The novel's title, referring to the kind of exotic dishes created for Western tastes served at such places (''rubbish, total lupsup, fit only for foreign devils''), on the other hand emphasizes the cunning character of such an assimilative process. Despite Chen's murder through the Triad society, a Chinese Mafia organization exploiting immigrant Chinese in its drug smuggling operations, and the extreme violence of the rivaling Mafia gangfights (that give evidence that Mo was once working as a part-time reporter for the *Boxing News*), *Sour Sweet* is an immensely comic novel. Mo manages to create a universe so exclusively Chinese that the reader may forget that the novel is actually set in London. Characters like Lily, Chen's headstrong wife with expert training in traditional temple boxing, or her sister Mui who builds up her knowledge about the British by watching soap operas, are memorable, wonderfully vivid characters. *Sour Sweet,* already successful as a novel, was also made into a film whose screenplay was written by Ian McEwan.

With the success of *Sour Sweet,* Mo's reputation as a novelist of excellence was established. *An Insular Possession,* published four years later and another Booker finalist, was accordingly blurbed in the North American editions as ''perhaps the most highly praised work of fiction published in England in 1986.'' *An Insular Possession,* however, differs in both complexity and ambition from Mo's first two books. Mo studied history at St John's College, Oxford, and his meticulous historical interest is evident in his vast narrative. The historical novel, set in Canton and Macao in the mid-nineteenth century (the time of the first Opium War and the founding of British Hong Kong), is also the closest Mo gets to postmodernism, showing history and fiction to be inseparably intertwined. *An Insular Possession* is an experimental narrative of multiplicities. Not enough that the quest for truth and the representation of reality are skeptically explored, also the novel's form as a mosaic of all kinds of ''historical'' documents—newspapers, diaries, letters, etc.—is held together by a scholarly Victorian-style omniscient narrator. In a famous passage by one of the two young American protagonists, Gideon Chase, the Western and the Eastern novel are contrasted as ''linear'' account of an individual (Western) and ''circular'' account of the life of a group (Eastern). Needless to say, *An Insular Possession* is both, and as such an intellectually demanding but very rewarding tour de force.

The Redundancy of Courage, both documentary fiction and a political thriller, stakes out new territory again. Set in a different part of Southeast Asia, on the island Danu (read East Timor) in the troublesome 1970s, Mo's forth novel is the first to forsake an omniscient narrator for a first-person account. Adolph Ng, of Chinese descent and as a homosexual graduate from the University of Toronto clearly marked as another of Mo's outsiders, describes the guerilla warfare after the brutal Malais (read Indonesian) invasion. Ng's conviction that ''there is no such thing as a hero'' is reflected in his own chameleon-like life in the jungle, but Ng is difficult to catch for the reader, too, through his sometimes nauseated, sometimes amused, sometimes wry comments on the incredible hardships of war. With this novel, Mo introduces to his work a very cynical point of view with regard to the West's perception and exploitation of the Third World, a point of view that prevails also in his two other 1990s novels. In *The Redundancy of Courage,* it is the enormous reality-shaping power of the mass media (already important in *An Insular Possession*) that Mo uncompromisingly explores. As Ng at one point bitterly observes, ''if it doesn't get on to the TV in the West, it hasn't happened,'' a statement given in the midst of a breathtaking account on the soldiers' desperation and agony. Even if the novel ends on a conciliatory note, *The Redundancy of Courage* is a less funny book than its predecessors, and replaces the trickster's cunning growth with a new word in Mo's vocabulary: resistance.

The trajectory of his 1995 novel *Brownout at Breadfruit Boulevard* is similar, although Mo, apparently annoyed with his literary agents and publishers, had left Vintage and founded his own imprint, Paddleless Press. The critical response treated *Brownout at Breadfruit Boulevard* more reservedly than his other novels, blaming the narrative's multiple focus (the point of view is shared by various characters) and loose structure on the lack of good editorial advise. This criticism may be overstated, but it is true that the (whether deliberately or not) clichéd characters are sacrificed to the novel's crass vulgarity. Mo himself has cheerfully described the first chapter as ''the filthiest of any book ever written,'' but also the rest of the book is entirely preoccupied with the excremental. The ''shower of shit'' with which the novel starts, is used as the dominant metaphor to describe the Philippines as torn between arcane business and violence, power games and selfishness, incomprehension between the cultures and-again—the press trying to control reality. The title of the conference around which the narrative revolves may be applied to the book itself: ''Cultural Plurality in a World of Ecological Limits.'' *Brownout at Breadfruit Boulevard,* though at times intensely funny and very self-conscious—for example, some of the Mafiosi from *Sour Sweet* appear again—is probably Mo's most uncompromising novel.

Renegade or Halo2, his latest novel to date, shows Mo back dealing with another of his typical miscreant protagonists, Sugar Rey Castro, educated by Jesuit brothers and embarking on a picaresque journey from Manila via Hong Kong and Bombay to Miami. The protagonist-narrator, an ethnic mixture of African-American and Malay Chinese roots, is also called 'Halo-Halo' (the reduplicated form indicates the plural in Indonesian languages) which refers to ''the many-hued and multi-textured confection of ice-cream, cereals, neon syrups, crystallised fruits, frosty shavings, leguminous preserves and bloated pulses that you find under different names all over South East Asia.'' Castro, the true-born multicultural boy, is not only notable for his intelligence but also for the ''elephant gun'' in his trousers, which gets him again and again into trouble. While the character formation through a series of extremely brutal events and the omnipresent wry humor connect *Renegade or Halo2* with Mo's earlier novels, the at times insistent display of the author's polyglottery and the somewhat bloated use of intertextual references (*A Portrait of the Artist as a Young Man* and *Midnight's Children* are just the most obvious) arguably make the book an over-rich Halo2 pudding itself.

Still, *Renegade or Halo2* proves once more Mo's status as a prolific and important literary voice of British fiction—even if the Anglo-Cantonese writer has recently moved back to Hong Kong after twenty years in London.

—Tobias Wachinger

MOMADAY, N(avarre) Scott

Nationality: American. **Born:** Lawton, Oklahoma, 27 February 1934. **Education:** The University of New Mexico, Albuquerque, A.B. 1958; Stanford University, California (creative writing fellow, 1959), A.M. 1960, Ph.D. 1963. **Family:** Married 1) Gaye Mangold in 1959 (divorced), three daughters; 2) Regina Heitzer in 1978, one daughter. **Career:** Assistant professor, 1963–67, and associate professor, 1967–69, University of California, Santa Barbara; professor of English and comparative literature, University of California, Berkeley, 1969–72; professor of English, Stanford University, 1972–80. Since 1980 professor of English and comparative literature, University of Arizona, Tucson. Professor, University of California Institute for the Humanities, 1970; Whittall Lecturer, Library of Congress, Washington, D.C., 1971; visiting professor, New Mexico State University, Las Cruces, 1972–73, State University of Moscow, Spring 1974, Columbia University, New York, 1979, and Princeton University, New Jersey, 1979; writer-in-residence, Southeastern University, Washington, D.C., 1985, and Aspen Writers' Conference, Colorado, 1986. Artist: has exhibited drawings and paintings. Since 1978 member of the Board of Trustees, Museum of the American Indian, New York. **Awards:** Academy of American Poets prize, 1962; Guggenheim grant, 1966; Pulitzer prize, 1969; American Academy award, 1970; Western Heritage award, 1974; Mondello prize (Italy), 1979; Western Literature Association award, 1983. D.H.L.: Central Michigan University, Mt. Pleasant, 1970; University of Massachusetts, Amherst, 1975; Yale University, New Haven, Connecticut, 1980; Hobart and William Smith Colleges, Geneva, New York, 1980; College of Santa Fe, New Mexico, 1982; D.Litt.: Lawrence University, Appleton, Wisconsin, 1971; University of Wisconsin, Milwaukee, 1976; College of Ganado, 1979; D.F.A.: Morningside College, Sioux City, Iowa, 1980. **Address:** Department of English, University of Arizona, Tucson, Arizona 85721, U.S.A.

PUBLICATIONS

Novels

House Made of Dawn. New York, Harper, 1968; London, Gollancz, 1969.
The Ancient Child. New York, Doubleday, 1989.
In the Bear's House. New York, St. Martin's Press, 1999.

Poetry

Angle of Geese and Other Poems. Boston, Godine, 1974.
Before an Old Painting of the Crucifixion, Carmel Mission, June 1960. San Francisco, Valenti Angelo, 1975.
The Gourd Dancer. New York, Harper, 1976.
In the Presence of the Sun: Stories and Poems, 1961–1991, illustrated by the author. New York, St. Martin's Press, 1992.

Other

Owl in the Cedar Tree (for children). Boston, Ginn, 1965.
The Journey of Tai-me (Kiowa Indian tales). Privately printed, 1967; revised edition, as *The Way to Rainy Mountain,* Albuquerque, University of New Mexico Press, 1969.
Colorado: Summer, Fall, Winter, Spring, photographs by David Muench. Chicago, Rand McNally, 1973.
The Names: A Memoir. New York, Harper, 1976.
Circle of Wonder: A Native American Christmas Story (for children). Santa Fe, New Mexico, Clear Light, 1994.
Editor, *The Complete Poems of Frederick Goddard Tuckerman.* New York, Oxford University Press, 1965.
Editor, *American Indian Authors.* Boston, Houghton Mifflin, 1976.
Editor, *A Coyote in the Garden,* by An Painter. Lewiston, Idaho, Confluence Press, 1988.
The Man Made of Words: Essays, Stories, Passages. New York, St. Martin's Press, 1997.

*

Manuscript Collection: Bancroft Library, University of California, Berkeley.

Critical Studies: *Four American Indian Literary Masters* by Alan R. Velie, Norman, University of Oklahoma Press, 1982; *N. Scott Momaday: The Cultural and Literary Background* by Matthias Schubnell, Norman, University of Oklahoma Press, 1986; *Approaches to Teaching Momaday's "The Way to Rainy Mountain"* edited by Kenneth M. Roemer, New York, Modern Language Association of America, 1988; *Ancestral Voice: Conversations with N. Scott Momaday* (includes bibliography) by Charles L. Woodard, Lincoln, University of Nebraska Press, 1989; *Landmarks of Healing: A Study of "House Made of Dawn"* by Susan Scarberry-Garcia, Albuquerque, University of New Mexico Press, 1990; *Place and Vision: The Function of Landscape in Native American Fiction* by Robert M. Nelson, New York, Lang, 1993; *Conversations with N. Scott Momaday,* edited by Matthias Schubnell, Jackson, University Press of Mississippi, 1997.

* * *

In a 1971 lecture at Colorado State University, N. Scott Momaday said:

> At one time in my life I suddenly realized that my father had grown up speaking a language that I didn't grow up speaking, that my forebears on his side made a migration from Canada along with Athapaskan peoples I knew nothing about, and so I determined to find something out about these things and in the process I acquired an identity; and it is an Indian identity.

In acquiring his own Indian identity, Momaday has also created two novels which help to define identity for many Native Americans. When Momaday's first novel, *House Made of Dawn,* received the

Pulitzer prize for fiction in 1969 it was the first major recognition for a work of Native American literature and a landmark for those seeking to understand ''Indian identity.''

House Made of Dawn is the story of Abel, a Native American caught between two worlds, the traditional world of Indian heritage and the white man's world. Momaday employs sharply drawn imagery, multiple points of view, flashbacks, journal entries and sermons, and passages in italic print to create a complex tapestry of myth and recollection. The novel begins with a one-page prologue which depicts Abel marked with ashes and running through the beautiful dawn of a New Mexico landscape. The prologue is a ritual celebration, but the novel is the tale of the path the character ran to bring him to that place.

The novel recounts Abel's return to the reservation after World War II; his affair with Angela St. John, a rich Anglo woman; and his conflict with an albino Indian named Juan Reyes Fragua, whom Abel murders. The novel goes on to depict Abel's life in Los Angeles after he is paroled from prison, his involvement with the Los Angeles Indian community, his friendship with Ben Benally, his intimate relationship with a sympathetic social worker named Milly, and his conflict with a corrupt policeman. After being badly beaten, Abel returns to the reservation and learns from his grandfather how to get beyond the pain of living. This book presents a Native American view of the world and of reality. Abel is damaged by the white man's world, but he ultimately is healed when he understands his true home rests within a place of harmony with the natural world, a ''house made of dawn.''

The themes of the healing force of nature and of the Indian caught between two worlds resurface in Momaday's second novel, *The Ancient Child.* The novel's primary character is Locke Setman, or Set, a Kiowa artist in San Francisco who has been raised as an Anglo. Set is a successful landscape artist but a personal crisis develops when his Indian identity begins to assert itself. As Set attempts to find his bearlike Kiowa identity he is aided by a nineteen-year-old medicine woman named Grey who takes him first to his Kiowa homeland and then to the Navajo reservation.

Like *House Made of Dawn, The Ancient Child* is a novel told in a complex manner. The book contains traditional Native American tales of bears and lost and transformed children, the legend of Billy the Kid, the evolution of a young Indian girl into womanhood, and lyrical descriptions of nature. At its heart, however, the novel is about the cultural crisis most Native Americans must face: how do ancient peoples whose collective memories recall a once intact and beautiful land cope with what that land and their lives have become?

Momaday's most vital message is that native cultures must endure. In the same way that Set is healed by Grey, American culture can learn to heal its shattered and broken self if respect for the land and land's people can be regained.

—Tom Colonnese

MOODY, Rick

Nationality: American. **Born:** 1962. **Education:** Brown University, Providence, Rhode Island, B.A.; Columbia University, New York, graduate writing program. **Awards:** Pushcart Press Editors' Book Award; O. Henry Award. **Address:** Brooklyn Heights, New York, U.S.A.

Publications

Novels

Garden State. Boston, Little, Brown, 1992.
The Ice Storm. Boston, Little, Brown, 1994.
Purple America. Boston, Little Brown, 1997.

Short Stories

The Ring of Brightest Angels around Heaven: A Novella and Stories. Boston, Little, Brown, 1995.

Other

Joyful Noise: The New Testament Revisited (editor, with Darcey Steinke). Boston, Little, Brown, 1997.
Hover (text), photographs by Gregory Crewdson. San Francisco, Artspace Books, 1998.
Contributor of essays, *Judith Schaechter: Heart Attacks* by Judith Tannenbaum. Philadelphia, University of Pennsylvania, 1995.

*

Film Adaptations: *The Ice Storm*, 1997.

* * *

Rick Moody is one of the most gifted American novelists of his generation. Born in New York City, Moody spent his childhood and youth in many northeastern American locations. The suburbs of New York City; Manchester; New Hampshire, where he attended St. Paul's School; Hoboken, New Jersey, where he lived after graduating from Brown University in Providence, Rhode Island; and Columbia University in New York City all appear in barely disguised form in his fiction. Like the work of other well-known East-Coast American writers (John Irving, John Updike), Moody's fiction is firmly rooted in, as well as written in response to, the urban, rural, and suburban landscapes of the area roughly bounded by New York City to the south and Boston to the north. His three novels, *Garden State*, *The Ice Storm*, and *Purple America*, and his short story collection, *The Ring of Brightest Angels around Heaven*, all published at a prolific pace within five years, create not only a distinct literary geography but also a fascinating temporal picture. Like the fiction of his contemporary, the Canadian novelist Douglas Coupland, Moody's fiction features protagonists of Moody's own generation. These are Americans (a word Moody often uses to ironic effect) who lived through the Vietnam War as pre-teens, came of age during the Reagan-era 1980s, and who are intensely aware of the significance of pop cultural references, right down to the significance of their own clothing.

Stylistically, Moody is an author who takes postmodernism for granted. He ends his short story collection *The Ring of Brightest Angels around Heaven* with a section called ''Primary Sources,'' which lists those books that have most influenced him. Conversant with Barthes, Derrida, Eco, Foucault, and Angela Carter among other theorists, Moody footnotes theirs and other books in places where they correlate to significant events of his own life. Thus, we read ''At the end of my drinking ... I started writing my first novel,'' and ''In 1987, I institutionalized myself.'' The line between Moody's life and his fiction is always a thin one, and Moody both encourages this tendency (as in ''Primary Sources'' and the introduction to the new edition of *Garden State*) and discourages it at the same time (as in the note before *Purple America* where he disavows comparison between his character Billie Raitliffe and his own mother). As a self-confessed ''writer of the nineties ... who beats a sentence to death, ten or twenty or thirty or even forty times on occasion, and then maybe cuts the sentence just the same'' (*Beat Writers at Work*, ed. George Plimpton, Harvill Press, 1999), Moody's choice to ally his fiction with his life is a conscious and fitting one, tied to his own vision of literature as an intrinsically hermeneutical enterprise. Another conscious stylistic choice is Moody's eschewing of standard North American quotation marks for European dashes to signal conversation, as well as his subtle use of italic script, most fully pronounced in *Purple America*: ''Dexter, it turns out, is spoiling for trouble. He's drunk too. Whatever the cause, *he rushes at Mac Kowalski*.'' Moody's stylistic innovation always turns the reader into an interpreter, the same situation in which many of Moody's characters find themselves.

Moody's first novel, *Garden State*, revolves around several characters in their early to mid- twenties, living in Haledon, New Jersey, in an unspecified time that feels a lot like the early 1980s. The plot follows Alice and her on- and off-again boyfriend, Dennis, and his half-brother Lane, who has just been released from a mental hospital after attempting suicide, as they make the difficult passage between an extended adolescence and adulthood. Assorted others, including the main characters' parents and friends, populate this first novel, which lays the groundwork for the rest of Moody's fiction. Patterns discernible in Moody's later work are first articulated in *Garden State*. These patterns include the failure and reconstitution of the American family, the influence of popular culture, especially music, the doubled always-present fear and attraction of institutionalization on one hand and of New York City on the other, the use of Christian imagery and metaphors, the disparity and congruence of rich and poor, and the structuring device of the ''one big event'': in *Garden State* a huge party that takes place in an abandoned factory, in *The Ice Storm* the event alluded to in the novel's title, and in *Purple America* the meltdown of a Connecticut nuclear reactor. *Garden State* ends with Alice and Lane together in New York City. They ''left off thinking about the past right then'' and ''With all that in front of them, they looked up.''

This upward movement—the happy ending—where the characters are able to make a break with the past, is echoed at the end of Moody's next novel, *The Ice Storm*. In the novel's final scene, Paul Hood, the novel's narrator, is met at the Stamford train station by his parents, Benjamin and Elena, and his sister, Wendy. He decides that it is time to break with the past: ''I have to leave him and his family there because after all this time, after twenty years, it's time I left.'' Ostensibly about the slow disintegration of a well-to-do American family in the early 1970s, *The Ice Storm* is also about the way fiction is written. The novel opens with the unidentified narrator's claim that the novel will be a ''comedy about a family I knew when I was growing up.'' The novel then proceeds to detail numerous incidents of marital strain between parents, and between parents and children, to the point where the reader forgets the narrator's insistence that the novel is a ''comedy.'' Moody's narrator both references and defamiliarizes classical literary theory by labeling the novel a comedy, and then figuratively links comedy with the genre of the comic book. Paul's version of comedy has the sky over Connecticut light up with ''A flaming figure four,'' signaling that the reader is to see the Hoods, the novel's ''Fantastic Four,'' as a comic book family whose adventures go on and on and on. Tampering also with the conventions of narrative voice, Moody creates a narrator who cannot restrain himself from giving the reader a lesson in the art of fiction. ''This congruency,'' he writes, ''—between Paul and his dad—is sort of like the congruency between me, the narrator of this story, the imaginer of all these consciousnesses of the past, and God.''

Moody's destabilizing of the omniscient narrator is short-lived. In his next novel, *Purple America*, Moody returns to the convention of third-person omniscient narration. The story of Dexter Raitliffe and his terminally ill mother, Billie Raitliffe, is told in the soothing tones of a narrator who revels in repetition. The stunning opening chapter of the novel proclaims that ''Whosoever knows the folds and complexities of his own mother's body, *he shall never die*,'' and goes on for four more pages to proclaim various acts of kindness and humanity—all prefaced by the construction ''Whosoever...''—proffered by Dexter, better known as Hex, to his mother Billie. Like his previous novels, *Purple America* takes as a given the breakdown in relations between members of a family, only this time it happens twice. Hex loses his father as a child, and then loses his stepfather Lou in his late thirties, the present setting of the novel. Hex's comedic attempt to reunite his second family is ultimately unresolved. It is Moody's use of repetition, on a thematic level (the two fathers, the two nuclear accidents) and on a linguistic level (Hex's stuttering, the narrator's poetic repetitions), that marks a distinct evolution in Moody's work. Moving away from the historically hermetically sealed worlds of *Garden State* and *The Ice Storm*, in *Purple America* Moody argues that the past and what comes after it exist in close relation to each other. The relatedness of what seems unrelated (a theme Moody earlier explored in his story ''The Ring of Brightest Angels around Heaven'') leaves the reader with the strange dual feeling of unease, and of comfort.

—Richard Almonte

MOORCOCK, Michael

Pseudonyms: Bill Barclay; Edward P. Bradbury; James Colvin; Hank Janson; Desmond Reid. **Nationality:** British. **Born:** Mitcham, Surrey, 18 December 1939. **Military Service:** Served in the Royal Air Force Training Corps. **Family:** Married 1) Hilary Bailey in 1962, two daughters and one son; 2) Jill Riches in 1978; 3) Linda Steel in 1983. **Career:** Editor, *Tarzan Adventures,* London, 1956–57, and Sexton Blake Library, Fleetway Publications, London, 1958–61; editor and writer for Liberal Party, 1962–63. Editor since 1964 and publisher since 1967, *New Worlds,* London. Since 1965 songwriter and member of various rock bands including Hawkwind, Deep Fix, and Blue Oyster Cult. **Awards:** British Science Fiction Association award, 1966; Nebula award 1967; Derleth award 1972, 1974, 1975, 1976; *Guardian* Fiction prize, 1977; Campbell Memorial award, 1979; World Fantasy award, 1979. Guest of Honor, World Fantasy

Convention, New York, 1976. **Agent:** c/o Giles Gordon, Curtis Brown Group, 28–29 Haymarket, London SW1Y 4SP, England.

PUBLICATIONS

Novels

Caribbean Crisis (as Desmond Reid, with James Cawthorn). London, Fleetway, 1962.

Stormbringer. London, Jenkins, 1965; New York, Lancer, 1967; revised edition, New York, DAW, 1977.

The Sundered Worlds. London, Compact, 1965; New York Paperback Library, 1966; as *The Blood Red Game,* London, Sphere, 1970.

The Fireclown. London, Compact, 1965; New York, Paperback Library, 1967; as *The Winds of Limbo,* Paperback Library, 1969.

The Twilight Man. London, Compact, 1966; New York, Berkley, 1970; as *The Shores of Death,* London, Sphere, 1970.

Printer's Devil (as Bill Barclay). London, Compact, 1966; revised edition, as *The Russian Intelligence,* as Michael Moorcock, Manchester, Savoy, 1980.

Somewhere in the Night (as Bill Barclay). London, Compact, 1966; revised edition, as *The Chinese Agent,* London, Hutchinson, and New York, Macmillan, 1970.

The Jewel in the Skull. New York, Lancer, 1967; London, Mayflower, 1969; revised edition, New York, DAW, 1977.

The Wrecks of Time. New York, Ace, 1967; revised edition, as *The Rituals of Infinity; or, The New Adventures of Doctor Faustus,* London Arrow, 1971; New York, DAW, 1978.

The Final Programme. New York, Avon, 1968; London, Allison and Busby, 1969; revised edition, London, Fontana, 1979.

Sorcerer's Amulet. New York, Lancer, 1968; as *The Mad God's Amulet,* London, Mayflower, 1969; revised edition, New York, DAW, 1977.

The Sword of the Dawn. New York, Lancer, 1968; London, Mayflower, 1969; revised edition, New York, DAW, 1977.

The Secret of the Runestaff. New York, Lancer, 1969; as *The Runestaff,* London, Mayflower, 1969; revised edition, New York, DAW, 1977.

The Ice Schooner. London, Sphere, and New York, Berkley, 1969; revised edition, London, Harrap, 1985.

Behold the Man. London, Allison and Busby, 1969; New York, Avon, 1970.

The Black Corridor, with Hilary Bailey. London, Mayflower, and New York, Ace, 1969.

The Eternal Champion. London, Mayflower, and New York, Dell, 1970; revised edition, New York, Harper, 1978.

Phoenix in Obsidian. London, Mayflower, 1970; as *The Silver Warriors,* New York, Dell, 1973.

A Cure for Cancer. London, Allison and Busby, and New York, Holt Rinehart, 1971; revised edition, London, Fontana, 1979.

The Warlord of the Air. London, New English Library, and New York, Ace, 1971.

The Swords Trilogy. New York, Berkley, 1977.

The Knight of the Swords. London, Mayflower, and New York, Berkley, 1971.

The Queen of the Swords. London, Mayflower, and New York, Berkley, 1971.

The King of the Swords. London, Mayflower, and New York, Berkley, 1971.

The Sleeping Sorceress. London, New English Library, 1971; New York, Lancer, 1972; revised edition, as *The Vanishing Tower,* New York, DAW, 1977.

Elric of Melniboné. London, Hutchinson, 1972; as *The Dreaming City,* New York, Lancer, 1972.

An Alien Heat. London, MacGibbon and Kee, and New York, Harper, 1972.

Breakfast in the Ruins: A Novel of Inhumanity. London, New English Library, 1972; New York, Random House, 1974.

The English Assassin. London, Allison and Busby, and New York, Harper, 1972; revised edition, London, Fontana, 1979.

The Chronicles of Corum. London, Grafton, 1986.

The Bull and the Spear. London Allison and Busby, and New York, Berkley, 1973.

The Oak and the Ram. London, Allison and Busby, and New York, Berkley, 1973.

The Sword and the Stallion. London, Allison and Busby, and New York, Berkley, 1974.

The Chronicles of Castle Brass. London, Granada, 1985.

Count Brass. London, Mayflower, 1973; New York, Dell, 1976.

The Champion of Garathorm. London, Mayflower, 1973.

The Quest for Tanelorn. London, Mayflower, 1975; New York, Dell, 1976.

The Land Leviathan. London, Quartet, and New York, Doubleday, 1974.

The Hollow Lands. New York, Harper, 1974; London, Hart Davis MacGibbon, 1975.

The Distant Suns, with Philip James. Llanfynydd, Dyfed, Unicorn Bookshop, 1975.

The Sailor on the Seas of Fate. London, Quartet, and New York, DAW, 1976.

The Adventures of Una Persson and Catherine Cornelius in the Twentieth Century. London, Quartet, 1976.

The End of All Songs. London, Hart Davis MacGibbon, and New York, Harper, 1976.

The Condition of Muzak. London, Allison and Busby, 1977; Boston, Gregg Press, 1978.

The Transformation of Miss Mavis Ming. London, W.H. Allen, 1977; as *Messiah at the End of Time,* New York, DAW, 1978.

The Cornelius Chronicles (omnibus). New York, Avon, 1977.

The Weird of the White Wolf. New York, DAW, 1977; London, Panther, 1984.

The Vanishing Tower. New York, DAW, 1977.

The Bane of the Black Sword. New York, DAW, 1977; London, Panther, 1984.

Gloriana; or, The Unfulfill'd Queen. London, Allison and Busby, 1978; New York, Avon, 1979.

The History of the Runestaff (collection). London, Hart Davis MacGibbon, 1979.

The Great Rock 'n' Roll Swindle. London, Virgin, 1980; revised edition as "Gold Diggers of 1977", in *Casablanca and Other Stories,* London, Gollancz, 1989.

The Golden Barge. Manchester, Savoy, and New York, DAW, 1980.

The Entropy Tango. London, New English Library, 1981.

The Steel Tsar. London, Mayflower, 1981; New York, DAW, 1982.

The War Hound and the World's Pain. New York, Timescape, 1981; London, New English Library, 1982.

Byzantium Endures. London, Secker and Warburg, 1981; New York, Random House, 1982.
The Brothel in Rösenstrasse. London, New English Library, 1982; New York, Carroll and Graf, 1987.
The Dancers at the End of Time (omnibus). London, Granada, 1983.
The Laughter of Carthage. London, Secker and Warburg, and New York, Random House, 1984.
The Crystal and the Amulet. Manchester, Savoy, 1986.
The Dragon in the Sword. New York, Ace, 1986; London, Grafton, 1987.
The City in the Autumn Stars. London, Grafton, 1986; New York, Ace, 1987.
Mother London. London, Secker and Warburg, 1988; New York, Harmony, 1989.
The Fortress of the Pearl. London, Gollancz, and New York, Ace, 1989.
The Revenge of the Rose. New York, Ace, and London, Grafton, 1991.
Blood: A Southern Fantasy. New York, W. Morrow, 1994.
Fabulous Harbors. New York, Avon Books, 1995.
The War Amongst The Angels: An Autobiographical Story. New York, Avon Books, 1997.

Novels as Edward P. Bradbury

Warrior of Mars. London, New English Library, 1981.
Warriors of Mars. London, Compact, 1965; New York, Lancer, 1966; as *The City of the Beast* (as Michael Moorcock), Lancer, 1970.
Blades of Mars. London, Compact, 1965; New York, Lancer, 1966; as *The Lord of the Spiders* (as Michael Moorcock), Lancer, 1970.
The Barbarians of Mars. London, Compact, 1965; New York, Lancer, 1966; as *The Masters of the Pit* (as Michael Moorcock), Lancer, 1970.

Short Stories

The Stealer of Souls and Other Stories. London, Spearman, 1963; New York, Lancer, 1967.
The Deep Fix (as James Colvin). London, Compact, 1966.
The Time Dweller. London, Hart Davis, 1969; New York, Berkley, 1971.
The Singing Citadel: Four Tales of Heroic Fantasy. London, Mayflower, and New York, Berkley, 1970.
The Jade Man's Eyes. Brighton, Unicorn Bookshop, 1973.
Elric: The Return to Melniboné (cartoon), illustrated by Philippe Druillet. Brighton, Unicorn Bookshop, 1973.
Moorcock's Book of Martyrs. London, Quartet, 1976; as *Dying for Tomorrow,* New York, DAW, 1978.
The Lives and Times of Jerry Cornelius. London, Allison and Busby, 1976; New York, Dale, n.d.
Legends from the End of Time. London, W.H. Allen, and New York, Harper, 1976.
My Experiences in the Third World War. Manchester, Savoy, 1980.
The Opium General and Other Stories. London, Harrap, 1984.
Elric at the End of Time: Fantasy Stories. London, New English Library, 1984; New York, DAW, 1985.
Casablanca and Other Stories. London, Gollancz, 1989.
Lunching With The Antichrist: A Family History: 1925–2015. Shingletown, California, Mark V. Ziesing, 1995.
Von Bek. Stone Mountain, Georgia, White Wolf, 1995.
Hawkmoon. Clarkston, Georgia, White Wolf, 1995.

Uncollected Short Stories

"The Girl Who Shot Sultry Kane" (as Hank Janson), in *Golden Nugget,* April 1965.
"The Museum of the Future," in *Daily Telegraph* (London), May 1990.
"The Ciarene Purse," in *Zenita,* June 1990.
"Colour," in *New Worlds* (London), 1991.

Plays

Screenplays: *The Land That Time Forgot,* with James Cawthorn, 1974.

Other

Sojan (for children). Manchester, Savoy, 1977.
Epic Pooh. London, British Fantasy Society, 1978.
The Retreat from Liberty: The Erosion of Democracy in Today's Britain. London, Zomba, 1983.
Letter from Hollywood, with Michael Foreman. London, Harrap, 1986.
Wizardry and Wild Romance: A Study of Epic Fantasy. London, Gollancz, 1987.
Editor, *The Best of New Worlds.* London, Compact, 1965.
Editor, *Best SF Stories from New Worlds 1–8.* London, Panther, 8 vols., 1967–74; New York, Berkley, 6 vols., 1968–71.
Editor, *The Traps of Time.* London, Rapp and Whiting, 1968.
Editor (anonymously), *The Inner Landscape.* London, Allison and Busby, 1969.
Editor, *New Worlds Quarterly 1–5.* London, Sphere, 5 vols., 1971–73; New York, Berkley, 4 vols., 1971–72.
Editor, with Langdon Jones, *The Nature of the Catastrophe.* London, Hutchinson, 1971.
Editor, with Charles Platt, *New Worlds 6.* London, Sphere, 1973; as *New Worlds 5,* New York, Avon, 1973.
Editor, *Before Armageddon: An Anthology of Victorian and Edwardian Imaginative Fiction Published Before 1914.* London, W.H. Allen, 1975.
Editor, *England Invaded: A Collection of Fantasy Fiction.* London, W.H. Allen, and New York, Ultramarine, 1977.
Editor, *New Worlds: An Anthology.* London, Fontana, 1983.
Editor, with James Cawthorn, *Fantasy: The 100 Best Books.* London, Xanadu, and New York, Carroll and Graf, 1988.
Ghostwriter: *The LSD Dossier,* by Roger Harris. London, Compact, 1966.

*

Bibliography: *Michael Moorcock: A Bibliography* by Andrew Harper and George McAulay, T-K Graphics, 1976.

Manuscript Collections: Bodleian Library, Oxford University; Sterling Library, Texas A & M University, College Station.

Critical Study: *Speaking of Science Fiction: The Paul Walker Interviews* edited by Paul Walker, Luna, 1978; *The Entropy Exhibition: Michael Moorcock and the British "New Wave" in Science*

Fiction by Colin Greenland, London, Routledge, 1983; *Michael Moorcock: A Reader's Guide* by John Davey, revised edition, London, privately printed, 1992.

Michael Moorcock comments:

My work varies so radically in type that I've no way of introducing it. I write very little science fiction, in my own view and that of most science fiction readers. My genre fiction is mostly fantasy.

Much of my work borrowed from the iconography and vocabulary of science fiction in the 1960s but I would not, for instance, classify the Jerry Cornelius tetralogy as a genre work while *The Dancers at the End of Time* though a comedy *is* generically science fiction.

Since I've worked hard to break down the classifications I'm uncomfortable with them being applied to my own stuff. In the past ten years most of my fiction has been nongeneric.

Cross-fertilisation—internationally—is always what I aim for in an edition. My own work owes as much to German *Schelmenroman* as to the English nineteenth-century novel and very little, to say, pulp science fiction.

* * *

> ''Invent phantoms? Fabulous beasts? Powerful Gods? Whole Cosmologies?'' said the astonished traveller. ''Are all these things, then unreal?''
>
> ''They're real enough,'' Corum replied. ''Reality, after all, is the easiest thing in the world to create.''
>
> (*The Chronicles of Corum*)

Corum's wit is a fitting introduction to the fictional world of Michael Moorcock. The paradox, ''reality is the easiest thing to create'' directs us to the astonishing fertility of Moorcock's imagination: Moorcock's work does indeed contain powerful gods, whole cosmologies, and fabulous beasts. The epigram also alerts us to the peculiarly persuasive nature of Moorcock's fiction. It is not of course reality that Moorcock creates in his books. His heroes, demigods, and monsters are spectacularly unlike anything we may recognise as reality. Yet his ideas attain ''reality'' because we, his readers, are willing to accept them as such: Moorcock is one of the most popular as well as the most prolific of contemporary fantasy writers.

He works quickly, wasting little effort on what Tolkien termed ''subcreation.'' Entire continents are created in the space of a paragraph; characters in a single line. Significantly, Moorcock's books do not have maps. Stories such as the Elric saga and *The History of the Runestaff* pare characterisation and setting to the bone, resulting in a fictional form which moves at breathtaking speed and consists of a series of action sequences. Such novels owe much to the art of graphic ''comic strip'' magazines. Our pleasure is not in the imaginative exploration of other worlds but in the imaginative experience of sensations which the fictional device of another world makes possible. Brilliant *tours de force* such as the ornithopters and beast masks of *The Jewel in the Skull* are never developed at length. The stories are simply moving too fast to allow this. Moorcock succeeds in this because he is able to draw on a wealth of conventions established by a generation of fantasy writers since Tolkien.

Many of these derive ultimately from the epic: the overall structure of protracted revenge or quest within which occurs an episodic series of adventures characterised by discovery of marvels, capture, escape, and intervention by patron gods. The influence of the epic even extends down to dialogue:

> I am Elric of Melniboné, last of a line of great sorcerer kings. This blade I wield will do more than kill you, friend demon. It will drink your soul and feed it to me. Perhaps you have heard of me by another name? ... soul thief?

The ritualised challenge with its declaration of name and lineage, the savouring of the exotic sounds of an alien language, and the riddling around the hero's identity, all stem directly from the epic.

From the conventions of this genre Moorcock derives a number of essential principles. Firstly, the struggle of good (law) against evil (chaos). Secondly, the extension of this struggle, which is centered on earth, into other planes or dimensions. Thirdly, the movement of characters and objects of power between these dimensions, bringing ''supernatural'' elements into the initial conflict. Fourthly, the central importance of the hero, who is the decisive force in the battle between law and chaos.

While of crucial importance in Moorcock's world, the hero is nonetheless an ambiguous figure, at once attractive and forbidding. Like the antihero of Gothic literature many of his protagonists bear some scar or stigma which serves as an emblem of their alienation from mankind. Elric is an Albino, Corum has lost a hand and an eye, Dorian Hawkmoon has a black jewel embedded in his forehead. These scars symbolise the alienated, slightly inhuman perspective with which we enter the narratives. The prologue of *The Dancers at the End of Time* describes its protagonists: ''Most of the old emotions had atrophied... . They had rivalry without jealously, affection without lust, malice without rage, kindness without pity.''

This dark edge to Moorcock's fantasy emerges vividly in his portrayal of women: women are whores, warrior queens, demonesses or lovers. But love for Moorcock's heroes is often contaminated by bitterness, betrayal, or bereavement. Elric has to slay his wife, Zarozina, in *Stormbringer,* and Corum is slain by Medhbh, the woman he loves, in *The Sword and the Stallion.* In the unrestrained Cornelius saga, the hero's love is both incestuous and necrophilic. Moorcock, then, both embraces and subverts the conventions of twentieth-century fantasy.

Among more than sixty novels, one, perhaps, can be singled out: *The City in the Autumn Stars.* The hero, Von Beck, enters the Mittelmarch, a hidden realm contiguous to Europe in which occult forces reign. Here he finds his dreams and nightmares becoming real. Driven by his search for the goddess-like Libussa, Duchess of Crete, he is unwillingly caught up in supernatural mysteries in which Lucifer struggles with God for the redemption of the earth.

Here the story is not simply one of adventure but of initiation. Symbols from ancient myth and from the unconscious are awoken and come alive: the labyrinth, the minotaur, and the hermaphrodite. Sequences of mystical and erotic union are conveyed in dream-like images and in a heightened poetic, quasi-biblical language. Moorcock creates a fantasy which takes its protagonist through spiritual struggle to eventual wholeness. The effect of this on the reader is intensified by the author's exceptional use of a first person narrator. The epigraph to the work suggests an intriguing comparison between fantasy fiction and magic. Both are arts that transform those who deal with them: ''At its deepest, this magic is concerned with the creative powers of the will.''

No essay on Moorcock would be complete without mention of the playfulness which affectionately undercuts all the conventions of the genre he employs. This extends from the experiments with chapter titles and typography in the Cornelius chronicles to the wry humour of his fantasy heroes: in *The Vanishing Tower* Ereköse asks, ''Why cannot I—we—ever be faced with a small problem, a domestic problem? Why are we forever involved with the destiny of the universe?

In *Blood,* a quartet of characters in the American South play a game of chance whereby they affect the fate of invented worlds. The book represents a summing-up of the large body of work that preceded it, and also marked the beginning of a sort of trilogy—though the second installment, *Fabulous Harbors,* is not a novel but a collection of short stories connected by narrative scenes. Together these help to form a glimpse of the ''multiverse'' Moorcock had been creating all along, and *The War Amongst the Angels* further defines this picture with scenes that stretch in space and time from the catacombs of Egypt to nineteenth-century England, and from events in World War II to the hills of Texas.

—Edmund Cusick

MOORE, Lorrie

Nationality: American. **Born:** Marie Lorena Moore in Glens Falls, New York, 13 January 1957. **Education:** St. Lawrence University, Canton, New York, 1974–78, B.A. (summa cum laude) 1978; Cornell University, Ithaca, New York, 1980–82, M.F.A. 1982. **Career:** Assistant professor, 1984–87, and since 1987 associate professor of English, University of Wisconsin, Madison. **Awards:** National Endowment for the Arts award, 1989; Rockefeller Foundation fellowship, 1989; Guggenheim fellowship, 1991; O. Henry award, 1998. **Agent:** Melanie Jackson Agency, 250 West 57th Street, New York, New York 10107. **Address:** Department of English, University of Wisconsin, 600 North Park Street, Madison, Wisconsin 53706, U.S.A.

PUBLICATIONS

Novel

Anagrams. New York, Knopf, 1986; London, Faber, 1987.
Who Will Run the Frog Hospital? New York, Knopf, and London, Faber, 1994.

Short Stories

Self-Help. New York, Knopf, and London, Faber, 1985.
Like Life. New York, Knopf, and London, Faber, 1990.
Birds of America: Stories. New York, Knopf, 1998.

Uncollected Short Stories

''Willing,'' in *Best American Short Stories 1991,* edited by Alice Adams and Katrina Kenison. Boston, Houghton Mifflin, 1991.
''Community Life,'' in *Best American Short Stories 1992.* Boston, Houghton Mifflin, 1992.
''Terrific Mother'' in *Best American Short Stories 1993.* Boston, Houghton Mifflin, 1993.

Other

The Forgotten Helper: A Christmas Story (for children), illustrated by T. Lewis. New York, Delacorte Press, 2000.

* * *

Lorrie Moore was a relative newcomer on the fiction scene in the late twentieth century. Her first book, *Self-Help,* a collection of stories, was her master's thesis at Cornell University and won her critical acclaim for its humorous parody of the popular self-help books of the time period. The collection was also well regarded for its experimentation with second-person point of view in fiction. In second person, the reader becomes the main character in the story, and it is because of this intrusion on the reader that it is usually avoided in the genre. By parodying the self-help manuals that were often more popular with general readers than fiction of the same period, Moore was able to create a collection of short pieces such as ''How to Become a Writer,'' ''The Kid's Guide to Divorce,'' and ''How to Be an Other Woman'' that did not offend readers yet at the same time held a mirror up to their experiences that reflected moments of self-recognition and insight which ironically are not found in how-to books, where many contemporary readers seek answers in negotiating life, but are revealed in good fiction.

Since this well-regarded debut, Moore's work has not garnered quite the same level of attention in literary circles and with the general reading public. She is not a particularly prolific writer and her subsequent story collections *Like Life* and *Birds of America* received more notice and acclaim than the novels, and sometimes her technical expertise wins at the expense of heart. However, the novels continue her theme of subverting readers' expectations in relation to nonfiction genres with contemporary humor, sharp wit, and increasing depth and poignancy.

The title of Moore's first novel, *Anagrams,* like *Self-Help,* suggests a very different kind of book than a work of fiction. Published between her first two collections of stories, the title suggests a book of puzzles or word plays or amusing coincidences of the anagram. Instead, Moore presents a novel of late-twentieth-century life in which the main character, Benna, a local nightclub singer, tries to ''make anagrams out of words that weren't anagrams.'' No matter how she tries, Benna cannot seem to rearrange the letters, the details of her life, to make something meaningful out of the experience of living it. She experiments in love with Gerard, her neighbor across the hall who writes operas and reveals more secrets about himself as the novel progresses, and with one of her poetry students. The novel has a stark, urban feel of isolation as Benna tries to form lasting relationships that seem doomed and moves increasingly toward imaginary rather than real others in her life. Interestingly, Moore experiments with point of view again in this novel, as though keeping a camera moving, shifting the reader off balance as she moves from first person to third omniscient. This technique causes the reader to sense Benna's lack of identity, loss of control, inability to form secure attachments, and her deepening despair. An odd scene of Benna and her brother toward the close of the novel seems unnecessary and inappropriate to the story and speaks to Moore's difficulty in sustaining the longer fictional form at this stage of her career.

The title *Who Will Run the Frog Hospital?* begs for a book that will answer that question, however unlikely such an answer to such a question might be. In contrast to Benna in *Anagrams,* Berie Carr is a middle-aged woman who is in a more secure place in her life and her relationships and can afford the luxury of a reflective mood about lost innocence and youth. This mature stance shows a development in Moore's work away from heavy reliance on technical artifice and toward the more lasting qualities of character development and story. Instead of anagrams, here is a tapestry, like Carol King's record that Berie and her girlhood friend Sils, about whom much of the novel turns, listen to in their bedrooms while dancing and fixing their hair. The girls worked at an amusement park called Storyland, in fact, and there is much about looking back with nostalgia in this novel to a time when innocence borders knowledge, just like their upstate New York town of Horsehearts borders Canada. The novel's title, in this case, suggests perhaps a children's story, and much of the book is about Berie's childhood and adolescence. In Paris, middle-aged Berie realizes that she no longer loves her husband, or believes that kissed frogs turn into princes, but the realization is not startling to her. Instead, the insight provides a channel for her to travel back down her own literal Memory Lane to recognize a place where she once experienced true beauty in the world as a young woman, if only for a moment.

Moore lapses away from third-person point of view to first in this novel only for a brief time, in flashback. One hopes that she will increasingly trust her talent for storytelling in the more traditional sense and will develop her longer fiction further along that path.

—Connie Ann Kirk

MOORHOUSE, Frank

Nationality: Australian. **Born:** Nowra, New South Wales, 21 December 1938. **Education:** The University of Queensland, 1959–61. **Military Service:** Served in the Australian Army and Reserves, 1957–59. **Family:** Divorced. **Career**: Journalist, Sydney *Telegraph,* 1956–59; editor, *Lockhart Review,* New South Wales, 1960, and *Australian Worker,* Sydney, 1962; assistant secretary, Workers' Educational Association, Sydney, 1963–65; union organizer, Australian Journalists' Association, 1966; editor, *City Voices,* Sydney, 1966; contributor and columnist, 1970–79, and nightclub writer, 1980, *Bulletin,* Sydney; co-founding editor, *Tabloid Story,* Sydney, 1972–74. Writer-in-residence, University of Melbourne and other Australian universities; travelled in Europe and Middle East, late 1980s; moved to France, 1991. Vice president, 1978–80, and president, 1979–82, Australian Society of Authors; chairman, Copyright Council of Australia, 1985. **Awards:** Lawson Short Story prize, 1970; National Book Council Banjo award for fiction, 1975; senior literary fellowship, 1976; *Age* Book of the Year, 1988; Australian Literature Society gold medal, 1989; South Australian Festival Award, 1993. **Member:** Order of Australia, 1985. **Address:** c/o Pan Books, 63–71 Balfour Street, Chippendale, New South Wales 2008, Australia.

Publications

Novel

Grand Days: A Novel. New York, Pantheon Books, and London, Picador, 1993.
Loose Living. Sydney, Picador, 1995.

Short Stories

Futility and Other Animals. Sydney, Powell, 1969.
The Americans, Baby. Sydney and London, Angus and Robertson, 1972.
The Electrical Experience. Sydney, Angus and Robertson, 1974.
Conference-ville. Sydney, Angus and Robertson, 1976.
Tales of Mystery and Romance. London, Angus and Robertson, 1977.
The Everlasting Secret Family and Other Secrets. Sydney and London, Angus and Robertson, 1980.
Selected Stories. Sydney and London, Angus and Robertson, 1982; as *The Coca Cola Kid: Selected Stories,* Sydney, Angus and Robertson, 1985.
Room Service: Comic Writings. Ringwood, Victoria, and London, Penguin, 1985; New York, Penguin, 1987.
Forty-Seventeen. Ringwood, Victoria, Penguin, and London, Faber, 1988; San Diego, Harcourt Brace, 1989.
Lateshows. Sydney, Pan, 1990.

Plays

Screenplays: *Between Wars,* 1974; *The Disappearance of Azaria Chamberlain,* 1984; *Conference-ville,* 1984; *The Coca-Cola Kid,* 1985; *The Everlasting Secret Family,* 1988

Television Plays: *Conference-ville,* 1984; *The Disappearance of Azaria Chamberlain,* 1984; *Time's Raging,* 1985.

Other

Editor, *Coast to Coast.* Sydney, Angus and Robertson, 1973.
Editor, *Days of Wine and Rage.* Ringwood, Victoria, Penguin, 1980.
Editor, *The State of the Art: The Mood of Contemporary Australia in Short Stories.* Ringwood, Victoria, Penguin, 1983.
Editor, *A Steele Rudd Selection: The Best Dad and Dave Stories, with Other Rudd Classics.* St. Lucia, University of Queensland Press, 1986.

*

Manuscript Collections: Fryer Library, University of Queensland, Brisbane; National Library of Australia, Canberra.

Critical Studies: ''The Short Stories of Wilding and Moorhouse'' by Carl Harrison-Ford, in *Southerly* (Sydney), vol. 33, 1974; ''Frank Moorhouse's Discontinuities'' by D. Anderson, in *Southerly* (Sydney), vol. 35, 1975; ''Some Developments in Short Fiction 1969–80'' by Bruce Clunies Ross, in *Australian Literary Studies* (Hobart, Tasmania), vol. 10, no. 2, 1981; interview in *Sideways from the Page* edited by J. Davidson, Melbourne, Fontana, 1983; ''The Thinker from the Bush'' by Humphrey McQueen, in *Gallipoli to Petrov,* Sydney, Hale and Iremonger, 1984; ''Form and Meaning in the Short Stories of Moorhouse'' by C. Kanaganayakam, in *World Literature Written in English,* vol. 25, no.1, 1985; interview in *Yacker 3: Australian Writers Talk About Their Work* by Candida Baker, 1989; ''The Short Story Cycles of Moorhouse'' by Gay Raines, in *Australian Literary Studies,* vol. 14, 1990.

Frank Moorhouse comments:

(1991) *Futility and Other Animals, The Americans, Baby, The Electrical Experience,* and *The Everlasting Secret Family* are described as ''discontinuous narratives'' and are experiments with interlocked and overlapped short stories. The individual books also overlap and characters recur.

* * *

Frank Moorhouse entered Australian fiction during the 1960s speaking a voice politically radical, witty, unabashedly intelligent, and—in a society engaged in widespread censorship—sexually explicit. Moorhouse and his contemporaries took on the hegemony of English culture as it was being played out in not quite postcolonial circumstances. They were a generation who, instead of sailing to London as soon as they were old enough and able, stayed in their homeland and remapped its literary space. At a time when fiction to most Australians meant social realist tales of the bush and rural life, Moorhouse wrote about his countrymen as an urban tribe changed utterly by the Americanization of its culture and by immigration which from World War II onward had altered the ethnic mix. Alert to the fracturing of social certainties, Moorhouse developed the structure he called ''discontinuous narrative.''

This phrase, the subtitle for his first three books, *Futility and Other Animals, The Americans, Baby,* and *The Electrical Experience,* called attention to the shape which remains characteristic of Moorhouse's fiction. His books of short stories are more cohesive than conventional collections, though their unity is never linear. Within meticulously constructed fictional locales, realistic in their surface detail, episodes are structured. Characters and incidents from one episode may reappear in other stories in the same volume, or turn up years later in some altogether different work. These repetitions are not continuities: Moorhouse's Australia is a world without underlying harmony, a world fragmented and isolating.

Reaction to the first volumes was mixed. Among Australians of Moorhouse's own generation, and those who were younger, were many admirers delighting in an audacity others found shocking and profoundly distasteful, as they did the social changes about which he wrote. In *The Americans, Baby* the milieu is a Sydney under-40 population who, hoping that being earnest or outrageous will make them feel real, are left saturated with anxiety instead. Carl, moving into the arms of the American journalist Paul Jonson, afterwards feels guilty, humiliated, trapped—though he will return. Throughout these stories dramatic tension develops between impulse, figured as sex in various combinations, and an obsessively cerebral approach to life, an approach which suffocates physicality and seems to offer nothing much more appealing than an ideologically correct dinner of baked potatoes with lemon, served in a beautiful dark wooden bowl beside a pile of coarse black bread. Refusing all social pieties, Moorhouse pushes against his audience's expectations of the territory a writer can inhabit while remaining ''serious.'' In the title story of *The Everlasting Secret Family,* a politician who has seduced a schoolboy brings to him years later his own son for initiation into a secret and unrecognized ''family.'' Some readers recoiled from a prose enfusing political allegory with detailed homoeroticism.

Moorhouse is undoubtedly one of Australia's best writers of the erotic; unexpectedly, he is also its most acute observer of bureaucratic forms and process. In *Conference-ville* he uses the conference as a social ritual during which people detached from their ordinary life become vulnerable. *Tales of Mystery and Romance* details the narrator's intricate relationship with a Sydney academic and affords an opportunity to chart university life. The narrator of these collections is so given to ironic detachment, self-deprecation, and world-weariness that the prose was threatened by the enervation portrayed. It is in the League Nations about which Moorhouse writes in *Grand Days* that he finds a bureaucracy and cast of characters sufficiently significant to sustain his focus on the tactics of life as played out in the workings of an organization. In this long novel, a departure in form from the earlier fiction though recognizably evolving from the discontinuous narrative, the young diplomat Edith Campbell Berry—like some American counterpart in a novel by Henry James—brings to Geneva an Australian innocence both attracted to and repelled by what she finds in Europe.

Though *Grand Days* won the South Australian Festival Award, it was judged insufficiently ''Australian'' to be considered for the important Miles Franklin prize, a decision hotly debated in the literary community and the newspapers. In any case, Frank Moorhouse has won many of the country's most prestigious literary prizes, and his contribution to letters has been recognized in the national honors list by his appointment as a Member of the Order of Australia, perhaps an ironic tribute to a persistently disturbing writer.

—Lucy Frost

MORRISON, Toni

Nationality: American. **Born:** Chloe Anthony Wofford, Lorain, Ohio, 18 February 1931. **Education:** Howard University, Washington, D.C., B.A. 1953; Cornell University, Ithaca, New York, M.A. 1955. **Family:** Married Harold Morrison in 1958 (divorced 1964); two sons. **Career:** Instructor in English, Texas Southern University, Houston, 1955–57, and Howard University, 1957–64; senior editor, Random House, publishers, New York, 1965–84; associate professor, State University of New York, Purchase, 1971–72; visiting lecturer, Yale University, New Haven, Connecticut, 1976–77, Rutgers University, New Brunswick, New Jersey, 1983–84, and Bard College, Annandale-on-Hudson, New York, 1986–88; Schweitzer Professor of the Humanities, State University of New York, Albany, 1984–89; Regents' Lecturer, University of California, Berkeley, 1987; Santagata Lecturer, Bowdoin College, Brunswick, Maine, 1987. Since 1989 Golheen Professor of the Humanities, Princeton University, New Jersey. **Awards:** American Academy award, 1977; National Book Critics Circle award, 1977; New York State Governor's award, 1985; Book of the Month Club award, 1986; Before Columbus Foundation award, 1988; Robert F. Kennedy award, 1988; Melcher award, 1988; Pulitzer prize, 1988; MLA Commonwealth award in literature, 1989;

Nobel prize, 1993, for literature; Pearl Buck award, 1994; Condorcet medal (Paris), 1994; Rhegium Julii prize, 1994, for literature; National Book Foundation Medal, 1996. Honorary degree: College of Saint Rose, Albany, 1987. **Agent:** International Creative Management, 40 West 57th Street, New York, New York 10019. **Address:** Department of Creative Writing, Princeton University, Princeton, New Jersey 08544, U.S.A.

Publications

Novels

The Bluest Eye. New York, Holt Rinehart, 1970; London, Chatto and Windus, 1980.
Sula. New York, Knopf, and London, Allen Lane, 1974.
Song of Solomon. New York, Knopf, 1977; London, Chatto and Windus, 1978.
Tar Baby. New York, Knopf, and London, Chatto and Windus, 1981.
Beloved. New York, Knopf, and London, Chatto and Windus, 1987.
Jazz. New York, Knopf, and London, Chatto and Windus, 1992.
Paradise. New York, Knopf, 1998.

Play

Dreaming Emmett (produced Albany, New York, 1986).

Other

Playing in the Dark: Whiteness and the Literary Imagination. Cambridge, Massachusetts, and London, Harvard University Press, 1992.
Conversations with Toni Morrison, edited by Danille Taylor-Guthrie. Jackson, University Press of Mississippi, 1994.
Lecture and Speech of Acceptance upon the Award of the Nobel Prize for Literature. London, Chatto and Windus, 1994.
Four Songs for Soprano, Cello, and Piano (poems), by Andre Previn. Bury St. Edmunds, Suffolk, England, Music Sales, 1995.
The Dancing Mind: Speech upon Acceptance of the National Book Foundation Medal for Distinguished Contribution to American Letters on the Sixth of November, Nineteen Hundred and Ninety-Xix. New York, Knopf, 1996.
The Big Box (for children), illustrated by Giselle Potter. New York, Hyperion Books for Children/Jump at the Sun, 1999.
Editor, *Race-ing Justice, En-gendering Power: Essays on Anita Hill, Clarence Thomas, and the Construction of Social Reality.* New York, Pantheon, 1992; London, Chatto and Windus, 1993.
Editor, *To Die for the People: The Writings of Huey P. Newton.* New York, Writers and Readers Publishing, 1995.

*

Film Adaptations: *Beloved,* 1998.

Bibliography: *Toni Morrison: An Annotated Bibliography* by David L. Middleton, New York, Garland, 1987.

Critical Studies: *New Dimensions of Spirituality: A Biracial and Bicultural Reading of the Novels of Toni Morrison* by Karla F.C. Holloway, Westport, Connecticut, Greenwood Press, 1987; *The Crime of Innocence in the Fiction of Toni Morrison* by Terry Otten, Columbia, University of Missouri Press, 1989; *Toni Morrison* by Wilfred D. Samuels and Clenora Hudson-Weems, Boston, Twayne, 1990; *Toni Morrison* edited by Harold Bloom, Chelsea House, 1990; *Fiction and Folklore: The Novels of Toni Morrison* by Trudier Harris, Knoxville, University of Tennessee Press, 1991; *Folk Roots and Mythic Wings in Sarah Orne Jewett and Toni Morrison: The Cultural Function of Narrative* by Marilyn Sanders Mobley, Baton Rouge and London, Louisiana State University Press, 1991; *Toni Morrison's Developing Class Consciousness* by Doreatha Drummond Mbalia, Selinsgrove, Susquehanna University Press, and London, Associated University Presses, 1991; *The Voices of Toni Morrison* by Barbara Hill Rigney, Columbus, Ohio State University Press, 1991; *The Novels of Toni Morrison: The Search for Self and Place Within the Community* by Patrick Bryce Bjork, New York, Lang, 1992; *The Dilemma of ''Double-Consciousness'': Toni Morrison's Novels* by Denise Heinze, Athens and London, University of Georgia Press, 1993; *Toni Morrison: Critical Perspectives Past and Present* edited by Henry Louis Gates Jr. and K.A. Appiah, New York, Amistad, 1993; *Toni Morrison* by Douglas Century, New York, Chelsea House, 1994; *Bridging the Americas: The Literature of Paule Marshall, Toni Morrison, and Gayl Jones* by Stelamaris Coser, Philadelphia, Temple University Press, 1994; *A World of Difference: An Inter-Cultural Study of Toni Morrison's Novels* by Wendy Harding and Jacky Martin, Westport, Greenwood Press, 1994; *The Discourse of Slavery: Aphra Behn to Toni Morrison,* edited by Carl Plasa and Betty J. Ring, London and New York, Routledge, 1994; *Toni Morrison* by Linden Peach, New York, St. Martin's Press, 1995; *Toni Morrison and the American Tradition: A Rhetorical Reading* by Herbert William Rice, New York, P. Lang, 1996; *Toni Morrison's Fiction* by Jan Furman, Columbia, South Carolina, University of South Carolina Press, 1996; *Toni Morrison: An Intricate Spectrum,* edited with an introduction by Alladi Uma, New Delhi, Arnold Associates, 1996; *Toni Morrison: Critical and Theoretical Approaches,* edited by Nancy J. Peterson, Baltimore, John Hopkins University Press, 1997; *Approaches to Teaching the Novels of Toni Morrison,* edited by Nellie Y. McKay and Kathryn Earle, New York, Modern Language Association of America, 1997; *The Female Bildungsroman by Toni Morrison and Maxine Hong Kingston: A Postmodern Reading* by Pin-chia Feng, New York, P. Lang, 1998; *Circles of Sorrow, Lines of Struggle: The Novels of Toni Morrison* by Gurleen Grewal, Baton Rouge, Louisiana State University Press, 1998; *Toni Morrison: A Critical Companion* by Missy Dehn Kubitschek, Westport, Connecticut, Greenwood Press, 1998; *The Novels of Toni Morrison: A Study in Race, Gender, and Class* by K. Sumana, New Delhi, Prestige Books, 1998; *Toni Morrison and Womanist Discourse* by Aoi Mori, New York, P. Lang, 1999; *The Broom Closet: Secret Meanings of Domesticity in Postfeminist Novels by Louise Erdrich, Mary Gordon, Toni Morrison, Marge Piercy, Jane Smiley, and Amy Tan* by Jeannette Batz Cooperman, New York, Peter Lang, 1999; *Prophets of Recognition: Ideology and the Individual in Novels by Ralph Ellison, Toni Morrison, Saul Bellow, and Eudora Welty* by Julia Eichelberger, Baton Rouge, Louisiana State University Press, 1999; *Quiet As It's Kept: Shame, Trauma, and Race in the Novels of Toni Morrison* by J. Brooks Bouson, Albany, State University of New York Press, 2000; *Toni Morrison,* edited and with an introduction by Harold Bloom, Broomall, PA, Chelsea House, 2000; *The Artist As Outsider in the Novels of Toni Morrison and Virginia Woolf* by Lisa Williams, Westport, Connecticut, Greenwood Press, 2000; *Toni Morrison*

Explained: A Reader's Road Map to the Novels by Ron David, New York, Random House, 2000; *Toni Morrison: Historical Perspectives and Literary Contexts* by Linden Peach, New York, St. Martin's Press, 2000.

* * *

A comparison of Toni Morrison with Joyce and Faulkner is irresistible. One dominant aspect of her work is an exhaustive, mythical exploration of place. Another is the search for the nexus of past and present. She is to the black milieu of Lorain what Joyce and Faulkner are to Dublin and Oxford, and her Medallion is as curiously fascinating as Anderson's Winesburg. Her stories translate a multiplicity of places, often superficially tawdry, into a rich cultural matrix. Likewise, the times of her forebears and herself in Ohio are a duration, not a chronology. She thus makes the legendary altogether new, and discovers in colloquial habit and naming the altogether legendary. Legend includes not only the tales of her black folk, but the myths of world literature. She has excluded Caucasians from her fiction more than Joyce and Faulkner have excluded ethnic ''others'' from theirs. But her focus on personality and character (in the moral sense) is indisputably universal. Her pervasive irony and paradox are not merely adroit but ethically motivated. At times they accentuate an erosion of the dignified, reliable courtlines of ancestral blacks, the more profound because it was maintained through the grossest depredations in American history. She is able to say of her contemporaries: ''We raised our children and reared our crops; we let infants grow, and property develop.'' It is a deep regard for craft—for verbal nuance, metaphor image, point of view—that enables Morrison not merely to discourse upon but to animate social process and existential crisis.

The Bluest Eye tells of the incestuous rape of 11-year-old Pecola Breedlove by her father. The girl's need to be loved (pushed to the extreme when she observes her mother, a ''domestic,'' heaping upon a little white girl affections Pecola has only dreamed of) takes the doomed form of a yearning for blue eyes. The insanity of this flight from reality comes to fruition after the death of the baby, when she actually believes herself to have acquired them. With her ubiquitous metaphor of flight, Morrison sums up this personal fate and the novel's powerful theme:

> The damage was total. She spent her days … walking up and down, up and down, her head jerking to the beat of a drummer so distant only she could hear. Elbows bent, hands on shoulders, she flailed her arms like a bird in an eternal, grotesquely futile effort to fly. Beating the air, a winged but grounded bird, intent on the blue void it could not reach—could not even see—but which filled the valleys of the mind.

We are led to conclude that the narrator, Claudia Macteer, and her sister Frieda probably dodged this perversion by directing an ordinate malice at their Shirley Temple dolls and by being born to a family that, though rough and austere, did know how to breed love.

Sula explores equally an extraordinary consciousness and the gap between generations. Sula Mae Peace and her grandmother, Eva, share a great deal in common. Both left the same home in Medallion's ''Bottom'' only to return and inhabit it in willful isolation. Both shun tender expressions of love. Both have authored another's death. But in her indifference to family bonds, Sula is her grandmother's opposite. Where Eva left to save her family, Sula left to indulge her fancy. Where Eva returned for her children (though only content alone on the second floor), Sula returned from boredom and put her grandmother in a home. Where Eva, with tragic awareness, ignited her son's drug-addicted body, Sula dropped the little boy ''Chicken'' to his death with a weird inadvertence. And where Eva maimed herself trying to save her flaming daughter Hannah, Sula watched her mother's immolation with distant curiosity.

Yet this portrait is not simply a paean to the old ways. There is sympathy for Sula because as a child she had misconceived Hannah's remark about her, ''I love her, I just don't like her,'' and because of her vain effort to save ''Chicken.'' Of that the narrator remarks that it has exorcised ''her one major feeling of responsibility.'' Moreover, her temperament blends ''Eva's arrogance and Hannah's self indulgence'' in an ''experimental life'' which itself seems a precondition for seeing and acting upon hard social truths. And finally, she seems like Pecola Breedlove, whose ''guilt'' mysteriously sanctified those around her. Sula performs the original Eve's purpose; as a community ''witch,'' she provides others with a scapegoat, a model of such evil conduct that their own is actually elevated thereby.

Song of Solomon is a work of enormous breadth. Macon and Ruth Dead complete an often devastating characterization of genteel blacks begun with Geraldine and Helene in the earlier novels. Self-serving and cool, their son ''Milkman'' has given full life to the family name. Burdened by his parents' merciless marriage and prompted by his saintly aunt, Pilate, he sets out for Virginia and the skeletons in his family closet. But lore steadily leads and yields to more interesting truth, in the form of persons who correct his myopic view. He discovers his dead grandmother, Sing, so called because she was half Indian, Singing Bird, but also the daughter of a white Virginian named Byrd. And he discovers his great-grandfather, Solomon, who once proudly flew the coop of slavery and about whom the country black kids still sing: ''O Solomon don't leave me.'' Song and flight make life endurable and beautiful in Morrison's world. Having discovered these true ancestors, Milkman forgets the mundane, taking his best friend Guitar's advice to heart: ''[If you] wanna fly, you got to give up the shit that weighs you down.'' The murderous conflict that had developed between the two (Guitar is a consummate study of an extremist racial approach toward which the novel displays both sympathy and disgust) is ended: ''For now [Milkman] knew what Shalimar knew: If you surrendered to the air, you could *ride* it.''

The design of *Tar Baby,* so allegorical and symbolic, probably overextends the mythic note of *Song of Solomon.* Folk legend is provided by the title, but elsewhere little is quite so down to earth and the supporting realism is undercut by both the fabulous Haitian settings and Morrison's anthropomorphizing of them. The key figures are Jadine and Son. Their union and divorce embody a black man's search for an authentic, natural past and a black woman's estrangement from it. Committed to materialistic white values, she ends by fondling her sealskin coat. He ends, more unbelievably than the airborne Milkman, by entering a jungle so humanoid that it ''make[s] the way easier for a certain kind of man,'' Morrison's archetype.

Beloved, properly, earned Morrison the Pulitzer prize. The plot entails the struggle of Sethe (Suggs), from the summer of 1873 to the spring of 1874, to bear the resurgent impact of her past, particularly the moment 18 years earlier when she had drawn a handsaw across the throat of her baby girl, named Beloved. She had done so rather than hand the child and her siblings to a vicious plantation manager who had come to Cincinnati, in the name of the ''Fugitive Bill,'' for the family of escaped Kentucky slaves. Once again using magic realism, Morrison simply allows the child's ghost to cross back into her mother's world, in the form of a living and troubled young woman. Readers will struggle to see it otherwise, but this seems the only viable interpretation of the latter-day Beloved. The plot moves constantly between the present in a spuriously free North and an exactingly drawn past in the South before the Civil War. The detail Morrison provides here about plantation existence for slaves, chain gang existence for black convicts, and the terrors of the runaway's passage to freedom is potently authentic. But all is cast in highly lyrical terms.

In 1992, Morrison offered her readers *Jazz,* a continuation of her look at excessive love, which began with maternal love in particular in *Beloved.* Set in America's Jazz Age, *Jazz* presents Joe and Violet Trace, a door-to-door salesman and hairdresser, respectively. Displaced after they are evicted from their home in Virginia and enchanted by their perception of Harlem, they migrate to New York in 1906 but quickly become ''people enthralled, then deceived by the music the world makes.'' Joe takes a teenage lover, Dorcas, who makes him ''so sad and happy he [shoots] her just to keep the feeling going'' after she jilts him. Violet tries to cut Dorcas's face at the funeral home and, after being forced to leave, runs home to free her primary companions, the birds she keeps in their home. Avoiding a strict chronology is typical for Morrison's work, but here, reading the narrative is often like listening to jazz music as it moves with seamless improvisations, unveiling not only the complexities of romantic love but also the disappointments many blacks faced upon migrating North in the early twentieth century.

In 1993, Morrison was honored with the Nobel Prize for Literature, making her the first African-American woman to receive the award. Her next novel, *Paradise,* again focuses on love, this time the love of God and of humans for one another, in the all-black community of Ruby, Oklahoma. This novel returns to fundamental themes of Morrison's work: a sense of place and the interconnectedness of past and present. The citizens of Ruby feel that their ''paradise,'' established by a group of freed slaves who found strength in their religious faith, is being corrupted by the ''outside.'' As the novel covers events between 1890 and 1976, Ruby faces an increasing amount of ''sin''—violence, disease, infidelity. As in *The Bluest Eye* and *Sula,* a society blind to its own inadequacies seeks a scapegoat; here, it finds the Convent, the refuge for five downtrodden and outcast women. In the conflict between traditional religion, symbolized by the Oven, and the unconventional ''magic'' which takes place at the Convent, the values of past and present do battle.

Structurally reminiscent of Faulkner's *As I Lay Dying, Paradise* is divided into sections according to narrative point of view, not chronology, leaving the reader to assemble the narrative as one would a puzzle. The novel begins with the culmination of Ruby's frustrations: an act of violence against the women of the Convent. The opening sentence of the novel reads, ''They shoot the white girl first.'' Using a tactic she uses in her obscure short story ''Recitatif,'' Morrison never explicitly reveals the race of the Convent's women but leaves the reader to decide: which woman is white? More importantly, however, the struggle to solve this riddle leads one to ponder other questions: in this particular act by the citizens of Ruby, is race relevant? Does the victim's race somehow justify her murderers or vilify them even more? Although Morrison often searches the issues particular to the black race, she is at her best in conundrums like this one. From *The Bluest Eye* to *Paradise,* her work compels readers to consider issues that involve race but also transcend it, as they often see their own world, and perhaps even themselves, reflected in the pages of each novel.

—David M. Heaton, updated by Melissa Simpson

MORTIMER, John (Clifford)

Nationality: British. **Born:** Hampstead, London, 21 April 1923. **Education:** Harrow School, Middlesex, 1937–40; Brasenose College, Oxford, 1940–42, B.A. 1947; called to the bar, 1948; Queen's Counsel, 1966; Master of the Bench, Inner Temple, 1975. **Military Service:** Served with the Crown Film Units as scriptwriter during World War II. **Family:** Married 1) Penelope Dimont in 1949 (divorced 1971, deceased 1999), one son and one daughter; 2) Penny Gollop in 1972, one daughter. **Career:** drama critic, *New Statesman, Evening Standard,* and *Observer,* 1972, all London; member of the National Theatre Board, 1968–88; president, Berkshire, Buckinghamshire, and Oxford Naturalists' Trust, from 1984; chairman, League of Dramatists; chairman of the council, Royal Society of Literature for 1989; chairman, Royal Court Theatre since 1990; president, Howard League for Penal Reform since 1991; chairman, the Royal Society of Literature since 1992. Lives in Henley-on-Thames, Oxfordshire. **Awards:** Italia prize, for radio play, 1958; Screenwriters Guild award, for television play, 1970; BAFTA award, for television series, 1980; *Yorkshire Post* award, 1983. D. Litt.: Susquehanna University, Selinsgrove, Pennsylvania, 1985; University of St. Andrews, Fife, 1987; University of Nottingham, 1989; LL.D.: Exeter University, 1986. C.B.E. (Commander, Order of the British Empire), 1986; knighted, 1998. **Agent:** Peters Fraser and Dunlop, 503–504 The Chambers, Chelsea Harbour, Lots Road, London SW10 0XF, England.

Publications

Novels

Charade. London, Lane, 1948.
Rumming Park. London, Lane, 1948.
Answer Yes or No. London, Lane, 1950; as *The Silver Hook,* New York, Morrow, 1950.
Like Men Betrayed. London, Collins, 1953; Philadelphia, Lippincott, 1954.
The Narrowing Stream. London, Collins, 1954; New York, Viking, 1989.
Three Winters. London, Collins, 1956.
Will Shakespeare: The Untold Story. London, Hodder and Stoughton, 1977; New York, Delacorte Press, 1978.
Paradise Postponed. London and New York, Viking, 1985.
Summer's Lease. London and New York, Viking, 1988.
Titmuss Regained. London and New York, Viking, 1990.
Dunster. London and New York, Viking Penguin, 1992.
Rumpole and the Angel of Death. New York, Viking, 1996.

Felix in the Underworld. New York, Viking, 1997.
The Sound of Trumpets. New York, Viking, 1999.

Short Stories

Rumpole. London, Allen Lane, 1980.
Rumpole of the Bailey. London, Penguin, 1978; New York, Penguin, 1980.
The Trials of Rumpole. London, Penguin, 1979; New York, Penguin, 1981.
Regina v. Rumpole. London, Allen Lane, 1981.
Rumpole's Return. London, Penguin, 1980; New York, Penguin, 1982.
Rumpole for the Defence. London, Penguin, 1982.
Rumpole and the Golden Thread. New York, Penguin, 1983.
The First Rumpole Omnibus (includes *Rumpole of the Bailey, The Trials of Rumpole, Rumpole's Return).* London, Penguin, 1983.
Rumpole's Last Case. London, Penguin, 1987; New York, Penguin, 1988.
The Second Rumpole Omnibus (includes *Rumpole for the Defence, Rumpole and the Golden Thread, Rumpole's Last Case).* London, Viking, 1987; New York, Penguin, 1988.
Rumpole and the Age of Miracles. London, Penguin, 1988; New York, Penguin, 1989.
Rumpole à la Carte. London and New York, Viking Penguin, 1990.
Rumpole on Trial. London and New York, Viking Penguin, 1992.
The Best of Rumpole. London and New York, Viking Penguin, 1993.
The Third Rumpole Omnibus (includes *Rumpole and the Age of Miracles, Rumpole a la Carte, Rumpole and the Angel of Death.)* London, Viking, and New York, Penguin, 1998.

Plays

The Dock Brief (broadcast 1957; produced London, 1958; New York, 1961). In *Three Plays,* 1958.
I Spy (broadcast 1957; produced Salisbury, Wiltshire, and Palm Beach, Florida, 1959). In *Three Plays,* 1958.
What Shall We Tell Caroline? (produced London, 1958; New York, 1961). In *Three Plays,* 1958.
Three Plays: The Dock Brief, What Shall We Tell Caroline?, I Spy. London, Elek, 1958; New York, Grove Press, 1962.
Call Me a Liar (televised 1958; produced London, 1968). In *Lunch Hour and Other Plays,* 1960; in *The Television Playwright: Ten Plays for B.B.C. Television,* edited by Michael Barry, New York, Hill and Wang, 1960. Sketches in *One to Another* (produced London, 1959). London, French, 1960.
The Wrong Side of the Park (produced London, 1960). London, Heinemann, 1960.
Lunch Hour (broadcast 1960; produced Salisbury, Wiltshire, 1960; London, 1961; New York, 1977). In *Lunch Hour and Other Plays* 1960; published separately, New York, French, 1961.
David and Broccoli (televised 1960). In *Lunch Hour and Other Plays,* 1960.
Lunch Hour and Other Plays (includes *Collect Your Hand Baggage, David and Broccoli, Call Me a Liar*). London, Methuen, 1960.
Collect Your Hand Baggage (produced Wuppertal, Germany, 1963). In *Lunch Hour and Other Plays,* 1960. Sketches in *One over the Eight* (produced London, 1961).
Two Stars for Comfort (produced London, 1962). London, Methuen, 1962.
A Voyage round My Father (broadcast 1963; produced London, 1970). London, Methuen, 1971. Sketches in *Changing Gear* (produced Nottingham, 1965).
A Flea in Her Ear, adaptation of a play by Feydeau (produced London, 1966; Tucson, Arizona, 1979). London and New York, French, 1967.
A Choice of Kings (televised 1966). In *Playbill Three,* edited by Alan Durband, London, Hutchinson, 1969.
The Judge (produced London, 1967). London, Methuen, 1967.
Desmond (televised 1968). In *The Best Short Plays 1971,* edited by Stanley Richards, Philadelphia, Chilton, 1971.
Cat Among the Pigeons, adaptation of a play by Feydeau (produced London, 1969; Milwaukee, 1971). New York, French, 1970.
Come As You Are: Four Short Plays (includes *Mill Hill, Bermondsey, Gloucester Road, Marble Arch)* (produced London, 1970). London, Methuen, 1971.
Five Plays (includes *The Dock Brief, What Shall We Tell Caroline?, I Spy, Lunch Hour, Collect Your Hand Baggage*). London, Methuen, 1970.
The Captain of Köpenick, adaptation of a play by Carl Zuckmayer (produced London, 1971). London, Methuen, 1971.
Conflicts, with others (produced London, 1971).
I, Claudius, adaptation of the novels *I, Claudius* and *Claudius the God* by Robert Graves (produced London, 1972).
Knightsbridge (televised 1972). London, French, 1973.
Collaborators (produced London, 1973). London, Eyre Methuen, 1973.
The Fear of Heaven (as *Mr. Lucy's Fear of Heaven,* broadcast 1976; as *The Fear of Heaven,* produced with *The Prince of Darkness* as *Heaven and Hell,* London, 1976). London, French, 1978.
Heaven and Hell (includes *The Fear of Heaven* and *The Prince of Darkness*) (produced London, 1976; revised version of *The Prince of Darkness,* as *The Bells of Hell* produced Richmond, Surrey, and London, 1977). *The Bells of Hell* published London, French, 1978.
The Lady from Maxim's, adaptation of a play by Feydeau (produced London, 1977). London, Heinemann, 1977.
John Mortimer's Casebook (includes *The Dock Brief, The Prince of Darkness, Interlude*) (produced London, 1982).
When That I Was (produced Ottawa, 1982).
Edwin (broadcast 1982). In *Edwin and Other Plays,* 1984.
A Little Hotel on the Side, adaptation of a play by Feydeau and Maurice Desvalliers (produced London, 1984). In *Three Boulevard Farces,* 1985.
Edwin and Other Plays (includes *Bermondsey, Marble Arch, The Fear of Heaven, The Prince of Darkness*). London, Penguin, 1984.
Three Boulevard Farces (includes *A Little Hotel on the Side, A Flea in Her Ear, The Lady from Maxim's*). London, Penguin, 1985.
Die Fledermaus, adaptation of the libretto by Henri Meihac and Ludovic Halévy, music by Johann Stauss (produced London, 1989). London, Viking, 1989.
A Christmas Carol, adaptation of the novel by Charles Dickens (produced London, 1994); published as *Charles Dickens' A Christmas Carol,* New York and London, S. French, 1995.

Screenplays: *Ferry to Hong Kong,* with Lewis Gilbert and Vernon Harris, 1959; *The Innocents,* with Truman Capote and William Archibald, 1961; *Guns of Darkness,* 1962; *I Thank a Fool,* with others, 1962; *Lunch Hour,* 1962; *The Running Man,* 1963; *Bunny Lake Is Missing,* with Penelope Mortimer, 1964; *A Flea in Her Ear,* 1967; *John and Mary,* 1969.; *Tea with Mussolini,* 1998.

Radio Plays: *Like Men Betrayed,* 1955; *No Hero,* 1955; *The Dock Brief,* 1957; *I Spy,* 1957; *Three Winters,* 1958; *Lunch Hour,* 1960; *The Encyclopedist,* 1961; *A Voyage round My Father,* 1963; *Personality Split,* 1964; *Education of an Englishman,* 1964; *A Rare Device,* 1965; *Mr. Luby's Fear of Heaven,* 1976; *Edwin,* 1982; *Rumpole,* from his own stories, 1988; *Glasnost,* 1988.

Television Plays: *Call Me a Liar,* 1958; *David and Broccoli,* 1960; *A Choice of Kings,* 1966; *The Exploding Azalea,* 1966; *The Head Waiter,* 1966; *Hughie,* 1967; *The Other Side,* 1967; *Desmond,* 1968; *Infidelity Took Place,* 1968; *Married Alive,* 1980; *Swiss Cottage,* 1972; *Knightsbridge,* 1972; *Rumpole of the Bailey,* 1975, and series, 1978, 1979, 1987, 1988; *A Little Place off the Edgware Road, The Blue Film, The Destructors, The Case for the Defence, Chagrin in Three Parts, The Invisible Japanese Gentlemen, Special Duties,* and *Mortmain,* all from stories by Graham Greene, 1975–76; *Will Shakespeare,* 1978; *Rumpole's Return,* 1980; *Unity,* from the book by David Pryce-Jones, 1981; *Brideshead Revisited,* from the novel by Evelyn Waugh 1981; *Edwin,* 1984; *The Ebony Tower,* from the story by John Fowles, 1984; *Paradise Postponed,* from his own novel, 1986; *Summer's Lease,* from his own novel, 1989; *The Waiting Room,* 1989; *Titmuss Regained,* 1991; *Cider with Rosie,* 1998; *Don Quixote,* 2000.

Other

No Moaning of the Bar (as Geoffrey Lincoln). London, Bles, 1957.

With Love and Lizards (travel), with Penelope Mortimer. London, Joseph, 1957.

Clinging to the Wreckage: A Part of Life (autobiography) . London, Weidenfeld and Nicolson, and New Haven, Connecticut, Ticknor and Fields, 1982.

Murderers and Other Friends (autobiography). London and New York, Viking Penguin, 1994.

In Character (interviews). London, Allen Lane, 1983.

The Liberty of the Citizen (lecture), with Franklin Thomas and Lord Hunt of Tanworth. London, Granada, 1983.

Character Parts (interviews). London, Viking, 1986.

Editor, with Harry Hodge and James H. Hodge, *Famous Trials.* London, Viking, and New York, Penguin, 1984.

Editor, *Great Law and Order Stories.* London, Bellew, 1990.

*

Manuscript Collections: Boston University; University of California, Los Angeles.

* * *

Now approaching eighty but showing no signs of reducing his considerable literary output, John Mortimer continues as one of England's best known living authors. His stories, novels, plays, film and television scripts, and autobiographical writing have won him both critical and popular success. Still best known for his engaging ''Rumpole of the Bailey'' stories, inspired by his own experiences as a working barrister, Mortimer has published two memoirs, *Clinging to the Wreckage* and *Murderers and Other Friends,* complementing the story only sketched in his early autobiographical television drama, *A Voyage round My Father.* He has also maintained a prolific output in fiction, publishing three installments in the ''Rapstone Chronicles'' series, a satiric look at English politics in the Thatcher and post-Thatcher era, and a number of free-standing novels about the manners and morals of contemporary English life.

In his earlier days, while still an active barrister, Mortimer wrote two novels which did not attract much attention: *Like Men Betrayed,* the story of a London solicitor whose son has misappropriated a client's investments, and *The Narrowing Stream* in which a young woman's murder disrupts the lives of an ordinary family. Though apprentice work, both novels take a characteristically perceptive view of English life and have many of the themes Mortimer would develop to better effect in his later novels.

Inspired perhaps by Evelyn Waugh, whose *Brideshead Revisited* Mortimer had adapted for television, Mortimer attempted his own novels of manners in the ''Rapstone Chronicles,'' beginning with *Paradise Postponed.* Using many of the conventions of Victorian and Edwardian novels, though with telling variations, Mortimer deftly weaves throughout his story sharp observations on the state of postwar England. When the revered liberal Rector of Rapstone Fanner, Simeon Simcox, dies leaving his entire estate to Leslie Titmuss, Conservative M.P. from Rapstone, his widow and his two sons attempt to understand their father's surprising bequest. Mortimer traces the story of the Simcox, Titmuss, and Fanner families, moving back and forth in time until at last family secrets are revealed and the inheritance explained. Along the way, Mortimer draws on familiar character types from earlier English novels, from the idealistic village Rector (reminiscent of Trollope's Septimus Harding) to any of Dickens's lower-class boys striving for acceptance in high society. In *Paradise Postponed,* however, the characters break their stereotypes. The seeming innocence of the rector is qualified at the end, and the working lad, Titmuss, at first treated sympathetically, proves to be utterly without scruple as he marries his way into the best family of the village on his climb up the ranks of the Thatcher government. Mortimer's own political leanings come through clearly. The leftists in the novel may be muddle-headed and ineffective, but they are never as mean-spirited as their right-wing opponents.

Following the success of *Paradise Postponed* and responding to the public's interest in the character of Leslie Titmuss, Mortimer continued his story in *Titmuss Regained.* Now a conservative government minister, Titmuss purchases the very Fanner Manor where his mother had worked as a servant and which in the earlier novel had represented unattainable social preeminence. But corporate developers are determined to reconstruct the village into a real estate agent's version of English rustic life. Mortimer is at his best describing the various factions involved in promoting or opposing the enterprise: developers, environmentalists, local politicians, even the villagers themselves—all revealed as self-seeking hypocrites. While his portrait of this cluster of peripheral characters is bitingly satiric, Mortimer is somewhat easier on his hero, and in his efforts to make his second marriage a success, he even wins back a measure of the sympathy we felt for Titmuss as a child in *Paradise Postponed.*

In the third novel in the series, *The Sound of Trumpets,* Leslie, now Lord Titmuss, having been swept out of office by the Labour Party victory, has retired to the country. Angry at the new Conservative leadership, he forms an alliance with an idealistic young politician, Terry Flitton, whose socialist political philosophy Titmuss softens into a more centrist, and electable, stance. But Flitton, having already betrayed his principles to get elected, is caught up in an extramarital affair with Agnes Simcox, reminding the dedicated Mortimer reader of the intricate romantic relationships chronicled in *Paradise Postponed.* The ensuing scandal ends Flitton's political career, but the novel ends sadly for Titmuss as well, as the master manipulator is left to face death alone. Whereas Mortimer's sympathies had been for the social welfare programs of the left, this bitter portrayal of English politics calls for a plague on both Tory and Labour houses.

For the same moral vision but a less pessimistic outlook, Mortimer has returned to more congenial subjects than contemporary politics. In *Summer's Lease* Mortimer draws on themes of the English abroad he had found in *Brideshead Revisited.* The setting is Tuscany, where an English family has leased a villa for the summer. The wife, Molly Pargenter, is determined to investigate the mysterious absence of their landlord, uncovering a complex web of relationships in which her family becomes entangled. As she comes to terms with what is happening around her, she finds that she must fight to save her own integrity and her marriage. Her father-in-law's irresponsible nonchalance beautifully contrasts Molly's determination to understand and control her life. While Mortimer's focus is still on English character types, the Italian surroundings depict those traits in sharper focus.

An incident involving the activities of English officers serving in Italy during World War II plays a role in *Dunster,* but the core of the novel is the relationship between the narrator, Philip Progmire, an accountant and amateur actor, and his old school nemesis, Richard Dunster, now a producer of television documentaries. The determined and dynamic but ruthless Dunster has accused Progmire's employer of a war crime, prompting a libel suit. Mortimer explores the comic effects of the contrast between Progmire and Dunster, though the reader may be too sympathetic to the long-suffering narrator to enjoy the humor in Dunster's reckless schemes. The conclusion of the war-crime plot, that even the best and the brightest are potential war criminals, may be too unsettling for what is essentially a comic novel.

For the more recent *Felix in the Underworld,* Mortimer describes two worlds he knows well, the criminal justice system and the publishing business. The main character, Felix Morsom, is a minor novelist once nominated for the Booker Prize and once compared to Chekhov. Criticized for writing stories about insignificant people to whom nothing ever happens, Felix finds himself, for the first time in his life, a celebrity, accused first in a paternity action and then in a gory murder. Mortimer is at his best describing police more interested in closing cases than in finding criminals, attorneys more concerned about their reputations than about justice, publishers more eager for profits than for literary merit. Felix, the mild-mannered observer of life, has to endure living among the homeless on the streets of London and a few weeks in prison before he is finally exonerated. The experience, however threatening, promises to improve his lonely, routine existence.

In the many genres and media he has used in his fifty-plus years of writing, Mortimer offers a view of humankind that is rarely comforting, but he manages to show us our worst side without condemning us. Like his Horace Rumpole, who has no romantic illusions about the criminals he defends, Mortimer is simultaneously harsh and forgiving. The first quality gives his work its import, the latter its appeal.

—Robert E. Lynch

MOSLEY, Nicholas

Nationality: British. **Born:** Lord Ravensdale in London, 25 June 1923; eldest son of Sir Oswald Mosley; became 3rd Baron Ravensdale, 1966; succeeded to the baronetcy of his father, 1980. **Education:** Eton College, Berkshire, 1937–42; Ballio College, Oxford, 1946–47. **Military Service:** Served in the Rifle Brigade, 1942–46; Captain; Military Cross, 1944. **Family:** Married 1) Rosemary Laura Salmond in 1947 (marriage dissolved 1974), three sons and one daughter; 2) Verity Elizabeth Bailey in 1974, one son. **Awards:** Whitbread Book of the Year award, 1990. Made a peer (Lord Ravensdale) in 1966. **Address:** 2 Gloucester Cresent, London NW1 7DS, England.

Publications

Novels

Spaces of the Dark. London, Hart Davis, 1951.

The Rainbearers. London, Weidenfeld and Nicolson, 1955.

Corruption. London, Weidenfeld and Nicolson, 1957; Boston, Little Brown, 1958.

Meeting Place. London, Weidenfeld and Nicolson, 1962.

Accident. London, Hodder and Stoughton, 1965; New York, Coward McCann, 1966.

Assassins. London, Hodder and Stoughton, 1966; New York, Coward McCann, 1967; revised edition, London, Minerva, 1993.

Impossible Object. London, Hodder and Stoughton, and New York, Coward McCann, 1969; revised edition, London, Minerva, 1993.

Natalie Natalia. London, Hodder and Stoughton, and New York, Coward McCann, 1971.

Catastrophe Practice: Plays for Not Acting, and *Cypher: A Novel* (includes *Skylight, Landfall, Cell*). London, Secker and Warburg, 1979; Elmwood Park, Illinois, Dalkey Archive Press, 1989; revised edition, London, Minerva, 1992.

Imago Bird. London, Secker and Warburg, 1980; Elmwood Park, Illinois, Dalkey Archive Press, 1989; revised edition, London, Minerva, 1991.

Serpent. London, Secker and Warburg, 1981; Elmwood Park, Illinois, Dalkey Archive Press, 1990; revised edition, London, Minerva, 1992.

Judith. London, Secker and Warburg, 1986; Elmwood Park, Illinois, Dalkey Archive Press, 1991.

Hopeful Monsters. London, Secker and Warburg, 1990; Elmwood Park, Illinois, Dalkey Archive Press, 1991.

Children of Darkness and Light. London, Secker & Warburg, 1996; Normal, Illinois, Dalkey Archive Press, 1997.

Plays

Screenplays: *The Assassination of Trotsky,* with Masolini d'Amico, 1972; *Impossible Object,* 1975.

Other

Life Drawing, with John Napper. London, Studio, 1954.
African Switchback (travel). London, Weidenfeld and Nicolson, 1958.
The Life of Raymond Raynes. London, Faith Press, 1961.
Experience and Religion: A Lay Essay in Theology. London, Hodder and Stoughton, 1965; Philadelphia, United Church Press, 1967.
The Assassination of Trotsky. London, Joseph, 1972.
Julian Grenfell: His Life and the Times of His Death 1888–1915. London, Weidenfeld and Nicolson, and New York, Holt Rinehart, 1976.
Rules of the Game: Sir Oswald and Lady Cynthia Mosley 1896–1933. London, Secker and Warburg, 1982; with *Beyond the Pale,* Elmwood Park, Illinois, Dalkey Archive Press, 1991.
Beyond the Pale: Sir Oswald Mosley and Family 1933–1980. London, Secker and Warburg, 1983; with *Rules of the Game,* Elmwood Park, Illinois, Dalkey Archive Press, 1991.
Efforts at Truth: An Autobiography. London, Secker and Warburg, 1994; Normal, Illinois, Dalkey Archive Press, 1995.
Editor, *The Faith: Instructions on the Christian Faith,* by Raymond Raynes. London, Faith Press, 1961.

*

Critical Studies: ''Nicholas Mosley Issue'' of *Review of Contemporary Fiction* (Elmwood Park, Illinois), vol. 2, no. 2, 1982.

Nicholas Mosley comments:

My novels are attempts to see how life works: I hope to learn from them.

* * *

Since 1951 Nicholas Mosley has published thirteen novels as well as a miscellaneous assortment of other books, notably biographies, and although his fiction has not won widespread popularity or much academic recognition, he is acknowledged in the literary world to be one of the most individual and innovative English novelists of his generation. What is most striking about his *oeuvre* as a whole is his ability to break free from one mode of writing and to experiment with something very different in his constant quest for appropriate forms and authentic expression. This adaptability is particularly interesting when viewed in light of the political career of his somewhat notorious father, Sir Oswald Mosely, who at one time or another during the 1920s and 1930s belonged to virtually every major political party in England before forming his own British Union of Fascists.

The novels the younger Mosely wrote during the 1950s form a distinct group and can be considered as the first phase in his growth as a writer. The three published novels of this decade, *Spaces of the Dark, The Rainbearers,* and *Corruption,* are essentially realistic in mode, although they explore beneath the level of character and society to locate a metaphysical or spiritual malaise in modern Western civilization. All three novels are mainly set in the postwar world, although they look back both directly and indirectly to the war itself, and not surprisingly they reveal the influence of the dominant European philosophical movement of the 1940s and 1950s, existentialism. *Spaces of the Dark* (a phrase from T.S. Elliot's ''Rhapsody on a Windy Night'') is an ambitious attempt at a tragic novel whose protagonist, Paul Shaun, is torn apart by guilt and angst as a result of a wartime incident in which he killed a close friend and fellow officer. The past again casts its shadow on the present in *The Rainbearers,* and, although this novel lacks the tragic intensity of his first novel, the emphasis is on unrealized potential, lost possibilities, and failure. *Corruption,* in which the Venetian setting plays an important part, is structurally and stylistically more complex than *Spaces of the Dark* and *The Rainbearers,* and differs from them in being a first-person narrative. The title could be that of a medieval morality play, and the characters in this analysis of modern decadence and corruption function symbolically as well as realistically. Until its later stages, *Corruption* emanates a similar type of doom-laden fatalism and pessimism as the earlier novels, but then there is a crucial episode in which the oppression and bleakness lift to produce an unexpectedly open ending rather than a tragic denouement. This shift, marked by the adoption of a simpler idiom, may be inconsistent but it dramatizes Mosley's subversion of his own tragic pretensions as he discovers light at the end of the existential tunnel his fiction had been probing in the 1950s.

Five years separate *Corruption* from his next novel, *Meeting Place,* a transitional novel inaugurating the second phase of his development, ending with *Natalie Natalia* in 1971. Mosley now discards many of the features of his previous novels, which had been long, exhaustively analytical, densely written (Henry James and William Faulkner are important influences), and sometimes convoluted to the point of turgidity. The prose is simpler, sentences and paragraphs shorter, and the style more visually immediate, indeed cinematic. Furthermore, the narrative method is elliptical, selective, and discontinuous, and involves intercutting between the various strands of the plot with its Murdochian network of relationships. Comedy, conspicuous by its absence from the earlier novels, plays an important part in *Meeting Place,* which also features a broader range of characters than its predecessors and is remarkable for its positive conclusion, embodying Mosley's new commitment to the possibilities of renewal, growth, and creativity. With *Meeting Place* Mosley liberated himself from his preoccupations of the 1950s and therefore prepared the way for his first major achievement, *Accident,* subsequently turned into a distinguished film by Joseph Losey using a screenplay by Harold Pinter. The story in *Accident* is very simple: a version of the eternal triangle narrated by an Oxford philosophy don, Stephen Jervis, who knows the three people involved. Mosley's way of telling the story, however, is highly original because the unorthodox style enacts both the indeterminacy of reality and the inevitable tentativeness of human attempts to apprehend it. By using verbal fragments and staccato rhythms, Mosley captures the disjointed, ambiguous, even contradictory nature of experience in a way that may owe something to the French *nouveau roman* and its underlying phenomenology. Yet although *Accident* begins with a death and incorporates disintegration and severed relationships, it is not pessimistic; the end, with the birth of a baby to the narrator's wife, looks forward, not back, and emphasizes continuity, not finality.

In *Assassins* Mosley applies the methods of *Accident* to the world of public affairs and politics by narrating the attempted assassination of an Eastern bloc leader in England. The subject matter is that of the political thriller, but Mosley completely transforms and revitalizes that genre without, however, achieving such subtlety and profundity as he did in *Accident.* The most difficult of the novels belonging to his second phase is *Impossible Object,* which at first sight seems to be a collection of short stories about love and marriage but proves to be a complex study in multiple viewpoint. By means of certain repetitions and patterns, Mosley provides his readers with a key to decode his collage of narratives and reassemble the fragments, but the reflexivity of the novel, as in *Accident,* draws attention to the impossibility of ever being able to fix or represent something as fluid and relativistic as reality. *Natalie Natalia,* one of Mosley's finest achievements, is less consciously experimental and more accessible than *Impossible Object,* but again displays his willingness to take risks with both language and narrative technique. The story line about a politician, Anthony Greville, and involving love, adultery, shame, and breakdown is unexceptional, but Mosley's way of treating familiar material is, as usual, startlingly different, and illuminates it in unexpected, mind-opening ways. The title, providing two names for the same woman, Greville's mistress, epitomizes Mosley's preoccupation with the enigmatic inconsistencies of life, because she is a living contradiction, both ravenous Natalie and angelic Natalia.

After *Natalie Natalia* Mosley published no fiction for eight years, and then in 1979 he launched by far his most ambitious project with *Catastrophe Practice,* initially intended to be the first of a group of seven novels, although he subsequently reduced the number to five. *Catastrophe Practice,* a compilation of three ''plays not for acting'' (with prefaces and a concluding essay) and a novella-length piece of fiction, is much more abstract than any of his other work. Catastrophe Theory is a mathematical attempt to account for discontinuities in the natural world: *Catastrophe Practice* is Mosley's attempt to create a literary form capable of encompassing and articulating the discontinuities of human experience. Superficially, the book is fragmented and dislocated, but by means of a complicated arrangement of correspondences and cross-references, including the appearance of the six principal characters in various guises in different sections, Mosley creates a form of unity out of apparent disunity and chaos. Running through *Catastrophe Practice* is a strain of polemic about the need to free consciousness, language, and art from the confines of convention, and also to rescue modern art from its devotion to versions of negativity—failure, disillusionment, pessimism, despair.

Mosley conceived the subsequent novels in the sequence to be self-contained yet interrelated books, each concentrating on one or two of the main figures in *Catastrophe Practice* itself. After the complexities of the very demanding *Catastrophe Practice, Imago Bird* is an immediately engaging and relatively straightforward novel, which presents a wide spectrum of contemporary life through the innocent eyes of its 18-year-old narrator, Bert. In trying to come to terms with the randomness of experience and to reconcile inner and outer reality, Bert apprehends the essential theatricality of adult life—how human beings allocate stereotyped parts to themselves and then proceed to act these out in a fictional illusion they mistake for reality. While believing themselves to be free, people, whether establishment politicians, media personalities, or dedicated revolutionaries, have imprisoned themselves in linguistic and behavioral conventions. *Imago Bird,* like its predecessor, is about the need to break out of the cage of false consciousness. *Serpent* is more intricate and less satisfactory than *Imago Bird.* Mosley interweaves a screenplay about the Jewish revolt against the Romans at Masada with contemporary events involving its writer, Jason, and a crisis in Israel. Parallels emerge between past and present, especially concerning the polarities of devotion and reason and of the individual and society. After *Serpent* Mosley temporarily shelved work on his large-scale project in order to write two books about his father, who had recently died, leaving all his papers to his son.

Five years after publishing *Serpent,* Mosley returned to his *Catastrophe Practice* series with *Judith,* and four years later completed the quintet of novels with the large-scale *Hopeful Monsters,* which deservedly won the Whitbread award, one of Britain's most prestigious literary prizes. *Judith* is cast in the form of three letters from Judith herself to other main characters in the sequence, each letter describing a separate episode in her life. At the narrative level there is a radical discontinuity between these episodes, but at a metaphorical level the narrative leaps can be interpreted as a progression towards a new conception of unity. Judith's training as an actress makes her particularly sensitive to the constantly shifting levels of stage or in life. Brecht's influence on Mosley's novel sequence is evident in Judith's awareness of the way in which people often speak as though in quotation marks. *Judith* is very much a novel about the enigma of human consciousness, including the consciousness of consciousness. The complex biblical symbolism, especially recurring references to the Garden of Eden, the Tree of Knowledge, and the story of Judith and Holofernes, develops motifs present in the earlier novels and points forward to *Hopeful Monsters.*

In this concluding novel Mosley ambitiously attempts to pursue the main themes of the sequence in relation to the political history of the twentieth century as well as to the history of science, especially the consequences of Einstein's theories. Major issues in the philosophy of language and the philosophy of science are interwoven with important historical events, as experienced by the two principal characters, Eleanor Anders and Max Ackerman, between whom the narrative alternates until the concluding section by a ''correlator'' (who turns out to be Jason). Eleanor's interest in anthropology and psychiatry and Max's in biology, theoretical physics, and cybernetics mean that crucial intellectual problems about the nature of matter, reality, subjectivity, and objectivity provide a way of interpreting the ideological and existential traumas of Europe, particularly between the two world wars. Mosley introduces such philosophers as Husserl, Heidegger, and Wittegenstein into the narrative as much as he introduces political figures like Rosa Luxemburg, Hitler, and Franco. Max's involvement in the Manhattan Project to develop nuclear weapons during World War II foregrounds the impossibility of an ivory-tower approach to scientific research, remote from ethical questions and political manipulation. As the culmination of the *Catastrophe Practice* sequence, *Hopeful Monsters* suggests an unorthodox way of coming to terms with the human condition in the twentieth century, facing up to the worst (the Spanish Civil War, Stalin's purges, the Nazi Holocaust) while not abandoning hope in human potentialities—a theme that, given his family history, must no doubt have special meaning for Mosley. Despite its length, *Hopeful Monsters* is one of Mosley's most accessible novels, possessing an urgent narrative drive that makes the high intellectual content palatable rather than indigestible. It is a novel of ideas in the best sense of the term. Many of the themes from the earlier book reappear in *Children of Darkness and Light,* though this time the focus is primarily spiritual rather than intellectual. Harry, an alcoholic journalist who once reported on alleged visitations by the Virgin Mary in the wartorn Balkans, now hears of similar appearances in Cumbria. Though these manifestations may be linked with nuclear pollution, there is also a possibility that the children who see the visions have, through mutation, become beings on a higher plane.

—Peter Lewis

MOSLEY, Walter

Nationality: American. **Born:** Los Angeles, California, 1952. **Education:** Attended Goddard College; received degree from Johnson State College; attended City College of the City University of New York, beginning 1985. **Family:** Married Joy Kellman. **Career:** Formerly a computer programmer; writer. Lives in New York. **Awards:** Shamus Award (Private Eye Writers of America), 1990. **Agent:** c/o W. W. Norton, 500 Fifth Avenue, New York, New York 10110, U.S.A.

PUBLICATIONS

Novels

Devil in a Blue Dress. New York, Norton, 1990.
A Red Death. New York, Norton, 1991.
White Butterfly. New York, Norton, 1992.
Black Betty. New York, Norton, 1994.
RL's Dream. New York, Norton, 1995.
Gone Fishin': An Easy Rawlins Novel. Black Classic Press, 1996.
A Little Yellow Dog: An Easy Rawlins Mystery. New York, Norton, 1996.
Blue Light: A Novel. Boston, Little, Brown, 1998.
Walkin' the Dog. Boston, Little Brown, 1999.

Short Stories

Always Outnumbered, Always Outgunned: The Socrates Fortlow Stories. New York, Norton, 1997.

Other

Workin' on the Chain Gang: Shaking off the Dead Hand of History. New York, Ballantine, 2000.
Contributor, *Los Angeles in Fiction: A Collection of Essays*, edited by David Fine. Albuquerque, University of New Mexico Press, 1995.
Contributor, *Mary Higgins Clark Presents The Plot Thickens.* Thorndike, Maine, Center Point Publishers, 2000.
Introduction, *The Stolen White Elephant and Other Detective Stories* by Mark Twain. New York, Oxford University Press, 1996.
Introduction and editor, with others, *Black Genius: African American Solutions to African American Problems.* New York, Norton, 1999.

*

Film Adaptations: *Devil in the Blue Dress*, 1995; *Always Outnumbered, Always Outgunned*, 1998.

Critical Studies: *Oil on the Waters: The Black Diaspora: Panel Discussions and Readings Exploring the African Diaspora through the Eyes of Its Artists* (sound recording), Washington, D.C., Library of Congress, 1995.

* * *

Although Walter Mosley first gained attention as the author of a series of detective novels featuring an African-American private eye in the Raymond Chandler tradition, in light of subsequent works it is now apparent that he is more than simply a genre writer. For example, though Easy Rawlins, Mosley's private detective, was introduced to readers in 1991 with the publication of *Devil in a Blue Dress*, followed in quick succession by four more appearances, Rawlins's first appearance was in a non-mystery novel, *Gone Fishin'*, written in 1988, though not published until 1997.

Gone Fishin' is a coming-of-age story centered around a trip made in 1939 by nineteen-year-old Easy Rawlins and his childhood friend Raymond Alexander (known as Mouse) from Houston to the Texas bayou town of Pariah. Childhood innocence gives way to painful lessons about mortality, friendship, and the heavy burden of guilt as Easy helplessly stands by and watches Mouse murder his stepfather, and then keeps quiet about it. At the end of the novel, Easy leaves Houston for a new life in Los Angeles, though his life there will continue to be complicated by the continuing presence of the recklessly dangerous Mouse.

Devil in a Blue Dress is set in 1948. Easy has just lost his job. When a white gangster offers him $100 to find a missing woman whom he believes is hiding somewhere in Watts, Easy, who needs the money to pay his mortgage, accepts the job. Trouble begins when friends of the missing woman begin turning up dead and Easy becomes a prime suspect in their murders. Easy, however, proves to be an effective detective, getting to the bottom of the mystery. He also discovers that being his own boss gives him a newfound confidence as a man—especially an African-American man in postwar America. In this and in subsequent novels in the series, Mosley also paints a colorful picture of Easy's world, taking his readers to places (e.g. neighborhood bars, local brothels, and community barbershops) heretofore largely absent from mainstream mystery fiction.

A Red Death picks up Easy's story five years later. Although he now owns three apartment buildings, Easy feels compelled to hide his ownership, posing instead as the maintenance man. But his ruse doesn't fool the IRS, who is after him for back taxes. When an FBI agent offers to fix his tax problems in return for whatever information he can uncover about a suspected Communist organizer working in a local black church, Easy once again finds himself in the role of detective.

As the series continues, life continues to grow more complicated for Easy. In *White Butterfly*, set in 1956, Easy, now married and the father of two (one of them a mute Mexican boy he saved from a life of child prostitution), still straddles the line between middle-class respectability (he now owns seven buildings, a secret he keeps even from his wife) and outlaw (he's jailed on suspicion of trying to extort money from his employer). Once again, though, he demonstrates his mettle as a detective, solving the case of the murder of a young white woman living in Watts. But his detective work takes its toll on his personal life, as his wife leaves, taking their daughter with her.

It's 1961, Kennedy's in the White House, Martin Luther King, Jr. is beginning to organize marches, and hope for black people is on the rise in *Black Betty*. But Easy's personal problems continue to weigh him down. He has to try to prevent Mouse from killing whoever sent him to jail, plus untangle an impossibly complicated mystery. The strain shows, and Easy's gloomy mood makes this the darkest novel in the series. At the end, he vows never again to get involved with the problems of others.

A Little Yellow Dog picks up Easy's story two years later, when he seems to have kept his promise: he's happily employed as head custodian at Sojourner Truth Junior High School and trying to raise his two adopted kids. But a sexual encounter with one of the school's teachers changes all that: her brother and his twin turn up dead, followed shortly by her own murder. Easy is left with her dog and a case that leads to more death and more pain. At the end of the novel, as the country grieves over the assassination of John F. Kennedy, Easy is left to grieve over the shooting of his friend Mouse and to agonize over his own guilt in that affair.

In the detective tradition established by Dashiell Hammett and Raymond Chandler, the private eye is usually portrayed as a loner working outside the system of organized law enforcement. But a black private detective like Easy is doubly marginalized, both by his profession and by his race. Race complicates his life in that the demands of justice are often at odds with the demands of his community, and though he often finds himself working for the police, he is never fully accepted by them—and his efforts on their behalf threaten his standing in his community. Mosley succeeds in expanding the bounds of the mystery genre by creating an unusual detective hero who is shown struggling with himself and with racial and class prejudices to make his place in the largely white world.

Ultimately, Easy has as much in common with a character like John Updike's Rabbit Angstrom as he does with the private eyes he's usually compared with. Like Updike, Mosley chronicles his hero's personal development in the context of the changing times. Also like Updike, Mosley is as interested in the slice of American life he portrays as he is in his hero. Easy is no simple hero; he's a flawed man in a flawed world. Mosley's genius is in creating believable portraits both of that man and of his world.

Mosley created a second series character, a tough ex-con named Socrates Fortlow, featured in two collections of stories, *Always Outnumbered, Always Outgunned* and *Walkin' the Dog*. Socrates spent twenty-seven years in an Indiana penitentiary for double murder. Out of prison for eight years and now living in a tiny apartment in Watts, his needs are few and his aims simple: after a lifetime of doing evil, he now wants to be a good man. Like his Greek namesake, Socrates is a philosopher in the fundamental sense of questioning how to live with dignity and integrity, even though circumstances and his troubled past sometimes make that effort difficult.

Written in simple and straightforward prose, perfectly matched to the character of Socrates, the stories display Mosley's skill in portraying realistically the demanding world of a down-and-outer like Socrates. They also celebrate the basic humanity of this fascinating fifty-eight-year-old supermarket bag boy seeking to atone for the past by striving against all odds to live a principled life.

Mosley's other two novels are also departures from the mystery genre with which he had first been identified. *RL's Dream* is a meditation on the blues. It tells the story of Atwater Wise, a blues guitar player known as Soupspoon. Fifty years ago, he played with legendary blues man Robert (''RL'') Johnson. Now dying of cancer in New York City, he strikes up an improbable friendship with an alcoholic white woman named Kiki. She rescues him from homelessness and helps him record his memories of the past. The best parts of the novel are Soupspoon's recollections of his early days in the Mississippi Delta juke joints where he learned to play the blues. By bringing to life those memories of a lifetime spent both living and singing the blues, Mosley celebrates the heartache and the poetry of the music of a people who, as he writes, ''carried the whole world on their shoulders and when they sighed it came out blues.''

An even more radical departure for Mosley is *Blue Light*, a science fiction novel that is his least successful book. Set in San Francisco in the 1960s, the novel is populated with otherworldly blue lights, graphic murders, and an evil presence known as Gray Man. Largely absent from this novel, however, is the one quality that has proven to be the hallmark of Mosley's best work: the realistic depiction of ordinary people struggling to live ordinary lives.

In his fictional portraits of a wide range of African Americans, Mosley chooses not to focus primarily on racism as a dominant theme. Rather than portraying black people in relation to whites, in other words as victims of racism, he is more interested in showing blacks simply living their lives, working hard, raising their children, trying to pay the bills. Out of such ordinary lives as these, Mosley has crafted some extraordinary American fiction.

—David Geherin

MUDROOROO

Also writes as Colin Johnson and Mudrooroo Narogin. **Nationality:** Australian. **Born:** East Cubbaling, Western Australia, 1938. **Education:** Brought up in a Roman Catholic orphanage. **Career:** Lived in India for 6 years, three as a Buddhist monk. Holds the Chair of Aboriginal Studies at Murdech University, Perth. **Awards:** Wieckhard prize, 1979; Western Australia Literary award, 1989; WA Premier's Book award, for most outstanding entry and for poetry, 1992; Australia Council Writer's grant, 1994. **Agent:** Iarune Little. **Address:** School of Humanities, Murdoch University, Murdoch, Western Australia 6150, Australia.

Publications

Novels

Doin' Wildcat (as Mudrooroo Narogin). South Yarra, Victoria, Hyland House, 1988.
Master of the Ghost Dreaming. Sydney, HarperCollins, 1991.
Wildcat Screaming. Sydney, HarperCollins, 1992.
The Kwinkan. Sydney, HarperCollins, 1993.
The Undying. Pymble, N.S.W., HarperCollins, 1998.
Underground. Pymble, Sydney, NSW, Angus & Robertson, 1999.

Novels as Colin Johnson

Wild Cat Falling. Sydney and London, Angus and Robertson, 1965.
Long Live Sandawara. Melbourne, Quartet, 1979; London, Quartet, 1980.
Doctor Wooreddy's Prescription for Enduring the Ending of the World. Melbourne, Hyland House, 1983.

Poetry

Dalwurra: The Black Bittern (as Colin Johnson). Nedlands, Western Australia, Centre for Studies in Australian Literature, 1988.
The Garden of Gethsemane. Melbourne, Hyland House, 1991.
Pacific Highway Boo-blooz: Country Poems. St. Lucia, Queensland, Australia, University of Queensland Press, 1996.

Other

Before the Invasion: Aboriginal Life to 1788 (as Colin Johnson), with Colin Bourke and Isobel White. Melbourne, Oxford University Press, 1980.
Writing from the Fringe (as Mudrooroo Narogin). South Yarra, Victoria, Hyland House, 1990.
The Mudrooroo/Mueller Project. Sydney, New South Wales University Press, 1993.
Aboriginal Mythology. London, Aquarian, 1994.
Us Mob: History, Culture, Struggle: An introduction to Indigenous Australia. Sydney and New York, Angus & Robertson, 1995.
Indigenous Literature of Australia/Milli Milli Wangka. South Melbourne, Victoria, Hyland House, 1997.

*

Critical Studies: *The Mudrooroo/Muller Project: A Theatrical Casebook,* edited by Gerhard Fischer. Kensington, NSW, Australia, New South Wales University Press, 1993; *Mudrooroo—A Critical Study* by Adam Shoemaker, Sydney, HarperCollins, 1994; *Doin' Mudrooroo: Elements of Style and Involvement in the Early Prose Fiction of Mudrooroo* by Greg Watson, Joensuu, Finland, Joensuun Yliopisto, 1997.

* * *

Colin Johnson's novels deal with the displacement of modern Aborigines and their inability either to find a place in white society or to hold to the traditional ways. His first novel was concerned with the world he knew growing up in Perth—a world of the bodgie subculture often in trouble with the law—while subsequent novels confront events from the Australian past and their implications for Aborigines today.

Wild Cat Falling portrays a cynical young Aborigine on his release after a prison sentence. One leitmotif of the novel is Beckett's *Waiting for Godot.* It is the absurdist view of a pointless world which appeals to the principal character as he moves among various groups in Perth, reticent and detached. He becomes involved in a burglary during which he shoots a policeman. Fleeing, he encounters an old Aborigine who represents both the lore of the Aboriginal and the moral center which he is seeking even while he thinks he is impervious to it. The conclusion sees him showing concern for the man he shot, and finding a glimmer of humanity even in the policeman who is arresting him.

A number of motifs in this novel reappear in the next, in particular the opposition between a directionless ''modern'' Aborigine and a decayed though still integral Elder. *Long Live Sandawara* is the story of a group of young Perth Aborigines whose sixteen-year-old leader, Alan, is keen to organize them to improve their opportunities, but his attempts to do so through the local Aboriginal leader get nowhere. Alan eventually leads the gang in a farcical raid on a bank during which all except himself are killed. Throughout the novel he has visited Noorak, who as a child saw the clash between an Aboriginal resistance fighter, Sandawara, and the whites. Noorak recounts the adventures of the past, and it is in emulation of these that Alan leads his ill-fated raid. Johnson treats the freedom fighters of the past with seriousness and dignity as true spiritual products of the soil. The sort of holistic integrity in Sandawara and his fighters contrasts strongly with the rootlessness of the modern characters. This is marked by different narrative styles, a sort of biblical cadence being used for the past events, while the modern story is told in a sometimes awkward historical present using a good deal of dialogue. Johnson has attempted to render in the one novel the ethos of two quite different genres, the epic past, and the problem-drama present. In this novel, the past offers to the present a model of what may be done to correct injustice. However, Johnson argues that more than Western guerrilla resistance is required—that to make anything of their lives modern Aborigines must re-establish contact with the centers of their cultural heritage. At the conclusion of the novel Alan leads the old man, Noorak, to the airport to fly north to their tribal country where he, Alan, will undergo initiation and Noorak will die contented.

The past in this novel is a time of glorious and inspiring resistance to the whites, invariably referred to as ''invaders.'' In Johnson's recent novel, history becomes less a source of political instruction than a crucible within which a philosophy of survival must be forged. *Doctor Wooreddy's Prescription for Enduring the Ending of the World* is concerned with the annihilation of the Tasmanian Aborigines in the first half of the 19th century. The controlling viewpoint is that of a learned man of the Bruny Island tribe who sees his land polluted by the aggressive practices of the whites. The focus of the novel is on Wooreddy's attempts to understand the processes of change where there had been no change before. Wooreddy is obsessed with the belief that he has been chosen to survive to see the imminent end of the world. This insight comes to him as a child when he sees his first sailing ship which he takes to be a floating island drawn by clouds from the domain of the evil spirit, *Ria Warawah.* Wooreddy's sense of being select enables him to avoid the worst pangs of outrage and regret as the dispossession of the Aborigines proceeds. He retreats into a fatalistic numbness which cannot be termed cowardice, for bravery and cowardice are no longer meaningful concepts.

Wooreddy's initial vision of the ship is balanced by a second vision which collapses the Manichean world-view which the Aborigines have held. In a sea cave to which he is led by a Port Phillip Aborigine he comes to see that instead of the traditional binary cosmology of a good spirit, *Great Ancestor,* and an opposing evil spirit, *Ria Warawah,* there is but one force which is primal and that all things are a manifestation of it. Johnson uses historical events and characters in this novel to investigate the state of doomed suspension in which the Aborigines found themselves after the arrival of the white man. Since there never was any chance of the Tasmanian Aborigines resisting the invaders, their world effectively ended from the appearance of the whites. From early in the novel the invading and polluting whites are seen as the embodiment of the evil spirit, *Ria Warawah,* but when the disjunction between him and the benevolent creator, *Great Ancestor,* is rejected by Wooreddy's second major vision the processes of history no longer allow the assignment of guilt. The whites are a force of history as much as a manifestation of the evil of man. Wooreddy is denied even the satisfaction of having someone to blame.

—Chris Tiffin

MUKHERJEE, Bharati

Nationality: Canadian. **Born:** Calcutta, India, 27 July 1940; became Canadian citizen, 1972. **Education:** Loreto Convent School, Calcutta; University of Calcutta, B.A. (honors) in English 1959; University of Baroda, Gujarat, M.A. 1961; University of Iowa, Iowa City, M.F.A. 1963; Ph.D. 1969. **Family:** Married Clark Blaise, *q.v.,* in 1963; two sons. **Career:** Instructor in English, Marquette University, Milwaukee, Wisconsin, 1964–65, and University of Wisconsin, Madison, 1965; lecturer, 1966–69, assistant professor, 1969–73, associate professor, 1973–78, and professor, 1978, McGill University, Montreal. Professor, Skidmore College, Saratoga Springs, New York; associate professor, Montclair State College, New Jersey, 1984–87; Queen's College, City University of New York, Flushing, 1987–89; professor, University of California, Berkeley, 1990–95. **Awards:** Canada Arts Council grant, 1973, 1977; Guggenheim fellowship, 1977; National Book Critics Circle award, 1989; Pushcart prize, 1999. **Agent:** Timothy Seldes, Russell and Volkening, 551 Fifth Avenue, New York, New York 10017, U.S.A.

Publications

Novels

The Tiger's Daughter. Boston, Houghton Mifflin, 1972; London, Chatto and Windus, 1973.
Wife. Boston, Houghton Mifflin, 1975; London, Penguin, 1987.
Jasmine. New York, Grove Weidenfeld, 1989; London, Virago Press, 1990.
The Holder of the World. New York, Knopf, and Chatto and Windus, 1993.
Leave It to Me. New York, Knopf, 1997.

Short Stories

Darkness. Toronto, Penguin, 1985.
The Middleman and Other Stories. New York, Grove Press, 1988; London, Virago Press, 1989.

Play

Screenplay: *Days and Nights in Calcutta,* with Clark Blaise, 1991.

Other

Kautilya's Concept of Diplomacy: A New Interpretation. Calcutta, Minerva, 1976.
Days and Nights in Calcutta, with Clark Blaise. New York, Doubleday, 1977; London, Penguin, 1986.
The Sorrow and the Terror: The Haunting Legacy of the Air India Tragedy, with Clark Blaise. Toronto, Viking, 1987.
Political Culture and Leadership in India: A Study of West Bengal. New Delhi, India, Mittal Publications, 1991.

*

Critical Studies: *Bharati Mukherjee: Critical Perspectives* edited by Emmanuel S. Nelson, New York, Garland Press, 1993; *Bharati Mukherjee* by Fakrul Alam, New York, Twayne Publishers, 1996; *The Fiction of Bharati Mukherjee: A Critical Symposium,* edited by R.K. Dhawan, New Delhi, Prestige, 1996.

* * *

Bharati Mukherjee is a versatile writer whose *oeuvre* includes five novels, two collections of short stories, some powerful essays, and two nonfiction books which she co-authored with her husband Clark Blaise. Her early work led to her being seen as a writer firmly enclosed in the bosom of Indian writing in English. But this was an embrace that Mukherjee herself sought to avoid. With the publication of *Darkness,* her third book of fiction, she convincingly declared her desire to be seen as a North American writer. In the hard-hitting introduction to this collection of stories Mukherjee explains this shift as "a movement away from the aloofness of expatriation, to the exuberance of immigration."

Mukherjee's early novels, *The Tiger's Daughter* and *Wife,* both published in the early 1970s, are novels about the isolation of Indian expatriates. A reading of *Days and Nights in Calcutta* reveals that there is a strong autobiographical element in *A Tiger's Daughter.* Tara Banerjee, like the Bharati Mukherjee of *Days and Nights in Calcutta,* is an outsider in India because of her decision to leave the subcontinent, to live in North America, and to marry an American, *mleccha* (outcaste) husband. On her return, Tara sees India through the eyes of a Western imagination rather than through her own childhood eyes. Her sense of alienation in Calcutta is symbolized by her regular visits to the Catelli-Continental Hotel, from where she views the turmoil of Calcutta from the safe heights of a tourist, cut off from the "real" India which seethes below her. Tara is no longer able to feel a part of her family, who belong to an old Bengal which is now lost to her, nor is she able to feel at ease with her old friends who, like her family, belong to a Calcutta which is rapidly fading, and who, in their different ways are as isolated as Tara from the beast beneath them. On another level, *The Tiger's Daughter* is an interesting response to E.M. Forster's *A Passage to India.*

The theme of expatriation and isolation which is handled with such assurance in *The Tiger's Daughter* is again treated in her second novel. In *Wife,* Dimple Dasgupta is married off to a young engineer, and soon finds herself emigrating to America. She finds her new life impossible to adjust to, and her attempts to become American—to learn to speak American-English by watching the television, for example—cause her to question her own cultural values, and even her own happiness. These are questions she might never have asked herself in Calcutta, and had she done so and found herself equally disillusioned, her solution, the novel suggests, would probably have been suicide. The infidelity and the murder which brings the novel to its shocking close are the alternatives with which Dimple's American experience has provided her.

Darkness is an important landmark for Mukherjee. It is in this book, her first collection of stories, that she begins to exchange the robes of an Indian expatriate writer for the new, but not borrowed robes of a North American writer who is an immigrant. The specifically Canadian stories in this collection continue to explore the painful world of the expatriate she writes about in *Wife*—indeed the story "Visitors" is a re-working of the essential elements of that novel. Other stories, though, explore North America through the alien voices of its various immigrant cultures—Italian, Latin American, Sri Lankan, as well as Indian. With *The Middleman and Other Stories* Mukherjee's exchange of mantles is complete. In these stories, sometimes with anger, often with violence, sometimes with comedy, often with tenderness, Mukherjee gives voice to the ''other'' within North America. The result is a broader, more detailed portrait of the North American immigrant experience than *Wife* or even the impressive stories in *Darkness* provide. ''The Management of Grief,'' which deals with the sorrow of the bereaved relatives of the victims of the 1985 Air India disaster, is perhaps the most moving story in the collection. The horror of that tragedy is dealt with in harrowing detail in Mukherjee's second nonfiction collaboration, *The Sorrow and the Terror.*

After a gap of fourteen years, Mukherjee made a welcome return to the novel form with the publication of *Jasmine,* which explores female identity through the story of an Indian peasant woman whose path takes her from the Punjab, to Florida, to New York, to Iowa, and as the novel draws to a close she is about to set off for California. With each new move the protagonist reinvents herself with a new name—Jyoti, Jasmine, Jase, Jane—and with each new name she moves closer to her dream of being an American, of belonging to the New World. Jasmine's ongoing journey is an effective device which highlights her rootless position and her search for identity. The move to California, which resonates with hope and invests her with the aspirations of America's early pioneers, suggests that Jasmine has finally found her identity in America, which, perhaps more than any other country, can contain her many identities without contradiction.

In *The Holder of the World,* her most accomplished work to date, Mukherjee turns her attention to one of the founding novels of the postcolonial American canon—Nathaniel Hawthorne's *The Scarlet Letter.* Reversing the usual binary opposition between occidental and oriental texts, Mukherjee presents Hawthorne's novel as one which has been written out of a knowledge of India. And in doing this Mukherjee has written herself (as an American whose roots are in India) into her text perhaps more effectively even than in the seemingly autobiographical *The Tiger's Daughter.* The novel is also interesting for the way it very subtly parodies the Western construct of India as a nation and the perception of Indians as a homogenous group.

In Mukherjee's most recent novel, *Leave It to Me,* some of the themes of her earlier fiction—notably identity and dislocation—are again important. And as in *Jasmine,* the central character of this novel goes through a series of incarnations as she is abandoned in India by her American hippie mother and Eurasian father, raised in Schenectady, New York, by her adoptive Italian-American parents, and then (in classic road movie style) moves to San Francisco to look for her birth mother. This novel is Mukherjee's most American work: an enigmatic and alarming meditation on the consequences of the America's recent past—the hippie culture of the 1960s, Vietnam—rather than a novel of dislocation in the diasporic sense of her earlier fiction. In this novel Mukherjee's shift from immigrant diasporic writer to multicultural writer is complete. However, it may be that Mukherjee has moved too far. Few of the characters are as convincing as those who populated her earlier works, and at times the level of coincidence works against this novel—as when, in a moment of epiphany, Debby reinvents herself as Devi Dee, without realizing that she has taken the name of the goddess after whom the Indian village of Devigaon, where she was born, is named.

Bharati Mukherjee is a writer who is at her best when she draws on her experiences of the Old World while writing with insight about the New World to which she now belongs. Her more recent books, particularly *The Holder of the World,* confirm that hers is an original voice at the cutting edge of American immigrant/multicultural literature.

—Ralph J. Crane

MULKERNS, Val

Nationality: Irish. **Born:** Dublin, Ireland, 1925. **Career:** Associate editor, *The Bell,* 1952–54; weekly columnist, *Evening Press,* until 1983; writer in residence, Mayo County Council, 1988; novelist, journalist, lecturer, and teacher of creative writing. **Awards:** A.I.B. Prize for literature, 1984. **Address:** 1 Monto Alto, Sorrento, Dalkey, County Dublin, Ireland.

PUBLICATIONS

Novels

A Time Outworn. London, Chatto & Windus, 1951; New York, Devin-Adair, 1952.
A Peacock Cry. London, Hodder & Stoughton, 1954.
The Summerhouse. London, J. Murray, 1984.
Very Like a Whale. London, J. Murray, 1986.

Short Stories

Antiquities: A Sequence of Short Stories. London, Deutsch, 1978.
An Idle Woman and Other Stories. Dublin, Poolbeg Press, 1980.
A Friend of Don Juan. London, J. Murray, 1988.

Other

Editor, *New Writings from the West.* Mayo County Council, 1988.
Introduction, *Hurrish: A Study* by Emily Lawless. Belfast, Northern Ireland, Appletree Press, 1992.

*

Critical Studies: *No Mean City?: The Image of Dublin in the Novels of Dermot Bolger, Roddy Doyle, and Val Mulkerns* by Ulrike Paschel. New York, P. Lang, 1998.

* * *

Val Mulkerns, born in 1925, has had what amounts to two separate publishing careers. In the 1950s, some of her short stories appeared in *The Bell* and she published two novels, *A Time Outworn* and *A Peacock Cry.* Subsequent published work, beginning with a short story collection, began to appear more than 20 years later, in 1978. Mulkerns's work examines the complexities of family relationships and conveys a strong sense of contemporary Irish life, especially for its women.

Although she later dismissed her first two novels as ''juvenile'' and refused to have them reprinted, they offer a window on an everyday Irish world of the 1950s that is rarely represented in literature. *A Time Outworn* tells the story of Maeve Cusack, a young woman who takes a job (arranged by a family friend) as librarian in a small town in Tipperary. She has not scored well enough on her exams to continue her education, but her boyfriend Diarmud remains in Dublin to continue his own studies. In Tipperary, she rooms in the same house as the schoolmaster, a Kerryman with radical ideas about society and language. When Maeve learns that one of her old school friends is pregnant by Diarmud, she breaks off the relationship with him. Her friend dies in childbirth; Maeve and the schoolmaster visit the Aran Isles. In a sentimental ending, Maeve drowns at age 20 when an ''Aran curragh capsized'' on her second holiday in the west. The novel examines some important contemporary issues—the fate of the Irish language, the division of the island into two separate countries, the role of Irish literary figures such as Joyce, Yeats, and Gregory—but it is often cliched and melodramatic.

Mulkerns's next novel, *A Peacock Cry*, is set mainly in the west of Ireland. The exception is a brief visit to Dublin, the occasion of a literary party with figures no doubt recognizable to those who knew literary Dublin in the 1950s. In this novel, Mulkerns brings an Englishman to the west of Ireland; he is the nephew of Dara Joyce, rough-hewn novelist of Syngean themes. The novel is flawed in several ways; the main obstacles for twenty-first century readers are its insularity (open prejudice against all things English, American, and Jewish) and the lack of credibility surrounding Dara Joyce. The novel only succeeds if readers can accept him as his devoted wife describes him—'''rare and splendid, a product of the purest and oldest form of Gaelic civilisation'''—but it also exposes him as a fraud in many ways, making such acceptance difficult.

After a long hiatus, Mulkerns published *Antiquities*. This book is a series of short stories about several generations of an Irish family. Not presented in chronological order, their connection only gradually becomes clear to the reader. The oldest setting is post-1916; the most recent is right up to the publication date. The stories examine family relations and question some of the Irish political verities endorsed by Mulkerns's earlier work. The return to violence that broke out in the late 1960s has cast a new, unpleasant light on those political platitudes. The interconnections among the stories, and between family life and politics, are sophisticated and finely wrought. After another collection of short stories, *An Idle Woman*, which takes on themes of familial neglect and cruelty, snobbery, inadequate middle-aged husbands and bored wives, Mulkerns published another novel, *The Summerhouse*. *The Summerhouse* is a short story writer's novel; although not containing separate stories, it is structured as a series of family narratives covering different time periods and told by various characters. The novel's main themes are the isolation of individuals and the dysfunctional nature of many families (especially their cruelty to those perceived as outsiders, often including children and spouses). The novel is interesting in part for the way Mulkerns uses the multiple narrators to represent conflicting explanations of actions and attitudes presented by different characters.

Her most important novel, *Very Like A Whale*, draws on her lifelong knowledge of Dublin. Mulkerns is a Dubliner, and in this novel she examines the city directly and at length. The main character, Ben, returns to Dublin after several years abroad and finds that both his family and the city itself have changed enormously in his absence. Ben takes a job at a northside school, and one of the novel's preoccupations is with the debased conditions of life he finds there. This territory has become known to many through Roddy Doyle's fiction, but Mulkerns examines it with a more serious eye. Dublin, by the 1980s, has lost much of its small-town character and has become more urban and faceless. The chaos and degradation wrought by drugs on the northside of Dublin is symptomatic of more widespread changes. Ben is made aware of other areas of change through his family; his parents have separated and both have new residences and new relationships, and his sister and brother-in-law are upwardly mobile young parents with an au pair and a fashionable home in what used to be artisans' cottages. Mulkerns's novel is an important addition to twentieth-century literature about Dublin.

After *Very Like A Whale*, Mulkerns published *A Friend of Don Juan*. Several of the stories in this collection are reprints from earlier publications. Mulkerns's outlook is expressed concisely in an introduction she wrote for an Emily Lawless reprint, *Hurrish*, in 1992. First, her introduction presents feminism as a necessary and inevitable response to certain arrogant male behaviors, and second, she describes the original appeal of Lawless's novel (in 1887) as that of ''a dispatch from the battlefield.'' Lawless's English readers, baffled by the social and political movements gaining force in Ireland at that time, could find some answers in her novel. Mulkerns observes that ''the Irish question'' has yet to be answered; in her own novels, she provides some insight into the social and political conditions of the second half of the twentieth century.

—Rosemary Johnsen

MUNONYE, John (Okechukwu)

Nationality: Nigerian. **Born:** Akokwa, 28 April 1929. **Education:** Christ the King College, Onitsha, 1943–47; University College, Ibadan, 1948–52, B.A. in classics and history 1952; Institute of Education, University of London, 1952–53, Cert. Ed. 1953. **Family:** Married Regina Nwokeji in 1957; one daughter and one son. **Career:** Education Officer, 1954–57, and Provincial Education Officer and Inspector of Education, 1958–70, Nigerian Ministry of Education; Principal, Advanced Teachers College, Oweri, 1970–73; Chief Inspector of Education, East Central State, 1973–76, and Imo State, 1976–77. Columnist, *Catholic Life* magazine, Lagos, and *Nigerian Statesman*, Owerri. Member of the Board of Directors, East Central State Broadcasting Service, Enugu, 1974–76. **Member:** Order of the Niger, 1980. **Agent:** David Higham Associates, 5–8 Lower John Street, London W1R 4HA, England. **Address:** P.O. Box 436 Orlu, Imo State, Nigeria.

PUBLICATIONS

Novels

The Only Son. London, Heinemann, 1966.
Obi. London, Heinemann, 1969.
Oil Man of Obange. London, Heinemann, 1971.
A Wreath for Maidens. London, Heinemann, 1973.
A Dancer of Fortune. London, Heinemann, 1974.
Bridge to a Wedding. London, Heinemann, 1978.
A Kind of Fool. Ibadan, Nigeria, Heinemann Educational, 1999.

Uncollected Short Stories

''Silent Child,'' in *Okike 4* (Amherst, Massachusetts), December 1973.
''Pack Pack Pack,'' in *Festac Anthology of Nigerian New Writing*. Lagos, Ministry of Information, 1977.
''Man of Wealth,'' in *Catholic Life* (Lagos), 1981.

''On a Sunday Morning,'' in *Catholic Life* (Lagos), 1982.
''Rogues,'' in *Catholic Life* (Lagos), 1985.

Other

Drills and Practice in English Language (textbook), with J. Cairns. Lagos, African Universities Press, 1966.

*

John Munonye comments:

(1991) All six of my novels are children of the land. Set in the Igbo area of Nigeria, they draw from the experiences of ordinary men and women, children too. The motif is the processes of change that started with the arrival of Christian missionaries some sixty years ago. Culture (''all the arts, beliefs, social institutions ... characteristic of a community'') had to shift ground. And the environment, sensitive in its own way, was transformed too. How did our ordinary men and women fare in it all? Is there anything of their authentic nature that could be said to have survived the stress? The earliest experiences, which are depicted in *The Only Son* and *Obi,* were severe and traumatic. Later, people came to live with the new state of things, and the result is *Bridge to a Wedding,* a novel of accommodation and reconciliation between traditional and modern. We do indeed need the bridge.

Oil Man of Obange is a relentless tragedy, a novel of confrontation on an individual scale. The Oil Man musters all his energy, zeal, optimism, and integrity towards improving his low social status. But did he consult the god of success? *A Wreath of Maidens* also deals with moral issues—on a wider canvas. The blood shed in the end is not, unfortunately, that of the protagonists: it is a novel of futility. *A Dancer of Fortune* proceeds on much lighter feet.

What next? The beautiful ones are not yet born—yes. But hope is one of man's sustaining gifts, a gift of the spirit. With it goes vision (without which a people perish) and commitment. Nothing shrill or didactic; no sermons; no protest.

* * *

Though he wrote six novels in one twelve year period, John Munonye has attracted surprisingly little critical attention. The reason is not far to seek: despite the intrinsically interesting material he works on, his craftsmanship and command of English have flagged noticeably since his earliest books. Yet, as a compassionate chronicler of the ways in which ordinary Eastern Nigerian people have been affected by historical and social change, he is a writer well worth reading. In his first and third novels, *The Only Son* and *Oil Man of Obange,* theme and treatment interlock admirably and reveal his competence at its best. Jeri, the petty trader in palm oil of *Oil Man of Obange,* pits his own elemental resources of courage, devotion, and physical strength against fate, accident, and malice to raise money for his children's schooling; Munonye subdues the narration rigorously to a stark recording of the everyday hardships of bare human existence that is still the lot of most Nigerians, indeed of the peoples of the Third World in general. With similar, though slightly less stringent, narrative austerity, *The Only Son* presents the privations of a self-reliant widow whose humble, sparse life is touched into tragic proportions by her simple courage and steadfastness: the relationship between Chiaku and her son is tenderly but unsentimentally handled, and, in their estrangement, when he seeks Western and Christian education, Munonye achieves a sympathetic insight into both sides of an irreconcilable clash of aspirations.

The Only Son is the first novel in Munonye's trilogy about the fortunes of one family, the twentieth-century descendants of the legendary Udemezue of Burning Eyes in the community of Umudiobia of ten villages and two. In *Obi* the fully Christianized son and his Christian wife return to Umudiobia to re-establish his father's *obi* or homestead, but the tensions between traditional custom and their new faith culminate in their flight into exile in a distant town. *Bridge to a Wedding* introduces them as the materially prosperous parents of six children and traces the patient and successful efforts of a highly respected Umudiobian to heal the feud between them and their village kinsfolk so that his son can marry their daughter. While these two novels share the attractive unifying theme of how African custom still operates upon the lives of ordinary Nigerians, for good and for ill, Munonye's concern with this theme, especially in *Bridge to a Wedding,* leads him into an often irritating discursiveness.

The virtue of Munonye's civil-war novel, *A Wreath for the Maidens,* rests upon his intimate knowledge of how the common people are affected for the worse by large historical events, despite the public rhetoric that accompanies them. Poor characterization and a tendency to wordiness do not vitiate the somber moral concern at the heart of this book. That it could so soon be followed by *A Dancer of Fortune,* with its apparent endorsement of mere individualist opportunism, is a disturbing measure of Munonye's increasing lack of self-criticism as a writer.

—Arthur Ravenscroft

MUNRO, Alice (Anne)

Nationality: Canadian. **Born:** Alice Anne Laidlaw, Wingham, Ontario, 10 July 1931. **Education:** Wingham public schools; University of Western Ontario, London, 1949–51. **Family:** Married 1) James Armstrong Munro in 1951 (separated 1972; divorced 1976), four daughters (one deceased); 2) Gerald Fremlin in 1976. Lived in Vancouver, 1951–63, Victoria, British Columbia, 1963–71, London, Ontario, 1972–75, and Clinton, Ontario, from 1976. **Career:** Writer-in-residence, University of Western Ontario, 1974–75, and University of British Columbia, Vancouver, 1980. **Awards:** Governor-General's award, 1969, 1978, 1987; B.C. Library Association Outstanding Fiction Writer's award, 1972; Great Lakes Colleges Association award, 1974; Province of Ontario Council for the Arts award, 1974; Canada-Australia literary prize, 1977; National Magazine Awards Foundation Gold Medal award, 1977, 1982; Foundation for the Advancement of Canadian Letters and Periodical Distributors of Canada Author's award, 1980; Marian Engel award, 1986; Canada Council Molson prize, 1991; Commonwealth Writers prize (Canada and Caribbean Region), 1991; Trillium Book award, 1991; Order of Ontario medal, 1994; Canada-Australia Literary Prize, 1994; Canadian Booksellers Association Author of the Year award, 1995; Giller Prize, 1998. D.Litt.: University of Western Ontario, 1976. **Address:** c/o Writers Union of Canada, 24 Ryerson Street, Toronto, Ontario M5T 2P4, Canada.

PUBLICATIONS

Novels

Lives of Girls and Women. Toronto, McGraw Hill Ryerson, 1971; New York, McGraw Hill, 1972; London, Allen Lane, 1973.
Queenie. London, Profile Books, 1999.

Short Stories

Dance of the Happy Shades. Toronto, Ryerson Press, 1968; New York, McGraw Hill, 1973; London, Allen Lane, 1974.
Something I've Been Meaning to Tell You: Thirteen Stories. Toronto, McGraw Hill Ryerson, and New York, McGraw Hill, 1974.
Personal Fictions, with others, edited by Michael Ondaatje. Toronto, Oxford University Press, 1977.
Who Do You Think You Are? Toronto, Macmillan, 1978; as *The Beggar Maid: Stories of Flo and Rose,* New York, Knopf, 1979; London, Allen Lane, 1980.
The Moons of Jupiter. Toronto, Macmillan, 1982; New York, Knopf, and London, Allen Lane, 1983.
The Progress of Love. Toronto, McClelland and Stewart, and New York, Knopf, 1986; London, Chatto and Windus, 1987.
Friend of My Youth. New York, Knopf, and London, Chatto and Windus, 1990.
A Wilderness Station. New York, Knopf, 1994.
Open Secrets. Toronto, McClelland & Stewart, New York, Alfred A. Knopf, and London, Chatto and Windus, 1994.
Selected Stories. New York, Knopf, 1996.
The Love of a Good Woman: Stories. New York, Knopf, 1998.

Plays

How I Met My Husband (televised 1974). Published in *The Play's the Thing,* edited by Tony Gifford, Toronto, Macmillan, 1976.

Television Plays: *A Trip to the Coast,* 1973; *Thanks for the Ride,* CBC, 1973; *How I Met My Husband,* 1974; *1847: The Irish* (*The Newcomers* series), 1978.

*

Bibliography: ''Alice Munro: A Checklist (To December 31, 1974)'' by D.E. Cook, in *Journal of Canadian Fiction* 16, 1976; ''Some Highly Subversive Activities: A Brief Polemic and a Checklist of Works on Alice Munro'' by J.R. (Tim) Struthers, in *Studies in Canadian Literature* 6, 1981; ''Munro, Alice (1931-)'' by Helen Hoy, in her *Modern English-Canadian Prose: A Guide to Information Sources,* Detroit, Gale Research, 1983; ''Alice Munro: An Annotated Bibliography'' by Robert Thacker, in *The Annotated Bibliography of Canada's Major Authors: Volume Five,* edited by Robert Lecker and Jack David, Downsview, Ontario, ECW Press, 1984; *The Alice Munro Papers First Accession: An Inventory of the Archive at The University of Calgary Libraries* compiled by Jean M. Moore and Jean F. Tener and edited by Apollonia Steele and Jean F. Tener, Calgary, University of Calgary Press, 1986; *The Alice Munro Papers Second Accession: An Inventory of the Archive at The University of Calgary Libraries* compiled by Jean M. Moore and edited by Apollonia Steele and Jean F. Tener, Calgary, University of Calgary Press, 1987; ''Munro, Alice (1931-)'' by Allan Weiss, in his *A Comprehensive Bibliography of English-Canadian Short Stories, 1950–1983,* Toronto, ECW Press, 1988.

Manuscript Collection: The University of Calgary Libraries, Alberta.

Critical Studies: ''A Conversation with Alice Munro'' in *Journal of Canadian Fiction* 1(4), 1972, and ''Casting Sad Spells: Alice Munro's 'Walker Brothers Cowboy''' in *Writers in Aspic,* Montreal, Vehicule Press, 1988, both by John Metcalf; ''Unconsummated Relationships: Isolation and Rejection in Alice Munro's Stories,'' in *World Literature Written in English,* 11(1), 1972, ''The Fiction of Alice Munro,'' in *Ploughshares* 4(3), 1978, and *Alice Munro and Her Works,* Toronto, ECW Press, 1985, all by Hallvard Dahlie; ''Alice Munro'' by Graeme Gibson, in his *Eleven Canadian Novelists: Interviewed by Graeme Gibson,* Toronto, House of Anansi Press, 1973; ''Alice Munro and the American South,'' in *Here and Now, The Canadian Novel,* edited by John Moss, vol. 1, Toronto, NC Press, 1978, and ''Reality and Ordering: The Growth of a Young Artist in *Lives of Girls and Women,*'' in *Modern Canadian Fiction,* Richmond, British Columbia, Open Learning Institute, 1980, both by J.R. (Tim) Struthers; ''Pronouns and Propositions: Alice Munro's *Something I've Been Meaning To Tell You,*'' by W.H. New, in his *Dreams of Speech and Violence: The Art of the Short Story in Canada and New Zealand,* Toronto, University of Toronto Press, 1987; ''Women's Lives: Alice Munro'' by Bronwen Wallace, in *The Human Elements: Critical Essays,* edited by David Helwig, Ottawa, Oberon Press, 1978; ''Alice Munro and James Joyce,'' in *Journal of Canadian Fiction,* 24, 1979, and *Alice Munro: Paradox and Parallel,* Edmonton, University of Alberta Press, 1987, both by W.R. Martin; '''Dull, Simple, Amazing and Unfathomable': Paradox and Double Vision in Alice Munro's Fiction,'' in *Studies in Canadian Literature* 5, 1980, and ''Alice Munro: 'Unforgettable, Indigestible Messages','' in *Journal of Canadian Studies,* 26(1), 1991, and '''Rose and Janet': Alice Munro's Metafiction,'' in *Canadian Literature,* 121, 1989, all by Helen Hoy; ''Alice Munro'' by Geoff Hancock, in his *Canadian Writers at Work: Interviews with Geoff Hancock,* Toronto, Oxford University Press, 1987; *Probable Fictions: Alice Munro's Narrative Acts* edited by Louis K. MacKendrick, Downsview, Ontario, ECW Press, 1983, and *Some Other Reality: Alice Munro's ''Something I've Been Meaning To Tell You''* by MacKendrick, Toronto, ECW Press, 1993; ''Three Jokers: The Shape of Alice Munro's Stories,'' in *Centre and Labyrinth: Essays in Honour of Northrop Frye,* edited by Eleanor Cook et al, Toronto, University of Toronto Press, 1983, and *The Other Country: Patterns in the Writing of Alice Munro,* Toronto, ECW Press, 1993, both by James Carscallen; *Alice Munro* by B. Pfaus, Ottawa, Golden Dog Press, 1984; *The Art of Alice Munro: Saying the Unsayable* edited by Judith Miller, Waterloo, Ontario, University of Waterloo Press, 1984; ''Connection: Alice Munro and Ontario,'' in *The American Review of Canadian Studies* 14, 1984, and ''Conferring Munro'' in *Essays on Canadian Writing* 34, 1987, ''Go Ask Alice: The Progress of Munro Criticism,'' in *Journal of Canadian Studies,* 26(2), 1991, all by Robert Thacker; '''What Happened to Marion?': Art and Reality in *Lives of Girls and Women*'' by Thomas E. Tausky, in *Studies in Canadian Literature,* 11(1), 1986; *Alice Munro* by E.D. Blodgett, Boston, Twayne/Hall, 1988; ''Alice Munro'' by Michelle Gadpaille, in her *The Canadian Short Story,* Toronto, Oxford University Press, 1988; *''The Other Side of Dailiness'': Photography in the Works of Alice Munro, Timothy Findley, Michael Ondaatje, and Margaret Laurence* by Lorraine M. York, Toronto, ECW Press, 1988; ''Alice Munro'' by W.J. Keith, in his *A Sense of*

Style: Studies in the Art of Fiction in English-Speaking Canada, Toronto, ECW Press, 1989; *Controlling the Uncontrollable: The Fiction of Alice Munro* by Ildiko de Papp Carrington, DeKalb, Northern Illinois University Press, 1989; *Dance of the Sexes: Art and Gender in the Fiction of Alice Munro* by Beverly J. Rasporich, Edmonton, University of Alberta Press, 1990; *Introducing Alice Munro's ''Lives of Girls and Women'': A Reader's Guide* by Neil K. Besner, Toronto, ECW Press, 1990; *Alice Munro: A Double Life* by Catherine Sheldrick Ross, Toronto, ECW Press, 1992; *Figuring Grief: Gallant, Munro, and the Poetics of Elegy* by Karen Smythe, Montreal, McGill-Queen's University Press, 1992; ''A Hopeful Sign: The Making of Metonymic Meaning in Munro's 'Meneseteung''' by Pam Houston, in *The Kenyon Review* 14.4, 1992; *Mothers and Other Clowns: The Stories of Alice Munro* by Magdalene Redekop, London, Routledge, 1992; *How Stories Mean* edited by John Metcalf and J.R. (Tim) Struthers, Erin, Ontario, Porcupine's Quill, 1993; ''Alice Munro: The Art of Fiction CXXXVII'' by Jean McCulloch and Mona Simpson, in *The Paris Review* 131, 1994; *The Tumble of Reason: Alice Munro's Discourse of Absence* by Ajay Heble, Toronto, University of Toronto Press, 1994; ''The Woman Out Back: Alice Munro's 'Meneseteung''' by Dermot McCarthy, in *Studies in Canadian Literature,* 19(1), 1994; ''A National Treasure: An Interview with Alice Munro'' by Pleuke Boyce and Ron Smith, in *O Canada 2,* edited by Cassandra Pybus, *Meanjin,* 54, 1995; *The Influence of Painting on Five Canadian Writers: Alice Munro, Hugh Hood, Timothy Findley, Margaret Atwood, and Michael Ondaatje* by John Cooke, Lewiston, New York, Edwin Mellen Press, 1996; *Alice Munro* by Coral Ann Howells, Manchester, England, and New York, Manchester University Press, 1998; *The Rest of the Story: Critical Essays on Alice Munro,* edited by Robert Thacker, Toronto, ECW Press, 1999.

Alice Munro comments:

(1982) I did promise to talk about using reality. ''Why, if Jubilee isn't Wingham, has it got a Shuter Street in it?'' people want to know. Why have I described somebody's real ceramic elephant sitting on the mantelpiece? I could say I get momentum from doing things like this. The fictional room, town, world, needs a bit of starter dough from the real world. It's a device to help the writer—at least it helps me—but it arouses a certain baulked fury in the people who really do live on Shuter Street and the lady who owns the ceramic elephant. ''Why do you put in something true and then go and tell lies?'' they say, and anybody who has been on the receiving end of this kind of thing knows how they feel.

''I do it for the sake of my art and to make this structure which encloses the soul of my story, that I've been telling you about,'' says the writer. ''That is more important than anything.'' Not to everybody it isn't.

So I can see there might be a case, once you've written the story and got the momentum, for going back and changing the elephant to a camel (though there's always a chance the lady might complain that you made a nasty camel out of a beautiful elephant), and changing Shuter Street to Blank Street. But what about the big chunks of reality, without which your story can't exist? In the story ''Royal Beatings,'' I use a big chunk of reality: the story of the butcher, and of the young men who may have been egged on to ''get'' him. This is a story out of an old newspaper; it really did happen in a town I know. There is no legal difficulty about using it because it has been printed in a newspaper, and besides, the people who figure in it are all long dead. But there is a difficulty about offending people in that town who would feel that use of this story is a deliberate exposure, taunt and insult. Other people who have no connection with the real happening would say ''Why write about anything so hideous?'' And lest you think that such an objection could only be raised by simple folk who read nothing but Harlequin Romances, let me tell you that one of the questions most frequently asked at universities is, ''Why do you write about things that are so depressing?'' People can accept almost any amount of ugliness if it is contained in a familiar formula, as it is on television, but when they come closer to their own place, their own lives, they are much offended by lack of editing.

There are ways I can defend myself against such objections. I can say, ''I do it in the interests of historical reality. That is what the old days were really like.'' Or, ''I do it to show the dark side of human nature, the beast let loose, the evil we can run up against in communities and families.'' In certain countries I could say, ''I do it to show how bad things were under the old system when there were prosperous butchers and young fellows hanging around livery stables and nobody thought about building a new society.'' But the fact is, the minute I say *to show* I am telling a lie. I don't do it to show anything. I put this story at the heart of my story because I need it there and it belongs there. It is the black room at the centre of the house with all other rooms leading to and away from it. That is all. A strange defence. Who told me to write this story? Who feels any need of it before it is written? I do. I do, so that I might grab off this piece of horrid reality and install it where I see fit, even if Hat Nettleton and his friends were still around to make me sorry.

* * *

Alice Munro is not an explicitly political or feminist writer, nor does she write autobiography. However, her stories are largely concerned with the struggle between rebellion and respectability; they dramatize the ''underbelly of relationships''; and in each collection we regularly see the same small-town, rural, Canadian setting where she grew up and continues to live ''because I live life here at a level of irritation which I would not achieve in a place that I knew less well.''

The stories are studies in perspective. They take family structures, neighborhoods, individuals, and groups of people, and show how they shift in the memory as they appear suddenly from an unexpected angle. Her characters move through layers of time and reality, and it is the gaps between those layers that reveal the power of Munro's fiction. ''There are no such things as big and little subjects,'' she has said. ''The major things, the evils, that exist in the world have a direct relationship to the evil that exists around a dining room table when people are doing things to each other.''

Her first book of stories, *Dance of the Happy Shades,* charts the adolescent discovery of love and fear. ''Boys and Girls'' deals with two recurring themes in Munro's stories: domestic power plays and the impossibility of the functional mother/daughter relationship. When a girl, whose mother was ''plotting to get me to stay in the house more, although she knew I hated it (*because* she knew I hated it) and keep me from working for my father'' cries, it is because ''she's only a girl.'' ''I didn't protest that, even in my heart. Maybe it was true.'' Early sexual experiences in ''Postcard'' and ''Thanks for the Ride'' provide the vehicle for exploring adult sexual deceit. Many of the stories in this collection present a recognizable physical world rendered impenetrable by the emotionally disaffected people attempting to exist in it.

Munro's first novel, *Lives of Girls and Women,* follows the life of Del Jordan, a woman struggling to avoid the obscurity made seemingly inevitable by growing up in a small town, Jubilee. As Del Jordan remembers the milestones of her emotional growth, we see her pursuing different ways of being ''endangered and desired.'' The novel is in a sense less satisfying than Munro's short stories; the form affords Del Jordan the opportunity to ''go out and take on all kinds of experiences ... and come back proud.'' But it does not make her any more complex a character than those who live in the short stories.

In the next collection of stories—*Something I've Been Meaning To Tell You*—the emphasis is on remembering, rather than projecting; on making sense of the past. *Something I've Been Meaning To Tell You* is one of Munro's bleaker collections, with disarray increasing through examination, rather than being resolved. In ''Winter Wind'' a character believes ''that we have some connections that cannot be investigated.''

Where many short story writers fall into the trap of making the form shrink to fit, Munro's stories bulge with details and density and are extended by the tensions and contradictions they generate. *Who Do You Think You Are?* is as much a novel as *Lives of Girls and Women;* it has the same episodic structure and offers ten ''moments'' from the life of Rose, who manages to leave the confines of her small town on a university scholarship. Neither Rose nor Del Jordan is able to ''shuck off'' fully the things they don't want, although Del affects some kind of certainty about what she does want. Rose, however, is often trapped by what the narrator in ''Simon's Luck'' calls ''those shifts of emphasis that throw the story line open to question, the disarrangements which demand new judgments and solutions, and throw the windows open on inappropriate unforgettable scenery.''

The Moons of Jupiter focuses on the nature of relationships between characters, rather than on the nature of the isolation these connections often seem to create in Munro's stories. Again, the contradictions between different levels of reality give these stories an atmosphere of threat: beneath the seemingly benign surface of experience real danger lurks. In ''The Moons of Jupiter'' the narrator describes ''various knowns and unknowns and horrific immensities.'' The connections dramatized in this collection —between cousins (''Chaddeleys and Flemings''), lovers (''Hard-Luck Stories,'' ''Accident''), or rest home companions (''Mrs. Cross and Mrs. Kidd'')—are undermined by personal deceits, or by ''the gap between what she wanted and what she could get,'' or by the overlap of need and want. ''Connection. That was what it was all about. A connection with the real, and prodigal, and dangerous world.'' In ''The Turkey Season,'' about relationships between women in a turkey factory, the protagonist explains how ''I got to the stage of backing off from the things I couldn't really know.''

Three subsequent collections of stories—*The Progress of Love, Friend of My Youth,* and *Open Secrets*—provide, perhaps, the best introduction to Munro's work. In *The Progress of Love* all the elements of her previous work combine in an orgy of dishonesty and dissatisfaction. Jesse, the teenage girl conducting an imaginary affair with an older man in ''Jesse and Meribeth,'' concedes ''I didn't at all mind the lying. Once I had taken the plunge into falsehood ... falsehood felt wonderfully comfortable.'' In ''Eskimo'' Mary Jo is having an affair with her married boss, Dr. Streeter, a man of ''incurable, calm, and decent sadness.... This sadness seems to come from obedience.'' In the title story the narrator realizes that ''Moments of kindness and reconciliation are worth having, even if the parting has to come sooner or later. I wonder if those moments aren't more valued, and deliberately gone after, in the setups some people like myself have now, than they were in those old marriages, where love and grudges could be growing underground, so confused and stubborn, it must have seemed they had forever.'' In ''Fits'' the apparent murder-suicide of a local couple provides such a moment for Peg and Robert: ''They needed something new to talk about. Now he felt more like going home.'' In these stories Munro draws the tensions between everyday dissatisfaction and its chaotic possibilities brilliantly. The characters' realizations of these consequences—and their bearing on their own existence—are always insidious, revealed in flashes of light.

In *Friend of My Youth* the stories are more personal in feeling, the writing more controlled, and the characters' lives more full of falsity. In ''Wigtime'' Margot is reduced to stalking her adulterous husband in a wig and leaving anonymous notes under his windscreen. Hazel in ''Hold Me Fast, Don't Let Me Pass'' is a widow in her 50s, taking a leave of absence, who scribbles in notebooks: ''It prevents the rise of panic.... This sort of panic had nothing to do with money or ticket arrangements, it had to do with a falling off of purpose, and the question why am I here?'' There is a note of elegy in these stories, but the changes of mood and the shifts in perspective betray the deceptive gentleness of Munro's writing. The daughter in ''Oh, What Avails'' reflects that her mother had formed in the children ''a delicate, special regard for themselves, which made them want to go out and grasp what they wanted, whether love or money.''

The eight darkly luminous stories in *Open Secrets* explore with increasing precision and wonder, with increasing graveness and love, the tensions and contradictions of the human condition. ''A Wilderness Station'' presents—through a group of letters and recollections by, and to, a variety of persons—the fictional biography of Annie Herron, a woman of somewhat uncertain beginning, middle, and end who reaches early adulthood and marries in the mid-nineteenth century and lives on into the twentieth. Following the seemingly accidental death of her husband while he is out working in the bush with his younger brother, Annie temporarily seeks refuge (of sorts) in a local Southwestern Ontario gaol for criminals and the insane and only gains retribution (of sorts) more than half a century later. The deeper historical note sounded in ''A Wilderness Station'' is reminiscent of ''Meneseteung,'' an overwhelmingly original fictional biography, from *Friend of My Youth,* about an invented nineteenth-century southwestern Ontario poetess named Almeda Joynt Roth. Like so many of Munro's later stories, but somehow more compellingly, ''Meneseteung'' fills and empties the reader in ways we associate with classical tragedy. This is not to say that her later stories are without comedy, for comedy represents an extremely important, and equally ritualistic, component of her work.

In ''Spaceships Have Landed''—a story describing the friendship, then and now, of two country girls —imaginative play and verbal play are crucial to Munro's achievement: ''And the worst thing was when Eunie launched into accounts that Rhea found both boring and infuriating, of murders and disasters and freakish events that she had heard about on the radio. Rhea was infuriated because she could not get Eunie to tell her whether these things had really happened, or even to make that distinction—as far as Rhea could tell—to herself. ''Was that on the news, Eunie? Was it a story? Were there people acting it in front of a microphone or was it reporting? Eunie! Was it real or was it a play?'' It was Rhea, never Eunie, who would get frazzled by these questions. Eunie would just get on her bicycle and ride away. 'Toodeley oodeley oo! See you in the zoo!''' What nonsense, we think—or is it? Might Eunie be seen to possess an understanding of the indivisibility of truth and imagination, seriousness and play, the natural and the supernatural, that surpasses Rhea's meagrely realistic, literal-minded understanding? Might Eunie be seen to represent some kind of metaphor, or an alter ego, for the artist?

In story after story, Munro reveals the exhilarating character of life itself, with all of life's surprising but inevitable interventions in the form of a death, unexpected visitors, an unusual letter, whatever. Such occurrences pervade Munro's later stories, fracturing each character's—and each reader's—expectations, rendering easy accommodations with life or art impossible. Moreover, from these interventions other actions unfailingly unfold. Increasingly in Munro's later stories, we see something of the quality that Eudora Welty (an acknowledged influence on Munro) admired in William Faulker: ''veracity and accuracy about the world'' that reveals both the comedy of being human and what Welty terms ''that comedy's adjoining terror.''

Perhaps Munro's stories should be read as a new kind of novel; not one after the other, but each allowed time to resonate in the reader's head. As Munro says: ''I want the stories to keep diminishing but not to be suddenly over with, so one is left with the central mystery of the story.''

—Juliette Bright, updated by J.R. (Tim) Struthers

MURNANE, Gerald

Nationality: Australian. **Born:** Melbourne, Victoria, in 1939. **Education:** The University of Melbourne, B.A. 1969. **Family:** Married; three sons. **Career:** Currently lecturer in creative writing, Victoria College, Melbourne. **Address:** 2 Falcon Street, Macleod, Victoria 3085, Australia.

PUBLICATIONS

Novels

Tamarisk Row. Melbourne, Heinemann, 1974.
A Lifetime on Clouds. Melbourne, Heinemann, 1976.
The Plains. Carlton, Victoria, Norstrilia Press, 1982; London, Penguin, 1984; New York, Braziller, 1985.
Landscape with Landscape. Carlton, Victoria, Norstrilia Press, 1985.
Inland. Richmond, Victoria, Heinemann, 1988; London, Faber, 1989.
Emerald Blue. Ringwood, Victoria, McPhee Gribble, 1995.

Short Stories

Velvet Waters. Ringwood, Victoria, McPhee Gribble, 1990.

Other

Editor, with Jenny Lee and Phillip Mead, *Temperament of Generations: Fifty Years of Writing in Meanjin.* Carlton, Victoria, Meanjin, 1990.

*

Critical Studies: *Gerald Murnane* edited by John Hanrahan, Footscrag, Victoria, Footscrag Foundation for Australian Studies, 1987; *Gerald Murnane* by Imre Salusinszky, Melbourne and Oxford, Oxford University Press, 1993.

* * *

Gerald Murnane began as a writer of confessedly autobiographical fiction of a talented but fairly conventional kind, but developed eventually into a writer who has been variously classified as postmodernist or fabulist and who has been described hyperbolically by at least one Australian critic as ''the most original writer this country has produced.'' *Tamarisk Row,* for instance, is a comparatively familiar story of growing up Catholic in the Australian countryside. Clement Killeaton lives in the town of Bassett. His father is a compulsive gambler and the family live in perpetual poverty. The boy inherits his father's love of gambling but converts it into an activity of the imagination. Already, though, there are signs of the direction which Murnane's fiction will eventually lead—in the constant references to maps and calendars, in the boy's substitution for the dull reality of numbers and figures images of his own devising and in the beginnings of the hypnotic absorption in his own imaginative processes.

Murnane's second novel *A Lifetime on Clouds* remains more or less in the realm of realism. It suffers, despite the witty treatment of its material from the fact that the material is very familiar, in Australia at least—the tormented nature of adolescent sexuality for Catholic-educated youths. More specifically it concerns masturbation and, *Portnoy's Complaint* not withstanding, there has probably never been any other novel which examines, explores, concerns itself with the subject so relentlessly and in such detail. What elements of fantasy are present are employed crudely, for example with the protagonist driving in Florida with Jayne, Marilyn, and Susan—whose identities can easily be guessed.

With *The Plains,* however, Murnane more or less abandons realism altogether to move in the direction of something best described by his own term of fable. None of the characters is named; there are hardly any references to specific places, though the city of Melbourne is mentioned with abhorrence; there are no personal relationships, little or no action and scarcely any dialogue except for one long series of lateral monologues which occasionally intersect as the plainsmen converse. The plains work on the level of myth or metaphor but the problem is to decide what they are a metaphor of. The plains, the novel seems to be saying, are the ''real'' Australia to which residents of Outer Australia or the coast flee in relief. *Landscape with Landscape,* the second of three successive works to have titles concerning landscape, confirms the movement towards a kind of metarealism, a fiction preoccupied with a kind of infinite regression, not the representation of reality but the exploration of modes of representing reality, through modes of exploring those modes ... etc. As the narrator of the fourth of the book's six sections puts it, ''I decided to include the poem below in this story when I understood that the young man who wrote it was not myself but a character in a work of fiction and that as soon as I began to write about him I became an author of fiction. (Since the previous sentence is part of a work of fiction a certain young man and the man he might have become are doubly difficult to image anywhere but in fiction. [The sentence just ended is also part of a work of fiction as is this sentence].'' The concern is not merely with experience as such but with the possibility of representing experience, the substitution of language for experience, the ways in which fiction and reality merge and become conflated. The self-consciousness and the preoccupation with writing itself—the inner landscape at the expense of the outer one—come out in the long parentheses, in the intertextual references and in the narrator/writer defining himself as writer. ''Now he seemed almost defined by the long shapely sentences in the pages on his desk … ''

Inland is constructed of some dozen or so unmarked sections, linked only by the probable presence of an identical yet nevertheless anonymous narrator, which become shorter and shorter and closer to home in scope. The opening words of the novel are: ''I am writing in the library of a manor-house in a village I prefer not to name, near the town of Kunmadaras, in Szolnok County.'' The narrator addresses and engages with the reader constantly, quickly establishing a self-conscious mode with his long, meditative, elaborate sentences; he mentions in particular his editor, Anne Kristaly Gunnarsen, who lives ''in the land of America, in the state of South Dakota, in Tripp County, in the town of Ideal'': America is yet another of Murnane's mythical landscapes. The landscape of Szolnok County seems to merge into that of South Dakota and then in turn to that of ''Melbourne county.'' The autobiographical references as well as allusions to Murnane's earlier work become more frequent. There are the same key motifs: maps and atlases, calendars, colours, references to suburbs. The constant allusions to Proust are both appropriate and justified. One of the many books that the novel refers to or quotes points to Proust's achievement in making France real for people who have never been there. Murnane is much concerned with the boundaries—or blurring of boundaries—of the real and the imagined and with the role of literature in mediating between them.

Velvet Waters is a collection of his shorter fiction dating back to 1972, and as one would expect is closely related to and refers back to his earlier writing. ''Stream System'' in fact is taken from an earlier version of *The Plains* but the stories in general deal with the same material and themes as the novels. Murnane's prose, in its almost ritualistically repetitive cadences and stylised simplicities, can seem like a strange combination of Proust and Calvino while the story ''Precious Bane'' is Borgesian in its preoccupation with a self-contained world of writing. Murnane can descend almost into self-parody at times, as in ''Finger Webb'' with its deliberately reiterated cadences ('The man in this story . . . The man in this story …') but some of the stories are among the most moving that he has ever written. ''When the Mice Failed to Arrive,'' for instance, cuts between past and present to offer a delicate portrait of the relationship between the narrator and his father, and the former's realisation of his failure with the students he loves, while ''Stream System'' becomes a poignantly retrospective act of self-understanding as the narrator recognises his failure to love his retarded brother.

—Laurie Clancy

MURRAY, Albert L.

Nationality: American. **Born:** Nokomis, Alabama, 12 June 1916. **Education:** Tuskegee Institute, B.S. 1939; New York University, M.A. 1948; postgraduate work at University of Michigan, 1940, Northwestern University, 1941, and University of Paris, 1950. **Military Service:** U.S. Air Force, 1943–62, including service during World War II; retired as major. **Family:** Married Mozelle Menefee in 1941; one daughter. **Career:** Instructor, Tuskegee Institute, 1940–43, 1946–51, director of College Little Theatre; lecturer, Graduate School of Journalism, Columbia University, 1968; O'Connor Professor of Literature, Colgate University, 1970, O'Connor Lecturer, 1973, professor of humanities, 1982; visiting professor of literature, University of Massachusetts, Boston, 1971; Paul Anthony Brick lecturer, University of Missouri, 1972; writer in residence, Emory University, Atlanta, 1978; adjunct associate professor of creative writing, Barnard College, 1981–83; Woodrow Wilson fellow, Drew University, 1983; Dupont visiting professor, Washington and Lee University, 1993; lecturer and participant in symposia. **Awards:** Lillian Smith award for fiction, 1974; Deems Taylor award for music criticism (ASCAP), 1976; Lincoln Center Directors Emeriti award, 1991; Literature Achievement award (National Book Critics Circle), 1997; Harper Lee award for Literary Excellence (Alabama Writer's Forum), 1998. Litt.D., Colgate University, 1975; Doctor of humane letters, Spring Hill College, 1996. **Address:** 45 West 132nd Street, New York, New York 10037, U.S.A.

Publications

Novels

Train Whistle Guitar. New York, McGraw, 1974.
The Spyglass Tree. New York, Pantheon, 1991.
The Seven League Boots. New York, Pantheon, 1996.

Plays

Television Programs: *Newport Jazz '90* (cowriter, with others). WETA-TV, 1990.

Other

The Omni-Americans: New Perspectives on Black Experience and American Culture (essays). Outerbridge & Dientsfrey, 1970; published as *The Omni-Americans: Some Alternatives to the Folklore of White Supremacy.* St. Paul, Minnesota, Vintage Book, 1983.
South to a Very Old Place (memoir). New York, McGraw, 1972.
The Hero and the Blues (lectures). Columbia, University of Missouri Press, 1973.
Stomping the Blues. New York, McGraw, 1976.
Good Morning Blues: The Autobiography of Count Basie (with Count Basie). New York, Random House, 1985.
Reflections on Logic, Politics, and Reality: A Challenge to the Sacred Consensus of Contemporary American Thinking. Riverdale, New York, Braimanna Publishers, 1989.
Contributor, *Alabama Bound: Contemporary Stories of a State,* edited by James E. Colquitt. Livingston, Alabama, Livingston Press, 1995.
The Blue Devils of Nada: A Contemporary American Approach to Aesthetic Statement. New York, Pantheon, 1996.
Romare Bearden in Black-and-White: Photomontage Projections, 1964. New York, Whitney Museum of American Art, 1997

* * *

Albert Murray has had a profound influence on American art since World War II. A brilliant cultural critic, novelist, essayist, and biographer, Murray's artistry is found in his description of the forms and meanings of the blues and jazz. Robert O'Meally explains that ''more than any other writer, he has taken on the complex task of naming the aspects of performances by blues-idiom musicians, and then of saying with precision what it is that makes such performances so irresistible to audiences and dancers, so definitive of their time and culture.'' Murray's works include *The Omni-Americans: New Perspectives on Black Experience and American Culture*, *South to a Very Old Place*, *Train Whistle Guitar*, *Stomping the Blues*, *The Spyglass Tree*, *The Seven League Boots*, and *The Blue Devils of Nada*.

Murray's first work, *The Omni-Americans*, is a clear defense of African-American culture found in a collection of essays, commentaries, and reviews dealing with politics, literature, and music. His next work, *South to a Very Old Place*, is an autobiographical memoir of his youth and a celebration of black culture. *The Hero and the Blues* is a collection of Murray's Paul Anthony Brick lectures at the University of Missouri on ethical implications of literary esthetics. *Train Whistle Guitar*, *The Spyglass Tree*, and *The Seven League Boots* constitute ''the Scooter trilogy.'' *Train Whistle Guitar* begins the saga of Scooter by telling the story of his childhood in the deep South of the 1920s. *The Spyglass Tree* then follows Murray's resilient, intelligent, vibrant, and universal protagonist to an imaginary Alabama college in the 1930s. The last novel in the trilogy, *The Seven League Boots*, recounts Scooter's experiences as a bass player in a touring jazz band following his graduation from college. During the Scooter trilogy, Murray also wrote *Stomping the Blues*, an examination of the redefinition of blues music and its connection to American culture, and *Good Morning Blues*, a biography of Count Basie. *The Blue Devils of Nada*, a more recent work, focuses on the creative process, what he calls ''the vernacular imperative for American aesthetics.''

In all of Murray's works, one encounters the people and places of the blues, and the author's theories on jazz and the blues seek to define a modern consciousness and create a new archetype of the American hero known as the ''blues hero.'' An opposition of the unhappy reality presented in the blues music with improvisation by the dancers, musicians, and even the music itself implies the role of the hero, who may not always win but who will most assuredly always go down swinging. According to Murray, ''the blues is not the creation of a crushed-spirited people. It's the product of a forward-looking, upward-striving people. Jazz is only possible in a climate of freedom.'' It is this elemental differentiation between the blues as a feeling of despondency and blues music, which brings people happiness by gathering them together to dance and sing and flirt and ''stomp'' the blues away, that is a reoccurring theme in Murray's work.

Murray not only writes about the blues and uses the music as a basis for his philosophy, he also imitates the art form in his prose, which Larry Neal calls the ''acoustical iconography'' of language. This musical emulation provides a unique framework for Murray's novels that are, according to O'Meally, ''arrangements of verbal vamps, breaks, riffs, choruses, and out choruses—rhythmically repeated figures analogous to … Basie's 'One O'Clock Jump' or Leadbelly's 'Good Morning Blues.''' In his long passages of dialogue and monologue, and in his lyric description, Murray's language dances across the page, intruding on the reader's awareness and impressing rhythmic order in the story. Through a unique creative process, Murray has found a way to actually write the blues.

Murray is regarded as one of the nation's best black Southern writers, yet he doesn't regard himself as such. Rather, he chooses to be known as an ''all American writer.'' Working to establish a foundation for a national identity, Murray describes the American culture as ''mulatto,'' a race of interrelated, multicolored people, and focuses on the irony of intolerance existing in a sophisticated society such as the United States. Whether he regards himself as a black writer or not, Murray has been a very real inspiration for several generations of African-American writers ever since he burst onto the scene with *The Omni Americans*, which challenged its readers to undertake the hard, honest work of accepting his vision of the mulatto culture. Accused in the past of fostering racism when he was, above all, attempting to transcend racial peripheries, Murray today offers his elegant ''blues aesthetic,'' steeped in black cultural tradition, for engaging in the turmoil of subsistence.

Murray is indisputably America's great literary practitioner of the blues idiom, the creator of a bold, new, elegant, lyrical style comprised of the black folk tradition, the Southern tradition of storytelling, the rumination of Faulkner, the wordplay of Joyce along with the cadences and idioms of African-American speech. Duke Ellington said it best when he once explained: ''Albert Murray is a man whose learning did not interfere with understanding. An authority on soul from the days of old, he is right on right back to back and commands respect. He doesn't have to look it up. He already knows. If you want to know, look him up. He is the unsquarest person I know.''

—Cathy Kelly Power

N

NAHAL, Chaman (Lal)

Nationality: Indian. **Born:** Sialkot (now in Pakistan), 2 August 1927. **Education:** The University of Delhi, M.A. in English 1948; University of Nottingham (British Council scholar), 1959–61, Ph.D. in English 1961. **Family:** Married Sudarshna Rani in 1955; two daughters. **Career:** Lecturer at universities in India, 1949–62; reader in English, Rajasthan University, Jaipur, 1962–63; reader in English, 1963–80, and professor of English, University of Delhi, 1980–92; visiting Fulbright Fellow, Princeton University, New Jersey, 1967–70; from 1971 visiting lecturer at several universities in the U.S.A., Malaysia, Japan, Singapore, Canada, and North Korea; fellow, Churchill College, Cambridge, 1991. Columnist (''Talking about Books''), *Indian Express,* New Delhi, 1966–73. **Awards:** Sahitya Academy award, 1977; Federation of Indian Publishers award, 1977, 1979. **Agent:** Margaret Hanbury, 27 Walcot Square, London SE11 4XB, England. **Address:** 2/1 Kalkaji Extension, New Delhi 110019, India.

PUBLICATIONS

Novels

My True Faces. New Delhi, Orient, 1973.
Into Another Dawn. New Delhi, Sterling, 1977.
The English Queens. New Delhi, Vision, 1979.
Sunrise in Fiji. New Delhi, Allied, 1988.
Azadi (Freedom). New Delhi, Arnold-Heinemann, and Boston, Houghton Mifflin, 1975; London, Deutsch, 1977.
The Crown and the Loincloth. New Delhi, Vikas, 1981.
The Salt of Life. New Delhi, Allied, 1990.
The Triumph of the Tricolour. New Delhi, Allied, 1993.
The Ghandi Quartet. New Delhi, Allied, 1993.

Short Stories

The Weird Dance and Other Stories. New Delhi, Arya, 1965.

Uncollected Short Stories

''Tons,'' in *The Statesman* (New Delhi), 12 June 1977.
''The Light on the Lake,'' in *Illustrated Weekly of India* (Bombay), 22 July 1984.
''The Take Over,'' in *Debonair* (Bombay), August 1985.

Other

Moby Dick (for children), adaptation of the novel by Melville. New Delhi, Eurasia, 1965.
A Conversation with J. Krishnamurti. New Delhi, Arya, 1965.
D.H. Lawrence: An Eastern View. South Brunswick, New Jersey, A.S. Barnes, and London, Yoseloff, 1971.
The Narrative Pattern in Ernest Hemingway's Fiction. New Delhi, Vikas, and Rutherford, New Jersey, Fairleigh Dickinson University Press, 1971.
The New Literatures in English. New Delhi, Allied, 1985.
Jawaharlal Nehru as a Man of Letters. New Delhi, Allied, 1990.
Editor, *Drugs and the Other Self: An Anthology of Spiritual Transformations.* New York, Harper, 1971.

*

Bibliography: In *The New Literatures in English,* 1985.

Critical Studies: *Commonwealth Literature in the Curriculum* edited by K.L. Goodwin, St. Lucia, University of Queensland Press, 1980; introduction by A. Komarov to *The Crown and the Loincloth,* Moscow, Raduga, 1984; *Three Contemporary Novelists: Khushwant Singh, Chaman Nahal, and Salman Rushdie* edited by R.K. Dhawan, New Delhi, Classical, 1985.

Chaman Nahal comments:

(1991) I have largely concerned myself with two themes in my novels; the individual vs. the joint family system in India, and my historical identity as an individual, as an Indian. For the latter theme I have drawn extensively on history, especially our freedom movement, 1915–47. *Azadi, The Crown and the Loincloth,* and *The Salt of Life* are part of a quartet on that theme; I'm working on the fourth volume of the quartet now. I use Gandhi as the ultimate symbol of that identity.

(1995) I am now working on a novel for children.

* * *

Chaman Nahal's distinction lies in writing about India without any touch of exoticism; he scrupulously avoids the stereotyped ''East'' of maharajahs, tigers and snakecharmers. The actual town of Delhi (in *My True Faces* and *The English Queens*) and the typical Punjabi town of Sialkot are presented vividly, and we get a good idea of middle-class life in India. *Azadi* is the best of the Indian-English novels written about the traumatic partition which accompanied Indian Independence in 1947. *The Crown and the Loincloth* and *The Salt of Life* portray Mahatma Gandhi as a complex character with human failings. *The English Queens* breaks new ground by using the comic mode to treat a problem which has concerned all Indians—the tendency of the educated elite in India to ape the West.

Nahal's first novel, *My True Faces,* adequately portrays the agony of a sensitive young man when he finds his wife and baby son missing. But the crisis seems to be too minor to warrant the heavy philosophical treatment, with the hero realizing at the end of the novel that all earthly manifestations are but faces of Krishna, and they are all his ''true faces.'' The involved language betrays the fact that it is the work of a scholarly professor of English.

Azadi (''Freedom''), which won the award of the Sahitya Akademi (India's national academy of letters), employs an entirely different style. It is a straightforward account of a rich Hindu grain merchant and his family. The novel begins in mid-1947 with the people of Sialkot (now in Pakistan) hearing the announcement regarding partition, but they refuse to believe that they now have to move. Nahal shows how Kanshi Ram the Hindu, Barkat Ali the Mohammedan, and Teja Singh the Sikh share the same Punjabi culture and language, and consider Sialkot their homeland. Meticulous attention to details and a firsthand knowledge of the life of the characters enable Nahal to make the plight of the refugees real to the reader. The novel ends with a sadly depleted family trying to begin life anew in Delhi. *Azadi* has none of the sensationalism of other novels about India's partition, such as Khushwant Singh's *Train to Pakistan* or Manohar Malgonkar's *A Bend in the Ganges.* Nahal shows the cruelty as well as the humanity of both sides. The novel also shows the maturing of Arun, Kanshi Ram's only son, but the account of his love, first for Nur, the Muslim girl left behind in Pakistan, and then for Chandni, a low-caste girl who is abducted on the way to India, is not as gripping as the rest of the novel.

Nahal's next novel, *Into Another Dawn,* is basically an East-West love story, set chiefly in the U.S.A. Nahal's fourth novel, *Sunrise in Fiji,* is a psychological study of Harivansh, a successful architect in his forties, who finds his personal life empty and meaningless. He goes to Fiji to bid for a building contract, and uses the break from routine to do some much needed soul-searching.

The English Queens is unique in Indian-English fiction; it is a very funny but hard-hitting satire against the elitism of the English-speaking groups in India, such as the officers of the defense forces, the *nouveau riche,* the highly placed civil servants, or Indians having foreign wives. Nahal unfolds a fantastic plot hatched by Lord Mountbatten, the last British Viceroy of India, to ensure India's subjugation to Britain. On the eve of handing over political power he prepares a charter for the ''safe transfer of linguistic power'' by which he gives the English language to India. To ''preserve, propagate and spread'' English in India he appoints six women in New Delhi to ''The Order of the Queens.'' Rekha, the daughter of one of these queens, horrifies them by wanting to marry a young man from a working-class slum; worse still, he wears Indian clothes and is an expert in Indian classical music. The novel takes a further fantastic turn when the bridegroom reveals himself as an avatar of Vishnu, who has come to destroy this pernicious second-hand English culture. He flies back to heaven with the charter, but it drops out of his hand accidentally, and comes back to continue its destructive work; perhaps even God cannot help India! Of course, Nahal is not against the English language as such; his satire is against the kind of Indian who thinks that it is shameful to know anything about his own culture. One wonders whether non-Indian readers would enjoy the book as much as Indians do, because much of the humor rests on topical allusions.

''The Gandhi Quartet'' covers three decades of Indian history, from 1915 to 1947. *Azadi,* which describes the last phase of the struggle for independence, was the first to be published. *The Crown and the Loincloth* is the first of three novels with Mahatma Gandhi as central character. Nahal presents Gandhi directly as well as in terms of the effect he has on the family of Thakur Shanti Nath, a landowner in a Punjabi village. This novel is set in the period from 1915 to 1922, and deals with many historical events such as Gandhi's return to India in 1915 and the Jallianwala Bagh massacre. Sunil, the landlord's son, and Sunil's wife Kusum are followers of Mahatma Gandhi. Sunil dies in 1922 while saving the Prince of Wales from an attack by terrorists, and Kusum joins Gandhi's ashram at Sabarmati with their young son Vikram. The second novel, *The Salt of Life,* centers on Gandhi's salt satyagraha of 1930. The heroine, Kusum, leaves the ashram when she gets married to Raja Vishal Chand, the ruler of a small princely state in the Himalayas. Her son Vikram stays on with Gandhi and participates in the Dandi march. When Vishal Chand dies, Kusum comes back to the ashram. *The Triumph of the Tricolour,* the third volume, deals with the Quit India movement of 1942. The narrative style of the later novels is quite complex, integrating Indian modes of storytelling with Western techniques like the stream-of-consciousness novel. But they lack the power of *Azadi,* which remains Nahal's best novel.

—Shyamala A. Narayan

NAIPAUL, (Sir) V(idiadhar) S(urajprasad)

Nationality: Trinidadian. **Born:** Trinidad, 17 August 1932; brother of the writer Shiva Naipaul. **Education:** Tranquillity Boys School, 1939–42; Queen's Royal College, Port of Spain, Trinidad, 1943–49; University College, Oxford, 1950–54, B.A. (honors) in English 1953. **Family:** Married Patricia Ann Hale in 1955. **Career:** Editor, ''Caribbean Voices,'' BBC, London, 1954–56; fiction reviewer, *New Statesman,* London, 1957–61; contributor to *New York Review of Books, New Statesman,* and other periodicals. **Awards:** Rhys Memorial prize, 1958; Maugham award 1961; Phoenix Trust award, 1962; Hawthornden prize, 1964; W.H. Smith literary award, 1968; Arts Council grant, 1969; Booker prize, 1971; Bennett award (*Hudson Review*), 1980; Jerusalem prize, 1983; T.S. Eliot award, 1986; Trinity Cross (Trinidad), 1989; James Tod Award, Maharana Mewar Foundation (India), 2000. D.Litt.: University of the West Indies, Trinidad, 1975; St. Andrews University, Fife, Scotland, 1979; Columbia University, New York, 1981; Cambridge University, 1983; London University, 1988; Oxford University, 1992. Honorary fellow, University College, Oxford, 1983. Knighted, 1990. **Agent:** Aitken and Stone Ltd., 29 Fernshaw Road, London SW10 0TG, England.

PUBLICATIONS

Novels

The Mystic Masseur. London, Deutsch, 1957; New York, Vanguard Press, 1959.
The Suffrage of Elvira. London, Deutsch, 1958; in *Three Novels,* New York, Knopf, 1982.
Miguel Street. London, Deutsch, 1959; New York, Vanguard Press, 1960.
A House for Mr. Biswas. London, Deutsch, 1961; New York, McGraw Hill, 1962.
Mr. Stone and the Knights Companion. London, Deutsch, 1963; New York, Macmillan, 1964.
The Mimic Men. London Deutsch, and New York, Macmillan, 1967.
In a Free State. London, Deutsch, and New York, Knopf, 1971.
Guerrillas. London, Deutsch, and New York, Knopf, 1975.
A Bend in the River. London, Deutsch, and New York, Knopf, 1979.
The Enigma of Arrival. London, Viking, and New York, Knopf, 1987.
A Way in the World. London, Heinemann, and New York, Knopf, 1994.

Short Stories

A Flag on the Island. London, Deutsch, 1967; New York, Macmillan, 1968.

Other

The Middle Passage: Impressions of Five Societies—British, French and Dutch—in the West Indies and South America. London, Deutsch, 1962; New York, Macmillan, 1963.
An Area of Darkness: An Experience of India. London, Deutsch, 1964; New York, Macmillan, 1965.
The Loss of El Dorado: A History. London, Deutsch, 1969; New York, Knopf, 1970; revised edition, London, Penguin, 1973.
The Overcrowded Barracoon and Other Articles. London, Deutsch, 1972; New York, Knopf, 1973.
India: A Wounded Civilization. London, Deutsch, and New York, Knopf, 1977.
The Return of Eva Perón, with *The Killings in Trinidad* (essays). London, Deutsch, and New York, Knopf, 1980.
A Congo Diary. Los Angeles, Sylvester and Orphanos, 1980.
Among the Believers: An Islamic Journey. London, Deutsch, and New York, Knopf, 1981.
Finding the Centre: Two Narratives. London, Deutsch, and New York, Knopf, 1984.
A Turn in the South. London, Viking, and New York, Knopf, 1989.
India: A Million Mutinies Now. London, Heinemann, 1990; New York, Viking, 1991.
Bombay: Gateway of India (text/conversations), photographs by Raghubir Singh. New York, Aperture, 1994.
Conversations with V.S. Naipaul, edited by Feroza Jussawalla. Jackson, University Press of Mississippi, 1997.
Beyond Belief: Islamic Excursions Among the Converted Peoples. New York, New York Review of Books, 2000.
Between Father and Son: Family Letters by V.S. Naipaul, edited by Gillon Aitken. New York, Knopf, 2000.

*

Bibliography: *V.S. Naipaul: A Selective Bibliography with Annotations* by Kelvin Jarvis, Metuchen, New Jersey, Scarecrow Press, 1989.

Critical Studies: By David Pryce-Jones, in *London Magazine,* May 1967; Karl Miller, in *Kenyon Review* (Gambier, Ohio), November 1967; *The West Indian Novel* by Kenneth Ramchand, London, Faber, and New York, Barnes and Noble, 1970; *V.S. Naipaul: An Introduction to His Work* by Paul Theroux, London, Deutsch, and New York, Africana, 1972; *V.S. Naipaul* by Robert D. Hamner, New York, Twayne, 1973, and *Critical Perspectives on V.S. Naipaul* edited by Hamner, Washington, D.C., Three Continents, 1977, London, Heinemann, 1979; *V.S. Naipaul* by William Walsh, Edinburgh, Oliver and Boyd, and New York, Barnes and Noble, 1973; *V.S. Naipaul: A Critical Introduction* by Landeg White, London, Macmillan, and New York, Barnes and Noble, 1975; *Paradoxes of Order: Some Perspectives on the Fiction of V.S. Naipaul* by Robert K. Morris, Columbia, University of Missouri Press, 1975; *V.S. Naipaul* by Michael Thorpe, London, Longman, 1976; *Four Contemporary Novelists* by Kerry McSweeney, Montreal, McGill-Queen's University Press, 1982, London, Scolar Press, 1983; *V.S. Naipaul: A Study in Expatriate Sensibility* by Sudha Rai, New Delhi, Arnold-Heinemann, 1982; *Contrary Awareness: A Critical Study of the Novels of V.S. Naipaul* by K.I. Madhusudana Rao, Madras, Centre for Research on New International Economic Order, 1982; *V.S. Naipaul: In Quest of the Enemy* by Anthony Boxill, Fredericton, New Brunswick, York Press, 1983; ''V.S. Naipaul Issue'' of *Modern Fiction Studies* (West Lafayette, Indiana), Autumn 1984; *The Fiction of V.S. Naipaul* by Nonditor Mason, Calcutta, World Press, 1986; *Journey Through Darkness: The Writing of V.S. Naipaul* by Peggy Nightingale, St. Lucia, University of Queensland Press, 1987; *The Web of Tradition: Uses of Allusion in V.S. Naipaul's Fiction* by John Thieme, Mundelstrup, Denmark, Dangaroo Press, and London, Hansib, 1987; *V.S. Naipaul* by Peter Hughes, London, Routledge, 1988; *V.S. Naipaul: A Materialist Reading* by Selwyn R. Cudjoe, Amherst, University of Massachusetts Press, 1988; *V.S. Naipaul* by Richard Kelly, New York, Continuum, 1989; *The Novels of V.S. Naipaul: A Study of Theme and Form* by Shashi Kamra, New Delhi, Prestige, 1990; *London Calling: V.S. Naipaul, Postcolonial Mandarin* by Rob Nixon, New York and Oxford, Oxford University Press, 1992; *On the Margins: The Art of Exile in V.S. Naipaul* by Timothy F. Weiss, Amherst, University of Massachusetts Press, 1992; *Irony in the Novels of R.K. Narayan and V.S. Naipaul* by K.N. Padmanabhan Nair, Trivandrum, S. India, CBH Communications, 1993; *Self and Colonial Desire: Travel Writings of V.S. Naipaul* by Wimal Dissanayake, New York, Lang, 1993; *V.S. Naipaul* by Bruce King, New York, St. Martin's Press, and Basingstoke, Macmillan, 1993; *V.S. Naipaul* by Fawzia Mustafa, Cambridge and New York, Cambridge University Press, 1995; *V.S. Naipaul: Displacement and Autobiography* by Judith Levy, New York, Garland, 1995; *The Novels of V.S. Naipaul: Quest for Order and Identity* by N. Ramadevi, New Delhi, Prestige Books, 1996; *V.S. Naipaul: A Critical Study* by Md. Akhtar Jamal Khan, New Delhi, Creative Books, 1998; *V.S. Naipaul* by Manjit Inder Singh, Jaipur, India, Rawat Publications, 1998.

V.S. Naipaul comments:

I feel that any statement I make about my own work would be misleading. The work is there: the reader must see what meaning, if any, the work has for him. All I would like to say is that I consider my nonfiction an integral part of my work.

* * *

V.S.Naipaul's central place in Caribbean, and indeed, world literature, has been hard won. His double honor in receiving a British knighthood and the Trinidad Trinity Cross are the fruits of an often painful search for identity across English and Caribbean cultures, in which fiction and autobiography constantly interact.

His work falls broadly into five phases. These are his early satirical writings; the major Trinidadian novels; works exploring a rootless existence ''in a free state''; the ambivalent recovery of a sense of place in *The Enigma of Arrival;* and later exploration of global cultures. *Miguel Street* was his first-written (though third-published) novel, begun in 1955 while Naipaul was freelancing for the BBC. It offers a gallery of vivid characters from Port of Spain, Trinidad, seen through the eyes of a growing child. It is an affectionate book, investing bizarre, almost caricatured figures with humanity: B. (Black) Wordsworth who spends his life trying to write one line; Laura who has many children by different men, but drives her daughter to suicide when she follows her mother's behavior; and Man Man, the religious enthusiast who asks to be crucified but is scandalized when bystanders begin throwing stones.

Naipaul omitted the section originally intended to implicate the boy-narrator directly in the narrative, leaving *Miguel Street* as a series of impressions rather than a novel. Nevertheless, it is one of his most attractive works, pointing to his achievement in the short stories published in *A Flag for the Island* (which includes the previously omitted story, ''The Enemy'') and elsewhere.

The Mystic Masseur is more complex and directly satirical. The anti-hero, Pandit Ganesh Ramsummair, through the fraudulent assumption of powers as a mystic and writer, rises from humble beginnings to the position of G. Ramsay Muir, Esq., M.B.E., Member of the Legislative Council. The satire on popular superstition and the unstable roots of political power in Trinidad is sharply focused by Ramsummair himself, who tells his story both in direct narrative and in the form of a suppressed diary, significantly called The Years of Guilt. *The Suffrage of Elvira Naipaul* again turns Naipaul's mordant satire on popular politics in Trinidad.

The early work was attacked by his fellow West Indian novelist George Lamming in 1960 as ''castrated satire,'' signaling the resentment many in the Caribbean felt against their most accomplished novelist until the late 1980s. Yet Naipaul's often scarifying account of the futility of West Indian culture grew out of an intense exploration of his own cultural roots, an ambivalence nowhere more clearly seen than in his major Caribbean novel, *A House for Mr. Biswas,* which owes much to the career of his own father, who became a journalist in Port of Spain.

The novel is mediated through the sensibility of Mohun Biswas. Born with an extra finger—at once an indicator of endemic bad luck and malnutrition—he reacts to his privations with a defensive and often self-destructive clowning. He has a genius for disaster—a childish flirtation leads to a marriage into the Tulsis, a predatory merchant family who wish to possess Biswas for the sake of his Brahmin status, and who embody all the values of vulgarity and possessive clannishness Biswas detests. Biswas, artistic by nature, can find an outlet for his talents only in sign-painting, and the creative reporting of sensational events for the island paper. Throughout the book his search for a house of his own is an attempt to find both independence and a meaning for his life, and the often hilarious account of petty island life is underpinned with a deeper sense of the essential loneliness of the human state. This is vividly intimated at the center of the book, when a hurricane blows Biswas's precarious house from around him, precipitating a moment of nervous breakdown. But by the end Biswas has his own (if heavily mortgaged) house, while the Tulsi family is disintegrating. A tender tragicomedy, the book becomes an epic of Trinidad life between the world wars.

After a comparatively unsuccessful sortie into English life with *Mr. Stone and the Knights Companion,* Naipaul returned to Caribbean themes in *The Mimic Men.* Set largely on the fictional island of Isabella, it narrates Ralph Kripalsingh's rise to power on fortunes acquired through Coca-Cola and real estate. Politics becomes a metaphor for the essential futility of the Caribbean predicament, based as Naipaul sees it on the ''mimicry'' of other cultures. Ralph's self-destructive career is set against the possibilities suggested by Ralph's father, who becomes a *sunyasi* (''holy man''), but Ralph comes to see this only at the end, when, in a lonely London boarding house, he seeks to shape the absurdity of his island history through the medium of writing. A rich, finely crafted novel, its final impact is lessened by its despair.

By 1967, Naipaul was a novelist of international stature, and, partly influenced by his travel and journalism, his fiction increasingly took on a world perspective. *In a Free State* is a thematically linked trio of stories, set between two diary entries of a Middle East tour. Its subjects are an Indian servant in the United States, West Indians in Britain, and an Englishman in an African state in revolution. The rich detail characteristic of the earlier books is stripped away, giving spare action and description—an image on a television set, a blank stare—momentous impact. The trauma underlying the loss of roots becomes universalized, and is conveyed with a disquieting energy.

Guerrillas, based on the factual journalism republished as *The Killings in Trinidad,* is set in a thinly disguised Trinidad on the brink of revolution. Jimmy Ahmed, Afro-Chinese, Muslim, and English-educated, attempts to organize a socialist commune, but is finally defeated by his own flawed vision and the self-defeating racial and social conflicts of the island. His tragedy is paralleled by that of Roche, a hero of the South African freedom struggle, who is tricked into confessing his moral disillusionment. Jane, an English girl, attempts to relate to both Roche and Ahmed, and is murdered. The novel reveals Naipaul at his bleakest.

Offering a richer imaginative impact, *A Bend in the River* is related to Naipaul's *A Congo Diary.* It masterfully recreates life in a contemporary central African state under a dictatorship, where race, education, and conflicting ideologies uneasily coexist with traditional African cultures. The political struggles are played out against the background of river, jungle, and forest peoples impervious to the changing cycles of history.

In 1984 Naipaul published *Finding the Centre,* two narratives, one directly about Naipaul's early experiences in London, the other a travelogue describing the African search for identity among the upheavals of the contemporary Ivory Coast. The highly individual use of travel autobiography to explore issues of culture and identity prepared the way for *The Enigma of Arrival.* Starting with Naipaul's experiences of coming to England from Trinidad with Indian ancestry, the work builds up an evocation of life in rural Wiltshire, as seen from a cottage in the grounds of an Edwardian mansion. As the narrative weaves a pattern of the seasons in the English countryside, one becomes aware of subtle links with patterns in Caribbean and Indian cultures. By coming to terms with the change, rhythms, and decay in rural England, the narrator comes to an intuitive understanding of his own predicament, an ambivalent sense that the journey in time and space is also ''the enigma of arrival.'' Resisting précis, the work takes Naipaul's work onto a further stage of experimentation and achievement.

Enigma of Arrival confirmed Naipaul's coming to terms with the Caribbean, and it coincided with his being received of state honors in Trinidad. But he was also a writer of the world. In a series of controversial travelogues, he examined the world of Islam (*Among the Believers*), the United States (*A Turn in the South*), and India (*A Million Mutinies Now*).

After seven years, Naipaul returned to novel writing with *A Way in the World.* The theme is the European contact with the Caribbean that he had explored in his early *The Loss of El Dorado.* But now history is presented in a multilayered work of fiction and autobiography. In it, Raleigh's sixteenth-century expedition to Guyana and Miranda's disastrous invasion of Cuba interact with the contemporary experience of expatriates in London, and revolutionary change and brutal death in East Africa. The work shifts effortlessly between historical periods and three continents, revealing correspondences that illuminate both past and present. Starting as an alienated postcolonial, Naipaul has evolved into a writer with a world perspective, whose constantly evolving literary skill has few rivals in contemporary fiction.

—Louis James

NARAYAN, R(asipuram) K(rishnaswamy)

Nationality: Indian. **Born:** Madras, 10 October 1906. **Education:** Collegiate High School, Mysore; Maharaja's College, Mysore, graduated 1930. **Family:** Married Rajam Narayan c. 1934 (died 1939); one daughter. **Career:** Teacher, then journalist, early 1930s; owner, Indian Thought Publications, Mysore. **Awards:** Sahitya Academy award, 1961; Padma Bhushan, India, 1964; National Association of Independent Schools award (U.S.A.), 1965; English-Speaking Union award, 1975; Royal Society of Literature Benson medal, 1980; Padma Vibhushan, India, 2000. Litt.D.: University of Leeds, Yorkshire, 1967; D.Litt.: University of Delhi; Sri Venkateswara University, Tirupati; University of Mysore. Fellow, Royal Society of Literature, 1980; honorary member American Academy, 1982. **Agent:** Anthony Sheil Associates Ltd., 43 Doughty Street, London WC1N 2LF, England. **Address:** 15 Vivekananda Road, Yadavagiri, Mysore 2, India.

PUBLICATIONS

Novels

Swami and Friends: A Novel of Malgudi. London, Hamish Hamilton, 1935; with *The Bachelor of Arts,* East Lansing, Michigan State College Press, 1954.
The Bachelor of Arts. London, Nelson, 1937; with *Swami and Friends,* East Lansing, Michigan State College Press, 1954.
The Dark Room. London, Macmillan, 1938.
The English Teacher. London, Eyre and Spottiswoode, 1945; as *Grateful to Life and Death,* East Lansing, Michigan State College Press, 1953.
Mr. Sampath. London, Eyre and Spottiswoode, 1949; as *The Printer of Malgudi,* East Lansing, Michigan State University Press, 1957.
The Financial Expert. London, Methuen, 1952; East Lansing, Michigan State College Press, 1953.
Waiting for the Mahatma. London, Methuen, and East Lansing, Michigan State College Press, 1955.
The Guide. Madras, Higginbothams, London, Methuen, and New York, Viking Press, 1958.
The Man-Eater of Malgudi. New York, Viking Press, 1961; London, Heinemann, 1962.
The Vendor of Sweets. New York, Viking Press, 1967; as *The Sweet-Vendor,* London, Bodley Head, 1967.
The Painter of Signs. New York, Viking Press, 1976; London, Heinemann, 1977.
A Tiger for Malgudi. London, Heinemann, and New York, Viking Press, 1983.
Talkative Man. London, Heinemann, 1986; New York, Viking, 1987.
The World of Nagaraj. London, Heinemann, and New York, Viking, 1990.

Short Stories

Malgudi Days. Mysore, Indian Thought, 1943.
Dodu and Other Stories. Mysore, Indian Thought, 1943.
Cyclone and Other Stories. Mysore, Indian Thought, 1944.
An Astrologer's Day and Other Stories. Mysore, Indian Thought, and London, Eyre and Spottiswoode, 1947.
Lawley Road. Mysore, Indian Thought, 1956.
A Horse and Two Goats. London, Bodley Head, and New York, Viking Press, 1970.
Old and New. Mysore, Indian Thought, 1981.
Malgudi Days (not same as 1943 book). London, Heinemann, and New York, Viking Press, 1982.
Under the Banyan Tree and Other Stories. London, Heinemann, and New York, Viking, 1985.
The Grandmother's Tale, with sketches by R.K. Laxman. Madras, Indian Thought, 1992; London, Heinemann, 1993; as *The Grandmother's Tale and Other Stories,* New York, Viking, 1994.
Salt & Sawdust: Stories and Table Talk. New Delhi, Penguin, 1993.

Uncollected Short Story

"The Cobbler and the God," in *Playboy* (Chicago), 1975.

Other

Mysore. Mysore, Government Branch Press, 1939.
Next Sunday: Sketches and Essays. Mysore, Indian Thought, 1956.
My Dateless Diary: A Journal of a Trip to the United States in October 1956. Mysore, Indian Thought Publications, 1960; New York and London, Penguin, 1988.
Gods, Demons, and Others. New York, Viking Press, 1964; London, Heinemann, 1965.
The Ramayana: A Shortened Modern Prose Version of the Indian Epic. New York, Viking Press, 1972; London, Chatto and Windus, 1973.
Reluctant Guru (essays). New Delhi, Hind, 1974.
My Days: A Memoir. New York, Viking Press, 1974; London, Chatto and Windus, 1975.
The Emerald Route (includes play *The Watchman of the Lake*). Bangalore, Government of Karnataka, 1977.
The Mahabharata: A Shortened Modern Prose Version of the Indian Epic. New York, Viking Press, and London, Heinemann, 1978.
A Writer's Nightmare: Selected Essays 1958–1988. New Delhi, Penguin, 1988; New York, Penguin, 1989.
A Story-Teller's World: Stories, Essays, Sketches. New Delhi, Penguin, 1989.
Editor, *Indian Thought: A Miscellany.* New Delhi, Penguin, 1997.

*

Manuscript Collection: Mugar Memorial Library, Boston University.

Critical Studies: *R.K. Narayan: A Critical Study of His Works* by Harish Raizada, New Delhi, Young Asia, 1969; *R.K. Narayan,* London, Longman, 1971, and *R.K. Narayan: A Critical Appreciation,* London, Heinemann, and Chicago, University of Chicago Press, 1982, both by William Walsh; *The Novels of R.K. Narayan* by Lakshmi Holmstrom, Calcutta, Writers Workshop, 1973; *R.K. Narayan,* New Delhi, Arnold-Heinemann, 1973, and *R.K. Narayan as Novelist,* New Delhi, B.R., 1988, both by P.S. Sundaram; *Perspectives on R.K. Narayan* edited by Atma Ram, Ghaziabad, Vimal, 1981; *R.K. Narayan: A Critical Spectrum* edited by Bhagwat S. Goyal, Meerut, Shalabh Book House, 1983; *The Ironic Vision: A Study of the Fiction of R.K. Narayan* by M.K. Naik, New Delhi, Sterling, 1983; *R.K. Narayan: His World and His Art* by Shiv K. Gilra, Meerut, Saru, 1984; *The Novels of R.K. Narayan* by Cynthia Vanden Driesen, Nedlands, University of Western Australia Centre for South and Southeast

Asian Studies, 1986; *A Critical Study of the Novels of R.K. Narayan* by J.K. Biswal, New Delhi, Nirmal, 1987; *Patterns of Myth and Reality: A Study in R.K. Narayan's Novels* by U.P. Sinha, New Delhi, Sandarbh, 1988; *The Language of Mulk Raj Anand, Raja Rao, and R.K. Narayan* by Reza Ahmad Nasimi, New Delhi, Capital, 1989; *Human Struggle in the Novels of R.K. Narayan* by Nazar Singh Sidhu, New Delhi, Bahri, 1992; *A Critical Study of the Novels of R.K. Narayan* by Nagendra nath Sharan, New Delhi, Classical, 1993; *Cultural Imperialism and the Indo-English Novel: Genre and Ideology in R.K. Narayan, Anita Desai, Kamala Markandaya, and Salman Rushdie* by Fawzia Afzal-Khan, University Park, Pennsylvania State University Press; *Indian Life and Problems in the Novels of Mulk Raj Anand, Faja Fao, and R.K. Narayan* by G.N. Agnihtri, Meerut, Shalabh Prakashan, 1993; *Irony in the Novels of R.K. Narayan and V.S. Naipaul* by K.N. Padmanabhan Nair, Trivandrum, S. India, CBH, 1993; *Major Themes in the Novels of R.K. Narayan* by R.M. Varma, New Delhi, Jainsons, 1993; *Message in Design: A Study of R.K. Narayan's Fiction* by P.S. Ramana, New Delhi, Harman, 1993; *R.K. Narayan: Contemporary Critical Perspectives* edited by Geoffrey Kain, East Lansing, Michigan State University Press, 1993; *R.K. Narayan's India: Myth and Reality* edited by Bhagwat S. Goyal, New Delhi, Sarup, 1993; *R.K. Narayan, Critical Perspectives,* edited by A. L. McLeod, New Delhi, Sterling Publishers, 1994; *Myths and Symbols in Raja Rao and R.K. Narayan: A Select Study* by Rajesh K. Pallan, Jalandhar, India, ABS Publications, 1994; *R.K. Narayan: A Painter of Modern India* by Michel Pousse, New York, P. Lang, 1995; *R.K. Narayan* by Susan Ram and N. Ram, New Delhi, Viking, 1996; *The Novels of R.K. Narayan: A Typological Study of Characters* by Ramesh Dnyate, New Delhi, Prestige, 1996; *Six Indian Novelists: Mulk Raj Anand, Raja Rao, R.K. Narayan, Balachandran Rajan, Kamala Markandaya, Anita Desai* by A.V. Suresh Kumar, New Delhi, Creative Books, 1996; *The Elusive Searchlight: The World of R.K. Narayan* by Mustafizur Rahman, Dhaka, Bangladesh, Popular Publishers, 1998; *The Novels of R.K. Narayan: A Critical Evaluation* by P.K. Singh, New Delhi, Atlantic Publishers and Distributors, 1999; *R.K. Narayan: A Study of His Female Characters* by K.K. Gaur, Delhi, S.S. Publishers, 2000.

* * *

No other twentieth-century novelist besides William Faulkner has so well succeeded in creating through a succession of novels an imagined community that microcosmically reflects the physical, intellectual, and spiritual qualities of a whole culture as has R.K. Narayan in his tales of the South Indian community of Malgudi. His stories have made a naive, highly emotional society half a world away as much a part of a reader's experience as Faulkner's novels have made the mad, decadent world of the red hills of Mississippi.

Narayan took longer than Faulkner to discover his metier, though all the Indian writer's novels have been largely set in Malgudi. With his third novel, *Sartoris* (1929), published when he was 32, Faulkner laid the cornerstone for his Yoknapatawpha saga of pride-doomed families. Narayan published four apprentice works based largely on reminiscences before producing, at the age of 43, *Mr. Sampath,* the first of the five most remarkable studies of flamboyant characters who electrified the sleepy city of Malgudi.

It is unlikely that anyone would have guessed that Narayan's first two novels were the work of a major artist. *Swami and Friends* is a kind of charming Indian *Penrod and Sam,* an episodic account of the adventures of two cricket-playing chums as they start high school. *The Bachelor of Arts* is another episodic account of a young man's graduating from college, experiencing a frustrating love affair, wandering about the country disconsolately, returning home to become an agent for a big city newspaper, and finally marrying under family auspices. His third novel, *The Dark Room,* he describes as dealing with a Hindu wife who submitted passively to an overbearing husband.

His work changed drastically with *The English Teacher,* a thinly veiled account of his own marriage and the event that most matured and shaped his character, the early death of his beloved wife. This novel begins like Narayan's earlier ones with episodic sketches of a young preparatory school teacher's relationships with his students, colleagues, and family. After the tragic death of the wife while househunting, however, the novel becomes a much deeper and more tightly unified work.

With his next novel, Narayan settled upon the kind of characters and narrative patterns that he was to employ in his five remarkable explorations of the fantastic agitations beneath the enervating surface of the life of Malgudi. Near the end of *Mr. Sampath,* Narayan observes of Srinivas, the principal character, that ''he felt he had been involved in a chaos of human relationships and activities.''

Nearly all of Narayan's subsequent novels involve characters and readers in such chaos. Srinivas is a rather aimless young man who has finally been driven by his family to choose a profession and who comes to Malgudi in 1938—when war clouds hang over the whole world—to found a newspaper that has ''nothing special to note about any war, past or future,'' but is ''only concerned with that war that is always going on—between man's inside and outside.'' He falls into the hands of a printer, Mr. Sampath, who takes a proprietary interest in the success of the paper, but who is lured from his printing trade into a film-producing venture. Even Srinivas is briefly tempted to abandon his paper and take up script writing. Despite frantic activity and great expenditures, however, the movie-making venture collapses. Only Srinivas emerges unscathed. He finds another printer and returns to publishing his paper, reflecting on one of the men involved in the catastrophe he has witnessed:

> throughout the centuries ... this group was always there: Ravi with his madness, his well-wishers with their panaceas and their apparatus of cure. Half the madness was his own doing, his lack of self-knowledge, his treachery to his own instincts as an artist, which had made him a battleground. Sooner or later he shook off his madness and realized his true identity—though not in one birth, at least in a series of them.

The passage is a key to understanding Narayan's major works and their relationship to Hindu philosophy; for the characters he focuses upon are those who are ''mad'' as a result of their lack of self-knowledge. Some must await another reincarnation; but some manage to shake off the madness and find their true identities.

One who must wait is the title character of *The Financial Expert,* Margayya, whom we meet sitting under a banyan tree assisting peasants in obtaining loans from a cooperative banking institution. The society's officers resent Margayya's activities, but his business flourishes until his spoiled young son throws into a sewer the book in which all accounts are kept. During a trip to collect a red lotus needed for a penitential ritual, Margayya meets Dr. Pal, a self-styled sociologist, who has written a pornographic manuscript based on the *Kama Sutra.* Margayya recoups his fortune by publishing it under the title

Domestic Harmony; then, embarrassed by the source of his new wealth, he goes back into a money-lending business that is based on withholding the interest from the first installment on the loan. He becomes so successful that he achieves an honored position in the community and recruits Dr. Pal to attract investors. The scheme collapses, however, when the son, who has been gambling with Dr. Pal, demands a share in the business; Margayya assaults Dr. Pal, who in turn discredits the money-lender with his investors. When investors demand their money back, both Margayya and his son are ruined and driven back into dealings with the peasants beneath the banyan tree.

Narayan's next novel, *Waiting for the Mahatma,* is one of his most noble-minded, but least successful. It tells, in the episodic manner of his earlier books, of the misadventures of two young disciples of Mahatma Gandhi during the master's long effort to free his native land. Written after Gandhi's assassination, the book is an admirable tribute, but the fictional characters are too sketchily developed to make it of more than historical interest.

Narayan next turned to the work that has generally been recognized as his most outstanding, *The Guide,* an extremely complicated tale of a confidence man turned saint. In flashbacks, we learn of the rise of Raju from food-seller in the Malgudi railroad station to manager and apparent husband of Rose, who becomes an extremely popular dancer, and his quick fall when he is jailed for forging her signature to a package of jewels. We meet him first, however, when he has installed himself in an abandoned temple after his release from jail and has begun to play the role of spiritual advisor to a peasant community that accepts him as a Mahatma. Gradually he comes to believe in the role he has created, and to relieve a drought he feels compelled to make a fifteen-day fast that he has suggested as an appropriate penance. As a great crowd gathers, he gains ''a peculiar strength'' from, for the first time in his life, ''learning the thrill of full application, outside money and love.'' Despite grave peril to his health he continues to fast until he feels that the rain is falling in the hills. The ending of this novel like that of *The English Teacher* is ambiguous: does Swami Raju die? do the rains come? Narayan tells us only, ''He sagged down''; but he has transcended the madness that once affected him and found a fulfillment denied the printer of Malgudi and the financial expert.

Such fulfillment is denied also Vasu, the fanatical taxidermist of *The Man-Eater of Malgudi,* Narayan's greatest picture of the madness that leads to self-destruction. After successfully flaunting his great strength about the community unchecked through a series of outrageous incidents, he finally devises a plot against Malgudi's beloved temple elephant. The beast seems doomed, but Vasu dies instead; and in one of the most spectacular conclusions to any of Narayan's works, the almost incredible but carefully foreshadowed way in which he destroyed himself is disclosed. In the complementary *The Vendor of Sweets* Narayan portrays a man who discovers his true identity. Jagan had been freed from patriarchal thralldom when he broke with his orthodox family and followed Mahatma Gandhi. His example, however, proves of no value to a son who prefers American ''get-rich-quick'' ideas to the self-sacrificial life Gandhi recommended. Jagan indulges the boy by selling sweetmeats to the luxury-loving community; but when the son gets into serious trouble, Jagan feels helpless. He abandons his business and retires to a decrepit garden of meditation. Having freed himself from successive bondages to parents, hero, and child, he finds a tranquillity unique to this point in Narayan's tales.

Only confusion, however, awaits the protagonist of *The Painter of Signs,* in which Narayan also deals boldly with a new India's urgent and controversial problem of population control. Raman, a highly traditional thiry-year-old bachelor, who took up signboard painting because he ''loved calligraphy,'' is cared for selflessly by his aunt until he meets Daisy, a dynamic propagandizer for birth control. When Raman induces Daisy to marry him, the aunt departs on a religious pilgrimage from which she does not expect to return. Then when Daisy discovers that she cannot give up her missionary work for marriage, Raman finds that he has destroyed his old life without creating a new one.

Reviewers accustomed to the down-to-earth manner of Narayan's ironic fictions were as disconcerted by *A Tiger for Malgudi* as the frantic villagers who are confronted by Raja, the tiger. Since Raja is the hero-narrator of the novel, Narayan seems to be abandoning reality for fantasy; but *A Tiger for Malgudi* is no traditional anthropomorphic beast fable. Drawing delicately on Hindu doctrines of reincarnation, Narayan depicts Raja as a creature with a soul, who lacks only the faculty of conversing with humans. His tale is told by those who learn to read his mind: the fictional master that saves Raja from the rest of the wryly depicted human community and the master of fiction who has conjured him up. The tale is of the overcoming of ''the potential of violence,'' with which, Raja's master observes, ''every creature is born.'' The seemingly whimsical history of a talking tiger thus expands into an ironic fable and prophecy about not just the recent troubled history of Narayan's own country, but of mankind generally. A wise and witty message from one who has aged serenely without missing the significance of a moment of his experiences, this novel should take its place among the most beatific visions of a century that has produced far more diabolical ones. It climaxes the achievement of the major Malgudi novels in depicting the soul's erratic progress from fanaticism toward the tranquil transcendence of the dusty streets of Malgudi.

—Warren French

NAROGIN, Mudrooroo

See MUDROOROO

NAYLOR, Gloria

Nationality: American. **Born:** New York City, 25 January 1950. **Education:** Brooklyn College, New York, B.A. in English 1981; Yale University, New Haven, Connecticut, 1981–83, M.A. in Afro-American Studies 1983. **Career:** Missionary for the Jehovah's Witnesses, New York, North Carolina, and Florida, 1968–75; telephone operator, New York City hotels, 1975–81. Writer-in-residence, Cummington Community of the Arts, Massachusetts, Summer 1983; visiting professor, George Washington University, Washington, D.C., 1983–84, University of Pennsylvania, Philadelphia, 1986, New York University, 1986, Princeton University, New Jersey, 1986–87, and Boston University, 1987; Fannie Hurst Visiting Professor, Brandeis University, Waltham, Massachusetts, 1988; United States Information Agency Cultural Exchange Lecturer, India, Fall 1985. Columnist, *New York Times,* 1986. Since 1988 judge, Book-of-the-Month Club. **Awards:** American Book award, 1983; National Endowment for the Arts fellowship, 1985; Guggenheim fellowship, 1988. **Address:** c/o One Way Productions, 638 Second Street, Brooklyn, New York 11215, U.S.A.

Publications

Novels

The Women of Brewster Place: A Novel in Seven Stories. New York, Viking Press, 1982; London, Hodder and Stoughton, 1983.
Linden Hills. New York, Ticknor and Fields, and London, Hodder and Stoughton, 1985.
Mama Day. New York, Ticknor and Fields, and London, Hutchinson, 1988.
Bailey's Café. New York, Harcourt Brace, 1992; London, Minerva, 1993.
The Men of Brewster Place. New York, Hyperion, 1998.

Uncollected Short Story

"Life on Beekman Place," in *Essence* (New York), March 1980.

Other

Editor, *Children of the Night: The Best Short Stories by Black Writers, 1967 to the Present.* Boston, Little, Brown, 1995.

*

Film Adaptations: *The Women of Brewster Place*, 1989.

Critical Studies: *Gloria Naylor: Critical Perspectives Past and Present* edited by Henry Louis Gates and K.A. Appiah, New York, Amistad, 1993; *Gloria Naylor: In Search of Sanctuary* by Virginia C. Fowler, New York, Twayne Publishers and London, Prentice Hall, 1996; *The Power of the Porch: The Storyteller's Craft in Zora Neale Hurston, Gloria Naylor, and Randall Kenan* by Trudier Harris, Athens, University of Georgia Press, 1996; *The Critical Response to Gloria Naylor,* edited by Sharon Felton and Michelle C. Loris, Westport, Connecticut, Greenwood Press, 1997; *Understanding Gloria Naylor* by Margaret Earley Whitt, Columbia, University of South Carolina Press, 1999; *Gloria Naylor: Strategy and Technique, Magic and Myth,* edited by Shirley A. Stave, Newark, University of Delaware Press, 2000.

Gloria Naylor comments:

I think of *The Women of Brewster Place* as a love letter to the black women of America—a celebration of their strength and endurance. *Linden Hills* is a cautionary tale—an example of the drastic results if a people forsake their ethnocentric identity under the pressure to assimilate into a mainstream society and seek its rewards.

* * *

Gloria Naylor has written several original and absorbing novels, among them *The Women of Brewster Place: A Novel in Seven Stories* (which won the American Book award for best first writing in 1983), *Linden Hills,* and *Mama Day.* Naylor's success lies, in part, in the intensity of her presentation of such social issues as poverty, racism, discrimination against homosexuals, the unequal treatment of women, the value of a sense of community among blacks, and the failure of some upper middle-class educated blacks to address racial problems and social injustice.

The Women of Brewster Place has a simple structure. Most of the scenes take place in the decaying apartment complex, Brewster Place. The dwellers expect to go nowhere else. The brick wall that closed their street several years earlier now separates them from the rest of the city and symbolizes their psychological and spiritual isolation. In the closing pages of the novel, one woman removes a brick that she thinks is stained with the blood of a resident recently gang-raped and left to die. Impulsively, the other women join her and collectively they tear down the wall, experiencing as they do so an inner regeneration, a sense of community and solidarity, and a rebirth of hope.

The novel includes seven narratives, each focusing on a woman and illuminating her present situation while abundant flashbacks recapitulate her earlier experience. The dominant woman in one chapter appears as a less important figure in several others, so that the entire book, consisting of related though not always consecutive episodes, emerges as a novel rather than as a collection of stories only. While each of the narratives has its own climax, the book builds toward the most threatening crises faced by the Brewster Place community: Ciel's starving herself almost to death in grief for her lost child, the antagonism that builds against two lesbian tenants, and the rape-murder of Lorraine, the lesbian elementary school teacher who has tried to help Kiswana (an idealistic radical) establish a closely organized community among the tenants. Through the suffering of Ciel and that of Lorraine, the other women achieve a new understanding of one another and deepened insight into the problems that confront them individually and collectively. The work considered as a novel gains unity through Naylor's use of a single setting, her concentration upon a small number of women in each narrative, her analysis of the major threats to the community in the tragedies of Ciel and Lorraine, and her resort to rituals of healing in which the characters join each other in expressing their human concern in acts rather than in words.

In *Linden Hills* Naylor again confines her scenes to one location, but her tone and outlook are more sardonic and pessimistic. In her castigation of middle-class black society, Naylor here finds little hope for renewal of spiritual values or for a development of communal responsibility or identity among the residents. Linden Hills blacks are ambitious and selfish; the richer ones live close to the bottom of the hillside; and richest of all is Luther Nedeed. For five generations Luther Nedeed has controlled Linden Hills real estate and also been the local mortician. Next to the Nedeed home and morgue lies the cemetery. The Nedeed wives in each generation have been so deprived of affection and companionship by their "frog-eyed" husbands that they looked forward finally only to death.

Linden Hills has a far more intricate narrative structure than Naylor's first novel. Two young poets, Willie and Lester, in the six days before Christmas earn gift money doing odd jobs. Most of the action is seen through their eyes, except for flashbacks related to the past experiences of the householders who employ them. As they journey further down the hillside each day, they encounter death, suicide, hypocrisy, exploitation, and treachery. The poets agonize and rage over the people who are living a meaningless, deathlike existence.

An additional narrative line appears in "inserts" in the text that interrupt the narration of the experiences of Willie and Lester during this week. The lines addressed directly to the reader reveal secret horrors unknown to Willie and Lester. Luther Nedeed, dissatisfied with the light skin of his infant son, has banished his wife, Willa, and their infant to his abandoned basement morgue, and he begins lowering food and water to her only after the infant has starved to death. In her desperate isolation, Willa searches for any sign of humanity. From day to day she discovers—and furtively reads—the secret notes recorded in diaries, letters, Bibles, and recipe books by the wives of Nedeed men since 1837. Sharing their tales of abuse, she feels their presence with her and gains strength to climb the stairs on Christmas Eve, carrying her dead son, and to confront her husband. At that moment the decorated tree bursts into flame and in the inferno that follows all traces of the Nedeeds disappear. No neighbor bothers to assist them or even to sound an alarm.

Naylor uses Dante's journey through the lower world in the symbolism that gives additional coherence and depth to the multiple plots. The powerful in Linden Hills resist spiritual illumination and prefer a life in Hell to a life in Paradise. They illustrate the principle underlying Dante's vision of those who inhabit the netherworld, ''Abandon hope, all ye who enter here.'' Naylor's work demonstrates that in hell all malefactors are concerned only with their own suffering, rather than with their guilt. Blacks in Linden Hills have the wealth and resources to attain self-awareness, love, and grace, but they are actually far less receptive to the promptings of the spirit than the poor women in Brewster Place, who are capable of spiritual illumination and conversion to a regenerate existence.

Naylor's third novel, *Mama Day,* shows a continued progression in her boldly imagined fiction. It recounts a love story of a good marriage that was sometimes far from calm, and it presents for the first time in her novels a kind, responsible, and interesting husband. Ophelia and George Andrews work in a small Manhattan engineering office and hesitantly fall in love, frequently fight, and finally learn to listen to each other by taking turns expressing themselves in long monologues. This continues even after one is in a grave and the other is sitting next to the grave. The novel speaks of the death in the early pages and what one might hear in the cemetery. The courtship and marriage are thus recounted for the reader after the marriage has been broken by death. They recall memories of the details of arguments, happy events, and of their childhood. The alternate passages in the book develop a kind of antiphonal poetry, with long questions and long answers. The love story is told in first person by the two narrators in alternating sections. Only occasionally and when another person appears in the story does the third-person omniscient narrator speak. The connected monologues begin in New York City and end in Willow Springs, a sea island where Ophelia (also called Cocoa and Baby Girl) was raised by her grandmother, Abigail, and her great-aunt, Miranda (Mama Day). George, abandoned as an infant in New York, grew up in a shelter for boys. He has learned to stress intellectuality and insist upon reason and provable facts. Cocoa values not only what she has been taught in college but also the folk wisdom of Mama Day and Abigail, their intuition, but not their connection with magic, conjure, or hexes.

The island of Willow Springs is connected by a bridge to both Georgia and South Carolina but is not a part of either state. The latter three-fourths of the novel takes place at Willow Springs. Most of the action in Willow Springs is narrated in the first-person voice of Mama Day, as are the philosophical or spiritual messages that Naylor seeks to convey. During their summer visit to the island both Cocoa and George are forced to compromise and both develop greater understanding. Cocoa, after violent confrontation and deadly illness, finds less need to insist on her own way. George, with greater difficulty, begins to acknowledge some kind of faith in Mama Day's power to heal and to respect both nature and the supernatural.

The folkways, celebrations, and eccentricities of the populace on the island provide an intriguing sequence of events, but the novel ends chaotically with a hurricane and flood that confuses intricate lines of the plots and their intersection. While the extensive symbolism leads the reader to search for mythic and universal truth in the novel, Naylor raises as many questions as answers. Although the ''Candle Walk,'' in which the villagers march to the bridge carrying lighted candles, is impressive, no one knows why they observe it. They know that something happened to free their ancestors in 1823, but are unsure how a slave named Sapphira Wade was able to marry the slave owner, get him to sign papers freeing all his slaves on the island, and then murder him. Mama Day and Abigail recognize that Baby Girl is a descendant of Sapphira and accept her aggressive and stubborn nature as inevitable, but they are concerned that she and George will never find peace.

In making a quilt for their wedding present, they consider protecting her by not including pieces of cloth that belonged to ''contrary'' women—only using remnants from women who were sheltered and timid. But they decide against this, because Mama Day thinks the broad experience of life is to be treasured rather than avoided. While they include scraps of cloth from women who broke men's hearts and who never found inner peace, they also choose a quilt pattern that is composed of interlocking rings, suggesting the support one woman needs from other women. Mama Day is supported by the community in the gift-giving that follows the Candle Walk. In recognition of the old woman's healing, midwifery, and sage advice throughout the past year, the people bring her provisions of every sort to be stored to last all through the next year.

But if the Candle Walk activities suggest an idyllic black community, Naylor negates this impression with her stories of vengeance, hexes, and curses and makes clear that the people consult not only Mama Day but also her rival in advising and healing—a man who is a fraud, a bootlegger, and a card shark. Mama Day's thoughts are shadowed by grief for her mother, who drowned herself, and Mama Day is responsible late in the story for the violent murder of a jealous woman who has poisoned Cocoa. George, though drawn to the family and community, values his urban life and job and seeks to swim through the flood to return ''beyond the bridge.'' If less carefully structured than Naylor's earlier novels, *Mama Day* is a rich and powerful novel that shows the influence of both Toni Morrison and Alice Walker in venturing beyond the natural into suggestions of the power of the supernatural and the spirit.

Bailey's Café is a place where a variety of people, each incomplete or hurting in his or her own way, come to find completion. Like a speakeasy, to enter it requires use of a code, but here the code is the blues, and Naylor has structured the novel like a sort of blues symphony. This polyphonic quality returns in *The Men of Brewster Place,* a sequel to *The Women of Brewster Place* that brings back the character of Ben, a janitor from the earlier novel, as both narrator and chorus.

—Margaret B. McDowell

NDEBELE, (Nimrod) Njabulo S(imakahle)

Nationality: South African. **Born:** Ladysmith, Natal Province, South Africa, 12 October 1913. **Education:** St. Peter's High School, Resettenvelle, Johannesburg, 1929–31; Amanzimtoti (Adams') College, 1933–34, earned teaching certificate; University of Witwatersrand, A.B. in Zulu language and political science 1948. **Career:** Assistant teacher, Khaiso Secondary School, 1935–45; assistant teacher, Madibane High School, Johannesburg, 1945–53; principal, Charterston High School, Nigel, 1953–57; inspector of schools, Middleburg Circuit, from 1957. **Awards:** Esther May Bedford prize, 1937, for *UGubudele namazimuzimu.*

PUBLICATIONS

Short Stories

Fools and Other Stories. Johannesburg, Raven Press, 1983; Harlow, Longman, 1985.

Play

UGubudele namazimuzimu. Johannesburg, University of Witwatersrand Press, 1941.

Other

Rediscovery of the Ordinary: Essays on South African Literature and Culture. Johannesburg, COSAW, 1991; Manchester, England, and New York, Manchester University Press, 1994.

Bonolo and the Peach Tree, illustrated by Vusi Malindi (for children). Johannesburg, Raven Press, 1992.

* * *

> The relationship between politics and art is by definition always mediated by reflection. We distinguish only between immediate action, on the one hand, and delayed action, on the other. We do not choose between politics and art: rather, we participate in the dialectic between them. To understand this is to understand the creative possibilities of both.

For Njabulo Simakahle Ndebele, the role art plays in political struggle has been central to both his artistic development and his pronouncements on South African literature. Western critics have welcomed Ndebele's finely crafted prose in *Fools and Other Stories* as a pleasant change from the didactic propagandeering of politically motivated literature. J. M. Coetzee invokes Dostoevsky and Chekhov. Certainly, Ndebele's tales, coupled with his essays, helped move South African literature beyond a stagnant ''protest literature'' obsessed with constructing ''a totally debased people whose only reason for existence is to receive the sympathy of the world.'' The tales are set in a location but eschew descriptions of overt racist tensions in favor of accounts of less sensational conflicts emerging from the range of inhabitants.

However, Ndebele has not left the political arena and entered a specious ''objective'' aestheticism. He does resist the narrow view that politically committed writing must identify and draw moral conclusions from oppression because, as he states in ''Beyond 'Protest,''' it can too easily lead to ''the simplification and trivialization of moral perception,'' thereby allowing ''the rhetoric of protest'' to replace ''paying critical attention to the concrete social, political details of that oppression.''

But rather than endorsing apoliticism, such concrete details broaden the writer's scope: ''Politics is not only the seizure of state power, it can also be the seizure of a woman's burial society in the township.'' Ndebele focuses his storyteller's gaze on these localized, everyday instances to build a sense of the human potential for resistance and intervention in the monoliths of political power.

In *Fools,* a young boy defies his parents' middle-class, Westernized values by refusing to play the great European masters on his violin. Another boy masters the fear of getting a vial of water for his sick mother from a local sorceress. In the title novella, a Boer cracks a whip preparatory to beating the narrator, a weak and abusive man, who realizes ''I knew then that his whip was all there was to him.'' In silently resisting, he thinks, ''my silence was my salvation; the silence of years of trying to say something without much understanding… . This would be the first silence that would carry meaning.'' Such limited epiphanies power Ndebele's creative work, which explores complex political issues through their manifestation in seemingly insignificant social contexts.

Ndebele demonstrates that literature crafted with a sophisticated awareness of the only metaphorical connection between ''narrative and the real world'' can nonetheless create and consolidate ''a subjective confidence which will enable people to have the will to go out with an inner commitment to smash the oppression that is keeping them down.'' Such a revitalizing of both the aesthetic and the political components of literary work imparts a significance to Ndebele's writing that resonates far beyond South Africa.

—Victoria Carchidi

NEUGEBOREN, Jay

Nationality: American. **Born:** New York City, 30 May 1938. **Education:** Columbia University, New York, B.A. 1959 (Phi Beta Kappa); Indiana University, Bloomington, M.A. 1963. **Family:** Married 1) Betsy Bendorf in 1964 (divorced 1983), three children; 2) Judy Karasik in 1985 (divorced 1987). **Career:** Junior executive trainee, General Motors Corporation, Indianapolis, 1960; English teacher, Saddle River Country Day School, New Jersey, 1961–62; teacher, New York City public high and junior high schools, 1963–66; preceptor in English, Columbia University, 1964–66; lecturer, Stanford University, California, 1966–67; assistant professor, State University of New York, Old Westbury, 1968–69. Since 1971 writer-in-residence, University of Massachusetts, Amherst. **Awards:** Bread Loaf Writers Conference De Voto fellowship, 1966; *Transatlantic Review* novella award, 1969; National Endowment for the Arts grant, 1973; Guggenheim fellowship, 1977; Massachusetts Council on the Arts fellowship, 1978; American Jewish Committee, best novel prize, 1981; Smilen-*Present Tense* award, 1982; PEN Syndicated Fiction prize, 1982–88 (6 prizes); National Endowment for the Arts fellowship, 1989. **Agent:** Richard Parks, 138 E. 16th St., New York, New York, 10003. **Address:** Department of English, University of Massachusetts, Box 30515, Amherst, Massachusetts 01003–0515, U.S.A.

PUBLICATIONS

Novels

Big Man. Boston, Houghton Mifflin, 1966.

Listen Ruben Fontanez. Boston, Houghton Mifflin, and London, Gollancz, 1968.

Sam's Legacy. New York, Holt Rinehart, 1974.
An Orphan's Tale. New York, Holt Rinehart, 1976.
The Stolen Jew. New York, Holt Rinehart, 1981.
Before My Life Began. New York, Simon and Schuster, 1985.

Short Stories

Corky's Brother and Other Stories. New York, Farrar Straus, 1969; London, Gollancz, 1970.
Penguin Modern Stories 3, with others. London, Penguin, 1970.
Don't Worry about the Kids: Stories. Amherst, Massachusetts, University of Massachusetts Press, 1997.

Uncollected Short Stories

''My Son, The Freedom Rider,'' in *Colorado Quarterly* (Boulder), Summer 1964.
''Connorsville, Virginia,'' in *Transatlantic Review* (London), Winter 1969.
''My Life and Death in the Negro American Baseball League: A Slave Narrative,'' in *Massachusetts Review* (Amherst), Summer 1973.
''The Place Kicking Specialists,'' in *Transatlantic Review* (London), Fall-Winter 1974.
''Monkeys and Cowboys,'' in *Present Tense* (New York), Summer 1976.
''A Worthy Cause,'' in *Willmore City 6–7* (Carlsbad, California), 1978.
''Uncle Nathan,'' in *Ploughshares* (Cambridge, Massachusetts), vol. 4, no. 4, 1978.
''His Violin,'' in *Atlantic* (Boston), November 1978.
''Kehilla,'' in *Present Tense* (New York), Winter 1978.
''Star of David,'' in *Tri-Quarterly* (Evanston, Illinois), Spring 1979.
''The St. Dominick's Game,'' in *Atlantic* (Boston), December 1979.
''Poppa's Books,'' in *Atlantic* (Boston), July 1980.
''Bonus Baby,'' in *John O'Hara Journal* (Pottsville, Pennsylvania), Fall 1980.
''Visiting Hour,'' in *Shenandoah* (Lexington, Virginia), Fall 1980.
''Noah's Song,'' in *Present Tense* (New York), Winter 1980.
''Daughter,'' in *Confrontation* (New York), Spring 1981.
''When the Cheering Turned to Sorrow,'' in *Inside Sports* (Evanston, Illinois), May 1981.
''Death and the Schoolyard,'' in *Boston Globe Magazine,* 3 May 1981.
''The 7th Room,'' in *Rendezvous* (Pocatello, Idaho) Summer 1981.
''Leaving Brooklyn,'' in *Literary Review* (Madison, New Jersey), Fall 1981.
''Jonathan,'' in *Tri-Quarterly* (Evanston, Illinois), Winter 1981.
''The Imported Man,'' in *Midstream* (New York), February 1982.
''The Golden Years,'' in *New England Review* (Hanover, New Hampshire), Spring 1982.
''Before the Camps,'' in *Congress Monthly* (New York), April 1982.
''Lev Kogan's Journey,'' in *Boston Globe Magazine,* 6 June 1982.
''The Year Between,'' in *Boston Review,* January 1983.
''On a Beach near Herzlia,'' in *The Ploughshares Reader,* edited by DeWitt Henry. Wainscott, New York, Pushcart Press, 1985.
''Cold Storage,'' in *Massachusetts Review* (Amherst), Spring 1985.
''Fix,'' in *Denver Quarterly,* Spring 1985.
''Stairs,'' in *Present Tense* (New York), Fall 1985.
''Abe's Room,'' in *Confrontation* (New York), Fall 1985.
''Drawing Home,'' in *San Francisco Chronicle,* 22 December 1985.
''1945,'' in *Floridian,* 5 September 1987.
''What Satisfaction Canst Thou Have Tonight?'' in *Columbia* (New York), October 1987.
''About Men,'' in *American Scholar* (Washington, D.C.), Winter 1987.
''High Concept,'' in *Confrontation* (Greenvale, New York), Spring 1988.
''Tolstoy in Maine,'' in *New Letters* (Kansas City), Spring 1988.
''Workers to Attention Please,'' in *Louder than Words,* edited by William Shore. New York, Vintage, 1989.
''How I Became an Orphan in 1947,'' in *Willow Springs* (Cheney, Washington), Spring 1989.
''Your Child Has Been Towed,'' in *Gettysburg Review* (Gettysburg, Pennsylvania), Autumn 1989.
''In Memory of Jane Fojarbi,'' in *Tikkun,* September 1989.
''Minor 6ths, Diminished 7ths,'' in *Gentlemen's Quarterly* (New York), June 1990.
''Overseas,'' in *Michigan Quarterly Review* (Ann Arbor), Summer 1990.
''Have You Visited Israel?'' in *New Letters* (Kansas City), Summer 1991.
''Dept. of Athletics,'' in *Conference Quarterly,* Winter 1992.
''What Is the Good Life?'' in *Gettysburg Review* (Gettysburg, Pennsylvania), Autumn 1992.
''Meanwhile Back on the Word,'' in *The American Scholar* (Washington, D.C.), Summer 1994.
''Where Do We Live Now?'' in *Tikkun,* September/October 1994.

Plays

The Edict (produced New York, 1981).

Radio Play: *The Stolen Jew,* 1980.

Television Play: *The Hollow Boy,* 1991.

Other

Parentheses: An Autobiographical Journey. New York, Dutton, 1970.
Poli: A Mexican Boy in Early Texas (for children). San Antonio, Texas, Corona, 1989.
Imagining Robert: My Brother, Madness, and Survival: A Memoir. New York, Morrow, 1997.
Transforming Madness: New Lives for People Living with Mental Illness. New York, William Morrow, 1999.
Editor, *The Story of ''Story'' Magazine: A Memoir,* by Martha Foley. New York, Norton, 1980.

*

Critical Studies: Statement by Ian Watt, in *Listen Ruben Fontanez,* London, Gollancz, 1968; ''Parentheses'' by Charles Moran, in *Massachusetts Review* (Amherst), Fall 1970; ''From Kerouac to Koch'' by Michael Willis, in *Columbia College Today* (New York), Winter-Spring 1971; ''A Decade of the Ethnic Fiction of Jay Neugeboren,'' in *Melus* (Los Angeles), Winter 1978 and article in *Twentieth-Century American-Jewish Fiction Writers* edited by Daniel Walden, Detroit, Gale, 1984, both by Cordelia Candelaria; interview with

Steven Goldleaf, in *Columbia College Today* (New York), December 1979, and "A Jew Without Portfolio" by Goldleaf, in *Partisan Review* (Boston), Summer 1983; interview in *Literary Review* (Madison, New Jersey), Fall 1981; "Wonderful Lies That Tell the Truth: Neugeboren Reviewed" by Peter Spackman in *Columbia* (New York), November 1981.

* * *

It is easy, perhaps too easy, to dismiss all American-Jewish novelists as confirmed self-haters, as "know-nothings" bent on turning Jewish life into a vulgar joke. In this respect, Jack Portnoy of Philip Roth's 1969 *Portnoy's Complaint* speaks up for those who have grown impatient with their belligerent sons: "Tell me something, do you know Talmud? Do you know history? … Do you know a single thing about the wonderful history and heritage of the saga of your people?" And while such charges are true enough about the likes of Alexander Portnoy—and his wise-cracking creator—they are no longer an accurate assessment of contemporary Jewish-American fiction. Writers like Cynthia Ozick, Arthur Cohen, and Hugh Nissenson have made mighty efforts on behalf of a Jewish aesthetic, one that would draw its sustenance from Jewish sources both wider and deeper than suburban assimilation. With *The Stolen Jew* Jay Neugeboren—a journeyman writer with a half-dozen volumes to his credit—adds himself to their number.

The Stolen Jew is a thick, complicated novel, but basically it is about the inextricable connections between personal memory and Jewish history, between the patterning that art makes possible and the insistencies of life, between an aging ex-writer named Nathan Malkin and his obligations to those, living and dead, who comprise his "family." The result is a novel-within-a-novel, as Nathan rewrites "The Stolen Jew," hoping to sell the manuscript at a high price on the Russian black market and, thus, to raise money to aid the refusniks. Whole chapters of Nathan's novel are interspersed with the Neugeboren's; each refracts upon the other. As Nathan puts it: "A true mosaic was made by shattering the original picture—and putting it together again." *The Stolen Jew* was selected as best novel of 1981 by the American Jewish Committee and, suddenly, Neugeboren became a writer to reckon with. As he himself suggests in a recent interview:

> In my early books [e.g. *Big Man* or *Listen Ruben Fontanez*], I used to pride myself on their "objective" quality. I mean, I don't think I'd ever done an autobiographical novel in a way that even anyone who knew me could feel. My books always seemed to be very much about other things. I think that was one way, in my own life, of not dealing with certain materials, potentially very rich materials, things that I do know about, but also material that I was afraid of, and felt I couldn't handle… . Now, with *The Stolen Jew* I've found a *subject,* a subject that comes from deep personal wells with me.

Before My Life Began is another installment in Neugeboren's continuing effect to combine aspects of traditional fiction (character, plot, naturalistic surface) with experimentation. As Neugeboren would have it, describing his new aesthetic manifesto, "I'd like to raise some of the questions some of the innovative writers are raising about the relation to art to life, but I would like to do it without losing the nineteenth-century novel—without losing character, history, story, the love of these things." In *The Stolen Jew* the result was as compelling as it was densely textured; with *Before My Life Began* one feels Neugeboren's ambition insisting too much:

> Oh you are so good *inside,* David, don't you know that? You're a truly good *and* strong person, and there aren't many of your kind left. It's just so hard for me to watch you walking through the world, pulled on from so many sides, without my being able to help. I keep wanting to run in front of you—the court Jester, yes?—so I can steer you away from Evil and Hate and Anger and Cruelty and all the forces of Darkness—so I can point you to the true path—to righteousness and to light and to happiness.

For an author who can capture speech rhythms so accurately, who can reduplicate the Brooklyn streets of his doomed protagonist, David Voloshin, so well, such flights through airy abstraction may strike one as embarrassing. *Before My Life Began* is the story of a man forced by circumstances to live "two" lives—one as the David Voloshin who grows up in Brooklyn during the years immediately after World War II; the other as Aaron Levin, a civil rights activist during the mid-1960s.

The problem with Neugeboren's ever-thickening plot is that David, as a character, gets lost in the process. Somewhere, despite the rich texture and the patches of lyrical prose, there is no "David" one can grab hold of. He reappears as Aaron Levin, Freedom School teacher and civil rights activist, a man out to do dangerously good work in the Deep South. Once again, Neugeboren has an admirable feel for that time, that place, but he cannot quite resist those moments when David/Aaron speculates abstractly about his situation:

> Sometimes, as now, he feels that his second life—all the years that have passed since he left Brooklyn, along with all the years to come—will only prove to be a rumination on his first life… . Why is it so, he wonders—that truth sometimes has the potential to destroy, while lies can save?

Given the displacement and wrenching dislocations of Neugeboren's protagonist, we are hardly surprised that he seeks pockets of respite. Unfortunately, Neugeboren protests too much about the happiness Voloshin/Levin presumably achieves. *Before My Life Began* ends in a litany of future tenses, of those movements back to a Brooklyn that will bring the novel—and David's life—full circle:

> He will take his boys to his old neighborhood and show them his street and his house and the courtyards and the alleyways. He can see the four small rooms of his apartment, can see himself walking through them with his boys, room by room. The rooms are clean and white and empty, freshly painted and full of pale morning light—the way they might have been, he thinks, before his life began.

Evidently one *can* go home again, at least in the final vision of *Before My Life Began.* In *Poli: A Mexican Boy in Early Texas,* Neugeboren departs from the urban Jewish landscape of his previous fiction to tell the tale of quite another young initiate—and in the genre of the juvenile book, this one suggested for grades seven upward. But if Neugeboren's last works of fiction suggest differing views of childhood—either recaptured or imagined out of whole cloth—his growing readership is, I suspect, much more interested in the treatments of adulthood that lie in Neugeboren's novels as yet unwritten.

—Sanford Pinsker

NGUGI WA THIONG'O

Formerly wrote as James T. Ngugi. **Nationality:** Kenyan. **Born:** Kamiriithu, near Limuru, Kiambu District, 5 January 1938. **Education:** Kamaandũra School, Limuru; Karing'a School, Maanguũ; Alliance High School, Kikuyu; University College, Kampala, Uganda (editor, *Penpoint*), 1959–63, B.A. 1963; Leeds University, Yorkshire, 1964–67, B.A. 1964. **Family:** Married Nyambura in 1961; five sons and three daughters. **Career:** Columnist (''As I See It''), early 1960s, and reporter, 1964, Nairobi *Daily Nation;* editor, *Zuka,* Nairobi, 1965–70; lecturer in English, University College, Nairobi, 1967–69; Fellow in Creative Writing, Makerere University, Kampala, 1969–70; visiting lecturer, Northwestern University, Evanston, Illinois, 1970–71; senior lecturer, associate professor, and chairman of the Department of Literature, University of Nairobi, 1972–77; imprisoned under Public Security Act, 1977–78; left Kenya, 1982; now lives in London. **Awards:** East African Literature Bureau award, 1964. **Address:** c/o Heinemann International, Halley Court, Jordan Hill, Oxford OX2 8EJ, England.

Publications

Novels

Weep Not, Child. London, Heinemann, 1964; New York, Collier, 1969.
The River Between. London, Heinemann, 1965.
A Grain of Wheat. London, Heinemann, 1967.
Petals of Blood. London, Heinemann, 1977; New York, Dutton, 1978.
Caitaani Mutharaba-ini (in Kikuyu). Nairobi, Heinemann, 1980; as *Devil on the Cross,* London, Heinemann, 1982.
Matigari (in Kikuyu). Nairobi, Heinemann, 1986; translated by Wangui wa Goro, London, Heinemann, 1989.

Short Stories

Secret Lives and Other Stories. London, Heinemann, and New York, Hill, 1975.

Plays

The Black Hermit (produced Kampala, Uganda, 1962; London, 1988). London, Heinemann, 1968.
This Time Tomorrow (broadcast 1967). Included in *This Time Tomorrow,* 1970.
This Time Tomorrow (includes *The Rebels* and *The Wound in the Heart*). Nairobi, East African Literature Bureau, 1970.
The Trial of Dedan Kimathi, with Micere Mugo (produced London, 1984). Nairobi, Heinemann, 1976; London, Heinemann, 1977.
Ngaahika Ndeenda (in Kikuyu), with Ngugi wa Mirii (produced Limuru, 1977). Nairobi, Heinemann, 1980; as *I Will Marry When I Want,* London, Heinemann, 1982.

Radio Play: *This Time Tomorrow,* 1967.

Other

Homecoming: Essays on African and Caribbean Literature, Culture, and Politics. London, Heinemann, 1972; New York, Hill, 1973.
The Independence of Africa and Cultural Decolonisation, with *The Poverty of African Historiography,* by A.E. Afigbo. Lagos, Afrografika, 1977.
Writers in Politics: Essays. London, Heinemann, 1981; published as *Writers in Politics: A Re-Engagement with Issues of Literature and Society.* Oxford, England and Portsmouth, New Hampshire, 1997.
Detained: A Writer's Prison Diary. London, Heinemann, 1981.
Education for a National Culture. Harare, Zimbabwe Publishing House, 1981.
Barrel of a Pen: Resistance to Repression in Neo-Colonial Kenya. London, New Beacon, and Trenton, New Jersey, Africa World Press, 1983.
Decolonising the Mind: The Politics of Language in African Literature. London, Currey, 1986.
Njamba Nene and the Cruel Chief (for children). Nairobi, Heinemann, 1986.
Njamba Nene's Pistol (for children). Nairobi, Heinemann, 1986.
Writing Against Neocolonialism. London, Vita, 1986.
Walter Rodney's Influence on the African Continent. London, Friends of Bogle, 1987.
Moving the Centre: The Struggle for Cultural Freedoms. London, Currey, and Portsmouth, New Hampshire, Heinemann, 1993.
Penpoints, Gunpoints, and Dreams, Toward a Critical Theory of the Arts and the State in Africa. Oxford, Clarendon Press and New York, Oxford University Press, 1998.

*

Bibliography: *Ngugi wa Thiong'o: A Bibliography of Primary and Secondary Sources 1957–1987* by Carol Sicherman, London, Zell, 1989.

Critical Studies: *Ngugi wa Thiong'o* by Clifford Robson, London, Macmillan, 1979, New York, St. Martin's Press, 1980; *An Introduction to the Writings of Ngugi* by G.D. Killam, London, Heinemann, 1980; *Ngugi wa Thiong'o: An Exploration of His Writings* by David Cook and Michael Okenimkpe, London, Heinemann, 1983; *East African Writing in English* by Angela Smith, London, Macmillan, 1989; *Ngugi wa Thiong'o: The Making of a Rebel: A Source Book in Kenyan Literature and Resistance* by Carol Sicherman, 1990; *The Novel as Transformation Myth: A Study of the Novels of Mongo Beti and Ngugi wa Thiong'o* by Kandioura Dram, Syracuse, New York, Syracuse University, 1990; *''Justice for the Oppressed—'': The Polictical Dimension in the Language Use of Ngugi wa Thiong'o* by Herta Meyer, Essen, Verlag Die Blaue Eule, 1991; *African Independence from Francophone and Anglophone Voices: A Comparative Study of the Post-Independence Novels by Ngugi and Sembene* by Clara Tsabedze, New York, Lang, 1994; *The Novels of Achebe and*

Ngugi: A Study in the Dialectics of Commitment by K. Indrasena Reddy, New Delhi, Prestige Books, 1994; *Postcolonial Literatures: Achebe, Ngugi, Desai, Walcott,* edited by Michael Parker and Roger Starkey, New York, St. Martin's Press, 1995; *Ngugi wa Thiong'o: Text and Contexts,* edited by Charles Cantalupo, Trenton, New Jersey, Africa World Press, 1995; *Politics As Fiction: The Novels of Ngugi wa Thiong'o* by Harish Narang, New Delhi, Creative Books, 1995; *Ngugi and African Post-colonial Narrative: The Novel as Oral Narrative in Multi-Genre Performance* by F. Odun Balogun, St-Hyacinthe, Quebec, World Heritage Press, 1997; *Ngugi wa Thiong'o: An Exploration of His Writings* by David Cook and Michael Okenimkpe, Oxford, J. Currey, 1997; Portsmouth, New Hampshire, Heinemann, 1997; *Post-Colonial African Fiction: The Crisis of Consciousness* by Mala Pandurang, Delhi, Pencraft International, 1997; *A Teacher's Guide to African Narratives* by Sara Talis O'Brien, Portsmouth, New Hampshire, Heinemann, 1998; *Ngugi's Novels and African History: Narrating the Nation* by James Ogude, London and Sterling, Virginia, Pluto Press, 1999; *Critical Essays: Achebe, Baldwin, Cullen, Ngugi, and Tutuola* by Sydney E. Onyeberechi, Hyattsville, Maryland, Rising Star Publishers, 1999; *Ngugi wa Thiong'o* by Simon Gikandi, Cambridge, England, and New York, Cambridge University Press, 2000; *Ngugi wa Thiong'o* by Oliver Lovesey, New York, Twayne Publishers, 2000.

* * *

Ngugi wa Thiong'o was a Kikuyu adolescent in Kenya during the Mau Mau Rebellion, and the events of those years, of the larger issues of black dispossession by white settlers, and of the history of the Kikuyu from pre-colonial times to the present, lie at the center of his novels and most of his short stories. He was the first Anglophone African writer to give in fiction a Kikuyu view of the bitter colonial war that the British called the Mau Mau Emergency—a healthy corrective to other fictional accounts, like Robert Ruark's, from a white man's point of view. Ngugi's attitudes to larger political questions are by no means unambiguous in his first two novels (hence some considerable uncertainty of craftsmanship in them) but what emerges clearly from *The River Between* (the first to be written, but the second published) is a deep sense of African deprivation and of the desire to win back a lost heritage. It is expressed in *Weep Not, Child* through Ngotho's religious attachment to the land of his ancestors taken from him by Mr. Howlands, and through his older sons' determination to fight for their lands by joining the Mau Mau. But Ngugi is also aware of another part of the African heritage diminished by white colonialism—the Kikuyu religion and tribal culture; it is this aspect of their disinheritance that figures particularly in *The River Between.*

The river is a symbol of sustenance and growth, but it also divides the christianized half of the tribe from the adherents of the traditional tribal ways, soon after the advent of colonialism. Waiyaki, the hero, is an idealistic youth, who dreams with messianic fervor of leading his people out of colonial tutelage, peacefully, by acquiring the white man's education. He would also reconcile the two religiously divided villages; though associated with the traditionalists, he loves a daughter of the fanatical Christian Kikuyu pastor. But Waiyaki's enthusiasm for Western education blinds him to political methods, and he is rejected by his people. The weakness of the novel is that Ngugi romanticizes and glamorizes Waiyaki: his tribal opponents are presented as vindictive personal enemies; their different political approach is not seriously considered.

Njoroge in *Weep Not, Child* is another self-centered youth with mission-school education and messianic ambitions, whose hopes are destroyed when his brothers' involvement in Mau Mau forces him out of school, but again self-centeredness is not part of any ironic regarding of the hero by the novelist. Yet *Weep Not, Child* is a better novel, for Ngugi develops some complexity of structure. There are ironic parallels between the African devotion to ancestral lands and the white settler's love of the soil he has acquired, with the opposed characters oblivious to their common human suffering. Such ironical treatment is a great advance in Ngugi's technique, as are the convincing portraits of subsidiary characters who betray the very values they struggle to achieve, or who suffer constant frustration.

A Grain of Wheat is a novel of mature outlook and much subtler technique. Ostensibly about the Uhuru celebrations of Kenya's independence in 1963, it keeps flashing back to individual sufferings in Mau Mau days. There is no single, central hero this time, but four major characters, each guilty of betraying himself and others when sorely tried in the Rebellion. Mugo, regarded by his people as a Mau Mau hero, has messianic visions before the Rebellion, but his jealousy of the real leader led him to betray him to the British. At last Ngugi is able to treat a messianic figure with detachment, but also with humane sympathy: the years of Mugo's lonely, conscience-ridden life are movingly conveyed. Other characters who also committed acts of betrayal painfully learn, first, the depths of utter disillusion, and then, the harrowing experience of coming to terms with their own limitations. Mugo's public confession brings *him* peace of mind, and helps *them* to face the future with some hope. A great strength of this finely orchestrated novel is Ngugi's skillful use of disrupted time sequence to indicate the interrelatedness of the characters' behavior in the Rebellion and the state of their lives (and of the nation) at Independence. Ngugi's maturity appears also in his sober attitude both to the struggle for, and attainment of, Independence; there are signs of the new African politicians already betraying the ordinary people who suffered under colonialism. Though a disturbing novel, it proclaims hope for the regenerative capabilities of ordinary human nature.

In his critical essays in *Homecoming,* Ngugi argues the vital social function of literature in Africa, and the Third World generally. In *Petals of Blood* he impressively puts this belief into practice. A convincing attack, often Marxist in language, upon neocolonialism in Independent Africa is achieved fictionally by indicating powerfully and effectively how the lives of dispossessed little people are all but broken by an imported capitalist system. The four major characters, each a misfit in Independent Kenyan society, have come to the distant village of Ilmorog to seek personal peace and modest new beginnings. Long associated with heroic Kikuyu legends, Ilmorog becomes a living presence in the novel. In the grip of prolonged drought, and ignored by the M.P. who had begged their votes, the desperate villagers undertake an epic march to the capital to lay their troubles before the authorities. Subsequently religious, political, and economic exploiters swarm upon Ilmorog to ''develop'' it, and using such devices as foreclosed loans eventually dispossess the local inhabitants and establish New Ilmorog. The ample detail with which Ngugi conveys the ruthless stripping of already deprived ordinary people gains power from a sophisticated narrative technique that enables Kenya's history since 1963 to be felt through the consciousness of its social victims. *Petals of Blood* is an angry novel but it does affirm the potentialities of native communality for a just, humane African polity.

With greater fervor of feeling and rhetoric, Ngugi renews in *Devil on the Cross* his attack upon neocolonial exploiters of ordinary

Kenyan people. The story of the economically and sexually exploited young woman, Warīīnga, is given some of the drama of fantasy by being told by "Gīcaandī Player, Prophet of Justice," a figure drawn from the oral tradition, who uses language emotively and didactically in ways reminiscent of Armah's novel *Two Thousand Seasons* (1973). While the device allows Ngugi to employ a variety of highly charged rhetorical modes, it is questionable whether he deploys them as convincingly as he might have. Would such a narrator use not only songs, incantations, the very idiom of oral tradition, but also echoes and parodies of Bible stories and biblical English, together with Marxist analysis and denunciation of capitalism? Ngugi doesn't seem to have tried very hard to disguise his authorial voice, or perhaps it is the effect of translating from his own original Kikuyu. While in *Devil on the Cross* he combines the biblical linguistic and moral flavor of his first two novels with the acerbic political tones of *Petals of Blood,* the cost is much wordy reiteration. Nevertheless, the catastrophic effects of the Western economic stranglehold on many African nations is starkly revealed in the misery of the destitute and starving and the monstrosity of the new Kenyan affluent class.

—Arthur Ravenscroft

Ní DHUIBHNE, Eilis

Also writes as Elizabeth O'Hara. **Nationality:** Irish. **Born:** Eilis Deeney in Walkinstown, Dublin, 22 February 1954. **Education:** University College Dublin, Ireland, B.A. 1974, M.Phil. 1976, Ph.D. 1982. **Family:** Married Bo Almquist in 1982; two sons. **Career:** Folklore collector, University College Dublin, Dublin, Ireland, 1978–80; assistant keeper, National Library, 1980–95; folklore lecturer, People's College, 1986–92; writer of books for children, 1990—. Lives in Dublin. **Awards:** Listowel Poetry Award, 1985; Art Council Bursary, 1986; Bisto Merit Award, 1994; Bisto Book of the Year, 1995; Readers' Association of Ireland Overall Winner, 1995.

Publications

Novels

The Bray House. Dublin, Attic Press, 1990.
The Dancers Dancing. Belfast, Blackstaff Press, 1999.

Fiction (for children, as Elizabeth O'Hara)

The Uncommon Cormorant, illustrations by Carol Betera. Swords, County Dublin, Ireland, Poolbeg Press, 1990.
Hugo and the Sunshine Girl. Dublin, Poolbeg, 1991.
The Hiring Fair. Dublin, Poolbeg, 1993.
Blaeberry Sunday. Dublin, Poolbeg, 1994.
Singles. Dublin, Basement Press, 1994.
Penny-Farthing Sally. Dublin, Poolbeg, 1996.

Short Stories

Blood and Water. Dublin, Attic Press, 1988.
Eating Women Is Not Recommended. Dublin, Attic, 1991.
The Inland Ice and Other Stories. Belfast, Blackstaff Press, 1997.

Plays

Dún na mBan Trí Thine, Peacock Theatre, Dublin, 1994.

Other

Voices on the Wind: Women Poets of the Celtic Twilight. Dublin, New Island Books, 1995.

* * *

That Eilis Ní Dhuibhne's literary work is heavily influenced by Irish culture and mythology is not surprising when one considers that this prolific short story writer and novelist also has an M.Phil. in Medieval Studies and a Ph.D. in Irish Folklore. Born in Walkinstown, Dublin, in 1954, Ní Dhuibhne has found much in Ireland to sustain her as a writer, and Ireland in turn has recognized her contribution favorably. Since the publication of her first collection of short stories, *Blood and Water*, Ní Dhuibhne has received numerous prizes including the Bistro Book of the Year Award, the Readers' Association of Ireland Award, the Listowel Writers' Week award, the Stewart Parker Drama Award, and an Oireachtas award. Her most recent novel, *The Dancers Dancing*, was the first Irish novel ever shortlisted for the influential Orange Prize for Fiction. Nothing if not versatile, Ní Dhuibhne has also published academic articles on folklore, written a play, *Dún na mBan Trí Thine*, which was staged at Dublin's Peacock Theatre, and edited an anthology of women's poetry from the Irish Revival, *Voices on the Wind*. She has also published a number of very successful children's books under the pseudonym Elizabeth O'Hara.

In her creative work Ní Dhuibhne considers universal themes through the specificity of Irish life and culture, particularly as they impact the lives of women. *Blood and Water* explores the lives of a number of women as they attempt to negotiate the politics of a tumultuous outer world, more often than not reflected in their fractured personal lives. In almost every story the female protagonist must confront the personal desires she has suppressed in the face of larger social desires or expectations, and attempt to generate a livable solution. *The Inland Ice and Other Stories* continues to juxtapose the lives of various women in order to expose their commonalities, all the while weaving throughout the short stories a mythological tale of a woman in pursuit of lost love. By framing the stories of different female characters with a folktale quest of passion, love, and loss—which balances success, disillusionment, and wisdom in its conclusion—Ní Dhuibhne draws attention to the sacrifices women have often made in the pursuit of passion, and draws attention to the very gendered stakes of love. *The Inland Ice and Other Stories* further questions the roles women have historically been expected to play in relationships and events defined by patriarchal conventions, including the project of nation building.

For Ní Dhuibhne, the politics of Ireland are inseparable from the construction of gender, sex, and class, and she is not afraid to engage these issues critically. Nowhere is this more apparent than in her most recent novel, *The Dancers Dancing*, where she explores the impact of these tensions on the lives of teenage girls in 1970s Ireland. As a diverse group of girls study Irish language and culture, they also confront a different definition of Ireland, one that predates the political strife by which they have defined their nation, and in turn, been defined as women. Deeply committed to Irish culture, Ní Dhuibhne is also just as deeply committed to feminist politics. Ní

Dhuibhne handles these themes however, with equal portions of wit, humor, and occasional fantastical elements, which render her writing accessible, original, entertaining, and never didactic. Currently Ní Dhuibhne is affirming her ongoing commitment to Irish culture by following her successful Irish language play *Dún na mBan Trí Thine*, with a collection of short stories written in Irish.

—Jennifer Harris

NORFOLK, Lawrence

Nationality: British. **Born:** 1963.

PUBLICATIONS

Novels

Lemprière's Dictionary. London, Sinclair Stevenson, and New York, Harmony, 1991.
Pope's Rhinoceros. London, Sinclair-Stevenson, 1996; New York, Harmony Books, 1996.

* * *

Lawrence Norfolk's formidable reputation rests upon a small collection of works. The success of *Lemprière's Dictionary,* an erudite, intricately designed, and densely textured novel, derives chiefly from its pastiche of literary forms and sensibilities even more varied than its range of geographical and temporal settings (from England to India, from 1600 to 1788). Impossible to classify (or summarize), the novel combines numerous genres—Gothic, Victorian, historical, adventure, mystery, detective, political thriller, and quest—in a decidedly postmodern (even postcolonial) way that strongly suggests the influence of writers such as Umberto Eco, Thomas Pynchon, and Peter Ackroyd.

Norfolk's protagonist is John Lemprière, a fictional version of the author of the well-known *Classical Dictionary* (1788). Building upon the relative dearth of information about the real Lemprière's life, Norfolk fashions his own version (a narrative ploy of considerable thematic import). His Lemprière is a myopic youth whose reading has addled his brain, causing him to see the myths he reads about come to life. Instead of correcting the problem, glasses only enable him to see all the better his father torn apart by his own hunting dogs, in the manner of Actaeon. Himself torn apart by guilt and the desire to solve the family mystery, Lemprière begins his exile/quest. Early in his wanderings, it is suggested that he write a dictionary as a form of therapy. Although it offers him a refuge from a series of baffling mysteries (and thus functions in much the same way the novel itself does for the similarly naive and escapist reader), the dictionary also serves a more sinister purpose. It is the ''signed confession'' linking its innocent author to a series of myth-inspired murders perpetrated by a shadowy Cabbala. It is this Cabbala, comprising descendants of François Lemprière's former business partners, that the hero believes he is searching out but has in fact been directing his efforts all along.

Norfolk's title recalls other, more famous dictionaries. Unlike Samuel Johnson's (1755), Norfolk's does not attempt to ''fix'' and ''preserve'' its subject. Like the *Oxford English Dictionary,* it is ''based upon historical principles'' that in the novel are to be understood semiotically rather than scientifically. As Norfolk explains in ''Bosnian Alphabet'' in the Spring 1993 issue of *Granta,* a dictionary is a very useful but also highly arbitrary means for organizing chaotic experience. It is also a way to organize a novel, as Walter Abish (*Alphabetical Africa*) and Milorad Pavic (*The Dictionary of the Khazars*) have demonstrated. And just as Pavic's novel exists in two forms, male and female, each with its own ending, so does Norfolk's: the longer, denser, more fantastic original English edition and the shorter American, with its greater ''forward momentum.'' Appropriately, *Lemprière's Dictionary* is filled with twins, metamorphoses, mistaken identities, and deliberate disguises and pretends to be a good many things that it is not, including a historical novel (about the East India Company, England's coming-of-age as a colonial power, the events leading up to the French Revolution, and so on). Even as the details are deployed to create a Jamesian ''sense of the past,'' they also serve as a set of facts, some real, some fictional, whose permutational possibilities allow for a seemingly endless series of rearrangement and reinterpretation, that may be understood as an instance of postmodern play or, more seriously, as Don DeLillo has said of his novel *Libra,* as a way of thinking about history, including the history of the novel).

Norfolk's novel repeatedly calls attention to the reading process: to how characters read or, more often, misread events and texts, sometimes, as in François's message to his partners still in the besieged city of La Rochelle, with disastrous consequences. The consequences for the novel and its readers are of course quite different, misinterpretation being the engine that drives them both. Reading a novel such as *Lemprière's Dictionary* becomes at times a highly self-conscious affair. What is said about characters and events often applies equally well to the novel itself. Like the Cabbala, it is ''a kind of joke, a huge prank'' turned serious; like the rumors of impending massacre, it is something that the reader, like the citizens of La Rochelle, perversely ''want to believe.'' It is as well a bog, a fraud, a game of chess, a conspiracy, a simulacrum (in the Baudrillardian sense, a postmodern image having no antecedent reality). Ultimately it resembles the creation of one of Lemprière's own mythical subjects, the master artificer Daedalus, maker of automata and labyrinths.

The title *The Pope's Rhinoceros* might seem metaphoric on first glance, but in fact it is quite literal, referring to an unsuccessful attempt by Portuguese explorers of the 16th century to bring a rhinoceros from Africa back to Rome as a gift for Pope Leo X. These facts, however, are merely a point of departure, and from there Norfolk takes readers on a ride that is as complex (in the view of some detractors, overly so) as it is intriguing.

—Robert A. Morace

NORMAN, Howard A.

Nationality: American. **Born:** Toledo, Ohio, 4 March 1949. **Education:** Graduated form Western Michigan University; graduate study at the Folklore Institute of Indiana University. **Family:** Married Jane Shore; one daughter. **Career:** Worked variously as a translator for the World Society for the Protection of Animals, as a member of a fire crew in Manitoba, Canada, and as a field naturalist; instructor in Native American literature, University of Maryland; translator and writer. **Agent:** Melanie Jackson Agency, 250 West 57th Street, Suite 1119, New York, New York 10107, U.S.A.

Publications

Novels

The Northern Lights. New York, Summit Books, 1987.
The Bird Artist. New York, Farrar, Straus, 1994.
The Museum Guard. New York, Farrar, Straus, 1998.

Fiction (for children)

The Owl Scatterer, illustrated by Michael McCurdy. Boston, Atlantic Monthly Press, 1986.
Who-Paddled-Backward-with-Trout, illustrated by Ed Young. Boston, Joy Street Books, 1987.
Reteller, *The Girl Who Dreamed Only Geese, and Other Tales of the Far North*, illustrated by Leo and Diane Dillon. New York, Harcourt, 1997.

Short Stories

Kiss in the Hotel Joseph Conrad, and Other Stories. New York, Summit Books, 1989.

Other

Compiler and translator *The Wishing Bone Cycle: Narrative Poems from the Swampy Cree Indians.* Stonehill Publishing, 1976; enlarged edition, Ross-Erikson, 1982.
Compiler and translator *Where the Chill Came From: Cree Windigo Tales and Journeys.* San Francisco, North Point Press, 1982.
Contributor, *Off the Beaten Path: Stories of Place*, edited by Joseph Barbato and Lisa Weinerman Horak. New York, North Point Press, 1998.
Editor, *Northern Tales: Traditional Stories of Eskimo and Indian Peoples*, New York, Pantheon Books, 1990.
Foreword, *Indian Tales* by Jaime de Angulo. New York, North Point Press, 1997.
Introduction, *Lafayette Life: Words and Images Since 1928* by Jane Donovan and Brian McClure. Washington, D.C., Historic Chevy Chase, D.C., 1999.
Reteller, *How Glooskap Outwits the Ice Giants, and Other Tales of the Maritime Indians*, wood engravings by Michael McCurdy. Boston, Little, Brown, 1989.
Reteller, *Trickster and the Fainting Bird*, illustrated by Tom Pohrt. San Diego, Harcourt Brace, 1999.
Translator *The Woe Shirt: Caribbean Folk Tales*, Paule Barton. Penmaen Press, 1980.

* * *

Howard Norman creates characters in the midst of transformation brought on by life's arbitrary occurrences, which most would label fate. These people are compelling, often humorous, slightly odd, and maddeningly introspective. As a result, Norman's novels are the kind that stick with the reader far after the book is finished. Maybe the best single word to describe his style is haunting.

Norman has set each of his novels in remote villages and towns in Canada. ''It is where my imagination, for better or worse, comes alive,'' he has said. The harsh Canadian landscapes are reflected in the mindset of the inhabitants. They are products of their environment and succumb to the unpredictability of life. On the wall in his tiny writing studio in the mountains of Vermont, Norman keeps an old Jewish proverb taped to his desk, ''Man makes plans, God laughs.''

A look into Norman's background exposes many of the themes he now includes in his fiction. He was born in Toledo, Ohio, in 1949, the son of parents who met in a Jewish orphanage. Norman experienced a difficult childhood growing up in Grand Rapids, Michigan. They were poor and an absentee father exacerbated their plight. Norman found solace in libraries and reading, especially the adventure stories of Jack London.

After the death of his best friend, Norman dropped out of high school and went to live with relatives in Toronto. While working in a brush-fire crew, he met Inuit and Cree Indians and developed a fascination with northern folktales. He studied the native languages and realized he wanted to become a writer.

After passing his high school equivalency exam, Norman enrolled in Western Michigan University, graduating with degrees in zoology and English. He later received a Master's degree at Indiana University in folklore. It was life as a freelance writer, however, that would serve as Norman's true education.

He returned to Canada and immersed himself in Indian culture, transcribing stories handed down through generations of Canadian Indians. As a freelancer, he took on every assignment he was offered, including documentaries for Canadian film companies and travel pieces. He moved around frequently and lived in the Arctic and Greenland. Somewhat a loner, Norman modeled naturalist and bird artist Edward Lear, and hoped also to become a bird artist, but readily admits his artistic ability wasn't up to par.

Norman turned his translation efforts into several books. In 1978, he published *The Wishing Bone Cycle: Narrative Poems from the Swampy Cree Indians.* Four years later, a collection of stories came out titled *Where the Chill Came From.* In 1994, he produced another book of translations, *Northern Tales: Traditional Stories of Eskimo and Indian Peoples.*

Norman later followed with two children's books, *How Glooskap Outwits the Ice Giants* and *The Girl Who Dreamed only Geese and Other Tales of the Far North.* Although his work in the North served as a wonderful literary apprenticeship, Norman eventually longed for a more normal life and a center that he did not have as a child or young adult.

After moving to Boston, Norman found his center when he met poet Jane Shore at a friend's house on Thanksgiving in 1981. The two dated and eventually married in 1984. It was Shore who pushed him to work on his novels. Norman was amazed at her dedication to poetry and impressive work ethic.

Norman began writing in earnest and submitted some pages to *Ploughshares*, which published them. This start propelled him toward the 1987 publication of *The Northern Lights*, a novel set in northern Manitoba. The book received vast critical acclaim. Even more surprising, since Norman was virtually unknown at the time, was the book's nomination for the National Book award.

The Northern Lights is a coming-of-age story of Noah Krainik and his best friend Pelly Bay (modeled after Norman's friend Paul, who died of a rare blood disease). Like Norman, Noah and his mother are abandoned by his father. The book is filled with quirky characters, Cree hunters, and self-righteous missionaries. Their world is a lonely one—harsh land with little contact with the outside world. When Pelly is killed in a freak accident, the novel shifts to present-day Toronto.

In 1989, Norman's short story collection *Kiss in the Hotel Joseph Conrad* was published. Set again in isolated upper Canada, the stories deal with unsettled characters who are forced to deal with extremes: temperature, age, feelings, distance—constants in all Norman's work. Forces out of control, mainly the frozen chill of winter, conspire against the characters. Although these people are generally misfits and oddballs, Norman treats their lives with tenderness and compassion.

Critics praised Norman's second novel, *The Bird Artist*, hailing it as ''one of the most perfect and original novels that I have read in years'' and noting that it ''glows like a nightlight in the reader's mind.'' The impetus for the novel developed in the late 1970s while Norman researched a documentary in a fishing village in Newfoundland. He stayed in a church annex that contained a watercolor mural of an ibis. After asking around, he discovered the artist had been acquitted of murder, but then lived as an outcast in the village. The basic blueprint of the novel was formed.

Once again set in Canada, the book explores tiny Witless Bay, Newfoundland, in 1911. It is the story of Fabian Vas, a bird artist who murders his mother's lover, the town lighthouse keeper. It is a tale filled with promiscuity, daily life, and murder. Witless Bay is the quintessential Norman setting: rocky, course, and isolated. The reader feels the tension of the story on every page, which Norman fills with a kind of inevitability. He shows that good people can be driven to do hideous things. *The Bird Artist* also captured a National Book award nomination.

Norman's 1998 novel *The Museum Guard* is the story of DeFoe Russet, an orphaned museum guard who desperately loves Imogen Linny, the caretaker of Halifax's Jewish cemetery. After a mysterious painting entitled ''Jewess on a Street in Amsterdam'' arrives at the museum, Linny starts believing her life is captured in the piece, and she teeters on the brink of insanity. Set in the late 1930s, the novel examines small-town life while also exploring how Hitler's menacing threat in Europe affects its protagonists.

Describing the work, Norman explained, ''I tried to write a novel that was very much about the sense of incipient doom.'' In contrast to his first two novels, *The Museum Guard* explores interior spaces, not the great Canadian spaces. Relationships are the central theme: Russet and his carousing uncle, Edward, who raised him; Linny and the two men; and ultimately the obsession that develops between Linny and the painting itself.

Norman is currently working on his next novel, *The Haunting of L.*, which he says is about faith, reason, and murder. It takes place in the late 1920s in Halifax and grew out of a photograph from the period that reportedly reveals Indian souls rising out of an airplane wreck.

In a brief fiction career, Norman has astounded readers with tales imbibing the mysticism, mystery, and stark contrasts of remote Canada, ultimately drawing on the Indian myths and folklore he learned traveling throughout the tundra. His characters yearn for a better life and search for the right path, always combating the inevitable forks that arise. Norman is a master storyteller, chronicling the lives of common people who deal with the good and bad coupled with human emotions.

—Bob Batchelor

NYE, Robert

Nationality: British. **Born:** London, 15 March 1939. **Education:** Dormans Land, Surrey; Hamlet Court, Westcliff, Essex; Southend High School, Essex. **Family:** Married 1) Judith Pratt in 1959 (divorced 1967), three sons; 2) Aileen Campbell in 1968, one daughter, one stepdaughter, and one stepson. **Career:** Since 1961 freelance writer: since 1967 poetry editor, the *Scotsman,* Edinburgh; since 1971 poetry critic, the *Times,* London. Writer-in-residence, University of Edinburgh, 1976–77. **Awards:** Eric Gregory award, 1963; Scottish Arts Council bursary, 1970, 1973, and publication award, 1970, 1976; James Kennaway Memorial award, 1970; *Guardian* Fiction prize, 1976; Hawthornden prize, 1977; Society of Authors' Travel scholarship, 1991. Fellow, Royal Society of Literature, 1977. **Agent:** Sheil Land Associates, 43 Doughty Street, London WC1N 2LF, England; or, Wallace Literary Agency, 177 East 70th Street, New York, New York 10021, U.S.A. **Address:** 2 Westbury Crescent, Wilton, Cork, Ireland.

PUBLICATIONS

Novels

Doubtfire. London, Calder and Boyars, 1967; New York, Hill and Wang, 1968.

Falstaff. London, Hamish Hamilton, and Boston, Little Brown, 1976.

Merlin. London, Hamish Hamilton, 1978; New York, Putnam, 1979.

Faust. London, Hamish Hamilton, 1980; New York, Putnam, 1981.

The Voyage of the Destiny. London, Hamish Hamilton, and New York, Putnam, 1982.

The Memoirs of Lord Byron. London, Hamish Hamilton, 1989.

The Life and Death of My Lord Gilles de Rais. London, Hamish Hamilton, 1990.

Mrs. Shakespeare: The Complete Works. London, Sinclair-Stevenson, 1993; New York, Arcade Publishing, 2000.

The Late Mr. Shakespeare. London, Chatto & Windus, 1998; New York, Arcade Publishing, 1999.

Short Stories

Tales I Told My Mother. London, Calder and Boyars, 1969; New York, Hill and Wang, 1970.

Penguin Modern Stories 6, with others. London, Penguin, 1970.

The Facts of Life and Other Fictions. London, Hamish Hamilton, 1983.

Uncollected Short Stories

Lines Review 38 (includes 4 stories, verse, and a film script) (Edinburgh), 1971.

Plays

Sawney Bean, with William Watson (produced Edinburgh, 1969; London, 1972; New York, 1982). London, Calder and Boyars, 1970.

Sisters (broadcast 1969; produced Edinburgh, 1973). Included in *Penthesilea, Fugue, and Sisters,* 1975.

Penthesilea, adaptation of the play by Heinrich von Kleist (broadcast 1971; produced London, 1983). Included in *Penthesilea, Fugue, and Sisters,* 1975.
The Seven Deadly Sins: A Mask, music by James Douglas (produced Stirling and Edinburgh, 1973). Rushden, Northamptonshire, Omphalos Press, 1974.
Mr. Poe (produced Edinburgh and London, 1974).
Penthesilea, Fugue, and Sisters. London, Calder and Boyars, 1975.

Radio Plays: *Sisters,* 1969; *A Bloody Stupit Hole,* 1970; *Reynolds, Reynolds,* 1971; *Penthesilea,* 1971; *The Devil's Jig,* music by Humphrey Searle, from a work by Thomas Mann, 1980.

Poetry

Juvenilia 1. Northwood, Middlesex, Scorpion Press, 1961.
Juvenilia 2. Lowestoft, Suffolk, Scorpion Press, 1963.
Darker Ends. London, Calder and Boyars, and New York, Hill and Wang, 1969.
Agnus Dei. Rushden, Northamptonshire, Sceptre Press, 1973.
Two Prayers. Richmond, Surrey, Keepsake Press, 1974.
Five Dreams. Rushden, Northamptonshire, Sceptre Press, 1974.
Divisions on a Ground. Manchester, Carcanet, 1976.
A Collection of Poems 1955–1988. London, Hamish Hamilton, 1989.
14 Poems. Cadognan, France, Editions Ottezec, 1994.
Henry James and Other Poems. Edgewood, Kentucky, Barth, 1995.
Collected Poems. London, Sinclair-Stevenson, 1995.

Other (for children)

Taliesin. London, Faber, 1966; New York, Hill and Wang, 1967.
March Has Horse's Ears. London, Faber, 1966; New York, Hill and Wang, 1967.
Bee Hunter: Adventures of Beowulf. London, Faber, 1968; as *Beowulf: A New Telling,* New York, Hill and Wang, 1968; as *Beowulf, The Bee Hunter,* Faber, 1972.
Wishing Gold. London, Macmillan, 1970; New York, Hill and Wang, 1971.
Poor Pumpkin. London, Macmillan, 1971; as *The Mathematical Princess and Other Stories,* New York, Hill and Wang, 1972.
Cricket: Three Stories. Indianapolis, Bobbs Merrill, 1975; as *Once upon Three Times,* London, Benn, 1978.
Out of the World and Back Again. London, Collins, 1977; as *Out of This World and Back Again,* Indianapolis, Bobbs Merrill, 1978.
The Bird of the Golden Land. London, Hamish Hamilton, 1980.
Harry Pay the Pirate. London, Hamish Hamilton, 1981.
Three Tales. London, Hamish Hamilton, 1983.
Lord Fox and Other Spine-Chilling Tales. London, Orion, 1995.

Other

Editor, *A Choice of Sir Walter Ralegh's Verse.* London, Faber, 1972.
Editor, *William Barnes: A Selection of His Poems.* Cheadle, Cheshire, Carcanet, 1972.
Editor, *A Choice of Swinburne's Verse.* London, Faber, 1973.
Editor, *The Faber Book of Sonnets.* London, Faber, 1976; as *A Book of Sonnets,* New York, Oxford University Press, 1976.
Editor, *The English Sermon 1750–1850.* Manchester, Carcanet, 1976.
Editor, *PEN New Poetry.* London, Quartet, 1986.
Editor, with Elizabeth Friedmann and Alan J. Clark, *First Awakenings: The Early Poems of Laura Riding.* Manchester, Carcanet, and New York, Persea books, 1992.
Editor, *A Selection of the Poems of Laura Riding.* Manchester, Carcanet, 1994.

*

Manuscript Collections: University of Edinburgh; University of Texas, Austin; National Library of Scotland, Edinburgh; Colgate University, Hamilton, New York.

* * *

A hallmark of Robert Nye's fiction has been his ability to harness the imagination to his will, to take the facts of everyday life and to transform them into fantastic happenings so that myth and reality become as one. The stories in *Tales I Told My Mother* rework the lives of literary personalities, and his first novel, *Doubtfire,* ranges in time and space between different worlds with remarkable ease and fluidity of style. Equally fantastic have been his children's novels which have followed faithfully C.S. Lewis's dictum that children's stories should be just as enjoyable to adults.

In later novels such as *Falstaff, Merlin, Faust,* and *The Voyage of the Destiny,* Nye created a quartet of loosely related myths from characters, real or imaginary, who exist in our collective pasts. The worlds that they people are dream-like and fabulous, half-caught, half-forgotten by the subconscious mind. And yet their darksome existence is lightened by Nye's ability to steer away from allegory by making their worlds new again and instantly recognizable: Falstaff lives in an England that is demonstrably fourteenth century, Merlin's world is one of medieval chivalry, and Faust knows a Europe shared by Luther and Calvin.

Falstaff, a novel of 100 chapters, tells the story of Sir John Falstaff—his relationship to the English aristocracy and to the giant of Cerne Abbas, his conduct at the siege of Kildare, his friendship with Prince Hal, and his prowess at the Battle of Agincourt. His adventures, often unlikely and scabrous, unfold before the reader's eyes like a medieval tapestry, and by the end of the novel he has been consumed by the myth he has created for himself, the eternal John Bull, both patriot and buffoon. Myth of a different kind lies at the heart of *Merlin* whose central character is at once the unmistakable Merlin of Sir Thomas Malory's *Le Morte D'Arthur* and at the same time an older, more cunning figure from Welsh vernacular literature and from the poetry of the twelfth-century French poet Robert de Boron, who created a Merlin capable of seeing both past and future and thus able to connect the ancient history of the Grail with the court of King Arthur.

Faust is the story of Dr. Faust's final forty days on Earth, having sold his soul to the devil, and it follows many of the themes of the previous two novels and expands on them: a delight in mixing myth with reality, an earthy eroticism, and a fast-moving dialogue that is both funny and deeply serious. Here the story is seen through the excited reaction of his servant Kit Wagner—a device which Nye was to repeat in *The Life and Death of My Lord Gilles de Rais.* The mythical strain was continued in *The Voyage of the Destiny* which tells the story of Sir Walter Raleigh, explorer, poet, adventurer, and favorite of Queen Elizabeth I. Raleigh himself is the narrator and his voice leads us through the three great voyages of his life: his return from the Americas, his journey through life, and the impending transition from life to death which gives the book its title. As in all

Nye's novels the writing is crisp and lucid, a mixture of scholarly anecdotes racily told and erudite low comedy.

However well crafted and ingenious these novels undoubtedly are, they pale before *The Life and Death of My Lord Gilles de Rais.* As with the other novels, it is based on a historical figure who has assumed mythical proportions: Gilles de Rais, one of the greatest French noblemen of the fifteenth century and a boon companion of Joan of Arc. Unlike *Falstaff* or *Merlin,* though, it has been stripped of literary extravagance and fine flourishes. One reason for the change of mood lies in the subject. Gilles was hanged and his body burned at Nantes in 1440 after he confessed to crimes ranging from pederasty to murder. The second reason, perhaps the more imperative of the two, is the overriding necessity to explore the nature of evil. Gilles has committed his crimes because he has allowed himself to be seduced by pride and vanity, two sins which he fails to recognize in himself. Over 140 children died at his hands, yet throughout his short life he believed that his behavior stood above the law.

All this becomes clear through the testimony of a priest called Blanchet who acts as the narrator and thereby distances the reader from the full horror of Gilles's crimes. This device also allows Blanchet to give his version of the truth, for he, too, was arraigned with Gilles but found not guilty. The other great character in the novel remains unseen: Joan of Arc, who provides Blanchet with the theme of redemption and Christian charity. In his earlier historical novels Nye established himself as one of the most inventive and adventurous of contemporary novelists, with an imagination of Rabelaisian proportions. In *The Life and Death of My Lord Gilles de Rais* he added to that wit and learning profound insights into the nature of evil and a deep understanding of matters Christian.

Two later novels offered fake-book biographies of the English-speaking world's greatest writer. In *Mrs. Shakespeare,* Anne Hathaway offers an insider's view of her husband, but the tale she tells is not nearly as intriguing as that of ''Robert Reynolds alias Pickleherring'' in *The Late Mr. Shakespeare.* An aging actor and a sort of Falstaff type himself, Pickleherring claims to remember all sorts of things about the Bard—including ''facts'' of questionable truth. The novel was well-timed, coming as it did hand-in-hand with *Shakespeare in Love* at the box office: the laughs in *The Late Mr. Shakespeare,* however, run an even wider gamut, with humor appealing to those with greater rather than lesser knowledge of the playwright's works.

—Trevor Royle

O

OATES, Joyce Carol

Pseudonym: Rosamond Smith. **Nationality:** American. **Born:** Millersport, New York, 16 June 1938. **Education:** Syracuse University, New York, 1956–60, B.A. in English 1960 (Phi Beta Kappa); University of Wisconsin, Madison, M.A. in English 1961; Rice University, Houston, 1961. **Family:** Married Raymond J. Smith in 1961. **Career:** Instructor, 1961–65, and assistant professor of English, 1965–67, University of Detroit; member of the Department of English, University of Windsor, Ontario, 1967–78. Since 1978 writer-in-residence, and currently Roger S. Berlind Distinguished Professor, Princeton University, New Jersey. Since 1974 publisher, with Raymond J. Smith, *Ontario Review,* Windsor, later Princeton. **Awards:** National Endowment for the Arts grant, 1966, 1968; Guggenheim fellowship, 1967; O. Henry award, 1967, 1973, and Special Award for Continuing Achievement, 1970, 1986; Rosenthal award, 1968; National Book award, 1970; Rea award, for short story, 1990; Bobst Lifetime Achievement award, 1990; Heideman award, 1990, for one-act play; Walt Whitman award, 1995. **Member:** American Academy, 1978. **Agent:** John Hawkins and Associates, 71 West 23rd Street, Suite 1600, New York, New York 10010. **Address:** Department of Creative Writing, Princeton University, 185 Nassau Street, Princeton, New Jersey 08540, U.S.A.

PUBLICATIONS

Novels

With Shuddering Fall. New York, Vanguard Press, 1964; London, Cape, 1965.
A Garden of Earthly Delights. New York, Vanguard Press, 1967; London, Gollancz, 1970.
Expensive People. New York, Vanguard Press, 1968; London, Gollancz, 1969.
Them. New York, Vanguard Press, 1969; London, Gollancz, 1971.
Wonderland. New York, Vanguard Press, 1971; London, Gollancz, 1972.
Do with Me What You Will. New York, Vanguard Press, 1973; London, Gollancz, 1974.
The Assassins: A Book of Hours. New York, Vanguard Press, 1975.
Childwold. New York, Vanguard Press, 1976; London, Gollancz, 1977.
Son of the Morning. New York, Vanguard Press, 1978; London, Gollancz, 1979.
Cybele. Santa Barbara, California, Black Sparrow Press, 1979.
Unholy Loves. New York, Vanguard Press, 1979; London, Gollancz, 1980.
Bellefleur. New York, Dutton, 1980; London, Cape, 1981.
Angel of Light. New York, Dutton, and London, Cape, 1981.
A Bloodsmoor Romance. New York, Dutton, 1982; London, Cape, 1983.
Mysteries of Winterthurn. New York, Dutton, and London, Cape, 1984.
Solstice. New York, Dutton, and London, Cape, 1985.
Marya: A Life. New York, Dutton, 1986; London, Cape, 1987.
You Must Remember This. New York, Dutton, 1987; London, Macmillan, 1988.
American Appetites. New York, Dutton, and London, Macmillan, 1989.
Because It Is Bitter, and Because It Is My Heart. New York, Dutton, 1990; London, Macmillan, 1991.
I Lock My Door upon Myself. New York, Ecco Press, 1990.
The Rise of Life on Earth. New York, New Directions, 1991.
Black Water. New York, Dutton, 1992.
Foxfire: Confessions of a Girl Gang. New York, Dutton, 1993.
What I Lived For. New York, Dutton, 1994.
Zombie. New York, Dutton, 1995.
First Love: A Gothic Tale, designed and illustrated by Barry Moser. Hopewell, New Jersey, Ecco Press, 1996.
Tenderness. Princeton, New Jersey, Ontario Review Press, 1996.
We Were the Mulvaneys. New York, Dutton, 1996.
Man Crazy. New York, Dutton, 1997.
My Heart Laid Bare. New York, Dutton, 1998.
Broke Heart Blues. New York, Dutton, 1999.
Blonde. Hopewell, New Jersey, Ecco Press, 2000.

Novels as Rosamond Smith

Lives of the Twins. New York, Simon and Schuster, 1987.
Soul-Mate. New York, Dutton, 1989.
Snake Eyes. New York, Dutton, 1992.
You Can't Catch Me. New York, Dutton, 1995.
Starr Bright Will Be With You Soon. New York, Dutton, 1999.

Short Stories

By the North Gate. New York, Vanguard Press, 1963.
Upon the Sweeping Flood and Other Stories. New York, Vanguard Press, 1966; London, Gollancz, 1973.
The Wheel of Love and Other Stories. New York, Vanguard Press, 1970; London, Gollancz, 1971.
Cupid and Psyche. New York, Albondocani Press, 1970.
Marriages and Infidelities. New York, Vanguard Press, 1972; London, Gollancz, 1974.
A Posthumous Sketch. Los Angeles, Black Sparrow Press, 1973.
The Girl. Cambridge, Massachusetts, Pomegranate Press, 1974.
Plagiarized Material (as Fernandes/Oates). Los Angeles, Black Sparrow Press, 1974.
The Goddess and Other Women. New York, Vanguard Press, 1974; London, Gollancz, 1975.
Where Are You Going, Where Have You Been? Stories of Young America. Greenwich, Connecticut, Fawcett, 1974.
The Hungry Ghosts: Seven Allusive Comedies. Los Angeles, Black Sparrow Press, 1974; Solihull, Warwickshire, Aquila, 1975.
The Seduction and Other Stories. Los Angeles, Black Sparrow Press, 1975.
The Poisoned Kiss and Other Stories from the Portuguese (as Fernandes/Oates). New York, Vanguard Press, 1975; London, Gollancz, 1976.

The Triumph of the Spider Monkey. Santa Barbara, California, Black Sparrow Press, 1976.
The Blessing. Santa Barbara, California, Black Sparrow Press, 1976.
Crossing the Border. New York, Vanguard Press, 1976; London, Gollancz, 1978.
Daisy. Santa Barbara, California, Black Sparrow Press, 1977.
Night-Side. New York, Vanguard Press, 1977; London, Gollancz, 1979.
A Sentimental Education. Los Angeles, Sylvester and Orphanos, 1978.
The Step-Father. Northridge, California, Lord John Press, 1978.
All the Good People I've Left Behind. Santa Barbara, California, Black Sparrow Press, 1979.
The Lamb of Abyssalia. Cambridge, Massachusetts, Pomegranate Press, 1979.
A Middle-Class Education. New York, Albondocani Press, 1980.
A Sentimental Education (collection). New York, Dutton, 1980; London, Cape, 1981.
Funland. Concord, New Hampshire, Ewert, 1983.
Last Days. New York, Dutton, 1984; London, Cape, 1985.
Wild Saturday and Other Stories. London, Dent, 1984.
Wild Nights. Athens, Ohio, Croissant, 1985.
Raven's Wing. New York, Dutton, 1986; London, Cape, 1987.
The Assignation. New York, Ecco Press, 1988.
Heat and Other Stories. New York, Dutton, 1991.
Where Is Here? Hopewell, New Jersey, Ecco, 1992.
Haunted: Tales of the Grotesque. New York, Dutton, 1994.
Will You Always Love Me? and Other Stories. New York, Dutton, 1996.
The Collector of Hearts: New Tales of the Grotesque. New York, Dutton, 1998.

Plays

The Sweet Enemy (produced New York, 1965).
Sunday Dinner (produced New York, 1970).
Ontological Proof of My Existence, music by George Prideaux (produced New York, 1972). Included in *Three Plays,* 1980.
Miracle Play (produced New York, 1973). Los Angeles, Black Sparrow Press, 1974.
Daisy (produced New York, 1980).
Three Plays (includes *Ontological Proof of My Existence, Miracle Play, The Triumph of the Spider Monkey*). Windsor, Ontario Review Press, 1980.
The Triumph of the Spider Monkey, from her own story (produced Los Angeles, 1985). Included in *Three Plays,* 1980.
Presque Isle, music by Paul Shapiro (produced New York, 1982).
Lechery, in *Faustus in Hell* (produced Princeton, New Jersey, 1985).
In Darkest America (*Tone Clusters* and *The Eclipse*) (produced Louisville, Kentucky, 1990; *The Eclipse* produced New York, 1990).
American Holiday (produced Los Angeles, 1990).
I Stand Before You Naked (produced New York, 1991).
How Do You Like Your Meat? (produced New Haven, Connecticut, 1991).
Twelve Plays. New York, Dutton, 1991.
Black (produced Williamstown, 1992).
The Secret Mirror (produced Philadelphia, 1992).
The Perfectionist (produced Princeton, New Jersey, 1993). In *The Perfectionist and Other Plays,* 1995.
The Truth-Teller (produced New York, 1995).
Here She Is! (produced Philadelphia, 1995).
The Perfectionist and Other Plays. Hopewell, New Jersey, Ecco, 1995.
New Plays. Princeton, New Jersey, Ontario Review Press, 1998.

Poetry

Women in Love and Other Poems. New York, Albondocani Press, 1968.
Anonymous Sins and Other Poems. Baton Rouge, Louisiana State University Press, 1969.
Love and Its Derangements. Baton Rouge, Louisiana State University Press, 1970.
Woman Is the Death of the Soul. Toronto, Coach House Press, 1970.
In Case of Accidental Death. Cambridge, Massachusetts, Pomegranate Press, 1972.
Wooded Forms. New York, Albondocani Press, 1972.
Angel Fire. Baton Rouge, Louisiana State University Press, 1973.
Dreaming America and Other Poems. New York, Aloe Editions, 1973.
The Fabulous Beasts. Baton Rouge, Louisiana State University Press, 1975.
Public Outcry. Pittsburgh, Slow Loris Press, 1976.
Season of Peril. Santa Barbara, California, Black Sparrow Press, 1977.
Abandoned Airfield 1977. Northridge, California, Lord John Press, 1977.
Snowfall. Northridge, California, Lord John Press, 1978.
Women Whose Lives Are Food, Men Whose Lives Are Money. Baton Rouge, Louisiana State University Press, 1978.
The Stone Orchard. Northridge, California, Lord John Press, 1980.
Celestial Timepiece. Dallas, Pressworks, 1980.
Nightless Nights: Nine Poems. Concord, New Hampshire, Ewert, 1981.
Invisible Woman: New and Selected Poems 1970–1982. Princeton, New Jersey, Ontario Review Press, 1982.
Luxury of Sin. Northridge, California, Lord John Press, 1984.
The Time Traveller: Poems 1983–1989. New York, Dutton, 1989.

Other

The Edge of Impossibility: Tragic Forms in Literature. New York, Vanguard Press, 1972; London, Gollancz, 1976.
The Hostile Sun: The Poetry of D.H. Lawrence. Los Angeles, Black Sparrow Press, 1973; Solihull, Warwickshire, Aquila, 1975.
New Heaven, New Earth: The Visionary Experience in Literature. New York, Vanguard Press, 1974; London, Gollancz, 1976.
The Stone Orchard. Northridge, California, Lord John Press, 1980.
Contraries: Essays. New York, Oxford University Press, 1981.
The Profane Art: Essays and Reviews. New York, Dutton, 1983.
Funland. Concord, New Hampshire, Ewert, 1983.
On Boxing, photographs by John Ranard. New York, Doubleday, and London, Bloomsbury, 1987; expanded edition, Hopewell, New Jersey, Ecco, 1994.
(Woman) Writer: Occasions and Opportunities. New York, Dutton, 1988.
Conversations with Joyce Carol Oates, edited by Lee Milazzo. Jackson, University Press of Mississippi, 1989.

George Bellows: American Artist. Hopewell, New Jersey, Ecco Press, 1995.
Come Meet Muffin (for children), illustrated by Mark Graham. Hopewell, New Jersey, Ecco Press, 1998.
Where I've Been, and Where I'm Going: Essays, Reviews, and Prose. New York, Plume, 1999.
Editor, *Scenes from American Life: Contemporary Short Fiction.* New York, Vanguard Press, 1973.
Editor, with Shannon Ravenel, *The Best American Short Stories 1979.* Boston, Houghton Mifflin, 1979.
Editor, *Night Walks: A Bedside Companion.* Princeton, New Jersey, Ontario Review Press, 1982.
Editor *First Person Singular: Writers on Their Craft.* Princeton, New Jersey, Ontario Review Press, 1983.
Editor, with Boyd Litzinger, *Story: Fictions Past and Present.* Lexington, Massachusetts, Heath, 1985.
Editor, with Daniel Halpern, *Reading the Fights* (on boxing). New York, Holt, 1988.
Editor, *The Essential Dickinson.* Hopewell, New Jersey, Ecco Press, 1996.
Editor, *American Gothic Tales.* New York, Plume, 1996.
Editor, *Tales of H.P. Lovecraft: Major Works.* Hopewell, New Jersey, Ecco Press, 1997.
Editor, with R.V. Cassill, *The Norton Anthology of Contemporary Fiction.* New York, Norton, 1998.
Editor, *Telling Stories: An Anthology for Writers.* New York, Norton, 1998.

*

Bibliography: *Joyce Carol Oates: An Annotated Bibliography* by Francine Lercangée, New York, Garland, 1986.

Manuscript Collection: Syracuse University, New York.

Critical Studies: *The Tragic Vision of Joyce Carol Oates* by Mary Kathryn Grant, Durham, North Carolina, Duke University Press, 1978; *Joyce Carol Oates* by Joanne V. Creighton, Boston, Twayne, 1979; *Critical Essays on Joyce Carol Oates* edited by Linda W. Wagner, Boston, Hall, 1979; *Dreaming America: Obsession and Transcendence in the Fiction of Joyce Carol Oates* by G.F. Waller, Baton Rouge, Louisiana State University Press, 1979; *Joyce Carol Oates* by Ellen G. Friedman, New York, Ungar, 1980; *Joyce Carol Oates's Short Stories: Between Tradition and Innovation* by Katherine Bastian, Bern, Switzerland, Lang, 1983; *Isolation and Contact: A Study of Character Relationships in Joyce Carol Oates's Short Stories 1963–1980* by Torborg Norman, Gothenburg, Studies in English, 1984; *The Image of the Intellectual in the Short Stories of Joyce Carol Oates* by Hermann Severin, New York, Lang, 1986; *Joyce Carol Oates: Artist in Residence* by Eileen Teper Bender, Bloomington, Indiana University Press, 1987; *Understanding Joyce Carol Oates* by Greg Johnson, Columbia, University of South Carolina Press, 1987; *Joyce Carol Oates: Novels of the Middle Years* by Joanne V. Creighton, New York, Twayne, 1992; *Joyce Carol Oates: A Study of the Short Fiction* by Greg Johnson, New York, Twayne Publishers and Toronto, Maxwell Macmillan Canada, 1994; *Lavish Self-Divisions: The Novels of Joyce Carol Oates* by Brenda Daly, Jackson, University Press of Mississippi, 1996; *Invisible Writer: A Biography of Joyce Carol Oates* by Greg Johnson, New York, Dutton, 1998; *Critical Reception of the Short Fiction by Joyce Carol Oates and Gabriele Wohmann* by Sigrid Mayer and Martha Hanscom, Columbia, South Carolina, Camden House, 1998.

* * *

Joyce Carol Oates is among the most able American novelists writing today and belongs in a long tradition of serious literary novelists who also had broad popular appeal, including her American predecessors, Edith Wharton and Henry James, as well as their British counterparts, George Eliot, Charles Dickens, and earlier, Fanny Burney. Some of her detractors have been suspicious of a writer whose productivity is nothing short of staggering, and they have tended to underestimate her talent, complaining of the looseness of her writing, the sensationalistic nature of many of her stories, and her lurid imagination.

Her recent books invite some comparisons with the writing of John Updike and Saul Bellow. She and Updike share an uncanny knack for understanding middle America, suburbia, and the temper of the times. Updike, too, shares Oates's delight in witches, although the two treat their subjects quite differently. Bellow and Oates have less in common, although both see themselves as novelists of ideas and both have written in a comedic and parodic style about the academy. Bellow is a wittier writer and the more elegant stylist. Both authors have very recently produced imaginative accounts of public figures, prompting critics to ponder the motives behind their choice of subject and to raise interesting questions about the relationship between a writer and real life and how those relationships translate themselves in fiction.

Bellow's novel, *Ravelstein,* and Oates's novel, *Blonde,* take as their subject Allan Bloom and Norma Jean Baker—''Marilyn Monroe,'' respectively. Both authors made their careers at universities and both fill their books with references and allusions to the world of ideas and literature. Bloom, the real man behind the fictive Ravelstein, was a professor in the Committee of Social Thought at the University of Chicago and a close friend of the author. He was heralded as the darling of the right wing conservatives when his book, *The Closing of the American Mind,* was at the height of its popularity. *Blonde*'s subject is the life of the very troubled woman-made-star and sex goddess, whose screen image circulated globally, receiving more adulation and attention than most any other star in this century. Oates is the latest of a number of famous artists and writers who have chosen to write about or paint Monroe, including Gloria Steinem, Norman Mailer, and Ed Paschke.

Oates's decision to write about Norma Jean Baker is not unexpected. It allows her to immerse herself in the distorted psychosexuality of the woman and write about the sex act with an abandon and graphic literalness that has increasingly become part of her style in recent writings. In *Zombie* she takes on the voice of a sexual-psychopathic serial killer, Quentin P. With chilling effect, she enters the mind of the killer, utterly devoid of conscience, assuming his stream-of-consciousness. She showed her interest in public figures earlier in *Black Water* where she treated the drowning at Chippaquiddick. Her taste for stories that make screaming headlines and haunt the public imagination for many years to come is one of her trademarks.

The process of myth making that transforms a life into ballads, legends, and stories has long fascinated her. She is intrigued by cult figures and the way they reflect the subterranean needs of their age. Her propensity to write about seemingly vacuous women, usually illegitimate, self-destructive, spoiled, beautiful, and empty, although often in fact, highly intelligent, has been in evidence since her very earliest novels.

Oates may have taken Marilyn for her subject in order to guarantee herself book sales, but a more important motive was probably her desire to write about a woman whose image as much as any other female star in American film—including such greats as Greta Garbo or Ingrid Bergmann—has captured the American psyche and achieved iconic proportions that ensure her a place in twentieth-century cultural history. The subject allows Oates to explore the ways in which a culture invents such icons. She tries empathetically to capture the psyche of the actual woman, whose life has been appropriated by the media and society, exposing what it must have felt like to inhabit her body and mind. This act of recuperation is precisely the kind of challenge that Oates the thinker has always found attractive.

Blonde has sparked a range of responses and in curious ways contributed to the view of Oates as a glib, often sloppy, writer, with too predictable, albeit grotesque and sometimes sleazy, an imagination. The book does have its fair share of anachronisms, inconsistencies, and erratic scholarship. Nonetheless, it brilliantly expresses the inner and outer life of this film goddess/whore and captures the world of Hollywood, California and New York and its school of Method Acting replete with all their personalities. The book's narrative structure is complex. Oates assumes many voices and perspectives in order to show, as Jean-Paul Sartre is quoted to say on the opening pages, how ''Genius is not a gift, but the way a person invents in desperate circumstances.''

Opening with the section ''Special Delivery'' in which a package is handed to Marilyn by Death in an early evening in Brentwood, California, on August 3, 1962, the novel chronicles Baker's life as a child, a girl, a woman, ''Marilyn,'' and her afterlife years. It concludes with her actual death, deciding to draw on one of the controversial accounts of Marilyn's last hours. She has Marilyn die at the hands of the Sharpshooter, an employee of the Agency, who inserts a lethal dose of Nembutal directly into her heart. Oates describes her book as fictive, in which she creates the radically distilled ''life'' of Monroe, collapsing twelve sets of foster parents into one frightening pair, and making other alterations, including her version of Monroe's death, to fit her needs as a novelist. As is her practice, she draws heavily on biographical sources on Marilyn and on the film-industry to give her book a richness of specificity that is characteristic of her best writing. She does not use original material or interviews since a determination of the facts of Marilyn's life is not of paramount importance. She does a superb job of studying film footage, photographs, and the famous nude poster and finding the exact words to call up the image and to describe Monroe's excitement and genius when in front of the camera.

She fully enters into her subject, penning some of Marilyn's poems and constructing the dialogues between Marilyn and her three husbands that have a ring of authenticity—the reader almost believes that these must really have been her words, the way she would talk with the Ex-Athlete, the Playwright, and the President, the names Oates assigns to Marilyn's two husbands, Joe DiMaggio and Arthur Miller, and her lover, John F. Kennedy. Two other screen presences, The Fair Prince and the Dark Prince, frame Oates's account of Norma Jean's life and explain, mythopoetically, the source of the child's love affair with her Magic Image in the mirror. The little girl sits in movie houses, watching these two enchanted creatures, awaiting their final perfect kiss, fearing there will be no closure, and wanting to be in life what she has seen in the movies, an image that has no other meaning beyond itself. Ultimately, it is Cass Chaplin whose final package to her practices a joke so cruel that only Nembutal can ease her. He is the doomed son of the silent movie star, Charlie Chaplin. It is Charlie Chaplin's dark eyes gazing out of a poster from *City-Lights* that lit up Norma Jean's world when she lived in squalor as a child with her mentally unstable, finally unfit, mother. This alcoholic, drug-besotted man with movie-star good looks is at once her kindred spirit in the novel and her cruel betrayer.

Bellow states that he wrote *Ravelstein* to honor a promise to his friend and colleague to write about him and give him immortality. The book also allowed him to more nakedly treat himself in fiction, under the guise of Chick, than he had done before, and it offered him a chance of write of his own near-death experience and his gratitude and love for his young wife. Most important, it expresses his love for not just the character in the book, but for the man whose life became his subject. In this sense, this last book of Bellow's is more revealing than any other. In Oates's case, the motive for the book must lie in her preoccupation with myths and how they express themselves in today's American culture and her desire to redeem Monroe from the unnatural, almost caricatured woman that circulates in late twentieth-century discourse. At a deeper level, her need to get way inside of Norma Jean Baker and her inventions, suggests that Oates's own writings, so full of inventions and fabulations, answer some urgent need to find words that can give expression to some fundamental truths—often unnamable or unspeakable until a writer finds words for them—about lived experience.

Any assessment of Oates's accomplishments should admit that the sheer quantity and range of her writing is impressive. In addition to her numerous novels since her first, *With Shuddering Fall,* she has written many volumes of short stories, poems, plays, and criticism. She usually writes about extraordinary people whose fanatical desire to compel life to conform to their vision finally becomes all consuming and self-destructive. Most frequently, these figures are imaginary. In *Blonde,* Oates totally invests herself in creating the inner life of the quintessential doomed woman, Marilyn Monroe. In all of these books, Oates relentlessly charts the disintegration of the self.

Son of the Morning offers perhaps her most shocking and gripping exploration of this theme. A Pentecostal preacher, Nathanael Vickery, witnesses seven visitations from the Lord, each more terrifying than the last. Nathanael is left with the knowledge that God has withdrawn himself and left him to sink back into oblivion and write the book of himself. In other novels, Oates moves beyond a vision in which man can free himself only through an explosion of violence. These novels work toward quieter endings in which her central protagonists survive and transcend their nightmarish experiences to construct more stable lives, integrating themselves into the social fabric.

In one of her recent novels, *Broke Heart Blues,* she tells the story of John Reddy Heart, an adolescent 1960s hero—a sort of combination of Jimmy Dean, Marlon Brando, and Elvis Presley—who is accused of murdering his mother's lover in her bed when he is sixteen years old. The novel covers more than thirty years and is written largely from the point of view of John Reddy Heart's idols. It includes a section where Heart finally unfolds his story, totally reframing the incidents of the night in question. He depicts a very different, and wholly innocent, man complete with his sense of self-sacrifice which has molded his life to the needs of the moment, where he has simply ''done what he had to do'' and allowed others, also, to ''do what they have to do.'' This novel has all the characteristics of Oates's writing at its best. Her sense of the period is uncanny and done with meticulous detail and a feel for the times, the dress codes, the popular music, the favorite films, and so on. She has an absolute flair for dialogue and a genius for types. Her characters come from an affluent upper-state New York suburb. Oates shows them caught up in each fad of their time. Each represents a type but is delineated with breathtaking originality. There are the boy-crazed screaming teenage girls, the elite, snobby group of popular boys and girls who had started school together in kindergarten, the acne-scarred, pimple-faced adolescents, the plain, pudgy-faced sad girl, the rowdies and the straights, and the fat girl nobody liked who was notorious for keeping her Death Chronicles. You cannot read about these characters without recalling your own teenage years and all the subsequent reunions. The novel's ending is a tour-de-force as Oates chronicles the final thirtieth reunion and all the misadventures as well as successes that attend it. It weirdly echoes the language and structure of James Joyce and Anthony Burgess in a way the reader will relish.

Oates also exploits the macabre. In *Black Water,* she delves into the consciousness and the experience of drowning in her imaginative recreation of the Teddy Kennedy/Mary Jo Kopechne incident at Chippaquiddick. In *Foxfire: Confessions of a Girl Gang,* Maddy-Monkey, the official chronicler of the gang, shares the secrets and rites of the gang. She dwells on the fateful year of 1956 when their crimes led to the notorious kidnapping and ransoming of Whitney Kellogg, Jr. Their leader, Legs Sadovsky, mysteriously disappeared never to be seen again, or at least the chronicler of the confessions is uncertain that a recent sighting has any validity. An even more disturbing portrait of a deranged mind appears in *Zombie,* reminiscent of Paul Theroux's shocking novel, *Chicago Loop,* published five years earlier and similarly offering the stream-of-consciousness of a perverted mind.

Oates's appetite as a writer is as voracious as the will of her most willful protagonists. She consumes and disgorges experience, her own and that of others. She has recast the visions and stories of numerous writers, exhibiting her debt to Dostoyevsky, Flaubert, Kafka, Mann, and Balzac while remaining firmly planted in the American realistic and naturalistic narrative traditions. She has imaginatively entered in the lives of Pentecostal preachers, children of the slums, a nineteenth-century detective, professors in academia, schoolteachers, artists, a drowned woman, and countless others.

Although there are Continental influences, her writing is thoroughly American, after the manner of Fitzgerald and Faulkner, Dreiser, Farrell, and Mailer. Faulkner's Yoknapatawpha County is her fictitious Eden County, set near Millersport, New York, where she lived as a child. Farrell's Chicago is her Detroit: Studs Lonigan is made over into Jules and Maureen Wendall in *Them.* Fitzgerald's Gatsby is her Jules, a man in love with the aloofness money brings, crazily hungry for Nadine, Daisy's counterpart in *Them.* Oates is fascinated with property and the violence it engenders in those obsessed with it. She struggles to write an American epic, built around a dynastic family that will express the American experience.

Bellefleur is her ambitious attempt at such an epic, an attempt that eluded the grasp of writers whose talents dwarf her—Melville and Twain, Faulkner and Bellow. *A Bloodsmoor Romance* and *Mysteries of Winterthurn* continue Oates's treatment of nineteenth-century and early twentieth-century America. Each imitates brilliantly the genre of the Gothic saga, the romance, and the detective novel respectively.

Oates is a storyteller of considerable gifts. She is also a writer's writer. In her novels of social and psychological realism, she reveals little interest in postmodern experimental modes, avoiding the dexterous verbal play and intricate parodic structures developed by John Barth, Thomas Pynchon, or Donald Barthelme. John Updike and Bellow are writers more to her tastes. She has also embarked on literary projects in which fabulation, invention, and intertextuality figure prominently. In these, her flair for irony and her playful, sometimes nasty, reimaginings of popular nineteenth-century genres are evident, but the novels remain ultimately stable in their meaning. They are not true works of deconstruction or postmodernity. She often writes with a social purpose out of concerns that are moral, psychological, and political. There are times, however, when the violence in her novels seems gratuitous and the work itself seems, finally, immoral. *Expensive People* is such a book.

Childwold and *Cybele* mark Oates's shift away from naturalism, with *The Assassins* figuring as a transitional, experimental work. The assassin who stalks Andrew Petrie, the one-time senator, is Andrew. The murderer is monistic thinking, the willful fixation upon one idea, be it religious, philosophical, or literary. It severs the individual from the community of man, isolating and destroying him. The monism encases its believer in isolation as total as that which Hugh experiences as a paralytic, breathing with the aid of an iron lung, without his sight. *Bellefleur* and *Unholy Loves*—few books could be less alike—testify to Oates's skill and range.

Bellefleur is a vast, sprawling book that weirdly welds the natural and the supernatural together to create a psychologically and imaginatively plausible history of six generations of the Bellefleur family from 1744 to the present. The book stretches the genre of American Gothic, including history in its domain. *Unholy Loves* is a tightly constructed, unified book: five chapters, five parties, it lays bare the soul of Brigit Stott, a recent divorcée, member of the English department, and a writer in a university modeled after Syracuse University, where Oates earned her undergraduate degree. *Unholy Loves* and *American Appetites* belong with Kingsley Amis's *Lucky Jim* and Iris Murdoch's *A Severed Head. Unholy Loves* contains scenes of erupting violence, but the general atmosphere is one of forced conviviality. Oates knows intimately the scandals of the university, the ambitions, the bitchiness, pomposity, petty jealousy, and colossal loneliness that are endemic to modern university life.

Marya: A Life and *Solstice* each extend Oates's treatment of teachers and academics. The first is in some ways an autobiographical book, treating in eleven disconnected episodes the life of a woman from her squalid origins to her rapid success as a writer. *Solstice* is an absorbing study of an obsessive relationship between Monica Jensen, a thirtyish divorcée and teacher in a private school in the wilds of Pennsylvania, and a much older, widowed, eccentric artist, Sheila Trask, whose self-dramatization and self-destructiveness ensnare Monica, binding her in a relationship as passionate and all-consuming as any Oates had earlier delineated.

Cybele and *Childwold* move away from the quasi-naturalistic fiction that dominated Oates's early writing. *Childwold* is lyrical. It is set in Eden County. Nature is mysterious and erotic and, in a Faulknerian manner, Oates celebrates the survivors. *Cybele* is more disturbing. Edwin Locke is the luckless victim of *Cybele,* the great goddess of nature who asks for nothing less than the life of this man who falls under her enchantment during his midlife crisis. She is a demanding goddess; he pays her the ultimate sacrifice when he allows himself to be consumed by his own passions. He confuses eros with love and falls. The action of *Cybele* is similar to that of *Do With Me What You Will.* However, love redeems Elena in the latter novel, whereas Edwin never experiences it. The narrative angle of *Cybele* shifts, reflecting Oates's desire to move more overtly into the realm of the demonic and the unconscious which dominate her novels *Bellefleur, A Bloodsmoor Romance,* and *Mysteries of Winterthurn.*

Much has been written about Oates's obsession with violence. Rape, incest, patricide, infanticide, self-mutilation, animal mutilation, suicide, wife beating, child abuse, murder, and drowning abound in her fiction. Sometimes the violence is gratuitous—too often it is sensational—but more often than one wants to admit, it demands to be confronted. Conceptions are violent in her fiction, blighting the children born of them. In *Them,* Jules is conceived in a coupling that results in the murder of his natural father by his mother's brother, leaving his mother bathed in the blood of her dead lover and hostage to the policemen whose help she seeks. The violence that marked his conception doggedly pursues him. Hopelessly drawn to Nadine, he finds himself the target of her gun after a night of lovemaking in which he could not satisfy her. Later, caught up in the chaos of the Detroit fires, he kills a man and paradoxically recovers himself.

Nathanael Vickery, the Pentecostal preacher of *Son of the Morning,* is a child born of his mother's rape. Lacking a father, he grows up believing he is God's child and that his will is not his own. The initiation that rids him of this delusion, leaving him a nullity, is a terrifying one. When God withdraws from this man he has inhabited for 35 years, Nathanael is left without words or gestures. He crawls off the platform where he had been preaching before thousands, numbering himself among the damned. Stephen, in *The Assassins,* and Jebediah, in *Bellefleur,* are similarly abandoned by the god of their willful self-creation. In *Bellefleur* Oates includes every one of the violent acts mentioned above and more. Germaine is one of the Bellefleurs who survives. Her father, Gideon, wrecks his vengeance on his past and his wife when he flies his plane into the Bellefleur Mansion, destroying it, himself, his wife, and her numerous followers. The special child he saves is the child whose chilling birth opens the book. She is born a biological freak, with the genitalia of a male twin protruding from her abdomen to be sliced off by her quick-thinking mother. Judith Rossner's *Attachments,* seems to have had an unfortunate influence on Oates's already sufficiently grotesque imagination.

A Bloodsmoor Romance is a nineteenth-century romance, narrated by a young virgin and chronicling the ''ignominious'' history of the five marriageable daughters of the Zinn family settled in the Bloodsmoor valley of Pennsylvania. More overtly feminist than Oates's earlier writings, this book has been described as the other side of *Little Women,* the tale it did not dare to tell. The style is turgid; the tale replete with the trademarks of historical romance-fainting virgins, a sudden abduction, ghosts, and the unspeakable evils of drink and dissipation. An odd mingling of myth and history, *A Bloodsmoor Romance* and its successor, *Mysteries of Winterthurn,* indulge Oates's excursions into Victoriana and humor.

Mysteries of Winterthurn disguises itself as a detective story told by an orotund, male connoisseur of criminal investigations while it probes the mystery of personality and religion. The detective-hero, Xavier Kilgarvan, confronts three bizarre cases, each separated by twelve years. The first begins when he is but a twelve-year-old boy, besmitten with his wayward cousin and caught up in a bizarre series of bedchamber murders, the first being the vampirish murder of a child. The second mystery, ''Devil's Half-Acre; or the Mystery of the 'Cruel Suitor,''' occurs twelve years later and involves a succession of butchered factory girls. The third case, ''The Blood-Stained Bridal Groom,'' involves an outbreak of frenzy in a disbeliever resulting in the death of a clergyman, his mother, and a female parishioner. The detective finally surrenders to brain fever and forgetfulness rather than know what Perdita, his wayward cousin, has done. The story dissolves into one of radical ambiguity in which guilt and innocence cannot be distinguished. All three of the sagas of nineteenth-century America are full of ghastly circumstances, authorial asides, quaint, baroque descriptions, extravagances, and morbid preoccupations. All three are pointedly feminist. All are stylistically indulgent.

After plumbing the depths of chaotic nightmares and the annihilation of the self, Oates, in the mid-1980s began to reconfigure her tragic vision, concentrating more on a character's capacity to survive and transcend. She revisits the naturalistic landscape of her earlier fiction but with some noteworthy differences. She continues to minutely depict American cultural history, returning to the era of the Depression in flashbacks in *You Must Remember This* and fleshing out her description of America between 1944 and 1956, complete with bomb shelters and civil defense drills, the adulation of Eisenhower, the Army-McCarthy hearings, and the electrocution of the Rosenbergs. In *I Lock the Door Upon Myself,* she imaginatively reenters a turn-of-the-century rural community, recounting the narrative of a willful white woman's defiant flight with a black itinerant water diviner. In *American Appetites,* the main action occurs in 1986. It is set in Hazelton-on-Hudson, New York, at the prestigious Institute for Independent Research in the Social Sciences, yet the book also captures the flavor of the 1980s. Returning to the vein of *Unholy Loves,* Oates satirizes the petty rivalries and pretensions of illustrious members of the American research university while she unfolds a terrifying story of an eruption of domestic violence that results in the death of the wife and criminal charges against her husband, the protagonist, Ian McCullough. *Foxfire* is set in upstate New York and the episodes recalled occur in the mid-1950s. Oates explores the sensibility and dreams of the young, impressionable, wild, bad adolescent girl. The story of the exploits of the girl gang members starts innocently enough but draws them into a world of thievery and prostitution and threatens to destroy them all when they act on their kidnapping plot.

The difference in the evolving sensibility of Oates lies in her handling of the aftermath of the violence unleashed in her novels. In *Because It Is Bitter, and Because It Is My Heart, You Must Remember This,* and *Foxfire,* the protagonists survive the brutal events that threaten to engulf them. In the first, Iris Courtney is both complicit in a black man's murder of an adolescent thug and a victim of her father's neglect and her mother's whorish, alcoholic life, and yet she endures to move beyond these events in her past. In the second, Enid, suicidal at the opening of the novel and suffering from anorexia nervosa, survives the protracted incestuous relationship with her uncle to marry and come to a forgiveness of those who hurt her. *American Appetites,* in some respects one of the most shocking novels she has written, also emerges from its dark night of the soul, portraying an altered man, but one capable of a complex moral understanding of the events that led to his accidental killing of his wife in the midst of a marital quarrel. Madeleine Faith Wirst is expelled from the Foxfire gang, miraculously paving the way for her to return to society, have a short marriage followed by divorce, get a university degree, and pursue a career as an astronomer's assistant, probing negative light in films of identical parts of the sky.

It is difficult to know what finally to say about Oates's reliance on violence. It is integral to her vision—and surely, it is all-too-much a part of American life, throughout this century. It rivets her action and often constellates her characters. It does not go away. Often it seems to mar her characterization, leaving motives ill defined and murky. The tensions unleashed by the violence threaten the boundaries of her art. But the violence is often believable and it does not let us forget. It stuns us, makes us wonder how the imagination that so clear-sightedly depicts it can remain so remarkable levelheaded and intact. In a book like *Blonde* the violence is so convincingly portrayed and so much a part of what we know of Norma Jean/''Marilyn'' that it is hard to dismiss its explanatory power. Critics continue to say that Oates is obsessively consumed with violence, reveling in its brutishness, caught in its senseless repetitions, salaciously reveling in its psycho-sexual dimensions, thrilled, somehow, by the recurring theme of domination and submission, discipline and punishment.

Oates's fascination with the sport of boxing has fueled the critical response to her writing that is so often colored by references to her gender and the body image of the woman herself. *Black Water* provides her with an occasion to reflect on the death penalty and the five ways in which it can be carried out in America. It is too easy and misguided to complain that she writes too much and too easily and that she exploits violence in her novels. She is a supreme teller of tales and her imagination never fails to startle the reader. The scene of domestic violence in *American Appetites,* the circumstances of the drowning in *Black Water,* the sex orgies and the nude photographing of Marilyn in *Blonde* are vivid, unforgettable, and original. The first two novels are importantly about crime and punishment, remorse and forgiveness. The latter scathingly indicts the industry, people, and society that created the circumstances in which a ''Marilyn'' can be made. Oates's excursions into a world of violence and hyperreality touch something little understood. Now that she is tunneling behind the violence, letting the reader see its mainsprings more fully, she makes clearer the end that justifies the experience. Oates is a writer who embarks on ambitious projects; her imagination is protean; her energies and curiosity seemingly boundless; and throughout all her writing, the reader detects her sharp intelligence, spirit of inquiry, and her zeal to tell a story.

—Carol Simpson Stern

O'BRIEN, Edna

Nationality: Irish. **Born:** Tuamgraney, County Clare, 15 December 1932. **Education:** National School, Scariff; Convent of Mercy, Loughrea; Pharmaceutical College of Dublin: licentiate, Pharmaceutical Society of Ireland. **Career:** practiced pharmacy briefly; novelist, playwright, and screenwriter. **Family:** Married Ernest Gebler in 1952 (marriage dissolved 1967); two sons. Lives in London. **Awards:** Kingsley Amis award, 1962; *Yorkshire Post* award, 1971. **Agent:** Robert Lescher, 155 East 71st St., New York, NY 10021, U.S.A. **Address:** Duncan Heath Associates, 162–170 Wardour St., London W1V 3AT, England.

PUBLICATIONS

Novels

The Country Girls. London, Hutchinson, and New York, Knopf, 1960.

The Lonely Girl. London, Cape, and New York, Random House, 1962; as *Girl with Green Eyes,* London, Penguin, 1964.

Girls in Their Married Bliss. London, Cape, 1964; New York, Simon and Schuster, 1968.

August Is a Wicked Month. London, Cape, and New York, Simon and Schuster, 1965.

Casualties of Peace. London, Cape, 1966; New York, Simon and Schuster, 1967.

A Pagan Place. London, Weidenfeld and Nicolson, and New York, Knopf, 1970.

Night. London, Weidenfeld and Nicolson, 1972; New York, Knopf, 1973.

Johnny I Hardly Knew You. London, Weidenfeld and Nicolson, 1977; as *I Hardly Knew You,* New York, Doubleday, 1978.

The Country Girls Trilogy and Epilogue. New York, Farrar Straus, 1986; London, Cape, 1987.

The High Road. London, Weidenfeld and Nicolson, and New York, Farrar Straus, 1988.

Time and Tide. New York, Farrar Straus Giroux; London, Penguin; and Toronto, HarperCollins, 1992.

An Edna O'Brien Reader (includes *August is a Wicked Month, Casualties of Peace,* and *Johnny I Hardly Knew You*). New York, Warner Books, 1994.

House of Splendid Isolation. New York, Farrar Straus Giroux, and London, Weidenfeld and Nicolson, 1994.

Down by the River. New York, Farrar, Straus and Giroux, 1997.

Wild Decembers. Boston, Houghton Mifflin, 2000.

Short Stories

The Love Object. London, Cape, 1968; New York, Knopf, 1969.

A Scandalous Woman and Other Stories. London, Weidenfeld and Nicolson, and New York, Harcourt Brace, 1974.

Mrs. Reinhardt and Other Stories. London, Weidenfeld and Nicolson, 1978; as *A Rose in the Heart,* New York, Doubleday, 1979.

Returning. London, Weidenfeld and Nicolson, 1982.

A Fanatic Heart: Selected Stories. New York, Farrar Straus, 1984; London, Weidenfeld and Nicolson, 1985.

Lantern Slides. London, Weidenfeld and Nicolson, and New York, Farrar Straus Giroux, 1990.

Plays

A Cheap Bunch of Nice Flowers (produced London, 1962). Published in *Plays of the Year 1962–1963,* London, Elek, and New York, Ungar, 1963.

The Wedding Dress (televised 1963). Published in *Mademoiselle* (New York), November 1963.

Zee & Co. (screenplay). London, Weidenfeld and Nicolson, 1971.

A Pagan Place, adaptation of her own novel (produced London, 1972; New Haven, Connecticut, 1974). London, Faber, 1973; Port Townsend, Washington, Graywolf Press, 1984.

The Gathering (produced Dublin, 1974; New York, 1977).

The Ladies (produced London, 1975).

Virginia (produced Stratford, Ontario, 1980; London and New York, 1981). London, Hogarth Press, and New York, Harcourt Brace, 1981.

Flesh and Blood (produced Bath, 1985; New York, 1986).

Madame Bovary, adaptation of the novel by Flaubert (produced Watford, Hertfordshire, 1987).

Screenplays: *Girl with Green Eyes,* 1964; *I Was Happy Here (Time Lost and Time Remembered),* with Desmond Davis, 1965; *Three into Two Won't Go,* 1969; *Zee & Co. (X, Y, & Zee),* 1972; *The Tempter,* with others, 1975; *The Country Girls,* 1984.

Television Plays: *The Wedding Dress,* 1963; *The Keys of the Café,* 1965; *Give My Love to the Pilchards,* 1965; *Which of These Two Ladies Is He Married To?,* 1967; *Nothing's Ever Over,* 1968; *Then and Now,* 1973; *Mrs. Reinhardt,* from her own story, 1981.

Poetry

On the Bone. Warwick, Greville Press, 1989.

Other (for children)

The Dazzle. London, Hodder and Stoughton, 1981.
A Christmas Treat. London, Hodder and Stoughton, 1982.
The Rescue. London, Hodder and Stoughton, 1983.
Tales for the Telling: Irish Folk and Fairy Tales. London, Joseph, and New York, Atheneum, 1986.

Other

Mother Ireland. London, Weidenfeld and Nicolson, and New York, Harcourt Brace, 1976.
Arabian Days, photographs by Gerard Klijn. New York, Horizon Press, and London, Quartet, 1977.
The Collected Edna O'Brien (miscellany). London, Collins, 1978.
James and Nora: A Portrait of Joyce's Marriage. Northridge, California, Lord John Press, 1981.
Vanishing Ireland, photographs by Richard Fitzgerald. London, Cape, 1986; New York, Potter, 1987.
James Joyce. New York, Viking Penguin, 1999.
Editor, *Some Irish Loving: A Selection.* London, Weidenfeld and Nicolson, and New York, Harper, 1979.

*

Critical Studies: *Edna O'Brien* by Grace Eckley, Lewisburg, Pennsylvania, Bucknell University Press, 1974.

Edna O'Brien comments:

I quote from two critics: William Trevor and John Berger.

A Pagan Place: ''Constitutes a reconstruction of a childhood experience which so far as I know, is unique in the English language. In this respect, though otherwise it is different, it invites comparison with Proust; a book whose genius is memory'' (Berger).

The Love Object: ''Rarely has a woman protested as eloquently as Edna O'Brien. In sorrow and compassion she keens over the living. More obviously now, despair is her province'' (Trevor).

My aim is to write books that in some way celebrate life and do justice to my emotions as well as form a connection with the reader, the unknown one.

* * *

The major theme of Edna O'Brien's fiction is the ineffable pain of loneliness, guilt, and loss. Her works record a bleak odyssey from naive optimism, through rancor, bitterness and hatred, to the scarred wisdom that comes from having wrestled with her suffering. Her insights into the conflicting dilemmas that beset women today have won her international acclaim.

Her fiction grows out of the trilogy which follows Caithleen and Baba from their initiation into life and love to their chilling disillusionment with both. At the outset, innocent and intelligent Caithleen Brady (Kate) wants every story to have a happy ending. Baba is so brazen that even her father, Mr. Brennan, prefers Kate: ''Poor Caithleen, you've always been Baba's tool.'' *The Country Girls* and its sequel represent a woman's version of a traditionally masculine motif: that of an ego tempted by an alter ego to enjoy forbidden fruit (like Faust and Mephistopheles). The entire trilogy operates around this theme. Kate has ''one mad eye,'' but her softness, daftness, and wantonness are not her essential nature. They come to her from an alter ego whose influence she is unable to resist. Baba promotes Kate's decisions, and the story follows their consequence: their expulsion from the convent school, an affair with Mr. Gentleman in *The Country Girls,* and an affair with Eugene Gaillard in *The Lonely Girl.* Because Kate is so influenced by her friend, she is always restless. She feels ''lonely'' without the weight of Eugene's body, but she cannot commit herself to him: ''Before she left Eugene she had often thought of being with other men—strange distant men who would beckon to her.'' She recognizes that she is disloyal to anyone who is ''real'' for her, and that what she yearns for is a ''shadow''—but she cannot stop herself. This weakness is reflected in the shift in narrative perspective. In *Girls in Their Married Bliss,* Baba, the temptress, has become the narrator and Kate, the ego, is correspondingly unable to determine her actions. She becomes increasingly introverted, afraid of giving herself: ''Life was a secret with the Self. The more one gave out the less there remained for the centre.'' The novel ends with Baba regretting the loss of ''some important region that they both knew nothing about.'' In the epilogue that O'Brien added when her trilogy was republished in 1986, Kate, utterly wasted by life, has committed suicide, and Baba, while waiting to meet the coffin at Waterloo Station, reflects on the conflict between her own desires and the emptiness of her own life. It is a bleak ending to what is still O'Brien's finest work.

The sense of being divided also lies at the heart of O'Brien's next novel. ''This is not me, I am not doing this,'' thinks Ellen, the heroine of *August Is a Wicked Month.* While the ''Not-I'' has her ''jaunt into iniquity''—a holiday in France following her separation—her son, on holiday with his father, is killed. Unable to discover an adequate reaction to the loss of part of her essential self, she returns to England, anxious only about whether she has contracted gonorrhea. Worry about the ''Not-I''—which proves needless— replaces concern about the ''I.'' This mechanism anticipates the next novel, *Casualties of Peace,* in which the insubstantial ego (Willa) is accidentally killed in place of the alter ego figure (Patsy). The motif is further explored in *Zee & Co.,* the only work in which it achieves even a tentative, though unstable, resolution.

The humor, so intrinsic to the early work, is gradually replaced by sharp and sometimes acid observations. But the most notable tendency in O'Brien's fiction is the progress from the ''realism'' of the trilogy to the introverted monologues, reminiscences, and reconstructions of her later work. The author has declared that her favorite is *A Pagan Place,* which tells the problems of a young girl very similar to Kate. Its second-person narrative voice is a bold but sometimes disconcerting device. *Night,* a disturbing and impressive novel, traces Mary Hooligan's reconstruction of her past. In *Johnny I Hardly Knew You,* bitterness and invective detract from its technical merits. *The High Road's* heroine, Anna, on holiday to a Spanish island to forget an affair, is drawn into a circle of characters that includes a waitress called Catalina, who falls in love with her. When Catalina's husband discovers this, he kills her. Anna, devastated by the realization that it might have been her that Juan meant to kill, determines to return to Ireland. For all the brilliance with which the various scenes are painted, this is an angry, claustrophobic book.

All these works rest on the assumption that there is an inevitable conflict between men's and women's needs, and that the only way for a woman to come to terms with this is to learn to be independent. At the end of *Girls in Their Married Bliss,* Kate says: ''What Baba doesn't know is that I'm finding my feet, and when I'm able to talk I imagine that I won't be alone.'' The subsequent novels represent ever bolder experiments in *talking*—that is, in narrative technique. They lean on words to ward off an increasingly desperate inner loneliness.

Her finest novel since *The Country Girls* is *Time and Tide,* which tells the story of Nell, who runs away from home to live with a man. Their marriage goes sour, he becomes brutal and tries to prevent her from having custody of their two sons. As they grow from children to young men, she struggles to discover a sense of her own identity. Pared of all inessentials, each of the short episodes takes a scalpel to the shattering ironies that pass for life.

House of Splendid Isolation, which is set in contemporary Ireland, represents a new direction in O'Brien's writing. McGreevy is a Republican activist on the run: he hides for a few days in the house of an elderly woman called Josie. The partisan is made subservient to the personal; the personal, to the integrity of motivation. It is a work infused by a numbed awareness of the waste of human worth. O'Brien's short stories are among her finest work. They explore very much the same ground as her novels—the various kinds of misfortune and loneliness that beset the lives of her Irish characters—and reverberate freely in the reader's imagination. Her weakness is that her characters can often seem only vehicles for the dilemmas that confront them. Her strength is the lyricism of her language. No other contemporary novelist has better captured, and with as much poignancy, the agony brought about by confused longings.

O'Brien's acknowledged major literary influences are William Faulkner, James Joyce, and Anton Chekhov. While her prose style often reveals a debt to Joycean sensuousness as well as to his prolixity, in her later novels themes she explores often approximate the concerns of Faulkner with life in the rural South. O'Brien's setting is rural village Irish life in *Down by the River* and mountainside remoteness in west Ireland in *Wild Decembers.* The rural dilemmas faced by Mary, the fourteen-year-old heroine of *Down by the River,* include the guilt laden dogma of her village church when she finds herself pregnant by her abusive father and the political agendas of those who would deny her an abortion. O'Brien based her novel on events in 1992 that led to political turmoil and a national referendum on abortion for those in distress, such as the heroine of O'Brien's novel. Fathers, church, state, judicial rulings, and anti-abortion foes represent an oppressive political system's response to a young girl's personal dilemma in this novel. As Mary flees from the reach of a grasping and exploitative system, O'Brien's characteristic pessimism about the possibilities of happiness gives way to hope and the possibility of community in those good people who rally to support Mary.

Wild Decembers focuses less on repression caused by church and state than it does on characters primal identification with the land itself. Here a land feud erupts between an Australian, Mick Bugler, returned to claim his ancestral Irish lands, and an Irishman Joseph Brennan and his devoted sister Brege Brennan. The tractor Mick introduces signals the clash between modernity and traditional ways of life, a conflict that cannot avoid catastrophe when Joseph's sister, Brege, falls in love with Mick. O'Brien's description of the tractor's first appearance captures both its appeal and its menace: ''Heraldic and unflagging it chugged up the mountain road, the sound, a new sound jarring in on the profoundly pensive landscape.'' Above it, crows are ''blackening the sky, fringed, soundless, auguring.'' Here O'Brien captures sensibilities and the values organizing those characters hearts and minds that she has not previously explored, marking a new direction in her work.

—Terence Dawson, updated by Roberta Schreyer

O'BRIEN, Tim

Nationality: American. **Born:** William Timothy O'Brien in Austin, Minnesota, 1 October 1946. **Education:** Macalaster College, St. Paul, Minnesota, B.A. in political science (summa cum laude) 1968; Harvard University, Cambridge, Massachusetts, 1970–76. **Military Service:** Served in the United States Army during the Vietnam war; discharged wounded 1970: Purple Heart. **Career:** Reporter, Washington *Post,* 1971–74. **Awards:** National Book award, 1978; National Endowment for the Arts award; Bread Loaf Writers Conference award; Heartland Award, 1990; Melcher Book Award, 1991. L.H.D., Miami University (Ohio), 1990. **Agent:** International Creative Management, 40 West 57th Street, New York, New York 10019, U.S.A.

Publications

Novels

Northern Lights. New York, Delacorte Press, and London, Calder and Boyars, 1975.

Going after Cacciato. New York, Delacorte Press, and London, Cape, 1978.

The Nuclear Age. Portland, Oregon, Press 22, 1981; London, Collins, 1986.

In the Lake of the Woods. Boston, Houghton Mifflin, 1994.

Tomcat in Love. New York, Broadway Books, 1998.

Short Stories

The Things They Carried. Boston, Houghton Mifflin, and London, Collins, 1990.

Uncollected Short Stories

''Keeping Watch by Night,'' in *Redbook* (New York), December 1976.

''Night March,'' in *Prize Stories of 1976,* edited by William Abrahams. New York, Doubleday, 1976.

''Fisherman,'' in *Esquire* (New York), October 1977.

''Calling Home,'' in *Redbook* (New York), December 1977.

''Speaking of Courage,'' in *Prize Stories of 1978,* edited by William Abrahams. New York, Doubleday, 1978.

''Civil Defense,'' in *Esquire* (New York), August 1980.

''The Ghost Soldiers,'' in *Prize Stories of 1982,* edited by William Abrahams. New York, Doubleday, 1982.

''Quantum Jumps,'' in *The Pushcart Prize 10,* edited by Bill Henderson. Wainscott, New York, Pushcart Press, 1985.

''Underground Tests,'' in *The Esquire Fiction Reader 2,* edited by Rust Hills and Tom Jenks. Green Harbor, Massachusetts, Wampeter Press, 1986.

''The Lives of the Dead,'' in *Esquire* (New York), January 1989.

''Sweetheart of the Song Tra Bong,'' in *Esquire* (New York), July 1989.

''In the Field,'' in *Gentlemen's Quarterly* (New York), December 1989.

''Enemies and Friends,'' in *Harper's* (New York), March 1990.

''Field Trip,'' in *McCall's* (New York), August 1990.

''Speaking of Courage,'' in *The Other Side of Heaven: Post-War Fiction by Vietnamese and American Writers,* edited by Wayne Karling. Williamatic, Connecticut, Curbstone Press, 1995.

Other

If I Die in a Combat Zone, Box Me Up and Ship Me Home (memoirs). New York, Delacorte Press, and London, Calder and Boyars, 1973; revised edition, Delacorte Press, 1979.

Speaking of Courage. Santa Barbara, California, Neville, 1980.

*

Critical Studies: ''Imagining the Real: The Fiction of Tim O'Brien'' by Daniel L. Zins, in *Hollins Critic* (Hollins College, Virginia), June 1986; ''Tim O'Brien's Myth of Courage'' by Milton J. Bates, in *Critique* (Washington, D.C.), Summer 1987; *Understanding Tim O'Brien* by Steven Kaplan, Columbia, University of South Carolina Press, 1994; *Tim O'Brien* by Tobey C. Herzog, New York, Twayne Publishers, 1997.

* * *

Looking back, it almost seems as if, during the 1970s and 1980s, in order to have a book acclaimed as one of the best pieces of writing to emerge from the Vietnam War, all an author needed to do was get it published. Whatever the reason for the hype, some highly commendable work was produced as a result of America's military misadventures in southeast Asia. Few writers contribute more than once to the list though, and few have really been able to forge much headway beyond their first couple of books. Tim O'Brien is the exception.

O'Brien's debut, *If I Die in a Combat Zone,* a collection of newspaper and magazine journalism supplemented by other articles, would have been enough to ensure him a lasting reputation as a gritty and reliable witness to some of the worst stupidity of the war in Vietnam. Anecdotal and sometimes jarring in its juxtaposition of Socratic dialogue and personal meditation, *If I Die in a Combat Zone* is a clear-sighted and unsensationalist account of one young enlistee's fears and aspirations. In no way does it prepare us for *Going after Cacciato,* O'Brien's intense, impressionistic, and impassioned fictionalization of the experiences of ordinary combat personnel in Vietnam. Here O'Brien's narrative stretches across Asia and Europe as the remaining members of a platoon hunt a deserter. Gradually it becomes evident that this epic chase is a graft of fantasy onto fact—Paul Berlin, the central character, and his colleagues follow their prey no further than a grassy knoll not far from their departure point. The subsequent developments are all the products of an imagination feverishly creating alternative scenarios to the horrors of a foot-soldier's daily existence. Reality becomes malleable as O'Brien weaves memorable sections of recalled events—sentry duty, ambush, patrol, and death—into the path of Cacciato's flight. Imagination is the metaphor for and means of survival—a theme that unites O'Brien's work.

Northern Lights brings together two brothers—one returned from Vietnam, the other homebound—and pitches them into a battle for life in the untamed Minnesotan Arrowhead country after a skiing trip goes disastrously wrong. In a not unexpected role reversal, Harvey, who has proved his manhood in battle, becomes utterly dependent upon Paul, who has ''flown a desk'' for the duration. O'Brien's portrayals of an impersonal but fiercely hostile winter wilderness and the oppressive atmosphere of a dying small town are vivid and impressive. *Northern Lights* also introduces us, somewhat ominously, to a bomb shelter dug by Harvey.

O'Brien's third novel, *The Nuclear Age,* draws that shelter out of the background and deposits it in a dominant position, in the middle (and beginning and end) of the plot. William Cowling, the narrator of this tale of paranoia and atrophied passion, has led a life determined by dread—the same interminable panic felt by O'Brien in Vietnam but modified into the more universal concept of the all-consuming terror of nuclear Armageddon. As a child he constructed a refuge in his basement out of a ping-pong table, surrounding it at one point with pencils purloined from school, in the belief that radiation from a nuclear explosion would not penetrate the ''lead.'' At college, Cowling's personal antibomb protests are mistaken for the actions of a putative politician, and he is soon embroiled in campus revolt, orchestrated by Sarah, the childhood sweetheart he never had. The primary motive of the hero is, however, self-preservation: ''She was out to change the world, I was out to survive it.'' As Cowling grows out of love with Sarah, so his concern with his imminent obliteration becomes more profound, and we join him, late at night, in his garden, obeying the ''voice'' of a hole that is telling him to dig or perish.

The Things They Carried, more short story cycle than novel, reads so much like a memoir that the author has to emphasize, in a subtitle and prefatory note, that what follows is ''a work of fiction.'' The intensely autobiographical tone of the stories is underscored by the presence of a first person narrator named Tim O'Brien. The stories that follow all attempt to come to terms with the narrator's Vietnam experience and frequently try to account for the purpose of telling or writing stories. ''How to Tell a True War Story'' begins with the assertion, ''This is true'' and, like many of the other stories in the collection, goes on to question what truth is. Truth and reality are even fuzzier in Vietnam than elsewhere, and examining how experience is converted into meaning matters more than trying to figure out what is real. Despite the narrator's playing with the notion of truth in stories, the reader comes away from these stories with a sense of the awful truth that was Vietnam, though we share the frustrations of the various storytellers, who will never quite be able to communicate their experience.

This frustration becomes the theme of O'Brien's next novel, *In the Lake of the Woods,* the story of John Wade, who goes into exile after losing a primary election for U.S. senate, and his wife Kathy, who disappears while they are in exile. The novel comprises various testimonies of people who knew John, the local authorities who suspect foul play, neighbors who try to comfort John after the disappearance, and other ''evidence'' in the form of documents chronicling Wade's life. Bringing it all together is a narrator who is self-conscious about his role as a writer, and his inability to ''know'' anything beyond direct personal experience. ''Evidence is not truth,'' he tells us in a footnote, ''and if you require solutions, you will have to look beyond these pages.'' Like the rest of O'Brien's work, this novel takes on Vietnam, yet more obliquely; Wade had been involved in the My Lai incident, and his experience there becomes part of the evidence in his case. The connection is clear enough: despite all of our various attempts to make sense of the disturbing side of human existence, our capacity to understand is limited. O'Brien has certainly not left the war behind, but he has gotten beyond the war itself and begun to delve into its long-term implications. He remains the most compelling voice to emerge from the Vietnam war, but he is also developing into a master of storytelling who is aware of his craft and of the necessity for its continuation.

—Ian McMechan, updated by D. Quentin Miller

O'CONNOR, Joseph

Nationality: Irish. **Born:** Dublin, Ireland, 1963. **Education:** University College, Dublin, B.A. 1986; briefly attended Oxford University. **Family:** Married. **Career:** Worked with British Nicaragua Solidarity Campaign, 1980s; journalist, screenwriter, writer for television, and author. Lives in Dublin. **Awards:** *Sunday Tribune* First Fiction Award, 1989; New Irish Writer of the Year Award, 1989; *Time Out* Magazine Writing Prize, 1990; Miramax Screenwriting Award, 1995; *In Dublin* Magazine Award for Best New Irish Play, 1995.

Publications

Novels

Cowboys and Indians. Dublin, Sinclair-Stevenson, 1991.
Desperadoes. London, Flamingo, 1993.
Finbar's Hotel (serial novel, with others), devised and edited by Dermot Bolger. Dublin, New Island Books, 1997.
The Salesman. London, Secker & Warburg, 1998; New York, Picador, 1999.

Short Stories

True Believers. London, Flamingo, 1992.

Plays

Red Roses and Petrol. Dublin, Project Arts Centre, 1995; London, Methuen, 1995.
The Weeping of Angels. Dublin, Gate Theatre, 1997.

Other

Even the Olives Are Bleeding: The Life and Times of Charles Donnelly. Dublin, New Island Books, 1992.
The Secret World of the Irish Male (humorous essays). Dublin, New Island Books, 1994.
Sweet Liberty: Travels in Irish America. London, Picador, 1996; Boulder, Colorado, Robert Rinehart Publishing, 1996.
The Irish Male at Home and Abroad (humorous essays). Dublin, New Island Books, 1996.

* * *

In the hard, laconic, yet strangely evocative prose of Joseph O'Connor, the modern novel has gained a new, intriguing individual voice. Choosing leading characters who are often unattractive and sometimes downright unpleasant, and tracing their adventures in gritty urban and rural wasteland settings, he writes without sentiment while at the same time involving the reader emotionally with his creations. This is nowhere more true than in his first, and arguably his finest, novel, *Cowboys and Indians*, where he follows the doomed efforts of Dublin student/musician Eddie Virago to make his name on the London punk rock scene. Handsome, confident Eddie with his outrageous Mohican hairstyle and outsized ego is one of a class of would-be leaders who graduated from University College only to find their achievements fall woefully short of their grandiose dreams. Like them, Eddie's ambitions are doomed to failure, his wisecracking ''cool'' exterior shielding the vulnerable, bewildered child of a broken marriage who struggles as vainly in his relationships as in his search for fame. First seen throwing up on the ferry from Dublin, he encounters the spiky exile Marion Mangan—surely one of the most shrewish, quarrelsome ''heroines'' ever created—and the pair embark on a tense, permanently fraught relationship that continues through most of the book. Through Eddie's eyes the reader takes in the soulless horror of Margaret Thatcher's Britain with its desert of industrial estates and aspiring yuppies with their banal management jargon, and glimpses the underside of the music scene in grimy clubs and out-of-town acid raves. O'Connor switches adroitly from London to Dublin to rural Donegal, one nightmare scenario following another as Eddie flounders in a morass of drink, drugs, and sex, his best efforts forever thwarted. His author presents him without excuses, showing his selfishness, his facility for easy face-saving lies, his ability to explain away his cowardice and stupidity. Yet for all that, it's impossible not to identify with him and want him to come through unscathed. As Marion's dark secret reveals itself and Eddie drifts closer to disaster, kidding himself all the while that things aren't so bad, the reader is drawn after him, dreading what lies ahead but hoping that somehow he's going to survive it. A powerful, accomplished work, *Cowboys and Indians* combines wry social comment and hard-hitting prose with frequent bursts of pathos and humor. With it, O'Connor established his reputation as a novelist and found the voice that informs his later writings.

Eddie Virago returns in the opening story of *True Believers*, where in ''Last of the Mohicans'' he impresses a fellow exile in 1980s London with his cool, assured style, undermined somewhat by his lowly status as hamburger salesman and unpublished author. In ''The Wizard of Oz'' an Irish youngster arrives from the Antipodes to be groomed by a slick, know-all Irish yuppie, only to discover in amusingly detailed fashion that the emperor has no clothes. Elsewhere, the author ranges from comedy through the unrequited love story of ''Ailsa'' to the atmospheric tension of ''The Long Way Home,'' where a fleeing husband picks up a mysterious hitch-hiker on a lonely country road. More often, his stories combine several of these aspects, as in ''The Bedouin Feast,'' where nightmare slapstick is blended with the wry sadness of betrayal, or the title story, where the death of a strange old woman signals the end of the narrator's childhood and the loss of his faith. Throughout, O'Connor matches sharp dialogue with adept character sketches, while making some probing comments of his own. This is certainly the case in ''The Hills Are Alive,'' which details the doomed love affair between a British soldier and an Irish Republican Army volunteer, their brief episodes of warmth and closeness blasted to destruction by two opposing armies, each believing itself to be in the right. The description of their funerals, both marked by gunshots over the grave and a man in a suit saying ''something about freedom,'' is a tragic epitaph to a struggle that has outlasted its early ideals. *True Believers*, with its sharply focused blend of incident and internalized thought, shows O'Connor the novelist as a skilful writer of short fiction.

His novel *Desperadoes* is set in war-ravaged Nicaragua, where at the height of the conflict between the Sandinista government and the Contra rebels Frank Little and his estranged wife Eleanor arrive to identify the body of their musician son Johnny. Discovering that the corpse is not their son, they set off without official permission into the war zone in the company of Johnny's old band, the Desperados de Amor, in the hope of finding him. O'Connor phases their adventures with neat flashback recollections from the lives of the Irish couple, detailing their passionate early love and its progression to a traumatic, disastrous marriage and separation. His vivid depiction of a country in the throes of civil war, where ordinary men and women struggle to carve out a threadbare existence in the face of death and devastation, is matched by his skill in revealing the complex natures of his characters and their tangled past. Johnny and the band members are drawn with neat, sharp strokes as the novel moves forward, but it is Frank and Eleanor who take center stage and who most engage the reader's attention. Hot-tempered, unreasonable, often exasperating in their stubbornness, they nevertheless emerge as strong, endearing creations. Through them O'Connor traces the tender shoots of love and ponders what happens to it when things go wrong. *Desperadoes* combines the pace of an action novel with deep psychological insight, and is a triumph for its author.

The Salesman is the story of Billy Sweeney, a seller of satellite dishes in the Dublin area, who in the summer of 1994 decides to take the law into his own hands. His beloved daughter Maeve, hospitalised and left in a coma by a gang of young robbers, lies on the brink of death, and one of her attackers has escaped from custody. Tracking the thug down, Sweeney plots his own revenge and eventually moves to execute it. Events, though, take several unexpected turns, and long before the story ends Billy is forced to a painful reconsideration of his motives and the meaning of his own life. Writing of these happenings in a diary addressed to his comatose child, Billy Sweeney emerges as an unhappy, driven man with a troubled past that—like that of Frank and Eleanor Little in *Desperadoes*—stems from his early love and wrecked marriage. His uneasy relationship with the escaped gangster Donal Quinn echoes that earlier partnership in its violent, rapid shifts of mood, and in the end is headed for horror and mayhem. Here, as in his earlier novels, the author indicates the blight of alcoholism and the drug culture, both of which are shown as ugly symptoms of a deeper underlying malaise. Powerful, often funny, and just as often heartbreakingly sad, *The Salesman* is a many-layered work that once more makes telling points while moving swiftly through its pages, and abounds with the customary one-liners—a waiting room is ''the colour of a cancerous lung,'' a stretch of road ''smooth as a politician's lies.'' Like the novels and stories that precede it, it confirms O'Connor's own significance as a leading modern writer in his native country and beyond.

—Geoff Sadler

O'FAOLAIN, Julia

Nationality: Irish. **Born:** London, England, 6 June 1932; daughter of the writer Sean O'Faolain. **Education:** The Sacred Heart Convent, Dublin; University College, Dublin, B.A. in French and Italian 1952, M.A. 1953; University of Rome; the Sorbonne, Paris. **Family:** Married Lauro Martines in 1957; one son. **Career:** Translator for Council of Europe, and worked as supply teacher and cook in London, 1955–57; instructor in French, Reed College, Portland, Oregon, and taught evening classes in Italian, Portland State University, 1957–61; teacher, Scuola Interpreti, Florence, 1962–65. Lives in London. **Awards:** Arts Council of Great Britain bursary, 1981. **Agent:** Deborah Rogers, Rogers Coleridge and White Ltd., 20 Powis Mews, London, W11 1JN, England; or, International Creative Management, 40 West 57th Street, New York, New York 10019, U.S.A.

PUBLICATIONS

Novels

Godded and Codded. London, Faber, 1970; as *Three Lovers,* New York, Coward McCann, 1971.

Women in the Wall. London, Faber, and New York, Viking Press, 1975.

No Country for Young Men. London, Allen Lane, 1980; New York, Carroll and Graf, 1987.

The Obedient Wife. London, Allen Lane, 1982; New York, Carroll and Graf, 1985.

The Irish Signorina. London, Viking, 1984; Bethesda, Maryland, Adler, 1986.

The Judas Cloth. London, Sinclair Stevenson, 1992.

Short Stories

We Might See Sights! and Other Stories. London, Faber, 1968.

Man in the Cellar. London, Faber, 1974.

Melancholy Baby and Other Stories. Dublin, Poolbeg Press, 1978.
Daughters of Passion. London, Penguin, 1982.

Other

Editor, with Lauro Martines, *Not in God's Image: Women in History from the Greeks to the Victorians.* London, Temple Smith, and New York, Harper, 1973.

Translator (as Julia Martines), *Two Memoirs of Renaissance Florence: The Diaries of Buonaccorso Pitti and Gregorio Dati,* edited by Gene Brucker. New York, Harper, 1967.

Translator, *A Man of Parts,* by Piero Chiara. Boston, Little Brown, 1968.

*

Critical Studies: *Two Decades of Irish Writing* edited by Douglas Dunn, Manchester, Carcanet, and Philadelphia, Dufour, 1975; ''The Irish Novel in Our Time'' edited by Patrick Rafroidi and Maurice Harmon, in *Publications de l'Université de Lille 3,* 1975–76; by O'Faolain, in *Contemporary Authors Autobiography Series 2* edited by Adele Sarkissian, Detroit, Gale, 1985; *Irish Women Writers* by Ann Owens Weekes, Lexington, University Press of Kentucky, 1990; articles by Thomas R. Moore and Laura B. Van Dale, in *Colby Quarterly* (Waterville, Maine), March 1991.

Julia O'Faolain comments:

I like fiction to be a Trojan horse. It can seem to be engineering an escape from alien realities but its true aim is to slip inside them and get their measure. Sly and demystificatory, it dismantles myths. This can arouse mixed feelings, for myths, though more interesting when taken apart, are grander while intact. But then ambivalence, it seems, is the nerve of narrative. Regret plus pleasure moves more than either can alone. Moreover, having grown up in a place where myth ran rampant, my native impulse is to cut through and past it.

(1995) Recently I have gone back to writing short stories, a notoriously tricky genre which should be able to condense enough light to burn through to the essence of things. I aim for realism and particularity, then try—nervously—to achieve a lift-off to some angle of vision from which my narrative will look different. The genre is prodigal in that it compresses what a novel would spin out, and risky, since it can misfire. When it works, there's nothing like it for catching the vibrancy of the evanescent. Just now the writers who seem to me to bring this off best are nearly all American and Canadian. A response to a need? Surely. The day they seize is so protean. Living, as I do, in London's slower tempo, I may be working against the odds.

* * *

There is something *déjà vu* about Julia O'Faolain's first novel, *Godded and Codded,* centring on the innocent Irish Sally's further education—in several senses—in Paris, not wholly redeemed by the book's uproarious comedy. The inevitably pregnant Sally's equally inevitable Christmas visit to her parents in Ireland covers even more familiar ground, as we are shown the circumstances that have made Sally what she is—that is, what she must react against. O'Faolain's earlier story ''A Pot of Soothing Herbs'' encapsulated this—the archetypal Irish virginal dilemma; the later story ''Lots of Ghastlies'' more adroitly transplants to an English bourgeois setting the theme of a return visit to the parental home. More interesting in *Godded and Codded* than the ''innocents abroad'' theme is the peripheral description of the underground activities of a group of Algerian students in Paris shortly before Independence. Irish expatriates provide much of the novel's burlesque comedy.

Her first collection, *We Might See Sights!,* is divided by O'Faolain into Irish and Italian stories. The outstanding story is ''Dies Irae,'' set in an Italian hairdresser's salon and perhaps influenced by Colette; to pacify an elderly Russian princess, the hairdresser points out signs of decay in the narrator, for whom a normally pleasant occasion becomes her *dies irae.* There is black comedy in the plight of the husband chained in the cellar by his wife, in the title story of *Man in the Cellar;* the story is told in letters and the final surprisingly affectionate letter from the decamped and mentally disturbed wife reveals how securely *invisible* chains are fastened on her. The didactic element is stronger in this later collection of stories, but is offset by these of out-of-the-way situations; ''This is My Body,'' for instance, set in a sixth-century convent, handles the female Irish writer's stock-in-trade of convent material from a new angle, which *Women in the Wall* also exploits.

In *Women in the Wall,* set in 6th-century Gaul, O'Faolain breathes life into a group of characters who—except two—existed in history, though as the author explains in her introduction, she departed from history in plotting. The monologue of the anchoress in the convent alternates with an account of the darkening political situation, bringing barbarism to the very convent walls; the two threads finally merge in the denouement. But even behind the convent walls, the nuns' lives are shown as often far from quiet, as O'Faolain probes the stresses of celibacy, its occasional abandonment and its link to mystical experience. Her description of nature is always vivid, especially here where she relies heavily on natural imagery to avoid anachronism.

O'Faolain also interweaves different narrative threads to provide explosive connections in *No Country for Young Men:* the death of an American Republican fundraiser in Ulster in 1922 casts a long shadow as an American ex-academic arrives in Ireland in 1979 to interview survivors of the 1920s Troubles for a film and so crosses paths with an old half-insane nun through his romantic entanglement with her married great-niece. This novel, shortlisted for the Booker prize, is O'Faolain's best novel to date, enabling her to deploy all her skills of allusively connecting social, cultural, historical, and economic insights. These electric interconnections are often wittily achieved, sometimes pivoting on linguistic humour. O'Faolain's style is so exciting that the reader may overlook the fact that her characters tend to share a similar wide-ranging, ironic perception, imposed by the style.

An outstanding illustration of the disadvantage of O'Faolain's brilliant style, notwithstanding that it provides a vivid impression of whatever society she's writing about, comes in *The Obedient Wife;* Carla is endowed by the author with witty dialogue and far-ranging ironic thought that seem too dazzling for the character as otherwise presented. An Italian living in California from where her husband has returned, supposedly temporarily, to Italy, Carla despite her paganism believes in the traditional role of the wife—or has been culturally brainwashed into believing in it. Yet, she becomes emotionally involved with a Catholic priest. Carla's relationship with her teenage son is especially well drawn, with empathy for both sides.

In *The Irish Signorina,* as in earlier books, the plot is engendered by the crisscrossing of intergenerational threads. A young Irish girl is invited by the dying Italian Marchesa Cavalcanti to stay in the villa where her mother had worked for the marchesa as a girl. Against the background of the Cavalcanti family's roots in the land and modern terrorism, complex webs of personal relationships, old and new, emerge. Though shorter than O'Faolain's previous novels, the economy and restraint that she here shows in dealing with her always interesting material illustrate her extraordinary stylistic development since her early writing. Returning to her ever-present Catholic themes in *The Judas Project,* O'Faolain portrayed the world of Pope Pius IX. Pius, who reigned in the mid-19th century, reacted to the uprising of 1848 by becoming an archconservative who promulgated the doctrines of Immaculate Conception and papal infallibility. The book is a powerful narrative, one that amply illustrates the punch which O'Faolain packs into each novel.

—Val Warner

O'HAGAN, Andrew

Nationality: Scottish. **Born:** Glasgow, Scotland, 1968 or 1969. **Career:** Former assistant editor, *London Review of Books;* writes for London *Daily Telegraph. Lives in London.*

PUBLICATIONS

Novels

Our Fathers. New York, Harcourt Brace, 1999.

Short Stories

Contributor, *The Junky's Christmas and Other Stories*, edited by Elisa Seagrave. New York, Serpent's Tail, 1994.

Other

The Missing (nonfiction). New York, New Press, 1996.

* * *

With one novel and one nonfiction book to his credit, Andrew O'Hagan has already established himself as a writer of some achievement and considerable promise. O'Hagan had begun to make a name for himself as a journalist and editor when his first book, *The Missing*, was published in 1996; this is a combination of family history, autobiography, and an exploration of a range of cases of people who mysteriously disappear from society, sometimes to reappear later in grim circumstances—as murder victims, for example—and sometimes to vanish without trace. In *The Missing*, O'Hagan tells the story of his grandfather, lost at sea in 1940, and of his own tough childhood in a working-class family that moved out from Glasgow's tenements to the new town of Irvine when he was three. Irvine represented the social hopes of city planners for a better life for the working class, but it continued to be marked by violence and gang warfare. *The Missing* won O'Hagan high praise; and his concern in that book with family history across the generations and with the failure of idealistic planning projects is carried through into his first novel, *Our Fathers*.

Our Fathers takes the form of a fictional family history narrated by Jamie Bawn, who travels from England to Scotland to pay a last visit to his grandfather, Hugh Bawn. The brutalist, run-down tower block in which Hugh lies dying is a symbol of his failed political aspirations, and more generally of the collapse of a certain kind of Utopian socialism. Once an admired civic leader dubbed ''Mr. Housing'' who wanted to provide proper, inexpensive homes for working-class people, Hugh is now held responsible for the trauma of the tower blocks and is under investigation for financial corruption. Ironically, Jamie works as an executive for a demolition firm that, among other things, razes tower blocks to the ground. As Jamie attends Hugh's deathbed and reflects on his grandfather's life, he also painfully recalls the lives of Robert, his own father, and Thomas, his great-grandfather. Thomas, moving from the country to the city, started to drink and was only saved from alcoholism by death in World War I. Robert, lacking Hugh's social concern, was also a heavy drinker who disappeared from view like the people O'Hagan wrote about in *The Missing*. It is the women who are left behind—Thomas's wife, Margaret, and Jamie's mother, Alice—who bravely take on the task of supporting their families. But Jamie's recollections result in a partial reconciliation both with his grandfather and with his father, whom he tracks down and rescues from the ranks of the missing; he also comes round to wishing for a family of his own, although he has earlier been trying to force his pregnant girlfriend to have an abortion in order to stop the transmission of unhappiness to future generations of Bawns. In *Our Fathers*, a particular family history in a harsh environment finally becomes a metaphor for the pains and possibilities of life itself.

Our Fathers is a powerful, serious work that tackles large themes with skill, if not with complete success. Despite the importance and interest of the stories that it tells, it lacks narrative drive; the potentially dramatic sequences are slowed down by poetic passages. O'Hagan has himself identified the Scottish lyrical tradition, represented by Lewis Grassic Gibbon, Neil Gunn, and Robert Louis Stevenson, as one of his fundamental inspirations, and criticism has detected in the prose of *Our Fathers* the influence of the contemporary Scottish poets John Burnside, Robert Crawford, and Douglas Dunn. But O'Hagan's first novel made a well-deserved impact and was one of the six works shortlisted for the 1999 Booker prize, the United Kingdom's most prestigious literary award for fiction. Still in his early thirties, O'Hagan is likely to produce further fiction and has the potential to become a substantial contemporary novelist.

—Nicolas Tredell

OKRI, Ben

Nationality: Nigerian. **Born:** Minna, 15 March 1959. **Education:** In Nigeria; at University of Essex, Colchester, B.A. in comparative literature. **Career:** Broadcaster, ''Network Africa,'' BBC World Service, 1984–85; poetry editor, *West Africa,* 1981–87. Full-time writer and reviewer for the *Guardian,* the *Observer,* and the *New Statesman,* all London. **Awards:** Commonwealth Prize for Africa, 1987; *Paris Review* Aga Khan prize, 1987, for fiction; Booker prize, 1991, for *The Famished Road.* **Address:** c/o Jonathan Cape, 20 Vauxhall Bridge Road, London SW1V 2SA, England.

PUBLICATIONS

Novels

Flowers and Shadows. London, Longman, 1980.
The Landscapes Within. London, Longman, 1981.
The Famished Road. London, Cape, 1991; New York, Talese, 1992.
Songs of Enchantment. London, Cape, and New York, Talese, 1993.
Astonishing the Gods. London, Phoenix House, 1995.
Dangerous Love. London, Phoenix House, 1996.
A Way of Being Free. London, Phoenix House, 1997.
Infinite Riches. London, Phoenix, 1999.

Short Stories

Incidents at the Shrine. London, Heinemann, 1986.
Stars of the New Curfew. London, Secker and Warburg, and New York, Viking, 1989.

Uncollected Short Stories

''The Dream-Vendor's August,'' in *Paris Review* (New York), Winter 1987.
''Disparities,'' in *Literary Review* (Madison, New Jersey), Fall 1990.

Poetry

An African Elegy. London, Cape, 1992.

*

Critical Studies: *Some African Voices of Our Time* by Ivor Agyeman-Duah. Accra, Ghana, Anansesem Publications, 1995; *Strategic Transformations in Nigerian Writing: Orality and History in the Work of Rev. Samuel Johnson, Amos Tutuola, Wole Soyinka and Ben Okri* by Ato Quayson, Oxford, J. Currey and Bloomington, Indiana University Press, 1997.

* * *

Ben Okri's writing career began early: his first novel, *Flowers and Shadows,* was published when he was 21. The novel recounts the growth into adulthood of Jeffia Okwe, the sensitive son of a corrupt and ruthless businessman and a woman who, from being ''beautiful, fresh'' with ''so much life and vigour,'' becomes a ''walking tragedy'' after the death of her husband. Jeffia's discovery of the nature of his father's business and his business associates is economically described and frequently the pathos of the characters—particularly Juliet, his father's former mistress—is all the more effective for its understatement. Okri is exceptionally deft at evoking moments and meetings fraught with emotion, such as Jeffia's tentative falling in love with Cynthia, a night nurse. The social context of a Nigerian town is effortlessly realised.

If *Flowers and Shadows* was a relatively conventional *Bildungsroman, The Landscapes Within,* Okri's next novel, takes a similarly conventional form and, as the title suggests, begins to stretch the imaginative properties it holds. The central character here is a solitary painter named Omovo, whose artistic vision leads him into conflict not only with his family and friends but also with the state. Social and political corruption are the condition and context of Omovo's artistic effort. If the clarity and precision of Okri's style owe something to Chinua Achebe, then his vision of social squalor and human degradation is as unflinching and as compassionate as that of Wole Soyinka. Omovo is actually described at one point, reading Soyinka's novel *The Interpreters,* whose title points up the social significance of his own artistic dedication. Omovo's tender love for Ifeyinwa, the wife of a neighbour, develops towards emotional disaster when she leaves their squalid township and wanders unwittingly to a senseless and anonymous death, shot by soldiers and dumped ''into the brackish stream nearby.'' The novel ends with Omovo picking his way ''slowly through the familiar darkness, alone.''

This turning out and movement away from conventional contexts is mirrored in Okri's next two books, both collections of short stories which develop the nightmare visions of nocturnal landscapes, filling them with the bodies of spirits, living and dead. *Incidents at the Shrine* is a slim volume of eight stories, each one a strong but unemphatic marvel. The stories are set in Nigeria during the Civil War, in London among the derelicts and the dispossessed, and in dream-worlds suffused with an African sensibility and experience of Britain in the 1980s, where a ruthless Conservative government oversees urban and industrial collapse. Hidden histories reveal themselves, disparities converge and prayers go crooked in an unkempt, deregulated world. Yet the pace and procedure of Okri's prose is undaunted. He maintains a fluent attention to realistic detail. He is still observant of those moments and places of ''very perceptible demarcation.'' *Stars of the New Curfew* opens with an epigraph by Christopher Okigbo: ''We carry in our worlds that flourish our worlds that have failed.'' The ''worlds that have failed'' resurface and submerge. In the title-story, a recalcitrant salesman is forced into dispensing fake ringworm medicines which actually multiply ringworm, then finds work with a new firm called ''CURES UNLIMITED.'' From describing the ''nightmare of salesmen'' Okri moves to depicting the ''salesman of nightmares.'' In both short story collections, Okri's visions have the vividness of hallucination.

The Famished Road expands the hallucinatory medium of the stories over the length of a 500-page novel. This is Okri's most haunting, entertaining, and challenging work to date. It is as if Soyinka and Amos Tutuola had coauthored a work with the South American ''magic realists'' Borges and Marquez, although there is also a singularly elegant lightness of touch and a constancy of pace.

The narrator is Azaro, a ''spirit-child'' who is still linked with the protean spirits that lie unborn behind or underneath creation's struggling forms. His innocuous naiveté, unquenchable curiosity, and endless thirst are unchecked by his adventures. His experience is articulated within a limited but shifting constellation of characters and places: his home and his parents; the shrewd, magisterial Madame Koto and her bar; the forest that surrounds the village; and the interstellar spaces into which his wayward imagination sails. Realistic details and dream-scenarios are syncopated and run together. The result is not counterpoint but a unique blend of physical, sensual, and creatural particularities within a radically unpredictable metaphysical context. The staple diet in Madam Koto's bar is hot pepper soup and palm wine. This scalds the palate and the imagination at the same time that it sustains both. The book is populated with grotesque and wonderful characters from the compound, the forest, the world beyond the forest, and the spirit world. We encounter a two-legged dog, a photographer, hundreds of rats, various parties of politicians, the motley inhabitants of Madame Koto's bar, Azaro's Dad (who becomes a champion boxer, a political revolutionist, and a fantastic storyteller), and his Mum, who hawks her wares around the streets of the compound to pay for food and ''ogogoro.''

Despite the unremitting grimness of much of what Okri describes, the lasting impression of *The Famished Road* is of the regenerative power of the imagination. Medicines are found for the harshest poisons; fevers rage and die; performances take their exultant forms and shift camp once again. Nevertheless, if the imagination is a source of future hope, it is often unreliable. Azaro's naive perceptiveness, his childlike wisdom and insouciance, undercut the potential banality in his ingenuous pronouncements. He accepts, with some scepticism, his Dad's judgements: ''The heart is bigger than a mountain. One human life is deeper than the ocean. Strange tribes and sea-monsters and mighty plants live in the rock-bed of our spirits. The whole of human history is an undiscovered continent deep in our souls.'' Azaro's response brings reality into perspective: ''A dream can be the highest point of a life.''

Songs of Enchantment returns to the world of Azaro, which is torn by the tension between political factions, and by Azaro's own personal turmoil. Okri's writing here is richly sensual: ''His limbs shook and he was bathed in radiance, as if his fit were a sweet juice that he was drinking, or as if it were sunlight to the feverish.'' Azaro appears once again in *Infinite Riches,* a novel featuring the characters and conflicts familiar to Okri's readers.

—Alan Riach

OLSEN, Tillie

Nationality: American. **Born:** Tillie Lerner, Omaha, Nebraska, 14 January 1912 or 1913. **Education:** Some high school. **Family:** Married Jack Olsen in 1943 (died); four daughters. **Career:** Has worked in the service, warehouse, and food processing industries, and as an office typist. Writer-in-residence, Amherst College, Massachusetts, 1969–70; visiting professor, Stanford University, California, Spring 1971; writer-in-residence, Massachusetts Institute of Technology, Cambridge, 1973; visiting professor, University of Massachusetts, Boston, 1974; visiting lecturer, University of California, San Diego, 1978; International Visiting Scholar, Norway, 1980; Hill Professor, University of Minnesota, Minneapolis, 1986; writer-in-residence, Amherst College; writer-in-residence, Kenyon College, Gambier, Ohio, 1987; Regents' professor, University of California, Los Angeles, 1988. Creative Writing fellow, Stanford University, 1956–57; fellow, Radcliffe Institute for Independent Study, Cambridge, Massachusetts, 1962–64. **Awards:** Ford grant, 1959; O. Henry award, 1961; American Academy award, 1975; Guggenheim fellowship, 1975; Unitarian Women's Federation award, 1980; National Endowment for the Humanities grant, 1966 and 1984; Bunting Institute fellowship, 1986; Nebraska Library Association Mari Sandoz award, 1991; Rea award, for distinguished contribution to the short story, 1994; Distinguished Achievement award, Western Literary Association, 1996. Doctor of Arts and Letters: University of Nebraska, Lincoln, 1979; D.Litt.: Knox College, Galesburg, Illinois, 1982; Hobart and William Smith College, Geneva, New York, 1984; Clark University, Worcester, Massachusetts, 1985; Albright College, Reading, Pennsylvania, 1986; Wooster College, Ohio, 1991; Mills College, 1995; Amherst College, Amherst, Massachusetts, 1998. ''Tillie Olsen Day'' observed in San Francisco, 1981. **Address:** 2333 Ward Street Rear, Berkeley, California 94705–1110, U.S.A.

PUBLICATIONS

Novel

Yonnondio: From the Thirties. New York, Delacorte Press, 1974; London, Faber, 1975.

Short Stories

Tell Me a Riddle: A Collection. Philadelphia, Lippincott, 1961; London, Faber, 1964.

Dream Vision. New York, Mother to Daughter, Daughter to Mother, n.d.

Uncollected Short Story

''Requa-I,'' in *The Best American Short Stories 1971,* edited by Martha Foley and David Burnett. Boston, Houghton Mifflin, 1971.

Other

Silences. New York, Delacorte Press, 1978; London, Virago Press, 1980.

Mothers and Daughters: That Special Quality: An Exploration in Photographs, with Julie Olsen-Edwards and Estelle Jussim. New York, Aperture, 1987.

Afterword, Life in the Iron Mills. Old Westbury, New York, Feminist Press, 1972.

The Word Made Flesh. Iowa City, Iowa Humanities Council, 1984.

Editor, *Mother to Daughter, Daughter to Mother: Mothers on Mothering.* Old Westbury, New York, Feminist Press, 1984; London, Virago Press, 1985.

*

Manuscript Collection: Berg Collection, New York Public Library; Stanford Library American Literature Archives, Stanford University, California.

Critical Studies: *Tillie Olsen* by Abigail Martin, Boise, Idaho, Boise State University, 1984; *Tillie Olsen and a Feminist Spiritual Vision* by Elaine Neil Orr, Jackson, University Press of Mississippi, 1987; *Tillie Olsen* by Abby Werlock and Mickey Pearlman, Boston, Twayne, 1991; *Protest and Possibility in the Writing of Tillie Olsen* by Mara Faulkner, Charlottesville and London, University Press of Virginia, 1993; *The Critical Response to Tillie Olsen* edited by Kay Hoyle Nelson and Nancy Huse, Westport, Connecticut, and London, Greenwood Press, 1994; *Listening to Silences* edited by Elaine Hedges and Shelley Fisher Fishkin, New York and Oxford, Oxford University Press, 1994; *Better Red: The Writing and Resistance of Tillie Olsen* *and Meridel Le Sueur* by Constance Coiner, New York, Oxford University Press, 1995; *Tillie Olsen: A Study of the Short Fiction* by Joanne Frye, Boston, Twayne, 1995; *Tell Me A Riddle* by Deborah Rosenfelt, Rutgers, Rutgers University Press, 1995; *Three Radical Women Writers: Class and Gender in Meridel Le Sueur, Tillie Olsen, and Josephine Herbst* by Nora Ruth Roberts, New York, Garland, 1996; *Women's Ethical Coming-of-Age: Adolescent Female Characters in the Prose Fiction of Tillie Olsen* by Agnes Toloczko Cardoni, Lanham, Maryland, University Press of America, 1997.

* * *

Tillie Olsen repeatedly expresses her conviction that literature is impoverished to the degree that creativity is not nourished and sustained in women and in people of the working class. Her speeches and essays on the waste of talent and on periods of aridity in the lives of authors, her long treatise on Rebecca Harding Davis's thwarted career following marriage, and her notes and quotations of this theme—collected over a period of 15 years—constitute *Silences.* Her own artistic recognition was postponed by the exigencies of making a living for herself and her children. She ''mislaid'' a novel for 35 years and wrote no story she thought worthy of publication until she was 43.

Tell Me a Riddle includes the three stories and the novella published between 1956 and 1960. ''Tell Me a Riddle'' centers on the antagonism which arises between two Jewish immigrants after their 37 years of marriage. In this novella Olsen reflects also upon the embarrassment and bewilderment of their married children as the ''gnarled roots'' of this marriage split apart. The wife's slow death from cancer greatly intensifies the conflict, but also dramatizes the love that remains only because it has become a habit. The wife returns in her delirium to their 1905 revolutionary activism, as her husband sighs, ''how we believed, how we belonged.'' Almost without plot, this novella demonstrates Olsen's artistry in characterization, dialogue, and sensory appeal, and it fully displays, as does all her fiction, her highly rhythmic and metaphorical use of language.

In the monologue ''I Stand Here Ironing'' a woman reviews the 19 years of her daughter's life and mourns those days which blighted the daughter's full ''flowering.'' Most intense are the mother's memories of being torn away from her infant in order to support her after they were abandoned. In ''Hey Sailor, What Ship?'' Whitey, a sailor, is given to drink and to buying admiration from the children of Lennie and Helen by giving them expensive gifts. Here he endures his last visit with his adopted family, with whom he has spent San Francisco shore leaves for years. The oldest daughter, embarrassed before her friends, turns in judgment upon the man who has brought a sense of adventure and romance to the family, while they have provided him some understanding and security over the years. In the elegiac close, Whitey pauses at the top of the third of seven hills to look back through the fog to the house with ''its eyes unshaded.'' In the story ''O Yes'' a 12-year-old black girl invites her white friend to her baptism. As the throb of voices and clapping and the swaying of bodies intensifies the congregation's religious fervor, the white child feels her senses assailed and faints. The next year in junior high, as rigid social patterns separate the two friends, she mourns the warmth and openness she felt momentarily at the baptism.

The novel *Yonnondio: From the Thirties,* which Olsen began at the age of 19 (when she was already a mother), she abandoned five years later, a few pages short of its close. The manuscript was found 35 years later, and in 1973, in ''arduous partnership'' with her younger self, Olsen selected, edited, and organized the fragments, but she could not write the ending or rewrite sections. The novel significantly adds to American fiction of the Depression years, and it provides remarkable evidence of Olsen's artistry in her early youth. Greatly impressive are the imagery, the use of smells and sounds, the rhythms which shift notably between the first two sections written from the view of the child Mazie, and the third section which emerges from the narrative consciousness of the mother, Mary Holbrook, dying gradually of exhaustion, childbearing, and malnutrition. The title of this novel is taken from Walt Whitman's ''Yonnondio'' and in Iroquois means a lament for the aborigines—the authors mourn the common folk who suffered greatly but left ''No picture, poem, statement, passing them to the future.'' During the course of the novel, Jim Holbrook moves from a Wyoming mine to a North Dakota tenant farm and finally to a Chicago or Omaha meat-packing plant with his wife and family. The zestful and imaginative Mazie in the early months of their life on the farm becomes ecstatically pantheistic in the style of Whitman's nature poetry, but in the city, in section three, she has lost her aspiration and much of her sensitivity and moves into the background in her bewilderment at her mother's illness and her father's increasing bad temper and dependence on alcohol. Critics generally acclaimed the novel, but several complained that Olsen gives her readers no mercy and that her work may be too painful for sustained reading and too unrelenting in its despair to allow characters to triumph through suffering.

—Margaret B. McDowell

O'NAN, Stewart

Nationality: American. **Born:** Pittsburgh, Pennsylvania, 4 February 1961. **Education:** Boston University, B.S. 1983; Cornell University, M.F.A. 1992. **Family:** Married Trudy Anne Southwick in 1984; one son, one daughter. **Career:** Test engineer, Grummann Aerospace Corporation, Bethpage, New York, 1984–88; writer. **Awards:** Ascent Fiction prize, 1988; Columbia Fiction award, 1989; Drue Heinz Prize for Literature, 1993; William Faulkner prize, 1993; named one of America's Best Young Novelists, *Granta,* 1996. **Agent:** Georges Borchardt, Inc., 136 East 57th Street, New York, New York 10022, U.S.A. **Address:** 407 Utica Street, Ithaca, New York 14850, U.S.A.

PUBLICATIONS

Novels

Snow Angels. New York, Doubleday, 1994.
The Names of the Dead. New York, Doubleday, 1996.
The Speed Queen. New York, Doubleday, 1997.
A World Away. New York, Henry Holt, 1998.
A Prayer for the Dying. New York, Henry Holt, 1999.
The Circus Fire. New York, Doubleday, 2000.

Short Stories

In the Walled City. Pittsburgh, University of Pittsburgh Press, 1993.

Other

Transmission. Colorado Springs, Colorado, Arjuna, 1987.
Editor, *On Writers and Writing* by John Gardner. Reading, Massachusetts, Addison-Wesley, 1994.
Editor, *The Vietnam Reader: The Definitive Collection of American Fiction and Nonfiction on the War.* New York, Anchor, 1998.

* * *

Stewart O'Nan calls himself a horror writer, although his novels have not been marketed as such. Indeed, the spread of O'Nan's reputation as a novelist has been complicated, perhaps slowed, by his admirable refusal to write to a niche market. Each of his novels differs in length, approach, and subject matter from the one before it. ''If there is an audience out there for me,'' O'Nan told *Publishers Weekly,* ''I want them to be surprised when the next book comes out.''

Yet a recurring truth of O'Nan's fictional universe, as in John Irving's, is that horrible things happen to people, often without warning or reason. The suffering protagonist of O'Nan's strongest novel, *A Prayer for the Dying,* observes, ''It's astonishing how quickly things fall apart.'' That the human responses to such horrors are infinitely varied helps explain the diversity of O'Nan's novels to date. It's as if O'Nan, a Grumman engineer before he turned to writing full time, were doggedly testing to destruction character after character, to see what shapes the fragments take.

Partially because his novels offer none of Irving's Dickensian comforts, no layers of Victorian-era Turkish delight to sweeten their horrors, O'Nan—like two of his novelist heroes, Flannery O'Connor and Stephen King—has been accused of coldness, of cruelty. But there is much to admire, too, in O'Nan's determination repeatedly to tackle the stark fact of mortality, and in his ability to do so with such chameleon-like virtuosity. Underscoring O'Nan's achievement as a novelist to date is another stark fact: he is not yet forty years old.

O'Nan's first novel, *Snow Angels,* details the tragic events leading up to the death of a dissatisfied young wife and mother, Annie Marchand, at the hands of her tormented husband, Glenn. Annie's decline and fall are narrated by a neighbor, Artie Parkinson, a teenager at the time of the events. For Artie, the story of Annie, his former baby sitter, is inextricably linked to his own coming of age—his parents ' divorce, his first fumbling romance, his complex feelings for this troubled but alluring older woman. O'Nan adopted a broader canvas in his next novel, *The Names of the Dead,* in which Vietnam veteran Larry Markham, already burdened by decades of guilt and by his attempts to salvage his unhappy marriage, finds himself and his family stalked by an even more troubled veteran, an ex-Special Forces psychopath named Creeley. The novel alternates the present-day story with chapters detailing Markham's Vietnam experience; the realism and power of these sequences are especially notable as O'Nan was still a child when the war ended.

As if in rebellion against the narrative complexity of his first two novels, O'Nan then produced *The Speed Queen,* the lean, mean, blackly comic Death Row memoir of a white-trash spree killer named Marjorie Standiford, whose nickname gives the novel its title. Marjorie is doggedly tape-recording her answers to 114 questions submitted by the unnamed best-selling horror writer who has contracted to write a non-fiction book about her bloody exploits; indeed, O'Nan's original title for the novel was *Dear Stephen King.* Marjorie's well-imagined voice and the somewhat tricky question-and-answer format—in which the reader is left to deduce the questions ''answered'' by the numbered sections—are ultimately more interesting than the glorified-outlaw plot, which Oliver Stone's film *Natural Born Killers* already had pushed about as far as it could go.

A World Away, O'Nan's much more deliberately paced fourth novel, echoes *The Names of the Dead* in its exploration of battlefields both foreign and domestic. The focus is on the World War II home front as represented by the Langer family. Both husband James and wife Anne are unfaithful; James's father is aged and infirm; adolescent son Jay is sullen and rebellious; and older son Rennie, who already has scandalized the family by becoming a conscientious objector, is now missing in action as a medic in the Pacific. Eventually Rennie comes home, as do his young wife and infant child, but the homecoming brings traumas of its own. O'Nan's working title was *Fear Itself,* perhaps an ironic comment on New Deal optimism; he describes the novel as an ''American pastoral'' in purposeful contrast to the gleaming excesses of *The Speed Queen.*

Yet the pastoral mode can hold horrors aplenty, as O'Nan abundantly demonstrates in his fifth novel, *A Prayer for the Dying*—inspired, O'Nan says, by Michael Lesy's haunting 1973 classic *Wisconsin Death Trip,* which documents the grim reality of small-town nineteenth-century America. Having in earlier novels probed the psychic scars of Vietnam and World War II veterans, O'Nan here focuses on Civil War veteran Jacob Hansen, who, despite traumatic, guilt-ridden flashbacks, has managed to establish a quiet, rewarding life with his wife and baby daughter in the small, isolated town of Friendship, Wisconsin—a town Jacob serves in three roles: sheriff, minister, and undertaker. Jacob soon has more than he can handle in each of these jobs, as a drifter's body turns out to be infected with diphtheria. The resulting epidemic kills most of the townsfolk, including Jacob's wife and daughter, and a rampaging forest fire claims those few spared by the disease. At novel's end, only Jacob is left to walk through the ruins of his town, his life and, perhaps, his faith.

Some readers found *A Prayer for the Dying* unbearably bleak, the book of Job minus the happy ending. Others were put off by O'Nan's uncharacteristic use of second-person narration, as Jacob essentially talks to himself as ''you'' throughout the novel. Some, too, complained about O'Nan's occasional Gothic excess, as when Jacob, deranged by grief, play-acts at happy domesticity with the corpses of his wife and daughter. Yet the risks O'Nan takes in *A Prayer for the Dying* are those of a first-rate novelist whose apprenticeship is over. The climactic fire that engulfs Friendship and a fleeing refugee-laden locomotive is a set piece worthy of Melville: suspenseful, poetic, thematically rich. Beautifully structured and imagined, filled with resonant imagery and compelling prose, *A Prayer for the Dying,* like the best fiction of O'Connor and King, lingers for months in the reader's head, continuing to disturb, to pose unanswerable questions about God, death, and fate. Readers may differ about what will become of Jacob amid the ashes, but few doubt that O'Nan will continue to enthrall, enrich, and disturb for many novels to come.

—Andy Duncan

ONDAATJE, (Philip) Michael

Nationality: Canadian. **Born:** Colombo, Ceylon (now Sri Lanka), 12 September 1943. **Education:** St. Thomas' College, Colombo; Dulwich College, London; Bishop's University, Lennoxville, Quebec, 1962–64; University of Toronto, B.A. 1965; Queen's University, Kingston, Ontario, M.A. 1967. **Family:** Married 1) Betty Kimbark in 1963, one daughter and one son; 2) Kim Jones (separated). **Career:** Taught at the University of Western Ontario, London, 1967–71. Since 1971 member of the Department of English, most recently a full professor, Glendon College, York University, Toronto. Visiting professor, University of Hawaii, Honolulu, summer 1979; Brown University, 1990. Editor, *Mongrel Broadsides.* **Awards:** Ralph Gustafson award, 1965; Epstein award, 1966; E.J. Pratt medal, 1966; President's medal, University of Western Ontario, 1967; Canada Council grant, 1968, 1977; Books in Canada First Novel award. 1977 Governor-General's Award for Poetry, 1979; Governor-General's Award for Fiction, 1971, 1980, 1992; Canada-Australia prize, 1980; Toronto Book award, 1988; Booker prize, 1992; Literary Lion award (New York Public Library), 1993. **Address:** Department of English, Glendon College, York University, 2275 Bayview Ave., Toronto, Ontario M4N 3M6, Canada.

PUBLICATIONS

Novels

Coming Through Slaughter. Toronto, Anansi, 1976; New York, Norton, 1977; London, Boyars, 1979.
In the Skin of a Lion. Toronto, McClelland and Stewart, New York, Knopf, and London, Secker and Warburg, 1987.
The English Patient. New York, Knopf, and London, Bloomsbury, 1992.
Anil's Ghost. New York, Knopf, 2000.

Plays

The Collected Works of Billy the Kid (produced Stratford, Ontario, 1973; New York, 1974; London, 1984).
Coming Through Slaughter, adaptation of his own novel (produced Toronto, 1980).

Poetry

The Dainty Monsters. Toronto, Coach House Press, 1967.
The Man with Seven Toes. Toronto, Coach House Press, 1969.
The Collected Works of Billy the Kid: Left Handed Poems. Toronto, Anansi, 1970; New York, Norton, 1974; London, Boyars, 1981.
Rat Jelly. Toronto, Coach House Press, 1973.
Elimination Dance. Ilderton, Ontario, Nairn Coldstream, 1978; revised edition, Ilderton, Brick, 1980.
There's a Trick with a Knife I'm Learning to Do: Poems 1963–1978. Toronto, McClelland and Stewart, and New York, Norton, 1979; as *Rat Jelly and Other Poems 1963–1978,* London, Boyars, 1980.
Secular Love. Toronto, Coach House Press, 1984; New York, Norton, 1985.
Two Poems. Milwaukee, Woodland Pattern, 1986.
The Cinnamon Peeler: Selected Poems. London, Pan, 1989; New York, Knopf, 1991.
Handwriting: Poems. New York, Knopf, 1999.

Other

Leonard Cohen. Toronto, McClelland and Stewart, 1970.
Claude Glass. Toronto, Coach House Press, 1979.
Tin Roof. Lantzville, British Columbia, Island, 1982.
Running in the Family. Toronto, McClelland and Stewart, and New York, Norton, 1982; London, Gollancz, 1983.
Editor, *The Broken Ark* (animal verse). Toronto, Oberon Press, 1971; revised edition, as *A Book of Beasts,* 1979.
Editor, *Personal Fictions: Stories by Munro, Wiebe, Thomas, and Blaise.* Toronto, Oxford University Press, 1977.
Editor, *The Long Poem Anthology.* Toronto, Coach House Press, 1979.
Editor, with Russell Banks and David Young, *Brushes with Greatness: An Anthology of Chance Encounters with Greatness.* Toronto, Coach House Press, 1989.
Editor, with Linda Spalding, *The Brick Anthology.* Toronto, Coach House Press, 1989.
Editor, *From Ink Lake: An Anthology of Canadian Stories.* New York, Viking, 1990.
Editor, *The Faber Book of Contemporary Canadian Short Stories.* London, Faber, 1990.

*

Bibliography: By Judith Brady, in *The Annotated Bibliography of Canada's Major Authors 6* edited by Robert Lecker and Jack David, Toronto, ECW Press, 1985.

Manuscript Collection: National Archives, Ottawa; Metropolitan Toronto Library.

Critical Studies: *Spider Blues: Essays on Michael Ondaatje* edited by Sam Solecki, Montreal, Véhicule Press, 1985; *Michael Ondaatje* by Douglas Barbour, New York, Twayne, 1993; *Discoveries of the Other: Alterity in the Work of Leonard Cohen, Hubert Aquin, Michael Ondaatje, and Nicole Brossard* by Winfried Siemerling, Toronto and Buffalo, University of Toronto Press, 1994.

Theatrical Activities: Director: **Films**—*Sons of Captain Poetry,* 1971; *Carry on Crime and Punishment,* 1972; *Royal Canadian Hounds,* 1973; *The Clinton Special,* 1974.

* * *

Award-winning author Michael Ondaatje's novels examine the internal workings of characters who struggle against and burst through that which makes people passive and which historically renders human experience programmatic and static. To this end, his style—for which two lines from his poem "The Linguistic War Between Men and Women" act as a perfect comment—is raw, stark, energetic: "Men never trail away. / They sweat adjective." It is more appropriate to talk of Ondaatje's fiction and its energetic qualities as proceeding through "scenes" rather than through episodes or chapters: his extensive work and interest in film informs his preoccupation with matters of shaping and form.

Through Ondaatje's prose the reader is taken beyond morality into a realm of human action and interaction. His protagonists take great risks because they cannot do otherwise: they are driven to break through the limitations of mediocrity in a personal anarchy that is often destructive to self and others. The fractured narrative *Coming Through Slaughter* traces the personal anarchy of jazz trumpet player Buddy Bolden and the perspectives on him of those who knew him best. Bolden was never recorded and "never professional in the brain," but he was hailed as a great and powerful innovator. Ondaatje molds the little-known facts of Bolden's life into a fictional yet ostensibly objective account of the years of his fame, from the moment in approximately 1900 (age twenty-two) he walks into a New Orleans parade playing his loud, moody jazz. In a manic push beyond the order and certainty by which he was always tormented, he goes insane while playing in a parade in 1907, and is committed to an asylum where he dies in 1931.

In the Skin of a Lion draws less on historical fact than any of his previous novels. For the first time he uses culturally marginalized and wholly fictional central characters—except for Ambrose Small—and draws out their mythic potential rather than relying on and reshaping a preexistent cultural myth or a historical figure. In this novel Ondaatje explores the pulse of physical labor and the life of an immigrant neighborhood in Toronto and Southwestern Ontario from 1900 to 1940, and reveals its sense of community, solidarity, and hatred of the solipsistic idle rich. The protagonist Patrick, like Buddy Bolden, "departs from the world," but unlike Bolden, he has a private revolution that eventually takes the form of public political action.

All of Ondaatje's "fictions" have a metafictional aspect: Patrick, like the police detective Webb in *Coming Through Slaughter,* like Ondaatje himself in *Running in the Family,* is the searcher-figure, analogous to the writer, who stands to an extent outside of "lived experience" observing, rooting out facts and "truths," trying to shape a coherent history, or story. Through these figures, Ondaatje inscribes the perspective of the history-writer and sets up a tension between their observing and others' experiencing. In his novels, Ondaatje himself becomes a kind of historiographer and underscores the fact that the observer's impulse to articulate, an impulse experienced almost as a physical drive, is necessary to history.

The English Patient might be considered a sequel to *In the Skin of a Lion.* It features characters from the previous novel—Hana (Patrick's daughter), Caravaggio the thief—and continues Ondaatje's alertness to the fundamental importance of writing history. But Ondaatje's novels are characterized so much by inner transformations of character, voice, and scene, that it would be against the tenor of his craft to presume rigid connections between them, or to read them in a sequential manner. Like the sands of the North African desert that feature so prominently, *The English Patient* is a novel about shape-shifting. Set in the final days of World War II, as the map of Europe is about to be redrawn and Hiroshima and Nagasaki are soon to be disfigured utterly, it depicts the lives of four characters in a derelict villa north of Florence. The English patient (whose Englishness is not secure) is an aircraft pilot burned beyond recognition. He is cared for by a shell-shocked Hana, a nurse in the Canadian forces. They are joined by Caravaggio and Kirpal Singh, who earns the nickname Kip. Caravaggio has been tortured and suffered the removal of his thumbs. The emphasis upon the damage that each of these three characters has suffered finds its contrast in Kip, a Sikh sapper who spends his days defusing the mines that litter the vicinity of the villa. Kip symbolizes the propensity to reverse potential destruction; Ondaatje's descriptions of his work are some of the most memorable in all his prose. Those passages depicting Kip defusing the complex circuitry of mines make you tremble with relief at his eventual success.

Kip's presence at the villa helps emphasize storytelling as a form of defusing, an act that makes approachable an incendiary past. Gradually, through the act of recounting their histories, each character clears a path through their pasts that allows them to remember in safety. Their stories resemble the tattered books in the villa's library: fragmentary, full of gaps and parentheses. Indeed, the importance of rewriting is a theme that emerges in the novel's structure. Ondaatje builds the narrative upon fragments of other texts, just as the English patient records his thoughts in the pages of an old copy of Herodotus's *Histories* that is similarly swollen and torn.

But the bombs that cannot be defused fall on Hiroshima and Nagasaki, and the novel is never far from this apocalypse. When Kip learns of the news on the radio in the novel's climactic scene, his response is to confront the English patient with a rifle, outraged at this latest "tremor of Western wisdom." This, it seems, is one historical experience that renders redundant the narratives of Western history—with their emphasis on civilization and progress. A new narrative of history is required, perhaps one the novel itself tries to fashion, that rends the fabric of existing history in its attempt to bear witness to the immensity of what has happened.

This attempt at writing history is again undertaken in Ondaatje's latest novel, *Anil's Ghost.* In this work, however, Ondaatje does not set his characters against a diminishing mid-century conflict but, instead, in the midst of a recent war that does not exhibit the geometric sweep of advancing fronts, nor antagonists that are readily identifiable. The conflict between the government, anti-government insurgents, and separatist guerrillas involved in the Sri Lankan civil war of the late 1980s and early 1990s envelops the story like the imperious monsoons that drench its combatants and obscure the landscape. The result is that the characters, amid the pervasive and bald-faced violence of this war, do not have the constant sanctuary of an Italian villa in which to assemble their fragmented stories. Anil, a foreign educated forensic anthropologist assigned to her homeland on a UN mission to investigate alleged war atrocities, discovers a suspicious skeleton with her secretive local colleague, Sarath. The careful descriptions of the evidence drawn by Anil's handling of the bones are as lyrical and compelling as Kip's meticulous maneuvers in *The English Patient.* However, evidence, like the fragmented scenes of the novel, does not point to an apprehensible truth in this conflict. Indeed, these characters tell their stories not by gathering the evidence of their lives, but by reaching into the unknowing that surrounds them and making, or sculpting a place for human encounter. Palipana, the blind epigraphist, lives his days making connections beyond the evidence of his former archeological research while searching for lice in his young caregiver's hair; Gamini, Sarath's brother, the peripatetic, shy doctor, is driven to insomnia and exhaustion by his irrepressible need to physically care for the wounded; even Sarath, who would not shake his brother's hand, learns to touch as he gives his life to the inscrutable machinery of government at the end in order to secure safe passage for Anil.

To a greater extent than *The English Patient,* war in its genocidal capacities is the central concern of this novel. War is an omnipresence that reveals itself in the novel's epigraphic scenes always removed from contextual certainty. In one such scene, a man is crucified to the pavement with common builder's nails. Similarly, later in the novel, an anonymous assassin, edging closer to the president on the street, flicks the switches under his shirt that will force Gamini from Sarath's bedside to tend to a burst of wounded in the hospital. We do not learn why the man was nailed to the road, nor do we learn the name of the assassin or the political motivation for his bomb. These fragmented moments are not given to us as evidence with which to logically apprehend the pulse of this conflict. Indeed, we are left to approach these horrific and emotional incidents the way that the artist in the novel's last few pages approaches the act of painting the Buddha's eyes. We can only see indirectly and we can only abide the "sweet touch from the world."

Ondaatje's writing of history in *Anil's Ghost* develops his interest in the observer's impulse to articulate, yet it qualifies it in a way that removes the assuredness of evidence and renders the characters either silent, as in the case of the departed Anil, or responsive to the intimate, ineffable corporeality of their surroundings. Stories become, as they are in his 1998 book of poetry, *Handwriting*—which is in many ways a companion piece to the novel—unspeakable scripts on leaves, on smoke, or dispersed gestures like a gathering of bones that point to different pasts.

—Diane Watson, revisions by John McLeod and Adam Dickinson

OSBORNE, David

See SILVERBERG, Robert

O'SULLIVAN, Vincent (Gerard)

Nationality: New Zealander. **Born:** Auckland, 28 September 1937. **Education:** University of Auckland, M.A. 1959; Lincoln College, Oxford, B.Litt. 1962. **Career:** Editor, *Comment,* Wellington, 1963–66; lecturer, Victoria University of Wellington; senior lecturer, Waikato University, Hamilton. Literary editor, *New Zealand Listener,* 1978–79. **Awards:** Commonwealth scholarship, 1960; Macmillan Brown prize, 1961; Jessie Mackay award, 1965, for *Our Burning Time;* Farmers Poetry prize, 1967. **Address:** Pukeroro, R.D. 3, Hamilton, New Zealand.

PUBLICATIONS

Novels

Miracle: A Romance. Dunedin, McIndoe, 1976.
The Boy, the Bridge, the River. Dunedin, McIndoe, 1978.
Let the River Stand. Auckland and Oxford, Oxford University Press, n.d.
Believers to the Bright Coast. Auckland, Penguin, 1998.

Short Stories

Dandy Edison for Lunch, and Other Stories. Dunedin, McIndoe, 1981.
The Snow in Spain. Wellington, Allen and Unwin, 1990.
Palms and Minarets: Selected Stories. Wellington, Victoria University Press, 1992.

Poetry

Our Burning Time. N.p., Prometheus, 1965.
Revenants. N.p., Prometheus, 1969.
Bearings. Wellington and London, Oxford University Press, 1973.
From the Indian Funeral. Dunedin, McIndoe, 1976.
Butcher and Co. Auckland and Oxford, Oxford University Press, 1977.
Brother Jonathan, Brother Kafka, with prints by John Drawbridge. Wellington and Oxford, Oxford University Press, 1980.
The Butcher Papers. Auckland and Oxford, Oxford University Press, 1982.
The Pilate Tapes. Auckland and Oxford, Oxford University Press, 1986.
Selected Poems. Auckland, Oxford University Press, 1992.
The Houses of Sin; with Poems. New York, Woodstock Books, 1995.
Seeing You Asked. Wellington, Victoria University Press, 1998.

Other

New Zealand Poetry in the Sixties. Wellington, Wellington Department of Education, 1973.
Katherine Mansfield's New Zealand. London, Muller, 1975.
James K. Baxter. Wellington and London, Oxford University Press, 1977.
Finding the Pattern, Solving the Problem: Katherine Mansfield, the New Zealand European. Wellington, Victoria University Press, 1989.
Editor, *An Anthology of Twentieth-Century New Zealand Poetry.* Auckland and London, Oxford University Press, 1970.
Editor, *New Zealand Short Stories: Third Series.* Wellington and London, Oxford University Press, 1975.
Editor, *The Aloe;* with *Prelude,* by Katherine Mansfield. Manchester, Carcanet, 1983.
Editor, with Margaret Scott, *The Collected Letters of Katherine Mansfield. Volume 1: 1903–1917.* Oxford, Clarendon Press, 1985.
Editor, *Collected Poems,* by Ursula Bethell. Auckland and Oxford, Oxford University Press, 1985.
Editor, with S.C. Harrex. *Kamala Das: A Selection with Essays on Her Work.* Adelaide, Centre for Research in the New Literature in English, 1986.
Editor, with Margaret Scott, *The Collected Letters of Katherine Mansfield. Volume 2: 1918–1919.* Oxford, Clarendon Press, 1987.
Editor, *The Unsparing Scourge: Australian Satirical Texts 1845–1860.* Nedlands, Western Australia, Centre for Studies in Australian Literature, University of Western Australia,1988.
Editor, *Katherine Mansfield: Selected Letters.* Oxford, Clarendon Press, 1989.
Editor, *The Poems of Katherine Mansfield.* Auckland and Oxford, Oxford University Press, 1990.
Editor, with Margaret Scott, *The Collected Letters of Katherine Mansfield. Volume 3: 1919–1920.* Oxford, Clarendon Press, 1993.

Editor, *The Oxford Book of New Zealand Short Stories.* Auckland and New York, Oxford University Press, 1994.

Editor, *New Zealand Stories.* Auckland and New York, Oxford University Press, 1997.

*

Critical Studies: *Two Wellington Poets: W.H. Oliver and Vincent O'Sullivan: A Critique* by F.W. Nielsen Wright, Wellington, Cultural and Political Booklets, 1997.

* * *

Vincent O'Sullivan's versatility as short story writer, poet, playwright, scholar, and editor makes him perhaps New Zealand's most literary "man for all seasons." He is not to be confused with the Aesthetic Movement's author of the same name: the Vincent O'Sullivan who was friend to Oscar Wilde and master of macabre British fiction. There is a connection, however, in that New Zealand's Vincent O'Sullivan wrote his M.A. thesis on Oscar Wilde for the University of New Zealand in 1959. He undoubtedly became aware of his predecessor during his scholarly research on Wilde, and often used a shortened version of his name, "Vince," to avoid confusion. Vince O'Sullivan was born in Auckland in 1937, a year prior to the death of Oscar Wilde's friend. His scholarly work on Wilde, Katherine Mansfield, and other New Zealand and Australian writers quantitatively surpasses the number of novels he wrote. His reputation as a novelist rests largely on one great book, *Let the River Stand,* a classic of New Zealand literature.

Let the River Stand has been acclaimed for the sustained excellence of the writing, its perceptive characterization, and its teasing, jigsaw structure. Ostensibly a historical, social-realist fiction of rural New Zealand society between the 1920s and 1950s, it moves from Waikato during the Depression to Tasmania and Spain with a complex narrative structure that has been compared to the work of James Joyce. Images resonate with exacting observations of events, places, and people to evoke feelings and memories that are layered with meaning over time and which invite symbolic interpretation. Through his hero, Alex McLeod, O'Sullivan revisits the masculine world of his short stories and verse, and through the mind of Collins/Schwarz, a failed boxer turned pig-raiser, he investigates the bleakly limited world of the besieged, marginal man.

Drawing from several local literary traditions and models, but predominantly from John Mulgan's archetypal motif of "man alone," O'Sullivan apotheosizes the fate of the outsider with Schwarz's death. At one point in the narrative, O'Sullivan introduces a character by the name of Johnson, who originated in John Mulgan's fiction. Other images of isolation reverberate throughout the novel. Alex is a loner whose youthful idealism drives him and his cousin, Rory, to fight in the Spanish Civil War. Later he and his communist wife, Bet, are ostracized by the rural community because of their socialist beliefs.

O'Sullivan's original treatment of a favorite Decadent Movement theme used by Wilde's friend, Vincent, adds an erotically charged element to the image of female purity in *Let the River Stand.* In the story, Barbara Trevaskis wears her white dress, which symbolizes female purity, to school instead of the regulation gym tunic. The maelstrom of repression and desire resulting from the white dress and its stimulation of masculine obsessions leads to tragedy due to a displaced romanticism. Images of the river, sunlight, and water described in the hospital scenes reinforce the theme of repressed sexual passion that has gone out of control.

O'Sullivan creates a discontinuous narrative of anticipation and deferral in which several stories and memories interact. He sustains the dramatic tension by playing with reader expectation of a linear, causal sequence. His technique of hinting at a central tragedy while sharply delineating contingent and peripheral events, as James Joyce did, is essential to the realism O'Sullivan's great novel achieves. The meanings of some episodes emerge like a film running backwards. The juxtaposition of time past against time present contributes to the novel's lyrical, sensuous texture. The subtle irony resulting from the mysterious silence of the accident victim in *Let the River Stand,* is a refinement of his lifelong fascination with literary wit and satire.

The social satire, *Miracle: A Romance,* predates the accomplishment of his masterpiece, which was completed relatively late in life—*Let the River Stand* was published in 1993. *Miracle: A Romance* satirizes major political and cultural icons in New Zealand society, including its politicians and its passion for rugby. O'Sullivan mocks national vices through the grotesque ruler, Mr. Sagwheel, and Stumpy Smith, a barman-turned-sports-ambassador to South Africa. By equating popular responses to the sporting success of the rugby champion, Miracle Hornbeam, with Ranfruly Shield's heralded accomplishment of renewed virginity despite nightly rape, he overlaps satire with fantasy.

In the introduction to a collection of nineteenth-century Australian satirical texts which he edited titled *The Unsparing Scourge,* O'Sullivan reveals how important the use of satire and Wilde-like wit is to his writing. He states that moral energy supplies the various strategies of wit, and that this type of wit, when "brought to bear on instances of depravity," gives literary texts their vigor and interest. Wit and satire, particularly in O'Sullivan's writing, often supply the comic elements in literature that permit reader acceptance of the fantastic and an open discussion of social taboos. This lively style of discourse circumvents the somewhat repressed nature attributed to New Zealanders.

Like his forebears, authors Maurice Duggan and Dan Davin, O'Sullivan has flavored the predominantly puritan, Protestant ethic of New Zealand social realism with an Irish-Catholic sensibility and wit. In *Miracle: A Romance,* O'Sullivan tries to merge a macabre humor with a story about Catholic miracles. To accomplish the seamless connections of the improbable, the incomprehensible, and the impossible, he utilizes an interlaced narrative technique in a novel which can be called a comedy of obsession, its momentum derived from a decentered, bizarre vision of society.

The techniques that constitute O'Sullivan's impressive style in the novels were honed in his numerous collections of short stories, including *Dandy Edison for Lunch, and Other Stories,* written while he was a creative writing fellow at Victoria University of Wellington. The short stories range across different cultures with diverse characters; yet O'Sullivan's focus on middle-class hypocrisy and his dispassionate portrayals of the underprivileged are both distinctive and convincing. Precise observation correlated to a low-key emotional register and an understated social vision bordering on the satiric are his hallmarks. Epiphanies are rare, and metaphor, when it occurs, functions as a principle of structure rather than of style. In his early stories, confrontations between his misfit heroes and the pretensions of bourgeois New Zealand society are underpinned by a recognition of loss or the hint of an alternative world view; in his later stories, he turns to social satire or black comedy.

One gets the sense that O'Sullivan makes distinctions in his aesthetic requirements for each genre he practices. For example, he does not impose a lyrical poetic style upon his fiction, despite numerous collections of poetry such as *Seeing You Asked,* published the same year as his latest novel, *Believers to the Bright Coast,* in 1998. His fictional themes of emotional repression, estrangement, and betrayal usually work by implication and by insight into motive and character. Pervasive images of concealment, lying, and dissimulation, which contrast to his narrators' masks of literal-minded obtuseness, derive from fiction writers he has studied rather than from an amalgam of inter-genre stylistics. New Zealand's literary ''man for all seasons'' is master of all precisely because he does not blur the boundaries between the genres he practices.

—Janet Wilson, updated by Hedwig Gorski

OZICK, Cynthia

Nationality: American. **Born:** New York City, 17 April 1928. **Education:** New York University, B.A. (cum laude) in English 1949 (Phi Beta Kappa); Ohio State University, Columbus, M.A. 1951. **Family:** Married Bernard Hallote in 1952; one daughter. **Career:** Instructor in English, New York University, 1964–65; Distinguished Artist-in-Residence, City University, New York, 1982; Phi Beta Kappa Orator, Harvard University, Cambridge, Massachusetts, 1985. Lives in New Rochelle, New York. **Awards:** National Endowment for the Arts fellowship, 1968; Wallant award, 1972; B'nai B'rith award, 1972; Jewish Book Council Epstein award, 1972, 1977; American Academy award, 1973; Hadassah Myrtle Wreath award, 1974; Lamport prize, 1980; Guggenheim fellowship, 1982; Strauss Living award, 1982–1987; Distinguished Alumnus award, New York University, 1984; Rea award, for short story, 1986; Lucy Martin Donnelly award, Bryn Mawr College, 1991–92; PEN/Spiegel-Diamonstein award for the Art of the Essay, 1997; Harold Washington Literary award, City of Chicago, 1997; John Cheever award, 1999. D.H.L.: Yeshiva University, New York, 1984; Hebrew Union College, Cincinnati, 1984; Williams College, Williamstown, Massachusetts, 1986; Hunter College, New York, 1987; Jewish Theological Seminary, New York, 1988; Adelphi University, Garden City, New York, 1988; State University of New York, 1989; Brandeis University, Waltham, Massachusetts, 1990; Bard College, Annandale-on-Hudson, New York, 1991; Skidmore College, 1992; Seton Hall University, 1999; Rutgers University, 1999. **Agent:** Raines and Raines, 71 Park Avenue, New York, New York 10016. **Address:** c/o Knopf Inc., 201 East 50th Street, New York, New York 10022, U.S.A.

PUBLICATIONS

Novels

Trust. New York, New American Library, 1966; London, MacGibbon and Kee, 1967.
The Cannibal Galaxy. New York, Knopf, 1983; London, Secker and Warburg, 1984.
The Messiah of Stockholm. New York, Knopf, and London, Deutsch, 1987.
The Puttermesser Papers. New York, Knopf, 1997.

Short Stories

The Pagan Rabbi and Other Stories. New York, Knopf, 1971; London, Secker and Warburg, 1972.
Bloodshed and Three Novellas. New York, Knopf, and London, Secker and Warburg, 1976.
Levitation: Five Fictions. New York, Knopf, and London, Secker and Warburg, 1982.
The Shawl: A Story and a Novella. New York, Knopf, 1989.

Uncollected Short Stories

''The Sense of Europe,'' in *Prairie Schooner* (Lincoln, Nebraska), June 1956.
''Stone,'' in *Botteghe Oscure* (Rome), Autumn 1957.
''The Laughter of Akiva,'' in *New Yorker,* 10 November 1980.
''At Fumicaro,'' in *New Yorker,* 6 August 1984.

Plays

Blue Light (produced Long Island, 1994).

Poetry

Epodes: First Poems, with woodcuts by Sidney Chafetz. N.p., 1992.

Other

Art and Ardor (essays). New York, Knopf, 1983.
Metaphor and Memory (essays). New York, Knopf, 1989.
What Henry James Knew, and Other Essays on Writers (essays). London, n.p. 1993.
A Cynthia Ozick Reader, edited by Elaine M. Kauvar. Bloomington, Indiana University Press, 1993.
Fame and Folly: Essays. New York, Knopf, 1996.
Quarrel and Quandary: Essays. New York, Knopf, 2000.

*

Bibliography: ''A Bibliography of Writings by Cynthia Ozick'' by Susan Currier and Daniel J. Cahill, in *Texas Studies in Literature and Language* (Austin), Summer 1983.

Critical Studies: ''The Art of Cynthia Ozick'' by Victor Strandberg, in *Texas Studies in Literature and Language* (Austin), Summer 1983; *Cynthia Ozick, Texas Studies in Literature and Language,* edited by Catherine Rainwater and William J. Scheick, University Press of Kentucky, 1983; *Contemporary American Women Writers: Narrative Strategies,* edited by Catherine Rainwater and William J. Scheick, University Press of Kentucky, 1985; *Crisis and Covenant: The Holocaust in American Jewish Fiction,* by Alan L. Berger, State University of New York, 1985; *Cynthia Ozick* edited by Harold Bloom, New York, Chelsea House, 1986, and *Cynthia Ozick: Modern Critical Views,* by Bloom, Chelsea Publishers, 1986; *The World of Cynthia Ozick: Studies in American Jewish Literature,* edited by Daniel Walden, Kent State University Press, 1987; *Since Flannery O'Conner: Essays on the Contemporary Short Story,* by Loren Logsdon and Charles W. Mayer, Western Illinois University Press, 1987; *The Uncompromising Fictions of Cynthia Ozick* by Sanford Pinsker, Columbia, University of Missouri Press, 1987; *Cynthia*

Ozick by Joseph Lowin, Boston, Twayne, 1988; *Understanding Cynthia Ozick* by Lawrence S. Friedman, University of South Carolina Press, 1991; *Cynthia Ozick: Tradition and Invention* by Elaine M. Kasuvar, Indiana University Press, 1993; *Greek Mind, Jewish Soul* by Victor Strandberg, University of Wisconsin Press, 1994; *Cynthia Ozick's Comic Art,* by Sarah Blacher Cohen, Indiana University Press, 1994; *Greek Mind/Jewish Soul: The Conflicted Art of Cynthia Ozick* by Victor Strandberg, Madison, Wisconsin, University of Wisconsin Press, 1994.

* * *

Cynthia Ozick has said that she began her first novel as an American writer and ended it six-and-a-half years later as a Jewish writer. Overarching this book, *Trust,* is a third cultural presence made manifest in the seductive appeal of the pagan Earth-gods, who have maintained their potency under various names from old Greek and Canaanite times to our own. Ozick's conviction regarding this insight is attested by her view of ''the issue of Hellenism-versus-Hebraism as the central quarrel of the West.'' Nevertheless, it was the American writer Henry James who most deeply stamped his image upon her youthful imagination. She wrote her master's thesis on parable in James's fiction, and spent seven apprentice years writing a never-published novel in the Jamesian manner, followed by almost as long a period working on the neo-Jamesian *Trust.*

Completed on the day President Kennedy was murdered, *Trust* was published in 1966 to a thin but highly favorable chorus of reviews. Its Jamesian elements are immediately evident in its style (''both mandarin and lapidary,'' Ozick calls it), its social milieu (a wealthy American family), its masking of greed and duplicity under an elegant surface of manners, and its international theme (half the book is set in Europe, half in America). The title itself is ironic to a Jamesian degree of complexity in that lack of trust affects every relationship from the familial (husband-wife, mother-daughter) to the theological (God's covenant having been broken in the Holocaust). What revives trust in the end is the young heroine's disavowal of her decaying cultural heritage (epitomized in her mother's crassly mis-spent trust fund) in favor of the spontaneous gods of nature—which is to say, her reversion to the ancient pagan ethos. Her discovery of that ethos in her lost father (who had sired her as his ''illegitimate issue'' and then was succeeded by unsatisfactory Christian and Jewish father figures) makes up the central plot line of this immense and densely written novel. In the end, her father's apotheosis as a fertility god (which she witnesses) occasions one of the most vividly imagined sexual encounters in American literature—an imagistic rendering of sensation that is perhaps Ozick's finest (and most difficult) artistic achievement.

Even while she was working on *Trust,* Ozick's fascination with the Pan vs. Moses theme (as a character in *Trust* calls it) gathered such force as to promulgate her next book, the collection of stories titled *The Pagan Rabbi.* Within the title story, Pan overcomes Moses when the rabbi couples with a dryad—in another vividly imagined sexual encounter—and then hangs himself from her tree, not in guilt but in pantheistic ecstasy. ''The molecules dance within all forms … and within the atoms dance still profounder sources of divine vitality. There is nothing that is Dead,'' says the rabbi's last testament. Behind this heretical hunger for the world's beauty lies the chief paradox, for Ozick, of the Jewish artist. ''The single most serviceable description of a Jew—as defined 'theologically'— … is someone who shuns idols,'' she has written; yet to create literature is to put oneself ''in competition, like a god, with the Creator,'' so that ''[art] too is turned into an idol.'' Ozick memorably transmutes this theme into fiction in her next book, *Bloodshed,* where the artist-as-idolator appears triumphant in ''Usurpation (Other People's Stories).'' Here the Jewish poet, so apostate as to have published a hymn to Apollo, ascends to the Olympic rather than Jewish afterworld in the end, totally rejecting his Jewish heritage. But though the God of Israel permits him to espouse the new identity, the Gentile gods do not: ''Then the taciturn little Canaanite idols call him, in the language of the spheres, kike.'' Flight from and coerced movement back toward Jewish identity is thus the unifying theme of the four tales in *Bloodshed,* with the Holocaust exerting the most powerful such coercive force. In ''A Mercenary'' a Polish Jew who survived the Holocaust tries to expunge his Jewishness by becoming United Nations ambassador for a black African nation, but he is subtly called Jew by his black aide and even by inanimate objects: his cigarette reminds him of Holocaust smoke; his ''white villa on the blue coast,'' of the ''bluish snow'' and ''snow-white hanging stars of Poland'' during his Holocaust period. Conversely, in the title story, ''Bloodshed,'' despair over the Holocaust prompts its Jewish protagonist to contemplate suicide, until he is rescued by a Holocaust survivor's powerful lesson that ''despair must be earned.''

The later stages of Ozick's career have featured two books of essays, *Art and Ardor* and *Metaphor and Memory,* which embrace a quarter-century of journal contributions. Many of these essays offer incisive insights into her imaginative writing, especially concerning the dilemmas of contemporary Jewish-American culture. Her later fiction explores those dilemmas in a transatlantic range of settings. *Levitation: Five Fictions,* set almost wholly in New York City, uses its title as a three-part pun for its opening story: levitation, levity, the priestly tribe of Levi. It portrays the Holocaust as an identity-defining event, levitating genuine Jews away from the pseudo- or de-Judaized Jews who remain below on ground level. The most expansive, ambitious, and original part of this collection is the Puttermesser-Xanthippe series, a new version of Pan vs. Moses. In this instance the Pan figure (Xanthippe) is a female golem chanted into existence by Puttermesser to save New York City, but in the end the Jewish lawgiver (Puttermesser has become mayor) must sorrowfully chant her charming friend back to a pile of mud after Xanthippe begins to inflame the whole city with illicit sexual hunger. An extensive sequel to this series, in which Puttermesser falls in love, has appeared in the *New Yorker* magazine.

The Cannibal Galaxy revives the Jamesian theme of interaction between Europe and America via a Holocaust survivor, Joseph Brill, who hopes to unite the best of both cultures in a Jewish-American educational program. Although his school, located in the Midwest, thrives financially, in the end the American culture (which may be the ''cannibal galaxy'') crushes out the European, in part because the high culture of Europe did not truly survive the Holocaust. *The Messiah of Stockholm,* the only Ozick novel set wholly in Europe, concerns the effort of Lars Andemening, a Swedish book reviewer, to verify his claim that Bruno Schulz (the real-life Polish Jew, murdered in 1942) is his father. Schulz's dichotomy between ''Cinnamon Shops'' and ''The Street of Crocodiles''—his best known story titles—repeats itself in Ozick's novel, as Andemening in the end is stripped of his energizing illusions (the comforting refuge of ''Cinnamon Shops'') and left to cope with the cold barrenness of reality (''The Street of Crocodiles''). And finally, *The Shawl*—Ozick's little book combining the stories ''The Shawl'' and ''Rosa''—plays off Jewish-American and Jewish-European cultures against each other, to the discredit of both. Rosa, a Holocaust survivor from Warsaw, relies on her high-class, assimilated Polish family heritage to assert her superiority over the degraded Jewish-American culture she experiences in New York and Miami. ''My Warsaw is not your Warsaw,'' she insists to Persky, her kindly but vulgar friend in Miami who had emigrated from the impoverished Warsaw ghetto before the war. Rosa's use of magic to invoke the spirit of her infant daughter (who had been murdered at Auschwitz) comprises yet another instance of the enticement of the pagan gods, tying Ozick's latest work to early books like *Trust* and *The Pagan Rabbi.*

Although Ozick's Jewish materials—including a sprinkling of Yiddish words on many pages—can create an initial impression of opacity, her general reading audience should not find her cultural heritage more difficult to apprehend than Faulkner's or Toni Morrison's materials. Through her greatly original and powerful expression of her Jewish ethos, Ozick contributes importantly to the larger American literary tradition.

—Victor Strandberg

P

PALEY, Grace

Nationality: American. **Born:** Grace Goodside in New York City, 11 December 1922. **Education:** Evander Childs High School, New York; Hunter College, New York, 1938–39. **Family:** Married 1) Jess Paley in 1942, one daughter and one son; 2) the playwright Robert Nichols in 1972. **Career:** Has taught at Columbia University, New York, and Syracuse University, New York. Since 1966 has taught at Sarah Lawrence College, Bronxville, New York, and since 1983 at City College, New York. New York State Author, 1986–88. **Awards:** Guggenheim grant, 1961; National Endowment for the Arts grant, 1966; American Academy award, 1970; Edith Wharton award, 1988, 1989; Rea Award for short story, 1993; Vermont Governor's award for Excellence in the Arts, 1993; award for contribution to Jewish culture, National Foundation. **Member:** American Academy, 1980. **Address:** Box 620, Thetford Hill, Vermont 05074, U.S.A.

PUBLICATIONS

Short Stories

The Little Disturbances of Man: Stories of Men and Women in Love. New York, Doubleday, 1959; London, Weidenfeld and Nicolson, 1960.

Enormous Changes at the Last Minute. New York, Farrar Straus, 1974; London, Deutsch, 1975.

Later the Same Day. New York, Farrar Straus, and London, Virago Press, 1985.

The Collected Stories. New York, Farrar Straus Giroux, 1994.

Uncollected Short Story

''Two Ways of Telling,'' in *Ms.* (New York), November-December 1990.

Poetry

Leaning Forward. Penobscot, Maine, Granite Press, 1985.

New and Collected Poems. Maine, Tilbury Press, 1991.

Begin Again: Collected Poems. New York, Farrar, Straus and Giroux, 2000.

Other

365 Reasons Not to Have Another War. Philadelphia and New York, New Society Publications—War Resisters' League, 1989.

Long Walks and Intimate Talks. New York, Feminist Press, 1991.

Conversations with Grace Paley, edited by Gerhard Bach and Blaine H. Hall. Jackson, University Press of Mississippi, 1997.

Just As I Thought (autobiography). New York, Farrar, Straus and Giroux, 1998.

*

Critical Studies: *Grace Paley: Illuminating the Dark Lives* by Jacqueline Taylor, Austin, University of Texas Press, 1990; *Grace Paley: A Study of the Short Fiction* by Neil Isaacs, Boston, Twayne, 1990.

* * *

The individuality of Grace Paley's voice—warm, comic, defensive, and without illusions—and the sophistication of her technique led to the reissue of her first collection of short stories, *The Little Disturbances of Man,* 10 years after it first appeared. Her stories, invariably set in New York and often with a Jewish background, depend especially on her ear for dialogue. Her realism, with a concision sometimes deliberately telescoped into the absurd, admits sudden surrealistic perceptions: ''A Subject of Childhood'' ends as the sun comes out above a woman being comforted by her child for the desertion of her lover: ''Then through the short fat fingers of my son, interred forever, like a black and white barred king in Alcatraz, my heart lit up in stripes.''

According to one character, who has risen above the slums of his childhood, the difficulties of a woman bringing up four children on her own in the New York slums are merely ''the little disturbances of man'' beside the real cataclysms of existence. All the stories in *Enormous Changes at the Last Minute* are set in these slums, but in *The Little Disturbances of Man* Paley ranges over the wider social strata, probing similar preoccupations of loneliness, lust, and escapism. ''An Irrevocable Diameter'' relates the forced marriage of Charles C. Charley to a rich teenager, less than half his age, who claimed to have seduced him. ''The Pale Pink Roast'' swings between farce and lyricism in a picture of a woman going to bed with her ex-husband immediately after her new marriage to a richer man.

Paley's concern in *The Little Disturbances of Man* with broken and shifting relationships where the women are dominant is even more important in *Enormous Changes.* For each of the unmarried or separated mothers, it is a question of whether her ''capacity for survival has not been overwhelmed by her susceptibility to abuse.'' There is also a new sense of commitment in *Enormous Changes,* where the key story is ''Faith in a Tree''; when the police break up a tiny demonstration against napalm-bombing in Vietnam, Faith's son defiantly writes up the demonstrators' slogan again. The story concludes: ''And I think that is exactly when events turned me around … directed … by my children's heartfelt brains, I thought more and more and every day about the world.''

Earlier in that story, Faith says of some of her neighbors, ''our four family units, as people are now called, are doomed to stand culturally still as this society moves on its caterpillar treads from ordinary affluent to absolute empire.'' These tenants crop up in other stories, some reappearing from *The Little Disturbances of Man.* ''An Interest in Life'' in the earlier book is retold from another character's angle as ''Distance'' in the later one: ''There is a long time in me between knowing and telling.''

The subject of ''Dreamer in a Dead Language'' in *Later the Same Day,* a father-daughter relationship is important in several stories in *Enormous Changes,* where in an introductory note the author states: ''Everyone in this book is imagined into life except the father. No matter what story he has to live in, he's my father… .''

Enormous Changes at the Last Minute is altogether darker in tone than *The Little Disturbances of Man:* the interplay of two generations is used to show the long shadow of ''the cruel history of Europe'' continuing to darken second-generation immigrant lives, while the ''last minute'' of the title refers to the nuclear threat. As the title suggests, *Later the Same Day* picks up these concerns where *Enormous Changes at the Last Minute* left off.

These later stories are set against a backcloth of the grass roots political struggle of the peace movement, although this is never intrusive in the stories but indissolubly meshed, as it must be, with the everyday concerns of semiadult and adult children, aging parents, and the sickness and death of middle-aged friends. The ''day'' of *Later the Same Day* is the dangerous contemporary moment in the life of the planet as the ''poor, dense, defenseless thing—rolls round and round. Living and dying are fastened to its surface and stuffed into its softer parts'' and also in Paley's life as she approaches old age. A striking example of her habitual crisscrossing of perceptions is the story ''Zagrowsky Tells,'' where the first-person narrator, an old Jew, tells Faith how his mentally handicapped daughter came to bear a black baby. Faith, the woman who continues to appear centrally in the stories, often in the first person, in this book is old enough to be ''remembering babies, those round, staring, day-in day-out companions of her youth''; now, her son and his stepfather are equal companions, in ''Listening.'' Celebrating precarious human relationships in a society, and a world, of dangerous inequalities, Grace Paley's voice is comically appalled and positive.

—Val Warner

PALLISER, Charles

Nationality: American and Irish. **Born:** the United States in December 1947. **Education:** Exeter College, Oxford, 1967–70, B.A. (honors) in English 1970; Wolfson College, Oxford, 1971–75, B.Litt. 1975. **Career:** Lecturer, Huddersfield Polytechnic, Yorkshire, 1972–74, and University of Strathclyde, Glasgow, 1974–90; visiting teacher in creative writing, Rutgers University, New Brunswick, New Jersey, 1986. **Awards:** American Academy award, 1991. **Agent:** Giles Gordon, Sheil and Associates, 43 Doughty Street, London WC2N 2LF, England; or, Diane Cleaver, Sanford J. Greenburger Associates, 55 Fifth Avenue, New York, New York 10003, U.S.A. **Address:** 78 Alkham Rd., London N16 6XF, England.

PUBLICATIONS

Novels

The Quincunx. Edinburgh, Canongate, 1989; New York, Ballantine, 1990.
The Sensationist. London, Cape, 1991.
Betrayals. New York, Ballantine, 1995.
The Unburied. New York, Farrar, Straus and Giroux, 1999.

*

Charles Palliser comments:

On the evidence of my first two novels I would suggest that what motivates me as a novelist is the idea of surprising the reader into a new perception of something. So *The Quincunx* at first appeals to the expectations the reader derives from his or her knowledge of Victorian fiction and social history, but then gradually undermines these expectations with its distinctively modernist elements—the irony, the moral neutrality, and the final impossibility of ever knowing the truth for sure. Much more straightforwardly, *The Sensationist* fragments and ''defamiliarizes'' the everyday experiences of living in a big modern city, using jump-cuts, elisions, and highly metaphorical language to stress the strangeness of so much that we take for granted. In terms of subject matter, I seem to be interested in people in extreme situations—a young boy starving in the streets of London in the 1820s or a young man under pressure and at the edge of a breakdown in the 1980s.

I suppose I'm reacting against the idea of the novel as an unproblematical reflection of shared experience. Instead I see it as a tool for making discoveries—not just on the part of the reader, but also myself. For one of the strongest motives that drives me to write is out of curiosity, and I write in order to find things out. In the most obvious sense, writing lets me research things I don't know about already. (I sometimes think it's no more than an excuse to read the books and visit the places and meet the people I am already interested in.) But in another sense, writing enables me—or, rather, requires me—to find out things I already know. It's a way of forcing myself to think hard about difficult issues, to try to go beyond the evasions and half-truths that I'm satisfied with in my own life but which are ruthlessly exposed within a novel.

Writing fiction, moreover, is one of the few occupations in which you never have to repeat yourself. Every challenge is new and so the solution to it is unprecedented. And unlike most other pursuits, the challenge is the one that you've created for yourself. There's an interesting paradox there, and I often think of Houdini having himself elaborately manacled, coffined, and then dropped into a river. Like Houdini, you have to want to go on taking risks and making things difficult for yourself. Otherwise there's no point in doing it.

* * *

Rarely has a first novel achieved the instant acclaim and the high sales enjoyed by Charles Palliser's *The Quincunx.* A big novel in the true sense of the word—it is over 800 pages long—it lacked the modesty and restricted ambition usually found in a writer's first offering. Instead, it appeared to aspire to the loftiness and the magnitude of a novel by Dickens or Wilkie Collins, both writers who are much admired by Palliser. The comparison is not fanciful for Palliser seems deliberately to have set out to write a Victorian-style novel, or at the very least a historical novel set in the 19th century, the great age of historical fiction. Certainly, his descriptions of the London underworld and of the moneymaking and industrialization that was overtaking London in the Victorian period are as vivid as anything to be found in *Bleak House* or *The Woman in White.* And like both Dickens and Collins, Palliser has a penchant for creating an intricate, even tortuous, plot which meanders through the narrative as ceaselessly as the main characters wander through the alleyways of London in search of hidden family secrets and lost inheritances.

At the heart of the novel is young John Huffman who is found living with his mother under the assumed name of Mellamphy. The small family is in hiding, but no reason is given for this state of affairs and attempts by John to unravel the secret are met with silence or obfuscation. Into this uneasy existence a sense of danger intrudes and John and his mother are forced to flee to London where poverty soon beckons. What follows is a tale of misunderstandings, criminal folly and corruption as mother and son attempt to enforce the codicil which will bring John into his rightful inheritance. A gallery of colorful characters is introduced into their lives, some for good, others for evil, and hope follows disaster until all the disparate elements in this rambling novel are disentangled in the final chapter. Throughout the novel Palliser holds the structure together in masterly fashion and his firm command of narrative allows the plot to unfold without ever running ahead of itself, no mean feat in a such an ambitious novel. A good example of his technique can be found in the episodes where his mother dies, and in the lunatic asylum where John comes face to face with his long-lost father.

Given the novel's range and scope and the author's unself-conscious use of Victorian literary themes it was hardly surprising that some critics dismissed *The Quincunx* as mere pastiche, an enjoyable read but one which only reproduced the big Victorian novel for a modern readership. There is some truth in the accusation but Palliser's ability to recreate scenes from Victorian life and his knowing awareness of the foibles of human behavior give this novel an existence of its own. By any reckoning it is an admirable achievement.

Palliser's second novel, *The Sensationist,* also broke most of the rules about what a novel should or should not be. Spare, intensely bleak and devoid of emotion, the prose has none of the literary embellishment and color which suffuses *The Quincunx.* Indeed, the casual reader would have been forgiven for thinking that the two novels had been written by different authors. Whereas John Huffman is painfully human in his reactions to life and suffers and celebrates accordingly, David, the ''sensationist'' of the title, is a man without heart, seemingly devoid of any recognizable human feeling. Here is a man who does not engage in life or even experience it; instead he moves through his existence without ever touching it or even being a part of it. A university lecturer in a hideously depicted Glasgow—all overbearing buildings and wasteland parks—he proceeds through a history of casual sexual couplings, all graphically described, yet all clearly depressing and meaningless, until, suddenly, he falls in love. The unexpected choice is Lucy, a painter with a young child, who resists his advances, thereby only adding strength to his attraction to her. With the roles reversed—David has always enjoyed easy sexual conquests—he is left mystified and tormented. Ultimately the relationship ends as unexpectedly as it began and David's last words mirror the sense of emptiness and withdrawal that dominates the novel: ''I don't know anything about that. You'll have to ask someone else.''

The appearance of both novels in quick succession introduced Palliser as a disturbing and quirky voice in modern fiction. In *The Sensationist* in particular he shows himself to be capable of capturing the artificiality of a life without roots, in which people are disfigured by their inability to make contact with their fellow human beings. It is as if he is saying that the sensationist, for all his easy conquests and his success in the academic field, is at heart an empty vessel, devoid of emotion or even the ability to nurture them.

—Trevor Royle

PARKS, Tim(othy) (Harold)

Nationality: English. **Born:** Manchester, England, 19 December 1954. **Education:** Cambridge University, B.A. 1977; Harvard University, M.A. 1979. **Family:** Married Rita Baldassarre in 1979; two sons, one daughter. **Career:** Writer, WGBH-Radio, Boston, 1978–79; telephone salesperson in London, England, 1979–81; language teacher in Verona, Italy, 1981; freelance translator in Verona, 1985; lector at University of Verona. **Awards:** Betty Trask award and Somerset Maugham award, both Society of Authors, both 1986; John Llewellyn Rhys Memorial prize, Book Trust, 1986.

Publications

Novels

Tongues of Flame. New York, Grove Press, 1985.
Loving Roger. New York, Grove Press, 1986.
Home Thoughts. New York, Grove Press, 1987.
Family Planning. New York, Grove Weidenfeld, 1989.
Cara Massimina. London, Hodder & Stoughton, 1990; published as *Juggling the Stars.* New York, Grove Press, 1993.
Goodness. New York, Grove Weidenfeld, 1991.
Shear. New York, Grove Press, 1994.
Mimi's Ghost. London, Secker & Warburg, 1995.
Europa. London, Secker & Warburg, 1997.
Destiny. London, Secker & Warburg, 2000.

Other

Italian Neighbors, Or, a Lapsed Anglo-Saxon in Verona. New York, Grove Weidenfeld, 1992.
An Italian Education: The Further Adventures of an Expatriate in Verona by Tim Parks. New York, Grove Press, 1995.
Translating Style: The English Modernists and Their Italian Translations. London and Washington, D.C., Cassell, 1998.
Adult-ery and Other Diversions (essays). New York, Arcade, 1999.
Translator, *Erotic Tales,* by Alberto Moravia. New York, Farrar, Straus, and Giroux, 1986.
Translator, *The Voyeur,* by Alberto Moravia. New York, Farrar Straus Giroux, 1987.
Translator, *Indian Nocturne: A Novella,* by Antonio Tabucchi. New York, New Directions, 1989.
Translator, *The Edge of the Horizon,* by Antonio Tabucchi. New York, New Directions, 1990.
Translator, *There Is a Place on Earth; A Woman in Birkenau,* by Giuliana Tedeschi. New York, Pantheon Books, 1992.
Translator, *The Marriage of Cadmus and Harmony,* by Roberto Calasso. New York, Knopf, 1993.
Translator, *The Road to San Giovanni,* by Italo Calvino. New York, Pantheon Books, 1993.
Translator, *Sweet Days of Discipline,* by Fleur Jaeggy. New York, New Directions, 1993.
Translator, *Vanishing Point; The Woman of Porto Pim; The Flying Creatures of Fra Angelico,* by Antonio Tabucchi. London, Vintage, 1993.
Translator, *Numbers in the Dark,* and Other Stories, by Italo Calvino. New York, Pantheon Books, 1995.

Translator, *Last Vanities,* by Fleur Jaeggy. New York, New Directions, 1998.

Translator, *Ka,* by Robert Calasso. New York, Knopf, 1998.

* * *

Tim Parks pairs his early novels either through techniques, as in the first person narrations of *Tongues of Flame* and *Loving Roger* and the epistolary *Home Thoughts* and *Family Planning*, or by genre, as in the thrillers *Cara Massimina* and *Mimi's Ghost*; in turn, they furnish recurring themes, voice, situation, props, or character traits for his later, less obviously paired, but more intense, intellectually complex novels such as *Europa* and *Destiny*.

At first, the prize-winning, autobiographical *Tongues of Flames*, narrated by Richard, fifteen-year-old son of the Reverend Bowan, could be a rite-of-passage novel about a traditional vicarage family whose rebellious older son, Adrian, embraces all the accouterments of the 1968 counterculture. Into this peaceful North London well-to-do parish, Parks introduces Curate Donald Rolandson and his ''Sword of the Spirit.'' Soon, the well-drawn characters populate a frenzied parish overwhelmed by religious fanaticism where ''Everybody was talking about Satan''; Adrian becomes the devil incarnate as they ''read'' the ''signs'' of his rebellion. Meanwhile, Richard, heretofore unresponsive while neutrally navigating his adolescence, is forced by an evangelist to opinions about religion and his sexuality at the church's annual Youth Fellowship, during which Adrian becomes the victim of a witch hunt and subsequent ritual exorcism—not an incident which triggers the familiar angst-ridden, comical (and this novel has comedy) coming-of-age epiphanies. Critics have paired this tightly written novel with *Catcher in the Rye;* Parks pairs it with his second prize-winning novel *Loving Roger*, which is narrated by Anna, a seemingly ordinary, but honest and perceptive, typist who lives with her parents, who obsessively mourn their son Brian.

As in *Tongues of Fire*, an intruder disturbs the boring equilibrium of their mundane world. Roger Cruikshank, an office executive, secretly takes up with Anna for sex, but more importantly, as a source of material for his writing—aspiring writers and language teachers inhabit Parks's early novels. Obsessed with Roger, Anna becomes pregnant but he becomes the selfish cad we all recognize from office politics; not only unfaithful during a business trip to America, he reduces Anna to single parenthood, despite his delight with the baby, for he has his career to consider. Opening with Anna's murder of Roger, the novel becomes a ''brilliant 'whydunnit''' as Parks contrasts Roger's banal diaries with Anna's perceptive understanding of them. Her self-analysis and self-assertion reveal that Parks has created a far from ordinary character, no doubt for she dispatches Roger with a kitchen knife.

Moving from first-person narration, multiple voices shape the next two novels through an exchange of letters. *Home Thoughts*, set in Verona, develops condensed scenarios of the frenzied, yet paradoxically paralyzed, lives of the heterogeneous British expatriate community, particularly Julia Helen Delaforce who, soon after her arrival, loses her job teaching English as a Second Language at the University of Verona; but Parks goes beyond his witty portrayal of petty academic politics (there is only one permanent job available). The novel's mixture of letters and narratives reveals both rationalized and real reasons why its characters are not in England—they have fled Thatcherism; they have fled self; they might go back; they might stay. Meanwhile their exile places them in an emotional limbo, their unaccustomed behavior perhaps protected by their anonymity. Julia has fled an impossible love affair with a married man with whom she exchanges letters and writes to others about. Parks incisively portrays his characters' vacillations no doubt because he is a keen observer who had lived near Verona for eight years and taught English at the University during the writing of this novel.

Family politics motivate the letters in *Family Planning* which expose the crazy, clever, Baldwin family selfishly denying their responsibility to care for schizophrenic Raymond, the elder brother of loser Garry, yuppie Graham, and academic drop-out Lorna. Mother and Father abdicate; he retreats to Algeria, she into madness having been goaded into attacking Raymond with a cake knife, but the vacuum left by their abdication sucks everybody into their whirlpool. Raymond participates in the letter writing campaign with death threats and pornographic notes, eventually denouncing family members as spies planted by the CIA. Who could blame him, for the letters which zip back and forth naturally reveal more than intended about their zany writers. Meanwhile family assets disintegrate as they argue over who will manage them. Parks's entertaining parody reads, according to Michael Dibdin, as if it were an Alan Ayckbourn play. But neither the actors nor the audience is listening.

Murder and Italy reoccur in perfect combination in the macabre comic thriller *Cara Massimina* (*Juggling the Stars* in America) and, four years later, its sequel *Mimi's Ghost.* A not-so-talented, underpaid English teacher turned petty thief, Morris Duckworth, yearns to climb the social ladder. He hatches a brilliant (to him) plan when sweet, wealthy Massimina, Mimi for short, unbeknownst to her strict family arrives at his door willing to run away; from their mock honeymoon trip, he mails ransom notes to her relatives. Simultaneously elated and terrified yet falling in love, while moving closer and closer to her murder, Morris rationalizes his actions through contemplation of his goodness. When Morris reappears in the sequel, he has achieved wealth through marrying Paola, Mimi's wanton older sister, yet is well on his way to becoming a serial killer; one critic compares him to Ted Bundy. But Mimi's ghost literally haunts Morris, by guiding, suggesting, manipulating his every move. Previously ruminating over what might be written about him, Morris now provides biographical material; at Mimi's ghost's urging, he develops a social conscious, befriending African immigrants and seeking redemption through religion, albeit kinky. The irresistible comedy of these witty novels set in a deftly drawn contemporary Italy deflects the horrific murder and mayhem necessary in this unconventional tale of a bumbling psychopath. George Crawley must also contemplate goodness, but, unlike Morris, George faces an agonizing moral dilemma. In *Goodness,* another first person narration, Parks again uses humor to treat a serious subject, in this case the morals and ethics surrounding birth deformities. His daughter Hilary, conceived to recharge a faltering marriage, is born severely handicapped; unsuccessful surgery heightens the dilemma. In the naive clarity of youth, George had rejected his Methodist upbringing and vowed ''I would never be gratuitously mean or violent, as Grandfather was, but then nor would I ever put up with anybody or any situation that made life unbearable, as Mother did. I would be honest ... and I would always chose the road that lead to a happy, healthy, normal life.'' Now a successful computer expert with a life that should by all rights be filled with satisfaction and normality, George discovers the ambiguity of life's choices. Religion and goodness clash with common sense as George agonizes over a solution. Critics praised Parks's ''rich understanding of human contradiction'' and his unsentimental approach to his topical subject.

Through George's adult male voice and situation, *Goodness* serves as a transition to *Shear*, *Europa*, and *Destiny*. Despite their one word titles and brevity (in pages and time span), these novels become more complex in both voice and stylistic approach as Parks reflects his protagonists' chaotic lives and resultant mental states. From novel to novel as his male protagonists increasingly lose control, Parks concurrently tightens his through denser plots, syntax, and sentence structures. These next novels have undertones of Greek myth and Beckettian pessimism coupled with variations on the style of the misanthropic Austrian Thomas Bernhard.

In the psychological thriller *Shear*, Parks unobtrusively combines knowledge garnered from years of translating magazines about stone quarries with impressions from his recent translation of Calasso's *The Marriage of Cadmus and Harmony.* Geologist Peter Nicholson intends to loll away a five day working vacation on a Mediterranean island with his young mistress Margaret. Instead, what should have been a cursory inspection for a pre-arranged negative report of a granite quarry operation turns into a Hitchcockian nightmare. Hazel Owen, widow of an Australian worker recently killed in the quarry, arrives with her seven-year-old daughter seeking revenge for what she believes is his murder; the voluptuous Thea, his official translator, lures Peter to afternoon trysts which are partially a set up so that her father, a connoisseur of Attic vases, can regulate damage control on the emerging conspiracy. Threats are made; people disappear. These dangerous external complications collide with the internal stresses of Peter's personal life. Although their marriage is crumbling, his wife faxes announcing her pregnancy but threatening abortion without Peter's immediate enthusiastic response; Margaret decides that they should no longer see each other upon their return, and his boss inexplicably orders Peter's immediate withdrawal from the inspection. ''Shear,'' a geological phenomenon, occurs when ''pressure is applied in at least two different and not diametrically opposite directions.'' Peter, who experiences life through geological analogies, inevitably transmutes into the suspect granite which he has been inspecting.

For Parks, *Shear* represents a creative turning point. To frame *Europa*, short-listed for the Booker prize, Parks again turns to personal experiences; here his early 1990s bus trip to the European Court of Justice in Strasbourg to protest discriminatory employment practices for foreign-language teachers, a familiar profession in Parks's novels. In this novel, divorced, 45-year-old English teacher Jerry Marlowe boards a similar bus in Milan, not to protect his job, but because he is unable to overcome his erotic obsession with ''her,'' his former French mistress and quasi leader of the miniature European Union riding the bus, which includes nubile student supporters, termed ''totties'' by leering Colin and equally lecherous, drunken Vikram Griffiths, a ''bi-minority'' Welshman of an Indian mother. Jerry's torrential inner monologue rails at the hypocrisy of his fellow travelers and obsesses on sex and his former mistress, whom he only names at novel's end in an effort not to dilute her power through mindless repetition, as has happened in the cliché-ridden ''Europe this and Euro that'' at which he sneers while ruminating about the lost classical world of the beautiful Europa. Jerry's torment can only lead to explosion; however, as Parks observes, ironically someone else's unpredictable explosion highlights self-indulgent Jerry's (and our) unawareness that others also suffer their private hells, perhaps more so. Certainly, this is true of Chris Burton, the famous writer of *Destiny*. Already edgy from living within, yet between, two cultures, Burton learns by phone in London of his schizophrenic son Marco's suicide in Turin. Immediately resolving to leave his aristocratic Italian wife, Burton begins a tortured (and torturous) journey from Heathrow via Turin to accompany his son's body for burial in Rome. And so for 72 hours, as Burton struggles to maintain at least outer control while trapped in public, the reader is trapped inside his grief stricken, fragile, jumbled mind, privy, as he rehearses his marriage, career, adopted daughter and son's life, to the simultaneous memories, anxieties, indigestion and body functions, decisions, anticipations, questions for an interview with disgraced prime minister Andreotti, and repressed secrets detonating in this novel's Joycean stream-of-consciousness. To gain this disturbing effect, Parks wrote, then sliced and moved sentences and clauses about to intercut Burton's thought patterns; the result is a difficult, but rewarding, novel to read. With this highly experimental novel, far more accomplished and intense than any of his others, Parks is correctly paired with Faulkner.

—Judith C. Kohl

PERRY, Anne

Nationality: British. **Born:** London, 28 October 1938. **Education:** Privately educated. **Career:** Has had a variety of jobs, including airline stewardess, 1962–64; assistant buyer, Newcastle upon Tyne, 1964–66; property underwriter, Muldoon and Adams, Los Angeles. Since 1972 full-time writer. Lived in California, 1967–72. **Agent:** Meg Davis, MBA Literary Agency Ltd., 45 Fitzroy Street, London W1P 5HR, England. **Address:** 1 Seafield, Portmabomack, Rossshire IY20 IYB, Scotland.

Publications

Novels (series: Charlotte and Thomas Pitt in all books except as indicated)

The Cater Street Hangman. New York, St. Martin's Press and London, Hale, 1979.

Callander Square. New York, St. Martin's Press, and London, Hale, 1980.

Paragon Walk. New York, St. Martin's Press, 1981.

Resurrection Row. New York, St. Martin's Press, 1981.

Rutland Place. New York, St. Martin's Press, 1983.

Bluegate Fields. New York, St. Martin's Press, 1984; London, Souvenir Press, 1992.

Death in the Devil's Acre. New York, St. Martin's Press, 1985; London, Souvenir Press, 1991.

Cardington Crescent. New York, St. Martin's Press, 1987; London, Souvenir Press, 1990.

Silence in Hanover Close. New York, St. Martin's Press, 1988; London, Souvenir Press, 1989.

Bethlehem Road. New York, St. Martin's Press, 1990; London, Souvenir Press, 1991.

Face of a Stranger (Monk William). New York, Fawcett, 1990; London, Headline, 1993.

A Dangerous Mourning (Monk William). New York, Fawcett, 1991; London, Headline, 1994.

Highgate Rise. New York, Fawcett, 1991; London, Souvenir Press, 1992.

Belgrave Square. New York, Fawcett, 1992; London, Souvenir Press, 1993.

Defend and Betray (Monk William). New York, Fawcett, and London, Headline, 1992.
Farriers' Lane. New York, Fawcett, 1993; London, Collins Crime, 1994.
A Sudden, Fearful Death (Monk William). New York, Fawcett, and London, Headline, 1993.
The Hyde Park Headsman. New York, Fawcett, 1994.
The Sins of the Wolf (Monk William). New York, Fawcett, and London, Headline, 1994.
Traitor's Gate. New York, Fawcett, 1995.
Cain His Brother. New York, Fawcett Columbine, 1995.
Pentecost Alley. New York, Fawcett Columbine, 1996.
Weighed in the Balance. New York, Fawcett Columbine, 1996.
Ashworth Hall. New York, Fawcett Columbine, 1997.
The Silent Cry. New York, Fawcett Columbine, 1997.
Brunswick Gardens. New York, Fawcett Columbine, 1998.
A Breach of Promise. New York, Fawcett Columbine, 1998.
The Twisted Root. New York, Fawcett Columbine, 1999.
Tathea. Salt Lake City, Utah, Shadow Mountain, 1999.
Half Moon Street. New York, Ballantine Books, 2000.

Uncollected Short Story

''Digby's First Case,'' in *Alfred Hitchcock's Mystery Magazine* (New York), February 1988.

*

Manuscript Collection: Mugar Memorial Library, Boston University.

Anne Perry comments:

(2000) I am an amateur historian in the sense that I write about other times purely because I enjoy it. It seems to me to be the best of all possible worlds to create characters and set them to play out their passions against whatever backdrop you like! The differences between their time and ours is a challenge which is fun to explore, and the exercise of transporting a drama from the present into another age brings into sharp relief what is transient and what is permanent, part of the core of human nature. The writing of each story then becomes a journey of discovery as to what is lasting, which values and passions are part of our own condition and are always worth addressing.

Mysteries have always fascinated a wide audience because they satisfy so much in us. They begin with the chaos of things having gone tragically wrong, work through finding facts about events and thus about people, emotions and finally piecing together a truth. Masks are stripped away—uniquely satisfying! Secrets are exposed, good and bad, funny and tragic. In the end we understand what happened and why, we see people and possibly society in sharper focus. In the best stories we see something of ourselves as well. And finally from chaos we untangle order and restore some kind of balance and justice, not always legal, but with a moral satisfaction.

* * *

Beginning with *The Cater Street Hangman* in 1978, Anne Perry has supplied readers of detective novels with an annual volume in either her Thomas and Charlotte Pitt series or her more recent William Monk-Hester Latterley mysteries. Because of her love of history, her novels are set in the mid- and late nineteenth century—Monk and Latterley in the 1850s, the Pitts in the 1880s and early 1890s—and she does her best to reconstruct the sights, smells, menus, costumes, and concerns of each.

Concurrently with the self-contained mystery of each novel is an ongoing development of the marriage of Charlotte Ellison, an outspoken young woman who ''lowers'' herself by marrying a police inspector, Thomas Pitt. They meet when her sister is murdered in the first novel, marry, and have two children in subsequent books. Pitt himself is falsely charged with murder in *Silence in Hanover Close,* enabling the reader to look inside the brutalities of a Victorian prison to which his superior officer, the power-server, Ballaret, is anxious to condemn him.

Charlotte, although she becomes proficient in housewifery, assists in her husband's investigations, at times without his knowledge. Aided by her own social *savoir faire* and by elegant borrowed clothes, Charlotte meets and probes the interests of upper-middle and upper-class suspects, accessories, and innocents. Pitt, a gamekeeper's son, whose education and accent are those of a gentleman, deals with more unsavory criminal classes—brothel-keepers, money-lenders, informers—often in dirty disguises. In more recent novels, Ballaret is replaced by the gentlemanly Drummond and, eventually, by Pitt himself, who prefers street work but is now able to give Charlotte something more than a working-class home.

These events, moving through some fifteen narratives of violent death, have accrued other ongoing personages: Charlotte's sister, Lady Emily, for example, whose first husband is murdered and who eventually marries Jack Radley, a successful candidate for Parliament. Emily, too, uses her social position to gather information for Pitt, especially when, bored with the seclusion demanded by widowhood, she impersonates a maid in the York household, which also allows Perry to show us the heavy demands made upon servants. Lady Vespasia, Emily's aunt by marriage, adds her aged beauty, superb gowns, and advanced social convictions to each case. Charlotte's father dies, but her mother finally loves and marries an actor; an elderly humor character, Charlotte's grandmother is repellently venomous in her brief appearances.

The mysteries these characters help to solve are identified by place-names—for example, *Rutland Place, Farrier's Lane, Paragon Walk, Traitor's Gate, The Hyde Park Headsman*—in which a group of well-born neighbors often supply a tightly knit community, secretly riddled with loves and hatreds. Few of Perry's murderers come from the working classes, and their crimes are frequently bizarre in conception, shocking in solution, or both. A mother kills two newborn children of her venereal-diseased, blackmailing husband; a man is crucified; a judge is poisoned by an opium-laden cigar at the theater; two homosexuals are found dead and naked together, a murder and suicide; a young girl has taken part in rites of black magic and is branded with a ''devil's mark''; another young girl kills her brother after he persuades her to abort their incestuously conceived child; and so on. Moreover, in two novels innocent men are hanged.

Several recent works have introduced the mysterious and seemingly omnipresent Inner Circle, ostensibly a secret society for doing good but really an intricate series of groups devoted to power, including the power of death. Pitt and Jack refuse to join but the Inner Circle's influence is difficult to combat. The other concern of Perry's latest novels is ''the African question,'' which involves the foreign office and the British-German race to colonize Africa.

By now Perry's fiction has settled into a pattern, although it still has surprises. Perhaps that is why she began the Monk-Latterley series in 1990 with a brilliantly conceived first volume, *The Face of a*

Stranger. It opens with Monk's amnesia from a cab accident, requiring him to discover who and what he is while trying to solve a tenuously leftover murder. In subsequent works, he still adds flashes of memory. He is thrown into the abrasive company of a former Crimean nurse, Hester Latterley, too anxious to initiate Florence Nightingale's reforms in English hospitals to be long employable in one. They are joined by Lady Callandra Daviot, a younger, untidy variant of Aunt Vespasia, and later by the admirable barrister, Oliver Rathbone. Crimes include child abuse and abortion. Like Pitt, Monk has an intolerable superior officer, Runcorn, who drives him into resigning from the force and setting up as a private detective.

Like the Pitt series, these novels have been praised for their fullness of Victorian detail, and their dialogue is generally more realistic than the stilted conversations of the drawing rooms that Charlotte visits. Perhaps Perry should read more Victorian fiction to sharpen her ear for the way people talked. At present this is the chief weakness of her determined historicity.

—Jane W. Stedman

PERUTZ, Kathrin

Pseudonym: Johanna Kingsley. **Nationality:** American. **Born:** New York City, 1 July 1939. **Education:** Barnard College, New York, B.A. 1960; New York University, M.A. 1966. **Family:** Married Michael Studdert-Kennedy in 1966; one son. **Career:** Lived in London, 1960–64. **Address:** 16 Avalon Road, Great Neck, Long Island, New York 10021, U.S.A.

Publications

Novels

The Garden. London, Heinemann, and New York, Atheneum, 1962.
A House on the Sound. London, Heinemann, 1964; New York, Coward McCann, 1965.
The Ghosts. London, Heinemann, 1966.
Mother Is a Country: A Popular Fantasy. New York, Harcourt Brace, and London, Heinemann, 1968.
Scents (as Johanna Kingsley). New York, Bantam, and London, Corgi, 1985.
Faces (as Johanna Kingsley, in collaboration). New York, Bantam, and London, Corgi, 1987.

Uncollected Short Story

''An American Success,'' in *Voices 2,* edited by Michael Ratcliffe. London, Joseph, 1965.

Other

Beyond the Looking Glass: America's Beauty Culture. New York, Morrow, 1970; as *Beyond the Looking Glass: Life in the Beauty Culture,* London, Hodder and Stoughton, 1970.
Marriage Is Hell: It's Better to Burn Than to Marry. New York, Morrow, 1972; as *The Marriage Fallacy: It's Better to Burn Than to Marry,* London, Hodder and Stoughton, 1972; as *Liberated Marriage,* New York, Pyramid, 1973.
Polly's Principles, with Polly Bergen. New York, Wyden, 1974.
I'd Love To, But What'll I Wear?, with Polly Bergen. New York, Wyden, 1977.
Reigning Passions: Leopold von Sacher-Masoch and the Hapsburg Empire. Philadelphia, Lippincott, and London, Weidenfeld and Nicolson, 1978.
Writing for Love and Money. Fayetteville, University of Arkansas Press, 1991.

*

Critical Studies: *Don't Never Forget* by Brigid Brophy, London, Cape, 1966, New York, Holt Rinehart, 1967; ''The Truth about Fiction'' by George P. Elliott, in *Holiday* (New York), March 1966.

Kathrin Perutz comments:

(1972) The only general theme (or background) of my books is America. *Mother Is a Country* is a direct parody of certain American dreams (the acquisition of power and the desire to become a commodity); *A House on the Sound* charts the distance from reality to where rich liberals have their camp. *Beyond the Looking Glass,* a nonfiction book often fictionalized, examines preoccupation with appearance in America, where people have the hope of seeming what they have not yet become, and where self-knowledge is replaced by concern over minutiae of deception.

My first three novels also concern sub-rosa relationships, the area of self that is undeveloped or suppressed. *The Garden* presents a love affair between two girls, not lesbian (both girls are young and boy-crazy), but of an essential intensity to contradict fears of not existing. *A House on the Sound* shows different manifestations of embryonic love—homosexuality, incest, masochism—never acknowledged by the characters. The two main characters of *The Ghosts* have not reconciled themselves to the sexual roles, male and female, they are supposed to play, and often parody or pervert these roles.

But mainly, each book has been my attempt to learn more of the craft. The first was a simple diary; the second tried, in six hours, to cut through time past and present, more similar to movie techniques than traditional flashbacks. The third book tried to give a sense of development, over the space of a year. The fourth, a satire, was deliberately ''surface,'' a board game played over true but generalized emotions. My fifth book presented problems of journalism, in organization of material, tone, pace, and the creation of a personal, but abstracted, narrator.

(1976) My last book, *Marriage Is Hell,* is an essay on the institution of marriage as it exists today in the West, particularly in America. It deals with the anachronism of marriage, its false expectations, its imprisonment of personality and distortion of both privacy and personal liberty. The book, which is strongly opinionated, attacks marriage from many perspectives—legal, historical, anthropological, sexual—and then goes on to suggest reform and finally a turning that will make marriage possible again. I consciously tried to keep the style loose and colloquial, the better to let readers argue with me, and literary experiment is superseded in this book by political, or pragmatic, aims.

* * *

Kathrin Perutz has a baroque spider-web sensibility; it is as exquisite as it is tough, and permits her to explore such matters as incest, sadomasochism, homosexuality, suicide, and murder with the delicacy of an appropriate dinner wine. It is the most pervasive force in her novels and the one that diminishes the importance of whatever flaws may appear in them as a consequence of her experimentation with form and theme.

The first novel, *The Garden,* is a straightforward first-person narrative of life at a small women's college in Massachusetts. Its treatment of the urge to put aside the burden of virginity becomes tedious, and the book is marked with jejune expressions (''O.K., Pats, shoot'') that may be true to dormitory life but are vexatious in a novel. Perutz handles the garden symbolism of the novel well, however; describes a memorably tender, vivacious relationship between Kath and the Blossom, the two principal characters; and, with perfect briskness of pace and lightness of tone, captures the banal essence of a party weekend at an American men's college probably better than any other writer has.

The Ghosts, Perutz's third novel, walks the maze of a love affair in which the participants—or combatants—Luke, an excessively cerebral writer, and Judith, an undercerebral but sensitive hairdresser, are haunted chiefly by Luke's dead father and an assortment of cast-off lovers. The deficiency of the volume is that there is no one with whom an audience would much care to identify. Luke is insatiably clinical toward the involvement, and he and Panda, a deep platonic love of his who befriends Judith, are sometimes mouthpieces discussing their actions and Judith's, and examining one of the immediate themes of the novel, abortion, and, of more general metaphysical interest, the nature of human action. The conception of the characters is acute; their mechanism, however, is too much exposed and not enough is left for the reader to infer. They are often pieces of an essay rather than people in a work of fiction. Judith is too pliable, too much prop for Luke, until the end, when she takes control of herself and Luke becomes more human. But that occurs too late to place the novel in balance.

Mother Is a Country is a satiric fantasy that strikes at the mass-produced, antiseptic, Saran-wrapped materialism in American life. That quality accounts for the death of the three main characters, and the most palpable reaction in the cosmically unfeeling nation is that ''a mother eagle in her nest flapped powerful wings and laid another egg.'' Though the book has been criticized for its superficiality of characterization, it can be argued that since superficial consumerism is primarily what the satire is about, John Scudely (a hero with much of the feeling of a Bellow character, but without the profundity) and the other characters are properly shallow. *Reigning Passions,* Perutz's fifth novel, has done nothing to enhance her reputation. It is a fictionalized account of the complex man who gave his name to masochism, and so flat are the nuances of his life made to seem that to get through the book it helps to have a fair dose of the affliction.

It was Perutz's second novel, *A House on the Sound,* that proved her excellence. She paints a dinner party of sham liberals on a small canvas with precise detail, probing through the word, the facial expression, the gesture, the nuance of conversation the variety of characters present and their secret relationships. In this and in her control of time through brief, illuminating flashbacks and staging of the moments of her characters, there is the clear echo—but just the echo—of Virginia Woolf.

—Alan R. Shucard

PETERKIEWICZ, Jerzy (Michal)

Nationality: British. **Born:** Fabianki, Poland, 29 September 1916; emigrated to England in 1940. **Education:** Dlugosz School, Wloclawek; University of Warsaw; University of St. Andrews, Scotland, M.A. in English and German 1944; King's College, London, Ph.D. 1947. **Family:** Married Christine Brooke-Rose, *q.v.,* in 1948 (divorced 1975). **Career:** Lecturer, 1950–64, reader, 1964–72, and professor of Polish language and literature, 1972–79, School of Slavonic and East European Studies, University of London. **Address:** 7 Lyndhurst Terrace, London NW3 5QA, England.

Publications

Novels

The Knotted Cord. London, Heinemann, 1953; New York, Roy, 1954.
Loot and Loyalty. London, Heinemann, 1955.
Future to Let. London, Heinemann, 1958; Philadelphia, Lippincott, 1959.
Isolation: A Novel in Five Acts. London, Heinemann, 1959; New York, Holt Rinehart, 1960.
The Quick and the Dead. London, Macmillan, 1961.
That Angel Burning at My Left Side. London, Macmillan, 1963.
Inner Circle. London, Macmillan, 1966.
Green Flows the Bile. London, Joseph, 1969.

Plays

Sami Swoi (produced London, 1949).
Scena ma trzy ściany. London, Wiadomości, 1974.

Poetry

Prowincja. Warsaw, 1936.
Wiersze i poematy. Warsaw, Prosto z Mostu, 1938.
Pokarm cierpki. London, Myśl Polska, 1943.
Pity poemat. Paris, Instytut Literacki, 1950.
Poematy londynskie i wiersze przedwojenne. Paris, Kultura, 1965.
Kula magiczna (Selected Poems). Warsaw, Ludowa Spóldzielnia, 1980.
Modlitwy intelektu. Warsaw, Pax, 1988.
Poezje wybrane. Warsaw, Ludowa Spóldzielnia, 1986.

Other

Znaki na niebie. London, Mildner, 1940.
Po chlopsku: Powieść. London, Mildner, 2 vols., 1941.
Umarli nie są bezbronni. Glasgow, Książnica, 1943.
Pogrzeb Europy. London, Mildner, 1946.
The Other Side of Silence: The Poet at the Limits of Language. London and New York, Oxford University Press, 1970.
The Third Adam. London, Oxford University Press, 1975.
Literatura polska w perspektywie europejskiej (essays translated from English). Warsaw, Państwowy Instytut, 1986.
Messianic Prophecy: A Case for Reappraisal. London, University of London Press, 1991.

In the Scales of Fate: An Autobiography. London, Boyars, 1993.

Editor, *Polish Prose and Verse.* London, Athlone Press, 1956.

Editor and Translator, *Antologia liryki angielskiej 1300–1950.* London, Veritas, 1958.

Editor and Translator, with Burns Singer, *Five Centuries of Polish Poetry 1450–1950.* London, Secker and Warburg, 1960; Philadelphia, Dufour, 1962; revised edition, with Jon Stallworthy, as *Five Centuries of Polish Poetry 1450–1970,* London and New York, Oxford University Press, 1970.

Editor and Translator, *Easter Vigil and Other Poems,* by Karol Wojtyla. London, Hutchinson, and New York, Random House, 1979.

Editor and Translator, *Collected Poems,* by Karol Wojtyla. London, Hutchinson, and New York, Random House, 1982.

Editor and Translator, *The Place Within: The Poetry of Pope John Paul II,* New York, Random House, 1994.

Translator, *Poezje Poems* by Karol Wojtyla. Warsaw, Literackie, 1998.

*

Critical Studies: In *New Statesman* (London), 10 October 1959; *Sunday Times Magazine* (London), 10 June 1962; ''Speaking of Writing'' by Peterkiewicz, in *The Times* (London), 9 January 1964; *Le Monde* (Paris), 28 June 1967; *The Novel Now* by Anthony Burgess, London, Faber, and New York, Norton, 1967, revised edition, Faber, 1971; by Peterkiewicz, in *Times Literary Supplement* (London), 30 July 1971; ''Three Conversations,'' in *New Literary History* (Charlottesville, Virginia), vol. 15, 1984.

Jerzy Peterkiewicz comments:

If titles are significant, *Isolation* and *Inner Circle* seem to be my representative novels, both structurally and thematically.

* * *

Three of Jerzy Peterkiewicz's last six novels are comic entertainments of a high order of literary craftsmanship; three others show a marked falling-off of standards. His first novels have little bearing on the later work. *The Knotted Cord* is a genuinely moving account of a peasant boyhood in Poland; its hero has to escape from many things, but particularly from the ''cord'' of the scratchy brown cassock that his pious mother has thrust him into, and from all that cord represents. The work is a ''first novel'' of promise, and it is a pity the Peterkiewicz has chosen not to develop or integrate into his later work a mode which might have provided a carbohydrate counterbalance to the sometimes too frothy champagne of the books which follow. *Loot and Loyalty* is a trivial and poorly constructed historical novel about a seventeenth-century Scots soldier of fortune exiled in Poland, and his connection with the ''false Dmitri.''

Future to Let, the first of the really successful books, is less ''mannerist'' by far than its successors. It is a very funny *roman à clef* on the tortured loves, English plots, and politics of contemporary Polish émigrés, chief among them Julian Atrament (''ink'' in Polish), quite unidentifiable, of course, but almost recognizable, whose ''escape to freedom'' by means of his St. Bernard dog is Peterkiewicz's finest comic turn. *Isolation,* probably his best book, parodies the erotic mystifications of a modern spy story with a skill that even the suggestions of deep meanings about the mutual isolation of sexuality, etc., cannot spoil. The Powell-esque (or Waugh-like) Commander Shrimp (alias Pennyworthing), faded semi-spy and bathetic con-man, is a great comic creation. *That Angel Burning at My Left Side* has some of the virtues of *The Knotted Cord;* it is realism with a light touch, of a boy growing up through World War II and postwar refugeehood, looking for father, country, and self. The gimmick of the ''angels'' grows tiresome, but descriptions of place and event and the hero himself are vivid and concrete—until the hero gets to England, and everything, including him, suddenly (and apparently inadvertently on the author's part) becomes less real.

The three unsuccessful works include *The Quick and the Dead,* a spoof ghost story and fantasy of serio-comic realism, involving among other things the amorous relations of the dead in Limbo, the suffering and repentance of ghosts (a somewhat Golding-like concept), with significance, apparently, but the coy handling of its basic situation makes for heavy reading. Still harder to read, but even more significant, is *Inner Circle* in which a three-layered story of Surface (the far future), Underground (present-day sub-Firbankian London), and Sky (a version of the Eden story), is held together by repeated ''circle'' and ''underground'' image patterns, and by analogous destinies. The themes and point-of-view games again make it seem almost like a collaboration between Golding, Burgess, and Arthur C. Clarke. Peterkiewicz's most recent novel, *Green Flows the Bile* is as tastelessly affected a social satire as its title would suggest. It recounts the last journey together of two ''fellow-travellers'' (in all senses), the Secretary, a ''political gigolo,'' and his employer, the ''senior prophet of the age … the travelling peace salesman.'' The comic travelogue is passable in places, but the political satire is either painfully obvious or intensely private; the two pitfalls that await the topical *roman à clef* have caught Peterkiewicz this time.

Peterkiewicz's heroes are almost all coyly hollow semi-comic shadow-men, pretending to contain abysses and seeking with morose jocularity for an ''identity'' to which they are fundamentally indifferent. Their human relationships are sketched with equal shallowness. Even the intrigues are lower Greeneland, territory more powerfully explored by Burgess, though at times Peterkiewicz is clearly aiming for the playful, complex ''meanings'' of a Chesterton, or a Woolf (*Orlando*), or a Nabokov, or for the light, horrid satire of a Waugh (*Scott-King's Modern Europe*). Stage metaphors, mirrors, masks, costumes, photographs, cute but pallid versions of Nabokovian artifices, crowd the pages of *Isolation,* in which mock-pornography and reciprocal voyeuristic spyings, slowly building up a posthumous portrait, bring to mind *Lolita* (courteously, or perhaps coincidentally, acknowledged in a parrot of that name) or *The Real Life of Sebastian Knight.* These are samples of tone, not assertions of source; but even the best of Peterkiewicz's work is marred by hearing continually whispered chords made up of the murmurs of other men's voices, almost as if he were unwilling to hear his own voice. His real talent for language and comedy is almost swamped by his need to be terribly à la mode in these six novels, and it is a pity, for, to paraphrase a comment he makes on one of his characters, ''his anonymous extraterritorial aura predicts at every step a possible eruption of personality.''

It may be that, for all the polished virtues and assurance of his better novels, Peterkiewicz will be remembered longest and known most widely for his critical essays and anthologies, and for his book *The Other Side of Silence,* in which he sensitively discusses some intricacies of modern literature and places Polish literature in their context. One would like, however, to have as well his views on his own Polish contemporaries, who are giving us one of the most flourishing of modern minor literatures. Perhaps in his criticism he has more truly earned the right than he has in his fiction, to the inevitable, and specious, comparison with Conrad, that other Polish man of letters who turned himself, in adult life, and not without success, into an English writer.

—Patricia Merivale

PETERS, Elizabeth

See MERTZ, Barbara

PETRAKIS, Harry Mark

Nationality: American. **Born:** St. Louis, Missouri, 5 June 1923. **Education:** The University of Illinois, Urbana, 1940–41. **Family:** Married Diane Perparos in 1945; three sons. **Career:** Has worked in steelmills, and as a real estate salesman, truck driver, and sales correspondent. Since 1960 freelance writer and lecturer. Taught at the Indiana University Writers Conference, Bloomington, 1964–65, 1970, 1974; McGuffey Visiting Lecturer, Ohio University, Athens, 1971; writer-in-residence, Chicago Public Library, 1976–77, and for the Chicago Board of Education, 1978–80; taught at Illinois Wesleyan University, Bloomington, 1978–79, Ball State University, Muncie, Indiana, 1978 and 1980, University of Wisconsin, Rhinelander, 1978–80, and University of Rochester, New York, 1979–80; Nikos Kazantzakis Professor, San Francisco State University, 1992. **Awards:** *Atlantic* Firsts award, 1957; Benjamin Franklin citation, 1957; Friends of American Writers award, 1964; Friends of Literature award, 1964; Carl Sandburg award, 1983; Ellis Island Medal of Honor, 1995. D.H.L.: University of Illinois, 1971; Governors State University, Park Forest South, Illinois, 1980; Hellenic College, Brookline, Massachusetts, 1984. L.H.D.: Roosevelt University, Chicago, 1987. **Address:** 80 East Road, Dune Acres, Chesterton, Indiana 46304, U.S.A.

Publications

Novels

Lion at My Heart. Boston, Little Brown, and London, Gollancz, 1959.
The Odyssey of Kostas Volakis. New York, McKay, 1963.
A Dream of Kings. New York, McKay, 1966; London, Barker, 1967.
In the Land of Morning. New York, McKay, 1973.
The Hour of the Bell. New York, Doubleday, 1976; London, Severn House, 1986.
Nick the Greek. New York, Doubleday, 1979; London, New English Library, 1980.
Days of Vengeance. New York, Doubleday, 1983; London, Sphere, 1985.
Ghost of the Sun. New York, St. Martin's Press, 1990.

Short Stories

Pericles on 31st Street. Chicago, Quadrangle, 1965.
The Waves of Night and Other Stories. New York, McKay, 1969.
A Petrakis Reader. New York, Doubleday, 1978.
Collected Stories. Chicago, Lake View Press, 1987.

Plays

Screenplays: *A Dream of Kings,* with Ian Hunter, 1969; *In the Land of Morning,* 1974; *Ghost of the Sun,* with John Petrakis, 1994.

Television Plays: *Pericles on 31st Street,* with Sam Peckinpah, from the story by Petrakis, and *The Judge,* with Bruce Geller (both in *Dick Powell Show*), 1961–62; *The Blue Hotel,* from the story by Stephen Crane, 1978; *Song of Songs,* with John Petrakis, from the story by Petrakis, 1994.

Other

The Founder's Touch: The Life of Paul Galvin of Motorola. New York, McGraw Hill, 1965.
Stelmark: A Family Recollection (autobiography). New York, McKay, 1970.
Reflections: A Writer's Life, A Writer's Work. Chicago, Lake View Press, 1983.
Tales of the Heart: Dreams and Memories of a Lifetime. Chicago, Ivan R. Dee, 1999.

*

Critical Studies: In *Old Northwest* (Oxford, Ohio), December 1976; interview in *Chicago Review,* Winter 1977; *Hellenes and Hellions* by Alexander Karanikas, Urbana, University of Illinios Press, 1981.

Harry Mark Petrakis comments:

(1991) My task now as I reach the threshold of seventy (how swiftly a lifetime has passed) is to find that language born of the years I have lived that expresses my vision now, a language that belongs to a mature age.

What I feel now is gratefulness because from an early age I was allowed to discover what I wished to do. For all the insecurities, my vocation has never failed to provide me those moments, however rare, when I could say with a figure in an old Greek chorus, ''still there surges within me a singing magic.''

* * *

In a book of personal recollections, *Stelmark,* Harry Mark Petrakis confirms what the reader of his novels would guess: that Petrakis is the son of Greek immigrants to the United States. He is in fact a second generation man who is intent on estimating the meaning of his presence in a country that is far from the Crete of his ancestors. To the territory of South Chicago, Petrakis's father, a Greek Orthodox priest, brought the recollections of a strange and noble sort of life where poverty was the foreground of an existence lived in an awesome setting of mountains and an equally demanding texture of ancient custom and suffering. As a young man, Petrakis was impressed by the interplay of his inheritance and the sections of American culture that he came into contact with in the land of promise: the narrow opportunities of a great and indifferent city, the materialism of Midwestern life as the immigrants encountered it and the continuation of the pride and violence that crossed the Atlantic with the Greek immigrants. It is this basic contrast between America as dreamed in the Cretan valleys and America as experienced by an ethnic minority that gives Petrakis his subject.

It is a subject full of challenges to Petrakis's novelistic imagination. And that imagination is equal to the passions, the disappointments, and the envies of the newcomers among whom, as a mediator and creator, Petrakis has lived his artistic life. He has created a striking company of persons who are, as Kurt Vonnegut has observed, at least 14 feet tall. These persons are swept by passions that are awesome when they are compared with the feebler desires and lesser dignities of men and women who have had several generations to adapt to the conditions of American life. The male figures still know the Greek versions of *omertà,* the Sicilian code of honor. These men act on the basis of personal pride and have loyalties that bind them less to American society than to family and a few close acquaintances. They have a sentimental vision of the cruel and impoverished land they—or their parents—fled. There is a dual center to their lives. One center is the church, whose ministers they respect, but whose teachings they put aside as having little to do with the lives of Greeks in South Chicago. The other center, more compulsive for them, is the world of cheap restaurants, backroom gambling dens that are full of con-men and bookies, and seedy offices above grocery stores where, as in *A Dream of Kings,* palms are read and advice is given to clients who do not know where to turn in a society that has scant tolerance for new arrivals. This male world has, in large part, a cold indifference for wives and mistresses; women are tolerated because men must have sons or because sexual desires must find expression. Sincere and deep affection is known to some of the men, as in *The Odyssey of Kostas Volakis.* But even so, the hopes of women remain alien to male concerns and are seldom respected or shared.

Mention of particular novels fills out this general description. *Lion at My Heart,* Petrakis's first novel, rehearses the fortunes of an immigrant household made up of a father and two sons. The father, with pride and suspicion, watches over the education and the marriages of his two sons, esteeming the son who takes a Greek wife and repudiating the son who marries ''outside.'' A priest, a familiar figure in the novels, intervenes to mollify the father's harshness. *The Odyssey of Kostas Volakis* tells a similar story. Kostas is a young Cretan man who married a slightly older woman for her dowry, which pays for the passage to America. The novel traces stages in Kostas's adjustment to his new land: his struggle as a restaurant owner, his overcoming of his illiteracy, and—most important—his final forgiveness of his murderer-son who has disgraced his family.

A Dream of Kings explores a slightly higher social level and tells of the life of Masoukas the palm-reader and consultant, half charlatan and half-concerned adviser, by turns a compulsive gambler and adulterer. But Masoukas's dreams are fixed on an ailing son, for whose cure everything must be sacrificed. A journey to the sacred land of Greece will restore the health of the child and, perhaps, of the father. In another novel with a Chicago setting, *In the Land of Morning,* Petrakis moves into the post-Vietnam American world where the shock of a veteran's return is gradually merged with the ongoing tumult of life in the community. All this is a passionate and sad human encounter which the reader can find elsewhere in Petrakis, as in the collections of short stories, *Pericles on 31st Street* and *The Waves of Night.* Petrakis circles back to such themes—Greeks in a strange land—in *Nick the Greek.* Here the hero, Nick Dandalos, comes to the United States in the 1920s and allows himself to be drawn into the gambling life of Chicago, all at the cost of a sound future and a happy love affair. Particularly strong are the gambling scenes which take readers back to a distant time in the Greek community.

A bit to one side is *The Hour of the Bell.* This novel is an account of the revolution that commenced in Greece in 1820 when a confused but finally successful revolt against Turkish power began. Instead of finding the usual cultural enclave in South Chicago, the reader moves back and forth over the tumultuous Greek landscape, which is seen through various eyes: those of military leaders, some savage, some resigned to years of violence; those of a priest who respects the humanity of the slaughtered Turks; and those of an educated young man who is trying to write the history of the confusion that surrounds him. With his usual power, Petrakis, as it were, adds the completing piece to the Greek-American puzzle that is his concern. *The Hour of the Bell* is the ''explanation'' of the pride and the harsh tauntings and the intermittent tenderness that the novels about South Chicago record.

It is a record that is made up of prose of varying textures: realistic and poetically fierce by turns. The result is an indispensable report and also an imaginative world that takes its place along with the works of fiction—Chekhov's and others—that, Petrakis tells us, used to make him weep as a youth.

—Harold H. Watts

PHILLIPS, Caryl

Nationality: British. **Born:** St. Kitts, West Indies, 13 March 1958; brought to England in 1958. **Education:** Schools in Leeds to 1974, and in Birmingham, 1974–76; Queen's College, Oxford, 1976–79, B.A. (honors) 1979. **Career:** Founding chairman, 1978, and artistic director, 1979, *Observer* Festival of Theatre, Oxford; resident dramatist, The Factory Arts Centre, London 1981–82; writer-in-residence, Mysore, India, 1987, and Stockholm University, Sweden, 1989. Visiting lecturer, University of Ghana, 1990; visiting lecturer, University of Poznan, Poland, 1991; visiting writer, Humber College, Toronto, 1992–93; visiting professor of English, New York University, 1993; writer-in-residence, National Institute of Education, Singapore, 1994; writing instructor, Arvon Foundation, England, since 1983; visiting writer, 1990–92, professor of English, 1994–98; writer-in-residence, Amherst College, Massachusetts, 1992—; Henry R. Luce professor of migration and social order, Barnard College, Columbia University, 1998—. Member of the Board of Directors, Bush Theatre, London, 1985–88; member, British Film Institute Production Board, London, 1985–88; honorary senior member, the University of Kent, England, 1985; board member, *The Caribbean Writer,* St. Croix, 1989. Consulting editor, Faber, Inc., 1992–94; contributing editor, *Bomb Magazine,* New York, 1993; consultant editor, Graywolf Press, Minneapolis, 1994. Lives in London. **Awards:** Arts Council of Great Britain Bursary in Drama, 1984; British Council Fiftieth Anniversary fellowship, 1984; Malcolm X Prize for Literature, 1985; Martin Luther King Memorial prize, 1987; Guggenheim fellowship, 1992; *Sunday Times* (London) Young Writer of the Year, 1992; Rockefeller Foundation Bellagio residency, 1994; James Tait Black Memorial prize, 1994; Lannan Literary award, 1994. Honorary M.A., Amherst College (Massachusetts), 1995. D.Univ, Leeds Metropolitan University, 1997. Named University of the West Indies Humanities Scholar of the Year, 1999. **Agent:** Anthony

Harwood, Curtis Brown Ltd., Haymarket House, 28/29 Haymarket, London SW1Y 4SP, England.

PUBLICATIONS

Novels

The Final Passage. London, Faber, 1985; New York, Penguin, 1990.
Higher Ground. London, Viking, 1986; New York, Viking, 1989.
A State of Independence. London, Faber, and New York, Farrar Straus, 1986.
Cambridge. London, Bloomsbury, 1991; New York, Knopf, 1992.
Crossing the River. London, Bloomsbury, and New York, Knopf, 1994.
The Nature of Blood. New York, Knopf, 1997.

Plays

Strange Fruit (produced Sheffield, 1980; London, 1982). Ambergate, Derbyshire, Amber Lane Press, 1981.
Where There Is Darkness (produced London, 1982). Ambergate, Derbyshire, Amber Lane Press, 1982.
The Shelter (produced London, 1983). Oxford, Amber Lane Press, 1984; New York, Applause, 1986.
The Wasted Years (broadcast 1984). In *Best Radio Plays of 1984,* London, Methuen, 1985.

Screenplay: *Playing Away,* 1986.

Radio Plays: *The Wasted Years,* 1984; *Crossing the River,* 1986; *The Prince of Africa,* 1987; *Writing Fiction,* 1991.

Television Plays: *The Hope and the Glory,* 1984; *The Record,* 1984; *Lost in Music,* 1985.

Other

The European Tribe (travel). London, Faber, and New York, Farrar Straus, 1987.
The Atlantic Sound. New York, Knopf, 2000.
Editor, *Extravagant Strangers: A Literature of Belonging.* New York, Vintage International, 1999.
Editor, *The Right Set: A Tennis Anthology.* New York, Vintage Books, 1999.

*

Critical Studies: ''Caryl Phillips Talks to Linton Kwesi Johnson'' in *The Race Today Review* (London), 1987; ''Caryl Phillips: Interview'' by Kay Saunders, *Kunapipi* (Denmark), vol. 9, no. 1, 1987; ''Interview with Caryl Phillips'' by Frank Birbalsingh, in *Displaced Persons* edited by Kirsten Holst Peterson and Anna Rutherford, Denmark, Dangeroo Press, 1988; ''The Slippery Bounds of Somewhere Else: Caryl Phillips's *The European Tribe*'' by Socorro Suarez in *Passage to Somewhere Else* edited by D. McDermott and S. Ballyn, Barcelona, PPU, 1988; ''Caryl Phillips'' by Mario Relich in *Contemporary Writers: The British Council,* London, 1989; ''On Dislocation and Connectedness in Caryl Phillips's Writing'' by H. Okazaki, in *The Literary Criterion* (Mysore, India), vol. 26, no. 3, 1991; ''The Fictional Works of Caryl Phillips'' by Charles P. Sarvan and Hasan Marhama, in *World Literature Today,* vol. 65, no. 1, Winter 1991; ''An Interview With Caryl Phillips'' by Graham Swift, in *Kunapipi* (Denmark), vol. 13, no. 3, 1991; ''Worlds Within: An Interview with Caryl Phillips,'' in *Callaloo,* vol. 14, no. 3, Fall 1991; ''Voyages into Otherness: Cambridge and Lucy'' by Benedicte Ledent, in *Kunapipi* (Denmark), vol. 14, no. 2, 1992; ''Caryl Phillips'' by Benedicte Ledent, in *Post-War Literatures in English* (Belgium, University of Liege), March 1993; ''Historical Fiction and Fictional History: Caryl Phillips's *Cambridge*'' by Evelyn O'Callaghan, in *Journal of Commonwealth Literature,* vol. 29, no. 2, 1993; ''The Unkindness of Strangers'' by Nadar Alexander Mousavizadeh, in *Transition,* issue 61, 1994; ''Caryl Phillips,'' in *Current Biography,* vol. 55, no. 7, 1994.

Caryl Phillips comments:

My dominant theme has been cultural and social dislocation, most commonly associated with a migratory experience.

* * *

Caryl Phillips writes novels of disinheritance, of rootlessness and impotence. They are works concerned with the human cost of inhumanity and ignorance, and in which the price is largely, but not uniquely, paid by black men and women. Phillips returns consistently to the themes of imposed or motiveless migration, of nostalgia for a homeland which does not exist, of betrayal and emptiness. His early novels depict loveless worlds, where characters are torn from or never know their family, where new loves and friendships stagnate, or die, or never begin. Yet, in *Crossing the River* of 1994, Phillips explores the possibility of love to redeem even the most desolate life and marks a shift from his earlier despondency.

In Phillips's early novels, rootless and disoriented characters search for or imagine their identities. In *The Final Passage,* the first and bleakest novel, Leila is a mulatto living on a Caribbean island in the 1950s. Culturally disenfranchised by mixed parentage, she imagines her parents other than they are in order to find her own identity. She dreams of her absent white father, perceiving him a financial benefactor and believing him real in order to discover herself. Yet Leila's mother, herself betrayed in youth by an incestuous rape, knows not nor cares which of her ''lovers'' fathered Leila, discerning instead that the child ''belonged to all of them and none of them.'' Leila craves her mother's friendship and, although she does not doubt her mother's love, she is in truth ''not to know that her mother had never wanted a child.'' The love this mother eventually gives is begrudging, bestowed as a reward for the direction given to her life by motherhood. It is not a love to cherish nor one from which to build self-knowledge. Leila is eventually granted an identity in London, a dismal place where the rivers ''were like dirty brown lines, full of empty bottles and cigarette ends, cardboard boxes and greying suds of pollution.'' Color is her identity and one which affords her only abuse, misuse or, at best, condescension. It proves an unbearable alternative to her island non-self and Leila finally allows life to dribble away.

In ''Heartland,'' the first chapter in *Higher Ground,* the narrator loses his identity by betraying his own people. Using his grasp of English, he collaborates with slave traders, acting as interpreter between them and village head men who part with their human future in exchange for a few trinkets. In his effort to evade physical bondage, he feigns assimilation with Englishness, apparently understanding English behavior better than that of his own people. He notices "inner stillness ... as a trait" of his native kin but not one with which he now identifies, and announces proudly that he has "finally mastered the art of forgetting—of murdering the memory" in order to leave his former self behind.

But his very language does not ring true. He is certainly clever, using English as a tool for discourse and imagery. Yet it is a disjointed use, clipped and unnatural. During the story's course he perceives reality. He learns that he is indeed "held captive" though his arms and legs move with deceptive freedom. Betrayed by a soldier "friend" for having a forbidden woman in his room, he is thrown into the bonds he had feared, but which ultimately release him to his brotherhood and his identity.

In Phillips's work, identity is also something which may be bestowed, changed, or taken away by the powerful. The powerless are either enticed, like Leila, from their only known home by some nebulous hope of change, or by the false promise of education (*A State of Independence*). The powerful may rip the impotent from their homes in a callous and cynical bid to perpetuate their own society and at the intentional expense of another. This is the fate of all four characters in *Higher Ground* and *Cambridge.* The loss of identity in this way is then compounded by the imposition of new names. In *Higher Ground,* Irena, an escapee from Nazism's elitist brutality, finds her name stolen by ignorance—an ignorance which is certain of its own precision: "It was now that the Irene-Irina-Irene-Irina-Irene-Irina-Irene problem would begin for English people were too lazy to bend their mouths or twist their tongues into unfamiliar shapes." This ignorance attempts to force her divorce with a past which she cannot, in fact, let go. She is a misfit, and turns in on herself, confused between past and present, and sure only that she has no future. Cambridge suffers three changes to his name. Two of these, Tom and Cambridge, are the products of a smug mid-18th century (by which time slavery has been abolished in law, but not in practice). Cambridge is twice torn from home and family, one African and one English, where he could act as an individual. His naming at these points resembles that of a dog, the single name pointedly affirming a position of inferiority which his masters intend to maintain.

In England, Cambridge finds his true identity. As David Henderson, a name bestowed without cynicism, he embraces Christianity. With a dearly loved white wife at his side, he is accepted, if begrudgingly, into society, and on an evangelical tour of England he encounters a merchant who "was commonly very pleasant to both my wife and myself, directing us with witty turns and fanciful stories, but never to the prejudice of religion or good taste." The merchant, an African trader with a retinue of servants, is surely amusing himself. But there is a glimpse that in time, David Henderson might achieve a social integration that would affirm his own confidence in this identity.

But a loving relationship which might grant security cannot last. David Henderson's wife dies in childbirth, and with her dies Henderson's tenuous credibility. Society will not allow him to perpetuate the myth of equality and, in trying to extend his mission to Africa, he is again taken captive to become the subjugated Cambridge.

Phillips's novel of 1994, *Crossing the River,* reworks these characteristic themes: slavery, identity, and desolation. But the scope is wider and more ambitious, and it offers a conclusion uncharacteristic of Phillips's previous work. *Crossing the River* concerns the selling into slavery of three children—Nash, Martha and Travis—by their father, when his crops fail and he is left with nothing. Their journey—the eponymous crossing of the river—takes them across space and time. Nash spends his slavery in America, undergoing a rigorous Christian education, and is returned to Africa by his "father," Edward Williams, under the Auspices of the American Colonisation Society, to assist in the Christian mission. Martha emerges in Virginia as a slave of the Hoffmans. When their financial difficulties make it impossible to keep her, Martha travels westward in search of the daughter from whom she was separated at an auction. Travis appears as an American GI stationed "somewhere in England" during World War II. His relationship with a local girl, Joyce, results in a child that Joyce is forced to give away. Their marriage is cut short by Travis's premature death.

The anomalies in space and time between the characters suggest that Phillips uses them to bear witness to the *legacy* of slavery, the many generations whose lives were shaped by that initial crossing of the river. Nash, Martha, and Travis are individual figures through whom the experiences of many lives are inferred. Their father is the voice of 18th-century Africa, and we join him in watching how those taken from him survive the fracturing of lives by sinking "hopeful roots into difficult soil." Their legacy is one of pain and desolation, but most important in this novel is the capacity for love and survival in times of immense difficulty. Nash rejects both the values of Christianity and the American dream, but takes what is positive from his education to contend for the rights of "the coloured man" in Liberia. Martha's quest for her lost family is achieved in her mind only, as she dies freezing in a doorway, dreaming of their reunion. But on her journey she has encountered people willing to help her, and in her final moments she is received into the care of a stranger. Although Travis is killed in action, his son, Greer, is emotionally and compellingly reunited with his mother in 1963.

Crossing the River is ultimately about the pain involved in revisiting the past, but also discovering there the persistence of positive values. It searches the centuries for brief moments of altruism and love. They may be exceptional and rare, but to ignore them is to give a distorted account of history. The children's father celebrates in the novel's final sentence how Nash, Martha, and Travis "arrived on the far bank of the river, loved." Such an affirmative ending makes the novel Phillips's bravest to date, and strikes a tentative note of hope absent from *Cambridge.*

Cambridge and *Crossing the River* are Phillips's most effective novels by far. While *Higher Ground* is thematically complete, it is a collection of fragmented stories, and indeed, both *The Final Passage* and *A State of Independence* read as long short stories rather than novels. The success of *Cambridge* is ensured by Phillips's use of narrators, first the mannered daughter of an English landowner and second, Cambridge himself. *Crossing the River* extends Phillips's skill in modulating between narrative voices across time and space without sacrificing thematic sophistication or becoming unnecessarily convoluted. Less easily comprehensible is his sixth novel, *The Nature of Blood,* a three-tiered narrative that includes the story of Eva, a Holocaust survivor; the tale of Othello told in first person; and a third-person account of anti-Semitic "blood-libel cult" killings in fifteenth-century Italy.

Also a successful playwright, Phillips writes with ease in this form and certainly to great effect.

—Pat Gordon-Smith, updated by John McLeod

PHILLIPS, Jayne Anne

Nationality: American. **Born:** Buckhannon, West Virginia, 19 July 1952. **Education:** West Virginia University, Morgantown, B.A. 1974; University of Iowa, Iowa City, M.F.A. 1978. **Family:** Married Mark Brian Stockman in 1985; one son and two stepsons. **Career:** Teaching fellow, M.F.A. Program, University of Iowa, Iowa City, 1977–78; lecturer, Humboldt State University, Arcata, California, 1978–79; fellow, Fine Arts Work Center, Provincetown, Massachusetts, 1979–80; assistant professor, Bunting Institute, Radcliffe College, Cambridge, Massachusetts, 1980–81; assistant professor of English, Boston University, 1982–83; visiting senior lecturer, Harvard University, 1990, 1993–94; writer in residence, Brandeis University, Waltham, Massachusetts, 1996. **Awards:** Pushcart prize, 1977, for *Sweethearts,* 1979, for short stories ''Home'' and Lechery,'' 1983, for short story ''How Mickey Made It''; National Endowment for the Arts grant, 1977, 1984; Coordinating Council of Literary Magazines Fels award, 1978, for *Sweethearts;* St. Lawrence award, 1978, for *Counting;* American Academy Kaufman award, 1980, for *Black Tickets;* O. Henry award, 1980, for ''Snow''; Bunting Institute fellowship, Radcliffe College, 1981; literature award, American Academy and Institute for Arts and Letters, 1997. **Agent:** c/o Lynn Nesbit, Janclow & Nesbit, 598 Madison Avenue, New York, New York 10022–1614, U.S.A.

Publications

Novel

Machine Dreams. New York, Dutton, and London, Faber, 1984.
Shelter. Boston, Houghton Mifflin, 1994; London, Faber, 1995.
MotherKind. New York, Knopf, 2000.

Short Stories

Sweethearts. Carrboro, North Carolina, Truck Press, 1976.
Counting. New York, Vehicle, 1978.
Black Tickets. New York, Delacorte Press, 1979; London, Allen Lane, 1980.
How Mickey Made It. St. Paul, Bookslinger Press, 1981.
Fast Lanes. New York, Vehicle, 1984; London, Faber, 1987.

Uncollected Short Stories

''Something That Happened,'' in *The Best American Short Stories 1979,* edited by Joyce Carol Oates and Shannon Ravenel. Boston, Houghton Mifflin, 1979.
''Bess,'' in *Esquire* (New York), August 1984.

* * *

Jayne Anne Phillips began as primarily a short story writer, though more recently she has concentrated mostly on the novel. Much of her early work was privately published, but *Black Tickets* is the first collection that introduced her to a wider audience. It contains no fewer than twenty-seven stories in its generously spaced 265 pages, but sixteen of these hardly amount to more than sketches, only one or two pages long. In her traditional disclaimer at the start of the book Phillips notes that ''Characters and voices in these stories began in what is real but became, in fact, dreams''; the word ''voices'' is particularly significant here as many of the stories, especially the shorter ones, seem like attempts at the creation and expression of a particular voice. They could almost be the product of assigned tasks at a creative writing course. ''Wedding Picture,'' for instance, is merely a description, less than a page long, of a photograph of a daughter's parents on their wedding day. It is hard to derive very much significance from this or a number of other short pieces. Often they are written in the first person, in a variety of different voices. ''Home,'' on the other hand, is not only a much more substantial story but a moving account of the relationship between a daughter and mother, a theme which comes up often in Phillips's work. The prose is spare, almost minimalist at times, with short sections, sparse dialogue. The two women argue over changing sexual mores but the bond between them is clear.

Relationships between a daughter and one or both of her parents come up in several stories but most impressively in ''The Heavenly Animal,'' in which a father can only express his love for his daughter by repeatedly offering to repair her car, and in ''Souvenir'' when a woman discovers her mother has fatal cancer and debates whether or not to tell her or, as her brother demands, conceal the news. Others concern runaway young girls, cocaine users, strippers, and young unmarried mothers. Phillips's vision is a darkly disturbing one. She concentrates on outsiders, those on the periphery of society, and especially the young and defenseless. The best story is the title one, a brilliant monologue by a man who has been dealing in drugs and been betrayed by the two people who introduced him into that world. Only slowly, as the story moves in reverse, do we find out the whole truth (or most of it) as to what has happened and why the narrator is in jail. It is a superbly sustained narrative, part protest, part plea, part love story. ''El Paso'' alternates between different voices, a device Phillips has come to use quite often.

Machine Dreams is Phillips's first novel and a considerably ambitious one. Using four narrative voices in alternating order, the novel tells the story of the marriage of Mitch and Jean Hampson, a couple who live in a small town in West Virginia, and their two children, Danner and Billy, born close together. It documents the slow corrosion of the marriage, with its eventual culmination in divorce, and finally, in a brilliantly written chapter, the tragic death of Billy in Vietnam. The concluding chapter, which goes oddly over much the material we have already become acquainted with, deals with the near madness of depression and rage which overcomes Danner after the death of her brother.

The private difficulties of the family are placed against the larger public issues affecting America in the forties through seventies—World War II and the defeat of the Japanese, the Korean war, civil rights marches, the Cuban missile crisis, and, above all, the Vietnam war, which finally impinges closely on the family. Mitch's letters home from the Pacific—so dull that they sound absolutely authentic—are juxtaposed against those of Billy twenty-five years later after he is conscripted to Vietnam. The novel shows the first fumbling attempts at sexual experience of Danner and Billy. Frequently it focuses on important occasions which should be of celebration—July 4, New Year's Eve—but treats them with irony. Three sections of the novel are actually headed ''Machine Dreams,'' and the novel is full of images of technology, most obviously in the Vietnam section. *Machine Dreams* is hard going at times but it is an impressive attempt to document the mores of American society over three decades in the way that John Updike was also doing at the same time and Don DeLillo attempted later.

Phillips's collection of short stories, *Fast Lanes,* repeated the success of *Black Tickets.* Again she experiments with different voices as in that of the twenty-eight-year-old man in ''How Mickey Made It,'' a story which had been privately published earlier. Another first person narrative, ''Rayme,'' tells the story of a disturbed girl, while ''Bluegill'' is an experiment in a kind of impressionistic, almost stream-of-consciousness style. Some of the material in the collection recalls *Machine Dreams;* ''Blue Moon'' deals with Billy and Danner and Billy's lover Kato from a different angle to the earlier work.

Shelter is set in Shelter County, West Virginia, in 1963. In this novel Phillips takes her device of multiple voices further than in *Machine Dreams.* The narrative has again four voices—Lenny and her sister Alma, Parson, and Buddy Carmody—but they alternate much more rapidly, with the novel being divided into forty-two sections. It is much more concentrated in time and essentially is built around one central, climactic incident—the killing of Buddy's stepfather Carmody by Buddy, during the ironically named Camp Shelter. There is a Faulknerian quality to *Shelter* with its highly idiomatic language and its concentration on strange sexual relationships, forms of religious belief that have gone awry, and the awakening knowledge of evil by young people. The same events are viewed from a multitude of angles and perspectives. Often characters spy on other characters, unknown to them. Of most importance is the perspective of Buddy, the young boy sexually assaulted by his stepfather, who struggles to understand and come to terms with the world. He watches Lenny and her friend Cap: ''Buddy would see them wherever they were, but they couldn't see him, he was invisible, spotted brown and green like the army guys in comic books.'' There is much less political content than in *Machine Dreams,* though some attention is paid to Mrs. Thompson-Warner and her deranged anti-Communism. Once again, Phillips employs sustained motifs—the bats who fly around in Turtle Hole, the rings that both Carmody and Buddy covet, snakes, the girl who was a fish.

Set not in West Virginia but in Boston, Phillips's most recent novel, *Motherkind,* is strikingly different from anything she has done previously. *Motherkind* focuses almost exclusively on the figure of Kate Tateman, a poet and teacher who is quite different from the underclass characters in many of the short stories. Kate is in the unusual position at the start of the novel of being about to give birth and become a mother for the first time, but also losing her own mother, who has been diagnosed with terminal cancer. Yet again, mother and daughter are extremely close while the estranged father remains on the periphery. Kate has to juggle her impending motherhood, her relationship with her new partner and his two rowdy sons by a previous marriage whose adjustment to the situation is made more difficult by the unrelenting hostility of her partner's ex-wife, and the arduous duty of taking painstaking care of her dying mother. There is no multitude of voices this time. The novel concentrates exclusively on Kate; Phillips cuts back and forth in time but almost the only perspective we see is hers and we learn what little we do about her mother Katherine, her divorced father, and her doctor-partner Matt through dialogue. The novel concentrates on and juxtaposes the simultaneous experiences in Kate's life—the joy and wonder she experiences in looking after her son and the corresponding agony as her mother slowly slips into unconsciousness. There is an almost documentary quality to the novel, a meticulous and at times almost ruthless recording of the experiences of birth, marriage and death, that is new in Phillips's work. The description of Katherine's last days and her growing alienation from those around her is particularly harrowing. Though there are hints that Kate showed some wildness when she was young, the figure we see in the novel behaves with exemplary patience and maturity, struggling to reconcile the various forces tugging at her in this celebration of banal domesticity.

—Laurie Clancy

PHILLIPS, Mike

Nationality: Guyanese-British. **Born:** Guyana (immigrated to Britain in 1956). **Education:** Attended school in Islington; studied for a degree, and later for a postgraduate degree, at other schools. **Career:** Worked variously in factories, garages, and at a post office; established a hostel for homeless black youths, Notting Hill, London; community activist, Manchester and Birmingham, England; journalist, 1970s—; teacher, University of Westminster. Lives in London, England. **Awards:** Silver Dagger award (Crime Writers' Association.)

Publications

Novels

Blood Rights. New York, St. Martin's Press, 1989.
The Late Candidate. New York, St. Martin's Press, 1990.
Point of Darkness: A Sam Dean Mystery. London, Michael Joseph, 1994; New York, St. Martin's Press, 1995.
An Image to Die For. New York, St. Martin's Press, 1997.
The Dancing Face. New York, HarperCollins, 1997.
A Shadow of Myself. New York, HarperCollins, 2000.

Short Stories

Smell of the Coast and Other Stories. London, Akira Press, 1987.

Other

Notting Hill in the Sixties (text), photography by Charlie Phillips. London, Lawrence & Wishart, 1991.
Windrush: The Irresistible Rise of Multi-Racial Britain (with Trevor Phillips). London, HarperCollins, 1998.

* * *

Mike Phillips writes from a consciously black British perspective while seeking to avoid the usual conventions of African and African-American writing. There is discrimination but no history of slavery on plantations or apartheid; there is a history of immigrants, outsiders who survive in and become part of a new society. Whether writing about black Britons or others, such as the Russians and Germans and a Ghanaian in *A Shadow of Myself,* Phillips is concerned with migrants, people who cross boundaries and take chances whether out of necessity, curiosity, or in search of a better life. Change, excitement, survival, and memory are major themes in his writing.

Although working within such popular commercial literary forms as the crime story and international thriller, Phillips is a serious writer with an analytical view of the world who sees people morally and sociologically; they are products of society but still have free will and make choices. Life consists of change and excitement, but disappoints our desires; it is necessary to learn from the past while moving on. Phillips has published two documentary studies, the mostly pictorial and nostalgic *Notting Hill in the Sixties* and *Windrush: The Irresistible Rise of Multi-Racial Britain*, both social histories of the West Indian community in England and its progress from postwar immigrants to a major influence in creating a multi-racial England.

Smell of the Coast and Other Stories consists of short stories mostly set outside England. In ''The Smell of the Coast'' the narrator is in East Africa and assumes that, as the people are black and the landscape is similar to the Caribbean, he is at home. He soon is actually and culturally lost. He does not understand the sexual mores of urbanized East African women, nor the usual social behavior of East Indians in Africa, and he does not understand Swahili. East Africa is one of many places where characters deceive themselves about black people in other societies before the character accepts being English. Phillips sets several stories in the United States which at first seems a paradise for black people who can rise to the top and become millionaires in sports and entertainment, and who are sought by prestigious colleges and who hold university professorships. It is a land of opportunities for West Indians, but the children of the immigrants lack the ambition of their parents, often live in black ghettos, and turn rapidly to drugs and crime. This is the other side of Black America in contrast to the millionaires, black separatism, and affirmative action.

Mostly set in the immigrant and ethnic areas of New York City, with a concluding chase to California and Arizona, *Point of Darkness*, one of his Sam Dean novels, contrasts the sense of community still found in black England with the everyone-for-oneself rat race of the United States where, despite talk of black brotherhood, it is dog eat dog. The United States is more corrupt, violent, and socially fragmented than England. For someone with Sam's moral sense and need to belong, England is home. Sam Dean is a black British freelance journalist who in the course of doing some minor job becomes aware of a larger mystery which he voluntarily risks his life to solve. Although he might seem an existentialist hero living by his own rules in a chaotic changing world, Sam is part of a community with social ties and he needs others to save him and solve his problems, although others can never be depended on and are themselves changing.

Blood Rights is the first of the Sam Dean novels. Sam, from Guyana, has been in England since his teens and is known for his newspaper columns and television appearances. He is divorced and has a long-term affair with Sophie, an Argentine photographer. They live separately and regard themselves as ''free'' to carry on other affairs provided that they engage in ''safe'' sex. Sam can speak and act tough and is good with his fists but dislikes violence. In the novels there is usually someone who does the violent dirty work for him. Sam is aware of the history of neighborhoods, of the problems faced by black youths—especially by young men—and how people are treated as stereotypes. He wants his son to have a knowledge of black British history, but his son has been raised by his white middle-class mother and, has little ability to comprehend the immigrant culture that Sam knows, with its history of poverty and racial hurts. Sam remembers a time when blacks in England always smiled at each other as they felt they were among white strangers.

People ignore how difficult it is for young black males to climb out of an environment of poverty and crime. The exploitation of and rejection by the British of their black past is represented in *Blood Rights* by Roy Akimbola Baker, the unacknowledged son of Greville Baker, a wealthy powerful Tory MP tipped to be in the next Cabinet. When an angry Roy learns the truth about his background, and goes to London to confront Greville, he tussles with the police, is jailed, and wants revenge. This soon gets out of hand when Roy's friend Winston turns out to be a vicious murderer. Roy helps Sam rescue Virginia, the daughter of Greville Baker, who has become a captive of Winston. The novel might be said to be an allegory of white and black Britain; history has made them part of a large extended family which will continue to hurt itself until it reaches some mutual recognition and accommodation.

Racism in Phillips's novels has social and psychological causes as well as economic. *The Late Candidate* concerns those in the running for nomination as the Labour Party's candidate for election to Parliament in a traditional Labour Party borough. The formerly white Labour Party controlled Local Council now consists of Indians, blacks, gays, lesbians, Marxists, and other interest groups. An older Irish group is still powerful but no longer dominates. Aston Edwards, a black member of the local borough council is a doubly late candidate as he was officially in the running and was killed, the police think by a younger black man who was having an affair with Aston's white wife. Walter Davis, a black spokesman for the borough Labour Party, turns out to be another late candidate as he is hoping to replace the dead Aston Edwards by gaining the support of the working class Irish group led by the Parker family. Davis knows about an investigation Aston was conducting before his death into the ways Parker's construction company had corrupted the Council, gaining a monopoly on contracts. When Walter is killed the police suspect a black man who has organized and runs a local youth center, a meeting place for petty drug dealing. Sam fears that the police will jump at the chance to build a case against the two black men, as love triangles and drug dealing fit black stereotypes, rather than look for the real culprits. Each lead concludes with Sam deciding that he does not have a candidate for the murderer of Aston until the one person who seems an unlikely suspect turns out to be the double murderer because of racial hatred which disguises his own insecurity and failures.

Life consists of false appearances, misleading representations, and fantasies of desire. It is also unfair. In *An Image to Die For* Sam's son talks of going to America as the white students do not see him as a person with similar private interests to their own; they stereotype him as a black victim only interested in racial matters. Sophie who has been photographing Arab women takes on their perspective and covers herself like an Arab woman; she talks about the safety it offers her from prying male eyes. By contrast Sarah, with whom Sam had an affair many years ago, asks him to work with his old friend Wyndham, who runs an independent TV film company and to whom she is married. Sam sleeps with her and hopes to protect her from the killer, but at the novel's conclusion Sarah turns out to be herself a killer who put the various events and murders in motion. She calmly tells Sam that even if he reports her to the police nothing can be proven and she won't go to prison, whereas he is the one likely to be in trouble. He calls the police anyway.

The Dancing Face returns to the question of black British identity. Most African-Americans and black Britons are racially mixed, brown rather than black, and know little about what Africa is really like. Gus is a brown Englishman whose West Indian father taught him that all blacks are Africans. He steals a famous ancient mask to dramatize the moral right of Africa to reparations. In contrast to Gus's idealism concerning Africa and bitterness towards white England, there is Dr. Okigbo, a vicious, powerful, corrupt businessman and politician who escaped from Nigeria after being imprisoned by a corrupt, violent, tyrannical military government. Okigbo financed the stealing of the mask, which he wants to use to negotiate his return to power. At the conclusion, Osman, a Nigerian studying in England, destroys the work of art and says, ''I turned my back on history.'' Osman served in the Nigerian army and saw opponents of the government massacred; he knows it is time to forget dreams of an ideal Africa as home, better to begin again in England.

—Bruce King

PIERCY, Marge

Nationality: American. **Born:** Detroit, Michigan, 31 March 1936. **Education:** The University of Michigan, Ann Arbor (Hopwood award, 1956, 1957), A.B. 1957; Northwestern University, Evanston, Illinois, M.A. 1958. **Family:** Married Ira Wood (third marriage) in 1982. **Career:** Instructor, Indiana University, Gary, 1960–62; poet-in-residence, University of Kansas, Lawrence, 1971; visiting lecturer, Thomas Jefferson College, Grand Valley State Colleges, Allendale, Michigan, 1975; visiting faculty, Women's Writers' Conference, Cazenovia College, New York, 1976, 1978, 1980; staff member, Fine Arts Work Center, Provincetown, Massachusetts, 1976–77; writer-in-residence, College of the Holy Cross, Worcester, Massachusetts, 1976; Butler Professor of Letters, State University of New York, Buffalo, 1977; Elliston Professor of Poetry, University of Cincinnati, 1986. Member of the board of directors, 1982–85, and of the advisory board since 1985, Coordinating Council of Literary Magazines; since 1988 poetry editor, *Tikkun* magazine, Oakland, California. **Awards:** Borestone Mountain award, 1968, 1974; National Endowment for the Arts grant, 1978; Rhode Island School of Design Faculty Association medal, 1985; Carolyn Kizer prize, 1986, 1990; Shaeffer Eaton-PEN New England award, 1989; New England Poetry Club Golden Rose, 1990; May Sarton award, 1991; Brit ha-Dorot award, Shalom Center, 1992; Arthur C. Clarke award, 1993; Notable Book award, American Library Association, 1997. **Agent:** Lois Wallace, Wallace Literary Agency, 177 East 70th Street, New York, New York 10021. **Address:** Box 1473, Wellfleet, Massachusetts 02667, U.S.A.

PUBLICATIONS

Novels

Going Down Fast. New York, Simon and Schuster, 1969.
Dance the Eagle to Sleep. New York, Doubleday, 1970; London, W.H. Allen, 1971.
Small Changes. New York, Doubleday, 1973; London, Penguin, 1987.
Woman on the Edge of Time. New York, Knopf, 1976; London, Women's Press, 1979.
The High Cost of Living. New York, Harper, 1978; London, Women's Press, 1979.
Vida. New York, Summit, and London, Women's Press, 1980.
Braided Lives. New York, Summit, and London, Allen Lane, 1982.
Fly Away Home. New York, Summit, and London, Chatto and Windus, 1984.
Gone to Soldiers. New York, Summit, and London, Joseph, 1987.
Summer People. New York, Summit, and London, Joseph, 1989.
He, She and It. New York, Knopf, 1991; as *Body of Glass,* London, Joseph, 1992.
The Longings of Women. New York, Fawcett, and London, Joseph, 1994.
City of Darkness, City of Light. New York, Fawcett Columbine, 1996.
Storm Tide (with Ira Wood). New York, Fawcett Columbine, 1998.
Three Women. New York, William Morrow, 1999.

Uncollected Short Stories

''Crossing over Jordan,'' in *Transatlantic Review* (London), Fall 1966.
''Love Me Tonight, God,'' in *Paris Review,* Summer 1968.
''A Dynastic Encounter,'' in *Aphra* (New York) Spring 1970.
''And I Went into the Garden of Love,'' in *Off Our Backs* (Washington, D.C.), Summer 1971.
''Do You Love Me?,'' in *Second Wave* (Cambridge, Massachusetts), vol. 1, no. 4, 1972.
''The Happiest Day of a Woman's Life,'' in *Works in Progress 7* (New York), 1972.
''Somebody Who Understands You,'' in *Moving Out* (Detroit), vol. 2, no. 2, 1972.
''Marriage Is a Matter of Give and Take,'' in *Boston Phoenix,* 3 July and 10 July 1973.
''Little Sister, Cat and Mouse,'' in *Second Wave* (Cambridge, Massachusetts), Fall 1973.
''God's Blood,'' in *Anon,* no. 8, 1974.
''Like a Great Door Closing Suddenly,'' in *Detroit Discovery,* March-April 1974.
''The Retreat,'' in *Provincetown Poets* (Provincetown, Massachusetts), vol. 2, nos. 2–3, 1976.
''What Can Be Had,'' in *Chrysalis 4* (San Diego, California), 1977.
''The Cowbird in the Eagles' Nest,'' in *Maenad,* Fall 1980.
''I Will Not Describe What I Did,'' in *Mother Jones* (San Francisco), February-March 1982.
''Spring in the Arboretum,'' in *Michigan Quarterly Review* (Ann Arbor), Winter 1982.
''Of Chilblains and Rotten Rutabagas,'' in *Lilith* (New York), Winter-Spring 1985.

Play

The Last White Class: A Play About Neighborhood Terror, with Ira Wood (produced Northampton, Massachusetts, 1978). Trumansburg, New York, Crossing Press, 1980.

Poetry

Breaking Camp. Middletown, Connecticut, Wesleyan University Press, 1968.
Hard Loving. Middletown, Connecticut, Wesleyan University Press, 1969.
A Work of Artifice. Detroit, Red Hanrahan Press, 1970.
4-Telling, with others. Trumansburg, New York, Crossing Press, 1971.
When the Drought Broke. Santa Barbara, California, Unicorn Press, 1971.

To Be of Use. New York, Doubleday, 1973.
Living in the Open. New York, Knopf, 1976.
The Twelve-Spoked Wheel Flashing. New York, Knopf, 1978.
The Moon Is Always Female. New York, Knopf, 1980.
Circles on the Water: Selected Poems. New York, Knopf, 1982.
Stone, Paper, Knife. New York, Knopf, and London, Pandora Press, 1983.
My Mother's Body. New York, Knopf, and London, Pandora Press, 1985.
Available Light. New York, Knopf, and London, Pandora Press, 1988.
Mars and Her Children. New York, Knopf, 1992.
Eight Chambers of the Heart. London, Penguin, 1995.
What Are Big Girls Made Of?: Poems. New York, Knopf, 1997.
The Art of Blessing the Day: Poems with a Jewish Theme. New York, Knopf, 1999.
Early Grrrl: The Early Poems of Marge Piercy. Wellfleet, Massachusetts, Leapfrog Press, 1999.

Recordings: *Marge Piercy: Poems,* 1969; *Laying Down the Tower,* Black Box, 1973; *Reclaiming Ourselves,* 1973; *At the Core,* 1976; *Reading and Thoughts,* Everett Edwards, 1976; *At the Core,* Watershed, 1976.

Other

The Grand Coolie Damn. Boston, New England Free Press, 1970.
Parti-Colored Blocks for a Quilt. Ann Arbor, University of Michigan Press, 1982.
The Earth Shines Secretly: A Book of Days. Cambridge, Massachusetts, Zoland Press, 1990.
Editor, *Early Ripening: Young Women's Poetry Now.* London and New York, Pandora Press, 1987.

*

Bibliography: In *Contemporary American Women Writers: Narrative Strategies* edited by Catherine Rainwater and William J. Scheick, Lexington, University Press of Kentucky, 1985; *Marge Piercy: An Annotated Bibliography by Patricia Doherty.* Westport, Connecticut, Greenwood Press, 1997.

Manuscript Collection: Harlan Hatcher Graduate Library, University of Michigan, Ann Arbor.

Critical Studies: ''Marge Piercy: A Collage'' by Nancy Scholar Zee, in *Oyez Review* (Berkeley, California), vol. 9, no. 1, 1975; *Ways of Knowing: Critical Essays on Marge Piercy* edited by Sue Walker and Eugenie Hamner, Mobile, Alabama, Negative Capability Press, 1986; *The Repair of the World: The Novels of Marge Piercy* by Kerstin W. Shands, Connecticut, Greenwood, 1994; *The Broom Closet: Secret Meanings of Domesticity in Postfeminist Novels by Louise Erdrich, Mary Gordon, Toni Morrison, Marge Piercy, Jane Smiley, and Amy Tan* by Jeannette Batz Cooperman, New York, Peter Lang, 1999.

Marge Piercy comments:

Each of my novels appears to me a different miniature world, in which the style, the language appropriate to the characters, is worked out of my understanding of them and their universe of action and discourse. My intention is always appropriateness, and when I do what is usually seen as ''fine writing,'' I do my best to strike it out. My impulse to autobiography is given ample play in my poetry, and thus has little reason to shape my novels. My novels divide into those which are placed in the present; those which are placed in speculative time; and those which occur entirely, or largely, in the past. My interest is always centered on the results of choice through time.

I start with a theme, and then work through character. Fiction is as old a habit of our species as poetry. It goes back to telling a tale, the first perceptions of pattern, and fiction is still about pattern in human life. For me, writing fiction issues from the impulse to tell the story of people who deserve to have their lives revealed, examined, clarified, to people who deserve to read good stories. To find ourselves spoken for in art gives dignity to our pain, our anger, our lust, our losses. I have been particularly although not exclusively concerned with the choices open to—or perceived to be open to—women of various eras, races, and classes. I am one of the few contemporary American novelists consciously and constantly preoccupied with social class and the economic underpinnings of decision and consequence.

In the end, I suspect my novels find readers because they create full characters easy to enter, no matter how hard they might be for the reader to identify within actuality, and because I try to tell a good story.

* * *

Marge Piercy is (with Lisa Alther) one of the best known of that group of American women writers who have created popular fictions about the changing face of radical America, and, in particular, about changing perceptions of and about women. Piercy writes about, and on behalf of, radical political causes, but her main interest is in (and she is most interesting on) sexual politics. Taken together her novels offer a feminist's eye-view of American history from World War II (*Gone to Soldiers*), through the 1950s (*Braided Lives*) to the heady days of 1960s student activism and anti-Vietnam war campaigns (treated retrospectively in *Vida*), and the raising of consciousness of the women's movement of the late 1960s and 1970s (*The High Cost of Living, Small Changes,* and *Fly Away Home*). *Summer People* is an affectionate (even self-indulgent) chronicle of a group of middle-aged people whose lives and values were shaped by the revolutions of the 1960s, and are now disturbed both by the passage of time and the more abrasive climate of the 1980s. At the very least these novels will provide the future social historian with an interesting perspective on radical chic and the countercultures of the mid-twentieth century. Indeed Piercy's novels are frequently quoted by feminists as documents in the history of the modern American women's movement. Among the most quoted in this context is *Small Changes,* which offers a guided tour of countercultural Boston as it charts the decline into marriage of the beautiful, clever, and independent Miriam, and the emergence of her friend Beth from an adolescent marriage into a new (consciousness-raised) sense of self.

These books are all loose baggy monsters, chunky blockbusters which mix together a variety of genres. Elements of the political thriller (*Vida*) are combined with love stories of various kinds. There are portraits of the artist at various stages of development (*Braided Lives* and *Summer People*), and stories of the late-adolescent quest for identity (*The High Cost of Living, Braided Lives,* and *Small Changes*). There are mystery, intrigue, alternative ''lifestyles,'' and above all sex, lots of it in all sorts of combinations. Piercy is no stylist. For the most part these are chronicle novels whose formal inventiveness is restricted to the frequent use of the flashback. Her aim seems to be to recreate the world-as-it-was and to draw her readers into it. Occasionally there seems to be an ironic gap between the reader's perceptions and those of the characters about whom she is reading. This is sometimes the result of Piercy's satiric focus on the way we lived then—whether the ''then'' be the dark ages of the 1950s or the sexual revolution of the 1960s. Indeed some of the funniest (but also the most depressing) writing focuses on the elaborately entwined, and constantly changing, patterns of relationships in the omni-sexual post-1960s (pre-AIDS) world. Sometimes, however, the ironic distance appears to derive from the author's failure to offer a satirical or critical focus on her characters and their attitudes, which increasingly, especially in novels such as *Small Changes* and *Vida,* look dated and naive. Nevertheless, these last-mentioned novels which focus on 1960s radicalism and the women's movement, also give a very powerful sense of what it must have been like to be caught up in the excitement and confusions of those times.

There seems to be a general consensus that by far the most interesting and accomplished of Piercy's novels is one of her earliest creations, *Woman on the Edge of Time.* This book is usually grouped with other feminist utopian or dystopian fantasies such as Ursula K. Le Guin's *The Dispossessed* and *The Left Hand of Darkness,* Joanna Russ's *The Female Man,* Angela Carter's *The Passion of New Eve,* and Margaret Atwood's *The Handmaid's Tale. Woman on the Edge of Time* is the story of Connie Ramos, a thirty-seven-year-old poor, Mexican-American woman, one of the have-nots who is defeated and discarded by a society which is geared towards the needs and interests of the haves. Her lover is killed, her daughter is taken away from her ''unstable'' mother, and Connie is incarcerated in a bleak public mental hospital where (as the pathway to release) she is subjected to a mind-control experiment involving electronic implantations in the brain. Connie is, however, also a ''catcher'' who is able to mind-travel—under the guidance of her ''natural'' Luciente—from the confines of the ''real'' world of her hospital ward to the possible future world of Metapoisset, a new and better society. In Metapoisset the likenesses of Connie's lover, and her daughter Angelina live on in a new, fruitful life in a world of social and ecological harmony. The class and gender roles of Connie's America have been dissolved. These roles are simply not known in Metapoisset, where sexual relationships and the nuclear family have been replaced by a collectivism that respects and preserves the individual self. In short, Metapoisset reverses the values of the world that oppresses Connie and her kind in the present. The competitive individualism which is the creed of bourgeois America become the antivalues of Metapoisset, where notions of evil ''center around power and greed—taking from other people their food, their liberty, their health, their land, their customs, their prides.''

Woman on the Edge of Time finely counterpoints the utopianism of Metapoisset with the dystopian realism with which Connie's actual world is represented. Metapoisset is used to make a critique of modern America, but it is also offered as a vindication of the enabling power of fantasy. Connie's fantasy is not the infantile ''womanish'' regression that she herself suspects at the beginning of her period as a ''catcher,'' but the vision of a new world of possibility which emphasizes human choice and agency. Like much contemporary feminist fantasy fiction *Woman on the Edge of Time* uses a science fiction genre to enact the vision of women overcoming oppressive social and psychological conditions by transcending both the physical and ideological constraints of patriarchal society. It is a profoundly disturbing, but also inspiriting novel.

Set during the French Revolution, *City of Darkness, City of Light* depicts the lives of three female revolutionaries, along with a number of historical figures: Danton, Robespierre, and the mathematician Caritat. A less lofty—and less successful—effort was *Storm Tide,* which Piercy cowrote with husband Ira Wood. The premise, at least, is an attractive one: a washed-up baseball star comes to a resort town, seduces the wife of a leading left-wing politician (who, when he learns of the affair, approves of it in progressive terms), and is persuaded by the same politician to run for a local office. Despite these details and others that accrue as the plot thickens, the book is lifeless in execution. In *Three Women,* however, Piercy offered a compelling portrait of three generations balancing political and personal commitments.

—Lyn Pykett, updated by Judson Knight

PLANTE, David (Robert)

Nationality: American. **Born:** Providence, Rhode Island, 4 March 1940. **Education:** Boston College, 1957–59, 1960–61, B.A. in French 1961; University of Louvain, Belgium, 1959–60. **Career:** Teacher, English School, Rome, 1961–62; guidebook writer, New York, 1962–64; teacher, Boston School of Modern Languages, 1964–65, and St. John's Preparatory School, Massachusetts, 1965–66; moved to England in 1966. Henfield Writing Fellow, University of East Anglia, Norwich, 1977; writer-in-residence, University of Tulsa, Oklahoma, 1979–82, Adelphi University, New York, 1989, and University of Quebec, Montreal, 1990; Visiting Fellow, Cambridge University, 1984–85; lecturer, Gorky Institute of Literature, Moscow, Autumn 1990. Lives in London. **Awards:** Arts Council bursary, 1977; American Academy award, 1983; Guggenheim grant, 1983. **Address:** Altken, Stone, and Wylie, 29 Fernshaw Rd., London SW10 0TG.

PUBLICATIONS

Novels

The Ghost of Henry James. London, Macdonald, and Boston, Gambit, 1970.
Slides. London, Macdonald, and Boston, Gambit, 1971.
Relatives. London, Cape, 1972; New York, Avon, 1974.
The Darkness of the Body. London, Cape, 1974.
Figures in Bright Air. London, Gollancz, 1976.
The Family. London, Gollancz, and New York, Farrar Straus, 1978.
The Country. London, Gollancz, and New York, Atheneum, 1981.
The Woods. London, Gollancz, and New York, Atheneum, 1982.
The Francoeur Family. London, Chatto and Windus, 1984.
The Foreigner. London, Chatto and Windus, and New York, Atheneum, 1984.
The Catholic. London, Chatto and Windus, 1985; New York, Atheneum, 1986.
The Native. London, Chatto and Windus, 1987; New York, Atheneum, 1988.

The Accident. New York, Ticknor and Fields, 1991.
Annunciation. New York, Ticknor and Fields, 1994.
The Age of Terror. New York, St. Martin's Press, 1999.

Short Stories

Penguin Modern Stories 1, with others. London, Penguin, 1969.
My Mother's Pearl Necklace. New York, Albondocani Press, 1987.

Uncollected Short Stories

"The Buried City," in *Transatlantic Review* (London), Spring 1967.
"The Tangled Centre," in *Modern Occasions* (Cambridge, Massachusetts), Spring 1971.
"Mr. Bonito," in *New Yorker,* 7 July 1980.
"The Student," in *Tri-Quarterly* (Evanston, Illinois), Fall 1982.
"Work," in *Prize Stories 1983: The O. Henry Awards,* edited by William Abrahams. New York, Doubleday, 1983.
"Paris, 1959," in *New Yorker,* 4 June 1984.
"The Crack," in *First Love / Last Love,* edited by Michael Denneny, Charles Ortleb, and Thomas Steele. New York, Putnam, 1985.
"A House of Women," in *New Yorker,* 28 April 1986.

Other

Difficult Women: A Memoir of Three. London, Gollancz, and New York, Atheneum, 1983.
Keith Milow: New Work. New York, Nohra Haime Gallery editions, 2000.

*

Bibliography: In *American Book Collector* (New York), November-December 1984.

Manuscript Collection: University of Tulsa, Oklahoma.

David Plante comments:

One of course always writes with an intention in mind, but it is what one cannot intend that is my fascination in writing. I know, all the while I am choosing my words, making as vivid as possible my descriptions, that there is something floating beneath my words and descriptions which has a will of its own, which sometimes rises up to meet my words and most often sinks away, and one can no more intend it than one can (to borrow an image from William James) turn up a bright light to see the darkness. The best one can do is allow it to well up, to give it space.

One is or isn't in touch with this sense, and one knows one is or isn't as matter of factly, as unmysteriously, as one knows one is happy or depressed. In touch with it, one writes "Mr. Stein woke to a room of shadows," and the sentence comes to life, evokes a deep world of associations, while out of touch with it the same sentence, "Mr. Stein woke to a room of shadows," is banal, dull, dead. The difference between good and bad writing is quite as simple as that.

How does one know one is in touch or not? One knows the signs, particular enough to be recognizable. For example, walking down a street most often I am unaware of the litter that's around me, or I am aware of it only to wish it weren't there. This past afternoon, however, walking along a sidewalk, I found myself studying, on the cement, a small printed target with three or four bullet holes blown through it, a match book printed with three spades, a page torn from a magazine, a parking lot ticket, an addressed envelope, and it seemed to me that everything I saw was indicative of much more than what it was—after all, just litter—was, because of its rich suggestiveness, beyond my imaginative grasp. I wanted to *write* about that target, match book, page, ticket, letter, and I wanted to with the similarly recognizable, similarly matter of fact urge one has when one wants to sneeze, *I was in touch with something.*

One is, at various times, *aware* that one has to sneeze, one is aware that one is sexually attracted to someone, one is aware that one must work and eat and sleep, and one is aware that there is a sense, informing things yet capable of being abstracted from them, which one hopes to be the essence of one's writing, which one hopes will bring one's words and one's world to life.

Sneezing is important, and making love is important, and working and eating and sleeping are important, and something else is also important, something longed for, something which is the whole purpose of my work. William James said: "It is, the reader will see, the reinstatement of the vague and inarticulate to its proper place in our mental life which I am so anxious to press on the attention."

* * *

Separateness and tension distinguish the writing of David Plante, his novels containing within themselves a complex balance of ambiguities. Beneath its unremarkable surface, his fiction seethes with an inner life sensed rather than observed, the books seeming to vibrate with half-heard resonances. The outer skin of the novels, crowded as they are with a succession of apparently trivial incidents, serves merely to mask the hidden conflicts waiting to explode, whose pulses travel upward to meet the consciousness of the reader.

The Ghost of Henry James explores the group identity of a family in New England, following through a series of abrupt transitions the subtle alteration in attitudes, the shifts of understanding that bind the members one to another despite their differences, and the trauma that ensues when the central character tries to break free of the rest. Lost without the family, he finds only madness and death, but from it comes a transformation and a reordering of the other lives as his ghostly presence pervades the final scenes. Plante pays homage to the author of *The Turn of the Screw,* both in his evocation of sinister New England landscapes and in a style which distinguishes the text as a separate entity from what it describes. *Slides* pursues the same theme, the group this time consisting of adolescent friends, and the violent climax an attempted suicide. The shade of Hawthorne is summoned here, the Gothic aspect of his writings recreated as Plante hints subtly at the conflict between freedom and unity, the sexuality repressed beneath an innate puritanism, in a carefully weighted language that throbs behind the matter-of-fact conversations and weekend outings that make up the action of the book.

The Darkness of the Body and *Figures in Bright Air* reveal a deeper probing beneath the surface. In them, Plante undertakes a detailed portrayal of obsessive states of mind, presenting through the charged love-hate relationships of his characters the destructive force of physical love, the body's threat to the innerness of the beloved, the need for the personality to retain separateness and distance. Love-making is shown as a death-struggle, a falling into a black pit. The world itself is broken down to intensely potent fragments, individuals perceived as geometric shapes that clash against each other. Elements of air and stone are balanced in opposition, mirrors of the narrator's inward struggle where art, like life, is set the incompatible tasks of all-embracing vision and the reduction of everything to nothing. Plante's finely poised language, his matching of stillness with explosive action, invest the surface with its necessary undercurrents of tension and release. In these works in particular, he appears to be striving towards the ideal of Flaubert, and later of Robbe-Grillet, of the perfect irreductible text as a self-sufficient entity from which nothing can be removed.

In his trilogy on the Francoeur family—*The Family, The Country,* and *The Woods*—Plante's expression is less elusive than before, drawing directly from his personal experience. *The Country* especially veers close to documentary at times, representing the author's sense of himself as a native of two countries, his French-speaking birthplace in Rhode Island, and the rest of the United States. His central character, Daniel Francoeur, discovers through the contact of the last days with his dying father an affinity between them, and beyond it a kinship with the father's long-dead Indian ancestors: ''My father was born, as I was, among the ghosts of a small community of people of strange blood. They were people who saw that they were born in darkness and would die in darkness, and who accepted that. They spoke, in their old French, in whispers, in the churchyard, among the gravestones, in the snow, and with them, silent, were squaws with papooses on their backs, and the woods began beyond the last row of gravestones. They were strange to me, and yet they were not strange.''

Daniel's transformation, the slow change that takes place in him as he witnesses the death of his father and cares for his aging mother, is movingly and simply described. Plante builds up through meetings and casual conversation the relationship between parents and brothers, the feuds and differences that strain the underlying unity. The brooding presence of the forest permeates the novel, but *The Country* is among the clearest of its author's works. Daniel's mother above all, with her hatred of sex and childbirth, explains much of the meaning behind the ''destructive love'' theme in previous writings.

With *The Woods* Plante forsakes documentary techniques, returning to a third-person narrative that explores Daniel's inner world, culminating in his adolescent lovemaking, again visualized as a violation. This approach is continued with *The Foreigner* and *The Catholic.* More ''fictionalized'' than some of the Francoeur trilogy, these novels contain a greater degree of violence and erotic force which blasts more often to the surface. Here, as in earlier works, the core of the book lies almost out of sight beneath the text, a white-hot magma that simmers under the skin.

—Geoff Sadler

PLUNKETT, James

Nationality: Irish. **Born:** James Plunkett Kelly in Dublin, 21 May 1920. **Education:** Synge Street Christian Brothers School, Dublin; Dublin College of Music. **Family:** Married Valerie Koblitz in 1945; one daughter and three sons. **Career:** Branch secretary, Workers Union of Ireland, 1946–55; assistant head of drama, Radio Eireann, Dublin, 1955–60; producer-director, 1961–68, head of features, 1969–71, and senior producer, 1974–85, Radio Telefis Eireann (Irish Television), Dublin. Council member, Society of Irish Playwrights, 1984–85. **Awards:** Irish Television award, 1964, 1966; *Yorkshire Post* award, 1969. **Member:** 1970, and president, 1980–82, Irish Academy of Letters; Toscaire (council member), Aosdana, 1981–85. **Agent:** Peters Fraser and Dunlop Group, 503–504 The Chambers, Chelsea Harbour, Lots Road, London SW10 0XF, England. **Address:** 29 Parnell Rd., Bray, County Wicklow, Ireland.

Publications

Novels

Strumpet City. London, Hutchinson, and New York, Delacorte Press, 1969.

The Gems She Wore: A Book of Irish Places. London, Hutchinson, 1972; New York, Holt Rinehart, 1973.

Farewell Companions. London, Hutchinson, 1977; New York, Coward McCann, 1978.

The Circus Animals. London, Hutchinson, 1990.

Short Stories

The Trusting and the Maimed, Other Irish Stories. New York, Devin Adair, 1955; London, Hutchinson, 1959.

Collected Short Stories. Dublin, Poolbeg Press, 1977.

Plays

Homecoming (broadcast 1954). Published in *The Bell* (Dublin), June 1954.

Big Jim (broadcast 1954). Dublin, O'Donnell, 1955.

The Risen People (produced Dublin, 1958; London, 1959; New York, 1978). Dublin, Co-op, 1978.

Radio Plays: *Dublin Fusilier,* 1952; *Mercy,* 1953; *Homecoming,* 1954; *Big Jim,* 1954; *Farewell Harper,* 1956.

Television Plays and Programs: *Memory Harbour,* 1963; *The Life and Times of Jimmy O'Dea,* 1964; *Portrait of a Poet,* 1965; *When Do You Die, Friend?,* 1966; *The Great O'Neill,* 1966; *Inis Fail,* 1971; *The State of the Nation,* 1972; *A Dash of Genius,* 1979; *That Solitary Man,* 1979; *The Wicklow Way,* 1980; *I Hear You Calling Me* (on John McCormack), 1984; *The Eagles and the Trumpets,* 1984; *One Man in His Time* (on Cyril Cusack), 1985.

Other

The Boy on the Back Wall and Other Essays. Dublin, Poolbeg Press, 1987.

*

Critical Studies: *Dublin and the Drama of Larkinism* by Godeleine Carpentier, Lille, France, Université de Lille, 1975; *Great Hatred,*

Little Room: The Irish Historical Novel by James Cahalan, Dublin, Gill and Macmillan, 1984.

* * *

Of his native Dublin, the city which forms the backdrop to his historical novel *Strumpet City,* James Plunkett has written: ''Despite its tensions and its tragedies, Dublin was a good city to grow up in. The sea was at its feet, its Georgian buildings gave it nobility, its squares and its expanses of water made it a place of openness and light and air.'' Something of that affection is immediately apparent in this first novel—and, indeed, Dublin appears as a character in its own right in just about everything he has written—for unlike James Joyce Plunkett did not feel compelled to leave his native city in order to put it into perspective.

Set in the angry years leading to World War I, *Strumpet City*'s first concern is with the downtrodden working classes; in particular Plunkett deals with the attempts of the trades union movement to win better conditions for its members. Standing like a colossus above his fellow men is the figure of Barney Mulhall, a trades union leader whom Plunkett based upon Barney Conway, in real life the right-hand man of the political activist Jim Larkin. The other characters are no less firmly drawn and each is created in the likeness of men whom Plunkett, himself once a trades union official, had known in Dublin: Fitz, the idealistic foreman who joins the strike, Pat his friend and sage adviser, Keever who turns traitor, and perhaps the most colorful of them all, ''Rashers'' Tierney, the poorest of the poor.

Although *Strumpet City* finds its truest voice in Plunkett's vivid creation of Dublin working-class life, it does not ignore other strata of society. The middle-class world of the Bradshaws is faithfully reproduced, as is the claustrophobic life led by the priests Father Giffley and O'Connor. As each character's story draws to its conclusion, all we are left with is Plunkett's faith in the essential decency of people if only they can escape from the snare of the human condition.

In *Farewell Companions* Plunkett moves ahead in time to the inter-war years. A younger generation has arrived to come to terms with a country which has broken its shackles with Britain: they have to face up to, and come to terms with, a different set of rules. As in its predecessor, politics are never far away from the main narrative line but here the arguments are polarized between the demands of sentimental nationalism and the airier ideals of international socialism. Tim McDonagh, the novel's central character, is based loosely on Plunkett himself, and his story plots the journey from the old world occupied by his parent's generation to the hopes and fears of an independent Ireland. Once again, the description of Dublin and the delineation of Irish working-class life is faultless, equaled only by Plunkett's uncanny ability to create a gallery of vivid characters, each with a story to tell. Given such a broad tapestry it is not surprising perhaps to discover some loose threads, and for many readers the novel's ending will come as an anticlimax. Unable to come to terms with the demands of industrial life, McDonagh opts out of the real world and takes holy orders, a limp conclusion that is out of keeping with the speculative intention of the first half of the novel.

The Circus Animals follows Dublin's story into the bleak postwar years when Ireland had to face up to a new economic and political dispensation as its more tempestuous history slipped into the past. As had become standard practice in the previous two novels about Dublin, Plunkett showed himself well able to mix fact and fiction to create a riveting period picture. The action is seen through the eyes of a young couple, Frank and Margaret McDonagh as they struggle to come to terms with married life in the restricted life of a modern Ireland where the Catholic faith seems increasingly out of place. Margaret, for example, wants to practice birth control, but inevitably her conscience is troubled by the church's teachings. Plunkett is particularly good at revealing his characters' feelings and at presenting them in a plausible way. Even his priests and nuns possess a rounded humanity despite the fact that they are portrayed as basically unsympathetic characters. Inevitably, Frank, a political cartoonist, is drawn into conflict with the more conservative elements of Irish society and has to struggle to keep his sense of artistic identity, hence perhaps the use of Yeats's poem in the epigraph: ''Now that my ladder's gone,/I must lie down where all the ladders start/In the foul rag and bone shop of the heart.'' As in the previous novels, too, the supporting characters are superbly realized, especially Lemuel Cox who acts both as mentor to Frank and interpreter of the action.

No understanding of the fictional world created by Plunkett is complete without reading his collection of short stories, *The Trusting and the Maimed,* the title story in particular giving a clue to the success of Plunkett's technique: the use of multiple voices and film-like scenes as he cuts from one character, one situation, one time, to another.

—Trevor Royle

POWERS, Richard

Nationality: American. **Born:** 1957. **Career:** Has been a computer professional. Currently a full-time writer. **Awards:** MacArthur grant, 1990–94; Lannan Literary award, 1999. **Address:** c/o William Morrow, 1350 Avenue of the Americas, New York, New York 10019, U.S.A.

Publications

Novels

Three Farmers on Their Way to a Dance. New York, Morrow, 1985; London, Weidenfeld and Nicolson, 1988.

Prisoner's Dilemma New York, Morrow, 1988; London, Weidenfeld and Nicolson, 1989.

Gold-Bug Variations. New York, Morrow, 1991; London, Scribner, 1992.

Operation Wandering Soul. New York, Morrow, 1993; London, Abacus, 1994.

Galatea 2.2. New York, Farrar Straus, 1995.

Gain. New York, Farrar, Straus, and Giroux, 1998.

Plowing the Dark. New York, Farrar, Straus and Giroux, 2000.

* * *

Recipient of a MacArthur ''genius grant'' in his mid-thirties, Richard Powers published five widely praised novels before the age of forty. Because of his historical subjects, including twentieth-century wars, and his scientific orientations, including cybernetics and biology, Powers has been most frequently compared to Thomas Pynchon, prodigy of an earlier generation. In his output and accessibility, Powers is more like Don DeLillo, with whom he shares interests in neurology and cognition, media such as photography and film, and the disasters of contemporary American life. Using autobiography to examine the sources and values of fictions, Powers also resembles John Barth and his invented doubles. "Crackpot realism"—a phrase from Powers's second novel—represents his combination of these older writers' postmodern methods and materials. What distinguishes Powers's work is his imaginative earnestness, this prodigy's premodern urge to impart his knowledge to readers.

To understand the mind of Powers, readers should begin with his later work and move backward. Like Barth's *Chimera* and DeLillo's *Mao II, Galatea 2.2* works close to the author's life: a novelist named Powers returns to the university where he learned to read literature and attempts to teach a computer the same skill. While exploring the nature of literary processing Powers comments on his novels, recalls his motives for writing, and remembers his first reader, his former lover. Synthesizing extremes of abstract intelligence and intimate revelation, *Galatea 2.2* is an excellent introduction to earlier generations of Powers's wordprocessing program.

Operation Wandering Soul, like Pynchon's *Vineland* and Barth's *Sabbatical,* is a moving story about recovery of health and a collection of stories about moving, the forced wandering of refugees. The novel's main characters are a resident and nurse in a Los Angeles children's ward, a collection point for the horrors of urban violence. As the doctor attempts to save bodies, the nurse comforts souls with fictions. Cut into the text are children's tales, such as the Pied Piper and Peter Pan, and anecdotes from the protagonists' childhoods. In the *Age of Abuse,* Powers asks, what stories should be told to children and what stories can the novelist tell to readers desensitized by daytime and nighttime television?

The Gold-Bug Variations is Powers's *Gravity's Rainbow* and *Ratner's Star,* an encyclopedic novel that twists together the recursive science of genetics and the recursive art of Bach. In this book about four-part variation, there are two love stories: genetics researchers in the 1950s, a librarian and art historian in the 1980s. As the contemporary characters investigate the earlier lives, *Gold-Bug* becomes a Poe-like tale of detection for the characters and a treasure hunt for readers, who learn only at book's end that it, like an offspring, has been spliced from the contemporary lovers' independent narrations. The literal and conceptual center of the novel is a section called "The Natural Kingdom," which celebrates life itself as a prodigy, unlikely as genius, both artfully regular and imaginatively accidental. In its understanding of sexual combination and cognitive mutation, *The Gold-Bug Variations* is, in my opinion, the most profound novel published in America since Joseph McElroy's *Women and Men* in 1987.

In *Operation Wandering Soul,* Powers treated the war in Vietnam and in city streets. In *Prisoner's Dilemma,* members of a Midwestern family of the 1980s are victims of the husband's and father's radiation exposure in World War II. Physically and perhaps mentally ill, Eddie Hobson, a high school history teacher, both imprisons and frees his four children with paradoxical mind games and an unreliable autobiography, a taped journal called "Hobstow" that mixes personal facts, Japanese internment, and Disney films. Told through the family members' six points of view, the novel authoritatively records domestic double binds and inventively recounts prewar and postwar history.

In *Prisoner's Dilemma,* Powers refers to the butterfly effect of chaos theory: "a butterfly flapping its wings in Peking ... alter[s] tomorrow's weather in Duluth." This unpredictable relation between small and large—personal and historical, mutation and code, biography and story, book and readership—coils through all of Powers's fiction. *Three Farmers on Their Way to a Dance* imagines the lives of the Europeans shown in August Sander's photo and connects the farmers to both World War I and a young computer journalist in Boston. Although *Three Farmers* has the intellectual range and global concern of Powers's later novels, it lacks their artistic ingenuity, their formal butterfly effects. For most contemporary writers, this first novel would have been an *Invisible Man* or *Catch-22.* But for Richard Powers, *Three Farmers* was just the beginning of his prodigious fiction.

Again like Pynchon and others, Powers explored the idea of environmental retribution—of Nature quite literally taking revenge on humankind for polluting it—in *Gain,* the story of a soap company, a woman's cancer, and 170 years of American life. An ambitious and intriguing, if not always successful, effort, it could only be topped by another novel, Powers's seventh, *Plowing the Dark.* This time the parallel stories are closer together, involving young prodigies at a virtual-reality software company on the one hand and a hostage in Beirut on the other. At least they are living in the same time period, yet the book provides Powers with a sufficiently large venue in which to examine issues as varied as the meaning of art, the end of the Cold War, and the implications of virtual-reality technology.

—Tom LeClair, updated by Judson Knight

POWNALL, David

Nationality: British. **Born:** Liverpool, 19 May 1938. **Education:** Lord Wandsworth College, Long Sutton, Hampshire, 1949–56; University of Keele, Staffordshire, 1956–60, B.A. (honors) 1960. **Family:** Married 1) Glenys Elsie Jones in 1961 (divorced 1971), one son; 2) Mary Ellen Ray in 1972, one son. **Career:** Personnel officer, Ford Motor Co., Dagenham, Essex, 1960–63; personnel manager, Anglo-American, Zambia, 1963–69; resident writer, Century Theatre touring group, 1970–72, and Duke's Playhouse, Lancaster, 1972–75; founder and resident writer, Paines Plough Theatre, Coventry, 1975–80. **Awards:** John Whiting award, for drama, 1982, 1986. Fellow, Royal Society of Literature, 1976. **Agent:** Andrew Hewson, John Johnson Ltd., 45–47 Clerkenwell Green, Clerkenwell House, London EC1R 0HT, England. **Address:** 136 Cranley Gardens, London N10 3AH, England.

PUBLICATIONS

Novels

The Raining Tree War. London, Faber, 1974.
African Horse. London, Faber, 1975.
God Perkins. London, Faber, 1977.
Light on a Honeycomb. London, Faber, 1978.
Beloved Latitudes. London, Gollancz, 1981.
The White Cutter. London, Gollancz, 1988; New York, Viking, 1989.
The Gardener. London, Gollancz, 1990.

Stagg and His Mother. London, Gollancz, 1991.
The Sphinx and the Sybarites. London, Sinclair-Stevenson, 1993.

Short Stories

My Organic Uncle and Other Stories. London, Faber, 1976.
The Composers Plays. London, Oberon Books, 1994.

Plays

As We Lie (produced Cheltenham, 1973). Zambia, Nkana-Kitwe, 1969.
How Does the Cuckoo Learn to Fly? (produced on tour, 1970).
How to Grow a Guerrilla (produced Preston, Lancashire, 1971).
All the World Should Be Taxed (produced Lancaster, 1971).
The Last of the Wizards (for children; produced Windermere, Cumbria, and London, 1972).
Gaunt (produced Lancaster, 1973).
Lions and Lambs (produced on Lancashire tour, 1973).
The Dream of Chief Crazy Horse (for children; produced Fleetwood, Lancashire, 1973). London, Faber, 1975.
Beauty and the Beast, music by Stephen Boxer (produced Lancaster, 1973).
The Human Cartoon Show (produced Lancaster, 1974).
Crates on Barrels (produced on Lancashire tour, 1974; London, 1984).
The Pro (produced London, 1975).
Lile Jimmy Williamson (produced Lancaster, 1975).
Buck Ruxton (produced Lancaster, 1975).
Ladybird, Ladybird (produced Edinburgh and London, 1976).
Music to Murder By (produced Canterbury, 1976; Miami, 1984). London, Faber, 1978.
A Tale of Two Town Halls (produced Lancaster, 1976).
Motocar, and Richard III, Part Two, music by Stephen Boxer (produced Edinburgh and London, 1977). London, Faber, 1979.
An Audience Called Edouard (produced London, 1978). London, Faber, 1979.
Seconds at the Fight for Madrid (produced Bristol, 1978).
Livingstone and Sechele (produced Edinburgh, 1978; London, 1980; New York, 1982).
Barricade (produced on tour, 1979).
Later (produced London, 1979).
The Hot Hello (produced Edinburgh, 1981).
Beef (produced London, 1981; New York, 1986). Published in *Best Radio Plays of 1981,* London, Methuen, 1982.
Master Class (produced Leicester, 1983; London and Washington, D.C., 1984; New York, 1986). London, Faber, 1983.
Pride and Prejudice, adaptation of the novel by Jane Austen (produced Leicester, 1983; New Haven, Connecticut, 1985; London, 1986).
Ploughboy Monday (broadcast 1985). Published in *Best Radio Plays of 1985,* London, Methuen, 1986.
The Viewing (produced London, 1987).
Black Star (produced Bolton, Lancashire, 1987).
The Edge (produced London, 1987).
King John's Jewel (produced Birmingham, 1987).
Rousseau's Tale (produced London, 1991).
My Father's House (1991).
Elgar's Rondo (1993).
Dreams and Censorship (1993).

Radio Plays: *Free Ferry,* 1972; *Free House,* 1973; *A Place in the Country,* 1974; *An Old New Year,* 1974; *Fences,* 1976; *Under the Wool,* 1976; *Back Stop,* 1977; *Butterfingers,* 1981; *The Mist People,* 1981; *Flos,* 1982; *Ploughboy Monday,* 1985; *Beloved Latitudes,* from his own novel, 1986; *The Bridge at Orbigo,* 1987; *A Matter of Style,* 1988; *Plato Not Nato,* 1990; *The Glossomaniacs,* 1990; *Bringing Up Nero,* 1991.

Television Plays: *High Tides,* 1976; *Mackerel Sky,* 1976; *Return Fare,* 1978; *Follow the River Down,* 1979; *Room for an Inward Light,* 1980; *The Sack Judies,* 1981; *Love's Labour* (*Maybury* series), 1983; *The Great White Mountain* (*Mountain Men* series), 1987; *Something to Remember You By,* 1991.

Poetry

An Eagle Each: Poems of the Lakes and Elsewhere, with Jack Hill. Carlisle, Cumbria, Arena, 1972.
Another Country. Liskeard, Cornwall, Harry Chambers/Peterloo Poets, 1978.

Other

Between Ribble and Lune: Scenes from the North-West, photographs by Arthur Thompson. London, Gollancz, 1980.
The Bunch from Bananas (for children). London, Gollancz, 1980; New York, Macmillan, 1981.
Nijinsky: Death of a Faun. London, Oberon Books, 1997.
Editor, with Gareth Pownall, *The Fisherman's Bedside Book.* London, Windward, 1980.

* * *

David Pownall's vision reveals and satirizes a world in microcosm. The favored territory for his early novels is the crammed, seething canvas peopled with grotesques, whose collective idiocy he lampoons in a style at once comic and macabre. Several of his books have African locations, and it is here—where technology rubs shoulders uneasily with tribal magic—that he appears most at home. Pownall utilizes a variety of literary techniques, subordinating them to a single individual utterance. His wit is caustic and pitiless, sparing no one, yet at times he shows glimpses of a touching faith in humanity.

The Raining Tree War depicts a power struggle between the ruthless president Mulombe and the Muntu religious cult under their prophetess Maud, an archetypal Earth-mother figure who claims to be the ''Wife of God.'' Maud embodies the strength of older African traditions, and constitutes a challenge to Mulombe's authority. Into their gradually intensifying conflict Pownall weaves the threads of other lives, following his eccentric characters through the turmoil of a comic-opera war. The ridiculous, mock-heroic climax of the government's attack on Maud's capital in the Bengweulu swamp is a *tour de force,* Pownall expertly juxtaposing the broadest slapstick with the most stygian of humor. In the aftermath of this lethal ''main event,'' the novel's conclusion is strangely poignant and moving. *The Raining Tree War* is an excellent work, skillfully handled in its action sequences, the thumbnail character sketches capably achieved.

African Horse uses the same location and several characters from the previous novel, but the main plot is devoted to the Englishman Hurl Halfcock and his search for an imagined animal ancestor. Hurl's odyssey through the bars, brothels, and house parties of the newly independent Zonkendavo provides a mixture of picaresque adventure and potent symbolism which Pownall continually ridicules en route. Confrontations abound, whether Hurl's battle with an Afrikaner rugby fifteen, or the more deeply layered duel between a power shovel operator and a crocodile in a colliery sump, while Hurl's weird metamorphosis into his ''animalself,'' for instance, is both absurd and convincing. *African Horse* amuses, but lacks the coherence of *The Raining Tree War,* which is the more satisfying novel of the two.

More impressive is *Light on a Honeycomb,* set in a fictional English town where for centuries insane people have been settled and rehabilitated, and which is now ruled by madmen. Pownall recreates the biblical concept of an upper and lower world, the ''honeycomb'' of limestone caverns with its shadowy dream-population of slaves, Irish laborers, and ancestral tribes overset by its modern counterpart run by lunatic businessmen and gangsters, typified by the spray-on carpet foam they use to hide the universe beneath their feet. The ''light'' is cast by Kevin, inmate of the mental hospital, who invokes the dormant ancestors to overthrow the world above as its rulers succumb to death and madness. *Light on a Honeycomb* is a striking success, Pownall's skills marshalled to full effect. Characterization is sure, with contrasting and symbolic portrayals, and the blending of scenes is ably rendered. The author's keen eye for the ridiculous touches coldly on landowners and ineffectual revolutionaries alike, both being shown as deluded simpletons unaware of the reality about to burst from the ground beneath them. Pownall compels the reader's attention, drawing him or her through a complex network of scenes to the light above, where a new world waits to be made. Perhaps the most controlled of his early works, *Light on a Honeycomb* must be ranked among his best.

Beloved Latitudes marks a departure for Pownall. Outwardly the most ''serious'' of his books, it also has the smallest cast. Presented in the form of a spoken autobiography, the story follows the career of an overthrown African dictator, recounted in prison to his English ''advisor'' and friend. Central to the novel is the close, lover-like relationship between the two men, and the tension of their conflicting personalities. Touches of humor brighten the work, but for once Pownall's mood is unusually sombre. *Beloved Latitudes* is a powerful, thought-provoking novel, whose visual strength is matched by the author's careful understatement.

The later novels show a startling advance on previous writings, Pownall revealing himself as a novelist of considerable depth and maturity, a world away from the barbed, satirical humor of his earlier fiction. *The White Cutter, The Gardener, Stagg and His Mother,* and *The Sphinx and the Sybarites* are epic and memorable creations which show a major fiction writer at the height of his powers. Complex, brooding works, they present a bleak, tragic vision while at the same time compelling the reader's attention with their subtlety and strength. Just as the early novels reveal their attraction to tribal societies, so the most impressive of the recent works are those set furthest back in historical time. *The White Cutter* explores the life of the great medieval builder Hedric Herbertson and his encounters with a world which defines itself as a constant struggle between Good and Evil spiritual forces. These manifest themselves in a variety of forms, notably the powerful ruling group of ''The Four'', whose actions determine much of Hedric's life, and whose mirror-image is found in a particularly dark, disturbing version of Robin Hood's Sherwood. Hedric, driven to crime and renunciation, is a brilliantly tragic figure, and his fate is echoed by that of the Greek diviner Kallias, who in *The Sphinx and the Sybarites* is called on to solve an apparent malaise at the heart of the rich city of Sybaris. Foreseeing the destruction of Sybaris in a nightmare vision, Kallias finds himself enmeshed in a merciless web of politics and warfare which ends in tragedy. Pownall's characters are unwilling pawns to gods and men, cynically manipulated and deceived as they progress painfully to a tragic resolution. The doomed love of Eric and Pauline in *The Gardener* and the fraught love-hate relationship of *Stagg and His Mother,* both dissolved by death, are further examples. Pownall's vision is unremittingly bleak, but his imaginative power and the skillful use of language compels the respect of the reader. These latest works establish him as not only an accomplished, but an important writer of fiction.

—Geoff Sadler

PRATCHETT, Terry

Nationality: British. **Born:** 1948. **Education:** Wycombe Technical High School. **Career:** Journalist in Buckinghamshire, Bristol, and Bath, then press officer, Central Electricity Board Western Region, until 1987. **Awards:** British Science Fiction award, 1990. Honorary degree, University of Warwick, 1999. Order of the British Empire (O.B.E.), 1998. **Agent:** Colin Smythe Ltd., P.O. Box 6, Gerrards Cross, Buckinghamshire SL9 8XA, England.

PUBLICATIONS

Novels (series: Discworld; Truckers/Bromeliad)

Carpet People. Gerrards Cross, Buckinghamshire, Smythe, 1971; revised edition, London, Doubleday, 1992.

The Dark Side of the Sun. Gerrards Cross, Buckinghamshire, Smythe, 1976.

Strata. Gerrards Cross, Buckinghamshire, Smythe, and New York, St. Martin's Press, 1981.

The Colour of Magic (Discworld). Gerrards Cross, Buckinghamshire, Smythe, and New York, St. Martin's Press, 1983.

The Light Fantastic (Discworld). Gerrard's Cross, Buckinghamshire, Smythe, and New York, St. Martin's Press, 1986.

Mort (Discworld). London, Gollancz, and New York, New American Library, 1987.

Sourcery (Discworld). London, Gollancz, 1988; New York, New American Library, 1989.

Pyramids (Discworld). London, Gollancz, and New York, Penguin, 1989.

Guards! Guards! (Discworld; with Gray Jolliffe). London, Gollancz, 1989; New York, Roc, 1991.

Truckers (first of the Truckers trilogy; in the U.S. as the Bromeliad trilogy). London, Doubleday, 1989; New York, Delacorte, 1990.

Eric (Discworld). London, Gollancz, 1989.

Good Omens: The Nice and Accurate Predictions of Agnes Nutter, Witch, with Neil Gaiman. London, Gollancz, and New York, Workman, 1990.

Moving Pictures (Discworld). London, Gollancz, 1990.

Diggers (Truckers/Bromeliad). London, Doubleday, and New York, Delacorte, 1990.
Wings (Truckers/Bromeliad; with Neil Gaiman). London, Doubleday, 1990; New York, Delacorte, 1991.
Reaper Man (Discworld). London, Gollancz, 1991.
Lords and Ladies. London, Gollancz, 1992.
Only You Can Save Mankind. London, Doubleday, 1992.
Small Gods (Discworld). London, Gollancz, and New York, HarperCollins, 1992.
Men at Arms (Discworld). London, Gollancz, 1993.
Johnny and the Dead. London, Doubleday, 1993.
Interesting Times. London, Gollancz, 1994.
Soul Music (Discworld). London, Gollancz, 1994; New York, HarperPrism, 1995.
The Witches Trilogy (Discworld). London, Gollancz, 1995.
Equal Rites (Discworld). London, Gollancz, 1986; New York, New American Library, 1987.
Wyrd Sisters. London, Gollancz, and New York, Penguin, 1988.
Witches Abroad. London, Gollancz, 1991.
Maskerade. London, Gollancz, 1995; New York, HarperPrism, 1997.
Feet of Clay (Discworld). New York, HarperPrism, 1996.
Jingo (Discworld). New York, HarperPrism, 1997.
Hogfather (Discworld). New York, HarperPrism, 1998.
Carpe Jugulum (Discworld). New York, HarperPrism, 1998.
The Last Continent (Discworld). New York, HarperPrism, 1999.
The First Discworld Novels (contains *The Colour of Magic* and *The Light Fantastic*). Gerrards Cross, Buckinghamshire, England, C. Smythe; Chester Springs, Pennsylvania, Dufour Editions, 1999.
The Truth. New York, HarperCollins, 2000.
The Fifth Elephant (Discworld). New York, HarperPrism, 2000.

Other

The Unadulterated Cat, with illustrations by Gray Jolliffe. London, Gollancz, 1989.
The Discworld Companion, with Stephen Briggs. London, Gollancz, 1994.

* * *

Terry Pratchett's texts are woven from the stuff of fantasy: wizards, witches, trolls, dwarves, gnomes, elves, demons, gods; magic spells, sudden space-and-time shifts, drastic metamorphoses. His fiction is both a hilarious parody of the fantasy genre, as represented by Tolkien and ''sword-and-sorcery'' novels, and a genuine contribution to it, in that it creates a rich, imaginative ''multiverse'' that absorbs and intrigues the reader. It shares with the strongest fantasy a concern with fundamental issues such as death, and it incorporates aspects of contemporary culture such as fast food and rock music. Pratchett has a witty, inventive style that draws attention to itself in an engaging way and that often seizes on a phrase drawn from common speech or from literature and brings out a buried or alternative meaning—as when Robert Frost's line ''good fences make good neighbors'' is applied to living next door to a receiver of stolen goods.

Pratchett's major corpus is the Discworld series of novels, which now number twenty-four. The Discworld is a flat disc, carried on the back of four giant elephants, who in turn stand on the shell of the huge turtle Great A'Tuin, swimming slowly through space. It is the ideal fantasy world for the postmodernist era, since its flatness means that its inhabitants have no truck with those ''global'' theories denounced by postmodernist thinkers. Its capital city is Ankh-Morpork, densely overpopulated, impossibly labyrinthine, and egregiously foul-smelling. The Discworld is full of stories that bear on our social and metaphysical concerns. In *Equal Rites,* for example, a dying wizard gives his staff of power to a baby who turns out to be a girl and grows up to become the first female wizard in the face of male prejudice and opposition. *Moving Pictures* looks at how cinema comes to the Discworld, whereas *Soul Music* charts the effects of a new and overwhelming form of rock music. In *Mort,* Death takes on an apprentice and tries to train him on the job, but the young man disturbs the order of the multiverse when he reprieves a young princess who is about to be assassinated. *Hogfather* affirms that human beings need fantasy to be human, and describes the attempts of the Auditors of Reality, who hate life, human beings above all, to destroy belief in the Hogfather, a kind of Discworld Santa Claus. *Jingo* is about the destructive results of excessive nationalism, as war threatens between Ankh-Morpork and the kingdom of Klatch when both lay claim to an island that has unexpectedly appeared between them. In *The Last Continent,* campus revolt takes a new form when books barricade themselves into the library of Unseen University.

Each of the Discworld novels is enjoyable and absorbing in its own right, with a range of character and incident and, usually, a strong and complex narrative structure, although some of the tales are more compelling than others, perhaps inevitably given Pratchett's large and rapid output. Taken together, these novels create an imaginative zone that is rich and strange, offering the reader both the pleasures of discovery, as new aspects are revealed, and of recognition, as familiar figures recur. Among the most notable of these are the Luggage, a travelling chest with hundreds of little legs, which follows its owner everywhere, proffering clean linen whenever he requires it and dealing ruthlessly with anyone or anything else that gets in its way; the Librarian of Unseen University who, having been inadvertently changed by magic into an orangutan, prefers to remain that way, since it simplifies life's philosophical problems and enables him to get by with only one utterance, ''Oook''; and Death, a tall skeleton who always speaks in capital letters but who turns out to be lonely, troubled, and strangely human. It is Death who, in *Hogfather,* tries to take the Hogfather's place after the Hogfather is ''severely reduced'' by the lessening belief of children in him. Pratchett is also good at creating engaging minor characters, such as Bilious, the ''oh God of Hangovers,'' in *Hogfather*—so named because the hungover always say ''oh God'' when he manifests himself—or the werewolf in *Feet of Clay* who, anticipating the change that occurs at the time of the full moon, suffers from PLT: pre-lunar tension.

Among Pratchett's other novels, particular mention should be made of *Only You Can Save Mankind, Johnny and the Dead,* and *Johnny and the Bomb,* which combine fantasy and science fiction with a realistic portrayal of a group of teenagers in a rundown English city. In *Only You Can Save Mankind,* Johnny Maxwell finds himself involved in a video game in which the aliens against whom he is fighting turn out to be real; the novel invokes and echoes the blurring of the distinction between image and reality in the Gulf War. *Johnny and the Dead* engages with the issue of the loss of the sense of the past in the postmodernist era: Johnny joins a campaign to save a local cemetery from redevelopment after he has discovered that he can see and talk to the people buried there. In *Johnny and the Bomb,* the past comes alive as a supermarket trolley serves as the time machine that carries Johnny and his friends back to 21 May 1941; the narrative skillfully interweaves the contrasting but connected events of a day in the Second World War and the same day in the 1990s.

Pratchett is a best-selling writer with an enormous and devoted following. He identifies his intended readership as "children of any age," and he has a large teenage and adult audience. But critical response to him has been mixed; his work enjoys the admiration of important contemporary novelists such as A.S. Byatt but it has also been judged to be formulaic and of low quality. The eclectic mixture of elements and the crossing of cultural boundaries in his fiction might mark it as postmodernist. But postmodernist work that has found critical acceptance tends to imply a knowing, distanced attitude toward the popular materials on which it draws, whereas Pratchett remains deeply rooted in those materials even as he parodies them; he thus challenges the postmodernist aesthetic as well as traditional cultural categories. Since *Johnny and the Bomb,* he has focused on producing further Discworld novels, most recently *Carpe Jugulum,* in which he employs vampires for the first time—they try to take over the small kingdom of Lancre and are resisted by its witches—and *The Fifth Elephant,* in which another recurrent Discworld character, the tough and tactless Samuel Vimes, captain of the Ankh-Morpork City Watch, is sent as an ambassador to the Northern principality of Uberwald and gets entangled with vampires, dwarves, and werewolves. While some readers and reviewers have felt that his inventiveness is flagging in these latest works, others have continued to applaud and enjoy them. Pratchett seems happy to devote most of his energies to the continuing creation of the Discworld and has no apparent aspiration towards being acknowledged as a serious writer; it will be interesting to see whether, in the twenty-first century, he continues to offer more of the same or strikes out in new directions.

—Nicolas Tredell

PRICE, (Edward) Reynolds

Nationality: American. **Born:** Macon, North Carolina, 1 February 1933. **Education:** Duke University, Durham, North Carolina, 1951–55 (Angier Duke scholar), A.B. (summa cum laude) 1955 (Phi Beta Kappa); Merton College, Oxford, 1955–58 (Rhodes scholar), B.Litt. 1958. **Career:** Member of the faculty since 1958, assistant professor, 1961–68, associate professor, 1968–72, professor of English, 1972–77, and since 1977, James B. Duke Professor, Duke University. Writer-in-residence, University of North Carolina, Chapel Hill, 1965, and Greensboro, 1971, and University of Kansas, Lawrence, 1967, 1969, 1980; Glasgow Professor, Washington and Lee University, Lexington, Virginia, 1971; member of the faculty, Salzburg Seminar on American Studies, 1977. Editor, the *Archive,* Durham, 1954–55. Since 1964 advisory editor, *Shenandoah,* Lexington, Virginia. Chair, National Endowment for the Arts Literature Advisory Panel, 1976. **Awards:** Faulkner Foundation prize, 1963; Guggenheim fellowship, 1964; National Association of Independent Schools award, 1964; National Endowment for the Arts fellowship, 1967; American Academy award, 1971; Bellamann Foundation award, 1976; Lillian Smith award, 1976; National Book Critics Circle award, 1987; Bobst award, 1988; R. Hunt Parker award, North Carolina Literary and Historical Society, 1991; Northcarolinana award, 1999. Litt.D.: St. Andrews Presbyterian College, Laurinburg, North Carolina, 1978; Wake Forest University, Winston-Salem, North Carolina, 1979; Washington and Lee University, 1991; Davidson College, 1992; Elon College, 1996. **Agent:** Harriet Wasserman Literary Agency, 137 East 36th Street, New York, New York 10016. **Address:** P.O. Box 99014, Durham, North Carolina 27706, U.S.A.

Publications

Novels

A Long and Happy Life. New York, Atheneum, and London, Chatto and Windus, 1962.

A Generous Man. New York, Atheneum, 1966; London, Chatto and Windus, 1967.

Love and Work. New York, Atheneum, and London, Chatto and Windus, 1968.

The Surface of Earth. New York, Atheneum, 1975; London, Arlington, 1978.

The Source of Light. New York, Atheneum, 1981.

Mustian (2 novels and a story). New York, Atheneum, 1983.

Kate Vaiden. New York, Atheneum, 1986; London, Chatto and Windus, 1987.

Good Hearts. New York, Atheneum, 1988.

The Tongues of Angels. New York, Atheneum, 1990.

Blue Calhoun. New York, Atheneum, 1992.

The Promise of Rest. New York, Scribner, 1995.

The Honest Account of a Memorable Life: An Apocryphal Gospel. Rocky Mount, North Carolina, Wesleyan College Press, 1994.

The Three Gospels. New York, Scribner, 1996.

Roxanna Slade. New York, Scribner, 1998.

Short Stories

The Names and Faces of Heroes. New York, Atheneum, and London, Chatto and Windus, 1963.

Permanent Errors. New York, Atheneum, 1970; London, Chatto and Windus, 1971.

Home Made. Rocky Mount, North Carolina Wesleyan College Press, 1990.

The Foreseeable Future: Three Long Stories. New York, Atheneum, 1991.

An Early Christmas. Rocky Mount, North Carolina Wesleyan College Press, 1992.

The Collected Stories. New York, Atheneum, 1993.

A Singular Family: Rosacoke and Her Kin. New York, Scribner, 1999.

Uncollected Short Stories

"Night and Day at Panacea," in *Harper's* (New York), August 1974.

"Commencing," in *Virginia Quarterly Review* (Charlottesville), Spring 1975.

"His Final Mother," in *New Yorker,* 21 May 1990.

"Two Useful Visits," in *Virginia Quarterly Review* (Charlottesville), Summer 1990.

"Serious Need," in *Esquire* (New York), November 1990.

"Full Day," in *Harper's* (New York), January 1991.

Plays

Early Dark (produced New York, 1978). New York, Atheneum, 1977.
Private Contentment. New York, Atheneum, 1984.
New Music: A Trilogy. New York, Theatre Communications, 1990.
Full Moon and Other Plays. New York, Theatre Communications, 1993.

Poetry

Late Warning: Four Poems. New York, Albondocani Press, 1968.
Torso of an Archaic Apollo—After Rilke. New York, Albondocani Press, 1969.
Lessons Learned: Seven Poems. New York, Albondocani Press, 1977.
Christ Child's Song at the End of the Night. Privately printed, 1978.
Nine Mysteries (Four Joyful, Four Sorrowful, One Glorious). Winston-Salem, North Carolina, Palaemon Press, 1979.
Vital Provisions. New York, Atheneum, 1982.
The Laws of Ice. New York, Atheneum, 1986.
The Use of Fire. New York, Atheneum, 1990.
The Collected Poems. New York, Scribner, 1997.

Other

The Thing Itself (address). Durham, North Carolina, Duke University Library, 1966.
Two Theophanies: Genesis 32 and John 21. Privately printed, 1971.
Things Themselves: Essays and Scenes. New York, Atheneum, 1972.
The Fourth Eclogue of Vergil. Privately printed, 1972.
An Apocryphal Hymn of Jesus. Privately printed, 1973.
Presence and Absence: Versions from the Bible. Bloomfield Hills, Michigan, Bruccoli Clark, 1973.
A Nativity from the Apocryphal Book of James. Privately printed, 1974.
Annuciation. Privately printed, 1975.
Conversations, with William Ray. Memphis, Memphis State University, 1976.
The Good News According to Mark. Privately printed, 1976.
Oracles: Six Versions from the Bible. Durham, North Carolina, Friends of the Duke University Library, 1977.
A Palpable God: Thirty Stories Translated from the Bible with an Essay on the Origins and Life of Narrative. New York, Atheneum, 1978.
Christ Child's Song at the End of the Night. Privately printed, 1978.
Question and Answer. Privately printed, 1979.
The Annual Heron. New York, Albondocani Press, 1980.
Country Mouse, City Mouse (essay). Rocky Mount, North Carolina, Friends of the Wesleyan College Library, 1981.
A Start (miscellany of early work). Winston-Salem, North Carolina, Palaemon Press, 1981.
A Common Room: Essays 1954–1987. New York, Atheneum, 1987.
Real Copies: Will Price, Crichton Davis, Phyllis Peacock, and More. Rocky Mount, North Carolina Wesleyan College Press, 1988.
Back Before Day. Rocky Mount, North Carolina Wesleyan College Press, 1989.
Clear Pictures: First Loves, First Guides. New York, Atheneum, 1989.
Conversations with Reynolds Price, edited by Jefferson Humphries. Jackson, University Press of Mississippi, 1991.
Michael Egerton (for children). Mankato, Minnesota, Creative Education, 1993.
A Whole New Life. New York, Atheneum, 1994.
Learning a Trade: A Craftsman's Notebook, 1955–1997. Durham, North Carolina, Duke University Press, 1998.
Letter to a Man in the Fire: Does God Exist and Does He Care? New York, Scribner, 1999.
A Perfect Friend (for children). New York, Atheneum Books for Young Readers, 2000.

*

Bibliography: *Reynolds Price: A Bibliography 1949–1984* by Stuart Wright and James L.W. West III, Charlottesville, University Press of Virginia, 1986.

Critical Studies: ''A Conversation with Reynolds Price'' by Wallace Kaufman, in *Shenandoah* (Lexington, Virginia), Summer 1966; ''The Reynolds Price Who Outgrew the Southern Pastoral'' by Theodore Solotaroff, in *Saturday Review* (New York), 26 September 1970; ''Love (and Marriage) in *A Long and Happy Life,*'' in *Twentieth Century Studies* (Los Angeles), January 1971; *Understanding Reynolds Price* by James A. Schiff, Columbia, South Carolina, University of South Carolina Press, 1996; *Critical Essays on Reynolds Price,* edited by James A. Schiff, New York, G.K. Hall; London, Prentice Hall International, 1998.

* * *

Reynolds Price has moved from detailed examination of North Carolina rural life to an intense concern with the artist's vision of reality. Beginning with the tragicomic saga of the Mustian family (the novels *A Long and Happy Life* and *A Generous Man,* and the story ''A Chain of Love,'' now collected in *Mustian*), he has come in *Love and Work* and *Permanent Errors* to wrestle with narrative forms closer to the bone. In the preface to *Permanent Errors* Price described his work as ''the attempt to isolate in a number of lives the central error of act, will, understanding which, once made, has been permanent, incurable, but whose diagnosis and palliation are the hopes of continuance.''

This applies to all Price's fiction. *A Long and Happy Life* is the inside story of Rosacoke Mustian, a country girl seeking a conventional life with an unconventional young man, Wesley Beavers. Her error is that she conceives ''a long and happy life'' only in the clichéd terms of romance, of settled-wedded-bliss tradition. She reviews her life, her family's life, is discontent, becomes pregnant by Wesley and finally comes to see him and herself in larger terms, terms of myth, in a Christmas pageant which shows her the complete (and divine) meanings of motherhood, birth, and love.

Myth becomes the vehicle of self-understanding more overtly in *A Generous Man,* which shows the Mustian family several years earlier. It describes an allegorical search for an escaped circus python, a giant serpent named Death, and the discovery of a lost treasure. Milo Mustian describes the stifling forces of convention which circumscribe their lives: ''it's what nine-tenths of the humans born since God said 'Adam!' have thought was a life, planned out for themselves—all my people, my Mama, my Daddy (it was what strangled him), Rosacoke …'' Only by transcending the everyday, by seeing human life in larger terms, can the individual escape the slow strangulation of "permanent errors" and find direction and meaning in existence.

Good Hearts updates and completes the saga of Rosacoke Mustian and Wesley Beavers, who have reached married middle age and the wisdom of accumulated domestic experience. Wesley, after 28 years of marriage to Rosacoke, suddenly leaves home. Both Wesley and Rosacoke learn about their unique needs and natures, especially their sexual temperaments, in this separation. By the end of the story they are reunited after realizing essential truths about the evolving physical and spiritual demands of love.

Price's fiction has become increasingly abstract and complex as he has moved to a more inward vision. From the first he has used sets of images and metaphors to suggest a mysterious or magical reality beyond his pastoral settings. He has deepened this metaphorical (and psychological) interest in *Love and Work* and *Permanent Errors,* where the protagonists are no longer the eccentric pastoral figures of the Mustian clan but are closer to Price's own viewpoint. Price's fiction has always dealt with confusion of the heart and alienation of the mind, but the recent work draws its images and symbols from Price's own experience—his family, a visit to Dachau prison camp, the writer's situation. The grotesqueness and unfamiliarity of the Mustian clan are replaced by more familiar and universal facts of contemporary life.

In *The Tongues of Angels,* Price creates a memoir-like *bildungsroman,* a story of adolescent initiation and adult epiphany, set in a Smoky Mountain summer camp. The novel explores directly the spiritual springs of art and the religious meaning of experience as an artist renders it. This is Price's most overt and effective disquisition on profound religious experience and memory as the basis of art.

In two large novels, *The Surface of Earth* and *The Source of Light,* Price is most ambitious. The narratives deal with a family saga encompassing the first half of our century and drawing from Price's own experience. The novels detail through letters, conversations, and lyrical soliloquies the Mayfield family and its cycle of birth, maturity and death as viewed by Rob Mayfield, who focuses the narratives. The family is more genteel than the Mustians, and these novels detail a world of important things and social valences. The search by Rob Mayfield for a sense of himself and for a peaceful reconciliation with his father's memory is an important mirror image of Rosacoke Mustian's growth into adulthood.

Love and death are polarities in Price's work—how to save life from death, how to prevent life from becoming deathly, stale, void of myth and magic. The theme appears most clearly in *A Generous Man,* when the Mustians set out to find and kill Death, the great serpent, and are finally told, "Death is dead." In the course of this magical hunt, Milo Mustian comes to understand what he must do to save himself from the slow death of a clichéd life; Rato Mustian, the wise fool, grapples with Death and escapes its coils through his cunning folly; Rosacoke moves from complete innocence to the dawn of maturity. In his later fiction Price has moved from symbols of external life to more internalized ones: sleep, dreams, a writer seeking a relationship between love and work, self and others, private life and shared life. Price's fiction describes the individual's perceptions of himself and of the realities around him, the uses of imagination. His characters travel on a quest for the potency of myth and the ability to transcend a closed vision of everyday reality. They move toward permanent truths through "permanent errors."

Blue Calhoun is, in essence, another story of permanent errors, the novel being an extended letter written by Blue to his granddaughter through which he hopes for penance. Blue has seen his life crumble: a relapsing alcoholic, his decline begins with an affair with sixteen-year-old Luna. For Blue, these errors move inexorably to tragedies for which he feels responsible, including the death of his wife and his daughter by cancer. The feeling of guilt pervades Price's work, as does the desire for absolution, and both center on the interweaving of death and love.

Any understanding of love in Price's work is necessarily connected to grief, loss, and death, so that in *The Promise of Rest,* just as in *Blue Calhoun,* Price draws to the center of his work a man whose life of errors works to uncover the truths offered by love even in the shadow of death. While *The Promise of Rest* details the final days of Wade Mayfield, the novel is more the unburdening of Wade's father Hutch and parallels Blue's unburdening of his past to his granddaughter. Hutch's mission to rescue Wade from isolation as he dies of AIDS is more a mission to revisit his own bisexual past and to understand the crumbling of his marriage and his disavowal of his African-American relationships.

Wade's gay relationship with an African American causes, literally and metaphorically, Hutch to reconnect with his past, with his errors, and to reconcile them with the fact of the death of his son. Hutch's various loves are at the center of the work, and each of those loves ends in a death: Hutch fails to reunite with Straw, his African-American friend with whom he had a gay relationship; Hutch's marriage to Ann ends in divorce; Wade, Hutch's only child, dies of AIDS. Each of these deaths are explorations of the love that once gave them life, of the relationships Hutch nurtured with different people in his life.

In *Roxanna Slade,* Price returns to a female narrative voice for the first time since *Kate Vaiden,* but the story, which reads variously as advice manual and extended elegy, parallels *Blue Calhoun*'s life narrative of love and death and the awful connections forged in the dark corners of the South. Indeed, Roxanna's life as told in the book literally begins with the death of Larkin Slade. Roxanna marries Larkin's brother, Palmer, and the two have a child, who is named after Larkin. The novel, told in the rambling, but forceful, narrative voice of Roxanna Slade, centers upon the complex relationships between black and white, male and female, and how those relationships affect others around them.

Palmer's illegitimate daughter, born by a poor African-American woman, becomes in almost Dickensian fashion the helpmate of Roxanna, and through the connections, Roxanna's life is laid bare. The narrative of Roxanna is self-consciously concerned with "telling it straight," and in large part, that purpose undergirds Price's work as a whole. While by no means a realist, Price uncovers the complexity that governs relationships and how love and death compete in a structuring reality. Price's works increasingly focus on the intensity of the relationships that govern lives, and how those relationships essentially change the realities of the world.

—William J. Schafer, updated by Roger Thompson

PRICE, Richard

Nationality: American. **Born:** New York, 12 October 1949. **Education:** Cornell University, B.S. 1971; Columbia University, graduate study, 1972–74, M.F.A. 1976; Stanford University, further graduate study, 1973. **Family:** Married Judy Hudson; two daughters. **Career:**

Lecturer in English as a second language, Hostos Community College, 1973; lecturer in urban affairs, New York University, 1973; lecturer in creative writing, State University of New York at Stony Brook, beginning 1974, New York University, 1974 and 1977, State University of New York at Binghamton, 1976, Hofstra University, 1978–79, and Yale University, 1980; screenwriter, actor, and producer. Lives in the Bronx, New York. **Awards:** *Playboy* Magazine Nonfiction Award, 1979. **Agent:** Brandt & Brandt, 1501 Broadway, New York, New York 10036, U.S.A.

PUBLICATIONS

Novels

The Wanderers. Boston, Houghton Mifflin, 1974.
Bloodbrothers. Boston, Houghton Mifflin, 1976.
Ladies' Man. Boston, Houghton Mifflin, 1978.
The Breaks. New York, Simon & Schuster, 1983.
Clockers. Boston, Houghton Mifflin, 1992.
Freedomland. New York, Broadway Books, 1998.

Plays

Screenplays: *Streets of Gold*, 1986; *The Color of Money*, Buena Vista Pictures, 1986; *Bad* (for Michael Jackson music video), 1987; *Rain Man* (uncredited), United Artists, 1988; *Sea of Love*, Universal Pictures, 1989; *New York Stories* (''Life Lessons'' segment), Buena Vista Pictures, 1989; *Night and the City*, Twentieth Century-Fox, 1992; *3 Screenplays,* Boston, Houghton Mifflin, 1993; *Mad Dog and Glory*, Universal Pictures, 1993; *Kiss of Death*, Twentieth Century-Fox, 1995; *Clockers* (with Spike Lee), Universal Pictures, 1995; *Money Train* (uncredited), Columbia Pictures, 1995; *Ransom*, Buena Vista Pictures, 1996; *Shaft* (and story), Paramount Pictures, 2000.

Other

Introduction and interview, *Men in the Cities, 1979–1982,* by Robert Longo. New York, Abrams, 1986.

*

Critical Studies: *Interview* (sound recording), with Kay Bonetti, Columbia, Missouri, American Audio Prose Library, 1982; *Richard Price, Novelist* (sound recording), Washington, D.C., National Public Radio, 1986.

* * *

Richard Price is a late-twentieth-century hybrid of Charles Dickens and Theodore Dreiser. His protagonists know both the destitution of David Copperfield and the craftiness of Sister Carrie. We may want to throw a little Upton Sinclair in the mix, too; Price's description of the risks and exploitation of the street drug dealer's life evoke comparisons to *The Jungle*'s slaughterhouse. Price's distinct trademark is his ear for street talk. He ably follows its changing lexicon, rhythms, and discourse communities in each of his novels, set in various New York City-area urban neighborhoods from the 1960s to the 1990s.

Price published *The Wanderers* when he was only twenty-four. This coming-of-age novel takes place in the multi-ethnic Bronx of the early–1960s. The Wanderers are a tight-knit group of Italian-American high school buddies, trying to survive parental abuse, teen pregnancy, and threats from rival gangs. They are an oxymoronic blend of tough and sensitive, which Price pulls off by avoiding sentimentality. At first Price's ''protagonist'' is collective. Richie, Joey, Eugene, Buddy, and Perry take on the threats of their ethically splintered high school together: the blacks, the all-Chinese gang, the mute Irish maniacs. The boys are gradually individualized by their personal plights; they become fathers, soldiers, desperados, on the road alone to success, failure, or the purgatory of the blue-collar working man's life.

Bloodbrothers' singular protagonist, eighteen-year-old Stony De Coco, is trying to decide what to do with his life. He can join the family construction business, work as a hospital aid with children, or go to college. His choices reflect three conflicting impulses: stay with the violent, gritty, hatred-ridden world he knows best; turn soft, helpful, ''feminine'' at the hospital, or attempt class mobility through higher education. Again Price lays claim to this proletariat coming-of-age story through the tough talk and brutality of street and home. At times Price relies too heavily on these devices for authenticity and emotional impact; the novel lacks more understated moments of character development.

In *Ladies' Man*, Price pulls away from the mean streets, a move that allows him to turn to other, more subtle means of characterization. Thirty-year-old Kenny Becker has made it out of the Bronx to become a household sprays salesman in Manhattan. His live-in girlfriend has just left him, and he's compelled to recapture the ruffian existence of his gang-member youth. The arena, though, is now the vacuous 1970s swinging singles scene. This scenario is far more bourgeois than those in Price's first two novels, yet Becker's lonely, wandering bachelor life is no less vividly portrayed than the tumultuous high school halls of *The Wanderers*. Furthermore, the relative quietude of a salesman's bachelorhood allows Price to concentrate on character rather than chaos. Price proves himself here to be more than a one-trick pony.

The Breaks is another study of a working-class youth trying to be upwardly mobile. Peter Keller has just graduated from college, the first of his family to do so. After being wait-listed at law school, he moves back home to Yonkers and works meaningless jobs that do little but distance him from his goal of becoming an attorney. He ends up moving back to his college town to teach English, where he contemplates another future vision of himself: becoming an actor and stand-up comedian. Peter is even more confused about his chance at class mobility than Stony was in *Bloodbrothers*. Peter got ''the break'' of going to college, the chance to live out the classic dream of having a better life than one's parents did. Though college initially offers him the freedom to ''be himself''—happy and unselfconscious—for the first time in his life, after graduation Peter finds he can't quite leave home. While living with his father in Yonkers, he suffers Oedipal longings for his stepmother. Once he leaves, he reinscribes this triangle onto an older colleague and his wife.

Price returns to the mean streets in *Clockers*, but character development is not sacrificed to the shock of the violence-ridden, illegal drug underworld setting. Strike, a black crack dealer, and Rocco, a white homicide cop, co-narrate the novel. Strike's brother, Victor, a young father working himself to the bone at two low-wage jobs, turns himself in for killing another neighborhood dealer. Rocco becomes obsessed with Strike and Victor, believing Victor is taking the rap for his brother's crime. Strike is indeed the bad boy, working for the neighborhood drug lord, luring a pre-teen boy into the racket with new sneakers, books, and adult male attention. But Strike is also a tortured soul with a stutter and a bleeding ulcer he treats by downing bottles of vanilla Yoo-Hoo. Rocco's late-career quest to nail the "right brother," we learn, is really about his yearning for moral order in the drug- and crime-torn world of his hometown of Dempsy, New Jersey. Strike, ironically, harbors the same desire, refusing to believe his do-good brother could kill. *Clockers* is a brilliant portrayal of the black inner city, Strike and Victor the two faces of a post-Civil Rights era "Native Son."

In *Freedomland*, the insular chaos of Dempsy becomes ground zero in a clash of racist mythologies. A young white woman tells the Dempsy police she was carjacked by a black man outside a housing project, her four-year-old son in the backseat. Racial tensions erupt between Dempsy and the adjacent, mostly white community, Gannon, and the media descends. The plot is based on the true story of Susan Smith, a white woman in South Carolina who drowned her two children, then told the world a black man had kidnapped them. Again Price uses blackness and whiteness as ironic mirrors for one another. The white mother, Brenda Martin, is exhausted and fragile and raising her son on her own, bearing the "single mother" moniker so many of her black neighbors are demonized for, yet she easily becomes a media victim-darling. The white cops of Gannon physically reinforce the black-white divide by sealing off and invading Dempsy. Meanwhile, black Dempsy detective Lorenzo Council ostensibly joins in this scouring of the mean streets, yet quietly explores Brenda Martin's own potential role in the crime. He is joined in his suspicions by Jesse Haus, a newspaper reporter from Dempsy's evening paper, who befriends Brenda as she investigates the woman's unstable world.

—Lisa A. Phillips

PROFUMO, David

Nationality: British. **Born:** London, 30 October 1955. **Education:** Eton College, 1968–73; Magdalen College, Oxford, B.A. and M.A. (with honors), both 1977. **Family:** Married 1) Valerie Hobson; 2) Helen Ann Fraser in 1980, two sons. **Career:** Assistant master of English, Eton College, Windsor, 1978, and The Royal School, Shrewsbury, 1978–79; part-time lecturer of English, King's College, London, 1981–83. Deputy editor, *The Fiction Magazine,* 1982–84. **Awards:** Geoffrey Faber Memorial prize, for *Sea Music,* 1989. **Agent:** Peters Fraser & Dunlop, The Chambers, Chelea Harbour, Lots Road, London SW10. **Address:** 24 Argyll Road, London W8, England.

Publications

Novels

Sea Music. London, Secker and Warburg, 1988.
The Weather in Iceland. London, Picador, 1993.

Uncollected Short Stories

"The Blind Man Eats Many Flies," in *Foreign Exchange,* edited by Julian Evans. London, Sphere, 1985.

Other

In Praise of Trout. London, Viking, 1989.
Editor, with Graham Swift, *The Magic Wheel: An Anthology of Fishing Literature.* London, Picador, 1985.

* * *

A keen and knowledgeable angler, David Profumo permeates his writing with his interest in fishing. *In Praise of Trout* is a personal account of this passion, in this case trout fishing. It details types of trout, the characteristics of their habitat, and the methods used to catch them. However, it is more than yet another treatise on trout angling for devotees, since it is related in informal and anecdotal fashion with the easy skill of a writer, as well as the fervent passion of an angler.

The advent of *The Magic Wheel: An Anthology of Fishing in Literature* edited by Profumo and Graham Swift, should therefore come as no surprise. It produces an interesting and compelling range of sources, to compile an unusual and intriguing collection of literary material on matters piscatorial. The collection goes much further than the obligatory homage to Izaak Walton, bringing together in chronological manner, such unlikely writers as Virginia Woolf, John Donne, Herodotus, George Orwell, Li Yu and John Gay among others. The introduction to the anthology provides an informative history of the representation of angling in diverse literary works from the ancient Greeks to Ted Hughes. It points out that this huge body of literary representation has a basis in the not infrequent correlations between fishing and acts of imagination as they have been conceived of by writers over the years: angling is "a mythopoeic activity, the shapes of its experience being representative of experience elsewhere." The idiosyncratic guiding principal of fishing as "a paradigm of the individual struggle," makes this anthology committed and earnest, yet equally something of a rewarding curiosity for the nonangler.

Such themes and preoccupations reemerge in Profumo's first novel *Sea Music* which appeared to general acclaim. Set on a remote western Scottish island in the early 1950s, it narrates the adventures of a public schoolboy, James Benson, on his summer holiday. His businessman father and an assortment of Tory friends have rented a hunting lodge for the summer, and they generally engage themselves in huntin'-shootin'-fishin' pursuits. The adults treat the islanders with colonial contempt and insouciance, preoccupied with their various sporting triumphs and business transactions, while passing the wine and port around the dining table. Enclosed in their conservative milieu, little attention is given to James by these people beyond a condescending pretense of interest. With his mother incarcerated in an asylum (for some action which is never entirely clear), and somewhat estranged from his distant, severe father and his father's friends, James finds himself lonely, alienated and isolated in the group.

In such circumstances, it is not surprising that James is drawn into a friendship with the lodge underkeeper Alec Campbell, one of the indigenous islanders, who takes him under his wing. He introduces James to his aunt Rachel, a woman with the reputed mystical properties of second sight, and with whom James becomes increasingly fascinated. It is Alec and Rachel who engage James's attention: with stories about the island's past; jaunts to different parts of the island; anecdotes about various natural phenomena like the bloodstone; myths and legends about the Three Sons of the North Wind, and Bride, the foster-mother of Christ. It is through Alec's friendship that James undergoes an initiation in various island rites sufficient for

Alec to acknowledge "You're an island boy now," in what appears to be all but an adoption of James as a surrogate son.

Profumo's writing is understated, working more by suggestion and hint than by emphatic declaration. It uses the Scottish islands as a gentle backdrop to the boy's unfolding consciousness, and the Gaelic language which marks the speech of the native inhabitants seems somewhat too "atmospheric" at times. Nevertheless, his novel constantly brings one back to water—the rivers and lochs of the island, the surrounding sea, and its animal life. The book is punctuated with James's initial observation of and contact with sea life: the "inky, arched backs" of lobsters; the jellyfish "like an egg poaching in a pan;" the skinning of a dead seal; the tense excitement of catching a trout; the surreptitious stealth in the night expedition to poach salmon; the compelling horror of finding a rotting monkey carcass on the shoreline. Profumo subtly brings his knowledge and love of fishing into the narrative and his dialogue between the portly Doctor and James about the art of making flies for fly-fishing; the descriptions of various fish throughout the holiday; and the lore attached to various fishing pursuits. This serves to give the narrative a delicate touch of depth, in a novel which is finely balanced between sketch and full portrait. Most of the characters are no more than suggestive types, from Mr. Benson's garrulous mistress Mrs. Walker who gushes and oozes affection throughout the novel, to the obsequious gamekeeper Willie Grant, who desires to rid himself of Alec Campbell and please the squirearchy.

It comes as something of a shock when James Benson dies in the final pages of the novel. He is diagnosed as having some form of blood disease, but the causes of death are inexact and there are symbolic and structural hints of some mysterious links with the illness Rachel suffered in the final days of James's vacation on the island. In the concluding scene, Alec launches a small leaf-boat on the sea and this returns the novel back to the realms of Scottish folk-myth which so riveted James in Rachel's company. The return to the sea also completes the symbolic dimension of the novel, with its fascination for the sound of water and the music of the sea. This first foray into fiction produces a compelling drama of childhood development, which provides a sympathetic depiction of a lonely and marginalized youth, whilst simultaneously acting as an oblique indictment of the class and community values of the English postwar bourgeoisie.

—Tim Woods

PROULX, E(dna) Annie

Nationality: American. **Born:** Norwich, Connecticut, 22 August 1935. **Education:** University of Vermont, Burlington, B.A. (cum laude), 1969 (Phi Beta Kappa); Sir George Williams University, Montreal, M.A., 1973. **Family:** Married James Hamilton Lang in 1969 (divorced 1990); three children. **Awards:** Kress Fellow, Harvard University, Boston, 1974; Vermont Council of the Arts fellowship, 1989, National Endowment for the Arts fellowship, 1991, Guggenheim Foundation fellowship, 1992; PEN/Faulkner award, 1993, for *Postcards;* National Book award, 1993, *Chicago Tribune* Heartland award, 1993, *Irish Times International* award, 1993, and Pulitzer prize, 1994, all for *The Shipping News*; Dos Passos Prize for Literature, 1996, for *Accordion Crimes*; National Magazine award, 1998, for "Brokeback Mountain." D.H.L.: University of Maine, Orono, 1994. **Address:** c/o Scribners Publishing Co., 866 Third Avenue, 7th floor, New York, New York 10022, U.S.A.

Publications

Novels

Postcards. New York, Scribner, 1992; London, Fourth Estate, 1993.
The Shipping News. New York, Scribner, 1993; London, Fourth Estate, 1994.
Accordion Crimes. New York, Scribner, 1996.

Short Stories

Heart Songs, and Other Stories. New York, Scribner, 1988; London, Flamingo, 1989.
Close Range: Wyoming Stories, watercolors by William Matthews. New York, Scribner, 1999.

Other

Sweet and Hard Cider: Making It, Using It, and Enjoying It, with Lew Nichols. Charlotte, Vermont, Garden Way, 1980; second edition, with Lew Nichols, Pownal, Vermont, Storey Communications, 1997.
"What'll You Take for It?": Back to Barter. Charlotte, Vermont, Garden Way, 1981.
The Complete Dairy Foods Cookbook: How to Make Everything from Cheese to Custard in Your Kitchen, with Lew Nichols. Emmaus, Pennsylvania, Rodale Press, 1982.
The Gardener's Journal and Record Book. Emmaus, Pennsylvania, Rodale Press, 1983.
Plan and Make Your Own Fences and Gates, Walkways, Walls and Drives. Emmaus, Pennsylvania, Rodale Press, 1983.
The Fine Art of Salad Gardening. Emmaus, Pennsylvania, Rodale Press, 1985.
The Gourmet Gardener: Growing Choice Fruits and Vegetables with Spectacular Results, illustrated by Robert Byrd. New York, Fawcett Columbine, 1987.

*

Annie Proulx comments:

(2000) All over this scratched and worn earth regional and rural cultures, the natural world, and the diversity of life itself are eroding and crumbling under terrific outside pressures. For more than a decade, through the medium of fiction, I have been trying to catch pieces of North American rural lives and ways squeezed in the pincers of change. For me everything begins with the great landscape—not scenery but soil and water, climate and weather, indigenous plant and animal life, geography and geology. Against this background human adaptation to, and exploitation of, that landscape in a particular time orders the personalities and characaters of my stories, shapes the stories themselves which must tumble out of the place portrayed. I am concerned as well with the growing gap between rural and urban attitudes and behavior, the rural perception of the economic forces that call out the marching orders.

* * *

Arguably one of the most exciting writers to come along in decades, E. Annie Proulx is hardly what one might call an overnight success. For nearly two decades, she worked as freelance journalist and was a writer of ''how-to'' books on assignment; meanwhile, stories bubbled inside her. They finally erupted in her first collection, *Heart Songs and Other Stories.* Set in a northern New England, a landscape that can only be described as ''severe,'' the nine stories gave evidence of greatness to follow. Their odd-sounding names and battered conditions were simultaneously a mirror of the landscape and of Proulx's own quirky humor.

Heart Songs was followed by *Postcards,* a novel that won the PEN/Faulkner Award for Fiction. In other hands Proulx's decision to launch each chapter with a postcard tied to Loyal Blood, an aimless wanderer who serves as the book's protagonist, would have been a disaster, but Proulx so integrates the furious pace of story with the dazzle of technique that the result seems at once aesthetically coherent and entirely effortless.

Moreover, in documenting the decline-and-fall of a small American farm, one that had been in the Blood family for generations, Proulx was driving toward the very heart of America itself. Not that she preaches her message in an overt, editorializing manner; rather, her fiction dramatizes the particularities of a time and place with the fury of a gothic vision.

Shipping News is also set in an essentially hostile environment: Killick-Claw, a remote coastal village in Newfoundland. Known for its sudden storms and icy seas, the setting seems as unlikely as the postcards faithfully reproduced in Proulx's earlier novel. However, the saga of Quoyle, a hapless journalist who returns to his Newfoundland family home when his faithless wife is killed in a car wreck, serves as the springboard for an ambitious, multilayered novel.

At the center of *The Shipping News* is both the column of maritime comings-and-goings that Quoyle writes for *The Gammy Bird* (Prouxl's hilarious send-up of a small town newspaper) and her protagonist's ongoing effort to pull his life together. As Proulx's delightfully quirky style makes clear, he has a long way to go:

> [He had] a great damp loaf of a body. At six he weighed eighty pounds. At sixteen he was buried under a casement of flesh. Head shaped like a crensaw, no neck, reddish hair ruched back. Features as bunched as kissed fingertips. Eyes the color of plastic. The monstrous chin, a freakish shelf jutting from the lower face.

As for *The Gammy Bird,* it specializes in car wrecks (''We run a front-page photo of a car wreck every week, whether we have a wreck or not''), sexual abuse stories garnered from the wire service, and the ''shipping news,'' the paper's effort to spread the good news that commerce still goes on in Killick-Claw.

Quoyle digs out of his disastrous past by digging into work and the strange community he encounters through it. Even more remarkable, what might have been the unrelenting tale of his perpetual loserhood takes a sharp turn at the end toward love. Not only does Quoyle's unlikely column become an unqualified success (rather like *The Shipping News* itself, which won a Pulitzer Prize), but Quoyle finds himself ''coiled'' in the grasp of the community in general and of Wavey Prowse in particular. That he marries her at the end seems as magical—given Quoyle's long history of estrangement—as Newfoundland. But that may well be Proulx's point: darkness, even dark comedy, may not be the final word. Rather,

> Water may be older than light, diamonds crack in hot goat's blood, mountaintops give off cold fire, forests appear in mid-ocean, it may happen that a crab is caught with the shadow of a hand on its back, that the wind be imprisoned in a bit of knotted string. And it may be that love sometimes occurs with pain or misery.

In Accordion Crimes, Proulx once again proved her ability to construct a powerful narrative on a rather modest framework. The idea, of tracing the progress of an object as it moves from owner to owner, is not a new one, but Proulx's execution is so deft, and her portrayals so varied, that in her hands it all seems fresh again. The object in question is the one suggested by the title, and the ''crimes'' are those ordinary and sometimes extraordinary ones that people commit in the course of living. The cast of characters, those who own the accordion at various times between the late-nineteenth and late-twentieth centuries, comprises an array of figures, many of them immigrants, all across the heartland of the United States. They bring with them the prejudices of their past, and gain new ones on these shores, but the universality of music unites them at weddings and at wakes. Whether describing the workings of the accordion itself or a violent scene at a lunch counter in the segregated South of the 1960s, Proulx brings to each detail a penetrating insight and an obvious love for her creations that ensure her work will remain readable for generations to come.

—Sanford Pinsker, updated by Judson Knight

PURDY, James (Otis)

Nationality: American. **Born:** near Fremont, Ohio, 14 July 1923. **Education:** The University of Chicago, 1941, 1946; University of Pueblo, Mexico. **Career:** Worked as an interpreter in Latin America, France, and Spain; taught at Lawrence College, Appleton, Wisconsin, 1949–53. Since 1953 full-time writer. Visiting professor, University of Tulsa, Oklahoma, 1977. **Awards:** American Academy award, 1958, 1993; Guggenheim fellowship, 1958, 1962; Ford fellowship, for drama, 1961; Morton Dauwen Zabel Fiction Award, American Academy of Arts and Letters, 1993; Oscar Williams and Gene Durwood Award for poetry and art, 1995. **Address:** 236 Henry Street, Brooklyn, New York 11201, U.S.A.

Publications

Novels

Malcolm. New York, Farrar Straus, 1959; London, Secker and Warburg, 1960.

The Nephew. New York, Farrar Straus, 1960; London, Secker and Warburg, 1961.

Cabot Wright Begins. New York, Farrar Straus, 1964; London Secker and Warburg, 1965.

Eustace Chisholm and the Works. New York, Farrar Straus, 1967; London, Cape, 1968.

Gertrude of Stony Island Avenue. New York, Morrow, 1997.

Sleepers in Moon-Crowned Valleys:
- *Jeremy's Version.* New York, Doubleday, 1970; London, Cape, 1971.
- *The House of the Solitary Maggot.* New York, Doubleday, 1974; London, Owen, 1986.

I Am Elijah Thrush. New York, Doubleday, and London, Cape, 1972.
Narrow Rooms. New York, Arbor House, 1978; Godalming, Surrey, Black Sheep, 1980.
Mourners Below. New York, Viking Press, 1981; London, Owen, 1984.
On Glory's Course. New York, Viking, 1984; London, Owen, 1985.
In the Hollow of His Hand. New York, Weidenfeld and Nicolson, 1986; London, Owen, 1988.
Garments the Living Wear. San Francisco, City Lights, and London, Owen, 1989.
Out with the Stars. London, Owen, 1993.
Kitty Blue (fairy tale). Utrecht, The Netherlands, Ballroom, 1993.

Short Stories

Don't Call Me by My Right Name and Other Stories. New York, William Frederick Press, 1956.
63: Dream Palace. New York, William Frederick Press, 1956; London, Gollancz, 1957.
Color of Darkness: Eleven Stories and a Novella. New York, New Directions, 1957; London, Secker and Warburg, 1961.
Children Is All (stories and plays). New York, New Directions, 1961; London, Secker and Warburg, 1963.
An Oyster Is a Wealthy Beast (story and poems). Los Angeles, Black Sparrow Press, 1967.
Mr. Evening: A Story and Nine Poems. Los Angeles, Black Sparrow Press, 1970.
A Day after the Fair: Collection of Play and Stories. New York, Note of Hand, 1977.
Sleep Tight. New York, Nadja, 1979.
The Candles of Your Eyes. New York, Nadja, 1985.
The Candles of Your Eyes and Thirteen Other Stories. New York, Weidenfeld, 1987; London, Owen, 1988.

Plays

Mr. Cough Syrup and the Phantom Sex, in *December* (Western Springs, Illinois), vol. 8, no. 1, 1960.
Cracks (produced New York, 1963).
Wedding Finger, in *New Direction 28.* New York, New Directions, 1974.
Two Plays (includes *A Day after the Fair* and *True*). Dallas, New London Press, 1979.
Proud Flesh: Four Short Plays (includes *Strong, Clearing in the Forest, Now, What Is It, Zach?*). Northridge, California, Lord John Press, 1980.
Scrap of Paper, and The Berry-Picker: Two Plays. Los Angeles, Sylvester and Orphans, 1981.
The Berry-Picker (produced New York, 1985). With *Scrap of Paper,* 1981.
Ruthanna Elder. New York, Zenith Winds, 1990.
In the Night of Time and Four Other Plays. Amsterdam, Polak and Van Genned.

Poetry

The Running Sun. New York, Paul Waner Press, 1971.
Sunshine Is an Only Child. New York, Aloe, 1973.
I Will Arrest the Bird That Has No Light. Northridge, California, Santa Susana Press, 1977.
Lessons and Complaints. New York, Nadja, 1978.
The Brooklyn Branding Parlors. New York, Contact II, 1986.
Collected Poems. Amsterdam, Polak and Van Genned, 1992.

*

Bibliography: By Jay Ladd, in *American Book Collector* (Ossining, New York), September-October 1981; *James Purdy: A Bibliography,* compiled by Jay L. Ladd. Columbus, Ohio State University Libraries, 1999.

Manuscript Collections: Yale University, New Haven, Connecticut; Ohio State University, Columbus.

Critical Studies: Introduction by David Daiches to *Malcolm,* 1959, by Edith Sitwell to *Color of Darkness,* London, Secker and Warburg, 1961, and by Tony Tanner to *Color of Darkness,* and *Malcolm,* New York, Doubleday, 1974; *The Not-Right House: Essays on James Purdy* by Bettina Schwarzchild, Columbia, University of Missouri Press, 1968; *City of Words,* London, Cape, and New York, Harper, 1971, and ''Birdsong,'' in *Partisan Review* (New Brunswick, New Jersey), Fall 1972, both by Tony Tanner; ''James Purdy on the Corruption of Innocents'' by Frank Baldanza, in *Contemporary Literature* (Madison, Wisconsin), 1974; interview with Fred Barron, in *Penthouse* (New York), July 1974; *James Purdy* by Henry Chupack, Boston, Twayne, 1975; *James Purdy* by Stephen D. Adams, London, Vision Press, and New York, Barnes and Noble, 1976; ''James Purdy and the Black Mask of Humanity'' by Joseph T. Skerrett, Jr., in *Melus* (Los Angeles), 1979.

James Purdy comments:

(1972) As I see it, my work is an exploration of the American soul conveyed in a style based on the rhythms and accents of American speech. From the beginning my work has been greeted with a persistent and even passionate hostility on the part of the New York literary establishment which tries to rule America's literary taste—and the world's. My early work was privately printed by friends. Dame Edith Sitwell read these works and persuaded Victor Gollancz to publish the book in England. Without her help I would never have been published in America and never heard of. The mediocrity of the American literary scene, as is evidenced in the *New York Times* and the creatures of the vast New York establishment, has tried to reduce me to starvation and silence. Yet as a matter of fact I believe my work is the most American of any writer writing today. My subject, as I said, is the exploration of the inside of my characters, or as John Cowper Powys put it, ''under the skin.'' The theme of American culture, American commercial culture, that is, is that man can be adjusted, that loudness and numbers are reality, and that to be ''in'' is to exist. My work is the furthest from this definition of ''reality.'' All individual thought and feeling have been silenced or ''doped'' in America today, and to be oneself is tantamount to non-existence. I see no difference between Russia and America; both are hideous failures, both enemies of the soul, both devourers of nature, and undisciplined disciplinarians who wallow in the unnatural. Anything in America is sacred which brings in money, and the consumers can easily be persuaded to move from their old crumbling Puritan ethic to belief in things like sexual stereotyping and coprophilia, provided and only provided these bring in money and notoriety. The one crime is to be oneself, unless it is a ''self'' approved and created by the commercial forces. Beneath this vast structure of madness, money, and anesthetic prostitution, is my own body of work.

I prefer not to give a biography since my biography is in my work, and I do not wish to communicate with anybody but individuals, for whom my work was written in the first place. I began writing completely in the dark, and so continue. Were I in a financial position to do so, I would never publish anything commercially, since the literary establishment can promote only lies, and the critics, newspapers, and public, having been fed on poison so long, are incapable of reading anything that is not an advertisement for their own destruction. The most applauded writers in America are those who seem to have been born in a television studio where words are hourly produced from baking tins. In New York City, where American speech is unknown, a writer such as myself is considered a foreigner. Clarity and idiomatic language are considered in fact mad, while the language of dope addicts and coprophiliacs is now standard ''American,'' approved for use by the dowagers who make best-sellers.

* * *

James Purdy is fascinated by the ''color of darkness.'' His stories and novels deal with consuming narcissism and they assume, consequently, that ''normal'' love is, for the most part, cruel and nightmarish.

In *Color of Darkness* he gives us many heroes who are confused, lonely, and freakish. They do not know how to love (or to be loved). They are afraid to commit themselves. We see them sitting in dark rooms or roaming city streets; we hear their silent screams. Fenton Riddleway is so tormented by love for Claire, his dying brother, in ''63: Dream Palace,'' the most impressive story in the collection, that he must kill him. The murder is the culmination of perverse love; it is perfectly in keeping with the ''not-rightness'' and rot of their dream palace.

In another collection, *Children Is All,* Purdy returns to the conflicts in family relationships. Often his heroes are orphans or bachelors. The narrator of ''Daddy Wold,'' for example, has seen his wife and child leave him; he turns for solace to the invisible ''daddy.'' He calls him on the ''trouble phone'', he rants, confesses, and rambles. But he is, finally, alone—except for the rats which crawl near him. ''Goodnight, Sweetheart,'' like all of the best stories, fuses the realistic (or cliché) dialogue and the fantastic incident. It begins with Pearl Miranda walking ''stark naked from her class-room in the George Washington'' to the house of Winston, a former pupil. Both are victims of love (or ''rape''); both cannot exist in the wolfish world. Unfortunately, they cannot even live with each other. As the story ends, they ''both muttered to themselves in the darkness as if they were separated by different rooms from one another.'' They pray for help.

Purdy's novels are more varied than his stories. (It is questionable whether they surpass the great achievement of the stories.) The hero of his first novel, *Malcolm,* searches for his father, hoping thereby to affirm his own identity and *name.* But, like Fenton Riddleway, he cannot exist as a ''person''—he becomes another shadow in the rotten city. He is manipulated by others; he is never understood completely, except as a mere reflection of their selfish demands. Malcolm is, to quote his lusty wife, ''a little bit of this and that,'' and when he dies—has he ever lived?—he apparently vanishes into thin air. *Malcolm* is a wonderfully strange mixture of comedy and pathos, and it alone asserts Purdy's impressive gifts as a novelist. Although it deals with the lack of substance in relationships—between human beings and the cosmos—it creates its own substantial texture largely as a result of Purdy's mixed, ''transformational'' style.

The Nephew is set in Rainbow Center, a small American town. (It is a change from the ''fairy-tale'' *Malcolm.*) It delights in clichés, minor scandals, and popular holidays; it is, at least superficially, a realistic picture of the middle Americans. But it represents Boyd and Alma (and Cliff, their missing nephew) in such a deceptive, complex way that ''local color'' changes subtly to universal darkness. When Alma discovers that she has never known Cliff (despite having lived with him for many years) and, consequently, realizes her own needs and dreams, she is depressed *and* exalted. She grasps the hard truth; she understands that we are all ''missing'' shadows; we live briefly and secretly. She accepts the significance of memorial days—the novel begins and ends on this holiday—and the ''faint delicious perfume'' of our lives before the court house clock strikes again. Thus *The Nephew,* like all of Purdy's novels, must be read closely (as Alma reads her nephew's life)—it presents two worlds and demands the recognition that only art can reconcile their differences.

Cabot Wright Begins is a savage satire on American life. It attacks the automatic, false, and empty values which make us treat people as *valuable objects.* Cabot Wright becomes a rapist because he can assert his identity only as a vital, pumping being. Later he runs away from the others—Bernie, Zoe, and Princeton—who want to trap and use his exotic past for their narcissistic ends. Cabot Wright begins to laugh and write; he rises from the ''deadly monotony of the human continuity'' when he lies on the ground, ''weeping a little from the pain of his laughter, a thread of drivel coming down from his mouth onto his pointed dimpled chin.'' Despite the cluttered sermons, this novel is brilliantly effective when its says ''HA!'' to the boredom of our daily routines. It is Purdy's blackest comedy.

Eustace Chisholm and the Works details the various strategies of lovers who refuse to acknowledge their own potentialities. The homosexuality which colored *Malcolm, The Nephew* and *''63: Dream Palace''* flourishes here. Daniel Haws, for example, cannot accept his love for Amos (except at the end); he flees from it into the Army. There he is ''satisfied'' by sadistic Captain Stadger in a powerfully detailed execution (or embrace?). These Army scenes are perhaps the most brutal ones in all of Purdy's fiction.

Eusatce Chisholm is a writer. He resembles Alma, Cabot Wright, and Bernie of *Cabot Wright Begins* in trying to solve the mysteries of love and will in the community, and, like them, he discovers that he cannot get to the heart of the matter. He *abdicates*—unlike Purdy himself—and turns instead to his wife for incredible love. He warms her with ''a kind of ravening love,'' knowing that they will probably ''consume'' each other in the future. He is saved only momentarily.

Jeremy's Version is the first part of an uncompleted trilogy called *Sleepers in Moon-Crowned Valleys,* but it stands alone. Jeremy is an adolescent who writes down the sermons, tales, and histories of Matthew Lacy. He is, therefore, the familiar character we have met before, but unlike the other earlier writers, he is more open, innocent and *human* than they are. He learns as he listens and transcribes.

Jeremy moves into the past. He becomes so involved with the family conflicts of the nineteenth-century Fergises—he identifies especially with Jethro, another adolescent writer—that at times he becomes a free-floating *spirit.* Thus he forces us to recognize that only by giving oneself to others can we survive and create. He offers hope. His ''version'' is finally a mellow, full, and sunny account, which indicates some new directions for Purdy's forthcoming novels.

The House of the Solitary Maggot, the second volume of the trilogy, presents different characters—Lady Bythwaite and her illegitimate sons—but it also assumes that love is a bloody mixture. The ''family'' is, again, a maggot-ridden, melodramatic structure. Thus this novel, a discontinuous part of the trilogy, parallels the first, implying a mythic, disturbing, general design; it offers few solutions and little hope for American society.

—Irving Malin

PYNCHON, Thomas

Nationality: American. **Born:** Glen Cove, New York, 8 May 1937. **Education:** Cornell University, Ithaca, New York, 1954–58, B.A. 1958. **Military Service:** Served in the United States Naval Reserve. **Career:** Former editorial writer, Boeing Aircraft, Seattle. **Awards:** Faulkner award, 1964; Rosenthal Memorial award, 1967; National Book award, 1974; American Academy Howells medal, 1975. **Agent:** Candida Donadio and Associates, 231 West 22nd Street, New York, New York 10011. **Address:** c/o Little Brown, 34 Beacon Street, Boston, Massachusetts 02106, U.S.A.

PUBLICATIONS

Novels

V. Philadelphia, Lippincott, and London, Cape, 1963.
The Crying of Lot 49. Philadelphia, Lippincott, 1966; London, Cape, 1967.
Gravity's Rainbow. New York, Viking Press, and London, Cape, 1973.
Vineland. Boston, Little Brown, and London, Secker and Warburg, 1990.
Mason & Dixon. New York, Henry Holt, 1997.

Short Stories

Mortality and Mercy in Vienna. London, Aloes, 1976.
Low-lands. London, Aloes, 1978.
The Secret Integration. London, Aloes, 1980.
The Small Rain. London, Aloes, 1980(?).
Slow Learner: Early Stories. Boston, Little Brown, 1984; London, Cape, 1985.

Other

A Journey into the Mind of Watts. London, Mouldwarp, 1983.
Deadly Sins, illustrations by Etienne Delessert. New York, Morrow, 1994.

*

Bibliography: *Thomas Pynchon: A Bibliography of Primary and Secondary Materials* by Clifford Mead, Elmwood Park, Illinois, Dalkey Archive Press, 1989.

Critical Studies: *Thomas Pynchon* by Joseph V. Slade, New York, Warner, 1974, and *Thomas Pynchon,* New York, Lang, 1990; *Mindful Pleasures: Essays on Thomas Pynchon* edited by George Levine and David Leverenz, Boston, Little Brown, 1976; *The Grim Phoenix: Reconstructing Thomas Pynchon* by William M. Plater, Bloomington, Indiana University Press, 1978; *Pynchon: A Collection of Critical Essays* edited by Edward Mendelson, Englewood Cliffs, New Jersey, Prentice Hall, 1978; *Pynchon: Creative Paranoia in Gravity's Rainbow* by Mark Richard Siegel, Port Washington, New York, Kennikat Press, 1978; *Thomas Pynchon: The Art of Allusion* by David Cowart, Carbondale, Southern Illinois University Press, 1980; *The Rainbow Quest of Thomas Pynchon* by Douglas A. Mackey, San Bernardino, California, Borgo Press, 1980; *Pynchon's Fictions: Thomas Pynchon and the Literature of Information* by John O. Stark, Athens, Ohio University Press, 1980; *A Reader's Guide to Gravity's Rainbow* by Douglas Fowler, Ann Arbor, Michigan, Ardis, 1980; *Critical Essays on Thomas Pynchon* edited by Richard Pearce, Boston, Hall, 1981; *Pynchon: The Voice of Ambiguity* by Thomas H. Schaub, Urbana, University of Illinois Press, 1981; *Thomas Pynchon* by Tony Tanner, London, Methuen, 1982; *Signs and Symptoms: Thomas Pynchon and the Contemporary World* by Peter L. Cooper, Berkeley, University of California Press, 1983; *Approaches to Gravity's Rainbow* edited by Charles Clerc, Columbus, Ohio State University Press, 1983; *Ideas of Order in the Novels of Thomas Pynchon* by Molly Hite, Columbus, Ohio State University Press, 1983; *The Style of Connectedness: Gravity's Rainbow and Thomas Pynchon* by Thomas Moore, Columbia, University of Missouri Press, 1987; *A Gravity's Rainbow Companion* by Steven C. Weisenburger, Athens, University of Georgia Press, 1988; *The Fictional Labyrinths of Thomas Pynchon* by David Seed, London, Macmillan, 1988; *A Hand to Turn the Time: The Menippean Satires of Thomas Pynchon* by Theodore D. Kharpertian, Rutherford, New Jersey, Fairleigh Dickinson University Press, 1989; *Writing Pynchon: Strategies in Fictional Analysis* by Alec McHoul and David Wills, London, Macmillan, 1990; *The Gnostic Pynchon* by Dwight Eddins, Bloomington, Indiana University Press, 1990; *Thomas Pynchon: Allusive Parables of Power* by John Dugdale, London, Macmillan, and New York, St. Martin's Press, 1990; *New Essays on ''The Crying of Lot 49''* edited by Patrick O'Donnell, Cambridge, Cambridge University Press, 1991; *The Postmodernist Allegories of Thomas Pynchon* by Deborah L. Madsen, New York, St. Martin's Press, and Leicester, Leicester University Press, 1991; *Marginal Forces/Cultural Centers: Tolson, Pynchon, and the Politics of the Canon* by Michael Bérubé, Ithaca, New York, Cornell University Press, 1992; *Thomas Pynchon* by Judith Chambers, New York, Twayne, 1992; *Pynchon's Poetics: Interfacing Theory and Text* by Hanjo Berressem, Urbana, University of Illinois Press, 1993; *The Vineland Papers: Critical Takes on Pynchon's Novel* edited by Geoffrey Green, Donald Greiner, and Larry McCaffery, Normal, Illinois, Dalkey Archive Press, 1994.

* * *

The legend of Thomas Pynchon—no photographs, no interviews, no public appearances—cannot help but ensure, and indeed has ensured over the last forty years, a kind of spectacular visibility to both the man and the fiction. Pynchon's collection of short prose and the five important novels he has written to date have garnered him a reputation as not only North America's finest contemporary writer, but also as the undisputed world heavyweight champion of postmodern prose. Pynchon's novels are exemplary postmodern texts: critiquing grand narratives; indulging in fierce, slapstick displays of irony; reveling in the meta-textual; and obsessing about popular culture. But his works are also indisputably stamped with the hallmarks of high modernism, and in particular with an old-school literary erudition. Pynchon's cultural reputation reflects his stunningly eclectic prose: this super-hip, super-cerebral style that is nuanced as much with rock 'n' roll as it is with Rainer Maria Rilke.

But while critics have identified Pynchon as a clear inheritor of modernist literary experiments, his books, for the most part, are also recognizably realist. Pynchon's favorite form is the meta-literary picaresque, and he regularly utilizes a conventional third-person narrator. In fact, his lack of interest in exaggerated formal experimentation may lend the greatest power to Pynchon's inimitable prose style: traditional and yet also surprisingly absurdist, paranoid, hilarious, manic, celebratory, labyrinthine, and yet always melancholic. Pynchon's works are deeply nostalgic—in search of lost time, not to mention countries, histories, ideologies, and modes of identity.

Pynchon and his *oeuvre* can perhaps be most appropriately figured in a post-World War II, and particularly post-Beat, landscape. This is an environment distinguished by both great paranoia and great hope, especially as these extremes relate to the technologization of modern American culture. Pynchon's first novel, *V.,* published in 1963, concerns itself with this very conundrum. How do modern subjects—literally marked by their own obsolescence (the two principal protagonists are named Profane and Stencil)—negotiate the modern dangers of a nihilistic, corrupt, degrading, and mechanized environment? The leitmotif of *V.* is the grail quest, and we follow Stencil as he searches for the protean character ''V.'' (at first encountered as a woman, but a woman who throughout the novel metamorphoses into numerous fictional and historical personages). As in all of Pynchon's novels, underlying *V.*'s wonderful comedy and searing political commentary is a focused meditation on the workings of history and religion. Stencil and Profane are not unlike characters in a Kenneth Patchen allegory: two likeable but ill-fated dudes in search of signs of higher morality—and yet forever at the whim of a cultural order simultaneously droll and belligerent.

These dire themes and Stooges-like predicaments also infect Pynchon's second novel, *The Crying of Lot 49.* The tale opens with Oedipa Maas, just home from a Tupperware party, receiving word that she has been named executor of a California real estate mogul's will. Though Pynchon has since dismissed this second novel as rushed, it is distinguished by some utterly brilliant passages of stream-of-consciousness writing. The extremely tight and engaging plot also involves itself with the key Pynchon themes: conspiracy, madness, history, drugs, machines, science, love, capitalism, information. Pynchon's work is clearly obsessed with and by information—the transmission, receiving, manipulating, and concealment of—and especially the tendency of ''information'' to spin towards nonsense. This chaotic tendency is directly related to Pynchon's infamous preoccupation with ''entropy'' as a cultural and intellectual metaphor.

The paradoxical line ''A screaming comes across the sky'' opens Pynchon's monumental, and indeed immortality-securing, 1973 work *Gravity's Rainbow.* This screaming, the reader learns, is the uncanny after-sound of a German V2 rocket: travelling faster than the speed of sound, it has already detonated somewhere in England. The entire novel, with its 400-plus characters, can be read as an epic attempt to come to terms with the horror of this one scientific phenomenon. Thus the V2, like entropy, is for Pynchon that haunting aberration, that modern thing that exists outside traditional systems of rationality, beyond cause and effect. As the ominous central metaphor for the novel, Pynchon capitalizes on the V2's transgressive power and ingeniously links the bombings with the sexual exploits of one GI, Tyrone Slothrop (the locations of *his* ''detonations'' predict those of the V2). Clearly, Pynchon's absurdist tendencies are still wildly at work here, and the novel contains some unparalleled humorous writing (witness the English-candy tasting scene at Mrs. Quoad's house in which Slothrop is forced to sample, among other goodies, orange-mayonnaise flavored chocolates). *Gravity's Rainbow* is, however, peopled with characters far more cynical and more fundamentally anxious (they are literally waiting for super-rockets to destroy them) than the schlemiels and goofballs that inhabit *V.* and *The Crying of Lot 49.*

It is critically customary to dismiss a plot synopsis of the sprawling *Gravity's Rainbow* as impossible, but the plot would appear less vital than Pynchon's actual writing—which is tour de force. For many readers, comparisons to Joyce's *Ulysses* are unavoidable because *Gravity's Rainbow* is an utterly self-assured and inventive exercise in poetic style. It boasts not only effortless writerly technique (narrative shifts from first- to second- to third-person; incantatory, dream-like passages; use of song lyrics; parodies of numerous literary genres) but also, like Joyce, a cocky certainty that a reader will be *patient* enough to settle into its vast and idiosyncratic language-world. And so it is probably more predictable than ironic that *Gravity's Rainbow,* a novel pathologically obsessed with hard-ons and their relationship to missiles and vice versa, should itself exist as one of the more explosive, can(n)on-ready texts of the postmodern period.

A crucial interval in the Pynchon literary biography belongs to the seventeen years that stretches from the publication of *Gravity's Rainbow* to the publication of Pynchon's follow-up novel, *Vineland,* in 1990. While Pynchon did publish *Slow Learner: Early Stories* in 1984 (a collection of his previously published short fiction), he had otherwise completely turned off, and dropped out from, the literary scene. Not surprisingly, these ''silent'' years guaranteed Pynchon's reputation as first-rate recluse and also, of course, vouchsafed that the publication of *Vineland* would be an international literary event—what could possibly, reviewers wondered, follow the American *Ulysses?* What appeared was an uproarious, somewhat canon-indifferent, pop-culture-saturated book—resembling more *The Crying of Lot 49* than *Gravity's Rainbow*—set in 1984 and concerning aging hippie Zoyd Wheeler and his Northern California adventures with the Federal government. Pynchon's prose throughout is, unlike the oblique and somber arabesques of *Gravity's Rainbow,* TV-fluid and pure stand-up: ''Zoyd headed down to Vineland Mall and rolled around the lot there for a while, smoking up half a joint he'd found in his pocket, before parking the rig and going into More Is Less, a discount store for larger-size women.'' If the soundtrack for *Gravity's Rainbow* is ''screaming,'' then the background music in *Vineland* is all rim-shots. Yet while Pynchon is good with a pun, he is also, like Joyce, remorselessly allusive and learned. In *Vineland,* however, a reader is asked not to be familiar with Sanskrit or Greek myth, but with the minutiae of contemporary culture: ninja lore; breakfast cereal trivia; the history of surfer culture; strip mall ambience; punk rock references etc. *Vineland* really predicts, or elucidates the directions of, the next generation of American po-mo writers—Nicholson Baker, Donald Antrim, David Foster Wallace, Jonathan Franzen—themselves also steeped in the so-called detritus of modern western civilization.

Pynchon's latest novel is the hefty, *Gravity's Rainbow*-sized *Mason & Dixon.* Wicks Cherrycoke is the eighteenth-century narrator and he charts the life and times of the famous astronomer and surveyor duo entrusted with cutting the North-South dividing Line across the United States. The work is implicitly metaphoric, infinitely preoccupied with historical demarcations; scientific systems; and with the transgressions of, or adherence to, ''categories'' generally. *Mason & Dixon* is also pastiche writing at its finest: Pynchon employs numerous Age-of-Sensibility style capitalized words and a note-perfect Floridity. There is certainly something of the irreverent, master puppeteer on display in the novel as Pynchon manipulates his characters through fraught historical terrain.

Thomas Pynchon is, even more so than his esteemed comrades John Barth or Robert Coover, *the* contemporary sensei of the postwar American novel. As the brightest literary all-star then—despite the legendary invisible man status—Pynchon remains formidably, brilliantly in one's face.

—Jake Kennedy

R

RAMPLING, Anne

See RICE, Anne

RANDALL, Robert

See SILVERBERG, Robert

RAPHAEL, Frederic (Michael)

Nationality: American. **Born:** Chicago, Illinois, 14 August 1931. **Education:** Charterhouse School, Godalming, Surrey; St. John's College, Cambridge, 1950–54 (Major Classics Scholar, 1950; Harper Wood Studentship, 1954), M.A. (honours) 1954. **Family:** Married Sylvia Betty Glatt in 1955; two sons and one daughter. **Career:** Since 1962 contributor, and fiction critic, 1962–65, *Sunday Times,* London. **Awards:** British Screen Writers award, 1965, 1966, 1967; British Academy award, 1965; Oscar, for screenplay, 1966; Royal Television Society Writer of the Year award, 1976; Ace Award, Best Film for Cable TV, 1990. Fellow, Royal Society of Literature, 1964. **Agent:** Sanford Gross Agency, 1015 Gayley Avenue, Suite 301, Los Angeles, California 90024–3424, U.S.A.

PUBLICATIONS

Novels

Obbligato. London, Macmillan, 1956.
The Earlsdon Way. London, Cassell, 1958.
The Limits of Love. London, Cassell, 1960; Philadelphia, Lippincott, 1961.
A Wild Surmise. London, Cassell, 1961; Philadelphia, Lippincott, 1962.
The Graduate Wife. London, Cassell, 1962.
The Trouble with England. London, Cassell, 1962.
Lindmann. London, Cassell, 1963; New York, Holt Rinehart, 1964.
Darling. London, Fontana, and New York, New American Library, 1965.
Orchestra and Beginners. London, Cape, 1967; New York, Viking Press, 1968.
Like Men Betrayed. London, Cape, 1970; New York, Viking Press, 1971.
Who Were You with Last Night? London, Cape, 1971.
April, June and November. London, Cape, 1972; Indianapolis, Bobbs Merrill, 1976.
Richard's Things. London, Cape, 1973; Indianapolis, Bobbs Merrill, 1975.
California Time. London, Cape, 1975; New York, Holt Rinehart, 1976.
The Glittering Prizes. London, Allen Lane, 1976; New York, St. Martin's Press, 1978.
Heaven and Earth. London, Cape, and New York, Beaufort, 1985.
After the War. London, Collins, 1988; New York, Viking, 1989.
The Hidden I: A Myth Revised. London and New York, Thames and Hudson, 1990.
A Double Life. London, Orion, 1993.
Old Scores. London, Orion, 1995.
The Necessity of Anti-Semitism. New York, St. Martin's Press, 1998.
Coast To Coast. North Haven, Connecticut, Catbird Press, 1999.

Short Stories

Sleeps Six. London, Cape, 1979.
Oxbridge Blues and Other Stories. London, Cape, 1980; Fayetteville, University of Arkansas Press, 1984.
Oxbridge Blues (includes *Sleeps Six* and *Oxbridge Blues and Other Stories*). London, Penguin, 1984.
Think of England. London, Cape, 1986; New York, Scribner, 1988.
The Latin Lover. London, Orion, 1994.

Plays

Lady at the Wheel, with Lucienne Hill, music and lyrics by Leslie Bricusse and Robin Beaumont (produced London, 1958).
A Man on the Bridge (produced Hornchurch, Essex, 1961).
The Island (for children), in *Eight Plays 2,* edited by Malcolm Stuart Fellows. London, Cassell, 1965.
Two for the Road (screenplay). London, Cape, and New York, Holt Rinehart, 1967.
An Early Life (produced Leicester, 1979).
The Serpent Son: Aeschylus: Oresteia, with Kenneth McLeish (televised 1979). London, Cambridge University Press, 1979.
From the Greek (produced Cambridge, 1979).

Screenplays: *Bachelor of Hearts,* with Leslie Bricusse, 1958; *Nothing But the Best,* 1963; *Darling,* 1965; *Two for the Road,* 1967; *Far from the Maddening Crowd,* 1967; *A Severed Head,* 1970; *Don't Bother to Knock* (*Why Bother to Knock*), with Denis Cannan and Frederic Gotfurt, 1971; *Daisy Miller,* 1974; *Richard's Things,* 1981; *The Man in the Brooks Brothers Shirt,* 1990; *Eyes Wide Shut* (with Stanley Kubrick; based on a novel by Arthur Schnitzler). New York, Warner Books, 1999.

Radio Writing: *The Daedalus Dimension,* 1979; *Death in Trieste,* 1981; *The Thought of Lydia,* 1988; *The Empty Jew,* 1994.

Television Plays: *The Executioners,* 1961; *Image of a Society,* from the novel by Roy Fuller, 1963; *The Trouble with England,* from his own novel, 1964; *The Glittering Prizes,* 1976; *Rogue Male,* from the novel by Geoffrey Household, 1976; *Something's Wrong,* 1978; *The Serpent Son,* with Kenneth McLeish, 1979; *Of Mycenae and Men,* with Kenneth McLeish, 1979; *School Play,* 1979; *The Best of Friends,* 1980; *Byron: A Personal Tour* (documentary, also narrator), 1981; *Oxbridge Blues,* 1984; *After the War* series, 1989.

Other

W. Somerset Maugham and His World. London, Thames and Hudson, and New York, Scribner, 1977; revised edition, Sphere, 1989.
Cracks in the Ice: Views and Reviews. London, W.H. Allen, 1979.

A List of Books: An Imaginary Library, with Kenneth McLeish. London, Mitchell Beazley, and New York, Harmony, 1981.
Byron. London, Thames and Hudson, 1982.
Of Gods and Men, with illustrations by Sarah Raphael. London, Folio Society, 1992.
France: The Four Seasons, with photographs by Michael Busselle. London, Pavilion, 1994.
Popper. New York, Routledge, 1999.
Eyes Wide Open: A Memoir of Stanley Kubrick. New York, Ballantine Books, 1999.
Editor, *Bookmarks.* London, Cape, 1975.
Translator, with Kenneth McLeish, *The Poems of Catullus.* London, Cape, 1978; Boston, Godine, 1979.
Translator, with Kenneth McLeish, *The Complete Plays of Aeschylus.* London, Methuen, 1991.
Translator, with Kenneth McLeish, *Medea,* by Euripides. London, Hern, 1994.

*

Critical Study: ''The Varied Universe of Frederic Raphael'' by Frederick P.W. McDowell in *Critique* (Minneapolis), Fall 1965.

Theatrical Activities: Director: **Television**—*Something's Wrong,* 1978; *He'll See You Now,* 1984; **Film—***The Man in the Brooks Brothers Shirt,* 1990.

Frederic Raphael comments:

Although in many ways I am the most marginal of Jews (I am agnostic in religion and wary of communities), I suppose it is honest to say that I would not be a novelist if it were not for the singular experiences of the Jewish people and for my sense of being, if not a direct participant, at least a witness, of them. My themes, if I have themes, are scarcely Jewish since I lack intimate knowledge of the practices and habits of those who live in so-called Jewish society. When I do come in contact with them I do not necessarily find them congenial. Yet, the Final Solution—its vulgarity no less than its brutality, its greedy malice no less than its murderous factories—lies always at the back of my mind even if I myself, as a child growing up in England, suffered nothing more than its bad breath blowing in my face from across the Channel. It may be an indulgence for anyone who did not have closer experience to claim personal acquaintance with the holocaust; it is equally frivolous to ignore it. It is too convenient a conclusion to dispose of the Jewish experience under the Germans (and the Austrians and the Poles and the Hungarians and the Ukrainians and the Russians, and the English and the Americans) as a sort of freakish explosion, a San Francisco earthquake of an event, a once-and-for-all catastrophe after which, in the comforter's cliché, one has to ''go on living.'' And yet, of course, one does.

For me, the novelist is, above all, the historian of conscience. How does the individual conscience—in other words, how do I—go on living in a world which gives the clearest possible testimony of the cruelty and indifference of man? How does one continue to worry about the nuances of personal life, about love, friendship, taste, and responsibility when all the signs are that man is essentially rapacious, vindictive, and stupid? I have no answers to these questions, nor do I pretend they are in themselves new; they have been asked often enough and yet one does live at a particular time and, despite all the elegant suggestions to the contrary, it seems to me that our time is still linear. Certain things are beyond change, others lie ahead.

The problem is, in a sense, of language. Only in language is it possible to assimilate horrors and yet to achieve something which is both clear and, in a sense, pure. The way in which man remembers meaningfully is by not refusing sense in his language to those things which most profoundly influence or instruct him. This might be an argument for writing either history or philosophy and in a way I tried to do this, but I am not an historian or a philosopher. An obsession with a particular instance of the human character and a desire no less than a tendency—to show the futility of generalisation in the face of the fatuous and magnanimous individuality of human beings, lead me to examine the world through dramatic and emotional states rather than through a study of documents or the analysis of trends. Beyond and through the tragic comes the comic—the comic which does not explode the tragic but defines it—and this interpenetration is only one example of the sort of ambiguities in which the novelist finds himself at home. These ambiguities reveal themselves in drama and I have always found that, in spite of the attractions of both the theatre and the cinema, the drama can be worked out at its most personal and in the most piercing fashion in fiction. Truth may be stranger than fiction but fiction is truer.

How loftily one speaks in such generalising terms as these. The actual impulses which start a book are, of course, less grand. They spring as much from a sense of one's own contradictions as from any perception of human inadequacy or follies. When one begins to speak in the first person it sounds like conceit but it is more often confession, at least at my age. I am conscious above all of being equipped to be a novelist because it is only in a multiplicity of characters that I can reconcile my own ragbag personality. When people speak of a crisis of identity, I remind them that we know very well who we are, where we are having dinner and with whom we are sleeping, yet when I consider myself I am less commonsensical.

I was born in Chicago of a British father and an American mother. Beyond them, my grandparents and great-grandparents branched off across the world like an airline network. I was educated at Charterhouse which, I am told, is a great English Public School, and at Cambridge. I was readily influenced both by the ethos of the English middle class and by the intellectual habits of a classical education. Although I now regret much of what I was told and some of what I learned, I cannot shrug off the influence of these places, nor am I certain that I would wish to do so. The conflict of values reveals itself in fiction in the conflict of characters. I am conscious of being foreign in England and I find myself at home to some extent in many other places, yet I cannot sever myself entirely from the country where I live or from the language in which I write. I am sickened by xenophobia and yet in many ways I fear what lies beyond me. I believe that reason is better than unreason and that intelligence is better than instinct but I have not always been impressed by the decency of those who are most intelligent or by the capacity for affection and love of those who are most reasonable.

Within the nooks and crannies of the great edifices of generalisation and judgement, the innocently guilty and the guiltily innocent scurry about carrying nuts to their families, seeking their pleasures, snapping at their enemies, and providing, for those who have eyes to see, the proof of the impossibility of final solutions to the human condition.

* * *

Frederic Raphael began with a slight novel, *Obbligato,* a satiric and mock-heroic account of the rise to fame of an improvising pop-singer. Literary merit is abundant, however, in Raphael's second book, *The Earlsdon Way,* a realistic novel about the futility of British suburban life and the ineffectual revolt against its mores undertaken by Edward Keggin and his daughter Karen.

The Limits of Love gained for Raphael wide and deserved recognition. Its protagonist, Paul Riesman, is a Jew divorced by his training and inclinations from his race. Because he will not recognize what is necessity for him, his Jewishness, he becomes a selfish, life-destroying man despite his continuing efforts to achieve identity. But Paul increasingly sees that love is a defeating force if it is limited to the personal sphere and if it rejects the community; and he finds in his mother-in-law, Hannah Adler, stability that he lacks and in her daughter Julia, his wife, flexibility and depth.

In *A Wild Surmise* Raphael used a technique of montage to reveal his protagonist, Robert Carn, gradually. Carn hopes to escape British conventions in San Roque and to find genuine value through the spontaneous, impassioned, disinterested self. Ultimately, he supplements his introspective endeavors with a commitment to others in his efforts, ostensibly unsuccessful, to save some Indians from being poisoned. The novel is powerful and evocative, especially as it charts the processes of Carn's mind and the subtleties of his psychic life.

Raphael has written a number of brief novels, ironically executed, which concentrate upon a moral problem and its significance for the chief characters. *The Trouble with England* develops the moral contrasts between two vacationing couples on the French Riviera; *The Graduate Wife* focuses upon the forward development of a priggish heroine to inner stability. *Who Were You with Last Night?* has, as first-person narrator, the disenchanted Charles Hanson, who is amusing as he deflates bourgeois values (sometimes his own), recounts his satisfactions and frustrations with wife and mistress, and analyzes the delicate balance existing between love and hate in intimate relationships. *Richard's Things* is a *tour de force,* suggesting the impermanence not only of the marital relationship but of life itself, as the piquant relationship between the wife of the now dead Richard and his mistress diminishes from its first ardor to something near hatred. *The Glittering Prizes* reveals Raphael's remarkable technical expertise and depth of emotional insight as he traces the unfolding lives after their graduation, of a group of Cambridge contemporaries. The chief of these, Adam Morris, is a novelist similar in temperament to Raphael himself. He is an ironically minded but aesthetically talented Jew whose temporary foray into the world of the mass media is engaging farce, meant also to define the difficulties that the serious artist encounters in holding fast to his genuine impulses.

The peak of Raphael's achievement in writing the experimental novel is *Lindmann.* A British civil servant, James Shepherd, connived in 1942 to prevent the *SS Broda* from landing in Turkey with its Jewish refugees. Shepherd, to expiate his guilt and to achieve self-definition, assumes the identity of Jacob Lindmann, one of the two survivors from the ship who later died from exposure. A certain chastity gives Shepherd as Lindmann his moral force, since he forgoes any kind of fulfillment for himself; and he is, by his spiritual tenacity, something more than the failure he judges himself to be. Through patience and love he tries to influence others to a course of moderation, toleration, consideration, and affection.

Orchestra and Beginners, Like Men Betrayed, April, June, and November, and *California Time* are also works of considerable scope. In *Orchestra and Beginners* Raphael analyzes the ineffectual decency and the effete decay which characterized British upper-middle-class society just prior to World War II. Linda Strauss suffers from the moral paralysis of the class into which as an American she has married but is sympathetically seen, even if she fails her husband at his military enlistment because of her intensely personal reactions to experience. Leonard, in turn, is too impersonal toward Linda. Paradoxically, Linda's passion and Leonard's critical intelligence are both needed in confronting the complexities of modern life.

Like *Men Betrayed* is about Greek and, by implication, English politics, and it is remarkable for penetrating the relationships between the individual's psyche and social institutions. Three main points in time contrapuntally organize the book: the Greece of the 1930s under the Marshal's moderate dictatorship; Greece during World War II when factional jealousies are only less intense than hatred for the Italians and Germans; and postwar Greece when a power struggle develops between the corrupt royalist regime and the leftist insurgents. Artemis Theodoros defects from the Royalists when government troops fail in World War II to support the leftist General Papavastrou against the Germans. The novel is subtle and complex as it traces Artemis's endeavors to reach spiritual and political truth. As the novel opens he is fleeing north to the frontier where supposedly his forces will reach asylum. Instead, he learns that they will be betrayed. He remains faithful to his inner standards, however, despite misunderstanding, violence, betrayal, imprisonment, and exile. In Artemis a deplorable waste of genius occurs. The integrity inherent in such a heroic man, however, is the resource which we will have to learn how to use to insure a revitalized polity, Raphael would seem to be saying.

April, June, and November, California Time, and *Heaven and Earth* are also novels about talented men whose creative energies are deflected either by weakness of will or by circumstances. In *April, June, and November* the liberal and magnetic Daniel Meyer is, in fact, capable of a heroism which he can never display to any purpose in his hedonistic, effete milieu. The football field rather than the political arena claims his intelligence and genius. In *California Time* Victor England is likewise a victim, but could he have ever achieved distinction in the cutthroat and standardless world of the motion pictures studios, a world which needs his creativity but which also humiliates him to the greatest possible extent? Raphael is frankly experimental in this novel, collapsing all of Victor's experience into the ongoing present and creating doubts in him as to the reality of his perceptions of the given moment, in a milieu in which the reality and the hallucination become barely distinguishable. In *Heaven and Earth* Gideon Shand is a good man whose happiness, prosperity, and integrity seem unassailable. Underneath, the irrational forces in himself and others lead, unexpectedly to him (and to the reader), to destruction and self-destruction. Life is at once tougher and more fragile than he had at first realized; and the implicit question raised in this novel, but not decisively answered, is whether a man like Gideon can survive the violent effects of these unconscious forces. In these three novels Raphael develops the tragedy of the man who cannot actualize his good intentions and give free expression to his genius, with the same density, elusiveness, and complication that characterize his fiction as a whole.

—Frederick P.W. McDowell

READ, Piers Paul

Nationality: British. **Born:** Beaconsfield, Buckinghamshire, 7 March 1941; son of the writer Herbert Read. **Education:** Gilling Castle, York, 1949–52; Ampleforth College, York, 1953–57; St. John's College, Cambridge, 1959–62, B.A. in history 1962, M.A. 1966. **Family:** Married Emily Boothby in 1967; two sons and two daughters. **Career:** sub-editor, *Times Literary Supplement,* London, 1964–65. Artist-in-residence, Ford Foundation, Berlin, 1963–64; adjunct professor of writing, Columbia University, New York, 1980; governor, Cardinal Manning Boys School; chair, Catholic Writers' Guild, 1993–97. **Awards:** Commonwealth Fund Harkness fellowship, 1967; Faber Memorial award, 1968; Hawthornden prize, 1969; Maugham award, 1970; Thomas More Association medal, 1974; Enid McLeod award, 1988; James Tait Black Memorial prize, 1988. Fellow, Royal Society of Literature, 1972. **Agent:** Aitken and Stone Ltd., 29 Fernshaw Road, London SW10 0TG. **Address:** 50 Portland Road, London W11 4LG, England.

PUBLICATIONS

Novels

Game in Heaven with Tussy Marx. London, Weidenfeld and Nicolson, and New York, McGraw Hill, 1966.
The Junkers. London, Secker and Warburg, 1968; New York, Knopf, 1969.
Monk Dawson. London, Secker and Warburg, 1969; Philadelphia, Lippincott, 1970.
The Professor's Daughter. London, Secker and Warburg-Alison Press, and Philadelphia, Lippincott, 1971.
The Upstart. London, Alison Press, and Philadelphia, Lippincott, 1973.
Polonaise. London, Alison Press, and Philadelphia, Lippincott, 1976.
A Married Man. London, Secker and Warburg, 1979; Philadelphia, Lippincott, 1980.
The Villa Golitsyn. London, Secker and Warburg, 1981; New York, Harper, 1982.
The Free Frenchman. London, Secker and Warburg, 1986; New York, Random House, 1987.
A Season in the West. London, Secker and Warburg, 1988; New York, Random House, 1989.
On the Third Day. London, Secker and Warburg, 1990; New York, Random House, 1991.
The Patriot. London, Weidenfeld & Nicolson, 1995; New York, Random House, 1996.
Knights of the Cross. London, Weidenfeld & Nicolson, 1997.

Uncollected Short Story

''Son and Heir,'' in *Winter's Tales 2* (new series), edited by Robin Baird-Smith. London, Constable, and New York, St. Martin's Press, 1986.

Plays

The Class War, in *Colloquialisms* (produced London, 1964).

Radio Plays: *The Family Firm,* 1970; *The House on Highbury Hill,* music by Julian Slade, 1971.

Television Plays: *Coincidence,* 1968; *The Childhood Friend,* 1974; *Margaret Clitheroe (Here I Stand* series), 1977.

Other

Alive! The Story of the Andes Survivors. London, Secker and Warburg, and Philadelphia, Lippincott, 1974.
The Train Robbers. London, Allen and Unwin-Alison Press, and Philadelphia, Lippincott, 1978.
Ablaze: The Story of Chernobyl. London, Secher and Warburg, and New York, Random House, 1993.

*

Critical Studies: Article by Philip Flynn, in *British Novelists Since 1960,* edited by Jay L. Halio, Detroit, Gale, 1983; ''The Novels of Piers Paul Read'' by C.J. Taylor, in *Spectator,* 23 February 1990.

* * *

Piers Paul Read once observed that he was much influenced by the novels of Graham Greene, and indeed, moral and political issues, ambiguity, belief, and skepticism are given considerable focus in his work. In *A Season in the West,* for example, the political decadence of Communist-ruled Czechoslovakia is contrasted with the moral decadence of the capitalist west. Even in the Communist east the right family and party connections can protect a dissident, while in England the defecting dissident discovers that the right family and class connections are also more significant than political idealism.

Like Greene, Read sets his novels in various locales besides England: Germany, France, the United States, and the Eastern bloc. Each country evinces a pronounced ambiguity to political aspirations and activism. The most altruistic theories and motives, while seemingly presenting utopian solutions, are marred by inherent human corruption and deficiencies. On the extreme is Nazism, examined by Read in *The Junkers.* Not only is there the unspeakable horror of the Holocaust itself, but there are the petty horrors as well: in Read's depiction, the snobbery and obsession with class differences so frequently associated with the English are in their own form characteristic of the Germans as well.

Even when the political cause is noble, as in *The Free Frenchman,* the pure goal of working for freedom from oppression is often thwarted and obfuscated by family differences, love entanglements, and human betrayals. Comrades working together in the Resistance movement cannot avoid disagreements and hostilities. In Read's fiction manifestations of Manichean conflict must always rage in every individual and situation. Read's world is one where integrity is often compromised, love and sex are ambivalent if not treacherous, and hedonism, honor, and cruelty co-exist. Quoting Pierre d'Harcourt, Read observes that ''the real enemy is within.'' The struggle between the sinner and the saint promises endless conflict. Even though one phase is in the ascendant, the other aspect makes progress on the imaginative plane so that this mixture and conflict will produce constant turmoil, and the yearning for betterment will continue to torment. In the fiction of Read we are reminded that all too often ''the devil is prince of the world ... He has powers too.''

Read reiterates this theme in numerous forms. As soon as humans involve themselves with other members of society, evil will intensify. Edward Dawson, the protagonist of one of Read's best novels, *Monk Dawson,* is a well-meaning, civilized man; but a decadent, sex-obsessed, and excessively materialistic society soon contaminates him with its folly. His ultimate decision to enter a monastery, while a symbol of personal salvation, is a scathing commentary on the hopelessness of attempting to find moral decency and stability in contemporary society. Basic kindness, integrity, and fair-minded behavior are regarded as anachronistic and naive. Read's world is a Greeneland, sometimes more flashy and dazzling than the atmosphere used by Greene, but nevertheless filled with treachery, hostility, disbelief, and despair.

Professor Henry Rutledge in *The Professor's Daughter* is trapped in a typical Read dilemma. He champions liberal and progressive ideas, yet ironically his death results from militant revolutionary activity carried out by some of his own graduate students. While politically Rutledge may be on the side of the angels, his own family is torn apart by alcoholism, prostitution, and attempted suicide. The mutual devotion between his favorite daughter and himself cannot withstand the chaos of 1960s activism. Read constantly stresses that twentieth-century life has shattered family values and cohesiveness and maintains that until some stability can be returned to the family unit, the pervasiveness of evil will increase uncontrollably.

There is hope in genuine repentance and atonement as Hilary Fletcher demonstrates in *The Upstart,* but repentance is a rare occurrence in today's world, and is not even considered a workable option by most of Read's characters.

Read is a born storyteller with a cold, dispassionate style that often yields ironic overtones. He invents plots which of themselves are intriguing. In *On the Third Day*, Israelis on an archeological dig in Jerusalem, used as camouflage to spy on Arab rebels, discover the 2000-year-old skeleton of a crucified man which has a nail through its feet, thorn marks on the skull, and evidence of a spear having pierced the rib cage. Is this possibly the remains of Christ?

Read has more than once been accused of contriving melodramatic plots based on sensational events; yet melodrama can be powerful and effective, and the nature of the characters, situation, and settings can justify some melodramatic aspects and treatment. At times he has turned from lofty considerations to pure entertainment, as in *The Patriot.* The plot is that of a purely traditional Cold War spy thriller, with the only alteration being the fact that this one is set at the end of the Cold War, in the Berlin of the early 1990s. The book was less than successful critically, however, suggesting that Read's talents are best applied for serious narratives. In his greatest novels, such as *Monk Dawson, The Junkers,* and *The Villa Golitsyn,* he handles vital themes with evident talent that establishes him as an important figure in contemporary fiction.

—Paul A. Doyle, updated by Judson Knight

RECHY, John (Francisco)

Nationality: American. **Born:** El Paso, Texas, 10 March 1934. **Education:** Texas Western College, El Paso, B.A.; New School for Social Research, New York. **Military Service:** Served in the United States Army. **Career:** Has taught creative writing at University of California, Occidental College, and University of Southern California, all Los Angeles. Lives in Los Angeles. **Awards:** Longview Foundation prize, 1961; National Endowment for the Arts grant, 1976. **Agent:** Georges Borchardt Inc., 136 East 57th Street, New York, New York 10022, USA.

PUBLICATIONS

Novels

City of Night. New York, Grove Press, 1963; London, MacGibbon and Kee, 1964.
Numbers. New York, Grove Press, 1967.
This Day's Death. New York, Grove Press, and London, MacGibbon and Kee, 1970.
The Vampires. New York, Grove Press, 1971.
The Fourth Angel. New York, Viking Press, and London, W.H. Allen, 1972.
Rushes. New York, Grove Press, 1979.
Bodies and Souls. New York, Carroll and Graf, 1983; London, W.H. Allen, 1984.
Marilyn's Daughter. New York, Carroll and Graf, 1988.
The Miraculous Day of Amalia Gómez. Boston, Little Brown, 1991.
Our Lady of Babylon. New York, Arcade, 1996.
The Coming of the Night. New York, Grove Press, 1999.

Plays

Momma As She Became—Not As She Was (produced New York, 1978).
Tigers Wild (produced New York, 1986).

Other

The Sexual Outlaw: A Documentary ... of Three Days and Nights in the Sexual Underground. New York, Grove Press, 1977; London, W.H. Allen, 1978.

*

Manuscript Collection: Boston University.

John Rechy comments:

Because my first novel, *City of Night,* was greeted by two personally assaultive reviews, one in "The New York Review of Books," the other in "The New Republic," both of which shrilly attacked the novel's salient subject (homosexuality and male-hustling) while ignoring its careful literary form, much of my subsequent work is still frequently mis-viewed, especially since those two reviews have been anthologized. I consider myself a literary writer, one attentive to structure and style as essential to meaning. Employing a variety of forms, I've explored many subjects, ranging from male-hustling (*City of Night, The Sexual Outlaw*) to the power of legend over myth as epitomized by Marilyn Monroe (*Marilyn's*

Daughter), to a day in the life of a Mexican-American woman (*The Miraculous Day of Amalia Gómez*) to a panoramic view of Los Angeles as a modern paradise of "lost angels" (*Bodies and Souls*). I wish that equal critical attention were paid to the literary aspects of my writing as, often—and years later—to the subject, only the subject, of my first novel.

* * *

Author of eleven novels, several plays, and one work of nonfiction, John Rechy's reputation was made by the publication of his first novel, *City of Night* (1963), in which, as one critic has put it, his "world is the heir of Hawthorne's. His characters inhabit a moral universe whose codes are as rigorous as Calvin's and whose cops are the vigilantes of a new unmerciful Salem." Throughout his career he has focused on the transgressive, sexual in particular, but also social, political, and emotional. He has often employed quasi-allegorical structures to convey such transgression, especially in *City of Night* and *Our Lady of Babylon* (1996). Landscapes are colored by social, political, and moral disintegration, stirrings of uncompleted searches for social identity, and looming disaster. As his career has progressed, however, Rechy's artistry has matured and he has been able to embed his primary themes in a wider variety of styles and approaches, including a traditional Mexican-American novel of poverty, parodies of enlightenment literature, and self-referential camp.

In Rechy's first two novels, *City of Night* and *Numbers* (1967), his "youngmen" are the fallen angels of an eternally inaccessible paradise, and their lives are characterized by a search for the eros that will at last become agape. That the search is frenetic is scarcely surprising; it has all the desperate urgency that characterizes the role of the sensitive American—the anguish of exile within one's own country. Although in *City of Night* Rechy never quite succeeds in conveying Francis Thompson's added sense of "dreadful," it is plain that the implication is there. New York, from the first page, is a metaphor city, a fairy city—in a sense like the London of Robert Louis Stevenson—where anything might happen. That is not to say that Rechy's urban fantasy has the caliber of James Purdy's. It is more limited in its focus. Its world is a moral world turned upside down, where the *Deus absconditus* is Priapus. The quest for that god is a never-ending and insatiable one, one in which the tyrants of the old moral order have all the destructive vindictiveness of Diocletian against the Christians.

However, neither *City of Night* nor *Numbers* (in spite of the deliberate "allegorical" pretensions of the former) often rises above what seem to be the masturbatory fantasies of an aging queen. In his third novel, *This Day's Death* (1969), Rechy gets beyond the labored dualisms of his first two—a catalogue of well-equipped muscleboys on the one hand and a labored novelistic artifice to contain it on the other. *This Day's Death* does indeed suffer from a somewhat contrivedly concealed central event and a time scheme that is sometimes confusing and tedious. Its *a la recherche de la virginite perdue*, however, is convincing in a way that is true of neither of the earliest novels. Rechy's New Mexico, like John Steinbeck's Oklahoma, is a small-town world of poverty and pain, the anguish of growth and the desire to break out. His California is the nightmare inversion of that desire—a world where the law is a monster devouring the innocents who nonetheless have a Genet-like fascination with its devious iniquities. And together these worlds, as commentaries on one another, form a larger moral universe than any Rechy has created before.

It is disenchanting, then, to find that in *The Vampires* (1971), the novel that succeeds *This Day's Death*, he returns to the world of gothic fiction with an overlay of baroque Satanism. *The Fourth Angel* (1973) suffers less from this, being set once again in the Southwest. But if its teenage characters are more "real," their problems are too much the stereotypes of the late 1960s to remain interesting, and their presentation is overly laced with sentimentality—"and so, suddenly, they're gentle children playing gentle children's games." *Rushes* (1979) and *Bodies and Souls* (1983) focus on the similar themes with which Rechy was identified through his early career, with varying success.

In *Marilyn's Daughter* (1988), Rechy enters the bizarre world of southern California cults, indulging a continuing fascination with a fall from grace and generally vain attempts to regain it. The story of a young woman from Texas who believes herself to be the daughter of Marilyn Monroe, the book suffers from an overreliance on a parody of maps of the stars homes. However, it signals a shift in Rechy's work toward the exploration of women's illusions and sexual and social victimization, which he would then explore in *The Miraculous Day of Amalia Gómez* (1991) and *Our Lady of Babylon*.

Despite the inclusion of several Mexican-American characters in his earlier work, *The Miraculous Day* is Rechy's most overtly Mexican-American fiction. It follows the tradition of the poor, victimized Hispanic woman in the Spanish-speaking ghetto who populates both the Northeast and the Southwest but whose story has been told only in 1990s literature. In it, Rechy no longer sets up the starkly dichotomous morality of alterity, his wont in early work, particularly in *City of Night* and *Numbers*. Amalia Gómez is a flawed individual within a flawed society, as delusive as many of her predecessors, mistake-prone, battered by circumstance and awaiting the confluence of illusion and miracle, either of which will satisfy her delusion. Rechy's maturing style allows a more nuanced prose than he had previously exhibited.

In *Our Lady of Babylon*, Rechy continues to explore the position of women as he did with young men in his early work, devolving an allegorical structure that removes his landscape far from the contemporary southwestern, urban world that has been his strength. Yet whereas Rechy's earlier use of allegory was fraught with earnestness, *Our Lady* is a cunningly camp parody of literary collective memory and the eighteenth-century eroticism of *Les liaisons dangereuses* and *La Princesse de Clèves*. His 1999 novel, *The Coming of the Night*, returns to many of the settings and themes of his earlier work, but reflects the much more mature, varied prose style that allows characters to exhibit flaws, an element often missing from his more allegorical early work about young men. It also finds a writer at the height of his powers experimenting with a continued parody of memory and desire in a camp, self-referential manner.

Because of his subject matter, Rechy has attracted most review and criticism from gay-oriented publications. Owing to the current development of the politics of inclusion, publication of the Mexican-American-themed *Amalia Gómez*, and the urging of Chicano critic Juan Bruce-Novoa, Rechy (whose full name is John Francisco Rechy-Flores) has recently attracted the attention of Chicano critics and bibliographers.

—D. D. C. Chambers, updated by Harold Augenbraum

REED, Ishmael (Scott)

Nationality: American. **Born:** Chattanooga, Tennessee, 22 February 1938. **Education:** Buffalo Technical High School; East High School, Buffalo, graduated 1956; University of Buffalo, 1956–60. **Family:** Married 1) Priscilla Rose in 1960 (separated 1963, divorced 1970), one daughter; 2) Carla Blank-Reed in 1970, one daughter. **Career:** Staff writer, *Empire Star Weekly,* Buffalo, 1960–62; freelance writer, New York, 1962–67; co-founder, *East Village Other,* New York, and *Advance,* Newark, New Jersey, 1965; teacher, St. Mark's in the Bowery prose workshop, New York, 1966. Since 1971 chair and president, Yardbird Publishing Company, editor, *Yardbird Reader,* 1972–76, since 1973 director, Reed Cannon and Johnson Communications, and since 1981 editor and publisher, with Al Young, *Quilt* magazine, all Berkeley, California. Since 1967 lecturer, University of California, Berkeley. Lecturer, University of Washington, Seattle, 1969–70, State University of New York, Buffalo, 1975, 1979, Sitka Community Association, Summer 1982, University of Arkansas, Fayetteville, 1982, Columbia University, New York, 1983, Harvard University, Cambridge, Massachusetts, 1987, and University of California, Santa Barbara, 1988. Visiting professor, Fall 1979, and since 1983 Associate Fellow of Calhoun House, Yale University, New Haven, Connecticut; visiting professor, Dartmouth College, Hanover, New Hampshire, 1980; since 1987 Associate Fellow, Harvard University Signet Society. Since 1976 president, Before Columbus Foundation. Chair, Berkeley Arts Commission, 1980, 1981. Associate editor, *American Book Review.* **Awards:** National Endowment for the Arts grant, 1974; Rosenthal Foundation award, 1975; Guggenheim fellowship, 1975; American Academy award, 1975; Michaux award, 1978; MacArthur fellow, 1998. **Agent:** Ellis J. Freedman, 415 Madison Avenue, New York, New York 10017, U.S.A.

PUBLICATIONS

Novels

The Free-Lance Pallbearers. New York, Doubleday, 1967; London, MacGibbon and Kee, 1968.
Yellow Back Radio Broke-Down. New York, Doubleday, 1969; London, Allison and Busby, 1971.
Mumbo-Jumbo. New York, Doubleday, 1972; London, Allison and Busby, 1989.
The Last Days of Louisiana Red. New York, Random House, 1974.
Flight to Canada. New York, Random House, 1976.
The Terrible Twos. New York, St. Martin's Press-Marek, 1982; London, Allison and Busby, 1990.
Reckless Eyeballing. New York, St. Martin's Press, 1986; London, Allison and Busby, 1989.
The Terrible Threes. New York, Atheneum, 1989.
Japanese by Spring. New York, Atheneum, 1993.

Poetry

Catechism of d neoamerican hoodoo church. London, Paul Breman, 1970.
Conjure: Selected Poems 1963–1970. Amherst, University of Massachusetts Press, 1972.
Chattanooga. New York, Random House, 1973.
A Secretary to the Spirits. New York, NOK, 1978.
New and Collected Poems. New York, Atheneum, 1988.

Other

The Rise, Fall and . . . ? of Adam Clayton Powell (as Emmett Coleman), with others. New York, Bee-Line, 1967.
Shrovetide in Old New Orleans (essays). New York, Doubleday, 1978.
God Made Alaska for the Indians. New York, Garland, 1982.
Cab Calloway Stands In for the Moon. Flint, Michigan, Bamberger, 1986.
Airing Dirty Laundry. Reading, Addison-Wesley, 1993.
The Reed Reader. New York, Basic Books, 2000.
Editor, *19 Necromancers from Now.* New York, Doubleday, 1970.
Editor, *Yardbird Reader* (annual). Berkeley, California, Yardbird, 5 vols., 1971–77.
Editor, with Al Young, *Yardbird Lives!* New York, Grove Press, 1978.
Editor, *Calafia: The California Poetry.* Berkeley, California, Yardbird, 1979.
Editor, with Al Young, *Quilt 2–3.* Berkeley, California, Reed and Young's Quilt, 2 vols., 1981–82.
Editor, *Writin' Is Fightin': Thirty-Seven Years of Boxing on Paper.* New York, Atheneum, 1988.
Editor, with Kathryn Trueblood and Shawn Wong, *The Before Columbus Foundation Fiction Anthology: Selections from the American Book Awards, 1980–1990.* New York, Norton, 1992.
Editor, *MultiAmerica: Essays on Cultural Wars and Cultural Peace.* New York, Viking, 1997.

*

Bibliography: ''Mapping Out the Gumbo Works: An Ishmael Reed Bibliography'' by Joe Weixlmann, Robert Fikes, Jr., and Ishmael Reed, in *Black American Literature Forum* (Terre Haute, Indiana), Spring 1978.

Critical Studies: ''Ishmael Reed Issue'' of *Review of Contemporary Fiction* (Elmwood Park, Illinois), vol. 4, no. 2, 1984; *Ishmael Reed and the New Black Aesthetic Critics* by Reginald Martin, New York, Macmillan, 1988; *Ishmael Reed* by Jay Boyer, Boise, Idaho, Boise State University, 1993; *Conversations with Ishmael Reed,* edited by Bruce Dick and Amritjit Singh. Jackson, University Press of Mississippi, 1995; *Ishmael Reed and the Ends of Race* by Patrick McGee, New York, St. Martin's Press, 1997; *The Critical Response to Ishmael Reed,* edited by Bruce Allen Dick with the Assistance of Pavel Zemliansky, Westport, Connecticut, Greenwood Press, 1999.

* * *

In an introduction to an essay collection, *Shrovetide in Old New Orleans,* Ishmael Reed says: ''Many people here called my fiction muddled, crazy, incoherent, because I've attempted in fiction the techniques and forms painters, dancers, film makers, musicians in the West have taken for granted for at least fifty years, and the artists of many other cultures, for thousands of years.'' Reed's strengths are enunciated here: flexible, vivid language ranging from street argot to lofty estheticism, experimentation with materials and means, and a deep awareness of the mythic roots of all cultures. Reed is an Afro-American ironist, but his gifts and insights are multicultural, multimedia.

Reed's early novels, *The Free-Lance Pallbearers* and *Yellow Back Radio Broke-Down,* are musical and mythical in conception and development. Using ''hoodoo'' as a system both of ideas and of language, Reed describes our world in terms of the hero and the prison of society. In *The Free-Lance Pallbearers* Bukka Doopeyduk is the epigonous hero fighting against **HARRY SAM**, which is the nation-state transformed into a monstrous personification, a dragon. In similar fashion, the Loop Garoo Kid of *Yellow Back Radio Broke-Down* is a shaman-hero (Loupe Garou=werewolf in Creole-French folklore) of a cowboy saga, in which the town of Yellow Back Radio is threatened by Drag Gibson, the stultifying force of the square world. The vaudevillian jokes, surrealism, and wordplays flow at *allegro* tempo.

In *Mumbo Jumbo* Reed concentrates on a mythic time (the 1920s) and magic places (New Orleans and Harlem) in U.S. culture. The ideas of hoodoo/voodoo and other Afro-American magic-religious cults figure in Reed's tapestry of the Jazz Age and the Harlem Renaissance. Reed describes the epic struggle between Jes Grew, the black cultural impulse, and the Atonists, i.e., the monotheistic Western tradition. In the narrative, Reed incorporates drawings, photographs, collages, and handwritten texts, along with many scholarly references.

The Last Days of Louisiana Red extends this mythology, bringing many of the same characters and ideas to Berkeley in the 1970s. ''Louisiana Red'' is the plague of modern technocratic-industrial culture:

> Louisiana Red was the way they related to one another, oppressed one another, maimed and murdered one another, carving one another while above their heads, fifty thousand feet, billionaires flew in custom-made jet planes equipped with saunas tennis courts swimming pools discotheques and meeting rooms decorated like the Merv Griffin show set.

In *Flight to Canada* Reed moves back to the mythos of slavery and the Civil War, applying the same wild, anachronistic expressionism to the central tragedy of the black American culture. In ironic, dramatic terms, Reed answers the ''cliometric'' revisers of history: ''Revisionists. Quantitative historians. What does a computer know? Can a computer feel? Make love? Can a computer feel passion?'' Quickskill tears off his shirt. ''Look at these scars. Look at them! All you see is their fruit, but their roots run deep. The roots are in my soul.''

The Terrible Twos is a comic-mythological tour de force, uniting elements of our culture's Christmas story—Dicken's ''A Christmas Carol,'' the legend of St. Nicholas, the commercial street-corner Santa Claus—into a bizarre satire on greed, racism and inhumanity. Reed chides the U.S. of the 1980s as a mindless, grasping two-year-old, an infant-giant draining the world of resources, hope, and compassion, hiding behind a phony costume of charity and concern. *The Terrible Threes* updates the sociopolitical allegory to summarize the hedonism, egocentricity, and fatuous self-satisfaction of the Reagan years. It focuses on the impact of TV evangelism, TV political advertising, paranoid militarism, and the all-pervasive role of sales pitches in contemporary America.

With *Reckless Eyeballing,* Reed returns to the elaborate mythology of racism in the idea of ''reckless eyeballing'' (i.e., ogling of white women by black men) as a ''crime.'' In his usual high-energy mix of history, folkore, contemporary observation and mythopoeic imagination, Reed investigates the way sexual mores and folklore have colluded with political expediency to stifle U.S. culture.

Reed's brilliant comic vision of American history brings together the basic ingredients of black culture in a rich musical-dramatic form. His expansion of language into a radically personal style points to the richness of that culture as a storytelling source. Reed's wide interests in traditions outside the received mainstream of ''Western Culture'' courses, in magic, myth, and ritual, make him one of the most forceful and persuasive novelists of the past twenty years.

—William J. Schafer

REID, Desmond

See MOORCOCK, Michael

RENDELL, Ruth (Barbara)

Pseudonym: Barbara Vine. **Nationality:** British. **Born:** Ruth Barbara Grasemann, London, 17 February 1930. **Education:** Loughton High School, Essex. **Family:** Married Donald Rendell in 1950 (divorced 1975); remarried in 1977; one son. **Career:** Reporter and sub-editor, *Express* and *Independent* newspapers, West Essex, 1948–52. **Awards:** Mystery Writers of America Edgar Allan Poe award, for short story, 1975, 1984; Crime Writers Association Silver Dagger award, 1984, and Gold Dagger award, 1976, 1986, 1987; Arts Council National Book award, 1981; Arts Council bursary, 1981; Popular Culture Association award, 1983; Sunday *Times* award for Literary Excellence, 1990. **Agent:** Peters Fraser and Dunlop, 503–504 The Chambers, Chelsea Harbour, Lots Road, London SW10 0XF. **Address:** Nussteads, Polstead, Colchester, Essex CO6 5DN, England.

PUBLICATIONS

Novels

From Doon with Death. London, Hutchinson, 1964; New York, Doubleday, 1965.

To Fear a Painted Devil. London, Long, and New York, Doubleday, 1965.

Vanity Dies Hard. London, Long, 1965; New York, Beagle, 1970; as *In Sickness and in Health,* New York, Doubleday, 1966.

A New Lease of Death. London, Long, and New York, Doubleday, 1967; as *Sins of the Fathers,* New York, Ballantine, 1970.

Wolf to the Slaughter. London, Long, 1967; New York, Doubleday, 1968.

The Secret House of Death. London, Long, 1968; New York, Doubleday, 1969.

The Best Man to Die. London, Long, 1969; New York, Doubleday, 1970.

A Guilty Thing Surprised. London, Hutchinson, and New York, Doubleday, 1970.
No More Dying Then. London, Hutchinson, 1971; New York, Doubleday, 1972.
One Across, Two Down. London, Hutchinson, and New York, Doubleday, 1971.
Murder Being Once Done. London, Hutchinson, and New York, Doubleday, 1972.
Some Lie and Some Die. London, Hutchinson, and New York, Doubleday, 1973.
The Face of Trespass. London, Hutchinson, and New York, Doubleday, 1974.
Shake Hands for Ever. London, Hutchinson, and New York, Doubleday, 1975.
A Demon in My View. London, Hutchinson, 1976; New York, Doubleday, 1977.
A Judgement in Stone. London, Hutchinson, 1977; New York, Doubleday, 1978.
A Sleeping Life. London, Hutchinson, and New York, Doubleday, 1978.
Make Death Love Me. London, Hutchinson, and New York, Doubleday, 1979.
The Lake of Darkness. London, Hutchinson, and New York, Doubleday, 1980.
Put On by Cunning. London, Hutchinson, 1981; as *Death Notes,* New York, Pantheon, 1981.
Master of the Moor. London, Hutchinson, and New York, Pantheon, 1982.
The Speaker of Mandarin. London, Hutchinson, and New York, Pantheon, 1983.
The Killing Doll. London, Hutchinson, and New York, Pantheon, 1984.
The Tree of Hands. London, Hutchinson, 1984; New York, Pantheon, 1985.
An Unkindness of Ravens. London, Hutchinson, and New York, Pantheon, 1985.
Live Flesh. London, Hutchinson, and New York, Pantheon, 1986.
A Warning to the Curious. London, Hutchinson, 1987.
Heartstones. London, Hutchinson, and New York, Harper, 1987.
Talking to Strange Men. London, Hutchinson, and New York, Harper, 1987.
Wexford: An Omnibus. London, Hutchinson, 1988.
The Veiled One. London, Hutchinson, and New York, Pantheon, 1988.
The Bridesmaid. London, Hutchinson, and New York, Mysterious Press, 1989.
The Fourth Wexford Omnibus. London, Hutchinson, 1990.
Going Wrong. London, Hutchinson, and New York, Mysterious Press, 1990.
The Fifth Wexford Omnibus. London, Hutchinson, 1991.
Kissing the Gunner's Daughter. London, Hutchinson, and New York, Mysterious Press, 1992.
The Crocodile Bird. London, Hutchinson, and New York, Crown, 1993.
Inspector Wexford. London, Cresset, 1993.
Simisola. London, Hutchinson, 1994.
The Keys to the Street. New York, Crown Publishers, 1996.
Road Rage. New York, Crown Publishers, 1997.
A Sight for Sore Eyes. New York, Crown, 1999.
Harm Done. New York, Crown, 1999.

Novels as Barbara Vine

The Dark-Adapted Eye. London, Viking, and New York, Bantam, 1986.
A Fatal Inversion. London, Viking, and New York, Bantam, 1987.
The House of Stairs. London, Viking, and New York, Crown, 1989.
Gallowglass. London, Viking, and New York, Crown, 1990.
King Solomon's Carpet. London, Viking, 1991.
Asta's Book. London, Viking, 1993.
No Night Is Too Long. London, Viking, 1994.

Short Stories

The Fallen Curtain and Other Stories. London, Hutchinson, and New York, Doubleday, 1976.
Means of Evil and Other Stories. London, Hutchinson, 1979; New York, Doubleday, 1980.
The Fever Tree and Other Stories. London, Hutchinson, and New York, Pantheon, 1982.
The New Girl Friend. London, Hutchinson, 1985; New York, Pantheon, 1986.
Collected Short Stories. London, Hutchinson, 1987; New York, Pantheon, 1988.
The Strawberry Tree (with *Flesh and Grass* by Helen Simpson). London, Pandora Press, 1990.
The Copper Peacock and Other Stories. London, Hutchinson, and New York, Mysterious Press, 1991.
Blood Lines: Long and Short Stories. New York, Crown Publishers, 1996.

Other

Ruth Rendell's Suffolk, photographs by Paul Bowden. London, Muller, 1989.
Editor, *A Warning to the Curious: The Ghost Stories of M.R. James.* London, Century Hutchinson, 1987; Boston, Godine, 1989.
Editor, with Colin Ward, *Undermining the Central Line.* London, Chatto and Windus, 1989.

*

Critical Studies: *From Agatha Christie to Ruth Rendell* by Susan Rowland, New York, St. Martin's Press, 2000.

* * *

In the thirty-plus years that have followed the publication of her debut ''Wexford'' novel *From Doon with Death* in 1964, Ruth Rendell has been writing fiction of a uniquely impressive kind. Incredibly prolific, with some fifty titles to her name, her work rate is more than matched by the high quality of her writing, and her novels and stories have secured her numerous awards while winning favor with readers and critics alike. Most of her books fall under the general heading of murder mystery or detective fiction, but to pigeon-hole her as a ''genre'' writer is to do both author and potential readers a disservice. In a real sense Rendell has created her own category, operating with great success on three fictional fronts—the ''Inspector Wexford'' detective series, the stand-alone novels produced under her own name and those written as Barbara Vine. Any one of these formidable streams of fiction would be enough to build her a lasting reputation; taken together, they put her in a class of her own.

Rendell's work is distinguished by strong characterization, assured plotting, compelling atmosphere and deep psychological insights. Her knowledge—of trees and plants and their properties, of Mozart opera, of literature and especially of human psychology—staggers with its range, while at the same time avoiding intrusiveness. *The Face of Trespass* for most of its length reads like a mainstream novel, Graham Lanceton's despised woodland retreat and curtailed love affair evoked with supreme skill, and one is almost one-third of the way through before the possibility of murder rears its head. Whatever else this may be, it certainly isn't ''genre fiction.'' Similar qualities distinguish *A Demon in My View* and *A Judgement in Stone,* where the author examines the thoughts and actions of two psychopathic killers. Rendell's sardonic humor is present throughout her writing, and vulgar or tasteless characters often suffer severely at her hands, but in *A Demon in My View* a more sensitive treatment is afforded to the strangler Arthur Johnson. Through his recollections she fits together the terrible blend of nature and nurture that has made him what he is, the vicious murderer hidden by a façade of neat dress and prim, austere behavior. A black humor surfaces with the arrival of fellow lodger and namesake Anthony Johnson, a student of psychology who scans texts on psychopathic personalities while a real-life killer walks the floor above him. Unlike Anthony Johnson, Rendell defines Arthur in human terms, and while one feels horror at his murderous acts it is possible to have a grudging sympathy for a man doomed to destruction by his own compulsive urges. Kindred personalities appear in several later novels, a murderous father and son ''tradition'' established in *The Master of the Moor,* while in *A Sight for Sore Eyes* a lethal partnership is formed by two individuals damaged in childhood. In *A Judgement in Stone* Eunice Parchman, starved of love as a child and cut off from the rest of the world by her inability to read and write, takes center stage. Eunice is harder to identify with, her evident lack of feeling defying any understanding of her as a person, but both she and her crazed ally Joan Smith are brought to fearful life on the page.

The series of novels and stories featuring Chief Inspector Wexford have proved enormously popular, and have been successfully screened on U.K. television with George Baker in the starring role. More conventionally ''detective fiction'' than her other works, their quality and individuality resists easy pigeon-holing. Like all her writing they are notable for superb plotlines, excellent atmosphere and memorable characters, not least Wexford and his ''Watson'' figure Inspector Mike Burden. The pair are marvelous foils for each other, the large, sometimes irascible Wexford whose painstaking deductions are allied to intuitive hunches striking sparks from his decent but stiff, by-the-book subordinate. This rapport enables their author to show Burden expounding one mistaken theory while babysitting his young son, and the unforgettable scene in ''Means of Evil'' where the straitlaced inspector cooks and serves Wexford shaggy-cap mushrooms and whisky in a vain attempt to solve a poisoning case. Once again Rendell impresses by her humanity, the ability to present her detectives and their families as people in their own right. The reader grieves with Burden over the death of his wife and shares his joy in a happy second marriage. When Wexford's wife Dora is kidnapped during a protest over an environmentally-damaging bypass in *Road Rage,* or his daughter Sylvia enters a refuge for battered wives in *Harm Done,* their trauma and that of their loved ones involves the reader with them. While the Wexford novels may not inhabit the deeper darkness that pervades Rendell's other writings, they nevertheless reflect the increasingly grim nature of modern society. Such topics as aggressive feminism (*An Unkindness of Ravens*), drugs, mass murder, and the blight of AIDs (*Kissing the Gunner's Daughter*), pedophilia, and lynch law (*Harm Done*) and the vulnerable lives of immigrant workers (*Simisola*) are brought into the weave of her novels and given thoughtful consideration without preaching or disturbing the movement of the plot. Here, as elsewhere in her work, she examines the formative experiences of her criminals, the often harmful effects of upbringing and chance encounters that lead to violence and murder.

Away from the Wexford canon, one is made aware of a potent, oppressive atmosphere of darkness and doom in which Rendell's characters find themselves trapped without hope of rescue. This atmosphere, evident in *A Demon in My View,* is equally apparent in the recent *A Sight for Sore Eyes.* Here Rendell explores through the warped mind of murderer Teddy Brex the poisonous results of parental love withheld. Denied true affection like Arthur and Eunice before him, Teddy shuns the world's ugliness to form a lethal alliance with his damaged soul-mate Francine, herself orphaned by murder. The horrors that follow are achieved with supreme skill, suspense and tension heightened to the final terrifying climax. As Barbara Vine, Rendell studies the effect of chance and circumstance on what we would regard as normal lives, the reaction of characters to sudden stresses and discoveries that lead to obsession and violence. In *A Fatal Inversion* the weak, easy-going Adam Verne-Smith attempts to set up a commune at the country house he has inherited in the summer of 1976, but his efforts come to grief when the runaway Zosie breaks into the charmed circle. Rendell studies the impact of the attractive, disturbed Zosie on the group, the plot moving with ever-rising tension to a brutal culmination. The aftermath, where years later the survivors are forced to confront past events, shows her at her most subtle and accomplished. In *No Night is Too Long* the study of three characters caught in a destructive triangular relationship is equaled by the author's description of the bleak Alaskan landscape. *The Chimney Sweeper's Boy* begins with the death of a respected author, whose daughter decides to write her own memoir of him only to discover that her father invented his past and was not the person he claimed to be. A powerful, disturbing narrative that uncovers those dark secrets so familiar to Rendell's readers, it shows the author at the height of her powers and set to continue her well-deserved success into the 21st century.

—Geoff Sadler

RICE, Anne

Pseudonyms: Anne Rampling; A.N. Roquelaure. **Nationality:** American. **Born:** Howard Allen O'Brien, New Orleans, Louisiana, 4 October 1941; name changed to Anne c.1947. **Education:** Texas Women's University, Denton, Texas, 1959–60; San Francisco State College (now University), California, B.A. 1964, M.A. 1971; graduate study at University of California, Berkeley, 1969–70. **Family:** Married Stan Rice in 1961; one daughter (deceased), and one son. **Career:** Has held a variety of jobs, including waitress, cook, theater usherette, and insurance claims examiner. Currently, a full-time writer. **Awards:** Joseph Henry Jackson award, honorable mention, 1970. **Address:** 1239 First St., New Orleans, Louisiana 70130, U.S.A.

Publications

Novels

The Feast of All Saints. New York, Simon and Schuster, 1980; Harmondsworth, Penguin, 1982.
Cry to Heaven. New York, Knopf, 1982; London, Chatto and Windus, 1990.
The Mummy: or Ramses the Damned. New York, Ballantine, and London, Chatto and Windus, 1989.
Vampire Chronicles:
Interview with the Vampire. New York, Knopf, and London, Raven, 1976.
The Vampire Lestat. New York, Ballantine, and London, Macdonald, 1985.
The Queen of the Damned. New York, Knopf, 1988; London, Macdonald, 1989.
The Vampire Armand. New York, Knopf, 1998.
The Witching Hour. New York, Knopf, 1990; London, Chatto and Windus, 1991.
The Tale of the Body Thief. New York, Knopf, and London, Chatto and Windus, 1992.
Lasher. New York, Knopf, and London, Chatto and Windus, 1993.
Taltos: Lives of the Mayfair Witches. New York, Knopf, and London, Chatto and Windus, 1994.
Memnoch the Devil. New York, Knopf, 1995.
Servant of the Bones. New York, Knopf, 1996.
Violin. New York, Alfred A. Knopf, 1997.
Pandora: New Tales of the Vampires. New York, Knopf, 1998.
Vittorio, the Vampire: New Tales of the Vampires. New York, Knopf, 1999.
Merrick. New York, Knopf, 2000.

Novels as Anne Rampling

Exit to Eden. New York, Arbor House, and London, Futura, 1985.
Belinda. New York, Arbor House, 1986; London, Macdonald, 1987.

Novels as A.N. Roquelaure

The Sleeping Beauty Trilogy. New York, New American Library/Dutton, 1999.
The Claiming of Sleeping Beauty. New York, Dutton, and London, Macdonald, 1983.
Beauty's Punishment. New York, Dutton, 1984.
Beauty's Release. New York, Dutton, 1985; London, Warner, 1994.

Plays

Screenplays: *Interview with the Vampire—the Vampire Chronicles.* Geffen Pictures, Warner Brothers, 1994.

Other

Conversations with Anne Rice, edited by Michael Riley. New York, Ballantine Books, 1996.
The Anne Rice Reader, edited by Katherine Ramsland. New York, Ballantine Books, 1997.

*

Critical Studies: *Prism of the Night: A Biography of Anne Rice* by Katherine M. Ramsland, New York, Dutton, 1991; *Anne Rice* by Bette B. Roberts, New York, Twayne, and Oxford, Maxwell Macmillan, 1994; *The Witches' Companion: The Official Guide to Anne Rice's Lives of the Mayfair Witches* by Katherine Ramsland, written in Cooperation with Anne Rice, New York, Ballantine Books, 1994; *Haunted City: An Unauthorized Guide to the Magical, Magnificent New Orleans of Anne Rice* by Joy Dickinson, Secaucus, New Jersey, Carol Publishing Group, 1995; *The Roquelaure Reader: A Companion To Anne Rice's Erotica* by Katherine Ramsland, New York, Plume, 1996; *The Unauthorized Anne Rice Companion,* edited by George Beahm, Kansas City, Missouri, Andrews and McMeel, 1996; *Writing Horror and the Body: The Fiction of Stephen King, Clive Barker, and Anne Rice* by Linda Badley, Westport, Connecticut, Greenwood Press, 1996; *Anne Rice: A Critical Companion* by Jennifer Smith, Westport, Connecticut, Greenwood Press, 1996; *The Gothic World of Anne Rice,* edited by Gary Hoppenstand and Ray B. Browne, Bowling Green, Ohio, Bowling Green State University Popular Press, 1996; *In the Shadow of the Vampire: Reflections from the World of Anne Rice* by Jana Marcus, New York, Thunder's Mouth Press, 1997.

* * *

Anne Rice has achieved considerable success with her imaginative forays into the occult, especially the lore of vampires and witches, the focal concerns of her two major sagas. In these books, Rice spins complex tales that weave through both time and space and the minds of her characters in intricate patterns that make her works fascinating. Rice combines literary genres and styles, meshing Romantic plots with erotic and pornographic imagery; gothic settings with ''glittering'' modern cities; and grotesque horror with abstract philosophical thought. Thus, Rice's stories of fantastic beings and supernatural phenomena reach beyond the traditional formulaic limitations of ''horror'' novels and delve into universal human themes such as the conflict between good and evil, the twentieth-century loss of faith in God and sense of isolation, the search for human identity and self-awareness, the longing for family ties and community, the fear of death and the human desire for love, power, and immortality.

Rice, in typical late twentieth-century fashion, gives voice to the marginal members of society, reveals the decline in religion and the family, and questions the modern values of rationalism, order, and science espoused in earlier vampire novels such as Bram Stoker's *Dracula* (1897). Rice's vampires experience crises of confidence and identity, as well as increased senses of loss and loneliness. These so-called ''monsters (or children) of the night'' are conflicted, sympathetic characters with whom we can identify. Plot-dilating passages of introverted and tormented inner questing blanket external action, as in Louis's confessional in *Interview with the Vampire,* the first of the author's popular Vampire Chronicles. Like many of Rice's succeeding works, it is a lengthy and intricate odyssey of self-discovery rather than a chronicle of sharply delineated action.

As in many modern texts of the twentieth century, Rice's heroes are, in fact, anti-heroes. In particular, Rice's vampires have lost many of the evil, monstrous qualities that characterize ''old-world'' vampires such as Dracula and, instead, represent more modern, existential beings who blur the line between good and evil. By telling the Vampire Chronicles from the vampire's point of view, Rice shifts the voice of the ''minority'' to the center of her story and makes it nearly impossible for us not to identify with vampires such as Louis, Lestat, and Armand. Rice uses her beautiful, desirable vampires to expose and reveal human evil in the world. In her novels, Rice blurs the lines between human and monster, questioning our natures and our so-called certainties.

Rice's vampires live, interact, and even fall in love with human characters, as in *The Vampire Armand* (Rice's latest addition to the Vampire Chronicles), in which Armand loves and protects two children, Benji and Sybelle. Vampires such as Lestat, Louis, Marius, and Armand live in modern cities, they attend operas and plays, appreciate, and even create, music, art, and literature. Lestat, in *The Vampire Lestat,* becomes a rock musician, Marius is an artist when he first meets Armand, and Armand opens and manages the ''Théâtre des Vampires'' in Paris. Rice's vampires are, on many levels, modern consumers and producers, they are very much in our midst and also somewhat heroic.

Not only are Rice's vampires physically attractive, but they are also younger, well-dressed, witty, and evoke our sympathies by speaking directly to us. Hence, Rice indicates that the threat to human life comes from within and is an integral, intimate element of the societies being depicted in her novels. Rice places gothic crypts, coffins, sinister houses, and a ''Théâtre des Vampires'' in the midst of modernity, indicating that our ''darker sides'' dwell within us and cannot be destroyed by the forces of science and rationalism. In all her novels, Rice prompts an exploration of these dark, irrational, ''forbidden'' forces and desires.

The narrative paths in Rice's novels are sometimes difficult to follow. They often evolve as narratives within narratives. For example, in *The Queen of the Damned,* the third vampire book, the plot weaves through the impressions of many characters. In this novel, Rice once again blurs the boundaries between good and evil, demonstrating how Akasha's goal of a peaceful world is warped into an evil, ritualistic bloodbath as she attempts to decimate the male population so that women may hold ultimate power in the world. As Lestat's coven converges and the history of Akasha the Queen unfolds, the reader is taken back and forth from the modern world to the dark recesses of pre-Egyptian antiquity. Lestat is merely the nominal narrator, who both introduces the story and ends its telling from a contemporary vantage point. In between, the story evolves through a series of ever-shifting narrative perspectives.

Rice's elaborate plots, however, enable her to comment through her immortal vampires and lingering ghosts on the impact of centuries-old historical developments and ancient cultures and religions. *Violin,* one of Rice's recent ghost novels, moves from nineteenth-century Vienna to modern New Orleans to Rio de Janeiro. In this novel, Rice renders a passionate, romantic telling of her love of music through the lives of three dangerous, seductive, and brilliant characters.

While most of Rice's novels are in some way historical, Rice has written two novels which fall under the genre of historical novel: *Cry to Heaven,* about castrati opera singers in eighteenth-century Italy, and *The Feast of All Saints,* about the ''Free People of Color'' in Louisiana before the Civil War. In *Cry to Heaven,* which may be her best work fashioned outside her sagas, Rice reveals her considerable range in subject matter, but in using a castrato hero, Tonio, and his teacher-mentor-lover, Guido, she does not stray from the themes that underlie all her more serious fiction. The lonely outcast's quest for an acceptable identity is the epicenter of most of her novels.

The Tale of the Body Thief, Rice's fourth book in the Vampire Chronicles, brings themes of human desire for immortality and human craving for power to the fore. Lestat, who nearly dies when he exchanges bodies with a human, realizes that his identity (or soul) has become inextricably linked to his immortal body and despite his initial desires to experience mortality, Lestat prefers to retain his immortality and supernatural powers. Not only does Lestat regain his body, but he then transforms his friend, David Talbot, into a vampire against his will—playing Mephistopheles to David Talbot's protesting Faust.

Rice's novels reveal a preoccupation with Christian ritual and codes. The vampiric act of drinking blood is often couched in imagery of the communion. In *Memnoch the Devil,* Rice's fifth Vampire Chronicle, Lestat journeys to Heaven and Hell, meets God and the Devil, witnesses Jesus's crucifixion, and even drinks Jesus's blood. In this book, as in her others, Rice prompts us to contemplate our very conceptions of Good and Evil. In *The Vampire Armand,* Armand—an icon painter in his youth—recommences Louis's and Lestat's search for God and their interrogation of religious faith and revelation.

A reader who is unsympathetic to Rice's convoluted plots, androgynous protagonists, gender-bending ideas, elaborate myth making, and the rhapsodic but cloying self-consciousness of her principal characters, can easily lose the direction of her narratives and grow impatient with her style. She is a prolix and at times very turgid writer. Yet her strengths lie precisely in that baroque style—in her sensual verbal panoply, her lush and exotic detail, her constant reference to the physicalness of her characters and their self-indulgent, fugitive, ''savage-garden'' existence.

As *The Mummy: or Ramses the Damned* reveals, without those full phantasmagoric trappings and inner focus, Rice's plots exploiting the occult may seem merely incredible, even faintly absurd. In that novel, intended or not, whimsy tempers credibility when Ramses the Damned and Cleopatra both quicken from the long dead into, respectively, an Edwardian gentleman and a roadster-driving, murderous nymphomaniac—all in the matter of a few hours. That is the stuff of a B-grade horror movie, from which the plot partially sprang.

Rice exploits the sensational without apology, whether eroticism, as in the novels written under her two pseudonyms, Anne Rampling and A.N. Roquelaure, or the occult, as in her two sagas. The exchange of blood is most often erotic in Rice's novels, and incestuous and homoerotic relationships are commonplace. Rice's Sleeping Beauty trilogy, published under the name A.N. Roquelaure, has been described as explicit sadomasochistic pornography. In these novels, Rice re-imagines Sleeping Beauty as a woman awakened and trained by her Prince and his mother (the Queen) in the sadomasochistic traditions of the land. The princess Beauty's training as a love-slave involves sexual degradation and abuse. Similarly, in *Exit to Eden,* published under the name Rampling, dominatrix Lisa works as a trainer at an exclusive resort where people engage in sadomasochistic fantasies. Finally, *Belinda,* also published under Rampling, is an erotic romance in which Belinda, a 16-year-old runaway, has an affair with Jeremy Walker, a 44-year-old artist. Jeremy risks his career and reputation in order to paint Belinda nude. Jeremy, who ventures into the realm of erotic art and succeeds, can be regarded as representative of Rice's own artistic foray into the realm of erotic and pornographic subject matter.

In fact, eroticism pervades all Rice's work, even in her novels focusing on androgynous characters, as in *Interview with the Vampire* and *The Vampire Lestat,* where it is either transmuted or barely suppressed. There it takes the form of homoeroticism and thinly veiled incest and pedophilia. In her vampire novels, Rice collapses gender boundaries and foregrounds homosexuality. Vampires, traditionally representatives of ''deviant'' or taboo sexuality are desirable and heroic in Rice's works, and thus convey a positive reading of homosexuality. In an age when minority issues and concerns have gained widespread attention, Rice's sympathetic portrayal of the homoerotic vampire has been readily popularized.

Even Rice's heterosexual, non-androgynous characters, are either sexually offbeat, caught up in the sadomasochistic bondage exploited in *Exit to Eden,* for example, or guilt ridden by taboos, as in her study of the Louisiana Creole culture in *The Feast of All Saints.* In the occult books, the erotic is often bound to the ubiquitous blood and flesh-tearing images. Yet, despite the author's gruesome images, horror and a sense of terror both seem oddly muted in her novels. There are lurid details, but none are very memorable, except, perhaps, the distinctly grotesque, as, when, for example, Maharet devours her own eyes in *The Queen of the Damned* or Cleopatra, in *The Mummy,* tries to disguise her gaping wounds as she searches for sexual prey.

Rice's novels are not simply about supernatural phenomena and fantastic creatures, but incorporate a wide range of social issues and themes. For example, in both the *Vampire* and *Witch Chronicles*, Rice explores issues of family unity and domesticity. In *Interview,* Louis, Lestat, and Claudia form the epitome of a dysfunctional vampire family and are ultimately, tragically, destroyed. In ''The Lives of the Mayfair Witches,'' Rice chronicles the Mayfair family history over thirteen generations, depicting a history of family trauma, unity, and division—as well as corruption and incest. Each Mayfair generation contains a witch who inherits the Mayfair fortune, mansion, and the company of the family demon, Lasher. Through the character of the thirteenth-generation witch, Rowan Mayfair, Rice conveys the importance of family ties. Rice uses details from her own life, home, and background to construct many of her settings and characters as, for example, in *The Witching Hour,* Michael Curry possesses much of Rice's own family background and the Mayfair family mansion is modeled after Rice's own home in the New Orleans Garden District.

Clearly, Rice, like Mary Shelley in *Frankenstein,* is less interested in chilling effects than in the minds of her dark, lost-soul characters and her evolving myths and themes. She is concerned with human liberation, sexual and otherwise, with human emotions ravaged by conflicting needs and with her recurring themes of nurturing and self-reconciliation in her pariah and androgynous protagonists. It is these elements, and not the supernatural, that give her novels their dense texture. While Rice has received mixed critical reception for her novels' convoluted plots and violent sexual imagery, popular support for her writing has been overwhelming. Readers revel in Rice's detailed histories, intricate settings, and sensual, conflicted characters, thus sustaining the author's considerable success and popularity.

—John W. Fiero, updated by Janna Nadler

RICHARDS, David

Nationality: Canadian. **Born:** Newcastle, New Brunswick, 17 October 1950. **Education:** Attended St. Thomas University. **Family:** Married Margaret McIntyre in 1971. **Awards:** Norma Epstein First Prize for Undergraduate Creative Writing, 1974; silver medal (Atlantic chapter of the Royal Society of the Arts), 1986–87; Governor General's award for fiction, 1988; Canadian Authors' Association award, 1991; Canada-Australia Writer's prize, 1993; Best Scriptwriter, New York International Film Festival, 1996. **Agent:** c/o McClelland and Stewart, 481 University Avenue, Suite 900, Toronto, Ontario M5G 2E9, Canada. **Address:** 376 King George Highway, Newcastle, New Brunswick, Canada.

Publications

Novels

The Coming of Winter. Ottawa, Oberon Press, 1974.
Blood Ties. Ottawa, Oberon Press, 1976.
Lives of Short Duration. Ottawa, Oberon Press, 1981.
Road to the Stilt House. Ottawa, Oberon Press, 1985.
Nights below Station Street. Toronto, McClelland & Stewart, 1987.
Evening Snow Will Bring Such Peace. Toronto, McClelland & Stewart, 1991.
For Those Who Hunt the Wounded Down. Toronto, McClelland & Stewart, 1993.
Hope in the Desperate House. Toronto, McClelland & Stewart, 1996.
The Bay of Love and Sorrows. Toronto, McClelland & Stewart, 1998.

Short Stories

Dancers at Night. Ottawa, Oberon Press, 1978.

Poetry

Small Heroics. New Brunswick Chap Books, 1973.

Other

A Lad from Brantford and Other Essays. Fredericton, Canada, Broken Jaw Press, 1995.
Lines on the Water: A Fisherman's Life on the Miramichi. Toronto, Doubleday Canada, 1998.

* * *

Since the publication of his earliest novels, *The Coming of Winter* and *Blood Ties*, David Adams Richards has emerged as one of the most distinct and powerfully human voices in contemporary Canadian fiction. Writing in a economical but rhythmic prose that captures effectively both the cadence and the suffocating reticence of his characters, Richards works toward hyper-realistic portrayals of the working-class communities scattered along New Brunswick's Miramichi River. Immediately accessible as independent works of fiction, these are also richly allusive novels that weave carefully rendered details, repetitions of image and language, and recurring characters into patterns that extend across the body of Richards's work. As he shows most eloquently in *Lives of Short Duration*, an intricately structured multigenerational novel focusing on the struggles and successes of the Packet family, these are stories that speak of a place and culture in which history runs deep, of towns in which the lives that have unfolded in the past continue to haunt those in the present.

In *For Those Who Hunt the Wounded Down*, perhaps the most accomplished of his novels (and one that the author himself adapted for film), Richards returns again to the Miramichi in order to complete the trilogy he began in 1988 with *Nights Below Station Street*, which won the Governor General's award for fiction, and continued with the story of the Basterache family in *Evening Snow Will Bring Such*

Peace. Set in the fall of 1989, *For Those Who Hunt the Wounded Down* recounts the final three months in the life of Jerry Bines, a character Richards first introduced in his 1985 novel, *Road to the Stilt House*. Now twenty-six years old, recently acquitted of murder, and separated from his deeply religious wife, Bines is back on the river, bringing with him an ominous potential for violence. As his cousin Adele comments uneasily after learning of his sudden reappearance in town: ''Something is going on—it's time on this river for something to happen once again.''

Gathered loosely around the oral history related to a nine-year-old boy, the tales of Bines's troubled past accumulate gradually in the novel, often being told and retold from a number of perspectives and through a variety of story-telling forms and chronological dislocations. As in most of Richards's novels, hunting-camp gossip, fragmented police reports, interviews, third-person recollections of first meetings, and memorable encounters continue to add layers to the myths that have built up around the life of the central characters: stories of a young Bines taken down to the old ice rink by a hobbled, mentally unbalanced father where he would fight with older boys so that his father might win a quart of wine; stories of hunting prowess, double-crosses and prison breaks, and crimes approved, committed, or planned, are all essential and oft-repeated parts of river lore.

Moving away from the tightly controlled, third-person narration that propelled the previous two books of the trilogy towards their dramatic conclusions, Richards turns to a multi-voiced structure for this novel, a decision that allows him to blend masterfully Bines's story with those of the people around him. Most prominent among these is the story of Adele Walsh. Sixteen and pregnant at the end of the first book of the trilogy, she is now married to Ralphie Pillar, who, despite his wife's warnings, is becoming enthralled with the power that lies behind Bines's infectious smile. Unable to forgive Bines for his involvement in the theft of a tractor-trailer three years earlier, Adele is nonetheless forced to confront the loyalty that she still feels towards him, a closeness grounded in a relationship that stretches across more than two decades.

It is the almost palpable tension between the violent power and vulnerability of men like Bines, John Delano (*The Coming of Winter*), and Packet Terri (*Lives of Short Duration*), that remains at the heart of the most effective of Richards's fiction. Writing against cultural stereotypes, he shuns the one dimensional in favor of poignant portraits of enigmatic men standing alone in a world that does not understand them, of men who frequently square themselves to enter into battles in which their daunting physical powers will be rendered all but useless. Like the alcoholism that haunts Joe Walsh in *Nights Below Station Street* or the river gossip that follows young Ivan Basterache to his grave, the pain of Bines's past cannot be beaten down with fists or tracked and killed in the woods of the river valley. It inevitably resurfaces to entangle and frustrate any attempts to move forward in the present, to find redemption within a culture all too willing to sacrifice them to any number of causes, and to find peace in a community that coincidentally fears and respects them.

Remaining outsiders capable of acts of disturbing and devastating violence, Richards's characters are never excluded from reaching out in spontaneous acts of tenderness and generosity. Nor are these totally grim lives emptied of all moments of humor. When asked how he feels after being caught in a self-detonated explosion that totally destroys his hunting camp, Bines, for example, delivers his answer with almost impeccable comic timing: ''None too pleased about it.''

Critics and reviewers have been less kind to Richards's later novels, *Hope in the Desperate Hour* and *The Bay of Love and Sorrows*. Although less astute criticisms (of Richards's determined emphasis on social realism in a postmodern world or of the limited appeal of his regional voice) can be easily countered, these later novels do suffer in comparison with the more consistent earlier works. In the later books, Richards's once-subtle treatment of the familiar themes of isolation, failed ambitions, false hopes, betrayal, and violence have been replaced, in part, by heavy-handed attacks on various social institutions (notably, the academy and popular media) and what he renders, inevitably, as a self-satisfied and often self-serving liberal middle class. Despite recent and not undeserved reservations, however, Richards's novels remain essential reading in a society becoming increasingly polarized along lines of faith, economic disparity, and political dogma. Invested with a passion and acuity that strip away false fronts of ideological or moral smugness, these are books that ask readers to think again about the dignity and spirit of people far removed from the urban centers, suburban sprawls, and picturesque towns that all too often dominate images of the contemporary world. These are not bleak stories, but stories that allow readers to shake hands with men like Jerry Bines, to look into their eyes and come away feeling a little uncomfortable, both with what we see and the lens through which we see it.

—Klay Dyer

RICHLER, Mordecai

Nationality: Canadian. **Born:** Montreal, 27 January 1931. **Education:** Attended Sir George Williams University, 1949–51. **Family:** Married Florence Wood in 1960; three sons, two daughters. **Career:** Freelance writer in Paris, France, 1952–53, London, England, 1954–72, and Montreal, 1972—; writer-in-residence, Sir George Williams University, 1968–69; visiting professor of English, Carleton University, 1972–74; member of editorial board, Book-of-the-Month Club, 1972—. **Awards:** President's medal for nonfiction (University of Western Ontario), 1959; *Paris Review* humor prize, 1967; Governor-General's literary award (Canada Council), 1968, 1971; *London Jewish Chronicle* literature award, 1972; Berlin Film Festival Golden Bear, 1974; Screenwriters Guild of America award, 1974; ACTRA Award for best television writer—drama (Academy of Canadian Cinema and Television), 1975; Book of the Year for Children award (Canadian Library Association), 1976; Ruth Schwartz Children's Book award, (Ontario Arts Council), 1976; *London Jewish Chronicle* H. H. Wingate award for fiction, 1981; Commonwealth Writers prize (Book Trust), 1990; Giller award, 1997; Stephen Leacock Award for Humor, 1998. **Agent:** Lynn Nesbit, International Creative Management, 40 West 57th Street, New York, New York 10019, U.S.A. **Address:** 1321 Sherbrooke Street West, Apartment 80C, Montreal, Quebec, Canada H3G 1J4.

PUBLICATIONS

Novels

The Acrobats. New York, Putnam, 1954; published as *Wicked We Love*. New York, Popular Library, 1955.
Son of a Smaller Hero, Toronto, Collins, 1955.
A Choice of Enemies. Toronto, Collins, 1957.
The Apprenticeship of Duddy Kravitz. Boston, Little, Brown, 1959.

The Incompatible Atuk. Toronto, McClelland & Stewart, 1963; published as *Stick Your Neck Out.* New York, Simon & Schuster, 1963.
Cocksure. New York, Simon & Schuster, 1968.
St. Urbain's Horseman. New York, Knopf, 1971.
Joshua Then and Now. New York, Knopf, 1980.
Solomon Gursky Was Here. New York, Viking, 1989.
Barney's Version. New York, Knopf, 1997.

Fiction (for children)

Jacob Two-Two Meets the Hooded Fang, illustrated by Fritz Wegner. New York, Knopf, 1975.
Jacob Two-Two and the Dinosaur, illustrated by Norman Eyolfson. New York, Knopf, 1987.
Jacob Two-Two's First Spy Case, illustrated by Michael Chesworth. New York, Farrar, Straus, 1997.

Short Stories

The Street: Stories. Toronto, McClelland & Stewart, 1969.

Plays

Duddy. Edmonton, Alberta, Citadel Theatre, 1984.

Radio Plays: *The Acrobats* (based on his novel of the same title), Toronto, Canadian Broadcasting Corporation (CBC), 1956; *Benny, the War in Europe, and Myerson's Daughter Bella*, Toronto, CBC, 1958; *The Spare Room*, Toronto, CBC, 1961; *Q for Quest* (excerpts from his fiction), Toronto, CBC, 1963; *It's Harder to Be Anybody*, Toronto, CBC, 1965; *Such Was St. Urbain Street*, Toronto, CBC, 1966; *The Wordsmith* (based on a short story), Toronto, CBC, 1979

Screenplays: *No Love for Johnnie* (with Nicholas Phipps), Embassy, 1962; *Tiara Tahiti* (with Geoffrey Cotterell and Ivan Foxwell), Rank, 1962; *The Wild and the Willing* (with Nicholas Phipps), Rank, 1962, released in the United States as *Young and Willing,* Universal, 1965; *Life at the Top*, Royal International, 1965; *The Apprenticeship of Duddy Kravitz,* Paramount, 1974; *Fun with Dick and Jane* (with David Giler and Jerry Belson), Bart/Palevsky, 1977; *Joshua Then and Now* (adapted from his novel of the same title), Twentieth Century-Fox, 1985.

Television Plays: *Friend of the People*, Toronto, CBC, 1957; *Paid in Full*, London, ATV, 1958; *The Trouble with Benny* (based on a short story), London, ABC, 1959; *The Apprenticeship of Duddy Kravitz* (based on his novel of the same title), Toronto, CBC, 1960; *The Fall of Mendel Krick*, London, British Broadcasting Corporation (BBC), 1963.

Other

Hunting Tigers under Glass: Essays and Reports. Toronto, McClelland & Stewart, 1969.
Shoveling Trouble (essays). Toronto, McClelland & Stewart, 1973.
Notes on an Endangered Species and Others (essays). New York, Knopf, 1974.
Creativity and the University (with Andre Fortier and Rollo May). Toronto, York University, 1975.
The Suit (animated filmstrip). National Film Board of Canada, 1976.
Images of Spain (text), photographs by Peter Christopher. New York, Norton, 1977.
The Great Comic Book Heroes and Other Essays. Toronto, McClelland & Stewart, 1978.
Home Sweet Home: My Canadian Album (essays). New York, Knopf, 1984, published as *Home Sweet Home,* New York, Penguin, 1985.
Broadsides: Reviews and Opinions. New York, Viking, 1990.
Oh Canada! Oh Quebec! Requiem for a Divided Country. New York, Knopf, 1992.
The Language of Signs. New York, McKay, 1992.
This Year in Jerusalem. New York, Knopf, 1994.
Belling the Cat: Essays, Reports, and Opinions. Toronto, Knopf Canada, 1998.
Editor, *Canadian Writing Today.* Magnolia, Manitoba, Peter Smith, 1970.
Editor, *The Best of Modern Humor.* New York, Knopf, 1984.
Editor, *Writers on World War II: An Anthology.* New York, Knopf, 1991.
Contributor, *A Climate Changed*, edited by B. W. Powe. New York, Mosaic Press, 1984.
Introduction, *The Innocents Abroad* by Mark Twain. New York, Oxford University Press, 1996.

*

Manuscript Collections: University of Calgary Library, Calgary, Alberta.

Critical Studies: *Literary History of Canada: Canadian Literature in English,* edited by Carl F. Klinck, et al. University of Toronto Press, 1965; *Hunting Tigers Under Glass: Essays and Reports* by Mordecai Richler, Toronto, McClelland & Stewart, 1969; *Mordecai Richler* by George Woodcock, Toronto, McClelland & Stewart, 1970; *Mordecai Richler,* edited by G. David Sheps, New York, McGraw Hill/Ryerson, 1971; *Articulating West* by W. H. New, New Press, 1972; *The Haunted Wilderness: The Gothic and Grotesque in Canadian Fiction* by Margot Northey, University of Toronto Press, 1976; *Mordecai Richler* by Victor J. Ramraj, Boston, Twayne, 1983; *Mordecai Richler* by Arnold E. Davidson, New York, F. Ungar, 1983; *Perspectives on Mordecai Richler,* edited by Michael Darling, Toronto, ECW Press, 1986; *Broadsides: Reviews and Opinions* by Mordecai Richler, New York, Viking, 1990; *Belling the Cat: Essays, Reports, and Opinions* by Mordecai Richler, Toronto, Knopf Canada, 1998.

* * *

In Canada Mordecai Richler is as well known for his acerbic ornery persona and his biting columns on the state of Quebec politics as he is for his numerous popular and critically acclaimed novels. Born to a second-generation Jewish family in Montreal, and raised in the working-class Jewish neighborhood associated with St. Urbain Street, Richler briefly attended Sir George Williams College before relocating to Paris, then England to work as a freelance journalist and scriptwriter. While he did not return to Montreal until 1972, the city and its people nevertheless retained pride of place in his imagination and writing, particularly those who populated his former neighborhood. Many of his novels trace the development of St. Urbain's inhabitants and former inhabitants as they negotiate the later half of the twentieth century facing rising and falling fortunes, shifting politics, the realities of aging, disillusionment, and betrayal. At the center of Richler's writing is usually a protagonist whose lapses in morals or conduct are nevertheless matched by the character's own sense of what is right, and his passionate howls of injustice at the world, even in the face of his own failings. Fiercely moral in his criticisms of the modern world and never afraid to ridicule that which he disdains or disapproves of, Richler's novels are often darkly humorous revelings in, and satirizations of, the less flattering side of human nature.

Richler's first novel, *The Acrobats*, was published to mixed reviews, though most acknowledged its power and intensity. At its center is André Bennett, a Montreal gentile who has fled to Spain to escape the guilt associated with his Jewish girlfriend's accidental death following an abortion gone awry. Carnivalesque in both style and setting, it foregrounds Richler's vicious satire, his flawed self-absorbed characters and their tendency to flee relationships and countries, and his preoccupation with relations between Jews and gentiles. Occurring during the festival of Saint Joseph, earthly father of Christ, the novel also foregrounds Richler's invocation of biblical sub-texts throughout his fiction. His second novel, *Son of a Smaller Hero*, continues these themes with its depiction of Noah Adler's merciless desire to escape the Montreal ghetto of his youth and what he perceives as its sanctimonious hypocrisy and claustrophobic insularity. In a critical dissection of the community he knows so well, Richler exposes the kinds of lies families and communities willfully propagate as a means of concealing their imperfections, insecurities, and petty jealousies. This dissection resulted in his being castigated by some as anti-Semitic, but time has proven that Richler's intensely moral criticism is not limited to a single caste or creed. In his next novel, *A Choice of Enemies*, Richler demonstrated this in his construction of a protagonist, Norman Price, whose latent anti-Semitism is indicative of his inability to discriminate between individuals as such, rather than as representatives of ideas or ideals. In a plot that can only be described as possessing the strained coincidence of Greek tragedies, Price discovers that the man whom he has befriended has not only cuckolded him but also killed his brother in a bar brawl. However, these characters are all revealed to be acting out their preordained fates as determined by their character, just as unable to alter or retrieve past possibilities as they are incapable of altering their essential being. In Richler, God alone is not to blame for this proscriptive fate; modern society is also implicated as morally tenuous and fundamentally unreliable. Brutally unflinching in his depiction of his characters' defects, Richler also characteristically does not ignore their darkly comic possibilities.

Despite the recognition accorded his first three novels, it was not until the 1959 publication of *The Apprenticeship of Duddy Kravitz* that Richler cemented his literary reputation. Both the plot and the irrepressible, morally bankrupt title character are maniacal forces with which to be reckoned. A classic anti-hero, Kravitz sacrifices his childhood to ambition and his personal relationships to commercial greed and exploitation. In Kravitz, Richler created one of his most believable and sustaining characters, a man obsessed with his grandfather's cliché, ''a man without land is nothing.'' The frenetic energy of the novel is sustained by astute characterization, exceptionally well-written dialogue, outrageous yet believable plot turns, and most of all a compelling depiction of place and community in its Montreal setting. It is not, however, enough to say that Montreal is the setting of this novel; as in much of Richler's work the city is a character in its own right.

Richler's next two novels, *The Incomparable Atuk* and *Cocksure*, shared the fast-paced outrageous energy and fantastical plot twists of *Duddy Kravitz* while also critiquing the mores of the modern world. *Atuk* features an Inuit poet whose critical success and popular reception results in his relocation to Toronto, where he exploits his fame and the urban fascination with his ethnic otherness for personal gain. Atuk soon abandons literature, importing relatives from Baffin Bay and setting up a sweatshop for the production of ''authentic'' Inuit sculpture. Rampant capitalism, racism, and greed abound in the world Atuk enters and quickly adopts. Deliciously satirical, *The Incomparable Atuk* caricatures the romantic pretensions of 1960s Canadian nationalism and its attempts to articulate an independent national identity. Still, critics did not warm to *Atuk*, reserving their praise for *Cocksure*, which received Canada's coveted Governor General's award. Set in urban London, England, the novel chronicles the take over of an established publishing firm by a reclusive Howard Hughes-like character via his henchmen. Canadian Mortimer Griffin must cope with the imposition of eccentric policies while surrounded by fantastical plots and people, all of which violate his own understanding of the world. While Griffin provides the moral core of the novel, he is not without flaws, and in his responses to events and individuals reveals the superficiality and hypocrisy of the 1960s sexual liberalism and racial integration that Richler pillories throughout the novel.

Both *Atuk* and *Cocksure* were written during creative breaks from Richler's composition of an ambitious, exceptionally complex work, *St. Urbain's Horseman*, nominated for the Booker prize and recipient of the Governor General's award. Richler not only returns to the Montreal of his childhood in this novel, he revisits aspects of his own life in imagining the internal life of an introspective protagonist, even going so far as to recycle portions of his published reminiscences. However, *St. Urbain's Horseman* is very much the story of Jake Hersh and the past he retreats to as a means of escaping his difficult present, which includes criminal charges of sexual misconduct. Central to Hersh's recollections is his legendary cousin, Joey, whose adventures in the Spanish Civil War and as a Nazi hunter transform him in Hersh's imagination into a personal Horseman who will avenge him. While ostensibly it is Hersh who is on trial, via his imagination he tries and punishes mankind at large for its crimes, ranging from Nazi activities to the trivialization of history. Ultimately he must recognize his image of the elusive Joey and become his own Horseman, yet Richler is clear to demonstrate that vengeance is not an uncomplicated moral act, nor are those who enact it necessarily heroic figures. The similarities between Hersh and the structure and protagonist of Richler's next novel, *Joshua Then and Now*, have not gone unnoted. Structurally dependent upon flashbacks, a technique crucial to Richler's fiction as of *St. Urbain's Horsemen*, the book addresses the toll of time, mortality, and the irretrievability of a past that continues to signify on the present. The Joshua in the title is a version of Jake Hersh ten years later, having returned to Montreal from living abroad. Equally preoccupied with history, its injustices, and the injustices done to historical fact by those seeking to alternately sanitize, mythologize, and popularize versions of it, Joshua seeks meaning in the chaos of history just as he seeks coherence in the tragicomic chaos of his daily life.

After almost a decade without publishing a novel, Richler returned to the forefront with the 1989 publication of surely his most outrageous work to date, *Solomon Gursky Was Here*. A subversive, irreverent send-up of Canadian history and the mythologies communities create about selves—Jewish or goyim—the titular character epitomizes Richler's playful attitude towards the likeable scoundrels and scalawags who populate his fiction. Solomon Gursky is a character by now familiar in Richler's fiction, the elusive figure who may or may not be dead, but whose presence continues to haunt and taunt those left behind. The descendent of another evasive figure, Ephraim Gursky, the lone survivor of the famed nineteenth-century shipwreck of the Erebus, both are equally mythologized by outsiders and themselves, and blur the line between fact and fiction. Richler further complicates this blurring, taking giddy liberties with the history and personalities of an actual Montreal Jewish family whose transformation from ruthless bootleggers to respectable liquor barons parallels that of the Gursky family. Given these entanglements, it is no coincidence that the image of the raven is central to this novel, as both a trickster figure in Canadian First Nations cultures, and a bird that feeds on the flesh of others. At the center of the novel is Moses Berger, who is alone in his understanding of the Gursky history, but unbelieved with his tales of impossible histories and filial and paternal betrayal and cannibalism. Nominated for the Booker prize, *Solomon Gursky* attests to Richler's ability to make improbable plots believable and irascible characters redeemable, all the while pondering the fate of a ''lost generation'' in a fragmentary immoral world.

It is in *Barney's Version*, though, that the ''lost generation'' with which so much of Richler's writing has been concerned assumes its final poignancy. Barney Panofsky, trivialized and misrepresented in the recently published memoirs of a former friend, is motivated to write his own version of his life in a final attempt to set the record straight. A thoroughly unreliable narrator from the beginning, Panofsky's veracity is finally challenged by his mental deterioration due to Alzheimer's. Panofsky progresses from having ''lost'' his purpose as a youth to having finally lost his grasp on his own life and history (if he indeed ever had it) as an adult. The culmination of over forty years of novel writing, *Barney's Version* revisits all of Richler's favorite themes—a now fading Montreal, Jewish-gentile relations, the search for values in a hostile world, generational tensions, biblical subtexts, national identity, elusive truths, mysterious characters, etc.—in a comic, touching, but never maudlin reflection on the life of one man.

Over the past two decades, in between the publications of his novels, Richler has put his chronically cantankerous self to work as a commentator on Quebec politics and the issue of separatism. In a political forum renowned for opinionated cranks, Richler has distinguished himself in his application of his moral vision and satirical tongue to critiquing the ridiculousness of the political situation. Still, in all of his comments, his longstanding love of and investment in Montreal remains evident. Recently, in an attempt to stave off the demise of English-language newspapers, Richler has expressed interest in buying the newspaper in the township where he spends his summer. As an accomplished novelist, writer of memoirs, children's author, and political and cultural commentator, the hat of publisher does not seem out of the realm of possibilities for Richler.

—Jennifer Harris

ROBBINS, Tom

Nationality: American. **Born:** Thomas Eugene Robbins in Blowing Rock, North Carolina, 22 July 1936. **Education:** High school in Warsaw, Virginia; Hargarve Military Academy; Washington and Lee University, Lexington, Virginia; Richmond Professional Institute (now Virginia Commonwealth University), graduated 1960. **Military Service:** Served in the United States Air Force in Korea. **Family:** Married Terrie Hemingway (divorced), married Alexa d'Avalon in 1995; one child. **Career:** Copy editor, Richmond *Times-Dispatch,* 1960–62, and Seattle *Times* and *Post-Intelligencer,* 1962–63; reviewer and art columnist, *Seattle Magazine,* and radio host, 1964–68. **Agent:** Phoebe Larmore, 228 Main Street, Venice, California 90291, USA.

Publications

Novels

Another Roadside Attraction. New York, Doubleday, 1971; London, W.H. Allen, 1973.
Even Cowgirls Get the Blues. Boston, Houghton Mifflin, 1976; London, Corgi, 1977.
Still Life with Woodpecker. New York, Bantam, and London, Sidgwick and Jackson, 1980.
Jitterbug Perfume. New York, Bantam, 1984.
Skinny Legs and All. New York, Bantam, 1990; London, Bantam, 1991.
Half Asleep in Frog Pajamas. New York, Bantam, 1994.
Fierce Invalids Home from Hot Climates. New York, Bantam Books, 2000.

Uncollected Short Story

''The Chink and the Clock People,'' in *The Best American Short Stories 1977,* edited by Martha Foley. Boston, Houghton Mifflin, 1977.

Other

Guy Anderson. Seattle, Gear Works Press, 1965.
Guy Anderson (exhibition catalogue), with William Ivey and Wallace S. Baldinger. Seattle, Seattle Art Museum, 1977.

*

Critical Studies: *Tom Robbins* by Mark Siegel, Boise, Idaho, Boise State University, 1980; *Tom Robbins: A Critical Companion* by Catherine E. Hoyser and Lorena Laura Stookey, Westport, Connecticut, Greenwood Press, 1997.

Tom Robbins comments:

I sometimes think of my serio-comic novels as cakes with files baked in them. If you choose, you can throw the file away and simply enjoy the cake. Or, you may use the file to saw through the iron bars erected by those forces in life that are forever trying to imprison us. Of course, if you aren't hip enough to know the file is there, you may end up with dental problems of an acute nature.

* * *

Although practically ignored by academic critics, except as an eccentric regionalist, Tom Robbins with his first two novels became the only American novelist since J.D. Salinger and Jack Kerouac in the 1950s to become a cult hero among disaffected college undergraduates.

Like Salinger—and Thomas Pynchon, who in an uncharacteristic move has publicly praised Robbins's second novel—the author lives in seclusion. He allows himself to be described only as "a student of art and religion" who "dropped out" to write fiction in a Washington State fishing village. Although Kerouac is the only author Robbins mentions in his novels, these more nearly resemble Salinger's Glass Family stories. The ostensible "author" frequently interrupts the stories; and, although the characters are more bizarre than Salinger's, they tend like his to be highly talkative, much given to self-analysis, lengthy confessions, and populist philosophical speculation.

Robbins's writing is even more bitterly anti-Establishment than Salinger's or Kerouac's; FBI and CIA violence and treachery and the conspiratorial practices of the Roman Catholic Church are his most frequent targets. Much of the action of *Another Roadside Attraction,* for example, deals with the involvement of Plucky Purcell (a regenade football player) in a secret order of monks that leads to his discovery during an earthquake of the mummified body of Jesus hidden in the Vatican catacombs. He brings his grotesque find to the "roadside attraction," a giant West Coast hot-dog stand operated by drop-out artist John Paul Ziller and his wife Amanda, an archetypal matriarchal figure. The principal movement of the story, narrated by Marx Marvelous, a skeptical scientific dropout from an East Coast think tank, is toward "light," toward a physical dissolution of the individual in his reunion with the sun, which Ziller describes to Marvelous as "the source of all biological energy, and ultimately ... the source of you." While Plucky debates how to use Christ's corpse to expose the hoax of Christian culture, Ziller steals it and sets off with it and his pet baboon on a space balloon for the "return to sunlight," which he had said was an "inevitability" he'd been "reckoning with." "Let Amanda by your pine cone," the novel concludes as a joyous tribute to her survival.

Even Cowgirls Get the Blues is longer, talkier, and more self-consciously whimsical than its predecessor. The first half of the novel dwells upon the picaresque adventures of Sissy Hankshaw, a born hitch-hiker with monstrous thumbs. Most of the second half is dominated by the "clock people," Indian refugees from the San Francisco earthquake, who have substituted rigid individual rituals for societal rituals. The two fantasies are united by events at the Rubber Rose Ranch, a wealthy women's retreat that is seized by insurgent cowgirls. Their brush with the government culminates in the Whooping Crane war, after the cowgirls disrupt the endangered species' migration by feeding them peyote. The convoluted story, which is related by an offbeat psychiatrist curiously named Robbins, winds up with the cranes circling the globe while Sissy is envisioned as the mother of a tribe of big-thumbed people in the "postcatastrophe" world.

Whimsy predominates in Robbins's third book, the short and relatively uncomplicated *Still Life with Woodpecker,* which counterpoints such trendy topics of the early 1980s as deposed royalty, red-headed bombers, and pyramid power to ask the plaintive question, "Who knows how to make love stay?" Robbins despairs of an answer during an era of distrust between the sexes, but an almost *Aida*-like ending hints at a way out of the dilemma.

Heavy-handed whimsy turns into sheer fantasy in *Jitterbug Perfume.* The action of this fourth novel focuses on Alobar, tribal king of a tiny, barbarous medieval city-state, who escapes the customary execution of the ruler at his first sign of aging to become for a thousand years a wanderer to exotic places who has learned the Bandaloop principles of immortal life. Interpolated into this bizarre pilgrimage are brief glimpses of life among the perfume-makers in contemporary Seattle, New Orleans, and Paris. This fable simply lays the groundwork for the climactic proclamation of Wiggs Dannyboy (a character reminiscent of Timothy Leary) a man that is on the verge of leaving behind his reptilian and mammalian consciousness to enter the phase of "floral consciousness," during which the production of sensorily stimulating perfumes will be his highest good. It is hard to tell how seriously to take this preachment; but if it isn't serious, there seems no point at all to the long stretches of Robbins's increasingly self-indulgent prose. As the title suggests, the whole production has the dated air of celebrating the culture of the flower children of the 1960s. These two later works have done little to sustain Robbins's position as guru to an underground cult.

Fierce Invalids Home from Hot Climates, Robbins's first novel in six years, proved that he still had a command of lush, sexy prose, but the author's use of contrived, bizarre plots—a CIA operative who loves underage girls goes to Peru and as the result of a curse is unable to let his feet touch the ground for fear of death—was wearing thin. Subsequent events, however, gave Robbins stalwarts ammunition against critics. The novel, released on May 2, 2000, contained speculation regarding the third secret imparted by the Virgin at Fatima. (In 1917, three Portuguese children reportedly had a vision of the Virgin Mary, who told them three secrets. The first two, "revealed" after the fact by the Church, allegedly concerned the events of the Russian Revolution and World War II.) The third secret remained unrevealed, however—until just a few days after the release of Robbins's novel, when Pope John Paul II stated that it concerned the 1981 assassination attempt against him. Robbins, who had suggested in his book that the third secret was that "the salvation of mankind would come from a source other than the church," emerged from his reclusive exile to speculate impishly on the pages of *Time* magazine: "I'd hate to accuse the Pope of reading my book," he said, "but 10 days after it's published, they reveal a long-held secret as something pretty wimpy and innocuous."

—Warren French, updated by Judson Knight

ROBERTS, Michèle (Brigitte)

Nationality: British. **Born:** Bushey, Hertfordshire, 20 May 1949. **Education:** Oxford University, B.A. (with honors) 1970; University of London Library Associate, 1972. **Career:** Has worked as a librarian, cook, teacher, cleaner, pregnancy counselor, and researcher; writer-in-residence, Lambeth Borough, London, 1981–82, and Bromley Borough, London, 1983–84. Poetry editor, *Spare Rib,* 1975–77, and

City Limits, 1981–83. **Awards:** *Gay News* Literary award, 1978, for *A Piece of the Night.* **Agent:** Caroline Dawnay, A.D. Peters, 10 Buckingham St., London W.C.2, England.

PUBLICATIONS

Novels

A Piece of the Night. London, Women's Press, 1978.
The Visitation. London, Women's Press, 1978.
The Wild Girl. London, Methuen, 1984.
The Book of Mrs. Noah. London, Methuen, 1987.
In the Red Kitchen. London, Methuen, 1990.
Psyche and the Hurricane. London, Methuen, 1991.
Daughters of the House. London, Virago, and New York, Morrow, 1992.
During Mother's Absence. London, Virago, 1993.
Flesh & Blood. London, Virago, 1994.
Impossible Saints. Hopewell, New Jersey, Ecco Press, 1998.
Fair Exchange. London, Little, Brown, 1999.

Short Stories

Tales I Tell My Mother, with Alison Fell . London, Journeyman Press, 1978.

Poetry

Licking the Bed Clean. N.p., 1978.
Smile, Smile, Smile, Smile. N.p., 1980.
Touch Papers, with Judith Karantris and Michelene Wandor. London, Allison and Busby, 1982.
The Mirror of the Mother: Selected Poems 1975–1985. London, Methuen, 1985.
All the Selves I Was: New and Selected Poems. London, Virago, 1995.

Other

Food, Sex and God: On Inspiration and Writing. London, Virago, 1998.
Editor, with Michelene Wandor, *Cutlasses and Earrings.* London, Playbooks, 1976.
Editor, with Sara Dunn and Blake Morrison, *Mind Readings: Writers' Journeys through Mental States.* London, Minerva, 1996.

* * *

Michèle Roberts is one of a group of novelists who emerged from 1970s British feminism and has become recognized as an important author concerned to represent the body, particularly the female body, in writing. Using realistic and non-realistic modes, Roberts has always been concerned to recover the lost body of the mother/female experience and female art. Influenced by both Freudian and Jungian theory, her novels seek out the unconscious as a creative force and explore ways of recuperating religious experience from patriarchal structures as Roberts reinterprets her Catholic heritage. All her novels engender their own authors using Christian, classical, artistic, and maternal myths to try to free female creativity from a patriarchal culture.

A Piece Of The Night, the first novel, strongly reflects the contemporary British feminist movement. In realistic form, it charts the career of Julie, insufficiently mothered, who marries in a state of dependence, is trapped into domesticity but finds liberation in lesbian love. Later novels give more space to problematic heterosexuality. This novel also struggles with problems of representing women in a radical way and finds Julie's Catholic heritage offers only images of repression, submission, and death, leaving women to feel themselves only ''a piece of the night.''

The next work, *The Visitation,* begins Roberts's project of rewriting Christian myth to figure the independent woman since it uses the New Testament friendship of Elizabeth and Mary (here Beth and Helen) to privilege the relationship of two heterosexual women and represent female creativity in motherhood and in writing. Beth becomes pregnant but the Virgin birth seems to be Helen's novel, possibly *The Visitation* itself. Just as religious myths are now available to be rewritten, so is the unconscious; dreams are a sustaining force for female selfhood. These two aspects of Roberts's style are particularly prominent in her next, most controversial, text, *The Wild Girl,* purporting to be the fifth Gospel as told by Mary Magdalen. This novel is a marvellous fusing of Roberts's theme of the meaningfulness of the female body, religious experience, and female authority as religious teacher, as author. Significantly influenced by feminist Jungians, it is structured around a sexual romance between Jesus and Mary Magdalen becoming a sacred marriage, an initiation into the unconscious which is also religious. Like the earlier two novels the form resembles a romance but the intensity of *The Wild Girl* also figures as tragedy. *The Book of Mrs. Noah* tries to escape the dual structure of romance and tragedy by containing a more multifarious plot, leaving realism for myth and fantasy and adopting comedy. At one level it continues earlier works by restructuring the Old Testament story of Noah's Ark, offering an Ark devoted to female writers. This brings in the contemporary narrative as the sibyls who visit the Ark are all representatives of the peculiar struggles of the female writer in a male-dominated society. They tell stories on the Ark that rewrite Christian heritage while Mrs. Noah, the narrator, ponders the fraught issue of motherhood. Much of the comedy of the Ark comes from the stowaway, the Voice of God, a male artist suffering from writer's block after his blockbuster, the Bible. This is a complex work suggesting for the first time that feminist problems cannot be solved easily but it asserts the healing power of the unconscious, here the Ark, as manifested in storytelling.

In The Red Kitchen, the fifth novel, returns to realism while investigating father-daughter bonds in a series of female histories linked by spiritualism, that female-dominated movement that preceded the birth of psychoanalysis. Based on a real case, Victorian Flora Milk has as a spirit guide Hat, an Egyptian princess who acquires power through incest with her father. Flora becomes involved with the middle-class patriarchal marriage of Minnie and William and with the mysterious death of their daughter. In turn, Flora haunts Hattie, a single woman living in her house in contemporary London who is a cookery writer because she has a vision of a giantess in a red kitchen (the repressed place of female creativity).

Perhaps Roberts's most successful novel is *Daughters of the House,* which mingles autobiography with a saint's life, using the story of Saint Therese of Lisieux. An intensely poetic piece, it tells the story of two cousins, Therese and Leonie, who spend summers together in post-war France. What comes up from the Catholic and historical repressions of the period is Leonie's archetypal visions of a ''red lady'' connected to the villagers' suppressed worship of a goddess. This causes the discovery of a grave, the murdered remains of Jews who had been betrayed by the priest. Therese also claims to have visions, but orthodox ones, and becomes a nun. The novel again privileges female relationships but here in a political context.

Flesh and Blood is an almost Gothic series of interlocking stories focusing on female sexual experience through history in France and Britain. *Impossible Saints* is an even more intricate offering, intertwining the lives of numerous women who tried to be saints with that of Josephine, a nun with a lust for life (and other things). Both books prove Roberts an important contemporary explorer of female identity and creativity, a dazzling sensualist in her writing, and an adept spinner of interwoven plot lines.

—S.A. Rowland, updated by Judson Knight

ROBINSON, Kim Stanley

Nationality: American. **Born:** Waukegan, Illinois, 23 March 1952. **Education:** University of California, San Diego, B.A. in literature, 1974, Ph.D. 1982; Boston University, M.A. in English 1975. **Family:** Married Lisa Howland Nowell in 1982. **Career:** Visiting lecturer, University of California, in Davis, 1982–84, 1985, and in San Diego, 1982, 1985. **Awards:** World Fantasy award, 1983; *SF Chronicle* award, 1984, 1992; *Locus* award, 1985, 1991, 1994, 1997; Nebula award, 1987, 1993, 1995; John W. Campbell Memorial award, 1991; Brit. Sci. Fiction award, 1993; Hugo award, 1994, 1997. **Address:** c/o Tor Books, 49 West 24th Street, 9th floor, New York, New York 10010, U.S.A.

PUBLICATIONS

Novels (series: Orange County)

The Wild Shore (Orange County). New York, Ace, 1984; London, Futura, 1985.
Icehenge. New York, Ace, 1984; London, Futura, 1985.
The Memory of Whiteness: A Scientific Romance. New York, Tor, 1985; London, Macdonald, 1986.
The Blind Geometer. New Castle, Virginia, Cheap Street, 1986; with *Return from Rainbow Bridge,* and *The New Atlantis,* by Ursula Le Guin, New York, Tor, 1989.
The Gold Coast (Orange County). New York, St. Martin's Press, and London, Macdonald, 1988.
Green Mars, with *A Meeting with Medusa,* by Arthur C. Clarke. New York, Tor, 1988; as *Green Mars,* London, HarperCollins, 1993.
Pacific Edge (Orange County). New York, Tor, and London, Unwin Hyman, 1990.
A Short, Sharp Shock. Shingletown, California, Siesing, 1990.
Down and Out in the Year 2000. London, Grafton, 1992.
Red Mars. London, HarperCollins, 1992; New York, Bantam, 1993.
Blue Mars. New York, Bantam Books, 1996.
Antarctica. New York, Bantam Books, 1998.
The Martians. New York, Bantam Books, 1999.

Short Stories

The Planet on the Table. New York, Tor, 1986; London, Futura, 1987.
Escape from Kathmandu. Eugene, Oregon, Axolotl Press, 1987; London, Unwin Hyman, 1990.
Remaking History, and Other Stories. New York, Tor, 1991.

Other

The Novels of Philip K. Dick. Ann Arbor, Michigan, UMI Research Press, 1984.
Editor, *Future Primitive: The New Ecotopias.* New York, Tor, 1994.

* * *

Kim Stanley Robinson is a writer of hard science fiction, a spiritual descendant of Jules Verne, and a writer most closely aligned with such writers of hard science fiction as Isaac Asimov. When Jules Verne disparaged the work of H.G. Wells by calling Wells an ''inventor,'' he defined a schism that divided science fiction writers into at least two camps: Verne considered himself to be a writer of ''extrapolative'' fiction, based in known and projected fact. He considered that writers of Well's camp ''invented'' material, making up whatever was necessary to create a good story. Kim Robinson is firmly within the Verne/Asimov/hard science fiction camp. Aside from the fact that all of science fiction is a branch of the larger category of fantasy, there is little that seems fantasy-like about Robinson's work. His knowledge of and use of science and technology in his fiction are impressive, and much of his work reads as if it were written the day after tomorrow.

Robinson first became familiar to science fiction readers with a series of books known as the *Orange County* trilogy. These books are not a ''trilogy'' in the sense of being connected by repeated characters or themes; they are connected largely by their Orange County, California, locale. The books are written in three science fiction traditions. *The Wild Shore,* the first of the books, is a post-nuclear holocaust novel. *The Gold Coast* is dystopian; *Pacific Edge* is utopian. The first of the books, *The Wild Shore,* is probably the weakest of the three, using as it does a rather self-conscious adolescent as its protagonist. In general, however, the books are well written and carefully researched. As an exercise they provide a beautifully done set of answers to the implicit questions in science fiction of ''What if the worst happens?'' and ''If we keep going this way, what becomes of us?'' and finally, ''Could we do this better, and if so, how?''

Robinson's early work, however, is surpassed by his *Mars* trilogy, a group of books which promises to make secure his reputation as a first-rate science fiction writer. The three books, *Red Mars, Green Mars,* and *Blue Mars,* are works of considerable depth and power. Robinson's work is indeed extrapolative in terms of science and technology, but also in terms of economics, politics, business, and social trends. Robinson's understanding of our society's inclinations in each of those areas provides fascinating reading. In contrast to many writers who focus on science to the exclusion of the political and social implications created by that science, Robinson explores many of the possibilities and problems inherent in scientific advance.

Unlike the *Orange County* trilogy, the *Mars* trilogy is connected by characters, plot lines, and chronology. Prospective readers would be advised to approach the books in sequence because the frequent references to preceding events tends to make them less comprehensible otherwise. The books are tied together by the ''first hundred,'' the first hundred colonists who landed on Mars. The colonists have been given longevity treatments which insure that they will live very long lives, and in spite of the fact that the books cover more than three hundred years, some of the first hundred survive through the final book, *Blue Mars.*

Two themes recur in Robinson's fiction, and both are explored in depth in the *Mars* trilogy. The first theme is the persistent nature of the human animal. In the *Mars* books as well as in other works, such as *The Memory of Whiteness,* he seems to consider that even if the human experience is moved to Mars or Jupiter or to any other planet, the human being remains the human being and, as such, behaves in human, therefore limited, ways. In the *Mars* books, factional and national differences on Earth are merely transferred to Mars. The fact of a new planet, of an interplanetary experience, does not erase them, though with time connections with Earth become weaker, in much the same way that connections of immigrants from the Old World lessened as they were integrated into the New World.

A second, related theme has to do with the ecological concerns of the Mars colonization groups. One segment of the population wants very much to keep Mars ''pure''; that is, they want to keep the planet much as it was when they first landed on it. A second, much larger group, wants to ''terraform'' the planet; that is, they want to make it like Earth, with a breathable atmosphere and living conditions comparable to those on Earth. One has only to read the titles of the books to understand which side prevails.

These same ecological concerns appear in *Antarctica,* a novel set on that remote continent. Robinson has spent time in Antarctica, and the novel reflects his first-hand knowledge. To some extent *Antarctica* is a microcosm of ecological concerns in other parts of the world. Conflicts between nations, corporations, and citizens with diverse views of the ''proper'' use of the Earth's natural resources all play a part in this study of life on the world's least-explored continent. Robinson has also done his homework on the history of Antarctic exploration; the early exploration of the continent is presented in enough detail to make clear that he knows whereof he writes.

Robinson does not stint on scientific detail, nor does he ''write down'' to those readers who might not be as well versed in science and technology as he. His fiction has been called ''dense'' because of his tendency to embrace a science-text style in description, but fans of the hard science fiction genre will undoubtedly be taken with his verisimilitude. Other readers may be less entranced by the somewhat repetitious descriptions of the Martian landscape. As with all good writers, Robinson plays to his strengths, and his knowledge of geology is clearly among those strengths.

In spite of his tendency to immerse the reader in scientific and technological detail, Robinson does not lose sight of the fact that he is writing a novel. Unlike those science fiction writers who focus on presenting ideas to the exclusion of in-depth character portrayal, Robinson creates strong, consistent, and believable characters. Those characters express views that pull the reader into their worlds with an arresting facility. Indeed, so adept is he at the expression of various viewpoints through the characters he creates that the reader would be very hard put to determine which of the viewpoints he might personally support. There are no sharp good versus evil delineations here, as is the case with *Star Wars*-type space operas; these are real people wrestling with real problems, and simple answers are not provided.

Any quibbles about Robinson's works are probably minor. For fans of the hard science fiction genre, his *Mars* trilogy may well set the standard by which interplanetary colonization novels will be judged in the future.

—June Harris

ROBINSON, Marilynne

Nationality: American. **Born:** Sandpoint, Idaho, in 1943. **Education:** Brown University, Providence, Rhode Island, B.A. in American literature; University of Washington, Seattle, M.A. and Ph.D. in English. **Family:** Married; two sons. Lives in Massachusetts. **Awards:** American Academy Rosenthal Foundation award, 1982; Hemingway Foundation award, 1982; PEN Essay Prize, 1999. **Address:** c/o Farrar Straus and Giroux Inc., 19 Union Square West, New York, New York 10003, USA.

Publications

Novel

Housekeeping. New York, Farrar Straus, 1980; London, Faber, 1981.

Uncollected Short Stories

''Orphans,'' in *Harper's* (New York), February 1981.
''Connie Bronson,'' in *Paris Review,* Summer-Fall 1986.

Other

Mother Country: Britain, The Nuclear State, and Nuclear Pollution. New York, Farrar Straus, and London, Faber, 1989.
The Death of Adam: Essays on Modern Thought. Boston, Houghton Mifflin, 1998.

* * *

Housekeeping is, for most people, a basic requirement, if only on the simplest level of maintaining shelter. Little chores become so routine that they are done without thinking: washing the dishes or clothes, sweeping, dusting, all take up time and energy that we disregard, write off. Not many of us can or would bother to total the hours spent in such minor labors, any more than we could tally up the hours spent in the bath; they are just necessary losses. Those hours are acceptably, if boringly, spent in the small acts that give our lives some structure, some normality. Changing the linens on Mondays, shopping on Thursdays, church on Sundays, accumulate to keep our lives from flapping loose out into the chaos, like a dress blown off the laundry line and clean away.

Marilynne Robinson's novel *Housekeeping* is about the collapse and abandonment of housekeeping and of the frail structure it provides. For Ruth, who tells the story, housekeeping is a phase of the past, disintegrated in a childhood of isolated women and the constant presence of a lake. Ruth and Lucille were little girls when their mother drove them to her home town on a mountain lake in Idaho. The town, with the macabre and ludicrous name of Fingerbone, is small, completely surrounded, with the lake on one side, and the mountains and forest on the others. As in all remote towns, the people know one another too well, and the closeness is oppressive: ''The people of Fingerbone and its environs were very much given to murder. And it seemed that for every pitiable crime there was an appalling accident. What with the lake and the railroads, and what with blizzards and floods and barn fires and forest fires and the general availability of shotguns and bear traps and homemade liquor and dynamite, what with the prevalence of loneliness and religion and the rages and ecstasies they induce, and the closeness of families, violence was inevitable.'' With long, slow sentences, Ruth tells how the mountains shut out light and the rest of the world, the forest holds darkness and danger, and the lake is a bowl of death. Never once is there any mention of ''natural beauty.''

The lake, the reason for the town's location, sits by, always in one's awareness, passive, a relentless presence. Ruth's first experience of the lake comes when, after dropping the girls off at the house of a grandmother they had never met, her mother drives her car off the cliffs and into the lake, drowning herself. Years earlier, a train had derailed and, plunging into the lake, drowned all aboard, including Ruth's grandfather. All of the dead remain in their underwater capsules. When the lake freezes, people go ice-skating. During the summer, Ruth and her sister play by it, fish in it. Slowly and undramatically, its importance grows. One winter, the snows melt but the lake does not, leaving the water to back up and flood the town. In Ruth's house, they move upstairs, letting the water take the downstairs, soaking furniture and curtains and sloshing against the walls. The whole town sits and waits, sodden, for the ice on the lake to melt so the water can flow home. ''The clashes and groans from the lake continued unabated, dreadful at night, and the sound of the night wind in the mountains was like one long indrawn breath. Downstairs the flood bumped and fumbled like a blind man in a strange house, but outside it hissed and trickled, like the pressure of water against your eardrums, and like the sounds you hear in the moment before you faint.''

There are no men in this story, no sweet romance, no subtle sexuality, and the women are quiet, solitary, odd. Ruth's mother rarely spoke to her children. After her suicide, the girls are cared for by a very old grandmother living in her memories. When the girls find her dead, two elderly aunts are summoned from Spokane, but they then track down another aunt, Sylvie, to take over. Desertions and deaths are recounted in Ruth's helpless, rarely angry tone of acceptance in the same way that she tells of a fishing trip with Lucille, or of Sylvie's strange, transient ways. Sylvie rummages in rubbish bins, eats only in the dark, saves all tins, never cleans anything, plays crazy eights during the flood. She does her best to care for the girls, but housekeeping and structure left her life long ago.

As they reach adolescence, Ruth begins to acquiesce to her fate, while Lucille begins to fight it. Lucille wants to dress cleanly, to have friends, be normal, learn housekeeping. In a final desertion, she moves in with her Home Economics teacher. Ruth is left to drift, having decided ''it is better to have nothing.''

Robinson's style itself is evocative of drifting and drifters' tales, with long, often poetic descriptions that suddenly snap back to the original point or deflect to a new, unrelated one. At times, Ruth's anger appears in harsher narrative: a cold realization about Lucille, snide comments about Fingerbone's church ladies, or one long tirade about Cain's betrayal of Abel, which seems slightly inappropriate in a book without men: betrayal exists among sisters as well. At times, too, the sneering is so rough as to seem more than could be felt by this bland girl who cannot tell the difference between what she has dreamed and what she has imagined. These are small flaws in a book that is so rich with thought and feeling that it compels the reader to slow down and truly read.

—Anne Morddel

ROBINSON, Peter

Nationality: Canadian. **Born:** Castleford, Yorkshire, 17 March 1950. **Education:** University of Ledds, B.A. 1974; University of Windsor, M.A. 1975; York University, Ph.D. 1983. **Family:** Married Janice Hyndman in 1984. **Awards:** Arthur Ellis award for Canadian crime novel of the year, 1992. **Address:** 30 Lawlor Ave., Toronto, Ontario M4E 3L7, Canada.

Publications

Novels

The Gallows View. Toronto, Viking, 1987; New York, Scribner, 1990.
A Dedicated Man. Toronto, Viking, 1988; New York, Scribner, 1991.
The Hanging Valley. Toronto, Viking, 1989; New York, Scribner, 1992.
A Necessary End. Toronto, Viking, 1990; New York, Scribner, 1992.
Caedmon's Song. Toronto, Viking, 1990.
Past Reason Hated. Toronto, Viking, 1991; New York, Scribner, 1993.
Wednesday's Child. Toronto, Viking, 1992; New York, Berkley, 1995.
Final Account. Toronto, Penguin, 1994; New York, Berkley, and London, Constable, 1995.
No Cure for Love. Toronto, Penguin, 1995.
Innocent Graves: An Inspector Banks Mystery. New York, Berkley Prime Crime, 1996.
Blood at the Root: An Inspector Banks Mystery. New York, Avon Books, 1997.
In a Dry Season. New York, Avon Twilight, 1999.
Cold Is the Grave. New York, William Morrow, 2000.

Short Stories

Not Safe After Dark and Other Stories. Norfolk, Virginia, Crippen & Landru Publishers, 1998.

* * *

Peter Robinson, who emigrated to Canada in 1974, is best known for his novels featuring Detective Chief Inspector Alan Banks of the

Eastvale Criminal Investigation Department, Yorkshire, England. In addition, Robinson has published several non-series novels, among them the psychological thriller *Caedmon's Song* and a police procedural set primarily in Los Angeles, *No Cure for Love.* In each case, Robinson combines what might be called ''psychological realism,'' or a focus on character and motivation, with thoughtful cultural commentary, particularly with respect to post-Thatcher England and its susceptibility to the values, tastes, and practices of urban America.

Robinson's Inspector Banks series is built around the character of Alan Banks and the quiet, methodical, and ruminative way in which he sets about solving crimes in the Yorkshire Dales with the assistance of his investigative team. Banks is relatively new to the Dales, having recently transferred from London in search of (ironically, given the number of murders that fall his way) a quieter professional life. He is married to an independent woman he genuinely enjoys and who challenges rather than acquiesces to him. A consummate family man, Banks runs miniature trains for relaxation, relishes his Sunday beef with Yorkshire pudding, and mourns his children's adolescent trajectory away from hearth and home. He enjoys a good working partnership with his superior, Detective Superintendent Gristhorpe, a gritty Yorkshireman who struggles to replicate the ancient technology of dry stone wall-building on his Dales farm. In employing cool logic, honed instinct, and sheer doggedness in pursuing his inquiries, and in avoiding violence for the most part, Inspector Banks is very much the classic police investigator—which is not surprising, given Robinson's acknowledgment of writers like Simenon, Maigret, and Christie as early influences upon his work.

Yet Banks is distinctive in the robust psychological contours that Robinson affords him. A working-class lad who had failed his ''eleven plus'' exams and barely escaped being shoehorned into a manual trade of little interest to him, Banks is acutely aware of his good luck but also of his lack of formal education. He hungers for knowledge and culture. He loves classical music, especially opera, and crams his home and his mind with the detritus of things he wishes he knew more about—from Dickens and winemaking to bird eggs and local geology. He has an instinct for ferreting out white-collar and class-motivated crime as a result of what Robinson calls a ''working-class chip on the shoulder'' and exploits what is second nature to him, that sense of cautious distrust that characterizes the perpetual outsider.

Indeed, as ''incomer'' to fictional Swainsdale (a composite, Robinson says, of the four main Yorkshire Dales), Banks is well positioned to see more clearly than longtime residents both its quixotic regional characteristics, such as the wry taciturnity of those raised in the Dales, and the simultaneous ways in which even remote Yorkshire is being invaded and eroded by the electronic juggernaut that is American popular culture. Tourism has become the main industry in Swainsdale, bringing trailer parks, campsites, snack bars, and tarted-up pubs to a town traditionally known for its ancient cross, its Norman church, and its Roman ruins. Against these relics of earlier invasions of Britain, Banks links the current importation of all things American (from the wearing of expensive hiking gear to the yuppie-style renovations of venerable Dales farmhouses) to an increase in violent crime in the Dales.

Yet the real danger that Banks points to is less the ubiquity of American popular culture and the inevitable urbanization of northern England than the habits and habits of mind that such changes signal. Swainsdale is moments by car from the cities of Leeds, Bradford, and York and no longer immune to the instant pleasures of contemporary city life, from fast food to satellite broadcasts to anonymous sex and its aftermath. Throw-away gratification is certainly an affront to traditional Yorkshire values of perseverance, deferral, and endurance. But the larger danger, Robinson suggests, is the way that electronic or ''virtual'' cultures increasingly blunt our capacity for thought and, especially, for separating illusion from reality.

In Robinson's novels, as in most crime fiction, it is camouflage, disguise, pretense, or masking that must be penetrated if the mystery is to be solved. The social issues change from novel to novel, and to move from *Gallows View* to *No Cure for Love* is to encounter teen crime, marital treachery, class privilege, police brutality, homophobia, child abuse, and organized crime in rapid succession. In the mystery that forms the plot of *Innocent Graves,* the eighth Inspector Banks novel, the suspects include a priest who may be gay, as well as a college lecturer with a taste for young girls. *Blood in the Root* draws on drugs, as well as the racial violence between neo-Nazis and Pakistani youth in London. On a personal note for Banks, the novel also sees his separation from his wife, and includes a scene in which he punches his officious superior, Constable Riddle. By the beginning of *In a Dry Season,* he is despondent, estranged from his children, and hitting the bottle. He finds solace in the arms of his female partner on the police force—and of course there's a mystery in there as well, but the story is at least as much concerned with the development of Banks as a character.

The common element in many of these books is the need—in the face of the many ways that the same thing or same person can be perceived—for a heightened ability to spot the illusion, the sleight-of-hand, that obscures ''reality.'' Robinson's is a conservative vision, just as crime fiction itself is a conservative genre, with its insistence upon ''knowing,'' upon solution and closure. What Robinson's fiction offers, whether in the Banks series or in his non-series novels such as *Caedmon's Song,* is a certain richness of cultural commentary and moral inquiry. In the face of a contemporary culture that (from a police perspective, at any rate) valorizes glamour and surface and over-tolerates greasy deals and unfettered greed, his fiction celebrates the will to dismember illusion while retaining one's basic decency and humanity—as in the case of the redoubtable Inspector Banks. It is an interesting and challenging response to the tumbling of old certainties that marks our time.

—Marilyn Rose, updated by Judson Knight

ROBISON, Mary

Nationality: American. **Born:** Mary Reiss in Washington, D.C., 14 January 1949. **Education:** Johns Hopkins University, Baltimore, M.A. 1977. **Family:** Married to James N. Robison. **Career:** From 1981, member of the Department of English, Harvard University, Cambridge, Massachusetts. Visiting lecturer, Ohio University, Athens, 1979–80; writer-in-residence, University of Southern Mississippi, Hattiesburg, 1980 and 1985, University of North Carolina, Greensboro, 1980, College of William and Mary, Williamsburg, Virginia, 1981, and Bennington College, Vermont, 1984, 1985; visiting assistant professor of Writing, Oberlin College, Ohio, 1984–85. **Awards:** Yaddo fellowship, 1978; Bread Loaf Writers Conference fellowship, 1979; Authors Guild award, 1979; Guggenheim fellowship, 1980. **Address:** c/o Andrew Wylie, Wylie, Aiken and Stone, Inc., 250 West 57th St., #2106, New York, New York 10107, USA.

PUBLICATIONS

Novel

Oh! New York, Knopf, 1981.

Short Stories

Days. New York, Knopf, 1979.
An Amateur's Guide to the Night. New York, Knopf, 1983.
Believe Them. New York, Knopf, 1988.
Subtraction. New York, Knopf, 1991.

*

Critical Studies: *Minimalism and the Short Story—Raymond Carver, Amy Hempel, and Mary Robison* by Cynthia Whitney Hallett. Lewiston, New York, E. Mellen Press, 1999.

* * *

Many readers have been introduced to Mary Robison's writing through her short stories in the *New Yorker.* She writes of people caught in a web of alienation and living amid the trivia of contemporary suburban America. Many of her characters seem cut off from events in their lives and their own innermost feelings. For example, in her novel, *Oh!,* Maureen and Howdy, the two adult children of Mr. Cleveland (a self-made, semi-retired millionaire) still live at home, passing the time drinking, complaining, watching TV, and vaguely trying to figure out what to do with their lives. At one point Maureen says ''I love this house ... I've never lived any place else. I couldn't be comfortable or feel safe anywhere else .... Yet I don't want to be stuck here the rest of my life .... Except I'm scared of going anywhere else. Of living out my days being poor.'' The narrator of one short story ''Smart'' is an unmarried, pregnant, thirty-six-year-old woman living alone in a seedy apartment. She spends her hours sitting, or getting up ''just to change a record or twist my spine, or to nibble some of the food my neighbor, Mrs. Sally Dixon, brought me.''

Robison's characters are often rootless and without ambition. They have difficulty making connections with anyone or anything. They live their lives in a holding pattern. Like Maureen and Howdy, few find anything that motivates them to improve their lives. One exception to this, however, is the seventeen-year-old protagonist of the title story in *An Amateur Guide to the Night.* Lindy lives with her divorced mother and her maternal grandfather. She works as a waitress, goes to school, and watches *Fright Night* with the family. But beyond that, Lindy has discovered for herself the beauty of the night sky, and armed with her star charts and telescope she explores the splendor of one of nature's most spectacular shows.

The narrative voice of Robison contains a stark, unmelodic poetry devoid of frills, usually brushing only the surface, describing rather than exploring. Although much can be learned in this way, the author's detachment from her characters has been a persistent criticism leveled at her work. A scene in a Robison story is like a snapshot. She has an eye for detail and tends to focus on mundane, ordinary events. The short story ''In the Woods'' has this: ''Evenings on the farm, Kenneth would grill steaks or chops outside and my sister and I would do the salad, sometimes corn. We'd open wine. We would cut up muskmelon. After eating, we'd sit on the long flagstone patio, with its view of yard and pond, and maybe drink a Scotch.''

The author's voice throughout is cool and meticulous. The reader watches along with the author as the story unfolds, slowly at times, just the same as it does in life. Sometimes the insight gleaned from this approach is no more discerning than when we observe strangers. Often, though, we catch a clear, penetrating glimpse into a person's heart and mind. At these times, despite the distancing, something quite profound is achieved. For example, in ''I Am Twenty-one'' a college student struggles with an essay question on an exam, watching the time pass, unable to answer all the questions. The young narrator is obviously under severe strain, something more than worry over a test, but only later do we understand the depth of her struggle to just keep going. She describes her apartment, a spartan arrangement except for one photograph, an eight-by-ten glossy of her parents in their youth. ''My folks (are) two and a half years gone,'' she says flatly yet meaningfully, and then talks of her visits to the scene of the accident.

Robison has a playwright's ear for dialogue. Her characters speak the way people really do, in fits and starts with half-formed thoughts and sentences. Their conversations center on common events. In ''Mirror'' the narrator visits her longtime friend, Lolly. The scene opens in a beauty parlor where these two are discussing the boredom of being there and problems associated with getting a permanent. At times, it might seem that these conversations go nowhere, but through these snippets of talk the essences of the characters evolve, and their values are revealed. Sometimes that revelation comes suddenly, as the meaningless chitchat abruptly becomes substantive. At one point Maureen (*Oh!*) and her seven-year-old daughter, Violet, are splashing in the child's pool. They are talking about the maid, Lola, when suddenly the conversation shifts to the topic of Maureen's mother. Maureen's resentment of her father and anguish over her mother's abandonment are poignantly revealed. She wants only to remember the good things about this woman and tells her daughter, ''You just remember when your grandpa talks about your grandma, no matter what he's saying, he's making it all up. Everything about drinking or about ranting and raving? That's all rubbish.''

Robison gives her readers vignettes of life that have power in their sparseness. Her scenes begin in the middle and stop, as if a TV were being switched on and off with the program in progress. The characters are talking, dreaming, or moving about when the reader arrives, and they continue as the reader exits. It is this ability to convince us that we are observing living, breathing people—who will proceed with their lives whether observed by the reader or not—that gives strength and power to Robison's writing.

—Patricia Altner

ROOKE, Daphne (Marie)

Nationality: British and South African. **Born:** Daphne Marie Pizzey in Boksburg, Transvaal, South Africa, 6 March 1914. **Education:** Durban Girls' High School. **Family:** Married Irvin Rooke in 1937; one daughter. Lived in Australia, 1946–53, and since 1965. **Awards:** Afrikaanse Pers Beperk prize, 1946. **Address:** 54 Regatta Court, Oyster Row, Cambridge CB5 8NS, England.

PUBLICATIONS

Novels

The Sea Hath Bounds. Johannesburg, A.P.B. Bookstore, 1946; as *A Grove of Fever Trees,* Boston, Houghton Mifflin, 1950; London, Cape, 1951.
Mittee. London, Gollancz, 1951; Boston, Houghton Mifflin, 1952.
Ratoons. London, Gollancz, and Boston, Houghton Mifflin, 1953.
Wizards' Country. London, Gollancz, and Boston, Houghton Mifflin, 1957.
Beti. London, Gollancz, and Boston, Houghton Mifflin, 1959.
A Lover for Estelle. London, Gollancz, and Boston, Houghton Mifflin, 1961.
The Greyling. London, Gollancz, 1962; New York, Reynal, 1963.
Diamond Jo. London, Gollancz, and New York, Reynal, 1965.
Boy on the Mountain. London, Gollancz, 1969.
Margaretha de la Porte. London, Gollancz, 1974.

Uncollected Short Stories

''The Deal,'' in *Woman* (Sydney), 26 June 1950.
''Emily,'' in *John Bull* (London), 1952.
''The Boundary Dog,'' in *John Bull* (London), 1957.
''The Friends,'' in *South African Stories,* edited by David Wright. London, Faber, and New York, Duell, 1960.
''Fikizolo,'' in *Over the Horizon.* London, Gollancz, 1960.
''There Lies Hidden … ,'' in *Optima* (Johannesburg), 1963.

Other (for children)

The South African Twins. London, Cape, 1953; as *Twins in South Africa,* Boston, Houghton Mifflin, 1955.
The Australian Twins. London, Cape, 1954; as *Twins in Australia,* Boston, Houghton Mifflin, 1956.
New Zealand Twins. London, Cape, 1957.
Double Ex! London, Gollancz, 1971.
A Horse of His Own. London, Gollancz, 1976.

*

Bibliography: *Daphne Rooke: Her Works and Selected Criticism: A Bibliography* by Helen Camburg, Johannesburg, University of the Witwatersrand, 1969.

Manuscript Collections: Mugar Memorial Library, Boston University; National English Literary Museum, Grahamstown, South Africa.

Critical Studies: By Orville Prescott, in *New York Times,* 1 March 1950; Dorothy Canfield Fisher, in *Book-of-the-Month News* (New York), January 1952; Sylvia Stallings, in *New York Herald Tribune,* 20 December 1953; *Illustrated London News,* 21 December 1957; *Saturday Review of Literature* (New York), 7 March 1959; *Chicago Tribune,* 26 February 1961; Paul Scott, in *Country Life* (London), 24 May 1962.

Daphne Rooke comments:

(1991) The places where I have lived have been most important to my writing. My early memories of the Transvaal are reflected in *Mittee. Ratoons* has for background the South Coast of Natal where I lived for many years on a sugar plantation. Zululand made a most profound impression on me: I lived there for years as a girl: *A Grove of Fever Trees, A Lover for Estelle,* and *Wizard's Country* all have Zululand for background. *Beti* is set in India and East Africa, and *Boy on the Mountain* in New Zealand. All are written in the first person.

There is a pattern of sorts in some of the South African works: the race of the narrator has an important bearing on the story. In *Mittee* the whole story hinges on the fact that the narrator Selina is a Colored girl; in *Ratoons* the narrator is an English-speaking South African girl who falls in love with an Afrikaner; in *Wizards' Country* the narrator is a Zulu; in *A Lover for Estelle* the narrator is an Afrikaans girl whose life is influenced by a sophisticated English-woman. I did not consciously set out to create this pattern; it was pointed out to me after I had written *Wizards' Country.*

All the stories, including those for children, are imaginative works but have a basis in fact. In *Wizards' Country* when writing about superstition I attempted to avoid the supernatural; for example, Benge is a hunchback and masquerades as a magic dwarf (the tokoloshi). In my short story for children, ''Fikizolo,'' the ingredients of a fairytale were actually present in Zululand: the two children were called a prince and princess, there was a real old witch, and Fikizolo himself was like a fabled beast, a cross between a donkey and a zebra!

* * *

Though Daphne Rooke's novels were favorably reviewed in journals such as the *Times Literary Supplement* when they first appeared in the 1950s and 1960s, they did not receive the same critical attention in her home country, South Africa. Since the more recent reissue of certain of her novels, Rooke's work has begun to be reassessed—not least because a novel such as *Mittee,* in dealing with sexuality and gender relations as well as race, touches upon themes currently being explored in terms of patriarchal discourse in colonial society.

The novels are striking a new generation of readers afresh with their unmistakable flavor of ''South African Gothic'': a startling mixture of the ordinary and the bizarre that appears to meet white/western subliminal expectations of Africa; a galloping plot so laden with incident that others might have spun two or three books from the same material; and an overwhelming response to landscape which tends to make it (as in Hardy or Emily Brontë) the most important character in the book, leaving the human ones to become strangely strident, even melodramatic and sentimental, in their efforts to be seen and heard.

Mittee centers upon a young Boer woman and her lifelong companion and servant Selina, a ''colored'' girl who is like a sister to Mittee but is never allowed to forget her place in Afrikaner society. Though she is ostensibly the narrator, in a sense Selina is the ''shadow'' of the Boer girl, as if the two characters were really one, and the underlying aim of relating their mutual struggles was to explore women's repression—and bitter revenge—in the Afrikaner world of the late nineteenth century.

Both Selina and Mittee love the same man, the Afrikaner Paul, who marries Mittee while using Selina. Both women suffer at his hands, and both exact their own revenge in a drama dwarfed by the harshness of the land and by the cruel course of the Boer War which overtakes their lives. But all is not solemn. Selina tells her story with the kind of humor that illuminates Olive Schreiner's *Story of an African Farm,* and details of vanished Boer customs and manners throng the pages with intentional comic effect. There is an inimitable lilt to the language of the characters, which is written with a strongly idiomatic Afrikaans flavor. Few beside Pauline Smith and short story writer Herman Charles Bosman have so effortlessly captured the particular note of the Afrikaner world: "Mittee called and called me again, her voice pitched on a note of anger. Ag what, let her call until she is black in the face, I thought, I won't wait on their table tonight. The way she carried on now that she was married, with Paul hanging after her as though she was gold." The dialogue is exact and often extremely funny; and Mittee's hero, the cultured English doctor Basil Castledene, is throughout the book designated as "Doctor Besil" in imitation of the flat Transvaal intonation of his name. All in all, the novel has the density of tapestry, richly and delightfully filled.

If there remains a critical suspicion that *Mittee* leans towards melodrama, Rooke's first novel, *A Grove of Fever Trees* (published internationally in 1950), is undeniably open to the accusation. Its narrator Danny is evil, not merely amoral: a twisted man through whose eyes we see the whole plot as if through strangely colored glass. The lurid light cast on the story of his doomed brother Edward and ironically named girlfriend Prudence, falls on a violence of passion and incident that would destroy a lesser book. What transforms the novel is the memorable evocation of its backdrop: an arid Zululand of ghostly fever trees and deadly poisonous snakes, the whole dominated by the mysterious peak Tshaneni, among the Lebombo Mountains. Such names are repeated like a litany, chanted to a presence more powerful than any human one could ever hope to be—or so Rooke seems to imply, as she dispatches her characters.

In *Ratoons,* set in a lusher Natal of canefields, tensions between white and black, Zulu and Indian are thrown up by the stormy plot as if by chance. What we chiefly remember is the sheer force of nature: floods, devastating fires, the "charred trash and the blackened stalks of the cane" from which the green of the new shoots, the ratoons, will spring after rain. Humanity appears to be shaped by this force, and sometimes swept away; human violence appears a vain attempt to assert control, born in rage and ending in a whimper.

In *A Lover for Estelle* the drought that grips the country mirrors the gradual attrition of the Kramer family's innocence even as it brings on their economic ruin. Once again the landscape dominates, impassive in its beauty: "We love this earth for nothing: the grassy plain and mountains are for whoever passes and our suffering or joy makes no mark on them."

If the novels contain an amount of violence that even today seems shocking, history has not disproved this view of southern Africa. Neither an academic nor a political writer, Rooke is content to be a storyteller. She succeeds magnificently, leaving the echoes to do their work—for, though you may forget the details of one of her novels, the particular atmosphere of each remains indelible in the memory.

—Lynne Bryer

ROQUELAURE, A.N.

See RICE, Anne

ROSSNER, Judith

Nationality: American. **Born:** Judith Perelman in New York City, 31 March 1935. **Education:** City College of New York, 1952–55. **Family:** Married 1) Robert Rossner in 1954 (divorced 1972), one daughter and one son; 2) Mort Persky (divorced 1983). Lives in New York City. **Address:** c/o Simon and Schuster, 1230 Avenue of the Americas, New York, New York 10020, U.S.A.

Publications

Novels

To the Precipice. New York, Morrow, 1966; London, Barker, 1977.
Nine Months in the Life of an Old Maid. New York, Dial Press, 1969; London, Weidenfeld and Nicolson, 1977.
Any Minute I Can Split. New York, McGraw Hill, 1972; London, Weidenfeld and Nicolson, 1977.
Looking for Mr. Goodbar. New York, Simon and Schuster, and London, Cape, 1975.
Attachments. New York, Simon and Schuster, and London, Cape, 1977.
Emmeline. New York, Simon and Schuster, and London, Cape, 1980.
August. Boston, Houghton Mifflin, and London, Cape, 1983.
His Little Women. New York, Simon and Schuster, and London, Sinclair Stevenson, 1990.
Olivia; or, The Weight of the Past. New York, Crown, 1994.
Perfidia. New York, Nan A. Talese, 1997.

Uncollected Short Stories

"Please Think of Me as a Friend," in *Ararat* (New York), Winter 1967.
"Voyage of the Earth Maiden," in *Cosmopolitan* (New York), May 1968.
"The Unfaithful Father," in *Mademoiselle* (New York), August 1986.

Other

What Kind of Feet Does a Bear Have? (for children). Indianapolis, Bobbs Merrill, 1963.

*

Manuscript Collection: Mugar Memorial Library, Boston University.

* * *

Judith Rossner's novels are concerned with women and relationships. In almost all of them, starting with *To the Precipice* in 1966 and continuing through *August* in 1983, the story opens with the protagonist's admission that the choices she has made, or not made, in life have been painfully wrong. In most cases, Rossner employs a first-person narrative to chronicle her protagonist's journey to self-discovery. The self-discovery never comes easily and it usually requires hard choices. Rossner's women are often outrageously self-indulgent and needy. They take their pride in thinking of themselves as hysterical types; they bemoan their maimed childhoods; they dwell upon their dreams and daydreams; and most have woken up one day to discover that their marriage of many years is hopelessly inadequate and must be abandoned if they are ever to have a chance to live as complete women with a self of their own. In the hands of a less able and inventive writer, this theme could quickly become banal. It is Rossner's interest in character and her flair for the grotesque and extravagant that carry her narratives. Many of her novels offer a clinical dissection of America's failed marriages and of a culture that has not permitted women to have a life apart from their children and husband. Almost all her books deal with women and their children, women and their sexual hunger, and women and their men. It is difficult to read her novels without keenly appreciating the depth of the psychological disorders which plague our era. Her novels travel from the quiescence and affluence of the 1950s, through the turbulence of the sexual and political upheavals in the mid-1960s, to the more mature feminism of the 1970s and early 1980s when women began to reassess their cry for independence and judge anew another set of sacrifices they have made in the pursuit of balancing the rival claims of mate, children, and work. Even in *Emmeline,* a novel which ostensibly takes the cotton mills in Lowell, Massachusetts in the early nineteenth century as its subject, Rossner makes the reader feel a twentieth-century feminist's outrage at the status of women and the plight of her heroine, a fourteen-year-old girl seduced by a mill foreman and later luckless enough to marry unwittingly her own son, the child she had given up for adoption some nineteen years earlier.

Rossner is intimately knowledgeable about women's dependency and her novels examine it with an often witty and ironic lens. She is thoroughly conversant with the world of what she calls her ''off-the-wall'' women and details in a most convincing way the world of the commune or the New York singles bar or the nineteenth-century mill town. She is immensely indebted to Freud, to the point that one entire novel, *August,* devotes itself to the month when psychiatrists vacation and patients struggle with the pains of withdrawal and transference while the analysts try to resist the tugs of counter-transference. She is heavily influenced by the writing of Doris Lessing, most particularly, *The Golden Notebook* and *The Children of Violence* series, as well as by Erica Jong's ribald *Fear of Flying.* Her writing is often sexually explicit, reveling in its own creation of women's fantasies, quick to celebrate multiple orgasms, and candid in its study of impotence and sexual indifference between married couples. She is savvy about the novel and its readership, exploiting her feminist subject and catering to the tastes of the New York/California sophisticate with an insatiable appetite for novels about neurotic women, free sex, and identity. She has also capitalized on the vogue for non-fiction, drawing on Truman Capote's *In Cold Blood* in her own clinical dissection of a rapist-murderer in *Looking for Mr. Goodbar* and upon the oral telling of Nettie Mitchell, a ninety-four-year-old woman who knew Emmeline when she herself was a child and Emmeline was an old woman. Whether she is exploring the victimization of Emmeline or Terry Dunne, the attractive, educated young schoolteacher of *Looking for Mr. Goodbar* whose sex with a stranger costs her her life, or whether she is analyzing the self-destructiveness of Ruth Kossoff in *To the Precipice,* or Nadine in *Attachments,* or Margaret in *Any Minute I Can Split,* or Dawn Henley in *August,* Rossner manages to make her reader recognize a part of themselves in her confused protagonists. Even when she is depicting with Rabelaisian humor some of the most grotesque scenes—the four-way orgy of Nadine and Dianne and the two joined Siamese twins Amos and Eddie in *Attachments,* or the scene where a 250-pound pregnant naked Margaret prances about her house, hardly raising an eyebrow among her husband's friends in *Any Minute I Can Split*—she is able to make her scene credible, illuminating, and capable of arousing our compassion. Understanding women in psychological *extremis,* Rossner can write ably about them.

In Rossner's early novels the women choose men for the wrong reasons and have their children also for wrong reasons. A goodly proportion of the novels chart the womens' bewildered emotional state in which they are afraid to leave the man they married but never loved, afraid to leave their children, and afraid to accept responsibility for the lives they have chosen and for the actions they belatedly recognized they must take. *To the Precipice* ends with the protagonist pregnant with her lover's child contemplating the difficult decisions she is going to have to confront when she finally acknowledges to her husband that this new child is not his. Knowing she may risk losing custody of her other children, knowing that she has already lost any chance of marrying her childhood lover, knowing that in all probability she might be simply a single mother, she has come to know that no matter what the pain and suffering she fears, she must not slip back into the depression-unto-death that she has previously succumbed to, but rather must face the difficulties ahead. Margaret, in *Any Minute I Can Split,* also learns self-respect. This woman, who flees her husband when she is nine months pregnant at the opening of the book and bears his children in a commune where he does not bother to visit her for many months, and who flirts with the notion of loving either the young hippie who has befriended her on the road, or the married guru of the commune, finally comes to terms with herself, her father, and her husband. Again, the novel leaves us uncertain whether Margaret will, in fact, remain with her husband. He, like the male protagonist in most of Rossner's novels, knows himself most imperfectly, but Margaret has come to recognize some of her own delusions and is herself determined to grow up even if her husband cannot. In *Attachments,* Nadine's needs and capacity for anomie are seemingly without limits. Marrying one of the freakish Siamese twins, and coercing her friend to marry the other so that the two women can remain together, Nadine lives in the circus atmosphere of her own making for more than thirteen years—through the birth of several children, the operation which separates the twins, the trials of her adolescent daughter, to her final decision to leave Amos and accept the guilt of knowing she had neither loved him when he was a freak, nor when he becomes normal. She has to go because she has now learned limits and it has become intolerable to live with the image of her own twisted, hopelessly vulnerable adolescent self. But in this novel, unlike the other two, the reader feels a terrible pity for the male protagonist and much more ambivalent about Nadine's decision.

Emmeline is a poignant book. It is written simply, capturing life in the industrial city of Lowell, and making us see how Emmeline's deprivations and innocence lead to her ruin. There is a sentimentality in the tale, but it is also simple and affecting. When the incest theme completes itself, there is a darkness reminiscent of Edith Wharton's *Ethan Frome.*

In *August* Rossner offers a full portrait of a divorced psychiatrist's life with her children and her lovers, not to mention her patients. In the other novels we see much of the moral confusion of broken households and much of the weight of despair alternating with boredom of the household which remain intact. *August,* although it traces the torturous childhood of Lulu Shinefeld's patient, Dawn, is a more compassionate and healing novel than any of the others. Dawn's life has more than its share of aberrations—after the tragic death of her parents, she has been raised by two lesbians, her surrogate parents, whose "divorce" when the novel opens drives Dawn into the arms of the analyst and many lovers. Nonetheless, despite the lurid details of Dawn's past which are recounted upon the analyst's couch as Dawn tries to recover her past, the novel itself is full of comic and affecting moments and the subplot about Dr. Shinefeld's private life is handled with humor and warmth. Ultimately, in this novel, both women mend, and, in the case of Dr. Shinefeld, we witness how life feels after she has mended and what life without a husband and with a career and children is actually like. The more affirmative character of this novel marks a greater maturity in its author.

His Little Women offers a feminist revisionist's response to Louisa May Alcott's *Little Women.* It counters the Victorian ideals of family, mother and sisterhood with its scathing examination of the broken family of the late twentieth century and its progeny. This new book is replete with divorces, rivalries between half-sisters and wives, and lurid accounts of the breakdown of the family. It offers a late twentieth-century critique of Alcott's novel. In *His Little Women,* the modern counterpart for Marmie is three different women, all connected by the fact that they have been married to the same man, Sam Pearlstein, the Papa March of this postmodern world. One of the Marmie figures is a neurasthenic, narcissistic movie star who coyly plays mistress to her husband, a Hollywood producer with four daughters from three wives. The bookish Jo March from Alcott's *Little Women* is transformed in *His Little Women* into Louisa, an ambitious woman, scarred by her father's neglect. Leaving her own family in order to be joined again with her natural father and ushered into his Hollywood world, Louisa becomes a best-selling novelist, penning a so-called "libelous" novel at the expense of her father and his extended family. It is probably no accident that this figure bears the first name of Alcott, thus commenting upon Alcott's relationship to her subject at the same time as it comments upon one of the characters in Alcott's book. It is difficult to tell who are Meg and Amy in Rossner's rereading of Alcott's novel and certainly Sam Pearlstein, the charismatic, Don Juan father is an unexpected counterpart to Mr. March. There is much in the novel that is more the stuff of pulp fiction and *Princess Daisy* than the work of a serious writer working in the literary traditions that gave rise to the much loved *Little Women.* Too much of Rossner's novel is preoccupied with the role of the writer, the license a writer can take with fact, and the personal costs of writing when the author is a woman, and a mother at that. Nonetheless, the book is funny in places. Its portrait of the Hollywood era of the big stars, producers, and paternalistic studio has a certain authentic ring to it. And like *August,* it is written heavily under the spell of Freud while simultaneously attacking him. *Perfidia* draws on contemporary themes—an abused daughter who ultimately kills her mother—and portrays them against the backdrop of 1970s decadence that had, by the end of the 1990s, become a staple of film if not fiction; but Rossner's unsympathetic portrayal of her characters gives readers few opportunities to bond with the story.

Rossner is an accomplished writer. She can spin a good tale; she can write a chilling, taut novel of suspense and murder or a raucous, bawdy tale of attachments. She writes mostly about women and her writing has further broken the silence that has shrouded so much of women's lives. Her accounts of pregnancy, sex with a stranger, the introduction of a man into a single-parent household, and women's needs explore areas of experience that have traditionally been ignored in the novel.

—Carol Simpson Stern

ROTH, Philip (Milton)

Nationality: American. **Born:** Newark, New Jersey, 19 March 1933. **Education:** Weequahic High School, New Jersey; Newark College, Rutgers University, 1950–51; Bucknell University, Lewisburg, Pennsylvania, 1951–54; A.B. 1954 (Phi Beta Kappa); University of Chicago, 1954–55, M.A. 1955. **Military Service:** Served in the United States Army, 1955–56. **Family:** Married 1) Margaret Martinson in 1959 (separated 1962; died 1968); 2) the actress Claire Bloom in 1990. **Career:** Instructor in English, University of Chicago, 1956–58; visiting writer, University of Iowa, Iowa City, 1960–62; writer-in-residence, Princeton University, New Jersey, 1962–64; visiting writer, State University of New York, Stony Brook, 1966, 1967, and University of Pennsylvania, Philadelphia, 1967–80. Since 1988 Distinguished Professor, Hunter College, New York. General editor, Writers from the Other Europe series, Penguin, publishers, London, 1975–80. Member of the Corporation of Yaddo, Saratoga Springs, New York. **Awards:** Houghton Mifflin literary fellowship, 1959; Guggenheim fellowship, 1959; National Book Award, 1960, 1995, for *Sabbath's Theater*; Daroff award, 1960; American Academy grant, 1960; O Henry award, 1960; Ford Foundation grant, for drama, 1965; Rockefeller fellowship, 1966; National Book Critics Circle award, 1988, for *The Counterlife,* 1992, for *Patrimony;* National Jewish Book award, 1988; PEN-Faulkner award, 1993, for *Operation Shylock*; National Medal of Arts, 1998; Pulitzer prize, 1998, for *American Pastoral;* Jewish Book Council Lifetime Achievement Award, 1999 Honorary degrees: Bucknell University, 1979; Bard College, Annandale-on-Hudson, New York, 1985; Rutgers University, New Brunswick, New Jersey, 1987; Columbia University, New York, 1987. **Member:** American Academy, 1970. **Address:** c/o Simon and Schuster, 1230 Avenue of the Americas, New York, New York 10020, U.S.A.

PUBLICATIONS

Novels

Letting Go. New York, Random House, and London, Deutsch, 1962.

When She Was Good. New York, Random House, and London, Cape, 1967.

Portnoy's Complaint. New York, Random House, and London, Cape, 1969.

Our Gang (Starring Tricky and His Friends). New York, Random House, and London, Cape, 1971.

The Breast. New York, Holt Rinehart, 1972; London, Cape, 1973; revised edition in *A Philip Roth Reader,* 1980.

The Great American Novel. New York, Holt Rinehart, and London, Cape, 1973.

My Life as a Man. New York, Holt Rinehart, and London, Cape, 1974.

The Professor of Desire. New York, Farrar Straus, 1977; London, Cape, 1978.

The Ghost Writer. New York, Farrar Straus, and London, Cape, 1979.

Zuckerman Unbound. New York, Farrar Straus, and London, Cape, 1981.

The Anatomy Lesson. New York, Farrar Straus, 1983; London, Cape, 1984.

The Prague Orgy. London, Cape, 1985.

Zuckerman Bound (includes *The Prague Orgy*). New York, Farrar Straus, 1985.

The Counterlife. New York, Farrar Straus, and London, Cape, 1987.
Deception. New York, Simon and Schuster, and London, Cape, 1990.
Operation Shylock: A Confession. New York, Simon and Schuster, and London, Cape, 1993.
Sabbath's Theater. Boston, Houghton Mifflin, 1995.
American Pastoral. Boston, Houghton Mifflin, 1997.
I Married a Communist. Boston, Houghton Mifflin, 1998.
The Human Stain. Boston, Houghton Mifflin, 2000.

Short Stories

Goodbye, Columbus, and Five Short Stories. Boston, Houghton Mifflin, and London, Deutsch, 1959.
Penguin Modern Stories 3, with others. London, Penguin, 1969.
Novotny's Pain. Los Angeles, Sylvester and Orphanos, 1980.

Uncollected Short Stories

''Philosophy, or Something Like That'' May 1952, ''The Box of Truths'' October 1952, ''The Fence'' May 1953, ''Armando and the Frauds'' October 1953, and ''The Final Delivery of Mr. Thorn'' May 1954, all in *Et Cetera* (Lewisburg, Pennsylvania).
''The Day It Snowed,'' in *Chicago Review,* Fall 1954.
''The Contest for Aaron Gold,'' in *Epoch* (Ithaca, New York), Fall 1955.
''Heard Melodies Are Sweeter,'' in *Esquire* (New York), August 1958.
''Expect the Vandals,'' in *Esquire* (New York), December 1958.
''The Love Vessel,'' in *Dial* (New York), Fall 1959.
''Good Girl,'' in *Cosmopolitan* (New York), May 1960.
''The Mistaken,'' in *American Judaism* (New York), Fall 1960.
''Psychoanalytic Special,'' in *Esquire* (New York), November 1963.
''On the Air,'' in *New American Review 10,* edited by Theodore Solotaroff. New York, New American Library, 1970.
''Smart Money,'' in *New Yorker,* 2 February 1981.
''His Mistress's Voice,'' in *Partisan Review* (Boston), vol. 53, no. 2, 1986.

Play

Television Play: *The Ghost Writer,* with Tristram Powell, from the novel by Roth, 1983.

Other

Reading Myself and Others. New York, Farrar Straus, and London, Cape, 1975; revised edition, London, Penguin, 1985.
A Philip Roth Reader. New York, Farrar Straus, 1980; London, Cape, 1981.
The Facts: A Novelist's Autobiography. New York, Farrar Straus, 1988; London, Cape, 1989.
Patrimony: A True Story. New York, Simon and Schuster, and London, Cape, 1991.
Conversations with Philip Roth, edited by George J. Searles. Jackson, University Press of Mississippi, 1992.
The Conversion of the Jews (for children). Mankato, Minnesota, Creative Education, 1993.
A Philip Roth Reader. London, Vintage, 1993.

*

Bibliography: *Philip Roth: A Bibliography* by Bernard F. Rodgers, Jr., Metuchen, New Jersey, Scarecrow Press, 1974; revised edition, 1984.

Manuscript Collection: Library of Congress, Washington, D.C.

Critical Studies: *Bernard Malamud and Philip Roth: A Critical Essay* by Glenn Meeter, Grand Rapids, Michigan, Eerdmans, 1968; ''The Journey of Philip Roth'' by Theodore Solotaroff, in *The Red Hot Vacuum,* New York, Atheneum, 1970; *The Fiction of Philip Roth* by John N. McDaniel, Haddonfield, New Jersey, Haddonfield House, 1974; *The Comedy That ''Hoits'': An Essay on the Fiction of Philip Roth* by Sanford Pinsker, Columbia, University of Missouri Press, 1975, and *Critical Essays on Philip Roth* edited by Pinsker, Boston, Twayne, 1982; *Philip Roth* by Bernard F. Rodgers, Jr., Boston, Twayne, 1978; ''Jewish Writers'' by Mark Shechner, in *The Harvard Guide to Contemporary American Writing* edited by Daniel Hoffman, Cambridge, Massachusetts, Harvard University Press, 1979; introduction by Martin Green to *A Philip Roth Reader,* New York, Farrar Straus, 1980, London, Cape, 1981; *Philip Roth* by Judith Paterson Jones and Guinevera A. Nance, New York, Ungar, 1981; *Philip Roth* by Hermione Lee, London, Methuen, 1982; *Reading Philip Roth* edited by A.Z. Milbauer and D.G. Watson, London, Macmillan, 1988; *Understanding Philip Roth* by Murray Baumgarten and Barbara Gottfried, Columbia, University of South Carolina Press, 1990; *Philip Roth Revisited* by Jay L. Halio, New York, Twayne, 1992; *Comic Sense: Reading Robert Coover, Stanley Elkin, Philip Roth* by Thomas Pughe, Basel, Birkhäuser, 1994; *Beyond Despair: Three Lectures and a Conversation with Philip Roth* by Aharon Appelfeld, translated by Jeffrey M. Green, New York, Fromm International, 1994; *Philip Roth and the Jews* by Alan Cooper, Albany, State University of New York Press, 1996; *Text/Countertext: Postmodern Paranoia in Samuel Beckett, Doris Lessing, and Philip Roth* by Marie A. Danziger, New York, P. Lang, 1996.

* * *

In the title of one of the best essays on Philip Roth, Alfred Kazin used the word ''toughminded.'' This quality pervades his novels, stories, and essays. Roth's unsparing portraits of Jews too adept at scheming and compromise have upset rabbis and Jewish organizations. His frank acknowledgment of such unmentionables as abortion, masturbation, and sexual calisthenics has alarmed some, but these irate—usually unliterary—responses seem only to have fueled his writing.

Roth has been most at ease with Jewish characters and settings. His ear is especially sensitive to the verbal rhythm and pulse beat of the second-generation American Jew who has recently abandoned the inner city for the suburbs. The stories in Roth's first book, *Goodbye, Columbus,* are almost all concerned with confrontations between Jews of radically different persuasions and temperaments. Thus Neil Klugman, in the title story, confronts the Jewish society of Short Hills, as represented by Brenda Patimkin and her family, where ''fruit grew in their refrigerator and sporting goods dropped from their trees!'' Neil's wrong-side-of-the-track Judaism fails to make the proper concessions and adjustments. In ''Eli, The Fanatic'' the assimilated Jews of another suburban community, Woodenton, employ the lawyer Eli Peck to force a Yeshivah to move elsewhere or at least to ''modernize.'' We see a skillful confrontation between the Talmudic logic of the Yeshivah's headmaster and the more worldly logic of Eli. Eli ends by donning the Hasidic garb of one of the Yeshivah instructors—which suggests to his fellow Jews of Woodenton the return of an earlier nervous breakdown. Jew is also pitted against Jew in ''The Conversion of the Jews,'' This time the questioning Jewish schoolboy Ozzie Freedman forces embarrassing ideological concessions from Rabbi Binder and the Jewish establishment when he threatens to jump from the roof of the synagogue. The stories in *Goodbye, Columbus* are brilliantly irreverent.

Roth's heterodoxy continues into his first novel, *Letting Go,* He enlarges the focus here to include not only the idiosyncrasies of the Jewish community but also of university faculties, charlatan abortionists, and ill-suited love relationships. Very little is left out. Gabe Wallach's ''I'' controls the early parts of the novel; then it recedes into a kind of background first-person and finally turns into a more respectably detached third-person. Wallach is the intruder who keeps moving in and out of delicate situations—always avoiding complete involvement—and so this changing of narrative focus is especially apt. He defines his position early in the novel: ''It was beginning to seem that toward those for whom I felt no strong sentiment, I gravitated; where sentiment existed, I ran.'' Wallach's years as a graduate student at the University of Iowa and as an instructor at the University of Chicago offer a rejection of his eastern seaboard Jewish background (born in New York, educated at Harvard). The first words of the novel are the deathbed letter of Gabe Wallach's mother. This letter, inadvertently tucked between the pages of his copy of James's *Portrait of a Lady,* starts Gabe off on the midwestern pilgrimage which involves the series of precarious relationships with Libby and Paul Herz and with Martha Reganhart. The terribly flawed Herz marriage somehow survives Gabe's ''meddling''; in fact, it is strengthened by the adoption of a child and by a spirited assertion of Judaism. Gabe Wallach's love affair with Martha Reganhart fares less well. Gabe speaks of himself in a final letter to Libby as an ''indecisive man'' who had had but ''one decisive moment.''

Roth also places his next novel, *When She Was Good,* in the midwest—this time a midwest without Jews. The texture of his writing changes markedly; it seems to flatten out, to become, as Theodore Solotaroff suggests, ''a language of scrupulous banality.'' The midwestern Protestantism which underlies the novel is threatened only by an adolescent flirtation with the Catholic Church by the heroine Lucy Nelson; this is lightly dismissed as ''all that Catholic hocus-pocus.'' Lucy's intolerance and uncomfortable moral provincialism manage to get in the way of her own marriage and that of her parents. She cannot put up with her husband's rather puerile brashness and incompetence or with her father's alcoholism.

Just as Roth was able to capture the special quality of the conversation of both first and second generation American Jews in *Goodbye, Columbus* and *Letting Go,* so in *When She Was Good* he manages handsomely with the cliché-ridden language of Main Street.

Portnoy's Complaint is a return, with a vengeance, to Roth's earlier manner. It seems to come out of the best pages of *Goodbye, Columbus* and *Letting Go.* Roth has settled here on all the things he knows how to do best, especially in his creation of the urban Jewish family with the mother at its moral center. *Portnoy's Complaint* is the staccato confession of Alexander Portnoy to his psychiatrist Dr. Spielvogel (who makes another appearance in *My Life As a Man*) in heavily free associative prose.

The novel begins with a section entitled ''The Most Unforgettable Character I've Met''; the reference is to Sophie Portnoy who dominates not only the family but also the ''confessions'' of her son. (She is in part anticipated by Aunt Gladys in ''Goodbye, Columbus'' and Paul Herz's mother in *Letting Go.*) She characteristically pushes to the background her perpetually constipated and henpecked husband and her pathetically unendowed daughter. The confrontation is between mother and son. The fiercely aggressive, domineering mother seems to win out since it is the son who does the confessing from the analyst's couch. Alex, however, gains some measure of revenge through sieges of masturbation in his youth and through affairs with gentiles (*shiksas*) in his more mature years. He masterfully uncovers chinks in his Jewish mother's armor by taunting her with his conquest of Christian girls and by abusing the family rabbi, but always at the expense of his own too active feelings of guilt. Everything in this novel, it would seem, ''can be traced to the bonds obtaining in the mother-child relationship.'' Jewish mothers, in the past few years, have presented a challenge to some of the best American Jewish novelists, like Wallace Markfield, Bruce Jay Friedman, and Herbert Gold. Probably the most realized and convincing of all is Sophie Portnoy.

Roth's versatility is very much in evidence in *Our Gang (Starring Tricky and His Friends),* he seems able to manage the rhetoric of political corruption quite as easily as the language of the Jewish urban dweller who has recently retreated to the suburbs. In *Our Gang* Roth takes on a formidable adversary, the Nixon administration: he carried a certain Trick E. Dixon from a press conference, an underground meeting with his ''coaches;'' an address to his ''fellow Americans,'' to an election speech—following his assassination—to his ''fellow Fallen'' in Hell. This speech ends with the revealing sentence: ''And let there be no mistake about it: if I am elected Devil, I intend to see Evil triumph in the end; I intend to see that our children, and our children's children, need never know the terrible scourge of Righteousness and Peace.'' Passages from Swift and Orwell appropriately serve as epigraphs for this novel.

The Breast, in certain ways, marks a return to *Portnoy's Complaint.* One might think of this novella—with its college professor narrator, David Alan Kepesh, who turns into a female breast—as a working out of certain fantasies suggested by *Portnoy* with some help from Kafka, Gogol, and Swift. The bookish hero cannot resist likening his peculiar condition to that of Kafka's Gregor Samsa who awakens to discover that he has turned into a huge bug or to that of Gogol's Kovalyov who awakens to find that he is missing his nose; he makes reference also to Swift's ''self-satisfied Houyhnhnms'' and to ''Gulliver among the Brobdingnags,'' in which country ''the king's maidservants had him walk out on their nipples for the fun of it.''

The Great American Novel seems to have little in common with the previous fiction. This baseball novel is Roth's contributions to a genre that has already attracted several other American Jewish writers, including Bernard Malamud and Mark Harris. It is filled with oblique references to a wide variety of literary works. Thus it begins with the sentence, ''Call me Smitty.'' A sensational pitcher goes under the name Gil Gamesh. American literature and baseball are occasionally brought together in uneasy confrontation; they make for strange bedfellows. This mock-heroic tone reinforces the sense of caricature and pastiche which runs through the novel. Roth holds up the myth of the Great American Novel to the same ridicule as the myth of the Great American Pastime.

My Life As a Man fits snugly into place in the main line of Philip Roth's development. The Jewish ingredients are less pronounced here than in *Goodbye, Columbus, Letting Go,* and *Portnoy's Complaint,* yet the ambience is unmistakably the same. The writer-hero of the novel, Peter Tarnopol, has much in common with Gabe Wallach, Alexander Portnoy, and David Alan Kepesh. Indeed he has the same bookish tendencies as Kepesh. Roth offers a clever variation on the novel-within-the-novel device as he prefaces the main part of his work, ''My True Story'' (Tarnopol's sustained confessional), with two of his protagonist's short stories. The ''useful fictions,'' as Roth calls these stories, have a great deal to do with Tarnopol's ''true story''; truth and fiction, it would seem, are ultimately interchangeable. *My Life As a Man* reveals Roth in his dual roles as novelist and critic. The narrative strategy allows for a good deal of theorizing about the nature of novel-writing and a certain amount of literary criticism.

The Professor of Desire and *The Ghost Writer,* both first-person novels, borrow as narrators characters who appeared in the earlier fiction. *The Professor of Desire,* like *The Breast,* is told by David Kepesh while Nathan Zuckerman, the central presence in the ''Useful Fictions'' section of *My Life As a Man,* narrates *The Ghost Writer. The Professor of Desire* offers an elaborate unfolding of Kepesh's *wanderjahre* in the years preceding his metamorphosis. The restless narrative starts and ends in the Catskills—the Jewish still point of the novel. The itinerary is dotted with literary and amorous ''excavations.'' Since his graduate school days at Stanford, Kepesh has been working intermittently on a book about romantic disillusionment in Chekhov's stories. A real and imagined Kafka occupies a central position in the Prague interlude. The amorous is even more in evidence than the literary, as Kepesh makes his way from a succession of girl friends, to a marriage and divorce, finally to a rather idyllic relationship with Claire Ovington.

The literary and the amorous are also strongly evident in *The Ghost Writer.* The novel turns about an odd triangular relationship, involving the narrator, Zuckerman, the renowned writer E.I. Lonoff, and a young lady who has served a kind of apprenticeship (literary and perhaps also sexual) at Lonoff's feet, Amy Bellette. Zuckerman, a youthful author, arrives at Lonoff's house at the beginning of this short novel, in retreat from his cloying Jewish parents and his Newark childhood. He is an onlooker, in much the same way as Styron's narrator in *Sophie's Choice,* as he tries to unravel the complications of a situation that couples the erotic with the literary. With some help from Henry James's *The Middle Years* and other literary texts, Zuckerman weaves a complex mosaic which turns Amy Bellette into the author of *The Diary of Anne Frank.* The mythological machinery he invents here is in a sense his work of art: the gesture which will make him worthy of becoming Lonoff's ''spiritual son'' and perhaps eventually Amy's sexual partner. In *The Ghost Writer* Roth seems to have moved his familiar literary baggage to a new setting, rural New England; with the change has come a minimizing of the ethnically Jewish world of the early fiction in favor of a broader Judaeo-Christian canvas.

The Ghost Writer can probably be read, as several reviewers have suggested, as being something of a *roman à clef:* with Zuckerman taking on many aspects of the young Roth, halfway through his first book, *Goodbye, Columbus,* looking for a Jewish literary patron and finding him in Lonoff, who is probably a composite figure with a heady dose of Bernard Malamud and a suspicion of Isaac Bashevis Singer and Isaac Babel. One can continue this kind of reading with *Zuckerman Unbound,* which takes place in 1969, thirteen years after the events of *The Ghost Writer.* Nathan Zuckerman, who has abdicated his role as narrator in this third-person novel, has just published a controversial best-seller, *Carnovsky,* which bears an uncanny resemblance to Roth's 1969 *Portnoy's Complaint.* (This title may offer an oblique reminder of I.J. Singer's *The Family Carnovsky* which, in its translation from the Yiddish, also appeared in 1969).

Zuckerman Unbound concerns the aftermath of this event as Zuckerman spends much of his time coping with the bittersweet smell of post-*Carnovsky* success, disentangling himself from his creature Gilbert Carnovsky, picking up the pieces of his most recent broken marriage. We see him during a variety of encounters: with his agent, his answering service, a beautiful Irish actress, members of his family, and a curious interloper named Alvin Pepler (who takes on the role of his ''double'' or ''secret sharer''). If the novel has an epiphany it occurs toward the end when Zuckerman flies to Miami to witness the death of his father, only to hear him pronounce, as his dying word, ''bastard''—unmistakably directed at his author son. Nathan's desperate litany in the final paragraph sums up the futility: ''You are no longer any man's son, you are no longer some good woman's husband, you are no longer your brother's brother, and you don't come from anywhere anymore, either.''

The Anatomy Lesson sounds an even more wrenching note of despair. Zuckerman, now forty years old, is unable to write and is forced to wear an orthopedic collar to support his neck; psychic pain combines with physical pain to make his life unbearable. The only reprieve is offered by the visits of four women who ''exercise'' (also exorcise) him on a ''playmat.'' The central text in *The Anatomy Lesson* is probably Mann's *The Magic Mountain,* which one of the woman reads to him; it serves something of the same purpose as *The Middle Years* did in *The Ghost Writer.* Alvin Pepler was a haunting presence throughout *Zuckerman Unbound,* but nothing quite as terrifying and obsessive as the literary critic Milton Appel proves to be here. (In another flirtation with the possibilities of *roman à clef,* Roth has modeled Appel after Irving Howe who had singularly harsh things to say about his work, including the devastating comment, in a December 1972 *Commentary* article, ''Philip Roth Reconsidered,'' that the cruelest thing would be to read *Portnoy's Complaint* twice.)

Zuckerman finally decides to renegotiate the circumstances of his life, as he leaves New York for Chicago: ''By nightfall his career as a writer would be officially over and the future as a physician underway.'' The closest he gets to a medical career is a long stay at a university hospital, first as patient, then as patient accompanying interns on their monotonous rounds.

Zuckerman Bound contains the three Zuckerman novels, now declared to be a trilogy, and an epilogue, the novella-length *The Prague Orgy.* This postlude offers segments from Zuckerman's notebooks, one from New York, dated 11 January 1976, the other two from Prague, dated February 4 and 5 of the same year. A seemingly revitalized Zuckerman leaves New York for Prague to recover the unpublished Yiddish stories of a certain Sisovsky, the father of a Czech writer he meets in New York; we are told that ''this is not the Yiddish of Sholem Aleichem. This is the Yiddish of Flaubert,'' Zuckerman does finally gain possession of this material only to have it confiscated before he leaves Prague. This failed mission seems to be linked to Kafka at every turn. The author of ''The Metamorphosis,'' for example, makes an intriguing appearance: ''*As Nathan Zuckerman awoke one morning from uneasy dreams he found himself transformed in his bed into a sweeper of floors in a railway café*'' (Roth's italics). This is not only the twentieth-century Prague of Kafka revisited but also perhaps the sixteenth-century Prague of the golem—the creation of the Maharal, Rabbi Jehuda Loew—who was to save the Jews from Czech atrocities. One can agree with Harold Bloom who sees *The Prague Orgy* as something of a summa, ''a kind of coda to all his [Roth's] fiction so far.''

Roth's Zuckermania continues into *The Counterlife,* which critics were quick to characterize as Roth's first serious flirtation with metafiction. David Denby expressed this as well as anybody when he spoke of Roth's having "abandoned narrative solidity altogether, reviving characters supposedly dead, allowing characters to review their fictional representation, folding fictions within fictions, becoming, in fact, an earnest writer of 'metafiction.'" Nathan Zuckerman and his brother Henry dominate the narrative which restlessly moves across the globe, with stops in New Jersey, Israel, and England. Among other unlikely occurrences, we see both Henry and Nathan returning from the dead after unsuccessful encounters with open-heart surgery. Toward the end of the novel, Nathan receives a long letter from his beloved Maria, which begins: "I'm leaving. I've left. I'm leaving you and I'm leaving the book ... I know characters rebelling against their author has been done before ..."

The Facts completes the task started by *The Counterlife* and emphatically brings Roth onto the postmodern scene, especially in the sense that distinctions between fact and fiction no longer apply. Roth brackets the memoir part of his narrative—five chapters and a prologue of seeming "factual" autobiography—with epistolary exchanges between himself and Nathan Zuckerman. Zuckerman's thiry-five-page letter, which concludes *The Facts,* is filled with the rebelliousness of the character turning on the author, a more realized example of the species than Maria's letter in *The Counterlife.* Nathan questions the nature of Roth's enterprise in postmodern language: "With autobiography there's always another text, a countertext, if you will, to the one presented. It's probably the most manipulative of all literary forms." In *The Facts,* fact and fiction seem to rub up against each other, blurring distinctions between the two.

Deception relies entirely on dialogue, dialogue rendered through quotation marks rather than Joycean dashes. We listen in on a babel of voices—often recycling material from the earlier novels—which allow the erotic to mingle freely with the aesthetic. One of the unnumbered, untitled chapters begins: "'This is the situation. Zuckerman, my character, dies. His young biographer is having lunch with somebody, and he's talking about his difficulties getting started with the book.'" The biographer's craft is discussed for several pages as fact and fiction once again seem to be on a collision course: "The Lonoff book turned out to be a critical biography, *Between Worlds, The Life of E.I. Lonoff.* The tentative title of the Zuckerman book is *Improvisations on a Self* ..."

Deception seems to thrive on *trompe l'oeil* effects. The author himself enters the frame of his novel and makes a number of revealing statements, such as "'I write fiction and I'm told it's autobiography, I write autobiography and I'm told it's fiction ...'" Or this metafictional insertion: "'I have been imagining myself, outside of my novel, having a love affair with a character inside my novel.'"

The Counterlife, The Facts, and *Deception* form a curious trilogy of artistic dissent. The presence of Nathan Zuckerman in all three makes one feel that he has emphatically replaced all those earlier literary alter egos, such as Gabe Wallach, Peter Tarnopol, and David Alan Kepesh.

The mid- to late 1990s saw a shower of novels and awards attending the apogee of Roth's career. In *Sabbath's Theater,* his portrayal of Mickey Sabbath, a failed theater owner and misanthrope almost worthy of Moliere, won Roth a National Book Award. *American Pastoral* exceeded its predecessors in all respects, a fact measured by its winning a Pulitzer: in this, perhaps Roth's greatest work, the unravelling of America in the mid-twentieth century takes on a highly personal dimension in the personae of the mild-mannered Swede Levov and his troubled daughter Merry. Much of the imagery in the earlier part of the book is as peaceful as the title suggests, and this makes the confrontation with the hatred, violence, and militancy of the 1960s all the more painful. Overcome by radical fervor—a fervor for which Roth has no sympathy, given the fact that it is turned against the very nation that nurtured their parents—Merry and her friends plant a bomb that kills an innocent man. Thus Swede and his family are forced "out of the longed-for American pastoral and into everything that is its antithesis and its enemy—into the fury, the violence and the desperation of the counter-pastoral—into the American berserk."

Here Roth has almost completely transcended the narrow ethnic confines of his earlier work. His characters happen to be Jewish in the same sense that Dostoyevsky's happen to be Russian: it is the world the author knows, and ethnic or national identity is integral to that world, but the message belongs to a much wider audience. After *American Pastoral,* Roth faltered with *I Married a Communist,* a book guilty of an unpardonable sin— it was boring—but he more than redeemed himself with *The Human Stain,* a work that proved the author as inventive and as capable of surprises as he has ever been.

—Melvin J. Friedman, updated by Judson Knight

ROY, Arundhati

Nationality: Indian. **Born:** Kerala, India, c. 1960. **Education:** Attended architectural school. **Career:** Sold cakes on a beach in Goa, India; worked as an architect; actress, screenwriter, and novelist. Lives in New Delhi, India. **Awards:** Booker prize, 1997. **Agent:** c/o Random House, 201 East 50th Street, New York, New York 10022, U.S.A.

PUBLICATIONS

Novels

The God of Small Things. New York, Random House, 1997.

Other

The Cost of Living. New York, Modern Library, 1999.

Introduction, *India: A Mosaic* by Ian Buruma; edited by Robert B. Silvers and Barbara Epstein. New York, New York Review Books, 2000.

*

Critical Studies: *Arundhati Roy, The Novelist Extraordinary,* edited by R. K. Dhawan, New Delhi, Prestige Books, 1999.

* * *

Arundhati Roy's *The God of Small Things* was one of the most remarkable and talked-about fiction débuts of the 1990s. Garnering enormous interest before publication for its million-dollar advance, and later for winning the Booker Prize, this inventive first novel garnered critical acclaim throughout the world. Like many Indian novelists of the past generation—including Salman Rushdie, Anita Desai, Amitav Ghosh, and Bharati Mukherjee—Roy addresses the theme of history and the individual; also like them she makes the political personal by framing it through the eyes of bewildered children as well as the wiser eyes of the psychologically bruised adults they become.

The twins at the center of the novel, brother Estha and sister Rahel, are seven in December, 1969, and 31 in May, 1994, when the novel opens. Alternating between the two time periods, the narrative explores the impact of the tragic drowning of Sophie Mol, a nine-year-old cousin visiting India from London. Her death in 1969 was part of a complex series of events that destroyed the extended family and caused the formerly inseparable twins to be parted for over twenty-four years. Following an unusual structure, Roy paints the broad strokes of the whole story in the first chapter. She then continues to circle around and around the central events, accumulating details and finally plunging into her narrative core at the end. This method is reflected in two striking images: of ''a funnel of mosquitoes, like an inverted dunce cap'' whining over people's heads, and especially the image of a group of bats that ''coalesced and blackened'' over the ''History House'' where key events take place, then suddenly plummet down through the ''History-hole'' in the roof. With its non-linear gathering, repetitions, and deferral of its most painful and ecstatic moments, Roy's intimate narrative reflects the logic of human memory sifting through the past to assess the damaged state of the present.

The story is both unsettlingly funny and brutally sad. Though primarily focused on a well-off but decadent anglophile family ''trapped outside their own history,'' it also offers a rich social portrait of a region (the state of Kerala in Southern India) combustive with repressed violence and historical tensions. The world's first democratically elected Communist government may be in power but the ''Edges, Borders, Boundaries, Brinks and Limits'' of ancient class and caste systems continue to divide Indians. However, the rules that enforce these divisions prompt some, like the twins' mother Ammu, to radically transgress them, breaking not only the laws of history but also ''the Love Laws ... that lay down who should be loved, and how.'' As in many Indian novels, *The God of Small Things* shows history making its first and most powerful inscriptions on the human body. Ammu outrages family and social proprieties by loving Velutha, a carpenter whom the family has patronized but steered clear of since he belongs to an ''Untouchable'' caste. Ammu is one of several sexual taboo-breakers in the novel; while transgressive eros is equated in her case with the kind of provocative radicalism that could shake up an ossified status quo, in the case of the Orangedrink Lemondrink Man sex is simply self-indulgent abuse of a child. Whether associated with transcendent or base pleasures, all such acts (with one exception) are shown to have damaging, violent effects. In the exception, Estha and Rahel as adults drift into a healing incestuous love, joining their bodies as the only way to bridge the distance and silence that have severed them for so long.

The novel's playful, ironic humor emerges through the quirky seven-year-old minds whose perspectives dominate, and through the novel's eccentric prose style. Reflecting in English the linguistic resources and habits of Malayalam (Kerala's vernacular), Roy's writing abounds in sentence fragments and one-line paragraphs, coinages formed by fusing or chopping up words (''thiswayandthat,'' ''Lay. Ter.'') and idiosyncratic capitalizations (''Who d'you love Most in the World?'') that reflect the youthful fixations of Estha and Rahel. Indeed, many capitalizations are anthropomorphized abstractions: an overwhelming force or event (History, Biology, the Return of Estha, the Loss of Sophie Moll) will be animated so that it may be brought down to size and pictured having its effects, moving potently through the twins' world like an unpredictable animal. Although many critics find Roy's exuberant style overwrought or precious, especially in its penchant for repeating key phrases and images, she makes a unique contribution to a long-standing literary tradition in India. Ever since Raja Rao's famous statement, made in 1938, that he aims ''to convey in a language that is not one's own the spirit that is one's own,'' Indian novelists have bent and twisted the English of their colonizers to reflect local speech-rhythms and patterns of thought.

Portraying the village of Ayemenem and its inhabitants as burdened by poisonous grievances and layers of dust and defeat that they cannot shake off, *The God of Small Things* dramatizes the destructive gap that separates those with an eye to the future, who aspire to transform history, and those with an eye to the past, who are content to wallow in its accumulated personal and social debris. The novel also reveals the hideous harm done to children not old enough to competently negotiate that gap—sinned-against innocents who fall into the chasm even as they are made to feel, guiltily, that they are the sinners who created it. Part love story, part political fable, part linguistic dazzle, and part psychological drama, *The God of Small Things* firmly establishes Arundhati Roy as a complex and original contemporary writer.

—John Clement Ball

RUBENS, Bernice (Ruth)

Nationality: British. **Born:** Cardiff, Wales, 26 July 1928. **Education:** Cardiff High School for Girls; University College of South Wales and Monmouthshire, Cardiff, 1944–47, B.A. (honours) in English 1947. **Family:** Married Rudi Nassauer in 1947; two daughters. **Career:** English teacher, Handsworth Grammar School for Boys, Birmingham, 1948–49. Since 1950 documentary film writer and director, for the United Nations and others. **Awards:** American Blue Ribbon Award, for filmmaking, 1968; Booker prize, 1970; Welsh Arts Council award, 1976. Fellow, University of Wales, Cardiff, 1982. **Address:** 16-A Belsize Park Gardens, London NW3 4LD, England.

PUBLICATIONS

Novels

Set on Edge. London, Eyre and Spottiswoode, 1960.
Madame Sousatzka. London, Eyre and Spottiswoode, 1962.
Mate in Three. London, Eyre and Spottiswoode, 1965.
The Elected Member. London, Eyre and Spottiswoode, 1969; as *Chosen People,* New York, Atheneum, 1969.
Sunday Best. London, Eyre and Spottiswoode, 1971; New York, Summit, 1980.
Go Tell the Lemming. London, Cape, 1973; New York, Washington Square Press, 1984.

I Sent a Letter to My Love. London, W.H. Allen, 1975; New York, St. Martin's Press, 1978.
The Ponsonby Post. London, W.H. Allen, 1977; New York, St. Martin's Press, 1978.
A Five Year Sentence. London, W.H. Allen, 1978; as *Favours,* New York, Summit, 1979.
Spring Sonata. London, W.H. Allen, 1979; New York, Warner, 1986.
Birds of Passage. London, Hamish Hamilton, 1981; New York, Summit, 1982.
Brothers. London, Hamish Hamilton, 1983; New York, Delacorte Press, 1984.
Mr. Wakefield's Crusade. London, Hamish Hamilton, and New York, Delacorte Press, 1985.
Our Father. London, Hamish Hamilton, and New York, Delacorte Press, 1987.
Kingdom Come. London, Hamish Hamilton, 1990.
A Solitary Grief. London, Sinclair Stevenson, 1991.
Mother Russia. London, Chapmans, 1992.
Autobiopsy. London, Sinclair Stevenson, 1993.
Yesterday in the Back Lane. London, Little, Brown, 1995.
The Waiting Game. London, Little, Brown, 1997.
I, Dreyfus. London, Little, Brown, 1999.

Plays

I Sent a Letter to My Love, adaptation of her own novel (produced New Haven, Connecticut, 1978; London, 1979).
Hijack. New York and London, French, 1993.

Screenplays (documentaries; also director): *One of the Family,* 1964; *Call Us By Name,* 1968; *Out of the Mouths,* 1970.

Television Play: *Third Party,* 1972.

*

Bernice Rubens comments:

(1972) I am never consciously aware of the actual matter of my work and never think about it unless the question is directly raised. There seems to be a terrible finality about assessing one's own work, because such an assessment might bind you to that evaluation forever. I am open to the most radical changes in my thinking and outlook. I hope it will be reflected in my work. My first four novels were essentially on Jewish themes in a Jewish environment, for in that environment I felt secure. My fifth novel, *Sunday Best,* was an attempt to challenge myself to step outside that familiarity. I noticed that my radical change of location did not involve as radical a change of style, which seems to remain simple, direct, always empty of what in school is called ''descriptive passages,'' for these frighten me. As to the matter of what I write about, I can only be general. I am concerned with the communication, or non-communication as is more often the case, between people and families. A general enough statement, and in this general sense my books will always be about that theme.

* * *

The salient feature of Bernice Ruben's writing is her maddening refusal to fit neatly into any single category, while proffering the same unchanging, unmistakably individual vision of humanity. Some of her novels approach sheer slapstick (*Set on Edge*), others a Hitchcockian murder story (*Mr. Wakefield's Crusade, Sunday Best*), others a case study of the strains of family life (*The Elected Member, Set on Edge, Spring Sonata, Brothers*), others again a comedy of manners (the expatriate set in *The Ponsonby Post,* a cruise in *Birds of Passage,* eccentric lodgers in *Madame Sousatzka*). The variety is considerable, but they all present the same picture of human misery, miscomprehension, of loneliness slipping into madness.

Her earlier novels pillory the claustrophobic closeness of Jewish family life, pointing an accusing finger at the Jewish matriarch with her devouring, ambitious mother love. Her first novel, *Set on Edge,* takes its title from the words of the prophet Ezekiel (''The fathers have eaten sour grapes, and the children's teeth are set on edge'') which ought to hang as a motto over any analyst's couch. Mrs. Sperber burdens her daughter Gladys with guilt, and at the close of the novel we watch Gladys taking over her mother's role as the accuser as well as the provider. Mrs. Crominski in *Madame Sousatzka,* Mrs. Zweck in *The Elected Member,* Sheila's mother and grandmother in *Spring Sonata* all provide good Laingian material, parading their maternal guilt. Indeed Bernice Rubens shows her *romans* to be very much *à thèse* here, particularly in her Booker prize winner, *The Elected Member,* with its epigraph from R.D. Laing himself (''If patients are *disturbed,* their families are *disturbing*'').

Her novelist's imagination, however, refuses to be circumscribed, and she turns away from the familiarity of Jewish life in North London to find the same tragicomedies of emotional crippling played out against a gentile background. The transvestite George Verrey Smith in *Sunday Best,* the lonely spinster Jean Hawkins in *A Five Year Sentence,* the sad homosexual Luke in *Mr. Wakefield's Crusade* are all walking wounded on the battlefield of life, maimed by a loveless childhood, free of guilt because they are the victims, the sinned against rather than the sinning.

Faces with such unspeakable misery, Rubens chooses to laugh, and her echoing laughter is truly shocking. She is a witty writer, with a brilliant sense of comedy: Jenny's client in *Madame Sousatzka,* in his shirtsleeves, masquerading as a carpenter; Mrs. Sperber in *Set on Edge* taking her rolled-up corset to bed with her like a child with a teddy bear; the parade of too many Hitlers at the fancy dress party in *Birds of Passage* (like ''the Hall of Mirrors in Berchtesgaden''), all these are very funny set pieces. There are many such moments of high comedy in Rubens's novels, but she is equally skilled in the use of sly verbal wit (Luke's comment on the ''posh deaths'' in *The Times,* Betty Knox in *Birds of Passage* asking her husband how many people had witnessed her humiliation ''as if he were responsible for the gate''). In her recent novel *Kingdom Come* Rubens returns to the Jewish theme but with a difference, telling the tale of Sabbotai Zvi, the founder of a seventeenth-century Middle Eastern messianic sect. The comic scenes, the flip echoes of the New Testament, oddly enhance the underlying terror of her story.

Like all witty writers she uses language with great care—if a single right word (like ''gate'' in the quotation above) is enough to make a reader laugh then words must be treated with proper respect. Her writing is spare, as befits the bleak landscape of her vision. Her sombre, plain sentences can be very moving (the chilling prayer that closes *The Elected Member,* ''Dear God, look after us cold and chosen ones,'' has such power). There is a striking absence of description. Although she provides those recognisable authentic touches that mark present-day novels—Alice's silk dungarees in

Birds of Passage, the shuffling post office queue in *Mr. Wakefield's Crusade*—her characters move against a blank background, almost faceless themselves. This technique, particularly remarkable in *Birds of Passage* where full descriptions are provided of the supporting cast and yet we never see the two protagonists, Ellen and Alice, is obviously deliberate. By blurring the faces she is calling our attention to the turmoil behind. It is the human mind and the human heart that interest her, and if her interest strikes us at times as chillingly clinical (as, again in *Birds of Passage,* in the description of the two women's reaction to rape: ''The women were reacting in diametrically opposed fashion to exactly the same agent, though neither knew of the other's connection'') then our shocked reaction is exactly what the author intended. Her purpose is to shock, as well as to amuse, and to achieve this dual purpose she will stop at nothing. Such deliberate excesses (as the episode of Betty Knox's soiled skirt in *Birds of Passage*) are of course all the more startling in a writer so much in control of her material.

To dwell only on her attention to her craft, however, is to present a false picture, for she is a writer of imagination, with a penchant for the bizarre, the grotesque. The fetus which refuses to be born, playing the fiddle and writing his diary in his mother's womb (*Spring Sonata*), is the product of no ordinary imagination, and comparisons with Gogol's *Nose* are not entirely out of place. The same rich imagination is at work on the plot of *Mr. Wakefield's Crusade* (over which the plump shadow of Alfred Hitchcock seems to hover) and on the domesticated madness of *A Five Year Sentence.* These are excesses of imagination, shocking and frightening as they are fully intended to be, for they are a part of Bernice Rubens's world in which the dullness of pain can only be broken by a loud laugh or a scream of terror.

With two epic novels, *Brothers* and *Mother Russia,* Bernice Rubens marked what was be a complete change in her subject matter and treatment of her characters. Rubens has put aside her cynical observations on society, but she has not lost her acute powers of analysis. Instead she projects compassion directly, rather than through accidents of farce or the comic. *Brothers* and *Mother Russia* particularly embody her new style and also show her gift in sustaining, very ably, the threads of extremely long narratives. Both have similarities in that they trace the progress of families and their paths of destiny. In *Brothers,* the Bindel family, who are Russian Jews, survive through each generation of various persecutions, from 1825 to the 1970s, because they learn the message that is passed on, that ''There is no cause on earth worth dying for… . Only in the name of love is Death worthy!'' The panorama is vast, taking in the Odessa, Wales, and Buchenwald. If at times the Bindel's accident of fate seems rather contrived to fit ''real'' historical events they are involved in, the cumulative effect of *Brothers* is a sensitive account of Jewish oppression.

Mother Russia, which opens in the year 1900 and ends in 1985, is both the history of two families and a twentieth-century history of Russia, the USSR, and the second Revolution of Gorbachev. Although extremely long, the appalling trials of Anna Larionov, formerly an aristocrat, and her peasant husband Sasha Volynin, who becomes a writer, are profoundly moving. Both born on the first day of the new century, on the Larionov estate, they are inseparable, even through family betrayal, Stalinism, and Siberia, until they return to die at the place they were born. ''All that matters'' Rubens writes, ''is the loving. Without it there is no beginning. And without a beginning there is little reason to reach for the end,'' emphasising her philosophy of *Brothers.*

A Solitary Grief is a tragedy about Doris, a Down's Syndrome baby, and the inability of her father, Dr. Crown, to look on her face. ''Physician heal thyself'' might be the hidden motto for this novel, for the father is a psychiatrist who has no ability to analyse himself. Both he and his daughter are victims, common enough Rubens characters, but Doris functions more ''normally'' than her father, until he murders her for complex reasons, involving the betrayal and death of a man society judged to be hideous because of excessive body hair. The details are grotesque, but instead of evoking a response of humour, as it would had it appeared in her earlier work, Rubens now rouses deep compassion. Less convincing because it moves in the realms of fantasy is *Autobiopsy,* where the brain of a dead world-famous novelist is kept in a freezer, and his hitherto past secret life, is syphoned off by a friend who plans to turn it into a book. The improbability of the plot perhaps strains the imagination, although if the book is a failure, it is a quite brilliant one.

—Hana Sambrook, updated by Geoffrey Elborn

RULE, Jane (Vance)

Nationality: Canadian. **Born:** Plainfield, New Jersey, United States, 28 March 1931. **Education:** Palo Alto High School, California; Mills College, Oakland, California (Ardella Mills award, 1952), 1948–52, B.A. in English 1952 (Phi Beta Kappa); University College, London, 1952–53; Stanford University, California, 1953. **Career:** Teacher of English and biology, Concord Academy, Massachusetts, 1954–56; assistant director of International House, 1958–59, intermittent lecturer in English, 1959–72, and guest lecturer in creative writing, 1972–73, University of British Columbia, Vancouver. Since 1974 full-time writer. **Awards:** Canada Council award, 1969, 1970; Canadian Authors Association prize, for short story, 1978, for novel, 1978; Gay Academic Union (USA) award, 1978; Fund for Human Dignity (USA) award, 1983. D.H.L., University of British Columbia, 1994. **Agent:** Georges Borchardt Inc., 136 East 57th Street, New York, New York 10022, USA. **Address:** The Fork, Route 1 S.19 C17, Galiano, British Columbia V0N 1P0, Canada.

PUBLICATIONS

Novels

Desert of the Heart. Toronto, Macmillan, and London, Secker and Warburg, 1964; Cleveland, World, 1965.

This Is Not for You. New York, McCall, 1970; London, Pandora Press, 1987.

Against the Season. New York, McCall, 1971; London, Davies, 1972.

The Young in One Another's Arms. New York, Doubleday, 1977; London, Pandora Press, 1990.

Contract with the World. New York, Harcourt Brace, 1980; London, Pandora Press, 1990.

Memory Board. Tallahassee, Florida, Naiad Press, and London, Pandora Press, 1987.

After the Fire. Tallahassee, Florida, Naiad Press, and London, Pandora Press, 1989.

Short Stories

Theme for Diverse Instruments. Vancouver, Talonbooks, 1975; Tallahassee, Florida, Naiad Press, 1990.
Outlander (includes essays). Tallahassee, Florida, Naiad Press, 1981.
Inland Passage and Other Stories. Tallahassee, Florida, Naiad Press, 1985.

Uncollected Short Stories

''Your Father and I,'' in *Housewife* (London), vol. 23, no. 8, 1961.
''No More Bargains,'' in *Redbook* (New York), September 1963.
''Three Letters to a Poet,'' in *Ladder* (Reno, Nevada), May-June 1968.
''Moving On,'' in *Redbook* (New York), June 1968.
''Houseguest,'' in *Ladder* (Reno, Nevada), January 1969.
''The List,'' in *Chatelaine* (Toronto), April 1969.
''Not an Ordinary Wife,'' in *Redbook* (New York), August 1969.
''Anyone Will Do,'' in *Redbook* (New York), October 1969.
''The Secretary Bird,'' in *Chatelaine* (Toronto), August 1972.
''The Bosom of the Family,'' in *75: New Canadian Stories,* edited by David Helwig and Joan Harcourt. Ottawa, Oberon Press, 1975.
''This Gathering,'' in *Canadian Fiction* (Vancouver) Autumn 1976.
''Pictures,'' in *Body Politic* (Toronto), December 1976-January 1977.
''The Sandwich Generation,'' in *Small Wonders,* edited by Robert Weaver. Toronto, CBC, 1982.
''Ashes, Ashes,'' in *New: West Coast Fiction.* Vancouver, Pulp Press, 1984.
''Blessed Are the Dead,'' in *The Vancouver Fiction Book,* edited by David Watmough. Winlaw, British Columbia, Polestar Press, 1985.

Other

Lesbian Images (history and criticism). New York, Doubleday, 1975; London, Davies, 1976.
A Hot-Eyed Moderate. Tallahassee, Florida, Naiad Press, 1985.
Detained at Customs: Jane Rule Testifies at the Little Sister's Trial. Vancouver, British Columbia, Lazara Press, 1995.

*

Manuscript Collection: University of British Columbia, Vancouver.

Critical Studies: ''Jane Rule and the Reviewers'' by Judith Niemi, in *Margins* (Milwaukee), vol. 8, no. 23, 1975; ''Jane Rule Issue'' of *Canadian Fiction* (Vancouver), Autumn 1976; interview with Michele Kort, in *rara avis* (Los Angeles), Summer-Fall 1981.

* * *

Jane Rule's writing is best known for its open exploration of unconventional human relationships, particularly lesbianism. Her first two novels contrast two different types of relations between women. *Desert of the Heart* traces, in alternating chapters, the lives of two women, widely separated by age and background, as they overcome their initial fear and prejudice and risk living together. *This Is Not for You,* the only one of Rule's novels to be narrated from a single perspective (it takes the form of an unmailed letter) follows the development of two women, friends from their California college days, who fail to break free of convention, so that their love for each other remains unfulfilled.

Rule's third novel branches out to embrace a larger cross-section of the human community. Set in a small American town, *Against the Season* explores the intersecting lives of a wider range of female and male characters, including a lame seventy-two-year-old spinster, two pregnant teenage girls from a home for ''unwed mothers,'' and a lesbian businesswoman of Greek descent. Although kinship, habit, and professional functions link some of the townspeople, Rule highlights the element of free choice in their social interactions, and her work extends the usual boundaries of romantic love to include the longings and desires of the elderly.

The tyranny of conventional morality, which marginalizes the handicapped and nonconforming, set against a more generous and innovative concept of community, which values human differences, is explored further in Rule's fourth and fifth novels, where multiple points of view again are used to reflect a non-hierarchical vision of society. *The Young in One Another's Arms* describes how the residents of a Vancouver boarding house—slated for demolition in a program of urban renewal—regroup around the owner, a crippled fifty-year-old woman, to form a voluntary four-generation ''family,'' related by bonds of affection rather than by legal or blood titles. They seek shelter from urban politics and an intrusive social order by working together to establish a restaurant as an experiment in communal living. *Contract with the World* describes the life and work of six different Vancouver artists or art dealers, all friends, who must confront philistinism, prejudice, and failure, and who suffer existential crises over their sexual and artistic identities, being homosexuals in a homophobic culture or artists in a barbarous climate.

Rule's short stories, collected in three books—*Theme for Diverse Instruments, Outlander,* and *Inland Passage*—present a similar diversity of emotional and sexual relationships. Again, despite her primary interest in female sexuality and identity, especially lesbianism, Rule does not ignore male and heterosexual perspectives. The characters' attempts at self-definition are sometimes frustrated, resulting in feelings of weakness, vulnerability, alienation, and even madness. However, most of the characters, in the end, manage to discover some means of integrating personal and social realities. The stories are set variously in England, the U.S., and West Coast Canada; but more significant than geographic location are the smaller domestic spaces or psychic ''houses'' which the characters inhabit, construct, or deconstruct. Arguably her best stories, ''Themes for Diverse Instruments'' and ''Outlander'' celebrate women's vitality and emphasize a recurring theme—that tolerance for a variety of lifestyles engenders a sense of community, thereby extending the creative potential of the group and of each of its members.

Rule's essays, many written for her column in the controversial paper *The Body Politic,* deal with various aspects of sexuality, morality, and literature, and are particularly valuable on the subject of lesbianism. Twelve essays appear alongside the short stories in *Outlander;* others have been collected in *Lesbian Images* and *A Hot-Eyed Moderate.* The former begins with an essay surveying attitudes to female sexuality over the centuries, condemning the prejudices fostered by churchmen and psychologists, and it contains searching studies of individual women writers such as Radclyffe Hall, May

Sarton, and Vita Sackville-West, and of the veiled forms through which they projected their love for other women. The latter is a collection of Rule's reflections, courageously honest and deeply personal, on her own life as a lesbian and a writer; in addition there are miscellaneous reviews and articles on topics such as pornography, censorship, morality in literature, homosexuals and children, and caring for the elderly.

In all her writing, Rule says, she has tried ''to speak the truth as I saw it,'' to present lesbians and homosexuals as ''not heroic or saintly but *real.*'' Refusing the strategies of evasion of many earlier women's texts, but equally resisting the separatist and utopian tendencies of some contemporary lesbian literature, Rule has been criticized by the gay community for not being political enough; she maintains, however, that ''literature is the citadel of the individual spirit which inspires rather than serves the body politic.'' Indeed, Rule's method has consistently been to treat homosexuality as a given, and then to explore ideas raised within that context. *Memory Board,* for instance, examines memory loss amid the backdrop of a lesbian love triangle, thus providing Rule an opportunity to develop another favorite theme, that of aging. In *After the Fire* the characters, five women living on one of the Golf Islands in British Columbia, represent a variety of ages, but their needs are similar, and transcend issues of ''mere'' sexuality.

—Wendy Robbins Keitner, updated by Judson Knight

RUMAKER, Michael

Nationality: American. **Born:** Philadelphia, Pennsylvania, 5 March 1932. **Education:** Rider College, Trenton, New Jersey; Black Mountain College, North Carolina, graduated 1955; Columbia University, New York, M.F.A. 1970. **Career:** Visiting writer-in-residence, State University of New York, Buffalo, 1967; Lecturer in Creative Writing, New School for Social Research, New York, 1967–71; writer-in-residence and Lecturer, City College of New York, 1969–71, 1985. **Awards:** Dell Publishing Foundation award, 1970. **Agent:** Harold Ober Associates, 425 Madison Avenue, New York, New York 10017. **Address:** 139 South Broadway, South Nyack, New York 10960, USA.

Publications

Novels

The Butterfly. New York, Scribner, 1962; London, Macdonald, 1968.
A Day and a Night at the Baths. Bolinas, California, Grey Fox Press, 1979; published in German as *Ein Tag und eine Nacht in der Sauna.* Berlin, Verlag rosa Winkel, 1995.
My First Satyrnalia. San Francisco, Grey Fox Press, 1981.
To Kill a Cardinal. Rocky Mount, North Carolina, Mann Kaye, 1992.
Pagan Days. Nyack, New York, Circumstantial Productions Publishing, 1999.

Short Stories

The Bar. San Francisco, Four Seasons, 1964.
Exit 3 and Other Stories. London, Penguin, 1966; as *Gringos and Other Stories,* New York, Grove Press, 1967; as *Gringos and Other Stories: A New Edition,* Rocky Mount, North Carolina, Mann Kaye, 1991.

Play

Schwul (Queers), translated by Wylf Teichmann and Dirk Mülder. Frankfurt, März, 1970.

Other

Prose 1, with Ed Dorn and Warren Tallman. San Francisco, Four Seasons, 1964.
Robert Duncan in San Francisco. San Francisco, Grey Fox Press, 1996.

*

Bibliography: By George F. Butterick, in *Athanor 6* (Clarkson, New York), Spring 1975.

Manuscript Collection: University of Connecticut, Storrs.

Critical Studies: ''The Use of the Unconscious in Writing'' by Rumaker, in *New American Story* edited by Donald Allen and Robert Creeley, New York, Grove Press, 1965; article by George F. Butterick, in *The Beats* edited by Ann Charters, Detroit, Gale, 1983.

Michael Rumaker comments:

Story can be, obliquely, a map of the unconscious, its terrain and peopling. The intense preoccupation with the physical, with the self and with story, sets up an involitional force which is the unconscious, its contents moving parallel with the known contents as the narrative progresses. A rhythm, as car gears meshing, grabbing and jibing, each causing the other to move, to prompt and to yield the substance and power of each—an absolute rhythm of movement, instantaneous, going …

* * *

Michael Rumaker's reputation rests upon an astonishingly small output, and a number of later efforts—among them *My First Satyrnalia, To Kill a Cardinal,* and *Pagan Days*—have failed to attract significant critical attention. Yet he demonstrates virtuosity, versatility, and sophistication, all traits which normally suggest the maturity of experience. Rumaker must be counted among postmodernists who deliberately call attention to the artifice of their writing: with these fellow-writers he achieves his effects mostly through style, especially in the brilliantly clear rendering of the world of objects, his created milieu regressing to primal states of being and manifestations of the unconscious. What sets him off from his counterparts is his willingness to work within the apparent constraints of traditional fiction, so that his stories may be mass-read (and perhaps misread) as easily as those of Stephen Crane or Mark Twain.

Rumaker is best within the short story form, particularly when writing of ''natural'' men in raw settings. His three best stories, ''Gringos,'' ''The Pipe,'' and ''The Desert,'' depict intuitive men—misfits, cast-offs, wanderers—who create temporary ''societies'' with each other which threaten imminently to explode. They fight, lust, drink, and sometimes kill each other, yet at their most bizarre or violent they remain intensely human, and, for that reason, are interesting, even likeable, though grotesque. In ''Gringos'' a young American named Jim teams up with a friendly, blustering sailor in a small Mexican town. Jim agrees to share the sailor's room and hospitality; they saunter through the streets, dodge the aggressive prostitutes, drink, turn down a young male prostitute and finally ''purchase'' a girl (sailor's treat). At the night's end, they are attacked by Mexicans with knives, but they fight them off and return home. Simply as experience, this account is brilliantly realized, but from the start the mutual hostility of the intruding Americans and the impoverished Mexicans, the sink-hole quality of the squalid town, the oppressive atmosphere of cripples, pornography, exploitation, and homosexuality all point to a descent into the hells of our own making. ''The Pipe'' is even more vividly a landscape of the unconscious, projecting myth and symbol without obtruding upon the bare narrative. Five men wait by the mouth of a huge pipe. A dredgeboat anchored in mid-river will soon blow submerged waste into their midst; these scavengers will then extract the pig-iron and other ''valuables'' in which they trade for a livelihood. Waiting, they tease and brag, swap stories, talk sex; the idiot-boy Billy amuses his companions with an elaborate re-enactment of finding an infant's legless corpse within the muck. The ''blow'' comes, the men scramble among tons of oozy waste and Sam and Alex (who had found the dead baby) quarrel over a disputed find. A sudden burst of violence and Sam is dead. Bunk, who was earlier denied a drink from the common bottle because of mouth-sores, brushes the swirling flies from Sam's wound and covers his head with a sack. As the men leave, the circling chicken hawks land near the pipe and strut among the slime toward the body. Two other impressive stories, entirely different in locale and plot, deal with a group of young thieves in Camden, and suggest an incipient novel which never materialized.

In *The Butterfly,* a twenty-eight-year-old man (emotionally, a seventeen-year-old boy) fearfully re-enters society after two years in a mental institution. Different again from Rumaker's other fiction, the novel's cloistered atmosphere and simple story line hazard the risk on each page of descending from pathos to bathos yet rarely do so. Jim moves from the loving protection of a sensitive doctor to his love affair with a Japanese girl; the love affair fails, but only because Eiko, too, is disturbed and, unlike Jim, is fearful of loving someone. His courage in risking further disappointment is rewarded when he meets Aice and their love develops without mishap. There are perhaps too many significant, detailed dream-sequences, and the novel abounds with symbols—yellow balloons rising to the sun, birds hunted by thoughtless boys, flat rocks skipping across streams—but the sensitivity of the protagonist and the aptness of the imagery sustain a novel as delicate as haiku. Rumaker here avoids dramatizing a subject intrinsically pregnant with drama and, as with his stories, invents the form and language necessary to his ends.

—Frank Campenni

RUSHDIE, (Ahmed) Salman

Nationality: British. **Born:** Bombay, India, 19 June 1947. **Education:** Cathedral School, Bombay; Rugby School, Warwickshire, 1961–65; King's College, Cambridge, 1965–68, M.A. (honours) in history 1968. **Family:** Married 1) Clarissa Luard in 1976 (divorced 1987), one son; 2) the writer Marianne Wiggins in 1988 (divorced 1993). **Career:** Worked in television in Pakistan and as actor in London, 1968–69; freelance advertising copywriter, London, 1970–81; council member, Institute of Contemporary Arts, London, from 1985. Sentenced to death for *The Satanic Verses* in a religious decree (*fatwa*) by Ayatollah Khomeini, and forced to go into hiding, February 1989. **Awards:** Arts Council bursary; Booker prize, 1981; English-Speaking Union award, 1981; James Tait Black Memorial prize, 1982; Foreign Book prize (France), 1985; Whitbread award, 1988, 1995; Writer's Guild prize for children's fiction, 1991; Kurt Tucholsky prize, 1992; Prix Colette, 1993; Booker of Bookers, 1993; State Prize for European Literature, 1994. Fellow, Royal Society of Literature, 1983. Honorary professor, Massachusetts Institute of Technology (MIT). **Agent:** Aitken Stone & Wylie Ltd., 29 Fernshaw Road, London SW10 OTG, England.

Publications

Novels

Grimus. London, Gollancz, 1975; New York, Overlook Press, 1979.
Midnight's Children. London, Cape, and New York, Knopf, 1981.
Shame. London, Cape, and New York, Knopf, 1983.
The Satanic Verses. London, Viking, 1988; New York, Viking, 1989.
The Moor's Last Sigh. New York, Pantheon Books, 1995.
The Ground Beneath Her Feet. New York, Henry Holt, 1999.

Short Stories

East, West: Stories. New York, Pantheon, 1994.

Uncollected Short Stories

''The Free Radio,'' in *Firebird 1,* edited by T.J. Binding. London, Penguin, 1982.
''The Prophet's Hair,'' in *The Penguin Book of Modern British Short Stories,* edited by Malcolm Bradbury. London, Viking, 1987; New York, Viking, 1988.
''Good Advice Is Rarer than Rubies,'' in *New Yorker,* 22 June 1987.
''Untime of the Imam,'' in *Harper's* (New York), December 1988.

Fiction (for children)

Haroun and the Sea of Stories. London, Granta, 1990; New York, Viking, 1991.

Plays

Television Writing: *The Painter and the Pest,* 1985; *The Riddle of Midnight,* 1988.

Other

The Jaguar Smile: A Nicaraguan Journey. London, Pan, and New York, Viking, 1987.
Is Nothing Sacred? (lecture). London, Granta, 1990.

Imaginary Homelands: Essays and Criticism 1981–1991. London, Granta, and New York, Viking, 1991.
The Wizard of Oz. London, BFI, 1992.
Conversations with Salman Rushdie, edited by Michael Reder. Jackson, University Press of Mississippi, 2000.

*

Bibliography: *The Salman Rushdie Bibliography: A Bibliography of Salman Rushdie's Work and Rushdie Criticism* by Joel Kuortti, Frankfurt am Main and New York, P. Lang, 1997.

Critical Studies: *Three Contemporary Novelists: Khushwant Singh, Chaman Nahal, and Salman Rushdie* edited by R.K. Dhawan, New Delhi, Classical, 1985; *The Perforated Sheet: Essays on Salman Rushdie's Art* by Uma Parameswaran, New Delhi, Affiliated East West Press, 1988; *The Rushdie File* edited by Lisa Appignanesi and Sara Maitland, London, Fourth Estate, 1989, Syracuse, New York, Syracuse University Press, 1990; *Salman Rushdie and the Third World: Myths of the Nation* by Timothy Brennan, London, Macmillan, 1989; *A Satanic Affair: Salman Rushdie and the Rage of Islam* by Malise Ruthven, London, Chatto and Windus, 1990; *The Rushdie Affair: The Novel, The Ayatollah, and the West* by Daniel Pipes, New York, Birch Lane Press, 1990; *Salman Rushdie: Sentenced to Death* by W.J. Weatherby, New York, Carroll and Graf, 1990; *Distorted Imagination: Lessons from the Rushdie Affair* by Ziauddin Sardar and Merryl Wyn Davies, London, Grey Seal, 1990; *The Novels of Salman Rushdie* edited by G.R. Tanefa and R.K. Dhawan, New Delhi, Indian Society for Commonwealth Studies, 1992; *Salman Rushdie* by James Harrison, New York, Twayne, 1992; *Salman Rushdie's Fiction: A Study* by Madhusudhana Rao, New Delhi, Sterling, 1992; *For Rushdie: A Collection of Essays by 100 Arabic and Muslim Writers,* New York, Braziller, 1994; *Reading Rushdie: Perspectives on the Fiction of Salman Rushdie,* edited by M.D. Fletcher, Atlanta, Rodopi, 1994; *Blasphemy: Verbal Offense Against the Sacred, from Moses to Salman Rushdie* by Leonard W. Levy, Chapel Hill, University of North Carolina Press, 1995; *Colonial and Post-colonial Discourse in the Novels of Yom Sang-Sop, Chinua Achebe, and Salman Rushdie* by Soonsik Kim, New York, P. Lang, 1996; *Salman Rushdie* by Catherine Cundy, Manchester, England, Manchester University Press, and New York, St. Martin's Press, 1996; *Salman Rushdie* by D.C.R.A. Goonetilleke, New York, St. Martin's Press, 1998; *Critical Essays on Salman Rushdie,* edited by M. Keith Booker, New York, G.K. Hall, 1999.

* * *

Rushdie's *Midnight's Children* is often credited with having made Magic Realism a popular style for postcolonial English-language fiction. His models were the German Gunther Grass and Colombian Gabriel Garcia Marquez. Written in a larger than life manner, mixing fact with fable, such novels suggest an allegory of recent political history with the fabulous events corresponding to public realities. The magic world of the folk imagination blends with the Western and Westernized modernity brought about by colonialism, imperialism, capitalism, and science. The older and modern explanations are often in conflict. Whereas *Midnight's Children* concerns the modern colonial history of India through the independence struggle up to the national emergency declared by Mrs. Ghandi in 1975, *Shame* tells a story based on the political infighting among leading politicians in post-Partition Pakistan. In both novels modern political history is partly told as, and found to be similar to, the folk tales and myths of the past. A writer with a marvelous imagination whose plots always surprise, and with an instantly recognizable manner and diction modeled on traits of Indian and Pakistani spoken English, someone who often puns in several languages, Rushdie is also abrasive and combative. On the liberal Left, and for a time flirting with Marxism, Rushdie attacks, usually by satirizing, parodying, and making grotesque, what he considers reactionary and feudal forces in society.

Behind each novel there is usually a central topic being examined. In *Shame* it is how notions of personal and family honor in Pakistani politics are related to the feelings of shame that cause a Pakistani family in England to kill its daughter for what it regards as sexual dishonor. The obviousness of his allusions has often brought him into trouble, making him the most famous writer of our time. Mrs. Ghandi as Prime Minister of India sued Rushdie in court for the suggestion in *Midnight's Children* that to insure her power she had her son killed, which the novel implied was continuing older feudal Indian dynastic practices and was part of the real politics of post-colonial India. *Shame* was banned in Pakistan for insulting the state and individuals. Then in *Satanic Verses,* a novel about fanaticism and terrorism, Rushdie was felt by some radical fundamentalist Muslims to have insulted Islam and a *fatwah* was declared that he must be killed. The novel remains banned in many countries.

Rushdie, who had studied Islamic history, had followed scholarly sources in retelling older stories about Mohammed's life, but his novel became a pawn in the mobilization of Islamic sentiment against the West and liberalism. Rushdie himself had said nothing; the passages which caused offense were the fantasies and dreams of a psychotic character in his novel. But as a result several publishing houses were bombed, translators killed, and Rushdie for many years remained hidden from public sight. The novel concerned such common Rushdie themes as the condition of exile, living in more than one language and culture, deracination, and the foreigner's feelings of alienation and fear. It implies that values are relative and that what becomes accepted history is arbitrary and regarded differently at various times and places. Its strongest satire was aimed at England, especially Margaret Thatcher's government, but also a London Black Power hustler. It concludes with what appears to be Rushdie's own imagined reconciliation with his father in Bombay; a reconciliation necessarily imagined as his family moved from Bombay to Pakistan after Indian independence.

Throughout his work there is nostalgia for the Bombay of his youth, a Bombay which is now called Mumbai, in an India which has now become three nations, India, Pakistan, and Bangladesh. Bombay, the most cosmopolitan city in India, a place where many tongues are spoken in mangled and marvelous mixtures, home of a thriving commercial film industry (''Bollywood''—which often figures in Rushdie's novels), is the home to which his imagination often returns. *East, West* includes ''The Courier,'' memories of his teenage years in England and refusing to choose between two cultures. Most of the short stories in *East, West* concern just such choices and conclude with some affirmation of Indian or Muslim values, affirmations which, coming as a surprise, seem ironic, even comic, as if the two cultures could not be reconciled.

Rushdie's later fiction suggests someone trying to come to terms with exile and accepting that the world has always been a place of migrancy and cross-cultural influences. At the conclusion of *The Moor's Last Sigh,* Moraes Zogoiby flees an apocalyptic Bombay of gang wars, bombings, and communal violence for Spain. There he is imprisoned by an enemy who forces him to write his personal and family history. The reader then turns back to the start of the novel which continues the narrator's flight and story, as Moraes nails pages of his tale to trees in an act which he sees as equivalent to Luther's theses, while recalling his mother's remark that he is full of feces. Moraes is the Moor of the title, although he is Jew, Christian, and Indian. His mother's side of the family is descended from the Portuguese who settled Goa and his father's side can trace its lineage to the Christian reconquest of Spain when both Moors and Jews were expelled. They have been Indian for centuries.

The Moor's Last Sigh is another version of *Midnight's Children* which used an improbable, fantastic family history as a way to retell the story of modern India from, in the earlier novel, the penetration of Western rationalism and science in the north during the late nineteenth-century through major events of the independence movement until the progressive vision of Nehru was destroyed by the emergence of a nativistic dynastic feudalism during the Emergency under Indira Gandhi. In *The Moor's Last Sigh* Indian history is told from the perspective of the South, with its many minorities, rather than the Hindu-Islamic North, and Indira's dynastic perversion of nationalism is supplanted by fanatical nativist thugs who violently destroy whatever they regard as non-Hindu. The wandering Jew has become the wandering Moor, symbolic of India's threatened minorities and the rejection of the Westernized elite that founded the nation. The narrator has become a homeless expatriate. World, national, and family history in this novel have autobiographical and literary foundations. Like Scheherazade the narrator has staved off execution by telling, or inventing, his *Thousand and One Nights.*

In *The Ground Beneath Her Feet* the myth of Orpheus and Eurydice is retold as two Indian lovers who become international rock stars symbolic of recent Western and post-colonial culture. This is Rushdie's New World novel, half of it set in New York, with some major events in Mexico. It is his most accessible novel, understandable without knowing Indian history and culture, as it alludes to or imitates cultural fashions of recent decades. The protests against the war in Vietnam, apocalyptic sci-fi novels, and grung rock are all there and all treated as equal. Instead of Bombay politicians he alludes to John and Yoko, Sid and Nancy. Curiously Rushdie's first novel, the widely disliked *Grimus,* was also a mixed bag of cultural fashions and allusions including sci-fi, American Indians and American history and popular culture, mythology, and movies. There, unlike *The Ground Beneath Her Feet,* the story was difficult to follow.

The first half of *The Ground Beneath Her Feet* is set in Bombay and reworks material from *Midnight's Children* and *The Moor's Last Sigh* concerning the late colonial period and the corrupt violent politics that followed independence. The perspective is that of the Parsis, a small minority that flourished for a century by adopting British ways, becoming the modernizers of India, who since independence have become increasingly threatened and marginalized.

Rai, the narrator (Rai the fusion of North African Arabic music with rock that is popular in France and Algeria), says that these are his last memories of Bombay. The main characters leave for England and then move on to New York (where Rushdie has been living in recent years). The shifts correspond somewhat to periods of Rushdie's own life, with the Beatles and well-known Chelsea people featuring in the early sections of the second half of the book. Rai, a photographer, joins the migration of British literati to New York, which he proclaims the center of the modern world while claiming that the USA is the world's bully. Rai holds politically correct opinions. While he gives his rock-and-rollers abusive and abusing poor-white-trash early lives, Rushdie says several times that no matter what they suffer it is not as bad as what African-Americans suffer. The social texture of this half of the novel thins badly. In the past Rushdie was criticized as sexist, so here we have two strong macho women rock-and-roll stars who have sex whenever, wherever, and with whomever they want, while the two men in their lives abstain and, although themselves famous artists, are softies. There are also a great lesbian guitarist and a great female drummer. The first half of *The Ground Beneath Her Feet* reads well. The second half is often Rushdie at his worst, making bad puns, opinionated, losing his story, and reducing life to a cartoon.

—Bruce King

RUSS, Joanna

Nationality: American. **Born:** New York City, 22 February 1937. **Education:** Cornell University, Ithaca, New York, B.A. 1957; Yale University School of Drama, New Haven, Connecticut, M.F.A. 1960. **Family:** Married Albert Amateau in 1963 (divorced 1967). **Career:** Lecturer in Speech, Queensborough Community College, New York, 1966–67; instructor, 1967–70, and assistant professor of English, 1970–72, Cornell University; assistant professor of English, State University of New York, Binghamton, 1972–73, 1974–75, and University of Colorado, Boulder, 1975–77. Associate professor, 1977–84, and professor of English, 1984–94, University of Washington, Seattle. Occasional book reviewer, *Fantasy and Science Fiction,* 1966–79, *The Village Voice, The Washington Post Book World, The Feminist Review of Books,* and others. Also essayist for *Science-Fiction Studies, Extrapolation, The Village Voice, Ms.,* and others. **Awards:** Nebula award, 1972, 1983; O. Henry award, 1977; National Endowment for the Humanities fellowship, 1974; Hugo award, 1983; *Locus* award, 1983; *Science Fiction Chronicle* award, 1983. **Agent:** Ellen Levine Literary Agency, 432 Park Avenue South, New York, New York 10016. **Address:** 8961 E. Lester St., Tucson, Arizona 85715, U.S.A.

Publications

Novels

Picnic on Paradise. New York, Ace, 1968; London, Macdonald, 1969.

And Chaos Died. New York, Ace, 1970.

The Female Man. New York, Bantam, 1975; London, Star, 1977.

We Who Are About to. . . . New York, Dell, 1977; London, Women's Press, 1987.

The Two of Them. New York, Berkley, 1978; London, Women's Press, 1986.

Kittatinny: A Tale of Magic. New York, Daughters, 1978.

On Strike Against God. New York, Out and Out, 1980; London, Women's Press, 1987.

Extra(Ordinary) People. New York, St. Martin's Press, 1984; London, Women's Press, 1985.

Short Stories

Alyx. Boston, Gregg Press, 1976.
The Adventures of Alyx. New York, Pocket Books, 1983; London, Women's Press, 1985.
The Zanzibar Cat. Sauk City, Wisconsin, Arkham House, 1983.
The Hidden Side of the Moon. New York, St. Martin's Press, 1987; London, Women's Press, 1989.

Play

Window Dressing, in *The New Women's Theatre,* edited by Honor Moore. New York, Random House, 1977.

Other

How to Suppress Women's Writing. Austin, University of Texas Press, 1983; London, Women's Press, 1984.
Magic Mommas, Trembling Sisters, Puritans and Perverts: Feminist Essays. Trumansburg, New York, Crossing Press, 1985.
To Write Like a Woman: Essays in Feminism and Science Fiction. Bloomington, Indiana University Press, 1995.
What Are We Fighting For?: Sex, Race, Class, and the Future of Feminism. New York, St. Martin's Press, 1998.

*

Critical Studies: Article by Marilyn Hacker, in *Chrysalis,* 4, 1977; article by Samuel Delany, in *Science-Fiction Studies,* 19, 3 November 1979; *In the Chinks of the World Machine: Feminism and Science Fiction* by Sarah Lefanu, London, Women's Press, 1988; *Feminist Utopias* by Frances Bartkowski, Lincoln, University of Nebraska, 1989.

*   *   *

The work of Joanna Russ is thematically unified and formally, generically, and stylistically diverse. She has written a number of novels that fall under the rubric of speculative fiction; she has written brilliant short stories; she has written what is called mainstream fiction (*On Strike Against God*). She has written in the genre of thematically related tales along the lines of Mary McCarthy's *The Company She Keeps* and John Horne Burns's *The Gallery (Extra[Ordinary] People*); she has written a fantasy, verging on lush fairy tale (*Kittatinny: A Tale of Magic*); she has written a closely reasoned and scholarly book, *How to Suppress Women's Writing,* and the very personal, peppery, and opinionated essays of *Magical Mommas, Trembling Sisters, Puritans and Perverts: Feminist Essays.*

Russ's underlying theme in all these works is empowerment: empowerment and powerlessness; aggression and negation. Other concerns that run through the body of her work include survival, alienation, loneliness, community, violence, sex roles, the nature of oppression both external and internal, the necessity and the nature of further civilization and what is gained and what is lost by its progress.

One advantage of working in a genre is that the plot must move along, and that discipline keeps Russ's springy intelligence anchored. If she resembles another writer, it is Swift: she is as angry, as disgusted, as playful, as often didactic, as airy at times and at times as crude, as intellectual. Appreciating the quality of outraged, clear-sighted pained intelligence at once incandescent and exacerbated, is one of the major experiences in reading her work. Her critical essays are often witty and savage. She has started frequent controversies with her criticism, partly because of her habit of saying what others may think but will not dare publish.

Russ gives a sense of speed in her narration. She is a master of pacing and often eliminates intermediate steps and decisions. She has the habit of starting *in medias res* and in a place and time the reader will simply have to deduce, whether we are on earth or elsewhere and what essentially is going on among all these articulate people. Sometimes she uses a jazzy style that gives a feeling of clever and controlled improvisation. This is not to suggest that the novels are, in fact, improvisations, for they are put together intricately in all their parts.

Another characteristic of Russ's style is the combination of serious, even dark concerns with wit. *The Female Man,* is studded with jokes, vaudeville routines, addresses to the reader, instructive vignettes, catalogues. Her short piece "Useful Phrases for the Tourist" is a stand-up comic routine. At the core of her humor is the perception of incongruity, absurdity.

She is precise in her characterization. In a sense, the four protagonists of *The Female Man,* Jeannine, Joanna, Jael, and Janet, are the same woman in four social contexts. Jeannine lives in a New York City where World War II never happened and which is only slowly emerging from a generations-long Depression. Joanna lives here and now. Janet lives in Whileaway, an all-female society far in the future after a plague has carried off the men. Jael is an agent and assassin from the near future, part of the "plague" that gives birth to bucolic Whileaway. They are all "the same woman," yet each (with the exception of Joanna) is sharply flavored and unmistakable in habits of thought, words, and movement. Alyx, a Greek thief from Alexandrian times, is the heroine of *Picnic on Paradise* and a number of short stories, extremely sharply etched. From the sexually ambiguous Victorian traveller of *Extra(Ordinary) People* to the brave and pragmatic young girl of *Kittatinny: A Tale of Magic,* Russ's works present a gallery of fully fleshed-out women of great diversity.

Russ is one of our best novelists of ideas because she possesses the traditional fictional virtues. She creates characters full of quirks, odd memories, hot little sexual nodes that make them believable. She embodies ideas in a fast-moving arc of action. Finally, she has wide emotional range, from savage indignation to broad humor, from the bleak to the lush, from extreme alienation (as in *We Who Are About to ...* , where the protagonist fights and kills for the right to die) to a warm and powerful projection of community (as in "Nobody's Home").

What Russ does not create is a world in which love conquers all—certainly not for her women. The push toward freedom, appetite, curiosity both intellectual and sensual, the desire to control and expand their own existence, figure far more importantly in the lives of her female characters than does traditional romance. In *The Two of Them* her protagonist Irene enjoys a long and satisfying emotional and sexual bond with her mentor Ernst. However, Ernst, besides being Irene's lover, is her limiting factor. As their goals diverge, he begins to use his power not to free but to confine her. Ultimately in order to save a young girl she has rescued and to preserve her own ability to act in accordance with her own values, she kills Ernst. A theme that Russ identifies in her own work and that of other contemporary feminist writers is the quest for the lost daughter, or the quest to save the daughter or young woman who will be true posterity.

One aspect of Russ's work that sometimes shocks is the place that violence holds in her fiction; not so much violence against women—a commonplace of our fiction as of our society—but violence by women. Russ is concerned with what price freedom and autonomy may exact. In her works violence is never glorified and never without consequence, but neither is it for long absent. Her women are as apt as her men to consider the full range of alternatives open to them in carrying out their will or their duty as they see it. Certainly nobody saves them unless they save themselves, which is often not possible. Hers are worlds in which there is frequently a wide range of nasty consequence to action, as to inaction.

Russ is a writer equally serious and entertaining. Although themes recur, she never repeats herself. Each book represents a new intellectual and literary voyage into darkness and light. In her collection *The Hidden Side of the Moon,* only a few tales (for instance, one about a unique solution to overpopulation and retirement) fall under the category of science fiction. Time is, however, quite elastic and variable in these stories. Many of them are fantasies on themes of family history and identity. A woman picks up a strange dirty little girl at the supermarket who turns out to be her own childhood; a woman tries to talk her mother out of marrying and giving birth to her, and rocks the same mother to sleep in an infant's body. George Sand encounters her literary destiny; Oscar Wilde rejects a second chance at respectability (long life as a nonentity). These stories from three decades are rich, varied, and an excellent introduction to a fascinating talent.

—Marge Piercy

S

SAHGAL, Nayantara (Pandit)

Nationality: Indian. **Born:** Allahabad, 10 May 1927. **Education:** Wellesley College, Massachusetts, 1943–47, B.A. in history 1947. **Family:** Married 1) Gautam Sahgal in 1949 (divorced 1967), three children; 2) E.N. Mangat Rai in 1979. **Career:** Scholar-in-residence, Southern Methodist University, Dallas, 1973, 1977; research scholar, Radcliffe Institute, Cambridge, Massachusetts, 1976; lecturer, University of Colorado semester-at-sea, 1979; fellow, Woodrow Wilson International Center, Washington, D.C., 1981, and National Humanities Center, North Carolina, 1983. Political journalist for Indian, American, and British newspapers; columnist, *Sunday Observer,* New Delhi. **Awards:** Sinclair prize, 1985; Sahitya Akademi award, 1987; Commonwealth Writers prize, 1987. Foreign honorary member, American Academy of Arts and Sciences, 1990. **Member:** United Nations Indian Delegation, New York, 1978. **Address:** 181-B Rajpur Road, Dehra Dun 248 009, Uttar Pradesh, India.

Publications

Novels

A Time to Be Happy. New York, Knopf, and London, Gollancz, 1958.
This Time of Morning. London, Gollancz, 1965; New York, Norton, 1966.
Storm in Chandigarh. New York, Norton, and London, Chatto and Windus, 1969.
The Day in Shadow. New Delhi, Vikas, 1971; New York, Norton, 1972; London, London Magazine Editions, 1975.
A Situation in New Delhi. London, London Magazine Editions, 1977.
Rich Like Us. London, Heinemann, 1985; New York, Norton, 1986.
Plans for Departure. New York, Norton, 1985; London, Heinemann, 1986.
Mistaken Identity. London, Heinemann, 1988; New York, New Directions, 1989.

Uncollected Short Stories

''The Promising Young Woman,'' in *Illustrated Weekly of India* (Bombay), January 1959.
''The Golden Afternoon,'' in *Illustrated Weekly of India* (Bombay), February 1959.
''The Trials of Siru,'' in *Triveni* (Madras), January 1967.
''The Girl in the Bookshop,'' in *Cosmopolitan* (London), September, 1973.
''Martand,'' in *London Magazine,* August-September 1974.
''Crucify Me,'' in *Indian Horizons* (New Delhi), October 1979.
''Earthy Love,'' in *Trafika* (Prague), Autumn 1993.

Other

Prison and Chocolate Cake (autobiography). New York, Knopf, and London, Gollancz, 1954.
From Fear Set Free (autobiography). London, Gollancz, 1962; New York, Norton, 1963.
The Freedom Movement in India. New Delhi, National Council of Educational Research and Training, 1970.
Sunlight Surround You, with Chandralekha Mehta and Rita Dar. Privately printed, 1970.
A Voice for Freedom. New Delhi, Hind, 1977.
Indira Gandhi's Emergence and Style. New Delhi, Vikas and Durham, North Carolina, Academic Press, 1978.
Indira Gandhi: Her Road to Power. New York, Ungar, 1982; London, Macdonald, 1983.
Relationship: Extracts from a Correspondence (with E.N. Mangat Rai). New Delhi, Kali for Women, 1994.
Point of View: A Personal Response to Life, Literature, and Politics. New Delhi, Prestige, 1997.

*

Bibliography: *Bibliography of Indian Writing in English 2* by Hilda Pontes, New Delhi, Concept, 1985.

Critical Studies: *Bridges of Literature* by M.L. Malhotra, Ajmer, Sunanda, 1971; essay by Sahgal, in *Adam* (London), August 1971; *Nayantara Sahgal and the Craft of Fiction* by Suresh Kohli, New Delhi, Vikas, 1972; *Nayantara Sahgal: A Study of Her Fiction and Non-Fiction 1954–1974* by A.V. Krishna Rao, Madras, Seshachalam, 1976; *Nayantara Sahgal* by Jasbir Jain, New Delhi, Arnold-Heinemann, 1978; interview with Nergis Dalal, in *Times of India Sunday Review* (New Delhi), 30 June 1985; ''Naryantara Sahgal's *Rich Like Us*'' by Shirley Chew, and ''The Search for Freedom in Indian Women's Writing'' by Ranjana Ash, both in *Motherlands,* edited by Susheil Nasta, London, Women's Press, 1992; ''The Crisis of Contemporary India and Nayantara Sahgal's Fiction'' by Makarnd Paranjape, in *World Literature Today,* Spring 1994; *Nayantara Sahgal* by Jasbir Jain, Jaipur, India, Printwell, 1994; *The Fiction of Nayantara Sahgal* by Manmohan Bhatnagar, New Delhi, Creative Books, 1996; *Woman's Space: The Mosaic World of Margaret Drabble and Nayantara Sahgal* by Sree Rashmi Talwar, New Delhi, Creative Books, 1997; *Microcosms of Modern India: A Study of the Novels of Nayantara Sahgal* by Madhuranthakam Narendra, New Delhi, Classical Pub. Co., 1998; *This Is No Place for a Woman: Nadine Gordimer, Nayantara Sahgal, Buchi Emecheta, and the Politics of Gender* by Joya Uraizee, Trenton, New Jersey, Africa World Press, 1999.

Nayantara Sahgal comments:

I am a novelist and a political journalist. My novels have a political background or political ambiance. I didn't plan it that way—I was dealing with people and situations—but looking back, each one seems to reflect the hopes and fears the political scene held out to us at the time.

I have a very strong emotional as well as intellectual attachment to my roots … I have certainly been plagued with wondering from time to time why I was born and what I'm doing here and why I haven't had to worry about my next meal when millions live lives of anxiety and drudgery. And then there is the problem of evil and pain. At times all that abstract conjecture has become very personal, with the need to atone for the terrible things people do to each other. Some of these matters fell into place for me when I gave up the struggle to be an atheist. Atheism—or agnosticism—is my general family background, but I am. a believer to the marrow of my bones, and much has become clearer to me since I faced the fact.

I see myself as both novelist and journalist. In the course of a lifetime one is many things, fiction is my abiding love, but I need to express myself on vital political issues. Political and social forces shape our lives. How can we be unaware of them? I believe there is a ''poetics of engagement'' where commitment and aesthetics meet and give each other beauty and power.

* * *

Most of Nayantara Sahgal's characters belong to the affluent upper class of Indian society. Sahgal sticks scrupulously to the people she knows intimately; she does not try to write about the caste-ridden middle class or the poor Indian villager just to conform with the accepted image of India. Her range of characters simplifies her technique; she does not have to struggle to present Indian conversation in English (a problem which bedevils many other Indian novelists writing in English) as most of her characters are the kind of people who would talk and think in English in real life.

Sahgal has a first-hand knowledge of politics and political figures in India, for she spent most of her childhood in Anand Bhawan, the ancestral home of the Nehrus in Allahabad. One could say that politics is in her blood—Jawaharlal Nehru was her mother's brother, while her father died because of an illness he suffered in prison when he was jailed for participating in India's freedom struggle. An important political event forms the background for each of her novels. Her first novel, *A Time to Be Happy,* presents the dawn of Indian independence. *This Time of Morning* comes later, when the initial euphoria has worn off, and things no longer look rosy. *Storm in Chandigarh* deals with the partition of the Punjab on linguistic lines just when the state had recovered from the trauma of the 1947 partition. *A Situation in New Delhi* presents the Indian capital faced with the After-Nehru-Who question; established politicians have given up all moral values, and the frustrated youth are becoming Naxalites (Communist extremists). But sometimes this political consciousness is not transmuted fully in artistic terms. Some of her characters are easily recognizable public figures: Kailash Sinha (Krishna Menon) in *This Time of Morning* or Shivraj (Jawaharlal Nehru) in *A Situation in New Delhi* are two examples. Her autobiographies, *Prison and Chocolate Cake* and *From Fear Set Free* are more satisfying than her earlier novels. An outstanding novel is *The Day in Shadow;* here personal concerns take precedence over politics. The heroine, Simrit Raman, a writer, is a divorcée (like Sahgal herself), and the novel shows the prejudice she faces in male-dominated Indian society. She grows close to Raj, an idealistic Member of Parliament, who shares her values, unlike her husband, who believes in money-making above all. Sahgal gives an authentic picture of high-level politicians and bureaucrats, wrapped up in their cocktail parties, worried more about themselves than about the problems which face the country. The mutual attraction between Simrit and Raj is not primarily sexual. As in her other novels, Sahgal suggests that marriage is not just a sexual relationship, it means companionship on equal terms. She pleads for a basic honesty in human relationships, whether they are between man and woman or the ruler and the ruled.

Because of her birth and upbringing, Sahgal makes an ideal spokesman for the western-educated Indian who finds it difficult to come to terms with India. As her character Sanad in *A Time to Be Happy* confesses, ''I don't belong entirely to India. I can't. My education, my upbringing, and my sense of values have all combined to make me unIndian… . Of course there can be no question of my belonging to any other country.'' Jawaharlal Nehru, too, had articulated the same problem when he wrote in his autobiography, ''I have become a queer mixture of the East and the West, out of place everywhere, at home nowhere. Perhaps my thoughts and approach to life are more akin to what is called Western than Eastern, but India clings to me as she does to all her children, in innumerable ways.'' This realization leads to a passionate concern with the Indian heritage and its meaning in the modern age; all of Sahgal's novels are concerned with the present decadence of India, and how creative use can be made of its past. It is this concern with the country which led her to protest against the Emergency imposed by her cousin Indira Gandhi when the majority of Indian writers preferred to keep silent. Her political acumen had led her to anticipate Mrs. Gandhi's action, and she had cautioned against it in her weekly newspaper column.

Rich Like Us, which won the Sinclair prize for fiction, is probably her best novel. Sahgal's searching look at India during the Emergency reveals that democracy and spirituality are only skin-deep. The murder of the narrator Sonali's great-grandmother in the name of *suttee,* the mutilation of the sharecropper because he asks for his due, the rape of the village women by the police because their menfolk dare to resist the landlord, and the murder of Rose, the large-hearted Englishwoman in New Delhi just because her frank talk is an embarrassment to her stepson Dev, are all described in an entirely credible manner. The narrative technique is interesting; the narrator is Sonali, but alternate chapters deal (in the third person) with her father Keshav's friend Ram, a businessman who loves Rose, so we get a dual perspective on events. The novel ends on a note of hope; in the midst of sycophancy, there are persons like Kishori Lal, a petty shopkeeper, who have the courage to protest against tyranny.

Sahgal's subsequent novels go back to the past. *Plans for Departure* has been hailed as a ''novel of ideas,'' though a less sympathetic reviewer has labelled it a ''backdated *Jewel in the Crown.*'' The usual Raj characters are present in the imaginary hill station of Himapur—the sympathetic British administrator, the missionary, the racist white woman out to uphold Imperialistic glory, the nationalist Indian leader etc. The heroine is Anna Hansen, a Danish woman on a visit to India, who makes her plans for departure when the shadows of World War I fall over Europe. She goes back to marry Nicholas Wyatt, the scion of an old English family. Anna's Indian experiences reach a kind of consummation when their son marries an Indian girl who is a political activist. The India of the early decades of this century is evoked more vividly in Sahgal's eighth novel, *Mistaken Identity,* which has a male narrator, just like her first novel, *A Time to Be Happy.* Bhushan Singh, the playboy son of the Raja of Vijaygarh, is on his way home from college in America in 1929 when he is arrested on a mistaken charge of sedition. He has to spend almost three years in jail, where his companions are idealistic followers of Mahatma Gandhi and militant trade union leaders, both trying to win freedom in their own ways; the hero's interaction with them is at times quite comic. These two later novels show Sahgal's continued preoccupation with India, though they lack the social commitment and contemporary relevance of *Rich Like Us.*

—Shyamala A. Narayan

ST. AUBIN de TERAN, Lisa

Nationality: British. **Born:** Lisa Rynveld, London, 2 October 1953. **Education:** Attended school in London. **Family:** Married 1) Jaime Teran, 1981 (divorced 1981), one daughter; 2) George MacBeth, 1981 (divorced 1986), one son; 3) Robbie Duff-Scott, 1989, one daughter. **Career:** Farmer of sugar cane, avocados, pears, and sheep, Venezuela, 1972–78. Since 1972, writer. **Awards:** Somerset Maugham award, 1983, for *The Long Way Home;* John Llewellyn Rhys memorial prize, 1983, for *Slow Train to Milan;* Eric Gregory award, 1983, for poetry. **Agent:** A.M. Heath, 79 St. Martins Lane, London WC2N 4AA, England. **Address:** 5437 Castello, Venesia, Italy; and 7 Canynge Aquare, Clifton, Bristol, England.

PUBLICATIONS

Novels

Keepers of the House. London, Cape, 1982; as *The Long Way Home,* New York, Harper and Row, and London, Cape, 1983.
The Slow Train to Milan. London, Cape, and New York, Harper and Row, 1983.
The Tiger. London, Cape, 1984.
The Bay of Silence. London, Cape, 1986.
Black Idol. London, Cape, 1987.
Joanna. London, Virago, 1990; New York, Carroll and Graf, 1991.
Nocturne. London, Hamilton, 1992; New York, St. Martin's Press, 1993.
The Palace. London, Macmillan, 1997, Hopewell, New Jersey, Ecco Press, 1999.

Short Stories

The Marble Mountain and Other Stories. London, Cape, 1989.
Southpaw: Short Stories. London, Virago Press, 1999.

Poetry

The Streak. Knotting, Martin Booth, 1980.
The High Place. London, Cape, 1985.

Other

Off the Rails: Memoirs of a Train Addict. London, Bloomsbury, 1989.
Landscape in Italy, with photographs by John Ferro Sims . London, Pavilion, 1989.
Venice: The Four Seasons, with photographs by Mick Lindberg. London, Pavilion, and New York, Clarkson Potter, 1992.
A Valley in Italy: Confessions of a House Addict. London, Hamilton, 1994; published as *A Valley in Italy: The Many Seasons of a Villa in Umbria,* New York, HarperCollins, 1994.
The Hacienda: A Memoir. Boston, Little Brown, 1997.
Editor, *Indiscreet Journeys: Stories of Women on the Road.* London, Virago, 1989; Boston, Faber, 1990.

* * *

Much of Lisa St. Aubin de Teran's early work was autobiographical, and chronologically the fictionalized events of *Keepers of the House,* although published first, followed her second novel, *The Slow Train to Milan.* St. Aubin de Teran is unusual for an English writer in setting her fiction abroad, often in Italy and South America. Her extraordinary sense of place, perhaps more obviously than her characterization, has made her work distinguished and memorable.

Little happens in *Keepers of the House,* which concerns the final decay of an old farmhouse, La Bebella, near Venezuela. The second last survivor of the Beltrán family, Diego, has married Lydia, an Englishwoman. They return to La Bebella, where years of drought and disease have gradually driven the servants away. Previously uncommunicative by nature, Diego slips into a deep depression and becomes a hermit-like recluse. Lydia has to manage the dilapidated farm and the uncertain avocado and sugar crops, despite being nearly defeated by the effect of the death of her newborn son. Lydia is sustained by Benito, an old retainer who relates to her two centuries of Beltrán family history. These exotic legends of this once powerful family are a rare imaginative achievement, and such writing has earned St. Aubin de Teran the accolade of the English Márquez. One learns little of Lydia or Diego, who is eventually paralyzed by a stroke; as in much of St. Aubin de Teran's writing, the past matters more than the present. The carefully detailed descriptive passages evoke a sympathy for the long-dead characters and their struggles. When the barren lands yield nothing more, Lydia abandons La Bebella when Benito dies, carrying her invalid husband to a jeep, to escape to a place of safety. Lydia, once again pregnant, has inherited a knowledge she can pass to her child. Only Diego's cousin, Christebal Beltrán, aged about 112, remains as a sentinel watching over the deserted valley.

The Slow Train to Milan has no plot, only a series of rather fantastic episodes about political exiles from South America on the run in Europe. The tone of the novel is casual, from the rapid marriage of Lisaveta, the sixteen-year-old narrator, to César, an amiable if self-centered eccentric. He and his exiled friends, Otto and Elias, are mysterious figures who shuffle aimlessly with Lisaveta between cities living in borrowed accommodations, pawning valuables for survival when their money runs outs, and fluctuating between the extremes of poverty and luxury. The uncomplaining, adventurous Lisaveta, though curious about her husband's past and his friends, rarely questions them and is content to be part of their unsettled existence, much of it spent on ''the slow train to Milan.'' The novel depends on the atmosphere of the innumerable contrasting places the travelers visit and people they encounter and the tension created by the constant fear that these exiles will be caught. The narrator identifies herself at least partly with St. Aubin de Teran and Lydia, remarking that she later grew avocados with her husband in the Andes.

The autobiographical element is less marked in *Tiger,* where the dominating character is Misia Schmutter, a murderous despot and head of her family, and her grandson, Lucien, whose course of life she influences even from beyond the grave. *Nocturne* is, perhaps, more plausible; it is a triumph of characterization and evocation of place. The setting is mainly in San Severino, a peasant village in Italy in the first decade of this century; this is where Alessandro Mezzanotte is born and lives until he dies. From the age of fifteen, Mezzanotte is obsessively in love with Valentina, a young gypsy who is part of a traveling fair. For some years he is compelled to travel from San Severino to be wherever the fair is, although his love is scorned by both families. Forced to be in Mussolini's army, Mezzanotte, previously handsome, is blinded and facially scarred and loses an arm when hit by a shell; he is pensioned off. His name, translating as

''Midnight,'' suggests his fate is preordained. However, his solitary life for the next fifty years is endurable because of his unshakable belief that Valentina will come to him, even in old age. Near the end of his life, Mezzanotte is looked after by a young army conscript, Stefano, whose own troubled life and character are deeply affected by the old man, who unburdens his secrets on the soldier. When Mezzanotte dies, Stefano finds Valentina's last letters, which the blind man could not read. To save his sanity, Mezzanotte had been told the reverse of Valentina's intentions. Unable to cope with his appearance, she had, in fact, finally written to say she had discarded Mezzanotte for someone else. *Nocturne* is poignant and haunting and is a further indication that St. Aubin de Teran has still much to say as a distinctive writer.

—Geoffrey Elborn

ST. OMER, Garth

Nationality: St. Lucian. **Born:** Castries, St. Lucia. **Education:** The University of the West Indies, Kingston, Jamaica, degree in French. **Career:** Has lived in France, Ghana, and England. **Address:** Department of English, University of California, Santa Barbara, California 93106–7150, U.S.A.

Publications

Novels

A Room on the Hill. London, Faber, 1968.
Nor Any Country. London, Faber, 1969.
J—, Black Bam and the Masqueraders. London, Faber, 1972.

Short Stories

Shades of Grey. London, Faber, 1968.

Uncollected Short Story

''Syrop,'' in *Introduction 2.* London, Faber, 1968.

* * *

Garth St. Omer creates characters filled with an unrest which they themselves cannot define or explain. It is a *malaise* of the islands which makes them hesitate even before opportunities which are apparently dazzling, which makes them hurt and abandon those they love, or turn aside from courses of action they have embarked on with every sign of conviction. The immediacy of his writing springs from the fact that he is so involved himself with this unrest that he is not yet able to distance or judge his heroes. The passion and the pain of these young island lives are fully conveyed, but it is perhaps this very lack of distance that makes his writing ideally suited to the novella form. His reputation was first made with ''Syrop,'' and the fact that he followed his first novel with a volume comprising two more novellas demonstrates his addiction to the form.

''Syrop'' is a harsh, tragic story of a family blighted by inexplicable misfortune, as well as by the poverty they share with their neighbors. Syrop, the young hero, differs from other St. Omer protagonists in that he doesn't live to carry his anguish and restlessness into adult life. He is smashed by a ship's propellers, diving for pennies on the very day he has been chosen to join the fishing crews, and on the eve of his much-loved brother's return from prison. John Lestrade, in St. Omer's first novel, *A Room on the Hill,* is older and tougher, but still haunted by intimate misfortunes and early deaths in his little island circle of relatives, friends and lovers. This book ends with a hard gesture towards departure, for it is increasingly obvious that all who stay in the island are doomed or lost, and Lestrade is determined to survive and transmute grief into action.

Of the two stories in *Shades of Grey* the first, ''The Lights on the Hill,'' is the more tightly organized. It starts at a moment of crisis in the hero's relationship with Thea, the beautiful and original girl whom he has long desired and who now loves him. Neither can explain the nature of this crisis and it can only cause pain to them both, yet Stephenson knows in his being that he must now leave her. The madman's cry from the asylum which punctuates this realization begins and ends the story. In between these cries (or are they the same?) St. Omer cross-cuts a number of short scenes from the hero's past in Jamaica and in his native St. Lucia. We see him charcoal-burning with his father and his illiterate brother Carl in the mountains, or seeking refuge with his mother in the empty barracks on the Morne after the Castries fire of 1948, or drifting into corruption, trial and dismissal as a petty official in the Civil Service. And we see the other affairs, some furtive and bourgeois, others casual and earthy, which have preceded all the phases of his rich relationship with Thea. Through it all we are conscious of the two lovers sitting on the hillside, smoking and talking in the darkness, numbed by their awareness that some force within him is sweeping them apart. The writing is full of sharp, perfectly registered dialogue. His narrative and descriptive passages are rendered throughout in short, rather spiky paragraphs and staccato sentences, which carry the same burden of unease as the lives they describe. The effect can occasionally be irritating for the reader who longs for a deeper and more measured breath. Again, it is a style for the novella rather than the novel, but it perfectly fits the peculiar and sustained tension of this story in which jobs, lives and love affairs are all snapped off before fruition.

The second story, ''Another Place Another Time,'' adopts a more chronological approach to a short period in the boyhood of its hero, Derek Charles. It lacks the originality and power of the first, but is full of a distinctive pain of its own. This pain stems largely from the sheer unlikeableness of this boy. He is priggish, snobbish, and jumpy, difficult to reach. He behaves brutally to Berthe, the simple girl whom he seduces and throws over. Yet we see in this society of few and roving males, of unfathered children, abortions, poverty and abandonment, how difficult it is for the growing child to find models by which to climb to maturity. It is as though leaving the island were an indispensable part of growing up, a *rite de passage* from which most of the initiates never return. The story is a cry from the forest of exile, a cry to which St. Omer fits the words of Shakespeare: ''How like a winter has my absence been/From thee.''

St. Omer is particularly good at rendering the speech of those who, though educated elsewhere, are still very close to the islands and unable to relate their living satisfactorily to any other place. The uncertainty of their position is registered in the groping movement of the sentences with which they seek to explain their lives. The handling of dialogue is less successful where it derives from the *patois* of St. Lucia, a dialect largely of French derivation for which St. Omer tries to find an English dialect equivalent. The shape and rhythm of this dialect are necessarily very different from those of *patois,* and the effect, despite an occasional ''oui'' or ''non'' at the end of a sentence, is vaguely West Indian rather than specifically St. Lucian. Yet it is hard to think of any more faithful alternative which would not leave most readers struggling.

To Peter Breville in *Nor Any Country,* as to all St. Omer's heroes, the memories of St. Lucia are the sore tooth which mars his enjoyment of more exotic pleasures and experiences. That nagging pain draws him at last to revisit the island in which he has left for eight years a scarcely-known wife, married only because of her pregnancy. Yet the return, which perhaps he hoped would be purgative, leads to a partial acceptance of what he is and has ever been. Phyllis is still there, still young, still open to his love and still able to awaken his lust. Peter's long-standing resentment of her existence is modified by what he sees of other lives forgotten during his absence. His brother Paul, who likewise impregnated a local girl, has become a special kind of island failure because of his refusal to marry her. The girl herself has committed suicide but her neglected son Michael has survived, whereas Peter's marriage has produced the mirror image of twins born and dead in his absence but a neglected wife who survives to challenge his egotism by her presence. At the end of his week-long visit Peter knows that he must take both Phyllis and Michael with him now. By this single gesture he will attempt to redeem the past. *Nor Any Country* thus ends on a more positive note than any of St. Omer's earlier writing. It stints nothing of the narrow fate attending those who stay in the islands. The failures lie steeped in rum and self-pity, while the few successes grow flashy and Americanized in their loud insecurity. Yet, when all this is said, it was the long-postponed return to the island which brought Peter Breville to his late maturity. For the last *rite de passage* is the reunification with one's origins, without which the cycle of exile can never be complete.

J—, Black Bam and the Masqueraders is a return to the themes and situations of *Nor Any Country,* with the same actors. The approach in this short novel is less naturalistic, intermingling long epistles from Paul (in St. Lucia) to Peter (in Europe), with snatches from the life of Peter in exile. There is far less memorable descriptive writing than in any of St. Omer's earlier work. The anguish of personal failure is as strong as ever, but this book gives off a powerful odor of decay. The actions, motives, and lost possibilities of the past are being raked over and examined yet again, but the novelist himself impresses us as a talent desperately in need of an entirely new subject.

—Gerald Moore

SALINGER, J(erome) D(avid)

Nationality: American. **Born:** New York City, 1 January 1919. **Education:** McBurney School, New York, 1932–34; Valley Forge Military Academy, Pennsylvania (editor, *Crossed Sabres*), 1934–36; New York University, 1937; Ursinus College, Collegetown, Pennsylvania, 1938; Columbia University, New York, 1939. **Military Service:** Served in the 4th Infantry Division of the United States Army, 1942–45: Staff Sergeant. **Family:** Married 1) Sylvia Salinger in 1945 (divorced 1946); 2) Claire Douglas in 1955 (divorced 1967), one daughter and one son. Has lived in New Hampshire since 1953. **Agent:** Dorothy Olding, Harold Ober Associates, 425 Madison Avenue, New York, New York 10017, U.S.A.

Publications

Novel

The Catcher in the Rye. Boston, Little Brown, and London, Hamish Hamilton, 1951.

Short Stories

Nine Stories. Boston, Little Brown, 1953; as *For Esmé—With Love and Squalor and Other Stories,* London, Hamish Hamilton, 1953.

Franny and Zooey. Boston, Little Brown, 1961; London, Heinemann, 1962.

Raise High the Roof Beam, Carpenters, and Seymour: An Introduction. Boston, Little Brown, and London, Heinemann, 1963.

Uncollected Short Stories

''The Young Folks,'' in *Story* (New York), March-April 1940.

''The Hang of It,'' in *Collier's* (Springfield, Ohio), 12 July 1941.

''The Heart of a Broken Story,'' in *Esquire* (New York), September 1941.

''Personal Notes on an Infantryman,'' in *Collier's* (Springfield, Ohio), 12 December 1942.

''The Varioni Brothers,'' in *Saturday Evening Post* (Philadelphia), 17 July 1943.

''Both Parties Concerned,'' in *Saturday Evening Post* (Philadelphia), 26 February 1944.

''Soft-Boiled Sergeant,'' in *Saturday Evening Post* (Philadelphia), 15 April 1944.

''Last Day of the Last Furlough,'' in *Saturday Evening Post* (Philadelphia), 15 July 1944.

''Once a Week Won't Kill You,'' in *Story* (New York), November-December 1944.

''A Boy in France,'' in *The Saturday Evening Post Stories 1942–45,* edited by Ben Hibbs. New York, Random House, 1945.

''Elaine,'' in *Story* (New York), March-April 1945.

''The Stranger,'' in *Collier's* (Springfield, Ohio), 1 December 1945.

''I'm Crazy,'' in *Collier's* (Springfield, Ohio), 22 December 1945.

''Slight Rebellion Off Madison,'' in *New Yorker,* 21 December 1946.

''A Young Girl in 1941 with No Waist at All,'' in *Mademoiselle* (New York), May 1947.

''The Inverted Forest,'' in *Cosmopolitan* (New York), December 1947.

''Blue Melody,'' in *Cosmopolitan* (New York), September 1948.

''The Long Debut of Lois Taggett,'' in *Story: The Fiction of the Forties,* edited by Whit and Hallie Burnett. New York, Dutton, 1949.

''A Girl I Knew,'' in *The Best American Short Stories 1949,* edited by Martha Foley. Boston, Houghton Mifflin, 1949.

''This Sandwich Has No Mayonnaise,'' in *The Armchair Esquire,* edited by Arnold Gingrich and L. Rust Hills. New York, Putnam, 1958.

"Hapworth 16, 1924," in *New Yorker*, 19 June 1965.
"Go See Eddie," in *Fiction: Form and Experience*, edited by William M. Jones. Lexington, Massachusetts, Heath, 1969.

*

Bibliography: *J.D. Salinger: A Thirty Year Bibliography 1938–1968* by Kenneth Starosciak, privately printed, 1971; *J.D. Salinger: An Annotated Bibliography 1938–1981* by Jack R. Sublette, New York, Garland, 1984.

Critical Studies (selection): *The Fiction of J.D. Salinger* by Frederick L. Gwynn and Joseph L. Blotner, Pittsburgh, University of Pittsburgh Press, 1958, London, Spearman, 1960; *Salinger: A Critical and Personal Portrait* edited by Henry Anatole Grunwald, New York, Harper, 1962, London, Owen, 1964; *J.D. Salinger and the Critics* edited by William F. Belcher and James W. Lee, Belmont, California, Wadsworth, 1962; *J.D. Salinger* by Warren French, New York, Twayne, 1963, revised edition, 1976, revised edition, as *J.D. Salinger Revisited,* 1988; *Studies in J.D. Salinger* edited by Marvin Laser and Norman Fruman, New York, Odyssey Press, 1963; *J.D. Salinger* by James E. Miller, Jr., Minneapolis, University of Minnesota Press, 1965; *J.D. Salinger: A Critical Essay* by Kenneth Hamilton, Grand Rapids, Michigan, Eerdmans, 1967; *Zen in the Art of J.D. Salinger* by Gerald Rosen, Berkeley, California, Creative Arts, 1977; *J.D. Salinger* by James Lundquist, New York, Ungar, 1979; *Salinger's Glass Stories as a Composite Novel* by Eberhard Alsen, Troy, New York, Whitston, 1984; *Brodie's Notes on J.D. Salinger's The Catcher in the Rye,* by Catherine Madinaveitia, London, Pan, 1987; *In Search of J.D. Salinger* by Ian Hamilton, London, Heinemann, and New York, Random House, 1988; *Critical Essays on Salinger's The Catcher in the Rye* edited by Joel Salzberg, Boston, Hall, 1990; *Holden Caulfield* edited by Harold Bloom, New York, Chelsea House, 1990; *Alienation in the Fiction of Carson McCullers, J.D. Salinger, and James Purdy* by Anil Kumar, Amritsar, Guru Nanak Dev University Press, 1991; *J.D. Salinger: A Study of the Short Fiction* by John Wenke, Boston, Twayne, 1991; *New Essays on The Catcher in the Rye* by Jack Salzman, Cambridge, Cambridge University Press, 1991; *The Catcher in the Rye: Innocence Under Pressure* by Sanford Pinsker, New York, Twayne, 1993; *J.D. Salinger,* edited by Harold Bloom, Broomall, Pennsylvania, Chelsea House Publishers, 1999.

* * *

In terms of subject matter, the fiction of J.D. Salinger falls into two groups. His most celebrated work, *The Catcher in the Rye,* tells of several days in the life of a young man, Holden Caulfield, after he has left the school from which he has been expelled; he wanders around New York City in a late-adolescent pursuit of contacts that will have meaning for him. The novel itself is Holden's meditation on these days some months later when he is confined to a West Coast clinic. The rest of Salinger's work, with the exception of some of the stories in *Nine Stories,* has for its subject elements drawn from the experience of the Glass family who live in New York. The parents, Les and Bessie, are retired vaudeville dancers; Les is Jewish in origin, Bessie Catholic—a fact that announces the merging of religious traditions effected in the lives of their children. The children, begotten over a considerable period of time, are seven in number. They are Seymour, a gifted poet; Buddy, a writer; Walker and Wake, twins—one killed in war, the other finally a priest; Boo Boo, a happily married daughter; and two much younger children, Franny and Zooey.

The diverse subject matter of Salinger's fiction tends, in retrospect, to coalesce. Holden Caulfield's parents, less loving and concerned than the Glass couple, have also begotten several children. But in Holden's case, there is only one child—a ten-year-old girl—to whom Holden can turn in his desperation.

But it is not just the mirror-image of subject matter that binds the Caulfield narrative together with the tales of the Glass family. There is a unity of tone and a prevailing interest that inform all of Salinger's narratives and that have made them appeal deeply to readers for decades. The tone and interest combine to produce a sad, often ironic meditation on the plight of young persons who are coming to maturity in a society where precise and guiding values are absent. This recurrent meditation, concealed in wrappings that are usually grotesque and farcical, has drawn readers to Salinger. His characters move through a "world they never made;" they address questions to that world and receive, for the most part, only a "dusty answer." Casual social contacts so nauseate Holden Caulfield, for example, that he is frequently at the point of vomiting. His quest for love is harassed by the sexual basis of love, and he is repelled. The only good relation in his life rests on the affection he feels for his younger sister; she is the one light in a wilderness of adult hypocrisy, lust, and perversion. In contrast, affection takes in a larger area in the Glass family chronicles; mutual esteem and concern bind the family together and somewhat offset the dreary vision of human relations in *The Catcher in the Rye.*

Perhaps one reason for this contrast is that, in *The Catcher in the Rye,* the narrative is presented from the point of view of Holden, a malleable, only half-conscious person. He moves in many directions, but none leads him toward the goals he aspires to. His teachers are "phonies;" the one in whom he puts some trust turns out to be a homosexual. His encounter with a prostitute gives him nothing, and his relations with girls of his class do not offer him the gift of comprehension. His parents are as deceived as he is about the proper use of the gift of life. As indicated, only his younger sister can offer him the love he needs, and she is too immature to counterbalance the panorama of insincerity that unfolds before Holden's eyes. So for Holden, all is in suspense—an effect that appealed strongly to Salinger's readers.

But for members of the Glass family, all is not fully in suspense. That gifted group of young people has indeed been badly shaken by the suicide of Seymour, their most gifted sibling. Thus, the central "mystery" which they must come to terms with is not Holden's general panorama of hypocrisy; the death and even more the remembered life of Seymour contain a secret that they are haunted by. The actual death of Seymour is briefly narrated in the story, "A Perfect Day for Bananafish," in *Nine Stories.* Later work, told from various points of view, relates the efforts of members of the Glass family to grasp and apply the eclectic religious truths that the memory of Seymour reminds them of. In none of these tales is there an effort to explain the suicide; this is a fact which the brothers and sisters accept rather than assess. What they do assess, in terms of their own later experience, is the teaching presence of Seymour as they recall it. In the two sections of *Franny and Zooey,* the two youngest members of the family reach out in directions that Seymour, in effect, has already pointed out. In "Franny" the heroine is obsessed by the "Jesus prayer'' which she has come across in the memoirs of a Russian monk; she does not know how to pray the prayer and is only aware that, until she does, all her other relations will be without meaning. In ''Zooey'' her charming brother helps her and himself to come to a grasp of what Seymour's existence had announced: repetition of the Jesus prayer transforms life that is contemptible into a constant act of love and reveals that a ''fat lady'' is indeed Christ—the ''fat lady'' and every other human being one encounters. In ''Raise High the Roof Beam, Carpenters''—told from the point of view of Buddy, the writing brother—the ridiculous circumstances of Seymour's wedding day are related: Seymour and his fiancée finally elope rather than endure an elaborate and empty wedding ceremony. Finally, in ''Seymour: An Introduction''—also told from the point of view of Buddy—all that can be recalled of Seymour is put down. Recalled are his mastery of the allusive oriental haiku and his even more important mastery of the process of extorting the greatest significance from trivial events (e.g., a game of marbles becomes a vehicle of Zen instruction).

It is undoubtedly the merging of Eastern and Western religious wisdom—the solution of the ''mystery'' of existence—that gives the work of Salinger its particular élan. In pursuit of what might be called the Seymour effect, the other Glasses consume innumerable packs of cigarettes and break out into perspiration when they find themselves in blind alleys. But the alleys occasionally open up, and fleeting vistas of human unity flash before the eyes. One can but hope that Holden Caulfield, in his later years, will meet one of the younger Glasses whose personal destinies swell to the proportions of regulative myth.

—Harold H. Watts

SALLIS, James

Nationality: American. **Born:** Helena, Arkansas, 21 December 1944. **Education:** Attended Tulane University, 1962–64. **Family:** Married Jane Rose in 1964; one son. **Career:** Former college instructor, publisher's reader, and magazine editor. **Agent:** c/o Meredith Bernstein, 470 West End Avenue, New York, New York 10023, U.S.A. **Address:** 2113 General Pershing, New Orleans, Louisiana 70115, U.S.A.

Publications

Novels

The Long-Legged Fly: A Novel. New York, Carroll & Graf, 1992.
Moth. New York, Carroll & Graf, 1993.
Black Hornet. New York, Carroll & Graf, 1994.
Renderings: A Novel. Black Heron Press, 1996.
Death Will Have Your Eyes: A Novel About Spies. New York, St. Martin's Press, 1997.
Eye of the Cricket: A Lew Griffin Novel. New York, Walker, 1997.
Bluebottle: A Lew Griffin Novel. New York, Walker, 1999.

Short Stories

A Few Last Words. London, Hart-Davis, 1969; New York, Macmillan, 1970.
Limits of the Sensible World. Host Publications, 1995.

Poetry

Sorrow's Kitchen: Poems. East Lansing, Michigan State University Press, 2000.

Other

Down Home: Country-Western. New York, Macmillan, 1971.
The Guitar Players: One Instrument and Its Masters in American Music. New York, Morrow, 1982.
Difficult Lives: Jim Thompson, David Goodis, Chester Himes. Brooklyn, New York, Gryphon, 1993.
Introduction, *A Case of Rape* by Chester Himes. New York, Carroll & Graf, 1994.
Gently into the Land of the Meateaters (essays). Seattle, Washington, Black Heron Press, 2000.
Editor, *The War Book.* New York, Dell, 1971.
Editor, *The Shores Beneath.* New York, Avon, 1971.
Editor, *Jazz Guitars: An Anthology.* New York, Morrow, 1984.
Editor, *Ash of Stars: On the Writing of Samuel R. Delaney.* Jackson, Mississippi, University Press of Mississippi, 1996.
Editor, *The Guitar in Jazz: An Anthology.* Lincoln, University of Nebraska Press, 1996.
Translator, *Saint Glinglin* by Raymond Queneau. Normal, Illinois, Dalkey Archive Press, 1993.

* * *

The novels of James Sallis exhibit the strong influence of the French New Novelists, who fashion structurally complex existential investigations, often using the methods and motifs of mere potboilers, a project Sallis himself has undertaken. While Sallis's own characters have more in common with the ambivalent ponderers of Michel Butor than with the dispassionate, depersonalized observers of Robbe-Grillet, Sallis shares both authors' preoccupations with changing perceptions and portrayals of time. But a larger shadow is cast across Sallis's novels by Camus's *L'Etranger.* Indeed, Camus's masterpiece is at least mentioned in each of Sallis's novels. With its depiction of the absurdity of the human condition through the context of the actions of a single, supremely alienated individual, *L'Etranger* can be seen as the ur-text against which all of Sallis's novels were anxiously created.

Sallis's novels share other anxious characteristics as well. In each, wounded male narrators relate their experiences in prose that is not so much allusive as it is full of direct references to other writers and their work. Such compulsive quoting can be seen as an appropriation of artistic authenticity that comes mostly from French literature, although Dostoevsky is also frequently mentioned, a fitting reference point for an author whose protagonists are mired in existential uneasiness.

But these references may also signal Sallis's attempt to create consciously-literate characters who apply their readings to their circumstances in ways that lend relevance to situations that are often bleak and even nihilistically shorn of meaning.

If neither of these interpretations is particularly insightful, nor are they mutually exclusive of each other, it may explain Sallis's curious place on the map of contemporary American letters. He is well regarded among aficionados of hard-boiled entertainments, who often review him in glowing terms that rank him with Raymond Chandler and Graham Greene. However, he has largely been ignored by academic critics, despite his prolific output, which includes short stories, poems, jazz criticism, a translation of a novel by Raymond Queneau, and a biography of Chester Himes.

Sallis's best-known works are a series of detective novels set in New Orleans. They feature Lew Griffin, an African-American amateur detective who, besides being an intermittently functioning alcoholic, is also a sometime teacher and novelist. In *The Long-Legged Fly*, the first and least formulaic novel of the series, the narrative opens with Griffin committing a murder that is only obliquely referred to again, which helps explain the pervasive sense of guilt that dogs Griffin throughout the subsequent three decades this short novel encompasses, detailing Griffin's handling of several missing-person's cases as well as his own swiftly changing fortunes.

Sallis's mysteries do not reach conclusions so much as merely end, confirming their narrators' forgone conclusions of absurdity by ending in ways that indict the very structures of the narratives they conclude. In this way, Sallis strives to subvert the contrived conventions of the genre, and of narrative literature itself, making of them emblems for much larger contrivances, such as assumptions about the redemptive nature of love or the purpose of life. In *Moth*, Griffin searches for the lost daughter of his long-time, now-deceased lover, a reformed prostitute who had married another man and spent the rest of her life doing social work. When Griffin finally locates this daughter, he helps her recover from drug addiction only to have her willfully run away again.

However, such attempted subversions are not always successful, often coming off as abrupt abandonments rather than earned realizations of futility. Sallis often employs a kind of deus ex machina ending in his novels, though his use of this device undermines structure rather than being an affirmation of meaning imparted from above. In *Black Hornet*, Lew Griffin's quest to find a sniper who has targeted white citizens of New Orleans ends when Griffin is literally told the address of the sniper by an acquaintance who has known the criminal's identity all along. When Griffin confronts the sniper, the criminal dies without revealing his identity while Griffin is credited with avenging the sniper's victims, though, in truth, the sniper's death was an accident and his reasons for killing have died with him. The mystery has ended, but it has not been solved.

Renderings is Sallis's only non-genre novel, the story of a writer who travels to a remote island to live in a settlement for some unspecified purpose, though he alludes to his trip being an ''expedition'' for which he is compiling a ''report'' that is ostensibly the novel itself. With its first-person, ruminative and highly provocative narration, *Renderings* invites comparisons with Dostoevsky's *Notes from Underground* and Ralph Ellison's *Invisible Man;* but *Renderings* has a tighter, almost microscopic focus, and its narrator's ruminations are less overtly topical. As this narrator revisits his past, which consists mostly of failed relationships with women, he does ruminate on such subjects as writing, the difference between the lyrical and narrative modes, and the novels of Dostoevsky. But the real subject of his thoughts is the struggle between past failures and present circumstances. Surreal details, such as people with animal heads, intrude on the narrative, highlighting its subjectivity by blurring the lines between experience and imagination. Indeed, this novel asks how much of experience is imagination, and its answer is solipsistic in the extreme. The narrator realizes that the essential alienation of individuals is insurmountable; spurred by some past trauma that may or may not have been the suicide of a lover, this man concludes that, while connection is impossible, we are compelled to try to communicate with one another. Hence, he writes, because we are ''unable to acknowledge silence.'' Thus, love, or our perception of love, is merely a coping mechanism with which we distract ourselves from the inevitable silence of impending death.

By the last half of *Renderings*, the narrator has embraced his solipsism, so that it becomes unclear whether or not the woman he has met at the settlement, and who has become his lover, is a real person, perhaps a fellow patient. She may instead be a ghost, or a figment of his imagination. Throughout the narrative, the sea has emerged as a symbol of the infinite unknowable, and the book ends with the narrator staring out at it, with his lover by his side, ''waiting for the end of the world.'' The novel seems to argue for an absurdity whose only obviation is through art, seemingly a central tenet of all of Sallis's fiction, but *Renderings* is troubling for not being particularly artistic. Rather, it is a rhetorical novel making an artistic argument, mustering the words of other writers as evidence without creating anything remotely sublime on its own.

In *Death Will Have Your Eyes*, Sallis creates a spy novel, incorporating the conventions of espionage tales to his central motif of a man coping with his dark past. David, a successful sculptor who was once a government assassin, is pressed back into service when one of his former colleagues begins committing murders whose purpose is unknown. Again, Sallis creates a super-literate protagonist whose ruminations take on existential connotations. And, as the episodes of the novel unfold in ways that both conform and then subvert the conventions of the spy genre as practiced by Ian Fleming and John le Carre, Sallis comes closer than in *Renderings* to the manifestation of his aesthetic that life is a nihilistic jumble that is best dealt with through creativity. David survives his final mission to again become, with the aid of his beautiful Gabrielle, a successful artist. It is not a particularly penetrating conclusion; it is a contrivance. But Sallis's hero knows it is, and that, it seems, makes all the difference. Like the condemned Meursault, David rejects the idea that his actions can be justified, therein finding the freedom, even at the moment of possible execution, to indulge them.

—J.J. Wylie

SAMS, Ferrol, Jr.

Nationality: American. **Born:** Fayetteville, Georgia, 26 September 1922. **Education:** Attended Mercer University; Emory University, M.D. 1949. **Military Service:** Served in military 1943–47. **Family:** Married Helen Fletcher in 1948; three sons, one daughter. **Career:** Physician in private practice, Fayetteville, Georgia, 1951—; instructor in creative writing, Emory University, Atlanta, 1991—. **Awards:** Townsend Prize for Fiction, 1991; D.Lit.: Mercer University, 1987, Emory University, 1992, Medical University of South Carolina, 1993, and Rhodes College, 1994. **Agent:** c/o Longstreet Press, 2140 Newmarket Parkway, Suite 118, Marietta, Georgia 30067, U.S.A. **Address:** 101 Yorktown Dr., Fayetteville, Georgia 30214, U.S.A.

PUBLICATIONS

Novels

Run with the Horsemen. Atlanta, Peachtree Publishers, 1982.
The Whisper of the River. Atlanta, Peachtree Publishers, 1984.
When All the World Was Young. Marietta, Georgia, Longstreet Press, 1991.

Short Stories

The Widow's Mite and Other Stories. Atlanta, Peachtree Publishers, 1987.
Epiphany: Stories. Marietta, Georgia, Longstreet Press, 1994.

Other

The Passing: Perspectives of Rural America (nonfiction), paintings by Jim Harrison. Marietta, Georgia, Longstreet Press, 1988; also published as *The Passing: Stories,* Marietta, Georgia, Longstreet Press, 1988.
Christmas Gift! (nonfiction). Marietta, Georgia, Longstreet Press, 1989.

* * *

Ferrol Sams, Jr., is an occupant of a dwindling, if not nonexistent, category of contemporary writers for whom writing is secondary to another occupation. Within a relatively short period of time, Sams has created a substantial body of work and has cemented himself as a significant voice in southern literature, all the while maintaining a successful medical practice with his wife Helen in Fayetteville, Georgia. Sams is best known for his colorful and accurate depictions of the early twentieth-century American South, representing a family-oriented lifestyle and community that is now disappearing in the name of progress and growth. Several of his works—both novels and short stories—have been adapted for the theater, and all of his works have been praised for their wry southern humor and for their introspective reflections on the nature of rural life, love, and sexuality. He has similarly been praised for his use of southern dialect and idiosyncrasies, and for richly developed characters. Though Sams has also produced nonfiction accounts of his early childhood, he is predominantly a fiction writer, and is best known for a trilogy of semi-autobiographical novels detailing his own youth and education in Georgia and his experiences in World War II.

At the age of fifty-eight, Sams revised private journals written earlier in his life, adapting and embellishing them to create his first novel. His trilogy begins with the work *Run with the Horsemen*, published in 1982. This novel, as with much of his work, is told from a first-person perspective, and the plot closely parallels the life of its author. The novel centers around a young prankster born in rural depression-era Georgia. Sams recounts his childhood through the voice of Porter Osborne, Jr. (Sams's own great-grandfather was named Porter), who is given the nickname ''Sambo,'' a name that had been given to Sams as a young farmboy born into a similar rural setting. Porter's varied, rustic adventures and shenanigans serve as a backdrop to explore and depict the early southern American scene. Besides presenting conditions of early southern families and the farming life, Sams has been praised for confronting issues of race and gender while neither embracing nor encouraging stereotypes in his characterizations.

The novel was warmly received by critics and the public, encouraging Sams to continue the tales of Porter as he left the farm and headed to the university in *The Whisper of the River*. Porter's journey to ''Willingham University'' parallels Sams own education at Mercer University, and exposes the young boy not only to traditional forms of learning and pedagogy, including a thorough introduction to canonical English literature, but also to the advanced sexual situations and challenges to accepted beliefs that come with further maturity and distance from home. The novel shows Porter questioning the Christianity taught in his childhood and, while he is still marked by the intelligence evident in the first novel, readers will also find him nevertheless engaging in his similarly characteristic pranks and escapades. Anyone who ended the series here might conclude that the smoking, sexually active, and rebellious Porter had affected a complete break from the stability of his home and family, although throughout the novel there is a ''whisper of the river'' to remind him of the stability of the land and its community, a familiar theme throughout Sams's work.

It is clear, at the end of *The Whisper of the River*, that a further novel is required to resolve both the approaching World War and Porter's process of maturation. Sams, however, was at first not entirely prepared to write that novel. Faced with writer's block on the longer project, he turned to producing other works. The result was a collection of short stories, *The Widow's Mite and Other Stories*, and two volumes of nonfiction childhood memoirs, *The Passing*, and *Christmas Gift!*. Although Sams has been given moderate criticism for his overabundant use of southern colloquialisms, these collections again exploit his knowledge of the southern homestead and southern traditions to good effect. In *The Widow's Mite*, he returns to biblical and spiritual subjects used in his previous novels, though the collection transcends the boundaries of the typical southern oral storytelling tradition. Sams employs varied dialects, perspectives, and narrative formats, including a story told from the perspective of a small girl, a nonfiction letter to a friend of Sams, and even contemporary tales that might be disturbing to those familiar with Sams's otherwise homespun narratives. The final story, ''Porphyria's Lover'' (referring to the Robert Browning poem of the same name), is a first-person confessional narrative that confronts entirely secular themes. The narrator of the story is an adulterous bisexual man who relates a tale of betrayal, sexual disease, and murder.

Despite the occasional profane morality tales, however, Sams is best known for the capricious, lighthearted nature of his fictional stories and nonfiction reflections. He is perhaps best recognized for his witty cataloging of southern behavior, and his reminiscences of southern traditions and communities that have now been erased or forgotten. *The Passing* argues for the value of small-town life, with its minimal traffic and earnest inhabitants, who have now gone the way of progress, swallowed in ''the avarice of politicians, the greed of developers,'' while *Christmas Gift!* celebrates the unity and love of Christmas traditions shared by the family—traditions of Christmas that survived and flourished even in the gift-deficient times of the economic Depression of Sams's youth.

The final novel in the trilogy of Porter Osborne, Jr., is entitled *When All the World Was Young*, a reference to G. K. Chesterton's poem ''Lepanto,'' cited throughout the novel. While the story is filled yet again with ribald tales of trickery and horseplay, the novel continues the trilogy's themes of maturity, spirituality, and community. Porter, ready to die for his country during World War II, soon confronts the deaths of those around him and learns about his own mortality. In response to this, his father writes in a letter from home, ''You are not becoming a man, you are a man.'' Porter also continues to confront the issue of his faith in God, finding at the end of the novel that doubt and faith are concepts that do not exist independent of one another. Another repetitive theme in the novel is the continuity and stability of the land; Porter carries a lump of red Georgia dirt in his shoes to remind himself of his home and his reasons for fighting. The novel ends with Porter's reflection that, even if he has not found himself in his journey, at least ''I sure as hell found America!''

Sams's work following the trilogy includes a book of three short stories given the collective title *Epiphany*. In this work, Sams furthers his experimentation with the short story format and also continues to write stories that readers will surely interpret as autobiographical in nature. The title story, ''Epiphany,'' involves an old, eccentric doctor whose relationship with a patient seems more like psychoanalysis than physical therapy, both men maturing by the end of the story. The subsequent stories in the collection explore the subject of enduring relationships between people (apparently Sams and his own wife), and connections between old and young, including observations on morality and slavery, which continue to be repetitive themes for Sams.

With few exceptions, Sams's work has been enthusiastically received by reviewers and the reading public. His detailed description of southern living reveals traditions and personalities that may be quickly and quietly passing from our world, and his writing urges a return to, and preservation of, the warmth of familial community. His work is influenced by the rich history of the South and by the literary history of England and America. Sams's narratives include tales of maturation, struggles with faith, blossoming sexuality, and, perhaps above all, idiomatic southern wit and wisdom. Though Sams is too recent an author to have received a great deal of literary criticism, his skill and craftsmanship has led many reviewers to place him among the best of contemporary southern writers.

—Steven J. Zani

SAVAGE, Thomas

Nationality: American. **Born:** Salt Lake City, Utah, 25 April 1915. **Education:** Colby College, B.A. 1940, M.A. 1955. **Family:** Married, 1939; two sons, one daughter. **Career:** Faculty member, Suffolk University, Boston, 1947–48; assistant professor, Brandeis University, 1949–55. **Awards:** Guggenheim fellowship, 1980; Northwest Booksellers award, 1989. **Agent:** Blanche Gregory, 2 Tudor City Place, New York, New York 10017, U.S.A.

PUBLICATIONS

Novels

The Pass. New York, Doubleday, 1944.
Lona Hanson. New York, Simon and Schuster, 1948.
A Bargain with God. New York, Simon and Schuster, 1953.
Trust in Chariots. New York, Random House, 1961.
The Power of the Dog. New York, Little Brown, and London, Chatto and Windus, 1967.
The Liar. New York, Little Brown, 1967.
Daddy's Girl. New York, Little Brown, 1970.
A Strange God. New York, Little Brown, 1974.
Midnight Line. New York, Little Brown, 1976.
I Heard My Sister Speak My Name. New York, Little Brown, 1977
Her Side of It. New York, Little Brown, 1981.
For Mary with Love. New York, Little Brown, 1983.
The Corner of Rife and Pacific. New York, Morrow, 1988.

*

Thomas Savage comments:

Mrs. Bridge, by Evan S. Connell, is one of the best novels I ever read. I was influenced by John Steinbeck, Robert Benchley, and Dorothy Parker. I was a history major, read little fiction, chiefly biography and history. I read S.J. Perelman.

I believe all organized religion is based on myths and is responsible for most of the horror in the world now and in the past. I think nothing will change much because of continuing, probably atavistic, superstition, ignorance, and greed. It's frightening that human beings continue to need scapegoats in order to justify themselves. I once made a speech somewhere and said, ''The more education you have, the less money you need.'' I still believe this. And if you don't have much education you'd damned well better have money.

* * *

Despite having spent most of his life on the Atlantic and Pacific coastlines, ''within sight of water,'' he says, Thomas Savage returns to the Montana valley of his youth as the setting for more than half of his novels. The people who settled and live in the geographic center of Savage's West (southwestern Montana and Idaho's Lemhi Valley) face hard work, harsh weather conditions, isolation, and rugged terrain. Against such a backdrop, Savage's western characters struggle to attain, maintain, or retain their individuality, family pride, love, success—and sometimes the land itself. One might expect people tested by such landscape to toughen themselves, both physically and emotionally, in order to survive; and though such characters do appear in Savage's work, he tends to focus most often on the more vulnerable citizens of his western ranching communities—the young and sensitive ''outsider,'' the woman who cannot cope with her circumstances, the man who fails himself and everyone else in his life through what Savage identifies as ''an inability to face unpleasantness.''

Although Savage says he writes fiction and not autobiography, he acknowledges the role that memory plays in his western fiction. As a youngster, Savage ''boarded out'' in Dillon, the town closest to the family ranch, while he attended school. In several novels, Dillon is transformed into Herndon or Grayling, and the experiences of the protagonists mirror those of the creator. There are also some ''stock'' fixtures in Savage's fictional household and domestic arrangements, such as the grandfather's clock that is ceremoniously wound once a week by the proprietor of the ranch or the home; the large cars (a Rolls-Royce; a Roamer) that Savage's businessmen and ranchers drive; the rings that wives of successful husbands wear as symbols of the family prosperity.

Several themes also resurface in many of Savage's novels, including that of the ''unsolicited kindness'' that is rewarded (sometimes years after the fact) at a time when the characters are most in need of the financial or emotional boost that is offered. Many of his female characters, be they located in the West or the East, lament the changes taking place in their lives or their surroundings; ''nothing's the same,'' Norma Reed says in *A Strange God* (1974), an eastern-setting novel. Her comment echoes the sentiments of a woman speaking her mind in Savage's first novel, *The Pass,* published thirty years earlier: ''All the new things, all the new ways, spoiled something.'' That ''something'' is the quality, the texture of life enjoyed by the characters before changes—what Martin Levin called ''the accidents of success and the accidents of failure'' in his *New York Times* review of *A Strange God* (25 August 1974)—occur. These changes can also sometimes be counted as losses, and loss is another familiar element in Savage's novels. Redemption or restoration is also possible for Savage's characters, however, and most of his novels do end on an optimistic note.

For Mary, with Love ends unhappily, it is true, but the novel—a tale of a social climber told by a childhood friend, Mary Skoning—is in part a morality tale, and thus the punishment of wrongdoing makes sense in this context. Likewise *The Corner of Rife and Pacific* involves a great deal of misfortune and injustice, as a kind and generous couple are dealt a hard blow, but again the underlying moral purpose in Savage's writing comes to the fore: kindness, he seems to be saying, is its own reward.

Savage identifies *Her Side of It,* the novel he wrote as a Guggenheim recipient in 1980, as his best work. (Ironically, his most commercially successful books, *Lona Hanson,* set in the West, and *A Bargain with God,* which takes place in Boston, are the two he feels least positive about in terms of artistic achievement.) The main character in *Her Side of It,* Liz Phillips, is a novelist, and Savage's narrator is able to comment on both the working life of a writer and on the achievement possible in that field of endeavor. In words that critics might apply to Savage's own work, he says that Phillips's novels ''promote a reader to search for answers ... and to find them. The search makes of life a sharper pleasure.''

—Sue Hart, updated by Judson Knight

SCHAEFFER, Susan Fromberg

Nationality: American. **Born:** Brooklyn, New York, 25 March 1941. **Education:** Simmons College, Boston; University of Chicago, 1958–66, B.A. 1961, M.A. 1963, Ph.D. 1966. **Family:** Married Neil J. Schaeffer in 1970; one son and one daughter. **Career:** Instructor in English, Wright Junior College, Chicago, 1964–65; instructor, 1965–66, and assistant professor of English, 1966–67, Illinois Institute of Technology, Chicago. Assistant Professor, 1967–71, associate professor, 1972–74, since 1974 professor of English, and since 1985 Broeklundian Professor, Brooklyn College. **Awards:** Wallant award, 1975; O. Henry award, 1980; St. Lawrence award, 1984; Guggenheim fellowship, 1984; *Centennial Review* award, for poetry, 1985. **Agent:** Janklow & Nesbit Associates, 598 Madison Avenue, New York, New York, 10022–1614, U.S.A. **Address:** Department of English, Brooklyn College, Brooklyn, New York 11210, U.S.A.

Publications

Novels

Falling. New York, Macmillan, 1973.
Anya. New York, Macmillan, 1974; London, Cassell, 1976.
Time in Its Flight. New York, Doubleday, 1978.
Love. New York, Dutton, 1981.
First Nights. New York, Knopf, and London, Hamish Hamilton, 1983.
The Madness of a Seduced Woman. New York, Dutton, 1983; London, Hamish Hamilton, 1984.
Mainland. New York, Simon and Schuster, and London, Hamish Hamilton, 1985.
The Injured Party. New York, St. Martin's Press, and London, Hamish Hamilton, 1986.
Buffalo Afternoon. New York, Knopf, and London, Hamish Hamilton, 1989.
The Golden Rope. New York, Knopf, 1996.
The Autobiography of Foudini M. Cat. New York, Knopf, 1997.

Short Stories

The Queen of Egypt. New York, Dutton, 1980.

Uncollected Short Stories

''In the Hospital and Elsewhere,'' in *Prairie Schooner* (Lincoln, Nebraska), Winter 1981–82.
''Virginia; or, A Single Girl,'' in *Prairie Schooner* (Lincoln, Nebraska), Fall 1983.

Poetry

The Witch and the Weather Report. New York, Seven Woods Press, 1972.
Granite Lady. New York, Macmillan, 1974.
The Rhymes and Runes of the Toad. New York, Macmillan, 1975.
Alphabet for the Lost Years. San Francisco, Gallimaufry, 1976.
The Red, White, and Blue Poem. Denver, The Ally, 1977.
The Bible of the Beasts of the Little Field. New York, Dutton, 1980.

Fiction (for children)

The Dragons of North Chittendon. New York, Simon and Schuster, 1986.
The Four Hoods and Great Dog. New York, St. Martin's Press, 1988.

*

Critical Studies: *Jewish American Women Writers* by Dorothy Bilik, Westport, Connecticut, Greenwood Press, 1995.

* * *

Susan Fromberg Schaeffer's novels, spanning sixteen years, are basically mainstream fictions that employ stream of consciousness, radical time shifts, and other modernist techniques, but only incidentally. Apparently she believes that the traditional form is adequate to her purposes, and she is right in so thinking. Schaeffer is mainly interested in exploring and illuminating the shapes of her characters' lives through presentation of the mundane details of their existences. Although she sometimes has her characters move through the larger contexts of historical times, and although she often offers elaborate explanations for behavior, her main strengths as a novelist are her ability to evoke the real quality of quotidian life and the particularities of emotional states.

Falling, Schaeffer's first novel, contains all her strengths and weaknesses as a writer. It is the story of Elizabeth Kamen, a graduate-school Jewish intellectual who suffers several near mental breakdowns, who has unfailingly bad judgment about the men in her life, and whose life is largely determined by her family background. In this and subsequent novels, the lives of characters are traced through their often harrowing childhoods which permanently stamp their personalities. As a child, Elizabeth had stolen a quarter to buy a doll, which her mother and grandmother demolished then hung on the wall to remind Elizabeth of her ''crime.'' This and other accounts, including events from her present life, are woven together in sessions with her psychiatrist. The aim is to arrest her falling and to get control of her life which, like others characters' lives, suffers from various kinds of slippage. But the human condition is to fall because, as Elizabeth's mother says in Elizabeth's dream. ''There is no bottom, there is only this falling,'' only motion and journey, as opposed to stasis and goal. Elizabeth's mother also asks, ''Can you swim, Elizabeth?'' ''Yes, Mother, if you hold, I'll kick.''

However, as a narrative *Falling* suffers from a peculiar stasis. The story is a series of vignettes or anecdotes that do not make up a single, satisfying narrative framework. This is not principally due to Schaeffer's abandoning traditional narrative technique; rather, the episodes are disjointed and without flow. As in other novels, characters are introduced only to show up later, after the reader has forgotten them; adding to the diffuseness that characterizes the entire novel. Yet the strengths of *Falling* remain. Schaeffer's skill as a poet saves many of the scenes; vivid images and descriptions help give the novel a heightened sense of life.

In *Anya* Schaeffer again concentrates on the incidental, even minute aspects of dailiness that are presented with the quality of a personal diary. The novel chronicles the life of Anya, a young Jewish woman in Poland, from the mid-1930s up to the present. Though the novel is partly set during the holocaust years, it is not really about the holocaust (descriptions of life before the Hitler years are among the most compelling in the novel), but about Anya whose life intersects, but is not principally affected by, social events of the time. Schaeffer almost always selects family history as more determinative of character and personality than culture or history. Again, life is the accretion of small things. Anya says, ''If you are going to learn a person's life, then, like learning a language, you must start with the little things, the little pictures, the tiny, square images, like rooms, that will grow into a film.'' To this must be added all of Anya's personal history, from naive, happy student to tough survivor in contemporary America. And Anya always draws on her former lives for strength, so the reader—more so than in *Falling*—experiences a more multi-dimensional character. It should be added that at the time Schaeffer was writing *Anya,* American-born Jewish novelists were more concerned with American social history than with the formation of a ''Jewishness'' as a response to the death camps and the World War II years. One thinks immediately of Bellow, say, as opposed to a writer like Cynthia Ozick. Now, of course, the holocaust has become an almost fashionable subject.

Love again details the potent, permanent effects of family and married lives, as opposed to culture and history. Esheal Luria is abandoned at the age of ten by his widowed mother after he has been rejected by his stepfather. He is rescued by a mysterious ''zenshima'' (witch) whose memory haunts him through adulthood and is in part responsible for his wanting, from childhood, ''to find an American woman and take care of her.'' Despite the fact that the novel is a saga of two Jewish immigrant families, the ultimate determinant is, as Luria's wife Emily puts it, the fact that we are ''only a new step in the continuing dance ... of the genes.'' Resembling at times an Isaac Bashevis Singer tale, *Anya* gains its strength through evocative detail, even the oddities of life lived away from the sweep of events. Emily's mother speaks for Schaeffer: ''I remember all those things, but now I don't like to save odd things. They take you over, all those books, cards, litter and pictures. They keep accumulating and it becomes a chore to sort them out and they pile up until they overwhelm you and then you get rid of them all.''

As though trying to escape the influence of Emily's mother's words, *The Madness of a Seduced Woman* is Schaeffer's attempt to understand a single life as compounded of personal history, woman's biology, psychiatry, and community standards. The novel is based on an actual murder trial in Vermont early in the century in which Agnes Dempster is tried for the murder of her rival and pronounced insane, largely on psychiatric testimony that Agnes's insanity resulted from ''the madness of a seduced woman.'' However, Schaeffer does not accept this judgment and painstakingly examines her motives (reminiscent of Joyce Carol Oates) as seen through the speculations of lawyers, friends, and her father. No firm conclusions are reached, except that no life may be understood exclusively by objective or subjective means. This process of examination is often numbing, especially since Agnes's life is more complicated than understood. Schaeffer, in this novel, does not allow the character's life to speak for itself; analyses and comment are often substituted for dramatization and the tale itself as an adequate vehicle for meaning.

Mainland, is in many ways a return to her more lighthearted first novel and to a less complex tale, whose theme is maturity. Eleanor, the main character, is a famous writer and professor, basically happy but almost obsessed by the moralistic voices of her dead grandmother and mother. The novel, comically delightful, avoids the diffuseness of much of her earlier work. The theme is expertly handled and the characterization fully realized. Before the novel's end Elizabeth realizes that her adulterous affair was necessary, so she forgives herself, realizing along the way that the dialogues in her head are only carry-overs from childhood and that ''maturity'' is a false ideal. Schaeffer demonstrates here that a less ambitious theme does not necessarily preclude a higher art.

—Peter Desy

SCHULBERG, Budd (Wilson)

Nationality: American. **Born:** New York City, 27 March 1914; son of the Hollywood film pioneer, B.P. Schulberg. **Education:** Los Angeles High School, 1928–31; Deerfield Academy, 1931–32; Dartmouth College, Hanover, New Hampshire, 1932–36, A.B. (cum laude) 1936 (Phi Beta Kappa). **Military Service:** Served in the United States Navy, 1943–46: Lieutenant. **Family:** Married 1) Virginia Ray in 1936 (divorced 1942), one daughter; 2) Victoria Anderson in 1943 (divorced 1964), two sons; 3) the actress Geraldine Brooks in 1964 (died 1977); 4) Betsy Anne Langman in 1979, one son and one daughter. **Career:** Screenwriter, Hollywood, 1936–39; in charge of photographic evidence for the Nuremberg trials; boxing editor, *Sports Illustrated,* New York, 1954. Has taught writing at Columbia University, New York, Phoenixville Veterans Hospital, University of the Streets, New York, Southampton College, New York, Darmouth College, and Hofstra University, Hempstead, New

York; founder, Watts Writers Workshop, Los Angeles, 1965. Since 1958 president, Schulberg Productions, New York; since 1970 founding chair, Frederick Douglass Creative Arts Center, New York. Member of the New York Council, Authors' Guild, 1958–60; since 1983 council member, Writers Guild. Lives in Westhampton Beach, New York. **Awards:** American Library Association award, New York Critics award, Foreign Correspondents award, Screen Writers Guild award, and Oscar, all for screenplay, 1955; Christopher award, 1956; German Film Critics award, for screenplay, 1958; Susie Humanitarian award, B'nai B'rith, 1966; Image award, NAACP, 1966; Journalism award, Dartmouth College, 1966; Merit award, Lotos Club, 1966; L.A. Community Service award, 1966; B'hai Human Rights award, 1968; special award for Watts Writers Workshop, New England Theater Conference, 1969; Heritage award, Deerfield Academy, 1986; Amistad award; award for work with black writers, Howard University; Prix Literaire, Deauville Festival; Westhampton Writers Lifetime Achievement award; World Boxing Association Living Legend award, 1990; Southampton Cultural Center 1st annual literature award, 1992; A.J. Leibling award, 1997. D.Litt.: Dartmouth College, 1960; Long Island University, Greenvale, New York, 1983; Hofstra University, 1985. **Address:** c/o Random House Inc., 201 East 50th Street, New York, New York 10022, U.S.A.

Publications

Novels

What Makes Sammy Run? New York, Random House, and London, Jarrolds, 1941.
The Harder They Fall. New York, Random House, and London, Lane, 1947; with a new foreword by the author, Chicago, Ivan R. Dee, 1996.
The Disenchanted. New York, Random House, 1950; London, Lane, 1951.
Waterfront. New York, Random House, 1955; London, Lane, 1956; as *On the Waterfront,* London, Corgi, 1959.
Sanctuary V. Cleveland, World, 1969; London, W.H. Allen, 1970.
Everything That Moves. New York, Doubleday, 1980; London, Robson, 1981.

Short Stories

Some Faces in the Crowd. New York, Random House, 1953; London, Lane, 1954.
Love, Action, Laughter, and Other Sad Tales. New York, Random House, 1989; London, Allison and Busby, 1992.

Plays

Hollywood Doctor (broadcast 1941). Published in *The Writer's Radio Theatre,* edited by Norman Weiser, New York, Harper, 1941.
Tomorrow, with Jerome Lawrence (radio play), in *Free World Theatre,* edited by Arch Oboler and Stephen Longstreet. New York, Random House, 1944.
The Pharmacist's Mate, in *The Best Television Plays 1950–1951,* edited by William I. Kauffman. New York, Merlin Press, 1952.
A Face in the Crowd: A Play for the Screen. New York, Random House, 1957.
Across the Everglades: A Play for the Screen. New York, Random House, 1958.
The Disenchanted, with Harvey Breit, adaptation of the novel by Schulberg (produced New York, 1958). New York, Random House, 1959.
What Makes Sammy Run?, with Stuart Schulberg, music by Ervin Drake, adaptation of the novel by Budd Schulberg (produced New York, 1964).
On the Waterfront: Original Story and Screenplay, edited by Matthew J. Bruccoli. Carbondale, Southern Illinois University Press, 1980.

Screenplays: *Little Orphan Annie,* with Samuel Ornitz and Endre Bohem, 1938; *Winter Carnival,* with Maurice Rapf and Lester Cole, 1939; *Weekend for Three,* with Dorothy Parker and Alan Campbell, 1941; *Government Girl,* with Dudley Nichols, 1943; *City Without Men,* with Martin Berkeley and W.L. River, 1943; *On the Waterfront,* 1954; *A Face in the Crowd,* 1957; *Wind Across the Everglades,* 1958; *Joe Louis—For All Time,* 1984.

Radio Play: *Hollywood Doctor,* 1941.

Television Play: *A Question of Honor,* 1982.

Other

Loser and Still Champion: Muhammad Ali. New York, Doubleday, and London, New English Library, 1972.
The Four Seasons of Success. New York, Doubleday, 1972; London, Robson, 1974; revised edition, as *Writers in America,* New York, Stein and Day, 1983.
Swan Watch, photographs by Geraldine Brooks. New York, Delacorte Press, and London, Robson, 1975.
Moving Pictures: Memories of a Hollywood Prince. New York, Stein and Day, 1981; London, Souvenir Press, 1982.
Sparring with Hemingway, and Other Legends of the Fight Game. Chicago, I.R. Dee, 1995.
Editor, *From the Ashes: The Voices of Watts.* New York, New American Library, 1967.

*

Manuscript Collections: Princeton University, New Jersey; Dartmouth College, Hanover, New Hampshire.

Critical Studies: interview in *Cineaste* (New York), 1981.

Budd Schulberg comments:

(1972) I was raised in Hollywood, in the middle of the film capital, and had an early education in the vicissitudes of success and failure. I became convinced, before I was out of high school, that the dynamics of success and failure were of earthquake proportions in American, and that Hollywood was only an exaggerated version of the American success drive. Undoubtedly this influenced my first novel, *What Makes Sammy Run?,* as it did *The Harder They Fall, The Disenchanted,* and many other things I have tried to write. I believe it is the prime American theme, prompting my essays on Sinclair Lewis, Scott Fitzgerald, William Saroyan, Nathanael West, Thomas Heggen, and John Steinbeck, all writers I knew well. I believe that the seasons of success and failure are more violent in America than anywhere else on earth. Witness only Herman Melville and Jack London, to name two of the victims.

I have been influenced by Mark Twain, by Frank Norris, Jack London, Upton Sinclair, John Steinbeck, and the social novelists. I believe in art, but I don't believe in art for art's sake; while despising the Soviet official societal writing, I believe in art for people's sake. I believe the novelist should be an artist cum sociologist. I think he should see his characters in social perspective. I think that is one of his obligations. At the same time, I think he also has an obligation to entertain. I think the novel should run on a double track. I am proud of the fact that *Uncle Tom's Cabin* and *The Jungle* and *The Grapes of Wrath* helped to change or at least alarm society. I am proud of the fact that books of mine, *Sammy,* or *On the Waterfront,* caught the public attention but also made it more aware of social sores, the corruption that springs from the original Adam Smith ideal of individuality. I think Ayn Rand tries to apply eighteenth-century ideals to twentieth-century problems—and I'm not sure they worked that well then. My flags are down: I believe in neither Smith nor Marx, in neither Nixon nor Mao nor the Soviet bureaucrats who persecute my fellow writers. There was a time when I was young when I sang the ''International.'' Who would have guessed that the ''International'' would result in the two largest countries in the world, both ''Socialist,'' brandishing lethal weapons at each other? As long as we can wonder and remember, speculate and (perhaps vainly) hope, we are not dead. The non- or anti-communist humanist writer of novels may be slightly out of style, but there are miles and decades and many books to go before he sleeps.

* * *

Budd Schulberg earned fame with his first and best novel, *What Makes Sammy Run?,* published in 1941 on the author's twenty-seventh birthday. This narrative of an obnoxious office boy's quick rise to head of a major motion picture studio threatened to become the author's type story for all his novels. *The Harder They Fall* told the pathetic story of the rise of Toro Molina to heavy-weight boxing champion, although ''El Toro'' is actually the victim of an ambitious, unscrupulous fight promoter named Nick Latka. Schulberg's *The Disenchanted* traced the doomed comeback attempt of Manley Halliday, a novelist and culture-hero of the 1920s now reduced to writing movie scenarios when sober. In these three early novels and many of the collected short stories of *Some Faces in the Crowd,* Schulberg is absorbed with the theme of rapid success and the psychic losses of public winners: compromise with self, betrayal by or of others, doubt, guilt, isolation, and fear haunt and shame his restless characters.

Schulberg's plots have frequently reflected the author's background as screenwriter and son of a Hollywood producer. Not surprisingly, many of his novels have been produced as movies, but his fourth novel, *Waterfront,* was a successful movie first, with the novel version a distinct improvement over the author's own scenario. After a fifteen year lapse, Schulberg returned to the novel with *Sanctuary V,* a melodramatic study of a failed revolution and the ruinous effects of sudden power. In this least successful novel, Justo Suarez, the provisional president of what is obviously Cuba, has fled from the corrupted revolutionary Angel Bello to take sanctuary in a corrupt embassy among corrupt or perverted refugees and jailer-hosts.

Not only is Angel Bello clearly Fidel Castro, earlier novels just as recognizably modeled their protagonists on real-life counterparts: the hapless, peasant-fighter Toro Molina is Primo Carnera, while Manley Halliday is Scott Fitzgerald, with whom Schulberg (''Shep'' in the book) had once worked on a Dartmouth winter carnival scenario. When Schulberg is not ''exposing'' Hollywood through memories of real-life counterparts or composites, he utilizes journalistic skill and thorough research for fictional exposés of the fight game (*Harder They Fall*) and the brutal life around New York harbor (*Waterfront*). Like most exposés, the novels exploit the most sensational elements, though Schulberg reveals an un-Hollywoodian preference for the seamy over the sexy. He does commit many other major ''Hollywood'' faults, employing gimmicks, stereotyped characters, sentimentality, and mechanical, reflex responses to life-situations in place of serious ideas or a personal vision.

With *Sammy,* however, even the faults seem appropriate. The snappy repartee and artificial dialogue brilliantly sum up the brittle, superficial world of 1930s Hollywood. The novel's fast pace, the picaresque audacity of the almost likable, conscienceless heel-hero, the predictable ending of the betrayer betrayed (and, implicitly, of the hunter about to be hunted) still add up, after fifty years, to one of the best Hollywood novels ever written. Like many other commercial writers, Schulberg knows that first-person is the easiest way to tell a story; he uses this form often and well, and in *What Makes Sammy Run?* he created a minor classic of this form and the Hollywood sub-genre.

—Frank Campenni

SCOTT, Rosie

Nationality: Australian-New Zealander. **Born:** Wellington, New Zealand, 1948 (has dual Australian and New Zealand citizenship). **Education:** Degrees in English and drama; M.A. in English. **Career:** Worked variously as waitress, fruit-picker, and script editor, as well as in social work, acting, publishing, and newspaper work. Lives in Sydney, Australia. **Awards:** Bruce Mason *Sunday Times* award.

PUBLICATIONS

Novels

Glory Days. Auckland, New Zealand, Penguin, 1988; Seattle, Washington, Seal Press, 1988.

Nights with Grace. Auckland, New Zealand, Heinemann, 1990; Melbourne, Australia, Minerva, 1991.

Feral City. Auckland, New Zealand, Reed Books, 1992.

Lives on Fire. Auckland, New Zealand, Hodder & Stoughton, 1993; St. Lucia, Queensland, Australia, University of Queensland Press, 1993.

Movie Dreams. Auckland, New Zealand, Tandem Press, 1995; St. Lucia, Queensland, Australia, University of Queensland Press, 1995.

Short Stories

Flesh and Blood. Auckland, New Zealand, Hard Echo Press, 1984.

Queen of Love and Other Stories. Auckland, New Zealand, Penguin, 1989; St. Lucia, Queensland, Australia, University of Queensland Press, 1993.

The Red Heart. Auckland, New Zealand, Vintage, 1999.

Plays

Say Thank You to the Lady. Auckland, New Zealand, Mercury Theatre Two, 1985.

Other

Contributor,*Nightmares in Paradise,* edited by Robyn Sheahan. St. Lucia, Queensland, Australia, University of Queensland Press,1995

* * *

Rosie Scott was born in Wellington, New Zealand in 1948 but moved to Queensland as a young woman. Although she published a collection of poetry and wrote a play that became the basis of a film in the 1980s, her first work of fiction, *Glory Days*, did not appear until she was forty. Since then she has become an extremely productive novelist.

Glory Days is narrated by a woman who is, in fact, named Glory Day. She is in many respects (including physically) a larger than life figure. Blues singer, painter of renown, heavy drinker, and pot smoker, center of a group of friends who attach themselves to her in Auckland, Glory attracts the hostility of a young woman named Roxy who has been modeling for her. Believing that she has somehow entered Glory's identity, Roxy stalks her, kidnaps her daughter, attacks her paintings, and eventually assaults her with a knife. *Glory Days* is an episodic, almost structureless novel, but it does end with the dramatic success of Glory's art exhibition and is convincing in its largely good-humored but realistic depiction of a certain underclass of New Zealand life. It was short-listed for the New Zealand National Book award.

Nights with Grace is a novella-length account of a seventeen-year old girl's first experience of sexual and romantic love on the eden-like Pacific island of Rarotonga. Opening with the abrupt sentence, ''The summer she turned seventeen, Grace spent a lot of her time dreaming,'' the work goes on to give a sensitive account of a delicate but inevitably doomed affair between the young girl and an attractive man who is visiting the island in order to investigate the effect of pesticides on the environment. Also caught up in the story is Grace's slatternly mother Mara—troubled relationships between mothers and daughters are common in Scott's fiction—who drinks heavily and sleeps around in defiance of the islanders' conventions. Scott says of Grace, ''She was making inroads into life even if her mother hadn't noticed. Her dreaminess only camouflaged intense mental processes. Her allegiances were to a private self that she never revealed to anyone, to the place where was born, and to certain people in her life.'' The novel captures this sense of private integrity and allegiance very well. Knowing that her lover Jack lives with another woman in New Zealand and that he will soon return there makes no difference to Grace, who is caught up in the intensity and certainty of her own feelings. As in much of Scott's work there is a fierce concentration on physical and sensual beauty.

The main character in *Lives on Fire* is Belle, a moderately successful actress, passionately in love with her builder husband Tyler and on holiday in Queensland away from the frenetic Sydney scene. Into their idyllic lives comes an extraordinarily beautiful woman named Sky, whom Belle had met briefly during the making of a film. But Sky soon turns out to have a past and a motive that will wreck the relationship between Belle and Tyler. Written in the first person, *Lives on Fire* is essentially an affirmative novel that reveals how a deeply wounded woman can recover her sense of self-worth by involving herself with other people. Stricken as she is, Belle rediscovers her relationship with her two children, is made aware of the deep affection her gay agent Nick holds for her, and above all immerses herself in working with a group of street kids in a touring theater. Like all of Scott's work it is a generous novel that prides selfless caring above everything sense.

The ''feral city'' of Scott's third novel is Auckland in the near but carefully unspecified future, a place teeming with homelessness, unemployment, street gangs, and drugs. This is a nightmarishly dystopian novel that savagely attacks the then-contemporary government policies of privatization and economic rationalism. Its protagonist, Faith, is a woman of thirty-eight who is returning to her roots in Auckland after a failed marriage, a drug addiction she has managed to overcome, and in general a not very successful life. In particular she is attempting to resume contact with her sister Violet. The details of a New Zealand set in the not-very-distant future are revealed slowly, subtly, though it is astonishing that Faith seems ignorant of what has been happening in the world. Despite the horrors Scott depicts and the grim ending, there is as always with Scott a deep feeling of affirmation and even optimism. Faith opens a bookshop, rescues and befriends a dog that was on the point of being tortured to death, begins to salvage something of her life as she slowly comes to realize the immensity of what her sister has been doing in leading protests against dehumanizing government policies. A youth leading a street gang proves to have unexpected depths to his personality. A rally against the deaths of homeless people draws a huge crowd, and there are intimations towards the end of the novel of the downfall of the current government and its replacement by a more humane one. *Feral City* is an uneven novel, its apocalyptic elements mingling uneasily with its satire, its evocation of a dark and disturbed society at war with its feelings of hope, but it is full of ideas and genuine feeling.

Like most of Scott's fiction, *Movie Dreams* is written in the first person, but this time the narrator is a male youth. Adan Loney breaks out of school in Brisbane and hitchhikes north to Cairns in order to free himself from what he feels is a stifling and claustrophobic existence. Talented, ambitious to make films, Adan is a kind of antipodean Holden Caulfied, disgusted with the world he lives in, shattered by the suicide of his close friend Lee, and harboring ambivalent feelings towards both his mother and his sister Jasmine. *Movie Dreams* is again a largely structureless, picaresque novel. Adan goes through a succession of experiences, meets a number of people, before once again setting off on the road, traveling even further north. The title refers to Adan's imaginative projections of himself into various, often unnamed but recognizable Hollywood films. In the end, the reader is limited by Adan's own limitations, confusions, and lack of understanding of some of the people with whom he comes into contact.

The stories in *Queen of Love* are for the most part fairly lightweight pieces, some of them hardly more than sketches, lacking the energy and virility of her novels. ''Journeys to the Edge of the World,'' for instance, is hardly more than a travel piece about the New Hebrides. Some of the stories seem to contain embryonic material for the later fiction. ''Warm Nights'' has a scene of the arrival of the narrator's mother that anticipates a similar event in *Nights with Grace*; another story is actually called ''Winter with Grace.'' ''Senseless Violets'' is also the title of the exhibition Glory puts on in *Glory Days*. ''Two Steps to Heaven,'' about a worker in the Paradise Bar, also anticipates some of the material from *Nights with Grace*. Several of the stories concern a social worker, deeply aware of how little she can do to alter the lives of the people in her care, whether they are prisoners or pensioners or, in one of the best stories, ''The Saving of Wok Tan,'' a refugee from the Vietnam War. The difficulty of the relationship between mothers and daughters again surfaces in a fine story with that title. In general, the stories display Scott's characteristically intense, sensual, and optimistic approach to life.

—Laurie Clancy

SEALY, I(rwin) Allan

Nationality: Indian. **Born:** Allahabad, India, 31 March 1951. **Education:** La Martiniere College; Delhi University, B.A. (with honors) in English 1971; Western Michigan University, B.A. (with honors) in English 1972, M.A. 1974. **Family:** Married Cushla Fitzsimmons, 1985. **Career:** Writer. **Award:** Commonwealth Writers' prize for best first book, 1989, for *The Trotter-Nama.* **Agent:** A.P. Watt, 20 John St., London WC1N 2DR, England. **Address:** D-101 Race Course, Dehra Dun, U.P.248001, India.

PUBLICATIONS

Novels

The Trotter-Nama: A Chronicle. New York, Knopf, and London, Viking, 1988.

Hero: A Fable. New Delhi, Viking, 1990; London, Secker and Warburg, 1991.

The Everest Hotel: A Calendar. New Delhi, IndiaInk, 1998.

Other

From Yukon to Yucatan: A Western Journey. London, Secker and Warburg, 1994.

* * *

Although I. Allan Sealy divides his time between India and New Zealand, he remains very much an Indian-English writer. Each of his novels to date, *The Trotter-Nama: A Chronicle, Hero: A Fable,* and *The Everest Hotel: A Calendar,* bring something distinctly Indian to what is, after all, a European literary form. In *The Trotter-Nama* Sealy adapts the Indian epic *nama* form (a form once used to flatter emperors, and ideally suited to Sealy's expansive and digressive style), whereas in *Hero* he transfers the formulaic ''masala movie'' of India's popular and prodigious film industry from celluloid to paper. In *The Everest Hotel* he continues his interest in the form of the novel (those colons are significant!) but leaves behind some of the more irksome postmodernist games that marked the earlier novels. What clearly links these three apparently disparate novels is Sealy's gift for storytelling.

In *The Trotter-Nama,* Sealy presents a history of India unreliably narrated by Eugene, the Seventh Trotter, a painter, and a chronicler of his Anglo-Indian family history, from its founding by the Great Trotter (a French mercenary soldier) in the eighteenth century through to the present day. Significantly, Eugene paints in a mock-Mughal style—a style in which perspective is often distorted, reflected in his role as historian. His story (and history) is centered on the predictably-named Trotter family seat of Sans Souci near Nakhlau (another name for Lucknow, and notably the one used by Kipling in his magnum opus, *Kim*); but as the Trotter family branches out across India and the world, Sealy is able to introduce postcolonial concerns such as identity, exile, and the diaspora into his fiction. Eugene Trotter's riotous chronicle, which recalls the work of both Sterne and Rabelais as well as recent postmodernist fictions, playfully flexes the boundaries of the novel to encompass maps, a family tree, and numerous digressions, interpolations, sections of verse, letters, recipes, household bills, authorial intrusions, and, on the cover, a miniaturist painting (by the author) which portrays all the major events of the novel.

In his second novel, *Hero,* Sealy moves away from the expansive style of *The Trotter-Nama* and directs his narrowed lens on India's pop-culture film world in an attempt to interpret the sub-continent through the unlikely, but surprisingly common Indian mix of politics and the cinema. Indeed, the novel borrows its structure from the masala movie mix—which is clearly outlined on the contents page. Again Sealy's interest in postmodernist games is evident from the outset. There is, for example, a skilled parody of structuralist theory in the opening section of the novel, which challenges theory as another tool of colonization. Literary allusions abound, as in the opening line of the novel: ''He stood six feet tall but it was his slouch that made him a hero,'' which clearly echoes the opening sentence of Joseph Conrad's *Lord Jim;* authorial intrusions are legion, and the many instructions which direct the gaze of the camera once more test the boundaries of the genre. Via the trope of the Bombay cinema, Sealy explores the nature of image, the portrayal of ''real life'' through image, and the relationship between ''reality'' and ''fiction.'' The novel is also a penetrating discourse on the nature of power, and an exposé of the corruption that has dogged recent Indian politics. All this is achieved through the story of Hero, a film superstar-cum-prime minister, whose story in many ways resembles that of Tamil Nadu's superstar of the popular cinema and erstwhile Chief Minister, M.G. Ramachandran. Hero's tale is told by his long-time sidekick, Zero, a Bombay scriptwriter, and, later, Hero's political speechwriter, whose presence (among other things) challenges any notion about the death of the author. In fact Sealy himself appears in the ''ENTRANCE,'' ''INTERMISSION,'' and ''EXIT'' sections of the novel, where he instructs the reader on how to read this fabulous novel (which is subtitled *a fable*).

The Everest Hotel begins with the arrival by train of Ritu, a young nun who has been sent ''for humbling'' to the small town of Drummondganj in the foothills of the Himalayas, and ends with her departure, again by train, exactly a year later (hence the subtitle). What we have in between is a slice of life and death: human experience explored in microcosm. Sealy's hotel is a perfect device for gathering together a small group of people in a limited space where human experience can be intensified. Along with four other nuns, Ritu is charged with looking after the geriatric inhabitants of the now faded Everest Hotel, including the lecherous ninety-year-old owner Jed, former mountaineer and collector of rare flowers who is now, in his more lucid moments, writing his own version of *The Book of the Dead.* The routine of the Hotel is interrupted on a number of occasions: first by the arrival of Ritu, then by the arrival of the

German neo-Nazi Inge, and finally by the arrival of the enigmatic orphan girl Masha, who is the catalyst for Ritu's departure. And all along there are the irregular visits of Jed's admirer, Brij, who brings a political dimension to the novel, as well as a challenge to Ritu's vocation.

Sealy has also written a work of nonfiction, *From Yukon to Yucatan: A Western Journey,* which recounts his journey across the North American continent following in the footsteps of its first people—from their landing place on the shores of the Arctic Sea down to the Gulf of Mexico. Of particular interest is his focus on the displaced people he meets along the way—Spaniards, Malaysians, and more.

Sealy is a writer to watch. His first two novels show that he is a writer who likes to challenge the borders of his preferred genre, and while his literary games may at times be distracting, for the most part he carries them off with consummate skill. His most recent novel, and most assured work to date, shows that he has found his form.

—Ralph J. Crane

SEE, Carolyn

Pseudonym: Monica Highland (with Lisa See and John Espey). **Nationality:** American. **Born:** Carolyn Penelope Laws, Pasadena, California, 13 January 1934. **Education:** Los Angeles City College, A.A.; California State University, Los Angeles, M.A., Ph.D. **Family:** 1) married Richard See, 1954 (divorced 1959), one daughter; 2) married Tom Sturak, 1961 (divorced 1969), one daughter; 3) lives with John Espey, since 1974. **Career:** Waitress, 1950s; teaching assistant, 1960s; professor of English, Loyola Marymount University, 1970–85; visiting professor of English, 1986–89, and adjunct professor of English, both University of California, Los Angeles. Book reviewer, *Los Angeles Times,* 1981–93; *New York Newsday,* 1990–92; and since 1993 *Washington Post.* President, PEN West International, 1990–91. **Awards:** Vesta award, 1989, for writing; Guggenheim fellowship in fiction, 1990–91; Lila Wallace teaching grant, 1992–93; Women's Care Cottage Apple award, 1991; *Los Angeles Times* Robert Kirsch body of work award, 1993. **Member:** National Book Critics Circle; Writers Guild of America. **Agent:** Anne Sibbold, Janklow Nesbit Agency, 589 Madison Ave., New York, New York 10022, U.S.A.

Publications

Novels

The Rest Is Done with Mirrors. New York, Little Brown, 1970.
Mothers, Daughters. New York, Coward McCann Geoghegan, 1977.
Rhine Maidens. New York, Coward McCann Geoghegan, 1980; Harmondsworth, Middlesex, Penguin, 1981.
Golden Days. New York, McGraw Hill, 1986; London, Century, 1987.
Making History. New York, Houghton Mifflin, 1991.
Dreaming: Hard Luck and Good Times in America. New York, Random House, 1995.

Novels as Monica Highland (with Lisa See and John Espey)

Lotus Land. New York, McGraw Hill, 1983.
110 Shanghai Road. New York, McGraw Hill, 1986.
Greeting from Southern California. New York, McGraw Hill, 1988.

Others

Blue Money: Pornography and the Pornographers. New York, Rawson, 1973.
Two Schools of Thought, with John Espey. Santa Barbara, California, Daniel, 1991.

*

Manuscript Collection: Special Collections, University of California, Los Angeles.

Carolyn See comments:

When I started to write I was relatively old, and lived in California. So I was the wrong sex, wrong age, wrong coast. Luckily I was too ignorant to know it. I've always had to write to make a living, and have a solid background in journalism from my father. My formal education more or less rolled off my back, critical theory means nothing to me, less than nothing.

I try to write about the larger world—nuclear war, the random nature of the universe, the oppression of the American underclass through drugs and drink. I've only written one ''lady'' novel, *Mothers, Daughters,* and I'm embarrassed for it. But I'm proud of the rest of my work.

* * *

Carolyn See's novels explore women's lives, broken relationships, and all things Californian. See has tackled the usual gamut of male-female romance, but she has also taken on the subjects of mothers, daughters, and aging in *Rhine Maidens;* female friendship, religious evangelism, and nuclear war in *Golden Days;* and international business, stepfamilies, and grieving in *Making History.* See uses strong first-person narration in her best work, some of which is rendered in diary form.

The Rest is Done With Mirrors, See's first novel (and generally not thought to be her best work), tells of two UCLA graduate students and their troubled relationships. Much of See's early work appears to be loosely biographical and deals with marital breakups. Her second novel, *Mothers, Daughters,* follows a divorced TV reporter, Ruth, as she negotiates a blossoming romance with Marc, the former beau of two of her female friends. Both the third-person narration and the plot are highly formulaic and plodding. See includes many cavalier references to her characters' acid trips and a great deal of humor, however, thus preventing the novel's easy categorization as mass-market romance.

With *Rhine Maidens,* See's masterful characterizations and clever dialogue emerge more fully formed. The story of the neurotic, stubborn Grace, left by several husbands and facing retirement alone, is coupled with that of her daughter, Garnet, a ''useless'' wealthy housewife who is into est and interior decorating. Garnet's story is presented as her assigned journal from the freshman composition class she has enrolled in to improve herself. Grace's narration is given as a would-be dialogue with the dead friend of her youth, Pearl. Both women unwillingly take stock of their failing and failed relationships with husbands and children.

The "Rhine maidens" of the title refers to a cruise on the Rhine River that Grace begrudgingly takes with the aging (and similarly alone) Edna. At novel's end, Grace, forever unable to have a good time, may in fact be letting go of her worries, and Garnet is poised to leave her rich housewife days behind her. The novel masterfully explores what happens when mothers and daughters not only don't get along but don't even like each other. Class conflicts and colliding generational values add further color.

Golden Days's title is taken from John Milton's *Paradise Lost,* and See's novel verges on religious allegory. It is no less gripping a tale for this feature. Readers follow gemologist Edith as she negotiates single parenting and teaches classes to prepare wealthy married women for their husbands' desertions by stockpiling jewels. Edith's reestablished friendship with Lorna, a caged housewife turned healer and evangelist, provides one of the most interesting story lines.

Women's friendships rarely receive short shrift from See. She writes:

> There was a basic inequality in the country I grew up and lived in. One man, one story. For women, it generally took two or even three to make one story… . This is partly the story of Lorna Villanelle and me; two ladies absolutely crazed with the secret thought that they were something special.

Everyone's "specialness" is seemingly leveled with the dropping of a nuclear bomb. See's novel, however, is one of hope and survival rather than mere despair—an ode to the sustenance of storytelling.

See's past efforts made use of "miracles," but *Making History* is the first to delve so deeply into the supernatural and into life after death. This novel deals with the functional yet vapid marriage of Jerry and Wynn and their family: Whitney (Wynn's teenage daughter by a first marriage), Tina, and Josh. Jerry's frequent business trips to Asia involve visits to prostitutes, written off as inconsequential infidelities. Wynn involves herself in the second-rate prep school her children attend and congratulates herself for having gotten out of a bad first marriage and into relative comfort. As Wynn remembers her father saying, however, "Life has a way of kicking the shit out of you." The novel involves fatal car accidents, friendships broken by grief, and marriages strained to the breaking point. As in *Golden Days,* however, See manages to hone the resilience in her characters while showing us the fragility of the order in our daily lives. *The Handyman* also calls up spiritual images: like Christ, protagonist Bob Hampton is a carpenter who goes around changing people's lives for the better. The oversexed Hampton would hardly be mistaken for the Savior, however, and the novel verges into over-the-top contrivance, but See manages to tie it all together with a story that also compellingly presents an L.A. of surprising beauty.

See is also a memoirist. With her partner, John Espey, she published *Two Schools of Thought: Some Tales of Learning and Romance,* reflections on Oxford (his) and UCLA (hers). She has also written an account of generations of her family's alcoholism, *Dreaming: Hard Luck and Good Times in America.* Furthermore, Espey, See's daughter Lisa See Kimball, and See have also joined forces to create the novels of Monica Highland, *Lotus Land* and *110 Shanghai Road.*

—Devoney Looser

SELBY, Hubert, Jr.

Nationality: American. **Born:** Brooklyn, New York, 23 July 1928. Educated in New York City public schools, including Peter Stuyvesant High School. **Military Service:** Served in the United States Merchant Marine, 1944–46. **Family:** Married 1) Inez Taylor in 1953 (divorced 1960), one daughter and one son; 2) Judith Lumino in 1964; 3) Suzanne Shaw in 1969, one daughter and one son. **Career:** Hospital patient, with tuberculosis, 1946–50; held various jobs, including seaman and insurance clerk, 1950–64. Lives in Los Angeles. **Member:** Writer's Guild of America, and Authors Guild. **Address:** c/o Grove Weidenfeld, 841 Broadway, New York, New York 10003–4793, U.S.A.

PUBLICATIONS

Novels

Last Exit to Brooklyn. New York, Grove Press, 1964; London, Calder and Boyars, 1966.
The Room. New York, Grove Press, 1971; London, Calder and Boyars, 1972.
The Demon. New York, Playboy Press, 1976; London, Boyars, 1977.
Requiem for a Dream. New York, Playboy Press, 1978; London, Boyars, 1979.
The Willow Tree. New York, Marion Boyars Publishers, 1998.

Short Stories

Song of the Silent Snow. New York, Grove Press, and London, Boyars, 1986.

Uncollected Short Stories

"Home for Christmas," in *Neon 2* (New York), 1956.
"Love/s Labour/s Lost," in *Black Mountain Review* (Black Mountain, North Carolina), Autumn 1957.
"Double Feature," in *Neon 4* (New York), 1959.
"Another Day, Another Dollar," in *New Directions 17.* New York, New Directions, 1961.
"A Penny for Your Thoughts," in *The Moderns,* edited by LeRoi Jones. New York, Corinth, 1963; London, MacGibbon and Kee, 1965.
"And Baby Makes Three," in *New American Story,* edited by Robert Creeley and Donald Allen. New York, Grove Press, 1965.
"Fat Phil's Day," in *Evergreen Review* (New York), August 1967.
"Happy Birthday," in *Evergreen Review* (New York), August 1969.

Plays

Screenplays: *Day and Night,* 1985; *Soldier of Fortune,* 1990.

*

Critical Studies: ''Hubert Selby Issue'' of *Review of Contemporary Fiction* (Elmwood Park, Illinois), vol. 1, no. 2, 1981; *Understanding Hubert Selby, Jr.* by James R. Giles, Columbia, University of South Carolina Press, 1998.

Hubert Selby, Jr., comments:

(1991) I write by ear. Music of line important. Want to put reader through emotional experience.

* * *

If *Last Exit to Brooklyn* and its ludicrous obscenity trial hadn't exhausted moralistic disgust, Hubert Selby, Jr.'s work could probably stand at the bench in perpetuity. The Seventh Circle of the Violent in Dante's *Inferno;* Gulliver upon the cancerous Brobdignagian breast; Genet's onanist reveries. These suggest Selby's fictive world. He is our eyewitness on the dead-ends of the daily. Stuck in the sick gut of the city, his camera fixes the disaffected masses and completes a picture begun with Crane's *Maggie.* On the other hand, his biblical epigraphs are both ironically and straightforwardly applicable. He is, then, at once a determinist and a moralist whose narratives are naturalistic fables. Consequently, his psychological landscape is more than social realism or a Hogarth satire could accommodate. It is a Bosch and Francis Bacon triptych. As the witness for the damned, Selby *is* mired in America's slime. But given a populace which could nod off on the Vietnam War, his ability to shock may be remarkable, even morally so.

The title of his first novel is taken from an expressway sign that overlooks a cemetery of solid concrete. The work thematically connects six tales of hopeless human isolation. Its people delude themselves with faith in family and ideal dreams of profound sexual communion. But Abraham's infidelity, angry remoteness, and, finally, sleep are domesticity. Tralala's rape is heterosexuality. ''Georgette's'' and Vinnie's bestiality is homosexuality. Casual and sadistic, the violent are little Eichmanns and Mengeles. In the background Selby works with a timeless symbology of darkness overwhelming light. This is conveyed to us by depth associations with *Ecclesiastes,* Poe's *Raven,* and our own disillusioned black ''Bird,'' Charlie Parker. It is only by viewing Selby in this context that we can grasp his preoccupation with drugs. He knows unequivocally the life-renouncing and futile lie at the heart of ''kind nepenthe.''

The Room shifts our focus from the sick social to the sick individual organism. Its sole province is the mind of a nameless paranoid schizophrenic, though Selby might resist terminology. The ''room'' is both a cell and the disconnected consciousness of the single character. Locked within each, he constructs antithetically lofty and brutal fantasies, but always out of a single-minded hatred of authority. Thus his imaginary revenges include delusions of magnanimity in which he self-sacrificially fights social injustice with the help of liberal lawyers. Conversely, they include totally dehumanizing tortures of police officers, sadistic acts which reduce his adversaries to canines. These are rendered with nauseating detail. Selby seems unwilling to attribute this state of mind to a sick society, an indifferent family, or a bad character. It is simply a *donnée,* and Selby's forte is neither sociological nor psychological reductionism but graphic presentation. The novel's unsavory force and its interest are considerably enhanced by the author's tactic of gliding constantly between an omniscient and a first person perspective.

The ''demon'' of Selby's third novel is sexual obsession and its mutations. It begins as womanizing so unalleviated that Harry White can sustain no connection, except tenuously to his career, with any other activity. (He cannot last out a softball game with friends or a party for his grandparents.) It ends with his murdering, on Palm Sunday, a Christlike Cardinal and his subsequent suicide. So the demoniacal obsession is larger than carnality, passing through debauchery and theft toward this ultimately exciting destructiveness which seems proof for Selby that ''The wages of sin is death.'' The novel's complementary epigraph is from *James* 1:15. At all times, whether White is fornicating or thieving, the demon exists as a physical tension so great that Harry hates whatever stands between himself and a feeling of exhausting gratification. But all respite from enslavement, including his marriage to Linda (the healthiest person Selby has drawn), is stop-gap. Only death does the job. As a study of the connection between sex and violence in the obsessive person, the book has merit. But the conclusion is unfortunately mystical in part, especially because the only psychological perspective is provided by an arrogant neo-Freudian simpleton. This straw man certainly doesn't exhaust more modestly agnostic interpretations of the events.

Requiem for a Dream is about hope ruined by narcotic habit. It sees America in terms of a pervasive dependence upon metaphorical and literal drugs. The widow Sara Goldfarb eats compulsively and lives a stuporously vicarious life through soap operas and TV game shows. Thinking she has a chance to appear in one and wanting to be appropriately svelte, she sees a physician who addicts her to Dexedrine. She ends up a skeletal and slavering schizoid in a mental hospital. Concurrently, her son Harry, his friend Tyrone Love, and Harry's lover, Marion, plot their own dreams' fulfillment's. All are sad clichés—and the trio are heroin addicts. From drug profits, Harry will build a coffeehouse for sensitive artists and writers where Marion's drawings will be admired; the black Tyrone will buy into the bliss of a modest suburb. But their endeavors only increase their addiction. Marion winds up in a sort of bisexual freak show working for her portion of bliss. Harry loses his arm from an infection and sinks into oblivion in a Miami hospital. Having gone south with Harry for a big pay-off, Tyrone gets to be brutalized by rednecks and thrown in prison. By now we have to ask if Selby Jr. has anything more to tell us along these lines.

—David M. Heaton

SELF, Will(iam)

Nationality: British. **Born:** London. **Family:** Married; two children. **Awards:** Geoffrey Faber Memorial prize, 1993, for *The Quantity Theory of Insanity.*

PUBLICATIONS

Novels

The Quantity Theory of Insanity: Together with Five Supporting Propositions. London, Bloomsbury, 1991; New York, Atlantic Monthly Press, 1995.

My Idea of Fun: A Cautionary Tale. London, Bloomsbury, 1993; New York, Atlantic Monthly Press, 1994.

Junk Mail. London, Bloomsbury, 1995.

A Story for Europe. London, Bloomsbury, 1996.

Great Apes. London, Bloomsbury, 1997; New York, Grove Press, 1997.
The Sweet Smell of Psychosis, illustrations by Martin Rowson. London, Bloomsbury, 1996; New York, Grove Press, 1999.
How the Dead Live. New York, Grove Press, 2000.

Short Stories

Cock and Bull (novellas). London, Bloomsbury, 1992; New York, Atlantic Monthly Press, 1993.
Grey Area, and Other Stories. London, Bloomsbury, 1994; New York, Grove Press, 1996.
Tough, Tough Toys for Tough, Tough Boys. New York, Grove Press, and London, Bloomsbury, 1998.

* * *

Will Self is a satirist on the order of Swift and Voltaire writing in the England of Malcolm Bradbury, David Lodge, and Martin Amis. Drawing on his experience as a heroin addict, a philosophy student at Oxford, and a cartoonist, he has crafted a style perfectly suited to his time and place. He pillories the absurdities of modern England and possesses a special genius for making the ridiculous appear credible. Passages of grotesque realism, horrific humor, and absurdist fantasy are delivered in an unnerving deadpan that manages to be at once sinister and slangy, erudite and wildly funny.

The stories in *The Quantity Theory of Insanity: With Five Supporting Propositions* introduce his chief targets. His English bear a curious resemblance to the Ur-Bororo, a ''relentlessly banal'' tribe bent upon ''boring one another still further.'' (As for Londoners, ''When you're dead,'' one narrator's dead mother explains, ''you move to another part of London, that's all there is to it.'') On Ward Nine for the ''metamad,'' therapists and patients exchange places according to Dr. Zack Busman's latest ''cost-effective'' theory. Busman, who reappears in several stories here and in *Grey Area,* serves as one of several representatives of pseudoscientific theories and Thatcherite economics that attract the author's special ire. The Quantitative Theory of Insanity, for example, proposes ''a fixed proportion of sanity available in any given society at any given time.'' In a brave new world where sanity is available on the time-share plan and (in ''Mono-Cellular'') plankton farmers sit down with Child Bankers to discuss investment opportunities in the adoption market, people have clearly lost the ability to think critically, to distinguish the genuine from the bogus, the important from the trivial, the morally monstrous from the financially feasible. They have (in *Grey Area*) lost a sense of ''Scale''; they are addicted to Inclusion, an antidepressant drug that makes them perfectly passive consumers indiscriminately interested in anything and everything.

The absurdity is even wilder in *Cock & Bull.* In the first of these two complementary stories, a submissive Carol discovers the joy of sex via masturbation, grows a penis, and sodomizes her husband to death, thus avenging past wrongs by becoming a grotesque version of masculinity at its very worst. In Self's daisy chain of dominance-submission plots, husband Dan is not the only one being diddled. The narrator finds himself first trapped and then raped on a train by a donnish gay-bashing anti-Semitic ancient mariner-like companion who turns out to be the fully metamorphosed Carol. The reader will undoubtedly empathize with the male narrator's feeling of female helplessness and complicity after having sat there ''like a prat, listening to a load of cock … and bull.'' Unlike ''Cock: A Novelette,'' ''Bull: A Farce'' begins in Kafkaesque fashion with the manly Bull waking up one morning to discover a vagina growing behind his left knee. His physician takes a more than clinical interest in the suddenly helpless Bull, who, busy discovering his female nature, is quickly seduced and soon abandoned. Foregoing suicide, he ends up a single parent in Wales, as complaisant now as Carol once was.

Sex is given an economic twist in *My Idea of Fun: A Cautionary Tale.* Self's novel takes its title from I. B. Singer and its underlying subject from Freud: the channeling of the sexual drive into primitive sadistic fantasies and postindustrial business ventures. With his split, ''borderline'' personality, the narrator-protagonist (first as *I* then as *he*) in effect resembles both Carol and Bull. However, unlike *Cock & Bull, My Idea of Fun: A Cautionary Tale* is polymorphously perverse, its satire more diffuse, its metamorphoses more numerous. The son of an absent father and an overprotective, class-conscious mother, Ian Wharton is an ''eidetiker'' who learns to use his psychological gift (or curse) for his own benefit as a marketeer under the tutelage of The Fat Controller. Either a real, if endlessly, metamorphosing person or a figment of Ian's disturbed imagination, The Fat Controller is most obviously a sinister version of the character in a series of children's books subsequently turned into a commercially successful TV series (with its own set of spin-off products) in Britain and America. Serving as Ian's ''personified id,'' The Fat Controller acts as the perfect guide for an age in which ''people had begun to feel less awkward about being greedy and of wanting more than their fair share.'' In this ''cautionary tale,'' eidetiking allows Ian and his tutor to indulge in their murderous fantasies without needing to act them out. In a Thatcherite world of relentless marketeering and postmodern simulacrum, of virtual reality and virtual money, all differences between the real and the imaginary may seem beside the point. It is, however, very much to the point of a writer whose display of stylistic effects and range of literary reference (from De Quincey and Dostoyevsky to Maurice Sendak and Thomas the Tank Engine) do not so much distract from as lend weight to the social consciousness that is at the heart of Will Self's pyrotechnic art.

The premise of a character waking up after a night of debauchery and finding that the rest of the world has turned into apes would, in the hands of Kafka, become a horrific tale; but with Self, who brought back the character of Simon Dykes from his short story ''Inclusion'' for *Great Apes,* it is a species of *de trop* satire. The stories of *Tough, Tough Toys for Tough, Tough Boys* succeed, to varying degrees, as humor; but *Sweet Smell of Psychosis* is unmistakably the genuine article. It is an old tale, that of the innocent come to the big city, but in Self's hands the story of how Richard Hermes succumbs to the charms of sexy Ursula Bently is made fresh. Particularly amusing is his portrayal of a media personality with the quite believable appellation of Bell: no surname or given name, just Bell. The Sealink Club they all inhabit is ''a dark, humid environment in which fungal tittle-tattle could swell overnight,'' and their London is a place in love with its own image in the mirror (not to mention the sweet smell of opium). Throughout it all, Self remains behind the scenes, pulling the strings and ensuring that everything will go as deliciously wrong as it can.

—Robert A. Morace, updated by Judson Knight

SELVADURAI, Shyam

Nationality: Sri Lankan (Ceylonese)-Canadian. **Born:** Colombo, Sri Lanka, 1963; immigrated to Canada, 1984. **Education:** York University, Toronto, B.F.A. **Career:** Novelist, essayist, and writer for television. **Awards:** Smithbooks/Books in Canada First Novel Award, 1997; Lambda Literary Award for gay men's fiction (Lambda Literary Foundation), 1997. **Agent:** William Morrow & Company, Inc., 1350 Avenue of the Americas, New York, New York 10019, U.S.A. **Address:** c/o McClelland & Stewart, 481 University Ave. #900, Toronto, Ontario, Canada M5G 2E9.

PUBLICATIONS

Novels

Funny Boy: A Novel in Six Stories. Toronto, McClelland & Stewart, 1994; as *Funny Boy: A Novel.* New York, Morrow, 1996.

Cinnamon Gardens. New York, Hyperion, 1999.

* * *

Like much recent South Asian diasporic fiction, the novels of Shyam Selvadurai share several thematic preoccupations: with the inherited legacy of the British colonial past; with the more recent strife caused by post-independence ethnic and religious divisions; with journeys of migration and return; with the rending of families by long suppressed secrets, generational conflicts, duties compelled, and traditions neglected. In this regard, Selvadurai's work has much in common with that of other South Asian-Canadian writers, including Neil Bisoondath (*A Casual Brutality, The Worlds Within Her*), Rohinton Mistry (*Such a Long Journey, A Fine Balance*), M. G. Vassanji, (*The Gunny Sack, The Book of Secrets*), Anita Rau Badami (*Tamarind Mem, The Hero's Walk*), and especially Michael Ondaatje (*Running in the Family, Anil's Ghost*), who, like Selvadurai, was born in Sri Lanka and emigrated to Canada at the age of nineteen. However, what is distinctive about Selvadurai's novels, and what sets them apart from the above list, is their skilful interweaving of issues of sexuality into the standard narrative of South Asian cultural dislocation.

Funny Boy, Selvadurai's first novel, was published in 1994 to immediate international acclaim. It won the W.H. Smith/Books in Canada First Novel Award, as well as a Lambda Literary Award for Best Work of Gay Fiction, and announced Selvadurai as a major new voice in Canadian, postcolonial, and gay literature. Set against the backdrop of growing tensions between Sri Lanka's Sinhalese and Tamil communities that culminated in the outbreak of civil war in 1983, the novel is a moving and scrupulously honest coming out story. Arjie Chelvaratnam, the cosseted son of prosperous Tamil hoteliers in Colombo, is not like the other boys in his large extended family; for one thing, when his cousins gather for childhood games of "bride-bride," he always likes to wear the sari. In an effort to curtail such eccentricities and teach his son "to become a man," Arjie's father sends him off to the Victoria Academy; there he meets Shehan, a Sinhalese boy about whom there is also something "funny."

The romance between Arjie and Shehan blooms furtively amidst the revelation of other family secrets, each progressively more violent in their repercussions: Arjie's glamorous aunt Radha clashes with his grandmother over her marriage prospects and her true love for a Sinhalese man; an Australian journalist murdered in Jaffna turns out to have been a former lover of Arjie's mother; and Jegan, whom Arjie's father "adopts" into the family and business, may or may not be a member of the Tamil Tigers. Throughout, Arjie's essential naivete and guilelessness makes him an ideal narrative filter for the explosive transformations he is witness to, both in the streets of Colombo and in his own bodily desires. This technique is most skilfully rendered by Selvadurai in the novel's concluding epilogue, a "Riot Journal" in which Arjie records the tumultuous events that have precipitated his family's imminent departure for Canada, as well as the poignant denouement of his relationship with Shehan.

Funny Boy is innovatively structured as "a novel in six stories." Arjie is the focalizing narrative consciousness of each, and to the extent that the book's plot traces, more or less linearly, his development through boyhood into young adulthood, it can be said that Selvadurai's writing achieves a cohesive unity. And yet, given that so much of the novel is concerned with the violent fracturing of cohesion, be it national, familial, or sexual, it seems only appropriate that its structure should likewise resist such a totalizing gesture. In this respect, *Funny Boy* bears examination alongside two similarly structured novels published by gay writers in Canada during this period: Wayson Choy's *The Jade Peony* (1995) and Derek McCormack's *Dark Rides* (1996). The interconnected "stories" in each novel add up to a cumulative portrait of adolescent identity formation (and especially the discontinuous links between sexual and ethnic identity in the cases of Selvadurai and Choy), at the same time as the silences and gaps between the stories point to the fact that the rendering of this portrait will never be complete or whole.

In *Cinnamon Gardens*, his second novel, Selvadurai goes back in time to the late 1920s, during the waning days of colonialism, when Sri Lanka was still Ceylon. The British government has just set up the Donoughmore Commission, in order to look at the possibility of transferring limited self-rule to the Ceylonese people. The Commission has sparked fierce debates among Colombo's wealthy Tamil families—most of whom live in the well-appointed suburb of Cinnamon Gardens—about what form this self-rule should take and to whom exactly the voting franchise should be extended (limited self-rule was eventually granted in 1931, but it would be another seventeen years before Ceylon/Sri Lanka achieved full independence).

Interestingly, Selvadurai also retreats somewhat in terms of form, modeling his novel more along the lines of nineteenth-century British examples of the genre. *Cinnamon Gardens* is a big book, sweeping in scope, grand in its ideas, and here it very much resembles the work of George Eliot, who serves as a sort of guiding spirit throughout the novel. Indeed, at one point we learn that Annalukshmi, Selvadurai's heroine, is reading *Silas Marner*; and a quotation from *Middlemarch* is used by Selvadurai as an epigraph to his novel. Annalukshmi, a fiercely intelligent and independent young woman who has scandalized her family by qualifying for her teacher's certificate and by espousing radical views on women's suffrage, is very much a Dorothea Brooke-figure. Both characters are externally public-spirited and progressive politically, working on behalf of others (Dorothea through housing, Annalukshmi through education); and both characters are deeply conflicted internally, unable to resolve the competing pulls of head and heart. To this end, Annalukshmi's immediate predicament concerns her family's desire for her to marry, a move that, in proper Ceylonese society of the time, would compel her to give up her teaching career. Much of the novel is taken up with a comic parading of potential suitors before Annalukshmi, all of whom fall impossibly short of her high standards. Partly through her own strength of will and partly through circumstance, Annalukshmi avoids making a match as disastrous as that between Dorothea and Edward Causabon; on the other hand, by the end of the novel neither has she found her Will Ladislaw.

Balendran, Annalukshmi's uncle and the novel's other principle protagonist, can likewise be compared with Eliot's Causabon. Both men have lived mostly unfulfilled lives, caught between thought and action, rationalization and passion. Like Causabon's unrealizable Key to All Mythologies, Balendran, we are told, has been working for some time on a study of Jaffna culture. Of even graver consequence, however, is the fact that for the past twenty years Balendran has submerged his own homosexual desires underneath a facade of respectable familial propriety. While a student at Oxford, Balendran fell in love with a white man, Richard Howland, but abandoned his lover and returned to Colombo to marry his cousin when his outraged father discovered the true nature of the relationship. Now, two decades later, Richard has come to Colombo to observe the Donoughmore Commission's proceedings, forcing Balendran to confront both his past and present duplicity. Here, in addition to Eliot, we see the influence of E. M Forster, especially in terms of Selvadurai's exploration of the attendant clashes between sexuality, colonialism, and class. We are told, for example, that early on in their relationship Richard and Balendran made a pilgrimage to visit Forster's great mentor, Edward Carpenter, author of *The Intermediate Sex* (Forster's *Maurice* was written soon after his own visit to the pioneering sexologist); moreover, late in the novel one of Annalukshmi's suitors presses upon her a copy of *A Passage to India*.

Cinnamon Gardens is, however, mostly Dickensian in its execution. Intricately plotted, sporting a huge cast of characters, and with all manner of secrets revealed, long-lost relatives returned, and penurious paupers rescued, Selvadurai uses humor and coincidence to explore some weighty issues: the suffragist movement, the classism inherent in the caste system, religious divisions, racial and sexual prejudice, and so on. On these issues, Selvadurai refuses to elevate anyone as moral spokesperson. All the characters in *Cinnamon Gardens* are flawed and compromised in some way. The progressive and much-admired headmistress of Annalukshmi's school, Miss Lawton, turns out to be a quiet racist and religious xenophobe, appalled that her adopted Tamil daughter, Nancy, has fallen in love with a poor Sinhalese Buddhist. Even Balendran, despite taking a climactic stand against his father, has failed to redress fully his treatment of Richard by the end of the novel. In this regard, Selvadurai's characters mirror the conflicts and contradictions inherent in Sri Lankan culture itself.

—Peter Dickinson

SETH, Vikram

Nationality: Indian. **Born:** Calcutta, India, 20 June 1952. **Education:** Doon School, India; Corups Christi College, Oxford, B.A. 1975; Stanford University, M.A. in economics 1979; Nanjing University, 1982. **Career:** Senior editor, Stanford University Press, 1985–86. **Awards:** Thomas Cook travel book award, 1983, for *From Heaven Lake;* Ingram Merrill fellowship, 1985–86; Commonwealth poetry prize, 1986; Guggenheim fellowship, 1986–87; Sahitya Akademi award, 1988. **Address:** c/o HarperCollins, 10 East 53rd St., New York, New York 10022–5299, U.S.A.

Publications

Novels

The Golden Gate: A Novel in Verse. New York, Random House, and London, Faber, 1986.

A Suitable Boy. New York, HarperCollins, and London, Phoenix, 1993.

An Equal Music. New York, Broadway Books, 1999.

Poetry

Mappings. Calcutta, Writers Workshop, 1981; London, Viking, 1994.

The Humble Administrator's Garden. Manchester, Carcanet, 1985.

All You Who Sleep Tonight (verse play). New York, Knopf, and London, Faber, 1990.

Beastly Tales from Here to There, illustrated by Ravi Shankar. New Delhi, Viking, 1992; New York, HarperCollins, 1994.

The Poems, 1981–1994. New Delhi, India and New York, Penguin Books, 1995.

Other

From Heaven Lake: Travels Through Sinkiang and Tibet. London, Chatto and Windus, 1983; Boston, Faber, 1986.

Arion and the Dolphin (for children), illustrated by Jane Ray. London, Orion Children's Books, 1994; New York, Dutton Children's Books, 1995.

Translator, *Three Chinese Poets: Translations of Poems by Wang Wei, Li Bai, and Du Fu.* New Delhi, Viking, and New York, HarperPerennial, 1992.

* * *

In poetry and interviews Vikram Seth has mocked experimental literature and romantic and extreme attitudes towards life. For him literature and life should be enjoyable, commonsensical, this worldly. For someone seemingly in favor on the conventional and practical, there is a Faustian side to his writing. His three novels have been virtuoso performances and for serious literature immensely successful with the reading public, and translated in many languages. Each novel has been very different from the others and has taken an older literary form in unexpected new dimensions. In our time when being avant-garde and shocking has become expected of the modern, Seth is a different kind of revolutionary, an extremely daring artist using older literary models and pretending to be an old-fashioned writer for the general reader. Yet such drawing on older artistic styles to create a contemporary literature is one characteristic fashion of our time and often termed the postmodern.

Although Indian he is also part of the new internationalism. Each of his novels is set in a different country. *The Golden Gate* was a high wire act pretending to be genial comedy. Set in a San Francisco of female rock musicians, gays, local radio stations, Berkeley, ''Just Desserts,'' and Italian wine makers, it seemed to be the great California novel, noting the fashions and distinctions of West Coast society and culture. Reading the novel was next best to living in San Francisco. At its heart was a common Seth theme, a relationship ruined by the extreme demands of a lover, and the woman's sensible choice of a good kind-hearted man in place of the miseries of an intense, agonizing love. The commonsense pleasures of enjoying each day are better than the pains that result from unrealizable desires. The novel, however, was verse, filled with amusing puns, and part of its fun was a difficult complicated regular rhyme scheme based on Alexander Puskin's eighteenth-century Russian epic poem *Eugene Onegin.* The verse form, a fourteen line stanza, and its amusing hipness meant the novel was a virtuoso display, a great show of what looked like effortlessly mastering a seemingly impossible poetic form. While the novel lacked depth of characters, that was part of Seth's message, avoid depth and misery, enjoy life while possible a day at a time. People ruin their lives with romantic ideas, excessive demands, obsessions, intolerance, rules, fanaticism, political ideals and causes.

A Suitable Boy uses the ''whom should she marry'' theme of many nineteenth-century novels to offer a portrait of the intricacies of northern Indian society during the 1950s. Its models are the realistic novels of Jane Austen, George Eliot, and Leo Tolstoy, with their range, depth, social detail, and examination of the ways of society, and it is said to be one of the longest novels in English. Following the intertwining lives of four upper-middle-class Hindustani families, *A Suitable Boy* moves from Calcutta through the Urdu-speaking region of Lucknow, Allahabad, and Benares to Delhi. It sketches a society from the untouchables through the new entrepreneurs to the Muslim Nawabs. Attention is given to such traditional trades as shoe-making and how they are threatened by foreign imports. The heroine, the daughter of a deceased senior government administrator, financially insecure, and dependent on the good will of others, falls in love with an unsuitable, brilliant Muslim intellectual but instead sensibly decides to marry a rather uncouth self-made businessman. He might be said to represent the new India which will replace the older Muslim and imitation British elites while avoiding Hindu fundamentalism. She also sensibly avoids marrying a witty sophisticated writer, who seems a bit like Seth himself, as he is too preoccupied with his own writing to make a good husband. The story can obviously be interpreted in terms of India which should put its future in the hands of practical businessman rather than fanatics, romantics, traditionalists, revolutionaries, and poets. Traditions should bring comfort and ease rather than become a source of foolishness, pride, fantasy, and violence.

In *An Equal Music* the message is similar, but the method and story deepen the treatment of character. Here Seth has taken the early twentieth-century European novel about the life of musicians and brought it up to date, set it in the contemporary world at a time when few schools in England still teach classical music, and when chamber music is losing its appeal and string quartets find it difficult to survive. This is partly a novel about economic survival as the world changes, but it is mainly about emotional survival as situations change; there is no love which cannot become destructive—excessive passions destroy.

The main story concerns a second violinist in an English string quartet who a decade earlier left his teacher, a great master of the Viennese school who tried to force his style and perspective about a solo career on his students. The English violinist is anti-authoritarian, having fought his lower-middle parents to pursue a career in music; he rebels, leaves Vienna, but also leaves a younger woman, a pianist who loves him. She breaks down, and on the rebound marries an American who gives her understanding and security. A decade later the violinist is still in love with her. They meet, have an affair, but she realizes that she is hurting her husband, risks hurting her child; the renewal of such passion can only destroy the life she and her husband have made. When she breaks off the affair, the violinist refuses to accept her wishes. For him there can be no friendship with her, only violent passion. In a funk with life he also quits the string quartet, destroying years of friendship, hard work, and the possibility of a breakthrough to fame and financial success—the quartet has recently had an offer from a major recording company. At the conclusion the quartet forgives him, and they reunite like a happy family, the quartet being the equivalent in this novel of a family of contrasting personalities who have learned to tolerate each other for their common good.

Although told by the violinist in an impressionistic manner like the motifs of music, with transformations into other keys, recapitulations, even a fugue-like poetic conclusion, the novel is filled with the detail usual to a Vikram Seth novel. The discussions of tunings, structuring a performance, violin makers, never feel out of place. That Seth has now written excellent books set in the U.S.A., India, England and a travel book about China, with American, Indian, and British central characters, suggests that national boundaries are falling to a new kind of international writer. Seth's own use of different literary models including hard to master difficult forms may suggest that despite his message of commonsense and comfort he enjoys great challenges if the hard work is likely to bring immediate fame and financial rewards.

—Bruce King

SETTLE, Mary Lee

Nationality: American. **Born:** Charleston, West Virginia, 29 July 1918. **Education:** Sweet Briar College, 1936–38. **Military Service:** Women's Auxiliary, R.A.F., 1942–43. **Family:** Married William Littleton Tazewell, 1978; has one son. **Career:** Editor, *Harper's Bazaar,* 1945; English correspondant, *Flair,* 1950–51; associate professor, Bard College, New York, 1956–76. Visiting lecturer, University of Virginia, 1978. **Awards:** Guggenheim fellow, 1958, 1960; Merrill Foundation award, 1975; National Book award, 1978, for *Blood Tie;* Janet Heidinger Kafka prize, 1983, for fiction; Academy award in literature, American Academy of Arts and Letters, 1994. **Address:** c/o Farrar Straus & Giroux, 19 Union Sq. W., New York, New York 10003–3304, U.S.A.

Publications

Novels

The Love Eaters. New York, Harper, and London, Heinemann, 1954.
The Kiss of Kin. New York, Harper, and London, Heinemann, 1955.
Fight Night on a Sweet Saturday (originally part of the Beulah Quintet). New York, Viking, 1964; London, Heinemann, 1965.
The Clam Shell. New York, Delacorte Press, and London, Bodley Head, 1971.
Blood Tie. Boston, Houghton Mifflin, 1977.
Celebration, illustrated by John Collier. New York, Farrar Straus, and London, Hutchinson, 1986.
Charley Bland. Franklin Center, Pennsylania, Franklin Library, 1989.
Choices. New York, Talese/Doubleday, 1995.
Beulah Quintet Series:
O Beulah Land. New York, Viking, and London, Heinemann, 1956.
Know Nothing. New York, Viking, 1960; London, Heinemann, 1961.

Prisons. New York, Putnam, 1973; as *The Long Road to Paradise,* London, Constable, 1974.
The Scapegoat. New York, Random House, 1980.
The Killing Ground. New York, Farrar Straus, 1982.

Uncollected Short Stories

''Congress Burney,'' in *Paris Review,* 7, 1954–55.
''The Old Wives' Tale,'' in *Harper's Magazine,* September 1955.
''Paragraph Eleven,'' in *The Girl in the Black Raincoat,* edited by George Garrett. New York, Duell, 1966.
''Coalburg, Virginia: One of the Lucky Ones,'' in *While Someone Else Is Eating,* edited by Earl Shorris. Garden City, Doubleday, 1984.

Other

All the Brave Promises: The Memories of Aircraft Woman 2nd Class 2146391. New York, Delacorte, and London, Heinemann, 1966.
The Story of Flight (for children), illustrated by George Evans. New York, Random House, 1967.
The Scopes Trial: The State of Tennessee v. John Thomas Scopes. New York, Watts, 1972.
Water World (for children). New York, Dutton, 1984.
Turkish Reflections: A Biography of a Place. New York, Prentice Hall, and London, Grafton, 1991.
Addie. Columbia, University of South Carolina Press, 1998.

*

Critical Studies: ''The Searching Voice and Vision of Mary Lee Settle'' by Peggy Bach, in *The Southern Review,* 20(4), October 1984; ''Mary Lee Settle and the Tradition of Historical Fiction,'' in *The South Atlantic Quarterly,* 86(3), Summer 1987, and ''Mary Lee Settle and the Critics'' in *Virginia Quarterly Review,* 65(3), Summer 1989, both by Brian Rosenberg; *Understanding Mary Lee Settle* by George Garrett, Columbia, University of South Carolina Press, 1988; ''Mary Lee Settle: 'Ambiguity of Steel''' by Jane Gentry Vance, in *American Women Writing Fiction: Memory, Identity, Family, Space,* edited by Mickey Pearlman, The University Press of Kentucky, 1989; *Mary Lee Settle's Beulah Quintet: The Price of Freedom* by Brian Rosenberg, Baton Rouge, Louisiana State University Press, 1991.

* * *

''First you're an unknown,'' Martin Myers once observed, ''then you write one book and you move up to obscurity.'' After more than a dozen books spread over four decades, Mary Lee Settle, one of the most large-minded of American novelists, still languishes in relative obscurity, and the fault lies with the prejudices of contemporary criticism.

Out of reviewers' compulsion to impose order by corralling art within the convenience of labels, Settle, like equally undervalued southerners Elizabeth Spencer and George Garrett, has been shoved under the blanket of ''southern writer,'' where she fails to meet imposed expectations. Why, critics demand, can't she be more baroque, like Faulkner, or tender, like Carson McCullers? Or, since her best-known work, the Beulah Quintet, is historical fiction, why can't Settle whisk us into the gothic romantic world of Margaret Mitchell?

Yet, Settle's fascination with the past, far from the exotic escapism of genre historical fiction, embodies nothing less than the quest to define the American character through a minute exploration of how it came to be formed. The picture that to this point emerges is a braided paradox: A national character shaped on the one side by hope and on the other by memory, each looking, Janus-like, in opposite directions, each guided by its own myth. On the one hand, Settle's America is founded by protean souls looking forward, to freedom, for a better life, willing to mortgage their past for a happier future. Simultaneously, its oedipal side wishes desperately to know who it is, which can only be discovered by learning where it came from.

The origins of the Beulah Quintet, which chronicles the saga of the Lacey, Catlett, and McKarkle families from the 1640s to 1980s, lie in the hero of the fourth-written of the quintet, *Promises.* Jonathan Church, fired by democratic passion for freedom, had rallied to Oliver Cromwell's rebellion against the Stuart monarchy. However, when he, like those later romantics who would at first cheer the French Revolution, grows disenchanted with Cromwell's own arrogance and refuses to bow before him, twenty-year-old Church is executed in 1649.

Church's illegitimate son (by Church's aunt) emigrates to that part of the Ohio River Valley in Virginia that would later become part of West Virginia. In *O Beulah Land,* set in the years preceding the American Revolution, Church's descendant, Jonathan Lacey, settles at Beulah and achieves for a time the vision of freedom of his English ancestor. Over ensuing decades, the Laceys blend into the melting pot Beulah had become, and Settle picks up their story next in *Know Nothing,* in which Johnny Catlett, master of Beulah Plantation, under family pressure fights for the Confederacy. The next Beulah novel, *The Scapegoat,* focusing on less than one day's time in 1912, provides a wealth of richly refracted inner experience in lives caught up in the early days of labor organizing at the Lacey family's Seven Stars Coal Mine. The final piece of the quintet, *The Killing Ground* (which expands upon and is meant to replace the earlier *Fight Night on a Sweet Saturday*), clarifies the pattern evolving over the whole as descendent/novelist Hannah McKarkle, whose books bear the same titles as Settle's, comes home to Canona, West Virginia (near Beulah and strikingly like Charleston) to investigate her brother Johnny's death and, while there, explain her novels.

Whereas Settle's first two novels, *Kiss of Kin* and *The Love Eaters,* were also set in Canona and contain characters who appear in the Beulah Quintet, her *Blood Tie,* winner of the 1978 National Book Award, is set in Turkey. Yet it, as well as the weaker *Celebration* (1986), shares the quintet's attention to the need to grasp the past, even the ancient past. So too do Settle's two most recent novels, quite possibly her best: *Charley Bland* and *Choices.* The outward shape of these novels could not be more different, the former being a close-up focusing on one small, ill-fated love affair, the latter a panoramic sweep over a long and remarkable life.

We know from the first pages of *Charley Bland* that the love affair between the unnamed narrator and Charley is doomed. The lovers are enmeshed in an inviolable triangle, where character lacks strength and compassion enough to permit love to survive. ''He won't marry you, you know, he never does,'' a woman calls out to the narrator. She'd known it from the start. In 1960, sixteen years after she'd run off with a British airman and become almost immediately widowed, the narrator returns to West Virginia.

Waiting there is the dissolute Charley Bland, the town's forty-five-year-old ladies' man. Two decades earlier, he had been the romanticized focus of her dreams. Back then it seemed ''all the wild roads led to Charley Bland… . He acted out our dreams of what we could hope to do when we grew up, if we only had the nerve.'' To her teenaged eyes, the ironically named Bland was so idealized that when he leapt into a pool ''his dive was so clean there was only a parting, not a splash.''

Though at thirty-five her eyes have matured, they gaze longingly on a past she had thus far rejected. She had cut herself off from her roots and feels desperate to return to them through Charley. He woos her (''Being with you is like being alone''). Knowing that Bland ''hated and used women,'' the narrator nevertheless yields both body and heart to him. But then there's Mrs. Bland, Charley's mother, the third corner of this most familiar of triangles. ''It is,'' the narrator says, ''the stuff of jokes, and comic strips, and suicides. It is the mother, and the son, and the woman, whether she is holy, whore, or wife.''

Mrs. Bland uses her ''charm like a blunt instrument,'' knowing this woman too will pass and become another autographed photo in the Bland attic, leaving herself at almost eighty to hold her middle-aged son as securely as any mother with her toddler on a leash. He must return to the mother who trained him in charm rather than character, a cripple caring for a cripple until her death.

Why, then, does the narrator remain in this hopeless love affair? She tells us, ''It is when the ordinary becomes luminous that we are transformed.'' Both Charley and Mrs. Bland are, to her adult vision, ordinary. Even their triangle is ordinary, if heartbreaking. Yet, she allows both the love affair and its tragic course to attain the quixotic luminosity her girlhood eyes would have given them because she feels a desperate need for transformation.

''I am a Southerner,'' she says, ''and there is bred in us, as carefully as if we were prize hounds, a sense of betrayal in leaving our roots.'' Charley Bland, the hero of her childhood, offers the hope of atonement. He ''made the past shine; what he promised without saying a word was neither of our real lives but some mutual hope. The part of me I had not let live was no longer rejected.'' Faced with a doomed love affair, she is nevertheless in a position where she can scarcely lose. She either fulfills her past with Charley or she gets betrayed, one betrayal atoning for another, and can put her past at peace.

The past of Melinda Kregg Dunston in Settle's *Choices* (1995), hardly needs to be put at peace, for hers has been an extraordinary and heroic life, which she recollects as spring dawns in 1993 and Melinda, eighty-two, lies dying on the Italian coast. In 1930 Richmond, Virginia, Melinda was a bright and lovely debutante in a world that doesn't reward belles for questioning too closely the established order. Surrounded by beaus who say things like ''don't worry about [exploited laborers]. Leave that to ugly women. You're much too beautiful to be high-minded,'' Melinda began as the naive product of a land where a mind is a terrible thing to waste on a girl.

Her father's suicide changes that. Hoping to leave his family safely rich with his insurance money, he instead turns Melinda away from safety and points her toward service, danger, and a lifetime of championing the oppressed. As she leaves Richmond, her Aunt Boodie extracts a promise that Melinda will keep: ''Do *everything,*'' Boodie urges.

First, Melinda becomes a Red Cross volunteer and crosses the Kentucky border to feed the starving families of coal miners. Trying to unionize, miners are starved, blacklisted, evicted, jailed, and shot by hired thugs. Melinda sees emaciated girls of twenty bent like old women and signs reading ''YOUR DOGS EAT BETTER THAN OUR KIDS,'' and she herself lands in jail for feeding the hungry. She has lost her innocence. And she has heard from a Kentucky widow another piece of life-defining advice: ''My husband used to say you can argy all day long, but when you wake up at three o'clock in the mornin a thing is either wrong or it's right, and either you take a drink or do something about it.''

That advice contains the key to the empathy that guides not only Melinda's life but the moral foundation of all of Settle's fiction. Melinda may be, in fact, the personification of all Settle most powerfully believes. The coal mines provide just the first of the battlefields Melinda enters to ''do something about it.'' In 1937, she sails for Spain to wage battle against Franco's fascism, a young woman who can speak Spanish, type, and drive ambulance trucks.

But even Kentucky's gunfire hadn't prepared her for the massive carnage she sees in Spain. Settle shows Melinda stepping over piles of corpses, working to exhaustion beside nuns with the hearts of Madonna and the mouths of sailors, rushing ''to take blood from the newly dead and pump it into the veins of the dying''—all in apparent futility, as Franco is copiously supplied by Hitler and Mussolini while the democracies stand idly by. But the British physician she marries reminds her what makes even a losing battle for justice essential: ''Tye said *anyway.* You do it anyway.''

Her remaining battles take on more muted, autumnal tones. But she fights them with every bit as much conviction. In London, Melinda comforts victims of V-2 bombings and supports her husband's efforts to launch the National Health Service. Melinda's last active battle fittingly takes place in her native south, in 1965 Mississippi, where she heads into the Deep South as a spy in her own country to find a missing cousin who'd been working for civil rights: ''I can go in disguise… . I'll be a white lady with a white mind and white gloves in a black Buick.'' The scene has changed, and it is now a woman in late middle age fighting, but the battle has always been the same, for the faces of hate, of fear at not being able to hold one's advantage, of rage at being blocked from the pursuit of happiness, are the same wherever she's been.

Though *Choices* is an eyewitness sojourn through the history of our century, the book's artistic magic, typically of Settle, lies in its details, how vividly she gives that history local habitations and names. More than that, though, we grow enrapt by Settle's richly human tapestry woven of wisdom, experience, and compassion around a woman whose heart seems to beat in constant sympathy with the hearts of others: ''The day her heart refused to creak and break a little,'' Melinda thinks, ''was the day she wanted to be dead.''

So, the study of the past has brought Settle to an understanding of the present as a place where the ongoing struggle for freedom and justice must always be fought because in that fight, even when it appears futile or even suicidal, lies the key to love and the meaning of life within the human community. In one way or another, all of Settle's most realized characters have sensed that. And the best of them, like Melinda Kregg Dunston, base their lives on it.

—Andy Solomon

SHAARA, Jeff

Nationality: American. **Born:** New Brunswick, New Jersey (son of well-known author Michael Shaara), 1952. **Education:** Florida State University, degree in criminology, 1974. **Family:** Wife's name is

Lynne. **Career:** Founder of rare coin business at age sixteen, eventually incorporated as Florida Coin Exchange, a retail business, sold company in 1988; became full- time writer. Divides his time between Florida and New York.

PUBLICATIONS

Novels

Gods and Generals. New York, Ballantine Books, 1996.
The Last Full Measure. New York, Ballantine Books, 1998.
Gone for Soldiers. New York, Ballantine Books, 2000.

* * *

Although he never intended to be a writer, after only four years of writing Jeff Shaara has proven to be one of the most popular and prolific American novelists at the turn of the twenty-first century. He is the son of Michael Shaara, winner of the 1975 Pulitzer Prize for his American Civil War novel, *The Killer Angels*, on which the film *Gettysburg* was based. During the filming of this movie in 1993, Shaara was approached about continuing his now-deceased father's legacy. His first book, *Gods and Generals*, was a prequel to his father's novel, and his second, *The Last Full Measure*, a sequel. Together, they form a trilogy with Shaara's father's novel at the center. While some critics perceive this framing of his father's writing as a form of tampering or exploitation, others align themselves with Shaara himself, who believes that he is continuing his father's legacy by telling the stories Michael Shaara was unable to tell before his death. Shaara's third novel, *Gone for Soldiers*, while not explicitly inter-textual with *The Killer Angels*, nevertheless returns to many of the same characters, examining their earlier participation in the Mexican-American War.

Shaara is reluctant to locate himself within a literary tradition, or cite any contemporary literary influences other than his father. Nevertheless, he is clearly a writer of historical fiction, as supported by his claim that his greatest influences are the writings of those historical figures with whom his books are concerned. His documentary style is complemented by his meticulous attention to the factual details of each historical event or period he chronicles. Simultaneously, his writing does not lack imagination, as he sifts through the history to retrieve the people who inhabited it, and bring them to life in a way traditional history making or telling does not. Shaara is aware that his writing must stand the test of the innumerable Civil War scholars and aficionados who read it, and is careful not to violate the accountability to the historical record he feels a writer imagining this period assumes. Shaara is also frank, however, about the profound emotional ties he feels to his characters and the very different kind of responsibility this almost spiritual connection entails for him as an author. Still, the inevitable comparison to Michael Shaara's work suggests that the son is more concerned with vividly and accurately documenting historical events, while the father was more deeply riveted by psychological themes, including the ability of the individual to grow and adapt when confronted with previously unimaginable tensions and conflicts, like the Civil War itself.

Gods and Generals, Shaara's first novel, was published to mixed reviews and tremendous commercial success, spending fifteen weeks on the *New York Times* bestseller list. The novel documents the first three years of the American Civil War as Shaara slowly threads together the lives of Generals Joshua Chamberlain, Stonewall Jackson, Winfield Scott Hancock, and Robert E. Lee. Quite believably, Shaara explores the ambivalence, ethics, loyalties, and disillusionment of each man, leading up to the Battle of Gettysburg—where Michael Shaara's novel takes over. Shaara's second novel, *The Last Full Measure*—also a commercial success—picks up after *The Killer Angels*, with Lee's retreat from Pennsylvania, and follows through to his surrender at Appomattox. With the introduction of Ulysses S. Grant, Shaara focuses his narrator's powers of omniscience on Lee and Grant as compelling examples of the North and South. His latest novel, *Gone for Soldiers*, also takes Lee as its subject, as it traces his evolution as a commander through the Mexican-American War.

Shaara is remarkable not just for achieving such tremendous success in such a short time, despite lacking previous writing experience, but also because he has been so remarkably successful in bringing his work to the public in a variety of forms. Each of his novels is being transformed into a cinematic version, with Shaara himself partner in a production company formed for that express purpose. He has also succeeded in bringing another of Michael Shaara's novels, *For Love of the Game*, to the screen in a movie of the same name. He is currently at work on a series on the American Revolutionary War and the American ''Founding Fathers.''

—Jennifer Harris

SHADBOLT, Maurice (Francis Richard)

Nationality: New Zealander. **Born:** Auckland, 4 June 1932. **Education:** Te Kuiti High School; Avondale College; University of Auckland. **Family:** Married 1) Gillian Heming in 1953, three sons and two daughters; 2) Barbara Magner in 1971; 3) Bridget Armstrong in 1978. **Career:** Journalist for various New Zealand publications, 1952–54; documentary scriptwriter and director for the New Zealand National Film Unit, 1954–57; full-time writer from 1957; lived in London and Spain, 1957–60, then returned to New Zealand. **Awards:** New Zealand Scholarship in Letters, 1959, 1970, 1982; Hubert Church Prose award, 1960; Katherine Mansfield award, 1963, 1967; University of Otago Robert Burns fellowship, 1963; National Association of Independent Schools award (U.S.A.), 1966; Freda Buckland award, 1969; Pacific Area Travel Association award, for non-fiction, 1971; James Wattie award, 1973, 1981, 1987; New Zealand Book award, 1981; Literary Fund travel bursary, 1988. C.B.E. (Commander, Order of the British Empire), 1989. **Agent:** Curtis Brown, 162–168 Regent Street, London W1R 5TA, England. **Address:** Box 60028, Titirangi, Auckland 7, New Zealand.

PUBLICATIONS

Novels

Among the Cinders. London, Eyre and Spottiswoode, and New York, Atheneum, 1965; revised edition, Auckland, Hodder and Stoughton, 1984.
This Summer's Dolphin. London, Cassell, and New York, Atheneum, 1969.
An Ear of the Dragon. London, Cassell, 1971.

Strangers and Journeys. London, Hodder and Stoughton, and New York, St. Martin's Press, 1972.

A Touch of Clay. London, Hodder and Stoughton, 1974.

Danger Zone. Auckland, Hodder and Stoughton, 1975; London, Hodder and Stoughton, 1976.

The Lovelock Version. Auckland and London, Hodder and Stoughton, 1980; New York, St. Martin's Press, 1981.

Season of the Jew. London, Hodder and Stoughton, 1986; New York, Norton, 1987.

Monday's Warriors. London, Hodder and Stoughton, 1990; Boston, Godine, 1992.

The House of Strife. London, Bloomsbury, 1993.

Short Stories

The New Zealanders: A Sequence of Stories. Christchurch, Whitcombe and Tombs, and London, Gollancz, 1959; New York, Atheneum, 1961.

Summer Fires and Winter Country. London, Eyre and Spottiswoode, 1963; New York, Atheneum, 1966.

The Presence of Music: Three Novellas. London, Cassell, 1967.

Figures in Light: Selected Stories. London, Hodder and Stoughton, 1979.

Dove on the Waters (novellas). Auckland, David Ling, 1996.

Selected Stories of Maurice Shadbolt, edited by Ralph Crane. Auckland, David Ling, 1998.

Play

Once on Chunuk Bair. Auckland, Hodder and Stoughton, 1982.

Other

New Zealand: Gift of the Sea, photographs by Brian Brake. Christchurch, Whitcombe and Tombs, 1963; revised edition, 1973; London, Hodder and Stoughton, 1991.

The Shell Guide to New Zealand. Christchurch, Whitcombe and Tombs, 1968; London, Joseph, 1969; revised edition, Whitcombe and Tombs, 1973; Joseph, 1976.

Isles of the South Pacific, with Olaf Ruhen. Washington, D.C., National Geographic Society, 1968.

Love and Legend: Some Twentieth Century New Zealanders. Auckland, Hodder and Stoughton, 1976.

Voices of Gallipoli. Auckland and London, Hodder and Stoughton, 1988.

Reader's Digest Guide to New Zealand, photographs by Brian Brake. Sydney, Reader's Digest, 1988.

One of Ben's: A New Zealand Medley (autobiography). Auckland, David Ling, 1993.

From the Edge of the Sky: A Memoir. Auckland, David Ling, 1999.

*

Bibliography: "A Bibliography of Maurice Shadbolt 1956–1984" by Murray Gadd, in *Journal of New Zealand Literature* (Dunedin), no. 2, 1984.

Critical Studies: by the author, in *Islands* (Auckland), June 1981; *Ending the Silences: Critical Essays on the Works of Maurice Shadbolt,* edited by Ralph J. Crane, Auckland, Hodder Moa Beckett, 1995.

Theatrical Activities: Actor: **Film:**—*Among the Cinders,* 1983.

Maurice Shadbolt comments:

I should like to say only that, as a man of my time and place, I have simply tried to make sense of both, in the course of a journey which allows no satisfying destination; my books might thus be seen as bottled messages tossed out at points along that journey. I know I might have been otherwise: I am frequently unsure why I write at all. But then I look from my study window out upon a bruised Eden, my country, and I begin again; there is no escape. My equivocal feeling for the country in which I happened to be born admits of no easy release in either a physical or literary sense. So I make, in diverse shapes, in stories and novels, my not always unhappy best of it. As a New Zealander, resident at the ragged edge of Western civilization, upon the last land of substance to be claimed by mankind, I often feel my involvement with the rest of the human race rather peripheral—as if upon a lonely floating raft. Yet fires lit upon the periphery may still illuminate the central and abiding concerns of man—the fires, I mean, which everywhere the human spirit ignites, and which everywhere shape the artist. So I make no apology. I might envy a Russian or an American—a Solzhenitsyn or a Mailer—his capacity to approach the giant themes of the twentieth century. But I would not wish, really, to be otherwise. For I have tried, beyond the particularities of time and place, to observe and examine those hungers and thirsts which remain constant in man; those hungers and thirsts which, in my peripheral position, may sometimes be more evident than elsewhere.

* * *

In a writing career which now stretches back over forty years Maurice Shadbolt has successfully turned his hand to short stories, drama, nonfiction, and autobiography, as well as the novels on which his reputation is likely to rest.

The stories in Shadbolt's first two books, *The New Zealanders: A Sequence of Stories* and *Summer Fires and Winter Country,* which chronicle New Zealand's social history during the first half of the twentieth century and beyond, demonstrate the close relationship which exists between Shadbolt's short stories and his longer fiction. In "Ben's Land," the impressive opening story of *Summer Fires and Winter Country,* for example, Shadbolt draws on his own family history, and introduces material which would later be reworked in his first novel, *Among the Cinders,* expanded in *The Lovelock Version,* and revisited again in his autobiographical work *One of Ben's.*

His first novel, *Among the Cinders,* uses the relationship between the adolescent Nick Flinders and his grandfather Hubert to explore New Zealand's history from the pioneering days to the 1950s. Here Shadbolt found a pattern for treating past and present that he would develop in later works, and established his preference for a cast of mainly male characters.

Shadbolt's next two novels, *This Summer's Dolphin* and *An Ear of the Dragon* are apprentice pieces with contemporary settings which see him casting around for a form. *This Summer's Dolphin* is a short novel inspired by the story of Opo the dolphin, whose presence at the beach of Opononi in New Zealand's far north one summer captured the imagination of the nation, while *An Ear of the Dragon* is a blatant reconstruction of the life of Renato Amato, which attracted considerable criticism when it appeared.

Strangers and Journeys, a loose and baggy monster of a novel which draws together many of the themes and characters of his earlier novels and stories, is essentially a contrast between the lives of two representative fathers and sons, and perhaps concludes a phase of Shadbolt's writing which began in the stories gathered in the first two collections. The earlier sections of the novel, which deal with the lives of the fathers as they battle against both the environment and the harsh economic times, is generally recognized as the strongest section of the novel. As the work moves closer to the present, to the city, and to the lives of the sons it tends to lose its focus somewhat.

A Touch of Clay and *Danger Zone,* two volumes in a projected but never completed trilogy of the 1970s, are further castings around for a form. *A Touch of Clay* continues Shadbolt's interest in the relationship between the artist (Paul Pike, a potter) and society, and the relationship between individuals and their environment. But perhaps the most significant aspect of this novel in terms of the progress of Shadbolt's writing is the nineteenth-century strand provided by Pike's grandfather's diaries. *Danger Zone,* like *This Summer's Dolphin* and *An Ear of the Dragon,* does not fit easily into the overall pattern of Shadbolt's oeuvre. It focuses on New Zealand's opposition to nuclear testing in the South Pacific, and is loosely based on Shadbolt's own voyage to Mururoa on board the protest vessel *Tamure* in 1972.

In 1980 Shadbolt published his first historical novel, *The Lovelock Version,* which marked a definite shift towards the nineteenth-century. Here for the first time the past is foregrounded in the stories of the three pioneering Lovelock brothers and their families, whose stories jointly depict the full panorama of New Zealand's nineteenth-century Pakeha (European) history. This novel, with its entertaining blend of metafiction and realism, sees Shadbolt the storyteller at his rollicking best.

Good though *The Lovelock Version* undoubtedly it, it is in the triptych of revisionist-historical novels which followed—*Season of the Jew, Monday's Warriors,* and *The House of Strife*—that Shadbolt found his form. These novels together add up to what is perhaps the most important work of historical fiction yet produced by a New Zealand writer. The first of the three novels in what is commonly referred to as Shadbolt's New Zealand Wars trilogy tells the story of Te Kooti's war, focussing in particular on his Poverty Bay campaigns of the 1860s; *Monday's Warriors,* also set in the 1860s, moves to Taranaki, and is concerned with Titokawaru's war and the story of the rebel American Kimball Bent; the final volume of the trilogy moves further back in time to the early years of the New Zealand Wars and the 1845–46 rebellion of Hone Heke. Common to each novel is a central Pakeha figure whose sympathies lie more with the Maori side than with the colonizers, and who provide Shadbolt with a apparently objective position from which to narrate the events of his stories.

Since the completion of his New Zealand Wars trilogy Shadbolt has turned his attention to autobiographical work, first in *One of Ben's: A New Zealand Medley,* a family history of national consequence which skillfully mixes the myths and legends of the Shadbolt tribe with those of Pakeha or post-colonization New Zealand, and more recently in *From the Edge of the Sky: A Memoir,* a more personal memoir which covers the years 1959–1976. He has also returned to the short story form after a gap of almost thirty years with *Dove on the Waters,* a consummate collection of three novella-length love stories that span the twentieth century.

Shadbolt is undoubtedly one of New Zealand's best known literary figures. And although he has had considerable success as a writer of short stories and autobiography as well as as a novelist, it is fair to say that his New Zealand Wars trilogy alone is enough to secure him a position as one of New Zealand's major writers.

—Ralph J. Crane

SHARPE, Tom

Nationality: British. **Born:** Thomas Ridley Sharpe in London, 30 March 1928. **Education:** Lancing College, Sussex, 1942–46; Pembroke College, Cambridge, 1948–51, M.A.; teacher's training, Cambridge University, 1962–63, P.C.G.E. 1963. **Military Service:** Served in the Royal Marines, 1946–48. **Family:** Married Nancy Anne Looper in 1969; three daughters. **Career:** Social worker, 1951–52, and teacher, 1952–56, Natal, South Africa; photographer, Pietermaritzburg, South Africa, 1956–61; deported from South Africa on political grounds, 1961; teacher, Aylesbury Secondary Modern School, Buckinghamshire, 1961; Lecturer in History, Cambridge College of Arts and Technology, 1963–71. Since 1971, full-time writer. **Agent:** Anthony Sheil Associates, 43 Doughty Street, London, WC1N 2LF. **Address:** 38 Tunwells Lane, Great Shelford, Cambridgeshire CB2 5LJ, England.

Publications

Novels

Riotous Assembly. London, Secker and Warburg, 1971; New York, Viking Press, 1972.

Indecent Exposure. London, Secker and Warburg, 1973; New York, Atlantic Monthly Press, 1987.

Porterhouse Blue. London, Secker and Warburg, and Englewood Cliffs, New Jersey, Prentice Hall, 1974.

Blott on the Landscape. London, Secker and Warburg, 1975; New York, Vintage, 1984.

Wilt. London, Secker and Warburg, 1976; New York, Vintage, 1984.

The Great Pursuit. London, Secker and Warburg, 1977; New York, Harper, 1984.

The Throwback. London, Secker and Warburg, 1978; New York, Vintage, 1984.

The Wilt Alternative. London, Secker and Warburg, 1979; New York, St. Martin's Press, 1981(?).

Ancestral Vices. London, Secker and Warburg, 1980.

Vintage Stuff. London, Secker and Warburg, 1982; New York, Vintage, 1984.

Wilt on High. London, Secker and Warburg, 1984; New York, Random House, 1985.

Grantchester Grind: A Porterhouse Chronicle. London, Secker & Warburg, 1995.

The Midden. London, A. Deutsch, Secker & Warburg, 1996; Woodstock, New York, Overlook Press, 1997.

Plays

The South African (produced London, 1961).

Television Play: *She Fell among Thieves,* from the novel by Dornford Yates, 1978.

* * *

Tom Sharpe's comic vision was formed under the pressure of state persecution strong enough to infuriate but not crush him. His initial satires on South Africa set the pattern for all his subsequent fiction. These early works draw their energy from the seditious author's deportation from South Africa in 1961.

Sharpe's first published novel, *Riotous Assembly,* is as funny as anything he has written. It has as its hero the tormented Anglophile policeman Kommandant Van Heerden. Van Heerden's feud with his scheming subordinate Verkramp (a fanatic Boer) and the murderous blunderings of Konstabel Els are one source of black merriment. Another is the degenerate world of the upper-class English colonials. Bungling authoritarian institutions and the English ruling class reappear as black beasts in all Sharpe's later novels. *Indecent Exposure* is a straight sequel, with the same principal characters as *Riotous Assembly* and the same ''Piemburg'' setting. Its comedy, however, is even broader. (At one point in the narrative the whole of Van Heerden's police force is subjected to electric shock therapy and converted to rampant homosexuality.)

After this novel, Sharpe evidently felt his South African vein was exhausted. *Porterhouse Blue* is set in a Cambridge college. Most of the plot revolves around the maneuverings of a reform and a reactionary faction. There is the usual play with comic ruthlessness and sexual perversions. (One comic climax has the quad full of inflated condoms.) In the largest sense, *Porterhouse Blue* can be read as a satire on English life, and its resistance to change. *Blott on the Landscape* is more straightforwardly funny. The central joke of the narrative is the modernization of Handyman Hall from stately home to theme park. The vivaciously homicidal lady of the house, Maude Lynchwood, is particularly well done.

With his next novel, *Wilt,* Sharpe created his most durable hero. The first in the series presents Henry Wilt as a henpecked and downtrodden lecturer at ''Fenland College'' (based transparently on the polytechnic where Sharpe himself taught). There is some effective incidental comedy on Wilt's futile attempts to educate a day release class of butchers (''Meat One''). But the main plot concerns Henry's involvement in suspected murder, following his witnessed disposal of a life-size sex doll which he accidentally came by. This leads to an epic struggle of will with the long-suffering Inspector Flint. Flint and Wilt reappear in *The Wilt Alternative,* which embroils the hero with international terrorists who mount a siege in his house. Wilt's murderously maternal wife Eva makes a notable comic appearance in this novel. *Wilt on High* (which brings in Greenham Common-style peace protesters) suggests that a whole saga may evolve around the misadventures of Sharpe's most likeable hero.

The Great Pursuit returns to the high Cambridge of *Porterhouse Blue.* The title plays on the titles of Cambridge critic F.R. Leavis's best known works. And Sharpe's novel is a jaundiced burlesque on the Leavisite disdain for merely popular literature. The story has a female don of austere critical rectitude who clandestinely writes pulp romance. An ingenuous acolyte, Peter Piper, is manipulated into fronting for her and undertakes an American promotional tour. Cantabrigian snobbishness and transatlantic vulgarity are comically opposed, with the usual fiendish plot complications.

The Throwback is a routine Sharpe comedy on the British rural gentry, and their inextinguishable capacity for survival even among the persecutions of a democratic age and modern world. *Ancestral Vices* has much the same theme. Walden Yapp, an American professor of demotic historiography, is hired to write the family history of the Petrefacts. In their native Vale of Bushampton, he discovers unspeakable sexual horrors underlying their prosperity. *Ancestral Vices* is probably the nastiest of Sharpe's novels, with some incredibly tasteless comedy on the subject of dwarves. But the rule of his fiction is that the more offensive to common decency, the funnier it is. *Vintage Stuff* finds Sharpe in the territory of the English public school. The novel climaxes in a chase across France, and a chateau siege. (Chases and sieges recur in many of Sharpe's narratives.) Again, the novel comically testifies to the indestructibility and the simultaneous awfulness of England's upper classes.

The main influence on Sharpe's fiction is clearly early Evelyn Waugh. Unlike the mature Waugh, Sharpe seems still to be waiting for something to believe in, to ballast the otherwise increasingly brittle negativities of his fiction. But for his admirers (they remain almost exclusively cis-Atlantic, incidentally) it is probably enough that he is consistently the most amusing novelist writing.

—John Sutherland

SHEED, Wilfrid (John Joseph)

Nationality: American. **Born:** London, England, 27 December 1930; emigrated to the United States in 1940. **Education:** Downside Academy, Bath; Lincoln College, Oxford, B.A. 1954, M.A. 1957. **Family:** Married Miriam Ungerer; three children. **Career:** Film critic, 1957–61, and associate editor, 1959–66, *Jubilee* magazine, New York; drama critic and book editor, *Commonweal* magazine, New York, 1964–67; film critic, *Esquire* magazine, New York, 1967–69; Visiting Lecturer in Creative Arts, Princeton University, New Jersey, 1970–71; columnist, *New York Times Book Review,* 1971–75. Judge, Book-of-the-Month Club, 1972–88. **Agent:** International Creative Management, 40 West 57th Street, New York, New York 10019. **Address:** Rysam and High Streets, Sag Harbor, New York 11963, U.S.A.

PUBLICATIONS

Novels

A Middle Class Education. Boston, Houghton Mifflin, 1960; London, Cassell, 1961.

The Hack. New York, Macmillan, and London, Cassell, 1963.

Square's Progress. New York, Farrar Straus, and London, Cassell, 1965.

Office Politics. New York, Farrar Straus, 1966; London, Cassell, 1967.

Max Jamison. New York, Farrar Straus, 1970; as *The Critic,* London, Weidenfeld and Nicolson, 1970.

People Will Always Be Kind. New York, Farrar Straus, 1973; London, Weidenfeld and Nicolson, 1974.

Transatlantic Blues. New York, Dutton, 1978; London, Sidgwick and Jackson, 1979.

The Boys of Winter. New York, Knopf, 1987.

Short Stories

The Blacking Factory, and Pennsylvania Gothic: A Short Novel and a Long Story. New York, Farrar Straus, 1968; London, Weidenfeld and Nicolson, 1969.

Other

Joseph. New York, Sheed and Ward, 1958.
The Morning After (essays). New York, Farrar Straus, 1971.
Three Mobs: Labor, Church and Mafia. New York, Sheed and Ward, 1974.
Muhammad Ali. New York, Crowell, and London, Weidenfeld and Nicolson, 1975.
The Good Word and Other Words (essays). New York, Dutton, 1978; London, Sidgwick and Jackson, 1979.
Clare Boothe Luce. New York, Dutton, and London, Weidenfeld and Nicolson, 1982.
Frank and Maisie: A Memoir with Parents. New York, Simon and Schuster, 1985; London, Chatto and Windus, 1986.
The Kennedy Legacy: A Generation Later, photographs by Jacques Lowe. New York and London, Viking, 1988.
Essays in Disguise. New York, Knopf, 1990.
Baseball and Lesser Sports. New York, HarperCollins, 1991.
My Life as a Fan. New York, Simon and Schuster, 1993.
In Love with Daylight: A Memoir of Recovery. New York, Simon & Schuster, 1995.
Editor, *Essays and Poems,* by G.K. Chesterton. London, Penguin, 1958.
Editor, *Sixteen Short Novels.* New York, Dutton, 1985.

* * *

Wilfrid Sheed is an acute cultural historian, critic, and satirist who has mapped out a special province of Anglo-American life as his own. His novels are polished comedies of manners on highly serious topics: the degeneracy of the ''communications industry'' in all its forms, the anxiety of Roman Catholics in a secularized society, the profound alienation of individuals who find themselves trapped between two cultures.

Beginning with *A Middle Class Education,* Sheed deals with the failure of both schooling and learning, especially the vaunted British public school and university system, a major target of satire recurring in *The Blacking Factory* and *Transatlantic Blues.* In *The Hack* Sheed combines two favorite subjects—the failure of the Roman Catholic church in the modern world and the variegated follies of modern communications media. The story tracks hapless Bert Flax, a freelance writer grinding out theological pulp for popular religious magazines. *Office Politics* focuses half of this theme on Gilbert Twining, a writer for a struggling popular magazine, in an extended study of self-deception in life and literature.

Behind the vaudevillian comic turns Sheed constructs are serious investigations of alienated, self-divided individuals in a world with little solace or aid. Fred and Alison Cope (who, of course, *can't* cope) in *Square's Progress* try to flee the confines of their middle-class educations and marriage for beat-bohemian-hippy freedoms, only to find the hip life as empty and sharp-cornered as suburbia. *Max Jamison* charts another hack writer's attempts to understand his own unravelling life. Max, a magazine critic, finds himself unable to reconcile his vocation with his desires, although writing criticism has been his life's goal: ''The difference between a critic and a reviewer is, I forget … I've always wanted to be a critic. Yes, really. Like wanting to be a dentist or an undertaker. Some kids are funny that way. No, ma'am, I have never wanted to write creatively. I was an unnatural little boy in many ways. The rumor that I used to torture flies probably contains some truth. I did write a poem once, in alexandrines, but I didn't much care for it. Yes, it's in my wallet now.''

People Will Always Be Kind observes the anomalies and aberrations of American politics in the early 1970s through a journalistic point of view, a mock-biography of an Irish Catholic presidential candidate feeling profound conflicts between religious, moral, and political realities. The novel is divided between a view of Brian Casey's personal and political life and the ruminations of a political hack writer, Sam Perkins, so Sheed again analyzes the failure of journalism, of writing, to capture the subtleties of life.

In *Transatlantic Blues* Sheed pulls together many early satiric themes. In some ways, the novel inverts and expands the brilliant short novel *The Blacking Factory,* detailing the schizophrenic development of Pendrid ''Monty'' Chatworth, a TV talk-show host educated in Britain and working in the U.S. Chatworth, a Roman Catholic, dictates the novel in the form of a sprawling mock-confession, a litany of the sins and disasters of his life. The conflicts between a British identity (Pendrid) and an American one (Monty), between high British culture (Oxford) and U.S. popular culture (TV ratings), between Catholicism and secular fame, make the novel painful as well as comic. Pendrid is another version of the ''hack writer,'' the ''office politician,'' the Anglo-American accepted in neither world, the Catholic who finds no solace in the church and who is rejected by the secular-Protestant culture in which he is immersed.

In *The Boys of Winter,* Sheed constructs a clever intellectual comedy based on analogies between writing, publishing, sexual pursuit, and sandlot softball. Set in a Long Island writer's haven, it chronicles a ''hot stove league'' of hack writers and their editor, Jonathan Oglethorpe, who organizes and coaches them to compete against a visiting Hollywood film crew. The skein of satire involves parallels between macho gamesmanship and schlock-merchandizing, a theme which provokes Sheed to some of his most penetrating analysis of American literary culture.

Sheed's acute ear for both British and American speech (and thought), his ability to parody popular idioms in journalism, his serious questions about education, the content of popular culture, the role of the Roman Catholic church in a secularized society all make him one of the most penetrating satirists of our day. His specific view of the world in which rootlessness, divorce, and flamboyant failure are imposed against the old values of work, stability, marriage, and modest success gives his novels a sharp edge and clarity, the bite of classic satire.

—William J. Schafer

SHIELDS, Carol

Nationality: Canadian and American. **Born:** Carol Warner, Oak Park, Illinois, 2 June 1935. **Education:** Hanover College, Indiana, 1953–57, A.B.; University of Ottawa, 1969–75, M.A. **Family:** Married Donald Shields, 1957; four daughters, one son. **Career:** Editorial assistant, *Canadian Slavonic Papers,* 1972–74; faculty member, University of Ottawa, 1976–77, and University of British Columbia, 1978–79. Since 1980, faculty member, University of Manitoba; since 1996, chancellor, University of Winnipeg. **Awards:** Canada Council grant, 1972, 1974, 1976; Canadian Authors Association prize, 1976, for *Small Ceremonies;* Marion Engel award, Writers' Development Trust, 1990; Governor General's award for fiction, 1993; National Book Critics Circle award, 1994; Canadian Book Sellers' award, 1994; Manitoba Book of the Year award, 1994; Pulitzer prize for fiction, 1995; National Book Critics Circle award, 1995. Honorary doctorate: University of Ottawa, 1995; Hanover College, 1996; Queen's University, 1996; University of Winnipeg, 1996; University of British Columbia, 1996; University of Western Ontario, 1997; University of Toronto, 1998; Concordia University, 1998. Order of Canada, 1998. **Agent:** Bella Pomer, 22 Shallmar Blvd., Toronto, Ontario M5N 2Z8, Canada. **Address:** 701–237 Wellington Cr., Winnipeg, Manitoba R3M 0A1, Canada.

PUBLICATIONS

Novels

Small Ceremonies. Toronto, McGraw Hill Ryerson, 1976; London, Fourth Estate, 1995; New York, Penguin, 1996.
The Box Garden. Toronto, McGraw Hill Ryerson, 1977; London, Fourth Estate, 1995; New York, Penguin, 1996.
Happenstance. Toronto, McGraw Hill Ryerson, 1980; with *A Fairly Conventional Woman,* London, Fourth Estate, 1993, New York, Viking, 1994.
A Fairly Conventional Woman. Toronto, Macmillan Canada, 1982; with *Happenstance,* London, Fourth Estate, 1993, New York, Viking, 1994.
Swann: A Mystery. Don Mills, Ontario, Stoddart, 1987; New York, Viking, 1989; London, Fourth Estate, 1992.
A Celibate Season, with Blanche Howard. Regina, Saskatchewan, Coteau, 1991.
The Republic of Love. Toronto, Random House Canada, New York, Viking, and London, Fourth Estate, 1992.
The Stone Diaries. Toronto, Random House Canada, and London, Fourth Estate, 1993; New York, Viking, 1994.
Mary Swann. London, Fourth Estate, 1996.
Larry's Party. New York, Viking, 1997.

Short Stories

Various Miracles. Don Mills, Ontario, Stoddart, 1985; New York, Viking, 1989; London, Fourth Estate, 1994.
The Orange Fish. Toronto, Random House Canada, 1989; New York, Viking, 1990.
Dressing Up for the Carnival. New York, Viking, 2000.

Plays

Arrivals and Departures. N.p., Blizzard, 1990.
Thirteen Hands. N.p., Blizzard, 1993.

Poetry

Others. Ottawa, Borealis Press, 1972.
Intersect. Ottawa, Borealis Press, 1974.
Coming to Canada. Ottawa, Carleton University Press, 1992.

Other

Susanna Moodie: Voice and Vision. Ottawa, Borealis Press, 1976.
Fashion, Power, Guilt, and the Charity of Families (with Catherine Shields). Winnipeg, Blizzard Publishing, 1995.
Anniversary: A Comedy (with Dave Williamson). Winnipeg, Blizzard Publishing, and Buffalo, New York, 1998.

*

Manuscript Collection: National Library of Canada.

Carol Shields comments:

My novels have centred on half a dozen concerns: the lives of women, notions of gender, the force of time, the genesis of art, synchronicity, the relationship of fiction and biography.

* * *

Carol Shields adds something to a traditional theme of contemporary women writers: the difficulty of negotiating the gender gap. She explores this territory with signature-style humor and optimism. She does not perceive the problem with any less acuity for her funniness; she only gives her characters a likable resilience. Her writing uses a form of black humor that incites a giggle just because it so categorically refuses to romanticize the situation. Absurdity, satire, paradox, and mistaken identity are also the source of much pleasure.

Small Ceremonies and *The Box Garden* are twin novels about women who are martyring, fussbudgety, stingy, widowed, emotional-blackmailing. There is a wickedly funny mother of two grown daughters; and the two daughters themselves, one married with kids and living a life that looks full and enviable to her single sister—one out west in Vancouver, the other back home near mom in Manitoba. One novel per sister. Although the married sister doesn't often think of the single one, the single sister's envy is palpable. Shields has been compared to Margaret Laurence—*Small Ceremonies* has even been seen as derivative of Margaret Laurence's *A Jest of God* and *The Fire Dwellers.* This comparison may be rooted in their Canadian stock, and their interest in the profundity of the mundane. In *Small Ceremonies,* once you have read the narrative of the lucky, married sister, you know her jealous sister's vision is skewed. The marriage isn't so rosy, communication isn't so flourishing, and romance isn't so hot as the sister thought.

This intertextuality makes good suspense and enriches the plot for one who reads both novels. Shields does not hide her derivativeness but rather makes the derivative nature of writing theme and plot the subject of many jokes throughout her canon. Her main characters are all writers of some description, and each one commits a fraud, an infringement, a plagiarism, or a distortion in the course of plying a trade. According to one of her characters, who has stolen the plot of his best-seller from a novel written by his graduate student (who in turn ripped it off from her former landlord), there are only seven plots in the world, so you might as well make use of them. The resemblance of *The Box Garden* and *Small Ceremonies* in plot and character to Laurence's early work affected this reader—a Canadianist—in a pleasurable, comforting way, somewhat like the feeling of the scholar when encountering the repetition of facts already familiar to her: the sense that she is beginning to know the field.

In the 1980s, Shields tried a new genre: mystery. With this shift in direction, her writing gained individuality and force. *Swann: A*

Mystery is a hilarious send-up of academics, biographers, critics, archivists, book collectors, and conferenciers. Each of the four main characters has an interest in deceased poet Mary Swann. Each one's literary interest is adulterated by his or her own ambitions. But someone is stealing, buying, and destroying all of the remaining Swann manuscripts and artifacts, making it difficult for the others to carry on the international Swann conference with dignity. Perhaps Shields's criminal is not as difficult for the reader to identify as those in the best of Sherlock Holmes or Agatha Christie, but what Shields provides is a romp through the corruptions of the book business and an exposé of the average psyche: the small lies that normal people tell, the little corners that they cut, and their rationalizations that help make their behavior seem acceptable in the context of the lonely, bookish lives they lead. ''Who would ever know?'' is the question, not ''Is this right or wrong?''

Shields's skills as a short story writer are strong, especially in the 1985 collection *Various Miracles,* though falter somewhat in *The Orange Fish,* published four years later. The first volume contains several gems. The subject about which Shields writes best is mother-daughter relationships that are full of ambivalence yet founded on unshakable love and understanding. The mother-daughter bond is so much more profound or real than the man-woman connection that the latter is nearly always a source of jest. Nor is the preference meant to show favoritism of the female; rather it honors the bonding of women and of motherhood while questioning the strength of most romantic female-male ties. Shields shows her characters, especially the ''sensitive one of the family,'' relating to, identifying with, and rebelling against their mothers but always returning later to seek them out, to question, to support, to respect, and to understand. Her latest collection of short fiction, *Dressing Up for the Carnival,* tells many stories about those who yearn to be successful artists and in one way or another come up short. ''The Scarf,'' for example, may at first be about a successful writer, but after lunch with a friend she discovers her own success may not be a direct comparison to her talent.

The Stone Diaries, which won the Pulitzer Prize and the Governor General's Award, is a rich portrayal of inner-bloom in Daisy Goodwill's later life. Daisy's early life is marred with difficulty—her mother dies in childbirth and her father is prone to disappearance. Daisy marries, but her husband commits suicide. She marries professor Barker Flett and she lives out her life with the humorous sarcasm and wit of a survivor. Daisy, a garden columnist, has a penchant for gossip, recipes, and other fragments of life congealed in a fluidity of prose. Much like Daisy, Shields enjoins the fragments of postmodern life with the sometimes monotonous rootedness of daily life. This remarkable tension is all the more served by a character of later years and great depth.

Shields's themes are typical of postmodern fiction: mother-daughter symbiosis; husband-wife estrangement; the inventiveness of the writer; the pretentiousness of the academy; loneliness and our anger at our aloneness; the role that chance plays in all encounters and happenings, good or bad. Her writer-protagonists are so literary that, in the end, they see their own selves as characters in a book. Successful feminist critic Sarah Maloney suddenly chooses marriage because she wants to live a good metaphor. Anatomizing her psyche, she says of ''the irrepressible Sarah,'' her academic self, ''Her awful energy seems to require too much of me, and I wonder: Where is her core? Does she even have a core? I want to live for a time without irony, without rhetoric, in a cool, solid metaphor. A conch shell, that would be nice.''

Shields herself cannot live without irony, a fact for which her readers should be grateful.

—Andy Solomon, updated by Maureen Aitken

SHREVE, Anita

Nationality: American. **Born:** Dedham, Massachusetts, 1946. **Education:** Tufts University. **Family:** Married; two children. **Career:** Journalist assigned to Nairobi, Kenya, late 1970s; writer for *US* magazine, *New York Times,* and *New York* magazine, New York; freelance writer, 1986—; has taught at Amherst College, Massachusetts. Lives in western Massachusetts. **Awards:** PEN/L. L. Winship Award; New England Book Award for Fiction.

Publications

Novels

Eden Close. New York, Harcourt, 1989.
Strange Fits of Passion. New York, Harcourt, 1991.
Where or When. New York, Harcourt, 1993.
Resistance. Boston, Little, Brown, 1995.
The Weight of Water. Boston, Little, Brown, 1997.
The Pilot's Wife. Boston, Little, Brown, 1998.
Fortune's Rocks. Boston, Little, Brown, 2000.

Other

Dr. Balter's Child Sense: Understanding and Handling the Common Problems of Infancy and Early Childhood (with Lawrence Balter). New York, Poseidon Press, 1985.
Dr. Balter's Baby Sense (with Lawrence Balter). New York, Poseidon Press, 1985.
Working Woman: A Guide to Fitness and Health (with Patricia Lone). St. Louis, Missouri, Mosby, 1986.
Remaking Motherhood: How Working Mothers Are Shaping Our Children's Future. New York, Viking, 1987.
Who's in Control?: Dr. Balter's Guide to Discipline without Combat (with Lawrence Balter). New York, Poseidon Press, 1988.
Women Together, Women Alone: The Legacy of the Consciousness-Raising Movement. New York, Viking, 1989.

* * *

Anita Shreve is not only an award-winning fiction writer, but she has also been recognized for her non-fiction works. In her non-fiction career, Shreve focuses in the area of women's studies and psychology, often examining important issues such as working and single mothers. In her novels, which are frequently set in New England, Shreve frequently juxtaposes the past and the present while weaving in a thread of mystery and suspense. Shreve is particularly interested in male/female relationships and repeatedly emphasizes the hardships of marriage, especially for women. In her first two novels, *Eden Close* and *Strange Fits of Passion*, Shreve examines the oppression of domestic abuse. Her next four novels—*Where or When*, *Resistance*, *The Weight of Water*, and *The Pilot's Wife*—explore the theme of adultery, while a subsequent novel, *Fortune's Rocks*, investigates scandal and disgrace in a wealthy New England family.

Eden Close and *Strange Fits of Passion* follow Shreve's usual pattern of mystery and intrigue. Both of these novels focus on how past events affect the present, while concentrating on domestic violence and undiscovered secrets that link the characters. While *Eden Close* examines violence against women in a non-political manner, *Strange Fits of Passion* takes a different approach. *Eden Close* tells the story of Andrew and Eden, who grew up next door to one another. When Eden is raped, the love between the two friends is postponed. While Eden is blinded and remains at home, Andrew goes to college and begins a career. It is only after Andrew returns home for his mother's funeral that their love is rekindled and Andrew goes in search of Eden's attacker.

Strange Fits of Passion, which also examines domestic violence, is told through a reporter's notes and a woman's letters from prison. The story opens with vague references to the murder of Maureen's abusive husband. A reporter, Helen Scofield, observes the imprisoned Maureen and composes a magazine piece about her life. *Strange Fits of Passion* was originally intended to be a non-fiction work. Shreve was especially attracted to the stories that domestic abuse survivors shared with her, and, when it was time to write the novel, she felt that she could more candidly portray the life of a battered woman through a fictitious narrator.

Where or When is the first of Shreve's four novels that discuss adultery. Sian and Charles, both unhappily married, awaken their old romance that began when they were young. This novel shifts between the viewpoints of the two main characters as they reveal their feelings about their current love affair and their past relationship. The novel has been criticized for being nothing more than a morality play, telling the universal story of sinners forced to pay for their transgressions.

Resistance also details adultery and the struggle with trust and betrayal. This text, set in Nazi-occupied Belgium, tells the story of a wounded American pilot, Ted Brice, who falls in love with the unhappily married Claire Daussois, who furnishes a safehouse for him during World War II. While this novel could fall into the familiar morality tale of good and evil, Shreve resurrects it with obscurities that could fall anywhere between the two categories.

Shreve's fifth novel, *The Weight of Water*, returns to her New England setting. Shreve originally recorded the idea for this work in a short story that was published in the *Cimarron Review* and many years later developed it into a full-length novel. The main character, Jean, is given the assignment of photographing the Isle of Shoals off the coast of New Hampshire, the scene of an infamous nineteenth-century double murder. Traveling to the island, Jean notices a romance developing between her husband and his brother's girlfriend. The text examines the problems in Jean's marriage and the ramifications of jealousy while paralleling modern day action with an 1873 double murder.

The Pilot's Wife, like *Resistance*, opens with a fallen aircraft, only in this case, it is a commercial jet and no one survives the crash. This terrible accident continues Shreve's theme of tragedy and betrayal. After Kathryn Lyons learns of the death of her husband, she discovers the mistress that he kept in England. *The Pilot's Wife* is truly about inner anguish and details one woman's emotional aftermath following the discovery of her husband's affair. Some critics have claimed that the book lacks a clear focus and declared that it is not apparent whether Shreve is writing a psychological study of women in crisis or a suspense romance.

Fortune's Rocks is set in the late nineteenth century. This novel has been compared to *Wuthering Heights*, but, like *The Pilot's Wife*, *Fortune's Rocks* has been criticized for its weak female characters and unsuccessful feminist message. Olympia Biddeford is the daughter of a wealthy Boston family. After spending the summer at her father's New Hampshire estate, Olympia is entranced by John Haskell. When she ends up pregnant, her father insists that she break off the relationship. Despite the main character's quest for independence, Olympia only overcomes her problems because of her family's wealth and societal status. She does not act independently, and, without her family, would probably fail.

With each novel, Shreve receives more critical and popular attention. While examining the struggle of the human heart, she manages to incorporate page-turning thrill and suspense. Shreve's stories of trust and betrayal will gain her the recognition she deserves because of her honest portrayal of human suffering and its aftermath.

—Marta Krogh

SIDHWA, Bapsi

Nationality: American (Pakistani exile, emigrated to United States, 1984). **Born:** Bapsi Bhandara, Karachi, Pakistan, 11 August 1938. **Education:** Kinnaird College for Women, B.A. 1956. **Family:** Married 1) Gustad Kermani, 1957 (died); 2) Noshir R. Sidhwa, 1963; has three children. **Career:** Conducted novel writing workshops, Rice University, 1984–86; assistant professor of creative writing, University of Houston, 1985. President, International Women's Club of Lahore, 1975–77. Pakistan's delegate to Asian Women's Congress, 1975. **Agent:** Elizabeth Grossman, Sterling Lord Literary Agency Inc., 1 Madison Ave, New York, New York 10021, U.S.A. **Address:** 1600 Massachusetts Ave., #603, Cambridge, Massachusetts 02138, U.S.A.

Publications

Novels

The Crow Eaters. Lahore, Pakistan, Imani Press, 1978; London, Cape, 1980; New York, St. Martin's Press, 1983.

The Bride. New York, St. Martin's Press, and London, Cape, 1983.

Ice-Candy-Man. London, Heinemann, 1988; as *Cracking India,* Minneapolis, Milkweed Editions, 1991.

An American Brat. Minneapolis, Milkweed Editions, 1993; London, Penguin, 1994.

*

Critical Studies: *Configurations of Exile: South Asian Writers and Their World* by Chelva Kanaganayakam, Toronto, TSAR, 1995; *The Novels of Bapsi Sidhwa,* edited by R.K. Dhawan and Novy Kapadia, New Delhi, Prestige Books, 1996.

* * *

With the publication of her third novel, *Ice-Candy-Man* (or *Cracking India*), Bapsi Sidhwa established herself as Pakistan's leading English-language novelist. Pakistan is the location of Sidhwa's first three novels, and in each there is a strong sense of place and community which she uses to examine the post-colonial Pakistani identity. In her novel *The American Brat* she shifts the predominant locale of her fiction from Lahore and Pakistan to various cities across America as she explores the Parsi/Pakistani diaspora. Multiple alternative voices are heard in Sidhwa's fiction through her choice of narrators and characters from Pakistan's minority communities—members of the Parsi religion, Kohistanis from Pakistan's Tribal Territories, and, perhaps most importantly, women.

Sidhwa's first three novels, although very different from one another, share what Anita Desai has described as "a passion for history and for truth telling." And in each her desire to understand the terrible events of the Partition of the Indian sub-continent in 1947 and the subsequent birth of Pakistan as a nation is evident. Her first-published novel, *The Crow Eaters,* is a delightfully rambunctious comedy in which Faredoon Junglewalla tells the story of his life and times from the turn of the century to the eve of Partition. In common with such a writer as Salman Rushdie, Sidhwa believes that in order to understand any single event it is necessary to consider the many events which led up to it. Like the author herself, Faredoon is a Parsi and his story takes the reader to the heart of that minority community. The focus on the Parsis, their rites, and customs, not only provides a rich subject in itself, but also an ideal vehicle for observing the history of India, and in particular the events played out between Hindus, Sikhs, and Muslims, from a detached yet intimate insider/outsider perspective. Through the contact Faredoon and his family have with other groups in India (including the British) a picture of the whole is skillfully created. But always, behind her panoramic canvas, history ticks away and moves the reader gradually but inexorably towards 1947.

Whereas *The Crow Eaters* ends with the horrors of Partition still to come, *The Bride* (or *The Pakistani Bride,* her second published novel, but actually written before *The Crow Eaters*) uses those horrors as its starting point, and thus focuses on the first chapter of Pakistan's history as an independent nation. In this novel Sidhwa again makes use of a detached and marginalized character from one of Pakistan's minority groups. She uses Qasim, a Kohistani tribesman, as her window onto the period of history she treats. After witnessing a brutal attack on a train of refugees (a common Partition motif), Qasim adopts a young girl left orphaned by the massacre. When, years later, he takes Zaitoon to his ancestral village to be married, Sidhwa demonstrates the extent of the cultural divisions which exist within the newly drawn political boundaries of Pakistan, and in doing so raises questions about the construction of national identity. Her focus on the relationship between dominant and minority communities in Pakistan is extended specifically to include gender relations, which indeed is a strong theme in all her fiction.

In both *The Crow Eaters* and *The Bride,* Partition is a significant event without being the main subject of either novel. But in *Ice-Candy-Man*—which is revisionist history of Partition from a Pakistani perspective, and major contribution to the growing list of novels which treat Partition—Sidhwa meets that terrible event head-on. Here Sidhwa returns to the Parsi community and chooses Lenny, a young Parsi girl with polio, as her narrator. The political and historical consciousness of her previous novels reaches a pinnacle in this novel, and the young narrator, naive, innocent, and free of the various prejudices an older narrator would be subject to, proves to be an ideal means of exposing the complexities of the period. The frequent intertextual referencing in *Ice-Candy-Man* is testament to Sidhwa's dual literary heritage, but more significantly, her use of Eugene O'Neill's play *The Iceman Cometh,* which provides both the title and the framework for *Ice-Candy-Man,* insists on the importance of fiction as a shaping force of history, and lends one more twist to Sidhwa's exploration of the nature of truth.

In her richly comic novel *An American Brat,* Sidhwa chronicles the departure of Feroza Ginwalla—a member of the Junglewalla clan first encountered in *The Crow Eaters*—from an increasingly fundamentalist Pakistan of the late 1970s and her subsequent exposure to American culture. More than simply the tale of a young girl coming of age, it shows Feroza coming to terms with her identity in the increasingly diasporic climate of the late twentieth century. Sidhwa convincingly handles the personal growth of her central character and the difficulties that arise when two cultures come into contact. This novel, with its focus on diaspora, is a logical extension of the interest in displacement and the clashes between communities which is present in all her previous three novels.

—Ralph J. Crane

SIGAL, Clancy

Nationality: American. **Born:** Chicago, Illinois, 6 September 1926. **Education:** The University of California, Los Angeles, B.A. in English 1950. Staff Sergeant in the United States Army Infantry, 1944–46. **Career:** Assistant to the Wage Coordinator, United Auto Workers, Detroit, 1946–47; story analyst, Columbia Pictures, Hollywood, 1952–54; agent, Jaffe Agency, Los Angeles, 1954–56. Member, Citizens Committee to Defend American Freedoms, Los Angeles, 1953–56, and Group 68, Americans in Britain Against the Indo-China War. Has lived in England since 1957. **Awards:** Houghton Mifflin Literary fellowship, 1962. **Agent:** Elaine Greene Ltd., 37 Goldhawk Road, London W12 8QQ. **Address:** 58 Willes Road, London N.W.5, England.

PUBLICATIONS

Novels

Weekend in Dinlock. Boston, Houghton Mifflin, and London, Secker and Warburg, 1960.
Going Away: A Report, A Memoir. Boston, Houghton Mifflin, 1962; London, Cape, 1963.
Zone of the Interior. New York, Crowell, 1976.
The Secret Defector. New York, HarperCollins, 1992.

Uncollected Short Story

"Doctor Marfa," in *Paris Review 35,* Fall 1965.

Play

Radio Play: *A Visit with Rose,* 1983.

* * *

Two documentary novels, *Weekend in Dinlock* and *Going Away,* have given Clancy Sigal a large reputation. These novels, imaginative fusions of autobiography, social history and fiction, convey a strong sense of time and place, a powerful feeling of reality.

Going Away (Sigal's first novel, though revised and published after *Weekend in Dinlock*) is subtitled ''A Report, A Memoir.'' It is a compendium of significant social and political observations, an ''American Studies'' novel answering the question, ''*What's it like in America these days?*'' The time is 1956, the opening days of the Hungarian Revolt, and the autobiographical narrator drives from Los Angeles to New York with the manuscript of a confessional novel, experiencing a nervous breakdown as he passes through America and reviews his past. It is an ''on-the-road'' novel, a pursuit of lost time, a gathering of the narrator's experiences and a diagnosis of America's spiritual and political malaise: ''For years, possibly since adolescence, I have dryly and studiously examined the indications of my own life as a clue to the country at large, as though reading a psychic thermometer.''

The narrator is half-Irish, half-Jewish, a radical ex-union-organizer, an ex-Hollywood-agent, an ex-soldier in Occupied Germany; by age twenty-nine he has led half a dozen full, complex lives and reached the end of his road in America. He realizes he must leave America in order to find it. He visits old friends and enemies, sees them in despair and collapse, so he flees his dead past encapsulated in an America of brutalizing forces—billboards, highways, movies, the blank, alienating face of capitalist culture.

Once in England, where he finished *Going Away,* Sigal also wrote a much smaller but beautifully articulated study of Yorkshire mines and miners, *Weekend in Dinlock.* A documentary study of a composite mining village in the midlands, the book compares favorably with George Orwell's classic *The Road to Wigan Pier.* It chronicles the miner's life in the nationalized mines and draws almost the same conclusion Orwell made a generation earlier—that mining is an atrocity, a deadening, dehumanizing torment on which all industrial civilization rests. The novel is also the story of Davie, a Lawrence-like young man who is both a gifted painter and a miner, caught between the need to paint, to escape Dinlock, and the powerful *machismo* ethic of the miners which demands that he stay on the job and prove himself at the coal face. Finally, the narrator leaves Davie wrestling with his irresolvable conflict, still trapped by Dinlock.

This brilliant small study is a logical extension of *Going Away.* The narrator has fled America and found in England's coal country yet another world of dehumanizing technology and alienated individuals. The wide-open feeling of crossing America (the loneliness of the land itself) is replaced by the paranoid claustrophobia of the mine shaft and the paranoid closed society of the provincial village. Both novels chronicle the pressures of modern life on the individual, both reflect Sigal's own history: ''I was a member, in good standing, of the Double Feature Generation: nothing new was startling to me.'' Sigal, in *Going Away,* gives the intense, confessional view of the 1950s in the backwash of McCarthyism, the collapse of the old left, and draws conclusions about his own sense of self: ''I see no salvation in personal relationships, in political action, or in any job I might undertake in society. Everything in me cries out that we are meaningless pieces of paste; everything in me hopes this is not the end of the story.''

Zone of the Interior carries forward Sigal's odyssey into the 1960s, exploring a subculture of artists and dropouts. An R.D. Laing-like protagonist observes the disintegration of culture and personality in British society of the time. The world has gone thoroughly mad, and the personal experience of insanity, first encountered in *Going Away,* seems less scarifying against a background of general disillusionment, drugs, and the cornucopia of therapeutic theories that promise personal salvation in the face of apocalypse. *The Secret Defector* carries forward earlier themes, portraying the progress of an American leftist writer named Gus Black through the England of the swinging sixties, the depressed and punkish seventies, and the Thatcherite eighties.

—William J. Schafer

SILKO, Leslie Marmon

Nationality: American. **Born:** 1948. **Education:** Board of Indian Affairs schools, Laguna, New Mexico, and a Catholic school in Albuquerque; University of New Mexico, Albuquerque, B.A. (summa cum laude) in English 1969; studied law briefly. **Family:** Has two sons. **Career:** Taught for 2 years at Navajo Community College, Tsaile, Arizona; lived in Ketchikan, Alaska, for 2 years; taught at University of New Mexico. Since 1978 professor of English, University of Arizona, Tucson. **Awards:** National Endowment for the Arts award, 1974; *Chicago Review* award, 1974; Pushcart prize, 1977; MacArthur Foundation grant, 1983. **Address:** Department of English, University of Arizona, Tucson, Arizona 85721, U.S.A.

PUBLICATIONS

Novel

Ceremony. New York, Viking Press, 1977.
Almanac of the Dead. New York, Simon and Schuster, 1991.
Gardens in the Dunes. New York, Scribner, 1999.

Uncollected Short Stories

''Bravura'' and ''Humaweepi, the Warrior Priest,'' in *The Man to Send Rain Clouds: Contemporary Stories by American Indians,* edited by Kenneth Rosen. New York, Viking Press, 1974.
''Laughing and Loving,'' in *Come to Power,* edited by Dick Lourie. Trumansburg, New York, Crossing Press, 1974.
''Private Property,'' in *Earth Power Coming,* edited by Simon J. Ortiz. Tsaile, Arizona, Navajo Community College Press, 1983.

Play

Lullaby, with Frank Chin, adaptation of the story by Silko (produced San Francisco, 1976).

Poetry

Laguna Woman. Greenfield Center, New York, Greenfield Review Press, 1974.
Storyteller (includes short stories). New York, Seaver, 1981.
Voices Under One Sky. Freedom, California, Crossing Press, 1994.
Rain. New York, Library Fellows of the Whitney Museum of American Art, Grenfell Press, 1996.

Other

The Delicacy and Strength of Lace: Letters Between Leslie Marmon Silko and James A. Wright, edited by Anne Wright. St. Paul, Minnesota, Graywolf Press, 1986.

Yellow Woman, edited by Melody Graulich. New Brunswick, New Jersey, Rutgers University Press, 1993.

Rooster and the Power of Love (correspondence). New York, Norton, 1995.

Yellow Woman and a Beauty of the Spirit: Essays on Native American Life Today. New York, Simon & Schuster, 1996.

Conversations with Leslie Marmon Silko, edited by Ellen L. Arnold. Jackson, University Press of Mississippi, 2000.

*

Manuscript Collection: University of Arizona, Tucson.

Critical Studies: *Leslie Marmon Silko* by Per Seyersted, Boise, Idaho, Boise State University, 1980; *Four American Indian Literary Masters* by Alan R. Velie, Norman, University of Oklahoma Press, 1982.

* * *

Through her works Leslie Marmon Silko has defined herself as a Native American writer, concentrating on ethnic themes, motifs, and genres. She had already established a minor reputation as a short story writer when she published her novel *Ceremony,* which, along with N. Scott Momaday's *House Made of Dawn,* is one of the two most important novels in modern Native American literature.

Like the earlier novel, *Ceremony* focuses on a young American Indian who, under somewhat similar circumstances, struggles to realign himself with traditional Indian culture and reservation life after having been torn away. Tayo, Silko's half-Laguna, half-Anglo protagonist, returns to his New Mexico reservation just after World War II. The horrors of the war against the Japanese in the Philippine jungles have led him to the brink of insanity and the mental ward of a veterans' hospital. Back home, he is in constant danger of succumbing to mental illness as he faces a sad, apparently hopeless life. His half-breed status among his own people and the legacy of shame from his promiscuous mother, now dead, exacerbate the pain of living among a dispossessed people who are constantly reminded of their lost heritage. He associates with fellow veterans who fill their meaningless lives with alcohol and anecdotes about their sexual exploits among white women during the war, and he observes Indian prostitutes and winos in scenes of skid-row squalor that remind him of his own ruined mother. Guided by Betonie, an old medicine man, Tayo finds a helpmeet in a sort of Indian earth-goddess figure and gradually proceeds through the series of mystical ceremonies and rituals that will make him whole again, and in the process he outwits the witchcraft of his evil antagonist Emo.

Storyteller, an anthology of tribal folk tales, short stories, family anecdotes, photographs, and poems, demonstrated Silko's continuing fascination with narrative, but fourteen years passed before she published her second novel, *Almanac of the Dead.* The reason for the interlude is obvious: *Almanac* is massive and ambitious. This apocalyptic novel, set in the unspecified present, describes the collapse of white European-American civilization and the resurgence of Native American peoples. It is divided into six sections: "The United States of America," "Mexico," "Africa," "The Americas," "The Fifth World", and "One World, Many Tribes." The main action begins at a heavily fortified ranch near Tucson, Arizona, and focuses on the characters Lecha and Zeta, sixty-year-old twin sisters of Mexican extraction and grand-daughters of Yoeme, a Yaqui woman who escaped a death sentence for sedition in 1918. Lecha is a psychic with visionary powers. Zeta, with Lecha's estranged son Ferro, directs an operation for smuggling drugs, illegal immigrants, and arms. The sisters inherit from Yoeme an ancient, fragmentary almanac of tribal narratives which, Yoeme believed, contains a mysterious power "that would bring all the tribal people of the Americas together to retake the land." The working out of this prophecy generates the novel's plot as a whole, and at the open-ended conclusion, a series of bombings and murders in Tucson coincides with a gathering of shamans and would-be revolutionaries while in Mexico an army of disfranchised Indians begins to march north. But in developing this overall scheme, Silko weaves together multiple interrelated tales and anecdotes, employing about seventy characters and a wide range of settings. The overall movement toward the destruction of decadent Western culture in North America is associated with the rapid decline of late capitalism predicted by Marx.

As a Native American writer, Silko deals with the usual dichotomies: white culture is cruel, artificial, dead, cut off from nature, based on greed; traditional Indian culture is holistic, natural, communal. However, Silko is by no means simple-minded in working within this framework of values, and she is a close observer of both nature and human nature.

Like many contemporary writers, Silko experiments with the narrative line, weaving in and out of chronological time as she explores the consciousness of her characters. However, her habitual use of what she takes to be the Indian concept of reality—or at least one's experience of reality—as narrative (or myth) enables her to avoid the morbid extremes of self-consciousness that can result from an analysis of the narrative process. She begins *Ceremony* with a description of Thought-Woman, the spider, "sitting in her room/ thinking of a story now/I'm telling you the story she is thinking." In *Almanac of the Dead* the visionary or mystical mode of storytelling is represented by the almanac itself, as well as by the visionary Lecha and by a character named Tacho, who offers prophecies about "The Reign of the Fire-Eye Macaw" (the present era).

The success of *Ceremony* was largely due to Silko's ability to deal convincingly with Indian traditions and myth while recognizing the demands of psychological realism and exercising a strict control over her narrative art. *Almanac of the Dead* is extremely ambitious but uneven and finally unsatisfying as a work of fiction: narrative control seems to break down toward the end of the novel as realism is sacrificed to apocalyptic vision.

Silko, of Laguna Pueblo, Mexican, and Anglo descent, has become more than a personal, tribal, or even regional writer: she is an important figure in Native American literature. As such, she writes for two audiences: the small group of readers who identify with her ethnic background and share her Indian sensibilities and the general readers who, regardless of their sympathy for Indian problems and concerns, find her works somewhat exotic. Indeed, this exotic quality provides a large part of their appeal. Silko herself reveals insights into her art of storytelling in the series of letters she exchanged with James Wright prior to that writer's death in 1980, published as *Delicacy and Strength of Lace.* Since the image of the Indian has always been problematic in American culture—with strong tendencies toward the mythic, either ''Devil'' or ''Noble Savage''—Silko, like other writers in her position, must be wary of appealing to easy sentimentality or other conventional responses.

One interesting development in literary criticism in recent years has been to place Silko and other Native American writers in the context of postcolonial, postmodern literature. Silko is said to be searching in her fiction for an alternative to both traditional Western, humanist discourse and the postmodern critique of that discourse (which denies the autonomous subject). From this point of view her project as a Native American writer has been to model a ''dynamic'' identity and redefine multiple possibilities of the subject. On the one hand, Silko obviously offers a powerful critique of the Western, ''imperial'' self that has worked toward the dominance and destruction of nature and native peoples. On the other hand, Silko has expressed biting criticism of fellow Native American novelist Louise Erdrich for her ''postmodern, so-called experimental influences.'' Silko remains committed to the referential dimension of literary language and to the shared, communal experience that she associates with Native American oral tradition.

—Clinton Machann

SILVERBERG, Robert

Pseudonyms: Walker Chapman; Ivar Jorgenson; Calvin M. Knox; David Osborne; Robert Randall; Lee Sebastian. **Nationality:** American. **Born:** New York City, 15 January 1935. **Education:** Columbia University, New York, A.B. 1956. **Family:** Married Barbara H. Brown in 1956. **Career:** Full-time writer: associate editor, *Amazing,* January 1969 issue, and associate editor, *Fantastic,* February-April 1969 issues. President, Science Fiction Writers of America, 1967–68. **Awards:** Hugo award, 1956, 1969; Nebula award, for story, 1969, 1971, 1974, for novel, 1971, for novella, 1985; Jupiter award, 1973; Prix Apollo, 1976; *Locus* award, 1981. Guest of Honor, 28th World Science Fiction Convention, 1970. **Agent:** Ralph Vicinanza, 432 Park Avenue South, Room 1205, New York, New York 10016, U.S.A.

Publications

Novels (series: Majipoor; Nidor)

The 13th Immortal. New York, Ace, 1957.
Master of Life and Death. New York, Ace, 1957; London, Sidgwick and Jackson, 1977.
The Shrouded Planet (Nidor; as Robert Randall, with Randall Garrett). New York, Gnome Press, 1957; London, Mayflower, 1964.
Invaders from Earth. New York, Ace, 1958; London, Sidgwick and Jackson, 1977.
Invincible Barriers (as David Osborne). New York, Avalon, 1958.
Stepsons of Terra. New York, Ace, 1958.
Aliens from Space (as David Osborne). New York, Avalon, 1958.
Starhaven (as Ivar Jorgenson). New York, Avalon, 1958.
The Dawning Light (Nidor; as Robert Randall, with Randall Garrett). New York, Gnome Press, 1959; London, Mayflower, 1964.
The Planet Killers. New York, Ace, 1959.
Collision Course. New York, Avalon, 1961.
The Seed of Earth. New York, Ace, 1962; London, Hamlyn, 1978.
Recalled to Life. New York, Lancer, 1962; revised edition, New York, Doubleday, 1972; London Gollancz, 1974.
The Silent Invaders. New York, Ace, 1963; London, Dobson, 1975.
Regan's Planet. New York, Pyramid, 1964.
A Pair from Space. New York, Belmont, 1965.
To Open the Sky. New York, Ballantine, 1967; London, Sphere, 1970.
Thorns. New York, Ballantine, 1967; London, Rapp and Whiting, 1969.
Those Who Watch. New York, New American Library, 1967; London, New English Library, 1977.
The Time-Hoppers. New York, Doubleday, 1967; London, Sidgwick and Jackson, 1968.
Planet of Death. New York, Holt Rinehart, 1967.
Hawksbill Station. New York, Doubleday, 1968; as *The Anvil of Time,* London, Sidgwick and Jackson, 1969.
The Masks of Time. New York, Ballantine, 1968; as *Vornan-19,* London, Sidgwick and Jackson, 1970.
Up the Line. New York, Ballantine, 1969; London, Gollancz, 1987.
Nightwings. New York, Avon, 1969; London, Sidgwick and Jackson, 1972.
To Live Again. New York, Doubleday, 1969; London, Sidgwick and Jackson, 1975.
Downward to the Earth. New York, Doubleday, 1970; London, Gollancz, 1977.
Tower of Glass. New York, Scribner, 1970; London, Panther, 1976.
A Robert Silverberg Omnibus. London, Sidgwick and Jackson, 1970.
The World Inside. New York, Doubleday, 1971; London, Millington, 1976.
A Time of Changes. New York, Doubleday, 1971; London, Gollancz, 1973.
Son of Man. New York, Ballantine, 1971; London, Panther, 1979.
The Book of Skulls. New York, Scribner, 1971; London, Gollancz, 1978.
Dying Inside. New York, Scribner, 1972; London, Sidgwick and Jackson, 1974.
The Second Trip. New York, Doubleday, 1972; London, Gollancz, 1979.
The Stochastic Man. New York, Harper, 1975; London, Gollancz, 1976.
Shadrach in the Furnace. Indianapolis, Bobbs Merrill, 1976; London, Gollancz, 1977.
Lord Valentine's Castle (Majipoor). New York, Harper, and London, Gollancz, 1980.
The Desert of Stolen Dreams. Columbia, Pennsylvania, Underwood Miller, 1981.
A Robert Silverberg Omnibus. New York, Harper, 1981.
Majipoor Chronicles. New York, Arbor House, and London, Gollancz, 1982.
Valentine Pontifex. New York, Arbor House, 1983; London, Gollancz, 1984.
Lord of Darkness. New York, Arbor House, and London, Gollancz, 1983.
The Conglomeroid Cocktail Party. New York, Arbor House, 1984; London, Gollancz, 1985.
Gilgamesh the King. New York, Arbor House, 1984; London, Gollancz, 1985.
Tom O'Bedlam. New York, Fine, 1985; London, Gollancz, 1986.
Sailing to Byzantium. Columbia, Pennsylvania, Underwood Miller, 1985.
Star of the Gypsies. New York, Fine, 1986; London, Gollancz, 1987.

At Winter's End. New York, Warner, and London, Gollancz, 1988.
The Secret Sharer (novella). Los Angeles, California, Underwood Miller, 1988.
The Mutant Season, with Karen Haber. New York, Doubleday, 1989.
Time Gate, with Bill Fawcett. New York, Baen, 1989.
To the Land of the Living. London, Gollancz, 1989; Norwalk, Connecticut, Easton Press, 1990.
The Queen of Springtime. London, Gollancz, 1989.
The New Springtime. New York, Warner, 1990.
Nightfall, with Isaac Asimov. New York, Doubleday, and London, Gollancz, 1990.
The Man in the Maze. London, Gollancz, 1990.
In Another Country, with *Vintage Season* by C.L. Moore. New York, Tor, 1990.
Child of Time, with Isaac Asimov. London, Gollancz, 1991.
The Face of the Waters. New York, Bantam, and London, Grafton, 1991.
The Ugly Little Boy, with Isaac Asimov. New York, Doubleday, 1992.
The Positronic Man, with Isaac Asimov. London, Gollancz, 1992; New York, Doubleday, 1993.
Kingdoms of the Wall. London, HarperCollins, 1992; New York, Bantam, 1993.
Thebes of the Hundred Gates. London, HarperCollins, 1993.
Hot Sky at Midnight. New York, Bantam, and London, HarperCollins, 1994.
The Mountains of Majipoor. New York, Bantam, and London, Macmillan, 1995.
Starborne. New York, Bantam Books, 1996.
Sorcerers of Majipoor. New York, N.Y., HarperPrism, 1997.
The Alien Years. New York, HarperPrism, 1998.
Lord Prestimion. New York, HarperPrism, 1999.

Novels as Calvin M. Knox

Lest We Forget Thee, Earth. New York, Ace, 1958.
The Plot Against Earth. New York, Ace, 1959.
One of Our Asteroids Is Missing. New York, Ace, 1964.

Short Stories

Next Stop the Stars. New York, Ace, 1962; London, Dobson, 1979.
Godling, Go Home! New York, Belmont, 1964.
To Worlds Beyond. Philadelphia, Chilton, 1965; London, Sphere, 1969.
Needle in a Timestack. New York, Ballantine, 1966; London, Sphere, 1967; revised edition, Sphere, 1979.
To Open the Sky. New York, Ballantine, 1967.
Dimension Thirteen. New York, Ballantine, 1969.
Parsecs and Parables. New York, Doubleday, 1970; London, Hale, 1973.
The Cube Root of Uncertainty. New York, Macmillan, 1970.
Moonferns and Starsongs. New York, Ballantine, 1971.
The Reality Trip and Other Implausibilities. New York, Ballantine, 1972.
Valley Beyond Time. New York, Dell, 1973.
Unfamiliar Territory. New York, Scribner, 1973; London, Gollancz, 1975.
Earth's Other Shadow. New York, New American Library, 1973; London, Millington, 1977.
Born with the Dead (three novellas). New York, Random House, 1974; London, Gollancz, 1975.
Sundance and Other Science Fiction Stories. Nashville, Nelson, 1974; London, Abelard Schuman, 1975.
The Feast of St. Dionysus. New York, Scribner, 1975; London, Gollancz, 1976.
The Shores of Tomorrow. Nashville, Nelson, 1976.
The Best of Robert Silverberg. New York, Pocket Books, 1976; London, Sidgwick and Jackson, 1977.
Capricorn Games. New York, Random House, 1976; London, Gollancz, 1978.
The Songs of Summer and Other Stories. London, Gollancz, 1979.
World of a Thousand Colors. New York, Arbor House, 1982.
Beyond the Safe Zone: Collected Short Fiction. New York, Fine, 1986.

Fiction (for children)

Revolt on Alpha C. New York, Crowell, 1955.
Starman's Quest. New York, Gnome Press, 1959.
Lost Race of Mars. Philadelphia, Winston, 1960.
Time of the Great Freeze. New York, Holt Rinehart, 1964.
Conquerors from the Darkness. New York, Holt Rinehart, 1965.
The Calibrated Alligator. New York, Holt Rinehart, 1969.
The Gate of Worlds. New York, Holt Rinehart, 1967; London, Gollancz, 1978.
Across a Billion Years. New York, Dial Press, 1969; London, Gollancz, 1977.
The Man in the Maze. New York, Avon, and London, Sidgwick and Jackson, 1969.
Three Survived. New York, Holt Rinehart, 1969.
World's Fair 1992. Chicago, Follett, 1970.
Sunrise on Mercury. Nashville, Nelson, 1975; London, Gollancz, 1983.
Project Pendulum. New York, Walker, 1987; London, Hutchinson, 1989.
Letters from Atlantis. New York, Atheneum, 1990.

Other (for children)

Treasures Beneath the Sea. Racine, Wisconsin, Whitman, 1960.
Lost Cities and Vanished Civilizations. Philadelphia, Chilton, 1962.
Sunken History: The Story of Underwater Archaeology. Philadelphia, Chilton, 1963.
Home of the Red Man: Indian North America Before Columbus. Greenwich, Connecticut, New York Graphic Society, 1963.
The Great Doctors. New York, Putnam, 1964.
The Man Who Found Nineveh: The Story of Austen Henry Layard. New York, Holt Rinehart, 1964; Kingswood, Surrey, World's Work, 1968.
The World of Coral. New York, Duell, 1965.
The Mask of Akhnaten. New York, Macmillan, 1965.
Socrates. New York, Putnam, 1965.
Niels Bohr, the Man Who Mapped the Atom. Philadelphia, Macrae Smith, 1965.
Forgotten by Time: A Book of Living Fossils. New York, Crowell, 1966.
Kublai Kahn, Lord of Xanadu (as Walker Chapman). Indianapolis, Bobbs Merrill, 1966.

Rivers (as Lee Sebastian). New York, Holt Rinehart, 1966.
To the Rock of Darius: The Story of Henry Rawlinson. New York, Holt Rinehart, 1966.
Four Men Who Changed the Universe. New York, Putnam, 1968.
The South Pole (as Lee Sebastian). New York, Holt Rinehart, 1968.
Bruce of the Blue Nile. New York, Holt Rinehart, 1969.

Other

First American into Space. Derby, Connecticut, Monarch, 1961.
The Fabulous Rockefellers. Derby, Connecticut, Monarch, 1963.
15 Battles That Changed the World. New York, Putnam, 1963.
Empires in the Dust. Philadelphia, Chilton, 1963.
Akhnaten, The Rebel Pharaoh. Philadelphia, Chilton, 1964.
Man Before Adam. Philadelphia, Macrae Smith, 1964.
The Loneliest Continent (as Walker Chapman). Greenwich, Connecticut, New York Graphic Society, 1965; London, Jarrolds, 1967.
Scientists and Scoundrels: A Book of Hoaxes. New York, Crowell, 1965.
The Old Ones: Indians of the American Southwest. Greenwich, Connecticut, New York Graphic Society, 1965.
Men Who Mastered the Atom. New York, Putnam, 1965.
The Great Wall of China. Philadelphia, Chilton, 1965.
Frontiers of Archaeology. Philadelphia, Chilton, 1966.
The Long Rampart: The Story of the Great Wall of China. Philadelphia, Chilton, 1966.
Bridges. Philadelphia, Macrae Smith, 1966.
The Dawn of Medicine. New York, Putnam, 1967.
The Adventures of Nat Palmer, Antarctic Explorer. New York, McGraw Hill, 1967.
The Auk, the Dodo, and the Oryx. New York, Crowell, 1967; Kingswood, Surrey, World's Work, 1969.
The Golden Dream: Seekers of El Dorado. Indianapolis, Bobbs Merrill, 1967.
Men Against Time: Salvage Archaeology in the United States. New York, Macmillan, 1967.
The Morning of Mankind. Greenwich, Connecticut, New York Graphic Society, 1967; Kingswood, Surrey, World's Work, 1970.
The World of the Rain Forest. New York, Meredith Press, 1967.
Light for the World: Edison and the Power Industry. Princeton, New Jersey, Van Nostrand, 1967.
Ghost Towns of the American West. New York, Crowell, 1968.
Mound Builders of Ancient America. Greenwich, Connecticut, New York Graphic Society, 1968.
Stormy Voyager: The Story of Charles Wilkes. Philadelphia, Lippincott, 1968.
The World of the Ocean Depths. New York, Meredith Press, 1968; Kingswood, Surrey, World's Work, 1970.
The Challenge of Climate: Man and His Environment. New York, Meredith Press, 1969; Kingswood, Surrey, World's Work, 1971.
Vanishing Giants: The Story of the Sequoias. New York, Simon and Schuster, 1969.
Wonders of Ancient Chinese Science. New York, Hawthorn, 1969.
The World of Space. New York, Meredith Press, 1969.
If I Forget Thee, O Jerusalem: American Jews and the State of Israel. New York, Morrow, 1970.
Mammoths, Mastodons, and Man. New York, McGraw Hill, 1970; Kingswood, Surrey, World's Work, 1972.
The Pueblo Revolt. New York, Weybright and Talley, 1970.
The Seven Wonders of the Ancient World (for children). New York, Crowell Collier, 1970.
Before the Sphinx. New York, Nelson, 1971.
Clocks for the Ages: How Scientists Date the Past. New York, Macmillan, 1971.
To the Western Shore: Growth of the United States 1776–1853. New York, Doubleday, 1971.
Into Space, with Arthur C. Clarke. New York, Harper, 1971.
John Muir: Prophet among the Glaciers. New York, Putnam, 1972.
The Longest Voyage: Circumnavigation in the Age of Discovery. Indianapolis, Bobbs Merrill, 1972.
The Realm of Prester John. New York, Doubleday, 1972.
The World Within the Ocean Wave. New York, Weybright and Talley, 1972.
The World Within the Tide Pool. New York, Weybright and Talley, 1972.
Drug Themes in Science Fiction. Rockville, Maryland, National Institute on Drug Abuse, 1974.
The Ultimate Dinosaur, with Byron Preiss, edited by Peter Dodson. New York, Bantam, 1992.
Reflections and Refractions: Thoughts on Science-Fiction, Science, and Other Matters. Grass Valley, California, Underwood Books, 1997.
Editor, *Great Adventures in Archaeology.* New York, Dial Press, 1964; London, Hale, 1966.
Editor, *Earthmen and Strangers.* New York, Duell, 1966.
Editor (as Walker Chapman), *Antarctic Conquest.* Indianapolis, Bobbs Merrill, 1966.
Editor, *Voyagers in Time.* New York, Meredith Press, 1967.
Editor, *Men and Machines.* New York, Meredith Press, 1968.
Editor, *Mind to Mind.* New York, Meredith Press, 1968.
Editor, *Tomorrow's Worlds.* New York, Meredith Press, 1969.
Editor, *Dark Stars.* New York, Ballantine, 1969; London, Ballantine, 1971.
Editor, *Three for Tomorrow.* New York, Meredith Press, 1969; London, Gollancz, 1970.
Editor, *The Mirror of Infinity: A Critics' Anthology of Science Fiction.* New York, Harper, 1970; London, Sidgwick and Jackson, 1971.
Editor, *Science Fiction Hall of Fame 1.* New York, Doubleday, 1970; London, Gollancz, 1971.
Editor, *The Ends of Time.* New York, Hawthorn, 1970.
Editor, *Great Short Novels of Science Fiction.* New York, Ballantine, 1970; London, Pan, 1971.
Editor, *Worlds of Maybe.* New York, Nelson, 1970.
Editor, *Alpha 1–9.* New York, Ballantine, 5 vols., 1970–74; New York, Berkley, 4 vols., 1975–78.
Editor, *Four Futures.* New York, Hawthorn, 1971.
Editor, *The Science Fiction Bestiary.* New York, Nelson, 1971.
Editor, *To the Stars.* New York, Hawthorn, 1971.
Editor, *New Dimensions 1–12* (vols. 11 and 12 edited with Marta Randall). New York, Doubleday, 3 vols., 1971–73; New York, New American Library, 1 vol., 1974; New York, Harper, 6 vols., 1975–80; New York, Pocket Books, 2 vols., 1980–81; *5–7* published London, Gollancz, 3 vols., 1976–77.
Editor, *The Day the Sun Stood Still.* Nashville, Nelson, 1972.
Editor, *Invaders from Space.* New York, Hawthorn, 1972.
Editor, *Beyond Control.* Nashville, Nelson, 1972; London, Sidgwick and Jackson, 1973.

Editor, *Deep Space.* Nashville, Nelson, 1973; London, Abelard Schuman, 1976.
Editor, *Chains of the Sea.* Nashville, Nelson, 1973.
Editor, *No Mind of Man.* New York, Hawthorn, 1973.
Editor, *Other Dimensions.* New York, Hawthorn, 1973.
Editor, *Three Trips in Time and Space.* New York, Hawthorn, 1973.
Editor, *Mutants.* Nashville, Nelson, 1974; London, Abelard Schuman, 1976.
Editor, *Threads of Time.* Nashville, Nelson, 1974; London, Millington, 1975.
Editor, *Infinite Jests.* Radnor, Pennsylvania, Chilton, 1974.
Editor, *Windows into Tomorrow.* New York, Hawthorn, 1974.
Editor, with Roger Elwood, *Epoch.* New York, Berkley, 1975.
Editor, *Explorers of Space.* Nashville, Nelson, 1975.
Editor, *The New Atlantis.* New York, Hawthorn, 1975.
Editor, *Strange Gifts.* Nashville, Nelson, 1975.
Editor, *The Aliens.* Nashville, Nelson, 1976.
Editor, *The Crystal Ship.* Nashville, Nelson, 1976; London, Millington, 1980.
Editor, *Triax.* Los Angeles, Pinnacle, 1977; London, Fontana, 1979.
Editor, *Trips in Time.* Nashville, Nelson, 1977; London, Hale, 1979.
Editor, *Earth Is the Strangest Planet.* Nashville, Nelson, 1977.
Editor, *Galactic Dreamers.* New York, Random House, 1977.
Editor, *The Infinite Web.* New York, Dial Press, 1977.
Editor, *The Androids Are Coming.* New York, Elsevier Nelson, 1979.
Editor, *Lost Worlds, Unknown Horizons.* New York, Elsevier Nelson, 1979.
Editor, *The Edge of Space.* New York, Elsevier Nelson, 1979.
Editor, with Martin H. Greenberg and Joseph D. Olander, *Car Sinister.* New York, Avon, 1979.
Editor, with Martin H. Greenberg and Joseph D. Olander, *Dawn of Time: Prehistory Through Science Fiction.* New York, Elsevier Nelson, 1979.
Editor, *The Best of New Dimensions.* New York, Simon and Schuster, 1979.
Editor, with Martin H. Greenberg, *The Arbor House Treasury of Modern Science Fiction.* New York, Arbor House, 1980; as *Great Science Fiction of the 20th Century,* New York, Avenel, 1987.
Editor, with Martin H. Greenberg, *The Arbor House Treasury of Great Science Fiction Short Novels.* New York, Arbor House, 1980; as *Worlds Imagined,* New York, Avenel, 1989.
Editor, with Martin H. Greenberg and Charles G. Waugh, *The Science Fictional Dinosaur.* New York, Avon, 1982.
Editor, *The Best of Randall Garrett.* New York, Pocket Books, 1982.
Editor, with Martin H. Greenberg, *The Arbor House Treasury of Science Fiction Masterpieces.* New York, Arbor House, 1983; as *Great Tales of Science Fiction,* New York, Galahad, 1985.
Editor, with Martin H. Greenberg, *Fantasy Hall of Fame.* New York, Arbor House, 1983; as *The Mammoth Book of Fantasy All-Time Greats,* London, Robinson, 1988.
Editor, *The Nebula Awards 18.* New York, Arbor House, 1983.
Editor, with Martin H. Greenberg, *The Time Travelers: A Science Fiction Quartet.* New York, Fine, 1985.
Editor, with Martin H. Greenberg and Charles G. Waugh, *Neanderthals.* New York, New American Library, 1987.
Editor, *Robert Silverberg's Worlds of Wonder.* New York, Warner, 1987; London, Gollancz, 1988.
Editor, with Karen Haber, *Universe 1.* New York, Doubleday, 1990.
Editor, with Martin H. Greenberg, *The Horror Hall of Fame.* New York, Carroll and Graf, 1991.
Editor, *Murasaki: A Novel in Six Parts,* by Poul Anderson. New York, Bantam, 1992; London, Grafton, 1993.
Editor, *A Century of Fantasy, 1980–1989.* New York, MJF Books, 1997.
Editor, *A Century of Science-Fiction, 1950–1959.* New York, MJF Books, 1997.
Editor, with Grania Davis, *The Avram Davidson Treasury: A Tribute Collection.* New York, Tor, 1998.
Editor, *Legends: Short Novels by the Masters of Modern Fantasy.* New York, Tor, 1998.
Editor, *Far Horizons: All New Tales from the Greatest Worlds of Science Fiction.* New York, Avon Eos, 1999.

*

Bibliography: In *Fantasy and Science Fiction* (New York), April 1974.

Manuscript Collection: Syracuse University, New York.

Critical Studies: ''Robert Silverberg Issue'' of *SF Commentary* (Melbourne), March 1977; *Robert Silverberg* by Thomas D. Clareson, Mercer Island, Washington, Starmont House, 1983; *Robert Silverberg's Many Trapdoors: Critical Essays on His Science Fiction* edited by Charles L. Elkins and Martin Harry Greenberg, Westport, Connecticut, Greenwood Press, 1992; *The Road to Castle Mount: The Science Fiction of Robert Silverberg* by Edgar L. Chapman, Westport, Connecticut, Greenwood Press, 1999.

* * *

Robert Silverberg is a masterly science fiction writer who has demonstrated the capacity of the genre to encompass and enrich the themes of the traditional realistic novel. He quickly developed the qualities that made him a very successful purveyor of commercial science fiction: the ability to grasp a reader's attention with his opening sentences, to sustain a compelling narrative, to evoke character and setting vividly and swiftly, to generate and elaborate fascinating ideas. He has carried these qualities into his later work, and they have been complemented, in his best novels and short stories, by characterization in depth and by a prose style that is rhythmically resourceful and rich in allusion and imagery.

Silverberg is especially concerned with time and death; with journeys to, and visions of, past and future; and with attempts to avoid or overcome mortality. For instance, *Recalled to Life,* by means of imaginative extrapolations from American society in the second half of the twentieth century, vividly dramatizes the social, political, and ethical consequences of the discovery of a scientific means of resurrecting the newly dead. *To Live Again* evokes a world that offers the wealthy not physical immortality but the survival, in recorded form, of a persona that can be transplanted into the mind of a living individual: The individual chooses the persona that will best complement her or him, but there is always the risk that the persona may take over. By means of a science fiction hypothesis, *To Live Again* recasts and extends the traditional theme of the divided self.

The Book of Skulls may be Silverberg's most powerful dramatization of the quest for immortality. Four American students—one Jewish, one gay, one a WASP, and one an upwardly mobile Kansas farmer's boy—set out on a journey to Arizona to find a sect they believe can grant them immortality. There is one drawback: Only two students will be eligible; they must kill the third student, and the fourth must kill himself. They do not know, however, who is to die and who is to be saved. The novel is a compelling combination of a science fiction story and a thriller, the suspense of which is increased by a narrative technique that alternates between first-person accounts by each student. This technique also enables Silverberg to offer complex psychological portrayals of each of his four protagonists.

The combination of complex psychological characterization with science fiction achieves possibly its greatest success in *Dying Inside,* a novel about a middle-aged Jewish telepath, David Selig, who is losing his powers. The novel combines memories of Selig's unhappy childhood and youth with an evocation of his present life, in which he ekes out a living by ghostwriting essays for students. Selig laments the loss of his gift, even though it has been more of a curse than a blessing, isolating him from his fellows and thwarting his hopes of forming enduring relationships. At times we might be reading a realistic novel; but the science fiction element adds an extra dimension, Selig's telepathic power serving as a metaphor for intensity of emotion and for a faculty of perception that makes one special but sets one apart.

Silverberg's fiction grew less intense in the 1970s, when he produced novels and short stories about the fantasy world of Majipoor and historical novels like *Lord of Darkness.* As he entered the 1990s, he could still produce very effective work, such as *Thebes of the Hundred Gates,* which combines elements of a science fiction story and an historical novel in its tale of a time traveler returning to ancient Thebes in search of two other travelers who have gone missing. Silverberg vividly evokes the sights, sounds, and smells of ancient Egypt, but the novel is more than a skillful rhetorical construction. It poses, once again, a question often raised in his previous work: whether to choose the past or the future. Some of his most notable earlier fiction, despite its pessimistic projections, ended on a progressive note: The choice was made for the future, despite all its perils. *Sorcerers of Majipoor,* the fifth novel in that series, concerns the question of who will succeed the Pontifex, ruler of Majipoor. Yet again the theme is the future, but in *The Alien Years,* which uses elements of Silverberg's 1986 short story ''The Pardoner's Tale,'' the future looks bleak indeed: invaded by hostile aliens, Earth is plunged into darkness as technology breaks down, and the Carmichael family is forced to survive in a mountain redoubt.

Although he has been highly praised, Silverberg has not won promotion to the ranks of a significant contemporary novelist as quickly and easily as some other science fiction writers, such as Philip K. Dick or William Gibson. His overwhelming productivity, as well as his continued willingness to publish fiction that is highly competent but not ostentatiously literary, may have inhibited the growth of his serious reputation. In the 1990s, however, it is possible to take stock of his work and to see that it comprises a substantial, and sometimes outstanding, contribution to modern fiction.

—Nicolas Tredell

SIMPSON, Mona

Nationality: American. **Born:** Green Bay, Wisconsin, 14 June 1957. **Education:** University of California, Berkeley, B.A. 1979; Columbia University, M.F.A. 1983. **Awards:** Guggenheim award, 1988; Whiting prize, 1989; Lila Wallace Readers Digest award, 1996–99; Hadder prize, Princeton University. **Agent:** Amanda Urban, International Creative Management, 40 West 57th St., New York, New York 10019, U.S.A.

Publications

Novels

Anywhere But Here. New York, Knopf, and London, Bloomsbury, 1986.
The Lost Father. New York, Knopf, and London, Faber, 1992.
A Regular Guy. New York, Knopf, 1996.
Off Keck Road. New York, Knopf, 2000.

* * *

In *Anywhere but Here* and *The Lost Father,* Mona Simpson has created characters who are oddly likable, benignly to profoundly troubled, and eerily familiar, though rarely predictable. Simpson fashions powerful, simple prose and tackles awkward subjects with straightforward grace. Her settings—though ranging from California to Egypt to New York—capture the manners and mores of the American Midwest, particularly exploring how ''heartland'' sensibilities mix with those of either coast. Her novels center on Wisconsin small-town life and the inhabitants who fled, searching for glamour and opportunity, as well as those who stayed in all of their mediocre and eccentric glory.

The primary narrator of *Anywhere But Here,* Ann Stevenson, lives out an adolescent tug-of-war with her unstable and needy mother, Adele. The novel's opening sentence, ''We fought,'' only scratches the surface of their bizarre rapport. Adele, abandoned by her husband, spends much of her adulthood chasing living beyond her means and emotionally abusing her daughter. The word ''abuse'' is never used in the novel, though Adele's habit of dropping Ann on the side of the highway and driving away (only to return in search of her an hour later) should qualify. It is often difficult to determine who is parenting whom.

Ann recognizes Adele's emotional and financial immaturity. But Adele sometimes becomes the more sympathetic character, as when we see her difficulties as a single mother, trying to provide her daughter with a cosmopolitan, advantaged life in California rather than an ordinary one in Racine. There are moments when it becomes difficult to approve of Ann as well. Readers are not left with an easy identification or an easy hatred.

Adele ostensibly leaves her kindly, aging mother's home to allow Ann to pursue a Hollywood acting career. In the process, she leaves a stale marriage with a washed-up figure skater in search of glamour in Beverly Hills. The title's lament of ''anywhere but here'' signals not only Adele's restlessness but Ann's, too. Adele and Ann's understanding of what it means to be ''have-nots'' among the ''haves''—and their attempts to pretend otherwise—provide many painful and humorous episodes. The novel is rightly acclaimed for its complex treatment of familial relationships and its keen rendering of mother-daughter bonds.

Simpson's second novel, *The Lost Father,* although still exploring the same modern family, shifts focus to a father-daughter relationship. This time Ann Stevenson is transformed into Mayan Amneh Atassi—her birthname, reflecting her Egyptian heritage. We hear very little from Adele during the course of the novel; she is primarily a reflection of Mayan's often self-destructive and fruitless quest for "Joh" Atassi, a washed up college professor, gambler, swindler, and ladies' man. Again, we follow Mayan's journey, this time from medical school to near madness, as she shuffles her loyalties and her priorities in search of lost origins.

This adult "An" is every bit as savvy and wise as the child. Her desire for the father she never had becomes the focal point for all of the other problems in her life. She questions her search for and wish for a father, but each time she gives it up the desire returns to consume her, poison her romantic relationships, and prevent her from feeling "normal." Mayan's wish for her father is never naive, however. She recognizes that finding her father may be "beside the point"—that she may not want him after all. We follow her hiring detectives, badgering distant relatives, and making friends with telephone operators. Mayan ruminates over her fear of being abandoned by men, her fragmented cultural heritage, and her status as a contemporary American middle-class white woman. She is obsessed with her beauty and weight, her ambition, and her intelligence, never sure precisely how each talent might be put to use or downplayed in the name of her desire to be "like anybody else."

Simpson's novels are remarkable for their unsentimental versions of contemporary womanhood. Her female narrators are strong characters but not invincible heroines; they are victimized but not merely victims. Simpson's prose is insightful but not preachy, eccentric but not outlandish, and entertaining but not simply comedic. Her novels read much more like memoir, providing readers with intricate and painful windows into her characters' psyches. With *A Regular Guy,* which retells the story of the biblical Genesis and Exodus through the tale of a slightly dysfunctional Silicon Valley family, Simpson showed her ability to extend her themes into a broader landscape. The project was an ambitious one, yet Simpson more than succeeded, primarily by relying on the underlying strengths that have served her so well throughout her career as a writer.

—Devoney Looser, updated by Judson Knight

SINCLAIR, Andrew (Annandale)

Nationality: British. **Born:** Oxford, 21 January 1935. **Education:** The Dragon School, Oxford; Eton College, Berkshire (King's scholar), 1948–53; Trinity College, Cambridge, 1955–58, B.A. (double 1st) in history, 1958; Churchill College, Cambridge, Ph.D. in American history 1962. **Military Service:** Served in the Coldstream Guards, 1953–55: Ensign. **Family:** Married 1) Marianne Alexandre in 1960 (divorced), one son; 2) Miranda Seymour in 1972 (divorced 1984), one son; 3) Sonia Lady Melchett in 1984. **Career:** Harkness fellow, Harvard University, Cambridge, Massachusetts, and Columbia University, New York, 1959–61; fellow and director of Historical Studies, Churchill College, Cambridge, 1961–63; fellow, American Council of Learned Societies, 1963–64; lecturer in American History, University College, London, 1965–67; managing director, Lorrimer Publishing Ltd., London, 1967–84, and Timon Films, 1969–95. **Awards:** Maugham award, 1967. Fellow, Royal Society of Literature, 1973; Fellow, Society of American Historians, 1974. **Address:** 16 Tite Street, London SW3 4HZ, England.

PUBLICATIONS

Novels

The Breaking of Bumbo. London, Faber, and New York, Simon and Schuster, 1959.
My Friend Judas. London, Faber, 1959; New York, Simon and Schuster, 1961.
The Project. London, Faber, and New York, Simon and Schuster, 1960.
The Hallelujah Bum. London, Faber, 1963; as *The Paradise Bum,* New York, Atheneum, 1963.
The Raker. London, Cape, and New York, Atheneum, 1964.
Gog. London, Weidenfeld and Nicolson, and New York, Macmillan, 1967.
Magog. London, Weidenfeld and Nicolson, and New York, Harper, 1972.
The Surrey Cat. London, Joseph, 1976; as *Cat,* London, Sphere, 1977.
A Patriot for Hire. London, Joseph, 1978.
The Facts in the Case of E.A. Poe. London, Weidenfeld and Nicolson, 1979; New York, Holt Rinehart, 1980.
Beau Bumbo. London, Weidenfeld and Nicolson, 1985.
King Ludd. London, Hodder and Stoughton, 1988.
The Far Corners of the Earth. London, Hodder and Stoughton, 1991.
The Strength of the Hills. London, Hodder and Stoughton, 1992.

Uncollected Short Stories

"To Kill a Loris," in *Texas Quarterly* (Austin), Autumn 1961.
"A Head for Monsieur Dimanche," in *Atlantic* (Boston), September 1962.
"The Atomic Band," in *Transatlantic Review 21* (London), Summer 1966.
"Twin," in *The Best of Granta.* London, Secker and Warburg, 1967.

Plays

My Friend Judas (produced London, 1959).
Adventures in the Skin Trade, adaptation of the work by Dylan Thomas (produced London, 1966; Washington, D.C., 1970). London, Dent, 1967; New York, New Directions, 1968.
Under Milk Wood (screenplay). London, Lorrimer, and New York, Simon and Schuster, 1972.
The Blue Angel, adaptation of the screenplay by Josef von Sternberg, music by Jeremy Sams (produced Liverpool, 1983).

Screenplays: *Before Winter Comes,* 1969; *The Breaking of Bumbo,* 1970; *Under Milk Wood,* 1972; *Blue Blood,* 1974; *Malachi's Grove* (*The Seaweed Children*), 1977.

Television Plays: *The Chocolate Tree,* 1963; *Old Soldiers,* 1964; *Martin Eden,* from the novel by Jack London, 1980.

Other

Prohibition: The Era of Excess. London, Faber, and Boston, Little Brown, 1962; as *Era of Excess,* New York, Harper, 1964.
The Available Man: The Life Behind the Masks of Warren Gamaliel Harding. New York, Macmillan, 1965.

The Better Half: The Emancipation of the American Woman. New York, Harper, 1965; London, Cape, 1966.

A Concise History of the United States. London, Thames and Hudson, and New York, Viking Press, 1967; revised edition, Thames and Hudson, 1970; London, Lorrimer, 1984.

The Last of the Best: The Aristocracy of Europe in the Twentieth Century. London, Weidenfeld and Nicolson, and New York, Macmillan, 1969.

Guevara. London, Fontana, and New York, Viking Press, 1970.

Dylan Thomas: Poet of His People. London, Joseph, 1975; as *Dylan Thomas: No Man More Magical,* New York, Holt Rinehart, 1975.

Inkydoo, The Wild Boy (for children). London, Abelard Schuman, 1976; as *Carina and the Wild Boy,* London, Beaver, 1977.

Jack: A Biography of Jack London. New York, Harper, 1977; London, Weidenfeld and Nicolson, 1978.

The Savage: A History of Misunderstanding. London, Weidenfeld and Nicolson, 1977.

John Ford: A Biography. London, Allen and Unwin, and New York, Dial Press, 1979.

Corsair: The Life of J. Pierpont Morgan. London, Weidenfeld and Nicolson, and Boston, Little Brown, 1981.

The Other Victoria: The Princess Royal and the Great Game of Europe. London, Weidenfeld and Nicolson, 1981; as *Royal Web,* New York, McGraw Hill, 1982.

Sir Walter Raleigh and the Age of Discovery. London, Penguin, 1984.

The Red and the Blue: Intelligence, Treason and the Universities. London, Weidenfeld and Nicolson, 1986; Boston, Little Brown, 1987.

Spiegel: The Man Behind the Pictures. London, Weidenfeld and Nicolson, 1987; Boston, Little Brown, 1988.

War Like a Wasp: The Lost Decade of the Forties. London, Hamish Hamilton, 1989; New York, Viking Hamilton, 1990.

The Need to Give: The Patrons and the Arts. London, Sinclair Stevenson, 1990.

The Naked Savage. London, Sinclair Stevenson, 1991.

The Sword and the Grail. New York, Crown, 1992; London, Century, 1993.

Francis Bacon: His Life and Violent Times. London, Sinclair Stevenson, 1993; New York, Crown, 1994.

In Love and Anger: A View of the 'Sixties. London, Sinclair Stevenson, 1994.

Arts and Cultures: The History of the 50 Years of the Arts Council of Great Britain. London, Sinclair Stevenson, 1995.

Jerusalem: The Endless Crusade. New York, Crown Publishers, 1995.

Arts and Cultures: The History of the 50 years of the Arts Council of Great Britain. London, Sinclair-Stevenson, 1995.

Che Guevara (with Carlos Olave). Phoenix Mill, Gloucestershire, England, Sutton, 1998.

The Discovery of the Grail. New York, Carroll & Graf, 1998.

Death by Fame: A Life of Elisabeth, Empress of Austria. New York, St. Martin's Press, 1999.

Editor, *GWTW* [Gone with the Wind]: *The Screenplay,* by Sidney Howard. London, Lorrimer, 1979.

Editor, *The Call of the Wild, White Fang, and Other Stories,* by Jack London. London, Penguin, 1981.

Editor, *The War Decade: An Anthology of the 1940s.* London, Hamish Hamilton, 1989.

Editor, *Greece: A Literary Companion.* London, John Murray, 1994.

Translator, *Selections from the Greek Anthology.* London, Weidenfeld and Nicolson, 1967; New York, Macmillan, 1968.

Translator, with Carlos P. Hansen, *Bolivian Diary: Ernesto ''Che'' Guevara.* London, Lorrimer, 1968.

Translator, with Marianne Alexandre, *La Grande Illusion* (scenario), by Jean Renoir. London, Lorrimer, 1968.

*

Critical Studies: *Old Lines, New Forces* edited by Robert K. Morris, Rutherford, New Jersey, Fairleigh Dickinson University Press, 1976.

Theatrical Activities: Director: **Films—***The Breaking of Bumbo, 1970; Under Milk Wood, 1972; Blue Blood, 1974..*

Andrew Sinclair comments:

I work between fact and fiction: history and biography, the novel and film. The one informs the other without confusion, I hope. Aging, I find myself admiring professionals, not philosophers. Like the Victorians I have found liberty in writing and in not working for wages. Freedom is having four jobs—and only on hire. Yet age is a stimulus to write only what I want to write, given the tick of time.

* * *

From the beginning Andrew Sinclair established himself as a writer of extraordinary fluency and copiousness, whether in fiction or in American social history. His early novels were light-hearted attempts to capture significant moments in the life of the 1950s: the misadventures of a young National Service officer in the Brigade of Guards in *The Breaking of Bumbo* (later adventures are recounted in *Beau Bumbo*), or life in Cambridge when traditional academic forms were coming apart at the seams in *My Friend Judas.* Sinclair's awareness of social nuance and his ready ear for changing forms of speech made him an effective observer, though at the cost of making these novels soon seem dated. *The Project* was a deliberate attempt to move to new ground—the moral fable and apocalyptic science fiction—but the result was wooden and contrived. In *The Hallelujah Bum* Sinclair returned to Ben Birt, the cheerfully iconoclastic hero of *My Friend Judas,* and thrust him into a thin but fast-moving narrative about driving across the United States in a stolen car. The book was partly a loving evocation of American landscape, and partly an example of a new fictional genre that emerged in the 1960s which showed the impact of America on a visiting Englishman.

Sinclair's next novel, *The Raker,* was a fresh endeavour to get away from the fictional recreation of personal experience, though it was still a projection of a personal obsession, in this case what Sinclair has described as a preoccupation with death. *The Raker* is, if anything, too nakedly allegorical, with a strong flavour of Gothic fantasy about it. But it brings together the separate vision of the novelist and the historian, and it is most powerful in its superimposition of the plague-ridden London of the seventeenth century on the modern metropolis. The preoccupation with history and myth in *The Raker* was fully worked out in *Gog.*

Compared with the latter, Sinclair dismisses his previous five novels as no more than ''experiments in style.'' ''Gog'' is a legendary giant of British mythology, personified in the novel by an enormous naked man washed up on the Scottish coast in the summer of 1945. The book is essentially a long picaresque account of his walk to London to claim his inheritance as a representative of the British people. On the way he has many fantastic adventures, some comic, some cruel, but all reflecting Sinclair's extraordinary imaginative exuberance. The journey takes him to many sacred places, such as York Minster, Glastonbury, and Stonehenge, and on one level the story is an exploration of the multi-layered past of England, almost like the excavation of an archaeological site. The richness of content is matched by a great variety of formal device: *Gog* draws on the techniques of the comic strip and the cinema, as well as those of the novel.

Magog, the sequel, which describes the life and times of Gog's villainous brother in postwar England, is much less interesting. Although an intelligent, inventive and entertaining piece of social satire, it has little of *Gog*'s mythic power. Weaker still was *King Ludd,* which completed the trilogy with a tale linking such diverse themes as the anti-technology Luddites and the development of the computer.

—Bernard Bergonzi, updated by Judson Knight

SINGH, Khushwant

Nationality: Indian. **Born:** Hadali, India (now Pakistan) 2 February 1915. **Education:** The Modern School, New Delhi; St. Stephen's College, New Delhi; Government College, Lahore, B.A. 1934; King's College, London, LL.B. 1938; called to the bar, Inner Temple, London, 1938. **Family:** Married Kaval Malik in 1939; one son and one daughter. **Career:** Practicing lawyer, High Court, Lahore, 1939–47; press attaché, Indian Foreign Service, in London and Ottawa, 1947–51; staff member, Department of Mass Communications, Unesco, Paris, 1954–56; editor, *Yejna,* an Indian government publication, New Delhi, 1956–58; visiting lecturer, Oxford University, 1965, University of Rochester, New York, 1965, Princeton University, New Jersey, 1967, University of Hawaii, Honolulu, 1967, and Swarthmore College, Pennsylvania, 1969; editor, *Illustrated Weekly of India,* Bombay, 1969–78; editor-in-chief, *National Herald,* New Delhi, 1978–79; chief editor, *New Delhi,* 1979–80; editor-in-chief, *Hindustan Times* and *Contour,* both New Delhi, 1980–83. Since 1980 member of the Indian Parliament. Head of the Indian Delegation, Manila Writers Conference, 1965. **Awards:** Rockefeller grant, 1966; Punjab Government grant, 1970; Mohan Singh award, Padma Bhushan, India, 1974. **Address:** 49-E Sujan Singh Park, New Delhi 110 003, Delhi, India.

PUBLICATIONS

Novels

Train to Pakistan. London, Chatto and Windus, 1956; New York, Grove Press, 1961; as *Mano Majra,* Grove Press, 1956.
I Shall Not Hear the Nightingale. New York, Grove Press, 1959; London, Calder, 1961.
The Company of Women. New Delhi and New York, Viking, 1999.

Short Stories

The Mark of Vishnu and Other Stories. London, Saturn Press, 1950.
The Voice of God and Other Stories. Bombay, Jaico, 1957.
A Bride for the Sahib and Other Stories. New Delhi, Hind, 1967.
Black Jasmine. Bombay, Jaico, 1971.
The Collected Stories. N.p., Ravi Dayal, 1989.

Play

Television Documentary: *Third World—Free Press* (also presenter; *Third Eye* series), 1982 (UK).

Other

The Sikhs. London, Allen and Unwin, and New York, Macmillan, 1953.
The Unending Trail. New Delhi, Rajkamal, 1957.
The Sikhs Today: Their Religion, History, Culture, Customs, and Way of Life. Bombay, Orient Longman, 1959; revised edition, 1964; revised edition, New Delhi, Sangam, 1976, 1985.
Fall of the Kingdom of the Punjab. Bombay, Orient Longman, 1962.
A History of the Sikhs 1469–1964. Princeton, New Jersey, Princeton University Press, and London, Oxford University Press, 2 vols., 1963–66.
Ranjit Singh: Maharajah of the Punjab 1780–1839. London, Allen and Unwin, 1963.
Not Wanted in Pakistan. New Delhi, Rajkamal, 1965.
Ghadar, 1915: India's First Armed Revolution, with Satindra Singh. New Delhi, R and K, 1966.
Homage to Guru Gobind Singh, with Suneet Veer Singh. Bombay, Jaico, 1966.
Shri Ram: A Biography, with Arun Joshi. London, Asia Publishing, 1968.
Religion of the Sikhs (lecture). Madras, University of Madras, 1968.
Khushwant Singh's India: A Mirror for Its Monsters and Monstrosities. Bombay, India Book House, 1969.
Khushwant Singh's View of India (lectures), edited by Rahul Singh. Bombay, India Book House, 1974.
Khushwant Singh on War and Peace in India, Pakistan, and Bangladesh, edited by Mala Singh. New Delhi, Hind, 1976.
Good People, Bad People, edited by Rahul Singh. New Delhi, Orient, 1977.
Khushwant Singh's India Without Humbug, edited by Rahul Singh. Bombay, India Book House, 1977.
Around the World with Khushwant Singh, edited by Rahul Singh. New Delhi, Orient, 1978.
Indira Gandhi Returns. New Delhi, Vision, 1979.
Editor's Page, edited by Rahul Singh. Bombay, India Book House, 1981.
We Indians. New Delhi, Orient, 1982.
Delhi: A Portrait. New Delhi and Oxford, Oxford University Press, 1983.
The Sikhs, photographs by Raghu Rai. Benares, Lustre Press, 1984.
Tragedy of the Punjab: Operation Bluestar and After, with Kuldip Nayar. New Delhi, Vision, 1984.
Many Faces of Communalism. Chandigarh, Centre for Research in Rural and Urban Development, 1985.
My Bleeding Punjab. New Delhi and London, UBSPD, 1992.
Women and Men in My Life. New Delhi, UBS Publishers' Distributors, 1995.
How the Sikhs Lost Their Kingdom. New Delhi, UBS Publishers' Distributors, 1996.
Editor, with Peter Russell, *A Note ... on G.V. Desani's "All about H. Hatterr" and "Hali."* London and Amsterdam, Szeben, 1952.

Editor, with Jaya Thadani, *Land of the Five Rivers: Stories of the Punjab.* Bombay, Jaico, 1965.
Editor, *Sunset of the Sikh Empire,* by Sita Ram Kohli. Bombay, Orient Longman, 1967.
Editor, *I Believe.* New Delhi, Hind, 1971.
Editor, *Love and Friendship.* New Delhi, Sterling, 1974.
Editor, with Qurratulain Hyder, *Stories from India.* New Delhi, Sterling, 1974.
Editor, *Gurus, Godmen, and Good People.* Bombay, Orient Longman, 1975.
Editor, with Shobha Dé, *Uncertain Liaisons: Sex, Strife and Togetherness in Urban India,* New Delhi and London, Viking, 1993.
Editor, with Syeda Saiyidain Hameed, *A Dream Turns Seventy-Five: The Modern School, 1920–1995.* New Delhi, Allied Publishers, 1995.
Editor, *A Brush with Life: An Autobiography,* by Satish Gujral. New Delhi, India, Penguin Books India, 1997.
Translator, *Jupji: The Sikh Morning Prayer.* London, Probsthain, 1959.
Translator, with M.A. Husain, *Umrao Jan Ada: Courtesan of Lucknow,* by Mohammed Ruswa. Bombay, Orient Longman, 1961.
Translator, *The Skeleton and Other Writings,* by Amrita Pritam. Bombay, Jaico, 1964.
Translator, *I Take This Woman,* by Rajinder Singh Bedi. New Delhi, Hind, 1967.
Translator, *Hymns of Guru Nanak.* Bombay, Orient Longman, 1969.
Translator, *Dreams in Debris: A Collection of Punjabi Short Stories,* by Satindra Singh. Bombay, Jaico, 1972.
Translator, with others, *Sacred Writings of the Sikhs.* London, Allen and Unwin, 1974.
Translator, with others, *Come Back, My Master, and Other Stories,* by K.S. Duggal. New Delhi, Bell, 1978.
Translator, *Shikwa and Jawab-i-Shikwa/Complaint and Answer: Iqbal's Dialogue with Allah.* New Delhi and Oxford, Oxford University Press, 1981.
Translator, *Amrita Pritam: Selected Poems.* New Delhi, Bharatiya Jnanpith, 1982.
Translator, *The Skeleton and That Man,* by Amrita Pritam. London, Oriental University Press, 1987.

*

Critical Studies: *Khushwant Singh* by V.A. Shahane, New York, Twayne, 1972; *Three Contemporary Novelists: Khushwant Singh, Chaman Nahal, and Salman Rushdie* by R.K. Dhawan, New Delhi, Classical, 1985; *A Man Called Khushwant Singh,* edited by Rohini Singh, New Delhi, UBS Publishers, 1996.

* * *

Although Khushwant Singh is a distinguished Sikh historian, his reputation as a fiction writer rests solely upon *Train to Pakistan,* a harrowing tale of events along the borders of the newly divided nations of India and Pakistan in the summer of 1947.

The atrocities that accompanied the division of these nations had an enormously depressing effect on a world that had just fought a long, bitter war to defeat practitioners of genocide. The somewhat artificial division of the subcontinent (the boundaries remain in dispute) had been strictly along religious lines: Pakistan was to be a nation of Moslems; India, of Hindus, Sikhs, and what Singh calls "pseudo Christians." There were, however, colonies of non-coreligionists left within each nation. Rather than settle down to peaceful coexistence or permit a passive exchange of populations, partisans on both sides set out on a violent campaign of annihilating the communities that were trapped on their ancestral lands beyond friendly borders.

Train to Pakistan is set against a background of this ruthless and senseless mass destruction. This powerful novel derives its title from a squalid border town, where a rail line crosses from India to Pakistan. At first this mixed community of Sikhs and Moslems is undisturbed by the violence that is breaking out elsewhere on the frontier, but inevitably it, too, is caught up in the mass hysteria as ominous "ghost trains" of slain Sikhs begin to arrive in town from across the border. Agitation for reprisals follows when the Moslems of the town are at last rounded up and fanatics urge the Sikhs of the community to kill their former neighbors as the train carrying them to Pakistan passes through town.

Singh's story contrasts the ineffectualness of the educated and ruling classes with the power of the violent and irrational peasants. Early in the story the town's only educated citizen, a Hindu money-lender, is gruesomely murdered by a band of Dacoity (professional bandits). Juggut Singh, a passionate Sikh farmer with a bad record, is suspected of the crime—though he played no part in it—and imprisoned; at the same time, an educated young former Sikh, Iqbal, comes to the community to agitate for a radical cause and is also imprisoned on suspicion of being a Moslem League agent. While these two are off the scene, the unlighted trains with their cargoes of dead begin to roll into town, and the agitation for reprisals begins. Both the young radical and a government commissioner, Hukum Chand, are unable to prevent the vicious plot against the fleeing Moslems from being carried out, and collapse emotionally; but in an extraordinary gesture of self-sacrifice, Juggut Singh—who had been in love with a Moslem girl—foils the plotters and allows the train to roll over his body "on to Pakistan."

Singh's terse fable suggests a profound disillusionment with the power of law, reason, and intellect in the face of elemental human passions. The philosophy that sparked his tale seems to be expressed through the thoughts of Iqbal, the young radical, as he realizes his helplessness and drifts off into a drugged sleep the night of the climactic incident of the train's passing: "If you look at things as they are … there does not seem to be a code either of man or God on which one can pattern one's conduct…. In such circumstances what can you do but cultivate an utter indifference to all values? Nothing matters." The same disillusioned tone characterizes Singh's second novel, *I Shall Not Hear the Nightingale,* but the rather wooden tale is almost overwhelmed by heavy-handed ironies. The action occurs about five years before that of the earlier novel, at a time when the British are expressing a willingness to get out of India once the Axis nations have been defeated in World War II. Sher Singh, the ambitious but lazy son of a Sikh senior magistrate, cannot decide between two worlds, "the one of security provided by his father … and the other full of applause that would come to him as the heroic leader of a band of terrorists." His dabblings in terrorism—actually abetted by a cynical young British civil servant—end in the pointless killing of a village leader, who has also been a political spy. Sher is suspected of the murder and imprisoned, but on the advice of his mother (when his father will not speak to him) he refuses to betray his companions. The British release him for lack of evidence, and he is honored as a kind of local hero—seemingly his political future is assured. His father is even honored by the British.

The novel takes a much dimmer view of the human capacity for compassion and self-sacrifice than *Train to Pakistan* (at one point Sher Singh reflects that "for him loyalties were not as important as the ability to get away with the impression of having them"), so that the novel ends not with the kind of thrilling gesture that its predecessor did, but with the obsequious magistrate, Sher Singh's father, sitting in the Britisher's garden observing, "As a famous English poet has said, 'All's well that ends well.'" The title of the book comes from Sher Singh's reply to his mother when she asks, "What will you get if the English leave this country?" He replies lyrically, "Spring will come to our barren land once more ... once more the nightingales will sing." Khushwant Singh evidently thinks not, if the land is to fall into such self-serving hands as Sher Singh's.

His ironic short stories resemble Angus Wilson's and express a similar disillusionment about man's rationality. Singh is a brilliant, sardonic observer of a world undergoing convulsive changes; and his novels provide a unique insight into one of the major political catastrophes of this century. His difficulties in fusing his editorial comments with the action in his stories, however, cause his novels to remain principally dramatized essays.

—Warren French

SIONIL JOSE, F(rancisco)

Nationality: Filipino. **Born:** Rosales, Pangasinan, 3 December 1924. **Education:** The University of Santo Tomas, Manila, Litt.B. 1949. **Family:** Married Teresita G. Jovellanos in 1949; five sons and two daughters. **Career:** Staff member, *Commonweal,* Manila, 1947–48; assistant editor, United States Information Agency, U.S. Embassy, Manila, 1948–49; associate editor, 1949–57, and managing editor, 1957–60, Manila *Times Sunday* magazine, and editor of Manila *Times* annual *Progress,* 1958–60; editor, *Comment* quarterly, Manila, 1956–62; managing editor, *Asia* magazine, Hong Kong, 1961–62; information officer, Colombo Plan Headquarters, Ceylon, 1962–64; correspondent, *Economist,* London, 1968–69. Since 1965 publisher, Solidaridad Publishing House, and general manager, Solidaridad Bookshop, since 1966 publisher and editor, *Solidarity* magazine, and since 1967 manager, Solidaridad Galleries, all Manila. Lecturer, Arellano University, 1962, University of the East graduate school, 1968, and De La Salle University, 1984–86, all Manila; writer-in-residence, National University of Singapore, 1987; visiting research scholar, Center for Southeast Asian Studies, Kyoto University, Japan, 1988. Consultant, Department of Agrarian Reform, 1968–79. Founder and national secretary, PEN Philippine Center, 1958. **Awards:** U.S. Department of State Smith-Mundt grant, 1955; Asia Foundation grant, 1960; National Press Club award, for journalism, 3 times; British Council grant, 1967; Palanca award, for journalism, 3 times, and for novel, 1981; ASPAC fellowship, 1971; Rockefeller Foundation Bellagio award, 1979; Cultural Center of the Philippines award, 1979; City of Manila award, 1979; Magsaysay award, 1980; East-West Center fellowship (Honolulu), 1981; International House of Japan fellowship, 1983; Outstanding Fulbrighters award, 1988, for literature; Cultural Center of the Philippines award, 1989, for literature. **Address:** Solidaridad Publishing House, 531 Padre Faura, Ermita P.O. Box 3959, Manila, Philippines.

Publications

Novels

The Pretenders. Manila, Solidaridad, 1962; published as *The Samsons: The Pretenders; and, Mass,* New York, Modern Library, 2000.
Tree. Manila, Solidaridad, 1978.
My Brother, My Executioner. Manila, New Day, 1979.
Mass. Amsterdam, Wereldvenster, 1982; London, Allen and Unwin, 1984; as *Mis,* Manila, Solidaridad, 1983.
Po-on. Manila, Solidaridad, 1985.
Ermita. Manila, Solidaridad, 1988.
Spiderman. Manila, Solidaridad, 1991.
Sin. Manila, Solidaridad, 1994; published as *Sins*, New York, Random House, 1996.
Dusk. New York, Modern Library, 1998.
Don Vincente: A Novel in Two Parts (contains *Tree* and *My Brother, My Executioner*). New York, Modern Library, 1999.

Short Stories

The Pretenders and Eight Short Stories. Manila, Regal, 1962.
The God Stealer and Other Stories. Manila, Solidaridad, 1968.
Waywaya and Other Short Stories from the Philippines. Hong Kong, Heinemann, 1980.
Two Filipino Women (novellas). Manila, New Day, 1982.
Platinum and Other Stories. Manila, Solidaridad, 1983.
Olvidon and Other Stories. Manila, Solidaridad, 1988.
Three Filipino Women (novellas) . New York, Random House, 1992.

Uncollected Short Stories

"The Chief Mourner" (serial), in *Women's Weekly* (Manila), 11 May-10 July 1953.
"The Balete Tree" (serial), in *Women's Weekly* (Manila), 4 March 1954–6 July 1956.

Poetry

Questions. Manila, Solidaridad, 1988.

Other

(*Selected Works*). Moscow, 1977.
A Filipino Agenda for the 21st Century. Manila, Solidaridad, 1987.
Conversations with F. Sionil Jose, edited by Miguel Bernad. Manila, Vera-Reyes, 1991.
In Search of the Word: Selected Essays of F. Sionil Jose. Manila, de la Salle University Press, 1998.
Editor, *Equinox 1.* Manila, Solidaridad, 1965.
Editor, *Asian PEN Anthology 1.* Manila, Solidaridad, 1966; New York, Taplinger, 1967.

*

Critical Studies: *F. Sionil Jose and His Fiction* edited by Alfredo T. Morales, Manila, Vera-Reyes, 1990.

* * *

F. Sionil Jose holds two distinctions in Philippine writing in English, indeed in Philippine writing in general. He is the only writer who has produced a series of novels that constitute an epic imaginative creation of a century of Philippine life, and he is perhaps the most widely known abroad, his writings having been translated into more foreign languages than those of any other Filipino writer. (The only exception would be that greatest of all Filipino writers and patriots, Jose Rizal, martyred in the struggle against Spanish domination.)

We are introduced to the early world of Sionil Jose in *Po-on.* The earliest novel in terms of chronology, it is set in the later decades of the 19th century during the decaying years of the Spanish empire. The latter still retained some struggling remnants of its colonial civil services, including some manorial lords in the plains of central Luzon island, descendants of the Basque and Spanish-Catalan settlers, served by immigrants from the deep Ilocano country up north. In one scene a Basque grandee comes to the town of Rosales, when the settlement is still unorganized, and designates the limits of his domain with his whip.

After the Philippine revolution, which saw the change of colonial masters from Spanish to American, no significant change occurred in the feudal relations of the agrarian economy. In fact, free trade was instituted between the Philippines and the United States, benefiting the native landowners and their hirelings and the leaders of industry and their subalterns while impoverishing the tenants of the land and the laborers in small-scale industries. Such relationships are examined in *Tree.* Despite all the injustices they suffered during the American colonial regime, when war came in December 1941, the tenants and their leaders decided to fight the Japanese invaders as guerrillas, hoping that at the end of the war they would be afforded improved living conditions.

My Brother, My Executioner occurs at this point in Sionil Jose's epic narrative. It deals with the activities of two half-brothers, one a dispossessed guerrilla. With more than enough property to keep his family in comfort, the bourgeois half-brother can afford to entertain liberal ideas and even consider embracing progressive ways, but his dispossessed half-brother avenges himself by destroying the more fortunate.

The master-servant, lord-slave relationship may also be found in the industrial world in Manila. One specific case is Antonio Samson in *The Pretenders.* Overcoming the disadvantages of rural birth, Samson manages to earn a doctorate at a prestigious New England university, afterwards planning to return to his hometown sweetheart, with whom he had fathered a child. Instead, he is snatched away by a powerful agro-industrial baron and married off to his socialite daughter. Samson is now made to move in elevated social circles and do work he had not prepared himself to do. He has frequent spats with his wife who, he discovers to his dismay, has been engaged in affairs with other men. Determined to end his shame, Samson throws himself under a train.

We are afforded a rich composite picture of the Philippines of the mid-to late twentieth century in *Mass,* which covers the years before and after the proclamation of martial law in 1972. A few of the old names reappear, but new characters emerge—student activists, women's liberation movement followers, drug addicts, intellectuals. The major character is the bastard son of Antonio Samson, Pepe Samson, now living in the slums of Tondo. He is a faithful follower of a former anti-Japanese Huk (Communist rebel) commander now devoted to local affairs, and a student leader at a university in Manila. A reform movement that started with protest at the increase in oil prices becomes a struggle for human rights, student rights, tenant's rights, women's liberation, and eventually a heterogeneous mass of protests manipulated by fraudulent leaders. After the failure of the intended uprising, one of the dedicated characters decides to return to central Luzon to seek his roots and build anew.

Sins looks back on the history of the Philippines during much of the twentieth century through the eyes of the amoral Don Carlos Corbello, or C.C., who took part in that history and, on his deathbed, is reaping much of what he sowed. *Dusk* jumps back to the time of the Spanish-American War, whose Philippine theatre (as opposed to the Cuban theatre) is largely unknown to most Americans. In the course of Sionil Jose's work, which calls to mind Balzac's ''Human Comedy'' if on a smaller scale, we get an increasingly defined picture of Philippine history over more than a century. We are shown all kinds of people, from the moral cowards to the fiercely heroic, from the ferociously greedy to the selflessly philanthropic. In the face of all the tragic events in their lives, many of the people in Sionil Jose's epic are still able to say ''We shall overcome.''

—Leopoldo Y. Yabes, updated by Judson Knight

SLAUGHTER, Carolyn

Nationality: British. **Born:** New Delhi, India, 7 January 1946. Educated in Botswana and England. **Family:** Married 1) Denis Pack-Beresford (divorced); 2) Daniel Cromer (divorced), one daughter and one son; 3) Kemp Battle, one daughter and one son. **Career:** Advertising copywriter, Garland Compton Ltd., 1966–68, Norman Craig and Kummel, 1969–71, Collett Dickenson and Pearce, 1971–72, Nadler Larimer and Cromer, 1972–74, all London. Freelance writer, 1974–85. **Awards:** Geoffrey Faber Memorial prize, 1977. **Address:** 2805 Main Street, Lawrenceville, New Jersey 08648, U.S.A.

Publications

Novels

The Story of the Weasel. London, Hart Davis, 1976; as *Relations,* New York, Mason Charter, 1977.
Columba. London, Hart Davis, 1977; New York, Panther House, 1979.
Magdalene. London, Hart Davis, 1978; New York, Evans, 1979.
Dreams of the Kalahari. London, Granada, 1981; New York, Scribner, 1987.
Heart of the River. London, Granada, 1982; New York, St. Martin's Press, 1983.
The Banquet. London, Allen Lane, 1983; New Haven, Connecticut, Ticknor and Fields, 1984.
A Perfect Woman. London, Allen Lane, 1984; New York, Ticknor and Fields, 1985.
The Innocents. London, Viking, and New York, Scribner, 1986.
The Widow. London, Heinemann, 1989.

* * *

She decided she'd read more than enough of those well-balanced, neatly clipped English parochial novels where the greatest excitement was reading the last page and being done with the damn thing.

(Heart of the River)

With this resolution, Constance, Caroline Slaughter's heroine, throws her paperback ''with a flabby flop'' into the swimming pool. It is not hard to see the author behind the character. Slaughter herself first grasps and then rejects the English paperback, casting off the norms of the genre, transmuting it with her own fierce emotional vitality. Her art sheds, easily but with far reaching consequences, the conventions of romantic fiction, creating novels which are characterized by a naked honesty which is at times almost confessional in its intimacy. While her themes are those of paperback romances—love, relationships, and the family—her quest for psychological reality leaves the art of idealization and euphemism far behind. Her art shatters the convenient collusion between romance writer and reader as to what human beings feel.

Slaughter portrays the dark knots of bitterness and vulnerability, pain and need, which lie within the individual psyche. Her vision strikes dramatic contrasts to fictional norms. One example of this is an unusual frankness in her treatment of sex. Another fictional taboo to be broken is that of monogamous love. Constance in *Heart of the River* (as Humphrey in *A Perfect Woman*) is torn by love for more than one person. The violence of our needs and our own inner contradictions destroy the easy assumptions about the consequences of falling in love.

The thirst for psychological honesty—and Slaughter is acutely psychologically aware—draws her work deeper and deeper into the inner wounds from which our compulsive emotions spring: the traumas of childhood and early sexual experience, the relationship with the mother, the secrets passed from one generation to another within the family. The epigraph to *Heart of the River,* from Eliot, is appropriate to all her work:

> We shall not cease from exploration
> And the end of all our exploring
> Will be to arrive where we started
> And know the place for the first time.

While not making explicit use of psychoanalysis, there is an impulse within Slaughter's work which parallels that of the analyst: the search for inner knowledge, for discovery of, and confrontation with, the secrets hidden within the self. Her plots are driven not only by the momentum of unfolding action, but by that of unfolding knowledge. As in classical tragedy, there is a pattern of concealment and revelation leading to eventual denouement and catharsis. At the climax of her novels are realizations: both in the sense of comprehension, and in the sense of fulfillment of what has long lain hidden. At the same time as characters approach the crisis of their lives they (and the reader) approach understanding of the seeds of that crisis, often sown far in the past. In *Heart of the River* Slaughter quotes Shiva Naipaul, ''To rediscover a lost past is to rediscover an essential part of the self.'' Such rediscovery however, as in *The Innocents* and *The Banquet,* can be destructive as well as enlightening.

As the analyst's sensitivity and acuteness are brought to bear on individuals, so Slaughter also scrutinizes tensions between people, particularly between lovers. *The Banquet* and *A Perfect Woman* show how our deepest needs become focused on the objects of erotic attraction; *The Widow* and *Heart of the River* demonstrate the violent battles which take place within relationships. We feel, too, the rage of the lover against those parts of the beloved which cannot be contained by a relationship. Such tension and mutual incomprehension are cleverly illustrated by Slaughter's technique of split narratives, where each of the protagonists tells a segment of story in turn.

The psychological conflicts which fascinate Slaughter find logical extension in the split personality of Bella in *The Widow.* Similarly, the psychological violence Slaughter records is writ large in the act of homicide; in men who kill women (Harold in *The Banquet*) and in women who kill men (Rebecca in *The Widow,* Zelda in *The Innocents*). The characters who commit these acts are not incomprehensible monsters: they are themselves the heroes and heroines, and their stories are recounted from within, and in their own words. They are acted upon by the same compulsions and passions which drive us all.

Slaughter's novels are at the same time love stories and dispatches from a war between women and men, a war for the goals of fulfillment and the satisfaction of emotional need. This war spills over into sexual politics. *The Widow* shows the dissociation between two personalities: Rebecca, an earthy, home-loving woman in floral dresses, and Bella, a severe, cerebral career-minded surgeon. The war is however primarily fought out between lovers. Constance's weary acknowledgment of ''the sadomasochistic cycle'' of her relationship highlights an underlying connection between love and pain. We, the readers, are implicated in this war, and are brought to identify with the characters who take it to its most violent extreme. In *The Banquet* Slaughter teases the reader with sensuous prose which anticipates the fulfillment of exquisite fantasies:

> Then she opened her lips and the red fruit disappeared into the wet dome of her mouth; he watched with intensity, as though at any moment he expected the pink flesh to cry out … the seductive breath of the warm strawberries pierced him with longing; the juices ran into the corners of her lips and it was agonizing not to kiss her.

The sheer eroticism of Harold's descriptions, and his sensitivity, draw us into his disturbed mind. Similarly in *The Widow,* Bella succeeds in showing that Joseph, the psychiatrist, is as incomplete and as broken as she is: that all face the same inner search and struggle for wholeness.

Slaughter's power to portray a particular place and culture is considerable, whether it be rich suburban life in Britain of the 1980s, or the heat and brutality of Africa in revolution. It is however in setting new standards of emotional veracity that her greatest achievement lies.

—Edmund Cusick

SMILEY, Jane

Nationality: American. **Born:** Los Angeles, 26 September 1949. **Education:** Vassar College, B.A. in English 1971; University of Iowa, M.A. 1975, M.F.A. 1976, Ph.D. 1978. **Family:** Married 1) John Whiston, 1970 (divorced 1975); 2) William Silag, 1978 (divorced), two daughters; 3) Stephen Mark Mortensen, 1987. **Career:** Assistant professor, 1981–84, associate professor, 1984–89, professor, 1989–90, distinguished Professor, 1992–96, Iowa State University. Visiting assistant professor, University of Iowa, 1981, 1987. **Awards:** Fulbright grant, 1976–77; Pushcart prize, 1977, for ''Jeffrey, Believe

Me''; NEA grant, 1978, 1987; O. Henry award, 1982, for ''The Pleasure of Her Company,'' 1985, for ''Lily,'' and 1988; Friends of American Writers prize, 1981; Pulitzer prize, 1992, and National Book Critics Circle award, 1992, both for *A Thousand Acres;* Midland Author's award, 1992; Heartland prize, 1992. **Address:** Department of English, Iowa State University, 201 Ross, Ames, Iowa 50011–1401, U.S.A.

PUBLICATIONS

Novels

Barn Blind. New York, Harper and Row, 1980; London, Flamingo, 1994.
At Paradise Gate. New York, Simon and Schuster, 1981.
Duplicate Keys. New York, Knopf, and London, Cape 1984.
Greenlanders. New York, Knopf, and London, Collins, 1988.
A Thousand Acres. New York, Knopf, and London, Flamingo, 1991.
Moo. New York, Knopf, and London, Flamingo, 1995.
The All-True Travels and Adventures of Lidie Newton. New York, Knopf, 1998.
Horse Heaven. New York, Knopf, 2000.

Short Stories

The Age of Grief. New York, Knopf, 1987; London, Collins, 1988.
Ordinary Love and Good Will (novellas) . New York, Knopf, 1989; London, Collins, 1990.
The Life of the Body, with linoleum cuts by Susan Nees. Minneapolis, Minnisota, Coffee House Press, 1990.

Other

Catskill Crafts: Artisans of the Catskill Mountains. New York, Crown, 1988.

*

Critical Studies: *Understanding Jane Smiley* by Neil Nakadate, [Columbia], University of South Carolina Press, 1999; *The Broom Closet: Secret Meanings of Domesticity in Postfeminist Novels by Louise Erdrich, Mary Gordon, Toni Morrison, Marge Piercy, Jane Smiley, and Amy Tan* by Jeannette Batz Cooperman, New York, Peter Lang, 1999.

* * *

Jane Smiley's congenial turf is the dailiness of daily life, as its domestic rhythms play themselves out in a variety of settings and circumstances. She writes, in short, about families—a subject that once occupied literature's very center but now seems ignored. That Smiley came to wide critical attention with *A Thousand Acres,* a novel that won her both a Pulitzer Prize and a National Circle Critics Award, is true enough, but it is even truer that earlier collections (*The Age of Grief* and *Ordinary Love & Good Will*) amply demonstrated that she could write beautifully about family members.

As a tale of a tyrannical father who resolves to divide his thousand-acre Iowa farm among his three daughters, only to slip into madness, curse his offspring, and venture out alone into a fearsome storm, Smiley's novel is filled with correlations to *King Lear*—not only in terms of allusion and plot but also in its inevitable arc toward tragedy. Generally speaking, reviewer-critics praised Smiley's large ambitions and infectious style, but some worried that the novel's schema was a bit *too* schematic. However, there are at least as many reasons to think of Dreiser's *Sister Carrie* or Arthur Miller's *The Death of a Salesman* as one turns the pages of Smiley's altogether engrossing novel.

Moreover, *King Lear* represents only a fraction of Smiley's concerns; others include farming as it has evolved into big business, dysfunctional families, and even dashes of feminist theory. Perhaps Smiley tried to pack too many disparate concerns between the covers of a single novel (a criticism that might also be made of *Moo,* her effort to squeeze a large land-grant university under the novelist's microscope), but it is clear that *A Thousand Acres* is a brava performance in ways that *Barn Blind, At Paradise Gate,* or even *The Greenlanders* are not. For in *A Thousand Acres,* the slow gathering of quotidian detail means to tackle large, existential questions: Not only what it means to be a true daughter but also, as Ron Carlson points out, ''what is the price to be paid for trying one's whole life to please a proud father who slenderly knows himself—who coveted his land the way he loved his daughters, not wisely but too well?''

By contrast, *Moo* asks what kind of institution is the American university in the 1990s, and it sets about making its estimates by focusing not so much on individual characters (several administrators, a handful of colorful professors, and a slice of students) within an academic setting as on the setting itself. ''What is a university?'' one of her characters asks, and the answer seems hazy at best. Indeed, the novel's main character is not a human being at all but rather a pig named Earl Butz. Like most of those feeding from the university's deep trough, Smiley's pig lives only to eat and then to eat some more. He is, in short, the deep secret hidden in the bowels of Moo University. As Provost Harstad puts it:

> Over the years … everyone around the university had given free reign to his or her desires, and the institution had, with a fine, trembling responsiveness, answered, ''Why not?'' It had become, more than anything, a vast network of interlocking wishes.

No doubt there will be those who resist Smiley's portrait of the university as hog heaven (''Unfair! Unfair!'' I can hear them muttering), just as there must have been those Iowa farmers who did not see their lives on the land accurately reflected in *A Thousand Acres.* But a novelist has other allegiances, and Smiley's commitment to the dictums of art has produced reams of extraordinary prose already and promises even more in the future.

—Sanford Pinsker

SMITH, Emma

Nationality: British. **Born:** Newquay, Cornwall, 21 August 1923. **Family:** Married R.L. Stewart-Jones in 1951 (died 1957); one son and one daughter. **Awards:** Atlantic award, 1947; Rhys Memorial prize, 1949; James Tait Black Memorial prize for *The Far Cry,* 1950.

Agent: Curtis Brown, 162–68 Regent Street, London W1R 5TB, England.

PUBLICATIONS

Novels

Maidens' Trip. London, Putnam, 1948.
The Far Cry. London, MacGibbon and Kee, 1949; New York, Random House, 1950.
The Opportunity of a Lifetime. London, Hamish Hamilton, 1978; New York, Doubleday, 1980.

Uncollected Short Stories

"A Surplus of Lettuces," in *The Real Thing,* edited by Peggy Woodford. London, Bodley Head, 1977.
"Mackerel," in *Misfits,* edited by Peggy Woodford. London, Bodley Head, 1984.

Fiction (for children)

Emily: The Story of a Traveller. London, Nelson, 1959; as *Emily: The Travelling Guinea Pig,* New York, McDowell Obolensky, 1959.
Out of Hand. London, Macmillan, 1963; New York, Harcourt Brace, 1964.
Emily's Voyage. London, Macmillan, and New York, Harcourt Brace, 1966.
No Way of Telling. London, Bodley Head, and New York, Atheneum, 1972.

Other

Village Children: A Soviet Experience. Moscow, Progress, 1982.

*

Emma Smith comments:

(1991) What one writes for children is quite as important as what one writes for adults, and I'm not at all sure it isn't more important; because what children read can color their feelings, and affect their behavior, for the rest of their lives. If they are sufficiently impressed, what they read is absorbed into themselves and becomes part of their own experience to an extent that can't be so after they've grown up. Consequently, everything I write for children is really full of secret messages and exhortations and warnings of what I think the whole of life, which lies ahead waiting for them, is all about, and what I think they're going to need in the way of equipment.

* * *

Emma Smith has published three novels and several books designed for the young. In all her work there are a precise creation of character, a sensitive response to setting, and a careful attention to detail.

Her first book, *Maidens' Trip,* set in England during World War II, is the story of three girls, Emma, Charity, and Nanette, who, during the manpower shortage, become "boaters" and guide their motorboat *Venus* and its "butty" *Adrane* over the network of locks and canals running through the heartland of the English countryside. Their adventures, observations, and problems make up the substance of the story as, without formal plot or characterizations, Smith manages to create a forward-moving, frequently suspenseful narrative. The adventures become misadventures as awkwardly at first, and later with more skill, the girls make the trip for supplies from London to Birmingham and back again. There are the physical hardships of rain and cold, blistered hands and aching backs; the hazards of machinery broken down, accidents with other boats, mud that sticks and locks that refuse to open. Charity is the housewife; Nanette, the coquette; Emma, the steady "professional" who directs the whole operation. The reality of the constant rain and cold with the contrasted coziness of the little cabin on the *Venus,* the ubiquitous steaming cups of tea, the hearty flavor of the cooking stew, and the sights and sounds of the loading docks form a background for the most memorable feature of the book—the characterization of the girls and their realization of the world of the "boaters," a world completely apart from that of a great nation at war. Even the brief appearance of a young soldier on leave is no more than a vague reminder of the danger and death in the world beyond. The other notable feature of the book is Smith's understanding of the three young girls forced by circumstances to deal with people and situations totally foreign to them. Each is a real person; not one of the three a stereotype of the adolescent. Each, however, at the same time is realized as young and immature.

Smith's second book, *The Far Cry,* is even more distinguished than *Maidens' Trip.* It is the story of an eccentric schoolmaster, Mr. Digby, who flees with his fourteen-year-old daughter, Teresa, to India and the sanctuary of his elder daughter, Ruth, to escape his estranged second wife, Teresa's mother. Their departure and trip across the ocean make up the first two sections of the book; the trip across India by train, the third. The fourth section is Ruth's as the reader discovers that she and her husband Edwin have not succeeded in resolving all the differences of their marriage. The last section is a kind of summary for Teresa when, confronted by the sudden horror of her father's death from a heart attack and Ruth's accidental death in Calcutta, she is obliged to become more mature than seems possible for her to be. Even at the end she "had yet to learn that the relationships of people are never established, are ever mutable…." All the principal characters are skillfully drawn: Mr. Digby, a failure as husband, father, and schoolmaster; Ruth, an exotic beauty without confidence in herself or her role as wife; Teresa, sensitive and perceptive, escaping from the repression of her unimaginative Aunt May; and Edwin, the young English tea planter who understands India and his tea workers far more than he does his beautiful wife Ruth.

The journey from England to India, the introduction of India itself, and the daily life of the tea plantation make up the chronology of the story. There is hardly a plot in the conventional definition of the term since there is little doubt from the beginning that Teresa and her father will escape her American mother. The real focus of the novel is on Teresa and her varying responses to the people she meets and the constantly shifting scenery she observes. Smith is especially good in realizing the detail of setting—the crowded life on board ship; the arresting picture of camels and their drivers at Port Suez, a kind of point in time for Teresa; the arrival at Bombay and the acquisition of their bearer, Sam; the long uncertain train trip in dirty cramped quarters; the English way of life Ruth has created in the midst of a tea plantation. The book is as full of the multitude of details as is reality itself, but each so skillfully chosen that it seems precisely right for the observation of the characters to whom it is assigned. *The Far Cry* is a beautifully sensitive novel of time, place, and character.

The Opportunity of a Lifetime was Smith's first adult novel for almost thirty years. It again centers on a young girl. In this case the heroine is a fifteen-year-old on a summer holiday in Cornwall in 1937. And again there are many finely wrought characters, a nice sense of time and place, and moving contrasts between innocence and betrayal. If Smith has chosen a rather limited range, her virtue is that she has done well what she set out to do, and her work shows an unusual sensitivity to people and a real artist's eye for detail.

—Annibel Jenkins

SMITH, Lee

Nationality: American. **Born:** Grundy, Virginia, 1 November 1944. **Education:** Hollins College, B.A. 1967; attended Sorbonne, University of Paris. **Family:** Married 1) James E. Seay in 1967; 2) Hal Crowther in 1985; one son, one daughter. **Career:** Feature writer, film critic, and editor of Sunday magazine, *Tuscaloosa News*, Tuscaloosa, Alabama, 1968–69; seventh-grade teacher, Harpeth Hall School, Nashville, Tennessee, 1971–73; teacher of language arts, Carolina Friends School, Durham, North Carolina, 1974–77; lecturer in creative writing, University of North Carolina, Chapel Hill, 1977–81; member of English department faculty, North Carolina State University, Raleigh, North Carolina, 1981—. **Awards:** O. Henry award, 1979, 1981; Sir Walter Raleigh award, 1984; North Carolina award for literature, 1985. **Agent:** Liz Darhansoff, 1220 Park Ave., New York, New York 10028, U.S.A. **Address:** English Department, North Carolina State University, Raleigh, North Carolina 27695–8105, U.S.A.

PUBLICATIONS

Novels

The Last Day the Dogbushes Bloomed. New York, Harper, 1968.
Something in the Wind. New York, Harper, 1971.
Fancy Strut. New York, Harper, 1973.
Black Mountain Breakdown. New York, Putnam, 1980.
Oral History New York, Putnam, 1983.
Family Linen. New York, Putnam, 1985.
Fair and Tender Ladies. New York, Putnam, 1988.
The Devil's Dream. New York, Putnam, 1992.
Saving Grace. New York, G.P. Putnam's Sons, 1995.
The Christmas Letters: A Novella. Chapel Hill, North Carolina, Algonquin Books, 1996.
News of the Spirit. New York, Putnam, 1997.

Short Stories

Cakewalk. New York, Putnam, 1980.
Me and My Baby View the Eclipse: Stories. New York, Putnam, 1990.

Other

Appalachian Portraits, photographs By Shelby Lee Adams. Jackson, University Press of Mississippi, 1993.
We Don't Love with Our Teeth. Portland, Oregon, Chinook Press, 1994.

*

Critical Studies: *Lee Smith* by Dorothy Combs Hill, New York, Twayne Publishers, 1992; *Gender Dynamics in the Fiction of Lee Smith: Examining Language and Narrative Strategies* by Rebecca Smith, San Francisco, International Scholars Publications, 1997; *Lee Smith, Annie Dillard, and the Hollins Group: A Genesis of Writers* by Nancy C. Parrish, Baton Rouge, Louisiana State University Press, 1998.

* * *

Lee Smith has repeatedly claimed that the story is the storyteller's, that people recounting the same event will tell it with drastically different details. The author of numerous novels and several collections of short stories, Smith tells the stories of the "other South": Appalachia, where, Smith writes in a recent article in *Women's Review of Books*, the only columns were on the Presbyterian church, where there was no once-landed aristocracy, and where there is a long tradition of storytelling and songwriting. As Smith's work has increasingly reflected Appalachian themes, even her novels have become more like collections of stories, stories told by Smith's remarkable narrators, whose varied perspectives on shared experiences undermine any sense of a controlling, transcendent narrative.

Smith's narrators/protagonists are primarily women, and their stories balance self-expression against their duties towards men, their children, and their families. Smith's first novel, *The Last Day the Dogbushes Bloomed*, is the story of Susan Tobey's ninth summer, when her mother leaves the family and Susan is raped. Her mother's departure fractures the traditionally southern narrative of chivalry through which Susan had understood her family. Soon afterwards, Susan gets caught up in another narrative: little Eugene's game of Iron Lung, in which Susan is the sick patient and Eugene and his imaginary friend Arthur are the Iron Lung. Susan realizes that this fiction is wrong, too, that she will be neither the omnipotent queen nor a sick, helpless girl, but where she will go from here is uncertain: she seems to face a kind of material reality, to abandon fictions, but she still perceives little Arthur, and she draws strength from a mythic vision of thirteen wondrous dogs who descend from the mountains.

In *Something in the Wind* and *Fancy Strut*, Smith again confronts the confining moors of traditional southern society, particularly as they confine southern women. In *Something in the Wind*, Brooke Kincaid is raised to be a southern lady, but at college she experiments with ideas and actions she believes are neither "southern" nor ladylike. Brooke's education at college seems to offer her a means of re-imagining herself: late in the novel, Brooke describes her friends' traditional wedding ceremony but laughs as she decides to pursue "new directions." In *Fancy Strut*, Smith satirizes society in a small southern town, Speed, Alabama. The name is ironic, as are the names of many of the characters: Manly Neighbor, for example, and Iona Flowers, who literally invents genteel details to grace the events she reports on in her social column. In laughing at southern social fictions, Smith reminds us that other directions are possible, but, as in her first novel, those directions remain uncharted.

In *Black Mountain Breakdown*, Smith begins a novelistic return to the ''other South,'' the Appalachians, though the novel explores familiar themes. Crystal Spangler confronts what Smith has told Edwin T. Arnold is a challenge typical of women: ''The way so many women, and I think particularly Southern women, are raised is to make themselves fit the image that other people set out for them.'' Crystal wins beauty contests and marries the football hero, fulfilling her mother's expectations of her, and she allows her husband to ''take care'' of her, sacrificing her extraordinary voice as a teacher. In almost every facet of her life, her voice and her desires remain unheard; even after her own uncle rapes her, no one credits her story. By the story's end, Crystal becomes literally catatonic. Though she is silenced, *Black Mountain Breakdown* contests the narrative that breaks down Crystal: Smith's close third-person perspective recounts Crystal's Appalachian voice, reminding us of an ''other South,'' and the narrative is disrupted by excerpts from the diary of one of Crystal's female ancestors: a voice that offers Crystal an example she does not grasp.

The voices of female ancestors explode into Smith's next work, *Oral History*: framed by a college student's project to research her Appalachian heritage are stories told by primarily Appalachian storytellers, beginning with Granny Younger's almost mythic account of the original Almarine Cantrell's encounter with Red Emmy and ending with Sally's earthy and delightful story, which begins, ''There's two things I like to do better than anything else in this world, even at my age and one of them is talk. You all can guess what the other is.'' In *Oral History*, the voices of strong female characters who can and do articulate their desires complement and compete with others' stories, including Richard Burbage's over-educated description of his experiment in Hoot Owl Holler and Rose Hibbitt's spiteful characterization of her failure to win Almarine's heart—the story that creates the local fiction of Hoot Owl Holler's curse. The end result, as Anne Goodwyn Jones has observed, is an absence at the heart of *Oral History* that is the absence of absolute truth, but everywhere else a wealth of character, stories, and meanings. Nonetheless, we never learn to what extent the knowledge enriches the student's life.

In perhaps a more optimistic novel, *Family Linen*, Smith employs a similar technique, organizing the perspectives of different family members who interact while the matriarch of the family is dying. The novel examines the relationships that hold families together, and it closes hopefully: with a wedding and with a significant change in Theresa, another of Smith's female college students. Theresa's new love and new motto, ''Irony sucks,'' suggests that she has connected with her family and renounced the detachment from life that is typical of Smith's least successful female characters.

In *Fair and Tender Ladies*, an epistolary novel, Smith presents a life's worth of letters penned by Ivy Rowe, who may be Smith's most richly described and extraordinary character. By the middle of the novel, Rowe has achieved the self-reflection to exclaim joyfully, ''I am beautiful,'' but her dying words demonstrate that her consciousness is centered in that beautiful body: ''Oh I was young then, and I walked in my body like a Queen.'' Rowe's goals, perspectives, and voice change throughout her long life, yet she sees herself and accepts herself, though her community labels her as ''ruint.'' By the novel's end, asked why she had written letters even to a sister long dead, Rowe responds, ''It was the writing of them, that signified,'' indicating that the meaning of the letters is more in the act than the product, more in the writer than in the words. Appropriately, *Fair and Tender Ladies* is more remarkable for its gritty and lyrical storytelling than for its plot. It, too, ends hopefully: Rowe's next-to-last letter is to another of Smith's aspiring educated women, Rowe's daughter Joli, who has taken a Ph.D. in English and still corresponds meaningfully with her mother.

In *The Devil's Dream*, Smith further emphasizes the lyricism of Appalachian storytelling, presenting the perspectives of the members of a mountain family whose roots parallel the development of country music. More obviously than elsewhere, in *The Devil's Dream*, Smith interweaves fiction and fact, family history and regional history, once again subverting categories of fiction and thereby emphasizing the role of the speaker, who gives it meaning. And again, in *The Devil's Dream*, we see a successful, articulate female character, Katie Cocker, a country rock star, whose daughter remains close to her. *Saving Grace*, Smith's subsequent work, examines the life of Florida Grace Shepherd, who abandons her domineering father's serpent-handling religion to marry Travis Word, who believes in salvation by work rather than by grace of God. Florida Grace eventually rejects Travis Word and his philosophies, returning to the beliefs of her youth—absent the influence of her father while she rediscovers a relationship to her dead mother.

In focusing upon modern southern womanhood, Smith writes in the tradition of Eudora Welty and evokes comparisons with the work of Bobbie Ann Mason and Kaye Gibbons. Her work demonstrates that concocting fictions is a part of everyone's life, that articulating desires and fears is an important part of understanding one's self and a particularly challenging aspect of life as a southern woman.

—Gary MacDonald

SMITH, Ray

Nationality: Canadian. **Born:** Cape Breton, Nova Scotia, 12 December 1941. **Education:** Dalhousie University, B.A. 1963. **Military Service:** Royal Canadian Air Force, 1959–64; became flying officer. **Family:** Married Anja Mechielsen. **Career:** Systems analyst, Manufacturer's Life, Toronto, Ontario, 1963–64; full-time writer, 1964–70; instructor in English, Loyola College, Montreal, Quebec, 1970; instructor in English, Dawson College, Montreal, 1971—. **Awards:** New Press award for best short fiction, 1985. **Address:** 11 Burton Avene, Westmount, Quebec, Canada H3Z 1J6.

Publications

Novels

Lord Nelson Tavern. Toronto, McClelland & Stewart, 1974.
A Night at the Opera. N.p., n.d.
The Man Who Loved Jane Austen. Erin, Ontario, Porcupine's Quill, 1999.

Short Stories

Cape Breton Is the Thought Control Centre of Canada. Toronto, Anansi Press, 1969.
Century. Toronto, Stoddart, 1986.

Plays

Lord Nelson Tavern (one-act play). Toronto, 1976.

Radio Plays: *Lord Nelson Tavern*. Toronto, Canadian Broadcasting Corporation, 1975.

Other

Contributor, *The New Romans*, edited by Al Purdy. Hurtig, 1968.
Contributor, *Sixteen by Twelve*, edited by John Metcalf. New York, Ryerson, 1970.
Contributor, *Great Canadian Short Stories*, edited by Alec Lucas. New York, Dell, 1971.
Contributor, *The Story So Far*, edited by George Bowering. Toronto, Coach House, 1971.
Contributor, *Seeing through Shuck*, edited by Richard Kostelanetz. New York, Ballantine, 1972.
Contributor, *The Narrative Voice*, edited by John Metcalf. New York, Ryerson, 1972.
Contributor, *Breakthrough Fictioneers*, edited by Richard Kostelanetz. Something Else, 1973.
Contributor, *Stories from Atlantic Canada*, edited by Kent Thompson. Macmillan, 1973.
Contributor, *Readings for Canadian Writing Students*, edited by Bill Schermbrucker. Capilano College, 1976.
Contributor, *East of Canada*, edited by Ray Fraser. Breakwater, 1976.
Contributor, *Here and Now: Best Canadian Stories*, edited by John Metcalf and Blaise. Oberon, 1977.
Contributor, *Fiction of Contemporary Canada*, edited by George Bowering. Toronto, Coach House, 1980.
Contributor, *The Cape Breton Collection*, edited by Lesley Choyce. Pottersfield, 1984.
Contributor, *The New Press Anthology: Best Canadian Short Fiction 1*, edited by John Metcalf and Rooke. General, 1984.
Contributor, *The New Press Anthology: Best Canadian Short Fiction 2*, edited by John Metcalf and Rooke. General, 1985.
Contributor, *The Montreal Storytellers: A Collection of Memoirs, Photographs, and Critical Essays*, edited by J. R. Struthers. Vehicule, 1985.

*

Critical Studies: *The Montreal Storytellers: A Collection of Memoirs, Photographs, and Critical Essays,* edited by J. R. Struthers, Vehicule, 1985.

* * *

For more than three decades, Ray Smith has occupied a distinctive position on the margins of the Canadian literary scene. His work is characterized by an interest in experimentation, but there is no discernible pattern of development. Each of his books is markedly different from the others, and none fits comfortably into the standard academic overviews of Canadian literature.

His first book, *Cape Breton Is the Thought Control Centre of Canada* (short fiction), is one of the earliest Canadian examples of experimental writing in the international tradition. (Of American writers, perhaps Donald Barthelme provides the closest analogue.) The relentless, witty interrogation of short story form underscores a parallel skepticism about received truths in other areas of life.

Smith's first novel, *Lord Nelson Tavern*, focuses on a group of about ten characters, most of whom have known each other from their student days. The first of its seven sections depicts that period of their lives as being relatively ordinary, but as their life stories unfold, their individual narratives become increasingly bizarre and exotic. One, for example, becomes a famous poet who marries an Oscar-winning actress. Another—the least likely—becomes a major player in a world-class drug smuggling operation; eventually he is murdered in accordance with Hollywood convention. A third becomes an internationally acclaimed artist, a fourth a producer of pornographic films, and so on.

Smith does not attempt to make such lives seem believable. Instead his interest is in exploring the voices of his characters, both spoken and written. Much of the book is in dialogue, and there are many unusually long speeches; two of the sections are transcriptions of diaries. Though many of the episodes involve comic exaggeration, the novel does address serious thematic issues, especially the nature of love and art, and the factors that promote and destroy them. Taken as a whole (and despite the sometimes frivolous and cynical rhetoric), *Lord Nelson Tavern* professes an almost Romantic faith in the validity of romantic love and the power of art to redeem human experience.

Century is a collection of six stories set at various times between 1893 and 1983 and in various places, mostly European. Connections are drawn among some of the protagonists (usually participants in the world of diplomacy), but in other respects the book is a mirror image of its predecessor. Smith here is interested in verisimilitude, as the stories' settings are presented in full (and clearly well-researched) detail. Thematically, the volume makes no clear assertions, as it leads its reader to contemplate the complexity, chaos, and absurdity of twentieth-century life. Collective madness is set against the sanity and dignity of certain individuals, but the focus is on questioning rather than affirmation.

A Night at the Opera, Smith's second novel, also reflects his fascination with history, though here his stance is more straightforwardly satirical. The setting is the fictional south German city of Waltherrott. Three narratives are played off against each other: the late-twentieth-century identity quest of one Herr Einzelturm, the director of the local transit authority; the story of the struggle, in 1848, of Carl Maria von Stumpf to compose his opera *Der Hosenkavalier*, which purports to mythologize the city's early history; and a document written by a medieval priest named Adalbert describing first-hand the events that inspired the opera (which, by Einzelturm's time, has become a local classic).

The titles of both the opera and the novel itself (with its reference to the Marx Brothers) suggest something of the slapstick, parodic tone, as Smith examines the ways in which mythologies are created and propagated out of social and personal need, with little regard for historical truth. Beyond that, Smith assumes the traditional role of the satirist, ridiculing the manifestations of folly (especially lust, greed, and pride) that remain constant over the centuries. Some sympathy is generated for all three protagonists, each of whom is (comparatively) an innocent in a world of fools and knaves. Though its concept is intriguing, the novel's impact is dulled by the fact that the general targets of its satire have been hit so easily and often before. (The local, German targets are essentially parabolic, it is broadly hinted.) There is something labored about using such complex machinery to skewer bourgeois complacency yet again.

The Man Who Loved Jane Austen is very different in tone and style. Smith uses standard realism to deliver a narrative set in Montreal in the late 1990s, against the backdrop of ongoing debate about whether the province of Quebec should secede from the Canadian confederation. The protagonist, Frank Wilson, an English instructor at a community college, feels angered and threatened by the separatist movement (as do all of the novel's other characters who express themselves on the subject). But the primary focus is on Frank's effort to retain custody of his two young sons after his wife's death, in the face of determined attempts by his in-laws to take them away from him. The personal and political themes—potential break-up of a family and of a country—are clearly meant to resonate with each other.

Frank is a believable and sympathetic figure, and Smith—for the first time in his career—has painstakingly delineated the mundane details of a daily life that is supremely ordinary rather than exceptional in some way. But most of the secondary characters are simplistically drawn, especially the in-laws, whose status as caricature villains weakens the novel's texture. Nor is Quebec nationalism given credible representation; a reader unfamiliar with Quebec history might be puzzled that so many otherwise sane people could be attracted to a cause that any reasonable person (in the context of this novel) must conclude is self-evidently without merit.

Smith's career has been spectacularly atypical. His first two books, perhaps because of their self-conscious experimentation, attracted some academic attention in the decade or so after their publication, but the next three have been virtually ignored both by academe and by the broader audience for literary fiction. In part this may be the result of a collective judgment about the quality of the work. But it may also be that Smith's fiction simply diverges too dramatically from what the Canadian reading public is used to. And the only thing certain about Smith's next book is that it will be significantly different from anything he has written to date.

—Lawrence Mathews

SMITH, Rosamond

See OATES, Joyce Carol

SOMERS, Jane

See LESSING, Doris (May)

SONTAG, Susan

Nationality: American. **Born:** New York City, 16 January 1933. **Education:** The University of California, Berkeley, 1948–49; University of Chicago, 1949–51, B.A. 1951; Harvard University, Cambridge, Massachusetts, 1954–57, M.A. 1955; St. Anne's College, Oxford, 1957. **Family:** Has one son. **Career:** Instructor in English, University of Connecticut, Storrs, 1953–54; Teaching Fellow in Philosophy, Harvard University, 1955–57; editor, *Commentary,* New York, 1959; Lecturer in Philosophy, City College of New York, and Sarah Lawrence College, Bronxville, New York, 1959–60; Instructor in Religion, Columbia University, New York, 1960–64; writer-in-residence, Rutgers University, New Brunswick, New Jersey, 1964–65. President, PEN American Center, 1987–89. Lives in New York City. **Awards:** American Association of University Women fellowship, 1957; Rockefeller fellowship, 1965, 1974; Guggenheim fellowship, 1966, 1975; American Academy award, 1976; Brandeis University Creative Arts award, 1976; Ingram Merrill Foundation award, 1976; National Book Critics Circle award, 1977; Academy of Sciences and Literature award (Mainz, Germany), 1979; MacArthur Foundation fellowship, 1990–95; Premio Malaparte award (Italy), 1992. **Member:** American Academy, 1979; Officer, Order of Arts and Letters (France), 1984. **Address:** c/o Wylie, Aitken & Stone, 250 West 57th Street, New York, New York 10107, U.S.A.

Publications

Novels

The Benefactor. New York, Farrar Straus, 1963; London, Eyre and Spottiswoode, 1964.
Death Kit. New York, Farrar Straus, 1967; London, Secker and Warburg, 1968.
The Volcano Lover. New York, Farrar Straus, and London, Cape, 1992.
In America. New York, Farrar, Straus and Giroux, 2000.

Short Stories

I, etcetera. New York, Farrar Straus, 1978; London, Gollancz, 1979.
The Way We Live Now, illustrated by Howard Hodgkin. New York, Farrar Straus, and London, Cape, 1991.

Uncollected Short Stories

"Man with a Pain," in *Harper's* (New York), April 1964.
"Description (of a Description)," in *Antaeus* (New York), Autumn 1984.
"The Letter Scene," in *The New Yorker,* 18 August 1986.
"Pilgrimage," in *The New Yorker,* 21 December 1987.

Plays

Duet for Cannibals (screenplay). New York, Farrar Straus, 1970; London, Allen Lane, 1974.
Brother Carl (screenplay). New York, Farrar Straus, 1974.
Alice in Bed. New York, Farrar Straus, 1993.

Screenplays: *Duet for Cannibals,* 1969; *Brother Carl,* 1971.

Other

Against Interpretation and Other Essays. New York, Farrar Straus, 1966; London, Eyre and Spottiswoode, 1967.
Trip to Hanoi. New York, Farrar Straus, and London, Panther, 1969.
Styles of Radical Will (essays). New York, Farrar Straus, and London, Secker and Warburg, 1969.
On Photography. New York, Farrar Straus, 1977; London, Allen Lane, 1978.
Illness as Metaphor. New York, Farrar Straus, 1978; London, Allen Lane, 1979.
Under the Sign of Saturn (essays). New York, Farrar Straus, 1980; London, Writers and Readers, 1983.
A Susan Sontag Reader. New York, Farrar Straus, 1982; London, Penguin, 1983.
Aids and Its Metaphors. New York, Farrar Straus, and London, Allen Lane, 1989.

Conversations with Susan Sontag, edited by Leland Poague. Jackson, University Press of Mississippi, 1995.

Women (text), photographs by Annie Leibovitz. New York, Random House, 1999.

Editor, *Selected Writings of Artaud,* translated by Helen Weaver. New York, Farrar Straus, 1976.

Editor, *A Barthes Reader.* New York, Hill and Wang, and London, Cape, 1982; as *Barthes: Selected Writings,* London, Fontana, 1983.

Editor, *Best American Essays: 1992.* New York, Ticknor and Fields, 1992.

Editor, with Danilo Kis, *Homo Poeticus.* New York, Farrar Straus, 1995.

*

Bibliography: *Susan Sontag: An Annotated Bibliography, 1948–1992* by Leland Poague and Kathy Parsons, New York, Garland, 2000.

Critical Studies: *Susan Sontag: The Elegiac Modernist* by Sohnya Sayres, New York, Routledge Chapman and Hall, 1989; *Susan Sontag: Mind as Passion* by Liam Kennedy, Manchester, England, Manchester University Press, and New York, St. Martin's Press, 1995; *Susan Sontag: The Making of an Icon* by Carl Rollyson and Lisa Paddock, New York, Norton, 2000.

Theatrical Activities: Director: **Plays**—*As You Desire Me* by Pirandello, Turin and Italian tour, 1979–80; *Jacques and His Master* by Milan Kundera, Cambridge, Massachusetts, 1985; *Waiting for Godot* by Samuel Beckett, Sarajevo, 1993–94. **Films**—*Duet for Cannibals,* 1969; *Brother Carl,* 1971; *Promised Lands* (documentary), 1974; *Unguided Tour,* 1983.

* * *

Traditionally readers have approached works of fiction as verbal structures which reveal and generally make statements about a preexisting ''real'' subject. The writer may represent his subject directly, ''imitating'' in accordance with conventional understandings about the probable behavior of the human and the natural order; or he may render his subject indirectly by presenting a metaphor which stands for and usually implies a generalization about the same reality. Thus traditional criticism was designed to judge the verisimilitude of fiction and to provide a way of understanding metaphor, allegory, and parable as symbolic statements. It is impossible, however, to discuss the fiction of Susan Sontag in critical terms derived from this essentially naturalistic tradition, just as Sontag herself has attempted to construct a new critical approach to do justice to those works of *avant-garde* artists whose rendering of the modern world she finds significant.

The tough, polemical essays collected in *Against Interpretation* and *Styles of Radical Will* are more impressive than Sontag's fiction thus far, which too often seems contrived to illustrate a doctrine. For Sontag, the final ''most liberating value of art'' is ''transparency,'' which means experiencing ''the luminousness of the thing in itself, of things being what they are.'' Interpretation, which seeks to replace the work with something else—usually historical, ethical or psychological paraphrase—is essentially ''revenge which the intellect takes upon art.'' To interpret is ''to impoverish, to deplete.'' Sontag's chief interest as a critic is the work of artists (especially film makers) whose work is misunderstood because it resists ''being reduced to a story.'' Thus Sontag observes that in his film *Persona* Bergman presents not a story, but ''something that is, in one sense, cruder, and, in another, more abstract: a body of material, a subject. The function of the subject or material may be as much its opacity, its multiplicity, as the ease with which it yields itself to being incarnated by a determinate plot or action.'' Deliberately frustrating any conventional attempt to determine ''what happens,'' the new novels and films are able, she maintains, to involve the audience ''more directly in other matters, for instance in the very processes of seeing and knowing.... The material presented can then be treated as a thematic resource, from which different (and perhaps concurrent) narrative structures can be derived as variations.'' The artist intends his work to remain ''partly encoded'': the truly modern consciousness challenges the supremacy of naturalism and univocal symbolism.

While vestiges of naturalistic situations remain in Sontag's fiction (her story ''The Will and the Way,'' for example, seems to be an allegory concerning the image of women in modern life), ''interpretation'' is by definition more or less irrelevant. *The Benefactor* is in its general outline a dream novel; its ''thematic resource'' is the problem of attaining selfhood and genuine freedom. Just as Sontag sees Montaigne's essays as ''dispassionate, varied explorations of the innumerable ways of being a self,'' the hero of *The Benefactor* uses his dreams as a means of achieving freedom. ''It seemed to me,'' Hippolyte concludes, ''all my life had been converging on the state of mind ... in which I would finally be reconciled to myself—myself as I really am, the self of my dreams. That reconciliation is what I take to be freedom.'' The device which keeps the reader from treating the novel as paraphrasable allegory is the deliberate ambiguity of the narrative frame: we are left to decide whether the narrative is an account of what happened or an account which is at least in part the construction of a mad Hippolyte whose dreams are symbolic transformations, in the usual Freudian sense, of ''what happened.'' Sontag owes a good deal to Sartre and Camus, but even more to the *auteurs* of *Last Year at Marienbad* and *L'Avventura. Death Kit* has as its concern the failure of a man who has no true self. ''Diddy, not really alive, had a life. Not really the same. Some people are their lives. Others, like Diddy, merely inhabit their lives.'' Diddy commits a murder, or thinks he commits a murder; there is no way of determining this, but what matters is how Diddy handles the possibility that he is a murderer, and how he tries to appropriate the self of a blind girl whom he selfishly ''loves.'' Out of the materials of his life Diddy assembles his death; out of his failure the reader may assemble an understanding of vanity, inauthenticity, and death. Wholly successful or not, *The Benefactor* and *Death Kit* are haunting works, effective to the degree to which the reader can accept Sontag's powerful arguments elsewhere about the exhaustion of the naturalistic tradition. As the American critic E.D. Hirsch puts it, ''Knowledge of ambiguity is not necessarily ambiguous knowledge.''

—Elmer Borklund

SORRENTINO, Gilbert

Nationality: American. **Born:** Brooklyn, New York, 27 April 1929. Educated in New York public schools; Brooklyn College, 1950–51, 1955–57. **Military Service:** Served in the United States Army

Medical Corps, 1951–53. **Family:** Married 1) Elsene Wiessner (divorced); 2) Vivian Victoria Ortiz; two sons and one daughter. **Career:** Re-insurance clerk, Fidelity and Casualty Company, New York, 1947–48; messenger, American Houses Inc., 1948–49; freight checker, Ace Assembly Agency, New York, 1954–56; packer, Bennett Brothers, New York, 1956–57; shipping room supervisor, Thermo-fax Sales, 1957–60. Editor, *Neon* magazine, 1956–60, and Grove Press, 1965–70, both New York; book editor, *Kulchur,* New York, 1961–63; taught at Columbia University, New York, 1965; Aspen Writers Workshop, Colorado, 1967; Sarah Lawrence College, Bronxville, New York, 1971–72; New School for Social Research, New York, 1976–79, 1980–82; Edwin S. Quain Professor of Literature, University of Scranton, Pennsylvania, 1979. Since 1982 professor of English, Stanford University, California. **Awards:** Guggenheim fellowship, 1973, 1987; National Endowment for the Arts grant, 1974, 1978; Fels award, 1975; Ariadne Foundation grant, 1975; Creative Artists Public Service grant, 1975; John Dos Passos prize, 1981; American Academy award, 1985; Lannan Literary award for fiction, 1992. **Agent:** Mel Berger, William Morris Agency, 1350 Avenue of the Americas, New York, New York 10019, U.S.A. **Address:** Department of English, Stanford University, Stanford, California 94305, U.S.A.

PUBLICATIONS

Novels

The Sky Changes. New York, Hill and Wang, 1966.
Steelwork. New York, Pantheon, 1970.
Imaginative Qualities of Actual Things. New York, Pantheon, 1971.
Splendide-Hôtel. New York, New Directions, 1973.
Mulligan Stew. New York, Grove Press, 1979; London, Boyars, 1980.
Aberration of Starlight. New York, Random House, 1980; London, Boyars, 1981.
Crystal Vision. Berkeley, California, North Point Press, 1981; London, Boyars, 1982.
Blue Pastoral. Berkeley, California, North Point Press, 1983; London, Boyars, 1985.
Odd Number. Berkeley, California, North Point Press, 1985.
Rose Theatre. Elmwood Park, Illinois, Dalkey Archive, 1987.
Misterioso. Elmwood Park, Illinois, Dalkey Archive, 1989.
Under the Shadow. Elmwood Park, Illinois, Dalkey Archive, 1991.
Red the Fiend. New York, Fromm International, 1995.
Pack of Lies. Normal, Illinois, Dalkey Archive Press, 1997.

Short Story

A Beehive Arranged on Human Principles (novella). New York, Grenfell Press, 1986.

Uncollected Short Stories

''The Moon in Its Flight,'' in *New American Review 13,* edited by Theodore Solotaroff. New York, Simon and Schuster, 1971.
''Land of Cotton,'' in *Harper's* (New York), November 1977.
''Decades,'' in *The Best American Short Stories 1978,* edited by Theodore Solotaroff and Shannon Ravenel. Boston, Houghton Mifflin, 1978.
''Chats with the Real McCoy,'' in *Atlantic* (Boston), March 1979.
''The Gala Cocktail Party,'' in *The Pushcart Prize 9,* edited by Bill Henderson. Wainscott, New York, Pushcart Press, 1984.

Play

Flawless Play Restored: The Masque of Fungo. Los Angeles, Black Sparrow Press, 1974.

Poetry

The Darkness Surrounds Us. Highlands, North Carolina, Jargon, 1960.
Black and White. New York, Totem, 1964.
The Perfect Fiction. New York, Norton, 1968.
Corrosive Sublimate. Los Angeles, Black Sparrow Press, 1971.
A Dozen Oranges. Santa Barbara, California, Black Sparrow Press, 1976.
White Sail. Santa Barbara, California, Black Sparrow Press, 1977.
The Orangery. Austin, University of Texas Press, 1978.
Selected Poems 1958–1980. Santa Barbara, California, Black Sparrow Press, 1981.

Other

Something Said (essays). Berkeley, California, North Point Press, 1984.
Translator, *Sulpiciae Elegidia/Elegiacs of Sulpicia.* Mount Horeb, Wisconsin, Perishable Press, 1977.

*

Bibliography: *Gilbert Sorrentino: A Descriptive Bibliography* by William McPheron, Elmwood Park, Illinois, Dalkey Archive, 1991.

Manuscript Collection: University of Delaware, Newark.

Critical Studies: ''Gilbert Sorrentino Issue'' of *Vort* (Silver Spring, Maryland), Fall 1974, and *Review of Contemporary Fiction* (Elmwood Park, Illinois), Fall 1981; *Fact, Fiction, and Representation: Four Novels by Gilbert Sorrentino* by Louis Mackey, Columbia, South Carolina, Camden House, 1997.

Gilbert Sorrentino comments:

My writing is the act of solving self-imposed problems.

* * *

Gilbert Sorrentino's novels are dedicated to several anti-traditional propositions: that space, rather than time, is the most revealing principle for narrative structure; that the physical texture of language, rather than its semantic properties, is the key to communication between a novelist and the reader; and that an awareness of the author's act of writing, rather than the willing suspension of disbelief, yields the greatest pleasure in experiencing a novel.

The Sky Changes and *Steelwork,* Sorrentino's earliest novels (from the days when he was still best known as a poet), are demonstrations of spatial order. The first is the record (told in block sections of separate narrative) of a protagonist's dissolving marriage, framed by an auto trip across the United States. Both the relationship and the journey would seem to imply a temporal order; but at several points Sorrentino self-consciously violates that order to show that the human imagination transcends simple chronology—the trip's emotional resolution comes as early as two-thirds through the cross-country journey. *Steelwork* is the spatial portrait of a Brooklyn neighborhood over two decades of human experience. On one street-corner, for example, the events of several years' distance are imaginatively rehearsed; and characters' lives are studied in a simultaneity of presence, although by the clock they have lived through much of their lives. Because space—the neighborhood—is the organizing principle, the chronology is deliberately scrambled, so that we move back and forth from 1951 to 1942 to 1949. As a result, the reader experiences the neighborhood as the spatial whole it would be for anyone who lived there all those years. Emotions and the imagination outstrip time.

Imaginative Qualities of Actual Things is Sorrentino's wildly comic exercise of his most self-apparent writing techniques. Ostensibly a *roman à clef* exposing the petty jealousies and seductions of the 1950s and 1960s New York art world, the book is in fact a demonstration of Sorrentino's pleasure in writing a novel. Characters' statements are undercut by rudely sarcastic footnotes; midway through a piece of exposition the author will stop and berate the reader for making him supply such petty details; and when the author hates a character, ludicrous scenes are devised for the unfortunate soul's humiliation and punishment. Throughout, the reader is aware that the real subject of this novel is not its mimicry of a projected real world, but instead the process of its own composition, which the reader witnesses firsthand.

Making fiction its own subject—not a representation of an illusionary world but instead its own artifice as added to the world, an aesthetic Sorrentino learned from his mentor, William Carlos Williams—is the achievement of *Splendide-Hôtel.* Its brief chapters are named after the successive letters of the alphabet, which provide the topics for composition—the capital letter A's on the page looking like flies on a wall, breeding in decay; the letter K reminding Sorrentino of the baseball score-card symbol for strike-out, and of a headline which spoke volumes just by saying ''K-K-K-Koufax!!!!''

In his fifth and most commercially successful work of fiction, *Mulligan Stew,* Sorrentino offers a full display of novelistic talents at work. Indeed, he wishes to surpass his previous efforts by showing all aspects of fiction writing, from the novelist's act of composition to his notebooks, letters, and even the personal thoughts of his characters. Borrowing his structure from Flann O'Brien's novel *At Swim-Two-Birds* (1939), Sorrentino invents an imaginary novelist named Anthony Lamont who is struggling to shore up a sagging career with an experimental novel, a piece of ''surfiction'' (Sorrentino despises the term) titled *Guinea Red.* A murder mystery, it features unabashedly miserable writing; Lamont keeps losing the murdered body and forgetting where he's placed the fatal wound, and the prose itself is dreadfully overwritten in a parody of low-brow style. The reader is also given access to Lamont's letters, notebooks, and journal entries. Midway through, his characters mutiny and seek ways to escape Lamont's leaden narrative and find work in a more promising repertoire. A massive novel which by its very bulk and meticulous range of styles immerses the reader in its own subject, *Mulligan Stew* is Sorrentino's fullest repertoire of writing talent.

Mulligan Stew exhausts the innovative techniques of 1960s fiction, and also clears the way for a new lyricism in Sorrentino's work. Whereas his earlier novels turned to poetic devices as a way of eclipsing the quotidian *Aberration of Starlight, Crystal Vision,* and *Blue Pastoral* are able to confront both experience and the act of writing directly.

Aberration of Starlight explains experience as a matter of point of view, fragmenting a summer's experience at a New Jersey vacation lodge into four narratives, much in the manner of William Faulkner's *The Sound and the Fury.* Sorrentino uses these distinct modes of vision in order to highlight language, especially how essentially stupid world views are, in the manner of Flaubert's *Dictionnaire des idées reçues,* created by and not just expressed through banalities of language. *Crystal Vision* embraces language directly, transcribing streetcorner conversations from the verbally rich Brooklyn of Sorrentino's youth, as the characters of his earlier *Steelwork* re-emerge from their ''world of light'' to speak directly. Their language expands the author's previous vision, showing how they have the vitality to survive on their own in fiction, without narrative's customary supporting devices. *Blue Pastoral* celebrates the stylistics of Blue Serge Gavotte as he creates a pastoral accompanying his journey from New York to San Francisco (a less lyrical trip once made west by the protagonist of *The Sky Changes*). Sorrentino takes the occasion to parody pastoral forms and satirize stock characters; much of his play consists in delighting with obviously bad writing. But with all conventions demolished by his earlier works, and with unconventionality itself made a sham by the achievement of *Mulligan Stew,* there seems little else for Sorrentino to do with the novel than continue to write it, even poorly.

Sorrentino's inward turn of narrative is confirmed by his practice in *Odd Number,* a brief (159-page) reinvestigation of how his earlier novel, *Imaginative Qualities of Actual Things,* might have been assembled. In the earlier work Sorrentino had used the well-established formal device of the *roman à clef* to structure his narrative; his use of footnotes and intrusively parenthetical remarks indicates that the form is barely able to contain his rage against some of these characters drawn from a lifestyle he was now rejecting. *Odd Number* transposes this volatility to the novel's form itself. Like *Aberration of Starlight,* the tale is told several times, but here the emphasis is even more on the uncertainty of events. The first time through the reader is given a question-and-answer dialogue, as in detective fashion the voice of the novel interrogates its own resources to discover exactly what has happened. This section's awkward and uncertain rhythm yields to a more fluently conversational account of the book's events—all of which originally transpired in *Imaginative Qualities of Actual Things,* now supplemented with coy references to Sorrentino's other novels. But the authority of part two yields to a cross examination of the documents themselves: the contents of dresser drawers, photographs, and other possessions which contradict certain assertions of both previous sections, virtually unmaking the novel which has been read. The novel, therefore, is no more reliable a report on the world than the self-conscious rage of Sorrentino's earlier version, a reminder that truth, if one cares for it, must be found beyond the fiction writer's practice no matter how it might be structured.

That the matters of *Imaginative Qualities*...can be extended infinitely across time and space is evident from Sorrentino's success with *Rose Theatre,* in which the female characters attempt to correct apparent misinformation from *Odd Number,* data now considered errant not because of any mistakes in that particular work but because the questions which generated it excluded certain possibilities of discourse. The very attempt to stabilize reality, however, adds a new dimension to its nature, which invites further uncertainties—a reminder of the continuously evolving nature of fiction, which in its struggles to provide a persuasive account of reality only confounds its unverifiable nature.

Sorrentino's trilogy of responses to *Imaginative Qualities ...* concludes with *Misterioso.* Here the narrative aspires toward the encyclopedic as a strategy for both inclusiveness and authority. Yet because previous facts can only be clarified by the introduction of new materials, verifiability still remains in dispute. That the novel is set in a supermarket implies both its structure and utility: there is no firm basis for its narrative, but rather a wide variety of materials from which to select, a treasury of stories one can choose according to fancy. Yet no one would ever try to draw conclusive substance from everything; there can even be narratives that threaten to distract by their intrusion, the resistance to which constitutes a sub-theme in itself. Simply to comprehend all that is possible remains the novel's goal, an activity reflecting on Sorrentino's activity in writing the initial work, a novel that can expand infinitely with each reconsideration.

—Jerome Klinkowitz

SOYINKA, Wole

Nationality: Nigerian. **Born:** Akinwande Oluwole Soyinka, in Abeokuta, 13 July 1934. **Education:** St. Peter's School, Ake, Abeokuta, 1938–43; Abeokuta Grammar School, 1944–45; Government College, Ibadan, 1946–50; University College, Ibadan (now University of Ibadan), 1952–54; University of Leeds, Yorkshire, 1954–57, B.A. (honors) in English. **Family:** Married; has children. **Career:** Play reader, Royal Court Theatre, London, 1957–59; Rockefeller Research Fellow in drama, University of Ibadan, 1961–62; lecturer in English, University of Ife, Ile-Ife, 1963–64; senior lecturer in English, University of Lagos, 1965–67; head of the department of theater arts, University of Ibadan, 1969–72 (appointment made in 1967); professor of comparative literature, and head of the department of dramatic arts, University of Ife, 1975–85. Visiting fellow, Churchill College, Cambridge, 1973–74; visiting professor, University of Ghana, Legon, 1973–74, University of Sheffield, 1974, Yale University, New Haven, Connecticut, 1979–80, and Cornell University, Ithaca, New York, 1986. Founding director, 1960 Masks Theatre, 1960, and Orisun Theatre, 1964, Lagos and Ibadan, and Unife Guerilla Theatre, Ile-Ife, 1978; co-editor, *Black Orpheus,* 1961–64; editor, *Transition* (later *Ch'indaba*) magazine, Accra, Ghana, 1975–77. Secretary-General, Union of Writers of the African Peoples, 1975. Tried and acquitted of armed robbery, 1965; political prisoner, detained by the Federal Military Government, Lagos and Kaduna, 1967–69. **Awards:** Dakar Festival award, 1966; John Whiting award, 1967; Jock Campbell award *(New Statesman),* for fiction, 1968; Nobel Prize for Literature, 1986; Benson Medal, 1990; Premio Letterario Internazionalle Mondello, 1990. D.Litt: University of Leeds, 1973, Yale University, University of Montpellier, France, University of Lagos, and University of Bayreuth, 1989. Fellow, Royal Society of Literature (U.K.); member, American Academy. Named Commander, Federal Republic of Nigeria, 1986, Order of La Legion d'Honneur, France, 1989, and Order of the Republic of Italy, 1990; Akogun of Isara, 1989; Akinlatun of Egbaland, 1990. **Agent:** Morton Leavy, Leavy Rosensweig and Hyman, 11 East 44th Street, New York, New York 10017; or Triharty (Nig.) Ltd. Agency Division, 4, Ola-ayeni Street, Ikeja, Lagos, Nigeria. (U.K. Correspondent: Cognix Ltd., Media Suite, 3 Tyers Gate, London SE1 3HX). **Address:** P.O. Box 935, Abeokuta, Nigeria.

PUBLICATIONS

Novels

The Interpreters. London, Deutsch, 1965; New York, Macmillan, 1970.

Season of Anomy. London, Collings, 1973; New York, Third Press, 1974.

Plays

The Swamp Dwellers (produced London, 1958; New York, 1968). Included in *Three Plays,* 1963; in *Five Plays,* 1964.

The Lion and the Jewel (produced Ibadan, 1959; London, 1966). Ibadan, London, and New York, Oxford University Press, 1963.

The Invention (produced London, 1959).

A Dance of the Forests (produced Lagos, 1960). Ibadan, London, and New York, Oxford University Press, 1963.

The Trials of Brother Jero (produced Ibadan, 1960; Cambridge, 1965; London, 1966; New York, 1967). Included in *Three Plays,* 1963; in *Five Plays,* 1964.

Camwood on the Leaves (broadcast 1960). London, Eyre Methuen, 1973; in *Camwood on the Leaves, and Before the Blackout,* 1974.

The Republican and The New Republican (satirical revues; produced Lagos, 1963).

Three Plays. Ibadan, Mbari, 1963; as *Three Short Plays,* London, Oxford University Press, 1969.

The Strong Breed (produced Ibadan, 1964; London, 1966; New York, 1967). Included in *Three Plays,* 1963; in *Five Plays,* 1964.

Childe Internationale (produced Ibadan, 1964). Ibadan, Fountain, 1987.

Kongi's Harvest (produced Ibadan, 1964; New York, 1968). Ibadan, London, and New York, Oxford University Press, 1967.

Five Plays: A Dance of the Forests, The Lion and the Jewel, The Swamp Dwellers, The Trials of Brother Jero, The Strong Breed. Ibadan, London, and New York, Oxford University Press, 1964.

Before the Blackout (produced Ibadan, 1965; Leeds, 1981). Ibadan, Orisun, 1971; in *Camwood on the Leaves, and Before the Blackout,* 1974.

The Road (produced London, 1965; also director: produced Chicago, 1984). Ibadan, London, and New York, Oxford University Press, 1965.

Rites of the Harmattan Solstice (produced Lagos, 1966).

Madmen and Specialists (produced Waterford, Connecticut, and New York, 1970; revised version, also director: produced Ibadan, 1971). London, Methuen, 1971; New York, Hill and Wang, 1972.

The Jero Plays: The Trials of Brother Jero, and Jero's Metamorphosis. London, Eyre Methuen, 1973.

Jero's Metamorphosis (produced Lagos, 1975). Included in *The Jero Plays,* 1973.

The Bacchae: A Communion Rite, adaptation of the play by Euripides (produced London, 1973). London, Eyre Methuen, 1973; New York, Norton, 1974.

Collected Plays: A Dance of the Forests, The Swamp Dwellers, The Strong Breed, The Road, The Bacchae. London and New York, Oxford University Press, 1973.
Collected Plays:The Lion and the Jewel, Kongi's Harvest, The Trials of Brother Jero, Jero's Metamorphosis, Madmen and Specialists. London and New York, Oxford University Press, 1974.
Camwood on the Leaves, and Before the Blackout: Two Short Plays. New York, Third Press, 1974.
Death and the King's Horseman (also director: produced Ile-Ife, 1976; Chicago, 1979; also director: produced New York, 1987). London, Eyre Methuen, 1975; New York, Norton, 1976.
Opera Wonyosi, adaptation of *The Threepenny Opera* by Brecht (also director: produced Ile-Ife, 1977). Bloomington, Indiana University Press, and London, Collings, 1981.
Golden Accord (produced Louisville, 1980).
Priority Projects (revue; produced on Nigeria tour, 1982).
Requiem for a Futurologist (also director: produced Ile-Ife, 1983). London, Collings, 1985.
A Play of Giants (also director: produced New Haven, Connecticut, 1984). London, Methuen, 1984.
Six Plays (includes *The Trials of Brother Jero, Jero's Metamorphosis, Camwood on the Leaves, Death and the King's Horseman, Madmen and Specialists, Opera Wonyosi*). London, Methuen. 1984.
From Zia with Love. London, Methuen, 1992
The Beatification of Area Boy: A Lagosian Kaleidoscope. London, Methuen Drama, 1995.

Screenplay: *Kongi's Harvest,* 1970.

Radio Plays: *Camwood on the Leaves,* 1960; *The Detainee,* 1965; *Die Still, Dr. Godspeak,* 1981; *A Scourge of Hyacinths,* 1990; *Nineteen Ninety-Four,* 1993.

Television Plays: *Joshua: A Nigerian Portrait,* 1962 (Canada); *Culture in Transition,* 1963 (USA).

Poetry

Idanre and Other Poems. London, Methuen, 1967; New York, Hill and Wang, 1968.
Poems from Prison. London, Collings, 1969.
A Shuttle in the Crypt. London, Eyre Methuen-Collings, and New York, Hill and Wang, 1972.
Ogun Abibimañ . London, Collings, 1976.
Mandela's Earth and Other Poems. New York, Random House, 1988; London, Deutsch, 1989.
Early Poems. New York, Oxford University Press, 1998.

Other

The Man Died: Prison Notes. London, Eyre Methuen-Collings, and New York, Harper, 1972.
In Person: Achebe, Awoonor, and Soyinka at the University of Washington. Seattle, University of Washington African Studies Program, 1975.
Myth, Literature, and the African World. London, Cambridge University Press, 1976.
Aké: The Years of Childhood (autobiography). London, Collings, 1981; New York, Vintage, 1983.
The Critic and Society (essay). Ile-Ife, University of Ife Press, 1981.
The Past Must Address Its Present (lecture). N.p., Nobel Foundation, 1986; as *This Past Must Address Its Present,* New York, Anson Phelps Institute, 1988.
Art, Dialogue and Outrage: Essays on Literature and Culture. Ibadan, New Horn, 1988.
Isara: A Voyage Around ''Essay.'' New York, Random House, 1989; London, Methuen, 1990.
Ibadan—The Penkelemes Years. London, Methuen, 1994.
The Open Sore of a Continent: A Personal Narrative of The Nigerian Crisis. New York, Oxford University Press, 1996.
The Burden of Memory, the Muse of Forgiveness. New York, Oxford University Press, 1999.
Editor, *Poems of Black Africa.* London, Secker and Warburg, and New York, Hill and Wang, 1975.
Translator, *The Forest of a Thousand Daemons: A Hunter's Saga,* by D.O. Fagunwa. London, Nelson, 1968; New York, Humanities Press, 1969.

*

Bibliography: *Wole Soyinka: A Bibliography* by B. Okpu, Lagos, Libriservice, 1984.

Critical Studies: *Wole Soyinka* by Gerald Moore, London, Evans, and New York, Africana, 1971, revised edition, Evans, 1978; *The Writing of Wole Soyinka* by Eldred D. Jones, London, Heinemann, 1973, revised edition, 1983, 2nd revised edition, London, Curry, 1988; *Three Nigerian Poets: A Critical Study of the Poetry of Soyinka, Clark, and Okigbo* by Nyong J. Udoeyop, Ibadan, Ibadan University Press, 1973; *Critical Perspectives on Wole Soyinka* edited by James Gibbs, Washington, D.C., Three Continents Press, 1980, London, Heinemann, 1981, and *Wole Soyinka* by Gibbs, London, Macmillan, and New York, Grove Press, 1986; *A Writer and His Gods: A Study of the Importance of Yoruba Myths and Religious Ideas in the Writing of Wole Soyinka* by Stephan Larsen, Stockholm, University of Stockholm, 1983; *Wole Soyinka: An Introduction to His Writing* by Obi Maduakar, London, Garland, 1986; *Before Our Very Eyes: Tribute to Wole Soyinka* edited by Dapo Adelugba, Ibadan, Spectrum, 1987; *Index of Subjects, Proverbs and Themes in the Writings of Wole Soyinka* by Greta M.K. Coger, New York, Greenwood, 1988; *Wole Soyinka Revisted* by Derek Wright, New York, Twayne, and Toronto, Maxwell Macmillan Canada, 1993; *The Politics of Wole Soyinka* by Tunde Adeniran, Ibadan, Nigeria, Fountain Publications, 1994; *Wole Soyinka and Yoruba Oral Tradition in Death and Theking's Horseman* by Bimpe Aboyade, Ibadan, Nigeria, Fountain Publications, 1994; *The Poetry of Wole Soyinka* by Tanure Ojaide, Lagos, Malthouse Press, 1994; *Some African Voices of Our Time* by Ivor Agyeman-Duah, Accra, Ghana, Anansesem Publications, 1995; *Understanding Wole Soyinka: Death and the King's Horseman* by A.O. Dasylva, Ibadan, Nigeria, Sam Bookman, 1996; *Strategic Transformations in Nigerian Writing: Orality and History in the Work of Rev. Samuel Johnson, Amos Tutuola, Wole Soyinka and Ben Okri* by Ato Quayson, Oxford, J. Currey, and Bloomington, Indiana University Press, 1997; *Form and Technique in the African Novel* by Olawale Awosika, Ibadan, Nigeria, Sam Bookman, 1997; *Ogun's Children: The Literature and Politics of Wole Soyinka Since* *the Nobel Prize,* edited by OnookomeOkome, Trenton, New Jersey, Africa World Press, 1999.

Theatrical Activities: Director: **Plays**—by Brecht, Chekhov, Clark, Easmon, Eseoghene, Ogunyemi, Shakespeare, Synge, and his own works; *L'Espace et la Magie,* Paris, 1972; *The Biko Inquest* by Jon Blair and Norman Fenton, Ile-Ife, 1978, and New York, 1980. Actor: **Plays**—Igwezu in *The Swamp Dwellers,* London, 1958; Obaneji and Forest Father in *A Dance of the Forests,* Lagos and Ibadan, 1960; Dauda Touray in *Dear Parent and Ogre* by R. Sarif Easmon, Ibadan, 1961; in *The Republican,* Lagos, 1963; **Film**—*Kongi's Harvest,* 1970; **Radio**—Konu in *The Detainee,* 1965.

* * *

Early in his career, Wole Soyinka produced two novels which distill several of the Nobel laureate's key themes. Both *The Interpreters* and *Season of Anomy* focus on the tensions and contradictions of post-colonial Nigerian society. They explore the social and political consequences of the uncomfortable coexistence of African and Western European values within a single cultural framework. Soyinka's characters try to affect various temporary (and often unsatisfying) resolutions in their lives, and to reconcile past to present, tradition to modernity, local life to global economies.

Soyinka's writing style has been criticized as overly erudite and unnecessarily allusive; in both his dialogue and his narration, he tends to blend references to Yoruba traditions (which would be inaccessible to Western readers and which require him to include a glossary in *The Interpreters*) and to European art and philosophy (which would be largely foreign, his critics have suggested, to his Nigerian readership). Soyinka's cultural politics push him to discover and to recover a distinctively African form of literary self-expression; however, his thought and writing have also been indelibly informed by Western traditions. The difficult, abstract textures of his prose emerge from a fluctuating position he establishes between these two cultural systems, as he attempts to negotiate his own uneasy compromise. In fact, that lack of ease or stability gives his writing its energy and its vital interest.

The Interpreters opens with a complex nightclub scene which sets the tone for the rest of the novel. Six friends, who represent various functions in contemporary Nigerian society (such as journalist, engineer, artist, and teacher), get drunk and discuss their lives. The dialogue, in keeping with their situation, is highly fluid, restless, and ironic. The time frame shifts from present to past, establishing resonances but also suggesting the interconnectedness of memory and action. Soyinka's narrative remains somewhat non-linear throughout the book, preferring to follow multiple threads of event and history. Various voices and perspectives interpenetrate, creating a verbal web rather than a monolithic, disciplined plot. Like his character Egbo, who cannot reconcile the demands of his native heritage with contemporary life, Soyinka tends to float between worlds, exploring the manifestations and consequences of that medial state without necessarily resolving his dilemma. The novel is often bitterly satiric, particularly through the character of Sagoe, whose pseudo-philosophy of ''voidancy'' (a scatology run amuck, not unlike that of Jonathan Swift) offers an ongoing misanthropic commentary on the corruption and absurdity of Nigerian society. Little escapes the novel's incisive harshness. Sekoni, the one idealist, is killed at the novel's midpoint, and the second half of the text finds no alternatives for social recovery or happiness. Symbolically, a schoolgirl whom Egbo has made pregnant offers some hope for new life, but she remains nameless and lost to Egbo himself. *The Interpreters* traces the dissolution and despair often brought about by post-colonial states of cultural hybridity and uncertainty.

While *Season of Anomy* also remains uncertain at its conclusion, it takes up the duplicitous situations of post-colonial life and attempts to suggest tentative social, political, and imaginative resolutions. The title refers both to the anarchy that comes with the violent political upheavals in the novel and to the yearly cycles of death and rebirth in nature. The narrative follows the attempts by Ofeyi, a marketing genius who works for a nameless cartel controlling the government, to subvert his employers' social and economic power by introducing a counter-philosophy he discovers at the agricultural community of Aiyéró, which is collectivist, peaceful, native, and benign. The five parts of the novel trace the slow vegetal spread of the indigenous ''way of life'' of Aiyéró, which leads to violence as ideologies of greed and corruption collide with grass-roots philosophy. The revolution appears to fail, although Soyinka also suggests that ''spores'' have been released among the people and that the possibility of betterment remains. The figure of Suberu, the prison guard who has thoughtlessly served the interests of corruption but later chooses to follow Ofeyi, represents such potential conversions. Iriyise, Ofeyi's kidnapped lover whom he sees as intimately and symbolically tied to the land and to Aiyéró, becomes sick and then lapses into a coma from which she has not emerged at the novel's close; her eventual rescue represents the possible healing of Africa in the wake of terrifying social upheavals, while her lack of consciousness suggests that all is not yet well. Soyinka's novel has been criticized for over-simplifying the political conflicts in post-colonial Nigeria, but he aims, at least, to advocate in his fiction a positive, forceful change for African society.

—Kevin McNeilly

SPARK, Muriel (Sarah)

Nationality: British. **Born:** Muriel Sarah Camberg in Edinburgh, 1 February 1918. **Education:** James Gillespie's School for Girls and Heriot Watt College, both Edinburgh. **Family:** Married S.O. Spark in 1937 (marriage dissolved by 1944); one son. **Career:** Worked in the Foreign Office Political Intelligence Department during World War II. General secretary, Poetry Society, and editor, *Poetry Review,* London, 1947–49. Lives in Rome. **Awards:** *Observer* story prize, 1951; Italia prize, for radio play, 1962; James Tait Black Memorial prize, for fiction, 1966; F.N.A.C. prize (France), 1987; Bram Stoker award, 1988; Royal Bank of Scotland—Saltire Society award, 1988; Ingersoll T.S. Eliot award, 1992; David Cohen British Literary prize, 1997; Gold Pen award, International PEN, 1998. D.Litt.: University of Strathclyde, Glasgow, 1971; University of Edinburgh, 1989; Aberdeen University, 1995; University of St. Andrews, 1998; University of Oxford, 1999. D.Univ.: Heriot-Watt University, 1995. C.Litt: Royal Society of Literature, 1991. Fellow, Royal Society of Literature, 1963; Honorary member: American Academy, 1978. O.B.E. (Officer, Order of the British Empire), 1967, Dame, Order of the British Empire, 1993; Officer, Order of Arts and Letters (France), 1988, Commander, 1996. **Agent:** David Higham Associates, 5–8 Lower John Street, London W1R 4HA, England.

PUBLICATIONS

Novels

The Comforters. London, Macmillan, and Philadelphia, Lippincott, 1957.
Robinson. London, Macmillan, and Philadelphia, Lippincott, 1958.
Memento Mori. London, Macmillan, and Philadelphia, Lippincott, 1959.
The Ballad of Peckham Rye. London, Macmillan, and Philadelphia, Lippincott, 1960.
The Bachelors. London, Macmillan, 1960; Philadelphia, Lippincott, 1961.
The Prime of Miss Jean Brodie. London, Macmillan, 1961; Philadelphia, Lippincott, 1962.
The Girls of Slender Means. London, Macmillan, and New York, Knopf, 1963.
The Mandelbaum Gate. London, Macmillan, and New York, Knopf, 1965.
The Public Image. London, Macmillan, and New York, Knopf, 1968.
The Driver's Seat. London, Macmillan, and New York, Knopf, 1970.
Not to Disturb. London, Macmillan, 1971; New York, Viking Press, 1972.
The Hothouse by the East River. London, Macmillan, and New York, Viking Press, 1973.
The Abbess of Crewe. London, Macmillan, and New York, Viking Press, 1974.
The Takeover. London, Macmillan, and New York, Viking Press, 1976.
Territorial Rights. London, Macmillan, and New York, Coward McCann, 1979.
Loitering with Intent. London, Bodley Head, and New York, Coward McCann, 1981.
The Only Problem. London, Bodley Head, and New York, Coward McCann, 1984.
A Far Cry from Kensington. London, Constable, and Boston, Houghton Mifflin, 1988.
Symposium. London, Constable, and Boston, Houghton Mifflin, 1990.
Omnibus I. London, Constable, 1993.
Omnibus II. London, Constable, 1994.
The Novels of Muriel Spark (collection). Boston, Houghton Mifflin, 1995.
Reality and Dreams. Boston, Houghton Mifflin, 1997.

Short Stories

The Go-Away Bird and Other Stories. London, Macmillan, 1958; Philadelphia, Lippincott, 1960.
Voices at Play (includes the radio plays *The Party Through the Wall, The Interview, The Dry River Bed, Danger Zone*). London, Macmillan, 1961; Philadelphia, Lippincott, 1962.
Collected Stories I. London, Macmillan, 1967; New York, Knopf, 1968.
Bang-Bang You're Dead and Other Stories. London, Granada, 1982.
The Stories of Muriel Spark. New York, Dutton, 1985; London, Bodley Head, 1987.
Open to the Public: New and Collected Stories. New York, New Directions, 1997.

Plays

Doctors of Philosophy (produced London, 1962). London, Macmillan, 1963; New York, Knopf, 1966.

Radio Plays: *The Party Through the Wall,* 1957; *The Interview,* 1958; *The Dry River Bed,* 1959; *The Ballad of Peckham Rye,* 1960; *Danger Zone,* 1961.

Poetry

The Fanfarlo and Other Verse. Aldington, Kent, Hand and Flower Press, 1952.
Collected Poems I. London, Macmillan, 1967; New York, Knopf, 1968.
Going Up to Sotheby's and Other Poems. London, Granada, 1982.

Other

Child of Light: A Reassessment of Mary Wollstonecraft Shelley. London, Tower Bridge, 1951; revised edition, as *Mary Shelley: A Biography,* New York, Dutton, 1987; London, Constable, 1988.
Emily Brontë: Her Life and Work, with Derek Stanford. London, Owen, 1953.
John Masefield. London, Nevill, 1953; revised edition, London, Hutchinson, 1991.
The Very Fine Clock (for children). New York, Knopf, 1968; London, Macmillan, 1969.
The French Window and the Small Telephone (for children). London, Colophon, 1993.
The Essence of the Brontës. London, Owen, 1993.
Curriculum Vitae. London, Constable, and Boston, Houghton Mifflin, 1993.
Editor, with David Stanford, *Tribute to Wordsworth.* London, Wingate, 1950.
Editor, *A Selection of Poems,* by Emily Brontë. London, Grey Walls Press, 1952.
Editor, with David Stanford, *My Best Mary: The Letters of Mary Shelley.* London, Wingate, 1953.
Editor, *The Brontë Letters.* London, Nevill, 1954; as *The Letters of the Brontës: A Selection,* Norman, University of Oklahoma Press, 1954.
Editor, with David Stanford, *Letters of John Henry Newman.* London, Owen, 1957.

*

Bibliography: *Iris Murdoch and Muriel Spark: A Bibliography* by Thomas T. Tominaga and Wilma Schneidermeyer, Metuchen, New Jersey, Scarecrow Press, 1976.

Critical Studies: *Muriel Spark: A Biographical and Critical Study* by Derek Stanford, Fontwell, Sussex, Centaur Press, 1963; *Muriel Spark* by Karl Malkoff, New York, Columbia University Press, 1968; *Muriel Spark* by Patricia Stubbs, London, Longman, 1973; *Muriel Spark* by Peter Kemp, London, Elek, 1974, New York, Barnes and Noble, 1975; *Muriel Spark* by Allan Massie, Edinburgh, Ramsay

Head Press, 1979; *The Faith and Fiction of Muriel Spark* by Ruth Whittaker, London, Macmillan, 1982, New York, St. Martin's Press, 1983; *Comedy and the Woman Writer: Woolf, Spark, and Feminism* by Judy Little, Lincoln, University of Nebraska Press, 1983; *Muriel Spark: An Odd Capacity for Vision* edited by Alan Bold, London, Vision Press, and New York, Barnes and Noble, 1984, and *Muriel Spark* by Bold, London, Methuen, 1986; *Muriel Spark* by Velma Bourgeois Richmond, New York, Ungar, 1984; *The Art of the Real: Muriel Spark's Novels* by Joseph Hynes, Rutherford, New Jersey, Fairleigh Dickinson University Press, 1988; *Muriel Spark* by Norman Page, London, Macmillan, 1990; *Vocation and Identity in the Fiction of Muriel Spark* by Rodney Stenning Edgecombe, Columbia, University of Missouri Press, 1990; *Re-Inventing Reality: Patterns and Characters in the Novels of Muriel Spark* by Mickey Pearlman, New York, P. Lang, 1996.

* * *

''Her prose is like a bird, darting from place to place, palpitating with nervous energy; but a bird with a bright beady eye and a sharp beak as well.'' Francis Hope's description crystallizes one important aspect of Muriel Spark's highly idiosyncratic talent. A late starter in the field of fiction, she had until early middle age published only conventional criticism and verse which gave little hint of her real gifts and future development. These were triumphantly released with the publication of *The Comforters* in 1957, and the spate of creative activity which followed, speedily establishing her reputation as a genuine original with a style and slant on life uniquely her own.

Spark spoke in an interview of her mind ''crowded with ideas, all teeming in disorder.'' In 1954 she had become a convert to Roman Catholicism; and she regards her religion primarily as a discipline for this prodigal fertility—''something to measure from,'' as she says, rather than a direct source of its inspiration. Yet her Catholicism pervasively colours a vision of life seen, in her own phrase, ''from a slight angle to the universe.'' For all her inventive energy, verve and panache, and glittering malice, this writer is profoundly preoccupied with metaphysical questions of good and evil. Like Angus Wilson, she is a moral fabulist of the contemporary scene who works through the medium of comedy; and like him, she is often most in earnest when at her most entertaining.

Her novels abound in Catholic characters, but these are by no means always on the side of the angels. In *The Comforters* they teeter on the brink of delusion, retreating from orthodoxy into eccentric extremes of quasi-religious experience satirized with the wicked acuteness with which she later pillories spiritualism in *The Bachelors,* focussing upon the trial of a medium for fraud. Religious hypocrites such as the self-consciously progressive couple in ''The Black Madonna'' are quite as likely to be her targets as rationalist unbelievers. Her awareness of the powers of darkness as a palpable force at work in the world is most effectively embodied in her study of Satanism in the suburbs, *The Ballad of Peckham Rye,* in the diabolic person and activities of an industrial welfare worker born with horns on his head.

Such manifestations of the supernatural in the midst of prosaic actuality are a central element in Spark's novels. Her fantasy, earthed in the everyday, is presented as not illusion but natural extension of the material scene: the product of ''that sort of mental squint,'' as she calls it, which perceives the credible co-existence of the uncanny with the most rational aspects of experience. Those who attempt to ignore or reject its reality—like the cynics staging their tawdry Nativity play and confounded by the avenging intervention of a real angel in ''The Seraph and the Zambesi,'' or the sceptical George trying to explain away the flying saucer of ''Miss Pinkerton's Apocalypse''—do so at their peril. Another short story, ''The Portobello Road,'' is narrated by the ghost of a girl who materializes to her murderer in the Saturday morning street market; while *Memento Mori,* in which a number of old people are the victims of a sinister anonymous telephone caller, is a mordant exercise in the macabre. It is subtly suggested that these events might well, for those who choose to believe so, have a straightforward psychological explanation. The ghostly visitant need be no more than an externalization of the murderer's guilty conscience belatedly returned to plague him; the grim practical joker of *Memento* (never finally traced by the police) may embody the insistent reminder of imminent mortality already present within each aged subconscious mind.

Spark's work was highly praised by Evelyn Waugh, whose influence is detectable in the quickfire satirical wit of what one critic called her ''machine-gun dialogue.'' The savage grotesqueries of early Waugh comedy are strongly recalled, too, by the chilling vein of heartlessness, even cruelty, in the violent ends to which so many Spark characters are remorselessly doomed: Needle, smothered in a haystack; the octogenarian Dame Letty, battered in her bed; Joanna Childe, bizarrely chanting passages from the Anglican liturgy as she burns to death; and the bored and loveless office worker of *The Driver's Seat* obsessively resolved to get herself killed in the most brutal fashion possible.

Yet if disaster and death haunt the pages of Spark's novels, her piquant humours are still more abundant. Although *The Girls of Slender Means* ends in tragedy, its portrayal of the impoverished inmates of a war-time hostel for young women of good family is as delectably funny as the depiction, in *The Bachelors,* of their gossipy male counterparts in London bedsitterland; or as the intrigues among nuns at a convent besieged by the media avid for ecclesiastical scandal in *The Abbess of Crewe.* Perhaps Spark's greatest comic triumph is her creation of the exuberant Edinburgh schoolmistress Jean Brodie, grooming her girls for living through an educationally unorthodox but headily exhilarating curriculum ranging from her heroes, Franco and Mussolini, to the love-lives of remarkable women of history, including her own.

Spark's narrative expertise is best exemplified in shorter forms, where her stylistic economy so often achieves a riveting intensity of impact. By contrast a longer, more ambitious book like *The Mandelbaum Gate,* about the adventures of a half-Jewish Catholic convert caught up in the divisions of warring Jerusalem, seems laboured and diffuse. Two novels, *The Takeover,* set during the 1970s but rooted in classical mythology, and *Territorial Rights,* have the Italian background which the author clearly finds a fruitful imaginative climate for exploring such themes as the exploitation of bogus religion and excessive wealth.

Loitering with Intent returns to her earlier London scene, and a time just after World War II. The composition of a struggling author's first novel is skilfully interwoven with her experiences in the employ of a bizarre society of pseudo-writers, whose grotesque fantasies, deceptions, and intrigues entertainingly reveal the possibilities of confusion between life and art. In *The Only Problem* the central character is a hapless scholar vainly seeking peace and seclusion in order to wrestle with interpreting the Book of Job. The daily problems of his own life increasingly impinge upon this task—not least the procession of modern counterparts of his biblical subject's comforters, or persecutors.

All these works wryly illustrate those characteristic qualities of sly, deadly wit in observing human oddity and weakness, the ingenious fusion of fact with fantasy and unpredictable surprise, and the underlying moral seriousness, which make Spark one of our most stimulating and quirkily individual novelists.

—Margaret Willy

SPENCE, Alan

Nationality: British. **Born:** Glasgow, 5 December 1947. **Education:** Glasgow University, 1966–69, and 1973–74. **Career:** Writer-in-residence, Glasgow University, 1975–77, Traverse Theatre, Edinburgh, 1982, Edinburgh District Council, 1986–87, and since 1990 Edinburgh University. **Address:** c/o Canongate Publishing, 16 Frederick Street, Edinburgh EH2 2HB, Scotland.

Publications

Novels

The Magic Flute. Edinburgh, Canongate, 1990.
Way to Go. London, Phoenix House, 1998.

Short Stories

Its Colours They Are Fine. London, Collins, 1977.
Stone Garden and Other Stories. London, Phoenix House, 1995.

Uncollected Short Stories

''Sailmaker,'' in *Modern Scottish Short Stories,* edited by Fred Urquhart and Giles Gordon. London, Hamish Hamilton, 1978; revised edition, London, Faber, 1982.
''The Rain Dance'' and ''Tinsel,'' in *Street of Stone,* edited by Moira Burgess and Hamish Whyte. Edinburgh, Salamander Press, 1985.

Plays

Sailmaker. Edinburgh, Salamander Press, 1982.
Space Invaders. Edinburgh, Salamander Press, 1983.
Change Days. London, Hodder and Stoughton, 1991.

Poetry

Plop! 15 Haiku. Glasgow, No Name Press, 1970.
Glasgow Zen. Glasgow, Print Studio Press, 1981.

Other

Crab and Lobster Fishing. N.p., Fishing News, 1989.

* * *

Alan Spence's reputation as a novelist and writer of short stories is much stronger in his native Scotland than elsewhere, but he deserves to be brought into greater prominence. His published output is not extensive, but his work as a writer-in-residence at the universities of Glasgow and Edinburgh and at the Traverse Theatre in Edinburgh has given him a much wider following than that for more prolific authors.

His first book, *Its Colours They Are Fine,* is a very intense and carefully crafted collection of short stories. Dealing powerfully with childhood and early adulthood in Glasgow through the 1950s and 1960s, it is a volume on which the author's own formative experiences seem to exert creative pressure. Its central concerns are made local by the emphasis on male, Protestant, working-class characters, but Spence's work is always illuminated and broadened by his perception of the spiritual dimension to everyday experience. To talk of influences may inevitably be belittling, but Spence in this book seems very much in the tradition of James Joyce, looking for the magical revealing moments in the lives of ordinary urban citizens. However, where the lives of Joyce's Dubliners are full of disappointment and disillusion, the lives of Spence's creations are more richly nuanced. In ''Tinsel,'' for example, a boy's excitement at putting up Christmas decorations is turned into a glimpse of a mysterious world of beauty and light which seems to overlap with the more mundane surroundings of a tenement flat in Govan. In ''Sheaves,'' the tensions between boyish rough and tumble and a dimly intuited holiness are worked out without pretention. The collection is consistently impressive for its willingness to take on a reverent mystical suggestiveness, influenced no doubt by the author's developed interest in the Indian spiritual teacher Sri Chinmoy. The recurring theme in the book is that at moments of ceremony, however local or fleeting, we may gain insight into greater cosmic forces. The best story is without any doubt ''The Rain Dance,'' which gives a beautifully modulated account of a Glasgow registry office wedding and all its attendant festivities, at once culturally specific and universal. Other stories deal with the lives of dispossessed and lonely characters, but Spence cannot manage the controlled outrage and vehemence of James Kelman, and occasionally his humane tolerance falls into sentimentality. Nonetheless, there are some truly exceptional pieces in this volume, and its sensibility is invigoratingly dignified and humane.

After an interval of thirteen years, in which Spence concentrated mostly on poetry and occasional radio pieces, his first novel, *The Magic Flute,* appeared. It returns to the concern with childhood which distinguished the earlier short stories, and revisits some of the episodes to construct a complex tale of the different paths various people take through their lives. It follows four Glasgow boys through more than twenty years, from the late 1950s to the early 1980s, and to some extent it could be seen alongside the more popular saga novels of, say, Margaret Drabble. But that would be a distortion of the book's main enterprise, as well as of its unmistakable seriousness of purpose. Spence is highly ambitious and intricate in this work, as he tries to weave a very elaborate pattern of divergence and convergence around his characters. Each one is taken to represent a plausible journey through difficult times, conducted with different degrees of sensitivity, integrity, and success. The narrative is sustained by a deft allusiveness, touching upon identifiable cultural and historical references, and encompassing other literary archetypes, like Mozart's opera and a wide range of ''quest'' stories. The novel is certainly a very impressive piece of design, its architecture skillfully created and maintained. Furthermore, it contains wonderfully evocative sketches of times and places, which readers of a certain age will find acute and haunting. However, it is unevenly imagined, with much greater care being taken in the presentation of the more sensitive figures of Tam and Brian, and rather less in the sketching of the violent Eddie and the spiritless George. And it has to be said that Spence's female characters remain too lifeless. Overall, *The Magic Flute* is an intermittently powerful and searching book, serious and humane in its treatment of its participants, with a high sense of purpose and intelligence, which also sprawls and drifts too much.

Spence is a writer whose continuing development should be closely followed. If he can find a way of integrating his exceptional perceptiveness and reverence for experience in a compelling extended narrative, he could be one of the most interesting and individual novelists in Britain. How many other writers would choose as their subject the undertaking industry of Glasgow, as he did in *Way to Go?* Added to the mix is an East-West theme, with a protagonist who returns from the Orient following the death of his father, and who takes over the family funeral parlor business with the intention of adding a certain Eastern flair to it.

—Ian A. Bell, updated by Judson Knight

SPENCER, Colin

Nationality: British. **Born:** London, 17 July 1933. **Education:** Brighton Grammar School, Selhurst; Brighton College of Art. **Military Service:** Served in the Royal Army Medical Corps, 1950–52. **Family:** Married Gillian Chapman in 1959 (divorced 1969); one son. **Career:** Paintings exhibited in Cambridge and London; costume designer. Chair, Writers Guild of Great Britain, 1982–83. **Agent:** Richard Scott Simon, Anthony Sheil Associates, 43 Doughty Street, London WC1N 2LF, England.

PUBLICATIONS

Novels

An Absurd Affair. London, Longman, 1961.
Generation:
Anarchists in Love. London, Eyre and Spottiswoode, 1963; as *The Anarchy of Love,* New York, Weybright and Talley, 1967.
The Tyranny of Love. London, Blond, and New York, Weybright and Talley, 1967.
Lovers in War. London, Blond, 1969.
The Victims of Love. London, Quartet, 1978.
Asylum. London, Blond, 1966.
Poppy, Mandragora, and the New Sex. London, Blond, 1966.
Panic. London, Secker and Warburg, 1971.
How the Greeks Kidnapped Mrs. Nixon. London, Quartet, 1974.

Uncollected Short Stories

''Nightworkers,'' in *London Magazine,* vol. 2, no. 12, 1955.
''An Alien World,'' in *London Magazine,* vol. 3, no. 6, 1956.
''Nymph and Shepherd,'' in *London Magazine,* vol. 6, no. 8, 1959.
''It's Anemones for Mabel,'' in *Transatlantic Review* (London), Spring 1963.
''The Room,'' in *Transatlantic Review* (London), Summer 1966.
''Carpaccio's Dream,'' in *Harpers and Queen* (London), December 1985.

Plays

The Ballad of the False Barman, music by Clifton Parker (produced London, 1966).
Spitting Image (produced London, 1968; New York, 1969). Published in *Plays and Players* (London), September 1968.
The Trial of St. George (produced London, 1972).
The Sphinx Mother (produced Salzburg, Austria, 1972).
Why Mrs. Neustadter Always Loses (produced London, 1972).
Keep It in the Family (produced London, 1978).
Lilith (produced Vienna, 1979).

Television Plays: *Flossie,* 1975; *Vandal Rule OK?* (documentary), 1977.

Other

Gourmet Cooking for Vegetarians. London, Deutsch, 1978.
Good and Healthy: A Vegetarian and Wholefood Cookbook. London, Robson, 1983; as *Vegetarian Wholefood Cookbook,* London, Panther, 1985.
Reports from Behind, with Chris Barlas, illustrated by Spencer. London, Enigma, 1984.
Cordon Vert: 52 Vegetarian Gourmet Dinner Party Menus. Wellingborough, Northamptonshire, Thorsons, 1985; Chicago, Contemporary, 1987.
Mediterranean Vegetarian Cooking. Wellingborough, Northamptonshire, Thorsons, 1986.
The New Vegetarian: The Ultimate Guide to Gourmet Cooking and Healthy Living. London, Elm Tree, 1986.
The Vegetarian's Healthy Diet Book, with Tom Sanders. London, Dunitz, 1986; as *The Vegetarian's Kitchen,* Tucson, Arizona, Body Press, 1986.
One-Course Feasts. London, Conran Octopus, 1986.
Feast for Health: A Gourmet Guide to Good Food. London, Dorling Kindersley, 1987.
Al Fresco: A Feast of Outdoor Entertaining. Wellingborough, Northamptonshire, Thorsons, 1987.
The Romantic Vegetarian. Wellingborough, Northamptonshire, Thorsons, 1988.
The Adventurous Vegetarian. London, Cassell, 1989.
Which of Us Two? The Story of a Love Affair. London, Viking, 1990.
The Heretic's Feast: A History of Vegetarianism. Pullisle, Fourth Estate, and New England University Press, 1992.
Homosexuality in History. New York, Harcourt Brace, 1995.
The Vegetable Book, photography by Linda Burgess. New York, Rizzoli, 1995.
The Gay Kama Sutra. New York, St. Martin's Press, 1997.
Editor, *Green Cuisine: The Guardian's Selection of the Best Vegetarian Recipes.* Wellingborough, Northamptonshire, Thorsons, 1986.

*

Critical Studies: Interview with Peter Burton, in *Transatlantic Review 35* (London), 1970.

Theatrical Activities: Director: **Play**—*Keep It in the Family,* London, 1978.

Colin Spencer comments:

I have the impression that my work taken as a whole can be confusing to a critic or a reader. Both the novels and the plays appear to be written in too many various styles; if this is true I make no apologies but will attempt an explanation. The main core of my work as a writer is found in the four volumes of the unfinished sequence of novels: *Generation.* This, in its simplest form is nothing but fictionalised autobiography—the line where fiction begins and reality ends is a philosophical enigma that continually fascinates me. The volumes are sagas of various families, their children and grandchildren, their marriages and relationships; their social context is firmly middle-class though in later volumes some of the characters move into the upper-middle stratas while others remain socially rootless. I have struggled in these books to make the characters and their backgrounds as true to what I have observed and experienced as my perception and recollection allow. For I believe that the novel form is unique in being as exact a mirror to our experience as is afforded in the whole range of art forms. For not only can the novel communicate the great obsessive passions, frustrations, and longings of individuals, but it can also conjure up a picture of all the myriad details—quite trivial in themselves—which at certain times affect major actions. In form I based these interrelating novels on the nineteenth-century tradition (it is a complicated story with many characters) but I have allowed myself within that framework to use all the literary experiments forged in the first half of this century. The characters that I have created from my experience and observation are not puppets; I cannot control and guide them into some preconceived aesthetic pattern, for they exist in life and in the narration I have to pursue and relate as truthfully as possible their own tragic mistakes, their comic failures and triumphs, their self-deceit and affirmation of life.

But in my plays there is no direct autobiographical experience: they are, like some of the other novels, satires on social problems that oppress individuals. I like to entertain in the theatre, to make an audience laugh but at the same time debate at the core of the work a serious and unresolved problem. The novels *Poppy, Mandragora, and the New Sex* and *How the Greeks Kidnapped Mrs. Nixon* also use comedy to expose gross injustice. *Panic* treats another subject, that of child assault, on the surface as a murder mystery, yet its main intention was to induce the reader to understand the psychological nature of the killer. I would dismiss my first novel, *An Absurd Affair,* as merely a public rehearsal in the craft of fiction. But there is one novel that falls outside any of the above categories—*Asylum.* The Oedipus myth has always fascinated me. (The play *The Sphinx Mother* is a contemporary account of the Jocasta figure refusing to commit suicide and struggling for final and complete possession of her son/husband.) Another myth, the Fall of Man, with its pervasive sense of original sin corroding free will seems for me with the Oedipus myth to have influenced the compulsive aspirations in Western culture for over two thousand years. In *Asylum* I created a plot, loosely based on a 19th-century American scandal, where I united both myths in the same family and set it in a hierarchic social commune, almost a science-fiction Asylum. I then tried to imply how our religious and judicial structure worked through arbitrary indifference and cruel repression. I might add that for large passages of the book I allowed myself the indulgence of writing in a style akin to poetic prose.

If I may sum up I would say that I feel my job as a writer is to state the truth in as vivid a manner as is possible and to involve the reader in a celebration of life, while uncovering the injustices that as individuals and as society we impose upon each other.

* * *

Colin Spencer's novels revel in the eccentric, the bizarre, and the grotesque while tending toward social commentary. His event-filled books examine human relationships buffeted by sexual antagonisms of various, extreme types. In depicting his frequently polymorphously perverse characters, Spencer plays a recurrent theme of protest against conventional mores and morality, although, perhaps unintentionally, the alternatives he presents hardly seem more satisfactory. With casts of almost Dickensian proportions and curiosity, he runs the gamut of sexual expression, particularly homosexual. Sympathetic understanding, graphic detail, and a fine talent for low comedy do not often, however, extend his narratives beyond the superficial or raise them from mere sensationalism to genuine significance. Nor does his tendency to have protagonist-spokesmen speechify make his arguments more appealing.

In *An Absurd Affair* Spencer sketches some telling scenes of marital dependence and oppression, but soon gives way to improbable melodrama. Conceited, petty, and dull, James dominates his immature, thoughtless child-wife, Sarah. Though he is undereducated and boring, James finds his wife inferior and her love of art beyond his comprehension. By accident, Sarah finds the negative of a "dirty" picture, and, to the prudish James's shock, she is fascinated. Undue influence by this "art," along with romantic infatuation and huge amounts of alcohol, leads the insecure woman into a ludicrous pursuit of a sadistic schoolteacher and finally into a delusory affair with a Sicilian gigolo. Though James rescues her, she finds she no longer loves him and declares her independence. For all Spencer's obvious and overdrawn psychologizing, both characters remain rather implausible caricatures in what is, indeed, an absurd affair, unredeemed by the crude poetic justice—or ladies' magazine moralizing—of its pat ending.

Of considerably more merit and interest are the volumes of the series *Generation,* a sizeable contribution to the large corpus of English novels examining life in reaction to post-World War II conditions, in this case a sprawling saga of the Simpson family from World War I through the 1960s. Shifting back and forth over the years, Spencer draws vivid, well-rounded portraits of several characteristic types, some of which develop into unique personalities; the ever more complicated alliances and misalliances of the heterogeneous Simpsons reveal a fascinating panorama of several social milieus. While realistic scenes are well-executed, the more emotional confrontations take on the unfortunate tone of a soap opera. And though characters occasionally mention and blame the war for their uncertain, disjointed worlds, its significance for their individual struggles is implied more than clearly stated.

Weaving in and out of the separate stories of the factional family members, friends, and lovers, Eddy Simpson's raunchy career, depicted in short, often raucous vignettes, becomes a central focus for understanding the wayward, amusing, and sometimes pathetic journeys in the novels. Crude and conscious only of his own desires, paterfamilias Eddy jokes, drinks, and womanizes. His Rabelaisian zest for life can be hilarious, but it is also ruinous for the rest of the Simpsons. Long-suffering wife Hester turns to religion, whose comforts are of little use to her artistic and volatile children Sundy and

Matthew. The major portions of the novels are devoted to their painful growing up and tortured adulthood.

Hetero-, homo-, and bi-sexual roles are played out in several combinations; in the convoluted course of the interconnected plots there is more changing of partners than in a country square dance. Sundy is most original. After dallying with lesbianism, she is caught briefly in an incestuous bond. She takes up with Reg, a handsome liar, self-proclaimed anarchist, and sometime rent-boy, aborts their illegitimate child, and finally, confusedly, marries him. After losing Reg to her brother Matthew, she leads a bohemian life with an unreliable publisher. Through tumultuous years, Matthews's reactions to his father's boorishness and cruelty alternate between dejection and desire for revenge, religious fanaticism and self-hatred. His homosexuality comes slowly to consciousness but not acceptance, and his ambivalence ends in a disastrous and mutually destructive marriage to a priggish, unstable shrew.

Along the way Spencer portrays lower-, middle-, and upper-class life, as well as the more baroque aspects of the homosexual world, with deftness and insight. Sometimes his prose sags, but generally Spencer's humor, irony, and use of contrast are skillful, allowing his themes to reveal themselves by inference. Perhaps his strongest points are made by the self-inflicted wounds of the ''anarchists'' whose intellectual poses ineffectually mask their adolescent, mixed-up libertinism.

Constructed in a fantastic mode, *Asylum* displays Spencer's penchant for the macabre. The patients in the ultra-modern insane asylum are prompted to act out their twisted pasts and perverse imaginings by the equally but scientifically demented psychiatrists (who are, in turn, directed by monstrous computers), before they are hunted and left to die. Spencer's surrealistic vision combines and curiously reworks *Oedipus* and the Book of Genesis through phantasmagoric permutations. In the confused dimension of illusion-reality, Cleo-Jocasta tries to work her incestuous vindictive will upon her priest-husband Max (Addams) through their dark-skinned son Carl, but Carl prefers the charms of his fair-skinned brother Angelo. While the inversions and embroidery of the Greek and Judaic myths are imaginative, their point is often as obscure as Cleo's mad history.

Perhaps Spencer's most mature work is his probing analysis of the mentality of the child molester in *Panic*. With the seamy Brighton underworld as a backdrop, the novel unfolds the wretched life of Woody and his mother Saffron May and their increasingly perverted relationship, culminating in the tragic child-murders. Spencer tells the gripping story through the voices of the major characters, carefully controlling the tensions to the last climactic moments. What was once used largely for shock value in earlier books, is now integral to theme and structure. Both killer and victims are revealed with sympathy from the inside, and even the freakish characters of the lesbian burglar Trigger and the wretched dwarf Jumbo emerge as strange but human beings.

—Joseph Parisi

SPENCER, Elizabeth

Nationality: American. **Born:** Carrollton, Mississippi, 19 July 1921. **Education:** Belhaven College, Jackson, Mississippi, 1938–42, A.B. 1942; Vanderbilt University, Nashville, 1942–43, M.A. 1943. **Family:** Married John Rusher in 1956. **Career:** Instructor, Northwest Mississippi Junior College, Senatobia, 1943–44, and Ward-Belmont College, Nashville, 1944–45; reporter, Nashville *Tennessean,* 1945–46; instructor, 1948–49, and instructor in creative writing, 1949–51, 1952–53, University of Mississippi, Oxford; Donnelly Fellow, Bryn Mawr College, Pennsylvania, 1962; creative writing fellow, University of North Carolina, Chapel Hill, 1969; writer-in-residence, Hollins College, Virginia, 1973. Member of the creative writing faculty, 1976–81, adjunct professor, 1981–86, Concordia University, Montreal; visiting professor, University of North Carolina, Chapel Hill, 1986–92. Charter member, 1987, vice-chancellor, 1993, Fellowship of Southern Writers. **Awards:** American Academy Recognition award, 1952, Rosenthal award, 1957, and Award of Merit Medal, 1983; Guggenheim fellowship, 1953; *Kenyon Review* fellowship, 1957; McGraw-Hill fiction award, 1960; Bellaman award, 1968; National Endowment for the Arts grant, 1982, and award, 1988; Salem award, 1992, for literature; Dos Passos award, 1992, for fiction; North Carolina Governor's award, 1994, for literature; Corrington award for literature, 1997; Richard Wright award for literature, 1997; Fortner award for Literature, 1998; award for nonfiction, Massachusetts Library Association, 1999; award for nonfiction, Mississippi Library Association, 1999. D.L.: Southwestern (now Rhodes) University, Memphis, 1968; LL.D.: Concordia University, Montreal, 1988; Litt.D.: University of the South, Sewanee, Tennessee, 1992; University of North Carolina, Chapel Hill, 1998; Belhaven College, 1999. **Member:** American Academy, 1985. **Agent:** Virginia Barber, 353 West 21st Street, New York, New York 10011, U.S.A. **Address:** 402 Longleaf Drive, Chapel Hill, North Carolina 27514, U.S.A.

Publications

Novels

Fire in the Morning. New York, Dodd Mead, 1948.
This Crooked Way. New York, Dodd Mead, and London, Gollancz, 1952.
The Voice at the Back Door. New York, McGraw Hill, 1956; London, Gollancz, 1957.
The Light in the Piazza. New York, McGraw Hill, 1960; London, Heinemann, 1961.
Knights and Dragons. New York, McGraw Hill, 1965; London, Heinemann, 1966.
No Place for an Angel. New York, McGraw Hill, 1967; London, Weidenfeld and Nicolson, 1968.
The Snare. New York, McGraw Hill, 1972.
The Salt Line. New York, Doubleday, 1984; London, Penguin, 1985.
The Night Travellers. New York, Viking, 1991.

Short Stories

Ship Island and Other Stories. New York, McGraw Hill, 1968; London, Weidenfeld and Nicolson, 1969.
The Stories of Elizabeth Spencer. New York, Doubleday, 1981; London, Penguin, 1983.
Marilee: Three Stories. Jackson, University Press of Mississippi, 1981.
The Mules. Winston-Salem, North Carolina, Palaemon Press, 1982.
Jack of Diamonds and Other Stories. New York, Viking, 1988.
On the Gulf. Jackson, University Press of Mississippi, 1991.

Uncollected Short Stories

''To the Watchers While Walking Home,'' in *Ontario Review* (Princeton, New Jersey), 1982.
''Madonna'' and ''Puzzle Poem,'' in *Hudson Review* (New York), Summer 1983.
''Up the Gatineau,'' in *Boulevard* (Philadelphia), Spring 1989.
''The Weekend Travellers,'' in *Story* (Cincinnati), Winter 1994.
''The Runaways,'' in *Antaeus* (Hopewell, New Jersey), Spring 1994.
''The Master of Shongalo,'' in *Southern Review* (Baton Rouge, Louisiana), Winter 1995.

Play

For Lease or Sale, in *Mississippi Writers 4: Reflection of Childhood and Youth,* edited by Dorothy Abbott. Jackson, University Press of Mississippi, 1991.

Other

Conversations with Elizabeth Spencer, edited by Peggy Whitman Prenshaw. Jackson, University Press of Mississippi, 1991.
Landscapes of the Heart: A Memoir. New York, Random House, 1998.

*

Bibliography: By Laura Barge, 1976, and by C.E. Lewis, 1994, both in *Mississippi Quarterly* (Starkville).

Manuscript Collections: National Library of Canada, Ottawa; University of Kentucky, Lexington.

Critical Studies: *Elizabeth Spencer* by Peggy Whitman Prenshaw, Boston, Twayne, 1985; *Self and Community in the Fiction of Elizabeth Spencer* by Terry Roberts, Baton Rouge, Louisiana State University Press, 1994.

Elizabeth Spencer comments:

I began writing down stories as soon as I learned how to write; that is, at about age six; before that, I made them up anyway and told them to anybody who was handy and would listen. Being a rural Southerner, a Mississippian, had a lot to do with it, I have been told, with this impulse and with the peculiar mystique, importance, which attached itself naturally thereto and enhanced it. We had been brought up on stories, those about local people, living and dead, and Bible narratives, believed also to be literally true, so that other stories read aloud—the Greek myths, for instance—while indicated as ''just'' stories, were only one slight remove from the ''real'' stories of the local scene and the Bible. So it was with history, for local event spilled into the history of the textbooks; my grandfather could remember the close of the Civil War, and my elder brother's nurse had been a slave. The whole world, then, was either entirely in the nature of stories or partook so deeply of stories as to be at every point inseparable from them. Even the novels we came later to read were mainly English nineteenth-century works which dealt with a culture similar to our own—we learned with no surprise that we had sprung from it.

Though I left the South in 1953, I still see the world and its primal motions as story, since story charts in time the heart's assertions and gives central place to the great human relationships. My first three novels, written or projected before I left the South, deal with people in that society who must as the true measure of themselves either alter it or come to terms with it. Years I spent in Italy and more recently in Canada have made me see the world in other than this fixed geography. The challenge to wring its stories from it became to me more difficult at the same time that it became more urgent that I and other writers should do so. A story may not be the only wrench one can hurl into the giant machine that seems bent on devouring us all, but is one of them. A story which has been tooled, shaped, and slicked up is neither real nor true—we know its nature and its straw insides. Only the real creature can satisfy, the one that is touchy and alive, dangerous to fool with. The search for such as these goes on with me continually, and I think for all real writers as well.

(1995) I returned to the South in 1986 and have found a not altogether different world, for the South can maintain its continuity better perhaps than most other areas. But the media and the electronic age are doing their work of restructuring, and enduring as a separate, recognizable region of the United States tests and will continue to test the considerable talents of southern writers. We remain, however, what we have always been—storytellers, some of the world's best.

* * *

Elizabeth Spencer's first three novels portray the upper middle class of her native Mississippi trapped between the decadent planter aristocrats and politically ambitious ''redneck'' bigots who were William Faulkner's special province. *Five in the Morning* (titled from Djuna Barnes's *Nightwood*) grimly depicts the effectiveness of petty greed in stifling a small community's vitality. The Gerrard family moved into Tarsus in the wake of Civil War disruptions and made themselves leading citizens through perjury and blackmail. Their machinations result, however, only in the destruction of almost everyone involved except one Gerrard son and a former schoolmate, son of one of the family's principal victims. These young men achieve a reconciliation when the Gerrard follows the many other people driven from the community and the other, Kinloch Armstrong, learns that his strength is the very ''strangeness'' he has always felt that allows him to transcend the squalor that engulfs the others. *This Crooked Way* is a less complex and more cynical tale about an opportunist who comes down from the hills to become a Delta planter. Amos Dudley has always dreamed of seeing a ladder of angels, but his inability to face reality results only in the wreckage of the lives of his family and most of those around him.

Spencer's most powerful novel, *The Voice at the Back Door,* bares the history of a well-educated and inherently decent young lawyer, Kerney Woolbright, who must sacrifice his integrity to win political preferment in his community. The novel contrasts Kerney's lying about his knowledge of an explosive situation involving a black man in order to assure his victory at the polls with the behavior of Duncan Harper, a truculently honest athlete—once idol of the community—who sacrifices a comfortable career to protect the man from ignorant bigotry.

After this chilling revelation of the corruption of competence and the persecution of decency, Spencer abandoned Mississippi for

Italy, which inspired two brief novels about women who escape abroad to victory. *The Light in the Piazza,* source of an unusually tasteful and subtle film, tensely relates an American mother's risky effort to marry her mentally retarded daughter to an attractive young Florentine despite her husband's misgivings and the Italian family's efforts to profit by the match. *Knights and Dragons* studies an American woman who has fled to Rome after her marriage collapses and who finds at last that human love demands too much of the individual to be worth the struggle, so that she frees herself—like Federico Fellini's Juliet of the Spirits—to become ''a companion to cloud and sky.''

After these short, intense international novels, Spencer returned by stages to the United States and, at last, Mississippi. *No Place for an Angel* chronicles against an international background (Washington-Florida, Rome-Sicily and elsewhere) the intricate interrelationships of two married couples and their sprawling families and a young American sculptor, who dreams like Amos Dudley of angels. One wife says of her husband, ''Jerry had to be great, and he almost made it.'' The novel is a mature, unsentimental account of characters that almost make it, only to find—as one put it—that ''life keeps turning into a vacuum,'' though the author tempers the bleakness by suggesting that these people's children may find happiness by wanting less. *The Snare* concentrates on a woman who does at last ''make it'' by never seeking greatness. Julia Garrett's life in a New Orleans that the novelist pictures with special skill has been a search on ''a many-branched road'' for an identity from the time that her aimless father abandons her in the arms of better-placed relatives. Frustrated in efforts to achieve mature relationships, Julia realizes herself at last not through the vision of an angel, but the person of her own very real child.

After a long period during which she experimented with a variety of short stories, Spencer returned to Mississippi's Gulf Coast in *The Salt Line;* but the region is no longer Faulkner's gothic south nor the transitory plastic America that materialized after World War II. *The Salt Line* occurs after Hurricane Camille, which in 1969 devastated the modernizing region. We witness efforts to rebuild principally through three survivors—two of whom were former friends as college professors, the other a petty gangster—through whose own lives hurricanes have passed. While they blame ''bad luck,'' they are what Scott Fitzgerald called ''careless people.'' Just as residents of the hurricane-prone areas return to waiting out seasons nervously, these leading characters return to their old ways. At the end of the novel, Spencer holds out the possibility of ''the bright redemption of love''; but the vision illuminating the novel is that love helps people endure, but not prevail. As Peggy Prenshaw points out, the Byronic central figure of *The Salt Line* faces the future asking the same question as Robert Frost's oven-bird—what to make of ''a diminished thing.''

With *The Night Travellers,* Spencer suggested one solution: take a Southern character and move her out of the South. The fact that Mary Kerr Harbison came from an aristocratic Southern family is only part of her story, though perhaps it informs some of her gullibility. Pulled into a deeply emotional relationship with a left-wing social activist, Jefferson Blaise, she is ultimately forced to go with him as a fugitive to Toronto. Their love is intense and almost all-powerful, and this makes the tragedy of their story all the more compelling.

—Warren French, updated by Judson Knight

STEAD, C(hristian) K(arlson)

Nationality: New Zealander. **Born:** Auckland, 17 October 1932. **Education:** Balmoral Intermediate School; Mount Albert Grammar School; Auckland University, B.A. 1954, M.A. (honors) 1955; Bristol University (Michael Hiatt Baker Scholar), Ph.D. 1961. **Family:** Married Kathleen Elizabeth Roberts in 1955; two daughters and one son. **Career:** Lecturer in English, University of New England, New South Wales, 1956–57; lecturer, 1960–61, senior lecturer, 1962–64, associate professor, 1964–67, professor of English, 1967–86, and emeritus professor since 1986, University of Auckland. Visiting fellow, University of Oxford, England, since 1996. Chair, New Zealand Literary Fund, 1972–75, and 1988–90, New Zealand Authors Fund. **Awards:** Poetry Awards Incorporated prize (U.S.A.), 1955; Readers award (*Landfall*), 1959; Katherine Mansfield award, for fiction and for essay, 1961, and fellowship, 1972; Nuffield traveling fellowship, 1965; Jessie Mackay poetry award, 1973; New Zealand Book award, for poetry, 1976, for fiction, 1986; New Zealand Arts Council scholarship, 1987, 1992; Queen's Medal, 1990. D.Litt.: University of Auckland, 1981. C.B.E. (Commander, Order of the British Empire), 1985. Fellow, Royal Society of Literature, 1996. **Address:** 37 Tohunga Crescent, Parnell, Auckland 1, New Zealand.

PUBLICATIONS

Novels

Smith's Dream. Auckland, Longman Paul, 1971; revised edition, 1973.

All Visitors Ashore. Auckland, Collins, and London, Harvill Press, 1984.

The Death of the Body. London, Collins, 1986.

Sister Hollywood. London, Collins, 1989; New York, St. Martin's Press, 1990.

The End of the Century at the End of the World. London, Harvill Press, 1992.

The Singing Whakapapa. Auckland, Penguin Books, 1994.

Villa Vittoria. New York, Penguin Books, 1997.

Short Stories

Five for the Symbol. Auckland, Longman Paul, 1981.

The Blind Blonde with Candles in Her Hair: Stories. Auckland, Penguin Books, 1998.

Uncollected Short Stories

''Concerning Alban Ashtree,'' in *London Magazine,* December 1983-January 1984.

''Ludwig and Jack,'' in *Rambling Jack 2,* August 1986.

''The Last Life of Clarry,'' in *Vital Writing: New Zealand Poems and Stories 1989–90,* edited by Andrew Mason. N.p., Godwit Press, 1990.

''A Short History of New Zealand,'' *Sport* (Wellington), May 1992.

''Sex in America,'' *Sport* (Wellington), March 1994.

''Of Angels and Oystercatchers,'' in *The Inward Sun,* edited by Elizabeth Alley. Wellington, Daphne Brasell Press, 1994.

Poetry

Whether the Will Is Free: Poems 1954–62. Auckland, Paul's Book Arcade, 1964.
Crossing the Bar. Auckland, Auckland University Press-Oxford University Press, 1972.
Quesada: Poems 1972–74. Auckland, The Shed, 1975.
Walking Westward. Auckland, The Shed, 1979.
Geographies. Auckland, Auckland University Press-Oxford University Press, 1982.
Poems of a Decade. Dunedin, Pilgrims South Press, 1983.
Paris. Auckland, Auckland University Press-Oxford University Press, 1984.
Between. Auckland, Auckland University Press, 1988.
Voices. Wellington, Government Printing Office, 1990.
Straw into Gold: Poems New and Selected. Auckland, Auckland University Press, 1997.

Other

The New Poetic: Yeats to Eliot. London, Hutchinson, 1964; New York, Harper, 1966.
In the Glass Case: Essays on New Zealand Literature. Auckland, Auckland University Press-Oxford University Press, 1981.
Pound, Yeats, Eliot and the Modernist Movement. London, Macmillan, and New Brunswick, New Jersey, Rutgers University Press, 1986.
Answering to the Language: Essays on Modern Writers. Auckland, Auckland University Press, 1989.
Editor, *New Zealand Short Stories: Second Series.* London, Oxford University Press, 1966.
Editor, *Measure for Measure: A Casebook.* London, Macmillan, 1971.
Editor, *The Letters and Journals of Katherine Mansfield: A Selection.* London, Allen Lane, 1977.
Editor, *Collected Stories,* by Maurice Duggan. Auckland, Auckland University Press-Oxford University Press, 1981.
Editor, with Elizabeth Smither and Kendrick Smithyman, *The New Gramophone Room: Poetry and Fiction.* Auckland, University of Auckland, 1985.
Editor, *The Faber Book of Contemporary South Pacific Stories.* London, Faber and Faber, 1994.

*

Manuscript Collection: Alexander Turnbull Library, Wellington.

Critical Studies: Ken Arvidson, in *Journal of New Zealand Literature 1,* 1983; interview with Michael Harlow, in *Landfall 132* (Christchurch), 1983; ''A Deckchair of Words'' in *Landfall 159* (Christchurch), September 1986, and ''Stead's Dream'' in *Landfall 163* (Christchurch), September 1987, both by Reginald Berry; ''Modernist Making and Self-Making'' by A. Walton Litz, in *Times Literary Supplement* (London), 10 October 1986; interview in *Talking About Ourselves,* edited by Harry Ricketts, Wellington, Mallinson Rendel, 1986; *Barbed Wire and Mirrors: Essays on New Zealand Prose* by Lawrence Jones, Dunedin, Otago University Press, 1987; *The Writer Written* by Jean-Pierre Durix, New York, Greenwood Press, 1987; *Leaving the Highway: Six Contemporary New Zealand Novelists* by Mark Williams, Auckland, Auckland University Press, 1990; *The Penguin History of New Zealand Literature* edited by Patrick Evans, Auckland, Penguin, 1990; *The Oxford History of New Zealand Literature* edited by Terry Stern, Oxford, 1991.

C.K. Stead comments:

For a good part of my writing life in New Zealand I have been known as a poet and critic who occasionally ventures into short stories; but in my own mind, since I began writing at the age of fourteen, I have thought of myself as a *writer.* It has never seemed to me that one had to choose between poetry and fiction (and there are honorable precedents—Goldsmith, for example, who also wrote plays; Thomas Hardy; and D.H. Lawrence). But novels require time; and until 1986, when I gave up my position as professor of English at the University of Auckland, my time was limited. As an academic I made poetry, in particular 20th-century poetry, my special field with the consequence that I could see my own work as a poet on a broad historical map. As a fiction writer I possess no such map and have proceeded more by instinct, or intuition, with the possible consequence that in fiction I may have been more original, or individual, or peculiar, than I have been as a poet.

Of my first two significant experiments in fiction, one ''A Race Apart,'' is a Mandarin comedy set in rural England, and the other, ''A Fitting Tribute,'' is a New Zealand fantasy and social satire about a man who achieves engineless flight and vanishes. Both have female first-person narrators. Both were published outside New Zealand, the first in England, the second in America (and the latter was almost at once translated into Spanish and Hungarian). These stories indicate, I think, an early preoccupation with the question of narrative voice and ''point of view.'' I was troubled (without knowing that this was a current preoccupation of theorists of fiction) about the question of the authority of the information fiction offers. Not its authenticity, or its truth; but rather the question, Who is supposed to be giving us this supposed information; what is its provenance? I was not much interested in current British and American fiction; but I read, for example, in translation, everything by the Italian Alberto Moravia and the Argentinian Jorge Luis Borges, writers whose approach to fiction seemed clever enough to overcome this problem of authority—Moravia by his intense clarity of ''seeing'' (in the sense both of visualizing and understanding) through the eyes of a single character, and Borges by signalling in various ways that fiction was a game with rules, an agreement between writer and reader to pretend that the story was true. These were sophistications I had already found in Fielding, Sterne, Emily Brontë, and Dickens, but which modern fiction writers in English (or those I tried to read in the 1950s and 1960s) had largely forgotten.

But it would be wrong to say that I thought clearly and historically about all this. I can now see, though I would not have seen it at the time, that what I wanted to do was to make the voice which gave the story its authority a part of the fiction; and the simplest—though certainly not the only, or always the best—way to do this, was first person narration. This is a problem which grows larger as the fiction expands in size, because it involves consistency of tone, of persona, of style, of manner; and a mercurial, or anyway protean temperament, such as suits the writer of lyric poems, must be damped down and made dependable and consistent in the writer of novels.

My other strong impulse in fiction has been the simple one towards narrative. I enjoy telling stories, and hearing stories well told, and admire narrative management, especially in places (such as Wordsworth's poems in *The Lyrical Ballads*) where it does its work largely unnoticed. The difference between Borges and his many recent imitators is that most of them acquire something of his sophistication without possessing any of his native skill as a storyteller.

I offer these remarks only as background, which the reader may find ways of applying to my novels and stories.

*   *   *

C.K. Stead quickly established himself as one of New Zealand's finest poets and also as a distinguished literary critic; his *The New Poetic* is a definitive account of the modernist movement in poetry that won for him an international reputation. However, he had always been interested in fiction as well. The stories in *Five for the Symbol,* for instance, range between 1959 and 1979 in composition. Since retiring from academic life in 1986 in order to devote himself full-time to writing he has continued to produce poetry and literary criticism as well as edit a number of volumes, but his output of fiction has increased considerably.

Stead has declared that he has always been concerned with "the question of the information fiction offers ... Who is supposed to be giving us this supposed information, what is its provenance?" After some fairly conventional stories such as "A Race Apart" and fantasies such as "A Fitting Tribute," which anticipates his first novel *Smith's Dream,* Stead ventured into a highly self-conscious, often self-referential kind of postmodernist fiction that questions the nature of fiction and storytelling itself. Most of his fiction is written in the first person, by narrators of doubtful integrity or who are simply bewildered or unsure, and very often goes back into a distant past to investigate the truth of accepted interpretations of events. In the story "The Town," Stead begins to play games, cutting between past and present, and employing the self-consciousness that characterizes much of his later fiction: "My name is Miller, Rod Miller," the narrator tells his audience. "Age thirty-eight, divorced, nationality New Zealander. And I am in France because ..." "A Quality of Life" concerns a well-known writer (his narrators are often writers) on the tiny Pacific island of Nova who decides to burn his most recent book, rather than publish it. He then sets out to explain why. The story is about himself as a student, falling in love for the first time with a young girl. She falls in love too easily, we are told: "I could sweep her off her feet in the course of an evening. But so could any young man who was reasonably presentable and sufficiently determined." But eventually, owing to mistakes that the narrator makes and that he recognizes now only retrospectively, she marries a rich but nondescript man.

Much of Stead's work is highly political, if only by implication; he is too intelligent a writer to hector his readers. The 1951 Wharfies' strike and the Holland government's declaration of emergency feature in several of his works, but in none more so than *All Visitors Ashore.* This is again the story of a young man's first ventures into love. Curl Skidmore is a third year arts student, a budding writer, perhaps to some extent a portrait of the author himself. He becomes involved in different ways with three women before losing all of them. The novel is a highly self-conscious act of recollection, moving from character to character, never staying with any one of them for long. There is a consciously cinematic quality to it, which would become even more pronounced in Stead's next novel, *The Death of the Body.* It is like a succession of pan shots, or perhaps sideways tracking shots as the novel shifts from scene to scene. A painter named Melior Farbro talks with the poet Rex Fairbain but each of them conducts a private monologue, oblivious of what the other person is saying. There are question and answer sections, direct addresses to both the characters and the reader. Slowly we learn the eventual fates of the characters. Melio's cartoon sequence is a failure, Curl becomes professor, like several of Stead's protagonists, Felice achieves fame as a singer, and Pat sails for London. It is a satiric but also affectionate portrait of the art scene in Auckland in 1951.

The Death of the Body is on the surface a comparatively conventional, enjoyable novel that combines two themes: that of the older, powerful academic who is having an affair with a post-graduate student, and a group of people who are running drugs. The two stories come together when police ask the professor, Harry Butler, if they can use his house in order survey their targets next door and he agrees—until he finds that he knows two of them personally. But Stead juxtaposes these against the idea of the narrator (who is also one of the characters) having difficulty writing the novel, or The Story as he calls it, breaking down often, and needing to call on his Muse, who turns out to be Uta, the wife of a Scandinavian Consul. This, in turn, allows Stead to make playful speculations about the nature of reality and its relationship to fiction. But Uta complicates further by being constitutionally unable to distinguish between fact and invention, so that she constantly imputes attitudes of the characters which she finds offensive to Harry himself. The narrative is frequently interrupted by the narrator's account of the difficulties he is having in continuing the narrative. The author makes it clear that he is inventing the characters and therefore that they could just as easily have taken quite different forms. The Story, as he calls it, at times assumes a life of its own and dictates events to the author. Even more consciously than he did in his previous novel, Stead employs cinematic techniques: "I've sometimes thought how you would begin if you were making a movie." He talks about his problems to the reader: "We have now to bring Larson Snow and Harry Butler together in the same room." He speculates, asks questions about his characters. Stead is, like most academics, very partial to puns and literary parodies. In this novel, one of his characters writes an undergraduate essay with the title "O Henry James Joyce Carey." In another, one of his characters says, "Wake drunken with thy knocking? I wouldst thou could."

Sister Hollywood is one of Stead's most attractive novels, as well as one of his most straightforward, though even here there are some tricks. It is the story of a young New Zealand woman named Edie Harper who suddenly and without explanation deserts her family, making no subsequent attempt to contact them. Again the story is told in the first person, by a narrator looking back many years later. In this case it is Edie's retired brother Bill, who sees her in two small parts in Hollywood films and finally looks her up. Bill's chapters are juxtaposed against those dealing with Edie, or Arlene as she has become in the late forties in Hollywood. Arlene has married a young Australian actor named Rocky Tamworth, and they go to Hollywood to pursue Rocky's career. However, he finds it impossible to gain a contract, partly due to difficulties with his accent, and though he becomes a good friend of Humphrey Bogart his frustration leads him into alcoholism. In contrast, Arlene becomes a big success without even trying. A job as secretary leads to a well-paid position as senior secretary to the famous producer Jesse Fischer, then to the brief screen appearances, scriptwriting, and an affair with Jesse. She does a good deal of work on a film called ''Shooting'' that stars Bogart and sounds remarkably like Nicholas Ray's ''In a Lonely Place''—which had not yet been made. Shortly after she tells Rocky, in dramatic circumstances, that she is pregnant, he is killed and she breaks off the affair. The story is mostly that of Arlene—Sister Hollywood—though we slowly learn that Bill too in a different way had a successful career, as Professor of English, becoming an expert in Keats. The novel takes in the activities of the House of Un-American Activities Committee and the execution of the Rosenbergs as well as the father's aspirations to become a Labour member of parliament, but otherwise the novel is largely a love story, lively, interesting, if fairly structureless. There are cameo appearances of real-life figures like Bogart, Grace Kelly, and ''Bert'' Brecht.

The Singing Whakapapa is probably Stead's most ambitious novel. It is an attempt to look at the history of one family over one hundred and fifty years and in that way to document much of New Zealand's history and especially the history of the complex relationship between the whites and the Maoris. The central character is Hugo Wolf Grady, married to Harriet (''Hat'') Enverson, and now a retired historian. In one of the novel's few jokes, Hugo or Hugh is married to Hat and has a passionate affair with a woman called Lid. Assisted by a young librarian, Jean-Anne Devantier, who he eventually discovers is his daughter by Lid, Hugh sets out to explore his family story, his ''singing whakapapa,'' going as far back to 1835 to the story of John Flatt, his great-great-great-grandfather. The novel is predictably skeptical about the notion of historical ''causes'' but offers the idea that a young girl Tarore, who was murdered by a Maori tribe, and with whom Flatt, we learn at the end, had an affair, is the cause of peace between warring Maori tribes. Stead uses (or invents) historical documents, has his two historians speculate and hypothesize, and in general reconstructs the history of the family over five generations.

Stead is an interesting and intelligent novelist whose experiments with form do not interfere with his determination to supply lively and gripping narratives.

—Laurie Clancy

STEFFLER, John (Earl)

Nationality: Canadian. **Born:** Toronto, Ontario, 13 November 1947. **Education:** University of Toronto, Ontario, 1967–71, B.A. in English 1971; University of Guelph, Ontario, 1972–74, M.A. in English 1974. **Family:** Married Shawn O'Hagan, 1970; one daughter and one son. **Career:** Since 1975 professor of English, Sir Wilfred Grenfell College, Memorial University of Newfoundland. **Awards:** Canada Council Arts grant, 1988, 1993; Newfoundland Arts Council Artist of the Year award, 1992; Smith Books/*Books in Canada* First Novel award, 1993; Thomas Raddall Atlantic Fiction award, 1993; Joseph S. Stauffer prize, 1993. **Member:** League of Canadian Poets. **Agent:** Susan Schulman Literary Agency, 454 West 44th St., New York, New York 10036, USA. **Address:** Department of English, Sir Wilfred Grenfell College, Corner Brook, Newfoundland A2H 6P9, Canada.

Publications

Novels

The Afterlife of George Cartwright. Toronto, McClelland and Stewart, 1992; New York, Holt, 1993.
That Night We Were Ravenous. Toronto, McClelland & Stewart, 1998.

Poetry

An Explanation of Yellow. Ottawa, Borealis Press, 1980.
The Grey Islands. Toronto, McClelland and Stewart, 1985.
The Wreckage of Play. Toronto, McClelland and Stewart, 1988.

Other

Flights of Magic (for children). Victoria, Press Porcepic, 1987.

*

Critical Studies: ''The Writings of John Steffler'' by James Harrison, *Brick,* 45, Winter 1993.

John Steffler comments:

I am essentially a poet. All my writing begins with immediate experience, the stuff of time and space. Without planning to, I find myself writing about the interaction of people and nature, people and landscape, the character of place. In the same way, I'm interested in how the past influences the present, how we live in a flow of time, a choir of ghosts. I am not interested in obeying the restrictions of traditional genres. My novel is part history, part fantasy, part poetry. We should feel free inside a work of literature. I like the pull of ''What happens next?'' in a story. I also like the pull of invention and surprise in the way a work is constructed.

* * *

John Steffler's first novel, *The Afterlife of George Cartwright,* comes out of the directions mapped by his considerable achievements in poetry and *The Grey Islands,* a diary mixture of poetry and prose describing a summer spent alone on a tiny island off the northeast shore of Newfoundland. In his early work, he demonstrated a mixture of preoccupation with the search for the inner self, a quiet center, and considerations of the effects of place on strangers, largely his own migration from Ontario to rugged Newfoundland. Quietly brilliant, *The Afterlife of George Cartwright* emerges from his reading of the real George Cartwright's 1792 journal and interleaves Steffler's fascination with Newfoundland-Labrador—the land and its history—with his concerns about personal destiny.

Cartwright, part of whose life was spent in the British army in Germany and India, wrote a journal of fact until December 1779 and then made up the later entries (which cover time when he was not actually in the Labrador he is describing) while barracks master of the Nottingham militia. Steffler is equally free with fact, mixing entries from the journal with entries of his own making and surrounding the journal with a richly imagined world of the Cartwright family and Britain, Germany, India, and Labrador. The whole is framed by the device of imagining Cartwright living on after his death, alone except for his hunting hawk and his horse as he wanders the English countryside and sometimes lets wandering omnibuses drive right through his hearty ghost (a ghost who enjoys decent cooking). The most extensive portion of the novel deals with Cartwright's creation of several settlements in Labrador and his sorrow when his Inuit mistress and her party die of smallpox after he has taken them to England. Cartwright was ever eager to learn in Labrador, survived the extreme challenges of that bleak yet sensational coast, and was among the first to befriend the native peoples. But his methods were often brutal, and through Mrs. Selby, Cartwright's housekeeper-mistress, Steffler introduces ideas about the blind rapacity of the colonial enterprise.

Besides the richly pictured eighteenth-century world of city and wilderness colony, the true center of this novel is the paradoxes surrounding Cartwright. Steffler pictures a man frozen in the amber of his era, unable to grasp the implications of fault in the greedy struggle for furs and timber. He is the imperfect traveler who brings all his values with him to impose upon an alien world and who freely treats its people as exhibits when he brings them to England. There is a wonderful heady mixture of distaste and admiration for Cartwright, and to make the mixture even more potent the George Cartwright of the Afterlife is no more aware of the paradoxes than the living one was.

The Afterlife of George Cartwright is a first novel of both promise and distinctive achievement. Like fellow poets Michael Ondaajte and Jane Urquhart before him, Steffler has chosen fiction to anatomize the Canadian past, which makes it luminous and at the same time raises paradoxes of power and personal morality that reflect sharply on the present.

—Peter Brigg

STEPHENS, Michael (Gregory)

Nationality: American. **Born:** Washington, D.C., 4 March 1946. **Education:** City College of New York, B.A. and M.A. 1976; Yale University, M.F.A. in drama 1979. **Family:** Married Okhee Stephens, 1974; one daughter. **Career:** Assistant professor of communications, Fordham University, 1979–85; lecturer, Columbia University, 1977–91; lecturer, Princeton University, 1987–91; lecturer, New York University, 1989–91, 1994–95; Gertz Professor of Writing, Alfred University, 1991. Public relations specialist, The Asia Society, 1992–93; Comptroller's Office, Audit Bureau of the City of New York, 1992. Since 1994 editor, *Flatiron News.* **Awards:** Fletcher Pratt Prose fellowship, Breadloaf Writers Conference, 1971; New York State Arts award, 1976; Associated Writing Programs award in creative nonfiction, 1993, for *Green Dreams.* **Address:** 520 West 110th St., #5C, New York, New York 10025, USA.

PUBLICATIONS

Novels

Season at Coole. New York, Dutton, 1972.
Still Life (novella) . New York, Kroesen, 1978.
Shipping Out (novella) . Cambridge, Massachusetts, Apple Wood, 1979.
The Brooklyn Book of the Dead. Normal, Illinois, Dalkey Archive, 1994.

Short Stories

Paragraphs. New York, Mulch Press, 1974.

Uncollected Short Stories

''Red Black and Whitey Greene,'' in *Provincetown Review,* 1968.
''The Hare Apparent,'' in *Evergreen Review,* February 1971.
''Prospecting,'' in *Evergreen Review,* May 1971.
''The Last Poetry Reading,'' in *Tri-Quarterly,* (26), 1973.
''Meat Lust,'' in *Broadway Boogie,* (2), 1974.
''Two Stories: 'Hemingway in Paris' and 'Mooney's Bartleby,''' in *Mulch,* (5), 1974.
''In Praise of Earwigs,'' in *The Falcon,* (13) Fall 1983.
''The Thug,'' in *North American Review,* 268(1), March 1983.
''In Memory,'' in *Kairos,* 1(3), 1984.
''MASH Bureau,'' in *Exquisite Corpse,* 3(9–10), September-October 1985.
Walking Papers,'' in *Other Voices,* 1(1), 1985.
''Eight Ruins,'' in *Exquisite Corpse,* 4(5–8), May-August 1986.
''The Fights,'' in *Ontario Review,* (25), Fall-Winter 1986–87.
''Bronx Fighter,'' in *Ontario Review,* (28), Spring-Summer 1988.
''Everlast,'' in *The Equator Hot Type Anthology.* New York, Scribner, 1988.
''Travels in Mexico,'' in *Hanging Loose,* (55), Fall 1989.
''The Sixth Man,'' in *Witness,* Spring 1989.
''Still Life with Anjou Pears,'' in *Fiction International,* 1990.
''Scrambled,'' in *Writ* (Toronto), Spring 1990.
''Tomato Cans,'' in *Writ* (Toronto), Summer 1991.
''Revenge,'' in *Manoa,* 3(2), Fall 1991.
''Five Jack Cool,'' in *The Black Pig, Imagining America,* edited by Wesley Brown and Amy Ling. New York, Persea, 1991.

Plays

Off-Season Rates (produced New Haven, Connecticut, 1978).
Cloud-Dream (produced New Haven, Connecticut, 1979).
Our Father (produced New York, 1984; London, 1985). In *Our Father and Other Plays,* 1995; published as *Our Father: A Play,* New York, Spuyten Duyvil, 1997.
Circles End (produced Cambridge, Massachusetts, 1985).
R & R (produced New York, 1985).
Horse (produced New York, 1986) . In *Kairos Magazine* (New York), 2(2), 1988.

Adam's Curse (produced New York, 1987).
Walking Papers (produced New York, 1987).
Cracow (produced New York, 1988).
Our Father and Other Plays. New York, Spuyten Duyvil, 1995.

Radio Plays: *Paragraphs,* 1978.

Poetry

Alcohol Poems. Binghamton, Loose Change Press, 1973.
Tangun Legend. Iowa City, Iowa, Seamark Press, 1978.
Circles End (includes prose) . New York, Spuyten Duyvil, 1982.
Translations. New York, Red Hanrahan, 1984.
Jigs and Reels. New York, Hanging Loose Press, 1992.
After Asia. New York, Spuyten Duyvil, 1993.

Other

The Dramaturgy of Style: Voice in Short Fiction. Carbondale, Southern Illinois University Press, 1986.
Lost in Seoul and Other Discoveries on the Korean Peninsula. New York, Random House, 1990.
Green Dreams: Essays Under the Influence of the Irish. Athens, University of Georgia Press, 1994.

*

Critical Studies: ''Interview with Michael Stephens'' by Jerome Klinkowitz, in *Tri-Quarterly,* 1975; ''Michael Stephens,'' by Klinkowitz, in his *The Life of Fiction,* Urbana, University of Illinois Press, 1977; by John O'Brien, in *Adrift,* Winter 1983–84.

Michael Stephens comments:

I am a writer comfortable with writing in many different genres of writing, but I always perceive of poetry being the essence of all my work. By that I don't mean a vague impressionism informing, say, my prose, but rather the rigorous linguistic pursuit of *le mot juste,* as Flaubert called it; and also being concise, emotionally charged in the language, seeing that every experience has its own unique rhythms, that there are no ideas but in things, as Dr. Williams wrote, and like Olson, that writing is about breath and syllable, even prose and playwriting. What else? Writing is a love affair, sometimes amorously beautiful, though often a dogged curse, just the way love is, its face always changing. As Yeats wrote, I see writing being cold and passionate, at once, and forever.

* * *

An Irish lyricism contesting with the harsher features of lower-middle-class American life has distinguished Michael Stephens's work from inception through maturity. As the child and grandchild of immigrants from Counties Clare and Mayo and raised in a large family where Irish-Americanism was both cultural treasure and battle flag, Stephens crafts a verbal song that contends with and eventually transforms the sordid details of dysfunctional social life into a magic realism that is ultimately redeeming of the creative self.

Season at Coole details just such a family. Gathering together for Christmas eve, its forces are at once centrifugal and centripetal, and from these contrary energies Stephens derives a structure that allows both descriptive coverage and exuberance of language. The circumstance at hand is so volatile that similes mix and collide in attempts to express it, particularly the enmity between the alcoholic father and his schizophrenic eldest son, ''for this Christmas he and the old man had decided to go off the edge of the planet like a brace of ducks in orange sauce together, a duet for father and son.'' Following an initial chapter that introduces the family and details the father's boozy, inept, and disconcerting violence, the novel continues with a chapter for each of the grown siblings, followed by briefer looks at the mother and the three youngest children off in their own world in attic rooms above. Each family member is seeking escape, pursuing it in such ways as madness, drugs, alcohol, crime, sex, art, alcohol-induced religious visions, physical training, prepubescent love, and sports. Matters are resolved when the mother and her children stand up to the father's attempt to functionalize them in their roles, divesting him of ''his excuses''—a technique with validity in therapy as well as in art.

Stephens followed this compactly written but large-scale first novel with an exercise in exquisite miniaturization, the novella *Still Life.* Beckettian in concept and slapstick in execution, it focuses its 90 spare pages on the attempt of a Buster Keaton-like protagonist, Buster Shigh (''pronounced 'Shee,' like the good people''), to shimmy up the drainpipe when drunk and locked out of his room. Rendered like a painted still life, there is little action other than this self-contained flurry that gets absolutely nowhere. Yet in the process Stephens's comic protagonist is all liveliness, proving that ''still, life goes on,'' an echo of Samuel Beckett's epigraph cited in *Season at Coole* that ''all is not then yet quite irrevocably lost.'' A second novella, *Shipping Out,* extends this Irish lyricism by mixing it with another element, the Hispanic, which the author had absorbed in his adopted upper West side Manhattan neighborhood. Here he creates a character named Rico O'Reilly, who, in working as a dishwasher on a trans-Atlantic liner, experiences the exotic life among ship hands beneath decks.

Even shorter prose works offer clues to Stephens's method, such as the physical sensuosity of language in *Paragraphs* and competing definitions of time in *Circles End.* Language as a body and one's body itself as a grammar of experience motivate the vignettes of *Jigs and Reels.* These concerns are studied in *The Dramaturgy of Style: Voice in Short Fiction,* a critical meditation on the role of voice in fiction. Autobiographically, *Lost in Seoul and Other Discoveries on the Korean Peninsula* characterizes the author's marriage into a happy Korean family as *Season at Coole* virtually inside out and upside down, whereas *Green Dreams: Essays Under the Influence of the Irish* reclaims his parents' heritage as well as his own, particularly its artistically linguistic features. ''I found the song of the savage and the antisocial, of the outlaw and even the misfit as tuneful as anything from the world of reason and responsibility and intelligence,'' Stephens writes.

> Even if my father did not write and could not sing and had not been in a battle for many years, I think perhaps there was more than a touch of that ancient, maniac Celt in him, and when he drank I knew he discovered that the sound of English was ridiculous and barbarian, that the only way to quell the thirst for the ancient words he no longer remembered—was to drink.

In *The Brooklyn Book of the Dead,* Michael Stephens draws on over two decades of work to produce what critics consider his masterpiece. In subject matter it is a sequel to *Season at Coole,* for 25 years afterwards the family is being once more reunited, this time for the father's wake and burial. This time chapters focus on the children's responses to the father's influence on what has become their lives; to some extent each can now appreciate how his crazed tyranny has forced them into a style of art in order to survive. Yet it is the innocent, hopeful second-youngest brother of the first novel, Terry, who is seen as the most desolate at the end of this narrative. Almost literally stripped naked and propelled not to an intended future but confusedly into the past, he is left crying piteously for the mother circumstances have denied him.

—Jerome Klinkowitz

STEPHENSON, Neal

Nationality: American. **Born:** Fort Meade, Maryland, 31 October 1959. **Education:** Boston University, B.A. 1981. **Family:** Married Ellen Marie Lackermann in 1985. **Career:** Teaching assistant in physics department, Boston University, 1979; research assistant, Ames Laboratory, U.S. Department of Energy, Ames, Iowa, 1978–79; researcher, Corporation for a Cleaner Commonwealth (environmental group), Boston, 1980; clerk in library, University of Iowa, Iowa City, 1981–83; writer. **Agent:** Liz Darhansoff, 1220 Park Avenue, New York, New York 10128, U.S.A.

PUBLICATIONS

Novels

The Big U. New York, Vintage, 1984.
Zodiac: The Eco-Thriller. New York, Atlantic Monthly Press, 1988.
Snow Crash. New York, Bantam, 1992.
The Diamond Age: Or, A Young Lady's Illustrated Primer. New York, Bantam, 1995.
Cryptonomicon. New York, Avon, 1999.

Other

In the Beginning ... Was the Command Line (nonfiction). New York, Avon, 1999.

* * *

Neal Stephenson has become the most prominent post-cyberpunk novelist, challenging and displacing the leading figure in the cyberpunk field, William Gibson. The post-cyberpunk novel takes for granted, and builds on, the key elements of Gibson's fictional world—cyberspace, virtual reality, and a degraded political, cultural, and social environment traversed by a lone, marginal hero. Stephenson's major novels are characterized by complex, multiple, interweaving plots; by a style that is generally lively and forceful, if sometimes banal; by a plethora of technological, mathematical, scientific, and cultural references that can become top-heavy; and by a bravura imagination that moves backwards and forwards in time, elaborating on actual historical events and extrapolating from current social trends into an imagined future. Stephenson has moved beyond the confines of genre or cult fiction to establish himself as a best-selling author who seems to catch the pace and style of a world that is being transformed by information technology.

After a first novel, *The Big U,* that made no impact, Stephenson produced an ecological thriller, *Zodiac,* featuring Sangamon Taylor, a campaigning chemist and a kind of environmental private eye who works for a Greenpeace-style environmental group, and who makes it his mission to expose large and powerful companies that dump toxic waste. Checking on the state of Boston Harbor, Taylor discovers a dangerous toxin that may destroy the whole earth—but when he tries publicly to identify the company responsible, all trace of the toxin disappears. The novel follows his quest to prove the company's culpability, a quest that involves—in what will become a characteristic Stephenson mix—businessmen, the FBI, Satanists, and the Mafia. In *Zodiac,* a compelling thriller combines with science fiction to produce a potent symbol of impending eco-catastrophe.

It was his third novel, *Snow Crash,* that established Stephenson as the key post-cyberpunk writer. From the opening pages, where a Deliverator, desperate to deliver a pizza within thirty minutes or suffer dire consequences from the Mafia, finds himself slowed down by a Kourier, a female skateboarder who has attached herself to his car with an electromagnet, we are in a fast-moving, feverish, fear-ridden future, in which the Internet has become the Metaverse, the Street has replaced the Information Superhighway, the USA has collapsed economically into a batch of city-states, and the Mafia, now an acceptable business organization but still able to instill deep fear, masterminds what is now a major industry—pizza delivery. The Deliverator—whose function in the novel is comically highlighted by his name, Hiro Protagonist—is also a freelance hacker and, in the Metaverse, a samurai swordsman, who sets out to find the source of a new drug, Snow Crash, that has destroyed the mind of Da5id [sic], Hiro's friend and the founder of the Metaverse protocol. Hiro is helped in this task by Y.T.—the skateboarder with the electromagnet—and the novel traces, somewhat schematically, the existential development of both these characters as it follows their dramatic adventures. As plot lines and cultural references proliferate—there is, for example, much use of Sumerian mythology in later chapters—Stephenson has some difficulty in holding his novel together and bringing it to a satisfying conclusion; but for much of the narrative his inventive power and the energy of his style sweeps the reader along. Of all Stephenson's novels so far, *Snow Crash* has attracted the greatest volume of critical commentary.

The Diamond Age; Or, a Young Lady's Illustrated Primer demonstrates Stephenson's interest in the past as well as the future, although it is the past reconstructed in the twenty-first century, where neo-Victorians rule Atlantis/Shanghai and the Confucian system of justice—in which the judge is also detective, jury, and sometimes executioner—still operates. But John Percival Hackworth, a nanotechnologist, creates an illicit copy of *A Young Lady's Illustrated Primer,* which, despite its very Victorian title, is intended to teach girls to think in an independent way. This copy gets into the hands of an orphan child, Nell, who uses it to educate herself. The novel interweaves passages from the *Primer* with a sensitive exploration of Nell's developing knowledge and understanding of the strange world she inhabits—a world that Hackworth, by creating a ''wet Net'' in the blood of the human race, hopes to transform. The novel is less hectic, more measured, than *Snow Crash;* but as in the earlier work, Stephenson finds it difficult to achieve a satisfactory ending. Once more, however, he carries the reader along for much of the story.

In 1999, Stephenson produced his most elaborate and complex novel yet, *Cryptonomicon,* which interweaves past and present and puts out threads towards possible futures. The two time zones in the novel are the 1940s and the 1990s. In World War II, mathematical genius Lawrence Waterhouse and U.S. marine and morphine addict Bobby Shaftoe—along with real-life gay mathematician Alan Turing—are members of Detachment 2702, an Allied group working to decipher Nazi communication codes while not letting the enemy know their codes have been cracked. In the 1990s, Randy Waterhouse, Lawrence's grandson, and Amy Shaftoe, Bobby's granddaughter, work together to create a haven for the free storage and exchange of data, and to search for gold that was once possessed by the Nazis. Although Stephenson handles the interweaving of the time zones well, he once more has problems in concluding a novel that is, as he himself says, a big tangle of interrelated themes: cryptography, language, computers, and money. This time, however, he plans a sequel, or perhaps a number of sequels, and he is already working on a novel called *Quicksilver*, once more concerned with cryptography but set 300 years ago. *Cryptonomicon* took Stephenson onto the best-seller charts and provoked comparisons with the works of Thomas Pynchon. This comparison is premature: Stephenson has not reached that rank yet, but it will be interesting to see whether he approaches it with *Quicksilver*.

—Nicolas Tredell

STERLING, Bruce

Nationality: American. **Born:** Brownsville, Texas, 14 April 1954. **Education:** Attended University of Texas at Austin, 1972–76. **Family:** Married Nancy Adell Baxter in 1979. **Career:** Proofreader, Texas Legislative Council, Austin, 1977–83; writer, 1983—. **Agent:** Writers House, Inc., 21 West 26th Street, New York, New York 10010, U.S.A.

Publications

Novels

Involution Ocean. New York, Berkley Publishing, 1977.
The Artificial Kid. New York, Harper, 1980.
Schismatrix. New York, Arbor House, 1985.
Burning Chrome. New York, Arbor House, 1986.
Islands in the Net. New York, Arbor House, 1988.
Crystal Express, illustrated by Rick Lieder. Sauk City, Wisconsin, Arkham House, 1989.
The Difference Engine (with William Gibson). New York, Bantam, 1990.
Heavy Weather. New York, Bantam, 1994.
Holy Fire. New York, Bantam, 1996.
The Artificial Kid. San Francisco, HardWired, 1997.
Distraction. New York, Bantam, 1998.
Zeitgeist. New York, Bantam, 2000.

Short Stories

Globalhead: Stories. Shingletown, California, Ziesing, 1992.
Schismatrix Plus (includes *Schismatrix* and other stories). New York, Ace Books, 1996.

Other

The Hacker Crackdown: Law and Disorder on the Electronic Frontier. New York, Bantam, 1992.
(With Hans Moravec and David Brin) *Thinking Robots, an Aware Internet, and Cyberpunk Librarians: The LITA President's Program*, edited by R. Bruce Miller and Milton T. Wolf. Chicago, Library and Information Technology Association, 1992.
Contributor, *Universe 13*, edited by Terry Carr, 1983.
Contributor, *Heatseeker*, edited by John Shirley. Scream/Press, 1989.
Contributor, *Semiotext(e) SF*, edited by Rudy Rucker, Peter Lambourne Wilson, and Robert Anton Wilson. Autonomedia, 1990.
Contributor, *Universe 1*, edited by Robert Silverberg and Karen Haber, Doubleday, 1990.
Contributor, *When the Music's Over*, edited by Lewis Shiner, Bantam Spectra, 1991.
Editor and contributor, *Mirrorshades: The Cyberpunk Anthology*. New York, Arbor House, 1986.
Foreword, *Cyberpunk Handbook: The Real Cyberpunk Fakebook* by St. Jude, R. U. Sirius, and Bart Nagel. New York, Random House, 1995.
Foreword, *Reality Check* by Brad Wieners and David Pescovitz. San Francisco, Hardwired, 1996.

*

Critical Studies: *Across the Wounded Galaxies: Interviews with Contemporary American Science Fiction Writers* by Larry McCaffrey, University of Illinois Press, 1990; *Science Fiction in the Real World* by Norman Spinrad, Southern Illinois University Press.1990.

* * *

Although Western culture is permeated with the narratives and iconography of science fiction, it is still relatively rare for an SF writer to be recognized outside the genre for work that remains within the genre. SF writers who ''break out'' into the mainstream, from Ray Bradbury and Kurt Vonnegut to Jonathan Lethem and Neal Stephenson, usually do so by producing work that, to one extent or another, drifts away from the materials of science fiction. There have been exceptions, such as Ursula Le Guin and Octavia Butler; to that list may be added the name of Bruce Sterling.

As the main voice, along with colleague and one-time collaborator William Gibson, of the ''cyberpunk'' movement in 1980s SF, Sterling promoted a worldview and aesthetic that strongly influenced the generation that came of age with the computer revolution, a worldview that, arguably, has had a greater impact on the world at large than on the literature of science fiction. Sterling has continued to chronicle the social and technological developments of that world through numerous journalistic pieces, including a book-length study of the computer ''underground,'' *The Hacker Crackdown*. However, his fiction, which in some ways never fit comfortably into the cyberpunk mold, has evolved both conceptually and aesthetically; his most recent novels may be ranked with the best the SF field has to offer. By the late 1990s, with featured articles on Sterling in such publications as *Time*, it was clear that Sterling's novels were beginning to be noticed not just as important science fiction, but also as important fiction.

Like many SF writers, Sterling started early: his first novel, *Involution Ocean*, appeared when the author was twenty-three. In this novel and *The Artificial Kid*, Sterling both revels in and undermines the materials of traditional far-future, space-faring SF. The narrator of *Involution Ocean* is on a whaling voyage in the dust seas of the planet Nullaqua, but he set sail because the whales of Nullaqua are the only source of his favorite recreational drug. The plot of *The Artificial Kid* revolves around competing scientific theories that spark a revolution on the planet Reverie, but the eponymous narrator is a ''combat artist'' resident in a ''Decriminalized Zone'' who surrounds himself with floating video cameras that record his every move for an appreciative audience. Both novels are glib and energetic. Sterling's third novel, *Schismatrix*, recalls the grand visions of Olaf Stapledon as it covers the multigenerational conflict between the Shapers, who modify their bodies through genetic engineering, and the Mechanists, who modify their bodies through non-biological prosthetics. Far more ambitious than his first two novels, *Schismatrix* is unapologetically dense in its detailed account of the transformation of humanity into something that is, if not non-human, then post-human.

Schismatrix marked the end of Sterling's consideration of far-future, off-world humanity. His next novel, *Islands in the Net*, began a series of books that, although unconnected in terms of setting and characters, all explore the possibilities of twenty-first-century Earth through protagonists who undergo some form of radical transformation, sometimes circumstantial, sometime physical and mental, sometimes both. Laura Webster in *Islands in the Net* is yanked from a comfortable existence as a rising star in a multinational corporation and thrust into a far less certain world of mercenaries and data pirates; Alex Unger, the protagonist of *Heavy Weather*, is kidnapped by a band of high-tech storm chasers; ninety-four-year-old Mia Ziemann of *Holy Fire*, after undergoing a comprehensive rejuvenation that partially wipes out her personality, wanders across Europe with the artistic underground of the late twenty-first century; Oscar Valparaiso of *Distraction*, born of a genetic experiment and so not fully human to begin with, must adapt himself to the human intricacies of being a political operative in the crumbling United States of the 2040s.

Like many classic SF writers, Sterling is often more concerned with cataloging the details of his various futures than with maintaining plot and character (although *Holy Fire* and *Distraction* offer impressively nuanced characterization of their protagonists). Unlike many other SF writers, he maintains a consistent and engaging narrative voice that manages to be both breezy and serious. Reading a Bruce Sterling novel is akin to listening to a kindly uncle rattle on about his weird and interesting travels, if the kindly uncle happened to be a cross between Arthur C. Clarke and Hunter S. Thompson. This marriage of shrewd extrapolation and hip sensibility is realized with particular brilliance in *Distraction*, Sterling's best novel to date and one of the best SF novels of the 1990s.

It should also be noted that, although Sterling's work is sometimes cited as ''postmodern'' science fiction, his novels are, relative to a William Burroughs or a Kathy Acker, quite conventionally written. And although his focus on the dynamics of radical personal transformation and its inevitable shattering of received categories certainly speaks to the concerns of postmodernism, Sterling's later work shows a subtle awareness of the difference between what is inevitable and what may be desirable. After battling illness through elaborate experimental treatments, Alex Unger discovers that ''genetically, I'm supposed to be a big fat blond guy''; after running on the cutting edge of art and technology, Mia Ziemann is able to pick up a camera and take her ''first true picture'' only after concluding that ''Machines were so evanescent … in their wake people stopped being people. But people didn't stop going on.''

This is not to say that Sterling has settled on a conservative determinism. But part of the astonishing energy of his novels derives from the tension between his detailing of the certainty of change and his apparent conviction that, once the radically transformed dust has settled, there will be a place for all, and all can, if they wish, find their place. Sterling has not yet turned fifty; we can only guess if he will maintain this relatively sanguine outlook, or if his future work will itself be marked by further radical transformation.

—F. Brett Cox

STERN, Daniel

Nationality: American. **Born:** New York, 18 January 1928. **Education:** Columbia University, The New School for Social Research, Julliard School of Music. **Military Service:** United States Army Infantry, 1946–47: staff sergeant. **Family:** Married 1963; one son. **Career:** Senior vice-president, managing director, McCann-Erickson, Advertising, 1964–69; vice-president advertising and publicity, Warner Bros. Motion Pictures, 1969–71; vice-president east coast, CBS Entertainment, 1979–86; director of humanities, 92nd Street Y, New York, 1986–88; president, Entertainment Division, McCaffrey & McCall, Advertising, 1989; professor of English, University of Houston, 1992–93. Since 1993 Cullen Distinguished Professor of English, University of Houston. Fellow, 1969, Boynton Professor in Creative Writing, 1975, visiting professor in letters and English, 1976–78, all Wesleyan University; visiting professor of creative writing, New York University Film School, 1981; Dyson Memorial Lecturer in the Humanities, Pace University, 1982 and 1984; literary director, Institute for Advanced Theatre Training and American Repertory Theatre, Harvard University, 1992. **Awards:** International Prix du Souvenir, 1978, for *Who Shall Live, Who Shall Die;* O. Henry prize, 1993, and Pushcart prize, 1993, both for ''A Hunger Artist by Franz Kafka''; City of Houston Recognition award for academic and literary distinction, 1993; Brazos prize for best short story, Texas Institute of Letters, 1996. . **Agent:** Borchardt Agency, 136 E. 57th St., New York, New York 10022, U.S.A.

Publications

Novels

The Girl with the Glass Heart. New York, Bobbs Merrill, 1957.
The Guests of Fame. New York, Ballantine, 1958.
Miss America. New York, Random House, 1959.
Who Shall Live, Who Shall Die. New York, Crown, 1963.
After the War. New York, Putnam, 1965.
The Suicide Academy. New York, McGraw Hill, and London, Allen, 1968.
The Rose Rabbi. New York, McGraw Hill, 1971.
Final Cut. New York, Viking, 1975.
An Urban Affair. New York, Simon and Schuster, 1980.

Short Stories

Twice Told Tales. N.p., Paris Review Editions, 1989.
Twice Upon a Time. New York, Norton, 1992.
One Day's Perfect Weather: More Twice Told Tales. Dallas, Southern Methodist University Press, 1999.

Uncollected Short Stories

"The Oven Bird by Robert Frost: A Story," in *Paris Review,* Spring 1995.
"Grievances and Griefs by Robert Frost: A Story," in *Boulevard,* Spring 1995.
"Comfort," in *American Short Fiction,* Spring 1995.

Plays

The Television Waiting Room. In *Playwrights Horizons,* 1987.

* * *

"All men are artists. After all, they have their lives." In just this way Daniel Stern opens his novel *The Rose Rabbi,* with an epigram that also serves as the story's thematic center, a terse, cryptic anchorhold that alone will finally make sense of the swirl of events that come to occupy Wolf Walker in the course of a day. Yet the epigram as thematic center is characteristic throughout Stern's fiction, revealing a central thesis at work in his aesthetic, whatever the story: life is always a problem in art. Whether it be art as the cinema (*Final Cut*), or the more practical sphere of urban planning (*An Urban Affair*), or art as theater (*Who Shall Live, Who Shall Die*), or art as language (*After the War, The Suicide Academy,* and *The Rose Rabbi*), for Daniel Stern art as form is elemental, imposed on a world otherwise chaotic without it, a form that molds and makes sense finally of lives and predicaments, and renders what is the ultimate concern of all Stern's fiction: redemption.

Fundamental to Stern's narrative approach in shaping the crises of his characters—crises that demand answers if life is to be lived at all in a world otherwise irrational and chaotic—is his concern with memory, and its function in time as a paradoxical force of both continuity and discontinuity. The paradox is detailed as a push and pull of what is past, impossible except as memory, and what is the present, equally impossible without some meaning rendered it by the past. We see this in *After the War* with especial clarity, where the protagonist, Richard Stone, back in New York after service in World War II, tries to live a life entirely in the present, a life of what he calls "disconnectedness," trying to escape memory, yet unable to escape the reality of a father who deserted him as a child. He tries to make sense of what happened to his close friend Jake, blown apart on the Italian front, the "brute fact," the "thingness" of Jake's dismembered body, evoking as it does the disconnectedness of Stone's present life as also "brute fact." The crisis that overcomes Richard Stone is thus life as aftermath, and how to live it.

Echoing the resolution finally achieved in *After the War,* Stern follows with two novels in the surrealist vein that take the matter further by illustrating the idea we can even create in the present the memory needed for just the necessary sense of making life as aftermath something purposeful. Thus the Wolf Walker of *The Rose Rabbi* can say on the occasion of his fortieth birthday, an occasion that propels the novel into action, that he was "eager to escape backward again, to be off to invent a past for the present." And he adds: "First, to invent myself, and then a locale." And in *The Suicide Academy* it is a dream of the other Wolf Walker which opens and propels that novel into action, of his former wife Jewel singing "Aprés un rève" by Fauré, and in particular the repetition of her singing "*reviens, reviens.*" It is a matter addressed still further, and in an entirely fresh way, by Stern's more recent venture into short fiction: *Twice Told Tales* and *Twice Upon a Time.* The magic and tension of "twice" designates every story a return, a mirror in aftermath of the story behind it and recreating it.

Yet nowhere does Stern achieve this vision more dramatically than in the dark, haunted pages of *Who Shall Live, Who Shall Die.* Nowhere is aftermath a more profound and oppressive entity, yet also an ultimate ground for choice, than in this story of two men, Judah Kramer and Carl Walkowitz, protagonist and antagonist, who survive the Holocaust and meet years later, becoming colleagues and yet at odds in the preparation of a Broadway play, *At the Gates,* directed by Kramer and set in a Nazi death camp much like that which the two men had known. But Kramer, to save his own family, had been responsible for the death of Walkowitz's family in that camp. It is evidence of the particularly close ties between this novel and the one that follows, *After the War,* that, as different as they are in many respects, the signal question which defines and drives the narrative of *After the War,* "Who will tell us how to lead our lives?," is the essential question of the earlier novel. And that the solution each man seeks to realize is finally enacted on a stage, with all the props of a concentration camp in place, and with all that is memory of the real camp years earlier impinging upon the moment as these two men face off, is a tour de force, and elevates *Who Shall Live, Who Shall Die* to a rare achievement in American letters.

—Eric Muirhead

STERN, Richard G(ustave)

Nationality: American. **Born:** New York City, 25 February 1928. **Education:** Stuyvesant High School; University of North Carolina, Chapel Hill, B.A. 1947 (Phi Beta Kappa); Harvard University, Cambridge, Massachusetts, M.A. 1949; University of Iowa, Iowa City, Ph.D. 1954. **Military Service:** Served as an educational adviser, United States Army, 1951–52. **Family:** Married 1) Gay Clark in 1950 (divorced 1972), three sons and one daughter; 2) Alane Rollings in 1985. **Career:** Lecturer, Jules Ferry College, Versailles, France, 1949–50; Lektor, University of Heidelberg, 1950–51; instructor, Connecticut College, New London, 1954–55. Assistant professor, 1956–61, associate professor, 1962–64, professor of English, 1965–91, and since 1991, Helen Regenstein Professor of English, University of Chicago. Visiting Lecturer, University of Venice, 1962–63; University of California, Santa Barbara, 1964; State University of New York, Buffalo, 1966; Harvard University, 1969; University of Nice, 1970; University of Urbino, 1977. **Awards:** Longwood fellowship, 1960; Friends of Literature award, 1963; Rockefeller fellowship, 1965; American Academy grant, 1968, and Award of Merit for the Novel Medal, 1985; National Endowment for the Arts grant, 1969; Guggenheim fellowship, 1977; Sandburg award, 1979; Chicago *Sun-Times* Book of the Year award, 1990; Heartland award, nonfiction book of year, 1995. **Address:** Department of English, University of Chicago, 1050 East 59th Street, Chicago, Illinois 60637, U.S.A.

Publications

Novels

Golk. New York, Criterion, and London, MacGibbon and Kee, 1960.
Europe; or, Up and Down with Schreiber and Baggish. New York, McGraw Hill, 1961; as *Europe; or, Up and Down with Baggish and Schreiber,* London, MacGibbon and Kee, 1962.
In Any Case. New York, McGraw Hill, 1962; London, MacGibbon and Kee, 1963; as *The Chaleur Network,* Sagaponack, New York, Second Chance Press, and London, Sidgwick and Jackson, 1981.
Stitch. New York, Harper, 1965; London, Hodder and Stoughton, 1967.
Other Men's Daughters. New York, Dutton, 1973; London, Hamish Hamilton, 1974.
Natural Shocks. New York, Coward McCann, and London, Sidgwick and Jackson, 1978.
A Father's Words. New York, Arbor House, 1986.
Shares and Other Fictions. New York, Delphinium Books, 1992.

Short Stories

Teeth, Dying, and Other Matters, and The Gamesman's Island: A Play. New York, Harper, and London, MacGibbon and Kee, 1964.
1968: A Short Novel, An Urban Idyll, Five Stories, and Two Trade Notes. New York, Holt Rinehart, 1970; London, Gollancz, 1971.
Packages. New York, Coward McCann, and London, Sidgwick and Jackson, 1980.
Noble Rot: Stories 1949–1988. New York, Grove Press, 1989.

Other

The Books in Fred Hampton's Apartment (essays). New York, Dutton, 1973; London, Hamish Hamilton, 1974.
The Invention of the Real. Athens, University of Georgia Press, 1982.
The Position of the Body (essays). Evanston, Illinois, Northwestern University Press, 1986.
One Person and Another: On Writers and Writing. Dallas, Baskerville, 1993.
Via Cracow and Beirut: A Survivor's Saga. London, Minerva Press, 1994.
A Sistermony. New York, Fine, 1995.
Editor, *Honey and Wax: Pleasures and Powers of Narrative: An Anthology.* Chicago, University of Chicago Press, 1966.

*

Manuscript Collection: Regenstein Library, University of Chicago.

Critical Studies: By Marcus Klein, in *Reporter* (Washington, D.C.), 1966; article by Hugh Kenner and interview with Robert Raeder, in *Chicago Review,* Summer 1966; ''Conversation with Richard Stern'' by Elliott Anderson and Milton Rosenberg, in *Chicago Review,* Winter 1980; ''On Richard Stern's Fiction'' by G. Murray and Mary Anne Tapp, in *Story Quarterly* (Northbrook, Illinois), Winter 1980; M. Harris, in *New Republic* (Washington, D.C.), March 1981; David Kubal, in *Hudson Review* (New York), Summer 1981; John Blades, in *Washington Post Book World,* November 1982; J. Spencer, in *Chicago Tribune,* 25 April 1985; James Schiffer, in *Dictionary of Literary Biography Yearbook: 1987,* Detroit, Gale, 1988; *Richard Stern* by James Schiffer, Boston, Twayne, 1993.

* * *

In a time when serious American fiction has tended towards extreme personal assertion and extravagance of manner, Richard G. Stern has been composing a body of work which is notable for its detailed craftsmanship, its intricacy, and its reticences. His novels and stories are neither lyrically confessional nor abstractly experimental. They are processes quite in the mode of an older tradition, in which character and event discover theme. In one and another incidental observation within his fiction, Stern has rejected both the idea of the novel as ''a roller coaster of distress and sympathy, love and desire,'' and the idea of the novel as a deliberate attack on formal expectations (*Europe*); he has addressed qualification to the view that a story is fully autonomous (see the sketch called ''Introductory'' in *1968*), but he has also rejected the idea of the author as solipsist (see ''Story-Making'' in *1968*). His own fiction accepts no extremities of technique and form. Its characteristic tone as well as its strategy of development is created by ironic modulations.

The tone and the technique are, moreover, exact functions of Stern's characteristic subject. The broad theme is the adjustment of private lives with public events. Typically, Stern's protagonist has been a passive, sensitive fellow, who is a little too old for adventuring, or a little too fat, or a little too fine-grained, but nonetheless possessing romantic inclinations. His latent disposition is tested when public event of one sort and another seeks him out. He is now forced to regard his own actions and the actions of others as moral events. And, typically, this protagonist has found himself engaged in a drama of betrayals, which have the effect of chastening his new ambitions as a public man. The end is his rather baffled, nonetheless scrupulous assessment of personal adventure. Between the beginning and the end, his motives are subjected to more and more contingencies. He has been lured from his innocent privacy into life, defined as public action which by its nature is dangerous and ambiguous. At the end he has sacrificed the self-protectedness with which he began, and he has also failed to discover an easy ground of general participation in life. His modest success is that he has become potentially moral.

Stern's first novel, *Golk,* is somewhat more spare and blatant in its actions than the fictions which follow, but it is otherwise exemplary. The hero is a thirty-seven-year-old boy, Herbert Hondorp, who lives with his widowed father in New York City. As he has done for most of the days of his life, he now spends his days wandering in and near Central Park, until on an occasion, abruptly, he is snared into public view and public occupation. The agent is a television program—''Golk''—which is created, precisely, by making public revelation of privacy. Ordinary, unwary people are caught by the television camera in prearranged, embarrassing situations. Stern's hero discovers that he likes not only the being caught, as do most of the Golk victims, but he also likes the catching. He takes a job with the television program, and not fortuitously at the same time he secures his first romance. Within this new situation there are moral implications, of course, but both ''Golk'' and Hondorp's romance are tentative and jesting. The novel then proceeds to raise the stakes of involvement: the program is transformed by its ambitious director into a device for political exposé, and Hondorp's romance becomes a marriage. This newer situation beckons and perhaps necessitates treacheries, which make it morally imperative that public involvement be terminated. Hondorp betrays the director of the program, in order to save the program—so he believes—from the fury of the political powers, and he thereby reduces it to vapidity. In a consequent narrative movement, his wife leaves him. Hondorp goes home at the end, "all trace of his ambition, and all desire for change gone absolutely and forever."

In his subsequent fictions, Stern has avoided such metaphorical ingenuity as the television program in *Golk,* and the lure to public action has been carefully limited to a matter of background or accident, but the area of his concerns has remained constant. In *Europe; or, Up and Down with Schreiber and Baggish,* the two protagonists are American civil employees in post-war occupied Germany. The pattern of their adventuring—despite the comic suggestion in the title of the novel—allows nothing implausible, and there are no sudden reversals. Realization is to be achieved, rather, through implied contrasts and comparisons. Schreiber is an aging sensitive gentleman who tries for intimate understanding of the ancient, bitter, guilty, and conquered people. Baggish is a shrewd young opportunist, who exploits the populace. Baggish succeeds, and Schreiber fails. *In Any Case* is the story of another aging American in post-war Europe, who is innocent for the reason that he has never sufficiently risked anything, his affections included. His testing comes when he is told that his son, dead in the war, was a traitor. In a belated and ironic act of love, he tries to prove that his son was really innocent, and he discovers that treachery is a vital ingredient of all social living. Although his son was indeed not guilty in the way supposed, everyone is a double agent.

His acceptance of that discovery provides the hero with the possibility of a modest participation in other people's lives. In his more recent fiction, Stern has apparently wanted to make that possibility more emphatic, by bringing historical and aesthetic confirmations to it. *Stitch* is in large part a *roman à clef* about one of the great modern traitors, Ezra Pound. The would-be disciple in the novel receives from the aged master, Stitch, lessons in the fusion of personality with civilization, and the consequence of expression in art. The background of the novel is Venice, which, from the muck of its history, raises its beauties. In the short novel Veni, Vidi … Wendt (included in *1968*), the protagonist is a composer who is writing an opera about modern love. The opera will extend backwards to include great love affairs of the past, which are founded on adulteries. The composer himself, meanwhile, realizes both his composition and his domestic love for wife and children only after experiments in romantic duplicity. The chief adventurer in *Other Men's Daughters* is a middle-aged professor of biology at Harvard. His life heretofore has been completely defined by such seeming ineluctabilities as filial ties, domestic habits, and the concretion of compromises, and the stern decencies of his New England ancestry. He betrays everything when he falls in love with a girl not much older than the eldest of his own children, and hopefully discovers, in nature, the justification for this treachery to nurture. In *Natural Shocks* Stern writes about a talented and successful journalist, which in this case is to say a man who with all decent goodwill has made a career of transforming private lives into public knowledge. The protagonist is now forced to confront the fact of death, alternately as a subject for journalism and as a domestic event, and he is thereby invited to learn the necessary treachery that is involved in his calling and also its ethical insufficiency. A true participation in life will require more strenuous sympathies, which he may or may not achieve.

The endings of Stern's fictions record an acquiescence at the most, and always something less than the assertion of a principle. The kind of realization that is in the novels makes it necessary that they be probationary and open-ended. They are by that, as well as by their detailed, persistent, and moderate account of human motives, in the great tradition of moral realism.

—Marcus Klein

STONE, Robert (Anthony)

Nationality: American. **Born:** Brooklyn, New York, 21 August 1937. **Education:** New York University, 1958–59; Stanford University, California (Stegner fellow, 1962). **Military Service:** Served in the United States Navy, 1955–58. **Family:** Married Janice G. Burr in 1959; one daughter and one son. **Career:** Editorial assistant, New York *Daily News,* 1958–60; writer-in-residence, Princeton University, New Jersey, 1971–72; taught at Amherst College, Massachusetts, 1972–75, 1977–78, Stanford University, 1979, University of Hawaii, Manoa, 1979–80, Harvard University, Cambridge, Massachusetts, 1981, University of California, Irvine, 1982, and San Diego, 1985, New York University, 1983, Princeton University, 1985; Johns Hopkins University, 1993–94; and since 1994, Yale University. **Awards:** Houghton Mifflin Literary fellowship, 1967; Faulkner Foundation award, 1967; Guggenheim grant, 1968; National Book award, 1975; Dos Passos prize, 1982; American Academy award, 1982; National Endowment for the Arts fellowship, 1983; Strauss Living award, 1987. **Agent:** Donadio and Ashworth, 121 West 27th Street, New York, New York 10001, U.S.A.

PUBLICATIONS

Novels

A Hall of Mirrors. Boston, Houghton Mifflin, 1967; London, Bodley Head, 1968.

Dog Soldiers. Boston, Houghton Mifflin, 1974; London, Secker and Warburg, 1975.

A Flag for Sunrise. New York, Knopf, and London, Secker and Warburg, 1981.

Children of Light. New York, Knopf, and London, Deutsch, 1986.

Outerbridge Reach. New York, Ticknor and Fields, and London, Deutsch, 1992.

Damascus Gate. Boston, Houghton Mifflin, 1998.

Short Stories

Bear and His Daughter: Stories. Boston, Houghton Mifflin, 1997.

Uncollected Short Stories

"Geraldine," in *Twenty Years of Stanford Short Stories,* edited by Wallace Stegner and Richard Scowcroft. Stanford, California, Stanford University Press, 1966.

"Farley the Sailor," in *Saturday Evening Post* (Philadelphia), 14 January 1967.

"Thunderbolts in Red, White, and Blue," in *Saturday Evening Post* (Philadelphia), 28 January 1967.

"A Hunter in the Morning," in *American Review 26,* edited by Theodore Solotaroff. New York, Bantam, 1977.

"WUSA," in *On the Job,* edited by William O'Rourke. New York, Vintage, 1977.

''War Stories,'' in *Harper's* (New York), May 1977.
''Not Scared of You,'' in *Gentlemen's Quarterly* (New York), March 1989.

Plays

Screenplays: *WUSA*, 1970; *Who'll Stop the Rain*, with Judith Rascoe, 1978.

Other

Images of War, edited by Julene Fischer. Boston, Boston Publishing Company, 1986.

*

Critical Studies: *Robert Stone* by Robert Solotaroff, New York, Twayne Publishers and Toronto, Maxwell Macmillan Canada, 1994.

* * *

Robert Stone combines old-fashioned concerns—the morality of human behavior, the responsibility of choice, the relationship between the individual and history—with topical interests—racism in the U.S., the war in Vietnam, American involvement in Latin-American revolutions—to produce fiction that is both emotionally engaging and thought provoking.

A Hall of Mirrors, Stone's first novel, tells the story of three rootless drifters whose paths converge in New Orleans: Rheinhardt, an alcoholic ex-musician; Geraldine, a battered woman; and Morgan Rainey, an idealistic social worker. Victims both of circumstance and of their own self-destructiveness, the trio is eventually caught up in an orgy of violence touched off by a patriotic rally sponsored by the owner of right-wing radio station WUSA, where Rheinhardt works. The final third of the novel is devoted to a nightmarish description of the rally and the ensuing riot (portrayed in almost hallucinatory language), which leaves nineteen persons dead. The apocalyptic conclusion is reminiscent of the movie premiere riot that ends Nathaniel West's *The Day of the Locust*, but Stone's version of Armageddon has its roots not so much in the unrealized longings of the alienated outsider as in the racism and fanatical right-wing extremism he sees poisoning American society in the 1960s.

Dog Soldiers centers on the desperate flight of Ray Hicks, an ex-marine, and Marge Converse, wife of Hicks's friend John Converse, a journalist on assignment in Vietnam, to escape the narcotics agents who are after the three kilos of heroin Hicks smuggled into California from Vietnam. Exciting as the narrative is, *Dog Soldiers* is much more than an adventure thriller, for by showing that the action is set in motion by events which have their origin in Vietnam where the novel begins, Stone links the madness of the war depicted in the early sections with the tragic fallout it has at home.

The novel begins with a quotation from Joseph Conrad's *Heart of Darkness*, a work which has strongly influenced *Dog Soldiers*. Like Conrad, who saw in Kurtz's ivory a symbol of man's ''rapacious and pitiless folly,'' Stone uses heroin as a symbol of his characters' obsessions and of the war's tragic cost. In Vietnam Converse finds himself, as Kurtz did in the African jungle, torn loose from all the conventional supports of civilized society. Afloat emotionally and morally, he turns to heroin as a way of asserting himself (''This is the first real thing I ever did in my life,'' he declares), but his decision will soon prove to have costly consequences as the heroin's deadly poison begins to spread.

Like *A Hall of Mirrors, Dog Soldiers* concludes with an apocalyptic finale, a shootout between Hicks and the federal agents pursuing him, the action punctuated by the recorded sounds of combat amplified over loudspeakers set up around the mountain compound where the scene occurs. By reminding the reader of the actual battle taking place in Vietnam, Stone underscores the relationship between the war in Asia and its consequences at home. Also, he makes the point that here, as in Vietnam, it is difficult to tell the good guys from the bad buys: Antheil, the government agent who ends up with the heroin at the end, decides to keep it and use it for his own profit. In Stone's view, there are no victors; everyone is corrupted by the poison.

A Flag for Sunrise is Stone's most ambitious and successful novel to date. Set in the fictional Central American country of Tecan, it features the stories of three Americans, each with his own reason for coming to the country: Sister Justin Feeney, a devoted young Roman Catholic nun who runs a local mission; Frank Holliwell, an anthropologist who declines the request of a CIA buddy to look into the situation at the mission, but whose curiosity compels him to go anyway; and Pablo Tabor, a paranoid, pill-popping soldier of fortune whose thirst for excitement leads to his involvement in the dangerous business of gun-running to the Tecanecan revolutionaries. Inexorably, the fates of all three Americans become intertwined, just as, Stone suggests, America itself has gotten itself involved in the fate of this ravaged little country.

The novel represents Stone's most effective attempt at incorporating political issues—here the economic, military, political, and cultural roles the U.S. is playing in Latin American countries—and personal ones—individual commitment and responsibility for one's actions. By examining a variety of motives ranging from the simple purity of Sr. Justin's desire to help the poor, a commitment for which she is willing to die, to Holliwell's feckless drifting, to the combination of ''circumstance, coincidence, impulse, and urging'' that has driven a host of other characters (e.g., whiskey priests, journalists, CIA agents, resort developers, soldiers of fortune) to Tecan, Stone exposes the reasons which have led the U.S. itself to an active involvement in the affairs of undeveloped countries like Tecan.

Children of Light, a satirical novel about Hollywood and filmmaking, fails to measure up to the best of that genre (i.e. novels like *Day of the Locust* or *Play It as It Lays*), nor does it measure up to Stone's previous books. The novel features some brilliant flashes of satire at Hollywood's expense, and Stone's ear for absurd dialogue among the film types is well-tuned. In actress Lu Anne Verger, Stone also paints an affecting portrait of a schizophrenic whose tormented psyche finally overwhelms her during the filming of Kate Chopin's *The Awakening* on location in Mexico. But talk largely replaces action in this novel and *Children of Light* lacks the dramatic intensity and moral dimension that characterizes Stone's best work.

Stone returns to familiar philosophical and moral territory in *Outerbridge Reach* as he continues to explore such weighty issues as truth, honesty, self-knowledge, and betrayal. Owen Browne is a fortyish copywriter and commercial spokesman for a pleasure boat manufacturer. He is unexpectedly presented with an opportunity for the kind of adventure he sees as an antidote to his mid-life restlessness when his company names him to sail their entry in a solo around-the-world race. Alone at sea, he encounters, like Kurtz in Conrad's *Heart of Darkness*, the awesome challenge of isolation. In the process he discovers hidden truths about himself that have dire consequences for him and profound repercussions for the two other principals in the novel: his wife Anne and Ron Strickland, a filmmaker shooting a documentary about Browne's adventure. As in all his best work, Stone's sure control over language, character, and narrative produces dramatic and ambitious fiction of the highest order.

Though the seven stories (written over a thirty-year period) collected in *Bear and His Daughter* lack the thematic complexity of Stone's novels, they too illustrate his gifts as a writer. The best of them (''Helping,'' ''Under the Pitons,'' and the title story) feature fascinating characters, powerful prose, and scenes fraught with tension, all hallmarks of Stone's longer fiction.

Stone's familiar apocalyptic themes find their perfect location in Jerusalem, the setting for *Damascus Gate.* The time is 1992 and the city is unsettled by political unrest (represented by the *intifada,* the Palestinian uprising against Israeli occupation, as well as a conspiracy to blow up the Islamic holy sites on the Temple Mount) and a steady influx of religious fanatics drawn to the Holy City in anticipation of the end of the millennium. At the center of the action is Christopher Lucas, an American writer researching a book on religious cults in the city. The novel features a much larger cast of characters than usual as Stone attempts to capture the crazy quilt of shifting religious identities and political alliances represented in the city. It is sometimes difficult to keep track of the diverse characters and their religious and political affiliations, which only serves to underscore the baffling complexity that characterizes Jerusalem. Stone's unwieldy cast of characters often overwhelms the narrative, with Lucas functioning more as a link connecting the disparate characters than as the central focus of the novel's moral and political themes, as Stone's protagonists ordinarily do. Ultimately, it is the city itself, brilliantly rendered in all its ancient beauty and contemporary mystery, that dominates the novel and it, rather than any of the characters, best symbolizes the confusing uncertainties of modern life that is Stone's recurring theme.

—David Geherin

STOW, (Julian) Randolph

Nationality: Australian. **Born:** Geraldton, Western Australia, 28 November 1935. **Education:** Geraldton Primary School, 1941–47; Geraldton High School, 1948–49; Guildford Church of England Grammar School, Perth, 1950–52; St. George's College, University of Western Australia, Perth, 1953–56, B.A. in French and English 1956, further study, 1961; University of Sydney, 1958. **Career:** Storeman at an Anglican mission, Wyndham, Western Australia, 1957; tutor in English, University of Adelaide, 1957; anthropological assistant, Papua New Guinea, 1959; lecturer in English, University of Leeds, Yorkshire, 1961–62, and University of Western Australia, 1963–64; Harkness Fellow, U.S.A., 1964–66; lived in New Mexico, Maine and Alaska and studied Indonesian language, Yale University; returned to England, 1966; lecturer in English and Fellow in commonwealth Literature, University of Leeds, 1968–69; lived in East Bergholt, Suffolk, 1969–81, and Harwich, Essex, from 1981. **Awards:** Australian Literature Society gold medal, 1957, 1958; Miles Franklin award, 1959; Harkness traveling fellowship, 1964–66; Britannica—Australia award, 1966; Grace Leven prize, 1969; Commonwealth Literary Fund grant, 1974; Patrick White award, 1979. **Agent:** Richard Scott Simon, Anthony Sheil Associates, 43 Doughty Street, London WC1N 2LF, England.

PUBLICATIONS

Novels

A Haunted Land. London, Macdonald, 1956; New York, Macmillan, 1957.
The Bystander. London, Macdonald, 1957.
To the Islands. London, Macdonald, 1958; Boston, Little Brown, 1959; revised edition, Sydney, Angus and Robertson, 1981; London, Secker and Warburg, and New York, Taplinger, 1982.
Tourmaline. London, Macdonald, 1963; New York, Taplinger, 1983.
The Merry-Go-Round in the Sea. London, Macdonald, 1965; New York, Morrow, 1966.
Visitants. London, Secker and Warburg, 1979; New York, Taplinger, 1981.
The Girl Green as Elderflower. London, Secker and Warburg, and New York, Viking Press, 1980.
The Suburbs of Hell. London, Secker and Warburg, and New York, Taplinger, 1984.

Plays (opera librettos, music by Sir Peter Maxwell Davies)

Eight Songs for a Mad King (produced London, 1969). London, Boosey and Hawkes, 1971.
Miss Donnithorne's Maggot (produced Adelaide, 1974). London, Boosey and Hawkes, 1977.

Poetry

Act One. London, Macdonald, 1957.
Outrider: Poems 1956–1962. London, Macdonald, 1962.
A Counterfeit Silence: Selected Poems. Sydney and London, Angus and Robertson, 1969.
Poetry from Australia: Pergamon Poets 6, with Judith Wright and William Hart-Smith, edited by Howard Sergeant. Oxford, Pergamon Press, 1969.

Recording: *Poets on Record 11,* University of Queensland, 1974.

Other

Midnite: The Story of a Wild Colonial Boy (for children). Melbourne, Cheshire, and London, Macdonald, 1967; Englewood Cliffs, New Jersey, Prentice Hall, 1968.
Visitants, Episodes from Other Novels, Poems, Stories, Interviews, and Essays, edited by Anthony J. Hassall. St. Lucia, University of Queensland Press, 1990.
Blood, Sea and Ice: Three English Explorers. Greenwich, National Maritime Museum, 1996.
Editor, *Australian Poetry 1964.* Sydney, Angus and Robertson, 1964.

*

Bibliography: *Randolph Stow: A Bibliography* by P.A. O'Brien, Adelaide, Libraries Board of South Australia, 1968; ''A Randolph Stow Bibliography'' by Rose Marie Beston, in *Literary Half-Yearly* (Mysore), July 1975.

Manuscript Collection: National Library of Australia, Canberra.

Critical Studies: ''Raw Material'' by Stow, in *Westerly* (Nedlands, Western Australia), 1961; ''The Quest for Permanence'' by Geoffrey Dutton, in *Journal of Commonwealth Literature* (Leeds, Yorkshire), September 1965; ''Outsider Looking Out'' by W.H. New, in *Critique* (Minneapolis), vol. 9, no. 1, 1967; ''Waste Places, Dry Souls'' by Jennifer Wightman, in *Meanjin* (Melbourne), June 1969; ''Voyager from Eden'' by Brandon Conron, in *Ariel (Canada)* (Calgary, Alberta), October 1970; *The Merry-Go-Round in the Sea* by Edriss Noall, Sydney, Scoutline, 1971; ''The Family Background and Literary Career of Randolph Stow'' by John B. Beston, in *Literary Half-Yearly* (Mysore), July 1975; *Randolph Stow* by Ray Willbanks, Boston, Twayne, 1978; ''Randolph Stow's *Visitants,*'' in *Australian Literary Studies* (Brisbane), October 1980, and *Strange Country: A Study of Randolph Stow,* St. Lucia, University of Queensland Press, 1986, both by Anthony J. Hassall.

* * *

The contrast between *The Merry-Go-Round in the Sea,* with its local ''realism,'' and *Tourmaline,* which makes a symbolic landscape out of Randolph Stow's native land, indicates the initial range of his fiction. *The Merry-Go-Round* by no means eschews symbolic patterns, but it emerges more directly from Australian national sensibilities. Stow's novel links the isolating impact that World War II had on the country with the older traditions of convict settlement and South Pacific paradise. (Stow is careful to debunk the easy myths which see convict and bushranger mateyness as the *sole* generative character trait *throughout* Australia; his comic children's book *Midnite: The Story of a Wild Colonial Boy,* about the triumphant adventures of a native bushranger and his gang—a cockatoo and a cat—delightfully overturns assorted local archetypes. Yet with linguistic playfulness it celebrates the spirit of the country as well, which serves as a reminder of the ambivalent blend of prison and paradise which has always provoked the Australian imagination.) For Rick Maplestead, in *The Merry-Go-Round,* imprisoned in Changi and then freed only to discover his bonds to history, family, mates, and mediocrity, there is no escape but flight. But as he and his young cousin Rob Coram (whose offshore vision gives the book its title) know, glimpses of paradise are illusory and attempts to inhabit them fraught with disappointment.

By focusing ultimately on the quests of the mind, the book recapitulates many of Stow's earlier themes. His first books, full of mad characters and melodramatic incidents, are the Gothic attempts of a young novelist to record his knowledge of power and passion, of the relation between man and landscape and the impact of belief on action. Not till these sensibilities were controlled by Stow's anthropological and historical commitments did they exert a powerful literary effect. *To the Islands* reduced the reliance on incident and traced instead the wanderings of a man through the desert of his belief, in search of the afterworld islands of aboriginal dream order. His soul, he discovers, ''is a strange country''—which seems at first to be no advance on what he began by knowing. Increasingly, however, that very state of suspended apprehension becomes the world that Stow tries to explore. *Tourmaline,* about a wasteland of that name, which welcomes a stranger as a water-diviner (who begins to clothe himself in such a role), only to be desolated and turn to another authority when he fails, provides an even more archetypal canvas. Consciously symbolic and heavily mannered in style, the book tries to evoke the world of symbol, the fleeting perceptions that symbols try to convey, rather than the realities of everyday event. The reiteration on the part of the Law, the narrator, that to describe a heritage as ''bitter'' is ''not to condemn it,'' urges readers also to consider what it is that he does not say, what it is that he cannot say.

Tarot, Tao, and Jungian commentary become means to fathom the deep intuitive communications of silence, but wordless understandings present problems for a writer to communicate. Later novels pursue the imaginative reaches of the reflective mind. *Visitants* explores Melanesian tribal life and traces its impact on Australians of different sensibilities; the novel is cast as a series of depositions at a legal inquiry, which prove unable entirely to explain the cultural other-worldliness. *The Girl Green as Elderflower* turns imaginative threat—the pressures of tropical disease and a foreign tongue upon a sensitive young man—into imaginative renewal; the young man, in Suffolk, reconciles himself with his heritage and his experience, and in a series of fables he writes out his recognition of the ways in which the unusual has always permeated the everyday. To admit to such flights of mind, he discovers, is to admit to a kind of health and a kind of love, and to win a ''paradise'' of a different, more fluid, perhaps freer, certainly more comic nature.

But in *The Suburbs of Hell* Stow's vision is once again more problematic. The novel tells of a series of murders among both insiders and outsiders in an isolated East Anglia village. Who is the culprit? Adapting the forms of popular fiction, the narrative contrives to suggest a number of possibilities—but settles on none. The novelist here is interested more in the nature of motive and interpretive response than he is in simply bringing a story to a conclusion. He probes what the pressure of fear and uncertainty does to an apparently stable society—an interest not without its sociological import. But he fastens particularly on the power of narrative, and on the sometimes insidious capacity that the impulse to create narrative has on the way people (readers included) encode and therefore enclose all human behavior around them.

—W.H. New

STRAIGHT, Susan

Nationality: American. **Born:** Riverside, California, 19 October 1960. **Education:** University of Southern California, B.A. 1981; University of Massachusetts at Amherst, M.F.A. 1984. **Family:** Married Dwayne Sims in 1983; two daughters. **Career:** Teacher of gang members, dropouts and refugees, Inland Empire Job Corps, 1984–85; teacher of recent refugees from southeast Asia, Lao Family Community, 1985–86; teacher of English, Riverside City College, 1986–89; lecturer in creative writing, University of California, Riverside, 1988—. **Awards:** Milkweed National Fiction Award, 1990; New Writers Award (Great Lakes Colleges Association), 1991. **Agent:** Richard Parks, 138 East 16th Street, Number 5B, New York, New York 10003, U.S.A.

Publications

Novels

Aquaboogie: A Novel in Stories. Minneapolis, Milkweed Editions, 1990.

I Been in Sorrow's Kitchen and Licked out All the Pots. New York, Hyperion, 1992.

Blacker Than a Thousand Midnights. New York, Hyperion, 1994.
The Gettin Place. New York, Hyperion, 1996.

Other

Bear E. Bear, illustrated by Marisabina Russo. New York, Hyperion Books for Children, 1995.

*

Susan Straight Comments:

I hope, like Faulkner and Morrison and others I admire who write about their homelands, to till my own little postage stamp of soil, my area of southern California. In each of my novels, in nearly every story, I hope to make the landscape I love, which frightens some and fascinates others, become immortal.

* * *

Susan Straight's fiction takes the themes first explored by Richard Wright—the racial oppression and internal torment of destitute, ghettoized African Americans—into 1990s southern California. Straight is white. She's an expert documentarian of this turf, though, because it is also hers. She has lived in mixed-race Riverside, California, all her life. The vividness of her work interrogates essentialist assumptions that America's racial divide makes writing from the point of view of ''the other'' impossible.

Straight is concerned with the conflicted space of the poor black neighborhood. The characters in the fictional Rio Seco in *Aquaboogie,* a collection of interrelated short stories, are both constricted by and wordlessly loyal to their Westside neighborhood. Westside has been shaped by racism and poverty, but it still holds the power of home. The outside world, even with its material and/or professional advantages, not only fails to offer an escape from racism, but also leads to existential isolation. In ''Off-Season,'' Rosa, a sportswriter, and Donnie, a basketball player, move from Westside to Hartford, Connecticut, a transition that so destabilizes Donnie that he beats his wife. Nacho, the protagonist of *Aquaboogie*'s title story, moves to western Massachusetts to go to art school. He supports himself by working as a janitor. He is so ostracized by his co-workers that he's distracted from his dream of becoming an artist, his thoughts turning instead to working with his father back in southern California, ''outside, pushing together piles of cut-smelling leaves and trimmings, steaming grass.'' But romanticizing home is exactly that. When, in ''Hollow,'' Nacho returns to the ''cut'' smell, he discovers that it comes from the land of a greedy white developer—whose next conquest is the home of Nacho's aunt.

Yet in *I Been in Sorrow's Kitchen and Licked Out All the Pots,* moving away from home eventually frees Marietta. It's a long, hard struggle, though. Marietta is from Pine Garden, South Carolina, where her taciturn nature doesn't fit in with the chatty ways of the Gullah-speaking community. She seeks her fortune in Charleston, gets pregnant with twin boys, and during their childhood bounces between the city and Pine Garden, working menial jobs, conscious of the civil rights movement broiling around her. Her boys' success as professional football players leads her to southern California, where her attention shifts to their careers, tainted by stress and steroids. Though Marietta finds the enlightened West Coast hardly that at times, she ends up making her home there. A fish out of water in Pine Garden, at least she can ''swim'' in southern California.

First introduced in *Aquaboogie*, Darnell Tucker in *Blacker Than a Thousand Midnights* isn't nearly as mobile. He is a hard-working black man, surrounded by the crime, drugs, poverty, and despair of his Rio Seco neighborhood. Despite his diligence, he is expected to self-destruct by both whites and blacks. As his father-in-law puts it, ''Every nigga got his own poison.'' All Darnell wants to do is work with the forestry department, fighting fires. The flame is a clear enemy compared to the tumultuous world and divided loyalties he feels in his neighborhood. But the fires take him away from his family for weeks at a time, and he eventually decides to stay in the more complex battle ground of Rio Seco. There, he makes do by developing a persona that bypasses blackness. Whites want Asians, not blacks, in charge of their lawn care, so Darnell puts out flyers of ''Tuan's Oriental Landscape Maintenance Service,'' answers the phone with a clipped accent, and sends himself out as the black employee of this fictional boss.

In *The Gettin Place*, the life of the Thompson clan is turned upside down when three dead bodies are found burning in a car on the family's property. Seventy-six-year-old Hosea and his sons are immediately suspected, and Hosea's unspoken past comes crashing down. At age six, he survived the 1921 race riots in Greenwood, a black neighborhood in Tulsa, Oklahoma. The ''sweet, blood-laden smoke'' drifting from the burning bodies on his property recalls that awful time, making an immediate, sensory link between the injustice of the riots—which started after a black man accidentally bumped a white woman in an elevator—and of being under suspicion for a crime he did not commit. It is as if, more than seventy years later, Hosea can't shed the retribution, however erroneously inspired, of the Greenwood riots. Sixty miles away, the Los Angeles riots begin, a reaction to another injustice against a black man, a conflagration born of the same rage Hosea and his son, Marcus, the narrator of the tale, cannot afford to express.

—Lisa A. Phillips

STYRON, William

Nationality: American. **Born:** Newport News, Virginia, 11 June 1925. **Education:** Christchurch School, Virginia; Davidson College, North Carolina, 1942–43; Duke University, Durham, North Carolina, 1943–44, 1946–47, B.A. 1947 (Phi Beta Kappa). **Military Service:** Served in the United States Marine Corps, 1944–45, 1951: 1st Lieutenant. **Family:** Married Rose Burgunder in 1953; three daughters and one son. **Career:** Associate editor, McGraw Hill, publishers, New York, 1947. Since 1952 advisory editor, *Paris Review,* Paris and New York; member of the editorial board, *American Scholar,* Washington, D.C., 1970–76. Since 1964 fellow, Silliman College, Yale University, New Haven, Connecticut. **Awards:** American Academy Prix de Rome, 1952; Pulitzer prize, 1968; Howells Medal, 1970; American Book award, 1980; Connecticut Arts award, 1984; Cino del Duca prize, 1985; MacDowell Medal, 1988; Bobst award, 1989; National Magazine award, 1990; National Medal of Arts, 1993; National Arts Club Medal of Honor, 1995; F. Scott Fitzgerald award, 1996. Litt.D.: Duke University, 1968; Davidson College, Davidson, North Carolina, 1986. **Member:** American Academy, American Academy of Arts and Sciences, and American Academy of Arts and Letters; Commander, Order of Arts and Letters (France), and Legion of Honor (France). **Address:** 12 Rucum Road, Roxbury, Connecticut 06783, U.S.A.

PUBLICATIONS

Novels

Lie Down in Darkness. Indianapolis, Bobbs Merrill, 1951; London, Hamish Hamilton, 1952.
The Long March. New York, Random House, 1956; London, Hamish Hamilton, 1962.
Set This House on Fire. New York, Random House, 1960; London, Hamish Hamilton, 1961.
The Confessions of Nat Turner. New York, Random House, 1967; London, Cape, 1968.
Sophie's Choice. New York, Random House, and London, Cape, 1979.

Short Story

Shadrach. Los Angeles, Sylvester and Orphanos, 1979.

Uncollected Short Stories

''Autumn,'' and ''Long Dark Road,'' in *One and Twenty,* edited by W.M. Blackburn. Durham, North Carolina, Duke University Press, 1945.
''Moments in Trieste,'' in *American Vanguard 1948,* edited by Charles I. Glicksburg. New York, Cambridge, 1948.
''The Enormous Window,'' in *American Vanguard 1950,* edited by Charles I. Glicksburg. New York, Cambridge, 1950.
''The McCabes,'' in *Paris Review 22,* Autumn-Winter 1959–60.
''Pie in the Sky,'' in *The Vintage Anthology of Science Fantasy,* edited by Christopher Cerf. New York, Random House, 1966.

Play

In the Clap Shack (produced New Haven, Connecticut, 1972). New York, Random House, 1973.

Other

The Four Seasons, illustrated by Harold Altman. University Park, Pennsylvania State University Press, 1965.
Admiral Robert Penn Warren and the Snows of Winter: A Tribute. Winston-Salem, North Carolina, Palaemon Press, 1978.
The Message of Auschwitz. Blacksburg, Virginia, Press de la Warr, 1979.
Against Fear. Winston-Salem, North Carolina, Palaemon Press, 1981.
As He Lay Dead, A Bitter Grief (on William Faulkner). New York, Albondocani Press, 1981.
This Quiet Dust and Other Writings. New York, Random House, 1982; London, Cape, 1983.
Conversations with William Styron (interviews), edited by James L.W. West III. Jackson, University Press of Mississippi, 1985.
Darkness Visible (memoirs). New York, Random House, 1990; London, Cape, 1991.
A Tidewater Morning (Three Tales from Youth). Helsinki, Eurographica, 1991; New York, Random House, 1993; London, Cape, 1994.
Editor, *Best Short Stories from the Paris Review.* New York, Dutton, 1959.

*

Film Adaptations: *Sophie's Choice*, 1982; *Shadrach*, 1998.

Bibliography: *William Styron: A Descriptive Bibliography* by James L.W. West III, Boston, Hall, 1977; *William Styron: A Reference Guide* by Jackson R. Bryer and Mary B. Hatem, Boston, Hall, 1978; *William Styron: An Annotated Bibliography of Criticism* by Philip W. Leon, Westport, Connecticut, Greenwood Press, 1978.

Manuscript Collections: Library of Congress, Washington, D.C.; Duke University, Durham, North Carolina.

Critical Studies: *William Styron* by Robert H. Fossum, Grand Rapids, Michigan, Eerdmans, 1968; *William Styron* by Cooper R. Mackin, Austin, Texas, Steck Vaughn, 1969; *William Styron* by Richard Pearce, Minneapolis, University of Minnesota Press, 1971; *William Styron* by Marc L. Ratner, New York, Twayne, 1972; *William Styron* by Melvin J. Friedman, Bowling Green, Ohio, Popular Press, 1974; *The Achievement of William Styron* edited by Irving Malin and Robert K. Morris, Athens, University of Georgia Press, 1975, revised edition, 1981; *Critical Essays on William Styron* edited by Arthur D. Casciato and James L.W. West III, Boston, Hall, 1982; *The Root of All Evil: The Thematic Unity of William Styron's Fiction* by John K. Crane, Columbia, University of South Carolina Press, 1985; *William Styron* by Judith Ruderman, New York, Ungar, 1989; *The Novels of William Styron* by Gavin Cologne-Brookes, Baton Rouge, Louisiana State University Press, 1995; *The Critical Response to William Styron,* edited by Daniel W. Ross, Westport, Connecticut, Greenwood Press, 1995; *Gynicide: Women in the Novels of William Styron* by David Hadaller, Madison, New Jersey, Fairleigh Dickinson University Press, 1996; *William Styron: A Life* by James L.W. West, III, New York, Random House, 1998.

* * *

Of the American novelists who have come onto the literary scene since the end of World War II, William Styron would seem to have worked most directly in the traditional ways of story-telling. As a writer from the American South, he was heir to a mode of fiction writing most notably developed by William Faulkner and practiced to striking effect by such fellow southerners as Robert Penn Warren, Thomas Wolfe, Eudora Welty, and Katherine Anne Porter. It involved—as the mode of Hemingway did not involve—a reliance upon the resources of a sounding rhetoric rather than upon understatement, a dependence upon the old religious universals (''love and honor and pity and pride and compassion and sacrifice,'' as Faulkner once termed them) rather than a suspicion of all such external moral formulations, and a profound belief in the reality of the past as importantly affecting present behavior—an ''historical sense,'' as contrasted with the dismissal of history as irrelevant and meaningless.

His first novel, *Lie Down in Darkness,* was strongly indebted to the example of Faulkner; Styron began it, he said, after reading Faulkner night and day for several weeks. Yet though Styron portrayed a young southern woman, Peyton Loftis, as she battled for love and sanity in a dreary family situation, doomed to defeat by her father's weak, self-pitying ineffectuality and her mother's hypocrisy and sadistic jealousy, and though the setting was a tidewater Virginia city among an effete upper-class society, what resulted was not finally Faulknerian. At bottom the causes of Styron's tragedy were familial, not dynastic; the deficiencies of Milton and Helen Loftis were not importantly those of decadent aristocracy whose concept of honor and pride has become empty posturing and self-indulgence, as they would have been for a writer such as Faulkner, but rather personal and psychological. When Peyton flees Virginia for New York City, there is little sense of her plight as representing isolation from the order and definition of a time and place that are no longer available. Instead, hers was a break for freedom, and the failure to make good the break is the result of the crippling conflict within her mind and heart imposed by the example of her parents, and which symbolizes the hatreds engendered by a society that does not know how to love. The suicide of Peyton Loftis represents a plunge into the moral abyss of a self-destructive modern world. Styron, in other words, wrote out of a tradition that taught him to measure his people and their society against the traditional values, and to see the absence of those values in their lives as tragic; but he did not depict that absence as a falling away from a more honorable, more ordered Southern historical past.

The success of *Lie Down in Darkness* was considerable, perhaps in part because a novel that could depict the modern situation as tragic, rather than merely pathetic, and could thus make use of the High Style of language to chronicle it, was all too rare. Styron followed it with *The Long March,* a novella set in a Marine Corps camp during the Korean War (Styron himself was briefly recalled to active duty in 1951). Depicting the irrationality of war and the military mentality, it demonstrates the dignity, and also the absurdity, of an individual's effort to achieve nobility amid chaos.

Eight years elapsed before Styron's second full-length novel, *Set This House on Fire.* The story of a Southern-born artist, Cass Kinsolving, who is unable to paint, and is married and living in Europe, it involved a man in spiritual bondage, undergoing a terrifying stay in the lower depths before winning his way back to sanity and creativity. In Paris, Rome, and the Italian town of Sambucco, Cass Kinsolving lives in an alcoholic daze, tortured by his inability to create, wandering about, drinking, pitying himself, doing everything except confronting his talent. The struggle is on existential terms. Kinsolving has sought to find a form for his art outside of himself, looking to the society and the people surrounding him for what could only be located within himself: the remorseless requirement of discovering how to love and be loved, and so to create.

Set This House on Fire encountered a generally hostile critical reception, to some extent because it was sprawling and untidy, occasionally overwritten, and therefore so very different from his well-made first novel. It seemed, too, even further removed than *Lie Down in Darkness* from the customary Southern milieu: not only were there no decaying families, no faithful black retainers, no blood-guilt, and no oversexed Southern matrons, but we are told very little about the protagonist's past, either familial or personal, that might explain how he got the way he was. Yet there *was* a past; but Styron gives it to a friend of Kinsolving's, Peter Leverett, who tells the story. The fact is that Leverett's failure to find definition in his Southern origins is what really accounts for Kinsolving's present-day plight. Styron apparently could not avoid grounding his tragedy in history one way or the other. And after Kinsolving has fought his way back to personal responsibility and creativity, he leaves Europe and returns to the South. There is thus a kind of circular movement involved in the first two novels. Peyton Loftis finds the Southern community impossible to live within and love within, and she goes to New York. Cass Kinsolving, equally at loose ends, goes abroad and conducts his struggle for identity and definition there, and then comes home to the South. He has had in effect to ratify the individual and social worth of his attitudes and values away from the place and the institutions of their origins, and make them his own, not something merely bequeathed automatically to him.

If so, it was not surprising that Styron's next and most controversial novel, *The Confessions of Nat Turner,* once again was set in the South—in Southside Virginia, no more than an hour's automobile drive from Port Warwick where Peyton Loftis grew up and Newport News, Virginia, where Styron was born and raised—and that it concerned itself squarely with the southern past, as exemplified in the presence and the role of the black man. For though *The Confessions of Nat Turner* is based upon a famous slave insurrection that took place in 1831, its implications involve race and racism, integration and separatism, and the use of violent means in order to achieve political and social ends. Styron's strategy, for what he termed his ''meditation upon history,'' was to tell his story from the viewpoint of the slave leader Nat Turner, of whose actual life almost nothing is known. Rather than restrict his protagonist's language, however, to that which a plantation slave in the early 19th-century might be expected to have used, Styron decided that the range and complexity of such a man's mind could not be adequately represented in any such primitive fashion, and he cast Nat Turner's reflections in the rich, allusive, polysyllabic mode of the early Victorian novel. Styron was thus able to have his slave leader utilize the resources of a sounding rhetoric in order to look beyond his immediate circumstance into the moral and ethical implications of his actions.

The initial critical verdict on *The Confessions of Nat Turner* was highly favorable, with such critics as Alfred Kazin, Philip Rahv, C. Vann Woodward, and others declaring it an impressive contribution both to contemporary American fiction and to the knowledge of slavery. Almost immediately, however, the book became embroiled in a controversy, not so much literary as sociological, which made both novel and novelist into a *cause célèbre.* For in presuming, as a white man, to portray the consciousness of a black revolutionist of a century-and-a-half ago, Styron came into collision with the impetus of the black separatist movement. His novel appeared at a time when the black American was straining as never before to assert his identity and his independence of white paternalism, and the result was that numerous black critics, together with some white sympathizers, began heaping abuse on Styron for his alleged racism, his alleged unwarranted liberties with historical ''fact,'' and his alleged projection of ''white liberal neuroses'' onto a revolutionary black leader's personality. A host of reviews and essays and even a book appeared in denunciation of Styron. Other critics rose to the rebuttal, and historians joined in to certify the authenticity of Styron's historical portrayal. The outcome has been a voluminous literature of controversy that may well interest future social historians almost as much as the Nat Turner insurrection itself.

In 1979 Styron entered the lists again with a lengthy novel on another controversial subject. *Sophie's Choice* involved the confrontation of a young and very autobiographically clued Virginian with a Polish refugee who has undergone the horrors of concentration camp existence, and her lover, a young New York Jew who is a brilliant conversationalist but turns out to be quite mad. Written very much in the mode of Thomas Wolfe's fiction of encounter with the metropolis,

Styron's novel records the growing helplessness of a youthful American in the face of a developing acquaintance with the enormity of human evil and irrationality. The novel drew much criticism for its excesses of rhetoric and the apparent irrelevance of much of its sexual material; in effect it would seem to imitate the author's own difficulties in coming to terms with the subject matter described. Yet it contains powerful sequences, and as always represents Styron's unwillingness to seek easy ways out or avoid central human problems.

—Louis D. Rubin, Jr.

SUKENICK, Ronald

Nationality: American. **Born:** Brooklyn, New York, 14 July 1932. **Education:** Cornell University, Ithaca, New York, B.A. 1955; Brandeis University, Waltham, Massachusetts, M.A. 1957, Ph.D. in English 1962. **Family:** Married Lynn Luria in 1961 (divorced). **Career:** Lecturer, Brandeis University, 1956–57, and Hofstra University, Hempstead, New York, 1961–62; part-time teacher, 1963–66; assistant professor of English, City College, New York, 1966–67, and Sarah Lawrence College, Bronxville, New York, 1968–69; writer-in-residence, Cornell University, 1969–70, and University of California, Irvine, 1970–72. Since 1975 professor of English, and director of the Publications Center, University of Colorado, Boulder. Taught at Université Paul Valéry, Montpellier, France, Fall 1979; Butler Professor of English, State University of New York, Buffalo, Spring 1981. Contributing editor, *Fiction International,* Canton, New York, 1970–84; chairman, Coordinating Council of Literary Magazines, 1975–77. Since 1974 founding member and co-director, Fiction Collective, New York; since 1977 founding publisher, *American Book Review,* New York; since 1989 editor, *Black Ice,* New York. **Awards:** Fulbright fellowship, 1958, 1984; Guggenheim fellowship, 1977; National Endowment for the Arts fellowship, 1980; Faculty fellowship, 1982; Coordinating Council of Literary Magazines award, for editing, 1985; Before Columbus Foundation award, 1988. **Address:** Department of English, University of Colorado, Boulder, Colorado 80309, U.S.A.

PUBLICATIONS

Novels

Up. New York, Dial Press, 1968.
Out. Chicago, Swallow Press, 1973.
98.6. New York, Fiction Collective, 1975.
Long Talking Bad Conditions Blues. New York, Fiction Collective, 1979.
Blown Away. Los Angeles, Sun and Moon Press, 1986.
Doggy Bag. Boulder, Colorado, Black Ice, 1994.
Mosaic Man. Normal, Illionis, FC2, 1999.

Short Stories

The Death of the Novel and Other Stories. New York, Dial Press, 1969.
A Postcard from ''The Endless Short Story'' (single story). Austin, Texas, Cold Mountain Press, 1974.
The Endless Short Story. New York, Fiction Collective, 1986.

Uncollected Short Stories

''One Every Minute,'' in *Carolina Quarterly* (Chapel Hill, North Carolina), Spring 1961.
''A Long Way from Nowhere,'' in *Epoch* (Ithaca, New York), Fall 1964.
''Extract from *The Fortune Teller,*'' in *Trema* (Paris), no. 2, 1977.

Other

Wallace Stevens: Musing the Obscure. New York, New York University Press, 1967.
In Form: Digressions Towards a Study of Composition. Carbondale, Southern Illinois University Press, 1985.
Down and In: Life in the Underground. New York, Morrow, 1987.
Narralogues: Truth in Fiction. Albany, State University of New York, 2000.
Editor, with Curtis White, *In the Slipstream: An FC2 Reader.* Normal, Illinois, FC2, 1999.

*

Critical Studies: ''Getting Real: Making It (Up) with Ronald Sukenick,'' in *Chicago Review,* Winter 1972, and ''Persuasive Account: Working It Out with Ronald Sukenick,'' in *Seeing Castaneda,* edited by Daniel Noel, New York, Putnam, 1976, both by Jerome Klinkowitz; ''Reading *Out*'' by Melvin J. Friedman, in *Fiction International 1* (Canton, New York), Fall 1973; ''Imagination and Perception'' (interview), in *The New Fiction: Interviews with Innovative American Writers* by Joe David Bellamy, Urbana, University of Illinois Press, 1974; ''Tales of Fictive Power: Dreaming and Imagining in Ronald Sukenick's Postmodern Fiction'' by Daniel Noel, in *Boundary 2* (Binghamton, New York), Fall 1976; ''Obscuring the Muse: The Mock-Autobiographies of Ronald Sukenick'' by Timothy Dow Adams, in *Critique* (Atlanta), vol. 20, no. 1, 1978; ''Way Out West: The Exploratory Fiction of Ronald Sukenick'' by Alan Cheuse, in *Itinerary Criticism 7* edited by Charles Crow, Bowling Green, Ohio, Bowling Green State University Press, 1978; *The Novel as Performance: The Fiction of Ronald Sukenick and Raymond Federman* by Jerzy Kutnik, Carbondale, Southern Illinois University Press, 1986.

Ronald Sukenick comments:
(1991) My fiction is not ''experimental.''

* * *

As the most representative example of the innovative writers who contributed to the transformation of both American fiction and its supporting culture, Ronald Sukenick has remained active for over three decades, not so much adapting to conditions as challenging and in some cases changing the literary, publishing, and academic worlds about him. As such, he suggests the activist role of his artistic generation; not content to be, like Ken Kesey, a seismograph of cultural shock and a barometer of radical change, Sukenick has undertaken a revolution himself, leading developments that have reformed the culture in and of which Americans write.

Like several key figures of the 1960s group of innovators, Sukenick earned a doctorate (in English from Brandeis University) and undertook a career as a university professor. His first book was a revision of his dissertation on the poet Wallace Stevens, and while not directly related to any theory or style of narrative does demonstrate Sukenick's affinity for writing that exercises imaginative control. Aware of how Stevens believed that ''a fiction is not an ideological formulation of belief but a statement of a favorable rapport with reality,'' Sukenick began his own efforts as a writer by following this code for ordering reality: ''not by imposing ideas on it but by discovering significant relations with it.'' The most significant section of *Wallace Stevens: Musing the Obscure* is collected in Sukenick's book of essays, *In Form: Digressions Towards a Study of Composition,* where it complements an aesthetic underlying the fictive art of an era.

Sukenick's first novel, *Up,* activates this imagination as the generating force for narrative. As a gesture toward suspending the suspension of disbelief, Sukenick names his narrator/protagonist ''Ronald Sukenick'' and has him doing many of the same things Sukenick did at the time: struggling to study and teach free of the inhibitions that had smothered academic life in the preceding age, working to complete a novel (titled *Up*), and trying to establish a rapport with the reality around him—a reality that includes the just-developing countercultural world of the New York's Lower East Side and the community of artists and hustlers who are his friends. Fantasy merits the same treatment as experience, and at one point Sukenick's protagonist teaches a lesson from Wallace Stevens to his class: that art is ''the invention of reality'' that seeks ''a vital connection with the world that, to stay alive, must be constantly reinvented to correspond with our truest feelings.'' *Up* is a *Bildungsroman* of just such a struggle, and by the end, when the artist has come to maturity, the point is not to celebrate this status but to appreciate how it is achieved.

The Death of the Novel and Other Stories collects a novella (from which the volume takes its title) and five short stories, all of which suggest various strategies for such imaginative connection with the world. ''The Death of the Novel'' is famous for its opening paragraph, a statement that not only sums up critically the eclipse of realistic fiction but, as the protagonist's lecture notes, propels him into a narrative experience that proves each point. Equally significant are ''Momentum'' and ''The Birds,'' two stories that propound Sukenick's belief, stated later in *In Form,* that fiction ''is not about experience but is more experience.'' The test of such work, which another essay from *In Form* compares to the anthropological tales of Carlos Castaneda, is the degree to which the teller can present ''a persuasive account.'' In league with how anthropologists understand the world, Sukenick argues that there is not one reality but only various accounts of it, the most convincing of which succeeds as the culture's model.

A cultural model for the revolutionary America of the late 1960s and early 1970s is provided in Sukenick's second novel, *Out.* Its structure draws on the vernacular American format of a cross-country journey with characters being formed and reshaped by their experiences along the way. Its East to West movement expresses both the historical settling of the Continent and the rhythm of increasing speed and opening up of space that the geography implies. To replicate this experience for the reader, Sukenick numbers his chapters backwards, starting with 10 and proceeding in the manner of a rocket-launch countdown; at the same time, each chapter reads more quickly, with chapter 10 offering 10-line blocks of print, chapter nine introducing a line of blank space for each nine lines of print, chapter eight adjusting the ratio to eight-to-two, and so forth until chapter one is rushing by with only one line of narrative for every nine of open space. Yet the novel, which has by now progressed to the near-vacancy of California, the virtual opposite of New York City's cluttered accumulation, has one more chapter: chapter zero, whose 10 lines of space and no lines of print at all send the reader spinning off into emptiness, much like the drag-racing cars in the James Dean film, *Rebel Without a Cause,* that speed out over the cliff into the nothingness beyond.

From the mid-1970s onwards Sukenick has devoted much of his energy to organizational causes, a commitment that has both biographical and artistic consequences. As a full professor at the University of Colorado, he attracted several key writers as faculty, including Clarence Major and Steve Katz. For a time he directed the Coordinating Council of Literary Magazines, working for grant support of alternative publishing venues; at the same time he became one of the founders of The Fiction Collective, a collaborative venture in which writers would fund their books' publication and therefore retain control of all phases of production, distribution, and sales. Working for equal reform in the profession of English, Sukenick became a member of the executive council of the Modern Language Association. His greatest impact, however, has been as publisher of *The American Book Review,* a tabloid dedicated to covering books neglected by the commercial reviews. He also began editing the magazine *Black Ice.*

His own novels began reflecting this increased social awareness and offered models for both resisting control by others and initiating personal reform. *98.6,* published in 1975, offers three models for society: an initial section which interpolates dreams interfacing ancient and postmodern worlds, a central narrative detailing the attempts of countercultural revolutionaries to establish a commune, and a third part devoted to a utopian venture in psychic consciousness called, with pun intended, ''the state of Israel.'' One of the author's most comically exuberant novels, *98.6* nevertheless answers critics' objections that innovative fiction was ignoring social and moral issues. Though ending in an exceedingly up-beat manner, its central indictment of the 1960s generation for failing to produce an enduring model is compelling (the title refers to the body temperature being monitored as a woman from the commune miscarries the child meant to be this world's future).

Sukenick's later works play with elements from realistic fiction in the service of just such social commentary, but always in ways that reaffirm the primacy of the imagination as the creative force in any world. *Long Talking Bad Conditions Blues* takes its form from a blues/jazz narrative, the style of composition Sukenick favors as proceeding by improvisation and being fueled by its own compositional energy. Set in Paris, where Sukenick owns an apartment and lives for a portion of each year, it is reminiscent of *Up* in that its world is created by not just a community but a central intelligence coming to terms with the experience of its being. *Blown Away* draws similar energy from the Colorado-California life the author has lived in the decades since leaving New York. Here the focus is on how Hollywood seeks to produce the country's imagination, a power based on the willing suspension of disbelief Sukenick scorns as the undoing of art. If audiences yield control of their imaginations, he argues, others will do their imagining for them—which means they will have no effective experience of life. *Blown Away* creates a culture suffering from just such imaginative stasis. Antidotes are found in the author's second collection of short stories, a book that bears the optimistic title *The Endless Short Story*—endless because the model is that of creation itself, on the order of Simon Rodia and his Watts Towers, an assemblage whose essence consists in a state of continual building from the detritus of an otherwise dead culture. Such rebuildings take the form of what Sukenick calls ''hyperfictions'' in the novel *Doggy Bag.* Here scenes from the global culture of European travel and international terrorism are played out within a cleverly comic language in which imaginatively dead citizens are not only called ''Zombies'' but are said to suffer from an unstoppable mind control plague called Zombie Immune Tolerance Syndrome, or ''ZITS.'' Thus life becomes atomized, everyone mounting his or her own private revolution in isolation from others, a condition the author calls ''the privatization of revolution.'' The counterforce to such stasis is to avoid rigidity by ''getting your mojo working,'' something the hyperfiction of *Doggy Bag* enacts. Though clearly recognizable as a satire of contemporary life, Sukenick's writing moves a step further by creating its own typologies, taxonomies, grammars, and eventually a language itself in which to comment on present conditions.

Respect for the genius of creation and a curiosity about the ways in which it functions motivated Sukenick's writing of *In Form: Digressions Toward a Study of Composition,* his commentary on the nature of postmodern narrative art, and *Down and In: Life in the Underground,* an autobiographical account of Sukenick's fascination with the transformative styles of literary art initiated in Greenwich Village and the East Village during the 1950s and early 1960s. Behind both studies is the example of Henry Miller, who in Paris a quarter-century before had learned how to deny ''official experience'' and shape both his life and art according to a more imaginative model. Such has been the imperative for all of Sukenick's work, in literature and in the professions of English and publishing alike.

—Jerome Klinkowitz

SWAN, Susan

Nationality: Canadian. **Born:** Midland, Ontario, 1945. **Education:** Havergal College, early 1960s; McGill University, B.A. 1967. **Career:** Writer and performer in theatre, 1970s; creative writing teacher, York University, Toronto. **Address:** Robarts Centre for Canadian Studies, York University, Toronto, Canada.

PUBLICATIONS

Novels

The Biggest Modern Woman in the World. Toronto, Lester & Orpen Dennys, 1983; New York, Ecco Press, 1986.
The Last of the Golden Girls. Toronto, Lester & Orpen Dennys, 1989; New York, Arcade Publishers, 1991.
The Wives of Bath. Toronto and New York, Knopf,1993.

Short Stories

Unfit for Paradise. Dingle Editions, 1982.
Stupid Boys Are Good to Relax With. N.p. 1996.

Plays

Queen of the Silver Blades, 1975.
Writing vs. Dance, 1977.
Down and In, 1978.
True Confessions of the Female Organs, 1978.
Poetry F.M., 1979.
X's and O's on the Longest Day of the Year, 1983.
Moral Passion, 1984.

Radio Plays: *The Collaborators*, Toronto, Canadian Broadcasting Corporation, 1974.

Television Plays: *Futurework*, Toronto, TVOntario, 1984.

Other

Contributor, *Best Canadian Short Stories.* Oberon, 1989.
Contributor*Hard Times.* Mercury Press, 1990.
Editor, with Margaret Dragu and Sarah Sheard, *Mothers Talk Back: Momz Radio.* Toronto, Coach House Press, 1991.

* * *

Coming from a career in journalism and presently teaching at York University in Toronto, Canadian writer Susan Swan has produced three novels and two volumes of short pieces to date. Her first publication, *Unfit for Paradise*, is a small group of short stories on the theme of Canadians traveling on tropical vacations. *The Biggest Modern Woman of the World* is her greatest success because it handles the transition of history into the mythic at the touchpoint of feminist issues, and in so doing joins the company of Jeanette Winterson's *Sexing the Cherry* and Margaret Atwood's *Alias Grace*. It professes to tell the story of the nineteenth-century Nova Scotia giantess Anna Swan (1846–1888), who was exhibited in New York by P. T. Barnum and later toured Britain and Europe before settling down in Seville, Ohio, to an uneasy married life with the Kentucky Giant. The story has a clever mix of narration, including Anna's own voice, her letters, other people's letters, ''testimonials,'' and fragments of poems and other documents. Anna's voice in particular is very cleverly presented, because the reader she is directly addressing is ostensibly her nineteenth-century listener, but in fact the quality of her observations are profoundly modern. While the story follows Anna's life in rough chronological sequence, its strength lies in the ironies set in motion by its title. Anna's experiences are precursors of the feminist moment of the late twentieth century, and her own narrative voice is a clever mixture of an educated nineteenth-century woman (the real Anna had extensive tutoring written into her contract with Barnum), a Nova Scotia Scots practical farmgirl, and a twentieth-century consciousness of how women feel themselves to be seen as strange and monstrous creatures. Anna says she intends to be ''… A Victorian lady who refused to be inconsequential.''

The novel is very direct about bodily functions and sexuality. Anna discovers that the Kentucky Giant is impotent and small, but she has two children with ''Judge'' Apollo Ingalls, her manager after she leaves Barnum. Anna's practicality and sharp eye for the world confound reader expectations of a giantess as a physical curiosity. In this witty and perceptive novel she emerges as an icon of ''modern'' womanhood, directing the reader to the personality rather than the body.

Swan's more recent books *The Last of the Golden Girls*, *The Wives of Bath*, and the short story collection *Stupid Boys Are Good to Relax With* are less coherent in tone and structure, but each has features that suggest that Swan is coming upon a style and form that may make her a first-rank writer.

The first half of *The Last of the Golden Girls*, subtitled ''Losing,'' takes place in 1959 on the shores of Georgian Bay (renamed U-Go-I-Go Sound), where fifteen-year-old Jude ''Dinger'' Bell and her friends Roberta ''Bobby'' Gallagher and Shelly Moffat are discovering themselves and sex. It has the strengths of good psychological perception and sensitivity to the pressures on the girls and their resulting struggles with parents, boys, and each other. Dinger is attempting to write romances, and she and Bobby are able to quote the sexual encounters from *Payton Place* and *Lady Chatterley's Lover*. But there are always overtones of a struggle for dominance, and the section ends when Bobby and Shelly trick Dinger into performing oral sex on Jay Manchester, the boy de jour, at a beach party, horribly shaming her and bringing the summer to a bitter end.

The second half of the novel, ''Winning,'' takes place ten years later when Bobby has married into the wealthy Cape family who own an island in the Sound. In this playground of the rich, Jude, now a journalist working on a book about the Cape family, is struggling with Shelly for the love of Child Cape, and Bobby is married to Bull Cape. Swan directs the section at ''you,'' whom she identifies as the reader, Old Voyeur Eyes, who she imagines as actually present in the scenes she depicts. Thus she can address the reader, correcting what she sees as their misconceptions of the situation. This self-conscious narrative position represents an increased maturity in Jude, and from this stance she chronicles a series of sexual struggles within the family and involving Jonah Prince, a rich Jew who is having an affair with Bobby. The section centers on a series of sexual exchanges and struggles. But the novel switches tone near the end and becomes awkwardly apocalyptic as atomic bombs explode and the Capes, plus an Indian swami Mrs. Cape has recruited, end up under the Sound in a strange double sphere that she has had built. These events simply run away from the focus on human personal experience that the book has been about, and there is finally no explanation for the section title ''Winning,'' and no resolution to the tangled lives that the voyeur reader has been watching. The unevenness of the plan for this novel overwhelms the energy of its narrative.

The Wives of Bath is much more coherent as a narrative and features Swan's most convincing character, Mary Beatrice ''Mouse'' Bradford, the slightly hunchbacked (she calls her hump Alice) daughter of a small-town physician. In this narrative she is sent to Huron Ladies College because her father Morley is nervous about bringing up a daughter and Mouse's stepmother Sal does not want her in the house. From the beginning we know that the trial of her roommate Pauline Sykes is underway, but the spectacular nature of her crime takes most of the retrospective narrative to emerge. The first-person narrative is intelligent, and Swan creates an edgy style that allows both a naturalistic representation of the young women at the school and overtones of caricature and even surrealism. Caricature emerges in the persons of the mistresses in the school and in aspects of school life, and surrealism in images of a former Victorian headmistress riding a gigantic three-wheeler. Mouse herself is a realist, almost a version of Anna Swan and Jude Bell. She sees her own situation clearly, and she has a wry eye for the world of the school. She copes with most things but is surprised by the discovery that Lewis, who is ostensibly Pauline's brother and who works on the grounds of the school, is in fact Pauline herself acting as a boy. Seeking her friendship, Mouse imitates male roles as well, but Pauline's behavior detonates into the pathological, leading to the brutal and bizarre conclusion of the novel.

The Wives of Bath, like *The Last of the Golden Girls* before it, lacks a unity of style. But unlike the unfitted compound parts of the earlier work the difficulty here may lie more with the reader than the author. Swan has found a tone for the narrative ''I'' of Mouse Bradford unlike any other woman's voice in fiction. If Mouse's bravado was removed, it would be like the voice of J. D. Salinger's Holden Caulfield—observant, sensitive, a touch cynical, and suffering through the shocks of discovering the intricacies of the world.

Stupid Boys Are Good to Relax With is a short story collection in two parts: Gutenberg Stories and Cyber Tales. The Cyber Tales are mytho-comic experiments in sexual politics featuring imagined emails between such luminaries as St. Paul, Hannibal, Catherine the Great, Marilyn Monroe, and Ariadne. Four of the Gutenberg Stories, however, extend the Mouse Bradford character from *The Wives of Bath*. Three of these are set before Wives, including the title story and ''The Stupid Boy Handbook,'' a teenager's guide to boys. ''The Unabridged Stupid Boy Handbook'' is Mouse's adult version of the same handbook, written at the age of thirty.

Swan's *oeuvre* to date is a mixture of success and promise. She seeks new narrative approaches, like the Old Voyeur Eyes character of the reader who is actually present in *The Last of the Golden Girls*, and the knowing young woman characters of Jude Bell and Mouse Bradford, but the voice of Anna Swan is to date her only assured, flexible, and coherent vehicle.

—Peter Brigg

SWIFT, Graham

Nationality: British. **Born:** London, 4 May 1949. **Education:** Dulwich College, 1960–67; Queens' College, Cambridge, 1967–70, B.A., M.A.; York University, 1970–73. Lives in London. **Awards:** Geoffrey Faber Memorial prize, 1983; *Guardian* Fiction prize, 1983; Royal Society of Literature Winifred Holtby award, 1984; Premio Grinzane Cavour (Italy), 1987; Prix du meilleur livre étranger (France), 1994; Booker prize, 1996. Fellow, Royal Society of Literature, 1984. **Agent:** A.P. Watt Ltd., 20 John Street, London WC1N 2DR, England.

PUBLICATIONS

Novels

The Sweet Shop Owner. London, Allen Lane, 1980; New York, Washington Square Press, 1985.
Shuttlecock. London, Allen Lane, 1981; New York, Washington Square Press, 1984.
Waterland. London, Heinemann, 1983; New York, Poseidon Press, 1984.
Out of This World. London, Viking, and New York, Poseidon Press, 1988.
Ever After. London, Picador, and New York, Knopf, 1992.
Last Orders. New York, Knopf, 1996.

Short Stories

Learning to Swim and Other Stories. London, London Magazine Editions, 1982; New York, Poseidon Press, 1985.

Other

Editor, with David Profumo, *The Magic Wheel: An Anthology of Fishing in Literature.* London, Picador, 1985.

*

Critical Studies: ''History and the 'Here and Now': The Novels of Graham Swift'' by Del Ivan Janik, in *Twentieth Century Literature* (Hempstead, New York) vol. 35, No. 1, 1989.

* * *

''Can it be a kindness not to tell what you see? And a blessing to be blind? And the best aid to human happiness that has ever been invented is a blanket of soft, white lies?'' asks one of the characters in *Out of This World.* These questions sound the central theme of Graham Swift's six novels: does human happiness depend on understanding or on feeling? While the question is asked as if for the first time in each novel, Swift's answer remains, with one exception, the same: ''soft, white lies'' are necessary to human happiness. In keeping with his belief that feelings matter more than understanding, Swift also adheres to a model of authorship that prioritizes self-expression above communication with readers.

The Sweet Shop Owner spans a single hot summer's day, the last day of the life of widowed shopkeeper Willy Chapman. Throughout much of the day Willy carries on an internal dialogue with his estranged daughter. He remembers his marriage to an unloving wife, Irene, who attempted to compensate by bearing him the child: ''You were her gift.'' His scholarly daughter has forsaken her father, and, according to Mrs. Cooper, won't return. Refusing to accept this, Willy quietly kills himself in the hope of finally reuniting with his daughter. ''Don't you see, you're no freer than before, no freer than I am? And the only thing that can dissolve history now is if, by a miracle, you come.''

A single suspicion brings about the climax of *Shuttlecock.* Immobilized by the heroic figure of his war spy father, Prentis, a Dead Crimes Investigator, bullies his wife and two sons. The suspicion that his father may have been a traitor has multiple effects. It frees Prentis: ''Something had collapsed around me; so I couldn't help, in the middle of the ruins, this strange feeling of release. I had escaped; I was free.'' The threat of the publicity of this suspicion also may have driven his father mad. The suspicion illustrates to Prentis the power—and the danger—of knowledge: ''I stared again at the file. I thought of the number of times I'd opened the cover of *Shuttlecock* hoping Dad would come out; hoping to hear his voice. Was I afraid that the allegations might be true—or that they might be false? And supposing, in some extraordinary way, that everything Quinn told me was concocted, was an elaborate hoax—if I never looked in the file, I would never know. I read the code letters over and over again. C9/E … And then suddenly I knew I wanted to be uncertain, I wanted to be in the dark.'' Rather than confirmation or denial of his father's betrayal, it is the suspicion—the ''soft, white lies''—that ultimately proves more valuable because it preserves the possibility of a heroic man.

Like Charles Dickens's *Great Expectations, Waterland* is a bildungsroman about a young boy from the Fens of East Anglia. Unlike other Swiftian characters, Tom Crick, the history teacher protagonist, is drawn to face the truth of his family's tortured history: ''I'm the one who had to ask questions, who had to dig up the truth (my recipe for emergencies: explain your way out).'' But the price Tom pays for his knowledge is high. His wife abducts a child. His half-brother commits suicide.

The split between understanding and feelings structures *Out of This World,* which is narrated through the alternating monologues of photographer, Harry Beech, and his estranged daughter, Sophie. The latter has forbidden cameras (a metaphor for realist understanding) in her house. We learn that Sophie glimpsed Harry photographing the wreck of the car bombing of his own father: ''I saw him first, then he saw me. He was like a man caught sleep-walking, not knowing how he could be doing what he was doing, as if it were all part of some deep, ingrained reflex. But just for a moment I saw this look on his face of deadly concentration. He hadn't seen me first because he'd been looking elsewhere, and his eyes had been jammed up against a camera.'' Appalled by her father's detachment, she has refused to speak to him for 10 years. At first Harry resists Sophie's point. Ultimately, Harry acknowledges that a lie reunited him with his estranged father. His father's lie, which shielded Harry from his wife's infidelity, demonstrated his father's love. Harry reciprocated by reaching out to his father: ''We strolled to the end of the terrace. As we turned, I wanted to do that simple but rare thing and take his arm… . He said, 'I've never told you, have I?'''

The split between understanding and feelings also structures *Ever After,* which is narrated through the alternating monologues of Victorian Darwinist Matthew Pearce and widowed English professor Billy Unwin. Whereas the Victorian Pearce sacrificed his wife and family to remain faithful to his Darwinist beliefs, Unwin would sacrifice the few beliefs he holds to bring back his deceased wife. ''I would believe or not believe anything, swallow any old make-belief, in order to have Ruth back. Whereas Matthew—Whereas this Pearce guy-'' After a seduction plot momentarily tempts Unwin to forget the memory of his wife, life no longer appears to be worth living to the professor, who attempts suicide. His revival leads him to the discovery that it is the ''soft, white lie'' of the memories of his wife that gives him a reason for living.

Like Faulkner's *As I Lay Dying,* the polyphonic *Last Orders* is narrated through the friends and family of a recently deceased man on the burial journey. Londoners Ray Johnson, Lenny Tate, Vic Tucker, Vince Dodds, and Amy Dodds are bound to the recently deceased Jack Dodds through decades of love, friendship, and secrets. Vince is Jack's adopted son, who ran away as a teenager. Ray fought with Jack in World War II, and has been in love with Jack's wife, Amy, for as many years. Amy remembers the foundering of her marriage as Jack refused to acknowledge their mentally retarded daughter: ''He won't mention June so I won't mention Ray. Fair dos. What you don't know can't hurt.'' Here the lies sometimes serve not only to protect, but also to create a better community. ''So when Vince Pritchett, but forget the Pritchett, dropped into my lap, into our lap,'' says Amy, ''I ought to have known it wouldn't help a bit, it wouldn't win him back. You can't make a real thing out of pretending hard.'' Regardless of her denial, it is through ''pretending hard'' that Amy has created a family: After years of resentment, Vince has reunited with his adopted parents.

The importance of ''soft, white lies'' is apparent in Swift's attitude towards authorship. Some authors write to communicate with their readers a necessary piece of social criticism, a rationale which has its roots in the Realist tradition of social responsibility. Other authors write to express themselves, a rationale which has its roots in the Romantic tradition of self-expression. A quote from Swift expresses the Romantic tenet that deep feeling is the essential ingredient of art: ''I am absolutely not a formalist, because what does matter to me are things as felt, and feeling seems at least to stand in opposition to form: form is to do with control and discipline, and feeling is to do with liberation... .''

While expressing himself may be Swift's intention as an author, it's suspect that this self-expression is ''liberation.'' After all, what kind of ''liberation'' can obsessively rewriting the same plot be called? Immobilized by the excessive expectations of her parents, Irene in *The Sweet Shop Owner* could neither fully reject, nor fully participate in her family life. Immobilized by the heroic figure of his father, Prentis in *Shuttlecock* is freed by the revelation that his father may have been a traitor to the English. Immobilized by the expectations of her father to become like her sanctified mother, Mary in *Waterland* goes mad. Sense a pattern here? Regardless of which book by Swift one chooses, one meets the same plot: an adult frozen in childhood must free him- or herself from the overpowering example of an idealized parent. The repetition of a single plot suggests that Swift has supported a rationale of writing as self-expression from necessity rather than from choice. Even if Swift had wanted to write for his audience, one wonders whether he could do so. As Swift has said, ''I write a lot by sheer instinct, groping around in the dark.''

Expressing himself may have been Swift's foremost aim, but communicating with his readers is a necessary aim of any author. Swift fails—as several reviewers' comments indicate—to communicate with his readers. Too many perspectives, none of which are authorized by the obfuscating narrator has been the frequent charge of reviewers. ''Mr. Swift is so committed to seeing around perspectives, undermining his own assertions, squeezing the narrator between the pincers of the past and present, being ironic at the expense of what somebody didn't know but somebody now does, that the effect he creates is rather like a three-ring circus,'' a *New York Times Book Review* critic said of *Waterland.* ''One yearns for a whiff of directness. ...'' Stephen Wall of the *London Review of Books* also protested that the multiple perspectives in *Ever After* were not resolved: ''Despite its manifestly humane intentions, the different areas of narrative interest in *Ever After* disperse, rather than concentrate attention. Although its varying strands are conscientiously knitted together ... they don't seem significantly to cohere.'' In failing to organize the multiple viewpoints, Swift violates the assumption that the author will provide a ''hierarchical organization of details.'' Instead, the reader is left alone to make meanings; a job she could have done without the reading of any of Swift's novels.

Why this refusal to guide his readers? An answer lies in Swift's admiration of ''vulnerability.'' Swift's characters are often proud to say, ''I don't know.'' In *Shuttlecock,* Prentis says: '''I don't know' . . . It seemed to me that this was an answer I would give, boldly, over and over again for the rest of my life.'' According to Swift, when an author shows the reader his vulnerability, he gains the reader's trust: ''An author ought to have authority ... It makes sure the reader trusts the writer ... Often that stems from the realization that the writer is prepared to show that vulnerability.'' When Swift has shown vulnerability, however, his reviewers have not trusted him. Just the opposite. Swift has said, ''I am desperate to avoid a sense of power derived from form.'' His fear of authority is indeed evident in his novels.

—Cynthia Cameros

T

TAN, Amy (Ruth)

Nationality: American. **Born:** Oakland, California, 19 February 1952. **Education:** San Jose State University, California, B.A. in linguistics and English, 1973, M.A. in linguistics, 1974; University of California, Berkley, 1974–76. **Family:** Married Louis M. DeMattei in 1974. **Career:** Specialist in language development, Alameda County Association for Mentally Retarded, Oakland, 1976–80; project director, MORE Project, San Francisco, 1980–81; reporter, managing editor, and associate publisher, *Emergency Room Reports,* 1981–83; technical writer, 1983–87. **Awards:** Commonwealth Club gold award, 1989, and Bay Area Book Reviewers award, 1990, both for *The Joy Luck Club;* Best American Essays award, 1991. Honorary D.H.L.: Dominican College, San Rafael, 1991. **Address:** c/o Penguin Putnam Inc., 375 Hudson Street, New York, New York 10014–3658, U.S.A.

PUBLICATIONS

Novels

The Joy Luck Club. New York, Putnam, and London, Heinemann, 1989.
The Kitchen God's Wife. New York, Putnam, and London, Collins, 1991.
The Hundred Secret Senses. New York, G.P. Putnam's Sons, 1995.

Play

Screenplay: *The Joy Luck Club,* 1993.

Other

The Moon Lady (for children). New York, Macmillan, 1992.
The Chinese Siamese Cat, illustrated by Gretchen Shields (for children). New York, Macmillan, and London, Hamilton, 1994.

*

Film Adaptation: *The Joy Luck Club,* 1993.

Critical Studies: *Amy Tan: A Critical Companion* by E.D. Huntley, Westport, Connecticut, Greenwood Press, 1998; *The Broom Closet: Secret Meanings of Domesticity in Postfeminist Novels by Louise Erdrich, Mary Gordon, Toni Morrison, Marge Piercy, Jane Smiley, and Amy Tan* by Jeannette Batz Cooperman, New York, Peter Lang, 1999; *Amy Tan,* edited and with an introduction by Harold Bloom, Philadelphia, Chelsea House Publishers, 2000.

* * *

When Amy Tan's first novel *The Joy Luck Club* appeared in 1989, there had been a long interval since the publication of any work on Chinese-American identity, a theme briefly and convincingly explored by Maxine Hong Kingston in *The Woman Warrior* and *China Men* in the previous decade. Both *The Joy Luck Club* and *The Kitchen God's Wife* use the framing device of mother-daughter relationships, a motif used in works of American novelists such as Alice Walker, Toni Morrison, Edith Wharton, and Anzia Yezierska to name just a few.

In this way Tan draws upon a familiar and comforting tradition for the Western reader. Strategically too this theme is central to Western women in that it explores the twin poles of the daughter's desire for individuation, wherein she demands an identity as separate from her mother. This clashes with her intense and fierce attachment to and sense of continuum with her mother's life. In this, Tan's pursuit of mother-daughter relationships, rather than father-son ones, reinscribes the woman in the interrogation of origins, a theme only explored via sons who are the ''legitimate'' heirs to any notion of origins.

Marianne Hirsch points out in *The Mother-Daughter Plot* of 1989, that the mother-daughter narrative varies from the traditional father-son relationship in that the former is marked with opposition and contradiction. She argues that the Western narrative of mother-daughter relationships is located in the Demeter-Persephone myth which enacts the daughter's unbreakable attachment to her mother which is constantly interrupted by her relationship to her husband. To this extent, the daughters Jing-Mei Woo (along with a host of others) in *The Joy Luck Club* and Pearl in *The Kitchen God's Wife* indicate the tremendous difficulties of individuation and the loss of the maternal.

In Tan's novels, mother-daughter dyads ultimately become a metaphor for the relationship between China and the U.S. In the early part of this century Anzia Yezierska had written immigrant novels where the mother and daughter embody the old country and the new world respectively and it is within this framework that Tan too explores the Chinese part of a Chinese-American identity. Thus mother-daughter relationships as well as its intersection with the inscription of the old country get played out in the overarching theme of identity. As first-generation Americans, Jing-Mei Woo and Pearl signify the assimilation that America requires whereas their mothers, as immigrants, embody a severe sense of displacement. Jing-Mei and Pearl's desire for individuation thus goes beyond a break from the mother. Their lives also mirror the ambiguous relationship that Chinese-Americans have with the two mother-countries, the U.S. and China. In a further turn of the screw, Tan shows Pearl's mother, Winnie, as a daughter, in China. This repetition of mothers as daughters prefigures in the characters of Ying-Ying St. Clair and An-Mei Hsu in *The Joy Luck Club.* In this foregrounding of mothers as daughters, Tan reveals her ploy, wherein she wrests this particular theme from the Western tradition and locates it squarely within China. The oriental other who functions as the object of inquiry of the West is revealed to be the maternal progenitor of a Western tradition.

The Hundred Secret Senses uses themes familiar from Tan's two earlier novels: of sisters, of China and America, of competition, of the stories one tells about one's past. Ultimately, the issues that Tan's novels raise are: Can one really assimilate? Does assimilation bring about equality or is the Chinese-American always in an inferior position within dominant American identity? Can one emphasize difference while maintaining equality? There is no resolution to these questions, but rather conclusions that always end in the mother-country, China. Kwan, one of the two protagonists in *The Hundred Secret Senses,* remains almost entirely Chinese, even though she came to America as a teenager. Her assimilated half-sister Olivia is impatient with her and with her stories of ghosts and dragons, but ultimately Kwan and her stories win her over—particularly after the two travel to China with Olivia's estranged husband Simon, and find themselves in danger.

In addition to her novels, Tan has written two works of children's fiction, *The Moon Lady* (an excerpt from *The Joy Luck Club*), and *The Chinese Siamese Cat,* both of which deal with clever daughters.

—Radhika Mohanram

TENNANT, Emma (Christina)

Has also written as Catherine Aydy. **Nationality:** British. **Born:** London, 20 October 1937. **Education:** St. Paul's Girls' School, London. **Family:** Has one son and two daughters. **Career:** Travel correspondent, *Queen,* London, 1963; features editor, *Vogue,* London, 1966; editor, *Bananas,* London, 1975–78. Since 1982 general editor, *In Verse,* London; since 1985 editor, Lives of Modern Women series, Viking, publishers, London. Fellow, Royal Society of Literature, 1982. **Address:** 141 Elgin Crescent, London W.11, England.

PUBLICATIONS

Novels

The Colour of Rain (as Catherine Aydy). London, Weidenfeld and Nicolson, 1964.
The Time of the Crack. London, Cape, 1973; as *The Crack,* London, Penguin, 1978.
The Last of the Country House Murders. London, Cape, 1974; New York, Nelson, 1976.
Hotel de Dream. London, Gollancz, 1976.
The Bad Sister. London, Gollancz, and New York, Coward McCann, 1978.
Wild Nights. London, Cape, 1979; New York, Harcourt Brace, 1980.
Alice Fell. London, Cape, 1980.
Queen of Stones. London, Cape, 1982.
Woman Beware Woman. London, Cape, 1983; as *The Half-Mother,* Boston, Little Brown, 1985.
Black Marina. London, Faber, 1985.
The Adventures of Robina, by Herself. London, Faber, 1986; New York, Persea, 1987.
Series: *The Cycle of the Sun*
The House of Hospitalities. London, Viking, 1987.
A Wedding of Cousins. London, Viking, 1988.
The Magic Drum. London, Viking, 1989.
Two Women of London: The Strange Case of Ms. Jekyll and Mrs. Hyde. London, Faber, 1989.
Sisters and Strangers. London, Grafton, 1990.
Faustine. London, Faber, 1991.
Pemberley; or, Pride and Prejudice Continued. New York, St. Martin's Press, 1993; as *Pemberley: A Sequel to Pride and Prejudice,* London, Hodder and Stoughton, 1993.
Tess. London, HarperCollins, 1993.
An Unequal Marriage; or, Pride and Prejudice Twenty Years Later. London, Sceptre, and New York, St. Martin's Press, 1994.
Travesties. London and Boston, Faber and Faber, 1995.
Emma in Love: Jane Austen's Emma Continued. London, Fourth Estate, 1996.

Uncollected Short Stories

''Mrs. Ragley,'' in *Listener* (London), 1973.
''Mrs. Barratt's Ghost,'' in *New Statesman* (London), 28 December 1973.
''Philomela,'' in *Bananas,* edited by Tennant. London, Quartet-Blond and Briggs, 1977.
''The Bed That Mick Built,'' in *New Stories 2,* edited by Derwent May and Alexis Lykiard. London, Arts Council, 1977.
''Cupboard Love,'' in *New Stories 4,* edited by Elaine Feinstein and Fay Weldon. London, Hutchinson, 1979.
''Tortoise-Shell Endpapers,'' in *Time Out* (London), 21 December 1979.
''The Frog Prints,'' in *London Tales,* edited by Julian Evans. London, Hamish Hamilton, 1983.
''The German in the Wood,'' in *London Review of Books,* 1984.

Play

Television Script: *Frankenstein's Baby,* 1990.

Other (for children)

The Boggart. London, Granada, 1980.
The Search for Treasure Island. London, Penguin, 1981.
The Ghost Child. London, Heinemann, 1984.
Dave's Secret Diary. London, Longman, 1991.

Other

The ABC of Writing. London, Faber, 1992.
Hooked Rugs (with Ann Davies). New York, Sterling, 1995.
Girlitude: A Memoir of the 50s and 60s. London, Jonathan Cape, 1999.
Strangers: A Family Romance (autobiography). New York, New Directions, 1999.
Burnt Diaries (memoir). Edinburgh, Canongate, 1999.
Editor, *Bananas.* London, Quartet-Blond and Briggs, 1977.
Editor, *Saturday Night Reader.* London, W.H. Allen, 1979.

*

Manuscript Collection: National Library of Scotland, Edinburgh.

Critical Studies: ''Emma Tennant, Hyper-Novelist'' by Gary Indiana, in *Village Voice Literary Supplement* (New York), May 1991.

* * *

Since the early 1970s, when she was in her mid-thirties, Emma Tennant has been a prolific novelist and has established herself as one of the leading British exponents of ''new fiction.'' This does not mean that she is an imitator of either the French *nouveaux romanciers* or the American post-modernists, although her work reveals an indebtedness to the methods and preoccupations of some of the latter. Like them, she employs parody and rewriting, is interested in the fictiveness of fiction, appropriates some science-fiction conventions, and exploits the possibilities of generic dislocation and mutation, especially the blending of realism and fantasy. Yet, although parallels can be cited and influences suggested, her work is strongly individual, the product of an intensely personal, even idiosyncratic, attempt to create an original type of highly imaginative fiction.

The first novel she published under her own name was *The Time of the Crack.* This futuristic fable about an ever-widening crack in the riverbed of the Thames is a fusion of black farce, wide-ranging satire, and apocalyptic vision. One reviewer described it as "Lewis Carroll technique applied to H.G. Wells material," but other names suggest themselves even more strongly, notably Orwell and Waugh. Like *Nineteen Eighty-Four, The Time of the Crack* is, in its bizarre way, a "condition of England" novel, projecting onto the immediate future current obsessions with decline and fall, and literalizing the metaphor of national disintegration. Stylistically, the book is characterized by a satirical panache recalling Waugh's early period, as Tennant mercilessly caricatures many aspects of contemporary society.

Her next novel, *The Last of the Country House Murders,* is also set in the near future—Britain after the Revolution—and in its oblique way is another "condition of England" novel. Again like Orwell, Tennant extrapolates from the present a possible picture of the future, but what makes this novel so different from other dystopias is her ingenious fusion of the novel of pessimistic prophecy with an amusing parodistic re-working of the country-house brand of detective fiction. Indeed, the book increasingly focuses on the small group of peculiar, virtually caricature figures who arrive at Woodiscombe Manor to participate in the murder mystery planned by the government as a tourist attraction; the wider social and national issues become more marginal than in *The Time of the Crack.* The result is bizarre comedy, replete with the eccentricities, foibles, and oddities that recur throughout her *oeuvre.*

Eccentricity also pervades the small hotel that provides the setting for *Hotel de Dream,* in which the dreams and fantasies of the few residents, one of whom is a romantic novelist, play a much more important part than the framework of waking reality. Reality itself dissolves into fantasy and vice versa, and the various dreams and fictions merge with one another to create a super-reality of the collective unconscious, in which the dreamers acquire new identities and the romantic novelist's imaginary characters become as real as their creator. While the book is certainly not lacking in the weird humour of her two previous books, and actually abounds in the grotesque, there is a shift away from satirical comedy in favour of psychological fantasy, from a broad perspective to a closed world. Even so, Tennant still provides a tangentially symbolic comment on the "condition of England" issue through her characters and their dream-selves.

In both *The Last of the Country House Murders* and *Hotel de Dream,* Tennant plays self-consciously with novelistic conventions, but in *The Bad Sister* she attempts something much more daring and ambitious—some would say foolhardy. She models the entire book very closely on a literary masterpiece, Hogg's *Confessions of a Justified Sinner.* While setting her novel in the present and locating only part of it in Scotland, she adheres to Hogg's highly original structure, adopts some of the main features of his plot, and retains his embodiment of the Devil, Gil-Martin, though in a peripheral role. However, she does alter the sex of the main characters, the equivalent of the Justified Sinner being Jane Wild and her evil genius being Meg rather than Gil-Martin. This change allows Tennant to introduce the subject of feminism and the contemporary phenomenon of female urban guerrillas, but the main focus is not social or political but psychological—the split personality of Jane under the influence of the obsessional Meg. Like Hogg, Tennant is concerned with human duality, fanaticism, the subjectivity of reality, and the possibility of possession, but she interprets these in a contemporary context, developing the theme of the schizoid nature of modern woman.

If *The Bad Sister* is imaginatively claustrophobic, her two subsequent novels, *Wild Nights* and *Alice Fell,* are even more so, the dividing line between reality and fantasy being increasingly blurred and ambiguous. In *Wild Nights,* for example, the child-narrator presents a vision of the world controlled by the imagination rather than reason, in which magic and enchantment are an integral part of nature. Seasonal symbolism and archetypal images play a vital part, and the action seems timeless and placeless despite being located in postwar Scotland and England. For the most part, the relatively few characters in this closed world are strange, eccentric beings, more mythical than social. *Alice Fell* is strikingly similar to *Wild Nights* in a number of these respects, despite the differences that arise from it being a third-person narration. Tennant sustains the obsessive visionary quality of both novels by brilliant and evocative writing, but she does so at a price. In moving so far from *The Time of the Crack,* she sacrifices some of her most attractive qualities as a novelist. Nevertheless, *Alice Fell,* a reworking of the myth of Persephone in terms of contemporary British society in a state of upheaval, is a most ambitious imaginative feat, even if the symbolism and archetypal characterization tend to be too intrusive.

Queen of Stones represents a move away from the cul-de-sac of poetic fiction into which Tennant was in danger of becoming trapped. After *The Time of the Crack,* Tennant's fiction in the 1970s had gradually become more intense, more introspective, and narrower in focus. There was a gain in the sheer virtuosity of her writing, but there was also a loss of the comedy and satire of *The Time of the Crack,* together with its panoramic sweep. Like *The Bad Sister, Queen of Stones* has a specific literary model, *Lord of the Flies* (itself an antidote to Ballantyne's *The Coral Island*), but Tennant does not provide such close parallels to Golding's novel as she does to Hogg's in her earlier book.

The most striking resemblance between *Queen of Stones* and *The Bad Sister* is Tennant's use of sex-reversal, substituting females for their male equivalents in her sources. A sponsored walk in Dorset goes terribly wrong when a group of girls are lost in appalling fog; cut off from their normal everyday surroundings and the adult world, like Golding's schoolboys, they create their own imaginative reality involving ritual and sacrifice. Tennant arrives at a conclusion not dissimilar from Golding's. In her next novel, *Woman Beware Woman,* Tennant again investigates the deeper mythic reality behind the appearances of social reality, the subconscious drives that shape reality itself, especially as they manifest themselves in women and their behaviour. The literary roots of *Woman Beware Woman* are less obvious than in *The Bad Sister* and *Queen of Stones,* but the close similarity to the title of Middleton's Jacobean revenge tragedy *Women Beware Women* suggests that Tennant is creating her own highly imaginative equivalent of a drama of thwarted love, resentment, suppressed passion, hatred and revenge as various people assemble in a quiet part of Ireland following the death of a distinguished literary man.

Political undercurrents are present in a number of Tennant's novels, but *Black Marina* is the most explicitly political. The setting is the imaginary island of St. James, adjacent to Grenada in the Caribbean; the time, Christmas Eve 1983, not long after the murderous real-life coup against Maurice Bishop's government in Grenada which precipitated American military intervention. During the day in which the novel is set St. James is expected to be the target of a similar Marxist-Leninist coup by a group of those involved in the attempt to seize power in Grenada. The subject-matter is topical and journalistic, but Tennant's handling of it is characteristically complex and far removed from orthodox social realism. The principal narrator, Holly Baker, an English woman who came to the island in the 1960s and stayed, gradually unfolds in piecemeal fashion the network of human relationships in St. James and England that has eventually precipitated the happenings of Christmas Eve 1983. As usual in Tennant's fiction, mythic elements lie just beneath the contemporary surface, and the title itself, alluding to Shakespeare's *Pericles* (Marina is the King's long-lost daughter) and Eliot's related Ariel poem ''Marina,'' points towards the most important of these, a daughter's quest for her father. Even so, *Black Marina* is something of a new departure for Tennant in setting and theme, and it confirms her ability to go on regenerating herself as a novelist.

The Adventures of Robina, by Herself is a lighter work in picaresque vein, but stylistically it is one of Tennant's most bravura performances, a brilliant display of sustained literary pastiche. Throughout she imitates the idiom Defoe adopts for his female narrators while wryly adapting it to accommodate her 20th-century concerns. After this ''imitation'' of Defoe, Tennant began work on something different again, a sequence of novels with the overall title *The Cycle of the Sun* that is intended to explore aspects of aristocratic and bohemian life in England from the 1950s to the 1980s, reflecting the major changes in the country's international role during these decades. So far two of these novels have appeared. In the first, *The House of Hospitalities,* Tennant introduces her central character Jenny going through a crisis of adolescence, while the second, *A Wedding of Cousins,* continues Jenny's confused life story four years later. Although Tennant's approach is essentially comic and satirical, there are elements of sadness and confusion at both social and individual levels. Despite the underlying realism of the sequence, Jenny's frequent inability to distinguish between reality and fantasy gives the novels a pervasive ambiguity typical of Tennant.

In 1989 Tennant published two novels outside the *The Cycle of the Sun* sequence, *Two Women of London: The Strange Case of Ms. Jerkyll and Mrs. Hyde* and *The Magic Drum,* both being crime stories of a characteristically eccentric and gothic kind. The subtitle of *Two Women of London, The Strange Case of Ms. Jekyll and Mrs. Hyde,* indicates that this is another of Tennant's reworkings of famous literary texts. Cast in fabular rather than realistic form, Tennant's tale of rape and murder in West London is a timely feminist adaptation of Robert Louis Stevenson's seminal exploration of the divided self, in which she examines the enormous pressure experienced by women in a violent, competitive society. The divided self she portrays reflects the divisions in a society where poverty and deprivation co-exist with conspicuous consumption and a ''loadsamoney'' philosophy. The subtext of the novel is highly political. By refurbishing an important Victorian work of fiction, Tennant radically subverts the ''Victorian values'' advocated by free-market and self-help politicians in the 1980s.

The Magic Drum is set in an isolated country house, Cressley Grange, the home of the cult feminist poet Muriel Cole before her suicide at the age of 32 (the same age as Sylvia Plath, to whom there are parallels and even references). Since Cole's death, her husband, also a famous poet, has turned the house into a shrine to her memory and a place of literary pilgrimage. The Grange has the potential for the kind of closed-world crime story favoured by such Golden Age authors as Agatha Christie, and there is certainly a mystery at the heart of the novel—a murder, too, if the main narrator, Catherine Treger, is to be believed. Yet the status of Catherine's diary entries for her five days of detective work at the Grange is uncertain. Do they provide a reliable, factual account or are they the imaginative outpourings of a disturbed mind? Is she observing reality or creating a ''reality'' of her own out of the materials of crime and gothic fiction? The ambiguous conclusion does not provide a clear answer. *The Magic Drum* is a teasingly enigmatic book in which Tennant remodels elements of crime fiction to examine the posthumous power exerted by the real-life equivalents of Cole, and to undermine commonsense assumptions about the meaning of ''reality.''

After *Two Women of London: The Strange Case of Ms. Jekyll and Mrs. Hyde* and *The Magic Drum,* Tennant did not return immediately to *The Cycle of the Sun* but published *Sisters and Strangers,* perhaps her most ambitious attempt to provide a comprehensive survey of the life-lies, contradictions and hypocrisies central to women's lives, both past and present. Although couched in the form of an a historical fable or *A Moral Tale,* as the subtitle puts it, *Sisters and Strangers* is, paradoxically, a history of woman. Within a fairy-tale format, Tennant retells the story of Eve in an imaginatively exuberant as well as incisively sardonic manner. The Genesis story is blended with 20th-century reality in a freewheeling, synchronic way that incorporates myth, legend, and fantasy as the narrative surveys the recurring roles offered to women, such as Harlot, Madonna, Courtesan, Bluestocking, and Witch (titles of some of the sections). For all its wit and inventiveness, *Sisters and Strangers* is a disturbing post-feminist analysis of the deceptions and self-deceptions, especially concerning love and romance, by which women are virtually forced to live if they are to survive at all.

During the 1990s, Tennant made a sharp turn away from the past, a move perhaps prefigured by her exploration of the 19th-century Jekyll and Hyde story. Her *Faustine* incorporated ideas from Goethe in a modern setting for a feminist retelling of *Faust.* There followed a series of sequels to Jane Austen: *Pemberley, An Unequal Marriage,* and *Emma in Love.* Unfortunately, the first two, which continued the story of Elizabeth Darcy (née Bennett) and Mr. Darcy from *Pride and Prejudice,* failed to replicate the joys of their precursor. The problem was that Tennant was writing in an entirely different time, and apparently thought it appropriate to picture Elizabeth discussing topics such as vaginal douches. Somewhat more successful was her sequel to *Emma,* but again Tennant faced the restrictions imposed by a theme that has existed at the margins, if not the center, of her work: time, and the changes time imposes on all of society.

—Peter Lewis, updated by Judson Knight

THAROOR, Shashi

Nationality: British. **Born:** London, 1956. **Education:** Delhi University, B.A. (with honors) 1975; Tufts University, M.A. 1976; M.A.L.D. 1977; Ph.D. 1978. **Career:** Assistant to the director of external affairs, 1978–79, public information officer, 1980–81, head of Singapore office, 1981–84, senior external affairs officer, 1985–87, executive assistant to the deputy high commissioner, 1987–89, all

United Nations High Commissioner for Refugees; special assistant to the undersecretary general for peacekeeping operations, 1989–96, executive assistant to the Secretary- General, United Nations, 1996–98. Since 1998, director of special projects, Office of the Secretary General, United Nations. **Awards:** Rajika Kripalani Young Journalist award, 1976; Federation of Indian Publishers and *Hindustan Times* Best Book of the Year, 1990, and Commonwealth Writers prize (Eurasian region), 1990, both for *The Great Indian Novel.*

PUBLICATIONS

Novels

The Great Indian Novel. New Delhi, Penguin, London, Viking, and New York, Arcade, 1989.

Show Business. New Delhi, Viking, 1991; New York, Arcade, 1992; London, Picador, 1994.

Short Stories

The Five-Dollar Smile: Fourteen Early Stories and a Farce in Two Acts. New Delhi, Viking, 1990; as *The Five-Dollar Smile and Other Stories,* New York, Arcade, 1993.

Other

Reasons of State: Political Development and India's Foreign Policy Under Indira Ghandi, 1966–1977. New Delhi, Vikas Publishing House, 1982.

India: From Midnight to the Millennium. New York, Arcade, 1997.

*

Critical Studies: *History-Fiction Interface in Indian English Novel: Mulk Raj Anand, Nayantara Sahgal, Salman Rushdie, Shashi Tharoor, O.V. Vijayan* by T.N. Dhar, New Delhi, Prestige, 1999.

* * *

Despite living and working overseas (in Switzerland and the United States) for much of his adult life, Shashi Tharoor's writing shares few of the concerns, such as identity, place, and displacement, that have become the stock-in-trade of writers of the Indian diaspora. *The Great Indian Novel* and *Show Business,* and a collection of early stories, *The Five-Dollar Smile: Fourteen Early Stories and a Farce in Two Acts,* have in common Tharoor's postmodernist interest in playing games with his readers. Indeed his taste for sometimes awful puns and his delight in elaborate wordplay is evident even in the early stories.

The title of Tharoor's first full-length work of fiction, *The Great Indian Novel,* immediately signposts his interest in language games. The title is at once a play on the elusive ''great American novel'' and a reference to the work which provides the framework of Tharoor's novel, India's greatest epic the *Mahabharata* (which roughly translated means ''great India''). In his retelling of modern Indian history and politics, Tharoor explores ground similar to that covered by Salman Rushdie in *Midnight's Children.* Yet though Tharoor's voice is evidently of the post-Rushdie generation of Indian writing in English, it remains distinct. In the novel, figures from the *Mahabharata* are recreated as characters who in turn represent figures from recent Indian history. Thus Bhishma from the *Mahabharata* becomes Ganga Datta (who is also a fictional representation of Mahatma Gandhi) in Tharoor's version of the epic. Similarly, Karna becomes Muhammad Ali Karna in the novel, and a figure who parallels Jinnah from modern history. And just as all the major figures from recent Indian history are included in Tharoor's novel, so all the major events are recorded too, though at times two or three historical events are condensed into a single fictional one.

But perhaps of even greater importance than the history and politics in this novel is Tharoor's interest in language. Through his many linguistic and literary games—such as the novel's self-reflexivity and the frequent spot-the-allusion games—Tharoor exposes the power of language as a tool of the colonial process while at the same time pointing the reader back to literature. History and politics, the novel seems to suggest, are best understood via literature (the *Mahabharata,* for example). This is a neat conceit which also privileges Tharoor's own text.

In *Show Business,* his second novel, Tharoor casts his satirical eye over Bollywood, India's popular, Bombay-based cinema industry. The novel closely follows the career of Ashok Banjara, an Indian film hero (who despite the mandatory disclaimers is clearly based on India's superstar of the screen, Amitabh Bacchan)—his rise to fame, his marriage to an up-and-coming young heroine, his many affairs, his vast wealth, his flirtation with politics, and so on. Interspersed with Ashok Banjara's own story and ultimately indistinguishable from it are the plots of the various films in which he stars. The novel is at once a comic tale about the Indian film industry, a homily on greed and ambition, and a highly entertaining look at the boundaries between fiction and reality (which in the celluloid world of Bollywood is surely all illusion anyway).

Tharoor's early stories—some of which he wrote as a teenager for Indian mass-circulation periodicals—and a two-act play have been published in *The Five-Dollar Smile.* The stories, which treat such issues as racism (''The Boutique''), hypocrisy (''The Temple Thief''), and gender stereotyping (''City Girl, Village Girl''), show signs of the language skills which Tharoor exploits to such great effect in *The Great Indian Novel.* ''Twenty-Two Months in the Life of a Dog'' is a short play about abuses of power during Indira Gandhi's Emergency which lacks the satirical and political bite of a novel like Nayantara Sahgal's *Rich Like Us,* which covers the same territory. Tharoor has also written a work of non-fiction, *Reasons of State: Political Development and India's Foreign Policy Under Indira Gandi, 1966–1977,* which examines the making of Indian foreign policy.

—Ralph J. Crane

THEROUX, Alexander (Louis)

Nationality: American. **Born:** Medford, Massachusetts, 17 August 1939; brother of Paul Theroux, *q.v.* **Education:** St. Joseph's Seminary, 1960–62; St. Francis College, Biddeford, Maine, B.A. 1964;

University of Virginia, Charlottesville (Woodrow Wilson fellow), M.A. 1965, Ph.D. 1968; Brasenose College, Oxford. **Career:** Instructor, University of Virginia, 1968; Fulbright lecturer, University of London, 1968–69; instructor, Longwood College, Farmville, Virginia, 1969–73, and Harvard University, Cambridge, Massachusetts, 1973–78; writer-in-residence, Phillips Academy, Andover, Massachusetts, 1978–83; visiting artist, Massachusetts Institute of Technology, Cambridge, from 1983. Currently member of the Department of English, Yale University, New Haven, Connecticut. **Awards:** National Endowment for the Arts grant, 1966; Academy of American Poets award, 1966; Encyclopaedia Britannica award, 1973; Guggenheim fellowship, 1974. **Address:** Department of English, Yale University, P.O. Box 3545, New Haven, Connecticut 06520, U.S.A.

PUBLICATIONS

Novels

Darconville's Cat. New York, Doubleday, 1981; London, Hamish Hamilton, 1983.
An Adultery. New York, Simon and Schuster, 1987; London, Hamish Hamilton, 1988.

Short Stories

Three Wogs. Boston, Gambit, 1972; London, Chatto and Windus-Wildwood House, 1973.

Uncollected Short Stories

''Fark Pooks,'' in *Esquire* (New York), August 1973.
''Scugnizzo's Pasta Co.,'' in *Encounter* (London), September 1974.
''Lynda Van Cats,'' in *The Pushcart Prize 1,* edited by Bill Henderson. Yonkers, New York, Pushcart Press, 1976.
''Finocchio; or, The Tale of a Man with a Long Nose,'' in *Massachusetts Review* (Amherst), Summer 1976.

Plays

Christmas Eve at the Gordon Crumms, in *Rapier,* Spring 1968.
The Sweethearts and Chagrin of Roland McGuffey, in *Rapier,* Winter 1968.
The Master's Oral (produced Cambridge, Massachusetts, 1974).
The Confessions of Mrs. Motherwell, in *Rapier,* Autumn 1976.

Poetry

The Lollipop Trollops and Other Poems. Normal, Illinois, Dalkey Archive Press, 1992.

Other (for children)

The Great Wheadle Tragedy. Boston, Godine, 1975.
The Schinocephalic Waif. Boston, Godine, 1975.
Master Snickup's Cloak. New York, Harper, and Limpsfield, Surrey, Dragon's World, 1979.

Other

Theroux Metaphrastes: An Essay on Literature. Boston, Godine, 1975.
The Primary Colors: Three Essays. New York, Holt. 1994.
The Secondary Colors: Three Essays. New York, Henry Holt, 1996.

*

Critical Studies: ''Alexander Theroux/Paul West Issue'' of *Review of Contemporary Fiction* (Elmwood Park, Illinois), Spring 1991.

* * *

Unlike his prolific brother Paul, whose travel books and novels supply readers the here and now with journalistic directness, Alexander Theroux is the soul of anachronism, a backwards literary history: unconcerned with modern markets, romantic in sensibility, neoclassical in aesthetic judgments, renaissance in learning and style, medieval in spirit. His line of descent recedes from game-playing Nabokov to the late-Victorian romance writer Baron Corvo, satirists Swift and Sterne, and encyclopedist Thomas Browne. For Theroux, observation of the present, whether the London of *Three Wogs* or the American eastern seaboard of *Darconville's Cat,* is the occasion for, not the purpose of, writing, an activity generated by a long memory of other writing. And yet, despite or, perhaps, because of his hyperliteracy—his esoteric allusions, archaic lexicon, elegant inversions, and orotund voice—the here and now are somehow defamiliarized, his artificial characters made curiously human, by his hermetic eccentricities.

Theroux's first book, *Three Wogs,* collects three long stories, each featuring an immigrant from the Empire clashing with a representative 1960s Londoner. In ''Mrs. Proby Gets Hers'' a widowed middle-class matron develops a paranoid and ultimately killing fear of an old shopkeeper from Hong Kong. ''Childe Roland'' exercises a stupid laborer's hatred for an educated Indian student. In ''The Wife of God'' an epicene Anglican priest selfishly attempts to stop his African choirmaster's marriage. The Britishers' pride and racism mask feelings of inferiority to and envy of the more energetic and even better-mannered ''wogs.'' While Theroux has innocent fun with his foreigners' malapropisms and misinformation, the English are savaged by their own smugly expressed pretensions and by the ironic punishments Theroux gives them at stories' ends. Wholly appropriate for the dilettante Reverend Which Therefore (sic) of ''The Wife of God,'' Theroux's stylistic contrivances sometimes overwhelm their satiric targets in the first two stories, manufacturing sentence to sentence wit but risking a reversal of sympathies for his characters from the present ''Age of Shoddy.''

Three Wogs was a startling debut, sufficiently noticed to be read by a character in *Darconville's Cat;* but it's this later book that earns Theroux prominent shelfspace in the Library of Literary Extravagance, the ''A'' range of alphabetical amusements, anomalies, anatomies, and artificial autobiographies. Theroux's predilections struggled within the constraints of the short story; here they are freed to create a 704-page, densely printed story of courtly love gone sour. A crazed character named Crucifer slightly scrambles the novel's strategy and achievement: ''Nothing exceeds like excess.''

According to an essay on the Theroux family by James Atlas (*New York Times Magazine,* 30 April 1978), Alexander was once engaged to and then jilted by one of his students at Longwood College. He vowed literary revenge, and she said ''Do your worst.'' *Darconville's Cat* is his best and worst, a very funny send-up of young love and a compendium of misogyny in which, says Atlas, Theroux doesn't change the name of the girl who disappointed him. The novel's writer-protagonist, Alaric Darconville, was, like Theroux, in and out of monasteries as a youth and taught at Harvard and a Virginia college for women. But as the very simple plot inches from first meeting through courtship to betrayal and bitterness, the parallels between life and art increasingly feel like literary hoaxing, a way to draw life-minded readers into worlds made of words. Once again, Crucifer seems to speak for Theroux, ''Love was the invention of the Provençal knight-poets to justify their verse.''

What's best about *Darconville's Cat* is the advantage Theroux takes of the tradition of The Book, the large storehouse of knowledge such as The Bible, *Gargantua,* or *Moby-Dick.* Elaboration is all. The reader who doesn't care for a chapter on college girls' late-night rap sessions or the dialogue in verse between Alaric and his beloved Isabel or a classical oration by Crucifer can skip ahead or back without losing essential continuity. There are learned disquisitions on love, hate, and the human ear; wonderful odd-lot lists; Shandyian japes such as a one-word chapter and a page of asterisks; and Swiftian renderings of small-town southern life, ranting religionists, academic foolery, and much more. The parts are all related but don't disappear into a whole, into an illusion of reality.

Darconville's Cat is boring and brilliant, both puerile and profound, self-indulgent and often cruel. Theroux lacks Thomas Pynchon's interest in this century and the popular humor of Gilbert Sorrentino's *Mulligan Stew,* the novel Theroux's most closely resembles. ''Madness,'' Darconville says of a book very like the one in which he is a character. But like that excessive anomaly of the 1950s, William Gaddis's *The Recognitions, Darconville's Cat* should find a dedicated following, readers with an appetite for ambition and literary aberration, for a prodigal art that, in Darconville's world, ''declassifies.''

—Thomas LeClair

THEROUX, Paul (Edward)

Nationality: American. **Born:** Medford, Massachusetts, 10 April 1941; brother of Alexander Theroux, *q.v.* **Education:** Medford High School; University of Maine, Orono, 1959–60; University of Massachusetts, Amherst, B.A. in English 1963. **Family:** Married Anne Castle in 1967 (divorced 1993), married Sheila Donnelly in 1995; two sons. **Career:** Lecturer, University of Urbino, Italy, 1963; Peace Corps lecturer, Soche Hill College, Limbe, Malawi, 1963–65; lecturer, Makerere University, Kampala, Uganda, 1965–68, and University of Singapore, 1968–71; writer-in-residence, University of Virginia, Charlottesville, 1972. **Awards:** *Playboy* award, 1971, 1977, 1979; American Academy award, 1977; Whitbread award, 1978; *Yorkshire Post* award, 1982; James Tait Black Memorial prize, 1982; Thomas Cook award, for travel book, 1989. D. Litt.: Tufts University, Medford, Massachusetts, 1980; Trinity College, Washington, D.C., 1980; University of Massachusetts, 1988. **Member:** Fellow, Royal Society of Literature, and Royal Geographical Society; American Academy, 1984. **Address:** c/o Hamish Hamilton Ltd., 27 Wright's Lane, London W8 5TZ, England.

Publications

Novels

Waldo. Boston, Houghton Mifflin, 1967; London, Bodley Head, 1968.
Fong and the Indians. Boston, Houghton Mifflin, 1968; London, Hamish Hamilton, 1976.
Girls at Play. Boston, Houghton Mifflin, and London, Bodley Head, 1969.
Murder in Mount Holly. London, Ross, 1969.
Jungle Lovers. Boston, Houghton Mifflin, and London, Bodley Head, 1971.
Saint Jack. London, Bodley Head, and Boston, Houghton Mifflin, 1973.
The Black House. London, Hamish Hamilton, and Boston, Houghton Mifflin, 1974.
The Family Arsenal. London, Hamish Hamilton, and Boston, Houghton Mifflin, 1976.
Picture Palace: A Novel. London, Hamish Hamilton, and Boston, Houghton Mifflin, 1978.
The Mosquito Coast. London, Hamish Hamilton, 1981; Boston, Houghton Mifflin, 1982.
Doctor Slaughter. London, Hamish Hamilton, 1984.
Half Moon Street: Two Short Novels (includes *Doctor Slaughter* and *Doctor DeMarr*). Boston, Houghton Mifflin, 1984.
O-Zone. London, Hamish Hamilton, and New York, Putnam, 1986.
My Secret History. London, Hamish Hamilton, and New York, Putnam, 1989.
Doctor DeMarr. London, Hutchinson, 1990.
Chicago Loop. London, Hamish Hamilton, 1990; New York, Random House, 1991.
Millroy the Magician. London, Hamish Hamilton, 1993; New York, Random House, 1994.
My Other Life. Boston, Houghton Mifflin, 1996.
Kowloon Tong. Boston, Houghton Mifflin, 1997.
The Collected Short Novels. London, Penguin Books, 1999.

Short Stories

Sinning with Annie and Other Stories. Boston, Houghton Mifflin, 1972; London, Hamish Hamilton, 1975.
The Consul's File. London, Hamish Hamilton, and Boston, Houghton Mifflin, 1977.
World's End and Other Stories. London, Hamish Hamilton, and Boston, Houghton Mifflin, 1980.
The London Embassy. London, Hamish Hamilton, 1982; Boston, Houghton Mifflin, 1983.
The Collected Stories. New York, Viking, 1997.

Plays

The Autumn Dog (produced New York, 1981).
The White Man's Burden. London, Hamish Hamilton, 1987.

Screenplay: *Saint Jack,* with Peter Bogdanovich and Howard Sackler, 1979.

Television Play: *The London Embassy,* from his own story, 1987.

Other

V.S. Naipaul: An Introduction to His Work. London, Deutsch, and New York, Africana, 1972.
The Great Railway Bazaar: By Train Through Asia. London, Hamish Hamilton, and Boston, Houghton Mifflin, 1975.
A Christmas Card (for children). London, Hamish Hamilton, and Boston, Houghton Mifflin, 1978.
The Old Patagonian Express: By Train Through the Americas. London, Hamish Hamilton, and Boston, Houghton Mifflin, 1979.
London Snow (for children). Salisbury, Wiltshire, Russell, 1979; Boston, Houghton Mifflin, 1980.
Sailing Through China. Salisbury, Wiltshire, Russell, 1983; Boston, Houghton Mifflin, 1984.
The Kingdom by the Sea: A Journey Around the Coast of Great Britain. London, Hamish Hamilton, and Boston, Houghton Mifflin, 1983.
Sunrise with Seamonsters: Travels and Discoveries 1964–1984. London, Hamish Hamilton, and Boston, Houghton Mifflin, 1985.
The Imperial Way: Making Tracks from Peshawar to Chittagong, photographs by Steve McCurry. London, Hamish Hamilton, and Boston, Houghton Mifflin, 1985.
Patagonia Revisited, with Bruce Chatwin. Salisbury, Wiltshire, Russell, 1985; Boston, Houghton Mifflin, 1986.
The Shortest Day of the Year: A Christmas Fantasy. Leamington, Warwickshire, Sixth Chamber Press, 1986.
Riding the Iron Rooster: By Train Through China. London, Hamish Hamilton, and New York, Putnam, 1988.
Travelling the World. London, Sinclair Stevenson, 1990.
The Happy Isles of Oceania: Paddling the Pacific. London, Hamish Hamilton, and New York, Putnam, 1992.
The Pillars of Hercules: A Grand Tour of the Mediterranean. New York, G.P. Putnam's Sons, 1995.
Down the Yangtze. London, Penguin, 1995.
Sir Vidia's Shadow: A Friendship Across Five Continents. Boston, Houghton Mifflin, 1998.
Fresh Air Fiend: Travel Writings, 1985–2000. Boston, Houghton Mifflin, 2000.

*

Paul Theroux comments:

(1986) Both in my fiction and non-fiction I have tried to write about the times in which I have lived. Although I have been resident in various countries for the past 25 years, and these countries have been the settings for my books, I consider myself an American writer. I have a strong homing instinct.

* * *

In his note to *My Other Life,* Paul Theroux writes that the book is ''the story of a life I could have lived had things been different—an imaginary memoir.'' This brief statement could summarize a general paradox that drives the overwhelming majority of Theroux's acclaimed novels and short stories, as well as his immensely popular travel accounts: a person can only discover and comment on ''the self'' by taking on the role of a stranger. In fact, encounters with the ''strange,'' both within and outside of the self, transform all of Theroux's narrators into travelers of sorts. Mingling the Gothic with the journalistic and the psychological with the geographical, Theroux blends the distant past with the distant present to comment on human nature, racism, colonialism, cultural identity, alienation from the natural world, and the hypocrisy of civilization. Like the author himself, the most compelling characters and settings in Theroux's novels seem to balance two identities—fiction and fact, sacred and secular, foreign and familiar, past and present, strange and mundane.

In both his fiction and nonfiction, Paul Theroux estranges the familiar by positioning Western (British and America) characters as outsiders in a foreign society or transforming Western landscapes into unfamiliar dystopias. Whether he is moving the New Englander to the Honduran Mosquito Coast, recounting his own journeys in his many travel narratives, or laying out an alien-infested O-Zone, he is fascinated by people and places who are out of sync.

In *Saint Jack,* Jack Flowers is an American expatriate who addresses the pathos and puzzlement of being an outsider in Singapore. *Kowloon Tong,* set against the backdrop of Hong Kong's reunification with China, features British expatriate Neville ''Blunt'' Mullard. Like Heather Monkhouse in *Girls at Play,* he seeks a Western lifestyle in a non-Western country. Although he was born in the colony and barely knows England, he lives a British lifestyle that is insulated from the Chinese culture around him (except for his visits to local ''blue hotel'' prostitutes and an affair with one of his employees). Both novels, one written early in Theroux's career and one written very recently, dislocate their Western characters to expose a common dilemma: their nostalgic constructions of Occidentalism are only at home when the characters are abroad.

In a novel like *O-Zone,* Theroux positions individual outsiders/strangers within an estranged landscape that stresses the alienating effects of technology and a separation from nature. The story follows seven wealthy couples and a boy living in 21-century America as they encounter literal aliens—Skells, Starkies, Trolls, Diggers, and Roaches—during a New Year's Eve holiday in The Outer Zone. In this dystopic future New York, civilization has proved unfriendly and residents are afraid to leave their fortress-like homes. Traveling in a strange, brutal, and primitive Missouri outback, the mixed bag of characters once again address duplicitous identities, culture clashes, and the introspective process of traveling outside metaphorical safety zones of all kinds.

In creating such dystopias, Theroux dislocates entire Western social structures and landscapes. *The Family Arsenal* follows American consul Valentine Hood through the strange and violent dynamics of an East London terrorist underground.

In the *Mosquito Coast,* megalomaniac Allie Fox decides to start a utopic new life in Honduras, away from the corruption of modern America. In a forced estrangement from civilization and materialism, he moves his wife and four children from Hatfield, Massachusetts, to a remote clearing on the Mosquito Coast, where their quest for paradise quickly leads to apocalyptic destruction. Like the wizard Millroy in *Millroy the Magician*—who embarks on an odyssey through America, preaching the wisdom of a whole food diet and performing magic tricks for an awestruck crowd—Allie Fox invents himself as a messiah and prophet against the backdrop of corrupt[ing] fast-food-addicted society. Both men seem bigger than life, embodying myth and history, salvation and destruction, illusion and reality.

Theroux also uses traditional Gothicism to achieve a sense of discomfort and uncertainty, as in *Girls at Play* and *The Black House.* In the first novel, a horrific chain of events forces characters to abandon their illusions about themselves. In the second, spectral illusions make the characters' surroundings seem horrific. *Girls at Play* revolves around three women in East Africa: Miss Poole, the headmistress of a girls' school; Heather Monkhouse, a promiscuous salesgirl from Croydon who dreams of being a high-class call girl; and Bettyjean Lebow, a naïve American from the Peace Corps. Black/white, East/West, male/female, civilized/savage collide as the women are faced with alien landscapes, vanishings, recurring nightmares, rape, and murder. In *The Black House,* anthropologist Alfred Munday returns to Dorset, England, after ten years in Uganda, where he ''lived closely with an alien people,'' only to find a ghostly ''foreigner'' in his own house. Munday has an affair with an apparition, Caroline, who occasionally possesses the body of his wife, Emma; he uses the local church hall for lectures on African circumcision ceremonies and weaponry; and the once separate worlds of England and Africa begin to blur and reflect each other. Recalling Sam Fong in *Fong and the Indians,* Calvin Muller and Marais in *Jungle Lovers,* and the three women in *Girls at Play,* Munday is the ultimate outsider. He is out of joint in both time and place, realizing that the balance between seemingly solid and disparate points in geography, history, and psychology is tenuous as best.

The conflicting forces in these novels—Western and Eastern, order and chaos, white and black, past and present, history and fantasy—also speak to the importance of some fundamental duality in each of Theroux's novels. This duality can be absolutely literal, as in the characters' double lives in *My Secret History* and *Chicago Loop,* or come through more subtly in the divided lives for characters like Maude Coffin Pratt in *Picture Palace* and the fictional Paul Theroux of *My Other Life.*

On the one hand, *My Secret History* traces the double life of Andre Parent—writer, traveler, and lover of women—through an all-American boyhood, libertinism in Africa, a dangerous secret life, marriage, and self-analysis. Similarly, *Chicago Loop* explores the double life of successful Chicago businessman Parker Jagoda, who is a health-conscious suburban model of propriety by day and a sexual serial killer in the city by night. Both novels recall the earlier *Half Moon Street,* which combines two novellas on the theme of double identity: *Doctor Slaughter* (set in England) and *Doctor DeMarr* (set in America). Doctor Slaughter is a research fellow in political sciences and part-time prostitute; Dr. Marr is a man who takes over the identity of his murdered twin brother. In each case, the duality of the characters reflects Theroux's literary preoccupation with identity and alienation.

In books like *Picture Palace: A Novel,* on the other hand, the duality is more complicated. At age seventy, world-famous photographer Maude Coffin Pratt travels through her past as she rummages through her life's work. Theroux uses her recollections, which exist somewhere between the past and the present, to address, once again, issues of paradoxical double identity. In fact, in a conversation with T.S. Eliot, Maude compares herself to Tiresias from *The Waste Land*—''throbbing between two lives''—to express her position between the estranged, fictional, visual world of her photographs and the mundane, factual, blind world in which she lives. Throughout her narrative, Pratt's incestuous desire for her brother, who prefers their sister, and her psychosomatic blindness again interrogate the recurring dynamics of sexual desire, perception, and reality.

Further complicating this idea of double identity, the fictional narrator (named Paul Theroux) in *My Other Life* recalls scenes that are similar to the ones from the author's biography, as he begins the story as a 23-year-old Peace Corps volunteer teaching English in Africa. Like the author, the narrator writes books titled *The Great Railway Bazaar* and *The Mosquito Coast,* teaches in Singapore, lives in London with his wife and children, and moves back to Massachusetts later in his life. Yet, Theroux blends fiction and nonfiction to estrange his own familiar biography and expose our presumptions about the two genres. In setting up this alter-ego, Theroux also hearkens back to the two white characters in *Jungle Lovers*—Calvin Mullet, a divorced insurance agent from Massachusetts, and Marais, a revolutionary intent on overthrowing a corrupt fascist regime—who were, according to Theroux, ''two opposing sides of [his] own personality.'' Like these characters, the fictional Theroux of *My Other Life* balances the author's contradictory impulses for security and upheaval, revealing the complicated relationship between autobiography, fiction, art, and reporting.

Like his travel narratives, Theroux's novels familiarize readers with the strange and violent. They interrogate arbitrary and capricious divisions in the modern world, and they blur the lines that define our assumptions about the city and the jungle, beauty and savagery, Self and Other.

—Christine Roth

THOMAS, Audrey (Grace)

Nationality: Canadian citizen. **Born:** Audrey Callahan in Binghamton, New York, 17 November 1935. Moved to Canada, 1959; lived in Kumasi, Ghana, 1964–66. **Education:** Smith College, Northampton, Massachusetts, B.A. 1957; University of British Columbia, Vancouver, M.A. in English 1963. **Family:** Married Ian Thomas in 1958 (divorced); three daughters. **Career:** Since 1990 visiting professor, Concordia University, Montreal. Scottish-Canadian Exchange Fellow, Edinburgh, 1985–86; writer-in-residence, University of Victoria, British Columbia, University of British Columbia, Vancouver, Simon Fraser University, Burnaby, British Columbia, and David Thompson University Centre, Nelson, British Columbia. **Awards:** Atlantic Firsts award, 1965; Canada Council grant, 1969, 1971, 1972, 1974, and Senior Arts grant, 1974, 1977, 1979, 1987, 1991, 1994; Marian Engel award, 1987; Canada-Australia Literary prize, 1990; Ethel Wilson award and BC Book prize, 1985, for *Intertidal Life,* 1991, for *Wild Blue Yonder,* and 1995, for *Coming Down From Wa.* Honorary doctorate: Simon Fraser University, 1994; University of British Columbia, 1994. **Address:** R.R. 2, Galiano, British Columbia V0N 1P0, Canada.

Publications

Novels

Mrs. Blood. Indianapolis, Bobbs Merrill, 1967.

Munchmeyer, and Prospero on the Island. Indianapolis, Bobbs Merrill, 1972.

Songs My Mother Taught Me. Indianapolis, Bobbs Merrill, 1973.

Blown Figures. Vancouver, Talonbooks, 1974; New York, Knopf, 1975.

Latakia. Vancouver, Talonbooks, 1979.
Intertidal Life. Toronto, Stoddart, 1984; New York, Beaufort, 1985.
Graven Images. Toronto, Penguin Canada, 1993.
Coming Down from Wa. Toronto and New York, Viking, 1995.
Isobel Gunn. Toronto, Viking, 1999.

Short Stories

Ten Green Bottles. Indianapolis, Bobbs Merrill, 1967.
Ladies and Escorts. Ottawa, Oberon Press, 1977.
Personal Fictions, with others, edited by Michael Ondaatje. Toronto, Oxford University Press, 1977.
Real Mothers. Vancouver, Talonbooks, 1981.
Two in the Bush and Other Stories. Toronto, McClelland and Stewart, 1981.
Goodbye Harold, Good Luck. Toronto, New York, and London, Viking, 1986.
The Wild Blue Yonder. Toronto, Viking, 1990.

Plays

Radio Plays: *Once Your Submarine Cable Is Gone . . .*, 1973; *Mrs. Blood,* from her own novel, 1975.

*

Manuscript Collection: National Library of Canada, Ottawa, Ontario.

Critical Studies: ''Audrey Thomas Issue'' of *Room of One's Own* (Vancouver), vol. 10, no. 3–4, 1986.

Audrey Thomas comments:

I write primarily about women—modern women with their particular dreams, delights, despairs. Also how these women relate to men and the terrible things we do to one another in the name of love. I am also interested in what happens to a person set down in a strange city or country, without a familiar environment, friends, or job to define him, when he must ask serious questions. Madness, too, interests me, and the delicate balance between sanity and madness.

I like to tell a good tale, and at the same time I like to make the reader work. I assume my readers will want to run a bit for their money.

* * *

Audrey Thomas, a prolific Canadian-American author, uses the knowledge that societal roles are all too often understood to be rigid and blameless, supported by the highest religious, political, and social authorities as a base from which to build her explorations of the possibilities and multiplicities that are in direct contention with this human pull toward the accepted ''norm'' within society's network of ideology. Her characters pull to the surface all that is unstable, relative, and questionable as they continually explore the arbitrary nature of gender and caste systems, the power struggles between men and women, and the complexities of attraction and passion that are ever present within both the text and within the life of the author herself. Her work, autobiographical in nature, displays an interest in feminism and a love of experimentation, both with language and with literary devices.

Thomas, a significant figure in Canadian feminist literature for more than thirty years, has been, on numerous occasions, ranked among the best in her field. In Thomas's fiction, gender, culture at large, and character form a complex mixture of contradictory and variable patterns that can be readily seen in her latest novel *Isobel Gunn,* published in 1999. Here, the hierarchy of selves is so confused and confusing, that while arranging the personality through division and category, it calls attention to the potential weakness in its own foundation as an ordering system. And, we find that the many voices present are hailing forth our ability to call into question a certain discourse, or way of thinking. The examples of real versus constructed ''realities'' in *Isobel Gunn* are numerous and varied and thus expose many of the ideological inconsistencies of societal roles in individualistic America.

Thomas has demonstrated in her quasi-autobiographical fictions how small the territory of incident need be for the writer to create a continent of psychological complexity. Such categories as novel, novella, and short story are not easily applied to Thomas's work, for continuities are always present, within and between genres. The short stories that form her first novel, *Ten Green Bottles,* for example, are closely interrelated; all of them are told by an unhappy female persona, so in the end the book takes on in one's mind the character of a sequence of psychologically linked incidents. More loosely, the later collections—*Ladies and Escorts; Real Mothers;* and *Goodbye Harold, Good Luck*—appear as true organic unities in their representation respectively of the pain and sadness in sexual relations and the reality of generational links.

Similarly, the two novellas published in a single volume, *Munchmeyer* and *Prospero on the Island,* are not in reality separate works. They are linked by the fact that *Munchmeyer* (itself a kind of mirror work in which it is hard to tell what is meant as plot and what is the novelist-hero's fantasizing) is presented as the novel that had been written by Miranda, the narrator in *Prospero on the Island,* and is being discussed by her with ''Prospero,'' an elderly painter friend who lives on the same British Columbian island. And the novels—*Mrs. Blood, Songs My Mother Taught Me, Latakia* and *Intertidal Life*—are in turn constructed within loose frameworks, so that structurally there are considerable resemblances between the groups of interrelated stories and the highly episodic novels.

It soon becomes evident that the structural principle of Thomas's fictions is one in which the psychological patterns take precedence over the aesthetic or self-consciously formal. The experience in them is, in merely physical terms, limited and largely repetitious; it also runs fairly closely parallel to Thomas's own life. She was born and brought up in upstate New York, spent time in England and Ghana, traveled in the Levant, and in recent years has been dividing her life between Vancouver and the nearby islands of the Gulf of Georgia, with their mixed population of aging English expatriates, writers, and artists.

In fictional terms it is equally interesting to observe that the central persona of the books appears to be the same, yet treated unchronologically. For example, a middle period book, *Songs My Mother Taught Me,* deals in a rather shapelessly flowing narrative with the childhood memories that already find their place as fleeting recollections in earlier stories. *Mrs. Blood,* which harrowingly evokes a somewhat perilous pregnancy in West Africa, also incorporates the persona's sentimental journeys in England. In the novella *Prospero on the Island* creation and memory meld together with the persona-now-turned novelist reflecting on the creative present to which all these pasts contribute.

As in the case of even the novella, *Munchmeyer* (the one item presented as totally fictitious), it is hard to tell when the actuality of the author's life merges into the invented narrative. An added complication arises from Thomas's acute sense of place, whose expression she has developed from book to book, so that in two of her more recent novels, *Latakia* and *Intertidal Life,* the evocations of the Levantine background and of the Pacific coast, respectively, become almost as important as the always frustrated and pathetic relationships between human beings.

There are no absolutes in Thomas's work. Instead, it is full of endless movements of giving and receiving. Each character, each word, reinscribes something; each constructs the web it tries to decipher. When lost in her worlds, one must pay attention to not only that which is visible and present, but to the non-text as well, the unknown that is always being conquered and always conquering, to that which lies beyond the boundaries of society, the silences. In these images of grotesque ideas of familial bonds and honor, in examples of love and selfishness, in battles between various kinds of truths and lies Thomas seems to reveal many of her perplexities about the society in which she lives, but she does not offer solutions to these internal and external contradictions. This, perhaps, is exactly what makes her novels, as well as her shorter works, timeless masterpieces of perpetual questioning.

—George Woodcock, updated by Tammy Bird

THOMAS, D(onald) M(ichael)

Nationality: British. **Born:** Redruth, Cornwall, 27 January 1935. **Education:** Redruth Grammar School; University High School, Melbourne; New College, Oxford, B.A. (honours) in English 1958, M.A. 1961. **Military Service:** Served in the British Army (national service), 1953–54. **Family:** Married twice; two sons and one daughter. **Career:** Teacher, Teignmouth Grammar School, Devon, 1959–63; senior lecturer in English, Hereford College of Education, 1964–78, visiting lecturer in English, Hamline University, St. Paul, Minnesota, 1967; lecturer in Creative Writing, American University, Washington, D.C., 1982. **Awards:** Richard Hillary Memorial prize, 1960; Arts Council award, for translation, 1975, Cholmondeley award, for poetry, 1978; *Guardian*—Gollancz Fantasy Novel prize, 1979; *Los Angeles Times* prize, for novel, 1980; Cheltenham prize, 1981; Silver Pen award, 1982. **Address:** The Coach House, Rashleigh Vale, Truro, Cornwall TR1 1TJ, England.

Publications

Novels

The Flute-Player. London, Gollancz, and New York, Dutton, 1979.
Birthstone. London, Gollancz, 1980.
The White Hotel. London, Gollancz, and New York, Viking Press, 1981.
Series: Russian Nights
 Ararat. London, Gollancz, and New York, Viking Press, 1983.
 Swallow. London, Gollancz, and New York, Viking, 1984.
Sphinx. London, Gollancz, 1986; New York, Viking, 1987.
 Summit. London, Gollancz, 1987; New York, Viking, 1988.
Lying Together. London, Gollancz, and New York, Viking, 1990.
Flying in to Love. London, Bloomsbury, 1991; New York, Carroll & Graf, 1995.
Pictures at an Exhibition. London, Bloomsbury, 1993; New York, Carroll & Graf, 1994.
Eating Pavlova. London, Bloomsbury, and New York, Carroll & Graf, 1994.
Lady with a Laptop. New York, Carroll & Graf, 1996.
Charlotte: The Final Journey of Jane Eyre. London, Duckworth, 2000.

Uncollected Short Stories

"Seeking a Suitable Donor," in *The New SF,* edited by Langdon Jones. London, Hutchinson, 1969.
"Labyrinth," in *New Worlds* (London), April 1969.

Plays

The White Hotel, adaptation of his own novel (produced Edinburgh, 1984).
Boris Godunov, adaptation of the play by Pushkin (broadcast 1984). Leamington, Warwickshire, Sixth Chamber Press, 1985.

Radio Plays: *You Will Hear Thunder,* 1981; *Boris Godunov,* 1984.

Poetry

Personal and Possessive. London, Outposts, 1964.
Penguin Modern Poets 11, with D.M. Black and Peter Redgrove. London, Penguin, 1968.
Two Voices. London, Cape Goliard Press, and New York, Grossman, 1968.
The Lover's Horoscope: Kinetic Poem. Laramie, Wyoming, Purple Sage, 1970.
Logan Stone. London, Cape Goliard Press, and New York, Grossman, 1971.
The Shaft. Gillingham, Kent, Arc, 1973.
Lilith-Prints. Cardiff, Second Aeon, 1974.
Symphony in Moscow. Richmond, Surrey, Keepsake Press, 1974.
Love and Other Deaths. London, Elek, 1975.
The Rock. Knotting, Bedfordshire, Sceptre Press, 1975.
Orpheus in Hell. Knotting, Bedfordshire, Sceptre Press, 1977.
The Honeymoon Voyage. London, Secker and Warburg, 1978.
Protest: A Poem after a Medieval Armenian Poem by Frik. Privately printed, 1980.
Dreaming in Bronze. London, Secker and Warburg, 1981.
Selected Poems. London, Secker and Warburg, and New York, Viking Press, 1983.
News from the Front, with Sylvia Kantaris. Todmorden, Lancashire, Arc, 1983.
The Puberty Tree, New & Selected Poems. Newcastle upon Tyne, Bloodaxe, 1992.

Other

The Devil and the Floral Dance (for children). London, Robson, 1978.
Memories and Hallucinations: An Autobiographical Excursion. London, Gollancz, and New York, Viking, 1988.

Alexander Solzhenitsyn: A Century in His Life. New York, St. Martin's Press, 1998.

Editor, *The Granite Kingdom: Poems of Cornwall.* Truro, Cornwall, Barton, 1970.

Editor, *Poetry in Crosslight.* London, Longman, 1975.

Editor, *Songs from the Earth: Selected Poems of John Harris, Cornish Miner, 1820–84.* Padstow, Cornwall, Lodenek Press, 1977.

Translator, *Requiem, and Poem Without a Hero,* by Anna Akhmatova. London, Elek, and Athens, Ohio University Press, 1979.

Translator, *Way of All the Earth,* by Anna Akhmatova. London, Secker and Warburg, and Athens, Ohio University Press, 1979.

Translator, *Invisible Threads,* by Evtushenko. New York, Macmillan, 1981.

Translator, *The Bronze Horseman and Other Poems,* by Pushkin. London, Secker and Warburg, and New York, Viking Press, 1982.

Translator, *A Dove in Santiago,* by Evtushenko. London, Secker and Warburg, 1982; New York, Viking Press, 1983.

Translator, *You Will Hear Thunder: Poems,* by Anna Akhmatova. London, Secker and Warburg, and Athens, Ohio University Press-Swallow Press, 1985; as *Selected Poems,* London, Penguin, 1988.

*

Manuscript Collection: University of Michigan, Ann Arbor.

* * *

D.M. Thomas began his writing career as a poet. His early work in this medium was ranged from the fantasy worlds of science fiction to what would become his trademark stocking-topped, suspender-belted, bawdy sensuality. Fiction turned out to be the more accommodating genre, though, for his unconventional combinations of forms: narrative, poetry, letters, historical documents that flirt with time and the nature of reality.

Thomas's first novel, *The Flute-Player,* is set in an unnamed city of chaos, probably in Russia; there are glimpses of Leningrad, and the book is dedicated to the dissident Russian poets Mandlestam, Pasternak, Akhmatova, and Tsvetayeva. Elena, a flute player, here is the embodiment of the persecuted creative spirit, endangered by the city's totalitarian regime. Her presence is often lost, though, in the novel's whirl of characters, fast-moving incidents, and mood changes.

Thomas's most critically acclaimed and popular novel, *The White Hotel,* maintains its thematic focus more forcefully. Lisa Erdman, an imagined patient of Sigmund Freud, expresses her hyperbolic and crudely masochistic sexual fantasies in the novel's famed opening poem. The perverted brutality of Erdman's desires is later paralleled by the perverted brutality of a world in which the horrors of Babi Yar can take place. Erdman's private desires, which cannot be fully deciphered or cured by psychoanalysis, are not so private after all. The right kind of manipulation can penetrate into the masses and harness the power of their own similarly violent impulses, with horrifying results.

Ararat and *Swallow,* the first two novels of Thomas's ''Russian Nights'' quartet, are free-wheeling and fantastical, involving a number of ''improvisatores.'' *Swallow* features an actual Olympiad of these extempore storytellers, whose rhyming narratives take up a large proportion of the novel. Through this poetry, Thomas explores the ways in which fiction is inspired by—or can create—reality; the improvisatores' stories are paralleled in their own lives and those of the people they encounter. The reader is never quite sure, nor is meant to be sure, where the frontiers of reality and fantasy lie, if indeed there are any frontiers. This dynamic often feels abstract, though, in contrast to the humanity portrayed in *The White Hotel.* The exception is *Swallow*'s ''autobiographical'' episodes, in which scenes from Thomas's (or his persona's) childhood are ingeniously interlaced with adapted passages from *King Solomon's Mines.*

The third novel in the ''Russian Nights'' quartet, *Sphinx,* feeds off *Ararat* and *Swallow,* extending their characters, plots, and the theme of the ''improvisatores.'' *Summit,* the last of the quartet, breaks from this in the ancient tradition of a serious trilogy being succeeded by a farcical or satirical coda. In the antics of a thinly disguised President O'Rielly and a Russian Grobichov, we have a couple of lampooning caricatures on the ''Spitting Image'' level. The novel is in fact an extended joke based mainly on O'Rielly's mental difficulties, including a delayed ratiocination that finds him answering a question, at least one before the question actually being asked. It is amusing, but wears a bit thin as it goes on.

After rounding off his trilogy/quartet in such a traditional manner, Thomas produced *Lying Together,* effectively extending the quartet into a quintet. The characters of the earlier books meet up at a writers' conference, once again taking up their roles as ''improvisatories.'' *Lying Together* has been described as ''pure satire/poetic fantasy/autobiography and dirty book'' all in one. In any case, this work, as its title suggests, makes fantasy and reality more indistinguishable than ever. Thomas is again a character, suggesting an autobiographical edge. The ''improvisions'' of the other characters in the book often seem more ''realistic'' than the characters who invent them, such as the lustful, menstruating, blind film producer who spends a deal of time groping about on the carpet for the tampons she has removed to accommodate her lover.

In *Flying in to Love,* Thomas returns to his earlier tactic of examining significant historical events through the prism of his fiction. The result is an ironic postmodern hatchet job of the Kennedy assassination. Thomas mocks the dizzying array of conspiracy theories and the ways they reveal Americans' sentimental attachment to the youthful prince of Camelot far more than their yearning for the truth. *We* heedlessly ''flew into Love'' with Kennedy, the novel's title a convenient play on Dallas' only airport at the time. Thomas deconstructs the object of our affections as a smarmy playboy, who shares Marilyn Monroe with his brother Bobby.

Thomas revisited the Holocaust in *Pictures at an Exhibition.* Thomas presents the disturbing conundrum of Galewski, a Czech inmate at Auschwitz, who is called upon to cure an SS officer's headaches. Galewski uses his understanding of Freud to help Dr. Lorenz, a doctor who performs brutal experiments on the camp inmates. Out of fear for his own life, though, Galewski cannot state the obvious: that mass murder just might weight on one's mind. Galewski survives the war to become a psychoanalyst, his patients recalling the painful moral evasions of his wartime ''apprenticeship'' for his profession. Galewski and Dr. Lorenz meet again in London, fifty years after the war, and the two must contend with the awful emotional legacy of the Holocaust. The gravity of this subject matter clashes bizarrely and often distractingly with his confusing pastiche style. It is as if Thomas is trying to point out that evil can be obscured by the nonsensical and even the surreal. Yet evil it remains, so we must learn to contend with it despite the chaos.

Much of Thomas's work is heavily invested in Freudian theories of sex, dreams, and sublimation. Thus it is no surprise that Thomas should turn to Freud's life as a subject for fiction in *Eating Pavlova.* Thomas's trademark tangle of narrative threads isn't as jarring here. After all, the book is about Freud, a man who immersed himself in the interpretation of the seemingly dissociative world of dreams. What's more, *Eating Pavlova*'s Freud is in his morphine-clouded, semi-conscious last days. The strongest narrative thread here is that of Freud's daughter Anna, who is so devoted to her father and his work that she'll analyze his dying dreams for him.

Lady with a Laptop finds Thomas mocking his own profession. Simon, his protagonist, is teaching a New Age writing workshop on the subpar Greek island of Skagathos. Simon takes a cheap and cynical delight in his students' lack of talent, but the joke is on him. His career has hit the skids. He's not even much of a flirt anymore. Teacher and students have a chance to be redeemed when they come up with a bizarre, sordid murder mystery in a team writing exercise. The lead author, Lucinda, ends up a murder victim herself. She is the necessary victim, it seems, of the work of writing fiction, for every story ends in death—if not a literal one, then a figurative one, the dying of possibility that comes with the dot at the end of the final sentence.

Writing is also thematic material in *Charlotte: The Final Journey of Jane Eyre.* Jane Eyre has fallen prey to metafictional impulses before. *Wide Sargasso Sea,* Jean Rhys's 1966 exploration of the subjectivity of Rochester's mad and exotic first wife, comments on the limits of the British literary imagination in the Victorian era. In Thomas's version, Miranda Stevenson, a literature professor, takes a somewhat different tact, aiming to ''bring out some of the repressed issues'' in Bronte's novel. Her Jane abandons Rochester after finding him sexually insufficient. She travels to the West Indies, where she finds a black lover who impregnates her. Authoress Miranda, meanwhile, is off on far kinkier journeys. If Jane's black lover was scandalous for her day, Miranda tests the sexual mores of her own time by having sex with a drag queen and parading in front of her father (who, like Rochester, is nearly blind) in her dead mother's lingerie and suspender belt.

—John Cotton, updated by Lisa A. Phillips

THORNTON, Lawrence

Nationality: American. **Born:** Pomona, California, 14 October 1937. **Education:** University of California, Santa Barbara, B.A. 1960, M.A. 1967, Ph.D. 1973. **Family:** Married Toni Clark in 1969. **Career:** Assistant professor of English, Montana State University, Bozeman, 1974–79, associate professor of English, 1980–84; visiting associate professor at University of California, Los Angeles, and University of California, Santa Barbara, 1984–88; writer in residence at University of California, Irvine, 1990; writer, 1990—. **Awards:** Ernest Hemingway Foundation award, 1988; best novel award (PEN Center USA West), 1988; silver medal (Commonwealth Club of California), 1988; Shirley Collier award (University of California, Los Angeles), 1988. **Agent:** Ned Leavitt, William Morris Agency, 1350 Avenue of the Americas, New York, New York 10019, U.S.A. **Address:** 603 West Eighth St., Claremont, California 91711, U.S.A.

Publications

Novels

Imagining Argentina. New York, Doubleday, 1987.
Under the Gypsy Moon. New York, Doubleday, 1990.
Marlow's Book. New York, Doubleday, 1991.
Ghost Woman. New York, Ticknor & Fields, 1992.
Naming the Spirits. New York, Doubleday, 1995.
Tales from the Blue Archives. New York, Doubleday, 1997.

Other

Unbodied Hope: Narcissism and the Modern Novel (criticism). Lewisburg, Pennsylvania, Bucknell University Press, 1984.

*

Lawrence Thornton comments:

(2000) All the novels bear the stigmata of magic realism, though ''The Argentina Trilogy'' is probably my purest work in the form. Writing straight, realistic fiction goes against my natural bent to manipulate the continuum of time and space to reveal the impact of political reality on people's lives. I seek the language of exposure, condemnation, courage, love to shape the tales that come my way, voices that are unlimited by convention.

* * *

Imagining Argentina, Lawrence Thornton's first and most absorbing novel, is set in Buenos Aires in the late 1970s, a time when a brutal military regime silenced dissidents and even the most innocent by kidnapping, imprisoning, torturing, and killing. Instead of merely presenting a repetitive description of such actions, Thornton ingeniously creates the narrative device of having a clairvoyant, Carlos Rueda, relate what has happened to many of the victims as their relatives come to sessions in his garden in the hope of learning some word of those who have suddenly disappeared. The story's narrator publishes an account of the atrocities in a French magazine and constantly interacts with Rueda. Rueda had run a Children's Theatre until it was closed by the authorities, and his interest in fancy and creation mingle effectively with his seemingly magical powers to see on some occasions past and present events otherwise unknown to the general public. Thornton's imaginative immersion in the material makes Rueda's revelations and insights convincing in the context. The novel possesses a strong narrative drive and a frequently poetic prose that adds a haunting aura to the stark, realistic content.

The musical flow in no way diminishes the horror involving *los desaparecidos*, those who mysteriously disappeared by the thousands. The monstrous brutality and viciousness of the generals is conveyed in all its terrifying results: sudden day and night seizures of people from their homes and even from the streets, detention camps, and the hidden killing fields. White-scarved women constantly parade in protest in the Plaza de Mayo seeking information about their lost families, although the majority of citizens go about their daily business totally unconcerned.

Naming the Spirits, the sequel to *Imagining Argentina*, begins with the mass killing of seized citizens in a remote grove in the pampas. One young teenage girl manages to escape and wanders speechless and uncertain of her identity because of shock and a gun wound. She is taken in by a couple whose own daughter has disappeared. Carlos Rueda explains what has doubtless happened to the silent and bewildered girl.

Thornton uses an especially clever technique of having the spirits from the mass grave speak in unison at various times hoping that the girl or some searching group can help locate their camouflaged graveyard. Short, set pieces—in effect inter-chapters—of monologues are also added to focus on some of the dead who explain their backgrounds and lives before they were arrested and executed.

Argentina's military dictatorship has now collapsed, and the new government has official international and local organizations actively seeking the location of the graves of the disappeared. There is a particularly intense effort underway to locate not only the hidden graves, but also to find those babies and young children whom the generals did not execute but gave to their supporters. The birth parents are now determined to find their offspring.

Thornton handles with convincing effect the spirits speaking from the grave and their deep communion with the girl who was almost killed with them. He blends realism and imaginative threads in an often elegiac, lyrical prose that adds further dimension to the horrors that have occurred as the whole world comes to realize what the rulers of Argentina have long denied.

Tales from the Blue Archives, the final section of the trilogy, focuses on Dolores Masson, who never gives up the search for her two grandsons who disappeared years before when their mother was seized by the military. Earlier in the trilogy we have witnessed the Ponce family, who once worked for one of the powerful generals, move rapidly from place to place to avoid discovery, since as a childless couple they had longed for children and had been illegally given Dolores's grandsons. Justice is eventually achieved, but by an improbable and melodramatic plot twist when the Ponces commit suicide after killing the general who had originally given them the babies.

Tales from the Blue Archives, while realistically portraying the children's disappearance and other aspects of the fascist rulers' regime, is the weakest link in the trilogy. The prose is rarely lyrical as this melancholy (blue) era is described. Further, the novel is so overfurnished with details and description that the reader is pushed into a somnolent mood.

This pronounced tendency toward excessive detail also diminishes Thornton's other novels: *Under the Gypsy Moon* and *Ghost Woman*. While evincing some flashes of style and the imaginative fancy that distinguished the first two volumes of the Argentine trilogy, these books do not retain the intensity of narrative interest. The stories are excessively padded but would perhaps be more successful as novellas. It is not that Thornton did not include potentially successfully poetic material—as with the many forced references to Garcia-Lorca in *Gypsy Moon* and the more integrated Indian myths and legends in *Ghost Woman*—but there is very little intriguing suspense.

There is also the issue of political overkill. One may understandably sympathize with Thornton's political views regarding Franco's Spain or the mistreatment suffered by Indian tribes in pioneering America, but more narrative force and presentation are needed to overcome what becomes, in Thornton's handling, overly obvious political tracts. Further, much of this material has been handled better by other writers. Think Hemingway, for example.

In *Imagining Argentina*, a decidedly memorable book, Thornton effectively blended imaginative details with stark realism while conveying a vital message. The medium and the message coalesced powerfully. When his message becomes over-labored in much of his other work, realism not only suffers but also narrative freshness and force.

—Paul A. Doyle

THUBRON, Colin (Gerald Dryden)

Nationality: British. **Born:** London, 14 June 1939. **Education:** Eton College, Berkshire, 1953–57. **Career:** Editorial assistant, Hutchinson, publishers, London, 1959–62; production editor, Macmillan, publishers, New York, 1964–65; since 1965 freelance documentary filmmaker and writer. **Awards:** PEN award, 1985; Thomas Cook award, for travel book, 1988; Hawthornden prize, 1989. **Agent:** Gillon Aitken and Stone, 29 Fernshaw Road, London SW10 0TG. **Address:** Garden Cottage, 27 St. Ann's Villas, London W11 4RT, England.

Publications

Novels

The God in the Mountain. London, Heinemann, and New York, Norton, 1977.

Emperor. London, Heinemann, 1978.

A Cruel Madness. London, Heinemann, 1984; New York, Atlantic Monthly Press, 1985.

Falling. London, Heinemann, 1989; New York, Atlantic Monthly Press, 1990.

Turning Back the Sun. London, Heinemann, 1991; New York, HarperPerennial, 1994.

Distance. London, Heinemann, 1996.

Uncollected Short Stories

"Nothing Has Changed," in *Firebird 4,* edited by R. Robertson. London, Penguin, 1985.

"The Ear," in *Foreign Exchange,* edited by Julian Evans. London, Sphere, 1985.

Plays

Radio Plays: *Emperor,* from his own novel, 1989; *A Cruel Madness,* from his own novel, 1991.

Other

Mirror to Damascus. London, Heinemann, 1967; Boston, Little Brown, 1968.

The Hills of Adonis: A Quest in Lebanon. London, Heinemann, 1968; Boston, Little Brown, 1969.

Jerusalem, photographs by Alistair Duncan. London, Heinemann, and Boston, Little Brown, 1969.

Journey into Cyprus. London, Heinemann, 1975.
Istanbul, with others. Amsterdam, Time-Life, 1978.
The Venetians, with others. Alexandria, Virginia, Time-Life, 1980.
The Ancient Mariners, with others. Alexandria, Virginia, Time-Life, 1981.
The Royal Opera House Covent Garden, photographs by Clive Boursnell. London, Hamish Hamilton, 1982.
Among the Russians. London, Heinemann, 1983; as *Where the Nights Are Longest: Travels by Car Through Western Russia.* New York, Random House, 1984.
Behind the Wall: A Journey Through China. London, Heinemann, 1987; New York, Atlantic Monthly Press, 1988.
The Silk Road China: Beyond the Celestial Kingdom. London, Pyramid, 1989.
The Lost Heart of Asia. London, Heinemann, and New York, HarperCollins, 1994.
In Siberia. New York, HarperCollins, 1999.

*

Colin Thubron comments:

My work as a novelist arises less from a fascination with plot or even character, than with the exploration of areas of experience which are distressing or (to me) unresolved. Hence the novels revolve around loss of religious faith, pain of love, enigma of memory; the gulf between ideal and reality.

* * *

Colin Thubron is well known as a travel writer but enjoys a growing reputation as a novelist. Thubron himself has stressed the distinction between his travel books, which focus away from himself on exterior landscapes, and the novels, which explore the strange interior landscape of the self. However, the novels are also intense love stories mainly ending in death. In three of them, the male protagonist kills the woman he loves most, though in widely differing circumstances. Part of the movement of the second novel, *Emperor* (it is set on a journey) is the Empress Fausta's realization that her husband will kill her and we are told in a postscript that this eventually happens. In *A Cruel Madness,* the man kills literally to touch his lover's heart, and *Falling* meditates about the mercy killing of a paralysed trapeze artist, Clara, by her lover, Mark.

Thubron claims retarded adolescence for his passive male heroes. The most deranged of the three, Daniel of *A Cruel Madness,* says he gives ''a plausible imitation of masculinity,'' and even Constantine, the *Emperor,* conquers while feeling unable to control his wife, his emotions, and his religion. This so called ''immaturity'' is Thubron's Romanticism, predominant in both his fiction and travel writing—a quest for something he says he knows intellectually is not there.

In the novels, the quest is contained within a love affair, pursuing a woman who tends to be idealized and who has an inaccessible part: a region the male hero cannot enter. The resulting frustration is most evidently dangerous in *A Cruel Madness,* set in a mental hospital. We become increasingly aware of the narrator's fantasy world, blamed on the shadowy Sophia, who closed herself to him. The same motif occurs in a simpler form in *The God in the Mountain:* Julian missed the early passionate surrender of Ekaterina because he was too immature to give himself to their relationship. Returning after many years, he finds her unhappily married, with that part of her closed to him, and unable to give herself fully now that he is ready. Fausta, in *Emperor,* is remote and cannot love her husband, perhaps through damage in childhood. A profound and continuing dependence is demonstrated between them, even though she realizes it will end in her death. *Falling* is a study in loving two women, and Mark the narrator finds parts of both unreachable. He comes to need most the independent Clara, who is culturally furthest from him (in the circus) and who chooses to leave him (in death): ''She acknowledged a human separateness which I never deeply accepted.''

Thubron's novels exhibit a tension between an intellectual unbeliever and a romantic quest for perfect fulfillment in love or in God. This duality influences the novel's structure as the plots increase the tension to a moment of tragic action (Julian goes to the mountain, Clara falls, Daniel strikes, Constantine has a vision) and then a release at the end, usually in death, where Romantic and ''realist'' are resolved. Thubron experiments with narrative forms, notably in *Emperor* with multiple narration from the journals, diaries, and letters of the major characters. Some accounts are omitted, ostensibly ''lost,'' ''damaged by rain'' etc., so what we have is an artful selection by the author disguised as historical chance.

This carefully arranged yet apparently wandering text is reinterpreted in *A Cruel Madness* and *Falling.* The former is narrated by a wandering mind but the novel is effectively organised to release significant information to the reader. *Falling* is similar, except that Mark is not mad but remembering in prison, and there is also the governing metaphor of the Fall. Clara, the swallow, falls literally, and disastrously because she won't use a safety net. Katherine makes a stained glass window of the Fall from heaven and all three fall in love, unsafely. *Turning Back the Sun* may offer hope in the romantic quest in sexual terms if not in the encounter with other cultures. Set in an unnamed colonial country, Rayner, a doctor, is exiled to a frontier town where ''savages'' roam, dangerous but also vulnerable. Romantically longing for his childhood home, ''the Capital,'' he loves Zoe, another of Thubron's heroines desired for their separateness, their intense selves. Rayner, unusually, avoids tragedy when he treats the demonized savages but cannot cure a mysterious skin disease blackening the white colonists. After repression and torture, a massacre of savages is averted when Rayner's army patrol witness their religious attempt to ''turn back the sun'' to restore an Eden before sin and death. Rayner is able to stay with Zoe but the novel's colonial themes are tentatively mapped rather than thoroughly explored. Yet this novel is characteristic of Thubron's work in its longing for intensity, beyond the well-trodden margins of safety.

—S.A. Rowland

TINDALL, Gillian (Elizabeth)

Nationality: British. **Born:** London, 4 May 1938. **Education:** Lady Margaret Hall, Oxford, B.A. (honours) in English, M.A. 1959. **Family:** Married Richard G. Lansdown in 1963; one son. **Career:** Freelance journalist since 1960. **Awards:** Mary Elgin prize, 1970; Maugham award, 1972. **Agent:** Curtis Brown, 28–29 Haymarket, London SW1Y 4SP, England.

PUBLICATIONS

Novels

No Name in the Street. London, Cassell, 1959; as *When We Had Other Names,* New York, Morrow, 1960.
The Water and the Sound. London, Cassell, 1961; New York, Morrow, 1962.
The Edge of the Paper. London, Cassell, 1963.
The Youngest. London, Secker and Warburg, 1967; New York, Walker, 1968.
Someone Else. London, Hodder and Stoughton, and New York, Walker, 1969.
Fly Away Home. London, Hodder and Stoughton, and New York, Walker, 1971.
The Traveller and His Child. London, Hodder and Stoughton, 1975.
The Intruder. London, Hodder and Stoughton, 1979.
Looking Forward. London, Hodder and Stoughton, 1983; New York, Arbor House, 1985.
To the City. London, Hutchinson, 1987.
Give Them All My Love. London, Hutchinson, 1989.
Spirit Weddings. London, Hutchinson, 1992.

Short Stories

Dances of Death: Short Stories on a Theme. London, Hodder and Stoughton, and New York, Walker, 1973.
The China Egg and Other Stories. London, Hodder and Stoughton, 1981.
Journey of a Lifetime and Other Stories. London, Hutchinson, 1990.

Play

Radio Play: *A Little Touch of Death,* 1985.

Other

A Handbook on Witches. London, Barker, 1965; New York, Atheneum, 1966.
The Born: Exile: George Gissing. London, Temple Smith, and New York, Harcourt Brace, 1974.
The Fields Beneath: The History of One London Village. London, Temple Smith, 1977.
City of Gold: A Biography of Bombay. London, Temple Smith, 1982; New York, Penguin, 1992.
Rosamond Lehmann: An Appreciation. London, Chatto and Windus, 1985.
Countries of the Mind: The Meaning of Place to Writers. London, Hogarth Press, 1991.
Célestine: Voices from a French Village. London, Sinclair Stevenson, 1995.
The Journey of Martin Nadaud: A Life and Turbulent Times. London, Chatto & Windus, 1999.

* * *

Gillian Tindall's first novel, *No Name in the Street,* was published soon after she graduated from Oxford, and its heroine, Jane, is 19 years old. However, it was not just another autobiographical first novel about teenagers, jazz, and ennui. Though concerned with bohemian life on the Left Bank in Paris, it is written in a lucid and formal prose, and the novel is straightforward, if unexpected in its movement and denouement.

Jane is a half-French visitor from England who falls in love with Vincent Lebert, a painter much older than herself. She lives happily with him till she discovers that Vincent is having a homosexual affair with an English boy, and finds herself pregnant. Up to this point, the novel is merely pleasant, chiefly because of its somewhat naive, but innocent and thorough, romanticism; from this point on, it develops a dramatic power which Tindall handles with striking maturity and dexterity. The contrast between the everyday materials she chooses to use, and the depth of the uses to which she puts them, marks all of Tindall's most successful work.

Her second novel, *The Water and the Sound,* is also about a young girl, Nadia, and about Bohemian life in Paris. Nadia hopes to find out the truth about her parents, both of whom died young. She has been told that her father was a poetic genius, wild in his private life; and that her mother had misguidedly attempted to save him from himself, having loved him so much that she had committed suicide the day after he died. Nadia interviews every person she can find who had known her parents: friends, enemies, literary critics, servants, doctors, gossips, all. Tindall's sketches of these people are memorable, and her allusive descriptions bring the atmosphere of Paris, with its night clubs and trendies, to vivid life. There is nothing notable about the story itself: it is interesting because of Tindall's delineation of her characters, her compassionate insight into their psychology. She masters her wealth of material by the sheer quality of her writing, welding together the similar but historically separate worlds of Nadia and her parents with unhurried aplomb.

The Youngest, too, is a kind of psychological detective story of the soul. Elizabeth, intelligent, sensitive, educated, articulate, gives birth to a deformed baby, whom she smothers. Tindall's novel explores the question of what sort of woman Elizabeth is. Increasingly disturbed, Elizabeth undergoes a hard journey of self-discovery, realizing that her response to her deformed baby has typified her response to life as a whole: she has consistently rejected her responsibility towards others in her absorption with herself and her towering effort to become "independent," and she has, without earlier realizing it or putting it in these terms, actually sacrificed her mother, sister, and husband to her own views and desires. Written in the mid-1960s, this implicit condemnation of the attitudes of the "me-generation" was highly unusual in the fiction of the time, and remains unusual in contemporary fiction. Possibly for this reason, the virtues of this novel were not as widely appreciated as they might have been. Tindall has always been keen to use symbolism, but it had not been wholly integrated into her earlier novels; here, however, the deformed baby provides a powerful symbol of Elizabeth herself, with her own character and actions triggering her self-discovery. The book was variously received; some people perceived it as a complex and insightful work, her best book so far; others thought of it as "intelligent but limited," as failing to subjugate a social problem to the art of fiction, and as a fictionalised documentary rather than a novel.

In *Fly Away Home* Antonia is a fairly sensitive, but not particularly intelligent woman nearing 30 and going through an emotional crisis. She is married to Marc, a well-to-do and thoroughly assimilated Parisian Jew; her two daughters are growing up and needing her less than they did. We share Antonia's journey of self-discovery through the diary she keeps from 1966 to 1968. This diary is one of Tindall's best achievements, revealing the pattern of Antonia's life with something of the surprising-but-inevitable quality of reality. Events that are outwardly dramatic (deaths, births, violent quarrels) rub shoulders with more internal, emotional dramas "which prepare themselves for years and then are abruptly revealed." Antonia is excited by the Israeli victories, and she cannot understand why Marc remains unelated, putting it down to his Jewish fear of involvement. However, when students take over the Sorbonne, Marc's youthful revolutionary romanticism is stirred and he does become enthusiastically involved; Antonia, on the other hand, finds herself unmoved by the excitement of the times, perceiving the events as obscure and senseless. Such moments come rarely in fiction, moments in which people who think they know each other discover, by their unexpected reactions to events, how little they know each other in reality. Such moments occur repeatedly in this novel—for example, in the different way that people regard Marc's brother Jean-Luc after his accidental death in Israel; or in Antonia's deepening understanding of her mother whom she had earlier regarded as a typical do-gooder, always rushing after the latest thing which might be considered progressive, without her activities actually making much positive impact; or in the change in Marc's attitude to his parents, from dutiful politeness to anger when they condemn the students as gangsters or, worse, as anarchists. Like all of Tindall's best novels, this is moving and tender in its portrayal of human relationships, exquisitely written, and packed with insights. These qualities are even more in evidence in the short stories in *Dances of Death: Short Stories on a Theme* and *The China Egg and Other Stories.*

The Traveller and His Child concerns the unusual theme of the paternal instinct. Robert, divorced by his appalling American wife for his inability to adjust to her orgasmic sexuality, finds that he misses his son Robbie terribly; so much, in fact, that he decides to kidnap another boy, the seven-year-old son of old friends. This is apparently done on impulse, though Tindall shows how his character and situation have been leading up to this moment through the years of his miserable childhood and unfortunate marriage. Robert's longing for his own son, now in America, and the way in which that unexpressed love and longing are focused on the boy, Pip, are convincingly narrated. In showing us Robert's heart, Tindall is showing us too the heart of the woman who steals someone else's baby from a pram. Robert is selfish as much as he is self-deceived but, on a desperate journey through France with the boy, he experiences fear and shame, and slowly gains insight. He realizes that he has caused overwhelming anguish, and that he has caused this anguish to people who have trusted him and for whom he cares. He sees that his action is unforgivable. Yet, miraculously, he is forgiven, by the child, by his friends, and—it is hinted—by himself.

In *Looking Forward* Tindall's protagonist is a childless gynaecologist concerned with finding ways of overcoming infertility. The book typifies the qualities of Tindall's less successful novels. The infertility is emblematic of the book itself: good intentions struggle against creative deficiency. Earnest, professional, and well researched, it lacks the germ of imaginative vitality which might be warmed to life by Tindall's brooding. This is partly due to an over-concern with formal cleverness. The characters—families and friends whose careers are charted through the first seven decades of this century—are relatively inert, but arranged in tableaux characteristic of the various periods in which the narrative is set. *To the City,* the tale of a young man saved from the Holocaust as a boy and now returning to Vienna after many years, suffers many of the weaknesses of its predecessor. Much stronger is *Give Them All My Love,* which uses flashbacks far more effectively than did *To the City.* The protagonist has murdered the man who killed his daughter, and now he sits in jail, remembering the events that got him there. It is a powerful and cinematic portrayal on Tindall's part.

What really interests Tindall and brings her characters to life are the emotional cores of people. Where she is content to let her heart lead her, Tindall's work comes alive; where she allows her considerable intellectual gifts too much play, she has not yet shown that she can embody her strong and subtle moral sense to produce impressive fictional work. This is not to deride her intellectual gifts, which are best evidenced by her non-fictional books. In all her books she has a highly accomplished style, and her fictional examination of current shibboleths is cool and penetrating. Unpretentious and unusual, she has an impeccable sense of the nuances of life.

—Prabhu S. Guptara, updated by Judson Knight

TINNISWOOD, Peter

Nationality: British. **Born:** Liverpool, 21 December 1936. **Education:** Sale County Grammar School, 1947–54; University of Manchester, 1954–57, B.A. 1957. **Family:** Married 1) in 1966, three children; 2) Liz Goulding, 1980. **Career:** Insurance clerk, Vienna, 1957; journalist, *Sheffield Star,* 1958–63, Thomson newspapers, London, 1964–65, *Cardiff Western Mail,* 1966–69, and *Liverpool Echo,* 1967. **Awards:** Authors Club award, 1969; Winifred Holtby prize, 1974; Welsh Arts Council bursary, 1974, and prize, 1975; Sony Radio award, 1988, for play; Writers' Guild Best Radio Comedy of the Year, 1991. Fellow, Royal Society of Literature, 1974. **Agent:** Jonathan Clowes Ltd., Iron Bridge House, Bridge Approach, London NW1 8BD, England.

Publications

Novels

A Touch of Daniel. London, Hodder and Stoughton, and New York, Doubleday, 1969.
Mog. London, Hodder and Stoughton, 1970.
I Didn't Know You Cared. London, Hodder and Stoughton, 1973.
Except You're a Bird. London, Hodder and Stoughton, 1974.
The Stirk of Stirk. London, Macmillan, 1974.
Shemerelda. London, Hodder and Stoughton, 1981.
The Home Front (novelization of TV series). London, Granada, 1982.
The Brigadier Down Under. London, Macmillan, 1983.
The Brigadier in Season. London, Macmillan, 1984.
The Brigadier's Brief Lives. London, Pan, 1984.
Call It a Canary. London, Macmillan, 1985.
The Brigadier's Tour. London, Pan, 1985.
Uncle Mort's North Country. London, Pavilion-Joseph, 1986.
Hayballs. London, Hutchinson, 1989.
Uncle Mort's South Country. London, Arrow, 1990.
Winston. London, Hutchinson, 1991.

Short Stories

Collected Tales from a Long Room. London, Hutchinson, 1982.
Tales from a Long Room. London, Arrow, 1981.
More Tales from a Long Room. London, Arrow, 1982.
Tales from Witney Scrotum. London, Pavilion-Joseph, 1987.

Uncollected Short Story

"Summer, New York, 1978—That's All," in *The After Midnight Ghost Book,* edited by James Hale. London, Hutchinson, 1980; New York, Watts, 1981.

Plays

The Investiture (produced Bristol, 1971).
Wilfred (produced London, 1979).
The Day the War Broke Out (produced London, 1981).
You Should See Us Now (produced Scarborough, 1981; London, 1983). London, French, 1983.
Steafel Variations (songs and sketches), with Keith Waterhouse and Dick Vosburgh (produced London, 1982).
At the End of the Day (produced Scarborough, 1984).
The Village Fete (broadcast 1987; produced Scarborough, 1991); New York, S. French, 1995.
Napoli Milionaria, adaptation of the play by Eduardo De Filippo (produced London, 1991).

Radio Plays and Features: *Hardluck Hall* series, with David Nobbs, 1964; *Sam's Wedding,* 1973; *The Bargeman's Comfort,* 1977; *A Touch of Daniel,* from his own novel, 1977; *The Umpire's Thoughts Regarding a Certain Murder,* 1979; *Jake and Myself,* 1979; *The Siege,* 1979; *A Gifted Child,* 1980; *Home Again* series, 1980; *An Occasional Day,* 1981; *Crossing the Frontier,* 1985; *The Village Fete,* 1987; *M.C.C.: The Fully Harmonious and Totally Unauthorised History,* 1987; *Winston* series, 1989–91; *A Small Union,* 1989; *Call It a Canary,* 1989; *The Sitters,* 1990; *I Always Take Long Walks,* 1991; *Two into Two,* 1992; *The Governor's Consory,* 1993; *Tales from the Brigadoon,* 1993; *Uncle Mot's Celtic Fringe,* 1994.

Television Plays and Features: scripts for *That Was the Week That Was* and *Not So Much a Programme* series, with David Nobbs; *Lance at Large* series, with David Nobbs, 1964; *The Signal Box of Grandpa Hudson,* with David Nobbs, 1966; *Never Say Die* series, 1970; *The Rule Book,* 1971; *The Diaries of Stoker Leishman,* 1972; *I Didn't Know You Cared,* 4 series, 1975–79; *Tales from a Long Room* series, 1980; *More Tales from a Long Room* series, 1982; *A Gifted Adult* and *At the Grammar* (*The Home Front* series), 1983; *South of the Border,* 1985; *Tinniswood's North Country,* 1987; *Uncle Mort's North Country* series, 1987–88; *Can You Hear Me, Mother?,* 1988; *Tinniswood Country,* 1989.

*

Critical Studies: In *New Review* (London), November 1974.

Peter Tinniswood comments:

I write very short sentences.

And very short paragraphs.

I try to make people laugh. I am a very serious writer, who has a gloomily optimistic outlook on life.

My books about the Brandon family contain all the above qualities.

* * *

Peter Tinniswood is a journalist, a television-script writer, and the author of a large number of popular novels and short stories. He is predominantly a highly skilled craftsman and his style reflects both his professional background and his own self-confessed northern English temperament. His works tend to be set in the north of England, thematically dependent on the northern ethos, informed by the happy morbidity of the stock comic conventions of the north, and filled with stock northern characters. Tinniswood is a great creator of the memorable character.

Many of Tinniswood's novels are continuations of the same characters. The Brigadier is the acerbic narrator of *Collected Tales from a Long Room, Tales from Witney Scrotum,* and all of those works bearing his name. He leaps from the pages bristling with the kind of prejudice which can only stem from a military background coupled with the thoroughly English belief that the game of cricket is the only proper foundation for all social, sexual, moral, and intellectual judgments. Since the ultimate test for such a mind lies not with the conquering of the Antarctic, with war, with art, nor yet with Margaret Thatcher's Britain, but takes place between Lancashire and Yorkshire every summer, a comic perspective is created for what might otherwise be considered serious. Similarly, in Tinniswood's work, the more working-class prejudices of the Brandon family form a comic filter through which the changing face of the north of England in recent decades can be viewed.

A Touch of Daniel, I Didn't Know You Cared and *Except You're a Bird,* all novels which feature the Brandon family, are potentially the most seriously comic of Tinniswood's novels and perhaps the most intrinsically northern. Les and Annie, Uncle Mort, who is Annie's brother, Carter, Les and Annie's son, and Pat, Carter's girlfriend and later his wife are all stock northern characters. The women feed the men with Yorkshire puddings, treacle tart, and porridge with brown sugar. They keep their blood clear with sulfur tablets, their bowels free with Gregory powder, their complexions clear with bile beans, and colds at bay with daily doses of halibut oil, wheat germ oil, cod-liver oil, and Virol. The men wait for the women to serve their food and grumble. "Isn't it rum the way women think catering's the way to a man's heart?" says Uncle Mort. "I don't like these onions" says Les, "They make me sweat." Carter, of the second generation, flirts with the idea of running away and freedom, as he flirts with the idea of sexuality with the voluptuous Linda Preston, but ultimately he wants neither: "I don't want to run away. I want to stay here. I want things to be simple and clear-cut like what they used to be. I want it to be like when I was a nipper. I didn't have to make no decisions then." The pathetic exploration of entrapment and futility is eschewed by Tinniswood in favor of the comic. Carter retreats into characteristically passive disobedience before his wife and his moments of introspection and self-knowledge are confined to conversations with Daniel, his much younger cousin who dies of pneumonia when Carter takes him out in the rain. Pat, who hopes by carefully rationing her sexuality to achieve her dream of a new house, a "young executive" lifestyle, and the attention she craves, is also disappointed. Even her pregnancy is offset by other events; a silver wedding, her mother's courtship, Uncle Mort and Olive Furnival, or Carter's football team. "It's not fair" says Pat, "Well what about me and baby? Why can't we have the field clear for ourselves? Why can't we have all the limelight?" The Brandons are, as they would say in the north, set in their ways.

The blighted lives of the Brandon family are played out against the slow erosion of a way of life. This is epitomized in the novels by the new housing estate on which Carter and Pat live, and by Uncle Mort's trenchant refusal to sell off his allotment to developers. The emphasis is placed not on the intrinsic seriousness of stunted lives and stunted relationships, but on imaginative verbal flights informed by the cheerful misery of stock northern humor. "Life's not worth living is it?" reflects Les. "No" agrees Uncle Mort, "I wish there were summat else you could do with it." Tinniswood is at his best when tossing words and logic about without reference to the actual living of life. In this sense his novels are not realistic, but rather full blown caricatures of northern life. It is a sense of humor not always easily exported however, and drove one New York Times book reviewer to declare that Tinniswood's work should be read when "ready for a good chuckle at the expense of old age, deformity, sickness and death...." Death is as sudden, frequent, and funny in Tinniswood's work, as sex is serious, infrequent and if possible to be avoided altogether.

The treatment of elementals in Tinniswood's work is entirely blasé. The form and style of his work allows their discussion to take place with all of the intensity normally accorded to the need for a nice cup of tea. When Uncle Mort says that Olive Furnival has been fatally injured falling off a bus, as was his wife, he is driven to consider that he "never did have much luck with public transport," "'Is your bust tender?' asks Mrs. Partington of the pregnant Pat. 'Yes' she replies. 'Well don't let Carter play with it.'" It is a style which will not ultimately cope with seriousness, not even that demanded by the good parody and satire. Thus *Shemerelda,* a satire on beautiful and spoilt American womanhood, fails insofar as it is unable to emulate and parody the form of the brief dialogue that has been perfected by those working in the tradition of Twain and Hemingway. *The Stirk of Stirk,* an attempt to parody the epic fable loses humor in the telling of a straight narrative, while the characters remain stereotypical and superficial. When seriousness is attempted in the Brandon novels, usually via Carter's moments of introspection, it allows the misogyny latent in stock northern humor, and therefore in most of Tinniswood's writing, to break through and reveal its unfortunate aspect. For the most part however the accent remains strictly on the comic. It is no accident that the Brandon household, when transferred to the timeless medium of the television situation comedy where neither change nor resolution are to be expected, have become something of a television classic. It is this medium which allows Tinniswood to excel.

—Jan Pilditch

TLALI, Miriam (Masoli)

Nationality: South African. **Born:** Doornfontein, Transvaal. **Education:** University of the Witwatersrand, Johannesburg. **Career:** Co-founder, *Staffrider* magazine; board member, Skotaville Press. **Address:** c/o Pandora Press, 77–85 Fulham Palace Road, London W6 8JB, England.

Publications

Novels

Muriel at Metropolitan. Johannesburg, Ravan Press, 1975; London, Longman, 1979.

Amandla. Johannesburg, Ravan Press, 1980.

Short Stories

Mihloti. Johannesburg, Skotaville, 1984.

Footprints in the Quag: Stories and Dialogues from Soweto. Cape Town, Philip, 1989; as *Soweto Stories,* London, Pandora Press, 1989.

* * *

Miriam Tlali was brought up in Sophiatown, that legendary community within Johannesburg which was razed because it was the sole area where Africans were permitted to take permanent title to land. She successfully completed high school and entered Witwatersrand University. A series of practical difficulties forced her to seek employment as a book-keeper/typist. This background makes it the more remarkable that she is one of the few black South African women who have been able to express their experiences and concerns in print. Her first publication, *Muriel at the Metropolitan,* seems largely autobiographical, the events deriving predominantly from her office experience. In spite of being so personal this is not pure autobiography, the events are embellished with considerable skill and the sequence of incidents is controlled by a deliberate, artistic structuring.

Metropolitan Radio is a shop that provides radios and furniture to Africans on tempting but greedy hire-purchase terms. The staff becomes a microcosm of the society and the characters are designed to become representative of the racial elements which make up this complex country. The owner, Mr. Bloch, is a Jew who displays all the traditional expectations of sharp dealing to make a barely legal extra profit. There are two white female cashiers; an overtly racist Afrikaaner Mrs. Stein and an English-speaking liberal Mrs. Kuhn, whose racism is more subtle but ultimately similar. Then there are the "coloured" mechanics, and below them, a variety of African drivers and attendants. They work together not very harmoniously, and from time to time, all express antagonistic inter-racial prejudice.

If one took this work too seriously, the people would become mere symbols. In particular the underlying anti-Semitism would be cruelly evident. Mr. Bloch would become a modern Shylock, always eager to make a rand/ducat at the expense of the ignorant and unfortunate Africans. But the entire work is based upon an attitude of extraordinary tolerance and amiability. Muriel enjoys her work. She likes her involvement with the business. Generally she even likes Mr. Bloch. Since she is employed as an office worker, a status usually reserved for Whites, and manages her duties every bit as efficiently as they do, she is inevitably treated disrespectfully and often blamed for errors the White staff have made. She is used and abused; and given the task, beneath White dignity, of coping with a series of very legitimate African complaints. Sometimes she helps, by explaining the dangerous results of compound interest and is accused of disloyalty to the company. Sometimes she finds herself unavoidably becoming a tool of Mr. Bloch's calculated exploitation. The surprising thing about this book is its tone. It is occasionally defiant as Muriel stands up to false accusations with articulate denials. But there is a strange tolerance and humor, a genuine acceptance that sees the racist extremes as absurd as they are threatening. She can laugh at the comic illiteracy of the African clients' letters without unkindness. She beautifully rises above the political and racial status that has been imposed on her by saying, ''I am just myself, just a person.'' It is this tolerant vein which sustains this work.

Eventually Miriam is offered the chance of a much better job. Government inspectors come and determine that the struggling immigrant employer cannot afford to build an ''African woman'' toilet. It is illegal for Muriel to share either African male or White women's facilities, therefore she cannot be employed. Although Muriel is denied her promotion, the explanation exposes the madness of the divisions imposed upon South African society. They are as ludicrous as wicked. Indicatively this book itself was immediately and even more absurdly ''banned'' by the government censors.

After *Muriel at Metropolitan* Tlali wrote a collection of short stories, *Mihloti,* some plays and essays. Her major work is a lengthy novel, *Amandla.* The title is chanted at public demonstrations and means power. This novel is very different from *Muriel* and displays no tolerance, rather, it takes a strongly committed and activist posture. The events take place in 1976 and such actual plot as there is, consists of a review of the circumstances of the Soweto rebellion against the imposition of Afrikaans in the African schools—the children's uprising. There is a single coherent aspect, violence imposed by the police, by troops, and by Africans against each other. Blood and shootings are a constant backdrop. There are various minimal sub-plots; a youthful love affair between the student leader Pholoso and his girlfriend Felleng which is aborted by his being driven to political activism by governmental persecution. There is an adulterous love relationship between the wife of the police sergeant and his subordinate. There is loving old Gramsy who contemplates the horrendous present from the warm sentiment of the past. There are other characters, too numerous to recall individually, who play their cameo roles but are forgotten against the main sweep of the story, which is political challenge against the existing regime. Many of such small incidents are portrayed with conviction. The language is colloquial and realistic, their concerns, though briefly detailed, connect to the local events at the true level of human consequence, the personal conflicts and miseries that are suffered. Unhappily these painful and tender circumstances are not the focal point of this novel in which the prime purpose is to make bitter political complaint about the appalling injustice of the South African system. In itself, this intention is legitimate enough. Hardly anyone would offer a defense of apartheid. But the writer of fiction must create a conviction in the reader by inventing realistic individuals who, by their acts, expose the social issues, and engage our imaginative sympathies. Richard Rive successfully acheived this with *Emergency.* Here Tlali prefers argument. Many will approve of her denunciations of this regime but the rhetoric in which it is conducted is full of improbably pompous speech and palpable jargon. The young students enforcing the trade boycott speak with an extreme formality before they pour the unacceptably purchased quarts of paint on the head of an unhappy man who sought only to renovate the walls of his house, and so politely explain why they must burn the new clothes an affectionate mother has bought for her children. One long section consists of nothing more than a debate between two characters, which is meant to educate the reader by making reference to the entire history of South African oppressive legislation detailing all the parliamentary enactments with their dates. Perhaps this has to be told. Many political scientists have expressed it more academically, but the inventor of fiction should give it life. Without that humanity the novel is stultified unless its admirers determine that its contents are of such supervening importance that the normal practices of fiction no longer apply. This is less novel than diatribe. At the same time it includes many enticing elements that show that Tlali is still a uniquely sensitive observer of the intolerably grotesque society in which she lives. When free from her perceived obligation to convince through denunciation and the political clichés which voice that stance, she still has all the qualities which will allow her to express with loving accuracy the human feelings of her people.

—John Povey

TÓIBÍN, Colm

Nationality: Irish. **Born:** Ireland, 1955. **Career:** Journalist and columnist for the *Dublin Sunday Independent,* beginning in 1985; essayist for *Esquire* (London), and *London Review of Books.* **Awards:** *Irish Times*—Aer Lingus International Fiction Prize, 1991; Encore Prize for best second novel published in Britain, 1992; E. M. Forster Award (American Academy of Arts and Letters), 1995. **Agent:** c/o Publicity Director, Penguin Books, 375 Hudson Street, New York, New York 10014. **Address:** 12 Upper Pembroke Street, Dublin 2, Ireland.

Publications

Novels

The South. London, Serpent's Tail, 1990; New York, Viking, 1991.

The Heather Blazing. London, Pan Books, 1992; New York, Viking, 1993.

The Story of the Night. London, Picador, 1996; New York, Henry Holt, 1997.

Finbar's Hotel (serial novel, with others), devised and edited by Dermot Bolger. London, Picador, 1997; San Diego, Harcourt Brace, 1999.

The Blackwater Lightship. London, Picador, 1999; New York, Scribner, 2000.

Other

Walking along the Border. London, Macdonald, 1987; as *Bad Blood: A Walk along the Irish Border.* London, Vintage, 1994.

Martyrs and Metaphors. Dublin, Raven Arts Press, 1987.

Homage to Barcelona. New York, Simon & Schuster, 1990; with a new introduction by the author, New York, Penguin, 1992.

The Trial of the Generals: Selected Journalism, 1980–1990. Dublin, Raven Arts Press, 1990.

Dubliners (travelogue), photographs by Tony O'Shea. London, Macdonald, 1990.

The Sign of the Cross: Travels in Catholic Europe. New York, Pantheon, 1994.

The Irish Famine. London, Profile Books, 1999.

The Modern Library: The Two Hundred Best Novels in English Since 1950 (with Carmen Callil). London, Picador, 1999.

Editor, *Seeing Is Believing: Moving Statues in Ireland.* Mountrath, Ireland, Pilgrim Press, 1985.

Editor, *Soho Square 6: New Writing from Ireland.* London, Bloomsbury, 1993; published as *New Writing from Ireland.* Winchester, Massachusetts, Faber & Faber, 1994.

Editor, *The Kilfenora Teaboy: A Study of Paul Durcan.* Dublin, New Island Books, 1996.

Editor, *The Penguin Book of Irish Fiction.* New York, Viking, 2000.

* * *

Colm Tóibín's four novels pose the issues of tone and style. If we call it the ''plain style,'' we will need to distinguish it from the ironic deadpan of Joyce's *Dubliners* or the deadbeat of Beckett's prose, to name two important antecedents for any Irish writer. But it is also different from the bravados of Gertrude Stein or Ernest Hemingway. We will find Tóibín's prose true to his characters rather than himself.

Not since Iris Murdoch's call in 1959 (''The Sublime and the Beautiful Revisited'') for novelists to write about characters unlike themselves have we seen so thorough a forgetting of authorial personhood in the novel. The central character of *The South* is Katherine Proctor, who leaves husband, child, and ancestral big house behind. While the ostensible breaking point for her is her husband's insistence that a poor neighbor be sued for damages against her wishes, we learn that her mother also left her husband, her child, and this house behind after they were burnt out in the troubles by their Catholic neighbors. We find out later how alien Katherine felt in her home, surrounded by a hostile class and culture. Katherine's flight to Barcelona is supported by her mother.

Katherine is a painter. She begins a relationship with another painter who has suffered incarceration and torture for his revolutionary activities during the Spanish Civil War. They begin a different kind of life for themselves, centered on their work. They leave Barcelona for an isolated mountain village and have a daughter, but Miguel cannot forget the war, and Katherine finds that they are occupying a battlefield in Miguel's past. When he retrieves a fellow anarchist to recuperate with them, it brings the police down on them, upsetting Miguel's own tenuous stability. In one of the most terrible scenes in the novel, Miguel (who does not drive) takes their daughter with him in the jeep, and has an accident fatal to them both.

But Katherine's past has not been expunged either. Early in their relationship, Miguel and Katherine meet an Irish painter, Michael Graves, who is from Katherine's town. His continued friendship keeps her from losing her Irish identity in Spain, and they return to Ireland together after Miguel dies. Katherine makes an elaborate peace with her son, now married. She resumes her painting and forges a quiet companionship with Graves, but these accommodations are not presented as equal to what she has lost.

The Heather Blazing opens onto Eamon Redmond, a High Court judge who will drive off to his holiday cottage with his wife, Carmen, after delivering a judgement in favor of a hospital discharging a handicapped child into the care of its impoverished parents. The novel recovers the childhood that brought him to such a distant relation to the pain of others, to his wife and children.

Chapters alternate (roughly) between Eamon's present and his past, when he grew up in Enniscorthy. His father, a schoolteacher, raised him alone. His father was a respected teacher and local historian. When he has a stroke and goes into the hospital, Eamon cannot remain at home—he must live with relatives and go to a trade school. When his father is able to return, Eamon suffers with his father's slurred speech and diminished capacity. He follows his father's political affiliation to Fianna Fáil, and meets his future wife while canvassing. His rise in the courts is not hampered by his politics.

Carmen tries to reach him, to make him talk to her, to keep less to himself. Unexpectedly, she has a stroke; he tends to her but later, she dies. Eamon must then deal with his grief over her passing. He gradually comes closer to his children and their families through his grandson. In a beautifully understated final episode, he becomes a companion to the boy by making him a basin of seawater to play in. At the end, they go to the shore to play in the sea, repeating a custom that Eamon shared with his father.

The Story of the Night is set in Argentina during the military dictatorship of the late 1970s and early 1980s. Richard Garay's irreconcilably British mother taught him English and associated herself with the British enclave in Buenos Aires. When his father dies, their diminished income forces them to vacate their apartment for the grudging charity of Argentinean relatives she has scorned. They can return only after his mother has drawn on the charity of the resident British for a job for herself and help with Richard's tuition.

Richard feels distant from his parents, his relatives, his schoolfellows, and his fellow English teachers at the school, but he is in love with Jorge Canetto, a fellow university student who asked him to teach him English. Richard and Jorge go for a holiday in Spain together, paid for by the Canettos, but Jorge is emphatically heterosexual in his company. As Argentina destabilizes during the Malvinas debacle, Jorge's father envisions himself as the next president. To access American support, he secures an invitation for Richard to a party given by Donald and Susan Ford, two CIA operatives. Richard's bilingualism proves invaluable to the Fords, and he is woven into the profiteering of denationalizing the oil industry as a consultant.

As Richard's world widens beyond his parents' flat and their furniture, which he has kept, he meets Pablo, Jorge's brother returned from San Francisco. Eventually Pablo agrees to move into a modern house Richard sublets.

Although Tóibín's fictional characters speak as sparely as he writes, it is only *The Story of the Night* that is told in first-person narrative. Perhaps only the full power of his understated prose can carry what one expects or fears for Richard and Pablo. Although years are never given, Pablo's description of San Francisco recounts the initial appearance of AIDS. Pablo inexplicably leaves Richard. In despair, Richard visits in New York with an acquaintance from the oil industry who gives him sex and cocaine without complications, but Richard's apparently allergic reaction to the drugs shows how well this narrator keeps from himself and his readers how sick he is. He barely gets home on the plane. He has AIDS as well, and he encounters Pablo in the doctor's office, also being treated. The full weight of Tóibín's investment in spareness across several novels pays for a dignity of suffering at the end of the novel, in the last words Richard has for us:

> We went into the house and closed the door behind us. He asked me to turn the heating on and said that he would go to bed for a while. Maybe, if he was well enough, I said, we could go back into the city in the evening and go to a movie. Maybe, he said, maybe we'll do that. He asked me to wake him in an hour or two if he was still asleep.

The Blackwater Lightship, shortlisted for the Booker Prize, leaves behind what threatened to be standard features of Tóibín's fiction as it adds the unexpected. The second novel quietly used the same area of Ireland (Enniscorthy) as his first, but his new novel consciously names properties and families from *The Heather Blazing*. Until we see more of his work, we cannot rule out the depressing idea that he has fallen to aspirations of an oeuvre and his own literary landscape. But the work itself is very fine, a new step, a more energetic narrating and listening to several characters good at telling their stories to each other, as if he had legacied his recognizably laconic prose style to Richard Garay's terminal narrative.

In the novel Helen's father died when she was a child, and her mother's need to tend him in the hospital in Dublin forged in Helen a separateness that she cannot relinquish. She lives her life as a principal of a comprehensive school, mother of two boys, and wife without allowing her mother to see any of it.

Her world apart is breached by a visitor who tells her that her brother Declan is near death from AIDS. Declan wants to leave the hospital to go to his grandmother's house in Cush (the locale detailed in *The Heather Blazing*). The grandmother Dora, her daughter Lily, and her granddaughter Helen must deal with Declan's friends and his life in the close area of a cliff-side cottage and the unremitting last stages of Declan's illness. When he inevitably must return to the hospital for treatment, each of the women has changed enough to come closer to each other.

—William Johnsen

TRAPIDO, Barbara

Nationality: British (emigrated from South Africa, 1963; granted British citizenship, 1968). **Born:** Barbara Schuddeboom, Capetown, South Africa, 5 November 1941. **Education:** University of Natal, South Africa, B.A. 1963; University of London, diploma in education, 1967. **Family:** Married Stanley Trapido, 1963; one daughter and one son. **Career:** English teacher, Greenwich Park School, London, 1964–67, and Sunderland College of Further Education, 1967–70. Since 1970, full-time writer. **Awards:** Whitbread Special prize for fiction, 1982, for *Brother of the More Famous Jack.* **Agent:** Felicity Bryan, 2A North Prade, Oxford OX2 6PE, England.

Publications

Novels

Brother of the More Famous Jack. London, Gollancz, and New York, Viking, 1982.
Noah's Ark. London, Gollancz, 1984; and New York, Watts, 1985.
Temples of Delight. London, Michael Joseph, 1990; New York, Grove Weidenfeld, 1991.
Juggling. London, Hamish Hamilton, 1994; New York, Penguin, 1995.
The Travelling Hornplayer. London, H. Hamilton, 1998; New York, Viking, 1999.

*

Barbara Trapido comments:

Funny/warm/satirical/slightly highbrow but accessible.

* * *

Barbara Trapido was born in South Africa in 1941, the daughter of dissident academic parents. She emigrated to England in 1963 and has lived in Oxford since 1971. Her first novel won a special prize in the Whitbread Awards in 1982 and was widely praised.

All Trapido's novels feature a dominating, unconventional older man. In the first three books he causes the heroine to fall in love with him or with the freedom from convention he represents; in the last he has something like the opposite effect. *In Brother of the More Famous Jack,* Katherine's friendship with her urbane philosophy teacher, Jacob Goldman, and his family gives her, living in suburban rectitude with her mother ''at the far reaches of the Northern line,'' an entre into a world in which passions are visibly displayed and strong views are essential. Katherine falls in love with a series of unsuitable men, but the uxorious Jacob is the real hero of the novel. A shaggy Jew from the East End, he is sexy, uninhibited, and refreshingly trenchant; when Katherine eventually finds a man worthy of her, it is with the most Jacob-like of his sons.

The eponymous Noah Glazer, in *Noah's Ark,* is an American. He is as uxorious and bossy and cocksure as Jacob but with a different accent and somewhat less charm. Effortlessly, he rescues vague Ali from a dreary existence as a single parent still under the thumb of her awful ex and marries her. But such dazzling rescues bring their own problems. Compliant Ali has never gotten over her first love. As she slowly comes to terms with him, with the country of her birth, South Africa, and also her talent for painting, her marriage almost founders. Noah, like Jacob, isn't a man to relish coming second. Ali is ultimately forgiven, though Noah has been softened by an inconvenient summer spent apart from her. Forgiveness, like marital happiness, is fragile.

By the third novel we know that the typical Trapido heroine is young, demure, clever, and ripe to be rescued by someone vivid and powerful by virtue of their subversive plain-speaking. In *Temples of Delight,* it is Jem, neither male nor Jewish nor even adult but nonetheless poised, Catholic, and well-read, who first rescues Alice. She is tall, scruffy, unconventional, given to flights of fancy (to disguise her humble origins), and believes in passion. Alice adores her and uses her as a touchstone—it is passion and not materialism that makes life worth living.

In *Temples of Delight,* Trapido uses attitudes toward food as an index of class and religion. Alice's friend Flora's appalling parents are so stingy that Flora is brought up to eat lumps of gristle and wear an overcoat indoors. Alice's mother treats Flora's family to a celebration meal in a restaurant. It is an episode of high comedy: Alice's builder father chats about bricks, Flora's father gropes Alice's mother and promptly dies of an unsuspected allergy to mussels, and the incontinent old grandmother piddles on the floor.

Though *Temples of Delight* uses the conventions of a school story, it includes elements of satire, melodrama (with some elements drawn from Mozart's *Magic Flute*), and comedy. The glue that sticks it together is psychological realism. Alice is fully drawn, though other characters, apart from Joe, the dominating male (this time Catholic and Italian-American), are lightly sketched. But when Joe arrives late in the novel—literally at Jem's deathbed—Alice, like Ali and Katherine before her, is ready to be swept off her feet.

Juggling is a sequel to *Temples of Delight* (though there are some inconsistencies with dates). It is more complex, full of unexpected twists and contrivances, and the women characters are its glory. Pamina is Jem's daughter, born by cesarean section while Jem lay dying. Christina was born early in Alice's marriage to Joe. But time moves on. Alice is less impressed by Joe than hitherto. As a teenager, Christina is filled with the need to rebel—both to quell Joe and to make her way in the world without his help. Abandoning her beloved sister, she finds a black, working-class replacement in the ebullient, capable Dulce. Alice also rebels, and there is an intricate, careful patterning of joinings-together and splittings-apart, of mistaken identities and disappearances, that mirrors the patterning of a Shakespearean comedy.

An undergraduate at Cambridge, Christina develops strong views on the Comedies. She has also learned more than the basics on relations between the sexes. ''In the conflict of gender, the women win the war of words, but the men will win the battle.'' Katherine, and Alice before her, clever though they were, spent their youth without discovering as much. The book's ending, ''frozen in a moment of precarious, brilliant symmetry,'' promises much for the future.

—Anne French

TREMAIN, Rose

Nationality: British. **Born:** Rose Thomson in London, 2 August 1943. **Education:** Frances Holland School, 1949–54; Crofton Grange School, 1954–60; the Sorbonne, Paris, 1960–61, diploma in literature 1962; University of East Anglia, Norwich, 1964–67, B.A. (honors) in English 1967. **Family:** Married 1) Jon Tremain in 1971 (divorced 1978), one daughter; 2) Jonathan Dudley in 1982 (divorced 1991). **Career:** Teacher, Lynhurst House School, London, 1968–70; assistant editor, British Printing Corporation, London, 1970–72; part-time research jobs, 1972–79; creative writing fellow, University of Essex, Wivenhoe, 1979–80. Since 1980 full-time writer and part-time lecturer in creative writing, University of East Anglia. **Awards:** Dylan Thomas prize, for short story, 1984; Giles Cooper award, for radio play, 1985; Angel Literary award, 1985, 1989; *Sunday Express* Book of the Year award, 1989; James Tait Black Memorial prize, 1993; Prix Femina étranger (France), 1994. Fellow, Royal Society of Literature, 1983. **Agent:** Richard Scott Simon, 43 Doughty Street, London WC1N 2LF. **Address:** 2 High House, South Avenue, Thorpe St. Andrew, Norwich NR7 0EZ, England.

PUBLICATIONS

Novels

Sadler's Birthday. London, Macdonald, 1976; New York, St. Martin's Press, 1977.
Letter to Sister Benedicta. London, Macdonald, 1978; New York, St. Martin's Press, 1979.
The Cupboard. London, Macdonald, 1981; New York, St. Martin's Press, 1982.
The Swimming Pool Season. London, Hamish Hamilton, and New York, Summit, 1985.
Restoration. London, Hamish Hamilton, 1989; New York, Viking, 1990.
Sacred Country. London, Sinclair Stevenson, 1993; New York, Atheneum, 1994.
The Way I Found Her. London, Sinclair-Stevenson, 1997; New York, Farrar, Straus, and Giroux, 1998.
Music and Silence. New York, Farrar, Straus, and Giroux, 2000.

Short Stories

The Colonel's Daughter and Other Stories. London, Hamish Hamilton, and New York, Summit, 1984.
The Garden of the Villa Mollini and Other Stories. London, Hamish Hamilton, 1987.
Evangelista's Fan. London, Sinclair Stevenson, 1994; published as *Evangelista's Fan and Other Stories,* Thorndike, Maine, Thorndike Press, 1995.
Collected Short Stories. London, Sinclair-Stevenson, 1996.

Plays

Mother's Day (produced London, 1980).
Yoga Class (produced Liverpool, 1981).
Temporary Shelter (broadcast 1984). Published in *Best Radio Plays of 1984,* Methuen, 1985.

Radio Plays: *The Wisest Fool,* 1976; *Dark Green,* 1977; *Blossom,* 1977; *Don't Be Cruel,* 1978; *Leavings,* 1978; *Down the Hill,* 1979; *Half Time,* 1980; *Hell and McLafferty,* 1982; *Temporary Shelter,* 1984; *The Birdcage,* 1984; *Will and Lou's Boy,* 1986; *The Kite Flyer,* 1987.

Television Plays: *Halleluiah, Mary Plum,* 1978; *Findings on a Late Afternoon,* 1980; *A Room for the Winter,* 1981; *Moving on the Edge,* 1983; *Daylight Robbery,* 1986.

Other

The Fight for Freedom for Women. New York, Ballantine, 1973.
Stalin: An Illustrated Biography. New York, Ballantine, 1975.
Journey to the Volcano (for children). London, Hamish Hamilton, 1985.

*

Rose Tremain comments:

Most interesting to me is my attempt to communicate ideas through many different forms of writing; this is allied to my belief that a writer who stays working in one form only risks becoming repetitive and stale. Hence, the large output of plays for radio and the three collections of short stories and children's novels.

I have strenuously resisted categorisation as a ''woman's writer'' and the notion that women should address themselves only to women's problems, as this strikes me as limiting and inhibiting, a kind of literary sexism in itself.

Themes that recur in my work are: dispossession, the effect of religious and exclusive ''clubs'' of all kinds on the individual's compassion, class antagonisms, solitariness, sexual bereavement, emotional bravery, and, above all, love.

* * *

A highly original, versatile writer, Rose Tremain explores past ages and the present time with equal conviction. The leading characters of her fictions, often first-person narrators, range from young children to the very old, and may be of either gender. At her best, her work combines wit and humor with a wistful, elegiac sadness.

Tremain's early novels are notable mainly for their unusual settings and unconventional leading characters. Of these, the first and most unlikely is Sadler, the decrepit old servant in *Sadler's Birthday* whose day is spent wandering the empty house willed to him by his gentry employers. Skillfully mingling his recollections with the routine visitors of the day—the vicar, the cleaning lady, a prying estate agent—the author outlines the events that have shaped Sadler's life, not least the repression of his feelings by the strait-jacket of domestic service. Sadler's unacknowledged longings for love and friendship are rendered all the more moving by Tremain's hard, unsentimental style. *Sadler's Birthday* is an accomplished work whose characters and conversations have the ring of truth, and the blend of incident and flashback is ably achieved. *Letter to Sister Benedicta* has as its narrator the fat middle-aged matron Ruby Constad. Living in the shadow of a successful husband and beautiful children, Ruby's life changes when her husband has a stroke and her children embark on an incestuous relationship. Faced by the challenge, Ruby emerges stronger than before, able to cope and find a new life of her own. Her experiences are described in her letters to the nun who raised her in India, and reveal not only her inner turmoil but her warmth and self-deprecating humor. In *The Cupboard*, an ambitious work spanning the twentieth century and both world wars, events are presented from two contrasting viewpoints. The neglected novelist Erica March, old and nearing death, is interviewed by Ralph, a failed hack journalist, and the novel unfolds her past and her innermost feelings in a series of conversations and quotations from her books. The dynamic life Erica has made for herself is contrasted with Ralph's futile, submissive existence, and as she prepares for death her example inspires him to his own kind of rebellion. Perhaps the least accessible of Tremain's works, *The Cupboard* has a richness of content that rewards a careful reading. In all three novels one feels that Tremain is setting herself a challenge to wring something of value from unpromising material. If so, it is a challenge she is more than able to meet.

The stories of *The Colonel's Daughter* and the novel *The Swimming Pool Season* move beyond central characters to encompass a network of inter-connected lives. The novel and the long title story of the collection have strong similarities. Written in a firm, direct present tense, they build to climax through a sequence of brief, sharply visualized incidents. Whether the criminal act of *The Colonel's Daughter* or the ill-fated venture of a swimming pool in a remote French village, each serves as a central point around which Tremain constructs the interwoven lives of her characters, events unfolding gradually and with deceptive stealth to emerge in eventual tragedy.

Tremain's eagerness to explore other forms—evidenced in her radio plays and her children's story *Journey to the Volcano*—is matched by continuing experiment and variety in her novels and short stories. *The Garden of the Villa Mollini* and *Evangelista's Fan* show a further honing of her talent for the shorter forms, with stories that explore the feelings and responses of her varied characters with brevity and assurance, her thoughtful prose compressing deep insights into a handful of pages.

Restoration, which marks a radical departure from previous work, is a historical rather than contemporary novel, but shares with *The Swimming Pool Season* the sense of interlocked lives, the slow workings of fate foreshadowed by a series of incidents akin to Joycean ''epiphanies.'' Robert Merivel, her narrator and another unlikely hero-figure, admits early on that ''I am also in the middle of a story which might have a variety of endings, some of them not entirely to my liking.'' Set during the reign of Charles II with its twin catastrophes the Great Plague and Great Fire of London, the novel examines Robert's career as ''King's Fool,'' his ennoblement, his downfall as the King's favor is withdrawn, and his efforts at reintegration. Tremain shows great skill in alternating a past-tense main narrative with crucial present-tense flashbacks, and explores the complex nature of her hero. Merivel mirrors his age in his early excess and later, uncertain efforts at renunciation, and stands at the heart of a fascinating epic novel. *Restoration*, whose title refers not only to the time but to Merivel's re-ordering of his own broken world, is a deep, many-layered work, and at all levels the author's touch is firm and assured. One of Tremain's most challenging novels, it is also one of her best. *Sacred Country* has her switching to the modern world. Set mainly in rural Norfolk and spanning the period 1950s-80s, it centers on the realization by Mary Ward that her true nature is male. Her odyssey to gender change and fulfillment as Martin Ward is echoed by the lives of her own troubled family and their neighbors. Their linked stories are tracked to eventual resolution, Martin's fulfillment in the U.S.A. contrasted with the death and despair of Sonny and Estelle in the mean-spirited Britain of Margaret Thatcher. Once again Tremain creates a rich, complex epic, crammed like *Restoration* with evocative symbols and talismans.

Recent novels show Tremain at the height of her powers, writing with equal mastery of current events and those of the 1600s. *The Way I Found Her* describes a series of events leading to violence and tragedy in the hot Paris summer of 1994, as seen through the eyes of a young boy in his early teens. The character of Lewis the young narrator is a triumph, the reader drawn into his inner world with its blend of adult fantasies and childhood fears and preoccupations. The mystery that envelops not only him but his translator mother, Valentina the famous Russian novelist and Lewis's secret obsession, existentialist roofer Didier, and others, progresses at speed through a thickening plot with ingenious clues culled from literary quotations in the pages of *Crime and Punishment* and *Le Grand Meaulnes* to a final, tragic conclusion. Tremain's superb style hooks the reader from the opening lines, the rapid pace sustained throughout. It is matched by an unforgettable vision of the hot summer city, its landmarks, colors, and scents. Swift-moving and deep, its dark secret leavened by frequent moments of humor, *The Way I Found Her* is a magnificent creation and arguably its author's finest work. *Music and Silence* returns to the seventeenth century in an ambitious novel that rivals *Restoration* in complexity and scope. Lutenist Peter Claire, who takes service with King Christian IV of Denmark, is adopted by the king as his ''angel.'' Claire, in his love for Emilia Tilsen, companion to the King's adulterous consort Kirsten Munk, is dogged by guilt over a past affair, while the King is haunted by the terrible death of his friend Bror Brorson, who Claire closely resembles. These themes are woven into a narrative that also contains incidents from the fraught existence of Emilia and her family, the rampant sex-life of Kirsten, Claire's musings on art and life, and the King's desperate attempts to save his impoverished realm by various ill-judged schemes. Once more Tremain brings the early period alive, action switching from Frederiksborg to Jutland to Norfolk and back again in a series of memorably vivid scenes. The story is told from multiple viewpoints, the author moving smoothly from first-person interior monologue to third-person narrative and from present to past tense without strain. The plot of *Music and Silence* expands to take in the nature of music and creative art, an examination of sensual pleasure, the dilemma of love versus duty, and references to alchemy, fairytale and miracles. The balanced, sedately paced prose fits perfectly, just as the faster-moving style matches *The Way I Found Her*. With these later works, Rose Tremain's writing attains an impressive peak.

—Geoff Sadler

TREVOR, William

Nationality: Irish. **Born:** Mitchelstown, County Cork, 24 May 1928. **Education:** St. Columba's College, Dublin, 1942–46; Trinity College, Dublin, B.A. 1950. **Family:** Married Jane Ryan in 1952; two sons. **Career:** History teacher, Armagh, Northern Ireland, 1951–53; art teacher, Rugby, England, 1953–55; sculptor in Somerset, 1955–60; advertising copywriter, Notley's, London, 1960–64. Lives in Devon, England. **Awards:** *Transatlantic Review* prize, for fiction, 1964; Hawthornden prize, for fiction, 1965; Society of Authors travelling fellowship, 1972; Allied Irish Banks prize, for fiction, 1976; Heinemann award, for fiction, 1976; Whitbread Award, 1976, 1983, Book of the Year, 1994; Irish Community prize, 1979; BAFTA award, for television play, 1983; *Sunday Express* Book of the Year, 1994. D.Litt.: University of Exeter, 1984; Trinity College, Dublin, 1986; D.Litt.: Queen's University, Belfast, 1989; National University, Cork, 1990. **Member:** Irish Academy of Letters. C.B.E. (Commander, Order of the British Empire), 1977. **Agent:** Peters Fraser and Dunlop Group, 503–504 The Chambers, Chelsea Harbour, Lots Road, London SW10 0FX, England; or, Sterling Lord Literistic Inc., 1 Madison Avenue, New York, New York 10010, U.S.A.

PUBLICATIONS

Novels

A Standard of Behaviour. London, Hutchinson, 1958.
The Old Boys. London, Bodley Head, and New York, Viking Press, 1964.
The Boarding-House. London, Bodley Head, and New York, Viking Press, 1965.
The Love Department. London, Bodley Head, 1966; New York, Viking Press, 1967.
Mrs. Eckdorf in O'Neill's Hotel. London, Bodley Head, 1969; New York, Viking Press, 1970.
Miss Gomez and the Brethren. London, Bodley Head, 1971.
Elizabeth Alone. London, Bodley Head, 1973; New York, Viking Press, 1974.
The Children of Dynmouth. London, Bodley Head, 1976; New York, Viking Press, 1977.
Other People's Worlds. London, Bodley Head, 1980; New York, Viking Press, 1981.
Fools of Fortune. London, Bodley Head, and New York, Viking Press, 1983.
The Silence in the Garden. London, Bodley Head, and New York, Viking, 1988.
Two Lives (includes *Reading Turgenev* and *My House in Umbria*). London and New York, Viking, 1991.
Juliet's Story. New York, Simon & Schuster Books for Young Readers, 1994.
Felicia's Journey. London and New York, Viking, 1995.
After Rain. New York, Viking, 1996.
Death in Summer. New York, Viking, 1998.
The Hill Bachelors. New York, Viking, 2000.

Short Stories

The Day We Got Drunk on Cake and Other Stories. London, Bodley Head, 1967; New York, Viking Press, 1968.
Penguin Modern Stories 8, with others. London, Penguin, 1971.
The Ballroom of Romance and Other Stories. London, Bodley Head, and New York, Viking Press, 1972.
The Last Lunch of the Season. London, Covent Garden Press, 1973.
Angels at the Ritz and Other Stories. London, Bodley Head, 1975; New York, Viking Press, 1976.
Lovers of Their Time and Other Stories. London, Bodley Head, 1978; New York, Viking Press, 1979.
The Distant Past and Other Stories. Dublin, Poolbeg Press, 1979.
Beyond the Pale and Other Stories. London, Bodley Head, 1981; New York, Viking Press, 1982.
The Stories of William Trevor. London and New York, Penguin, 1983.
The News from Ireland and Other Stories. London, Bodley Head, and New York, Viking, 1986.
Nights at the Alexandra (novella). London, Century Hutchinson, and New York, Harper, 1987.
Family Sins and Other Stories. London, Bodley Head, and New York, Viking, 1990.
Trio: Three Stories from Cheltenham (novellas, with Jane Gardam and Rose Tremain). London, Penguin Books, 1993.
Outside Ireland: Selected Stories. London, Penguin Books, 1995.
Cocktails at Doney's and Other Stories, edited by Giles Gordon. London, Bloomsbury, 1996.
Ireland: Selected Stories. New York, Penguin Books, 1998.

Plays

The Elephant's Foot (produced Nottingham, 1965).
The Girl (televised 1967; produced London, 1968). London, French, 1968.
A Night with Mrs. da Tanka (televised 1968; produced London, 1972). London, French, 1972.
Going Home (broadcast 1970; produced London, 1972). London, French, 1972.
The Old Boys, adaptation of his own novel (produced London, 1971). London, Davis Poynter, 1971.
A Perfect Relationship (broadcast 1973; produced London, 1973). London, Burnham House, 1976.
The 57th Saturday (produced London, 1973).
Marriages (produced London, 1973). London, French, 1973.
Scenes from an Album (broadcast 1975; produced Dublin, 1981). Dublin, Co-op, 1981.
Beyond the Pale (broadcast 1980). Published in *Best Radio Plays of 1980,* London, Eyre Methuen, 1981.
Autumn Sunshine adaptation of his own story (televised 1981; broadcast 1982). Published in *Best Radio Plays of 1982,* London, Methuen, 1983.

Radio Plays: *The Penthouse Apartment,* 1968; *Going Home,* 1970; *The Boarding House,* from his own novel, 1971; *A Perfect Relationship,* 1973; *Scenes from an Album,* 1975; *Attracta,* 1977; *Beyond the Pale,* 1980; *The Blue Dress,* 1981; *Travellers,* 1982; *Autumn Sunshine,* 1982; *The News from Ireland,* from his own story, 1986; *Events at Drimaghleen,* 1988; *Running Away,* 1988.

Television Plays: *The Baby-Sitter,* 1965; *Walk's End,* 1966; *The Girl,* 1967; *A Night with Mrs. da Tanka,* 1968; *The Mark-2 Wife,* 1969; *The Italian Table,* 1970; *The Grass Widows,* 1971; *O Fat White Woman,* 1972; *The Schoolroom,* 1972; *Access to the Children,* 1973; *The General's Day,* 1973; *Miss Fanshawe's Story,* 1973; *An Imaginative Woman,* from a story by Thomas Hardy, 1973; *Love Affair,* 1974; *Eleanor,* 1974; *Mrs. Acland's Ghosts,* 1975; *The Statue and the Rose,* 1975; *Two Gentle People,* from a story by Graham Greene, 1975; *The Nicest Man in the World,* 1976; *Afternoon Dancing,* 1976; *The Love of a Good Woman,* from his own story, 1976; *The Girl Who Saw a Tiger,* 1976; *Last Wishes,* 1978; *Another Weekend,* 1978; *Memories,* 1978; *Matilda's England,* 1979; *The Old Curiosity Shop,* from the novel by Dickens, 1979; *Secret Orchards,* from works by J.R. Ackerley and Diana Petre, 1980; *The Happy Autumn Fields,* from a story by Elizabeth Bowen, 1980; *Elizabeth Alone,* from his own novel, 1981; *Autumn Sunshine,* from his own story, 1981; *The Ballroom of Romance,* from his own story, 1982; *Mrs. Silly* (*All for Love* series), 1983; *One of Ourselves,* 1983; *Broken Homes,* from his own story, 1985; *The Children of Dynmouth,* from his own novel, 1987; *August Saturday,* from his own novel, 1990; *Events at Drimaleen,* from his own story, 1992.

Other

Old School Ties (miscellany). London, Lemon Tree Press, 1976.

A Writer's Ireland: Landscape in Literature. London, Thames and Hudson, and New York, Viking, 1984.

Excursions in the Real World. London, Hutchinson, and New York, Knopf, 1994.

Editor, *The Oxford Book of Irish Short Stories.* Oxford and New York, Oxford University Press, 1989.

*

Manuscript Collections: University of Tulsa, Oklahoma.

Critical Studies: ''William Trevor's System of Correspondences,'' in *Massachusetts Review* (Amherst), Autumn 1987, and *William Trevor,* New York, Twayne, 1993, both by Kristin Morrison; *William Trevor: A Study of His Fiction* by Gregory A. Schirmer, London, Routledge, 1990; *William Trevor: A Study of the Short Fiction* by Suzanne Morrow Paulson, New York, Twayne, 1993; *William Trevor: The Writer and His Work* by Dolores MacKenna. Dublin, New Island, 1999.

* * *

William Trevor's celebrated writing career has largely been spent exploring the intersection of corruption and the human heart. His interest in moral vagaries and deluded, vulnerable characters speak to readers often through dark humor and acerbic perception. With over 30 published works—including fiction, short stories and non-fiction—Trevor is considered one of the greatest living short story writers and novelists, and his last few novels, especially, have been highly acclaimed.

Trevor's early works, dating back into the 1960s, mark a blooming affection for characters in bad relationships and down-and-out-predicaments. *The Old Boys* and *The Boarding-House* are filled with colorful characters drawn from London life. But these eccentricities are not the sort to be taken lightly. They sometimes disguise motives that set characters against one another in wicked and often-comical fashion. The comedy tends to disguise the kinds of evil that ultimately show through—a mask that Trevor becomes more concerned with in his later fiction. Mr. Jaraby's ambition to become president of the Old Boys Association of his school is hardly diabolical, and the extent to which he is willing to go to insure his election is as funny as it is outlandish. But as we learn more and more about him and his ambition, aspects of his private life—particularly his attitude towards his wife and son—reveal a sinister side to his nature that even his worst enemy, Mr. Nox, does not suspect. At the end, defeated in ways he had not anticipated, Mr. Jaraby is left alone with his wife who, though she counsels hope, rightly questions, ''Has hell begun, is that it?'' and urges, ''Come now, how shall we prove we are not dead?''

William Wagner Bird's death at the beginning of *The Boarding-House* provides one answer to Mrs. Jaraby's question. He leaves a will that bequeaths his boarding-house, occupied by an odd assortment of individuals of both sexes, to two of its most vigorous enemies, Studdy and Nurse Clock, both of them senior residents. Studdy is a petty con artist whose success in stealing one of Nurse Clock's elderly patients away from her has heightened the rivalry and ugliness between the pair. The specific condition of the bequest—that they make no changes in the residents or staff—puts them in an awkward position, but not for long. Like many of Trevor's less reputable characters, they are extremely acquisitive and quickly see that they have more to gain by working together than by working against each other. Unholy alliance though it may be, they systematically try to rid themselves of those strange and solitary inmates in whose hearts Mr. Bird believed he had kindled some comfort by bringing them together in his ''great institution in the south-western suburbs of London.'' By attempting to disrupt the careful arrangement Bird had created and cultivated, they finally destroy everything else, as from his grave Mr. Bird takes his revenge—in the person of a deranged and dispossessed resident who believes he is taking revenge on *him.*

Timothy Gedge in *The Children of Dynmouth* is a younger version of Mr. Studdy, and, being younger, displays the causes of his behavior more clearly. An unwanted child, neglected at home by his working mother and sister and abandoned by his father, Gedge finds in others' lives not so much vicarious pleasures as sources of information and feelings that feed his diseased imagination. These help him to blackmail various townspeople, even those once kindly disposed towards him. While his demands are seemingly innocuous—a wedding dress, a dog's-tooth suit, a discarded tin bath—his means to secure those ends are entirely vicious, masked by a false heartiness and cheer that belie his true feelings. Ironically—and Trevor is a master of irony—what he invents to piece out his knowledge often comes close to the truth, close enough in any case to cause considerable anguish and hurt, for example, to Commander and Mrs. Abigail, who for years—ever since they first got married—have been living a lie; or to Stephen and Kate, whose parents—Stephen's father and Kate's mother—have just been married and are off on a honeymoon, leaving their children to begin a difficult adjustment to a new family life. In these and other relationships, Gedge pretends to a friendship that none of the others feels, and that tends to drive him into greater fantasies—and greater invasions of their privacy. His worse invasions, however, are those of the human heart—until he is stopped by someone who recognizes what he is doing and whose wife, through understanding Gedge's plight, puts away her own discontents and concerns herself more fully with her family's future—and his, too.

This somewhat upbeat ending should not be overemphasized—though subsequent novels also show an effort to overcome despair and pathos, optimism is always very qualified in Trevor's fiction and very hard-won, as his many short stories also reveal. *Other People's Worlds* and *Fools of Fortune,* give a good idea of just how high the costs can be. Francis Tyte, another descendant of Studdy in Trevor's own rogue's gallery, is a very attractive young man who works as an actor in bit parts and in making commercials. Even more than Timothy Gedge, he has been victimized in his youth by a male boarder in his parents' home, a debt-collector who draws Francis into what one of his later benefactors aptly describes as a ''bitter world.'' Since that time, Francis has also turned into a debt-collector of sorts, like Studdy and Gedge reaping from others what he regards as his due. Already married to an elderly dressmaker in Folkestone who has thrown him out, he later meets Julia, 14 years his senior, who becomes infatuated with him and agrees to marry him and give him her jewelry. Their Italian honeymoon lasts a single day, during which Francis tells Julia everything, including the daughter he has fathered with Doris Smith, a poor shopgirl in Fulham, 12 years earlier. He absconds with the jewels and is not heard from again. But Julia is drawn into Dorrie Smith's world as well as Francis's other circles, including that of the aged parents he has long since abandoned in a retirement home. Despite the humiliation and despondency she naturally suffers because of her folly, Julia becomes more and more deeply involved in the shambles of others' lives Francis has left behind him. Once a devout Catholic, she nearly loses her faith altogether. But Dorrie's joy in more than one sense finally becomes Francis's own, as Gedge becomes Lavinia Featherston's. Drawn into other people's worlds and the messes they contain, she learns to value more her own, but not with smugness. The pain she has experienced has made her invulnerable to that and more truly compassionate than she had ever been before.

Fools of Fortune deepens the focus and the tone displayed in all of these novels, as Trevor resorts to first-person narrative and tells a story of revenge and retribution from several points of view. His eccentrics are still present, but here subordinated to their proper functions in a novel that spans the present century and deals with the perennial conflict between the Irish and their erstwhile British masters. Actually, the narrative goes back to the 19th century, when Irish Protestant William Quinton married English Anna Woodcombe and brought her to live in Kilneagh, County Cork. Two generations later, when for the third time a Quinton had taken a Woodcombe for his bride, Kilneagh is burned down by Black and Tans under the leadership of a Liverpool sergeant named Rudnick. Young Willie and his widowed mother survive the ordeal, but when years afterward Eve Quinton commits suicide—an alcoholic, she never recovered from the disaster—Willie decides to exact his revenge upon Rudnick. Just before he does so, he falls in love with yet another Woodcombe, Marianne, and fathers a child. But he is forced to spend most of the rest of his life in lonely exile, while Marianne and their daughter Imelda are taken in by Willie's aging aunts at what is left of Kilneagh. Anglo-Irish himself, Trevor has for many years lived in England and only occasionally attempted to treat the people and the landscapes of his native land in his fiction. In his short story ''Attracta,'' about an elderly Protestant schoolteacher in a village near Cork, he sketched out some of the same themes he developed more fully in *Fools of Fortune.* But in ''Matilda's England'' he shows how the atrocities of the past and their impact upon the present are by no means limited to a single time or place or series of events.

Two more recent works, *The Silence in the Garden,* and his novella, *Nights at the Alexandra,* tend to bear out this trend. Both are set in Ireland, where Trevor grew up, and both reflect the elegiac tone that has grown more pronounced in his later work. *Nights at the Alexandra* looks back to the boyhood of a 58-year-old bachelor and the strange infatuation he felt for a beautiful and rather mysterious woman, Frau Messinger, an Englishwoman married to a German and brought to live in Ireland as World War II began. Isolated from the rest of the townsfolk in their home, Cloverhill, Frau Messinger befriends Harry, the narrator, who quickly falls under her spell. To provide some entertainment for his wife as well as for the townsfolk, Herr Messinger decides to establish a cinema, but it takes a long time to build, and meanwhile Frau Messinger falls ill. She dies shortly after the cinema opens and Harry is employed by her husband to help run it. Eventually he inherits the movie house, which at first was extremely popular. As the customers gradually stop coming, he closes it, just as Cloverhill is closed up when Herr Messinger leaves after his wife's death, and Harry is left to look after the boarded windows and her grave. In the end, he refuses to take a good offer for the place from a business partnership that would turn it into a furniture store.

The Silence in the Garden is a more complex and fully developed novel that uses several narrative techniques, including flashbacks and diary entries. Futile and misdirected love are part of the story, but so are senseless violence, superstition, family pride, and war. The novel is related from several viewpoints: the spinster Sarah Pollexfen's, a poor relation who comes to work at Carriglas, first as a governess, later as a companion to family duenna, old Mrs. Rolleston; Tom, son of the parlor maid (later cook) Brigid, whose intended husband, the butler Linchy, was killed in a Black and Tan ambush intended for the Rolleston men, Lionel and John James; Villana, granddaughter of Mrs. Rolleston, whose engagement to Sarah's brother, Hugh, is suddenly and mysteriously broken off shortly after Linchy's murder. Other Rollestons and townsfolk populate the novel; for example, Colonel Rolleston, Mrs. Rolleston's son and Villana's father, killed at Passchendaele; his sons, Lionel and John James; Finnamore Balt, the pedantic and elderly lawyer who eventually marries Villana; Mrs. Moledy, a widow who runs a boarding house, where she carries on a long liaison with John James, her ''king,'' and who puts in an uninvited and comical appearance at Villana and Finnamore's wedding at Carriglas.

But the real protagonist of the novel is Ireland and her long unhappy history of Protestant landowners and Catholic servants and tenant farmers. If during the Great Famine an earlier generation of Rollestons had taken pity and forgiven rents, the later generation is still largely despised. As an example, when a bridge is proposed and built between the mainland and the island on which Carriglas is situated, it is named after Cornelius Dowley, the man responsible for Linchy's death but otherwise regarded as a hero of the struggle against the British. Over the course of the present century, Carriglas falls into disuse and disrepair, as one by one the Rollestons die out or leave, and only Tom is left. He inherits what is left of the estate, the old house whose value lies mainly in the valuable lead of its roof, and a little land—too little to make farming profitable. Although his would-be fiance, Esmeralda Coyne, thinks it would make a good resort hotel, Tom shows little interest in her or her idea, and the novel ends, like *Nights at the Alexandra,* with Tom likely to remain a bachelor and the old house steadily disintegrating.

In *Death in Summer*, Trevor creates a suspenseful tale ripe with elegant language and a subtlety readers have come to expect. Thaddeus Davenant has buried his wife, Letitia, who died in a freak accident. Letitia was a compassionate soul, though her nature was lost on Thaddeus, who married the woman for her money. His true and only affection is for his baby. After many interviews with less-than-qualified nannies, he even agrees to let Letitia's mother move in rather than risk any mishaps with his child. Though Thaddeus is a chilly sort, he manages to gain the affection of Pettie, one of the many nannies rejected for a position in Thaddeus's home. Pettie seems to be the oppositional force to Thaddeus's wintry nature. Having been deprived of love as a girl, she is ravenous for it now with Thaddeus. But is her affection so strong that she would kidnap the one person Thaddeus does love? Trevor's literary teeth are sharper than ever, and he is one of the top heirs to the Anglo-Irish tradition in fiction that has provided a wealth of talent. Trevor's legacy, both in its penchant for human evil and his gentle, luscious prose, make him a writer of insight and remarkable compassion.

—Jay L. Halio, updated by Maureen Aitken

TROLLOPE, Joanna

Also writes as Caroline Harvey. **Nationality:** English. **Born:** England, 9 December 1943. **Education:** Oxford University, M.A. 1965. **Family:** Married David Roger William Potter in 1966; two daughters. **Career:** Associated with Foreign Office, London, 1965–67; worked as an English teacher for twelve years and in the children's clothing business. Lives in Hampshire, England. **Awards:** Historical Novel of the Year Award (Romantic Novelists Association), 1979; Elizabeth Goudge Historical Award, 1980. **Agent:** Georges Borchardt, Inc., 136 East 57th Street, New York, New York 10022, U.S.A.

PUBLICATIONS

Novels

Eliza Stanhope. London, Hutchinson, 1978; New York, Dutton, 1979.
Parson Harding's Daughter. London, Hutchinson, 1979, as *Mistaken Virtues.* New York, Dutton, 1980.
Leaves from the Valley. New York, St. Martin's, 1980.
The Steps of the Sun. New York, St. Martin's, 1984.
The Taverners' Place. New York, St. Martin's, 1986.
A Village Affair. New York, Harper, 1989.
A Passionate Man. London, Bloomsbury, 1990.
The Rector's Wife. London, Bloomsbury, 1991; New York, Random House, 1994.
Trollope Omnibus: A Village Affair, A Passionate Man, The Rector's Wife. London, Bloomsbury, 1992.
The Men and the Girls. New York, Random House, 1992.
The Choir. London, Black Swan, 1992; New York, Random House, 1995.
A Spanish Lover. London, Bloomsbury, 1993; New York, Random House, 1997.
The Best of Friends. London, Bloomsbury, 1995; New York, Viking, 1998.
Next of Kin. London, Bloomsbury, 1996.
Other People's Children. New York, Viking, 1999.
The Brass Dolphin (as Caroline Harvey). New York, Viking, 1999.
Marrying the Mistress. New York, Viking, 2000.
Legacy of Love (as Caroline Harvey). New York, Viking, 2000.

Recordings

A Second Legacy, 1995.
The City of Gems, 1995.

Other

Britannia's Daughters: Women of the British Empire. London, Hutchinson, 1983.
Introduction, *An Illustrated Autobiography: Including How the 'Mastiffs' Went to Iceland* by Anthony Trollope. Glouchester, England, A. Sutton, 1987; Wolfeboro, New Hampshire, A. Sutton, 1987.
Foreword, *Life, Death and Art: The Medieval Stained Glass of Fairford Parish Church: A Multimedia Exploration*, edited by Sarah Brown and Lindsay MacDonald. Stoud, Gloucestershire, England, Sutton Publishing, 1997.
Foreword, *Starting from Glasgow* by Rosemary Trollope. Stoud, Gloucestershire, England, Sutton Publishing, 1998.

* * *

A popular author best known for her novels exploring the complexities of modern life, Joanna Trollope began her published career as a writer of historical fiction. The action of *Eliza Stanhope* takes place on the battlefield of Waterloo, where its heroine assists the surgeons in tending wounded soldiers, among them her cavalry officer lover, and displays the author's knowledge of the period. In *Parson Harding's Daughter*, perhaps Trollope's best known historical work, Catherine Harding makes the journey to Calcutta to meet a prospective husband who turns out to be an alcoholic, and their failing marriage is further endangered when she falls in love with another man. These, and her later historical novels—*Leaves from the Valley, City of Gems, The Steps of the Sun*—are all clearly the work of an assured, capable writer and give the impression of being thoroughly researched. As ''Caroline Harvey'' Trollope has also ventured effectively into the family saga, and in *Legacy of Love* and *Second Legacy* she traces the lives of several generations of women from Victorian times to the present day. From the late 1980s onwards she has continued to produce historical novels together with her contemporary works. One of the most ambitious is *The Taverners' Place*, whose story spans seven generations of rural landowners from 1870 to 1939 in a single volume. More recently, *The Brass Dolphin* depicts the adventures of a young woman in Malta during World War II, and is projected as the first of a series of novels. A talented historical writer whose work has been compared with that of Georgette Heyer, Trollope's gifts in this field are undeniable, but one cannot help feeling that she is at her best in her contemporary novels.

The Choir established Trollope's reputation as a writer concerned with modern life and relationships. With it she broke fresh ground, taking her writing to a different level and establishing a recognizable individual style. Set in the cathedral city of Aldminster, the action centers on the power struggle between the Dean and local headmaster Alex Fry to decide the fate of the choir. The Dean is pressing for its disbandment as a means of raising funds to repair the cathedral, and the intrigues that follow are shown from multiple viewpoints. As well as the Dean and Fry, these include Helen Ashworth (who turns from a failing marriage to a new life with choirmaster Leo Beckford), her choirboy son Henry and her father-in-law, Labour Party councillor Frank Ashworth. The cathedral city setting and ecclesiastical intrigue recall the Barchester chronicles of her Victorian ancestor Anthony Trollope, who would probably have enjoyed reading the novel. Trollope handles her maze of plotlines in a deft, memorable fashion, the love affair of Helen and Leo neatly intertwined with Henry's emergence as a ''star'' with a hit record that saves the choir, Frank's bitter struggles with the council, and the maneuvering in higher ecclesiastical circles. Eventual resolution falls short of the ''happy ending,'' the saving of the choir counter-balanced by the losses suffered by other characters. Still one of her most impressive creations, *The Choir* reveals Trollope as an accomplished modern novelist with a voice of her own.

A Village Affair marks a departure from *The Choir*, with Trollope choosing a small rural community as the setting for the action. Her account of the love affair between two women—one a conventional middle-class housewife, the other an aggressive, outspoken ''high-flyer''—examines the relationship and its effect on the village with a perceptive restraint and confirms the author's reputation. A similar country village provides the background in *The Rector's Wife*, where Anna Bouverie (whose name brings Flaubert's Emma Bovary to mind) is faced by the need to find an identity of her own distinct from ''the rector's wife'' of the title. When her husband, disappointed in his bid for promotion, turns away from her to bury himself in parish duties, Anna makes a bid for independence that leads to their eventual separation. *The Rector's Wife* ranks with *The Choir* and *A Village Affair* and shows Trollope's skill in probing the complications of modern life. All three novels have been successfully televised in the United Kingdom.

In *The Men and the Girls* Trollope examines the relationships of two young women whose partners are both older men. Sudden career changes, illness, and a random accident bring disruption into their lives and lead to radical alteration and re-adjustment. As in *The Choir*, Trollope handles a large cast with skill and assurance, and her conclusion matches triumph with tragedy. The central characters of *A Spanish Lover* are twin sisters, the successful married mother and career woman Lizzie and unattached, unsatisfied Frances. The action of the novel brings a sudden reversal of roles as Lizzie encounters business and domestic problems while her sister finds fulfillment with the married Spanish lover of the title. Trollope describes a difficult situation with a light, sympathetic style that allows the characters to speak for themselves, and once again the story is resolved only by a painful adaptation to changed circumstances. *The Best of Friends* again shows her ability to control a large and varied group of characters, its story dealing with two families whose lives are disrupted when one couple separate, and the effect on children and other relatives. Trollope produces a sensitive portrayal of the nature of love and its impact on several different generations, and further confirms her mastery of the form. This ability to present the action from multiple viewpoints is also evident in *Next of Kin*, where a sequence of events in a remote farming community leads to a violent suicide and its aftermath. Trollope draws a stark picture of the farmer's life—its isolation, the unbearable economic pressures, and their effect on individual relationships. Her skill in handling the ''cast of thousands'' has never been better demonstrated than in *Other People's Children*, the plot of which includes a complex network of relationships centered on the role of the step-parent and step-child. Here, action is perceived at different times by the natural mother, the step-mother, a would-be stepmother, and the children of the families involved. Trollope presents her characters sympathetically, without hiding the shortcomings that render them more believable. Her latest modern novel, *Marrying the Mistress*, once more addresses the theme of beginning life afresh after earlier, failed relationships, and displays her familiar qualities.

In these contemporary works Trollope explores love and loss with a clear, unwavering but sensitive perception, and is at her most compelling.

—Geoff Sadler

TUOHY, Frank

Nationality: British. **Born:** John Francis Tuohy in Uckfield, Sussex, 2 May 1925. **Education:** Stowe School, Buckinghamshire; King's College, Cambridge, 1943–46, B.A. (honours) 1946. **Career:** Lecturer, Turku University, Finland, 1947–48; professor of English language and literature, University of São Paulo, Brazil, 1950–56; contract professor, Jagiellonian University, Krakow, Poland, 1958–60; visiting professor, Waseda University, Tokyo, 1964–67; visiting professor and writer-in-residence, Purdue University, Lafayette, Indiana, 1970–71, 1976, 1980; visiting professor, Rikkyo University, Tokyo, 1983–89. **Awards:** Katherine Mansfield-Menton prize, 1959; Society of Authors Travelling fellowship, 1963; James Tait Black Memorial prize, 1965; Faber Memorial prize, 1965; E.M. Forster award (U.S.A.), 1972; Heinemann award, 1979, for *Live Bait*; Bennett award (*Hudson Review*), 1994. D.Litt.: Purdue University 1987. Fellow, Royal Society of Literature, 1965. **Agent:** Peters Fraser and Dunlop, 503–504 The Chambers, Chelsea Harbour, Lots Road, London SW10 0XF. **Address:** Shatwell Cottage, Yarlington, near Wincanton, Somerset BA9 8DL, England.

Publications

Novels

The Animal Game. London, Macmillan, and New York, Scribner, 1957.

The Warm Nights of January. London, Macmillan, 1960.

The Ice Saints. London, Macmillan, and New York, Scribner, 1964.

Short Stories

The Admiral and the Nuns with Other Stories. London, Macmillan, 1962; New York, Scribner, 1963.

Fingers in the Door. London, Macmillan, and New York, Scribner, 1970.

Live Bait and Other Stories. London, Macmillan, 1978; New York, Holt Rinehart, 1979.

The Collected Stories. London, Macmillan, and New York, Holt Rinehart, 1984.

Play

Television Play: *The Japanese Student,* 1973.

Other

Portugal. London, Thames and Hudson, and New York, Viking Press, 1970.

Yeats (biography). London, Macmillan, and New York, Macmillan, 1976; as *Yeats: An Illustrated Biography,* London, Herbert Press, 1991.

*

Critical Studies: ''Foreign Bodies: The Fiction of Frank Tuohy'' by John Millors, in *London Magazine,* n.s.18, February 1979.

Frank Tuohy comments:

Most of what I write seems to start off with the interaction between two cultures, modes of behaviour, ways of living, etc. Sometimes this confrontation is between a foreigner and an alien environment, sometimes between groups in that environment itself. For me, the sense of displacement, loss, anxiety which happens to people derives from the world outside them, in their relationships with that world. If I thought of it as starting inside, as being a part of the Self, I probably would not write at all.

* * *

The novels and short stories of Frank Tuohy are marked by a strong sense of social reality. They are set in various places—England, Brazil, Poland—and give one a vivid sense of the physical place: the climate, landscape, local customs. Against the backdrop of special place, the drama of the characters' lives unfolds. In the short stories interest focuses usually on intense personal encounters in which the protagonist is made to face some unpleasant decision or harsh truth about himself or people close to him. These stories, sharply etched and intensely though quietly dramatic, have no apparent underlying theme. It is the revelation itself, the exquisitely rendered but ''painful bite down on the rotten tooth of fact,'' to borrow a phrase from Tuohy, that one is meant to savor.

In his novels and longer stories there are the same sharp awareness of external reality and savoring of unpleasant fact, but there is also clearly a discernible moral structure. The writer's sympathies are with those who suffer and respond, who are capable of loyalty and self-abnegation. His dislike is for characters who, protected by money, indulge their appetites at the expense of those socially or culturally inferior or morally more sensitive.

The protagonist of Tuohy's first novel, *The Animal Game,* is Robin Morris, a young Englishman working in São Paulo, who encounters the beautiful corrupt daughter of a Brazilian aristocrat. Morris is attracted to this woman but is saved at the end of the novel from a relationship which, one sees, would have been sterile, self-indulgent, and ultimately destructive. Tuohy's moral sense is even more fully involved in his second novel about Brazil, *The Warm Nights of January,* which also deals with self-indulgence and sexual corruption. *The Ice Saints* takes place in Poland, some time after the Stalinist ''thaw.'' Here the protagonist, an attractive, pleasant, but inexperienced and pampered young English woman visits her married sister and Polish brother-in-law with the idea of rescuing their son from what she regards as a grim and depressing existence, and taking him back to England to live. Although we are at first allowed to identify with the young woman's point of view (the horrors of Polish life are vividly presented), we are made to see, finally, the moral superiority of the Polish brother-in-law whose human qualities outweigh his lack of polish and urbanity.

Tuohy's stories and novels are written in a style that is compressed and economical yet remarkably evocative. One has the immediate sense of a physical world vividly and objectively presented and yet one also feels, but unobtrusively, the authorial presence choosing and arranging for judgmental effect.

—W.J. Stuckey

TYLER, Anne

Nationality: American. **Born:** Minneapolis, Minnesota, 25 October 1941. **Education:** Duke University, Durham, North Carolina, 1958–61, B.A. 1961; Columbia University, New York, 1961–62. **Family:** Married Taghi Modarressi in 1963 (deceased 1997); two daughters. **Career:** Russian bibliographer, Duke University Library, 1962–63; assistant to the librarian, McGill University Law Library, Montreal, 1964–65. **Awards:** American Academy award, 1977; Janet Kafka prize, 1981; PEN Faulkner award, 1983; National Book Critics Circle award, 1986; Pulitzer prize, 1989. **Agent:** Russell and Volkening Inc., 50 West 29th Street, New York, New York 10001. **Address:** 222 Tunbridge Road, Baltimore, Maryland 21212, U.S.A.

PUBLICATIONS

Novels

If Morning Ever Comes. New York, Knopf, 1964; London, Chatto and Windus, 1965.

The Tin Can Tree. New York, Knopf, 1965; London, Macmillan, 1966.

A Slipping-Down Life. New York, Knopf, 1970; London, Severn House, 1983.

The Clock Winder. New York, Knopf, 1972; London, Chatto and Windus, 1973.

Celestial Navigation. New York, Knopf, 1974; London, Chatto and Windus, 1975.

Searching for Caleb. New York, Knopf, and London, Chatto and Windus, 1976.

Earthly Possessions. New York, Knopf, and London, Chatto and Windus, 1977.

Morgan's Passing. New York, Knopf, and London, Chatto and Windus, 1980.

Dinner at the Homesick Restaurant. New York, Knopf, and London, Chatto and Windus, 1982.

The Accidental Tourist. New York, Knopf, and London, Chatto and Windus, 1985.

Breathing Lessons. New York, Knopf, 1988; London, Chatto and Windus, 1989.

Saint Maybe. New York, Knopf, and London, Chatto and Windus, 1991.

Ladder of Years. New York, Knopf, 1995.

A Patchwork Planet. New York, Knopf, 1998.

Uncollected Short Stories

"I Play Kings," in *Seventeen* (New York), August 1963.
"Street of Bugles," in *Saturday Evening Post* (Philadelphia), 30 November 1963.
"Nobody Answers the Door," in *Antioch Review* (Yellow Springs, Ohio), Fall 1964.
"I'm Not Going to Ask You Again," in *Harper's* (New York), September 1965.
"Everything But Roses," in *Reporter* (New York), 23 September 1965.
"As the Earth Gets Old," in *New Yorker,* 29 October 1966.
"Feather Behind the Rock," in *New Yorker,* 12 August 1967.
"Flaw in the Crust of the Earth," in *Reporter* (New York), 2 November 1967.
"Common Courtesies," in *McCall's* (New York), June 1968.
"With All Flags Flying," in *Redbook* (New York), June 1971.
"Bride in the Boatyard," in *McCall's* (New York), June 1972.
"Respect," in *Mademoiselle* (New York), June 1972.
"Misstep of the Mind," in *Seventeen* (New York), October 1972.
"Knack for Languages," in *New Yorker,* 13 January 1975.
"Some Sign That I Ever Made You Happy," in *McCall's* (New York), October 1975.
"Your Place Is Empty," in *New Yorker,* 22 November 1976.
"Holding Things Together," in *New Yorker,* 24 January 1977.
"Average Waves in Unprotected Waters," in *New Yorker,* 28 February 1977.
"Foot-Footing On," in *Mademoiselle* (New York), November 1977.
"The Geologist's Maid," in *Stories of the Modern South,* edited by Ben Forkner and Patrick Samway. New York, Penguin, 1981.
"Laps," in *Parents' Magazine* (New York), August 1981.
"The Country Cook," in *Harper's* (New York), March 1982.
"Teenage Wasteland," in *The Editors' Choice 1,* edited by George E. Murphy, Jr. New York, Bantam, 1985.
"Rerun," in *New Yorker,* 4 July 1988.
"A Street of Bugles," in *Saturday Evening Post* (Indianapolis), July-August 1989.
"A Woman Like a Fieldstone House," in *Louder than Words,* edited by William Shore. New York, Vintage, 1989.

Other

Tumble Tower (for children). New York, Orchard, 1993.
Editor, with Shannon Ravenel, *The Best American Short Stories 1983.* Boston, Houghton Mifflin, 1983; as *The Year's Best American Short Stories,* London, Severn House, 1984.
Editor, with Shannon Ravenel, *Best of the South: From Ten Years of New Stories from the South.* Chapel Hill, North Carolina, Algonquin Books of Chapel Hill, 1996.

*

Film Adaptations: *The Accidental Tourist,* 1988.

Bibliography: *Anne Tyler: A Bio-Bibliography* by Robert W. Croft, Westport, Connecticut, Greenwood Press, 1995.

Critical Studies: *Art and the Accidental in Anne Tyler* by Joseph C. Voelker, Jackson, University Press of Mississippi, 1989; *The Temporal Horizon: A Study of the Theme of Time in Anne Tyler's Major Novels* by Karin Linton, Uppsala, Sweden, Studia Anglistica, 1989; *The Fiction of Anne Tyler* edited by C. Ralph Stephens, Jackson, University Press of Mississippi, 1990; *Understanding Anne Tyler* by Alice Hall Petty, Columbia, University of South Carolina Press, 1990; *Anne Tyler as Novelist,* edited by Dale Salwak, Iowa City, University of Iowa Press, 1994; *Moving On: The Heroines of Shirley Ann Grau, Anne Tyler, and Gail Godwin* by Susan S. Kissel, Bowling Green, Ohio, Bowling Green State University Popular Press, 1996; *An Anne Tyler Companion* by Robert W. Croft, Westport, Connecticut, Greenwood Press, 1998; *Anne Tyler: A Critical Companion* by Paul Bail, Westport, Connecticut, Greenwood Press, 1998.

* * *

Anne Tyler's novels do not create cosmic waves but have quietly and carefully, for over a third of a century, attempted to illustrate the struggle between asserting one's individual identity versus functioning in a role within the American middle-class family. Perhaps it is because Tyler seems to place such importance on the role of family or because her settings stay primarily around the city and suburbs of Baltimore, Maryland, or perhaps critics do not see her pushing the boundaries enough. In any case, despite a Pulitzer Prize in 1989 for *Breathing Lessons* and a National Book Critics Circle Award, Tyler's work is chronically appreciated but not heralded by critics. Nevertheless, she is a prolific and popular writer. Her tendency to use humor to create colorful characters and place them into fairly ordinary circumstances has gained her a loyal readership and prompted comparisons to Eudora Welty, an American writer whose work she claims as an influence.

In *Morgan's Passing,* for instance, Morgan appears to be a well-adjusted family man. Inside, however, we discover he is struggling with what he sees as the madhouse he lives in—the goings on of his seven daughters and their friends are driving him over the edge. He attempts to cope through the use of costume and impersonation. Alternately, he becomes a tugboat captain, doctor, politician, clerk at a fish market, priest, and others. Morgan's home is not his haven, so he has to find shelter at his office at Cullen Hardware, and this refuge of changing identities within the world of work is reminiscent of Walter Mitty.

The quirky character in *Breathing Lessons* is Junie, Ira's sister. Like Jeremy in *Celestial Navigation,* Junie does not like to leave home. Ira's wife, Maggie, decides to help her break out of her shell by performing a makeover routine on her, from makeup to clothes. Like Morgan, Junie seems to draw courage from this disguised identity in the outside world. Unlike Morgan, however, Junie will only leave home with Ira at her side because as family, he represents a part of home going out with her.

In *Dinner at the Homesick Restaurant,* Ezra tries to create a family atmosphere at the restaurant that he feels is missing at home. In this novel, again there is a juxtaposition of the individual, the family, and the outside world of work and commerce. Tyler admits and demonstrates that the three do not always easily cohabit. In *The Accidental Tourist,* it takes another eccentric character, Muriel Pritchett, the dog trainer, to bring Macon Leary out of his sheltered world in which traveling is simply for business, not pleasure.

Delia Grinstead, in *Ladder of Years,* leaves her sheltered life in a much different way. If readers suspect Tyler is only capable of writing in a her self-established pattern, this novel marks a shift from the dependence on the quirky character device to an exploration of every family members' fantasy—what if I just walked right out that door and never came back? While at the beach, that is just what forty-year-old Delia does, finally settling in a small town in Delaware to find the self she never knew by living all of her adult life in the same house in which she grew up. As Tyler matures, so does her writing, and one wonders whether she may be one of the best chroniclers of the problems women born in mid-twentieth century America and living in the domestic sphere face in later life.

With *A Patchwork Planet,* Tyler returned to her familiar pattern, however. This time, she attempts to write from the point of view of Barnaby Gaitlin, a thirty-year-old loser who takes care of eccentric old people. In this novel, it is not so much a character from within a family doing the searching as it is a character without family searching for a home. While one wishes Tyler would venture out from her own protective sphere of character patterns, one cannot help but praise her for taking advantage of exploring what seems like every possible angle on the struggles of the individual inside and outside the shelter of home and family. Perhaps with the perspective of an elder spokesperson in the years ahead, she will offer new insights that only someone who has worked on a subject for many years can contribute to our understanding of this very ordinary, but vital aspect of the human condition.

—Connie Ann Kirk

U

UNSWORTH, Barry (Forster)

Nationality: British. **Born:** Durham, England, 10 August 1930. **Education:** University of Manchester, B.A. (with honors in English) 1951. **Military Service:** British Army, Royal Corps of Signals, 1951–53: second lieutenant. **Family:** 1) married Valerie Moor, 1959 (marriage dissolved, 1991) three daughters; 2) Aira Pohjanvaara-Buffa, 1992. **Career:** Lecturer in English, Norwood Technical College, 1960 and 1963–65; lecturer in English for British Council, University of Athens, Greece, 1960–63. Since 1965 lecturer in English for British Council, University of Istanbul, Turkey. **Awards:** Royal Society of Literature-Heinemann award for literature, 1974, for *Mooncranker's Gift;* Booker prize, 1992, for *Sacred Hunger.* **Address:** c/o Hamish Hamilton, 22 Wright's Lane, London W8 5TZ, England.

PUBLICATIONS

Novels

The Partnership. London, Hutchinson, 1966.
The Greeks Have a Word for It. London, Hutchinson, 1967.
The Hide. London, Gollancz, 1970.
Mooncranker's Gift. London, Allen, 1973; New York, Houghton Mifflin, 1974.
The Big Day. London, Michael Joseph, 1976; New York, Mason/Charter, 1977.
Pascali's Island. London, Michael Joseph; as *The Idol Hunter,* New York, Simon and Schuster, 1980.
The Rage of the Vulture. London, Granada, 1982; New York, Houghton Mifflin, 1983.
Stone Virgin. London, Hamilton, 1985; New York, Houghton Mifflin, 1986.
Sugar and Rum. London, Hamilton, 1988.
Sacred Hunger. London, Hamilton, and New York, Doubleday, 1992.
Morality Play. New York, N.A. Talese, 1995.
After Hannibal. New York, N.A. Talese, 1997.
Losing Nelson. New York, N.A. Talese, 1999.

Other

The Student's Book of English: A Complete Coursebook and Grammar to Advanced Intermediate Level, with John Lennox Cook and Amorey Gethin. Oxford, Blackwell, 1981.
Novels and Novelists in the 1990's. London, Random House, 1993.

*　*　*

Barry Unsworth's fiction offers powerful and closely observed explorations of human relationships in which desire is entangled with exploitation and with potential, and sometimes actual, violence. In his first novel, *The Partnership,* the association of two business partners is complicated and eventually destroyed by the repressed homoerotic attraction that one of them has for the other, and in *The Hide,* a semiarticulate gardener is pressured by his dominating friend into arranging the rape of a young woman. Both of these early works are set in England in modern times, and their close focus on the relationships they portray largely excludes explicit engagement with wider concerns; but in Unsworth's most characteristic work, such relationships are placed in broader geographical, political, and historical contexts. *Pascali's Island* and *The Rage of the Vulture* go back to the last throes of the Ottoman Empire in 1908; *Stone Virgin* takes place in Venice, partly in the 15th century, partly in the 18th century, and partly in the later 20th century; *Sacred Hunger,* set in the 18th century, moves from the British port of Liverpool to a slave ship, the Guinea Coast, and Florida; *Morality Play* returns to northeast England in the 14th century, in a bitter time of plague, famine, poverty, and anarchy; the location of *After Hannibal* is the idyllic landscape of modern Umbria in Italy, but, as the novel's title indicates, we are reminded of its bloody past, when Hannibal massacred the Roman army or the homicidal Baglioni family ruled in the Renaissance; the narrator of *Losing Nelson* is a late 20th-century biographer who finds it hard to come to terms with the fact that his hero, Admiral Lord Horatio Nelson, tricked the Neapolitan Jacobean rebels in 1799 and sent them to their deaths.

A recurrent concern of Unsworth's novels is the link between the relationships of his characters and the artifacts and representations that they make, display, observe, exchange, or desire. In *The Partnership,* for example, the pixies turned out by one of the partners, Foley, provide the staple of the business, whereas the seraphs and cherubs he also makes represent his desire for independence and finally become the object of his partner's violence. *Pascali's Island* sets up a complex relationship between a marble head of a woman that is fraudulently claimed to have been found on an archaeological site, a bronze male statue, which is actually buried on the site and provokes a fatal attempt at theft, and a wax model of a saint that topples down during the ceremony of his Assumption. The central motif of *Stone Virgin* is a carved Venetian Madonna that is first fashioned by Girolamo, a Piedmontese stonecutter; is subsequently discovered after three hundred years by a rake called Ziani; and finally, in 1972, falls into the hands of an English conservation expert, Simon Raikes. The ambiguity of the artifact—as both a product and a denial of mortality—is forcefully encapsulated in *Mooncranker's Gift,* where the "gift" of the title is a bandaged effigy of the crucified Christ that is in fact made of sausage meat and turns rotten and stinking. Artifacts take on a range of symbolic functions in Unsworth's novels, and they link up with his other concerns, such as voyeurism, in *The Hide,* or the commodification of human beings, in *Sacred Hunger. After Hannibal* examines the way in which houses may become objects of desire, focusing on a group of people who come from the United Kingdom, the United States, and Germany to buy a house in Umbria—as Unsworth himself did after *Sacred Hunger* won the Booker Prize, the UK's best known literary award. The dream of a house, one of the characters reflects, is unlike any other dream of ownership because the dream of a way of life goes with it.

Theatrical representation is a key theme of *Morality Play,* as its title suggests. Unsworth's tale of a group of strolling players in medieval England provides a fascinating recreation of the stagecraft and theatrical philosophy of the Middle Ages and dramatizes the question of the relationship between art and life when the players decide, in order to try to increase their audience, to re-enact the recent murder of a twelve-year-old boy, for which a local woman is soon to be executed. The divide between representation and reality gives way as the woman's guilt is called into question and the actors don masks to play out a real event. On and off stage, things are not what they appear to be. *Losing Nelson* focuses on biographical and historical representation, on its protagonist's attempt to recreate and exculpate a truly heroic Nelson with whom he strongly identifies: the novel sharply examines the relationship between the truths that we may desire from history and biography and the truths which they may actually yield.

At his best, Unsworth has a precise, nuanced, and rhythmically accomplished style that enables him to register psychological complexity sensitively and evocatively to render time and place. Some of his novels, such as *The Greeks Have a Word for It,* employ an omniscient narrator, allowing for movement between the minds of different characters for dramatic effect; in other novels, for instance *Pascali's Island,* the story is told in the first person, whereas *Stone Virgin* combines third-person with some first-person narration. The novels are skillfully structured to maintain narrative interest—for example, *Morality Play* is, among other things, a compulsively readable mystery tale—and to provide a range of perspectives on their themes and symbols.

Whether he writes of the past or present, Unsworth demonstrates that he has the realist novelist's ability to bring places, people, and situations before us in a convincing and immediate way. But he also demonstrates a postmodernist awareness of the way in which fiction—and, to some extent, history and biography—construct the reality they supposedly convey. *Sugar and Rum,* which portrays a novelist who wants to write a novel about the Liverpool slave trade but is suffering from writer's block, provides a kind of metafictional commentary on the book that follows it, *Sacred Hunger.* Despite its vivid medieval detail, *Morality Play,* like some of William Golding's novels, can be read as a kind of fable for the present. *Losing Nelson* explores the obsessions and compulsions that may enter into the writing of historical biography. Unsworth has made a major contribution to reviving the historical novel as a serious form both by writing powerful historical novels but also by raising questions, in his fiction, about how and why we represent the past. He has also, in both his historical and present-day fictions, shown the need to engage with the past in order adequately to portray and understand the present; for example, *Sacred Hunger* confronts an area of Britain's imperial past, its involvement with the slave trade, which is a deeply repressed but still potent subtext in contemporary British debates about immigration and national identity. Unsworth has become an increasingly accomplished and ambitious novelist, whose work constitutes an exciting and wide-ranging exploration of human complexity in the past and present.

—Nicolas Tredell

UPDIKE, John (Hoyer)

Nationality: American. Born in Shillington, Pennsylvania, 18 March 1932. Educated at public schools in Shillington; Harvard University, Cambridge, Massachusetts, A.B. (summa cum laude) 1954; Ruskin School of Drawing and Fine Arts, Oxford (Knox fellow), 1954–55. Married 1) Mary Pennington in 1953 (marriage dissolved), two daughters and two sons; 2) Martha Bernhard in 1977. **Career:**staff reporter, *New Yorker*, 1955–57. Recipient: Guggenheim fellowship, 1959; Rosenthal award, 1960; National Book award, 1964; O. Henry award, 1966; Foreign Book prize (France), 1966; New England Poetry Club Golden Rose, 1979, MacDowell medal, 1981; Pulitzer prize, 1982, 1991; American Book award, 1982; National Book Critics Circle award, for fiction, 1982, 1991, for criticism, 1982; Union League Club Abraham Lincoln award, 1982; National Arts Club Medal of Honor, 1984; PEN/Faulkner award, 1988; National Medal of the Arts, 1989; Pulitzer Prize, 1991; National Book Critics Circle award, 1991; Harvard Arts medal, 1998; National Book Foundation award, Lifetime Achievement, 1998. Member, American Academy, 1976. **Address:** Beverly Farms, Beverly, Massachusetts 01915, U.S.A.

PUBLICATIONS

Novels

The Poorhouse Fair. New York, Knopf, and London, Gollancz, 1959
Rabbit, Run. New York, Knopf, 1960; London, Deutsch, 1961
The Centaur . New York, Knopf, and London, Deutsch, 1963.
Of the Farm. New York, Knopf, 1965.
Couples. New York, Knopf, and London, Deutsch, 1968
Rabbit Redux. New York, Knopf, 1971; London, Deutsch, 1972.
A Month of Sundays. New York, Knopf, and London, Deutsch, 1975.
Marry Me: A Romance. New York, Knopf, 1976; London, Deutsch, 1977.
The Coup. New York, Knopf, 1978; London, Deutsch, 1979.
Rabbit Is Rich. New York, Knopf, 1981; London, Deutsch, 1982.
The Witches of Eastwick. New York, Knopf, and London, Deutsch, 1984.
Roger's Version. New York, Knopf, and London, Deutsch, 1986.
S. New York, Knopf, and London Deutsch, 1988.
Rabbit at Rest. New York, Knopf, 1990; London, Deutsch, 1991.
Memories of the Ford Administration. New York, Knopf, 1992; London, Hamish Hamilton, 1993.
Brazil. New York, Knopf, and London, Hamish Hamilton, 1994.
Rabbit Angstrom: A Tetralogy. New York, Knopf, 1995.
In the Beauty of the Lilies. New York, Knopf, 1996.
Toward the End of Time. New York, Knopf, 1997.
Bech at Bay: A Quasi-novel. New York, Knopf, 1998.
Gertrude and Claudius. New York, Knopf, 2000.

Short Stories

The Same Door. New York, Knopf, 1959; London, Deutsch, 1962.
Pigeon Feathers and Other Stories. New York, Knopf, and London, Deutsch, 1962.
Olinger Stories: A Selection. New York, Knopf, 1964.
The Music School. New York, Knopf, 1966; London, Deutsch, 1967.
Penguin Modern Stories 2, with others. London, Penguin, 1969.
Bech: A Book. New York, Knopf, and London, Deutsch, 1970.
The Indian. Marvin, South Dakota, Blue Cloud Abbey, 1971.
Museums and Women and Other Stories. New York, Knopf, 1972; London, Deutsch, 1973.
Warm Wine: An Idyll. New York, Albondocani Press, 1973.

Couples: A Short Story. Cambridge, Massachusetts, Halty Ferguson, 1976.
Too Far to Go: The Maples Stories. New York, Knopf, 1979; London, Deutsch, 1980.
Three Illuminations in the Life of an American Author. New York, Targ, 1979.
The Chaste Planet. Worcester, Massachusetts, Metacom Press, 1980.
The Beloved. Nothridge, California, Lord John Press, 1982.
Bech Is Back. New York, Knopf, 1982; London, Deutsch, 1982.
Getting Older. Helsinki, Eurographica, 1985.
Going Abroad. Helsinki, Eurographica, 1987
Trust Me. New York, Knopf, and London, Deutsch, 1987.
The Afterlife. Leamington, Warwickshire, Sixth Chamber Press, 1987.
Baby's First Step. Huntington Beach, California, Cahill, 1993.
The Afterlife and Other Stories. New York, Knopf, and London, Hamish Hamilton, 1994.
Licks of Love: Short Stories and a Sequel, ''Rabbit Remembered.'' New York, Knopf, 2000.

Uncollected Short Stories

''Morocco,'' in *Atlantic* (Boston), November 1979.

Plays

Three Tests from Early Ipswich: A Pageant. Ipswich, Massachusetts, 17th Century Day Committee, 1968.
Buchanan Dying. New York, Knopf, and London, Deutsch, 1974.

Verse

The Carpentered Hen and Other Tame Creatures. New York, Harper, 1958; as *Hoping for a Hoopoe,* London, Gollancz, 1959.
Telephone Poles and Other Poems. New York, Knopf, and London, Deutsch, 1963.
Verse. New York, Fawcett, 1965.
Dogs Death. Cambridge, Massachusetts, Lowell House, 1965.
The Angels. Pensacola, Florida, King and Queen Press, 1968.
Bath after Sailing. Monroe, Connecticut, Pendulum Press, 1968.
Midpoint and Other Poems. New York, Knopf, and London, Deutsch, 1969.
Seventy Poems. London, Penguin, 1972.
Six Poems. New York, Aloe, 1973.
Query. New York, Albondocani Press, 1974.
Cunts (*Upon Receiving the Swingers Life Club Memberships Solicitation*). New York, Hallman, 1974.
Tossing and Turning. New York, Knopf, and London, Deutsch, 1977.
Sixteen Sonnets. Cambridge, Massachusetts, Halty Ferguson, 1979.
An Oddly Lovely Day Alone. Richmond, Virginia, Waves Press, 1979.
Five Poems. Cleveland Bits Press, 1980.
Spring Trio. Winston-Salem, North Carolina, Palaemon Press, 1982.
Jester's Dozen. Northridge, California, Lord John Press, 1984.
Facing Nature. New York, Knopf, 1985; London, Deutsch, 1986.
A Pear Like a Potato. Northridge, California, Santa Susana Press, 1986.
Two Sonnets. Austin, Texas, Wind River Press, 1987.
Collected Poems, 1953–1993. New York, Knopf, and London, Hamish Hamilton, 1993.

Other

The Magic Flute (for children), with Warren Chappell. New York, Knopf, 1962.
The Ring (for children), with Warren Chappell. New York, Knopf, 1964.
Assorted Prose. New York, Knopf, and London, Deutsch, 1965.
A Child's Calendar. New York, Knopf, 1965.
On Meeting Authors. Newburyport, Massachusetts, Wickford Press, 1968.
Bottom's Dream: Adapted from William Shakespeare's ''A Midsummer Nights Dream'' (for children). New York, Knopf, 1969.
A Good Place. New York, Aloe, 1973.
Picked-Up Pieces. New York, Knopf, 1975; London, Deutsch, 1976.
Hub Fans Bid Kid Adieu. Northridge, California, Lord John Press, 1977.
Talk from the Fifties. Northridge, California, Lord John Press, 1979.
Ego and Art in Walt Whitman. New York, Targ, 1980.
People One Knows: Interviews with Insufficiently Famous Americans. Northridge, California, Lord John Press, 1980.
Invasion of the Book Envelopes. Concord, New Hampshire, Ewert, 1981.
Hawthorne's Creed. New York, Targ, 1981.
Hugging the Shore: Essays and Criticism. New York, Knopf, 1983; London, Deutsch, 1984.
Confessions of a Wild Bore (essay). Newton, Iowa, Tamazunchale Press, 1984.
Emersonianism (lecture). Cleveland, Bits Press, 1984.
The Art of Adding and the Art of Taking Away: Selections from John Updike's Manuscripts, edited by Elizabeth A. Falsey. Cambridge, Massachusetts, Harvard College Library, 1987.
Self-Consciousness: Memoirs. New York, Knopf, and London, Deutsch, 1989.
Just Looking: Essays on Art. New York, Knopf, and London, Deutsch, 1989.
Odd Jobs: Essays and Criticism. New York, Knopf, and London, Deutsch, 1991.
Concerts at Castle Hill. Northridge, California, Lord John Press, 1993.
The Twelve Terrors of Christmas. New York, Gotham Book Mart, 1993.
Golf Dreams: Writings on Golf, drawings by Paul Szep. New York, Knopf, 1996.
A & P, edited by Wendy Perkins. Fort Worth, Texas, Harcourt Brace College Publishers, 1998.
More Matter: Essays and Criticism. New York, Knopf, 1999.
Editor, *Pens and Needles,* by David Levine. Boston, Gambit, 1970.
Editor, with Shannon Ravenel, *The Best American Short Stories 1984.* Boston, Houghton Mifflin, 1984; as *The Year's Best American Short Stories,* London, Severn House, 1985.
Editor, *A Century of Arts and Letters: The History of the National Institute of Arts and Letters and the American Academy of Arts and Letters as Told, Decade by Decade, by Eleven Members.* New York, Columbia University Press, 1998.

*

Bibliography: *John Updike: A Bibliography* by C. Clarke Taylor, Kent, Ohio, Kent State University Press, 1968; *An Annotated Bibliography of John Updike Criticism 1967–1973, and a Checklist of His*

Works by Michael A. Olivas, New York, Garland, 1975; *John Updike: A Comprehensive Bibliography with Selected Annotations* by Elizabeth A. Gearhart, Norwood, Pennsylvania, Norwood Editions, 1978; *John Updike: A Bibliography, 1967–1993,* compiled by Jack De Bellis, foreword by John Updike, Westport, Connecticut, Greenwood Press, 1994.

Manuscript Collection: Harvard University, Cambridge, Massachusetts.

Critical Studies: interviews in *Life* (New York), 4 November 1966, *Paris Review*, Winter 1968, and *New York Times Book Review,* 10 April 1977; *John Updike* by Charles T. Samuels, Minneapolis, University of Minnesota Press, 1969; *The Elements of John Updike* by Alice and Kenneth Hamilton, Grand Rapids, Michigan, Eerdmans, 1970; *Pastoral and Anti-Pastoral Elements in John Updike's Fiction* by Larry E. Taylor, Carbondale, Southern Illinois University Press, 1971; *John Updike: Yea Sayings* by Rachael C. Burchard, Carbondale, Southern Illinois University Press, 1971; *John Updike* by Robert Detweiler, New York, Twayne, 1972, revised edition, 1984; *Rainstorms and Fire: Ritual in the Novels of John Updike* by Edward P. Vargo, Port Washington, New York, Kennikat Press, 1973; *Fighters and Lovers: Theme in the Novels of John Updike* by Joyce B. Markle, New York, New York University Press, 1973; *John Updike: A Collection of Critical Essays* by Suzanne H. Uphaus, New York, Ungar, 1980; *The Other John Updike: Poems/Short Stories/Prose/Play,* 1981, and *John Updike's Novels,* 1984, both by Donald J. Greiner, Athens, Ohio University Press; *John Updike's Images of America* by Philip H. Vaughan, Reseda, California, Mojave, 1981; *Married Men and Magic Tricks: John Updike's Erotic Heroes* by Elizabeth Tallent, Berkeley, California, Creative Arts, 1982; *Critical Essays on John Updike* edited by William R. Macnaughton, Boston, Hall, 1982; *John Updike* by Judie Newman, London, Macmillan, 1988; *Conversations with John Updike* edited by James Plath, Jackson, Mississippi, University Press, 1994; *John Updike Revisited* by James A. Schiff, New York, Twayne Publishers, 1998; *John Updike and Religion: The Sense of the Sacred and The Motions of Grace,* edited by James Yerkes, Grand Rapids, Michigan, W.B. Eerdmans, 1999; *The John Updike Encyclopedia* by Jack De Bellis, Westport, Connecticut, Greenwood Press, 2000; *John Updike,* edited by Harold Bloom, Philadelphia, Chelsea House Publishers, 2000.

John Updike comments:

In over thirty years as a professional writer I have tried to give my experience of life imaginative embodiment in novels, short stories, and poems. Art is, as I understand it, reality passed through a human mind, and this secondary creation remains for me unfailingly interesting and challenging.

* * *

For over forty years, Updike has been regularly producing his novels about small town and suburban middle class Americans—in short, ordinary people—and their messy domestic lives. He writes with relish, caring, and precision of their marriages and remarriages, sexual trysts, and their struggles to make sense of themselves. Births, deaths, infidelities, and failures fill his pages. Violence, blessedly, is rarely present. Most often, the books chart the way his protagonists adjust their dreams to more nearly match reality. What mark, he wonders, do such people's lives finally make? He is adept at describing the day-to-day existence of suburban bridge players who cultivate their roses, trim their hedges, feed their faces, tidy their homes, maintain contact with children and grandchildren and ''socioeconomically identical acquaintances,'' and travel to Florida and to Maine in suitable seasons, to paraphrase Updike. He also captures specific time periods in our history: the 1950s, the cold war, the Eisenhower and Kennedy eras, and Truman's America. Allegorically, the Nixon term in the White House lies behind *The Coup,* a novel set in Africa. Buchanan's aborted presidency and the Ford administration have also been treated. He adopts various voices, writing from a woman's perspective as well as a man's; using present tense to tell some tales; writing at once from the perspective of a Protestant, ex-basketball star, Harry Angstrom, living in rural Pennsylvania, while at other times employing the persona of his alter-ego, Henry Bech, unmarried, childless, and Jewish, suffering from writer's block and settled in Manhattan.

In his first novel, *The Poorhouse Fair,* he took an old people's home as his subject and experimented with the form of the anti-novel. At the time, readers were startled that such a young man would write so knowingly about the old people, his grandfather's generation. In a sense, his career has come full circle. In 1997 he published *Toward the End of Time,* where he assumes the voice of Ben Turnbull, a sixty-six year old, twice married, retired investment counselor, living in Massachusetts in the year 2020. America has been reduced to a commonwealth, complete with new currency, brought about by a Sino-American Conflict that dissolved the government, collapsed the national economy, decimated the population, and resulted in social chaos. Only the criminal elements have the resources left to rule. Ben's journal recounts the happenings of a difficult year when he is preoccupied by sex and aging, only to find he has prostate cancer. He suffers the indignities and pain of surgery and the consequent incontinence and impotence that follow. He revisits his past, his life with his first wife, Perdita, and with his second wife, the ravishing, strong-willed, dynamic, Gloria, who is determined to have him kill the deer that are ruining her roses, yew bushes, and the euonymus hedge over by the driveway. There are blank spots in his thinking and his journal captures his daily life, often leaving the reader uncertain whether the facts he recounts are true or imagined. In typical Updike form, the novelist fleshes out Ben's mind, recounting his fascination with recent scientific theories about parallel universes that have branched from this moment of measurement. Often he seems to enter one or another of these other ''many worlds.'' Ben also ruminates on Neanderthal man, the Biblical past, St. Paul and his crisis theology, his own personal ancestry, and looks forward into future time.

True also to form, Updike offers an unblinking account of the processes of aging and Ben's numerous infirmities, capturing his fears and joys, the toll age exacts and the hopes it awakens. Ben insists that his wife is worried about whether she or he will die first, priming him with vitamins by day while by night, dreaming of his death. Later he marvels at her loyalty and bravery in the face of his illness, at the same time he refuses to minimize his discomforts—his ''rumbling, spurting bowels'' and his diapers—or her level-headed, self-centered and self-protective ways. His olfactory sense is heightened—all stinks and messes are minutely described. He fears for the sanity of his mind and wonders how much he has forgotten. In one of his fantasies that seems to be real, he purchases the favors of a young prostitute, relishing the numerous ways he can take her, the cunnilingus and fellatio they can practice, his desire to slap her too decisively in the midst of sex, the pleasure he takes in talking crudely to her, addressing her as his "bitch," "whore," and "working-class doxy," but bringing her into his house as his so-called "wife" during a period of time when he claims that his wife has disappeared and he seems uncertain whether he has shot her in his attempt to get rid of the deer, or whether she is simply misplaced or has left him.

This novel and his latest book, *Gertrude and Claudius,* compare with other "last works" of such great writers as Shakespeare or Yeats in that the vision shifts, mellows, while the writer employs new forms and an altered style to reflect the wisdom and insights that come with age. Shakespeare completed his life with three "last plays," *Cymbeline, The Winter's Tale,* and *The Tempest.* In each, he abandons the form of the tragedy, replacing it with romance. In *The Winter's Tale* the central action of an entire tragedy is compressed into the opening act. Later, sixteen years passes, a child grows up, a statue comes to life, and Leontes, the jealous king of the first act regains a wife. In later poetry of Yeats, the poet continues his celebration of the world of artifice and Byzantium, but acknowledges in "The Circus Animals' Desertion" that all inspiration starts in "the foul rag-and-bone shop of the heart." Updike also relies more on romance and myth in his latest novels while at the same time reveling in the powers of the body and sex and probing philosophical questions about the nature of life, time, and religion. Even as the physical body visibly decays, the protagonist's hunger is not only undiminished, it is heightened, and the spirit of experimentation and a craving for plenty is abundant. Many of the passages explicitly describing sex recall the excesses of sexuality expressed in "The Wild Old Wicked Man" and other late poems by Yeats. The bizarre grotesqueries that also figure in *Toward the End of Time* have an oddness akin to the monstrous scene in *Cymbeline* where Imogen cradles the headless body of Cloten in her arms, mistaking him for her beloved Posthumous. The manner in which Updike condenses material that earlier had engrossed him, and lingers on descriptive passages of a bucolic texture while taking extreme liberties with time also make the comparison apt.

Updike has often drawn on myth and fairy tales in his novels and reworked the stories of others. The St. Stephen story figures prominently in *The Poorhouse Fair* and reappears in *Toward the End of Time. The Centaur* uses the Chiron version of the Hercules myth, alternately telling the tale of George Caldwell, a teacher and the Chiron figure, and the Centaur. The subject of *Rabbit, Run,* the first novel in his tetralogy, is based on Beatrix Potter's *Tale of Peter Rabbit.* In *The Witches of Eastwick,* Updike looks at the lives of three modern day divorcées, seeing the similarities between their predicament and those of witches and their covens. Darryl Van Horne is the devil in this work. Therefore, it is not unexpected to find him theorizing in *Toward the End of Time* that several worlds and different time periods may exist simultaneously and offering glimpses into these alternate worlds or earlier times.

His habit of rewriting stories from the perspectives of different characters is also one of his trademarks. He has written a trilogy of novels based on Nathaniel Hawthorne's, *The Scarlet Letter.* In Updike's case, *A Month of Sundays* tells the story of the adulterous minister, Marshfield, from his point of view and offers a parody of the triangle in Hawthorne's tale; in *Roger's Version* we are given the betrayed husband's perspective and Updike explores the theme of the unknowability of God; *S.* completes the trilogy providing the view of the adulterous woman, Hawthorne's Hester Prynne.

His decision to write a novel about the lives of Gertrude, Claudius, Hamlet Senior, and Hamlet immediately prior to where the action opens in Shakespeare's play is almost expected. I should hasten to mention that the central figures appear under different names in different parts of the book, a topic that bears further comment later.

Updike has long marveled at the talents of James Joyce, understanding his need to write his own variant of Shakespeare's story and the Hamlet material in his masterwork, *Ulysses.* Joyce uses Stephen to spin his erudite explanation of Shakespeare's relationship to his creations, both the real children he bore in life and those he invented in his writings. He is familiar with Tom Stoppard's *Rosencrantz and Guildenstern are Dead,* also based on the Hamlet legend. Updike, ever the researcher and inventive in the interests of his art, fashions his novel in three parts and presents Gertrude's story. In Part I of his book, he turns to a late-twelfth-century Latin account of the ancient Hamlet legend in *Historia Danica* of Saxo Grammaticus that was first printed in Paris in 1514. In Part II, he uses alternate spellings of the central figures' names, drawing on another version of the Saxo tale, François de Belleforest's, *Histoires tragiques,* that appeared prior to Shakespeare's *Hamlet* and was republished in English in 1608, probably as a result of the popularity of Shakespeare's play. In Part III, he concludes his novel, drawing on the so-called *Ur-Hamlet,* generally attributed to Thomas Kyd that was acquired by Shakespeare's company and served as the source of his play. Updike achieves a marvelous sense of ancient history and times, largely by dint of employing the ancient spellings of the names of the central characters and by imitating the style of an old Danish legend in his writing. For example, Gerutha is Gertrude in Part I, Horwendil is Hamlet Senior, Feng is Claudius, and Corambis is Polonius, coming originally from a German variant of the ancient tale. Hamlet first emerges as Amleth. He recounts the tale whereby Rorik (Gertrude's father) pledges Gerutha to Horwendil, co-governor of Jutland, who has slain the tormentor of Denmark's coast, the feared King Koll of Norway, giving him the funeral he required while butchering the slain man's sister, as his brother, Feng (read Claudius) is fighting on behalf of the Holy Roman Emperor and whoring in far away lands. Updike takes sheer delight in writing this ancient saga with a thoroughly contemporary twist, and his stylistic touches show him at his best.

The book also seems to be a vehicle to answer some of his feminist critics who have faulted Updike for the way he treats women. He has been accused of constantly treating women as broads, airheads, often amoral. Some feminists loathed *The Witches of Eastwick,* resenting Updike's treatment of the three female women, their philosophies of life, their forays into lesbianism, their fascination with and seduction by Horne. In *Gertrude and Claudius* Hamlet is depicted as a cold, unloving son and Gertrude's affair with Claudius is traced to her ambivalence towards Hamlet Senior, a man whom she was obliged to marry by her father after he had conquered the King Koll.

Updike's style in this book is beguiling: he adopts the tone of an earlier age, proffering the story from Gertrude's perspective and capturing her domesticity, her boredom, her yearning to be truly needed by her husband and lord, not simply taken by him through his authority and used to produce heirs. His treatment of Gertrude's sense of guilt once she has taken her husband's brother to her bed and her desire to remain ignorant of Claudius's ultimate crime while harboring the truth just below her levels of consciousness is convincing. His grasp of Polonius, Hamlet, and Ophelia also seems fresh. Given how much has been written about this play of Shakespeare's, it is hard to imagine that a writer could offer another plausible reading, appropriate to the late twentieth century. Updike has managed to do this in a manner that will delight the reader.

One of the virtues of Updike's talent is that so many of his books are memorable. The tetralogy of books that take Harry Angstrom as their protagonist, namely *Rabbit Run, Rabbit Redux, Rabbit is Rich,* and *Rabbit at Rest,* assured Updike his place as one of America's best contemporary writers. He aspires to a quality of writing he finds in Iris Murdoch, Muriel Spark, Henry Green, Saul Bellow, and Philip Roth and it is fair to say that he has achieved that goal. The freshness of his characters, the truth of his vision, and his ability to describe exactly events, places, people, and feelings are all evident in this very American collection. In *Couples,* his wildly popular novel of wife-swapping among suburbanites, he ensured that his audience would remember him as one of the very finest describers of sex, belonging alongside Vladimir Nabokov, Philip Roth, Henry Miller, and Jack Kerouac, writers whom he invokes when he discusses how sex is depicted in this pornographic age of ours. Of course, D.H. Lawrence and James Joyce are the writers that first convinced him that sex must assume a central place in any writing that purports to capture life. His books on Bech, too, show us a writer in his prime, and they have the virtue of permitting him to write in the character and mind of someone like himself, although very dissimilar in certain ways, rather than constraining him to have to imagine the consciousness of a less well-educated, less privileged Middle-American. Finally, his recent writing, although continuing in veins he opened earlier, continues to surprise and please their reader.

—Carol Simpson Stern

UPWARD, Edward (Falaise)

Nationality: British. **Born:** Romford, Essex, 9 September 1903. **Education:** Repton School, Derby, 1917–21; Corpus Christi College, Cambridge (Chancellors's medal for English verse), 1922–24, M.A. 1925. **Family:** Married to Hilda Maude Percival; one son and one daughter. **Career:** Schoolmaster, 1928–62; Member of the Editorial Board, the *Ploughshare,* London, 1936–39. Lives in Sandown, Isle of Wight. **Address:** c/o Heinemann Ltd., 81 Fulham Road, London SW3 6RB, England.

Publications

Novels

Journey to the Border. London, Hogarth Press, 1938; revised edition, London, Enitharmon Press, 1994; Chester Springs, Pennsylvania, Dufour Editions, 1994.

In the Thirties. London, Heinemann, 1962.

The Rotten Elements. London, Heinemann, 1969.

The Spiral Ascent (includes *In the Thirties, The Rotten Elements, No Home But the Struggle*). London, Heinemann, 1977.

Short Stories

The Night and Other Stories. London, Heinemann, 1967.

The Railway Accident and Other Stories. London, Heinemann, 1969.

The Mortmere Stories (with Christopher Isherwood). London, Enitharmon Press and Chester Springs, Pennsylvania, Dufour Editions, 1994.

The Scenic Railway. London, Enitharmon Press and Chester Springs, Pennsylvania, Dufour Editions, 1997.

Uncollected Short Story

''The Theft,'' in *Colours of a New Day: Writing for South Africa,* edited by Sarah Lefnau and Stephen Hayward. London, Lawrence and Wishart, and New York, Pantheon, 1990.

Poetry

Buddha. London, Cambridge University Press, 1924.

Other

An Unmentionable Man. London, Enitharmon Press, Dufour Editions, 1994.

Christopher Isherwood: Notes in Remembrance of a Friendship. London, Enitharmon, 1996.

*

Manuscript Collection: British Library, London.

Critical Studies: *The Destructive Element: A Study of Modern Writers and Beliefs* by Stephen Spender, London, Cape, 1935, Boston, Houghton Mifflin, 1936; introduction by W.H. Sellers to *The Railway Accident and Other Stories,* 1969; article by Upward, in *London Magazine,* June 1969; *Leben und Werk von Edward Upward* by Dieter Mensen, unpublished thesis, Berlin, Free University, 1976; *Aestheticism and Political Commitment in the Works of Edward Upward* by Clarke Thayer, unpublished thesis, Tulsa, Oklahoma, University of Tulsa, 1981; *History and Value* by Frank Kermode, Oxford, Oxford University Press, 1988.

* * *

Edward Upward as a young writer in the 1930s achieved a great reputation, was indeed something of a legend, among a number of writers of his own age and younger. Christopher Isherwood told in *Lions and Shadows* how he and Upward (called Chalmers in Isherwood's book) at Cambridge invented a fantasy world they called Mortmere which paralleled and parodied the world about them. Mortmere seems to have been at once sinister and comic, partly surrealist and partly Gothic. That it had affinities with Auden's early poetry, influenced as it was by Freud, seems clear, and something of it seems to merge in the plays Isherwood wrote in collaboration with Auden, notably *The Dog Beneath the Skin.* Upward, however, overtly pursued the vein of fantasy in his fiction, but was even then politically committed in the cause of Marxism. The central character of *Journey to the Border* is a middle-class young man employed as a tutor in the house of a rich man; he is constantly struggling against the implications and ignominies of his position but is unable to resolve them. He is persuaded against his will to accompany his employer to a race-meeting. On the way, and while there, he experiences a series of hallucinations that mount in intensity and are the counterparts of the debate going on in his mind. By the end of the novel he is forced to realize that the only solution to this problem, the only way to reality, is for him to identify himself with the working-class struggle.

When the novel was first published, reviewers read the influence of Kafka into it. This is not much apparent now, if it ever existed. Upward's novel is much less complex than those in simple allegory. Nevertheless, the voltage of imaginative work is admirably sustained. It remains a brilliant experimental novel of a very unusual kind.

Upward published nothing for twenty-five years, and then in 1962 published *In the Thirties* (followed by *The Rotten Elements* and, as a complete trilogy incorporating *No Home But the Struggle, The Spiral Ascent*). These novels are based, it is impossible not to think, on the author's own life. *In the Thirties* describes the stages by which a young middle-class man comes to Communism. In a sense, the theme is that of *Journey to the Border,* but the treatment is entirely different. Fantasy has been replaced by literal realism, which is also the vein of later volumes of the trilogy. In *The Rotten Elements* the hero of the earlier novel, a school teacher now married, finds himself compelled in the years immediately after the war to leave the Communist Party, not because he has lost his political faith but because for him and his wife the British Communist Party, under the influence of Moscow, has deviated from Marxism-Leninism. *No Home But the Struggle* shows them recommitted to the campaign for nuclear disarmament. The trilogy lacks the literary interest of *Journey to the Border,* but it has an anguish of its own and a documentary quality which suggests that, though it may not be read in the future for its artistic value, it will be essential reading for scholars concerned with the role of the Communist party in Britain.

—Walter Allen

V

VANDERHAEGHE, Guy

Nationality: Canadian. **Born:** Esterhazy, Saskatchewan, 5 April 1951. **Education:** University of Saskatchewan, Saskatoon, B.A. 1972, M.A. 1975; University of Regina, B.Ed. 1978. **Family:** Married Margaret Elizabeth Nagel in 1972. **Career:** Archivist, University of Saskatchewan, Saskatoon, 1973–75; Editor, *Journal of Orthomolecular Medicine,* Regina, Saskatchewan, 1976–78; high school English and history teacher, Herbert, Saskatchewan, 1978–79; Researcher, Access Consulting (health care consultants), Saskatoon, 1979–81; writer, 1981—; writer-in-residence, Saskatoon Public Library, 1983–84. Lives in Saskatoon, Saskatchewan, Canada.**Awards:** Governor General's award for English fiction, 1982, 1996. **Agent:** c/o Writers Union of Canada, 24 Ryerson Ave., Toronto, Ontario, Canada M5T 2P3.

Publications

Novels

My Present Age. Toronto, Macmillan of Canada, 1984; Ticknor & Fields, 1985.

Homesick. Toronto, McClelland & Stewart, 1989; Ticknor & Fields, 1990.

The Englishman's Boy. New York, Picador USA, 1997.

Short Stories

Man Descending. Toronto, Macmillan of Canada, 1982; New York, Ticknor & Fields, 1985.

The Trouble with Heroes. Ottawa, Borealis Press, 1983.

Things as They Are? Short Stories. Toronto, McClelland & Stewart, 1992.

Plays

I Had a Job I Liked, Once: A Play. Saskatoon, Saskatchewan, Fifth House, 1992.

Other

Dancock's Dance. Winnipeg, Manitoba, Blizzard Publishers, 1996.

Contributor, *Aurora: New Canadian Writing.* New York, Doubleday, 1978.

Contributor, *Aurora: New Canadian Writing.* New York, Doubleday, 1979.

Contributor, *Aurora: New Canadian Writing.* New York, Doubleday, 1980.

Contributor, *Sundogs: Stories from Saskatchewan*, edited by Robert Kroetsch. Moose Jaw, Saskatchewan, Thunder Creek Publishing Cooperative, 1980.

Contributor, *Best Canadian Short Stories.* Oberon Press, 1980.

Contributor, *Best American Short Stories,* 1982.

Contributor, *Myths and Voices: Contemporary Canadian Fiction,* edited by David Lampe. Fredonia, New York, White Pine Press, 1993.

*   *   *

Having established himself on the Canadian literary scene on the strengths of such story collections as *Man Descending*, for which he was awarded the Governor General's award in 1982, and *The Trouble with Heroes*, Guy Vanderhaeghe turned to the novel form in 1984 with *My Present Age*. Pivoting on the quixotic quest of Ed, a character from his earlier stories who sets off to find a wife who has abandoned him, this is a story that is equal parts journey to the past and exploration of the future. More importantly, Ed's sometimes comic (mis)adventures prove an opportunity for extended exploration of many of the themes and issues that Vanderhaeghe probes in the strongest of his shorter fictions: the complex influences of time and place on the lives of individuals and communities; questions of what constitutes a hero and an act of heroism in the postmodern world; the moral implications of a cultural tendency toward stultifying self-deceptions; and the resiliency of the human spirit and the ability of individuals to search out spiritual and emotional nourishment in even the bleakest of environments.

Similar questions and struggles are revisited in *Homesick*, Vanderhaeghe's second novel, as the widow Vera Monkman works toward reconciling herself with her own father and the prairie town in which she lives. With clear affiliations with the works of such antecedent prairie novelists as Margaret Laurence (the Manawaka books) and Sinclair Ross (notably *As for Me and My House*), it is a story that reveals a community torn between an intense, almost obsessive yearning for a sense of home and an equally powerful fear of the realities of the harsh geography in which they find themselves.

Although both novels were well received by critics and reviewers, it was Vanderhaeghe's third book, the richly textured *The Englishman's Boy*, that secured him a position in the upper ranks of Canadian novelists. Awarded the Governor General's award and nominated for the prestigious Giller prize, it is a carefully crafted narrative that weaves together two causally linked stories: one of a little known late nineteenth-century massacre of an encampment of Assiniboine by a group of white wolf hunters (based on an actual event in Canadian history), the other of a 1920s Hollywood mogul's determination to renarrate the details of the event in support of his megalomaniacal, and degradingly revisionist, goals. Connecting these two historical threads is Harry Vincent, a Canadian expatriate and frustrated writer hired by the mogul to find an infamous ''Indian fighter,'' Shorty McAdoo, who might (or might not) hold the key to the many mysteries clouding the historical ''truth'' of the slaughter. Myopic and passive, Vincent proves the ideal witness to the increasingly sinister events that unfold in the novel; drawn deeper and deeper into the story of the Cypress Hills massacre, he proves a less than astute reader of the events that unfold around him. Developing slowly and with careful attention to subtle ironies and to the rhythms and nuances of language, *The Englishman's Boy* forces other readers (those of the novel proper) to confront questions of how they come to know the past, and how, via a traditional cultural commitment to such abstractions as historical truth and objectivity, each of us is to varying degrees complicit in the attitudes and policies that help sustain the machineries of exploitation and institutional repression serving the present.

—Klay Dyer

VANSITTART, Peter

Nationality: British. **Born:** Bedford, 27 August 1920. **Education:** Marlborough House School; Haileybury College, Hertford; Worcester College, Oxford (major scholar in modern history). **Career:** Director, Burgess School, London, 1947–59; formerly, publisher, Park Editions, London. **Awards:** Society of Authors travelling scholarship, 1969; Arts Council bursary, 1981, 1984. Fellow, Royal Society of Literature, 1985. **Agent:** Sheil and Associates Ltd., 43 Doughty Street, London WC1N 2LF. **Address:** 9 Upper Park Road, London N.W.3; or, Little Manor, Kersey, Ipswich, Suffolk, England.

PUBLICATIONS

Novels

I Am the World. London, Chatto and Windus, 1942.
Enemies. London, Chapman and Hall, 1947.
The Overseer. London, Chapman and Hall, 1949.
Broken Canes. London, Lane, 1950.
A Verdict of Treason. London, Lane, 1952.
A Little Madness. London, Lane, 1953.
The Game and the Ground. London, Reinhardt, 1956; New York, Abelard Schuman, 1957.
Orders of Chivalry. London, Bodley Head, 1958; New York, Abelard Schuman, 1959.
The Tournament. London, Bodley Head, 1959; New York, Walker, 1961.
A Sort of Forgetting. London, Bodley Head, 1960.
Carolina. London, New English Library, 1961.
Sources of Unrest. London, Bodley Head, 1962.
The Friends of God. London, Macmillan, 1963; as *The Siege,* New York, Walker, 1963.
The Lost Lands. London, Macmillan, and New York, Walker, 1964.
The Story Teller. London, Owen, 1968.
Pastimes of a Red Summer. London, Owen, 1969.
Landlord. London, Owen, 1970.
Quintet. London, Owen, 1976.
Lancelot. London, Owen, 1978.
The Death of Robin Hood. London, Owen, 1981.
Harry. London, Park, 1981.
Three Six Seven. London, Owen, 1983.
Aspects of Feeling. London, Owen, 1986.
Parsifal. London, Owen, 1988; Chester Springs, Pennsylvania, Dufour, 1989.
The Wall. London, Owen, 1990.
A Choice of Murder. London, Owen, 1992.
A Safe Conduct. London, Owen, 1995; Chester Springs, Pennsylvania, 1995.

Other

The Dark Tower: Tales from the Past (for children). London, Macdonald, 1965; New York, Crowell, 1969.
The Shadow Land: More Stories from the Past (for children). London, Macdonald, 1967.
Green Knights, Black Angels: The Mosaic of History (for children). London, Macmillan, 1969.
Vladivostok (essay). London, Covent Garden Press, 1972.
Dictators. London, Studio Vista, 1973.
Worlds and Underworlds: Anglo-European History Through the Centuries. London, Owen, 1974.
Flakes of History. London, Park, 1978.
The Ancient Mariner and the Old Sailor: Delights and Uses of Words. London, Centre for Policy Studies, 1985.
Paths from a White Horse: A Writer's Memoir. London, Quartet, 1985.
London: A Literary Companion. London, Murray, 1992.
In the Fifties. London, Murray, 1995.
In Memory of England: A Novelist's View of History. London, John Murray, 1998.
Survival Tactics: A Literary Life. London and Chester Springs, Pennsylvania, P. Owen, 1999.
Editor, *Voices from the Great War.* London, Cape, 1981; New York, Watts, 1984.
Editor, *Voices: 1870–1914.* London, Cape, 1984; New York, Watts, 1985.
Editor, *John Masefield's Letters from the Front 1915–1917.* London, Constable, 1984; New York, Watts, 1985.
Editor, *Happy and Glorious! An Anthology of Royalty.* London, Collins, 1988.
Editor, *Voices of the Revolution.* London, Collins, 1989.
Editor, *Kipps,* by H.G. Wells. London, Everyman, 1993.

*

Peter Vansittart comments:

Though I have published non-fiction, novels alone excite my ambitions; not plays, short stories, poems, manifestos, sermons. My novels have been appreciated, if not always enjoyed, more by critics than the reading public, which shows no sign of enjoying them at all. This must be partly due to my obsession with language and speculation at the expense of narrative, however much I relish narrative in others. Today I take narrative more seriously, though still relying, perhaps over-relying, on descriptive colour, unexpected imagery, the bizarre and curious, no formula for popular success. *The Game and the Ground, The Tournament, Lancelot,* and *Quintet,* have succeeded the most in expressing initial vision and valid situation in fairly accessible terms. Others—*A Verdict of Treason, A Sort of Forgetting*—had interesting and provocative material, clumsily handled. *The Story Teller,* my own favourite, failed through excess of ambition, *A Little Madness* and *Sources of Unrest,* through too little.

My novels range in time from the second millennium BC, to AD 1986. They share the effect of time, and the apparently forgotten or exterminated on the present, time transmuting, distorting, travestying, ridiculing facts and ideas, loves and hates, generous institutions and renowned reputations. I was long impressed by the woeful distinction between the historical Macbeth and Shakespeare's: by the swift transformation of E.M. Forster's very English Mrs. Moore into an Indian goddess. Such phenomena relate very immediately to my own work, in which myth can be all too real, and the real degenerate into fantasy.

* * *

In his memoirs, *Paths from a White Horse,* Peter Vansittart comments enlighteningly on the genre with which he is most closely associated, the historical novel. He knows that it has come to be disdained by many readers because of its long tradition of crude sentimentality and easy picturesqueness, with language that is either over-spiced with random archaism in vocabulary and syntax or else bled white for the sake of coining a supposedly timeless idiom. Worst of all, the desire to present the ''facts'' is too often allowed to come between the novelist and his primary duty of creating significant fictions. Though Vansittart is uncommonly well informed about history, it has never been his intention to attempt to rehabilitate the historical novel by basing his work on a sounder foundation of scholarship. Instead, appreciating that the objects and methods of history and fiction are distinct, for all that the starting point in both enterprises is a serious contemplation of the past, he is content to leave research and verification to the historians and claims for novelists the right to speculate over the facts that are available. He argues that he is entitled to let his imagination brood over events, situations, and characters, discovering by poetic insight mythic continuities that could be too daring for academic minds. This can happen in especially interesting ways when the past is reflected through the personalities of highly individualised characters whose outlook necessarily colours every interpretation of what is related. For Vansittart, the historical novel is, moreover, not exclusively concerned with the depiction of the past. Far more excitingly, he always presents past and present as a continuity, and while relishing the otherness of remote ages and of the people who lived through them, he makes his historical fiction a vehicle for an alert commentary on our present discontents.

The Death of Robin Hood, for instance, is an ambitious attempt to unify experiences by portraying a huge tract of time, with fantasy and realism mingled to create myth. First comes a spell-binding evocation of the forest in primal times when strange rites are already seen as failing to arrest the processes of change and decay. The second part of the novel, ''John in the Castle,'' depicts the paranoid terrors of a tyrant who cowers behind stone walls, dreading the prospect of conflict with the unruly bands that have taken refuge in the forest. Here there is fine descriptive writing, but it is John's state of mind that is the centre of attention. Next, not pausing to make the linkage explicit, Vansittart moves on to the Luddite riots of 1811 when Nottinghamshire workers rose up and smashed the new machines that were taking away their livelihood and then, as the forces of repression gathered, ran off in droves into the forest. Finally, reverting to the environment he had portrayed with satiric verve in *Broken Canes,* Vansittart shows the old values under attack in the closed world of an independent school just before the outbreak of World War II. With its abrupt transitions, *The Death of Robin Hood* can be puzzling, but the immediacy of the emotions and the vividness of the scenes carry the reader along. *Lancelot* is more straightforward. It takes as its starting point Field-Marshal Wavell's observation that ''Arthur was probably a grim figure in a grim, un-romantic struggle in a dark period of history,'' and, once again, it presents within a framework of exciting events an enquiry into the meaning of change and apparent decay. *Three Six Seven* is set in A.D. 367, a year of cataclysm for Roman Britain.

Parsifal is a novel that has some affinities with *The Death of Robin Hood.* The cryptic first chapter makes an explicit reference to Richard Wagner, but then the narrative doubles back to present, in chronological sequence, a series of portrayals of the Arthurian quasi-hero through the ages, from a curiously indeterminate prehistorical era to the fall of the Nazis. With his precise choice of vocabulary and tight-lipped style, Vansittart, without here trying very often for pictorial effects, creates compelling fiction. It evokes a world sadly out of joint, with legendary and literary elements curiously combined and with the extraordinary blend of reinterpreted myth and remorseless psychological realism which is the hallmark of Vansittart's historical novels.

Vansittart is by no means only a historical novelist, and his gift for description and his disabused insight into human motivations are equally well revealed in the portrayal of the life of the bourgeoisie in modern times in such novels as *Quintet.* The first of its five parts is set in Africa in the immediate post-war era when Britain was shedding its colonial responsibilities, and institutional decay is generally the framework within which flawed human beings pursue their complex ways.

As well as presenting a personal vision of man's lot and exploring the possibilities of narrative technique in challenging fashion, Vansittart possesses a most distinguished prose style. Provided every thought of complacent exuberance and lush imagery is banished, it might well be called poetic, for here there is a rare regard for the communicative power of the exact word in precisely the right place. Nouns in particular he values, not cluttering them with adjectives but letting them stand stark and unmodified to convey meaning. This gives an impression of elemental vigour which is apt in *Lancelot,* for example, and the tight-lipped statements suggest pressures that can be held in check only with difficulty just as dark hints leave us to draw dire conclusions for ourselves. In *The Death of Robin Hood* the prose, which is very stylised at first, becomes more and more relaxed as we move towards modern times, though Vansittart continues to use words with scrupulous care for their effect. In his novels there is humour too, but usually the laughter is uneasy, in situations that are becoming uncomfortable. Quite a prolific novelist, Vansittart has kept a voice that is distinctively his own.

The title of *A Choice of Murder* might lead one to guess it is a genre mystery, but in Vansittart's hands it is far from it. The protagonist is Timoleon of Syracuse, an actual historical figure who in the fourth century B.C. liberated his home in Sicily from Carthaginian domination. He also murdered his older brother, and the author examines his life to find out why. *A Safe Conduct* jumps forward to the eve of the Renaissance in Germany, again focusing on a real person. The heretic Hans Bohm was, along with contemporary Thomas Munzer, a precursor of twentieth-century political radicalism; in Vansittart's version, however, he becomes one who prepares the way for a more powerful prince, Albrecht.

—Christopher Smith, updated by Judson Knight

VASSANJI, M(oyez) G.

Nationality: Canadian (originally Kenyan, emigrated to United State, 1970; emigrated to Canada, 1978). **Born:** Nairobi, Kenya, 30 May 1950. **Education:** Massachusetts Institute of Technology, B.S. 1974; University of Pennsylvania, Ph.D. 1978. **Family:** Married Nurjehan

Aziz; one child. **Career:** Affiliated with Atomic Energy of Canada at Chalk River power station, 1978–80; research associate and lecturer in physics, 1980–89. Since 1989 full-time writer. **Agent:** Peter Livingston Associates, Inc., 89 Collier St., Toronto, Ontario M4W 1M2, Canada.

PUBLICATIONS

Novels

The Gunny Sack. Oxford, Heinemann International, 1989.
No New Land. Toronto, McClelland and Stewart, 1991.
The Book of Secrets. Toronto, McClelland & Stewart, 1994; New York, Picador, 1996.
Amriika. Toronto, McClelland & Stewart, 1999.

Short Stories

Uhuru Street. Heinemann International, 1991.

Other

A Meeting of Streams: South Asian Canadian Literature. Toronto, TSAR, 1985.
Editor, *The Journey Prize Anthology: Short Fiction from the Best of Canada's New Writers.* Toronto, McClelland & Stewart, 1995.

* * *

As a storyteller, M.G. Vassanji is fascinated with the often elliptical forms that stories can take and with the vestiges of experience (tangible and otherwise) that connect individuals and communities to them. And, as is often the case, it is this willingness to explore continually the boundaries of form that is at once the principal strength and weakness of his fiction.

Illustrative of this tension is *The Gunny Sack,* an episodic generational novel set, like all the strongest of Vassanji's writing, in and against the multicultural panorama of East Africa. Engaging a structure that reflects the randomness of reaching into a bag of treasures, he organizes this narrative around the artifacts that the book's narrator, Salim, recovers from an almost mythical repository passed to him by a great-aunt. Forever being ordered and reordered by the holder of the bag, each wisp of memory elicits any number of stories about one extended family's arrival and existence in this story-rich country. Considered individually, these episodes take many shapes—fables of community, lyrical remembrances of family, and recollections of political events. Considered cumulatively, they intermingle, though not always smoothly, to form a lush polyphony, an exploration of place and character that avoids flat archetypes and the subsumption of individual voices in any grand pattern of history or myth. Indeed, at times the genealogical details that accumulate with each subsequent episode threaten to become frustratingly labyrinthine.

This occasional awkwardness dissipates when Vassanji shifts form for his only short fiction collection, *Uhuru Street,* the sixteen linked stories that share a number of characters and episodes with *The Gunny Sack.* More traditional in style than his longer fiction, these are economical, but nonetheless vivid, evocations of the anxious movement of East Africa from the final days of colonial rule to the harsh realities of newfound independence. In the strongest inclusions, "All Worlds Are Possible Now," in which a man endeavors to reclaim a sense of place and self during a trip "home," and the bittersweet remembrances of "The London-returned," Vassanji's control of the story format creates a novelistic collection that moves almost seamlessly across the frontiers of geography and history to speak of stories at once individual and collective, singular and diverse.

Moving from the fluidity of *The Gunny Sack* and the interdependence that characterizes linked stories, Vassanji finds the form for *The Book of Secrets,* his most accomplished work of fiction, in a more fixed trace of the past: the 1913 diary of a colonial administrator, Corbin, that is discovered hidden in a shopkeeper's backroom in modern Dares Salaam. Lent to Pius Fernandes, a retired teacher whose own notebook entries also become part of the novel, the diary becomes the centerpiece in a quest to (re)construct the enigmatic family history believed to be concealed in its pages. Although the dual presence of diary and notebook suggests a certain precision to the notation and relationship of the times, places, and events that shape this story, Vassanji reveals both to be versions of the titular book of secrets, necessarily incomplete records of experiences that have no witnesses and of questions that remain unanswered—and perhaps unanswerable. Who exactly is the beautiful Shamsi woman, Mariamu, whom Corbin rescues from a potentially fatal exorcism? And what exactly is the nature of their intensely intimate relationship? Is it passion that inspires her to steal the Englishman's personal journal or something darker? Indeed, such questions accumulate with dazzling frequency.

An intriguing palimpsest of vernacular, historical, and cultural discourses, *The Book of Secrets* also foregrounds the themes and ideas that recur throughout Vassanji's fiction: notions of history and memory; inquiries into how much one can (and dare) know about the past; ideas of home and community as they extend across time and space; and the insidious legacies of colonialism, war, race prejudice, and religious intolerance. And though these books suggest that a relatively harmonious coexistence of peoples and cultures is at least possible, and at best vital, in the modern world, the potential for conflict is omnipresent. Institutional hypocrisy and racism, family feuds, petty jealousies, and sexual exploitation are never far from the surface of Vassanji's narratives. At times, this undercurrent of discord erupts in viciousness, notably in the violence of the Kurtz-like Maynard (*The Book of Secrets*), in the frequent convergence of commerce and sexual exploitation ("For a Shilling"), and in the racially motivated murder that symbolizes the changing times in "What Good Times We Had." Indeed, it is the image that ends this story, a tableau of death in which the brutalized victim hangs by her feet from a tree branch, that resonates in a number of subsequent stories in the Uhuru cycle. In *The Book of Secrets* and in stories like "The Beggar" and "Alzira," though, the immediate threat of confrontation is replaced or diffused by sudden and unexpected acts of kindness, allowing questions of dignity, humanity, and love to be invoked as optimistic counterpoints to the darker shadows that ripple through the lives of his characters and the stories they tell.

A writer whose most evocative works are distinguished by luxurious subtleties and a lightness of touch, Vassanji does allow his narratives to slide, on occasion, toward a heavy-handed characterization and somewhat stilted dialogue. Too often in his more traditionally structured novels—*No New Land* and the ambitious *Amriika*—Vassanji sacrifices explorations of nuanced character and story in favor of examining what might be best described as the anthropological or sociological tensions confronting immigrants drawn to the uneasy promise of a future in North America. Tracing the struggles of an idealistic young African who leaves home in 1968 to attend an American college, *Amriika*, for example, engages the backdrop of three tumultuous decades in American history, a period of anti-war protests, radicalized politics, sexual openness, and spiritual quests. The rich potentialities of setting are unable to sustain a story burdened, in this case, by a narrator whose presence remains nebulous and whose life journeys never lead to the kind of profound introspection that lift the stories of Fernandes, Salim, and others off the page.

Drawing often, as he does, on the specificities of East Africa has led to obvious comparisons with such novelists as Abdulrazak Gurnah, and in a less localized sense, with fellow Canadians Rohinton Mistry and Michael Ondaatje. Although such comparisons do tend to oversimplify the works of each writer, they also point to the fact that Vassanji has established himself as a writer whose novels continue to expand our understanding of stories, of the powers (and dangers) of borders, and of the common threads that connect readers and writers regardless of where they were born or where they reside.

—Klay Dyer

VIDAL, Gore

Pseudonym: Edgar Box. **Nationality:** American. **Born:** Eugene Luther Gore Vidal, Jr. in West Point, New York, 3 October 1925. **Education:** Los Alamos School, New Mexico, 1939–40; Phillips Exeter Academy, New Hampshire, 1940–43. **Military Service:** Served in the United States Army, 1943–46: Warrant Officer. **Career:** Editor, E.P. Dutton, publishers, New York, 1946. Lived in Antigua, Guatemala, 1947–49, and Italy, 1967–76; member, advisory board, *Partisan Review,* New Brunswick, New Jersey, 1960–71; Democratic-Liberal candidate for Congress, New York, 1960; member, President's Advisory Committee on the Arts, 1961–63; co-chairman, New Party, 1968–71. **Awards:** Mystery Writers of America award, for television play, 1954; Cannes Film Critics award, for screenplay, 1964; National Book Critics Circle award, for criticism, 1983; National Book award for nonfiction, 1993; Chevalier de l'Ordre des Arts et des Lettres, France, 1995. **Address:** La Rondinaia, Ravello, Salerno, Italy; or c/o Random House Inc., 201 East 50th Street, New York, New York 10022, U.S.A.

Publications

Novels

Williwaw. New York, Dutton, 1946; London, Panther, 1965.
In a Yellow Wood. New York, Dutton, 1947; London, New English Library, 1967.
The City and the Pillar. New York, Dutton, 1948; London, Lehmann, 1949; revised edition, Dutton, and London, Heinemann, 1965; revised, with a new preface by the author, published as *The City and the Pillar and Seven Early Stories,* New York, Random House, 1995.
The Season of Comfort. New York, Dutton, 1949.
Dark Green, Bright Red. New York, Dutton, and London, Lehmann, 1950.
A Search for the King: A Twelfth Century Legend. New York, Dutton, 1950; London, New English Library, 1967.
The Judgment of Paris. New York, Dutton, 1952; London, Heinemann, 1953; revised edition, Boston, Little Brown, 1965; Heinemann, 1966.
Messiah. New York, Dutton, 1954; London, Heinemann, 1955; revised edition, Boston, Little Brown, 1965; Heinemann, 1968.
Three: Williwaw, A Thirsty Evil, Julian the Apostate. New York, New American Library, 1962.
Julian. Boston, Little Brown, and London, Heinemann, 1964.
Washington, D.C. Boston, Little Brown, and London, Heinemann, 1967.
Myra Breckinridge. Boston, Little Brown, and London, Blond, 1968.
Two Sisters: A Memoir in the Form of a Novel. Boston, Little Brown, and London, Heinemann, 1970.
Burr. New York, Random House, 1973; London, Heinemann, 1974.
Myron. New York, Random House, 1974; London, Heinemann, 1975.
1876. New York, Random House, and London, Heinemann, 1976.
Kalki. New York, Random House, and London, Heinemann, 1978.
Creation. New York, Random House, and London, Heinemann, 1981.
Duluth. New York, Random House, and London, Heinemann, 1983.
Lincoln. New York, Random House, and London, Heinemann, 1984.
Empire. New York, Random House, and London, Deutsch, 1987.
Hollywood: A Novel of American in the 1920s. New York, Random House, and London, Deutsch, 1990.
Live from Golgotha. New York, Random House, 1992.
The Smithsonian Institution. New York, Random House, 1998.
The Golden Age. New York, Doubleday, 2000.

Novels as Edgar Box

Death in the Fifth Position. New York, Dutton, 1952; London, Heinemann, 1954.
Death Before Bedtime. New York, Dutton, 1953; London, Heinemann, 1954.
Death Likes It Hot. New York, Dutton, 1954; London, Heinemann, 1955.

Short Stories

A Thirsty Evil: Seven Short Stories. New York, Zero Press, 1956; London, Heinemann, 1958.

Plays

Visit to a Small Planet (televised 1955). Included in *Visit to a Small Planet and Other Television Plays,* 1956; revised version (produced New York, 1957; London, 1960), Boston, Little Brown, 1957; in *Three Plays,* 1962.
Honor (televised 1956). Published in *Television Plays for Writers: Eight Television Plays,* edited by A.S. Burack, Boston, The Writer, 1957; revised version as *On the March to the Sea: A Southron Comedy* (produced Bonn, Germany, 1961), in *Three Plays,* 1962.
Visit to a Small Planet and Other Television Plays (includes *Barn Burning, Dark Possession, The Death of Billy the Kid, A Sense of Justice, Smoke, Summer Pavilion, The Turn of the Screw*). Boston, Little Brown, 1956.
The Best Man: A Play about Politics (produced New York, 1960). Boston, Little Brown, 1960; in *Three Plays,* 1962.

Three Plays (includes *Visit to a Small Planet, The Best Man, On the March to the Sea*). London, Heinemann, 1962.
Romulus: A New Comedy, adaptation of a play by Friedrich Dürrenmatt (produced New York, 1962). New York, Dramatists Play Service, 1962.
Weekend (produced New York, 1968). New York, Dramatists Play Service, 1968.
An Evening with Richard Nixon and ... (produced New York, 1972). New York, Random House, 1972.

Screenplays: *The Catered Affair,* 1956; *I Accuse,* 1958; *The Scapegoat,* with Robert Hamer, 1959; *Suddenly, Last Summer,* with Tennessee Williams, 1959; *The Best Man,* 1964; *Is Paris Burning?,* with Francis Ford Coppola, 1966; *Last of the Mobile Hot-Shots,* 1970; *The Sicilian,* 1970; *Gore Vidal's Billy the Kid,* 1989.

Television Plays: *Barn Burning,* from the story by Faulkner, 1954; *Dark Possession,* 1954; *Smoke,* from the story by Faulkner, 1954; *Visit to a Small Planet,* 1955; *The Death of Billy the Kid,* 1955; *A Sense of Justice,* 1955; *Summer Pavillion,* 1955; *The Turn of the Screw,* from the story by Henry James, 1955; *Honor,* 1956; *The Indestructible Mr. Gore,* 1960; *Vidal in Venice* (documentary), 1985; *Dress Gray,* from the novel by Lucian K. Truscott IV, 1986.

Other

Rocking the Boat (essays). Boston, Little Brown, 1962; London, Heinemann, 1963.
Sex, Death, and Money (essays). New York, Bantam, 1968.
Reflections upon a Sinking Ship (essays). Boston, Little Brown, and London, Heinemann, 1969.
Homage to Daniel Shays: Collected Essays 1952–1972. New York, Random House, 1972; as *Collected Essays 1952–1972,* London, Heinemann, 1974.
Matters of Fact and of Fiction: Essays 1973–1976. New York, Random House, and London, Heinemann, 1977.
Sex Is Politics and Vice Versa (essay). Los Angeles, Sylvester and Orphanos, 1979.
Views from a Window: Conversations with Gore Vidal, with Robert J. Stanton. Secaucus, New Jersey, Lyle Stuart, 1980.
The Second American Revolution and Other Essays 1976–1982. New York, Random House, 1982; as *Pink Triangle and Yellow Star and Other Essays,* London, Heinemann, 1982.
Vidal in Venice, edited by George Armstrong, photographs by Tore Gill. New York, Summit, and London, Weidenfeld and Nicolson, 1985.
Armegeddon? Essays 1983–1987. London, Deutsch, 1987; as *At Home,* New York, Random House, 1988.
A View from the Diners Club. London, Deutsch, 1991.
The Decline and Fall of the American Empire. Berkeley, California, Odonian Press, 1992.
Screening History. Cambridge, Harvard University Press, and London, Deutsch, 1992.
United States: Essays, 1952–1992. New York, Random House, and London, Deutsch, 1993.
Palimpsest: A Memoir. New York, Random House, 1995.
The American Presidency. Monroe, Maine, Odonian Press, 1998.
Virgin Islands, a Dependency of United States: Essays 1992–1997. London, Abacus, 1998.
The Essential Vidal, edited by Fred Kaplan. New York, Random House, 1999.
Gore Vidal, Sexually Speaking: Collected Sex Writings, edited by Donald Weise. San Francisco, Cleis, 1999.
Editor, *Best Television Plays.* New York, Ballantine, 1956.

*

Bibliography: *Gore Vidal: A Primary and Secondary Bibliography* by Robert J. Stanton, Boston, Hall, and London, Prior, 1978.

Manuscript Collection: University of Wisconsin, Madison.

Critical Studies: *Gore Vidal* by Ray Lewis White, New York, Twayne, 1968; *The Apostate Angel: A Critical Study of Gore Vidal* by Bernard F. Dick, New York, Random House, 1974; *Gore Vidal* by Robert F. Kiernan, New York, Ungar, 1982; *Gore Vidal: Writer Against the Grain* edited by Jay Parini, New York, Columbia University Press, and London, Deutsch, 1992; *Gore Vidal: A Critical Companion* by Susan Baker and Curtis S. Gibson, Westport, Connecticut, Greenwood Press, 1997; *Gore Vidal: A Biography* by Fred Kaplan, New York, Doubleday, 1999.

* * *

Gore Vidal has been called ''our wild man of the literary left.'' He has lent his political savvy to monumental historical fiction projects such as the American Chronicle series which spans the history of the United States from the Revolution to the post-World War II years. The six novels arch from Hollywood to Washington, D.C., with a large cast of fictional and historical characters in a panorama of American politics interpreted by the intellectually adroit mind and drawn with the irreverent hand of a sophisticated and ironic observer. Vidal's oeuvre is not limited to historical fiction, however, as he has turned his attentions to doomsday fictions, playfully pornographic novels, a pseudonymous series of detective stories, and science fiction, as well as essays and plays. Always relevant, often funny, undeniably astute, Vidal's tone purposefully drifts into cynicism and his style into satire whenever possible.

Vidal's first novel, *Williwaw,* published in 1946, is set on an army transport vessel laying a course among the Aleutian Islands during World War II. The story about seven self-absorbed men whose enforced closeness results in a homicide about which no one really cares was written when Vidal was nineteen years old. Of more lasting interest among the early novels is his third published in 1948, *The City and the Pillar,* about a young man's gradual discovery that he is homosexual. The stark, unsentimental examination of his main character's sexual identity shocked the public, and the five novels which followed, including the somewhat redemptive *Messiah,* a savagely apocalyptic novel about merchandising a savior, were commercial failures. The rest, which were coolly received by critics, include *In a Yellow Wood,* a glimpse into the Manhattan demimonde; *The Season of Comfort; A Search for the King: A Twelfth Century Legend,* the first of Vidal's historical novels; and *The Judgment of Paris,* a campy updating of the Greek myth.

After a successful period of writing dramatic scripts for television, film, and the stage during the 1950s and 1960s, he published one of his most enduring early novels, *Julian,* in 1964. Vidal's first major novel purports to be the Emperor Julian's autobiographical memoir and private journal. The sympathetic fictional portrait is of Julian the Apostate, the fourth-century pagan Roman emperor who opposed Christianity. In scenes complexly imagined and impressively researched, Vidal recreates Julian's path from Christianity to Mithraism and from philosophy to military science. The novel is rewarding for its rich historicity and for the interplay of Julian's elevated discourse with the witty phrase-making of Priscus and the pedantry of Libanius, the editors of Julian's memoirs. Its ventriloquistic mode of narration became a proven formula for Vidal's most accomplished fiction.

Washington, D.C., published in 1967, is the first novel of a sequence and offers an illuminating portrait of the republic from the time of the New Deal to the McCarthy era. Widely regarded as Vidal's ultimate comment on how the American political system degrades those who participate in it, the novel traces the fortunes James Burden Day, a conservative senator eyeing the presidency, Clay Overbury, a congressional aide, and Blaise Sanford, a newspaper magnate. The novel follows the power and the money as the power mongers of the nation's capital transform the United States into ''possibly the last empire on earth.'' As national events from Pearl Harbor to Korea stage themselves in the background, the histrionic characters prove the importance of image and the Hollywood style in the success of politics.

The theme of how public opinion is shaped by movies is fleshed out in *Hollywood: A Novel of America in the 1920s,* which begins with the fall of William Randolph Hearst on the eve of American involvement in the First World War and ends shortly after the mysterious death of Warren G. Harding, who is replaced by the taciturn Calvin Coolidge. It covers the scandals involving Roscoe ''Fatty'' Arbuckle and William Desmond Taylor, and a youthful Franklin Delano Roosevelt with his mistress, Lucy Mercer. It is the fifth in the biography of the United States series covering a period when Hollywood tries to shape public opinion on behalf of the powerful, and America exercises its world power.

The third novel in the sequence, *1876,* is a sardonic centennial celebration of the nation's birth in which an old man named Charlie Schuyler returns from Europe to New York for the first time since 1837 and travels about the country in the service of a newspaper. Everywhere he sees violence and mendacity lurking behind the patriotic scrim of the nation's centenary—particularly in the scandals of the Grant administration and the bitterly contested Hayes-Tilden presidential election.

The centerpiece of the series, and one of Vidal's best novels, is *Burr,* an account of Aaron Burr's last days as written by the young Charlie Schuyler, whom Vidal imagines Burr employing and befriending. Schuyler's interest in Burr's life encourages the older man to give his written account of the early days of the republic—a compelling, gossipy account in which the Founding Fathers are little more than despoilers of infant America. The alternation of Burr's own narrative with Schuyler's worshipful memoir results in a composite portrait of Burr as both an unregenerate adventurer and an elegant arbiter of political style. It also shows Vidal at his best: iconoclastic, anecdotal, intellectually and stylistically agile.

In a duo of confections entitled *Myra Breckinridge* and *Myron,* Vidal indulges freely the taste for camp extravagance evident in his work as early as *The Season of Comfort. Myra Breckinridge* takes the form of a journal that the eponymous Myra begins when she arrives in Hollywood after a sex-change operation. Firm in her belief that film is the only art and militant in her devotion to Hollywood's Golden Age, she is no less imperious in her determination to realign the sexes—a determination rooted in her former life as Myron. The results are gaudily offensive, climaxing in her rape of a chauvinistic young man and ending (to her chagrin) in her accidental reversion into Myron. *Myron* picks up the story five years later when Myron falls into his television and discovers himself on a Hollywood set in 1948. As the novel progresses, Myra and Myron alternately commandeer the Breckinridge psyche, Myra bent on saving Hollywood from television, Myron on defeating Myra's revisionist imperative. Although not to everyone's taste, the books are enormously rich—a comedic feast of styles and sexualities, invention and invective. Their charm is considerable.

Vidal's greatest success in recent years has been in the historical mode. In *Creation* his central character and narrator is a fictional diplomat named Cyrus Spitama (a grandson of Zoroaster), who cuts a broad swath through the Persian-Greek wars and recounts fascinating meetings with the Buddha, Master Li, Confucius, and a host of kindred figures. Revisionist speculations and tantalizing ''what ifs'' energize what amounts to a Cook's Tour of the fifth century. If *Lincoln* overshadows *Creation,* it overshadows very nearly everything else in Vidal's oeuvre. A compelling, thoughtful, and well-researched portrait of America's sixteenth president, it renders his tragic Civil War years through candid viewpoints of his family, his political rivals, and even his future assassins. The result is a rare fusion of monumentality and intimacy, quite distinct from the idealized portraits created by romantic nationalism.

Vidal's historical novels move through time and the lives of famous personages with the breathless anticipation of good fictional epics, yet he continues to explore a variety of modes. *Kalki* is a mordant doomsday novel, narrated with odd restraint by a bisexual aviatrix, the personal pilot of a Vietnam veteran who exterminates the human race in a belief that he is the last avatar of Vishnu. Because of its emotional coolness, the story fails to engage except in scattered passages, as does the story in *Duluth,* a broad parody of law-and-order consciousness in middle America during the 1980s of the Reagan era. More interesting stylistically than these novels is the undervalued *Two Sisters: A Memoir in the Form of a Novel,* a Chinese box of narrations in which each narrative replicates a single story-line encapsulated in a screenplay at the heart of the novel.

The Smithsonian Institution is a recent, light foray into science fiction, time travel, historical costume romance, and Vidal's familiar political satire. The love story woven through the text is between Gore Vidal and the main character, who is Jimmie Trimble, based on Vidal's friend killed on Iwo Jima in March 1, 1945. In a whimsical revision of his personal history, Vidal rescues his lover from the destruction of one of the bloodiest battles fought in the Pacific. His novel surpasses the trivial material produced in the fantasy/science fiction genre while using its conventions. The story is driven by that powerfully brilliant and original mind which produced the Empire narratives.

The greatness of Vidal's fiction lies not only with its extraordinary range but with its small-scale effects: witty, autobiographical indiscretions; aphoristic nuggets, firm and toothsome; a fine interplay of the demonic and the mannered. Indeed, he must be regarded as one of the most important stylists of contemporary American prose. His ear for cadence and his touch with syntax are sure, and few can equal his ability to layer a sentence with wit and to temper it with intelligence. His book list survives in popular reprints despite the government's consistent attacks on left-wing politics and the public taboo against homosexuality.

—Robert F. Kiernan, updated by Hedwig Gorski

VIRAMONTES, Helena Maria

Nationality: American. **Born:** East Los Angeles, 26 February 1954. **Education:** Immaculate Heart College, B.A., 1975; attended University of California at Irvine. **Family:** Two children. **Career:** Teaches at Cornell University. **Awards:** *Statement Magazine* first prize for fiction (California State University), 1977, 1978; first prize for fiction (University of California at Irvine Chicano Literary Contest), 1979. **Agent:** c/o Dutton/Signet, 375 Hudson Street, New York, New York 10014, U.S.A.

PUBLICATIONS

Novels

Under the Feet of Jesus. New York, Dutton, 1995.
Their Dogs Came with Them. New York, Dutton, 2000.

Short Stories

The Moths and Other Stories. Houston, Texas, Arte Publico Press, 1985.
Paris Rats in E.L.A. N.p. 1993.

Other

Chicana Creativity and Criticism: Charting New Frontiers in American Literature (co-editor, with Maria Herrera-Sobek). Houston, Texas, Arte Publico Press, 1988.
Chicana (W)Rites: On Word and Film (co-editor, with Maria Herrera-Sobek). Berkeley, California, Third Woman Press, 1995.
Contributor, *Cuentos: Short Stories by Latinas.* Kitchen Table/Women of Color Press, 1983.
Contributor, *Woman of Her Word*, edited by Evangelina Vigil. Houston, Texas, Arte Publico Press, 1984.
Contributor, *Breaking Boundaries: Latina Writings and Critical Readings*, edited by Asuncion Horno-Delgado, Eliana Ortego, Nina M. Scott, and Nancy Saporta Sternbach. Amherst, University of Massachusetts Press, 1989.
Contributor, *New Chicana/Chicano Writing*, edited by Charles M. Tatum. Tucson, University of Arizona Press, 1992.

* * *

Helena Maria Viramontes is committed to exploring creative representations of Chicana women in the contemporary United States. As an academic she has co-edited with Maria Herrera-Sobek two anthologies that examine the imaginative output of Chicana women and its political implications: *Chicana Creativity and Criticism: Charting New Frontiers in American Literature* and *Chicana (W)Rites: On Word and Film*. As an author of fiction, Viramontes has published two novels and two collections of short pieces. *The Moths and Other Stories*, *Paris Rats in E.L.A.*, *Under the Feet of Jesus* and *Their Dogs Came with Them* all focus on the lives of Chicana women and their relationships, both in the familial realm and in American society at large.

Viramontes no sooner began to publish than she began to receive accolades for her writing style and the sensitive depiction of her characters' internal conflicts. By 1979 she had received two awards from the literary magazine *Statement* and another from the University of California at Irvine for her short stories. *The Moths and Other Stories*, published after her enrollment in UC Irvine's creative writing program, emphasizes her dedication to providing counter narratives to popular representations of Chicana women, as does *Paris Rats in E.L.A.*, her second story collection. Exploring the impact of sexual discrimination in their lives—both from within their communities and without—as well as the racial discrimination and disproportionate levels of poverty to which Chicana women are prone, Viramontes' stories provide a window into the interior lives of women too often overlooked by mainstream society. That their culture can be both sustaining and debilitating is crucial to Viramontes' fiction: the paternalism of American Imperialism is certainly critiqued, but not without a similar awareness of the damaging patriarchal impulse in Chicano culture. How these forces overlap and impact the lives of Chicana mothers, daughters, and wives is thematically central in these stories.

Her first novel, *Under the Feet of Jesus*, is a sustained examination of the themes established in *The Moths and Other Stories* through the life of a thirteen-year-old migrant worker, Estella, and her family. Viramontes' much remarked upon lyrical language evokes not only Estella's enthusiasm, defiance, and dreams for the future, but also her dissatisfaction with her present life of discrimination, frustration, labor, and poverty. Through the stream of consciousness style Viramontes so often employs, the reader is also provided with compelling glimpses into the interior world of Estella's mother, Petra, defeated and betrayed by a life to which she seems condemned, and Estella's step-father, who contemplates escaping his responsibility by abandoning his family. Viramontes, as the daughter of former cotton-pickers, brings both a personal and political commitment to representing the difficult lives of migrant workers and combating their erasure in popular representations of California. Distinctly American in subject matter and content, *Under the Feet of Jesus* is particular to the lives of her subjects, while also providing a basis for a critique of the organization and distribution of power in American society at large.

Their Dogs Came with Them, Viramontes' second novel, remains thematically consistent with her previous work, while moving from the rural setting of *Under the Feet of Jesus* to the urban East Los Angeles of the 1960s. Her characters do not have access to the political resources that would allow them to contest the impeding destruction of their neighborhood in order to construct a new freeway: in this novel urban renewal and development become synonymous with urban dislocation, denial, and destruction. Not merely a portrait of one family, *Their Dogs Came with Them* is both a requiem for, and celebration of, a community on the verge of eradication and dispersal. Nevertheless, a sense of a precedent for cultural continuity and survival is established in Viramontes' evocation of other historical colonial impositions on the Chicano people. The ancestral myths invoked by different characters find parallels in their knowledge that this moment in history will one day too assume mythic proportions. This communal experience and history is a unifying force in a narrative of a world populated by wildly disparate, never stereotypical characters, ranging from gang girls and boys to the devoutly faithful, the intellectually brilliant, and the physically—or more often emotionally—challenged.

Viramontes continues to be recognized for her wok, having received a National Endowment for the Arts fellowship, and the John Dos Passos prize in literature. Her social commitment to Chicano/a culture and peoples has kept pace with this recognition, not only through her fiction, but also in her advising Chicano/a students and aspiring writers through her work at Cornell University, where she is an Assistant Professor of Literature.

—Jennifer Harris

VIRTUE, Noel

Nationality: New Zealander. **Born:** 1947. **Career:** Formerly a zookeeper. Since 1987 a writer. **Address:** David Bolt Associates, 12 Heath Drive, Send, Surrey GU23 7ED, England.

PUBLICATIONS

Novels

The Redemption of Elsdon Bird. London, Owen, and New York, Grove Press, 1987.
Then Upon the Evil Season. London, Owen, 1988.
In the Country of Salvation. Auckland, Random Century, and London, Hutchinson, 1990.
Always the Islands of Memory. London, Hutchinson, 1991.
The Eye of the Everlasting Angel. London, Owen, 1992.
Sandspit Crossing. London, Owen, 1993.
The Transfiguration of Martha Friend. Auckland and New York, Vintage, 1996.
Losing Alice. Auckland, Random House New Zealand, 1999.

Other

Among the Animals: A Zookeeper's Story. London, Owen, 1988.
Once a Brethren Boy. (autobiography). Auckland, Vintage, 1995.

* * *

A latecomer to novel writing, Noel Virtue has made a small but definite name for himself in contemporary New Zealand fiction. He has been in residence in the United Kingdom for much of his career, but returned to New Zealand in 1995 to launch his autobiography, *Once a Brethren Boy,* at New Zealand's first Gay and Lesbian Writing Festival, which was held at Auckland College of Education. Virtue was a catalyst for the Man to Man Gay and Lesbian Writing Festival designed to increase the visibility of lesbian and gay writing with publishers and the general public, and to provide motivation and support for aspiring writers.

Much of Virtue's fiction deals with a very peculiar family life which is psychologically brutal due to religious fanaticism. Britain's newly acclaimed novelist, Jeanette Winterston, portrays her self-discovery as a lesbian woman in a similarly constricting and religiously irrational home in her breakthrough book, *Oranges Are Not the Only Fruit.* Virtue's approach to his fictional narratives about similar self-discoveries in an non-receptive, even hostile, environment differ from Winterston's postmodernism. His style and form are conservative, which is, perhaps, an aesthetic concession to the conservatism ingrained during his childhood. Nevertheless, the contrast of the conservative style to the liberal nature of the authorial narrative lends a powerful, even disturbing, tension that never ceases.

The Redemption of Elsdon Bird, Virtue's first work, is to my mind his most successful. In libraries it is often classed as teenage fiction, but this designation is misleading, as the emotions and themes it deals with are distinctly adult. Written in a spare, vivid style, it tells the story of a lonely youngster whose upbringing at the hands of ''holy roller'' parents is strange and nightmarish. Isolated by his family's religious convictions, Elsdon is the subject of constant physical abuse. He is systematically deprived of everyone and everything he loves, and at the conclusion of the book, he faces life alone. The story's plot development of such extreme personal loss would be almost unbearable were it not for the protagonist's poignantly cheerful character.

Critics have been fascinated by the contrasting elements in Elsdon Bird, such as the victim's cheerful optimism and innocence despite his heartless environment, and the cruel irony of evil in religiosity in most of Virtue's other work. They find a saintly virtue in the author's courage to redeem passion from the control of hypocritical and close-minded Bible thumpers. The price Virtue pays for his sincerity is a socially inbred guilt about who he is. In a 1990 interview, Virtue suggests that he is ''dogged by hellfire and brimstone.''

One can surmise that Virtue's reluctance to present his life and sincere beliefs caused most of the delays in the onset of his public life as an author. For many years, he worked as a zookeeper. These years are chronicled in his 1988 book, *Among the Animals: A Zookeeper's Story.* Anonymity, however, always rewards fiction writers with the ability to eavesdrop on the lives and speech of those around them. Virtue's skilled use of New Zealand slang is specific evidence of this, especially in combination with Elsdon Bird's innocent way of speaking in the debut novel, which is both comic and touching. It is the character's own innocent optimism that will rescue him from the concluding despair in the story's end.

Then Upon the Evil Season continues the themes of violence and religious mania. As in the earlier novel the focus is on a child, in this case a teenager, Lubin, who must cope with his parent's fundamentalist belief and the persecution they invite. Mixed in with this burdensome family life, there is a murder and two unusual animals, an ostrich and a dolphin, whose natural goodness serves to highlight man's cruelty and greed. It is a more ambitious novel than *The Redemption of Elsdon Bird* because the plot is much more complex and the number of significant characters is greatly increased. For these reasons, *Then Upon the Evil Season* is less successful than the first novel, for it lacks the earlier book's intensity. The characters—some are animal and some are human—seem to be allegorical figures designed for readers in their teens, but may appear to be stereotypes to adult readers.

With *In the Country of Salvation,* Virtue has attempted to write a properly adult novel, one that deals with several different lives over a long period of time. The main focus, once again, is on a lonely child, Billy, whose upbringing at the hands of religiously obsessed parents causes him much unhappiness, driving him to attempt suicide. Billy, as it happens, has a double cross to bear in that he is homosexual; however, all of the family members are injured and suffering in some real or imagined ways, until all achieve some kind of a redemptive state of forgiveness. This third novel is more ambitious than the first two, and some say that Virtue sometimes fails to sustain interest in a lengthy narrative. To some extent the problem lies with the characters themselves: lacking Elsdon's touching optimism, their unhappiness is more grueling than affecting. Another problem is that the focus of the novel is too diffuse. Subplots involving Colin and Seddon, Billy's older brothers, are interesting but tend to distract from, rather than complement, Billy's agony. Despite its flaws, *In the Country of Salvation* does have its moments.

Virtue's books gain in mastery as he continues to explore religious mania and the suffering it inflicts upon children. He has published five books since 1991 in addition to his autobiography. They include *Always the Islands of Memory, The Eye of the Everlasting Angel, Sandspit Crossing, The Transfiguration of Martha Friend,* and *Losing Alice.* The most recent additions to Virtue's oeuvre continue in the development of his perspicacious voice, one that is moral and decent without the negative impositions of zealous religion.

—John O'Leary, updated by Hedwig Gorski

VOLLMANN, William T.

Nationality: American. **Born:** Santa Monica, California, 28 July 1959. **Education:** Attended Deep Springs College, 1977–79; Cornell University, B.A. 1981; graduate study at University of California, Berkeley, 1982–83. **Career:** Founder, CoTangent Press; writer. **Awards:** Ludwig Vogelstein award, 1987; Whiting Writers' award, 1988; Shiva Naipaul Memorial prize, 1989; PEN Center USA West Literary award, 1997. **Agent:** c/o Viking-Penguin, 375 Hudson Street, New York, New York 10014, U.S.A.

PUBLICATIONS

Novels

You Bright and Risen Angels: A Cartoon. New York, Atheneum, 1987.

Seven Dreams: A Book of North American Landscapes, Volume 1, *The Ice-Shirt,* New York, Viking, 1990; Volume 2, *Fathers and Crows,* New York, Viking, 1992; Volume 6, *The Rifles,* New York, Viking, 1993.

Whores for Gloria; or, Everything Was Beautiful until the Girls Got Anxious (documentary novel). London, Pan-Picador, 1991; New York, Pantheon, 1992.

Butterfly Stories: A Novel. New York, Grove/Atlantic, 1993.

The Royal Family. New York, Viking, 2000.

Short Stories

The Rainbow Stories. New York, Atheneum, 1989.

Thirteen Stories and Thirteen Epitaphs. London, Deutsch, 1991; New York, Grove, 1994.

The Atlas: People, Places, and Visions. New York, Viking, 1996.

Other

An Afghanistan Picture Show: Or, How I Saved the World (memoir). New York, Farrar, Straus, 1992.

Open All Night (text), photographs by Ken Miller. Woodstock, New York, Overlook Press, 1995.

* * *

William T. Vollmann is the prodigiously prolific author of several novels, collections of short stories, and numerous nonfiction articles for *The New Yorker, Spin,* and other publications. Like others of his contemporaries labeled ''postmodernists,'' Vollmann refuses to distinguish between fiction, journalism, autobiography, and fantasy, preferring instead to travel among genres in his work.

Temperamentally, Vollmann's fiction is most often described as alienated and lonely. His characters—prostitutes, street people, skinheads—are culled from the margins of society, and his stories unfold through finely drawn scenes of lust and violence rendered in prose at once poetic and clinical. Indeed, Vollmann has been accused of moral ambiguity in his work, in part because of this style of writing and in part because of his apparent reluctance to remark on the physical and spiritual brutality he often depicts. His collection *The Atlas,* and in particular the story ''Under the Grass,'' provides a stirring counterpoint, however. The story begins with the 1968 drowning of Vollmann's sister, as the author characteristically embeds autobiographical detail into a work of fiction, and includes an extended mediation on death and guilt, responsibility and pain, and finally on the genesis of his own empathy for and identification with the doomed.

The oeuvre of Vollmann may be divided into two categories: his historical works and what might be best described as his ''extreme fiction.'' Like other postmodern novelists before him—Don DeLillo and E.L. Doctorow, for instance—Vollmann's outlook seems to be shaped by philosophy's pronouncement of the death of the metanarrative, and in particular by the idea that history itself is an imaginative construct, a fiction. This sensibility is evident throughout Vollmann's historical novels, which critics have called ''historiographic metafiction.''

In his *Seven Dreams: A Book of North American Landscapes,* which is a planned series of seven volumes, Vollmann explores the contingency of history and colonialism and, most especially, the Western self's construction of the indigenous Other. In the three volumes completed, Vollmann effects a remarkable fusion of historiography, confessional poetry, anthropology, philosophy, and sociology. Each book is meticulously researched, and one can only marvel at the extent of Vollmann's polymath interests. In volume one, *The Ice-Shirt,* he examines the tenth-century Norse landings in Greenland; in volume two, *Fathers and Crows,* the French settlement of what would become Canada; and in volume six, *The Rifles,* the Canadian government's relocation of the Intuits to the Arctic Circle in the 1950s.

The second category of Vollmann's work is the extreme fiction, his portraits of the marginalized and his excursions into the sexual fringes of society. Characteristic is *Butterfly Stories,* in which Vollmann follows the protagonist—known to the reader first as ''the butterfly boy,'' then later ''the journalist'' and finally ''the husband''—through a travel narrative that empties into the killing fields of Cambodia. There he falls in love with a prostitute, Vanna. The journalist returns to California HIV-positive and dreams of bringing Vanna to America, but he is killed by the Khmer Rouge as he tries to re-enter Cambodia.

Vollmann has argued that what propels his fiction is the inescapable innateness of sex and violence in all people. And yet he has also said that what drives him most is the desire to construct beautiful sentences.

—Michele S. Shauf

VONNEGUT, Kurt, Jr.

Nationality: American. **Born:** Indianapolis, Indiana, 11 November 1922. **Education:** Shortridge High School, Indianapolis, 1936–40; Cornell University, Ithaca, New York, 1940–42; Carnegie Institute, Pittsburgh, 1943; University of Chicago, 1945–47. **Military Service:** Served in the United States Army Infantry, 1942–45: Purple Heart. **Family:** Married 1) Jane Marie Cox in 1945 (divorced 1979), one son and two daughters, and three adopted sons; 2) the photographer Jill Krementz in 1979, one daughter. **Career:** Police reporter, Chicago City News Bureau, 1946; worked in public relations for the General Electric Company, Schenectady, New York, 1947–50. Since 1950 freelance writer. After 1965, teacher, Hopefield School, Sandwich, Massachusetts. Visiting lecturer, Writers Workshop, University of Iowa, Iowa City, 1965–67, and Harvard University, Cambridge, Massachusetts, 1970–71; visiting professor, City University of New York, 1973–74. **Awards:** Guggenheim fellowship, 1967; American Academy grant, 1970. M.A.: University of Chicago, 1971; D.Litt.: Hobart and William Smith Colleges, Geneva, New York, 1974. **Member:** American Academy, 1973. Lives in New York City. **Address:** c/o Donald C. Farber, Tanner Gilbert Propp and Sterner, 99 Park Avenue, 25th Floor, New York, New York 10016, U.S.A.

PUBLICATIONS

Novels

Player Piano. New York, Scribner, 1952; London, Macmillan, 1953; as *Utopia 14,* New York, Bantam, 1954.
The Sirens of Titan. New York, Dell, 1959; London, Gollancz, 1962.
Mother Night. New York, Fawcett, 1962; London, Cape, 1968.
Cat's Cradle. New York, Holt Rinehart, and London, Gollancz, 1963.
God Bless You, Mr. Rosewater; or, Pearls Before Swine. New York, Holt Rinehart, and London, Cape, 1965.
Slaughterhouse-Five; or, The Children's Crusade. New York, Delacorte Press, 1969; London, Cape, 1970.
Breakfast of Champions; or, Goodbye, Blue Monday. New York, Delacorte Press, and London, Cape, 1973.
Slapstick; or, Lonesome No More! New York, Delacorte Press, and London, Cape, 1976.
Jailbird. New York, Delacorte Press, and London, Cape, 1979.
Deadeye Dick. New York, Delacorte Press, 1982; London, Cape, 1983.
Galápagos. New York, Delacorte Press, and London, Cape, 1985.
Bluebeard. New York, Delacorte Press, 1987; London, Cape, 1988.
Hocus Pocus; or, What's the Hurry, Son? New York, Putnam, and London, Cape, 1990.
Three Complete Novels. New York, Wings Books, 1995.
Timequake. New York, G.P. Putnam's, 1997.

Short Stories

Canary in a Cat House. New York, Fawcett, 1961.
Welcome to the Monkey House: A Collection of Short Works. New York, Delacorte Press, 1968; London, Cape, 1969.
Bagombo Snuff Box: Uncollected Short Fiction. New York, G.P. Putnam's Sons, 1999.

Plays

Happy Birthday, Wanda June (as *Penelope,* produced Cape Cod, Massachusetts, 1960; revised version, as *Happy Birthday, Wanda June,* produced New York, 1970; London, 1977). New York, Delacorte Press, 1970; London, Cape, 1973.
The Very First Christmas Morning, in *Better Homes and Gardens* (Des Moines, Iowa), December 1962.
Between Time and Timbuktu; or, Prometheus-5: A Space Fantasy (televised 1972; produced New York, 1976). New York, Delacorte Press, 1972; London, Panther, 1975.
Fortitude, in *Wampeters, Foma, and Granfalloons,* 1974.
Timesteps (produced Edinburgh, 1979).
God Bless You, Mr. Rosewater, adaptation of his own novel (produced New York, 1979).

Television Plays: *Auf Wiedersehen,* with Valentine Davies, 1958; *Between Time and Timbuktu,* 1972.

Other

Wampeters, Foma, and Granfalloons: Opinions. New York, Delacorte Press, 1974; London Cape, 1975.
Sun Moon Star. New York, Harper, and London, Hutchinson, 1980.
Palm Sunday: An Autobiographical Collage. New York, Delacorte Press, and London, Cape, 1981.
Nothing Is Lost Save Honor: Two Essays. Jackson, Mississippi, Nouveau Press, 1984.
Conversations with Kurt Vonnegut, edited by William Rodney Allen. Jackson, University Press of Mississippi, 1988.
Fates Worse than Death: An Autobiographical Collage of the 1980s. New York, Putnam, 1991.
Like Shaking Hands with God: A Conversation about Writing (with Lee Stringer). New York, Seven Stories Press, 1999.
God Bless You, Dr. Kevorkian. New York, Seven Stories Press, 2000.

*

Bibliography: *Kurt Vonnegut: A Comprehensive Bibliography* by Asa B. Pieratt, Jr., Julie Huffman-Klinkowitz, and Jerome Klinkowitz, Hamden, Connecticut, Archon, 1987.

Critical Studies: *Kurt Vonnegut, Jr.,* by Peter J. Reed, New York, Warner, 1972; *Kurt Vonnegut: Fantasist of Fire and Ice* by David H. Goldsmith, Bowling Green, Ohio, Popular Press, 1972; *The Vonnegut Statement* edited by Jerome Klinkowitz and John Somer, New York, Delacorte Press, 1973, London, Panther, 1975, *Vonnegut in America: An Introduction to the Life and Work of Kurt Vonnegut* edited by Klinkowitz and Donald L. Lawler, New York, Delacorte Press, 1977, *Kurt Vonnegut,* London, Methuen, 1982 and *Slaughterhouse Five: Reforming the Novel and the World,* Boston, Twayne, 1990, both by Klinkowitz; *Kurt Vonnegut, Jr.* by Stanley Schatt, Boston, Twayne, 1976; *Kurt Vonnegut* by James Lundquist, New York, Ungar, 1977; *Vonnegut: A Preface to His Novels* by Richard Giannone, Port Washington, New York, Kennikat Press, 1977; *Kurt Vonnegut: The Gospel from Outer Space* by Clark Mayo, San Bernardino, California, Borgo Press, 1977; *Vonnegut's Duty-Dance with Death: Theme and Structure in Slaughterhouse-Five* by Monica Loeb, Ume[ao], Sweden, Ume[ao] Studies in the Humanities, 1979; *Critical Essays on Kurt Vonnegut* edited by Robert Merrill, Boston, Hall, 1990; *Forever*

Pursuing Genesis: The Myth of Eden in the Novels of Kurt Vonnegut by Leonard Mustazza, Lewisburg, Pennsylvania, Bucknell University Press, 1990; *Understanding Kurt Vonnegut* by William Rodney Allen, Columbia, University of South Carolina Press, 1991; *Kurt Vonnegut* by Donald E. Morse, San Bernardino, California, Borgo Press, 1992; *Critical Response to Kurt Vonnegut* edited by Leonard Mustazza, Westport, Connecticut, Greenwood Press, 1994; *Sanity Plea: Schizophrenia in the Novels of Kurt Vonnegut* by Lawrence R. Broer, Tuscaloosa, University of Alabama Press, 1994; *Kurt Vonnegut, Jr.'s Slaughterhouse-Five,* edited by Tonnvane Wiswell and M. Fogiel, illustrations by Matteo DeCosmo, Piscataway, New Jersey, Research & Education Association, 1996; *The Short Fiction of Kurt Vonnegut* by Peter J. Reed, Westport, Connecticut, Greenwood Press, 1997; *Chaos Theory and the Interpretation of Literary Texts: The Case of Kurt Vonnegut* by Kevin A. Boon, Lewiston, New York, Edwin Mellen Press, 1997; *Wholeness Restored: Love of Symmetry as a Shaping Force in the Writings of Henry James, Kurt Vonnegut, Samuel Butler and Raymond Chandler* by Ralf Norrman, Frankfurt am Main and New York, P. Lang, 1998; *Kurt Vonnegut,* edited by Harold Bloom, Philadelphia, Chelsea House Publishers, 2000.

* * *

During the 1960s Kurt Vonnegut emerged as one of the most influential and provocative writers of fiction in America. His writing, indeed, constitutes an unremitting protest against horrors of the 20th century—the disastrous wars, the deterioration of the environment, and the dehumanization of the individual in a society dominated by science and technology. Such protest is by no means new in literature. The peculiar force of Vonnegut's voice may be traced to its complete contemporaneity. Fantasy (usually of the science variety), black humor, a keen sense of the absurd are the ingredients of his novels and stories.

Vonnegut has described himself as "a total pessimist." And indeed his writing offers little except wry laughter to counteract despair. This is certainly true of his first novel, *Player Piano.* The time of the story is the not-too-distant future and the place is an industrial city, Ilium, New York, which serves as the setting for much of Vonnegut's fiction and which resembles Schenectady, New York, where Vonnegut once worked in public relations. In the novel not only the local industry but industries throughout the nation have been completely mechanized. Machines supplant human workers because machines make fewer errors. All national policy is determined by huge computers located in Mammoth Cave. A small elite of scientists are in charge of all production. The masses, who are provided with all material necessities and comforts, including an impressive array of gadgetry, serve in either military or work battalions. Acutely aware of their dehumanization and worthlessness except as consumers of the huge output of the machines, the common people revolt under the leadership of a preacher and several renegade scientists. Though the revolt in Ilium, at least, is successful and many of the objectionable machines are destroyed, Vonnegut denies his readers any sense of satisfaction. He records that the rebels destroyed not only obnoxious machinery but also useful and necessary technological devices such as sewage disposal plants. Also, they soon began to tinker with the unneeded machines with a view to making them operative again. In the face of such inveterate stupidity the leaders suicidally surrender to the government forces.

An obvious question arises: Why should Vonnegut or his readers concern themselves with the dehumanization of apparent morons? What, indeed, is there to be dehumanized? An answer is not readily forthcoming, but perhaps Vonnegut believes that there is some value in trying to save humanity from its own stupidity. In each novel there is at least one person who is aware of human folly, and thus is living proof that intellectual blindness is not universal. More frequently than not, these discerning individuals are reformers, as in *Player Piano,* who make self-sacrificing efforts to improve the lot of their fellow beings. Thus *The Sirens of Titan,* which in plot is a rather conventional example of science fiction with an interplanetary setting, has as its reformer a man who, having been rendered immortal, omniscient, and virtually omnipotent by entrapment in a "chrono-synclastic-infundibulum," sets about uniting all nations of the world in bonds of brotherhood by staging an abortive attack against the earth by Martians. The latter are earthlings abducted to Mars and converted to automatons by the insertion in their skulls of radio antennae through which orders are transmitted from a central directorate. These unfortunates are thus subjected to ruthless dehumanization and exploitation, but for a worthwhile end. The scheme is successful; the earth becomes united after the defeat of the Martians and the unity is cemented by the establishment of a new religion—the Church of God the Utterly Indifferent. The happy outcome is somewhat clouded, however, by the revelation that all human history has been determined by the trivial needs of the inhabitants of the planet Tralfamadore in one of the more remote galaxies.

Cat's Cradle and *God Bless You, Mr. Rosewater; or, Pearls Before Swine* also focus upon the efforts of altruistic individuals to alleviate misery. *Cat's Cradle* presents an entirely new religion, Bokonism, (named for its founder, Bokonon), much of the doctrine of which is written in Calypso verse. According to Bokonism religion *should* be an opiate; its function is to deceive and, by deceiving, make people happy. It teaches that God directs human destinies and that humankind is sacred, and it promotes an ethic of love, which believers manifest by pressing the soles of their feet against those of fellow believers. Bokonism was founded and flourished on a Caribbean island oppressed by a Duvalier-type dictator. It flourished because it was outlawed, for, according to *Cat's Cradle* at least, a religion functions most vigorously when opposed to the existing social order. There can be no doubt that Bokonism brings relief to the wretched islanders, the final horror of whose existence is that of being congealed, along with the rest of the world, by ice-nine, a discovery of an Ilium scientist. *God Bless You, Mr. Rosewater; or, Goodbye, Blue Monday* recounts the efforts of an enormously wealthy man to alleviate human misery through the more or less random disbursement of the Rosewater Foundation's almost limitless funds.

Two other novels, *Mother Night* and *Slaughterhouse-Five; or, The Children's Crysade,* both of which focus on World War II, contain no such reformers or philanthropists. In these the protagonists are never really in a position to be altruistic, even though they wish to be. In *Mother Night* Howard W. Campbell, Jr., serves schizophrenically as the Nazis' chief English-language radio propagandist at the same time that he is one of the allies' most effective spies. Years after the war he finds himself in an Israeli prison awaiting trial along with Adolf Eichmann. Here he commits suicide, even though a bizarre turn of events has ensured his acquittal. He realizes that one who has played his dual roles has betrayed beyond recovery his own humanity—a realization achieved by few Vonnegut characters in analogous situations.

Slaughterhouse-Five; or, The Children's Crusade, perhaps Vonnegut's most impressive novel, presents two characters who can see beneath the surface to the tragic realities of human history but make no attempt to bring about a change. These are the author himself, who is a frequent commentator, and the protagonist, Billy Pilgrim. The central event is the fire-bombing of Dresden—a catastrophe that Vonnegut had witnessed as a prisoner of war. Billy Pilgrim's liberating insights are the outgrowth of his being freed from the prison of time and, as a result, seeing the past, present and future as one and coexistent. One consequent realization is that death is an illusion. Though his periods of release from time occur on earth, their significance is explained to him by inhabitants of the distant planet Tralfamadore, to which he is transported on a Tralfamadorian spaceship. Though Billy finds no way to improve the tragically absurd condition of humanity, he does arrive at an understanding of it and a resultant deepening of compassion.

Four novels after *Slaughterhouse-Five—Breakfast of Champions; or, Goodbye, Blue Monday, Slapstick; or, Lonesome No More!, Jailbird,* and *Deadeye Dick*—continue to satirize human folly in its contemporary manifestations, still relying on fantasy, black humor, and the absurd as tools of satire. Yet their tone differs from that of the earlier fiction. The seriousness of theme and, above all, the compassion implicit in such books as *Cat's Cradle* and *Slaughterhouse-Five* are all but absent. *Slapstick; or, Lonesome No More!,* indeed, would be appropriate as a title for any of the four. Fun and wit and laughs aplenty are not lacking, but thought is in short supply. The clown has shoved aside the thinker. But in the novel following these four, *Galápagos,* Vonnegut achieves a more subtle and more effective irony. For an epigraph he quotes from Anne Frank's *Diary:* ''In spite of everything, I still believe people are really good at heart.'' Though Vonnegut, or the narrator, declares that he agrees with this statement, the characters and events in the novel provide overwhelming evidence that most people are evil at heart. According to the novel, human beings have used their ''big brains''—evolution's prized gift—to destroy themselves and the world they live in. But when, by a fantastic series of events that only Vonnegut could dream up, the human species is reduced to only ten individuals marooned on the Galápagos Islands, a reverse process of evolution sets in, the ''big brains'' disappear, and after a million years the human species is transformed into a gentle, seal-like mammal which actually is ''good at heart.''

In *Galápagos* there is a haunting quality that is not sustained in two later novels—*Bluebeard* and *Hocus Pocus; or, What's the Hurry, Son?* The protagonist in *Bluebeard* is an artist, one of the founders of the abstract expressionist school of painting but later a fanatical representationalist. His great opus, which he keeps locked in a potato barn on Long Island, is an eight-by-sixty-four foot depiction of a World War II scene, presenting each object and every one of innumerable men and women in the minutest detail. Most of the satire, which is gentler than in most of Vonnegut's work, is directed against artists and writers, though peripherally other matters such as war and genocide are dealt with. *Hocus Pocus; or, What's the Hurray, Son?* roams over a wider field of ills: the deterioration of American education, the ''buying of America'' by the Japanese, the Vietnam war, the prison system, and racism.

The narrator of *Hocus Pocus* remarks: ''All I ever wanted to overthrow was ignorance and self-serving fantasies.'' Later he asserts: ''The truth can be very funny in an awful way, especially as it relates to greed and hypocrisy.'' These two statements admirably sum up Vonnegut's intention and tone in most of his fiction. To achieve his purposes (and perhaps to carry along readers with short attention spans) he employs a technique, especially in his later novels, of breaking his narratives into brief sections of no more than a paragraph, in which he recounts an anecdote that more often than not ends with a punch line. The effect somewhat resembles the performance of a stage or television comedian, though with Vonnegut there is an underlying seriousness.

Timequake was Vonnegut's first novel after a seven-year silence—and, as he revealed publicly, it was to mark the end of his career. Actually, ''novel'' is a bit of a strong word to apply to what is really a collection of observations, or sketches for a novel, that Vonnegut's sci-fi writer alter-ego Kilgore Trout would have written if he'd gotten around to it. The premise is that ''a sudden glitch in the space-time continuum'' has forced everyone to repeat the period from 1991 to 2001 without being able to change a thing.

On 30 January 2000, fire struck Vonnegut's New York brownstone; he suffered smoke inhalation, but survived.

—Perry D. Westbrook, updated by Judson Knight

W

WAGONER, David (Russell)

Nationality: American. **Born:** Massillon, Ohio, 5 June 1926. **Education:** Pennsylvania State University, University Park, B.A. 1947; Indiana University, Bloomington, M.A. in English 1949. **Military Service:** Served in the United States Navy, 1944–46. **Family:** Married 1) Patricia Parrot in 1961 (divorced 1982); 2) Robin Heather Seyfried in 1982. **Career:** Instructor, DePauw University, Greencastle, Indiana, 1949–50, and Pennsylvania State University, 1950–53; assistant professor, 1954–57, associate professor, 1958–66, and since 1966 professor of English, University of Washington, Seattle. Elliston Professor of Poetry, University of Cincinnati, 1968; editor, Princeton University Press Contemporary Poetry Series, 1977–81. Since 1966 editor, *Poetry Northwest,* Seattle; since 1983 poetry editor, University of Missouri Press, Columbia. **Awards:** Guggenheim fellowship, 1956; Ford fellowship, for drama, 1964; American Academy grant, 1967; Morton Dauwen Zabel prize, 1967; National Endowment for the Arts grant, 1969; Oscar Blumenthal prize, 1974; Fels prize, 1975; Eunice Tietjens Memorial prize, 1977; Sherwood Anderson award, 1980; English-Speaking Union prize, 1980 (*Poetry,* Chicago); Union League prize, 1987; Ruth Lilly Poetry prize, 1991; Levinson prize, 1994. Chancellor, Academy of American Poets, 1978. **Address:** English Department, University of Washington, Seattle, Washington 98195, U.S.A; or 5416 154th Place, S.W., Edmonds, Washington 98026, U.S.A.

PUBLICATIONS

Novels

The Man in the Middle. New York, Harcourt Brace, 1954; London, Gollancz, 1955.
Money, Money, Money. New York, Harcourt Brace, 1955.
Rock. New York, Viking Press, 1958.
The Escape Artist. New York, Farrar Straus, and London, Gollancz, 1965.
Baby, Come On Inside. New York, Farrar Straus, 1968.
Where Is My Wandering Boy Tonight? New York, Farrar Straus, 1970.
The Road to Many a Wonder. New York, Farrar Straus, 1974.
Tracker. Boston, Little Brown, 1975.
Whole Hog. Boston, Little Brown, 1976.
The Hanging Garden. Boston, Little Brown, 1980; London, Hale, 1982.

Uncollected Short Stories

"Afternoon on the Ground," in *Prairie Schooner* (Lincoln, Nebraska), Fall 1978.
"Mr. Wallender's Romance," in *Hudson Review* (New York), Spring 1979.
"Cornet Solo," in *Boston Globe Magazine,* 20 May 1979.
"The Water Strider," in *Boston Globe Magazine,* 14 October 1979.
"Fly Boy," in *Ohio Review 25* (Athens), 1980.
"The Bird Watcher," in *Georgia Review* (Athens), Spring 1980.
"Snake Hunt," in *Western Humanities Review* (Salt Lake City), Winter 1980.
"Magic Night at the Reformatory," in *Shenandoah* (Lexington, Virginia), vol. 34, no. 4, 1981.
"The Sparrow," in *Epoch* (Ithaca, New York), Spring 1981.
"Mermaid," in *Western Humanities Review* (Salt Lake City), Summer 1981.
"Wild Goose Chase," in *Necessary Fictions,* edited by Stanley W. Lindberg and Stephen Corey. Athens, University of Georgia Press, 1986.
"The Land of the Dead," in *Georgia Review* (Athens), Summer 1987.
"The Riding Lesson," in *Southwest Review* (Dallas), Autumn 1987.

Plays

Any Eye for an Eye for an Eye (produced Seattle, 1973).

Screenplays: *The Escape Artist,* 1981.

Poetry

Dry Sun, Dry Wind. Bloomington, Indiana University Press, 1953.
A Place to Stand. Bloomington, Indiana University Press, 1958.
Poems. Portland, Oregon, Portland Art Museum, 1959.
The Nesting Ground. Bloomington, Indiana University Press, 1963.
Five Poets of the Pacific Northwest, with others, edited by Robin Skelton. Seattle, University of Washington Press, 1964.
Staying Alive. Bloomington, Indiana University Press, 1966.
New and Selected Poems. Bloomington, Indiana University Press, 1969.
Working Against Time. London, Rapp and Whiting, 1970.
Riverbed. Bloomington, Indiana University Press, 1972.
Sleeping in the Woods. Bloomington, Indiana University Press, 1974.
A Guide to Dungeness Spit. Port Townsend, Washington, Graywolf Press, 1975.
Travelling Light. Port Townsend, Washington, Graywolf Press, 1976.
Collected Poems 1956–1976. Bloomington, Indiana University Press, 1976.
Who Shall Be the Sun? Poems Based on the Lore, Legends, and Myths of Northwest Coast and Plateau Indians. Bloomington, Indiana University Press, 1978.
In Broken Country. Boston, Little Brown, 1979.
Landfall. Boston, Little Brown, 1981.
First Light. Boston, Little Brown, 1983.
Through the Forest: New and Selected Poems 1977–1987. New York, Atlantic Monthly Press, 1987.
Walt Whitman Bathing. Champaign, University of Illinois Press, 1996.

Other

Editor, *Straw for the Fire: From the Notebooks of Theodore Roethke 1943–1963.* New York, Doubleday, 1972.

*

Manuscript Collections: Olin Library, Washington University, St. Louis; University of Washington, Seattle.

Critical Studies: ''David Wagoner's Fiction: In the Mills of Satan'' by William J. Schafer in *Critique* (Minneapolis), vol. 9, no. 1, 1965; ''It Dawns on Us That We Must Come Apart,'' in *Alone with America* by Richard Howard, New York, Atheneum, 1969, London, Thames and Hudson, 1970, revised edition, Atheneum, 1980; ''An Interview with David Wagoner,'' in *Crazy Horse 12* (Marshall, Minnesota), 1972; ''A Conversation with David Wagoner,'' in *Yes* (Avoca, New York), vol. 4, no. 1, 1973; ''On David Wagoner,'' in *Salmagundi* (Saratoga Springs, New York), Spring-Summer 1973, and ''Pelting Dark Windows,'' in *Parnassus* (New York), Spring-Summer 1977, both by Sanford Pinsker; *David Wagoner* by Ron McFarland, Boise, Idaho, Boise State University, 1989; *The World of David Wagoner* by Ron McFarland, Moscow, Idaho, University of Idaho Press, 1997.

David Wagoner comments:

It is almost impossible for me to comment coherently on my own fiction, except to say that I began writing poetry first and received early encouragement as a writer of fiction from Edward J. Nicols at Penn State and Peter Taylor at Indiana University, and later from Malcolm Cowley at Viking Press and Catherine Carver who was then at Harcourt Brace. I seem to have a penchant for what might be called serious farce, but whether farce can stand the serious strains I put on it, I must leave to others to say. I also recognize my tendency to write what I believe critics call ''initiation'' novels. I tend to dramatize or write in scenes rather than to be discursive. One clear theme would seem to be the would-be innocent protagonist *vs.* the corrupt city, perhaps a result of my having grown up between Chicago and Gary, Indiana, where the most sophisticated and effective forms of pollution were first perfected.

*   *   *

In his novels, David Wagoner has pursued the themes of innocence and corruption, of the connections between past, present and future, of the individual trapped in a violent society. The novels depict individuals corrupted by modern urban life, protagonists essentially innocent and helpless damaged by the pressures of family and further maimed by society. Wagoner skillfully uses Dickensian comedy and drama to create a tragic myth of man stripped and abandoned by his parents and his fellows yet struggling to survive and to remain intact.

The Man in the Middle and *Money, Money, Money* describe helpless, childlike adults caught up in criminal machinations. *The Escape Artist* and *Where Is My Wandering Boy Tonight?* treat the same theme from the viewpoint of juvenile protagonists. Each novel involves criminals and corrupt politicians who pursue and persecute an innocent victim. There is a strong element of picaresque comedy in this drama of innocence adapting to a wicked world. The later novels also develop a complex sexual theme revolving around an Oedipal relationship—a child confronted and fascinated by a destructive mother figure. Each of the protagonists must overcome this infantile sexual bondage before he is free to live wholly, just as each must learn the depth of the world's wickedness before he can shed his infantile social innocence.

The Road to Many a Wonder continues Wagoner's comedy of nineteenth-century America (begun in *Where Is My Wandering Boy Tonight?*) and his parable of innocence and the frontier. In it a gold-seeker, Isaac Bender, succeeds by the most improbable means, his questing innocence overcoming the money-corruption of the gold rush and the Hobbesian savagery of the raw West. The novel is marked by a comic sweetness and light that offsets the bleak portraiture of venal American character-types.

Tracker and *Whole Hog* extend Wagoner's story of the frontier and the wild west by focusing on the uncertainties of the pioneer spirit, the fragility of familial and social relations and the ultimate triumph of intelligent virtue over mindless evil. Both tales revolve around juvenile protagonists (Wagoner's type of innocence) who learn by painful experience to outwit a lawless adult world.

In *Rock* and *Baby, Come On Inside* Wagoner deals with the destructiveness of family life and the crippling effects of the past. Both stories concentrate on the conflict between leaving home and returning home: ''You can't go home again'' vs. ''You *must* go home again.'' In each novel, the protagonist tries to recapture his past, to find a home place, but ends in confusion and further exile.

A recurrent pattern in Wagoner's novels is that of pursuit and flight, a nightmarish sense of implacable evil, and a recurrent scene is a metaphorical return to the womb, to primordial shelter. Charlie Bell in *The Man in the Middle* spends a night in a railway coin locker. Willy Grier is left in a garbage can in *Money, Money, Money.* Danny Masters in *The Escape Artist* hides out in a Goodwill Industries collection box and a US mailbox. The pattern of flight and hiding, a fragile individual pursued by a terrifying nemesis, occurs in a comic context—cynical wit and slapstick farce—for the dreamlike or mythic dimension of Wagoner's novels derives from their mixed tone. The stories encompass suspense, adventure, comedy, pathos, and a strong sense of the social and political life of midwestern cities.

In *The Hanging Garden* Wagoner returns to a detective-story format of homicidal insanity defeated by a man who is basically good but worn from personal and political struggle. Returning to nature (a holiday cottage), the protagonist is confronted with ''natural evil'' in the form of a sadistic killer. The tale becomes a description of survival of the intelligent, cultured man faced with the most primitive forces of the human psyche.

Wagoner's tragicomedies of violence achieve effects somewhat like François Truffaut's *Shoot the Piano Player.* The mixture of naiveté, tough-guy dialogue, violence, thriller action, and insight into complex states of mind creates a fantasy world as an accurate analog for contemporary urban life. Danny Masters, in *The Escape Artist,* muses on violence and trickery and how to escape them:

> Danny felt his own life shut inside him, keeping as quiet as it could, shying away. Nobody should be able to break anybody open like a nut and clean out the insides, but some people did it, and he would never let them come close. That was why getting away was important, getting out, getting loose, because they had to make you sit still long enough so they could crack you open, otherwise it spoiled their aim. They were no good with moving targets, no good if you weren't where they thought you were. They knew a lot of tricks, and that was why you had to keep ahead of them, and then if you got a big enough lead, you could afford to let them know who you were, taunting them from a distance yet always ready to change shape to fool them.

Wagoner's novels reflect society's torments and traps and also explore the paths to freedom—self-understanding, imagination, and the uses of experience. While they detail corruption and destruction, they also reflect innocence and virtue. The possibilities in this world are tragic and comic, and the inevitable price of survival is loss of innocence.

—William J. Schafer

WAKEFIELD, Dan

Nationality: American. **Born:** Indianapolis, Indiana, 21 May 1932. **Education:** Shortridge High School, Indianapolis, graduated 1950; Indiana University, Bloomington, 1950–51; Columbia University, New York, 1951–55, B.A. (honors) in English 1955. **Career:** News editor, *Princeton Packet,* New Jersey, 1955; research assistant to C. Wright Mills, Columbia University, 1955; staff writer, the *Nation,* New York, 1956–61; contributing editor, *Atlantic Monthly,* Boston, 1968–82; since 1992 contributing writer, *GQ Magazine.* Since 1983 co-chairperson of religious education, King's Chapel, Boston. Visiting lecturer, University of Massachusetts, Boston, 1965–67, 1981, Bread Loaf Writers Conference, Middlebury, Vermont, 1966, 1968, 1970, University of Illinois, Urbana, 1968, University of Iowa, Iowa City, 1972, and Emerson College, Boston, 1982–83. Distinguished visiting writer, Florida International University, 1995. Creator and story consultant, *James at 15* series, NBC Television, 1977–78. Since 1994, Board of Directors, National Writers Union. **Awards:** Bread Loaf Writers Conference De Voto fellowship, 1957; Nieman Foundation fellowship, for journalism, Harvard University, 1963; Rockefeller grant, 1968; National Endowment for the Arts award, for ''A Visit from Granny,'' 1966, for unknown, 1968; Golden Eagle award, for screenplay, 1983. *Going All the Way* was a selection at Sundance Film Festival, 1997. **Address:** King's Chapel, 64 Beacon Street, Boston, Massachusetts 02108, U.S.A.

Publications

Novels

Going All the Way. New York, Delacorte Press, 1970; London, Weidenfeld and Nicholson, 1971.
Starting Over. New York, Delacorte Press, 1973; London, Hart Davis MacGibbon, 1974.
Home Free. New York, Delacorte Press, and London, Hart Davis MacGibbon, 1977.
Under the Apple Tree. New York, Delacorte Press, 1982.
Selling Out. Boston, Little Brown, 1985.

Uncollected Short Stories

''The Rich Girl,'' in *Playboy,* September 1965.
''Autumn Full of Apples,'' in *The Best American Short Stories 1966,* edited by Martha Foley and David Burnett. Boston, Houghton Mifflin, 1966.
''A Visit from Granny,'' in *American Literary Anthology #2,* 1966.
''Full Moon in Sagittarius,'' in *Atlantic,* Boston, January 1973.

Plays

Television Films: *James at 15,* 1977; *The Seduction of Miss Leona,* 1980; *The Innocents Abroad,* from the novel by Mark Twain, 1983.

Screenplays: *Going All the Way*, 1997

Other

Island in the City: The World of Spanish Harlem. Boston, Houghton Mifflin, 1959.
Revolt in the South. New York, Grove Press, 1961.
Between the Lines: A Reporter's Personal Journey Through Public Events. New York, New American Library, 1965.
Supernation at Peace and War. Boston, Little Brown, 1968.
All Her Children: The Making of a Soap Opera. New York, Doubleday, 1976.
Returning: A Spiritual Journey. New York, Doubleday, 1988.
The Story of Your Life: Writing a Spiritual Autobiography. Boston, Beacon Press, 1990.
New York in the Fifties. Boston, Houghton Mifflin, 1991.
Expect a Miracle. San Francisco, HarperSanFrancisco, 1995.
Creating from the Spirit: Living Each Day As a Creative Act. New York, Ballantine Books, 1996.
How Do We Know When It's God?: A Spiritual Memoir. Boston, Little, Brown, 1999.
Editor, *The Addict: An Anthology.* New York, Fawcett, 1963.

*

Manuscript Collection: Mugar Memorial Library, Boston University.

Film Adaptation: *Going All the Way,* 1997.

Critical Studies: *The New American Novel of Manners: The Fiction of Richard Yates, Dan Wakefield, and Thomas McGuane* by Jerome Klinkowitz, Athens, University of Georgia Press, 1986; ''Remembering the '50s'': Three Spiritual Mentors'' by James Wall, in *The Christian Century,* 109(19), 3–10 June 1992.

Dan Wakefield comments:

I believe in the novel as story, entertainment, and communication—as if those elements could be separated! One of my college English professors defined the novel as ''how it was with a group of people.'' I believe it is that and more. I want my novels to convey interior as well as social truth. I want them to enable readers to appreciate how other people felt, to make connections among human beings in all their diversity and in their alikeness as well. I love it when readers recognize some aspect of themselves in one of my characters and thus feel ''I am not the only one!'' who experienced some particular type of pain or joy. I try to write the way my characters think, the way they would express themselves, and I fear this attempt to be ''plain'' and open is sometimes misconstrued as an inability to write in a more self-consciously ''literary'' style. So be it. My aim is to convey the perception of the people I write about. I write about people I love, and in so doing I wish to honor them and celebrate our common humanity.

* * *

Dan Wakefield had already established himself as a feature journalist a decade before writing his first novel, but the unique style of his journalistic writing would lay the groundwork for his fiction. *Island in the City: The World of Spanish Harlem, Revolt in the South, Between the Lines,* and *Supernation at Peace and War,* were pioneering efforts in a field which became known as ''The New Journalism.'' Sacrificing the distance and objectivity of conventional journalism, Wakefield found the best way to write about an issue was to immerse himself within it and then write about himself. Thus he lived inside the poverty of New York City's Spanish Harlem, experienced first-hand the civil rights movements in the American south, and travelled from coast to coast talking with common citizens about the state of their nation. Moreover, the New Journalism used the techniques of realistic fiction, including characterization, narrative development, imagery, and symbolism to tell its story—conventions which had recently been discarded by the innovative novelists who wished their fiction to practice no such structuring illusions. As a result, by 1970 Wakefield was prepared to write a new American novel of manners, using the traditional form of fiction to express the new semiotics of culture he had experienced firsthand as a New Journalist.

A strong sense of how the signs of culture operate pervades Wakefield's fiction, and his novels provide an excellent cross-section of the development of American manners since World War II. *Going All the Way* shows two young men returning to their homes in Indianapolis after serving in the Korean War. Anxious for their own lives to begin, they face the obstacles of being fettered by their parent's obsolescent manners and by the confusions, sexual and otherwise, being wrought by their exuberant young manhood. The times are changing as well, and within this kaleidoscope of radically different values Sonny and Gunner attempt to sort out new trends in dress, music, and social conduct. That matters do not improve with age is shown in *Starting Over,* in which a recently divorced advertising executive refashions his life in a new city, with a new profession and friends. An entirely new system of manners takes over, with innovations such as the single-person's lonely Sunday and holidays providing difficult tests of adjustment. His protagonist's mind, however, proves to be a *tabula rasa* upon which any suggestion can be planted. Therefore, readers can find an index to the manners of the times (the late 1960s and early 1970s in America) simply by watching the hero's reactions. The novel closes with him drifting into another marriage, with everyone telling him how lucky he is, as he stares wistfully after a young woman on the beach.

In Wakefield's first two novels his characters are richly imprinted by their social environment. That the radically changing times may have exhausted themselves and become as blank as the tablets of his characters is suggested by Wakefield's third novel, *Home Free.* Change has its rhythms and dynamics, and in this case the author shows how he can employ periods of lull and regression just as effectively. The protagonist begins college but is swept away by the countercultural movement of the times. When this movement fizzles out to its entropic end, he is cast adrift on a sea of nothingness. His stimuli have been ethereal—often just the suggestive lyrics of popular music—and when faced with reality, he has little ability to respond. He crosses America, but in a parody of Jack Kerouac's *On the Road,* for instead of energy Wakefield's hero draws on ennui. He winds up at the extreme edge of America, on the beach outside Los Angeles, where he lives in a situation as blank as a movie screen:

> His life.
>
> He'd walked into it like walking up the aisle of a movie and melting into the screen and becoming part of the picture, the story, finding out what happened as you went along, knowing from the beginning how it would end but not when. Then he'd be standing on the stage feeling silly and strange with the screen dark and the houselights on. Bright. He'd be blinking, trying to find his way out. In the meantime this was his life.

Under the Apple Tree and *Selling Out* are much fuller works because Wakefield again builds his fiction from the materials of popular culture, rather than from their lack. The first, set in a small Illinois town during the years of World War II, traces the maturation of a young boy as his older brother goes off to fight and the home community responds with a semiotic riot of patriotic support. The novel's action is a study of reading habits, as the war's far-off action is translated to the ''home front'' by means of advertisements, promotional campaigns, and instructive attitudes. Their signal nature is perfectly matched to the boy's innocence, and as he grows up so do popular notions toward the conflict. His own understanding of sexuality and human relations parallels this cultural development as his own ability to read his brother's and future sister-in-law's emotions rises from the comic-book level to the sophisticated.

Selling Out shows Wakefield's semiotic method in high relief, because the novel constitutes a test of it. His central character is a short-story writer named Perry Moss, who experiments with a new medium (film writing) in a new environment (Hollywood). Wakefield is judicially precise in his contrast of the bi-coastal and intermedia realities, as Perry finds the jet ride from Boston to Los Angeles has taken him into an entirely different world. The contrasts are shown to good purpose, not simply for their own value but for what they contribute to an understanding of Perry's fatal attempt at change. Yet his true allegiances remain to the printed word and life in New England, and when he returns to them at the end it is with a heightened sense of appreciation which his west coast adventures have made so obvious.

Based as it is upon self-evidently autobiographical materials, *Selling Out* paves the way for Wakefield's subsequent work in what he calls ''spiritual autobiography.'' *Returning: A Spiritual Journey* documents his commercial success in Hollywood and chronicles his physical breakdown from the stress it entailed. To this point the book parallels *Selling Out.* Yet where *Selling Out* ends, with the protagonist's return to New England, *Returning* begins its major work, that of detailing the restorative powers Wakefield found in a spiritual understanding of himself. It is the employment of theological and not just intellectual elements that makes such a ''return'' possible, and in *The Story of Your Life* Wakefield presents a workable program for combining narrative activity with spiritual understanding as a way of constructing one's life as a meaningful work. Such patterns appear in his own canon, as *New York in the Fifties* not only summarizes his own involvement with the writers and thinkers of that era but investigates his own artistic growth; as such, it serves as the legwork for a novel in progress, set in the same time and region.

Wakefield knows that man is the sign-making animal, and his appreciation of the semiosis by which human life is conducted makes him ably qualified to describe how life is lived in America today.

—Jerome Klinkowitz

WALKER, Alice (Malsenior)

Nationality: American. **Born:** Eatonton, Georgia, 9 February 1944. **Education:** Spelman College, Atlanta, 1961–63; Sarah Lawrence College, Bronxville, New York, 1963–65, B.A. 1965. **Family:** Married Melvyn R. Leventhal in 1967 (divorced 1976); one daughter. **Career:** Voter registration and Head Start program worker, Mississippi, and with New York City Department of Welfare, mid-1960s; teacher, Jackson State College, 1968–69, and Tougaloo College, 1970–71, both Mississippi; lecturer, Wellesley College, Cambridge, Massachusetts, 1972–73, and University of Massachusetts, Boston, 1972–73; associate professor of English, Yale University, New Haven, Connecticut, after 1977. Distinguished Writer, University of California, Berkeley, Spring 1982; Fannie Hurst Professor, Brandeis University, Waltham, Massachusetts, Fall 1982. Co-founder and publisher, Wild Trees Press, Navarro, California, 1984–88. **Awards:** Bread Loaf Writers Conference scholarship, 1966; *American Scholar* prize, for essay, 1967; Merrill fellowship, 1967; MacDowell fellowship, 1967, 1977; Radcliffe Institute fellowship, 1971; Lillian Smith award, for poetry, 1973; American Academy Rosenthal award, 1974; National Endowment for the Arts grant, 1977; Guggenheim grant, 1978; American Book award, 1983; Pulitzer prize, 1983; O. Henry award, 1986; Nora Astorga Leadership award, 1989; Fred Cody award for lifetime achievement, Bay Area Book Reviewers Association, 1990; Freedom to Write award, PEN Center USA West, 1990; Shelia award, Tubman African American Museum, 1998. Ph.D.: Russell Sage College, Troy, New York, 1972; D.H.L.: University of Massachusetts, Amherst, 1983. Lives in San Francisco. **Address:** c/o Harcourt Brace Jovanovich Inc., 1250 Sixth Avenue, San Diego, California 92101, U.S.A.

PUBLICATIONS

Novels

The Third Life of Grange Copeland. New York, Harcourt Brace, 1970; London, Women's Press, 1985.
Meridian. New York, Harcourt Brace, and London, Deutsch, 1976.
The Color Purple. New York, Harcourt Brace, 1982; London, Women's Press, 1983.
The Temple of My Familiar. San Diego, Harcourt Brace, and London, Women's Press, 1989.
Possessing the Secret of Joy. New York, Harcourt Brace, and London, Cape, 1992.
By the Light of My Father's Smile. New York, Random House, 1998.

Short Stories

In Love and Trouble: Stories of Black Women. New York, Harcourt Brace, 1973; London, Women's Press, 1984.
You Can't Keep a Good Woman Down. New York, Harcourt Brace, 1981; London, Women's Press, 1982.
Complete Short Stories, London, Women's Press, n.d.
Everyday Use, edited by Barbara T. Christian. New Brunswick, Rutgers University Press, 1994.

Uncollected Short Stories

"Cuddling," in *Essence* (New York), July 1985.
"Kindred Spirits," in *Prize Stories 1986,* edited by William Abrahams. New York, Doubleday, 1986.

Poetry

Once. New York, Harcourt Brace, 1968; London, Women's Press, 1986.
Five Poems. Detroit, Broadside Press, 1972.
Revolutionary Petunias and Other Poems. New York, Harcourt Brace, 1973; London, Women's Press, 1988.
Good Night, Willie Lee, I'll See You in the Morning. New York, Dial Press, 1979; London, Women's Press, 1987.
Horses Make a Landscape Look More Beautiful. New York, Harcourt Brace, 1984; London, Women's Press, 1985.
Her Blue Body Everything We Know: Earthling Poems 1965–1990. San Diego, Harcourt Brace, and London, Women's Press, 1991.

Other (for children)

Langston Hughes, American Poet (biography). New York, Crowell, 1974.
To Hell with Dying. San Diego, Harcourt Brace, and London, Hodder and Stoughton, 1988.
Finding the Green Stone. San Diego, Harcourt Brace, and London, Hodder and Stoughton, 1991.

Other

In Search of Our Mothers' Gardens: Womanist Prose. New York, Harcourt Brace, 1983; London, Women's Press, 1984.
Living by the Word: Selected Writings 1973–1987. San Diego, Harcourt Brace, and London, Women's Press, 1988.
Warrior Marks: Female Genital Mutilation and the Sexual Blinding of Women, with Pratibha Parmar. New York, Harcourt Brace, 1993.
The Same River Twice: Honoring the Difficult, A Meditation on Life, Spirit, Art, and the Making of The Film The Color Purple, Ten Years Later. New York, Scribner, 1996.
Alice Walker Banned. San Francisco, Aunt Lute Books, 1996.
Anything We Love Can Be Saved: A Writer's Activism. New York, Random House, 1997.
The Way Forward Is with a Broken Heart. New York, Random House, 2000.
Editor, *I Love Myself When I Am Laughing ... and Then Again When I Am Looking Mean and Impressive: A Zora Neale Hurston Reader.* Old Westbury, New York, Feminist Press, 1979.

*

Bibliography: *Alice Malsenior Walker: An Annotated Bibliography 1968–1986* by Louis H. Pratt and Darnell D. Pratt, Westport, Connecticut, Meckler, 1988; *Alice Walker: An Annotated Bibliography 1968–1986* by Erma Davis Banks and Keith Byerman, London, Garland, 1989.

Critical Studies: *Brodie's Notes on Alice Walker's "The Color Purple"* by Marion Picton, London, Pan, 1991; *Alice Walker* by Conna Histy Winchell, New York, Twayne, 1992; *Alice Walker* by Tony Gentry, New York, Chelsea, 1993; *Alice Walker and Zora Neale Hurston: The Common Bond* edited by Lillie P. Howard, Westport, Connecticut, and London, Greedwood Press, 1993; *Alice Walker: Critical Perspectives Past and Present* edited by Henry Louis Gates and K.A. Appiah, New York, Amistad, 1993; *Black Feminist Consciousness* by Kashinath Ranveer, Jaipur, India, Printwell, 1995; *The Voices of African American Women: The Use of Narrative and Authorial Voice in the Works of Harriet Jacobs, Zora Neale Hurston, and Alice Walker* by Yvonne Johnson, New York, P. Lang, 1998; *Critical Essays on Alice Walker,* edited by Ikenna Dieke, Westport, Connecticut, Greenwood Press, 1999; *Alice Walker* by Maria Lauret, New York, St. Martin's Press, 1999; *Alice Walker: Freedom Writer* by Caroline Lazo, Minneapolis, Lerner Publications, 2000; *Alice Walker,* edited by Harold Bloom, Philadelphia, Pennsylvania, Chelsea House Publishers, 2000; *Alice Walker in the Classroom: Living by the Word* by Carol Jago, Urbana, Illinois, National Council of Teachers of English, 2000.

* * *

With the publication of a single startling novel, *The Color Purple,* Alice Walker almost single-handedly brought the struggle of the African-American female into public view for the general reading audience in the United States. It paved the way for later novels like Toni Morrison's *Beloved,* to which it is often compared, to find a wider and more willing readership among audiences of all ethnic backgrounds.

While none of her novels since that one have achieved quite the same level of notoriety or are so frequently taught in schools and universities, there is no doubt that Walker's prolific and persistent political, cultural, and spiritual journeys through writing have engaged a national dialogue about important issues such as women's rights, race, and identity. Walker is an activist in each of the political, cultural, and spiritual spheres, as her many nonfiction titles attest. Her novels thus far include *The Third Life of Grange Copeland* and *Meridian,* which appeared before *The Color Purple,* and *The Temple of My Familiar, Possessing the Secret of Joy,* and *By the Light of My Father's Smile,* which appeared afterward. In her novels, as well as in her short fiction, essays, and poetry, Walker's activism is prevalent. In the novels, however, this activism runs the risk of didacticism. In other words, some of Walker's novels work more successfully as stories than others do.

Her second novel, *Meridian,* is a story about a civil rights activist from the 1960s and what happens to her during and after the movement on a personal level. In this novel, the political movement causes some real-life changes in Meridian, the protagonist. For example, she leaves her husband and child to join the movement with Truman, and she is given a scholarship as a result of her involvement. The struggles of the movement become even more complex, however, when they become personal and things do not always go as Meridian plans. Truman deserts her for a white woman, and college requires too much conformity. People in the movement change sides and loyalties are put into question. In some ways, Walker seems to be questioning the value of political activism throughout this book in a healthy sort of way. However, the reader considers these larger questions as a result of Meridian's experiences, not as a result of an imposing hand of the author.

Walker turned to the cultural sphere in *The Color Purple.* Celie survives incest and domestic abuse to gain more and more confidence in her own abilities and talents. In many ways, the novel is a classic American rags to riches story of sorts, which may account in part for the reason it, and the feature film made of the story, remain popular. However, Celie's voice throughout the novel is most engaging and creative on Walker's part. In a way much like James Joyce's *Portrait of the Artist as a Young Man,* the reader can chart Celie's progress and growth through her narrative of her own story. While some coincidences seem unlikely in the story (e.g. Celie gaining the inheritance just in time to make her happy by the end of the novel), the voice that was found not only by Celie, but by many silent late-twentieth-century women who were reading her story, easily overcomes the novel's occasional flaws.

Possessing the Secret of Joy contains a character who appears briefly in *The Color Purple,* but the novel itself is not as successful and represents the other type of Walker novel, where activism dominates story. Celie's daughter-in-law, Tashi, the young African woman married to Adam, suffers female circumcision in Africa and later returns to murder the woman who did it, M'Lissa. The novel takes a strong stand against the practice of female circumcision and becomes almost an argumentative essay against the practice rather than a story about Tashi's experience.

If Walker is social critic in *Secret of Joy,* she becomes a medium of sorts in an earlier, longer novel, *The Temple of My Familiar.* The book is about memory and family history being handed down, and the multiplicity of voices in the novel both fascinates and frustrates critics. Many find form surpassing content, which again distracts from the story at hand.

Unfortunately, the trend to move away from sound storytelling continues in *By the Light of My Father's Smile.* In a final act that might be prophetic to Walker's work, novelist Susannah becomes a human sacrifice and dies along with her books. The scene appears to be either a subconscious act of placing writers on some kind of martyr's pyre in terms of their activism, or Walker's attempt to kill off the novelist she feels may be dying a slow death anyway within her own creative energies. One can only wonder what will happen to Walker's dead activist novelist, whether she will resurrect or enjoy an afterlife returning to good storytelling.

—Connie Ann Kirk

WALLACE, David Foster

Nationality: American. **Born:** Ithaca, New York, 21 February 1962. **Education:** Amherst College, A.B. 1985; University of Arizona, M.F.A. 1987. **Career:** Associate professor of English, 1993—. **Awards:** Whiting Writers' Award (Mrs. Giles Whiting Foundation), 1987; John Traine Humor Prize (*Paris Review*), 1988; Illinois Arts Council Award for Non-Fiction, 1989; Quality Paperback Book Club's New Voices Award in Fiction, 1991; Lannan Foundation

Award for Literature, 1996. **Agent:** Frederick Hill Associates, 1842 Union Street, San Francisco, California 94123, U.S.A.

PUBLICATIONS

Novels

The Broom of the System. New York, Viking, 1987.
Infinite Jest. Boston, Little, Brown, 1996.

Short Stories

Girl with Curious Hair. New York, Penguin, 1988.
Brief Interviews with Hideous Men. Boston, Little, Brown, 1999.

Other

Signifying Rappers: Rap and Race in the Urban Present (with Mark Costello). New York, Ecco Press, 1990.
A Supposedly Fun Thing I'll Never Do Again: Essays and Arguments. Boston, Little, Brown, 1997.
Contributor, *Innovations: An Anthology of Modern and Contemporary Fiction*, edited by Robert L. McLaughlin. Normal, Illinois, Dalkey Archive Press, 1998.

* * *

David Foster Wallace has arguably become America's most well known younger—that is, under forty—writer, due largely to his mammoth novel, *Infinite Jest.* Though Wallace had already published a novel, *The Broom of the System*, and a collection of short stories, *Girl with Curious Hair*, before *Infinite Jest* appeared, it was with this last work that Wallace began to be favorably compared with such luminaries as Thomas Pynchon and William Gaddis. Like that of these two predecessors, Wallace's work is ambitious and sprawling, by turns epicomical and philosophical.

Wallace's meganovel—extending over one thousand pages, with over one hundred pages of endnotes—is, like so much fiction of the postwar era, an amalgam of highbrow and lowbrow, literature and pop culture. Set in the vaguely near future in which time itself is identified by corporate sponsors (the ''Year of the Depend Adult Undergarment''), *Infinite Jest* revolves, mobius-strip-like, around two institutional settings, the elite Enfield Tennis Academy and the Ennett House Drug and Alcohol Recovery facility. While apparently situated at opposite ends of the social strata, the two settings mirror each other and what Wallace diagnoses as our peculiar modern malaise. As Wallace begins to probe the lives of the tennis prodigies at Enfield, who are there to prepare for the professional circuit or ''The Show,'' and the histories of Ennett's addicts, he slowly reveals the inescapability of cultural conditioning. Whether it is the dysfunctional families of affluence who train their children in the spiritually deadening mores of privilege or the media complex that trains consumers in the likewise deadening ''pleasure'' of entertainment, all are trapped in the circularity of escapism and the contemporary obsession ''with watching and being watched.''

Like Pynchon's most expansive work, *Infinite Jest* makes no attempt to refuse the language and tone of techno-scientific discourse, especially as it is incorporated into vernacular language. Wallace seems to eschew the lyrical at all costs and instead finds eloquence, such as it is, in the flat euphemism and advertising-speak that so characterize American English at the millennium. Indeed, some critics describe Wallace, like William T. Vollmann and Richard Powers, as a distinctly information-age writer, one who has interiorized the decenteredness of the database and the pacing of hyperlinking to such a degree that his fiction feels more like information generation than literary fiction, with no discernible main character but instead an architecture of characters attached by tangential associations and prolonged riffs of uncertain meaning. Wallace himself refers to this stylization as ''radical realism,'' because it is not intended as a postmodern experiment with the novel but as a mimetic reflection of American morality circa 2000.

Nevertheless, Wallace's plot structures in particular share a great deal with the novels we have come to regard as high postmodernism, Pynchon's *Gravity's Rainbow*, for instance. His almost inscrutable web of conspiracies and counter-conspiracies are virtually second-nature to postmodern readers, and his philosophical concerns about the fragmented self, the impossibility of communication, and the omnivorousness of capitalism are all well-worn themes explored extensively by postmodern philosophers such as Frederic Jameson.

Wallace followed *Infinite Jest* with *A Supposedly Funny Thing I'll Never Do Again*, an anthology of essays and travel pieces, and *Brief Interviews with Hideous Men*, a collection of short stories.

—Michele S. Shauf

WARNER, Marina

Nationality: British. **Born:** London, 9 November 1946. **Education:** Lady Margaret Hall, Oxford, B.A. in modern languages 1963, M.A. 1964. **Family:** Married 1) William Shawcross in 1972 (marriage dissolved 1981), one son; 2) John Dewe Mathews in 1981. **Career:** Getty Scholar, 1987–88; Tinbergen Professor, Erasmus University, Rotterdam, the Netherlands, 1991. Visiting professor, University of Ulster, 1994–95; Queen Mary and Westfield College, University of London, 1994. **Awards:** PEN award, 1988; Commonwealth Writers prize, 1989. Since 1985, Fellow Royal Society of Literature. **Agent:** Rogers, Coleridge, and White, 20 Powis Mews, London W11 1NJ, England.

PUBLICATIONS

Novels

In a Dark Wood. London, Weidenfeld and Nicolson, and New York, Knopf, 1977.
The Skating Party. London, Weidenfeld and Nicolson, 1982; New York, Atheneum, 1984.
The Lost Father. London, Chatto and Windus, 1988; New York, Simon and Schuster, 1989.
Indigo. London, Chatto and Windus, 1992; New York, Simon and Schuster, 1993.

Short Stories

The Mermaids in the Basement. London, Chatto and Windus, 1993.

Plays

The Legs of the Queen of Sheba (libretto), music by Julian Grant (produced London, 1991).

Television Play: *Tell Me More,* 1991.

Other

The Dragon Empress: The Life and Times of Tz-u-hsi, 1835–1908, Empress Dowager of China. London, Weidenfeld and Nicolson, and New York, Macmillan, 1972.

Alone of All Her Sex: The Myth and Cult of the Virgin Mary. London, Weidenfeld and Nicolson, 1976; New York, Vintage, 1983.

Queen Victoria's Sketchbook. London, Macmillan, and New York, Crown 1979.

The Crack in the Teacup: Britain in the 20th Century (for children). London, Deutsch, and New York, Clarion, 1979.

Joan of Arc: The Image of Female Heroism. London, Weidenfeld and Nicolson, and New York, Knopf, 1981.

The Impossible Day [Night, Bath, Rocket] (for children). London, Methuen, 4 vols., 1981–82.

The Wobbly Tooth (for children). London, Deutsch, 1984.

Monuments and Maidens: The Allegory of the Female Form. London, Weidenfeld and Nicolson, and New York, Atheneum, 1985.

Into the Dangerous World (pamphlet). London, Chatto and Windus, 1989.

From the Beast to the Blonde: On Fairy Tales and Their Tellers. London, Chatto and Windus, 1994; New York, Farrar Straus, 1995.

Managing Monsters: Six Myths of Our Time. London, Vintage, 1994; published as *Six Myths of Our Time: Little Angels, Little Monsters, Beautiful Beasts, and More,* New York, Vintage, 1995.

The Book of Signs and Symbols. New York, DK Publishing, 1996.

No Go the Bogeyman: Scaring, Lulling, and Making Mock. New York, Farrar, Straus, and Giroux, 1999.

Editor, *Wonder Tales.* London, Chatto and Windus, 1994; New York, Farrar, Straus and Giroux, 1996.

* * *

Marina Warner is a historian and author of several studies of mythology. Historical events—real or imaginary—and mythological symbols pervade the worlds in which her novels take place, literally as well as subliminally.

In Warner's first novel, *In a Dark Wood,* Gabriel Namier, a Jesuit priest, is studying and writing an account of the life of another Jesuit Father who was involved in a mission to China in the seventeenth century. The two men's worlds, separated by three centuries, converge, both in outer circumstance—Gabriel, too, has lived in China, and the Catholic church of his time, like that of the seventeenth century, is internally divided—and on a more personal level. Gabriel's subject was accused by his rivals of homosexuality and in the course of the novel Gabriel himself develops an obsession, albeit not overtly homosexual, with a young man.

In *The Skating Party,* it is not the distant past that provides a point of reference, although one central motif of the book—a cycle of frescoes discovered in a secret room in the Vatican—does provide a symbol of the patterns of male-female relationship which are enacted by Warner's characters. The story within this story is instead a more recent event, a witch-hunting ritual to which the central characters of the novel were personal witnesses, and the distance is provided not by time but by the fact that it took place in a very different country and culture.

Warner's novel *The Lost Father* is similar to *In a Dark Wood,* in that past and present are linked in the form of a historical account, a story within a story; here the narrator is writing a novel set in southern Italy, based on her own family's history, and the external and the internal narratives are shared by several characters. Warner uses the device to make a point about the fallacious nature of history—or the historical novel—itself. The narrator's imagination is captured by one dimly-remembered and ill-documented episode of family legend. When this is thrown into doubt, the reader is reminded that the narrator's portrayal of the family and its characters, however vivid and convincing, is nothing more than fiction.

More often, however, comparison between the past and the present only serves to show that human nature is a constant that transcends time and cultural differences. The dominant subject of Warner's novels is the family, and other characters are almost always seen in the context of their relationship to the family's members. *In a Dark Wood* shows the barriers that exist between different members of the same family. In *The Skating Party,* father and son are distanced, initially by lack of mutual interests and later by sexual rivalry, and the novel shows how wide the generation gap really is. The Pittagora family, the subject of *The Lost Father,* is closely knit and the relationships between mother and daughter and between sisters are warm and compassionate, but this emphasizes all the more strongly the absence of the ''lost father'' of the title. In all three novels, these barriers and gaps are aggravated, if not created, by an intruder. However, the relationships between Warner's characters are seldom straightforward and unambiguous; by the end of *In a Dark Wood,* Oliver is no longer Gabriel's object of temptation but is seen in the more positive role of Gabriel's niece's lover. Viola, of *The Skating Party,* whose husband is obsessed with Katy, sees the girl not only as a threat but also as someone deserving compassion.

In *The Lost Father,* with its Southern Italian setting, Warner is aided by the fact that her often highly poetic language does not jar with twentieth-century English vernacular in the way that it does in her first two novels, and does not give the impression of a gratuitous display of erudition, as it occasionally does in *In a Dark Wood.* Her meticulous description of detail, too, is at its best in this novel, where it brings to life the Italy of the last century and makes it as vivid and immediate as present-day London. Moreover, the intrusive and occasionally condescending voice of the author as omniscient narrator, which throughout the first novel breaks in to reveal and explain the characters' thoughts and motives rather than revealing them through their own words and actions, in the latest novel has been replaced by the voice of a fictional narrator, through whom both the world in which she lives, as well as the world about which she writes, are seen, and whose humour and understanding of her characters contribute much to the success of the novel.

This increasing complexity of narrative structure and density of descriptive detail is seen still more clearly in *Indigo,* which draws together many of the motifs of Warner's earlier work in an impressively rich and complex book, in which the distancing effect of other times and other cultures once again both establishes and undermines parallels. Starting from the mythical Caribbean island of Shakespeare's *Tempest,* the novel is a meditation on colonialism and its consequences, and a story of displacement and the silencing of the dispossessed. Warner recreates the story of Sycorac, Caliban, and

Ariel in the sixteenth century, whose place in the island is usurped by the coming of Europeans intent on profit; in the twentieth century, the Everard family, descendants of those earlier settlers who have dominated the island's culture through the intervening centuries, are themselves suffering the dislocation and exile of those whose place in the world and understanding of themselves has been fundamentally disrupted. Conflict invades the family, which, a microcosm of the processes of imperialism, can no longer displace its own internal contradictions onto the colonized world: husband and wife, parent and child, master/mistress and servant, all exist in tension and instability.

This novel perhaps most successfully unites Warner's intellectual and imaginative languages, drawing on fantasy and romance as well as on realism, in an intricately elaborate and sensuous prose. Myth and history, and the relations between them, are fundamental: the myths people live by, colonists and others, are placed alongside alternative and unacknowledged versions of truth. Warner's later non-fiction too has been closely concerned with myths and monsters; her collected short stories, *The Mermaids in the Basement,* reiterates these preoccupations. Many of these tales are retellings of familiar myths and histories, set in the contemporary world or in dialogue with it. ''The Legs of the Queen of Sheba,'' for instance, moves between a woman trying to be one of the boys at a conference in Jerusalem, and the Queen of Sheba trying to hold her own in conversation with Solomon: two women struggling for their own speech in a man's world and a man's language. Several are inspired by paintings, reinforcing the powerfully visual quality of Warner's writing. Once again, too, the intense bonds of family life are crucial, as the book's sections make plain: ''Mothers & Sisters,'' ''Husbands & Lovers,'' and ''Fathers & Daughters.'' These are clearly tales of women's perspectives (however variously), written mostly in the first person; here Warner is occasionally less persuasive, and her attempts to occupy more distant identities not always successful.

Nonetheless, Warner's is a voice of increasing assurance and power in contemporary British fiction. And how many authors have been mentioned in a song by the group Dire Straits? The reference was an oblique one: ''Lady writer on the TV / talk about the Virgin Mary....'' But given the fact that the song came out in 1979, when Warner had recently been promoting her book *Alone of All Her Sex,* the line was most likely about her. ''I wish I could claim something of more distinction in terms of popular culture,'' she laughed in a 1999 interview with *Time* magazine, ''but I don't know that I can.'' Her books, on the other hand, have contributed a great deal.

—Jessica Griffin, revisions by Katharine Hodgkin and Judson Knight

WATERHOUSE, Keith (Spencer)

Nationality: British. **Born:** Leeds, Yorkshire, 6 February 1929. **Education:** Osmondthorpe Council Schools, Leeds. **Military Service:** Served in the Royal Air Force. **Family:** Married 1) Joan Foster in 1951 (divorced 1968), one son and two daughters; 2) Stella Bingham (divorced 1989). **Career:** Since 1950 freelance journalist and writer in Leeds and London; columnist, *Daily Mirror,* 1970–86, and *Daily Mail* since 1986, both London. **Awards:** (for journalism): Granada award, 1970, and special award, 1982; IPC award, 1970, 1973; British Press award, 1978; *Evening Standard* award, for play, 1991. Honorary Fellow, Leeds Polytechnic. Fellow, Royal Society of Literature. **Member:** Kingman Committee on Teaching of English Language, 1987–88. **Agent:** David Higham Associates, 5–8 Lower John Street, London W1; (theatrical) London Management Ltd., 235–241 Regent Street, London W1. **Address:** 29 Kenway Road, London SW5 ORP, England.

PUBLICATIONS

Novels

There Is a Happy Land. London, Joseph, 1957.
Billy Liar. London, Joseph, 1959; New York, Norton, 1960.
Jubb. London, Joseph, 1963; New York, Putnam, 1964.
The Bucket Shop. London, Joseph, 1968; as *Everything Must Go,* New York, Putnam, 1969.
Billy Liar on the Moon. London, Joseph, 1975; New York, Putnam, 1976.
Office Life. London, Joseph, 1978.
Maggie Muggins; or, Spring in Earl's Court. London, Joseph, 1981.
In the Mood. London, Joseph, 1983.
Thinks. London, Joseph, 1984.
Our Song. London, Hodder and Stoughton, 1988.
Bimbo. London, Hodder and Stoughton, 1990.
Unsweet Charity. London, Hodder and Stoughton, 1992.
Good Grief. London, Sceptre, 1997.

Plays

Billy Liar, with Willis Hall, adaptation of the novel by Waterhouse (produced London, 1960; Los Angeles and New York, 1963). London, Joseph, 1960; New York, Norton, 1961.
Celebration: The Wedding and The Funeral, with Willis Hall (produced Nottingham and London, 1961). London, Joseph, 1961.
England, Our England, with Willis Hall, music by Dudley Moore (produced London, 1962). London, Evans, 1964.
Squat Betty, with Willis Hall (produced London, 1962; New York, 1964). Included in *The Sponge Room, and Squat Betty,* 1963.
The Sponge Room, with Willis Hall (produced Nottingham and London, 1962; New York, 1964). Included in *The Sponge Room, and Squat Betty,* 1963; in *Modern Short Plays from Broadway and London,* edited by Stanley Richards, New York, Random House, 1969.
All Things Bright and Beautiful, with Willis Hall (produced Bristol and London, 1962). London, Joseph, 1963.
The Sponge Room, and Squat Betty, with Willis Hall. London, Evans, 1963.
Come Laughing Home, with Willis Hall (as *They Called the Bastard Stephen,* produced Bristol, 1964; as *Come Laughing Home,* produced Wimbledon, 1965). London, Evans, 1965.
Say Who You Are, with Willis Hall (produced Guildford, Surrey, and London, 1965). London, Evans, 1966; as *Help Stamp Out Marriage* (produced New York, 1966), New York, French, 1966.
Joey, Joey, with Willis Hall, music by Ron Moody (produced Manchester and London, 1966).
Whoops-a-Daisy, with Willis Hall (produced Nottingham, 1968). London, French, 1978.
Children's Day, with Willis Hall (produced Edinburgh and London, 1969). London, French, 1975.

Who's Who, with Willis Hall (produced Coventry, 1971; London, 1973). London, French, 1974.

Saturday, Sunday, Monday, with Willis Hall, adaptation of a play by Eduardo De Filippo (produced London, 1973; New York, 1974). London, Heinemann, 1974.

The Card, with Willis Hall, music and lyrics by Tony Hatch and Jackie Trent, adaptation of the novel by Arnold Bennett (produced Bristol and London, 1973).

Filumena, with Willis Hall, adaptation of a play by Eduardo De Filippo (produced London, 1977; New York, 1980). London, Heinemann, 1978.

Worzel Gummidge (for children), with Willis Hall, music by Denis King, adaptation of stories by Barbara Euphan Todd (produced Birmingham, 1980; London, 1981). London, French 1984.

Steafel Variations (songs and sketches), with Peter Tinniswood and Dick Vosburgh (produced London, 1982).

Lost Empires, with Willis Hall, music by Denis King, adaptation of the novel by J.B. Priestley (produced Darlington, County Durham, 1985).

Mr. and Mrs. Nobody, adaptation of *The Diary of a Nobody* by George and Weedon Grossmith (produced London, 1986).

Budgie, with Willis Hall, music by Mort Shuman, lyrics by Don Black (produced London, 1988).

Jeffrey Bernard Is Unwell (produced Brighton and London, 1989). London and New York, French, 1991.

Bookends, adaptation of *The Marsh Marlowe Letters* by Craig Brown (produced London, 1990).

Jeffrey Bernard Is Unwell, with *Mr. and Mrs. Nobody* and *Bookends.* London, Penguin, 1992.

Our Song, adaptation of his own novel. London, French, 1993.

Screenplays, with Willis Hall: *Whistle Down the Wind,* 1961; *The Valiant,* 1962; *A Kind of Loving,* 1963; *Billy Liar,* 1963; *West Eleven,* 1963; *Man in the Middle,* 1963; *Pretty Polly* (*A Matter of Innocence*), 1967; *Lock Up Your Daughters,* 1969.

Radio Plays: *The Town That Wouldn't Vote,* 1951; *There Is a Happy Land,* 1962; *The Woolen Bank Forgeries,* 1964; *The Last Phone-In,* 1976; *The Big Broadcast of 1922,* 1979.

Television Plays: *The Warmonger,* 1970; *The Upchat Line* series, 1977; *The Upchat Connection* series, 1978; *Charlie Muffin,* from novels by Brian Freemantle, 1979; *West End Tales* series, 1981; *The Happy Apple* series, from play by Jack Pulman, 1983; *This Office Life,* from his own novel, 1984; *Charters and Caldicott,* 1985; *The Great Paper Chase,* from the book *Slip Up* by Anthony Delaro, 1988; *Andy Capp* series, 1988; with Willis Hall— *Happy Moorings,* 1963; *How Many Angels,* 1964; *Inside George Webley* series, 1968; *Queenie's Castle* series, 1970; *Budgie* series, 1971–72; *The Upper Crusts* series, 1973; *Three's Company* series, 1973; *By Endeavour Alone,* 1973; *Briefer Encounter,* 1977; *Public Lives,* 1979; *Worzel Gummidge* series, from stories by Barbara Euphan Todd, 1979.

Other

The Café Royal: Ninety Years of Bohemia, with Guy Deghy. London, Hutchinson, 1955.

How to Avoid Matrimony: The Layman's Guide to the Laywoman, with Guy Deghy (as Herald Froy). London, Muller, 1957.

Britain's Voice Abroad, with Paul Cave. London, Daily Mirror Newspapers, 1957.

The Future of Television. London, Daily Mirror Newspapers, 1958.

How to Survive Matrimony, with Guy Deghy (as Herald Froy). London, Muller, 1958.

The Joneses: How to Keep Up with Them, with Guy Deghy (as Lee Gibb). London, Muller, 1959.

Can This Be Love?, with Guy Deghy (as Herald Froy). London, Muller, 1960.

Maybe You're Just Inferior: Head-Shrinking for Fun and Profit, with Guy Deghy (as Herald Froy). London, Muller, 1961.

The Higher Jones, with Guy Deghy (as Lee Gibb). London, Muller, 1961.

O Mistress Mine: or, How to Go Roaming, with Guy Deghy (as Herald Froy). London, Barker, 1962.

The Passing of the Third-Floor Buck (*Punch* sketches). London, Joseph, 1974.

Mondays, Thursdays (*Daily Mirror* columns). London, Joseph, 1976.

Rhubard, Rhubard, and Other Noises (*Daily Mirror* columns). London, Joseph, 1979.

The Television Adventures [and *More Television Adventures*] *of Worzel Gummidge* (for children), with Willis Hall. London, Penguin, 2 vols., 1979; complete edition, as *Worzel Gummidge's Television Adventures,* London, Kestrel, 1981.

Worzel Gummidge at the Fair (for children), with Willis Hall. London, Penguin, 1980.

Worzel Gummidge Goes to the Seaside (for children), with Willis Hall. London, Penguin, 1980.

The Trials of Worzel Gummidge (for children), with Willis Hall. London, Penguin, 1980.

Worzel's Birthday (for children), with Willis Hall. London, Penguin, 1981.

New Television Adventures of Worzel Gummidge and Aunt Sally (for children), with Willis Hall. London, Sparrow, 1981.

Daily Mirror Style. London, Mirror Books, 1981; revised, edition as *Waterhouse on Newspaper Style,* London, Viking, 1989.

Fanny Peculiar (*Punch* columns). London, Joseph, 1983.

Mrs. Pooter's Diary. London, Joseph, 1983.

The Irish Adventures of Worzel Gummidge (for children), with Willis Hall. London, Severn House, 1984.

Waterhouse at Large (journalism). London, Joseph, 1985.

The Collected Letters of a Nobody (Including Mr. Pooter's Advice to His Son). London, Joseph, 1986.

The Theory and Practice of Lunch. London, Joseph, 1986.

Worzel Gummidge Down Under (for children), with Willis Hall. London, Collins, 1987.

The Theory and Practice of Travel. London, Hodder and Stoughton, 1989.

English Our English (and How to Sing It). London, Viking, 1991.

Sharon & Tracy & the Rest: The Best of Keith Waterhouse in the Daily Mail. London, Hodder and Stoughton, 1992.

City Lights: A Street Life. London, Hodder and Stoughton, 1994.

Streets Ahead: Life After City Lights. London, Hodder & Stoughton, 1995.

Editor, with Willis Hall, *Writers' Theatre.* London, Heinemann, 1967.

* * *

Keith Waterhouse's fiction is distinguished by a sharp comic sense, a facility that works on closely polished verbal, imagistic, and logical incongruities. For example, in the well-known *Billy Liar,* a character who is one of the two owners of the funeral establishment where Billy works, a man who keeps a copy of Evelyn Waugh's *The Loved One* on his desk in order to get new ideas and who looks forward to the day when all coffins will be made of fiberglass, is introduced: ''He was, for a start, only about twenty-five years old, although grown old with quick experience, like forced rhubarb,'' In *Billy Liar on the Moon,* a sequel to *Billy Liar* that both takes place and was written about fifteen years after the original, and which moves Billy from his Yorkshire locale of the late 1950s to a carefully designed community of shopping malls, motels, and perplexing one-way streets that lead only to motorways, a new housing estate is a ''suburb of the moon'' with ''a Legoland of crescents and culs-de-sac with green Lego roofs and red Lego chimney stacks.'' In *The Bucket Shop* Waterhouse depicts the bumbling, self-deceptive owner of a tatty antique shop, unsuccessful alike in his business, his adulteries, and his efforts to make his wife and his nine-year-old daughter, Melisande, fit his trendy definitions of ''interesting'' people. After a long passage developing Melisande's fantasies about herself, Waterhouse adds, ''She had William's gift for candid self-assessment.'' That kind of reductive comment, like the discordant contemporary images, the play with clichés, and the exploitation of grammatical incongruities, suggest comparisons with the comic prose of Evelyn Waugh.

Waterhouse builds his verbal texture on plots that often begin with a kind of adolescent humor. Billy, in *Billy Liar,* invents highly improbable and inconsistent stories, weaving a net of public and fantastic lies that is bound to be discovered by parents, bosses, and the three girlfriends to whom he is simultaneously engaged. He is full of elaborate compulsions: if he can suck a mint without breaking it or if he walks in certain complex patterns he feels he will escape the consequences of his stories. He is also a powerful leader in his fantasy land of Ambrosia. The point of view of the young boy in Waterhouse's first novel, *There Is a Happy Land,* is even more childlike. The boy plays at being blind, drunk, or maimed, mimics all his elders and delights in calling out cheeky statements that annoy or embarrass adults. Neither child nor adolescent, the central character in *Jubb,* a rent-collector and youth-club leader in a planned ''New Town,'' is also full of grandiose schemes that others always see through and mimics others' accepted pieties. All these characters, inventive, iconoclastic, and living almost wholly within their disordered imaginations, assault an adult world that pretends it's stable.

Underneath the texture of mimicry and iconoclasm, Waterhouse sometimes gradually shows a world far more sinister than the one suggested by the escapades of adolescent humor. As *There is a Happy Land* develops, the tone shifts and the boy recognizes the sexuality, perversion, evil, and violence (including the murder of a young girl) in the abandoned quarries and behind the picture-windows of the lower-middle-class housing estate. The character of Jubb himself is gradually revealed as psychotic. Behind his fantasies and comic compulsions is the sexual impotence that has led him to become a peeping Tom, a pyromaniac, and a murderer. In *The Bucket Shop* William's incompetent management of money and women, as well as his incapacity to deal with the consequences of his fantasies, leads to the suicide of a dependent actress. Sometimes, as the humor fades from Waterhouse's novels, it leaves a melodramatic revelation of perverse and horrible humanity.

Later novels, generally set in the anonymous world of London, focus satire or an understated pathos on more restricted treatments of contemporary life. *Office Life* centers on a worker made redundant who is absorbed into the modern corporation where everyone is sustained in a network of gossip, affairs, and shuffling papers, and nothing is produced or accomplished. *Maggie Muggins: or, Spring in Earl's Court* chronicles a day in the life of Maggie, born Margaret Moon, a promiscuous and alcoholic drifter in London for the past 10 years in revolt from a square, stable Doncaster family. During the day, she learns of a close friend's suicide, her father's decision to marry and start a new family, and the fact that the father of her aborted baby could have married her, yet the clever prose, satirizing the social services and any pretense to reform, finally and tersely establishes her ratchety integrity and capacity to survive. *Thinks* is more experimental technically. Concentrating, as a deliberate fictional device, on the anxieties and fantasies in the mind of the central character, without reporting what he says, the novel charts the pressures on the last, long day of Edgar Bapty's life. Through train journeys, a visit to his doctor, a job interview he only dimly realizes he has fumbled, thoughts of his three former wives, numerous heavy meals, a visit to a prostitute, and several recognition's of his own sexual incapacity, Bapty's thoughts and fears build to ''a magnificent Hallelujah chorus of sustained and bellowing rage'' before his fatal heart attack. The compressed focus and the sharp writing give these novels immediacy and vitality.

The two novels concerning Billy Liar are lighter than Waterhouse's other fiction, although the persona of Billy represents Waterhouse's only perspective that attempts to alter circumstance. Billy lies less to cover horror or perversion than ''to relieve the monotony of living on the moon,'' where the moon is his arid contemporary civic and domestic life. Both novels, as satire, also ridicule the parochial: in *Billy Liar* the target is, equally, romanticizing an old, rugged Yorkshire tradition and the ''new'' world of coffee bars, record shops, and the winner of the Miss Stradhoughton contest who delivers ''whole sentences ready-packed in disposable tinfoil wrapper''; in *Billy Liar on the Moon* the target is civic pride, all the contemporary designs and shapes applied to experience and undermined both by their implicit fatuity and old-fashioned corruption. In both novels, Billy, the comic, the spinner of fantasies, uses the vision of ''London'' as his potential escape from provincial dullness, ineptitude, and self-seeking.

That any ''real London'' is no answer for Waterhouse is clear from other novels such as *The Bucket Shop, Office Life,* and *Maggie Muggins.* Yet the point in both books about Billy Liar is that he cannot, more than momentarily in the second book, manage the break to London, cannot do more than mimic, scoff, and invent within the limited world he is dependent on. Both as satire and as a potential means of revealing some deeply thought or felt version of experience, Waterhouse's comedy is thin, a covering for the sense of horror in experience in *Jubb* or *Thinks,* in which the latent pain seems unmanageable and unchangeable. Continuing themes explored in the preceding works, *Our Song* depicts a failed love affair between a married adman and a much younger girl in his office. The office also provides a setting of sorts for *Unsweet Charity,* a satire on the world of public relations and fundraising campaigns.

All the novels seem staged (and Waterhouse, in conjunction with Willis Hall, has written a number of plays characterized by sharply witty dialogue and clever invention). As Billy himself says, in *Billy Liar on the Moon,* he is still only a ''juvenile lead'' in a ''comedy,'' not the central character in a ''tragedy'' he imagines, not equipped for any part in a drama of ''real life.'' At the end of the novel, he returns to Ambrosia. Whatever the incapacities of his characters to alter or transcend experience, Waterhouse is invariably an excellent mimic, often cogent and terse, and has created a comic prose and a sense of the involuted logic of systematic fantasy that are strikingly effective and enjoyable.

—James Gindin

WATMOUGH, David

Nationality: Canadian. **Born:** London, England, 17 August 1926; became Canadian citizen in 1963. **Education:** Coopers' Company School, London, 1937–43; King's College, University of London, 1945–49, degree in theology. **Military Service:** Served in the Royal Navy, 1944–45. **Career:** Reporter, *Cornish Guardian,* Bodmin, Cornwall, 1943–44; editor, Holy Cross Press, New York, 1953–54; talks producer, BBC Third Programme, London, 1955; editor, Ace Books, London, 1956; feature writer and critic, San Francisco *Examiner,* 1957–60; arts and theater critic, Vancouver *Sun,* 1964–67; host of *Artslib,* weekly television show, 1979–80. Since 1991 arts columnist, *Step* magazine, Vancouver; since 1993 book reviewer and columnist for *Xtra West,* Vancouver, British Columbia. **Awards:** Canada Council senior arts grant, 1976, 1986; Province of British Columbia Arts award, for creative writing, 1994–95. **Agent:** Robert Drake, 1218 Saint Paul Street, Baltimore, Maryland 21202, U.S.A. **Address:** 3358 West First Avenue, Vancouver, British Columbia V6R 1G4, Canada.

PUBLICATIONS

Novels

No More into the Garden. New York, Doubleday, 1978.
The Year of Fears. Toronto, Mosaic Press, 1988.
Families. Stamford, Connecticut, Knights Press, 1990.
Thy Mother's Glass. Toronto and New York, HarperCollins, 1992.
The Time of the Kingfishers. Vancouver, Arsenal Pulp, 1994.
Hunting with Diana. Vancouver, Arsenal Pulp Press, 1996.

Short Stories

Ashes for Easter and Other Monodramas. Vancouver, Talonbooks, 1972.
Love and the Waiting Game: Eleven Stories. Ottawa, Oberon Press, 1975.
From a Cornish Landscape. Padstow, Cornwall, Lodenek Press, 1975.
The Connecticut Countess. Trumansburg, New York, Crossing Press, 1984.
Fury. Ottawa, Oberon Press, 1984.
Vibrations in Time. Toronto, Mosaic Press, 1986.

Uncollected Short Stories

''The Wounded Christmas Choirboy,'' in *Canadian Short Stories.* Kingston, Ontario, Quarry Press, 1990.
''Eurydice, May I Kiss the Cop?,'' in *Certain Voices.* Boston, Alyson, 1991.
''Thank You Siegfried Sassoon,'' in *Indivisible.* New York, New American Library, 1991.
''Wedding Dress for a Greek Groom,'' in *Queeries.* Vancouver, 1993.
''Cool Cats on the Internet,'' in *Modern Words.* San Francisco, 1994.
''Maiden Voyage,'' in *Sayme.* Boston, 1994.
''Leonard,'' in *Church Wellesley Review.* Toronto, 1994.
''Secrets of Diomedes,'' in the *Gay Review.* Toronto, 1995.

Plays

Friedhof (produced Vancouver, 1966). Included in *Names for the Numbered Years,* 1967.
Do You Remember One September Afternoon? (produced Vancouver, 1966). Included in *Names for the Numbered Years,* 1967.
Names for the Numbered Years: Three Plays (includes *Do You Remember One September Afternoon?, Friedhof, My Mother's House Has Too Many Rooms*). Vancouver, Bau-Xi Gallery, 1967.

Other

A Church Renascent: A Study of Modern French Catholicism. London, SPCK, 1951.
The Unlikely Pioneer: Building Opera from the Pacific Through the Prairies. Toronto, Mosaic Press, 1986.
Editor, *Vancouver Fiction.* Winlaw, British Columbia, Polestar Press, 1985.

*

Critical Studies: ''The Novel That Never Ends: David Watmough's Reminiscent Fictions,'' in *The World of Canadian Writing* by George Woodcock, Vancouver, Douglas and McIntyre, and Seattle, University of Washington Press, 1980; in *The Oxford Companion to Canadian Literature* edited by William Toye, Toronto, Oxford, and New York, Oxford University Press, 1983; article by Jerry Wasserman, in *Canadian Writers since 1960* 1st series, edited by W.H. New, Detroit, Gale, 1986; ''The Human Whole'' by Kate Sirluck, in *Canadian Literature* (Vancouver), Winter 1990.

David Watmough comments:

In a very real sense I regard each successive volume of my fiction as part of an ongoing ''novel'' that will not be complete until I can no longer write. My work is an attempt to chronicle the private history of one man of Cornish ancestry living as a Canadian through the twentieth century. My fictional protagonist, Davey Bryant, is depicted in childhood, adolescence, maturity, and, currently, middle age. If the work finally succeeds then it will be because I have been able to muster the kind of candor and honesty that such a confessional narrative demands. Another feature of the work is the depiction of private history—including the most intimate sexual and psychological detail—against the backdrop of public events.

(1995) Although I continue to write through my protagonist, Davey Bryant, I have recently branched out and in my current stories [*Hunting with Diana*] have him tell of experiences inspired by Greek myth and classical legend but refashioned and shown on the Internet via his P.C. monitor. The eventual collection of connected fictions will be entitled *Odysseys on the Internet.*

*   *   *

The name of Proust often comes up when the Canadian fiction writer David Watmough is discussed, and though Watmough is no imitator of Proust, the affinities between the two are clear. Both are concerned with memory and its transforming power, and both tend to transmute their own memories into the stuff of fiction. Watmough has written several volumes of short stories, notably *Ashes for Easter* (his first), *Love and the Waiting Game,* and *The Connecticut Countess,* and also a trio of open-ended novels, (*No More into the Garden, The Year of Fears,* and *Families*).

Watmough's claim is that for the past two decades he has really been engaged in writing a single novel that will take a lifetime to complete. It is a claim that must be taken seriously, for the same central character, Davey Bryant, appears in almost all the fiction Watmough writes, whether it is short stories, novels, or the spoken and semi-dramatic fictions he calls monodramas.

Though this is no exact sense fictionalized autobiography, Davey Bryant does in many ways resemble Watmough in the same way as some of his experiences parallel his creator's. Yet the character stands apart, observed with irony and candour. But the observation is from within as well as without, and each story, each chapter of a novel, is a confession of ambivalent acts, ambivalent motives, for the screen between the straight and the gay world constantly wavers and dissolves and forms again.

In a way the saga of Davey Bryant is in the classic tradition of modernist fiction—a portrait of the artist as a young but aging man or dog. We follow him from his boyhood to middle age. But real life—from which so much undoubtedly comes—is modified by memory and changed by art, and Watmough's fictions walk a variety of tightropes, between actuality and truth, between the oral and the written mode.

These fictions are all essentially ironic, with the initial nostalgia of the vision always underlaid by the nagging memory, the jarring truth that provokes the nostalgia. Some of the most telling stories are those that evoke moments of folly or unworthiness which stir similar recollections in the reader to those the writer experiences, or, alternatively, make him uneasy because of the perilous closeness of the predicaments—frequently homosexual—that are delineated by the possibilities of his own life.

In the novels, especially, Davey Bryant is shown as both the victim of ludicrous circumstances and the perpetrator of petty moral atrocities. The victim is always seen to be seeking victory, and most personal relationships are marred by a cruelty that degrades one or other of the participants.

The recurrent themes are united on another level by a pervading elegiac consciousness; in the novel *No More into the Garden,* for example, the longed-for garden that is never re-entered is in one sense the Cornwall of childhood happiness, and in another the state of collective innocence that all men seek to recover. The garden, however, can become ''a harvest of threats.'' By the novel's end the fullness of life is balanced by ever-present death, for as the mind expands in consciousness the physical possibilities narrow. Here, for Watmough, is the irony and also the elegy. But the garden survives in the Proustian reality, and even in a later collection of stories, *Fury,* there is a return to the world of childhood with all its innocence and brutality.

Later novels have taken the narrating hero through the successive lustra of inner development and outward adventure as Davey metamorphoses from the boy of the original stories to the middle-aged man of *Families. The Year of Fears,* for example, concerns the period of the Vietnam War when Davey lives in the pre-AIDS gay culture of California. When we come to *Families* he is settled in Vancouver, a city which not only has a considerable gay world, but also a good deal of friendly and mutually tolerant interaction between the gay and the straight communities. And here Davey seems at least to have found his special role, not only as a chronicler-participant of the gay world, but also as a kind of mediator among his friends: as if, like the celibacy of a priest, his different sexual role has given him a privileged position as a kind of emotional middle man in what turns out to be a multisexual world. The problems he encounters, and often dabbles in, give a serious cast to the novel, but the threat of solemnity is dispelled by an ironic, self-deprecating manner, in which gossip is used, rather as Proust used it, for revelation as much as diversion. Watmough has—and I say this approvingly rather than pejoratively—a talent for the trivial. He knows how to use it for the maximum ironic effect, and how to temper the dynamics of structure by beginning and ending his novel, as it were, in mid-thought. *Families* ends with two friends, a heterosexual woman and a homosexual man, in a semi-rural park:

> There, where the gravel at the lake's edge gave way to a grass bank, we sat down in the October sun and stretched our legs. This time we saw no kingfishers.

It looks like an anti-climax; in fact it is continuity, tying in a cord from the past, yet paradoxically opening to an as yet unrevealed but perhaps already lived future. By contrast, *Thy Mother's Glass* goes far, far back, to Davey's origins in Cornwall as the son of an overbearing, lesbian mother. He grows up, serves in the Navy during World War II, and is brought up on charges for homosexuality. The short stories of *Hunting with Diana* move toward the future again, with Davey now seventy-one years old and living in Vancouver with his lover, Ken, and their cat. He spends his late-night hours chatting on the Internet, and comes in contact with an array of characters who resemble figures from Greek mythology.

—George Woodcock

WELCH, James

Nationality: American. **Born:** Browning, Montana, in 1940. **Education:** The University of Montana, Missoula, B.A.; Northern Montana College, Harve. **Awards:** National Endowment for the Arts grant, 1969; Los Angeles *Times* prize, for *Fools Crow,* 1987. **Address:** Roseacres Farm, Route 6, Missoula, Montana 59801, U.S.A.

Publications

Novels

Winter in the Blood. New York, Harper, 1974.
The Death of Jim Loney. New York, Harper, 1979; London, Gollancz, 1980.
Fools Crow. New York, Viking, 1986.
The Indian Lawyer. New York, Norton, 1990.
The Heartsong of Charging Elk. New York, Doubleday, 2000.

Poetry

Riding the Earthboy 40. Cleveland, World, 1971; revised edition, New York, Harper, 1975.

Other

Killing Custer: The Battle of the Little Bighorn and the Fate of the Plains Indians, with Paul Stekler. New York, Norton, 1994.
Editor, with Ripley S. Hugg and Lois M. Welch, *The Real West Marginal Way: A Poet's Autobiography,* by Richard Hugo. New York, Norton, 1986.

*

Critical Studies: *Four American Indian Literary Masters* by Alan R. Velie, Norman, University of Oklahoma Press, 1982; *James Welch* by Peter Wild, Boise, Idaho, Boise State University 1983; ''Beyond Myth: Welch's *Winter in the Blood*'' by Jack Brenner, in *Under the Sun: Myth and Realism in Western American Literature* edited by Barbara Howard Meldrum, Troy, New York, Whitston, 1985; ''Beyond Assimilation: James Welch and the Indian Dilemma'' by David M. Craig, in *North Dakota Quarterly* (Grand Forks), Spring 1985; ''Variations on a Theme: Traditions and Temporal Structure in the Novels of James Welch'' by Roberta Orlandini, in *South Dakota Review* (Vermillion), Autumn 1988; *Place and Vision: The Function of Landscape in Native American Fiction* by Robert M. Nelson, New York, Lang, 1993; *Understanding James Welch* by Ron McFarland, Columbia, University of South Carolina Press, 2000.

* * *

James Welch has described himself as both an ''Indian writer'' and ''an Indian who writes.'' This double vision of American Indian experience as unique and yet representative is at the heart of his first four novels, all set in or around reservation Montana and all revolving around protagonists, like Welch himself, of Blackfeet ancestry. Perhaps this is no more than saying that, like any good writer, Welch arrives at the universal through the particular. But the particular—the stresses and strains of Native American culture in uneasy contact with the culture that nearly destroyed it—has not much figured as a theme in serious American fiction. Welch has helped to change that, and he has done so without resort to sentimentality or preachiness.

Winter in the Blood, his first novel, takes up a week or so in the life of its unnamed narrator, a Thirty-two-year-old Blackfeet man suffering from a malaise he can neither understand nor escape from. There is no plot to speak of; the novel simply follows the narrator as he works for a few days as a farm-hand on his step-father's property, quizzes his strong-willed mother about the past, pursues an ex-girlfriend he does not really want to find into the bars and streets of small-town Montana, gets into a minor brawl, and sleeps with a couple of white women. If there is any hope in this grim depiction of aimlessness and anomie it occurs toward the end, when the narrator recognizes a dignified, blind, and ancient Blackfeet man named Yellow Calf as his grandfather and the savior of his family line. But this ''opening onto light'' that Reynolds Price thought the emotional climax of the novel is closed up in the equally emblematic scene that follows, in which the narrator fails to rescue a cow from a suffocating death in a mudhole. Indeed, a powerful sense of alienation seems to grip Welch as much as his narrator; in the conjunction of the personal and the cultural that might explain such desolation, Welch leans a little too heavily on the latter, and a faintly deterministic air clings to the narrator's stoic despair. Welch's taut prose, dark humor, and sharp, laconic dialogue, so much admired by the book's critics, do not finally save *Winter in the Blood* from a congealment of its own.

The alienation of the principal character is taken to its logical conclusion in *The Death of Jim Loney* with his suicide. Actually, Loney's death is a sort of ritualistic murder that he wills upon himself, but that this death is the only form of affirmation available to him suggests the impasse that Welch had worked himself into. Moreover, the novel suffers from some surprisingly clumsy dialogue and unfinished characterization, notably in the two women in Loney's life; his girlfriend Rhea, a white school teacher from Texas, and his sister Kate, a successful education official in Washington, D.C. Loney himself seems like a slightly older, more depressed version of the narrator of *Winter in the Blood.* A half-breed at home neither in the White nor in the Indian world, he knows that there is ''no real love in his life; that somehow, at some time, everything had gone dreadfully wrong.'' Since the second novel is almost as plotless as the first, there is little for Loney to do but drink and brood and watch passively as his girlfriend and sister try, but fail, to rescue his spirit.

If *The Death of Jim Loney* was an impasse, *Fools Crow* was one way out. This long, historical novel concerning a tribe of Blackfeet (Pikuni) in northern Montana in the terrible years after the Civil War, was a major departure for Welch and an unusual instance of a story told entirely from within the Indians' point of view. In *Fools Crow* Whites (Napikwans) are at most a marginal, though threatening, presence and the interpenetration of myth, religion, and daily life takes place with perfect matter-of-factness. For example the young warrior Fools Crow is guided on a solitary trip to the mountains by Raven, at once an ordinary bird and a trickster spirit. Such scenes effectively dispense with traditional notions of verisimilitude and involve the reader in a different kind of imaginative re-creation.

Welch's protagonist, though a brave warrior and a loving husband and provider, is not immune to the self-doubt and spiritual agony that afflict his two predecessors. But the existential uncertainty experienced by Fools Crow is motivated as much by forces from without as from within. In the course of the novel the Blackfeet are plagued by internal dissension, hunger, small pox, renegade tribespeople, and finally a massacre by white soldiers. Fools Crow's struggle for self knowledge enables him to withstand these shocks to his psyche and to take upon himself as much of the burden of his people as he can. This ethical awareness, new to Welch's fiction, impresses at least as much as his always vivid sense of the Montana landscape and his use of the Blackfeet's animistic speech patterns to describe it. If he does not always succeed in transcribing the Indians' metaphoric language into an unforced, conversational English, the somewhat wooden dialogue is a small price to pay for a novel that dares to forgo irony and narrative detachment in order to represent the harsh and beautiful traditions of the plains Indians at the moment those traditions began to unravel.

In its use of deliberately commercial formulas, *The Indian Lawyer* was a further departure for Welch. It reads fast, has a suspenseful plot, and even includes a few modest sex scenes. Far from representing a compromised artistry, however, *The Indian Lawyer* shows how well Welch can use commercial formulas to crest an entertainment of a very serious kind. The Indian lawyer is Sylvester Yellow Calf, who, at thirty-five, has risen above a childhood of deprivation and segregation to become the most promising member of an important law firm in Helena and the leading Democratic candidate for a vacant congressional seat. Suspense is generated by a blackmail attempt against Sylvester engineered by a vengeful prison inmate whose request for parole Sylvester, as a member of the State Board of Pardons, had denied. In fact, the blackmail threat, involving Sylvester's affair with the wife of the inmate, is hard to take seriously; even in conservative Montana, unmarried candidates for political office do not generally lose elections for having a sex life. But Welch arranges the mechanics of the blackmailing skillfully and Sylvester's affair with the lonely, unsophisticated Patti Ann is more than touching; here the more typical polarities of racial power are reversed, but the blue-collar white woman and the worldly, successful Indian share an experience of exclusion that allows them to transcend, if only with each other, constraints of race and class. Perhaps the novel's greatest strength is the characterization of Sylvester himself: a full-blooded Blackfeet both proud of and uncomfortable with his heritage, a liberal and idealist whose decision to run for congress is, as he well knows, exactly as selfish as it is selfless. The novel's ambiguous ending seems far more just than Jim Loney's weirdly affirmative death wish. Sylvester opts out of the race and commits himself to pro bono work for Indian water rights, but he is still competing fiercely against himself. Whether he has reconciled his own spiritual needs with the exigencies of social and moral responsibility is a question Welch does not attempt to answer. Impressive as his first novel is, it is not a question Welch would have thought to ask of the intense and intensely self-absorbed narrator of *Winter in the Blood.*

During the mid- to late 1990s, Welch moved increasingly into fact-based narrative, producing not only *Killing Custer,* an account of the Little Big Horn from the winners' viewpoint, but *The Heartsong of Charging Elk,* a novel based on the experience of an Oglala Sioux man who held a job with Buffalo Bill's Wild West Show.

—Stephen Akey

WELDON, Fay

Nationality: British. **Born:** Fay Birkinshaw in Alvechurch, Worcestershire, 22 September 1931; grew up in New Zealand. **Education:** Girls' High School, Christchurch; Hampstead Girls' High School, London; University of St. Andrews, Fife, 1949–52, M.A. in economics and psychology 1952. D. Litt, University of Bath, 1988, University of St. Andrews, 1992. **Family:** Married Ron Weldon in 1960 (marriage ended), married Nicholas Fox in 1994; four sons. **Career:** writer for the Foreign Office and *Daily Mirror,* both London, late 1950s; later worked in advertising. **Awards:** Writers Guild award, for radio play, 1973; Giles Cooper award, for radio play, 1978; Society of Authors traveling scholarship, 1981; Los Angeles *Times* award, for fiction, 1989. D.Litt: University of St. Andrews, 1990. Lives in London. **Agent:** Ed Victor, 6 Bayley St., London WC1B 3HB; Casarotto Company, National House, 62–66 Wardour Street, London W1V 3HP, England.

Publications

Novels

The Fat Woman's Joke. London, MacGibbon and Kee, 1967; as ... *and the Wife Ran Away,* New York, McKay, 1968.

Down among the Women. London, Heinemann, 1971; New York, St. Martin's Press, 1972.

Female Friends. London, Heinemann, and New York, St. Martin's Press, 1975.

Remember Me. London, Hodder and Stoughton, and New York, Random House, 1976.

Words of Advice. New York, Random House, 1977; as *Little Sisters,* London, Hodder and Stoughton, 1978.

Praxis. London, Hodder and Stoughton, and New York, Summit, 1978.

Puffball. London, Hodder and Stoughton, and New York, Summit, 1980.

The President's Child. London, Hodder and Stoughton, 1982; New York, Doubleday, 1983.

The Life and Loves of a She-Devil. London, Hodder and Stoughton, 1983; New York, Pantheon, 1984.

The Shrapnel Academy. London, Hodder and Stoughton, 1986; New York, Viking, 1987.

The Heart of the Country. London, Hutchinson, 1987; New York, Viking, 1988.

The Hearts and Lives of Men. London, Heinemann, 1987; New York, Viking, 1988.

Leader of the Band. London, Hodder and Stoughton, 1988; New York, Viking, 1989.

The Cloning of Joanna May. London, Collins, 1989; New York, Viking, 1990.
Darcy's Utopia. London, Collins, 1990; New York, Viking, 1991.
Life Force. London, Collins, and New York, Viking, 1992.
Affliction. London, Collins, 1994; as *Trouble,* New York, Viking, 1994.
Splitting: A Novel. New York, Grove Atlantic, 1994.
Worst Fears. New York, Atlantic Monthly Press, 1996.
Big Girls Don't Cry. New York, Atlantic Monthly Press, 1997.
Rhode Island Blues. New York, Atlantic Monthly Press, 2000.

Short Stories

Watching Me, Watching You. London, Hodder and Stoughton, and New York, Summit, 1981.
Polaris and Other Stories. London, Hodder and Stoughton, 1985; New York, Penguin, 1989.
The Rules of Life (novella). London, Hutchinson, and New York, Harper, 1987.
Moon over Minneapolis. London, Harper Collins, 1991.
Wicked Women: A Collection of Short Stories. London, Flamingo, 1995; New York, Atlantic Monthly Press, 1997.
Angel, All Innocence, and Other Stories. London, Bloomsbury, 1995.
A Hard Time to Be a Father. New York, St. Martin's Press, 1999.

Uncollected Short Stories

"Ind Aff; or, Out of Love in Sarajevo," in *Best Short Stories 1989,* edited by Giles Gordon and David Hughes. London, Heinemann, 1989; as *The Best English Short Stories 1989,* New York, Norton, 1989.

Plays

Permanence, in *We Who Are about to …* , later called *Mixed Doubles* (produced London, 1969). London, Methuen, 1970.
Time Hurries On, in *Scene Scripts,* edited by Michael Marland. London, Longman, 1972.
Words of Advice (produced London, 1974). London, French, 1974.
Friends (produced Richmond, Surrey, 1975).
Moving House (produced Farnham, Surrey, 1976).
Mr. Director (produced Richmond, Surrey, 1978).
Polaris (broadcast 1978). Published in *Best Radio Plays of 1978,* London, Eyre Methuen, 1979.
Action Replay (produced Birmingham, 1978; as *Love Among the Women,* produced Vancouver, 1982). London, French, 1980.
I Love My Love (broadcast 1981; produced Richmond, Surrey, 1982). London, French, 1984.
After the Prize (produced New York, 1981; as *Word Worm,* produced Newbury, Berkshire, 1984).
Jane Eyre, adaptation of the novel by Charlotte Brontë (produced Birmingham, 1986).
The Hole in the Top of the World (produced Richmond, Surrey, 1987).
Someone Like You, music by Petula Clark and Dee Shipman (produced London, 1990).

Radio Plays: *Spider,* 1973; *Housebreaker,* 1973; *Mr. Fox and Mr. First,* 1974; *The Doctor's Wife,* 1975; *Polaris,* 1978; *Weekend,* 1979; *All the Bells of Paradise,* 1979; *I Love My Love,* 1981; *The Hole in the Top of the World,* 1993.

Television Plays: *Wife in a Blonde Wig,* 1966; *A Catching Complaint,* 1966; *The Fat Woman's Tale,* 1966; *What About Me,* 1967; *Dr. De Waldon's Therapy,* 1967; *Goodnight Mrs. Dill,* 1967; *The 45th Unmarried Mother,* 1967; *Fall of the Goat,* 1967; *Ruined Houses,* 1968; *Venus Rising,* 1968; *The Three Wives of Felix Hull,* 1968; *Hippy Hippy Who Cares,* 1968; *£13083,* 1968; *The Loophole,* 1969; *Smokescreen,* 1969; *Poor Mother,* 1970; *Office Party,* 1970; *On Trial* (*Upstairs, Downstairs,* series), 1971; *Old Man's Hat,* 1972; *A Splinter of Ice,* 1972; *Hands,* 1972; *The Lament of an Unmarried Father,* 1972; *A Nice Rest,* 1972; *Comfortable Words,* 1973; *Desirous of Change,* 1973; *In Memoriam,* 1974; *Poor Baby,* 1975; *The Terrible Tale of Timothy Bagshott,* 1975; *Aunt Tatty,* from the story by Elizabeth Bowen, 1975; *Act of Rape,* 1977; *Married Love* (*Six Women* series), 1977; *Act of Hypocrisy* (*Jubilee* series), 1977; *Chickabiddy* (*Send in the Girls* series), 1978; *Pride and Prejudice,* from the novel by Jane Austen, 1980; *Honey Ann,* 1980; *Life for Christine,* 1980; *Watching Me, Watching You* (*Leap in the Dark* series), 1980; *Little Mrs. Perkins,* from a story by Penelope Mortimer, 1982; *Redundant! or, The Wife's Revenge,* 1983; *Out of the Undertow,* 1984; *Bright Smiles* (*Time for Murder* series), 1985; *Zoe's Fever* (*Ladies in Charge* series), 1986; *A Dangerous Kind of Love* (*Mountain Men* series), 1986; *Heart of the Country* serial, 1987.

Other

Simple Steps to Public Life, with Pamela Anderson and Mary Stott. London, Virago Press, 1980.
Letters to Alice: On First Reading Jane Austen. London, Joseph, 1984; New York, Taplinger, 1985.
Rebecca West. London and New York, Viking, 1985.
Wolf the Mechanical Dog (for children). London, Collins, 1988.
Sacred Cows. London, Chatto and Windus, 1989.
Party Puddle (for children). London, Collins, 1989.
Godless in Eden: A Book of Essays. London, Flamingo, 1999.
Editor, with Elaine Feinstein, *New Stories 4.* London, Hutchinson, 1979.

*

Critical Studies: *Fay Weldon* by Lana Faulks, New York, Twayne Publishers, 1998.

* * *

Fay Weldon's concern began as personal relationships in contemporary society, focusing on women, especially as mothers, and thus widening to take in relationships between the generations: "By our children, you shall know us." She amusingly traces long chains of cause and effect, inexorable as Greek tragedy, stemming from both conscious and unconscious motivation, and from chance circumstances. She looks at society with devastating clearsightedness, showing how good may spring from selfishness, evil from altruism.

Weldon's unique narrative style highlights the contradiction between free will which her characters, like us, assume and the conditioning which we know we undergo. Her characters are continually referred to by their names, where English style would normally use a pronoun, and addressed directly in the second person by the author and assessed by her—''Lucky Lily'' the author appraises a leading character in *Remember Me,* where she also ''translates'' passages of the characters' dialogue into what they *mean,* rather than say. In *The Hearts and Lives of Men* the author continually buttonholes ''Reader.'' Weldon's apparently disingenuous surface, with her own paragraphing lay-out, is underpinned by a whole battery of ironic devices, indicating the limitations on her characters'—and our—autonomy from cradle to grave. In *Puffball* this process is pushed back before the cradle, with sections ''Inside Liffey'' about the growth of the fetus and its conditioning via the circumstances of the mother's life.

The Fat Woman's Joke, Weldon's first novel, follows a greedy couple on a diet: this novel originated as a television play, and Weldon hadn't fully developed her unique style. Her characteristic plangent note, that the worst can happen and does, is accompanied by a muted optimism, especially in her novels' endings: gradual progress occurs, at least for the majority if not for the unfortunate individual. *Down among the Women* concludes ''We are the last of the women''—that is, the half of the population defined earlier as living ''at floor level, washing and wiping.''

Weldon's feminism colors all her work, and is powerful when she doesn't shrink from detailing the faults of individual women, or the way women exploit what advantages the system yields them. Men are the exploiting sex because the system favors them, and they take for granted the *status quo.* In *Female Friends,* focusing on three women friends and their mothers, Grace is shown as worthless, until perhaps the end, while Oliver and Patrick take what the system offers—and more.

The machinery of plot in *Remember Me* is ostensibly supernatural, as a dead divorced wife haunts her ex-husband's second *ménage.* Weldon's apparent reliance on the supernatural may seem unsatisfactory both here and in *Puffball,* where pregnant Liffey is ''overlooked'' by the local witch. But in both novels the psychology suggests something of Marjorie's realization about her ''haunted'' home in *Female Friends:* ''it was me haunting myself, sending myself messages.''

In *Little Sisters* (*Words of Advice* in the U.S.) Weldon turned to the very rich. This black comedy centers melodramatically on the wheelchair-bound Gemma, narrator of the story within a story. Weldon also uses this device in *The Fat Woman's Joke, Praxis, The President's Child,* and *Darcy's Utopia.* The story-within-a-story device enables her to run different time-sequences simultaneously, emphasizing the interlocking of cause and effect between the generations, and also to highlight our imperfect understanding and information, through each individual's partial perception.

Praxis charts the life of a woman who served a prison sentence for killing ''a poor little half-witted'' baby, as we learn from one of the first-person chapters alternating at the start of the novel with the third-person chapters that subsequently take over. *Puffball,* about Liffey's pregnancy in Somerset while her husband remains working in London, is as strongly feminist, incorporating much information about female physiology and pregnancy. In *The President's Child* Isabel, the mother of an American presidential candidate's illegitimate child, is ruthlessly hunted in a parody of a thriller. *The Life and Loves of a She-Devil* describes Ruth's remorseless revenge on the bestseller writer who ''stole'' her husband.

Two of Weldon's collections of short stories, *Watching Me, Watching You* and *Polaris and Other Stories,* are mainly concerned with men exploiting women in different domestic settings: an exception, the title story of the latter, is the best. Its antiwar theme is continued in *The Shrapnel Academy:* over the snowbound weekend of the Academy's prestigious Wellington Lecture, the contemporary ''servant problem'' with a largely Third World staff escalates into a ''local'' nuclear explosion. Chapters of military history, describing warfare's ''development,'' break up the story.

The Hearts and Lives of Men, set against the 1960s swinging London art market, more frothily charts the marriages—mainly to each other—of a trendy pair and the fraught childhood of their kidnapped daughter. In *The Heart of the Country* Sonia, now in a psychiatric hospital, explains her attempts to help Natalie, suddenly abandoned by her husband. Weldon parades the countryside's problems, from pesticides to the withdrawal of buses.

As one of the dead able to ''re-wind'' their life-stories, Gabriella reviews her lovers in the novella *The Rules of Life* set in 2004. In *Leader of the Band* ''Starlady Sandra,'' incidentally the result of a genetic experiment, abandons astronomy, TV program, and husband to accompany ''mad Jack the trumpet-player'' and his jazz band on tour in France.

The Cloning of Joanne May, set in the present day, shows Joanna secretly cloned by her husband, so that she has four sisters, young enough to be her daughters—all brought together by the plot. *Darcy's Utopia* is structured by the device of two journalists interviewing the notorious Mrs. Darcy, wife of an imprisoned government economic adviser; the journalists also have an affair. Despite much space, Darcy's ideas for a money-less and permissive society remain arbitrary and contradictory.

Although Weldon has widened her range, and has always used techniques of ''alienation'' to encourage the reader to think as well as feel, she has also increasingly relied on her unique narrative techniques, with her often deliberately intrusive authorial voice, to sustain each novel. In *Big Girls Don't Cry,* Weldon's twentieth novel, she pokes fun at the feminist movement—or as it was called in 1971, the setting of the book, ''women's lib.'' The stories in *A Hard Time to Be a Father* are also characteristically impish, giving notice to Weldon fans that they will not be disappointed.

—Val Warner, updated by Judson Knight

WELSH, Irvine

Nationality: Scottish. **Born:** Edinburgh, Scotland, 1958. **Education:** Heriot-Watt University, M.B.A. **Career:** Worked at various jobs, including television repairman, musician, and software consultant;

writer, 1993—. **Agent:** c/o Jonathan Cape, 20 Vauxhall Bridge Road, London SW1V 2SA, England.

Publications

Novels

Trainspotting. London, Secker & Warburg, 1993; New York, Norton, 1996.
Marabou Stork Nightmares: A Novel. London, J. Cape, 1995; New York, Norton, 1996.
Filth: A Novel. New York, Norton, 1998.

Short Stories

The Acid House. London, J. Cape; New York, Norton, 1995.
Ecstasy: Three Chemical Romances. New York, Norton, 1996.

Plays

Screenplays: *The Acid House: A Screen Play.* London, Methuen Film, 1999.

Other

The Wedding: New Pictures from the Continuing ''Living Room'' Series (text), photographs by Nick Waplington. New York, Aperture, 1996.
You'll Have Had Your Hole. London, Methuen Film, 1998.
Contributor, *Intoxication: An Anthology of Stimulant-Based Writing.* New York, Serpent's Tail, 1998.

* * *

In terms of its influence, Irvine Welsh's phenomenally successful first novel, *Trainspotting*, can be compared to Salman Rushdie's Booker Prize-winning *Midnight's Children.* Just as Rushdie's novel enlivened the somewhat insular, even moribund ''English novel'' by introducing a higher degree of postcolonial consciousness and postmodern play, *Trainspotting* has vastly expanded the nature and visibility of British fiction in general and Scottish fiction in particular. Originally issued by a small Edinburgh publisher in 1993, *Trainspotting* resonated with readers, and its reputation spread by word-of-mouth, largely in the British youth culture. The novel was soon reissued by a major London publisher and nominated for the Booker Prize. The acclaim, and notoriety, along with that of James Kelman's *How Late It Was, How Late* (winner of the 1994 Booker Prize), focused attention on the renaissance in Scottish writing that included established writers such as Kelman and Alisdair Gray, younger, consummate stylists Janice Galloway, A. L. Kennedy, and Candia McWilliam, and the rougher crowd of Alan Warner, Duncan McLean, Laura Hird, and Welsh. Following the success of *Trainspotting* (Welsh's novel as well as adaptations by Danny Boyle's film and Harry Gibson for stage), anthologies of Scottish and youth-based fiction flooded a literary market that expanded to include rave clubs and the ''chemical generation'' for whom Welsh soon became unofficial poet laureate. Against the excessive romanticizing of Scotland in the blockbuster films *Rob Roy* and *Braveheart* and the commercial success of the decidedly artsy, upscale Edinburgh Festival, Welsh offered a blackly humorous and stylistically energizing look at how the other half lives. For all its stylistic flair and cinematic structure, *Trainspotting* is in some ways a work in the naturalist tradition, both in its use of Edinburgh dialect and its preoccupation with social ills. These include, most obviously, heroin use and HIV infection as well as a dysfunctional social welfare system, a socially destructive capitalist ethos, a Scottish national character heavily dependent on drinking, violence, and sexual abuse of women, the lingering effects of English colonization, and most importantly, the demoralization and disaffiliation of Scottish youth.

The world of *Trainspotting*, the Edinburgh of Leith and Muirhouse, is a world without beliefs and without illusions, in which the phrase ''choose life'' has all the authenticity of a government-sponsored ad campaign. Although it has in style and subject a certain affinity to the heroin fictions of Alexander Trocchi and William S. Burroughs, *Trainspotting* is nonetheless a highly original work: unsparing and unsentimental on the one hand, stylistically brilliant on the other, not only in its at-times-fantastical depiction of ''the life-taking elixir,'' ''ma beautiful heroine's tender caresses,'' but in the compact, slangy brilliance of individual lines, such as ''Lizzie is a shag extraordinaire, but has a temper like a sailor and a castrating stare.'' Although it slips rapidly and without warning in and out of various characters' first-person narratives, *Trainspotting* focuses on Mark Renton, who realizes that in a world in which carpe diem has been taken to the furthest extreme, both in the drug-subculture and in a Britain made in Margaret Thatcher's image, a world in which there are ''Nae friends, in this game. Jist associates,'' the only escape lies in betrayal.

After *Trainspotting*, Welsh's two collections of short fiction were assured success, especially given their titles and suitably garish cover art. Although stylistically less interesting and innovative than *Trainspotting*, *Acid House* (21 stories and novella) extends the range of Welsh's examination of (some would say exploitation of) the social ills affecting Euro-youth. *Ecstasy*'s three hastily written novellas are weaker but interesting nonetheless, not for the violence and grossness with which Welsh is often criticized but for a surprising streak of sentimentality, carefully controlled in *Marabou Stork Nightmares*, all but overwhelming in *Filth.* Set in Scotland and Africa and dealing with various forms of exploitation (colonialism, racism, sexism, sexual abuse of women and children), *Marabou Stork Nightmares* is Welsh's most ambitious novel. The narrative literally—typographically—travels up into the hospitalized, semi-comatose narrator's semi-consciousness and at times down deeper into memory, dream, nightmare, and overdose-induced hallucination. The character of Roy Strang tries unsuccessfully to escape his past (including his part in a brutal gang-rape) via a third-rate adventure story involving stalking and exterminating Strang's symbol of ''evil incarnate,'' the exceptionally ugly and predatory Marabou stork, symbol too of Strang's self-loathing. The novel's complexity puts Welsh's efforts to explain if not quite excuse Roy's actions in perspective. The same cannot be said for *Filth*, which often reads like an episode of *Prime Suspect* as written by the makers of *Friday the 13th* under the influence of fellow Scottish writers Ian Rankin and Robert Louis Stevenson (*Jekyll and Hyde*). Bruce Robertson is a detective for whom abuse of power is a way of life—a frighteningly lonely life, it turns out. Unfortunately, Robertson's appalling isolation is all but overwhelmed by Welsh's crude approach (however deliberate some or all of it may be) and, once again, an equally appalling sentimentality when it comes to explaining (if not quite exonerating) Robertson's personality and behavior. Although the subject of much criticism for its cover—a pig wearing a constable's helmet—*Filth*—like the tapeworm-shaped passages that devour its host's narrative right on the page—tries too hard both to offend and explain. Whatever its aesthetic weaknesses, *Filth* evidences Welsh's willingness to address topics of concern to his mainly youthful audience in ways and forms sure to shock and even offend the general public: in his widely read novels and short stories; in the ''blasphemous'' film version of three *Acid House* stories (for which Welsh wrote the screenplay); in *Headstate*, a theater piece performed at rave clubs; and *You'll Have Had Your Hole*, a contemporary Jacobean revenge play set in an abandoned recording studio in Edinburgh.

—Robert Morace

WELTY, Eudora (Alice)

Nationality: American. **Born:** Jackson, Mississippi, 13 April 1909. **Education:** Mississippi State College for Women, Columbus, 1925–27; University of Wisconsin, Madison, B.A. 1929; Columbia University School for Advertising, New York, 1930–31. **Career:** Part-time journalist, 1931–32; publicity agent, Works Progress Administration (WPA), 1933–36; staff member, *New York Times Book Review,* during World War II. Honorary Consultant in American Letters, Library of Congress, Washington, D.C., 1958. **Awards:** Bread Loaf Writers Conference fellowship, 1940; O. Henry award, 1942, 1943, 1968; Guggenheim fellowship, 1942, 1948; American Academy grant, 1944, Howells Medal, 1955, and gold medal, 1972; Ford fellowship, for drama; Brandeis University Creative Arts award, 1965; Edward MacDowell medal 1970; Pulitzer prize, 1973; National Medal for Literature, 1980; Presidential Medal of Freedom, 1980; American Book award, for paperback, 1983; Bobst award, 1984; Common Wealth award, 1984; Mystery Writers of America award, 1985; National Medal of Arts, 1987; National Endowment for the Arts Award, 1989; National Book Foundation Medal, 1991; Charles Frankel prize, 1992; French Legion of Honor, 1996. D.Litt.: Denison University, Granville, Ohio, 1971; Smith College, Northampton, Massachusetts; University of Wisconsin, Madison; University of the South, Sewanee, Tennessee; Washington and Lee University, Lexington, Virginia. **Member:** American Academy, 1971; Chevalier, Order of Arts and Letters (France), 1987. **Address:** 1119 Pinehurst Street, Jackson, Mississippi 39202, U.S.A.

Publications

Novels

The Robber Bridegroom. New York, Doubleday, 1942; London, Lane, 1944.
Delta Wedding. New York, Harcourt Brace, 1946; London, Lane, 1947.
The Ponder Heart. New York, Harcourt Brace, and London, Hamish Hamilton, 1954.
Losing Battles. New York, Random House, 1970; London, Virago Press, 1982.
The Optimist's Daughter. New York, Random House, 1972; London, Deutsch, 1973.
Complete Novels. New York, Library of America, 1998.

Short Stories

A Curtain of Green. New York, Doubleday, 1941; London, Lane, 1943.
The Wide Net and Other Stories. New York, Harcourt Brace, 1943; London, Lane, 1945.
Music from Spain. Greenville, Mississippi, Levee Press, 1948.
The Golden Apples. New York, Harcourt Brace, 1949; London, Lane, 1950.
Selected Stories. New York, Modern Library, 1954.
The Bride of Innisfallen and Other Stories. New York, Harcourt Brace, and London, Hamish Hamilton, 1955.
Thirteen Stories, edited by Ruth M. Vande Kieft. New York, Harcourt Brace, 1965.
The Collected Stories of Eudora Welty. New York, Harcourt Brace, 1980; London, Boyars, 1981.
Moon Lake and Other Stories. Franklin Center, Pennsylvania, Franklin Library 1980.
Retreat. Jackson, Mississippi, Palaemon Press, 1981.
Stories, Essays and Memoir. New York, Library of America, 1998.
The First Story. Jackson, University Press of Mississippi, 1999.

Poetry

A Flock of Guinea Hens Seen from a Car. New York, Albondocani Press, 1970.

Other

Short Stories (essay). New York, Harcourt Brace, 1949.
Place in Fiction. New York, House of Books, 1957.
Three Papers on Fiction. Northampton, Massachusetts, Smith College, 1962.
The Shoe Bird (for children). New York, Harcourt Brace, 1964.
A Sweet Devouring (on children's literature). New York, Albondocani Press, 1969.
One Time, One Place: Mississippi in the Depression: A Snapshot Album. New York, Random House, 1971.
A Pageant of Birds. New York, Albondocani Press, 1975.
Fairy Tale of the Natchez Trace. Jackson, Mississippi Historical Society, 1975.
The Eye of the Story: Selected Essays and Reviews. New York, Random House, 1978; London, Virago Press, 1987.
Ida M'Toy (memoir). Urbana, University of Illinois Press, 1979.
Miracles of Perception: The Art of Willa Cather, with Alfred Knopf and Yehudi Menuhin. Charlottesville, Virginia, Alderman Library, 1980.
Conversations with Eudora Welty, edited by Peggy Whitman Prenshaw. Jackson, University Press of Mississippi, 1984.
One Writer's Beginnings. Cambridge, Massachusetts, Harvard University Press, 1984; London, Faber, 1985.
Photographs. Jackson, University Press of Mississippi, 1989.
A Worn Path (for children). Mankato, Minnesota, Creative Education, 1991.

A Writer's Eye: Collected Book Reviews, edited by Pearl Amelia McHaney. Jackson, University Press of Mississippi, 1994.
Country Churchyards. Jackson, University Press of Mississippi, 2000.
Editor, with Ronald A. Sharp, *The Norton Book of Friendship.* New York, Norton, 1991.

*

Bibliography: In *Mississippi Quarterly* (Mississippi State), Fall 1973, and *Eudora Welty—A Bibliography of Her Work,* Jackson, University Press of Mississippi, 1994, both by Noel Polk; *Eudora Welty: A Reference Guide* by Victor H. Thompson, Boston, Hall, 1976; *Eudora Welty: A Critical Bibliography* by Bethany C. Swearingen, Jackson, University Press of Mississippi, 1984; *The Welty Collection: A Guide to the Eudora Welty Manuscripts and Documents at the Mississippi Department of Archives and History* by Suzanne Marrs, Jackson, University Press of Mississippi, 1988.

Manuscript Collection: Mississippi Department of Archives and History, Jackson.

Critical Studies (selection): *Eudora Welty* by Ruth M. Vande Kieft, New York, Twayne, 1962, revised edition, 1986; *A Season of Dreams: The Fiction of Eudora Welty* by Alfred Appel, Jr., Baton Rouge, Louisiana State University Press, 1965; *Eudora Welty* by Joseph A. Bryant, Jr., Minneapolis, University of Minnesota Press, 1968; *The Rhetoric of Eudora Welty's Short Stories* by Zelma Turner Howard, Jackson, University Press of Mississippi, 1973; *A Still Moment: Essays on the Art of Eudora Welty* edited by John F. Desmond, Metuchen, New Jersey, Scarecrow Press, 1978; *Eudora Welty: Critical Essays* edited by Peggy Whitman Prenshaw, Jackson, University Press of Mississippi, 1979; *Eudora Welty: A Form of Thanks* edited by Ann J. Abadie and Louis D. Dollarhide, Jackson, University Press of Mississippi, 1979; *Eudora Welty's Achievement of Order* by Michael Kreyling, Baton Rouge, Louisiana State University Press, 1980; *Eudora Welty* by Elizabeth Evans, New York, Ungar, 1981; *Tissue of Lies: Eudora Welty and the Southern Romance* by Jennifer L. Randisi, Boston, University Press of America, 1982; *Eudora Welty's Chronicle: A Story of Mississippi Life* by Albert J. Devlin, Jackson, University Press of Mississippi, 1983, and *Welty: A Life in Literature* edited by Devlin, University Press of Mississippi, 1988; *With Ears Opening Like Morning Glories: Eudora Welty and the Love of Storytelling* by Carol S. Manning, Westport, Connecticut, Greenwood Press, 1985; *Eudora Welty* by Louise Westling, London, Macmillan, 1989; *Eudora Welty: Eye of the Storyteller* edited by Dawn Trouard, Kent, Ohio, Kent State University Press, 1989; *Eudora Welty: Seeing Black and White* by Robert MacNeil, Jackson, University Press of Mississippi, 1990; *Serious Daring from Within: Female Narrative Strategies in Eudora Welty's Novels* by Franziska Gygax, New York, Greenwood, 1990; *Eudora Welty: Seeing Black and White* by Robert MacNeil, Jackson, University Press of Mississippi, 1990; *The Heart of the Story: Eudora Welty's Short Fiction* by Peter Schmidt, Jackson, University Press of Mississippi, 1991; *The Critical Response to Eudora Welty's Fiction* by Laurie Champion, Westport, Connecticut, Greenwood Press, 1994; *Daughter of the Swan: Love and Knowledge in Eudora Welty's Fiction* by Gail Mortimer (Gail Linda), Athens, University of Georgia Press, 1994; *The Dragon's Blood: Feminist Intertextuality in Eudora Welty's ''The Golden Apples''* by Rebecca Mark, Jackson, University Press of Mississippi, 1994; *Eudora Welty's Aesthetics of Place* by Jan Nordby Gretlund, Newark, University of Delaware Press, 1994; *The Still Moment* by Paul Binding, London, Virago, 1994; *More Conversations with Eudora Welty,* edited by Peggy Whitman Prenshaw, Jackson, University Press of Mississippi, 1996; *A Reader's Guide to the Short Stories of Eudora Welty* by Diane R. Pingatore, New York, G.K. Hall, and London, Prentice Hall International, 1996; *Eudora Welty and Virginia Woolf: Gender, Genre, and Influence* by Suzan Harrison, Baton Rouge, Louisiana State University Press, 1997; *Eudora Welty: A Study of the Short Fiction* by Carol Ann Johnston, New York, Twayne Publishers, and London, Prentice Hall International, 1997; *The Late Novels of Eudora Welty,* edited by Jan Nordby Gretlund and Karl-Heinz Westarp, Columbia, University of South Carolina Press, 1998; *Understanding Eudora Welty* by Michael Kreyling, Columbia, University of South Carolina Press, 1999; *Eudora Welty,* edited by Harold Bloom, Broomall, Pennsylvania, Chelsea House Publishers, 1999; *Eudora Welty: Writers' Reflections Upon First Reading Welty,* edited by Pearl Amelia McHaney, Athens, Georgia, Hill Street Press, 1999; *Prophets of Recognition: Ideology and the Individual in Novels by Ralph Ellison, Toni Morrison, Saul Bellow, and Eudora Welty* by Julia Eichelberger, Baton Rouge, Louisiana State University Press, 1999; *Eudora Welty and Politics: Did the Writer Crusade?,* edited by Harriet Pollack and Suzanne Marrs, Baton Rouge, Louisiana State University Press, 2000.

* * *

For Peggy Whitman Prenshaw's collection of tributes, I described Eudora Welty as a rare phenomenon in American letters, ''a civilized writer.'' To explain my meaning, I must turn to Ruth M. Vande Kieft's introduction to the revised version of her *Eudora Welty.* Though Vande Kieft does not employ my term, she explains that as an artist Welty ''does not seem to have felt any deep personal alienation from her culture, made no strong protests about the encroachment of industrialism or passing of the old order.'' Unlike the modernists, she is a writer who has accepted, as the price of civilization, its discontents.

This acceptance finds form in her still too much neglected first novel, *The Robber Bridegroom,* which comes as close as any American fiction to providing a myth of the nation's maturing as, with the passing of the frontier, the wilderness gives way to the mercantile state. ''All things are double,'' planter Clement Musgrove observes ruefully as his own pastoral world that has replaced the Indian wild gives way in its turn to urban society. As for Jamie Lockhart, the two-faced hero of this serio-comic fantasy, Welty notes that ''the outward transfer from bandit to merchant had been almost too easy to count it a change at all.'' The transformation is only cosmetic; merchants use the same gifts as bandits to operate legally in polite society.

Even in her first published story, ''Death of a Traveling Salesman,'' Welty had subtly countered the Wastelanders of the 1920s and 1930s by counterpointing the death of the titular figure (that Arthur Miller would later confirm as emblematic of the dying world) with a Promethean bringer of fire as head of a family just emerging from barbarism to give promise of civilization's renewal.

The kind of memorable stories collected in Welty's first book, *A Curtain of Green*—''Why I Live at the P.O.,'' ''Petrified Man,'' ''A Visit of Charity,'' and the lilting jazz text ''Powerhouse''—had been enthusiastically received by Cleanth Brook's and Robert Penn Warren's *Southern Review,* house organ of the New Criticism that flourished on ironic portrayals of the differences between people's expectations and their fulfillment. Unlike other writers, however, Welty was able to expand her vision with changing times. With two stories in her next collection, *The Wide Net,* employing such historical figures as Aaron Burr (''First Love'') and the bandit Murrell, the Man of God Lorenzo Dow, and the naturalist Audubon in ''A Still Moment,'' Welty seemed embarked (as in *The Robber Bridegroom*) on creating a mythology that earlier aspirants had failed to produce for the emerging nation. In ''A Still Moment'' she had indeed captured as tellingly as Melville in *Billy Budd* the awful cost of civilization in the destruction of beauty as the quiet naturalist-artist horrifies the two wild men into whose company he has fallen by his cool shooting of a beautiful heron to use as a model for a painting.

Welty did not linger in the distant past, but returned with her next novel, *Delta Wedding,* to the world where she best found her voice (as she describes the climactic step in her development in the autobiographical *One Writer's Beginnings*), the Mississippi of her own lifetime where outsiders were beginning to challenge the rule of imperiously aristocratic family-clans that had dominated the society. Against the most tranquil background that Welty could summon up, she depicts the struggle of an uncle's bride and a niece's groom from what the Fairchilds regard as an inferior class to claim their spouses from a deeply loving but overprotective and tradition-ridden family.

Family dominates also *The Golden Apples.* Welty includes this work in her *Collected Stories,* but it is really what Forrest Ingram calls ''a short-story cycle,'' a novel composed of tales that can be read individually but that gain additional meaning when considered in relationship to each other. Welty explains in *One Writer's Beginnings* how stories that she had originally written about various characters ''under different names, at different periods in their lives, in situations not yet interlocking but ready for it,'' grew into ''a shadowing of Greek mythological figures, gods and heroes that wander in various guises, at various times, in and out, emblems of the characters' heady dreams.'' Focused on ''one location already evoked,'' the portentously named town of Morgana, Mississippi, the meandering tales demonstrate how these provincial versions of universal types, though some wander afar and some stay at home, all return at last to their origins.

Despite the principle of the eternal return seemingly underlying this story-sequence, Welty over the next decade began casting about to evoke what she regards as supremely important in fiction, ''a sense of place,'' about somewhere beyond contemporary Mississippi—the Civil War in ''The Burning,'' the Mississippi delta beyond New Orleans in ''No Place for You, My Love,'' and dreamlike regions as far afield as Italy and Cork, Ireland, in ''Going to Naples'' and ''The Bride of Innisfallen,'' in the stories collected in the volume named for the last mentioned. None of these experiments, however, had quite the authenticity of a story included with them, ''Ladies in Spring,'' and the separately published novelette *The Ponder Heart,* both of which take place in the rural Mississippi to which Welty returned, like her characters in *The Golden Apples,* after wandering.

The Ponder Heart, which went on to become a successful play after first being published in its entirety in one issue of the *New Yorker,* exemplifies the narrative form Welty handles with the most consummate skill, the first-person monologue of a figure with whom she by no means identifies, but whose mind she can read and whose words she can capture with the skill of the mockingbird, mimicking the sounds of its Southern ''place.'' This tale, told by a busybody small-town hotel-keeper about the surprising outcome of the trial of her elderly uncle Daniel Ponder for literally tickling his teenaged bride to death, appropriately won the William Dean Howells award of the American Academy of Arts and Letters for the most distinguished work of American fiction for the years 1950 to 1955; for it was Howells who had in *The Rise of Silas Lapham* laid down the challenge to American writers to which Welty's work has become the major response, ''... it is certain that our manners and customs go for more in life than our qualities. The price that we pay for civilization is the fine yet impassable differentiation of these. Perhaps we pay too much.'' Whatever Welty's views of Howell's last speculation, after her triumphs with *The Ponder Heart,* she settled down to working in the same vein for fifteen years as she was preoccupied with her longest and most complex novel, *Losing Battles,* the chronicle in many voices (that she reads aloud magically) of the reunion of an immense clan of subsistence farmers in one of the poorest backwoods regions of the northeast Mississippi hills. In part *Losing Battles* returns (as does later *The Optimist's Daughter*) to the story of an outside bride's attempts to rescue (as she sees it) the husband for whom she has given up her own ambitions to improve her place in the world from the clutches of his dependent family. As the story takes shape, however, Julia Mortimer—the kind of schoolteacher whom Welty admits in *One Writer's Beginnings* she has most often written about, although she dies beyond the principal scenes of the novel during the day and a half of its action—takes over as the focal figure. She is the embodiment of the enlightened disciplinarian who, though constantly losing battles, has never surrendered in the war to share her illumination with her charges in the waste land at the margin of civilization. A marvelous mixture of comedy and pathos, the long folk-like tale is a remarkable tribute to the indomitability of the human spirit, especially the female spirit in the role that Howells celebrated as the poised guardian of civilized culture.

The writing of the novel was interrupted by two of Welty's most powerful stories that did not appear in book form until her stories were collected in 1980. ''Where Is the Voice Coming From?,'' written in a single night after the shooting of civil rights leader Medgar Evers, is the internal monologue of his killer, for which, Welty explains in *One Writer's Beginnings,* she entered ''into the mind and inside the skin of a character who could hardly have been more alien or repugnant to me.'' ''The Demonstrators'' is an almost equally harrowing account of a small community's white doctor's involvement in some sordid affairs of the blacks during the years of the civil rights crises that he perceives necessitate the transformation of his traditional community. Most remarkable about the two stories is their revelation of the intensity that the most crucial experiences of her ''place'' can evoke from her.

Perhaps under the impact of such recent events, even Welty's good humor and civilized virtues have been sorely tried, as is suggested by her most recent novel, *The Optimist's Daughter,* in which she reverts to the ironic mode of her earliest stories to depict the plight of a woman who has lost her beloved husband, her mother, and her father as she is deprived of her inheritance and driven out of her home place by her father's young second wife, a redneck (never Welty's term) from Texas (envisioned here as beyond the edge of civilization). Despite all the honors that Welty has justifiably received and despite her avowal in *One Writer's Beginnings* that ''Of all my strong emotions, anger is the one least responsible for my work,'' the ironically titled *The Optimist's Daughter* seems an acknowledgment that like Julia Mortimer, she and her society have been fighting losing battles, although the struggle has been worthwhile in honoring what she describes as her reverence for ''the holiness of life.''

—Warren French

WENDT, Albert

Nationality: Samoan. **Born:** Apia, Western Samoa, 27 October 1939; member of the Aiga Sa-Tuala. **Education:** New Plymouth Boys High School, New Zealand, graduated 1957; Ardmore Teacher's College, diploma in teaching, 1959; Victoria University, Wellington, 1960–64, M.A. (honours) in history 1964. **Family:** Married Jennifer Elizabeth Whyte in 1964; two daughters and one son. **Career:** Teacher, 1964–69, and principal, 1969–73, Samoa College, Apia; senior lecturer, 1974–75, assistant director of Extension Services, 1976–77, and professor of pacific literature, 1982–87, University of the South Pacific, Suva, Fiji. Since 1988 professor of English, University of Auckland. Director, University of the South Pacific Centre, Apia, Western Samoa, after 1978. Editor, *Bulletin,* now *Samoa Times,* Apia, 1966, and Mana Publications, Suva, Fiji, 1974–80. Coordinator, Unesco Program on Oceanic Cultures, 1975–79. **Awards:** *Landfall* prize, 1963; Wattie award, 1980. **Agent:** Tim Curnow, Curtis Brown (Australia) Pty. Ltd., 27 Union Street, Paddington, New South Wales 2021, Australia. **Address:** Department of English, University of Auckland, Private Bag 92019, Auckland 1, New Zealand.

PUBLICATIONS

Novels

Sons for the Return Home. Auckland, Longman Paul, 1973; London, Penguin, 1987; Honolulu, University of Hawaii Press, 1996.

Pouliuli. Auckland, Longman Paul, 1977; Honolulu, University Press of Hawaii, 1980; London, Penguin, 1987.

Leaves of the Banyan Tree. Auckland, Longman Paul, 1979; London, Allen Lane, 1980; as *The Banyan,* New York, Doubleday, 1984.

Ola. Auckland, Penguin, 1990; Honolulu, University of Hawaii Press, 1995.

Black Rainbow. Auckland, Penguin, 1991; Honolulu, University of Hawaii Press, 1995.

Photographs. Auckland, Auckland University Press, 1995.

Short Stories

Flying-Fox in a Freedom Tree. Auckland, Longman Paul, 1974; Honolulu, University of Hawaii Press, 1999.

The Birth and Death of the Miracle Man. London and New York, Viking, 1986.

Plays

Comes the Revolution (produced Suva, Fiji, 1972).

The Contract (produced Apia, Western Samoa, 1972).

Poetry

Inside Us the Dead: Poems 1961 to 1974. Auckland, Longman Paul, 1976.

Shaman of Visions. Auckland, Auckland University Press, 1984; Oxford, Oxford University Press, 1985.

Other

Editor, *Some Modern Poetry from Fiji* [Western Samoa, *the New Hebrides, the Solomon Islands, Vanuatu*]. Suva, Fiji, Mana, 5 vols., 1974–75.

Editor, *Lali: A Pacific Anthology.* Auckland, Longman Paul, 1980.

Editor, *Nuanua: A Pacific Anthology.* Auckland, Auckland University Press, 1995; published as *Nuanua: Pacific Writing in English Since 1980,* Honolulu, University of Hawaii Press, 1995.

*

Critical Studies: ''Towards a New Oceania'' by Wendt, in *Mana Review* (Suva, Fiji), January 1976; chapter on Wendt in *South Pacific Literature: From Myth to Fabulation* by Subramani, Suya, Fiji, University of the South Pacific, 1985; *Albert Wendt and Samoan Identity* by Sina Va'ai, Apia, Samoa, NUS Publications, 1997.

* * *

As the Samoan novelist, short story writer, and poet Albert Wendt has said, he ''belongs to two worlds in almost every way.'' For more than a decade after his early teens he experienced the difficulties of adapting himself to an alien culture in New Zealand, and his return to Samoa gave rise to a process of readjustment both to his ancestral past and to the post-independence present of his country. His writing stems in some measure from this bi-cultural predicament. It is a return to and a quest for the roots of his being. Significantly enough, *Inside Us the Dead* is the title of his volume of poems.

If his novels and short stories are the work of a self-acknowledged literary pioneer, they are much more than a welcome indication that a Polynesian literature is developing in the southwest Pacific. However difficult it may be to assess the ultimate value of productions for which in many important ways no firm basis for comparison exists, it is nonetheless clear that they achieve distinction as explorations of human relations and a way of life that have almost escaped the attention of romantic or racist outlanders.

Sons for the Return Home, Wendt's first novel, was published many years after his own return to Western Samoa. The simplicity of its plot and language is in marked contrast to the ambiguities and ironies of the pursuit of selfhood that, interwoven with a Samoan myth, provides the theme and gives substance and meaning to the narrative. Because it is mainly concerned with a Samoan family living in New Zealand, the fa'a Samoa or the Samoan way of life becomes an integral part of the novel's structure and not an intrusive element requiring unnecessary explanation. The doubts and difficulties implicit in the theme are developed in terms of incident and human relationship, and the disillusion experienced after ''the return home'' becomes the novel's climax, which offers no easy solution to the personal problems arising from cultural shock.

Wendt's later publications are centred on the extended families in the villages of Samoa, but they contain little to suggest that they are guidebooks to an exotic and romantic island-world. In the short stories of *Flying-Fox in a Freedom Tree,* in *Pouliuli,* and in the three parts of *Leaves of the Banyan Tree* the quest for identity, the attempt to discover the true self caught between the claims of contending cultures, and the search for a precarious freedom from the dictates of competing orthodoxies are raised to a higher level. They are not merely the consequences of racial disharmony, but originate in the basic conditions of human existence. The flying-fox hangs upside-down in the freedom tree. The powerful head of an extended family rejects his past, repudiates his present, and in advanced old age seeks freedom in Pouliuli, in darkness. The rise and fall of another titled head of an aiga in *Leaves of the Banyan Tree,* with his lust for power and his imitation of Papalagi (European) ways, may be related to the social pollution of the islands but have their source in a deeper corruption.

This long and powerful novel explores in myth and legend, in traditional social structure, and in the changing post-independence present not only what has happened to the fa'a Samoa, but what has happened to human beings. The comedy and the tragedy, the violence, the horror and the glory of human life, together with man's desperate search for the meaning of existence, are localised in a village setting populated by an extraordinary variety of characters. The middle section of an expanded version of *Flying-Fox in a Freedom Tree,* the novella that gives its title to the earlier volume of short stories, becomes an essential and thoroughly coordinated part of the whole book, linking the first section, ''God, Money, and Success,'' to the third, ''Funerals and Heirs,'' of this saga of a Samoan village.

The Birth and Death of the Miracle Man is a divergence from Wendt's earlier writings. Where in previous works Wendt's protagonists struggled to find a place for themselves in a society that suppressed individualism, in *Birth and Death* communal values, parent-child relationships, and a strong familial structure are emphasized. Particularly prevalent are the relationships between fathers and sons. ''A Talent,'' ''Elena's Son,'' and ''The Balloonfish and the Armadillo'' deal with fathers who have failed in their obligations and sons who are held hostage by unreasonable expectations, both of their fathers and of themselves. Occasionally a story like ''Hamlet'' verges on the sentimental, but most of the tales in this collection leave the reader with an affecting, memorable impression, entirely in keeping with Wendt's belief that the fa'a Samoa is best presented by Samoans themselves.

Ola, a novel, delves into issues concerning the creative process. A Samoan word that functions as both noun and verb, Ola means ''life'' and ''to create life.'' It is these two merging concepts that the author tinkers with in the novel. When a biographer begins to rearrange Olamaiileoti Farou Monroe's letters, diaries, and poems, he finds that he has begun to reconstruct an entirely singular existence. Particularly effective is the chapter ''Crocodile,'' which captures the conflict between public fictions and private realities. The schoolgirl Ola gets a glimpse of this conflict after sharing a moment of empathy with a middle-aged schoolteacher who had been previously shrouded in myth and innuendo.

Black Rainbow, Wendt's next novel, adopts the devices of science fiction to advocate cultural differentness. Set in a futuristic New Zealand, ala Orwell's *1984, Black Rainbow* addresses the relationship between postcolonialism and postmodernism, contending that the creation of a national literature is a kind of colonialization itself—the imposition of a criteria on something that should be fluid. Through humor and a willful mixing of Anglo and Samoan popular culture, Wendt challenges the idea of a ''pure culture,'' untainted by the outside world. Culture is not immutable, the novel suggests, but constantly in flux—modified and enhanced by outside influences. Taking as its subtext a lithograph by Maori artist Ralph Hotere, which protests nuclear testing in the South Pacific, the novel also explores the legacy of cultural imperialism and the effects of progress on the Polynesian Garden of Eden.

As a Polynesian writer Wendt has not been satisfied to produce fiction that has entertainment value alone or to exploit the fa'a Samoa for the benefit of the foreign tourist. His aim has been far more ambitious, and he has taken greater risks. If at times he lays himself open to adverse critical comment and his intentions have not always been realised, his achievement is nonetheless impressive. He has set a standard that augurs well for the future.

—H. Winston Rhodes, updated by Lynda Schrecengost

WESLEY, Mary

Nationality: British. **Born:** Mary Farmar in Englefield Green, Berkshire, 24 June 1912. **Education:** Queen's College, London, 1928–39; London School of Economics, 1931–32. **Family:** Married 1) Lord Swinfen in 1937 (divorced 1944), two sons; 2) Eric Siepmann in 1951, one son. **Career:** Staff member, War Office, London, 1939–41. C.B.E. (Commander, Order of the British Empire), 1995. **Address:** c/o Bantam Press, 61–63 Uxbridge Road, London W5 5SA, England.

Publications

Novels

The Sixth Seal. London, Macdonald, 1969; New York, Stein and Day, 1971.
Jumping the Queue. London, Macmillan, 1983; New York, Penguin, 1988.
Haphazard House. London, Dent, 1983.
The Camomile Lawn. London, Macmillan, 1984; New York, Summit, 1985.
Harnessing Peacocks. London, Macmillan, 1985; New York, Scribner, 1986.
The Vacillations of Poppy Carew. London, Macmillan, 1986; New York, Penguin, 1988.
Not That Sort of Girl. London, Macmillan, 1987; New York, Viking, 1988.
Second Fiddle. London, Macmillan, 1988; New York, Viking, 1989.
A Sensible Life. London, Bantam, and New York, Viking, 1990.
A Dubious Legacy. London, Bantam, 1992; New York, Viking, 1993.
An Imaginative Experience. London, Bantam, 1994; New York, Viking, 1995.
Part of the Furniture. New York, Viking, 1996.

Other (for children)

Speaking Terms. London, Faber, 1969; Boston, Gambit, 1971.

* * *

Mary Wesley's popularity can be traced in part to the humor, sensitivity, and wit with which she handles her characters and plots. Depicting quintessentially British middle-class life she creates fast moving, tightly constructed scenarios written in simple yet evocative language. The frankness with which she deals with her subject matter has led one critic to comment that Wesley "... has reached an age when she can say dangerous or naughty things without shocking." All seven of her novels deal with seemingly taboo subjects such as incest, matricide, suicide, and prostitution; love, sex, and death are dominant themes throughout.

The female protagonists of her books are misfits—eccentric, for the most part independent women who live on the periphery of the middle-class world so often described. Matilda Poliport, the central figure in Wesley's first novel, *Jumping the Queue* begins this trend of characterization. Matilda comes from a comparatively privileged world, she resides in the South West of England (a favorite setting for Wesley's books), and she is alone. Recently widowed at the opening of the book, Matilda meticulously plans her suicide, only to be thwarted by the entrance of Hugh, a fugitive from the police. Also contemplating suicide, Hugh is instead taken home by Matilda and life begins again for them both.

Jumping the Queue is original and often maliciously witty. In common with Wesley's later novels the plot contains a series of sub-plots, farcical scenes, and bitter twists. We find for example that Tom, Matilda's much idolized husband, was in reality having an incestuous relationship with his daughter and was also involved in drug smuggling and espionage. Perhaps most shocking of all is the discovery that Matilda is aware of some if not all of these occurrences. Although the novel is filled with black humor it also possesses moments of extreme sadness and poignancy, the most surprising of which is Matilda's successful suicide at the end of the book. In this respect the novel differs from the author's other works which have somewhat happier endings. Even in *Second Fiddle*, which ends with the protagonist Laura walking away from the men who love her, there is some semblance of hope as the reader knows that Laura is a capable and strong woman, a survivor. However, Matilda dies completely disillusioned, having lost everything she ever cared for, even her dignity in death.

The Camomile Lawn introduces the colorful Calypso Grant, who reappears in four of the later works. Set initially during World War II, the book follows the fortunes and relationships of five cousins, Oliver, Polly, Calypso, Walter and Sophie over a period of forty years. Sex is a dominant theme, and the war becomes the liberating factor in allowing the female characters in particular the freedom to experiment with their own sexuality. Hence we find Polly enjoying a relationship with twin brothers, one or both of whom father her children, and Calypso and Sophie embark on a series of affairs. Sophie is the misfit child (a common character in Wesley's books) who at the beginning of the book is hopelessly in love with Oliver, a love which endures and which is finally consummated four decades later.

The theme of a lasting love that finally wins through is a favored one in Wesley's work occurring in *Harnessing Peacocks, Not That Sort of Girl,* and *A Sensible Life.* In *Not That Sort of Girl* the central figure, Rose, rejects her beloved yet impoverished Mylo Cooper for the staid and rich Ned Peel. Over the next forty years she remains faithful to both men; Ned, her husband, and Mylo her lover. When Ned dies, Rose and Mylo finally marry, their love having survived marriages, births, and deaths. Similarly, in *Harnessing Peacocks* Hebe falls pregnant at the beginning of the book then rediscovers and falls in love with the father of her son some seventeen years later. Hebe is probably one of the most likable of Wesley's female characters. Running away from her grandparents, who plan to force her to have an abortion, Hebe instead becomes first a cook and then a prostitute who sells her favors for vast amounts of money in order to school her son Silas. Hebe is independent, pragmatic, and very much in control of the men who pass through her life.

Laura, the protagonist in *Second Fiddle,* shares with Hebe her attraction for men. Both women are mysterious and unattainable, Hebe because of the nature of her work and Laura because of her avoidance of entanglement. Although Wesley never actually states it, through suggestion and innuendo the reader concludes that Laura is the product of an incestuous relationship between her mother and uncle, the twins Emily and Nicholas Thornby. To complicate matters further we find that Laura has also been sexually abused by Nicholas, who if not her father is certainly her uncle. Laura is a strange character who the reader never really knows. Combining strength with surprising vulnerability she embarks on a relationship with a 23-year-old would-be writer and inevitably falls in love with him. Choosing to be alone she ends the relationship and rejects the two men who love her.

Poppy Carew in *The Vacillations of Poppy Carew* advocates pleasure over commitment. Left a great deal of money by her milkman father (also an inveterate but successful gambler) Poppy is suddenly thrust into a completely new world. Moving from North Africa to the South West of England, the novel is crammed with charming and vital characters, sub-plots and petty intrigues. Although Poppy, like Laura, rejects the man who loves her (the pig farmer Willie Guthrie) she finally realizes that she can have both pleasure and commitment with him. Thus, unlike Laura, Poppy decides to take the risk.

Flora, the pivotal character in *A Sensible Life,* combines the independence of Laura and Hebe with the awkwardness of the young Sophie. Sojourning with her parents in Dinard in 1926 the ten-year-old Flora meets and falls in love with three young men, Cosmo, Hubert, and Felix. Rejected by her parents who consider her a misfit in the same way that Laura, Sophie, and Hebe are considered strange by their parents, guardians and grandparents, Flora turns instead to the three men for love and attention. Over a period of forty years (a popular time span in Wesley's books) she explores her feelings for all of them and ends up with Cosmo.

Wesley's other works include *The Sixth Seal,* an apocalyptic and frightening vision of the world. *Haphazard House* which focuses on an eccentric painter and his family, who go to live in an old and haunted house in the country, and differs from Wesley's other works in that the reader receives a much more personal account of events as seen through the eyes of the narrator Lisa. Wesley has also written a children's book called *Speaking Terms,* in which a group of children learn to understand and speak to the animals through a bullfinch named Mr. Bull. Charmingly written and illustrated, the message of the book is essentially conservationist. *An Imaginative Experience,* produced when the author was well into her eighties, depicts a romantic triangle of good man/good woman/bad man, and does so in such a deft and delightful fashion that one's major complaint is the book's length—too short. *Part of the Furniture,* a tale of May-December romance set against the backdrop of World War II, is perhaps even more delightful.

Several of these later works mark a departure for Wesley: stylistically her use of language is still concise and simple, yet her sentence structure is shorter in these books, and her use of dialogue more extensive. Thematically several of the topics tackled in the later novels—love, death, and age—also occur in these books, and her characters retain their sense of individuality, humor, and eccentricity.

Wesley's books show a great understanding of human nature. Young and old alike are depicted with sensitivity, perception, and wit. The combination of a frank style, rich and complex plots, and a concise and simple use of language create extremely charming and readable books.

—Aruna Vasudevan, updated by Judson Knight

WEST, Anthony C(athcart Muir)

Nationality: Irish. **Born:** County Down, Northern Ireland, 1 July 1910. **Military Service:** Served in the Royal Air Force Pathfinder Force during World War II: air observer and navigator bomber. **Family:** Married Olive Mary Burr in 1940; 11 children. **Awards:** Atlantic award, 1946. **Address:** c/o Midland Bank Ltd., Castle St., Beaumaris, Anglesey, Gwynedd LL58 8AR, Wales.

Publications

Novels

The Native Moment. New York, McDowell Obolensky, 1959; London, MacGibbon and Kee, 1961.
Rebel to Judgment. New York, Obolensky, 1962.
The Ferret Fancier. London, MacGibbon and Kee, 1963; New York, Simon and Schuster, 1965.
As Towns with Fire. London, MacGibbon and Kee, 1968; New York, Knopf, 1970.

Short Stories

River's End and Other Stories. New York, McDowell Obolensky, 1958; London, MacGibbon and Kee, 1960.
All the King's Horses and Other Stories. Dublin, Poolbeg Press, 1981.

*

Critical Studies: *Forces and Themes in Ulster Fiction* by John Wilson Foster, Dublin, Gill and Macmillan, 1974; *Celtic, Christian, Socialist: The Novels of Anthony C. West* by Audrey S. Eyler, Rutherford, New Jersey, Fairleigh Dickinson University Press, 1993.

Anthony C. West comments:

I have a creative and an a-political interest in the human condition, wherever and however it may be found, with the incorrigible hope for social harmony and world tolerance.

* * *

The fiction of Anthony C. West is filled with poignant and great tenderness, yet it is not just lyric. The main characters of his novels are all very much attuned to nature, yet *in* the world if not entirely *of* it. He handles scenes of childhood well, yet his children grow up. *As Towns with Fire,* his latest novel, creates a focus, almost a culmination, for *The Native Moment* and *The Ferret Fancier.*

As Towns with Fire is the portrait of a man and a war. Beginning New Year's Eve, 1939, it traces the experiences of Christopher MacMannan, an Irishman who has settled in London to train himself as a writer, to the day of his discharge from the R.A.F. after the war has ended. During this time he has done odd jobs and worked with the A.R.P., married, had two children, gone to Belfast where he suffered employment, unemployment, and air raids, joined the Air Force, and flown many missions as observer in Mosquitoes.

There is almost too much in this book, but all of it is good. The war scenes are vivid and suspenseful. There is a charming lyric episode when MacMannan camps out in the hills of Northern Ireland. There is mystery in that, although a long flashback traces his childhood in detail, his history stops when he leaves school; however, references throughout the story imply that between then and the beginning of the story proper, he had traveled widely and saved enough money for a free year in London, at the same time maturing without losing the sensitivity he had as a child. He refuses to submit his poetry for publication until it reaches some form of perfection known only to him. There is some sort of symbolism in his efforts to protect little ducks from the cruelty of thoughtless children.

A similar affinity with nature is in *The Native Moment,* an account of the day Simon Green goes to Dublin with a live eel in a pail; because London sales have dropped off, he is seeking an Irish market for the eels that abound in the northern lakes. He gets drunk, sleeps with a prostitute, is disappointed in a meeting with an old friend, and resolves to marry a girl made pregnant by her uncle. Yet so long as he can keep the eel alive, changing its water regularly he survives his crises. *The Ferret Fancier* is a pastoral in which the same kind of sensitive character is given a ferret as a pet when a child.

West has been compared with Joyce and Beckett, and if one does not seek word play or the broadly comic, it is possible to see the comparison. But in his feeling for nature, for the persons and places of the Irish countryside, he adds another ingredient. For all of their accomplishments this century, Irish writers have tended to be parochially Irish, or write mainly of urban settings or rural settings, but rarely both. West has broken through this barrier.

—William Bittner

WEST, Paul (Noden)

Nationality: American. **Born:** Eckington, Derbyshire, England, 23 February 1930; moved to the United States, 1961; became citizen, 1971. **Education:** The University of Birmingham, 1947–50, B.A. (1st class honours) 1950; Oxford University, 1950–52; Columbia University, New York, M.A. 1953. **Military Service:** Served in the Royal Air Force, 1954–57: flight lieutenant. **Career:** Assistant professor, 1957–58, and associate professor of English, 1959–62, Memorial University of Newfoundland, St. John's. Associate professor, 1962–68, professor of English and comparative literature, and senior fellow, 1968–94, and since 1994, emeritus professor of English, Institute for the Arts and Humanistic Studies, Pennsylvania State University, University Park. Visiting professor of comparative literature, University of Wisconsin, Madison, 1965–66; Pratt Lecturer, Memorial University of Newfoundland, 1970; Crawshaw Professor of Literature, Colgate University, Hamilton, New York, Fall 1972; Virginia Woolf Lecturer, University of Tulsa, Oklahoma, 1973; Melvin Hill Visiting Professor, Hobart and William Smith Colleges, Geneva, New York, Fall 1974; writer-in-residence, Wichita State University, Kansas, 1982, and University of Arizona, Tucson, 1984; visiting professor, Cornell University, Ithaca, New York, 1986. Contributor to *New Statesman,* London, 1954–62. Since 1962 regular contributor to *New York Times Book Review* and *Washington Post*

Book World. **Awards:** Canada Council Senior fellowship, 1960; Guggenheim fellowship, 1962; Aga Khan prize (*Paris Review*), 1974; National Endowment for the Arts fellowship, 1980, 1985; Hazlett Memorial award, 1981; American Academy award, 1985; Pushcart prize, 1987, 1991; New York Public Library Literary Lion award, 1987; Best American Essays award, 1990; Outstanding Achievement medal, Pennsylvania State University, 1991; Grand Prix Halpérine-Kaminsky for Best Foreign Book, 1992; Lannan prize, for fiction, 1993; Distinguished Teaching award, Joint Graduate Schools of the Northeast, 1993. **Agent:** Elaine Markson, 44 Greenwich Avenue, New York, New York 10011, U.S.A.

PUBLICATIONS

Novels

A Quality of Mercy. London, Chatto and Windus, 1961.
Tenement of Clay. London, Hutchinson, 1965.
Alley Jaggers. London, Hutchinson, and New York, Harper, 1966.
I'm Expecting to Live Quite Soon. New York, Harper, 1970; London, Gollancz, 1971.
Caliban's Filibuster. New York, Doubleday, 1971.
Bela Lugosi's White Christmas. London, Gollancz, and New York, Harper, 1972.
Colonel Mint. New York, Dutton, 1972; London, Calder and Boyars, 1973.
Gala. New York, Harper, 1976.
The Very Rich Hours of Count von Stauffenberg. New York, Harper, 1980.
Rat Man of Paris. New York, Doubleday, 1986; London, Paladin, 1988.
The Place in Flowers Where Pollen Rests. New York, Doubleday, 1988.
Lord Byron's Daughter. New York, Doubleday, 1989.
The Women of Whitechapel and Jack the Ripper. New York, Random House, 1991.
Love's Mansion. New York, Random House, 1992.
The Tent of Orange Mist. New York, Scribner, 1995.
Sporting with Amaryllis. Woodstock, New York, Overlook Press, 1996.
Terrestrials. New York, Scribner, 1997.
Life with Swan. New York, Scribner, 1999.
O.K.: The Corral, the Earps, and Doc Holliday. New York, Scribner, 2000.

Short Stories

The Universe and Other Fictions. New York, Overlook Press, 1988.

Uncollected Short Stories

"The Man Who Ate the Zeitgeist," in *London Magazine,* April-May 1971.
"Invitation to a Vasectomy," in *Words* (Boston), Summer 1973.
"The Wet-God's Macho," in *Remington Review* (Elizabeth, New Jersey), Spring 1974.
"The Monocycle," in *Carleton Miscellany* (Northfield, Minnesota), Spring 1975.
"Gustav Holst Composes Himself," in *New Directions 33.* New York, New Directions, 1976.
"Field Day for a Boy Soldier," in *Iowa Review* (Iowa City), Spring 1979.
"Dewey Canyon," in *Conjunctions* (New York), Spring 1982.
"The Destroyer of Delight," in *Paris Review,* Spring 1983.
"He Who Wears the Pee of the Tiger," in *Tri-Quarterly* (Evanston, Illinois), Spring 1984.
"Hopi," in *Kenyon Review* (Gambier, Ohio), Fall 1986.

Poetry

(*Poems*). Oxford, Fantasy Press, 1952.
The Spellbound Horses. Toronto, Ryerson Press, 1960.
The Snow Leopard. London, Hutchinson, 1964; New York, Harcourt Brace, 1965.

Other

The Fossils of Piety: Literary Humanism in Decline. New York, Vantage Press, 1959.
The Growth of the Novel. Toronto, Canadian Broadcasting Corporation, 1959.
Byron and the Spoiler's Art. London, Chatto and Windus, and New York, St. Martin's Press, 1960.
The Modern Novel. London, Hutchinson, 1963; New York, Hillary House, 1965.
I, Said the Sparrow (autobiography). London, Hutchinson, 1963.
Robert Penn Warren. Minneapolis, University of Minnesota Press, 1964; London, Oxford University Press, 1965.
The Wine of Absurdity: Essays in Literature and Consolation. University Park, Pennsylvania State University Press, 1966.
Words for a Deaf Daughter. London, Gollancz, 1969; New York, Harper, 1970.
Doubt and Dylan Thomas (lecture). St. John's, Newfoundland, Memorial University, 1970.
Out of My Depths: A Swimmer in the Universe. New York, Doubleday, 1983.
Sheer Fiction. New Paltz, New York, McPherson, 1987; *Sheer Fiction II,* 1991; *Sheer Fiction III,* 1994.
Portable People. New York, Paris Review Editions, 1991.
Duets (text), photographs by James Kiernan. New York, Random House, 1994.
A Stroke of Genius. New York, Viking, 1995.
My Mother's Music. New York, Viking, 1996.
The Secret Lives of Words. New York, Harcourt, 2000.
The Dry Danube: A Hitler Forgery. New York, New Directions, 2000.

*

Manuscript Collections: Pattee Library, Pennsylvania State University, University Park.

Critical Studies: By John W. Aldridge, in *Kenyon Review* (Gambier, Ohio), September 1966; *New Literary History* (Charlottesville, Virginia), Spring 1970 and Spring 1976: "The Writer's Situation II" in *New American Review 10,* New York, New American Library, 1970, and "In Defense of Purple Prose," in *New York Times,* 15 December 1985, both by West; interview with George Plimpton, in *Caliban's*

Filibuster, 1971; article by Brian McLaughlin, in *British Novelists since 1960* edited by Jay L. Halio, Detroit, Gale, 1983; ''Alexander Theroux / Paul West Issue'' of *Review of Contemporary Fiction* (Elmwood Park, Illinois), Spring 1991; *Understanding Paul West* by David Madden, Columbia, University of South Carolina Press, 1994.

Paul West comments:

Looking back, I see myself as a late starter who, between thirty and forty, in a sustained and intensive spell of application, set down half a lifetime's pondering and moved from a restless contentment with criticism and fairly orthodox fiction to an almost Fellini-like point of view.

Imagination, as I see it, is an alembic in limbo; it invents, and what it invents has to be added to the sum of Creation—even though nothing imagination invents is wholly its own. I think the realistic novel has served its turn. Fiction has to reclaim some of its ancient privileges, which writers like Lucian and Nashe and Rabelais and Grimmelshausen exploited to the full. I think that only the plasticity of a free-ranging imagination can do justice to late-twentieth-century man who, as incomplete as man ever was, keeps on arming himself with increasing amounts of data which, as ever, mean nothing at all.

My own fiction I have come to see as—I want it to be—a kind of linear mosaic, which is what my second novel, *Tenement of Clay,* was in a rudimentary form and which two others—*The Very Rich Hours of Count von Stauffenberg* and *Rat Man of Paris*—are in a much more advanced and demanding way. Actually, since both vocabulary and syntax are themselves fictive I don't regard my autobiographical writing as essentially different from my fiction: they're both part of the mosaic I invent.

* * *

For excellent reasons, Camden, the central character in Paul West's uneven, faintly gothic first novel, *A Quality of Mercy,* feels that ''what was wrong was not that life was too much but that it was just too many. There was powder in the wind when there should have been crystals immune from every wind.... Life was an unknown and unknowable quantity.'' Although now, more than twenty-five years later, West's fiction has grown so rich and apparently diverse that good readers will be suspicious of generalizations, it is still possible to see him as an artist working out unexpected variations on the theme Camden hints at indirectly; the problem of contingency. The final human tragedy, Santayana coolly observes, lies in our awareness that everything might just as well have been otherwise, in our consciousness that we are accidental creatures gratuitously existing in random places and forms. We might have been Caesar or we might have been a victim of the Holocaust; and in times when few can go on believing that angels were destined to be angels and stones stones, this can be a devastating insight. There are writers—Sartre, for example—who are in fact appalled by the idea; there are writers like Wallace Stevens and Iris Murdoch who are often exhilarated by the inexplicable variety of being; and there are also a few writers, like Nabokov and West, who veer back and forth eloquently but uneasily between delight and disgust.

A good many of West's characters live condemned to this awareness of contingency, and to make matters worse, condemned to exist in exotic and unlovely forms. The archetypal figure is Caliban, an artist of sorts, howling for justice or at least freedom. In *A Quality of Mercy* there is Camden; in *Tenement of Clay* there are Lazarus, the defiant dwarf, and his mentor, Papa Nick, failed saint and keeper of a flophouse whose inmates he tries to reconcile to ''the truth of life,'' and in helping them to swallow that truth to learn, himself, the proper ''angle of drinking.'' In *Caliban's Filibuster,* there is Cal, the failed writer, and in West's finest novel Count von Stauffenberg, who must go on suffering beyond the grave for his failures. But clearest of all there is Alley Jaggers. At the start of that novel, Alley, longing for some dimly perceived beauty, is ''enclosed and embattled but not closed up and defeated,'' but by the end he is both defeated and literally locked away. In *Bela Lugosi's White Christmas* Alley provides what is probably West's bitterest cry of rage:

> I never applied for admission to your so-called universe. I was kidnapped into it from a better place ... where it is more *optional* than it is here and now, about the time old God Almighty was in a poxdoctoring dither, not sure which day was which, and wondering why the bejesus he got involved with the whole thing in the first place.... My own feeling is this, in case you care, want it for your little black book: if only He'd kept at it all through the seventh day and maybe for all of the next week, we'd all of us be better off. It's just the same as saying the world—your so-called universe—is just a wee bit carelessly put together, fundamentally, firmamentally, fucked up, there being whole armies of folks with club foots, hare lips, folks with spines open to the fresh air and brains blown up as big as hunchback's humps, not to mention the deaf and the blind and the straightforward deformed, the slobberers and slaverers, the daft and St. Vitus dancers, the monkey-faced and the Siamese twins, folks whose hands grow out from their shoulders and folks with no especial sex at all. Don't tell me that twenty sets of quints can make up for all that. Why, it's like asking a pharmacist for an aspirin and getting gunpowder instead. Better to scrap it in the first place if he couldn't get it right or couldn't make up his mind ... Whatever blueprint there was, well, it was just a bit smudged. There ought to be laws against great minds bringing universes into being just for fun. There: that's AJ's first book of the bible; I could have done better myself once I'd gotten the sun to co-operate.

''Blow it all up then?'' asks Alley's equally failed analyst, to which Alley replies, ''*I* would, except I'd be loth to give your old universe a helping hand with a dead hand of my own.'' It is natural enough to wonder where this view of things comes from, and tempting to conclude that it grew from West's experiences with his own deaf, brain-damaged daughter, Mandy. In such cases a parent's first response is often to ignore the handicap, to make it ''go away''—or to make it go away by making the child go away. But there is another possible response: to see the handicap as a special kind of gift, and while trying to eliminate it still to ''learn its nature by heart, as a caution.'' *Words for a Deaf Daughter* is the astonishing account of West's infinitely patient attempts to understand the world in which Mandy is enclosed but not, if he can help it, defeated; to grasp, by imaginative participation, the ''super-sensitivity'' which such children often possess. The ''caution,'' that is, the lesson, turns out to be an awareness of just how arbitrary our definitions of sense and madness can be. The world West and his readers learn to look at through Mandy's eyes is a world in which things are seen with cleansed perception.

Words for a Deaf Daughter is ''fact''; *Gala* is ''fiction,'' or, as West puts it, ''the scenario of a wish-fulfillment,'' in which an adolescent Mandy comes to visit her father in America and finally speaks to him. The importance of this wish-fulfillment is central to West's fiction and makes it imperative to remember that something like Alley's cry of rage is not really West's own cry. For all of the pain which these characters must endure, West sees that act of expression, of imaginative creation, as an act of defiance and achievement, a substantial addition to the sum of existing things. In a 1971 interview he remarked:

> What a gratuitous universe it is, anyway; what a bloody surd ... what with such defectives as waltzing mice, axolotls that should become salamanders but don't, children born without one of the human senses. Not that I'm harping on the universe's lapses rather than its norms; no, what impresses me finally is the scope for error within the constancy of the general set-up contrasted with the power to imagine things as otherwise—to rectify, to deform. What is man? He's the creature imaginative enough to ask that question. And although I know that the imagination had always to start with something not its own—hasn't *complete* underivedness—it can generate much pearl from little grit.

In *The Wine of Absurdity* he states even more emphatically that the imagination is ''the only restorative each man has that is entirely his own ... Imagination, trite and presumptuous as it may seem to express the fact, is the only source of meaning our lives can have.'' Thus imagining Mandy's visit and making her speak is a triumphant act; and having so imagined, West reports that ''I can begin sentences with an *I* again, not so much glad or proud as astounded to be here on this planet as myself and not as a peppermint starfish, a thistle, an emu, a bit of quartz. Or a doorknob.'' It is the artist's imagination, then, which can turn Camden's irritating powder into crystals—if, of course, the artist has anything like West's drive and dazzling verbal resources.

—Elmer Borklund

WHARTON, William

Name is a pseudonym. **Nationality:** American. **Born:** Phildalphia, Pennsylvania, 7 November 1925. **Education:** The University of California, Los Angeles. **Military Service:** Served in the United States Army Infantry, 1943–47. **Family:** Married; four children (one deceased). **Career:** Teacher, 1950–60; since 1960, full-time painter and writer. **Awards:** American Book award, 1980. **Address:** B.P. 18 Port Marly 78, France.

PUBLICATIONS

Novels

Birdy. New York, Knopf, and London, Cape, 1979.
Dad. New York, Knopf, and London, Cape, 1981.
A Midnight Clear. New York, Knopf, and London, Cape, 1982.
Scumbler. New York, Knopf, and London, Cape, 1984.
Pride. New York, Knopf, 1985; London, Cape, 1986.
Tidings. New York, Holt, 1987; London, Cape, 1988.
Franky Furbo. New York, Holt, and London, Cape, 1989.
Last Lovers. New York, Farrar Straus, and London, Granta, 1991.
Wrongful Deaths. London, Granta, 1995.

Other

Ever After: A Father's True Story. New York, Newmarket Press, 1995.
Houseboat on the Seine. New York, Newmarket Press, 1996.

*

Film Adaptations: *Birdy,* 2000.

William Wharton comments:

Fantasy and intimacy are two main thrusts of my work. I usually write in the first person, continuous present to eliminate the artificial barrier of time and teller. One, too often, finds fiction told in the third person, past. It is a remnant from the ''presidium'' of the theatre, separating players, participants, from audience. I want to, as much as possible, dissolve that barrier from my work.

I use multiple print faces whenever possible to minimize referrals (He said, she said, Harry said), or narrative actions inserted merely to establish speaker.

I work from idea, to create stimulating, challenging dialogue with the reader, not merely to entertain. I write only about things I know, so there is often an aura of autobiography in the work. Actually the reader should be seduced to the material, so, in a sense, it is biography.

(1995) I think we are living in the age of the literate illiterate, that is, they have been taught to read, but don't. Probably the responsibility can be placed on schools, TV, and films. The wonder of creating a personal world from words in a dialogue with the writer is being lost. Too bad.

* * *

In *Birdy,* William Wharton's first novel, the title character longs to fly. But this is only part of his larger goal. Birdy seeks a way to ''know'' his life without ''knowledge,'' to move toward a free and unselfconscious life more in tune with the rhythms of the world and nature than the life offered him as a human male. Much of *Birdy* is taken up with meticulous descriptions of the life cycles of pigeons and canaries. It is from living as closely as possible with these birds that Birdy hopes to learn how to live his ideal life. Set in contrast to Birdy is his friend Alfonso, a wrestler who is looking to ''pin'' the world any way he can to gain revenge or some advantage. Both Birdy and Alfonso are drawn into World War II, and the horror of the war drives Birdy out of his human self. He begins imitating a baby bird waiting to be fed. It is Alfonso, himself damaged—physically, where it can most harm his image of himself—who tries to ''feed'' Birdy what he needs to know to be willing to become human again, though Alfonso is in no hurry to rejoin the race, either. So much of *Birdy* is taken up with the minute particulars of the lives of the birds that Alfonso's story is only sketchily told and this asymmetry of bird life over human life makes for tedious reading at times.

Birdy's greatest happiness during his time of involvement with his birds comes not from his attempts to fly, but during the nesting time when he helps the young birds survive and learn to fly. Birdy's involvement with the canaries is centered on the female he calls ''Birdie.'' (He names her dark, violent mate ''Alfonso.'') Birdy identifies strongly with the bird's nurturing side, envies her her female role. This is a thread that is part of several other Wharton characters, most notably the title character in *Scumbler.* Scum, as he calls himself, is an aging American painter living with his family in Paris. Scum at times wishes he were a woman, even telling one young woman to teach him how to love her ''as a woman would.'' Scum rents out a string of apartments, rooms, and shelters he has fixed up. He calls these his ''nests.'' (He also thinks of his paintings as ''nests'' or ''hideouts.'') Scum, like Birdy, attempts to recreate his own existence: ''I'm always trying to design my life ... it has to be lived on purpose with purpose.'' His purpose in life is as much nesting and nurturing (though his own children hardly figure in the novel at all) as it is painting. Like *Birdy, Scumbler* is episodic, almost Quixotic, and relies on a string of epiphanies rather than on any plot resolution for its effect. Both novels end abruptly, with visions of the title characters' personal Utopias.

Dad is Wharton's most conventional novel, the story of three generations of men in a family. The oldest man is dying even while enjoying a period of restored youth; his son watches and thinks of himself as ''next in line,'' while the third, not yet out of his teens, is impatient to get on with his life out from under the cautionary umbrella of his father's wishes for him. The grandfather is a grand character, full of life and honest surprise, but the others are little more than place holders, stock figures used to illustrate the contrasts Wharton wants to establish. *Dad* is Wharton's longest novel, but brings little new insight to the generational conflict.

Set at the beginning of the Battle of the Bulge, *A Midnight Clear* is at once Wharton's most direct and believable novel and that which most clearly illustrates the absurdity of human conflict. Two groups of soldiers, one American, one German, are holed up in a mountain valley. Using a snowman, a scarecrow, and a Christmas tree the two sides communicate their desire for peace with one another. Against all their best efforts death and war descend on the scene. Wharton's always meticulous prose takes on a hardboiled sound in *A Midnight Clear:* ''My being squad leader is also another story. It's another story the way *Peter Rabbit* is another story from *Crime and Punishment.*''

In *Pride* Wharton's efforts at using a nonhuman way of life to throw light on human moral questions is much more successful than in *Birdy.* The novel is set in 1938, as the Depression is easing up and unions are working their way into more industries. The young narrator's father is being threatened by union-breakers. The family travels to the sea shore while the father sorts out his thoughts. While they are there a lion escapes from a boardwalk sideshow and kills a man who has tortured him. The double meaning of the word ''pride''—honor and the family group—is manipulated by Wharton to parallel the lion's condition with that of the father. The lion, whose pride(s) has been destroyed, goes to his death because he has nowhere else to go. The father gathers his pride(s) and sets off on a course of self-reliance.

A personal tragedy in 1988 informs *Ever After,* a narrative nonfiction account of the circumstances surrounding the fatal accident that took from Wharton his daughter Kate, her husband Bert, and their two children. Parts of the book are written in first person as Kate. *Last Lovers,* written in the aftermath of his loss, is a painful novel with a glimmer of hope: an American expatriate painter, down and out in Paris, finds love and fulfillment with a homeless woman two decades his senior.

—William C. Bamberger

WHITE, Edmund Valentine, III

Nationality: American. **Born:** Cincinnati, Ohio, 13 January 1940. **Education:** The University of Michigan, Ann Arbor (Hopwood award, 1961, 1962), B.A. 1962. **Career:** Staff writer, *Time,* 1962–79, and editor, *Saturday Review,* 1972–73, both New York; assistant professor, Johns Hopkins University, Baltimore, 1977–79; adjunct professor, Columbia University, New York, 1981–83, and instructor in creative writing, Yale University, New Haven, Connecticut. Executive director, Institute for the Humanities, New York 1981–82. **Awards:** Ingram Merrill grant, 1973, 1978; Guggenheim fellowship, 1983; American Academy award, 1983; recipient Chevalier de l'ordre des Arts et Lettres, 1993; National Book Critics Circle award, 1994. **Agent:** Maxine Groffsky, 2 Fifth Avenue, New York, New York 10011, U.S.A.

Publications

Novels

Forgetting Elena. New York, Random House, 1973.
Nocturnes for the King of Naples. New York, St. Martin's Press, 1978; London, Deutsch, 1980.
A Boy's Own Story. New York, Dutton, 1982; London, Picador, 1983.
Caracole. New York, Dutton, 1985; London, Pan, 1986.
The Beautiful Room Is Empty. New York, Knopf, and London, Picador, 1988.
The Farewell Symphony. New York, Knopf, 1997.
The Married Man: A Love Story. New York, Knopf, 2000.

Short Stories

The Darker Proof: Stories from a Crisis, with Adam Mars-Jones. London, Faber, 1987.
Skinned Alive. London, Chatto and Windus, 1995; New York, Knopf, 1995.

Other

When Zeppelins Flew, with Peter Wood. New York, Time/Life, 1969.
The First Man, with Dale Browne. New York, Time/Life, 1973.
States of Desire: Travels in Gay America. New York, Dutton, and London, Deutsch, 1980.
Genet: A Biography. New York, Knopf, and London, Chatto and Windus, 1993.
The Burning Library, edited by David Bergman. New York, Knopf, 1994.
Sketches from Memory: People and Places in the Heart of Our Paris, illustrated by Hubert Sorin. London, Chatto and Windus, 1994; published as *Our Paris: Sketches from Memory,* New York, Knopf, 1995.

Altars (text), photographs by Mapplethorpe. New York, Random House, 1995.

Marcel Proust. New York, Viking, 1999.

Editor, with Charles Silverstein, *The Joy of Gay Sex: An Intimate Guide for Gay Men to the Pleasures of a Gay Lifestyle.* New York, Crown, 1977.

Editor, *The Faber Book of Gay Short Fiction.* London, Faber, 1991; Boston, Faber, 1992.

Editor, *The Selected Writings of Jean Genet.* Hopewell, New Jersey, Ecco, 1993.

*

Critical Studies: *Edmund White: The Burning World* by Stephen Barber, New York, St. Martin's Press, 1999.

* * *

Elegant and explicit writing, gay characters, economic elitism, AIDS. Edmund White's large appeal may be due to the wild and wide convergence of these many issues over his thirty-year writing career. His voice eloquently articulates the gay community's trajectory from oppression and indecisiveness through self-definition and, finally, toward liberation. His poetry, nonfiction, and fiction has garnered a cultivating and curious audience who see White as a witness to gay culture during rocky decades when AIDS, homosexual stereotypes, and protests for gay rights seemed to balloon in mainstream American consciousness.

White is a prolific writer. His numerous nonfictional works include *States of Desire: Travels in Gay America* and *The Joy of Gay Sex* (co-authored with Dr. Charles Silverstein). Several essays (in particular, ''The Artist and AIDS'') and magazine pieces have established his reputation as that of an urbane and insightful commentator on contemporary social and political issues.

His books, including *Forgetting Elana, Nocturnes for the King of Naples, A Boy's Own Story, The Beautiful Room Is Empty,* and *The Married Man,* as well as a co-written collection of short stories about AIDS, reveal a love of poetic language. His writing has an erotic, sensuous quality and his images, like his phrases, are extravagant and memorable. An ethos of homoeroticism permeates almost every aspect of his fictional art; it informs his diction and gives shape to his plots. In the opening paragraphs of *Nocturnes for the King of Naples,* for example, images of water and darkness swirl rapturously around images of violence and unrequited love:

> A young man leans with one shoulder against the wall, and his slender body remains motionless against the huge open slab of night sky and night water behind him ... On the other side of the water, lights trace senseless paths up across hills, lash-marks left by an amateur whip. He turns toward me a look of hope tempered by discretion ... I have failed to interest him. He turns back to his river as though it were the masterpiece and I the retreating guard.

A central theme in White's work is that of sexual maturation and of breaking away. Part of this maturation is individual, as in the case of his male protagonists who must break away from the repressive confines of their bourgeois families in order to express their own sexuality. But there is also the case of the American gay community, which had to break away from various regimes of oppression in order to find a geographical and linguistic terrain in which to explore its desires. This concern with personal and communal histories informs his two most successful novels to date: *A Boy's Own Story* and its sequel *The Beautiful Room Is Empty.* Together these novels, as a sort of homosexual Bildungsroman, describe the progression of a young unnamed male narrator from a state of confusion and immaturity to an acceptance of his homosexual identity on the very night that the Stonewall riots rocked the heterosexual establishment in New York City in 1969, thus ushering in the contemporary gay liberation movement. On the night of the riots, White's narrator, finds himself proudly anticipating the day ''gays might someday constitute a community rather than a diagnosis.''

Because of White's personal concern with the social and political dynamics of the gay community, his novels frequently have an autobiographical element to them. They are usually written in the first-person and parallel personal events in his own life, such as fraught relationships with fathers and male lovers, a desire to have a literary career, and a sardonic outlook on the foibles of middle-class America. His narrators frequently find solace from their own self-internalized condemnation of homosexuality in their writing, as, for example, does the unnamed narrator in *The Beautiful Room Is Empty:* ''there was another reason to write: to redeem the sin of my life by turning it into the virtue of art.'' Many of White's novels are artistic parables and they describe an individual's exploration of his literary and sexual identities.

In White's fiction, art and reality are frequently inseparable. His novels celebrate the polymorphous potentiality of contemporary gay relationships and lifestyles with their capacity to move between friendships and love relationships; and they explore the creative energy found in a minority group's ability to invent its own personal and erotic language and identity amidst overwhelming social and literary oppression.

Because nearly every story in White's collection *Skinned Alive* addresses the topic of AIDS, there is a new tenderness in the relationships, a closeness between the couples involved, and a quiet acceptance of life, threatened as it may be. The raunchy details of sex, which was a constant and vital factor in White's writing, is still present, but muted, and the celebration he writes of most often is the joy of being alive.

His latest book, *The Married Man* turns its attention once again to AIDS. When Austin, in his fifties, meets the young and married Julien in Paris, the twosome entangle themselves in French culture and lovemaking. Austin is HIV positive, and when Julien contracts AIDS, the two travel through Nice, Venice, Rome, and carry with them the biological reality of death and its profound sorrow. The book has been recognized for its immense detail and mature perspective towards love.

—Thomas Hastings, revisions by Geoffrey Elborn and Maureen Aitken

WIDEMAN, John Edgar

Nationality: American. **Born:** Washington, D.C., 14 June 1941. **Education:** Schools in Pittsburgh; University of Pennsylvania, Philadelphia (Franklin scholar), B.A. 1963 (Phi Beta Kappa); New College, Oxford (Rhodes scholar, 1963; Thouron fellow, 1963–66), B.Phil. 1966; University of Iowa, Iowa City (Kent fellow), 1966–67.

Family: Married Judith Ann Goldman in 1965; two sons and one daughter. **Career:** Member of the Department of English, Howard University, Washington, D.C., 1965; instructor to associate professor of English, 1966–74, assistant basketball coach, 1968–72, and director of the Afro-American Studies Program, 1971–73, University of Pennsylvania; professor of English, University of Wyoming, Laramie, 1974–85. Since 1986 professor of English, University of Massachusetts, Amherst. Phi Beta Kappa Lecturer, 1976. **Awards:** PEN/Faulkner award, 1984, 1991; Lannan award, 1991; MacArthur fellowship, 1993; Rea prize, 1998. D.Litt.: University of Pennsylvania, 1985. **Agent:** Wylie Aitken and Stone Inc., 250 West 57th Street, Suite 2106, New York, New York 10107. **Address:** Department of English, University of Massachusetts, Amherst, Massachusetts 01003, U.S.A.

Publications

Novels

A Glance Away. New York, Harcourt Brace, 1967; London, Allison and Busby, 1986.
Hurry Home. New York, Harcourt Brace, 1970.
The Lynchers. New York, Harcourt Brace, 1973.
Damballah. New York, Avon, 1981; London, Allison and Busby, 1984.
Hiding Place. New York, Avon, 1981; London, Allison and Busby, 1984.
Sent for You Yesterday. New York, Avon, 1983; London, Allison and Busby, 1984.
Reuben. New York, Holt, 1987; London, Viking, 1988.
Philadelphia Fire. New York, Holt, 1990; London, Viking, 1991.
The Homewood Books. Pittsburgh, University of Pittsburgh Press, 1992.
Identities: Three Novels. New York, H. Holt, 1994.
Two Cities. Boston, Houghton Mifflin, 1998.

Short Stories

Fever: Twelve Stories. New York, Holt, 1989.
The Stories of John Edgar Wideman. New York, Pantheon, 1992; as *All Stories Are True,* London, Picador, and New York, Vintage, 1993.

Uncollected Short Story

"Concert," in *Georgia Review* (Athens), Fall 1989.

Other

Brothers and Keepers (memoirs). New York, Holt Rinehart, 1984; London, Allison and Busby, 1985.
Fatheralong: A Meditation on Fathers and Sons, Race and Society. New York, Pantheon, 1994.

*

Critical Studies: *Blackness and Modernism: The Literary Career of John Edgar Wideman* by James W. Coleman, Jackson, University Press of Mississippi, 1989; *John Edgar Wideman: Reclaiming the African Personality* by Doreatha Drummond Mbalia, Selinsgrove, Susquehanna University Press, and London, Associated University Presses, 1995; *Stories of Resilience in Childhood: The Narratives of Maya Angelou, Maxine Hong Kingston, Richard Rodrigues, John Edgar Wideman, and Tobias Wolff* by Daniel D. Challener, New York, Garland, 1997; *Conversations with John Edgar Wideman,* edited by Bonnie Tu Smith, Jackson, University Press of Mississippi, 1998; *John Edgar Wideman: A Study of the Short Fiction* by Keith E. Byerman, New York, Twayne Publishers, 1998.

* * *

Following the publication of the Homewood trilogy, the *New York Times* proclaimed John Edgar Wideman, "one of America's premier writers of fiction." The winner of two PEN/Faulkner awards, Wideman is also one of the most prolific writers of his generation. Though he has published nine novels, several short story collections (including *Fever* and *All Stories Are True*), two works of nonfiction (*Brothers and Keepers* and *Fatheralong*), and numerous essays, Wideman's work still receives very little critical attention.

Most available criticism surrounds the Homewood trilogy: *Damballah, Hiding Place,* and *Sent for You Yesterday.* The works are set in the Homewood section of Pittsburgh where Wideman was raised. Often compared to William Faulkner's Yoknapatawpha, the Homewood stories center on the Lawson family, past and present, and the community. Throughout Wideman's work, he examines the connections between family and history. Committed to making certain that "all the stories" are told, Wideman infuses his writing with the style of jazz. His novels are polyphonic and improvisational; genres and discourses blend; and stories and characters are repeated, but played a different way each time. Wideman's riffing style illuminates the diversity of African-American experience, and the inadequacies of traditional narrative in capturing that experience. The necessity of sharing known and unknown stories in order to combat the marginalized portrait of African Americans in history and in the popular imagination is one of Wideman's most important thematic concerns.

These themes and techniques can be found in the first novel, *A Glance Away.* Eddie Lawson has returned home from a southern rehabilitation clinic. His home is an unidentified northern city, and the inversion of the historical migration of African Americans to the "promised land" is a trope for the writer's journey to his roots. Another character in the novel is Robert Thurley, a white professor who tries to connect with Lawson but is unable. Wideman has said that the character of Thurley was influenced by T.S. Eliot. Thurley's inability to communicate to others in the work represents the failure of the dominant ideology to sustain African-American life. Another voice in the novel is Brother, an albino African American. Brother is a storyteller; he can remember the stories of the Lawson family, even when Eddie cannot. Eddie has "glanced away" from his family and community, and the result is alienation.

The theme of the alienated African-American intellectual is further examined in Wideman's second novel, *Hurry Home.* The main character is Cecil Braithwaite, a lawyer who abandons his wife and travels to Europe and Africa. The reader is uncertain whether or not Braithwaite actually takes his journey or if it occurs only in his mind. The novel opens with the epigraph, the "pain of being two." Braithwaite's journey (real or imagined) is a reflection of a deeply embedded double-consciousness. He finds that he cannot connect to the history of Europe, and when he travels to Africa (an inverted image of the Middle Passage), Braithwaite discovers that he's alienated there as well.

The Lynchers also examines the weight of African-American history. The opening pages of the novel document the history of lynching in America. The novel begins with four men planning to subvert this history by killing a white policeman. The act, a "lynching in black face," will, according to the group's leader bring the community together. Wideman often suggests that symbolic ritual can be a healthy way to combat racism. But here the inversion of lynching is portrayed as a self-destructive act. In order to lynch the policeman, the conspirators must kill his African-American girlfriend. It is even suggested that her child may have to die. These acts against the community, and the inability of the conspirators to re-imagine their lives using their own stories and rituals, doom the plan to failure. Only one of the conspirators, Thomas Wilkerson, sees that the men are merely mimicking the hatred and violence that is illustrated in the preface. Wilkerson, a history teacher, finally realizes that the only way to remedy the disease of racism is through family and the sharing of stories.

The importance of family stories is at the heart of the three works that make up the Homewood trilogy. *Damballah,* a short story cycle, offers past and present vignettes about the Lawson family as well as those of the neighborhood of Homewood. The family is connected through space and time through the stories. The titular tale is set in the early days of American slavery. Its central character, Orion, is an African who will not give up his traditions. Orion could be a Lawson ancestor or any African-American family's, suggesting that "family" extends to race. Wideman opens the work with a description of the god, Damballah (a symbol of family and history), a begat chart of the Lawson family, and a letter to his brother, Robby. The stories are "letters" to Robby; their purpose is to keep him connected to the family while he is in jail.

Robby's fictional counterpart, Tommy, appears not only in *Damballah,* but also in *Hiding Place.* The novel follows Tommy while he is on the run from the law. He flees to Bruston Hill, the place where Homewood and the family began. The only family living there now is Mother Bess, who has run away from the world, isolating herself in a cabin. Tommy's brother, a writer, has also "run away" from Homewood to Wyoming. The theme of flight permeates the novel, inverting the image of fugitive slaves. These characters are not running to anything; they are "hiding." It is not until Tommy decides to turn himself in that Mother Bess sees that she must go back down the hill to her family and reconnect.

Sent for You Yesterday follows three generations of Homewood: John French and Albert Wilkes; Carl Lawson, Lucy, and Brother Tate; and Carl's nephew, John. We see again the character of Brother, the albino who appeared in *A Glance Away.* While not a continuation of that character, this Brother is a variation on a theme. Wilkes, a musician, is a catalyst for most of the novel's action. His death haunts the community, particularly Carl, Lucy, and Brother. Wilkes's blues music had been a sustaining force for Homewood, and after he is gone the neighborhood forgets their music and their past. The last pages of the novel offer hope that stories will be remembered and shared again as John begins to dance to a song he once knew as a child.

The novel *Reuben* is also set in Homewood. Reuben, the title character, is a lawyer in the neighborhood. He is a revision of the alienated intellectual figure that appears in many of Wideman's other novels. Unlike those characters, Reuben refuses to flee from his suffering. His office is a trailer in the middle of Homewood, from which he advises the community. Reuben's search for a twin brother who may be in jail is reminiscent of Wideman's nonfiction work, *Brothers and Keepers.* However, it is never clear if the brother even exists; the brother may be another version of Reuben.

Philadelphia Fire is based on the MOVE house bombing in Philadelphia. The novel intertwines the voices of Cudjoe, a writer, and Wideman, as the author and as a character. This virtuoso novel blends multiple texts and discourses from history to *The Tempest.* These are the voices that the African-American writer must confront and revise. In many ways, the novel is about writing and history, but it is also the story of lost children: Simba, a survivor of the bombing, and Wideman's son.

The Cattle Killing also revises texts. The novel revisits Wideman's short story, "Fever," about the yellow fever epidemic in Philadelphia in 1793. A neo-slave narrative, the novel is set in eighteenth century and contemporary Philadelphia, as well as Africa and England. Episodes in the novel are filtered through the central character, an unnamed African-American preacher who wanders the diseased city. The preacher tells stories to an ailing woman, who is possibly an African spirit, to soothe her fever and his rage. The stories are a lifeline to the past and to the African-American community. The "fever" is also the symbolic epidemic of racism that has plagued this country since its inception.

Wideman's latest work, *Two Cities,* connects its characters through shared suffering. Three characters voice the text: Kassima, Robert, and Mr. Mallory, a photographer. It is Mallory who links the two cities, Philadelphia and Pittsburgh, together. He uses his "double-exposed" photographs to express the lives of people who the world has silenced. Like all of Wideman's work, the novel embraces the necessity to address the silences of the African-American community, to let all the voices be heard. The repeated image of lost children in each of the novels stands as a warning of a future that could be lost if the past is not remembered.

—Tracie Church Guzzio

WIEBE, Rudy (Henry)

Nationality: Canadian. **Born:** Fairholme, Saskatchewan, 4 October 1934. **Education:** Alberta Mennonite High School; University of Alberta, Edmonton, 1953–56, 1958–60 (International Nickel graduate fellow, 1958–59; Queen Elizabeth graduate fellow, 1959–60), B.A. 1956, M.A. 1960; University of Tübingen, Germany (Rotary fellow), 1957–58; University of Manitoba, Winnipeg, 1961; University of Iowa, Iowa City, 1964. **Family:** Married Tena F. Isaak in 1958; one daughter and two sons. **Career:** Research officer, Glenbow Foundation, Calgary, 1956; foreign service officer, Ottawa, 1960; high school teacher, Selkirk, Manitoba, 1961; editor, Mennonite Brethren *Herald,* Winnipeg, 1962–63; assistant professor of English, Goshen College, Indiana, 1963–67. Assistant professor, 1967–70, associate professor, 1970–77, professor of English, University of Alberta, 1977–92; since 1992, professor emeritus. **Awards:** Canada Council arts scholarship, 1964, award, 1971; Governor General's award for fiction, 1973, 1994; grant, 1977; Lorne Pierce medal, 1987. D.Litt.: University of Winnipeg, Manitoba, 1986; Wilfred Laurier University, 1991. LLD: Brock University, 1991. **Address:** 5315–143 St., Edmonton, Alberta T6H 4E3, Canada.

PUBLICATIONS

Novels

Peace Shall Destroy Many. Toronto, McClelland and Stewart, 1962; Grand Rapids, Michigan, Eerdmans, 1964.
First and Vital Candle. Toronto, McClelland and Stewart, and Grand Rapids, Michigan, Eerdmans, 1966.
The Blue Mountains of China. Toronto, McClelland and Stewart, and Grand Rapids, Michigan, Eerdmans, 1970.
The Temptations of Big Bear. Toronto, McClelland and Stewart, 1973; Athens, Ohio University Press, 2000.
The Scorched-Wood People. Toronto, McClelland and Stewart, 1977.
The Mad Trapper. Toronto, McClelland and Stewart, 1977.
My Lovely Enemy. Toronto, McClelland and Stewart, 1983.
A Discovery of Strangers. Toronto, Knopf, 1994.

Short Stories

Where Is the Voice Coming From? Toronto, McClelland and Stewart, 1974.
Personal Fictions, with others, edited by Michael Ondaatje. Toronto, Oxford University Press, 1977.
Alberta: A Celebration, edited by Tom Radford. Edmonton, Alberta, Hurtig, 1979.
The Angel of the Tar Sands and Other Stories. Toronto, McClelland and Stewart, 1982.
River of Stone: Fictions and Memories. Toronto, Vintage Books, 1995.

Play

Far as the Eye Can See, with Theatre Passe Muraille. Edmonton, Alberta, NeWest Press, 1977.

Other

A Voice in the Land: Essays by and about Rudy Wiebe, edited by W.J. Keith. Edmonton, Alberta, NeWest Press, 1981.
Playing Dead: A Contemplation Concerning the Arctic. Edmonton, Alberta, NeWest Press, 1989.
Silence: The Word and the Sacred (essays). Waterloo, Ontario, Wilfrid Laurier University Press, 1989.
Chinook Christmas (for children), illustrated by David More. Red Deer College Press, 1993.
Stolen Life: The Journey of a Cree Woman. Toronto, Knopf Canada, 1998; Athens, Ohio, Swallow Press, 2000.
Editor, *The Story-Makers: A Selection of Modern Short Stories.* Toronto, Macmillan, 1970.
Editor, *Stories from Western Canada: A Selection.* Toronto, Macmillan, 1972.
Editor, with Andreas Schroeder, *Stories from Pacific and Arctic Canada: A Selection.* Toronto, Macmillan, 1974.
Editor, *Double Vision: An Anthology of Twentieth-Century Stories in English.* Toronto, Macmillan, 1976.
Editor, *Getting Here: Stories.* Edmonton, Alberta, NeWest Press, 1977.
Editor, with Aritha van Herk, *More Stories from Western Canada.* Toronto, Macmillan, 1980.
Editor, with Aritha van Herk and Leah Flater, *West of Fiction.* Edmonton, Alberton, NeWest Press, 1982.
Editor, with Bob Beal, *War in the West: Voices of the 1885 Rebellion.* Toronto, McClelland and Stewart, 1985.

*

Manuscript Collection: University of Calgary Library, Alberta.

Critical Studies: *The Comedians: Hugh Hood and Rudy Wiebe* by Patricia A. Morley, Toronto, Clarke Irwin, 1977; *Epic Fiction: The Art of Rudy Wiebe* by W.J. Keith, Edmonton, University of Alberta Press, 1981; articles in *A Voice in the Land,* 1981, and *Journal of Commonwealth Literature* (Edinburgh), 19(1), 1984.

Rudy Wiebe comments:

I believe that the worlds of fiction—story—should provide pleasure of as many kinds as possible to the reader; I believe fiction must be precisely, peculiarly rooted in a particular place, in particular people; I believe writing fiction is as serious, as responsible an activity as I can ever perform. Therefore in my fiction I try to explore the world that I know: the land and people of western Canada; from my particular world view: a radical Jesus-oriented Christianity.

* * *

Canada's foremost Mennonite writer, and one of the most innovative writers of historical fiction today, Rudy Wiebe, has consistently addressed far-reaching moral, social, and spiritual questions through narratives that focus on specific, rigorously researched, historical moments. Of his eight major novels to date, three—*Peace Shall Destroy Many, The Blue Mountains of China,* and *My Lovely Enemy*—focus directly on Mennonite communities in Canada and elsewhere; the remaining five—*First and Vital Candle, The Mad Trapper, The Temptations of Big Bear, The Scorched-Wood People, A Discovery of Strangers* (and to some extent, *My Lovely Enemy*)—examine the encroachments of white society on traditional Native American, Métis, and Inuit ways of life.

Irrespective of their differences, Wiebe's works are all thematically informed by his radical Mennonite faith, and his plots are all set in motion by what, in the title of his latest work, he calls "a discovery of strangers." Wiebe emphasizes the extent to which traditional indigenous and Mennonite communities were separated from the rest of humanity by barriers of space, language, culture, and, most importantly, religious belief. Day-to-day life in these communities was organized in accordance with religious and moral certainties, which, having solidified into fixed codes of conduct, remained for many years unquestioned. However, in each of Wiebe's novels, the boundaries of a closed community are broken open. Traditional cultural practices and religious certainties are either directly challenged from without or are exposed, as a result of external pressures, to threats that are latent within. In either case, a period of spiritual and moral disorientation ensues, in which the protagonist's most fundamental beliefs and values are tested.

Wiebe subjects his readers also to forces of disorientation. As his career progresses, he departs more and more from the conventions of narrative realism. *The Blue Mountains of China, The Temptations of Big Bear, My Lovely Enemy,* and (to a lesser extent) *A Discovery of Strangers* are fragmented, multi-voiced, stylistically heterogeneous narratives in which Wiebe "re-writes" existing historical documents and religious texts by inserting them into new verbal contexts. Perhaps because he is so acutely aware that meanings are intertextually generated, Wiebe continually tests the textual foundations of historical and religious certainty.

At times, Wiebe's Mennonite rhetoric intrudes awkwardly into his narratives, as in *First and Vital Candle* or in the end of *The Blue Mountains of China.* But Wiebe, in fact, addresses this very problem in *First and Vital Candle* and *My Lovely Enemy,* where he dramatizes the unsavory politics of Christian proselytizing. Mindful that his readership is not a congregation to be browbeaten, but a diverse community to be drawn into active dialogue with his texts, Wiebe has developed various intricate modes of indirect address. The main characters in both *First and Vital Candle* and *The Mad Trapper* escape to the seclusion of the Arctic. Abe Ross, from *First and Vital Candle,* eventually finds a new community while Albert Johnson severs all human contact, leaving mysterious his past, motives, and even identity.

Those of Wiebe's novels that are concerned with Canada's indigenous peoples are readable as post-colonial historical metafictions. They dramatize the power of communications technologies—writing, print, photography, telegraphy, film, computers, and other electronic media—as instruments of colonial and neo-imperial domination. Yet, in the process of recounting history from various indigenous perspectives, Wiebe also articulates Mennonite religious, social, and ecological values. In so doing, he has attracted accusations of cultural appropriation.

Throughout his writing career, Wiebe has concerned himself with the exploration of the mystery and variety of love. After touching rather awkwardly on love and divine grace in *First and Vital Candle,* Wiebe's exploration of love becomes at once more philosophical and more physically explicit, a quality that has provoked objections to his manner of representing women and female sexuality. In *My Lovely Enemy,* passionate sexual love works as a metaphor through which Wiebe revivifies the familiar Christian abstraction of God's redemptive love for humanity. In *A Discovery of Strangers,* Wiebe develops an extended metaphor of colonized woman: as the first Franklin expedition advances across the far northern landscape, the beautiful face of Birdseye, a Tetsot'ine woman of great prophetic wisdom, is progressively corroded by disease. Birdseye's fifteen-year-old daughter, Greenstockings, an object of universal male desire, embodies the virgin territory men struggle to possess. Miraculously, given the structural imbalance of power that exists between them, two strangers—Greenstockings and the English midshipman Robert Hood—come momentarily together as lovers by mutual agreement. Although Wiebe does not openly articulate his Mennonite beliefs in *A Discovery of Strangers,* they hover behind his representation of Tetsot'ine understandings of life as a divine gift and of human beings as spiritually connected with each other and with all living things by sacred ties of mutual physical dependence.

While Wiebe is best known for his novels, he is also skilled in other areas of literature. He is the author of several collections of short stories including *The Angel of the Tar Sands and Other Stories, River of Stone: Fictions and Memories, Alberta: A Celebration,* and *Where Is the Voice Coming From?* In *Alberta: A Celebration,* Wiebe uses a slightly different approach than in his other short story collections. In this work, Wiebe examines the legend of Albert Johnson and attempts to give a new perspective to the Canadian past by combining photographs with accounts of local places and their unique legends.

Wiebe has also composed a play, *Far As the Eye Can See,* and a children's book entitled *Chinook Christmas,* in which he writes about Coaldale, Alberta, a small community that he moved to in 1947. Wiebe's most recent work is *Stolen Life: The Journey of a Cree Woman.* This book, which is a chronicle of justice and injustice, tells the true story of the great-great-granddaughter of Cree Chief Big Bear, Yvonne Johnson, who was placed behind bars after being charged with murder. While this work is nonfiction, many critics have claimed that the text reads like a mystery novel. In his writing, Wiebe is successful at uniting realism with passion and reviving the past, so that it can be seen in a fresh light.

—Penny van Toorn, updated by Marta Krogh

WIER, Allen

Nationality: American. **Born:** San Antonio, Texas, 9 September 1946. **Education:** Baylor University, B.A. 1968; Louisiana State University, M.A. 1970; Bowling Green State University, M.F.A. 1974. **Family:** Married 1) Dara Dixon in 1969 (divorced 1983); 2) Donnie Holloway in 1984; one son. **Career:** Yard clerk, Kansas City Southern Railroad, 1966–67; laborer, All-Tex Ranch Supply, Waco, Texas, 1967–68; instructor in English, Longwood College, Farmville, Virginia, 1970–72; assistant professor of English, Carnegie-Mellon University, Pittsburgh, Pennsylvania, 1974–75; assistant professor of English, Hollins College, Virginia, 1975–79; associate professor and later professor, University of Alabama, Tuscaloosa, 1980–94; professor, University of Tennessee, Knoxville, 1994—. **Awards:** Robert Penn Warren Award (Fellowship of Southern Writers), 1997. **Agent:** Irene Tumulty, Julian Bach Literary Agency, Inc., 3 East 48th Street, New York, New York 10017, U.S.A. **Address:** Department of English, University of Tennessee, 103 McClung Tower, Knoxville, Tennessee 37996–0430, U.S.A.

PUBLICATIONS

Novels

Blanco. Baton Rouge, Louisiana State University Press, 1978.
Departing as Air: A Novel. New York, Simon & Schuster, 1983.
A Place for Outlaws. New York, Harper, 1989.

Short Stories

Things about to Disappear. Baton Rouge, Louisiana State University Press, 1978.

Other

Editor with Don Hendrie, Jr., *Voicelust: Eight Contemporary Fiction Writers on Style.* Lincoln, University of Nebraska Press, 1985.
Editor, *Walking on Water and Other Stories.* Tuscaloosa, University of Alabama Press, 1996.
Introduction, *Bad Man Blues: A Portable George Garrett.* Dallas, Texas, Southern Methodist University Press, 1998.

* * *

Allen Wier is one of the finest novelists to emerge from the American Southwest, and yet his novels transcend regional boundaries in their reflection upon human loneliness, the improbability of real human connections, and the tenuousness of life itself. Evocative of the works of such masters as William Goyen and Katherine Anne Porter, Wier's novels depict realistic characters whose stories become melanges of memory, imagination, and event that question the very nature of reality, of past and future. *Blanco*, Wier's first novel, is named after a real town in the Texas Hill Country north of San Antonio, but its spiritual setting is that of the American small town peopled by inhabitants who are isolated from one another and thereby dwell in their own death-obsessed imaginations. *Departing as Air* moves into a more exotic landscape, both literal and symbolic, shifting in time and memory from the frozen World War II landscape of Kansas, through Texas, to the fragrant, lush, and magical setting of Mexico, where memory and imagination become indistinguishable. *A Place for Outlaws*, Wier's most realistic and traditional novel, follows the life of Julia Marrs from its uncertain beginning to a sort of spiritual triumph in maturity and existential freedom. In all three novels, Wier's understanding of human frailty tempered by an affirmation of tragic nobility establishes him as a major voice in contemporary American fiction.

Blanco—in Spanish the word for white, blank, or empty—depicts the lives of Eunice Marrs, her son Turk, daughter June, and son-in-law Cage. Turk, at forty-five, still lives with Eunice, or Momma, as she is most often called, a passive-aggressive widow who spends much of her time on the phone discussing the illnesses and deaths of other people and predicting the certainty of her own death. Turk has not yet found his niche in life, nor has he been able to declare his love for Sally, his old sweetheart who has already outlived or divorced three husbands. Between husbands, Sally amuses herself with Turk, but would not in the words of Eunice, marry Turk ''if it harelipped the governor.'' Married but not connected to Cage, June floats in the pink landscape of her imagination, subliminally aware that she may have health problems, foreshadowed by a surreal pre-marital exam at the public health department, and, later, by the rotting pink Christmas tree in her pink living room. Both Turk and June have trouble sorting reality—the past, even the present—from fantasy. When Turk realizes that the past is ''a made-up story no more real than the future,'' he articulates one of the central motifs of Wier's fiction—life and time are ephemeral, shifting, fragile as the Texas landscape that Cage and his business associates are developing at lightning speed.

In *Departing as Air*, a novel that could be called magical realism, Wier intensifies his use of imagination as an alternate reality that blends with memory to shape the past of his principal character, Jessie. Aging now, Jessie tries to reconstruct the major events of her life as she studies old photographs of Camel, a man she has loved, followed to Mexico, and lost, in a way concealed or obscured by the juxtaposition of memory and imagination. When Jessie's first husband, Marlin, a man old enough to be her father, dies of a gallbladder ailment, Jessie is free to follow Camel to Mexico, where he has gone to buy cut flowers for a wholesale florist in Texas. The memory of Marlin plagues Jessie as if she has murdered him, and once in Mexico she confesses the imagined crime to a priest even though she is not Catholic. Jessie's imagination, reflected in the photographs she takes and the lush Mexican setting, shapes the novel with visions of horror and beauty, of madness and love. But Jessie's visions, or memories, are also tactile, concrete; they resonate with the smell of burnt coffee from the grocery bag of a beautiful woman electrocuted in a freak street accident, the soft feel of a pair of elegant alligator shoes. Jessie's memory cannot, or does not, isolate the loss of Camel. He is seized deep in the jungle by Mexican soldiers; he joins a renegade priest in search of his former wife, Miss Minnesota, whose body has disappeared from her casket after the plane transporting it crashes between North Dakota and Minnesota; he develops lung cancer. In the world of the novel, the most realistic ''memory'' is the least plausible. Camel has appeared in Jessie's life as if out of thin air and he departs as air. Experience cannot be grasped, lives not possessed, not even in the photographs that stir memory.

A Place for Outlaws returns to the more traditional form of the realistic novel. *Outlaws* tells the story of a self-reliant woman, Julia Marrs, the name if not the character repeated from *Blanco*. After her mother dies, Julia is raised first by her fundamentalist grandmother, Huldah, then by her flighty Aunt Annabelle, who is as much of a child as is Julia. Although she is twice orphaned, Julia is loved in both homes and grows into a capable young woman. Engaged to Larry Otto, the son of a wealthy cotton farmer, Julia is introduced to Avery Marrs, and her life at once changes. In the dislocation of World War II, Julia marries Avery and begins to live what might appear to be a charmed life with their son Cole. When tragedy comes Julia's way, she does not falter. But in Wier's fiction, life is never clean, never neat. Julia's charmed life, and Cole's as well, develops a dark side, a flirtation with danger, with violence that seems to pervade American culture. A professor of American studies at a university in Alabama, Cole is caught up in a drama fraught with estranged husbands and guns that leads him back into his mother's life and more violence. That Cole and Julia transcend speaks to the Biblical beginnings of the novel, to questions of redemption, and eventually to Julia's acceptance of existential freedom and responsibility. In many ways, *A Place for Outlaws* is Wier's most compelling novel because Julia Marrs, her fallibility, and her decency in a not-too-decent world, resonate through its pages. *Outlaws* draws on Wier's skill as a first-rate storyteller and his strong eye for character.

Wier's fictional landscapes, inner and outer, are constructed with insight and craft. Certainly his three novels, together with his short story collection *Things about to Disappear*, and his writings on contemporary fiction earn him a place among the finest of contemporary American writers.

—Celia M. Kingsbury

WIGGINS, Marianne

Nationality: American. **Born:** Lancaster, Pennsylvania, 8 November 1947. **Family:** Married 1) Brian Porzak in 1965 (divorced 1970), one daughter; 2) Salman Rushdie in 1988 (marriage ended). **Agent:** Wylie, Aitken & Stone, Suite 2106, 250 West 57th Street, New York, New York 10107, U.S.A.

Publications

Novels

Babe. New York, Avon, 1975.
Went South. New York, Delacorte, 1980.
Separate Checks. New York, Random House, 1984.
John Dollar. New York, Harper, 1989.

Eveless Eden. New York, HarperCollins, 1995.
Almost Heaven. New York, Crown, 1998.

Short Stories

Herself in Love and Other Stories. New York, Viking, 1987.
Learning Urdu. New York, Harper, 1990.
Bet They'll Miss Us When We're Gone. New York, HarperCollins, 1991.

Other

Introduction, *Other Edens* by Nick Waplington. New York, Aperture, 1994.
Contributor, *From the Heart: The Power of Photography, A Collector's Choice* by Adam D. Weinberg. New York, Aperture, 1998.

* * *

Few would describe Marianne Wiggins's writing as the gentle, delicate sort. Her fierce, satiric wit and bold characters are legendary practice throughout her four novels and two works of short fiction. Wiggins seems to relish the edgy, bizarre characters wielding their way through divorces and odd relationships. The American writer who has spent a great deal of her writing life in Britain, richly straddles the complex personal lives of her characters with political climates of colonialism, patriarchy, and supremacy. These strong characters often get caught in the maelstrom of these conditions, and try to extract themselves from the ensuing confinements.

Wiggins's early books captured some attention for their quirky-traited characters. Her first book *Babe*, was published in 1975, and set the tone for a future emphasis on edgy dispositions. Maggie Novak has a bizarre tendency to call everyone Babe, much to the discomfort of her lover. Novak is a divorcee who also seems overly impressed by her own observations. While Novak's circumstances may not be the best, her vitality as a character, and her assuredness create an energy that is infectious. But it's the mix of character tendencies—habits and self-indulgences—that make Novak compelling, and seem to be a foundation of character complexity that Wiggins relies on in future novels.

Went South is another story of problematic love, but in this novel the central character, Megan Rosen, suffers from too much comfort. Rosen lives on a New Jersey mini-farm with her child and her husband. But her husband is obsessed with money, and Rosen begins to see her life as much like the mini-farm—a miniature existence without much in the way of challenge. Her ennui comes to a climax and Megan, the woman destined for a life of fading beauty, finds herself wrenched from her own fate, and heading south for adventure.

Wiggins's interest in bold characters sometimes gets her into trouble. *Separate Checks* was judged by critics as writing that pushed too far into the extreme. The novel involves Ellery McQueen, a thirty-three-year-old actress who writes down experiences as a sort of therapy. But when the reader learns there are no men in the McQueen family because they have supposedly been eaten by the women of this matriarchy, it is easy to see Ellery is not the only one in need of therapy. Ellery was named after her mother, a mystery writer. The book is at times funny, but sometimes muddled down with too many risks. The title comes from the Last Supper cafe, where the waiter asks if a meal will be on separate checks.

After two praised story collections (*Herself in Love* and *Bet They'll Miss Us When We're Gone*) Wiggins went on to write her most hailed book to date: *John Dollar.* This book has often been compared to *Lord of the Flies,* except with a gender switch. In the novel, Charlotte Lewes has lost her husband in World War I and travels to Rangoon, Burma, to offer an act of Christian service. She begins to teach there, but service isn't her only interest. Charlotte also takes on sailor John Dollar as a lover. In a trip to the Amdaman Islands with schoolgirls, an accident leaves them stranded on an island. Dollar, who is a god-like figure to the girls, is left paralyzed. But the girls' descent from initial observance sinks quickly into cannibalism, and subversion. Critics agree that this devouring of John Dollar satirically pokes fun at colonialism and Western dominance. The book's large acclaim speaks to a more streamlined plot in *John Dollar* than in previous Wiggins works, and a graceful language contrasting barbarous events.

Wiggins's most recent book, *Almost Heaven* was published in 1998 to a mixed response. Holden Garfield, a war corespondent still recovering from his stint in Bosnia flees back to the United States and finds a woman suffering from traumatic amnesia after the loss of her family. Melanie also happens to be the sister of Holden's friend Noah John. The name is a satirical hint at the cause of fierce weather in the United States. The book's atmospheric focus touches on the chaotic conditions of our current world political order.

—Maureen Aitken

WILDING, Michael

Nationality: British. **Born:** Worcester, 5 January 1942. **Education:** Royal Grammar School, Worcester, 1950–59; Lincoln College, Oxford (editor, *Isis,* 1962), B.A. 1963, M.A. 1968. **Career:** Primary school teacher, Spetchley, Worcestershire, 1960; lecturer in English, University of Sydney, 1963–66; assistant lecturer, 1967–68, and lecturer in English, 1968, University of Birmingham. Senior lecturer, 1969–72, reader in English, 1972–93, and since 1993 professor in English and Australian literature, University of Sydney. Visiting professor, University of California, Santa Barbara, 1987; George Watson Visiting Fellow, University of Queensland, St. Lucia, 1989. Editor, *Balcony,* Sydney, 1965–69, and *Tabloid Story,* Sydney, 1972–76; general editor, Asian and Pacific Writing series, University of Queensland Press, 1972–82; director, Wild and Woolley, publishers, Sydney, 1974–79; editor, *Post-Modern Writing,* Sydney, 1979–81; currently Australian editor, *Stand Magazine,* U.K. Since 1971 Australian editor, *Stand,* Newcastle-upon-Tyne. Fellow, Australian Academy of Humanities, 1988. **Awards:** Australia Council senior fellowship, 1978. D.Litt., University of Sydney, 1996. **Address:** Department of English, University of Sydney, Sydney, New South Wales 2006, Australia.

PUBLICATIONS

Novels

Living Together. St. Lucia, University of Queensland Press, 1974.
The Short Story Embassy. Sydney, Wild and Woolley, 1975.
Pacific Highway. Sydney, Hale and Iremonger, 1982.

The Paraguayan Experiment. Ringwood, Victoria, and London, Penguin, 1985.
Book of the Reading. Sydney, Pope, 1994.
Wildest Dreams. St. Lucia, Queensland, University of Queensland Press, 1998.

Short Stories

Aspects of the Dying Process. St. Lucia, University of Queensland Press, 1972.
The West Midland Underground. St. Lucia, University of Queensland Press, 1975.
Scenic Drive. Sydney, Wild and Woolley, 1976.
The Phallic Forest. Sydney, Wild and Woolley, 1978.
Reading the Signs. Sydney, Hale and Iremonger, 1984.
The Man of Slow Feeling: Selected Short Stories. Ringwood, Victoria, Penguin, 1985.
Under Saturn: Four Stories. Moorebank, New South Wales, Black Swan, 1988.
Great Climate. London, Faber, 1990; as *Her Most Bizarre Sexual Experience,* New York, Norton, 1991.
This Is for You. Sydney, Angus and Rotokun, 1994.
Somewhere New: New and Selected Stories. Rockhampton, Queensland, Central Queensland University Press 1996.

Plays

Screenplay: *The Phallic Forest,* 1972.

Television Play: *Reading the Signs,* 1988.

Other

Milton's Paradise Lost. Sydney, Sydney University Press, 1969.
Cultural Policy in Great Britain, with Michael Green. Paris, Unesco, 1970.
Marcus Clarke. Melbourne and London, Oxford University Press, 1977.
Political Fictions. London, Routledge, 1980.
Dragons Teeth: Literature and Politics in the English Revolution. Oxford, Clarendon Press, 1987.
The Radical Tradition: Lawson, Furphy, Stead. Townsville, Foundation for Australian Literary Studies, 1993.
Social Visions. Sydney, Sydney Studies in Society and Culture, 1993.
Editor, with Charles Higham, *Australians Abroad: An Anthology.* Melbourne, Cheshire, 1967.
Editor, *Three Tales,* by Henry James. Sydney, Hicks Smith, 1967.
Editor, *Marvell: Modern Judgements.* London, Macmillan, 1969; Nashville, Aurora, 1970.
Editor, with others, *We Took Their Orders and Are Dead: An Anti-War Anthology.* Sydney, Ure Smith, 1971.
Editor, *The Portable Marcus Clarke.* St. Lucia, University of Queensland Press, 1976.
Editor, with Stephen Knight, *The Radical Reader.* Sydney, Wild and Woolley, 1977.
Editor, *The Tabloid Story Pocket Book.* Sydney, Wild and Woolley, 1978.
Editor, *The Workingman's Paradise,* by William Lane. Sydney, Sydney University Press, 1980.
Editor, *Stories,* by Marcus Clarke. Sydney, Hale and Iremonger, 1983.
Editor, with Rudi Krausmann, *Air Mail from Down Under.* Vienna, Gangan, 1990.
Editor, *The Oxford Book of Australian Short Stories.* Melbourne, Oxford University Press, 1994; New York, Oxton, 1995.
Editor, with Mabel Lee, *History, Literature, and Society, Essays in Honour of S.N. Mukherjee.* Leichhardt, Australia, Sydney Association for Studies in Society and Culture, 1997.

*

Critical Studies: "The Short Stories of Wilding and Moorhouse" by Carl Harrison-Ford, in *Southerly* (Sydney), 33, 1973; interviews with Rudi Krausmann, in *Aspect,* 1, 1975, David Albahari, in *Australian Literary Studies* (Hobart, Tasmania), 9, 1980, Kevin Brophy and Myron Lysenko, in *Going Down Swinging,* 3, 1982, Giulia Giuffre, in *Southerly* (Sydney), 46, 1986, and Peter Lewis, in *Stand* (Newcastle-upon-Tyne), 32, 1991; "Recent Developments in Australian Writing, with Particular Reference to Short Fiction" by Brian Kiernan, in *Caliban* (Toulouse), 14, 1977; "The New Novel" by Leon Cantrell, in *Studies in the Recent Australian Novel* edited by K.G. Hamilton, St. Lucia, University of Queensland Press, 1978; "Uncertainty and Subversion in the Australian Novel," in *Pacific Moana Quarterly* (Hamilton, New Zealand), 4, 1979, and "Character and Environment in Some Recent Australian Fiction," in *Waves* (Downsview, Ontario), 7, 1979, both by Ken Gelder; "Laszlo's Testament, or Structuring the Past and Sketching the Present in Contemporary Short Fiction," in *Kunapipi 1* (Aarhus, Denmark), 1979, "A New Version of Pastoral," in *Australian Literary Studies* (Hobart, Tasmania), 11, 1983, and "Paradise, Politics, and Fiction: The Writing of Michael Wilding," in *Meanjin* (Melbourne), 45, 1986, all by Bruce Clunies Ross; "The New Writing, Whodunnit?" by G.M. Gillard, in *Meanjin* (Melbourne), 40, 1981; "Michael Wilding: Post-Modernism and the Australian Literary Heritage" by Hans Hauge, in *Overland* (Melbourne), 96, 1984; "Lost and Found: Narrative and Description in Michael Wilding's 'What It Was Like, Sometimes'" by Simone Vauthier, in *Journal of the Short Story in English* (Angers, France), 12, 1989; *The New Diversity: Australian Fiction 1970–1988* by Ken Gelder and Paul Salzman, Fitzroy, Victoria, McPhee Gribble, 1989; "Koka Kola Kulture" by Don Graham in *Southwest Review* (Dallas, Texas), 78, Spring 1993; "Frank Moorhouse and Michael Wilding and Internationalism" by Frank Parigi, in *Antipodes* (Austin, Texas) 8, June 1994; "Talking with Michael Wilding" by Nadezda Obradovic, in *Antipodes* (Austin, Texas) 8, June 1994.

* * *

Michael Wilding is one of a "new generation" of writers in Australia who began publishing in the early 1970s. Impelled to political action by Australia's involvement in the Vietnam war, Wilding has also protested in his writings against censorship, conservative social values, and a subservience to American cultural imperialism.

In the first of his collections of stories *Aspects of the Dying Process,* an English persona is attracted and bemused in several stories by the hedonistic Sydney youth culture which he encounters. The title suggests the ''dying'' as an immigrant changes color with his new culture and extinguishes to some degree the old, and is a pun also on his sexual initiation rites. D.H. Lawrence and Henry James have left their mark on the writer's early style, in its rendering of the impulses and withdrawals of an observer who is not yet a participant in the new life. *The West Midland Underground,* Wilding's second volume of stories, has a free-wheeling variety of narrative modes and settings which include England, Greece, the United States, and Australia. In ''Canal Run'' a boy's claustrophobic world is evident in images of the English industrial midlands; at the center of frustration is a thwarted sexuality: ''Thinking back it is hard to see exactly when one's consciousness of sex began and became a desire for, a whole youth's looking for, fulfillment. Then, though, there was only a strong sense of sin and shame and dirt; no lyricism, and none of the hatred. It was wrong and furtive and C stream; which was another way of saying lower class.'' Most stories in *The Phallic Forest* energetically flout ''normal'' sexual and social mores, or celebrate alternatives; and in a later collection, *Reading the Signs,* a more reflective consciousness draws on a background of class awareness for sharp and penetrating observations of appearance and behavior. In Wilding's later work the term ''Midlander'' connotes the circumscribed spirit, against which all his writings rebel.

Wilding's first novel, *Living Together,* relates the exploits, and fantasies, of young men and women cohabiting in inner suburban Sydney. The traumas of Martin, Paul, and Ann (second names are unimportant) are related with wit and verve as they paint and decorate their house and have sex, joints, or drink with neighbors and visitors. (In a later novel, a character comments that the Pill introduced ''a whole new anthropology'' for the writer.) The strongest character is the irenic Ann, who, after leaving her outrageously chauvinist partner Martin half way through the novel, returns at the end to give his life some shape and order. The men are weaker and more ambivalent. Paul, the author's alter ego, has taken his sexual apprenticeship, but is unsure of his future directions. Martin's scenario of the house as a sort of ''cultural center'' is never realized; its most memorable visits are two female grotesques, the ever-ready next-door neighbor Mrs. Bilham, and Gretel Mann, of ''cavernous appetite,'' who helps Paul out of his innocence. Late in the novel Paul has decided that ''Change is the only aphrodisiac.'' The literary progenitor of this urban comedy of the 1970s is perhaps Thomas Love Peacock, whose miscellaneous parties of odd characters in English country houses also mix satire and romance, but where the treatment of sex is much more circumspect.

Wilding's second novel, *The Short Story Embassy,* and his third, *Pacific Highway,* contain insights into the literary process. The ''Embassy,'' situated ''halfway to the north'' on Australia's east coast, approximates to the ''cultural center'' envisaged by Martin in *Living Together.* The juxtaposition of culture and nature is a source of comedy, as in this version of ''pot pastoral'': ''The people traveling up from the south rested there and stripped off and got their bodies brown before going on to the full north. They lay around by creeks and wove garlands of bush flowers around each other. They made daisy-chains around their necks and twined poppies in their pubic hairs. The cows came and gazed on them and licked them and they licked each other.''

Here, as elsewhere, Wilding is both lyrical and amused; he celebrates the new freedoms and is affectionately ironic about them. While whimsy sometimes predominates, a sharper irony is evident in observations about characters' literary outlooks and values. The middle-aged Laszlo, for instance, possessively jealous of his lover, Valda, puzzles over his generation of radicals, who read Tom Paine, while hers has been ''turned on'' to astrology. To Valda, Laszio seems to use books as ''leaning posts.'' *The Short Story Embassy* quizzically examines the ''new'' experimental literature of process and locates its enemy as the Thought Police. But this is Kafka without the menace. The visitor, Tichborne, who mysteriously leaves the Embassy, may be one of the enemy (his name is a reminder of the famous Tichborne impersonation case), but his departure lacks consequence. There is paranoia aplenty in this novel but ''plot'' in the conventional sense is missing.

The pastoral element is paramount in *Pacific Highway.* In some respects it is a 1980s version of Vance Palmer's *The Passage* (1930), in which a rural holiday retreat on the Pacific Ocean is destroyed by ''progress'' and ''development.'' But the tone and style of the two novels differ markedly. In *Pacific Highway* the attempt by the narrator and his girlfriend, Lily, to recreate an idyllic world of innocence among friends who will live off the land, re-cycling their waste, is confronted by a censorious, authoritarian regime. This household (two young women and a man), is differentiated from other ''hippies'' by being middle-class and theoretical: escapees from the midlands. Confrontations with the wider society are often presented as wry comedy: for instance, how does a household with idealistic communist notions rationalize its employment of a cleaning woman? Another dimension is the love story—of the narrator and Lily—which contains some fine lyrical passages.

A search for utopia, implicit elsewhere, is the explicit theme of Wilding's fourth novel, *The Paraguayan Experiment.* The novel marks a departure for Wilding, who uses historical documents in his firm narration of the story of the New Australia movement. Disillusioned with the economic depression and social repression in Australia in the 1890s, William Lane led a group of 400 men, women, and children to found a New Australia in Paraguay. Using letters (especially Lane's), memos, and official documents, Wilding builds a lively account of this historic precursor to the idealistic communalists of the 1970s. Anachronisms in dialogue and commentary are evident, but these seem deliberate: in certain respects, which Wilding does not wish to conceal, this was a parable for the 1980s. Hence many of the issues which have obsessed this writer—the creation of alternative human settlements, the clash between individual and group needs, sexual politics, the use of drugs—are evident in this tale of a previous era in Australian history. In form and style, this novel shows Wilding's continuing interest in literary experimentation and is rich in humor, fantasy, and social observation.

The stories in *This Is for You* suggest that Wilding's themes have begun to seem a bit dated—too much a part of the 1960s (and the twentieth century in general), and thus outmoded for a world entering a new millennium. *Wildest Dreams* is, on the one hand, a memoir, but it is also a novel featuring Wilding's alter-ego Graham. Again the focus is on issues that for many other people were settled long ago: Vietnam, Marxism, drugs, and the beatnik lifestyle.

—Bruce Bennett, updated by Judson Knight

WILKINS, Damien

Nationality: New Zealander. **Born:** 1963. **Awards:** Heinemann Reed fiction award, 1989; New Zealand book award for fiction, 1993.

PUBLICATIONS

Novels

The Miserables. Wellington, New Zealand, Victoria University Press, and New York, Harcourt Brace, 1993.

Little Masters. Wellington, New Zealand, Victoria University Press, 1996; New York, Holt, 1997.

Short Stories

The Veteran Perils. Auckland, New Zealand, Heinemann Reed, 1990.

Poetry

The Idles. Wellington, New Zealand, Victoria University Press, 1993.

* * *

Damien Wilkins is part of a new generation of New Zealand writers who came of age in the midst of a surge of literary production in their home country, just as New Zealand literature was beginning to gain significant recognition internationally. With the 1990 publication of his collection of short stories, *The Veteran Perils*, Wilkins himself emerged as a writer of the late ''post-Provincial'' period, loosely characterized by its acknowledgement of international exchanges and its engagement with post-modernism and post-colonialism. He certainly meets these informal criteria in his creative work.

Wilkins's first novel, *The Miserables*, was published in 1993 to critical acclaim, winning the New Zealand book award for fiction. A classic bildungsroman, the novel traces the return of its protagonist, Healey, to Wellington, New Zealand, for the funeral of his grandfather. The return to his birthplace is accompanied by the return of memories, emotions, and the revelation of a self suppressed. But the self is more than suppressed, it is also dislocated, and as Healey revisits his memories of previous journeys undertaken, his dislocation is gradually displaced by a sense of place and a grounding that previously eluded him. In a creative triumph, Wilkins's imagining of Healey gains coherence precisely by abandoning all linear pretenses at coherence, as Healey slides in and out of memories and recognitions triggered by the encountering of places, or interactions with family members gathered for the funeral. However, in *The Miserables* there are no strategically placed epiphanies, denouements, or climaxes that will satisfy the lazy reader. Instead, Wilkins has engaged in a project of cartography that demands thoughtful contemplation on the part of the reader.

In his second novel, *Little Masters*, published in 1996, Wilkins makes his expectations of the reader more apparent. The novel opens with a scene of a therapy session, which we learn is taped and shared with the parents of the analyzed, forcing them to witness and consider the details of her life. This analyzed subject, who does not recur in the novel as a character, nevertheless sets the tone of the novel, and continues to signify on the story throughout in ways that are not immediately apparent. Wilkins, ever playful, further extends this metaphor of analysis by embedding other literary texts—a short story and a radio play—in the novel and creating dialogue in which his characters analyze their significance and meaning.

Thematic and stylistic similarities abound between the two novels. Both are fragmentary and episodic, spanning continents and history in their non-linear narratives. However, *Little Masters* is more ambitious, weaving together the narratives of several characters, all suffering a kind of spiritual dislocation. At the center of the novel are two New Zealanders in England, dissatisfied with the transnational lives they lead. One, Adrian, is the child of refugees liberated from a Polish camp at the end of World War II and relocated to New Zealand. As such, Adrian embodies several key themes that permeate that novel, including the residual effects of the trauma of war as manifested in the children of those who survive. As the dislocated son of dislocated parents who has a dislocated child himself, Adrian also draws attention to how the meaning of one's life is shifted by the experience of being a transnational subject. In order to achieve any grounding in the midst of this chaos of the unfamiliar and foreign, Wilkins's characters reconsider their primary relationships—families, lovers—as a means of staying their current sense of disorientation in their relationships with others. However, while his first novel closed with an invocation of tenderness, these notes in Wilkins are not uncomplicated: *Little Masters* also closes with an act of tenderness, but it is coupled with acts of innocent destruction and the presence of death.

As a graduate of the Victoria University of Wellington's creative writing course, and a former writing student at Washington University who also worked in London's publishing industry before returning to Wellington, Wilkins is widely recognized as a force to be reckoned with in the future of New Zealand literature. Not only a novelist, Wilkins has also published a book of poetry, *The Idles*, and written for television.

—Jennifer Harris

WILLIAMS, John A(lfred)

Nationality: American. **Born:** Jackson, Mississippi, 5 December 1925. **Education:** Central High School, Syracuse, New York; Syracuse University, A.B. 1950. **Military Service:** Served in the United States Navy, 1943–46. **Family:** Married 1) Carolyn Clopton in 1947 (divorced), two sons; 2) Lorrain Isaac in 1965, one son. **Career:** Member of the public relations department, Doug Johnson Associates, Syracuse, 1952–54, and Arthur P. Jacobs Company; staff member, CBS, Hollywood and New York, 1954–55; publicity director, Comet Press Books, New York, 1955–56; publisher and editor, *Negro Market Newsletter,* New York, 1956–57; assistant to the editor, Abelard-Schuman, publishers, New York, 1957–58; director of information, American Committee on Africa, New York, 1958; European correspondent, *Ebony* and *Jet* magazines, 1958–59; announcer, WOV Radio, New York, 1959; Africa correspondent, *Newsweek,* New York, 1964–65. Regents' Lecturer, University of California, Santa Barbara, 1972; Distinguished Professor of English, LaGuardia Community College, City University of New York, 1973–78; visiting professor, University of Hawaii, Honolulu, Summer 1974, Boston University, 1978–79, and New York University, 1986–87. Professor of English, 1979–90, Paul Robeson Professor of

English, 1990–94, and since 1994 professor emeritus, Rutgers University, Newark, New Jersey. Bard Center Fellow, Bard College, 1994–95. Member of the Editorial Board, *Audience*, Boston, 1970–72; contributing editor, *American Journal*, New York, 1972. **Awards:** American Academy grant, 1962; Syracuse University Outstanding Achievement award, 1970; National Endowment for the Arts grant, 1977; Rutgers University Lindback award, 1982; Before Columbus Foundation award, 1983; American Book award, 1998. Litt.D.: Southeastern Massachusetts University, North Dartmouth, 1978; Syracuse University, 1995. **Agent:** Barbara Hogenson Agency, 19 W. 44th St., New York, New York 10036. **Address:** 693 Forest Avenue, Teaneck, New Jersey 07666, U.S.A.

PUBLICATIONS

Novels

The Angry Ones. New York, Ace, 1960; as *One for New York,* Chatham, New Jersey, Chatham Bookseller, 1975.
Night Song. New York, Farrar Straus, 1961; London, Collins, 1962.
Sissie. New York, Farrar Straus, 1963; as *Journey Out of Anger,* London, Eyre and Spottiswoode, 1968.
The Man Who Cried I Am. Boston, Little Brown, 1967; London, Eyre and Spottiswoode, 1968.
Sons of Darkness, Sons of Light. Boston, Little Brown, 1969; London, Eyre and Spottiswoode, 1970.
Captain Blackman. New York, Doubleday, 1975.
Mothersill and the Foxes. New York, Doubleday, 1975.
The Junior Bachelor Society. New York, Doubleday, 1976.
!Click Song. Boston, Houghton Mifflin, 1982.
The Berhama Account. Far Hills, New Jersey, New Horizon Press, 1985.
Jacob's Ladder. New York, Thunder's Mouth Press, 1987.
Clifford's Blues. Minneapolis, Coffee House Press, 1998.

Other

Africa: Her History, Lands, and People. New York, Cooper Square, 1962.
The Protectors (on narcotics agents; as J. Dennis Gregory), with Harry J. Anslinger. New York, Farrar Straus, 1964.
This Is My Country, Too. New York, New American Library, 1965; London, New English Library, 1966.
The Most Native of Sons: A Biography of Richard Wright. New York, Doubleday, 1970.
The King God Didn't Save: Reflections on the Life and Death of Martin Luther King, Jr. New York, Coward McCann, 1970; London, Eyre and Spottiswoode, 1971.
Flashbacks: A Twenty-Year Diary of Article Writing. New York, Doubleday, 1973.
Minorities in the City. New York, Harper, 1975.
If I Stop I'll Die: The Comedy and Tragedy of Richard Pryor, with Dennis A. Williams. New York, Thunder's Mouth Press, 1991.
Flashbacks 2: A Diary of Article Writing. Westport, Connecticut, Orange Ball Press, 1991.
Editor, *The Angry Black.* New York, Lancer, 1962.
Editor, *Beyond the Angry Black.* New York, Cooper Square, 1967.
Editor with Charles F. Harries, *Amistad I* and *II.* New York, Knopf, 2 vols., 1970–71.
Editor, with Gilbert H. Muller, *The McGraw Hill Introduction to Literature.* New York, McGraw Hill, 1985.
Editor, with Gilbert H. Muller, *Bridges: Literature Across Cultures.* New York, McGraw Hill, 1994.
Editor, *Ways In: Approaches to Reading and Writing about Literature.* New York, McGraw Hill, 1994.
Editor, *Introduction to Literature 2/e.* New York, McGraw Hill, 1995.

*

Manuscript Collections: Syracuse University, New York; Rochester University, New York.

Critical Studies: *America as Seen by a Black Man* by Robert T. Haley, unpublished thesis, San Jose State College, California, 1971; ''The Art of John A. Williams'' by John O'Brien, in *American Scholar* (Washington, D.C.), Summer 1973; *The Evolution of a Black Writer: John A. Williams* by Earl Cash, New York, Third Press, 1974; *American Fictions 1940–1980* by Frederick R. Karl, New York, Harper, 1983; *John A. Williams* by Gilbert H. Muller, Boston, Twayne, 1984; article by James L. de Jongh, in *Afro-American Fiction Writers after 1955* edited by Thadious M. Davis and Trudier Harris, Detroit, Gale, 1984.

John A. Williams comments:

I think art has always been political and has served political ends more graciously than those of the muses. I consider myself to be a political novelist and writer to the extent that I am always aware of the social insufficiencies which are a result of political manipulation. The greatest art has always been social-political, and in that sense I could be considered striving along traditional paths.

* * *

An essayist, novelist, anthologist, poet, and biographer, John Alfred Williams is the author of nearly twenty books including a dozen novels that span four decades. With so diverse an oeuvre, it is helpful to group Williams's novels into particular phases, representative of the author's maturing vision of his principle theme—the tension between black experience and American ideology, portrayed against the backdrop of history.

The first phase comprises, *The Angry Ones* (*One for New York*), *Night Song,* and *Sissie,* and marks a semi-autobiographical focus. Tracing its protagonist's employment as a publicity director for a vanity press, *The Angry Ones* explores the hypocrisy of corporate America, the vanishing of the American dream, the psychological complexities surrounding interracial sex, and the black writer's challenge to maintain cultural integrity in an exploitative society. The main character, Steve Hill, leads a life that resembles Williams's. After leaving the navy, Williams worked in New York's burgeoning publishing industry. In *Night Song* Williams expands the narrow, first person focus of the first novel by relaying point of view through three distinct, though equally tragic protagonists: Richie ''Eagle'' Stokes, a decaying, self-destructive jazz musician; David Hillary, a self-pitying, ex college professor; and Keel Robinson, a former preacher. A study in nocturnal landscapes and the symbolic portrayal of mental desuetude, the novel draws from the mythic life of Charlie ''Bird'' Parker and pioneers what would later become the subgenre of ''jazz fiction.'' The novel also concerns the decay of social optimism, miscegenation, and the gaps between white and black America. These early novels also lay the important sociopolitical groundwork that undergirds all of Williams's work. This is perhaps especially true of *Sissie* with its relentless framing of individual characters against a politically charged history. A grand biography of the Joplin family's struggle over several generations, *Sissie* testifies to Williams's growing skill with a complex form of narrative time mechanics that has been likened to Faulkner, and which would later be put to effective use in *The Man Who Cried I Am.* In this first phase, Williams dramatizes black social struggle, but suggests the possibility of success in characters who do not resort to violence or reactionary politics, as they strive to reconcile their idealisms with the brutal facts of an oppressive racial system.

It is in the second phase that Williams reverses this political orientation. Now characters do realize the necessity of acquiring a heightened political and historical consciousness in order to not only succeed, but to survive in America. Written after being ruthlessly passed over for a promised *Prix de Rome* from the American Academy of Arts and Letters, the highly political novels of the second phase articulate most clearly the rage of the "angry black" and show the author's movement away from the image of the black protagonist struggling for confirmation of his self-worth. In *The Man Who Cried I Am,* a novel that has been called his masterpiece, Williams creates Max Reddick, a black writer who becomes a "success" in the white world, but who eventually asks himself "was it worth what it cost?" Reddick's final confirmation of "self" comes not from the white world, but from a metaphysical, interior space where the fact of existence outweighs the superficiality of race: "All you ever want to do is remind me that I am black. But, goddamn it, I also am," exclaims Reddick famously. Few writers match Williams in destroying the illusions of the black man as a victim subjugated by the pressures of racial injustice in the Western world. Slowly dying from rectal cancer, Reddick eventually learns of a secret plan kept by the American government. In times of emergency, the King Alfred plan calls for a mass detention and imprisoning of African Americans. Finally, after tragically realizing the impossibility of national identity, Reddick dies having stumbled across this information. *The Man Who Cried I Am* delivers perhaps the bleakest commentary on the incommensurability of national inclusiveness and national racist agendas, while plotting the convergence of tumultuous historical and cultural forces on the figure of the African American. In *Sons of Darkness, Sons of Light* Eugene Browning mulls over the advantages of knowing his past. But it is with reason and without anger, that Browning, after coming to the conclusion that civil rights and freedom marches would not bring justice to blacks, employs Mafia tactics in the assassination of a policeman guilty of killing a sixteen-year-old black boy. Novels of the rage period advertise the heightened sense of group conscious, self-resolve, and resourcefulness needed by blacks to eliminate racial injustices. *Captain Blackman* confronts American history from a military perspective. A Vietnam officer and also a teacher of military history, Abraham Blackman drifts back in time to recount black experiences in early American wars. In Blackman, the novel presents an allegorical figure of the black soldier, a paradoxical icon of heroism and national belonging, but also an object of hateful scorn to generals and politicians. At times the novel merges into historical nonfiction, as Williams inserts little-known but heavily documented letters which reveal the racism of such leaders as Teddy Roosevelt and Abraham Lincoln with starling clarity. All of the novels of the second phase register the need to both come to terms with history and to struggle against it.

With the publication of *Mothersill and the Foxes* and *The Junior Bachelor Society,* Williams enters a brief third phase noted for sexual parody, a modified politics, and technical complexity. Breaking away from traditional narrative modes, Williams experiments with postmodernism to relate the sexual odyssey of Odell Mothersill and the "foxes" whom he courts. The novel broaches bizarre sexual scenarios—incest, voyeurism, masturbation—in an uneven variety of techniques, ranging from surrealistic parody to pastoral fairy tale. Ludicrous, naturalistic, and absurdist, the novel's scenes of sexuality often devolve to horrific grotesques, which like the many allusions to grotesque art, comment on the macabre lack of emotion regarding sexuality and corporeality in Mothersill's picaresque world. *The Junior Bachelor Society* returns to the multi-character plot structure of Williams's earlier novels, as it cross cuts among the lives of its nine aging protagonists, who attend a hometown reunion in celebration of a former high school coach. Reminiscent of *Sissie* in its poignant portrayal of individuals striving against a repressive social order and in its concern for interpersonal relationships, the novel focuses on varieties of middle class and blue collar, late middle-aged, African-American masculinity. While investigating the vexed role that sports play in American culture and in the black imagination, the novel also stresses the relationship between physical contests and success in life.

In his fourth phase, Williams seems to reinvest in the political and social themes of his first two stages, but now through sharply drawn characters whose interior conflicts mirror the external political forces shaping history. *!Click Song, The Berhama Account, Jacobs Ladder,* and *Clifford's Blues* return to techniques that investigate the dynamics of storytelling while conveying a deeply political, increasingly global consciousness.

!Click Song reprises a character central to Williams's fiction, the black novelist. An obvious literary descendent of Max Reddick, Cato Douglass must bear the humiliating racism that drives the publishing industry as he develops relationships with his three sons, each from different wives: one white, one black, and one in Spain. Behind his scathing bitterness, Douglass shields an essentially artistic, deeply philosophic mind, which cleaves to its productions, both artistic and filial, in order to shore up some defense against the abuses of the literary establishment. *The Berhama Account* is a tale of international political intrigue and the panacea of romantic love. Another multi-plot story of personal optimism, the novel concerns a fake assassination, the political struggle of a Caribbean nation, and a re-ignited love affair that heals a journalist recovering from cancer. Although *The Berhama Account* evidences a global awareness of racist power dynamics, it finally expresses a degree of hope and possibility through love that is unparalleled in Williams's other novels. *Jacob's Ladder* turns to Africa and the specific problems in nation building that Fasseke, the newly installed president of Pandemi, faces. When African-American war hero Henry Jacob arrives to help Fasseke, much of the resulting dialogue between them explores the diasporic tensions separating Africans from African Americans. The novel critiques colonial history, slavery, and inter-African prejudice, while responding to American culture from a post-colonial vantage point. No less historically sophisticated is *Clifford's Blues,* which recounts in journal format the experiences of Clifford Pepperidge, an itinerant, homosexual, black American jazz musician who finds himself interred by the Nazis in Dachau. To stay alive, Clifford assembles a jazz band with other prisoners to entertain the Nazi officers. Like *Captain Blackman, Clifford's Blues* is an informative novel built upon exacting historical research of blacks in concentration camps, but its vivid, somber prose prevents it from waxing didactic. As with *Sissie, Night*

Song, and *The Junior Bachelor Society, Clifford's Blues* eloquently dramatizes the individual's triumph of will in the face of great adversity, and thus transcends the thematics of American racial injustices to evoke a wider sense of historical barbarity and heroism.

—Michael A. Chaney

WILLIS, Connie

Nationality: American. **Born:** Constance Elaine, Denver, Colorado, 31 December 1945. **Education:** University of Northern Colorado, B.A. in English and elementary education. **Family:** Married Courtney Wayne Willis, 1967; one daughter. **Career:** Elementary school teacher, 1967–68, and junior high teacher, 1968–69, Branford, Connecticut, public schools. **Awards:** Nebula award, 1982, and Hugo award, 1982, both for *Fire Watch;* 1982 for ''A Letter from the Clearys''; Nebula award, 1988, and Hugo award, 1988, both for *The Last of the Winnebagos;* Campbell Memorial award for best science fiction novel, 1988, for *Lincoln's Dreams;* Nebula award, 1989 for ''At the Rialto''; Nebula award, 1992, Locus award, 1992, and Hugo award, 1993, both for ''Even the Queen''; Nebula award, 1992, Locus award, 1992, and Hugo award, 1993, both for *Doomsday Book;* Locus award, 1993, for *Impossible Things,* 1993, for ''Close Encounter''; Hugo award, 1994, for ''Death on the Nile''; Hugo award, 1997, for *The Soul Selects;* Hugo award, 1999, for *To Say Nothing of the Dog.* **Agent:** Ralph Vicinanza, 111 Eighth Ave., Suite 1501, New York, New York 10011, U.S.A. **Address:** 1716 Thirteenth Ave., Greeley, Colorado 80631, U.S.A.

PUBLICATIONS

Novels

Water Witch, with Cynthia Felice. New York, Ace Berkeley, 1980.
Lincoln's Dreams. New York, Bantam, 1986.
Light Raid, with Cynthia Felice. New York, Ace Berkeley, 1988.
Doomsday Book. New York, Bantam, and Hodder and Stoughton, 1992.
Impossible Things. New York, Bantam, 1994.
Uncharted Territory. New York, Bantam, and Hodder and Stoughton, 1994.
Remake. New York, Bantam, 1995.
Bellwether. New York, Bantam Books, 1996.
Promised Land (with Cynthia Felice). New York, Ace Books, 1997.
To Say Nothing of the Dog; Or, How We Found the Bishop's Bird Stump at Last. New York, Bantam Books, 1997.

Short Stories

Fire Watch. New York, Bluejay, 1985.
Miracle, and Other Christmas Stories. New York, Bantam Books, 1999.

*

Connie Willis comments:

I first fell in love with science fiction at age thirteen, when I read Robert A. Heinlein's *Have Space Suit, Will Travel.* That's not unusual. Science fiction and adolescence have a lot in common: love of adventure, love of ideas, boundless enthusiasm for the universe. For many readers, it's only an infatuation, but for me it has turned into a lifelong love affair, I think because the medium of science fiction is ideal for the stories I want to tell and the themes I want to write about.

I find that looking at things obliquely, through the disguise of other places, other times, cuts through not only the reader's prejudices and defenses but my own and makes it possible to look clearly at our own world, our own faces. And the conventions of science fiction—Martians, time travel, robots—carry within them the themes that matter most to me. Time travel, especially, with its built-in resonances of grief and loss and regret, I could write about forever. After all these years, I still come to science fiction with that same shock of joy and recognition that I did at thirteen.

* * *

Connie Willis is one of the most beloved and respected writers in the field of science fiction. For her novels and short fiction, Willis has earned more Hugo and Nebula awards—the two major prizes given by readers and writers of science fiction and fantasy—than any other author. She is a noted humorist; her comical works are satirical while expressing great warmth. Often overshadowing the screwball antics and witty dialogue is a keen sympathy for the human condition, filling her novels with heart-wrenching pain.

Willis's earliest novels, *Water Witch* and *Light Raid,* were written with Cynthia Felice; they are generally considered slight and implausible. However, *Fire Watch,* her first short story collection, reveals Willis's talents for both humor and tragedy. The titular story, ''Fire Watch'' (1982), a Hugo and Nebula winner, is indicative of the themes and concerns which recur in her fiction. In the twenty-first century, time travel technology permits history students to visit the era of their studies. The protagonist is sent back to London during the Blitz of World War II, a period that fascinates Willis. Working with the volunteers who attempt to save St. Paul's Cathedral from the Luftwaffe, he learns that history is not a matter of textbook statistics but of living people, laboring side by side to save what they love, with their many species of courage and weakness.

Willis's first solo novel, *Lincoln's Dreams,* winner of the John W. Campbell Memorial award for best science fiction novel, is another story of history and (after a fashion) time travel. This remarkable debut investigates the horror with which the American Civil War continues to haunt us—as Willis says in her foreword, it disturbs us like a cry for help, or a dream, so that we still puzzle over its meaning. The first-person narrator, Jeff Johnston, is a researcher for an author of historical novels. Well-versed in Civil War minutiae and piecing together the story of Traveller, the noble-hearted horse of the noble-hearted general Robert E. Lee, he is only partly prepared to meet Annie, a woman suffering terrible nightmares. Jeff falls in love with this attractive and fragile woman as she tells him of her dreams. They hold no meaning for her, but Jeff recognizes the details as incidents from General Lee's actual memories. To learn the meaning of this extraordinary psychic link, Jeff escorts Annie on a tour of the Southern battlefields. He hopes to break the link by explaining to Annie the tragedies Lee and his men endured, but Annie determines to ''finish the dreams'' and exorcise Lee's guilt so that he may literally rest in peace. Jeff's discovery of the courage and ultimate fate of Traveller reveal to him his own connection to the inexorable replay of Lee's life and death. With immensely sympathetic characterization and vivid presentation of the horrors of war, *Lincoln's Dreams* is an unforgettable drama of love, loyalty, and duty.

Doomsday Book and *To Say Nothing of the Dog, or, How We Found the Bishop's Bird Stump At Last* are set in the same world as ''Fire Watch.'' In the former, set in 2054, history student Kivrin wishes to visit medieval Oxford for her practicum. However, the time-travel time technician has fallen suddenly ill with an unknown virus, and in his delirium he accidentally sends her to 1384, the year of the Black Death.

Doomsday Book, which also won both Hugo and Nebula awards, alternates between the two timelines, showing that human nature is much the same in each era, as both sets of characters must cope with an apocalyptic plague and ensuing panic. Kivrin seems doomed to die in the past, grieving as the villagers who have succored her succumb, one after another, to bubonic plague, because there is no way that she can signal her friend Professor Dunworthy that she is in the wrong place and time. The sweet and wise Dunworthy, however, has reasoned this out, and struggles with idiotic bureaucracy and social chaos to do everything he can to bring her back. Through mesmerizing adventure and dialogue, Willis works out her theme of the psychological response to the end of the world, portraying religious faith, helplessness, and incredible heroism.

A couple of collections, *Impossible Things* and *Futures Imperfect,* and the short novels *Remake, Uncharted Territory,* and *Bellwether,* followed *Doomsday Book. Remake* is a satire about censorship, presenting a future in which classic films are edited to the point of meaninglessness to remove any scenes showing sexual innuendo, drinking, smoking, or other immoral activities. The protagonists, two star-crossed lovers seeking their big break in a Hollywood that is ironically, sickeningly corrupt, long for the days when movies told real stories with real actors. *Uncharted Territory* parodies many science fiction clichés in its portrayal of a daring exploration of another planet, a mapping project that is bedeviled by ridiculous regulations and fussily bureaucratic aliens. Its more important themes, also comically treated, concern love, sex, and gender roles. *Bellwether* is a screwball romance between a woman who studies fads and a chaos theorist who arrive at a cynical revelation of how human bellwethers start trends.

To Say Nothing of the Dog, Willis's next ''big'' novel, is as ambitious as *Doomsday Book,* though not nearly as soul wrenching. A cheerful homage to Jerome K. Jerome's *Three Men in a Boat,* the novel documents a time-traveler's misadventures in a madcap tour of Victorian England. The plot involves a quest to find something called a bird-stump, but weaving through the antics is a satirical needle pointing out the puritanical (or Victorian) morality of the United States in the 1990s. It won the Nebula award in 1998.

Willis's fiction is not unlike that of Mark Twain's—very funny, often savage, and deeply compassionate. Her satire targets petty bureaucrats, hypocrites, and control freaks who make life miserable for others. Her protagonists are often middle-aged women wondering what happened to their happily-ever-afters and still seeking romance, or young people struggling to find love and preserve beauty while hampered by busybodies. Throughout her fiction there sounds a sorrowful note of loss and destruction, but Willis is optimistic that kindness and loyalty will always, if not prevail, then at least burn brightly in the metaphorical night of war, plague, and vicious stupidity. Her fans live in anticipation of her coming works, for, at whatever length, they always guarantee a good read.

—Fiona Kelleghan

WILSON, A(ndrew) N(orman)

Nationality: British. **Born:** Stone, Staffordshire, 27 October 1950. **Education:** Rugby School, Warwickshire, 1964–69; New College, Oxford (Chancellor's Essay prize, 1971; Ellerton Theological prize, 1975), 1969–72, M.A.; studied for priesthood, 1973–74. **Family:** Married 1) Katherine Duncan-Jones in 1971 (divorced 1990), two daughters; 2) Ruth Guilding. **Career:** Assistant master, Merchant Taylors' School, London, 1975–76; lecturer, St. Hugh's College, Oxford, 1976–82, and New College, 1977–80; literary editor, the *Spectator,* London, 1981–83. Presenter, *Eminent Victorians* television series, 1989. **Awards:** Rhys Memorial prize, for fiction, 1978, for biography, 1981; Maugham award, 1981; Arts Council National Book award, 1981; Southern Arts prize, 1981; W.H. Smith Literary award, 1983; Whitbread prize, for biography, 1988. Fellow, Royal Society of Literature, 1981. **Agent:** Peters Fraser and Dunlop, 503–504 The Chambers, Chelsea Harbour, Lots Road, London SW10 0XF. **Address:** 21 Arlington Rd., London NW1 7ER, England.

PUBLICATIONS

Novels

The Sweets of Pimlico. London, Secker and Warburg, 1977; New York, Penguin, 1989.
Unguarded Hours. London, Secker and Warburg, 1978.
Kindly Light. London, Secker and Warburg, 1979.
The Healing Art. London, Secker and Warburg, 1980; New York, Penguin, 1988.
Who Was Oswald Fish? London, Secker and Warburg, 1981; New York, Penguin, 1988.
Wise Virgin. London, Secker and Warburg, 1982; New York, Viking Press, 1983.
Scandal; or, Priscilla's Kindness. London, Hamish Hamilton, 1983; New York, Viking, 1984.
Gentlemen in England: A Vision. London, Hamish Hamilton, 1985; New York, Viking, 1986.
Love Unknown. London, Hamish Hamilton, 1986; New York, Viking, 1987.
Incline Our Hearts. London, Hamish Hamilton, 1988; New York, Viking, 1989.
A Bottle in the Smoke. London, Sinclair Stevenson, 1989; New York, Viking, 1990.
Daughters of Albion. London, Sinclair Stevenson, 1991; New York, Viking, 1992.
The Vicar of Sorrows. London, Sinclair Stevenson, 1993; New York, Norton, 1994.
Hearing Voices. London, Sinclair-Stevenson, 1995; New York, W.W. Norton, 1996.
A Watch in the Night. London, Sinclair-Stevenson, 1996.
Dream Children. New York, W.W. Norton, 1998.

Poetry

Lilibet: An Account in Verse of the Early Years of the Queen until the Time of Her Accession. London, Blond and Briggs, 1984.

Other (for children)

Stray. London, Walker Books, 1987; New York, Orchard, 1989.
The Tabitha Stories. London, Walker Books, 1988; as *Tabitha,* New York, Orchard, 1989.
Hazel the Guinea-Pig. London, Walker Books, 1989; Cambridge, Massachusetts, Candlewick Press, 1992.

Other

The Laird of Abbotsford: A View of Sir Walter Scott. Oxford and New York, Oxford University Press, 1980.
The Life of John Milton. Oxford and New York, Oxford University Press, 1983.
Hilaire Belloc. London, Hamish Hamilton, and New York, Atheneum, 1984.
How Can We Know? An Essay on the Christian Religion. London, Hamish Hamilton, and New York, Atheneum, 1985.
The Church in Crisis, with Charles Moore and Gavin Stamp. London, Hodder and Stoughton, 1986.
Landscape in France, photographs by Charlie Waite. London, Elm Tree, 1987; New York, St. Martin's Press, 1988.
Penfriends from Porlock: Essay and Reviews 1977–1986. London, Hamish Hamilton, 1988; New York, Norton, 1989.
Tolstoy: A Biography. London, Hamish Hamilton, and New York, Norton, 1988.
Eminent Victorians. London, BBC Publications, 1989; New York, Norton, 1990.
C.S. Lewis: A Biography. London, Collins, and New York, Norton, 1990.
Against Religion. London, Chatto and Windus, 1990.
Jesus. London, Sinclair Stevenson, 1992.
The Rise and Fall of the House of Windsor. London, Sinclair Stevenson, and New York, Norton, 1993.
Paul: The Mind of the Apostle. New York, W.W. Norton, 1997.
God's Funeral. New York, W.W. Norton, 1999.
Editor, *Ivanhoe,* by Scott. London, Penguin, 1982.
Editor, *Dracula,* by Bram Stoker. Oxford, Oxford University Press, 1983.
Editor, *Essays by Divers Hand 44.* Woodbridge, Suffolk, Boydell and Brewer, 1986.
Editor, *The Lion and the Honeycomb: The Religious Writings of Tolstoy.* London, Collins, and New York, Harper, 1987.
Editor, *John Henry Newman: Prayers, Poems, and Meditations.* London, SPCK, 1989; New York, Crossroad, 1990.
Editor, *The Faber Book of Church and Clergy.* London, Faber, 1992.
Editor, *The Faber Book of London.* London, Faber, 1994.
Editor, *The Norton Book of London.* New York, Norton, 1994.

* * *

A. N. Wilson is a prolific writer who has produced seventeen novels, biographies of Sir Walter Scott, Milton, Hilaire Belloc, Tolstoy, and C.S. Lewis, controversial accounts of Jesus and St. Paul, studies of religion, and many polemical articles. As a novelist, his territory is a familiar one in British fiction; the world of the English middle and upper middle classes, as represented primarily by Oxbridge graduates, London intellectuals, and Anglican clergymen. To some extent, his technique resembles the satire and black comedy of Evelyn Waugh and Ronald Firbank but he is generally a gentler, more affectionate writer with a capacity to evoke both love and, in his later work, the depths of despair. By his own account, he is a one-draft writer, who does not spend time revising; and this sometimes shows in the prose of his fiction; but he nonetheless has the ability to bring scenes and characters vividly and economically before the reader and he can be very funny; as some of his nonfiction books might suggest, however, he is also concerned to explore in his novels serious ethical and theological issues.

His first novel, *The Sweets of Pimlico,* is a comic and touching debut that traces the relationship between Evelyn Tradescant, a young upper middle-class Cambridge graduate teaching in London, and the elderly and enigmatic Baron Theo Gormann. It was followed by *Unguarded Hours* and *Kindly Light,* highly entertaining comedies that recount the embarrassments and exploits of Norman Shotover, a shy, awkward Cambridge graduate who becomes an Anglican priest, gets mixed up with lots of girls, jumps off a cathedral tower with a hang glider, joins the CIA—the Catholic Institute of Alfonso—and plunges into a host of other improbable roles. Though relatively lightweight, Wilson's second and third novels do raise questions about the nature of modern religious institutions. The vein of comic satire is mined more substantially in *Who Was Oswald Fish?* which combines strong characterization, farce, parody, and astute observation of social change—the novel runs from the victory of Conservative leader Edward Heath in the British General Election of 1970 to that of Margaret Thatcher in 1979. Deeper emotional depths are sounded in *The Healing Art* and *Wise Virgin; The Healing Art* presents alternating narratives of two women whose X-rays have been confused at a cancer clinic, so that one of them, Pamela, believes, mistakenly, that she has but a short time to live, and the other, Dorothy, believes, again incorrectly, that she is cancer-free. Pamela, her mind concentrated by the prospect of imminent death, seeks to behave less selfishly and to develop the sort of kindness that comes more readily to Dorothy. *Wise Virgin* explores the relationship between a medieval scholar, nearing fifty, who has lost his sight, his young female research assistant who wants to marry him, and his daughter, who is herself discovering the possibilities of love. Both these novels demonstrate Wilson's capacity to combine comedy, bleakness, and tenderness in a potent and moving mixture.

Scandal is coarser black comedy, focusing on a prostitute, Bernadette Woolley, and an ambitious politician, Derek Blore, who considers treason and murder in order to save himself from damaging revelations about his masochistic indulgences. But Wilson's excursions into London lowlife in this novel are unconvincing; in particular, he is unable to find an appropriate tone for the portrayal of Bernadette and his representation of her becomes rather heartless and caricatural. *Gentlemen in England* is an indulgent but enjoyable voyage back to the Victorian era to explore generational conflicts as the cosmopolitan Marvo Chatterway disrupts the Nettleship family, and its younger members are drawn to the religion of art and to apocalyptic Christianity. Wilson returns to the modern comedy of manners with *Love Unknown,* which follows the fortunes of three women, Monica, Belinda, and Richeldis, who, twenty years before, shared a London flat, went their separate ways, and now find that their different lives are not wholly satisfactory.

Wilson's next novel broke down the barrier between his adult and children's writing: *Stray* is the vividly written autobiography of Pufftail, an alley cat, and it can be read with pleasure by all ages. It was followed by the ambitious work *The Vicar of Sorrows,* in which a clergyman who has lost his faith and his love for his wife finds himself engulfed by crisis after his mother dies and he falls for a New Age traveler. Comedy here is combined with somber renderings of emotional and spiritual distress that show Wilson moving further into the dark territory he had begun to explore in *The Healing Art* and *Wise Virgin.* The novel that appeared after *The Vicar of Sorrows* is perhaps his most powerful and disturbing to date: *Dream Children* takes up the theme of pedophilia in its account of the sexual relationship between Oliver Gold, an admired philosopher who has not realized his potential for greatness, and Bobs, a sensitive, affectionate prepubertal girl. The novel is daring in the way it evokes sympathy for Oliver even as it demonstrates the appalling nature of child abuse.

The novels *Incline Our Hearts, A Bottle in the Smoke, Daughters of Albion, Hearing Voices,* and *A Watch in the Night,* which comprise the novel sequence ''The Lampitt Chronicles,'' stand somewhat apart from Wilson's other fiction, although they share its combination of comedy and seriousness. The narrator of the quintet is the orphan Julian Ramsay, who grows up in a Norfolk vicarage, goes through prep school, public school, National Service, and eventually becomes an actor. The novels turn on Ramsay's quest for the truth about the life and death of the Edwardian writer, James Petworth Lampitt, and on the way in which the same facts may be differently interpreted—concerns that link up with Wilson's own biographical writing. The sequence moves through a range of settings in London, New York, Italy and Venice, covers a time-span that stretches from the 1930s to early in the twenty-first century, and deploys a considerable variety of characters, some of whom are thinly disguised versions of actual people. It has been compared to Anthony Powell's twelve-novel sequence, *A Dance to the Music of Time,* but this comparison is exaggerated; in contrast to Powell, we hear too much of the narrator's voice and other potentially significant characters are not given space to develop. Nonetheless, the series is admirably ambitious and richly interesting.

Wilson has now produced a substantial body of fiction. His gift for comedy ensures that his novels are consistently entertaining; but as his career has progressed, he has also shown a capacity to develop his range, to tackle large and serious themes, and to respond to contemporary social concerns, despite his initial reputation as a ''young fogey'' opposed to modern attitudes. Although he enjoys a high reputation as a biographer, Wilson feels that fiction can present truths that elude biography and history; and his novels can be seen to constitute an engaging and insightful exploration of the nature of middle and upper middle-class British identity as it encounters the complex pressures of the later twentieth century.

—Nicolas Tredell

WINTERSON, Jeanette

Nationality: British. **Born:** Lancashire in 1959. **Education:** St. Catherine's College, Oxford. **Awards:** Whitbread award, 1985; John Llewellyn Rhys Memorial prize, 1987. **Address:** c/o Bloomsbury, 2 Soho Square, London W1V 5DE, England.

PUBLICATIONS

Novels

Oranges Are Not the Only Fruit. London, Pandora Press, 1985; New York, Atlantic Monthly Press, 1987.
Boating for Beginners. London, Methuen, 1985.
The Passion. London, Bloomsbury, 1987; New York, Atlantic Monthly Press, 1988.
Sexing the Cherry. London, Bloomsbury, and New York, Atlantic Monthly Press, 1989.
Written on the Body. London, Cape, 1992; New York, Knopf, 1993.
Art and Lies. London, Cape, 1994; New York, Knopf, 1995.
Gut Symmetries. New York, Knopf, 1997.
The PowerBook. New York, Knopf, 2000.

Short Stories

The World and Other Places. New York, Knopf, 1999.

Uncollected Short Stories

''Orion,'' in *Winter's Tales 4* (new series), edited by Robin Baird-Smith. London, Constable, and New York, St. Martin's Press, 1988.
''The Green Man,'' in *The New Yorker,* 26 June-3 July 1995.

Plays

Radio Plays: *Static,* 1988.

Television Plays: *Oranges Are Not the Only Fruit* (series), from her own novel, 1990.

Other

Fit for the Future: The Guide for Women Who Want to Live Well. London, Pandora Press, 1986.
Art Objects: Critical Essays. London, Cape, and New York, Knopf, 1995.
Editor, *Passion Fruit: Romantic Fiction with a Twist.* London, Pandora Press, 1986.

*

Critical Studies: *So Far So Linear: Responses to the Work of Jeanette Winterson* by Christopher Pressler. Nottingham, England, Paupers' Press, 1997.

* * *

Jeanette Winterson is often described as one of the most controversial yet innovative fiction writers in contemporary English literature. Her promising beginnings as a young talent have been rounded off in the past decade and a half by an increasingly general acclaim. Her fiction has entered the literary canon but still resists categorization.

Winterson's is a dense epigrammatic prose rich in beautiful images and flights of fancy. Her fiction brings in a play of signifiers that result in a continuous deferral of meaning that suggests a number of alternative readings. While abounding in experimental narrative techniques and decentering strategies that have been associated with postmodernist writings, Winterson's texts also show a dialogic relationship with the modernist tradition, especially with Virginia Woolf, T. S. Eliot, and James Joyce—as manifest in her volume of essays *Art Objects*. Winterson self-consciously questions the mechanisms by which narrative texts are produced and partakes of a clear penchant for fantasy, magical realism, and the fabulous. Postmodernist techniques, modernist tradition, metafiction, and magical realism are, however, mere instruments that Winterson deftly combines with a strong political commitment aimed at subverting socio-cultural power structures and, ultimately, at appropriating traditionally male-defined concepts for her lesbian politics.

Winterson began her literary career by reinventing herself in fiction. *Oranges Are Not the Only Fruit* is her only explicitly lesbian text to date. Not surprisingly, it has been widely understood as autobiographical: it tells the story of an adopted girl, significantly called Jeanette, growing up a lesbian inside a strict religious community. *Oranges* is both the most obvious example of Winterson's realist impulse and her first conscious attempt at deconstructing the opposition reality/fiction. Her rewriting the novel into a television script completed this Indian rope trick, which allowed the flesh-and-blood author to disappear behind a double fictionalization. Reading, or watching, *Oranges* as simply autobiographical would be, then, to disregard the complexity of layers that lie behind Jeanette's/Jess's story. *Oranges* manipulates several of the monologic narratives on which mainstream culture rests. It tells the story of Jeanette's quest for subjectivity and (homo)sexuality but rejects the traditional appropriation of the theory of the subject by the masculine and emphasizes instead the mother-daughter bonding as a counter-narrative of conventional masculine bondage that highlights female specificity and gender difference.

Boating for Beginners is euphemistically called an early work, despite its having been published immediately after *Oranges*. This disdainful attitude of the critics has been fuelled by Winterson herself, who regrets having written this ''comic book'' and separates it from her fiction experiment. Full of funny sketches, *Boating* rewrites another Biblical episode, the Flood and Noah's Ark. In Winterson's fiction, God has not created men, it is Noah that makes God ''by accident out of a piece of gateau and a giant electric toaster.'' Told by a homodiegetic adolescent female narrator, Gloria, who struggles to find her own identity in a world of distorted fictions that pass for unquestionable realities, the story has many issues in common with *Oranges*. It is, above all, a demystification of religion, romantic love, and heterosexuality. Gloria, together with the reader, learns to distrust all these long-established truths and to re-evaluate the neglected potential of storytelling.

''Stories were all we had,'' says Henri, the male protagonist of Winterson's *The Passion*, which together with *Sexing the Cherry* constitute two examples of ''historiographic metafiction.'' In these two novels Winterson expands on her quarrel with the nature of time, the instability of the self, love and desire, narrative, and historical discourse that she had initiated in *Oranges*: ''History should be a hammock for swinging and a game for playing, the way cats play. Claw it, chew it, rearrange it.'' If history is discourse, the notions of objectivity and verisimilitude no longer hold. History is shown to be subjective, limited, biased and open to revision and recontextualization. *The Passion* is situated in the aftermath of the French Revolution and the rise and fall of Napoleon Bonaparte. It combines the life stories of two character-narrators, Henri, a French soldier-cook from the ranks and files of Bonaparte, and Villanelle, a Venetian bisexual woman who has webbed feet like the men in her society. Set in Puritan England in the years of the English Civil War, the Great Plague, and the Great Fire of London, *Sexing the Cherry* is also told by two different voices, the Rabelaisian Dog Woman—a sublime portrait of excess that was prefigured by Jeanette's mother in *Oranges*—and Jordan, a foundling brought by the river to the childless Dog Woman, who travels both physically and mentally in search of his flying self—represented in the story by Fortunata, one of the Twelve Dancing Princesses. In both texts Winterson blends high and low art by pairing T. S. Eliot's *Four Quartets* with Tarot cards and fairy tales. By means of intertextuality, Winterson exposes linguistic and narrative conventions and provides alternative versions of history that focus on groups of people who have been marginalized by official history.

Written on the Body explores the nature of love, desire, and sexuality at the same time as it experiments with the limits of narrative by taking structure away. Having proved in her previous fictions that there is no such thing as a univocal fixed sexual identity, Winterson's character-narrator is unnamed and ungendered. Its story—an obsessive passion for a married woman, Louise, who has decided to leave her husband, a cancer-researcher, but who may be dying from leukemia—is not set in a particular place or time. There is no suspense because the whole story is already revealed in the first pages of the book. *Written on the Body* is Winterson's proof that a story should not be reduced to its plot, that conventions and clichés in narrative do not make good books just as conventions and clichés are useless when talking about love. Winterson's account of abnegation and loss in *Written on the Body* is an overt critique of romance narratives with their long established sexual roles, their happy endings, and their formulaic expressions. Winterson demonstrates that true love is original and poetic even when the lover resorts to anatomy textbooks for its imagery.

The nature of love, time, and art are again at the core of *Art and Lies*, a difficult book that has received the harshest criticism together with the most passionate acclamation of the author's oeuvre. The book is a time travel experience for the reader, who shares a high-speed train with Picasso, a young artist escaping from a sexually and emotionally abusive family; Handel, a disillusioned priest turned breast surgeon; and Sappho, the historical poet who, like Woolf's *Orlando*, has been alive since antiquity. As the title suggests, *Art and Lies* is more of a philosophical digression about art as artifice and invention than a story in the traditional sense of the term. It criticizes the Platonic notion of art as mimesis and reverences the power of the word. For Winterson art and, by extension, literature, do not simply reflect reality but construct it in and through language. Therefore art and literature not only have the potential but also the responsibility to change givens by opening up endless, more comprehensive possibilities.

Literature becomes multi-dimensional and cosmic in *Gut Symmetries*. Like *Art and Lies* the story is told by three different voices, each giving a particular version of the ''events.'' Stella and Jove are a married couple but they ''live on different planets.'' Stella refuses passion because feelings are always painful. Jove is a renowned physicist who works in a new model of the cosmos and lectures on time travel and ''The World and Other Places.'' Alice, also a physicist, brings in a double love affair as she falls in love with both Jove and Stella. Stella, Jove, and Alice are placed in a floating space, a boat, where everything is unstable. There is no conventional plotline, characters are not too convincing, and there is no passion in their love affairs. Passion, though, oozes from Winterson's dense poetic writing, which sublimates the eternal love triangle by making it a part of physics' Grand Unified Theory, the metaphor contained in the title of the book. *Gut Symmetries* is structured by Tarot cards, alchemy, and cabalistic theology, on the one hand, and by quantum physics and geometry on the other. The result seems to be a world that is both real and virtual, material and philosophical.

Apart from being the title of Jove's lecture in *Gut Symmetries, The World and Other Places* is Winterson's only collection of short stories, an open window to Winterson's creative trajectory. Written over a period of twelve years beginning soon after the publication of *Oranges*, these stories chart Winterson's preoccupation with the nature of time, the nature of love in its multiple forms, the search for the self as journey or quest, and the figure of the outsider either in the form of a stranger or because a character is marginalized by society. All these are not only key issues but also leitmotifs in each of Winterson's fictions. It is not surprising, then, that some of these stories prefigure Winterson's major books. ''The Three Friends'' is an especially significant example in this respect because it is an interlude in *Gut Symmetries* and resonates with echoes of *The Passion* and *Sexing the Cherry*. Like Jove, Winterson keeps on experimenting on a new model of the cosmos free from the constricting power of gravity. Her fiction transports her readers into a space where time is suspended. Her critical poise, her wonderful way with words, and her ability for outrageous humor are all at the service of feeling and imagination.

—Mar Asensio-Aróstegui

WINTON, Tim

Nationality: Australian. **Born:** Karrinyup, Western Australia, 1960. **Education:** Western Australian Institute of Technology. **Awards:** *Australian*/Vogel award, 1981, for *An Open Swimmer;* Miles Franklin award, 1984, for *Shallows;* Deo Gloria award, 1991, WA Premiers award, 1991, National Book Council's Banjo award, 1992, and Miles Franklin award, 1992, all for *Cloudstreet.* **Address:** c/o Pan Macmillan, Level 18, St. Martin's Tower, 31 Market St., Sydney, New South Wales 2000, Australia.

PUBLICATIONS

Novels

An Open Swimmer. Sydney, Allen and Unwin, 1982.
Shallows. Sydney, Unwin, 1985; London, Weidenfeld and Nicolson, and New York, Atheneum, 1986.
That Eye, the Sky. Melbourne, McPhee Gribble, New York, Atheneum, and London, Weidenfeld and Nicolson, 1986.
In the Winter Dark. Melbourne, McPhee Gribble, 1988; London, Weidenfeld and Nicolson, 1989.
Cloudstreet. London, Picador, 1991; Saint Paul, Minnisota, Graywolf Press, 1992.
The Riders. New York, Scribner, and London, Picador, 1995.
Blueback: A Contemporary Fable. New York, Scribner, 1997.

Short Stories

Scission. Fitzroy, Victoria, McPhee Gribble, 1985; as *Scission and Other Stories,* London, Weidenfeld and Nicolson, 1987.
Minimum of Two. Fitzroy, Victoria, McPhee Gribble, 1987; New York, Atheneum, and London, Weidenfeld and Nicolson, 1988.
Blood and Water. London, Picador, 1993.

Other

Jesse (for children). N.p., 1989.
Lockie Leonard, Human Torpedo (for children). N.p., Bodley Head, 1990; Boston, Little Brown, 1991.
Local Colour: Travels in Australia, with Bill Bachman. London, Allen and Unwin, 1994.

* * *

Tim Winton is perhaps the most precocious and prolific novelist Australia has yet produced. Born in 1960, he published his first novel, *An Open Swimmer,* at the age of twenty-two and has subsequently gone on to publish more than a dozen books of fiction, including several for children. *An Open Swimmer* seems, like much of Winton's early fiction, to have been influenced by Hemingway, though Winton denies this and says he owes far more to fellow western Australian writer Randolph Stow. Its protagonist Jerra, short for Jeremiah, is a former admirer of *The Old Man and the Sea,* to which there are two references, and the novel takes laconicism almost to the point of silence. At one point the author even acknowledges this: ''It was apathetic conversation, even for them.'' Not just Jerra and his mate Sean but all of the handful of characters in the novel speak in monosyllables, sparingly dished out, and the laconicism is carried over into the narrative voice of the novel as well. The spare, unadorned factuality of the writing is fleshed out with a few pervasive metaphors, the most important of which is the pearl that can sometimes be found in a kingfisher's head when it is cut open, but the theme of the novel is unclear, unless it is Jerra's sexual traumas, perhaps unwillingness to embrace the world of adulthood generally. As with much of Winton's work, the most interesting element is the preoccupation with landscape and especially seascape.

Set in the town of Angelus in the southern part of western Australia, Winton's second novel, *Shallows* (which won the Miles Franklin Award for best Australian novel of the year), deals with the conflict between whalers and a band of environmentalists who set out to disrupt the already dying industry. As *The Old Man and the Sea* provided a kind of reference point for the earlier novel, so *Moby-Dick* does for this. The novel cuts deliberately from character to character, as *Shallows* alternated between past and present. There are the young couple, Cleveland and Queenie Cookson, Queenie's father Daniel Coupar, the egregious Des Pustling and his reluctant girlfriend Marion Lowell, and the aged Presbyterian clergyman William Pell. There is a prologue set in 1831, and Winton also makes use of the diary of Daniel Coupart's grandfather, Nathaniel, which has been given to Cleve. The central conflict is between Cleve and Queenie but it springs up almost too quickly for plausibility and is dissolved at the end in a similarly peremptory manner. In the course of the narrative

Queenie becomes steadily stronger while Cleve deteriorates morally, so that their final upbeat reunion, with Queenie pregnant by him, seems to have an imposed quality. The vision of life the novel offers is perhaps best summed up by Daniel Coupar: ''It's having the choices that kills a man. It's the best and the worst. You get to choose and you get to regret. Almost guaranteed to bugger it up. And sometimes not.''

Jerra reappears in *Scission,* Winton's first collection of short stories. The epigraphs, this time coming from *The Book of Job* and *East Coker,* suggest the increasing importance of Christian belief in Winton's work. Again the style is spare, restrained, attempting to suggest or imply unstated significances; most of the stories are very short. Domesticity—of a young couple, of father and son—and especially its fragility is often the main concern. In the final, title story, the preoccupation with ''scissions'' of various kinds is taken even into the writing itself, its style and structure acting out the sense of a mind incapable of ordering its experience. The rather awkward title of *That Eye, the Sky* refers to those who have aspiration or faith. The sky or its absence is constantly referred to throughout the novel: ''I go out and look at the sky but it's blank; no stars, nothing,'' the novel's twelve-year-old narrator, Morton (''Ort'') Flack, says despairingly at one point near the end. No matter. This is the most explicitly Christian of Winton's works to date, the culmination of the movement that led to the affirmations in many of the stories in *Scission.* There is literally a *deus ex machina* in the unlikely person of Henry Warburton, former poet and hippy and now evangelist and car thief as well as the seducer of Ort's renegade sister, Tegwyn, with whom he flees at the end of the novel. When Henry finally runs away for the second time and the family discovers that the car he brought back has been stolen, all would seem to be lost, but it is then that Ort experiences his epiphany. He sees his stricken father: ''His eyes are open and they're on me and smiling as I come in shouting 'God! God! God!' His face is shining. I'm shaking all over. 'God! God! God!'''

The title of *Minimum of Two,* Winton's second collection of stories, refers to the sentence a rapist receives in the title story—''five years with a minimum before parole of two.'' Although one of the longest, at fifteen pages, it is also one of the weakest stories in this rather undernourished collection, the strongest point of which is its continuity with Winton's earlier fiction. In ''Laps,'' for instance, we meet Queenie Cookson and her husband seven years after the events narrated in *Shallows.* More commonly, the protagonists are Jerra and, by implication, in ''A Measure of Eloquence,'' his wife Rachel, their son Sam, and friends Ann and Philip. The story ''Gravity'' refers directly to when the honeymooning couple stayed in Jerra's shack. Jerra himself is now something of a mess. After trying to make it as a musician he seems burned-out, living off the dole, resentful of his parents and full of self-pity. The final story takes us back in time to the agonizingly painful birth of Sam. ''Blood and Water'' reminds us of the dedication of the book to Winton's wife and child in its graphic, impressionist account of childbirth. Elsewhere, though, the prose takes on the familiar cadences of Hemingway, as in this passage from ''Forest Winter'': ''He had been broken once before, years back, when he was still half a boy, and he knew that when you were beaten properly, you didn't get up; you had to wait for some obscure grace to put you together, and there was no guarantee it would come by a second time.'' That ''obscure grace'' is the key to Winton's vision.

In the Winter Dark is unusual among Winton's fiction, a short, barely novella-length account by an old man of a series of horrifying events that took place almost a year ago. Of the four people involved, two are now dead, the narrator Maurice Stubbs is tortured by incessant nightmares, and Murray Jaccob, his neighbor in the isolated valley known as the Sink, is drinking himself to death. Something or someone, we slowly learn, has been killing and disemboweling the animals in the area, but when Maurice and his wife, Jaccob, and a pregnant young woman named Ronnie collaborate to hunt it down they are unsuccessful, as their own private fears and guilts from the past take over. The novel is a skillful study in suspense.

Cloudstreet, perhaps Winton's most impressive and substantial novel, won him a second Miles Franklin Award. It is the most ambitious of his works, not only in terms of its length and in the time it covers (roughly 1943 to 1964), but also in its extraordinary gallery of characters and in the stylistic experiments that are new to Winton's fiction and seem to move him almost into the realms of magic realism. The novel is the story of two families named Lamb and Pickles (Winton has a lot of fun with names in this novel), who move into a huge house at no. 1 Cloud Street and bicker and love their way through two decades of Australian history. Lester and Oriel Lamb are God-fearing people who give thanks to the Lord when their son Fish comes back from drowning—except that not all of Fish Lamb has come back, his brain having been left behind in the sea. Sam and Dolly Pickles, on the other hand, are a feckless couple who fail to prosper. Sam loses most of the fingers of one hand in an episode of violence characteristic of this novel and takes to gambling; Dolly is an alcoholic. Winton covers the history of both sets of parents and their numerous offspring in numerous short episodes, some comic, others near tragic.

The style of the novel varies. There are sections written in the present tense, sudden bursts of lyricism, passages of interior monologue, and a great deal of slightly heightened Australian vernacular. Winton is also fond of bizarre and incongruous juxtapositions, often of a comically macabre kind: ''His mother came in to find him stuffing the old boy's dentures in. He stopped rigid, they exchanged looks, and it appeared with the upper plate the way it was, that the old man had died eating a small piano.'' There are also ventures into fabulism: the house in which they live gives out sighs, a pig speaks in Pentecostal tongues, a woman sets up house in a tent in the backyard. If there is a sustaining theme running through the novel it is the various views of chance and the contingent that the two families hold. For Sam Pickles, luck is ''the shifty shadow of God,'' which ''you do your best to stay out of the way of.'' Whereas with the Lambs, there is ''making luck, the hardest ... yacker there is.''

The Riders is Winton's most baffling novel, though it is also quite exhilarating to read. A young Australian man named Scully labors in the novel's first section to restore a house in Ireland that he has bought on the whim of his wife. He is sustained in his labor by the thought of her imminent arrival as well as that of their seven-year-old daughter, Billie, but when he finally gets to the airport only his daughter is there, too traumatized to explain what has happened. The rest of the novel is concerned with Scully's demented chase all over Europe—Greece, Italy, France, Holland, England—in search of his missing wife, a search that is finally left unresolved.

Winton's account of Scully's quest is as electrifying as it is implausible. Scully himself may embody all the possibilities, play all the roles that his creator suggests—''working-class boofhead with a wife who married beneath herself,'' ''hairy bohemian with a beautiful family,'' ''mongrel expat with the homesick twang and ambitious missus,'' ''poor decent-hearted bastard who couldn't see the roof coming down on his head.'' It is not possible to decide who or what he is because his behavior and personality change from moment to moment as he is violently propelled through the next series of dramatic events. Whatever he is, he behaves with a quite exceptional stupidity that, like much else in this novel, remains as mysterious as the imagery of the night riders that runs through the novel.

Blueback: A Contemporary Fable is the story of a boy and a blue grouper, the title character. It is not so much a novel as a tract, a call for environmental responsibility, and the spare, clean quality of Winton's language here is not helped by the use of preachy messages such as "there was nothing in nature as cruel and savage as a greedy human being." Yet this book, too, contains themes common to Winton's best work. The motif of the quest or the odyssey is present in most of his fiction, especially as it concerns the quest in search of the self. Also central is the tension between a sense of the importance of chance and the contingent in life and the wavering faith in some kind of force that imposes order upon the universe. Perhaps this is what Winton's protagonist senses in the riders he glimpses again at the end of the novel: "He knew them now and he saw that they would be here every night seen and unseen, patient, dogged faithful in all weathers and all worlds, waiting for something promised, something that was plainly their due, but he knew that as surely as he felt Billie tugging on him, curling her fingers in his and pulling them easily away, that he would not be among them and must never be, in life or death."

—Laurie Clancy, updated by Judson Knight

WOIWODE, Larry (Alfred)

Nationality: American. **Born:** Carrington, North Dakota, 30 October 1941. **Education:** University of Illinois, Urbana, 1959–64, A.A. 1964. **Family:** Married Carole Ann Peterson in 1965; four children. **Career:** Actor in Miami and New York, 1964–65; writer-in-residence, University of Wisconsin, Madison, 1973–74; visiting professor, Wheaton College, Illinois, summers 1981 and 1984; visiting professor, 1983–84, professor of English, 1984–88, director of the Writing Program, 1985–88, and co-director of the semester in London program, Spring 1988, State University of New York, Binghamton. Since 1988 professor of English, Beth-El Institute for the Arts and Sciences, Carson, North Dakota. Since 1978 farmer-rancher in western North Dakota, raising grains, sheep, and quarter horses. **Awards:** MacDowell fellowship, 1965; Faulkner Foundation award, 1969; Guggenheim fellowship, 1971; American Academy award, 1980; *Southern Review* award, for *The Neumiller Stories,* 1990; Aga Khan prize (*Paris Review*), 1990; John Dos Passos prize, for a literary body of work, 1991; Award of Merit, American Academy of Arts and Letters, 1995. D.Litt.: North Dakota State University, Fargo, 1977. **Agent:** Candida Donadio and Associates, 231 West 22nd Street, New York, New York 10011, U.S.A. **Address:** Route 1, Box 57, Mott, North Dakota, 57646, U.S.A.

Publications

Novels

What I'm Going to Do, I Think. New York, Farrar Straus, 1969; London, Weidenfeld and Nicholson, 1970.
Beyond the Bedroom Wall: A Family Album. New York, Farrar Straus, 1975.
Poppa John. New York, Farrar Straus, 1981.
Born Brothers. New York, Farrar Straus, 1988.
Indian Affairs. New York, Atheneum/Macmillan, 1991.

Short Stories

The Neumiller Stories. New York, Farrar Straus, 1989.
Silent Passengers. New York, Atheneum/Macmillan, 1993.

Uncollected Short Story

"Summer Storms," in *Paris Review,* Spring 1990.

Poetry

Poetry North: Five North Dakota Poets, with others. Fargo, North Dakota Institute for Regional Studies, 1970.
Even Tide. New York, Farrar Straus, 1977.

Other

Acts. San Francisco, HarperSanFrancisco, 1993.
What I Think I Did: A Season of Survival in Two Acts (memoir). New York, Basic Books, 2000.
The Aristocrat of the West: Biography of Harold Schafer. Fargo, North Dakota Institute for Regional Studies, 2000.

*

Manuscript Collection: Allen Memorial Library, Valley City State University, North Dakota.

Larry Woiwode comments:

(1981) I believe that prose should be set down so that the readers sees through it to the book's essential action: a fireplace screen behind which the blaze burns, as I've expressed it elsewhere. Yet I work in my books to make the prose do as much as it is able, in realms of rhythm, imagery, and underlying sound. If this seems a paradox, it perhaps is; it sometimes feels so as I work. But I believe that our language, and its heritage, is too rich to be relegated to the utilitarian. Besides trying to keep up on contemporaries and present trends, I like to read in the century of our language's flowering, in the Elizabethans and metaphysical poets, for instance, and all of the early novelists and novels, such as *Pilgrim's Progress.* Its structure is still valid and its language full of sparks.

In my books I try to convey the contours and textures of life as it's lived. Each book is a separate entity with its special demands, since each is lived by a different character, or series of them. The rhythm of every sentence of the six-hundred-and-some pages of *Beyond the Bedroom Wall* is modulated to fit the voice that speaks it. Or there was a conscious attempt to make this so. What I want to do in my fiction, with the help of the prose I work at, is to keep all of the reader's senses informed on every moment that he lives within a certain character's skin. This world we breathe. I expect a reader to emerge from my work affected, if not with a change of heart.

* * *

Larry Woiwode's second novel, *Beyond the Bedroom Wall,* is sure to be ranked as one of the great achievements of American fiction of the 1970s. It is a midwestern novel, an American novel, a universal novel. It spans four generations, and could be set in almost any century. The book's significant events emerge out of the natural histories of human beings. It is about births and deaths, love and courtship, joy and grief, motherhood and fatherhood, childhood, adolescence, old age. It is about strength of character, spoiled character, redeemed character. It is about hardship and work, competence and incompetence, faith and distrust. It is about provincial bigotry and the lot of a Catholic family in a town of Methodists. It is about enduring.

Otto Neumiller emigrated from Germany in 1881. He went all the way to the Dakota plain, where he prospered and then lost most of what he had gained. In his old age, he is lonely and envied and unloved by his neighbors. His son Charles returns to the homestead to attend him at his death. In one of the book's finest chapters, Woiwode shows Charles at work making his father's coffin, lovingly washing and dressing his father's body, burying him in the unhallowed ground of the farm he loved. Like his father, Charles Neumiller has been a devout Catholic all his life; and so is Charles's son Martin. Most of the novel is the story of Martin, his wife Alpha, who dies at 34, and their six children. The older children, the fourth generation, are off on their own in the 1970s.

The great strength of this novel is in Woiwode's rendering of the commonplace. The Neumiller family may be a bit more intelligent and may perhaps possess more fortitude than the average family, but they are not particularly special. In addition to the virtues, there certainly are waywardness, carelessness, and ill-considered, impulsive behavior among them. Indeed, one of the beautiful ironies in the novel is that it is the ill-considered decision of Martin, usually so steady and prudent, to move his family from North Dakota to Illinois that brings disaster to the family, including ultimately his beloved wife's death. But the fabric of the novel is made of such scenes as the father's telling stories to his children, the father's being overcome with frustration and kicking one of his sons viciously, the acting out of guilt feelings brought on by the nearly fatal illness of a child. An important motif running through the novel is the family's emotional involvement with each of the various houses in which they live.

The marriage of Martin and Alpha is old-fashioned and ordinary. Except for what is done by acts of nature, it is a marriage that is not susceptible to disruption. This man and this woman become totally entangled with each other, and regardless of what befalls them they cannot imagine themselves married to anyone else. To Martin and Alpha, marriage is for better or for worse, forever.

Even in bulk Woiwode's first novel, *What I'm Going to Do, I Think,* is not half the novel that *Beyond the Bedroom Wall* is. It has a small cast of characters, with the focus rarely leaving Chris or Ellen; it does not range over generations, but is concerned with only a few seasons in the lives of its young couple. It is lyrical and symbolic; unfortunately it is also murky. Its central situation is commonplace: the young woman is pregnant and the couple marry. They take an extended honeymoon at an isolated lodge up in northern Michigan. Only then does the nature of the commitment he has made become real to Chris. He is not single anymore; he must take account of another person. He is uncertain about which emotions to share and which to conceal. He experiences much anger, resentment, and frustration, but he does not know what to do with such feelings in the new context. Their physical relationship is different under the blanket of marriage; expectation, disappointment, jealously, and fulfillment have a new texture. Neither Chris nor Ellen has had an appropriate model for the roles of husband and wife; Chris, especially, suffers as a result.

Both had unusual childhoods. Ellen's parents were killed in an accident, and she has been raised by four grandparents. Chris's alienation from his parents is so severe that he hardly ever thinks of them; he does not invite them to his wedding, and he does not attend his mother's funeral. It is the quality of Chris's earlier life that is suggested by the title of the novel. The words are part of a remark made by his father when Chris has hurt himself being clumsy at a chore. What his father thinks he is going to do is get himself a new kid.

The child Ellen is carrying is born dead. When Ellen calls her grandmother for consolation, she is told that this is the ''wages of sin.'' Chris and Ellen do not have another child. The novel ends with the suggestion that Chris always will be a troubled man and that the marriage will not bring fulfillment or much joy to husband or wife. The lives of Chris and Ellen will never have the richness of the lives of Martin and Alpha. Standing by itself, the earlier novel does not have a meaning that clearly emerges from the interaction of character and plot. When it is put beside *Beyond the Bedroom Wall,* its theme is quite clear: without firm familial commitments, modern life will exact constant feelings of despair and loss.

In *Indian Affairs,* Woiwode picks up where he left off in his very first novel. It is seven years later, and Chris and Ellen are having normal marital problems. The general plot is interesting, but the many subplots are distracting and unnecessary. Woiwode's collection of stories *Silent Passengers* deals, once again, with midwestern family stories. Readers can see many threads of father-son relationships and how they influence other family members.

At his best, Woiwode renders the commonplace with such emotional and psychological truth that all the reader's capacity for empathy and compassion is tapped. Woiwode often demonstrates marvelous descriptive power; at his best, his readers see and feel and learn with him, making easy transfers of their fictional experience to their own lives.

—Paul Marx, updated by Loretta Cobb

WOLFE, Tom

Nationality: American. **Born:** Thomas Kennerly Wolfe, Jr. in Richmond, Virginia, 2 March 1930. **Education:** Washington and Lee University, Lexington, Virginia, A.B. (cum laude) 1951; Yale University, New Haven, Connecticut, Ph.D. 1957. **Family:** Married Sheila Berger Wolfe in 1978; one daughter and one son. **Career:** Reporter, Springfield *Union,* Massachusetts, 1956–59, Washington *Post,* 1959–62, and New York, *Herald Tribune,* 1962–66; writer, New York *World Journal Tribune,* 1966–67. **Awards:** American Book award, 1980; Columbia award, for journalism, 1980; National Sculpture Society citation for art history, 1980; John Dos Passos award, 1984; Gari Melchers medal, 1986; Benjamin Pierce Cheney medal, Eastern Washington University, 1986; Washington Irving medal, St. Nicholas Society, 1986; Theodore Roosevelt medal, Theodore Roosevelt Association, 1990; Wilbur Cross medal, Yale Graduate School Alumni Association, 1990; St. Louis Literary award, 1990; Quinnipiac College Presidential award, 1993. D.Litt.: Washington and Lee University, 1974; St. Andrews Presbyterian College, 1990; Johns Hopkins University, 1990; University of Richmond, 1993. Honorary D.F.A: Minneapolis College of Art, 1971; School of Visual Arts, 1987. L.H.D: Virginia Commonwealth University,

1983; Southampton College, 1984; Randolph-Macon College, 1988; Manhattanville College, 1988; Longwood College, 1989. **Agent:** Lynn Nesbit, Janklow and Nesbit, 598 Madison Avenue, New York, New York 10022, U.S.A.

PUBLICATIONS

Novels

The Bonfire of the Vanities. New York, Farrar Straus, 1987; London, Cape, 1988.
A Man In Full. New York, Farrar, Straus and Giroux, 1998.

Uncollected Short Stories

''The Commercial,'' in *Esquire* (New York), October 1975.
''2020 A.D.,'' in *Esquire* (New York), January 1985.

Plays

Screenplays: *Almost Heroes* (with Mark Nutter and Boiyd Hale). Warner Brothers, 1998.

Other

The Kandy-Kolored Tangerine Flake Streamline Baby (essays). New York, Farrar Straus, 1965; London, Cape, 1966.
The Electric Kool-Aid Acid Test. New York, Farrar Straus, and London, Weidenfeld and Nicolson, 1968.
The Pump House Gang (essays). New York, Farrar Straus, 1968; as *The Mid-Atlantic Man and Other New Breeds in England and America,* London, Weidenfeld and Nicolson, 1969.
Radical Chic and Mau-Mauing the Flak Catchers. New York, Farrar Straus, 1970; London, Joseph, 1971.
The Painted Word. New York, Farrar Straus, 1975.
Mauve Gloves and Madmen, Clutter and Vine, and Other Stories (essays). New York, Farrar Straus, 1976.
The Right Stuff. New York, Farrar Straus, and London, Cape, 1979.
In Our Time (essays). New York, Farrar Straus, 1980.
From Bauhaus to Our House. New York, Farrar Straus, 1981; London, Cape, 1982.
Editor, with E.W. Johnson, *The New Journalism.* New York, Harper, 1973; London, Pan, 1975.

*

Critical Studies: ''Tom Wolfe's Vanities'' by Joseph Epstein, in *New Criterion* (New York), February 1988; *Tom Wolfe* by William McKeen, New York, Twayne Publishers, 1995.

* * *

In a world concerned with high tech gadgetry, the Internet, and the latest IPO, Tom Wolfe is a true literary superstar. His 1998 novel, *A Man in Full,* had a first printing of 1.2 million copies and was nominated for the National Book Award a month before it was even released. The subsequent buzz surrounding Wolfe's tale of high society life in Atlanta reached deafening levels and propelled the book to the top of every bestseller list.

But, the inevitable backlash against someone with Wolfe's selling power is intense. In fact, some of America's foremost writers, including John Updike, Norman Mailer, and John Irving, all took Wolfe to task for *A Man in Full.* Their comments centered on whether Wolfe's work was literature or merely entertainment. For his part, Wolfe responded with his typical acerbic wit, telling the New York Post, ''The lead dog is the one they always try to bite in the ass.'' The literary feud is one that will assuredly be played out for years to come.

Perhaps part of Wolfe's enduring popularity is that he exudes charisma, style, and an inherent coolness that most authors cannot duplicate. He is a master at spotting the next trend or finding the perfect words to describe the big picture and big events, like dubbing the 1970s ''The Me Decade.'' He made his reputation by investigating subjects that have since become part of the national popular culture pantheon, like the acid tripping days of the 1960s and fighter pilots in *The Right Stuff.*

By the early 1960s, Wolfe was already the most famous journalist of his day and chief proponent of ''New Journalism,'' which held that good reporting should have as much style and flair as a work of fiction. In fact, Wolfe lambasted novelists for studying their own ''gullets,'' instead of tackling the larger issues that make up the grand spectacle of modern life. Decades later, assessing his criticism of the modern novel, Wolfe said, ''I said if the novel is to survive, it will have to be a form that will be known as a documentary or journalistic novel, based on deep and heavy reporting. In my humble opinion, I have been absolutely right.''

Leaving journalism behind, Wolfe joined the novelists to show them how it should be done. In 1987, he debuted with *The Bonfire of the Vanities,* a work every bit as wide in scope and weighty in content as some of the heavy-wrought productions against which he had once railed. The book though, represents more an exploitation of the novel form than a homage to it, and, in its hurtling Technicolor progress through a world in which the horrible maxim is ''All for one and one for all and lots for oneself!'' settled a few unanswered questions about the nature of Wolfe's output.

The Electric Kool-Aid Acid Test, upon which his original reputation rested, was not so much reportage as biographical improvisation. While it relied more heavily on historical fact than most novels, and was every jumpy inch as distorted and disjointed as the hallucinogenically-induced experiences it sought to describe.

Ultimately, Wolfe's first novel-length outing was utterly dependent on his own imaginative vibrancy. Valuable not only as an insight into the addled consciousness of fellow experimentalist Ken Kesey, Wolfe's tract remains, in all its fragmentary, speeding glory, the outstanding document of 1960s counterculture. Not only an exploration into the wild lifestyle of Kesey's Merry Pranksters, but a catalogue of the pressures which caused the embryonic hippie movement to self-combust.

Wolfe's writing in subsequent years honed new journalism's thick stew of style and content. The reader is invited to trace the growth of Wolfe's technique and the development of a highly intuitive perceptive gift, whether it is eyeing California's junior surf bums as they chill out on the extra-good vibe of being independent at 14 and living in low-rent garages, journeying through America's car-customizing shops and small-town racetracks, or cresting the adrenal wave of being very young and hip in swinging London.

During the 1970s, Wolfe's inquisitive ardor seems to have diminished somewhat. Fixing his attention on other areas of criticism,

Wolfe turned in some surprisingly flat period pieces. In *Mauve Gloves and Madmen, Clutter and Vine,* however, he enjoyed a renaissance. Kicking off with a ritual dismemberment of a major author, and ending with a prophetic tale about the selfishness and ruthlessness of Manhattan cab-hailers, Wolfe roamed, among other things, through a dissertation on one woman's hemorrhoids, the story of a Navy pilot risking his life on a daily basis over North Vietnam, and a genuinely funny piece of short fiction concerning one black athlete's efforts to make a conscionable perfume commercial.

In 1979, entering yet another brain-warping space, Wolfe produced an effortless and enthralling, warts and all history of America's launch into the stars. *The Right Stuff,* borne out of Wolfe's ''ordinary curiosity'' remains his best-written and most complete book, consummately encapsulating, in all seriousness, the adventurous spirit of the age. As in previous works, functioning on the intimate level of fraternity tale—Tom, the clever brother, is the wise spectator, while the rest of the gang goes off running and jumping into colorful and phenomenal dangers; in this case, sitting atop a huge stick of dynamite, waiting ''for someone to light the fuse.'' A must for vicarious thrill seekers everywhere (although not as appealing, probably to animal rights activists), *The Right Stuff* is Wolfe's second absolutely indispensable book—as vital to the social historian as the reader with only the most limited interest in space flight.

The Bonfire of the Vanities, like everything Wolfe has done, seeks to hold up a mirror to contemporary life and shout ''There! That's what it's like.'' Sherman McCoy's noisy descent from a cloud of privilege and wealth into the purgatorial netherworld of New York's criminal justice system is fitting reward for his participation in ''the greed storm'' of the consumerist 1980s.

Wolfe's incisive political awareness, his desire to penetrate the ''thickening democratic façade'' is equally as urgent as in his earlier denunciation of white liberal angst *Radical Chic* (further, his understanding of what makes the underclasses tick is piercing). McCoy, a cartoon-like central character is pitched on a spiraling express ride into the deepest, most decrepit tunnels of urban deprivation, becoming the victim of the startling contrast between what he is capable of possessing and what others cannot hope to touch. McCoy's culpability matters little: it is significant only that he is suitably placed to become a totemic sacrifice in a political game. For this fact alone, Wolfe finally offers him a ragged salvation while damning most everyone else.

A Man in Full is the story of Atlanta real estate magnate Charlie Croker, who has overextended his means building an edge-city tower to himself, ''Croker Concourse,'' that no one wants to rent. Croker stands on the verge of losing everything. The story also intertwines the fates of a blue-collar worker in one of Croker's plants, a black Georgia Tech football star, and plenty of lawyers, bankers, and politicians.

Like all of Wolfe's oeuvre, *A Man in Full* attacks the 1990s with vigor. Wolfe's satirical eye is fixed on Croker's 29,000-acre quail-hunting plantation, his trophy wife, and vacuous associates. But, throughout the book, the author also tackles race relations, the decline of urban neighborhoods, rap music, and suburban life. In short, Wolfe allows the reader to glimpse the modern world as it exists, both its foibles and triumphs.

Wolfe has held tenure as arbiter of style, master of the idiom, observer and interpreter of signs, symbols, and portents for more than four decades. He is a rare individual who actually laid out a bodacious blueprint for changing modern literature, and then showed us that it could be done through his own masterful works.

Despite the ongoing quarrel with his colleagues, Wolfe must be regarded as one of the top novelists of the twentieth century. It will be interesting to see whether young writers take his advice and move toward journalistic novels. While the book world eagerly anticipates the next big author, it will be difficult for someone to duplicate the success of Wolfe.

—Ian McMechan, updated by Bob Batchelor

WOLFF, Tobias (Jonathan Ansell)

Nationality: American. **Born:** Birmingham, Alabama, 19 June 1945. **Education:** Hill School, 1964; Oxford University, B.A. 1972, M.A. 1975; Stanford University, California, M.A. 1977. **Military Service:** Served in the United States Army, 1964–68: Lieutenant. **Family:** Married Catherine Dolores Spohn in 1975; two sons and one daughter. **Career:** Jones Lecturer in creative writing, Stanford University, (Stegner fellow), 1975–78; since 1980 Peck Professor of English, Syracuse University, New York. **Awards:** National Endowment fellowship, 1978, 1985; Rinehart grant, 1979; O. Henry award, for short story, 1980, 1981, 1985; St. Lawrence award, 1981; Guggenheim fellowship, 1982; PEN/Faulkner award, 1985; Rea award, for short story, 1989; Whiting Foundation award, 1990; Lila Wallace-Reader's Digest award, 1994; Lyndhurst Foundation award, 1994; Esquire-Volvo-Waterstone's award, 1994. **Agent:** Amanda Urban, International Creative Management, 40 West 57th Street, New York, New York 10019.

Publications

Novel

The Barracks Thief. New York, Ecco Press, 1984; London, Cape, 1987.

Short Stories

In the Garden of the North American Martyrs. New York, Ecco Press, 1981; as *Hunters in the Snow,* London, Cape, 1982.
Back in the World. Boston, Houghton Mifflin, 1985.
The Night in Question: Stories. New York, Knopf, 1996.

Uncollected Short Stories

''The Other Miller,'' in *The Best American Short Stories 1987,* edited by Ann Beattie and Shannon Ravenel. Boston, Houghton Mifflin, 1987.
''Smorgasbord,'' in *The Best American Short Stories 1988,* edited by Mark Helprin and Shannon Ravenel. Boston, Houghton Mifflin, 1988.
''Migraine,'' in *Antaeus* (New York), Spring-Autumn, 1990.
''Sanity,'' in *Atlantic* (Boston), December 1990.

Other

Ugly Rumours. London, Allen and Unwin, 1975.
This Boy's Life: A Memoir. New York, Atlantic Monthly Press, and London, Bloomsbury, 1989.

In Pharaoh's Army: Memories of the Lost War. New York, Knopf, and London, Bloomsbury, 1994.
Editor, *Matters of Life and Death: New American Short Stories.* Green Harbor, Massachusetts, Wampeter Press, 1983.
Editor, *The Short Stories of Anton Chekhov.* New York, Bantam, 1987.
Editor, *Best American Short Stories, 1994.* New York, Houghton Mifflin, 1994.
Editor, *The Vintage Book of Contemporary American Short Stories.* New York, Vintage, 1994.
Editor, *Writers Harvest 3.* New York, Dell, 2000.

*

Critical Studies: *Stories of Resilience in Childhood: The Narratives of Maya Angelou, Maxine Hong Kingston, Richard Rodrigues, John Edgar Wideman, and Tobias Wolff* by Daniel D. Challener, New York, Garland, 1997.

Tobias Wolff comments:

Writers are the worst interpreters of their own work. If their fiction is any good, it should be saying things they weren't aware of.

* * *

Tobias Wolff writes with a sparsity and clarity typical of the voices of the best writers of his generation, realists of the ilk of Raymond Carver, Richard Ford, William Kittredge, Jayne Anne Phillips, Mary Robison, and Stephanie Vaughan, all of whom are represented in *Matters of Life and Death,* an anthology of contemporary American short stories which Wolff put together in the early 1980s. In explaining his choices, Wolff wrote that in the stories "I heard something that I couldn't ignore, some notes of menace or hope or warning or appeal or awe; and in the matter of the stories themselves, the people who inhabit them and what they do, I saw something that I couldn't look away from."

The same should be said of Wolff's work. Every story, the novella *The Barracks Thief,* and the memoir *This Boy's Life* go right to the heart. Nowhere is there a slack page; Wolff writes as if each work were the only one he will every publish. He has admitted in interviews to being a relentless reviser. *The Barracks Thief,* scarcely a novella, was once a manuscript of several hundred pages. In the stories collected in *In the Garden of the North American Martyrs* and *Back in the World,* character development is quick and vivid, background material rare, as if Wolff has always kept clear in his mind Hemingway's axiom that stories get their energy from what is left unsaid. The result is a rather modest output. After fifteen years of publishing, all of Wolff's work could easily be contained in a single volume of 600 pages. But this hypothetical volume would say as much if not more than any other conceivable work about the generation of American men born in the decade after World War II.

The men in Wolff's stories have fathers and uncles who fought and won in the good war; their own war is a squalid and ambiguous affair that went on and on in a very hot place, and the themes of these fictions are deceit, betrayal, failure, and self-loathing, and the queer persistence of fellow-feeling in spite of all of these. Wolff was himself a member of the Special Forces and had a tour of duty in Vietnam. Yet nowhere has he written—not yet, anyway—of combat or his service in Southeast Asia. Instead the war is insinuated, providing the future with menace, or the past with ambivalence and depth. In other words, unconfronted, unobtruded, the Vietnam war remains in Wolff's fiction what it is for most men of his age, non-combatants as well as soldiers, the great shaping force that can never quite be understood, much less expunged. Consequently, many of Wolff's characters seemed surprised who they have become, survivors of a catastrophe who have become dependent on safety. As the narrator of *The Barracks Thief* puts it:

> I didn't set out to be what I am ... I'm a conscientious man, a responsible man, maybe even what you'd call a good man—I hope so. But I'm also a careful man, addicted to comfort, with an eye for the safe course. My neighbors appreciate me because they know I will never give my lawn over to the cultivation of marijuana, or send my wife weeping to their doorsteps at three o'clock in the morning, or expect them to be my friends. I am content with my life most of the time.

Comfort, however, scarcely describes the experience of reading Wolff's fiction. Instead, the reader is made uneasy by characters whose actions, often for the best of motives, lead them into error and excess. In "Hunters in the Snow" Tub and Frank rediscover their friendship while Kenny, bleeding or freezing to death, lies neglected in the back of the pick-up truck. In "Coming Attractions," a sister risks her life trying to get a bicycle out of the deep end of a swimming pool. In "Dessert Breakdown, 1968" a man nearly abandons his wife and children on a whim. And in "The Rich Brother," a man leaves his ineffectual younger brother by the side of a highway in the cold and an almost absolute darkness. Driving all of Wolff's fiction is the dynamism derived from the irreconcilable difference between who we might like to be and who our actions reveal us to be.

In *This Boy's Life,* an autobiography of his adolescence, Wolff writes "It takes a childish or corrupt imagination to make symbols of other people," and the comment affords an important insight into Wolff's aesthetic and ethical aims. For all of their economy, Wolff's works are never glib or shallow. They are never didactic, and the characters who inhabit them speak and act on their own in settings that are precisely and efficiently conceived. The plots move quickly, and since characters are never arrested and made to stand for something, reading Wolff is a headlong sort of business, wholly free of the artificial and emphatic closures of more ponderous writing. Invariably Wolff leaves the fate of his characters open. This can be exhilarating; however oblique the strike, we feel that we have made contact with the honest sufferings and joys of real people.

—Mark A.R. Facknitz

WRIGHT, Charles (Stevenson)

Nationality: American. **Born:** New Franklin, Missouri, 4 June 1932. Educated in public schools in New Franklin and Sedalia, Missouri. **Military Service:** Served in the United States Army, in Korea, 1952–54. **Career:** Stockboy in St. Louis, late 1950s; then freelance writer: columnist ("Wright's World"), *Village Voice,* New York. Lives in New York City. **Address:** c/o Farrar, Straus and Giroux, 19 Union Square West, New York, New York 10003, U.S.A.

PUBLICATIONS

Novels

The Messenger. New York, Farrar Straus, 1963; London, Souvenir Press, 1964.
The Wig: A Mirror Image. New York, Farrar Straus, 1966; London, Souvenir Press, 1967.
Absolutely Nothing to Get Alarmed About. New York, Farrar Straus, 1973.

Uncollected Short Stories

''A New Day,'' in *The Best Short Stories by Negro Writers,* edited by Langston Hughes. Boston, Little Brown, 1967.
''Sonny and the Sailor,'' in *Negro Digest* (Chicago), August 1968.
''Mr. Stein,'' in *Black American Literature Forum* (Terre Haute, Indiana), Summer 1989.

*

Charles Wright comments:

(1972) Numbers. One number has always walked through the front door of my mind. But when I was writing my first book, *The Messenger,* I did not think of numbers. I was very bitter at the time. *The Messenger* was simply a money roof. I was amused at its success. Mini-popular first published thing. A pleasant dream with the frame of reality.

The Wig was my life. And as I write this on a night of the last week in April of 1971—I have no regrets. Let me explain: A year after the publication of *The Messenger* I was thinking of that folkloric, second novel, and began a rough draft of a novel about a group of Black men, very much like the Black Panthers. But, in 1963, America was not ready for *that* type of novel, nor were they ready for *The Wig.* Ah! That is the first horror hors d'oeuvre. My agent, Candida Donadio, said: ''This is a novel. Write it.'' I will tell you quite simply … that I was afraid that I could not sustain the thing for say … fifty pages.

Now it was another year, another country (Morocco). Frightened, I returned to the states and rewrote *The Wig* in twenty-nine days … the best days of my life. The basic plot was the same but most of it was new. Thinking, working, like seven and, yes, sometimes fourteen hours a day. It took me less than three hours to make the final changes before the publishers accepted. I was *hot* … hot for *National Desire* … a short N. West-type of novel very much like *The Wig,* although *Race* would not have been the theme.

And.

And. Many things have happened to me and to my country since then. The country has always been like this, I suppose. I only know that something left me. As a result … I haven't written a novel in six years. I remember Langston Hughes saying: ''Write another nice, little book like *The Messenger.* White folks don't like to know that Negros can write books like that.'' Ah, yes … dear, dead Friend. Then. Yes. Another *Messenger.* And, what follows? Something that I've always wanted to do, something different … say an action packed Hemingway novel and then say … a Sackville-West novel. All I've ever wanted was a home by the sea and to be a good writer.

* * *

The literary output of Charles Wright has been slight in volume and promising, but not always effective, in practice. Wright's three small ''novels'' are each the size of Nathanael West novels, and they reflect the same mordant wit, yearning despair, and surrealistic lunacy of vintage West. Wright's world, however, is essentially a race-twisted society of black grotesques, of crippled lovers and dish-washer poets whose lives of wine, whores, and junkie-songs spell slow murder in white America.

The Messenger, The Wig, and *Absolutely Nothing to Get Alarmed About* portray an Inferno-world of sexual deviates: prostitutes (male and female), pimps, transvestites, poseurs, flower-children, sadistic cops. We meet not only lovers but pretenders, false black friends who set you up, genteel female perverts, white liberals whose children suddenly snarl ''nigger,'' beloved black musicians who betray their heritage to gain white favor. Each novel centers around the efforts of a young protagonist (''Charles Stevenson'' in the first and ''Charles Wright'' in the third novel) to cope with city life, where literally and metaphorically the protagonists prostitute themselves to survive. Each must dissemble, disguise, and sell himself; each finds the gimmicks and the humbling tricks to hustle an existence.

In *The Messenger,* which is heavily autobiographical, a young writer, Charles Stevenson (Wright's full name is Charles Stevenson Wright), stumbles to find himself, moving from the South to the army to New York. As a writer, he knows he must feel and record; his literal job as messenger is unimportant compared to his literary obligation to spread the word about life. As a black, however, he is torn between his compassion for outcast blacks and his emotional shield compounded of numbness, indifference, and cynicism. Although the writing occasionally slips into clichés or strained metaphor, style is the novel's chief attraction and is marvelously wedded to content. The writing is terse, the narrator-hero's manner laconic and usually guarded. Most episodes are deliberately inconclusive and undeveloped, sketchy vignettes that affect the narrator more than he acknowledges. Deeply touching are the few pages in which the spiritually exhausted young veteran is united with his warm, righteous grandmother, while his athletic command performance in a southern police station is outrageously comic and brilliantly symbolic of racial debasement.

If *The Messenger* seems like a patch-quilt of styles and moods, *The Wig* is more consistent in tone and mood, but regrettably so. For Wright's second novel goes all-out as black comedy, but despite its wildness it is more black, or malicious, than comic. There is a similar gallery of transvestites and other disguise-wearing freaks in quest of identity without guilt, failure, or self-hatred, but they are portrayed without hope or compassion. The hero, Lester Jefferson, is, like all the other blacks, on the make: he has conked and curled his Afro hair into a beautiful white ''wig'' that will open the doors to the Great (White) Society. Alas, he doesn't make it but we are not even sorry, for neither he nor the author reaches Ellison's solution that ''visibility'' begins with confronting and accepting one's truly created self. There are two or three successful comic achievements: Jimmy Wishbone, who once ''kept 100 million colored people contented for years'' as a Stepin Fetchit type in movies and who now wants to sue white society and redeem his lost fleet of Cadillacs; and Lester himself, crawling the streets in a feathery chicken-suit as employee of the Southern Fried Chicken King.

The last exchange of dialogue in *The Messenger* goes: '''Charles, what's wrong?' 'Nothing,' I said. 'Absolutely nothing.''' Wright's latest novelistic autobiography, *Absolutely Nothing to Get Alarmed About,* picks up from its predecessor's conclusion, although the locale has moved from mid-Manhattan to the Lower East Side. The mood if more uniformly despairing, with only a few attempts at the pathos and yearning of *The Messenger* or the caustic hilarity of *The Wig*. In place of the homosexual-junkie nightmare world of *The Messenger,* Wright's metaphor of our foundering American culture is here the yellow-black-white world of the Bowery. Appropriate to their original publication in New York's *Village Voice,* many chapters echo the vivid tone and the felt immediacy of ''new journalism'' prose.

—Frank Campenni

WURLITZER, Rudolph

Nationality: American. **Born:** 1937. **Awards:** *Atlantic* Firsts award, 1966. **Address:** c/o Knopf Inc., 201 East 50th Street, New York, New York 10022, U.S.A.

Publications

Novels

Nog. New York, Random House, 1969; as *The Octopus,* London, Weidenfeld and Nicolson, 1969.
Flats. New York, Dutton, 1970; London, Gollancz, 1971.
Quake. New York, Dutton, 1972; London, Pan, 1985.
Slow Fade. New York, Knopf, 1984; London, Pan, 1985.
Walker (novelization of screenplay). New York, Perennial Library, 1987.

Uncollected Short Story

''Boiler Room,'' in *Atlantic* (Boston), March 1966.

Plays

Two-Lane Blacktop (screenplay), with Will Corry. New York, Award, 1971.

Screenplays: *Two-Lane Blacktop,* with Will Corry, 1971; *Glen and Randa,* with Lorenzo Mans and Jim McBride, 1971; *Pat Garrett and Billy the Kid,* 1973; *Walker,* 1989; *Voyager,* 1991.

Other

Hard Travel to Sacred Places. Boston, Shambhala, 1994.

*

Critical Studies: *Rudolph Wurlitzer, American Novelist and Screenwriter* by David Seed, Lewiston, New York, Mellen Press, 1991.

Theatrical Activities: Actor: **Films**—*Two-Lane Blacktop,* 1971; *Pat Garrett and Billy the Kid,* 1973.

* * *

Rudolph Wurlitzer's novels represent a determined attempt to escape the materials of narrative. Unwilling to suspend disbelief and create a representative world of people, places, and ideals, he discards the conventions of mimetic storytelling in favor of a flat-out style of direct address which in his later novels slowly modulates into a more naturalized manner, yet never one that attempts to counterfeit a world. Instead, Wurlitzer's later work draws upon certain artifices of conduct which by virtue of long use have a structure which appears to be naturally made. In either case, the novelist is excused from proposing an enabling structure for his work; from first to last, Wurlitzer's novels speak with their own sense of authority, pretending to be nothing other than they are.

Nog and *Flats* are alternately diverse and spare works which rely upon the narrator's direct address for their substance and direction. Mirror-images of the same artistic vision, these novels contrast wild geographic narrative with a Beckett-like stasis of character, mood, and location, yet each ending with the same sense of voice alone. Even coherent character yields to this presence of mere voice, since in the first work Wurlitzer's narrator sometimes talks about Nog as a distinct person (''Nog, he was apparently of Finnish extraction, was one of those semi-religious lunatics you see wandering around the Sierras on bread and tea, or gulping down peyote in Nevada with the Indians'') and other times speaks as Nog himself, while the narrator of *Flats* proposes a similar exchange of identities with a person he has met and has been describing. The effect of such shimmering exchanges is to efface any sense of represented identity, establishing the narrative voice as a pure speaking sound which draws its sense of character from what is being described. In *Nog* this iridescence becomes geographical, as the narrator's voice yields to the on-running panorama of place, from the desert American southwest, through the Pacific and the Panama Canal, to the eastern seaboard and New York City. *Flats* presents the precise opposite of this range, but not of this tendency: the narrator sits within a small square of wasteland, vocally defending his space against all interlopers. He and they are named by their apparent home towns—''Call me Memphis,'' he introduces himself—but in their little square of desert they are motionless and without any identities all the same. All that exists is their voice, which is the text of Wurlitzer's novel.

Thematically, Wurlitzer argues against representation as well. Nog prizes silence and is proud not to divulge information to other characters (and therefore to the reader): ''No history,'' he remarks, ''therefore no bondage.'' Rather than act, he makes lists, because ''Lists don't need direction.'' *Flats* elevates this theme to phenomenological proportion, refusing to grasp events lest their surface take shape. ''I don't care to look around, having disappeared in all directions,'' the narrator admits, refusing any identity at all. ''There is only my momentum,'' which is the text's own movement. And even this is reductive: ''I want to say the same words over and over. I want just the sound. I want to fill up what space I am with one note … I want a sound that is not involved with beginning or ending.'' Wurlitzer's subsequent novels, *Quake* and *Slow Fade,* maintain their author's spare sense of prose, but now a textually self-conscious situation relieves the burden of flat narration. In *Quake* it is an earth tremor which by devastating the landscape erases any sense of conventional continuity; as the artifices of normal behavior crumble, the narrator is free to establish his own voice as the sole reality of his story. ''The words around us blurred and carried no definition,'' and so his voice is the only anchor of authority. Yet the unreality unleashed by the earthquake is only a destruction of conventionality; what is now revealed is that ''this day has given expression to what has always been latent within us.'' By the novel's end the narrator is reduced to guttural sounds, his own ability to articulate having been destroyed with the world around him. Yet even before this it has proven to be a talent whose time has been eclipsed.

Slow Fade is ostensibly Wurlitzer's most conventional work, as it is set securely within a recognizable world and is peopled by characters whose consistency of motive and behavior qualifies them for the most realistic fiction. But as with *Quake,* the author's choice of circumstance allows for purely self-conscious narrative, since here the action involves scriptwriting and filming, two undertakings which lend a textual self-appearance to the novel. As the stories of film director Wesley Hardin, his children, and his intrusive entrepreneur evolve, the narrative becomes less a document of their lives than a series of filters and indirect analyses, as events are perceived not as themselves but with references to scenes in films. This sense of intertextuality is enhanced by Wes's desire to learn the fate of his daughter, which he pursues by paying his son to write a film script which fictionalizes the details yet encodes the answer to his question. Yet as his son writes the script, he pauses to question his father about their relationship and to sort out the memory of his own wife's life and death. Soon so many layers of textuality have been sedimented upon the basic story that only text (and not any representations) remain. The climax of this layering occurs when Wes Hardin aborts his own film project and becomes the subject of a *cinema-verité* work encompassing his own breakdown as occasioned by his daughter's loss. In this respect the role of the entrepreneur A.D. Ballou, becomes instrumental. What happens in the world, Wurlitzer concludes, is due to direct action but by the manipulation of texts. As A.D. Ballou produces Hardin's autobiographical movie, so too does the reader produce the narrators' texts. Without either act, nothing would happen, and therefore Wurlitzer's novels place as little as possible in the way of this readerly action.

With *Walker,* Wurlitzer combines his novelist's role with his screenwriting activities to produce a work far different from the usual novelization of a film. The story itself is based on history, evoking the colorful career of the mid-nineteenth-century American adventurer William Walker as a way of providing not just a colorful narrative about Nicaragua during those years but a metaphoric commentary on American involvement in that country during the 1980s. Walker was a freebooting entrepreneur who made use of the business interests of Cornelius Vanderbilt in installing himself as President of Nicaragua, a position he held from 1855 through 1857. That his empire fell and he was eventually executed by a Honduran firing squad does not detract from his sense of ambition and idealism, tempered by the current reader's appreciation that such motives have often led to disasters in American foreign policy and the most unconscionable exploitation of foreign lands. In presenting this work Wurlitzer provides a fictive narrative, but supplements it with both historical and Walker's autobiographical accounts; these are then framed with shooting notes, production journals, and interviews with the filmmakers.

—Jerome Klinkowitz

Y

YAFFE, James

Nationality: American. **Born:** Chicago, Illinois, 31 March 1927. **Education:** Fieldston School, graduated 1944; Yale University, New Haven, Connecticut, 1944–48, B.A. (summa cum laude) 1948 (Phi Beta Kappa). **Military Service:** Served in the United States Navy, 1945–46. **Family:** Married Elaine Gordon in 1964; two daughters and one son. **Career:** Since 1968 member of the Department of English, currently professor of English, and since 1981 Director of General Studies, Colorado College, Colorado Springs. **Awards:** National Endowment for the Arts award, for drama, 1968. **Address:** 1215 North Cascade Avenue, Colorado Springs, Colorado 80903, U.S.A.

Publications

Novels

The Good-for-Nothing. Boston, Little Brown, and London, Constable, 1953.
What's the Big Hurry? Boston, Little Brown, 1954; as *Angry Uncle Dan,* London, Constable, 1955.
Nothing But the Night. Boston, Little Brown, 1957; London, Cape, 1958.
Mister Margolies. New York, Random House, 1962.
Nobody Does You Any Favors. New York, Putnam, 1966.
The Voyage of the Franz Joseph. New York, Putnam, 1970.
Saul and Morris, Worlds Apart. New York, Holt Rinehart, 1982.
A Nice Murder for Mom. New York, St. Martin's Press, 1988.
Mom Meets Her Maker. New York, St. Martin's Press, 1990.
Mom Doth Murder Sleep. New York, St. Martin's Press, 1991.
Mom Among the Liars. New York, St. Martin's Press, 1993.

Short Stories

Poor Cousin Evelyn. Boston, Little Brown, 1951; London, Constable, 1952.
My Mother, the Detective: The Complete "Mom" Short Stories. Norfolk, Virginia, Crippen and Landru Publishers, 1997.

Uncollected Short Stories

"On the Brink," in *The Queen's Awards 8,* edited by Ellery Queen. Boston, Little Brown, and London, Gollancz, 1953.
"One of the Family," in *The Queen's Awards 11,* edited by Ellery Queen. New York, Simon and Schuster, and London, Collins, 1956.
"The Problem of the Emperor's Mushrooms," in *All But Impossible!,* edited by Edward D. Hoch. New Haven, Connecticut, Ticknor and Fields, 1981; London, Hale, 1983.
"D.I.C. (Department of Impossible Crimes)," in *Ellery Queen's Book of First Appearances,* edited by Ellery Queen and Eleanor Sullivan. New York, Dial Press, 1982.

Plays

The Deadly Game, adaptation of a novel by Friedrich Dürrenmatt (produced New York, 1960; London, 1967). New York, Dramatists Play Service, 1960.
This Year's Genie (for children), in *Eight Plays 2,* edited by Malcolm Stuart Fellows. London, Cassell, 1965.
Ivory Tower, with Jerome Weidman (produced Ann Arbor, Michigan, 1968). New York, Dramatists Play Service, 1969.
Cliffhanger (as *Immorality Play,* produced Atlanta, 1983; as *Cliffhanger,* produced New York, 1985). New York, Dramatists Play Service, 1985.

Television Plays: for *U.S. Steel Hour, Studio One, G.E. Theater, Frontiers of Faith, The Defenders, Breaking Point, Alfred Hitchcock Presents, The Doctors and the Nurses,* and other series, 1953–67.

Other

The American Jews. New York, Random House, 1968.
So Sue Me! The Story of a Community Court. New York, Saturday Review Press, 1972.

*

James Yaffe comments:

(1991) For me, to write novels has been to create characters and to combine and juxtapose those characters, involve them in confrontations, place them in situations which challenge them, strengthen them, destroy them, transform them, test their mettle—and out of a variety of such characters, to build a world. Where do I get the raw material for my characters? From my own experience, of course—mostly from my experience of the world I was born and brought up in, the world of middle-class, second- and third-generation Jews living in New York, Chicago, Los Angeles, I have chosen to write about this world because I know it instinctively and subliminally, because it was part of me before I was old enough to doubt my perceptions.

But I have always tried to treat this experience not analytically or sociologically or philosophically but novelistically—that is, by imagining, and trying to re-create, the world as seen through each character's eyes. The greatest novelists, it seems to me, are those who succeed in merging their personalities with the lives and feelings of their people. This is the special ability shared by writers as different as Tolstoy and Jane Austen, Trollope and Joyce (to mention a few of my favorites). The attempt to follow their example may be presumptuous and doomed to failure, but it is also inevitable for anybody who wants to write novels.

* * *

James Yaffe is considered a leading novelist of middle-class Jewish life in America. His early collection of short stories (*Poor Cousin Evelyn*) and his first novel (*The Good-for-Nothing*) are essentially drawing room comedies set in New York. As in the novels of Jane Austen, whom Yaffe admits a special fondness for, small conflicts are closely scrutinized within a closed society—in Yaffe's case, the Jewish family, with all its attendant social hierarchies, its patriarchs, its strong-men and its failures, its pressures of shame and guilt applied by loved ones to safeguard conformity and tradition. In these earlier works, characters are simply drawn and situations directly presented, largely through dialogue.

A recurring Yaffe theme involves the ''dreamer,'' an impractical or artistically oriented individual confronted with pressures to survive in a competitive business world of the shady deals and opportunism. In *The Good-for-Nothing* this conflict is represented by two brothers, apparently very different from each other, yet mutually dependent. The one is college-educated and totally ineffectual in the business world, a charming sycophant. The other, a Certified Public Accountant, supports him, but in so doing restricts his own life. As they interact, it becomes unclear which is the ''good for nothing,'' which the success or the failure: in different ways, both are unwilling to face responsibilities or the possibility of failure. Self-righteousness and self-indulgence, like sentimentality, are both forms of escape, excuses for not taking risks.

In a later novel, *Mister Margolies,* this pattern of self-deception is advanced to the point where the manipulation of reality becomes a life-style. Stanley Margolies, defeated in his early attempt to become a concert pianist, yet unable to give up totally his dreams of a poetic life, withdraws into a world of fantasies. The reality of business and competition crashes in on this, and he withdraws deeper, erecting more elaborate defenses. Yaffe's ''dreamers'' create worlds which are both sad and poetic, but they are not the demonic Rose-gardens of the totally mad. They are the tiny fantasies of little men, dreams reinforced by sympathetic and condescending friends with whom they still retain some form of contact.

Yaffe avoids several stereotypes popular in much contemporary Jewish literature: the dominant Jewish Mother, and the Jew-Gentile confrontation, particularly in matters sexual, as an expression of, or as a means of resolving feelings of inferiority. In general, he maintains a comic narrative tone—some of the scenes are funny—and though his characters are forever lecturing each other, their messages are frequently as confused as they are. The novels themselves preach little other than a deep compassion for the small man and his hopes.

The theme of the dreamer in search of his vision makes a terrifying appearance in *Nothing But the Night,* which is based on the Nathan Leopold-Richard Loeb murder case of 1924, and the celebrated defense by Clarence Darrow. The case history is seen through the eyes of one of the young men, not as an investigation of the criminal mind, but as a study of a lonely and creative child. As in Chekhov, Yaffe's characters take their emotions very seriously and ponder them deeply. They are often trapped by their own visions and the pressures to succeed imposed from outside. In their struggle to hold on to their dreams, they are destroyed, transformed, and occasionally liberated. An example of the latter is presented in *Nobody Does You Any Favors,* which despite its 1940s cinema-sounding title is perhaps his best novel. As opposed to the earlier New York novels which suggest short stories in their structural focus on a single event, *Nobody Does You Any Favors* with its time span of roughly forty years allows for an extended development and growth in character. The confrontation between father and son is drawn with an understanding and passion valid beyond a scene of very special terror and insight. Certainly this novel is a significant contribution to American literature of the twentieth century.

The Voyage of the Franz Joseph represented an epic departure from his usual drawing room style. Like *Nothing But the Night,* it is based on an historical event, the sailing of the German liner *St. Louis* in 1939 with a thousand Jewish refugees searching for a homeland.

—Paul Seiko Chihara

YAMANAKA, Lois-Ann

Nationality: American. **Born:** Ho'olchua, Molokai, Hawaii, 7 September 1961. **Education:** University of Hawaii at Manoa, B.Ed. 1983, M.Ed. 1987. **Family:** Married—husband's name John; one son. **Career:** Language arts resource teacher and English teacher, Hawaii Department of Education; writer. Lives in Honolulu, Hawaii. **Awards:** Pushcart prize, 1993; Elliot Cades award for literature, 1993; Asian American Studies National Book award, 1994 (prize revoked); Pushcart Prize, 1994; Rona Jaffe award for women writers, 1996.

Publications

Novels

Wild Meat and the Bully Burgers. New York, Farrar, Straus, 1996.
Blu's Hanging. New York, Farrar, Straus, 1997.
Heads by Harry. New York, Farrar, Straus, 1999.
Name Me Nobody (juvenile fiction). New York, Hyperion, 1999.

Short Stories

Saturday Night at the Pahala Theatre (verse novellas). Honolulu, Hawaii, Bamboo Ridge Press, 1993.

Other

Contributor, *Transnational Asia Pacific: Gender, Culture, and the Public Sphere*, edited by Shirley Geok-lin Lim, Larry E. Smith, and Wimal Dissanayake. Urbana, University of Illinois Press, 1999.

* * *

Lois-Ann Yamanaka's writing is uncontrovertibly controversial. She did not set out to be controversial; indeed, she didn't even set out to be a writer. It was while Yamanaka was working as a schoolteacher in her native Hawaii that she observed her students writing poetry, and realized that she, too, was capable of creative writing. After returning to the University of Hawaii to study writing, Yamanaka has gone on to become one of that state's best known novelists, as well as a vocal proponent of Hawaiian Creole English, the pidgin spoken by many of the islands' working-class residents and in which Yamanaka often writes. This dialect is a combination of English, Japanese, and Philippine, and as a teacher Yamanaka was warned against using it in the working-class school in which she taught. As a writer she found her first collection, *Saturday Night at the Pahala Theatre*, banned by the Hawaii school system.

This attempt to suppress and assimilate minority cultures is precisely what Yamanaka is writing against in her novels. The descendant of Japanese agricultural workers and the daughter of educators, she grew up in the sugar-plantation town of Pahala, where pidgin was her native tongue. The sense of alienation and difference she felt from predominantly white, mainstream urban culture and its values has become the nucleus of much of her fiction. Her first collection, *Saturday Night at the Pahala Theatre*, explores that sense of difference through poetic narratives, critiquing race and gender relations in small-town Hawaii, while affirming the linguistic power of pidgin to do so. Awarded the Association for Asian American Studies National Book award, the Elliot Cades award for literature, and a Pushcart prize, the book more importantly reflected the lives of a segment of the Hawaiian population predominantly absent in the mainstream, the working-class Japanese segment from which Yamanaka hails. For Yamanaka, writing about a world erased in popular representations of Hawaii, and in the language of that world, is a fundamentally political act.

It is this close-knit Japanese world that Yamanaka has continued to explore in her adult novels to date, a loosely woven trilogy about coming of age in contemporary Hawaii. *Wild Meat and the Bully Burgers* inaugurates this triptych with the story of young Lovey Nariyoshi, whose desire for blond hair is just one of the many examples of her internalization of mainstream society's privileging of white middle-class culture. Set in 1970s rural Hilo, Lovey's reality does not mirror the conformist suburban fantasy of which she dreams. Instead, her family is poor and eccentric, in addition to being culturally marginalized. Her sense of cultural alienation is reinforced by schoolteachers who disparage her dialect and culture, classifying Lovey as slow. Through a series of vignettes, we witness Lovey's struggle, alternately comic and poignant, to establish a sense of self-worth as she moves into adolescence. That Yamanaka has written this story in pidgin is the final vindication of Lovey and the world she represents.

Yamanaka's second novel, *Blu's Hanging*, is admittedly the bleakest of the trio. After the death of their mother, three siblings attempt to negotiate an unremittingly severe world of poverty, violence, racism, and exploitation. As their father struggles to make ends meet, twelve-year old Ivah attempts to assume her mother's responsibilities, but can not provide the kinds of love and support necessary for her younger siblings or herself. While the children's energy is unavoidably infectious, their particular vulnerability is equally obvious, and the brother, Blu, is raped by a neighbor, just as Ivah is preparing to leave the family to attend boarding school. The children's father reads this departure as a form of betrayal and abandonment, and initially blames Ivah for her brother's victimization. Both the rape and its fallout are crucial for scholars of Yamanaka. The tension between Ivah and her father stemming from the rape is indicative of a thematic preoccupation in Yamanaka's works with Japanese-American father-daughter relations. In her work, Yamanaka often explores the emotional distancing, elisions, and reticence—as well as the moments of revelation and understanding—that characterize this particular familial bond.

However, the rape of Blu in *Blu's Hanging* is important not only for its fallout, or relevance to the narrative, but also for the political upheaval that resulted in regards to Yamanaka's work and literary reputation. That Blu is raped by a Filipino neighbor, Uncle Paulo, led to charges of racism that ultimately resulted in the Association for Asian American Studies revoking the fiction prize it had awarded the book—both acts occurring on the same day. Yamanaka's previous publications also came under fire, particularly a piece in *Saturday Night at the Pahala Theatre* where a youngster recounts being warned about Filipinos practicing cannibalism. While the passage appears ironic in context—there is also a warning that if you borrow someone's deodorant, you might catch their body order, or if you make faces you will get Japanese eyes—out of context, and with the history of Filipino-Japanese tension in Hawaii, it appears problematic. Likewise, that Uncle Paulo is the representative Filipino in the text, and not a fully developed character, is also troublesome. However, Uncle Paulo is not the only deviant adult in the novel, and the others are all Japanese. It is even rumored, according to Ivah, that his family hides their part Japanese heritage. Nevertheless, the passionate controversy ignited by the AAAS award and the decision to revoke it is very real, and it remains to be seen if or how Yamanaka will respond in her future writing.

Blu's Hanging was followed by the lighter and less controversial *Heads by Harry*, the last in Yamanaka's Hawaiian coming-of-age trilogy. In this novel her protagonists are older, and even reach adulthood, but still belong to the tight-knit family unit whose dynamics Yamanaka loves to explore and expose in her writing. The Yagyuus are uproarious in their eccentricities and antics, but genuine in their love for each other, which remains constant despite their individual attempts to achieve independence. The father-daughter relationship is again investigated through the eldest daughter, Toni, and the father whose taxidermy business she will inherit, as the only son—the flamboyant Sheldon—has chosen to open up a hair salon. Despite the family's propensity to misadventures, Yamanaka endows Toni, Sheldon, and the manipulative favorite, Bunny, with a sense of dignity and individuality that allows them to transcend easy categorization or stereotypes. Sheldon may be a gay hairdresser, but he is also an entrepreneur whose love of his family causes him to remain in Hilo and set up shop next door to his father's business. Nor is he a ''token'' character in Yamanaka's fiction; indeed, butch girl cousins and friends abound, and are central to the narrative of her 1999 children's novel, *Name Me Nobody*, which explores racism, poverty, discrimination, and sexuality with the same unflinching gaze as her adult novels.

In addition to her novels for adults and children, Yamanaka's works *Saturday Night at the Pahala Theatre* and *Wild Meat and the Bully Burgers* have both been produced as plays by Kuma Kahua. Yamanaka has weathered all criticism well, and remains committed to the use of pidgin and the importance of continuing to write about the experiences of her community, while insisting on the necessity of remaining true to the integrity of the characters and their experience, no matter how unpopular that experience may be.

—Jennifer Harris

YGLESIAS, Helen

Nationality: American. **Born:** Helen Bassine in New York City, 29 March 1915. **Family:** Married 1) Bernard Cole in 1938 (divorced 1950), one son and one daughter; 2) Jose Yglesias in 1950 (divorced 1992, deceased 1995); one son. **Career:** Literary editor, the *Nation*, New York, 1965–69; Visiting Professor, Columbia University School of the Arts, New York, 1973, and University of Iowa Writers Workshop, Iowa City, 1980. **Awards:** Houghton Mifflin Literary fellowship, 1972. LHD: University of Maine, 1996. **Address:** 123 W. 13th Street, No. 311, New York, New York 10011–7801, U.S.A.

Publications

Novels

How She Died. Boston, Houghton Mifflin, 1972; London, Heinemann, 1973.
Family Feeling. New York, Dial Press, 1976; London, Hodder and Stoughton, 1977.
Sweetsir. New York, Simon and Schuster, and London, Hodder and Stoughton, 1981.
The Saviors. Boston, Houghton Mifflin, 1987.
The Girls. Harrison, New York, Delphinium Books, 1999.

Uncollected Short Stories

''Semi-Private,'' in *New Yorker,* 5 February 1972.
''Kaddish and Other Matters,'' in *New Yorker,* 6 May 1974.
''Liar, Liar,'' in *Seventeen* (New York), February 1976.

Other

Starting: Early, Anew, Over, and Late. New York, Rawson Wade, 1978.
Isabel Bishop. New York, Rizzoli, 1989.

* * *

The novels of Helen Yglesias were written from her 54th year onwards. As she notes in her book of meditations, *Starting: Early, Anew, Over, and Late,* she had already had an active career of book reviewing and editorial work; she was for a time the literary editor of the *Nation.* Yglesias's account of her career and of the careers of other men and women in *Starting* shows that a recurrent pattern in her novels is an expression of her own sense of what a proper career for a person is. Each person has, as the many conversations with others in *Starting* shows, the opportunity to discover his or her ''true self'' and initiate actions that allow that self to unfold. Or, alternately, to turn aside and spend the years in conformity to the expectations of a group and thus court defeat and stultification. As Yglesias asks in the Introduction to *Starting:* ''Is there 'a true self'? Does it indeed exist and does its existence matter? Is there measurable damage in human and social terms when an impostor inhabits the corner of space and time reserved for a unique self—whatever that is? To do what one has always wanted to do—to be what one has always wanted to be—what does that mean?''

In the body of her book Yglesias devotes space to her own life as a young Jewish intellectual bucking the waves of indifference she met in the 1930s; it is a story that is repeated in her second novel, *Family Feeling.* She also relates the ''starting'' of her son, the novelist Rafael Yglesias, who, in his mid-teens, withdrew from society to realize *his* artistic destiny. And Yglesias moves on to many others whose diverse destinies are marked by the urgent questioning she directed at her own life. With a sort of modesty she remarks of herself: ''I admit to a vast general ignorance of things physical, technological, mythical, religious, and political-social.'' Such remarks indicate the drive behind the novels, and they also suggest the areas that are left for other novelists to handle. The Yglesias novels are tales of struggle: chiefly female struggle in a society that imposes on such struggle a terminology invented by males. Yglesias is a connoisseur of the successes and failures that women like her heroines—and one supposes, herself—meet. These struggles are often well realized and convince not so much by their general truth as by the mass of detail that is clustering at center-stage. This gives the novels an effect of conviction that cannot be overlooked. Occasionally Yglesias abandons this area for theoretical speculation; she endows a heroine with her own former or present political loyalties and her own esthetic preferences, and the novels become temporarily less vivid. But the textures that are impelling are soon re-established.

Family Feeling is the novel that is a rough equivalent (and a successful one) to the story Yglesias tells in the opening section of *Starting. Sweetsir* is a negative version of the successful struggles in *Family Feeling;* the efforts of the heroine of *Sweetsir* commence and recommence but never move very far from the point where the repeated departures take place: the heroine's desire to be something, to realize in the relations of love some amorphous inner power that the heroine senses but cannot express. In contrast, the heroine of *Family Feeling* has an abundance of words to apply to each twist and turn of *her* journey. Yglesias's first novel, *How She Died,* is an account of a woman whose ''starting'' and its consequences lie somewhere between the distinct success and the grim failures related in the other two novels. The heroine of *How She Died,* Jean, devotes herself to a dying woman, has a love-affair with the woman's husband, neglects her own children, and realizes that her political ardor has brought her little reason for pride.

The other two novels, as suggested, are more decisive in their impact. *Family Feeling* reproduces the complex history of an immigrant Jewish family: a family that starts in poverty and that ends—for some of the members at least—in considerable prosperity and personal satisfaction. Barry Goddard is a son who ends as the owner of vast enterprises *and* an apartment that overlooks Central Park. Anne, whose intelligence is usually (but not always) the center of the story, follows a different course, one which leads her through social protest, literary projects that occasionally distract the reader, and finally to several years of a happy marriage with a WASP magazine editor who finds the Jewishness of Anne's family a constant diversion. The main concern of the moving narrative is not the social and personal goods that various characters grasp; it is the panorama of endless struggle—of ''starting'' and then achieving a continuation that is sometimes wasteful and sometimes admirable.

Such continuations do not appear in *Sweetsir.* This long and minutely executed novel, in which many pages are devoted to the details of legal procedures, begins with a domestic battle between Sally and Morgan Sweetsir, a battle that ends when Sally pushes a knife into the body of her brutal husband. Attention thus engages, the reader is conducted through the considerable number of years that brought Sally Sweetsir to her fatal confrontation. If one chooses to wonder why Sally's many ''startings'' go nowhere in particular, answers arise again and again. Sally comes from a lower-class milieu where there is no such tradition of struggle and survival as that which gave strength to Anne Goddard in *Family Feeling.* Sally has almost no words to put to her desires, the desires that take her through two marriages and into the law courts. And she lacks the intelligence to direct the sexuality and the ambition that come and go in her. And quite beyond her control are the crudity and insensitivity of the two males in her life. It is no surprise that in Sally's ''world'' (as assembled by Yglesias) Sally does not have to pay a social penalty for her ''crime.'' Her long list of failures to ''start'' constitutes a sufficient punishment.

Yglesias describes her novel writing as "a happiness I could only liken to the happiness of love." Such happiness is open to the reader in long stretches of *Family Feeling.* And its absence is keenly felt elsewhere in the work of Yglesias.

—Harold H. Watts

YOUNG, Al(bert) (James)

Nationality: American. **Born:** Ocean Springs, Mississippi, 31 May 1939. **Education:** The University of Michigan, Ann Arbor (co-editor, *Generation* magazine), 1957–61; Stanford University, California (Stegner Creative Writing fellow), 1966–67; University of California, Berkeley, A.B. in Spanish 1969. **Family:** Married Arline June Belch in 1963; one son. **Career:** Freelance musician, 1958–64; disc jockey, KJAZ-FM, Alameda, California, 1961–65; instructor and linguistic consultant, San Francisco Neighborhood Youth Corps Writing Workshop, 1968–69; writing instructor, San Francisco Museum of Art Teenage Workshop, 1968–69; Jones Lecturer in creative writing, Stanford University, 1969–74; screenwriter, Laser Films, New York, 1972, Stigwood Corporation, London and New York, 1972, Verdon Productions, Hollywood, 1976, First Artists Ltd., Burbank, California, 1976–77, and Universal, Hollywood, 1979; writer-in-residence, University of Washington, Seattle, 1981–82. Since 1979 director, Associated Writing Programs. Founding editor, *Loveletter,* San Francisco, 1966–68. Since 1972 co-editor, *Yardbird Reader,* Berkeley, California; contributing editor, since 1972, *Changes,* New York, and since 1973, *Umoja,* New Mexico; since 1981 editor and publisher, with Ishmael Reed, *Quilt* magazine, Berkeley; vice-president, Yardbird Publishing Cooperative. **Awards:** National Endowment for the Arts grant, 1968, 1969, 1974; San Francisco Foundation Joseph Henry Jackson award, 1969; Guggenheim fellowship, 1974; Pushcart prize, 1980; Before Columbus Foundation award, 1982. **Agent:** International Creative Management, 40 West 57th Street, New York, New York 10019. **Address:** 514 Bryant St., Palo Alto, California 94301, U.S.A.

PUBLICATIONS

Novels

Snakes. New York, Holt Rinehart, 1970; London, Sidgwick and Jackson, 1971.
Who Is Angelina? New York, Holt Rinehart, 1975; London, Sidgwick and Jackson, 1978.
Sitting Pretty. New York, Holt Rinehart, 1976.
Ask Me Now. New York, McGraw Hill, and London, Sidgwick and Jackson, 1980.
Seduction by Light. New York, Delta, 1988; London, Mandarin, 1989.
Straight No Chaser. Berkeley, California, Creative Arts Book, 1994.

Uncollected Short Stories

"My Old Buddy Shakes, Alas, and Grandmama Claude," in *Nexus* (San Francisco), May-June 1965.
"The Question Man and Why I Dropped Out," in *Nexus* (San Francisco), November-December 1965.
"Chicken Hawk's Dream," in *Stanford Short Stories 1968,* edited by Wallace Stegner and Richard Scowcroft. Stanford, California, Stanford University Press, 1968.
"Moon Watching by Lake Chapala," in *Aldebaran Review 3* (Berkeley, California), 1968.

Plays

Screenplays: *Nigger,* 1972; *Sparkle,* 1972.

Poetry

Dancing. New York, Corinth, 1969.
The Song Turning Back into Itself. New York, Holt Rinehart, 1971.
Some Recent Fiction. San Francisco, San Francisco Book Company, 1974.
Geography of the Near Past. New York, Holt Rinehart, 1976.
The Blues Don't Change: New and Selected Poems. Baton Rouge, Louisiana State University Press, 1982.
Heaven: Collected Poems 1958–1988. Berkeley, California, Creative Arts, 1989.
Heaven: Collected Poems 1956–1990. Berkeley, California, Creative Arts, 1992.

Recording: *By Heart and by Ear,* Watershed, 1986.

Other

Bodies and Soul: Musical Memoirs. Berkeley, California, Creative Arts, 1981.
Kinds of Blue: Musical Memoirs. Berkeley, California, Creative Arts, 1984.
Things Ain't What They Used to Be: Musical Memoirs. Berkeley, California, Creative Arts, 1987.
Mingus/Mingus: Two Memoirs, with Janet Coleman. Berkeley, California, Creative Arts, 1989.
Drowning in the Sea of Love: Musical Memoirs. Hopewell, New Jersey, Ecco Press, 1995.
Editor, with Ishmael Reed, *Yardbird Lives!* New York, Grove Press, 1978.
Editor, with Ishmael Reed, *Quilt 2–3.* Berkeley, California, Reed and Young's Quilt, 2 vols., 1981–82.
Editor, *African American Literature: A Brief Introduction and Anthology.* New York, HarperCollins College Publishers, 1996.

* * *

In his story "Chicken Hawk's Dream" Al Young tells of a young man who believes that as magically as in a dream he might become a jazz artist. Failing to bring even a sound out of a borrowed horn, Chicken Hawk retreats into dope and alcohol, but his delusion persists so that when the narrator meets him later on a Detroit street corner Chicken Hawk says that he is off to New York to cut a record—just as soon as he gets his instrument out of the pawnshop. The dream of Chicken Hawk with its refusal of discipline and lack of nerve represents a version of what Young terms "art as hustle." It is not titillation, he says in a "Statement on Aesthetics, Poetics, Kinetics" (in *New Black Voices,* 1972), but the touching of human beings so that both toucher and touched are changed that matters most in art as in life. Touch may be magical but before all else it is the sign of willingness to engage actual life.

Through the metaphor of touch and repudiation of attitudinizing Young explains most of his literary practice. His novels gain much of their force from his ability to limn the texture of experience. Precise detailing of speech demonstrates how individuals play roles uniquely significant to those with whom they have personal relationships, including readers; and ways of seeing, talking, becoming, in short, ways of expressing the feel of life's touch, engender the books' movement.

In his first novel, *Snakes,* Young infuses the traditional narrative of adolescent growth with a principle of fluidity affecting every aspect of structure, style, and theme. MC, whose journey to maturity is the story's subject, gets turned on to modern jazz, an art of process which illustrates that personality itself may derive from music. Stylistically the book is largely constructed out of raps, oral performances by MC's friends, and reminiscences of his grandmother. The first concur with the performance of improvisational music to convey the importance of expressive response; the latter carry process into biographical temporality where memory of past events maintains influence in the present. Style and structure together support Young's theme of the struggle to be free, outlined in MC's thoughts on a bus to New York where he, unlike Chicken Hawk, will cut a record: ''For the first time in my life I don't feel trapped; I don't feel free either but I don't feel trapped and I'm going to try and make this feeling last for as long as I can.''

Who Is Angelina? picks up Young's theme in the story of a young woman who must regain the sense of not being trapped. In one answer to the question posed by the title, Angelina finds herself, in the words of a Pepsi-drinking fortune teller, poised between freedom to choose what she wishes and weaknesses which hold her back. A return to roots among family and neighborhood renews a sense of love for origins in Angelina but also demonstrates that she has no choice but to accept her distinct individuality; and to make the best of it, she must learn to move with awareness through her own becoming. Young allows Angelina to try transcendental meditation as a means of renewal, but her crucial realization of self occurs as it must, in the context of mundane experience. In a tussle with a purse snatcher she impulsively ventilates feelings of outrage that offend the liberal sentiments of friends and bystanders. Thereby she wipes out, for herself, the illusions one gains by living second-hand.

A year in the life of Sidney J. Prettymon, known as Sitting Pretty or sometimes plain Sit, provides the story line for Young's third novel. Sit's literary cousin is Langston Hughes's Jesse B. Semple, a.k.a. Simple. By the world's reckoning both Sit and Simple are ordinary men, but each has a philosophy and style that raises him above the average. In Sit's case the philosophy involves getting by without harming others and without succumbing to the values that will compromise integrity or happiness; thus, living is an improvisational performance. Rendered in the voice of Sit the novel *Sitting Pretty* works as the prose equivalent of an Afro-American musical composition alternatively echoing the situations of blues and celebratory riffs that are unique to the character's expressive style. Sit, jogging through the streets of Palo Alto, putting his two cents worth in on a radio talk show, caring deeply for his former wife in her time of trouble and his children when they don't even know they have problems, is a triumphant creation who deserves a place in the popular imagination right alongside Simple and probably, as Wallace Stegner suggested, Huckleberry Finn too.

Like Ishmael Reed, his colleague in *Yardbird* enterprises, Young is impatient with expectations that black writers should show their ethnicity in some predictable or stereotypical way. O.O. Gabugah the militant poet was Young's satirical treatment of such message writing, and O.O. makes an appearance in *Sitting Pretty* also. Usually, though, Young makes his point, as in *Ask Me Now,* by unselfconscious narrative of the human trials of his characters. What makes the books black is that the people, such as Woody Knight, the retired basketball player of his most recent novel, are granted a broad range of experience in which they talk and touch others in the style of black culture. That style permits comedy right along with tribulation, the sort of love that yields happy endings and the losses that create frustration and anger. Reviewers loaded with prescriptions for the ethnic author and critics who want the message straight can be displeased, but Young's art will persist as a loving treatment of the versions of human process that are its source and subject.

—John M. Reilly

YURICK, Sol

Nationality: American. **Born:** New York City, 18 January 1925. **Education:** New York University, A.B. 1950; Brooklyn College, New York, M.A. 1961. **Military Service:** Served in the United States Army, 1944–45. **Family:** Married Adrienne Lash in 1958; one daughter. **Career:** Librarian, New York University, 1945–53; social investigator, New York City Department of Welfare, 1954–59. Since 1959 fulltime writer. Lives in Brooklyn, New York. **Awards:** Guggenheim fellowship, 1972. **Agent:** Georges Borchardt Inc., 136 East 57th Street, New York, New York 10022, U.S.A. **Address:** c/o Morrow, 105 Madison Ave., New York, New York 10016, U.S.A.

PUBLICATIONS

Novels

The Warriors. New York, Holt Rinehart, 1965; London, W.H. Allen, 1966.

Fertig. New York, Simon and Schuster, and London, W.H. Allen, 1966.

The Bag. New York, Simon and Schuster, 1968; London, Gollancz, 1970.

An Island Death. New York, Harper, 1975.

Richard A. New York, Arbor House, and London, Methuen, 1982.

Short Stories

Someone Just Like You. New York, Harper, 1972; London, Gollancz, 1973.

Other

Editor, *Voices of Brooklyn: An Anthology.* Chicago, American Library Association, 1973.

*

Manuscript Collection: Tanument Library, New York University.

*   *   *

Taken singly, each of Sol Yurick's works constitutes a substantial contribution to the growing body of contemporary fiction that depicts the American megalopolis in perpetual crisis. Taken together, his novels make up the most compelling vision available to us (in fiction or in non-fiction) of the most nightmarish megalopolis of all: New York now. Yurick is (as surely befits someone who was involved for several years in attempting to construct a sound theoretical and practical base for action on the American left) not interested in formal experimentation in the novel for the novel's own sake. Yet neither is he a polemicist with little sense of artistic form. He is an extreme rarity: a social critic with broad theoretical and ''street level'' experience. Yet, he is at the same time an erudite novelist with solid historical knowledge of the genre and great skill in handling the form. In a deliberate and obviously self-conscious way, he consistently attempts to close the gap between the biblical and classical Greek world so often alluded to in his works and the world of welfare, of murder, and of political power plays, the three major elements in his portrait of New York today.

The Warriors is a novel about a decimated New York teenage gang whom we first met on hostile ''turf'' on their way back to their ''homeland'' after a gang conference which has just ended in attempted murder. The opening scene is prefaced by an epigraph drawn from Xenophon: ''My friends, these people whom you see are the last obstacle which stops us from being where we have so long struggled to be. We ought, if we could, to eat them up alive.'' The anabasis of Hinton (the gang artist), Lunkface, Bimbo, The Junior, and Hector is filled with memories of Ismael, leader of the Delancey Thrones, organizer of the citywide gang conference, and victim of the violence with which the conference had come to an abrupt close. ''Ismael,'' we are told, ''had the impassive face of a Spanish grandee, the purple-black color of an uncontaminated African, and the dreams of an Alexander, a Cyrus, a Napolean.'' He will return in *The Bag* as a saturnine figure (now with only one eye), a dope pusher, rent collector for a slum landlord (Faust), and stockpiler of rifles, waiting for that moment when the downtrodden of the city will rise up and use these arms to kill their ancient oppressors. Ismael is not alone in his reappearance. Though seemingly selfcontained when read singly, the novels (much like those of Faulkner) shade from one into another. The gang artist, Hinton in *The Warriors,* reappears, for instance, as a major figure in *The Bag*. Hinton's mother, Minnie (permanently on welfare and having a new ''lover''), and his brother the addict, Alonso, minor figures at the end of Hinton's anabasis, also return but now as full-fledged characters in *The Bag.*

In contrast to the lower depths of *The Warriors* and part of *The Bag, Fertig* appears at first to be an exploration of a strictly middle-class New York Jewish milieu. But the death of Fertig's son as a result of indifference on the part of the staff of a New York hospital triggers such a paroxysm of grief that Fertig cold-bloodedly murders some seven people involved however tenuously in his son's death. As mass murderer, Fertig is then thrust into the company of the criminals, madmen, and junkies who populate Yurick's other two novels. We are also given our first view of the political elite of this mythical New York: Judge Mabel Crossland whose thighs have encompassed every prominent jurist in New York in her climb to the judgeship; Fertig's lawyer, Royboy, the small but handsome sexual athlete, with multiple obligations to his female admirers (including Mabel Crossland) on his way to becoming Senator Roy, a character whom we then meet in *The Bag;* and Irving Hockstaff, king-maker, the man who indirectly runs the whole political apparatus of the city. A pawn in the political games of the mighty. Fertig and Fertig's trial are painfully reminiscent of *An American Tragedy.*

The evocation in *Fertig* of another classic work of literature is an integral part of Yurick's aesthetic and political methodology. The book is shaped as a contemporary replay of a recurrent phenomenon; the destruction of ''the little man'' by the power elite. Fertig's name comments ironically on a phenomenon that never ends. Likewise Ismael and Faust in *The Bag* are conscious restatements on a theme as old as poverty. Minnie (referred to by Yurick as a black Cybele and as the Wyf of Bath) loves Alpha (Fertig or Omega's opposite?) who has left his wife, Helen. They share the world with Faust (a figure drawn not only from Goethe but from Kosinski's *The Painted Bird*), with Faust's daughter, the lesbian Eve, and with Faust's ambitious urban renewal project: Rebirth. Finally, Rebirth and all the little men and women are crushed as the ghetto detonates despite the best efforts of the man from Agape (love, affection), the master of the government's counter-insurgency game plan. We know with Yurick at the end of *The Bag* (though it is never explicitly stated) that the future of this city that is all cities lies not with the Ismael's and others who seek social improvement but with the Royboys and the Hockstaffs. It is they who seem to believe: ''It didn't matter how many people you killed so long as you contained it [the revolution] and cooled it and co-opted it and made it run smoothly.'' So it has always been says Yurick and so it will be: Alpha and Agape are Omega and Fertig. The end of Ismael in *The Bag* returns us not only to Ismael at the beginning of *The Warriors* but to the ancient admonition drawn from the *Anabasis.* The ''homeland'' lies permanently within sight but beyond reach. There is some doubt that, all his aesthetic skill and political acumen notwithstanding, Yurick will ever get us any closer, but his portrayal of anabasis itself is worthy of comparison with its ancient counterpart.

—John Fuegi

NOTES ON ADVISERS AND CONTRIBUTORS

ABNEY, Lisa. Assistant professor of English and director of the Louisiana Folklife Center at Northwestern State University; research interests in folklore, sociolinguistics, and southern literature; currently working on a collection of essays regarding Louisiana writers from 1865–1945 (with Suzanne Green), and conducting linguistic survey of north Louisiana (to be completed in 2002). Editor (with Green) of *Songs of the New South: Writing Contemporary Louisiana*, 2001. **Essay:** Clyde Edgerton.

ABUNASSER, Rima. Doctoral candidate, University of North Texas, Denton. Specializes in English literature with a focus on eighteenth-century British literature and postcolonial theory. **Essay:** Nadine Gordimer.

AITKEN, Maureen. Teacher at University of Michigan, Ann Arbor. Author of short fiction published in various literary journals; winner of Fish Short Story Prize (Ireland). **Essays:** Octavia E. Butler; Carol Shields; William Trevor; Edmund White; Marianne Wiggins.

AKEY, Stephen. Freelance writer. **Essays:** Paul Auster; James Welch.

ALLEN, Walter. Critic and novelist. Author of *The English Novel: A Short Critical History*, 1954; *Tradition and Dream: The English and American Novel from the Twenties to Our Time,* 1965; and other critical studies. Died 1994. **Essay:** Edward Upward.

ALMONTE, Richard. Doctoral candidate in English, McMaster University, Hamilton, Ontario; marketing director, Insomniac Press, Toronto. Author of two editions of nineteenth-century Black Canadian texts and an essay on Blackness in Canadian literature. **Essays:** Peter Ackroyd; Rick Moody.

ALTNER, Patricia. Librarian, Department of Defense, Washington, D.C. Reviewer of historical fiction for *Library Journal*; associate editor of *This Year's Scholarship in Science Fiction, Fantasy, and Horror.* **Essays:** Carol Hill; Mary Robison.

ANDERSEN, Richard. James Thurber writer-in-residence, Ohio State University, Columbus. Author of critical studies of William Goldman and Robert Coover, and four novels—*Muckaluck, Straight Cut Ditch, On the Run*, and *The Reluctant Hero*. **Essay:** William Goldman.

ANG, Susan. Faculty member, Department of English Language and Literature, National University of Singapore. **Essay:** Catherine Lim.

ASENSIO-ARÓSTEGUI, Mar. Assistant lecturer of English language and English literature at the University of La Rioja, Spain. She has completed an M.A. in studies in fiction at the University of East Anglia, Great Britain, and is currently about to finish her Ph.D. thesis on Jeanette Winterson's fiction of the 1980s. Her published work includes articles on Doris Lessing, Jeanette Winterson, Woody Allen, Ridley Scott and Peter Weir. **Essay:** Jeanette Winterson.

AUBERT, Alvin. Professor emeritus of English, Wayne State University, Detroit; founding editor of *Obsidian* magazine, now *Obsidian II*. Author of five books of poetry—*Against the Blues*, 1972; *Feeling Through*, 1975; *South Louisiana*, 1985; *If Winter Come*, 1994; and *Harlem Wrestler*, 1995. **Essay:** Ernest J. Gaines.

AUGENBRAUM, Harold. Director, The Mercantile Library of New York and its Center for World Literature. Author of *Growing Up Latino* (co-edited with Ilan Stavans); *The Latino Reader*; and *U.S. Latino Literature: A Critical Guide for Students and Teachers* (both co-edited with Margarite Fernández Olmos). Editor of forthcoming *Norton Anthology of Latino Literature of the United States*. **Essays:** Cristina Garcia; Oscar Hijuelos; John Rechy.

BAKERMAN, Jane S. Professor of English emerita, Indiana State University, Terre Haute. Author of numerous critical essays, interviews, and reviews; adviser and contributor, *American Women Writers 1–4*; and *Twentieth-Century Crime and Mystery Writers*, 1991. Co-author of *The Adolescent in the Novel After 1960*. Editor of *Adolescent Female Portraits in the American Novel 1961–1981* (with Mary Jean DeMarr), 1983; and *And Then There Were Nine: More Women of Mystery*, 1984. **Essay:** Lisa Alther.

BALL, John Clement. Associate professor of English, University of New Brunswick, Fredericton, New Brunswick. Author of articles on postcolonial and Canadian literature. Editor of *Studies in Canadian Literature*. **Essays:** Andre Alexis; Amitav Ghosh; Arundhati Roy.

BAMBERGER, William C. Editor and publisher of Bamberger Books, Flint, Michigan. Author of *A Jealousy for Aesop*, 1988; *William Eastlake: High Desert Interlocutor* (forthcoming); criticism in *Review of Contemporary Fiction*; and fiction in *CoEvolution*, *Ascent*, and other periodicals. **Essays:** Barry Hannah; Alice Hoffman; Diane Johnson; Steve Katz; David Madden; William Wharton.

BARNES, John. Reader in English, La Trobe University, Bundoora, Victoria; editor of *Meridian*. Author of *Henry Kingsley and Colonial Fiction*, 1971; and articles on Hal Porter and Patrick White. **Essay:** Peter Cowan.

BATCHELOR, Bob. Writer at UpStart Communications, a division of Fleishman-Hillard. His work has appeared in dbusiness.com, Office.com, Voter.com and many other online and off-line publications. He is a contributing editor at *Inside Business* magazine and the author of the forthcoming *The 1900s: American History through Culture* (Greenwood). **Essays:** Howard Norman; Tom Wolfe.

BELL, Ian A. Professor of English, University of Wales, Swansea. Author of *Defoe's Fiction*, 1985; and *Literature and Crime in Augustan England*, 1991. Editor, with Graham Daldry, *Watching the Detectives: Essays in Crime Fiction*, 1990; and *Henry Fielding*, 1994. **Essays:** James Kelman; Alan Spence.

BELLMAN, Samuel I. Professor of English, California State University; freelance writer and critic. **Essay:** Alan Cheuse.

BENNETT, Bruce. Professor of English, University College, University of New South Wales, Australian Defense Force Academy, Canberra. Formerly editor of *Westerly: A Quarterly Review*, and director of the Center for Studies in Australian Literature, University of Western Australia. Author of *Place, Region and Community*, 1985; and *An Australian Compass*, 1991. Editor of *European Relations*, 1985; *A Sense of Exile*, 1988; *Myths, Heroes and Anti-Heroes*, 1992; books of critical essays on Australian authors; and anthologies of Australian and postcolonial literatures. **Essays:** Alex Miller; Michael Wilding.

BERGONZI, Bernard. Emeritus professor of English, University of Warwick, Coventry. Author of a novel, *The Roman Persuasion*, 1981; and several books on modern literature and criticism, of which the most recent are *Exploding English*, 1990; *Wartime and Aftermath*,

1993; and *David Lodge*, 1995. **Essays:** David Lodge; Julian Mitchell; Andrew Sinclair.

BIRD, Tammy. General education coordinator and distance education coordinator, ECPI College of Technology, Virginia Beach, Virginia. Research interests center around women's writing and women's literary history; American literature; feminist theory and pedagogy; rhetoric/composition; implementation of virtual-based communication in classrooms and the effects of hypertext documentation in literary research and analysis. **Essays:** Phyllis Gotlieb; Audrey Thomas.

BIRNEY, Earle. Formerly regents professor in creative writing, University of California, Irvine; past editor of *Canadian Forum*, *Canadian Poetry Magazine*, *Prism International*, and *New American and Canadian Poetry.* Author of more than 20 books of poetry (most recently *Copernican Fix*, 1985); two novels (*Turvey: A Military Picaresque*, 1949 [revised 1977] and *Down the Long Table*, 1955); short stories (*Big Bird in the Bush: Selected Stories and Sketches*, 1978); plays for stage and radio, and critical studies on creative writing. Editor of selections of poetry by Canadian writers.

BITTNER, William. Late professor of English, Acadia University, Wolfville, Nova Scotia. Author of *Poe: A Biography*; *The Novels of Waldo Frank*; and of articles in *Atlantic Monthly*, *The Nation*, *Saturday Review*, *New York Post*, and other periodicals. Died 1977. **Essay:** Anthony C. West.

BORDEN, William. Chester Fritz Distinguished Professor of English, University of North Dakota, Grand Forks. Author of the novel *Superstoe*, 1968; and plays, including *The Last Prostitute*, 1982; and *Loon Dance*, 1983. **Essay:** William Melvin Kelley.

BORKLUND, Elmer. Professor of English, Pennsylvania State University, University Park. Former associate editor of *Chicago Review.* Author of *Contemporary Literary Critics*, 1977 (2nd edition 1982); and of articles in *Modern Philology*, *Commentary*, *New York Herald-Tribune Book Week*, and *Journal of General Education.* **Essays:** Mavis Gallant; Susan Sontag; Paul West.

BRADBURY, Malcolm. See his own entry. **Essay:** William Cooper.

BRADFORD, M.E. Professor of English and American studies, University of Dallas; member of the editorial board of *Modern Age.* Author of *Rumours of Mortality: An Introduction to Allen Tate*, 1967; *A Better Guide Than Reason*, 1980; *Generations of the Faithful Heart: On the Literature of the South*, 1982; *A Worthy Company: Brief Lives of the Framers of the Constitution*, 1982; *Remembering Who We Are: Observations of a Southern Conservative*, 1985; *The Reactionary Imperative: Essays Literary and Political*, 1989; and of articles in *Bear, Man, and God*, 1971; *Allen Tate and His Work*, 1971; and *Sewanee Review*, *National Review*, *Southern Review*, and other periodicals. Editor of *The Form Discovered: Essays on the Achievement of Andrew Lytle*, 1973. **Essay:** Madison Jones.

BREITINGER, Eckhard. Associate professor, Institute for African Studies, Bayreuth University; former instructor at University of the West Indies (Jamaica), UST in Kumasi (Ghana), Makerere University (Uganda), and additional universities in Africa and Europe. Author of publications on the 18th-century novel, American radio drama, and African and Caribbean literature, mainly on theatre. Translator of plays into German; assembled theatre photographs in exhibitions shown in Africa, Europe, and the United States. **Essays:** Nuruddin Farah; Abdulrazak Gurnah.

BRIGG, Peter. Associate professor of English, University of Guelph, Guelph, Ontario. Author of *J.G. Ballard* and *A Shanghai Year*; chapters in volumes on Ursula K. Le Guin, Arthur C. Clarke, and Robertson Davies; articles in *Science Fiction Studies*, *Extrapolation*, *Mosaic*, *Foundation*, *English Studies in Canada*, *Canadian Literature*, *World Literature Written in English*, *Canadian Drama*, and *Educational Theatre Journal*; and encyclopedia entries in *Survey of Science Fiction Literature*, *Twentieth-Century Science Fiction Writers*, *Survey of Modern Fantasy Literature*, and *The International Dictionary of the Theatre*. **Essays:** Ursula Hegi; Michael Ignatieff; Anne Michaels; John Steffler; Susan Swan.

BRIGHT, Juliette. Freelance writer and journalist. **Essays:** Alice Munro.

BROUGHTON, W.S. Senior lecturer in English, Massey University, Palmerston North, New Zealand; member of New Zealand Literary Fund Advisory Committee, 1985–90. **Essay:** Owen Marshall.

BROWN, Lloyd W. Member of the Department of Comparative Literature, University of Southern California, Los Angeles. Author of *West Indian Poetry*, 1978 (revised 1984); *Amiri Baraka*, 1980; and *Women Writers in Black Africa*, 1981. Editor of *The Black Writer in Africa and the Americas*, 1973. **Essays:** Austin C. Clarke; Roy A.K. Heath; Marion Patrick Jones.

BROWN, Richard. Senior lecturer in English, University of Leeds; co-editor of *James Joyce Broadsheet.* Author of *James Joyce*, 1992; and *James Joyce and Sexuality*, 1985. **Essays:** Martin Amis; Julian Barnes.

BRYER, Lynne. Publisher, Chameleon Press, Cape Town; former critic and journalist; responsible for rediscovering and reissuing Daphne Rooke's South African novels in that country. Author of *The British Settlers of 1820*, 1986. **Essay:** Daphne Rooke.

BUCKNALL, Harry. English language teacher and freelance writer. **Essay:** Charles Johnson.

BURGESS, Anthony. Novelist and critic; author of *A Clockwork Orange*, 1962, among numerous other novels and works of nonfiction. Died 1993.

BUXTON, Jackie. Doctoral candidate in English, York University, Toronto. Dissertation on the contemporary historical novel. Author of articles on various aspects of contemporary fiction in *Contemporary Literature* and *English Studies in Canada.* **Essays:** Margaret Atwood; Witi Ihimaera.

BYERMAN, Keith. Professor, Department of English, Indiana State University, Terre Haute. Author of *Fingering the Jagged Grain: Tradition and Form in Recent Black Fiction*, 1986; *Alice Walker: An Annotated Bibliography* (with Erma Banks), 1989; *Seizing the Word: History, Art, and Self in the Work of W.E.B. DuBois*, 1994; *The Short Fiction of John Edgar Wideman*, 1998; and numerous book and journal articles on African-American and Southern literature.

CADOGAN, Mary. Secretary of an educational trust, governor of an international school, and freelance writer. Author of three books on popular literature with Patricia Craig—*You're a Brick, Angela!*, 1976; *Women and Children First*, 1978; and *The Lady Investigates*,

1981—three volumes of *The Charles Hamilton Companion* (with John Wernham), 1976–82; *The Morcove Companion* (with Tommy Keen), 1981; *From Wharton Lodge to Linton Hall: The Charles Hamilton Christmas Companion* (with Tommy Keen), 1984; *Richmal Crompton: The Woman Behind William*, 1986; *Frank Richards: The Chap Behind the Chums*, 1988; and *The William Companion*, 1990. **Essay:** Gillian Freeman.

CAMEROS, Cynthia. Teacher at Montclair State University, New Jersey. Author of reviews in *Modern Fiction Studies* and *Kirkus Reviews*. **Essays:** Penelope Lively; Graham Swift.

CAMPENNI, Frank. Associate professor of English, University of Wisconsin, Milwaukee. Author of articles and reviews in periodicals. **Essays:** Howard Fast; Irvin Faust; Mark Mirsky; Michael Rumaker; Budd Schulberg; Charles Wright.

CANEPARI-LABIB, Michela. Researcher of English literature. Born in Italy and educated at the University of Pavia (Italy) and the University of Sussex (United Kingdom). After she was awarded her first degree, she moved to the South of England, where she has lived ever since. She has combined teaching with translating and writing, publishing on both contemporary authors and topical issues of a literary and theoretical nature. She is the author of *Word-Worlds: Language, Identity and Reality in the Work of Christine Brooke-Rose*. **Essay:** Christine Brooke-Rose.

CARCHIDI, Victoria. Teaches postcolonial literature and media studies at Massey University, Palmerston North, New Zealand. **Essays:** Lois McMaster Bujold; Shimmer Chinodya; Njabulo Ndebele.

CHAMBERS, D.D.C. Associate professor of English, Trinity College, Toronto. Editor of two book of poetry by Thomas Traherne, and *A Few Friends: Poems for Thom Gunn's 60th Birthday*, 1989. **Essay:** John Rechy.

CHANEY, Michael A. Doctoral candidate in English with a minor in African American Studies at Indiana University. His dissertation explores antebellum cultural intersections of slave narratives and race spectacles with travel literature and ethnography. Chaney has written on nineteenth-century sentimentalism in the *American Transcendental Quarterly*; and has written reviews for *Post Modern Culture* and *African American Review*. **Essays:** Wesley Brown; Trey Ellis; Festus Iyayi; Jamal Majhoub; John A. Williams.

CHEW, Shirley. Lecturer in English, University of Leeds. Editor of *Selected Poems: Arthur Hugh Clough*, 1987. **Essay:** Patricia Grace.

CHIHARA, Paul Seiko. Associate professor of Music, University of California, Los Angeles. Composer of numerous works, including *Driftwood* (string quartet), 1969; *Forest Music for Orchestra*, 1970; and music for ballets and films. Author of "Revolution and Music," 1970; and other essays. **Essay:** James Yaffe.

CLANCY, Laurie. Reader in English, La Trobe University, Bundoora, Victoria. Author of three novels: *A Collapsible Man*, 1975; *Perfect Love*, 1983; and *The Wild Life Reserve*, 1994; two collections of short stories: *The Wife Specialist*, 1978; and *City to City*, 1988; and critical works on Christina Stead, Xavier Herbert, and Vladimir Nabokov, as well as *A Reader's Guide to Australian Fiction*, 1992. **Essays:** Glenda Adams; Thea Astley; Murray Bail; Brian Castro; Robert Coover; Blanche d'Alpuget; Sara Dowse; Beverley Farmer; David Foster; Kate Grenville; Rodney Hall; Shirley Hazzard; Janette Turner Hospital; Elizabeth Jolley; Neil Jordon; Victor Kelleher; C.J. Koch; Peter Mathers; Roger McDonald; Gerald Murnane; Jayne Ann Phillips; Rosie Scott; C.K. Stead; Tim Winton.

CLARK, Anderson. Associate professor of English and director of the International English Institute, Belmont College, Nashville. **Essay:** Shelby Foote.

COALE, Sam. Professor of English, Wheaton College, Norton, Massachusetts. Author of *Hawthorne's Shadow: American Romance from Melville to Miller*, 1985; and *William Styron Revisited*, 1991. **Essay:** James Lee Burke.

COBB, Loretta. Director emeritus of the Harbert Writing Center, University of Montevallo; freelance writer and editor, and columnist for *The Birmingham News*. **Essays:** Barry Hannah; Ward Just; W.P. Kinsella; Larry Woiwode.

COLONNESE, Tom. Teacher at Northern Arizona University, Flagstaff; program director for Native Americans for Community Action, and Native American Social Service Agency. Author of *American Indian Novelists: An Annotated Critical Bibliography* (with Louis Owens), 1985; and *Dictionary of American Indian Novelists* (forthcoming). **Essays:** Jim Harrison; Jay McInerney; Larry McMurtry; N. Scott Momaday.

COOKE, Judy. Freelance writer and editor, London. Editor of *The Best of Fiction Magazine* (with Elizabeth Bunster), 1986; and *Passions and Reflections: A Collection of 20th-Century Women's Fiction*, 1991. **Essays:** A.L. Barker; Jennifer Dawson; Maureen Duffy; Neil Jordan.

CORBALLIS, Richard. Senior lecturer in English, Massey University, Palmerston North, New Zealand. Author of *Stoppard: The Mystery and the Clockwork*, 1984; and *Introducing Witi Ihimaera* (with Simon Garrett), 1984. Editor of *George Chapman's Minor Translations: A Critical Edition of His Renderings of Musaeus, Hesiod and Juvenal*, 1984. **Essays:** Alan Duff; Stevan Eldred-Grigg; Patricia Grace; Keri Hulme.

COTTON, John. Author of many books of poetry—collections include *Old Movies and Other Poems*, 1971; *The Day Book*, 1983; *The Storyville Portraits*, 1984; *The Poetry File*, 1988; and *Here's Looking at You Kid*, 1990—and of *British Poetry since 1965*, 1973. **Essays:** Brian Aldiss; Maggie Gee; D.M. Thomas.

COX, F. Brett. Teaches literature and writing and is director of the Alabama Center for Literary Arts, Alabama Southern College, Monroeville, Alabama. Author of fiction and criticism in *New England Quarterly*, *The New York Review of Science Fiction*, *Century Magazine*, *The Robert Frost Encyclopedia*, *Baltimore Sun*, and elsewhere. **Essays:** Mark Childress; Edwidge Danticat; William Gay; William Gibson; Bruce Sterling.

CRANE, Ralph J. Senior lecturer in English, University of Waikato, Hamilton, New Zealand. Teaches colonial and postcolonial literatures. Author of *Inventing India: A History of India in English-Language Fiction*, 1992; *Ruth Prawer Jhabvala*, 1992; and *Troubled Pleasures: The Fiction of J.G. Farrell* (with Jennifer Livett), 1997. Editor of collections of essays on Ruth Prawer Jhabvala, Maurice Shadbolt, Nayantara Sahgal, J.G. Farrell, and Indian diaspora writing. Since 1994 he has been chairperson of the South Pacific Association for Commonwealth Literature and Language Studies (SPACLALS) and co- editor of the association's journal, *Span*. **Essays:** Anita Desai; Ruth Prawer Jhabvala; Bharati Mukherjee; I. Allan Sealy; Maurice Shadbolt; Bapsi Sidhwa; Shashi Tharoor.

CUSHMAN, Susan E. Doctoral candidate, Lehigh University, Pennsylvania. Specializes in twentieth-century American literature and teaches English and women's studies. Dissertation on postmodern trends in American autobiography, in particular the contributions that bicultural writers Maxine Hong Kingston, Leslie Marmon Silko, and Gloria Anzaldua have made to the genre. **Essay:** Sandra Cisneros.

CUSICK, Edmund. Lecturer in English, Liverpool Polytechnic; formerly assistant editor of *Shorter Oxford English Dictionary*. Author of "Macdonald and Jung," in *The Gold Thread*, 1991. **Essays:** Michael Moorcock; Carolyn Slaughter.

DANIEL, Helen. Freelance critic and reviewer. Author of *Double Agent: David Ireland and His Work*, 1982; and *Liars: Australian New Novelists*, 1988. Editor of *Australian Book Review*, and the books *Expressway*, 1989; *The Good Reading Guide: Australian Fiction 1968-1988*, 1989; and *Millennium*, 1991. **Essay:** Marion Campbell.

DAWSON, Terence. Lecturer in English, National University of Singapore. Author of numerous articles on both English and French literature. **Essay:** Edna O'Brien.

D'CRUZ, Doreen. Lecturer in English, Massey University, Palmerston North, New Zealand. **Essay:** Barbara Anderson.

de KOCK, Leon. Lecturer in English, University of South Africa, Pretoria. **Essays:** André Brink; Nadine Gordimer; Christopher Hope.

DELREZ, Marc. Teaches English literature at the University of Liege. Author of articles on David Malouf, Randolph Stow, and Janet Frame; and a forthcoming monograph on Janet Frame. **Essay:** David Malouf.

DESY, Peter. Member of the Department of English, Ohio University, Lancaster. Author of fiction and poetry in many journals and anthologies. **Essays:** Denis Johnson; W.P. Kinsella; Susan Fromberg Schaeffer.

deVILLE, Susie. Production editor and freelance writer. Contributor to *Travelers' Quarterly*. **Essay:** Festus Iyayi.

DICKINSON, Adam. Doctoral candidate at the University of Alberta with research interests in contemporary Canadian and American literature and ethics. **Essay:** Michael Ondaatje.

DICKINSON, Peter. Teaches in the English department and Critical Studies in Sexuality Program at the University of British Columbia. Author of *Here is Queer: Nationalisms, Sexualities, and the Literatures of Canada*, 1999. **Essays:** Stephen Gray; Tomson Highway; Shyam Selvadurai.

DILLARD, R.H.W. Professor of English and chairman of the graduate program in Contemporary Literature and Creative Writing, Hollins College, Virginia; editor of *Hollins Critic*. Author of four books of poetry (most recently *The Greeting: New and Selected Poems*, 1981); two novels *The Book of Chances*, 1974; and *The First Man on the Sun*, 1983; a screenplay; and of *Horror Films*, 1976; and *Understanding George Garrett*, 1988. Editor of two collections of essays. **Essay:** George Garrett.

DOYLE, Paul A. Professor of English, Nassau Community College, State University of New York, Garden City; editor, *Evelyn Waugh Newsletter and Studies* and *Nassau Review*. Author of *Sean O'Faolain*, 1968; *Introduction to Paul Vincent Carroll*, 1971; *Liam O'Flaherty*, 1971; *Guide to Basic Information Sources in English Literature*, 1976; *Pearl S. Buck*, 1980; *A Reader's Companion to the Novels and Short Stories of Evelyn Waugh*, 1988; of bibliographies of O'Flaherty and Waugh; and *A Concordance to the Collected Poems of James Joyce*, 1966; co-author of *Early American Trains*, 1993. Editor of *Alexander Pope's Iliad: An Examination*, 1960. **Essays:** John Ed Bradley; Thomas Flanagan; Piers Paul Read.

DRABBLE, Margaret. See her own entry.

DRIVER, Dorothy. Senior lecturer in English, University of Cape Town, South Africa; South African correspondent to the *Journal of Commonwealth Literature*. Author of *Pauline Smith and the Crisis of Daughterhood* (forthcoming) and of numerous articles on writing by South African women. Editor of *The Little Karoo* by Pauline Smith, 1983.

DUCKWORTH, Deborah. Formerly instructor in English and English as a Second Language, Louisiana State University, Baton Rouge. **Essay:** Elaine Dundy.

DUNCAN, Andy. Teaches creative writing, composition, and literature at the University of Alabama. Author of *Beluthahatchie and Other Stories*, 2000; fiction in *Asimov's*, *Event Horizon*, *Realms of Fantasy*, *Weird Tales*, *Starlight 1*, and Stephen Jones's *Best New Horror* series; and has been nominated for the Hugo, Nebula, Campbell, and International Horror Guild awards. Also author of critical essays in *FEMSPEC, The New York Review of Science Fiction,* and *North Carolina Literary Review*. **Essays:** Randall Kenan; Stewart O'Nan.

DURSO, Patricia Keefe. Independent scholar; teacher of English and creative writing at various universities. Author of articles on American women writers in various publications, including the *Colby Quarterly*, *In Process: A Journal of African-American and African Diasporan Literature and Culture*, and *Anglophone Literature* (forthcoming). Research interests in ethnicity and race; compiled special issue on "whiteness" for *Modern Language Studies*. **Essay:** Gish Jen.

DWELLE, Josh. Master's degree candidate, University of North Texas, Denton. Specializes in twentieth-century American literature. **Essays:** Cormac McCarthy; Ian McEwan.

DYER, Klay. Assistant professor, Department of English and Canadian Studies, Brock University, Ontario; academic advisor to the Early Canadiana Online digitalization project. Author of articles on Canadian literature and culture. Contributing editor for *Journal of Canadian Poetry* and *Harpweaver*. **Essays:** George Bowering; Bonnie Burnard; David Adams Richards; Guy Vanderhaeghe; M.G. Vassanji.

EDMANDS, Ursula. Former lecturer in English, Leeds Polytechnic; now with Sheffield City Council. **Essays:** C.J. Driver; Dan Jacobson.

EISINGER, Chester E. Former professor of English, Purdue University, Lafayette, Indiana; now retired. Author of *Fiction of the Forties*, 1963; and articles in *Proletarian Writers of the Thirties*, 1968; and *Saturday Review*. Editor of *The 1940's: Profile of a Nation* *in Crisis*, 1969. **Essays:** Louis Auchincloss; William H. Gass; Shirley Ann Grau.

ELBORN, Geoffrey. Freelance writer and critic. **Essays:** Peter Ackroyd; John Banville; Pat Barker; William Boyd; Sebastian Faulks; Alan Hollinghurst; Bernice Rubens; Lisa St. Aubin de Teran; Edmund White.

FACKNITZ, Mark A.R. Lecturer in English, James Madison University, Harrisonburg, Virginia. **Essay:** Tobias Wolff.

FERRAN, Peter. Professor, Rochester Institute of Technology. **Essay:** James Ellroy.

FERRELL, Keith. Novelist, nonfiction writer, and speaker. Author of more than a dozen books and over 1,000 articles. Dozens of public and media appearances to his credit. From 1990 until 1996 he was editor-in-chief of *OMNI Magazine*, and oversaw the migration of the magazine to the Internet, the first major publication to do so. His novel *Passing Judgment* was published in 1996; other books include biographies of H.G. Wells and Ernest Hemingway. A new novel should appear in 2000. **Essays:** Greg Bear; Gregory Benford.

FIEDLER, Leslie A. Critic and novelist. Clemens Chair Professor, Department of English, State University of New York, Buffalo. Author of *Love and Death in the American Novel*, 1960; *No! In Thunder*, 1960; *What Was Literature? Class Culture and Mass Society*, 1982; and other works of criticism.

FIERO, John W. Professor of English, University of Southwestern Louisiana, Lafayette; director of creative writing and the Deep South Writers Conference. Author of several plays and articles on Bertolt Brecht, Anton Chehkov, Max Frisch, Ernest Gaines, A.R. Gurney, Jr., Bret Harte, Preston Jones, Ben Jonson, Franz Kafka, Terrence McNally, William Saroyan, and Kurt Vonnegut, Jr. **Essay:** Anne Rice.

FOSTER, Ruel E. Benedum Professor of American Literature, West Virginia University, Morgantown. Author of *Work in Progress*, 1948; *William Faulkner: A Critical Appraisal*, 1951; *Elizabeth Madox Roberts, American Novelist* (with Harry Modean Campbell), 1956; and *Jesse Stuart*, 1968. **Essay:** John Knowles.

FRANKS, Jill. Faculty member, Department of English, University of British Columbia; freelance writer and critic. **Essays:** Ama Ata Aidoo; Rosellen Brown; Susan Minot.

FRENCH, Anne. Managing editor, Museum of New Zealand, Wellington. Author of four books of poetry—*All Cretans Are Liars*, 1987; *The Male as Evader*, 1988; *Cabin Fever*, 1990; and *Seven Days on Mykonos*, 1993. Contributor to *The Oxford Companion to Contemporary Poetry*, *The Oxford Companion to New Zealand Literature*, and *The Routledge Encyclopaedia of Commonwealth Literature*. **Essay:** Barbara Trapido.

FRENCH, Warren. Professor of English and director of the Centre for American Studies, Indiana University-Purdue University, Indianapolis, retired 1986; member of the editorial board, *American Literature* and *Twentieth-Century Literature*; editor of the American Authors series for Twayne publishers. Author of *John Steinbeck*, 1961; *Frank Norris*, 1962; *J.D. Salinger*, 1963 (revised 1976); *A Companion to "The Grapes of Wrath,"* 1963; *The Social Novel at the End of an Era*, 1966; *The South in Film*, 1981; *Jack Kerouac*, 1986; and a series on American literature: *The Thirties*, 1967; *The Forties*, 1968; *The Fifties*, 1971; and *The Twenties*, 1975. **Essays:** R.K. Narayan; Tom Robbins; Khushwant Singh; Elizabeth Spencer; Eudora Welty.

FRIEDMAN, Melvin J. Professor of comparative literature, University of Wisconsin, Milwaukee; advisory editor of *Journal of Popular Culture*, *Studies in the Novel*, *Renascence*, *Journal of American Culture*, *Studies in American Fiction*, *Fer de Lance*, *Contemporary Literature*, *Journal of Beckett Studies*, *International Fiction Review*, *Arete*, *Yiddish*, *Journal of Modern Literature*, and *Studies in American Jewish Literature*. Author of *Stream of Consciousness: A Study in Literary Method*, 1955. Author or editor of works about Beckett, Flannery O'Connor, Styron, Ezra Pound, Catholic novelists, and Ionesco. **Essays:** Wallace Markfield; Philip Roth.

FROST, Lucy. Senior lecturer in English, La Trobe University, Bundoora, Victoria. Author of *No Place for a Nervous Lady: Voices from the Australian Bush*, 1984; *A Face in the Glass: The Journal and Life of Annie Baxter Dawbin*, 1992; and articles on nineteenth- and twentieth-century literature and culture. **Essays:** Marion Halligan; Frank Moorhouse.

FUEGI, John. Professor and director of the comparative literature program, University of Maryland, College Park; managing editor, *Brecht Yearbook*. Author of *The Wall* (documentary film), 1961; *The Essential Brecht*, 1972; and *Bertolt Brecht: Chaos According to Plan*. Editor of *Brecht Today*, 3 vols., 1972–74. **Essay:** Sol Yurick.

FULLER, Roy. Poet, novelist, and critic. Died 1991.

GALLOWAY, David. Chair of American studies, University of the Ruhr, Bochum, West Germany. Author of *The Absurd Hero in American Fiction*, 1966 (revised 1970 and 1981); *Henry James*, 1967; *Edward Lewis Wallant*, 1979; and four novels—the most recent being *Tamsen*, 1983. Editor of *The Selected Writings of Edgar Allan Poe*, 1967; *Ten Modern American Short Stories*, 1968; *Calamus*, 1982; and *The Other Poe: Comedies and Satires*, 1983. **Essay:** Evan Hunter.

GAUTHIER, Tim. Doctoral candidate, University of Nevada, Las Vegas. Dissertation addresses the idea of history in the British novel of the 1980s and 1990s. Research interests extend to contemporary literature in general, including Irish and Canadian, and the evolution of the short-story sequence. **Essays:** Shane Connaughton; Michael Cunningham.

GEARHART, Stephannie S. Instructor of English, English Department, Lehigh University, Bethlehem, Pennsylvania. **Essays:** Russell Banks; Chitra Banerjee Divakaruni.

GEHERIN, David. Professor of English, Eastern Michigan University, Ypsilanti. Author of several articles and four books on mystery fiction: *Sons of Sam Spade*, *John D. MacDonald*, *The American Private Eye*, and *Elmore Leonard*. Teaches courses in twentieth-century literature and on mystery and detective fiction. **Essays:** Frederick Barthelme; Arthur Hailey; Elmore Leonard; Walter Mosley; Robert Stone.

GINDIN, James. Late professor of English, University of Michigan, Ann Arbor. Author of *Postwar British Fiction*, 1962; *Harvest of a Quiet Eye: The Novel of Compassion*, 1971; *The English Climate: An Excursion into a Biography of John Gals Worthy*, 1979; *John Galsworthy's Life and Art: An Alien's Fortress*, 1986; and *William Golding*, 1988. Editor of *The Return of the Native*, by Hardy, 1969.

Died. **Essays:** John Bowen; Malcolm Bradbury; David Cook; Lionel Davidson; Margaret Drabble; John Fowles; Thomas Hinde; Elizabeth Jane Howard; Norman Mailer; Keith Waterhouse.

GOONETILLEKE, D.C.R.A. Senior professor and department head of English, University of Kelaniya, Sri Lanka; world chair, Association for Commonwealth Literature and Language Studies; vice-chair, International Federation for Modern Languages and Literatures. Author of *Developing Countries in British Fiction*, 1977; *Between Culture: Essays on Literature, Language and Education*, 1987; *Images of the Raj: South Asia in the Literature of the Empire*, 1988; and *Joseph Conrad: Beyond Culture and Background*, 1990. Editor of *Heart of Darkness* by Joseph Conrad, 1995; and of anthologies of Sri Lankan poetry, fiction, and drama.

GORDON, Lois. Professor of English and comparative literature, Fairleigh Dickinson University, Teaneck, New Jersey. Author of Stratagems to *Uncover Nakedness: The Dramas of Harold Pinter*, 1969; *Donald Barthelme*, 1981; *Robert Coover: The Universal Fictionmaking Process*, 1983; *American Chronicle: Six Decades in American Life, 1920–1979*, 1987; *Harold Pinter: A Casebook*, 1990; *American Chronicle: Seven Decades in American Life, 1920–1989*, 1990; *The Columbia Chronicles of American Life, 1910–1995*, 1995; and articles on Faulkner, T.S. Eliot, Beckett, Philip Roth, Arthur Miller, and other writers. **Essays:** Ann Beattie; Erica Jong.

GORDON-SMITH, Pat. Commissioning editor and freelance writer. **Essay:** Caryl Phillips.

GORSKI, Hedwig. Doctoral candidate, University of Louisiana, Lafayette; poet, dramatist, journalist, and screenplay writer. Dissertation on Wislawa Szymborska. **Essays:** James Lee Burke; Maurice Gee; Aidan Higgins; Christopher Hope; Tana Jamowitz; Fiona Kidman; Sue McCauley; Larry McMurtry; Vincent O'Sullivan; Gore Vidal; Noel Virtue.

GRACIAS, Marian. Doctoral candidate, University of British Columbia, Vancouver, specializing in gender studies and postcolonialism. **Essay:** David Dabydeen.

GRAHAM, Colin. Lecturer in Irish Writing, Queen's University of Belfast. Author of *Ideologies of Epic*, 1998. **Essays:** Roddy Doyle; Hanif Kureishi; John McGahern.

GREEN, Suzanne Disheroon. Assistant professor of American literature, Northwestern State University. Co-author of *Kate Chopin: An Annotated Bibliography of Critical Works*, 1999; and *At Fault by Kate Chopin: A Scholarly Edition with Background Readings* (with David J. Caudle), 2001; and *Songs of the New South: Writing Contemporary Louisiana* (with Lisa Abney), 2001. Author of numerous articles on Southern writers, including "How Edna Escaped: The Life is a Journey Conceptual Metaphor in The Awakening" in *The Poetics of Cognition*. **Essays:** Kaye Gibbons; Erica Jong.

GREGORY, Sinda. Associate professor of English and comparative literature, San Diego State University. Author of numerous books and essays about contemporary fiction, including *Private Investigations: The Work of Dashiell Hammett* and *Alive and Writing: Interviews with American Authors of the 1980s* (with Larry McCaffery). Contributed an interview with Marianne Hauser to *Some Other Frequency: Interviews with Contemporary American Innovative Fiction Writers* by McCaffery, 1995. **Essay:** Marianne Hauser.

GRELLA, George. Associate professor of English, Rochester University, New York. Author of studies of Ian Fleming, Ross Macdonald, and John le Carré in *New Republic*; and articles on the detective novel, film, and popular culture. **Essays:** Len Deighton; J.P. Donleavy; John Gregory Dunne; John Irving.

GRIFFIN, Jessica. Editor and freelance writer. **Essay:** Marina Warner.

GUERARD, Albert. See his own entry.

GUPTARA, Prabhu S. Freelance writer, lecturer, and broadcaster. Author of *Indian Spirituality*, 1984; and *Black British Literature: An Annotated Bibliography*, 1986. Editor of *Third Eye: The Prospects of Third World Film*, 1986; and *The Lotus: An Anthology of Contemporary Indian Religious Poetry in English*, 1988. **Essay:** Gillian Tindall.

GUTTENBERG, Laurie Schwartz. Faculty member, Nassau Community College, Suffolk Community College, S.U.N.Y. College at Farmingdale, Syosset Central Schools. **Essay:** Joanne Greenberg.

GUZZIO, Tracie Church. Assistant professor of English, State University of New York, Plattsburgh. Specializes in African-American Literature. **Essay:** John Edgar Wideman.

HALIO, Jay L. Professor of English, University of Delaware, Newark; chair of the editorial board, University of Delaware Press. Author of *Angus Wilson*, 1964; and *Understanding Shakespeare's Plays in Performance*, 1988. Editor of *British Novelists since 1960*, 1983; *Critical Essays on Angus Wilson*, 1985; and *As You Like It: An Annotated Bibliography 1940–1980* (with Barbara C. Millard). **Essay:** William Trevor.

HALL, James B. See his own entry. **Essay:** R.V. Cassill.

HALL, Joan Wylie. Instructor in English, University of Mississippi, Jackson. Author of *Shirley Jackson: A Study of the Short Fiction* (forthcoming); and articles on Francis Bacon, William Faulkner, and Willa Cather. **Essay:** Marilyn French.

HANRAHAN, John. Freelance writer and critic. **Essays:** Liam Davison.

HARRIS, Jennifer. Doctoral candidate in English, York University, Toronto. Author of several articles in Canadian feminist journals. Associate editor of *Alphabet City* and co-editor of a forthcoming issue of the *Canadian Review of American Studies* titled "Blackness and the 49th Parallel." **Essays:** Leland Bardwell; Erna Brodber; Austin C. Clarke; Jack Hodgins; Mick Jackson; Jamaica Kincaid; Earl Lovelace; Terry McMillan; James McNeish; Eilis Ní Dhuibhne; Mordecai Richler; Jeff Shaara; Helena Maria Viramontes; Damien Wilkins; Lois-Ann Yamanaka.

HARRIS, June. Associate professor of teaching and teacher education, University of Arizona-South, Sierra Vista. **Essays:** John Grisham; Kim Stanley Robinson.

HART, James A. Late emeritus professor of English, University of British Columbia, Vancouver; former member of the editorial board, *Canadian Review of American Studies* and *English Studies in Canada*. Author of articles on Alan Seeger, Allen Tate, George Sylvester Viereck, and Joyce Kilmer in *Dictionary of Literary Biography*, vols. 45 and 54, 1986, 1987. Died. **Essay:** Edward Hoagland.

HART, Sue. Professor of English, Montana State University, Billings. Author of *Thomas and Elizabeth Savage*, chapters in *Women in*

Western American Literature, *Visions of War*, and *Willa Cather: Family and Community*, and of numerous critical essays and reviews. **Essay:** Thomas Savage.

HASTINGS, Thomas. Doctoral candidate, Department of English, York University, Toronto. **Essays:** Alan Hollinghurst; Edmund White.

HAWKES, John. Novelist, playwright, and poet. Author of *The Cannibal*, 1949; *The Lime Twig*, 1961; *Second Skin*, 1964; *Adventures in the Alaskan Skin Trade*, 1985; *Whistlejacket*, 1988; and others. Died 1998.

HEATON, David M. Associate professor of English, and University Ombudsman, Ohio University, Athens. Author of poetry; poetry translations; and articles on Ted Hughes, Alan Sillitoe, Stanley Plumly, Alan Stephens, Ben Belitt, Marvin Bell, Jon Anderson, and George P. Elliott. **Essays:** Frederick Busch; Joan Didion; Toni Morrison; Hubert Selby, Jr.

HERBERT, John. Freelance writer. **Essay:** E.L. Doctorow.

HERGENHAN, Laurie. Reader in English, University of Queensland, Brisbane; editor of *Australian Literary Studies*. Author of *Unnatural Lives*, 1983. Editor of *The Australian Short Story*, 1986.

HERMANN, Michelle. Doctoral candidate in English, University of Chicago, Illinois; visiting lecturer in English, Swarthmore College, Pennsylvania. **Essay:** Jeannette Armstrong.

HILL, Susan. See her own entry.

HODGKIN, Katharine. Faculty member, Department of English, University of Wales, Swansea. Author of articles on contemporary women writers, including Janet Frame. **Essay:** Marina Warner.

HOLM, Janis Butler. Associate professor of English, Ohio University, Athens. Author of articles on cultural theory and Tudor conduct books. Editor of *The Mirrhor of Modesty* by Giovanni Bruto, 1987. **Essay:** Gayl Jones.

IKIN, Van. Lecturer in English, University of Western Australia, Nedlands. Editor of the journal *Science Fiction: A Review of Speculative Literature*; and the books *Australian Science Fiction*, 1982; and *Glass Reptile Breakout and Other Australian Speculative Stories*, 1990. **Essays:** Robert Drewe; David Ireland.

JAMES, Louis. Professor of English and American literature. Keynes College, University of Kent, Canterbury. Author of *The Islands in Between*, 1968; *Fiction for the Working Man 1830–50*, 1974; *Jean Rhys*, 1978; and *Writers from the Caribbean*, 1990. Editor of *Print and the People 1819–1851*, 1976; and *Performance and Politics in Popular Drama: Aspects of Popular Entertainment in Theatre, Film and Television* (with others), 1980. **Essays:** Nicholas Hasluck; V.S. Naipaul.

JEFFARES, A. Norman. Professor emeritus of English Studies, University of Stirling, Scotland; general editor of the Macmillan Histories of Literature series and the York Classics series; co-editor of the Macmillan anthologies of English literature; past editor of *A Review of English Studies* and *Ariel*. Author of *Yeats: Man and Poet*, 1949 (revised 1962); *Seven Centuries of Poetry*, 1956; *Oliver Goldsmith*, 1959; *Gogarty*, 1961; *George Moore*, 1965; *A Critical Commentary on She Stoops to Conquer*, 1966; *A Commentary on the Collected Poems*, 1968; and *Collected Plays*, with A.S. Knowland, 1975; *Yeats, Anglo-Irish Literature*, 1982; *A New Commentary on the Poems of W. B. Yeats*, 1984; and *W. B. Yeats: A New Biography*, 1988. Editor of *Scott's Mind and Art*, 1969; *Restoration Comedy*, 1974; *Yeats: The Critical Heritage*, 1977; *Poems of W.B. Yeats: A New Selection*, 1984; *Yeats's Poems*, 1989; *Yeats the European*, 1989; *Yeats's Vision*, 1990; *Swift: The Selected Poems*, 1992; *Ireland's Women* (with Brendan Kennelly and Katie Donovan), 1994; and *Images of Imaginations*, 1995. Formerly chair of the Literature Section of the Scottish Arts Council for the Study of Anglo-Irish Literature. **Essay:** John le Carré.

JEFFREY, David K. Professor and head of the English department, James Madison University, Harrisonburg, Virginia; formerly co-editor of *Southern Humanities Review*. Editor of *Grit's Triumph: Essays on the Works of Harry Crews*, 1983. Author of numerous articles on Harry Crews, Edgar Allan Poe, Tobias Smollett, Alexander Pope, Herman Melville, and contemporary mystery writers. **Essay:** Ellen Douglas.

JENKINS, Annibel. Associate professor of English, Georgia Institute of Technology, Atlanta. Author of *Nicholas Rowe*, 1977. **Essay:** Emma Smith.

JENKINS, Ron. Lecturer in English, University of British Columbia. Author of articles on Graeme Gibson, Paul Theroux, Thomas Pynchon, Laurence Sterne, and George Peele. **Essays:** Graeme Gibson; Joy Kogawa.

JOHNSEN, Rosemary E. Member of the National Coalition of Independent Scholars. Author of essays on Edith Wharton, Grant Richards, Patrick Hamilton, and Miriam Grace Monfredo. Currently working on a book-length study of feminist historical crime fiction. **Essays:** Maeve Kelly; Deirdre Madden; Val Mulkern.

JOHNSEN, William A. Professor of English, Michigan State University, East Lansing. Author of publications on Irish, British, and European literature as well as critical theory. Author of numerous book and journal articles. **Essays:** Wilton Barnhardt; Dermot Bolger; Dermot Healy; Colm Tóibín.

KEATING, H.R.F. Crime novelist and critic. Author of the Inspector Ghote series including, most recently, *The Body in the Billiard Room*, 1987; *Dead on Time*, 1988; *Inspector Ghote, His Life and Crimes*, 1989; and *Doing Wrong*, 1994; of three novels as Evelyn Hervey: *The Governess*, 1984; *The Man of Gold*, 1985; and *Into the Valley of Death*, 1986; and of critical works including *Writing Crime Fiction*, 1986; *Crime and Mystery: The 100 Best Books*, 1987; and *The Bedside Companion to Crime*, 1989. Editor of *Agatha Christie: First Lady of Crime*, 1977; *Whodunit? A Guide to Crime, Suspense, and Spy Fiction*, 1982; and *The Best of Father Brown*, 1987. **Essays:** Dick Francis; Arun Joshi.

KEITH, Margaret. Freelance writer and researcher; also an actress and director. **Essays:** Hugh Hood; Norman Levine.

KEITNER, Wendy Robbins. Associate professor of English, University of New Brunswick, Frederiction. **Essay:** Jane Rule.

KELLEGHAN, Fiona. Librarian and associate professor at the University of Miami, Richter Library. Author of *Mike Resnick: An Annotated Bibliography and Guide to His Work*, 2000; articles and reviews in *Science-Fiction Studies*, *ParaDoxa*, *Extrapolation*, *The*

New York Review of Science Fiction, and *Nova Express*; and published essays and chapters in numerous reference works, including *St. James Guide to Science Fiction Writers*, *St. James Guide to Crime & Mystery Writers*, *Magill's Guide to Science Fiction and Fantasy Literature*, *Cyclopedia of World Authors*, *Fantasy and Horror: A Critical and Historical Guide*, and *Twentieth-Century Literary Movements Dictionary*. **Essays:** Ray Bradbury; Robert Olen Butler; Sebastian Faulks; Mark Helprin; Gwyneth Jones; Jonathan Lethem; Connie Willis.

KEMP, Sandra. Lecturer in English literature, University of Glasgow. Author of *Kipling's Hidden Narratives*, 1988. Editor of *Selected Stories*, 1987; and *Debits and Credits*, 1988, both by Kipling. **Essay:** Eva Figes.

KENDLE, Burton. Professor of English, Roosevelt University, Chicago. Author of articles on D.H. Lawrence, John Cheever, William March, Tennessee Williams, and others, and on screenwriting. **Essays:** Isabel Colegate; Alan Lelchuk.

KENNEDY, Jake. Doctoral candidate in English literature, McMaster University, Hamilton, Ontario. Dissertation concerns Marcel Duchamp and literary modernism. **Essays:** John Berger; Hilary Mantel; Thomas Pynchon.

KENNEDY, Liam. Lecturer in History, Department of American and Canadian Studies, University of Birmingham. Editor of *Economic Theory of Co-operative Enterprises: Selected Readings*, 1983; and *An Economic History of Ulster, 1820–1940* (with Philip Ollerenshaw), 1985. **Essay:** William Kennedy.

KHAIR, Tabish. Teacher at Copenhagen University. Author of six books, including *Where Parallel Lines Meet*, 2000; and *Babu Fictions: A Study of Contemporary Indian English Fiction* (forthcoming). **Essay:** Sunetra Gupta.

KIERNAN, Robert F. Associate professor of English, Manhattan College, Bronx, New York. Former associate editor of *Literary Research Newsletter*. Author of *Katherine Anne Porter and Carson McCullers: A Reference Guide*, 1976; *Gore Vidal*, 1982; *American Writing since 1945: A Critical Survey*, 1983; *Noel Coward*, 1986; and *Frivolity Unbound: Six Masters of the Camp Novel*, 1990. **Essay:** Gore Vidal.

KING, Bruce. Freelance writer and editor; Albert S. Johnston professor of English, University of North Alabama, Florence; has taught at universities in the United States, France, Israel, Nigeria, Canada, England, and New Zealand. Co-editor of Macmillan Modern Dramatists series. Author of *Dryden's Major Plays*, 1966; *Marvell's Allegorical Poetry*, 1977; *New English Literatures: Cultural Nationalism in a Changing World*, 1980; *A History of Seventeenth-Century English Literature*, 1982; *Modern Indian Poetry in English*, 1987; *Three Indian Poets: Ezekiel, Ramanujan and Moraes*, 1990; *V. S. Naipaul*, 1993; *Derek Walcott and West Indian Drama*, 1995; and other books. Editor of *Introduction to Nigerian Literature*, 1971; *Literatures of the World in English*, 1974; *A Celebration of Black and African Writing*, 1976; and *West Indian Literature*, 1979. **Essays:** Mike Phillips; Salman Rushdie; Vikram Seth.

KINGSBURY, Celia M. Kingsbury teaches in the English Department at Florida State University. Her area of specialization is World War I literature and cultural studies. She has published articles in *Conradiana* and *Modern Fiction Studies*. **Essay:** Allen Wier.

KIRK, Connie Ann. Writer, poet, and scholar of various topics in American literature, including American narratives, Emily Dickinson, and children's literature; teaches at Mansfield University, Pennsylvania. **Essays:** Louise Erdrich; Bobbie Ann Mason; Lorrie Moore; Anne Tyler; Alice Walker.

KLAUS, H. Gustav. Part-time professor of English, University of Osnabrück, and visiting professor, University of Halle, both Germany. Author of *Caudwell im Kontext*, 1978; and *The Literature of Labour: Two Hundred Years of Working-Class Writing*, 1985. Editor of *Gulliver: German-English Yearbook*, 1976–82; *The Socialist Novel in Britain: Towards the Recovery of a Tradition*, 1982; and *The Rise of Socialist Fiction 1880–1914*, 1987. **Essay:** Barry Hines.

KLEIN, Marcus. Professor of English, State University of New York, Buffalo. Author of *After Alienation: American Novels at Mid-Century*, 1964; and *Foreigners: The Making of American Literature 1900–1940*, 1981. Editor of *The American Novel since World War II*, 1969; and, with Robert Pack, of *Literature for Composition on the Theme of Innocence and Experience*, 1966; and *Short Stories: Classic, Modern, Contemporary*, 1967. **Essay:** Richard G. Stern.

KLINKOWITZ, Jerome. Professor of English, University of Northern Iowa, Cedar Falls. Author of *Kurt Vonnegut Jr.: A Descriptive Bibliography* (with Asa B. Pieratt, Jr.), 1974; *Literary Disruptions*, 1975 (revised 1980); *Donald Barthelme: A Comprehensive Bibliography* (with others), 1977; *The Life of Fiction*, 1977; *Kurt Vonnegut*, 1980; *The Practice of Fiction in America*, 1980; *The American 1960's*, 1980; *Peter Handke and the Postmodern Transformation* (with James Knowlton), 1983; *The Self-Apparent Word*, 1984; *Literary Subversions*, 1985; *The New American Novel of Manners*, 1986; *Kurt Vonnegut: A Comprehensive Bibliography* (with Judie Huffman-Klinkowitz), 1987; *A Short Season and Other Stories* (as Jerry Klinkowitz), 1988; *Rosenberg, Barthes, Hassan: The Postmodern Habit of Thought*, 1988; *Their Finest Hours: Narratives of the RAF and Lufiwaffe in World War II*, 1989; *Slaughterhouse-Five: Reforming the Novel and the World*, 1990; *Listen, Gerry Mulligan: An Aural Narrative in Jazz*, 1991; *Donald Barthelme: An Exhibition*, 1991; *Structuring the Voice*, 1992; and *Basepaths* (as Jerry Klinkowitz), 1995. Editor of *Innovative Fiction*, 1972; *The Vonnegut Statement*, 1973; and *Writing under Fire: Stories of the Vietnam War*, 1978 (all with John Somers); *Vonnegut in America* (with Donald L. Lawler), 1977; *The Diaries of Willard Motley*, 1979; *Nathaniel Hawthorne*, 1984; and *Writing Baseball*, 1991. **Essays:** Jonathan Baumbach; Stephen Dixon; Kenneth Gangemi; Clarence Major; Thomas McGuane; Gilbert Sorrentino; Michael Stephens; Ronald Sukenick; Dan Wakefield; Rudolph Wurltitzer.

KNIGHT, Judson. Freelance writer; co-owner of The Knight Agency, a firm specializing in literary sales and marketing. Author of *Ancient Civilizations* and *Medieval Reference Library*, 2000; *Abbey Road to Zapple Records: A Beatles Encyclopedia*, 1999; volumes in the UXL series *Slavery Throughout History*, 2000, and *African American Biography*, 1998; and three chapters in *Don't Fence Me In: An Anecdotal Biography of Lewis Grizzard by Those Who Knew Him Best*, 1995. Contributor to more than a dozen reference series published by Gale. **Essays:** Bret Easton Ellis; Michael Frayn; Marilyn French; Marge Piercy; Richard Powers; E. Annie Proulx; Piers Paul Read; Tom Robbins; Michèle Roberts; Peter Robinson; Philip Roth; Jane Rule; Thomas Savage; Will Self; Mona Simpson; Andrew Sinclair; F. Sionil Jose; Elizabeth Spencer; Alan Spence; Emma

Tennant; Gillian Tindall; Peter Vansittart; Kurt Vonnegut, Jr.; Fay Weldon; Mary Wesley; Michael Wilding; Tom Winton.

KOHL, Judith C. Professor emeritus of English and Humanities, Dutchess Community College (SUNY); freelance writer. Former teacher at Exploring Transfer Program, Vassar College (also served on its board of directors), Marist College's Center for Lifetime Studies, and Washington College's Academy of Lifelong Learning, Chestertown, Maryland. Author of "Talk of the Towns" for the *Kent County News* (Maryland) and contributor to *Contemporary Novelists* (6th edition); *An Encyclopedia of British Women Writers*, 1988, 1998; *Southern Writers*, 1999; *Lesbian Histories and Cultures*, 2000; and *The World Encyclopedia of Censorship* (forthcoming), among others. **Essays:** Anita Brookner; David Guterson; Barbara Kingsolver; Hilary Masters; Alice McDermott; Tim Parks.

KORGES, James. Freelance writer. Editor of *Critique: Studies in Modern Fiction*, 1962–70. Author of *Erskine Caldwell*, 1969. Died 1975.

KORINKOVA, Iva. Doctoral candidate at the University of North Texas. She focuses on contemporary American literature, American culture studies, and feminism. She translates from English to Czech; she has published her translation of the book *Quentin Tarantino: Shooting from the Hip* and several articles by Bruce Sterling. **Essay:** Rita Mae Brown.

KROGH, Marta. Graduate student in American literature, University of North Texas, Denton. **Essays:** Kristin Hunter; Anita Shreve; Rudy Wiebe.

LANE, Suzanne. Teacher, Expository Writing Program, Harvard University. Specializes in contemporary African-American literature. **Essays:** Charles Johnson; Gayl Jones; Chang-rae Lee.

LANKFORD, Ryan. Teaches English at Auburn University, Alabama. **Essay:** Harry Crews.

LAUER, Josh. Freelance editor and writer, Lauer InfoText, Inc. Associate editor of *Science and Its Times: Understanding the Social Significance of Scientific Discovery* (7 vols., Gale, 2000–01). Contributing editor for *Contemporary Literary Criticism* (Gale).

LAY, Mary M. Associate professor of liberal studies, Clarkson University, Potsdam, New York. Author of *Strategies for Technical Writing: A Rhetoric with Readings*, 1982; and articles on Margaret Drabble and Henry James. **Essays:** Gail Godwin; Maureen Howard.

LECKER, Robert. Associate professor of English, McGill University, Montreal; editor of the journal *Essays on Canadian Writing*. Author of *On the Line: Readings in the Short Fiction of Clark Blaise, John Metcalf and Hugh Hood*, 1982; *Robert Kroetsch*, 1986; and *Another I: The Fictions of Clark Blaise*, 1988. Editor of *The New Canadian Anthology: Poetry and Short Fiction in English* (with Jack David), 1988; and several works on Canadian literature; co-editor of the series *The Annotated Bibliography of Canada's Major Authors* and *Canadian Writers and Their Works*. **Essays:** Clark Blaise; John Metcalf.

LeCLAIR, Thomas. Professor of English, University of Cincinnati. Author of *In the Loop*, 1987; *The Art of Excess: Mastery in Contemporary American Fiction*, 1989; and of articles on contemporary fiction in *Tri-Quarterly, Contemporary Literature*, and other journals; and reviews in *New York Times Book Review, New Republic, Washington Post*, and other periodicals. Editor, with Larry McCaffery, *Anything Can Happen: Interviews with Contemporary American Novelists*, 1983. **Essays:** Richard Powers; Alexander Theroux.

LEE, Hermione. Lecturer in English, University of York. Presenter, Book Four television programme, 1982–85. Author of *The Novels of Virginia Woolf*, 1977; *Elizabeth Bowen: An Estimation*, 1981; *Philip Roth*, 1982; *Willa Cather: A Life Saved Up*, 1989; and introductions to works by Flannery O'Connor, Edith Oliver, Antonia White, Bowen, Woolf, and Cather. Editor of *Stevie Smith: A Selection*, 1983; *The Duke's Children* by Trollope, 1983; *The Secret Self: Short Stories by Women*, 2 vols., 1985–87; *The Mulberry Tree: Writings of Elizabeth Bowen*, 1986; and *The Short Stories of Willa Cather*, 1989.

LEHMANN, John. Founding editor of *New Writing, Daylight, Penguin New Writing, The London Magazine* and the BBC's *New Soundings*. Author of poetry, including *The Reader at Night*, 1974; fiction, including *In the Purely Pagan Sense*, 1976; and *In My Own Time: Memoirs of a Literary Life, Thrown to the Woolfs: Leonard and Virginia Woolf and the Hogarth Press*, 1978; *Rupert Brooke: His Life and His Legend*, 1981; *The English Poets of the First World War*, 1981; *Three Literary Friendships: Byron and Shelley, Rimbaud and Verlaine, Robert Frost and Edward Thomas*, 1983; and *Christopher Isherwood: A Personal Memoir*, 1987. Editor of *The Penguin New Writing 1940–50* (with John Fuller), 1985; and *Vienna: A Travellers' Companion* (with Richard Bassett), 1988. Died 1987.

LEIGH, Chris. Freelance writer. Author of numerous articles about American literature, Henry James, and Robert Penn Warren. **Essay:** William Cobb.

LEMBERGER, Michal. Doctoral candidate, University of California, Los Angeles. Dissertation on the use of Biblical themes in twentieth-century American poetry. **Essay:** Elizabeth Knox.

LEVIN, Harry. Irving Babbitt Professor of Comparative Literature, Harvard University, Cambridge, Massachusetts. Author of many critical books, including *The Myth of the Golden Age in the Renaissance, Grounds for Comparison, Shakespeare and the Revolution of the Times*, 1976; *Memories of the Moderns*, 1981; and *Playboys and Killjoys: An Essay on the Theory and Practice of Comedy*, 1987.

LEWIS, Peter. Reader in English, University of Durham. Author of *John Gay: The Beggar's Opera*, 1976; *Orwell: The Road to 1984*, 1981; *John le Carré*, 1984; *Fielding's Burlesque Drama*, 1987; *Eric Ambler*, 1990; and *The National: A Dream Made Concrete*, 1990. Editor of *The Beggar's Opera* by John Gay, 1973; *Poems '74* (anthology of Anglo-Welsh poetry), 1974; *Papers of the Radio Literature Conference 1977*, 1978; *Radio Drama*, 1981; and *John Gay and the Scriblerians* (with Nigel Wood), 1988. **Essays:** Peter Ackroyd; Paul Bailey; Maurice Gee; Nicholas Mosley; Emma Tennant.

LINDBERG, Stanley W. Editor of *The Georgia Review* and professor of English, University of Georgia, Athens. Author of *The Annotated McGuffey*, 1976; *Van Nostrand's Plain English Handbook* (with others), 1980; and co-author of *The Nature of Copyright*, 1991. Editor of *The Plays of Frederick Reynolds*, 3 vols., 1983; *Keener Sounds: Selected Poems from the Georgia Review* (with Stephen Corey), 1986; and *The Legacy of Erskine Caldwell*, 1989. **Essays:** Jack Matthews.

LINDSAY, Jack. Author of more than 100 books, including fiction, verse, and plays, and critical studies of William Blake, Mulk Raj

Anand, Charles Dickens, George Meredith, William Morris, and others. Editor of works by Robert Herrick, Morris, J.M.W. Turner, and anthologies of poetry; and translator of Greek and Roman texts. Died 1990. **Essay:** James Aldridge.

LIVETT, Jennifer. Lecturer in English, University of Tasmania. **Essay:** Russell Hoban.

LODGE, David. See his own entry.

LOOSER, Devoney. Assistant professor of English and Women's Studies, Indiana State University. Author of numerous articles on women's literature and feminist theory. Editor, *Jane Austen and Discourses of Feminism*, 1995. **Essays:** Carolyn See; Mona Simpson.

LOW, Gail. Teacher of postcolonial and contemporary British and American literatures in English, University of Dundee, Scotland. Author of *White Skins/Black Masks*, 1996, and publications in *New Formations, Research into African Literatures, Kunapipi* and *Women: A Cultural Review*. **Essay:** Fred D'Aguiar.

LUCAS, John. Professor and head of the Department of English and Drama, Loughborough University, Leicestershire; advisory editor, *Victorian Studies, Literature and History*, and *Journal of European Studies*. Author of *Tradition and Tolerance in 19th-Century Fiction*, 1966; *The Melancholy Man: A Study of Dickens's Novels*, 1970; *Arnold Bennett*, 1975; *Egitssaga: The Poems*, 1975; *The Literature of Change: Studies in the Nineteenth-Century Provincial Novel*, 1977; *The 1930's: Challenge to Orthodoxy*, 1978; *Romantic to Moderns: Literature: Essays and Ideas of Culture, 1750–1900*, 1982; *Moderns and Contemporaries: Novelists, Poets, Critics*, 1985; *Modern English Poetry from Hardy to Hughes*, 1986; *Studying Grosz on the Bus*, 1989; and *England and Englishness*, 1990. Editor of *Literature and Politics in the Nineteenth-Century*, 1971; and of works by George Crabbe and Jane Austen. **Essay:** Barry Cole.

LYNCH, Robert E. Professor of English, New Jersey Institute of Technology, Newark. Author of *Professional Writing*, 1993; and articles in *The Reader's Encyclopedia of Shakespeare*, 1966; and *The Reader's Encyclopedia of World Drama*, 1969. Editor of *The Example of Science: An Approach to College Composition*, 1981. **Essays:** Frederick Forsyth; Thomas Keneally; Leonard Michaels; John Mortimer.

MACDONALD, Andrew. Associate professor at Loyola University, New Orleans, Louisiana. Author of numerous articles on popular culture concerns and three books: *Howard Fast*, 1996; and, with Gina Macdonald and MaryAnn Sheridan, *Shapeshifting: Images of Native Americans in Recent Popular Fiction*, 2000, and *Shaman or Sherlock? The Native American Detective*, 2001. **Essay:** Andrei Codrescu.

MacDONALD, Gary D. Writer and teacher of English at Auburn University, Alabama, where he studies nineteenth-century American literature. **Essay:** Lee Smith.

MacDONALD, Gina. Author of numerous articles and reference entries for Buccoli Press, Salem Press, and St. James Press, and four books:*James Clavell*, 1995; *Robert Ludlum*, 1996; and, with Andrew Macdonald and MaryAnn Sheridan, *Shapeshifting: Images of Native Americans in Recent Popular Fiction*, 2000, and *Shaman or Sherlock? The Native American Detective*, 2001. **Essays:** Sherman Alexie; Barbara Mertz.

MACHANN, Clinton. Associate professor of English, Texas A & M University, College Station. Author of *Krásná Amerika: A Study of the Texas Czechs 1851–1939*, 1983; *Jason Jackson* (a novel), 1993; *The Essential Matthew Arnold*, 1993; *The Genre of Autobiography in Victorian Literature*, 1994; and numerous articles on British and American literature. Editor of *Matthew Arnold in His Time and Ours* (with Forrest D. Burt), 1988; *Katherine Anne Porter and Texas: An Uneasy Relationship*, 1990; *Czech Voices: Stories from the Amerikan narodní kalendár*, 1991; and *Selected Letters of Matthew Arnold* (with Forrest D. Burt), 1993. **Essay:** Leslie Marmon Silko.

MADDEN, David. See his own entry.

MAKOWSKY, Veronica. Professor of English, University of Connecticut. Author of *Caroline Gordon: A Biography*, 1989; *Susan Glaspell's Century of American Women*, 1993; and articles on southern and other American writers. **Essay:** Doris Betts.

MALIN, Irving. Professor of English, City College of the City University of New York. Author of *William Faulkner: An Interpretation*, 1957; *New American Gothic*, 1962; *Jews and Americans*, 1965; *Saul Bellow's Fiction*, 1969; *Nathanael West's Novels*, 1972; and *Isaac Bashevis Singer*, 1972. Editor of casebooks and collections of essays on Bellow, Capote, Styron, Singer, and McCullers, and of *Psychoanalysis and American Fiction* and *Contemporary American-Jewish Literature*. **Essay:** James Purdy.

MARX, Paul. Professor of English, University of New Haven, Connecticut. Editor of *12 Short Story Writers*, 1970. **Essays:** Richard Ford; Larry Woiwode.

MATHEWS, Lawrence. Teaches English at Memorial University, Newfoundland. **Essay:** Ray Smith.

MATHIAS, Roland. Poet and critic; former editor of *Anglo-Welsh Review*, and former chairman of the Welsh Arts Council Literature Committee. Author of seven books of poetry (most recently *Burning Brambles: Selected Poems 1944–1979*, 1983); a collection of short stories; and studies of Vernon Watkins, John Cowper Powys, and Anglo-Welsh literature. Editor of *Anglo-Welsh Poetry 1480–1980* (with Raymond Garlick), 1984; works by Welsh authors; and a collection of essays on David Jones. **Essay:** Emyr Humphreys.

McCORMICK, John. Emeritus professor of comparative literature, Rutgers University, New Brunswick, New Jersey. Author of *Catastrophe and Imagination* (on the modern novel), 1957; *The Complete Aficionada*, 1967; *American Literature 1919–1932: A Comparative History*, 1971; *Fiction as Knowledge*, 1975; *George Santayana: A Biography*, 1987; and *Wolfe, Malraux, Hesse: A Study in Creative Vitality*, 1987. **Essay:** Sybille Bedford.

McDOWELL, Frederick P.W. Professor of English, University of Iowa, Iowa City. Author of *Ellen Glasgow and the Ironic Art of Fiction*, 1960; *Elizabeth Madox Roberts*, 1963; *Caroline Gordon*, 1966; *Forster: An Annotated Bibliography of Writings about Him*, 1976; *E.M. Forster*, 1982; and articles on Shaw and Robert Penn Warren. **Essays:** Melvyn Bragg; Frederic Raphael.

McDOWELL, Margaret B. Professor of rhetoric and women's Studies, University of Iowa, Iowa City. Author of *Edith Wharton*, 1975 (revised 1990); and *Carson McCullers*, 1980. **Essays:** Ellen Gilchrist; Jamaica Kincaid; Gloria Naylor; Tillie Olsen.

McLEOD, John. Lecturer in English, LSU College of Higher Education, Southampton. **Essays:** Michael Ondaatje; Caryl Phillips.

McMECHAN, Ian. Freelance writer. Author of articles on contemporary crime fiction. **Essays:** Madison Smartt Bell; Tama Janowitz; Tim O'Brien; Tom Wolfe.

McNEILLY, Kevin. Faculty member, Department of English, University of British Columbia; freelance writer and critic. **Essays:** Jeannette Armstrong; Thomas King; Wole Soyinka.

MEPHAM, John. Freelance writer and teacher of philosophy and literature, Bennington College, Vermont. Co-author of *Issues in Marxist Philosophy,* 4 vols., 1979; author of *To the Lighthouse by Virginia Woolf* (study guide), 1987; *Virginia Woolf: A Literary Life,* 1991; and *Virginia Woolf: State of the Art,* 1991; and of many articles on philosophy and literature. **Essay:** Gabriel Josipovici.

MERIVALE, Patricia. Professor of English, University of British Columbia, Vancouver. Author of *Pan the Goat-God: His Myth in Modern Times;* and of articles in *Harvard Studies in Comparative Literature* and other periodicals. **Essay:** Jerzy Peterkiewicz.

MIELKE, Robert E. Assistant Professor of English, Northeast Missouri State University, Kirksville. Author of *The Riddle of the Painful Earth: Suffering and Society in W.D. Howells's Major Writings of the Early 1890's*; and articles in *Northwest Review, Paintbrush*; and other journals. **Essay:** J.G. Ballard.

MILLER, D. Quentin. Freelance writer; creative writing instructor and doctoral candidate in English, University of Connecticut, Storrs. **Essays:** Cormac McCarthy; Tim O'Brien.

MILNES, Stephen. Doctoral candidate, University of British Columbia. **Essay:** Sky Lee.

MOHANRAM, Radhika. Lecturer, Department of Women's Studies, University of Waikato, New Zealand. Author of articles on New Zealand postcolonial feminism. Co-editor of *Postcolonial Discourse and Changing Cultural Contexts* (forthcoming), and *English Postcoloniality: Literatures from around the World* (forthcoming). **Essays:** Upamanyu Chatterjee; Amy Tan.

MONTROSE, David. Freelance writer. Regular reviewer for the *Times Literary Supplement.* **Essay:** William Boyd.

MOORE, Gerald. Editor of the Modern African Writers series. Former Professor of English, University of Jos, Nigeria. Author of *The Chosen Tongue,* 1969; *Wole Soyinka,* 1971 (revised 1978); and *Twelve African Writers,* 1980. Editor, with Ulli Beier, of *The Penguin Book of Modern African Poetry,* 1984. **Essays:** Elechi Amadi; George Lamming; Garth St. Omer.

MOORE, Harry T. Research professor of English emeritus, Southern Illinois University, Carbondale; editor of the Crosscurrents/ Modern Critiques series. Author and editor of many books, including studies of Lawrence, Steinbeck, Forster, Rilke, Durrell, and James. Died 1981. **Essay:** Francis Stuart.

MORACE, Robert A. Teacher at Daemen College, Amherst, New York. Author of *The Dialogic Novels of Malcolm Bradbury and David Lodge, John Gardner: An Annotated Secondary Bibliography,* and numerous essays on contemporary literature, including most recently "The Life and Times of Ariel Dorfman's *Death and the Maiden.*" Co-editor (with Kathryn Van Spanckeren) of *John Gardner: Critical Perspectives.* **Essays:** Malcolm Bradbury; Tibor Fischer; Janice Galloway; Nick Hornby; Carole Maso; Candia McWilliam; Rohinton Mistry; Lawrence Norfolk; Will Self; Irvine Welsh.

MORDDEL, Anne. Freelance writer. **Essays:** Mervyn Jones; Marilynne Robinson.

MORPURGO, J.E. Emeritus professor of American literature, University of Leeds. Author and editor of many books, including *The Pelican History of the United States,* 1955 (third edition 1970); *Master of None: An Autobiography,* 1990; and volumes on Cooper, Lamb, Trelawny, Cobbett, Barnes Wallis, Margery Allingham, the publisher Allen Lane, and on Athens, Venice, and rugby football.

MOSS, Laura. Assistant professor of postcolonial literature and theory at the University of Manitoba. Research and teaching interests include the literatures of Canada, Southern Africa, Nigeria, India, Trinidad, New Zealand, and Australia; performance and politics; multiculturalism in Canada; and the intersection of race and gender studies. Recent publications include work on Chinua Achebe, Ngugi, Ian Wedde, Rohinton Mistry, Salman Rushdie, and postcolonial theory. She is currently editing a critical edition of Frances Brooke's early epistolary novel *The History of Emily Montague.* **Essays:** Peter Carey; Timothy Findley; Thomas King; Ann-Marie MacDonald.

MUIRHEAD, Eric. Member of the English faculty and director of creative writing, San Jacinto College, Pasadena, Texas. Author of poetry and short stories in journals and anthologies. **Essay:** Daniel Stern.

MURPHY, Graham J. Doctoral candidate in English literature, University of Alberta; instructor at Seneca College, Toronto. Dissertation: *Cy(ber)borg Netizens: (Re)Configuring the Post/Human Body in the Cultural Intersections of ScyberFiction and Cyberspace.* Author of material on *Tarzan* comic books, N. Katherine Hayles' *How We Became Posthuman,* and Pierre Lévy's *Collective Intelligence.* Co-editor of *Paddy Whacking: The Irish in Popular Literature of the Early American Republic.* **Essays:** Arthur C. Clarke; Samuel R. Delany.

MURRAY, Heather. Independent scholar and critic; co-editor of the *Journal of New Zealand Literature.* Author of *Double Lives: Women in the Stories of Katherine Mansfield.* **Essays:** Marilyn Duckworth; Stephanie Johnson.

MURRAY-SMITH, Stephen. Reader in education, University of Melbourne. Founding editor of *Overland*; and former editor of *Melbourne Studies in Education.* Author of *Henry Lawson,* 1962 (2nd edition 1975); *Mission to the Islands,* 1979; and *Indirections,* 1981. Editor of *The Tracks We Travel,* 1953; *An Overland Muster,* 1965; *His Natural Life* by Marcus Clarke, 1970; *Classic Australian Short Stories* (with Judah Waten), 1974; and *The Dictionary of Australian Quotations,* 1984.

NADLER, Janna Z. Doctoral candidate, McMaster University, Hamilton, Ontario. Research interests include Canadian fiction and the figure of the child in contemporary Canadian immigrant fiction.**Essay:** Anne Rice.

NARAYAN, Shyamala A. Lecturer in English, Ranchi Women's College, India. Author of *Sudhin N. Ghose,* 1973; *Raja Rao: The Man and His Work,* 1988; and studies of Nissim Ezekiel, Amitav Ghosh,

Salman Rushdie, Shashi Tharoor, and other Indian writers; and reviews in *Indian Literature, The Hindu, Journal of Indian Writing in English,* and other periodicals. Compiler of the Indian section of "The Bibliography of Commonwealth Literature" published annually in *Journal of Commonwealth Literature.* **Essays:** Mulk Raj Anand; Sasthi Brata; Shashi Deshpande; Chaman Nahal; Nayantara Sahgal.

NEW, W.H. Professor of English, University of British Columbia, Vancouver. Author and editor of numerous books on postcolonial subjects, including *Dreams of Speech and Violence: The Art of the Short Story in Canada and New Zealand; Land Sliding: Imagining Space, Presence, and Power in Canadian Writing; A History of Canadian Literature; Borderlands;* and *Reading Mansfield and Metaphors of Form.* Also the author of several books of poetry, including *Science Lessons, Raucous, Stone Rain* (forthcoming), and *Vanilla Gorilla* (for children). **Essays:** Janet Frame; Zulfikar Ghose; Randolph Stow.

NEWMAN, Judie. Lecturer in English, University of Newcastle upon Tyne. Author of *Saul Bellow and History,* 1984; *John Updike,* 1988; and *Nadine Gordimer,* 1988. Editor of *Gred: A Tale of the Great Dismal Swamp* by Harriet Beecher Stowe, 1992. **Essay:** Mary Gordon.

NORRIS, Leslie. Poet and lecturer. Christensen Fellow in the Humanities, Brigham Young University, Salt Lake City. Author of several books of poetry including *Sliding and Other Stories,* 1976; *Walking the White Fields,* 1980; *The Girl from Cardigan: Sixteen Stories,* 1989; and a study of Glyn Jones. Editor of a translation of *The Mabinogion* and of books on Vernon Watkins and Andrew Young; and translator of *The Sonnets of Orpheus* by Rilke (with Alan Keele), 1989. **Essay:** Glyn Jones.

NOWAK, Maril. Lecturer in English, Rochester Institute of Technology and Hobart and William Smith Colleges. **Essay:** Doris Grumbach.

NYE, Robert. See his own entry. **Essay:** Alan Burns.

O'BRIEN, Liam. Freelance writer.**Essay:** Howard Jacobson.

O'HEARN, D.J. Sub-dean, Faculty of Arts, University of Melbourne. Author of articles on Australian literature; regular fiction reviewer for Melbourne *Age* and Sydney *Australian.* Died 1993. **Essay:** Morris Lurie.

O'LEARY, John. Freelance writer. **Essays:** Ron Hansen; Noel Virtue.

ORR, Leonard. Associate professor of English and Liberal Arts Coordinator, Washington State University, Richland. Author of ten books, including *Research in Critical Theory Since 1965,* 1989; *A Dictionary of Critical Theory,* 1991; *Problems and Poetics of the Nonaristotelian Novel,* 1991; *Yeats and Postmodernism,* 1991; *Critical Essays on Samuel Taylor Coleridge,* 1994; *A Joseph Conrad Companion,* 1999; and numerous book and journal essays. Editor of *International Review of Modernism.*

ORTEGO, James. Doctoral candidate and teacher, University of Louisiana, Lafayette. Specializes in the study of medieval and Renaissance literature as well as the modern novel written in English. **Essay:** Bernard MacLaverty.

OZICK, Cynthia. See her own entry.

PACEY, Desmond. Late vice-president (academic), University of New Brunswick, Fredericton. Author of *Frederick Philip Grove,* 1945; *Creative Writing in Canada,* 1952 (revised 1962); *The Picnic and Other Stories,* 1958; *Our Literary Heritage,* 1968; and *Essays in Canadian Criticism,* 1969. Editor of *A Book of Canadian Stories,* 1947; and *Ten Canadian Poets,* 1958. Died 1975.

PAGE, Malcolm. Professor of English, Simon Fraser University, Burnaby, British Columbia. Author of *John Arden,* 1984; *Richard II,* 1987; *Howard's End,* 1993. Editor of the volumes in the Writers on File series on John Arden, Alan Ayckbourn, David Edgar, Michael Frayn, David Hare, John Osborne, Harold Pinter, Peter Shaffer, and Tom Stoppard. **Essay:** Michael Frayn.

PARISI, Joseph. Editor-in-chief of *Poetry* magazine, Chicago. Author of *Viewers' Guide to "Voices and Visions,"* 1987; and *Marianne Moore: The Art of a Modernist,* 1990. Editor of *The "Poetry" Anthology 1912–1977* (with Daryl Hine), 1978. **Essays:** Janet Burroway; Colin Spencer.

PEHOWSKI, Marian. Freelance writer and critic. Has taught comparative literature or journalism at five universities. **Essay:** Hortense Calisher.

PENNER, Tom. Doctoral candidate, University of Alberta. Research interests hinge upon the liminal performance of identity within Canadian multicultural literatures. **Essay:** Kazuo Ishiguro.

PERKINS, George. Professor of English, Eastern Michigan University, Ypsilanti. Author or editor of *Writing Clear Prose,* 1964; *Varieties of Prose,* 1966; *The Theory of the American Novel,* 1970; *Realistic American Short Fiction,* 1972; *American Poetic Theory,* 1972; *The Harper Handbook to Literature* (with others), 1985; *The Practical Imagination* (with others), 1987; *Contemporary American Literature* (with Barbara Perkins), 1988; *The American Tradition in Literature* (with others), seventh edition, 1990; and *Reader's Encyclopedia of American Literature* (with Barbara Perkins and Phil Leininger), 1991. **Essay:** Robert Gover.

PHILLIPS, Lisa A. Writer and public radio reporter. She has taught writing and earned her M.F.A at the University of Pittsburgh. **Essays:** Frederick Busch; Richard Ford; Abby Frucht; Richard Price; Susan Straight; D.M. Thomas.

PIERCY, Marge. See her own entry. **Essay:** Joanna Russ.

PILDITCH, Jan. Lecturer in English, University of Waikato, Hamilton, New Zealand. **Essay:** Peter Tinniswood.

PINSKER, Sanford. Shadek Humanities Professor, Franklin and Marshall College, Lancaster, Pennsylvania. Author of *The Schlemiel as Metaphor: Studies in the Yiddish and American-Jewish Novel,* 1971; *The Comedy That "Hoits": An Essay on the Fiction of Philip Roth,* 1975; *Still Life and Other Poems,* 1975; *The Languages of Joseph Conrad,* 1978; *Between Two Worlds: The American Novel in the 1960's,* 1978; *Memory Breaks Off and Other Poems,* 1984; *Conversations with Contemporary American Writers,* 1985; *The Uncompromising Fictions of Cynthia Ozick,* 1987; *Bearing the Bad News: Contemporary American Literature and Culture,* 1990; *Jewish-American Fiction, 1917–1987,* 1992; *The Catcher in the Rye: Innocence Under Pressure,* 1993; and many articles on contemporary fiction. Editor of *Critical Essays on Philip Roth,* 1982; and *America and the Holocaust* (with Jack Fischel), 1984. **Essays:** T. C. Boyle;

David Bradley; Bruce Jay Friedman; Johanna Kaplan; Maxine Hong Kingston; Jay Neugeboren; E. Annie Proulx, Jane Smiley.

PORTALES, Marco. Associate professor of literature, University of Houston, Clear Lake; associate editor of *MELUS.* Author of *Youth and Age in American Literature,* 1989; and articles on Virginia Woolf, Henry James, Twain, Kate Chopin, Sarah Orne Jewett, Chicano and Native American writers, and other subjects. **Essay:** Rudolfo A. Anaya.

PORTER, Hal. Fiction writer, poet, and playwright. Author of three novels (*A Handful of Pennies, The Tilted Cross, The Right Thing*); several collections of short stories (*Selected Stories,* 1971); four plays; three books of poetry; three volumes of autobiography; and other non-fiction; a general selection, *Hal Porter,* was published in 1980. Died 1984.

POVEY, John. Teacher of English as a second language and applied linguistics, Los Angeles, California. Editor of *A Sociolinguistic Profile of Urban Centers in Cameroon* (with others), 1983. **Essays:** Chinua Achebe; Miriam Tlali.

POWELL, Anthony. Writer. Noted for his landmark series titled "A Dance to the Music of Time," comprising twelve novels.

POWER, Cathy Kelly. Teacher, English Department, Alabama Southern Community College; assistant director for the Alabama Center for Literary Arts; project director for the Alabama Writers Symposium. **Essay:** Albert Murray.

POYNTING, Jeremy. Lecturer, Thomas Danby College, Leeds. Author of articles in *Journal of Commonwealth Literature, Journal of South Asian Literature, World Literature Written in English, Kyk-over-Al,* and other periodicals. **Essays:** Michael Anthony; Ralph de Boissière.

PRICE, Joanna. Lecturer, Liverpool John Moores University. **Essays:** Bret Easton Ellis; A.L. Kennedy.

PURDY, Elizabeth. Political scientist and freelance writer. **Essay:** Winston Groom.

PYKETT, Lyn. Senior lecturer in English, University College of Wales, Aberystwyth. Author of *Emily Brontë,* 1989; and of articles on contemporary fiction in *Critical Quarterly, New Welsh Review,* and *Watching the Detectives* edited by Ian A. Bell and Graham Daldry, 1990. **Essays:** Anita Brookner; Marge Piercy.

QUIGLY, Isabel. Freelance writer and critic. Author of the novel *The Eye of Heaven,* 1955; *The Heirs of Tom Brown: The English School Story,* 1982; a book on Charlie Chaplin; and many articles and reviews in *The Times, The Guardian,* and other periodicals. Editor, with Susan Hill, of *New Stories 5,* 1980. Translator of works of European fiction and non-fiction. **Essay:** Winston Graham.

RAVENSCROFT, Arthur. Late senior lecturer in English, University of Leeds; founding editor, *Journal of Commonwealth Literature,* 1965–79. Author of *Chinua Achebe,* 1969 (revised 1977); *Nigerian Writers and the African Past,* 1978; *A Guide to Twentieth-Century English, Irish and Commonwealth Literature* (with Harry Blamires and Peter Quartermain), 1983; and "Teaching Words" in *African Literature,* 1986. Translator, with C.K. Johnman, of *Journal of Jan van Riebeeck,* vol. 3, 1958. Died 1989. **Essays:** I.N.C. Aniebo; Ahmed Essop; John Munonye; Ngugi wa Thiong'o.

RAY, Sandra. Novelist and freelance writer. **Essays:** Louis Auchincloss; Alice Hoffman.

REILLY, John M. Professor of English, State University of New York, Albany. Author of many articles on African-American literature, popular crime writing, and social fiction, and bibliographical essays in *Black American Writers,* 1978; and *American Literary Scholarship.* Editor of *Richard Wright: The Critical Reception,* 1978; and the reference book *Twentieth-Century Crime and Mystery Writers,* 1980 (2nd edition 1985). **Essays:** Kristin Hunter; Paule Marshall; Peter Matthiessen; Al Young.

REISMAN, Jessica. Writer of fiction, screenplays, and nonfiction; research associate at the University of Texas, Austin. Author of works in various publications, including the magazines *Realms of Fantasy* and *The Third Alternative.* **Essays:** Andrea Barrett; Gita Mehta.

REXROTH, Kenneth. Poet and critic; lecturer at the University of California, Santa Barbara. Author of many books of verse (including *The Morning Star,* 1979); plays (*Beyond the Mountains,* 1951); and non-fiction (including *The Elastic Retort,* 1973; and *Communalism,* 1975). Editor of several collections of poetry and translator of works by Asian, European, and classical authors. Died 1982.

RHODES, H. Winston. Late professor of English, University of Canterbury, Christchurch, New Zealand. Co-founder of *Tomorrow* and *New Zealand Monthly Review.* Author of *New Zealand Fiction since 1945,* 1968; *Frank Surgeson,* 1969; *New Zealand Novels,* 1969; *Frederick Sinclaire: A Memoir,* 1984; and other books. Editor of six volumes of Rewi Alley's prose and poetry and *I Saw in My Dream* by Sargeson, 1976. Died 1987. **Essay:** Albert Wendt.

RIACH, Alan. Senior lecturer in English, University of Waikato, Hamilton, New Zealand. Author of three collections of poetry: *The Folding Map,* 1990; *An Open Return,* 1991; and *Hugh MacDiarmid's Epic Poetry,* 1991. Editor of *The Radical Imagination: Lectures and Talks* by Wilson Harris; *Selected Poems* and *Selected Prose* by Hugh MacDiarmid; and general editor of *Collected Works* by Hugh MacDiarmid. **Essays:** Wilson Harris; Ben Okri.

ROBERTSON, Karen. Visiting assistant professor of English, Vassar College, Poughkeepsie, New York. Author of articles on Renaissance revenge tragedy. Editor of the forthcoming books *Sexuality and Politics in Renaissance Drama* (with Carole Levin) and John Pikeryng's *Horestes* (with Jodi George). **Essay:** Maeve Binchy.

ROSE, Marilyn. Associate professor, Department of English, and Director, Canadian Studies Program, Brock University, St. Catharines, Ontario. Author of various articles, papers, and encyclopedia entries on Canadian fiction and poetry, as well as a number of papers on Canadian detective fiction. **Essay:** Peter Robinson.

ROSS, Alan. Editor of *London Magazine* and managing director of London Magazine Editions. Author of several books of poetry, including *Death Valley,* 1980; and of critical works, travel books, and books for children. Editor of works by John Gay and Lawrence Durrell and of several anthologies. Translator of four French works.

ROSSET, Barney. Former president of Grove Press, Inc. Editor of *Evergreen Review Reader 1 and 2,* 1979.

ROTH, Christine. Doctoral candidate, University of Florida. Specializes in Victorian studies and travel narratives. Dissertation on the cult of the little girl in late nineteenth-century England. **Essay:** Paul Theroux.

ROWLAND, S. A. Freelance writer. **Essays:** Michèle Roberts; Colin Thubron.

ROYLE, Trevor. Freelance writer and broadcaster; literary editor of *Scotland on Sunday.* Author of *We'll Support You Ever More: The Impertinent Saga of Scottish Fitba',* with Ian Archer, 1976; *Jock Tamson's Bairns: Essays on a Scots Childhood,* 1977; *Precipitous City: The Story of Literary Edinburgh,* 1980; *Death Before Dishonour: The True Story of Fighting Mac,* 1982; *The Macmillan Companion to Scottish Literature,* 1983; *James and Jim: The Biography of James Kennaway,* 1983; *The Kitchener Enigma,* 1985; *The Best Years of Their Lives: The National Service Experience 1945– 63,* 1986; *War Report: The War Correspondent's View of Battle from the Crimea to the Falklands,* 1987; *The Last Days of the Raj,* 1989; *Anatomy of a Regiment,* 1990; and *In Flanders Fields: Scottish Poetry and Prose of the First World War,* 1991; and many articles in journals. Editor of *A Dictionary of Military Quotations,* 1990. **Essays**: Richard Adams; Stan Barstow; Nina Bawden; Jonathan Coe; Ronald Frame; Brian Glanville; Giles Gordon; Alasdair Gray; Clifford Haney; Robin Jenkins; Benedict Kiely; Allan Massie; Robert Nye; Charles Palliser; James Plunkett.

RUBIN, Alan. Doctoral candidate in English at Lehigh University, Bethlehem, Pennsylvania. **Essay:** Martin Amis.

RUBIN, Louis D., Jr. Professor of English, University of North Carolina, Chapel Hill; general editor, Southern Literary Studies series; co-editor, *Southern Literary Journal.* Author and editor of many books, including the novel *The Golden Weather,* 1961; and *William Elliott Shoots a Bear,* 1975; *The Wary Fugitives: Four Poets and the South,* 1978; *The American South: Portrait of a Culture,* 1979; *The Even-Tempered Angler,* 1983; *A Gallery of Southerners,* 1984; *The Literary South,* 1986; *An Apple for My Teacher,* 1987; and *The Edge of the Swamp,* 1989. **Essay:** William Styron.

SADLER, Geoff. Assistant librarian, local studies, Chesterfield, Derbvshire. Author of western novels (as Jeff Sadler), including, most recently *Hangrope Journey,* 1994; and (as Wes Calhoun) *Sierra Trail,* 1993; the *Justus* trilogy of planation novels (as Geoffrey Sadler), 1982; a 5-volume history of Chesterfield librarians 1879–1944; *Around Shirebrook,* 1994; and *Journey to Freedom* (with Antoni Snarski), 1990. Editor of the reference book *Twentieth-Century Western Writers,* 2nd edition, 1991. **Essays:** Stan Barstow; Rachel Billington; Clare Boylan; Michael Crichton; Desmond Hogan; David Plante; David Pownall; Ruth Rendell; Rose Tremain.

SAMBROOK, Hana. Freelance editor and writer. Author of study guides to *The Tenant of Wildfell Hall, Lark Rise to Candleford, Victory, My Family and Other Animals,* and *Sylvia Plath: Selected Works.* **Essays:** Janice Elliott; Margaret Forster; Hilary Mantel; Bernice Rubens.

SANDERS, David. Emeritus professor of English, Harvey Mudd College, Claremont, California. Author of *John Hersey,* 1967; *John Dos Passos: A Comprehensive Bibliography,* 1987; *John Hersey, Revisited,* 1990. **Essay:** Vance Bourjaily.

SANDERSON, Stewart. Honorary Harold Orton Fellow, University of Leeds, now retired; former chair of the literature committee, Scottish Arts Council. Author of *Ernest Hemingway,* 1961 (revised 1970); and of many articles on British and comparative folklore and ethnology, and on modern literature. Editor of *The Secret Common-Wealth* by Robert Kirk, 1976; *The Linguistic Atlas of England* (with others), 1978; *Studies in Linguistic Geography,* 1985; and *World Maps: A Dialect Atlas of England,* 1987. **Essay:** Dorothy Dunnett.

SCHAFER, William J. Professor of English, Berea College, Kentucky. Author of articles on David Wagoner, Mark Harris, and Ralph Ellison in *Critique* and *Satire Newsletter.* Editor of *The William Nelson Reader,* 1989. **Essays:** Elliott Baker; Stephen Becker; Thomas Berger; Harry Crews; Nell Dunn; David Ely; Mark Harris; Reynolds Price; Ishmael Reed; Wilfrid Sheed; Clancy Sigal; David Wagoner.

SCHLAGER, Neil. President, Schlager Information Group, Inc. Editor of *St. James Press Gay and Lesbian Almanac* (St. James Press), 1998, *Best Literature By and About Blacks* (Gale), 2000, and *Science and Its Times: Understanding the Social Significance of Scientific Discovery* (7 vols., Gale), 2000–01.

SCHORER, Mark. Late professor of English, University of California, Berkeley. Author of three novels, three collections of short stories, and several critical works, including studies of Blake, Lawrence, and Sinclair Lewis. Editor of anthologies of fiction and literary criticism and of works by Capote and Lawrence. Died 1977.

SCHRECENGOST, Lynda D. Freelance writer and editor. **Essays:** Boman Desai; Kelvin Christopher James; Ursula K. Le Guin; Albert Wendt.

SCHREYER, Roberta. Associate professor, English and Communication Department, State University of New York, Potsdam. Teaches a wide range of courses, including women and literature and psychology and literature. **Essays:** Margaret Forster; Edna O'Brien.

SEMPLE, Linda. Writer, and owner of Silver Moon Women's Bookshop, London. Author of *A Suitable Job for a Woman: Women Mystery Writers,* 1990; and many articles and reviews on women writers. **Essay:** Rita Mae Brown.

SHAUF, Michele S. Assistant professor, School of Literature, Communication, and Culture, Georgia Institute of Technology, Atlanta. **Essays:** Dorothy Allison; Wilma Dykeman; Percy Everett; Hugo Hamilton; Jane Hamilton; William T. Vollmann; David Foster Wallace.

SHUCARD, Alan R. Professor of English, University of Wisconsin-Parkside, Kenosha. General editor of the English Section of Twayne's Critical History of Poetry series. Author of three books on poetry, a study of Countee Cullen, 1984; *American Poetry: The Puritans Through Walt Whitman,* 1988; and *Modern American Poetry, 1865'1950* (with Fred Moramarco and William Sullivan), 1989; as well as numerous articles on American poetry and fiction. **Essay:** Kathrin Perutz.

SIMPSON, Melissa. Freelance writer. **Essays:** Pat Conroy; Toni Morrison.

SMALLMAN, Victoria A. Doctoral candidate at McMaster University, Hamilton, Ontario. **Essay:** Patrick McCabe.

SMITH, Angela. Director, Centre of Commonwealth Studies, University of Stirling, Scotland. Author of *East African Writing in English,* 1989; the chapter on writing in Mauritius in *The Writing of East and Central Africa* edited by G.D. Killam, 1985; and of study guides to *Wuthering Heights, Persuasion,* and *Voss.* **Essay:** Ayi Kwei Armah.

SMITH, Christopher. Senior lecturer, School of Modern Languages and European History, University of East Anglia, Norwich; editor of *Seventeenth-Century French Studies.* Author of *Alabaster, Bikinis and Calvados: An ABC of Toponymous Words,* 1985; *Jean Anouilh: Life, Work, Criticism,* 1985; and many articles and reviews of the performing arts. Editor of works by Antoine de Montchrestien, Jean de la Taille, and Pierre Matthieu. **Essays:** Buchi Emecheta; Peter Vansittart.

SMITH, Curtis C. Professor of humanities, University of Houston, Clear Lake. Author of *Olaf Stapledon: A Bibliography* (with Harvey J. Satty), 1984. Editor of the reference book *Twentieth-Century Science-Fiction Writers,* 1981 (2nd edition, 1986). **Essay:** Ursula K. LeGuin.

SOLOMON, Andy. Professor of English, University of Tampa; fiction editor of *The Tampa Review;* regular book critic for the *New York Times, Washington Post, Chicago Tribune, Boston Globe, Los Angeles Times, San Francisco Chronicle, Miami Herald,* and *St. Petersburg Times*; book commentator and essayist on National Public Radio. Author of fiction, poetry, and articles in the *Atlantic, Boulevard,* and *New Orleans Review.* **Essays:** Madison Smartt Bell; Mary Lee Settle; Carol Shields.

SOLOMON, Eric. Professor of English, San Francisco State University. Author of *Stephen Crane in England,* 1963; *Stephen Crane: From Parody to Realism,* 1966; and many articles on 19th- and 20th-century British and American fiction. Editor of *The Faded Banners,* 1960; and *The Critic Agonistes,* 1985. **Essay:** Albert Guerard.

SPARKS, Tabitha. Doctoral candidate, University of Washington; teaches literature and cultural studies at Georgia Institute of Technology. Dissertation on Victorian literature. **Essays:** Mary Beckett; Carolyn Chute.

STEDMAN, Jane W. Emeritus professor of English, Roosevelt University, Chicago. Author of *W.S. Gilbert: A Classic Victorian and His Theatre,* 1995; and poems, articles, and reviews in anthologies of Victorian studies, scholarly journals, literary periodicals, and *Opera News.* Editor of *Gilbert Before Sullivan: Six Comic Plays,* 1967. **Essays:** P.D. James; Ira Levin; Anne Perry.

STEEMSON, Caroline. Tutor in women's studies and women's history, University of Waikato, Hamilton, New Zealand. **Essay:** Sue McCauley.

STEIN, Mark. Teaching fellow at Johann Wolfgang Goethe Universität (Frankfurt) and a research assistant at University of Kent (Canterbury). Research interests are postcolonial and diaspora theory, and British cultural studies. Author of essays on Black British, African and West Indian literatures in the journals *Wasafiri, Kunapipi,* and several edited collections. Co-editor of *Can the Subaltern Be Read? Acolit Special,* 1996. **Essay:** Jackie Kay.

STERN, Carol Simpson. Professor and Chair of the Department of Performance Studies, Northwestern University, Evanston, Illinois. Former Dean of The Graduate School, Northwestern University. Former President of the American Association of University Professors. Held numerous positions on the Councils and Boards of The American Association of University Professors, Council of Graduate Schools, National Communication Association, Northwestern University Press, Museum of Contemporary Art, and others. Author of *Performance: Texts and Contexts* (with Bruce Henderson), 1993. Regular contributor to *Contemporary Novelists, Contemporary Poets, Contemporary Dramatists, Reference Guide to Short Fiction, British Mystery and Thriller Writers Since, 1940, Dictionary of Literary Biography* (volume 87), and *Twentieth Century Crime and Mystery Writers.* Contributed articles to *Communication Quarterly, Victorian Studies, English Literature in Transition, Literature in Performance,* and other journals. Contributor of a chapter to *Academic Freedom: An Everyday Concern,* edited by Ernst Benjamin, 1995. **Essays:** Doris Lessing; Joyce Carol Oates; Judith Rossner; John Updike.

STEVENS, James R. Master, Confederation College, Thunder Bay, Ontario. Author of *Sacred Legends of the Sandy Lake Cree,* 1971; *Paddy Wilson's Gold Fever,* 1976; *Legends from the Forest,* 1985; and *Killing the Shamen,* 1985. **Essay:** Fred Bodsworth.

STONEHILL, Brian. Associate professor of English, Pomona College, Claremont, California; formerly fiction editor for the Chicago *Review.* Author of *The Self-Conscious Novel: Artifice in Fiction from Joyce to Pynchon,* 1988; and articles and reviews for the Los Angeles *Times* and the Washington *Post.* **Essays:** Harry Mathews; Joseph McElroy.

STRANDBERG, Victor. Professor of English, Duke University, Durham, North Carolina. Author of *A Colder Fire: The Poetry of Robert Penn Warren,* 1965; *The Poetic Vision of Robert Penn Warren,* 1977; *A Faulkner Overview: Six Perspectives,* 1981; *Religious Psychology in American Literature: A Study in the Relevance of William James,* 1981; and "The Art of Cynthia Ozick" in *Texas Studies in Literature and Language,* Summer 1983. **Essay:** Cynthia Ozick.

STRUTHERS, J.R. Faculty member, Department of English, University of Guelph. Author of numerous articles in books and periodicals, including essays, interviews, and bibliographies of Hugh Hood and Alice Munro. Editor of *Before the Flood: Our Exagmination round His Factification for Incamination of Hugh Hood's Work in Progress,* 1979; *The Montreal Story Tellers,* 1985; *Origins,* 1985; *New Directions from Old,* 1991; *The Possibilities of Story,* 2 vols., 1992; *Canadian Classics* (with John Metcalf), 1993; and *How Stories Mean* (with John Metcalf), 1993. **Essays:** Jack Hodgins; Hugh Hood; Alice Munro.

STUCKEY, W.J. Professor of English, Purdue University, Lafayette, Indiana; founding editor of *Minnesota Review,* acting editor of *Modern Fiction Studies,* and associate editor of *Journal of Narrative Technique.* Author of *Pulitzer Prize Novels,* 1966 (revised 1980); and *Caroline Gordon,* 1972. **Essay:** Frank Tuohy.

SULLIVAN, Maggi R. Lecturer in English, Finger Lakes Community College, Canandaigua, New York; freelance writer. Editor of a two-volume series on local history. **Essay:** Allan Gurganis.

SUMMERS, Judith. Freelance writer. Author of two novels (*Dear Sister,* 1985; and *I, Gloria Gold,* 1988); and of *Soho: A History of London's Most Colourful Neighbourhood,* 1989. **Essay:** Zoë Fairbairns.

SUTHERLAND, Fraser. Freelance writer; managing editor of *Books in Canada* magazine. Author of several books, including *The Style of Innocence: A Study of Hemingway and Callaghan,* 1972; *Madwomen* (poetry), 1978; *John Glassco: An Essay and Bibliography,* 1984;

Whitefaces (poetry), 1986; *The History of Canadian Magazines,* 1988; and of fiction, poetry, and criticism in journals and anthologies. **Essay:** Douglas Glover.

SUTHERLAND, John. Professor of English, California Institute of Technology, Pasadena. Author of *Fiction and the Fiction Industry,* 1978; *Bestsellers: Popular Fiction of the 1970's,* 1980; *Offensive Literature: Decensorship in Britain,* 1982; *The Longman Companion to Victorian Fiction,* 1988 (as *The Sanford Companion to Victorian Fiction,* 1989); and *Mrs. Humphry Ward: Eminent Victorian, Pre-eminent Edwardian,* 1990. Editor of works by Jack London, Thackeray, and Trollope. **Essay:** Tom Sharpe.

SWINFORD, Dean. Doctoral candidate in English at the University of Florida. **Essay:** J. G. Ballard.

SYKES, Arlene. Senior Lecturer in English, University of Queensland, Brisbane. Formerly editor in the Drama Department, Australian Broadcasting Commission. Author of *Harold Pinter,* 1970; and of articles on modern drama and Australian fiction. Editor of *Five Plays for Radio* and four other anthologies of Australian plays. **Essay:** Jessica Anderson.

TACON, Shana. Postgraduate student, Department of English, University of Queensland, Australia; researching Pacific women's writing. **Essay:** Barbara Anderson.

TALLEY, Sharon. Recently completed a Ph.D. in American literature at the University of North Texas and currently teaches English at Texas A&M University-Corpus Christi. Her particular interests include nineteenth- and twentieth-century American literature, death in literature, and nonfiction prose studies. **Essay:** Saul Bellow.

TANNER, Tony. Reader in English, King's College, Cambridge. Author of books on Conrad and Bellow and of *The Reign of Wonder: Naivety and Reality in American Literature,* 1965; *City of Words: American Fiction 1950–1970,* 1971; *Adultery in the Novel,* 1980; *Thomas Pynchon,* 1982; *Henry James: The Writer and His Work,* 1985; *Jane Austen,* 1986; and *Scenes of Nature, Signs of Men,* 1987. Editor of works by Jane Austen, Henry James, and Herman Melville, and of a collection of essays on James.

TAYLOR, Anna-Marie. Lecturer in drama, University of Wales, Swansea; freelance theatre critic. Author of numerous articles on contemporary literature and European drama. **Essays:** Kazuo Ishiguro; Alison Lurie.

THIEME, John. Professor and head of English Studies, South Bank University, London; previously taught at the Universities of Guyana, North London, and Hull. Author of numerous articles on postcolonial writing, particularly Caribbean, Canadian, and Indian literatures; books include *The Web of Tradition: Uses of Allusion in V.S. Naipaul's Fiction,* 1987; *The Arnold Anthology of Post-Colonial Literatures in English,* 1996; and *Derek Walcott,* 1999. Articles Editor for *The Journal of Commonwealth Literature* and General Editor of the Manchester University Press Contemporary World Writers Series. **Essay:** Robert Kroetsch.

THOMPSON, Roger. Assistant professor of American Literature, Virginia Military Institute. Specializes in nineteenth-century American literature and rhetorical theory, with an emphasis on the American Renaissance. **Essay:** Reynolds Price.

TIDWELL, Drew. Master's candidate, University of North Texas, Denton. **Essay:** Jay McInerney.

TIFFIN, Chris. Senior lecturer in English, University of Queensland, Brisbane. Author of articles on Australian and Pacific literatures. Editor of *South Pacific Images,* 1978; *South Pacific Stories* (with H.M. Tiffin), 1980; and *Rosa Praed, 1851–1935: A Bibliography,* 1989. **Essays:** Helen Garner; Colin Johnson.

TOOMEY, Philippa. Staff member, *The Times,* London. Regular reviewer for *The Times, The Tablet, Home and Country,* and other periodicals. **Essay:** Alice Thomas Ellis.

TOULSON, Shirley. Poet and freelance writer. Author of several books of poems, and of guidebooks and studies of rural history, regional folklore, and Celtic history, most recently *The Celtic Alternative,* 1987; *Walking Round Wales,* 1988; and *The Companion Guide to Devon,* 1991. **Essays:** David Hughes; Bernard Kops; Stanley Middleton.

TREDELL, Nicolas. Teaches literature and cultural and film studies at Sussex University, England. Contributor to numerous literary journals in the United Kingdom and United States. Author or editor of eleven books, including *Uncancelled Challenge: The Work of Raymond Williams,* 1990; *The Critical Decade: Culture in Crisis,* 1993; *Conversations with Critics: Interviews with Leading Figures in Literary Criticism,* 1994; and *The Fiction of Martin Amis,* 2000. Currently working on a study called *Notes Towards a Definition of Digital Culture* and editing *The Icon Critical History of Film Theory.* **Essays:** David Caute; J.M. Coetzee; Douglas Coupland; Louis de Bernières; Kinky Friedman; Stephen King; William Kotzwinkle; Andrew O'Hagan; Terry Pratchett; Robert Silverberg; Neal Stephenson; Barry Unsworth; A.N. Wilson.

TRUESDALE, C.W. Poet, short story writer, and essayist; founding editor and publisher of *New Rivers Press.* **Essay:** Jon Hassler.

TUERK, Richard. Professor of literature and languages, East Texas State University, Commerce. Author of *Central Still: Circle and Sphere in Thoreau's Prose,* 1975; and essays on Jewish-American literature, Emerson, Jacob Riis, and Twain. **Essay:** John Barth.

van TOORN, Penny. Postdoctoral research fellow, Department of English, University of Sydney. Author of *Rudy Wiebe and the Historicity of the Word,* 1995; and articles on postcolonial literatures and theory. Co-editor of *Speaking Positions: Aboriginality, Gender and Ethnicity in Australian Cultural Studies,* 1995. **Essays:** Neil Bissoondath; Rudy Wiebe.

VASUDEVAN, Aruna. Freelance writer. **Essay:** Mary Wesley.

VOGLER, Thomas A. Professor of English and comparative literature, and chair of the Humanities Institute, University of California, Santa Cruz. Author of *Preludes to Vision,* 1970; *Unnam'd Forms: Blake and Textuality* (with Nelson Hilton), 1986; and numerous essays on poetry and fiction of the 18th to 20th centuries. **Essays:** William Gibson; Ken Kesey.

WACHINGER, Tobias. Doctoral candidate, University of Munich, Germany. Dissertation on contemporary writers positioning themselves in a cultural space in-between. Author of essays on the modern city novel, postcolonial Englishness, the politics of food in Indian writing, as well as on Salman Rushdie, Peter Ackroyd, and Christopher Hope. **Essays:** Julian Barnes; Romesh Gunesekera; Timothy Mo.

WALSH, William. Emeritus professor of Commonwealth literature, University of Leeds. Author of *The Use of Imagination: Educational Thought and the Literary Mind,* 1959; *A Human Idiom: Literature and Humanity,* 1964; *Coleridge: The Work and the Relevance,* 1967; *A Manifold Voice: Studies in Commonwealth Literature,* 1970; *R. K. Narayan,* 1971;*Commonwealth Literature,* 1973; *V.S. Naipaul,* 1973; *D.J. Enright: Poet of Humanism,* 1974; *Patrick White's Fiction,* 1977; *F.R. Leavis,* 1980; *R.K. Narayan: A Critical Appreciation,* 1982; and *Indian Literature in English,* 1990. Editor of *Readings in Commonwealth Literature,* 1974. **Essay:** Kamala Markandaya.

WARNER, Val. Freelance writer. Author of two books of poetry: *Under the Penthouse,* 1973; and *Before Lunch,*1986; and short stories, articles, and reviews in periodicals. Editor of *Charlotte Mew: Collected Poems and Prose,* 1981. Translator of *Centenary Corbière,* 1974. **Essays:** Beryl Bainbridge; Philip Callow; Elaine Feinstein; Francis King; Adam Mars-Jones; Elizabeth Mavor; Julia O'Faolain; Grace Paley; Fay Weldon.

WATSON, Diane. Lecturer in English, University of British Columbia, Vancouver. **Essays:** John Berger; Michael Ondaatje.

WATTS, Harold H. Emeritus professor of English, Purdue University, West Lafayette, Indiana. Author of *The Modern Reader's Guide to the Bible,* 1949; *Ezra Pound and the Cantos,* 1951; *Hound and Quarry,* 1953; *The Modern Reader's Guide to Religions,* 1964; and *Aldous Huxley,* 1969. **Essays:** Frederick Buechner; Herbert Gold; William Maxwell; Harry Mark Petrakis; J.D. Salinger; Helen Yglesias.

WELDON, Fay. See her own entry.

WESTBROOK, Perry D. Emeritus professor of English, State University of New York, Albany. Author of *Acres of Flint: Writers of Rural New England,* 1951; *Biography of an Island,* 1958; *The Greatness of Man: An Essay on Dostoevsky and Whitman,* 1961; *Mary Ellen Chase,* 1966; *Mary Wilkins Freeman,* 1967; *John Burroughs,* 1974; *William Bradford,* 1978. *Free Will and Determinism in American Literature,* 1979; *The New England Town in Fact and Fiction,* 1982; and *A Literary History of New England,* 1988. **Essay:** Kurt Vonnegut, Jr.

WHITE, Jon Manchip. Author and former Lindsay Young Professor of English, University of Tennessee, Knoxville. Author of numerous novels, short fiction, and historical essays. **Essay:** Nicholas Delbanco.

WILCOX, Leonard. Head of the American Studies Department at the University of Canterbury in Christchurch, New Zealand. He has written on postmodernism and its relationship to American fiction and drama, and is editor of *Rereading Shepard: Contemporary Essays on the Plays of Sam Shepard.* He has also written on American intellectual history and is the author of *V.F. Calverton: Radical in the American Grain.* **Essay:** Don DeLillo.

WILLIAMS, Mark. Lecturer in English, University of Waikato, Hamilton, New Zealand. Editor of *New Zealand Poetry 1972–86,* 1987.

WILLY, Margaret. Lecturer for the British Council, and at the City Literary Institute and Morley College, London. Author of two books of poetry: *The Invisible Sun,* 1946; and *Every Star a Tongue,* 1951; and several critical books, including studies of Chaucer, Traherne, Fielding, Browning, Crashaw, Vaughan, Emily Brontë, and English diarists. Editor of two anthologies and of plays by Goldsmith. **Essays:** Susan Hill; Muriel Spark.

WILSON, Janet. Faculty member, Department of English, University of Otago. **Essays:** Russell Haley; Fiona Kidman; Vincent O'Sullivan.

WITHERUP, Bill. Freelance book reviewer and critic. Author of two collections of poetry: *Black Ash, Orange Fire* and *Men at Work.* Contributing editor to *Atomic Ghosts: Poets Respond to the Nuclear Age,* 1995. **Essay:** James B. Hall.

WOOD, Michael. Professor of English, University of Exeter, Devon. Author of *Stendhal,* 1971; and *America in the Movies,* 1975; and articles in *New York Review of Books, London Review of Books,* and other periodicals.

WOODCOCK, George. Freelance writer, lecturer, and editor. Author of poetry (*Collected Poems,* 1983); plays; travel books; biographies; autobiographies (*Letter to the Past,* 1982; and *Beyond the Blue Mountains,* 1987); and works on history and politics; critical works include *William Godwin,* 1946; *The Incomparable Aphra,* 1948; *The Paradox of Oscar Wilde,* 1949; *The Crystal Spirit* (on Orwell), 1966; *Hugh MacLennan,* 1969; *Odysseus Ever Returning: Canadian Writers and Writing,* 1970; *Mordecai Richler,* 1970; *Dawn and the Darkest Hour* (on Aldous Huxley), 1972; *Herbert Read,* 1972; *Thomas Merton,* 1978; *The World of Canadian Writers,* 1980; *Northern Spring: The Flowering of Canadian Literature,* 1987; *A Social History of Canada,* 1988; and *The Century That Made Us: Canada 1814–1914,* 1989. Editor of anthologies and of works by Charles Lamb, Malcolm Lowry, Wyndham Lewis, Hardy, Meredith, and others. Died 1995. **Essays:** Jack Hodgins; Audrey Thomas; David Watmough.

WOODS, Tim. Lecturer in English, University College of Wales, Aberystwyth. **Essays:** Patrick McGrath; David Profumo.

WOOLF, Michael. Director of the Council on International Education Exchange, London. Author of "Exploding the Genre: The Crime Fiction of Jerome Charyn," in *American Crime Fiction,* 1988. **Essay:** Jerome Charyn.

WYLIE, J.J. Writer; graduate of University of Nevada, Las Vegas, where he studied under novelists Richard Wiley and Douglas Unger. **Essays:** Richard Bausch; Jim Crace; Alex Garland; Patrick McCabe; Steven Millhauser; James Sallis.

YABES, Leopoldo Y. Late professor emeritus of literature and Philippine studies, University of the Philippines, Quezon City. Author of more than 20 books and numerous essays and articles; books include *The University and the Fear of Ideas,* 1956; *Philippine Literature in English,* 1958; *The Filipino Struggle for Intellectual Freedon,* 1959; *Jose Rizal on His Centenary,* 1963; *The Ordeal of a Man of Academe,* 1967; and *Graduate Education at the University of the Philippines,* 1975. Editor of many books, including *Philippine Short Stories,* 2 vols., 1975–81. Former editor of *Philippine Social Sciences and Humanities Review.* Died 1988. **Essay:** F. Sionil Jose.

ZANI, Steven. Assistant professor in English and Foreign Languages, Lamar University, Beaumont, Texas. Specializes in Romanticism and literary theory. **Essay:** Ferrol Sams.

ZWICKER, Heather. Faculty member, Department of English, University of Alberta, Edmonton. **Essay:** Daphne Marlatt.

NATIONALITY INDEX

Below is the list of entrants divided by nationality. The nationalities were chosen largely from information supplied by entrants. A small number of entrants submitted two nationalities (e.g., American and British) and thus are listed under both. It should be noted that "British" was used for all English entrants and for any other British entrant who chose that designation over a more specific one, such as "Scottish."

American

Sherman Joseph Alexie, Jr.
Dorothy E. Allison
Lisa Alther
Rudolfo A. Anaya
Louis Auchincloss
Paul Auster
Elliott Baker
Russell Banks
Wilton Barnhardt
Andrea Barrett
John Barth
Frederick Barthelme
Jonathan Baumbach
Richard Bausch
Gregory Dale Bear
Ann Beattie
Stephen Becker
Madison Smartt Bell
Saul Bellow
Gregory Albert Benford
Thomas Berger
Doris Betts
Vance Bourjaily
T. Coraghessan Boyle
Ray Bradbury
David Bradley
John Ed Bradley
Rita Mae Brown
Rosellen Brown
Wesley Brown
Frederick Buechner
Lois McMaster Bujold
James Lee Burke
Janet Burroway
Frederick Busch
Octavia Estelle Butler
Robert Olen Butler, Jr.
Hortense Calisher
R.V. Cassill
Jerome Charyn
Alan Cheuse
Mark Childress
Carolyn Chute
Sandra Cisneros
William Cobb
Andrei Codrescu
Pat Conroy
Robert Coover
Harry Crews
Michael Crichton
Michael Cunningham
Edwidge Danticat
Samuel R. Delany
Nicholas Franklin Delbanco
Don DeLillo
Boman Desai
Joan Didion
Chitra Banerjee Divakaruni
Stephen Dixon
E.L. Doctorow
Ellen Douglas
Elaine Dundy
John Gregory Dunne
Wilma Dykeman
Clyde Carlyle Edgerton
Bret Easton Ellis
Trey Ellis
James Ellroy
David Ely
Louise Erdrich
Percival L. Everett
Howard Fast
Irvin Faust
Thomas Flanagan
Shelby Foote
Richard Ford
Marilyn French
Bruce Jay Friedman
Kinky Friedman
Abby Frucht
Ernest J. Gaines
Kenneth Gangemi
Cristina Garcia
George Garrett
William H. Gass
William Gay
Kaye Gibbons
William Gibson
Ellen Gilchrist
Gail Godwin
Herbert Gold
William Goldman
Mary Gordon
Robert Gover
Shirley Ann Grau
Joanne Greenberg
John Grisham
Winston Groom
Doris Grumbach
Albert Guerard
Allan Gurganis
David Guterson
James B. Hall
Jane Hamilton
Barry Hannah
Mark Harris
Jim Harrison
Jon Hassler
Shirley Hazzard
Ursula Hegi
Mark Helprin
Oscar Hijuelos
Carol Hill
Edward Hoagland
Russell Hoban
Alice Hoffman
Maureen Howard
Evan Hunter
Kristin Hunter
John Irving
Tama Janowitz
Gish Jen
Ruth Prawer Jhabvala
Charles Johnson
Denis Johnson
Diane Johnson
Gayl Jones
Madison Jones
Erica Jong
Ward Just
Johanna Kaplan
Steve Katz
William Melvin Kelley
Randall Kenan
William Kennedy
Ken Kesey
Jamaica Kincaid
Stephen King
Barbara Kingsolver
Maxine Hong Kingston
John Knowles
William Kotzwinkle
Chang-rae Lee
Ursula K. Le Guin
Alan Lelchuk
Elmore Leonard
Jonathan Lethem
Ira Levin
Alison Lurie
David Madden
Norman Mailer
Clarence Major
Wallace Markfield
Paule Marshall
Carole Maso
Bobbie Ann Mason
Hilary Masters
Harry Mathews
Jack Matthews
Peter Matthiessen
William Maxwell

Cormac McCarthy
Alice McDermott
Joseph McElroy
Thomas McGuane, III
Jay McInerney
Terry McMillan
Larry McMurtry
Barbara Mertz
Leonard Michaels
Steven Millhauser
Susan Minot
Mark Mirsky
N. Scott Momaday
Rick Moody
Lorrie Moore
Toni Morrison
Walter Mosley
Albert L. Murray
Gloria Naylor
Jay Neugeboren
Howard A. Norman
Joyce Carol Oates
Tim O'Brien
Tillie Olsen
Stewart O'Nan
Cynthia Ozick
Grace Paley
Kathrin Perutz
Harry Mark Petrakis
Jayne Anne Phillips
Marge Piercy
David Plante
Richard Powers
Reynolds Price
Richard Price
E. Annie Proulx
James Purdy
Thomas Pynchon
Frederic Raphael
John Rechy
Ishmael Reed
Anne Rice
Tom Robbins
Kim Stanley Robinson
Marilynne Robinson
Mary Robison
Judith Rossner
Philip Roth
Michael Rumaker
Joanna Russ
J.D. Salinger
James Sallis
Ferrol Sams, Jr.
Thomas Savage
Susan Fromberg Schaeffer
Budd Schulberg
Carolyn See
Hubert Selby, Jr.
Mary Lee Settle
Jeff Shaara
Wilfrid Sheed
Carol Shields
Anita Shreve
Clancy Sigal
Leslie Marmon Silko
Robert Silverberg
Mona Simpson
Jane Smiley
Lee Smith
Susan Sontag
Gilbert Sorrentino
Elizabeth Spencer
Michael Stephens
Neal Stephenson
Bruce Sterling
Daniel Stern
Richard G. Stern
Robert Stone
Susan Straight
William Styron
Ronald Sukenick
Amy Tan
Alexander Theroux
Paul Theroux
Lawrence Thornton
Anne Tyler
John Updike
Gore Vidal
Helena Maria Viramontes
William T. Vollmann
Kurt Vonnegut, Jr.
David Wagoner
Dan Wakefield
Alice Walker
David Foster Wallace
James Welch
Eudora Welty
Paul West
William Wharton
Edmund Valentine White, III
John Edgar Wideman
Allen Wier
Marianne Wiggins
John A. Williams
Connie Willis
Larry Woiwode
Tom Wolfe
Tobias Wolff
Charles Wright
Rudolph Wurlitzer
James Yaffe
Lois-Ann Yamanaka
Helen Yglesias
Al Young
Sol Yurick

Australian

Glenda Adams
James Aldridge
Jessica Anderson
Thea Astley
Murray Bail
Marion Campbell
Peter Carey
Brian Castro
Peter Cowan
Blanche d'Alpuget
Liam Davison
Ralph de Boissière
Dale Sara Dowse
Robert Drewe
Beverley Farmer
David Foster
Helen Garner
Kate Grenville
Marion Halligan
Elizabeth Harrower
Nicholas Hasluck
Janette Turner Hospital
David Ireland
Elizabeth Jolley
Victor Kelleher
Thomas Keneally
C.J. Koch
Morris Lurie
David Malouf
Peter Mathers
Roger McDonald
Alex Miller
Frank Moorhouse
Mudrooroo
Gerald Murnane
Randolph Stow
Tim Winton

Barbadian

Austin C. Clarke
George Lamming

British

Peter Ackroyd
Richard Adams
Brian Aldiss
Martin Amis
Paul Bailey
Beryl Bainbridge
J.G. Ballard
A.L. Barker
Pat Barker
Julian Barnes
Stan Barstow
Nina Bawden
Sybille Bedford
John Berger
Rachel Billington
John Bowen
William Boyd
Malcolm Bradbury
Melvyn Bragg
Sasthi Brata
Christine Brooke-Rose
Anita Brookner

Alan Burns
Philip Callow
David Caute
Arthur C. Clarke
Jonathan Coe
Barry Cole
Isabel Colegate
David Cook
William Cooper
Jim Crace
David Dabydeen
Fred D'Aguiar
Lionel Davidson
Jennifer Dawson
Louis de Bernières
Len Deighton
Margaret Drabble
C.J. Driver
Maureen Duffy
Nell Dunn
Dorothy Dunnett
Janice Elliott
Alice Thomas Ellis
Buchi Emecheta
Zoë Fairbairns
Sebastian Faulks
Elaine Feinstein
Eva Figes
Tibor Fischer
Margaret Forster
Frederick Forsyth
John Fowles
Ronald Frame
Dick Francis
Michael Frayn
Gillian Freeman
Alex Garland
Maggie Gee
Zulfikar Ghose
Brian Glanville
Giles Gordon
Winston Graham
Abdulrazak S. Gurnah
Russell Haley
Rodney Hall
Clifford Hanley
Wilson Harris
Susan Hill
Thomas Hinde
Barry Hines
Alan Hollinghurst
Nick Hornby
Elizabeth Jane Howard
David Hughes
Emyr Humphreys
Kazuo Ishiguro
Mick Jackson
Dan Jacobson
Howard Jacobson
P.D. James
Robin Jenkins
Glyn Jones
Gwyneth A. Jones
Mervyn Jones
Gabriel Josipovici
Francis King
Bernard Kops
Hanif Kureishi
John le Carré
Doris Lessing
Penelope Lively
David Lodge
Jamal Mahjoub
Hilary Mantel
Adam Mars-Jones
Allan Massie
Elizabeth Mavor
Ian McEwan
Patrick McGrath
Candia McWilliam
Stanley Middleton
Julian Mitchell
Timothy Mo
Michael Moorcock
John Mortimer
Nicholas Mosley
Lawrence Norfolk
Robert Nye
Tim Parks
Anne Perry
Jerzy Peterkiewicz
Caryl Phillips
Mike Phillips
David Pownall
Terry Pratchett
David Profumo
Piers Paul Read
Ruth Rendell
Michèle Roberts
Bernice Rubens
Salman Rushdie
Lisa St. Aubin de Teran
Will Self
Tom Sharpe
Andrew Sinclair
Carolyn Slaughter
Emma Smith
Muriel Spark
Alan Spence
Colin Spencer
Graham Swift
Emma Tennant
Shashi Tharoor
D.M. Thomas
Colin Thubron
Gillian Tindall
Peter Tinniswood
Barbara Trapido
Rose Tremain
Joanna Trollope
Frank Tuohy
Barry Unsworth
Edward Upward
Peter Vansittart
Marina Warner
Keith Waterhouse
Fay Weldon
Mary Wesley
Michael Wilding
A.N. Wilson
Jeanette Winterson

Canadian

André Alexis
Jeannette Armstrong
Margaret Atwood
Clark Blaise
Fred Bodsworth
George Bowering
Bonnie Burnard
Douglas Coupland
Timothy Findley
Mavis Gallant
Graeme Gibson
Douglas Glover
Phyllis Fay Gotlieb
Arthur Hailey
Tomson Highway
Jack Hodgins
Hugh Hood
Michael Ignatieff
Thomas King
W.P. Kinsella
Joy Kogawa
Robert Kroetsch
Sky Lee
Norman Levine
Ann-Marie MacDonald
John Metcalf
Anne Michaels
Bharati Mukherjee
Alice Munro
Michael Ondaatje
David Richards
Mordecai Richler
Peter Robinson
Jane Rule
Shyam Selvadurai
Ray Smith
John Steffler
Susan Swan
Audrey Thomas
Guy Vanderhaeghe
David Watmough
Rudy Wiebe

French

Marianne Hauser

Ghanaian

Ama Ata Aidoo
Ayi Kwei Armah

Guyanese
Roy A.K. Heath
Pauline Melville
Mike Phillips

Indian
Mulk Raj Anand
Upamanyu Chatterjee
Anita Desai
Shashi Deshpande
Ahmed Essop
Amitav Ghosh
Sunetra Gupta
Arun Joshi
Kamala Markandaya
Gita Mehta
Rohinton Mistry
Chaman Nahal
R.K. Narayan
Arundhati Roy
Nayantara Sahgal
I. Allan Sealy
Vikram Seth
Khushwant Singh

Irish
John Banville
Leland Bardwell
Maeve Binchy
Dermot Bolger
Clare Boylan
J.P. Donleavy
Roddy Doyle
Hugo Hamilton
Dermot Healy
Aidan Higgins
Desmond Hogan
Jennifer Johnston
Neil Jordan
Maeve Kelly
Benedict Kiely
Bernard MacLaverty
Patrick McCabe
John McGahern
Val Mulkerns
Eilis Ní Dhuibhne
Edna O'Brien
Joseph O'Connor
Julia O'Faolain
Charles Palliser
James Plunkett
Colm Tóibín
William Trevor
Anthony C. West

Jamaican
Erna Brodber

Kenyan
Ngugi wa Thiong'o
M.G. Vassanji

Malaysian
Daphne Marlatt

New Zealander
Barbara Anderson
Marilyn Duckworth
Alan Duff
Stevan Eldred-Grigg
Janet Frame
Maurice Gee
Patricia Grace
Keri Hulme
Witi Ihimaera
Stephanie Johnson
Fiona Kidman
Elizabeth Knox
Owen Marshall
Sue McCauley
James McNeish
Vincent O'Sullivan
Rosie Scott
Maurice Shadbolt
C.K. Stead
Noel Virtue
Damien Wilkins

Nigerian
Chinua Achebe
Elechi Amadi
I.N.C. Aniebo
Festus Iyayi
John Munonye
Ben Okri
Wole Soyinka

Northern Irish
Mary Beckett
Shane Connaughton
Deirdre Madden

Pakistani
Bapsi Sidhwa

Philippine
F. Sionil Jose

Saint Lucian
Garth St. Omer

Samoan
Albert Wendt

Scottish
Janice Galloway
Alasdair Gray
Jackie Kay
James Kelman
A. L. Kennedy
Andrew O'Hagan
Irvine Welsh

Singaporean
Catherine Lim

Somali
Nuruddin Farah

South African
André Brink
J.M. Coetzee
Nadine Gordimer
Stephen Gray
Christopher Hope
Njabulo S. Ndebele
Daphne Rooke
Miriam Tlali

Sri Lankan
Romesh Gunesekera

Sudanese
Jamal Mahjoub

Trinidadian
Michael Anthony
Neil Bissoondath
Kelvin Christopher James
Marion Patrick Jones
Earl Lovelace
V.S. Naipaul

Zimbabwean
Shimmer Chinodya

TITLE INDEX

The following list includes the titles of all books listed in the Novels and Short Stories (designated "s") sections of the entries in the book. The name in parenthesis is meant to direct the user to the appropriate entry, where full publication information is given.

Abbess of Crewe (Spark), 1974
Aberration of Starlight (Sorrentino), 1981
About a Boy (Hornby), 1998
About a Marriage (Gordon), 1972
About Harry Towns (Friedman), 1975
About My Table, and Other Stories (s Delbanco), 1983
Absent Friends (s Busch), 1989
Absolute Hero (Humphreys), 1986
Absolutely Nothing to Get Alarmed About (Wright), 1973
Absurd Affair (Spencer), 1961
Accident (Mosley), 1966
Accident (Plante), 1991
Accidental Tourist (Tyler), 1985
Accidental Woman (Coe), 1987
According to Mark (Lively), 1985
Accordion Crimes (Proulx), 1996
Ace of Diamonds Gang (s Marshall), 1993
Acid House (s Welsh), 1995
Acolyte (Astley), 1972
Acrobats (Richler), 1954
Across the Black Waters (Anand), 1940
Across the Bridge: Stories (s Gallant), 1993
Across the Sea Wall (Koch), 1982
Across the Sea of Stars (Clarke), 1959
Across the Sea of Suns (Benford), 1984
Act of Darkness (King), 1983
Act of Terror (Brink), 1991
Action (King), 1978
Actual (Bellow), 1997
Adah's Story (Emecheta), 1983
Adaptable Man (Frame), 1965
Admiral and the Nuns with Other Stories (s Tuohy), 1963
Admiring Silence (Gurnah), 1996
Adult Entertainment (s Metcalf), 1989
Adultery (Theroux), 1988
Adulthood Rites: Xenogenesis (Butler), 1988
Adventures of Alyx (s Russ), 1985
Adventures of Augie March (Bellow), 1995
Adventures of Christian Rosy Cross (Foster), 1986
Adventures of Robina, by Herself (Tennant), 1987
Adventures of Una Persson and Catherine Cornelius in the Twentieth Century (Moorcock, as Bradbury, E.), 1976
Advertisements for Myself (s Mailer), 1961
Aesop's Forest (s Coover), 1986
Affair to Remember (Cassill), 1957
Affliction (Banks), 1990
Affliction (Weldon), 1994
Africa and After (s Kelleher), 1983
African Horse (Pownall), 1975
African Stories (s Lessing), 1965
African Trilogy (Achebe), 1988
After a Fashion (Middleton), 1987
After China (Castro), 1992
After-Dinner's Sleep (Middleton), 1986
After Goliath (Cassill), 1985
After Hannibal (Unsworth), 1997
After Julius (Howard), 1966
After Lazarus: A Filmscript (s Coover), 1980
After Rain (Trevor), 1996
After Rome, Africa (Glanville), 1959
After the Act (Graham), 1966
After the Fire (Rule), 1989
After the Rain (Bowen), 1959
After the War (Raphael), 1989
After the War (Stern), 1965
After Z-Hour (Knox), 1987
Afterlife (s Updike), 1987
Afterlife and Other Stories (s Updike), 1994
Afterlife of George Cartwright (Steffler), 1993
Afternoon of a Good Woman (Bawden), 1977
Against Infinity (Benford), 1983
Against the Dark (Middleton), 1998
Against the Fall of Night (Clarke), 1953
Against the Season (Rule), 1972
Agatha (Colegate), 1973
Age (Aldiss), 1967
Age (Calisher), 1987
Age of Consent (Greenberg), 1987
Age of Grief (s Smiley), 1988
Age of Iron (Coetzee), 1990
Age of Miracles: Stories (s Gilchrist), 1995
Age of Terror (Plante), 1999
Age of the Rainmakers (s Harris), 1971
Agent (Hinde), 1974
Agrippa's Daughter (Fast, as Cunningham), 1965
Agüero Sisters (Garcia), 1997
Ahmed and the Oblivion Machines: A Fable (Bradbury), 1998
Air and Angels (Hill), 1991
Air That Kills (King), 1948
Air We Breathe (Josipovici), 1981
Airframe (Crichton, as Lange), 1996
Airport (Hailey), 1968
Airs of Earth (s Aldiss), 1963
Airships (s Hannah), 1991
Alabaster Egg (Freeman), 1971
Albany Trio: Three Novels from the Albany Cycle (Kennedy), 1996
Albatross and Other Stories (s Hill), 1975
Alberta: A Celebration (s Wiebe), 1979
Albert's Memorial (Cook), 1972
Alburquerque (Anaya), 1992
Alder Tree (Jones), 1982
Alias Grace (Atwood), 1996
Alibi (Kroetsch), 1983
Alice (Fast, as Cunningham), 1965
Alice Fell (Tennant), 1980
Alice in Thunderland: A Feminist Fairytale (Kelly), 1993
Alien Heat (Moorcock, as Bradbury, E.), 1972
Alien Years (Silverberg, as Knox), 1998
Aliens from Space (Silverberg, as Knox), 1958
All Done with Mirrors (Haley), 1999
All Gone: 18 Short Stories (s Dixon), 1990

All My Friends Are Going to Be Strangers (McMurtry), 1973
All-Night Visitors (Major), 1969
All Souls' Rising (Bell), 1995
All That Glitters (Anthony), 1981
All the Days and Nights: The Collected Stories of William Maxwell (s Maxwell), 1995
All the Good People I've Left Behind (s Oates, as Smith, R.), 1979
All the King's Horses and Other Stories (s West), 1981
All the Nice Girls (Anderson), 1994
All the Pretty Horses (McCarthy), 1993
All the Tenderness Left in the World: Short Stories (s Johnson), 1993
All Things Nice (Billington), 1969
All Tomorrow's Parties (Gibson), 1999
All-True Travels and Adventures of Lidie Newton (Smiley), 1998
All Visitors Ashore (Stead), 1984
All We Need of Hell (Crews), 1987
All You Need (Feinstein), 1991
Alley Jaggers (West), 1966
Alleys of Eden (Butler), 1981
Alligator Report (s Kinsella), 1985
Ally Ally Aster (Jones), 1981
Almost Heaven (Wiggins), 1998
Alone (Farmer), 1980
Along the Arno (Glanville), 1957
Already Dead: A California Gothic (Johnson), 1997
Altered States (Brookner), 1996
Always Coming Home (Le Guin), 1986
Always Home and Other Stories (s Ely), 1991
Always Outnumbered, Always Outgunned: The Socrates Fortlow Stories (s Mosley), 1997
Always the Islands of Memory (Virtue), 1991
Alyx (s Russ), 1976
Amalgamemnon (Brooke-Rose), 1994
Amandla (Tlali), 1980
Amateur's Guide to the Night (s Robison), 1983
Amberstone Exit (Feinstein), 1972
Ambition and Love (Just), 1994
Ambrose's Vision: Sketches Towards the Creation of a Cathedral (Gordon), 1980
American: A Middle Western Legend (Fast, as Cunningham), 1949
American Ambassador (Just), 1987
American Appetites (Oates, as Smith, R.), 1989
American Blues (Just), 1984
American Brat (Sidhwa), 1994
American Dad (Janowitz), 1988
American Dream (Mailer), 1965
American Experience (s Mathews), 1991
American Marriage (Masters), 1969
American Mischief (Lelchuk), 1973
American Pastoral (Roth), 1997
American Psycho (Ellis), 1991
American Scrapbook (Charyn), 1969
American Woman in the Chinese Hat (Maso), 1994
Americana (DeLillo), 1990
Americans, Baby (s Moorhouse), 1972
Ammie, Come Home (Mertz, as Michaels), 1969
Amnesia Moon (Lethem), 1995
Amnesty (Dowse), 1993
Among the Cinders (Shadbolt), 1984
Amongst Thistles and Thorns (Clarke), 1965
Amongst Women (McGahern), 1990
Amriika (Vassanji), 1999
Amsterdam (McEwan), 1999
Ana Historic (Marlatt), 1990
Anabasis: A Journey to the Interior (Gilchrist), 1994
Anatomy Lesson (Roth), 1984
Ancestor Game (Miller), 1994
Ancestral Vices (Sharpe), 1980
Anchor Tree (Humphreys), 1980
Ancient Child (Momaday), 1989
Ancient Evenings (Mailer), 1983
Ancient History (McElroy), 1971
And Chaos Died (Russ), 1970
And We Were Young (Baker), 1980
Andromeda Strain (Crichton, as Lange), 1969
Anemones (Howard), 1998
Angel, All Innocence, and Other Stories (s Weldon), 1995
Angel at the Gate (Harris), 1982
Angel Landing (Hoffman), 1982
Angel of Light (Oates, as Smith, R.), 1981
Angel of the Tar Sands and Other Stories (s Wiebe), 1982
Angel on the Roof: The Stories of Russell Banks (s Banks), 2000
Angelica's Grotto (Hoban), 1999
Angell, Pearl and Little God (Graham), 1970
Angels (Johnson), 1984
Angels at the Ritz and Other Stories (s Trevor), 1976
Angels Falling (Elliott), 1969
Angled Road (Levine), 1952
Angry Brigade: A Documentary Novel (Burns), 1973
Angry Ones (Williams), 1960
Angry Tide: A Novel of Cornwall 1798–1799 (Graham), 1978
Anil's Ghost (Ondaatje), 2000
Animal Dreams (Kingsolver), 1990
Animal Game (Tuohy), 1957
Anna Apparent (Bawden), 1972
Anna Papers (Gilchrist), 1989
Annie, Gwen, Lily, Pam, and Tulip (s Kincaid), 1986
Annie John (Kincaid), 1985
Anniversary and Other Stories (s Auchincloss), 1999
Annunciation (Gilchrist), 1984
Annunciation (Plante), 1994
Anonymity of Sacrifice (Aniebo), 1974
Another Family Christmas: A Collection of Short Stories (s Boylan), 1997
Another Flesh (Callow), 1989
Another Part of the City (Hunter), 1986
Another Part of the Wood (Bainbridge), 1980
Another Roadside Attraction (Robbins), 1973
Another Street, Another Dance (Hanley, as Calvin), 1984
Another World (Barker), 1999
Another You (Beattie), 1995
Answer Yes or No (Mortimer), 1950
Ant Colony (King), 1991
Antarctica (Robinson), 1998
Antelope Wife (Erdrich), 1998
Anthills of the Savannah (Achebe), 1988
Antipodes (s Malouf), 1985

Antiquities: A Sequence of Short Stories (s Mulkerns), 1978
Anvil of Stars (Bear), 1992
Any Excuse for a Party: Selected Stories (s Barker), 1991
Any Minute I Can Split (Rossner), 1977
Any Woman's Blues (Jong), 1990
Anya (Schaeffer), 1976
Anything for Billy (McMurtry), 1989
Anywhere But Here (Simpson), 1986
Apology for a Hero (Barker), 1950
Apostles of Light (Douglas), 1973
Apple of the Eye (Middleton), 1970
Apprentice (Joshi), 1975
Apprenticeship of Duddy Kravitz (Richler), 1959
April, June and November (Raphael), 1976
April Morning (Fast, as Cunningham), 1961
April Robin Murders (Hunter), 1959
Aquaboogie: A Novel in Stories (Straight), 1990
Arcadia (Crace), 1992
Archimedes and the Seagle (Ireland), 1987
Are You Listening Rabbi Löw (Donleavy), 1988
Are You Mine? (Frucht), 1993
Aren't You Happy for Me? and Other Stories (s Bausch), 1995
Armadillo (Boyd), 1998
Armadillos and Old Lace (Friedman), 1994
Armstrong Trilogy (Heath), 1994
Around the Mountain: Scenes from Montreal Life (s Hood), 1967
Arranged Marriage: Stories (s Divakaruni), 1995
Arrow of God (Achebe), 1967
Art and Lies (Winterson), 1995
Art Lover (Maso), 1990
Arthur Rex: A Legendary Novel (Berger), 1979
Artifact (Benford), 1985
Artificial Kid (Sterling), 1980
Artist Type (Glanville), 1968
Artist of the Floating World (Ishiguro), 1986
As Far as You Can Go (Mitchell), 1963
As She Climbed Across the Table (Lethem), 1997
As Summers Die (Groom), 1980
As Towns with Fire (West), 1970
Ascent to Omai (Harris), 1970
Ash on an Old Man's Sleeve (King), 1996
Ashes for Easter and Other Monodramas (s Watmough), 1972
Ashworth Hall (Perry), 1997
Ask Me Now (Young), 1980
Ask Me Tomorrow (Barstow), 1962
Aspects of Feeling (Vansittart), 1986
Aspects of the Dying Process (s Wilding), 1972
Assassin Who Gave Up His Gun (Fast, as Cunningham), 1970
Assassins (Mosley), 1993
Assassins: A Book of Hours (Oates, as Smith, R.), 1975
Assignation (s Oates, as Smith, R.), 1988
Asta's Book (Rendell, as Vine), 1993
Astonishing the Gods (Okri), 1995
Astrologer's Day and Other Stories (s Narayan), 1947
Asya (Ignatieff), 1991
Asylum (McGrath), 1997
At Fever Pitch (Caute), 1961
At Paradise Gate (Smiley), 1981
At Play in the Fields of the Lord (Matthiessen), 1966
At Risk (Hoffman), 1988
At the Bottom of the River (s Kincaid), 1984
At the Jerusalem (Bailey), 1967
At Weddings and Wakes (McDermott), 1991
At Winter's End (Silverberg, as Knox), 1988
Athena (Banville), 1995
Atlantis: Three Tales (s Delany), 1995
Atlas: People, Places, and Visions (s Vollmann), 1996
Atonement, and Other Stories (s Auchincloss), 1997
Atonement of Ashley Morden (Bodsworth), 1964
Atrocity Exhibition (s Ballard), 1970
Attachments (Rossner), 1977
August (Rossner), 1983
August Is a Wicked Month (O'Brien), 1965
August Nights (s Hood), 1985
Augustus: The Memoirs of the Emperor (Massie), 1986
Aureole (Maso), 1996
Autobiography of Foudini M. Cat (Schaeffer), 1997
Autobiography of Miss Jane Pittman (Gaines), 1973
Autobiography of My Mother (Brown), 1976
Autobiography of My Mother (Kincaid), 1996
Autobiopsy (Rubens), 1993
Autumn Manoeuvres (Bragg), 1978
Autumn People (s Bradbury), 1965
Ava (Maso), 1993
Awaiting Court Martial (s Iyayi), 1996
Awake for Mourning (Kops), 1958
Awakening of George Darroch (Jenkins), 1985
Awfully Big Adventure (Bainbridge), 1991
Ax (Hunter), 1964
Azadi (Nahal), 1977

B (Figes), 1972
Babble (Baumbach), 1976
Babe (Wiggins), 1975
Babel (Burns), 1970
Babel-17 (Delany), 1976
Baby, Come On Inside (Wagoner), 1968
Baby No-Eyes (Grace), 1998
Baby Sitters (Caute), 1978
Baby's First Step (s Updike), 1993
Bachelor of Arts (Narayan), 1937
Bachelors (Spark), 1961
Bachman Books: Four Early Novels (King), 1996
Back in the World (s Wolff), 1985
Backward Place (Jhabvala), 1965
Bad Lot and Other Stories (s Glanville), 1977
Bad Music (McCauley), 1990
Bad Sister (Tennant), 1978
Bad Streak and Other Stories (s Glanville), 1961
Badlands (Kroetsch), 1983
Bag (Yurick), 1970
Bag of Bones (King), 1998
Bagombo Snuff Box: Uncollected Short Fiction (s Vonnegut), 1999
Bailey's Café (Naylor), 1993
Balcony of Europe (Higgins), 1972
Ball of Malt and Madame Butterfly (s Kiely), 1973
Ballad of Beta-2 (Delany), 1965
Ballad of Beta-2, and Empire Star (Delany), 1977
Ballad of Erinungarah (Foster), 1997

Ballad of Peckham Rye (Spark), 1960
Ballad of the Public Trustee (s Kinsella), 1982
Ballroom of Romance and Other Stories (s Trevor), 1972
Bandits (Leonard), 1987
Bane of the Black Sword (Moorcock, as Bradbury, E.), 1984
Bang the Drum Slowly, by Henry W. Wiggen: Certain of His Enthusiasms Restrained (Harris), 1956
Bang-Bang You're Dead and Other Stories (s Spark), 1982
Banished Misfortune (s Healy), 1982
Banker (Francis), 1983
Bankrupts (Glanville), 1958
Banquet (Slaughter), 1984
Bar (s Rumaker), 1964
Barbarians of Mars (Moorcock, as Bradbury, E.), 1966
Barbarous Tongue (Duckworth), 1963
Barbary Shore (Mailer), 1952
Barber's Trade Union and Other Stories (s Anand), 1944
Barclay Family Theatre (s Hodgins), 1981
Barefoot in the Head (Aldiss), 1970
Bargain with God (Savage), 1953
Barking at Butterflies, and Other Stories (s Hunter), 2000
Barking Man and Other Stories (s Bell), 1990
Barn Blind (Smiley), 1994
Barney's Version (Richler), 1997
Barnum Museum: Stories (s Millhauser), 1997
Barracks (McGahern), 1964
Barrayar (Bujold), 1991
Barrytown Trilogy (Doyle), 1992
Bastard out of Carolina (Allison), 1992
Bats Out of Hell (s Hannah), 1993
Battle for Christabel (Forster), 1991
Baumgartner's Bombay (Desai), 1989
Bay of Contented Man (s Drewe), 1991
Bay of Love and Sorrows (Richards), 1998
Bay of Noon (Hazzard), 1970
Bay of Silence (St. Aubin de Teran), 1986
Be Buried in the Rain (Mertz, as Michaels), 1986
Be Cool (Leonard), 1999
Beach (Garland), 1997
Beach Music (Conroy), 1995
Beachmasters (Astley), 1986
Bean Trees (Kingsolver), 1988
Beans of Egypt, Maine (Chute), 1985
Bear and His Daughter: Stories (s Stone), 1997
Bear Went over the Mountain (Kotzwinkle), 1996
Bearded Ladies (s Grenville), 1984
Bear's Fantasies: Six Stories in Old Paradigms (s Bear), 1992
Beast God Forgot to Invent: Novellas (Harrison), 2000
Beast of Heaven (Kelleher), 1984
Beastly Beatitudes of Balthazar B (Donleavy), 1969
Beasts of the Southern Wild (s Betts), 1973
Beau Bumbo (Sinclair), 1985
Beautiful (Billington), 1974
Beautiful Greed (Madden), 1961
Beautiful Room Is Empty (White), 1988
Beautiful Visit (Howard), 1950
Beautiful Words (Jones), 1979
Beauty and the Beast (Hunter), 1983
Beautyful Ones Are Not Yet Born (Armah), 1969
Beauty's Punishment (Rice, as Roquelaure), 1984
Beauty's Release (Rice, as Roquelaure), 1994
Because It Is Bitter, and Because It Is My Heart (Oates, as Smith, R.), 1991
Because the Night (Ellroy), 1987
Bech: A Book (s Updike), 1970
Bech at Bay: A Quasi-novel (Updike), 1998
Bech Is Back (s Updike), 1982
Becket Factor (Anthony), 1990
Bedrock (Alther), 1990
Beehive Arranged on Human Principles (s Sorrentino), 1986
Beet Queen (Erdrich), 1987
Before and After (Brown), 1993
Before My Life Began (Neugeboren), 1985
Before My Time (Howard), 1975
Before She Met Me (Barnes, as Kavanagh), 1986
Beggar My Neighbour (s Jacobson), 1964
Beginners (Jacobson), 1966
Beginning to End (Middleton), 1991
Beginnings: Samplings from a Long Apprenticeship: Novels Which Were Imagined, Written, Re-Written, Submitted, Rejected, Abandoned, and Supplanted (s Hodgins), 1983
Beheading and Other Stories (s Hunter), 1971
Behold the Man (Moorcock, as Bradbury, E.), 1970
Being Dead (Crace), 2000
Being Invisible (Berger), 1988
Bela Lugosi's White Christmas (West), 1972
Belfast Woman and Other Stories (s Beckett), 1980
Belgrave Square (Perry), 1993
Believe Them (s Robison), 1988
Believers to the Bright Coast (O'Sullivan), 1998
Belinda (Rice, as Roquelaure), 1987
Bellarmine Jug (Hasluck), 1984
Bellarosa Connection (s Bellow), 1989
Bellefleur (Oates, as Smith, R.), 1981
Bellwether (Willis), 1996
Bellydancer (Lee), 1994
Beloved (Morrison), 1987
Beloved (s Updike), 1982
Beloved Latitudes (Pownall), 1981
Ben, in the World: The Sequel to the Fifth Child (Lessing), 2000
Bend in the River (Naipaul), 1979
Benefactor (Sontag), 1964
Benefits (Fairbairns), 1982
Berhama Account (Williams), 1985
Berlin Game (Deighton), 1984
Beside Myself (Haley), 1990
Best Man to Die (Rendell, as Vine), 1970
Best of Friends (Humphreys), 1978
Best of Friends (Trollope), 1998
Best of Rumpole (s Mortimer), 1993
Best There Ever Was (Bradley), 1990
Bet They'll Miss Us When We're Gone (s Wiggins), 1991
Bethlehem Road (Perry), 1991
Beti (Rooke), 1959
Betrayals (Palliser), 1995
Bettany's Book (Keneally), 1999
Better Times Than These (Groom), 1978
Betting Man (s Glanville), 1969
Between (Brooke-Rose), 1968
Between Tears and Laughter (s Anand), 1973

Beyond Heaven's River (Bear), 1980
Beyond the Bedroom Wall: A Family Album (Woiwode), 1975
Beyond the Blue Mountains (Lively), 1997
Beyond the Bridge (Matthews), 1970
Beyond the Fall of Night (Benford), 1990
Beyond the Fall of Night (Clarke), 1990
Beyond the Pale and Other Stories (s Trevor), 1982
Beyond the Safe Zone: Collected Short Fiction (s Silverberg, as Knox), 1986
Big as Life (Doctorow), 1966
Big Bazoohley (Carey), 1995
Big Bounce (Leonard), 1969
Big Day (Unsworth), 1977
Big Dipper (Billington), 1970
Big Fix (Hunter), 1952
Big Girls Don't Cry (Weldon), 1997
Big Glass (Josipovici), 1991
Big Heart (Anand), 1980
Big Man (Hunter), 1978
Big Man (Neugeboren), 1966
Big Picture: Stories (s Everett), 1996
Big Season (Gee), 1962
Big U (Stephenson), 1984
Bigamist's Daughter (McDermott), 1982
Bigger Light (Clarke), 1975
Biggest Modern Woman in the World (Swan), 1986
Bijou (Madden), 1974
Billenium and Other Stories (s Ballard), 1962
Billie Dyer and Other Stories (s Maxwell), 1992
Billion-Dollar Brain (Deighton), 1966
Billy Bathgate (Doctorow), 1989
Billy Liar (Waterhouse), 1960
Billy Liar on the Moon (Waterhouse), 1976
Billy Phelan's Greatest Game (Kennedy), 1983
Bimbo (Waterhouse), 1990
Binary (Crichton, as Lange), 1972
Binding Vine (Deshpande), 1994
Bingo (Brown), 1988
Bingo Palace (Erdrich), 1994
Birchbark House (Erdrich), 1999
Birchwood (Banville), 1973
Bird (Hinde), 1970
Bird Artist (Norman), 1994
Bird of Night (Hill), 1973
Birdcage (Bowen), 1962
Birds of America: Stories (s Moore), 1998
Birds of Passage (Rubens), 1982
Birds of the Air (Ellis), 1981
Birds of the Innocent Wood (Madden), 1988
Birds on the Trees (Bawden), 1995
Birdsong (Faulks), 1993
Birdy (Wharton), 1979
Birth and Death of the Miracle Man (s Wendt), 1986
Birth of a Hero (Gold), 1951
Birthday Boys (Bainbridge), 1994
Birthstone (Thomas), 1980
Bit of Singing and Dancing (s Hill), 1973
Bitter Knowledge (s Matthews), 1964
Black Album (Kureishi), 1995
Black Angels (s Friedman), 1967
Black Baby (Boylan), 1989
Black Betty (Mosley), 1994
Black Butterfly (s Hannah), 1982
Black Cherry Blues (Burke), 1990
Black Cloud, White Cloud (s Douglas), 1963
Black Corridor (Moorcock, as Bradbury, E.), 1969
Black Dogs (McEwan), 1992
Black Hornet (Sallis), 1994
Black House (Theroux), 1974
Black Idol (St. Aubin de Teran), 1987
Black Jasmine (s Singh), 1971
Black Madonna (s Lessing), 1966
Black Marina (Tennant), 1985
Black Marsden: A Tabula Rasa Comedy (Harris), 1972
Black Moon: A Novel of Cornwall 1794–1795 (Graham), 1974
Black Mountain Breakdown (Smith), 1980
Black Prince and Other Stories (s Grau), 1956
Black Rainbow (Mertz, as Michaels), 1983
Black Rainbow (Wendt), 1995
Black Swan (s Hope), 1987
Black Tickets (s Phillips), 1980
Black Tower (James), 1975
Black Water (Oates, as Smith, R.), 1992
Blackboard Jungle (Hunter), 1955
Blacker Than a Thousand Midnights (Straight), 1994
Blacking Factory, and Pennsylvania Gothic: A Short Novel and a Long Story (s Sheed), 1969
Blackmailer (Colegate), 1958
Blackwater Lightship (Tóibín), 2000
Blades of Mars (Moorcock, as Bradbury, E.), 1966
Blake (Ackroyd), 1996
Blanco (Wier), 1978
Blast from the Past (Friedman), 1998
Bleeding Heart (French), 1980
Bless Me, Ultima (Anaya), 1972
Blessed Assurance: A Moral Tale (s Gurganis), 1990
Blessing (s Oates, as Smith, R.), 1976
Blind Assassin (Atwood), 2000
Blind Blonde with Candles in Her Hair: Stories (s Stead), 1998
Blind Geometer (Robinson), 1986
Blind Understanding (Middleton), 1982
Blinder (Hines), 1966
Bliss (Carey), 1981
Bliss Body (Callow), 1969
Bloch and Bradbury (s Bradbury), 1969
Blonde (Oates, as Smith, R.), 2000
Blood (s Galloway), 1991
Blood: A Southern Fantasy (Moorcock, as Bradbury, E.), 1994
Blood and Water (s Ní Dhuibhne), 1988
Blood and Water (s Winton), 1993
Blood and Water and Other Tales (s McGrath), 1989
Blood at the Root: An Inspector Banks Mystery (Robinson), 1997
Blood Countess (Codrescu), 1995
Blood Lines: Long and Short Stories (s Rendell, as Vine), 1996
Blood Meridian; or, The Evening Redness in the West (McCarthy), 1989
Blood Music (Bear), 1985
Blood on the Moon (Ellroy), 1985
Blood Red, Sister Rose (Keneally), 1974
Blood Relatives (Hunter), 1976

Blood Rights (Phillips), 1989
Blood Sport (Francis), 1968
Blood, Tears & Folly (Deighton), 1993
Blood Tie (Settle), 1977
Blood Ties (Richards), 1976
Bloodbrothers (Price), 1976
Bloodchild and Other Stories (s Butler), 1995
Bloodfather (Ireland), 1988
Bloodline (s Gaines), 1968
Bloodshed and Three Novellas (s Ozick), 1976
Bloodsmoor Romance (Oates, as Smith, R.), 1983
Blosseville File (Hasluck), 1992
Blott on the Landscape (Sharpe), 1984
Blow Your House Down (Barker), 1984
Blown Away (Sukenick), 1986
Blown Figures (Thomas), 1975
Blue Afternoon (Boyd), 1995
Blue Apes (Gotlieb), 1995
Blue Bed (s Jones), 1938
Blue Blood (Eldred-Grigg), 1997
Blue Calhoun (Price), 1992
Blue-Eyed Buddhist and Other Stories (s Gilchrist), 1990
Blue-Eyed Shan (Becker), 1982
Blue Eyes (Charyn), 1975
Blue Guitar (Hasluck), 1980
Blue Hill Avenue (Mirsky), 1972
Blue Light: A Novel (Mosley), 1998
Blue Mars (Robinson), 1996
Blue Mountains of China (Wiebe), 1970
Blue Pastoral (Sorrentino), 1985
Blueback: A Contemporary Fable (Winton), 1997
Bluebeard (Vonnegut), 1988
Bluebeard's Egg and Other Stories (s Atwood), 1987
Bluebottle: A Lew Griffin Novel (Sallis), 1999
Bluegate Fields (Perry), 1992
Bluejay's Dance (Erdrich), 1995
Bluest Eye (Morrison), 1980
Bluette (Frame), 1990
Blu's Hanging (Yamanaka), 1997
B-movie (Barstow), 1987
Boarding-House (Trevor), 1965
Boat Load of Home Folk (Astley), 1983
Boating for Beginners (Winterson), 1985
Bob the Gambler (Barthelme), 1997
Bobby-Soxer (Calisher), 1986
Bodies and Souls (Rechy), 1984
Bodily Harm (Atwood), 1982
Bodily Harm (Billington), 1993
Body (Crews), 1990
Body of Martin Aguilera (Everett), 1994
Body of Water: A Year's Notebook (s Farmer), 1990
Bodysurfers (s Drewe), 1984
Bogeyman (Forster), 1966
Bohemians: John Reed and His Friends (Cheuse), 1982
Bolt (Francis), 1987
Bomber (Deighton), 1970
Bonds of Attachment (Humphreys), 1991
Bone by Bone (Matthiessen), 1999
Bone People (Hulme), 1985
Bonecrack (Francis), 1972
Bonfire of the Vanities (Wolfe), 1988
Boo (Conroy), 1970
Book Class (Auchincloss), 1984
Book of Bebb (Buechner), 1979
Book of Brian Aldiss (s Aldiss), 1972
Book of Common Prayer (Didion), 1977
Book of Daniel (Doctorow), 1996
Book of Evidence (Banville), 1990
Book of Jamaica (Banks), 1980
Book of Knowledge (Grumbach), 1995
Book of Mrs. Noah (Roberts), 1987
Book of Ruth (Hamilton), 1988
Book of Secrets (Kidman), 1987
Book of Secrets (Vassanji), 1996
Book of Skulls (Silverberg, as Knox), 1978
Book of the Reading (Wilding), 1994
Boomerang (Hannah), 1989
Border (Feinstein), 1989
Border Station (Connaughton), 1989
Border Trilogy (McCarthy), 1999
Borderline (Hospital), 1985
Borders of Infinity (Bujold), 1989
Born Brothers (Woiwode), 1988
Born Indian (s Kinsella), 1981
Born of Man (Gray), 1989
Born with the Dead (s Silverberg, as Knox), 1975
Bornholm Night-Ferry (Higgins), 1983
Borrower of the Night (Mertz, as Michaels), 1974
Both Sides of the Moon (Duff), 1998
Bottle Factory Outing (Bainbridge), 1975
Bottle in the Smoke (Wilson), 1990
Bounty Hunters (Leonard), 1956
Bow Down to Nul (Aldiss), 1960
Box Garden (Shields), 1996
Box Socials (Kinsella), 1992
Boy on the Mountain (Rooke), 1969
Boy, the Bridge, the River (O'Sullivan), 1978
Boys and Girls Together (Goldman), 1965
Boys from Brazil (Levin), 1976
Boys in the Island (Koch), 1974
Boys of Winter (Sheed), 1987
Boy's Own Story (White), 1983
Braided Lives (Piercy), 1982
Brass Dolphin (Trollope), 1999
Bray House (Ní Dhuibhne), 1990
Brazen Prison (Middleton), 1971
Brazil (Updike), 1994
Brazzaville Beach (Boyd), 1991
Breach of Promise (Perry), 1998
Bread (Hunter), 1974
Break In (Francis), 1986
Breakfast in the Ruins: A Novel of Inhumanity (Moorcock, as Bradbury, E.), 1974
Breakfast of Champions; or, Goodbye, Blue Monday (Vonnegut), 1973
Breakfast on Pluto (McCabe), 1998
Breaking of Bumbo (Sinclair), 1959
Breaks (Price), 1983
Breast (Roth), 1973
Breath, Eyes, Memory (Danticat), 1994

Breathing Lessons (Tyler), 1989
Breathing Trouble and Other Stories (s Busch), 1974
Breed of Women (Kidman), 1988
Brendan (Buechner), 1987
Brethren (Grisham), 2000
Briar Rose (Coover), 1996
Bride (Sidhwa), 1983
Bride Price (Emecheta), 1976
Bride for the Sahib and Other Stories (s Singh), 1967
Bride of Innisfallen and Other Stories (s Welty), 1955
Bride of Lowther Fell: A Romance (Forster), 1981
Bridesmaid (Rendell, as Vine), 1989
Bridge Builder's Story (Fast, as Cunningham), 1995
Bridge of Lost Desire (Delany), 1987
Bridge to a Wedding (Munonye), 1978
Bridgeport Bus (Howard), 1965
Brief Conversation and Other Stories (s Lovelace), 1988
Brief Hours (Middleton), 1997
Brief Interviews with Hideous Men (s Wallace), 1999
Brief Lives (Brookner), 1991
Briefing for a Decent into Hell (Lessing), 1971
Brigadier Down Under (Tinniswood), 1983
Brigadier in Season (Tinniswood), 1984
Brigadier's Brief Lives (Tinniswood), 1984
Brigadier's Tour (Tinniswood), 1985
Bright Center of Heaven (Maxwell), 1934
Bright Lights, Big City (McInerney), 1985
Bright Road to El Dorado (Anthony), 1982
Brightfount Diaries (Aldiss), 1955
Brightness Falls (McInerney), 1993
Brighton Belle and Other Stories (s King), 1968
Brill among the Ruins (Bourjaily), 1971
Bring Larks and Heroes (Keneally), 1968
Bring Me the Head of Rona Barrett (s Gover), 1981
British Museum Is Falling Down (Lodge), 1967
Broke Heart Blues (Oates, as Smith, R.), 1999
Broken Canes (Vansittart), 1950
Broken Ground (Hodgins), 1998
Brooklyn Book of the Dead (Stephens), 1994
Brooklyn Boy (Lelchuk), 1989
Broom of the System (Wallace), 1987
Brothel in Rösenstrasse (Moorcock, as Bradbury, E.), 1987
Brother Frank's Gospel Hour, and Other Stories (s Kinsella), 1996
Brother of the More Famous Jack (Trapido), 1982
Brothers (Barthelme), 1993
Brothers (Goldman), 1986
Brothers (Rubens), 1984
Brothers in Arms (Bujold), 1989
Brothers in Confidence (Madden), 1972
Brothers of the Head (Aldiss), 1978
Brothers of the Head, and Where the Lines Converge (Aldiss), 1979
Brother's Tale (Barstow), 1980
Brown Girl, Brownstones (Marshall), 1960
Brownout on Breadfruit Boulevard (Mo), 1995
Brown's Requiem (Ellroy), 1984
Brunswick Gardens (Perry), 1998
Bubble (Anand), 1988
Buccaneer (Cassill), 1958
Bucket Shop (Waterhouse), 1968
Buddha of Suburbia (Kureishi), 1990
Budding Prospects: A Pastoral (Boyle), 1984
Buddwing (Hunter), 1964
Buffalo Afternoon (Schaeffer), 1989
Buffalo Gals and Other Animal Presences (s Le Guin), 1987
Buffalo Gals, Won't You Come Out Tonight (Le Guin), 1994
Buffalo Girls (McMurtry), 1991
Bulibasha (Ihimaera), 1994
Bull and the Spear (Moorcock, as Bradbury, E.), 1973
Burger's Daughter (Gordimer), 1979
Buried Land (Jones), 1963
Burn (Ireland), 1975
Burn (s Kelman), 1991
Burning (Johnson), 1971
Burning Angel (Burke), 1995
Burning Book (Gee), 1984
Burning Boy (Gee), 1990
Burning Chrome (Sterling), 1986
Burning House (s Beattie), 1983
Burning Water (Bowering), 1980
Burning World (Ballard), 1964
Burr (Vidal, as Box), 1974
Busconductor Hines (Kelman), 1984
Bushwhacked Piano (McGuane), 1989
Busted Scotch: Selected Stories (s Kelman), 1997
Buster (Burns), 1972
But for Bunter (Hughes), 1985
But We Are Exiles (Kroetsch), 1966
Butcher Boy (McCabe), 1993
Buttercup Chain (Elliott), 1967
Butterfly (Rumaker), 1968
Butterfly Plague (Findley), 1970
Butterfly Stories: A Novel (Vollmann), 1993
Buzzards (Burroway), 1970
By the Light of My Father's Smile (Walker), 1998
By the North Gate (s Oates, as Smith, R.), 1963
By the Shores of Gitchee Gumee (Janowitz), 1996
By the Waters of Whitechapel (Kops), 1970
Bye-Bye, Blackbird (Desai), 1971
Bystander (Guerard), 1959
Bystander (Stow), 1957
Byzantium Endures (Moorcock, as Bradbury, E.), 1982

Cabal and Other Stories (s Gilchrist), 2000
Cabin Fever (Jolley), 1991
Cabot Wright Begins (Purdy), 1965
Cadillac Jack (McMurtry), 1982
Cadillac Jukebox (Burke), 1996
Caedmon's Song (Robinson), 1990
Caesar (Massie), 1994
Cage (Hinde), 1962
Cain His Brother (Perry), 1995
Caitaani Mutharaba-ini (Ngugi wa Thiong'o), 1980
Cakewalk (s Smith), 1980
Cal (MacLaverty), 1983
Calcutta Chromosome: A Novel of Fevers, Delirium and Discovery (Ghosh), 1995
Caliban's Filibuster (West), 1971
California Time (Raphael), 1976

Call It a Canary (Tinniswood), 1985
Call for a Miracle (Kiely), 1951
Call for the Dead (le Carré), 1962
Call of Fife and Drum: Three Novels of the Revolution (Fast, as Cunningham), 1987
Callander Square (Perry), 1980
Caltrop's Desire (Gray), 1980
Calypso (Hunter), 1979
Cambridge (Phillips), 1992
Camelot Caper (Mertz, as Michaels), 1976
Cameo (Graham), 1988
Camera Always Lies (Hood), 1967
Camomile Lawn (Wesley), 1985
Campaign (Freeman), 1963
Can We Talk, and Other Stories (s Chinodya), 1998
Canary in a Cat House (s Vonnegut), 1961
Candace and Other Stories (s Cheuse), 1980
Candles of Your Eyes (s Purdy), 1985
Candles of Your Eyes and Thirteen Other Stories (s Purdy), 1988
Cannibal Galaxy (Ozick), 1984
Cannibal in Manhattan (Janowitz), 1988
Canopy of Time (s Aldiss), 1959
Can't Quit You, Baby (Douglas), 1990
Cape Breton Is the Thought Control Centre of Canada (s Smith), 1969
Capital (Duffy), 1976
Caprice (Bowering), 1987
Caprice and Rondo (Dunnett), 1998
Capricorn Games (s Silverberg, as Knox), 1978
Captain Blackman (Williams), 1975
Captain Corelli's Mandolin (de Bernières), 1994
Captain Kidd (Charyn), 1999
Captain Maximus (s Hannah), 1985
Captain with the Whiskers (Kiely), 1961
Captains and the Kings (Johnston), 1972
Captive in the Land (Aldridge), 1963
Captives of the Flame (Delany), 1963
Captivity Captive (Hall), 1988
Car (Crews), 1973
Cara Massimina (Parks), 1990
Caracole (White), 1986
Cardington Crescent (Perry), 1990
Cards of the Gambler: A Folktale (Kiely), 1953
Caribbean Crisis (Moorcock, as Bradbury, E.), 1962
Carn (McCabe), 1997
Carnival (Harris), 1985
Carnival Trilogy (Harris), 1993
Carolina (Vansittart), 1961
Carpathians (Frame), 1988
Carpe Jugulum (Pratchett), 1998
Carpet People (Pratchett), 1992
Carrie: A Novel of a Girl with a Frightening Power (King), 1991
Carrier (Mahjoub), 1998
Cartesian Sonata and Other Novellas (Gass), 1998
Casablanca and Other Stories (s Moorcock, as Bradbury, E.), 1989
Case Examined (Barker), 1965
Case of Knives (McWilliam), 1988
Case of Lone Star (Friedman), 1987
Case of Need (Crichton, as Lange), 1968
Case of the Kidnapped Angel (Fast, as Cunningham), 1983
Case of the Murdered Mackenzie (Fast, as Cunningham), 1985
Case of the One-Penny Orange (Fast, as Cunningham), 1978
Case of the Poisoned Eclairs (Fast, as Cunningham), 1980
Case of the Russian Diplomat (Fast, as Cunningham), 1979
Case of the Sliding Pool (Fast, as Cunningham), 1982
Casino and Other Stories (s Burnard), 1994
Cassandra Singing (Madden), 1969
Casual Acquaintance and Other Stories (s Barstow), 1976
Casual Brutality (Bissoondath), 1989
Casualties of Peace (O'Brien), 1967
Cat and the King (Auchincloss), 1981
Cat Chaser (Leonard), 1986
Cat Man (Hoagland), 1956
Cat on the Scent (Brown), 1999
Catacomb (Glanville), 1988
Catalysts (Middleton), 1994
Catastrophe Practice: Plays for Not Acting (Mosley), 1992
Cater Street Hangman (Perry), 1979
Catfish Man: A Conjured Life (Charyn), 1980
Catherine Carmier (Gaines), 1966
Catherine Wheel (Harrower), 1960
Catholic (Plante), 1986
Cat's Cradle (Vonnegut), 1963
Cat's Eye (Atwood), 1989
Cave with Echoes (Elliott), 1962
Cavedweller (Allison), 1998
Caverns (Kesey), 1990
Celebration (Crews), 1998
Celebration (Settle), 1986
Celebrations (Burns), 1967
Celestial Navigation (Tyler), 1975
Celibate Season (Shields), 1991
Cement Garden (McEwan), 1978
Centaur (Updike), 1963
Centigrade 233 (Benford), 1990
Central Line (s Binchy), 1978
Centre of the Green (Bowen), 1960
Century (s Smith), 1986
Century's Daughter (Barker), 1986
Certain Age (Janowitz), 1999
Certain Justice (James), 1997
Cetaganda: A Vorkosigan Adventure (Bujold), 1996
Chain of Voices (Brink), 1982
Chamber (Grisham), 1994
Chamber Music (Grumbach), 1979
Champagne Barn (s Levine), 1985
Champion of Garathorm (Moorcock, as Bradbury, E.), 1973
Chancer (Kelman), 1985
Chaneysville Incident (Bradley), 1986
Change (Duffy), 1987
Change and Decay in All Around I See (Massie), 1978
Change Here for Babylon (Bawden), 1955
Change for the Better (Hill), 1969
Change for the Better (s Mathers), 1984
Change of Climate (Mantel), 1994
Change of Heart (Humphreys), 1951
Changeling (Jenkins), 1958
Changes: A Love Story (Aidoo), 1993
Changes and Chances (Middleton), 1990

Changing Places: A Tale of Two Campuses (Lodge), 1979
Changing the Past (Berger), 1990
Chant of Jimmie Blacksmith (Keneally), 1972
Chantic Bird (Ireland), 1968
Charade (Mortimer), 1948
Charades (Hospital), 1988
Charisma Campaigns (Matthews), 1972
Charity (Deighton), 1996
Charley Bland (Settle), 1989
Charlie in the House of Rue (s Coover), 1980
Charlotte Gray (Faulks), 1999
Charming Billy (McDermott), 1998
Charms for the Easy Life (Gibbons), 1993
Chaste Planet (s Updike), 1980
Chateau (Maxwell), 1961
Chatterton (Ackroyd), 1988
Checkmate (Dunnett), 1997
Chelsea Murders (Davidson), 1978
Chez Charlotte and Emily (Baumbach), 1979
Chicago Loop (Theroux), 1991
Chieftain's Carnival and Other Stories (s Anthony), 1993
Child in Time (McEwan), 1987
Child of God (McCarthy), 1975
Child of Time (Silverberg, as Knox), 1991
Childhood: A Novel (Alexis), 1998
Childhood's End (Clarke), 1954
Child's Play, with Eustace and the Prowler (Malouf), 1982
Children (Fast, as Cunningham), 1947
Children in the Woods: New and Selected Stories (s Busch), 1994
Children Is All (s Purdy), 1963
Children of Darkness and Light (Mosley), 1997
Children of Dynmouth (Trevor), 1977
Children of Light (Stone), 1986
Children of Lir: Stories from Ireland (s Hogan), 1981
Children of Men (James), 1993
Children of the Rose (Feinstein), 1975
Children's Bach (Garner), 1984
Childwold (Oates, as Smith, R.), 1977
Chiller (Benford), 1993
Chilly Scenes of Winter (Beattie), 1976
Chimera (s Barth), 1974
China Egg and Other Stories (s Tindall), 1981
Chinese Bandit (Becker), 1976
Chisholms: A Novel of the Journey West (Hunter), 1976
Choice of Enemies (Richler), 1957
Choice of Murder (Vansittart), 1992
Choices (Settle), 1995
Choir (Trollope), 1995
Choir Invisible (Hauser), 1959
Chosen Instrument (Hanley, as Calvin), 1969
Chosen Place, The Timeless People (Marshall), 1970
Christine (King), 1983
Christine/Annette (Guerard), 1985
Christmas at Fontaine's (Kotzwinkle), 1982
Christmas Letters: A Novella (Smith), 1996
Christmas Tree (Johnston), 1982
Chroma and Other Stories (s Barthelme), 1989
Chronicles of Castle Brass (Moorcock, as Bradbury, E.), 1985
Chronicles of Corum (Moorcock, as Bradbury, E.), 1986
Chronopolis and Other Stories (s Ballard), 1971
Cider House Rules (Irving), 1985
Cigarettes (Mathews), 1988
Cimarron Rose: A Novel (Burke), 1997
Cinderella (Hunter), 1986
Cinnamon Gardens (Selvadurai), 1999
Circle (Feinstein), 1970
Circle Home (Hoagland), 1960
Circle of Friends (Binchy), 1991
Circle of Friends (Mitchell), 1967
Circle of Reason (Ghosh), 1986
Circles of Deceit (Bawden), 1987
Circus Animals (Plunkett), 1990
Circus Fire (O'Nan), 2000
Cities of the Plain (McCarthy), 1998
Citizen Sidel (Charyn), 1999
Citizen Tom Paine (Fast, as Cunningham), 1946
City and the Pillar (Vidal, as Box), 1948
City and the River (Joshi), 1990
City in the Autumn Stars (Moorcock, as Bradbury, E.), 1987
City of a Thousand Suns (Delany), 1969
City of Darkness, City of Light (Piercy), 1996
City of Discontent: An Interpretive Biography of Vachel Lindsay, Being Also the Story of Springfield, Illinois, USA, and of the Love of the Poet for That City, That State, and That Nation, by Henry W. Wiggen (Harris), 1952
City of Glass (Auster), 1985
City of God (Doctorow), 2000
City of Gold (Deighton), 1992
City of Illusions (Le Guin), 1971
City of Night (Rechy), 1964
City of the Mind (Lively), 1991
City of Women (Ireland), 1981
City Primeval: High Noon in Detroit (Leonard), 1981
City Tales (s Hoagland), 1986
Civil Campaign: A Comedy of Biology and Manners (Bujold), 1999
Civil Wars: A Novel (Brown), 1984
Claiming of Sleeping Beauty (Rice, as Roquelaure), 1983
Clam Shell (Settle), 1971
Clandestine (Ellroy), 1984
Clarkton (Fast, as Cunningham), 1947
Clay's Ark (Butler), 1984
Clear Light of Day (Desai), 1980
Clem Anderson (Cassill), 1960
Clemmons (Masters), 1985
Cleopatra's Sister (Lively), 1993
! Click Song (Williams), 1982
Client (Grisham), 1993
Clifford's Blues (Williams), 1998
Cliffs of Fall and Other Stories (s Hazzard), 1963
Clipped Wings (Callow), 1964
Clock Winder (Tyler), 1973
Clockers (Price), 1992
Cloning of Joanna May (Weldon), 1990
Close Range: Wyoming Stories (s Proulx), 1999
Close-Up (Deighton), 1972
Closed Eye (Brookner), 1991
Closing (Fairbairns), 1988
Closing Arguments (Busch), 1991

Cloudsplitter (Banks), 1998
Cloudstreet (Winton), 1992
Coast To Coast (Raphael), 1999
Cocaine Nights (Ballard), 1998
Cock and Bull (s Self), 1993
Cock Robin; or, A Fight for Male Survival (Billington), 1972
Cockles of the Heart (Halligan), 1996
Cocksure (Richler), 1968
Cocktails at Doney's and Other Stories (s Trevor), 1996
Coda (Astley), 1995
Coffee, Cigarettes and A Run in the Park (s Butler), 1996
Coffer Dams (Markandaya), 1969
Cold Country (Dawson), 1965
Cold Gradations (Middleton), 1972
Cold Ground Was My Bed Last Night (s Garrett), 1964
Cold Is the Grave (Robinson), 2000
Collected African Stories (s Lessing), 1981
Collector (Fowles), 1963
Collector Collector (Fischer), 1997
Collector of Hearts: New Tales of the Grotesque (s Oates, as Smith, R.), 1998
Collision Course (Silverberg, as Knox), 1961
Colonel Mint (West), 1973
Colonel's Daughter and Other Stories (s Tremain), 1984
Color of Darkness (s Purdy), 1961
Color of Light (Goldman), 1984
Color of the Sky (Cowan), 1986
Color Purple (Walker), 1983
Colour of Magic (Pratchett), 1983
Colour of Rain (Tennant), 1964
Columba (Slaughter), 1979
Comanche Moon (McMurtry), 1997
Come to Grief (Francis), 1995
Come Up and Be Dead (Deshpande), 1985
Come Winter (Hunter), 1973
Comeback (Francis), 1991
Comedy of the White Dog (s Gray), 1979
Comfort of Strangers (McEwan), 1981
Comforters (Spark), 1957
Comic (Glanville), 1975
Coming Down from Wa (Thomas), 1995
Coming from Behind (Jacobson), 1984
Coming Home (Jones), 1986
Coming of Age at the Y (Cobb), 1984
Coming of the Night (Rechy), 1999
Coming of Winter (Richards), 1974
Coming Through Slaughter (Ondaatje), 1979
Commandant (Anderson), 1975
Commitments (Doyle), 1989
Common Pasture (Masters), 1967
Common People (Callow), 1958
Communion (Gibson), 1971
Companions of the Day and Night (Harris), 1975
Company of Women (Gordon), 1981
Company of Women (Singh), 1999
Compass Error (Bedford), 1969
Compass Rose (s Le Guin), 1983
Composers Plays (s Pownall), 1994
Comrade Jacob (Caute), 1962
Con Man (Hunter), 1960
Conceived in Liberty: A Novel of Valley Forge (Fast, as Cunningham), 1939
Concentric Circles (Bowering), 1977
Concerning Virgins (s Boylan), 1989
Concrete Island (Ballard), 1974
Concubine (Amadi), 1966
Condition of Muzak (Moorcock, as Bradbury, E.), 1978
Conditions of Faith (Miller), 2000
Condor Passes (Grau), 1972
Cone-Gatherers (Jenkins), 1981
Confederates (Keneally), 1980
Conference-ville (s Moorhouse), 1976
Confession of a Lover (Anand), 1988
Confessions of a Spent Youth (Bourjaily), 1961
Confessions of an Indian Woman Eater (Brata), 1971
Confessions of Josef Baisz (Jacobson), 1979
Confessions of Nat Turner (Styron), 1968
Confusion (Howard), 1993
Conglomeroid Cocktail Party (Silverberg, as Knox), 1985
Congo (Crichton, as Lange), 1981
Congressman Who Loved Flaubert: 21 Stories and Novellas (s Just), 1973
Connecticut Countess (s Watmough), 1984
Conservationist (Gordimer), 1975
Consider Sappho Burning (Delbanco), 1969
Consul's File (s Theroux), 1977
Contemporary Portraits and Other Stories (s Bail), 1975
Continent (s Crace), 1987
Continental Drift (Banks), 1985
Contract (Iyayi), 1982
Contract with the World (Rule), 1990
Contradictions (Ghose), 1966
Contre-Jour: A Triptych after Pierre Bonnard (Josipovici), 1986
Control (Goldman), 1982
Convention (s Coover), 1982
Conversations at Curlow Creek (Malouf), 1996
Conversations in Another Room (Josipovici), 1984
Conversions (Mathews), 1962
Convict: A Novel (Burke), 1995
Coolie (Anand), 1936
Cooper (Masters), 1987
Cop Hater (Hunter), 1958
Copenhagen Connection (Mertz, as Michaels), 1983
Copper Beach (Binchy), 1993
Copper Peacock and Other Stories (s Rendell, as Vine), 1991
Cordelia (Graham), 1950
Corker's Freedom (Berger), 1993
Corky's Brother and Other Stories (s Neugeboren), 1970
Cornelius Chronicles (Moorcock, as Bradbury, E.), 1977
Corner of Rife and Pacific (Savage), 1988
Corona (Bear), 1984
Corregidora (Jones), 1988
Corroboree: A Book of Nonsense (Gangemi), 1977
Corruption (Mosley), 1958
Corruption and Other Stories (s Lively), 1984
Cosm (Benford), 1998
Cosmo Cosmolino (Garner), 1993
Count Brass (Moorcock, as Bradbury, E.), 1976
Count Zero (Gibson), 1986
Countdown (Ghosh), 1999

Counterlife (Roth), 1987
Counting (s Phillips), 1978
Counting House (Dabydeen), 1996
Country (Plante), 1981
Country Ahead of Us, the Country Behind (s Guterson), 1989
Country Cooking and Other Stories (s Mathews), 1980
Country Cousin (Auchincloss), 1978
Country Girls (O'Brien), 1960
Country Girls Trilogy and Epilogue (O'Brien), 1987
Country Without Music (Hasluck), 1990
Countrymen of Bones (Butler), 1983
Coup (Updike), 1979
Couple (s Gordon), 1978
Couples (Updike), 1968
Couples: A Short Story (s Updike), 1976
Courts of Love: Stories (s Gilchrist), 1996
Cousins (Grace), 1992
Covenant with Death (Becker), 1965
Cover Her Face (James), 1966
Cow in the House and Nine Other Stories (s Kiely), 1978
Cowboys and Indians (O'Connor), 1991
Coyote Columbus Story (King), 1992
Cradle (Clarke), 1988
Craft Slices (Bowering), 1985
Crash (Ballard), 1973
Crazy Horse (McMurtry), 1999
Crazy in Alabama (Childress), 1993
Crazy in Berlin (Berger), 1958
Crazy Women (s Matthews), 1985
Creamy and Delicious: Eat My Words (in Other Words) (s Katz), 1970
Creation (Vidal, as Box), 1981
Credo (Bragg), 1996
Cricket in the Road and Other Stories (s Anthony), 1973
Crime Story (Gee), 1995
Crimes of Conscience (s Gordimer), 1991
Crimes of Neglect (Johnson), 1992
Criminal Conversation (Hunter), 1994
Crocodile Bird (Rendell, as Vine), 1993
Crocodile on the Sandbank (Mertz, as Michaels), 1976
Cross Channel (Barnes, as Kavanagh), 1996
Crossing (Fast, as Cunningham), 1972
Crossing (McCarthy), 1994
Crossing the Border (s Oates, as Smith, R.), 1978
Crossing the River (Phillips), 1994
Crow Eaters (Sidhwa), 1983
Crown and the Loincloth (Nahal), 1981
Crown Jewel (de Boissière), 1981
Crown of Columbus (Erdrich), 1991
Cruel Madness (Thubron), 1985
Cry in the Jungle Bar (Drewe), 1981
Cry of Absence (Jones), 1972
Cry of Crickets (Glanville), 1970
Cry, The Peacock (Desai), 1963
Cry to Heaven (Rice, as Roquelaure), 1990
Crying Child (Mertz, as Michaels), 1973
Crying of Lot 49 (Pynchon), 1967
Crying Out Loud (Cook), 1988
Cryptonomicon (Stephenson), 1999
Crystal and the Amulet (Moorcock, as Bradbury, E.), 1986
Crystal Express (Sterling), 1989
Crystal Rooms (Bragg), 1992
Crystal Vision (Sorrentino), 1982
Crystal World (Ballard), 1966
Cuba Libre (Leonard), 1998
Cube Root of Uncertainty (s Silverberg, as Knox), 1970
Cujo (King), 1981
Culp (s Gass), 1985
Cumbrian Trilogy (Bragg), 1984
Cupboard (Tremain), 1982
Cupid and Psyche (s Oates, as Smith, R.), 1970
Cure for Cancer (Moorcock, as Bradbury, E.), 1979
Cure for Dreams (Gibbons), 1991
Curious Street (Hogan), 1984
Current Climate (Friedman), 1989
Curse of the Pharaohs (Mertz, as Michaels), 1982
Curtain of Green (s Welty), 1943
Custodian (s Hill), 1972
Custom House (King), 1962
Cut Me In (Hunter), 1960
Cut-Rate Kingdom (Keneally), 1984
Cuts: A Very Short Novel (Bradbury), 1987
Cutting Lisa (Everett), 1986
Cutting Stone (Burroway), 1992
Cybele (Oates, as Smith, R.), 1979
Cycle of the Werewolf (King), 1983
Cyclone and Other Stories (s Narayan), 1944
Cynthia (Fast, as Cunningham), 1969

Da Silva da Silva's Cultivated Wilderness, and Genesis of the Clowns (Harris), 1977
Dad (Wharton), 1981
Daddy's Girl (Savage), 1970
Daddy's Girls (Fairbairns), 1991
Daisy (s Oates, as Smith, R.), 1977
Dalva (Harrison), 1989
Damascus Gate (Stone), 1998
Damballah (Wideman), 1984
Dames' Delight (Forster), 1964
Dan Lemo and the Limehouse Golem (Ackroyd), 1994
Dance in the Sun (Jacobson), 1956
Dance Me Outside (s Kinsella), 1986
Dance of the Happy Shades (s Munro), 1974
Dance the Eagle to Sleep (Piercy), 1971
Dancer from the Dance (Burroway), 1968
Dancer of Fortune (Munonye), 1974
Dancers at Night (s Richards), 1978
Dancers at the End of Time (Moorcock, as Bradbury, E.), 1983
Dancers Dancing (Ní Dhuibhne), 1999
Dancers on the Shore (s Kelley), 1965
Dances of Death: Short Stories on a Theme (s Tindall), 1973
Dancing Face (Phillips), 1997
Dancing Girls and Other Stories (s Atwood), 1982
Dancing on Coral (Adams), 1988
Dandelion Wine (s Bradbury), 1999
Dandy Edison for Lunch, and Other Stories (s O'Sullivan), 1981
Danger (Francis), 1984
Danger Zone (Shadbolt), 1976
Dangerous Friend (Just), 1999
Dangerous Love (Okri), 1996

Dangerous Mourning (Perry), 1994
Dangerous Pawn (Graham), 1937
Dangling Man (Bellow), 1946
Daniel Martin (Fowles), 1977
Danny Hill: Memoirs of a Prominent Gentleman (King), 1977
Darconville's Cat (Theroux), 1983
Darcy's Utopia (Weldon), 1991
Dark (McGahern), 1966
Dark-Adapted Eye (Rendell, as Vine), 1986
Dark Carnival (s Bradbury), 1948
Dark Dominion (Hauser), 1947
Dark Duet (Mertz, as Michaels), 1983
Dark Glasses (s Hood), 1976
Dark Glasses (King), 1956
Dark Green, Bright Red (Vidal, as Box), 1950
Dark Half (King), 1989
Dark Holds No Terrors (Deshpande), 1980
Dark Lady (Auchincloss), 1977
Dark Light Years (Aldiss), 1964
Dark on the Other Side (Mertz, as Michaels), 1973
Dark Places (Grenville), 1994
Dark Room (Narayan), 1938
Dark Side of the Sun (Pratchett), 1976
Dark Tower: The Gunslinger (King), 1976
Dark Tower II: The Drawing of the Three (King), 1989
Dark Tower III: The Waste Lands (King), 1991
Dark Tower IV: Wizard and Glass (King), 1997
Dark Visions (s King), 1989
Darker Proof: Stories from a Crisis (s Mars-Jones), 1987
Darker Proof: Stories from a Crisis (s White), 1987
Darkest England (Hope), 1996
Darkness (s Mukherjee), 1985
Darkness of the Body (Plante), 1974
Darktown Strutters (Brown), 1994
Darling (Raphael), 1965
Darlin' Bill: A Love Story of the Wild West (Charyn), 1980
Darwin's Radio (Bear), 1999
Daughter Buffalo (Frame), 1973
Daughters (Marshall), 1992
Daughters of Albion (Wilson), 1992
Daughters of Passion (s O'Faolain), 1982
Daughters of the House (Roberts), 1992
David and Charles (Desai), 1990
Dawn: Xenogenesis (Butler), 1987
Dawning Light (Silverberg, as Knox), 1964
Day after the Fair: Collection of Play and Stories (s Purdy), 1977
Day and a Night at the Baths (Rumaker), 1979
Day Daddy Died (Burns), 1981
Day Hemingway Died (s Marshall), 1984
Day in Shadow (Sahgal), 1975
Day It Rained Forever (s Bradbury), 1959
Day of Creation (Ballard), 1988
Day of Forever (s Ballard), 1967
Day of the Jackal (Forsyth), 1971
Day Superman Died (s Kesey), 1980
Day the Call Came (Hinde), 1965
Day the Men Went to Town: 16 Stories by Women from Cape Breton (s MacDonald), 1999
Day We Got Drunk on Cake and Other Stories (s Trevor), 1968
Daylight (Feinstein), 1997
Daymaker (Jones), 1987
Daymare (Hinde), 1980
Days (Figes), 1974
Days (s Robison), 1979
Days of Vengeance (Petrakis), 1985
Daysman (Middleton), 1984
Dead Babies (Amis), 1976
Dead Cert (Francis), 1962
Dead Man's Walk (McMurtry), 1995
Dead of the House (Greenberg), 1972
Dead School (McCabe), 1995
Dead Sea Cipher (Mertz, as Michaels), 1975
Dead Zone (King), 1979
Deadeye Dick (Vonnegut), 1983
Deadline for Love and Other Stories (s Lim), 1992
DeAlfonce Tennis: The Superlative Game of Eccentric Champions: Its History, Accoutrements, Conduct, Rules and Regimen (Donleavy), 1985
Dealing; or, the Berkeley-to-Boston Forty-Brick Lost-Bag Blues (Crichton, as Lange), 1971
Dean's December (Bellow), 1982
Dean's List (Hassler), 1997
Dear Deceit (Brooke-Rose), 1961
Dear Future (D'Aguiar), 1996
Dear James (Hassler), 1993
Dear Miss Mansfield: A Tribute to Kathleen Mansfield Beauchamp (s Ihimaera), 1990
Death Before Bedtime (Vidal, as Box), 1954
Death in Summer (Trevor), 1998
Death in the Devil's Acre (Perry), 1991
Death in the Fifth Position (Vidal, as Box), 1954
Death Is a Lonely Business (Bradbury), 1986
Death Kit (Sontag), 1968
Death Likes It Hot (Vidal, as Box), 1955
Death of Fathers (Driver), 1972
Death of Jim Loney (Welch), 1980
Death of Men (Massie), 1982
Death of Robin Hood (Vansittart), 1981
Death of a Hero (Anand), 1963
Death of a Tango King (Charyn), 1998
Death of an Expert Witness (James), 1977
Death of the Body (Stead), 1986
Death of the Fox (Garrett), 1972
Death of the Novel and Other Stories (s Sukenick), 1969
Death Will Have Your Eyes: A Novel About Spies (Sallis), 1997
Debatable Land (McWilliam), 1994
Deceits of Time (Colegate), 1988
Deceiver (Forsyth), 1991
Deception (Roth), 1990
Decider (Francis), 1993
Declarations of War (s Deighton), 1971
Decline of the West (Caute), 1966
Dedicated Man (Robinson), 1991
Deeds of the Disturber (Mertz, as Michaels), 1988
Deep Fix (s Moorcock, as Bradbury, E.), 1966
Deep Green Sea (Butler), 1997
Deep Range (Clarke), 1957
Deeper Than the Darkness (Benford), 1970
Deer Park (Mailer), 1957
Defend and Betray (Perry), 1992

Defiance (Maso), 1998
Delta Wedding (Welty), 1947
Dem (Kelley), 1967
Demelza: A Novel of Cornwall 1788–1790 (Graham), 1953
Democracy (Didion), 1984
Demon (Selby), 1977
Demon Box (Kesey), 1986
Demon in My View (Rendell, as Vine), 1977
Departing as Air: A Novel (Wier), 1983
Descant for Gossips (Astley), 1960
Descend Again (Burroway), 1960
Descent of Man (s Boyle), 1980
Desert of Stolen Dreams (Silverberg, as Knox), 1981
Desert of the Heart (Rule), 1965
Desert Rose (McMurtry), 1985
Despair and Other Stories of Ottawa (s Alexis), 1994
Desperadoes (s Barstow), 1961
Desperadoes (O'Connor), 1993
Desperation (King), 1996
Destination Biafra (Emecheta), 1982
Destinies of Darcy Dancer, Gentleman (Donleavy), 1978
Destiny (Parks), 2000
Destiny of Nathalie "X" (s Boyd), 1995
Detective (Hailey), 1997
Deuce (Butler), 1989
Devices and Desires (James), 1990
Devil by the Sea (Bawden), 1976
Devil in a Blue Dress (Mosley), 1990
Devil-May-Care (Mertz, as Michaels), 1978
Devil's Alternative (Forsyth), 1980
Devil's Dream (Smith), 1992
Devil's Valley (Brink), 1999
Dew in the Morning (Chinodya), 1982
Dhalgren (Delany), 1977
Diamond (Glanville), 1962
Diamond Age: Or, A Young Lady's Illustrated Primer (Stephenson), 1995
Diamond Dust: Stories (s Desai), 2000
Diamond Jo (Rooke), 1965
Diamondback Dog (Bowering), 1998
Diamonds at the Bottom of the Sea and Other Stories (s Hogan), 1979
Diaries of Jane Somers (Lessing), 1984
Diary of a Good Neighbour (Lessing), 1983
Diary of a Yuppie (Auchincloss), 1987
Dick (Friedman), 1971
Die ambassadeur (Brink), 1963
Die Eerste lewe van Adamastor (s Brink), 1988
Die eindelose weë (Brink), 1960
Die for Love (Mertz, as Michaels), 1985
Die gebondenes (Brink), 1959
Die meul teen die hang (s Brink), 1958
Difference Engine (Sterling), 1990
Difference Engine (Gibson), 1991
Different Drummer (Kelley), 1963
Different Kinds of Love (s Bardwell), 1987
Different Seasons (King), 1982
Diggers (Pratchett), 1990
Digging (Dowse), 1996
Digging Up the Mountains (s Bissoondath), 1986
Dimension Thirteen (s Silverberg, as Knox), 1969
Dinner Along the Amazon (s Findley), 1985
Dinner at the Homesick Restaurant (Tyler), 1982
Dinosaur Junction (Jones), 1992
Dinosaur Summer (Bear), 1997
Dinosaur Tales (s Bradbury), 1983
Diplomat (Aldridge), 1950
Director's Wife and Other Stories (s Glanville), 1963
Dirty Bird Blues (Major), 1996
Dirty Friends (s Lurie), 1983
Dirty Tricks (s Matthews), 1990
Disaffection (Kelman), 1989
Disappearance (Dabydeen), 1993
Disappearing Acts (McMillan), 1989
Disappearing Moon Cafe (Lee), 1991
Disaster Area (s Ballard), 1967
Disclosure (Crichton, as Lange), 1994
Discovery of Strangers (Wiebe), 1994
Disenchanted (Schulberg), 1951
Disgrace (Coetzee), 2000
Dislocations (s Hospital), 1988
Disobedience: A Novel (Hamilton), 2000
Disorderly Conduct (Duckworth), 1984
Disorderly Knights (Dunnett), 1997
Dispossessed: An Ambiguous Utopia (Le Guin), 1974
Disquiet and Peace (Cooper), 1957
Dissent of Dominick Shapiro (Kops), 1967
Distance (Thubron), 1996
Distant Likeness (Bailey), 1973
Distant Past and Other Stories (s Trevor), 1979
Distant Stars (s Delany), 1981
Distant Suns (Moorcock, as Bradbury, E.), 1975
Distortions (s Beattie), 1976
Distraction (Sterling), 1998
Distractions (Middleton), 1975
Disturbing Influence (Mitchell), 1962
Divided World: Selected Stories (s Marshall), 1989
Dividing Stream (King), 1951
Divine Endurance (Jones), 1984
Dixie City Jam (Burke), 1994
Dixon Cornbelt League and Other Baseball Stories (s Kinsella), 1993
DNA Business (Hanley, as Calvin), 1967
Do, Lord, Remember Me (Garrett), 1965
Do Me a Favour (Hill), 1963
Do Unto Others (Hunter), 2000
Do with Me What You Will (Oates, as Smith, R.), 1974
Doctor Cobb's Game (Cassill), 1969
Doctor Copernicus (Banville), 1976
Doctor Criminale (Bradbury), 1993
Doctor DeMarr (Theroux), 1990
Doctor Fielder's Common Sense (Cole), 1972
Dr. Haggard's Disease (McGrath), 1993
Doctor Lopez (Baker), 1995
Dr. Orwell and Mr. Blair (Caute), 1994
Doctor Rat (Kotzwinkle), 1976
Doctor Slaughter (Theroux), 1984
Doctor Sleep (Bell), 1991
Doctor Wooreddy's Prescription for Enduring the Ending of the World (Mudrooroo, as Johnson), 1983

Dodu and Other Stories (s Narayan), 1943
Dog Attempts to Drown Man in Saskatoon (s Glover), 1985
Dog Rock: A Postal Pastoral (Foster), 1985
Dog Soldiers (Stone), 1975
Dog Tags (Becker), 1974
Doggy Bag (Sukenick), 1994
Dogs Enjoy the Morning (Kiely), 1968
Dogs of War (Forsyth), 1974
Dogs Think That Every Day Is Christmas (Bradbury), 1997
Doin' Wildcat (Mudrooroo, as Johnson), 1988
Doll (Hunter), 1966
Dolley: A Novel of Dolley Madison in Love and War (Brown), 1994
Dolly (Brookner), 1994
Dolly and the Bird of Paradise (Dunnett), 1984
Dolly and the Cookie Bird (Dunnett), 1970
Dolly and the Doctor Bird (Dunnett), 1971
Dolly and the Nanny Bird (Dunnett), 1982
Dolly and the Singing Bird (Dunnett), 1968
Dolly and the Starry Bird (Dunnett), 1973
Dolores Claiborne (King), 1993
Dolphin Connection (Bainbridge), 1991
Domestic Animal (King), 1970
Domestic Particulars: A Family Chronicle (s Busch), 1976
Don Vincente: A Novel in Two Parts (Sionil Jose), 1999
Don't Call Me by My Right Name and Other Stories (s Purdy), 1956
Don't Crowd Me (Hunter), 1960
Don't Tell Anyone (Busch), 2000
Don't Worry about the Kids: Stories (s Neugeboren), 1997
Doors (Hunter), 1976
Dormitory Women (Cassill), 1953
Dottie (Gurnah), 1990
Double God (Kelleher), 1994
Double Life (Raphael), 1993
Double-Wolf (Castro), 1991
Double Yoke (Emecheta), 1983
Doubleman (Koch), 1986
Doubtfire (Nye), 1968
Dove of the East, and Other Stories (s Helprin), 1975
Dove on the Waters (s Shadbolt), 1996
Down among the Women (Weldon), 1972
Down: An Explanation (Fairbairns), 1969
Down and Out in the Year 2000 (Robinson), 1992
Down by the River (O'Brien), 1997
Down in the City (Harrower), 1957
Downtown (Hunter), 1989
Downward to the Earth (Silverberg, as Knox), 1977
Dracula Unbound (Aldiss), 1991
Dragon Can't Dance (Lovelace), 1981
Dragon in the Sword (Moorcock, as Bradbury, E.), 1987
Drakenstein (Gray), 1994
Dream Children (s Godwin), 1977
Dream Children (Wilson), 1998
Dream More Luminous than Love: The Yandilli Trilogy (Hall), 1995
Dream of a Beast (Jordan), 1989
Dream of Kings (Petrakis), 1967
Dream Sleepers and Other Stories (s Grace), 1980
Dream Stuff: Stories (s Malouf), 2000
Dream Swimmer (Ihimaera), 1997
Dreamer (Johnson), 1998
Dreamerika! A Surrealist Fantasy (Burns), 1972
Dreamers (Feinstein), 1994
Dreamhouse (Grenville), 1987
Dreaming (Gold), 1988
Dreaming in Cuban (Garcia), 1992
Dreaming: Hard Luck and Good Times in America (See, as Highland), 1995
Dreams of the Kalahari (Slaughter), 1987
Dreams Surround Us: Fiction and Poetry (s Metcalf), 1977
Dreamweaver's Dilemma: Stories and Essays (s Bujold), 1995
Dressing Up for the Carnival (s Shields), 2000
Dressmaker (Bainbridge), 1973
Drift (Castro), 1994
Drift (s Cowan), 1944
Driftglass: 10 Tales of Speculative Fiction (s Delany), 1978
Driver's Seat (Spark), 1970
Driving Blind (Bradbury), 1997
Driving Force (Francis), 1992
Drop of Patience (Kelley), 1966
Drowned World (Ballard), 1963
Drowner (Drewe), 1997
Drowning Season (Hoffman), 1979
Drug of Choice (Crichton, as Lange), 1970
Drunk with Love (s Gilchrist), 1987
Dry White Season (Brink), 1980
Drylands: A Book for the World's Last Reader (Astley), 1999
D-Tours (Baumbach), 1998
Duane's Depressed (McMurtry), 1999
Dubious Legacy (Wesley), 1993
Dubious Persuasions (s Matthews), 1981
Dublin 4 (s Binchy), 1983
Dublin People (s Binchy), 1993
Dublin Where the Palm Trees Grow (Hamilton), 1996
Dud Avocado (Dundy), 1958
Duffy (Barnes, as Kavanagh), 1986
Duluth (Vidal, as Box), 1983
Dunfords Travels Everywheres (Kelley), 1970
Dunster (Mortimer), 1992
Duplicate Keys (Smiley), 1984
During Mother's Absence (Roberts), 1993
Dusk (Sionil Jose), 1998
Dusklands (Coetzee), 1985
Dust on the Paw (Jenkins), 1961
Dust to Dust: Stories (s Findley), 1997
Dutch Shea, Jr. (Dunne), 1982
Dutiful Daughter (Keneally), 1971
Dwarves of Death (Coe), 1990
Dying, In Other Words (Gee), 1984
Dying Inside (Silverberg, as Knox), 1974
Dying of the Light (Glanville), 1976

Eagle and the Chickens and Other Stories (s Aidoo), 1986
Eagle Eye (Calisher), 1973
Eagle on the Coin (Cassill), 1950
Ear of the Dragon (Shadbolt), 1971
Earlsdon Way (Raphael), 1958
Early Christmas (s Price), 1992
Early Harvest (s Bear), 1988

Earthlight (Clarke), 1998
Earthly Possessions (Tyler), 1977
Earth's Other Shadow (s Silverberg, as Knox), 1977
Earthsea (Le Guin), 1977
Earthsong (Kelleher), 1997
Earthworks (Aldiss), 1966
East into Upper East: Plain Tales from New York and New Delhi (s Jhabvala), 1998
East Is East (Boyle), 1991
East of the Mountains (Guterson), 1999
East, West: Stories (s Rushdie), 1994
Easter Egg Hunt (Freeman), 1981
Easter Man (a Play) and Six Stories (s Hunter), 1972
Easy Go (Crichton, as Lange), 1972
Eater: A Novel (Benford), 2000
Eaters of the Dead: The Manuscript of Ibn Fadlan, Relating His Experiences with the Northmen in A.D. 922 (Crichton, as Lange), 1976
Eating People Is Wrong (Bradbury), 1960
Eating Women Is Not Recommended (s Ní Dhuibhne), 1991
Ebony Tower: Collected Novellas (s Fowles), 1974
Echo Chamber (Josipovici), 1980
Echo House (Just), 1997
Echoes (Binchy), 1986
Ecstasy of Dr. Miriam Garner (Feinstein), 1976
Ecstasy: Three Chemical Romances (s Welsh), 1996
Eden Close (Shreve), 1989
Edge (Francis), 1989
Edge of the Alphabet (Frame), 1962
Edge of the City (Hogan), 1994
Edge of the Paper (Tindall), 1963
Edible Woman (Atwood), 1996
Edna O'Brien Reader (O'Brien), 1994
Education of Oscar Fairfax (Auchincloss), 1995
Education of Patrick Silver (Charyn), 1976
Edwin Mullhouse: The Life and Death of an American Writer (Millhauser), 1972
Eight Black Horses (Hunter), 1985
Eight Months on Ghazzah Street (Mantel), 1997
1876 (Vidal, as Box), 1976
Eighty Million Eyes (Hunter), 1966
Eighty-Minute Hour (Aldiss), 1974
Einstein Intersection (Delany), 1968
Einstein's Monsters: Five Stories (s Amis), 1987
Eisenhower, My Eisenhower (Charyn), 1971
El Bronx (Charyn), 1997
Elected Member (Rubens), 1969
Electric City and Other Stories (s Grace), 1987
Electrical Experience (s Moorhouse), 1974
Elegy for a Revolutionary (Driver), 1970
Elephant Bangs Train (s Kotzwinkle), 1971
Eleven Million Mile High Dancer (Hill), 1985
Eliza Stanhope (Trollope), 1979
Elizabeth Alone (Trevor), 1974
Elizabethan Trilogy (Garrett), 1998
Ellen Foster (Gibbons), 1987
Ellis Island and Other Stories (s Helprin), 1981
Elric at the End of Time: Fantasy Stories (s Moorcock, as Bradbury, E.), 1985
Elric of Melniboné (Moorcock, as Bradbury, E.), 1972
Elric: The Return to Melniboné (s Moorcock, as Bradbury, E.), 1973
Elsinore (Charyn), 1991
Elvis, Jesus, and Coca Cola (Friedman), 1993
Elvis over England (Hines), 1999
Embezzler (Auchincloss), 1966
Emerald Blue (Murnane), 1995
Emergency Exit (Major), 1979
Emigrants (Lamming), 1955
Emily's Shoes (Bolger), 1992
Emma Who Saved My Life (Barnhardt), 1989
Emmeline (Rossner), 1980
Empathy Experiment (Foster), 1977
Emperor (Essop), 1984
Emperor (Thubron), 1978
Emperor, Swords, Pentacles (Gotlieb), 1981
Empire (Vidal, as Box), 1987
Empire: A Visual Novel (Delany), 1978
Empire of the Sun (Ballard), 1984
Empire Star (Delany), 1966
Empress of the Splendid Season (Hijuelos), 1999
Empty Hours (s Hunter), 1963
Empty Street (s Cowan), 1965
Em's Story (Kelleher), 1988
Enchanted Night: A Novella (Millhauser), 1999
Enclosure (Hill), 1961
Encounter (s Brata), 1978
Encounters with the Element Man (s Atwood), 1982
End of All Songs (Moorcock, as Bradbury, E.), 1976
End of My Life (Bourjaily), 1963
End of the Century at the End of the World (Stead), 1992
End of the Hunt (Flanagan), 1994
End of the Road (Barth), 1967
End of the World and Other Stories (s Gallant), 1974
End Zone (DeLillo), 1973
Endless Short Story (s Sukenick), 1986
Ends and Means (Middleton), 1977
Enduring Love (McEwan), 1998
Eneaux troubles (Bowering), 1982
Enemies (Vansittart), 1947
Enemies: A Novel about Friendship (Gordon), 1977
Enemies of the System (Aldiss), 1978
England, England (Barnes, as Kavanagh), 1999
English Assassin (Moorcock, as Bradbury, E.), 1979
English, August: An Indian Story (Chatterjee), 1988
English Music (Ackroyd), 1993
English Patient (Ondaatje), 1992
English Queens (Nahal), 1979
English Teacher (Narayan), 1945
Englishman's Boy (Vanderhaeghe), 1997
Enigma of Arrival (Naipaul), 1987
Enormous Changes at the Last Minute (s Paley), 1975
Enquiry (Francis), 1971
Entered from the Sun (Garrett), 1990
Enthusiast (s Crews), 1981
Entrance to Porlock (Buechner), 1970
Entropy Tango (Moorcock, as Bradbury, E.), 1981
Entry into Jerusalem (Middleton), 1989
Eon (Bear), 1985
Epiphany: Stories (s Sams), 1994

Equal Music (Seth), 1999
Equal Rites (Pratchett), 1987
Equinox (Figes), 1966
Eric (Pratchett), 1989
Ermita (Sionil Jose), 1988
Errata (Bowering), 1988
Escape Artist (Wagoner), 1965
Escape from Five Shadows (Leonard), 1957
Escape from Kathmandu (s Robinson), 1990
Escape Plans (Jones), 1986
Escape to Reality (s Foster), 1977
Esmond in India (Jhabvala), 1958
Estrangement (Amadi), 1986
E.T., the Extra-Terrestrial Storybook (Kotzwinkle), 1982
E.T., the Storybook of the Green Planet: A New Storybook (Kotzwinkle), 1985
Eternal Champion (Moorcock, as Bradbury, E.), 1978
Eternity (Bear), 1988
Ethan of Athos (Bujold), 1986
Eucalyptus (Bail), 1998
Europa (Parks), 1997
Europe after the Rain (Burns), 1970
Europe; or, Up and Down with Schreiber and Baggish (Stern), 1961
Eustace Chisholm and the Works (Purdy), 1968
Evangelista's Fan (s Tremain), 1994
Eva's Man (Jones), 1976
Eveless Eden (Wiggins), 1995
Even Cowgirls Get the Blues (Robbins), 1977
Even the Wicked (Hunter), 1979
Evening (Minot), 1998
Evening and the Morning and the Night (Butler), 1991
Evening Class (Binchy), 1996
Evening News (Hailey), 1990
Evening of Adam (Ellis), 1994
Evening of the Holiday (Hazzard), 1966
Evening Performance: New and Selected Short Stories (s Garrett), 1985
Evening Snow Will Bring Such Peace (Richards), 1991
Evensong (Godwin), 1999
Ever After (Swift), 1992
Ever-Interesting Topic (Cooper), 1953
Everest Hotel: A Calendar (Sealy), 1998
Everlasting Secret Family and Other Secrets (s Moorhouse), 1980
Every Day Is Mother's Day (Mantel), 2000
Every Little Crook and Nanny (Hunter), 1972
Every Man for Himself (Bainbridge), 1996
Everyday Use (s Walker), 1994
Everything That Moves (Schulberg), 1981
Everything You Need (Kennedy), 1999
Evidence of Love (Grau), 1977
Evidence of Love (Jacobson), 1960
Evil Sleep! (Hunter), 1952
Exagggerations of Peter Prince (Katz), 1968
Except You're a Bird (Tinniswood), 1974
Excommunication (s Aldiss), 1975
Exile (Jones), 1970
Exile (Kotzwinkle), 1987
Exiles (Guerard), 1963
Exit Lady Masham (Auchincloss), 1984
Exit 3 and Other Stories (Rumaker), 1966
Exit to Eden (Rice, as Roquelaure), 1985
Expatriates (Jenkins), 1971
Expedition to Earth (s Clarke), 1998
Expensive Habits (Howard), 1986
Expensive People (Oates, as Smith, R.), 1969
Expensive Place to Die (Deighton), 1967
Experience of India (s Jhabvala), 1972
Experiment in Love (Mantel), 1996
Explorations (Dykeman), 1984
Explosions on the Sun (s Duckworth), 1989
Extra(Ordinary) People (Russ), 1985
Extreme Magic: A Novella and Other Stories (s Calisher), 1964
Eye in the Door (Barker), 1994
Eye of the Cricket: A Lew Griffin Novel (Sallis), 1997
Eye of the Everlasting Angel (Virtue), 1992
Eye of the Heron (Le Guin), 1983
Eye of the Scarecrow (Harris), 1965
Eyes (Burroway), 1966
Eyes of the Dragon (King), 1987

Fabulous Harbors (Moorcock, as Bradbury, E.), 1995
Face of a Stranger (Perry), 1993
Face of the Waters (Silverberg, as Knox), 1991
Face of Trespass (Rendell, as Vine), 1974
Face to Face (s Gordimer), 1949
Faces (Perutz), 1987
Faces in the Water (Frame), 1962
Facts in the Case of E.A. Poe (Sinclair), 1980
Facts of Life and Other Fictions (s Nye), 1983
Fahrenheit 451 (Bradbury), 1997
Fair and Tender Ladies (Smith), 1988
Fair Exchange (Roberts), 1999
Fair Game (Johnson), 1965
Fairly Conventional Woman (Shields), 1982
Fairly Good Time (Gallant), 1970
Fairy Tale (Ellis), 1998
Fairy Tale of New York (Donleavy), 1973
Faith (Deighton), 1994
Faith and the Good Thing (Johnson), 1974
Fall and Rise (Dixon), 1985
Fall of Innocence (Freeman), 1956
Fall of Kelvin Walker: A Fable of the Sixties (Gray), 1986
Fall of Moondust (Clarke), 1961
Fall of the Towers (Delany), 1971
Fall on Your Knees (MacDonald), 1996
Fallen Angel (Fast, as Cunningham), 1952
Fallen Curtain and Other Stories (s Rendell, as Vine), 1976
Falling (Schaeffer), 1973
Falling (Thubron), 1990
Falling Free (Bujold), 1988
Falling in Place (Beattie), 1981
Falling Slowly (Brookner), 1999
False Entry (Calisher), 1962
False Gods (s Auchincloss), 1993
Falstaff (Nye), 1976
Familiar Passions (Bawden), 1979
Families (Watmough), 1990
Family (Plante), 1978
Family: A Novel in the Form of a Memoir (Gold), 1983

Family and Friends (Brookner), 1985
Family Arsenal (Theroux), 1976
Family Feeling (Yglesias), 1977
Family Life (Banks), 1975
Family Linen (Smith), 1985
Family Madness (Keneally), 1986
Family Man (s Charyn), 1995
Family Money (Bawden), 1991
Family Planning (Parks), 1989
Family Sins and Other Stories (s Trevor), 1990
Family Trust (Just), 1978
Family's Affairs (Douglas), 1994
Famished Road (Okri), 1992
Famous Last Words (Findley), 1987
Fan Man (Kotzwinkle), 1974
Fanatic Heart: Selected Stories (s O'Brien), 1985
Fancy Man (McCauley), 1996
Fancy Strut (Smith), 1973
Fanny, Being the True History of the Adventures of Fanny Hackabout-Jones (Jong), 1980
Far Corners of the Earth (Sinclair), 1991
Far Cry (Smith), 1950
Far Cry from Bowmore and Other Stories (s Jenkins), 1973
Far Cry from Kensington (Spark), 1988
Far Family (Dykeman), 1966
Far from the City of Class and Other Stories (s Friedman), 1963
Far from the Sea (Hunter), 1983
Far Journey of Oudin (Harris), 1961
Far Side of Victory (Greenberg), 1983
Far Tortuga (Matthiessen), 1989
Farai's Girls (Chinodya), 1984
Farewell Companions (Plunkett), 1978
Farewell, Fond Dreams (s Gordon), 1975
Farewell Symphony (White), 1997
Farewell to Prague (Hogan), 1995
Farmer (Harrison), 1993
Farming of Bones (Danticat), 1998
Farriers' Lane (Perry), 1994
Farthest Shore (Le Guin), 1973
Fast Lanes (s Phillips), 1987
Fasting, Feasting (Desai), 2000
Fat Man in History (s Carey), 1980
Fat Woman's Joke (Weldon), 1967
Fata Morgana (Kotzwinkle), 1977
Fatal Inversion (Rendell, as Vine), 1987
Fathers: A Novel in the Form of a Memoir (Gold), 1967
Father and Other Stories (s Cassill), 1965
Father Melancholy's Daughter (Godwin), 1991
Fathering (Delbanco), 1973
Father's Day (Goldman), 1971
Father's Kisses (Friedman), 1996
Father's Music (Bolger), 1997
Father's Words (Stern), 1986
Fatima's Scarf (Caute), 1998
Faust (Nye), 1981
Favourite of the Gods (Bedford), 1963
Fear (Keneally), 1965
Fear Man (Jones), 1995
Fear of Flying (Jong), 1974
Feast of All Saints (Rice, as Roquelaure), 1982
Feast of St. Dionysus (s Silverberg, as Knox), 1976
Feast of Snakes (Crews), 1977
Feather Crowns (Mason), 1993
Feeding the Ghosts (D'Aguiar), 1999
Feeling in the Air (Hughes), 1957
Feet of Clay (Pratchett), 1996
Felicia's Journey (Trevor), 1995
Felix in the Underworld (Mortimer), 1997
Fellow Passengers: A Novel in Portraits (Auchincloss), 1990
Fellow Passengers: Collected Stories (s Jolley), 1997
Felo de Se (Higgins), 1960
Female Friends (Weldon), 1975
Female Man (Russ), 1977
Femina Real (s Barker), 1971
Fencepost Chronicles (s Kinsella), 1987
Fenella Phizackerley (Forster), 1971
Feral City (Scott), 1992
Fergus Lamont (Jenkins), 1979
Ferret Fancier (West), 1965
Fertig (Yurick), 1966
Feud (Berger), 1984
Fever Tree and Other Stories (s Rendell, as Vine), 1982
Fever: Twelve Stories (s Wideman), 1989
Few Last Words (s Sallis), 1970
Fiddle City (Barnes, as Kavanagh), 1986
Field of Scarlet Poppies (Dawson), 1979
Field of Thirteen (s Francis), 1998
Fierce Invalids Home from Hot Climates (Robbins), 2000
15 x 3 (s Cassill), 1957
15 x 3 (s Gold), 1957
15 x 3 (s Hall), 1957
Fifth Child (Lessing), 1988
Fifth Elephant (Pratchett), 2000
Fifth Wexford Omnibus (Rendell, as Vine), 1991
Fifty-Two Pickup (Leonard), 1974
Fight Night on a Sweet Saturday (Settle), 1965
Fighting Back (Bowen), 1989
Fighting with Shadows; or, Sciamachy (Healy), 1984
Figure of Fun (Jenkins), 1974
Figures in Bright Air (Plante), 1976
Figures in Light: Selected Stories (s Shadbolt), 1979
File on Stanley Patton Buchta (Faust), 1970
Filth: A Novel (Welsh), 1998
Filthy Lucre (Bainbridge), 1986
Final Account (Robinson), 1995
Final Beast (Buechner), 1965
Final Cut (Stern), 1975
Final Diagnosis (Hailey), 1960
Final Fate of the Alligators (s Hoagland), 1992
Final Passage (Phillips), 1990
Final Payments (Gordon), 1978
Final Programme (Moorcock, as Bradbury, E.), 1979
Financial Expert (Narayan), 1953
Financiers (Glanville), 1972
Finbar's Hotel (Johnston), 1997
Finbar's Hotel (O'Connor), 1997
Finbar's Hotel (Tóibín), 1997
Finbar's Hotel (Doyle), 1997
Find the Changeling (Benford), 1980
Fine Balance (Mistry), 1996

Fine Madness (Baker), 1964
Fingers in the Door (s Tuohy), 1970
Finished Man (Garrett), 1960
Finishing School (Godwin), 1985
Fire Dancer (Kelleher), 1996
Fire Eaters (Cobb), 1994
Fire in the Morning (Spencer), 1948
Fire on the Mountain (Desai), 1977
Fire Watch (s Willis), 1985
Fireclown (Moorcock, as Bradbury, E.), 1967
Fireflies (Hoffman), 1997
Firefly Summer (Binchy), 1988
Fireman's Wife and Other Stories (s Bausch), 1990
Firestarter (King), 1980
Firewalkers: A Memoir (King), 1956
Firm (Grisham), 1991
First and Vital Candle (Wiebe), 1966
First Discworld Novels (Pratchett), 1999
First Life of Adamastor (Brink), 1993
First Light (Ackroyd), 1989
First Love: A Gothic Tale (Oates, as Smith, R.), 1996
First Love, Last Rites (s McEwan), 1975
First Nights (Schaeffer), 1983
First Rumpole Omnibus (s Mortimer), 1983
First Signs (Hines), 1972
First Story (s Welty), 1999
First Winter of My Married Life (s Gass), 1979
Fisher King (Marshall), 2000
Fisherman of the Inland Sea: Science Fiction Stories (s Le Guin), 1994
Fiskadoro (Johnson), 1985
Fist of God (Forsyth), 1994
Five Acre Virgin and Other Stories (s Jolley), 1976
Five-Dollar Smile: Fourteen Early Stories and a Farce in Two Acts (s Tharoor), 1990
Five for the Symbol (s Stead), 1981
Five Legs (Gibson), 1969
Five Minutes in Heaven (Alther), 1995
Five: Short Novels (s Lessing), 1953
Five Stories (s Kinsella), 1987
Five Tales (s Maxwell), 1988
Five Thousand and One Nights (s Lively), 1997
Five Year Sentence (Rubens), 1978
Flag for Sunrise (Stone), 1981
Flag on the Island (s Naipaul), 1968
Flame (Cassill), 1980
Flaming Corsage (Kennedy), 1996
Flats (Wurlitzer), 1971
Flaubert's Parrot (Barnes, as Kavanagh), 1985
Flesh and Blood (Cunningham), 1995
Flesh and Blood (Humphreys), 1974
Flesh & Blood (Roberts), 1994
Flesh and Blood (s Scott), 1984
Flesh and Gold (Gotlieb), 1998
Flesh of Morning (Callow), 1971
Flesheaters (Ireland), 1972
Flight from Nevèrÿon (Delany), 1989
Flight into Danger (Hailey), 1958
Flight to Canada (Reed), 1976
Flights (s King), 1973
Flights of Angels: Stories (s Gilchrist), 1998
Fling with a Demon Lover (James), 1996
Floating Opera (Barth), 1968
Floating in My Mother's Palm (Hegi), 1990
Floatplane Notebooks (Edgerton), 1988
Florrie's Girls (Kelly), 1989
Florry of Washington Heights (Katz), 1989
Flowerdust (Jones), 1995
Flowers and Shadows (Okri), 1980
Fludd (Mantel), 1989
Flute-Player (Thomas), 1979
Fly Away Home (Piercy), 1984
Fly Away Home (Tindall), 1971
Fly Away Peter (Malouf), 1982
Fly in the Ointment (Ellis), 1989
Flycatcher and Other Stories (s Bowering), 1974
Flying a Red Kite (s Hood), 1962
Flying Finish (Francis), 1967
Flying-Fox in a Freedom Tree (s Wendt), 1999
Flying Hero Class (Keneally), 1991
Flying Home (Lurie), 1982
Flynn: A Novelisation (McDonald), 1992
Foe (Coetzee), 1987
Folded Leaf (Maxwell), 1946
Folk Tales and Fantasies (s Anthony), 1976
Follow Me Down (Foote), 1951
Folly (Minot), 1992
Fong and the Indians (Theroux), 1976
Fooling (s Duckworth), 1994
Fool's Alphabet (Faulks), 1992
Fools and Other Stories (s Ndebele), 1985
Fools Crow (Welch), 1986
Fools of Fortune (Trevor), 1983
Fool's Sanctuary (Johnston), 1988
Foot of Clive (Berger), 1962
Footprints in the Quag: Stories and Dialogues from Soweto (s Tlali), 1989
For Her Dark Skin (Everett), 1989
For Kicks (Francis), 1965
For Mary with Love (Savage), 1983
For the Good of the Company (Hinde), 1961
For Those Who Hunt the Wounded Down (Richards), 1993
For Want of a Nail (Bragg), 1965
Foreign Affairs (Lurie), 1985
Foreign Bodies (s Aldiss), 1981
Foreign Devils (Faust), 1973
Foreign Woman (s Kidman), 1993
Foreigner (Joshi), 1968
Foreigner (Plante), 1984
Foreseeable Future: Three Long Stories (s Price), 1991
Forest of the Night (Jones), 1961
Forfeit (Francis), 1969
Forge of God (Bear), 1987
Forgetting Elena (White), 1973
Forgotten Life (Aldiss), 1989
Forgotten Story (Graham), 1945
Forms of Water (Barrett), 1993
Forrest Gump (Groom), 1986
Fortress of the Pearl (Moorcock, as Bradbury, E.), 1989
Fortune (Drewe), 1987

Fortune Is a Woman (Graham), 1953
Fortune's Daughter (Hoffman), 1985
Fortune's Rocks (Shreve), 2000
Forty Lashes Less One (Leonard), 1972
Forty-Seventeen (s Moorhouse), 1989
43 Fictions (s Katz), 1991
Foundation and Chaos (Bear), 1998
Foundation's Fear (Benford), 1997
Founder's Praise (Greenberg), 1976
Fountains of Paradise (Clarke), 1979
Four Banks of the River of Space (Harris), 1990
Four-Dimensional Nightmare (s Ballard), 1963
Four-Grated City (Lessing), 1969
Four Past Midnight (s King), 1990
Four Stories (s Josipovici), 1977
Four Swans: A Novel of Cornwall 1795–1797 (Graham), 1977
Four Ways to Forgiveness (Le Guin), 1995
Fourteen Sisters of Emilio Montez O'Brien (Hijuelos), 1993
Fourth Angel (Rechy), 1972
Fourth Protocol (Forsyth), 1984
Fourth Wexford Omnibus (Rendell, as Vine), 1990
Fowler's Snare (Dawson), 1962
Foxfire: Confessions of a Girl Gang (Oates, as Smith, R.), 1993
Foxybaby (Jolley), 1986
Fragments (Armah), 1975
Francoeur Family (Plante), 1984
Frankenstein Unbound (Aldiss), 1974
Franklin Scare (Charyn), 1977
Franky Furbo (Wharton), 1989
Franny and Zooey (s Salinger), 1962
Fraud (Brookner), 1994
Freaky Deaky (Leonard), 1988
Free Frenchman (Read), 1987
Free-Lance Pallbearers (Reed), 1968
Freedom Road (Fast, as Cunningham), 1946
Freedomland (Price), 1998
Fremder (Hoban), 1996
French Lieutenant's Woman (Fowles), 1969
Frenzy (Everett), 1997
Frequent Flyer (Friedman), 1989
Friday's Footprint and Other Stories (s Gordimer), 1960
Friend from England (Brookner), 1988
Friend of Don Juan (s Mulkerns), 1988
Friend of My Youth (s Munro), 1990
Friend of the Earth (Boyle), 2000
Friends: More Will and Magna Stories (s Dixon), 1990
Friends of God (Vansittart), 1963
Frog (s Dixon), 1991
From a Cornish Landscape (s Watmough), 1975
From a Crooked Rib (Farah), 1970
From a Seaside Town (Levine), 1970
From Doon with Death (Rendell, as Vine), 1965
From the Fifteenth District: A Novella and Eight Short Stories (s Gallant), 1979
From the Heat of the Day (Heath), 1979
From the Oceans, From the Stars (Clarke), 1962
From the Realm of Morpheus (Millhauser), 1986
Frozen Music (s King), 1988
Fruit Man, the Meat Man, and the Manager (s Hood), 1971
Fruit of the Month (s Frucht), 1988
Fugitive Pieces (Michaels), 1997
Fun & Games (s Major), 1990
Funeral in Berlin (Deighton), 1965
Funland (s Oates, as Smith, R.), 1983
Funny Boy: A Novel in Six Stories (Selvadurai), 1994
Furious Gulf (Benford), 1994
Further Adventures of Slugger McBatt (s Kinsella), 1988
Further Inquiry (Kesey), 1990
Fury (s Watmough), 1984
Futility and Other Animals (s Moorhouse), 1969
Future to Let (Peterkiewicz), 1959
Fuzz (Hunter), 1968

G (Berger), 1972
Gabrielle: An Entertainment (Guerard), 1992
Gabriel's Lament (Bailey), 1987
Gain (Powers), 1998
Gala (West), 1976
Galápagos (Vonnegut), 1985
Galatea 2.2 (Powers), 1995
Gallowglass (Rendell, as Vine), 1990
Gallows View (Robinson), 1990
Game and the Ground (Vansittart), 1957
Game in Heaven with Tussy Marx (Read), 1966
Game Men Play (Bourjaily), 1980
Game of Kings (Dunnett), 1997
Game of Patience (King), 1974
Game of Thirty (Kotzwinkle), 1994
Game of Touch (Hood), 1970
Game, Set and Match (Deighton), 1989
Gamekeeper (Hines), 1975
Games at Twilight and Other Stories (s Desai), 1980
Games of Chance: The Interviewer, The Investigator (Hinde), 1967
Games of Choice (Gee), 1976
Games of the Strong (Adams), 1989
Games Were Coming (Anthony), 1968
Gap in the Spectrum (Duckworth), 1959
Garbage (Dixon), 1988
Garden (Perutz), 1962
Garden of Earthly Delights (Oates, as Smith, R.), 1970
Garden of Rama (Clarke), 1991
Garden of the Villa Mollini and Other Stories (s Tremain), 1987
Garden State (Moody), 1992
Gardener (Pownall), 1990
Gardens of Fire (Eldred-Grigg), 1993
Garish Day (Billington), 1986
Garrick Year (Drabble), 1965
Gates (Johnston), 1973
Gates of Ivory (Drabble), 1991
Gathering of Old Men (Gaines), 1984
Gemini (Dunnett), 2000
Gems She Wore: A Book of Irish Places (Plunkett), 1973
General Ludd (Metcalf), 1980
Generally a Virgin (Hinde), 1972
Generation X: Tales for an Accelerated Culture (Coupland), 1991
Generous Man (Price), 1967
Genetha (Heath), 1981
Genoese Fancy (Hughes), 1979
Gentle Insurrection (s Betts), 1954

Gentleman and Ladies (Hill), 1969
Gentleman Death (Gibson), 1993
Gentlemen in England: A Vision (Wilson), 1986
George Beneath a Paper Moon (Bawden), 1974
Georges' Wife (Jolley), 1993
Georgy Girl (Forster), 1966
Gerald's Game (King), 1992
Gerald's Party (Coover), 1986
Geronimo Rex (Hannah), 1972
Gertrude and Claudius (Updike), 2000
Gertrude of Stony Island Avenue (Purdy), 1997
Gesture Life (Lee), 1999
Get Ready for Battle (Jhabvala), 1963
Get Shorty (Leonard), 1990
Gettin Place (Straight), 1996
Getting It Right (Howard), 1982
Getting Older (s Updike), 1985
Getting Pretty on the Table (Gover), 1975
Getting Through (s McGahern), 1980
Ghandi Quartet (Nahal), 1993
Ghost Dance (Maso), 1987
Ghost from the Grand Banks (Clarke), 1990
Ghost of Henry James (Plante), 1970
Ghost of the Sun (Petrakis), 1990
Ghost Road (Barker), 1995
Ghost Town (Coover), 1998
Ghost Woman (Thornton), 1992
Ghost Writer (Roth), 1979
Ghostly Populations (s Matthews), 1987
Ghosts (Auster), 1986
Ghosts (Banville), 1993
Ghosts (Figes), 1988
Ghosts (Hunter), 1980
Ghosts (Perutz), 1966
Giant, O'Brien (Mantel), 1998
Giant's Chair (Graham), 1938
Gift (Humphreys), 1963
Gift of a Daughter (Humphreys), 1998
Gift of Stones (Crace), 1989
Giggler Treatment (Doyle), 2000
Giles Goat-Boy; or, The Revised New Syllabus (Barth), 1967
Gilgamesh the King (Silverberg, as Knox), 1985
Ginger Man (Donleavy), 1965
Ginger, You're Barmy (Lodge), 1965
Girl (s Oates, as Smith, R.), 1974
Girl at the Lion d'Or (Faulks), 1999
Girl Green as Elderflower (Stow), 1980
Girl in Gingham (Metcalf), 1978
Girl in Landscape (Lethem), 1998
Girl in a Swing (Adams), 1980
Girl of Forty (Gold), 1986
Girl on a Bicycle: A Novel (Bardwell), 1977
Girl Who Can and Other Stories (s Aidoo), 1997
Girl Who Loved Tom Gordon (King), 1999
Girl with a Monkey (Astley), 1987
Girl with a Monkey: New and Selected Stories (s Michaels), 2000
Girl with Curious Hair (s Wallace), 1988
Girl with Red Hair (Gordon), 1974
Girl with the Glass Heart (Stern), 1957
Girlfriend in a Coma (Coupland), 1998
Girls (Busch), 1997
Girls (Yglesias), 1999
Girls: A Story of Village Life (Bowen), 1987
Girls at Play (Theroux), 1969
Girls at War (s Achebe), 1973
Girls High (Anderson), 1991
Girls in Their Married Bliss (O'Brien), 1968
Girls of Slender Means (Spark), 1963
Give the Boys a Great Big Hand (Hunter), 1962
Give Them All My Love (Tindall), 1989
Give Them Stones (Beckett), 1987
Give Us This Day (Barstow), 1989
Giver (Cole), 1971
Glad Eye and Other Stories (s Barstow), 1984
Glade within the Grove (Foster), 1996
Glamorama (Ellis), 1999
Glamour and the Sea (Knox), 1996
Glance Away (Wideman), 1986
Glass Alembic (Feinstein), 1973
Glass Canoe (Ireland), 1976
Glass Lake (Binchy), 1995
Glass Palace (Ghosh), 2000
Glass People (Godwin), 1972
Glass Whittler: And Other Stories (s Johnson), 1989
Glass Zoo (McNeish), 1976
Glassblower's Breath (Gupta), 1993
Glide Path (Clarke), 1969
Glimpse of Sion's Glory (s Colegate), 1985
Glittering Prizes (Raphael), 1978
Glitz (Leonard), 1985
Globalhead: Stories (s Sterling), 1992
Gloriana (Moorcock, as Bradbury, E.), 1979
Glorious Morning, Comrade (s Gee), 1975
Glory Days (Scott), 1988
Glyph (Everett), 1999
Go-Away Bird and Other Stories (s Spark), 1960
Go Tell the Lemming (Rubens), 1984
Go the Distance: Baseball Stories (s Kinsella), 1995
Go When You See the Green Man Walking (s Brooke-Rose), 1970
Goalkeepers Are Crazy: A Collection of Football Stories (s Glanville), 1964
Goat's Song (Healy), 1995
God Bless John Wayne (Friedman), 1995
God Bless You, Mr. Rosewater; or, Pearls Before Swine (Vonnegut), 1965
God Bless the Child (Hunter), 1965
God-Fearer (Jacobson), 1993
God in the Mountain (Thubron), 1977
God of Small Things (Roy), 1997
God Perkins (Pownall), 1977
God Stealer and Other Stories (s Sionil Jose), 1968
Godded and Codded (O'Faolain), 1970
Goddess and Other Women (s Oates, as Smith, R.), 1975
Godling, Go Home! (s Silverberg, as Knox), 1964
Godmother (Elliott), 1967
Godric (Buechner), 1981
Gods and Generals (Shaara), 1996
God's Country (Everett), 1994

God's Own Country (s Kiely), 1993
Gog (Sinclair), 1967
Going Abroad (s Updike), 1987
Going after Cacciato (O'Brien), 1978
Going All the Way (Wakefield), 1971
Going Away: A Report, A Memoir (Sigal), 1963
Going Down Fast (Piercy), 1969
Going Down Slow (Metcalf), 1972
Going for Mr. Big (Gover), 1979
Going Places (s Michaels), 1970
Going to Jerusalem (Charyn), 1968
Going to the Dogs (Barnes, as Kavanagh), 1987
Going to the Moon (Callow), 1968
Going West (Gee), 1992
Going Wrong (Rendell, as Vine), 1990
Gold and Sand (s Aldridge), 1960
Gold-Bug Variations (Powers), 1992
Gold Coast (Leonard), 1982
Gold Coast (Robinson), 1988
Golden Age (Vidal, as Box), 2000
Golden Apples (s Welty), 1950
Golden Apples of the Sun (s Bradbury), 1953
Golden Barge (Moorcock, as Bradbury, E.), 1980
Golden Calves (Auchincloss), 1989
Golden Days (See, as Highland), 1987
Golden Dress (Halligan), 1999
Golden Evening (Middleton), 1968
Golden Gate: A Novel in Verse (Seth), 1986
Golden Honeycomb (Markandaya), 1977
Golden Notebook (Lessing), 1962
Golden River (Fast, as Cunningham), 1960
Golden Rope (Schaeffer), 1996
Golden States (Cunningham), 1984
Goldilocks (Hunter), 1978
Golk (Stern), 1960
Gone Fishin': An Easy Rawlins Novel (Mosley), 1996
Gone for Good (Childress), 1998
Gone for Soldiers (Shaara), 2000
Gone Indian (Kroetsch), 1973
Gone the Sun (Groom), 1988
Gone to Soldiers (Piercy), 1987
Good Bones (s Atwood), 1993
Good Day to Die (Harrison), 1993
Good Evening Mr. and Mrs. America, and All the Ships at Sea (Bausch), 1996
Good-for-Nothing (Yaffe), 1953
Good Grief (Waterhouse), 1997
Good Hearts (Price), 1988
Good Help (s Gurganis), 1988
Good House (Burnard), 1999
Good Husband (Godwin), 1994
Good Man in Africa (Boyd), 1982
Good Omens: The Nice and Accurate Predictions of Agnes Nutter, Witch (Pratchett), 1990
Good Policeman (Charyn), 1991
Good Scent from a Strange Mountain: Stories (s Butler), 1992
Good Terrorist (Lessing), 1985
Good Times (s Kelman), 1999
Goodbye, Columbus, and Five Short Stories (s Roth), 1959
Goodbye Harold, Good Luck (s Thomas), 1986
Goodbye Mickey Mouse (Deighton), 1982
Goodbye Un-America (Aldridge), 1979
Goodness (Parks), 1991
Gooseboy (Barker), 1987
Gor Saga (Duffy), 1982
Gospel (Barnhardt), 1993
Gospel According to the Son (Mailer), 1997
Gospel Singer (Crews), 1968
Goss Women (Cassill), 1975
Gossip from the Forest (Keneally), 1976
Gould: A Novel in Two Novels (Dixon), 1997
Goy (Harris), 1970
Grace (Gee), 1989
Grace Abounding (Howard), 1984
Grace Notes (MacLaverty), 1997
Graduate Wife (Raphael), 1962
Grain of Truth (Bawden), 1968
Grain of Truth (Hasluck), 1994
Grain of Wheat (Ngugi wa Thiong'o), 1967
Grand Opening (Hassler), 1987
Grandmothers' Club (Cheuse), 1986
Grandmother's Pigeon (Erdrich), 1996
Grandmother's Tale (s Narayan), 1993
Grantchester Grind: A Porterhouse Chronicle (Sharpe), 1995
Granted Wishes (s Berger), 1984
Grass Is Singing (Lessing), 1950
Grasse, 3/23/66 (Delbanco), 1968
Grave Descend (Crichton, as Lange), 1970
Graven Images (Thomas), 1993
Graveyard for Lunatics: Another Tale of Two Cities (Bradbury), 1990
Gravity's Rainbow (Pynchon), 1973
Greasy Lake and Other Stories (s Boyle), 1985
Great American Jackpot (Gold), 1971
Great American Novel (Roth), 1973
Great Apes (Self), 1997
Great Climate (s Wilding), 1990
Great Fake Book (Bourjaily), 1987
Great Fire of London (Ackroyd), 1988
Great Indian Novel (Tharoor), 1989
Great Jones Street (DeLillo), 1974
Great Occasion (Colegate), 1962
Great Ponds (Amadi), 1973
Great Profundo and Other Stories (s MacLaverty), 1988
Great Pursuit (Sharpe), 1984
Great Realizations (Hood), 1997
Great Rock 'n' Roll Swindle (Moorcock, as Bradbury, E.), 1977
Great Santini (Conroy), 1976
Great Sky River (Benford), 1987
Great Train Robbery (Crichton, as Lange), 1975
Great World (Malouf), 1991
Great World and Timothy Colt (Auchincloss), 1957
Greek Fire (Graham), 1958
Greeks Have a Word for It (Unsworth), 1967
Green Days by the River (Anthony), 1967
Green Equinox (Mavor), 1973
Green Flash (Graham), 1987
Green Flows the Bile (Peterkiewicz), 1969
Green Grass, Running Water (King), 1993
Green Journey (Hassler), 1986

Green Mars (Robinson), 1988
Green Mile (King), 1996
Green Shadows, White Whale (Bradbury), 1992
Green Water, Green Sky (Gallant), 1960
Greenlanders (Smiley), 1988
Greenwich Killing Time (Friedman), 1986
Greeting from Southern California (See, as Highland), 1988
Grey Area, and Other Stories (s Self), 1996
Grey Beginning (Mertz, as Michaels), 1986
Greybeard (Aldiss), 1964
Greygallows (Mertz, as Michaels), 1973
Greyhound for Breakfast (s Kelman), 1987
Greyling (Rooke), 1963
Grimus (Rushdie), 1979
Grisly Wife (Hall), 1993
Grotesque (McGrath), 1989
Ground Beneath Her Feet (Rushdie), 1999
Grove of Eagles (Graham), 1964
Guards! Guards! (Pratchett), 1991
Guerrillas (Naipaul), 1975
Guest of Honour (Gordimer), 1971
Guests of Fame (Stern), 1958
Guests of War (Jenkins), 1956
Guide (Narayan), 1958
Guide to Animal Behaviour (s Glover), 1991
Guilty Thing Surprised (Rendell, as Vine), 1970
Gump & Co (Groom), 1995
Gun, With Occasional Music (Lethem), 1994
Gunny Sack (Vassanji), 1989
Guns (Hunter), 1977
Gunsights (Leonard), 1979
Gut Symmetries (Winterson), 1997
Guyana Quartet (Harris), 1985
Gwendolen (Emecheta), 1989
Gypsy's Curse (Crews), 1975

Habit of Loving (s Lessing), 1957
Hack (Sheed), 1963
Ha-Ha (Dawson), 1961
Hail, Hail, The Gang's All Here! (Hunter), 1971
Hail to the Chief (Hunter), 1973
Hair o' the Chine (s Coover), 1979
Hajji and Other Stories (s Essop), 1978
Half a Heart (Brown), 2000
Half Asleep in Frog Pajamas (Robbins), 1994
Half Moon Street (Perry), 2000
Half Moon Street: Two Short Novels (Theroux), 1984
Half of Paradise (Burke), 1995
Hall of Mirrors (Stone), 1968
Hallelujah Bum (Sinclair), 1963
Hamilton Stark (Banks), 1978
Hammer of God (Clarke), 1993
Hammertown Tales (s Masters), 1987
Hand at the Shutter (s King), 1996
Hand-Reared Boy (Aldiss), 1970
Hand That Feeds You: A Satiric Nightmare (Hasluck), 1982
Handful of Rice (Markandaya), 1966
Handmaid's Tale (Atwood), 1986
Hanged Man in the Garden (Halligan), 1989
Hanger Stout, Awake! (Matthews), 1967
Hanging Garden (Wagoner), 1982
Hanging Tree (Massie), 1990
Hanging Valley (Robinson), 1992
Haphazard House (Wesley), 1983
Happenstance (Shields), 1980
Happy as Larry (Hinde), 1958
Happy Endings (Cook), 1974
Happy for the Child (Jenkins), 1953
Happy Marriage and Other Stories (s Cassill), 1967
Happy New Year, Herbie, and Other Stories (s Hunter), 1965
Happy Times (s Lurie), 1969
Harald, Claudia, and Their Son Duncan (Gordimer), 1996
Hard Blue Sky (Grau), 1959
Hard Feelings and Other Stories (s King), 1976
Hard Time to Be a Father (s Weldon), 1999
Harder They Fall (Schulberg), 1996
Hardfought (Bear), 1988
Hardwater Country (s Busch), 1979
Harland's Half Acre (Malouf), 1984
Harlot's Ghost (Mailer), 1991
Harlot's Progress (Dabydeen), 1999
Harm Done (Rendell, as Vine), 1999
Harnessing Peacocks (Wesley), 1986
Harriet Said (Bainbridge), 1973
Harris's Requiem (Middleton), 1960
Harry (Vansittart), 1981
Harry and Catherine (Busch), 1990
Harry Reunited (Cobb), 1995
Harry's Fragments: A Novel of International Puzzlement (Bowering), 1990
Harvest of Thorns (Chinodya), 1991
Hassan's Tower (s Drabble), 1980
Hat on the Letter O and Other Stories (s Hasluck), 1978
Haunt (Barker), 1999
Haunted Land (Stow), 1957
Haunted: Tales of the Grotesque (s Oates, as Smith, R.), 1994
Haunting of Jessica Raven (Jones), 1994
Have the Men Had Enough? (Forster), 1989
Hawaii One Summer (Kingston), 1998
Hawk Is Dying (Crews), 1974
Hawkmoon (s Moorcock, as Bradbury, E.), 1995
Hawksbill Station (Silverberg, as Knox), 1968
Hawksmoor (Ackroyd), 1986
Hayballs (Tinniswood), 1989
He, She and It (Piercy), 1991
He Who Hesitates (Hunter), 1965
He/She (Gold), 1982
Headbanger (Hamilton), 1996
Headhunter (Findley), 1994
Heading West (Betts), 1981
Headlong (Frayn), 1999
Heads (Bear), 1990
Heads by Harry (Yamanaka), 1999
Healers (Armah), 1979
Healing (Jones), 1998
Healing Art (Wilson), 1988
Health and Happiness (Johnson), 1991
Hear and Forgive (Humphreys), 1953
Hearing Voices (Wilson), 1996
Heart of Aztlán (Anaya), 1976

Heart of It (Hines), 1994
Heart of Red Iron (Gotlieb), 1989
Heart of the Comet (Benford), 1986
Heart of the Country (Weldon), 1988
Heart of the River (Slaughter), 1983
Heart Songs, and Other Stories (s Proulx), 1989
Heartland (Harris), 1964
Hearts and Lives of Men (Weldon), 1988
Hearts in Atlantis (King), 1999
Hearts of Wood, and Other Timeless Tales (s Kotzwinkle), 1986
Heart's Wild Surf (Johnson), 1996
Heartsong of Charging Elk (Welch), 2000
Heartstones (Rendell, as Vine), 1987
Heartwood (Burke), 1999
Heat (Goldman), 1985
Heat and Dust (Jhabvala), 1976
Heat and Other Stories (s Oates, as Smith, R.), 1991
Heat Wave (Lively), 1996
Heather Blazing (Tóibín), 1993
Heaven and Earth (Raphael), 1985
Heaven's Prisoners (Burke), 1990
Heavy Feather (Barker), 1979
Heavy Water and Other Stories (s Amis), 1999
Heavy Weather (Sterling), 1994
Heckler (Hunter), 1962
Hegira (Bear), 1979
Helen (Fast, as Cunningham), 1967
Helen Blake (Jones), 1955
Helliconia Spring (Aldiss), 1982
Helliconia Summer (Aldiss), 1983
Helliconia Trilogy (Aldiss), 1985
Helliconia Winter (Aldiss), 1985
Hello America (Ballard), 1981
Helsingør Station and Other Departures: Fictions and Autobiographies 1956–1989 (s Higgins), 1989
Henderson the Rain King (Bellow), 1959
Henry James' Midnight Song (Hill), 1993
Henry Sows the Wind (Glanville), 1954
Her Infinite Variety (Auchincloss), 2000
Her Mother's Daughter (French), 1987
Her Side of It (Savage), 1981
Her Story (Jacobson), 1987
Here Goes Kitten (Gover), 1965
Here I Stay (Mertz, as Michaels), 1985
Here on Earth (Hoffman), 1997
Here Today (Fairbairns), 1984
Hermes 3000 (Kotzwinkle), 1972
Hermit King (Cobb), 1987
Hero: A Fable (Sealy), 1991
Heroes (Iyayi), 1986
Heroes of the Empty View (Aldridge), 1954
Herr Nightingale and the Satin Woman (Kotzwinkle), 1978
Herself in Love and Other Stories (s Wiggins), 1987
Herzog (Bellow), 1965
Hessian (Fast, as Cunningham), 1973
Hey Jack! (Hannah), 1987
Hidden I: A Myth Revised (Raphael), 1990
Hidden in the Heart (Jacobson), 1991
Hidden Ones (Jones), 1988
Hidden Side of the Moon (s Russ), 1989
Hidden Symptoms (Madden), 1986
Hide (Unsworth), 1970
Hiding Place (Wideman), 1984
High (Hinde), 1969
High Cost of Living (Piercy), 1979
High Crimes and Misdemeanors (s Greenberg), 1980
High Fidelity (Hornby), 1995
High Ground and Other Stories (s McGahern), 1987
High Hearts (Brown), 1986
High Lonesome (Hannah), 1996
High-Rise (Ballard), 1977
High Road (O'Brien), 1988
High Stakes (Francis), 1976
Higher Ground (Phillips), 1989
Highgate Rise (Perry), 1992
Highways to a War (Koch), 1995
Hill Bachelors (Trevor), 2000
Hills of Apollo Bay (Cowan), 1989
Him They Compelled (Middleton), 1964
Him with His Foot in His Mouth and Other Stories (s Bellow), 1984
Hind's Kidnap: A Pastoral on Familiar Airs (McElroy), 1970
Hired Man (Bragg), 1970
His Little Women (Rossner), 1990
His Mistress's Voice (Freeman), 1999
History Maker (Gray), 1995
History Man (Bradbury), 1976
History of the Ginger Man (Donleavy), 1994
History of the Runestaff (Moorcock, as Bradbury, E.), 1979
History of the World in 10 1/2 Chapters (Barnes, as Kavanagh), 1989
Hitting the Wall: Two Novellas (s Foster), 1989
Hocus Pocus; or, What's the Hurry, Son? (Vonnegut), 1990
Hogfather (Pratchett), 1998
Hogg (Delany), 1998
Holden's Performance (Bail), 1987
Holder of the World (Mukherjee), 1993
Holding On (Jones), 1973
Holiday (Middleton), 1974
Hollow Lands (Moorcock, as Bradbury, E.), 1975
Hollywood: A Novel of American in the 1920s (Vidal, as Box), 1990
Hollywood Nocturnes (s Ellroy), 1994
Holy Fire (Sterling), 1996
Holy Pictures (Boylan), 1983
Holy Tree (Jenkins), 1969
Hombre (Leonard), 1961
Home at the End of the World (Cunningham), 1990
Home Free (Wakefield), 1977
Home Front (Tinniswood), 1982
Home Is the Exile (Masters), 1996
Home Made (s Price), 1990
Home Repairs (Ellis), 1993
Home Rule (Boylan), 1993
Home Thoughts (Parks), 1987
Home Time (s Farmer), 1985
Home Truths: Selected Canadian Stories (s Gallant), 1985
Homeland and Other Stories (s Kingsolver), 1989
Homesick (Vanderhaeghe), 1990
Homesickness (Bail), 1999

Homewood Books (Wideman), 1992
Honest Account of a Memorable Life: An Apocryphal Gospel (Price), 1994
Honey Seems Bitter (Kiely), 1954
Honor, Power, Riches, Fame and the Love of Women (Just), 1979
Honorable Men (Auchincloss), 1986
Honorary Patron (Hodgins), 1987
Honour, and Other People's Children: Two Stories (s Garner), 1982
Honourable Schoolboy (le Carré), 1977
Hope (Deighton), 1995
Hope in the Desperate House (Richards), 1996
Hopeful Monsters (Mosley), 1991
Horatio Stubbs Saga (Aldiss), 1985
Horse and Two Goats (s Narayan), 1970
Horse Heaven (Smiley), 2000
Horse under Water (Deighton), 1968
Horsefly (Hoffman), 2000
Horsehair Sofa (Hughes), 1961
Horseman, Pass By (McMurtry), 1961
Horse's Head (Hunter), 1968
Hosanna Man (Callow), 1956
Hospital Wedding (s Dawson), 1978
Hot Jazz Trio (Kotzwinkle), 1989
Hot Money (Francis), 1988
Hot Month (Hanley, as Calvin), 1967
Hot Sky at Midnight (Silverberg, as Knox), 1994
Hotel (Hailey), 1965
Hotel de Dream (Tennant), 1976
Hotel du Lac (Brookner), 1985
Hotel in the Jungle (Guerard), 1995
Hotel New Hampshire (Irving), 1981
Hothouse by the East River (Spark), 1973
Hottentot Room (Hope), 1987
Hottest Night of the Year (s Adams), 1989
Hound of Earth (Bourjaily), 1956
Hour of the Bell (Petrakis), 1986
Hours (Cunningham), 1998
House (Bardwell), 1984
House for Mr. Biswas (Naipaul), 1962
House Guest (Anderson), 1995
House Gun (Gordimer), 1998
House in the Light (Farmer), 1995
House Made of Dawn (Momaday), 1969
House of Doctor Dee (Ackroyd), 1993
House of Five Talents (Auchincloss), 1961
House of Many Shadows (Mertz, as Michaels), 1975
House of Sleep (Coe), 1998
House of Splendid Isolation (O'Brien), 1994
House of Stairs (Rendell, as Vine), 1989
House of Strife (Shadbolt), 1993
House of the Prophet (Auchincloss), 1980
House on Coliseum Street (Grau), 1961
House on Mango Street (Cisneros), 1984
House on the Sound (Perutz), 1965
House That Jack Built (Hunter), 1988
House That Jack Built (Kelleher), 1994
House with the Stained-Glass Windows (Graham), 1934
Houseguest (Berger), 1989
Householder (Jhabvala), 1960
Houses of Stone (Mertz, as Michaels), 1993
Housespy (Duffy), 1978
How Far Can You Go? (Lodge), 1980
How I Became a Holy Mother and Other Stories (s Jhabvala), 1976
How Late It Was, How Late (Kelman), 1994
How Many Miles to Babylon? (Johnston), 1974
How Mickey Made It (s Phillips), 1981
How She Died (Yglesias), 1973
How Stella Got Her Groove Back (McMillan), 1996
How the Dead Live (Self), 2000
How to Save Your Own Life (Jong), 1977
Hoyt's Child (Cassill), 1976
Human Element and Other Stories (s Barstow), 1969
Human Stain (Roth), 2000
Humboldt's Gift (Bellow), 1975
100 Scenes from Married Life: A Selection (Gordon), 1976
Hundred Secret Senses (Tan), 1995
Hungering Shame (Cassill), 1956
Hungry Ghosts: Seven Allusive Comedies (s Oates, as Smith, R.), 1975
Hunt (Bragg), 1972
Hunted (Guerard), 1947
Hunted (Leonard), 1978
Hunter (Aldridge), 1951
Hunter and the Trap (Fast, as Cunningham), 1967
Hunting the Wild Pineapple (s Astley), 1991
Hunting with Diana (Watmough), 1996
Hurricane Hazel and Other Stories (s Atwood), 1986
Hurry Home (Wideman), 1970
Hyde Park Headsman (Perry), 1994

I Am the World (Vansittart), 1942
I Been in Sorrow's Kitchen and Licked out All the Pots (Straight), 1992
I Cannot Get You Close Enough: Three Novellas (s Gilchrist), 1991
I Come as a Thief (Auchincloss), 1973
I Didn't Know You Cared (Tinniswood), 1973
I Don't Want to Know Anyone Too Well: 15 Stories (s Levine), 1971
I, Dreyfus (Rubens), 1999
I, etcetera (s Sontag), 1979
I Heard My Sister Speak My Name (Savage), 1977
I Like Being Killed: Stories (s Fischer), 2000
I Like 'em Tough (s Hunter), 1958
I Like It Better Now (s Hall), 1992
I Lock My Door upon Myself (Oates, as Smith, R.), 1990
I Married a Communist (Roth), 1998
I Sent a Letter to My Love (Rubens), 1978
I Shall Not Hear the Nightingale (Singh), 1961
I Sing the Body Electric! (s Bradbury), 1970
I Think We Should Go into the Jungle (s Anderson), 1993
I Want (Dunn), 1972
I Want to Go to Moscow: A Lay (Duffy), 1973
I Wanted a Year Without Fall (Busch), 1971
I Wish He Would Not Die (Aldridge), 1958
I Would Have Saved Them If I Could (s Michaels), 1975
Ice (Hunter), 1983

Ice Age (Drabble), 1977
Ice-Candy-Man (Sidhwa), 1988
Ice-Cream War (Boyd), 1983
Ice House (Bawden), 1983
Ice People (Gee), 1998
Ice Saints (Tuohy), 1964
Ice Schooner (Moorcock, as Bradbury, E.), 1985
Ice Storm (Moody), 1994
Icehenge (Robinson), 1985
Icon (Forsyth), 1996
Idea of Perfection (Grenville), 1999
Identifying the Object (s Jones), 1993
Identities: Three Novels (Wideman), 1994
Idle Woman and Other Stories (s Mulkerns), 1980
Idoru (Gibson), 1996
If I Die Today (Deshpande), 1982
If I Were Me (Blaise), 1997
If Morning Ever Comes (Tyler), 1965
If the Old Could— (Lessing), 1984
If the River Was Whiskey (s Boyle), 1989
If the Stars Are Gods (Benford), 1977
If Wishes Were Horses (Kinsella), 1996
Ikon Maker (Hogan), 1979
Illumination Night (Hoffman), 1987
Illuminations (Duffy), 1991
Illusionist (Johnston), 1995
Illusionist and Other Fictions (s Gordon), 1978
Illustrated Man (s Bradbury), 1997
Illywhacker (Carey), 1985
Image to Die For (Phillips), 1997
Imaginary Friends (Lurie), 1967
Imaginary Life (Malouf), 1978
Imaginary Toys (Mitchell), 1961
Imaginative Experience (Wesley), 1995
Imaginative Qualities of Actual Things (Sorrentino), 1971
Imagining Argentina (Thornton), 1987
Imaginings of Sand (Brink), 1996
Imago (Butler), 1989
Imago Bird (Mosley), 1991
Immortality at Any Price (Cooper), 1991
Imperial Earth (Clarke), 1976
Imperial German Dinner Service (Hughes), 1983
Impersonators (Anderson), 1980
Impossible Man and Other Stories (s Ballard), 1966
Impossible Object (Mosley), 1993
Impossible Saints (Roberts), 1998
Impossible Things (Willis), 1994
In a Dark Wood (Warner), 1977
In a Dry Season (Robinson), 1999
In a Free State (Naipaul), 1971
In a Harbour Green (Kiely), 1950
In a Hotel Garden (Josipovici), 1995
In a Strange Land (Middleton), 1979
In a Yellow Wood (Vidal, as Box), 1967
In Alien Flesh (Benford), 1986
In Alien Flesh (s Benford), 1986
In America (Sontag), 2000
In Another Country (Silverberg, as Knox), 1990
In Any Case (Stern), 1963
In Bed One Night and Other Brief Encounters (s Coover), 1983
In Between the Sheets (s McEwan), 1979
In Country (Mason), 1986
In Custody (Desai), 1985
In Her Day (Brown), 1976
In High Places (Hailey), 1962
In Honour Bound (Bawden), 1961
In Love and Trouble: Stories of Black Women (s Walker), 1984
In Lower Town (s Levine), 1977
In Memory of Junior: A Novel (Edgerton), 1992
In My Father's Den (Gee), 1972
In My Father's House (Gaines), 1978
In Our Nature: Stories of Wilderness (s Atwood), 2000
In Search of Love and Beauty (Jhabvala), 1983
In the Absence of Angels (s Calisher), 1953
In the Bear's House (Momaday), 1999
In the Beauty of the Lilies (Updike), 1996
In the Briar Patch (s Garrett), 1961
In the Castle of My Skin (Lamming), 1953
In the City of Fear (Just), 1982
In the Country of Last Things (Auster), 1988
In the Country of Salvation (Virtue), 1990
In the Ditch (Emecheta), 1972
In the Electric Mist with Confederate Dead (Burke), 1993
In the Fertile Land (s Josipovici), 1987
In the Frame (Francis), 1978
In the Garden of the North American Martyrs (s Wolff), 1981
In the Heart of the Country (Coetzee), 1977
In the Heart of the Heart of the Country and Other Stories (s Gass), 1969
In the Heat of the Day (Anthony), 1996
In the Hour of Signs (Mahjoub), 1996
In the Lake of the Woods (O'Brien), 1994
In the Land of Dreamy Dreams: Short Fiction (s Gilchrist), 1982
In the Land of Morning (Petrakis), 1973
In the Middle Distance (Delbanco), 1971
In the Mood (Waterhouse), 1983
In the Name of Mercy (Delbanco), 1995
In the Night Season: A Novel (Bausch), 1998
In the Ocean of Night (Benford), 1977
In the Palace of the Movie King (Calisher), 1993
In the Penny Arcade (s Millhauser), 1986
In the Red Kitchen (Roberts), 1990
In the Skin of a Lion (Ondaatje), 1987
In the Slammer with Carol Smith (Calisher), 1997
In the Springtime of the Year (Hill), 1974
In the Thirties (Upward), 1962
In the Walled City (s O'Nan), 1993
In the Winter Dark (Winton), 1989
In This City (s Clarke), 1992
In This Sign (Greenberg), 1970
In Transit: Twenty Stories (s Gallant), 1990
Incidents at the Shrine (s Okri), 1986
Incidents in the Rue Laugier (Brookner), 1996
Incline Our Hearts (Wilson), 1989
Incompatible Atuk (Richler), 1963
Incurable (Dunn), 1971
Indecent Exposure (Sharpe), 1987
Independence Day (Ford), 1995
Independent Woman (Fast, as Cunningham), 1997
Indian (s Updike), 1971

Indian Affairs (Woiwode), 1991
Indian Killer (Alexie), 1998
Indian Lawyer (Welch), 1990
Indian Summer (Knowles), 1966
Indifferent Children (Auchincloss), 1947
Indigo (Warner), 1993
Indirect Method and Other Stories (s King), 1980
Infinite Jest (Wallace), 1996
Infinite Rehearsal (Harris), 1987
Infinite Riches (Okri), 1999
Infinity Concerto (Bear), 1984
Information (Amis), 1995
Informers (Ellis), 1994
Injured Party (Dundy), 1974
Injured Party (Schaeffer), 1986
Injury Time (Bainbridge), 1978
Injustice Collectors (s Auchincloss), 1951
Ink Truck (Kennedy), 1970
Inklings: Selected Stories (s Jacobson), 1973
Inland (Murnane), 1989
Inland Ice and Other Stories (s Ní Dhuibhne), 1997
Inland Passage and Other Stories (s Rule), 1985
Inn at the Edge of the World (Ellis), 1990
Inner Circle (Peterkiewicz), 1966
Innocence of Age (Bissoondath), 1992
Innocent (Jones), 1957
Innocent (McEwan), 1990
Innocent Blood (James), 1980
Innocent Cities (Hodgins), 1990
Innocent Graves: An Inspector Banks Mystery (Robinson), 1996
Innocents (Slaughter), 1986
Innocents: Variations on a Theme (s Barker), 1948
Inside the Wardrobe: 20 Stories (s Lurie), 1978
Insomnia (King), 1994
Inspector Wexford (Rendell, as Vine), 1993
Instant in the Wind (Brink), 1977
Insular Possession (Mo), 1987
Intangibles Inc. (s Aldiss), 1969
Intended (Dabydeen), 1991
Intensive Care (Frame), 1971
Interceptor Pilot (Gangemi), 1980
Interesting Times (Pratchett), 1994
Interpreters (Soyinka), 1970
Interstate (Dixon), 1995
Intertidal Life (Thomas), 1985
Intimacy (Kureishi), 1999
Into Another Dawn (Nahal), 1977
Into the Dark (Kelleher), 1999
Into the Darkness (Mertz, as Michaels), 1990
Into the Fog (Graham), 1935
Into Their Labours (Berger), 1992
Introduction (s Mitchell), 1960
Intruder (Tindall), 1979
Intrusion and Other Stories (s Deshpande), 1994
Intrusions (Hegi), 1981
Invaders from Earth (Silverberg, as Knox), 1977
Inventing Memory: A Novel of Mothers and Daughters (Jong), 1997
Invention of the World (Hodgins), 1978
Inventory (Josipovici), 1968
Invincible Barriers (Silverberg, as Knox), 1958
Invisible Mending (Busch), 1984
Invisible Worm (Johnston), 1993
Involution Ocean (Sterling), 1977
Iowa Baseball Confederacy (Kinsella), 1986
Ipcress File (Deighton), 1963
I'm Cannon—For Hire (Hunter), 1959
I'm Expecting to Live Quite Soon (West), 1971
I'm the King of the Castle (Hill), 1970
Ireland: Selected Stories (s Trevor), 1998
Irish Signorina (O'Faolain), 1986
Ironweed (Kennedy), 1984
Isaac Quartet (Charyn), 1984
Island Death (Yurick), 1975
Island of Apples (Jones), 1992
Islands in the Net (Sterling), 1988
Isobars (s Hospital), 1992
Isobel Gunn (Thomas), 1999
Isolation: A Novel in Five Acts (Peterkiewicz), 1960
Isolation Booth (s Hood), 1991
It (King), 1986
It Could Be You (McCauley), 1997
It Looked Like For Ever (Harris), 1979
It Was Dark (s Deshpande), 1986
It Was the Nightingale (s Deshpande), 1986
Italian Gadget (Hanley, as Calvin), 1966
Italian Wife (Humphreys), 1958
Item from the Late News (Astley), 1984
Its Colours They Are Fine (s Spence), 1977
It's Different Abroad (Hanley, as Calvin), 1963
It's Raining in Mango: Pictures from a Family Album (Astley), 1988
Itsuka (Kogawa), 1993
Ivory Swing (Hospital), 1983

J—, Black Bam and the Masqueraders (St. Omer), 1972
Jack and the Beanstalk (Hunter), 1984
Jack Gance (Just), 1989
Jack in the Box (Kotzwinkle), 1980
Jack Maggs (Carey), 1998
Jack of Diamonds and Other Stories (s Spencer), 1988
Jack Orkney (s Lessing), 1978
Jack Would Be a Gentleman (Freeman), 1959
Jackal's Head (Mertz, as Michaels), 1969
Jacklighting (s Beattie), 1981
Jacko (Keneally), 1993
Jacob's Ladder (Williams), 1987
Jade Man's Eyes (s Moorcock, as Bradbury, E.), 1973
Jailbird (Vonnegut), 1979
Jalamanta: A Message from the Desert (Anaya), 1996
Jane and Louisa Will Soon Come Home (Brodber), 1980
Janine (Callow), 1977
Japanese by Spring (Reed), 1993
Japanese Girl and Other Stories (s Graham), 1972
Japanese Umbrella and Other Stories (s King), 1964
Jasmine (Mukherjee), 1990
Jazz (Morrison), 1992
J.C. Kitten Trilogy (Gover), 1982
J.C. Saves (Gover), 1979
Jeremiah 8:20 (Hill), 1970

Jeremy Poldark: A Novel of Cornwall 1790–1791 (Graham), 1950
Jerusalem the Golden (Drabble), 1967
Jesus' Son (s Johnson), 1992
Jewel in the Skull (Moorcock, as Bradbury, E.), 1977
Jewel of the Moon (s Kotzwinkle), 1985
Jewels of Aptor (Delany), 1977
Jigsaw (Hunter), 1970
Jigsaw: An Unsentimental Education (Bedford), 1989
Jim Dandy (Faust), 1994
Jingo (Pratchett), 1997
Jitterbug Perfume (Robbins), 1984
Joan Makes History (Grenville), 1988
Joanna (St. Aubin de Teran), 1991
Joanna's Luck (Jones), 1984
Joby (Barstow), 1964
John and Mary (Jones), 1967
John Brown's Body (Barker), 1969
John Dollar (Wiggins), 1989
John Ross: The True Story (Gray), 1987
Johnno (Malouf), 1978
Johnny and the Dead (Pratchett), 1993
Johnny I Hardly Knew You (O'Brien), 1977
Johnny Mnemonic (Gibson), 1995
John's Wife (Coover), 1996
Jones (Humphreys), 1984
Jordan County: A Landscape in Narrative (Foote), 1954
Joseph (Jones), 1970
Joseph Winter's Patronage (Cole), 1969
Josh Lawton (Bragg), 1972
Joshua Then and Now (Richler), 1980
Journal from Ellipsia (Calisher), 1966
Journal of the Flood Year (Ely), 1992
Journalist (Mathews), 1994
Journey Home (Bolger), 1990
Journey of a Lifetime and Other Stories (s Tindall), 1990
Journey to Ithaca (Desai), 1995
Journey to the Border (Upward), 1994
Journey to the Seven Streams (s Kiely), 1963
Journey Within (Aniebo), 1978
Joy (McNeish), 1982
Joy Luck Club (Tan), 1989
Joy-Ride and After (s Barker), 1964
Joys of Motherhood (Emecheta), 1979
J'Ouvert Morning (Jones), 1976
Jubb (Waterhouse), 1964
Judas Cloth (O'Faolain), 1992
Judasland (Dawson), 1989
Judgement Day (Lively), 1981
Judgement in Stone (Rendell, as Vine), 1978
Judgment of Dragons (Gotlieb), 1980
Judgment of Paris (Vidal, as Box), 1966
Judith (Mosley), 1991
Juggling (Trapido), 1995
Juice (Becker), 1959
Julian (Vidal, as Box), 1964
Juliet's Story (Trevor), 1994
Julip (Harrison), 1994
July's People (Gordimer), 1981
Jumping Ship and Other Stories (s James), 1992
Jumping the Queue (Wesley), 1988
Jungle Kids (s Hunter), 1956
Jungle Lovers (Theroux), 1971
Junior Bachelor Society (Williams), 1976
Junk Mail (Self), 1995
Junkers (Read), 1969
Junky's Christmas and Other Stories (s O'Hagan), 1994
Jupiter Project (Benford), 1980
Jurassic Park (Crichton, as Lange), 1991
Just Duffy (Jenkins), 1988
Just Exchange (Middleton), 1962
Just Like a Lady (Bawden), 1960
Just Relations (Hall), 1983
Just You Wait and See (Barstow), 1986

Kairos (Jones), 1988
Kalki (Vidal, as Box), 1978
Karate Is a Thing of the Spirit (Crews), 1972
Kate Vaiden (Price), 1987
Kayhut: A Warrior's Odyssey (Metcalf), 1998
Keep the Change (McGuane), 1990
Keepers of the House (Grau), 1964
Keepers of the House (St. Aubin de Teran), 1982
Keepsakes and Other Stories (s Hassler), 1999
Kehinde (Emecheta), 1994
Kennis van die aand (Brink), 1973
Kepler (Banville), 1983
Kestrel for a Knave (Hines), 1968
Keys of Chance (Graham), 1939
Keys to the Street (Rendell, as Vine), 1996
K-Factor (Caute), 1983
Killer Diller (Edgerton), 1991
Killer on the Road (Ellroy), 1986
Killer's Choice (Hunter), 1960
Killer's Payoff (Hunter), 1960
Killer's Wedge (Hunter), 1961
Killing Doll (Rendell, as Vine), 1984
Killing Everybody (Harris), 1973
Killing Mister Watson (Matthiessen), 1990
Killing Time (Berger), 1968
Killshot (Leonard), 1989
Kind of Fool (Munonye), 1999
Kind of Loving (Barstow), 1961
Kind of Loving: The Vic Brown Trilogy (Barstow), 1981
Kind of Marriage (Emecheta), 1986
Kindling (Elliott), 1970
Kindly Light (Wilson), 1979
Kindness Cup (Astley), 1974
Kindness of Women (Ballard), 1991
Kindred (Butler), 1988
Kinflicks (Alther), 1976
Kinfolks (Hunter), 1996
King, a Street Story (Berger), 1999
King David (Massie), 1995
King Death's Garden (Jones), 1986
King Hereafter (Dunnett), 1982
King Ludd (Sinclair), 1988
King of Babylon Shall Not Come Against You (Garrett), 1996
King of Hackney Marshes and Other Stories (s Glanville), 1965
King of the Mountain (s Garrett), 1959

King of the Swords (Moorcock, as Bradbury, E.), 1971
King Solomon's Carpet (Rendell, as Vine), 1991
Kingdom Come (Bragg), 1980
Kingdom Come (Rubens), 1990
Kingdom of the Cats (Gotlieb), 1983
Kingdoms of the Wall (Silverberg, as Knox), 1993
Kingfisher Come Home: The Complete Maori Stories (s Ihimaera), 1995
King's Persons (Greenberg), 1963
King's Ransom (Hunter), 1961
Kinky Friedman Crime Club (Friedman), 1992
Kiss (Hunter), 1992
Kiss Before Dying (Levin), 1954
Kiss in the Hotel Joseph Conrad, and Other Stories (s Norman), 1989
Kiss of Kin (Settle), 1955
Kiss of the Fur Queen (Highway), 1998
Kisses of the Enemy (Hall), 1989
Kissing America (Glanville), 1985
Kissing the Gunner's Daughter (Rendell, as Vine), 1992
Kitchen God's Wife (Tan), 1991
Kittatinny: A Tale of Magic (Russ), 1978
Kitty and Virgil (Bailey), 2000
Kleinzeit (Hoban), 1974
Klynt's Law (Baker), 1976
Knife Thrower and Other Stories (s Millhauser), 1998
Knight of the Swords (Moorcock, as Bradbury, E.), 1971
Knights and Dragons (Spencer), 1966
Knights of the Cross (Read), 1997
Knock-Down (Francis), 1975
Knockout Artist (Crews), 1988
Knot (Figes), 1996
Knotted Cord (Peterkiewicz), 1954
Kolymsky Heights (Davidson), 1994
Komarr: A Miles Vorkosigan Adventure (Bujold), 1998
Konek Landing (Figes), 1969
Kowloon Tong (Theroux), 1997
Krik? Krak! (s Danticat), 1995
Kruger's Alp (Hope), 1985
Kwaku; or, The Man Who Could Not Keep His Mouth Shut (Heath), 1982
Kwinkan (Mudrooroo, as Johnson), 1993

La Vie Passionée of Rodney Buckthorne: A Tale of the Great American's Last Rally and Curious Death (Cassill), 1968
LaBrava (Leonard), 1984
Labors of Love (Cassill), 1980
Ladder of Years (Tyler), 1995
Ladies (Grumbach), 1984
Ladies and Escorts (s Thomas), 1977
Ladies' Man (Price), 1978
Lady Chatterley's Confession (Feinstein), 1995
Lady Killer (Hunter), 1961
Lady, Lady, I Did It! (Hunter), 1963
Lady of Situations (Auchincloss), 1991
Lady Oracle (Atwood), 1977
Lady Who Sold Furniture (s Metcalf), 1970
Lady's Maid (Forster), 1991
Lagoon: Stories (s Frame), 1952
Lajwanti and Other Stories (s Anand), 1966
Lake of Darkness (Rendell, as Vine), 1980
Lakestown Rebellion (Hunter), 1978
Lamb (MacLaverty), 1980
Lamb of Abyssalia (s Oates, as Smith, R.), 1979
Lament on the Death of a Master of Arts (Anand), 1939
Lanark: A Life in Four Books (Gray), 1981
Lancelot (Vansittart), 1978
Land Leviathan (Moorcock, as Bradbury, E.), 1974
Land Without Stars (Kiely), 1946
Landing on the Sun (Frayn), 1991
Landlocked (Lessing), 1965
Landlord (Hunter), 1970
Landlord (Vansittart), 1970
Landscape with Landscape (Murnane), 1985
Landscapes Within (Okri), 1981
Langrishe, Go Down (Higgins), 1966
Languages of Love (Brooke-Rose), 1957
Lantern Lecture and Other Stories (s Mars-Jones), 1981
Lantern Slides (s O'Brien), 1990
Lanterns Across the Snow (s Hill), 1988
Larry's Party (Shields), 1997
Last Barricade (Jones), 1953
Last Burden (Chatterjee), 1993
Last Circus, and The Electrocution (s Bradbury), 1980
Last Continent (Pratchett), 1999
Last Dance (Hunter), 1999
Last Day the Dogbushes Bloomed (Smith), 1968
Last Days (s Oates, as Smith, R.), 1985
Last Days of Louisiana Red (Reed), 1974
Last Exile (Aldridge), 1961
Last Exit to Brooklyn (Selby), 1966
Last Frontier (Fast, as Cunningham), 1948
Last Full Measure (Shaara), 1998
Last Go Round (Kesey), 1994
Last Good Time (Bausch), 1984
Last Labyrinth (Joshi), 1981
Last Lovers (Wharton), 1991
Last Lunch of the Season (s Trevor), 1973
Last Magician (Hospital), 1992
Last Mandarin (Becker), 1979
Last Man's Head (Anderson), 1970
Last of the Country House Murders (Tennant), 1976
Last of the Crazy People (Findley), 1967
Last of the Curlews (Bodsworth), 1995
Last of the Golden Girls (Swan), 1991
Last of the Pleasure Gardens (King), 1965
Last of the Savages (McInerney), 1996
Last Orders (Swift), 1996
Last Orders and Other Stories (s Aldiss), 1989
Last Peacock (Massie), 1980
Last Picture Show (McMurtry), 1972
Last Resort (Lurie), 1998
Last Resorts (Boylan), 1986
Last Shot (Hamilton), 1992
Last Spin and Other Stories (s Hunter), 1960
Last Stand at Saber River (Leonard), 1959
Last Summer (Hunter), 1969
Last Testament of Oscar Wilde (Ackroyd), 1983
Last Thing He Wanted (Didion), 1996
Last Things (Jones), 1989

Last Voyage of Somebody the Sailor (Barth), 1991
Latakia (Thomas), 1979
Late Bourgeois World (Gordimer), 1966
Late Candidate (Phillips), 1990
Late Child (McMurtry), 1995
Late Mr. Shakespeare (Nye), 1999
Latecomers (Brookner), 1989
Later the Same Day (s Paley), 1985
Lateshows (s Moorhouse), 1990
Lathe of Heaven (Le Guin), 1972
Latin Lover (s Raphael), 1994
Laughter of Carthage (Moorcock, as Bradbury, E.), 1984
Law at Randado (Leonard), 1957
Law for the Lion (Auchincloss), 1953
Lawley Road (s Narayan), 1956
Lay Down My Sword and Shield (Burke), 1971
Le Divorce (Johnson), 1997
Le Mariage (Johnson), 2000
Leader (Freeman), 1966
Leader of the Band (Weldon), 1989
Lean Tales (s Gray), 1985
Lean Tales (s Kelman), 1985
Learning Lark (Jones), 1960
Learning Urdu (s Wiggins), 1990
Learning to Swim and Other Stories (s Swift), 1985
Leather Boys (Freeman), 1962
Leather Wings (Duckworth), 1995
Leave It to Me (Mukherjee), 1997
Leaves from the Valley (Trollope), 1980
Leaves of the Banyan Tree (Wendt), 1980
Leaves on Grey (Hogan), 1980
Leavetaking (McGahern), 1984
Leaving Cheyenne (McMurtry), 1972
Left Bank of Desire (Cassill), 1955
Left Hand of Darkness (Le Guin), 1994
Legacy (Bear), 1995
Legacy (Bedford), 1957
Legacy and Other Stories (s Deshpande), 1978
Legacy of Love (Trollope), 2000
Legend in Green Velvet (Mertz, as Michaels), 1976
Legend of La Llorona (Anaya), 1984
Legends from the End of Time (s Moorcock, as Bradbury, E.), 1976
Legends of the Fall (Harrison), 1980
Legs (Kennedy), 1976
Leila (Donleavy), 1983
Leila (Jenkins), 1995
Lemprière's Dictionary (Norfolk), 1991
Less Than Zero (Ellis), 1985
Lesson Before Dying (Gaines), 1993
Lesson in Music (s Hauser), 1964
Lest We Forget Thee, Earth (Silverberg, as Knox), 1958
Lestriad (Katz), 1987
Let the Dead Bury Their Dead and Other Stories (s Kenan), 1992
Letourneau's Used Auto Parts (Chute), 1988
Let's Fall in Love (Hill), 1975
Let's Hear It for a Beautiful Guy and Other Works of Short Fiction (s Friedman), 1984
Let's Hear It for the Deaf Man (Hunter), 1973
Letter Left to Me (McElroy), 1988
Letter to Our Son (s Carey), 1994
Letter to Peachtree and Nine Other Stories (s Kiely), 1988
Letter to Sister Benedicta (Tremain), 1979
Letters (Barth), 1980
Letting Go (Roth), 1962
Leviathan (Auster), 1992
Levitation: Five Fictions (s Ozick), 1982
Lewis Percy (Brookner), 1990
Liar (Savage), 1967
Liberty Man (Freeman), 1955
Libra (DeLillo), 1988
Licks of Love: Short Stories and a Sequel, "Rabbit Remembered" (s Updike), 2000
Licorice: A Novel (Frucht), 1990
Lie Down in Darkness (Styron), 1952
Lies and Stories (s Adams), 1976
Life after God (s Coupland), 1994
Life and Death of My Lord Gilles de Rais (Nye), 1990
Life and Loves of a She-Devil (Weldon), 1984
Life and Times of Captain N (Glover), 1993
Life and Times of Major Fiction (s Baumbach), 1987
Life and Times of Michael K (Coetzee), 1984
Life Before Death (Frucht), 1997
Life Before Man (Atwood), 1980
Life Force (Weldon), 1992
Life in the West (Aldiss), 1990
Life of Her Own, and Other Stories (s Kelly), 1976
Life of the Body (s Smiley), 1990
Life Stories (s Barker), 1981
Life with Swan (West), 1999
Lifetime Burning (Douglas), 1983
Lifetime on Clouds (Murnane), 1976
Light (Figes), 1983
Light a Penny Candle (Binchy), 1983
Light Can Be Both Wave and Particle (s Gilchrist), 1990
Light Fantastic (Pratchett), 1986
Light in the Piazza (Spencer), 1961
Light of Other Days (Clarke), 2000
Light on a Honeycomb (Pownall), 1978
Light Possessed (Cheuse), 1990
Light Years (Gee), 1986
Light Years (Howard), 1990
Lightning (Hunter), 1984
Like Birds, Like Fishes and Other Stories (s Jhabvala), 1964
Like Life (s Moore), 1990
Like Love (Hunter), 1964
Like Men Betrayed (Mortimer), 1954
Like Men Betrayed (Raphael), 1971
Lilac Bus (s Binchy), 1992
Lilac and Flag: An Old Wives' Tale of a City (Berger), 1991
Lilacs Out of the Dead Land (Billington), 1972
Lilian's Story (Grenville), 1986
Lilith's Brood (Butler), 2000
Limits of Love (Raphael), 1961
Limits of the Sensible World (s Sallis), 1995
Lincoln (Vidal, as Box), 1984
Lincoln's Dreams (Willis), 1986
Linden Hills (Naylor), 1985
Lindmann (Raphael), 1964
Lines of Flight (Campbell), 1985

Lion at My Heart (Petrakis), 1959
Lion Country (Buechner), 1971
Lion in the Valley (Mertz, as Michaels), 1987
Lion of Boaz-Jachin and Jachin-Boaz (Hoban), 1973
Lion of Comarre, and Against the Fall of Night (Clarke), 1970
Lions of the Grunewald (Higgins), 1993
Lisa (Cooper), 1937
Listen Ruben Fontanez (Neugeboren), 1968
Literary Woman (s Beckett), 1991
Little Angel Street (Charyn), 1994
Little Big Man (Berger), 1965
Little Book (Hughes), 1996
Little Disturbances of Man (s Paley), 1960
Little Drummer Girl (le Carré), 1983
Little Ironies: Stories of Singapore (s Lim), 1978
Little Kingdom (Humphreys), 1946
Little Kingdoms: Three Novellas (s Millhauser), 1993
Little Love, A Little Learning (Bawden), 1966
Little Madness (Vansittart), 1953
Little Masters (Wilkins), 1997
Little Stranger (McWilliam), 1989
Little Walls (Graham), 1955
Little Yellow Dog: An Easy Rawlins Mystery (Mosley), 1996
Live and Learn (Middleton), 1996
Live as Family (Fairbairns), 1968
Live Bait and Other Stories (s Tuohy), 1979
Live Bodies (Gee), 1998
Live Flesh (Rendell, as Vine), 1986
Live from Golgotha (Vidal, as Box), 1992
Lives and Times of Jerry Cornelius (s Moorcock, as Bradbury, E.), 1976
Lives of Girls and Women (Munro), 1973
Lives of Short Duration (Richards), 1981
Lives of the Poets: Six Stories and a Novella (s Doctorow), 1985
Lives of the Twins (Oates, as Smith, R.), 1987
Lives on Fire (Scott), 1993
Living Hothouse (s Halligan), 1988
Living in the Maniototo (Frame), 1981
Living Together (Wilding), 1974
Livingstone's Companions (s Gordimer), 1972
Lizzie (Hunter), 1984
Lobola vir die lewe (Brink), 1962
Local Colour (Gray), 1975
Local Girls (Hoffman), 1999
Locked Room (Auster), 1987
Lodestar Project (Bradley), 1986
Loitering with Intent (Spark), 1981
Lona Hanson (Savage), 1948
London Embassy (s Theroux), 1983
London Fields (Amis), 1990
London Jungle Adventures of Charlie Hope (Lurie), 1968
London Match (Deighton), 1986
London Observed: Stories and Sketches (s Lessing), 1992
London Transports (s Binchy), 1986
Londoners: An Elegy (Duffy), 1983
Lone Ranger and Tonto Fistfight in Heaven (s Alexie), 1994
Lonely Girl (O'Brien), 1962
Lonesome Dove (McMurtry), 1986
Long after Midnight (s Bradbury), 1977
Long Afternoon of Earth (Aldiss), 1962
Long and Happy Life (Price), 1962
Long Day's Dying (Buechner), 1951
Long Home (Gay), 1999
Long Hot Summer (Anderson), 1999
Long Lankin (s Banville), 1970
Long-Legged Fly: A Novel (Sallis), 1992
Long Live Sandawara (Mudrooroo, as Johnson), 1980
Long Made Short (s Dixon), 1993
Long March (Styron), 1962
Long Prospect (Harrower), 1958
Long Talking Bad Conditions Blues (Sukenick), 1979
Long Time No See (Hunter), 1977
Long View (Howard), 1956
Long Walk (King), 1979
Long Way from Home (Busch), 1993
Long Way from London (s Jacobson), 1958
Long Way to Shiloh (Davidson), 1966
Long Weekend with Marcel Proust: Seven Stories and a Novel (Frame), 1986
Longest Memory (D'Aguiar), 1995
Longings of Women (Piercy), 1994
Longleg (Adams), 1992
Longshot (Francis), 1990
Look at Me (Brookner), 1983
Looking Forward (Tindall), 1985
Looking for Mr. Goodbar (Rossner), 1975
Looking for the Possible Dance (Kennedy), 1993
Looking-Glass War (le Carré), 1965
Lookout Cartridge (McElroy), 1974
Looks and Smiles (Hines), 1981
Loon Lake (Doctorow), 1980
Loopdoppies: Nog dopstories (s Brink), 1984
Loose Lips (Brown), 1999
Loot and Loyalty (Peterkiewicz), 1955
Lord Byron's Daughter (West), 1989
Lord Nelson Tavern (Smith), 1974
Lord of Darkness (Silverberg, as Knox), 1983
Lord of the Dawn: The Legend of Quetzalcoatl (Anaya), 1987
Lord Prestimion (Silverberg, as Knox), 1999
Lord Richard's Passion (Jones), 1974
Lord Valentine's Castle (Silverberg, as Knox), 1980
Lords and Ladies (Pratchett), 1992
Lords of Discipline (Conroy), 1980
Losing Alice (Virtue), 1999
Losing Battles (Welty), 1982
Losing Nelson (Unsworth), 1999
Lost and Old Rivers: Stories (s Cheuse), 1998
Lost Child and Other Stories (s Anand), 1934
Lost Children (Gee), 1994
Lost Father (Simpson), 1992
Lost Father (Warner), 1989
Lost Get-Back Boogie (Burke), 1986
Lost in the Funhouse: Fiction for Print, Tape, Live Voice (s Barth), 1969
Lost Lands (Vansittart), 1964
Lost Man's River (Matthiessen), 1997
Lost Possessions (Hulme), 1985
Lost upon the Roundabouts (s Barker), 1964
Lost World: A Novel (Crichton, as Lange), 1995
Lotus Land (See, as Highland), 1983

Louisiana (Brodber), 1997
Love (Schaeffer), 1981
Love, Action, Laughter, and Other Sad Tales (s Schulberg), 1992
Love, Again: A Novel (Lessing), 1996
Love Always (Beattie), 1985
Love and Friendship (Lurie), 1962
Love and Glory (Bragg), 1983
Love and Like (s Gold), 1961
Love and Obits (Bradley), 1992
Love and the Waiting Game: Eleven Stories (s Watmough), 1975
Love and Will: Twenty Stories (s Dixon), 1989
Love and Work (Price), 1968
Love Child (Duffy), 1971
Love Child (Freeman), 1984
Love, Dad (Hunter), 1981
Love Department (Trevor), 1967
Love Eaters (Settle), 1954
Love Feast (Buechner), 1975
Love from Everybody (Hanley, as Calvin), 1959
Love Hunter (Hassler), 1981
Love in a Blue Time (Kureishi), 1997
Love in a Dry Season (Foote), 1951
Love Is a Fervent Fire (Jenkins), 1959
Love Is Not Love and Other Stories (s Glanville), 1985
Love Life (s Mason), 1989
Love Medicine (Erdrich), 1985
Love Object (s O'Brien), 1969
Love of a Good Woman: Stories (s Munro), 1998
Love of Innocence (Jenkins), 1963
Love on the Coast (Cooper), 1973
Love Song of J. Edgar Hoover (Friedman), 1996
Love Songs of Nathan J. Swirsky (s Hope), 1993
Love Talker (Mertz, as Michaels), 1981
Love Test (Hamilton), 1995
Love Unknown (Wilson), 1987
Lovelock (McNeish), 1986
Lovelock Version (Shadbolt), 1981
Love's Mansion (West), 1992
Lover for Estelle (Rooke), 1961
Lover's Almanac (Howard), 1998
Lovers and Cohorts: Twenty-Seven Stories (s Gold), 1986
Lovers' Knots (Halligan), 1995
Lovers of Their Time and Other Stories (s Trevor), 1979
Lovesong (Jolley), 1997
Loving Attitudes (Billington), 1988
Loving Brecht (Feinstein), 1992
Loving Cup: A Novel of Cornwall 1813–1815 (Graham), 1985
Loving Hands at Home (Johnson), 1969
Loving Roger (Parks), 1986
Loving Ways (Gee), 1996
Low-Flying Aircraft and Other Stories (s Ballard), 1976
Low-lands (s Pynchon), 1978
Lucid Stars (Barrett), 1988
Lucy (Kincaid), 1991
Lullaby (Hunter), 1987
Lunar Attractions (Blaise), 1979
Lunching With The Antichrist: A Family History: 1925–2015 (s Moorcock, as Bradbury, E.), 1995
Lunderston Tales (s Jenkins), 1996
Lust and Other Stories (s Minot), 1989
Lustful Summer (Cassill), 1958
Lusts (Blaise), 1983
Lydia (Fast, as Cunningham), 1965
Lying Days (Gordimer), 1953
Lying in Bed (Harris), 1984
Lying Low (Johnson), 1979
Lynchers (Wideman), 1973
Lynx Hunter and Other Stories (s Marshall), 1987

Machineries of Joy (s Bradbury), 1964
Macken Charm (Hodgins), 1995
Mackenzie (McNeish), 1970
Mackenzie Affair (McNeish), 1972
Mad and Bad Fairies (s Kelly), 1987
Mad·Man (Delany), 1994
Mad River and Other Stories (s Glover), 1981
Mad Trapper (Wiebe), 1977
Madame Sousatzka (Rubens), 1962
Madness (Lurie), 1991
Madness of a Seduced Woman (Schaeffer), 1984
Magdalene (Slaughter), 1979
Maggie Muggins; or, Spring in Earl's Court (Waterhouse), 1981
Maggot (Fowles), 1985
Magic (Goldman), 1976
Magic and Fate: Being the Not Quite Believable Adventures of Sissie Slipper (Billington), 1996
Magic Flute (Spence), 1990
Magic of the Past (s Aldiss), 1987
Magic Striptease (s Garrett), 1973
Magic Time (Kinsella), 1998
Magic Will: Stories and Essays of a Decade (s Gold), 1971
Magician's Girl (Grumbach), 1987
Magician's Wife (Charyn), 1988
Magnolia (Callow), 1994
Magog (Sinclair), 1972
Magus (Fowles), 1978
Maia (Adams), 1985
Maid of Buttermere (Bragg), 1987
Maidens' Trip (Smith), 1948
Mainland (Schaeffer), 1985
Majipoor Chronicles (Silverberg, as Knox), 1982
Major (Hughes), 1965
Make Death Love Me (Rendell, as Vine), 1979
Making Good Again (Davidson), 1968
Making History (See, as Highland), 1991
Making of the Representative for Planet 8 (Lessing), 1982
Making Time (Howard), 1991
Malacia Tapestry (Aldiss), 1977
Malafrena (Le Guin), 1980
Malcolm (Purdy), 1960
Male Cross-Dresser Support Group (Janowitz), 1992
Male Response (Aldiss), 1963
Malgudi Days (s Narayan), 1943
Mama (McMillan), 1987
Mama Day (Naylor), 1988
Mambo Kings Play Songs of Love (Hijuelos), 1989
MAMista (Deighton), 1991
Man and His World (s Blaise), 1992
Man and Two Women (s Lessing), 1963
Man Come Home (Heath), 1974

Man Crazy (Oates, as Smith, R.), 1997
Man Descending (s Vanderhaeghe), 1985
Man-Eater of Malgudi (Narayan), 1962
Man from the Creeks (Kroetsch), 1998
Man In Full (Wolfe), 1998
Man in the Cellar (s O'Faolain), 1974
Man in the Maze (Silverberg, as Knox), 1990
Man in the Middle (Wagoner), 1955
Man Made of Smoke (Middleton), 1973
Man of Power (Colegate), 1960
Man of Slow Feeling: Selected Short Stories (s Wilding), 1985
Man of the Market: Short Stories (s Aniebo), 1994
Man of the People (Achebe), 1966
Man on Fire (Cassill), 1957
Man on Stage: Play Stories (s Dixon), 1996
Man on the Rock (King), 1958
Man to Conjure With (Baumbach), 1966
Man Who Cried I Am (Williams), 1968
Man Who Grew Younger and Other Stories (s Charyn), 1967
Man Who Invented Tomorrow (Hughes), 1968
Man Who Knew Kennedy (Bourjaily), 1967
Man Who Loved Jane Austen (Smith), 1999
Man Who Was Not With It (Gold), 1965
Man Who Wasn't There (Barker), 1990
Mandarin Summer (Kidman), 1981
Mandelbaum Gate (Spark), 1965
Maniac Responsible (Gover), 1964
Man's Estate (Humphreys), 1956
Mantissa (Fowles), 1982
Manual Labor (Busch), 1974
Manuscript for Murder (Masters), 1987
Mao II (DeLillo), 1991
Map of the World (Hamilton), 1994
Maquisard: A Christmas Tale (Guerard), 1946
Mara and Dann: An Adventure by Doris Lessing (Lessing), 1999
Marabou Stork Nightmares: A Novel (Welsh), 1996
Marathon Man (Goldman), 1975
Marble Mountain and Other Stories (s St. Aubin de Teran), 1989
Margaretha de la Porte (Rooke), 1974
Margie (Fast, as Cunningham), 1968
Maria's Girls (Charyn), 1994
Marilee: Three Stories (s Spencer), 1981
Marilyn the Wild (Charyn), 1990
Marilyn's Daughter (Rechy), 1988
Marital Rites (Forster), 1982
Mark of Vishnu and Other Stories (s Singh), 1950
Marlow's Book (Thornton), 1991
Marnie (Graham), 1961
Marriage Machine (Freeman), 1975
Marriages Between Zones Three, Four, and Five (Lessing), 1980
Marriages and Infidelities (s Oates, as Smith, R.), 1974
Married Alive (Duckworth), 1985
Married Man (Read), 1980
Married Man: A Love Story (White), 2000
Married Past Redemption (Middleton), 1993
Marry Me: A Romance (Updike), 1977
Marrying the Mistress (Trollope), 2000
Martha Peake: A Novel of the Revolution (McGrath), 2000
Martha Quest (Lessing), 1952
Martian Chronicles (s Bradbury), 1950
Martian Race (Benford), 1999
Martians (Robinson), 1999
Martin Dressler: The Tale of an American Dreamer (Millhauser), 1996
Martlet's Tale (Delbanco), 1966
Mary, Mary (Hunter), 1992
Mary Swann (Shields), 1996
Marya: A Life (Oates, as Smith, R.), 1987
Maskerade (Pratchett), 1997
Masks of Time (Silverberg, as Knox), 1968
Mason & Dixon (Pynchon), 1997
Mass (Sionil Jose), 1984
Master Georgie: A Novel (Bainbridge), 1998
Master of Big Jingles and Other Stories (s Marshall), 1982
Master of Blacktower (Mertz, as Michaels), 1967
Master of Life and Death (Silverberg, as Knox), 1977
Master of Petersburg (Coetzee), 1994
Master of the Crossroads (Bell), 2000
Master of the Ghost Dreaming (Mudrooroo, as Johnson), 1991
Master of the Moor (Rendell, as Vine), 1982
Matchbox House (Duckworth), 1961
Mate in Three (Rubens), 1965
Mates of Mars (Foster), 1991
Matigari (Ngugi wa Thiong'o), 1989
Matriarch (Ihimaera), 1986
Matter of Conviction (Hunter), 1959
Matter of Time (Deshpande), 1999
Matter's End (s Benford), 1991
Matters of Chance (s Feinstein), 1972
Matthew and Sheila (Jenkins), 1999
Mavis Belfrage: A Romantic Tale, with Five Shorter Tales (Gray), 1996
Max Jamison (Sheed), 1970
Maximum Bob (Leonard), 1991
Mayo Sergeant (Hall), 1967
McBain Brief (s Hunter), 1983
McBain's Ladies: The Women of the 87th Precinct (s Hunter), 1988
McBain's Ladies Too (s Hunter), 1990
McGrotty and Ludmilla; or, The Harbinger Report (Gray), 1990
McGuffin (Bowen), 1985
Me and Hitch (Hunter), 1997
Me and My Baby View the Eclipse: Stories (s Smith), 1990
Me and My Mom (Hauser), 1993
Me, the Moon, and Elvis Presley (Hope), 1997
Means of Evil and Other Stories (s Rendell, as Vine), 1980
Medicine for Melancholy (s Bradbury), 1959
Medicine River (King), 1989
Medusa Frequency (Hoban), 1987
Meet My Maker the Mad Molecule (s Donleavy), 1965
Meeting Evil (Berger), 1992
Meeting Place (Mosley), 1962
Meeting Point (Clarke), 1972
Meeting with Medusa (s Clarke), 1988
Mefisto (Banville), 1989
Megan's Two Houses: A Story of Adjustment (Jong), 1996
Melancholy Baby and Other Stories (s O'Faolain), 1978
Memento Mori (Spark), 1959
Memoir from Antproof Case (Helprin), 1995
Memoirs of a New Man (Cooper), 1966

Memoirs of a Survivor (Lessing), 1975
Memoirs of Lord Byron (Nye), 1989
Memoirs of the Late Mr. Ashley: An American Comedy (Hauser), 1986
Memories of Dying (Hughes), 1976
Memories of Rain (Gupta), 1992
Memories of the Ford Administration (Updike), 1993
Memories of the Space Age (s Ballard), 1988
Memory (Bujold), 1996
Memory Board (Rule), 1987
Memory of Departure (Gurnah), 1987
Memory of Elephants (Desai), 1988
Memory of Murder (s Bradbury), 1984
Memory of Whiteness: A Scientific Romance (Robinson), 1986
Men and Angels (Gordon), 1985
Men and the Girls (Trollope), 1992
Men at Arms (Pratchett), 1993
Men of Brewster Place (Naylor), 1998
Merciless Ladies (Graham), 1980
Meridian (Walker), 1976
Merlin (Nye), 1979
Mermaids in the Basement (s Warner), 1993
Merry-Go-Round in the Sea (Stow), 1966
Merry Men (Chute), 1994
Message from Harpo (Duckworth), 1989
Messenger (Wright), 1964
Messiah (Codrescu), 1999
Messiah (Vidal, as Box), 1968
Messiah of Stockholm (Ozick), 1987
Messiah of the Last Days (Driver), 1974
Metroland (Barnes, as Kavanagh), 1981
Mexico Set (Deighton), 1985
Micky Darlin' (Kelleher), 1992
Microcosm (Duffy), 1966
Microserfs (Coupland), 1995
Midden (Sharpe), 1997
Middle-Class Education (s Oates, as Smith, R.), 1980
Middle Class Education (Sheed), 1961
Middle Ground (Drabble), 1980
Middle Kingdom (Barrett), 1991
Middle Passage (Johnson), 1991
Middleman and Other Stories (s Mukherjee), 1989
Middlemen: A Satire (Brooke-Rose), 1961
Middling: Chapters in the Life of Ellie Toms (Barker), 1967
Midnight All Day (s Kureishi), 1999
Midnight Clear (Wharton), 1982
Midnight Examiner (Kotzwinkle), 1989
Midnight Line (Savage), 1976
Midnight Magic: Selected Stories of Bobbie Ann Mason (s Mason), 1998
Midnight Turning Gray (s Matthiessen), 1984
Midnight's Children (Rushdie), 1981
Mighty Walzer (Jacobson), 1999
Migration of Ghosts (s Melville), 1998
Migrations (Josipovici), 1977
Miguel Street (Naipaul), 1960
Mihloti (s Tlali), 1984
Milk (s Farmer), 1983
Milk and Honey (Jolley), 1987
Miller's Dance: A Novel of Cornwall 1812–1813 (Graham), 1983
Millie (Fast, as Cunningham), 1975
Millroy the Magician (Theroux), 1994
Millstone (Drabble), 1966
Mimic Men (Naipaul), 1967
Mimi's Ghost (Parks), 1995
Mind of My Mind (Butler), 1977
Mind to Murder (James), 1967
Minimum of Two (s Winton), 1988
Ministry of Hope (Heath), 1997
Miracle: A Romance (O'Sullivan), 1976
Miracle, and Other Christmas Stories (s Willis), 1999
Miracle and Other Stories (s Deshpande), 1986
Miraculous Day of Amalia Gómez (Rechy), 1991
Miranda Must Die (Hanley, as Calvin), 1968
Miriam at Thirty-four (Lelchuk), 1975
Miriam in Her Forties (Lelchuk), 1985
Mirror Dance (Bujold), 1993
Mirror on the Floor (Bowering), 1967
Misalliance (Brookner), 1986
Miscellany Two (s Humphreys), 1981
Mischief (Hunter), 1993
Miserables (Wilkins), 1993
Misery (King), 1987
Miskien nooit: 'n Somerspel (Brink), 1967
Miss America (Stern), 1959
Miss Gomez and the Brethren (Trevor), 1971
Miss Hobbema Pageant (s Kinsella), 1989
Ms. Muffet and Others: A Funny, Sassy, Heretical Collection of Feminist Fairytales (s Kelly), 1986
Miss Owen-Owen Is at Home (Forster), 1969
Miss Peabody's Inheritance (Jolley), 1985
Miss Wyoming (Coupland), 1999
Missing Person (Grumbach), 1981
Missing Persons (Cook), 1986
Missionaries (Jenkins), 1957
Mist in the Mirror (Hill), 1993
Mistaken Identity (Sahgal), 1989
Mr. Armitage Isn't Back Yet (Jones), 1971
Mr. Bedford and the Muses (s Godwin), 1984
Mr. Bone's Retreat (Forster), 1971
Mr. Darwin's Shooter (McDonald), 1998
Mr. Evening: A Story and Nine Poems (s Purdy), 1970
Mr. Field's Daughter: A Novel (Bausch), 1989
Mr. Halliday and the Circus Master (McNeish), 1996
Mr. Ives' Christmas (Hijuelos), 1995
Mr. Majestyk (Leonard), 1986
Mister Margolies (Yaffe), 1962
Mr. Nicholas (Ely), 1975
Mr. Nicholas (Hinde), 1953
Mr. Sammler's Planet (Bellow), 1996
Mr. Sampath (Narayan), 1949
Mr. Scobie's Riddle (Jolley), 1985
Mr. Spaceman (Butler), 2000
Mr. Stone and the Knights Companion (Naipaul), 1964
Mr. Vertigo (Auster), 1994
Mr. Wakefield's Crusade (Rubens), 1985
Mister White Eyes (Gold), 1985
Mr. Wrong (s Howard), 1976
Misterioso (Sorrentino), 1989
Mrs. de Winter (Hill), 1993

Mrs Dixon and Friend (s Kidman), 1982
Mrs. Blood (Thomas), 1967
Mrs. Eckdorf in O'Neill's Hotel (Trevor), 1970
Mistress of Spices (Divakaruni), 1997
Mrs. Reinhardt and Other Stories (s O'Brien), 1978
Mrs. Shakespeare: The Complete Works (Nye), 2000
Mittee (Rooke), 1952
Mobiles (s Cowan), 1979
Mobius the Stripper: Stories and Short Plays (s Josipovici), 1974
Moccasin Telegraph and Other Indian Tales (s Kinsella), 1985
Mockery in Arms (Aldridge), 1975
Model Behavior: A Novel and 7 Stories (McInerney), 1998
Mog (Tinniswood), 1970
Mom Among the Liars (Yaffe), 1993
Mom Doth Murder Sleep (Yaffe), 1991
Mom Meets Her Maker (Yaffe), 1990
Moment of Eclipse (s Aldiss), 1972
Moment under the Moment (Hoban), 1992
Mona in the Promised Land (Jen), 1996
Mona Lisa Overdrive (Gibson), 1988
Monday Voices (Greenberg), 1965
Monday's Warriors (Shadbolt), 1992
Mondo Desperado: A Serial Novel (McCabe), 1999
Money: A Suicide Note (Amis), 1985
Money, Money, Money (Wagoner), 1955
Moneychangers (Hailey), 1975
Monique (Hauser), 1934
Monk Dawson (Read), 1970
Monkey Grip (Garner), 1981
Monkey King (Mo), 1980
Monkeys (Minot), 1986
Monkeys in the Dark (d'Alpuget), 1980
Monkfish Moon (s Gunesekera), 1992
Monopolies of Loss (s Mars-Jones), 1993
Monsieur Teste in America and Other Instances of Realism (s Codrescu), 1987
Montezuma's Man (Charyn), 1993
Month of Sundays (Updike), 1975
Moo (Smiley), 1995
Moo Pak (Josipovici), 1995
Moon Deluxe (s Barthelme), 1984
Moon Lake and Other Stories (s Welty), 1980
Moon over Minneapolis (s Weldon), 1991
Moon Palace (Auster), 1990
Moon Tiger (Lively), 1988
Mooncranker's Gift (Unsworth), 1974
Moonferns and Starsongs (s Silverberg, as Knox), 1971
Moonlight into Marzipan (Gupta), 1995
Moonlite (Foster), 1987
Moons of Jupiter (s Munro), 1983
Moonshine War (Leonard), 1970
Moorcock's Book of Martyrs (s Moorcock, as Bradbury, E.), 1976
Moor's Last Sigh (Rushdie), 1995
Morality Play (Unsworth), 1995
More Die of Heartbreak (Bellow), 1987
More Tales I Tell My Mother (s Fairbairns), 1987
Moreau's Other Island (Aldiss), 1980
Morgan's Passing (Tyler), 1980
Morning Face (Anand), 1986
Morning for Flamingoes (Burke), 1993
Morning in Antibes (Knowles), 1962
Moroccan Traffic (Dunnett), 1991
Mort (Pratchett), 1987
Mortality and Mercy in Vienna (s Pynchon), 1976
Mortmere Stories (s Upward), 1994
Mosaic Man (Sukenick), 1999
Mosby's Memoirs and Other Stories (s Bellow), 1969
Moscow Gold (Caute), 1980
Moses, Prince of Egypt (Fast, as Cunningham), 1959
Moses the Lawgiver (Keneally), 1975
Mosquito (Jones), 1999
Mosquito Coast (Theroux), 1982
Moth (Sallis), 1993
Mother and Two Daughters (Godwin), 1982
Mother Can You Hear Me? (Forster), 1979
Mother Is a Country: A Popular Fantasy (Perutz), 1968
Mother London (Moorcock, as Bradbury, E.), 1989
Mother Night (Vonnegut), 1968
Mother Russia (Rubens), 1992
Motherless Brooklyn (Lethem), 1999
Mothers and Daughters (Hunter), 1961
Mothers' Boys (Forster), 1994
Mothers, Daughters (See, as Highland), 1977
Mother's Girl (Feinstein), 1988
Mother's Kisses (Friedman), 1965
Mothersill and the Foxes (Williams), 1975
Moths and Other Stories (s Viramontes), 1985
Motorbike (Kops), 1962
Mountains of Majipoor (Silverberg, as Knox), 1995
Mourning Thief and Other Stories (s Hogan), 1987
Movie Dreams (Scott), 1995
Movies (s Dixon), 1983
Moving Mars (Bear), 1993
Moving On (McMurtry), 1971
Moving Out (Garner), 1983
Moving Parts (Katz), 1977
Moving Pictures (Pratchett), 1990
Mugger (Hunter), 1959
Mulching of America (Crews), 1995
Mules (s Spencer), 1982
Mulligan Stew (Sorrentino), 1980
Multiple Effects of Rainshadow (Astley), 1996
Multiple Orgasms (s Markfield), 1977
Mum (Eldred-Grigg), 1995
Mum and Mr. Armitage: Selected Stories (s Bainbridge), 1987
Mumbo-Jumbo (Reed), 1989
Mummy Case (Mertz, as Michaels), 1986
Mummy: or Ramses the Damned (Rice, as Roquelaure), 1989
Munchmeyer, and Prospero on the Island (Thomas), 1972
Murder at Monticello; or, Old Sins (Brown), 1994
Murder Being Once Done (Rendell, as Vine), 1972
Murder in Mount Holly (Theroux), 1969
Murder in the Dark: Short Fictions and Prose Poems (s Atwood), 1984
Murder in the Navy (Hunter), 1955
Murder of Aziz Khan (Ghose), 1969
Murder of Quality (le Carré), 1963
Murder on the Prowl (Brown), 1998
Murder, She Meowed (Brown), 1996

Murderer (Heath), 1992
Murders of Richard III (Mertz, as Michaels), 1989
Muriel at Metropolitan (Tlali), 1979
Museum Guard (Norman), 1998
Museums and Women and Other Stories (s Updike), 1973
Music and Silence (Tremain), 2000
Music from Spain (s Welty), 1948
Music of Chance (Auster), 1991
Music on Clinton Street (McCabe), 1986
Music School (s Updike), 1967
Musical Chairs (Friedman), 1991
Mustian (Price), 1983
Mutant Season (Silverberg, as Knox), 1989
Mutual Friend (Busch), 1978
Mutuwhenua: The Moon Sleeps (Grace), 1988
My Amputations (Major), 1986
My Brother, My Executioner (Sionil Jose), 1979
My Brother Tom (Aldridge), 1966
My Chocolate Redeemer (Hope), 1989
My Experiences in the Third World War (s Moorcock, as Bradbury, E.), 1980
My Father More or Less (Baumbach), 1982
My Father's Moon (Jolley), 1989
My First Satyrnalia (Rumaker), 1981
My Friend Judas (Sinclair), 1961
My Glorious Brothers (Fast, as Cunningham), 1950
My Hard Heart: Selected Fiction (s Garner), 1998
My Heart Is Broken: Eight Stories and a Short Novel (s Gallant), 1964
My Heart Laid Bare (Oates, as Smith, R.), 1998
My Idea of Fun: A Cautionary Tale (Self), 1994
My Juliet (Bradley), 2000
My Life as a Man (Roth), 1974
My Life, Starring Dara Falcon (Beattie), 1997
My Lovely Enemy (Wiebe), 1983
My Mother, the Detective: The Complete "Mom" Short Stories (s Yaffe), 1997
My Mother's Pearl Necklace (s Plante), 1987
My Name Is Paradiso (McNeish), 1995
My Organic Uncle and Other Stories (s Pownall), 1976
My Other Life (Theroux), 1996
My Present Age (Vanderhaeghe), 1985
My Pretty Pony (s King), 1989
My Secret History (Theroux), 1989
My Silver Shoes (Dunn), 1996
My Sister's Keeper (Cassill), 1961
My Son's Story (Gordimer), 1990
My Summer with George (French), 1996
My True Faces (Nahal), 1973
My Turn Next (Graham), 1942
Myal (Brodber), 1988
Myra Breckinridge (Vidal, as Box), 1968
Myron (Vidal, as Box), 1975
Mysteries of Motion (Calisher), 1983
Mysteries of Winterthurn (Oates, as Smith, R.), 1984
Mystic Masseur (Naipaul), 1959
Myths of the Near Future (s Ballard), 1982

'n Emmertjie wyn: 'n versameling dopstories (s Brink), 1981
Nail on the Head (s Boylan), 1985
Naive and Sentimental Lover (le Carré), 1972
Naked and the Dead (Mailer), 1998
Naked in Garden Hills (Crews), 1969
Naked Morning (Cassill), 1957
Naked Needle (Farah), 1976
Naked Once More (Mertz, as Michaels), 1990
Name Me Nobody (Yamanaka), 1999
Name of the World (Johnson), 2000
Names (DeLillo), 1983
Names and Faces of Heroes (s Price), 1963
Names of the Dead (O'Nan), 1996
Naming the Spirits (Thornton), 1995
Narcissa and Other Fables (s Auchincloss), 1983
Narrowing Stream (Mortimer), 1989
Nashville 1864: The Dying of the Light: A Novel (Jones), 1997
Natalie Natalia (Mosley), 1971
National Winner (Humphreys), 1971
Native (Plante), 1988
Native Ground (s Callow), 1959
Native Moment (West), 1961
Native Speaker (Lee), 1995
Natives (s Humphreys), 1968
Natives of My Person (Lamming), 1972
Natural Curiosity (Drabble), 1989
Natural History (Howard), 1992
Natural Selection (Barthelme), 1990
Natural Shocks (Stern), 1978
Nature of Blood (Phillips), 1997
Nature of Passion (Jhabvala), 1957
Navigation of a Rainmaker: An Apocalyptic Vision of War-Torn Africa (Mahjoub), 1989
Nazi Lady: The Diaries of Elisabeth von Stahlenberg 1933–1948 (Freeman), 1978
Neanderthal Planet (s Aldiss), 1970
Necessary End (Robinson), 1992
Necessary Treasons (Kelly), 1985
Necessity of Anti-Semitism (Raphael), 1998
Nectar in a Sieve (Markandaya), 1955
Needful Things (King), 1991
Needle (King), 1976
Needle in a Timestack (s Silverberg, as Knox), 1979
Needle's Eye (Drabble), 1972
Negotiator (Forsyth), 1989
Neighbors (Berger), 1981
Nelly's Version (Figes), 1988
Neon Rain (Burke), 1989
Nephew (Purdy), 1961
Nerve (Bragg), 1971
Nerve (Francis), 1964
Net of Jewels (Gilchrist), 1992
Neumiller Stories (s Woiwode), 1989
Neuromancer (Gibson), 1994
Never Again (King), 1948
Never Die (Hannah), 1991
Never Look Back (Glanville), 1980
Nevèrÿona; or, The Tale of Signs and Cities (Delany), 1989
New Arrivals, Old Encounters: Twelve Stories (s Aldiss), 1980
New Confessions (Boyd), 1988
New Country (s Cowan), 1976
New Dominion (Jhabvala), 1972

New Girl Friend (s Rendell, as Vine), 1986
New Lease of Death (Rendell, as Vine), 1967
New Net Goes Fishing (s Ihimaera), 1978
New Orleans of Possibilities (s Madden), 1982
New Shirt (Hogan), 1986
New Springtime (Silverberg, as Knox), 1990
New Town (Jones), 1953
New World (s Banks), 1978
New York Trilogy (Auster), 1990
New Yorkers (Calisher), 1970
New Zealanders: A Sequence of Stories (s Shadbolt), 1961
News (Delbanco), 1970
News from Ireland and Other Stories (s Trevor), 1986
News from Nowhere (Caute), 1986
News from the City of the Sun (Colegate), 1979
News from the Sun (s Ballard), 1982
News of the Spirit (Smith), 1997
Newspaper of Claremont Street (Jolley), 1988
Newsreel (Faust), 1980
Newton Letter: An Interlude (Banville), 1987
Next (Brooke-Rose), 1998
Next of Kin (Barstow), 1991
Next of Kin (Trollope), 1996
Next Stop the Stars (s Silverberg, as Knox), 1979
Next to Nature, Art (Lively), 1982
Niccolò Rising (Dunnett), 1986
Nice Change (Bawden), 1997
Nice Friendly Town (Hanley, as Calvin), 1967
Nice Murder for Mom (Yaffe), 1988
Nice Work (Lodge), 1989
Nicholson at Large (Just), 1975
Nick the Greek (Petrakis), 1980
Night (O'Brien), 1973
Night and Other Stories (s Upward), 1967
Night at the Movies; or, You Must Remember This (s Coover), 1987
Night-Book (Kotzwinkle), 1974
Night Geometry and the Garscadden Trains (s Kennedy), 1990
Night in Question: Stories (s Wolff), 1996
Night in Tunisia and Other Stories (s Jordan), 1979
Night Inspector (Busch), 1999
Night Journey (Graham), 1968
Night Journey (Guerard), 1951
Night Manager (le Carré), 1993
Night of Four Hundred Rabbits (Mertz, as Michaels), 1971
Night of Wenceslas (Davidson), 1961
Night School (Cassill), 1961
Night Shift (Bolger), 1985
Night Shift (s King), 1978
Night-Side (s Oates, as Smith, R.), 1979
Night Song (Williams), 1962
Night Train (Amis), 1997
Night Travellers (Spencer), 1991
Night We Ate the Sparrow: A Memoir and Fourteen Stories (s Lurie), 1985
Night Without Stars (Graham), 1950
Nightfall (Silverberg, as Knox), 1990
Nightlines (Jordan), 1995
Nightlines (s McGahern), 1971
Nightmares & Dreamscapes (s King), 1993
Nights at the Alexandra (s Trevor), 1987
Nights below Station Street (Richards), 1987
Nights in the Gardens of Spain (Ihimaera), 1995
Nights with Grace (Scott), 1991
Nightspawn (Banville), 1971
Nightwatchmen (Hannah), 1973
Nightwings (Silverberg, as Knox), 1972
NIMROD Conspiracy (Jones), 1999
Nine African Stories (s Lessing), 1968
Nine Billion Names of God: The Best Short Stories of Arthur C. Clarke (s Clarke), 1967
Nine Men Who Laughed (s Clarke), 1986
Nine Months in the Life of an Old Maid (Rossner), 1977
Nine Women (s Grau), 1986
1982, Janine (Gray), 1984
1915: A Novel (McDonald), 1980
1968: A Short Novel, An Urban Idyll, Five Stories, and Two Trade Notes (s Stern), 1971
Ninety Double Martinis (Hinde), 1963
98.6 (Sukenick), 1975
Ninety-Two in the Shade (McGuane), 1974
NO (Major), 1973
No Comebacks: Collected Short Stories (s Forsyth), 1982
No Country for Young Men (O'Faolain), 1987
No Cure for Love (Robinson), 1995
No Exit: An Adventure (Graham), 1940
No Longer at Ease (Achebe), 1961
No More Dying Then (Rendell, as Vine), 1972
No More into the Garden (Watmough), 1978
No More Mister Nice Guy (Jacobson), 1998
No Name in the Street (Tindall), 1959
No New Land (Vassanji), 1991
No Night Is Too Long (Rendell, as Vine), 1994
No Place for an Angel (Spencer), 1968
No Reck'ning Made (Greenberg), 1993
No Relief (s Dixon), 1976
No Retreat (Bowen), 1994
No Saddles for Kangaroos (de Boissière), 1964
No Sweetness Here (s Aidoo), 1971
No Time to Be Young (Jones), 1952
No Way To Treat a Lady (Goldman), 1968
No Witchcraft for Sale: Stories and Short Novels (s Lessing), 1956
No Word of Love (s Barker), 1985
Noah's Ark (Trapido), 1985
Noble Rot: Stories 1949–1988 (s Stern), 1989
Nobody Does You Any Favors (Yaffe), 1966
Nobody Knew They Were There (Hunter), 1972
Nobody's Angel (McGuane), 1982
Nobody's Fault (Jones), 1977
Nocturne (St. Aubin de Teran), 1993
Nocturnes for the King of Naples (White), 1980
Nog (Wurlitzer), 1969
Noise from the Zoo (s Elliott), 1991
Non-Stop (Aldiss), 1958
None Genuine Without This Signature (s Hood), 1980
None to Accompany Me (Gordimer), 1994
Noorjehan and Other Stories (s Essop), 1990
Nor Any Country (St. Omer), 1969
North American Education (s Blaise), 1973

North of Hope (Hassler), 1990
North South West: Three Novellas (s Foster), 1973
North Wind (Jones), 1996
Northern Lights (Norman), 1987
Northern Lights (O'Brien), 1975
Not a Word about Nightingales (Howard), 1962
Not Being Miriam (Campbell), 1989
Not by the Door (Hall), 1954
Not for Publication and Other Stories (s Gordimer), 1965
Not Just for Christmas (Doyle), 1999
Not Not While the Giro and Other Stories (s Kelman), 1983
Not Safe After Dark and Other Stories (s Robinson), 1998
Not That Sort of Girl (Wesley), 1988
Not to Disturb (Spark), 1972
Not Wanted on the Voyage (Findley), 1985
Nothing But Blue Skies (McGuane), 1992
Nothing But the Best (Hanley, as Calvin), 1964
Nothing But the Night (Yaffe), 1958
Nothing Happens in Carmincross (Kiely), 1985
Nothing Is Black (Madden), 1994
Nothing Missing But the Samovar and Other Stories (s Lively), 1978
Nova (Delany), 1969
Novelette with Other Stories (s Barker), 1951
Novellas of Hortense Calisher (Calisher), 1997
Novels of Muriel Spark (Spark), 1995
Novotny's Pain (s Roth), 1980
Now (Josipovici), 1998
Now Playing in Canterbury (Bourjaily), 1976
Now That You're Back (s Kennedy), 1994
Now You Know (Frayn), 1993
Nowhere (Berger), 1986
Nowhere City (Lurie), 1966
Nowhere Man (Markandaya), 1973
Nuclear Age (O'Brien), 1986
Numbers (Rechy), 1967
Nurses' Quarters (Cassill), 1962

O Master Caliban! (Gotlieb), 1976
O Singapore!: Stories in Celebration (s Lim), 1989
Oak and the Ram (Moorcock, as Bradbury, E.), 1973
Obasan (Kogawa), 1994
Obbligato (Raphael), 1956
Obedient Wife (O'Faolain), 1985
Obi (Munonye), 1969
Occam's Razor (Duffy), 1993
Occasion for Loving (Gordimer), 1963
Occasion of Sin (Billington), 1983
Occupation (Caute), 1972
October Country (s Bradbury), 1996
Odd Flamingo (Bawden), 1954
Odd Girl Out (Howard), 1972
Odd Number (Sorrentino), 1985
Odd Woman (Godwin), 1975
Odds Against (Francis), 1966
Odds On (Crichton, as Lange), 1966
Odessa File (Forsyth), 1972
Odyssey of Kostas Volakis (Petrakis), 1963
Of Age and Innocence (Lamming), 1981
Of Love and Dust (Gaines), 1968
Of Many Men (Aldridge), 1946
Of Space-Time and the River (Benford), 1985
Of Such Small Differences (Greenberg), 1988
Of the Farm (Updike), 1965
Of Time and Stars: The Worlds of Arthur C. Clarke (s Clarke), 1972
Of Wives, Talismans and the Dead (s Aniebo), 1983
Off Keck Road (Simpson), 2000
Office Life (Waterhouse), 1978
Office Politics (Sheed), 1967
Oil Man of Obange (Munonye), 1971
O.K.: The Corral, the Earps, and Doc Holliday (West), 2000
Ola (Wendt), 1995
Old and New (s Narayan), 1981
Old Army Game: A Novel and Stories (Garrett), 1994
Old Boys (Trevor), 1964
Old Jest (Johnston), 1980
Old Man and Me (Dundy), 1964
Old Man at the Railroad Crossing and Other Tales (s Maxwell), 1966
Old Pub Near the Angel (s Kelman), 1973
Old Scores (Delbanco), 1997
Old Scores (Raphael), 1995
Old Soldier (Bourjaily), 1990
Old Soldiers (Bailey), 1980
Old Woman and the Cow (Anand), 1960
Oldest Man, and Other Timeless Stories (s Kotzwinkle), 1971
Olinger Stories: A Selection (s Updike), 1964
Olivia; or, The Weight of the Past (Rossner), 1994
Olt (Gangemi), 1969
Olvidon and Other Stories (s Sionil Jose), 1988
Olympian (Glanville), 1969
Omensetter's Luck (Gass), 1967
On Distant Ground (Butler), 1985
On Keeping Women (Calisher), 1977
On Margate Sands (Kops), 1978
On Strike Against God (Russ), 1987
On the Big Wind (Madden), 1980
On the Contrary (Brink), 1994
On the Darkening Green (Charyn), 1965
On the Eve of Uncertain Tomorrows (s Bissoondath), 1990
On the Gulf (s Spencer), 1991
On the Last Day (Jones), 1958
On the Occasion of My Last Afternoon (Gibbons), 1998
On the River Styx and Other Stories (s Matthiessen), 1989
On the Road with the Archangel (Buechner), 1997
On the Third Day (Read), 1991
On the Yankee Station and Other Stories (s Boyd), 1988
On with the Story: Stories (s Barth), 1996
Once in Europa (Berger), 1989
Once Upon a Droshky (Charyn), 1964
Once Upon a Time: A Floating Opera (Barth), 1994
Once Were Warriors (Duff), 1995
One Across, Two Down (Rendell, as Vine), 1971
One and Only (King), 1994
One by One in the Darkness (Madden), 1996
One Day's Perfect Weather: More Twice Told Tales (s Stern), 1999
One Flew over the Cuckoo's Nest (Kesey), 1963
One Generation (Heath), 1981

One Good Story, That One (s King), 1993
One Hundred Dollar Misunderstanding (Gover), 1962
158-Pound Marriage (Irving), 1980
110 Shanghai Road (See, as Highland), 1986
One Is a Wanderer: Selected Stories (s King), 1986
One Last Glimpse (Aldridge), 1977
One Night in Winter (Massie), 1984
One Night Out Stealing (Duff), 1992
One of Our Asteroids Is Missing (Silverberg, as Knox), 1964
One of the Wattle Birds (Anderson), 1994
One Way Ticket (s Levine), 1961
Onion Eaters (Donleavy), 1971
Only (Groom), 1984
Only Child: A Simple Story of Heaven and Hell (Dunn), 1978
Only Children (Lurie), 1979
Only Problem (Spark), 1984
Only Son (Munonye), 1966
Only When I Larf (Deighton), 1968
Only You Can Save Mankind (Pratchett), 1992
Oom Kootjie Emmer (s Brink), 1973
Oom Kootjie Emmer en die nuwe bedeling: 'n stinkstorie (s Brink), 1983
Open Heart (Buechner), 1972
Open Secrets (Humphreys), 1988
Open Secrets (s Munro), 1994
Open Swimmer (Winton), 1982
Open to the Public: New and Collected Stories (s Spark), 1997
Opening Nights (Burroway), 1985
Operation Shylock: A Confession (Roth), 1993
Operation Wandering Soul (Powers), 1994
Opium General and Other Stories (s Moorcock, as Bradbury, E.), 1984
Opportunity of a Lifetime (Smith), 1980
Optimist (Gold), 1959
Optimist's Daughter (Welty), 1973
Or Else, the Lightning God and Other Stories (s Lim), 1980
Oracles and Miracles (Eldred-Grigg), 1987
Oral History (Smith), 1983
Orange Fish (s Shields), 1990
Orange Horses (s Kelly), 1990
Oranges Are Not the Only Fruit (Winterson), 1987
Orchard Keeper (McCarthy), 1994
Orchard Street (Gee), 1998
Orchard Thieves (Jolley), 1995
Orchestra and Beginners (Raphael), 1968
Orders of Chivalry (Vansittart), 1959
Ordinary Love and Good Will (s Smiley), 1990
Ordinary Lunacy (Anderson), 1964
Orealla (Heath), 1984
Orgie (Brink), 1965
Origin of the Brunists (Coover), 2000
Origin of Waves (Clarke), 1997
Original Bliss (Kennedy), 1997
Original Sin (James), 1995
Original Sins (Alther), 1981
Orlando at the Brazen Threshold (Colegate), 1971
Orlando King (Colegate), 1969
Orlando Trilogy (Colegate), 1984
Orphan's Tale (Neugeboren), 1976
Orrie's Story (Berger), 1990
Orsinian Tales (s Le Guin), 1977
Oscar and Lucinda (Carey), 1988
Osiris Rising: A Novel of Africa Past, Present, and Future (Armah), 1995
Other Halves (McCauley), 1985
Other Men's Daughters (Stern), 1974
Other Names (Fairbairns), 1998
Other Paris (s Gallant), 1957
Other People: A Mystery Story (Amis), 1981
Other People's Children (Trollope), 1999
Other People's Lives (s Kaplan), 1975
Other People's Worlds (Trevor), 1981
Other Side (Gordon), 1990
Other Side (Middleton), 1980
Other Side of the Fire (Ellis), 1983
Other Side of the Sky (s Clarke), 1961
Other Women (Alther), 1985
Our Father (French), 1995
Our Father (Hinde), 1976
Our Father (Rubens), 1987
Our Fathers (O'Hagan), 1999
Our Game (le Carré), 1995
Our Gang (Starring Tricky and His Friends) (Roth), 1971
Our House in the Last World (Hijuelos), 1983
Our Lady of Babylon (Rechy), 1996
Our Sister Killjoy; or, Reflections from a Black-Eyed Squint (Aidoo), 1979
Our Song (Waterhouse), 1988
Our Sunshine (Drewe), 1991
Out (Brooke-Rose), 1964
Out (Sukenick), 1973
Out of India: Selected Stories (s Jhabvala), 1987
Out of Ireland (Koch), 1999
Out of Sight (Leonard), 1996
Out of the Shelter (Lodge), 1989
Out of This World (Swift), 1988
Outcasts (Becker), 1967
Outer Dark (McCarthy), 1994
Outerbridge Reach (Stone), 1992
Outfoxed (Brown), 2000
Outlander (s Rule), 1981
Outrageous Behaviour: Best Stories (s Lurie), 1985
Outside Ireland: Selected Stories (s Trevor), 1995
Outside the House of Baal (Humphreys), 1965
Over by the River and Other Stories (s Maxwell), 1977
Over the Fence Is Out (Duckworth), 1969
Overhead in a Balloon: Stories of Paris (s Gallant), 1987
Overload (Hailey), 1979
Overloaded Man (s Ballard), 1967
Overseer (Vansittart), 1949
Owls Do Cry (Frame), 1961
Oxbridge Blues (s Raphael), 1984
Oxbridge Blues and Other Stories (s Raphael), 1984
Oxherding Tale (Johnson), 1995
Oyster (Hospital), 1998
Oyster Is a Wealthy Beast (s Purdy), 1967
O-Zone (Theroux), 1986

Pacific Edge (Robinson), 1990
Pacific Highway (Wilding), 1982

Pack of Cards: Stories 1978–86 (s Lively), 1989
Pack of Lies (Sorrentino), 1997
Packages (s Stern), 1980
Paddy Clarke Ha Ha Ha (Doyle), 1993
Paddy's Puzzle (Kidman), 1985
Pagan Babies (Leonard), 2000
Pagan Days (Rumaker), 1999
Pagan Place (O'Brien), 1970
Pagan Rabbi and Other Stories (s Ozick), 1972
Painted Desert (Barthelme), 1995
Painted Devil (Billington), 1975
Painted Turtle: Woman with Guitar (Major), 1988
Painter of Our Time (Berger), 1959
Painter of Signs (Narayan), 1977
Painter's Confessions (Callow), 1989
Pair from Space (Silverberg, as Knox), 1965
Palace (St. Aubin de Teran), 1999
Palace of Strangers (Masters), 1971
Palace of the Peacock (Harris), 1960
Pale Blue Crochet Coathanger Cover (Foster), 1988
Pale View of Hills (Ishiguro), 1982
Palms and Minarets: Selected Stories (s O'Sullivan), 1992
Palomino (Jolley), 1987
Pan Beat (Jones), 1973
Panama (McGuane), 1978
Panna Maria (Charyn), 1982
Paper Dragon (Hunter), 1967
Parable of the Sower (Butler), 1995
Parable of the Talents (Butler), 1998
Parachutes and Kisses (Jong), 1984
Paradise (Gurnah), 1994
Paradise (Morrison), 1998
Paradise Man (Charyn), 1988
Paradise News (Lodge), 1991
Paradise Postponed (Mortimer), 1985
Paradox Players (Duffy), 1968
Paragon (Knowles), 1971
Paragon Walk (Perry), 1981
Paragraphs (s Stephens), 1974
Paraguayan Experiment (Wilding), 1985
Paremata (Knox), 1989
Parents From Space (Bowering), 1994
Paris Rats in E.L.A (s Viramontes), 1993
Park (Forster), 1968
Park City: New and Selected Stories (s Beattie), 1998
Parsecs and Parables (s Silverberg, as Knox), 1973
Parsifal (Vansittart), 1989
Parson Harding's Daughter (Trollope), 1979
Part of the Furniture (Wesley), 1996
Partisans (Matthiessen), 1956
Partner (Grisham), 1997
Partners (Auchincloss), 1974
Partners (Kops), 1975
Partnership (Unsworth), 1966
Pascali's Island (Unsworth), 1980
Pass (Savage), 1944
Passage through Gehenna (Jones), 1978
Passenger (Keneally), 1979
Passing On (Lively), 1990
Passion (Winterson), 1988
Passionate Man (Trollope), 1990
Passionate Past of Gloria Gaye (Kops), 1972
Passport to Eternity and Other Stories (s Ballard), 1963
Past (Jordan), 1980
Past Must Alter (Guerard), 1938
Past Reason Hated (Robinson), 1993
Pastimes of a Red Summer (Vansittart), 1969
Patchwork Planet (Tyler), 1998
Patrimonies (s Cassill), 1988
Patriot (Read), 1996
Patriot for Hire (Sinclair), 1978
Patriot's Dream (Mertz, as Michaels), 1978
Patternmaster (Butler), 1976
Pawing through the Past (Brown), 2000
Pawn in Frankincense (Dunnett), 1997
Pay Dirt, or, Adventures at Ash Lawn (Brown), 1995
Peace Breaks Out (Knowles), 1981
Peace Shall Destroy Many (Wiebe), 1964
Peacock Cry (Mulkerns), 1954
Peacocks: And Other Stories (s Anderson), 1997
Peacock's Tail (Hoagland), 1965
Peeping Tom (Jacobson), 1985
Pegnitz Junction: A Novella and Five Short Stories (s Gallant), 1974
Pelican Brief (Grisham), 1992
Penelope (Fast, as Cunningham), 1966
Penelope's Hat (Frame), 1991
Penelope's Island (McNeish), 1990
Penny Wars (Baker), 1969
Pentecost Alley (Perry), 1996
People Will Always Be Kind (Sheed), 1974
People in Glass Houses: Portraits from Organization Life (Hazzard), 1967
Percy, Bob, and Assenpoop (Baker), 1999
Perfect Happiness (Billington), 1996
Perfect Happiness (Lively), 1984
Perfect Spy (le Carré), 1986
Perfect Woman (Slaughter), 1985
Perfectionists (Godwin), 1971
Perfidia (Rossner), 1997
Pericles on 31st Street (s Petrakis), 1965
Permanent Errors (s Price), 1971
Perpetual Motion (Gibson), 1982
Persian Nights (Johnson), 1987
Pet Sematary (King), 1983
Petals of Blood (Ngugi wa Thiong'o), 1978
Pete and Shirley: The Great Tar Heel Novel (Edgerton), 1995
Peter Smart's Confessions (Bailey), 1977
Petrakis Reader (s Petrakis), 1978
Phallic Forest (s Wilding), 1978
Phantom of Manhattan (Forsyth), 1999
Philadelphia Fire (Wideman), 1991
Phineas: Six Stories (s Knowles), 1968
Phoenix Café (Jones), 1998
Phoenix in Obsidian (Moorcock, as Bradbury, E.), 1970
Photocopies (Berger), 1996
Photographs (Wendt), 1995
Phyllis (Fast, as Cunningham), 1962
Piano Man's Daughter (Findley), 1995
Picnic on Paradise (Russ), 1969

Picture Palace: A Novel (Theroux), 1978
Picturegoers (Lodge), 1960
Pictures from an Exhibition (s Gordon), 1970
Pictures of the Journey Back (Matthews), 1973
Picturing Will (Beattie), 1991
Piece of My Heart (Ford), 1987
Piece of the Night (Roberts), 1978
Pig Earth (Berger), 1980
Pigeon Feathers and Other Stories (s Updike), 1962
Pigs in Heaven (Kingsolver), 1993
Pilgermann (Hoban), 1983
Pilgrim (Findley), 1999
Pilgrim's Way (Gurnah), 1988
Pillars of Gold (Ellis), 2000
Pilot's Wife (Shreve), 1998
Pinocchio in Venice (s Coover), 1991
Pinocchio's Nose (Charyn), 1983
Place Among People (Hall), 1975
Place at Whitton (Keneally), 1965
Place for Outlaws (Wier), 1989
Place in England (Bragg), 1971
Place in Flowers Where Pollen Rests (West), 1988
Place in the City (Fast, as Cunningham), 1937
Place Like Home (Hinde), 1962
Place of Birth (s Farmer), 1990
Place of Greater Safety (Mantel), 1993
Place to Die (s Bowering), 1973
Place to Stand (Middleton), 1992
Plagiarized Material (s Oates, as Smith, R.), 1974
Plague Dogs (Adams), 1978
Plains (Murnane), 1985
Planet Killers (Silverberg, as Knox), 1959
Planet of Death (Silverberg, as Knox), 1967
Planet of Exile (Le Guin), 1972
Planet on the Table (s Robinson), 1987
Plans for Departure (Sahgal), 1986
Platinum and Other Stories (s Sionil Jose), 1983
Platitudes (Ellis), 1988
Plato Papers: A Prophecy (Ackroyd), 2000
Play and Other Stories (s Dixon), 1988
Play It as It Lays (Didion), 1971
Player Piano (Vonnegut), 1953
Players (DeLillo), 1991
Playing the Game (Lelchuk), 1995
Playland (Dunne), 1995
Playmaker (Keneally), 1987
Pleasure City (Markandaya), 1982
Pleasure-Dome (Madden), 1979
Pledge for the Earth (Callow), 1960
Plot Against Earth (Silverberg, as Knox), 1959
Plowing the Dark (Powers), 2000
Plumbum (Foster), 1983
Plus (McElroy), 1977
Po-on (Sionil Jose), 1985
Pocock and Pitt (Baker), 1972
Poet and Dancer (Jhabvala), 1993
Point of Darkness: A Sam Dean Mystery (Phillips), 1995
Poison (Hunter), 1987
Poison Chasers (Hanley, as Calvin), 1971
Poison Pen (Garrett), 1986
Poisoned Kiss and Other Stories from the Portuguese (s Oates, as Smith, R.), 1976
Poisonwood Bible (Kingsolver), 1998
Polaris and Other Stories (s Weldon), 1989
Political Fable (s Coover), 1980
Polly's Ghost: A Novel (Frucht), 2000
Polonaise (Read), 1976
Pomare (Knox), 1994
Pomeroy (Castro), 1991
Ponder Heart (Welty), 1954
Ponsonby Post (Rubens), 1978
Poor Cousin Evelyn (s Yaffe), 1952
Poor Cow (Dunn), 1967
Poor Devils (Ely), 1970
Poor Things (Gray), 1993
Poorboy at the Party (Gover), 1966
Poorhouse Fair (Updike), 1959
Pope's Rhinoceros (Norfolk), 1996
Poppa John (Woiwode), 1981
Porcupine (Barnes, as Kavanagh), 1992
Pork Butcher (Hughes), 1985
Pornographer (McGahern), 1979
Porterhouse Blue (Sharpe), 1974
Portnoy's Complaint (Roth), 1969
Portrait in Brownstone (Auchincloss), 1962
Portrait of a Romantic (Millhauser), 1977
Portrait of the Artist's Wife (Anderson), 1993
Posh (Katz), 1971
Positronic Man (Silverberg, as Knox), 1993
Possessing the Secret of Joy (Walker), 1992
Possession (Delbanco), 1977
Possession (Markandaya), 1963
Postcard from "The Endless Short Story" (s Sukenick), 1974
Postcards (Proulx), 1993
Postcards from Surfers (s Garner), 1989
Posthumous Sketch (s Oates, as Smith, R.), 1973
Potiki (Grace), 1995
Pouliuli (Wendt), 1987
Pounamu, Pounamu (s Ihimaera), 1973
Poverty Castle (Jenkins), 1991
Power (Fast, as Cunningham), 1963
Power and Light (Hannah), 1983
Power of Darkness (McGahern), 1991
Power of Darkness and Other Stories (s Anand), 1958
Power of the Dog (Savage), 1967
PowerBook (Winterson), 2000
Powerhouse (Jones), 1997
Powers of Attorney (s Auchincloss), 1963
Practical Heart (s Gurganis), 1993
Practical Magic (Hoffman), 1995
Prague Orgy (Roth), 1985
Praisesong for the Widow (Marshall), 1983
Praxis (Weldon), 1978
Prayer for Owen Meany (Irving), 1989
Prayer for the Dying (O'Nan), 1999
Precious (Glover), 1984
Precious Gift (Bowen), 1992
Prelude to Mars (Clarke), 1965
Prelude to Space (Clarke), 1953
Presence of Music: Three Novellas (s Shadbolt), 1967

Present (Josipovici), 1975
President (Cassill), 1964
President's Child (Weldon), 1983
Pretenders (Sionil Jose), 1962
Pretenders and Eight Short Stories (s Sionil Jose), 1962
Pretty Boy Floyd (McMurtry), 1995
Pretty Leslie (Cassill), 1964
Price of Coal (Hines), 1979
Price of Diamonds (Jacobson), 1958
Pricksongs and Descants (s Coover), 2000
Pride (Wharton), 1986
Primal Urge (Aldiss), 1967
Prime Minister (Clarke), 1978
Prime of Miss Jean Brodie (Spark), 1962
Prince Ishmael (Hauser), 1964
Prince of Darkness (Mertz, as Michaels), 1971
Prince of Tides (Conroy), 1986
Princess Bride (Goldman), 1975
Printer's Devil (Moorcock, as Bradbury, E.), 1966
Prisoner's Dilemma (Powers), 1989
Prissy (Hanley, as Calvin), 1978
Private Life of an Indian Prince (Anand), 1970
Private Life of Axie Reed (Knowles), 1986
Private Papers (Forster), 1986
Private Parts and Other Tales (s Hope), 1982
Private View (Brookner), 1994
Privileged Conversation (Hunter), 1996
Proceedings of the Rabble (Mirsky), 1970
Professor of Desire (Roth), 1978
Professor's Daughter (Read), 1971
Progress of Love (s Munro), 1987
Project (Sinclair), 1960
Promise of Rest (Price), 1995
Promised Land (Willis), 1997
Pronto (Leonard), 1993
Proof (Francis), 1985
Proper Marriage (Lessing), 1954
Property Of (Hoffman), 1978
Prospect Before Us (Gold), 1954
Protective Footwear: Stories and Fables by George Bowering (s Bowering), 1978
Proud and the Free (Fast, as Cunningham), 1952
Proud Empires (Clarke), 1986
Proud Garments (Anderson), 1996
Providence (Brookner), 1984
Provinces of Night (Gay), 2001
Prowler (Campbell), 1999
Prowlers (Gee), 1987
Proxopera (Kiely), 1987
Psyche and the Hurricane (Roberts), 1991
Psychlone (Bear), 1979
Public Burning (Coover), 1978
Public Image (Spark), 1968
Puffball (Weldon), 1980
Pulling Faces (Duckworth), 1987
Punishments (King), 1990
Puppeteer (Kroetsch), 1993
Pure Land (Foster), 1985
Purple America (Moody), 1997
Purple Cane Road (Burke), 2000
Pursuit of Happiness (Jones), 1976
Pursuit of the Prodigal (Auchincloss), 1960
Pusher (Hunter), 1959
Puss in Boots (Hunter), 1987
Put On by Cunning (Rendell, as Vine), 1981
Puttermesser Papers (Ozick), 1997
Putting the Boot In (Barnes, as Kavanagh), 1985
Pyramids (Pratchett), 1989

Quake (Wurlitzer), 1985
Quality of Mercy (West), 1961
Quantity Theory of Insanity: Together with Five Supporting Propositions (Self), 1995
Quarantine (Crace), 1997
Quarantine (Hasluck), 1979
Queen of Angels (Bear), 1990
Queen of Egypt (s Schaeffer), 1980
Queen of Love and Other Stories (s Scott), 1993
Queen of Springtime (Silverberg, as Knox), 1989
Queen of Stones (Tennant), 1982
Queen of Swords (Kotzwinkle), 1983
Queen of the Swords (Moorcock, as Bradbury, E.), 1971
Queenie (Calisher), 1973
Queenie (Munro), 1999
Queens' Play (Dunnett), 1997
Quest for Karla (le Carré), 1982
Quest for Tanelorn (Moorcock, as Bradbury, E.), 1976
Question (Clarke), 1999
Question of Loyalties (Massie), 1989
Quick and the Dead (Peterkiewicz), 1961
Quicker Than the Eye (Bradbury), 1996
Quiet Life (Bainbridge), 1977
Quincunx (Palliser), 1990
Quinn's Book (Kennedy), 1988
Quintet (Vansittart), 1976
Quite Contrary (s Dixon), 1979

Rabbit Angstrom: A Tetralogy (Updike), 1995
Rabbit at Rest (Updike), 1991
Rabbit Is Rich (Updike), 1982
Rabbit Redux (Updike), 1972
Rabbit, Run (Updike), 1961
Race of Scorpions (Dunnett), 1990
Race Rock (Matthiessen), 1955
Racers to the Sun (Hall), 1962
Rachel Papers (Amis), 1974
Radiant Way (Drabble), 1987
Radical Surgery (Markfield), 1991
Raditzer (Matthiessen), 1962
Rage (King), 1977
Rage of the Vulture (Unsworth), 1983
Ragged Lion (Massie), 1994
Raging Calm (Barstow), 1968
Ragtime (Doctorow), 1975
Railway Accident and Other Stories (s Upward), 1969
Railway Police, and The Last Trolley Ride (Calisher), 1966
Railway Station Man (Johnston), 1985
Rain Ascends (Kogawa), 1995
Rain Barrel and Other Stories (s Bowering), 1994

Rainbearers (Mosley), 1955
Rainbirds (Frame), 1968
Rainbow Stories (s Vollmann), 1989
Raining Tree War (Pownall), 1974
Rainmaker (Grisham), 1995
Raise High the Roof Beam, Carpenters, and Seymour: An Introduction (s Salinger), 1963
Raj (Mehta), 1989
Raker (Sinclair), 1964
Rama Revealed (Clarke), 1993
Rama II (Clarke), 1989
Raney (Edgerton), 1985
Rangoon (s Barthelme), 1970
Ransom (McInerney), 1986
Rape of Shavi (Emecheta), 1985
Rape of Tamar (Jacobson), 1970
Rappaport (Lurie), 1967
Rappaport's Revenge (Lurie), 1973
Rare and Endangered Species: A Novella and Stories (s Bausch), 1994
Rat Man of Paris (West), 1988
Rat Race (Francis), 1971
Rates of Exchange (Bradbury), 1983
Ratner's Star (DeLillo), 1991
Ratoons (Rooke), 1953
Ravelstein (Bellow), 2000
Raven's Wing (s Oates, as Smith, R.), 1987
Raw Silk (Burroway), 1977
Ray (Hannah), 1981
Reach for Tomorrow (s Clarke), 1998
Reaching Tin River (Astley), 1990
Reading the Signs (s Wilding), 1984
Real Illusions: A Selection of Family Lies and Biographical Fictions in Which the Ancestral Dead Also Play Their Part (s Haley), 1985
Real Mothers (s Thomas), 1981
Real People (Lurie), 1970
Real Presence: A Novel (Bausch), 1980
Reality and Dreams (Spark), 1997
Reality Trip and Other Implausibilities (s Silverberg, as Knox), 1972
Realms of Gold (Drabble), 1975
Reaper Man (Pratchett), 1991
Rearguard Actions (Aniebo), 1998
Rebel Powers (Bausch), 1993
Rebel to Judgment (West), 1962
Recalled to Life (Silverberg, as Knox), 1974
Reckless Eyeballing (Reed), 1989
Recovery (Middleton), 1988
Rector of Justin (Auchincloss), 1965
Rector's Wife (Trollope), 1994
Red Adam (Mirsky), 1989
Red Death (Mosley), 1991
Red-Haired Bitch (Hanley, as Calvin), 1969
Red Heart (s Scott), 1999
Red Mars (Robinson), 1993
Red the Fiend (Sorrentino), 1995
Red, White and Blue (Dunne), 1987
Red Wolf, Red Wolf (s Kinsella), 1990
Redback (Jacobson), 1987
Redemption (Fast, as Cunningham), 1999
Redemption of Elsdon Bird (Virtue), 1987
Redeye: A Western (Edgerton), 1995
Redoubt (Mavor), 1967
Redundancy of Courage (Mo), 1991
Reef (Gunesekera), 1995
Reena and Other Stories (s Marshall), 1983
Refiner's Fire: The Life and Adventures of Marshall Pearl, a Foundling (Helprin), 1977
Reflections on the Golden Bed (s Anand), 1947
Reflex (Francis), 1981
Reflex and Bone Structure (Major), 1975
Regan's Planet (Silverberg, as Knox), 1964
Regeneration (Barker), 1992
Regeneration Trilogy (Barker), 1996
Regiment of Women (Berger), 1974
Regina v. Rumpole (s Mortimer), 1981
Regular Guy (Simpson), 1996
Regulators (King), 1996
Reinhart in Love (Berger), 1963
Reinhart's Women (Berger), 1982
Relation of My Imprisonment (Banks), 1983
Relative Successes (Barker), 1984
Relatives (Plante), 1974
Reluctant Dictator (Glanville), 1952
Remains of the Day (Ishiguro), 1989
Remake (Brooke-Rose), 1996
Remake (Willis), 1995
Remaking History, and Other Stories (s Robinson), 1991
Remember Me (Weldon), 1976
Remembering Babylon (Malouf), 1993
Remembering Light and Stone (Madden), 1992
Remembrance Day (Aldiss), 1993
Renderings: A Novel (Sallis), 1996
Rendezvous in Haiti (Becker), 1987
Rendezvous with Rama (Clarke), 1973
Renegade or Halo2 (Mo), 1999
Repentance of Lorraine (Codrescu), 1976
Report on Probability A (Aldiss), 1969
Republic of Love (Shields), 1992
Requiem for a Dream (Selby), 1979
Reruns (Baumbach), 1974
Reservation Blues (Alexie), 1995
Reservoir and Other Stories (s Frame), 1966
Reservoir: Stories and Sketches (s Frame), 1963
Resident Alien (s Blaise), 1986
Resistance (Shreve), 1995
Rest for the Wicked (Duckworth), 1986
Rest in Pieces (Brown), 1992
Rest Is Done with Mirrors (See, as Highland), 1970
Rest of Life: Three Novellas (s Gordon), 1993
Restitution (Duffy), 1998
Restoration (Tremain), 1990
Resurrection Row (Perry), 1981
Resurrection at Sorrow Hill (Harris), 1993
Resurrection of Joseph Bourne; or, A Word or Two on Those Port Annie Miracles (Hodgins), 1979
Resuscitation of a Hanged Man (Johnson), 1991
Retreat (s Welty), 1981
Retreat to Innocence (Lessing), 1959

Return Journey (s Binchy), 1996
Return of Ansel Gibbs (Buechner), 1958
Return of Little Big Man (Berger), 1999
Return of Service (s Baumbach), 1979
Return the Innocent Earth (Dykeman), 1973
Return to (Delany), 1994
Returning (s O'Brien), 1982
Reuben (Wideman), 1988
Revenge of the Rose (Moorcock, as Bradbury, E.), 1991
Revolutions of the Night (Burns), 1986
Revolving Door (Jones), 1973
Rhéa (Cooper), 1937
Rhine Maidens (See, as Highland), 1981
Rhoda: A Life in Stories (s Gilchrist), 1995
Rhode Island Blues (Weldon), 2000
Rich Like Us (Sahgal), 1986
Richard A (Yurick), 1982
Richard's Things (Raphael), 1975
Richter 10 (Clarke), 1996
Ricochet Baby (Kidman), 1996
Riddle of John Rowe (Graham), 1935
Riddley Walker (Hoban), 1998
Ride Out (Foote), 1996
Riders (Winton), 1995
Riding Shotgun (Brown), 1996
Riding the Bullet (King), 2000
Riding the Rap (Leonard), 1995
Right Here, Right Now (Ellis), 1999
Right True End (Barstow), 1976
Rights of Desire (Brink), 2000
Ring of Brightest Angels around Heaven: A Novella and Stories (s Moody), 1995
Ringed Castle (Dunnett), 1997
Rio Grande Fall (Anaya), 1996
Riotous Assembly (Sharpe), 1972
Ripple From the Storm (Lessing), 1958
Rise of Gerry Logan (Glanville), 1965
Rise of Life on Earth (Oates, as Smith, R.), 1991
Rising Sun (Crichton, as Lange), 1992
Risk (Francis), 1994
Rite of Passage (s Greenberg), 1972
Riven Rock (Boyle), 1998
River Between (Ngugi wa Thiong'o), 1965
River King (Hoffman), 2000
River of Stone: Fictions and Memories (s Wiebe), 1995
River Sutra (Mehta), 1993
River to Pickle Beach (Betts), 1995
River Town (Keneally), 1995
River's End and Other Stories (s West), 1960
RL's Dream (Mosley), 1995
Road (Anand), 1987
Road Home (Harrison), 1998
Road Rage (Rendell, as Vine), 1997
Road to Lichfield (Lively), 1991
Road to Many a Wonder (Wagoner), 1974
Road to the Stilt House (Richards), 1985
Road to Wellville (Boyle), 1993
Roadkill (Friedman), 1997
Roads (McMurtry), 2000
Roadwalkers (Grau), 1994
Roadwork: A Novel of the First Energy Crisis (King), 1981
Roar Lion Roar and Other Stories (s Faust), 1965
Robber Bride (Atwood), 1993
Robber Bridegroom (Welty), 1944
Robert Crews (Berger), 1994
Robinson (Spark), 1958
Rocannon's World (Le Guin), 1972
Rock (Wagoner), 1958
Rock Cried Out (Douglas), 1994
Rock Springs (s Ford), 1988
Roger's Version (Updike), 1986
Roman Marriage (Glanville), 1967
Romance of the Equator: Best Fantasy Stories (s Aldiss), 1990
Romantic Egoists: A Reflection in Eight Minutes (s Auchincloss), 1954
Rooi (s Brink), 1965
Rookery Blues (Hassler), 1995
Room (Selby), 1972
Room for a Single Lady (Boylan), 1997
Room on the Hill (St. Omer), 1968
Room Service: Comic Writings (s Moorhouse), 1987
Roots and Shadows (Deshpande), 1983
Rose Madder (King), 1995
Rose of Tibet (Davidson), 1962
Rose Rabbi (Stern), 1971
Rose Theatre (Sorrentino), 1987
Rosemary's Baby (Levin), 1967
Ross Poldark: A Novel of Cornwall 1783–1787 (Graham), 1945
Rotten Elements (Upward), 1969
Rough Wallaby (McDonald), 1995
Rounds (Busch), 1980
Roxanna Slade (Price), 1998
Royal Family (Vollmann), 2000
Rubyfruit Jungle (Brown), 1978
Rude Awakening (Aldiss), 1979
Rufus at the Door and Other Stories (s Hassler), 2000
Ruins (Aldiss), 1987
Rule of the Bone (Banks), 1995
Rules of Attraction (Ellis), 1988
Rules of Life (s Weldon), 1987
Rum and Coca-Cola (de Boissière), 1984
Rum Punch (Leonard), 1992
Rumming Park (Mortimer), 1948
Rumours of Rain (Brink), 1978
Rumpelstiltskin (Hunter), 1981
Rumpole (s Mortimer), 1980
Rumpole à la Carte (s Mortimer), 1990
Rumpole and the Age of Miracles (s Mortimer), 1989
Rumpole and the Angel of Death (Mortimer), 1996
Rumpole and the Golden Thread (s Mortimer), 1983
Rumpole for the Defence (s Mortimer), 1982
Rumpole of the Bailey (s Mortimer), 1980
Rumpole on Trial (s Mortimer), 1992
Rumpole's Last Case (s Mortimer), 1988
Rumpole's Return (s Mortimer), 1982
Run Across the Island (Cole), 1968
Run of the Country (Connaughton), 1992
Run River (Didion), 1994
Run with the Horsemen (Sams), 1982
Runaway Black (Hunter), 1957

Runaway Jury (Grisham), 1996
Running Dog (DeLillo), 1979
Running from Legs and Other Stories (s Hunter), 2000
Running Man (King), 1982
Running Nicely (s Lurie), 1979
Running Wild (Ballard), 1989
Rushes (Rechy), 1979
Rushing to Paradise (Ballard), 1995
Russia House (le Carré), 1989
Russian Interpreter (Frayn), 1966
Rutland Place (Perry), 1983

S (Updike), 1988
Sabbath's Theater (Roth), 1995
Sabbatical: A Romance (Barth), 1982
Sacred Country (Tremain), 1994
Sacred Hunger (Unsworth), 1992
Sacrificial Egg and Other Stories (s Achebe), 1962
Sad Bastard (Hamilton), 1998
Saddest Summer of Samuel S (Donleavy), 1967
Sadie When She Died (Hunter), 1972
Sadler's Birthday (Tremain), 1977
Safe Conduct (Vansittart), 1995
Sailing Bright Eternity (Benford), 1995
Sailing to Byzantium (Silverberg, as Knox), 1985
Sailor on the Seas of Fate (Moorcock, as Bradbury, E.), 1976
Sailor Song (Kesey), 1993
Saint Jack (Theroux), 1973
Saint Maybe (Tyler), 1991
St. Urbain's Horseman (Richler), 1971
Salem's Lot (King), 1991
Salesman (O'Connor), 1999
Saliva Tree and Other Strange Growths (s Aldiss), 1966
Sally (Fast, as Cunningham), 1967
Salt (Gold), 1964
Salt (Lovelace), 1997
Salt & Sawdust: Stories and Table Talk (s Narayan), 1993
Salt Dancers (Hegi), 1995
Salt Line (Spencer), 1985
Salt of Life (Nahal), 1990
Salt of the Earth (Humphreys), 1985
Samantha (Fast, as Cunningham), 1968
Same Door (s Updike), 1962
Sam's Legacy (Neugeboren), 1974
Sanctuary V (Schulberg), 1970
Sandglass (Gunesekera), 1999
Sandmouth People (Frame), 1987
Sandra Street and Other Stories (s Anthony), 1973
Sands of Mars (Clarke), 1952
Sandspit Crossing (Virtue), 1993
Santa Barbara Stories (s Boyle), 1998
Sapphires (Dowse), 1994
Sarah Conley (Gilchrist), 1997
Saratoga, Hot (s Calisher), 1985
Sardana Dancers (Jenkins), 1964
Sassafras (Matthews), 1983
Satanic Verses (Rushdie), 1989
Saturday Night at the Pahala Theatre (s Yamanaka), 1993
Saul and Morris, Worlds Apart (Yaffe), 1982
Sauna Bath Mysteries and Other Stories (s Haley), 1978
Savage Crows (Drewe), 1976
Save Me, Joe Louis (Bell), 1993
Saving Grace (Smith), 1995
Saviors (Yglesias), 1987
Saw (Katz), 1972
Scales of Gold (Dunnett), 1992
Scandal; or, Priscilla's Kindness (Wilson), 1984
Scandalous Woman and Other Stories (s O'Brien), 1974
Scar Lover (Crews), 1992
Scar Tissue (Ignatieff), 1994
Scarborough Fear (Duffy), 1982
Scarlet Thread (Betts), 1964
Scars (s Kinsella), 1978
Scenes from a Receding Past (Higgins), 1977
Scenes from Bourgeois Life (s Jones), 1976
Scenes from Later Life (Cooper), 1983
Scenes from Life (Cooper), 1961
Scenes from Married Life (Cooper), 1961
Scenes from Married Life, and Scenes from Later Life (Cooper), 1984
Scenes from Metropolitan Life (Cooper), 1982
Scenes from Provincial Life (Cooper), 1950
Scenes from Provincial Life, and Scenes from Metropolitan Life (Cooper), 1983
Scenic Drive (s Wilding), 1976
Scenic Railway (s Upward), 1997
Scented Gardens for the Blind (Frame), 1964
Scents (Perutz), 1985
Schemetime (Dowse), 1990
Schindler's Ark (Keneally), 1982
Schismatrix (Sterling), 1985
Schismatrix Plus (s Sterling), 1996
Schoolmaster (Lovelace), 1968
Schultz (Donleavy), 1980
Scission (s Winton), 1985
Scorched-Wood People (Wiebe), 1977
Scratch One (Crichton, as Lange), 1967
Scumbler (Wharton), 1984
Sea Change (Howard), 1960
Sea Eagle (Aldridge), 1944
Sea Hath Bounds (Rooke), 1946
Sea King's Daughter (Mertz, as Michaels), 1977
Sea Music (Profumo), 1988
Seal Woman (Farmer), 1992
Sealed with a Loving Kiss (Hughes), 1959
Search for Rita (Cole), 1970
Search for the King: A Twelfth Century Legend (Vidal, as Box), 1967
Search the Shadows (Mertz, as Michaels), 1988
Searching for Caleb (Tyler), 1976
Searching for Survivors (s Banks), 1975
Searoad (s Le Guin), 1992
Season at Coole (Stephens), 1972
Season in Purgatory (Keneally), 1977
Season in the West (Read), 1989
Season of Adventure (Lamming), 1999
Season of Anomy (Soyinka), 1974
Season of Comfort (Vidal, as Box), 1949
Season of Delight (Greenberg), 1981
Season of the Jew (Shadbolt), 1987

Season of the Stranger (Becker), 1951
Season of the Strangler (Jones), 1982
Season with Eros (s Barstow), 1971
Seasons' Difference (Buechner), 1952
Seasons in Flight (s Aldiss), 1986
Second Best (Cook), 1991
Second Bridegroom (Hall), 1991
Second Chance (s Auchincloss), 1971
Second-Class Citizen (Emecheta), 1975
Second Ending (Hunter), 1956
Second Fiddle (Wesley), 1989
Second Home (Glanville), 1966
Second Inheritance (Bragg), 1967
Second Life (Bolger), 1994
Second Marriage (Barthelme), 1985
Second Nature (Hoffman), 1994
Second Rumpole Omnibus (s Mortimer), 1988
Second Trip (Silverberg, as Knox), 1979
Second Wind (Francis), 1999
Seconds (Ely), 1964
Secret Defector (Sigal), 1992
Secret Harmonies (Barrett), 1989
Secret House of Death (Rendell, as Vine), 1969
Secret Integration (s Pynchon), 1980
Secret Isaac (Charyn), 1978
Secret Ladder (Harris), 1963
Secret Lives (s King), 1991
Secret Lives and Other Stories (s Ngugi wa Thiong'o), 1975
Secret of This Book: 20 Odd Stories (s Aldiss), 1995
Secret of the Northern Lights (s Kinsella), 1998
Secret of the Runestaff (Moorcock, as Bradbury, E.), 1969
Secret Pilgrim (le Carré), 1991
Secret Sharer (Silverberg, as Knox), 1988
Secret Table (s Mirsky), 1975
Secrets (James), 1993
Secrets and Other Stories (s MacLaverty), 1984
Secrets and Surprises (s Beattie), 1979
Seduction: A Book of Stories (s Barker), 1994
Seduction and Other Stories (s Oates, as Smith, R.), 1975
Seduction by Light (Young), 1989
Seduction of Mrs. Pendlebury (Forster), 1974
See Them Die (Hunter), 1963
Seed (Cowan), 1966
Seed of Earth (Silverberg, as Knox), 1978
Seeing Red (Duckworth), 1993
Seize the Day, with Three Short Stories and a One-Act Play (s Bellow), 1957
Selected Declarations of Dependence (s Mathews), 1977
Self-Help (s Moore), 1985
Self-Made Brain Surgeon, and Other Stories (s Harris), 1999
Self Possession (Halligan), 1987
Selling Out (Wakefield), 1985
Send War in Our Time, O Lord (Driver), 1970
Señor Vivo and the Coca Lord (de Bernières), 1991
Sensationist (Palliser), 1991
Sensible Life (Wesley), 1990
Sensuous Guru: The Making of a Mystic President (Brata), 1980
Sent for You Yesterday (Wideman), 1984
Sentimental Agents (Lessing), 1983
Sentimental Education (s Oates, as Smith, R.), 1978
Sentinel (s Clarke), 1985
Sentries (Hunter), 1965
Separate Checks (Wiggins), 1984
Separate Development (Hope), 1981
Separate Hours (Baumbach), 1990
Separate Peace (Knowles), 1999
September September (Foote), 1978
Serenissima: A Novel of Venice (Jong), 1987
Serenity House (Hope), 1992
Serious Woman (Middleton), 1961
Serpent (Mosley), 1992
Serpent Mage (Bear), 1986
Service of Clouds (Hill), 1999
Set of Wives (Jones), 1965
Set on Edge (Rubens), 1960
Set This House on Fire (Styron), 1961
Setting Free the Bears (Irving), 1979
Settle Down Simon Katz (Kops), 1973
Settlement (Haley), 1986
Seven Ages (Figes), 1987
Seven Books for Grossman (Lurie), 1983
Seven Dreams: A Book of North American Landscapes (Vollmann), 1990
Seven League Boots (Murray), 1996
Seven Rivers West (Hoagland), 1986
Seven Summers: The Story of an Indian Childhood (Anand), 1951
Seven Tales and a Fable (s Jones), 1995
Seven Wives: A Romance (Baumbach), 1994
Seventh Babe (Charyn), 1979
Seventh Heaven (Hoffman), 1991
Seventh Sinner (Mertz, as Michaels), 1975
Sexing the Cherry (Winterson), 1989
Shades of Grey (s St. Omer), 1968
Shadow Baby (Forster), 1996
Shadow Bride (Heath), 1988
Shadow Knows (Johnson), 1975
Shadow Knows (s Madden), 1970
Shadow Lines (Ghosh), 1989
Shadow Master (Feinstein), 1979
Shadow of Myself (Phillips), 2000
Shadow of a Shadow of a Dream: Love Stories of Singapore (s Lim), 1987
Shadow Play in India (Hauser), 1937
Shadows on Our Skin (Johnston), 1978
Shadrach (s Styron), 1979
Shadrach in the Furnace (Silverberg, as Knox), 1977
Shake Hands for Ever (Rendell, as Vine), 1975
Shallows (Winton), 1986
Shaman Winter (Anaya), 1999
Shame (Rushdie), 1983
Shampoo Planet (Coupland), 1992
Shanghai Incident (Becker), 1956
Shape Shifter: Stories (s Melville), 1990
Shardik (Adams), 1975
Shards of Honor (Bujold), 1986
Shards of Memory (Jhabvala), 1995
Shares and Other Fictions (Stern), 1992
Sharp Teeth of Love (Betts), 1997
Sharpshooter: A Novel of the Civil War (Madden), 1996

Shattered Silk (Mertz, as Michaels), 1987
Shawl: A Story and a Novella (s Ozick), 1989
She and He (Brata), 1973
She Took My Arm As If She Loved Me (Gold), 1997
Shear (Parks), 1994
Shemerelda (Tinniswood), 1981
Shepherd (Forsyth), 1976
Sherbrookes (Delbanco), 1978
Shikasta (Lessing), 1979
Shiloh (Foote), 1952
Shiloh and Other Stories (s Mason), 1985
Shining (King), 1991
Shining City (Eldred-Grigg), 1991
Ship Fever and Other Stories (s Barrett), 1996
Ship Island and Other Stories (s Spencer), 1969
Ship Rock, A Place: From Women and Men, A Novel in Progress (McElroy), 1980
Ship on the Coin: A Fable of the Bourgeoisie (Hall), 1972
Shipping News (Proulx), 1994
Shipping Out (Stephens), 1979
Shipwreck Party (s Davison), 1989
Shirley (Fast, as Cunningham), 1964
Shiva Descending (Benford), 1980
Shoeless Joe (Kinsella), 1988
Shoeless Joe Jackson Comes to Iowa (s Kinsella), 1993
Shoot! (Bowering), 1994
Shooting Party (Colegate), 1981
Shooting the Stars (s Metcalf), 1993
Shores of Tomorrow (s Silverberg, as Knox), 1976
Short Answer (Middleton), 1958
Short Hall: New and Collected Stories (s Hall), 1980
Short History of a Prince: A Novel (Hamilton), 1998
Short Sad Book (Bowering), 1977
Short, Sharp Shock (Robinson), 1990
Short Story Embassy (Wilding), 1975
Short Tales from the Nightshift (s Kelman), 1978
Short Throat, the Tender Mouth (Grumbach), 1964
Short Time to Live (Jones), 1981
Short Walk in the Rain (s Hood), 1989
Shotgun (Hunter), 1969
Show Business (Tharoor), 1994
Show World: A Novel (Barnhardt), 1998
Shrapnel Academy (Weldon), 1987
Shrinking: The Beginning of My Own Ending (Lelchuk), 1978
Shroud for a Nightingale (James), 1971
Shrouded Planet (Silverberg, as Knox), 1964
Shuttlecock (Swift), 1984
Sight for Sore Eyes (Rendell, as Vine), 1999
Sights Unseen (Gibbons), 1995
Signals of Distress (Crace), 1995
Signed with Their Honour (Aldridge), 1942
Silas Timberman (Fast, as Cunningham), 1955
Silence in Hanover Close (Perry), 1989
Silence in the Garden (Trevor), 1988
Silence of Desire (Markandaya), 1960
Silence of Llano (s Anaya), 1982
Silent Areas (s Feinstein), 1980
Silent Cry (Perry), 1997
Silent Gondoliers (Goldman), 1984
Silent Invaders (Silverberg, as Knox), 1975
Silent Passengers (s Woiwode), 1993
Silent Terror (Ellroy), 1990
Silhouette in Scarlet (Mertz, as Michaels), 1984
Silken Net (Bragg), 1974
Silver City (Dowse), 1984
Silver Wedding (s Binchy), 1989
Simisola (Rendell, as Vine), 1994
Simon's Night (Hassler), 1979
Simple Gifts (Greenberg), 1986
Sin (Sionil Jose), 1994
Sin Eater (Ellis), 1977
Sin of Colour (Gupta), 1999
Singing Citadel: Four Tales of Heroic Fantasy (s Moorcock, as Bradbury, E.), 1970
Singing Head (Elliott), 1968
Singing Whakapapa (Stead), 1994
Single & Single (le Carré), 1999
Single Eye (Duffy), 1964
Singular Family: Rosacoke and Her Kin (s Price), 1999
Singular Man (Donleavy), 1964
Singular Pleasures (s Mathews), 1988
Sinking of the Odradek Stadium and Other Novels (Mathews), 1985
Sinning with Annie and Other Stories (s Theroux), 1975
Sins of the Father (Massie), 1991
Sins of the Wolf (Perry), 1994
Siren Celia (Eldred-Grigg), 1989
Sirens of Titan (Vonnegut), 1962
Sirian Experiments (Lessing), 1980
Sissie (Williams), 1963
Sister Hollywood (Stead), 1990
Sister of My Heart (Divakaruni), 1999
Sisters (s Bear), 1992
Sitters (Miller), 1995
Sitting Pretty (Young), 1976
Situation in New Delhi (Sahgal), 1977
Six Feet of the Country (s Gordimer), 1956
Six of One (Brown), 1979
Sixth Seal (Wesley), 1971
63: Dream Palace (s Purdy), 1957
Skating Party (Warner), 1984
Skeleton in the Cupboard (Ellis), 1988
Skinned Alive (s White), 1995
Skinny Island: More Tales of Manhattan (s Auchincloss), 1988
Skinny Legs and All (Robbins), 1991
Skull Beneath the Skin (James), 1982
Sky Changes (Sorrentino), 1966
Sky People (s Grace), 1994
Skybreaker (Jones), 1990
Slap (McDonald), 1996
Slapstick; or, Lonesome No More! (Vonnegut), 1976
Slash (Armstrong), 1998
/ (Bear), 1997
Slaughterhouse-Five; or, The Children's Crusade (Vonnegut), 1970
Slave (Amadi), 1978
Slave Girl (Emecheta), 1977
Slave Trade (Gold), 1979
Slaves of New York (s Janowitz), 1987
Slay-Ride (Francis), 1973

Sleep: Stories (s Dixon), 1999
Sleep Tight (s Purdy), 1979
Sleepers of Roraima (s Harris), 1970
Sleeping Beauty Trilogy (Rice, as Roquelaure), 1999
Sleeping Life (Rendell, as Vine), 1978
Sleeping Partner (Graham), 1956
Sleeping Sorceress (Moorcock, as Bradbury, E.), 1972
Sleeps Six (s Raphael), 1979
Sleepside Story (s Bear), 1987
Slides (Plante), 1971
Slipping-Down Life (Tyler), 1983
Slipstream (McDonald), 1982
Sliver (Levin), 1991
Slow Digestions of the Night (Crace), 1995
Slow Fade (Wurlitzer), 1985
Slow Learner: Early Stories (s Pynchon), 1985
Slow Natives (Astley), 1967
Slow Train to Milan (St. Aubin de Teran), 1983
Small Bang (Calisher), 1992
Small Ceremonies (Shields), 1996
Small Changes (Piercy), 1987
Small Gods (Pratchett), 1992
Small Rain (Delbanco), 1975
Small Rain (s Pynchon), 1980
Small Remedies (Deshpande), 2000
Small Town in Germany (le Carré), 1968
Small World: An Academic Romance (Lodge), 1985
Smell of the Coast and Other Stories (s Phillips), 1987
Smile (Bradbury), 1991
Smiley's People (le Carré), 1980
Smith's Dream (Stead), 1973
Smith's Gazelle (Davidson), 1971
Smithsonian Institution (Vidal, as Box), 1998
Smoke (Bradley), 1994
Smoke and Mirrors (Mertz, as Michaels), 1989
Smokescreen (Francis), 1972
Smuggler's Bible (McElroy), 1968
Snake Eyes (Oates, as Smith, R.), 1992
Snakes (Young), 1971
Snap (Frucht), 1988
Snapper (Doyle), 1992
Snare (Spencer), 1972
Sneaky People (Berger), 1980
Snow Angels (O'Nan), 1994
Snow Crash (Stephenson), 1992
Snow Falling on Cedars (Guterson), 1994
Snow in Spain (s O'Sullivan), 1990
Snow Man (Chute), 1999
Snow White and Rose Red (Hunter), 1985
Snowman, Snowman: Fables and Fantasies (s Frame), 1963
So Gaily Sings the Lark (Jenkins), 1951
So Hurt and Humiliated and Other Stories (s King), 1959
So I Am Glad (Kennedy), 1995
So Long as You Both Shall Live (Hunter), 1976
So Long, See You Tomorrow (Maxwell), 1989
Soft Voice of the Serpent and Other Stories (s Gordimer), 1953
Soldier Erect; or, Further Adventures of the Hand-Reared Boy (Aldiss), 1971
Soldier in the Rain (Goldman), 1960
Soldier of the Great War (Helprin), 1991
Soldier of the Revolution (Just), 1970
Soldier's Embrace (s Gordimer), 1980
Soldier's Joy (Bell), 1989
Soldier's Return (Bragg), 1999
Solitary Child (Bawden), 1966
Solitary Grief (Rubens), 1991
Solomon Gursky Was Here (Richler), 1989
Solstice (Oates, as Smith, R.), 1985
Some Can Whistle (McMurtry), 1990
Some Faces in the Crowd (s Schulberg), 1954
Some Inner Fury (Markandaya), 1956
Some Kind of Grace (Jenkins), 1960
Some Lie and Some Die (Rendell, as Vine), 1973
Some Love (Callow), 1991
Some Monday for Sure (s Gordimer), 1976
Somebody's Darling (McMurtry), 1978
Someone Else (Tindall), 1969
Someone in the House (Mertz, as Michaels), 1983
Someone Just Like You (s Yurick), 1973
Someone to Watch Over Me: Stories (s Bausch), 1999
Something about a Soldier (Harris), 1958
Something Happened Here (s Levine), 1991
Something in Disguise (Howard), 1970
Something in the Wind (Smith), 1971
Something I've Been Meaning to Tell You (s Munro), 1974
Something Leather (Gray), 1991
Something Out There (s Gordimer), 1984
Something to Be Desired (McGuane), 1985
Something to Remember Me By: Three Tales (s Bellow), 1991
Something Wicked This Way Comes (Bradbury), 1963
Sometimes a Great Notion (Kesey), 1966
Sometimes I Live in the Country (Busch), 1986
Somewhere East of Life (Aldiss), 1994
Somewhere in the Night (Moorcock, as Bradbury, E.), 1966
Somewhere New: New and Selected Stories (s Wilding), 1996
Somnambulists (Elliott), 1964
Son of a Smaller Hero (Richler), 1955
Son of Laughter (Buechner), 1993
Son of Man (Silverberg, as Knox), 1979
Son of Rosemary: The Sequel to Rosemary's Baby (Levin), 1998
Son of the Circus (Irving), 1994
Son of the Morning (Oates, as Smith, R.), 1979
Son of the Morning and Other Stories (s Gotlieb), 1983
Song of Solomon (Morrison), 1978
Song of the Silent Snow (s Selby), 1986
Songs My Mother Taught Me (Thomas), 1973
Songs of Distant Earth (Clarke), 1986
Songs of Earth and Power (Bear), 1992
Songs of Enchantment (Okri), 1993
Songs of Summer and Other Stories (s Silverberg, as Knox), 1979
Sons (Hunter), 1970
Sons for the Return Home (Wendt), 1996
Sons of Darkness, Sons of Light (Williams), 1970
Sons of the Wolf (Mertz, as Michaels), 1968
Sophie's Choice (Styron), 1979
Sorcerer's Amulet (Moorcock, as Bradbury, E.), 1968
Sorcerer's Apprentice: Tales and Conjuration (s Johnson), 1988
Sorcerers of Majipoor (Silverberg, as Knox), 1997
Sort of Forgetting (Vansittart), 1960

Sot-Weed Factor (Barth), 1967
Soul Clap Hands and Sing (s Marshall), 1962
Soul-Mate (Oates, as Smith, R.), 1989
Soul Music (Pratchett), 1995
Souls Raised from the Dead (Betts), 1994
Sound of Trumpets (Mortimer), 1999
Soundings (Davison), 1993
Sour Sweet (Mo), 1985
Source of Embarrassment (Barker), 1974
Source of Light (Price), 1981
Sourcery (Pratchett), 1989
Sources of Unrest (Vansittart), 1962
South (Tóibín), 1991
South Street (Bradley), 1975
South Will Rise at Noon (Glover), 1989
Southern Discomfort (Brown), 1983
Southern Family (Godwin), 1987
Southpaw: by Henry W. Wiggen: Punctuation Inserted and Spelling Greatly Improved (Harris), 1953
Southpaw: Short Stories (s St. Aubin de Teran), 1999
Space, Time, and Nathaniel: Presciences (s Aldiss), 1957
Spaces of the Dark (Mosley), 1951
Spanish Lover (Trollope), 1997
Spanking Watson: A Novel (Friedman), 1999
Spanking the Maid (Coover), 1987
Sparrow's Fall (Bodsworth), 1967
Spartacus (Fast, as Cunningham), 1952
Speaker of Mandarin (Rendell, as Vine), 1983
Special Flower (Gee), 1965
Speed (Harris), 1990
Speed Queen (O'Nan), 1997
Spence + Lila (Mason), 1989
Spending: A Utopian Divertimento (Gordon), 1998
Sphere (Crichton, as Lange), 1987
Sphinx and the Sybarites (Pownall), 1993
Spider (McGrath), 1991
Spider Cup (Halligan), 1990
Spiderman (Sionil Jose), 1991
Spiderweb (Lively), 1999
Spiked Heel (Hunter), 1957
Spiral Ascent (Upward), 1977
Spirit Ring (Bujold), 1992
Spirit Weddings (Tindall), 1992
Spirits and Other Stories (s Bausch), 1987
Spit Delaney's Island: Selected Stories (s Hodgins), 1976
Splendide-Hôtel (Sorrentino), 1973
Split Images (Leonard), 1983
Splitting: A Novel (Weldon), 1994
Spoils of Flowers (Grumbach), 1962
Sport of Nature (Gordimer), 1987
Sporting Club (McGuane), 1969
Sporting Proposition (Aldridge), 1973
Sporting with Amaryllis (West), 1996
Sportswriter (Ford), 1986
Spreading Fires (Knowles), 1974
Spring of Souls (Cobb), 1999
Spring of the Ram (Dunnett), 1988
Spring Sonata (Rubens), 1986
Spy Hook (Deighton), 1988
Spy Line (Deighton), 1989
Spy Sinker (Deighton), 1990
Spy Story (Deighton), 1974
Spy Who Came In from the Cold (le Carré), 1964
Spyglass Tree (Murray), 1991
Square's Progress (Sheed), 1965
Squeak: A Biography of NPA 1978A 203 (Bowen), 1984
Squeeze Play (Auster), 1984
SS-GB: Nazi-Occupied Britain 1941 (Deighton), 1979
Stagg and His Mother (Pownall), 1991
Staggerford (Hassler), 1977
Stained White Radiance (Burke), 1993
Stand (King), 1978
Stand We at Last (Fairbairns), 1983
Standard Dreaming (Calisher), 1972
Standard of Behaviour (Trevor), 1958
Star Called Henry (Doyle), 1999
Star in the Family (Faust), 1975
Star Invaders (s King), 1964
Star of the Gypsies (Silverberg, as Knox), 1987
Star Wars: Rogue Planet (Bear), 2000
Starborne (Silverberg, as Knox), 1996
Starcarbon: A Meditation on Love (Gilchrist), 1994
Starhaven (Silverberg, as Knox), 1958
Staring at the Sun (Barnes, as Kavanagh), 1987
Starr Bright Will Be With You Soon (Oates, as Smith, R.), 1999
Stars and Bars (Boyd), 1985
Stars at Noon (Johnson), 1987
Stars in My Pocket Like Grains of Sand (Delany), 1984
Stars of the New Curfew (s Okri), 1989
Starswarm (s Aldiss), 1979
Start in Life (Brookner), 1981
Starting Over (Wakefield), 1974
State of Independence (Phillips), 1986
State of Ireland (s Kiely), 1982
State of Siege (Frame), 1967
State Ward (Duff), 1994
Statement Against Corpses (s Ghose), 1964
States of Emergency (Brink), 1989
Statesman's Game (Aldridge), 1966
Statues in a Garden (Colegate), 1966
Steagle (Faust), 1966
Stealer of Souls and Other Stories (s Moorcock, as Bradbury, E.), 1967
Steel Tsar (Moorcock, as Bradbury, E.), 1982
Steelwork (Sorrentino), 1970
Step-Father (s Oates, as Smith, R.), 1978
Stepford Wives (Levin), 1972
Stephanie (Graham), 1993
Stephen King's Skeleton Crew (s King), 1985
Stepper (Castro), 1997
Stepping Westward (Bradbury), 1995
Steps of the Sun (Trollope), 1984
Stepsons of Terra (Silverberg, as Knox), 1958
Stern (Friedman), 1963
Stick (Leonard), 1984
Still Life (Stephens), 1978
Still Life with Woodpecker (Robbins), 1980
Still Waters (Middleton), 1976
Stillness (Delbanco), 1980
Stirk of Stirk (Tinniswood), 1974

Stitch (Stern), 1967
Stochastic Man (Silverberg, as Knox), 1976
Stolen Jew (Neugeboren), 1981
Stolen Past (Knowles), 1984
Stolen Stories (s Katz), 1984
Stone Diaries (Shields), 1994
Stone Garden and Other Stories (s Spence), 1995
Stone Virgin (Unsworth), 1986
Stones (s Findley), 1990
Stones from the River (Hegi), 1994
Stories from the Warm Zone and Sydney Stories (s Anderson), 1988
Stories of Misbegotten Love (s Gold), 1985
Storm (Buechner), 1998
Storm in Chandigarh (Sahgal), 1969
Storm of Fortune (Clarke), 1973
Storm Tide (Piercy), 1998
Stormbringer (Moorcock, as Bradbury, E.), 1977
Story for Europe (Self), 1996
Story of a Non-Marrying Man and Other Stories (s Lessing), 1972
Story of Lola Gregg (Fast, as Cunningham), 1957
Story of My Desire (Callow), 1976
Story of My Life (McInerney), 1988
Story of the Night (Tóibín), 1997
Story of the Weasel (Slaughter), 1976
Story Teller (Vansittart), 1968
Storyboard (Bowen), 1960
Storyhood as We Know It and Other Tales (s Matthews), 1993
Storyman (Kelleher), 1996
Straight (Francis), 1989
Straight Cut (Bell), 1987
Straight No Chaser (Young), 1994
Straits of Messina (Delany), 1989
Strange Case of Billy Biswas (Joshi), 1971
Strange Fits of Passion (Shreve), 1991
Strange God (Savage), 1974
Strange Meeting (Hill), 1972
Strange One (Bodsworth), 1960
Strange Yesterday (Fast, as Cunningham), 1934
Stranger from the Sea: A Novel of Cornwall 1810–1811 (Graham), 1982
Strangers (Jones), 1974
Strangers and Journeys (Shadbolt), 1972
Strangers Meeting (Graham), 1939
Strangers When We Meet (Hunter), 1958
Strata (Pratchett), 1981
Strawberry Boy (Dawson), 1976
Strawberry Tree (s Rendell, as Vine), 1990
Street Games (s Brown), 1974
Street Lawyer (Grisham), 1998
Street of the Five Moons (Mertz, as Michaels), 1988
Street: Stories (s Richler), 1969
Streets of Conflict (Anthony), 1976
Streets of Gold (Hunter), 1975
Streets of Laredo (McMurtry), 1994
Strength of Stones (Bear), 1981
Strength of the Hills (Sinclair), 1992
Strickland: A Romance (Masters), 1990
String (Lurie), 1995
Stringer (Just), 1974
Strong Medicine (Hailey), 1984
Stronger Climate: Nine Stories (s Jhabvala), 1969
Struggles of Albert Woods (Cooper), 1953
Strumpet City (Plunkett), 1969
Studhorse Man (Kroetsch), 1970
Studmuffin (Duckworth), 2000
Stupid Boys Are Good to Relax With (s Swan), 1996
Subscript (Brooke-Rose), 1999
Subtraction (s Robison), 1991
Suburbs of Hell (Stow), 1984
Subway to New York (Callow), 1979
Success (Amis), 1987
Success (s Masters), 1992
Success Stories (s Banks), 1986
Succession: A Novel of Elizabeth and James (Garrett), 1983
Such (Brooke-Rose), 1966
Such a Long Journey (Mistry), 1991
Such a Pretty, Pretty Girl (Groom), 1999
Such Was the Season (Major), 1987
Sudden Death (Brown), 1983
Sudden, Fearful Death (Perry), 1993
Sudden Times (Healy), 2000
Suder (Everett), 1983
Suffrage of Elvira (Naipaul), 1958
Sugar and Rum (Unsworth), 1988
Sugar Cane (Bailey), 1993
Sugar Mother (Jolley), 1989
Suicide Academy (Stern), 1968
Suicide Hill (Ellroy), 1988
Suicide's Wife (Madden), 1978
Suitable Boy (Seth), 1993
Sula (Morrison), 1974
Summer (Cowan), 1964
Summer Before the Dark (Lessing), 1973
Summer Bird-Cage (Drabble), 1964
Summer Fires and Winter Country (s Shadbolt), 1966
Summer in the Greenhouse (Mavor), 1960
Summer of the Dragon (Mertz, as Michaels), 1980
Summer of the Royal Visit (Colegate), 1992
Summer People (Piercy), 1989
Summerhouse (Mulkerns), 1984
Summerhouse Trilogy (Ellis), 1994
Summering: A Book of Short Stories (s Greenberg), 1966
Summer's Lease (Mortimer), 1988
Sun Between Their Feet (s Lessing), 1973
Sun Chemist (Davidson), 1976
Sun Dogs (Butler), 1982
Sun on the Wall: Three Novels (Frame), 1994
Sunburst (Gotlieb), 1978
Sundance and Other Science Fiction Stories (s Silverberg, as Knox), 1975
Sunday Best (Rubens), 1980
Sundered Worlds (Moorcock, as Bradbury, E.), 1966
Sundog: The story of an American foreman, Robert Corvus Strang, as told to Jim Harrison (Harrison), 1985
Sunrise in Fiji (Nahal), 1988
Sunrise with Sea Monster (Jordan), 1995
Sunrising (Cook), 1986
Sunset Limited (Burke), 1998

Superman III (Kotzwinkle), 1983
Supper Waltz Wilson and Other New Zealand Stories (s Marshall), 1979
Surface of Earth (Price), 1978
Surfacing (Atwood), 1973
Surrey Cat (Sinclair), 1976
Surrogate City (Hamilton), 1990
Survivor (Butler), 1978
Survivor (Jones), 1968
Survivor (Keneally), 1970
Survivor: A Selection of Stories (s Joshi), 1975
Survivors (Feinstein), 1991
Survivors (Hunter), 1975
Survivors of the Crossing (Clarke), 1964
Suspects (Berger), 1996
Suspended Sentences (s Guerard), 1999
Suttree (McCarthy), 1980
Swag (Leonard), 1986
Swami and Friends: A Novel of Malgudi (Narayan), 1935
Swann: A Mystery (Shields), 1992
Swanny's Ways (Katz), 1995
Sweet Dreams (Frayn), 1974
Sweet Hereafter: A Novel (Banks), 1992
Sweet Shop Owner (Swift), 1985
Sweet Smell of Psychosis (Self), 1999
Sweet William (Bainbridge), 1976
Sweethearts (s Phillips), 1976
Sweets of Pimlico (Wilson), 1989
Sweetsir (Yglesias), 1981
Swiftie the Magician (Gold), 1975
Swimmer in the Secret Sea (Kotzwinkle), 1975
Swimming Pool Season (Tremain), 1985
Switch (Leonard), 1979
Sword and the Miracle (Bragg), 1996
Sword and the Sickle (Anand), 1942
Sword and the Stallion (Moorcock, as Bradbury, E.), 1974
Sword of the Dawn (Moorcock, as Bradbury, E.), 1977
Swords Trilogy (Moorcock, as Bradbury, E.), 1977
Sybil (Auchincloss), 1952
Sycamore Tree (Brooke-Rose), 1959
Sylvia (Fast, as Cunningham), 1962
Symposium (Spark), 1990
System (Hanley, as Calvin), 1962

Tabloid Dreams (s Butler), 1996
Tailor of Panama (le Carré), 1996
Take Me Back: A Novel (Bausch), 1981
Take My Life (Graham), 1967
Take This Man (Busch), 1981
Take Two Popes (Hanley, as Calvin), 1972
Taken (Marlatt), 1996
Takeover (Spark), 1976
Taking Shelter (Anderson), 1990
Tale for the Mirror: A Novella and Other Stories (s Calisher), 1963
Tale Maker (Harris), 1994
Tale of Asa Bean (Matthews), 1971
Tales from Firozsha Baag (s Mistry), 1992
Tales from Planet Earth (s Clarke), 1990
Tales from Watership Down (Adams), 1996
Tales from the Blue Archives (Thornton), 1997
Tales from the Empty Notebook (s Kotzwinkle), 1996
Tales from the White Hart (s Clarke), 1998
Tales I Tell My Mother (s Fairbairns), 1980
Tales I Tell My Mother (s Roberts), 1978
Tales I Told My Mother (s Nye), 1970
Tales of (s Delany), 1988
Tales of Burning Love (Erdrich), 1996
Tales of Manhattan (s Auchincloss), 1967
Tales of Mystery and Romance (s Moorhouse), 1977
Tales of Ten Worlds (s Clarke), 1963
Tales of Yesteryear (Auchincloss), 1994
Tales of the Ohio Land (s Matthews), 1978
Tales Told by an Idiot: Selected Short Stories (s Anand), 1999
Talisman (King), 1984
Talk Stories (s Kincaid), 2000
Talkative Man (Narayan), 1987
Talking It Over (Barnes, as Kavanagh), 1991
Talking Room (Hauser), 1976
Talking to Strange Men (Rendell, as Vine), 1987
Tall Houses in Winter (Betts), 1955
Tall Hunter (Fast, as Cunningham), 1942
Tall Woman (Dykeman), 1962
Tamarisk Row (Murnane), 1974
Tangents (s Bear), 1989
Tangi (Ihimaera), 1973
Tar Baby (Charyn), 1973
Tar Baby (Morrison), 1981
Tara Road (Binchy), 1996
Taste for Death (James), 1986
Taste of Sin (Cassill), 1959
Taste of Too Much (Hanley, as Calvin), 1960
Tathea (Perry), 1999
Taverners' Place (Trollope), 1986
Tawa (Knox), 1998
Tax Inspector (Carey), 1992
Teach Me to Fly, Skyfighter! and Other Stories (s Lee), 1983
Tear His Head Off His Shoulders (Dunn), 1975
Teeth, Dying, and Other Matters, and The Gamesman's Island: A Play (s Stern), 1964
Teeth of My Father (s Metcalf), 1975
Tehanu: The Last Book of Earthsea (Le Guin), 1990
Teitlebaum's Window (Markfield), 1971
Tell Me a Riddle: A Collection (s Olsen), 1964
Telling of Lies (Findley), 1988
Tempest (Cassill), 1959
Tempest of Clemenza (Adams), 1996
Temple of Flora (Mavor), 1961
Temple of Gold (Goldman), 1957
Temple of My Familiar (Walker), 1989
Temples of Delight (Trapido), 1991
Temporary Shelter (s Gordon), 1987
Temptations of Big Bear (Wiebe), 2000
Ten Green Bottles (s Thomas), 1967
Ten Indians (Bell), 1996
Ten Plus One (Hunter), 1964
10 Lb. Penalty (Francis), 1997
Ten Tales Tall and True (s Gray), 1994
Tenancy (Figes), 1993
Tenants (Cowan), 1994

Tenants of Time (Flanagan), 1988
Tender (Childress), 1990
Tender Mercies (Brown), 1979
Tenderness (Oates, as Smith, R.), 1996
Tenement of Clay (West), 1965
Tennessee Waltz and Other Stories (s Cheuse), 1990
Tennis Handsome (Hannah), 1983
Tent of Orange Mist (West), 1995
Terminal Beach (s Ballard), 1993
Terminal Man (Crichton, as Lange), 1972
Termination Rock (Freeman), 1989
Terms of Endearment (McMurtry), 1999
Terms of Reference (Middleton), 1966
Terrestrials (West), 1997
Terrible Threes (Reed), 1989
Terrible Twos (Reed), 1990
Territorial Rights (Spark), 1979
Tesseract (Garland), 1999
Testament (Grisham), 1999
Testostero (Foster), 1987
Texasville (McMurtry), 1987
Textermination (Brooke-Rose), 1991
Textures of Life (Calisher), 1963
That Angel Burning at My Left Side (Peterkiewicz), 1963
That Bad Woman (s Boylan), 1995
That Darcy, That Dancer, That Gentleman (Donleavy), 1991
That Eye, the Sky (Winton), 1986
That London Winter (Bardwell), 1981
That Long Silence (Deshpande), 1988
That Night (McDermott), 1987
That Night We Were Ravenous (Steffler), 1998
That Year in Paris (Jones), 1988
That's How It Was (Duffy), 1984
Thebes of the Hundred Gates (Silverberg, as Knox), 1993
Theft (s Bellow), 1989
Their Dogs Came with Them (Viramontes), 2000
Them (Oates, as Smith, R.), 1971
Theme for Diverse Instruments (s Rule), 1990
Then Again (McCauley), 1987
Then Upon the Evil Season (Virtue), 1988
Theo and Matilda (Billington), 1991
Therapy (Lodge), 1995
There Are No Elders (s Clarke), 1994
There Is a Happy Land (Waterhouse), 1957
There Was an Ancient House (Kiely), 1955
There We Have Been (Bardwell), 1989
Therefore Be Bold (Gold), 1962
These Enchanted Woods (Massie), 1993
They Came like Swallows (Maxwell), 1937
They Do Return (s Lim), 1983
They Fly at Ciron (Delany), 1993
They Whisper (Butler), 1994
Thin Ice (s Levine), 1980
Thing He Loves and Other Stories (s Glanville), 1973
Thing of It Is… (Goldman), 1967
Things about to Disappear (s Wier), 1978
Things as They Are? Short Stories (s Vanderhaeghe), 1992
Things Fall Apart (Achebe), 1992
Things They Carried (s O'Brien), 1990
Think of England (s Raphael), 1988
Thinks (Waterhouse), 1984
Thinner (King), 1984
Third Life of Grange Copeland (Walker), 1985
Third Rumpole Omnibus (s Mortimer), 1998
Thirsty Evil: Seven Short Stories (s Vidal, as Box), 1958
Thirteen Stories and Thirteen Epitaphs (s Vollmann), 1994
13th Immortal (Silverberg, as Knox), 1957
30: Pieces of a Novel (Dixon), 1999
This Crooked Way (Spencer), 1952
This Day's Death (Rechy), 1970
This Is Not for You (Rule), 1987
This Is for You (s Wilding), 1994
This Perfect Day (Levin), 1970
This Summer's Dolphin (Shadbolt), 1969
This Thing Don't Lead to Heaven (Crews), 1970
This Time of Morning (Sahgal), 1966
This Was the Old Chief's Country (s Lessing), 1952
This Year It Will Be Different and Other Stories: A Christmas Treasury (s Binchy), 1996
Thistle and the Grail (Jenkins), 1954
Thorns (Silverberg, as Knox), 1969
Those Who Watch (Silverberg, as Knox), 1977
Thou Worm, Jacob (Mirsky), 1967
Thought Gang (Fischer), 1995
Thousand Acres (Smiley), 1991
Three Blind Mice (Hunter), 1990
Three Cheers for the Paraclete (Keneally), 1969
Three Continents (Jhabvala), 1987
Three Farmers on Their Way to a Dance (Powers), 1988
Three Filipino Women (s Sionil Jose), 1992
Three Gospels (Price), 1996
Three Lives (s Auchincloss), 1994
Three Marriages (Cooper), 1946
Three Six Seven (Vansittart), 1983
3001: The Final Odyssey (Clarke), 1997
Three: Williwaw, A Thirsty Evil, Julian the Apostate (Vidal, as Box), 1962
Three Winters (Mortimer), 1956
Three Wogs (s Theroux), 1973
Three Women (Piercy), 1999
Thrill of the Grass (s Kinsella), 1985
Through the Wilderness (s Jacobson), 1968
Throwback (Sharpe), 1984
Thru (Brooke-Rose), 1975
Thy Mother's Glass (Watmough), 1992
Tiberius (Massie), 1990
Ticket for a Seamstitch, by Henry W. Wiggen: But Polished for the Printer (Harris), 1957
Tides of Light (Benford), 1989
Tides of Lust (Delany), 1979
Tidewater Tales: A Novel (Barth), 1988
Tidings (Wharton), 1988
Tiger (St. Aubin de Teran), 1984
Tiger for Malgudi (Narayan), 1983
Tiger in the Tiger Pit (Hospital), 1984
Tiger of Gold (Jenkins), 1962
Tiger's Daughter (Mukherjee), 1973
'Til Death (Hunter), 1961
Timbuktu (Auster), 1999
Time and Tide (O'Brien), 1992

Time Dweller (s Moorcock, as Bradbury, E.), 1971
Time Gate (Silverberg, as Knox), 1989
Time-Hoppers (Silverberg, as Knox), 1968
Time in Its Flight (Schaeffer), 1978
Time of Changes (Silverberg, as Knox), 1973
Time of Our Darkness (Gray), 1988
Time of Our Time (Mailer), 1998
Time of the Crack (Tennant), 1973
Time of the Kingfishers (Watmough), 1994
Time Out (s Ely), 1969
Time Outworn (Mulkerns), 1952
Time to Be Happy (Sahgal), 1958
Time to Dance (Bragg), 1991
Time to Dance and Other Stories (s MacLaverty), 1982
Time to Go (s Dixon), 1984
Time to Kill (Grisham), 1993
Time Will Darken It (Maxwell), 1949
Timeline (Crichton, as Lange), 1999
Time's Arrow; or, The Nature of the Offence (Amis), 1991
Time's Rub (Benford), 1984
Timequake (Vonnegut), 1997
Timescape (Benford), 1980
Tin Can Tree (Tyler), 1966
Tin Men (Frayn), 1966
Tinker, Tailor, Soldier, Spy (le Carré), 1974
Tins and Other Stories (s Cowan), 1973
Tinsel (Goldman), 1979
Tirra Lirra by the River (Anderson), 1984
Tisch (Dixon), 2000
Titmuss Regained (Mortimer), 1990
Tivington Nott (Miller), 1989
Tlooth (Mathews), 1987
TNT for Two (Hall), 1956
To an Early Grave (Markfield), 1965
To Fear a Painted Devil (Rendell, as Vine), 1965
To Kill a Cardinal (Rumaker), 1992
To Lie with Lions (Dunnett), 1996
To Live Again (Silverberg, as Knox), 1975
To Morrow Now Occurs Again (Gover), 1975
To Open the Sky (Silverberg, as Knox), 1970
To Open the Sky (s Silverberg, as Knox), 1967
To Recollect a Cloud of Ghosts: Christmas in England (s Garrett), 1979
To Say Nothing of the Dog; Or, How We Found the Bishop's Bird Stump at Last (Willis), 1997
To Sing Strange Songs (s Bradbury), 1979
To Skin a Cat (s McGuane), 1987
To the Bright and Shining Sun (Burke), 1995
To the City (Tindall), 1987
To the Dark Tower (King), 1946
To the Hermitage (Bradbury), 2000
To the Hilt (Francis), 1996
To the Islands (Stow), 1982
To the Land of the Living (Silverberg, as Knox), 1990
To the Precipice (Rossner), 1977
To the Wedding (Berger), 1995
To the Winds (Jones), 1996
To Whom She Will (Jhabvala), 1955
To Worlds Beyond (s Silverberg, as Knox), 1969
Toast to the Lord (Jenkins), 1972
Today the Struggle (Jones), 1978
Todd Andrews to the Author (s Barth), 1979
Tokyo Woes (Friedman), 1986
Tom O'Bedlam (Silverberg, as Knox), 1986
Tombs of Atuan (Le Guin), 1972
Tomcat in Love (O'Brien), 1998
Tommyknockers (King), 1987
Tomorrow Midnight (s Bradbury), 1966
Tomorrow We Save the Orphans (s Marshall), 1992
Tomorrow's World (Hunter), 1956
Tongues of Angels (Price), 1990
Tongues of Flame (Parks), 1985
Too Far to Go: The Maples Stories (s Updike), 1980
Too Late (Dixon), 1978
Too Late American Boyhood Blues (s Busch), 1984
Torquemada (Fast, as Cunningham), 1967
Tortilla Curtain (Boyle), 1995
Tortoise by Candlelight (Bawden), 1963
Tortuga (Anaya), 1979
Touch (Leonard), 1988
Touch of Clay (Shadbolt), 1974
Touch of Daniel (Tinniswood), 1969
Touch of Love (Coe), 1989
Tough Guys Don't Dance (Mailer), 1984
Tough, Tough Toys for Tough, Tough Boys (s Self), 1998
Toughest Indian in the World: Stories (s Alexie), 2000
Tour (Ely), 1967
Tourmaline (Stow), 1983
Tournament (Foote), 1949
Tournament (Vansittart), 1961
Toward the End of Time (Updike), 1997
Toward the Sea (Middleton), 1995
Towards Asmara (Keneally), 1989
Towards the End of the Morning (Frayn), 1967
Tower of Glass (Silverberg, as Knox), 1976
Towers of Toron (Delany), 1968
Town and Country Lovers (s Gordimer), 1980
Toy Epic (Humphreys), 1958
Toynbee Convector (s Bradbury), 1989
Tracer (Barthelme), 1986
Tracker (Wagoner), 1975
Tracks (Erdrich), 1988
Tractor and the Corn Goddess and Other Stories (s Anand), 1947
Tragic Magic (Brown), 1978
Trailerpark (s Banks), 1981
Train to Pakistan (Singh), 1961
Train Whistle Guitar (Murray), 1974
Trainspotting (Welsh), 1996
Traitor's Gate (Perry), 1995
Transatlantic Blues (Sheed), 1979
Transfer Station (s Haley), 1989
Transfiguration of Martha Friend (Virtue), 1996
Transformation of Miss Mavis Ming (Moorcock, as Bradbury, E.), 1977
Transformations (Jones), 1988
Transit of Venus (Hazzard), 1980
Transit to Narcissus: A Facsimile of the Original Typescript (Mailer), 1978
Translator (Just), 1991
Trap (Jacobson), 1955

Trap (Mathers), 1970
Trash (s Allison), 1988
Traveller (Adams), 1989
Traveller and His Child (Tindall), 1975
Travelling Entertainer and Other Stories (s Jolley), 1979
Travelling Hornplayer (Trapido), 1999
Travels of Maudie Tipstaff (Forster), 1967
Treasure (Knox), 1992
Treasure Hunt (Buechner), 1978
Treasures of Time (Lively), 1979
Tree (Sionil Jose), 1978
Tree of Hands (Rendell, as Vine), 1985
Tree of Knowledge (Figes), 1991
Tree of the Sun (Harris), 1978
Tremor (Graham), 1995
Trespasses (Bailey), 1971
Trial Run (Francis), 1979
Trials of Rumpole (s Mortimer), 1981
Tribal Justice (s Blaise), 1974
Trick of It (Frayn), 1990
Trick of the Light (Faulks), 1984
Trigger (Clarke), 1999
Trina (Cooper), 1934
Trio: Three Stories from Cheltenham (s Trevor), 1993
Tripmaster Monkey, His Fake Book (Kingston), 1989
Triton (Delany), 1977
Triumph of the Spider Monkey (s Oates, as Smith, R.), 1976
Triumph of the Tricolour (Nahal), 1993
Trojan Gold (Mertz, as Michaels), 1987
Trot: A Novel of Suspense (Ely), 1964
Trotter-Nama: A Chronicle (Sealy), 1988
Trouble in Bugland: A Collection of Inspector Mantis Mysteries (s Kotzwinkle), 1983
Trouble with England (Raphael), 1962
Trouble with Heroes (s Vanderhaeghe), 1983
Troublesome Offspring of Cardinal Guzman (de Bernières), 1994
Trout in the Turnhole (Kiely), 1995
Truant State (Hasluck), 1988
Truckers (Pratchett), 1990
True Believers (s O'Connor), 1992
True Confessions (Dunne), 1978
True Love (Gold), 1984
True Stars (Kidman), 1990
True Story of Lola MacKellar (Aldridge), 1992
Trumpet (Kay), 1998
Trumpet to the World (Harris), 1946
Trust (Ozick), 1967
Trust in Chariots (Savage), 1961
Trust Me (s Updike), 1987
Trusting and the Maimed, Other Irish Stories (s Plunkett), 1959
Truth (Pratchett), 2000
Truth about Lorin Jones (Lurie), 1988
Truth and Bright Water (King), 2000
Truth: Four Stories I Am Finally Old Enough to Tell (s Douglas), 1998
Truth Will Not Help Us: Embroidery on an Historical Theme (Bowen), 1956
Trying to Save Piggy Snead (s Irving), 1993
Tumatumari (Harris), 1968
Tumbled House (Graham), 1960
Tunnel (Gass), 1995
Tupelo Nights (Bradley), 1988
Tupolev Too Far (s Aldiss), 1994
Turning Back the Sun (Thubron), 1994
Turtle Beach (d'Alpuget), 1981
Turtle Diary (Hoban), 1976
Turtle Moon (Hoffman), 1992
Twenty-One: Selected Stories (s Just), 1990
27th Kingdom (Ellis), 1999
Twice Shy (Francis), 1982
Twice Told Tales (s Stern), 1989
Twice Twenty Two (s Bradbury), 1966
Twice Upon a Time (s Stern), 1992
Twilight Man (Moorcock, as Bradbury, E.), 1970
Twinkle, Twinkle, Little Spy (Deighton), 1976
Twisted Root (Perry), 1999
Twisted Sword: A Novel of Cornwall 1815–1816 (Graham), 1991
Two (s Crews), 1984
Two Against One (Barthelme), 1989
Two Brothers (Middleton), 1978
Two Brothers, Running: Seventeen Stories and a Movie (s Lurie), 1990
Two Cities (Wideman), 1998
Two Dead Girls (King), 1996
Two Filipino Women (s Sionil Jose), 1982
Two for Texas (Burke), 1995
Two in the Bush and Other Stories (s Thomas), 1981
Two Leaves and a Bud (Anand), 1954
Two Lives (Trevor), 1991
Two Moons (Johnston), 1998
Two of Them (Russ), 1986
Two Sisters: A Memoir in the Form of a Novel (Vidal, as Box), 1970
2001: A Space Odyssey (Clarke), 1994
Two Thousand Seasons (Armah), 1980
2061: Odyssey Three (Clarke), 1988
2010: Odyssey Two (Clarke), 1982
Two Valleys (Fast, as Cunningham), 1934
Two Virgins (Markandaya), 1974
Two Women and Their Man (Jones), 1982
Two's Company (Middleton), 1963
Typical American (Jen), 1991

Ugly Little Boy (Silverberg, as Knox), 1992
Uhuru Street (s Vassanji), 1991
Ultimate Good Luck (Ford), 1989
Umbrella Man (Gordon), 1971
Unburied (Palliser), 1999
Uncharted Territory (Willis), 1994
Uncle Mort's North Country (Tinniswood), 1986
Uncle Mort's South Country (Tinniswood), 1990
Unconditional Surrender (Humphreys), 1996
Unconsoled (Ishiguro), 1995
Under Saturn: Four Stories (s Wilding), 1988
Under the Apple Tree (Wakefield), 1982
Under the Banyan Tree and Other Stories (s Narayan), 1985
Under the Feet of Jesus (Viramontes), 1995
Under the Frog (Fischer), 1994
Under the Gypsy Moon (Thornton), 1990
Under the Shadow (Sorrentino), 1991

Under the Skin (Bawden), 1964
Under the Wheel (Benford), 1987
Underground (Mudrooroo, as Johnson), 1999
Underground Christmas (Hassler), 1999
Underground Man (Jackson), 1997
Underwood and After (Frame), 1991
Underworld (DeLillo), 1997
Undiscovered Country (Mitchell), 1970
Undue Influence (Brookner), 2000
Undying (Mudrooroo, as Johnson), 1998
Unearned Pleasures and Other Stories (s Hegi), 1988
Unearthing Suite (s Atwood), 1983
Unexplained Laughter (Ellis), 1987
Unfamiliar Territory (s Silverberg, as Knox), 1975
Unfinished Business (Hines), 1983
Unfit for Paradise (s Swan), 1982
Unguarded Hours (Wilson), 1978
Unhealthful Air (Baker), 1988
Unholy Loves (Oates, as Smith, R.), 1980
Unicorn Hunt (Dunnett), 1994
Union Street (Barker), 1983
Universal Baseball Association, Inc., J. Henry Waugh, Prop (Coover), 1970
Universe and Other Fictions (s West), 1988
Unkindness of Ravens (Rendell, as Vine), 1985
Unknown Industrial Prisoner (Ireland), 1971
Unknown Man No. 89 (Leonard), 1977
Unknown Soldier (Cassill), 1991
Unlawful Entry (Duckworth), 1992
Unlikely Stories, Mostly (s Gray), 1984
Unlimited Dream Company (Ballard), 1979
Unmarried Woman (Hill), 1978
Unnatural Causes (James), 1967
Unploughed Land (s Cowan), 1958
Unrequited Loves (s Baker), 1974
Unsuitable Friends (s Kidman), 1988
Unsuitable Job for a Woman (James), 1973
Unsweet Charity (Waterhouse), 1992
Untouchable (Anand), 1970
Untouchable (Banville), 1997
Untouchable Juli (Aldridge), 1976
Unusual Life of Tristan Smith (Carey), 1995
Unvanquished (Fast, as Cunningham), 1947
Up (Sukenick), 1968
Up the Junction (s Dunn), 2000
Up the Line (Silverberg, as Knox), 1987
Upon the Sweeping Flood and Other Stories (s Oates, as Smith, R.), 1973
Upstairs People (Dawson), 1988
Upstart (Read), 1973
Urban Affair (Stern), 1980
Us He Devours (s Hall), 1964

V (Pynchon), 1963
V for Victor (Childress), 1984
Vacant Places (Middleton), 1990
Vacant Possession (Mantel), 2000
Vacillations of Poppy Carew (Wesley), 1988
Valdez Is Coming (Leonard), 1970
Valentine Pontifex (Silverberg, as Knox), 1984
Valley Beyond Time (s Silverberg, as Knox), 1973
Valley of Decision (Middleton), 1987
Valley, The City, The Village (Jones), 1956
Vampires (Rechy), 1971
Van (Doyle), 1992
Vanguard from Alpha (Aldiss), 1959
Vanish with the Rose (Mertz, as Michaels), 1992
Vanishing Ladies (Hunter), 1961
Vanishing Points (s Astley), 1995
Vanishing Tower (Moorcock, as Bradbury, E.), 1977
Vanity Dies Hard (Rendell, as Vine), 1970
Various Miracles (s Shields), 1994
Vegas: A Memoir of a Dark Season (Dunne), 1974
Veiled One (Rendell, as Vine), 1988
Vein of Riches (Knowles), 1978
Velodrome (Davison), 1988
Velvet Waters (s Murnane), 1990
Vendor of Sweets (Narayan), 1967
Venging (s Bear), 1992
Venom Business (Crichton, as Lange), 1969
Ventriloquist's Tale (Melville), 1997
Venus Envy (Brown), 1993
Venus Hunters (s Ballard), 1980
Venus in Sparta (Auchincloss), 1958
Verbivore (Brooke-Rose), 1990
Verdict of Treason (Vansittart), 1952
Vermilion Sands (s Ballard), 1973
Veronica and the Gongora Passion (s Ghose), 1998
Veronica; or, The Two Nations (Caute), 1990
Very Like a Whale (Mulkerns), 1986
Very Model of a Man (Jacobson), 1994
Very Old Bones (Kennedy), 1992
Very Private Life (Frayn), 1968
Very Proper Death (Hospital), 1991
Very Rich Hours of Count von Stauffenberg (West), 1980
Very Scotch Affair (Jenkins), 1968
Vespers (Hunter), 1990
Veteran Perils (s Wilkins), 1990
Vibrations in Time (s Watmough), 1986
Vicar of Sorrows (Wilson), 1994
Victim (Bellow), 1948
Victim of the Aurora (Keneally), 1978
Victoria Line (s Binchy), 1980
Victory over Japan (s Gilchrist), 1985
Vida (Piercy), 1980
Villa Golitsyn (Read), 1982
Villa Vittoria (Stead), 1997
Village (Anand), 1939
Village (Hinde), 1966
Village Affair (Trollope), 1989
Vineland (Pynchon), 1990
Vintage Bradbury (s Bradbury), 1965
Vintage Stuff (Sharpe), 1984
Vintner's Luck (Knox), 1998
Violated (Bourjaily), 1962
Violence (Bausch), 1992
Violence (Iyayi), 1979
Violent Stars (Gotlieb), 1999
Violent Ward (Deighton), 1993
Violet Clay (Godwin), 1978

Virtual Light (Gibson), 1993
Virtuous Woman (Gibbons), 1989
Visible People (Gray), 1977
Vision of Emma Blau (Hegi), 2000
Visionary: The Life Story of Flicker of the Serpentine (s Le Guin), 1984
Visitants (Stow), 1981
Visitation (Essop), 1980
Visitation (Roberts), 1978
Visitation of Spirits (Kenan), 1989
Visiting Cards (King), 1990
Visitors (Brookner), 1997
Vital Parts (Berger), 1971
Voice at the Back Door (Spencer), 1957
Voice of God and Other Stories (s Singh), 1957
Voice of a Stranger (Humphreys), 1949
Voices (s Cowan), 1988
Voices at Play (s Spark), 1962
Voices from the River (Kelleher), 1991
Voices in an Empty Room (King), 1984
Voices in the City (Desai), 1965
Voices of Time and Other Stories (s Ballard), 1992
Volcano Lover (Sontag), 1992
Volcanoes from Puebla (Gangemi), 1979
Von Bek (s Moorcock, as Bradbury, E.), 1995
Vor Game (Bujold), 1990
Vorkosigan's Game (Bujold), 1990
Voyage of the Destiny (Nye), 1982
Voyage of the Franz Joseph (Yaffe), 1970
Voyage of the Narwhal (Barrett), 1998

Wabash (Butler), 1987
Wabash Factor (Fast, as Cunningham), 1987
Wages of Virtue (Middleton), 1969
Waiariki (s Grace), 1975
Wait for What Will Come (Mertz, as Michaels), 1980
Wait Till I Tell You (s McWilliam), 1997
Waiting for Cordelia (Gold), 1978
Waiting for the Barbarians (Coetzee), 1982
Waiting for the End of the World (Bell), 1985
Waiting for the Mahatma (Narayan), 1955
Waiting Game (Rubens), 1997
Waiting Room (Harris), 1967
Waiting to Exhale (McMillan), 1992
Wake Up, Stupid (Harris), 1960
Waking (Figes), 1982
Waldo (Theroux), 1968
Walk Me to the Distance (Everett), 1985
Walk Proud (Hunter), 1979
Walk Through Fire (Cobb), 1992
Walker (Wurlitzer), 1987
Walker in Shadows (Mertz, as Michaels), 1981
Walking Across Egypt (Edgerton), 1987
Walking Davis (Ely), 1972
Walking My Mistress in Deauville: A Novella and Nine Stories (s Frame), 1992
Walking Naked (Bawden), 1982
Walking Stick (Graham), 1967
Walking the Dog and Other Stories (s MacLaverty), 1995
Walkin' the Dog (Mosley), 1999
Wall (Vansittart), 1990
Wall of the Plague (Brink), 1985
Wall of the Sky, the Wall of the Eye: Stories (s Lethem), 1996
Walter (Cook), 1985
Walter and June (Cook), 1989
Wanderers (Price), 1974
War Amongst The Angels: An Autobiographical Story (Moorcock, as Bradbury, E.), 1997
War and War (Barthelme), 1971
War Babies (Busch), 1988
War Between the Tates (Lurie), 1974
War Child (Gray), 1993
War Cries over Avenue C (Charyn), 1986
War Crimes (s Carey), 1979
War Fever (s Ballard), 1991
War Hound and the World's Pain (Moorcock, as Bradbury, E.), 1982
War of Don Emmanuel's Nether Parts (de Bernières), 1991
Warleggan: A Novel of Cornwall 1792–1793 (Graham), 1953
Warlock (Harrison), 1981
Warlord of the Air (Moorcock, as Bradbury, E.), 1971
Warm Nights of January (Tuohy), 1960
Warm Wine: An Idyll (s Updike), 1973
Warning to the Curious (Rendell, as Vine), 1987
Warrior of Mars (Moorcock, as Bradbury, E.), 1981
Warriors (Yurick), 1966
Warrior's Apprentice (Bujold), 1986
Warriors of Mars (Moorcock, as Bradbury, E.), 1966
Wars (Findley), 1978
Washington, D.C (Vidal, as Box), 1967
Washington Square Ensemble (Bell), 1983
Watch in the Night (Wilson), 1996
Watch Tower (Harrower), 1966
Watchers on the Shore (Barstow), 1967
Watchfires (Auchincloss), 1982
Watching Me, Watching You (s Weldon), 1981
Watching Mrs. Gordon and Other Stories (s Frame), 1985
Watching the Climbers on the Mountain (Miller), 1988
Water and the Sound (Tindall), 1962
Water Is Wide (Conroy), 1972
Water Is Wide (s Le Guin), 1976
Water Man (McDonald), 1993
Water-Method Man (Irving), 1980
Water Music (Boyle), 1982
Water Music (s Jones), 1944
Water Pourer (s Coover), 1972
Water Witch (Willis), 1980
Water with Berries (Lamming), 1972
Waterfall (Drabble), 1969
Waterfront (Schulberg), 1956
Waterland (Swift), 1984
Waters of Thirst (Mars-Jones), 1994
Watershed (Everett), 1996
Watership Down (Adams), 1974
Waterworks (Doctorow), 1994
Watson's Apology (Bainbridge), 1985
Waves Behind the Boat (King), 1967
Waves of Night and Other Stories (s Petrakis), 1969
Way I Found Her (Tremain), 1998
Way in the World (Naipaul), 1994

Way of Being Free (Okri), 1997
Way of Life and Other Stories (s Jacobson), 1971
Way to Go (Spence), 1998
Way We Live Now (s Sontag), 1991
Waywaya and Other Short Stories from the Philippines (s Sionil Jose), 1980
We Are for the Dark: Six Ghost Stories (s Howard), 1951
We Could Do Worse (Benford), 1988
We Might See Sights! and Other Stories (s O'Faolain), 1968
We Were the Mulvaneys (Oates, as Smith, R.), 1996
We Who Are About to. . . (Russ), 1987
Weather and Women Treat Me Fair: Stories (s Everett), 1989
Weather in Iceland (Profumo), 1993
Wednesday's Child (Robinson), 1995
Weekend in Dinlock (Sigal), 1960
Weekend with Claude (Bainbridge), 1982
Weep Not, Child (Ngugi wa Thiong'o), 1969
Weighed in the Balance (Perry), 1996
Weight of Water (Shreve), 1997
Weird Dance and Other Stories (s Nahal), 1965
Weird of the White Wolf (Moorcock, as Bradbury, E.), 1984
Welcome to Hard Times (Doctorow), 1960
Welcome to Tangier (Lurie), 1997
Welcome to the Monkey House: A Collection of Short Works (s Vonnegut), 1969
Well (Jolley), 1986
Well-Dressed Explorer (Astley), 1988
Welsh Heirs (s Jones), 1977
Went South (Wiggins), 1980
West Block (Dowse), 1983
West Midland Underground (s Wilding), 1975
Westworld (Crichton, as Lange), 1974
Wexford: An Omnibus (Rendell, as Vine), 1988
Whale Rider (Ihimaera), 1988
Whanau (Ihimaera), 1975
What a Carve Up! (Coe), 1994
What Becomes of the Broken Hearted? (Duff), 1996
What Comes Next (Baumbach), 1968
What I Lived For (Oates, as Smith, R.), 1994
What I'm Going to Do, I Think (Woiwode), 1970
What Makes Sammy Run? (Schulberg), 1941
What Remains (Delbanco), 2000
What the Crow Said (Kroetsch), 1978
What Was Mine and Other Stories (s Beattie), 1991
Whatever Happened to Gloomy Gus of the Chicago Bears? (s Coover), 1988
What's the Big Hurry? (Yaffe), 1954
Wheel of Love and Other Stories (s Oates, as Smith, R.), 1971
Wheels (Hailey), 1971
When All the World Was Young (Sams), 1991
When He Was Free and Young and He Used to Wear Silks (s Clarke), 1973
When She Was Good (Roth), 1967
When the Cat's Away (Friedman), 1988
When the War Is Over (Becker), 1970
When We Were Orphans (Ishiguro), 2000
When Women Rule (s Clarke), 1985
Where Are You Going, Where Have You Been? Stories of Young America (s Oates, as Smith, R.), 1974
Where Are the Snows (Gee), 1992
Where Is Here? (s Oates, as Smith, R.), 1992
Where Is My Wandering Boy Tonight? (Wagoner), 1970
Where Is the Voice Coming From? (s Wiebe), 1974
Where or When (Shreve), 1993
Where Shall We Go This Summer? (Desai), 1975
Where the Dreams Cross (Douglas), 1968
Where the Road Goes (Greenberg), 1998
Where There's Smoke (Hunter), 1975
Where Trouble Sleeps: A Novel (Edgerton), 1997
Where You'll Find Me and Other Stories (s Beattie), 1987
Which Ones Are the Enemy? (Garrett), 1962
While Gods Are Falling (Lovelace), 1966
Whip Hand (Francis), 1980
Whisper of the River (Sams), 1984
Whispering in Shadows (Armstrong), 1999
Whistler (Johnson), 1998
White Butterfly (Mosley), 1992
White Cutter (Pownall), 1989
White Eye (d'Alpuget), 1994
White Father (Mitchell), 1965
White Figure, White Ground (Hood), 1964
White Horses (Hoffman), 1983
White Hotel (Thomas), 1981
White Noise (DeLillo), 1986
White People: Stories and Novellas (s Gurganis), 1991
White Queen (Jones), 1993
White Rat (s Jones), 1977
White Solitaire (Mavor), 1988
White Woman (Davison), 1994
Who Calls the Tune (Bawden), 1953
Who Do You Think You Are? (s Munro), 1978
Who Do You Think You Are? Stories and Parodies (s Bradbury), 1984
Who Is Angelina? (Young), 1978
Who Is Teddy Villanova? (Berger), 1977
Who Shall Live, Who Shall Die (Stern), 1963
Who Was Oswald Fish? (Wilson), 1988
Who Were You with Last Night? (Raphael), 1971
Whole Armour (Harris), 1962
Whole Hog (Wagoner), 1976
Who's Irish?: Stories (s Jen), 1999
Whores for Gloria; or, Everything Was Beautiful until the Girls Got Anxious (Vollmann), 1992
Why Are We in Vietnam? (Mailer), 1969
Why Are We So Blest? (Armah), 1975
Why Do You Live So Far Away? A Novella and Six Stories (s Levine), 1984
Why I Can't Talk on the Telephone (s Codrescu), 1972
Why I Want to Fuck Ronald Reagan (s Ballard), 1968
Why Should I Have All the Grief? (Gotlieb), 1969
Wicked Women: A Collection of Short Stories (s Weldon), 1997
Wide Net and Other Stories (s Welty), 1945
Widow (King), 1957
Widow (Slaughter), 1989
Widow for One Year (Irving), 1998
Widows (Hunter), 1991
Widow's Mite and Other Stories (s Sams), 1987
Wier and Pouce (Katz), 1984
Wife (Mukherjee), 1987
Wife Next Door (Cassill), 1960

Wig: A Mirror Image (Wright), 1967
Wild Blue Yonder (s Thomas), 1990
Wild Cat Falling (Mudrooroo, as Johnson), 1965
Wild Decembers (O'Brien), 2000
Wild Girl (Roberts), 1984
Wild Horses (Francis), 1994
Wild Meat and the Bully Burgers (Yamanaka), 1996
Wild Nights (s Oates, as Smith, R.), 1985
Wild Nights (Tennant), 1980
Wild Saturday and Other Stories (s Oates, as Smith, R.), 1984
Wild Seed (Butler), 1980
Wild Shore (Robinson), 1985
Wild Surmise (Raphael), 1962
Wildcat Screaming (Mudrooroo, as Johnson), 1992
Wilderness Station (s Munro), 1994
Wilderness Tips (s Atwood), 1991
Wildest Dreams (Wilding), 1998
Wildlife (Ford), 1990
Will Shakespeare: The Untold Story (Mortimer), 1978
Will You Always Love Me? and Other Stories (s Oates, as Smith, R.), 1996
Willie Masters' Lonesome Wife (Gass), 1971
Williwaw (Vidal, as Box), 1965
Willow Tree (Selby), 1998
Willy Remembers (Faust), 1971
Wilt (Sharpe), 1984
Wilt Alternative (Sharpe), 1981
Wilt on High (Sharpe), 1985
Wind from a Burning Woman (s Bear), 1983
Wind from Nowhere (Ballard), 1967
Wind from the Sun: Stories of the Space Age (s Clarke), 1972
Wind Shifting West (s Grau), 1974
Windeater/Te Kaihau (s Hulme), 1987
Window in Mrs. X's Place (s Cowan), 1987
Wind's Twelve Quarters (s Le Guin), 1976
Wine of Astonishment (Lovelace), 1984
Wings (Pratchett), 1991
Wings of Dust (Mahjoub), 1994
Wings of the Falcon (Mertz, as Michaels), 1979
Winston (Tinniswood), 1991
Winston Affair (Fast, as Cunningham), 1960
Winter (Deighton), 1987
Winter Doves (Cook), 1985
Winter Garden (Bainbridge), 1981
Winter Helen Dropped By (Kinsella), 1995
Winter in Jerusalem (d'Alpuget), 1986
Winter in July (s Lessing), 1966
Winter in the Blood (Welch), 1974
Winter Journey (Colegate), 1995
Winter Journey (Figes), 1968
Winter Journey (Frame), 1986
Wintering (Kelleher), 1990
Winter's Tale (Helprin), 1983
Winthrop Covenant (Auchincloss), 1976
Wise Virgin (Wilson), 1983
Wish You Were Here (Brown), 1990
Wishbone (Halligan), 1994
Witch (Mertz, as Michaels), 1975
Witch of Exmoor (Drabble), 1996
Witches Abroad (Pratchett), 1991
Witches of Eastwick (Updike), 1984
Witches Trilogy (Pratchett), 1995
With Cat for Comforter (Bradbury), 1997
With Shuddering Fall (Oates, as Smith, R.), 1965
With the Snow Queen and Other Stories (s Greenberg), 1991
Without a City Wall (Bragg), 1969
Without a Hero (s Boyle), 1994
Without Motive (Graham), 1936
Wives of Bath (Swan), 1993
Wizard of Earthsea (Le Guin), 1971
Wizards' Country (Rooke), 1957
Wizard's Daughter (Mertz, as Michaels), 1982
Wizard's Tide (Buechner), 1990
Wolf (Harrison), 1993
Wolf to the Slaughter (Rendell, as Vine), 1968
Woman Beware Woman (Tennant), 1983
Woman Hollering Creek and Other Stories (s Cisneros), 1991
Woman in a Lampshade (s Jolley), 1986
Woman in Black: A Ghost Story (Hill), 1986
Woman in the Mirror (Graham), 1975
Woman Lit by Fireflies (Harrison), 1991
Woman of Judah: A Novel and Fifteen Stories (Frame), 1989
Woman of My Age (Bawden), 1967
Woman of the Future (Ireland), 1980
Woman of the Inner Sea (Keneally), 1993
Woman on the Edge of Time (Piercy), 1979
Woman Who Talked to Herself (Barker), 1989
Woman Who Walked into Doors (Doyle), 1996
Woman Who Was God (King), 1988
Woman with a Poet (s Callow), 1983
Woman's Age (Billington), 1980
Woman's Book of Superlatives (s Lim), 1993
Woman's Daughter (Bolger), 1991
Women and Ghosts (s Lurie), 1994
Women and Men (McElroy), 1987
Women in the Wall (O'Faolain), 1975
Women of Brewster Place: A Novel in Seven Stories (Naylor), 1983
Women of Influence (s Burnard), 1988
Women of Whitechapel and Jack the Ripper (West), 1991
Women with Men: Three Stories (s Ford), 1997
Women's Hour (Caute), 1991
Women's Room (French), 1978
Wonder-Worker (Jacobson), 1974
Wonderland (Oates, as Smith, R.), 1972
Woods (Plante), 1982
Word for World Is Forest (Le Guin), 1977
Words (Josipovici), 1971
Words of Advice (Weldon), 1977
Words of My Roaring (Kroetsch), 1966
Work (Dixon), 1977
World According to Garp (Irving), 1978
World and Other Places (s Winterson), 1999
World Away (O'Nan), 1998
World Elsewhere (Bowen), 1967
World Inside (Silverberg, as Knox), 1976
World Made of Fire (Childress), 1984
World of a Thousand Colors (s Silverberg, as Knox), 1982
World of Nagaraj (Narayan), 1990
World of Profit (Auchincloss), 1969

World of Strangers (Gordimer), 1958
World's End (Boyle), 1988
World's End and Other Stories (s Theroux), 1980
World's Fair (Doctorow), 1986
Worlds of Exile and Illusion (s Le Guin), 1996
Worlds within Her (Bissoondath), 1998
Worry Box (s Halligan), 1993
Worst Fears (Weldon), 1996
Wort Papers (Mathers), 1973
Would-Be Saint (Jenkins), 1980
Wound of Love (Cassill), 1956
Wounds (Duffy), 1969
Wreath for Garibaldi and Other Stories (s Garrett), 1969
Wreath for Maidens (Munonye), 1973
Wrecks of Time (Moorcock, as Bradbury, E.), 1967
Writer's Trade, and Other Stories (s Delbanco), 1990
Written on the Body (Winterson), 1993
Wrongful Deaths (Wharton), 1995
Wyrd Sisters (Pratchett), 1988

Xorandor (Brooke-Rose), 1988
XPD (Deighton), 1981

Y Tri Llais (Humphreys), 1958
Year Before Yesterday (Aldiss), 1987
Year in San Fernando (Anthony), 1996
Year of Fears (Watmough), 1988
Year of Living Dangerously (Koch), 1979
Year of Silence (Bell), 1987
Year of the French (Flanagan), 1979
Year of the Hot Jock and Other Stories (s Faust), 1985
Yellow Back Radio Broke-Down (Reed), 1971
Yes from No-Man's Land (Kops), 1966
Yesterday in the Back Lane (Rubens), 1995
Yesterday's Spy (Deighton), 1975
You Are Now Entering the Human Heart (s Frame), 1984
You Bright and Risen Angels: A Cartoon (Vollmann), 1987
You Can't Catch Me (Oates, as Smith, R.), 1995
You Can't Get There from Here (Hood), 1984
You Can't Keep a Good Woman Down (s Walker), 1982
You Could Live If They Let You (Markfield), 1974
You Must Remember This (Oates, as Smith, R.), 1988
You Want the Right Frame of Reference (Cooper), 1971
Young Adolf (Bainbridge), 1979
Young in One Another's Arms (Rule), 1990
Young Miles (Bujold), 1997
Young People (Cooper), 1958
Youngest (Tindall), 1968
You'll Catch Your Death (s Hood), 1992
Your Turn to Curtsy, My Turn to Bow (Goldman), 1958
You're Not Alone: A Doctor's Diary (Cooper), 1976
Yours (Callow), 1972

Zanzibar Cat (s Russ), 1983
Zeitgeist (Sterling), 2000
Zeke and Ned (McMurtry), 1997
Zeph (Barker), 1992
Zero Cool (Crichton, as Lange), 1972
Zero db and Other Stories (s Bell), 1987
Zia Summer (Anaya), 1995
Zodiac: The Eco-Thriller (Stephenson), 1988
Zombie (Oates, as Smith, R.), 1995
Zone of the Interior (Sigal), 1976
Zuckerman Bound (Roth), 1985
Zuckerman Unbound (Roth), 1981
Zulu and the Zeide (s Jacobson), 1959

ISBN 1-55862-408-2
90000
9 781558 624085